(ex·ploring) SERIES

1. Investigating in a systematic way: examining. 2. Searching into or ranging over for the purpose of discovery.

USED

Microsoft®

Office 2016

VOLUME 1

Series Editor **Mary Anne Poatsy**

Mulbery | Krebs | Hogan | Cameron | Davidson | Lau | Lawson | Williams

Series Created by Dr. Robert T. Grauer

D0024467

PEARSON

Boston   Columbus   Indianapolis   New York   San Francisco   Hoboken
Amsterdam   Cape Town   Dubai   London   Madrid   Milan   Munich   Paris   Montréal   Toronto
Delhi   Mexico City   São Paulo   Sydney   Hong Kong   Seoul   Singapore   Taipei   Tokyo

Vice President of Career Skills: Andrew Gilfillan
Senior Editor: Samantha Lewis
Team Lead, Project Management: Laura Burgess
Project Manager: Laura Karahalis
Program Manager: Emily Biberger
Development Editor: Barbara Stover
Editorial Assistant: Michael Campbell
Director of Product Marketing: Maggie Waples
Director of Field Marketing: Leigh Ann Sims
Product Marketing Manager: Kaylee Carlson
Field Marketing Managers: Molly Schmidt & Joanna Sabella
Marketing Coordinator: Susan Osterlitz
Senior Operations Specialist: Diane Peirano
Senior Art Director: Diane Ernsberger
Interior and Cover Design: Diane Ernsberger
Cover Photo: Courtesy of Shutterstock® Images
Associate Director of Design: Blair Brown
Senior Product Strategy Manager: Eric Hakanson
Product Manager, MyITLab: Zachary Alexander
Media Producer, MyITLab: Jaimie Noy
Digital Project Manager, MyITLab: Becca Lowe
Media Project Manager, Production: John Cassar
Full-Service Project Management: Jenna Vittorioso, Lumina Datamatics, Inc.
Composition: Lumina Datamatics, Inc.
Efficacy Curriculum Manager: Jessica Sieminski

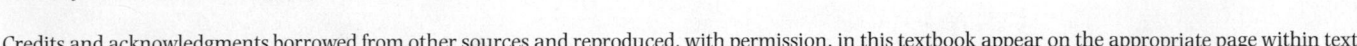

Credits and acknowledgments borrowed from other sources and reproduced, with permission, in this textbook appear on the appropriate page within text.

Library of Congress Control Number: 2015948028

10 9 8 7 6 5 4 3 2 1

ISBN 10:   0-13-432079-4
ISBN 13: 978-0-13-432079-3

Dedications

For my husband, Ted, who unselfishly continues to take on more than his share to support me throughout the process; and for my children, Laura, Carolyn, and Teddy, whose encouragement and love have been inspiring.

Mary Anne Poatsy

I dedicate this book in memory to Grandpa Herman Hort, who dedicated his life to his family and to the education field as a teacher and administrator. He inspired a daughter and several grandchildren to become passionate educators and provide quality curriculum to students.

Keith Mulbery

For my children for all of believing in me, encouraging me, and supporting me. Thank you Marshall Krebs, Jaron Krebs, Jenalee Krebs Behle, and Michelle Krebs. To my writing mentor, Dr. Keith Mulbery, for the same reasons.

Cynthia Krebs

I dedicate this work to my wonderful family—my husband, Paul, and my daughters, Jenn and Alli. You have made this adventure possible with your support, encouragement, and love. You inspire me!

Lynn Hogan

I dedicate this book to my wife Anny, for supporting me through the writing process, to my nieces Daniela and Gabriela, who someday will be old enough to think it is cool their names are in a book, and to my students, who make a career in teaching fulfilling. May you all go forward, change the world and inspire others.

Eric Cameron

I dedicate this book in loving memory of my grandfather Laurence L. Leggett. A passionate lifelong educator, gifted musician, and incredible role model. I will never forget our time together. I strive every day to make you proud.

Jason Davidson

I dedicate this book to my only child, Catherine Shen, who taught me that there is another wonderful life outside of my work. My life has been more fulfilling and exciting with her in it. I also dedicate this book to the loving memory of my dog, Harry, who was by my side, through thick and thin, for 16 years. I miss him dearly every day.

Linda K. Lau

This book is dedicated to my children and to my students to inspire them to never give up and to always keep reaching for their dreams.

Rebecca Lawson

I offer thanks to my family and colleagues who have supported me on this journey. I would like to dedicate the work I have performed toward this undertaking to my little grandson, Yonason Meir (known for now as Mei-Mei), who as his name suggests, is the illumination in my life.

Jerri Williams

To my husband Dan, whose encouragement, patience, and love helped make this endeavor possible. Thank you for taking on the many additional tasks at home so that I could focus on writing.

Amy Rutledge

About the Authors

Mary Anne Poatsy, Series Editor, Windows 10 Author

Mary Anne is a senior faculty member at Montgomery County Community College, teaching various computer application and concepts courses in face-to-face and online environments. She holds a B.A. in Psychology and Education from Mount Holyoke College and an M.B.A. in Finance from Northwestern University's Kellogg Graduate School of Management.

Mary Anne has more than 12 years of educational experience. She is currently adjunct faculty at Gwynedd-Mercy College and Montgomery County Community College. She has also taught at Bucks County Community College and Muhlenberg College, as well as conducted personal training. Before teaching, she was Vice President at Shearson Lehman in the Municipal Bond Investment Banking Department.

Dr. Keith Mulbery, Excel Author

Dr. Keith Mulbery is the Department Chair and a Professor in the Information Systems and Technology Department at Utah Valley University (UVU), where he currently teaches systems analysis and design, and global and ethical issues in information systems and technology. He has also taught computer applications, C# programming, and management information systems. Keith served as Interim Associate Dean, School of Computing, in the College of Technology and Computing at UVU.

Keith received the Utah Valley State College Board of Trustees Award of Excellence in 2001, School of Technology and Computing Scholar Award in 2007, and School of Technology and Computing Teaching Award in 2008. He has authored more than 17 textbooks, served as Series Editor for the Exploring Office 2007 series, and served as developmental editor on two textbooks for the Essentials Office 2000 series. He is frequently asked to give presentations and workshops on Microsoft Office Excel at various education conferences.

Keith received his B.S. and M.Ed. in Business Education from Southwestern Oklahoma State University and earned his Ph.D. in Education with an emphasis in Business Information Systems at Utah State University. His dissertation topic was computer-assisted instruction using Prentice Hall's Train and Assess IT program (the predecessor to MyITLab) to supplement traditional instruction in basic computer proficiency courses.

Cynthia Krebs, PowerPoint Author

Cynthia Krebs is the Program Director of Business and Marketing Education at Utah Valley University. She is a tenured professor in the Information Systems and Technology Department at UVU where she teaches the Methods of Teaching Business, Marketing, and Digital Technology course to future teachers, as well as classes in basic computer applications and business proficiency applications. She holds a B.S and M.S. in Business Education with an emphasis in Economic Education. Cynthia has received numerous awards, and has presented extensively at the local, regional, and national levels as well as consulting with government organizations and businesses.

Cynthia lives by a peaceful creek I in Springville, Utah. When she isn't teaching or writing, she enjoys spending time with her children, spoiling her grandchildren Ava, Bode, Solee, Morgan, and Preslee. She loves traveling and reading.

Lynn Hogan, Word Author

Lynn Hogan teaches at the University of North Alabama, providing instruction in the area of computer applications. With over 30 years of educational experience at the community college and university level, Lynn has taught applications, programming, and concepts courses in both online and classroom environments. She received an M.B.A. from the University of North Alabama and a Ph.D. from the University of Alabama.

Lynn is a co-author of Practical Computing and has served on the authoring team of Your Office as well as the Exploring Office 2010 series. She resides in Alabama with her husband and two daughters.

Eric Cameron, Access Author

Eric Cameron is a tenured Associate Professor at Passaic County Community College, where he has taught in the Computer and Information Sciences department since 2001. He holds an M.S. in Computer Science and a B.S. degree in Computer Science with minors in Mathematics and Physics, both from Montclair State University. He currently co-chairs the College's General Education committee and served as a member of the College's Academic Assessment, College Writing, and Educational Technology committees at various points. Eric has also developed degrees in Graphic Design and Medical Informatics for the College. Eric previously worked as a software engineer both as a full-time employee and contractor, most recently for ITT/Exelis (now part of Harris Corporation).

This is Eric's fourth publication for Pearson, after authoring Web 2.0 and Windows 8 books in the Your Office series and co-authoring the Exploring Access 2013 text.

Jason Davidson, Excel Author

Jason Davidson is a faculty member in the College of Business at Butler University, where he teaches Advanced Web Design, Data Networks, Data Analysis and Business Modeling, and introductory information systems courses. He is the co-author of Exploring Microsoft Excel 2013 Comprehensive, Exploring Microsoft Office 2013 Volume 2, Exploring Microsoft Office 2013 Plus, and Exploring VBA for Microsoft Office 2013.

With a background in media development, prior to joining the faculty at Butler, he worked in the technical publishing industry. Along with teaching, he currently serves as an IT consultant for regional businesses in the Indianapolis area. He holds a B.A. in Telecommunication Arts from Butler University and an M.B.A. from Morehead State University. He lives in Indianapolis, Indiana, and in his free time enjoys road biking, photography, and spending time with his family.

Dr. Linda K. Lau, Word Author

Since 1994, Dr. Linda K. Lau is a Management Information Systems (MIS) faculty at the College of Business and Economics, Longwood University, located in Farmville, Virginia. She received the Outstanding Academic Advisor Award in 2006. Besides teaching and advising, Linda has authored and co-authored numerous journal and conference articles and textbooks, edited two books, and sat on several editorial boards. Her current research interest focuses on cyber security and forensics, and she is the associate editor for the Journal of Digital Forensics, Security and Law (JDFSL). Linda earned her Ph.D. from Rensselaer Polytechnic Institute in 1993, and her MBA and Bachelor of Science from Illinois State University in 1987 and 1986, respectively. In her younger days, Linda worked as a flight attendant for Singapore International Airlines for six years before coming to America to pursue her academic dream. She also worked as a financial consultant with Salomon Smith Barney from 1999–2000 before returning to the academic world. Linda resides in Richmond with her family.

Rebecca Lawson, PowerPoint Author

Rebecca Lawson is a professor in the Computer Information Technologies program at Lansing Community College. She coordinates the curriculum, develops the instructional materials, and teaches for the E-Business curriculum. She also serves as the Online Faculty Coordinator at the Center for Teaching Excellence at LCC. In that role, she develops and facilitates online workshops for faculty learning to teach online. Her major areas of interest include online curriculum quality assurance, the review and development of printed and online instructional materials, the assessment of computer and Internet literacy skill levels to facilitate student retention, and the use of social networking tools to support learning in blended and online learning environments.

Jerri Williams, Access Author

Jerri Williams is a Senior Instructor at Montgomery County Community College in Pennsylvania. Jerri also works as an independent corporate trainer, technical editor, and content developer. She is interested in travel, cooking, movies, and tending to her colonial farmhouse. Jerri is married, and is the mother of two daughters, Holly (an Accounting graduate and full-time mother to an adorable son, Meir) and Gwyneth (a corporate defense attorney). Jerri and Gareth live in the suburbs of Philadelphia. They enjoy their home and garden, and spending time with family and good friends.

Amy Rutledge, Common Features Author

Amy Rutledge is a Special Instructor of Management Information Systems at Oakland University in Rochester, Michigan. She coordinates academic programs in Microsoft Office applications and introductory management information systems courses for the School of Business Administration. Before joining Oakland University as an instructor, Amy spent several years working for a music distribution company and automotive manufacturer in various corporate roles including IT project management. She holds a B.S. in Business Administration specializing in Management Information Systems, and a B.A. in French Modern Language and Literature. She holds an M.B.A from Oakland University. She resides in Michigan with her husband, Dan and daughters Emma and Jane.

Dr. Robert T. Grauer, Creator of the Exploring Series

Bob Grauer is an Associate Professor in the Department of Computer Information Systems at the University of Miami, where he is a multiple winner of the Outstanding Teaching Award in the School of Business, most recently in 2009. He has written numerous COBOL texts and is the vision behind the Exploring Office series, with more than three million books in print. His work has been translated into three foreign languages and is used in all aspects of higher education at both national and international levels. Bob Grauer has consulted for several major corporations including IBM and American Express. He received his Ph.D. in Operations Research in 1972 from the Polytechnic Institute of Brooklyn.

Brief Contents

Contents

Microsoft Office Word 2016

Microsoft Office PowerPoint 2016

■ CHAPTER ONE Introduction to PowerPoint: Creating a Basic Presentation 924

■ CHAPTER TWO Presentation Development: Planning and Preparing a Presentation 990

■ CHAPTER THREE Presentation Design: Illustrations and Infographics 1042

CHAPTER FOUR **Enhancing with Multimedia:** PowerPoint Rich Media Tools 1116

Application Capstone Exercises

Acknowledgments

The Exploring team would like to acknowledge and thank all the reviewers who helped us throughout the years by providing us with their invaluable comments, suggestions, and constructive criticism.

Adriana Lumpkin
Midland College

Alan S. Abrahams
Virginia Tech

Alexandre C. Probst
Colorado Christian University

Ali Berrached
University of Houston–Downtown

Allen Alexander
Delaware Technical & Community College

Andrea Marchese
Maritime College, State University of New York

Andrew Blitz
Broward College; Edison State College

Angel Norman
University of Tennessee, Knoxville

Angela Clark
University of South Alabama

Ann Rovetto
Horry-Georgetown Technical College

Astrid Todd
Guilford Technical Community College

Audrey Gillant
Maritime College, State University of New York

Barbara Stover
Marion Technical College

Barbara Tollinger
Sinclair Community College

Ben Brahim Taha
Auburn University

Beverly Amer
Northern Arizona University

Beverly Fite
Amarillo College

Biswadip Ghosh
Metropolitan State University of Denver

Bonita Volker
Tidewater Community College

Bonnie Homan
San Francisco State University

Brad West
Sinclair Community College

Brian Powell
West Virginia University

Carol Buser
Owens Community College

Carol Roberts
University of Maine

Carolyn Barren
Macomb Community College

Carolyn Borne
Louisiana State University

Cathy Poyner
Truman State University

Charles Hodgson
Delgado Community College

Chen Zhang
Bryant University

Cheri Higgins
Illinois State University

Cheryl Brown
Delgado Community College

Cheryl Hinds
Norfolk State University

Cheryl Sypniewski
Macomb Community College

Chris Robinson
Northwest State Community College

Cindy Herbert
Metropolitan Community College–Longview

Craig J. Peterson
American InterContinental University

Dana Hooper
University of Alabama

Dana Johnson
North Dakota State University

Daniela Marghitu
Auburn University

David Noel
University of Central Oklahoma

David Pulis
Maritime College, State University of New York

David Thornton
Jacksonville State University

Dawn Medlin
Appalachian State University

Debby Keen
University of Kentucky

Debra Chapman
University of South Alabama

Debra Hoffman
Southeast Missouri State University

Derrick Huang
Florida Atlantic University

Diana Baran
Henry Ford Community College

Diane Cassidy
The University of North Carolina at Charlotte

Diane L. Smith
Henry Ford Community College

Dick Hewer
Ferris State College

Don Danner
San Francisco State University

Don Hoggan
Solano College

Don Riggs
SUNY Schenectady County Community College

Doncho Petkov
Eastern Connecticut State University

Donna Ehrhart
State University of New York at Brockport

Elaine Crable
Xavier University

Elizabeth Duett
Delgado Community College

Erhan Uskup
Houston Community College–Northwest

Eric Martin
University of Tennessee

Erika Nadas
Wilbur Wright College

Floyd Winters
Manatee Community College

Frank Lucente
Westmoreland County Community College

G. Jan Wilms
Union University

Gail Cope
Sinclair Community College

Gary DeLorenzo
California University of Pennsylvania

Gary Garrison
Belmont University

Gary McFall
Purdue University

George Cassidy
Sussex County Community College

Gerald Braun
Xavier University

Gerald Burgess
Western New Mexico University

Gladys Swindler
Fort Hays State University

Hector Frausto
California State University
Los Angeles

Heith Hennel
Valencia Community College

Henry Rudzinski
Central Connecticut State University

Irene Joos
La Roche College

Iwona Rusin
Baker College; Davenport University

J. Roberto Guzman
San Diego Mesa College

Jacqueline D. Lawson
Henry Ford Community College

Jakie Brown Jr.
Stevenson University

James Brown
Central Washington University

James Powers
University of Southern Indiana

Jane Stam
Onondaga Community College

Janet Bringhurst
Utah State University

Jean Welsh
Lansing Community College

Jeanette Dix
Ivy Tech Community College

Jennifer Day
Sinclair Community College

Jill Canine
Ivy Tech Community College

Jill Young
Southeast Missouri State University

Jim Chaffee
The University of Iowa Tippie College of Business

Joanne Lazirko
University of Wisconsin–Milwaukee

Jodi Milliner
Kansas State University

John Hollenbeck
Blue Ridge Community College

John Seydel
Arkansas State University

Judith A. Scheeren
Westmoreland County Community College

Judith Brown
The University of Memphis

Juliana Cypert
Tarrant County College

Kamaljeet Sanghera
George Mason University

Karen Priestly
Northern Virginia Community College

Karen Ravan
Spartanburg Community College

Karen Tracey
Central Connecticut State University

Kathleen Brenan
Ashland University

Ken Busbee
Houston Community College

Kent Foster
Winthrop University

Kevin Anderson
Solano Community College

Kim Wright
The University of Alabama

Kristen Hockman
University of Missouri–Columbia

Kristi Smith
Allegany College of Maryland

Laura Marcoulides
Fullerton College

Laura McManamon
University of Dayton

Laurence Boxer
Niagara University

Leanne Chun
Leeward Community College

Lee McClain
Western Washington University

Linda D. Collins
Mesa Community College

Linda Johnsonius
Murray State University

Linda Lau
Longwood University

Linda Theus
Jackson State Community College

Linda Williams
Marion Technical College

Lisa Miller
University of Central Oklahoma

Lister Horn
Pensacola Junior College

Lixin Tao
Pace University

Loraine Miller
Cayuga Community College

Lori Kielty
Central Florida Community College

Lorna Wells
Salt Lake Community College

Lorraine Sauchin
Duquesne University

Lucy Parakhovnik
California State University, Northridge

Lynn Keane
University of South Carolina

Lynn Mancini
Delaware Technical Community College

Mackinzee Escamilla
South Plains College

Marcia Welch
Highline Community College

Margaret McManus
Northwest Florida State College

Margaret Warrick
Allan Hancock College

Marilyn Hibbert
Salt Lake Community College

Mark Choman
Luzerne County Community College

Maryann Clark
University of New Hampshire

Mary Beth Tarver
Northwestern State University

Mary Duncan
University of Missouri–St. Louis

Melissa Nemeth
Indiana University-Purdue University Indianapolis

Melody Alexander
Ball State University

Michael Douglas
University of Arkansas at Little Rock

Michael Dunklebarger
Alamance Community College

Michael G. Skaff
College of the Sequoias

Michele Budnovitch
Pennsylvania College of Technology

Mike Jochen
East Stroudsburg University

Mike Michaelson
Palomar College

Mike Scroggins
Missouri State University

Mimi Spain
Southern Maine Community College

Muhammed Badamas
Morgan State University

NaLisa Brown
University of the Ozarks

Nancy Grant
Community College of Allegheny County–
South Campus

Nanette Lareau
University of Arkansas Community
College–Morrilton

Nikia Robinson
Indian River State University

Pam Brune
Chattanooga State Community College

Pam Uhlenkamp
Iowa Central Community College

Patrick Smith
Marshall Community and Technical College

Paul Addison
Ivy Tech Community College

Paula Ruby
Arkansas State University

Peggy Burrus
Red Rocks Community College

Peter Ross
SUNY Albany

Philip H. Nielson
Salt Lake Community College

Philip Valvalides
Guilford Technical Community College

Ralph Hooper
University of Alabama

Ranette Halverson
Midwestern State University

Richard Blamer
John Carroll University

Richard Cacace
Pensacola Junior College

Richard Hewer
Ferris State University

Richard Sellers
Hill College

Rob Murray
Ivy Tech Community College

Robert Banta
Macomb Community College

Robert Dušek
Northern Virginia Community College

Robert G. Phipps Jr.
West Virginia University

Robert Sindt
Johnson County Community College

Robert Warren
Delgado Community College

Rocky Belcher
Sinclair Community College

Roger Pick
University of Missouri at Kansas City

Ronnie Creel
Troy University

Rosalie Westerberg
Clover Park Technical College

Ruth Neal
Navarro College

Sandra Thomas
Troy University

Sheila Gionfriddo
Luzerne County Community College

Sherrie Geitgey
Northwest State Community College

Sherry Lenhart
Terra Community College

Sophia Wilberscheid
Indian River State College

Sophie Lee
California State University,
Long Beach

Stacy Johnson
Iowa Central Community College

Stephanie Kramer
Northwest State Community College

Stephen Z. Jourdan
Auburn University at Montgomery

Steven Schwarz
Raritan Valley Community College

Sue A. McCrory
Missouri State University

Sumathy Chandrashekar
Salisbury University

Susan Fuschetto
Cerritos College

Susan Medlin
UNC Charlotte

Susan N. Dozier
Tidewater Community College

Suzan Spitzberg
Oakton Community College

Suzanne M. Jeska
County College of Morris

Sven Aelterman
Troy University

Sy Hirsch
Sacred Heart University

Sylvia Brown
Midland College

Tanya Patrick
Clackamas Community College

Terri Holly
Indian River State College

Terry Ray Rigsby
Hill College

Thomas Rienzo
Western Michigan University

Tina Johnson
Midwestern State University

Tommy Lu
Delaware Technical Community College

Troy S. Cash
Northwest Arkansas Community College

Vicki Robertson
Southwest Tennessee Community

Vickie Pickett
Midland College

Weifeng Chen
California University of Pennsylvania

Wes Anthony
Houston Community College

William Ayen
University of Colorado at Colorado Springs

Wilma Andrews
Virginia Commonwealth University

Yvonne Galusha
University of Iowa

Special thanks to our content development and technical team:

Barbara Stover

Julie Boyles

Lisa Bucki

Lori Damanti

Sallie Dodson

Patti Hammerle

Jean Insigna

Elizabeth Lockley

Joyce Nielsen

Janet Pickard

Linda Pogue

Steven Rubin

Mara Zebest

Preface

The Exploring Series and You

Exploring is Pearson's Office Application series that requires students like you to think "beyond the point and click." In this edition, we have worked to restructure the Exploring experience around the way you, today's modern student, actually use your resources.

The goal of Exploring is, as it has always been, to go farther than teaching just the steps to accomplish a task—the series provides the theoretical foundation for you to understand when and why to apply a skill. As a result, you achieve a deeper understanding of each application and can apply this critical thinking beyond Office and the classroom.

The How & Why of This Revision

Outcomes matter. Whether it's getting a good grade in this course, learning how to use Excel so students can be successful in other courses, or learning a specific skill that will make learners successful in a future job, everyone has an outcome in mind. And outcomes matter. That is why we revised our chapter opener to focus on the outcomes students will achieve by working through each Exploring chapter. These are coupled with objectives and skills, providing a map students can follow to get everything they need from each chapter.

Critical Thinking and Collaboration are essential 21st century skills. Students want and need to be successful in their future careers—so we used motivating case studies to show relevance of these skills to future careers and incorporated Soft Skills, Collaboration, and Analysis Cases with Critical Thinking steps in this edition to set students up for success in the future.

Students today read, prepare, and study differently than students used to. Students use textbooks like a tool—they want to easily identify what they need to know and learn it efficiently. We have added key features such as Tasks Lists (in purple), Step Icons, Hands-On Exercise Videos, and tracked everything via page numbers that allow efficient navigation, creating a map students can easily follow.

Students are exposed to technology. The new edition of Exploring moves beyond the basics of the software at a faster pace, without sacrificing coverage of the fundamental skills that students need to know.

Students are diverse. Students can be any age, any gender, any race, with any level of ability or learning style. With this in mind, we broadened our definition of "student resources" to include physical Student Reference cards, Hands-On Exercise videos to provide a secondary lecture-like option of review; and MyITLab, the most powerful and most ADA-compliant online homework and assessment tool around with a direct 1:1 content match with the Exploring Series. Exploring will be accessible to all students, regardless of learning style.

Providing You with a Map to Success to Move Beyond the Point and Click

All of these changes and additions will provide students an easy and efficient path to follow to be successful in this course, regardless of where they start at the beginning of this course. Our goal is to keep students engaged in both the hands-on and conceptual sides, helping achieve a higher level of understanding that will guarantee success in this course and in a future career.

In addition to the vision and experience of the series creator, Robert T. Grauer, we have assembled a tremendously talented team of Office Applications authors who have devoted themselves to teaching the ins and outs of Microsoft Word, Excel, Access, and PowerPoint. Led in this edition by series editor Mary Anne Poatsy, the whole team is dedicated to the Exploring mission of moving students **beyond the point and click**.

Key Features

The **How/Why Approach** helps students move beyond the point and click to a true understanding of how to apply Microsoft Office skills.

- **White Pages/Yellow Pages** clearly distinguish the theory (white pages) from the skills covered in the Hands-On Exercises (yellow pages) so students always know what they are supposed to be doing and why.

- **Case Study** presents a scenario for the chapter, creating a story that ties the Hands-On Exercises together.

- **Hands-On Exercise Videos** are tied to each Hands-On Exercise and walk students through the steps of the exercise while weaving in conceptual information related to the Case Study and the objectives as a whole.

The **Outcomes focus** allows students and instructors to know the higher-level learning goals and how those are achieved through discreet objectives and skills.

- **Outcomes** presented at the beginning of each chapter identify the learning goals for students and instructors.

- **Enhanced Objective Mapping** enables students to follow a directed path through each chapter, from the objectives list at the chapter opener through the exercises at the end of the chapter.
  - **Objectives List:** This provides a simple list of key objectives covered in the chapter. This includes page numbers so students can skip between objectives where they feel they need the most help.
  - **Step Icons:** These icons appear in the white pages and reference the step numbers in the Hands-On Exercises, providing a correlation between the two so students can easily find conceptual help when they are working hands-on and need a refresher.
  - **Quick Concepts Check:** A series of questions that appear briefly at the end of each white page section. These questions cover the most essential concepts in the white pages required for students to be successful in working the Hands-On Exercises. Page numbers are included for easy reference to help students locate the answers.
  - **Chapter Objectives Review:** Appears toward the end of the chapter and reviews all important concepts throughout the chapter. Newly designed in an easy-to-read bulleted format.

- **MOS Certification Guide** for instructors and students to direct anyone interested in prepping for the MOS exam to the specific locations to find all content required for the test.

End-of-Chapter Exercises offer instructors several options for assessment. Each chapter has approximately 11–12 exercises ranging from multiple choice questions to open-ended projects.

Watch the Video for this Hands-On Exercise!

- **Multiple Choice, Key Terms Matching, Practice Exercises, Mid-Level Exercises, Beyond the Classroom Exercises, and Capstone Exercises** appear at the end of all chapters.
  - **Enhanced Mid-Level Exercises** include a **Creative Case** (for PowerPoint and Word), which allows students some flexibility and creativity, not being bound by a definitive solution, and an **Analysis Case** (for Excel and Access), which requires students to interpret the data they are using to answer an analytic question, as well as **Discover Steps**, which encourage students to use Help or to problem-solve to accomplish a task.

- **Application Capstone** exercises are included in the book to allow instructors to test students on the entire contents of a single application.

ANALYSIS CASE

CREATIVE CASE

Resources

Instructor Resources

The Instructor's Resource Center, available at **www.pearsonhighered.com**, includes the following:

- **Instructor Manual** provides one-stop-shop for instructors, including an overview of all available resources, teaching tips, as well as student data and solution files for every exercise.

- **Solution Files with Scorecards** assist with grading the Hands-On Exercises and end-of-chapter exercises.

- **Prepared Exams** allow instructors to assess all skills covered in a chapter with a single project.

- **Rubrics** for Mid-Level Creative Cases and Beyond the Classroom Cases in Microsoft Word format enable instructors to customize the assignments for their classes.

- **PowerPoint Presentations** with notes for each chapter are included for out-of-class study or review.

- **Multiple Choice, Key Term Matching, and Quick Concepts Check Answer Keys**

- **Test Bank** provides objective-based questions for every chapter.

- **Scripted Lectures** offer an in-class lecture guide for instructors to mirror the Hands-On Exercises.

- **Syllabus Templates**
  - Outcomes, Objectives, and Skills List
  - Assignment Sheet
  - File Guide

Student Resources

Student Data Files

Access your student data files needed to complete the exercises in this textbook at **www.pearsonhighered.com/exploring**.

Available in MyITLab

- **Hands-On Exercise Videos** allow students to review and study the concepts taught in the Hands-On Exercises.
- **Audio PowerPoints** provide a lecture review of the chapter content, and include narration.
- **Multiple Choice quizzes** enable you to test concepts you have learned by answering auto-graded questions.
- **Book-specific 1:1 Simulations** allow students to practice in the simulated Microsoft Office 2016 environment using hi-fidelity, HTML5 simulations that directly match the content in the Hands-On Exercises.
- **eText** available in some MyITLab courses and includes links to videos, student data files, and other learning aids.
- **Book-specific 1:1 Grader Projects** allow students to complete end of chapter Capstone Exercises live in Microsoft Office 2016 and receive immediate feedback on their performance through various reports.

(ex·ploring)

SERIES

1. Investigating in a systematic way: examining. 2. Searching into or ranging over for the purpose of discovery.

Microsoft®

Office 2016

VOLUME 1

Windows 10

Working with an Operating System

LEARNING OUTCOMES:
- You will manage the Windows 10 environment through the desktop and other components.
- You will organize files and folders using Windows 10 features and tools.

OBJECTIVES & SKILLS: After you read this chapter, you will be able to:

CASE STUDY | Cedar Grove Elementary School

Your good friend recently graduated with a degree in elementary education and now is excited to begin her first job as a fifth-grade teacher at Cedar Grove Elementary School. The school has a computer lab for all students as well as a computer system in each classroom. The school acquired the computers through a state technology grant so they are new models running Windows 10. Your friend's lesson plans must include a unit on operating system basics and an introduction to application software. Because you have a degree in computer information systems, she has called on you for assistance with the lesson plans.

You cannot assume that all students are exposed to computers at home, especially to those configured with Windows 10. Your material will need to include very basic instruction on Windows 10, along with a general overview of file management. Your friend must complete her lesson plans right away, so you are on a short timeline but are excited about helping students learn!

Getting Started with Microsoft® Windows® 10

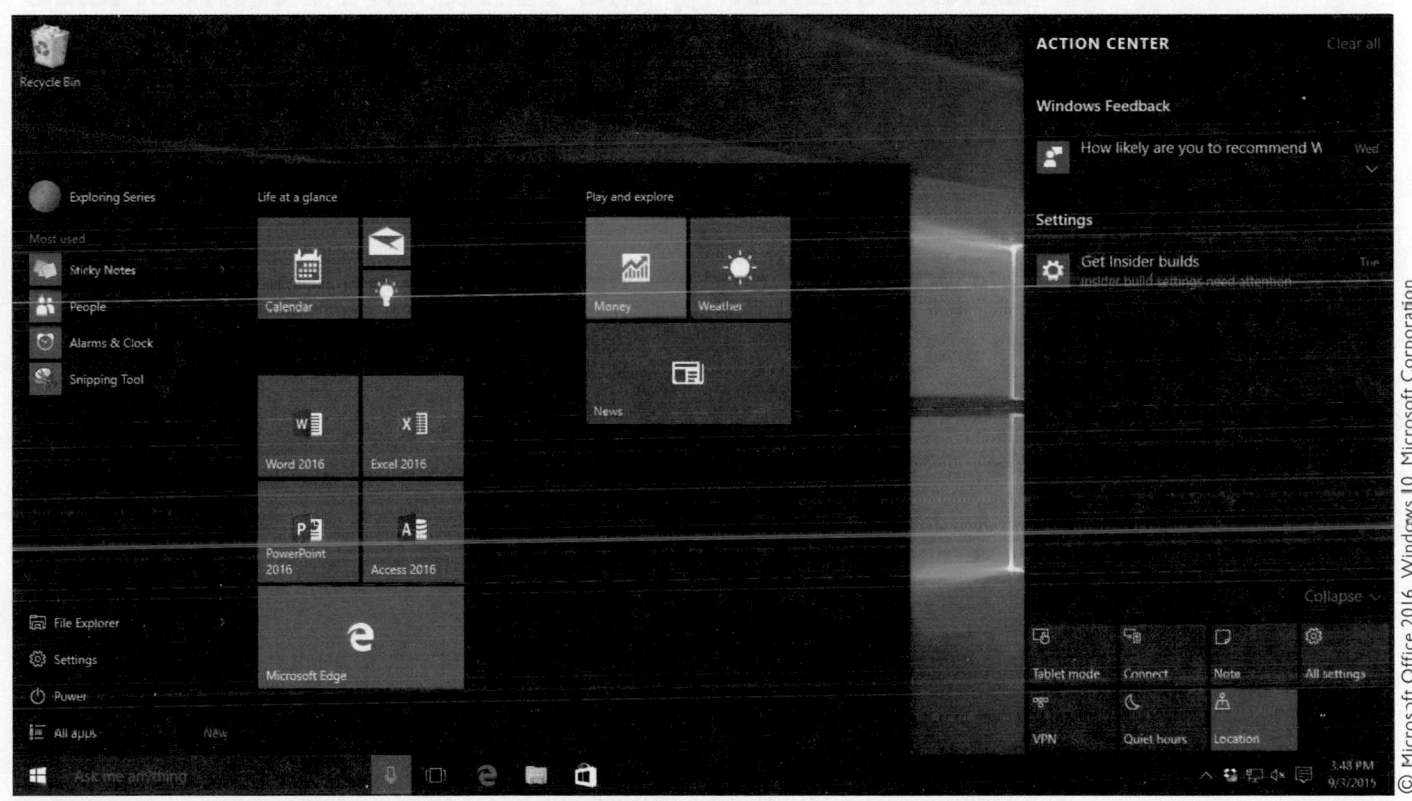

FIGURE 1.1 Cedar Grove Elementary School Windows 10 Start Menu

CASE STUDY | Cedar Grove Elementary School

Starting File	File to be Submitted
Blank Word document	win01h3Windows10_LastFirst

Windows 10 Fundamentals

There are two types of software on your computer: application software and system software. Application software are programs you use for email, gaming, social networking, and digital photo management. Application software also includes productivity software such as word processing, spreadsheet, and presentation applications. As essential as these application programs may be to you for entertainment or for accomplishing a specific task, system software is the essential software that the computer needs. Without system software, your computer could not function. System software includes the operating system and utility programs, and helps to run application software, manage your files, and manage system resources and other computer activities.

In this section, you will learn how to work with the features of the Windows 10 operating system. In particular, you will learn how to set up a Microsoft account if you do not have one established already, and start and shut down Windows. You will also learn how to configure the Start menu and taskbar to manage programs and apps.

Understanding the Windows 10 Interface

Windows 10 is the latest version of Microsoft's operating system and is available for desktops, laptops, cell phones, and tablet computers. Windows 10 has made changes that facilitate computer use, both on touch and non-touch devices. Because you are likely to encounter Windows 10 on computers and mobile devices at school, work, and home, it is well worth your time to explore and learn how to use it, as well as its computer management and security features.

Sign In to a Microsoft Account

When you start your computer, Windows 10 opens to the Lock screen that displays an image (which you can personalize with your own image) and the date and time. Clicking on the Lock screen brings you to the sign in page where you log in using your Microsoft account username (email address) and password. To use any Microsoft services such as Outlook.com, Xbox Live®, OneDrive®, and Office Online, you need to create a free Microsoft account.

If you already have a OneDrive, Xbox Live, or Outlook.com account, use that account to sign in. If you do not have a Microsoft account, you will need to create one to use Windows 10. A Microsoft account gives you a consistent experience across any device you sign into with your Microsoft account. In addition, you get access to Office Online and OneDrive (with free cloud storage), and all your information syncs across all your devices.

To sign up for a Microsoft account, complete the following steps:

1. Open any Web browser, type signup.live.com as the URL, and then click Sign up now.
2. Fill out the form by typing your first and last name. Your user name will be an email address. You can use an existing email address, or you can get a new email address by clicking *Or get a new email address*.
3. Create a password that has at least 8 characters. To create a strong password, use a combination of upper and lowercase letters, at least one number and one other character (such as an asterisk or exclamation point).
4. Fill out the rest of the form, and then click Create account.

Access Sleep and Power Settings

To save battery life on your laptop, tablet, or smartphone, or for more energy efficiency, Windows will go to *sleep* after a pre-determined period of inactivity. Sleep is a power-saving state that puts your work and settings in memory and draws a small amount of power that allows your computer to resume full-power operation quickly.

To manage the Sleep settings, complete the following steps:

1. Click the Start icon or press the Windows key to open the Start menu.
2. Click Settings on the Start menu, click System, and then click Power & sleep.
3. Select the desired level of inactivity from either of the following options:
   - Screen: to determine when the Screen turns off on battery power or when plugged in
   - Sleep: to determine when the PC goes to sleep on battery power or when plugged in

Eventually, you will want to shut down Windows and turn off your computer. To do so, from the Start menu, click Power. Selecting Restart will turn off and immediately restart Windows. This is a "warm boot." To power down completely, click Power and then select Shut down.

Explore the Windows 10 Start Menu

After signing in, you should see the same screen configuration no matter what Windows 10 device you are using, because your Microsoft account stores your preferences and settings for your Start menu on the Internet. For instance, your laptop computer, your home computer, and even your Windows smartphone should look the same.

Initially, your computer displays the primary working area: the *desktop*. If you were used to working on a system running Windows 8, you will notice that there is not a Start screen and a desktop. Instead, the desktop is the primary working area of Windows 10, and the Windows 10 *Start menu* provides the main access to all programs and features on your computer.

There are three different ways to accomplish tasks in Windows 10:

- Use a mouse
- Touch the screen (on touch-enabled devices)
- Use keystrokes

The method you use depends on the type of device you are using and, largely, on your personal preferences. In this text, we will focus mainly on mouse and keystroke commands. If you are using a touch-screen device, you should refer to the new touch gestures shown in Figure 1.2. For instance, when an instruction in this text says to click a screen element, you would tap the screen element with your finger on a touch-screen device.

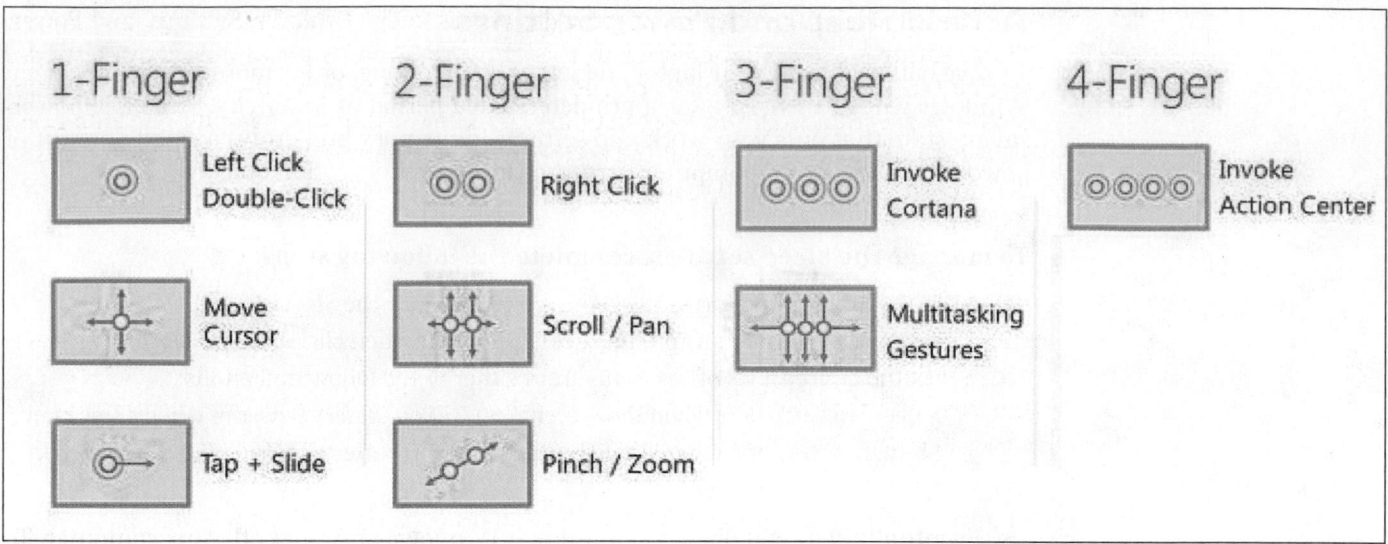

FIGURE 1.2 Touch Gestures in Windows 10

Precision Touchpad Overview, Windows 10 Overview Slideshow, PowerPoint Online

Open the Start menu by clicking the Start icon in the bottom left corner of the desktop or by pressing the Windows key on the keyboard. The Start menu, as shown in Figure 1.3, has two areas. The right side has the same look as the metro (or modern) view first introduced in Windows 8 with block icons, called **tiles**. Tiles represent installed programs and Windows apps (such as Weather, Skype, and Money). Tiles can also represent files, folders, or other items related to your computer. If there are more tiles on the Start menu than displayed, use the scroll bar on the right. You can launch Windows 10 apps and programs by clicking or tapping a tile on the Start menu.

> **TIP: STICKY NOTE APP**
> Sticky Notes is a useful Windows accessory application. Use Sticky Notes as you would a paper sticky note, recording to-do lists, phone numbers, or anything else. Your notes display on the desktop. Sticky Notes is found in the Windows Accessories folder in All apps. Click New Note to add another note, click Delete Note to delete a note, and right-click a note to change the color.

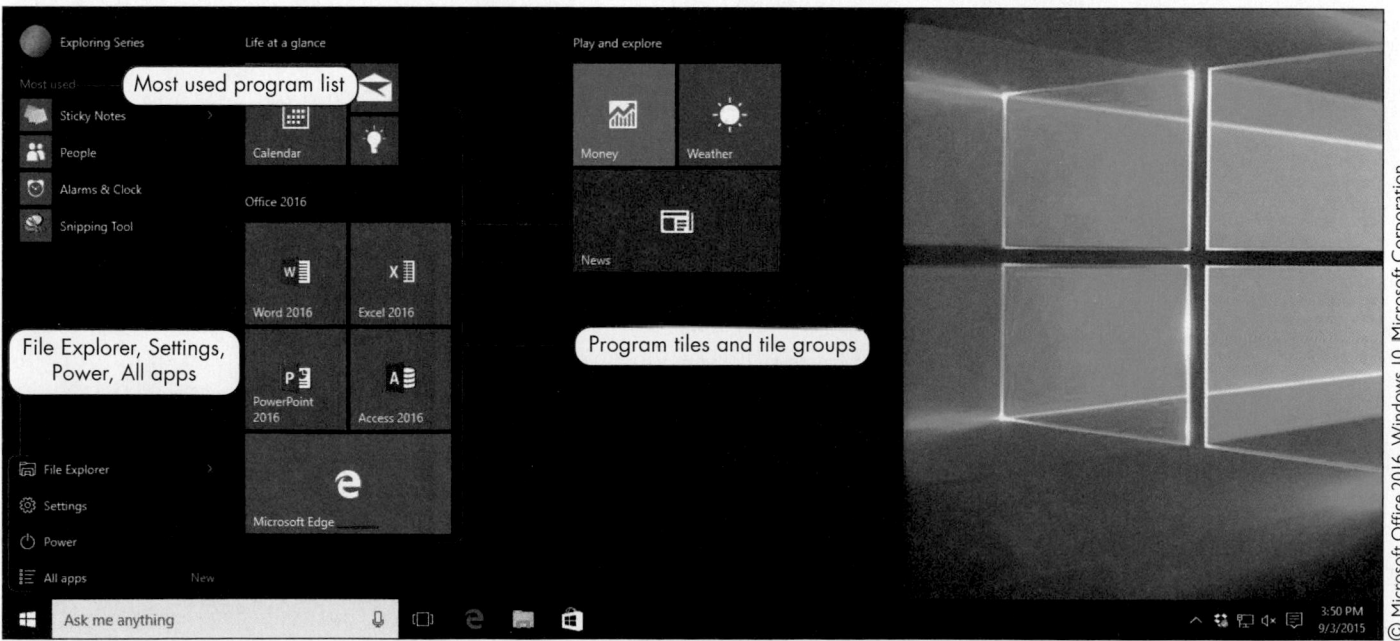

FIGURE 1.3 Windows 10 Start Menu

© Microsoft Office 2016, Windows 10, Microsoft Corporation

The left side of the Start menu provides access to File Explorer, Settings, and Power. These features are discussed later in this chapter. There is also a separate *Most used* section that contains a list of apps and programs you use every day. However, you can remove a program from the Most used list by right-clicking the icon and selecting *Don't show in this list*. Click *All apps* at the bottom of the left pane, and the left pane changes to display a list of all installed apps and programs on your computer, in alphabetical order.

Configure the Start Menu

STEP 1 ➤➤ You may want to customize the Start menu so you can use it most efficiently. It is easy to add and remove, resize, and move application tiles on the Start menu, as well as to group tiles, and name the groups. You can also display tiles to access folders or other areas of the computer that you use frequently. You **pin**, or add, a tile to the Start menu to make it easier to access the application.

To pin an application to the Start menu, complete the following steps:

1. Display the Start menu by clicking the Start icon or by pressing the Windows key on your keyboard.
2. Click All apps and find the application that you want to pin to the Start menu.
3. Right-click the app name and select Pin to Start. (You may also choose Pin to taskbar. The taskbar is discussed later in this chapter.)

A tile for the app displays on the Start menu. The new tile is added to the very end of your app tiles, so you may have to scroll down to find the tile you added. Once on the Start menu, the size of a tile can be modified.

To resize a tile on the Start menu, complete the following steps:

1. Right-click the tile and point to Resize.
2. Select from the list of available sizes: Small, Medium, Wide, or Large.

You may also have some tiles that you do not want on the Start menu. These might be programs or applications that appear on the Start menu by default, or tiles you added but now want to remove. Removing (or unpinning) an application is just as easy as adding one.

To unpin an application from the Start menu, complete the following steps:

1. Right-click the tile you want to remove from the Start menu.
2. Click Unpin from Start.

Tiles on the Start menu are organized in groups separated by a small amount of dividing space, as shown in Figure 1.3. You can easily move tiles from one group to another by clicking a tile and dragging it into another group. You can reorder groups by clicking the group name and dragging the group to its new location. You can also give any group of tiles a meaningful name.

To create a new group of tiles, complete the following steps:

1. Click and drag the first tile for the new group to the space above or below an existing tile group. An empty bar displays, indicating where the new group will be located.
2. Release the mouse button, and the tile will now be in its own new group.

Explore the Taskbar

At the bottom of the Windows desktop is the *taskbar*. The taskbar is the horizontal bar that displays open application icons, the *Notification area*, the *search box*, and any pinned apps or programs. The Notification area, at the far right of the taskbar, includes the clock and a group of icons that relate to a status of a setting or program. The search box, located on the left side of the taskbar, can be used to search your computer for programs, folders and files saved on your computer, as well as to get results from the Web. The search box is also home to Cortana, the personal digital assistant. Cortana is discussed later in this chapter.

Every open program has a corresponding icon on the taskbar. You can move from one program to another by clicking the program's icon on the taskbar. Figure 1.4 shows two windows open on the desktop, with corresponding taskbar program icons. A blue line displays under the open program icons. Although several windows can be open at one time, only one is active. The active program icon is shaded with a lighter blue background. When you right-click a program icon, you open the *Jump List* (see Figure 1.4). A Jump List is a list of program-specific shortcuts to recently opened files, the program name, an option to pin or unpin an item, and a Close windows option.

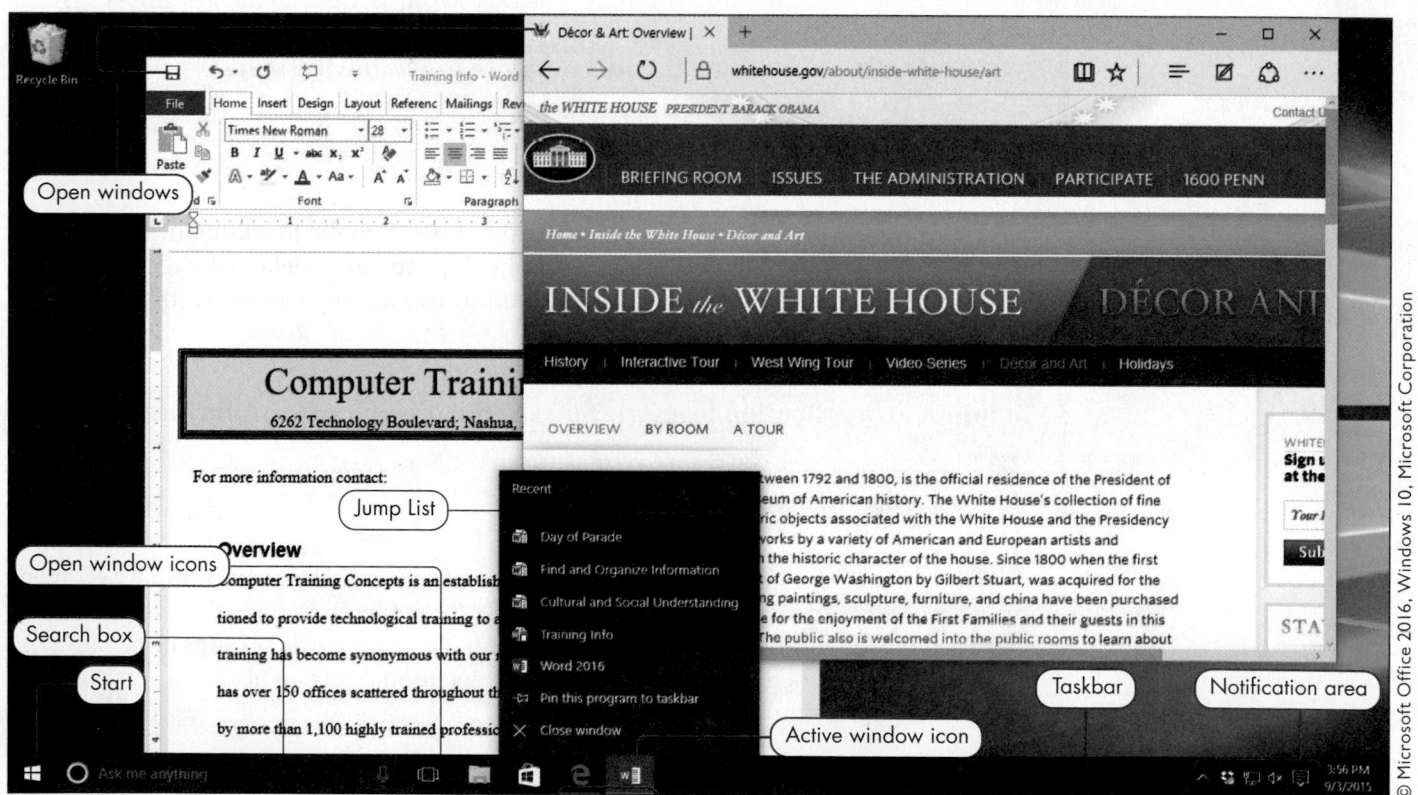

FIGURE 1.4 Desktop with Open Windows

Similar to pinning an app or program to the Start menu, you can place, or pin, icons of frequently used programs or websites on the taskbar for faster access. When you pin a program or website to the taskbar, its associated icon becomes a permanent part of the taskbar. You can then open the program or website by clicking its icon.

To pin to the taskbar a program that is not already open, complete the following steps:

1. Locate the program in All apps.
2. Right-click the program name.
3. Click Pin to taskbar.

To pin to the taskbar a program that is already open, complete the following steps:

1. Right-click the program icon on the taskbar.
2. Click Pin this program to taskbar.

You will find the Notification area (refer to Figure 1.4) on the right side of the taskbar. This area contains system icons, including Clock, Volume, OneDrive, and Action Center. The Notification area and what icons display in the Notification area are discussed later in this chapter.

Identify Desktop Components

The desktop in Windows 10 looks very much like the desktop in previous versions of Windows. On the desktop, *icons* represent links to programs, files, folders, or other items related to your computer (see Figure 1.5). Although the Start menu is meant to provide quick access to programs, files and folders you use most often, you can easily add and remove icons so that the desktop includes items that are important to you or that you access often.

The Recycle Bin icon displays by default on the Windows 10 desktop. The **Recycle Bin** is temporary storage for deleted files from the computer's hard drive or OneDrive. Files in the Recycle Bin are not permanently erased from the system until you right-click the Recycle Bin icon and select Empty Recycle Bin. Therefore, if you delete a file by mistake, it can be restored. The exception is if the file was from an external storage device such as a flash drive. When you delete files from an external storage device, they are permanently deleted.

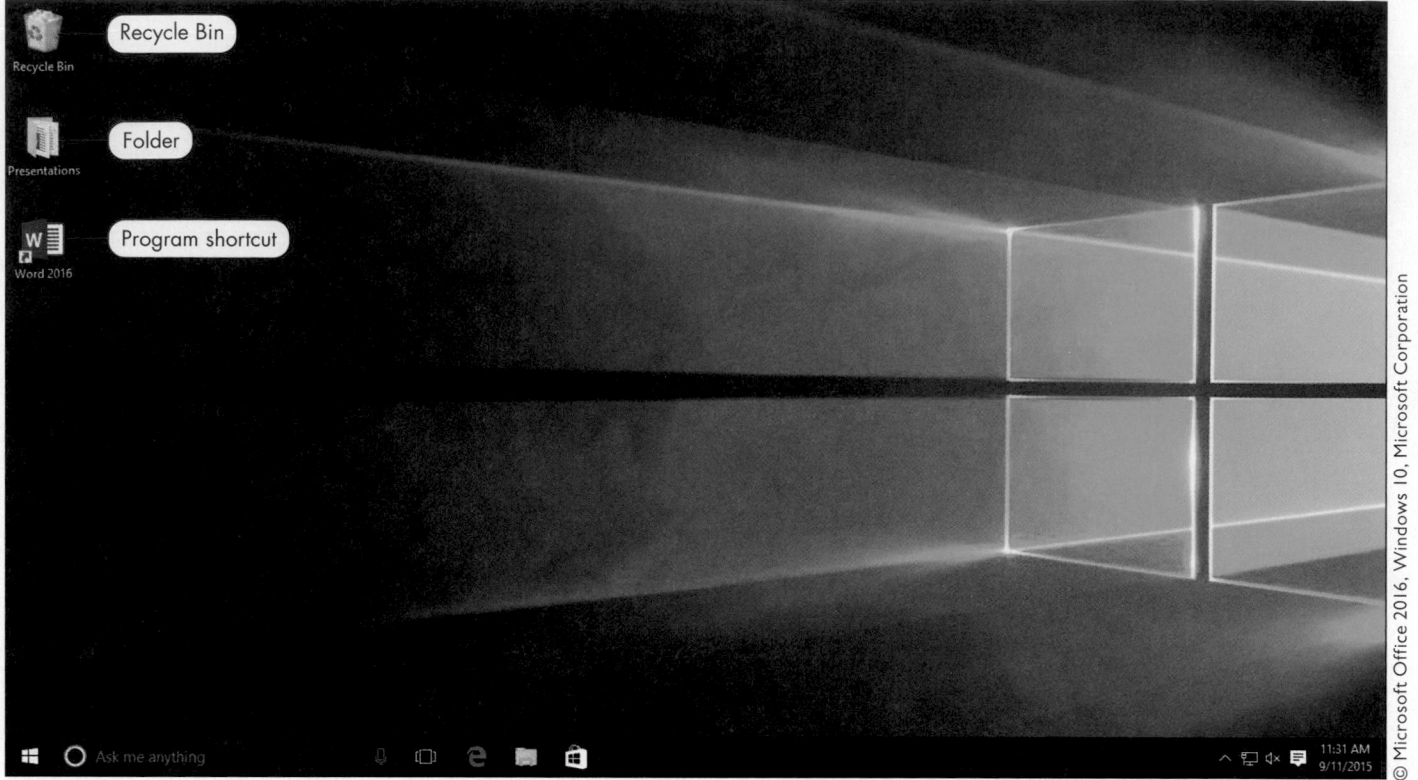

FIGURE 1.5 Desktop Components

Some icons that have a small arrow in the bottom-left corner are *shortcuts* that provide a link to programs. All other icons on the desktop are added when you save a file to the desktop. If you save files to the desktop, you should organize them in desktop folders so you can easily find related files.

To add a program or folder shortcut icon to the desktop, complete the following steps:

1. Right-click an empty area of the desktop, point to New, and then click Shortcut.
2. Click Browse and navigate to the folder that contains the program for which you wish to create a shortcut.
3. Click the program file and click OK.
4. Click Next. Type a name for the shortcut in the box
5. Click Finish to place the shortcut icon on your desktop.

You can also add a folder directly to the desktop by right-clicking an empty area of the desktop, pointing to New, and then selecting Folder. Or, if there is an existing folder you want to add to the desktop, open File Explorer, right-click the folder, choose Send to, and then select Desktop (create shortcut) from the menu.

To delete or rename icons on the desktop, complete one of the following steps:

- Right-click the icon you want to delete, and click Delete. Deleting a program shortcut icon does not remove or uninstall the program. You just remove the desktop shortcut to the program.
- Right-click the icon you want to rename, and click Rename. Type the new name and press Enter.

Customize the Desktop

For a little variety, you can customize the desktop with a different background color or theme. You can even include a slide show of favorite photos to display when your computer is idle. Customizing the desktop can be fun and creative. Windows 10 provides a wide selection of background and color choices.

The Personalization category in Settings gives you options to change the desktop background, lock screen image, or to select a different theme.

Managing and Using the Desktop and Components

The main purpose of the Start menu is to provide access to programs and apps. To launch an app or program from the Start menu, click the app tile. **Windows apps**, such as Weather, Sports, or Money, are programs that are displayed full screen without borders or many controls. This simpler design provides a viewing advantage on devices with smaller screens such as smartphones and tablets. Controls and settings are contained on app bars, such as the Address bar, which appear at the top or bottom of the opened app. Installed programs such as Microsoft Word or Google Chrome are applications that are more complex. They generally have multiple features and can perform multiple tasks.

Using the taskbar, you can move among open windows with ease, but Windows provides additional methods to switch easily between open programs and files. Windows makes it easy to move, resize, and close windows, as well as to arrange windows automatically, even snapping them quickly to the desktop borders.

Use Task View

STEP 2 ›› It is quite possible that you will have more than one application or program window open at any time, and may need to quickly switch between the various open windows or want to see two or more open windows at the same time. **Task View** allows you to view all the tasks you are working on in one glance (see Figure 1.6). For example, you might have Microsoft Word, PowerPoint, and Edge all open because you are creating a presentation from your latest research paper and are doing some extra Internet research. To see all three windows at once, click the Task View icon next to the search box in the taskbar, and thumbnail previews of all open applications display. Click on any of the thumbnails to switch to that application.

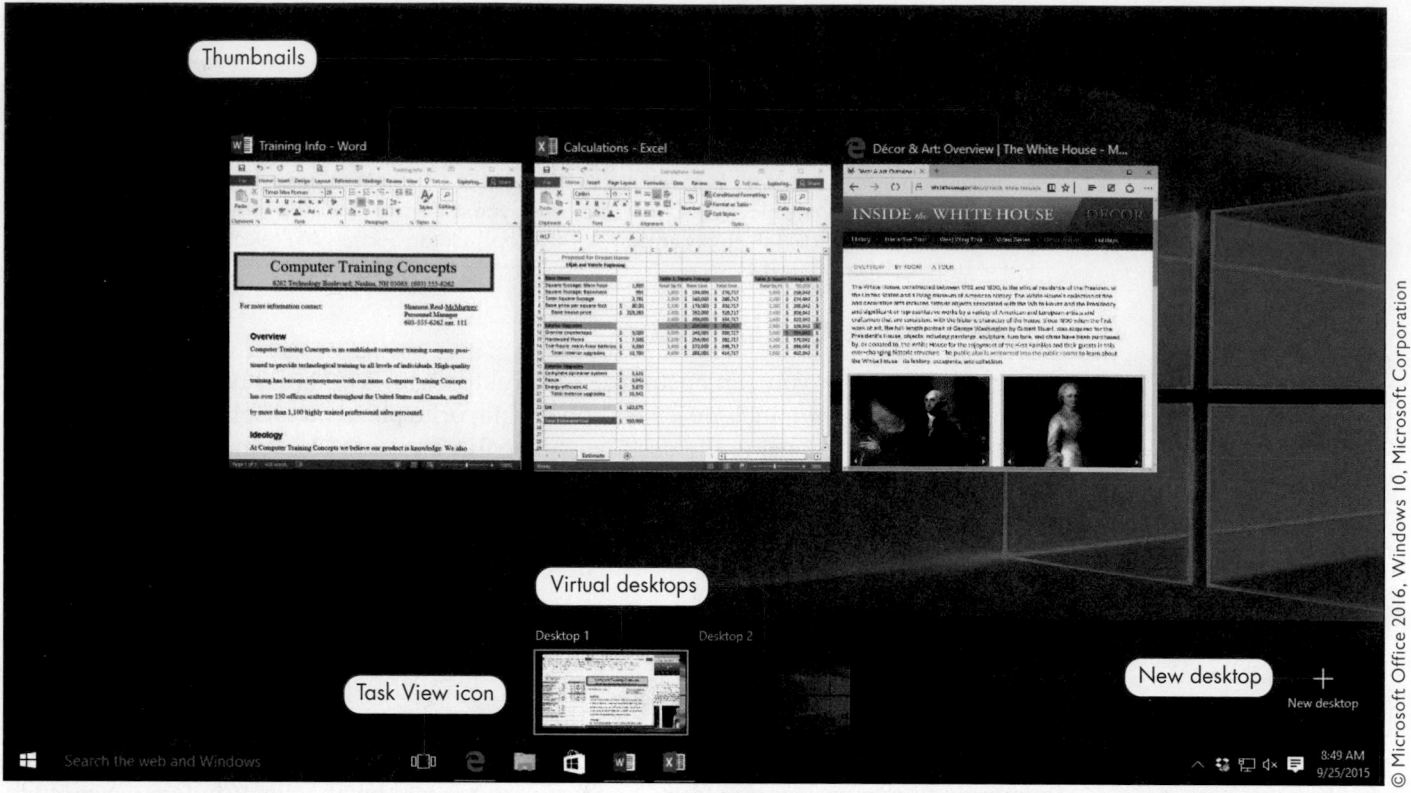

FIGURE 1.6 Task View

TIP: ALT+TAB
You can use the keyboard to cycle through all open windows. Press and hold Alt on the keyboard and repeatedly press Tab. Release Alt when the window that you want to display is selected.

Create a Virtual Desktop

Task View also enables you to create **_virtual desktops_** (refer to Figure 1.6). A virtual desktop is a way to organize and access groups of windows for different purposes. For example, when you do your schoolwork, you might have your school's learning management system (such as Blackboard or Desire to Learn), your school's email account, and MyITLab open. When you are not working on schoolwork, you might have several social media accounts open, perhaps a video game, and maybe Netflix or YouTube running. Using Task View, you can group these applications into virtual desktops, so that you can quickly switch between your "school" desktop and your "entertainment" desktop.

To create a new virtual desktop and move applications between desktops, complete the following steps:

1. Click Task View on the taskbar, and click New desktop in the lower right corner of your screen. You will then see a thumbnail preview of the new desktop (Desktop 2) alongside the current desktop (in this case, Desktop 1). Once the new desktop is created, you will need to populate it with applications by moving applications from one desktop to another.
2. Click Desktop 1, and then click Task View.
3. Drag a thumbnail of the application you want to move from Desktop 1 to Desktop 2. Alternatively, right-click a thumbnail preview of any open application in Desktop 1, point to Move to, and either select an existing virtual desktop or create a new desktop.
4. Repeat as needed to create a new virtual desktop.

To delete a virtual desktop, click Task View, point to the top right corner of the desktop thumbnail you want to delete, and click the Close button.

Identify Window Components

When you launch a folder, file, or application, the results are displayed in a window. All windows share common elements, including a title bar and controls, as shown in Figure 1.7. Although each window's contents vary, those common elements make it easy for you to manage windows so that you make the best use of your time and computer resources.

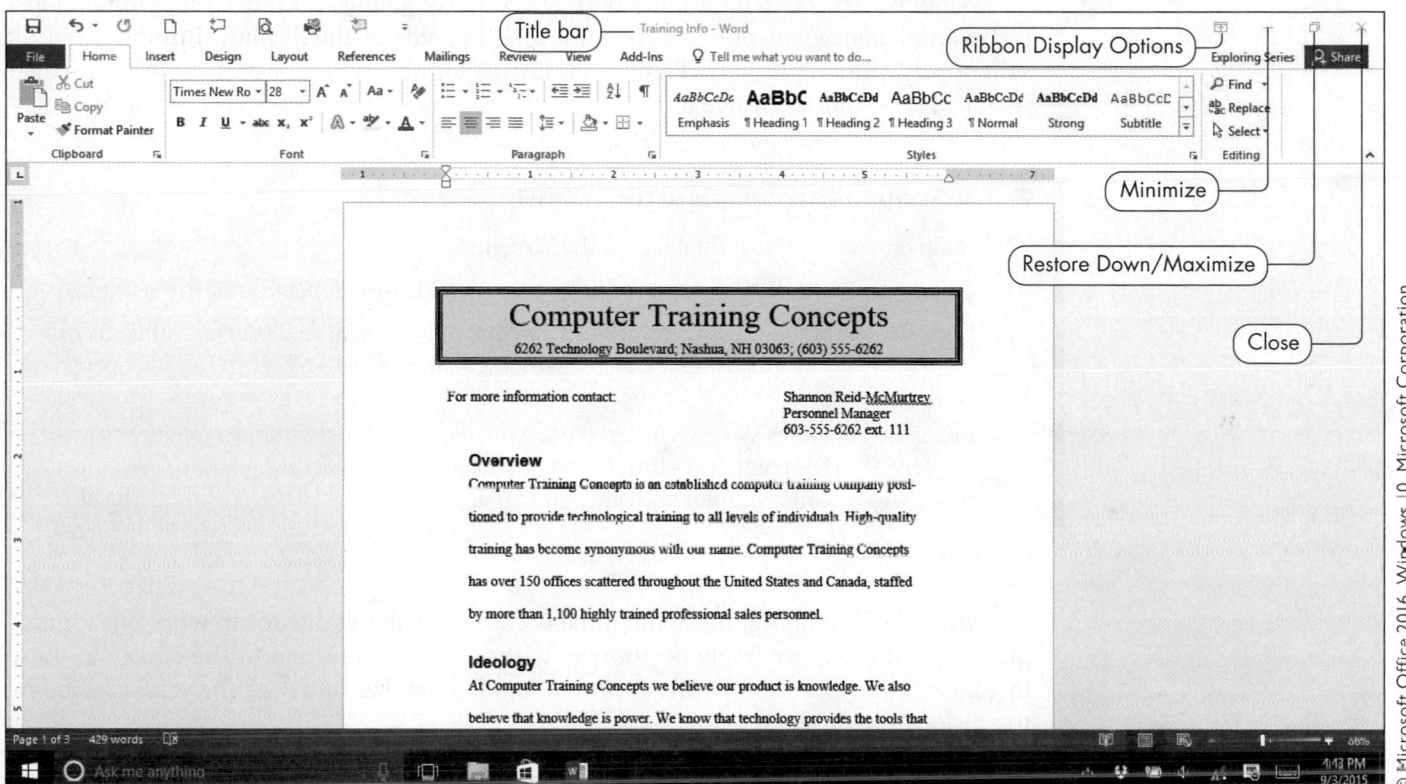

FIGURE 1.7 Common Window Components

The *title bar* is the long bar at the top of each window. The title bar always displays the name of the file and program displayed in the open window. Controls are found on the right side of the title bar. These controls enable you to manage the Ribbon display as well as to minimize, maximize (or restore down), or close any open window.

The Ribbon Display Options control enables you to hide the Ribbon, show only the Ribbon tabs, or to show the Ribbon tabs and commands all the time.

The Minimize control, represented by a horizontal line, when clicked hides a window from view, but does not close it. You can click on the taskbar icon to view the window again.

The next control shares two functions, depending on the current size of the window. When a window is full size, Restore Down, represented by two overlapping boxes, displays. When a window is open, but less than full size, Maximize, represented by a small box, displays. Clicking Restore Down returns a window to the size it was before the window was maximized; clicking Maximize brings a window to full size. You can also maximize or restore down a window by double-clicking the title bar of the open window.

The Close control, represented by an X, when clicked closes a window. When you close a window, you remove the file or program from the computer's random access memory (RAM). RAM is temporary (or volatile) storage, meaning files stored in RAM are not permanently saved. To save a file so you can access it later, the file must be saved to a permanent storage device such as the computer's hard drive or a flash drive, or to

OneDrive or other Web-based storage. If you have not saved a file, or any changes that you have made to a saved file that you are closing, Windows 10 will prompt you to save it.

Snap, Move, and Resize Windows

STEP 3 ▶▶ Multitasking involves working with multiple open windows at the same time, and this often requires moving or resizing windows so you can see each window. If multiple windows are open, you will need to know how to switch between windows and how to rearrange them. Windows 7 introduced "snapping" windows—displaying two windows side by side by snapping them to the left and right sides of the screen.

Windows 10 goes a bit further with Snap Assist, giving you more snapping options. For example, once you snap one window to either side of the display, thumbnails of all other open windows display (Figure 1.8) giving you the option of easily selecting which window(s) to snap alongside it.

> **To use Snap Assist, complete the following steps:**
>
> 1. Snap one window to either side of the screen.
>
>   Thumbnails of all other open windows display on the open portion of the screen.
>
> 2. Click the thumbnail you want to snap, or click in a blank area if you do not want to snap any of the choices. The selected window will snap into place, filling the open screen area.
>
> 3. Press the Windows key plus an arrow key once windows are snapped to either side of the screen to snap windows into corners. You can snap two, three, or four windows using this technique. Alternatively, you can drag a window to the corner of the screen.

Instead of snapping, there might be occasions when you want to work with multiple files that are more freely positioned, without snapping them to the edges. In these instances, you can restore down a window, modify the size, and drag the smaller window to any location on the screen.

> **To move or resize a window, you must first click Restore Down and then complete one of the following steps:**
>
> - Click and drag the title bar to move a window.
> - Point to the border of a window you want to resize, until the pointer becomes a double-headed arrow. Click and drag the edge of a window to make the window larger or smaller. If the pointer is on a corner of the window, forming a diagonal double-headed arrow, the height and width of the window will resize at the same time.

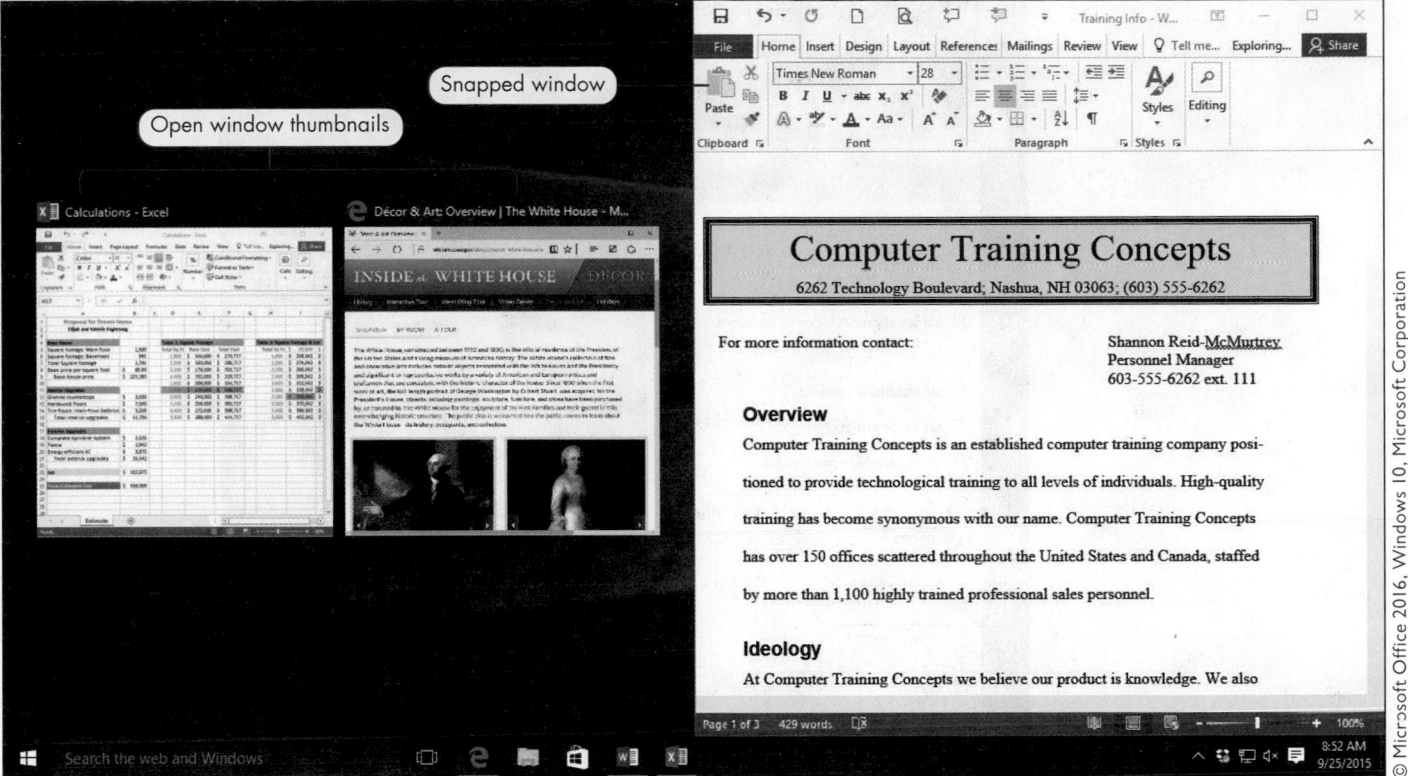

Labels on figure:
- Open window thumbnails
- Snapped window

FIGURE 1.8 Snap Assist

You might prefer to arrange your windows automatically in a cascading fashion, vertically stacked, or next to each other. In that case, right-click an empty part of the taskbar. Then, click Cascade windows, Show windows stacked, or Show windows side by side.

Using Windows 10 Search Features

The new design of Windows 10 makes it easy to organize and find the most used programs, files and folders on either the Start menu, taskbar, or desktop. However, there will always be situations that require you to find a feature or file that you do not often use, and are not certain of its location, or you may need to find information on the Web. In those cases, you will need to use Windows 10 search features.

Use the Search Box

STEP 4 ⟩⟩ To the right of the Start button is the search box. You can use this search feature to search the Web and to search your "stuff" in Windows. When you begin typing into the search box, suggested results begin to display with a list of applications, folders, and documents, as well as Web resources that relate to the search terms you have entered (see Figure 1.9).

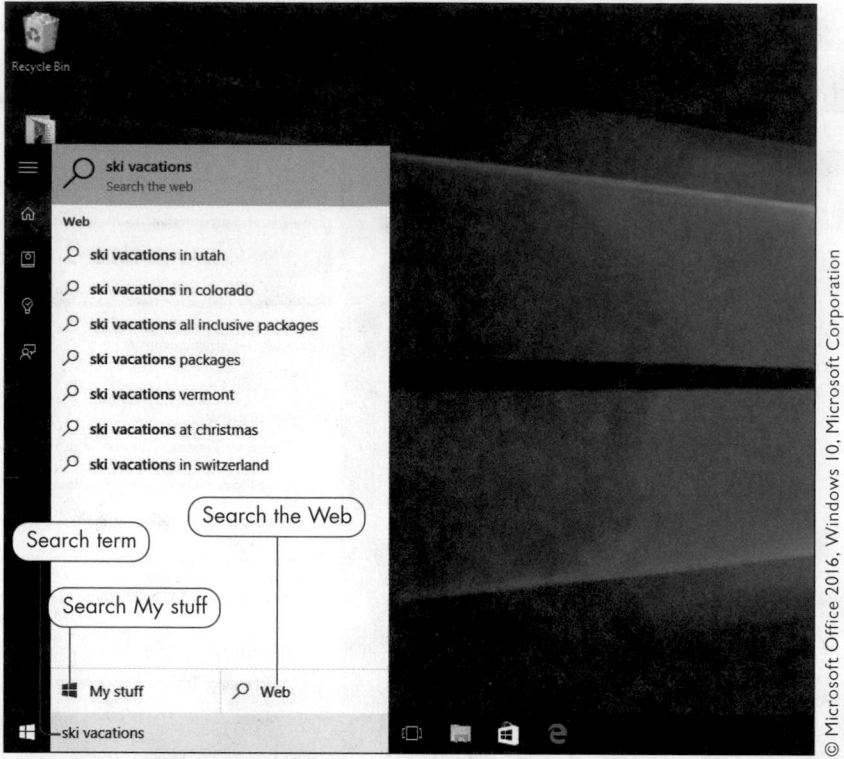

FIGURE 1.9 The Search Box

Use Cortana

If you have logged into Windows with your Microsoft account, you can use **Cortana**, Microsoft's personal assistant. Cortana is integrated into the search box and can assist you with reminders, calendar tasks, and can even tell jokes. You must initiate Cortana first, by giving her your name, and allowing her access to your information. Then, if your PC is equipped with a microphone, you begin talking to Cortana by saying, "Hey, Cortana." If no microphone is available, you can type all your questions.

Get Help

STEP 5 ❯❯ No longer do you have to go to a separate location on your computer, or use a different app, to get help. Cortana and the search box are your primary resources for help and support for Windows and other Microsoft related questions. Just type into the search box, or ask Cortana, and whether the answer is found in a file, an app, on the Web, or somewhere else, a list of possible results will display. Search results may also display how-to information and videos from Microsoft. You can even type the name of an app to open it right away. Finally, Cortana can help you with routine tasks such as turning on Airplane mode, just ask her!

Manage the Cortana Notebook and Settings

The more you use Cortana, the more she adapts to your personal needs and routines. When you initiate Cortana, you agree to let her collect and use some personal information that she has obtained from data on your PC (such as your location, contacts, info from email, browser history, search history, and calendar details). Once you set up Cortana, your data and information is managed in the Notebook. You can modify what Cortana remembers (or turn Cortana off altogether) in the Notebook. The Notebook contains categories that have been added by default, such as Eat & Drink, Events, Finance, and Getting around (see Figure 1.10).

To view or modify what is in the Notebook, complete the following steps:

1. Click the search box, and then click Notebook from the menu on the left.
2. Click any category to change a setting or add more information to the Notebook.

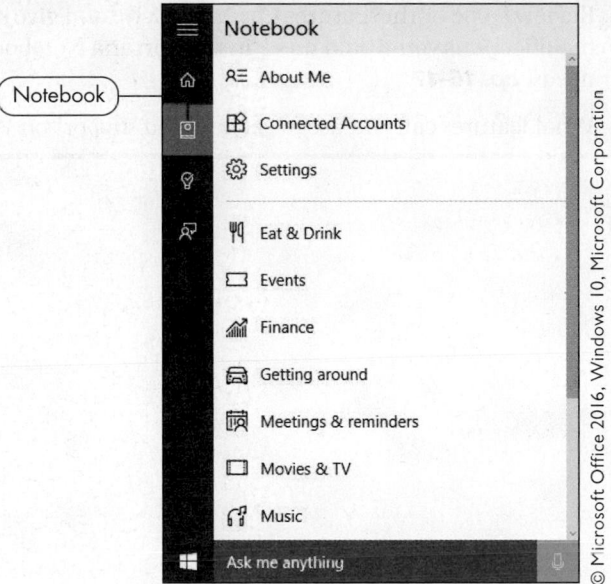

FIGURE 1.10 Modifying the Cortana Notebook

Once you have modified the settings, and you launch Cortana, the Home page shows a daily glance that reflects your personal settings such as the weather in your location, the scores of your favorite sports teams, your calendar events, and even how much time it will take to get to work or school based on current traffic.

You can modify other items such as Reminders, Places, and Music directly from the Cortana menu (see Figure 1.11).

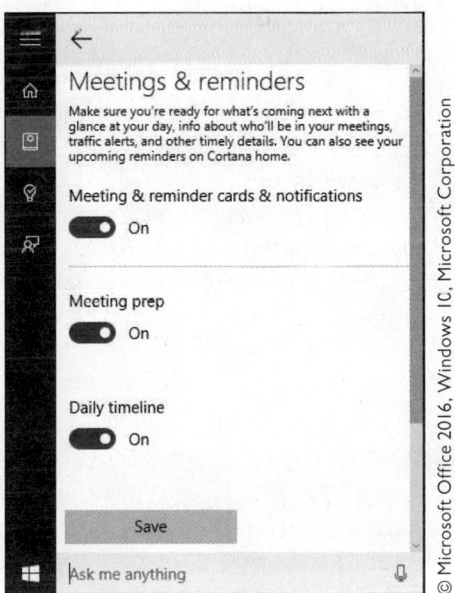

FIGURE 1.11 Cortana Notebook Menu Item

Quick Concepts ✓

1. Describe the features on the Start menu, and explain the various ways in which the Start menu can be customized. *pp. 5–8*

2. Explain what a virtual desktop is, and give an example of how you would use virtual desktops for school, work, or entertainment. *p. 12*

3. Review some of the features Cortana offers, and give some specific examples of modifications you would make in the Cortana Notebook to reflect your personal needs. *pp. 16–17*

4. What features can you use to get help and support on Windows 10? *p. 16*

Hands-On Exercise

Watch the Video
for This Hands-On
Exercise!

MyITLab®
Topic-Based
Training

Skills covered: Pin an App to Start Menu • Create Start Menu Group • Rename Start Menu Group • Move Tile • Resize Tile • Pin an App to the Taskbar • Create Virtual Desktop • Minimize, Close, Restore Down, Maximize • Snap Windows • Search Using Cortana • Manage Cortana Settings • Get Help

1 Windows 10 Fundamentals

Tomorrow, you will meet with the Cedar Grove class to present an introduction to Windows 10. You plan to lead the students through a few basics of working with the operating system, including managing the Start menu and navigating among different open windows. Above all, you want to keep it simple so that you encourage class enthusiasm.

STEP 1 ›› CONFIGURE THE START MENU AND EXPLORE THE TASKBAR

You want to emphasize the importance of the Start menu as the location starting point for all Windows 10 apps and programs. Students will practice launching, managing, and closing Windows 10 apps and programs. Students will modify the Start menu by creating a new group and moving a tile into the group. Lastly, students will add program icons to the taskbar. Refer to Figure 1.12 as you complete Step 1.

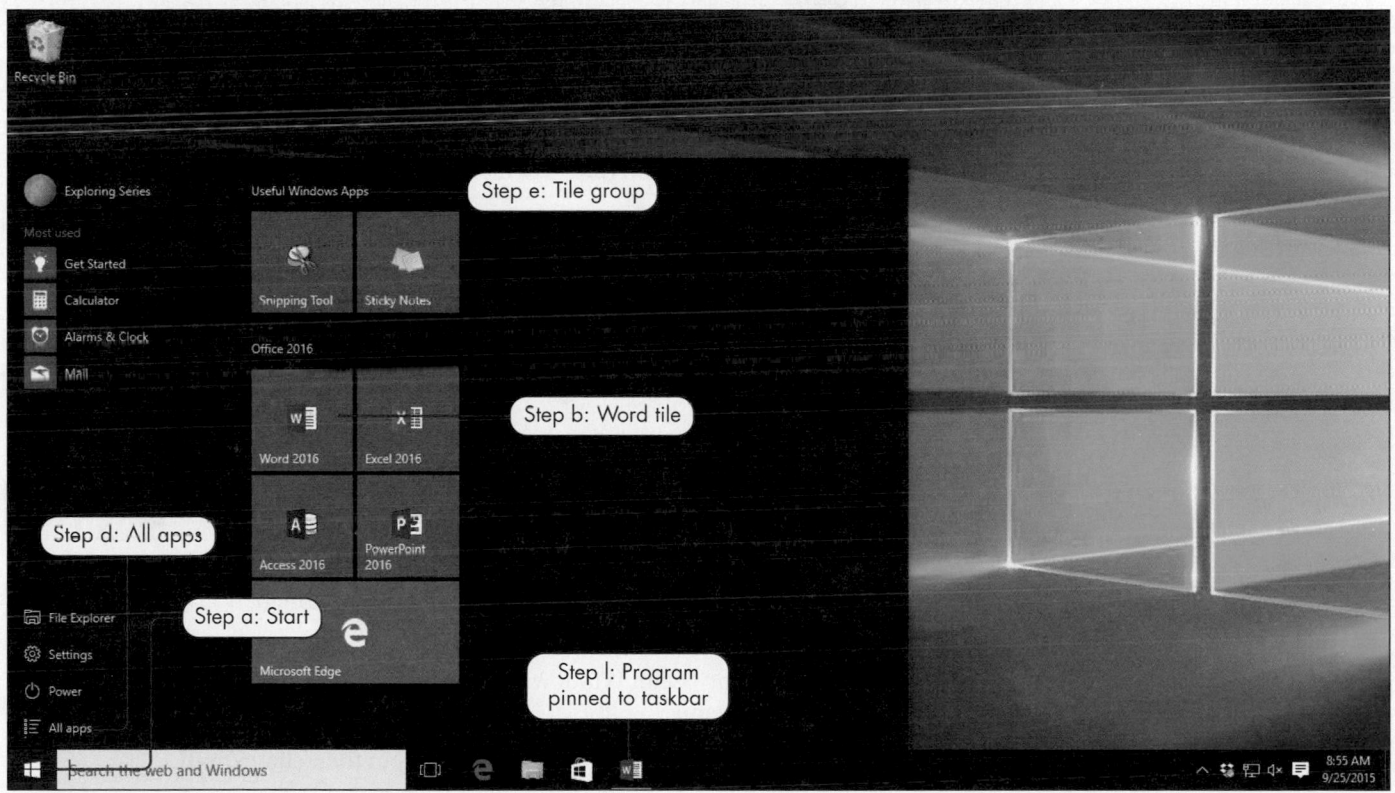

FIGURE 1.12 Customizing the Start Menu and Taskbar

    a. Click **Start** on the taskbar (or alternatively, press the Windows key on the keyboard).

       The Start menu displays.

    b. Click **Word 2016** on the Start menu, and click **Blank document**.

c. Click **File**, select **Save As**, and then click **Browse.** Navigate to the location of your homework files. Click in the **File name box** and type **win01h1Windows10_LastFirst**, replacing LastFirst with your own last name and first name in the File name box. Click **Save** to save the document.

When you save files, use your last and first names. For example, as the Windows 10 author, I would name my document "win01h1Windows10_PoatsyMaryAnne."

You will capture screenshots of your progress in this exercise and paste them into this document to submit to your instructor.

d. Click the **Start menu**, click **All apps**, and then scroll down to locate the Windows Accessories folder. Click the **arrow** to display the contents of the Windows Accessories folder, and then locate Snipping Tool. Right-click **Snipping Tool**, and select **Pin to Start**.

The Snipping Tool tile displays on the Start menu. You will use the Snipping Tool in a later exercise.

e. Point in the blank space just above the Snipping Tool tile and click to open a name box. Type **Useful Windows Apps**, and press **Enter**.

You have created a new group on the Start menu that includes the Snipping Tool.

f. Click **All apps**, open the Windows Accessories folder, right-click **Sticky Notes** and select **Pin to Start**.

The Sticky Notes tile is added to the Start menu.

g. Drag the Sticky Notes tile into the Useful Windows Apps group you just created.

The new group has two tiles.

h. Drag the **title bar** of the Useful Windows Apps group so that the new group is at the top left corner of the Start menu tiles section.

You have repositioned the Useful Windows Apps group to a place that is more easily accessible on the Start menu.

i. Right-click the **Snipping Tool tile**, point to **Resize**, and then click **Small**.

You have resized the Snipping Tool tile so that it is smaller.

j. Right-click the **Snipping Tool tile** again, point to **Resize**, and then click **Medium**.

You realize that you like the larger tile, so you resized it back to the larger size.

k. Keep the Start menu open, press **PrtSc** on your keyboard, click **Word** on the taskbar, and then press **Ctrl+V** on your keyboard. Click **Save** on the Quick Access Toolbar in the upper left corner of the Word window.

You have captured an image of your screen and pasted it into a Word document.

l. Right-click **Word** on the taskbar, and click **Pin this program to taskbar**.

Right-clicking an icon on the taskbar opens the Jump List and the option to pin the program to the taskbar.

m. Display the Word Jump List again, press **PrtSc**, click the **Word window**, press **Enter** twice, and then press **Ctrl+V**.

n. Save the document.

STEP 2 ›› USE TASK VIEW AND CREATE A VIRTUAL DESKTOP

Not only do you want students to understand the basics of managing apps and windows, but also you know they will enjoy customizing the Start menu. Refer to Figure 1.13 as you complete Step 2.

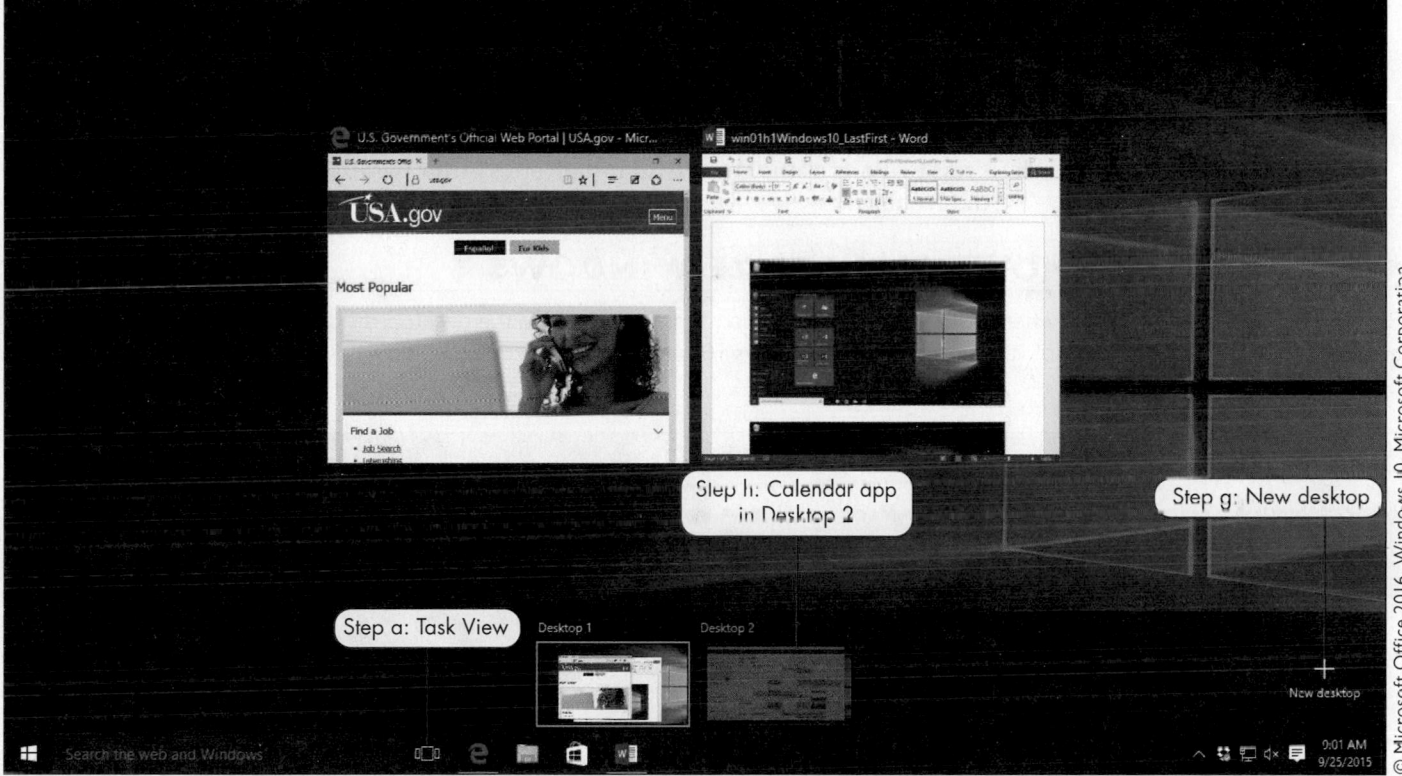

FIGURE 1.13 Task View and Virtual Desktops

a. Click **Minimize** (the horizontal line button) in the top right corner of the Word window. Click **Task View** on the taskbar.

A large thumbnail of the Word window displays.

b. Click the **Word thumbnail** to activate the Word window.

c. Open the **Start menu**, and click **Microsoft Edge** in the Most used section of the Start menu, type **usa.gov** in the Address bar, and then press **Enter**.

You have opened the Microsoft Edge browser application and navigated to usa.gov, the United States government's official Web portal.

> **TROUBLESHOOTING:** Microsoft Edge may not be in the Most used section of the Start menu. It may be on the Start menu or click All apps, and then scroll to locate Microsoft Edge. Alternatively, type Microsoft Edge in Cortana.

d. Click **Start** to return to the Start menu.

e. Click the **Calendar tile** on the Start menu.

You have now launched the Calendar app. The calendar may not have any data in it, unless you have previously entered items in the Calendar app.

> **TROUBLESHOOTING:** If the Calendar app is not on the Start menu, click another Windows 10 app such as Sports, Money, or Weather.

f. Click **Task View**.

The Calendar, Microsoft Edge, and Word thumbnails display on the desktop.

g. Click **New desktop** on the bottom right corner of the desktop.

Two desktop thumbnails display at the bottom of the desktop. Desktop 1 thumbnail displays the three open apps. The Desktop 2 thumbnail is blank.

h. Point to the **Desktop 1 thumbnail** to display thumbnails of the three open apps on Desktop 1. Drag the Calendar thumbnail to Desktop 2.

i. Press **PrtSc**, click the **Word thumbnail**, press **Enter** twice, and then press **Ctrl+V**. Save the document.

STEP 3 ⟫ SNAP, MOVE, AND RESIZE WINDOWS

Because there will be occasions when several windows are open simultaneously on the desktop, students should know how to arrange them. You will show them various ways that Windows 10 can help arrange open windows. Refer to Figure 1.14 as you complete Step 3.

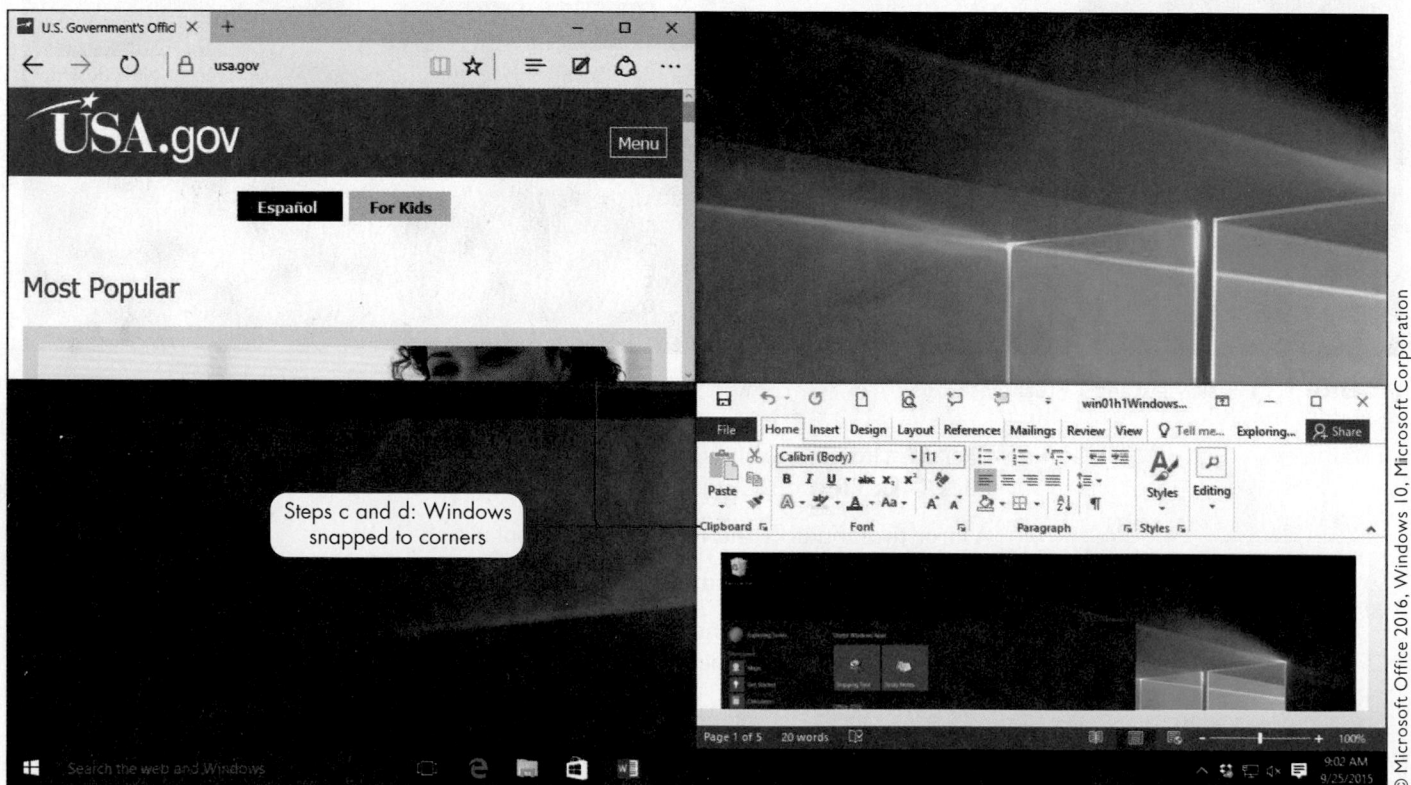

FIGURE 1.14 Arrange Windows Using Snap

a. Click and hold the left mouse button on the **title bar** of the Word window. Drag the window to the far right of the screen until you see an outline of the window display. Release the mouse button.

The Word window snaps to the right side of the display, and a thumbnail of the Microsoft Edge window is in the left side of the display.

b. Click the **Microsoft Edge thumbnail**.

The Microsoft Edge window automatically snaps to the left side of the display.

c. Press and hold the **Windows key**, and then press ⬆ to snap the Microsoft Edge window to the top left corner.

d. Click the **Word window**, press and hold the **Windows key**, and then press ⬇.

The Word window snaps to the bottom right corner.

e. Press **PrtSc**, click **Maximize** on the Word window, press **Enter** twice, and then press **Ctrl+V**. Right-click **Microsoft Edge** on the taskbar, click **Close window**.

f. Save and close the Word file.

Since Cortana is a cool feature of Windows 10, you want students to learn how to use it. You will show the students how to use Cortana to search for a file, schedule a reminder, and even how to tell a joke. Refer to Figure 1.15 as you complete Step 4.

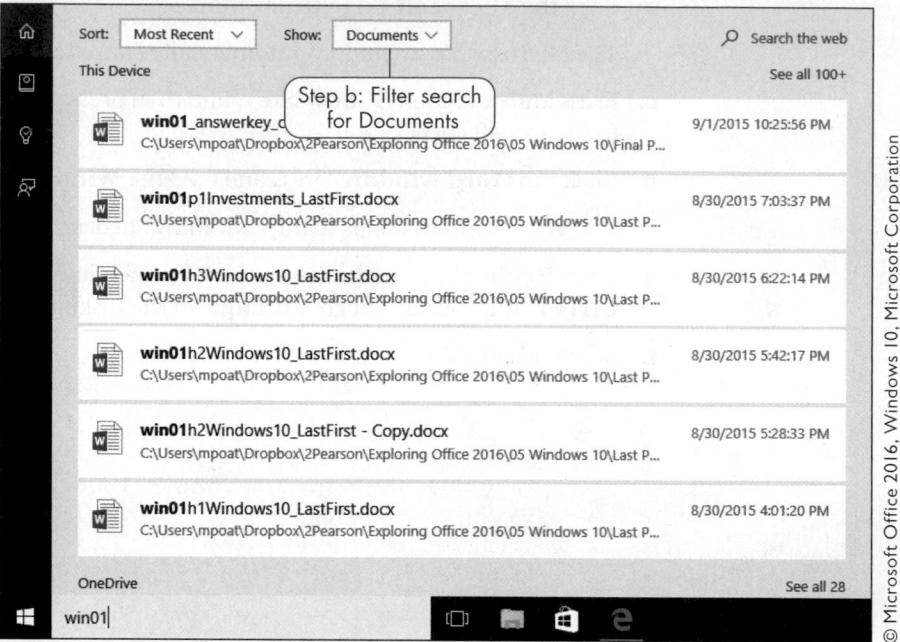

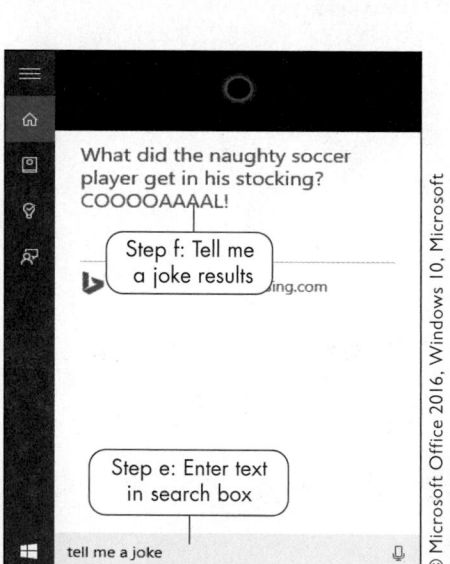

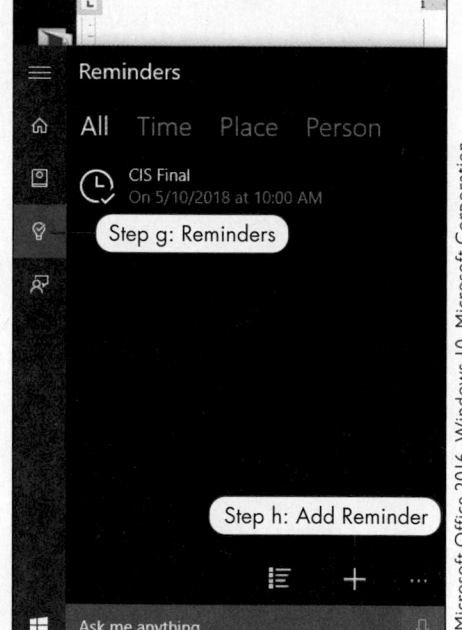

FIGURE 1.15 Cortana

a. Click the **search box**, and type **win01**. Click **My stuff**.

A list of settings, applications, files, and folders that are stored on your PC that contain "win01" in the name displays.

b. Click the **Sort arrow**, select **Most Recent**, click the **Show arrow**, and then select **Documents**.

Filter enables you to narrow the search results to items in a specific category. In this case, you only want to display results that are documents.

c. Press **PrtSc**, and click **win01h1Windows10_LastFirst** (it will show your own last and first names) that displays in the search results to open the document you have created with this Hands-On Exercise.

d. Press **Ctrl+End**, press **Enter** twice, and then press **Ctrl+V**. Save the file and minimize Word.

e. Click the **search box**, type **tell me a joke**, and then press **Enter**.

Cortana will display a response.

> **TROUBLESHOOTING:** You may need to initiate Cortana prior to completing Step e.

f. Press **PrtSc**, click **Word** on the taskbar, press **Enter** twice, and then press **Ctrl+V**. Save the file and minimize Word.

g. Click the **search box**, and then click **Reminders** in the Cortana menu.

Reminders display, listing any reminders you might already have.

h. Click the **plus sign**, click **Remember to** and type **CIS Final**, click **Time** and select **10:00 AM**, click the **check mark**, click **Today** (or it might say Tomorrow depending on the time of day you are completing this exercise), and then select **May 10, 2018**. (Alternatively, you can type the actual date and time of your class final.) Click the **check mark** again. Click **Remind**.

i. Press **PrtSc**, click **Word** on the taskbar, press **Enter** twice, and then press **Ctrl+V**. Save the document and minimize Word.

As students in your class progress to middle and high school, they may have opportunities to use laptops for class work. They also are likely to find themselves in locations where they can connect to the Internet wirelessly. Using that example, you will help the class understand how to search for information on finding and safely connecting to an available wireless network. Refer to Figure 1.16 as you complete Step 5.

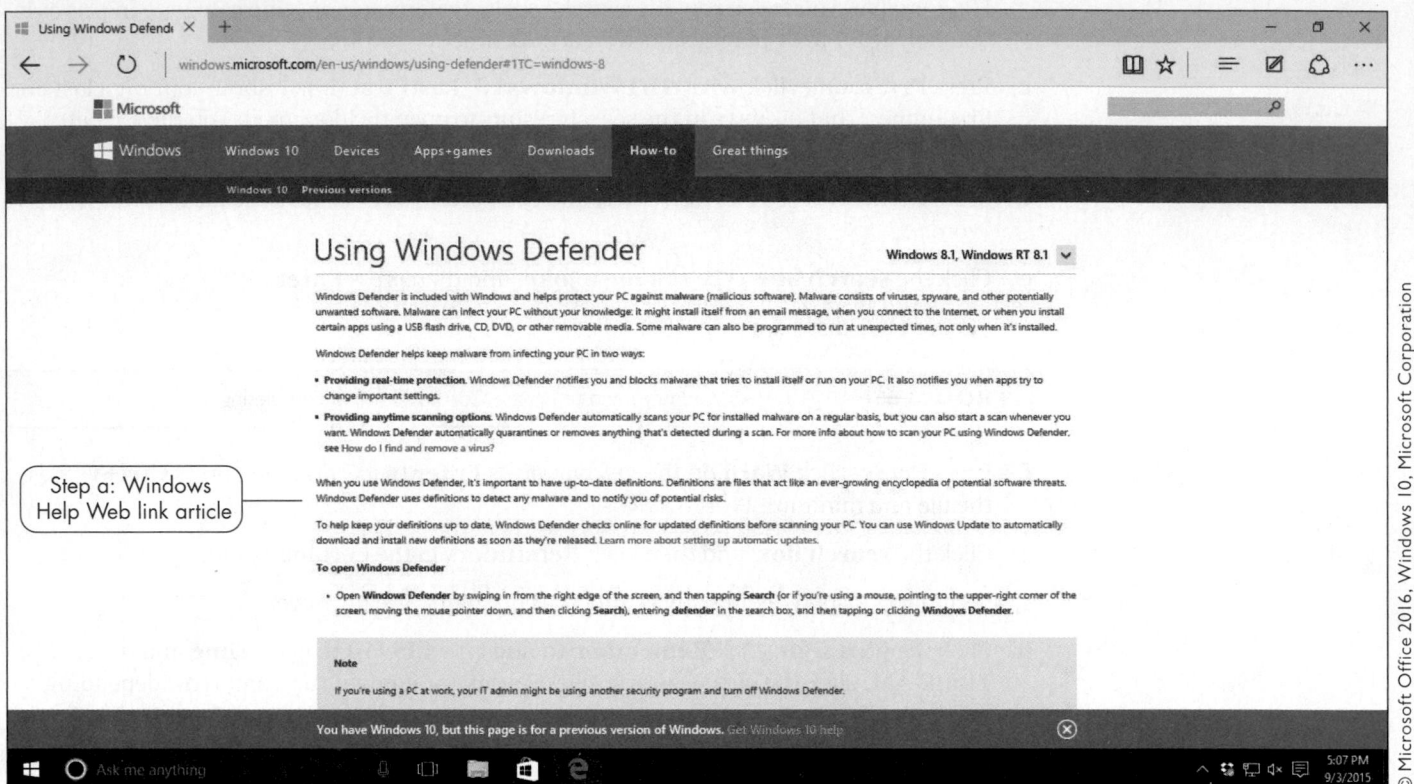

FIGURE 1.16 Windows Help

a. Click the **search box**, and type **Why use Windows Defender?** Press **Enter**. Select the Using Windows Defender – Windows Help Web link, and read the topic.

> **TROUBLESHOOTING:** If the webpage displays with a message, "Hi there - you're looking for Windows 10 info! We put that stuff in a new spot." Find new content for the new Windows by browsing our top categories and trending topics. Click the link, and then click Protect your PC and read the information.

b. Click the **Start menu**, click the **Snipping Tool tile**, click the **New arrow**, and then select **Full-screen Snip**.

The Snipping Tool window displays with an image of your screen.

c. Click **Word** on the taskbar, press **Enter** twice, and then press **Ctrl+V**.

d. Press **Enter**, then, in your own words, type why you should use Windows Defender, and the two ways it helps protect your PC. Save the file. Minimize the Word and Snipping Tool windows.

e. Click the **search box** and type **File History help**. Press **Enter**. At the top of the Bing results, click **Videos**, and click **Restore files or folders using File History – Windows Help** link. Watch the video.

f. Take a full-screen snip of your screen with the video information still displayed, click **Word** on the taskbar, press **Enter** twice, and then press **Ctrl+V**. Save the file.

g. Type **restore files** in the search box, and then click **Restore your files with File History – Control Panel**. Click **Snipping Tool** on the taskbar, click **New**, click the **New arrow**, and then click **Full-screen Snip**. Click **Word** on the taskbar, press **Enter** twice, and then press **Ctrl+V**.

h. Save the document. Keep the document open if you plan to continue with the next Hands-On Exercise. If not, close the document, and exit Word. Close all other windows.

File Management

One of the main functions of Windows is *file management*, which provides an organizational structure to your computer's contents. Windows organizes the drives, folders, and files of your computer in a hierarchical structure. The hard drive is represented as the C: drive and is where most programs and files are permanently stored. A unique letter (D, E, F, and so on) identifies other storage devices, such as a DVD drive, external hard drive, or flash drive, when they are connected to the computer.

In this section, you will learn how to use File Explorer to manage your files and folders. You will also learn how to create a folder; then open, rename, and delete folders, so that you can better organize your files; and how to move or copy files between different folders. Lastly, you will learn how to compress and extract files and folders.

Using File Explorer

File Explorer is an app that you can use to create folders and manage folders and files across various storage locations: your PC, online storage, and external storage devices such as a flash drive or backup drive. File Explorer displays the organizational hierarchy of storage locations, folders, and files so you can locate files more easily. Often, related files are organized together into folders. A folder structure can occur across several levels, so you can create folders within other folders—called subfolders—arranged according to purpose. The most common analogy for File Explorer is that of a filing cabinet in which common documents and files are located within a single drawer (in this case a storage location), and then further grouped and organized by folders, often multiple layers of folders.

Understand the File Explorer Interface

Windows 10 has made it very easy to access File Explorer by incorporating an icon on the taskbar and in the Start menu. If you use File Explorer a lot, an icon may also display in the Most used section of the Start menu.

Figure 1.17 shows and Table 1.1 further describes the various functional areas of the File Explorer interface.

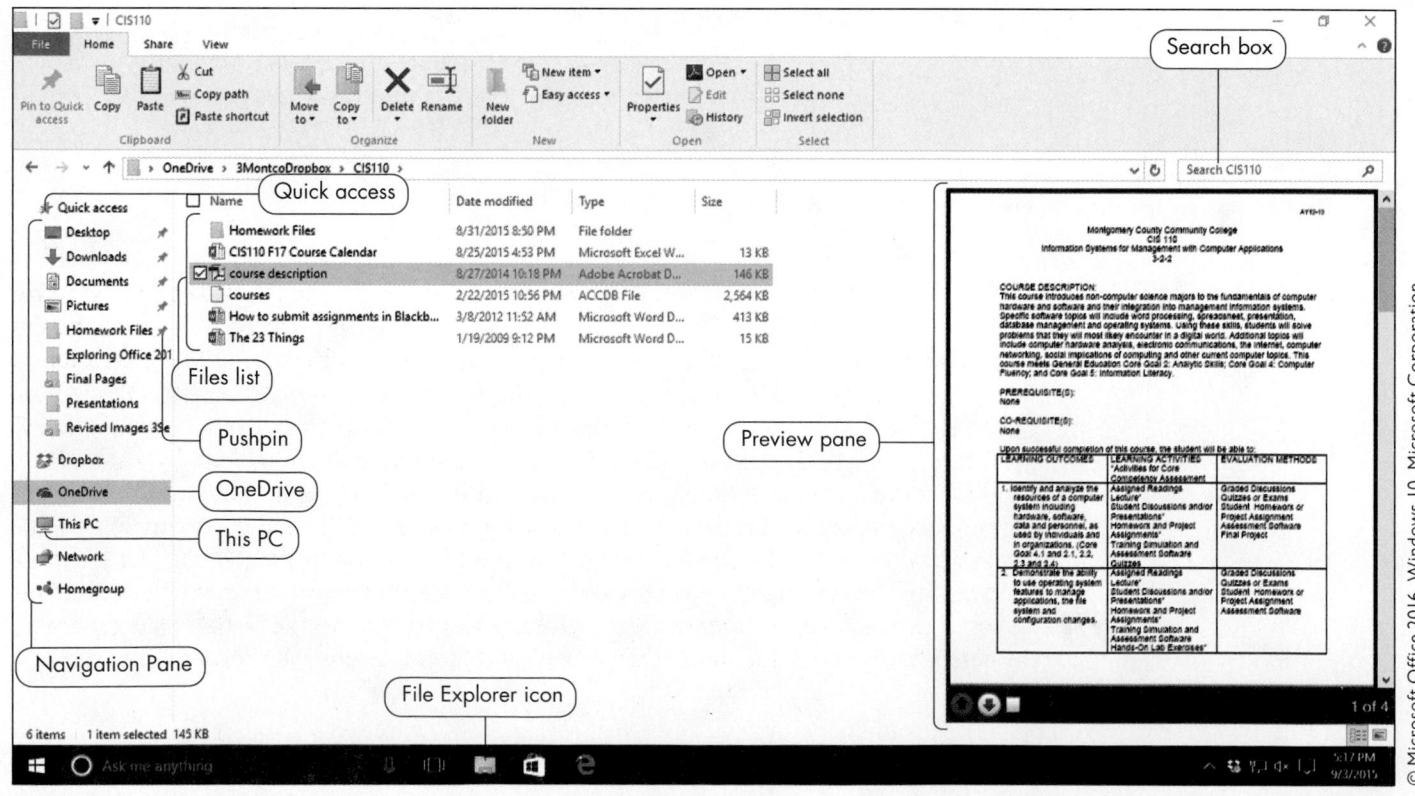

FIGURE 1.17 File Explorer

TABLE 1.1	File Explorer Interface
Ribbon	The Ribbon includes tabs and commands that are relevant to the currently selected item. If you are working with a music file, the Ribbon commands might include one for burning to a CD, whereas if you have selected a document, the Ribbon would enable you to open or share the file.
Back, Forward, and Up navigation arrows	Use these commands to visit previously opened folders. Use the Up command to open the parent folder for the current location.
Address bar	The Address bar enables you to navigate to other folders within File Explorer.
Search box	Find files and folders by typing descriptive text in the search box. Windows immediately begins a search after you type the first character, further narrowing results as you type. You can search the entire contents of File Explorer, or conduct a more directed search by first selecting a folder or drive.
Navigation Pane	The Navigation Pane contains Quick access, OneDrive, This PC, and Network. Click the arrow next to any of these content groups in the Navigation Pane to display contents and to manage files housed within a selected folder. Click any folder in the Navigation Pane to display the contained files.
Quick access	Quick access, as its name implies, provides immediate access to those files and folders that you use most often.
File list	The File list shows the contents of the currently selected folder or storage location. Files and folders can display in a variety of layouts that either show detailed information about the specific file or folder, or just file or folder names with small-, medium-, or large-sized icons. The icon is associated with the type of file or folder. For example, all Word documents will bear the W in a blue box icon.
Details pane	Displays the properties of the file or folder. Common properties include information such as the author name and the date the file was last modified. Details pane does not display by default, but displays after clicking the View tab and then clicking Details pane in the Panes group.
Preview pane	The Preview pane provides a snapshot of a selected file's contents (but not the contents of a selected folder). You can see file contents before actually opening the file. This pane can be displayed by clicking the View tab and then clicking Preview pane in the Panes group.

Use the View Tab on the Ribbon

File Explorer has a Ribbon, like all the Office applications. Use the View tab to customize what displays on File Explorer. For example, you might want to modify the size of the file and folder icons, or you might want additional details about displayed files and folders. Using the settings in the Layout group on the View tab, you can determine the size of icons by selecting Small, Medium, Large, or Extra Large icons. The Details layout will list the files and folder with other relevant information such as Date modified, Type, and Size. The List layout shows the file names without added detail, whereas Tiles and Content layouts are useful to show file thumbnails and varying levels of file details. If you want additional detail, such as who the file or folder is shared with and its availability, click Details pane on the View tab. To show a preview of a file, click Preview pane on the View tab. You can change the width of a pane by positioning the pointer on the border that separates the panes to display a double-headed arrow, and then dragging the border left or right.

Use and Modify Quick Access

When you launch File Explorer, it opens to the **Quick access** section on the Navigation Pane by default. Quick access contains shortcuts to the folders you use most often. Although certain folders such as Downloads, Desktop, Documents, and Pictures are pinned to Quick access by default, you can unpin any of those, and pin others, to meet your particular needs. A pushpin icon identifies a pinned folder (refer to Figure 1.17). If you have upgraded your system from Windows 7 or 8, all the folders in your Favorites list are added to Quick access automatically.

To pin (or unpin) a folder to Quick access, complete one of the following steps:

- Right-click the folder, and select Pin to (or Unpin from) Quick access.
- Select the folder to pin and then click Pin to Quick access on the Home tab. Clicking this button with a selected pinned folder does not unpin the folder, however.

Also displayed in Quick access is a list of Recent files. These files are the most frequently used files. As files are added, the less used files on the list are removed to make room for the new files, but you can remove any file from the Recent files list by right-clicking the file and selecting Remove from Quick access.

Use the Search Box in File Explorer

Occasionally, even the most organized person will need to search for a file or folder. While Cortana may be a convenient way to search for files and folders, you can only filter the results by type of file. When you use the search box in File Explorer, you can search only the contents of a specific folder, thus limiting the results; or you can Search an entire drive for a broader search. You can then further sort the results by file type or date modified to continue to locate the specific file or folder.

To search for a file or folder, complete the following steps:

1. Click the drive or folder in the Navigation Pane you want to search.
2. Type the search term in the search box.

Once you click in the File Explorer search box, the Search Tools tab displays. The Search Tools tab enables you to do the following:

- refine your search results by Date, Kind, Size, or Other properties
- revise the search location to include subfolders, the entire PC or another location
- save a search if you tend to conduct the same search repeatedly

Navigate File Explorer

The Navigation Pane is an easy way to move between folders and storage locations in File Explorer. As mentioned above, the Navigation Pane consists of four main areas: Quick access, OneDrive, This PC, and Network. **OneDrive** is Microsoft's cloud storage system.

Saving files to OneDrive, saves them to a Web-based location (OneDrive.com) and syncs them across all Windows devices. Sign in with your Microsoft account to access your files from any Internet-connected computer or mobile device. Changes you make will sync with the cloud, keeping your files up-to-date everywhere. Use File Explorer to access your OneDrive and to create new folders and organize existing folders.

> **TIP: CHOOSE WHAT TO SYNC**
>
> If you need to save space on your hard drive, sync just those OneDrive folders that you really use most often. Those folders or files you choose to stop syncing will not display in the OneDrive folder in File Explorer, but will remain in OneDrive and can be accessed from the OneDrive website. To choose which folders to sync, right-click the OneDrive icon in the Notification area on the taskbar. Click Settings, click the Choose folders tab, and then click Choose folders. Uncheck those folders you do not want to sync and display in File Explorer. Only checked folders will sync.

Files stored to This PC are saved onto the hard drive, and are accessible only when working on that particular device. Documents, Music, Pictures, Videos, and Downloads are standard library folders in the This PC area of File Explorer. Clicking on Network in the Navigation Pane displays all networked devices such as gaming and entertainment systems, printers, and other networked computers.

Clicking the arrow on the left side of these main storage areas in the Navigation Pane expands or collapses the folder to show or hide the folders and documents within each group. When you select a file or folder, the location of that file or folder is displayed in the Address bar (see Figure 1.18).

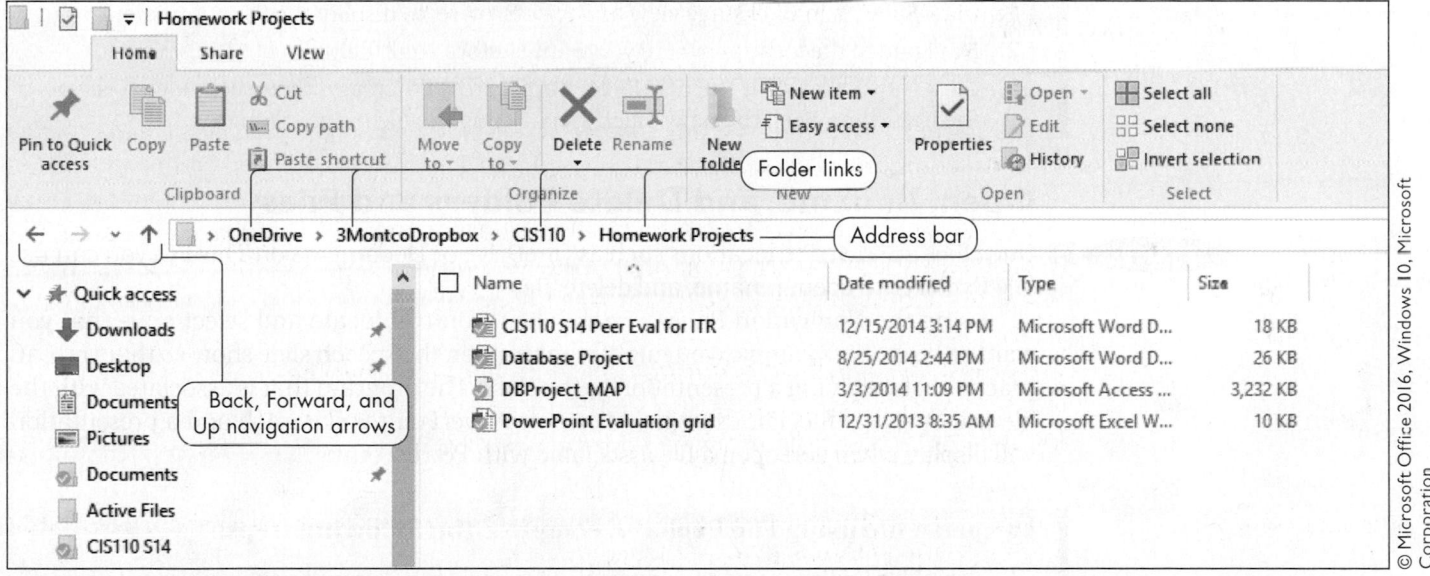

FIGURE 1.18 The Address Bar in File Explorer

The Address bar is located under the Ribbon, and displays the current location of a selected file or folder as a series of links and arrows. Next to the Address bar are the Back, Forward, and Up navigation arrows. These arrows help to move up or down the links in the location shown in the Address bar. Alternatively, you can click on any of the links in the Address bar to jump directly to the location. You can use the Address bar to navigate to a particular location (i.e., to Documents or Quick access), or you can click in any of the arrows between the folder links to view any subfolders. You can also use the Address bar to move files and folders to different locations. This and other ways to work with files and folders are covered in the next section.

Working with Files and Folders

STEP 1 ▶▶ As you work with software to create a file, such as when you type a report using Word, your primary concern will be saving the file so that you can retrieve it later. Grouping related files into folders helps to keep files organized. If you have created an appropriate and well-named folder structure, you can save the file in a location that is easy to find.

You can use File Explorer to create a folder structure, providing descriptive names and placing the folders in a well-organized hierarchy.

To create a folder in File Explorer, complete the following steps:

1. Open File Explorer, and then click OneDrive or any other location such as the hard drive or flash drive, in the Navigation Pane.
2. Click the Home tab on the Ribbon, and then click New folder in the New group.
3. Type the new folder name and press Enter. Repeat the process to create additional folders.

Undoubtedly, you will occasionally find that you have just created a file but have no appropriate folder in which to save the file. For example, you might have just finished the slide show for your speech class but have forgotten first to create a speech folder for your assignments. For those occasions, you can create a folder from within the software application at the time you are saving a file.

To create a folder as you save a file, complete the following steps:

1. Click Save As in Backstage view and click Browse, to display the Save As dialog box.
2. Navigate to the location where you want to store your file.
3. Click New folder, type the new folder name, press Enter, and then click Open to save the name and open the new folder. After typing the file name, click Save.

Open, Rename, and Delete Folders and Files

STEP 2 ▶▶ Once files are saved to locations such as OneDrive or Documents on This PC, you can use File Explorer to open, rename, and delete files.

Using the Navigation Pane or search box, you can locate and select a file that you want to open. For example, you might want to open the speech slide show so that you can practice before giving a presentation to the class. The program that is associated with the file will open the file. For example, Microsoft PowerPoint will launch and a presentation will display when you open a file associated with PowerPoint.

To open a file using File Explorer, complete the following steps:

1. Open File Explorer, and then navigate to the folder that contains the desired file. The file will display in the File list.
2. Enable the Preview pane from the View tab, and click the file name in the File list to preview the contents of a file before opening it.
3. Double-click the file.

At times, you may want to give a different name to a file or folder than the one that you originally gave it. Or perhaps you made a typographical mistake when you entered the name as you saved the file. In these situations, you can rename the file or folder.

To rename a file or folder, complete one of the following steps:

- Right-click the file or folder and select Rename. Type the new name and press Enter.
- Click the name twice—but much more slowly than a double-click. Type the new name and press Enter.
- Click a file or folder once to select it, click the Home tab, and then select Rename in the Organize group. Type the new name and press Enter.

It is much easier to delete a folder or file than it is to recover it if you remove it by mistake. Therefore, be very careful when deleting items so that you are sure of your intentions before proceeding. When you delete a folder, all subfolders and all files within the folder are also removed. If you are certain you want to remove a folder or file, the process is simple.

To delete a file or folder, complete one of the following steps:

- Right-click the item, click Delete, and then click Yes if asked to confirm removal to the Recycle Bin.
- Click to select the item, click the Home tab, and then click Delete in the Organize group.

Recall that items are placed in the Recycle Bin only if you are deleting them from a hard drive. Files and folders deleted from a removable storage medium, such as a flash drive, are immediately and permanently deleted, with no easy method of retrieval.

Selecting, Copying, and Moving Multiple Files and Folders

STEP 3 ❯❯ You will select folders and files when you need to rename, delete, copy, or paste them, or open files and folders so that you can view the contents. Click a file or folder to select it; double-click a file or folder (in the File list) to open it.

Select Multiple Files and Folders

To apply an operation to several files at once, such as deleting or moving them, you will select all of them. You can select several files and folders, regardless of whether they are adjacent to each other in the File list. Suppose that your digital pictures are contained in the Pictures folder. You might want to delete some of the pictures because you want to clear up some hard drive space.

To select multiple files or folders, complete the following steps:

1. Open File Explorer and click the desired folder or storage location.
2. Locate the desired files in the File list, and do one of the following:
   - Select the first file, press and hold Shift, and then click the last file to select adjacent files. All consecutive files will be highlighted, indicating that they are selected. At that point, you can delete, copy, or move the selected files at the same time.
   - Click the first file or folder, and press and hold Ctrl while you click all desired non-adjacent files or folders, releasing Ctrl only when you have finished selecting all the necessary files or folders. At that point, you can delete, copy, or move the selected files at the same time.
   - Open the folder, press and hold Ctrl, and then press A on the keyboard to select all items in a folder or disk drive. You can also click the Home tab, and in the Select group, click Select all to select all items. At that point, you can delete, copy, or move the selected files at the same time.

Copy and Move Files and Folders

When you copy or move a folder, you affect both the folder and any files that it contains. You can move or copy a folder or file to another location on the same drive or to another drive. If your purpose is to make a backup, or copy, of an important file or folder, you will probably want to copy it to an external drive or to OneDrive.

To move or copy an item in File Explorer, complete the following steps:

1. Right-click the item(s) and select either Cut (to move) or Copy on the shortcut menu.
2. Locate the destination drive or folder in the Navigation Pane, right-click the destination drive or folder, and then click Paste.

Compressing Files and Folders

STEP 4 ›› Sometimes you have an extremely large file, such as a video file that you want to email or upload to the Internet. Or, you might have a group of files, such as a bunch of pictures that you want to share with friends or family, but you do not want to send them as individual attachments. You can compress a file or zip multiple files together into a single compressed folder. A *compressed (zipped) folder* or file, takes up less space, is easier to email or to upload to OneDrive or another online storage site, and facilitates sharing a group of files.

Create a Compressed Folder

Using the Zip tool in File Explorer makes it easy to create a compressed folder. When compressing a file or folder, the compressed folder is created in the same location and takes on the same name as the file or folder. However, if you are compressing a group of files, it may be best to first put them in a folder and give that folder a meaningful name. Otherwise, the zipped folder will take the name of one of the documents in the folder. Of course, you can always rename a zipped folder, using the same methods described above for renaming a file or folder. The zipped file or folder does not replace the original files.

To compress a file or folder, complete the following series of steps:

1. Open File Explorer, and select the file, group of files, or folder in the File list that you want to compress.
2. Click the Share tab, and then click Zip in the Send group. A compressed folder is created and placed in the same folder location along with the original files or folder. Alternatively, right-click the selected files or folder, select Send to, and click Compressed (zipped) folder.

Once a compressed folder is created, you can add additional files to the folder without having to undo and redo the zipping process. Just drag new files into the compressed folder.

Extract Files from a Compressed Folder

You might have received or downloaded a compressed file or folder, such as the data files from this book, and need to unzip the folder and extract the files.

> **To unzip (extract) files or folders from a compressed folder, complete the following steps:**
>
> 1. Open File Explorer, and select the compressed folder.
> 2. Click the Extract tab, click Extract all, and if necessary, click Browse to select a destination where you want the individual files to be located. The individual files, by default, are saved to the same location as the zipped folder. Click Extract.

TIP: EXTRACTING FILES FROM A DOWNLOADED ZIP FOLDER

If you are extracting files from a folder you have downloaded from the Web, you should ensure your files are saved in a meaningful location. Otherwise, they may end up in the Downloads folder.

Extracting files does not remove the compressed folder from your computer. The compressed folder will remain until you decide to delete it.

Quick Concepts

5. The File Explorer interface has several functional areas. Name them and identify their characteristics. **pp. 28–29**

6. Describe why it might be more efficient to use the search box in File Explorer than the search box on the taskbar to look for a file. **p. 30**

7. You want to delete several files, but the files are not consecutively listed in File Explorer. Describe two different methods you could use to select and delete them. **p. 33**

8. Explain at least two circumstances in which file compression would be useful. **p. 34**

Hands-On Exercises

Watch the Video for This Hands-On Exercise!

MyITLab® Topic-Based Training

Skills covered: Create Folders • Pin a Folder to Quick Access • Rename a Folder • Delete a Folder • Copy a File • Move a Folder • Compress a Folder • Extract Files from a Compressed Folder

2 File Management

You have discussed with the students the importance of good file management, now you want to show them how easy it is to use File Explorer to organize and manage their files. You first have them create and pin a folder to Quick access, then you have them modify some folder names so they are more meaningful. Lastly, you show the students how to extract files from a compressed folder and move them to one of the previously created folders.

STEP 1 ›› CREATE FOLDERS AND PIN A FOLDER TO QUICK ACCESS

Your friend tells you that she would like to have all the files the students are working on saved in one folder so it is easy for everyone to access in the future. Refer to Figure 1.19 as you complete Step 1.

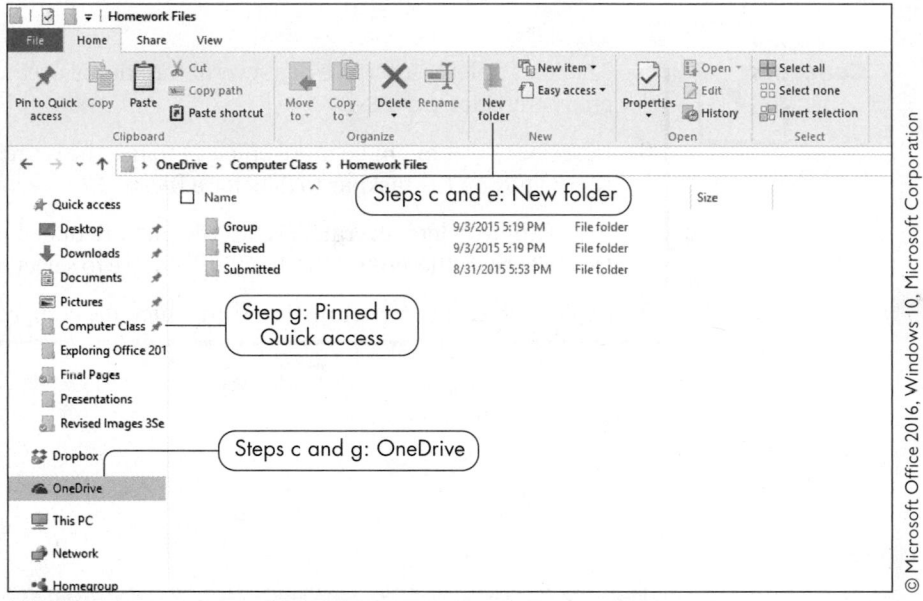

FIGURE 1.19 Create a Folder and Pin to Quick Access

a. Open *win01h1Windows10_LastFirst* if you closed it at the end of Hands-On Exercise 1 and save it as **win01h2Windows10_LastFirst**, changing h1 to h2. Keep the document open and maximized.

> **TROUBLESHOOTING:** If you make any major mistakes in this exercise, you can close the file, open *win01h1Windows10_LastFirst* again, and then start this exercise over.

b. Click **File Explorer** on the taskbar and maximize the window.

c. Click **OneDrive** in the Navigation Pane. Click **New folder** in the New group, type **Computer Class**, and then press **Enter**.

   You create a folder where you can organize subfolders and files for the students and your friend, and all the learning materials they generate for their computer class.

> **TROUBLESHOOTING:** If OneDrive does not display in the Navigation Pane, click This PC and create a new folder in Documents.

d. Double-click the **Computer Class folder** in the File list. The Address bar at the top of the File Explorer window should show that it is the currently selected folder.

e. Click **New folder** in the New group on the Home tab, type **Data Files**, and then press **Enter**. Repeat the process to create another folder, and name it **Homework Files**.

   You create two subfolders of the Computer Class folder. One to contain the data files the students will need to begin some of their computer work, and another to keep track of homework files they have completed.

f. Check the Address bar to make sure Computer Class is still the current folder. Navigate to and then double-click the **Homework Files folder** in the Navigation Pane. Right-click in a blank area of the File list, point to **New**, and then click **Folder**. Type **Submitted** and press **Enter**. Using either technique in this step, create two more folders named **Group** and **Revised**.

   To subdivide the Homework Files folder further, you create three subfolders, one to hold homework files that have been submitted, one for revised homework files, and one for homework files from group projects.

g. Click **OneDrive** in the Navigation Pane, and locate the Computer Class folder in the File list. Right-click the **Computer Class folder**, and select **Pin to Quick access**.

   The Computer Class folder displays in the Quick access area of File Explorer.

h. Double-click the **Computer Class folder** in Quick access, and double-click the **Homework Files folder** in the Files list.

i. Click **Snipping Tool** on the taskbar, click the **New arrow**, and click **Full-screen Snip**. Click **Word** on the taskbar, press **Ctrl+End**, press **Enter** twice, and then press **Ctrl+V**.

j. Save the document. Minimize the Word and Snipping Tool windows.

STEP 2 ⟫ **RENAME AND DELETE A FOLDER**

As often happens, you find that the folder structure you created is not exactly what you need. You will remove the Revised folder and will rename the Data Files folder to better describe the contents. Refer to Figure 1.20 as you complete Step 2.

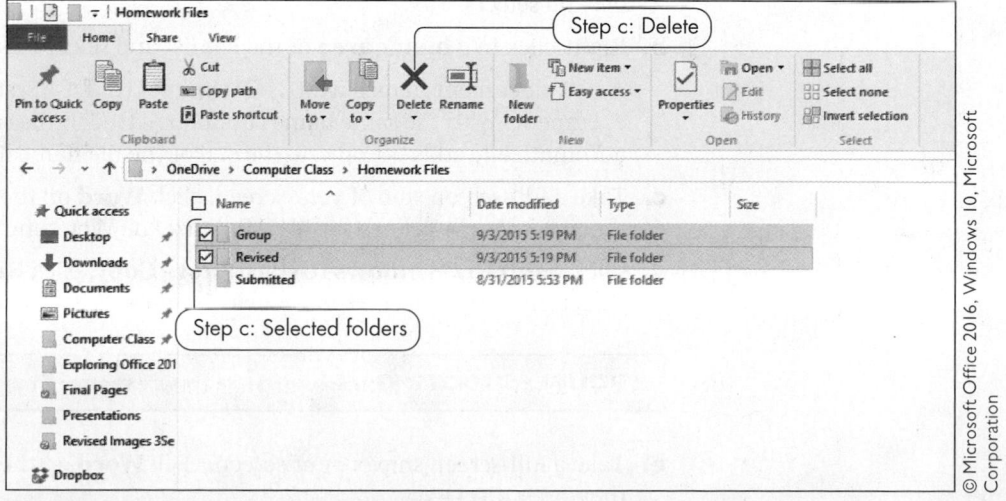

FIGURE 1.20 Rename and Delete a Folder

a. Double-click the **Computer Class folder** in Quick access.

b. Right-click the **Data Files folder**, click **Rename**, type **Starting Files**, and then press **Enter**.

Your friend thinks that her students will understand the term Starting Files better than Data Files, so you rename the folder.

c. Double-click the **Homework Files folder**. Click the check box next to **Revised** and **Group**. Both folders are selected. Click **Delete** in the Organize group. If asked to confirm the deletion, click **Yes**. Click **Computer Class** in the Address bar.

> **TROUBLESHOOTING:** If check boxes do not display next to the folder name, click the View tab, and click to select *Item check boxes* in the Show/hide group.

You decide that dividing the homework folder into revised and group subfolders is not necessary, so you deleted both folders.

d. Take a full-screen snip of your screen, click **Word** on the taskbar, press **Enter** twice, and then press **Ctrl+V**.

e. Save the document. Minimize the Word and Snipping Tool windows.

STEP 3 ›› SELECT AND COPY FILES

You want to show students how to copy a file, so in anticipation of completing the next assignment, you have them copy and rename the current homework file on which they are working. Refer to Figure 1.21 as you complete Step 3.

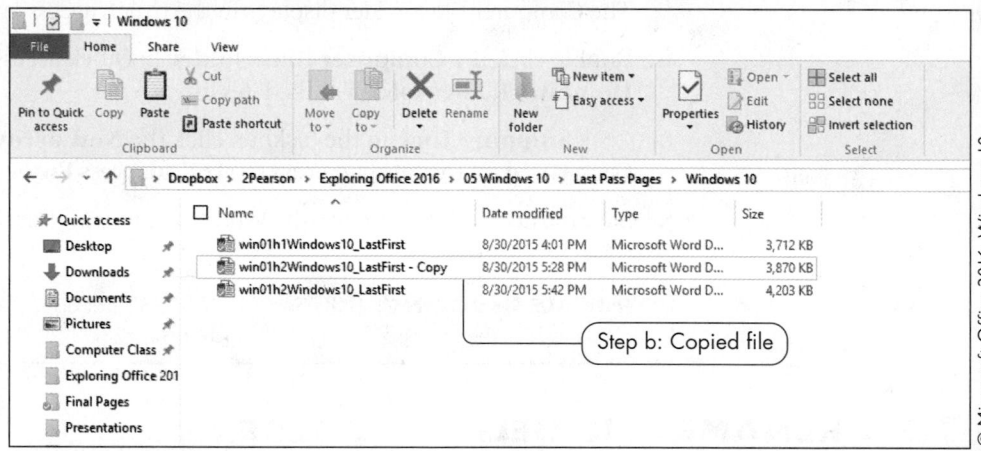

FIGURE 1.21 Select and Copy Files

a. Navigate to the location where you saved win01h2Windows10_LastFirst. Right-click the file and select **Copy**.

b. Right-click in a **blank area** of the File list and select **Paste**.

A new document named win01h2Windows10_LastFirst - Copy displays. Two documents with the same name cannot be saved in the same location, so Windows automatically adds "- Copy" to the end of the file name to differentiate the two files.

c. Take a full-screen snip of your screen, click **Word** on the taskbar, press **Enter** twice, and then press **Ctrl+V**. Save the file. Minimize the Word and Snipping Tool windows.

d. Click **win01h2Windows10_LastFirst - Copy**, click **Rename** on the Home tab, and then rename the file as **Homework_Images**. Press **Enter**.

> **TROUBLESHOOTING:** Be sure the file you are renaming has - Copy in the file name.

e. Take a full-screen snip of your screen, click **Word** on the taskbar, press **Enter** twice, and then press **Ctrl+V**.

f. Save the document. Minimize the Word and Snipping Tool windows.

You want to show the students how to compress a group of files into a zipped folder and then move the zipped folder to a new location. You will then have the students extract the files from the zipped folder. Refer to Figure 1.22 as you complete Step 4.

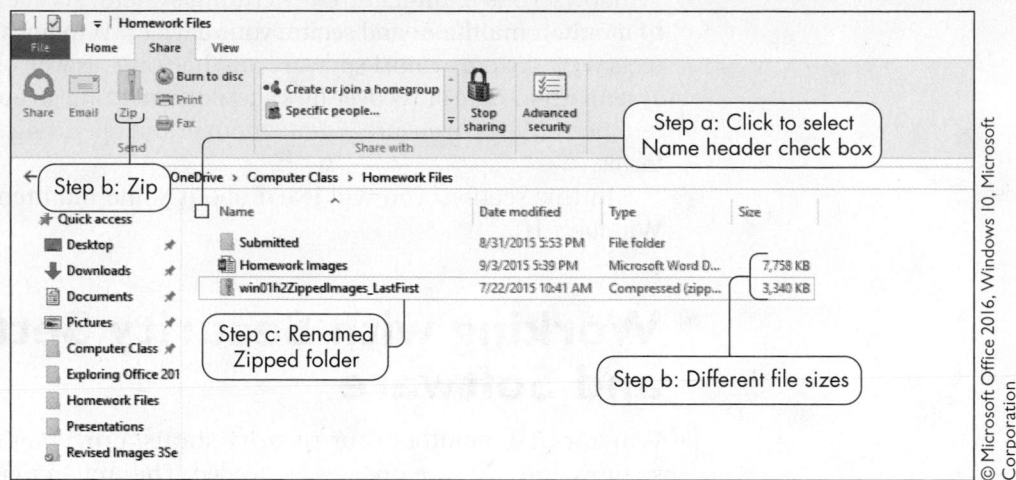

FIGURE 1.22 Compress and Extract Files

a. Click the **check box** next to the Name header in the File list in File Explorer to select both documents.

> **TROUBLESHOOTING:** If more than the two documents display in the File list, click the check box to select each individual file.

b. Click the **Share tab**, click **Zip**, and then press **Enter**.

A new zipped folder is created. Because the files were not in a separate folder, the zipped folder is named after one of the files. You will to rename the zipped folder.

c. Right-click the **zipped folder**, and click **Rename**. Type **Windows 10 Homework**, and press **Enter**.

d. Click the **Windows 10 Homework zipped folder**, press **Ctrl**, and then drag the folder to the Computer Class folder in Quick access.

A ScreenTip will display Copy to Computer Class. Note: If you wanted to move the zipped folder, you would just drag the folder to the new location.

e. Double-click the **Computer Class folder** in Quick access, and then double-click the **Windows 10 Homework zipped folder**.

The Compressed Folder Tools tab displays on the Ribbon, and the two files contained in the zipped folder display in the File list.

f. Take a full-screen snip of your screen, click **Word** on the taskbar, press **Enter** twice, and then press **Ctrl+V**. Save the file. Minimize the Word and Snipping Tool windows.

g. Click **Extract all**, and then click **Extract**.

You do not need to browse, as you want the new files to stay in the Computer Class folder.

h. Click **Computer Class** on the Address bar and note that the Windows 10 Homework zipped folder and the Windows 10 Homework folder are both in the Computer Class folder.

i. Take a full-screen snip of your screen, click **Word** on the taskbar, press **Enter** twice, and then press **Ctrl+V**. Close the Snipping Tool and close File Explorer. Click **No** if asked to save changes to the snip.

j. Save the document. Keep the document open if you plan to continue with the next Hands-On Exercise. If not, close the document, and exit Word. Close all other windows.

Windows System and Security Features

Windows 10 is a full-featured operating system. As such, it includes utilities that help to monitor, maintain, and secure your devices. Windows 10 contains software that protects your system against spyware and hacking, as well as utilities that help to keep your system up-to-date or recover files should something go awry. It also includes some maintenance utilities to ensure your computer and operating system continue to run in good form.

In this section, you will learn about some maintenance and security features in Windows 10.

Working with Security Settings and Software

Windows 10 monitors your security status, providing recommendations for security settings and software updates as needed. The Action Center provides a central location where you can access any status notifications and alerts. Windows 10 includes basic security features such as Window Defender and firewall software.

Understand the Action Center

STEP 1 ▶▶ Windows 10 checks your system for various maintenance and security settings, providing notifications and recommending action through the *Action Center* when necessary. A major purpose of the Action Center is to provide important status information. Status information could include the detection of new devices, the availability of software updates, or recommended maintenance and security tasks. When the status of a monitored item changes, a pop-up message in an alert box displays near the Notification area. You can click the message to perform the recommended task. If you are not working on your computer at the time the pop-up message appears, the Action Center icon, located in the Notification area of the taskbar, will turn opaque indicating that there are new notifications waiting for you. Click the Action Center icon in the Notification area (see Figure 1.23) to display the Action Center alerts box. Once clicked, the Action Center icon will become clear or "empty."

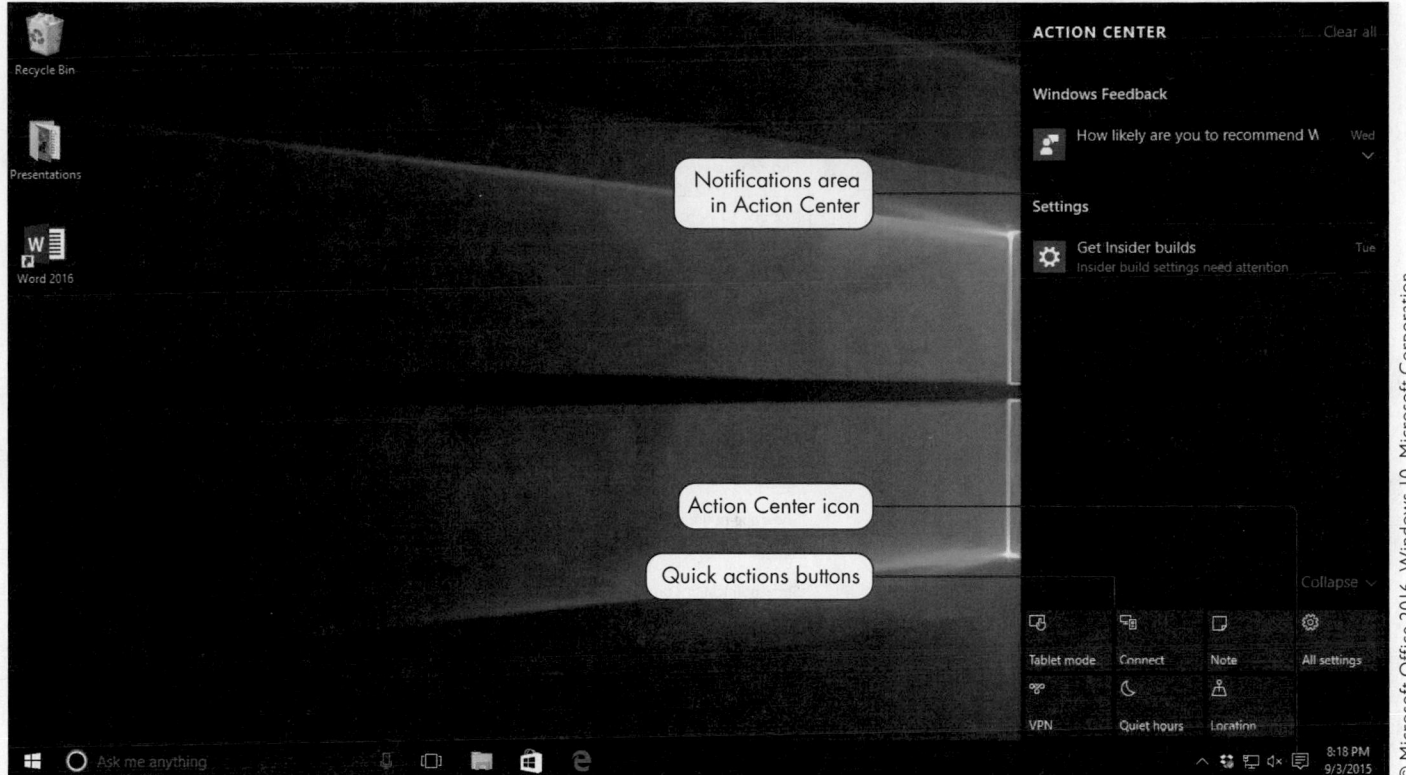

FIGURE 1.23 Action Center

The Action Center consists of two parts: the Notifications area at the top and Quick actions buttons at the bottom (refer to Figure 1.23). The Action Center runs across all your Windows devices. Therefore, in the Notifications area, you will see notifications from various apps, including Facebook, Twitter, and your email account, as well as from apps that might only be on your Windows phone or tablet. You can delete notifications by group (i.e. all your Twitter notifications) or you can delete individual notifications by pointing to the group or individual notification name and then clicking the "X" that displays. Lastly, you can click Clear All at the top of the Notifications area. Be mindful that Clear All will delete all notifications on all your Windows devices, not just the device on which you are currently working.

In the bottom of the Action Center are quick action buttons such as a Tablet mode toggle button, a button to connect your media devices, a link to All settings, a link to the Display settings, and toggle buttons for Location and Wi-Fi. Click Expand to see more quick actions such as toggle buttons for VPN and Rotation lock. Note that some buttons, such as Airplane mode or Rotation lock, will only display on mobile devices.

> **To change the Quick action buttons in the Action Center, complete the following steps:**
>
> 1. Click the All settings button in the Action Center (or click Settings from the Start menu).
> 2. Click System, and then Notifications & actions. In the Quick actions area (see Figure 1.24), four icons display, indicating the quick actions that will display in the Action Center.
> 3. Click any of the icons to change any or all of the actions, and then select another action from the displayed menu.

Also from the Notifications & actions menu, you can choose which icons will always display in the Notification area on the taskbar by clicking *Select which icons appear on the taskbar*.

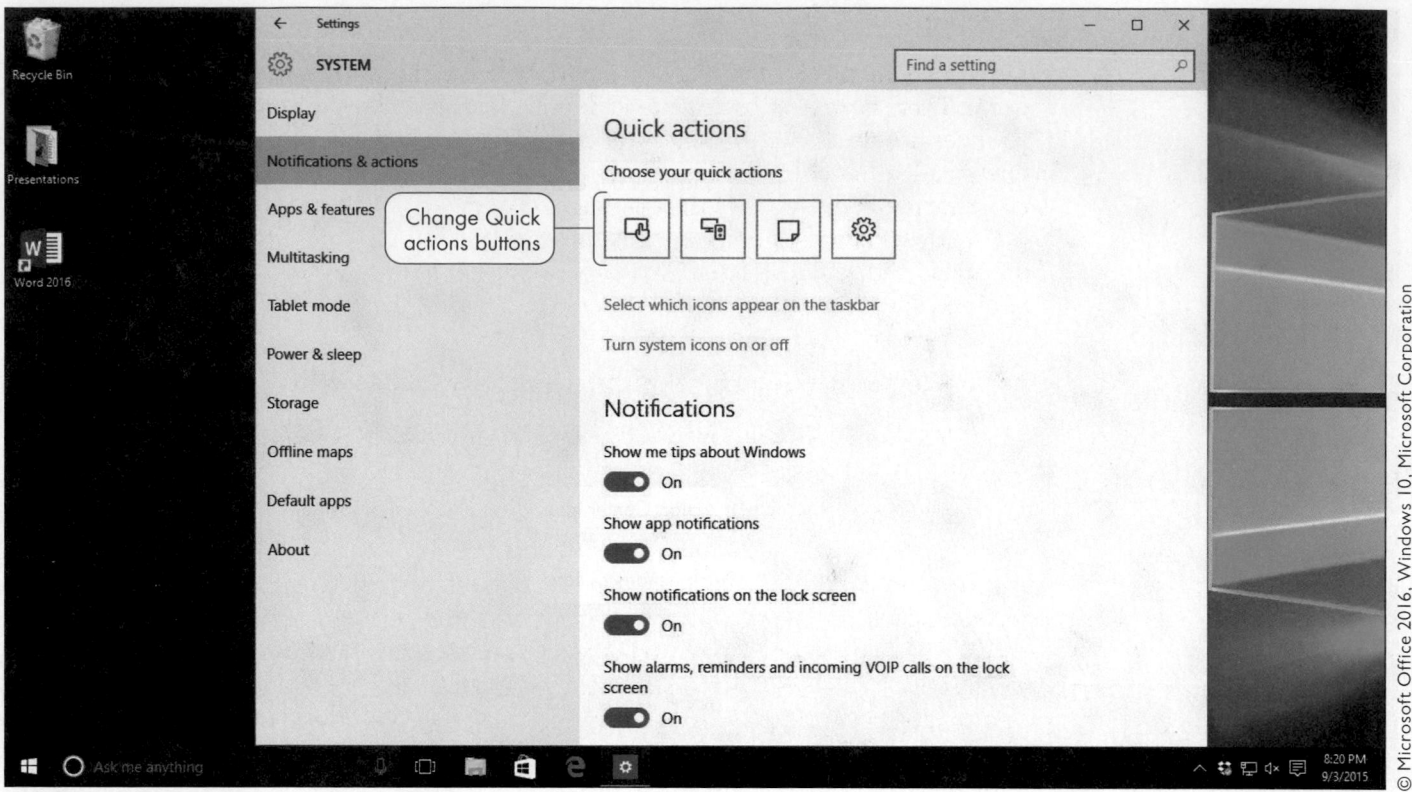

FIGURE 1.24 Modifying the Quick Actions Buttons

Use File History

Many things can accidently happen to your files. You might mistakenly delete a file or a file might become corrupted, meaning it is damaged and therefore unusable by your software programs. Windows *File History* is a utility that will continuously make copies of your important files so that you can recover them if you ever encounter a file problem. In order for you to take advantage of the File History feature, you need to ensure that File History is turned on and that a storage area, such as a separate partition of your hard drive, an external drive, or cloud storage such as OneDrive, has been selected as the back-up location.

To access File History, complete the following steps:

1. Right-click Start, and select Control Panel.
2. Select System and Security, and then click File History.

File History will save files to a drive that you designate, such as an external hard drive or a separate partition (section) of your computer's internal hard drive. To set up File History for the first time, you must first designate the drive where File History will store the file backups. Click *Select drive* in the File History window to see a list of drives connected to your computer. If you need to set up a drive, click *Add network location*. Once you have selected a drive, click the *Run now* link to back up your files. As long as File History is on, it will automatically back up your personal files on your PC. If there are some folders that you do not feel need backing up, such as the Downloads folder, you can exclude them by clicking Exclude folders. Click Advanced settings to choose how often you want the backup to run and how long your saved versions are kept.

If you want to restore files after one or more have been lost, you can use the Restore feature in File History. Unlike many other restore applications, once you begin the restore process, you can browse to a specific file or folder and see all versions of the selected folder or individual file. You can then navigate to the desired version by clicking on Previous or Next and click Restore to bring it back to its original location.

Access Windows Update

Microsoft constantly identifies ways to enhance Windows security or fix problems that occur. There is no need to download or purchase an updated operating system each time changes are necessary; instead, you can simply make sure that your computer is set to download automatically any updates (fixes). *Windows Update* provides a means to initiating such modifications to the operating system.

Microsoft strongly recommends that you configure your computer to automatically download and install updates. That way, you do not have to remember to check for updates or manually download them. This is the default setting for Windows Update in Windows 10.

To check your settings for updates, complete the following steps:

1. Select Settings on the Start menu, and click Update & security.
2. Click Windows Update.
3. Click Check for updates.

You can have Windows both download and install updates automatically (strongly recommended), only download updates but let you install them, or never check for updates.

If you want to check for updates for other Microsoft products, such as Microsoft Office, open Windows Update and click the *Change settings* link. Then in the Change settings dialog box, under Microsoft Update, check *Give me updates for other Microsoft products when I update Windows.*

Use Windows Defender

Viruses and spyware can be installed on your computer without your knowledge when you connect to the Internet, open an email message, or when you install certain apps using a flash drive or other removable media. Spyware and viruses can do many unpleasant things such as:

- Keep track of websites you visit
- Change browser settings to direct you to dangerous websites
- Record keystrokes for stealing sensitive information
- Erase or corrupt files on your hard drive

Obviously, viruses and spyware are unwelcome and potential security risks. *Windows Defender* is antispyware and antivirus software. It identifies and removes malware such as viruses and spyware. Windows Defender can be set to run with real-time protection, which means that it is always on to guard against threats, alerting you when malicious programs attempt to install themselves or change your computer settings. You can also schedule routine scans so that Windows Defender checks your system for malicious software.

To open Windows Defender, complete the following steps:

1. Open the Start menu, and click All apps.
2. Click Windows System, and then click Windows Defender.

Alternatively, type Defender in the search box, and then click the corresponding link at the top of the Results list. This opens up the Windows Defender dialog box, and from there you can determine the type of Scan (Quick, Full, Custom) you want to perform.

Use Windows Firewall

STEP 2 ›› Windows 10 also includes a *firewall*, a software program that helps to protect against unauthorized access (hacking) to your computer. Although Windows Defender and Windows Firewall provide basic protection, many computer users opt for the purchase of third-party software, such as Norton Internet Security, to provide an even greater level of protection.

When you work with the Internet, there is always a possibility that a hacker could disable your computer or view its contents. To keep that from occurring, it is imperative that you use firewall software. Windows 10 includes firewall software that is turned on by default when the operating system is installed. It protects against unauthorized traffic, both incoming and outgoing. That means that other people, computers, or programs do not have authorization to communicate with your computer unless you give permission. In addition, programs on your system are unable to communicate online unless you approve them.

Periodically, you might want to check to make sure your firewall has not been turned off accidentally. If you have another security program installed, such as Norton Internet Security, it has its own firewall software and therefore may recommend that Windows Firewall be turned off. This is because two active firewall programs can sometimes interfere with each other. But you should ensure that one firewall program is turned on at all times.

To access Windows Firewall, complete the following steps:

1. Open the Start menu, and then click Settings.
2. Type Firewall in Settings search box, and then click Windows Firewall. Alternatively, type Firewall in the search box, and select the top box in the search results.
3. Click Turn Windows Firewall on or off. You can then adjust other Firewall settings. Table 1.2 describes the Firewall settings that can be customized.

TABLE 1.2 Microsoft Firewall Settings

Setting	Description
Turn on Windows Firewall	Selected to be on by default to block most apps from receiving information through the firewall. You can add an app to a list of allowable apps.
Block all incoming connections	This setting, when turned on, blocks all unsolicited attempts to connect to your PC, even from those allowed apps. Consider turning this on when you are working in public places such as the airport or hotel. Turning this on does not affect your ability to use email and view most webpages.
Notify me when Windows Firewall blocks a new app	Selecting this option will allow you to unblock an app the Firewall has blocked.
Turn off Windows Firewall (not recommended)	Turn off Windows Firewall only if you have a separate security program, such as Norton or McAfee, running on your PC.

Working with Administrative Tools

One of the functions of the operating system is to manage computer resources such as the central processing unit (CPU) and random access memory (RAM). It is useful to have a good understanding of how well the CPU, RAM, and other computer resources are working so you can take preventative actions, such as upgrading the amount of RAM in your system, or freeing up or acquiring more hard drive capacity, if necessary. Windows 10 provides some tools that can help you monitor computer resources.

Use Task Manager

Task Manager displays the programs and processes that are running on your computer. When a program is not responding, you can use Task Manager to close it.

To view how the computer is performing, click the Performance tab. Leave this box open as you work, so you can see how your actions affect computer resources.

Monitor System Resources

The ***Resource Monitor*** displays how the computer is using its key components, including the CPU and RAM. Use the search box to access the Resource Monitor, or click the Windows Administrative Tools folder in All apps. By clicking on each tab in the Resource Monitor window, you can view in real-time the system resources as they are being used. For example, click the Memory tab to view how RAM is being used (see Figure 1.25). The chart at the bottom displays the total amount of memory installed, what is currently being used, what is on reserve (cached), and what is currently available. Click between CPU and Memory to view how your actions affect the utilization of these components. For example, as you work, if the CPU performance nears or exceeds 50% utilization, that means you are using most or all of the CPU's capabilities. At maximum, or near maximum utilization, your computer might not run as efficiently. Unfortunately, there is not an easy way to upgrade your CPU, so if you want greater performance, it might be time to get a new computer with a faster CPU. You can also monitor memory (RAM) utilization. If you find you are using most of your memory resources, it might be possible to add additional RAM to your computer. If you cannot add additional RAM, then again, it might be time for a computer that offers greater RAM capacity.

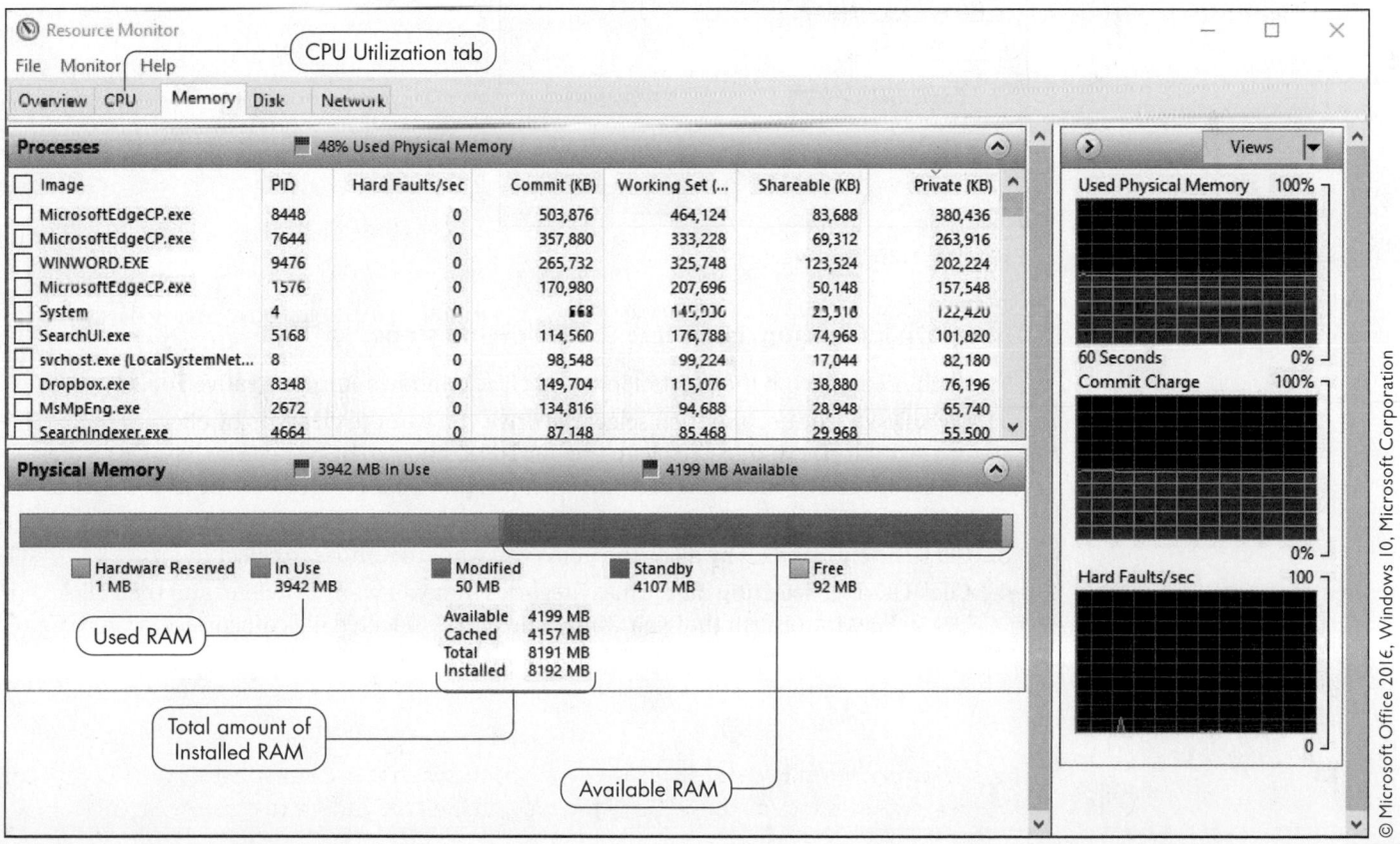

FIGURE 1.25 Resource Monitor

Use Disk Cleanup

STEP 3 ▶▶ Every now and then it is a good idea to do some internal "spring cleaning" on your computer. Over time, your computer system can accumulate many unnecessary files and program fragments that ultimately end up affecting computer performance. Some of these files accumulate in the Recycle Bin. Recall that deleted files from the hard disk go to the Recycle Bin but are not completely deleted from the system until the Recycle Bin is emptied. Windows often creates temporary files that temporarily store data. Usually Windows deletes these files automatically, but some remain. There are also files in Downloads that are not necessary anymore, such as small plug-ins and applets; or there are temporary files created when you use the Internet. The *Disk Cleanup* tool helps to free up space on your hard drive by searching for, and removing, any or all of these unnecessary files (see Figure 1.26). You can choose which types of files to delete. Read the description of the selected items if you do not understand what the files are. For additional information, you can click View files to see a list of files that will be deleted. The total amount of disk space gained is displayed below the Files to delete box.

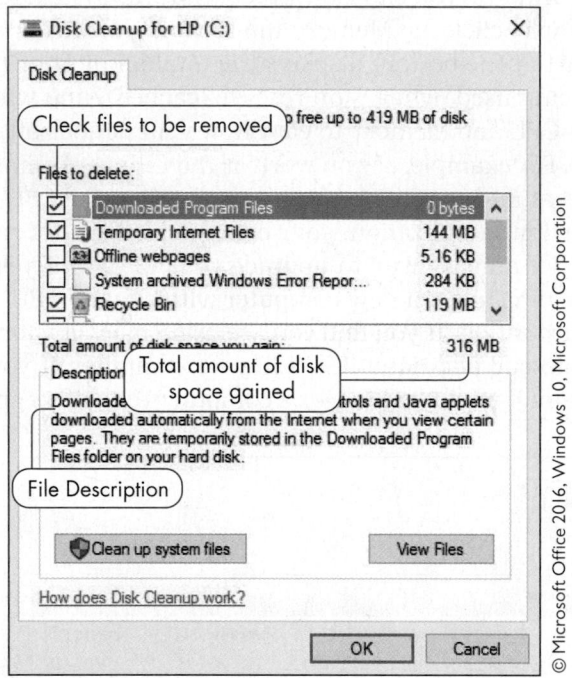

FIGURE 1.26 Disk Cleanup

To run Disk Cleanup, complete the following steps:

1. Click All apps from the Start menu, and click Windows Administrative Tools.

2. Click Disk Cleanup, and then select the drive you want to clean up by clicking the arrow in the Drives box. To clean the hard disk, choose the (C:) drive. Click OK. Note: If you only have one drive, the scan will start immediately without the need to select a drive.

3. Click the check boxes by all of the items you want to remove to select them.

4. Click OK after selecting all the file categories that you want to delete, and then click Delete Files to confirm that you want to delete the selected file categories.

Get Remote Assistance

Undoubtedly, you will have trouble with your computer at some time and need some assistance. You might consider getting someone to help you by letting him or her connect to your computer remotely to determine the problem. Of course, you will only want to ask someone that you trust because that person will temporarily have access to your files.

To allow Remote Assistance in Windows 10, complete the following steps:

1. Type Remote Access in the search box, and press Enter. The System Properties dialog box displays with the Remote tab selected.
2. Ensure that the Allow Remote Assistance connections to this computer check box is selected.

If the person who is helping you is also using Windows 10, you can use a method called Easy Connect. The first time you use Easy Connect to request assistance, you will receive a password that you then give to the person offering assistance. Using that password, the helper can remotely connect to your computer and exchange information. Thereafter, a password is not necessary—you simply click the contact information for the helper to initiate a session. If the person providing assistance is using an earlier Windows operating system (such as Windows 8.1), you can use an invitation file, which is a file that you create that is sent (usually by email) to the person offering assistance. The invitation file includes a password that is used to connect the two computers.

Quick Concepts

9. Describe the Action Center and the function it serves. **pp. 40–42**

10. Describe why you might use File History, and how it differs from other restore applications. **p. 42**

11. Describe the utilities you would use to monitor and manage computer resources, such as the CPU and RAM. **p. 45**

12. Describe the types of files that can be removed with Disk Cleanup. **p. 45**

Hands-On Exercise

Watch the Video for This Hands-On Exercise!

MyITLab®
Topic-Based Training

Skills covered: Use the Action Center • Modify Firewall Settings • Use Disk Cleanup

3 Windows System and Security Features

Windows is a gateway to using application software. You know that the fifth-grade students are most interested in the fun things that can be done with software. You want to excite them about having fun with a computer, but you also want them to understand that along with the fun comes some need to maintain the computer. They also need to understand the concerns about security and privacy. You also want the students to be confident in their ability but well aware that help is available when they need it. In this section of your demonstration, you will encourage them to understand how they can perform some basic maintenance tasks. You will also show them features in Windows that can help address security concerns. Lastly, you will show them how easy it is to get help should they need assistance or reminders of how to work with Windows.

STEP 1 ›› USE THE ACTION CENTER

The Action Center will occasionally display messages regarding security and privacy settings. You want the Cedar Grove students to be aware of how important those messages are, so you will show them how to use the Action Center. Refer to Figure 1.27 as you complete Step 1.

> **TROUBLESHOOTING:** If you are working in a campus lab, you might not have access to the Action Center or Windows Update. In that case, you should skip this Hands-On Exercise.

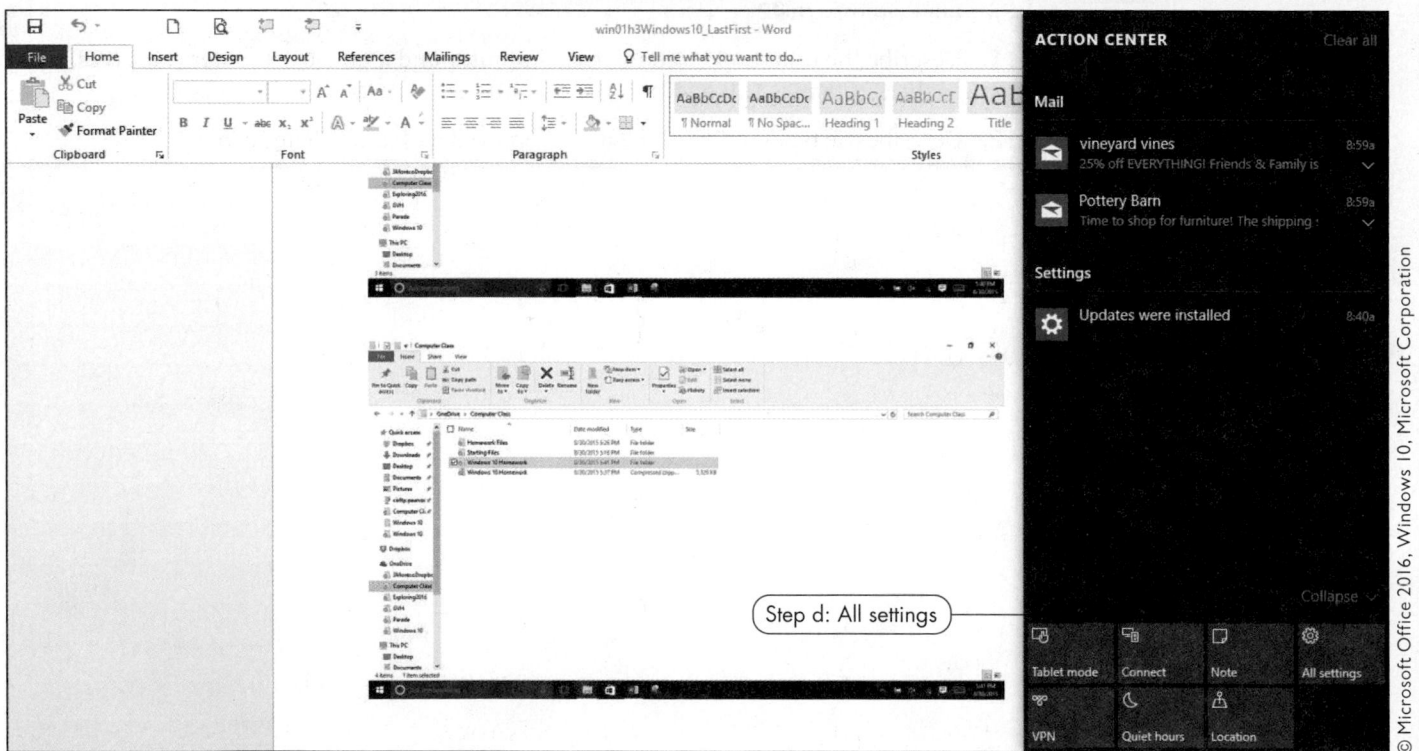

FIGURE 1.27 The Action Center

a. Open *win01h2Windows10_LastFirst* if you closed it at the end of Hands-On Exercise 2 and save it as **win01h3Windows10_LastFirst**, changing h2 to h3. Keep the document open and maximized.

b. Click **Action Center** in the Notification area on the taskbar.

Although any alerts displayed on your computer may vary from those shown in Figure 1.27, the general appearance should be similar.

c. Press **PtrSc**, click **Word** on the taskbar, press **Ctrl+End**, press **Enter** twice, and then press **Ctrl+V**. Save the file. Minimize Word.

d. Click **Action Center**, click **All settings**, click **System**, and then click **Notifications & actions**. Press **PtrSc**, click **Word** on the taskbar, press **Enter** twice, and then press **Ctrl+V**. Save the file. Minimize Word.

e. Click the **Back arrow** in the upper left of the Settings window, and then click **Update & security**.

Windows Update displays.

f. Click **Check for updates**.

g. Press **PtrSc**, click **Word** on the taskbar, press **Enter** twice, and then press **Ctrl+V**. Save the document. Minimize Word and close the Settings window.

STEP 2 ›› MODIFY FIREWALL SETTINGS

Although you do not expect the students to understand completely how firewalls work, you do want them to know that Windows includes a firewall and that they can manage firewall settings. Refer to Figure 1.28 as you complete Step 2.

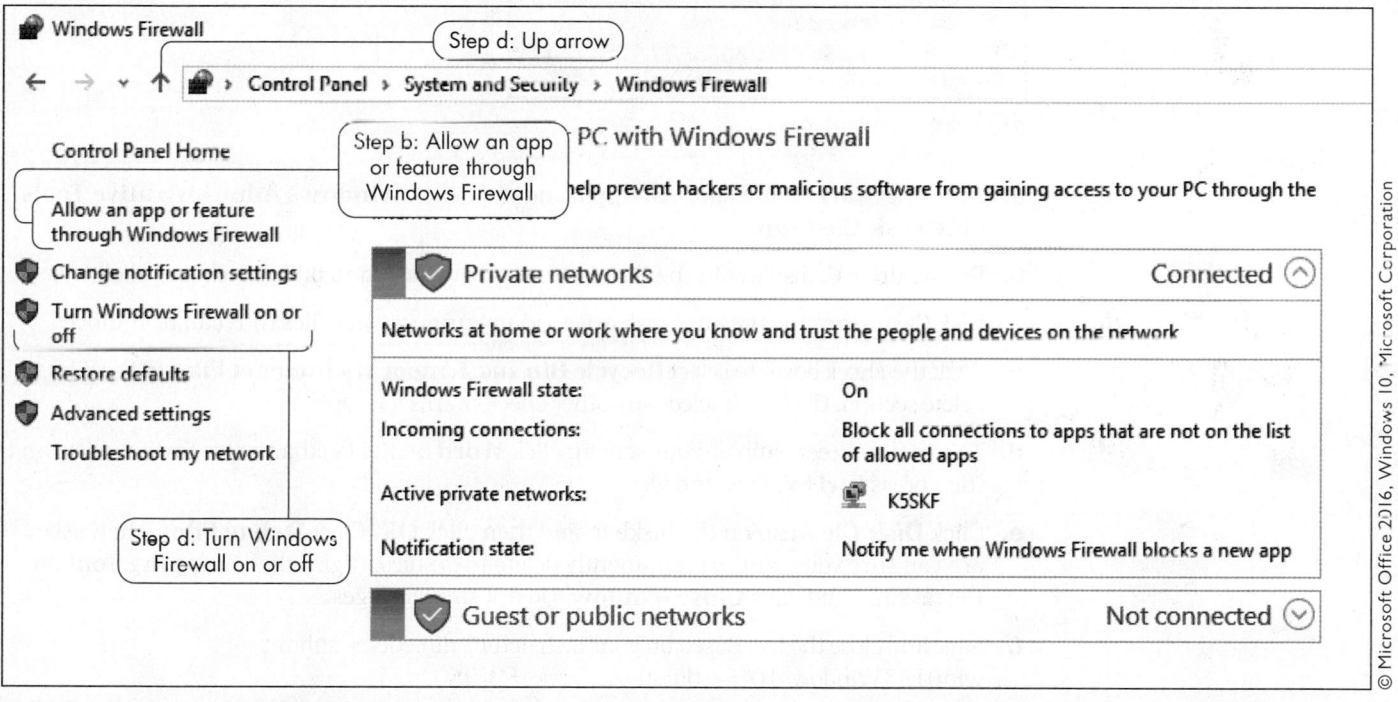

FIGURE 1.28 Modify Firewall Settings

a. Type **Firewall** in the search box, and then select **Windows Firewall - Control Panel**.

b. Click **Allow an App or feature through Windows Firewall**.

c. Take a full-screen snip of your screen, click **Word** on the taskbar, press **Enter** twice, and then press **Ctrl+V**. Minimize Word and the Snipping Tool windows.

d. Click the **up arrow** to return to main screen of Windows Firewall, and click **Turn Windows Firewall on or off**. Note the checkmarks.

e. Take a full-screen snip of your screen, click **Word** on the taskbar, press **Enter** twice, and then press **Ctrl+V**. Save the document. Minimize the Word and the Snipping Tool windows.

f. Click **Cancel**, and then close the Windows Firewall window.

You want to stress how important it is to run routine maintenance tasks on the computer. In addition to periodically wiping down the keyboard and monitor, you tell the students they should run the Disk Cleanup utility to remove unnecessary files that have accumulated. Refer to Figure 1.29 as you complete Step 3.

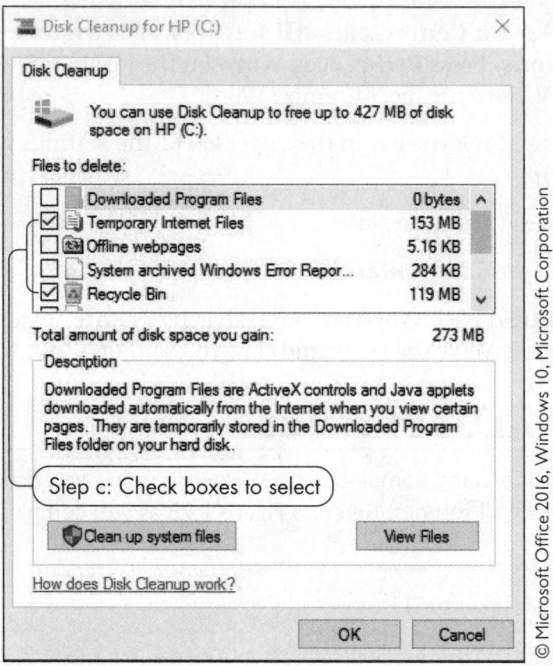

FIGURE 1.29 Disk Cleanup

a. Open the **Start** menu, click **All apps**, and then click **Windows Administrative Tools**. Click **Disk Cleanup**.

b. Ensure drive C: displays in the Disk cleanup: Drive Selection dialog box, and click **OK**.

Disk Cleanup scans the hard disk drive for any unnecessary files that can be removed.

c. Click the check boxes to select **Recycle Bin** and **Temporary Internet Files** in the Files to delete section. Click to deselect any other check marks.

d. Take a full-screen snip of your screen, click **Word** on the taskbar, press **Enter** twice, and then press **Ctrl+V**. Save the file.

e. Click **Disk Cleanup** on the taskbar, and then click **OK**. Click **Delete Files** when asked are you sure you want to permanently delete these files. Right-click **Snipping Tool** on the taskbar, and click **Close window**. Do not save changes.

f. Save and close the file. Based on your instructor's directions, submit win01h3Windows10_LastFirst.

Chapter Objectives Review

After reading this chapter, you have accomplished the following objectives:

1. Understand the Windows 10 Interface

- Sign in to a Microsoft account: A Microsoft account is necessary to use any Microsoft Services, including logging into Windows 10.
- Access sleep and power settings: Windows will go to sleep, a power-saving state, after a pre-determined period of inactivity. Restarting the computer is a warm boot. To power down the computer completely, choose Shut down.
- Explore the Windows 10 Start menu: The desktop is the primary working area that displays when you log into Windows. The Start menu is accessed by clicking the Start button on the taskbar. The Start menu has program tiles that can be arranged in groups, a Most used list of frequently used programs, and access to File Explorer, Documents, Settings, and Power. Clicking All apps changes the left panel of the Start menu to a list of all programs installed on the device.
- Configure the Start menu: You can easily add and remove tiles from the Windows 10 Start menu. Adding a tile to the Start menu or an icon to the taskbar is known as pinning. You can organize the tiles into groups by dragging them around the screen. You can also assign appropriate names for each group of tiles. Tiles can be resized and removed from the Start menu.
- Explore the taskbar: The taskbar displays icons of open programs, as well as Start, the search box, and the Notification area. A Task View enables you to view all current tasks in one glance. Frequently used programs can be pinned to the taskbar. Right-clicking an open program icon on the taskbar opens a Jump List.
- Identify desktop components: On the desktop, icons represent links to programs, files, folder, or other items related to your computer. The Recycle Bin is temporary storage for deleted files. Shortcuts are icons to program files.
- Customize the desktop: You can customize the desktop with a different background color or theme.

2. Manage and Use the Desktop and Components

- Use Task View: Task View enables you to see all open windows, and to organize them into separate workspaces.
- Create a virtual desktop: Virtual desktops help to organize and access groups of windows for different purposes.
- Identify windows components: Windows can be moved, resized, stacked, or snapped into position so that multiple windows are easier to work with and identify.
- Snap, move, and resize windows: You can display up to four Windows 10 apps at a time using Snap and Snap Assist. Dialog boxes are windows that display when a program requires user interaction.

3. Use Windows 10 Search Features

- Use the search box: A search box, incorporated into the taskbar for easy access, is used to search the Web and the device. If you are looking for help or specific answers, you can type search keyword(s) in the search box and then click any resulting links.
- Use Cortana: When enabled, Cortana, Microsoft's personal assistant, can assist with tasks such as reminders and directions, provide a news feed, as well as search the Web and the device. Cortana's settings are managed through the Cortana Notebook.
- Get help: Cortana and the search box are the primary resources for help and support for Windows and other Microsoft-related questions.
- Manage the Cortana Notebook and settings: You can add or modify your preferences in Cortana Notebook. As you use Cortana, she will adapt to your preferences and be able to better predict your needs.

4. Use File Explorer

- File Explorer is an app used to create and manage folders and files across various storage locations on your PC, online storage, external storage, and networks.
- Understand the File Explorer interface: File Explorer displays the organizational hierarchy of storage locations, folders, and files.
- Use the View tab on the Ribbon: The View tab contains controls that manage how files and folders are displayed in File Explorer.
- Use and modify Quick access: Quick access is a new feature of File Explorer that contains shortcuts to folders you use most often. Folders can be pinned and removed from Quick access.
- Use the search box in File Explorer: Use the search box in File Explorer to search for specific files and folders. Results can be filtered by type, date modified, or other properties for further search refinement.
- Navigate File Explorer: The Navigation Pane is used to move between folders and storage locations. Clicking next to each main area in the Navigation Pane expands or collapses the folder to show or hide contents.
- Working with files and folders: Grouping related files into folders helps keep them organized and easier to locate.
- Open, rename, and delete folders and files: Click on a file or folder to open it, right-click and select Rename to give the folder or file a different name, right-click and select Delete to remove the file or folder from File Explorer.

5. **Select, Copy, and Move Multiple Files and Folders**

- Select multiple files and folders: Select adjacent files while pressing the Shift key. Select non-adjacent files while pressing the Ctrl key. Alternatively, click the check box next to each item to select.
- Copy and move file and folders: Files and folders can be copied and moved by dragging to a new location, as needed.

6. **Compress Files and Folders**

- Create a compressed folder: Compress a folder or a group of files using the Zip tool to facilitate sending a large file or a group of files using email or uploading to the Web.
- Extract files from a compressed folder: To unzip, use the the Extract all feature on the Extract tab.

7. **Work with Security Settings and Software**

- Understand the Action Center: The Action Center monitors the status of your security and maintenance settings, alerting you when maintenance tasks (such as backing up your system) are overlooked or when your security is at risk (for example, when antivirus software is out of date).
- Use File History: The File History utility can be configured to automatically make backups of your important files while you work.

- Access Windows Update: Windows Update provides a means to push modifications and fixes made to the operating system to the computer.
- Use Windows Defender: Windows Defender, an antivirus and antispyware program, is included with Windows and works to identify and remove malicious software.
- Use Windows firewall: A Windows firewall protects against unauthorized access to your computer from outside entities and prohibits unauthorized programs from accessing your computer without your permission.

8. **Work with Administrative Tools**

- Use Task Manager: Task Manager displays programs and processes that are running on your computer. Task Manager can be used to close a program when it is not responding.
- Monitor system resources: Resource Monitor displays how the computer is using its key components, including the CPU and RAM.
- Use Disk Cleanup: Disk Cleanup is used to remove unnecessary files from the computer that can slow down system performance.
- Get remote assistance: Remote assistance allows a third party to take control of your device.

Key Terms Matching

Match the key terms with their definitions. Write the key term letter by the appropriate numbered definition.

a. Action Center

b. Compressed (zipped) folder

c. Cortana

d. Desktop

e. Disk Cleanup

f. File Explorer

g. File History

h. File management

i. Notification area

j. OneDrive

k. Pin

l. Quick access

m. Search box

n. Start menu

o. Task Manager

p. Task View

q. Taskbar

r. Tile

s. Virtual desktop

t. Windows Defender

1. _____ An administrative tool in Windows that is used to remove unnecessary files from the computer. **p. 46**

2. _____ Primary working area of Windows 10. **p. 5**

3. _____ A utility in Windows that continuously makes copies of your important files so that you can recover them if you encounter a file problem. **p. 42**

4. _____ Microsoft's cloud storage system. **p. 30**

5. _____ A folder that uses less drive space and can be transferred or shared with other users more quickly. **p. 34**

6. _____ A component of File Explorer that contains shortcuts to the most frequently used folders. **p. 30**

7. _____ The main access to all programs and features on your computer. **p. 5**

8. _____ The Windows 10 personal assistant that helps search the Web and your PC, and can also assist with reminders, tasks, and other activities. **p. 16**

9. _____ The means of providing an organizational structure to file and folders. **p. 28**

10. _____ Detects and removes viruses and spyware. **p. 43**

11. _____ Displays the programs and processes that are running on your computer. It is also used to close a non-responding program. **p. 44**

12. _____ Located on the taskbar, provides a convenient way to search your computer or the Web. **p. 8**

13. _____ Provides status information, notifications, and recommended actions for various maintenance and security settings. **p. 40**

14. _____ Horizontal bar at the bottom of the desktop that displays open applications, the Notification area, the search box, and pinned apps or programs. **p. 8**

15. _____ Provides system status alerts in pop-up boxes. **p. 8**

16. _____ A process to add a tile to the Start menu or an icon to the taskbar. **p. 7**

17. _____ A block icon on the Start menu that represents a program or app. **p. 6**

18. _____ A way to organize and access groups of windows for different purposes. **p. 12**

19. _____ The Windows app that is used to create folders and manage files and folders across various storage locations. **p. 28**

20. _____ Feature on the taskbar that enables the user to view thumbnail previews of all open tasks in one glance. **p. 11**

Multiple Choice

1. The Windows 10 feature that alerts you to any maintenance or security concerns is the:

   (a) Action Center.
   (b) Security Center.
   (c) Windows Defender.
   (d) Control Panel.

2. Snapping apps means that you:

   (a) Minimize all open apps simultaneously so that the Start menu displays.
   (b) Auto arrange all open apps so that they are of uniform size.
   (c) Manually reposition all open apps so that you can see the content of each.
   (d) Fix an app window(s) to either side or the corners of the screen.

3. What phrase is spoken to use Cortana?

   (a) Hey, Cortana
   (b) Wake up, Cortana
   (c) No specific phrase is necessary.
   (d) You cannot speak to Cortana.

4. Apps or programs on the Start menu are represented by rectangular icons known as:

   (a) Gadgets.
   (b) Tiles.
   (c) Thumbnails.
   (d) Boxes.

5. What feature is used to organize and access groups of open windows for different purposes, such as Schoolwork and Entertainment?

   (a) Windows Defender
   (b) Windows desktop
   (c) Virtual desktop
   (d) Task Manager

6. Which of the following best describes the Action Center?

   (a) Removes unnecessary files from the computer
   (b) Includes the clock and other icons that relate to the status or setting of a program
   (c) Contains shortcuts to the most frequently used folders
   (d) Provides status information, notifications, and recommended actions

7. Adding a tile to the Start menu or an icon to the taskbar is known as:

   (a) Snapping.
   (b) Snipping.
   (c) Pinning.
   (d) Tacking.

8. Which of the following is a method of switching between open windows?

   (a) Alt+Tab
   (b) Task View
   (c) Both A and B
   (d) Neither A nor B

9. When you restore down a window, you:

   (a) Keep it open, but remove it from view.
   (b) Make the window smaller, but keep it displayed on the desktop.
   (c) Minimize the window's height but leave its width unchanged.
   (d) Minimize the window's width but leave its height unchanged.

10. When you enter search keywords in the search box of File Explorer and the OneDrive option is selected:

    (a) The search is limited to that specific location.
    (b) The search cannot be further narrowed.
    (c) The search is automatically expanded to include every folder on the hard drive.
    (d) The search is limited to the selected location but can be expanded if you like.

Practice Exercises

1 Investments

FROM SCRATCH 🥤

You have some extra funds accumulating in your savings account. You want to begin investing, but before you take the plunge, you decide to watch a few stocks and learn more about them. You also want to take advantage of some Microsoft apps to read more about the stock market and investing, in general. You create and add tiles to a new group on your Start menu and also create a separate desktop for your investment activities, so you can easily come back to all the material. Refer to Figure 1.30 as you complete the exercise.

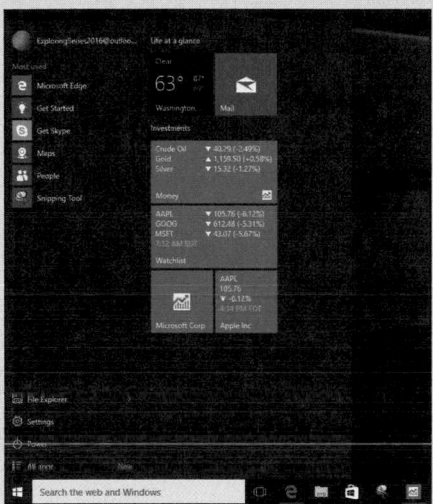 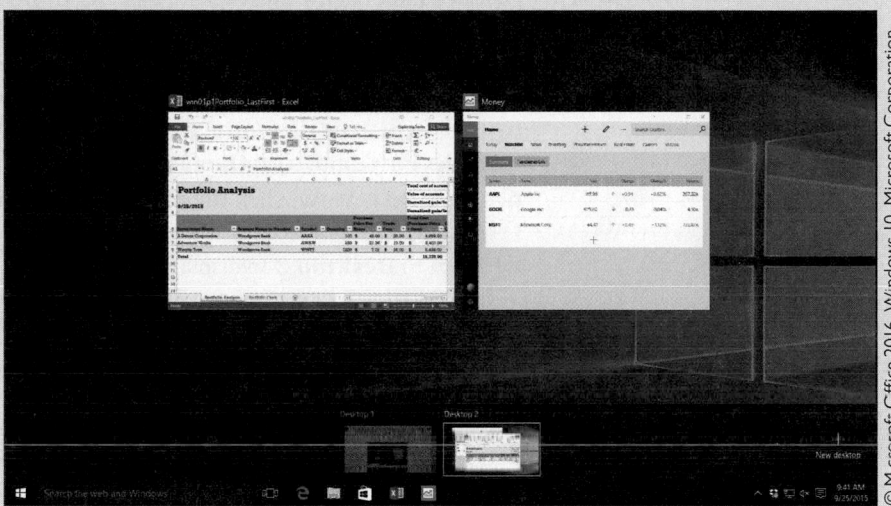

FIGURE 1.30 Investments Start Menu and Virtual Desktops

a. Open a Blank Word document, and save it as **win01p1Investments_LastFirst**. Minimize the window.

b. Click the **search box**, type **Money**, right-click **Money Trusted Windows Store app** that displays at the top of the results list, and then click **Pin to Start**.

> **TROUBLESHOOTING:** If the Money app is already pinned to start, skip to the next step.

c. Click **Start**, and move the Money tile to a blank area on the Start menu.

d. Point above the Money tile to display the Name group box, click inside the box, type **Investments**, and then press **Enter**.

   You have created a new group.

e. Click **Money**, and then click **Watchlist** from the top menu. Click **Add to Watchlist** (the plus sign), and then type **MSFT**, and press **Enter**. (Note: MSFT might already be added to the Watchlist.) Repeat this step to add **GOOG** and **AAPL**.

> **TROUBLESHOOTING:** If MSFT is the first stock begin added to the Watchlist, click Add a favorite in the middle of the screen. .

f. Click **Pin to Start** 📌 to pin the Watchlist to the Start menu. Click **Close**.

g. Click **MSFT** on the Watchlist, and click **Pin to Start**. Click the **Back arrow**. Repeat for **AAPL**. Minimize Money.

h. Click **Start**, and notice the three new tiles you have added. Drag the three new tiles into the Investments group.

i. Right-click the **Money tile**, and click **Resize**, and then select **Wide**. Resize the Watchlist tile to **Wide**.

j. Drag to arrange the tiles within the Investments group to match the arrangement in Figure 1.30.

k. Press **PrtSc**, click **Word** on the taskbar, and then press **Ctrl+V**. Save the document and minimize Word.

l. Click **Start**, and click the **Watchlist** tile.

m. Open Cortana, click the **Notebook icon**, and click **Finance**. In the Stocks you're tracking section, click **GOOG**, and click the **trashcan icon** to remove GOOG from the Watchlist.

n. Click **Excel** in the Start menu, type **Portfolio Analysis** in the Search for online templates box. Select the template that results, and click **Create**.

o. Click **File**, click **Save As**, click **Browse**, and then click **Documents** in the This PC folder. Check that This PC>Documents displays in the Address bar.

p. Type **win01p1Portfolio_LastFirst** in the File name box, click **New folder**, and name the folder **Portfolio**, click **Open**, and then click **Save**. Minimize Excel.

q. Open **Task View**, click the **plus sign** to create a new desktop, and then drag the Excel and Money thumbnails to Desktop 2.

r. Point to **Desktop 2** to display two thumbnails. Click **PrtSc**, point to **Desktop 1**, click **Word**, press **Enter** twice, and then press **Ctrl+V**. Save the document.

s. Click **Close** to delete Desktop 2, and close Excel. Open File Explorer, click **Documents** in the Quick access or This PC section, right-click the **Portfolio folder**, and then click **Pin to Quick access**.

t. Right-click **Portfolio** in the Documents folder and rename it as **Investments**.
Notice that the folder name also changes in Quick access.

u. Press **PrtSc**, click **Word**, press **Enter** twice, and then press **Ctrl+V**. Save the document.

v. Click **Start**, click **Settings**, type **Firewall** in the Find a setting search box, and then click **Windows Firewall**. Click **Turn Windows Firewall on or off**, and then in the Public network settings, click to select **Block all incoming connections, including those in the list of allowed apps**.

w. Press **PrtSc**, click **Word**, press **Enter** twice, and then press **Ctrl+V**. Save the document and minimize Word.

x. Click **Cancel**, close the Windows Firewall window, and then close the Settings window.

y. Save and close the file. Based on your instructor's directions, submit win01p1Investments_ LastFirst. Close any other open windows.

2 Planning a Trip

FROM SCRATCH

You and your family want to take a road trip through some National Parks. You volunteer to begin planning. You start by opening the Calendar app to block out the desired week, and then open the Map app to help with the navigation. You pin both apps to the Start menu, and place them in a new group. You also create a new desktop in which to display them. You create a folder and pin it to Quick access, so everyone in the family can easily find the folder and save their ideas. Your friend visited some National Parks last year and sent you her photos in a zipped folder. You move them to the new folder, and then extract the pictures so your family can better access them. You use Disk Cleanup to make sure your computer remains in tip-top shape. Refer to Figure 1.31 as you complete the exercise.

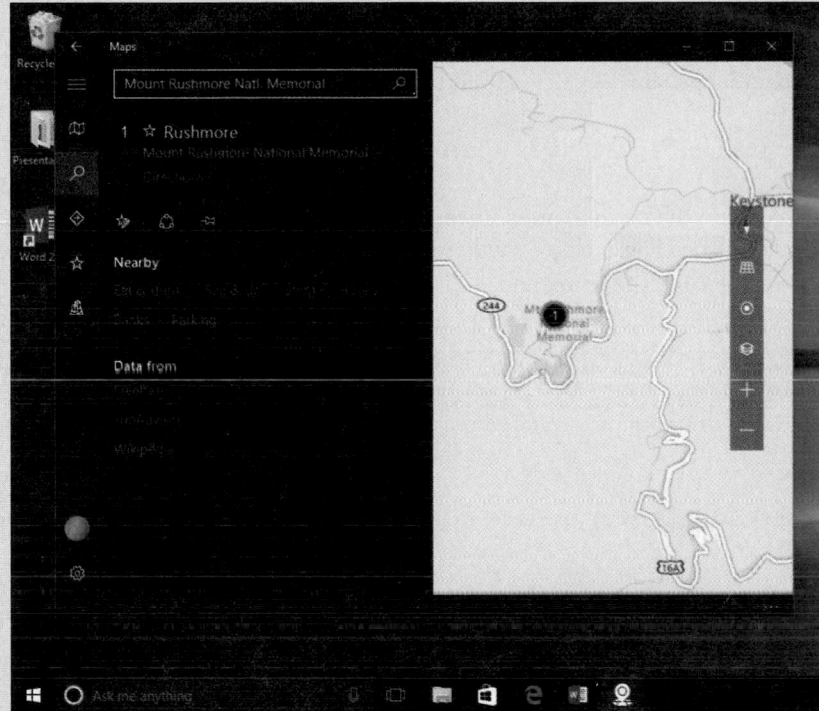 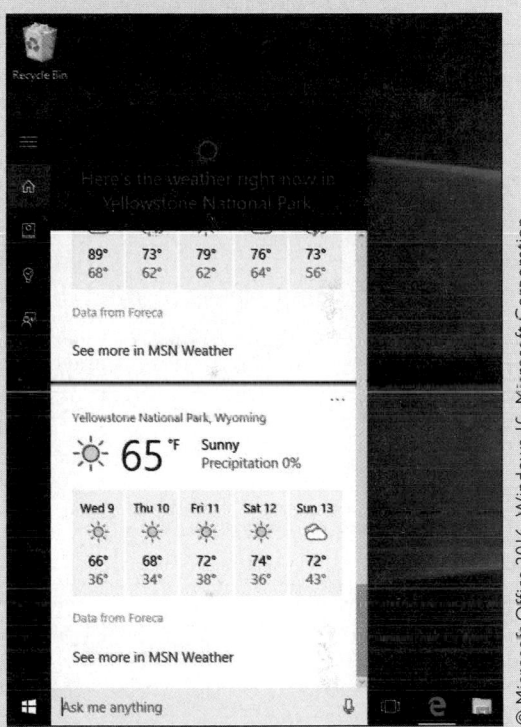

FIGURE 1.31 Planning a Trip

a. Start **Word**, create a **Blank document**, and then save the document as **win01p2Vacation_ LastFirst**. Keep the document open.

b. Click **Start**, click **All apps**, and scroll to find **Calendar**. Right-click and select **Pin to Start**. Note: If Calendar app is already on the Start menu, skip to the next step.

c. Click **Start**, click the **Calendar app**, click **New event**, click in the Event name box, and type **Family Vacation**. Click **Start**, and type **June 01, 2018**. Click **End**, and type **June 14, 2018**. Click to select the **All day box**, click the **Show As: box**, select **Tentative**, click the **Reminder box**, and then select **None**.

> **TROUBLESHOOTING:** If you have never worked with the Calendar app before, you might need to click Welcome, and confirm an email account before working with the application.

d. Press **PrtSc**, click **Word** on the taskbar, and then click inside a blank area of the document. Press **Ctrl+V**, click **Save**, and then minimize Word. Click **Save & Close** on the Calendar app. Close Calendar.

e. Click **Start**, click **All apps**, and scroll to find **Maps**, if it is not already on the Start menu. Right-click and select **Pin to Start**.

f. Open **Maps**, type **Yellowstone National Park**, select the entry in the resulting list, click the **Star** (Add to Favorites), type **Yellowstone** in the Nickname box, and then click **Save**. Repeat for **Grand Teton National Park**, using **Teton** as the Nickname, and **Mount Rushmore National Memorial**, using **Rushmore** as the Nickname.

g. Press **PrtSc**, click **Word**, press **Enter** twice, press **Ctrl+V**, click **Save,** and then minimize the Word document. Close Maps.

h. Open **File Explorer**, click **Documents** (in either This PC or Quick access), and then click **New folder** on the Home tab in the New group. Name the folder **Vacation**. Press **Enter**. Click **Pin to Quick access** in the Clipboard group.

i. Navigate to your student data files, and locate the *win01p2Pictures* zipped folder. Click the zipped folder, press and hold **Ctrl**, and drag it to the Vacation folder you pinned to Quick access.

j. Click **Vacation** in Quick access, click the **win01p2Pictures zipped folder**, click the **Extract tab**, and then click **Extract all**. Click **Extract**.

k. Click **Vacation** in the Address bar, click the **zipped win01p2Pictures folder** in the File list, and then click **Delete**.

l. Double-click to open the **win01p2Pictures folder** so the thumbnail images display in the File list.

m. Press **PrtSc**, click **Word** on the taskbar, press **Enter** twice, press **Ctrl+V**, and then save the Word document. Close all open File Explorer windows.

n. Click the **search box**, type **Disk Cleanup**, and then click **Disk Cleanup Desktop app**.

o. Click **OK** to run Disk Cleanup on the C: drive, and then in the results, click to select **Recycle Bin** and deselect all other check boxes.

p. Press **PrtSc**, click **Word**, press **Enter** twice, press **Ctrl+V**.

q. Save and close the file. Based on your instructor's directions submit win01p2Vacation_LastFirst.

Mid-Level Exercises

1 5K Pound Run

 **FROM SCRATCH**

To satisfy your community outreach graduation requirement, you and a friend have decided to organize a 5K run to benefit the regional animal rescue society. You are responsible for organizing the paperwork and pulling together the details. To start, you use Windows 10 to organize the various apps and files so you can easily find and work with all that you need at any time.

a. Start **Word**, create a **Blank document**, and it save as **win01m1Race_LastFirst**.

b. Type **5K Pound Run**, and press **Enter** twice. Save the file.

c. Pin Word to the taskbar.

d. Locate the Calendar app and Map app in All apps, and pin both to the Start menu.

e. Put the Maps and Calendar apps in a new group on the Start menu, and name the group **5K Race**.

f. Pin the Sticky Notes app to the Start menu, and add it to the 5K Race group.

g. Use PrtSc to capture a screenshot of the Start menu, and paste it in the win01m1Race_LastFirst document.

h. Use the search box to find information on the Web about 5K races in your area in April. Click any link that displays a list of races. Take a screenshot of the Web results, copy and paste to the Word document.

i. Open File Explorer, create a new folder where you save your student files named **5KPoundRun**, and then pin the folder to Quick access.

j. Create subfolders in the 5KPoundRun folder, and name them: **Sponsors**, **Permissions**, **Promotions**, **Registration**, and **Follow-Up**. Rename the Registration folder to **Participants**.

k. Click **Word** on the taskbar, click **File**, and then click **New**. Type **Seasonal Event Flyer (Spring)** in the templates search box. Click **Create**, and then save to the Promotions folder as **win01m1Flyer_LastFirst**.

 **DISCOVER**

l. Add the tag **5KPound Run** to win01m1Flyer_LastFirst. Take a screenshot to show the tag, copy and paste to the win01m1Race_LastFirst document. Save the flyer.

m. Create a new virtual desktop (Desktop 2), and drag the flyer into Desktop 2 in Task View. Display the contents of Desktop 2, and then take a screenshot and paste the screenshot into win01m1Race_LastFirst.

n. Compress the 5KPoundRun folder and rename it **win01m1PoundRun_LastFirst**.

o. Open the Action Center. Take a screenshot of the Action Center. Paste the screenshot into win01m1Race_LastFirst.

p. Save and close the file. Based on your instructor's directions, submit win01m1Race_LastFirst and win01m1PoundRun_LastFirst.

2 Junk Business

 **FROM SCRATCH**

You and a college friend were asked to reconfigure some old computers for an inner city after school club. Because you had a few spare parts and some hardware expertise, you rebuilt several computers and installed Windows 10. Now you will check the system of each computer to verify that it is workable and configured correctly. Assume the computer you are working on to complete this exercise is the computer you rebuilt.

a. Open Word, create a Blank document, and save the file as **win01m2Junk_LastFirst**. Snap Word to the left side of your screen.

b. Open the Action Center. Press **PrtSc** to capture a screen image of the Action Center. In Word, type **Step b:**. Press **Enter**, and press **Ctrl+V** to paste the screen. Underneath the image, describe any Notifications that display. Save the document. Close the Action Center.

c. Type **Resource Monitor** in the search box. Pin Resource Monitor to the Start menu. Open Resource Monitor, and click the **Memory tab**. Snap the Resource Monitor window to the right side of your screen. Click **Word** on the taskbar, press **Enter** twice, type **Step c:**, press **Enter**, and then list the amount of memory *In Use*, *Standby*, *Free*, and *Installed*. Add a sentence that comments on whether the amount of memory in the system seems sufficient. Close the Resource Monitor. Save the Word document.

d. Pin Disk Cleanup to the Start menu. Type **Windows Accessories** as a new group name, in the Start menu, and drag **Disk Cleanup** and **Resource Monitor** to the group. Take a screenshot of the Start menu, open Word, type **Step d:**, and then paste the screenshot.

e. Open File Explorer, and create a new folder in Documents named **Client Invoices**. Pin the Client Invoices folder to Quick access, and then open the Client Invoices folder. Take a screenshot of File Explorer, open Word, type **Step e:**, and then paste the screenshot.

f. Save and close the file. Based on your instructor's directions, submit win01m2Junk_LastFirst.

Beyond the Classroom

Speech Class Notes

GENERAL CASE

For your speech class, you must develop a speech that teaches how to do something. Because Windows 10 is a relatively new operating system, you decide to demonstrate some of its features. You will use Word to record a few notes that will help you make your presentation. After completing your notes, save the document as **win01b1Speech_ LastFirst**. Listing your points in numerical order, provide directions to the class on the following:

- Customize the Start menu.
- Pin programs to the taskbar and the Start menu.
- Use the search box to find and open a program that you think is installed on your computer and to get help on an item related to Windows 10.
- Use Cortana.
- Use the Action Center.

Based on your instructor's directions, submit win01b1Speech_LastFirst.

Computer Security Report

DISASTER RECOVERY

You depend on a laptop computer for most of what you do and you would be lost should you lose your laptop or the data and programs on it. A recent scare, when you temporarily misplaced the laptop, has led you to consider precautions you can take to make sure your computer and its data are protected. You will use the search box and Cortana to explore some suggestions for protecting your laptop. Create a report that describes how you would secure your laptop and the data, programs, and personal information on your laptop against harm. Consider virus protection software, cloud storage options, backup and recovery software and hardware, and ways to protect and secure your hardware. Use Word to record the report, save the report as **win01b2Protection LastFirst**, and submit as directed by your instructor.

Capstone Exercise

For your Entrepreneurial class, BUS401, you are planning a new business as the ongoing project. Since you will be working with many of the same apps and documents throughout the semester, you decide to use many of the new Windows 10 features to help you stay organized and be as efficient as possible.

Work with the Start Menu

To start things off, you want to pin a few apps to the Start menu that you know you will be working with consistently throughout the semester. You will put them in a group and give the group a meaningful name.

a. Open a new Word document and save it as **win01c1Business_LastFirst**.

b. Locate and pin to the Start menu, the Calculator app, the Snipping Tool, Word 2016, and Excel 2016.

c. Pin Word 2016 and the Snipping Tool to the taskbar.

d. Create a new group on the Start menu, name it **Business Apps**, and move the apps you added to the Start menu in Step b to this group.

e. Resize the Calculator app and the Snipping Tool tiles to Small. Keep Word 2016 and Excel 2016 tiles to Medium. Arrange the tiles so the Word and Excel tiles are next to each other, and the Calculator and Snipping Tool tiles are below the Word and Excel tiles.

f. Take a screenshot of the Start menu. Paste the screenshot to win01c1Business_LastFirst.

Use Task View and Virtual Desktops

There are a few Excel and Word files that you will be using for this project. So that you can get to them easily, you put them onto a separate desktop.

a. Open Word and search for a Business Plan template. Select the first template, named Business plan. Create and save the document as **win01c1BusinessPlan_LastFirst**.

b. Open Excel and search for a Profit and Loss template. Select the first template, named Profit and Loss Statement. Save the workbook as **win01c1ProfitLoss_LastFirst**.

c. Create a new virtual desktop (Desktop 2) and drag the Excel and Word files created in Steps a and b above to Desktop 2. Keep win01c1Business_LastFirst in Desktop 1.

d. Display Desktop 2, and snap the Word document to the left and the Excel workbook to the right of the screen and take a screenshot.

e. Display Desktop 1, and paste the screenshot to win01c1Business_LastFirst.

Use Cortana and the Search Box

One of the first things you need to do for your business is to write a Mission Statement. You use the search box to find information on Mission Statements, and then use Cortana to set up a reminder for you to talk to your professor about this, as well.

a. Type **how to write a mission statement** in the search box. Open the Entrepreneur.com link (or a similar link). Drag the browser window to Desktop 2.

b. Display Desktop 2, and then using the Windows and arrow keys, snap the browser window to the lower left corner, and the Word window to the upper left corner.

c. Use Cortana in Desktop 2 to add a reminder to meet with your professor. Choose a day and time next week.

d. Take a screenshot of Desktop 2 and Cortana Reminders. Display Desktop 1, and paste the screenshot to win01c1Business_LastFirst.

e. Close all windows in Desktop 2.

Use File Explorer

Although using virtual desktops helps to organize your active documents, you want to create a good file management structure so all your Entrepreneurial class documents are in one place and easy to access throughout the semester. You use File Explorer to create folders and pin one folder to Quick access.

a. Open File Explorer, and open the Documents folder in This PC. Create a new folder named **BUS401**. Pin this folder to Quick access.

b. Open the BUS401 folder, and create three new folders named **Business Plan Documents**, **Financial Statements**, and **Marketing Info**.

c. Take a screenshot of File Explorer and paste the screenshot to win01c1Business_LastFirst.

Work with Files and Folders

With the new folder structure set up, you reorganize your existing files. You then compress the BUS401 folder so you can more easily share it with your professor and others.

a. Save the win01c1ProfitLoss_LastFirst workbook to the Financial Statements folder, and move win01c1BusinessPlan_LastFirst to the Business Plan Documents folder.

b. Compress the BUS401 folder, and rename the folder **win01c1BUS401_LastFirst**.

Use the Action Center and Administrative Tools

One of the other components of the BUS401 project is to create a marketing video. You know creating and editing a video uses lots of computer processing and memory, so you check the status of your system resources to see if this will be the best computer to use going forward. You also want to check the Action Center for any new notifications.

a. Open Resource Monitor. Click the **Memory tab**, use the Snipping Tool to take a Rectangular Snip of the Resource Monitor window, and then paste it into win01c1Business_LastFirst.

b. Click the **CPU tab**, and then use the Snipping Tool to take a Rectangular Snip of the Resource Monitor window and paste it into win01c1Business_LastFirst. Close the Resource Monitor.

c. Open the Action Center. Take a screenshot, and paste the screenshot in to win01c1Business_LastFirst.

d. Save and close the document. Based on your instructor's directions, submit win01c1Business_LastFirst and win01c1BUS401_LastFirst.

Office 2016 Common Features

LEARNING OUTCOME You will apply skills common across the Microsoft Office suite to create and format documents and edit content in Office 2016 applications.

OBJECTIVES & SKILLS: After you read this chapter, you will be able to:

CASE STUDY | Spotted Begonia Art Gallery

You are an administrative assistant for Spotted Begonia, a local art gallery. The gallery does a lot of community outreach and tries to help local artists develop a network of clients and supporters. Local schools are invited to bring students to the gallery for enrichment programs.

As the administrative assistant for Spotted Begonia, you are responsible for overseeing the production of documents, spreadsheets, newspaper articles, and presentations that will be used to increase public awareness of the gallery. Other clerical assistants who are familiar with Microsoft Office will prepare the promotional materials, and you will proofread, make necessary corrections, adjust page layouts, save and print documents, and identify appropriate templates to simplify tasks. Your experience with Microsoft Office 2016 is limited, but you know that certain fundamental tasks that are common to Word, Excel, and PowerPoint will help you accomplish your oversight task. You are excited to get started with your work!

Taking the First Step

CHAPTER 1

Konstantin Chagin/
Shutterstock

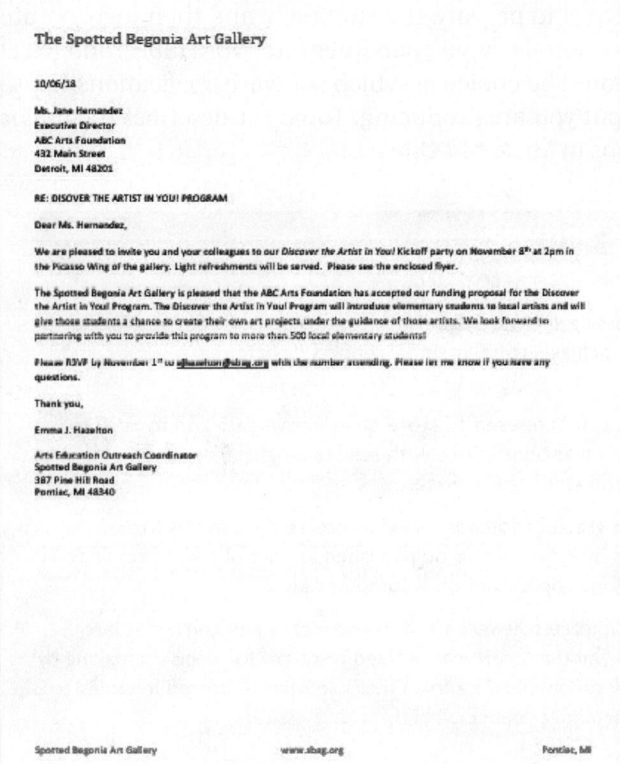

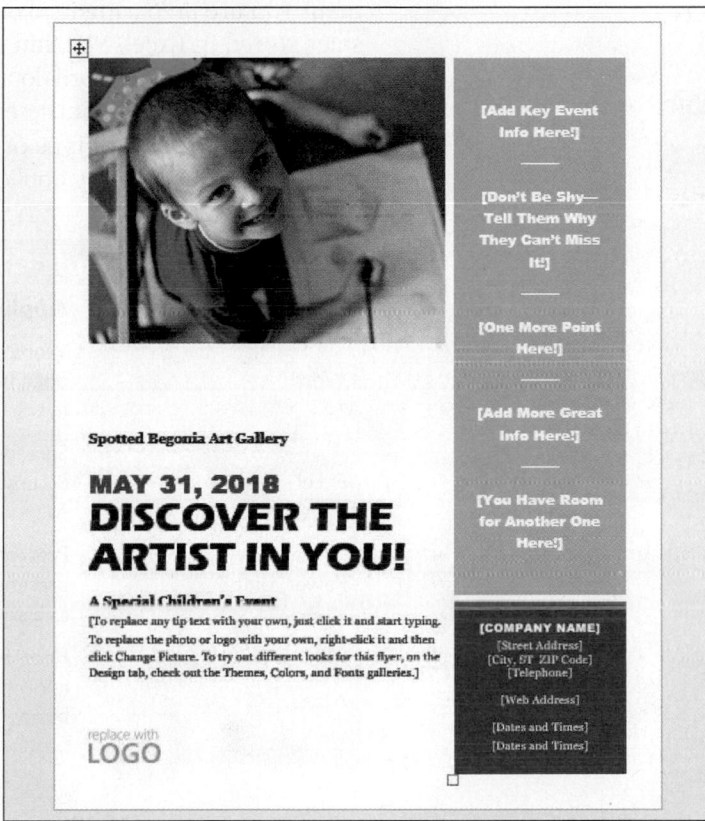

Word 2016, Windows 10, Microsoft Corporation

FIGURE 1.1 Spotted Begonia Art Gallery Memo and Flyer

CASE STUDY | Spotted Begonia Art Gallery

Starting Files	Files to be Submitted
f01h1Letter	f01h2Flyer_LastFirst
f01h2Flyer	f01h3Letter_LastFirst
Blank document	

Getting Started with Office Applications

Organizations around the world rely heavily on Microsoft Office software to produce documents, spreadsheets, presentations, and databases. **Microsoft Office** is a productivity software suite including a set of software applications, each one specializing in a particular type of output. You can use **Word** to produce all sorts of documents, including memos, newsletters, forms, tables, and brochures. **Excel** makes it easy to organize records, financial transactions, and business information in the form of worksheets. With **PowerPoint**, you can create dynamic presentations to inform and persuade audiences. **Access** is a relational database software application that enables you to record and link data, query databases, and create forms and reports.

You will sometimes find that you need to use two or more Office applications to produce your intended output. You might, for example, find that an annual report document you are preparing in Word for an art gallery should also include a chart of recent sales stored in Excel. You can use Excel to prepare the summary and then incorporate the worksheet in the Word document. Similarly, you can integrate Word tables and Excel charts into a PowerPoint presentation. The choice of which software applications to use really depends on what type of output you are producing. Table 1.1 describes the major tasks of the four primary applications in Microsoft Office.

TABLE 1.1 Microsoft Office Software	
Office 2016 Product	**Application Characteristics**
Word	Word processing software used with text to create, edit, and format documents such as letters, memos, reports, brochures, resumes, and flyers.
Excel	Spreadsheet software used to store quantitative data and to perform accurate and rapid calculations with results ranging from simple budgets to financial and statistical analyses.
PowerPoint	Presentation graphics software used to create slide shows for presentation by a speaker, to be published as part of a website, or to run as a stand-alone application on a computer kiosk.
Access	Relational database software used to store data and convert it into information. Database software is used primarily for decision making by businesses that compile data from multiple records stored in tables to produce informative reports.

Pearson Education, Inc.

As you become familiar with Microsoft Office, you will find that although each software application produces a specific type of output, all applications share common features. Such commonality gives a similar feel to each software application so that learning and working with Office software products is easy.

In this section, you will learn how to open an application, log in with your Microsoft account, and open and save a file. You will also learn to identify features common to Office software applications, including interface components such as the Ribbon, Backstage view, and the Quick Access Toolbar. You will experience Live Preview. You will learn how to get help with an application. You will also learn how to search for and install Office add-ins.

Starting an Office Application

STEP 1 ❱❱ Microsoft Office applications are launched from the Start menu. Click the Start button, and then click the app tile for the application in which you want to work. If the application tile is not on the Start menu, you can open the program from All apps, or alternatively, you can click in the search box on the task bar, type the name of the program, and press Enter. The program will open automatically.

Change Your Microsoft Account

Although you can log in to Windows as a local network user, you can also log in using a Microsoft account. When you have a Microsoft account, you can sign in to any Windows computer and you will be able to access the saved settings associated with your Microsoft account. That means the computer will have the same familiar look that you are used to seeing on other computers and devices. Your Microsoft account will automatically sign in to all of the apps and services that use a Microsoft account as the authentication. You can also save your sign-in credentials for other websites that you frequently visit. If you share your computer with another user, each user can have access to his own Microsoft account; you can easily switch between accounts so you can access your own files.

To switch between accounts in an application such as Word, complete the following steps:

1. Click the profile name at the top-right of the application.
2. Select Switch account. Select an account from the list, if the account has already been added to the computer, or add a new account.

Logging in with your Microsoft account also provides additional benefits such as being connected to all of Microsoft's resources on the Internet. These resources include a free Outlook email account and access to OneDrive cloud storage. *Cloud storage* is a technology used to store files and to work with programs that are stored in a central location on the Internet. *OneDrive* is an app used to store, access, and share files and folders. It is accessible using an installed desktop app or as cloud storage using a Web address. For Office applications, OneDrive is the default location for saving files. Documents saved in OneDrive are accessible from any computer that has an Internet connection. As long as the document has been saved in OneDrive, the most recent version of the document will be accessible when you log in from any computer connected to the Internet. Moreover, files and folders stored on the computer's hard drive or saved on a portable storage device can be synced with those on the OneDrive account.

OneDrive enables you to collaborate with others. You can easily share your documents with others or edit a document on which you are collaborating. You can even work with others simultaneously on the same document.

Working with Files

When working with an Office application, you can begin by opening an existing file that has already been saved to a storage medium, or you can begin work on a new file. When you open an application within Office, you can select a template to use as you begin working on a new file.

Create a New File

After opening an Office application, such as Word, Excel, or PowerPoint, you will be presented with template choices. Click Blank document (workbook, presentation, etc.) to start a new blank file. Perhaps you are already working with a document in an Office application but want to create a new file.

To create a new Office file, complete the following steps:

1. Click the File tab and click New.
2. Click Blank.

Open a File

STEP 2 ❯❯ You will often work with a file, save it, and then continue the project at a later time. To open an existing file, you can click a location such as This PC or OneDrive and navigate to the folder or drive where your document is stored. Once you make your way to the file to be opened, double-click the file name to open the file (see Figure 1.2).

To open a file, complete the following steps:

1. Open the application.
2. Click Open Other Documents (Workbooks, etc.).
3. Click the location for your file (such as This PC or OneDrive).
4. Navigate to the folder or drive and double-click the file to open it.

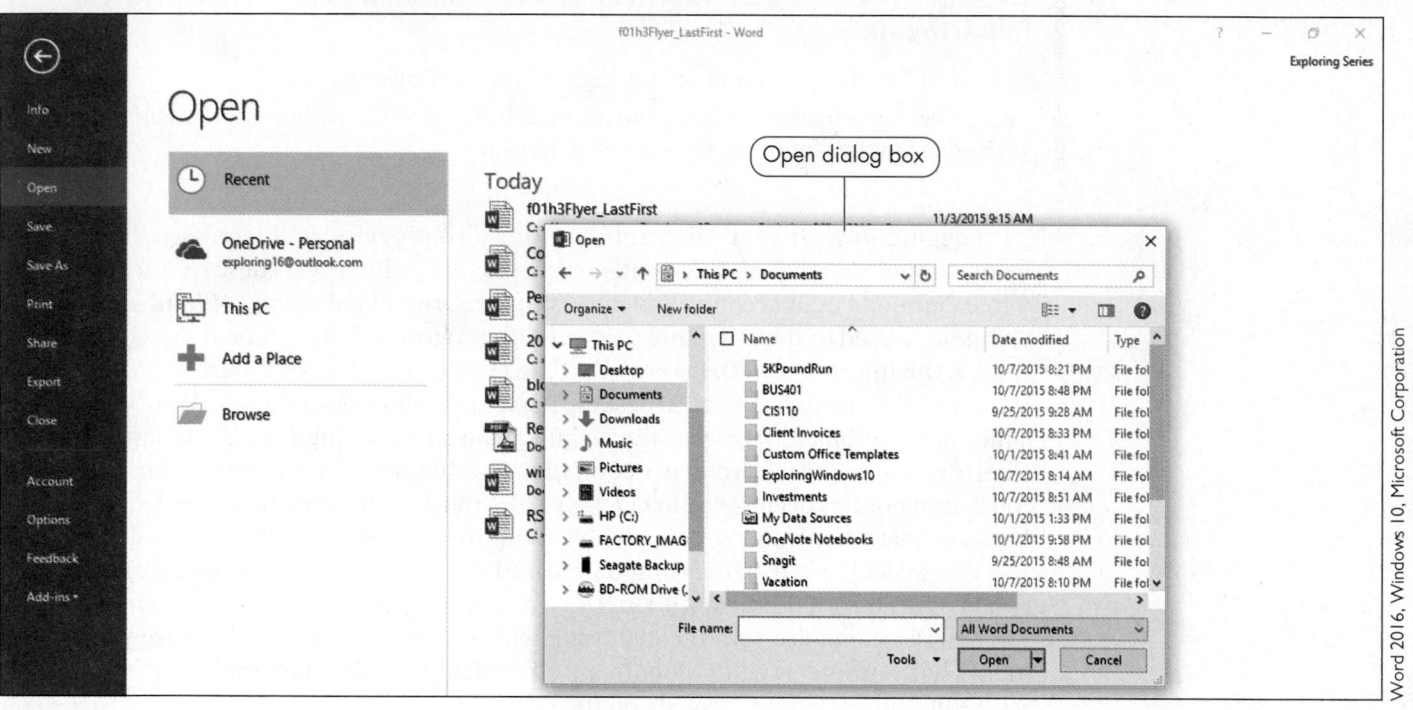

FIGURE 1.2 The Open Dialog Box

Office simplifies the task of reopening the file by providing a Recent documents list with links to your most recently opened files. Previously saved files, such as the data files for this book, are available in the Recent documents list, shown in Figure 1.3. If you just opened the application, the recent list displays at the left. If you do not see your file listed, you can click the link to Open Other Documents (or Workbooks, Presentations, etc.)

To access the Recent documents list, complete the following steps:

1. Open the application.
2. Click any file listed in the Recent documents list to open that document.

The list constantly changes to reflect only the most recently opened files, so if it has been quite some time since you worked with a particular file, you might have to browse for your file instead of using the Recent documents list to open the file.

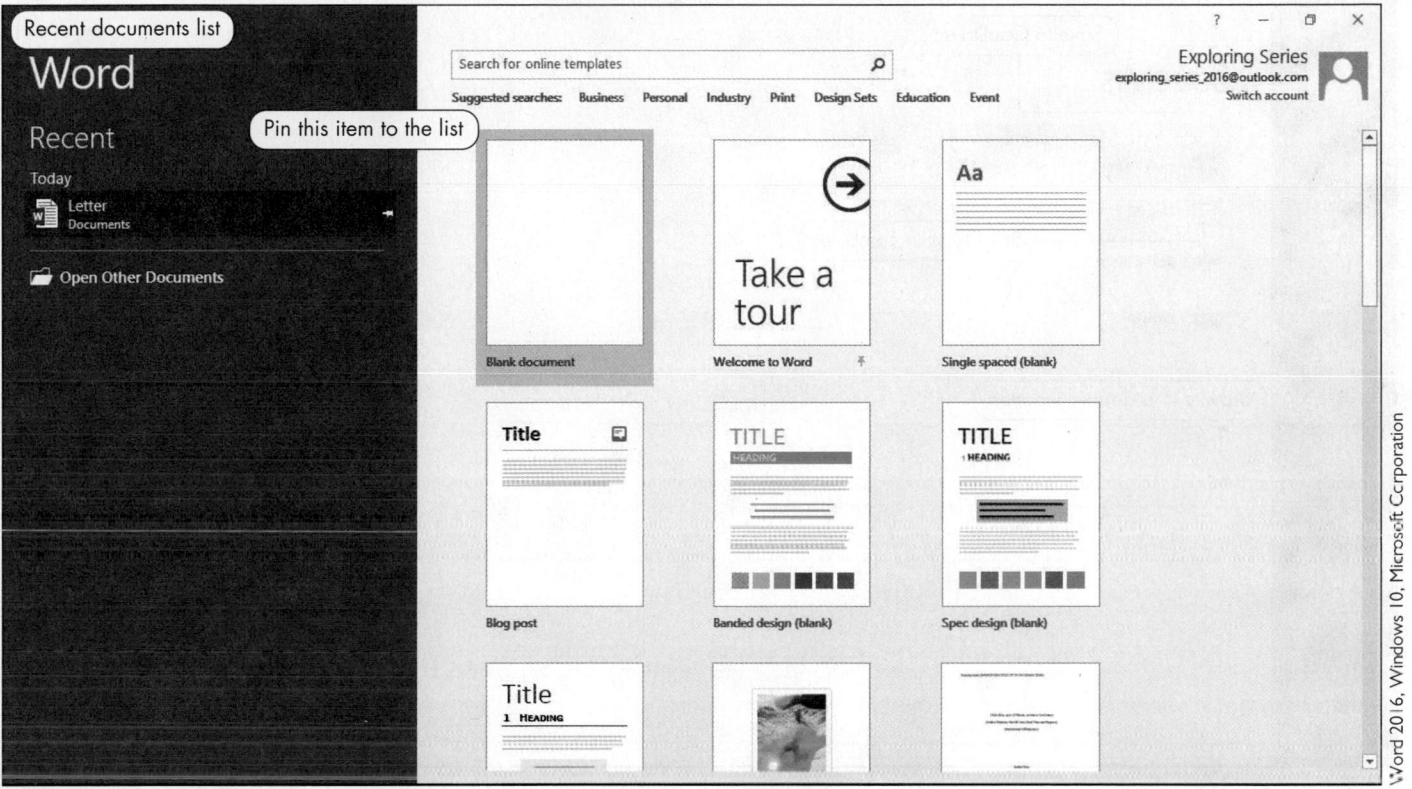

FIGURE 1.3 Recent Documents List

Save a File

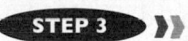 Saving a file enables you to later open it for additional updates or reference. Files are saved to a storage medium such as a hard drive, CD, flash drive, or to the cloud on OneDrive.

The first time that you save a file, you should indicate where the file will be saved and assign a file name. Of course, you will want to save the file in an appropriately named folder so that you can find it easily later. Thereafter, you can quickly save the file with the same settings, or you can change one or more of those settings, perhaps saving the file to a different storage device as a backup copy. Figure 1.4 shows a typical Save As pane for Office that enables you to select a location before saving the file.

It is easy to save a previously saved file with its current name and file location; click the Save icon on Quick Access Toolbar. There are instances where you may want to rename the file or save it to a different location. For example, you might reuse an event flyer for another event and simply update some of the details for the new event.

To save a file with a different name and/or file location, complete the following steps:

1. Click the File tab.
2. Click Save As.
3. Select a location or click Browse to navigate to the desired file storage location.
4. Type the file name.
5. Click Save.

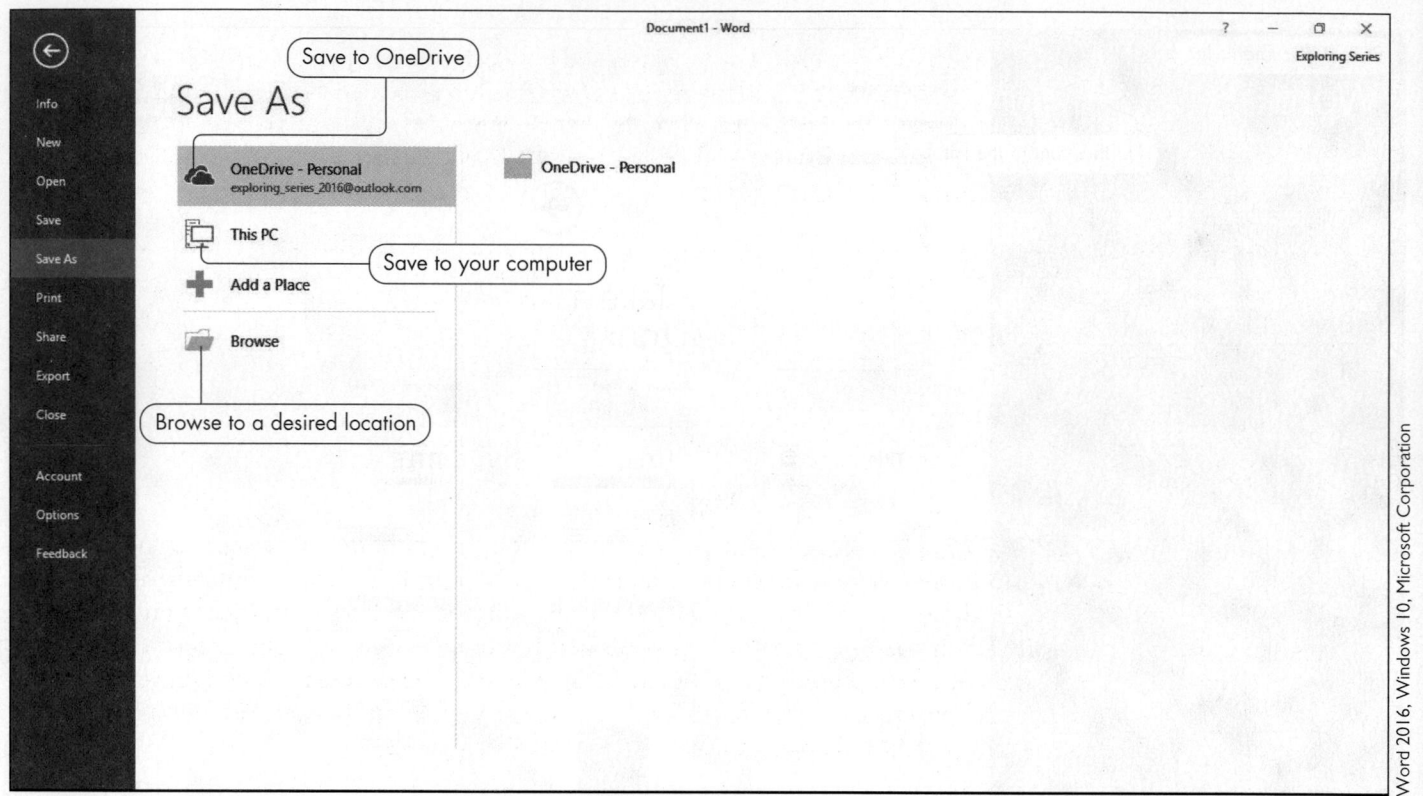

FIGURE 1.4 Save As in Backstage View

As previously mentioned, signing in to your Microsoft account enables you to save files to OneDrive and access them from virtually anywhere. To save a file to your OneDrive account follow the same steps as saving a file to your hard drive but select OneDrive and then the desired storage location on your OneDrive. You must be connected to the Internet in order to complete this action.

Using Common Interface Components

When you open any Office application you will first notice the title bar and Ribbon. The *title bar* identifies the current file name and the application in which you are working. It also includes Ribbon display options and control buttons that enable you to minimize, restore down, or close the application window (see Figure 1.5). The Quick Access Toolbar, on the left side of the title bar, enables you to save the file, and undo or redo editing. Located just below the title bar is the Ribbon. The **Ribbon** is the command center of Office applications. It is the long bar located just beneath the title bar, containing tabs, groups, and commands.

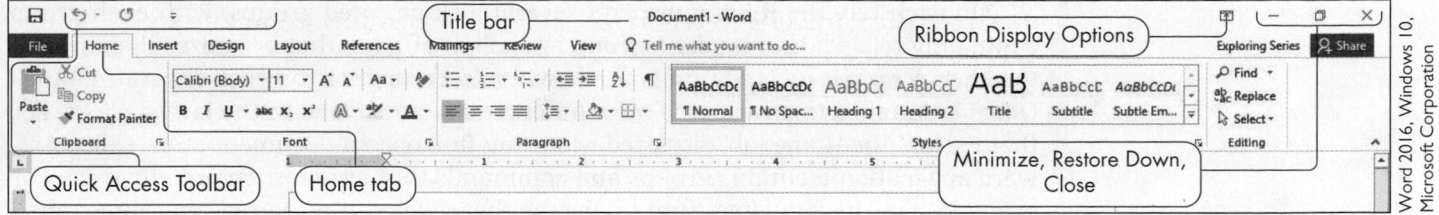

FIGURE 1.5 The Title Bar and Quick Access Toolbar

Use the Ribbon

The Ribbon is composed of tabs. Each **tab** is designed to appear much like a tab on a file folder, with the active tab highlighted. The File tab is located at the far left of the Ribbon. The File tab provides access to Backstage view which contains Save and Print, as well as additional functions. Other tabs on the Ribbon enable you to modify a file. The active tab in Figure 1.6 is the Home tab.

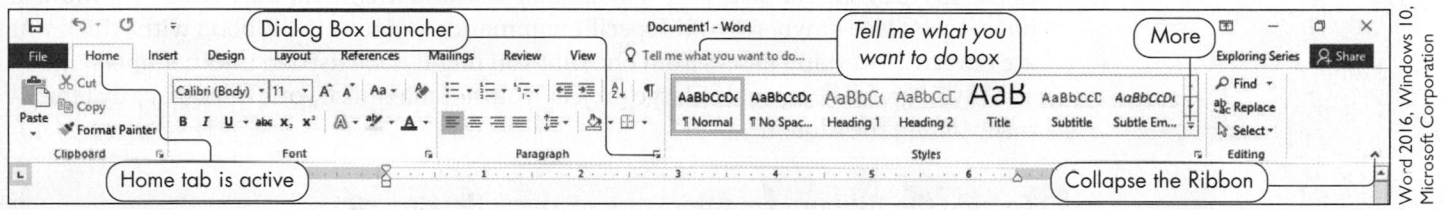

FIGURE 1.6 The Ribbon

Office applications enable you to work with objects such as images, shapes, charts, and tables. When you include such objects in a project, they are considered separate components that you can manage independently. To work with an object, you must select it. When you select an object, the Ribbon is modified to include one or more **contextual tabs** that contain groups of commands related to the selected object. Figure 1.7 shows a contextual tab related to a selected picture in a Word document. When you click away from the selected object, the contextual tab disappears.

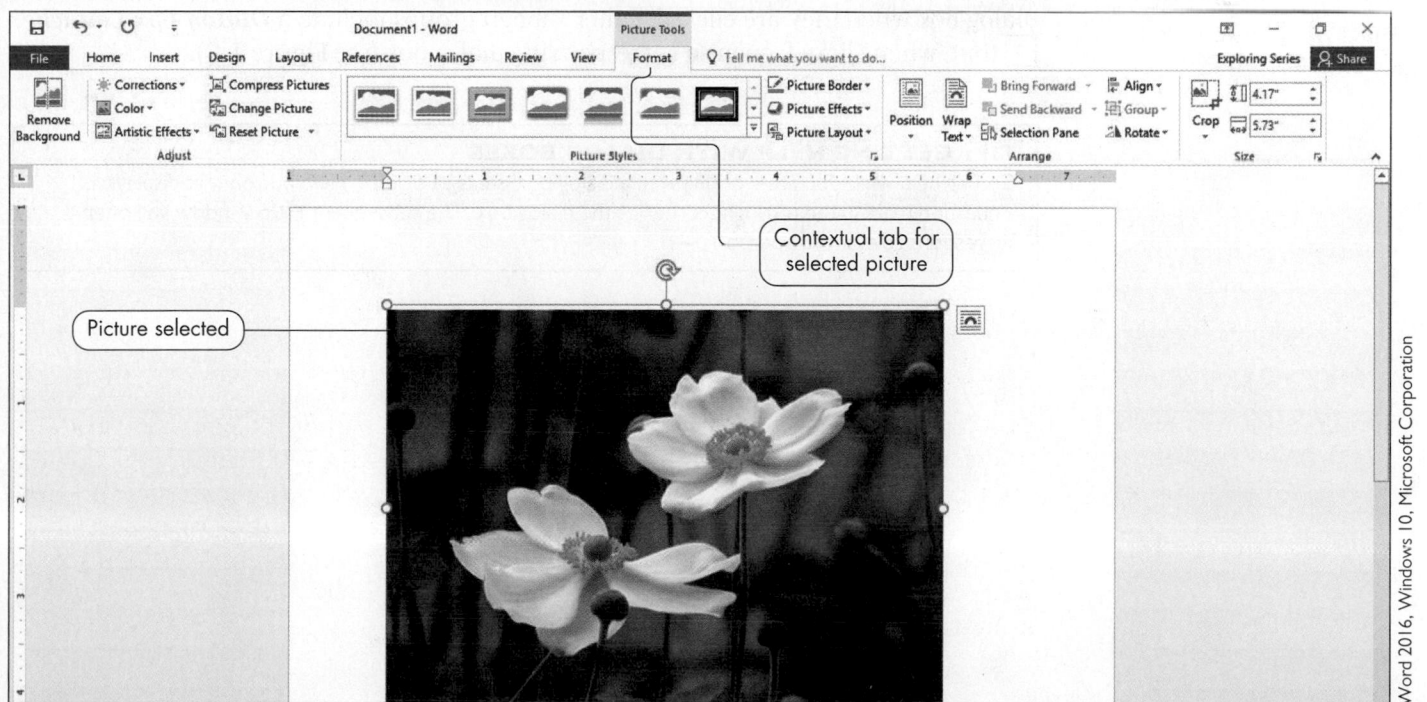

FIGURE 1.7 A Contextual Tab

On each tab, the Ribbon displays several task-oriented groups, with each group containing related commands. A **group** is a subset of a tab that organizes similar tasks together. A **command** is a button or area within a group that you click to perform tasks. Office is designed to provide the most functionality possible with the fewest clicks. For that reason, the Home tab, displayed when you first open a document in an Office software application, contains groups and commands that are most commonly used. For example, because you often want to change the way text is displayed, the Home tab in each Office application includes a Font group with commands related to modifying text. Similarly, other tabs contain groups of related actions, or commands, many of which are unique to the particular Office application.

Word, PowerPoint, Excel, and Access all share a similar Ribbon structure. Although the specific tabs, groups, and commands vary among the Office programs, the way in which you use the Ribbon and the descriptive nature of tab titles is the same regardless of which program you are using. For example, if you want to insert a chart in Excel, a header in Word, or a shape in PowerPoint, you will click the Insert tab in any of those programs. The first thing that you should do as you begin to work with an Office application is to study the Ribbon. Take a look at all tabs and their contents. That way, you will have a good idea of where to find specific commands and how the Ribbon with which you are currently working differs from one that you might have used in another application.

If you are working with a large project, you can maximize your workspace by temporarily hiding the Ribbon.

To hide the Ribbon, complete one of the following steps:

- Double-click the active tab to hide the Ribbon.
- Click Collapse the Ribbon (refer to Figure 1.6), located at the right side of the Ribbon.

To unhide the Ribbon, double-click any tab to redisplay the Ribbon.

Some actions do not display on the Ribbon because they are not as commonly used, but are related to commands displayed on the Ribbon. For example, you might want to change the background of a PowerPoint slide to include a picture. In that case, you will work with a **dialog box** that provides access to more precise, but less frequently used, commands. Figure 1.8 shows the Font dialog box in Word. Some commands display a dialog box when they are clicked. Other Ribbon groups include a **Dialog Box Launcher** that, when clicked, opens a corresponding dialog box (see Figure 1.8).

TIP: GETTING HELP WITH DIALOG BOXES

Getting help while you are working with a dialog box is easy. Click the Help button that displays as a question mark in the top-right corner of the dialog box. The subsequent Help window will offer suggestions relevant to your task.

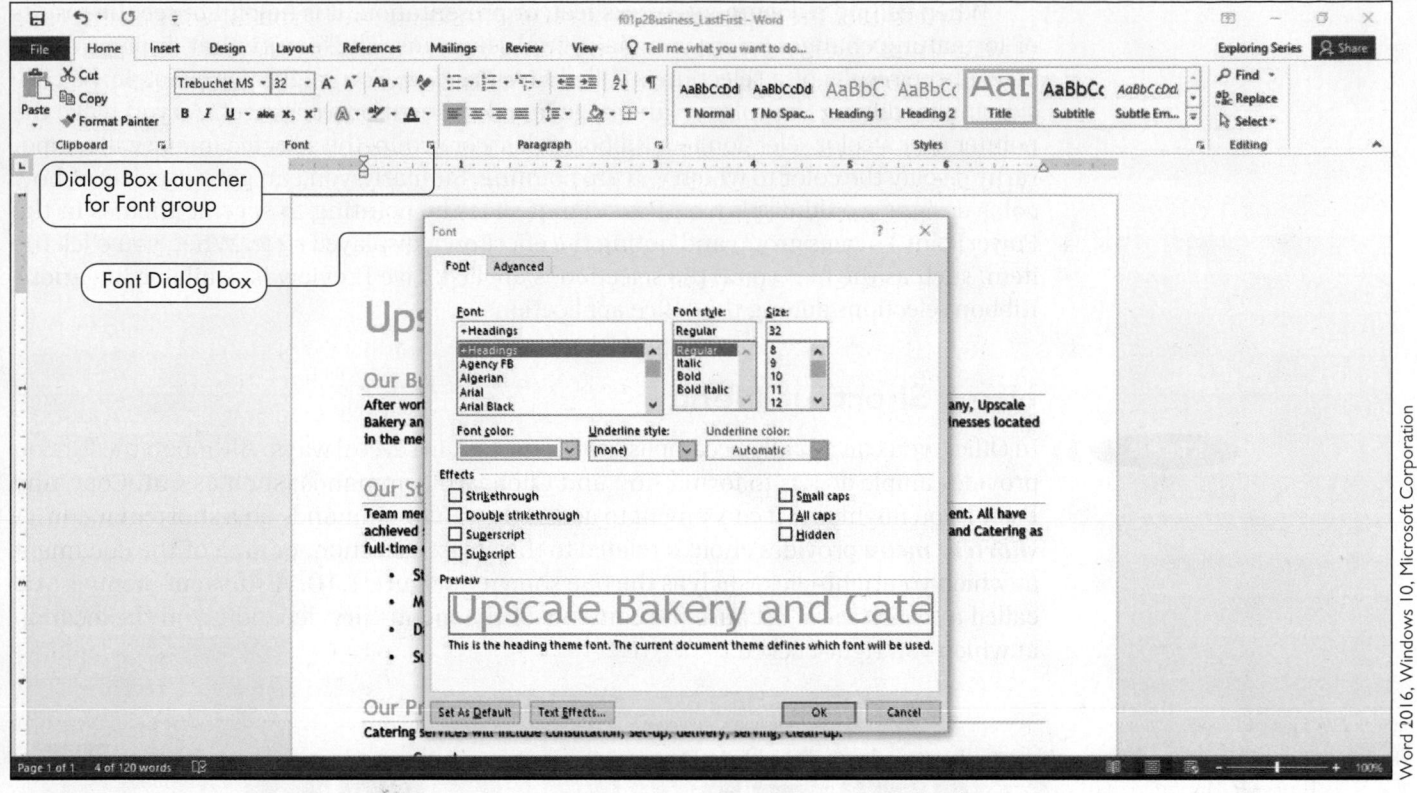

FIGURE 1.8 The Font Dialog Box

The Ribbon contains many selections and commands, but some selections are too numerous to include in the Ribbon's limited space. For example, Word provides far more text styles than it can easily display at once, so additional styles are available in a *gallery*. A gallery also provides a choice of Excel chart styles and PowerPoint transitions. Figure 1.9 shows an example of a PowerPoint Themes gallery. Most often, you can display a gallery of additional choices by clicking the More button ⊒ (refer to Figure 1.6) that is found in some Ribbon selections.

FIGURE 1.9 The Themes Gallery in PowerPoint

When editing a document, worksheet, or presentation, it is helpful to see the results of formatting changes before you make final selections. The feature that displays a preview of the results of a selection is called **Live Preview**. You might, for example, be considering modifying the color of an image in a document or worksheet. As you place the pointer over a color selection in a Ribbon gallery or group, the selected image will temporarily display the color to which you are pointing. Similarly, you can get a preview of how color designs would display on PowerPoint slides by pointing to specific themes in the PowerPoint Themes group and noting the effect on a displayed slide. When you click the item, such as the font color, the selection is applied. Live Preview is available in various Ribbon selections among the Office applications.

Use a Shortcut Menu

STEP 4 ›› In Office, you can usually accomplish the same task in several ways. Although the Ribbon provides ample access to formatting and Clipboard commands (such as Cut, Copy, and Paste), you might find it convenient to access the same commands on a shortcut menu. A **shortcut menu** provides choices related to the object, selection, or area of the document at which you right-click, such as the one shown in Figure 1.10. A shortcut menu is also called a *context menu* because the contents of the menu vary depending on the location at which you right-clicked.

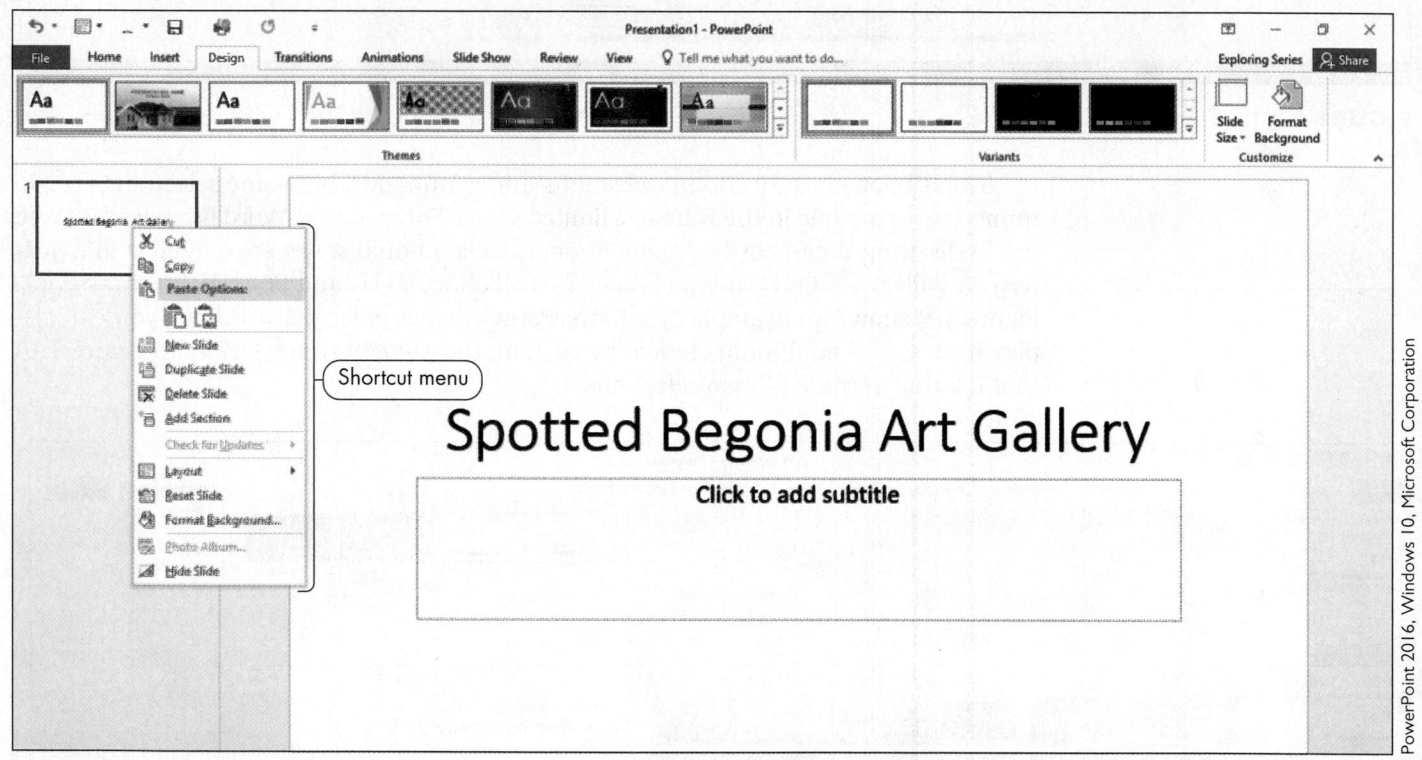

FIGURE 1.10 A Shortcut Menu in PowerPoint

Use Keyboard Shortcuts

You might find that you prefer to use keyboard shortcuts, which are keyboard equivalents for software commands, when they are available. Universal keyboard shortcuts in Office include Ctrl+C (Copy), Ctrl+X (Cut), Ctrl+V (Paste), and Ctrl+Z (Undo). To move to the beginning of a Word document, to cell A1 in Excel, or to the first PowerPoint slide, press Ctrl+Home. To move to the end of those items, press Ctrl+End. There are many other keyboard shortcuts. To discover a keyboard shortcut for a commonly used command, press

Alt to display Key Tips for commands available on the Ribbon and Quick Access Toolbar. You can press the letter or number corresponding to Ribbon commands to invoke the action from the keyboard. Press Alt again to remove the Key Tips.

TIP: USING RIBBON COMMANDS WITH ARROWS

Some commands, such as Paste in the Clipboard group, contain two parts: the main command and an arrow. The arrow may be below or to the right of the command, depending on the command, window size, or screen resolution. Instructions in the *Exploring* series use the command name to instruct you to click the main command to perform the default action (e.g., Click Paste). Instructions include the word *arrow* when you need to select the arrow to access an additional option (e.g., Click the Paste arrow).

Customize the Ribbon

The Ribbon provides access to commands to develop, edit, save, share, and print documents. Office applications enable users to personalize the Ribbon, giving them easier access to a frequently used set of commands that are unique to them or their business. You can create and name custom tabs on the Ribbon, add groups of commands to custom or existing tabs, and alter the positioning of tabs on the Ribbon (see Figure 1.11). By default, the command list displays popular commands associated with other tabs (e.g. Paste, Delete, Save As), but all available commands can be displayed in the list's respective menu. The custom tabs are unique to the Office program in which they are created. You can add and remove Ribbon tabs, as well as rename them.

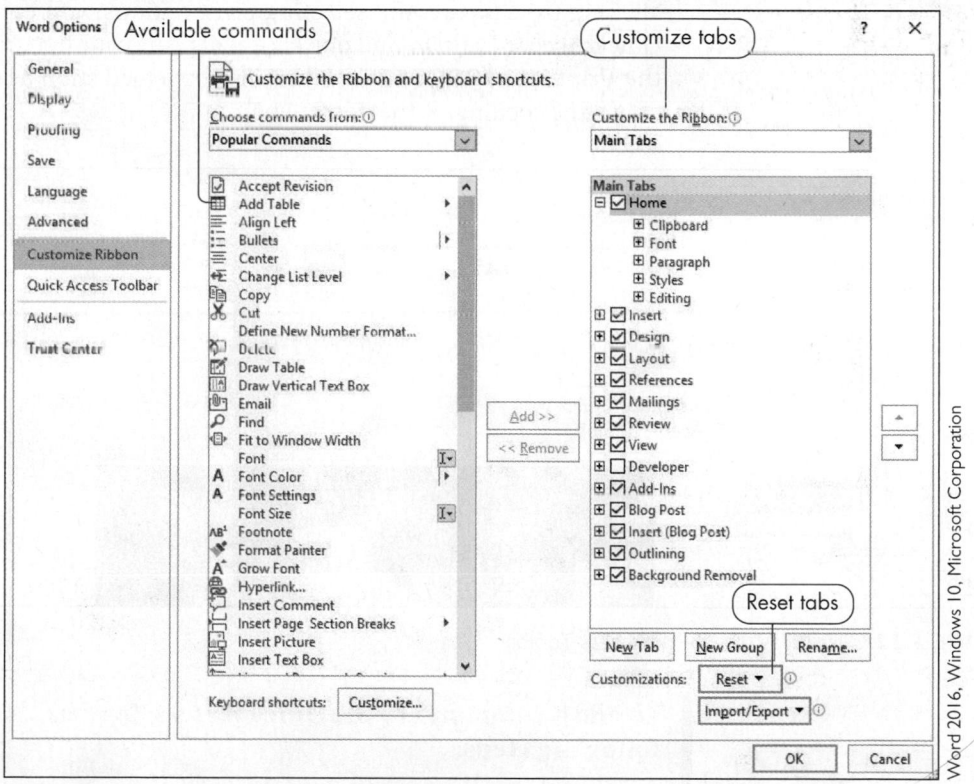

FIGURE 1.11 Customize the Ribbon in Word

To customize the Ribbon, complete the following steps:

1. Click the File tab and click Options.
2. Click Customize Ribbon. By deselecting a tab name, you can remove it from the Ribbon. Later, you can select it again to redisplay it.
3. Click a tab name and click Rename to change the name of the tab.
4. Type a new name and press Enter.

To return to showing all of the original tabs, click Reset and click Reset all customizations (refer to Figure 1.11).

Use the Quick Access Toolbar

The *Quick Access Toolbar*, located at the top-left corner of any Office application window (refer to Figure 1.5), provides one-click access to commonly executed tasks such as saving a file or undoing recent actions. By default, the Quick Access Toolbar includes buttons for saving a file and for undoing or redoing recent actions. You can recover from a mistake by clicking Undo on the Quick Access Toolbar. If you click the arrow beside Undo—known as the Undo arrow—you can select from a list of previous actions in order of occurrence. The Undo list is not maintained when you close a file or exit the application, so you can only erase an action that took place during the current Office session. Similar to Undo, you can also Redo (or Replace) an action that you have just undone. You can also customize the Quick Access Toolbar to include buttons you frequently use for commands such as printing or opening files. Because the Quick Access Toolbar is onscreen at all times, the most commonly accessed tasks are just a click away.

Customize the Quick Access Toolbar

There are certain actions in an Office application that you use often, and for more convenient access, you can add a button for each action to the Quick Access Toolbar (see Figure 1.12). One such action you may want to add is a Quick Print button. Rather than clicking the File tab and selecting print options, you can add a Quick Print icon to the Quick Access Toolbar, and one click will print your document with the default settings of the Print area. Other buttons can also be added such as Spelling & Grammar to quickly check the spelling of the document.

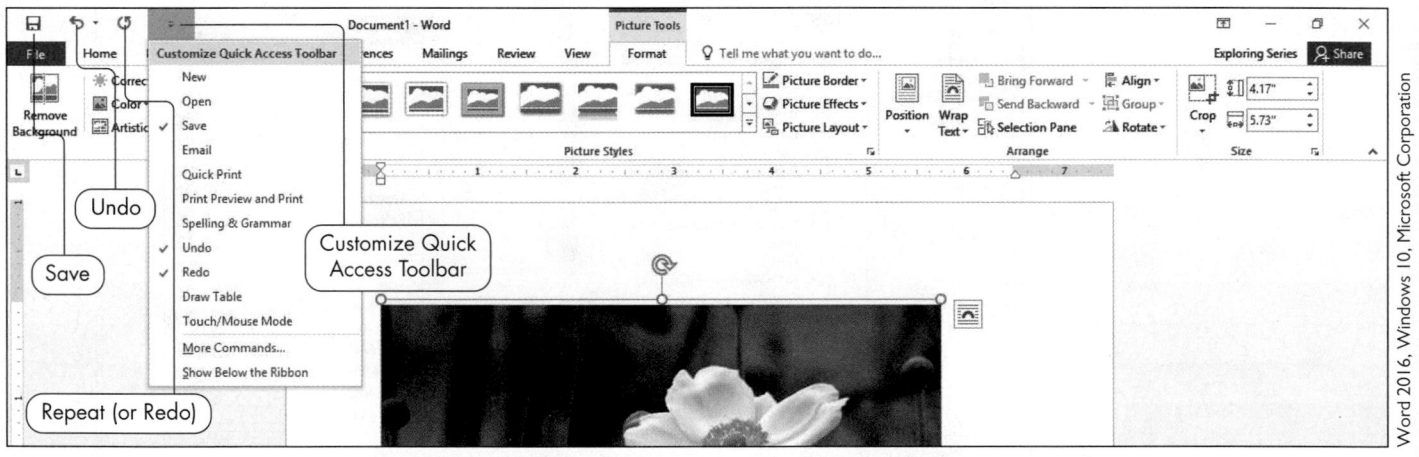

FIGURE 1.12 Customize the Quick Access Toolbar

> **To add a command to the Quick Access Toolbar, complete one of the following steps:**
> - Click Customize Quick Access Toolbar and then click More Commands near the bottom of the menu options. Then, select commands from a list and click Add.
> - Right-click the command on the Ribbon and click Add to Quick Access Toolbar.

Similarly, remove a command from the Quick Access Toolbar by right-clicking the icon on the Quick Access Toolbar and clicking *Remove from Quick Access Toolbar*. If you want to display the Quick Access Toolbar beneath the Ribbon, click *Customize Quick Access Toolbar* and click *Show Below the Ribbon*.

Getting Help

One of the most frustrating things about learning new software is determining how to complete a task. Microsoft includes comprehensive help with Office so that you are less likely to feel such frustration. As you work with any Office application, you can access help online as well as within the current software installation.

Use the *Tell me what you want to do* Box

STEP 5 New to Office 2016 is the *Tell me what you want to do* box. The **Tell me what you want to do box**, located to the right of the last tab (see Figure 1.13), not only enables you to search for help and information about a command or task you want to perform, but it will also present you with a shortcut directly to that command and in some instances (like Bold) it will complete the action for you. Perhaps you want to find an instance of a word in your document and replace it with another word but cannot locate the command on the Ribbon. You can type *find and replace* in the *Tell me what you want to do* box and a list of commands related to the skill will display. For example, in Figure 1.13, you see that Replace displays as an option in the list. If you click this option, the Find and Replace dialog box opens without you having to locate the button to do so.

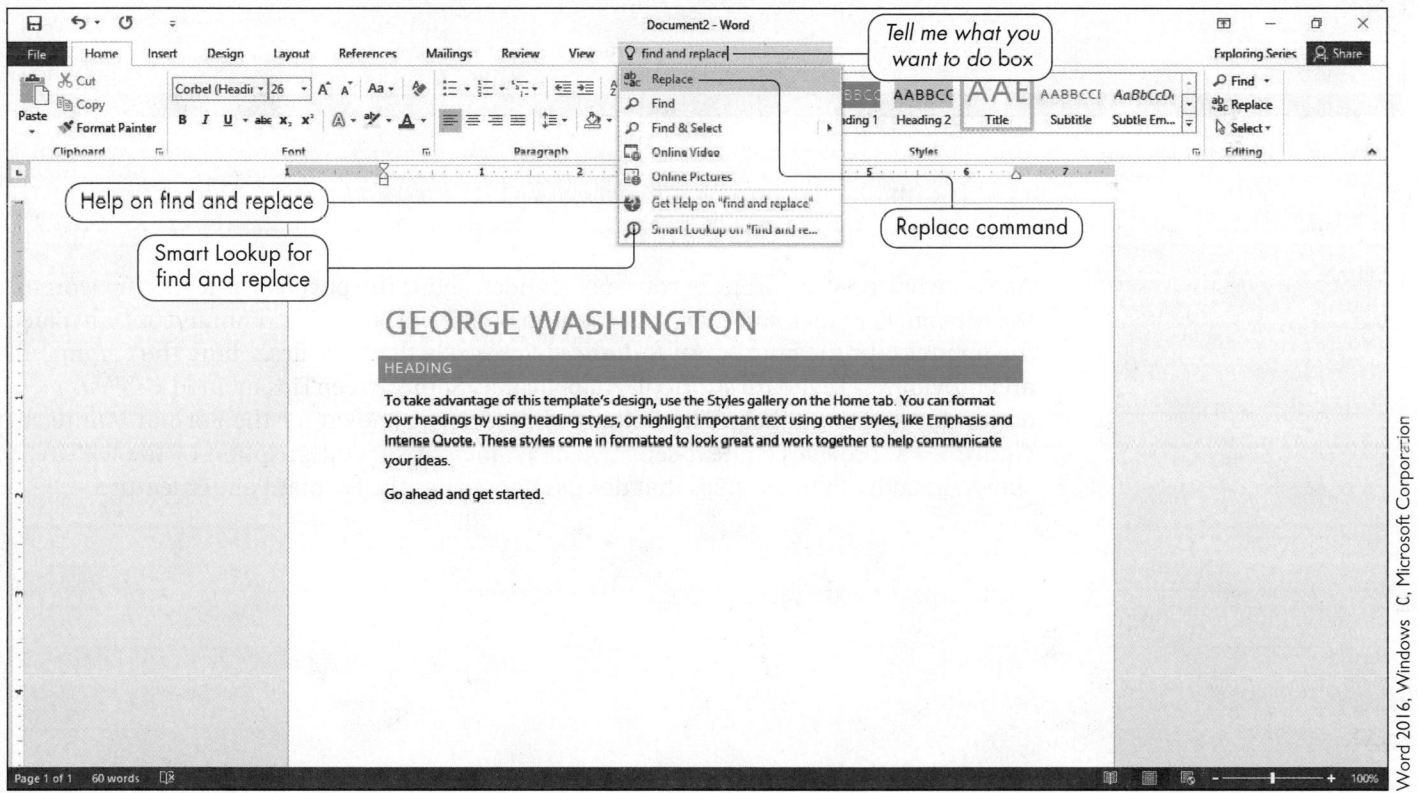

FIGURE 1.13 The *Tell me what you want to do* Box

Should you want to read about the feature instead of apply it, you can click *Get Help on "find and replace"* option, which will open Office Help for the feature. Another new feature is Smart Lookup. This feature opens the Insights pane that shows results from a Bing search on the task description typed in the box (see Figure 1.14). **Smart Lookup** provides information about tasks or commands in Office, and can also be used to search for general information on a topic such as *President George Washington*. Smart Lookup is also available on the shortcut menu when you right-click text.

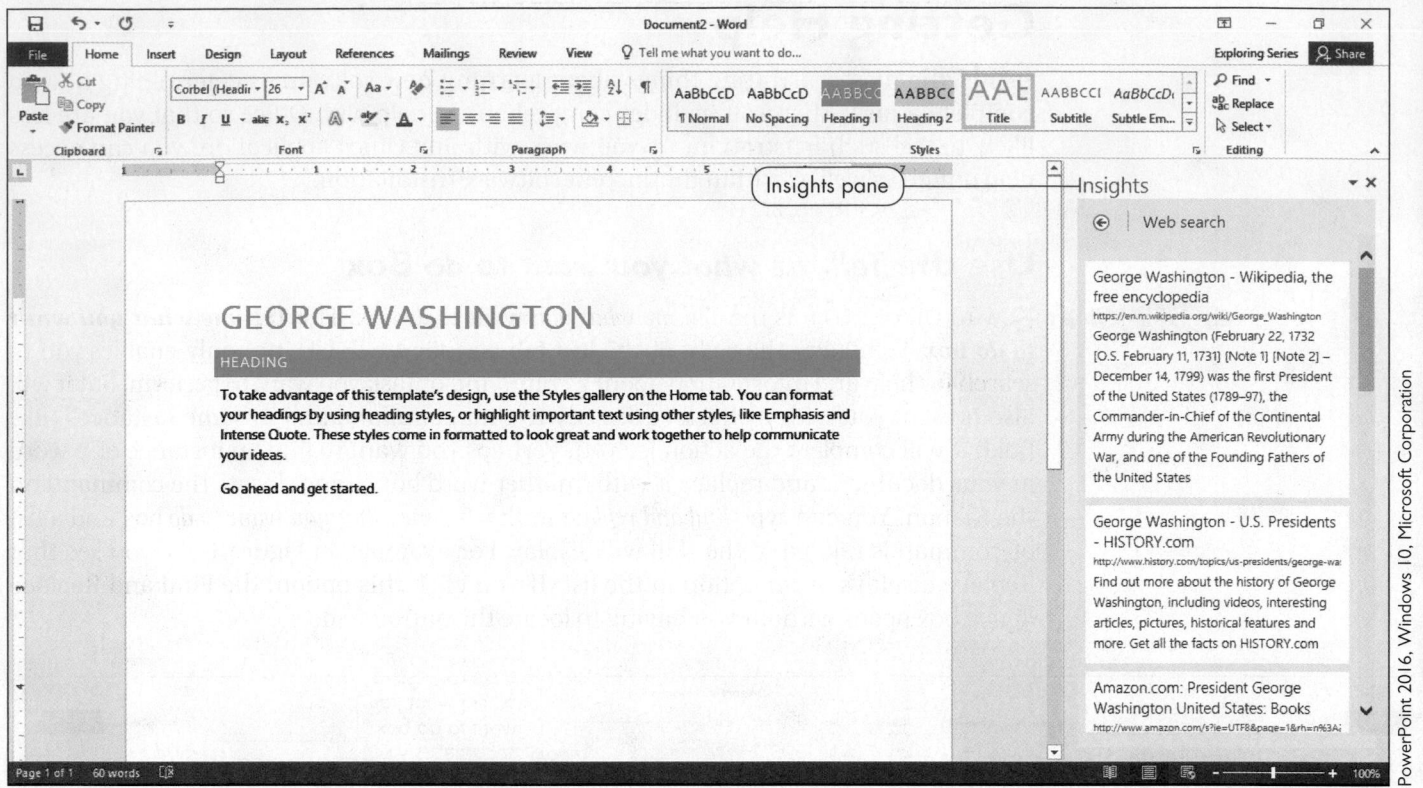

FIGURE 1.14 Smart Lookup

Use Enhanced ScreenTips

As you work on your projects you may wonder about the purpose of a specific icon on the Ribbon. For quick summary information on the purpose of a command button, place the pointer over the button. An ***Enhanced ScreenTip*** displays, describing the command, and providing a keyboard shortcut, if applicable. Some ScreenTips include a *Tell me more* option for additional help. The Enhanced ScreenTip, shown for the Format Painter in Figure 1.15, provides context-sensitive assistance. A short description of the feature is shown in addition to the steps that discuss how to use the Format Painter feature.

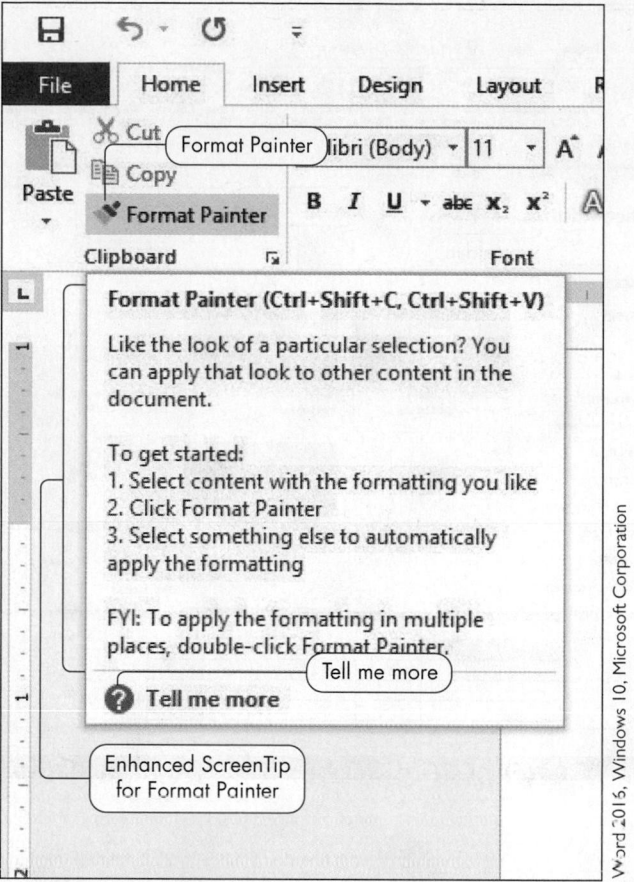

FIGURE 1.15 Enhanced ScreenTip

Installing Add-ins

Sometimes it is helpful to extend the functionality of Office programs by adding a Microsoft or third-party add-in to the program. An *add-in* is a custom program or additional command that extends the functionality of a Microsoft Office program (see Figure 1.16). Some add-ins are available for free while others may have a cost associated with them. For example, in PowerPoint you could add a Poll Everywhere poll that enables you to interact with your audience by having them respond to a question you have asked. The audience's electronic responses will appear on a slide as a real-time graph or word cloud. In Excel, add-ins provide additional functionality that can help with statistics and data mining.

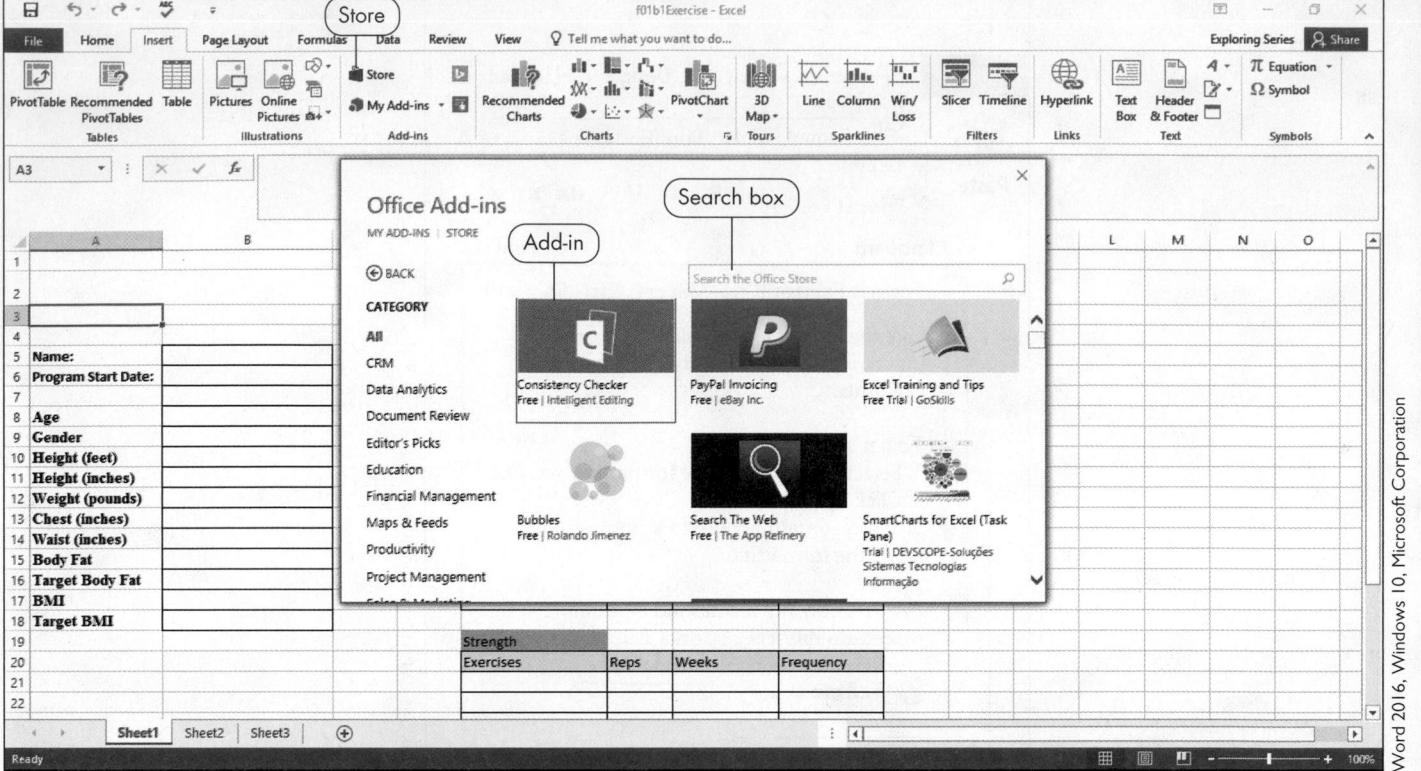

FIGURE 1.16 Add-Ins for Excel

To search for and install an add-in from the Microsoft Store, complete the following steps:

1. Click the Insert tab.
2. Click Store (refer to Figure 1.16). Browse the list of add-ins or use the search box.
3. Click the add-in. A box will display with information about the add-in such as its purpose, the cost (if any), and information it may access.
4. Click Trust It to add the add-in to your application. The newly added add-in will be available for future use in the My Add-ins list located on the Insert tab.

Quick Concepts

1. What are the benefits of logging in with your Microsoft account? *p. 67*
2. What is the purpose of the Quick Access Toolbar? *p. 76*
3. You are having trouble completing a task in Microsoft Word. What are some of the Office application features you could use to assist you in getting help with that task? *pp. 77–79*

Hands-On Exercises

Watch the Video for this Hands-On Exercise!

MyITLab®
HOE1 Training

1 Getting Started with Office Applications

The Spotted Begonia Art Gallery just hired several new clerical assistants to help you develop materials for the various activities coming up throughout the year. A coworker sent you a letter and asked for your assistance in making a few minor formatting changes. The letter is to thank the ABC Arts Foundation for its generous donation to the *Discover the Artist in You!* program and to invite them to the program's kickoff party. To begin, you will open Word and then open an existing document. You will use the Shortcut menu to make simple changes to the document. Finally, you will use the *Tell me what you want to do* box to apply a style to the first line of text.

STEP 1 ›› OPEN A MICROSOFT OFFICE APPLICATION

You start Microsoft Word from the Windows Start menu. Refer to Figure 1.17 as you complete Step 1.

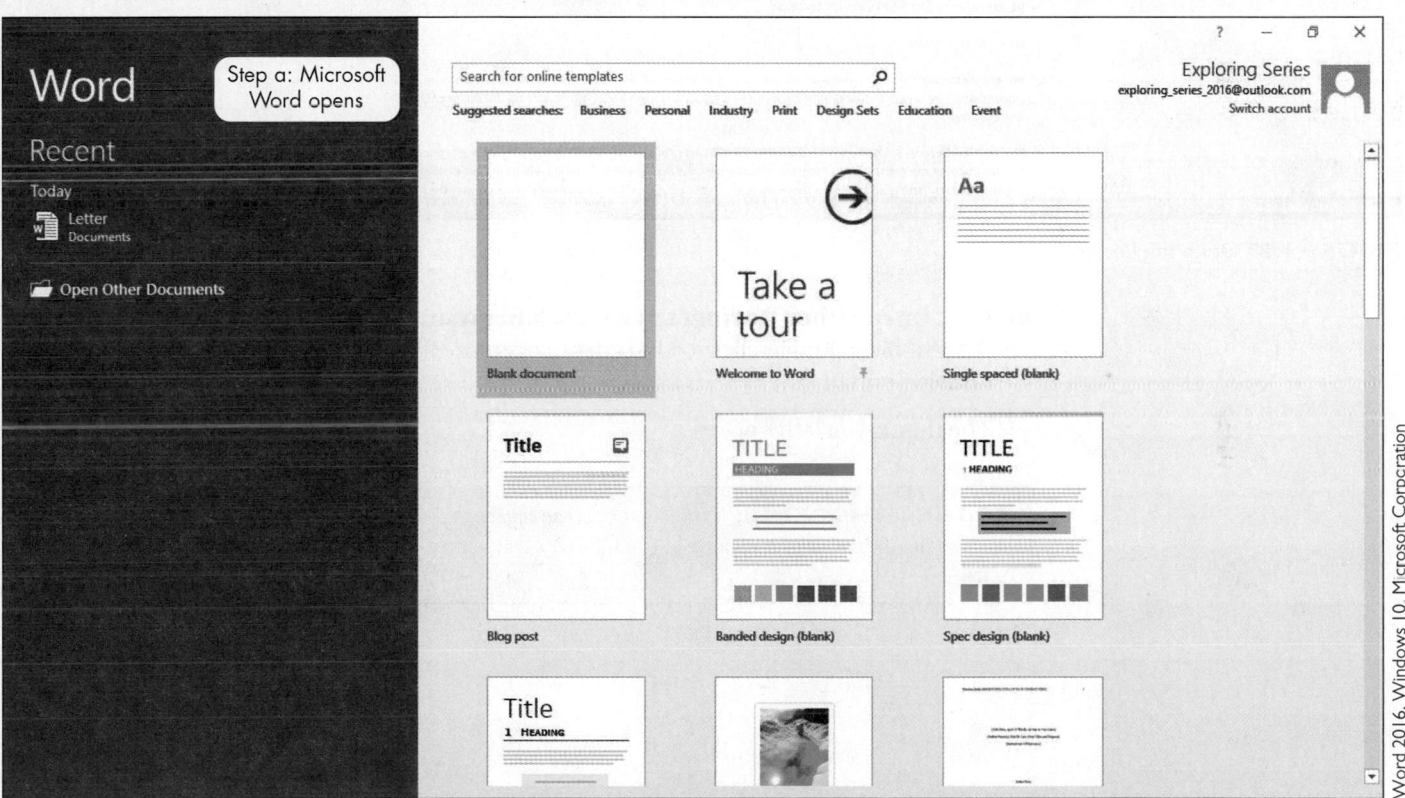

FIGURE 1.17 Open Word

a. Start your computer and log into your Microsoft account. On the Start menu, click **All apps** and click **Word 2016**.

Microsoft Word displays.

You open a thank-you letter that you will later modify. Refer to Figure 1.18 as you complete Step 2.

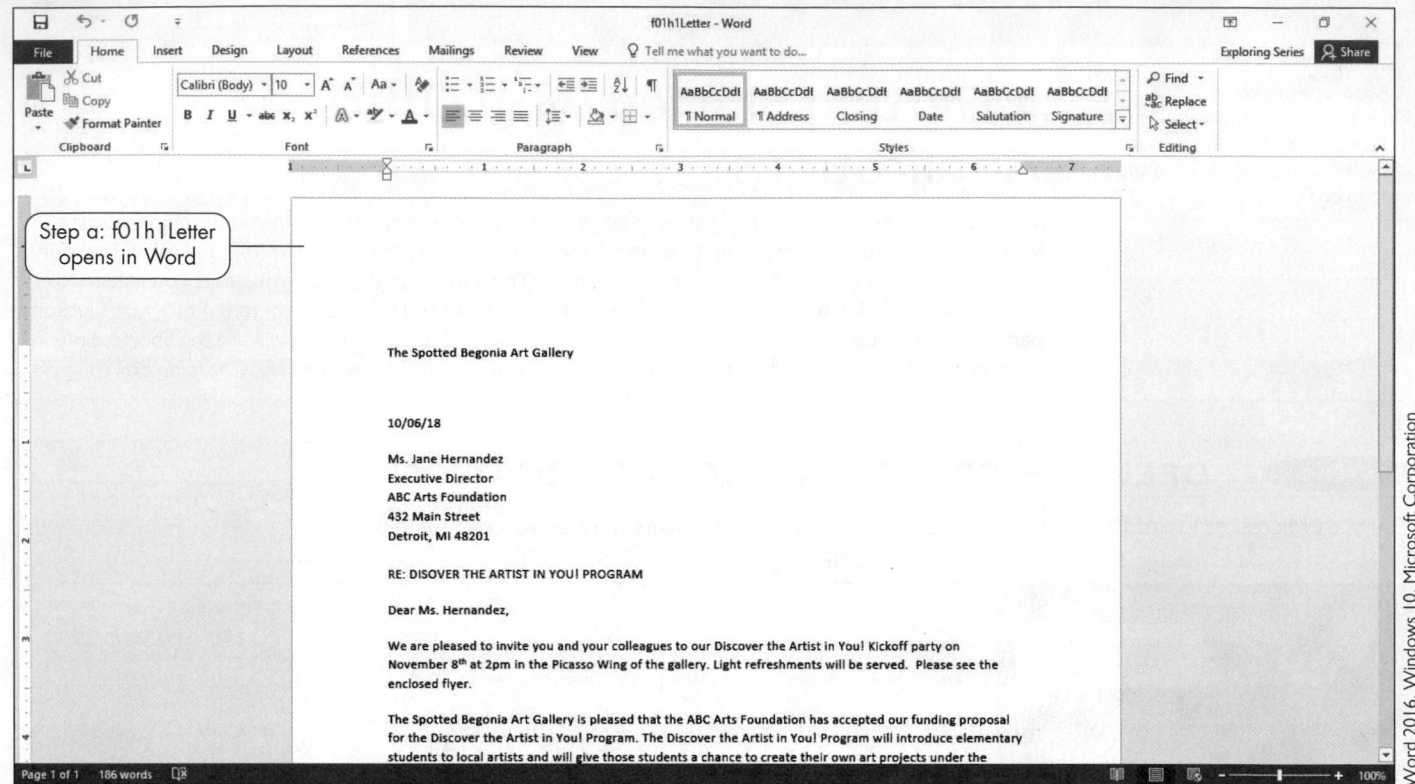

Step a: f01h1Letter opens in Word

FIGURE 1.18 Open the Letter

a. Click **Open Other Documents** and click **Browse**. Navigate to the location of your student files. Double-click *f01h1Letter* to open the file shown in Figure 1.18. Click Enable Content.

The thank-you letter opens.

> **TROUBLESHOOTING:** When you open an file from the student files associated with this book, you will need to enable the content. You may be confident of the trustworthiness of the files for this book.

You save the document with a different name, to preserve the original file. Refer to Figure 1.19 as you complete Step 3.

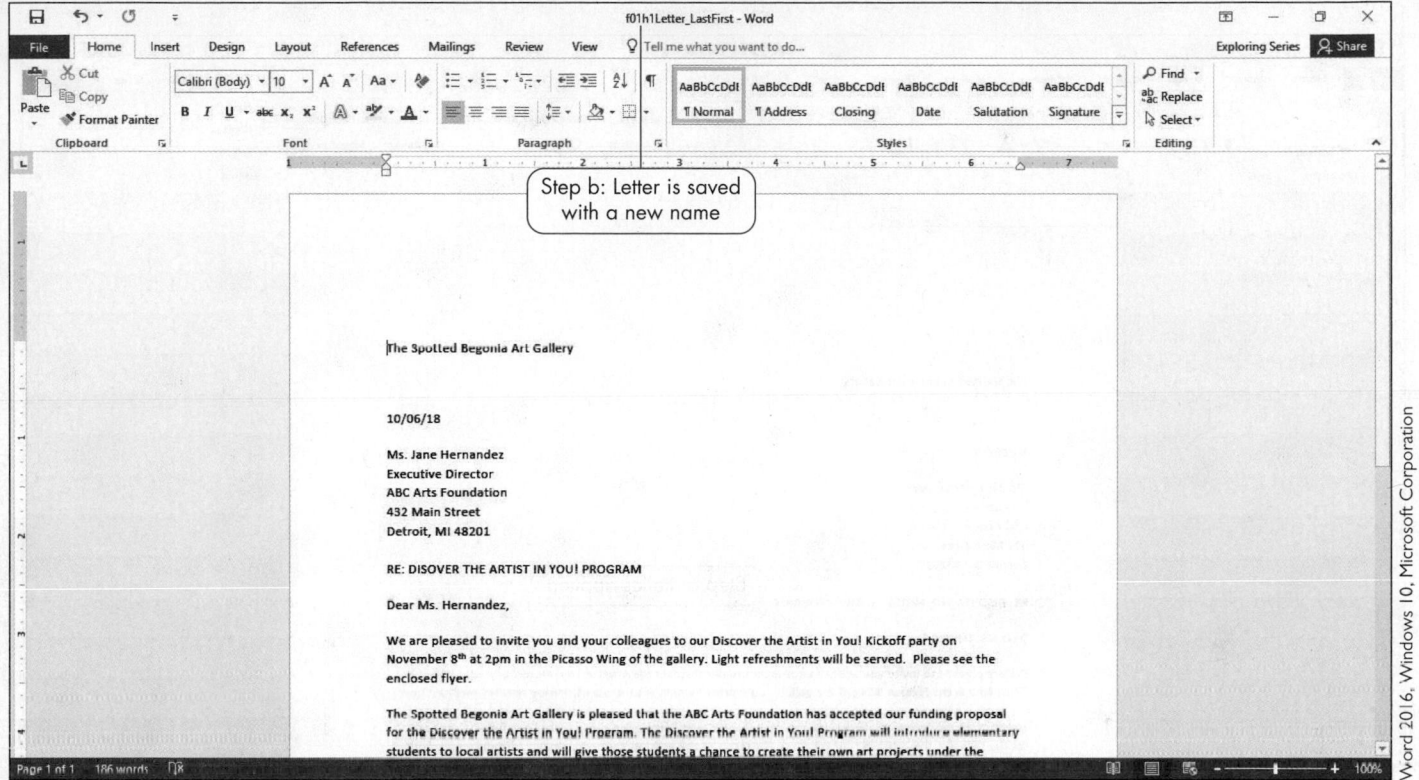

FIGURE 1.19 Save the Letter with a New Name

a. Click the **File tab**, click **Save As**, and then click **Browse** to display the Save As dialog box. Click **This PC** or click the location where you are saving your files.

b. Click in the **File name box** and type **f01h1Letter_LastFirst**.

When you save files, use your last and first names. For example, as the Common Features author, I would name my document "f01h1Letter_RutledgeAmy".

> **TROUBLESHOOTING:** If you make any major mistakes in this exercise, you can close the file, open *f01h1Letter* again, and then start this exercise over.

c. Click **Save**.

The file is now saved as f01h1Letter_LastFirst. You can check the title bar of the workbook to confirm that the file has been saved with the correct name.

You would like to apply italics to the *Discover the Artist in You!* text in the first sentence of the letter. You will select the text and use the shortcut menu to apply italics to the text. Refer to Figure 1.20 as you complete Step 4.

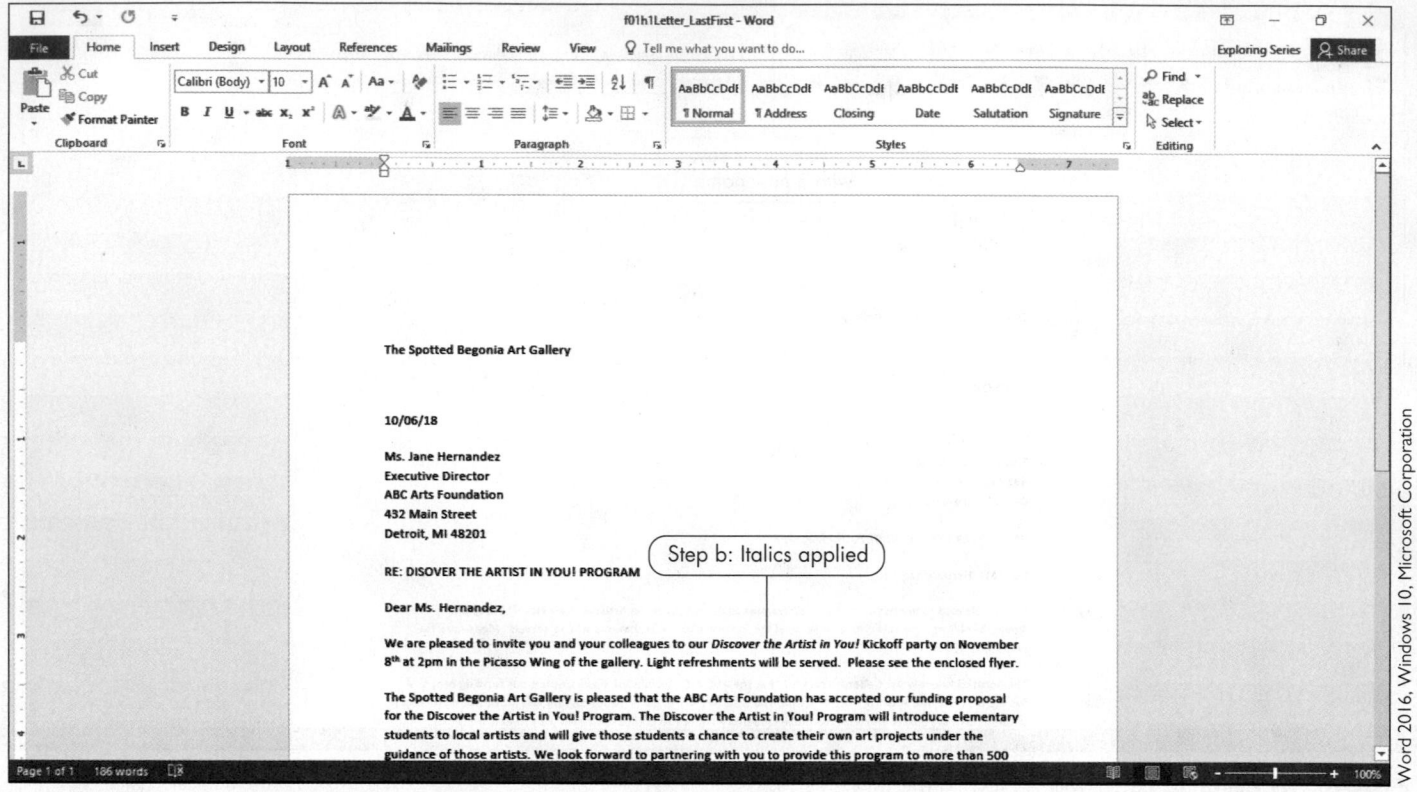

FIGURE 1.20 Apply Italics Using the Shortcut Menu

a. Select the text **Discover the Artist in You!** in the first sentence of the letter that starts with *We are pleased*.

The text is selected.

b. Right-click the selected text. Click **Font** on the Shortcut menu. Click **Italic** under Font style, and click **OK**.

Italics is applied to the text.

c. Click **Save** on the Quick Access Toolbar.

You would like to apply a style to the first line in the letter. Since you do not know how to complete the task, you use the *Tell me what you want to do* box to search for and apply the change. Refer to Figure 1.21 as you complete Step 5.

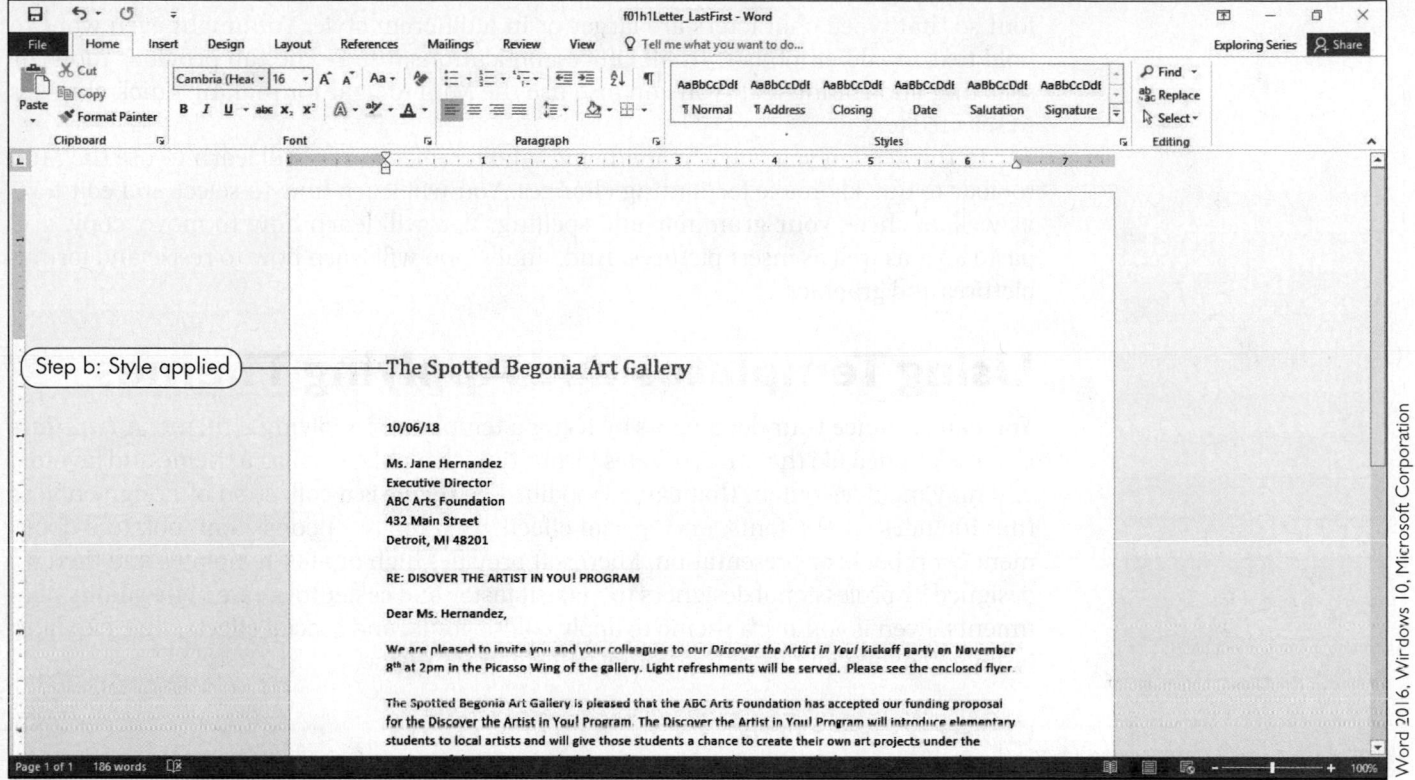

FIGURE 1.21 Change the Text Style Using the *Tell me what you want to do* Box

a. Triple-click the entire first line of the letter that starts with *The Spotted Begonia Art Gallery* to select it. Click the ***Tell me what you want to do*** **box**, and type **heading 1**.

A list of options appears below the box.

b. Click **Promote to Heading 1** to apply the style to the selected text.

The Heading 1 style is applied to the text.

c. Save the document. Keep the document open if you plan to continue with the next Hands-On Exercise. If not, save and close the workbook, and exit Word.

Format Document Content

After creating a document, worksheet, or presentation, you will probably want to make some formatting changes. You might prefer to center a title, or maybe you think that certain budget worksheet totals should be formatted as currency. You can change the font so that typed characters are larger or in a different style. You might even want to bold text to add emphasis. In all Office applications, the Home tab provides tools for selecting and editing text. You can also use the Mini toolbar for making quick changes to selected text.

In this section you will explore themes and templates. You will learn to use the Mini toolbar to quickly make formatting changes. You will learn how to select and edit text, as well as check your grammar and spelling. You will learn how to move, copy, and paste text, as well as insert pictures. And, finally, you will learn how to resize and format pictures and graphics.

Using Templates and Applying Themes

You can enhance your documents by using a template or applying a theme. A ***template*** is a predesigned file that incorporates formatting elements, such as a theme and layouts, and may include content that can be modified. A ***theme*** is a collection of design choices that includes colors, fonts, and special effects used to give a consistent look to a document, workbook, or presentation. Microsoft provides high quality templates and themes, designed by professional designers to make it faster and easier to create high-quality documents. Even if you use a theme to apply colors, fonts, and special effects, they can later be changed individually or to a completely different theme.

Open a Template

STEP 1 ▶▶ You can access a template in any of the Office applications (see Figure 1.22). Even if you know only a little bit about the software, you could then make a few changes so that the file would accurately represent your specific needs. The document also would be prepared much more quickly than if you designed it yourself from a blank file. For example, you might want to prepare a home budget using an Excel template, such as the Family monthly budget planner template, that is available by typing *Budget* in the *Suggested searches* template list.

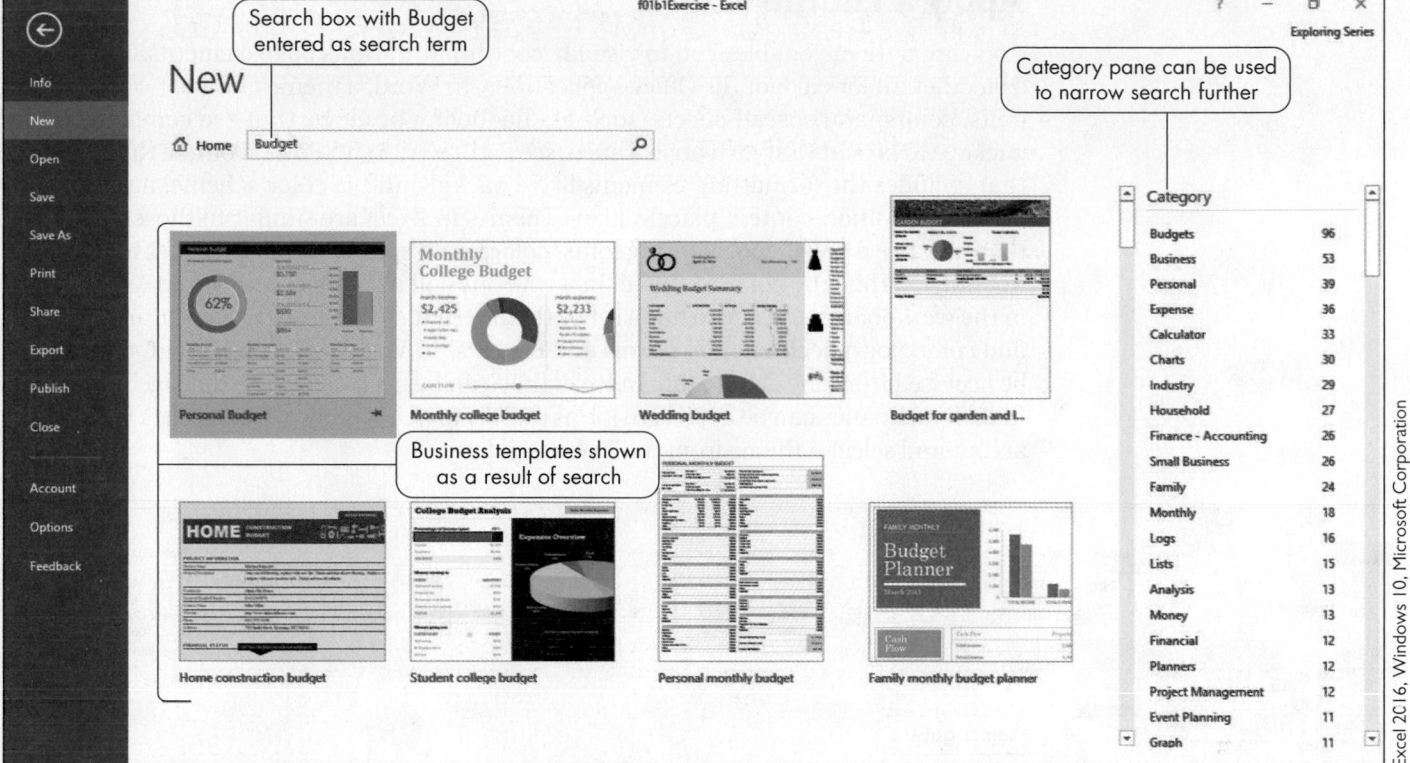

FIGURE 1.22 Templates in Excel

The Templates list is comprised of template groups available within each Office application. The search box enables you to locate other templates that are available online. When you click one of the Suggested searches, additional choices are displayed. Once you select a template, you can view more information about the template including author information, a general overview about the template, and additional views (if applicable).

To search for and use a template, complete the following steps:

1. Open the Microsoft application with which you will be working.
2. Type a search term in the *Search for online templates box*, or click one of the Suggested search terms.
3. Scroll through the template options or use the pane at the right to narrow your search further.
4. Select a template, and review its information in the window that opens.
5. Click Create to open the template in the application.

A Help window may display along with the worksheet template. Read it for more information about the template, or close it to continue working.

Apply a Theme

Applying a theme enables you to visually coordinate various page elements. Themes are a bit different for each of the Office applications. In Word, a theme is a set of coordinating fonts, colors, and special effects, such as shadowing or glows that are combined into a package to provide a stylish appearance (see Figure 1.23). In PowerPoint, a theme is a file that includes the formatting elements like a background, a color scheme, and slide layouts that position content placeholders. Themes in Excel are similar to those in Word in that they are a set of coordinating fonts, colors, and special effects. Themes in Excel will not only change the color of the fill in a cell, but will also affect any SmartArt or charts in the workbook. Access also has a set of themes that coordinate the appearance of fonts and colors for objects such as Forms and Reports. In Word and PowerPoint, themes can be accessed from the Design tab. In Excel they can be accessed from the Page Layout tab. In Access, themes can be applied to forms and reports. To apply a theme, click the Themes arrow, and select a theme from the Themes gallery.

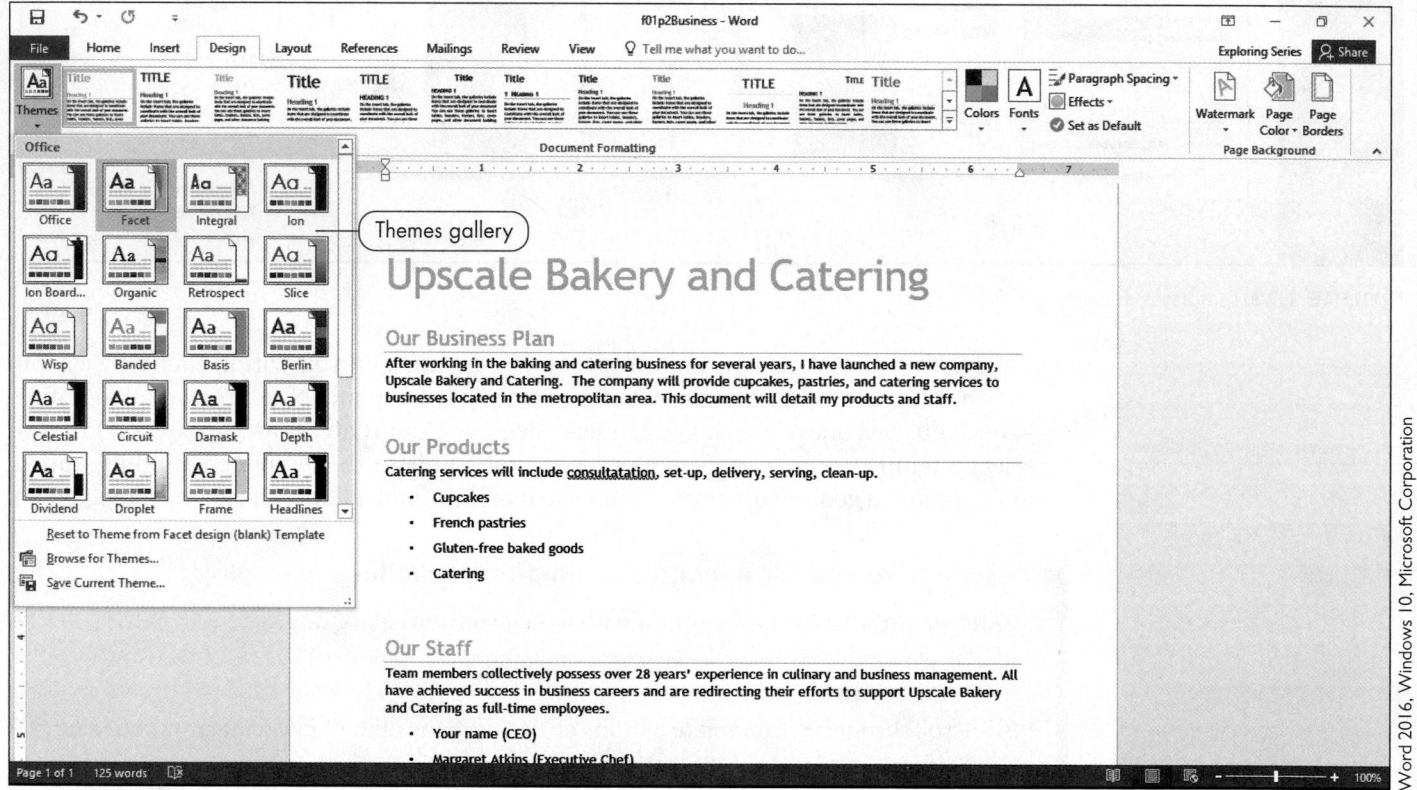

FIGURE 1.23 Themes in Word

Modifying Text

Formatting and modifying text in documents, worksheets, or presentations is an essential function when using Office applications. Centering a title, formatting cells, or changing the font color or size are tasks that occur frequently. In all Office applications, the Home tab provides tools for editing selected text. You can also use the Mini toolbar for making quick changes to selected text.

Select Text

STEP 2 Before making any changes to existing text or numbers, you must first select the characters. A general rule that you should commit to memory is "Select, then do." A foolproof way to select text or numbers is to place the pointer before the first character of the text you want to select, and then drag to highlight the intended selection. Before you drag, be sure that the pointer takes on the shape of the letter *I*, called the *I-beam* $\boxed{\text{I}}$. Although other methods for selecting exist, if you remember only one way, it should be the click-and-drag method. If your attempted selection falls short of highlighting the intended area, or perhaps highlights too much, click outside the selection and try again.

Sometimes it can be difficult to precisely select a small amount of text, such as a single word or sentence. Other times, the task can be overwhelming large, such as when selecting an entire 550-page document. In either case there are shortcuts to selecting text. The shortcuts shown in Table 1.2 are primarily applicable to text in Word and PowerPoint. When working with Excel, you will more often need to select multiple cells. To select multiple cells, drag the intended selection when the pointer displays as a large white plus sign $\boxed{+}$.

TABLE 1.2 Shortcut Selection in Word and PowerPoint

Item Selected	Action
One word	Double-click the word.
One line of text	Place the pointer at the left of the line, in the margin area. When the pointer changes to a right-pointing arrow, click to select the line.
One sentence	Press and hold Ctrl, and click in the sentence to select it.
One paragraph	Triple-click in the paragraph.
One character to the left of the insertion point	Press and hold Shift, and press the left arrow on the keyboard.
One character to the right of the insertion point	Press and hold Shift, and press the right arrow on the keyboard.
Entire document	Press and hold Ctrl, and press A on the keyboard.

Pearson Education, Inc.

Once you have selected the desired text, besides applying formatting, you can delete or simply type over to replace the text.

Edit Text

At times, you will want to make the font size larger or smaller, change the font color, or apply other font attributes. For example, if you are creating a handout for a gallery show opening, you may want to apply a different font to emphasize key information such as dates and times. Because such changes are commonplace, Office places those formatting commands in many convenient places within each Office application.

You can find the most common formatting commands in the Font group on the Home tab. As noted earlier, Word, Excel, and PowerPoint all share very similar Font groups that provide access to tasks related to changing the character font. Remember that you can place the pointer over any command icon to view a summary of the icon's purpose, so although the icons might at first appear cryptic, you can use the pointer to quickly determine the purpose and applicability to your desired text change.

The way characters display onscreen or print in documents, including qualities such as size, spacing, and shape, is determined by the font. Office applications have a default font, Calibri, which is the font that will be in effect unless you change it. Other font attributes include bold, italic, and font color, all of which can be applied to selected text. Some formatting commands, such as Bold and Italic, are called ***toggle commands***. They act somewhat like light switches that you can turn on and off. Once you have applied bold formatting to text, the Bold command is highlighted on the Ribbon when that text is selected again. To undo bold formatting, click Bold again.

If you want to apply a different font to a section of your project for added emphasis or interest, you can make the change by selecting a font from within the Font group on the Home tab. You can also change the font by selecting from the Mini toolbar.

If the font change that you plan to make is not included as a choice on either the Home tab or the Mini toolbar, you can find what you are looking for in the Font dialog box. Click the Dialog Box Launcher in the bottom-right corner of the Font group. Figure 1.24 shows a sample Font dialog box. Because the Font dialog box provides many formatting choices in one window, you can make several changes at once. Depending on the application, the contents of the Font dialog box vary slightly, but the purpose is consistent—providing access to choices related to modifying characters.

FIGURE 1.24 The Font Dialog Box

Use the Mini Toolbar

You have learned that you can always use commands on the Home tab of the Ribbon to change selected text within a document, worksheet, or presentation. Although using the Ribbon to select commands is simple enough, the **Mini toolbar** provides an even faster way to accomplish some of the same formatting changes. When you select any amount of text within a worksheet, document, or presentation, move the pointer slightly within the selection to display the Mini toolbar (see Figure 1.25). The Mini toolbar provides access to the most common formatting selections, such as bold or italic, or font type or color. Unlike the Quick Access Toolbar, the Mini toolbar is not customizable, which means that you cannot add or remove options from the toolbar.

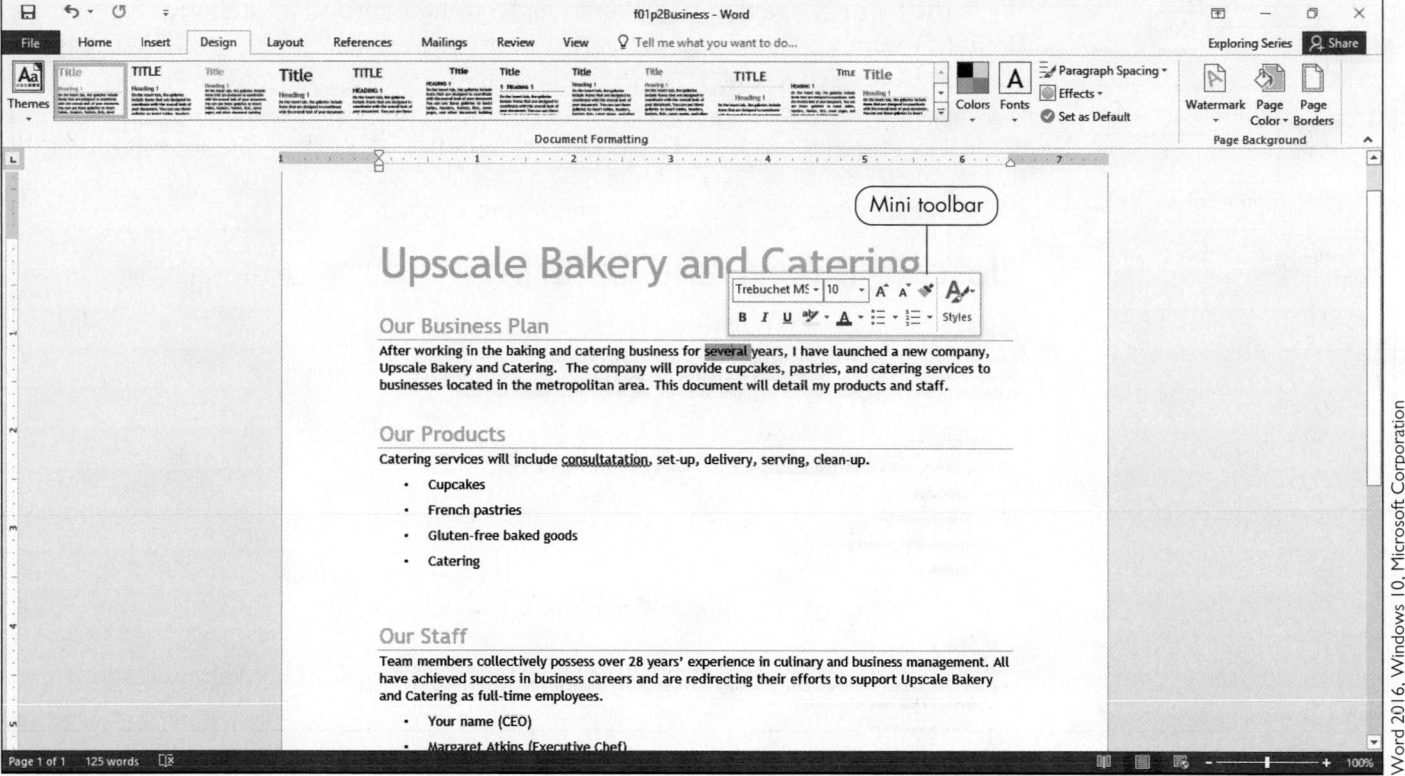

FIGURE 1.25 The Mini Toolbar

The Mini toolbar is displayed only when text is selected. The closer the pointer is to the Mini toolbar, the darker the toolbar becomes. As you move the pointer away from the selected text, the Mini toolbar eventually fades away. If the Mini toolbar is no longer displayed, you can right-click the selection to make the Mini toolbar appear again. To make selections from the Mini toolbar, click a command on the toolbar. To temporarily remove the Mini toolbar from view, press Esc.

> **To permanently disable the Mini toolbar so that it does not display in any open file when text is selected, complete the following steps:**
>
> 1. Click the File tab and click Options.
> 2. Click General.
> 3. Click the *Show Mini toolbar on selection* check box to deselect it.
> 4. Click OK.

Copy Formats with Format Painter

STEP 3 ❯❯ Using **Format Painter**, you can copy all formatting from one area to another in Word, PowerPoint, and Excel (see Figure 1.26). If, for example, a heading in Word includes multiple formatting features, you will save time by copying the entire set of formatting options to the other headings. In so doing, you will ensure the consistency of formatting for all headings because they will appear exactly alike.

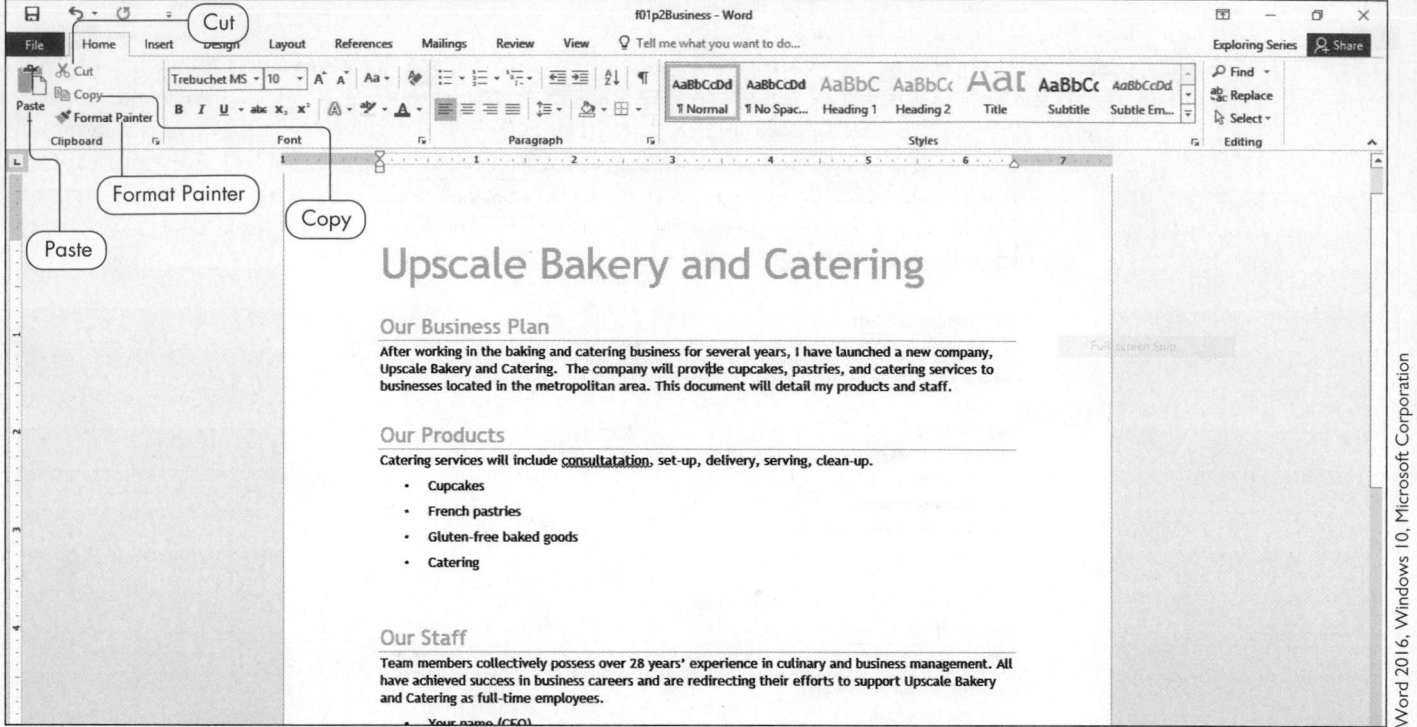

FIGURE 1.26 Format Painter

> **To copy a format, complete the following steps:**
> 1. Select the text containing the desired format.
> 2. Single-click Format Painter if you want to copy the format to only one other selection. If, however, you plan to copy the same format to multiple areas, double-click Format Painter.
> 3. Select the area to which the copied format should be applied.

If you single-clicked Format Painter to copy the format to one other selection, Format Painter turns off once the formatting has been applied. If you double-clicked Format Painter to copy the format to multiple locations, continue selecting text in various locations to apply the format. Then, to turn off Format Painter, click Format Painter again or press Esc.

Relocating Text

On occasion, you will want to relocate a section of text from one area to another. Suppose that you have included text on a PowerPoint slide that you believe would be more appropriate on a different slide. Or perhaps an Excel formula should be copied from one cell to another because both cells should be totaled in the same manner. You can move the slide text or copy the Excel formula by using the cut, copy, and paste features found in the Clipboard group on the Home tab. The Office **Clipboard** is an area of memory reserved to temporarily hold selections that have been cut or copied and allows you to paste the selections. When the computer is shut down or loses power, the contents of the Clipboard are erased, so it is important to finalize the paste procedure during the current session.

Cut, Copy, and Paste Text

STEP 4 >> To *cut* means to remove a selection from the original location and place it in the Office Clipboard. To *copy* means to duplicate a selection from the original location and place a copy in the Office Clipboard. Although the Clipboard can hold up to 24 items at one time, the usual procedure is to paste the cut or copied selection to its final destination fairly quickly. To *paste* means to place a cut or copied selection into another location. In addition to using the Clipboard group icons, you can also cut, copy, and paste in any of the ways listed in Table 1.3.

TABLE 1.3	Cut, Copy, and Paste Options
Command	**Actions**
Cut	• Click Cut in Clipboard group. • Right-click selection and select Cut. • Press Ctrl+X.
Copy	• Click Copy in Clipboard group. • Right-click selection and select Copy. • Press Ctrl+C.
Paste	• Click in destination location and select Paste in Clipboard group. • Click in destination location and press Ctrl+V. • Click Clipboard Dialog Box Launcher to open Clipboard pane. Click in destination location. With Clipboard pane open, click arrow beside intended selection and select Paste.

Pearson Education, Inc.

To cut or copy text, complete the following steps:

1. Select the text you want to cut or copy.
2. Click the appropriate icon in the Clipboard group either to cut or copy the selection. Remember that cut or copied text is actually placed in the Clipboard, remaining there even after you paste it to another location. It is important to note that you can paste the same item multiple times, because it will remain in the Clipboard until you power down your computer or until the Clipboard exceeds 24 items.
3. Click the location where you want the cut or copied text to be placed. The location can be in the current file or in another open file within any Office application.
4. Click Paste in the Clipboard group on the Home tab.

When you paste text you may not want to paste the text with all of its formatting. In some instances, you may want to paste only the text, unformatted, so that it fits in with the formatting of its new location. When pasting text, there are several options available and those options will depend on the program you are using.

Use the Office Clipboard

When you cut or copy selections, they are placed in the Office Clipboard. Regardless of which Office application you are using, you can view the Clipboard by clicking the Clipboard Dialog Box Launcher, as shown in Figure 1.27.

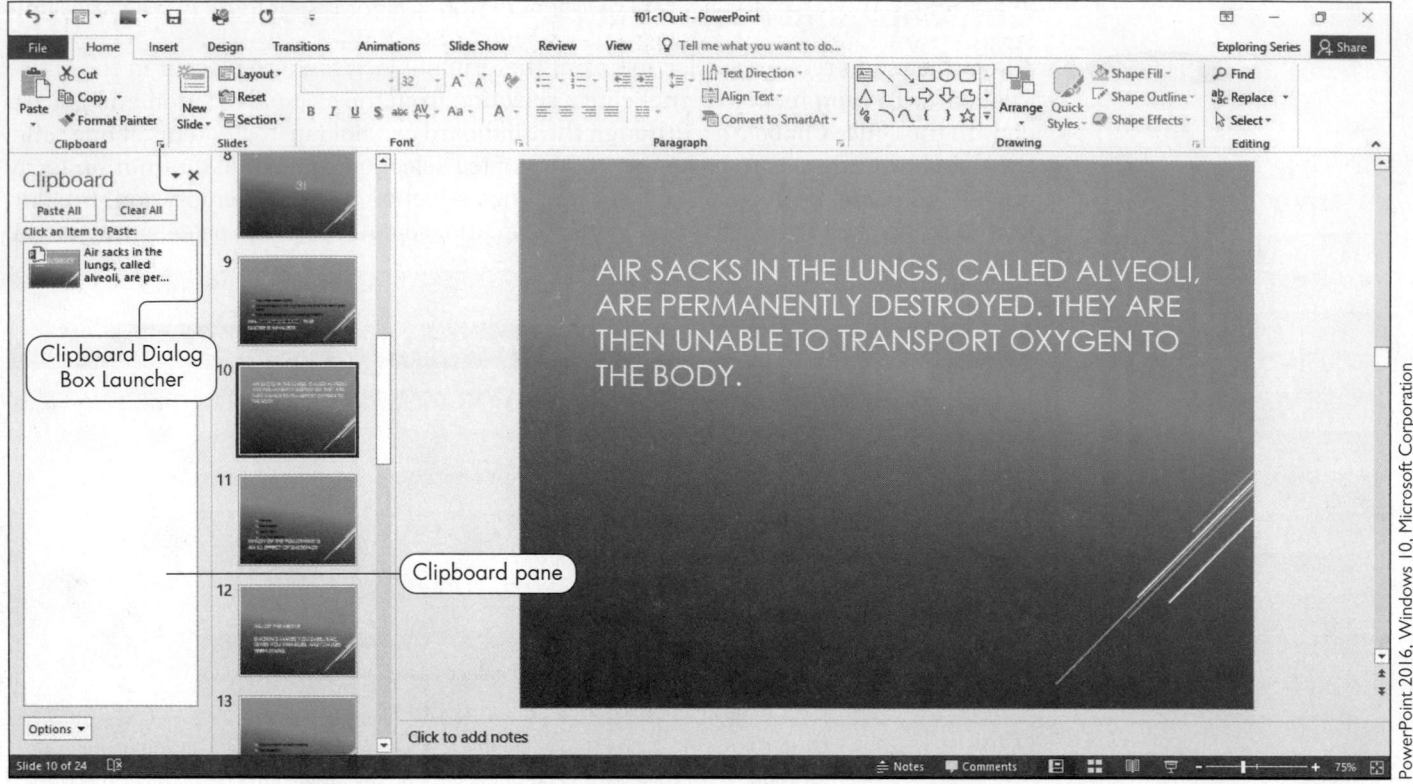

FIGURE 1.27 The Office Clipboard

Unless you specify otherwise when beginning a paste operation, the most recently added Clipboard item is pasted. You can, however, select an item from the Clipboard pane to paste. Click the item in the list to add it to the document. You can also delete items from the Clipboard by clicking the arrow next to the selection in the Clipboard pane and then clicking Delete. You can remove all items from the Clipboard by clicking Clear All. The Options button in the Clipboard pane enables you to control when and where the Clipboard is displayed. Close the Clipboard pane by clicking the Close ☒ button in the top-right corner of the pane or by clicking the arrow in the title bar of the Clipboard pane and selecting Close.

Checking Spelling and Grammar

 As you create or edit a file you will want to make sure no spelling or grammatical errors exist. You will also be concerned with wording, being sure to select words or phrases that best represent the purpose of the document, worksheet, or presentation. On occasion, you might even find yourself at a loss for an appropriate word. Word, Excel, and PowerPoint all provide standard tools for proofreading, including a spelling and grammar checker and thesaurus.

Word and PowerPoint check your spelling and grammar as you type. If a word is unrecognized, it is flagged as misspelled or grammatically incorrect. Even though Excel does not check your spelling as you type, it is important to run the spelling checker in Excel. Excel's spelling checker will review charts, pivot tables, and other reports that all need to be spelled correctly. Misspellings are identified with a red wavy underline, grammatical problems are underlined in green, and word usage errors (such as using bear instead of bare) have a blue underline.

To check the spelling for an entire file, complete the following steps:

1. Click the Review tab.
2. Click Spelling and Grammar.

Beginning at the top of the document, each identified error is highlighted in a pane similar to Figure 1.28. You can then choose how to address the problem by making a selection from the options in the pane.

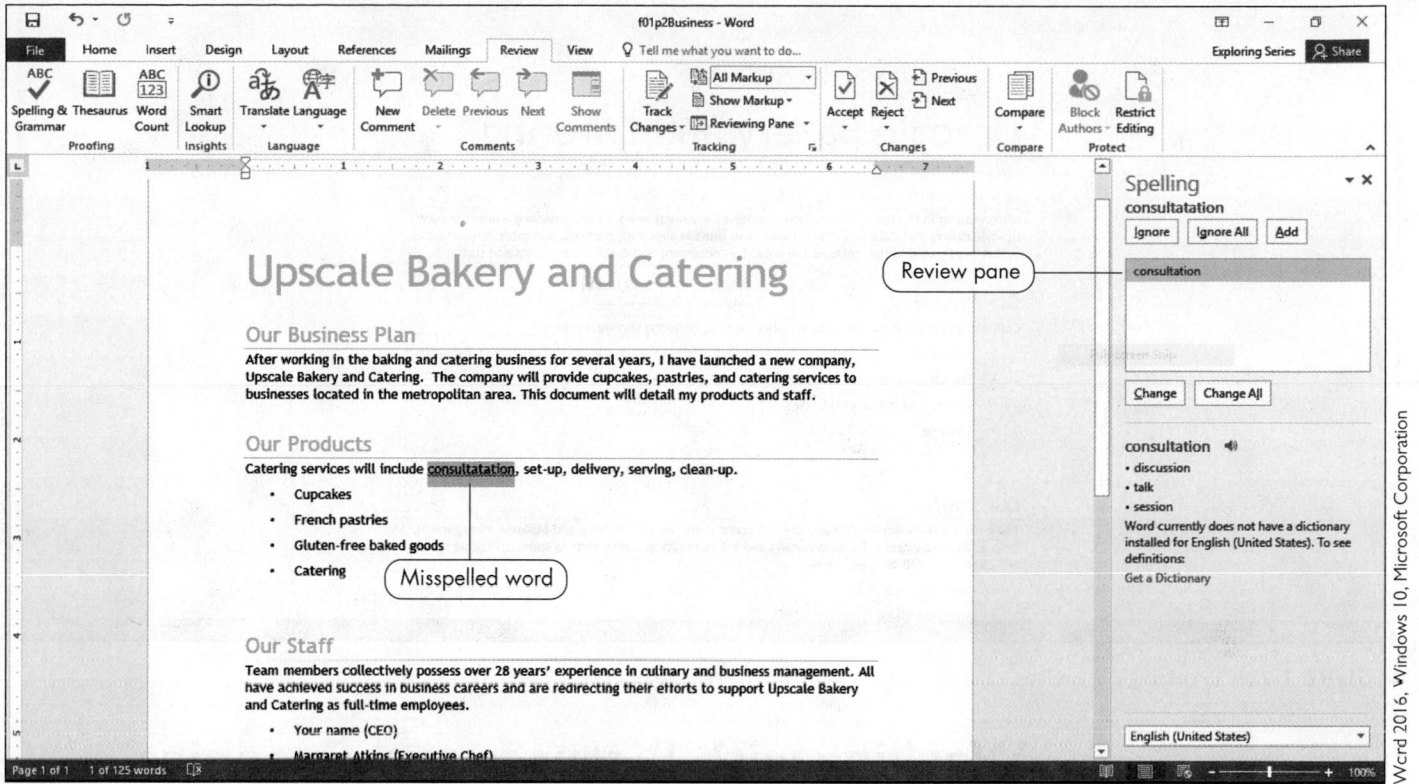

FIGURE 1.28 Checking for Spelling and Grammatical Errors

If the word or phrase is truly in error—that is, it is not a person's name or an unusual term that is not in the application's dictionary—you can correct it manually, or you can let the software correct it for you. If you right-click a word or phrase that is identified as a mistake, you will see a shortcut menu similar to that shown in Figure 1.29. If the Office dictionary makes a suggestion with the correct spelling, you can click to accept the suggestion and make the change. If a grammatical rule is violated, you will have an opportunity to select a correction. However, if the text is actually correct, you can click Ignore or Ignore All (to bypass all occurrences of the flagged error in the current document). Click *Add to Dictionary* if you want the word to be considered correct whenever it appears in any document. Similar selections on a shortcut menu enable you to ignore grammatical mistakes if they are not errors.

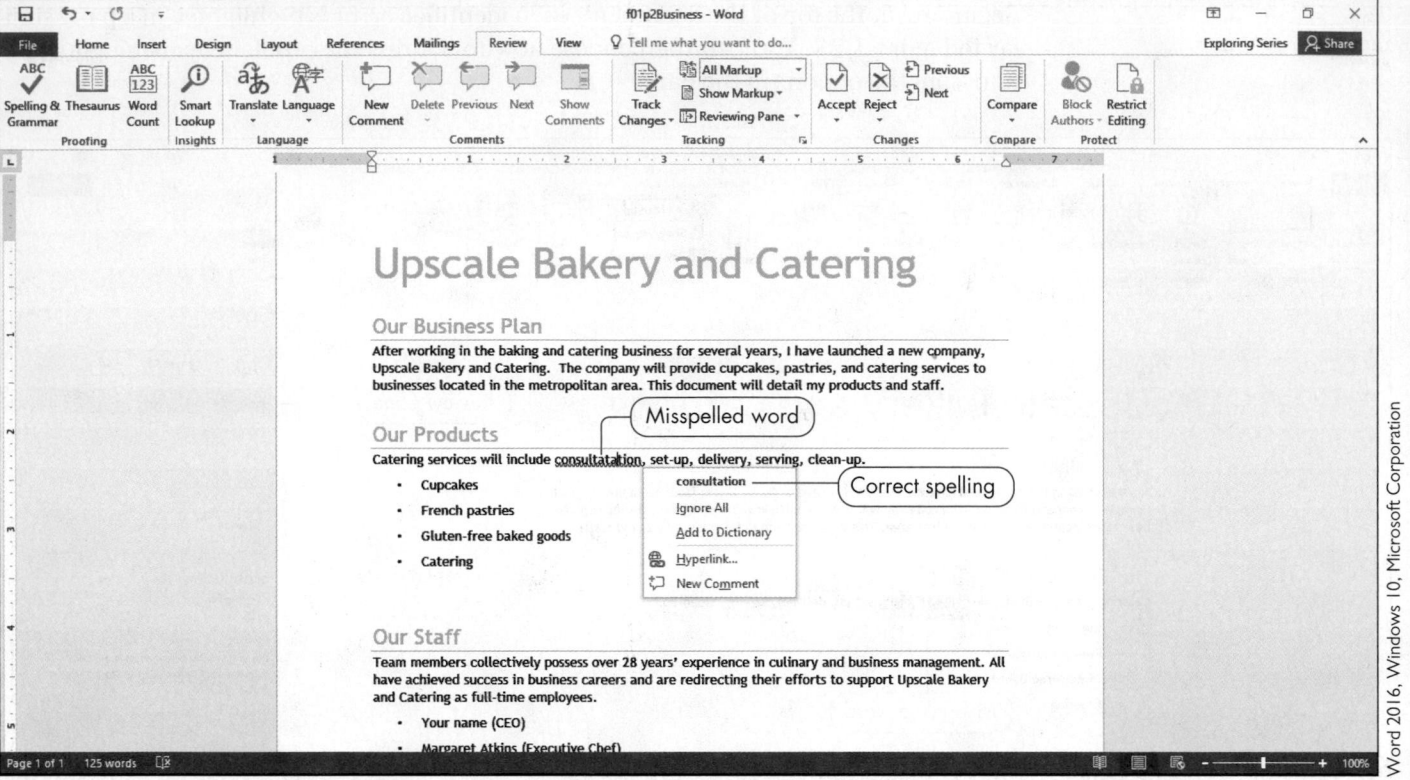

FIGURE 1.29 Correcting Misspelling

Working with Pictures and Graphics

Documents, worksheets, and presentations can include much more than just words and numbers. You can add energy and additional description to a project by including pictures and other graphic elements. Although a ***picture*** is usually just that—a digital photo—it is actually defined as a graphic element.

Insert Pictures and Graphics

 You can insert pictures from your own library of digital photos you have saved on your hard drive, OneDrive, or another storage medium, or you can initiate a Bing Image Search for online pictures directly inside the Office program you are using. The Bing search filters are set to use the Creative Commons license system. These are images and drawings that can be used more freely than images from websites. You should read the Creative Commons license for each image you use to avoid copyright infringement. You can also insert a picture from social media sites, such as Facebook, by clicking the Facebook icon at the bottom of the Online Pictures dialog box.

> **To insert an online picture from a Bing Image Search, complete the following steps:**
>
> 1. Click in the file where you want the picture to be placed.
> 2. Click the Insert tab.
> 3. Click Online Pictures in the Illustrations group.
> 4. Type a search term in the Bing Image Search box and press Enter.
> 5. Select your desired image and click Insert (see Figure 1.30).

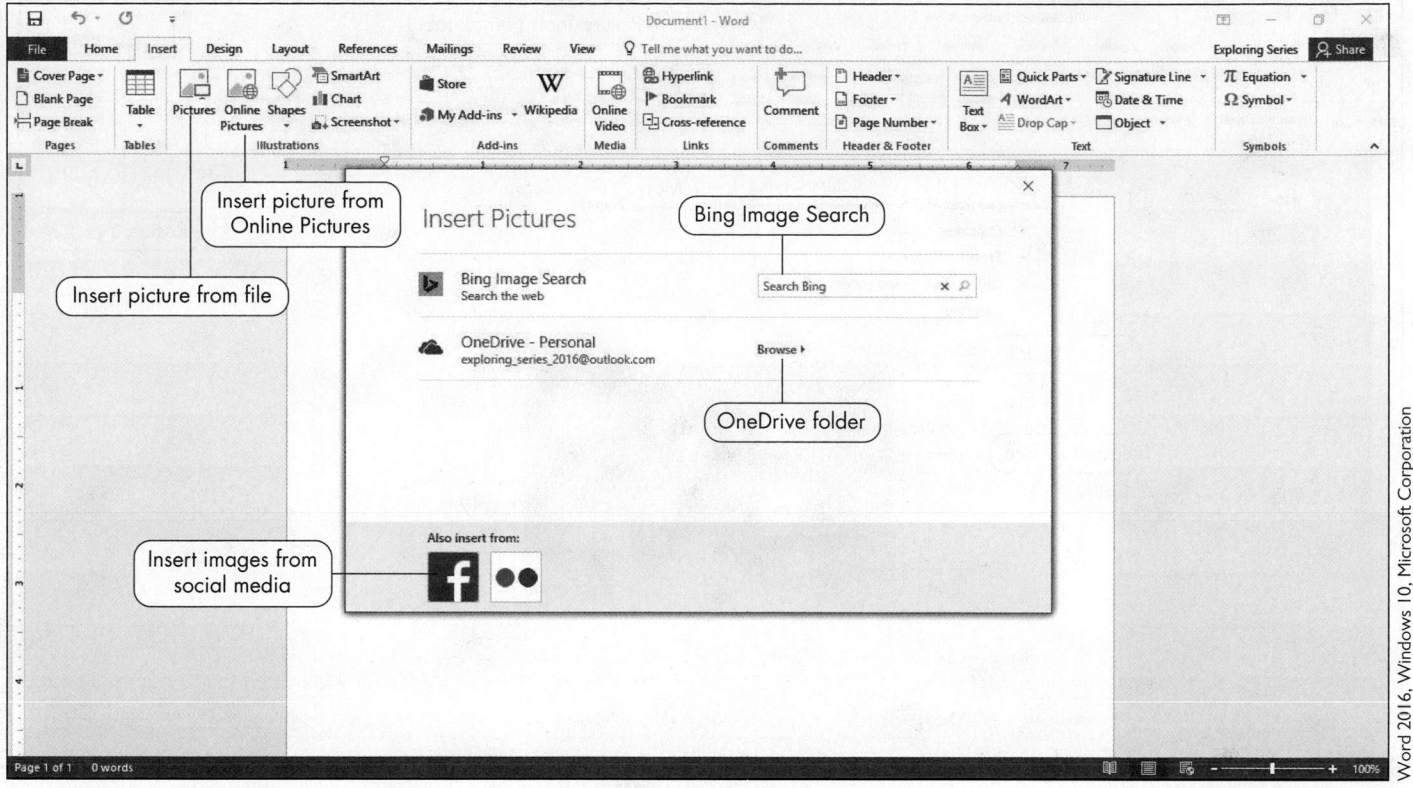

FIGURE I.30 Inserting Online Pictures

To insert a picture from a file stored on your computer, complete the following steps:

1. Click in the file where you want the picture to be placed.
2. Click the Insert tab.
3. Click Pictures in the Illustrations group to search for a file located on your computer.
4. Locate the file and select it. Click Insert at the bottom of the dialog box to insert the file into your document.

Resize and Format Pictures and Graphics

You have learned how to add a picture to your document, but quite often, a picture is inserted in a size that is too large or too small for your purposes. To resize a picture, you can drag a corner sizing handle. You should never resize a picture by dragging a center sizing handle, as doing so would skew the picture. You can also resize a picture by adjusting settings in the Size group of the Picture Tools Format tab. When a picture is selected, the Picture Tools Format tab includes options for modifying a picture (see Figure 1.31). You can apply a picture style or effect, as well as add a picture border, from selections in the Picture Styles group. Click More (see Figure 1.31) to view a gallery of picture styles. As you point to a style, the style is shown in Live Preview, but the style is not applied until you click it. Options in the Adjust group simplify changing a color scheme, applying creative artistic effects, and even adjusting the brightness, contrast, and sharpness of an image.

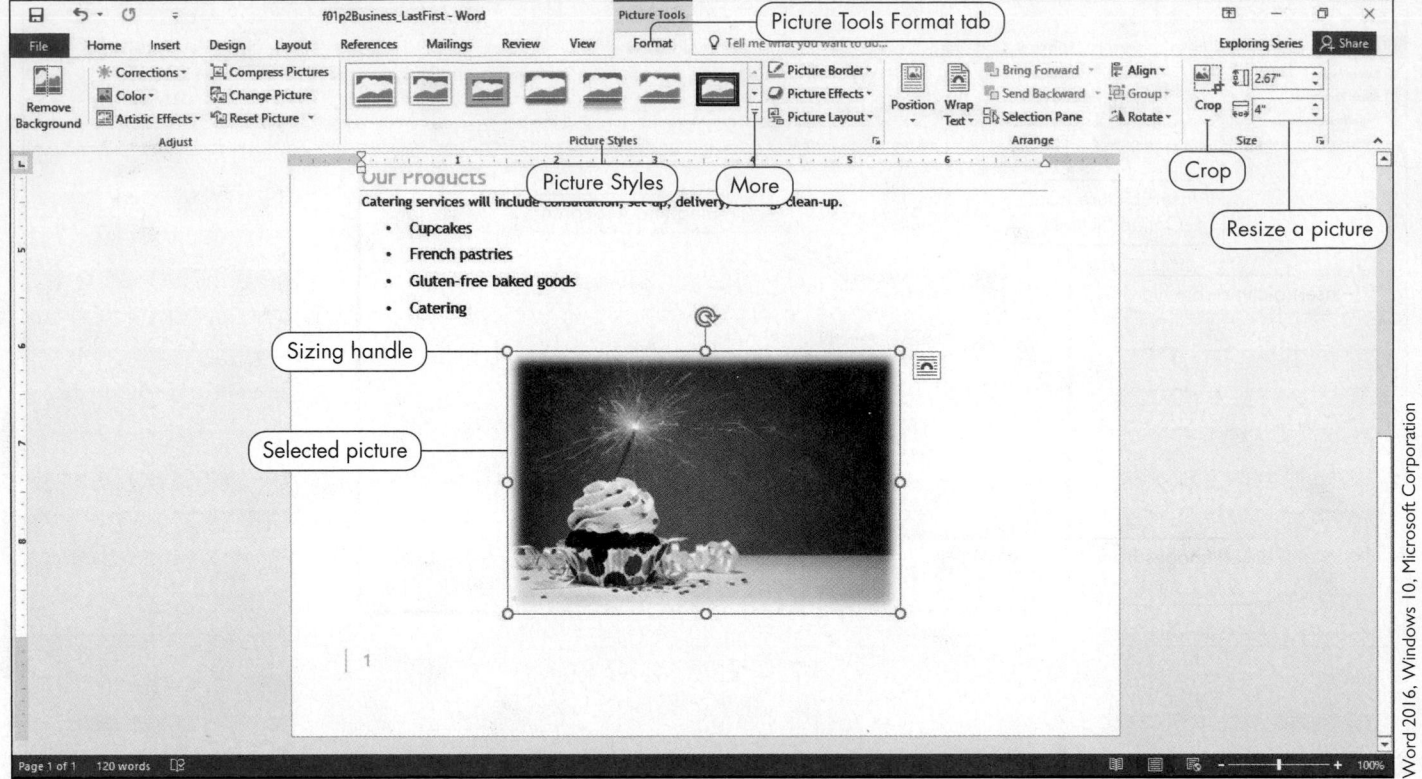

FIGURE 1.31 Formatting a Picture

If a picture contains more detail than is necessary, you can crop it, which is the process of trimming edges that you do not want to display. The Crop tool is located on the Picture Tools Format tab (refer to Figure 1.31). Even though cropping enables you to adjust the amount of a picture that displays, it does not actually delete the portions that are cropped out unless you actually compress the picture. Therefore, you can later recover parts of the picture, if necessary. Cropping a picture does not reduce the file size of the picture or the document in which it displays.

Quick Concepts

4. What is the difference between a theme and a template? *p. 86*

5. Give an example of when Format Painter could be used. *p. 91*

6. When will an Office application identify a word as misspelled that is not actually misspelled? *p. 95*

Hands-On Exercises

Watch the Video for this Hands-On Exercise!

MyITLab®
HOE2 Training

Skills covered: Open a Template • Select Text • Edit Text • Use the Mini Toolbar • Format Painter • Cut, Copy, and Paste Text • Check Spelling and Grammar • Insert a Picture

2 Format Document Content

As the administrative assistant for the Spotted Begonia Art Gallery, you want to create a flyer to announce the *Discover the Artist in You!* kickoff event. You decide to use a template to help you get started more quickly. You will modify the flyer created with the template by adding and editing text and a photo.

STEP 1 ▶▶ OPEN A TEMPLATE

To expedite the process of creating a flyer, you will review the templates that are available in Microsoft Word. You search for flyers and finally choose one that is appropriate for the gallery, knowing that you will be able to replace the photos with your own. Refer to Figure 1.32 as you complete Step 1.

Step b: Flyer template opened

Word 2016, Windows 10, Microsoft Corporation

FIGURE 1.32 Use a Template

a. Start Word. In the *Search for online templates* box type the search term **event flyer** to search for event flyer templates Click **Search**.

Your search results in a selection of event flyer templates.

b. Locate the event flyer template in Figure 1.32 and click to select it. The template appears in a preview. Click **Create** to open the flyer template.

The flyer template that you selected opens in Word.

> **TROUBLESHOOTING:** If you do not find the template in the figure, you may access the template from the student data files – *f01h2Flyer*.

c. Click **Save** on the Quick Access Toolbar. Save the document as **f01h2Flyer_LastFirst**. Because this is the first time to save the flyer file, the Save button on the Quick Access Toolbar opens a dialog box in which you must indicate the location of the file and the file name.

STEP 2 ⟫ SELECT AND EDIT TEXT

You will replace the template text to create the flyer, adding information such as a title, date, and description. After adding the text to the document, you will modify the organization name in the flyer so it is more like the logo text. Refer to Figure 1.33 as you complete Step 2.

[Add Key Event Info Here!]

[Don't Be Shy—Tell Them Why They Can't Miss It!]

[One More Point Here!]

[Add More Great Info Here!]

[You Have Room for Another One Here!]

Step a: Text added

Step c: 26 font size applied

Step b: Eras Bold ITC font applied

MAY 31, 2018
DISCOVER THE ARTIST IN YOU!
Spotted Begonia Art Gallery

A Special Childrens Event
[To replace any tip text with your own, just click it and start typing. To replace the photo or logo with your own, right-click it and then

[COMPANY NAME]

Word 2016, Windows 10, Microsoft Corporation

FIGURE 1.33 Select and Edit Text

a. Click the [Date] **placeholder** in the main body of the text and type **May 31, 2018** in the placeholder. Click the [Event Title Here] **placeholder** and type **Discover the Artist in You!** in the placeholder. Press **Enter** and continue typing **Spotted Begonia Art Gallery**. Click the [Event Description Heading] **placeholder** and type **A Special Childrens Event**. (Ignore the misspelling at this time.)

You modify the placeholders to customize the flyer for your purposes.

b. Point to the text **Discover the Artist in You!** until the pointer becomes an I-beam. Click and drag to select the text. Click the **Font arrow** on the Mini toolbar. Select **Eras Bold ITC**.

The font is changed.

c. Select the text, **May 31, 2018**. Click the **Font Size arrow** on the Mini toolbar. Select **26** on the Font Size menu.

The font size is changed to 26 pt.

d. Click Save on the Quick Access Toolbar to save the document.

You want the gallery name font to match that of the event description heading in the flyer. You recently learned about using the Format Painter tool to quickly apply font attributes to text. Refer to Figure 1.34 as you complete Step 3.

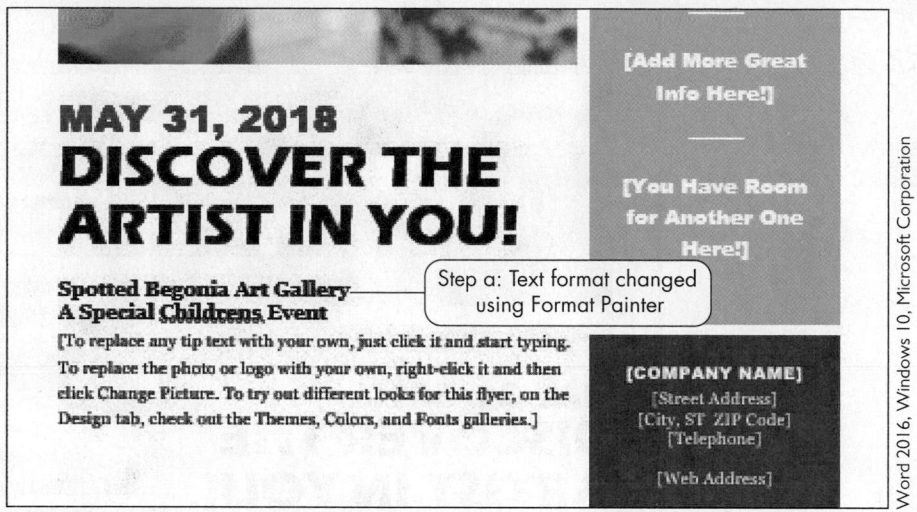

FIGURE 1.34 Use Format Painter

a. Click the **Home tab**. Select the text **A Special Childrens Event**, and click **Format Painter** in the Clipboard group. Drag to select the text **Spotted Begonia Art Gallery**.

The text is now modified to match the font and size of the event description heading.

b. Save the document.

You decide that one of the paragraphs in the flyer would be best near the end of the document. You cut the paragraph and paste it in the new location. Refer to Figure 1.35 as you complete Step 4.

FIGURE 1.35 Move Text

a. Point to the text **Spotted Begonia Art Gallery** until the pointer becomes an I-beam. Click and drag to select the text. Press **Ctrl+X**.

The paragraph text is cut from the document and placed in the Office Clipboard.

b. Click before the word *May*. Press **Ctrl+V** to paste the previously cut text.

The text is now moved above the event date.

c. Save the document.

Because this flyer will be seen by the public, it is important to check the spelling and grammar for your document. Refer to Figure 1.36 as you complete Step 5.

FIGURE 1.36 Check Spelling and Grammar

a. Press **Ctrl+Home**. Click the **Review tab**, and click **Spelling & Grammar**. in the Proofing group Click **Change** to accept the suggested change to *Children's* in the Spelling pane. Click **OK** to close the dialog box.

The spelling and grammar check is complete.

b. Save the document.

You want to add an image saved on your computer that was taken at a previous children's event held at the gallery. Refer to Figure 1.37 as you complete Step 6.

FIGURE 1.37 Insert Picture

a. Click the **image** to select it. Click the **Insert tab** and then click **Pictures**. Browse to your student data files and locate the *f01h2Art* picture file. Click **Insert**.

The child's image is inserted into the flyer and replaces the template image of the children with ice cream.

b. Save and close the document. You will submit this file to your instructor at the end of the last Hands-On Exercise.

Modify Document Layout and Properties

When working with a document, at some point you must get it ready for distribution and/or printing. Before you send a document or print it, you will want to view the final product to make sure that your margins and page layout are as they should be.

In this section you will learn about Backstage view and explore how to view and edit document properties. You will learn about views and how to change a document view to suit your needs. Additionally, you will learn how to modify the page layout including page orientation and margins as well as how to add headers and footers. Finally, you will explore Print Preview and the various printing options available to you.

Using Backstage View

Backstage view is a component of Office that provides a concise collection of commands related to a file. Using Backstage view, you can view or specify settings related to protection, permissions, versions, and properties. A file's properties include the author, file size, permissions, and date modified. Backstage view also includes options for customizing program settings, signing in to your Office account, and exiting the application. You can create a new document, as well as open, save, print, share, export, and close files using Backstage view. Backstage view also enables you to exit the application.

Click the File tab to see Backstage view (see Figure 1.38). Backstage view will occupy the entire application window, hiding the file with which you are working. You can return to the application in a couple of ways. Either click the Back arrow in the top-left corner or press Esc on the keyboard.

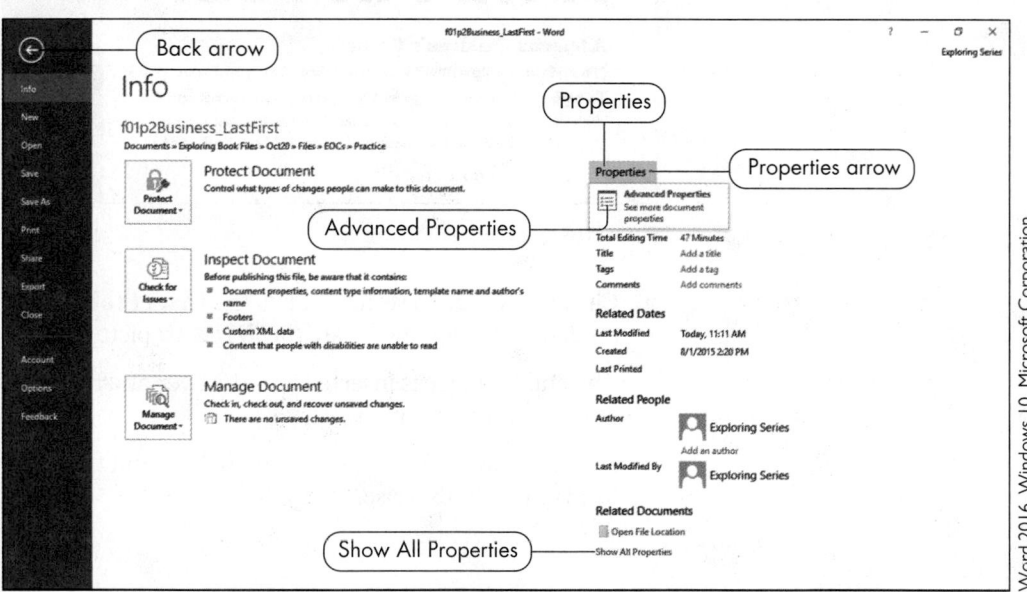

FIGURE 1.38 Backstage View and Document Properties

Customize Application Options

General settings in the Office application in which you are working can also be custom-ized (see Figure 1.39). For example, you can change the AutoRecover settings, a feature that enables Word to recover a previous version of a document, such as the location and save frequency. You can alter how formatting, spelling, and grammar are checked by the application such as ignoring words in all uppercase letters. You can also modify the AutoCorrect feature. Additionally, you can change the language in which the application is displayed or the language for spelling and grammar checking, which may be helpful for a language course.

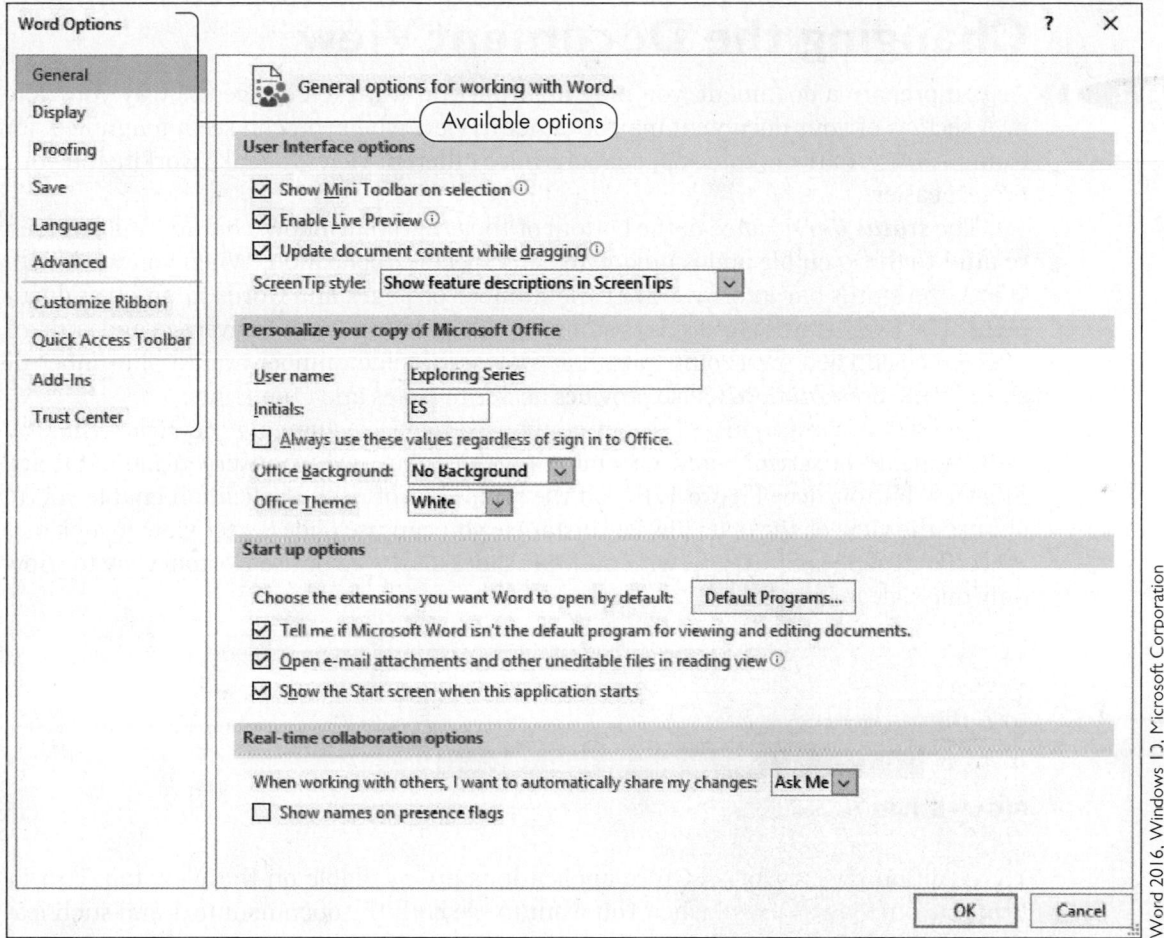

FIGURE 1.39 Application Options in Word

> **To customize an Office application, complete the following steps:**
> 1. Click the File tab.
> 2. Click Options and select the option of your choice.
> 3. Click OK.

View and Edit Document Properties

STEP 1 It is good to include information that identifies a document, such as the author, document purpose, intended audience, or general comments. Those data elements, or metadata, are saved with the document, but do not appear in the document as it displays onscreen or is printed. You can use the Document Properties, located in Backstage view, to display descriptive information. You can even search for a file based on metadata you assign a doc-ument. For example, suppose you apply a tag of *Picasso* to all documents you create that are associated with that particular artist. Later, you can use that keyword as a search term, locating all associated documents. Statistical information related to the current document such as file size, number of pages, and total words are located on the Info page of Backstage view. You can modify some document information, such as adding a title or comments, but for more possibilities, display the Advanced Properties (refer to Figure 1.38).

> **To display the Advanced Properties, complete the following steps:**
>
> 1. Click the File tab.
> 2. Click the Properties arrow on the Info page.

Changing the Document View

STEP 2 ❱❱ As you prepare a document, you may find that you want to change the way you view it. A section of your document may be easier to view when you can see it magnified, for example. Alternatively, some applications have different views to make working on your project easier.

The **status bar**, located at the bottom of the program window, contains information relative to the open file and is unique to each specific application. When you work with Word, the status bar informs you of the number of pages and words in an open document. The Excel status bar displays summary information, such as average and sum, of selected cells. The PowerPoint status bar shows the slide number and total number of slides in the presentation. It also provides access to Notes and Comments.

The status bar also includes commonly used tools for changing the **view**—the way a file appears onscreen—and for changing the zoom size of onscreen file contents. The view buttons (see Figure 1.40) on the status bar of each application enable you to change the view of the open file. For instance, you can use Slide Sorter view to look at a PowerPoint slide presentation with multiple slides displayed or use Normal view to show only one slide in large size.

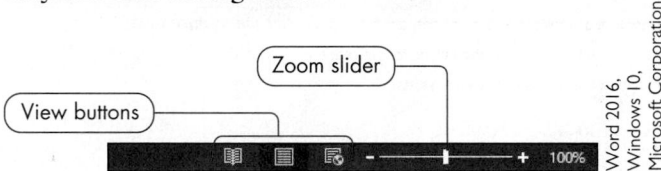

FIGURE 1.40 The Status Bar

Additional views for all Office applications are available on the View tab. Word's Print Layout view is useful when you want to see both the document text and such features as margins and page breaks. Web Layout view is useful to see what the page would look like on the Internet. Read Mode view provides a clean look that displays just the content without the Ribbon or margins. It is ideal for use on a tablet where the screen may be smaller than on a laptop or computer. PowerPoint, Excel, and Access also provide other unique view options. As you learn more about Office applications, you will become aware of the views that are specific to each application.

The **Zoom slider** is a horizontal bar on the bottom-right side of the status bar that enables you to increase or decrease the size of the document onscreen. You can drag the tab along the slider in either direction to increase or decrease the magnification of the file (refer to Figure 1.40). Be aware, however, that changing the size of text onscreen does not change the font size when the file is printed or saved.

Changing the Page Layout

When you prepare a document or worksheet, you are concerned with the way the project appears onscreen and possibly in print. The Layout tab in Word and the Page Layout tab in Excel provide access to a full range of options such as margin settings and page orientation. PowerPoint does not have a Page Layout tab, since its primary purpose is displaying contents onscreen rather than in print.

Because a document or workbook is most often designed to be printed, you may need to adjust margins and change the page orientation for the best display. In addition, perhaps the document or spreadsheet should be centered on the page vertically or the text should be aligned in columns. You will find these and other common page settings in the Page Setup group on the Layout (or Page Layout) tab. For less common settings, such as determining whether headers should print on odd or even pages, you use the Page Setup dialog box.

Change Margins

STEP 3 ▶▶ A ***margin*** is the area of blank space that displays to the left, right, top, and bottom of a document or worksheet. Margins display when you are in Print Layout or Page Layout view, or in Backstage view previewing a document to print. As shown in Figure 1.41, you can change the margins by clicking Margins in the Page Setup group. You can also change margins in the Print area on Backstage view.

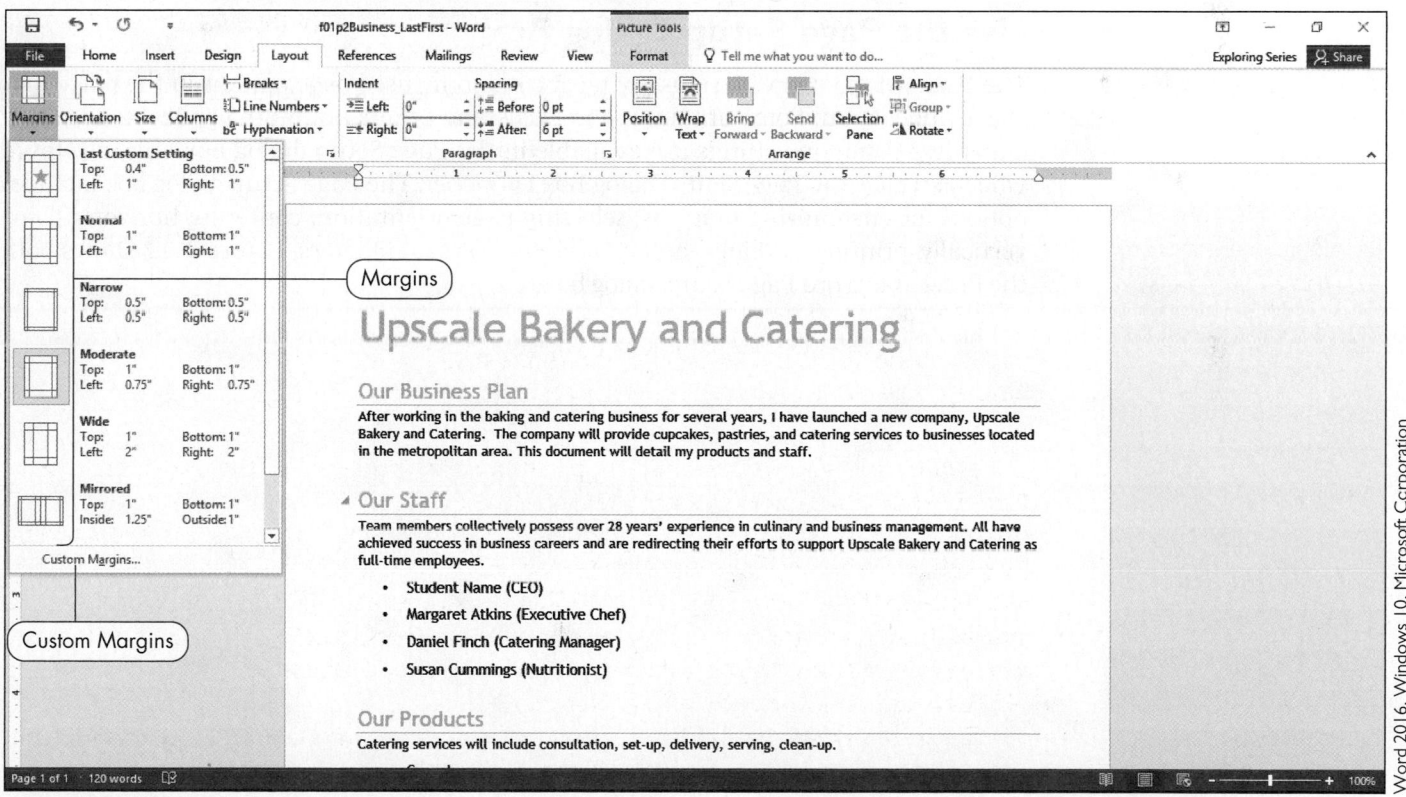

FIGURE 1.41 Page Margins in Word

To change margins in Word and Excel, complete the following steps:

1. Click the Layout (or Page Layout) tab.
2. Click Margins in the Page Setup group.
3. Select a preset margin option or click Custom Margins (refer to Figure 1.41) to display the Page Setup dialog box where you can apply custom margin settings.
4. Click OK to accept the settings and close the dialog box.

Change Page Orientation

Documents and worksheets can be displayed in different page orientations. A page displayed or printed in *portrait orientation* is taller than it is wide. A page in *landscape orientation* is wider than it is tall. Word documents are usually more attractive displayed in portrait orientation, whereas Excel worksheets are often more suited to landscape orientation.

To change the page orientation, complete the following steps:

1. Click the Layout (or Page Layout) tab.
2. Click Orientation in the Page Setup group.
3. Select Portrait or Landscape.

Orientation is also an option in the Print area of Backstage view.

Use the Page Setup Dialog Box

The Page Setup group contains the most commonly used page options in the particular Office application. Some are unique to Excel, and others are more applicable to Word. Other less common settings are available in the Page Setup dialog box only, displayed when you click the Page Setup Dialog Box Launcher. The Page Setup dialog box includes options for customizing margins, selecting page orientation, centering horizontally or vertically, printing gridlines, and creating headers and footers. Figure 1.42 shows both the Excel and Word Page Setup dialog boxes.

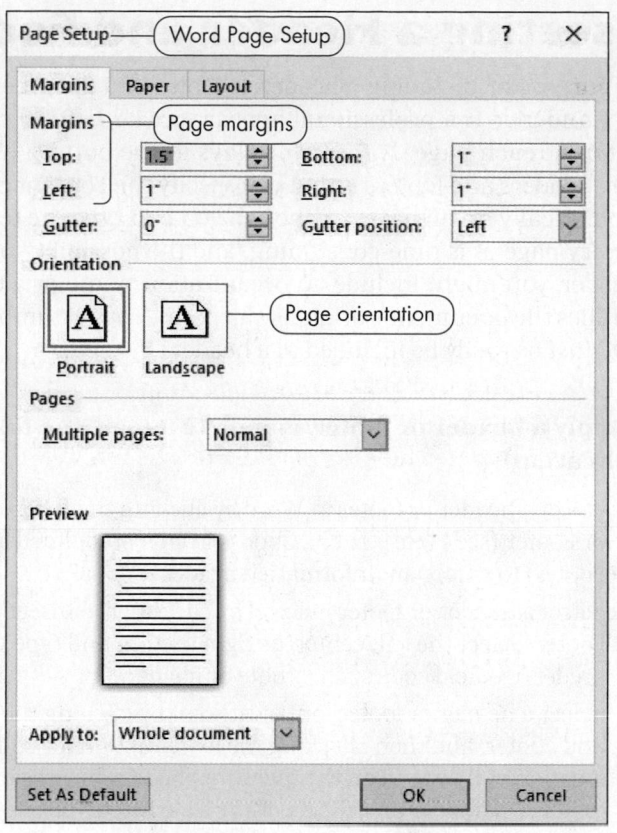

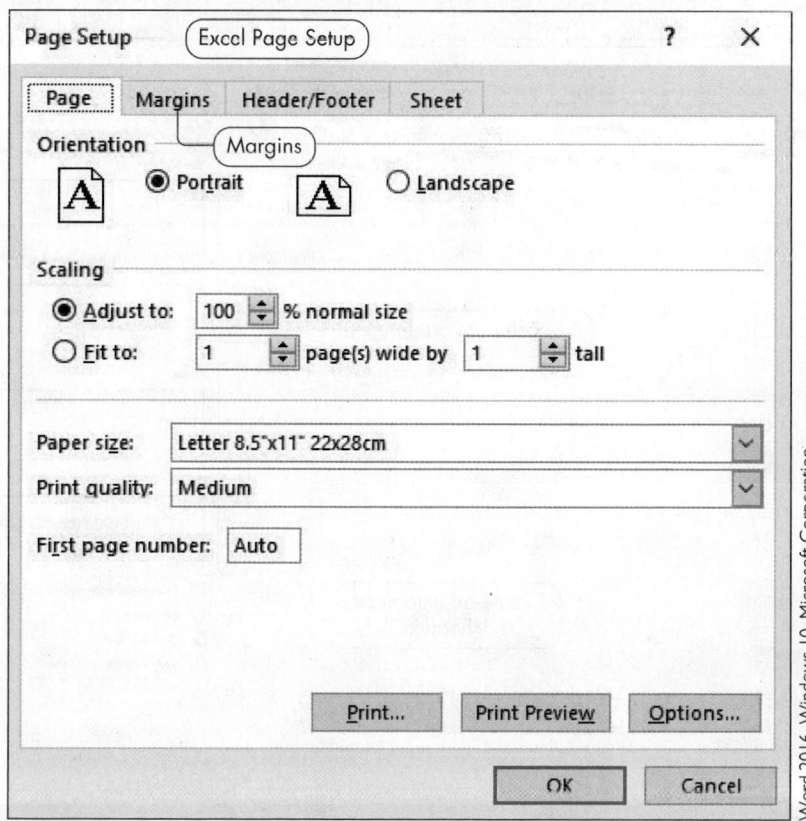

FIGURE 1.42 Page Setup Dialog Boxes in Word and Excel

Word 2016, Windows 10, Microsoft Corporation

Inserting a Header and Footer

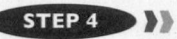

STEP 4 ›› The purpose of including a header or footer in a document is to better identify the document and give it a professional appearance. A ***header*** consists of one or more lines at the top of each page. A ***footer*** displays at the bottom of each page. One advantage of using headers and footers is that you specify the content only once, after which it displays automatically on all pages. Although you can type the text yourself at the top or bottom of every page, it is time-consuming, and the possibility of making a mistake is great. As a header, you might include an organization name or a class number so that each page identifies the document's origin or purpose. A page number is a typical footer, although it could just as easily be included in a header.

To apply a header or footer, complete one of the following steps (based on the application):

- Select a header or footer in Word by clicking the Insert tab and then clicking Header or Footer (see Figure 1.43). Choose from a predefined list, or click Edit Header (or Edit Footer) to create an unformatted header or footer.
- Select a header or footer in Excel by clicking the Insert tab and clicking Header and Footer. Select the left, center, or right section and type your own footer or use a predefined field code such as date or file name.
- Select a header or footer for PowerPoint by clicking the Insert tab, clicking Header and Footer, and then checking the footer option for slides. In PowerPoint, a footer's location will depend on the theme applied to the presentation. For some themes, the footer will appear on the side of the slide rather than at the bottom. Headers and footers are available for Notes and Handouts as well.

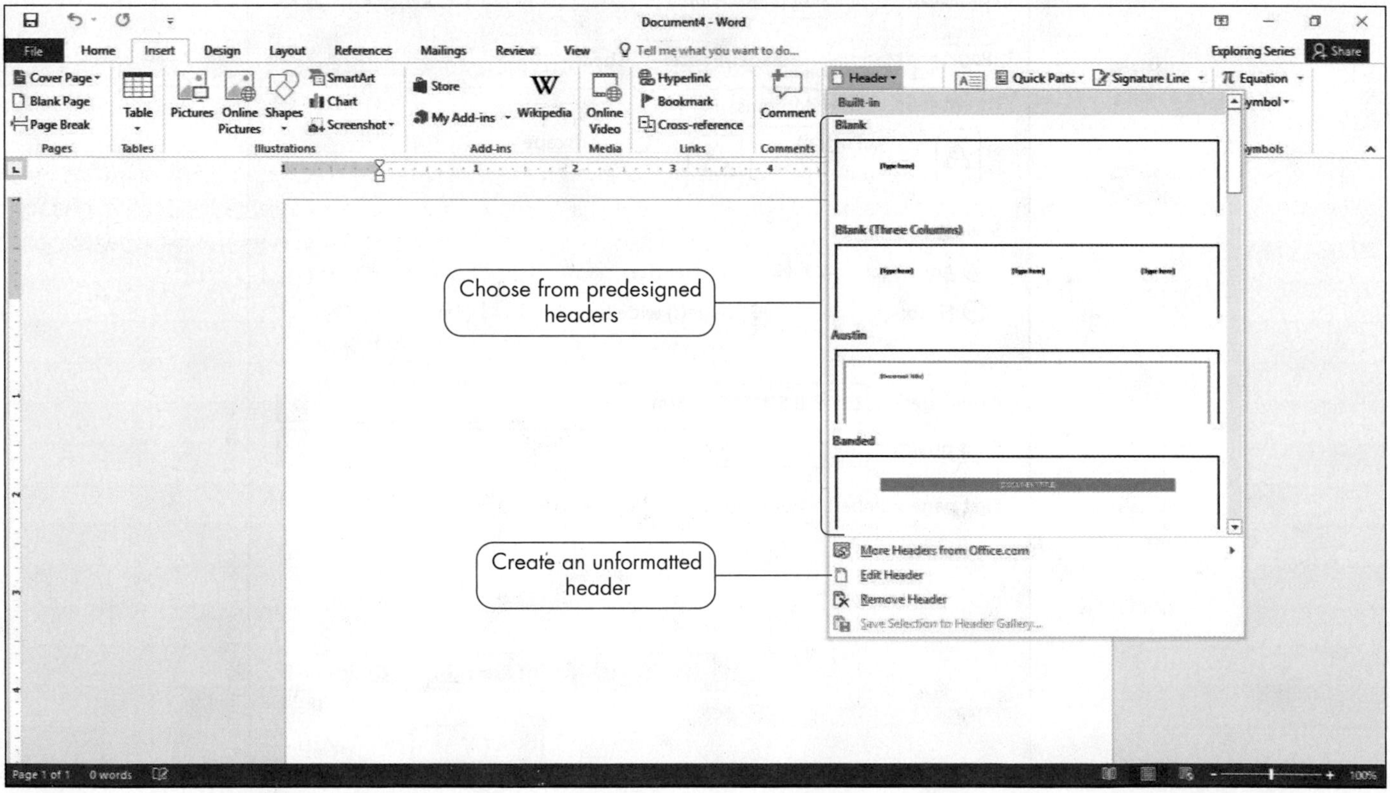

Word 2016, Windows 10, Microsoft Corporation

FIGURE 1.43 Insert Header in Word

After typing a header or footer, it can be formatted like any other text. It can be formatted in any font or font size. In Word or Excel, when you want to leave the header and footer area and return to the document, click Close Header and Footer (see Figure 1.44).

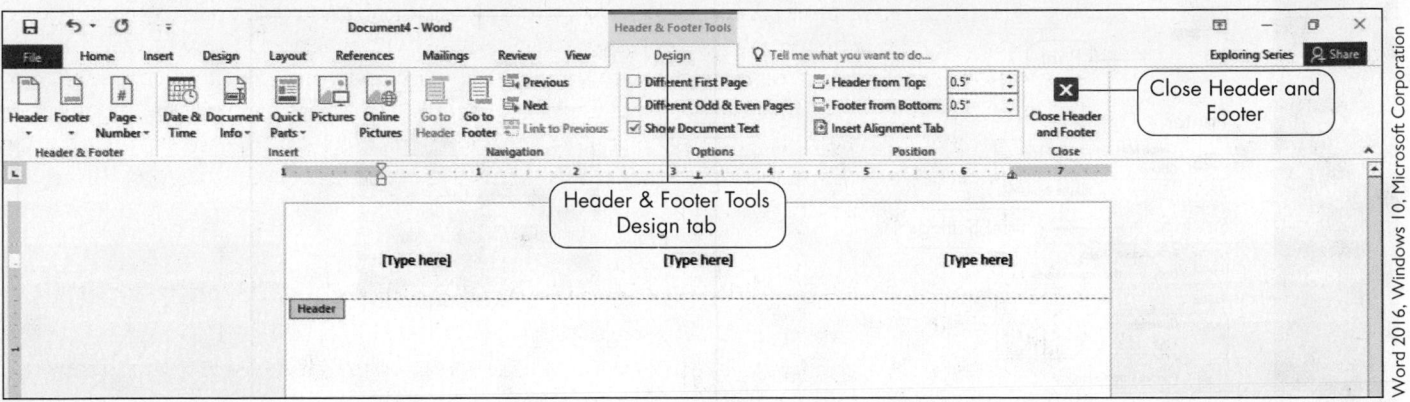

FIGURE 1.44 Close Header and Footer

Previewing and Printing a File

STEP 5 ▶▶ When you want to print an Office file, you can select from various print options, including the number of copies and the specific pages to print. It is a good idea to take a look at how your document or worksheet will appear before you print it. The Print Preview feature of Office enables you to do just that. In the Print Preview pane, you will see all items, including any headers, footers, graphics, and special formatting.

To view a file before printing, complete the following steps:

1. Click the File tab.
2. Click Print.

The subsequent Backstage view shows the file preview on the right, with print settings located in the center of the Backstage screen. Figure 1.45 shows a typical Backstage Print view. If you know that the page setup is correct and that there are no unique print settings to select, you can simply print without adjusting any print settings.

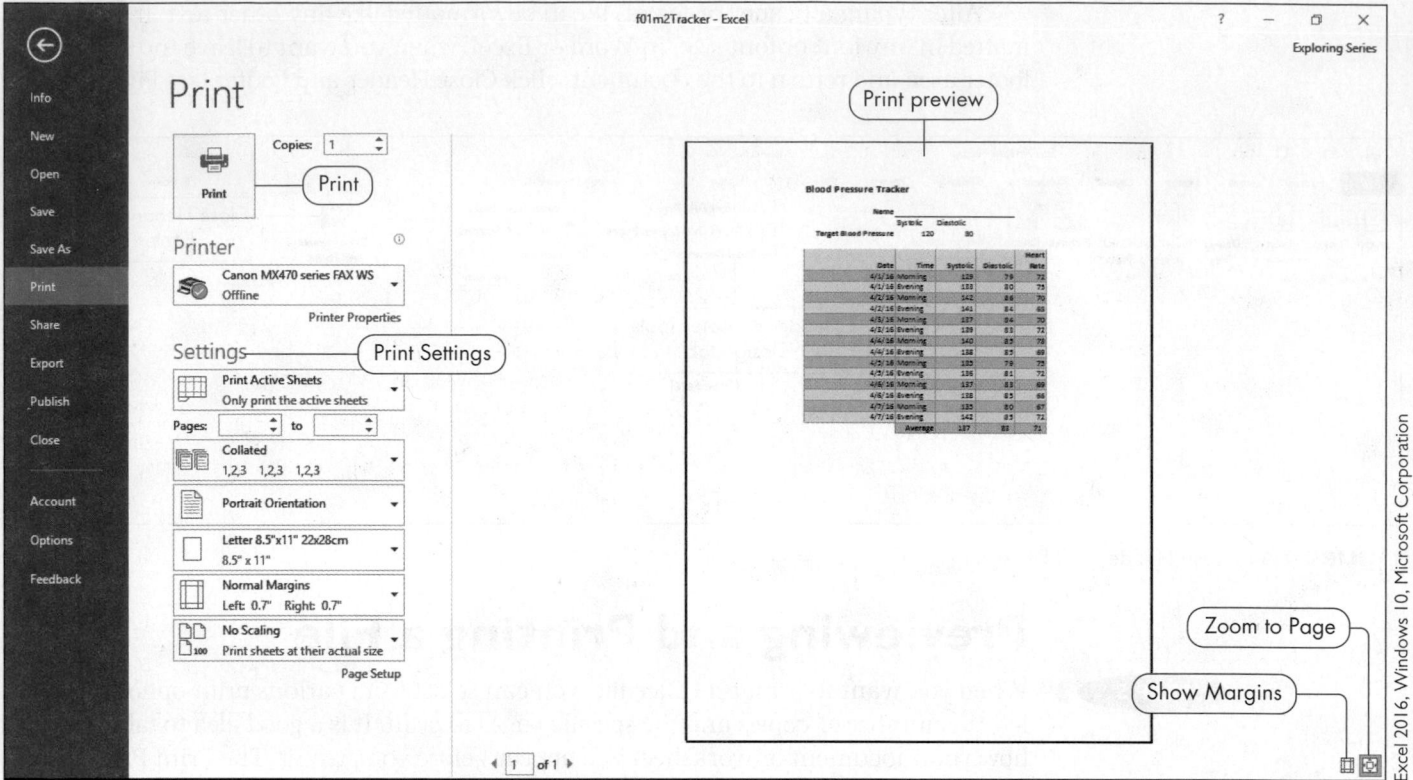

FIGURE 1.45 Backstage Print View in Excel

Options to show the margins (*Show Margins*) and to increase the size of the print preview (*Zoom to Page*) are found on the bottom-right corner of the preview (refer to Figure 1.45). Remember that increasing the font size by adjusting the zoom applies to the current display only; it does not actually increase the font size when the file is printed or saved. To return the preview to its original view, click *Zoom to Page* once more.

Other options in the Backstage Print view vary depending on the application in which you are working. For example, PowerPoint's Backstage Print view includes options for printing slides and handouts in various configurations and colors, whereas Excel's focuses on worksheet selections and Word's includes document options. Regardless of the Office application, you will be able to access Settings options from Backstage view, including page orientation (landscape or portrait), margins, and paper size. To print a file, click the Print button (refer to Figure 1.45).

Quick Concepts

7. What functions and features are included in Backstage view? *p. 104*

8. Why would you need to change the view of a document? *p. 106*

9. What is the purpose of a header or footer? *p. 110*

Hands-On Exercises

Watch the Video for this Hands-On Exercise!

MyITLab®
HOE3 Training

Skills covered: Enter Document Properties • Change the Document View • Change Margins • Insert a Footer • Preview a File • Change Page Orientation

3 Modify Document Layout and Properties

You continue to work on the thank-you letter you previously started. As the administrative assistant for the Spotted Begonia Art Gallery, you must be able to search for and find documents previously created. You know that by adding tags to your letter you will more easily be able to find it at a later time. You will review and add document properties, and prepare the document to print and distribute by changing the page setup. Additionally, you will add a footer with Spotted Begonia's information. Finally, you will explore printing options, and save the letter.

STEP 1 ›› ENTER DOCUMENT PROPERTIES

You will add document properties, which will help you locate the file when performing a search of your hard drive. Refer to Figure 1.46 as you complete Step 1.

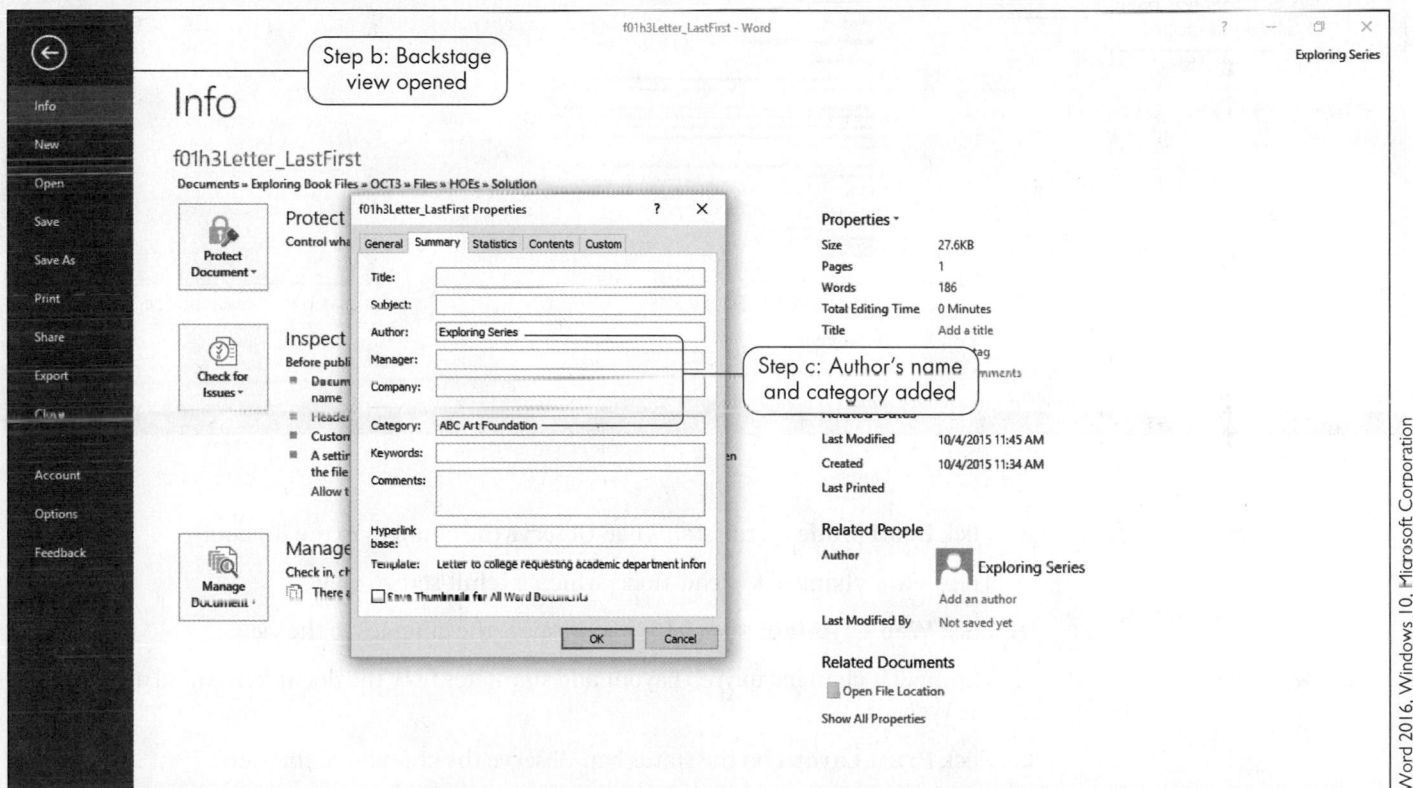

FIGURE 1.46 Backstage View

a. Open *f01h1Letter_LastFirst* if you closed it at the end of Hands-On Exercise 1, and save it as **f01h3Letter_LastFirst**, changing h1 to h3.

The letter is now open in Word.

b. Click the **File tab** and click **Properties** at the top-right of Backstage view. Click **Advanced Properties**.

The Properties dialog box opens so you can make changes.

    c. Select the **Author box** and type your first and last name. Select the **Category box** and type **ABC Art Foundation**. Click **OK**.

       You added the Author and Category properties to your document.

    d. Save the document.

STEP 2 ›› CHANGE THE DOCUMENT VIEW

To get a better perspective on your letter, you want to explore the various document views available in Word. Refer to Figure 1.47 as you complete Step 2.

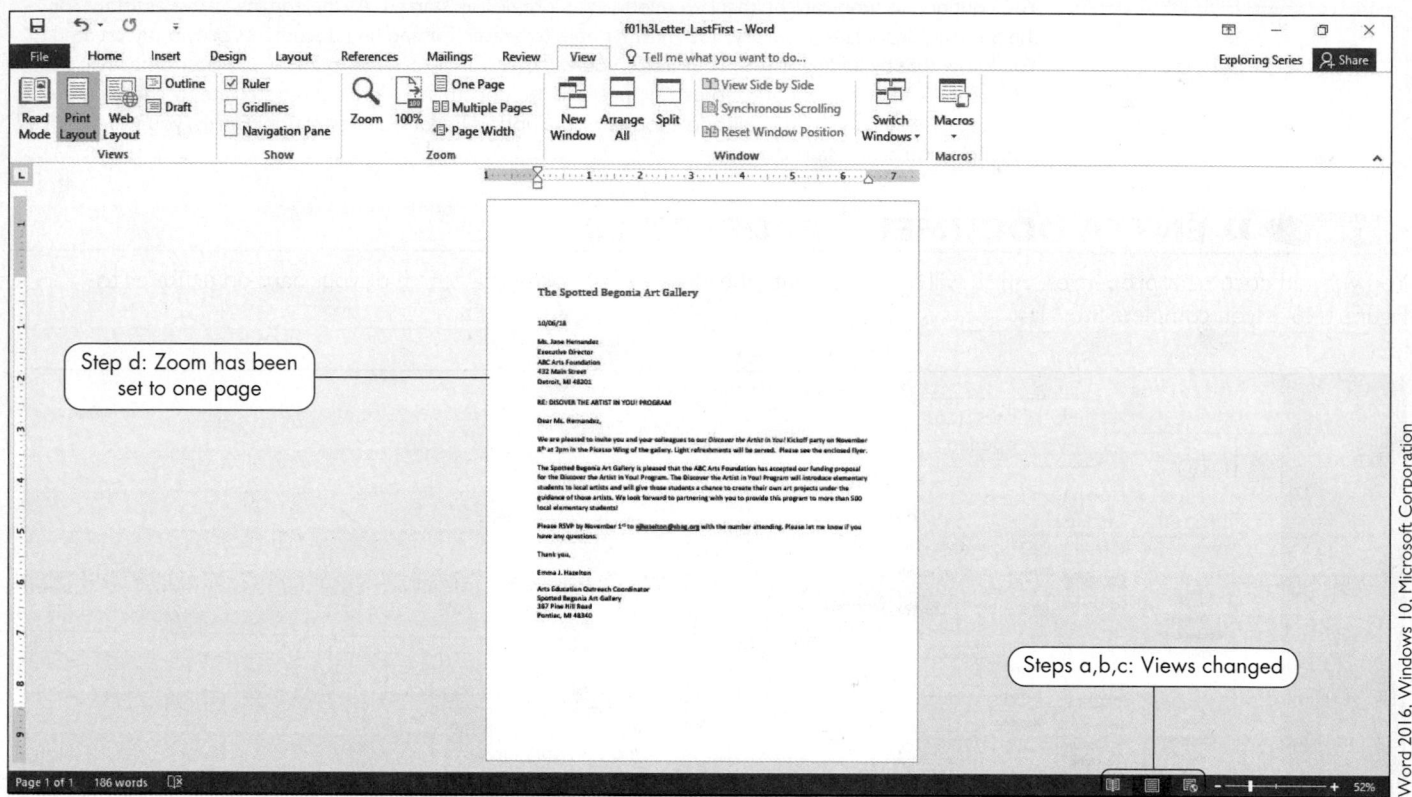

FIGURE 1.47 Change the Document View

    a. Click **Read Mode** on the status bar. Observe the changes to the Ribbon.

       The view is changed to Read Mode, which is a full-screen view.

    b. Click **Web Layout** on the status bar. Observe the changes to the view.

       The view is changed to Web Layout and simulates how the document would appear on the Web.

    c. Click **Print Layout** on the status bar. Observe the changes to the view.

       The document has returned to Print Layout view.

    d. Click the **View tab** and click **Zoom** in the Zoom group. Click the **One Page option**. Click **OK**.

       The entire letter is displayed.

While the letter was displayed in One Page zoom, you observed that the margins were too large. You will change the margins so they are narrower. Refer to Figure 1.48 as you complete Step 3.

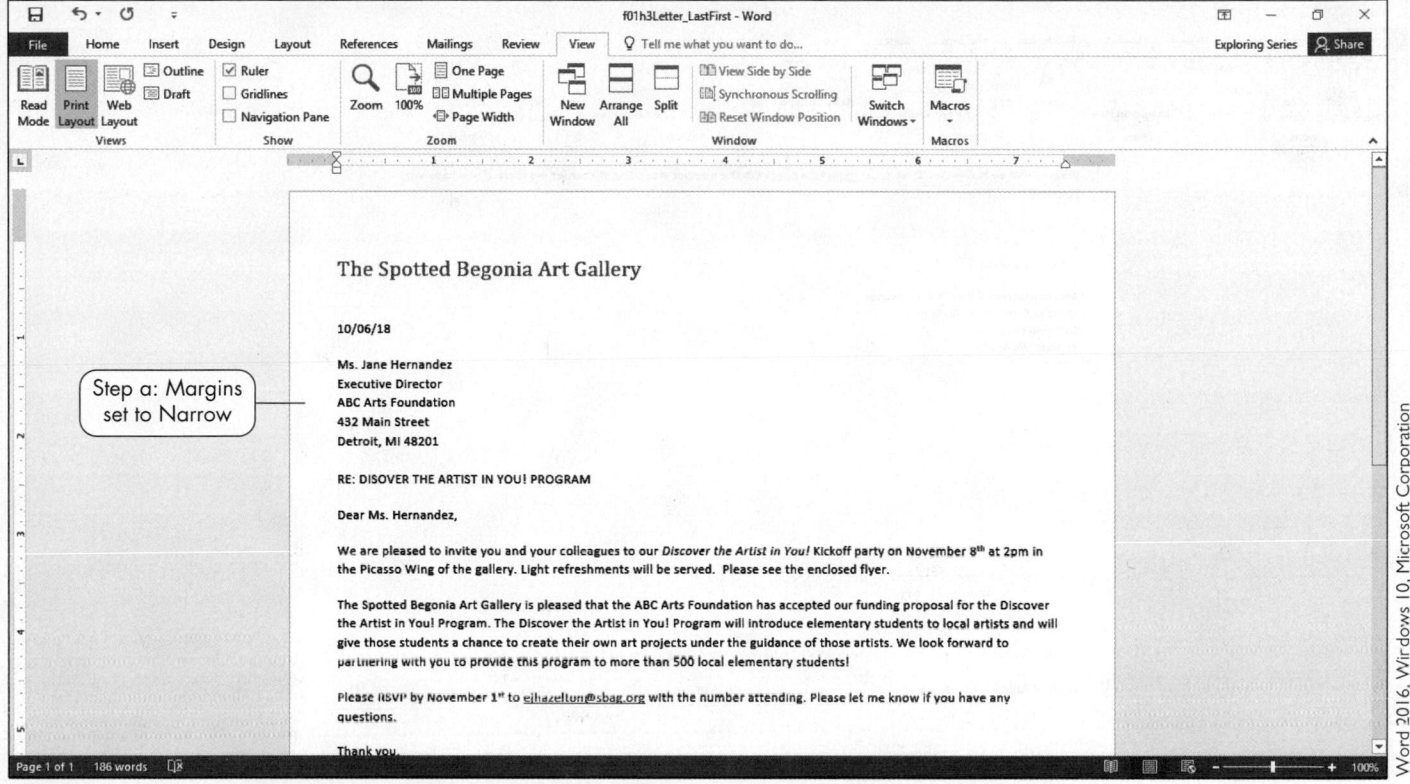

FIGURE 1.48 Change Margins

a. Click the **Layout tab** and click **Margins** in the Page Setup group. Select **Narrow**. Observe the changes.

   The document margins were changed to Narrow.

b. Click the **View tab** and click **100%** in the Zoom group.

   The document returns to its previous view.

c. Save the document.

Additional information such as a phone number and website need to be added to the letter. You decide to add these to the letter as a footer. Refer to Figure 1.49 as you complete Step 4.

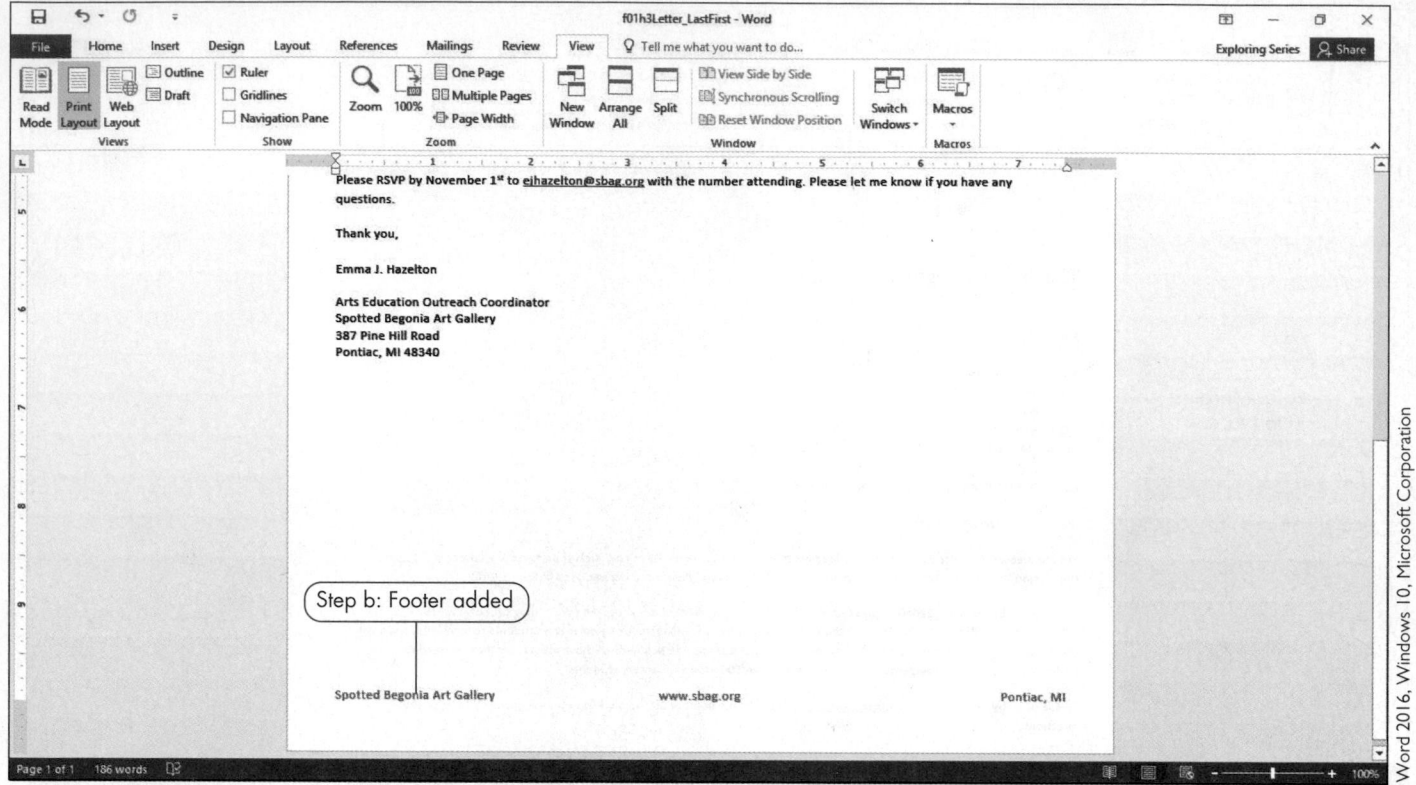

FIGURE 1.49 Footer

a. Click the **Insert tab** and click **Footer** in the Header & Footer group. Click the **Blank (three columns)** footer.

The document opens in Header and Footer view. You select a footer with little formatting.

b. Click **[Type here]** on the far left of the footer. Type **Spotted Begonia Art Gallery** in that placeholder. Click **[Type here]** in the center of the footer. Type **www.sbag.org** in that placeholder. Click **[Type here]** on the far right of the footer. Type **Pontiac, MI** in that placeholder. On the Header & Footer Tools Design tab, click **Close Header and Footer** in the Close group.

The footer information is entered.

c. Save the document.

You have reviewed and finalized the letter, so you will print the document so it can be sent to its recipient. You will first preview the document as it will appear when printed. Refer to Figure 1.50 as you complete Step 5.

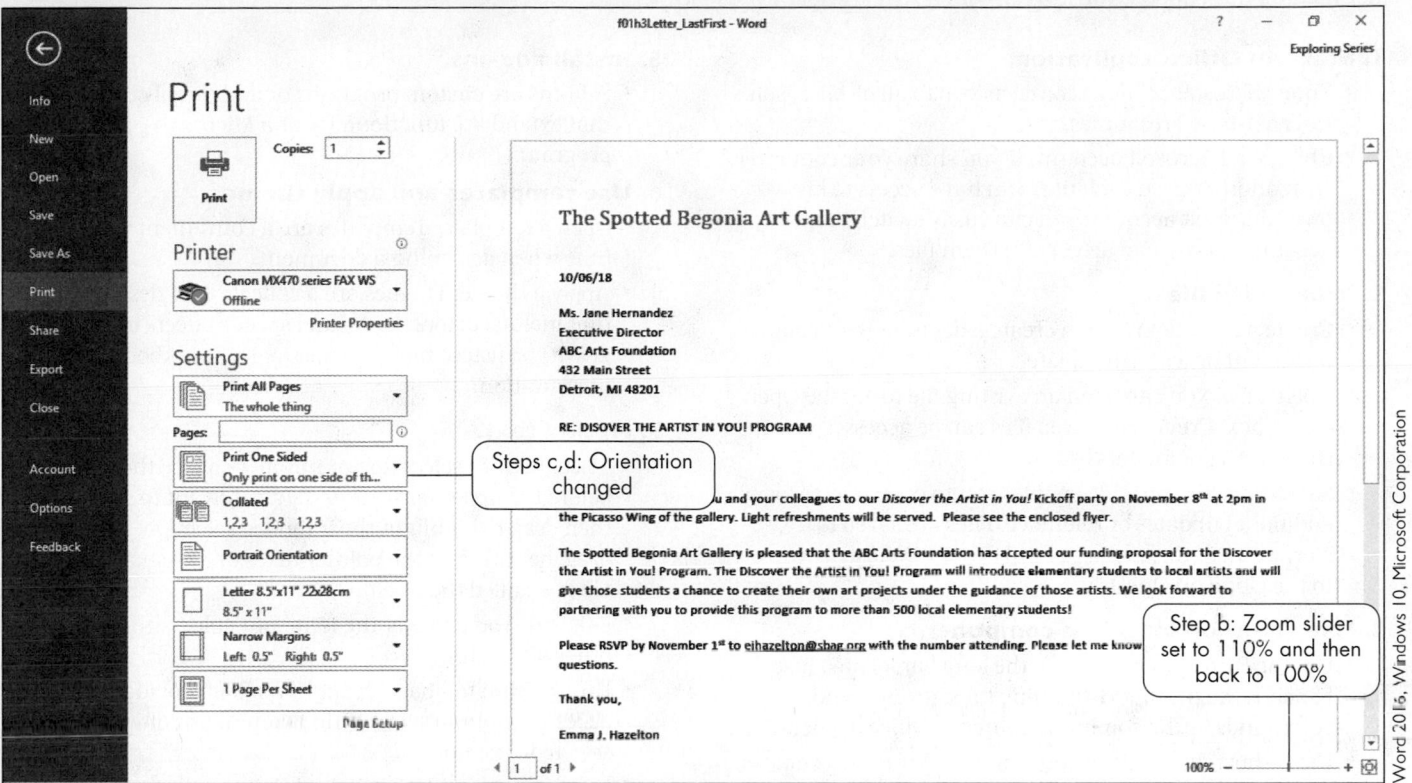

FIGURE 1.50 Backstage Print View

a. Click the **File tab** and click **Print**.

It is always a good idea to check the way a file will look when printed before actually printing it.

b. Drag the **Zoom slider on the status bar** to increase the document view to 110%. Click **Zoom to Page** 🖼 (located at the far right of the status bar).

Your print preview returns to the original size.

c. Click **Portrait Orientation** in the Settings area. Click **Landscape Orientation**.

The letter appears in a wider and shorter view.

d. Return to Portrait Orientation to see the original view.

You decide that the flyer is more attractive in portrait orientation, so you return to that setting.

e. Save and close the file. Based on your instructor's directions, submit the following:

f01h2Flyer_LastFirst

f01h3Letter_LastFirst

Chapter Objectives Review

After reading this chapter, you have accomplished the following objectives:

1. Start an Office application.
- Your Microsoft account connects you to all of Microsoft's Internet-based resources.
- Change a Microsoft account: If you share your computer with another user, each user can have access to his own Microsoft account; you can easily switch between accounts so you can access your own files.

2. Work with files.
- Create a new file: You can create a document as a blank document or with a template.
- Open a file: You can open an existing file using the Open dialog box. Previously saved files can be accessed using the Recent documents list.
- Save a file: Saving a file enables you to open it later for additional updates or reference. Files are saved to a storage medium such as a hard drive, CD, flash drive, or to the cloud on OneDrive.

3. Use common interface components.
- Use the Ribbon: The Ribbon, the long bar located just beneath the title bar containing tabs, groups, and commands, is the command center of Office applications.
- Use a shortcut menu: A shortcut menu provides choices related to the object, selection, or area of the document on which you right-click.
- Use keyboard shortcuts: Keyboard shortcuts are keyboard equivalents for software commands. Universal keyboard shortcuts in Office include Ctrl+C (Copy), Ctrl+X (Cut), Ctrl+V (Paste), and Ctrl+Z (Undo).
- Customize the Ribbon: You can personalize the Ribbon in your Office applications, giving you easier access to a frequently used set of commands that are unique to you or your business.
- Use the Quick Access Toolbar: The Quick Access Toolbar, located at the top-left corner of any Office application window, provides one-click access to commonly executed tasks such as saving a file or undoing recent actions.
- Customize the Quick Access Toolbar: You use certain actions in an Office application often, and for more convenient access, you can add a button for each action to the Quick Access Toolbar.

4. Get help.
- Use the *Tell me what you want to do* box: The *Tell me what you want to do* box not only links to online resources and technical support but also provides quick access to functions.
- Use Enhanced ScreenTips: An Enhanced ScreenTip describes a command and provides a keyboard shortcut, if applicable.

5. Install add-ins.
- Add-ins are custom programs or additional commands that extend the functionality of a Microsoft Office program.

6. Use templates and apply themes.
- Open a template: Templates are a convenient way to save time when designing a document.
- Apply a theme: Themes are a collection of design choices that include colors, fonts, and special effects used to give a consistent look to a document, workbook, or presentation.

7. Modify text.
- Select text: To select text or numbers, place the pointer before the first character or digit you want to select, and then drag to highlight the intended selection. Before you drag, be sure that the pointer takes on the shape of the letter *I*, called the I-beam.
- Edit text: You can edit the font, font color, size, and many other attributes.
- Use the Mini toolbar: The Mini toolbar provides instant access to common formatting commands after text is selected.
- Copy formats with the Format Painter: Easily apply formatting from one selection to another by using Format Painter.

8. Relocate text.
- Cut, copy, and paste text: To cut means to remove a selection from the original location and place it in the Office Clipboard. To copy means to duplicate a selection from the original location and place a copy in the Office Clipboard. To paste means to place a cut or copied selection into another location.
- Use the Office Clipboard: When you cut or copy selections, they are placed in the Office Clipboard. You can paste the same item multiple times; it will remain in the Clipboard until you power down your computer or until the Clipboard exceeds 24 items.

9. Check spelling and grammar.
- Office applications check and mark spelling and grammar errors as you type for later correction. The Thesaurus enables you to search for synonyms.

10. Work with pictures and Graphics.
- Insert pictures and graphics: You can insert pictures from your own library of digital photos you have saved on your hard drive, OneDrive, or another storage medium, or you can initiate a Bing search for online pictures directly inside the Office program you are using.
- Resize and format pictures and graphics: To resize a picture, drag a corner sizing handle; never resize a picture by dragging a center sizing handle. You can apply

a picture style or effect, as well as add a picture border, from selections in the Picture Styles group.

11. Use Backstage view.

- Customize application options: You can customize general settings in the Office application in which you are working, such as AutoRecover settings and location and save frequency.
- View and edit document properties: Information that identifies a document, such as the author, document purpose, intended audience, or general comments can be added to the document's properties. Those data elements are saved with the document, but do not appear in the document as it displays onscreen or is printed.

12. Change the document view.

- The status bar provides information relative to the open file and quick access to View and Zoom level options. Each application has a set of views specific to the application.

13. Change the page layout.

- Change margins: A margin is the area of blank space that displays to the left, right, top, and bottom of a document or worksheet.

- Change page orientation: Documents and worksheets can be displayed in different page orientations. Portrait orientation is taller than it is wide; landscape orientation is wider than it is tall.
- Use the Page Setup dialog box: The Page Setup dialog box includes options for customizing margins, selecting page orientation, centering horizontally or vertically, printing gridlines, and creating headers and footers.

14. Insert a header and footer.

- A footer displays at the bottom of each page.
- A header consists of one or more lines at the top of each page.

15. Preview and print a file.

- It is important to review your file before printing.
- Print options can be set in Backstage view and include page orientation, the number of copies, and the specific pages to print.

Key Terms Matching

Match the key terms with their definitions. Write the key term letter by the appropriate numbered definition.

a. Access
b. Add-in
c. Clipboard
d. Backstage view
e. Cloud storage
f. Format Painter
g. Footer
h. Group
i. Header
j. Margin

k. Microsoft Office
l. Mini toolbar
m. OneDrive
n. Quick Access Toolbar
o. Ribbon
p. Status bar
q. Tab
r. *Tell me what you want to do* box
s. Template
t. Theme

1. _____ A tool that copies all formatting from one area to another. **p. 91**

2. _____ Stores up to 24 cut or copied selections for use later on in your computing session. **p. 93**

3. _____ A task-oriented section of the Ribbon that contains related commands. **p. 72**

4. _____ An online app used to store, access, and share files and folders. **p. 67**

5. _____ Custom programs or additional commands that extend the functionality of a Microsoft Office program. **p. 79**

6. _____ A component of Office that provides a concise collection of commands related to an open file and includes save and print options. **p. 104**

7. _____ A tool that displays near selected text that contains formatting commands. **p. 90**

8. _____ Relational database software used to store data and convert it into information. **p. 66**

9. _____ Consists of one or more lines at the bottom of each page. **p. 110**

10. _____ A predesigned file that incorporates formatting elements, such as a theme and layouts, and may include content that can be modified. **p. 86**

11. _____ A collection of design choices that includes colors, fonts, and special effects used to give a consistent look to a document, workbook, or presentation. **p. 86**

12. _____ A component of the Ribbon that is designed to appear much like a tab on a file folder. **p. 71**

13. _____ Provides handy access to commonly executed tasks such as saving a file and undoing recent actions. **p. 76**

14. _____ The long bar at the bottom of the screen that houses the Zoom slider and various View buttons. **p. 106**

15. _____ A productivity software suite including a set of software applications, each one specializing in a particular type of output. **p. 66**

16. _____ Allows you to search for help and information about a command or task you want to perform, and will also present you with a shortcut directly to that command. **p. 77**

17. _____ The long bar located just beneath the title bar containing tabs, groups, and commands. **p. 70**

18. _____ The area of blank space that displays to the left, right, top, and bottom of a document or worksheet **p. 107**

19. _____ A technology used to store files and to work with programs that are stored in a central location on the Internet. **p. 67**

20. _____ Consists of one or more lines at the top of each page. **p. 110**

Multiple Choice

1. The Recent documents list shows documents that have been previously:
   - (a) Printed.
   - (b) Opened.
   - (c) Saved in an earlier software version.
   - (d) Deleted.

2. In Word or PowerPoint a quick way to select an entire paragraph is to:
   - (a) Place the pointer at the left of the line, in the margin area, and click.
   - (b) Triple-click inside the paragraph.
   - (c) Double-click at the beginning of the paragraph.
   - (d) Press Ctrl+C inside the paragraph.

3. When you want to copy the format of a selection but not the content, you should:
   - (a) Double-click Copy in the Clipboard group.
   - (b) Right-click the selection and click Copy.
   - (c) Click Copy Format in the Clipboard group.
   - (d) Click Format Painter in the Clipboard group.

4. Which of the following is *not* a benefit of using OneDrive?
   - (a) Save your folders and files to the cloud.
   - (b) Share your files and folders with others.
   - (c) Hold video conferences with others.
   - (d) Simultaneously work on the same document with others.

5. What does a red wavy underline in a document, spreadsheet, or presentation mean?
   - (a) A word is misspelled or not recognized by the Office dictionary.
   - (b) A grammatical mistake exists.
   - (c) An apparent word usage mistake exists.
   - (d) A word has been replaced with a synonym.

6. Which of the following is *true* about headers and footers?
   - (a) They can be inserted from the Design tab.
   - (b) Headers and footers only appear on the last page of a document.
   - (c) Headers appear at the top of a document.
   - (d) Only page numbers can be included in a header or footer.

7. Live Preview:
   - (a) Opens a predesigned document or spreadsheet that is relevant to your task.
   - (b) Provides a preview of the results of a choice you are considering before you make a final selection.
   - (c) Provides a preview of an upcoming Office version.
   - (d) Enlarges the font onscreen.

8. You can get help when working with an Office application in which one of the following areas?
   - (a) The *Tell me what you want to do* box
   - (b) Status bar
   - (c) Backstage view
   - (d) Quick Access Toolbar

9. In PowerPoint, a file that includes formatting elements such as a background, a color scheme, and slide layout is a:
   - (a) Theme.
   - (b) Template.
   - (c) Scheme.
   - (d) Variant.

10. A document or worksheet printed in landscape orientation is:
    - (a) Taller than it is wide.
    - (b) Wider than it is tall.
    - (c) A document with 2" left and right margins.
    - (d) A document with 2" top and bottom margins.

Practice Exercises

1 | Designing Webpages

You have been asked to make a presentation to the local business association. With the mayor's renewed emphasis on growing the local economy, many businesses are interested in establishing a Web presence. The business owners would like to know a little bit more about how webpages are designed. In preparation for the presentation, you will proofread and edit your PowerPoint file. You decide to insert an image to enhance your presentation. Refer to Figure 1.51 as you complete this exercise.

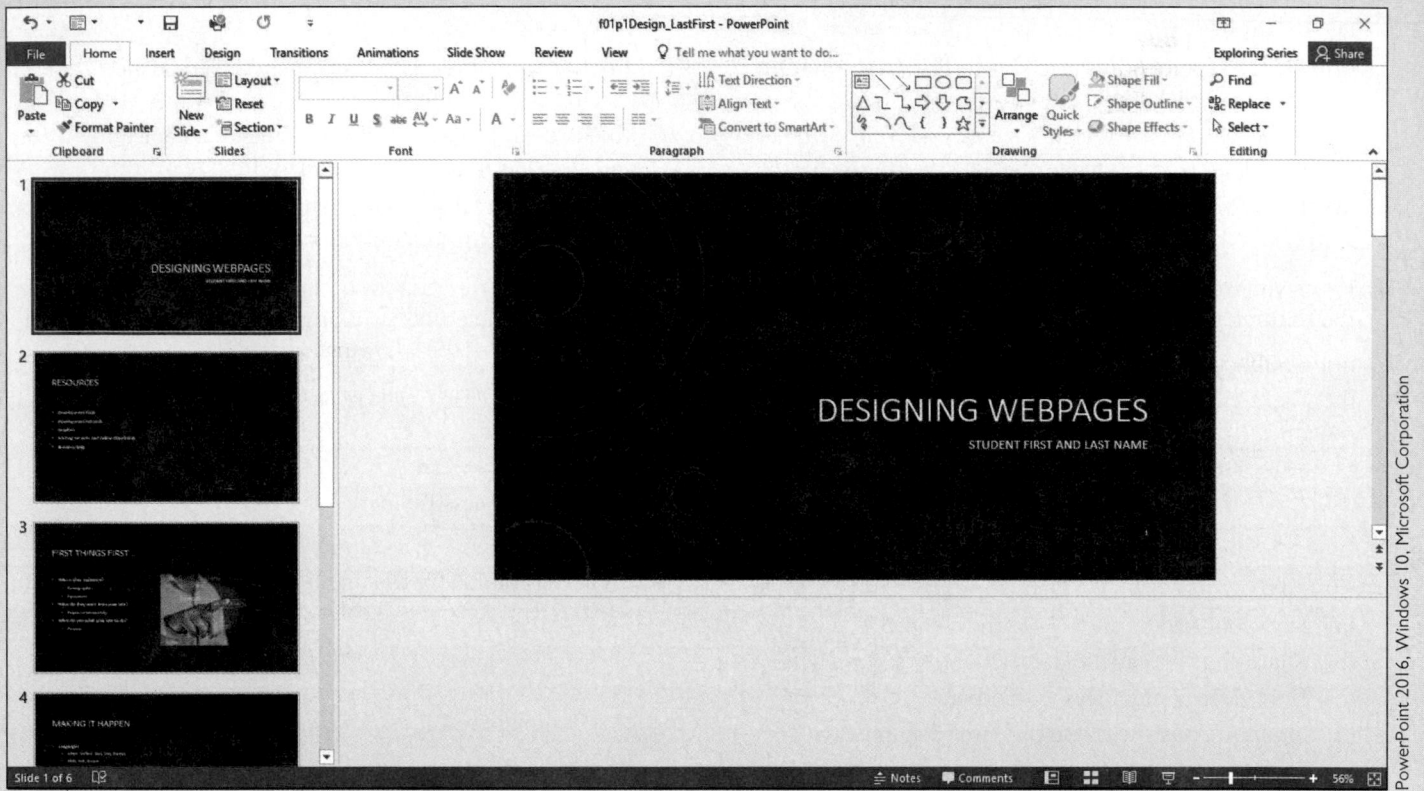

FIGURE 1.51 Designing Webpages Presentation

a. Open *f01p1Design*. Click the **File tab**, click **Save As**, and save the file as **f01p1Design_LastFirst**.

b. Ensure that Slide 1 is visible, select the text *Firstname Lastname*, and type your own first and last names. Click an empty area of the slide to cancel the selection.

c. Click the **Design tab**, then click the **Celestial theme** in the Themes group to apply it to all slides.

d. Click the **Review tab** and click **Spelling** in the Proofing group. In the Spelling pane, click **Change** or **Ignore** to make changes as needed. Most identified misspellings should be changed. The words *KompoZer* and *Nvu* are not misspelled, so you should ignore them when they are flagged. Click **OK** when you have finished checking spelling.

e. Click the **Slide Show tab**. Click **From Beginning** in the Start Slide Show group. Click each slide to view the show and press **Esc** when you reach the last slide, slide 6.

f. Click **Slide 2** in the Slides pane on the left. Triple-click to select the **Other tools** text on the slide and press **Backspace** on the keyboard to delete the text.

g. Click **Slide 4** in the Slides pane. Triple-click to select the **FrontPage, Nvu** text and press **Backspace** to delete the text.

h. Click the **Insert tab**. Click **Header & Footer** in the Text group. Click the **Slide number check box** to select it and click **Apply to All**.

i. Press **Ctrl+End** to place the insertion point at the end of *Templates* on Slide 4 and press **Enter**. Type **Database Connectivity** to create a new bulleted item.

j. Click **Slide 3** in the Slides pane. Click the **Insert tab** and click **Pictures** in the Images group. Browse to the student data files, locate and select *f01p1website*, and then click **Insert**.

k. Click the **Shape height box** in the Size group on the Picture Tools Format tab. Type **4** and then press Enter.

l. Click **Slide 6** in the Slides pane. Click the **Insert tab**, and then click **Store** in the Add-ins group. In the search box, type **multiple response poll**. Press **Enter**. The add-in will resize if the window or resolution is small.

m. Click the **Multiple Response Poll** and then click **Trust It** to insert it into the slide.

n. Click the **Insert question here text box** in the poll window, and type **Do you have a website?**

o. Click the first **Insert option here text box** and type **Yes**. Click the second **Insert option here text box** and type **No**. Click **Preview** in the poll window.

p. Click the **File tab** and click **Print**. Click the **Full Page Slides arrow** and click **6 Slides Horizontal** to see a preview of all of the slides as a handout. Click the **Back arrow**.

q. Click **Slide 1** in the Slides pane to move to the beginning of the presentation.

r. Drag the **Zoom slider** on the status bar to the right to **130%** to magnify the text. Use the **Zoom slider** to move to **60%**.

s. Save and close the file. Based on your instructor's directions, submit f01p1Design_LastFirst.

You have always been interested in baking and have worked in the field for several years. You now have an opportunity to devote yourself full time to your career as the CEO of a company dedicated to baking cupcakes and pastries, and to catering. One of the first steps in getting the business off the ground is developing a business plan so that you can request financial support. You will use Word to develop your business plan. Refer to Figure 1.52 as you complete this exercise.

a. Open *f01p2Business*. Click the **File tab**, click **Save As**, and save the file as **f01p2Business_LastFirst**.

b. Click the **Review tab** and click **Spelling & Grammar** in the Proofing group. Click **Change** for all suggestions and then click OK.

c. Select the paragraphs beginning with *Our Staff* and ending with *(Nutritionist)*. Click the **Home tab** and click **Cut** in the Clipboard group. Click to the left of *Our Products* and click **Paste**.

Upscale Bakery and Catering

Our Business Plan

After working in the baking and catering business for several years, I have launched a new company, Upscale Bakery and Catering. The company will provide cupcakes, pastries, and catering services to businesses located in the metropolitan area. This document will detail my products and staff.

Our Staff

Team members collectively possess over 28 years' experience in culinary and business management. All have achieved success in business careers and are redirecting their efforts to support Upscale Bakery and Catering as full-time employees.

- Student Name (CEO)
- Margaret Atkins (Executive Chef)
- Daniel Finch (Catering Manager)
- Susan Cummings (Nutritionist)

Our Products

Catering services will include consultation, set-up, delivery, serving, clean-up.

- Cupcakes
- French pastries
- Gluten-free baked goods
- Catering

1

Word 2016, Windows 10, Microsoft Corporation

FIGURE 1.52 Upscale Bakery Business Plan

d. Select the text **Your name** in the first bullet in the *Our Staff* section and replace it with your first and last names. Select the entire bullet list, click the **Font Size arrow** and then click **11**.

e. Double-click **Format Painter** in the Clipboard group on the Home tab. Drag the Format Painter pointer to change the other *Our Staff* bullets' font size to **11 pt**. Drag across all four *Our Products* bullets. Click Format Painter to deselect it.

f. Click the ***Tell me what you want to do* box**, and type **Footer**. Click **Add a Footer** scroll to locate the **Sideline footer**, click to add it to the page. Click **Close Header and Footer** on the Header & Footer Tools Design tab.

g. Select the last line in the document, which says *Insert and position picture here*, and press **Delete**. Click the **Insert tab** and click **Online Pictures** in the Illustrations group.

- Click in the **Bing Image Search box**, type **Cupcakes**, and then press **Enter**.
- Select any cupcake image and click **Insert**. Do not deselect the image.

> **TROUBLESHOOTING:** If you are unable to find a cupcake image in the Bing Image Search then you can use f01p2Cupcake from the student data files.

- Ensure the **Picture Tools Format tab** is active, and in the Picture Styles group, click the **Soft Edge Rectangle**.
- Click the **Shape width box** in the Size group and change the width to **4**.
- Click outside the picture.

h. Click the **File tab**. In the Properties section, add the tag **Business Plan**. Add your first and last name to the Author property.

i. Click **Print** in Backstage view. Change Normal Margins to **Moderate Margins**. Click the **Back arrow**.

j. Click the **picture** and click **Center** in the Paragraph group on the Home tab.

k. Save and close the file. Based on your instructor's directions, submit f01p2Business_LastFirst.

Mid-Level Exercises

1 Reference Letter

You are an instructor at a local community college. A student asked you to provide her with a letter of reference for a job application. You have used Word to prepare the letter, but now you want to make a few changes before it is finalized.

a. Open *f01m1RefLetter* and save it as **f01m1RefLetter_LastFirst**.

b. Select the date and point to several font sizes on the Mini toolbar. Use Live Preview to compare them. Click **11**.

c. Change the rest of the letter (below the date) to font size 11.

d. Apply bold to the student's name, *Stacy VanPatten*, in the first sentence.

e. Customize the Quick Access Toolbar so that a Spelling and Grammar button is added.

f. Use the button you just added to correct all errors using Spelling & Grammar. Stacy's last name is spelled correctly.

g. Select the word *intelligent* in the second paragraph, and use the Thesaurus to find a synonym. Replace *intelligent* with **gifted**. Change the word *an* to **a** just before the new word. Close the Thesaurus.

h. Add the tag **reference letter** to the Properties for the file in Backstage view.

i. Move the last paragraph—beginning with *In my opinion*—to position it before the second paragraph—beginning with *Stacy is a gifted*.

j. Move the insertion point to the beginning of the document.

k. Change the margins to **Narrow**.

l. Preview the document as it will appear when printed.

m. Save and close the file. Based on your instructor's directions, submit f01m1RefLetter_LastFirst.

2 Medical Monitoring

You are enrolled in a Health Informatics program of study in which you learn to manage databases related to health fields. For a class project, your instructor requires that you monitor your blood pressure, recording your findings in an Excel worksheet. You have recorded the week's data and will now make a few changes before printing the worksheet for submission.

a. Open *f01m2Tracker* and save it as **f01m2Tracker_LastFirst**.

b. Preview the worksheet as it will appear when printed. Change the orientation of the worksheet to **Landscape**. Close the Preview.

c. Click in the cell to the right of *Name* and type your first and last names. Press **Enter**.

d. Change the font of the text in **cell C1** to **Verdana**. Use Live Preview to try some font sizes. Change the font size to **20**.

e. Add the Spelling and Grammar feature to the Quick Access Toolbar, and then check the spelling for the worksheet to ensure that there are no errors.

 **DISCOVER**

f. Get help on showing decimal places. You want to increase the decimal places for the values in **cells E22, F22,** and **G22** so that each value shows one place to the right of the decimal. Select the cells and then use the *Tell me what you want to do* box to immediately apply the changes. You might use **Increase Decimals** as a search term. When you find the answer, increase the decimal places to **1**.

 **DISCOVER**

g. Click **cell A1** and insert an Online Picture of your choice related to blood pressure. Resize and position the picture so that it displays in an attractive manner. Apply the **Soft Edges** picture effect to the image and set to **5 pt**.

h. Change the page margins to **Wide**.

i. Insert a footer with the page number in the center of the spreadsheet footer area. Click on any cell in the worksheet.

j. Change the View to **Normal**.

k. Open Backstage view and adjust print settings to print two copies. You will not actually print two copies unless directed by your instructor.

l. Save and close the file. Based on your instructor's directions, submit f01m2Tracker_LastFirst.

3 Today's Musical Artists

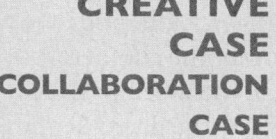
CREATIVE CASE
COLLABORATION CASE

With a few of your classmates, you will use PowerPoint to create a single presentation on your favorite musical artists. Each student must create at least one slide and then all of the slides will be added to the presentation. Because everyone's schedule is varied, you will use your OneDrive to pass the presentation file among the group.

a. Designate one student to create a new presentation and save it as **f01m3Music_GroupName**.

b. Add your group member names to the Author Properties in Backstage view.

c. Add a theme to the presentation.

d. Add one slide that contains the name of an artist, the genre, and two or three interesting facts about the artist.

e. Insert a picture of the artist or clip art that represents the artist.

f. Put your name on the slide that you created. Save the presentation.

g. Pass the presentation to the next student so that he or she can perform the same tasks in Steps d–f and save the presentation before passing it on to the next student. Continue until all group members have created a slide in the presentation.

h. Save and close the file. Based on your instructor's directions, submit f01m3Music_GroupName.

Beyond the Classroom

Fitness Planner
GENERAL CASE ✓

You will use Microsoft Excel to develop a fitness planner. Open *f01b1Exercise* and save it as **f01b1Exercise_LastFirst**. Because the fitness planner is a template, the exercise categories are listed, but without actual data. You will personalize the planner. Change the orientation to **Landscape**. Move the contents of **cell A2** (*Exercise Planner*) to **cell A1**. Click **cell A8** and use Format Painter to copy the format of that selection to **cells A5** and **A6**. Increase the font size of **cell A1** to **A18**. Use the *Tell me what you want to do* box to learn how to insert a header and put your name in the header. Begin the fitness planner, entering at least one activity in each category (warm-up, aerobics, strength, and cooldown). Insert a picture from a Bing Image Search that is appropriate for the planner. You may want to use **exercise** as your search term. Check the spelling in the workbook. Add the tag **Exercise Planner** to the Properties in Backstage view. Review the document in Print Preview. Ensure that the tracker fits on a single sheet of paper when printed. Resize the image if necessary to fit on the page. Save and close the file. Based on your instructor's directions, submit f01b1Exercise_LastFirst.

Household Records
DISASTER RECOVERY ✚
FROM SCRATCH

Use Microsoft Excel to create a detailed (fictional) record of valuables in your household. In case of burglary or disaster, an insurance claim is expedited if you are able to itemize what was lost along with identifying information such as serial numbers. You will then make a copy of the record on another storage device for safekeeping outside your home (in case your home is destroyed by a fire or weather-related catastrophe). Design a worksheet listing at least five fictional appliances and pieces of electronic equipment along with the serial number of each. Change the orientation to **Landscape**. Use the *Tell me what you want to do* box to learn how to insert a header and put your name in the header. Return to Normal view. Insert a picture from a Bing Image Search that is appropriate for the record. You may want to use **appliances** as your search term. Review the document in Print Preview. Ensure that the records fit on a single sheet of paper when printed. Move and resize the image as necessary so that it fits on the page when printed. Check the spelling in the workbook. Add the tag **Disaster Recovery** to the Properties in Backstage view. Save the workbook as **f01b2Household_LastFirst**. Save and close the file. Based on your instructor's directions, submit f01b2Household_LastFirst.

Capstone Exercise

You are a member of the Student Government Association (SGA) at your college. As a community project, the SGA is sponsoring a Stop Smoking drive designed to provide information on the health risks posed by smoking cigarettes and to offer solutions to those who want to quit. The SGA has partnered with the local branch of the American Cancer Society as well as the outreach program of the local hospital to sponsor free educational awareness seminars. As the secretary for the SGA, you will help prepare a PowerPoint presentation that will be displayed on screens around campus and used in student seminars. The PowerPoint presentation has come back from the reviewers with only one comment: A reviewer suggested that you spell out Centers for Disease Control and Prevention, instead of abbreviating it. You will use Microsoft Office to help with those tasks.

Open and Save Files

You will open, review, and save a PowerPoint presentation.

a. Open *f01c1Quit* and save it as **f01c1Quit_LastFirst**.

Select Text, Move Text, and Format Text

A reviewer commented that you should modify the text on slide 12. The last sentence in the paragraph should be first since it is the answer to the question on the previous slide. You also add emphasis to the sentence.

a. Click **Slide 12**, and select the text **Just one cigarette – for some people**.

b. Cut the selected text and then paste it at the beginning of the paragraph.

c. Use the Mini toolbar to apply **Italics** to the text *Just one cigarette – for some people*.

Apply a Theme and Change the View

There is a blank theme for the slides, so you apply a different theme to the presentation.

a. Apply the **Metropolitan** theme to the presentation.

b. Change the View to Slide Sorter. Click **Slide 2** and drag to move Slide 2 to the end of the presentation. It will become the last slide (Slide 22).

c. Return to Normal view.

Insert and Modify a Picture

You will add a picture to the first slide and then resize it and position it.

a. Click **Slide 1**, and insert an online picture appropriate for the topic of **smoking**.

b. Resize the picture and reposition it.

c. Click outside the picture to deselect it.

Use the *Tell me what you want to do* Box

A reviewer suggested that you spell out Centers for Disease Control and Prevention, instead of abbreviating it. You know that there is a find and replace option to do this but you cannot remember where it is. You use the *Tell me what you want to do* box to help you with this function. You then replace the text.

a. Use the *Tell me what you want to do* box to search **replace**.

b. Use the results from your search to find a function that will find and then replace the single occurrence of *CDC* with **Centers for Disease Control and Prevention**.

Customize the Quick Access Toolbar

You often preview and print your presentations and find it would be easier to have a button on the Quick Access Toolbar to do so. You customize the toolbar by adding this shortcut.

a. Add the Print Preview button to the Quick Access Toolbar.

b. Add the Print button to the Quick Access Toolbar.

Use Print Preview, Change Print Layout, and Print

To get an idea of how the presentation will look when printed, you will preview the presentation. You decide to print the slides so that two slides will appear on one page.

a. Preview the document as it will appear when printed.

b. Change the Print Layout to **2 Slides** (under the Handouts section).

c. Preview the document as it will appear when printed.

d. Adjust the print settings to print two copies. You will not actually print two copies unless directed by your instructor.

Check Spelling and Change View

Before you call the presentation complete, you will correct any spelling errors and view the presentation as a slide show.

a. Check the spelling. The word *hairlike* is not misspelled, so it should not be corrected.

b. View the slide show. Click after reviewing the last slide to return to the presentation.

c. Save and close the file. Based on your instructor's directions, submit f01c1Quit_LastFirst.

Introduction to Word

LEARNING OUTCOME You will develop a document using features of Microsoft Word.

OBJECTIVES & SKILLS: After you read this chapter, you will be able to:

CASE STUDY | Swan Creek National Wildlife Refuge

You are fascinated with wildlife in its natural habitat. For that reason, you are excited to work with Swan Creek National Wildlife Refuge, assigned the task of promoting the refuge's educational outreach programs. Emily Traynom, Swan Creek's site director, is concerned that children in the city have little opportunity to interact with nature. She fears that a generation of children will mature into adults with little appreciation of the role of our country's natural resources in the overall balance of nature. Her passion is encouraging students to visit Swan Creek and become actively involved in environmental activities.

Ms. Traynom envisions summer day camps where children explore the wildlife refuge and participate in learning activities. She asked you to use your expertise in Microsoft Word to produce documents such as flyers, brochures, memos, contracts, and letters. You will design and produce an article about a series of summer camps available to children from 5th through 8th grades. From a rough draft, you will create an attractive document for distribution to schools.

CHAPTER 1

Organizing a Document

Emily Traynool, Director
Swan Creek National Wildlife Refuge
89467 Mill Creek Road
Hastings, PA 19092

July 21, 2018

RE: Summer Day Camp Program at Swan Creek

As an educator in our community, you are sure to be interested in an opportunity for your students to learn at Swan Creek National Wildlife Refuge this summer. I hope you will encourage your students who are rising 5th through 8th graders to join us for a few days this summer. The day camp program, which is described on the following page, is an effort to instill an appreciation for our environment, all in an engaging and fun atmosphere. Funded through a grant from the Nature Federation, the program is free to campers; however, space is limited, so please encourage early registration.

I, or a member of my staff, will be happy to visit your classroom to promote the refuge and to answer questions or assign registration for the summer day camp program. Feel free to copy and distribute the article on the following page. We hope to hear from you soon and look forward to working with your students this summer!

Swan Creek National Wildlife Refuge

What: Swan Creek National Wildlife Refuge Day Camp

When: Week-Long Day Camps from July 5-August 21, 2018

Where: Swan Creek National Wildlife Refuge (at the headquarters)

Open to: 5th through 8th Grade Students

When was the last time you spent an afternoon immersed in nature, experiencing sights and sounds you could never enjoy in the city? Did you know there are 38 different types of birds native to our area, all of which you can find at Swan Creek National Wildlife Refuge? The refuge backwaters are home to beavers, mallard ducks, geese, largemouth bass, and slider turtles, among many other inhabitants. What better way to spend a few days this summer than with us at the refuge, experiencing nature at its finest?

Swan Creek National Wildlife Refuge is offering a series of week-long day camps this summer, designed for children who are rising fifth through eighth graders. The series of wildlife camps will begin on June 15, with the last camp ending on August 6. Children will participate in informative seminars and nature observations led by wildlife rangers. On nature hikes through the refuge, camp participants will explore a native forest comprised of trees and forestry indigenous to the area. Other activities include hiking along the raised boardwalk through the sunken forest, identifying wildlife from the refuge observation center, and participating in nature photography classes. The first 50 campers to register will receive a Striker™ backpack, compliments of Swan Creek!

Explore nature

Learn to identify native plants and wildlife

Take digital photos

Participate in nature seminars

Enjoy relaxing days at the refuge

For further information, or to register, please contact:

Melinda Gifford, Events Coordinator

(660) 555-5578

mgifford@scnwf.org

U.S. Fish and Wildlife Service
w01h3Refuge_LastFirst.docx

FIGURE 1.1 Swan Creek Documents

CASE STUDY | Swan Creek National Wildlife Refuge

Starting Files	Files to be Submitted
Blank document	w01h1Planner_LastFirst
w01h1Camps	w01h2Flyer_LastFirst
w01h2Letter	w01h3NewEmployee_LastFirst
w01h3NewEmployee	w01h3Refuge_LastFirst

Introduction to Word Processing

Word processing software, often called a word processor, is one of the most commonly used types of software in homes, schools, and businesses. People around the world—students, office assistants, managers, and professionals in all fields—use word processing programs such as **Microsoft Word** for a variety of tasks. Microsoft Word 2016, included in the Microsoft Office suite of software, is the most current version of the popular word processor. You can create letters, reports, research papers, newsletters, brochures, and all sorts of documents with Word. You can even create and send email, produce webpages, post to social media sites, and update blogs with Word. Figure 1.2 shows examples of documents created in Word. If a project requires collaboration online or between offices, Word makes it easy to share documents, track changes, view comments, and efficiently produce a document to which several authors can contribute. By using Word to create a research paper, you can easily create citations, a bibliography, a table of contents, a cover page, an index, and other reference pages. To enhance a document, you can change colors, add interesting styles of text, insert graphics, and use tables to present data. With emphasis on saving documents to the cloud, Word enables you to share these documents with others or access them from any device. Word is a comprehensive word processing solution, to say the least.

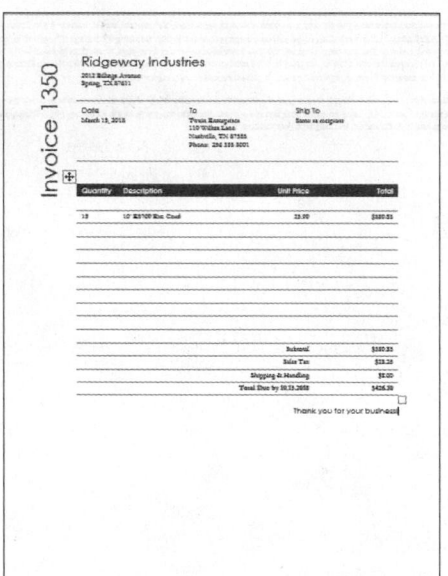

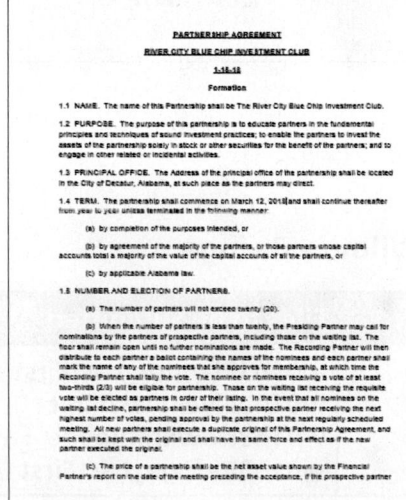

Word 2016, Windows 10, Microsoft Corporation

FIGURE 1.2 Sample Word Processing Documents

Communicating through the written word is an important, in fact, vital, task for any business or organization. Word processing software, such as Word, simplifies the technical task of preparing documents, but a word processor does not replace the writer. Be careful when phrasing a document so you are sure it is appropriate for the intended audience. Always remember that once you distribute a document, either on paper or electronically, you cannot retract the words. Therefore, you should never send a document that you have not carefully checked several times to be sure it conveys your message in the best way possible. Also, you cannot depend completely on a word processor to identify all spelling and grammatical errors, so be sure to proofread every document you create closely. Although several word processors, including Word, provide predesigned documents (called templates) that include basic layouts for various tasks, it is ultimately up to you to compose well-worded documents. The role of business communication, including the written word, in the success or failure of a business cannot be overemphasized.

In this section, you will explore Word's interface, learn how to create and save a document, explore the use of templates, and perform basic editing operations. You will learn how to move around in a document and to review spelling and word usage. Using Word options, you will explore ways to customize Word to suit your preferences, and you will learn to customize the Ribbon and the Quick Access Toolbar.

Beginning and Editing a Document

When you open Word, your screen will be similar to Figure 1.3. You can create a blank document, or you can select from several categories of templates. Recently viewed files are shown on the left, for ease of access should you want to open any again.

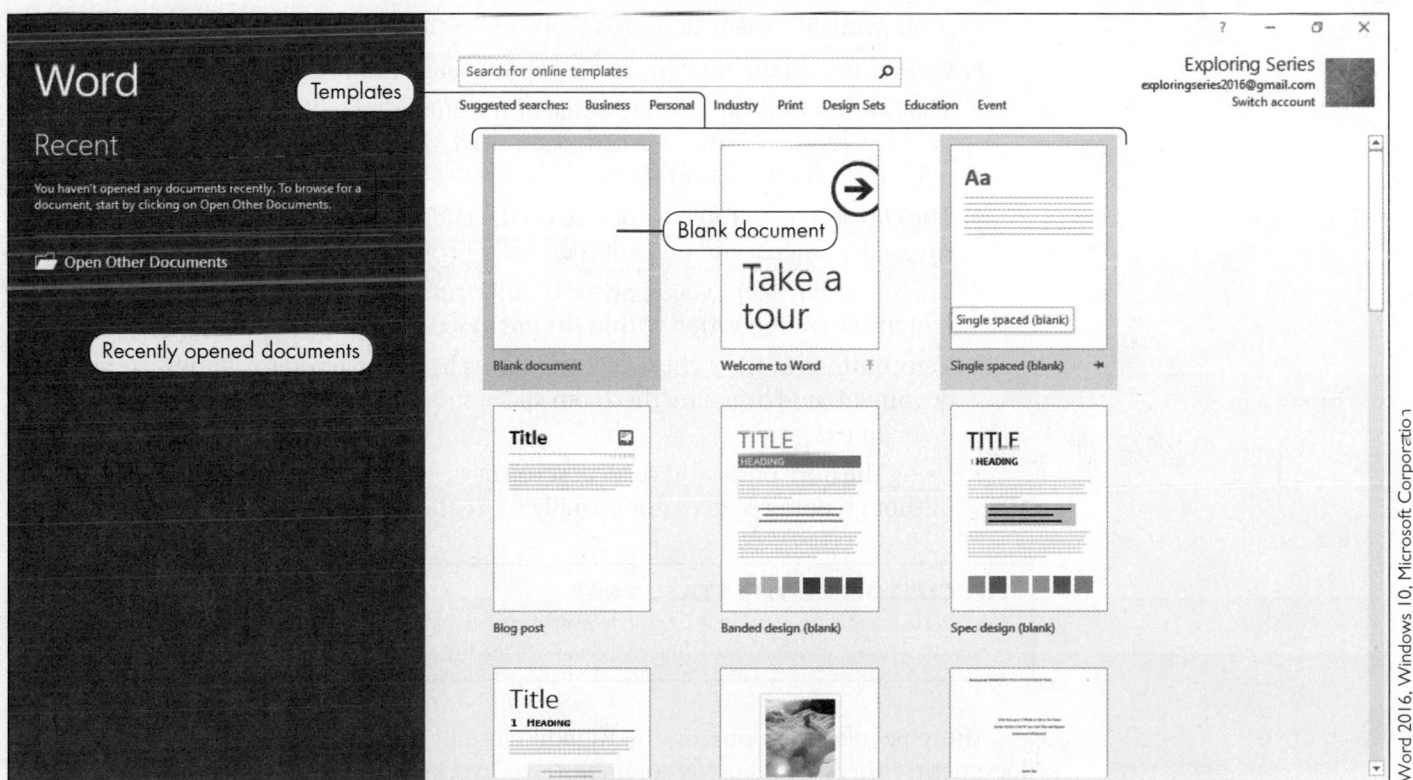

FIGURE 1.3 Word Document Options

To begin a blank document, click Blank document (or simply press Enter, if Blank document is selected). Word provides a clean, uncluttered area in which to type, with minimal distraction at the sides and across the top. Word provides a large, almost borderless area for your document. Figure 1.4 shows a typical Word document.

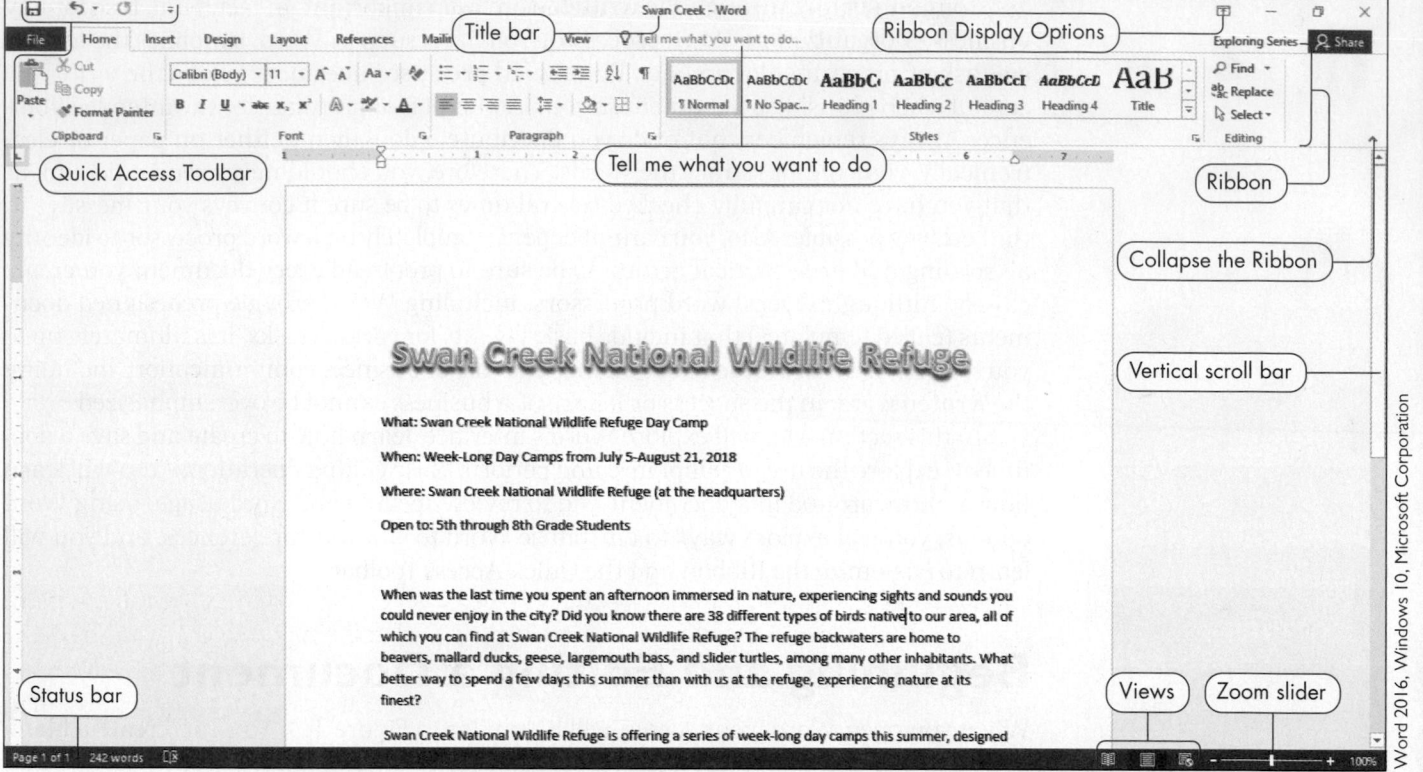

FIGURE 1.4 Word Components

The following list briefly describes Word's basic features:

- Commands on the Ribbon enable you to create, modify, and enhance documents.
- The title bar indicates the file name of the current document and includes Windows control buttons and access to *Tell Me*, a search tool that enables you to tell Word what you want to do.
- The Quick Access Toolbar, located on the left side of the title bar, makes it easy to save a document, and undo or redo recent commands.
- The status bar keeps you apprised of information such as word and page count, and the current position within the document.
- View buttons at the right side of the status bar enable you to change the view of a document, and dragging the Zoom slider enlarges or reduces the onscreen size of a document.
- Using the horizontal and vertical scroll bars, you can scroll through a document (although doing so does not actually move the insertion point).

TIP: CUSTOMIZE THE STATUS BAR
You can customize the status bar to include even more items of information. Right-click an empty area of the status bar and select one or more items from the list.

Many people enjoy having the Ribbon close at hand when developing or editing a document. Others might prefer an uncluttered workspace, free of distractions. When the Ribbon is removed from view, tabs remain displayed, but all detail beneath them is hidden, resulting in a large amount of uncluttered typing space.

To temporarily remove the Ribbon from view, complete one of the following steps:

- Click Collapse the Ribbon (refer to Figure 1.4).
- Double-click a tab on the Ribbon.

To display the Ribbon again, complete one of the following steps:

- Click Ribbon Display Options and click Show Tabs and Commands.
- Double-click a tab on the Ribbon.

TIP: USE THE TELL ME FEATURE

New to Microsoft Word 2016, the Tell Me feature not only provides support on how to do something, it can actually do it for you. For example, if you want to check spelling in a document, but do not know how, you can type *check spelling* in the Tell me what you want to do box (refer to Figure 1.4) and then select the command from a subsequent menu. Word actually checks spelling at that point.

Ribbon Display Options (refer to Figure 1.4) enables you to adjust the Ribbon view. You can choose to hide the Ribbon, providing a clear document space in which to edit or read a document. Click at the top of the Ribbon to show it again. You can also choose to show only the Ribbon tabs. Click a tab to display its options. Finally, you can choose to show all Ribbon tabs and commands, which is the default.

Create a Document

To create a blank document, click Blank document when Word opens (refer to Figure 1.3). As you type text, you will not need to think about how much text can fit on one line or how sentences progress from one line to the next. Word's ***word wrap*** feature automatically pushes words to the next line when you reach the right margin.

Word wrap is closely associated with another concept: the hard return and soft return. A hard return is created when you press Enter at the end of a line or paragraph. A soft return is created by Word as it wraps text from one line to the next. The locations of soft returns change automatically as text is inserted or deleted, or as page features or settings, such as objects or margins, are added or changed. Soft returns are not considered characters and cannot be deleted. However, a hard return is actually a nonprinting character, that you can delete, if necessary. To display nonprinting characters, such as hard returns (also called paragraph marks) and tabs, click Show/Hide ¶ (see Figure 1.5). Just as you delete any other character by pressing Backspace or Delete (depending on whether the insertion point is positioned to the right or left of the item to remove), you can delete a paragraph mark. To remove the display of nonprinting characters, click Show/Hide again.

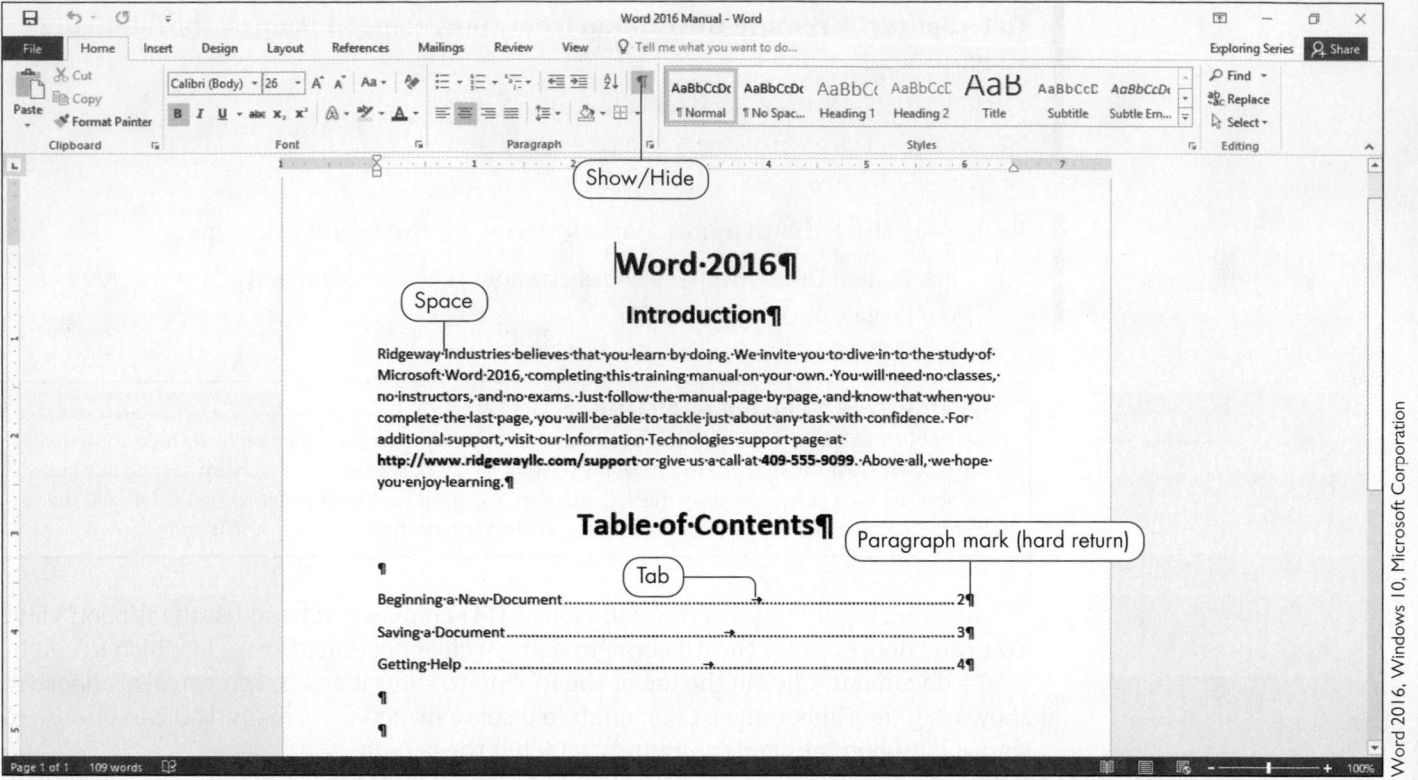

FIGURE 1.5 Displaying Nonprinting Characters

As you work with Word, you must understand that Word's definition of a paragraph and your definition are not likely to be the same. You would probably define a paragraph as a related set of sentences, which is correct in a literary sense. When the subject or direction of thought changes, a new paragraph begins. However, Word defines a paragraph as text that ends in a hard return. Even a blank line, created by pressing Enter, is considered a paragraph. Therefore, as a Word student, you will consider every line that ends in a hard return a paragraph. When you press Enter, a paragraph mark is displayed in the document if you choose to show nonprinting characters (refer to Figure 1.5).

In addition to the nonprinting mark that Word inserts when you press Enter, other nonprinting characters are inserted when you press keys such as Tab or the Spacebar. Click Show/Hide in the Paragraph group on the Home tab to reveal all nonprinting characters in a document. Why would you want to display nonprinting characters? Nonprinting characters are generally not viewed when working in a document and will not be included when a document is printed, but they can assist you with troubleshooting a document and modifying its appearance before printing or distributing. For example, if lines in a document end awkwardly, some not even extending to the right margin, you can click Show/Hide to display nonprinting characters and check for the presence of poorly placed, or perhaps unnecessary, hard returns. Deleting the hard returns might realign the document so that lines end in better fashion.

Reuse Text

STEP 1 You might find occasion to reuse text from a previously created document. For example, a memo to employees describing new insurance benefits might borrow wording from another document describing the same benefits to company retirees. In that case, you would simply insert text from a saved document into the new memo.

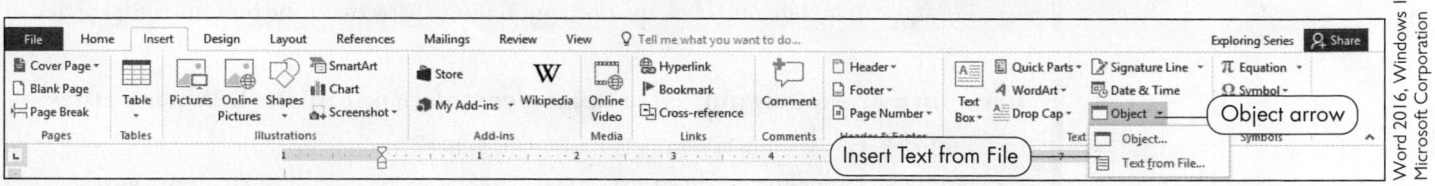

To insert text from another document, complete the following steps:

1. Position the insertion point where the inserted text is to be placed.
2. Click the Insert tab. Click the Object arrow (see Figure 1.6).
3. Click Text from File.
4. Navigate to the location of the source document and double-click the file name.

FIGURE 1.6 Inserting Text from Another File

Use a Template

STEP 2 ❯❯ Developing a new document can be difficult. With that in mind, the developers of Word have included a library of **_templates_** from which you can select a predesigned document. You can then modify the document to suit your needs. Categories of templates are displayed when you first open Word, or when you click the File tab and click New. In addition to local templates—those that are available offline with a typical Word installation—Microsoft provides many more online. All of those templates are displayed or searchable within Word, as shown in Figure 1.7. Microsoft continually updates content in the template library, so you are assured of having access to all the latest templates each time you open Word.

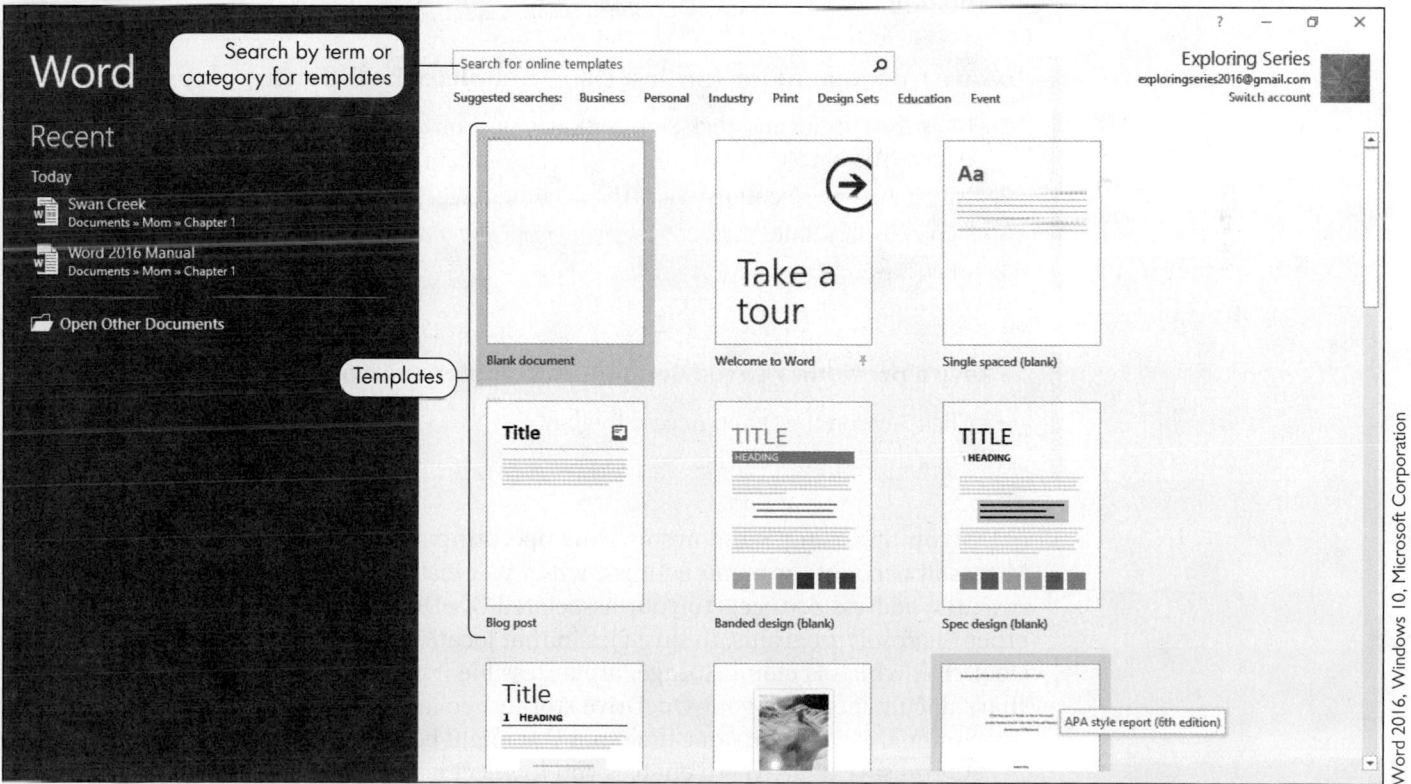

FIGURE 1.7 Working with Templates

Some templates are likely to become your favorites. Because you will want quick access to those templates, you can pin them to the top of the templates menu so they will always be available.

> **To pin a template, complete one of the following steps:**
> - Right-click a favorite template and click Pin to list.
> - Point to a template and click the horizontal Pin to list icon at the bottom-right corner.

> **To unpin a previously pinned template, complete one of the following steps:**
> - Right-click a previously pinned template and click Unpin from list.
> - Point to a template and click the vertical Unpin from list icon at the bottom-right corner.

Save a Document

Saving a document makes it possible for you to access it later for editing, sharing, or printing. In fact, it is a good idea not to wait until a document is complete to save it, but to save a document periodically as you develop it. That way, you risk losing only what you created or edited since the last save operation if you experience a disruption of power. Word recognizes not only the need to save files, but also the need to make them available on any device you might have access to and the need to share documents with others so you can collaborate on projects. To make that possible, Word encourages you to save documents to the cloud. It is always a good idea, however, to save an important document in several places—perhaps a hard drive or flash drive—so that you always have a backup copy.

> **To save a document for the first time, complete the following steps:**
> 1. Click the File tab and click Save (or Save As). You can instead click Save on the Quick Access Toolbar.
> 2. Navigate to the location where the document will be saved.
> 3. Type the file name.
> 4. Click Save.

> **To save a previously saved document, complete one of the following steps:**
> - Click Save on the Quick Access Toolbar.
> - Click the File tab and click Save.

If you are using Windows as your operating system, you most likely provided a Microsoft account, or email address, when you installed the operating system. In that case, the address connects to your associated OneDrive storage and enables Word, and other Microsoft programs, to save files in that location by default. Files that are saved on OneDrive, which is cloud storage, are accessible from mobile devices. If you choose to share documents from your OneDrive storage, collaborators can easily access and edit them online, even at the same time that you might be editing the document online.

As you save a file, Word enables you to select a location to which to save. Although OneDrive is the default, you can select another drive on your computer (see Figure 1.8).

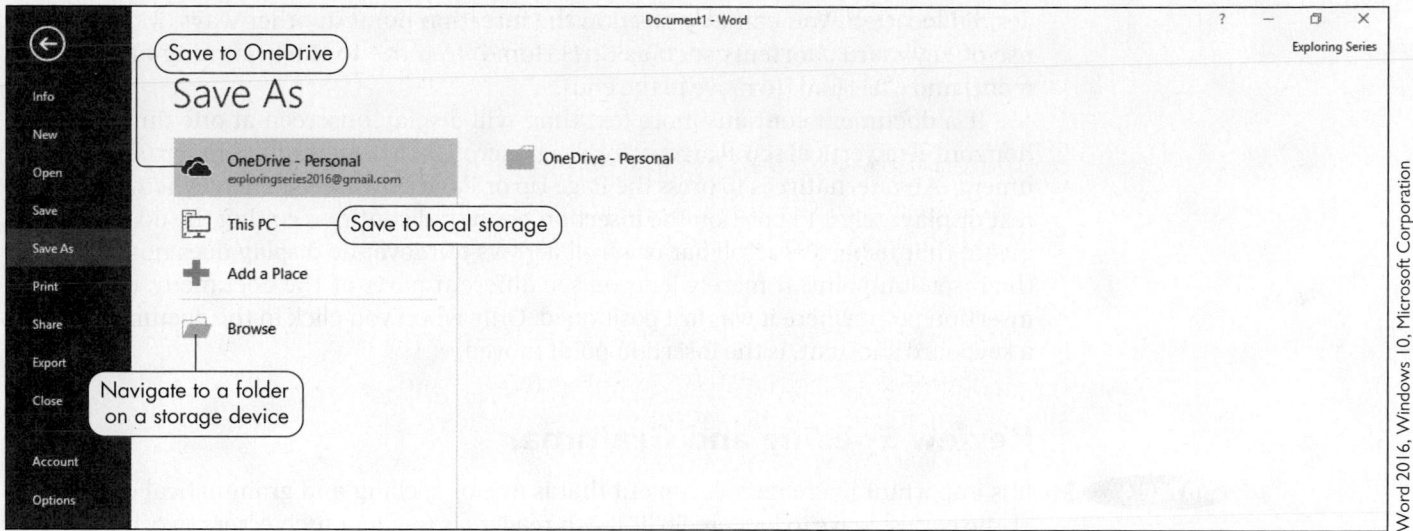

FIGURE 1.8 Saving a Word Document

Open a Document

After saving a document, you can open it later when you start Word and either select the document from the Recent list, or click Open Other Documents and navigate to the saved file. Word remembers the position of the insertion point when you previously saved the file and suggests that you return to that same location (see Figure 1.9). Just click the link to return, or ignore it if you want to work somewhere else in the document.

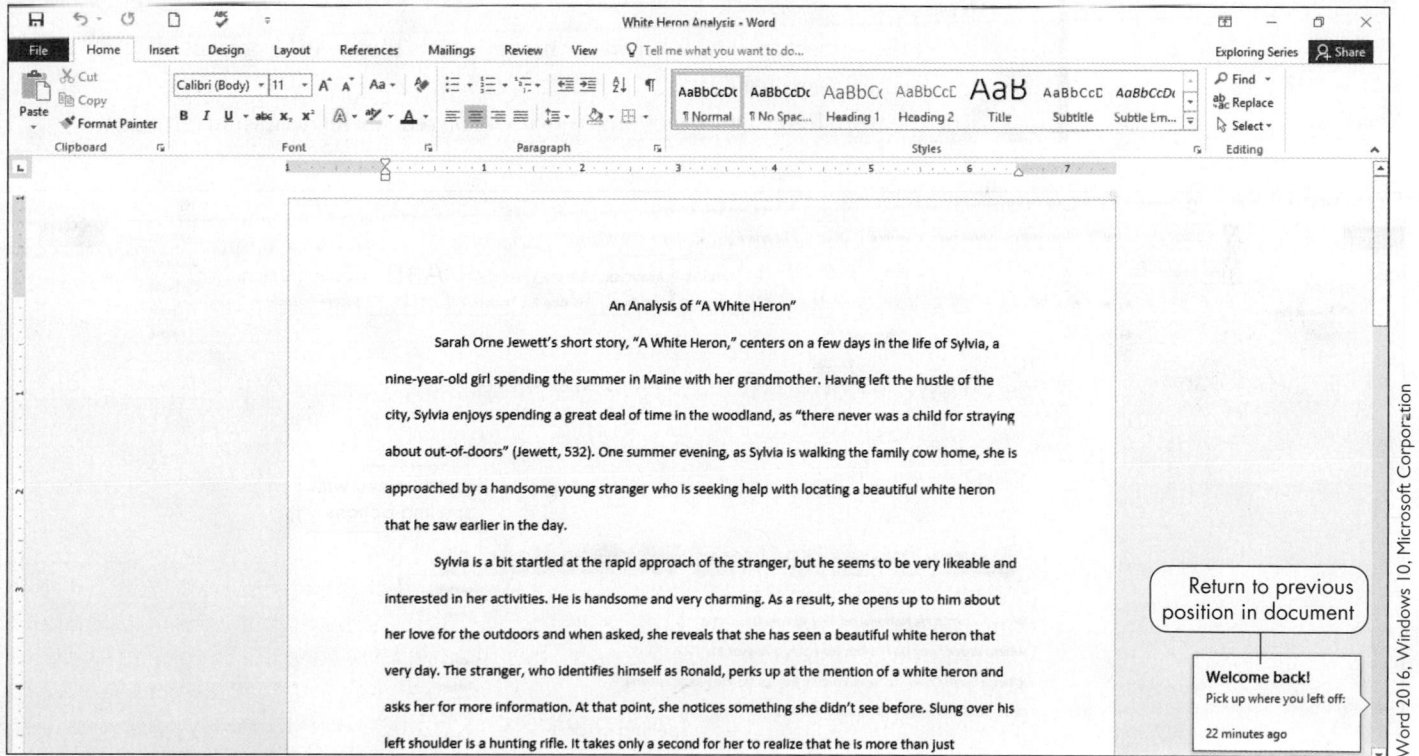

FIGURE 1.9 Returning to a Previous Position

Insert Text and Navigate a Document

STEP 3 ›› The *insertion point* indicates where the text you type will be placed. It is important to remain aware of the location of the insertion point and to know how to move it to control where text is typed. Most often, you will move the insertion point by simply clicking the desired location. You can also position the insertion point in other ways, including the use of keyboard shortcuts such as Ctrl+Home (to move to the beginning of the document) and Ctrl+End (to move to the end).

If a document contains more text than will display onscreen at one time, click the horizontal or vertical scroll arrows (or drag a scroll bar) to view different parts of the document. An alternative is to press the Page Up or Page Down keys. Then, when the desired text displays, click to position the insertion point and continue editing the document. Be aware that using the scroll bar or scroll arrows to move the display does not reposition the insertion point. It merely lets you see different parts of the document, leaving the insertion point where it was last positioned. Only when you click in the document, or use a keyboard shortcut, is the insertion point moved.

Review Spelling and Grammar

STEP 4 >> It is important to create a document that is free of spelling and grammatical errors. One of the easiest ways to lose credibility with readers is to allow such errors to occur. Choose words that are appropriate and that best convey your intentions in writing or editing a document. Word provides tools on the Review tab that simplify the tasks of reviewing a document for errors, identifying proper wording, and providing insight into unfamiliar words.

A word considered by Word to be misspelled is underlined with a red wavy line. A possible grammatical mistake or word usage error is underlined in blue. Both types of errors are shown in Figure 1.10.

> **To correct possible spelling, grammatical, or word usage errors in a document, right-click an underlined error and complete one of the following steps:**
>
> - Select the correct spelling from one or more options that may be presented.
> - Ignore the misspelled word.
> - Add the word to the Office dictionary so it will be recognized as a valid term.

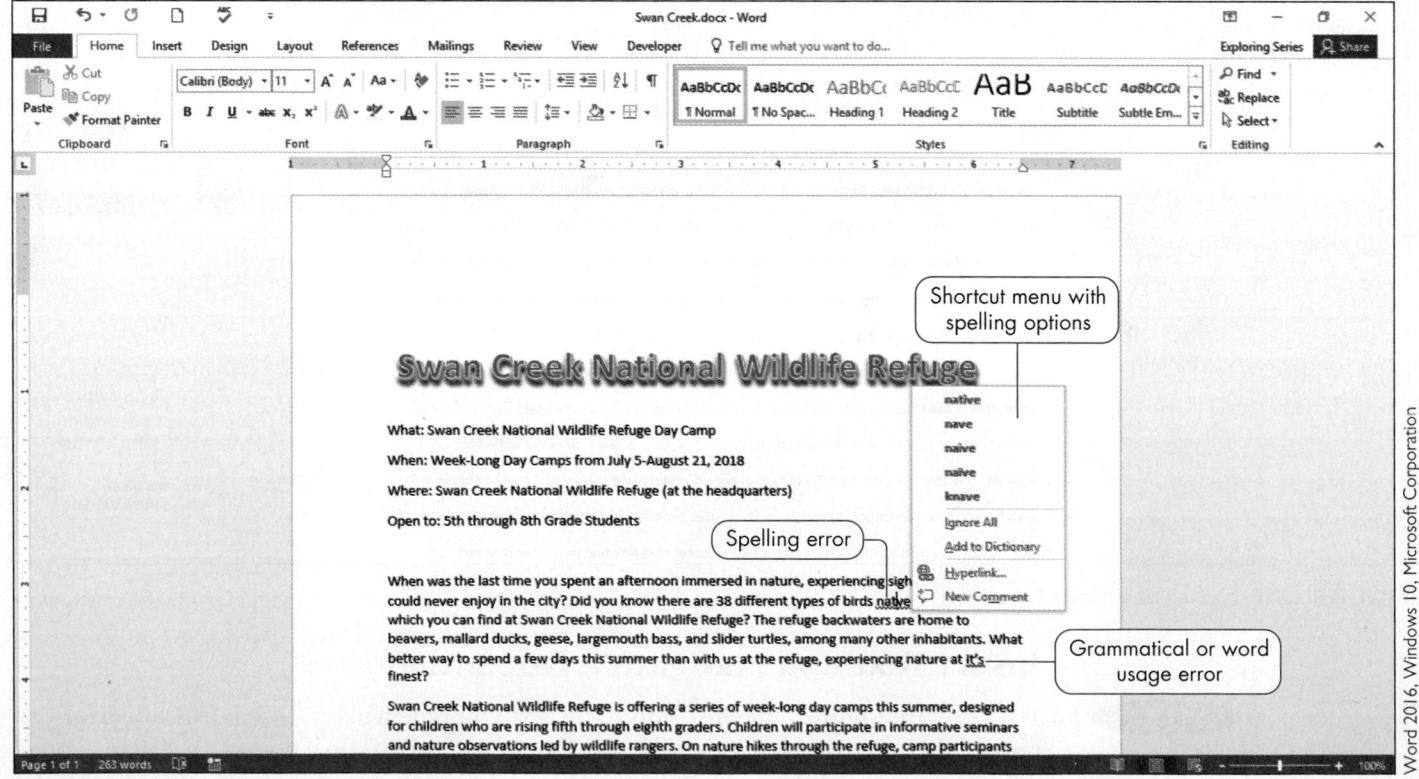

FIGURE 1.10 Correcting Spelling and Grammatical Errors

Correcting each error by right-clicking can become time-consuming, especially if the mistakes are many. In that case, Word can check an entire document, pausing at each identified error so that you can determine whether to correct or ignore the problem.

To check an entire document for spelling and grammatical errors, complete the following steps:

1. Click the Review tab and click Spelling & Grammar in the Proofing group (see Figure 1.11).
2. Review each error as it is presented, selecting an identified correction or ignoring the error if it is actually correct (as might be the case with a name or medical term). If a correct spelling is not presented, and a word is actually misspelled, you can manually make the correction.

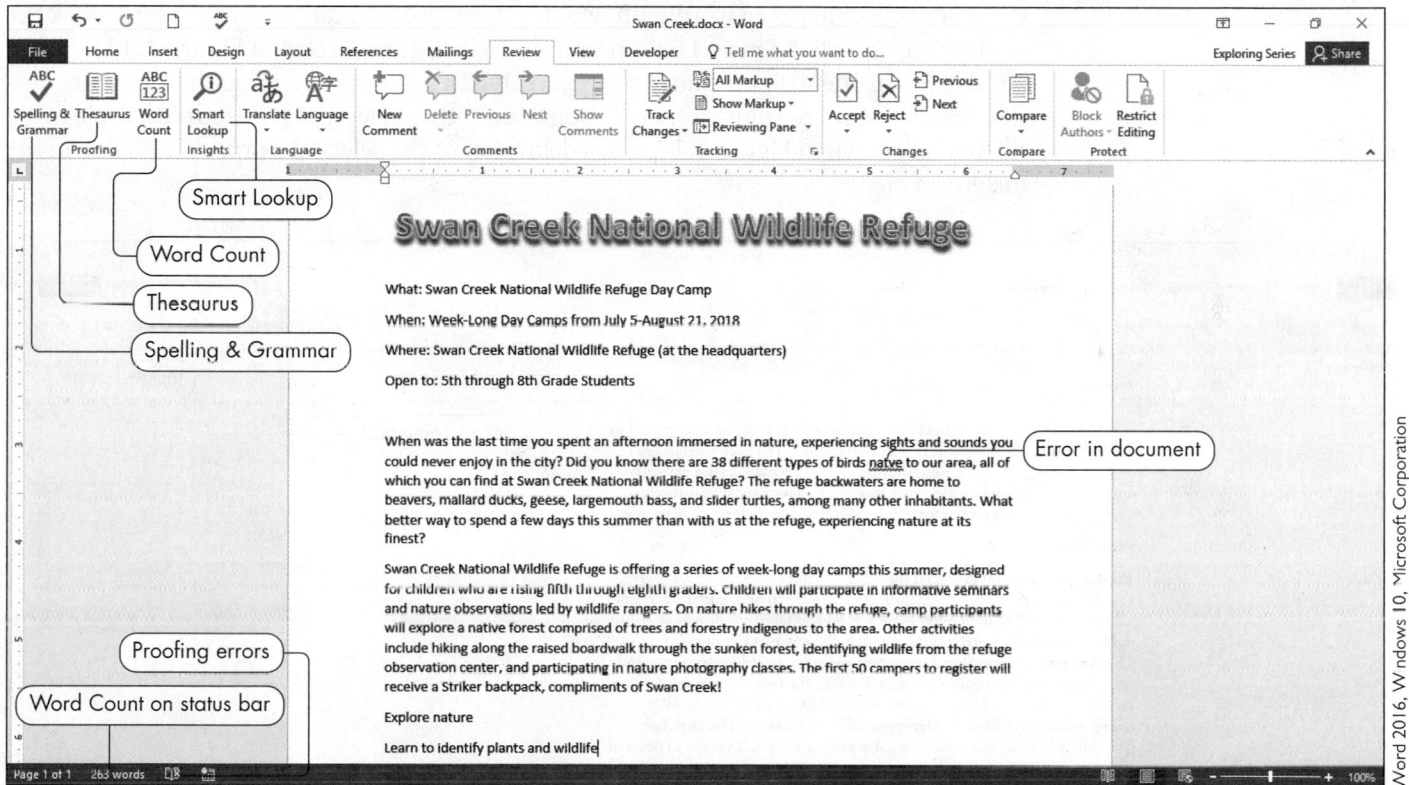

FIGURE 1.11 Options for Proofing a Document

For even quicker error identification, check the Proofing errors icon on the status bar (refer to Figure 1.11). By default, Word automatically checks the entire open document for spelling, grammatical, and word usage errors, displaying an *X* on the Proofing errors icon if errors are found. Click the Proofing errors icon to either change or ignore all errors, one at a time. If, instead, you see a check mark on the Proofing errors icon, the document appears to be error free. The document in Figure 1.11 contains errors, as indicated by the *X* on the Proofing errors icon.

Never depend completely on Word to catch all errors; always proofread a document yourself. For example, typing the word *fee* when you meant to type *free* is not an error that Word would typically catch, because *fee* is not actually misspelled and might not be flagged as a word usage error, depending upon the sentence context.

Words do not always come easily. Occasionally, you might need to find a synonym (a word with the same meaning as another) for a particular word. Word provides a handy **thesaurus** for just such an occasion.

> **To select a synonym, complete one of the following steps:**
>
> - Select a word in a document and click the Review tab. Click Thesaurus (refer to Figure 1.11), click the arrow beside a synonym, and then click Insert.
> - Right-click a word and click Synonyms. Select from a group of synonyms.

TIP: COUNTING WORDS

Occasionally, you might need to know how many words are included in a document, or in a selected portion of a document. For example, your English instructor might require a minimum word count for an essay. Click the Review tab and click Word Count (refer to Figure 1.11) to get a quick summary of words, characters, lines, pages, and paragraphs. Document word count is often displayed on the status bar as well.

Especially when editing or collaborating on a document created by someone else, you might come across a word with which you are unfamiliar. Select the word; click the Review tab and click Smart Lookup in the Insights group (refer to Figure 1.11). Smart Lookup opens the Insights pane (see Figure 1.12). **Insights** is a pane that presents outside resources, such as images, definitions, and other references. Resources display in a sidebar, as shown in Figure 1.12. For a definition of the selected word, click Define in the Insights pane.

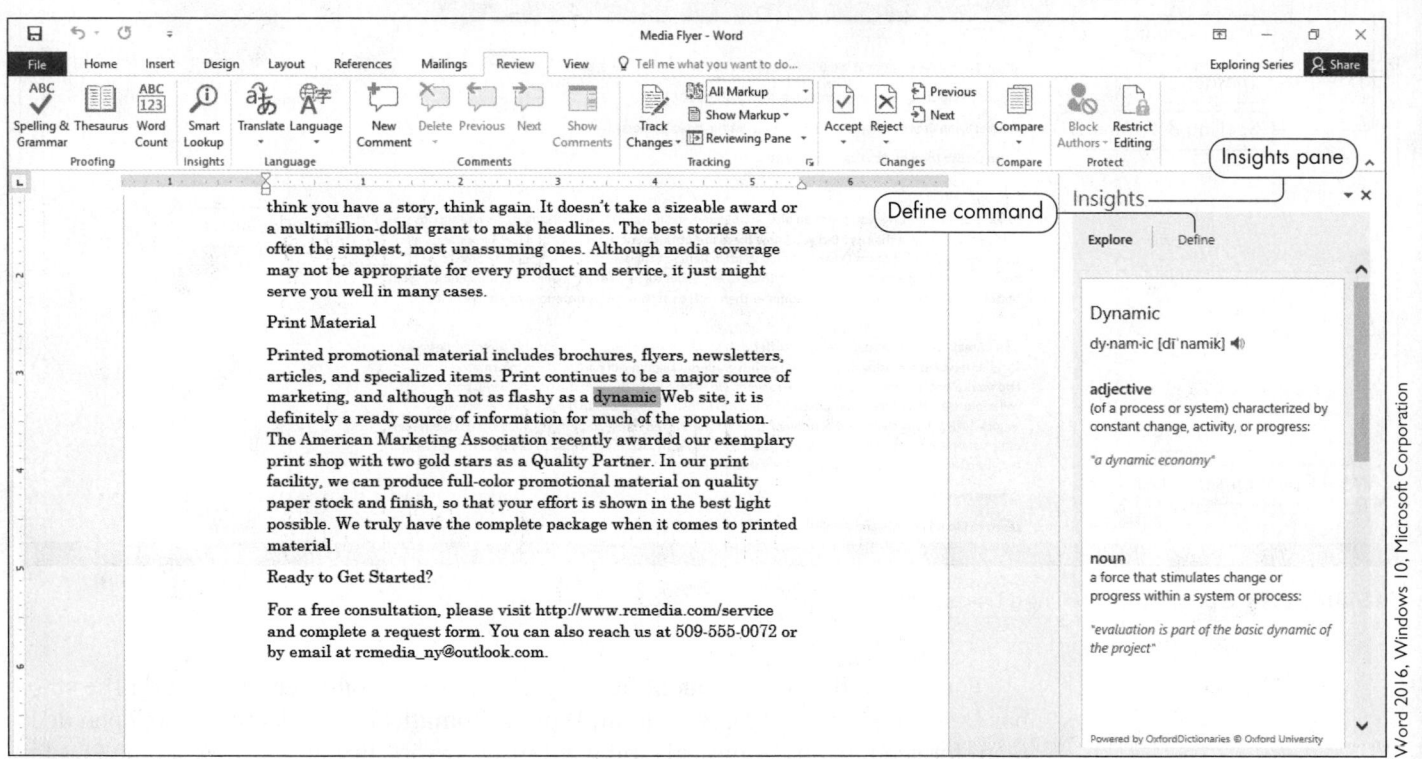

FIGURE 1.12 Using the Insights Pane

Customizing Word

As installed, Word is immediately useful. However, you might find options that you would prefer to customize, add, or remove from the document window. You might prefer that the Ribbon be organized differently, or it might be helpful to add frequently used commands to the Quick Access Toolbar for ease of access. These and other options are available for customization within Word.

Explore Word Options

STEP 5)) By default, certain Word settings are determined and in place when you begin a Word document. For example, unless you specify otherwise, Word will automatically check spelling as you type. Similarly, the Mini toolbar will automatically display when text is selected. Although those and other settings are most likely what you will prefer, there may be occasions when you want to change them. When you change Word options, you change them for all documents—not just the currently open file.

> **TIP: SETTING WORD OPTIONS**
> Word options that you change will remain in effect until you change them again, even after Word is closed and reopened. Keep in mind that if you are working in a school computer lab, you might not have permission to change options permanently.

To modify Word options, complete the following steps:

1. Click the File tab and click Options.
2. Select from categories and options, as shown in Figure 1.13.

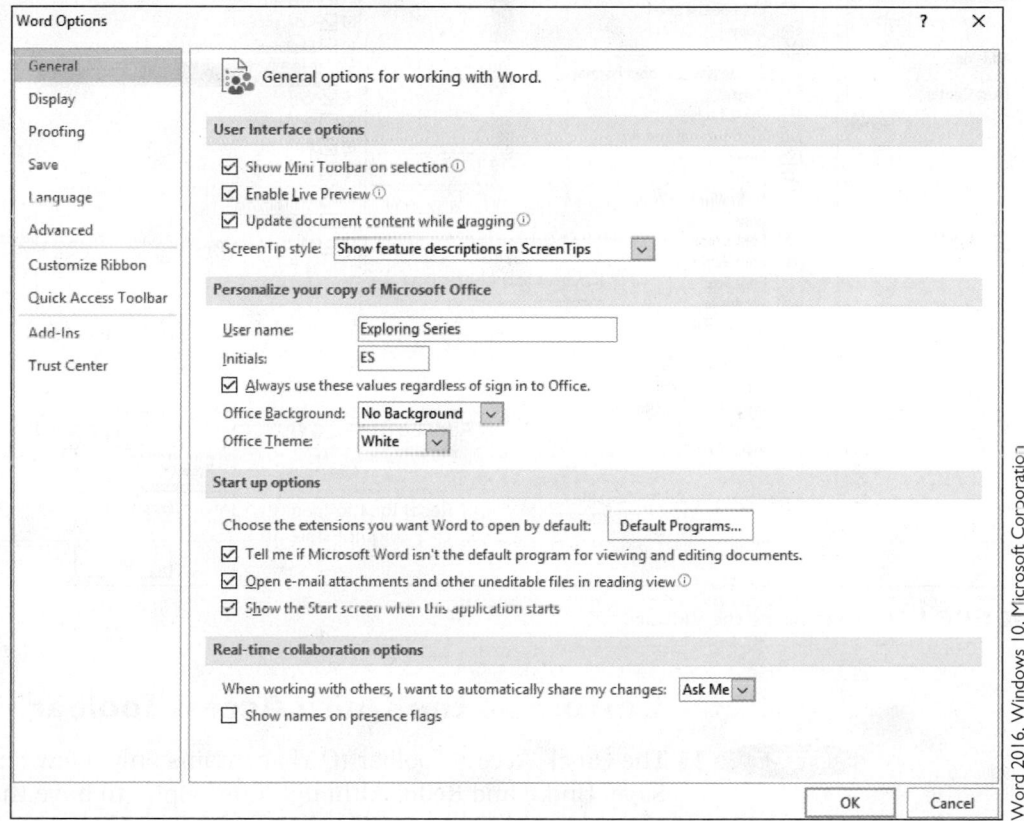

FIGURE 1.13 Accessing Word Options

Customize the Ribbon

STEP 6)) The Word Ribbon provides access to commands that make it easy to develop, edit, save, share, and print documents. If necessary, you can add and remove Ribbon tabs, as well as rename them.

To customize the Ribbon, complete the following steps:

1. Click the File tab and click Options.
2. Click Customize Ribbon.
3. Choose from the following options, as shown in Figure 1.14:
   - To add or remove a tab, select or deselect the tab name check box.
   - To change the name of a current tab, click Rename.
   - To reset the Ribbon to the original tabs, click Reset, and then click Reset all customizations.

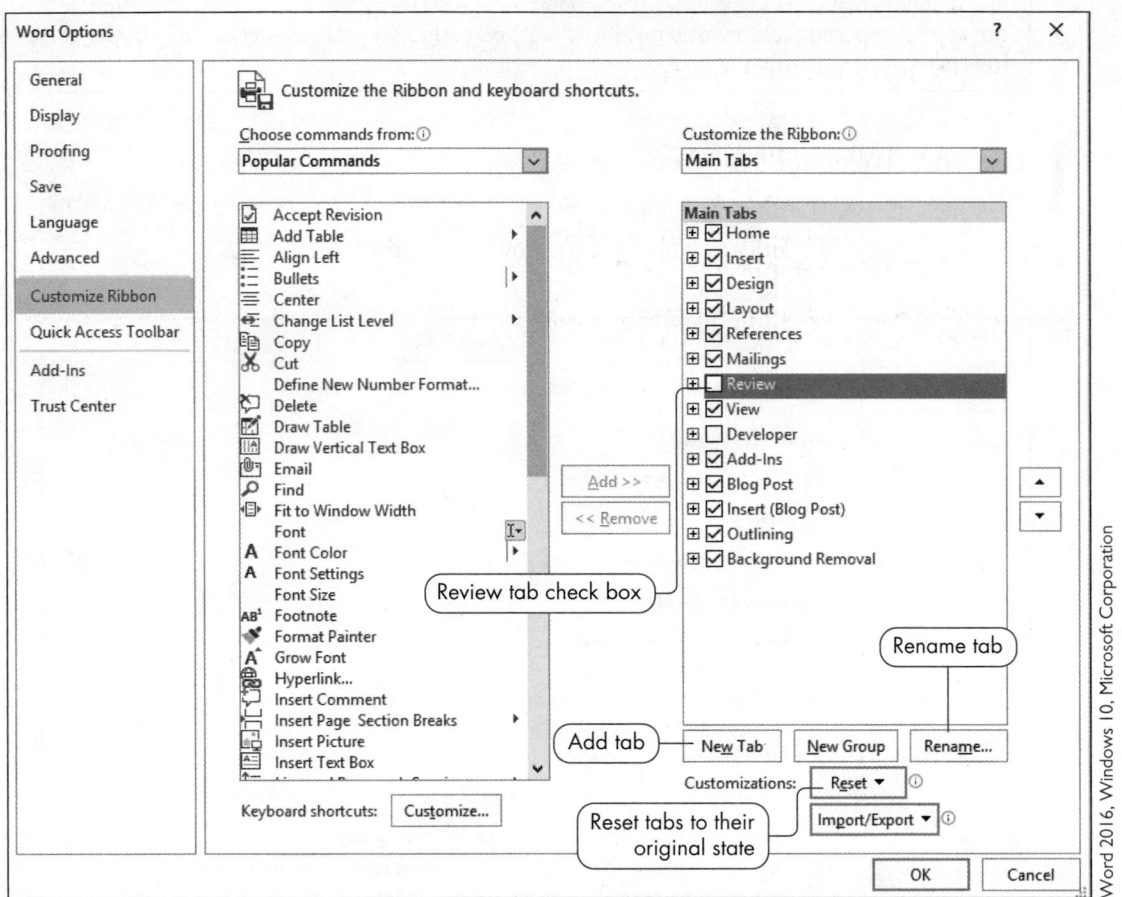

FIGURE 1.14 Customizing the Ribbon

Customize the Quick Access Toolbar

STEP 7 ❯❯ The Quick Access Toolbar (QAT) contains only a few commands by default, including Save, Undo, and Redo. Although it is helpful to have those options close at hand, you might want to include even more on the QAT. You can even remove commands that you do not use often.

To customize the QAT, complete one of the following steps:

- Click Customize Quick Access Toolbar (see Figure 1.15) and select from a menu of options.
- Right-click a Ribbon command and click Add to Quick Access Toolbar.

To remove a command from the QAT, right-click the command on the QAT and select Remove from Quick Access Toolbar.

Word 2016, Windows 10, Microsoft Corporation

FIGURE 1.15 Customizing the Quick Access Toolbar

Quick Concepts

1. Explain how the way you are likely to define a paragraph and the way Word defines a paragraph can differ. *p. 136*

2. Provide at least two advantages of using OneDrive as a storage location for your documents. *p. 138*

3. It is very important to check a document for spelling, grammatical, and word usage errors. However, Word might not identify every error in a document. Why not? Provide an example of an error that Word might not identify. *p. 141*

4. Describe an advantage of using Word templates to begin document production. *p. 137*

Hands-On Exercises

Watch the Video for this Hands-On Exercise!

MyITLab®
HOE1 Training

Skills covered: Create a Document • Save a Document • Use a Template • Insert Text and Navigate a Document • Review Spelling and Grammar • Explore Word Options • Customize the Ribbon • Customize the Quick Access Toolbar

1 Introduction to Word Processing

As an office assistant working with the wildlife refuge, you prepare a document publicizing the summer day camps at Swan Creek. Your supervisor provided a few paragraphs that you modify, creating an article for distribution to schools in the area. You also open a document from a template, and create an event planner. Because you plan to use the office computer for future projects as well, you explore ways to customize Word for ease of use.

STEP 1 >> CREATE AND SAVE A DOCUMENT

As you create a new document, you insert text provided by your supervisor and then save the document for later editing. Refer to Figure 1.16 as you complete Step 1.

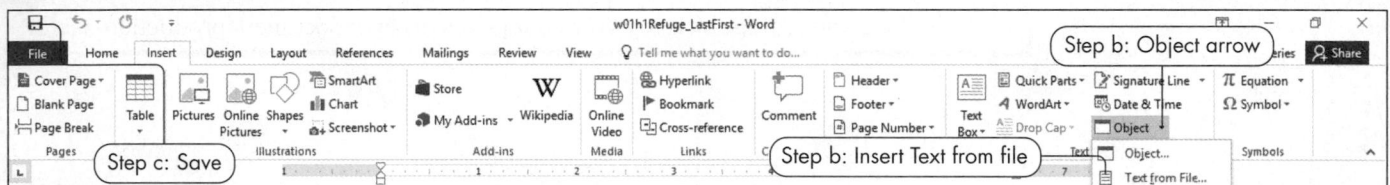

FIGURE 1.16 Beginning a Document

Word 2016, Windows 10, Microsoft Corporation

a. Open Word. Click **Blank document**. Click **Save** on the Quick Access Toolbar. In the right pane, click the location where you save your files, or click **Browse** and navigate to the location. Change the file name to **w01h1Refuge_LastFirst**. Click **Save**.

When you save files, use your last and first names. For example, as the Word author, I would name my document "w01h1Refuge_HoganLynn."

b. Click the **Insert tab** and click the **Object arrow**. Click **Text from File**. Navigate to your student data files for this chapter and double-click *w01h1Camps*. Press **Ctrl+Home** to move the insertion point to the beginning of the document.

c. Click **Save** on the Quick Access Toolbar.

This saves the document without changing the name or the location where it is saved.

d. Click the **File tab** and click **Close**.

You close the document. You will use this document again later in this Hands-On Exercise.

As a multitasker, you are accustomed to working with several projects at once. Ms. Traynom, your supervisor, asks that you print an event planner. She must often juggle tasks, and needs a document that will help organize them. You know that Word provides event planner templates, so you locate one. Refer to Figure 1.17 as you complete Step 2.

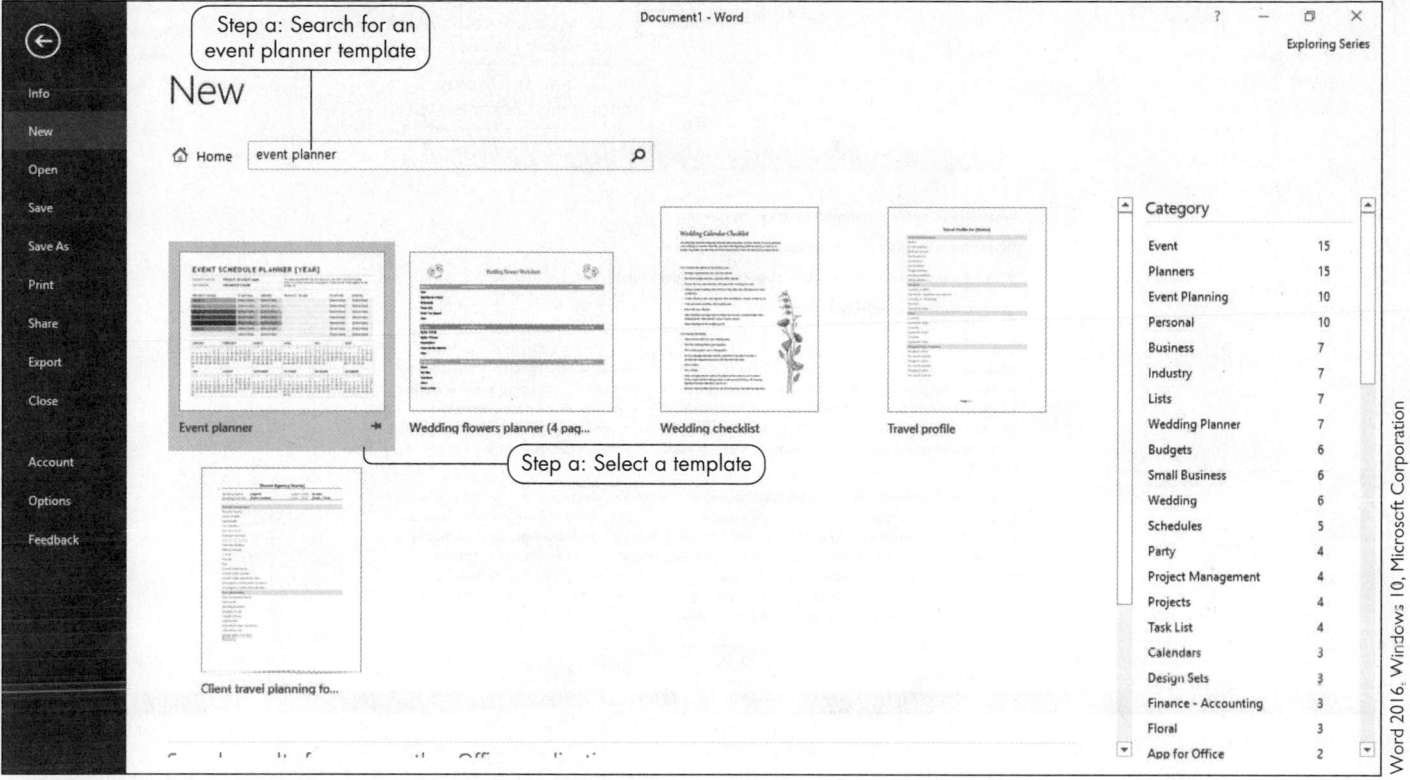

FIGURE 1.17 Working with a Template

a. Click the **File tab** and click **New**. Click the **Search for online templates box** and type **event planner**. Press **Enter**. Click **Event Planner**.

> **TROUBLESHOOTING:** The event planner template is only available if you are currently connected to the Internet.

b. Click **Create**. Click **OK**, repeatedly if necessary, to accept settings from any subsequent dialog boxes related to scheduling that may open. Save the planner as **w01h1Planner_LastFirst**.

c. Click the **File tab** and click **Close**.

Although Ms. Traynom provided you with a good start, you add a bit more detail to the w01h1Refuge_LastFirst article. Refer to Figure 1.18 as you complete Step 3.

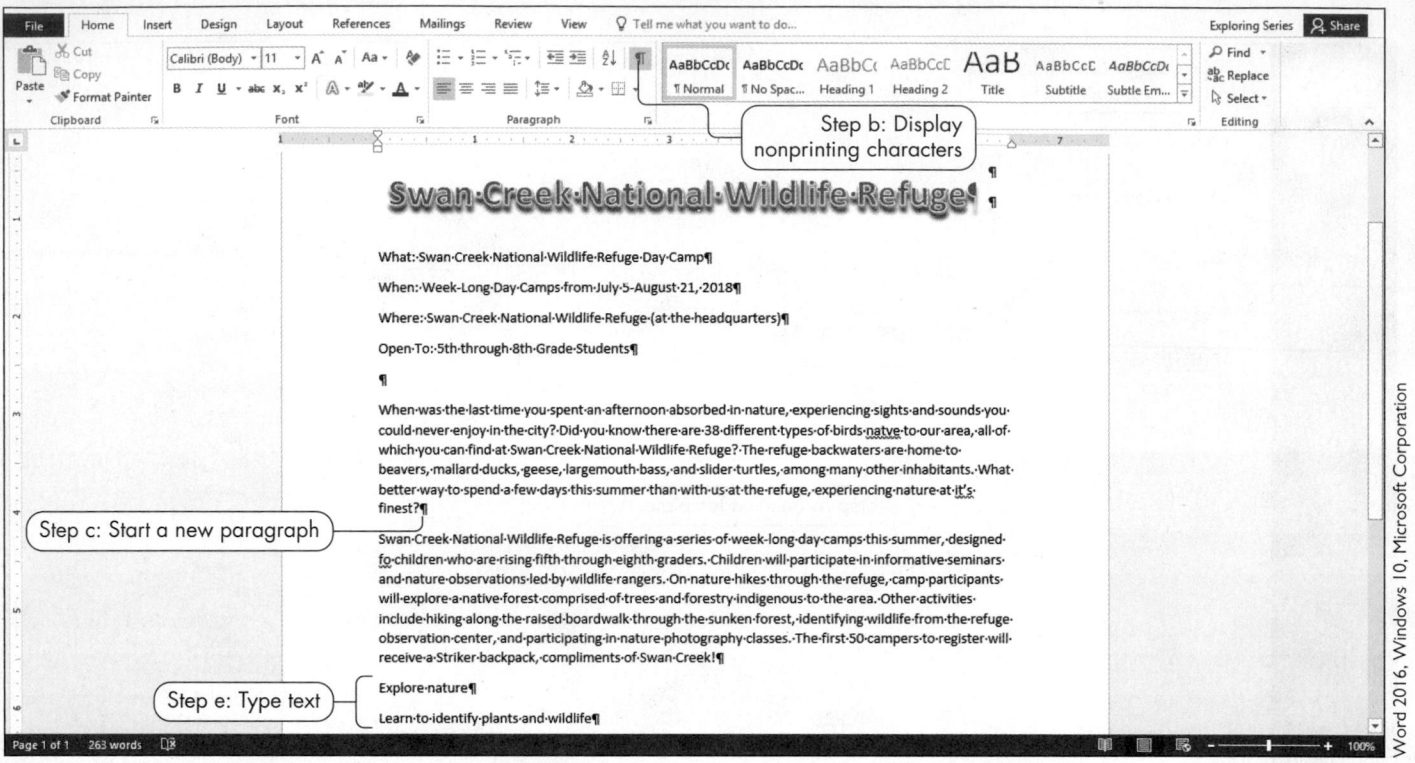

FIGURE 1.18 Editing a Document

a. Click the **File tab** and click **Open**. In the Recent list, click **w01h1Refuge_LastFirst**.

b. Click **Show/Hide** in the Paragraph group to display nonprinting formatting marks (unless they are already displayed).

c. Click after the sentence ending in *finest?*—immediately after the question mark and before the nonprinting space character at the end of the fourth sentence in the body text. Press **Enter**. Press **Delete**.

> **TROUBLESHOOTING:** There will be no space before Swan if you clicked after the space instead of before it when you pressed Enter. In that case, there is no space to delete, so leave the text as is.

d. Scroll down and click after *Creek!*—immediately after the exclamation point after the second body paragraph—and press **Enter**.

e. Type the following text, pressing **Enter** at the end of each line:

explore nature

learn to identify native plants and wildlife

take digital photos

participate in nature seminars

enjoy relaxing days at the refuge

As you type each line, the first letter is automatically capitalized.

f. Press **Ctrl+End**. Press **Delete**.

The final paragraph mark is deleted and the second blank page is removed.

g. Save the document.

STEP 4 ▶▶ REVIEW SPELLING AND GRAMMAR

As you continue to develop the article, you check for spelling, grammar, and word usage mistakes. You also identify a synonym and get a definition. Refer to Figure 1.19 as you complete Step 4.

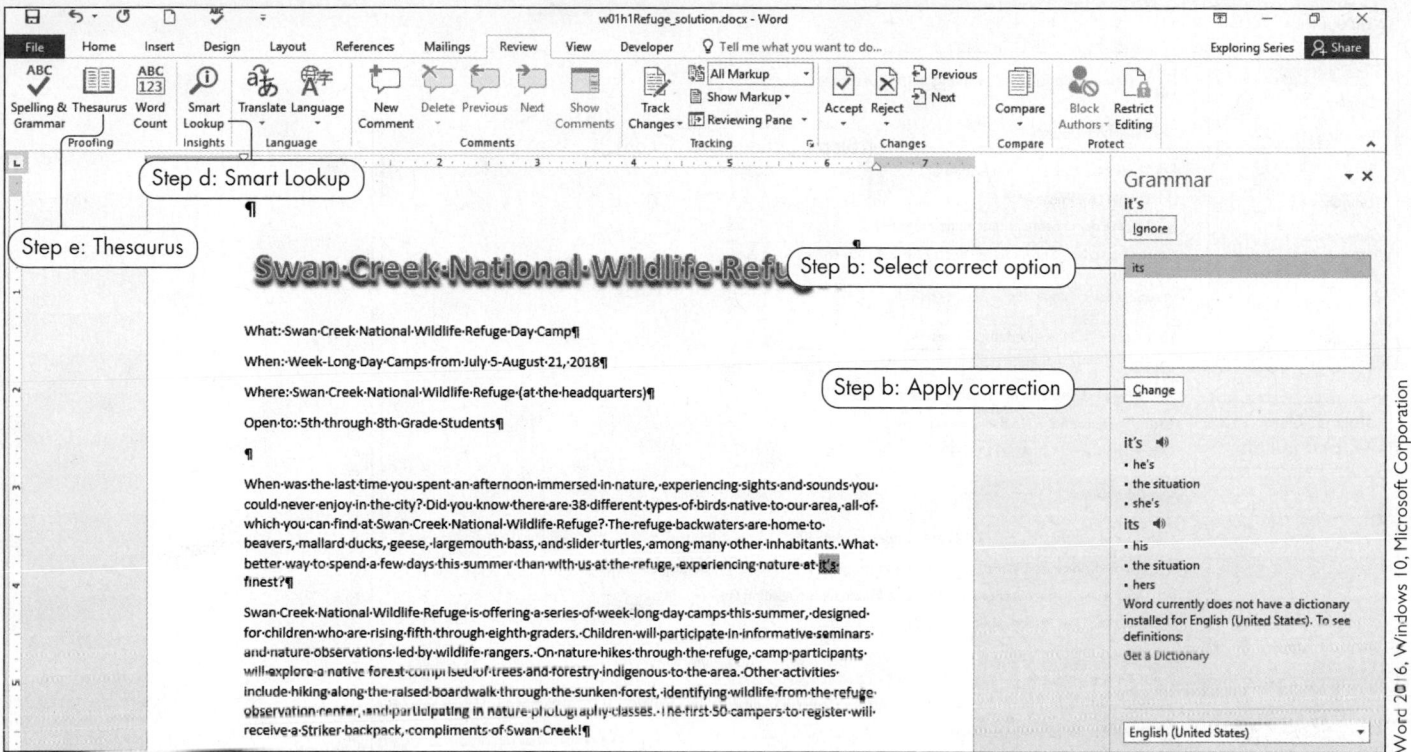

FIGURE 1.19 Proofing a Document

a. Press **Ctrl+Home**. Right-click the red underlined word **natve** in the second line of the first body paragraph in the document. Click **native** on the shortcut menu.

b. Click the **Review tab** and click **Spelling & Grammar** in the Proofing group. As each error is presented, click to select the correct option. The word *birds* is not possessive, so ignore the suggested error. The word **it's** should not include an apostrophe, so ensure the correct option is selected (refer to Figure 1.19) and click **Change**. The word *fo* should be **for**. Click **OK** when the check is complete.

c. Read through the document. At least one error in the document is not identified as a spelling or word usage error by Word. Identify and correct the error.

d. Select the word *immersed* in the first sentence of the first body paragraph. Click **Smart Lookup** in the Insights group. Click **Define** in the Insights pane.

Resources related to the selected word are shown in the Insights pane on the right. A definition is also available.

> **TROUBLESHOOTING:** If the Insights pane has not been used before, you may have to respond to a privacy prompt before the Insights pane will open.

e. Close the Insights pane. With the word *immersed* still selected, click **Thesaurus** in the Proofing group. Point to the word *absorbed*, click the arrow at the right, and then select **Insert**.

> **TROUBLESHOOTING:** If you click the word *absorbed* instead of the arrow at the right, you will be presented with related word choices, but the word will not be inserted. Click the back arrow at the top of the Thesaurus pane, and repeat step e.

f. Close the Thesaurus pane. Save the document.

You explore some Word options that enable you to customize the computer assigned to you at the refuge. Such customization ensures that Word is configured to suit your preferences. Refer to Figure 1.20 as you complete Step 5.

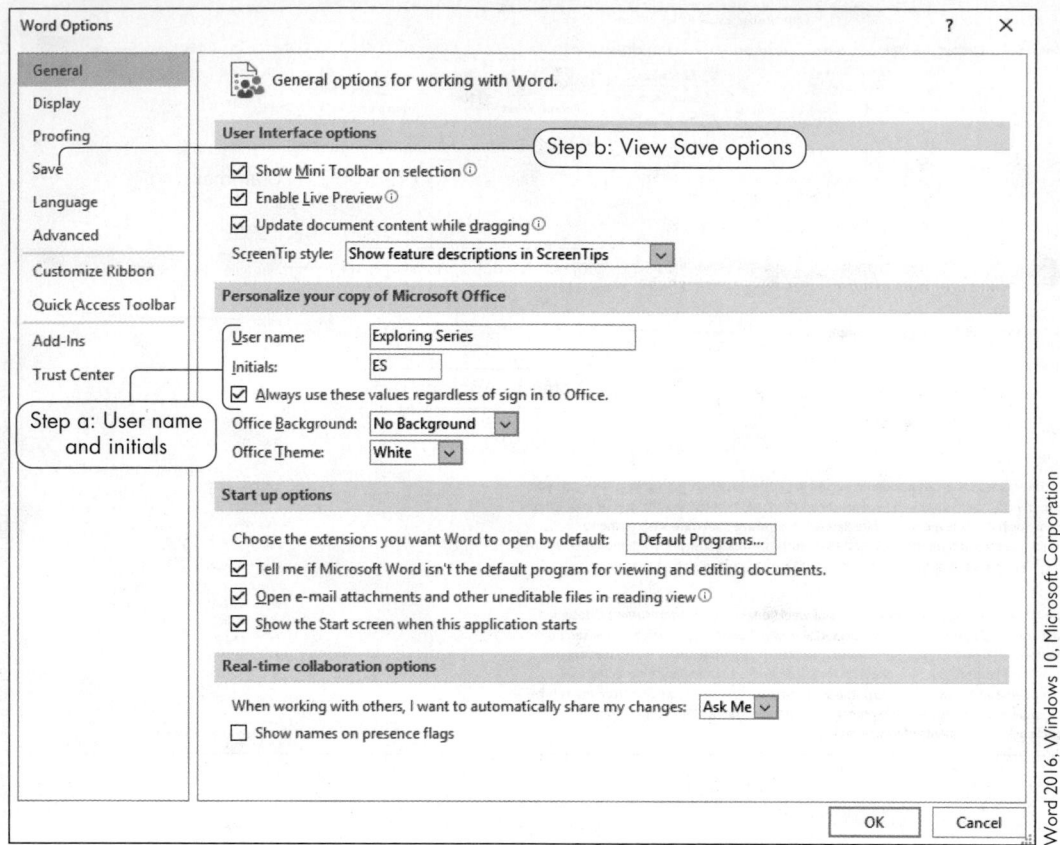

FIGURE 1.20 Exploring Word Options

a. Click the **File tab** and click **Options**. Ensure that the General category in the left pane is selected.

Note that you can change the User name and Initials that identify you as the author of documents you create. Because you might be working in a computer lab, you do not actually change anything at this time.

b. Click **Save** in the left pane of the Word Options dialog box.

Note that you can adjust the AutoRecover time, a feature covered later in this chapter, by typing in the text box, replacing existing text, or by clicking the up or down arrow repeatedly.

c. Click **Cancel**, so you do not actually make changes.

As you continue to explore ways to customize Word preferences, you identify Ribbon tabs that you can add or remove. Refer to Figure 1.21 as you complete Step 6.

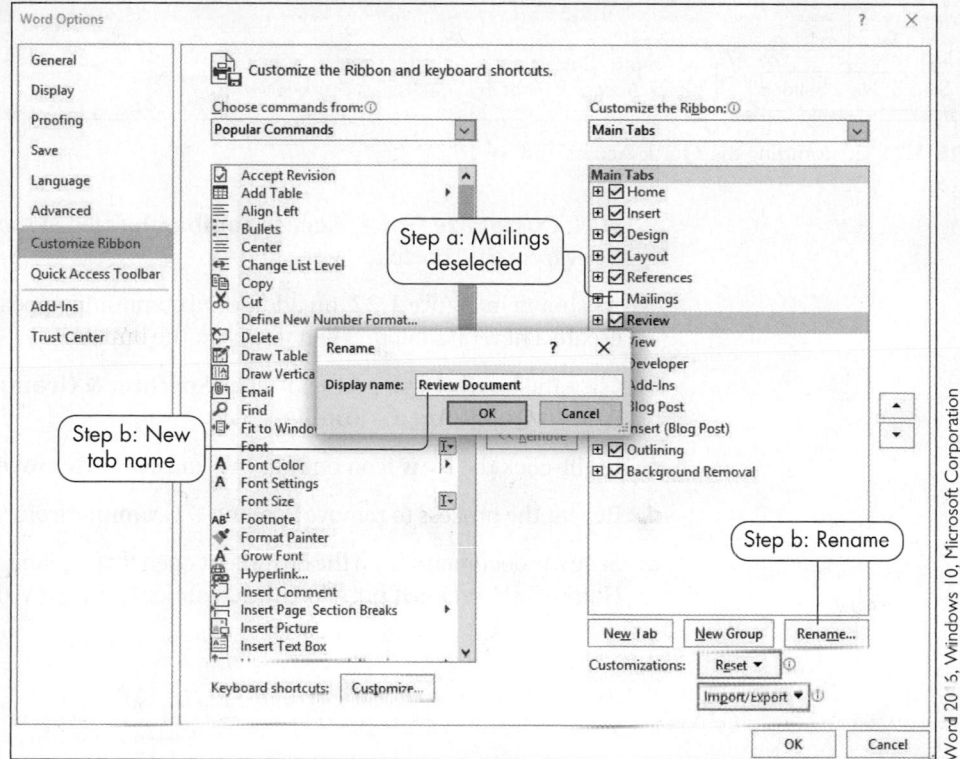

FIGURE 1.21 Customizing the Ribbon

a. Click the **File tab** and click **Options**. Click **Customize Ribbon** in the left pane. Click the **Mailings check box** under Main Tabs to deselect the item.

> **TROUBLESHOOTING:** If Mailings is not deselected, you clicked the word Mailings instead of the check box next to it. Click the Mailings check box.

b. Click **Review** under Main Tabs (click the word **Review**, not the check mark beside the word). Click **Rename** (located beneath the list of Main Tabs) and type **Review Document**—but do not click OK.

c. Click **Cancel**, so that changes to the Ribbon are not saved to a lab computer. Click **Cancel** again.

You customize the Quick Access Toolbar to include commands that you use often. Refer to Figure 1.22 as you complete Step 7.

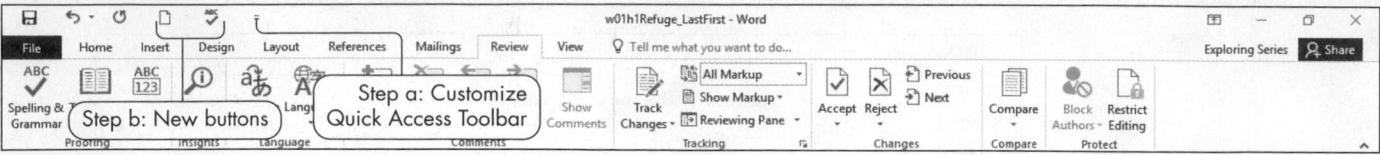

FIGURE 1.22 Customizing the Quick Access Toolbar

Word 2016, Windows 10, Microsoft Corporation

a. Click **Customize Quick Access Toolbar**, located at the right side of the QAT, and select **New** from the shortcut menu.

As shown in Figure 1.22, an additional command appears on the QAT, enabling you to create a new document when you click the button.

b. Click the **Review tab** and right-click **Spelling & Grammar** in the Proofing group. Click **Add to Quick Access Toolbar**.

c. Right-click the **New** icon on the QAT and select **Remove from Quick Access Toolbar**.

d. Repeat the process to remove Spelling & Grammar from the Quick Access Toolbar.

e. Save the document. Keep the document open if you plan to continue with the next Hands-On Exercise. If not, close the document and exit Word.

Document Organization

Most often, the reason for creating a document is for others to read; therefore, the document should be designed to meet the needs of the reading audience. It should not only be well worded and structured, but also might include features that better identify it, such as headers, footers, and watermarks. A watermark is text or graphics that displays behind text. In addition, adjusting margins and changing page orientation might better suit a document's purposes and improve its readability. Depending on its purpose, a document might need to fit on one page, or it could be very lengthy.

Before printing or saving a document, review it to ensure that it is attractive and appropriately organized. Word has various views, including Read Mode, Print Layout, Web Layout, Outline, and Draft, that you can use to get a good feel for the way the entire document looks, regardless of its length. The view selected can also give a snapshot of overall document organization so you can be assured that the document is well structured and makes all points. Using options on the View tab on the Ribbon, you can display a document in various ways, showing all pages, only one page, or zooming to a larger view, among other selections.

In this section, you will explore features that improve readability, and you will learn to change the view of a document.

Using Features That Improve Readability

Choosing your words carefully will result in a well-worded document. However, no matter how well worded, a document that is not organized in an attractive manner so that it is easy to read and understand is not likely to impress an audience. Consider not only the content, but also how a document will look when printed or displayed. Special features that can improve readability, such as headers, footers, and symbols, are located on Word's Insert tab. Other settings, such as margins, page orientation, and paper size, are found on the Layout tab. The Design tab provides access to watermarks, which can help convey the purpose or originator of a document.

Insert Headers and Footers

STEP 1 ›› *Headers* and *footers* can give a professional appearance to a document. A header consists of one or more lines at the top of each page. A footer displays at the bottom of each page. Typically, the purpose of including a header or footer is to better identify the document. As a header, you might include an organization name or a class number so that each page identifies the document's origin or purpose. A page number is a typical footer, although it could just as easily be included as a header.

One advantage of using headers and footers is that you have to specify the content only once, after which it displays automatically on all pages. Although you can type the text yourself at the top or bottom of every page, it is time-consuming, and the possibility of making a mistake is great.

To insert a header or footer, complete one of the following steps:

- Click the Insert tab and click Header (or Footer) in the Header & Footer group. Select from a gallery of predefined header or footer styles or click Edit Header (or Edit Footer) as shown in Figure 1.23 to create an unformatted header or footer.
- Double-click in the header or footer area to open a header or footer.

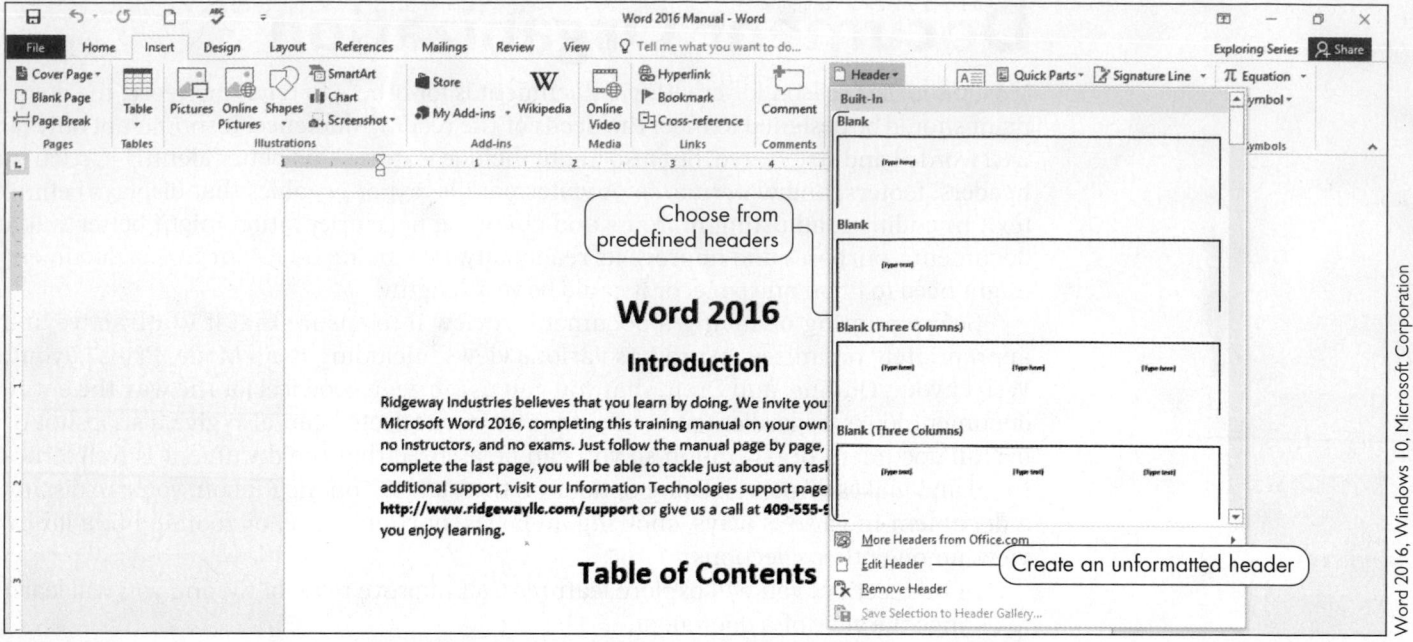

FIGURE 1.23 Inserting a Header

To close a header or footer, complete one of the following steps:

- Click Close Header and Footer to leave the header and footer area and return to the document (see Figure 1.24).
- Double-click in the document.

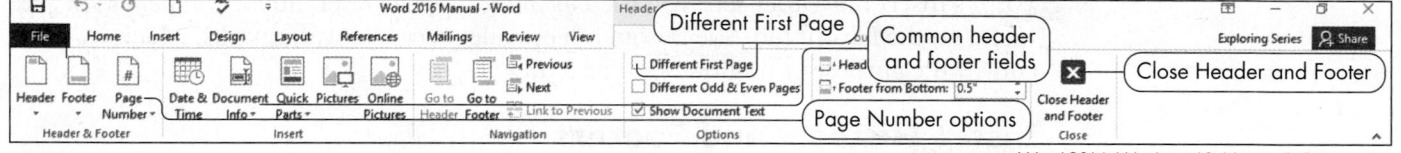

FIGURE 1.24 Header and Footer Fields and Options

Word 2016, Windows 10, Microsoft Corporation

A header or footer can be formatted like any other text. It can be center-, left-, or right-aligned, and formatted in any font or font size. When working with a header or footer, the main body text of the document is grayed out temporarily. When you return to the document, the body text is active, but the header or footer text is dim.

Word provides fields, such as author, date, and file name, that you can include in headers and footers. Some header and footer fields, such as page numbers, will actually change from one page to the next. Other fields, such as author name and date, will remain constant. Regardless, selecting fields (instead of typing the actual data) simplifies the task of creating headers and footers. Some of the most frequently accessed fields, such as Date & Time and Page Number, are available on the Header & Footer Tools Design contextual tab as separate commands (refer to Figure 1.24). Others, including Author, File Name, and Document Title, are available when you click Document Info in the Insert group (see Figure 1.25). Depending on the field selected, you might have to indicate a specific format and/or placement. For example, you could display the date as Monday, August 12, 2018, or you might direct that a page number is centered. Document Info also includes a Field option, which provides access to a complete list of fields from which to choose. The same fields are available when you click Quick Parts in the Insert group and click Field.

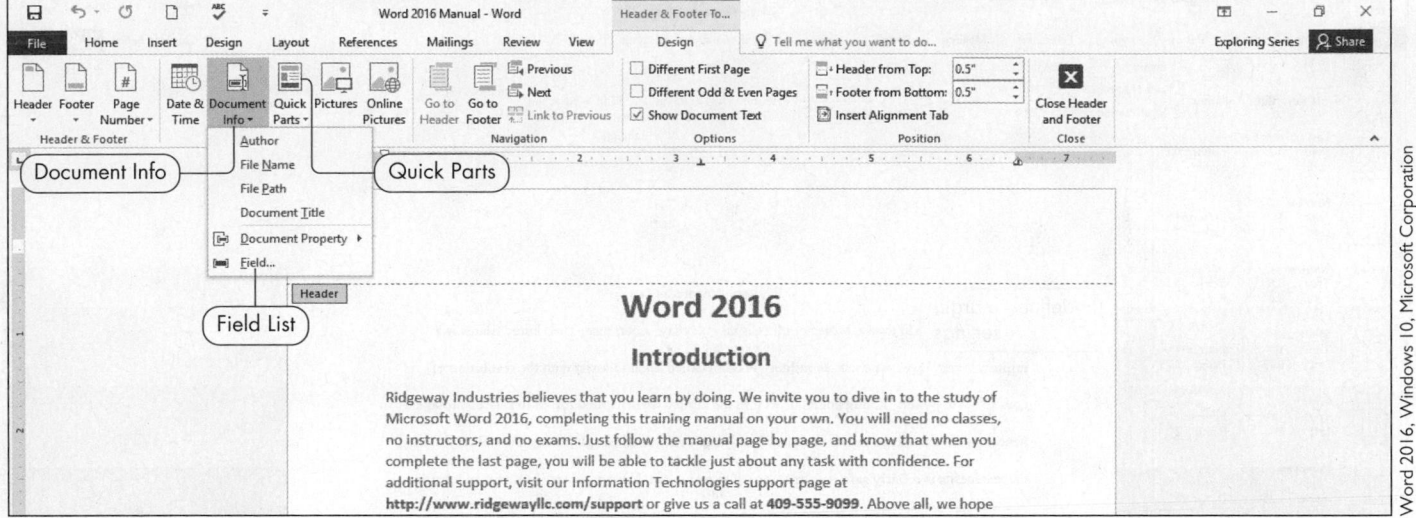

FIGURE 1.25 Inserting Header and Footer Fields

TIP: REMOVING A HEADER FROM THE FIRST PAGE

Occasionally, you will want a header or footer on all pages except the first, such as when the first page is a report's cover page. In that case, select Different First Page (refer to Figure 1.24) in the Options group on the Header & Footer Tools Design tab (when a header or footer is selected).

Adjust Margins

STEP 2 ⟫ Although a 1" margin all around the document is the default setting, you can easily adjust one or more margins for a particular document. You might adjust margins for several reasons. You can change a document's appearance and readability, perhaps even causing it to fit attractively on one page, by changing margins. Also, a style manual, such as you might use in an English class, will require certain margins for the preparation of papers and publications.

To change margins, complete one of the following steps:

- Click the Layout tab and click Margins in the Page Setup group. Select from one of the predefined margin settings (see Figure 1.26) or click Custom Margins to adjust each margin (left, right, top, and bottom) individually.
- Click the File tab and click Print. Click Normal Margins (or the previous margin setting) to change one or more margins.

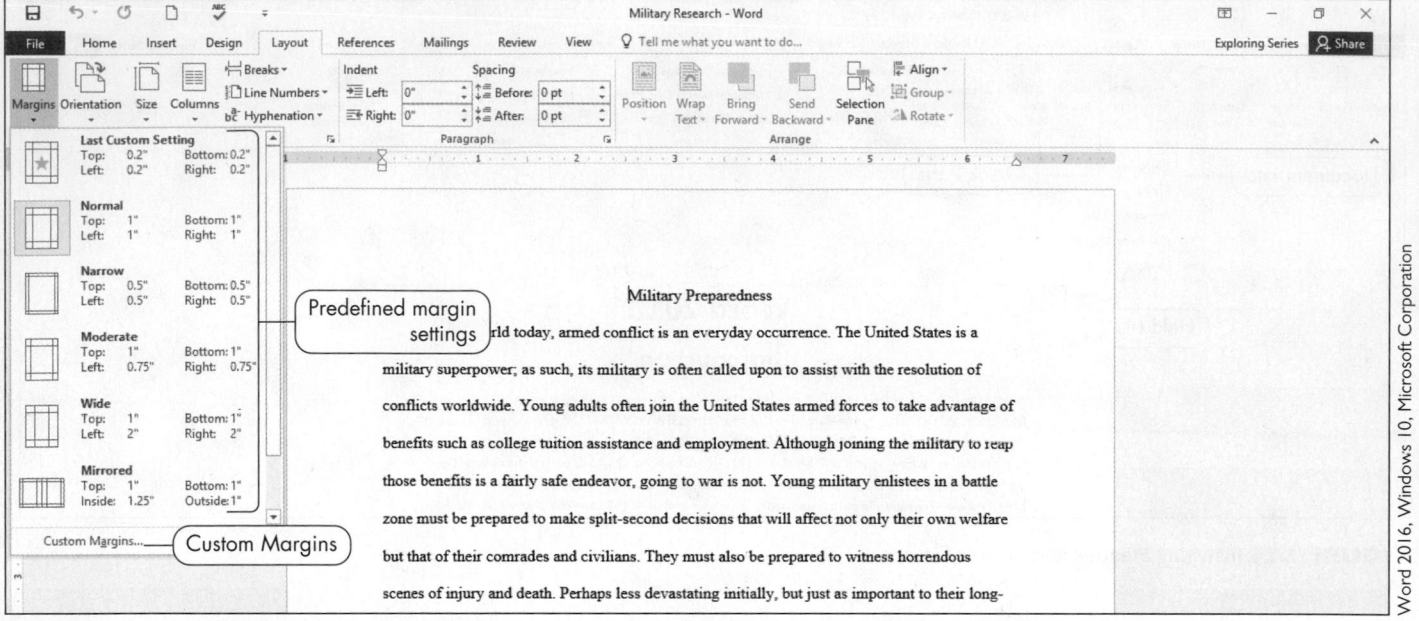

FIGURE 1.26 Setting Margins

Change Page Orientation

STEP 3 ❯❯ Some documents are better suited for portrait orientation, whereas others are more attractive in landscape. For example, certificates are typically designed in landscape orientation; letters and memos are more often in portrait orientation.

> **To change orientation, complete one of the following steps:**
>
> - Click Orientation on the Layout tab to select either Portrait or Landscape.
> - Click Margins on the Layout tab and click Custom Margins to display the Page Setup dialog box (see Figure 1.27). Select either Portrait or Landscape.
> - Click the File tab, click Print, and then click Portrait Orientation (or Landscape Orientation if the document is in landscape orientation). Select either Portrait Orientation or Landscape Orientation.

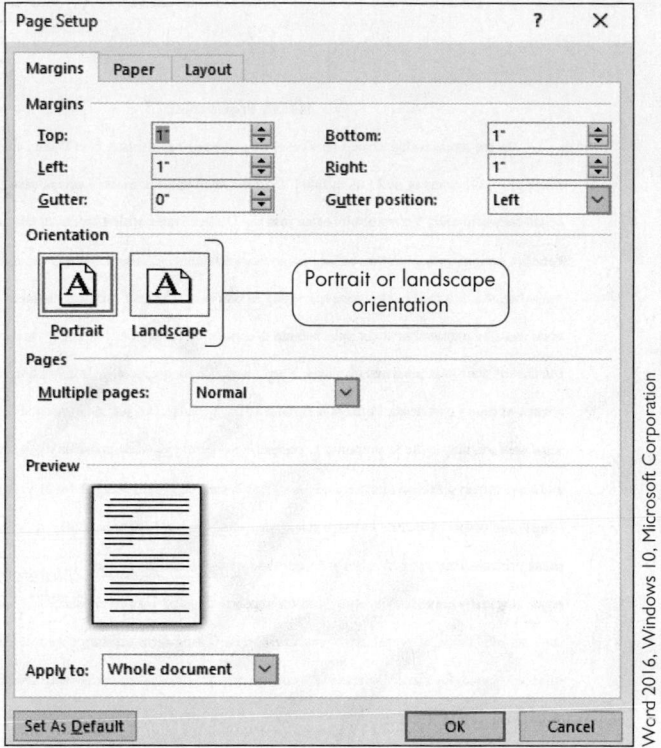

FIGURE 1.27 Changing Page Orientation

Insert a Watermark

STEP 4 ❱❱ A *watermark*, which is text or a graphic that displays behind text on a page, is often used to include a very light, washed-out logo for a company within a document, or to indicate the status of the document. For example, a watermark displaying Draft indicates that the document is not in final form. The document shown in Figure 1.28 contains a watermark. Watermarks do not display on a document that is saved as a webpage, nor will they display in Word's Web Layout view (discussed later in this chapter).

> **To insert a watermark, complete the following steps:**
> 1. Click the Design tab and click Watermark in the Page Background group.
> 2. Select from predesigned styles or click Custom Watermark to create your own.

> **To remove a previously created watermark (for example, when a draft becomes final), complete the following steps:**
> 1. Click the Design tab and click Watermark in the Page Background group.
> 2. Click Remove Watermark.

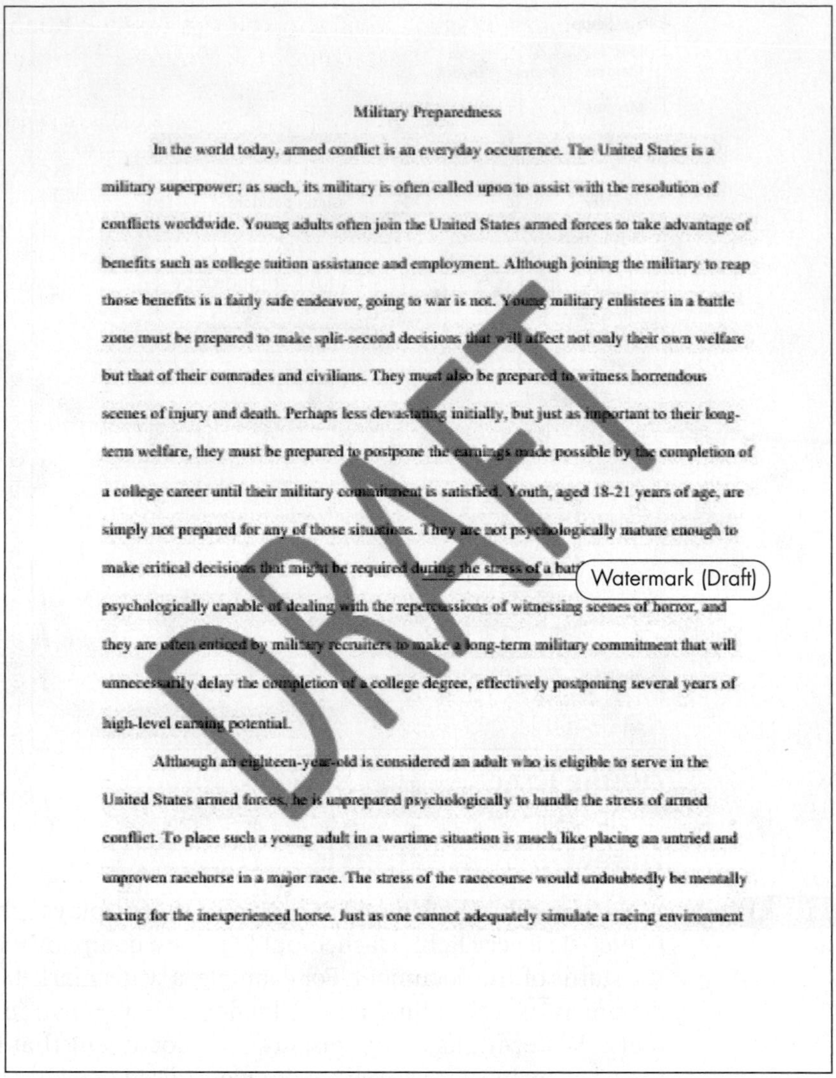

Military Preparedness

In the world today, armed conflict is an everyday occurrence. The United States is a military superpower; as such, its military is often called upon to assist with the resolution of conflicts worldwide. Young adults often join the United States armed forces to take advantage of benefits such as college tuition assistance and employment. Although joining the military to reap those benefits is a fairly safe endeavor, going to war is not. Young military enlistees in a battle zone must be prepared to make split-second decisions that will affect not only their own welfare but that of their comrades and civilians. They must also be prepared to witness horrendous scenes of injury and death. Perhaps less devastating initially, but just as important to their long-term welfare, they must be prepared to postpone the earnings made possible by the completion of a college career until their military commitment is satisfied. Youth, aged 18-21 years of age, are simply not prepared for any of those situations. They are not psychologically mature enough to make critical decisions that might be required during the stress of a bat... psychologically capable of dealing with the repercussions of witnessing scenes of horror, and they are often enticed by military recruiters to make a long-term military commitment that will unnecessarily delay the completion of a college degree, effectively postponing several years of high-level earning potential.

Although an eighteen-year-old is considered an adult who is eligible to serve in the United States armed forces, he is unprepared psychologically to handle the stress of armed conflict. To place such a young adult in a wartime situation is much like placing an untried and unproven racehorse in a major race. The stress of the racecourse would undoubtedly be mentally taxing for the inexperienced horse. Just as one cannot adequately simulate a racing environment

Watermark (Draft)

Word 2016, Windows 10, Microsoft Corporation

FIGURE 1.28 Using a Watermark

TIP: FORMATTING A WATERMARK

In designing a custom watermark, you can select or change a watermark's color, size, font, and text. In addition, you can include a picture as a watermark.

Insert a Symbol

STEP 5 ❱❱ A *symbol* is text, a graphic, or a foreign language character that can be inserted into a document. Some symbols, such as $ and #, are located on the keyboard; however, others are only available from Word's collection of symbols. Symbols such as © and ™ can be an integral part of a document; in fact, those particular symbols are necessary to properly acknowledge a source or product. Because they are typically not located on the keyboard, you need to find them in Word's library of symbols or use a shortcut key combination, if available.

Some symbols serve a very practical purpose. For example, it is unlikely you will want a hyphenated word to be divided between lines in a document. In that case, instead of typing a simple hyphen between words, you can insert a nonbreaking hyphen, which is available as a symbol. Similarly, you can insert a nonbreaking space when you do not want words divided between lines. For example, a person's first name on one line followed by the last name on the next line is not a very attractive placement. Instead, make the space between the words a nonbreaking space by inserting the symbol, so the names are never divided. Mathematical symbols, foreign currency marks, and popular emoticons are also available in Word's symbol library.

A typical Microsoft Office installation includes a wide variety of fonts. Depending upon the font selected (normal text is shown in Figure 1.29), your symbol choices will vary. Fonts such as Wingdings, Webdings, and Symbol contain a wealth of special symbols, many of which are actually pictures.

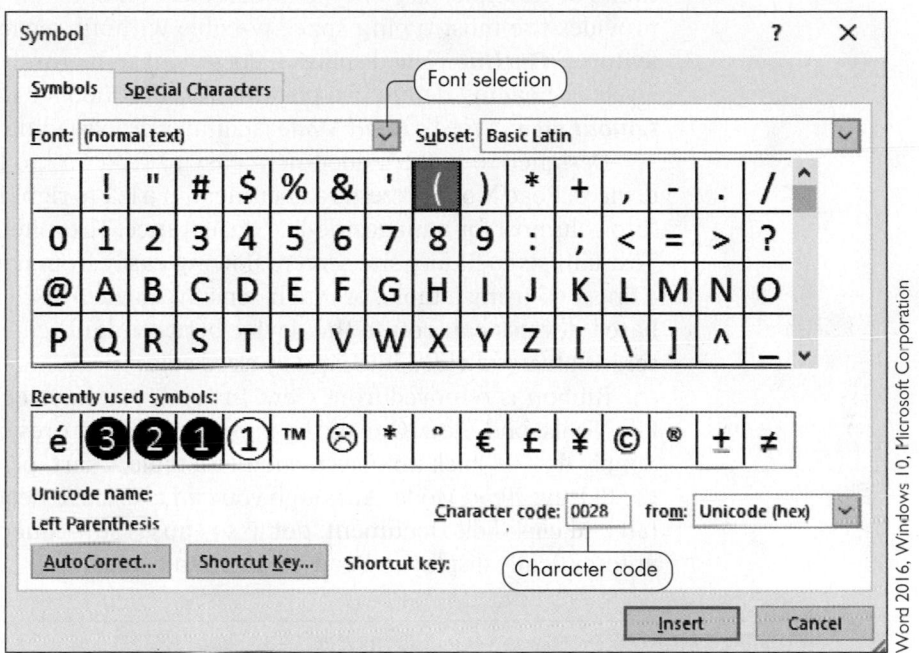

FIGURE 1.29 Selecting a Symbol

To select and insert a symbol, complete the following steps:

1. Click the Insert tab and click Symbol in the Symbols group.
2. Click More Symbols.
3. Select a symbol or click Special Characters and select from the list.
4. Click Insert. Click Close to close the dialog box.

Each symbol is assigned a character code. If you know the character code, you can type the code (refer to Figure 1.29) instead of searching for the symbol itself.

TIP: USING SYMBOL SHORTCUTS
Some symbols, such as © and ™, are included in Word's list of AutoCorrect entries. When you type (c), Word will automatically "correct" it to display ©. Type (tm), and Word shows ™.

Viewing a Document in Different Ways

Developing a document is a creative process. As you create, edit, or review a project, you will want to view the document in various ways. Word provides a view that enables you to see a document as it will print, as well as views that maximize typing space by removing page features. You might review a document in a magazine-type format for ease of reading, or perhaps a hierarchical view of headings and subheadings would help you better understand and proof the structure of a document. The ability to zoom in on text and objects can make a document easier to proofread, while viewing a document page by page helps you manage page flow—perhaps drawing attention to awkward page endings or beginnings. Taking advantage of the various views and view settings in Word, you will find it easy to create attractive, well-worded, and error-free documents.

Select a Document View

When you begin a new document, you see the top, bottom, left, and right margins. The default document view is called **Print Layout view**. You can choose to view a document differently, which is something you might do if you are at a different step in its production. For example, as you type or edit a document, you might prefer **Draft view**, which provides the most typing space possible without regard to margins and special page features. **Outline view** displays a document in hierarchical fashion, clearly delineating levels of heading detail. If a document is destined for the Web, you can view it in **Web Layout view**. Word's **Read Mode** facilitates proofreading and comprehension.

Designed to make a document easy to read and to facilitate access across multiple devices, Read Mode presents a document in a left to right flow, automatically splitting text into columns, for a magazine-like appearance. Text often displays in a two-page format. Text adjusts to fit any size screen, flowing easily from page to page with a simple flick of a finger (if using a tablet or touch-sensitive device) or click of the mouse. Users of touch-based devices can rotate the device between landscape and portrait modes, with the screen always divided into equally sized columns. When in Read Mode (see Figure 1.30), the Ribbon is removed from view. Instead, you have access to only three menu items: File, Tools, and View. One of the most exciting features of Read Mode is object zooming. Simply double-click an object, such as a table, chart, picture, or video, to zoom in. Press Esc to leave Read Mode. Although you can also leave Read Mode when you click the View tab and click Edit Document, doing so causes subsequently opened Word documents to automatically display in Read Mode when opened.

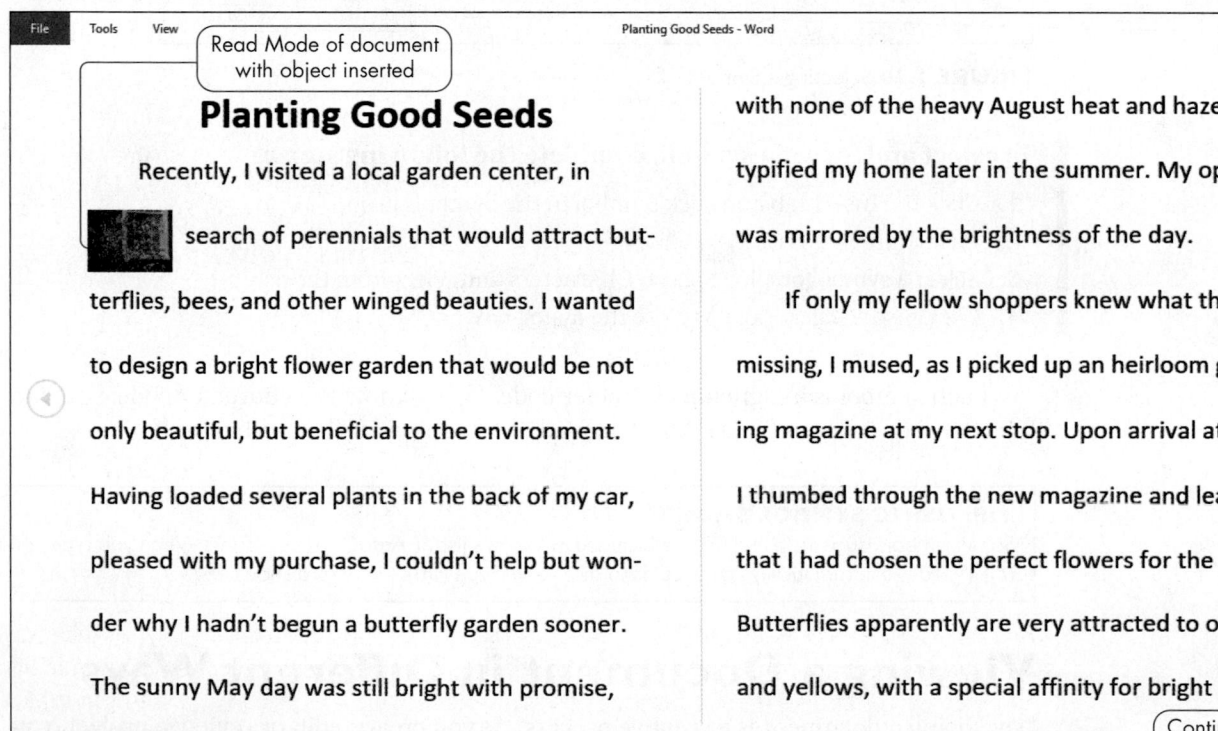

FIGURE 1.30 Word's Read Mode

To change a document's view, click the View tab and select a view from the Views group (see Figure 1.31). Although slightly more limited in choice, the status bar also provides views to choose from (Read Mode, Print Layout, and Web Layout). Word views are summarized in Table 1.1.

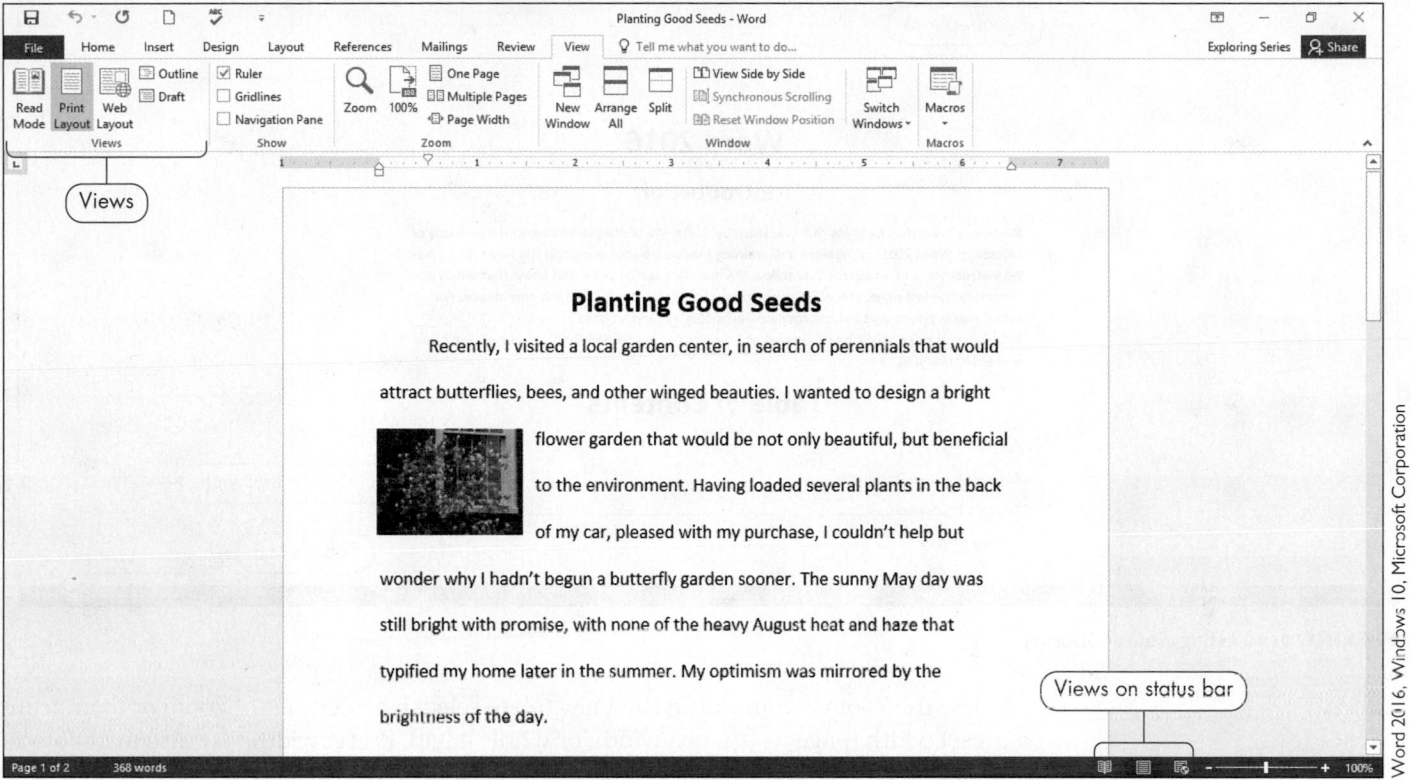

FIGURE 1.31 Word Views

TABLE 1.1	Word Views
View	**Appearance**
Read Mode	Primarily used for reading, with a document shown in pages, much like a magazine. The Ribbon is hidden, with only a limited number of menu selections shown.
Print Layout	Shows margins, headers, footers, graphics, and other page features—much like a document will look when printed.
Web Layout	Shows a document as it would appear on a webpage.
Outline	Shows level of organization and detail. You can collapse or expand detail to show only what is necessary. Often used as a springboard for a table of contents or a PowerPoint summary.
Draft	Provides the most space possible for typing. It does not show margins, headers, or other features, but it does include the Ribbon.

Change the Zoom Setting

Regardless of the view selected, you can use Word's zoom feature to enlarge or reduce the view of text. Unlike zooming in on an object in Read Mode, the zoom feature available on the View tab enables you to enlarge text, not objects or videos. Enlarging text might make a document easier to read and proofread. However, changing the size of text onscreen does not actually change the font size of a document. Zooming in or out is simply a temporary change to the way a document appears onscreen. The View tab includes options that change the onscreen size of a document (see Figure 1.32). You can also enlarge or reduce the view of text by dragging the Zoom slider on the status bar. Click Zoom In and Zoom Out on the status bar to change the view incrementally by 10% for each click.

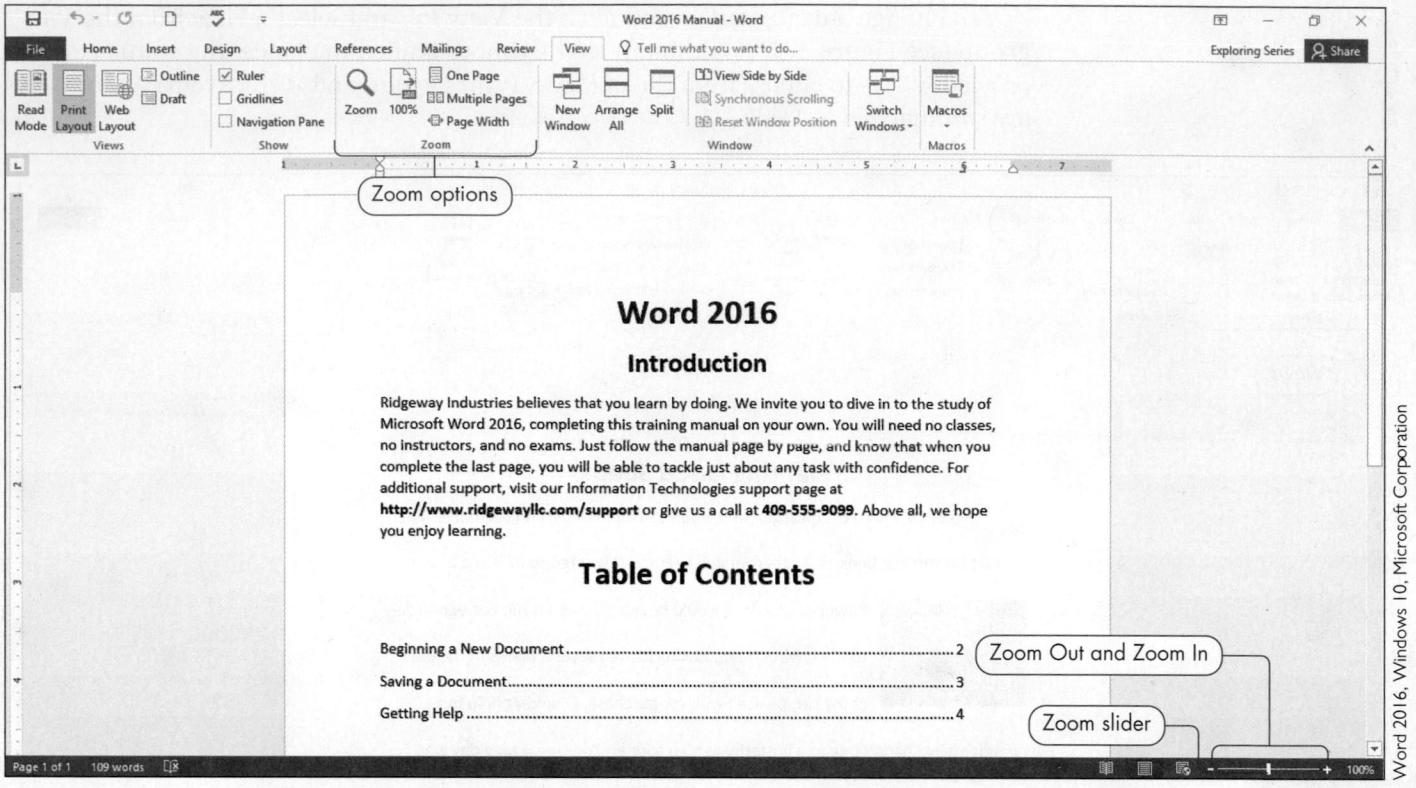

FIGURE 1.32 Using Zoom Options

Use the Zoom command on the View tab to select a percentage of zoom or to indicate a preset width (page width, text width, or whole page). Preset widths are also available as individual options in the Zoom group on the View tab (refer to Figure 1.32).

View a Document and Manage Page Flow

STEP 6 ▶▶ Document lengths can vary greatly. A research paper might span 20 pages, whereas a memo is seldom more than a few pages (most often, only one). Obviously, it is easier to view a memo onscreen than an entire research paper. Even so, Word enables you to get a good feel for the way a document will look when printed or distributed, regardless of document length.

Before printing, it is a good idea to view a document in its entirety. One way to do that is to click the File tab and click Print. A document is shown one page at a time in Print Preview (see Figure 1.33). Click the Next Page or Previous Page navigation arrow to proceed forward or backward in pages. You can also view a document by using options on the View tab (refer to Figure 1.32). Clicking One Page provides a snapshot of the current page, while Multiple Pages shows pages of a multiple-page document side by side (and on separate rows, in the case of more than two pages).

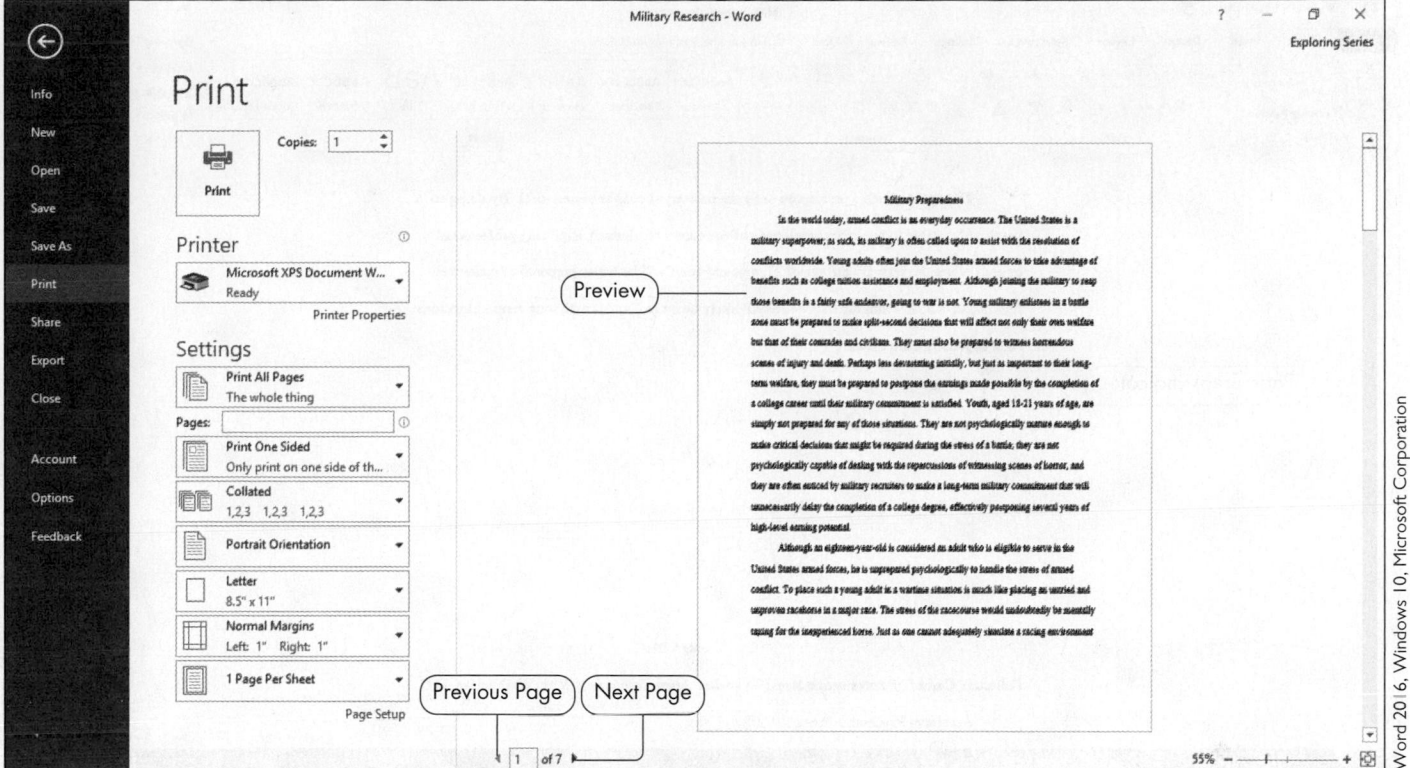

FIGURE 1.33 Previewing a Document

Occasionally, a page will end poorly—perhaps with a heading shown alone at the bottom of a page or with a paragraph split awkwardly between pages. Or perhaps it is necessary to begin a new page after a table of contents, so that other pages follow in the order they should. In those cases, you must manage page flow by forcing a page break where it would not normally occur.

> **To insert a page break, click where the page break is to be placed and complete one of the following:**
>
> - Press Ctrl+Enter.
> - Click the Layout tab, click Breaks, and then select Page.

With nonprinting characters shown, you will see the Page Break designation (see Figure 1.34). To remove a page break, click the Page Break indicator and press Delete.

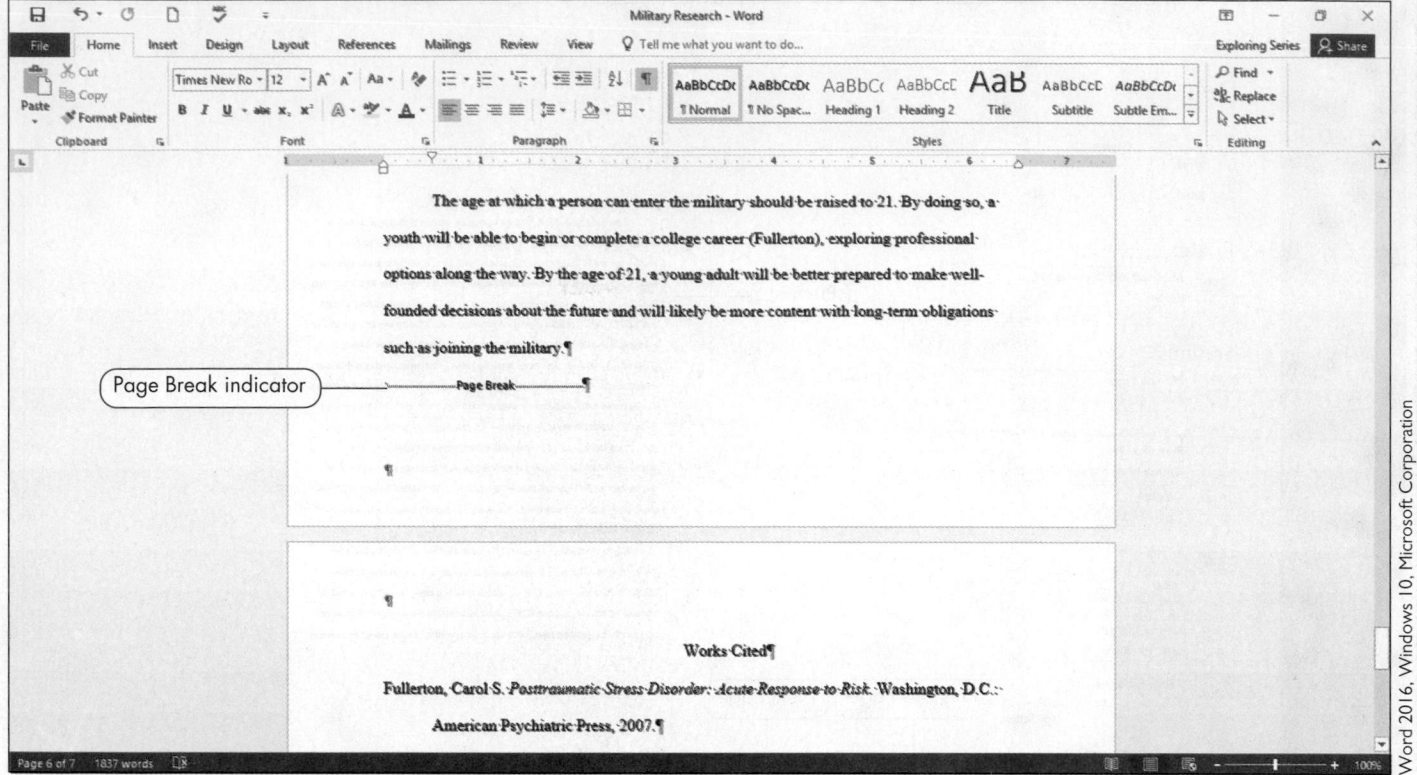

The age at which a person can enter the military should be raised to 21. By doing so, a youth will be able to begin or complete a college career (Fullerton), exploring professional options along the way. By the age of 21, a young adult will be better prepared to make well-founded decisions about the future and will likely be more content with long-term obligations such as joining the military.¶

————————Page Break————————¶

Page Break indicator

¶

¶

Works Cited¶

Fullerton, Carol S. *Posttraumatic Stress Disorder: Acute Response to Risk.* Washington, D.C.: American Psychiatric Press, 2007.¶

Page 6 of 7   1837 words

FIGURE 1.34 Inserting a Page Break

Quick Concepts

5. Some header and footer items, such as author name and file name, serve to identify the document and its origin. Other header and footer fields portray data that changes. Provide at least two examples of fields that contain variable data. When would you want to exclude headers and footers from the first page of a document, and how would you do that? *p. 154*

6. A watermark is often in the form of text, such as the word Draft, which indicates that a document is not in its final form. What other text and/or graphic watermarks might you include in a document? *p. 157*

7. The status bar includes selections that change a document view. Compare and contrast the view selections on the status bar. *p. 161*

8. Before printing a multiple-page research paper, you will check it onscreen to determine how text flows from one page to the next, assuring attractive page endings (no heading shown alone at the end of a page, for example). How would you force a page break before a solo heading that occurs at the bottom of a page? *p. 163*

Hands-On Exercises

Watch the Video for this Hands-On Exercise!

MyITLab®
HOE2 Training

Skills covered: Insert Headers and Footers • Adjust Margins • Change Page Orientation • Insert a Watermark • Insert a Symbol • Select a Document View • View a Document • Change the Zoom Setting • Manage Page Flow

2 Document Organization

You are almost ready to submit a draft of the summer day camp article to your supervisor for approval. After inserting a footer to identify the document as originating with the U.S. Fish and Wildlife Service, you adjust the margins and determine the best page orientation for the document. Next, you insert a watermark to indicate it is a draft document. Finally, you review the document for overall appearance and page flow.

STEP 1 ›› INSERT HEADERS AND FOOTERS

You insert a footer to identify the article as a publication of the U.S. Fish and Wildlife Service. The footer also includes the file name. Refer to Figure 1.35 as you complete Step 1.

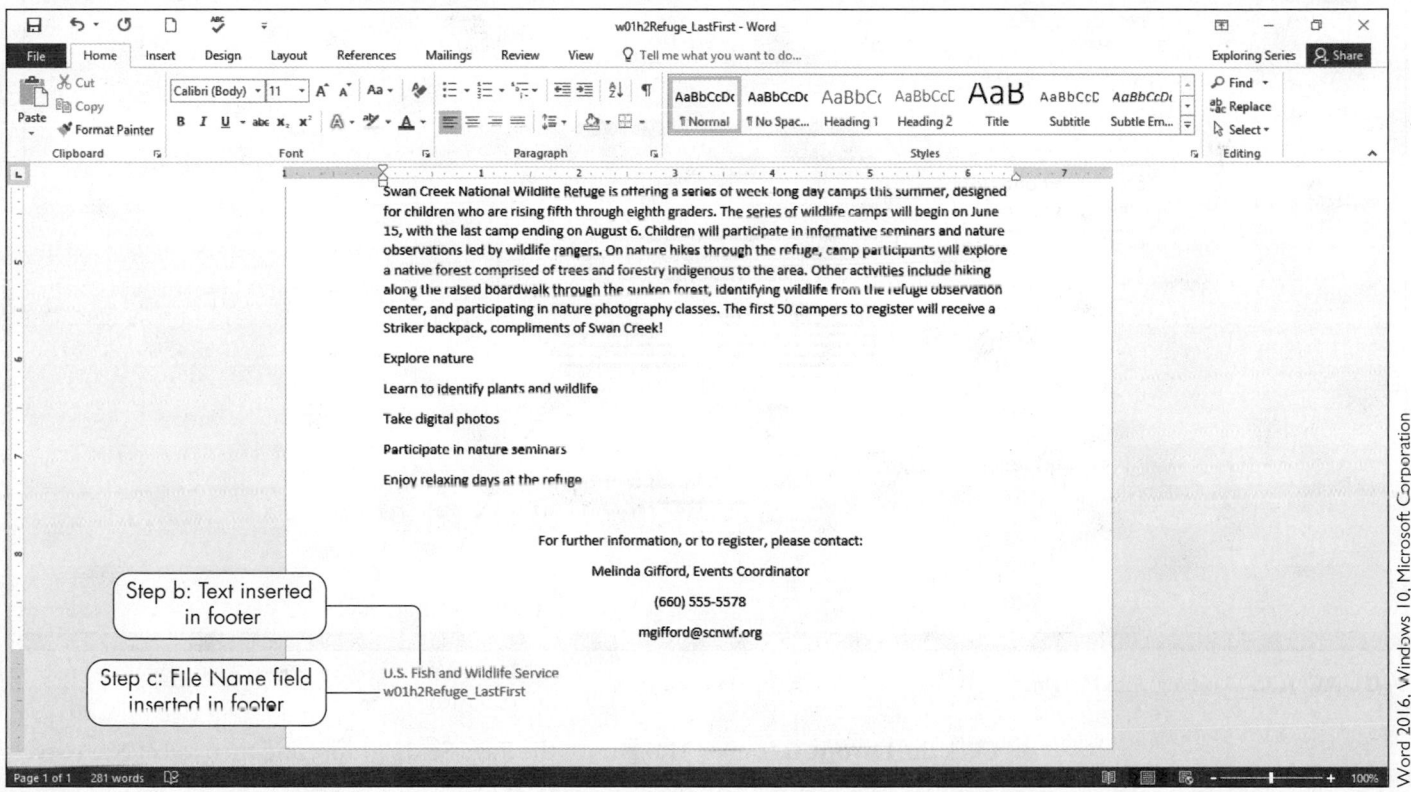

Step b: Text inserted in footer

Step c: File Name field inserted in footer

Word 2016, Windows 10, Microsoft Corporation

FIGURE 1.35 Designing a Footer

a. Open *w01h1Refuge_LastFirst* if you closed it at the end of Hands-On Exercise 1 and save it as **w01h2Refuge_LastFirst**, changing h1 to h2.

> **TROUBLESHOOTING:** If you make any major mistakes in this exercise, you can close the file, open *w01h1Refuge_LastFirst* again, and then start this exercise over.

b. Click the **Insert tab**, click **Footer** in the Header & Footer group, and then select **Edit Footer**. Type **U.S. Fish and Wildlife Service**. Press **Enter**.

> **TROUBLESHOOTING:** If you selected a predefined footer instead of clicking Edit Footer, click Undo on the Quick Access Toolbar and repeat Step b.

c. Click **Document Info** in the Insert group and select **File Name**.

d. Click **Close Header and Footer** in the Close group.

e. Click after the first sentence of the second body paragraph, ending with *through eighth graders.* Be sure to click after the period ending the sentence. Press **Spacebar** and type the following sentence: **The series of wildlife camps will begin on June 15, with the last camp ending on August 6.**

f. Save the document.

STEP 2 ⟫ ADJUST MARGINS

The article fits on one page, but you anticipate adding text. You suspect that with narrower margins, you might be able to add text while making sure the article requires only one page. You experiment with a few margin settings. Refer to Figure 1.36 as you complete Step 2.

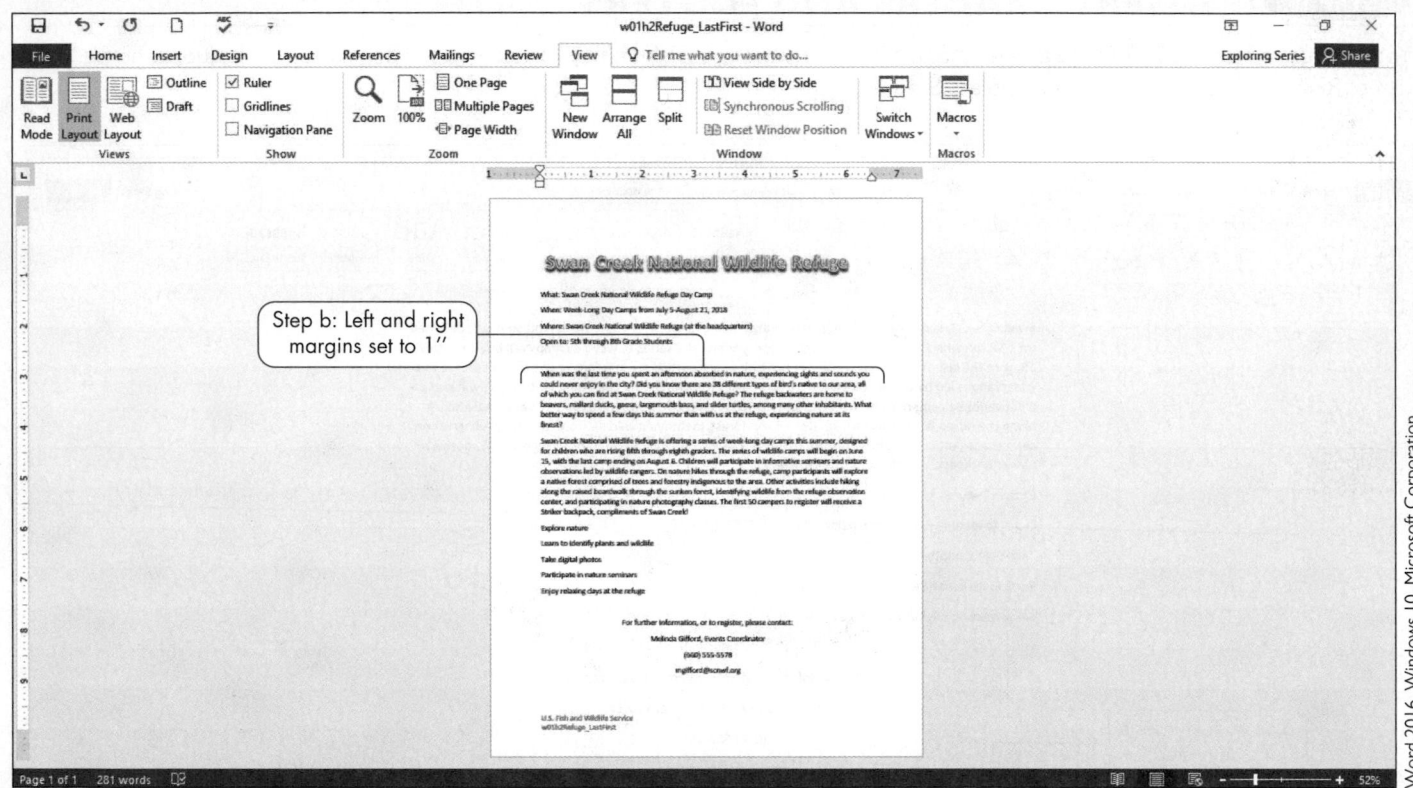

Step b: Left and right margins set to 1″

Word 2016, Windows 10, Microsoft Corporation

FIGURE 1.36 Working with Margins

a. Click the **Layout tab**, click **Margins** in the Page Setup group, and then select **Narrow**.

At a glance, you determine the right and left margins are too narrow, so you adjust them.

b. Click **Margins** and select **Custom Margins**. Adjust the Left and Right margins to **1"** and click **OK**.

c. Click the **View tab** and click **One Page** in the Zoom group.

The document appears to be well positioned on the page, with room for a small amount of additional text, if necessary.

d. Save the document.

Ms. Traynom asked you to prepare an abbreviated version of the article, retaining only the most pertinent information. You prepare and save the shortened version, but you also retain the lengthier version. The shortened article provides a snapshot of the summer activity in an at-a-glance format. Refer to Figure 1.37 as you complete Step 3.

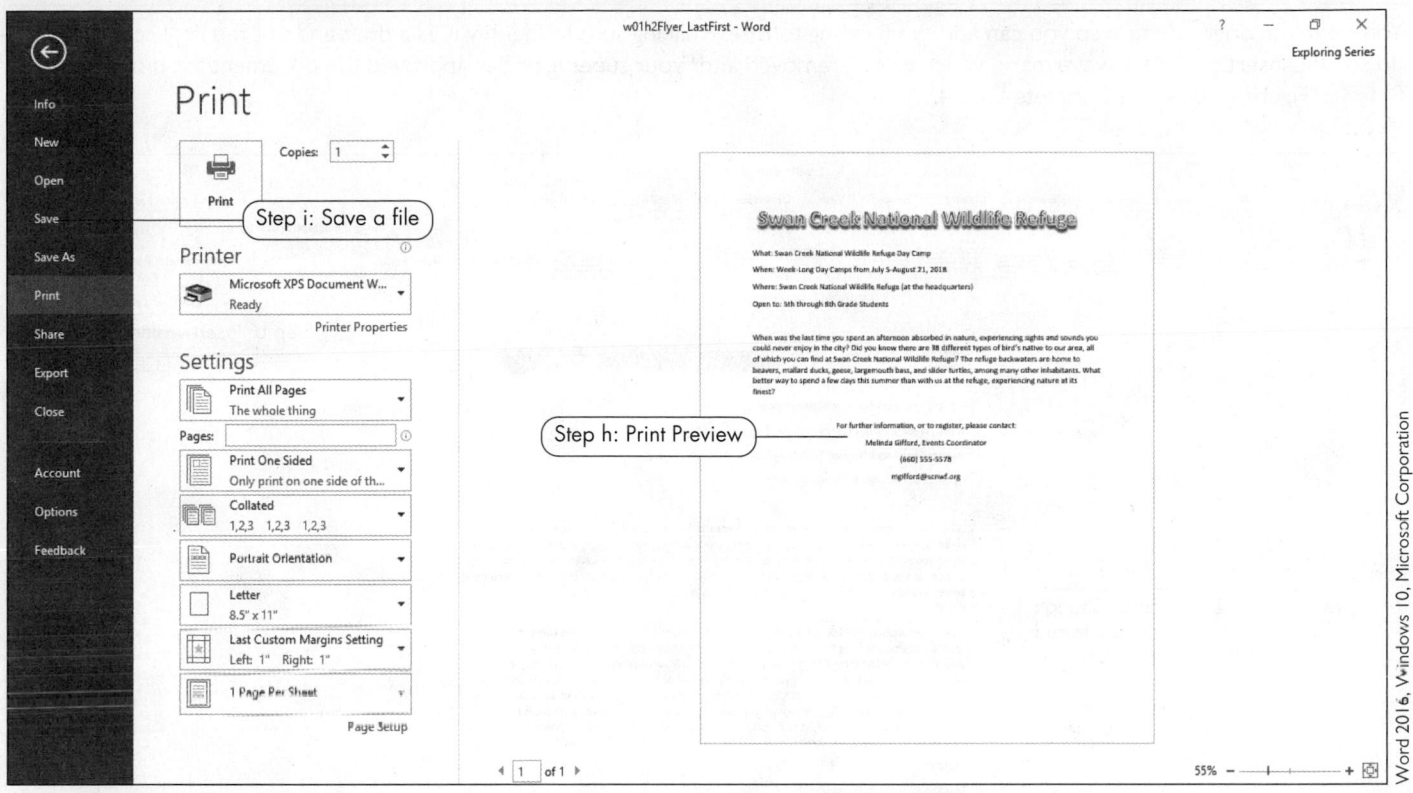

FIGURE 1.37 Previewing a Document

a. Click **100%** in the Zoom group on the View tab.

b. Ensure that nonprinting characters display. If they do not, click **Show/Hide** in the Paragraph group on the Home tab.

c. Triple-click in the second body paragraph, beginning with *Swan Creek National Wildlife Refuge is offering*, to select the entire paragraph and press **Delete** to remove the paragraph.

d. Delete the single-line paragraphs near the end of the document, beginning with *Explore nature* and ending with *Enjoy relaxing days at the refuge.*

e. Click the **File tab** and click **Save As**. Save the file as **w01h2Flyer_LastFirst**.

Because the document is a shortened version of the original, you save it with a different name.

f. Click the **Layout tab** and click **Orientation** in the Page Setup group. Click **Landscape**. Click the **View tab** and click **One Page**. Click **Undo** on the Quick Access Toolbar.

You had suspected the shortened document would be more attractive in landscape orientation. However, since the appearance did not improve, you return to portrait orientation.

g. Select **100%**. Scroll down and double-click in the footer area. Select both footer lines and press **Delete** to remove the footer. Double-click in the document to close the footer.

The flyer does not require a footer so you remove it.

h. Click the **File tab** and click **Print**. Check the document preview to confirm that the footer is removed.

> **i.** Click **Save** in the left pane. Click the **File tab** and click **Close**.
>
> You close the flyer without exiting Word.

STEP 4 ›› **INSERT A WATERMARK**

You open the original article so you can add the finishing touches, making sure to identify it as a draft and not the final copy. To do so, you insert a DRAFT watermark, which can be removed after your supervisor has approved the document for distribution. Refer to Figure 1.38 as you complete Step 4.

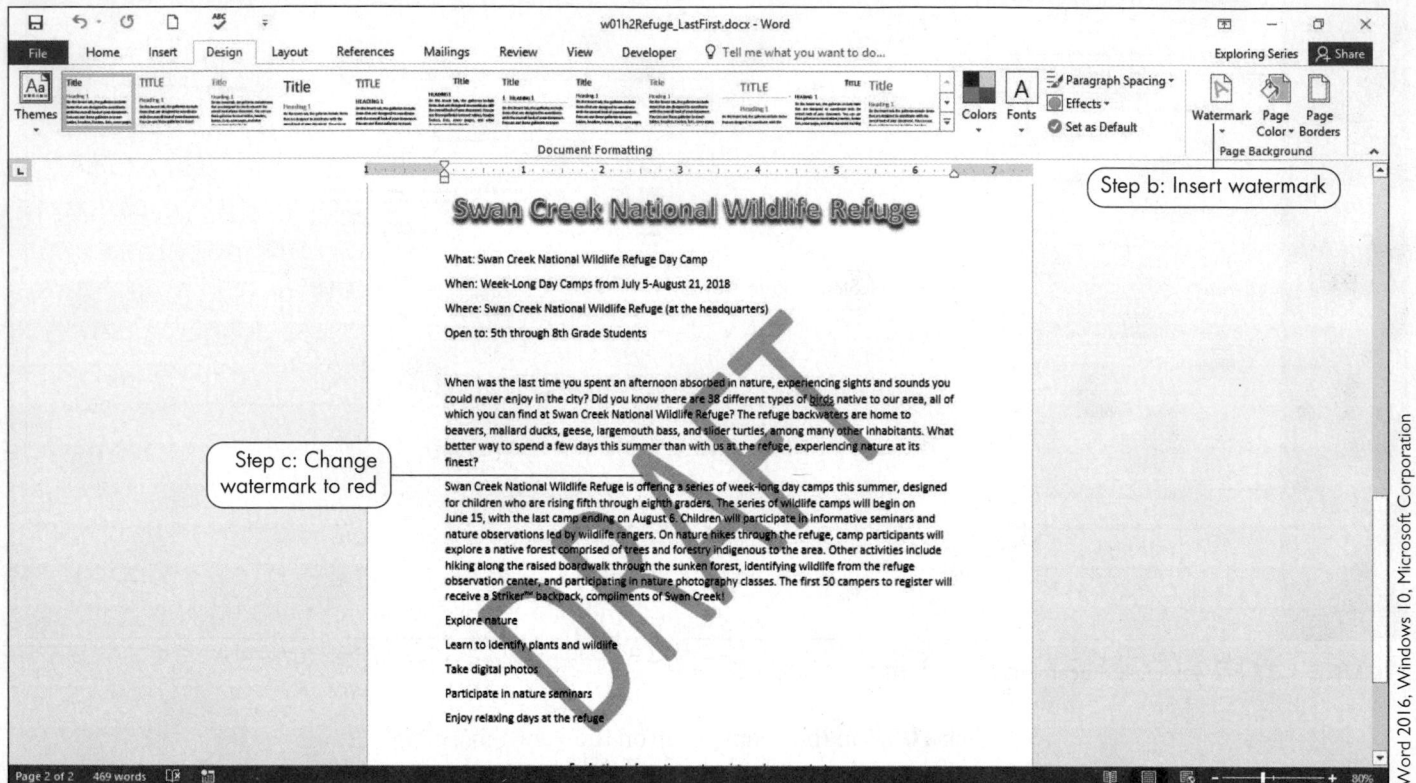

FIGURE 1.38 Inserting a Watermark

> **a.** Click the **File tab** and click **Open**. Select **w01h2Refuge_LastFirst** in the list of Recent Documents.
>
> **b.** Click the **Design** tab and click **Watermark** in the Page Background group. Scroll through the gallery of watermarks and click **DRAFT 1** (under Disclaimers).
>
> **c.** Click **Watermark** again and select **Custom Watermark**. Click the **Color arrow** in the Printed Watermark dialog box and click **Red** (under Standard Colors). Click **OK**.
>
> The watermark is not as visible as you would like, so you change the color.
>
> **d.** Save the document.

The article you are preparing will be placed in numerous public venues, primarily schools. Given the widespread distribution of the document, you must consider any legality, such as appropriate recognition of name brands or proprietary mentions, by inserting a trademark symbol. You also ensure that words flow as they should, with no awkward or unintended breaks between words that should remain together. Refer to Figure 1.39 as you complete Step 5.

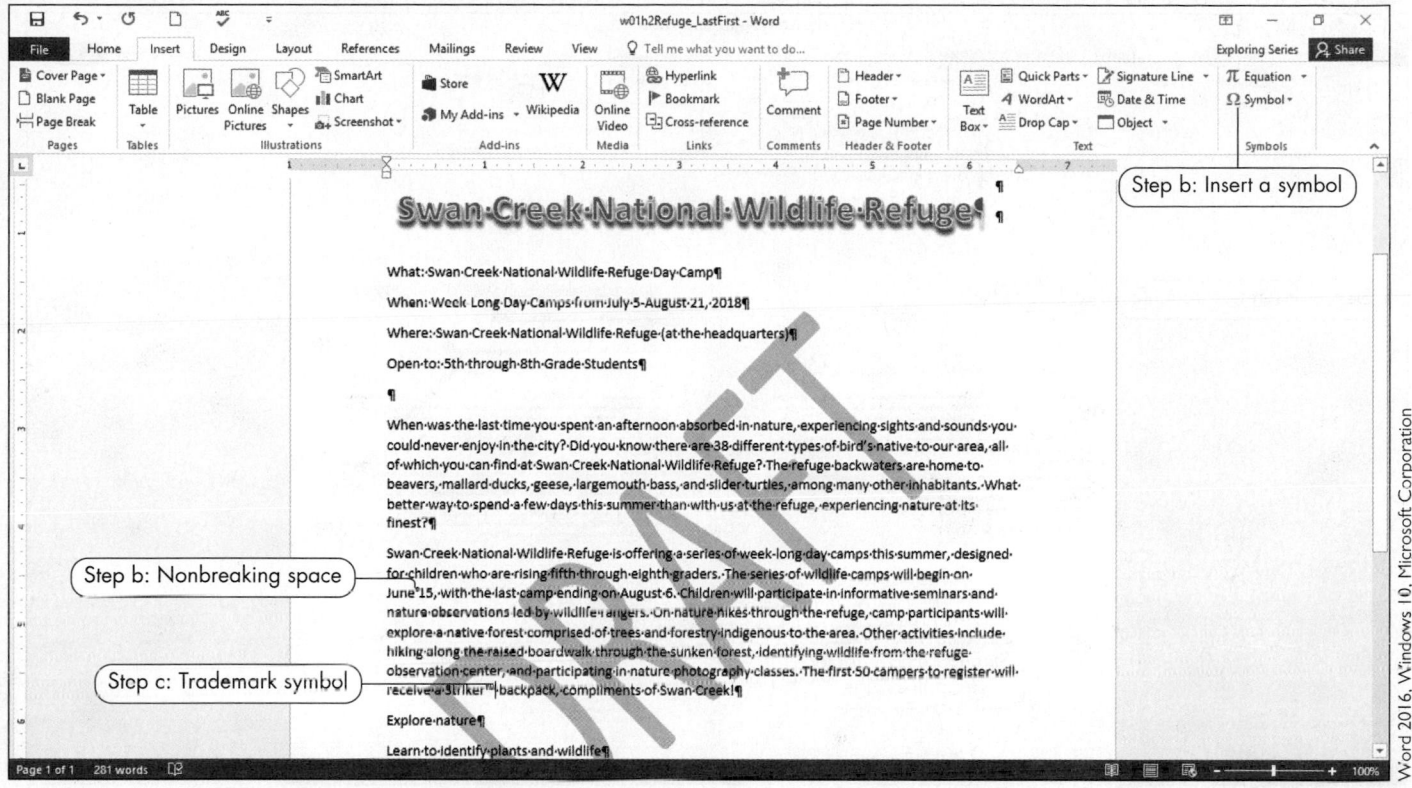

FIGURE 1.39 Working with Symbols

a. Click after the word *June* on the second line in the second body paragraph. Make sure you have placed the insertion point before the space following the word *June*. Press **Delete** to remove the space.

b. Click the **Insert tab** and click **Symbol** in the Symbols group. Click **More Symbols**. Click the **Special Characters tab**. Click **Nonbreaking Space**. Click **Insert** and click **Close**.

Regardless of where the line ends, you want to make sure the phrase June 15 is not separated, with the month on one line and the day on the following line. Therefore, you insert a nonbreaking space.

c. Click after the word *Striker* in the last sentence of the same paragraph. Click **Symbol** in the Symbols group and click **More Symbols**. Click **Special Characters**. Click **Trademark** to insert the Trademark symbol. Click **Insert** and click **Close**.

You use the Trademark symbol to indicate that Striker is a brand name.

d. Save the document.

Ms. Traynom provided you with a cover letter to include with the article. You incorporate the letter text into the article as the first page, remove the footer from the first page, proofread the document, and ensure that both pages are attractively designed. Refer to Figure 1.40 as you complete Step 6.

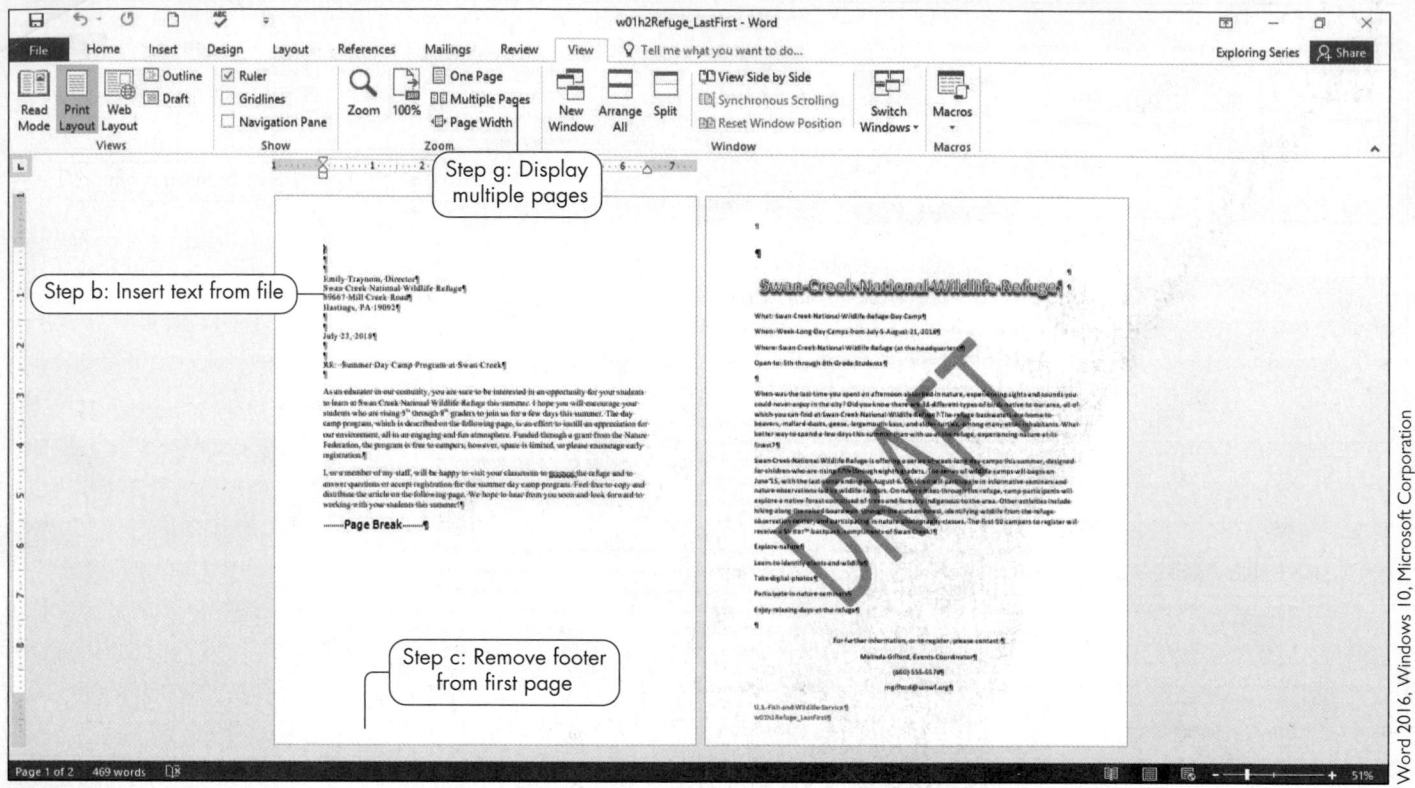

FIGURE 1.40 Modifying and Viewing a Multi-Page Document

a. Press **Ctrl+Home** to position the insertion point at the top of the article. Press **Ctrl+Enter** to insert a blank page at the top. Press **Ctrl+Home** to move to the top of the new page.

Note that both the watermark and the footer display on the new page. That is because those features are designed to appear by default on all pages of a document.

b. Click the **Insert tab** and click the **Object arrow** in the Text group. Click **Text from File**. Navigate to *w01h2Letter* in your student data files and double-click the file name.

c. Double-click in the footer area of the first page. Click **Different First Page** in the Options group of the Header & Footer Tools Design tab.

You indicate that the watermark and footer are not to appear on the first page, but will remain on all others.

d. Click **Close Header and Footer** in the Close group.

e. Press **Ctrl+Home**. Click the **View tab** and click **Zoom** in the Zoom group. Click in the **Percent box** and change the Zoom to **125%**. Click **OK**.

f. Scroll through the document, proofreading for spelling and grammatical errors. Right-click any underlined error and either correct or ignore it. Manually correct any errors that Word has not flagged. Press **Ctrl+Home**.

g. Click **Multiple Pages** in the Zoom group.

h. Click the **File tab** and click **Print**. Click **Next Page** (the arrow that follows 1 of 2 at the bottom of the screen) to view the article. Click **Previous Page** to return to the letter.

i. Click **Back** ⬅ to return to the document. Click **100%** in the Zoom group. Ensure the insertion point is at the top of the document, and press **Enter** three times to move the text down the page.

The letter appears to be too high on the page, so you move the text down a bit.

j. Click the **File tab** and click **Print**.

The first page is better situated on the page, with additional space at the top.

k. Save the document. Keep the document open if you plan to continue with the next Hands-On Exercise. If not, close the document and exit Word.

Document Settings and Properties

After you organize your document and make all the formatting changes you desire, you save the document in its final form and prepare it for use by others. You can take advantage of features in Word that enable you to manipulate the file in a variety of ways, such as identifying features that are not compatible with older versions of Word, saving in a format that is compatible with older versions, and including information about the file that does not display in the document. For example, you can include an author name, subject, and even keywords—all information that does not display in the content of the document but further identifies the file, and can be used as a basis on which to search for or categorize the document later. Because you are well aware of the importance of saving files, and even making backup copies of those files, you will explore backup options.

In this section, you will explore ways to prepare a document for distribution, including saving in a format compatible with earlier versions of Word, converting a file created in an earlier version to Office 2016, checking for sensitive information included in a file, making backup copies of important documents, and working with print options. In addition, you will learn to customize and print document properties.

Modifying Document Properties

Occasionally, you might want to include information to identify a document, such as author, document purpose, intended audience, or general comments. Those data elements, or ***document properties***, are saved with the document, but do not appear in the document as it displays onscreen or is printed. You can easily modify document properties to include identifying or descriptive information. Using a document property as a search keyword, or tag, you can even search for a particular file. For example, suppose you apply a keyword of *CIS 225* to all documents you create that are associated with that particular college class. Later, you can use that keyword as a search term, locating all associated documents.

Customize Document Properties

STEP 1 ▶▶ For statistical information related to the current document, click the File tab. Data such as file size, number of pages, and total words are presented in the right pane on the Info window (see Figure 1.41). You can modify some document information in this view, such as adding a title, tags, or comments, but for more possibilities, click Properties and click Advanced Properties (see Figure 1.42). You can then navigate through the Advanced Properties dialog box, adding or modifying properties. When you save the document, Word saves this information with the document.

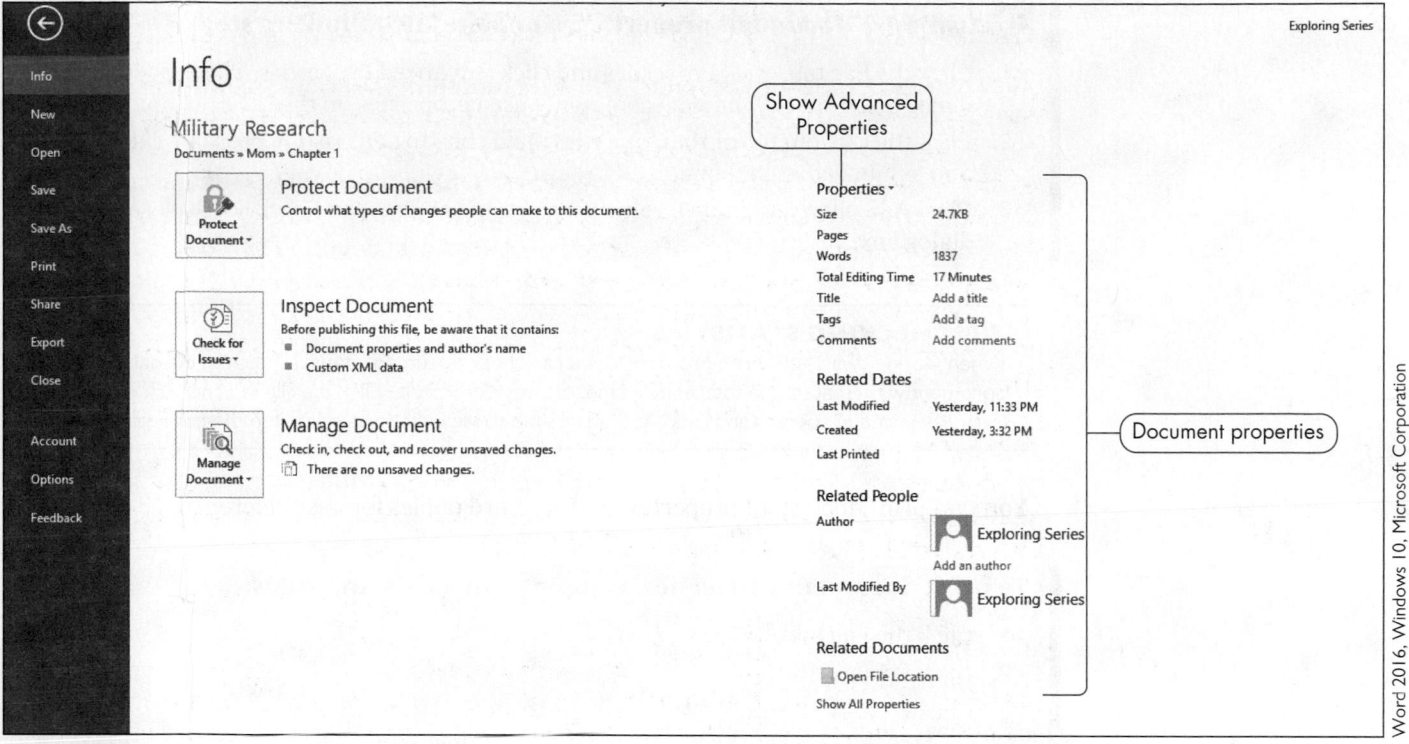

FIGURE 1.41 Displaying Document Properties

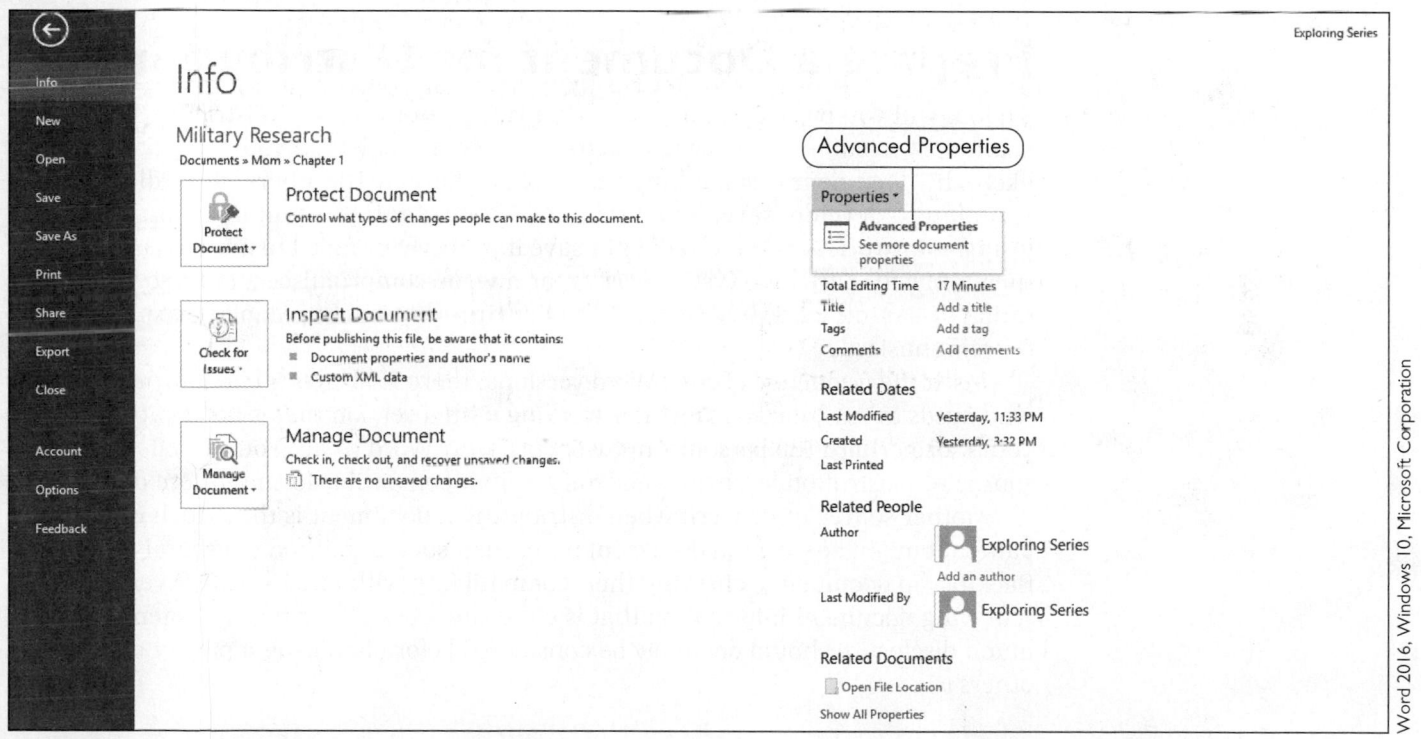

FIGURE 1.42 Selecting Advanced Properties

You may want to add or change document properties by including specific items such as a subject, department, or a particular project name. For example, you could add a *Date completed* property and specify an exact date for reference. This date would reflect the completion date, not the date the file was last saved. You also might create a field to track company information such as warehouse location or product numbers.

To customize document properties, complete the following steps:

1. Click the File tab. Click Properties and click Advanced Properties. The Properties dialog box displays, showing commonly used properties on the General tab.
2. Click the Custom tab of the Properties dialog box to add custom property categories and assign values to them.
3. Click Add, after assigning a value to a custom category, and click OK to close the dialog box.

TIP: CHECKING STATISTICS

When working with Advanced Properties, you can check document statistics, such as the date the document was created, the total editing time, or the word count. Click the File tab and click Properties. Click Advanced Properties and click the Statistics tab to view statistics related to the current document.

You can print document properties to store hard copies for easy reference.

To print document properties, complete the following steps:

1. Click the File tab.
2. Click Print.
3. Click Print All Pages.
4. Click Document Info.
5. Click Print.

Prepare a Document for Distribution

Seldom will you prepare a document that you do not intend to distribute. Whether it is a report to submit to your instructor or a memo on which you collaborated, most likely the document is something that will be shared with others. Regardless of how you plan to develop, save, and distribute a document, you will not want to chance losing your work because you did not save it properly or failed to make a backup copy. Inevitably, files are lost, systems crash, or a virus compromises a disk. So the importance of saving work frequently and ensuring that backup copies exist cannot be overemphasized.

With the frequency of new Word versions, there is always a chance that someone who needs to read your document is working with a version that is not compatible with yours, or perhaps the person is not working with Word at all. You can eliminate that source of frustration by saving a document in a compatible format before distributing it. Another source of concern when distributing a document is the hidden or personal data that might be stored in document properties, such as author, or general comments. Backing up documents, ensuring their compatibility with other software versions, and removing document information that is either unnecessary or has the potential for too much disclosure should definitely be considered before finalizing a project or allowing others to see it.

Ensure Document Compatibility

STEP 2 ›› If you plan to distribute a Word document to others, you should ensure that they will be able to open the document regardless of which version of Word they are using. Users of Word 2007-2013 will be able to open a document saved in Word 2016 format, but some Word 2016 features might be disabled. In that case, you can check a document for compatibility, to determine which features, if any, will be unavailable in an earlier version. If the recipient of a document you are distributing is using Word 2003 or earlier, you can save the document in a Word format that the earlier version can open. You might also consider saving a file in Rich Text Format (RTF) or Portable Document Format (PDF), which adds even more flexibility, as such a file can be opened by other software in addition to Word. Be aware, however, that doing so might compromise the document somewhat because other software versions might not be able to accommodate all of the current Word version's special features.

To save a Word 2016 document as another document type, complete the following steps:

1. Click the File tab and click Save As.
2. Navigate to the location to which you want to save the document.
3. Provide a file name and click the Save as type arrow (see Figure 1.43).
4. Select another file format and click Save.

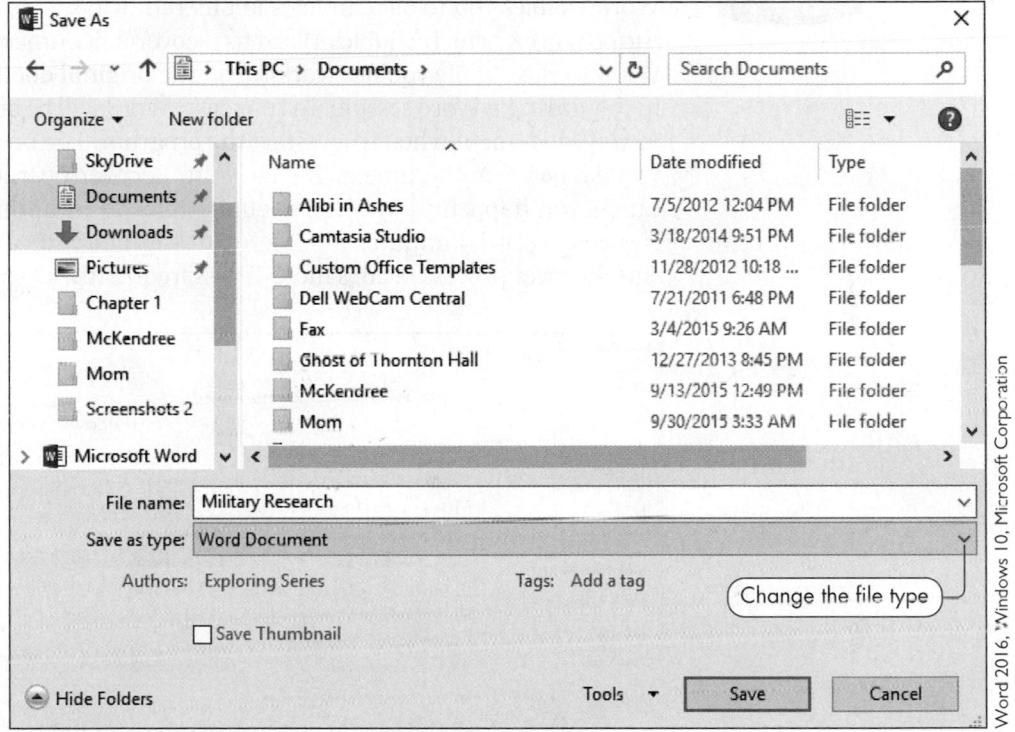

FIGURE 1.43 Saving as a Different File Type

Occasionally, you might receive a Word document that was created in an earlier Word version. In that case, the words *Compatibility Mode* are included in the title bar, advising you that some of Word 2016's features will not be available or viewable in the document. While in Compatibility Mode, you might not be able to use new and enhanced features of the most current Word version; by keeping the file in Compatibility Mode, you ensure that people with earlier Word versions will still have full editing capability when they receive the document. Word simplifies the process of converting a Word document to the newest version.

To convert a document to Word 2016, complete the following steps:

1. Click the File tab.
2. Click Convert (beside Compatibility Mode). The Convert option will not be displayed if the file is currently in Office 2016 format.
3. Click OK.

Before distributing a document, you can check it for compatibility, ensuring that it can be read in its entirety by users of earlier Word versions.

> **To check a document for compatibility, complete the following steps:**
>
> 1. Click the File tab.
> 2. Click Check for Issues (beside Inspect Document).
> 3. Click Check Compatibility.
> 4. Click *Select versions to show* and then select one or more versions of Word to check (or simply leave them all selected). Click *Select versions to show* again to close the list.
> 5. Read the summary of features that are incompatible, and click OK.

Understand Backup Options

STEP 3 ▶▶ Word enables you to back up files in different ways. One option is to use a feature called ***AutoRecover***, which enables Word to recover a document if an application error causes Word to close while you are working on the original document or if your computer loses power during a Word session. In that case, Word will be able to recover a previous version of your document when you restart the program. The only work you will lose is anything you did between the time of the last AutoRecover operation and the time of the crash, unless you happen to save the document in the meantime. By default, file information is saved every 10 minutes (see Figure 1.44), but you can adjust the setting so that the AutoRecover process occurs more or less frequently.

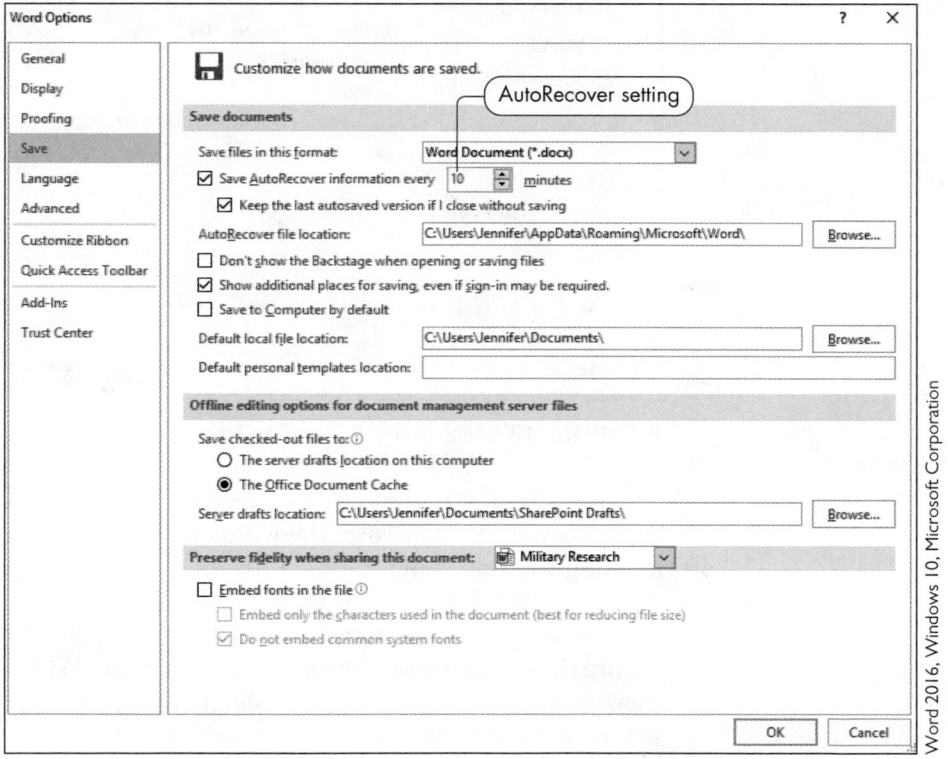

FIGURE 1.44 The AutoRecover Feature

You can also configure Word to create a backup copy each time a document is saved. Although the setting to always create a backup copy is not enabled by default, you can enable it from Word Options in the Advanced category. Even so, creating frequent backup copies can slow your system and may not be altogether necessary, given the excellent File History facility provided by Windows 10. As an additional safety net, though, you can certainly enable Word to create backup copies of documents.

To enable an automatic backup, complete the following steps:

1. Click the File tab.
2. Click Options.
3. Click Advanced.
4. Scroll to the Save group and select *Always create backup copy*. Click OK.

Run the Document Inspector

STEP 4 ❱❱ Before you send or give a document to another person, you should run the ***Document Inspector*** to reveal any hidden or personal data in the file. For privacy or security reasons, you might want to remove certain items contained in the document such as author name, comments made by one or more people who have access to the document, or document server locations. Word's Document Inspector will check for and enable you to remove various types of identifying information, including:

- Comments, revisions, versions, and annotations
- Document properties and personal information
- Custom XML data
- Headers, footers, and watermarks
- Invisible content
- Hidden text

Because some information removed by the Document Inspector cannot be recovered with the Undo command, you should save a copy of your original document, using a different name, prior to inspecting the document.

To inspect a document, complete the following steps:

1. Click the File tab.
2. Click Check for Issues.
3. Click Inspect Document.
4. Respond if a dialog box appears, by clicking Yes if you have not saved the file and want to do so (or clicking No if you have already saved the file).
5. Confirm the types of content you want to check in the Document Inspector dialog box (see Figure 1.45). Deselect any categories you do not want to check.
6. Click Inspect to begin the process. When the check is complete, Word lists the results and enables you to choose whether to remove the content from the document. For example, if you are distributing a document to others, you might want to remove all document properties and personal information. In that case, you can instruct the Document Inspector to remove such content.

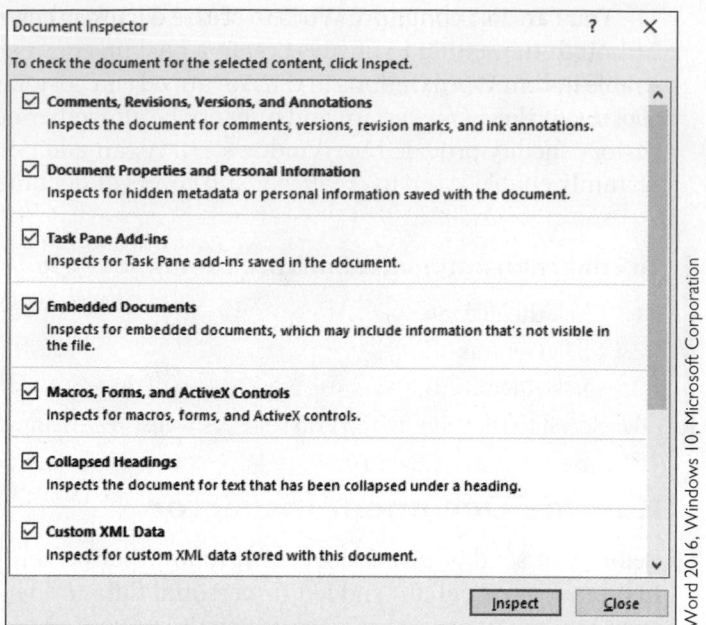

FIGURE 1.45 Inspecting a Document

Select Print Options

Although by default, Word prints one copy of an entire document, you might find it necessary to print multiple copies, or only a few pages. Those settings and others are available when you click the File tab and click Print. The Print settings shown in Figure 1.46 enable you to select the number of copies, the pages or range of pages to print, the printer to use, whether to collate pages, whether to print on only one side of the paper, and how many pages to print per sheet. In addition, you can adjust page orientation, paper size, and even customize a document's margins—all by paying attention to print options. Please note that the wording of some print options will vary, depending on whether you have previously selected the option and indicated a custom setting.

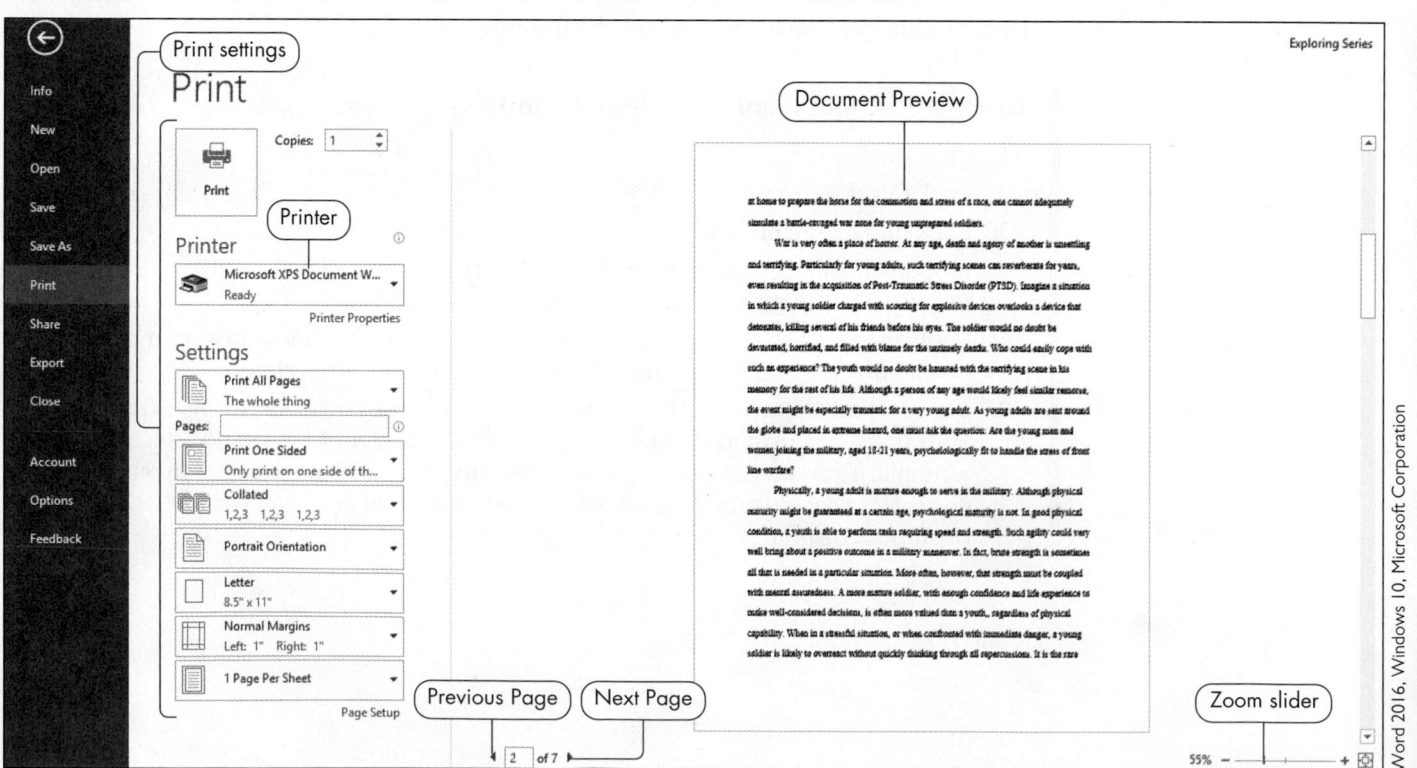

FIGURE 1.46 Word Print Settings

Print options display to the left of the document preview (refer to Figure 1.46). You can click the Next Page or Previous Page navigation arrow to move among pages in the document preview. You can also drag the Zoom slider to enlarge or reduce the size of the document preview.

Quick Concepts

9. A coworker who uses Office 2007 has sent you a document for review. When you open the document, the words *[Compatibility Mode]* display in the title bar after the file name. Is there any reason you might want to remove the document from Compatibility Mode? And if so, how would you convert the document to the format used by Word 2016? *p. 175*

10. Describe the process of using Word options to ensure that backup copies are automatically created. *p. 176*

11. Before distributing a document, how would you remove any personally identifying information, such as author and comments? *p. 177*

12. Before printing pages 3 through 5 of the current document, you want to preview the document and then print only those pages. In a separate print procedure, you also want to print document properties that are associated with the current document. What steps would you follow to preview and print those pages? *p. 178*

Hands-On Exercises

 Watch the Video for this Hands-On Exercise!

 MyITLab® HOE3 Training

Skills covered: Customize Document Properties • Print Document Properties • Ensure Document Compatibility • Understand Backup Options • Run the Document Inspector • Select Print Options

3 Document Settings and Properties

As the office assistant for Swan Creek National Wildlife Refuge, you are responsible for the security, management, and backup of the organization's documents. The article promoting the summer day camps is ready for final approval. Before that happens, however, you will check it one last time, making sure it is saved in a format that others can read. You will also ensure that you have sufficient backup copies. You also want to include appropriate document properties for additional identification, and you will consider print options. Privacy and security are to be considered as well, so you check for identifiers that should be removed before distributing the document.

STEP 1 ›› CUSTOMIZE AND PRINT DOCUMENT PROPERTIES

You assign document properties to the summer camp document to identify its author and purpose. You also create an additional property to record a project identifier. Finally, you prepare to print document properties. Refer to Figure 1.47 as you complete Step 1.

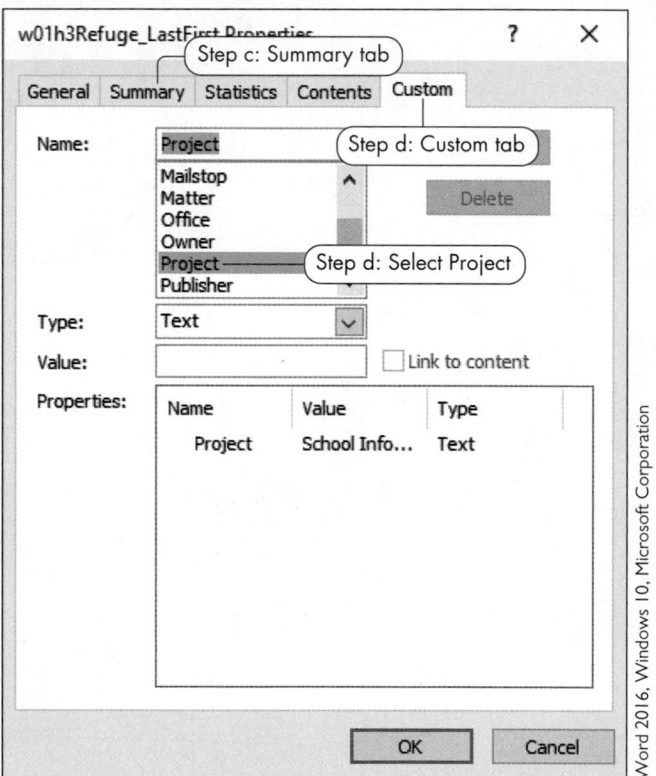

FIGURE 1.47 Customizing Document Properties

a. Open *w01h2Refuge_LastFirst* if you closed it at the end of Hands-On Exercise 2 and save it as **w01h3Refuge_LastFirst**, changing h2 to h3.

b. Click the **File tab**, click **Properties** in the right pane, and then click **Advanced Properties**.

The Properties dialog box displays.

c. Click the **Summary tab**. Ensure that the Author box contains your name. Click one time in the **Comments box** and type **Summer Camp Information**.

d. Create a custom property by completing the following steps:

- Click the **Custom tab** and scroll to select **Project** in the **Name list**.
- Type **School Information** in the **Value box**, as shown in Figure 1.47, and click **Add**.
- Click **OK** to close the dialog box.

You want to catalog the documents you create for Swan Creek National Wildlife Refuge, and one way to do that is to assign a project identifier using the custom properties that are stored with each document. Because you set up a custom field, you can later perform searches and find all documents in that Project category.

e. Click **Print**, click **Print All Pages**, and then click **Document Info** (under the Document Info heading). If your computer is in communication with, or connected to, a printer, click **Print**. Otherwise, continue without printing.

STEP 2 »» ENSURE DOCUMENT COMPATIBILITY

You know Ms. Traynom is anxious to review a copy of this document; however, she has not yet upgraded to Office 2016. Instead, her office computer has Office 2007 installed. To make sure she can open and read the document, you check the document for compatibility with earlier Word versions. Refer to Figure 1.48 as you complete Step 2.

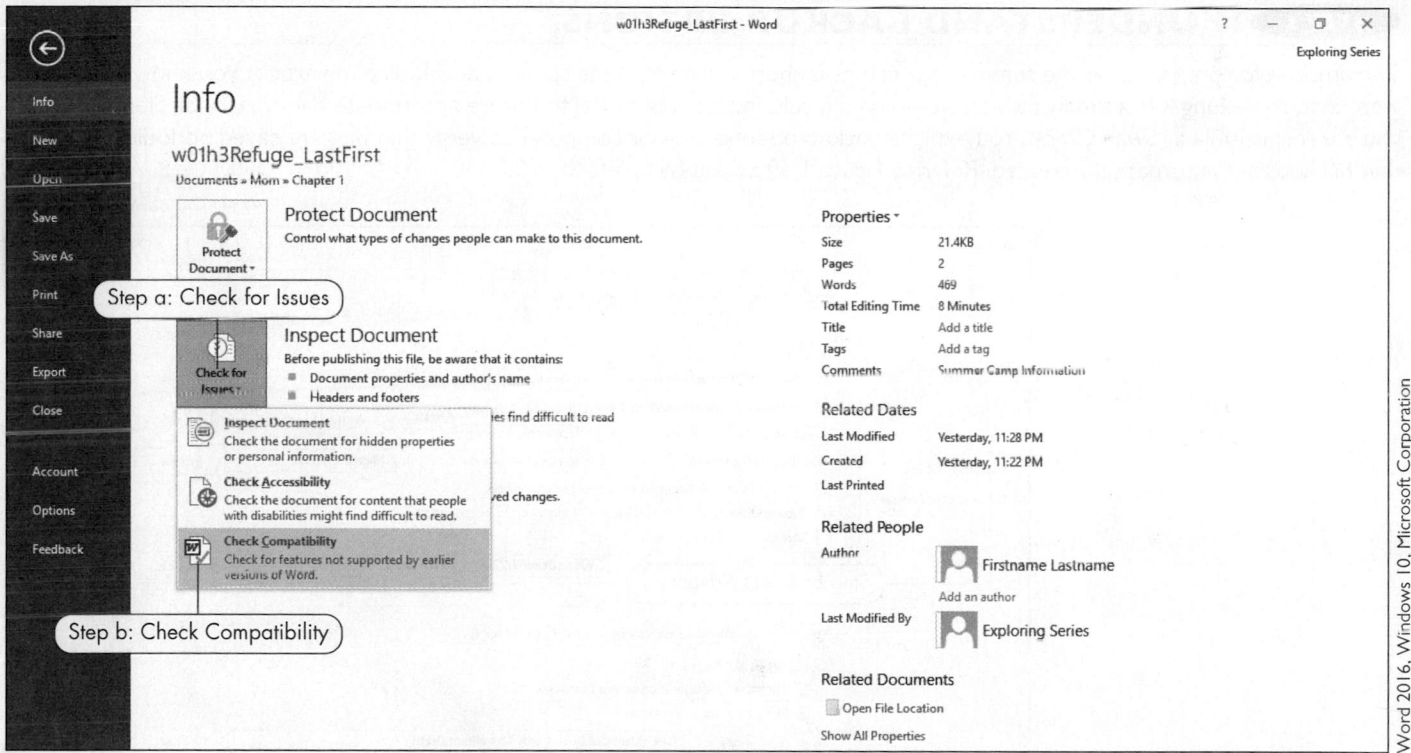

FIGURE 1.48 Check for Compatibility

a. Click the **File tab**, if necessary. Ensure that the Info window is displayed and click **Check for Issues** (beside Inspect Document).

b. Click **Check Compatibility**. Click **Select versions to show** and deselect **Word 97-2003** to ensure only Word 2007 and Word 2010 are selected.

Note that some formatting features are not supported and will not be available in the version you are preparing for Ms. Traynom.

c. Click **OK**. Save the document.

Because the compatibility issues are few and are restricted to what appear to be minor text effects, you feel confident that Ms. Traynom will be able to open the document in Word 2007.

d. Click the **File tab** and click **Close**.

The personnel director has prepared a draft of a memo introducing a new employee. He asked you to proof the document and prepare it for printing. However, he created and saved the memo using Word 2007.

e. Open *w01h3NewEmployee* from the student data files.

The title bar displays [Compatibility Mode] following the file name *w01h3NewEmployee*, indicating that it is not a file saved with a recent version of Word.

f. Click the **File tab** and click **Convert** (beside Compatibility Mode). A message box displays explaining the consequences of upgrading the document. Click **OK**.

The file is converted to the newest Word format. The Compatibility Mode designation is removed from the title bar.

g. Save the document as **w01h3NewEmployee_LastFirst**.

STEP 3 ›› UNDERSTAND BACKUP OPTIONS

The timeline for preparing for the summer day camps is short. Given the time spent in developing the article, you know that if it were lost, recreating it in a timely fashion would be difficult. In fact, it is critical to ensure appropriate backups for all files for which you are responsible at Swan Creek. You explore backup options on your computer to verify that files are saved periodically and that backups are automatically created. Refer to Figure 1.49 as you complete Step 3.

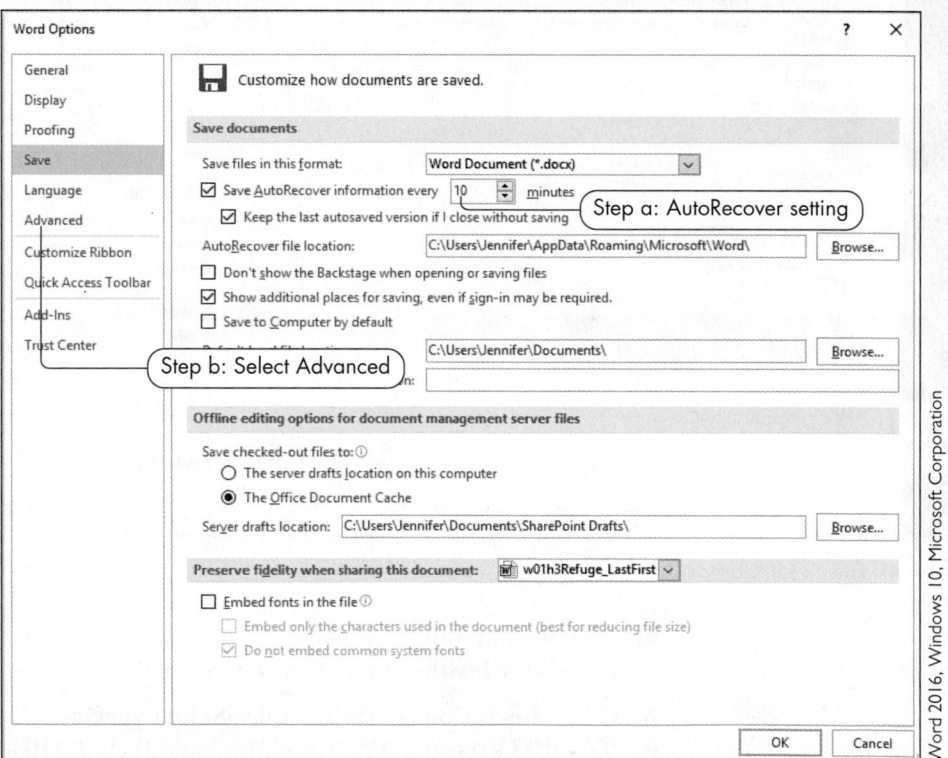

FIGURE 1.49 Exploring Backup and Save Options

a. Click the **File tab** and click **Options**. Click **Save** in the left pane of the Word Options dialog box. If *Save AutoRecover information every* is checked, note the number of minutes between saves.

b. Click **Advanced** in the left pane. Scroll to the Save area and ensure that *Always create backup copy* is not selected.

You do not select the setting at this time because you are likely to be in a school computer lab.

c. Click **Cancel**. Close the document.

STEP 4 ⟫ RUN THE DOCUMENT INSPECTOR AND SELECT PRINT OPTIONS

Before distributing the article, you run the Document Inspector to identify any information that should first be removed. You also prepare to print the document. Refer to Figure 1.50 as you complete Step 4.

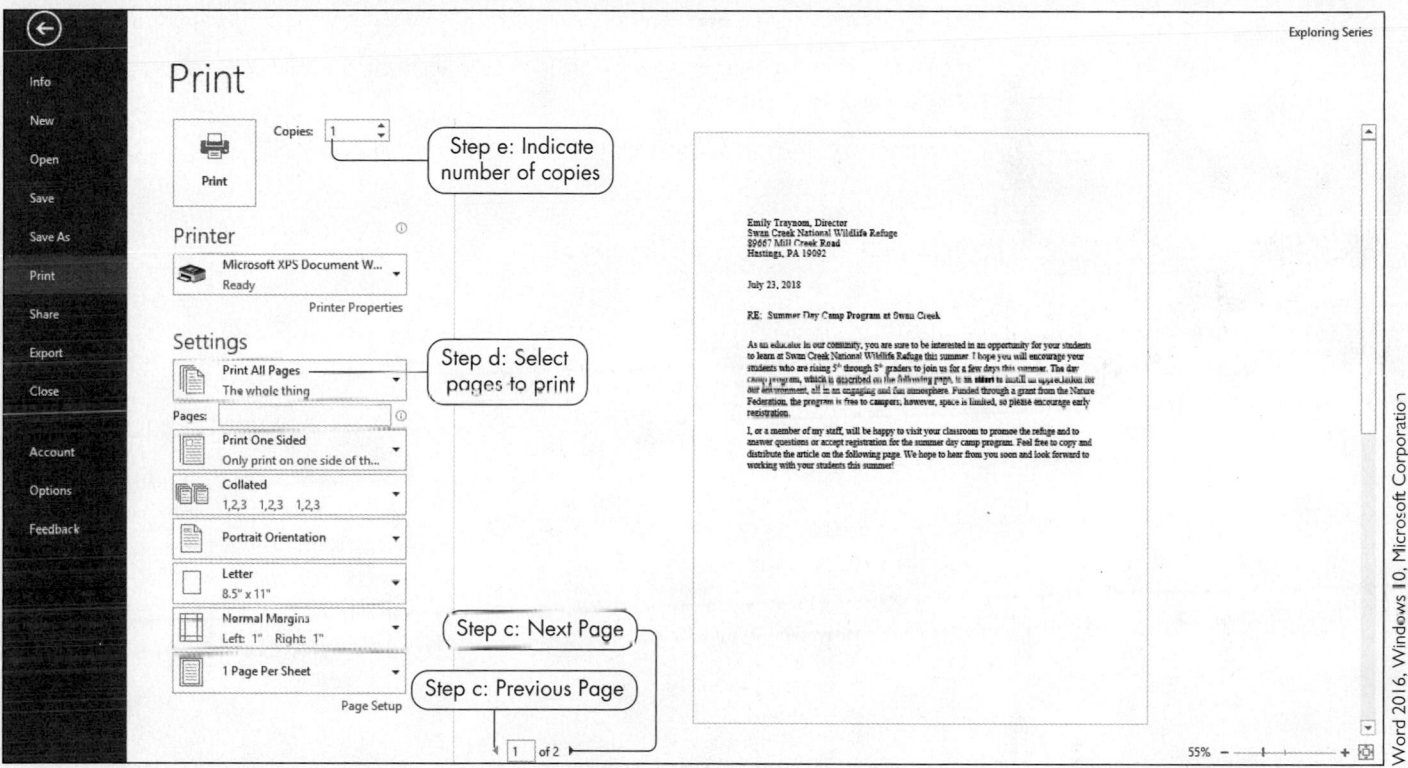

FIGURE 1.50 Working with Print Options

a. Open *w01h3Refuge_LastFirst*. Click the **File tab** and click **Check for Issues** (beside Inspect Document). Click **Inspect Document**. Click **Inspect**.

You check for document areas that might display sensitive information. The inspection suggests that the category of Document Properties and Personal Information contains identifying data, as does that of Headers, Footers, and Watermarks.

b. Click **Remove All** beside Document Properties and Personal Information. Click **Close**.

You determine that it would be best to remove all document properties, but you leave headers, footers, and watermarks.

c. Click **Print**. Click **Next Page** to view the next page. Click **Previous Page** to return to the first page.

d. Click in the **Pages box** below **Print All Pages**. Type **2**.

You indicate that you want to print page 2 only.

e. Click the **Copies up arrow** repeatedly to print five copies.

You indicate that you want to print five copies of page 2.

f. Press **Esc** to return to the document without printing.

g. Save and close the file. Based on your instructor's directions, submit the following:
w01h3Refuge_LastFirst
w01h1Planner_LastFirst
w01h2Flyer_LastFirst
w01h3NewEmployee_LastFirst

Chapter Objectives Review

After reading this chapter, you have accomplished the following objectives:

1. Begin and edit a document.

- Use a template: Predesigned documents save time by providing a starting point.
- Create a document: Create a blank document by clicking Blank document when Word opens.
- Reuse text: Text from previously created documents can be inserted in another document.
- Save a document: Saving a document makes it possible to access it later for editing, sharing, or printing.
- Open a document: Open a saved document by selecting the document from the Recent Documents list or browsing for other documents.
- Insert text and navigate a document: The insertion point indicates where the text you type will be placed. Use scroll bars or keyboard shortcuts to move around in a document.
- Review spelling and grammar: Use the Review tab to make sure all documents are free of typographical and grammatical errors.

2. Customize Word.

- Explore Word options: Word options are global settings you can select, such as whether to check spelling automatically, or where to save a file by default.
- Customize the Ribbon: Customize the Ribbon, using Word Options, to add, remove, or rename Ribbon tabs and commands.
- Customize the Quick Access Toolbar: The Quick Access Toolbar contains a few commands by default, but you can add more.

3. Use features that improve readability.

- Insert headers and footers: Headers and footers provide information, such as page number and organization name, in the top and bottom margins of a document.
- Adjust margins: You can change margins, selecting predefined settings or creating your own.
- Change page orientation: Select Landscape to show a document that is wider than it is tall, or Portrait to show a document taller than it is wide.

- Insert a watermark: A watermark is text or a graphic that displays behind text to identify such items as a document's purpose, owner, or status.
- Insert a symbol: A symbol is typically a character or graphic that is not found on the keyboard, such as ©.

4. View a document in different ways.

- Select a document view: A view is the way a document displays onscreen; available Word views include Print Layout, Read Mode, Outline, Web Layout, and Draft.
- Change the zoom setting: By changing the zoom setting, you can enlarge or reduce text size onscreen.
- View a document and manage page flow: Forcing a page break is useful to divide document sections (for example, to separate a cover page from other report pages), or to better manage page flow so that pages do not end awkwardly.

5. Modify document properties.

- Customize document properties: Document properties are items you can add to a document to further describe it, such as author, keywords, and comments.

6. Prepare a document for distribution.

- Ensure document compatibility: Using Word 2016, you can convert documents to the most recent version and you can also ensure a document's compatibility with earlier versions.
- Understand backup options: Backup options include AutoRecover and the ability always to create a backup copy of a saved document.
- Run the Document Inspector: Word's Document Inspector reveals any hidden or personal data in a file and enables you to remove sensitive information.
- Select print options: Using Word's print options, you can specify the pages to print, the number of copies, and various other print selections.

Key Terms Matching

Match the key terms with their definitions. Write the key term letter by the appropriate numbered definition.

a. AutoRecover
b. Document Inspector
c. Draft view
d. Header and Footer
e. Insertion point
f. Insights
g. Microsoft Word
h. Outline view

i. Print Layout view
j. Read Mode
k. Symbol
l. Template
m. Thesaurus
n. Watermark
o. Word processing software
p. Word wrap

I. _____ Text or graphic that displays behind text. **p. 157**

2. _____ A structural view of a document or presentation that can be collapsed or expanded as necessary. **p. 160**

3. _____ The feature that automatically moves words to the next line if they do not fit on the current line. **p. 135**

4. _____ The feature that enables Word to recover a previous version of a document. **p. 176**

5. _____ A computer application, such as Microsoft Word, used primarily with text to create, edit, and format documents. **p. 132**

6. _____ View in which text reflows to screen-sized pages to make it easier to read. **p. 160**

7. _____ Word processing application included in the Microsoft Office software suite. **p. 132**

8. _____ A predesigned document that may include formats that can be modified. **p. 137**

9. _____ View that closely resembles the way a document will look when printed. **p. 160**

10. _____ A character or graphic not normally included on a keyboard. **p. 158**

11. _____ A feature that checks for and removes certain hidden and personal information from a document. **p. 177**

12. _____ Information that displays at the top or bottom of each document page. **p. 153**

13. _____ View that shows a great deal of document space, but no margins, headers, footers, or other special features. **p. 160**

14. _____ Blinking bar that indicates where text that you next type will appear. **p. 139**

15. _____ Pane that displays when you click Smart Lookup, enabling you to access outside resources, such as images, definitions, and other items for a selected word. **p. 142**

16. _____ Tool that enables you to find a synonym for a selected word. **p. 141**

Multiple Choice

1. The view that presents a document in screen-sized pages with two shown at a time, for ease of comprehension and sharing, is:

   (a) Read Mode.
   (b) Print Layout view.
   (c) Draft view.
   (d) Full Screen Mode.

2. The Document Inspector is useful when you want to:

   (a) Troubleshoot a document, identifying and adjusting nonprinting characters.
   (b) Reveal any hidden or personal data in the file so that it can be removed, if necessary.
   (c) Check the document for spelling and grammatical errors.
   (d) Adjust page layout.

3. To keep a date, such as June 15, from being separated between lines of a document, where the word June might display on one line, with 15 on the next, you could:

   (a) Insert a soft return between June and 15.
   (b) Insert an Em dash symbol before the word June.
   (c) Insert a hard return after 15.
   (d) Insert a nonbreaking space symbol between June and 15.

4. The pane that displays images, resources, and definitions of a selected word is:

   (a) Insights.
   (b) Thesaurus.
   (c) Document Properties.
   (d) Read Mode.

5. Suppose you find that a heading within a report is displayed at the end of a page, with remaining text in that section placed on the next page. To keep the heading with the text, you would position the insertion point before the heading and then:

   (a) Press Ctrl+Enter.
   (b) Click the Layout tab, click Breaks, and then select Line Numbers.
   (c) Insert a soft return.
   (d) Press Ctrl+Page Down.

6. You need to generate a printed calendar quickly. You can use Word to accomplish that by using a predesigned document called a:

   (a) Pattern.
   (b) View.
   (c) Template.
   (d) Shell.

7. One reason to display nonprinting characters is to:

   (a) Simplify the process of converting a document to an earlier Word version.
   (b) Enable spell checking on the document.
   (c) Enable document properties to be added to a document.
   (d) Assist with troubleshooting a document and modifying its appearance.

8. You have just opened a document provided by a coworker, and the title bar includes not only the file name but also the words Compatibility Mode. What does that mean?

   (a) The file was created in an earlier version of Word but saved as a Word 2016 file.
   (b) The file was created using another operating system, but opened under a version of Windows.
   (c) Word has placed the document in read-only mode, which means you will not be able to edit it.
   (d) The file was created in an earlier version of Word and might not be able to accommodate newer Word 2016 features unless you convert it.

9. To identify a document as a draft, and not in final form, which of the following would you mostly likely add to the document?

   (a) Symbol
   (b) Watermark
   (c) Template
   (d) Document property

10. One reason to use a header or footer is because:

   (a) The header or footer becomes a document property that can be used to search for the document later.
   (b) You only have to specify the content once, after which it displays automatically on all pages.
   (c) Most writing style guides require both headers and footers.
   (d) Headers and footers are required for all professional documents.

Practice Exercises

1 River City Media

Having recently graduated from college with a marketing degree, you are employed by River City Media as a marketing specialist. River City Media provides promotional material in a variety of ways, including print, Web communications, photography, and news releases. It is your job to promote River City Media so that it attracts a large number of new and recurring contracts seeking support with the marketing of products and services. One of your first tasks is updating printed material that describes the specific services that River City Media offers to prospective clients. You modify a brief description of services, first converting the document from an earlier version of Word, in which it was originally saved, to the most current. Refer to Figure 1.51 as you complete this exercise.

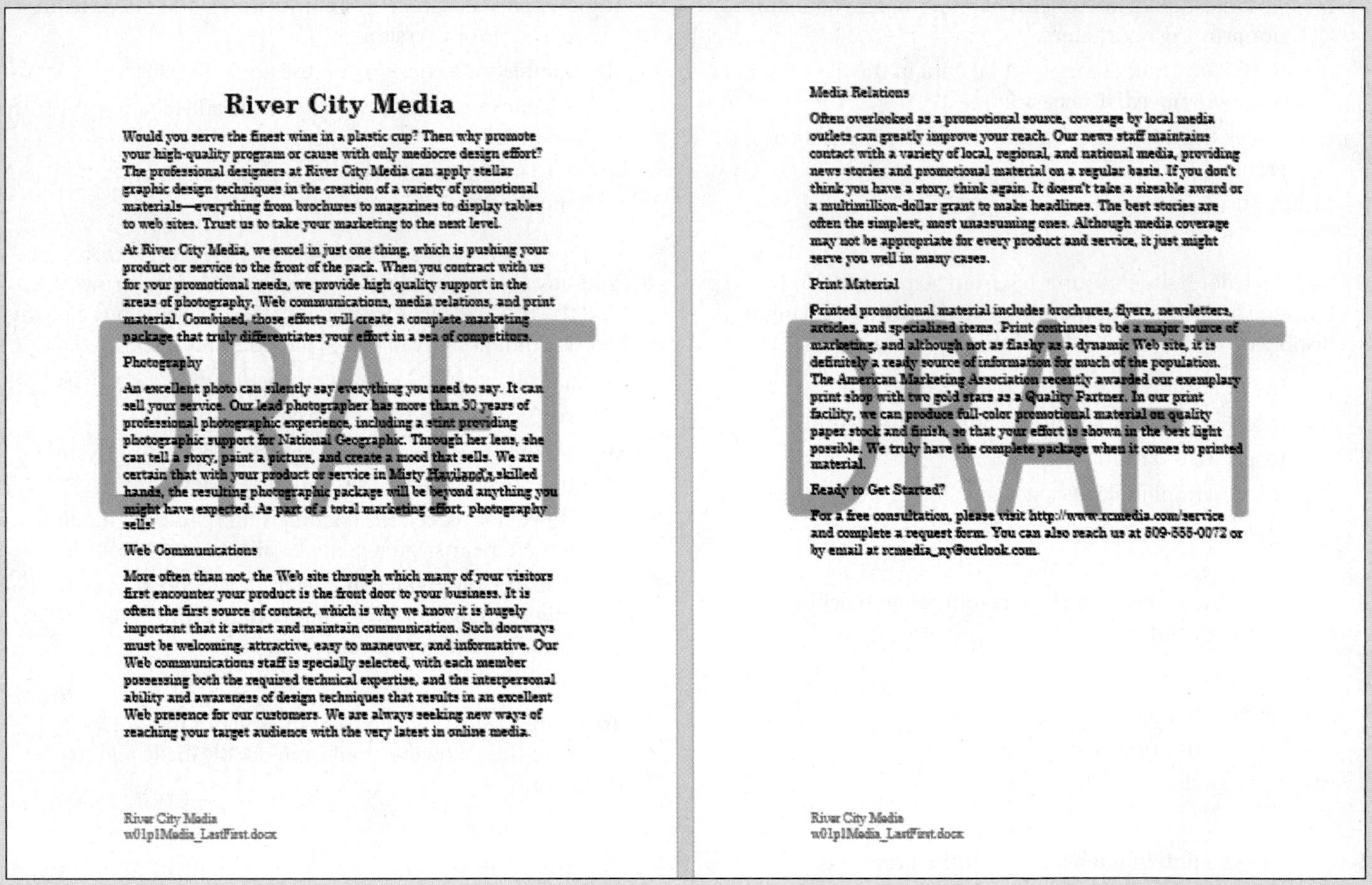

River City Media

Would you serve the finest wine in a plastic cup? Then why promote your high-quality program or cause with only mediocre design effort? The professional designers at River City Media can apply stellar graphic design techniques in the creation of a variety of promotional materials—everything from brochures to magazines to display tables to web sites. Trust us to take your marketing to the next level.

At River City Media, we excel in just one thing, which is pushing your product or service to the front of the pack. When you contract with us for your promotional needs, we provide high quality support in the areas of photography, Web communications, media relations, and print material. Combined, those efforts will create a complete marketing package that truly differentiates your effort in a sea of competitors.

Photography

An excellent photo can silently say everything you need to say. It can sell your service. Our lead photographer has more than 30 years of professional photographic experience, including a stint providing photographic support for National Geographic. Through her lens, she can tell a story, paint a picture, and create a mood that sells. We are certain that with your product or service in Misty Haviland's skilled hands, the resulting photographic package will be beyond anything you might have expected. As part of a total marketing effort, photography sells!

Web Communications

More often than not, the Web site through which many of your visitors first encounter your product is the front door to your business. It is often the first source of contact, which is why we know it is hugely important that it attract and maintain communication. Such doorways must be welcoming, attractive, easy to maneuver, and informative. Our Web communications staff is specially selected, with each member possessing both the required technical expertise, and the interpersonal ability and awareness of design techniques that results in an excellent Web presence for our customers. We are always seeking new ways of reaching your target audience with the very latest in online media.

River City Media
w01p1Media_LastFirst.docx

Media Relations

Often overlooked as a promotional source, coverage by local media outlets can greatly improve your reach. Our news staff maintains contact with a variety of local, regional, and national media, providing news stories and promotional material on a regular basis. If you don't think you have a story, think again. It doesn't take a sizeable award or a multimillion-dollar grant to make headlines. The best stories are often the simplest, most unassuming ones. Although media coverage may not be appropriate for every product and service, it just might serve you well in many cases.

Print Material

Printed promotional material includes brochures, flyers, newsletters, articles, and specialized items. Print continues to be a major source of marketing, and although not as flashy as a dynamic Web site, it is definitely a ready source of information for much of the population. The American Marketing Association recently awarded our exemplary print shop with two gold stars as a Quality Partner. In our print facility, we can produce full-color promotional material on quality paper stock and finish, so that your effort is shown in the best light possible. We truly have the complete package when it comes to printed material.

Ready to Get Started?

For a free consultation, please visit http://www.rcmedia.com/service and complete a request form. You can also reach us at 809-555-0072 or by email at rcmedia_ny@outlook.com.

River City Media
w01p1Media_LastFirst.docx

FIGURE 1.51 River City Media Draft

a. Open the *w01p1Media* document.

The words [*Compatibility Mode*] in the title bar inform you the document was created in an earlier version of Word.

b. Click the **File tab**, and then click **Save As**. Change the file name to **w01p1Media_LastFirst**. Click in the **Save as type box** and select **Word Document**. Click **Save**. You will be presented with a dialog box letting you know the document will be upgraded to the newest file format. Click **OK**.

c. Ensure that nonprinting characters are displayed by clicking Show/Hide in the paragraph group on the Home tab. Press **Ctrl+Home** to ensure that the insertion point is at the beginning of the document. Check the document for errors:

- Click the **Review tab** and click **Spelling & Grammar** in the Proofing group. The photographer's name is Haviland, so it is not misspelled. Click **Ignore**.
- Correct any identified spelling or grammatical errors. Click **OK** when the check is complete.
- Review the document again, checking for errors the spell check might have missed.

d. Double-click to select the word **maneuver** in the paragraph under the *Web Communications* heading. Click **Smart Lookup** in the Insights group. Scroll through the Insights pane to view information related to the selected word. Close the Insights pane.

e. Double-click **capable** in the paragraph under the *Photography* heading. Click **Thesaurus** in the Proofing group. Locate the word *skilled* in the Thesaurus pane, click its arrow, and then click **Insert**. Close the Thesaurus pane.

f. Make the following edits in the document:
- Select the words **When they are** from the second body paragraph on the first page and press **Delete**.
- Capitalize the word *Combined* in the same sentence.
- Rearrange the words *We at River City Media* in the same paragraph, so they read **At River City Media, we** (including a comma after the word *Media*).

g. Click after the word **materials** in the first body paragraph on the first page. Delete the following hyphen. Click the **Insert tab** and click **Symbol** in the Symbols group. Click **More Symbols**. Click the **Special Characters tab**. Ensure that Em Dash is selected. Click **Insert** and click **Close**. Click after the word **National** in the paragraph under the *Photography* heading and delete the following space. Press **Ctrl+Shift+Space** to insert a nonbreaking space, ensuring that the magazine title will not be divided between lines. Similarly, insert a nonbreaking space between **Misty** and **Haviland** so the photographer's name will not be divided between lines.

h. Click the **Design tab** and click **Watermark** in the Page Background group. Scroll through the watermarks and click **Draft 2**. Click **Watermark**, click **Custom Watermark**, and then click the **Semitransparent check box** to deselect it. Click **Color**, select **Blue Accent 5** (first row, ninth column under Theme Colors), and then click **OK**. You have inserted a watermark that indicates the document is not yet final.

i. Set up a footer:
- Click the **Insert tab** and click **Footer** in the Header & Footer group.
- Click **Edit Footer**. Type **River City Media** and press **Enter**.
- Click **Document Info** on the Header & Footer Tools Design tab and select **File Name**.
- Click **Close Header and Footer** (or double-click in the body of the document).

j. Adjust the left and right margins:
- Click the **Layout tab** and click **Margins** in the Page Setup Group.
- Click **Custom Margins**.
- Change the left and right margins to **1.5"**. Click **OK**.
- Click the **View tab** and click **Multiple Pages** in the Zoom group to see how the text is lining up on the pages.

k. Click before the **Media Relations** heading at the bottom of the first page and press **Ctrl+Enter** to insert a page break.

l. Press **Ctrl+Home**. Click **Read Mode** in the Views group. Click the arrow on the right to move from one page to the next. Press **Esc** to return to the previous document view. Click **100%** in the Zoom group. Save the document.

m. Click the **File tab** and click **Check for Issues**. Click **Inspect Document** and click **Inspect**. Click **Remove All** beside Document Properties and Personal Information and click **Close**.

n. Check the document for compatibility with earlier Word versions:
- Click **Check for Issues** and click **Check Compatibility**.
- Click **Select versions to show** and make sure that all earlier Word versions are selected.
- Click **Select versions to show** again to close the list. No compatibility issues are found.
- Click **OK**.

o. Click **Save** on the Quick Access Toolbar to save the document.

p. Close the file. Based on your instructor's directions, submit w01p1Media_LastFirst.

2 Working Space

You and a friend formed a partnership in which you help small businesses and independent workers procure temporary office space. Called Working Space, your company relies heavily on social media to advertise the business and obtain clients. As the company grows, and you hire more employees, you are finding it necessary to delegate much of the social media contact to others. Even so, you know that it is very important that the company maintain an appropriate and effective social media presence. Therefore, you use Word to develop a brief summary of expectations related to the use of social media to promote the business. Refer to Figure 1.52 as you complete this exercise.

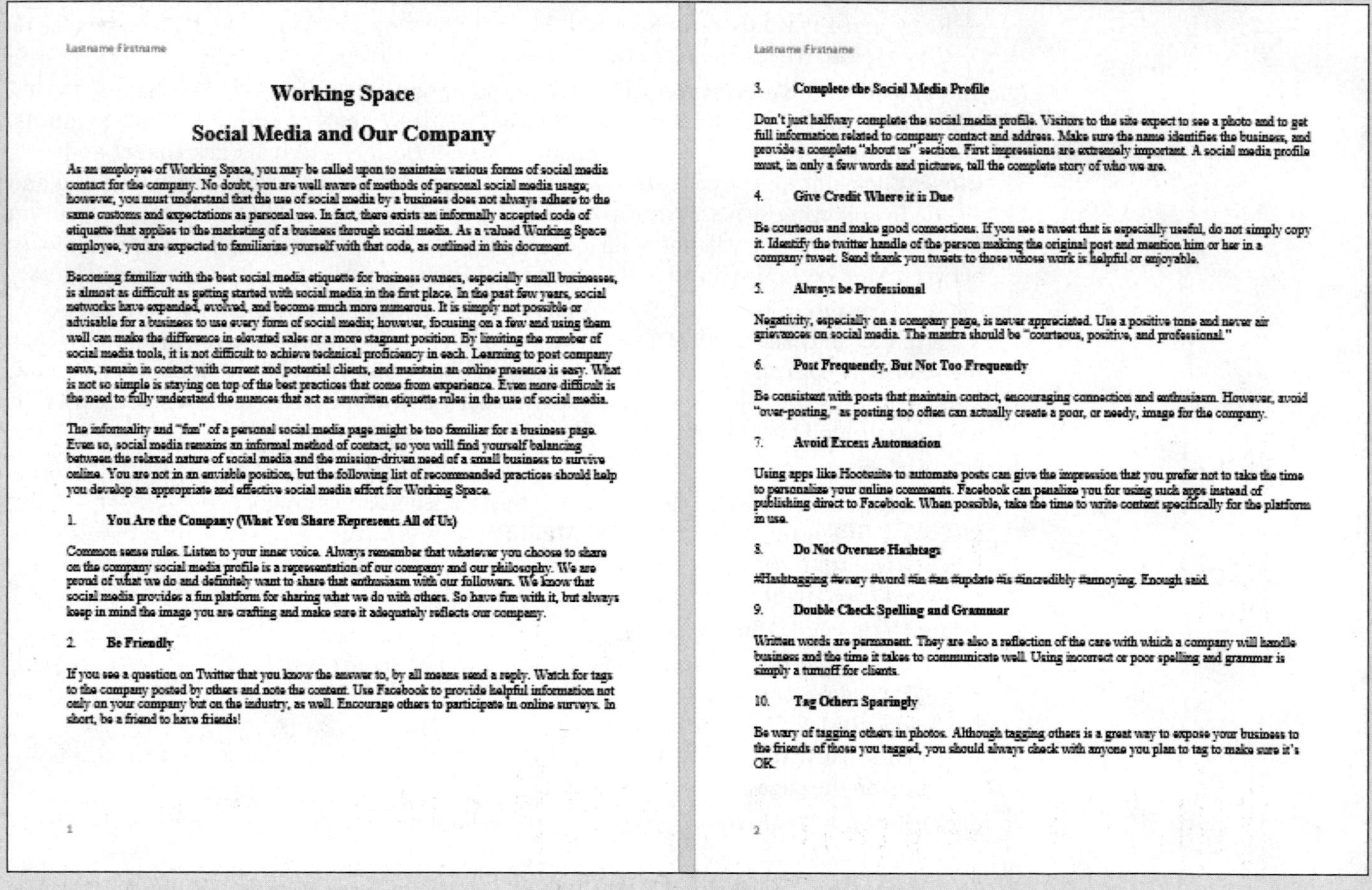
Lastname Firstname

Working Space

Social Media and Our Company

As an employee of Working Space, you may be called upon to maintain various forms of social media contact for the company. No doubt, you are well aware of methods of personal social media usage; however, you must understand that the use of social media by a business does not always adhere to the same customs and expectations as personal use. In fact, there exists an informally accepted code of etiquette that applies to the marketing of a business through social media. As a valued Working Space employee, you are expected to familiarize yourself with that code, as outlined in this document.

Becoming familiar with the best social media etiquette for business owners, especially small businesses, is almost as difficult as getting started with social media in the first place. In the past few years, social networks have expanded, evolved, and become much more numerous. It is simply not possible or advisable for a business to use every form of social media; however, focusing on a few and using them well can make the difference in elevated sales or a more stagnant position. By limiting the number of social media tools, it is not difficult to achieve technical proficiency in each. Learning to post company news, remain in contact with current and potential clients, and maintain an online presence is easy. What is not so simple is staying on top of the best practices that come from experience. Even more difficult is the need to fully understand the nuances that act as unwritten etiquette rules in the use of social media.

The informality and "fun" of a personal social media page might be too familiar for a business page. Even so, social media remains an informal method of contact, so you will find yourself balancing between the relaxed nature of social media and the mission-driven need of a small business to survive online. You are not in an enviable position, but the following list of recommended practices should help you develop an appropriate and effective social media effort for Working Space.

1. **You Are the Company (What You Share Represents All of Us)**

Common sense rules. Listen to your inner voice. Always remember that whatever you choose to share on the company social media profile is a representation of our company and our philosophy. We are proud of what we do and definitely want to share that enthusiasm with our followers. We know that social media provides a fun platform for sharing what we do with others. So have fun with it, but always keep in mind the image you are crafting and make sure it adequately reflects our company.

2. **Be Friendly**

If you see a question on Twitter that you know the answer to, by all means send a reply. Watch for tags to the company posted by others and note the content. Use Facebook to provide helpful information not only on your company but on the industry, as well. Encourage others to participate in online surveys. In short, be a friend to have friends!

1

Lastname Firstname

3. **Complete the Social Media Profile**

Don't just halfway complete the social media profile. Visitors to the site expect to see a photo and to get full information related to company contact and address. Make sure the name identifies the business, and provide a complete "about us" section. First impressions are extremely important. A social media profile must, in only a few words and pictures, tell the complete story of who we are.

4. **Give Credit Where it is Due**

Be courteous and make good connections. If you see a tweet that is especially useful, do not simply copy it. Identify the twitter handle of the person making the original post and mention him or her in a company tweet. Send thank you tweets to those whose work is helpful or enjoyable.

5. **Always be Professional**

Negativity, especially on a company page, is never appreciated. Use a positive tone and never air grievances on social media. The mantra should be "courteous, positive, and professional."

6. **Post Frequently, But Not Too Frequently**

Be consistent with posts that maintain contact, encouraging connection and enthusiasm. However, avoid "over-posting," as posting too often can actually create a poor, or needy, image for the company.

7. **Avoid Excess Automation**

Using apps like Hootsuite to automate posts can give the impression that you prefer not to take the time to personalize your online comments. Facebook can penalize you for using such apps instead of publishing direct to Facebook. When possible, take the time to write content specifically for the platform in use.

8. **Do Not Overuse Hashtags**

#Hashtagging #every #word #in #an #update #is #incredibly #annoying. Enough said.

9. **Double Check Spelling and Grammar**

Written words are permanent. They are also a reflection of the care with which a company will handle business and the time it takes to communicate well. Using incorrect or poor spelling and grammar is simply a turnoff for clients.

10. **Tag Others Sparingly**

Be wary of tagging others in photos. Although tagging others is a great way to expose your business to the friends of those you tagged, you should always check with anyone you plan to tag to make sure it's OK.

2

Word 2016, Windows 10, Microsoft Corporation

FIGURE 1.52 Working Space Document

a. Open *w01p2Social* and save it as **w01p2Social_LastFirst**.
b. Press **Ctrl+End** to move the insertion point to the end of the document. Press **Enter**. Click the **Insert tab** and click the **Object arrow** in the Text group. Click **Text from File**. Locate and double-click *w01p2Tips*.
c. Click the **View tab** and click **Multiple Pages** in the Zoom group. Note that very little text is shown on the last page.
d. Adjust the margins:
   - Click the **Layout tab**. Click **Margins** in the Page Setup group.
   - Click **Custom Margins**.
   - Change the left and right margins to **0.5"**. Click **OK**. Confirm that the document now fits on two pages.
   - Click the **View tab** and click **100%** in the Zoom group.

e. Insert a footer:
  - Click the **Insert tab** and click **Footer** in the Header & Footer group.
  - Click **Edit Footer**.
  - Click **Page Number** in the Header & Footer group, point to **Current Position**, and then click **Plain Number**.
  - Double-click in the current page of the document to close the footer.

f. Press **Ctrl+Home** to move to the beginning of the document and double-click in the Header area (top margin). Type your first name and last name. Double-click in the current page of the document to close the header.

g. Click the **File tab** and click **Print**. Click **Next Page** to view the next page. Click **Previous Page**. Note that the last line on the first page is a numbered item that is separated from its contents on the next page. Click **Back** (the arrow at the top left) to return to the document.

h. Ensure that nonprinting characters are displayed. Click before the number 3 on the last line of the first page. Press **Ctrl+Enter** to insert a page break.

i. Edit the text as follows:
  - Remove the words *develop or* from the first sentence of the first body paragraph on the first page. Ensure that only one space remains between the words *to* and *maintain*.
  - Locate the words *also are* in the paragraph under the heading *Double Check Spelling and Grammar* on the second page. Reverse those words so the sentence reads **are also** instead of *also are*.

j. Press **Ctrl+Home**. Click the **Review tab** and click **Spelling & Grammar** in the Proofing group. Correct any identified errors, if they are actual errors. The words *Hootsuite* and *Hashtagging* are correct and should not be changed. Click **OK** when the spelling check is complete.

k. Press **Ctrl+Home**. Click the **View tab** and click **Multiple Pages** in the Zoom group.

l. Adjust the left and right margins:
  - Click **100%** in the Zoom group.
  - Click the **Layout tab** and click **Margins** in the Page Setup group.
  - Click **Moderate**.

m. Preview the document. Press **Ctrl+End** and delete the blank paragraph mark that is forcing a third page. Ensure that the document now spans only two pages. Save the document.

n. Click the **File tab**, click **Check for Issues**, and then click **Check Compatibility**. Ensure that all versions of Word are checked. There are no compatibility issues with earlier Word versions, so click **OK**.

o. Click the **File tab**. Click **Check for Issues**, click **Inspect Document**, click **No**, and then click **Inspect**. Click **Close** after you view the results.

p. Click **Print**. Click in the **Pages box** under Print All Pages and type **2** to indicate that you want to print only the second page. Because you are likely in a lab setting, you will not print the pages.

q. Press **Esc** to return to the document. Save and close the file. Based on your instructor's direction, submit w01p2Social_LastFirst.

Mid-Level Exercises

1 Runners at Heart

A local cross-country team, Runners at Heart, is comprised of people who are recovering from a heart ailment or who support the cause of fitness for former heart patients. A half marathon is coming up in five months, and the Runners at Heart cross-country team wants to be prepared. A half marathon is a run/walk of 13.1 miles. You and others have researched tips on preparing for a half marathon and compiled a brief guide. You have begun a document containing a few of those tips, and have collected ideas from other club members as well. You finalize the document and make it available in plenty of time for the runners to prepare.

a. Open *w01m1Running* and save it as **w01m1Running_LastFirst**.

b. Move to the end of the document and press **Enter**. Insert text from *w01m1Guide*.

c. Display nonprinting characters if they are not already shown. View each page of the document and note that the first page ends awkwardly, with a single heading at the bottom. Insert a page break before the *What to wear* heading.

d. Correct any headings that are not capitalized appropriately. Headings should be changed to **Choose a Plan**, **Run Quality Miles**, **Cross-train**, **Prepare Mentally**, **Train with Others**, **Do Your Research**, **Rest**, and **What to Wear**.

e. Insert a hard return before each heading except What To Wear (beginning with *Choose a Plan* and ending with *Rest*) to increase the space between them.

DISCOVER

f. Remove the page break before the *What to Wear* heading.

g. View the document and insert a page break, wherever a heading stands alone.

h. Identify synonyms for the word *regimen* in the *Choose a Plan* section. Insert the word **schedule**. Close the Thesaurus pane. Check for spelling and word usage errors, correcting any that are identified. The brand of clothing is correctly spelled *Dri-Fit*. Proofread the document carefully to identify any errors that Word might have missed. Review the word *resistance* in the *Cross-train* section using the Smart Lookup tool. Close the Insights pane.

i. Insert a page number footer as a **Plain Number** in the current position (on the left side of the footer). As a header, include the file name as a field.

j. Select the hyphen between the words *long* and *distance* in the paragraph following *Training Tips for a Half Marathon*. Insert a Nonbreaking Hyphen. Insert a trademark symbol immediately after the words *Nike Dri-Fit* (before the period) in the *What to Wear* section.

k. Add a horizontal draft watermark. The watermark should be clearly visible (not semitransparent), and colored **Dark Blue**.

l. Change the page orientation to **Landscape**. Preview the document to determine if the orientation is appropriate. Delete the page break before the *Do Your Research* heading. Remove one of the blank paragraphs before the *Do Your Research* heading. Change the zoom to **100%**. Save the document.

m. Access Advanced Properties and replace the current author with your first and last names. In the Comments section, type **Tips for a Half Marathon**. Remove any information in the Company box.

n. Preview the document. Print the document properties if approved by your instructor.

o. Save and close the file. Based on your instructor's directions, submit w01m1Running_LastFirst.

2 Backyard Bonanza

With a degree in horticulture, you have recently been employed to work with Backyard Bonanza, a local outdoor living business specializing in garden gifts, statuary, outdoor fireplaces, landscaping materials, and pavers. The first Friday of each month, Backyard Bonanza participates in a downtown event in which vendors, artists, and musicians set up areas to perform or display products. To encourage those passing by to visit the store, you prepare a document describing a few do-it-yourself backyard projects—all of which can be completed with the help of products sold at Backyard

Bonanza. The document is well underway, but you modify it slightly, making sure it is attractive and ready for distribution at the next event.

a. Open *w01m2Backyard*. The document was originally saved in an earlier version of Word, so you should save it as a Word Document with the file name of **w01m2Backyard_LastFirst**. Agree that the upgrade should proceed, if asked.

b. Display nonprinting characters. Preview the document to get a feel for the text flow. Change the orientation to **Portrait**. Change the view to **One Page**.

c. Return to **100%** view. Add a page number footer. The page number should be placed at the **Bottom** with the **Plain Number 2** selection. Close the footer.

d. Insert text from *w01m2Fish* at the end of the document.

e. Scroll to the top of page 2. Change the word *Create* to **Build**.

f. Check the document for spelling and grammatical errors. The word *Delite* is not misspelled as it is a brand name. Because there is no correct suggestion for the misuse of the word *layer*, you will need to manually change it. (Hint: You can ignore the error and then return to manually correct the mistake.) Proofread the document to identify and correct errors that Word might have missed.

g. Preview the document and note the small amount of text on page 3. Change margins to **Narrow**.

h. Insert a page break so that *Build a Backyard Fish Pond* begins on a new page.

i. View the document in Read Mode. Return to Print Layout view. Display the document in **100%** zoom.

j. Click after the word **noticed** on page 2 and before the comma in the third sentence of the first body paragraph of directions. Remove the comma and the following space, and insert an **Em Dash**. On page 1, click after the words **Paving Delite**, but before the closing parenthesis (in the first paragraph of directions under *What to do:*). Insert a trademark symbol.

 **DISCOVER**

k. Add a watermark with the text **Backyard Bonanza** shown in Red. The watermark should be horizontal and semitransparent.

l. List **Backyard Bonanza** as the author in Document Properties. The subject is **Backyard Projects**.

m. Run the Compatibility Checker to make sure the file is compatible with earlier Word versions.

n. Save and close the file. Based on your instructor's directions, submit w01m2Backyard_LastFirst.

3 College Events

COLLABORATION CASE

FROM SCRATCH

You and a group of your fellow students are assigned the project of preparing a document describing several upcoming events at your college or university. Identify a few events to highlight, and assign each event to a student. Although each student will conduct independent research on an event, all event descriptions will be collected and combined into one document for submission to your instructor. To complete the project:

a. Identify a unique name for the group (perhaps assigned by your instructor).

b. Identify events (perhaps conduct research online) and assign one event to each student.

c. Each student will collect information on the event (general description, location, cost, etc.).

d. Compose a cover letter to the instructor, identifying group members and noting events to be included in the document. The cover letter should be attractive and error free.

e. Insert a page break at the end of the cover letter so that the first event description begins on a new page.

f. Save the document to OneDrive as **w01m3Events_GroupName** (replacing GroupName with the actual group name). Go to http://onedrive.live.com, sign in, and then open *w01m3Events_GroupName*. Click **Share** and click **Get a link**. Click **Shorten link** to get a shorter version of the URL. Provide the URL to group members so each member can access and edit the file.

g. Each group member will access the file from the URL. When the document opens, click **Edit Document**, and then click **Edit in Word**. Click Yes, if advised of a possibility of viruses. Enter any login information (Microsoft account credentials) and edit the document to add event information. When a description is complete, insert a hard return so that the next description begins on a new page. Click **Save** on the Quick Access Toolbar to save the document back to OneDrive.

h. Based on your instructor's directions, submit w01m3Events_GroupName.

Beyond the Classroom

Dream Destination

GENERAL CASE

FROM SCRATCH

You work with a local radio station that will award a dream vacation of one week in a resort area to a lucky listener. Select a destination and conduct some research to determine approximately how much it will cost your employer to make the vacation available. What travel arrangements are possible? What type of accommodations do you recommend? What activities are there to enjoy in the area, and what are some outstanding restaurants? Prepare a one- to two-page document, outlining what you think are the best selling points for the area and approximately how much the travel and hotel accommodations will cost the radio station. Because the document is for internal distribution in draft format, you do not need to be overly concerned with format. However, you should use skills from this chapter to properly identify the document (headers, footers, and watermarks) and to position it on the page. The document should be error free. Modify document properties to include yourself as the author. Save the file as **w01b1Vacation_LastFirst**. Close the file and based on your instructor's directions, submit w01b1Vacation_LastFirst.

Logo Policy

DISASTER RECOVERY

Open *w01b2Policy* and save it as a Word 2016 file with the file name **w01b2Policy LastFirst**. The document was started by an office assistant, but was not finished. You must complete the document, ensuring that it is error free and attractive. The current header includes a page number at the top right. Remove the page number from the header and create a footer with a centered page number instead. Remove the word *copyright* anywhere it appears in the document and replace it with the copyright symbol. Show nonprinting characters and remove any unnecessary or improperly placed paragraph marks. Insert hard returns where necessary to better space paragraphs. The hyphenated word *non-Association* should not be divided between lines, so use a nonbreaking hyphen. Modify document properties to include yourself as the author and assign relevant keywords. Finally, use a watermark to indicate that the document is not in final form. Save the document as a Word 2016 file and as a separate Word 97-2003 document with the same file name. Based on your instructor's directions, submit w01b2Policy_LastFirst.doc and w01b1Policy_LastFirst.docx.

Capstone Exercise

As a travel editor for a regional magazine, you are responsible for the preparation of material related to destinations and special events. Your staff often prepares material on specific areas, and you edit and combine the submissions into attractive documents for publication. In this case, you collect information to spotlight a couple of destinations in the Southeast. A deadline is looming so you use Word to produce an attractive article.

Spelling, Margins, Watermarks, and Editing

Nothing detracts from content more than spelling and grammatical errors. Since this article is destined for print, it must be error free. You check it for errors and manually proofread it. Additionally, you find it necessary to adjust margins to improve readability and you edit the content. Finally, a watermark indicates that this is not the final version.

a. Open *w01c1Travel* and save it as **w01c1Travel_LastFirst**.

b. Position the insertion point at the end of the document. On a new line, insert text from *w01c1Texas*.

c. Use Word's Spelling & Grammar checker to identify any spelling or word usage errors. All names are spelled correctly, so ignore any errors related to a name. Select the word *quaint* in the third paragraph on the first page. Use the thesaurus to identify synonyms. Insert the word **charming** instead. Close the Thesaurus pane. Proofread the document to ensure that there are no other errors.

d. Change the left and right margins to **1"**.

e. Insert a diagonal watermark that displays **Draft**. Color the watermark blue and leave semitransparency on.

f. Display nonprinting characters. Remove the hard return at the end of the third paragraph on the first page (ending in *guest rooms*). Insert a space. Change the number *200* in the sixth paragraph on the first page to *300*. Change the word *offer* in the last paragraph on the first page to **feature**. Change the word *it's* in the last paragraph on the second page to **it is**. The fourth paragraph on the first page incorrectly describes *The Cloister* as *The Cloisters*. Edit the paragraph to remove the *s* from the end of the resort name each place it occurs in the paragraph.

Headers, Footers, Symbols, and Features That Improve Readability

You number the pages and include a descriptive header. You also ensure that each destination appears on its own page (or set of pages). Finally, you use several symbols to improve readability and to ensure proper credit.

a. Create a page number footer, centered at the bottom of each page. Create a header with **Southeastern Living** on the left. On a second line in the header, insert the document file name.

b. Edit the header to include a copyright symbol before the words *Southeastern Living*.

c. At a couple of locations throughout the document, a hyphenated phrase is incorrectly separated at the end of a line. Replace the dash separating those divided words with a nonbreaking hyphen. Similarly, replace the space after the first name *Addison* with a nonbreaking space so that the full name is not divided.

d. Insert a page break before the fifth paragraph on the first page.

e. View the document as Multiple Pages to get a feel for the flow of text. Because the text is a bit too high on the page, change the top margin to **2"**. Return the view to **100%**. Save the document.

Set Properties and Finalize Document

As the document nears completion, you adjust document properties to include yourself as the author and to apply descriptive keywords. You also save the document in a format that ensures others will be able to read it. Finally you ensure compatibility with earlier Word versions.

a. Save the document in Rich Text Format as **w01c1Travel_LastFirst**. Save the document again as a Word Document with the same file name. Replace the existing file and agree to the upgrade.

b. Save the document. Run the Compatibility Checker for all previous Word versions. Inspect the document and remove all document properties and personal information.

c. Add **Travel**, **Texas**, and **Georgia** to the Keywords field in the document properties. List your first name and last name as the Author.

d. Preview the document.

e. Save and close the file. Based on your instructor's directions, submit w01c1Travel_LastFirst (the RTF document) and w01c1Travel_LastFirst (the Word document).

Word

Document Presentation

LEARNING OUTCOME You will modify a Word document with formatting, styles, and objects.

OBJECTIVES & SKILLS: After you read this chapter, you will be able to:

CASE STUDY | Phillips Studio L Photography

Having recently opened your own photography studio, you are engaged in marketing the business. Not only do you hope to attract customers from the local community who want photos of special events, but you will also offer classes in basic photography for interested amateur photographers. In addition, you have designed a website to promote the business and to provide details on upcoming events and classes. The business is not large enough yet to employ an office staff, so much of the work of developing promotional material falls on you.

Among other projects, you are currently developing material to include in a quarterly mailing to people who have expressed an interest in upcoming studio events. You have prepared a rough draft of a newsletter describing photography basics—a document that must be formatted and properly organized before it is distributed to people on your mailing list. You will modify the document to ensure attractive line and paragraph spacing, and you will format text to draw attention to pertinent points. Formatted in columns, the document will be easy to read. The newsletter is somewhat informal, and you will make appropriate use of color, borders, and pictures so that it is well received by your audience.

Editing and Formatting

FIGURE 2.1 Phillips Studio L Photography Document

CASE STUDY | Phillips Studio L Photography

Starting File	File to be Submitted
w02h1Studio	**w02h3Studio_LastFirst**

Text and Paragraph Formatting

When you format text, you change the way it looks. Your goal in designing a document is to ensure that it is well received and understood by an audience of readers. Seldom will your first attempt at designing a document be the only time you work with it. Inevitably, you will identify text that should be reworded or emphasized differently, paragraphs that might be more attractive in another alignment, or the need to bold, underline, or use italics to call attention to selected text. As you develop a document, or after reopening a previously completed document, you can make all these modifications and more. That process is called *formatting*.

In this section, you will learn to change font and font size, and format text with character attributes, such as bold, underline, and italics. At the paragraph level, you will adjust paragraph and line spacing, set tab stops, change alignment, and apply bullets and numbering.

Applying Font Attributes

A *font* is a combination of typeface and type style. The font you select should reinforce the message of the text without calling attention to itself, and it should be consistent with the information you want to convey. For example, a paper prepared for a professional purpose, such as a resume, should have a standard font, such as Times New Roman, instead of one that looks casual or frilly, such as Freestyle Spirit or French Script MT. Additionally, you will want to minimize the variety of fonts in a document to maintain a professional look. Typically, you should use three or fewer fonts within a document. Headings might be formatted in one font, while body text is shown in another. This arrangement is the default for Word. However, Word allows you to format text in a variety of ways. Not only can you change a font, but you can apply text attributes, such as bold, italic, or underline, to selected text, or to text that you are about to type. Several of the most commonly used text formatting commands are located in the Font group on the Home tab.

Select Font Options

When you begin a new, blank document, the default font for the body of the document is Calibri 11 pt, which you can change for the current document if you like. To change the font for selected text, or for a document you are beginning, click the Font arrow and select a font from those displayed (see Figure 2.2). Each font shown is a sample of the actual font. With text selected, you can point to any font in the list, without clicking, to see a preview of the way selected text will look in that particular font. *Live Preview* enables you to select text and see the effects without clicking.

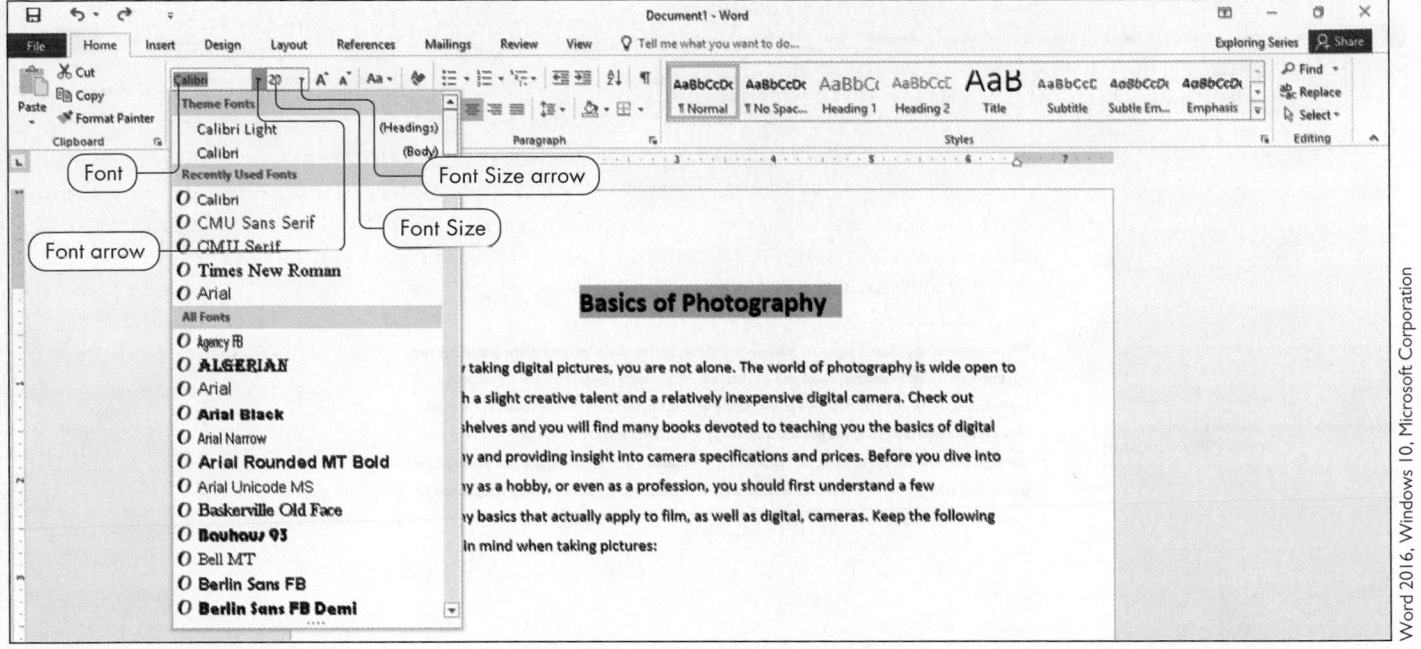

FIGURE 2.2 Select a Font and Font Size

You can also change font size when you click the Font Size arrow (refer to Figure 2.2) and select a point size. Each point size is equivalent to 1/72 of an inch; therefore, the larger the point size, the larger the font. A document often contains various sizes of the same font. For example, a document that includes levels of headings and subheadings might have major headings formatted in a larger point size than lesser headings.

A definitive characteristic of any font is the presence or absence of serifs, thin lines that begin and end the main strokes of each letter. A ***serif font*** contains a thin line or extension at the top and bottom of the primary strokes on characters. Times New Roman is an example of a serif font. A ***sans serif font*** (*sans* from the French word meaning *without*) does not contain the thin lines on characters. Calibri is a sans serif font.

Serifs help the eye connect one letter with the next and generally are used with large amounts of text. The paragraphs in this book, for example, are set in a serif font. Body text of newspapers and magazines is usually formatted in a serif font, as well. A sans serif font, such as Calibri, Arial, or Verdana, is more effective with smaller amounts of text such as titles, headlines, corporate logos, and webpages. For example, the heading *Select Font Options*, at the beginning of this section, is set in a sans serif font. Web developers often prefer a sans serif font because the extra strokes that begin and end letters in a serif font can blur or fade into a webpage, making it difficult to read. Examples of serif and sans serif fonts are shown in Figure 2.3.

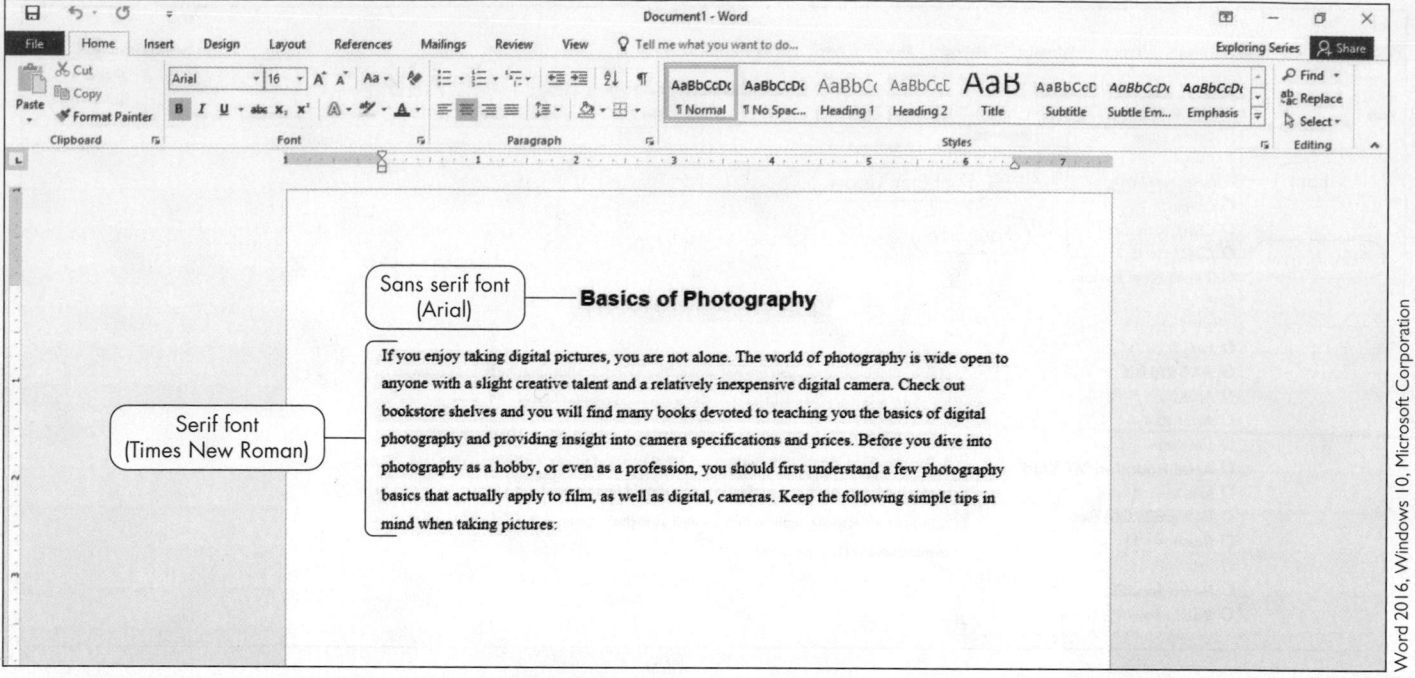

FIGURE 2.3 Serif and Sans Serif Fonts

TIP: FONT FOR BUSINESS DOCUMENTS

Most business documents are best formatted in 11- or 12-point serif font. A good choice is Times New Roman. A document designed for display on the Web is attractive in a blocky sans serif font, such as Arial, regardless of point size.

A second characteristic of a font is whether it is monospaced or proportional. A monospaced font (such as Courier New) uses the same amount of horizontal space for every character regardless of its width. Monospaced fonts are used in tables and financial projections where text must be precisely aligned, one character underneath another. A proportional font (such as Times New Roman or Arial) allocates space according to the width of the character. For example, the lowercase *m* is wider than the lowercase *i*. Proportional fonts create a professional appearance and are appropriate for most documents, such as research papers, status reports, and letters.

A typical Word installation includes support for TrueType and OpenType fonts. A TrueType font can be scaled to any size. Any output device, such as a printer, that Windows supports can recognize a TrueType font. An OpenType font is an advanced form of font that is designed for all platforms, including Windows and Macintosh. OpenType fonts incorporate a greater extension of the basic character set. Most fonts included in a typical Word installation are OpenType.

Change Text Appearance

Commonly accessed commands related to font settings are located in the Font group on the Home tab (see Figure 2.4). Word enables you to bold, underline, and italicize text, apply text highlighting, change font color, and work with various text effects and other formatting options from commands in the Font group. For even more choices, click the Font Dialog Box Launcher in the Font group and select from additional formatting commands available in the Font dialog box (see Figure 2.5). With text selected, you will see the Mini toolbar (see Figure 2.6) when you move the pointer near the selection, making it more convenient to quickly select a format (instead of locating it on the Ribbon or using a keyboard shortcut).

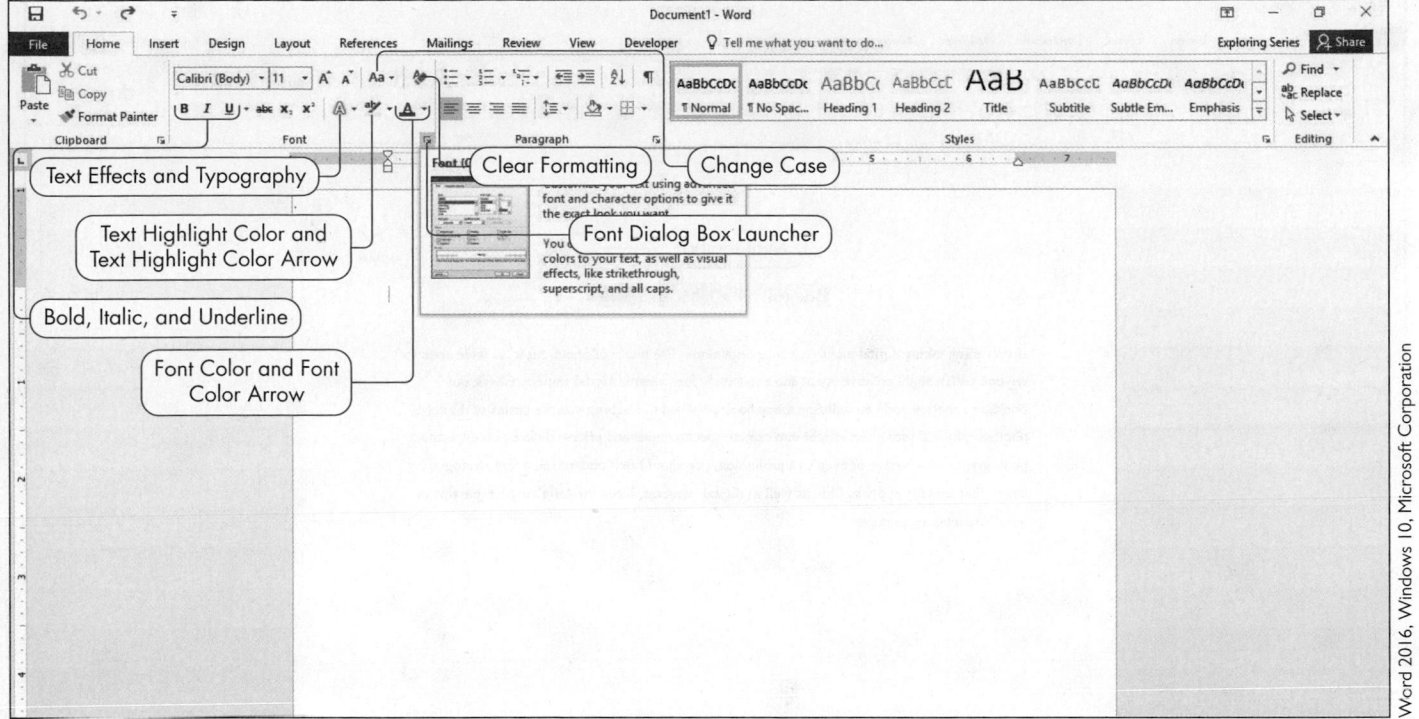

FIGURE 2.4 Font Commands

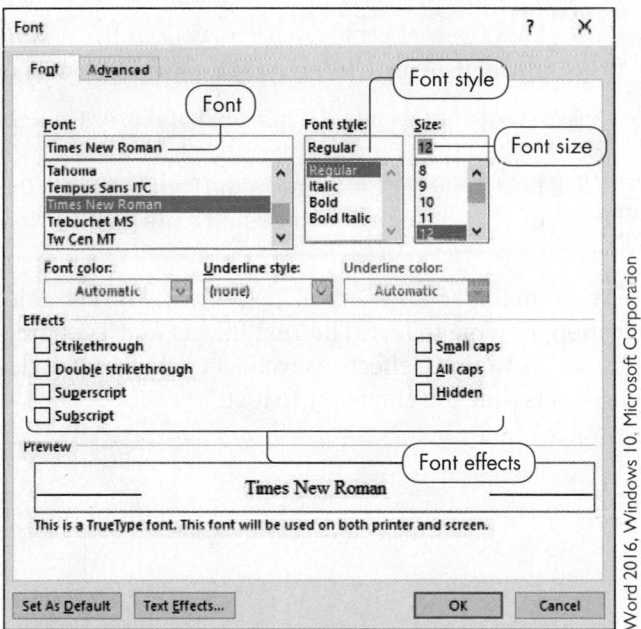

FIGURE 2.5 Font Dialog Box

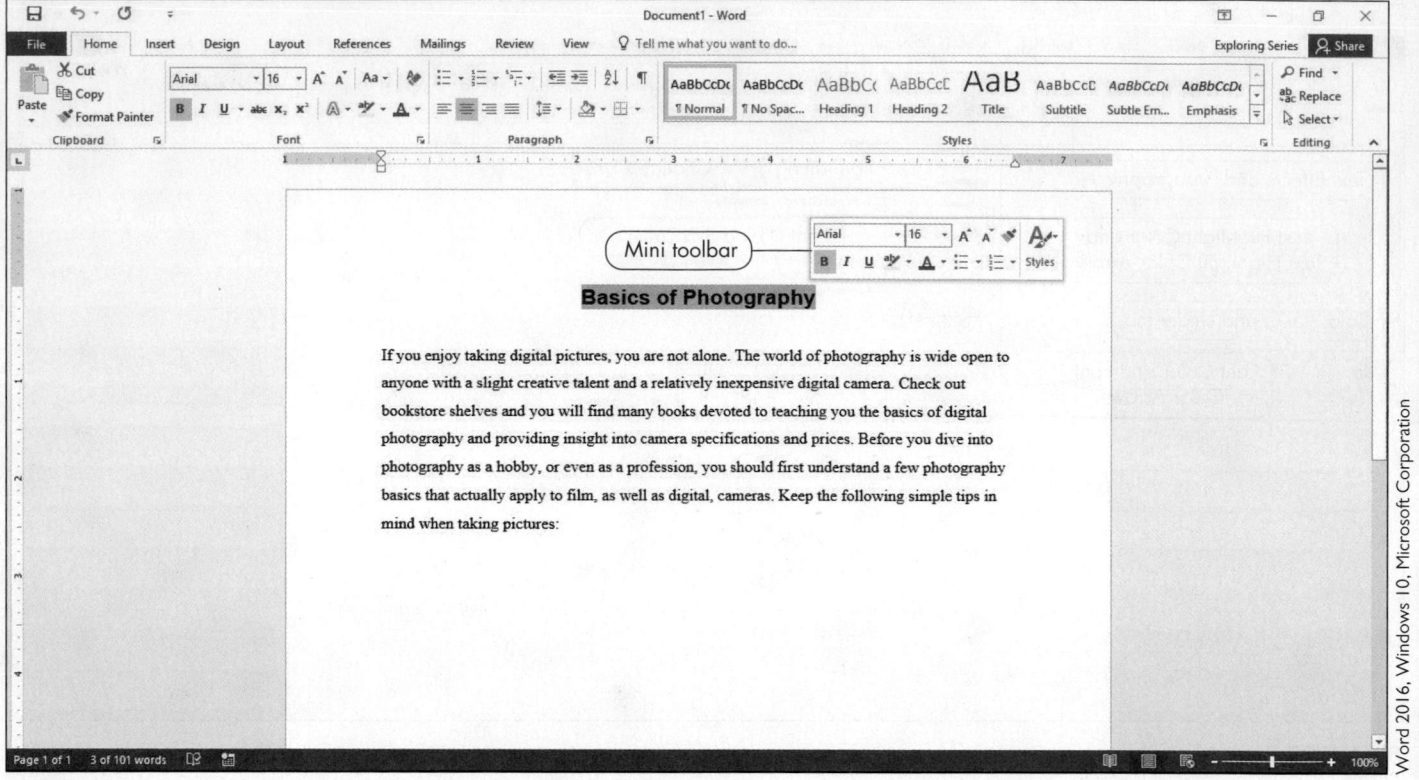

FIGURE 2.6 Mini Toolbar

To bold, underline, or italicize text, complete one of the following steps:

- Select text to be formatted. Click Bold, Italic, or Underline in the Font group on the Home tab.
- Click Bold, Italic, or Underline in the Font group on the Home tab and type text to be formatted. Click the same command to turn off the formatting effect.

Word includes a variety of text effects that enable you to add a shadow, outline, reflection, or glow to text. The Text Effects and Typography gallery (see Figure 2.7) provides access to those effects as well as to WordArt styles, number styles, ligatures, and stylistic sets that you can apply to text.

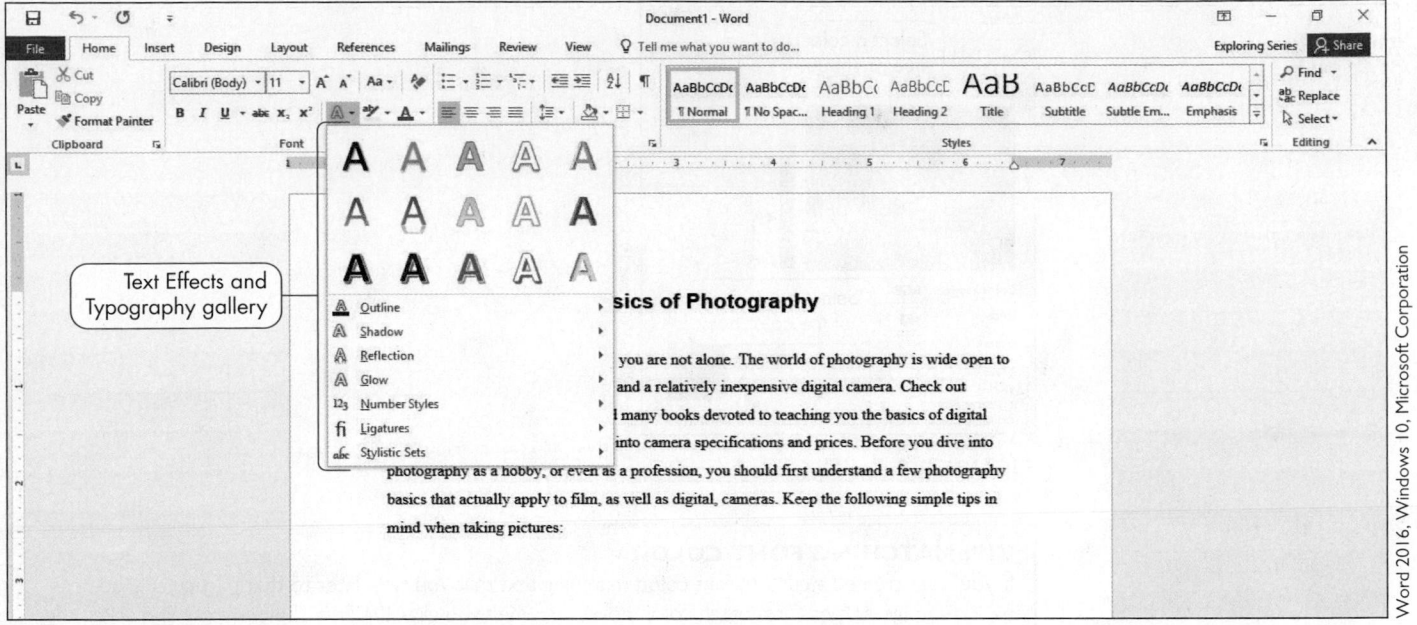

FIGURE 2.7 Text Effects and Typography Gallery

A ligature is two letters that are crafted together into a single character, or glyph. For example, you often see the letters *f* and *i* bound together in a ligature. A stylistic set is a collection of letter styles that you can apply to OpenType fonts. Some fonts include more stylistic sets than others. To explore advanced font settings, click the Font Dialog Box Launcher (refer to Figure 2.4) and click the Advanced tab (refer to Figure 2.5). Select a ligature and stylistic set. Stylistic sets and ligatures are often used in the preparation of formal documents such as wedding invitations.

As a student, you are likely to highlight important parts of textbooks, magazine articles, and other documents. You probably use a highlighting marker to shade parts of text you want to remember or to which you want to draw attention. Word provides an equivalent tool with which you can highlight text you want to stand out or to locate easily—the Text Highlight Color command, located in the Font group on the Home tab (refer to Figure 2.4).

To highlight text *before* selecting it, complete the following steps:

1. Click Text Highlight Color to select the current highlight color or click the Text Highlight Color arrow and choose another color. The pointer resembles a pen when you move it over the document.
2. Drag across text to highlight it.
3. Click Text Highlight Color or press Esc to stop highlighting.

To highlight text *after* selecting it, click Text Highlight Color or click the Text Highlight Color arrow and choose another color. You can remove highlights in the same manner, except that you will select No Color.

When creating a document, you must consider when and how to capitalize. Titles are occasionally in all caps, sentences begin with a capital letter, and headings typically capitalize each key word. Use the Change Case option in the Font group on the Home tab to quickly change the capitalization of document text (refer to Figure 2.4).

By default, text is shown in black as you type a document. For a bit of interest, or to draw attention to text within a document, you can change the font color of previously typed text or of text that you are about to type. Click the Font Color arrow (refer to Figure 2.4) and select from a gallery of colors. For even more choices, click More Colors and select from a variety of hues or shades. As shown in Figure 2.8, you can click the Custom tab in the Colors dialog box and click to select a color hue, while honing in on a variation of that hue by dragging along a continuum.

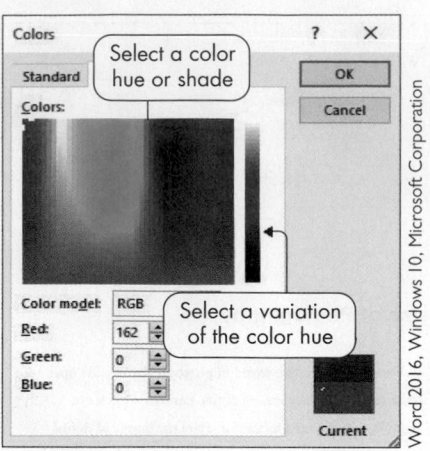

FIGURE 2.8 Apply a Custom Color

> **TIP: MATCHING FONT COLOR**
> If you have created a custom font color, matching text that you type later to that particular shade can be a challenge. It is easy to match color, however, when you click the Font Color arrow and select the shade from the Recent Colors area.

Formatting a Paragraph

Formatting selected text is only one way to alter the appearance of a document. You can also change the alignment, indentation, tab stops, or line spacing for any paragraph within the document. Recall that Word defines a paragraph as text followed by a hard return, or even a hard return on a line by itself (indicating a blank paragraph). You can include borders or shading for added emphasis around selected paragraphs, and you can number paragraphs or enhance them with bullets. The Paragraph group on the Home tab contains several paragraph formatting commands (see Figure 2.9). If you are formatting only one paragraph, you do not have to select the entire paragraph. Simply click to place the insertion point within the paragraph and apply a paragraph format. However, if you are formatting several paragraphs, you must select them before formatting.

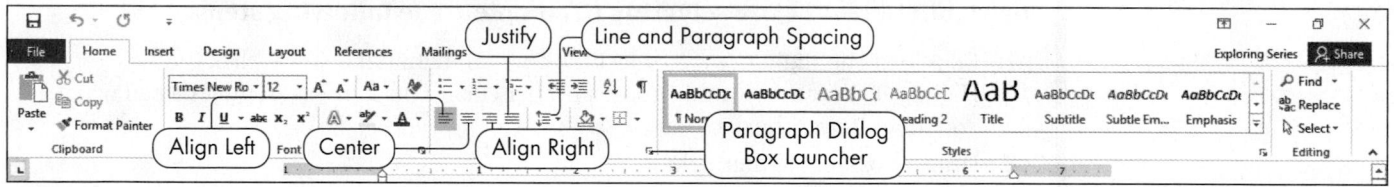

FIGURE 2.9 Paragraph Commands

Word 2016, Windows 10, Microsoft Corporation

Select Paragraph Alignment

Alignment refers to how the text is positioned relative to the margins. ***Left alignment*** is the most common alignment, often seen in letters, reports, and memos. When you begin a new blank Word document, paragraphs are left aligned by default. Text begins evenly at the left margin and ends in an uneven ("ragged") right edge. The opposite of left alignment is ***right alignment***, a setting in which text is aligned at the right margin with a ragged left edge. Short lines including dates, figure captions, and headers are often right aligned. A ***center alignment*** positions text horizontally in the center of a line, with an equal distance from both the left and right margins. Report titles and major headings are typically centered. Finally, ***justified alignment*** spreads text evenly between the left and right margins so that text begins at the left margin and ends uniformly at the right margin. Newspaper and magazine articles are often justified. Such text alignment often causes awkward spacing as text is stretched to fit evenly between margins. Figure 2.10 shows examples of paragraph alignments.

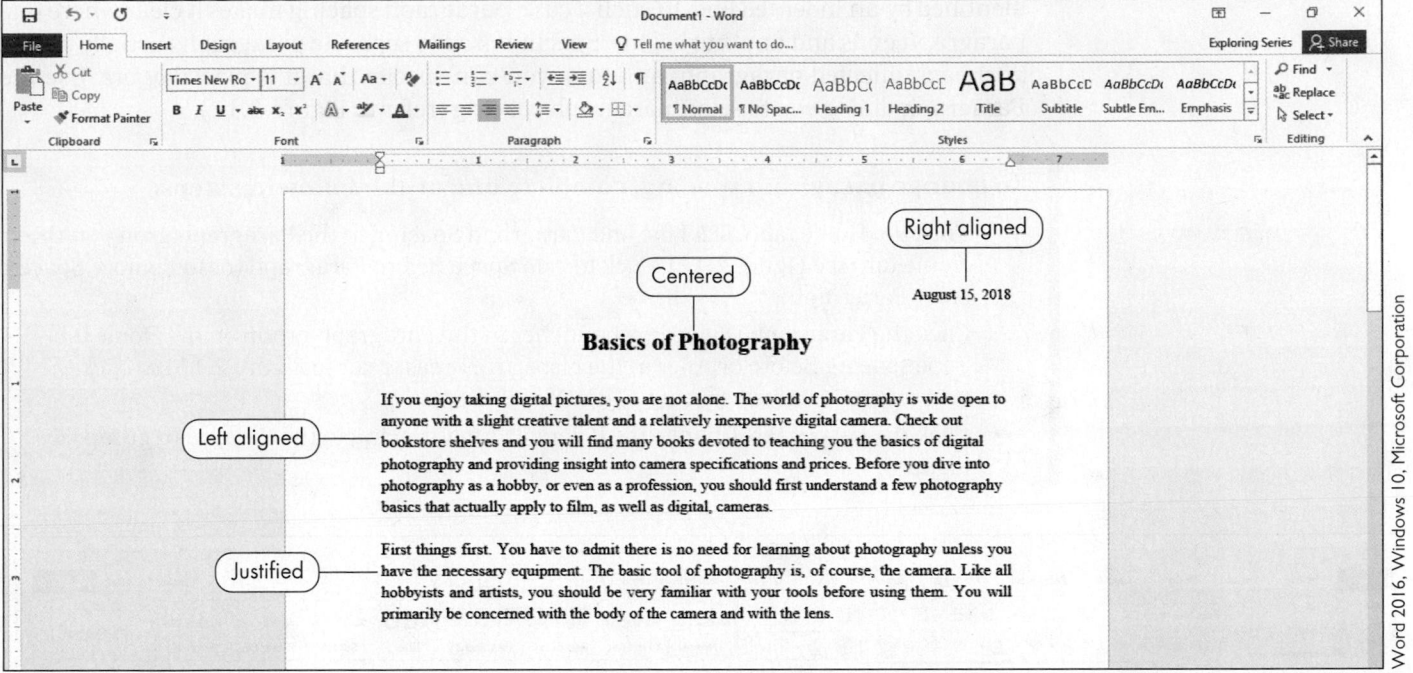

FIGURE 2.10 Paragraph Alignment

To change paragraph alignment, select text (or click to position the insertion point in a paragraph, if only one paragraph is to be affected) and select an alignment from the Paragraph group on the Home tab (refer to Figure 2.9). You can also change alignment by making a selection from the Paragraph dialog box (see Figure 2.11), which opens when you click the Paragraph Dialog Box Launcher (refer to Figure 2.9).

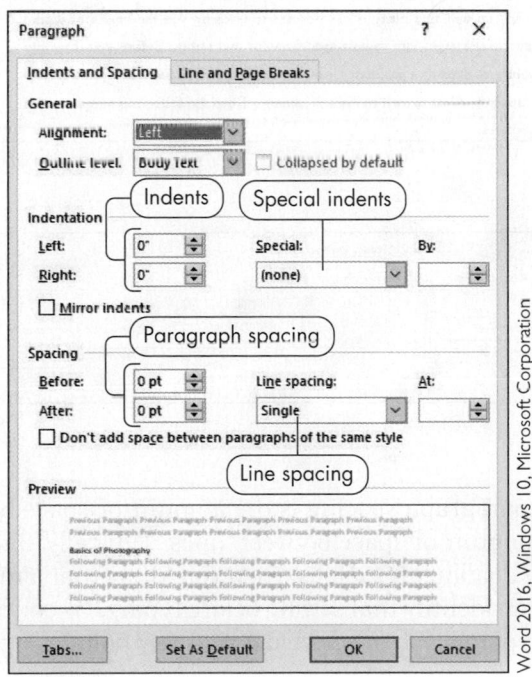

FIGURE 2.11 Paragraph Dialog Box

Select Line and Paragraph Spacing

Paragraph spacing is the amount of space between paragraphs, measured in points. (Recall that one point is 1/72 of an inch.) Paragraph spacing is a good way to differentiate between paragraphs, especially if the beginning of each paragraph is not clearly identified by an indented line. In such a case, paragraph spacing makes it clear where one paragraph ends and another begins. Spacing used to separate paragraphs usually comes *after* each affected paragraph, although you can specify that it is placed *before*. Use the Paragraph dialog box to select paragraph spacing (refer to Figure 2.11).

To change paragraph spacing, complete one of the following steps:

- Click the Home tab. Click Line and Paragraph Spacing in the Paragraph group on the Home tab (see Figure 2.12). Click to Add Space Before Paragraph (or to Remove Space After Paragraph).
- Click the Paragraph Dialog Box Launcher in the Paragraph group on the Home tab. Type spacing Before or After in the respective areas (refer to Figure 2.11) or click the spin arrows to adjust spacing. Click OK.
- Click the Layout tab. Change the Before or After spacing in the Paragraph group (see Figure 2.13).

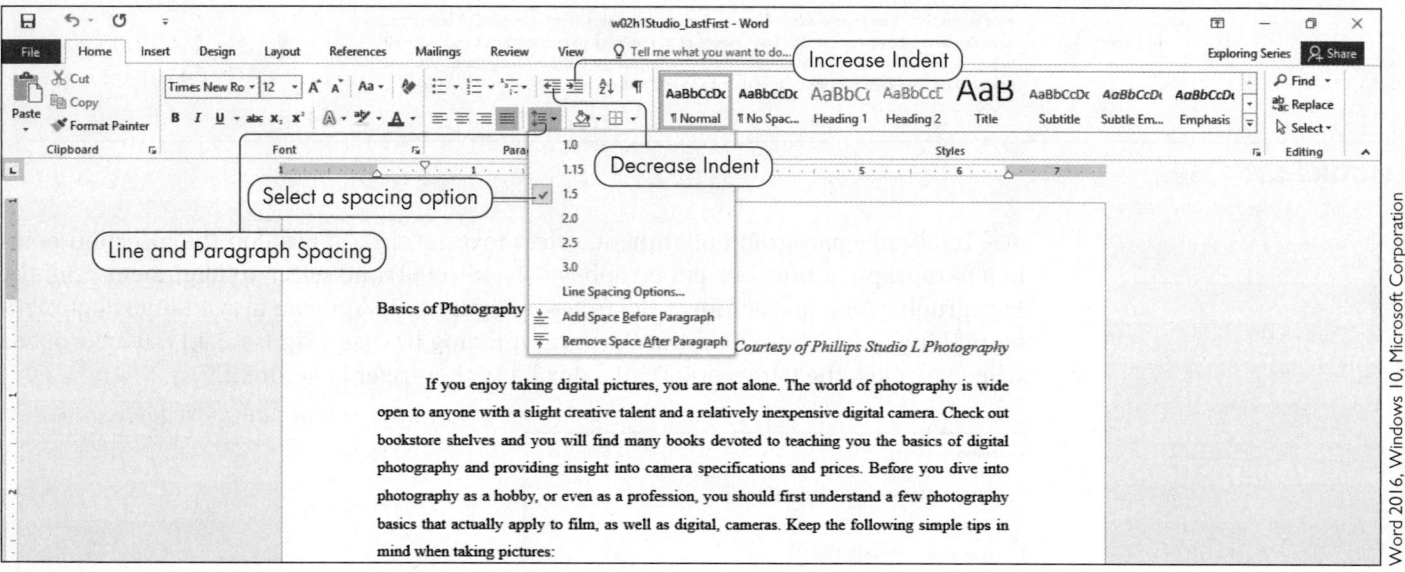

FIGURE 2.12 Spacing Options

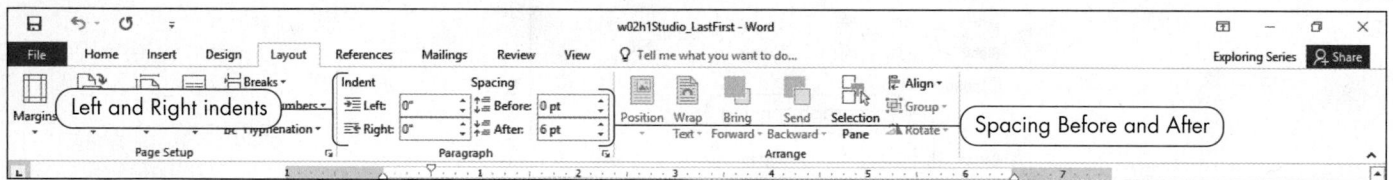

Word 2016, Windows 10, Microsoft Corporation

FIGURE 2.13 Paragraph Spacing and Indents

Just as paragraph spacing is the amount of space between paragraphs, **line spacing** is the amount of space between lines. Typically, line spacing is determined before beginning a document, such as when you know that a research paper should be double-spaced, so you identify that setting before typing. Of course, you can change line spacing of a current paragraph or selected text at any point as well.

To change the line spacing, complete one of the following steps:

- Click the Home tab. Click Line and Paragraph Spacing (refer to Figure 2.12). Select the line spacing you want to use or click Line Spacing Options for more choices.
- Click the Paragraph Dialog Box Launcher on the Home tab. Click the Line spacing arrow and select spacing (refer to Figure 2.11). Click OK.

The most common line spacing options are single, double, or 1.5 lines. Word provides those options and more. From the Paragraph dialog box (refer to Figure 2.11), you can select Exactly, At Least, or Multiple. To specify an exact point size for spacing, select Exactly. If you select At Least, you will indicate a minimum line spacing size while allowing Word to adjust the height, if necessary, to accommodate such features as drop caps (oversized letters that sometimes begin paragraphs). The Multiple setting enables you to select a line spacing interval other than single, double, or 1.5 lines.

Select Indents

STEP 2 An **indent** is a setting associated with how part of a paragraph is distanced from one or more margins. One of the most common indents is a **first line indent**, in which the first line of each paragraph is set off from the left margin. For instance, your English instructor might require that the first line of each paragraph in a writing assignment is indented 0.5" from the left margin, which is a typical first line indent. If you have ever prepared a bibliography for a research paper, you have most likely specified a **hanging indent**, where the first line of a source begins at the left margin, but all other lines in the source are indented. Indenting an entire paragraph from the left margin is a **left indent**, while indenting an entire paragraph from the right margin is a **right indent**. A lengthy quote is often set apart by indenting from both the left and right margins.

Using the Paragraph dialog box (refer to Figure 2.11), you can select an indent setting for one or more paragraphs. First line and hanging indents are considered special indents. You can select left and right indents from either the Paragraph dialog box or from the Paragraph group on the Layout tab (refer to Figure 2.13).

You can use the Word ruler to set indents. If the ruler does not display above the document space, click the View tab and click Ruler (see Figure 2.14). The three-part indicator at the left side of the ruler enables you to set a left indent, a hanging indent, or a first line indent. Drag the desired indent along the ruler to apply the indent to the current paragraph (or selected paragraphs). Figure 2.14 shows the first line indent moved to the 0.5" mark, resulting in the first line of a paragraph being indented by 0.5".

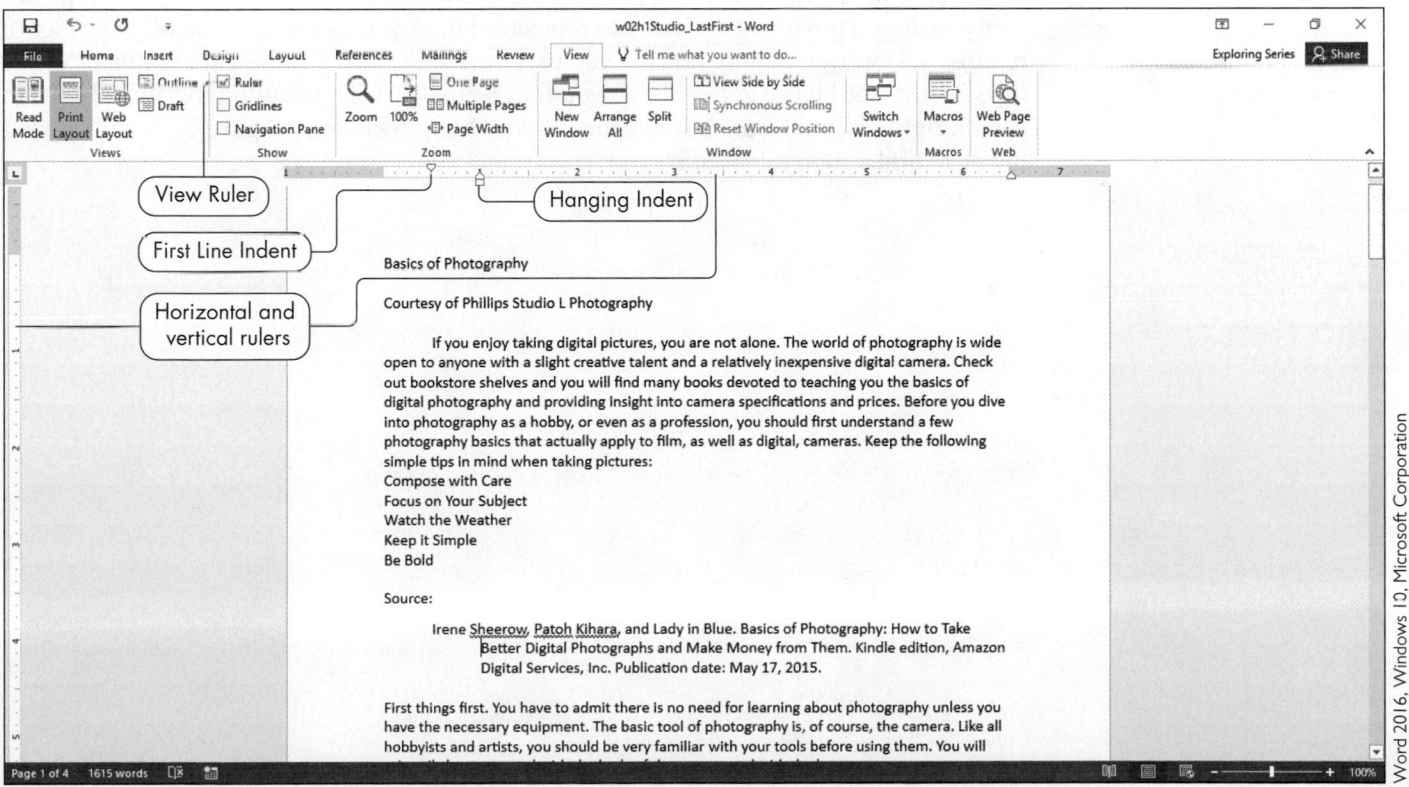

FIGURE 2.14 Set Indents on the Ruler

Set Tab Stops

STEP 3 ▶▶ A **tab stop** is a marker that specifies a position for aligning text. By using tab stops, you can easily arrange text in columns or position text a certain distance from the left or right margins. Tabs enable you to add organization to a document, arranging text in easy-to-read columns. A table of contents is an example of tabbed text, as is a restaurant menu. The most common tab stops are left, right, center, and decimal. By default, a left tab is set every 0.5" when you start a new document. Each time you press Tab on the keyboard, the insertion point will move to the right by 0.5". Typically, you would set a first line indent or simply press Tab to indent the first line of each new paragraph within a document. Table 2.1 describes the types of tabs.

TABLE 2.1	Tab Markers	
Tab Icon on Ruler	**Type of Tab**	**Function**
⌊	Left	Sets the start position on the left, so as you type text moves to the right of the tab setting.
⊥	Center	Sets the middle point of the text you type. Whatever you type will be centered on that tab setting.
⌐	Right	Sets the start position on the right, so as you type text moves to the left of that tab setting and aligns on the right.
⊥	Decimal	Aligns numbers on a decimal point. Regardless of how long the number, each number lines up with the decimal point in the same position.
		Bar	This tab does not position text or decimals but inserts a vertical bar at the tab setting. This bar is useful as a separator for text printed on the same line.

Pearson Education, Inc.

Tab stops that you set override default tabs. For example, suppose you set a left tab at 1". That means the default tab of 0.5" is no longer in effect. The easiest way to set tab stops is to use the ruler. You may click a position on the ruler to set a tab stop. You can also drag a tab along the ruler to reposition it, or you can drag a tab off the ruler to remove it. However, a more precise way to set tab stops is to use the Tabs dialog box. The tab selector (see Figure 2.15) allows you to repeatedly cycle through tabs, including left, center, right, decimal, bar, first line indent, and hanging indent. Figure 2.15 shows a left tab at 1" and a right tab at 5.5".

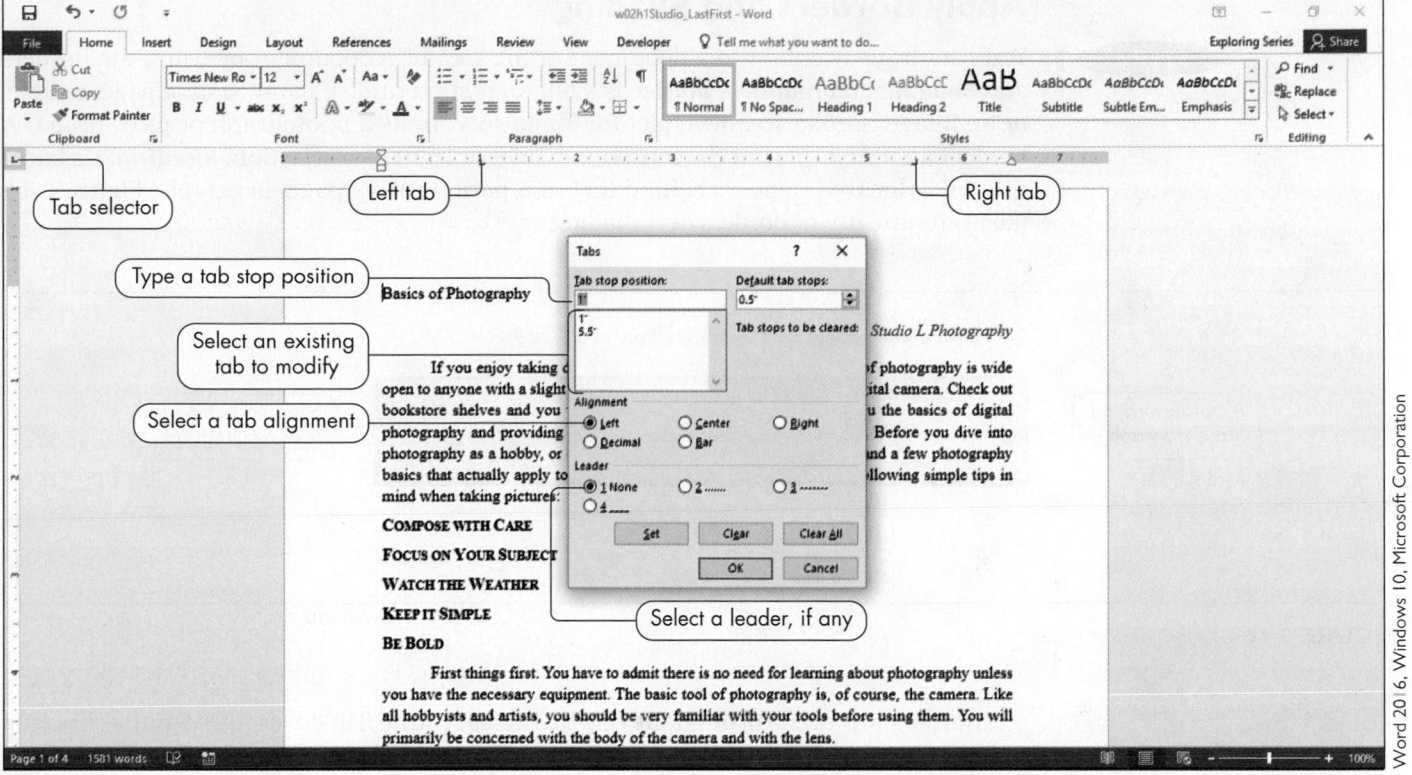

FIGURE 2.15 Set Tab Stops

TIP: MANAGE TAB STOPS

Tab stops can be inserted and applied in two ways. First, you can select text and then set the tab stops, which applies tabs to the selected text. Second, you can set a tab stop and then type text, which applies tab stops to text typed after setting tabs.

To include leaders (the series of dots or hyphens that leads the reader's eye across the page to connect two columns of information), use the Tabs dialog box, shown in Figure 2.15. The row of dots that typically connects a food item with its price on a restaurant menu is an example of a leader.

To set a tab with a leader, complete the following steps:

1. Click the Paragraph Dialog Box Launcher in the Paragraph group on the Home tab and click Tabs from the Indents and Spacing tab. Alternatively, double-click a tab on the ruler.
2. Type the location where you want to set the tab. The number you type is assumed to be in inches, so typing *2* would place a tab at 2".
3. Select a tab alignment (Left, Right, etc.).
4. Specify a leader.
5. Click OK (or click Set and continue specifying tabs).

TIP: DELETING TAB STOPS

To manually delete a tab stop you have set, select the text first, then simply drag the tab stop off the ruler. An alternative is to click the Paragraph Dialog Box Launcher, click Tabs, select the tab (in the Tab stop position box), and then click Clear. Click OK.

Apply Borders and Shading

STEP 4 ▶▶ You can draw attention to a document or an area of a document by using the Borders and Shading command. A ***border*** is a line that surrounds a paragraph, a page, a table, or an image, similar to how a picture frame surrounds a photograph or piece of art. A border can also display at the top, bottom, left, or right of a selection. ***Shading*** is a background color that appears behind text in a paragraph, a page, or a table. Figure 2.16 illustrates the use of borders and shading.

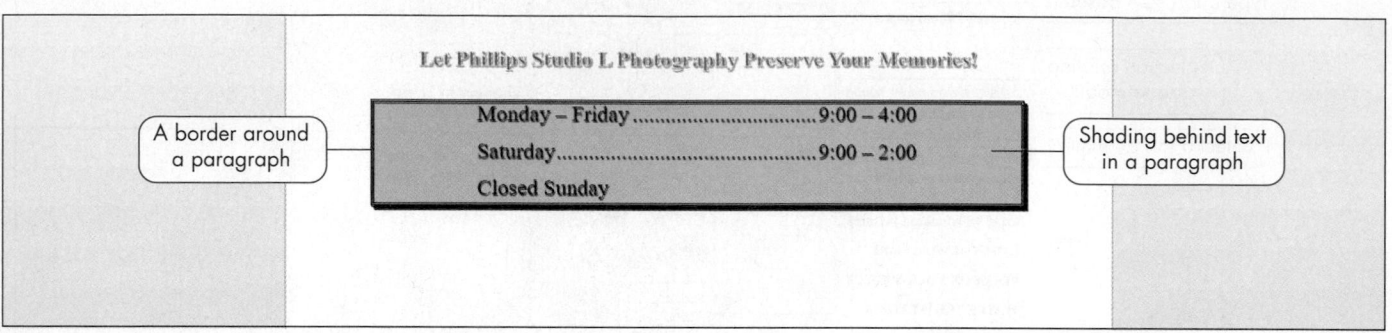

FIGURE 2.16 Borders and Shading

Word 2016, Windows 10, Microsoft Corporation

Borders are used throughout this text to surround Tip boxes and Troubleshooting areas. You might surround a particular paragraph with a border, possibly even shading the paragraph, to set it apart from other text on the page, drawing the reader's attention to its contents. You must first select all paragraphs to which you will apply the border or shading formats. If you have not selected text, any border or shading you identify will be applied to the paragraph in which the insertion point is located.

When you click the Borders arrow in the Paragraph group on the Home tab and select Borders and Shading, the Borders and Shading dialog box displays (see Figure 2.17). There are three tabs in the dialog box: Borders, Page Border, and Shading. The paragraph border settings are on the Borders tab. Besides the None setting, you can format your borders using a Box, Shadow, 3-D, or Custom format. A Box border places a uniform border around a paragraph. A Shadow border places thicker lines at the right and bottom of the bordered area. The 3-D border, on the other hand, adds more dimension to the border. The Custom border enables the user to select a specific style, color, width, and side. The Preview area displays a diagram of the border options that you select.

To apply a paragraph border to selected text, complete the following steps:

1. Select text. Click the Borders arrow in the Paragraph group on the Home tab.
2. Click Borders and Shading. Ensure that the Borders tab is selected.
3. Select the border setting of your choice (see Figure 2.17).
4. Select the style of the line of your choice.
5. Select the color for the border.
6. Select the width of the border.
7. Click OK.

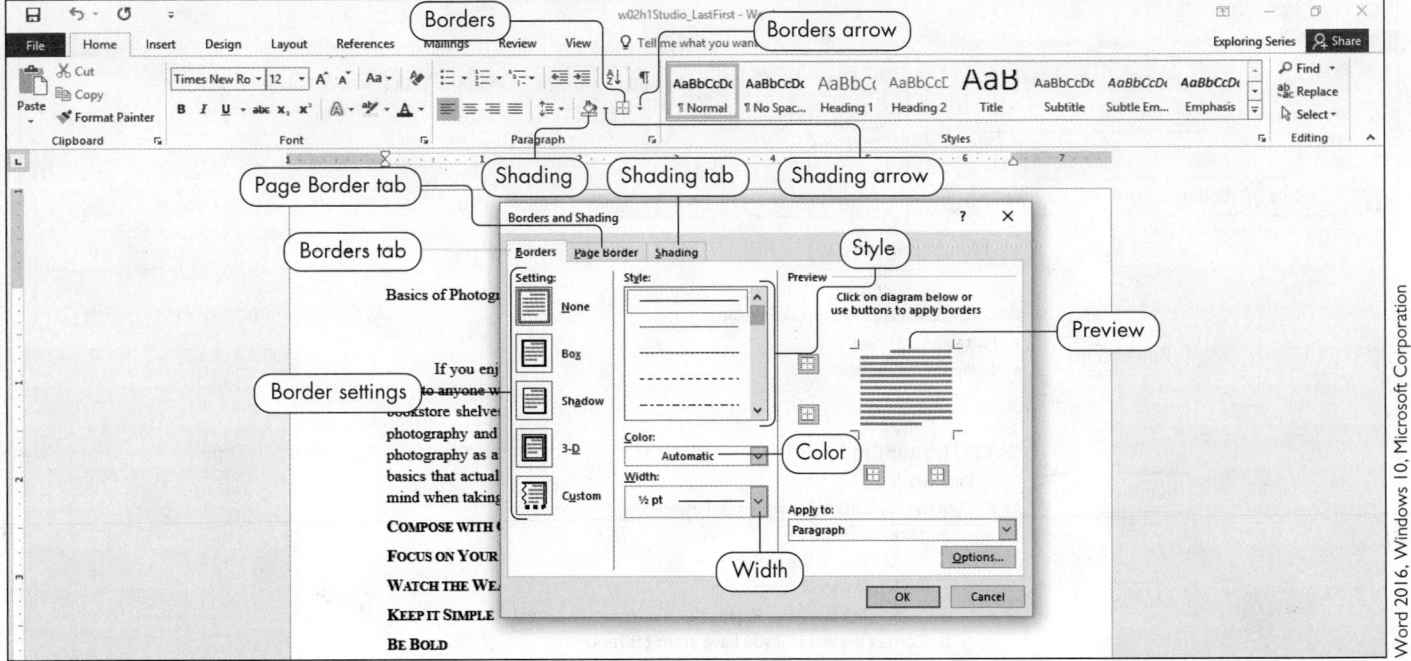

FIGURE 2.17 Select a Border

The Page Border tab in the Borders and Shading dialog box provides controls that you use to place a decorative border around one or more selected pages. As with a paragraph border, you can place the border around the entire page, or you can select one or more sides. The Page Border tab also provides an additional option to use a preselected image as a border instead of ordinary lines. Note that it is appropriate to use page borders on documents such as flyers, newsletters, and invitations, but not on formal documents such as research papers and professional reports.

> **To apply shading to one or more selected paragraphs, complete the following steps:**
>
> 1. Click the Shading arrow in the Paragraph group on the Home tab.
> 2. Select a solid color, or a lighter or darker variation of the color, for the shaded background. Or, click More Colors for even more selections. You can also select shading from the Shading tab of the Borders and Shading dialog box (see Figure 2.17).
> 3. Click OK.

Create Bulleted and Numbered Lists

STEP 5 ❯❯ A list organizes information by topic or in a sequence. Use a ***numbered list*** if the list is a sequence of steps. If the list is not of a sequential nature, but is a simple itemization of points, use a ***bulleted list*** (see Figure 2.18). The numerical sequence in a numbered list is automatically updated to accommodate additions or deletions, which means that if you add or remove items, the list items are renumbered. A multilevel list extends a numbered or bulleted list to several levels, and it, too, is updated automatically when topics are added or deleted. You create each of these lists from the Paragraph group on the Home tab.

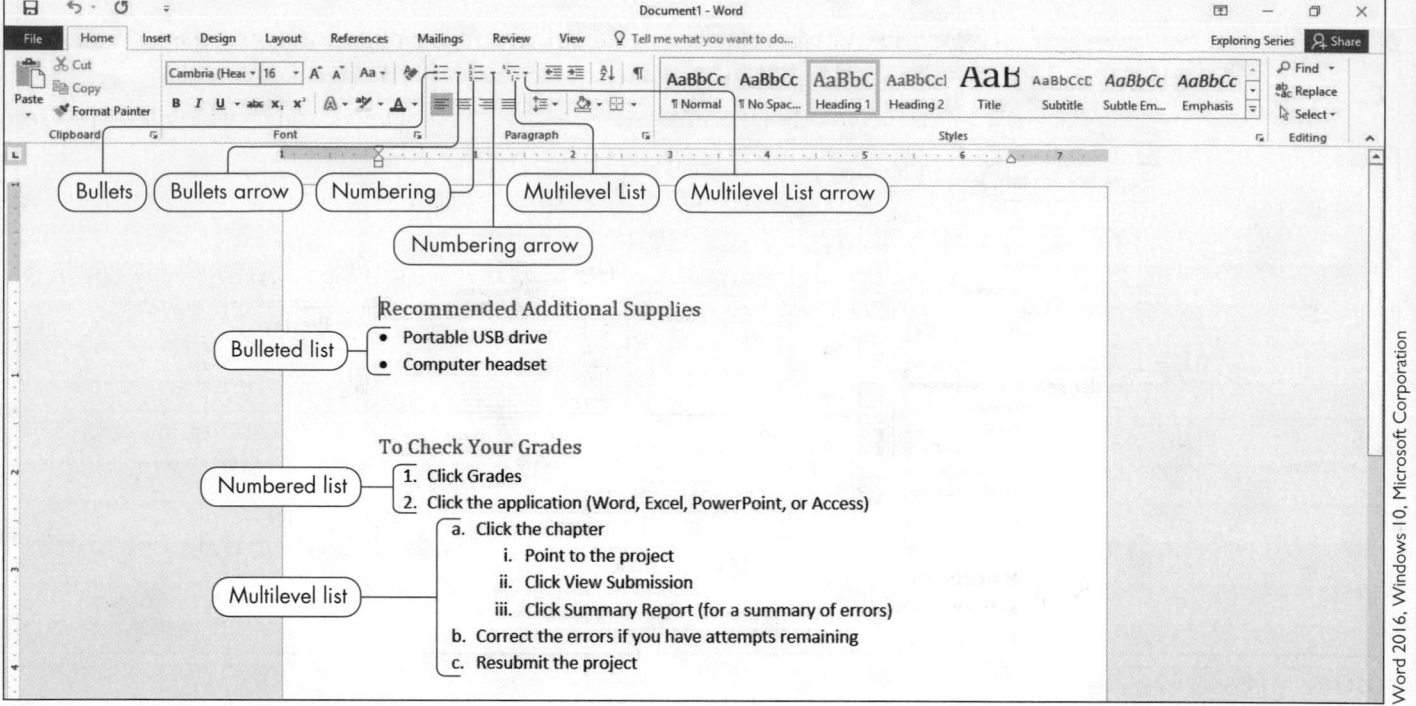

FIGURE 2.18 Bullets and Numbering

To apply bullets, numbering, or multiple levels to a list, complete the following steps:

1. Select the items to be bulleted or numbered.
2. Complete one of the following steps:
   - Click Bullets (or Numbering) to apply the default bullet or numbering style.
   - Click the Bullets (or Numbering) arrow in the Paragraph group on the Home tab and point to one of the predefined symbols or numbering styles in the library. A preview of the style will display in your document. Click the style you want to use.
   - Click Multilevel List and select a style to apply multiple levels to a list.

You can also apply bullets or numbering before you type the items by clicking Bullets (or Numbering), typing the list items, and clicking Bullets (or Numbering) again to turn off the toggle.

To define a new bullet or customize the formatting (such as color or special effect) of a selected bullet, complete the following steps:

1. Click the Bullets arrow in the Paragraph group on the Home tab.
2. Click Define New Bullet.
3. Make selections from the Define New Bullet dialog box.
4. Click OK.

> **TIP: RENUMBERING A LIST**
> Especially when creating several numbered lists in a document, you might find that Word continues the numbering sequence from one list to the next, when your intention was to begin numbering each list at 1. To restart numbering at a new value, right-click the item that is not numbered correctly, and click Restart at 1. Alternatively, you can click the Numbering arrow and select Set Numbering Value. Indicate a starting value in the subsequent dialog box and click OK.

Quick Concepts

1. Describe the difference between a serif and sans serif font. Give examples of when you might use each. *p. 201*

2. What could cause the larger space between lines of bullets, and how would you correct it so that the bulleted items are single spaced? *p. 208*

3. If you use Word to create a restaurant menu, what type of tabs would you use, and approximately how would you space them? *p. 211*

4. You are preparing a document with a list of items to bring for an upcoming camping trip. What Word feature could you use to draw attention to the list? *p. 213*

Hands-On Exercises

Watch the Video for this Hands-On Exercise!

MyITLab®
HOE1 Training

Skills covered: Select Font Options • Change Text Appearance • Select Paragraph Alignment • Select Paragraph Spacing • Select Indents • Set Tab Stops • Apply Borders and Shading • Create Bulleted and Numbered Lists

1 Text and Paragraph Formatting

The newsletter you are developing needs a lot of work. You want to format it so it is much easier to read. After selecting an appropriate font and font size, you will emphasize selected text with bold and italic text formatting. Paragraphs must be spaced so they are easy to read. You know that to be effective, a document must capture the reader's attention while conveying a message. You will begin the process of formatting and preparing the newsletter in this exercise.

STEP 1 ›› SELECT FONT OPTIONS AND CHANGE TEXT APPEARANCE

The newsletter will be printed and distributed by mail. As a printed document, you know that certain font options are better suited for reading. Specifically, you want to use a serif font in an easy-to-read size. Refer to Figure 2.19 as you complete Step 1.

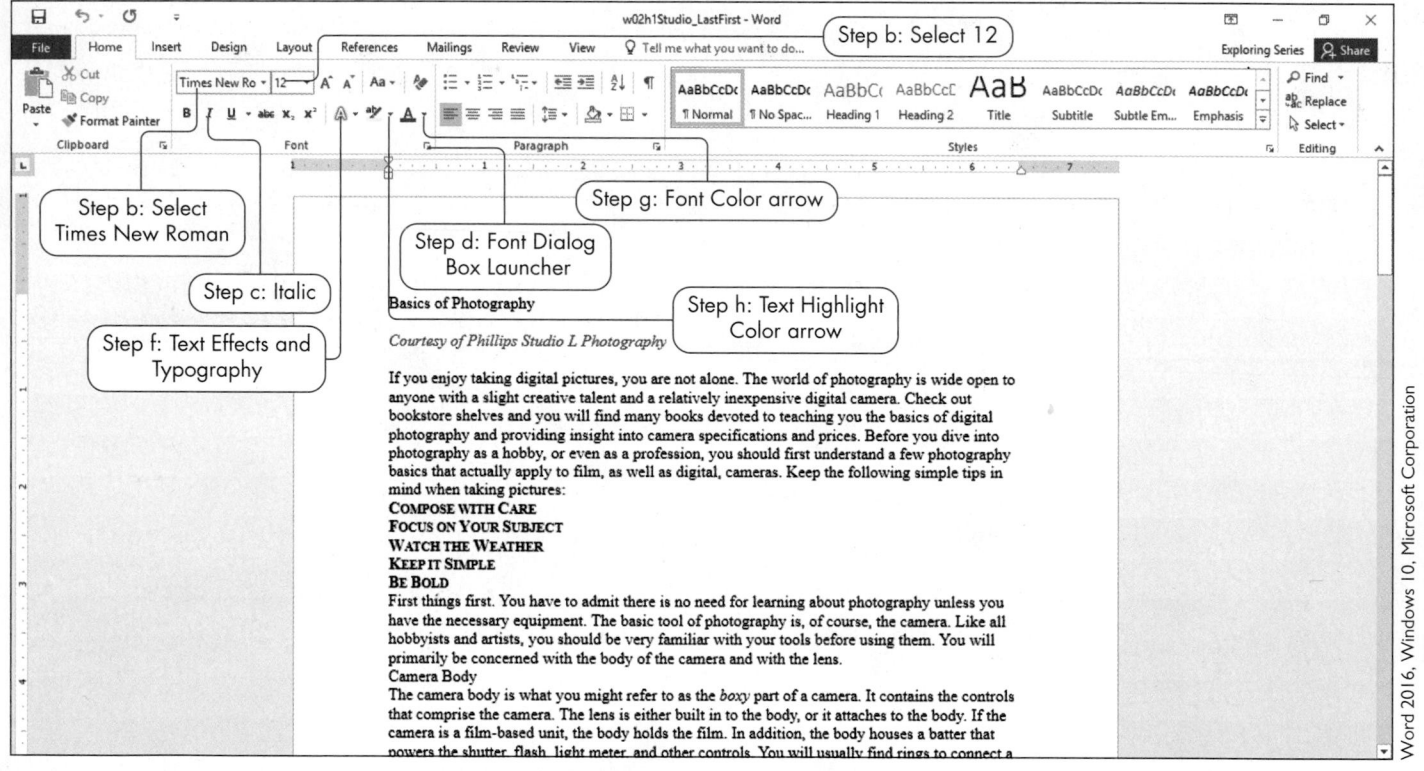

FIGURE 2.19 Format Text

a. Open *w02h1Studio* and save it as **w02h1Studio_LastFirst**.

> **TROUBLESHOOTING:** If you make any major mistakes in this exercise, you can close the file, open *w02h1Studio* again, and then start this exercise over.

b. Press **Ctrl+A** to select all of the text in the document. Click the **Font arrow** in the Font group on the Home tab and scroll to select **Times New Roman**. Click the **Font Size arrow** in the Font group and select **12**.

You use a 12-pt serif font on the whole document because it is easier to read in print.

c. Select the second paragraph in the document, *Courtesy of Phillips Studio L Photography*. Click **Italic** on the Mini toolbar. Locate and double-click **boxy** in the paragraph below Camera Body. Click **Italic** in the Font group.

> **TROUBLESHOOTING:** If the Mini toolbar does not display or disappears, click Italic in the Font group on the Home tab.

d. Select the five paragraphs beginning with *Compose with Care* and ending with *Be Bold*. Click the **Font Dialog Box Launcher** in the Font group.

The Font dialog box displays with font options.

e. Ensure that the Font tab is displayed in the Font dialog box, and click **Bold** in the Font style box. Click to select the **Small caps check box** under Effects. Click **OK**.

f. Press **Ctrl+End** to move the insertion point to the end of the document. Select the last paragraph in the document, *Let Phillips Studio L Photography Preserve Your Memories!* Click **Text Effects and Typography** in the Font group. Select **Fill – Blue, Accent 1, Outline – Background 1, Hard Shadow – Accent 1** (third row, third column). Change the font size of the selected text to **16**. Click anywhere to deselect the text.

g. Press **Ctrl+Home** to position the insertion point at the beginning of the document. Select the second paragraph in the document, *Courtesy of Phillips Studio L Photography*. Click the **Font Color arrow** and select **Blue, Accent 5, Darker 25%** (fifth row, ninth column).

h. Select the words *you should consider how to become a better photographer* in the paragraph under the *Composition* heading. Click the **Text Highlight Color arrow** and select **Yellow**.

i. Press **Ctrl+Home**. Click the **Review tab** and click **Spelling & Grammar** in the Proofing group to check spelling and grammar. Ignore any possible grammatical errors, but correct spelling mistakes.

j. Save the document.

STEP 2 ›› **SELECT PARAGRAPH ALIGNMENT, SPACING, AND INDENT**

The lines of the newsletter are too close together. It is difficult to tell where one paragraph ends and the next begins, and the layout of the text is not very pleasing. Overall, you will adjust line and paragraph spacing, and apply indents where necessary. Refer to Figure 2.20 as you complete Step 2.

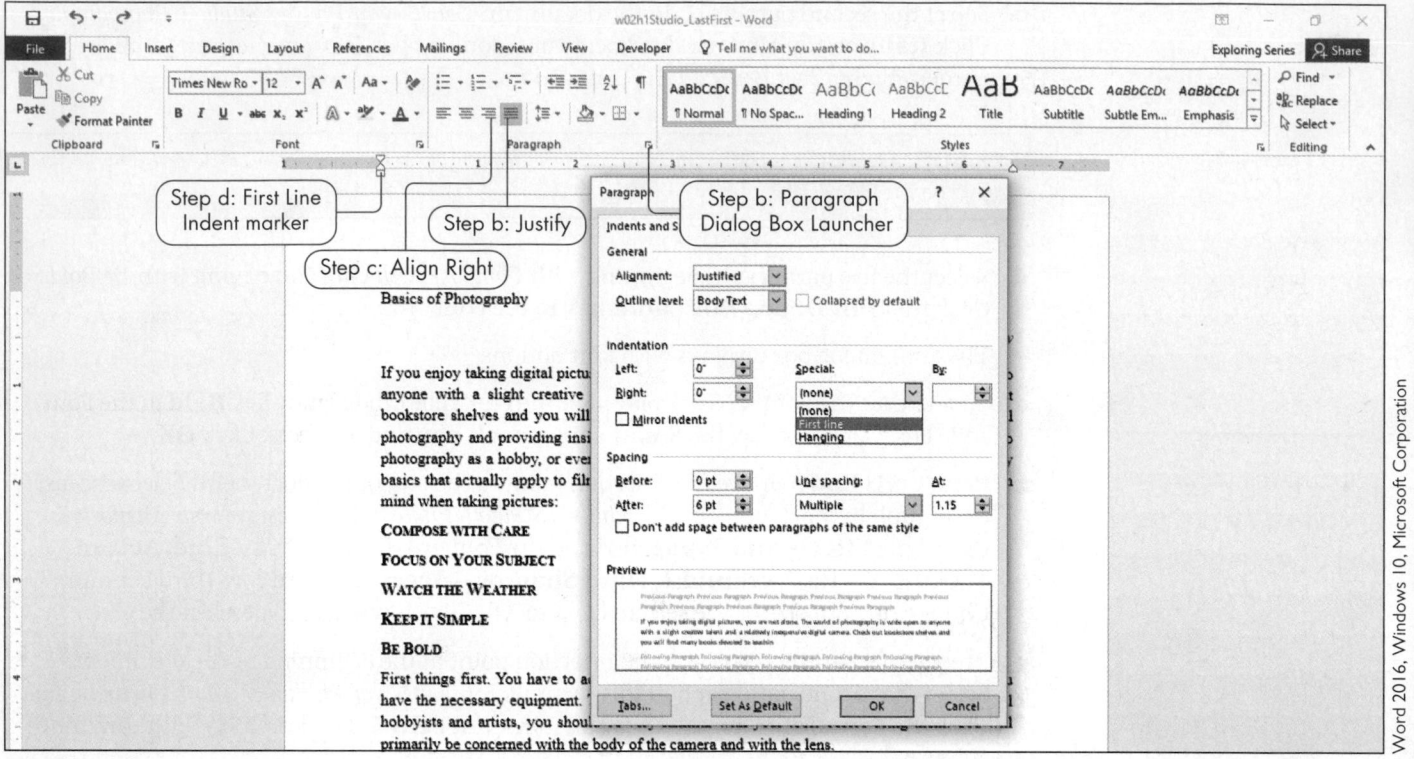

FIGURE 2.20 Adjust Spacing and Indents

a. Select most of the document beginning with the sentence *If you enjoy taking digital pictures* and ending with *emotion expressed before even greeting Santa*. Click the **Home tab**. Click **Line and Paragraph Spacing** in the Paragraph group. Select **1.15**. Do not deselect the text.

All lines within the selected text are spaced by 1.15.

b. Click **Justify** in the Paragraph group. Click the **Paragraph Dialog Box Launcher**. With the Indents and Spacing tab selected, click the **After spin arrow** in the Spacing section to increase spacing after to **6 pt**. Click **OK**. Click anywhere to deselect the text.

You have placed 6 pt spacing after each paragraph in the selected area. Selected paragraphs are also aligned with justify, which means text is evenly distributed between the left and right margins.

c. Press **Ctrl+End**. Click anywhere on the last paragraph in the document, *Let Phillips Studio L Photography Preserve Your Memories!* Click **Center** in the Paragraph group. Press **Ctrl+Home**. Click anywhere on the second line of text in the document, *Courtesy of Phillips Studio L Photography*. Click **Align Right** in the Paragraph group.

d. Click the **View tab**, and click the **Ruler check box** in the Show group to select it. Click anywhere in the first body paragraph, beginning with *If you enjoy taking digital pictures*. Click the **Home tab**, and click the **Paragraph Dialog Box Launcher**. Click the **Special arrow** in the Indentation group and select **First line**. Click **OK**. Click anywhere in the paragraph beginning with *First things first*. Position the pointer on the First Line Indent marker on the ruler and drag the marker to the **0.5"** mark on the horizontal ruler.

The first line of both multiline paragraphs that begin the document are indented by 0.5 inches.

e. Save the document.

You realize that you left off the studio hours and want to include them at the end of the document. Refer to Figure 2.21 as you complete Step 3.

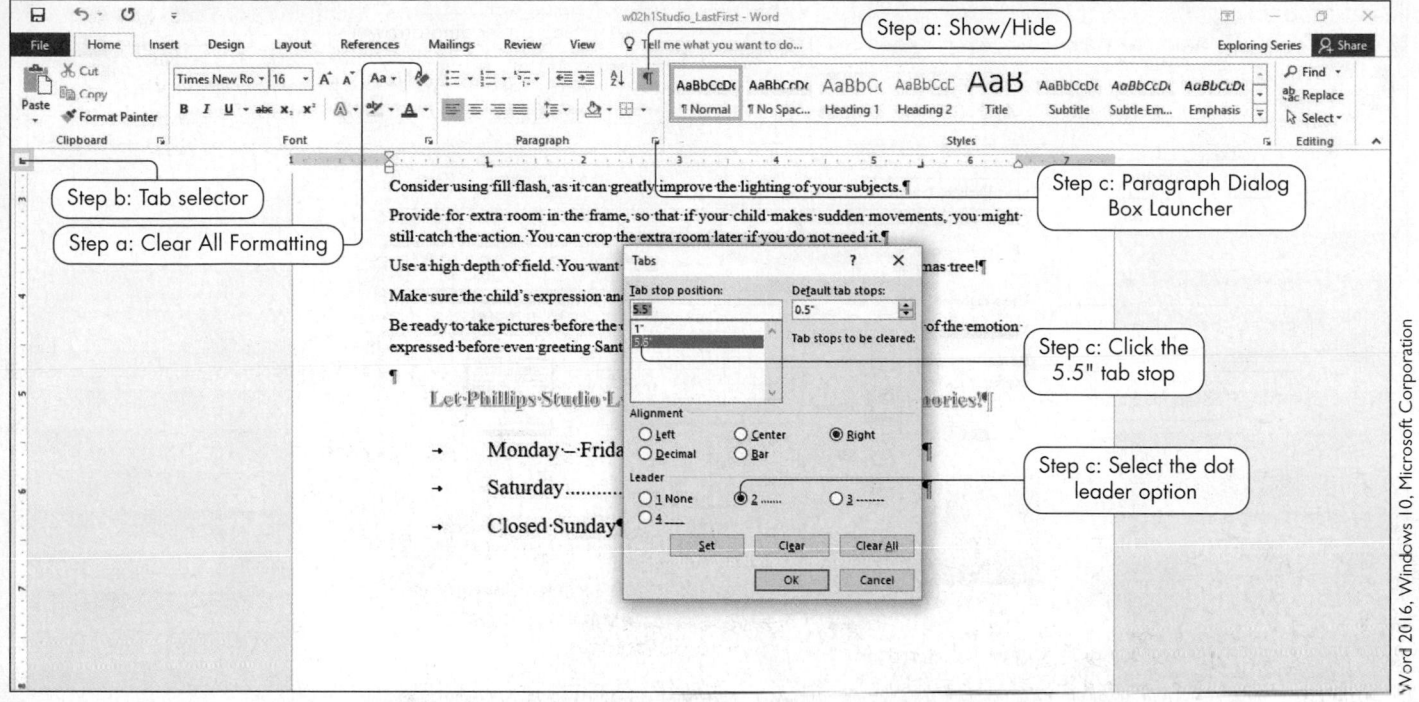

FIGURE 2.21 Set Tab Stops

a. Press **Ctrl+End**. Click **Show/Hide** in the Paragraph group to display nonprinting characters. Press **Enter** twice. Click **Clear All Formatting** in the Font group on the Home tab. Select **Times New Roman font** and **16 pt size**.

You clicked Clear All Formatting so that the text effect formatting from the line above the insertion point is not carried forward to text that you will type next.

b. Ensure the tab selector (shown at the top of the vertical ruler) specifies a Left Tab and click at **1"** on the ruler. Click the **tab selector** twice to select a Right Tab and click at **5.5"** on the ruler.

You set a left tab at 1" and a right tab at 5.5".

> **TROUBLESHOOTING:** If the tabs you set are incorrectly placed on the ruler, click Undo in the Quick Access Toolbar and repeat Step b. You can also simply drag a tab off the ruler to remove it, or drag it along the ruler to reposition it.

c. Click the **Paragraph Dialog Box Launcher** and click **Tabs** at the bottom-left corner. Click **5.5"** in the Tab stop position box. Click **2** in the Leader section and click **OK**.

You modified the right tab to include dot leaders, which means dots will display before text at the right tab.

d. Press **Tab**. Type **Monday – Friday** and press **Tab**. Type **9:00 – 4:00**. Press **Enter**. Press **Tab**. Type **Saturday** and press **Tab**. Type **9:00 – 2:00**. Press **Enter**. Press **Tab**. Type **Closed Sunday**.

e. Save the document.

To draw attention to the business hours, you will shade and border the information you typed. Refer to Figure 2.22 as you complete Step 4.

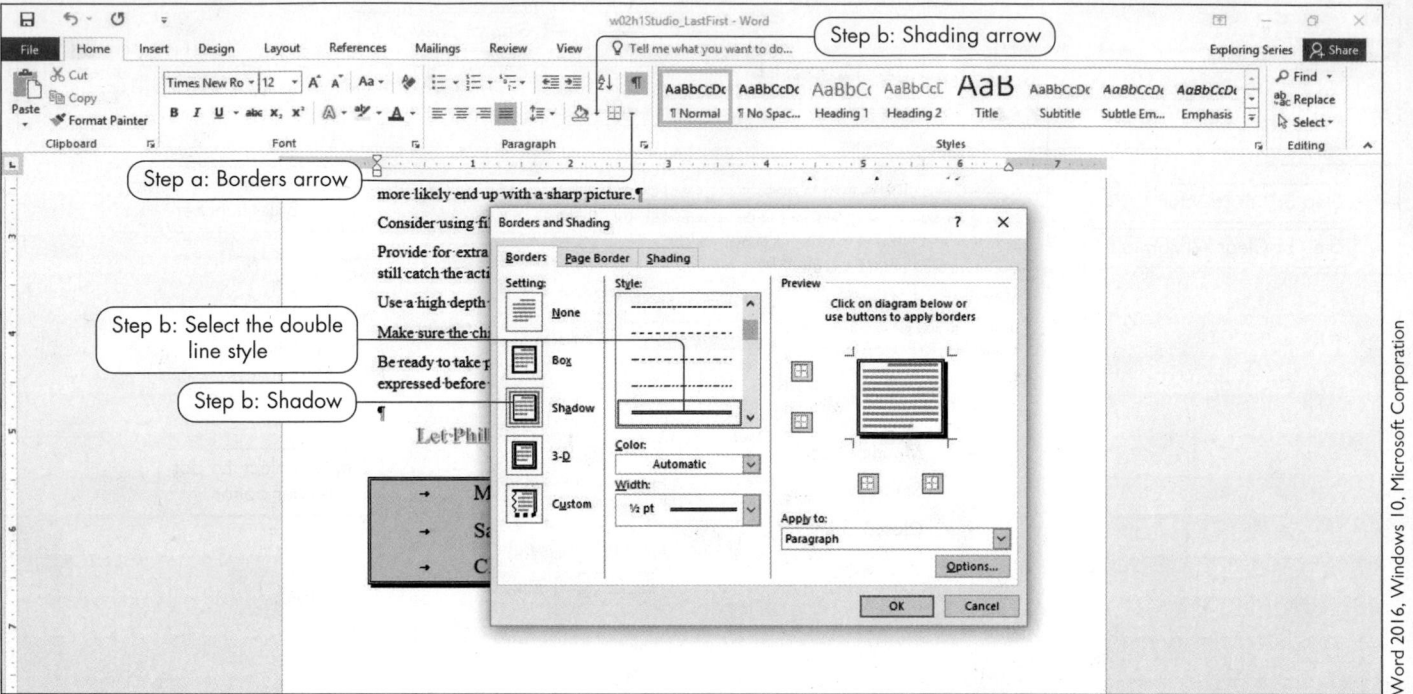

FIGURE 2.22 Apply Borders and Shade Text

a. Select the three paragraphs at the end of the document, beginning with *Monday – Friday* and ending with *Closed Sunday*. Click the **Borders arrow** in the Paragraph group on the Home tab and select **Borders and Shading**.

> **TROUBLESHOOTING:** If you click Borders instead of the Borders arrow, you will not see the Borders and Shading dialog box and the most recent border will be applied to selected text. Click Undo on the Quick Access Toolbar, click the Borders arrow, and then click Borders and Shading.

b. Click **Shadow** in the Setting section. Scroll through the Style box and select the seventh style—**double line**. Click **OK**. Do not deselect the text. Click the **Shading arrow** and select **Blue, Accent 1, Lighter 60%** (third row, fifth column). Click anywhere to deselect the text.

Studio hours are bordered and shaded.

c. Save the document.

At several points in the newsletter, you include either a list of items or a sequence of steps. You will add bullets to the lists and number the steps. Refer to Figure 2.23 as you complete Step 5.

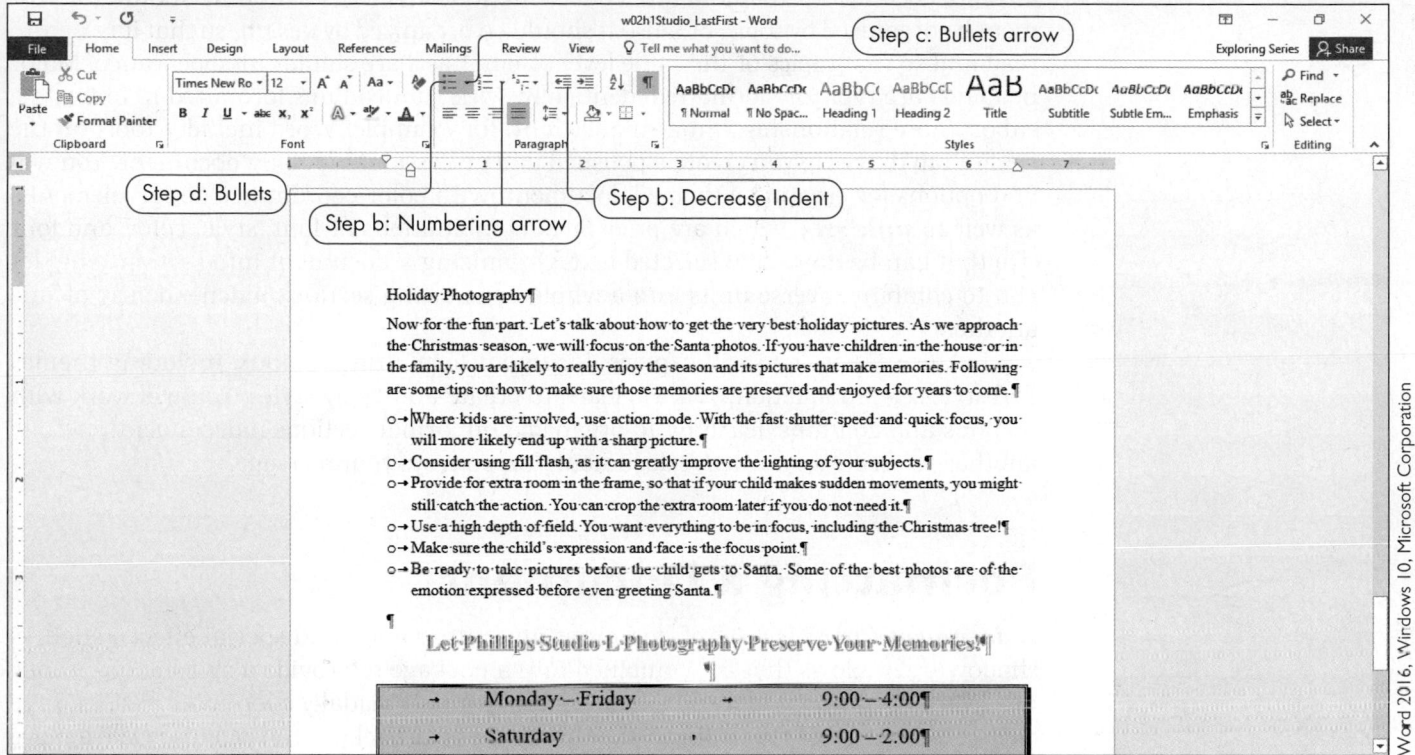

FIGURE 2.23 Add Bullets and Numbers

a. Press **Ctrl+Home**. Select the five boldfaced paragraphs, beginning with *Compose with Care* and ending with *Be Bold*.

b. Click the **Numbering arrow** and select the **Number Alignment** showing each number followed by a right parenthesis. Click **Decrease Indent** in the Paragraph group to move the numbered items to the left margin. Click anywhere to deselect the text.

c. Scroll to the second page and select the four paragraphs following the sentence *Depth of field is determined by several factors:*, beginning with *Aperture/F-Stop* and ending with *Point of View*. Click the **Bullets arrow** and select the **hollow round bullet**. Decrease the indent to move the selected text to the left margin. Deselect the text.

d. Press **Ctrl+End** and select the six paragraphs above the last line of text, beginning with *Where kids are involved*, and ending with *even greeting Santa*. Click **Bullets** to apply a hollow round bullet to the selected paragraphs. Decrease the indent so the bullets begin at the left margin.

Clicking Bullets applied the most recently selected bullet style to selected text. You did not have to click the Bullets arrow and select from the Bullet Library.

e. Save the document. Keep the document open if you plan to continue with the next Hands-On Exercise. If not, close the document, and exit Word.

Document Appearance

The overall appearance and organization of a document is the first opportunity to effectively convey your message to readers. You should ensure that a document is formatted attractively with coordinated and consistent style elements. Not only should a document be organized by topic, but also it should be organized by design, so that it is easy to read and so that topics of the same level of emphasis are similar in appearance. Major headings are typically formatted identically, with subheadings formatted to indicate a subordinate relationship—in a smaller font, for example. Word includes tools on the Design tab that help you create a polished and professional-looking document. You will find options for creating a themed document, with color-coordinated design elements, as well as *style sets*, which are predefined combinations of font, style, color, and font size that can be applied to selected text. Organizing a document into sections enables you to combine diverse units into a whole, formatting sections independently of one another.

In this section, you will explore document formatting options, including themes and style sets. In addition, you will learn to create and apply styles. You will work with sections and columns, learning to organize and format sections independently of one another, to create an attractive document that conveys your message.

Formatting a Document

A *document theme* is a set of coordinating fonts, colors, and special effects, such as shadowing or glows that are combined into a package to provide a stylish appearance in a Word document. Applying a theme enables you to visually coordinate various page elements. In some cases, adding a page border or page background can also yield a more attractive and effective document. All these design options are available on the Design tab. As you consider ways to organize a document, you might find it necessary to divide it into sections, with each section arranged or formatted independently of others. For example, a cover page (or section) might be centered vertically, while all other pages are aligned at the top. By arranging text in columns, you can easily create an attractive newsletter or brochure. The Layout tab facilitates the use of sections and formatting in columns. When formatting a document, you should always keep in mind the document's purpose and its intended audience. Whereas a newsletter might use more color and playful text and design effects, a legal document should be more conservative. With the broad range of document formatting options available in Word, you can be as playful or conservative as necessary.

Select a Document Theme

STEP 1 ⟫ When you select a theme for a document, a unified set of design elements, including font style, color, and special effects, is applied to the entire document. The Design tab includes selections related to themes (see Figure 2.24). A new blank Word document is based on a theme by default—the Office theme.

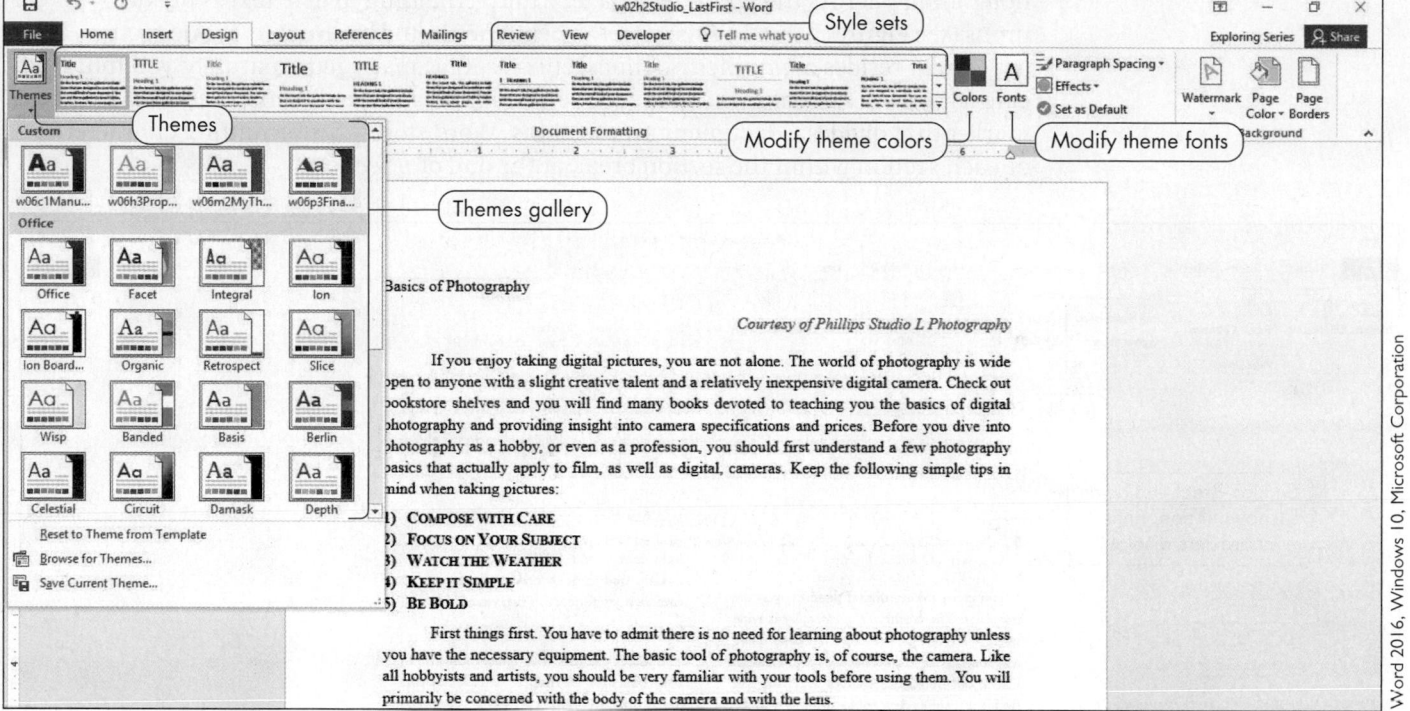

FIGURE 2.24 Design Tab

Themes are located in the Document Formatting group on the Design tab (refer to Figure 2.24). You can choose from a variety of themes from Themes in the Document Formatting group. You can change the style, color, font, paragraph spacing, and effects of any theme by selecting a different option within the Document Formatting group.

To change a document's theme, complete the following steps:

1. Click Themes in the Document Formatting group on the Design tab.
2. Point to each theme in the Themes gallery to display a preview of the effect on the document. Depending on document features and color selections already in place, you might not see an immediate change when previewing a theme.
3. Click a theme to select it.

To modify a color or font selection in a theme, complete the following steps:

1. Click Colors or Fonts in the Document Formatting group on the Design tab. Each group of coordinated colors or font selections is summarized and identified by a unique name.
2. Click to select a color or font group to adjust the selected theme in the document.

To apply theme effects to objects in a document, complete the following steps:

1. Click Effects in the Document Formatting group on the Design tab.
2. Select an effect from the gallery.

Work with Sections

It sometimes becomes necessary to vary the layout of a document within a page or between pages, and incorporate sections into a document. A section is a part of a document that contains its own page format settings, such as those for margins, columns, and orientation. To have text on the same page accommodating both single column and two-column text, break it into sections. For instance, a headline of an article might center horizontally across the width of a page, while remaining article text is divided into columns (see Figure 2.25). In this case, the headline should be situated in one section, while article text resides in another. So that sections can be managed separately, you must indicate with section breaks where one section ends and another begins. A **section break** is a marker that divides a document into sections. Word stores the formatting characteristics of each section within the section break at the end of a section.

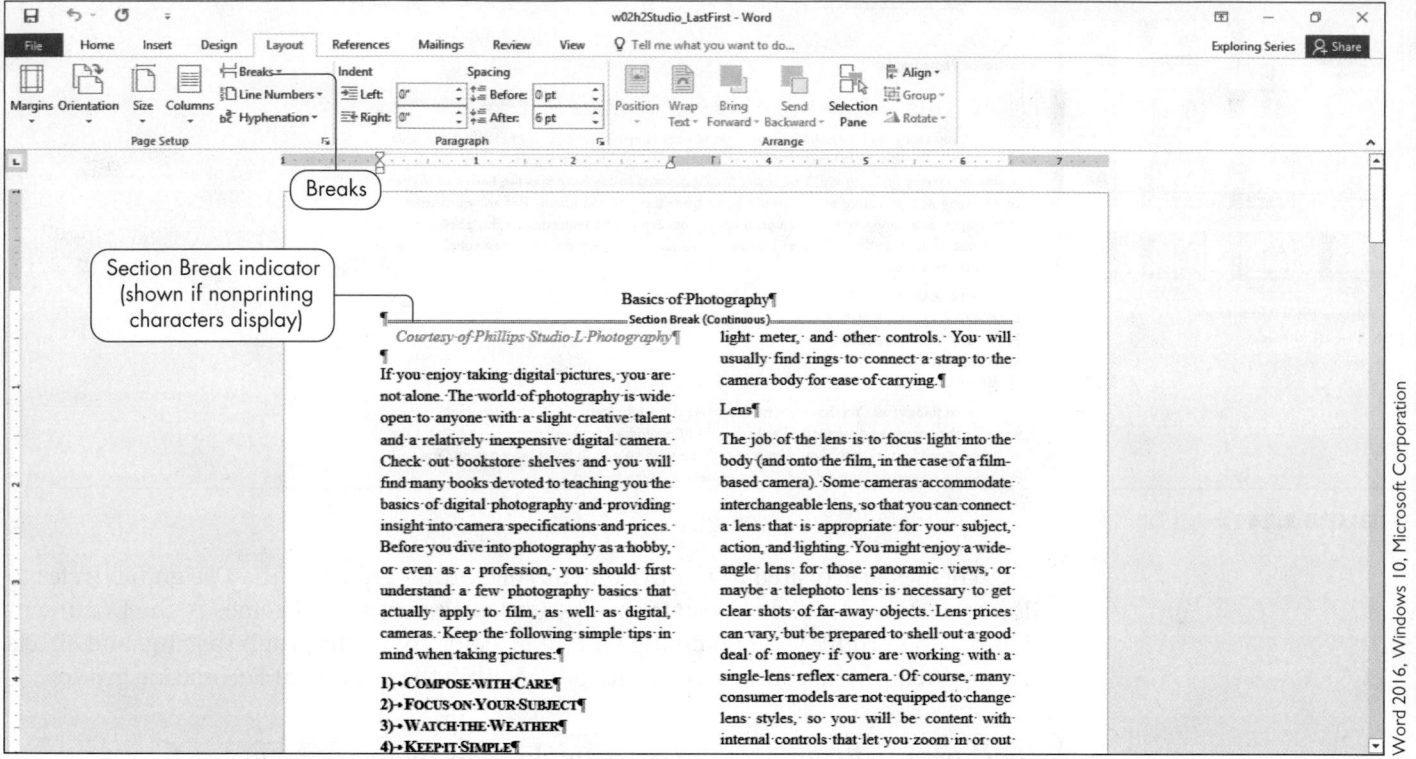

FIGURE 2.25 Select and Display a Section Break

There are four types of section breaks, as shown in Table 2.2. Before inserting a break, the insertion point should be at the point where the break is to occur. You can select a section break type from the Layout tab and click Breaks in the Page Setup group to apply the break.

TABLE 2.2 Section Breaks

Type	Text that follows ...	Use to ...
Next Page	must begin at the top of the next page.	force a chapter to start at the top of a page.
Continuous	can continue on the same page.	format text in the middle of the page into columns.
Even Page	must begin at the top of the next even-numbered page.	force a chapter to begin at the top of an even-numbered page.
Odd Page	must begin at the top of the next odd-numbered page.	force a chapter to begin at the top of an odd-numbered page.

To place a section break in a document, complete the following steps:

1. Click at the location where the section break should occur.
2. Click the Layout tab. Click Breaks in the Page Setup group.
3. Select a section break type (see Table 2.2). If nonprinting characters display, you will see a section break (refer to Figure 2.25).

If you delete a section break, you also delete the formatting for that section, causing the text above the break to assume the formatting characteristics of the following section. To delete a section break, click the section break indicator (refer to Figure 2.25) and press Delete.

Format Text into Columns

STEP 2 ⟩⟩ ***Columns*** format a document or section of a document into side-by-side vertical blocks in which the text flows down the first column and continues at the top of the next column.

To format text into columns, complete the following steps:

1. Click at the location where you want to start formatting the text into columns.
2. Click the Layout tab and click Columns in the Page Setup group.
3. Specify the number of columns or select More Columns to display the Columns dialog box. The Columns dialog box (see Figure 2.26) provides options for setting the number of columns and spacing between columns.
4. Click OK.

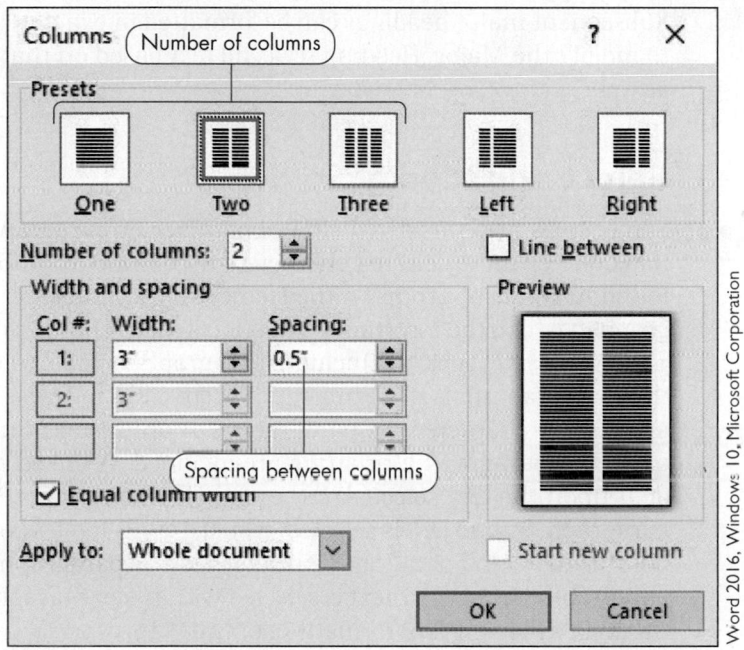

FIGURE 2.26 Columns Dialog Box

Having created a two-column document, you should preview the document to ensure an attractive arrangement of columns. Try to avoid columns that end awkwardly, such as a column heading at the bottom of one column with remaining text continuing at the top of the next column. In addition, columns should be somewhat balanced, if possible, so that one column is not far more lengthy than the next. To remedy these kinds of issues, a column break may be necessary.

To insert a column break, complete the following steps:

1. Click in the document where the break is to occur.
2. Click the Layout tab, click Breaks, and then click Column in the Page Breaks section.

With nonprinting characters displayed, you will see the Column break indicator at the location where one column ends and the next begins.

Applying Styles

As you complete reports, assignments, and other projects, you probably apply the same text, paragraph, table, and list formatting for similar documents. Instead of formatting each element of each document individually, you can create your own custom format for each element—called a style—to save time in designing titles, headings, and paragraphs. A *style* is a named collection of formatting characteristics. A characteristic of a professional document is uniform formatting. All major headings look the same, with uniform subheadings. Even paragraphs can be styled to lend consistency to a document. If styles are appropriately assigned, Word can automatically generate reference pages such as a table of contents and indexes.

Styles automate the formatting process and provide a consistent appearance to a document. It is possible to store any type of character or paragraph formatting within a style, and once a style is defined, you can apply it to any element within a document to produce identical formatting. Word provides a gallery of styles from which you can choose, or you can create your own style. For example, having formatted a major report heading with various settings, such as font type, color, and size, you can create a style from the heading, calling it Major_Heading. The next time you type a major heading, simply apply the Major_Heading style so that the two headings are identical in format. Subsequent major headings can be formatted in exactly the same way. If you later decide to modify the Major_Heading style, all text based on that style will automatically adjust as well.

Select and Modify Styles

STEP 3 ⟩⟩ Some styles are considered either character or paragraph styles. A character style formats one or more selected characters within a paragraph, often applying font formats found in the Font group on the Home tab. A paragraph style changes the entire paragraph in which the insertion point is located, or changes multiple selected paragraphs. A paragraph style typically includes paragraph formats found in the Paragraph group on the Home tab, such as alignment, line spacing, indents, tabs, and borders. Other styles are neither character nor paragraph, but are instead linked styles in which both character and paragraph formatting are included. A linked style applies formatting dependent upon the text selected. For example, when the insertion point is located within a paragraph, but no text is selected, a linked style applies both font characteristics (such as bold or italic) and paragraph formats (such as paragraph and line spacing) to the entire paragraph. However, if text is selected within a paragraph when a linked style is applied, the style will apply font formatting only.

By default, the Normal style is applied to new Word documents. Normal style is a paragraph style with specific font and paragraph formatting. If that style is not appropriate for a document you are developing, you can select another style from Word's Style gallery. The most frequently accessed styles are shown in the Styles group on the Home tab (see Figure 2.27).

To apply a style to selected text or to an existing paragraph, complete the following steps:

1. Select the text or place the insertion point within the paragraph.
2. Click a style in the Styles group on the Home tab. Click the More arrow for more styles.
3. Click the Styles Dialog Box Launcher (see Figure 2.27) to display the Styles pane for more choices.
4. Click to select a style.

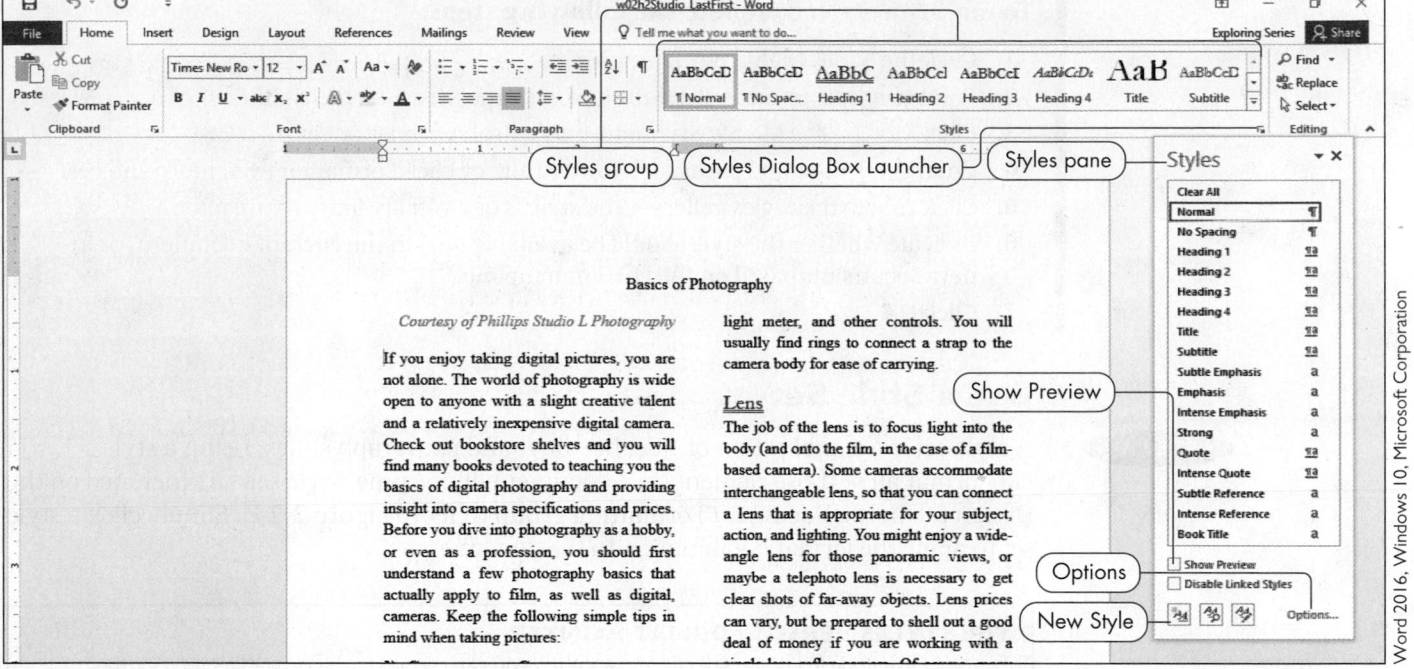

FIGURE 2.27 Styles

Modifying a style, or even creating a new style, affects only the current document, by default. However, you can cause the style to be available to all documents that are based on the current template when you select *New documents based on this template* in the Modify Style dialog box (see Figure 2.28). Unless you make that selection, however, the changes are not carried over to new documents you create or to others that you open. As an example, the specifications for the Title style are shown in Figure 2.28.

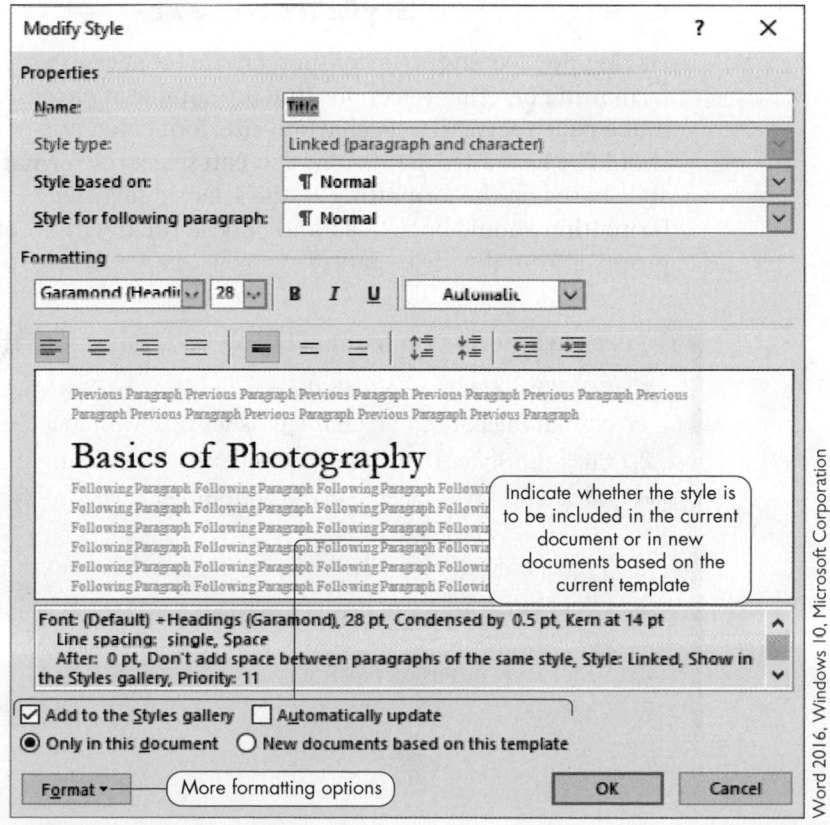

FIGURE 2.28 Modify a Style

To modify a style, complete the following steps:

1. Click the Styles Dialog Box Launcher.
2. Point to a style in the Styles pane and click the arrow on the right.
3. Click Modify. The Modify Style dialog box displays (refer to Figure 2.28).
4. Change any font and paragraph formatting, or click Format for even more choices.
5. Click Add to the Styles gallery if the style is one you are likely to use often.
6. Indicate whether the style should be available only in the current document, or in new documents based on the current template.
7. Click OK.

Use a Style Set

STEP 4 ❯❯ A style set is a combination of title, heading, and paragraph styles. Using a style set, you can format all of those elements in a document at one time. Style sets are included on the Design tab in the Document Formatting group (refer to Figure 2.24). Simply click a style set to apply the format combination to the document.

TIP: STYLES VERSUS FORMAT PAINTER

To copy formatting from one selection to another, you can certainly use Format Painter. Another alternative is to create a new style from the selection and apply it to additional text. Both processes seem to produce the same results. However, unlike changes made using Format Painter, a style remains available in both the current document and in other documents based on the same template, if you indicate that preference when you create the style. That way, the same formatting changes can be applied repeatedly in various documents or positions within the same document, even after a document is closed and reopened. Formatting changes made as a result of using Format Painter are not available later. Also, styles that indicate a hierarchy (such as Heading 1, Heading 2) can be used to prepare a table of contents or outline.

Create a New Style from Text

Having applied several formatting characteristics to text, you might want to repeat that formatting on other selections that are similar in purpose. For example, suppose you format a page title with a specific font size, font color, and bordering. Subsequent page titles should be formatted identically. You can select the formatted page title and create a new style based on the formatting of the selected text. Then select the next title to which the formatting should be applied and choose the newly created style name from the Styles group or from the Styles pane.

To create a new style from existing text, complete the following steps:

1. Select the text from which the new style should be created or click in a paragraph containing paragraph characteristics you want to include in the new style.
2. Click the Styles Dialog Box Launcher (refer to Figure 2.27) to open the Styles pane.
3. Click New Style, located in the bottom-left corner of the Styles pane (refer to Figure 2.27).
4. Type a name for the new style. Do not use the name of an existing style.
5. Click the Style type arrow and select a style type (Paragraph, Character, or Linked, among others).
6. Adjust any other formatting to fit your needs.
7. Click OK.

Use Outline View

STEP 5 » One benefit of applying styles to headings in a long document is the ability to use those headings to view the document in Outline view, making it easier to view and modify the organization of a long document. Outline view in Word displays a document in various levels of detail, according to heading styles applied in a document. Figure 2.29 shows Outline view of a document in which major headings were formatted in Heading 1 style, with subheadings in Headings 2 and 3 style. You can modify the heading styles to suit your preference. To select a level to view, perhaps only first-level headings, click All Levels (beside Show Level) and select a level. You can display the document in Outline view by clicking the View tab, and clicking Outline in the Views group.

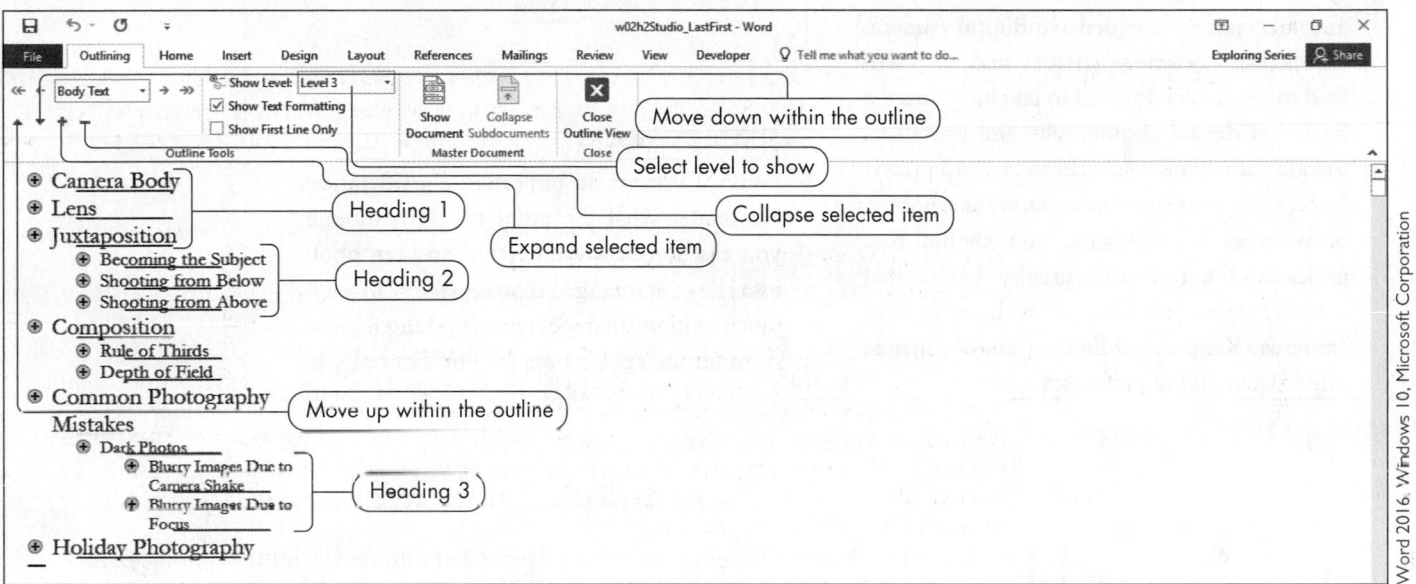

FIGURE 2.29 Outline View

Use Outline view to glimpse or confirm a document's structure. Especially when developing lengthy reports, you will want to make sure headings are shown at the correct level of detail. A document shown in Outline view can also be easily converted to a PowerPoint presentation, with Heading 1 becoming the slide titles, and lower levels becoming bullets on each slide. Also, a table of contents is automatically generated when you click Table of Contents on the References tab.

To collapse or expand a single heading, click the heading in Outline view and click the plus (+) sign (to expand) or the minus (−) sign (to collapse) on the Ribbon. For example, having clicked text formatted as Heading 1, click + to show any lower-level headings associated with the particular heading (refer to Figure 2.29). Text other than that associated with the selected heading will remain unaffected. As shown in Figure 2.29, you can move a heading (along with all associated subheadings) up or down in the document. In Outline view, you can also drag the plus (+) or minus (−) sign beside a heading to move the entire group, including all sublevels, to another location.

You can quickly move through a document in Outline view and to restructure a document. If the levels are collapsed so that body text does not display, you will click a heading to move quickly to that section, and change the view to Print Layout or another view. The document will expand, and the insertion point will be in the section identified by the heading you clicked. Using Outline view to move through a lengthy document can save a great deal of time because it is not necessary to page through a document looking for a particular section heading. You can also use Outline view to restructure a document. Simply drag and drop a heading to reposition it within a document, or use the Move Up or Move Down buttons. If subheadings are associated, they will move with the heading as well.

In Print Layout view, you can quickly collapse everything except the section with which you want to work. Point to a heading and click the small triangle that displays beside the heading (see Figure 2.30) to collapse or expand the following body text and sublevels. Collapsing text in that manner is a handy way to provide your readers with a summary.

Section Break (Continuous)

Courtesy of Phillips Studio L Photography

If you enjoy taking digital pictures, you are not alone. The world of photography is wide open to anyone with a slight creative talent and a relatively inexpensive digital camera. Check out bookstore shelves and you will find many books devoted to teaching you the basics of digital photography and providing insight into camera specifications and prices. Before you dive into photography as a hobby, or even as a profession, you should first understand a few photography basics that actually apply to film, as well as digital, cameras. Keep the following simple tips in mind when taking pictures:

houses a batter that powers the shutter, flash, light meter, and other controls. You will usually find rings to connect a strap to the camera body for ease of carrying.

Collapse or expand view

Lens

Juxtaposition

Point of view is an important consideration. No matter what the point of view, though, you can sometimes change a ho-hum photo into a stunning masterpiece through juxtaposition. Juxtaposition is taking a photo from an unexpected angle. For example, an eye-level photo of a bird is much more

Word 2016, Windows 10, Microsoft Corporation

FIGURE 2.30 Expand and Collapse Detail

Quick Concepts

5. Describe why a document may need to be divided into two or more sections. **p. 223**

6. How do you insert a column break into a Word document? **p. 225**

7. What is the benefit of using styles when formatting several different areas of text? **p. 226**

8. How is the concept of styles related to Outline view? **p. 229**

Hands-On Exercises

Skills covered: Select a Document Theme • Work with Sections • Format Text into Columns • Select and Modify Styles • Use a Style Set • Create a New Style from Text • Use Outline View

2 Document Appearance

The next step in preparing the photography newsletter for distribution is to apply document formatting to several areas of the document that will make it easier to read. By applying a theme and formatting the document in columns, you will add to the visual appeal. Using styles, you can ensure consistent formatting of document text. Finally, you will check the document's organization by viewing it in Outline view.

STEP 1 ➤➤ SELECT A DOCUMENT THEME

A document theme provides color and font coordination, simplifying your design task. You will apply a document theme to the newsletter as a simple way to ensure that yours is an attractive document with well-coordinated features. Refer to Figure 2.31 as you complete Step 1.

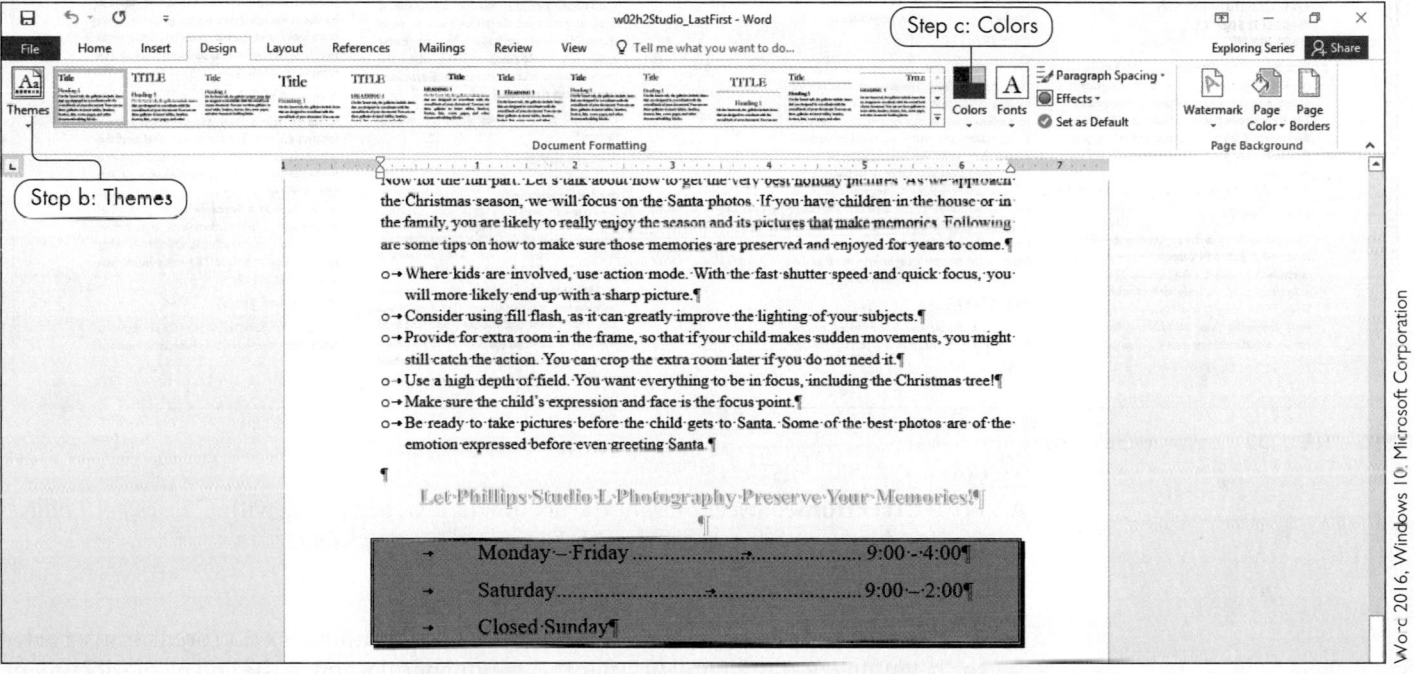

FIGURE 2.31 Apply a Document Theme

a. Open *w02h1Studio_LastFirst* if you closed it at the end of Hands-On Exercise 1, and save it as **w02h2Studio_LastFirst**, changing h1 to h2.

b. Press **Ctrl+Home**. Click the **Design tab** and click **Themes** in the Document Formatting group. Select **Organic**.

   Note the color change applied to the second paragraph of the document, *Courtesy of Phillips Studio L Photography*.

c. Click **Colors** in the Document Formatting group and select **Violet II**.

   The second paragraph of the document, *Courtesy of Phillips Studio L Photography*, has changed colors because you selected a new color scheme within the theme. The table of studio hours on the last page of the document also changed colors.

d. Save the document.

The document should be formatted as a newsletter. Most often, newsletters display in columns, so you will apply columns to the newsletter. A few items, such as the newsletter heading and the store hours at the end of the document, should be centered horizontally across the page instead of within a column. Using sections, you will format those items differently from column text. Refer to Figure 2.32 as you complete Step 2.

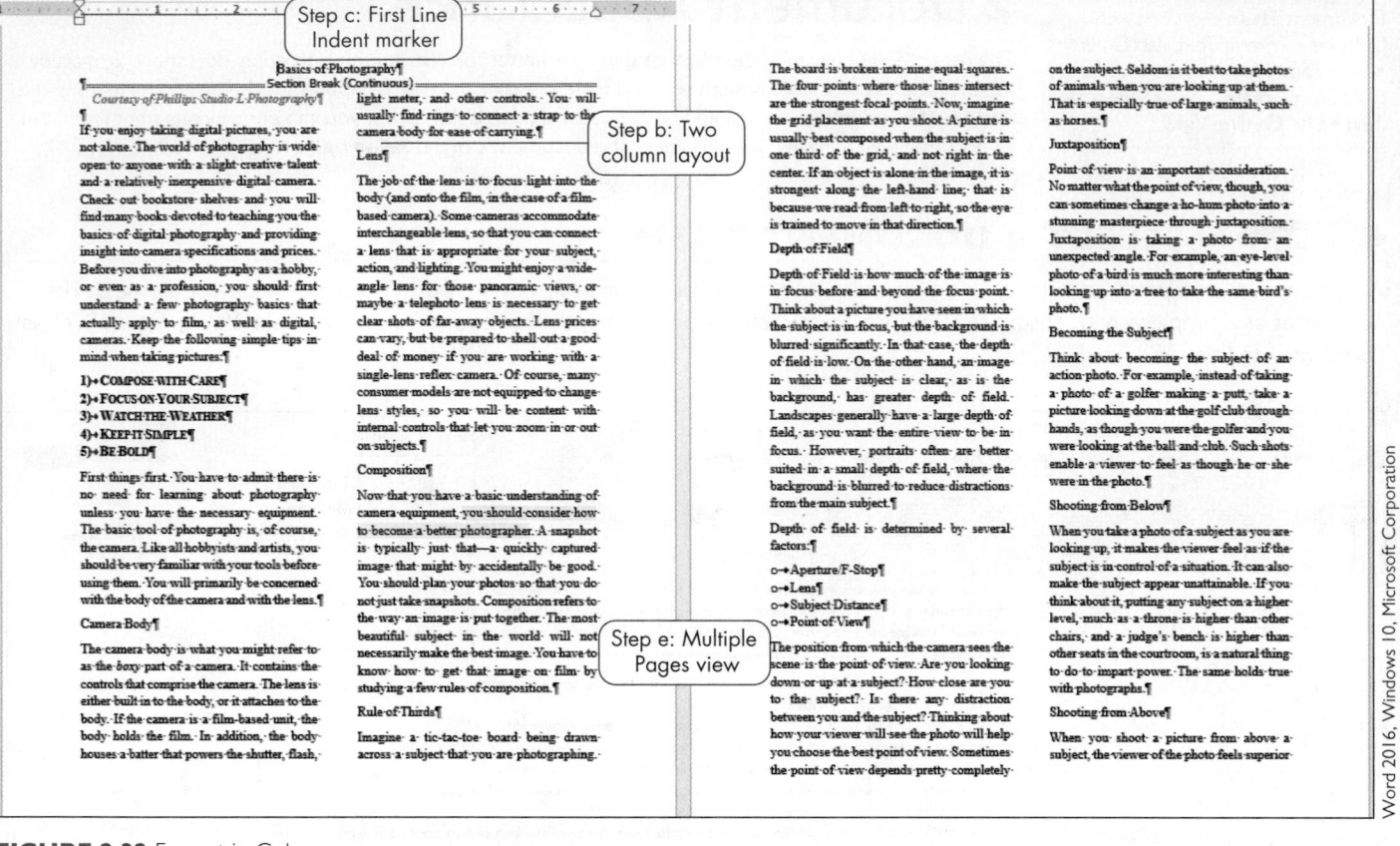

FIGURE 2.32 Format in Columns

a. Press **Ctrl+Home**. Select most of the document text, beginning with *Courtesy of Phillips Studio L Photography* and ending with *before even greeting Santa*.

b. Click the **Layout tab** and click **Columns**. Select **Two**.

The selected text is formatted into two columns. A continuous section break is inserted at the beginning of the document, after the document title, and at the end of the document (before the line that precedes the shaded box). The document now has three sections: The title, the middle with the two-column text, and the end.

c. Press **Ctrl+Home**. Click anywhere on the line containing *Basics of Photography*. Click the **Home tab** and click **Center** in the Paragraph group. Click anywhere in the paragraph beginning with *If you enjoy taking digital pictures*. Drag the **First Line Indent marker** on the ruler back to the left margin.

The title of the newsletter is centered horizontally. The first line indent is removed from the first multiline paragraph in the newsletter.

d. Click anywhere in the paragraph beginning with *First things first*. Drag the **First Line Indent marker** to the left margin to remove the indent.

e. Click the **View tab** and click **Multiple Pages** in the Zoom group. Scroll down to view all pages, getting an idea of how text is positioned on all pages. Click **100%** in the Zoom group.

f. Save the document.

The newsletter is improving in appearance, but you note that the headings (Camera Body, Lens, Composition, etc.) are not as evident as they should be. Also, some headings are subordinate to others, and should be identified accordingly. You will apply heading styles to headings in the newsletter to resolve these issues. Refer to Figure 2.33 as you complete Step 3.

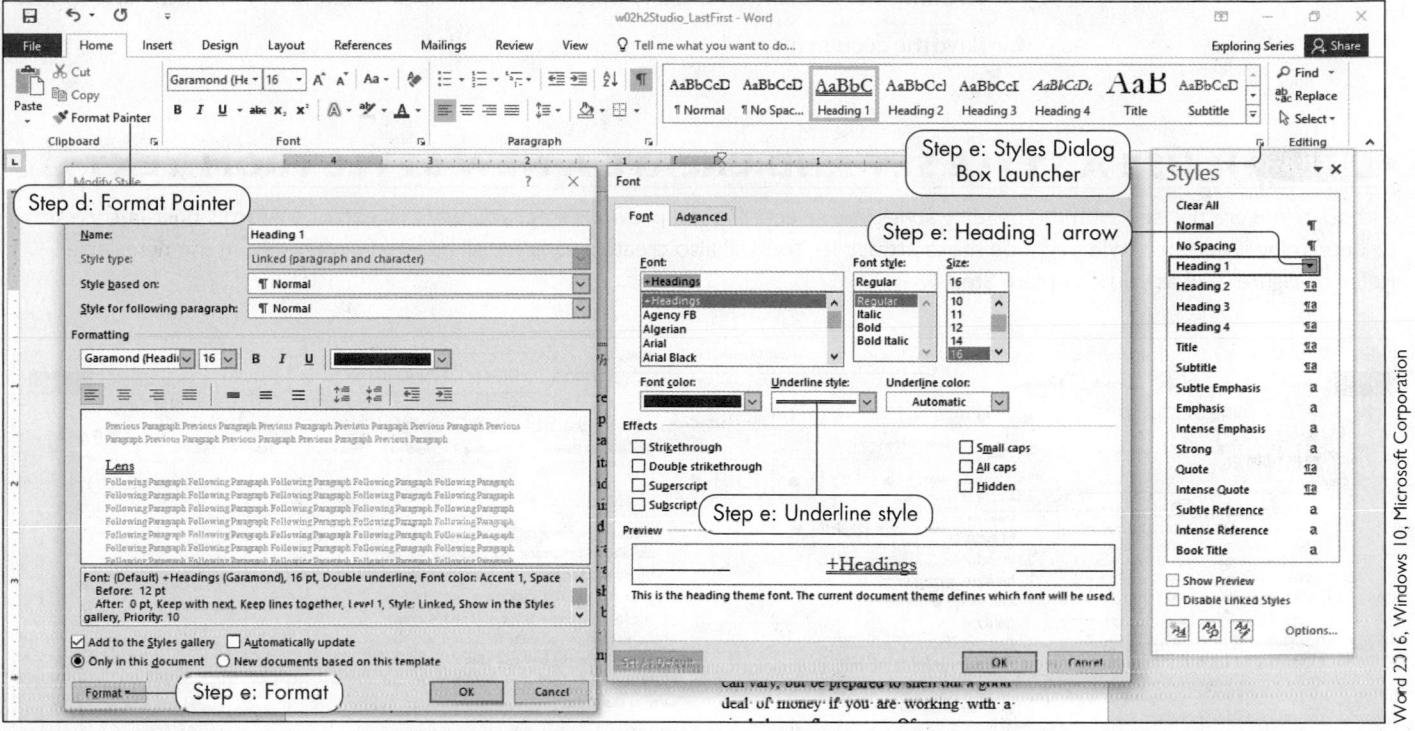

FIGURE 2.33 Work with Styles

a. Select the text **Camera Body** on the first page of the newsletter. Click the **Home tab** and select **Heading 1** in the Styles group. On the same page, in the column on the right, select **Lens** and apply **Heading 1**. Select **Composition** and apply **Heading 1**.

b. Apply **Heading 1** to *Juxtaposition, Common Photography Mistakes*, and *Holiday Photography* on the second and third pages of the newsletter.

c. Select **Rule of Thirds** on the first page, and press and hold **Ctrl** on the keyboard as you also select **Depth of Field**, **Becoming the Subject**, **Shooting from Below**, and **Shooting from Above** on the second page. Release Ctrl. Click **Heading 2** in the Styles group on the Home tab. Do not deselect text.

d. Double-click **Format Painter** in the Clipboard group. Select **Dark Photos** on the third page. Select **Blurry Images**. Press **Esc**. Select **Blurry Images Due to Focus** on the third page. Click **Heading 3** in the Styles group. Select **Blurry Images Due to Camera Shake** on the third page and apply the **Heading 3** style.

TROUBLESHOOTING: If you do not see Heading 3 in the Styles group, click More in the Styles group and select Heading 3.

Using Format Painter, you copied the format of the Heading 2 style to a few headings. Headings throughout the newsletter are formatted according to their hierarchy, with major headings in Heading 1 style and others in correct order beneath the first level.

e. Click the **Styles Dialog Box Launcher** to display the Styles pane. Point to **Heading 1** and click the **Heading 1 arrow**. Click **Modify**. Click **Format** in the Modify Style dialog box and click **Font**. Click the **Underline style arrow** and click the second underline style (double underline). Click **OK**. Click **OK** again.

You modified Heading 1 style to include a double underline. Every heading formatted in Heading 1 style is automatically updated to include an underline. Close the Styles pane.

f. Save the document.

STEP 4 ▶▶ **USE A STYLE SET AND CREATE A NEW STYLE FROM TEXT**

Although you are pleased with the heading styles you selected in the previous step, you want to explore Word's built-in style sets to determine if another style might be more attractive. You will also create a style for all bulleted paragraphs in the newsletter. Refer to Figure 2.34 as you complete Step 4.

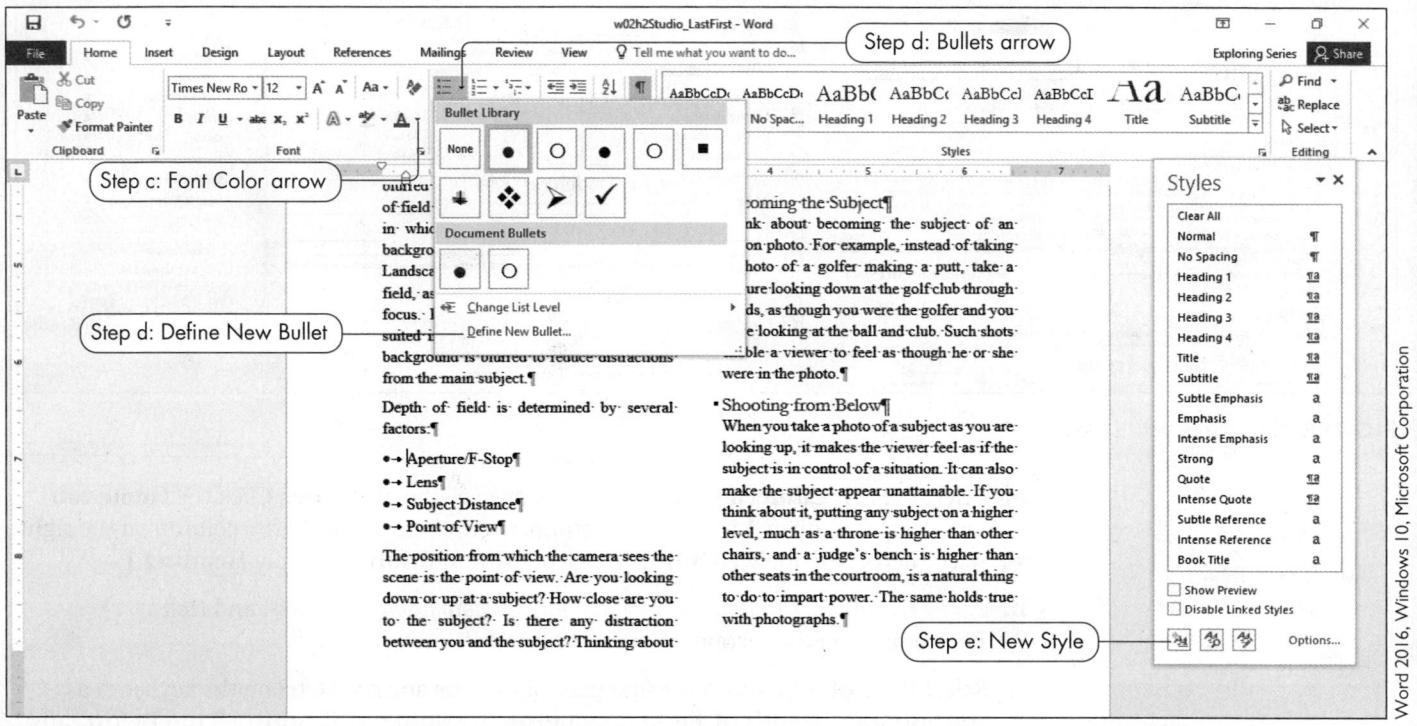

FIGURE 2.34 Use a Style Set

a. Press **Ctrl+Home**. Click the **Design tab**. Point to any style set in the Document Formatting group, without clicking, to view the effect on the document. Specifically, see how the previewed style affects the Lens heading shown in the right column. Click the **More arrow** beside the style sets and select **Lines (Simple)**.

When you apply a style set, headings are formatted according to the style settings, overriding any formatting characteristics you might have set earlier.

b. Click the **View tab** and click **One Page** in the Zoom group to view the first page.

Note that the format of the major headings—Camera Body, Lens, and Composition—has been modified, removing the underline you set earlier, and now displays the format of the Lines (Simple) style set.

c. Click **100%** in the Zoom group. Select the second paragraph in the document, *Courtesy of Phillips Studio L Photography*. Click the **Home tab**. Click the **Font Color arrow** and select **Plum, Accent 1, Darker 25%** (fifth row, fifth column).

You select a coordinating text color for the second line in the document.

d. Scroll to the second page and click anywhere in the bulleted paragraph containing the text *Aperture/F-Stop*. Click the **Bullets arrow** and select a solid round black bullet. Click the **Bullets arrow** and click **Define New Bullet**. Click **Font**. Click the **Font color arrow** and select **Plum, Accent 1, Darker 25%**. Click **OK**. Click **OK** again.

Having modified the format of one bulleted item, you will create a style from that format to apply to all other bulleted items in the document.

e. Click **New Style** in the Styles pane. Type **Bullet Paragraph** in the Name box and click **OK**.

You should see a new style in the Styles pane titled Bullet Paragraph.

f. Select the three bulleted paragraphs below *Aperture/F-Stop* and click **Bullet Paragraph** in the Styles pane. Scroll to the third page, select the three bulleted paragraphs at the bottom of the right column, and then click **Bullet Paragraph** in the Styles pane. Scroll to the fourth page, select the three bulleted paragraphs at the top of the page (in both columns), and then apply the **Bullet Paragraph style**. Close the Styles pane.

g. Save the document.

STEP 5 ›› **USE OUTLINE VIEW**

The newsletter spans four pages, with headings identifying various levels of detail. You will check to make sure you have formatted headings according to the correct hierarchy. To do so, you will view the newsletter in Outline view. Refer to Figure 2.35 as you complete Step 5.

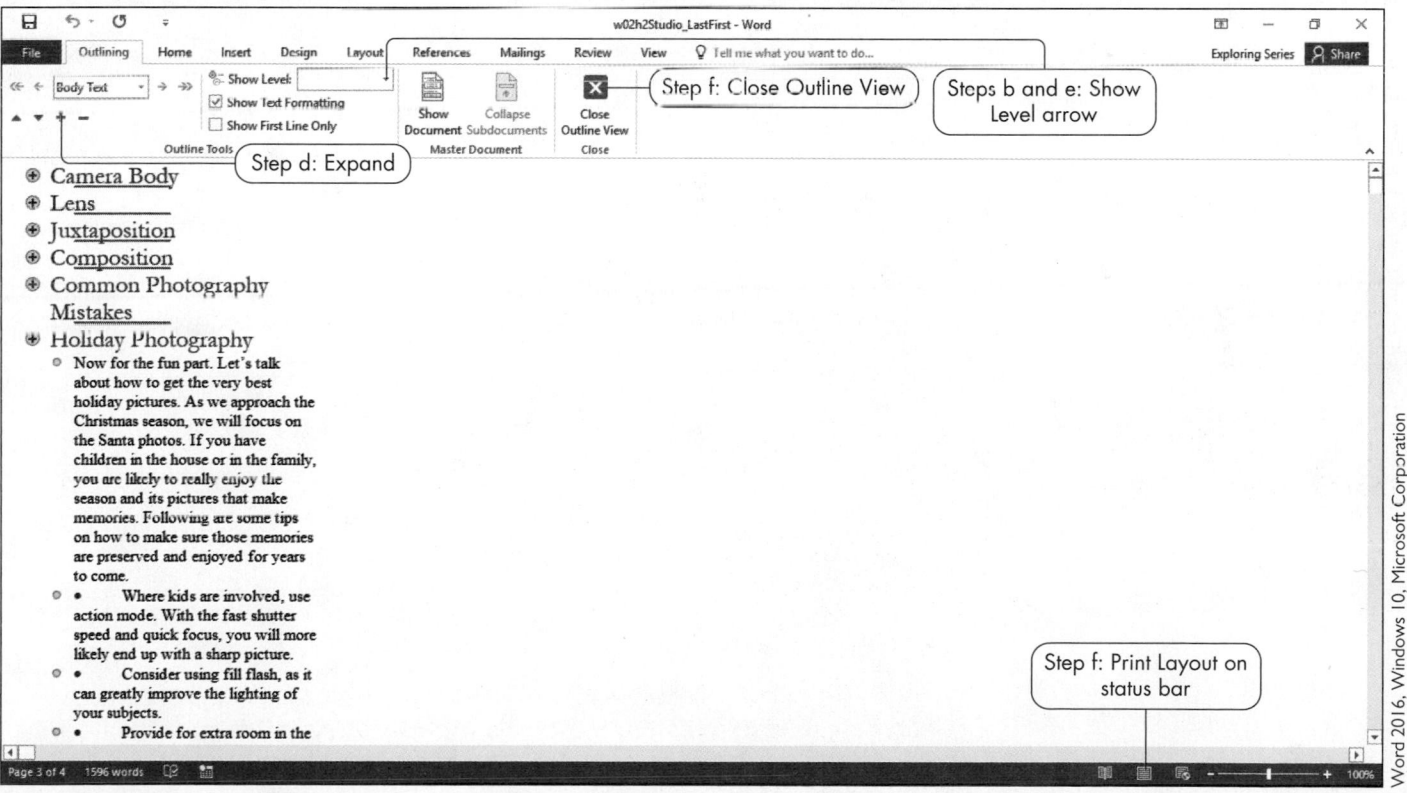

FIGURE 2.35 View an Outline

a. Press **Ctrl+Home**. Click the **View tab** and click **Outline** in the Views group. Scroll down slightly to see the first major heading (with a plus (+) sign on the left)—Camera Body.

b. Click the **Show Level arrow** and click **Level 3**.

You formatted headings in the newsletter as headings, in three levels of detail. Because you did so, you are able to view the document structure according to the hierarchy of headings.

c. Position the pointer on the plus (+) sign that precedes *Blurry Images Due to Camera Shake* (so the pointer becomes a four-headed arrow). Drag the heading above the preceding level (*Blurry Images Due to Focus*). When you see a small black triangle above the preceding level, release the mouse button to reposition the section.

d. Use the same procedure as in Step c to move the *Juxtaposition* section above *Composition*. Click **Expand** in the Outline Tools group to view the content of the *Juxtaposition* section.

e. Click the **Show Level arrow** and select **Level 1** to display Level 1 headings only. Select **Holiday Photography** and click **Expand** in the Outline Tools group.

The *Holiday Photography* section is expanded. Other Level 1 headings remain collapsed.

f. Click **Close Outline View** in the Close group on the Outlining tab. If both columns do not display, click **Print Layout** on the status bar.

g. Save the document. Keep the document open if you plan to continue with the next Hands-On Exercise. If not, save and close the document, and exit Word.

Objects

An **object** is an item that can be individually selected and manipulated within a document. Objects, such as pictures, text boxes, tables, and other graphic types, are often included in documents to add interest or convey a point (see Figure 2.36). A **text box** is a bordered area you can use to draw attention to specific text. Newsletters typically include pictures and other decorative elements to liven up what might otherwise be a somewhat mundane document. As you work with a document, you can conduct a quick search for appropriate pictures and graphics online—all without ever leaving your document workspace.

FIGURE 2.36 Word Objects

One thing all objects have in common is that they can be selected and worked with independently of surrounding text. You can resize them, add special effects, and even move them to other locations within the document. Word includes convenient text wrapping controls so that you can quickly adjust the way text wraps around an object. With Live Layout and alignment guides, you can easily line up pictures and other diagrams with existing text.

In this section, you will explore the use of objects in a Word document. Specifically, you will learn to include pictures, searching for them online as well as obtaining them from your own storage device. You will learn to create impressive text displays with WordArt. You will create text boxes, as well.

Inserting and Formatting Objects

Objects, such as pictures and illustrations, can be selected from the Web or a storage device. You can create other objects, such as WordArt, text boxes, charts, and tables. When you insert an object, it is automatically selected so that you can manipulate it independently of surrounding text. An additional tab displays on the Ribbon with options related to the selected object, making it easy to quickly modify and enhance an object.

Insert a Picture

STEP 1 » A **picture** is a graphic image, such as a drawing or photograph. You can insert pictures in a document from your own library of digital pictures you have saved, or you can access abundant picture resources from the Internet. For instance, you can use Bing Image Search in Word to conduct a Web search to locate picture possibilities. Finding and inserting a picture is only the first step in the process. Once incorporated into your document, a picture can be resized and modified with special borders and artistic effects. Other options enable you to easily align a picture with surrounding text, rotate or crop it if necessary, and even recolor it so it blends in with an existing color scheme.

If you do not have a picture already saved on your computer, you can go online to locate a suitable image. The picture is inserted directly from the Web, after which you can resize and reposition it. You can also insert images from Facebook and Flickr.

To insert an online picture, complete the following steps:

1. Click to place the insertion point in the document in the location where the picture is to be inserted.
2. Click the Insert tab and click Online Pictures (see Figure 2.37).
3. Complete one of the following steps:
   - Use Bing Image Search:
     1. Click in the Bing Image Search box.
     2. Type a search term (for example, type *school* to identify school-related images), and press Enter.
     3. Review any relevant licensing information, if presented, and select an image. Alternatively, click a link to expand the search.
     4. Click Insert.
   - Use OneDrive:
     1. Click Browse.
     2. Navigate to the folder containing the picture you want to insert.
     3. Click the picture and click Insert.

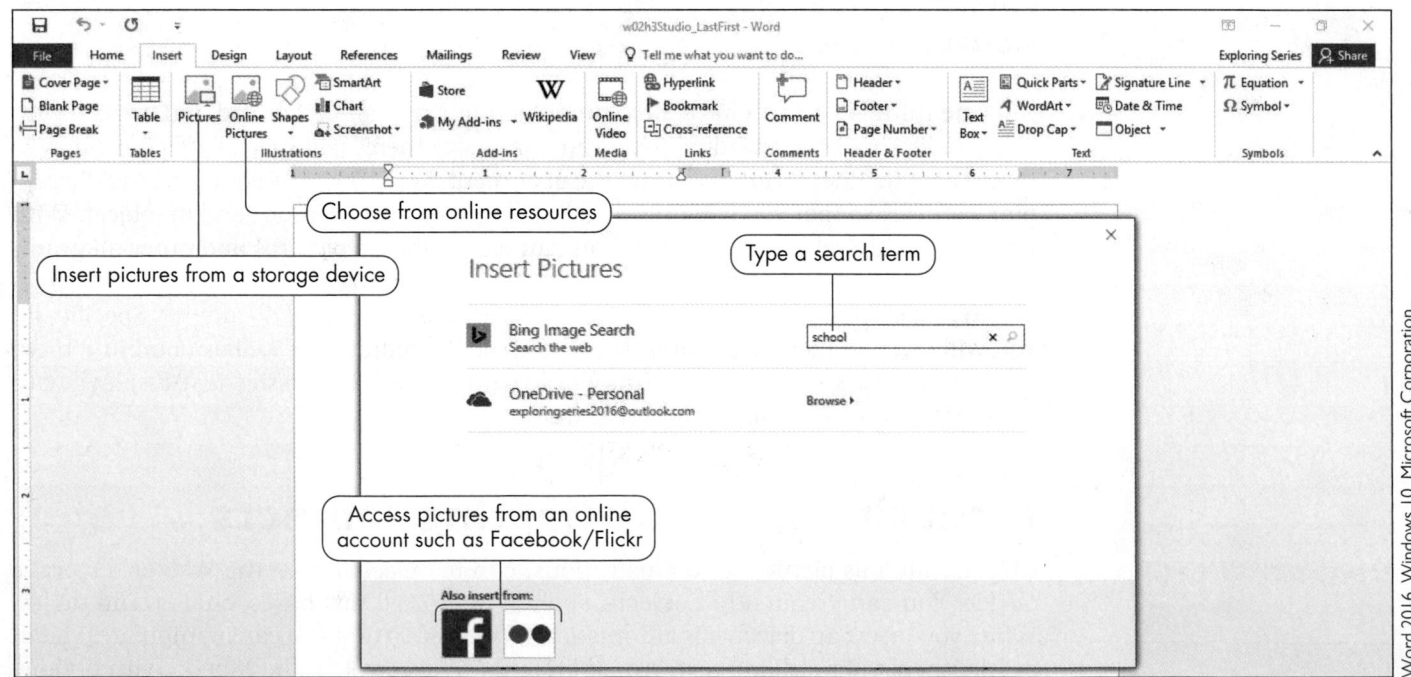

FIGURE 2.37 Insert an Online Picture

If you enjoy taking digital pictures, you most likely have a great many of your pictures saved to a storage device you can access with a computer. Suppose you are using Word to prepare a flyer or newsletter. In that case, you might want to insert one or more of your pictures into the document, which is a simple process.

To insert pictures from a storage device, complete the following steps:

1. Position the insertion point in the document where the picture is to be inserted.
2. Click the Insert tab, and click Pictures in the Illustrations group (refer to Figure 2.37).
3. Navigate to the folder in which your photos are stored.
4. Select a photo to insert, and click Insert.

Move, Align, and Resize a Picture

STEP 2 >> A new Ribbon tab, with one or more associated tabs beneath it, is added to the Ribbon when you insert and select an object. When a picture is selected, the Format tab displays, and includes settings and selections related to the inserted picture, as shown in Figure 2.38.

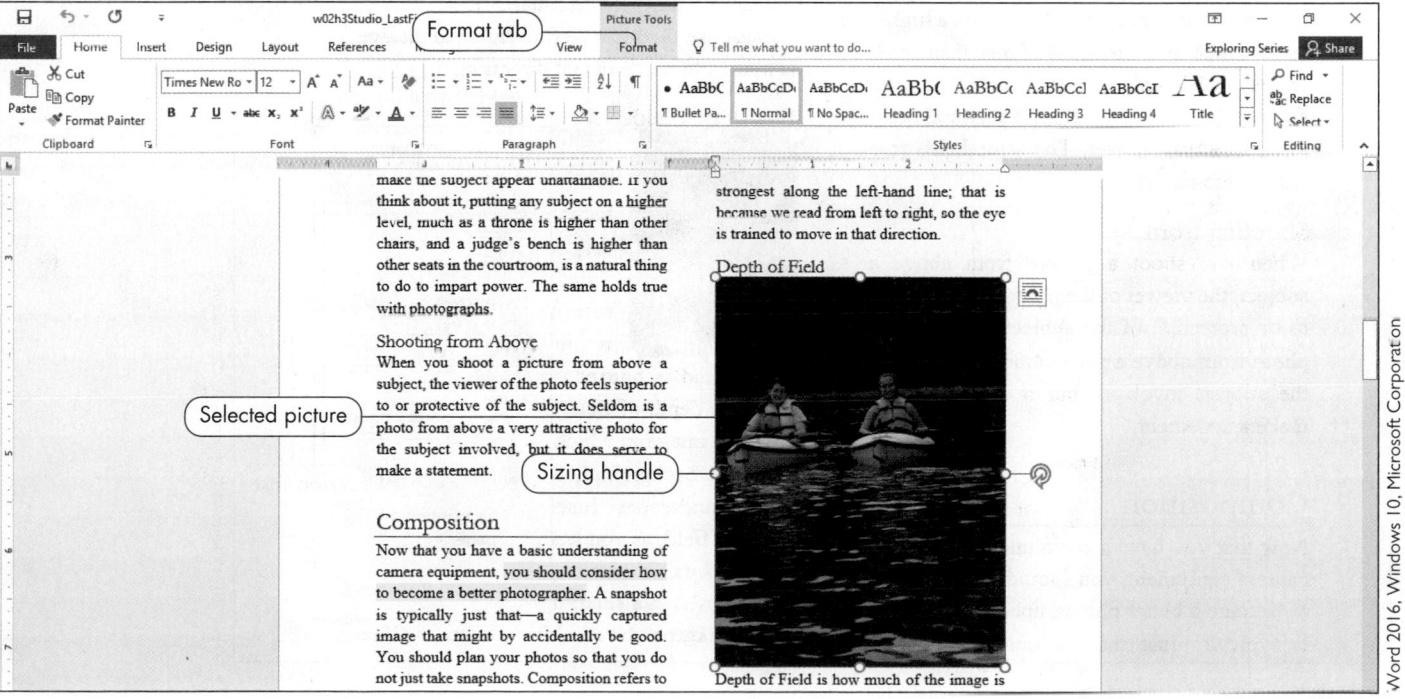

FIGURE 2.38 Format Tab

Word 2016, Windows 10, Microsoft Corporation

Although an inserted picture is considered a separate object, you will want to position it so that it flows well with document text and does not appear to be a separate unit. One way to make that happen is to wrap text around the picture. The Format tab includes Wrap Text in the Arrange group (refer to Figure 2.38). You can select from the text wrapping styles shown in Table 2.3 when you click Wrap Text. You can also choose to allow the object to move with text as text is added or deleted, or you can keep the object in the same place on the page, regardless of text changes.

TABLE 2.3	Text Wrap Options
Type	**Effect**
In Line with Text	The image is part of the line of text in which it is inserted. Typically, text wraps above and below the object.
Square	Text wraps on all sides of an object, following an invisible square.
Tight	Text follows the shape of the object, but does not overlap the object.
Through	Text follows the shape of the object, filling any open spaces in the shape.
Top and Bottom	Text flows above and below the borders of the object.
Behind Text	The object is positioned behind text. Both the object and text are visible (unless the fill color exactly matches the text color).
In Front of Text	The object is positioned in front of text, often obscuring the text.

Pearson Education, Inc.

Word has a feature that simplifies text wrapping around an object—Layout Options. Located next to a selected object, the Layout Options control (see Figure 2.39) includes the same selections shown in Table 2.3. The close proximity of the control to the selected object makes it easy to quickly adjust text wrapping.

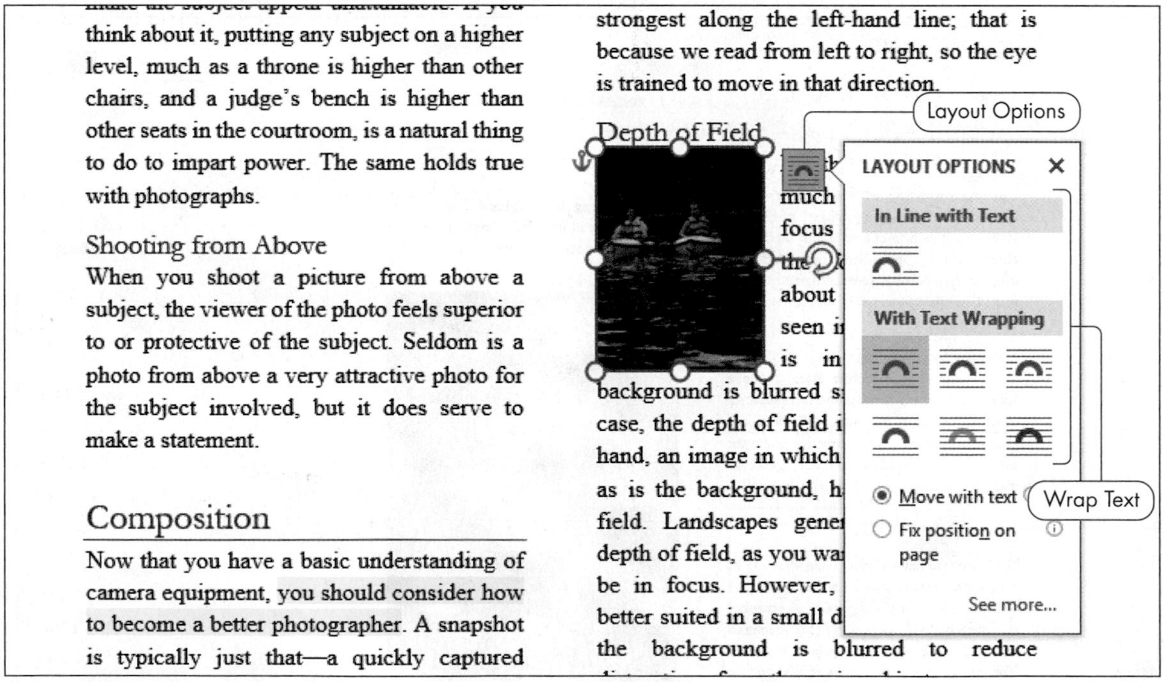

FIGURE 2.39 Layout Options

Word has two interesting features to assist you as you wrap text: Live Layout and alignment guides. **Live Layout** enables you to watch text flow around an object as you move it, so you can position the object exactly as you want it. **Alignment guides** are horizontal or vertical green bars that appear as you drag an object, so you can line up an object with text or with another object. The green alignment guide shown in Figure 2.40 helps align the picture object with paragraph text.

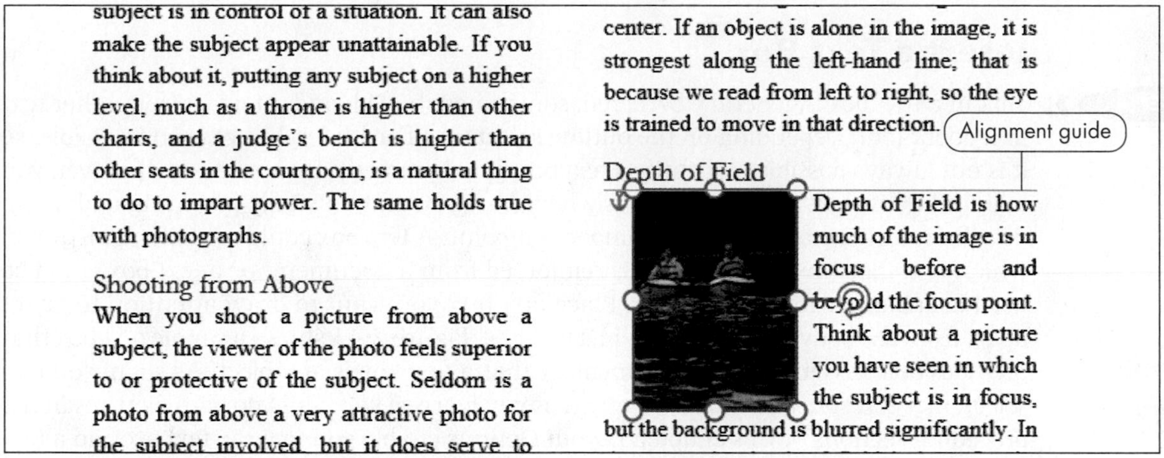

subject is in control of a situation. It can also make the subject appear unattainable. If you think about it, putting any subject on a higher level, much as a throne is higher than other chairs, and a judge's bench is higher than other seats in the courtroom, is a natural thing to do to impart power. The same holds true with photographs.

Shooting from Above
When you shoot a picture from above a subject, the viewer of the photo feels superior to or protective of the subject. Seldom is a photo from above a very attractive photo for the subject involved, but it does serve to

center. If an object is alone in the image, it is strongest along the left-hand line; that is because we read from left to right, so the eye is trained to move in that direction.

Depth of Field
Depth of Field is how much of the image is in focus before and beyond the focus point. Think about a picture you have seen in which the subject is in focus, but the background is blurred significantly. In

Alignment guide

Word 2016, Windows 10, Microsoft Corporation

FIGURE 2.40 Alignment Guides

Often, a picture is inserted in a size that is too large or too small for your purposes. To resize a picture, you can drag a corner **sizing handle**, which is a series of faint dots on the outside border of a selected object. (Resizing a picture by dragging a center sizing handle is generally not recommended, as doing so skews the picture.) You can also resize a picture by adjusting settings in the Size group of the Format tab (refer to Figure 2.38).

Modify a Picture

STEP 3 ⟫ The Format tab includes options for modifying a picture. You can apply a picture style or effect, as well as add a picture border, from selections in the Picture Styles group. Click the More arrow (refer to Figure 2.38) to view a gallery of picture styles. As you point to a style, the style is shown in Live Preview, but the style is not applied until you click it. Options in the Adjust group simplify changing a color scheme, applying creative artistic effects, and even adjusting the brightness, contrast, and sharpness of an image.

If a picture contains more detail than is necessary, you can **crop** it, which is the process of trimming edges that you do not want to display. The Crop tool is located on the Format tab (refer to Figure 2.38). Even though cropping enables you to adjust the amount of a picture that displays, it does not actually delete the portions that are cropped out. Therefore, you can later restore parts of the picture, if necessary. Note that this means also that cropping a picture does not reduce the file size of the picture or of the Word document in which it displays.

Other common adjustments to a picture include contrast and/or brightness. Adjusting contrast increases or decreases the difference in dark and light areas of the image. Adjusting brightness lightens or darkens the overall image. These adjustments often are made on a picture taken with a digital camera in poor lighting or if a picture is too bright or dull to match other objects in your document. The Brightness/Contrast adjustment is available when you click Corrections in the Adjust group on the Format tab (refer to Figure 2.38).

Insert a Text Box

STEP 4 ›› Text in a text box is generally bordered, sometimes shaded, and set apart from other text in a document. Depending on the outline selected, a border might not even be visible, so it is not always possible to identify a text box in a document. In most cases, however, you will find a text box as a conspicuously boxed area of text—usually providing additional details or drawing attention to an important point. A text box could contain a pull quote, which is a short text excerpt that is reinforced from a document, or a text box could be used as a banner for a newsletter. Place any text you want to draw attention to or set apart from the body of a document in a text box. Figure 2.41 shows a simple text box that provides business information. Remember that a text box is an object. As such, you can select, move, resize, and modify it, much as you learned you could do with pictures in the preceding sections of this chapter. Layout Options enable you to wrap text around a text box, and alignment guides assist with positioning a text box within existing text.

Basics of Photography

Courtesy of Phillips Studio L Photography

psl@geotech.net
610-555-0021

Text box

either built in to the body, or it attaches to the body. If the camera is a film-based unit, the body holds the film. In addition, the body houses a batter that powers the shutter, flash, light meter, and other controls. You will usually find rings to connect a strap to the camera body for ease of carrying.

If you enjoy taking digital pictures, you are not alone. The world of photography is wide

Word 2016, Windows 10, Microsoft Corporation

FIGURE 2.41 Text Box

To insert a text box, complete the following steps:

1. Click the Insert tab.
2. Click Text Box in the Text group.
3. Click Draw Text Box or select a predefined text box style (see Figure 2.42).
4. Drag to draw a box (unless you selected a predefined text box style, in which case, the text box will be automatically drawn). The dimensions of the text box are not that critical, as you can adjust the size using the Ribbon.
5. Type text in the text box.

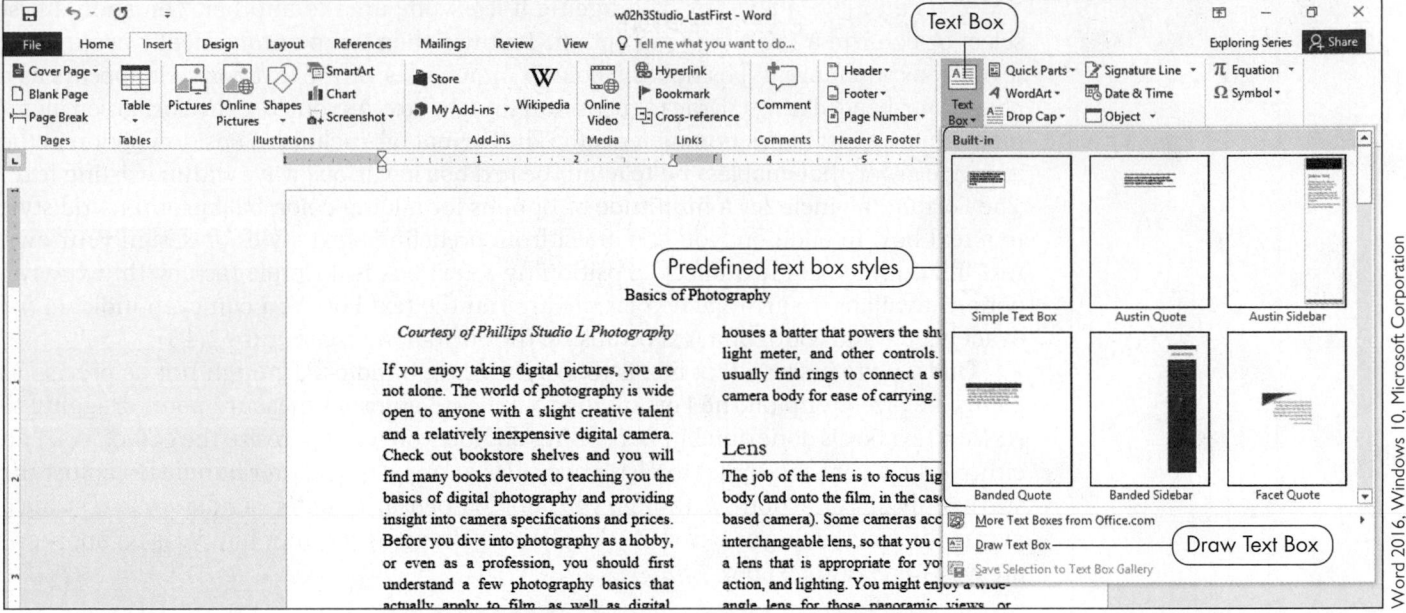

FIGURE 2.42 Draw a Text Box

> **TIP: FORMATTING TEXT IN A TEXT BOX**
> Before formatting text in a text box, you should select the text to be affected. To do so, drag to select the text to be formatted. Or, if you want to select all text, you might appreciate learning a shortcut. You can select all of the text when you click the dashed border surrounding the text box (when the pointer is a small four-headed shape). The dashed line should become solid, indicating that all text is selected. At that point, any formatting selections you make related to text are applied to all text in the text box.

Modify, Move, and Resize a Text Box

You can be as creative as you like when designing a text box. Options on the Format tab enable you to add color and definition to a text box with shape fill and outline selections, or select from a gallery of shape styles. Select text within a text box and select an alignment option on the Home tab to left-align, right-align, center, or justify text.

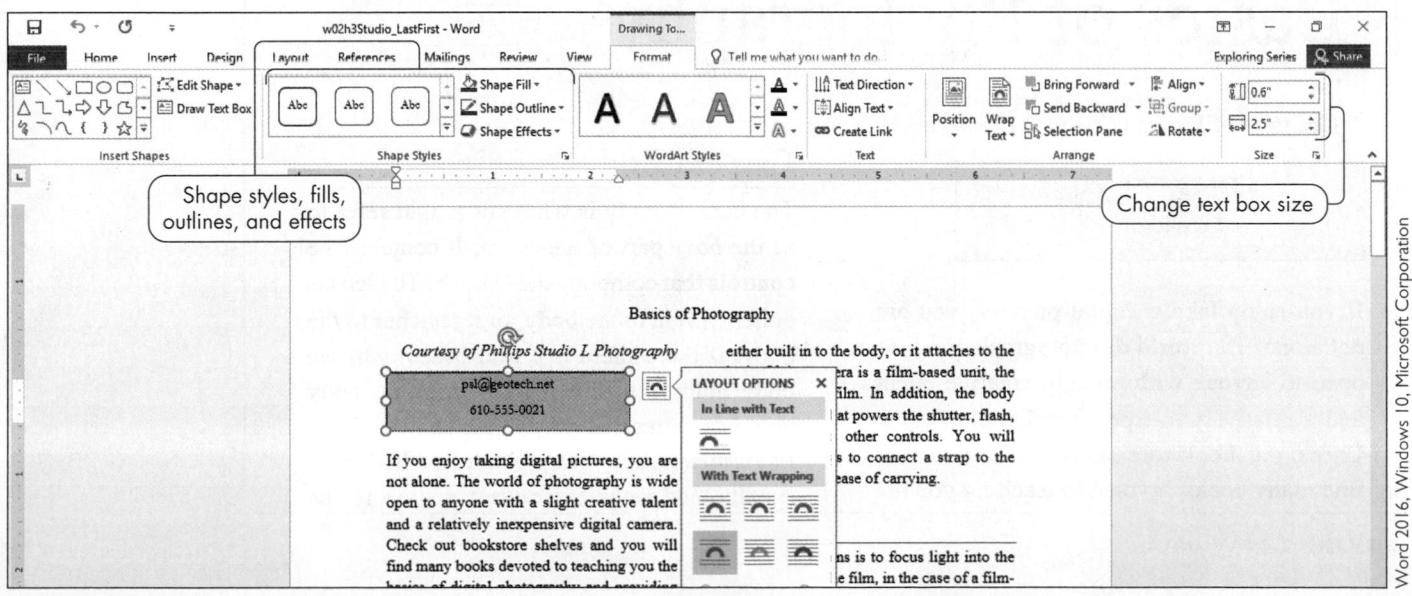

FIGURE 2.43 Modify a Text Box

You can move a text box by dragging it from one area to another. You should first select or confirm a text wrapping option. Text will then wrap automatically around the text box as you move it. Position the pointer on a border of the text box so it appears as a black, four-headed arrow. Drag to reposition the text box. As you drag the box, green alignment guides assist in positioning it neatly. The Format tab includes a Position option in the Arrange group that enables you to align the text box in various ways within existing text. The Format tab includes a multitude of options for adding color, background, and style to a text box. In addition, you can select from predefined text styles or design your own text fill, outline, and text effects. Positioning a text box is a simple task, with text wrap options available to arrange text evenly around the text box. You can even indicate the exact height and width of a text box using the Format tab (see Figure 2.43).

One way to resize a text box is to drag a sizing handle. Although not as precise as using the Size group on the Format tab to indicate an exact measurement, dragging to resize a text box is done quickly. Depending on how you want to resize the object, you can either drag a corner handle (to resize two sides at once) or a center handle (to adjust the size in only one direction). Although you should not drag a center handle when resizing a picture (because doing so will skew the picture), dragging a center handle is an appropriate way to resize a text box.

Insert WordArt

STEP 5 ❯❯ **WordArt** is a feature that modifies text to include special effects, including colors, shadows, gradients, and 3-D effects (see Figure 2.44). It is a quick way to format text so that it is vibrant and eye-catching. Of course, WordArt is not appropriate for all documents, especially more conservative business correspondence, but it can give life to newsletters, flyers, and other more informal projects, especially when applied to headings and titles. WordArt is well suited for single lines, such as document headings, where the larger print and text design draws attention and adds style to a document title. However, it is not appropriate for body text, because a WordArt object is managed independently of surrounding text and cannot be formatted as a document (with specific margins, headers, footers, etc.). In addition, if WordArt were incorporated into body text, the more ornate text design would adversely affect the readability of the document.

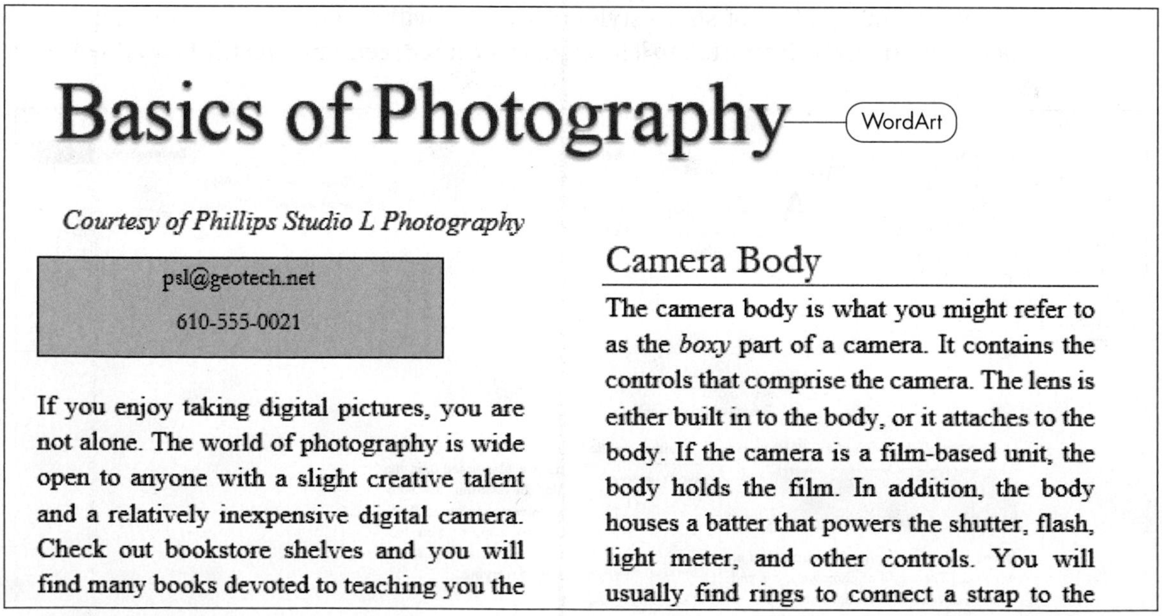

Basics of Photography (WordArt)

Courtesy of Phillips Studio L Photography

psl@geotech.net
610-555-0021

If you enjoy taking digital pictures, you are not alone. The world of photography is wide open to anyone with a slight creative talent and a relatively inexpensive digital camera. Check out bookstore shelves and you will find many books devoted to teaching you the

Camera Body

The camera body is what you might refer to as the *boxy* part of a camera. It contains the controls that comprise the camera. The lens is either built in to the body, or it attaches to the body. If the camera is a film-based unit, the body holds the film. In addition, the body houses a batter that powers the shutter, flash, light meter, and other controls. You will usually find rings to connect a strap to the

Word 2016, Windows 10, Microsoft Corporation

FIGURE 2.44 WordArt

You can format existing text as WordArt, or you can insert new WordArt text into a document. WordArt is considered an object; as such, the preceding discussion related to positioning pictures and text boxes applies to WordArt as well. Also, Live Layout and alignment guides are available to facilitate ease of positioning, and you can select a text wrapping style with layout options.

To format existing text as WordArt, complete the following steps:

1. Select text to be formatted.
2. Click the Insert tab.
3. Click WordArt in the Text group.
4. Select a WordArt style.

To insert new text as WordArt, complete the following steps:

1. Place the insertion point at the point where WordArt should appear.
2. Click the Insert tab.
3. Click WordArt in the Text group.
4. Select a WordArt style.
5. Type text.

Depending upon the purpose of a document and its intended audience, objects such as pictures, text boxes, and WordArt can help convey a message and add interest. As you learn to incorporate objects visually within a document so that they appear to flow seamlessly within existing text, you will find it easy to create attractive, informative documents that contain an element of design apart from simple text.

Quick Concepts

9. How would you determine what type of text wrapping to use when positioning a picture in a document? *p. 240*

10. Describe two methods to modify the height and width of a picture. *p. 241*

11. How does a text box differ from simple shaded text? *p. 242*

12. Why is WordArt most often used to format headings or titles, and not text in the body of a document? *p. 244*

Hands-On Exercises

Watch the Video for this Hands-On Exercise!

MyITLab®
HOE3 Training

3 Objects

You will add interest to the newsletter by including pictures that illustrate points, a text box with business information, and WordArt that livens up the newsletter heading.

STEP 1 ›› INSERT A PICTURE

You will include pictures in the newsletter to represent photographs shot from various angles, as well as holiday graphics. The pictures will be formatted with appropriate picture styles and effects and positioned within existing text. Refer to Figure 2.45 as you complete Step 1.

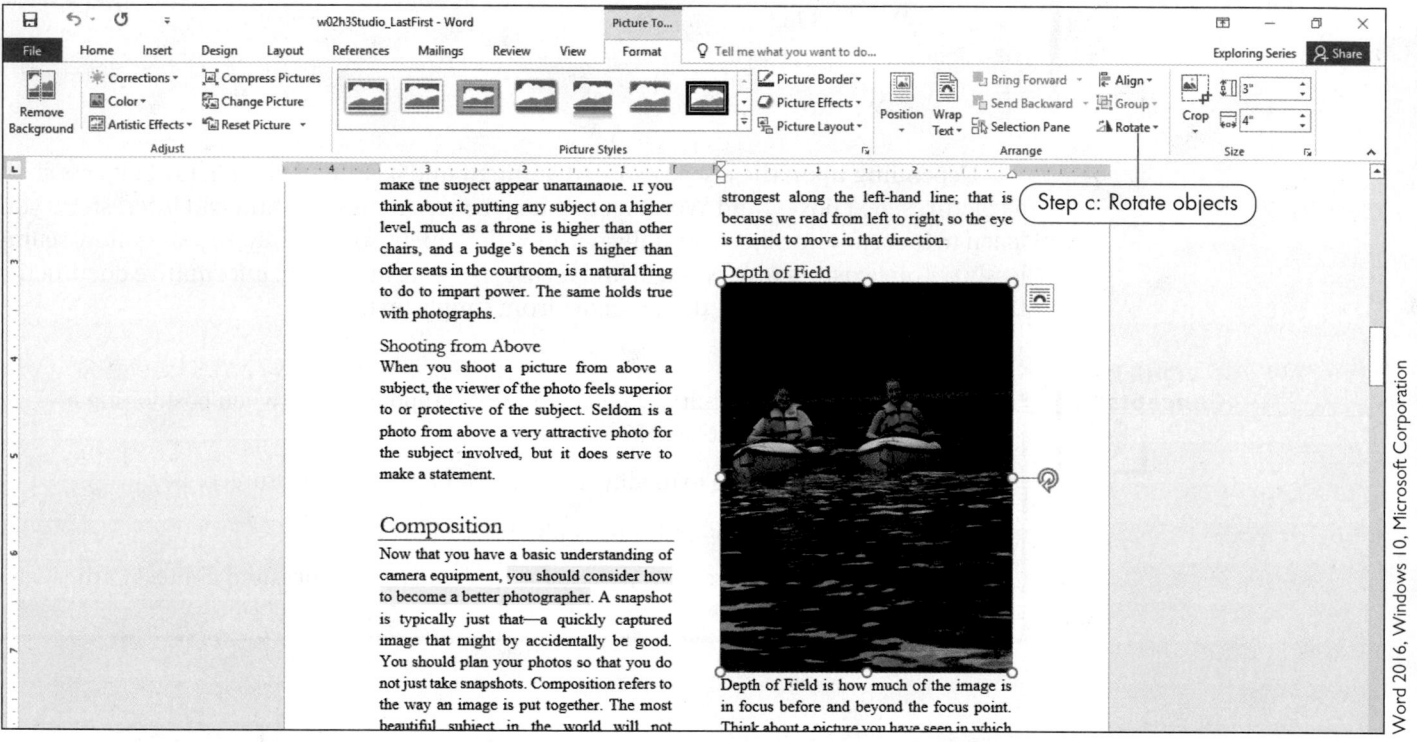

FIGURE 2.45 Insert and Rotate a Picture

a. Open *w02h2Studio_LastFirst* if you closed it at the end of Hands-On Exercise 2, and save it as **w02h3Studio_LastFirst**, changing h2 to h3.

b. Scroll to the second page of the document and click to place the insertion point before the words *Depth of Field is how much of the image*. Click the **Insert tab** and click **Pictures** in the Illustrations group. Navigate to the location of your student data files and double-click *w02h3Kayak*.

The picture is inserted, but must be rotated.

c. Ensure the picture selected (surrounded by a border and sizing handles), click **Rotate Objects** in the Arrange group on the Format tab, and click **Rotate Right 90°**. Click outside the picture to deselect it.

> **TROUBLESHOOTING:** If you do not see Rotate Objects or the Format tab, click the picture to select it and then click the Format tab.

d. Scroll to the third page and click to place the insertion point before *The most common reason for a blurred image* under the *Blurry Images Due to Focus* heading. Click the **Insert tab**, click **Pictures** in the Illustrations group, and then double-click *w02h3Float* in your student data files. Rotate the picture to the right. Click outside the picture to deselect it.

> **TROUBLESHOOTING:** The placement of the picture will vary, so it is OK if it is not positioned directly below the *Blurry Images Due to Focus* heading. You will move it later.

e. Scroll to the *Holiday Photography* section and click to place the insertion point before *Now for the fun part*. Click the **Insert tab**. Click **Online Pictures** in the Illustrations group. In the Bing Image Search box, type **Ski** and press **Enter**. Select the picture shown in Figure 2.47 (or one that is very similar). Click **Insert**.

The picture is placed within or very near the *Holiday Photography* section. You will reposition it and resize it later.

f. Save the document.

STEP 2 ▶▶ MOVE, ALIGN, AND RESIZE A PICTURE

The pictures you inserted are a bit large, so you will resize them. You will also position them within the column and select an appropriate text wrapping style. Refer to Figure 2.46 and Figure 2.47 as you complete Step 2.

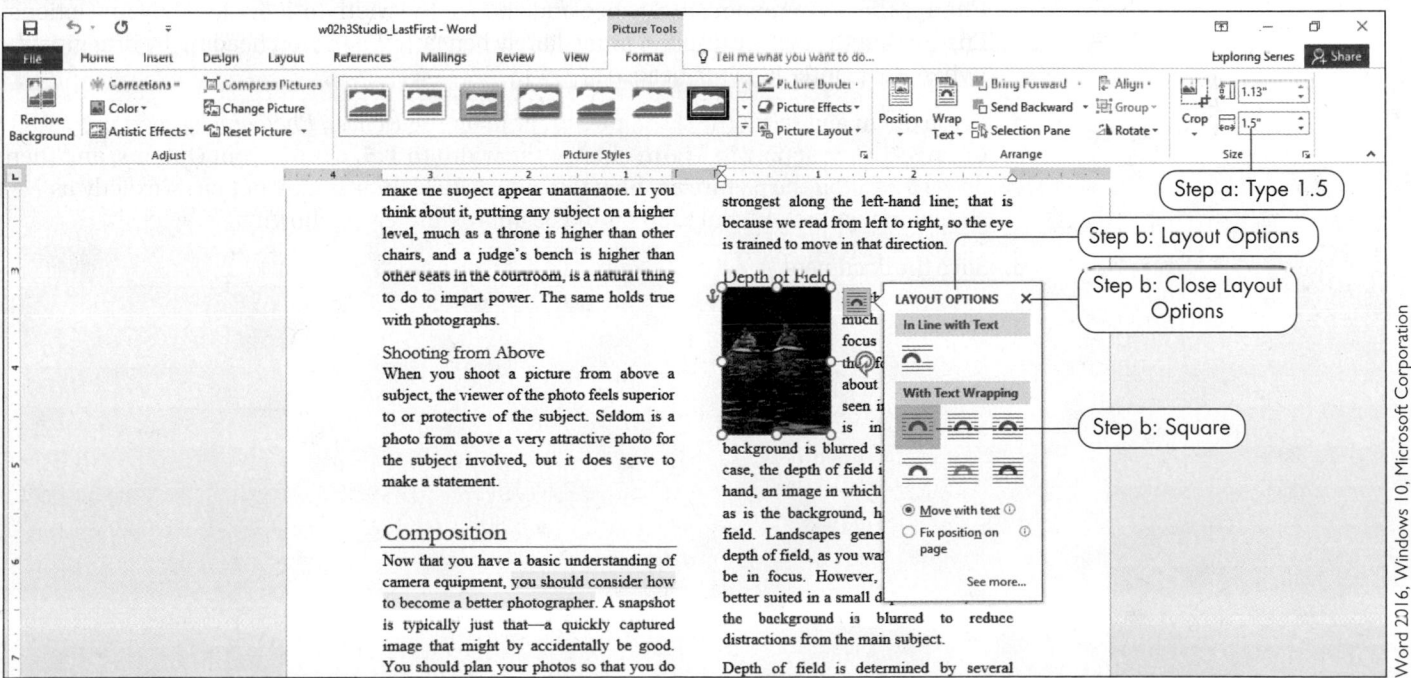

FIGURE 2.46 Resize, Move, and Align Pictures

Holiday Photography   Step d: Tight

Now for the fun part. Let's talk about how to get the very best holiday pictures. As we approach the Christmas season, we will focus on the Santa photos. If you have children in the house or in the family, you are likely to really enjoy the season and its pictures that make memories. Following are some tips on how to make sure those memories are preserved and enjoyed for years to come.

Word 2016, Windows 10, Microsoft Corporation

FIGURE 2.47 Insert and Rotate Pictures

a. Scroll up and click to select the picture near the *Depth of Field* section. Click in the **Width box** in the Size group on the Format tab and type **1.5**. Press **Enter**.

By default, the Lock aspect ratio setting is on, which means that when you change a dimension—either width or height—of a picture, the other dimension is automatically adjusted as well. To confirm or deselect the Lock aspect ratio, click the Size Dialog Box Launcher and adjust the setting in the Layout dialog box. Unless you deselect the setting, you cannot change both width and height distinctly from each other, as that would skew the picture.

b. Click **Layout Options** (beside the selected picture) and select **Square** (first selection under *With Text Wrapping*). Close Layout Options. Check the placement of the image with that shown in Figure 2.46, and adjust if necessary.

c. Scroll down and select the second picture, near the *Blurry Images Due to Focus* heading. Change the text wrapping to **Square** and change the width to **1.5**. Close Layout Options. Ensure that the picture displays immediately beneath the section heading by dragging it (when the pointer is a four-headed arrow).

d. Scroll down and select the ski picture in, or near, the *Holiday Photography* section. Change text wrapping to **Tight**, change the width to **1.5**, close Layout Options, and then drag to position the picture as shown in Figure 2.47. Words may not wrap exactly as shown in Figure 2.47, but they should be approximately as shown.

e. Save the document.

You will apply a picture style and picture effects to the pictures included in the newsletter. You will also crop a picture to remove unnecessary detail. Refer to Figure 2.48 and Figure 2.49 as you complete Step 3.

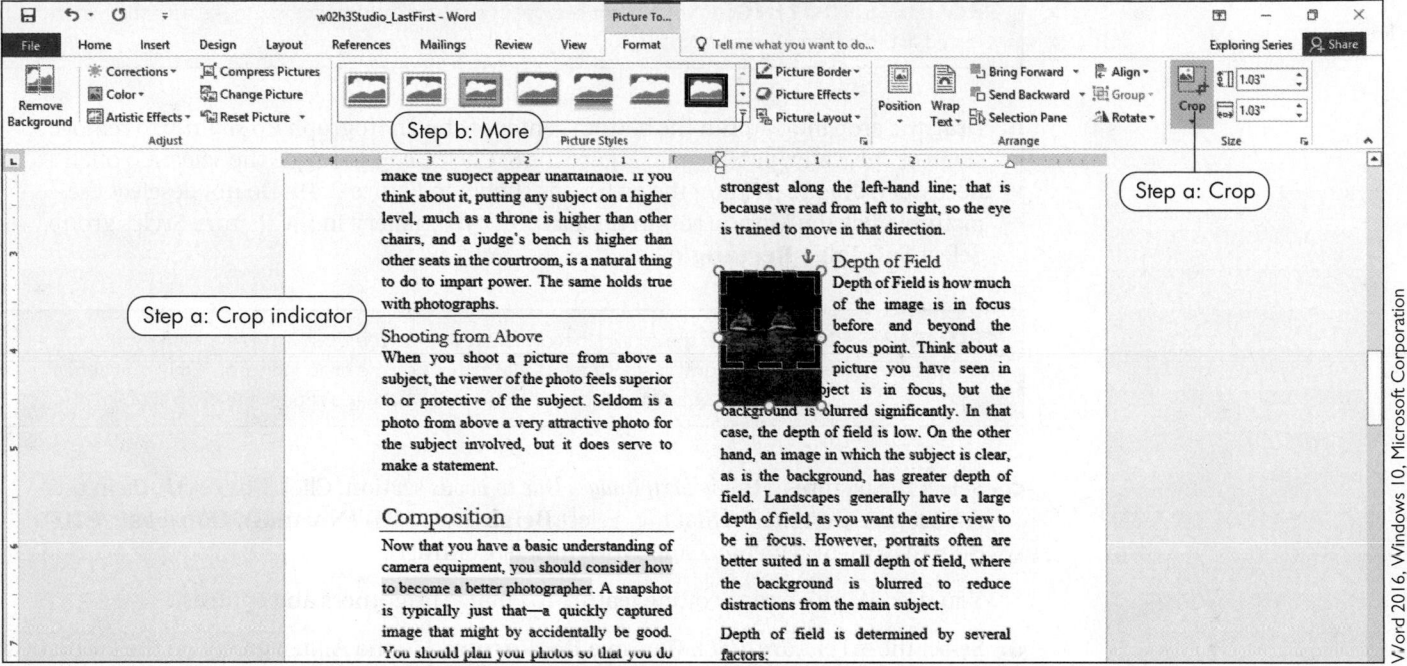

FIGURE 2.48 Crop a Picture

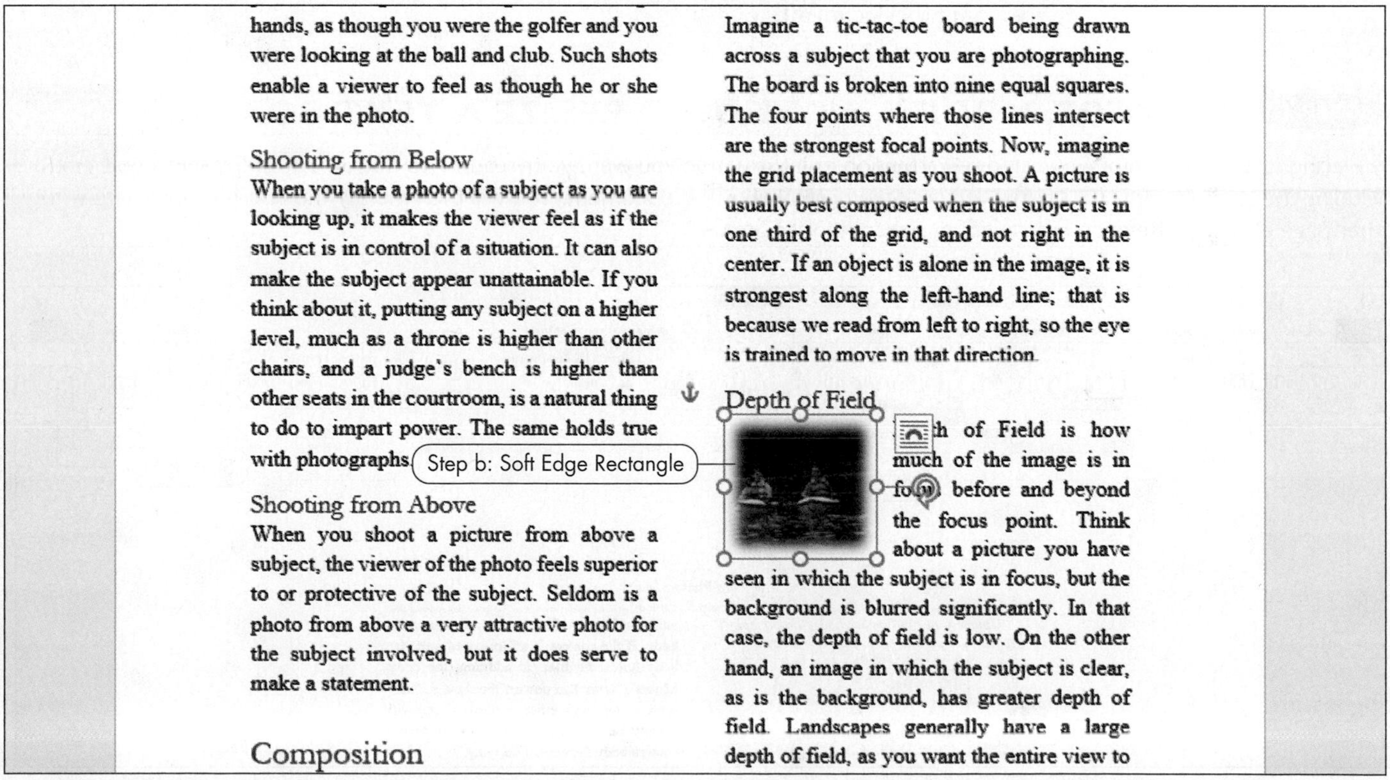

FIGURE 2.49 Select a Picture Style

a. Select the picture in the *Depth of Field* section. Click **Crop** in the Size group on the Format tab. (Be sure to click Crop, not the Crop arrow.)

The crop indicator consists of dark thick lines around the selected picture.

> **TROUBLESHOOTING:** If you do not see options related to the picture, make sure the picture is selected and click the Format tab.

b. Drag the crop indicator in the bottom center of the photograph up slightly to remove some of the water, as shown in Figure 2.48. Click **Crop** to toggle the selection off. If necessary, drag to position the picture as shown in Figure 2.49. Do not deselect the picture. Click the More arrow in the Picture Styles gallery in the Picture Styles group. Select **Soft Edge Rectangle**.

> **TROUBLESHOOTING:** If the picture becomes skewed as you drag, instead of simply shading the water to remove, you are dragging a sizing handle instead of the crop indicator. Only drag when the pointer is a thick black T, not a two-headed arrow. Click Undo and repeat the crop action.

c. Select the picture in the *Blurry Images Due to Focus* section. Click **Corrections** in the Adjust group on the Format tab. Select **Brightness: 0% (Normal), Contrast: +20%** (fourth row, third column under Brightness/Contrast).

You used Word's image editing feature to change brightness and contrast.

d. Select the ski picture. Click **Remove Background** in the Adjust group on the Format tab. Wait a few seconds until the background is shaded in magenta. Click **Keep Changes**. Deselect the picture.

e. Save the document.

STEP 4 »» INSERT, MODIFY, MOVE, AND RESIZE A TEXT BOX

By placing text in a text box, you can draw attention to information you want your readers to notice. You will insert a text box, including the studio's contact information, near the beginning of the document. You will then modify the text to coordinate with other page elements. Refer to Figure 2.50 as you complete Step 4.

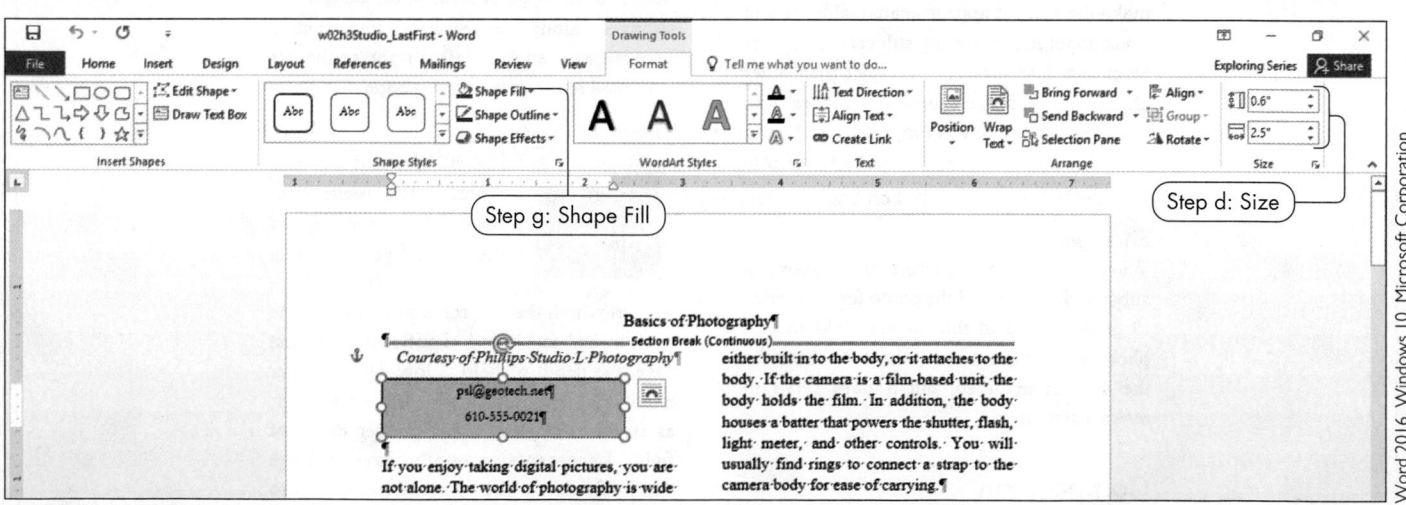

FIGURE 2.50 Insert a Text Box

a. Press **Ctrl+Home**. Click **Show/Hide** in the Paragraph group on the Home tab to ensure that nonprinting characters display.

b. Click the **Insert tab** and click **Text Box** in the Text group. Click **Draw Text Box**. Point to the blank paragraph mark below *Courtesy of Phillips Studio L Photography* and drag to draw a small box. The dimensions are not important, as you will resize the text box later.

A small text box is drawn in the document.

c. Click **Layout Options** (beside the text box) and select **Top and Bottom** (second row, first column under Text Wrapping). Close Layout Options.

Text wraps above and below the text box.

d. Click the **Height box** in the Size group on the Format tab and type **0.6**. Click the Width box and type **2.5**. Press **Enter**.

e. Click in the text box to position the insertion point. Type **psl@geotech.net** and press **Enter**. Type **610-555-0021**. Right-click the underlined email link in the text box and select **Remove Hyperlink**.

f. Click the dashed line surrounding the text box to make it solid, so that all text in the text box is selected (although it is not shaded). Click the **Home tab** and click **Center** in the Paragraph group.

All text is centered in the text box.

g. Click the **Format tab**. Click **Shape Fill** in the Shape Styles group. Select **Plum, Accent 1, Lighter 80%** (second row, fifth column).

The text box background is shaded to match the document theme.

h. Position the pointer near a border of the text box so that the pointer appears as a four-headed arrow. Drag to the left edge of the column, until the green alignment guide indicates the text box is aligned at that edge. Release the mouse button. The text box should appear as shown in Figure 2.50.

i. Save the document.

The newsletter is near completion, but you need to work with the heading—*Basics of Photography*. You will format the heading with WordArt to add some visual appeal. Refer to Figure 2.51 as you complete Step 5.

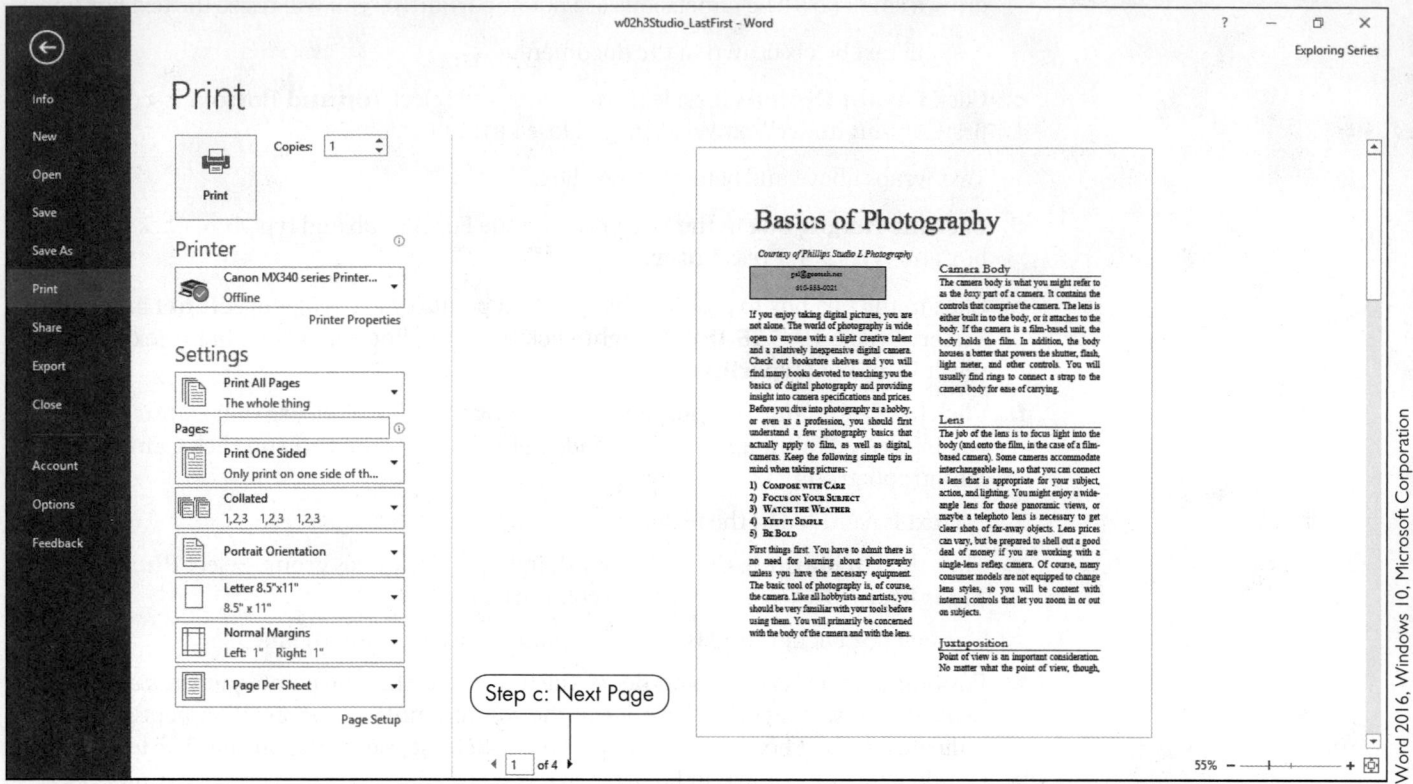

FIGURE 2.51 Insert WordArt

a. Select *Basics of Photography* on the first line of the newsletter, including the following paragraph mark. Be careful not to select the Section Break indicator following the paragraph mark. Click the **Insert tab** and click **WordArt** in the Text group. Select **Fill – Plum, Accent 1, Shadow** (first row, second column).

> **TROUBLESHOOTING:** If you do not see a Section Break indicator, click Show/Hide in the Paragraph group on the Home tab to display the nonprinting characters.

The heading is formatted in WordArt, in a shade that coordinates with other text formatting in the newsletter.

b. Click **Layout Options** and click **Top and Bottom**. Close Layout Options.

c. Click outside the WordArt object to deselect it. Click the **File tab** and click **Print**. The first page shows in preview in the right pane (refer to Figure 2.51). Click **Next Page** (at the bottom of the preview page) to move to the next page.

d. Save and close the file. Based on your instructor's directions, submit w02h3Studio_LastFirst.

Chapter Objectives Review

After reading this chapter, you have accomplished the following objectives:

I. Apply font attributes.

- Select font options: Font options include serif or sans serif fonts, as well as monospaced or proportional fonts. The Font group on the Home tab contains all the font selections.
- Change text appearance: Format characters by applying bold, italics, underline, font color, text highlighting, and text effects.

2. Format a paragraph.

- Select paragraph alignment: Align paragraphs to be left or right aligned, centered, or justified.
- Select line and paragraph spacing: Line spacing refers to the amount of space between lines within a paragraph, whereas paragraph spacing is the amount of space between paragraphs.
- Select indents: Options for indenting paragraphs include left indent, right indent, hanging indent, and first line indent.
- Set tab stops: Use tabs to indent the first line of the paragraph, or to arrange text in columns, including leaders if desired.
- Apply borders and shading: Borders and shading draw attention to selected paragraphs.
- Create bulleted and numbered lists: Itemized lists can be set apart from other text with bullets, while sequential lists are formatted with numbers.

3. Format a document.

- Select a document theme: Use a theme to create a color-coordinated document, with page elements based on theme settings.
- Work with sections: Divide a document into sections, so that each area can be formatted independently of others.
- Format text into columns: Some documents, such as newsletters, are formatted in two or more columns.

4. Apply styles.

- Select and modify styles: Styles enable you to apply identical formatting to page features, such as headings. When a style is modified, changes apply to all text formatted in that style.
- Use a style set: Select a style set to quickly format page elements, such as headers and paragraph text.
- Create a new style from text: Format text and create a style from the text so that formatting characteristics can be easily applied to other text in the document.
- Use Outline view: Expand and collapse sections, view document structure, and easily rearrange document sections in Outline view.

5. Insert and format objects.

- Insert a picture: Insert pictures from online sources or from a storage device connected to your computer.
- Move, align, and resize a picture: Reposition objects easily using Live Layout and alignment guides. You can also resize objects and wrap text around objects.
- Modify a picture: Apply a picture style or effect, adjust the color, contrast, and brightness of a picture, and crop a picture to modify a picture's appearance.
- Insert a text box: Include text in a bordered area by inserting a text box. You can format a text box with shape styles and effects, and you can align text within a text box.
- Modify, move, and resize a text box: As an object, a text box can be modified, moved, and resized with options on the Format tab.
- Insert WordArt: A WordArt object displays text with special effects, such as color, size, gradient, and 3-D appearance.

Key Terms Matching

Match the key terms with their definitions. Write the key term letter by the appropriate numbered definition.

a. Alignment guide
b. Border
c. Bulleted list
d. Column
e. Document theme
f. First line indent
g. Font
h. Indent
i. Line spacing
j. Live Preview

k. Object
l. Paragraph spacing
m. Picture
n. Section break
o. Sizing handle
p. Style
q. Style set
r. Tab stop
s. Text box
t. WordArt

1. _____ A feature that modifies text to include special effects, such as color, shadow, gradient, and 3-D appearance. **p. 244**

2. _____ A series of faint dots on the outside border of a selected object; enables the user to adjust the height and width of the object. **p. 241**

3. _____ A list of points that is not sequential. **p. 213**

4. _____ An item, such as a picture or text box, that can be individually selected and manipulated. **p. 237**

5. _____ A unified set of design elements, including font style, color, and special effects, that is applied to an entire document. **p. 222**

6. _____ A typeface or complete set of characters. **p. 200**

7. _____ A named collection of formatting characteristics that can be applied to characters or paragraphs. **p. 226**

8. _____ A mark that indicates the location to indent only the first line in a paragraph. **p. 209**

9. _____ The horizontal or vertical green bar that appears as you move an object, assisting with lining up an object. **p. 241**

10. _____ A combination of title, heading, and paragraph styles that can be used to format all of those elements at one time. **p. 222**

11. _____ A format that separates document text into side-by-side vertical blocks, often used in newsletters. **p. 225**

12. _____ A line that surrounds a paragraph or a page. **p. 212**

13. _____ The amount of space before or after a paragraph. **p. 207**

14. _____ An Office feature that provides a preview of the results of a selection when you point to it. **p. 200**

15. _____ The vertical space between the lines in a paragraph. **p. 208**

16. _____ An indicator that divides a document into parts, enabling different formatting in each section. **p. 224**

17. _____ A boxed object that can be bordered and shaded, providing space for text. **p. 237**

18. _____ A marker that specifies the position for aligning text, sometimes including a leader. **p. 210**

19. _____ A graphic file that is obtained from the Internet or a storage device. **p. 238**

20. _____ A setting associated with the way a paragraph is distanced from one or more margins. **p. 209**

Multiple Choice

1. How does a document theme differ from a style?

   (a) A theme applies an overall design to a document, with no requirement that any text is selected. A style applies formatting characteristics to selected text or to a current paragraph.

   (b) A theme applies color-coordinated design to selected page elements. A style applies formatting to an entire document.

   (c) A theme and a style are actually the same feature.

   (d) A theme applies font characteristics, whereas a style applies paragraph formatting.

2. To identify a series of sequential steps to several levels, you could use:

   (a) Tabs.

   (b) A bulleted list.

   (c) A multilevel list.

   (d) A numbered list.

3. The feature that is a collection of formatting characteristics that can be applied to text or paragraphs is:

   (a) WordArt.

   (b) Themes.

   (c) Style.

   (d) Text box.

4. What kind of indent is often used in preparing a bibliography for a research paper?

   (a) First line indent

   (b) Hanging indent

   (c) Right indent

   (d) Left indent

5. To draw attention to such items as contact information or store hours, you could place text in a bordered area called a:

   (a) Text box.

   (b) Dot leader.

   (c) Section.

   (d) Tabbed indent.

6. To divide a document into side-by-side vertical blocks so that the text flows down one side and then continues at the top of the other side, you can use a(n):

   (a) Column.

   (b) Indent.

   (c) Section break.

   (d) Page break.

7. If you select text and apply a linked style, what happens?

   (a) Paragraph formats are applied, but not character formats.

   (b) Both paragraph and character formats are applied.

   (c) Linked formats are applied.

   (d) Character formats are applied, but not paragraph formats.

8. Having applied a particular heading style to several headings within a document, you modify the style to include bold and italic font formatting. What happens to the headings that were previously formatted in that style, and why?

   (a) They remain as they are. Changes in style affect only text typed from that point forward.

   (b) They remain as they are. You cannot modify a style that has already been applied to text in the current document.

   (c) They are updated to reflect the modified heading style settings. When a heading style is modified, all text formatted in that style is updated.

   (d) Each heading reverts to its original setting. When you modify styles, you make them unavailable to previously formatted styles.

9. Which of the following statements is FALSE regarding Outline view?

   (a) It simplifies the application of formatting to entire sections.

   (b) It streamlines the process of applying heading styles to selected text.

   (c) It color coordinates various heading levels.

   (d) It allows you to easily convert the outline to a PowerPoint presentation.

10. The feature that simplifies text wrapping around an object is:

    (a) The alignment guide.

    (b) Live Layout.

    (c) Live Preview.

    (d) Layout Options.

Practice Exercises

1 Campus Safety

You are the office assistant for the police department at a local university. As a service to students, staff, and the community, the police department publishes a campus safety guide, available both in print and online. With national emphasis on homeland security, and local incidents of theft and robbery, it is obvious that the safety guide should be updated and distributed. You will work with a draft document, formatting it to make it more attractive and ready for print. Refer to Figure 2.52 as you complete this exercise.

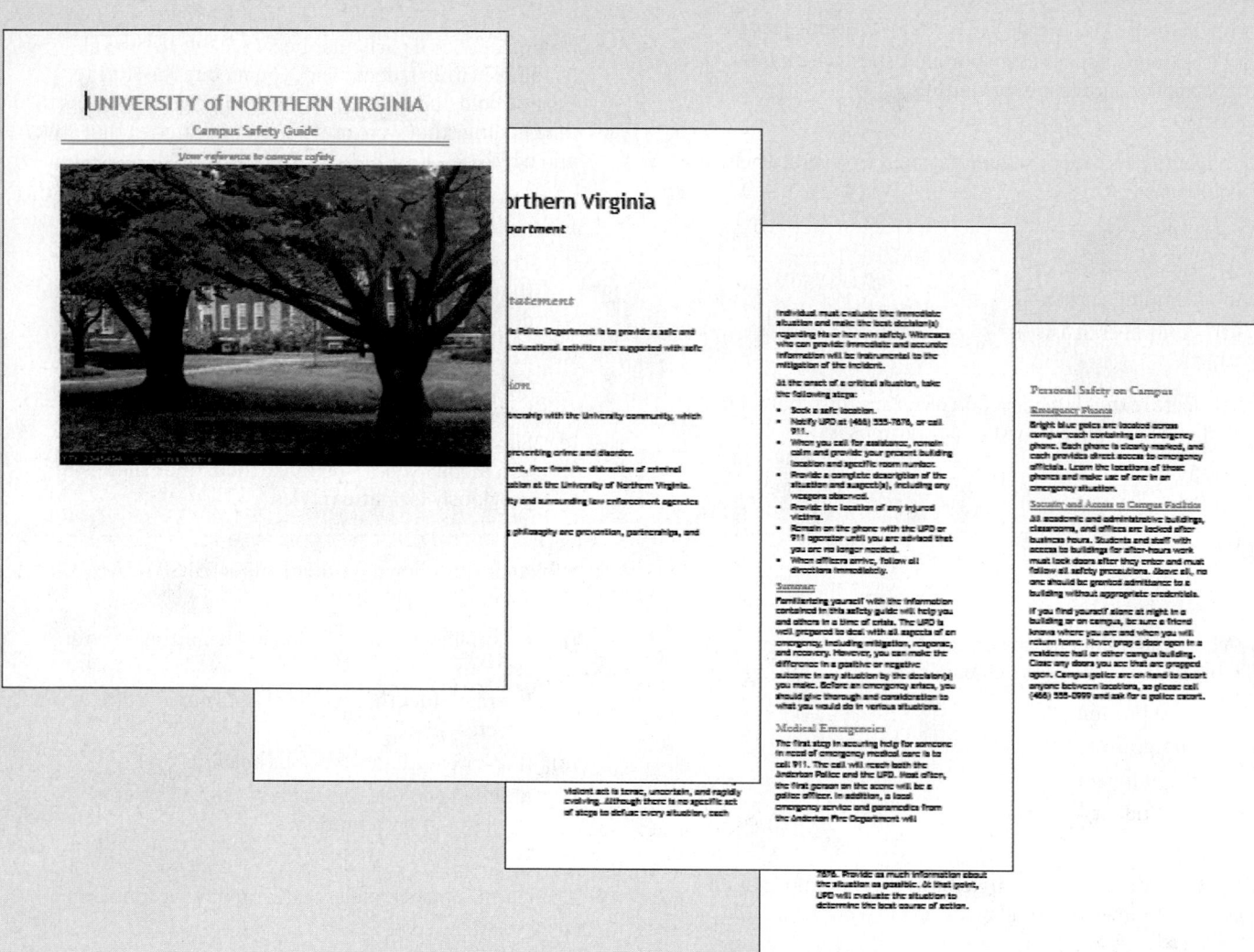

FIGURE 2.52 Format a Document

a. Open *w02p1Campus* and save the document as **w02p1Campus_LastFirst**. Click **Show/Hide** in the Paragraph group to ensure nonprinting characters are displayed.

b. Click the **Design tab**. Click **Themes** in the Document Formatting group and select **Ion Boardroom**. Click **Colors** in the Document Formatting group and select **Green Yellow**. Click **Fonts** in the Document Formatting group and select **Garamond TrebuchetMs**.

c. Click the **Home tab**. Select the first line in the document and click **Center** in the Paragraph group. Click the **Font Color arrow** in the Font group and select **Green, Accent 3**. Click the **Font Size arrow** and select **26**. Click **Change Case** in the Font group and select **UPPERCASE**. Double-click **of** in the first line in the document, click **Change Case**, and then select **lowercase**. Select the second line in the document. Center the line, change the font color to **Green, Accent 3**, change the font size to **16**, and then change the case to **Capitalize Each Word**. Do not deselect the text.

d. Click the **Borders arrow** in the Paragraph group and click **Borders and Shading**. Click **Custom** in the Setting section of the Borders and Shading dialog box. Click the **Color arrow** and select **Green, Accent 3**. Scroll through styles in the Style box and select the seventh style (double line). Click the **Width arrow** and select **1 1/2 pt**. Click **Bottom** in the Preview group and click **OK**.

e. Select the line containing the text *Your reference to campus safety*. Click **Font Color** on the Mini toolbar to apply the most recent font color selection. Use either the Mini toolbar or selections on the Home tab to change the font to **Lucida Calligraphy** and center the selection.

f. Click at the end of the currently selected line to position the insertion point immediately after *Your reference to campus safety*. Click the **Insert tab** and click **Pictures** in the Illustrations group. Navigate to the location of your student data files and double-click *w02p1Campus*.

g. Click **Height** in the Size group on the Format tab and type **5**. Press **Enter**. Click **Corrections** in the Adjust group and select **Brightness: 0% (Normal), Contrast: +20%** under Brightness/Contrast.

h. Click before the words *University of Northern Virginia* immediately below the picture and press **Ctrl+Enter** to insert a manual page break. Scroll up and select the first line on page 1 of the document. Click the **Home tab**, and click **Format Painter** in the Clipboard group. Scroll to the second page and select the first line (*University of Northern Virginia*) to copy the formatting. (Note that the Format Painter does not copy the All Caps format.) Change the font color of the selected line to **Black, Text 1**.

i. Select the second line on page 2, containing the text *Police Department*. Apply **Center**, **Bold**, and **Italic** to the selection. Change the font size to **16 pt**. Select text in the document beginning with *Mission Statement* and ending with *prevention, partnerships, and problem solving* (on the same page). Click **Line and Paragraph Spacing** in the Paragraph group and select **1.5**. Click the **Paragraph Dialog Box Launcher** and change Spacing After to **6 pt**. Click **OK**. Click to position the insertion point after the words *Police Department* and press **Enter** twice.

j. Select the *Mission Statement* heading near the top of page 2 and change the font color to **Green, Accent 3**. Center the selection and change the font size to **16** and the font to **Lucida Calligraphy**. Copy the format of the selection to the *Vision* heading on the same page. Insert a page break after the sentence ending with the words *problem solving* on page 2.

k. Select the paragraphs on page 2 beginning with *University police officers are committed to* and ending with *prevention, partnerships, and problem solving*. Click the **Bullets arrow** in the Paragraph group and select the square filled bullet. Click **Decrease Indent** in the Paragraph group to move the bullets to the left margin.

l. Scroll to page 3. Click the **Styles Dialog Box Launcher**. Complete the following steps to apply styles to selected text.

- Click in the line containing *Emergency Notifications*. Click **Heading 1** in the Styles pane. Scroll down and apply the Heading 1 style to the headings *Personal Safety*, *Medical Emergencies*, *Fire Emergencies*, *Homeland Security*, and *Personal Safety on Campus*.
- Click in the line on page 4 containing the text *Summary*. Click **Heading 2** in the Styles pane. Scroll down and apply Heading 2 style to the headings *Security and Access to Campus Facilities* and *Emergency Phones*.

m. Point to Heading 2 in the Styles pane, and click the **Heading 2 arrow**. Click **Modify**. Click **Underline** and click **OK**.

The Heading 2 style is modified to include an underline. All text previously formatted in the Heading 2 style now includes an underline.

n. Scroll to page 3 and select the five paragraphs in the *Emergency Notifications* section, beginning with *Phone* and ending with *provide additional information*. Apply square filled bullets to the selection. Decrease indent to the left margin. Click **New Style** in the Styles pane, type **Bulleted Text** in the Name box, and then click **OK**.

o. Select the seven paragraphs in the *Personal Safety* section, beginning with *Seek a safe location* and ending with *follow all directions immediately*. Click **Bulleted Text** in the Styles pane to apply the style to the selection. Apply the same style to the seven paragraphs in the *Medical Emergencies* section, beginning with *The victim should not be moved* and ending with *information is needed*. Close the Styles pane.

p. Press **Ctrl+Home** to move to the beginning of the document. Spell check the document. The word *of* in the university name is correct in lowercase, so do not correct it.

q. Scroll to page 3 and select all text beginning with *The University of Northern Virginia* and ending at the end of the document. Click the **Layout tab**, click **Columns**, and then select **Two**. Click the **View tab** and click **Multiple Pages** in the Zoom group to view pages of the document. Scroll up or down to check the document for text positioning and any awkward column endings. Click **100%** in the Zoom group.

r. Click **Outline** in the Views group. Click the **Show Level arrow** in the Outline Tools group and click **Level 1**. Click the plus (**+**) sign beside *Personal Safety on Campus* and click **Expand** in the Outline Tools group. Point to the plus (**+**) sign beside *Emergency Phones* and drag to position the *Emergency Phones* section above *Security and Access to Campus Facilities*. Click **Print Layout** on the status bar.

s. Press **Ctrl+Home** to move to the beginning of the document. Click **Show/Hide** in the Paragraph group to turn off the nonprinting characters feature. Click the **File tab** and click **Print** to preview the document. Click **Next Page** to move through the pages of the document. Click **Back** at the top-left corner of the screen to leave print preview.

t. Compare your work to Figure 2.52. Save and close the file. Based on your instructor's directions, submit w02p1Campus_LastFirst.

2 Drug Abuse

The local community center recently received a grant from the state to educate young people on the danger of drug addiction. You have been hired by the local community center to oversee this project. The primary purpose of the project is to develop materials on drug addiction, educate teenagers on the dangers of abusing illegal drugs, and warn them about the long-term repercussions of drug dependency. You will make presentations to various groups around the city, including high schools, civic clubs, and student organizations. Besides a PowerPoint presentation to support your discussions, you will also distribute research articles, flyers, and brochures to help convey the message. One such document, a summary of medical facts regarding drug abuse, is near completion. It is in need of proofreading, formatting, and a few other features that will result in a polished handout for your next presentation. Refer to Figure 2.53 as you complete this exercise.

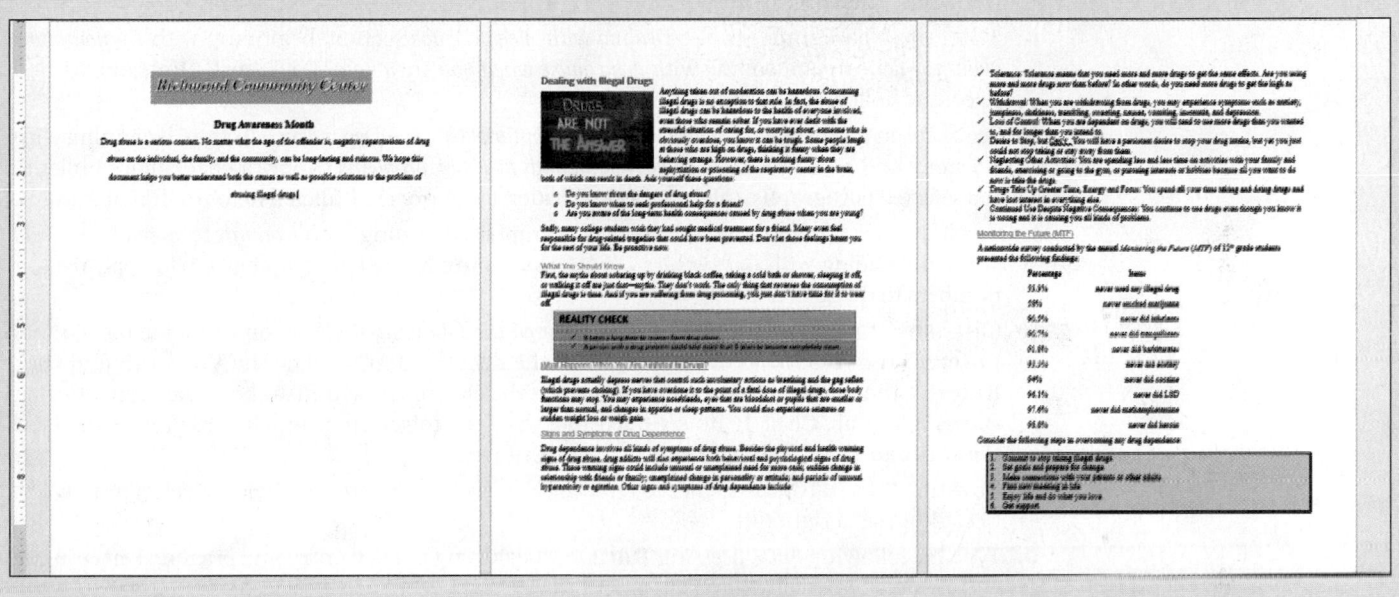

FIGURE 2.53 Finish a Handout

a. Open *w02p2Drug* and save it as **w02p2Drug_LastFirst**.

b. Click the **Home tab** and click **Show/Hide** if nonprinting characters are not displayed. Press **Ctrl+A** to select all document text. Click the **Font arrow** and select **Times New Roman**. Click anywhere to deselect the text. Check the document for spelling and grammatical errors. Ignore the identified grammatical mistake on page 2.

c. Press **Ctrl+Home** to move to the beginning of the document. Select the first line in the document, *Richmond Community Center*. Click the **Insert tab** and select **WordArt** in the Text group. Click **Fill – Black, Text 1, Outline – Background 1, Hard Shadow – Background 1** (third row, first column). Ensure that the text is still selected. Click the **Shape Fill arrow** in the Shape Styles group on the Format tab. Select **White, Background 1, Darker 25%** (fourth row, first column). Click the **Home tab** and change the font size to **24**.

d. Click **Layout Options** and click **Top and Bottom**. Close Layout Options. Point to the WordArt object and drag to visually center it. You should drag when the pointer resembles a four-headed arrow.

e. Select the second line in the document, *Drug Awareness Month*. When you select the text, the WordArt is also selected because it is anchored to the selected paragraph. Center and bold the selected text and change the font size to **14**.

f. Click anywhere in the first paragraph that begins *Drug abuse is a serious concern*. Center the paragraph. Click **Line and Paragraph Spacing** in the Paragraph group and select **2.0**. Click before the paragraph mark ending the paragraph that begins *Drug abuse is a serious concern*.

Click the **Layout tab** and click **Breaks**. Click **Next Page** in the Section Breaks group. Press **Delete** to remove the paragraph mark at the top of page 2.

g. Click the **Home tab**. Select the first line on page 2, *Dealing with Illegal Drugs*. Click **Heading 1** in the Styles group. Select *What You Should Know* and select **Heading 2**.

h. Select *What Happens When You Are Addicted to Drugs?* Change the font to **Arial**, click **Underline** in the Font group, click the **Font Color arrow**, and change the font color to **Blue, Accent 1**. Click the **Styles Dialog Box Launcher**. Click **New Style**. Type **Lower Item** in the Name box and click **OK**. Select the heading *Signs and Symptoms of Drug Dependence*. Click **Lower Item** in the Styles pane to apply the newly created style to the selected text. Apply the same format to the heading *Monitoring the Future (MTF)*.

i. Point to Heading 1 in the Styles pane and click the **Heading 1 arrow**. Click **Modify**. Click **Bold** and click **OK**. Scroll up, if necessary, to see that the heading *Dealing with Illegal Drugs* is bold. Close the Styles pane.

j. Select three paragraphs in the *Dealing with Illegal Drugs* section, beginning with *Do you know about the dangers* and ending with *drug abuse when you are young?* Click the **Bullets arrow** and select the hollow round bullet.

k. Select seven paragraphs in the *Signs and Symptoms of Drug Dependence* section, beginning with *Tolerance* and ending with *it is causing you all kinds of problems*. Apply a check mark bullet to the selected paragraphs. Click **Decrease Indent** to move the bulleted items to the left margin.

l. Scroll to page 3 and select the last six paragraphs, beginning with *Commit to stop taking illegal drugs* and ending with *Get support*. Click **Numbering** in the Paragraph group to apply default numbers to the selection.

m. Click after the sentence ending with *presented the following findings*: on the same page. Press **Enter**. If the ruler is not displayed above the document area, click the **View tab** and click **Ruler** in the Show group. Ensure that the tab selector, shown just above the vertical ruler, shows a left tab. Click **1"** to set a left tab. Click **3"** to set another left tab. Press **Tab**. Type **Percentage**. Press **Tab**. Type **Items**. Press **Enter**.

n. Drag the 3" left tab off the ruler to remove it. Click the **tab selector** twice to select a right tab. Click **4"** to set a right tab.

o. Type the following data, pressing **Tab** at the beginning of each entry and pressing **Enter** at the end of each line except the last line:

53.3%	never used any illegal drug
58%	never smoked marijuana
90.5%	never did inhalants
90.7%	never did tranquilizers
91.8%	never did barbiturates
93.5%	never did ecstasy
94%	never did cocaine
96.1%	never did LSD
97.6%	never did methamphetamine
98.8%	never did heroin

p. Scroll to page 2 and click before the first sentence in the *Dealing with Illegal Drugs* section. Click the **Insert tab** and click **Online Pictures** in the Illustrations group. Type **say no to drugs** in the Bing Image Search box. Press **Enter**. Double-click the image shown in Figure 2.53 (or select one very similar if it is unavailable). Change the height of the picture to **1.5** in the Size group on the Format tab. Click **Layout Options** and select **Square**. Close Layout Options. Drag to position the image as shown in Figure 2.53.

q. Press **Ctrl+End** to move to the end of the document. Select the six numbered paragraphs. Click the **Home tab** and click the **Borders arrow** in the Paragraph group. Click **Borders and Shading**. Click **Shadow** in the Setting section. Click the **Shading tab**. Click the **Color arrow** in the Fill section and select **White, Background 1, Darker 15%**. Click **OK**.

r. Click after the last sentence in the *What You Should Know* section. Click the **Insert tab** and click **Text Box** in the Text group. Click **Draw Text Box**. Drag to draw a box approximately 1" high and 6" wide below the *What You Should Know* section. Adjust the height to **1"** and the width to **6"** exactly in the Size group on the Format tab. Click **Layout Options**. Click **Top and Bottom**. Click to place the insertion point in the text box.

s. Click the **Home tab** and click **Bold** in the Font group. Change the font size to **16**. Type **REALITY CHECK** and press **Enter**. Click **Line and Paragraph Spacing** in the Paragraph group and click **1.0**. Click the **Paragraph Dialog Box Launcher**. Change Paragraph Spacing After to **0 pt**. Click **OK**. Change the font size to **10**. Type the following, pressing **Enter** after each line:

It takes a long time to recover from drug abuse.
A person with a drug problem could take more than 5 years to become completely clean.

t. Apply check mark bullets to the two sentences you just typed. Click the **Format tab**. Click the **More arrow** in the Shape Styles group. Select **Subtle Effect – Blue, Accent 5** (fourth row, sixth column). Point in the text box so that the pointer displays as a four-headed arrow. Drag to position the text box as shown in Figure 2.53. Click **Show/Hide** in the Paragraph group to turn off the nonprinting characters feature.

u. Save and close the file. Based on your instructor's directions, submit w02p2Drug_LastFirst.

Mid-Level Exercises

1 Balloon Festival

As chair of the Mount Sedona Balloon Festival, you are responsible for promoting the upcoming event. You have begun a document providing details on the festival. You plan to distribute the document both in print and online. First, you must format the document to make it more attractive and well designed. You will use styles, bullets, and line and paragraph spacing to coordinate various parts of the document. In addition, you will add interest by including objects, such as pictures, text boxes, and WordArt.

a. Open *w02m1Balloons* and save it as **w02m1Balloons_LastFirst**.

b. Change the document theme to **Slice**. Select the first line in the document, *Mount Sedona Hot Air Balloon Festival*. Insert WordArt, selecting **Fill – Dark Purple, Accent 2, Outline – Accent 2** (first row, third column). Change the font size of the WordArt object to **20**.

c. Wrap text around the WordArt object as **Top and Bottom**. Format the WordArt object with Shape Style **Subtle Effect – Dark Purple, Accent 2** (fourth row, third column). Visually center the WordArt object on the first line of the document.

d. Select the second line in the document, *See the Canyon From On High!* Center and bold the text and apply a font color of **Dark Purple, Accent 2**.

e. Select the remaining text on page 1, beginning with *May 26-27, 2018* and ending with *on the festival grounds*. Format the selected text into two columns. Insert a page break (not a section break) after the sentence ending with *on the festival grounds*. Change the font of the columned text on page 1 to **Century Schoolbook**.

f. Check spelling and grammar—the word *Ballumination* is not misspelled (for the purposes of this document). Also, ignore *From* in the second paragraph on page 1.

g. Click in the third line on page 1—May 26-27, 2018—and right align it. Select all columned text, including the line containing festival dates, and select a line spacing of **1.5** and paragraph spacing after of **6 pt**. Insert a column break before the paragraph beginning with *And don't forget the dogs!*

h. Click to place the insertion point before the paragraph beginning *As for the kids*. Insert an online picture from Bing Image Search relating to hot air balloons. Size the picture with a height of **1.5"**. Select **Square text wrapping** and a picture style of **Rotated, White**. Position the picture so that it is on the left side of the paragraph beginning with *As for the kids*, but still in the right column.

 i. Select the picture and recolor it to coordinate with the purple theme of the document. Choose an artistic effect of **Photocopy**.

j. Scroll to page 3 and select the heading, *When is the best time to see balloons?* Bold the selection and change the font color to **Dark Purple, Accent 2**. Do not deselect the heading. Open the Styles pane and create a new style named **Questions**. Apply the **Questions style** to other questions (headings) on page 3.

k. Scroll to page 4 and apply solid round bullets to the first nine paragraphs on the page. Decrease the indent so the bullets begin at the left margin. With the bulleted items selected, click the **Bullets arrow** and click **Define New Bullet**. Click **Font** and change the font color to **Dark Purple, Accent 2**. Click **OK**. Click **OK** again.

l. Insert a page break (not a section break) before the heading *How can I plan for the best experience?* on page 3.

m. Select the schedule of items under the heading *Saturday (5/26/18)*, beginning with *6:00 AM* and ending with *Balloon Glow*. Set a left tab at **1"**. Press **Tab** twice to move selected paragraphs to the left tab. Select the schedule of items under *Sunday (5/27/18)*, set a left tab at **1"**, and then tab twice for selected paragraphs.

n. Save and close the file. Based on your instructor's directions, submit w02m1Balloons_LastFirst.

2 Johnson Orthodontics

CREATIVE CASE

You are the office manager for Dr. Johnson, an orthodontist for children, who periodically conducts informational sessions for his young patients. You have written a letter to children in the neighborhood reminding them about the upcoming monthly session, but you want to make the letter more professional looking. You decide to use paragraph formatting such as alignment, paragraph spacing, borders and shading, and bullets that describe some of the fun activities of the day. You also want to add Dr. Johnson's email address and an appropriate image to the letter.

a. Open the document *w02m2Orthodontics* and save it as **w02m2Orthodontics_LastFirst**.

b. Change the capitalization of the recipient *ms. samantha smith* and her address so that each word is capitalized and the state abbreviation displays in uppercase. Also capitalize her first name in the salutation. Change Dr. Johnson's name to your full name in the signature block. Type your email address (or a fictitious email address) on the next line below your name.

c. Show nonprinting characters, if they are not already displayed. Apply **Justify alignment** to body paragraphs beginning with *On behalf* and ending with *July 12*. At the paragraph mark under the first body paragraph, create a bulleted list, selecting a bullet of your choice. Type the following items in the bulleted list. Do not press Enter after the last item in the list.

> **Participating in the dental crossword puzzle challenge**
> **Writing a convincing letter to the tooth fairy**
> **Digging through the dental treasure chest**
> **Finding hidden toothbrushes in the dental office**

d. Select text from the salutation *Dear Samantha:* through the last paragraph that ends with *seeing you on July 12*. Set **12 pt Spacing After paragraph**. Remove the paragraph mark just after the *Dear Samantha* paragraph.

e. Select *Dr. Johnson Orthodontics Office* in the first paragraph and apply small caps.

f. Select the italicized lines of text that give date, time, and location of the meeting. Remove the italics, do not deselect the text, and then complete the following:

- Increase left and right indents to **1.25** and set **0 pt Spacing After paragraph**.
- Apply a **double-line box border** with the color **Green, Accent 4, Darker 50%** and a line width of **3/4 pt**. Shade selected text with the **Green, Accent 4, Lighter 40% shading color**.
- Delete the extra tab formatting marks to the left of the lines containing *July 12, 2018; 4:00 p.m.*; and *Dr. Johnson Orthodontics Office* to align them with other text in the bordered area.
- Remove the paragraph mark before the paragraph that begins with *Please call our office*.

g. Click the line containing the text *Glen Allen, VA 23059*, and set **12 pt Spacing After** the paragraph. Click the line containing *Sincerely* and set **6 pt Spacing Before** the paragraph. Add **6 pt Spacing Before** the paragraph beginning with the text *Dr. Johnson is pleased to let you know*.

h. Select the entire document and change the font to **12-pt Bookman Old Style**.

i. Move to the beginning of the document. Search online for a picture related to **tooth**. Insert the picture and apply a square text wrap. Position the picture in the top-right corner of the document, just below the header area. Resize the graphic to **1.1"** high. Apply the **Bevel Perspective Left, White picture style** (fourth row, third column).

j. Move to the end of the document. Insert a Next Page section break. Change the orientation to **Landscape**. Change Paragraph Spacing After to **6 pt**. Change the font size to **14**. Center the first line. Type **Lake George Water Park Fun Day!** Press **Enter** and type **July 7, 2018**. Press **Enter** and change the alignment to **Left**. Change the font size to **12**. Set a left tab at **2"** and a right tab at **7"**. Type the following text, with the first column at the 2" tab and the next column at the 7" tab. Do not press Enter after typing the last line.

Check-in	9:00
Water slide	9:30-11:00
Lunch at the pavilion	11:00-12:00
Wave pool	12:00-2:00
Bungee	2:00-3:00
Parent pickup at the gate	3:00-3:30

k. Select **Lake George Water Park Fun Day!** on page 2 and insert WordArt with the style **Fill – Aqua, Accent 1, Outline – Background 1, Hard Shadow – Accent 1** (third row, third column). Wrap text around the WordArt object at **Top and Bottom**, change the font size of the WordArt object to **24**, and drag to center the object horizontally on the first line.

l. Select the tabbed text, beginning with *Check-in* and ending with *3:00-3:30*. Modify the 7" right tab to include a dot leader.

m. Change the theme to **Integral**. Check spelling and grammar, correcting any errors and ignoring those that are not errors. Turn off the nonprinting characters feature.

n. Save and close the file. Based on your instructor's directions, submit w02m2Orthodontics_LastFirst.

3 A Music CD Cover

COLLABORATION CASE

FROM SCRATCH

You play bass guitar with a local band, Twilight Hour. You love playing with the band, but you also enjoy the business side of music, and plan to pursue a career in music production. To that end, you are completing requirements for a B.S. degree. This semester, you are participating in a seminar on music marketing and production. You are in a group that is required to design the front and back of a CD cover for a band, real or fictitious, and your group decides to create a cover for your band. You will begin a document and share it with members of the group, who will each contribute to the CD cover. Your group will first locate a music CD case to use as a model. The front of the CD typically displays the band or artist name, along with a graphic or background design.

Before continuing with this case, all group members must have a Microsoft account. An account can be obtained at www.outlook.com.

a. One person in your group will complete the following two steps:
   • Open a new Word document. Include the group name in the header. Click the **File tab** and click **Share**. Click **Save to Cloud** and click the **OneDrive link**. Select a recently accessed folder, or click **Browse**, and navigate to, or create, another folder.
   • Change the file name to **w02m3Cover_GroupName** and click **Save**. Click **Share** and then click **Get a Sharing Link**. Click **Create Link** beside the Edit Link section. Share the link with group members so that they can access the document online.

b. Each group member will enter the link in a browser to access the shared document. When the document opens in Word Online, click **Edit Document** and click **Edit in Word**.
   • One or more group members will focus on developing the front cover, including WordArt, pictures, and/or text boxes where appropriate. Use font and paragraph formatting, as needed, to produce an attractive front cover. The front cover should occupy the first page, or first section, of the shared document. Save the document often, ensuring the save location is OneDrive.
   • One or more group members will focus on the back cover, including a list of songs, numbered and in two columns. In addition, give attention to the design of text and headings, formatting all items to produce an attractive back cover. The back cover will occupy the second page, or second section, of the shared document. Save the document often, ensuring the save location is OneDrive.
   • The dimensions of the final document will not necessarily be that of an actual CD. You are concerned with the design only.

c. The final version of the CD cover should be saved to OneDrive. Close the file. Based on your instructor's directions, submit w02m3Cover_GroupName.

Beyond the Classroom

Invitation

GENERAL CASE

FROM SCRATCH

Search the Internet for an upcoming local event at your school or in your community and produce the perfect invitation. You can invite people to a charity ball, a fun run, or a fraternity or sorority party. Your color printer and abundance of fancy fonts, as well as your ability to insert page borders, enable you to do anything a professional printer can do. Save your work as **w02b1Invitation_LastFirst**, and close the file. Based on your instructor's directions, submit w02b1Invitation_LastFirst.

Fundraising Letter

DISASTER RECOVERY

Each year, you update a letter to several community partners soliciting support for an auction. The auction raises funds for your organization, and your letter should impress your supporters. Open *w02b2Auction* and notice how unprofessional and unorganized the document looks so far. You must make changes immediately to improve the appearance. Consider replacing much of the formatting that is in place now and instead using columns for auction items, bullets to draw attention to the list of forms, page borders, and pictures or images—and that is just for starters! Save your work as **w02b2Auction_LastFirst** and close the file. Based on your instructor's directions, submit w02b2Auction_LastFirst.

Capstone Exercise

This semester you are enrolled in a personal finance course at your local university. One of the assignments is to write a research paper about investing. You conducted research on the various types of investing instruments, and wrote a final draft of the report. Now your research paper requires formatting to enhance readability and important information; and you will use skills from this chapter to format multiple levels of headings, arrange and space text, and insert graphics.

Applying Styles

This document is ready for enhancements, and the Styles feature is a good tool that enables you to add them quickly and easily.

a. Open *w02c1Finance* and save it as **w02c1Finance_LastFirst**.

b. Press **Ctrl+Home**. Create a paragraph style named **Title_Page_1** with these formats: **22-pt** font size and **Dark Blue, Text 2, Darker 50%** font color. Ensure that this style is applied to the first line of the document, *Personal Finance:*.

c. Select the second line, *Understanding the Investment Instruments*. Change the font size to **16** and apply a font color of **Dark Blue, Text 2, Darker 50%**.

d. Click the line following *Updated by:* and type your first and last names. Change the capitalization for your name to uppercase.

e. Select the remainder of the text in the document that follows your name, starting with *Personal Finance*. Justify the alignment of all paragraphs and change line spacing to **1.15**. Place the insertion point on the left side of the title *Personal Finance* (below your name) and insert a page break (not a section break).

f. Apply **Heading 1 style** to *Personal Finance* at the top of page 2. Apply **Heading 2 style** to paragraph headings, including *Introduction, Equity Stocks, Bonds, Mutual Funds, U.S. Treasury Bills, Fixed Deposits, Sources,* and *Conclusion*.

g. Modify the Heading 2 style to use **Dark Red** font color.

Formatting the Paragraphs

Next, you will apply paragraph formatting to the document. These format options will further increase the readability and attractiveness of your document.

a. Apply a bulleted list format for the six-item list in the third paragraph of the *Introduction* section. Use the symbol of a diamond.

b. Select the second body paragraph in the *Introduction* section, which begins with *The best time to prepare for your retirement*, and apply these formats: **0.6"** left and right indents, **6 pt** spacing after the paragraph, **boxed 1 1/2 pt border** using the color **Dark Blue, Text 2, Darker 25%**, and the shading color **Dark Blue, Text 2, Lighter 80%**.

c. Apply the numbered list format (1., 2., 3.) to the three types of bonds in the *Bonds* section.

d. Select the three quotes by Warren Buffet and the *Source:* paragraph in the *Equity Stocks* section and display them in two columns with a line between the columns.

e. Insert the hyperlinks for all the five sources listed in the *Sources* section.

Inserting Graphics

To put the finishing touches on your document, you will add graphics that enhance the explanations given in some paragraphs.

a. Insert the picture file *w02c1Bull* at the beginning of the line that contains *The major stock market* in the *Equity Stocks* section. Change the height of the picture to **3"**. Change text wrapping to **Top and Bottom**. Center the graphic horizontally. Apply the **Rounded Diagonal Corner, White picture style**. Position the picture so that it appears below the *Equity Stocks* heading.

b. Insert the picture file *w02c1Bear* at the beginning of the line that begins with *If you want something a little less risky than stocks* in the *Bonds* section. Change the height of the picture to **3"**. Ensure that text wrapping is **Top and Bottom**, position the picture so it appears immediately above the line beginning *U.S. Treasury bills and government*. Apply **Offset Center Shadow Picture Effect** (second row, second column under *Outer*) to the graphic. Position the picture so that it appears below the *Bonds* heading.

c. Spell check and review the entire document—no author names are misspelled.

d. Display the document in Outline view. Collapse all paragraphs so only lines formatted as Heading 1 or Heading 2 display. Move the *Sources* section to below the *Conclusion* section. Close Outline view.

e. Save and close the file. Based on your instructor's directions, submit w02c1Finance_LastFirst.

Document Productivity

LEARNING OUTCOMES

- You will demonstrate how tables are used to organize and present information.
- You will apply mail merge to create personalized letters and mailing labels.

OBJECTIVES & SKILLS: After you read this chapter, you will be able to:

CASE STUDY | Traylor University Economic Impact Study

As director of marketing and research for Traylor University, a mid-sized university in northwest Nebraska, you have been involved with an economic impact study during the past year. The study is designed to measure as closely as possible the contribution of the university to the local and state economy. An evaluation of data led university researchers to conclude that Traylor University serves as a critical economic driver in the local community and, to a lesser extent, the state of Nebraska. It is your job to summarize those findings and see that they are accurately reflected in the final report.

Your assistant has prepared a draft of an executive summary that you will present to the board of trustees, outlining the major findings and conclusions. The best way to present some of the data analysis will be through tables, which your assistant is not very familiar with, so you will take responsibility for that phase of the summary preparation. You will send an executive summary, along with a cover letter, to community and university leaders. You will use Word's mail merge feature to prepare personalized letters and mailing labels.

Working with Tables and Mail Merge

Table 2 presents impact sources, with a description of each.

Table 2 – Impact Sources	
Source	**Description**
Capital Investment	New construction expenditures, creating additional...
	...he local
	...eeded to

Key Findings

Primary data utilized in this analysis was obtained from the Traylor University's Office of Research and Development. Data included capital expenditures, operational expenditures, jobs data, payroll and benefits information, and taxes. We took a decidedly conservative approach in the analysis and determination of key findings. Not unexpectedly, study findings compare favorably to other top

...tatewide tax
...ral part of the
...e and local
...22.4 million in
...ax revenues that

...terms of

	rage of
	tal
	41.83%
	29.69%
	12.98%
	8.01%
	7.59%

October 15, 2018

Dr. Holly Lowe
Lowe & Assoc.
459 Hwy. 34
Ogalala, NE 68604

Dear Dr. Lowe:

Traylor University is making a difference in the local community and in the state of Nebraska, as confirmed by the results of the recently completed biannual economic impact study. As a member of the Traylor University Board of Trustees, you can be assured that you are leading a stellar university—one that contributes millions of dollars to the economy of the state each year, and one that is improving the lives of the state's populace.

The attached executive summary provides a snapshot of the university's monetary effect on its service area and the state. The expanded report will be printed and available at the November board meeting. As you review the executive summary, please let me know of any questions or suggestions.

Sincerely,

Melinda Roberts, Executive Director
Office of Marketing and Research
Traylor University

Word 2016, Windows 10, Microsoft Corporation

FIGURE 3.1 Traylor University Documents

CASE STUDY | Traylor University Economic Impact Study

Starting Files	Files to be Submitted
w03h1Traylor w03h2KeyFindings w03h2Text w03h3Letter	w03h2Traylor_LastFirst w03h3Merge_LastFirst

Tables

A *table* is a grid of columns and rows that organizes data. As shown in Figure 3.2, a table is typically configured with headings in the first row and related data in following rows. The intersection of each column and row is a *cell*, in which you can type data. A table is an excellent format in which to summarize numeric data because you can easily align numbers and even include formulas to sum or average numbers in a column or row. Text can be included in a table as well. Although you can use tabs to align text in columns in a Word document, you might find it quicker to create a table than to set tabs, and you have more control over format and design when using a table.

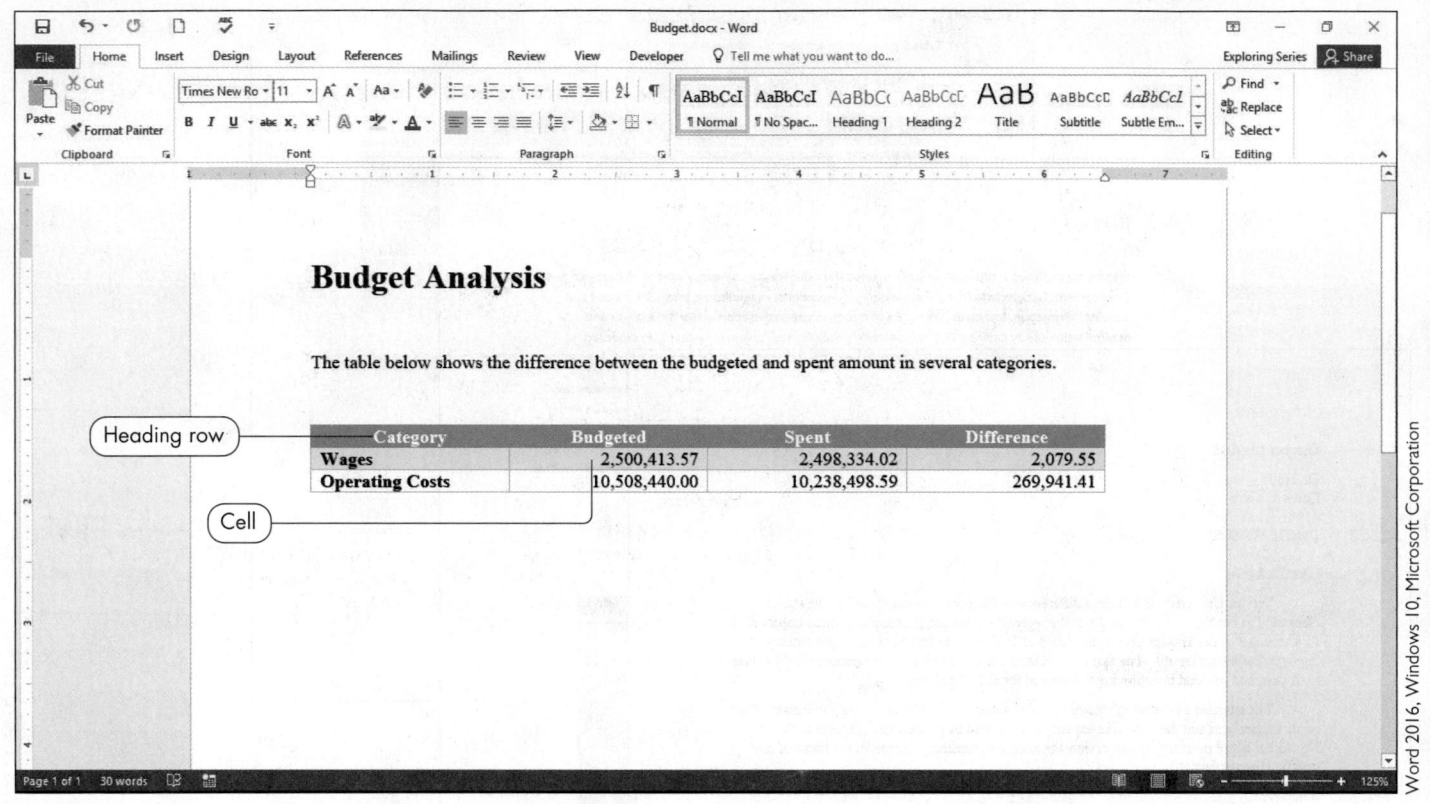

FIGURE 3.2 A Word Table

Word's Table feature is a comprehensive but easy-to-use tool, enabling you to insert a table, add and remove rows and columns, format table elements, include formulas to summarize numbers in a table, and customize borders and shading. You can always change a table, or format it differently, even after it is developed.

In this section, you will learn to insert a table. After positioning the table within a document, you will explore inserting and deleting columns and rows, merging and splitting cells, and adjusting row height and column width. Using table styles, you will modify the appearance of a table, and you will adjust table position and alignment.

Inserting a Table

Inserting a table in a document is an easy task. You can either create a table with uniformly spaced rows and columns, or you can draw a table with the pointer, creating rows and columns of varying heights and widths. Regardless of how a table is created, you can always change table settings so that rows and columns fit the data included in the table.

When you work with a table, you specify the number of columns and rows that should be included. For example, the table shown in Figure 3.2 is a 4 × 3 table, which means it contains 4 columns and 3 rows.

Create or Draw a Table

STEP 1 ›› A table is an object; as such, it can be selected and manipulated independently of surrounding text. Inserting a table is a process that requires only a few steps.

To insert a table with identically sized rows and columns, complete the following steps:

1. Click the Insert tab.
2. Click Table in the Tables group.
3. Complete one of the following steps:
   - Drag to select the number of columns or rows to include in the table, as shown in Figure 3.3. Click in the bottom-right cell of the selection.
   - Click Insert Table to display the Insert Table dialog box, where you can indicate the number of rows and columns you want to include. Click OK.
   - Click Quick Table to insert a predesigned table.

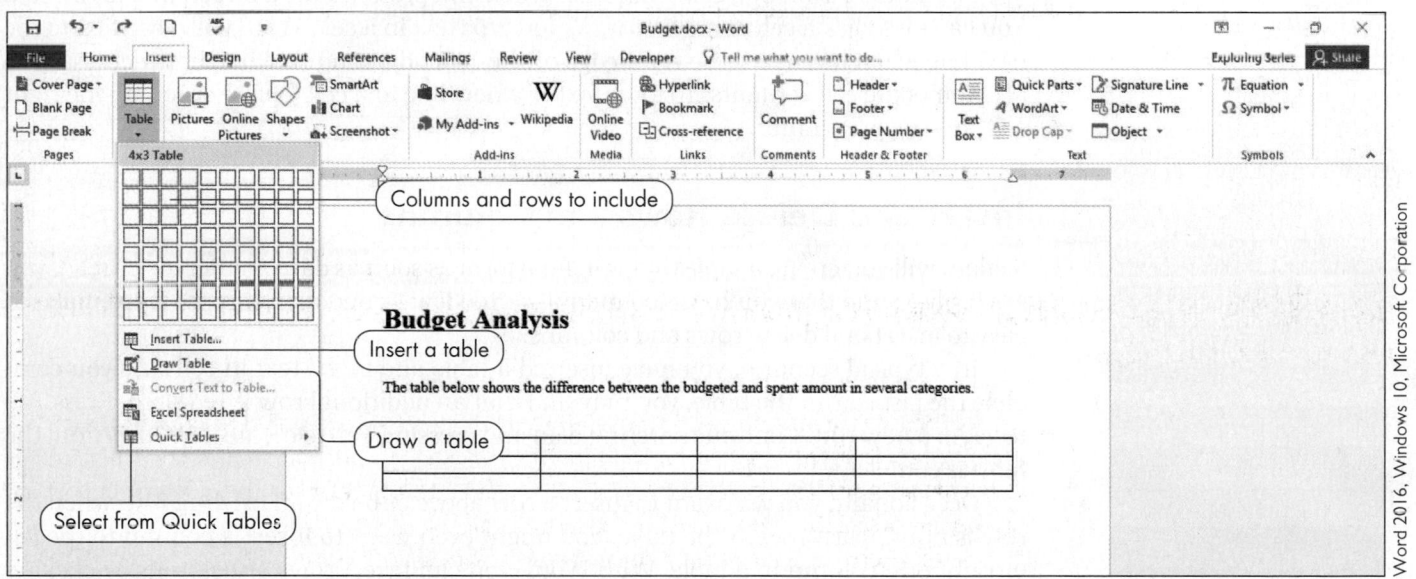

FIGURE 3.3 Inserting a Table

Instead of inserting a table by indicating the number of columns or rows to include, as described in the previous set of steps, you can draw a table. You might choose to draw a table if you know that rows and/or columns should have varying heights or widths. It is sometimes easier to draw rows and columns of varying dimensions when a table is created rather than to modify the dimensions later, as would be necessary if you used Word to create evenly distributed columns and rows.

> **To draw a table, complete the following steps:**
>
> 1. Click the Insert tab and click Table in the Tables group.
> 2. Click Draw Table. As you move the pointer over the document, it resembles a pencil.
> 3. Drag a rectangle and then draw horizontal and vertical lines to create rows and columns within the rectangular table space.
> 4. Press Esc when the table is complete.

Regardless of whether you draw a table or insert a table of identically sized columns or rows, you can erase one or more grid lines within the table.

> **To erase one or more grid lines, complete the following steps:**
>
> 1. Click anywhere in the table.
> 2. Click Eraser in the Draw group on the Table Tools Layout tab (see Figure 3.4). Click a grid line to erase.
> 3. Press Esc when all lines that you want to remove are erased.

After the table structure is created, you can enter characters, numbers, or graphics in cells, moving from one cell to another when you press Tab or a directional arrow key. You can also click a cell to move to it. As you type text in a cell, Word will wrap text to the next line when it reaches the right edge of the cell, adjusting row height if necessary to accommodate cell contents. To force text to a new line in a cell (before reaching the right cell border), press Enter.

Insert and Delete Rows and Columns

Seldom will you create a table that is in final form as soon as data is entered. Instead, you are likely to find that you have too many—or too few—rows or columns. Word makes it easy to insert and delete rows and columns.

In a typical scenario, you have inserted a table and typed text in cells. As you complete the last row in the table, you may find that an additional row is required. Press Tab to begin a new row. Continue entering data and pressing Tab to create new rows until the table is complete.

Occasionally, you will want to insert a row above or below an existing row, when the row is not the last row in the table. You might even want to insert a column to the left or right of a column in a table. With Word, you can insert rows or columns by clicking an *insert control* that displays when you point to the edge of a row or column gridline, as shown in Figure 3.4. To insert several rows or columns, drag to select the number of rows or columns to insert, and click the insert control.

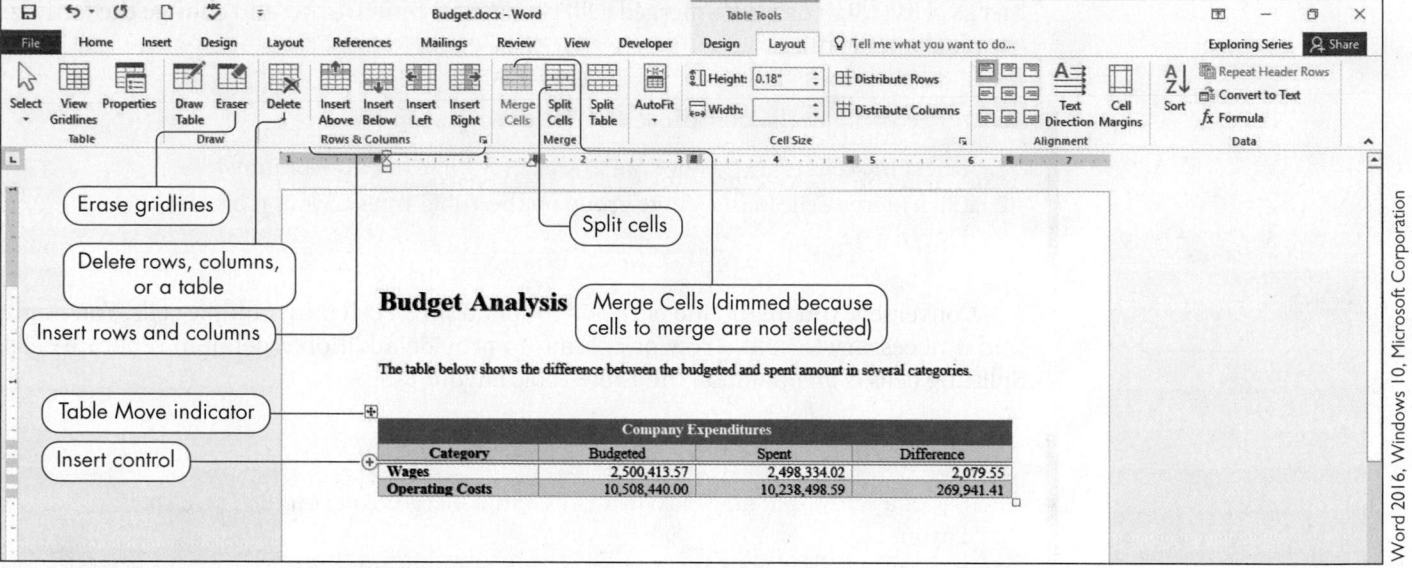

FIGURE 3.4 Working with Rows and Columns

Although it is convenient to use the insert control to insert rows and columns, the Table Tools Layout tab includes more comprehensive options that enable you to easily insert both columns and rows. Select from options in the Rows & Columns group, shown in Figure 3.4, to insert rows or columns.

To delete an entire row or column (not merely the cell contents of a row or column), complete the following steps:

1. Select the row or column to delete (or drag to select multiple rows or columns). To select the row or column, position the pointer just outside the left edge of a row or just above the top edge of a column and click.
2. Click Delete in the Rows & Columns group (refer to Figure 3.4) and click Delete Rows or Delete Columns. Alternatively, right-click a selection and choose Delete Rows or Delete Columns.

> **TIP: DELETE CELL CONTENTS**
> To delete cell contents without removing a row or column, position the pointer just inside the left edge of the cell so that the pointer appears as a small right-directed black arrow. Click to select all cell contents (or drag to select contents of multiple adjacent cells). Press Delete.

To delete a table, complete the following steps:

1. Click the Table Move indicator (visible at the top left corner of the table when you move the pointer over any cell in the table or click a cell in the table), shown in Figure 3.4.
2. Click Delete in the Rows & Columns group on the Table Tools Layout tab and click Delete Table. Alternatively, you can right-click any cell and select Delete Table.

Merge and Split Cells

STEP 2 ›› The first row of the table shown in Figure 3.4 is actually a merged cell. When several cells are combined into one, the new cell is considered a merged cell. If you want to place a title across the top of a table or center a label over columns or rows of data, you can merge cells. Align data in a merged cell, perhaps by centering it, and change the font size to create a table title.

To merge table cells, complete the following steps:

1. Select the cells to merge (or drag to select multiple rows or columns).
2. Click Merge Cells in the Merge group on the Table Tools Layout tab (refer to Figure 3.4).

Conversely, you might find occasion to split a single cell into multiple cells. You might find it necessary to split a row or column to provide additional detail in separate cells. Splitting cells is an option on the Table Tools Layout tab.

To split a cell, complete the following steps:

1. Select a cell to split and click Split Cells in the Merge group on the Table Tools Layout tab.
2. Respond to selections in the Split Cells dialog box and click OK.

Change Row Height and Column Width

When you create a table by inserting it, Word builds a grid with evenly spaced columns and rows. When text that you type requires more than one row within a cell, Word automatically wraps the text and adjusts row height to accommodate the entry. Row height is the vertical distance from the top to the bottom of a row, whereas column width is the horizontal space from the left to the right edge of a column. On occasion, you might want to manually adjust row height or column width to modify the appearance of a table, perhaps making it more readable or more attractive. Increasing row height can better fit a header that has been enlarged for emphasis. You might increase column width to display a wide area of text, such as a first and last name, to prevent wrapping of text in a cell.

You can distribute selected columns and rows to ensure that they are the same height and/or width. Simply select the columns and rows to affect and click Distribute Rows (or Distribute Columns) in the Cell Size group on the Table Tools Layout tab. Distributing rows and columns is an easy way to ensure uniformity within a table.

A simple, but not very precise way to change row height or column width is to position the pointer on a border so that it displays as a double-headed arrow and drag to increase or reduce height or width. For more precision, you can use Ribbon commands to adjust row height or column width.

To change row height or column width, complete the following steps:

1. Select a row or column to be adjusted (or select multiple rows or columns).
2. Change the row height or column width in the Cell Size group on the Table Tools Layout tab. Alternatively, you can right-click the selected row or column and select Table Properties on the shortcut menu. Then click the Column tab or Row tab and indicate a measurement in inches, as shown in Figure 3.5.

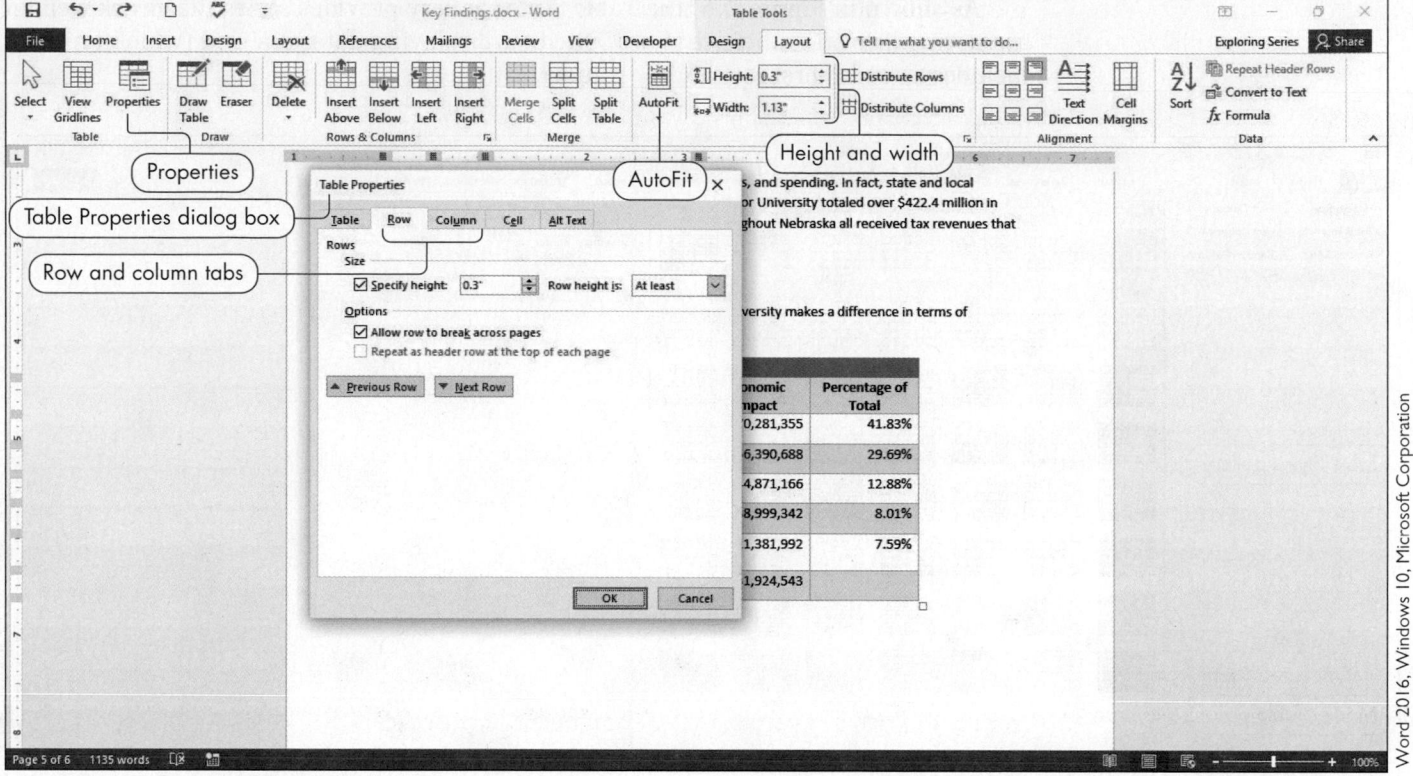

FIGURE 3.5 Changing Row Height and Column Width

Instead of adjusting individual columns and rows, you can let Word format a table with column and row dimensions that accommodate all cell entries. The feature, called AutoFit, automatically adjusts rows and columns.

To AutoFit rows and columns, complete the following steps:

1. Click in any table cell and click AutoFit in the Cell Size group on the Table Tools Layout tab (refer to Figure 3.5).
2. Click AutoFit Contents. Columns and rows are automatically adjusted.

Formatting a Table

After a table is inserted in a document, you can enhance its appearance by applying coordinated colors, borders, shading, and other design elements. Edit text within a table by underlining, boldfacing, or italicizing it. You can also align text within cells by selecting an alignment from the Alignment group on the Table Tools Layout tab. Lists or series within cells can be bulleted or numbered, and you can indent table text. Use the Properties control on the Table Tools Layout tab, or right-click a table and select Table Properties, to reposition a table by centering it horizontally or vertically, or simply drag a table to change its position on the page.

Apply Table Styles

STEP 3 ›› Word provides several predesigned *table styles* that contain borders, shading, font sizes, and other attributes that enhance the readability of a document. Use a table style when:

- You want to create a color-coordinated, professional document.
- You are coordinating a table with elements of Word, Excel, or PowerPoint files, so that the table can be shared among the Office applications.
- You do not have time to design your own custom borders and shading.

As shown in Figure 3.6, the Table Styles gallery provides styles that work well for presenting lists and others that are suited for displaying data in a grid (which typically includes a shaded first row and/or column with headings).

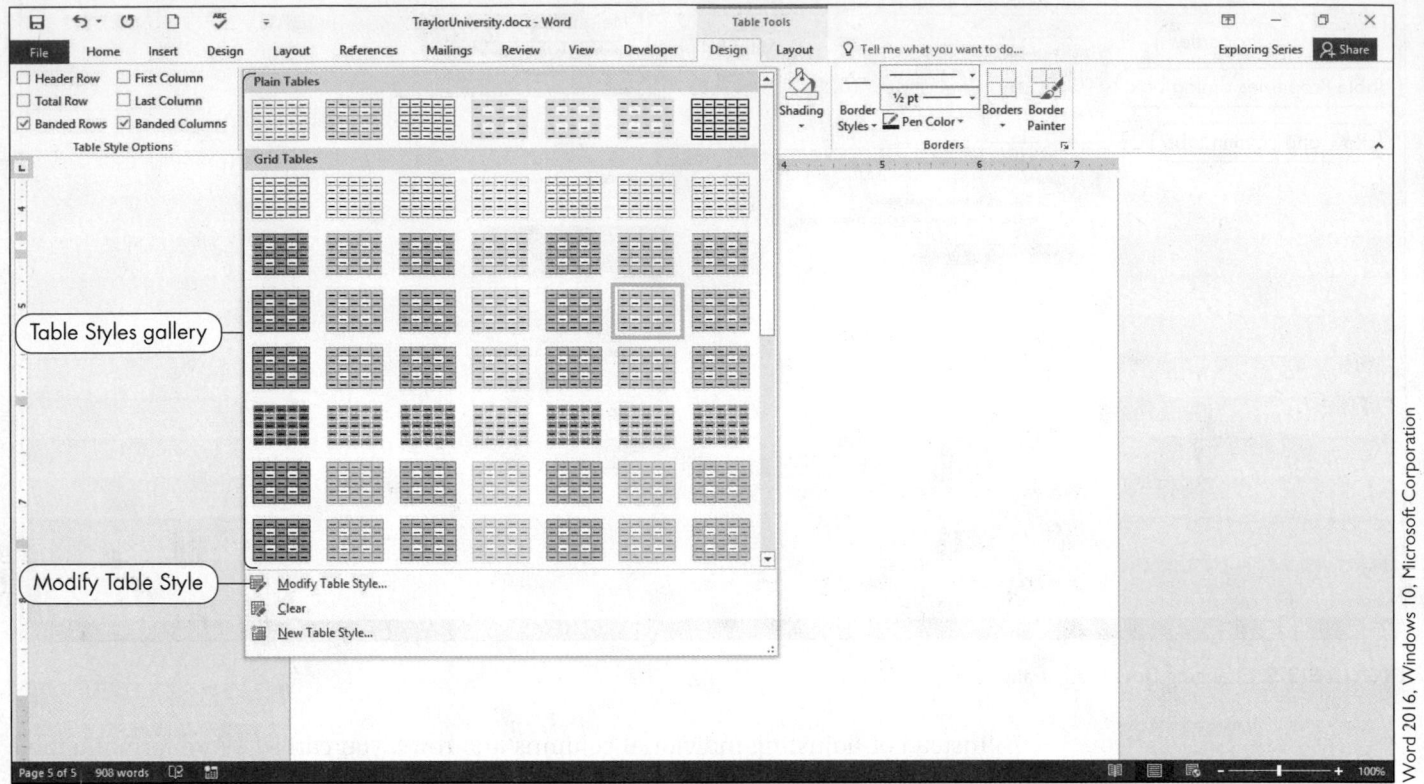

FIGURE 3.6 Working with Table Styles

To apply a table style, complete the following steps:

1. Click anywhere in a table. Click the Table Tools Design tab.
2. Select a style from the Table Styles group (refer to Figure 3.6) or click More for additional choices. When you point to a style in the gallery, Live Preview shows the result of the style selection in the table.

TIP: MODIFY A TABLE STYLE

Having selected a table style, you can modify it when you click Modify Table Style (refer to Figure 3.6) and adjust the format in the Modify Table Style dialog box. As you modify a table style, you can apply changes to the entire table or to elements such as the header row. In that way, you can adjust a style so that it better suits your purposes for the current table as well as for others that are based on the style. Save the changes for use in the current document only, or in new documents based on the current template.

Adjust Table Position and Alignment

Table alignment refers to the horizontal position of a table between the left and right document margins. When you insert a table, Word automatically aligns it at the left margin, although you can change the alignment, choosing to center the table or align it at the right margin.

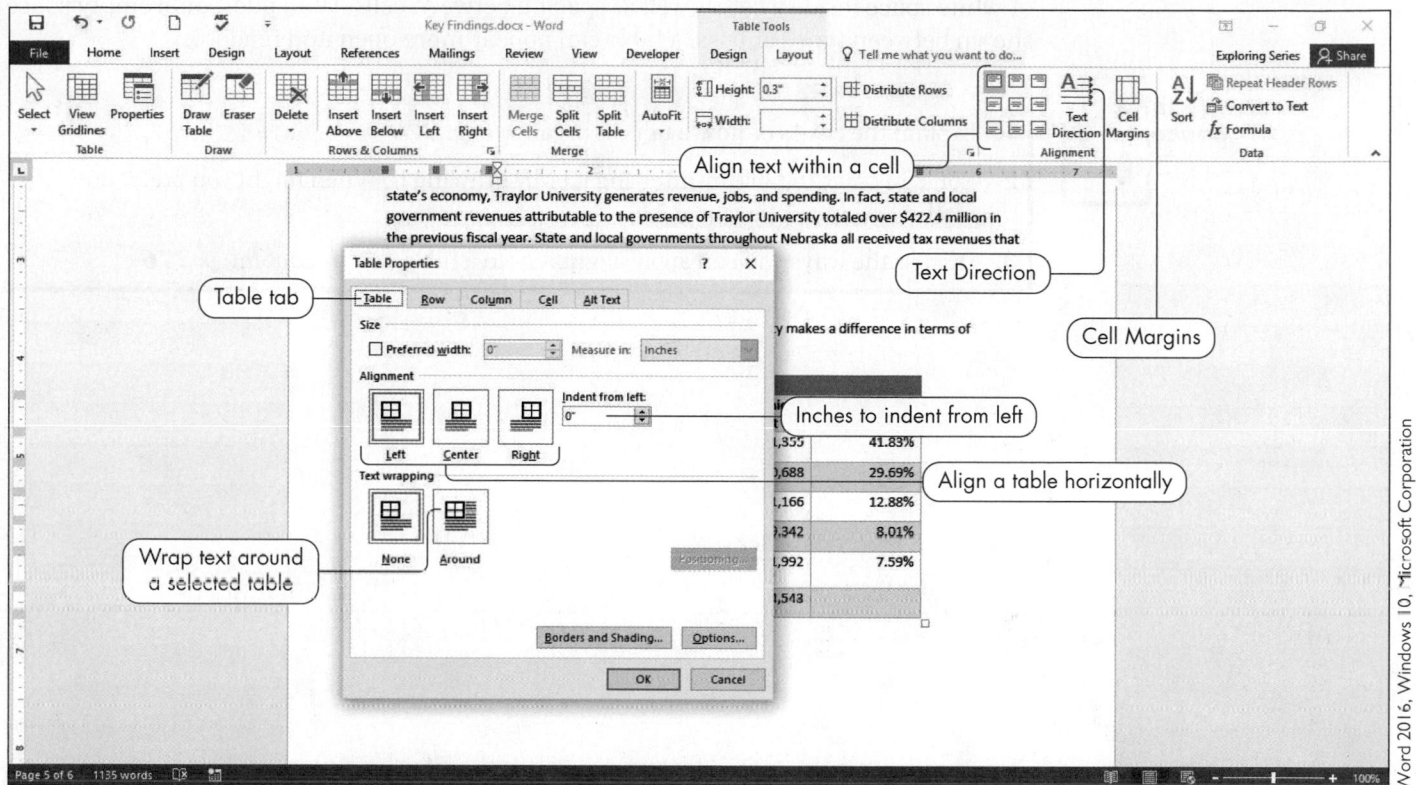

FIGURE 3.7 Adjusting Table and Text Alignment

You can move a table to any location within the document when you drag the Table Move handle. As you move the table, a dashed border displays, indicating the position of the table. Release the mouse button to position the table.

Especially when working with a small table that does not require much document space, you might find it useful to wrap text around the table so that the table is better incorporated visually into the document. On the Table tab of the Table Properties dialog box, select Around in the Text wrapping section (refer to Figure 3.7) to wrap text around a table. Text will wrap on the right side of a left-aligned table, on both sides of a centered table, and on the left side of a right-aligned table. If you select None in the Text wrapping section, text is prevented from wrapping, ensuring that text displays only at the top and bottom of a table.

Text within cells can be aligned as well. To align text in a cell, click the cell and select an alignment option in the Alignment group on the Table Tools Layout tab. You can align cell contents both vertically and horizontally within the current cell, as indicated in Figure 3.7.

Format Table Text

Text within a cell can be formatted just as any other text in a document. Select text to format and apply one or more font attributes such as font type, font size, underline, bold-face, or italics. Although you can drag text to select it, you can also quickly select all cell contents when you click just inside the left edge of a cell. Select a font attribute to apply to the selected cell text.

By default, text within a cell is oriented horizontally so that it reads from left to right. On occasion, you might want to change that direction. Lengthy column headings can be oriented vertically, so that they require less space. Or perhaps a table includes a row of cells repeating a telephone number, with each cell designed to be ripped off of a printed document. Such cells are often in a vertical format for ease of removal. To change cell orientation, click Text Direction in the Alignment group on the Table Tools Layout tab (refer to Figure 3.7). Each time you click the Text Direction option, text in the current cell or selection rotates.

The Cell Margins command in the Alignment group enables you to adjust the amount of white space inside a cell as well as spacing between cells. With additional empty space shown between typed entries, a table can appear more open and readable.

Quick Concepts

1. Explain the basics of how a table is organized. ***p. 270***

2. You can create a table by inserting it or by drawing it. When might you prefer one method over the other? ***p. 271***

3. Discuss the ways you can apply alignment to a table and its content. ***p. 276***

Hands-On Exercises

Watch the Video
for this Hands-On
Exercise!

MyITLab®
HOE1 Training

Skills covered: Create or Draw
a Table • Insert and Delete Rows
and Columns • Merge and Split Cells
• Change Row Height and Column
Width • Apply Table Styles • Adjust
Table Position and Alignment •
Format Table Text

1 Tables

The executive summary is the first section of the complete economic impact report for Traylor University. Although the summary is already well organized, the data analysis part of the summary needs some attention. Specifically, you develop tables to organize major findings.

STEP 1 ≫ CREATE A TABLE AND INSERT AND DELETE ROWS AND COLUMNS

You create a couple of tables to summarize study findings, including those tables in the executive summary. As you develop the tables, you find it necessary to insert rows to accommodate additional data and to delete columns that are not actually required. Refer to Figure 3.8 as you complete Step 1.

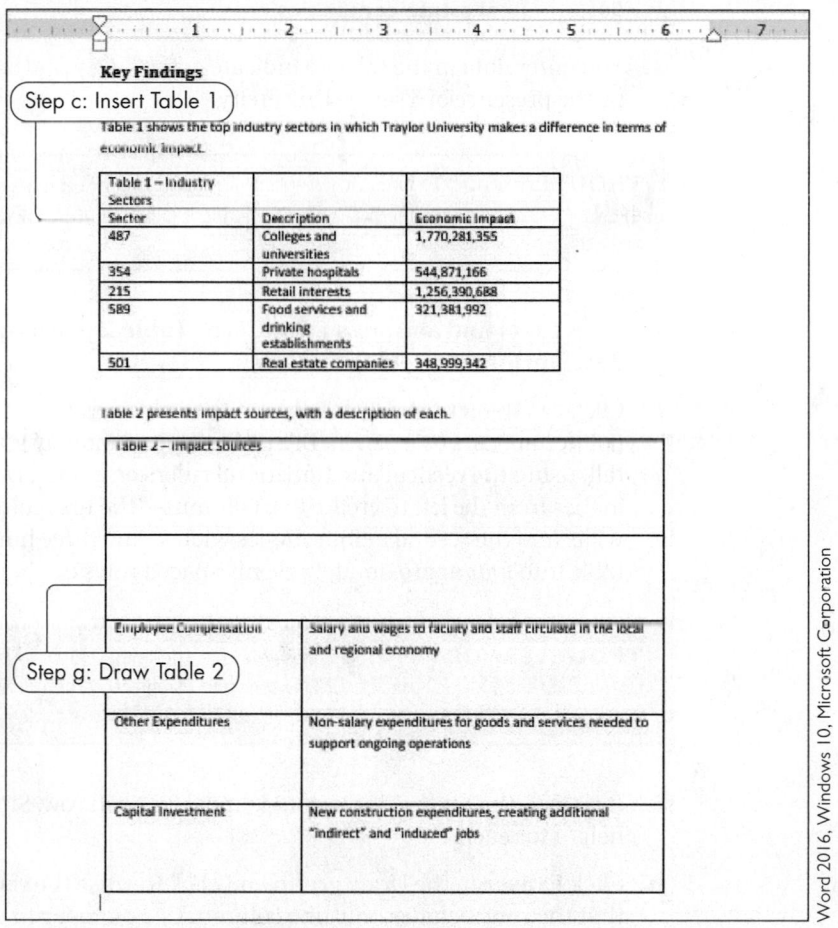

FIGURE 3.8 Report Tables

a. Open *w03h1Traylor* and save it as **w03h1Traylor_LastFirst**.

> **TROUBLESHOOTING:** If you make any major mistakes in this exercise, you can close the file, open *w03h1Traylor* again and then start this exercise over.

b. Click the **View tab** and ensure that Ruler is selected in the Show group. Scroll through the document to view its contents. Press **Ctrl+End** to move to the end of the document. Type **Table 1 shows the top industry sectors in which Traylor University makes a difference in terms of economic impact**. Press **Enter**.

c. Click the **Insert tab** and click **Table** in the Tables group. Drag to select a four-column by five-row table and click in the **bottom-right cell** of the selection.

A four-column by five-row table is inserted. The insertion point is located in the top-left cell.

d. Type **Sector** and press **Tab**. Type **Description** and press **Tab**. Type **Category**, press **Tab**, and then type **Economic Impact**.

e. Press **Tab** and type the following entries, tabbing between each item, but not tabbing after the last cell on the last row. Text will wrap, where necessary, in each cell.

487	**Colleges and universities**	**Education**	**1,770,281,355**
354	**Private hospitals**	**Health**	**544,871,166**
589	**Food services and drinking establishments**	**Retail**	**321,381,992**
501	**Real estate companies**	**Land**	**348,999,342**

You enter data in the table to indicate community and state interests positively impacted by the presence of Traylor University.

> **TROUBLESHOOTING:** If you press Tab after the last entry, a new row is created. Click Undo. If the insertion point returns to a new line within a cell instead of advancing to another cell or row, you pressed Enter instead of Tab between entries. Press Backspace and press Tab.

f. Press **Ctrl+End** and press **Enter**. Type **Table 2 presents impact sources, with a description of each**. Press **Enter**.

g. Click the **Insert tab**, click **Table** in the Tables group, and then click **Draw Table**. The pointer appears as a pencil. Drag a box approximately six inches wide and four inches tall, using the vertical and horizontal rulers as guides. Draw one vertical grid line at two inches from the left to create two columns—the first column approximately two inches wide, and the second at four inches wide. Draw three horizontal grid lines to divide the table into four approximately evenly spaced rows of about one inch each. Press **Esc**.

> **TROUBLESHOOTING:** It is possible that the lines you draw to form the table are in a color or style other than black. That occurs if someone using the same computer previously selected a different pen color. For this exercise, it will not matter what color the table borders are.

It is OK if the row height is not identical for each row. Simply approximate the required height for each.

h. Click **Eraser** in the Draw group and click to erase the vertical gridline in the first row, so that the row includes only one column. Click **Eraser** to toggle off the eraser or press **Esc**.

> **TROUBLESHOOTING:** If you make any mistakes while erasing gridlines, press Esc. Click Undo to undo your actions.

i. Ensure the insertion point is located in the first row, type **Table 2 - Impact Sources**. (Do not type the period.) Press **Tab** and complete the table as follows (do not press Tab at the end of the last entry):

Employee Compensation	**Salary and wages to faculty and staff circulate in the local and regional economy**
Other Expenditures	**Non-salary expenditures for goods and services needed to support ongoing operations**
Capital Investment	**New construction expenditures, creating additional "indirect" and "induced" jobs**

Text you type may wrap within a cell. You will resize the columns later, so leave the text as it appears.

j. Position the pointer just above the Category column in Table 1, so that the pointer resembles a downward-directed black arrow. Click to select the column. Click **Delete** in the Rows & Columns group on the Table Tools Layout tab and select **Delete Columns**.

k. Click anywhere in **row 1** of Table 1. Click **Insert Above** in the Rows & Columns group. Click in the **first cell** in the new row and type **Table 1 - Top Industry Sectors**. (Do not type the period.)

l. Point to the left edge of the horizontal gridline dividing Sector 354 from 589 to display an insert control. Click the **+** indicator on the end of the insert control to insert a new row. Click the **first cell** in the new row and type the following. Press **Tab** between cells. Do not press Tab after the last entry.

215	**Retail interests**	**1,256,390,688**

m. Click anywhere in **Table 2** to select the table. Point to the grid line dividing rows 1 and 2, and click the **insert control** to insert a row above row 2 (*Employee Compensation*). Leave the row blank, for now.

> **TROUBLESHOOTING:** Depending upon the size of the rows you drew for Table 2, it is possible that Table 2 spans two pages, with the last row shown on a separate page. You will correct that in the following step.

n. Check spelling and correct any errors. The *Salida* campus is spelled correctly. Save the document.

STEP 2 » MERGE AND SPLIT CELLS AND CHANGE ROW HEIGHT AND COLUMN WIDTH

As you work with the tables in the executive summary, you notice that the first row of Table 1 is not very attractive. The title in that row should not be limited to one small cell. More uniformity of row height and column width might also improve the appearance of Table 2, and you want to add data to the second row. You explore ways to modify both tables by merging and splitting cells and changing row height and column width. Refer to Figure 3.9 as you complete Step 2.

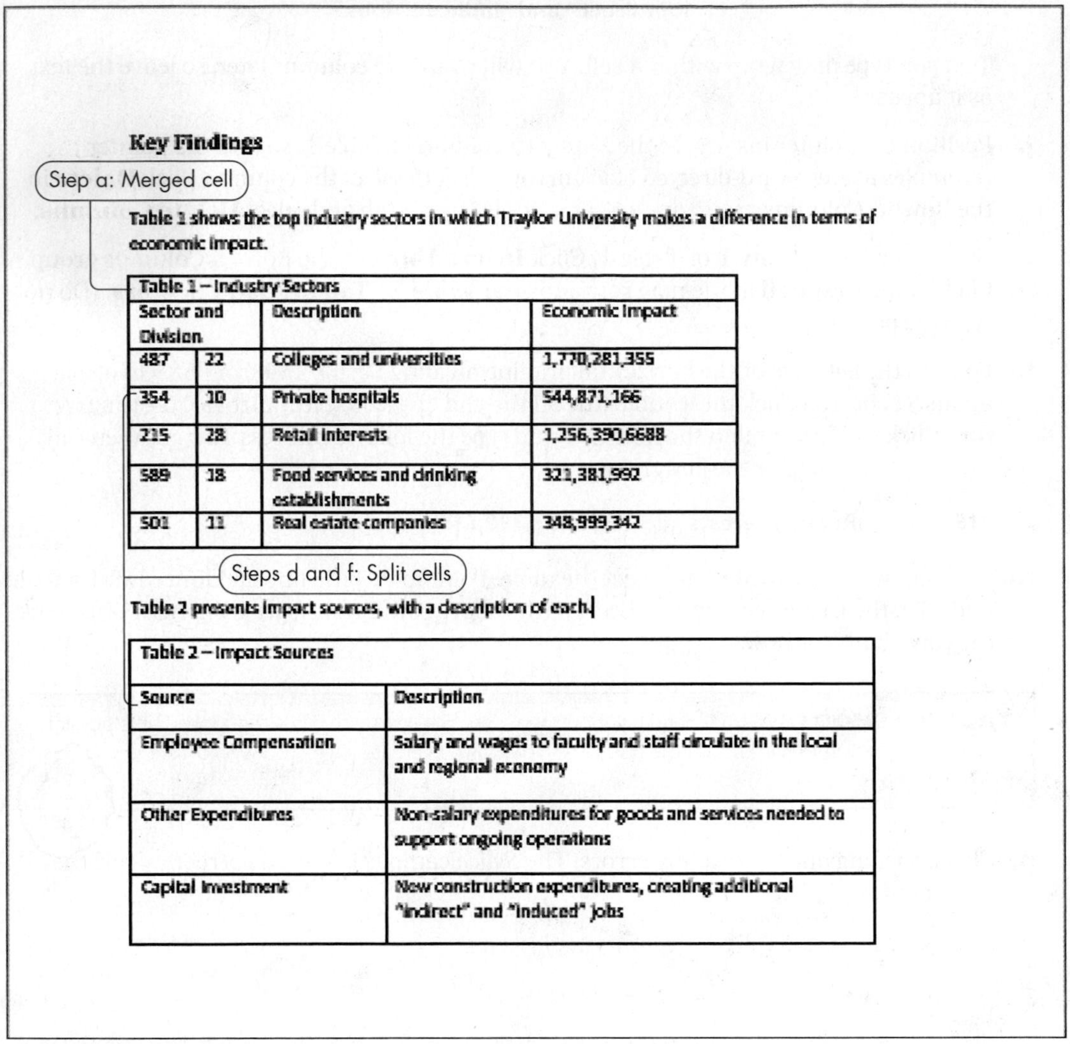

Key Findings

Step a: Merged cell

Table 1 shows the top industry sectors in which Traylor University makes a difference in terms of economic impact.

Table 1 – Industry Sectors			
Sector and Division		Description	Economic Impact
487	22	Colleges and universities	1,770,281,355
354	10	Private hospitals	544,871,166
215	28	Retail interests	1,256,390,6688
589	18	Food services and drinking establishments	321,381,992
501	11	Real estate companies	348,999,342

Steps d and f: Split cells

Table 2 presents impact sources, with a description of each.

Table 2 – Impact Sources	
Source	Description
Employee Compensation	Salary and wages to faculty and staff circulate in the local and regional economy
Other Expenditures	Non-salary expenditures for goods and services needed to support ongoing operations
Capital Investment	New construction expenditures, creating additional "indirect" and "induced" jobs

Word 2016, Windows 10, Microsoft Corporation

FIGURE 3.9 Merged and Split Cells

a. Position the pointer just outside the left edge of the first row of Table 1, so that it resembles a right-directed diagonal arrow. Click to select **row 1**. Click **Merge Cells** in the Merge group on the Table Tools Layout tab.

You merge the cells in row 1 to create one cell in which text can be better positioned across the table.

b. Position the pointer in row 2 on the border between the first and second column of Table 1. The pointer appears as a double-headed arrow. Drag to the left to reduce the column width to approximately 1 inch to better accommodate the contents of the column.

c. Position the pointer just outside the left edge of row 2 in Table 1 and drag down to select row 2 as well as all remaining rows. With the Table Tools Layout tab selected, click the **top spin arrow** beside Height in the Cell Size group to change the height to **0.3"**.

Row height of rows 2, 3, 4, 5, and 7 is adjusted to 0.3". However, because text wraps in row 6, the height of that row is not adjusted to 0.3". Click anywhere in the table to deselect text.

> **TROUBLESHOOTING:** If items in the first column are selected instead of every cell in every row, you selected cells instead of rows. Repeat Step c, making sure to position the pointer outside the table and very near the left edge.

The first column of Table 1 lists a sector in which an area of economic impact is identified. Each sector should be further identified by a division, which you now add.

d. Position the pointer just inside the left edge of the third row of Table 1 (containing *487*). The pointer should resemble a right-directed black arrow. Drag down to select the contents of the first column in row 3 as well as all remaining rows in that column. Click **Split Cells** in the Merge group. Check to ensure that *2* displays as the number of columns and *5* displays as the number of rows. Make necessary adjustments. Deselect **Merge cells before split**. Click **OK**.

You split column 1 into two columns so that the first column includes the sector, and the second will contain the associated division.

> **TROUBLESHOOTING:** If all sector numbers appear in the first cell, instead of remaining in separate cells, you did not deselect Merge cells before split. Click Undo and repeat Step d.

e. Click in the **first cell** on the second row in Table 1 (containing Sector). Type **and Division** after *Sector*. Ensure that a space is included between the words *Sector* and *Division*. Type the data underneath the heading as follows, using Figure 3.9 as a guide:

487	22
354	10
215	28
589	18
501	11

f. Click in the **second row** of Table 2. Click **Split Cells** in the Merge group. Ensure that 2 displays as the number of columns and 1 displays as the number of rows. Click **OK**. Place the pointer on the vertical gridline dividing the two columns in row 2. The pointer displays as a double-headed arrow. Click and drag to the left to align the gridline with the vertical gridline in row 3.

g. Type **Source**. Press **Tab**. Type **Description**.

h. Click the **Table Move handle** (at the top-left corner of Table 2) to select the entire table. Click the **bottom spin arrow** beside Height in the Cell Size group to reduce the height to **0.01"**.

Row height of all rows in Table 2 is reduced, resulting in a more attractive table.

i. Save the document.

The tables included in the Key Findings section are complete with respect to content, but you realize that they could be far more attractive with a bit of color and appropriate shading. You explore Word's gallery of table styles. You also bold and center column headings and explore aligning the tables horizontally on the page. Refer to Figure 3.10 as you complete Step 3.

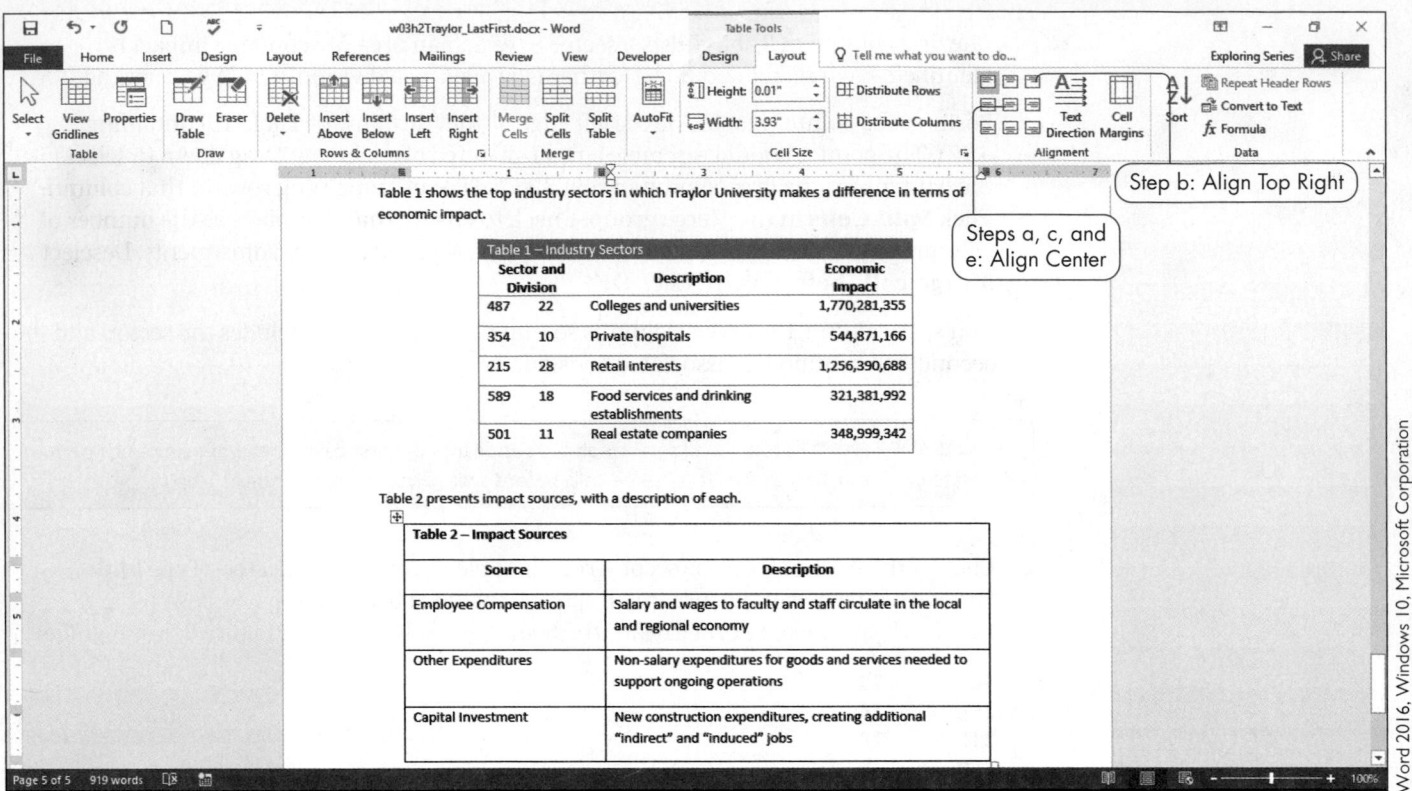

FIGURE 3.10 Formatting and Aligning a Table

a. Select the **second row** in Table 1. Click **Align Center** in the Alignment group on the Table Tools Layout tab.

Text in row 2 is centered both vertically and horizontally within each cell.

b. Select the **cells containing numbers** in the rightmost column of Table 1 (beginning with 1,770,281,355 and ending with 348,999,342). Click **Align Top Right** in the Alignment group. Click anywhere to deselect the cells. Position the pointer on the right border of the rightmost column of Table 1 so that it resembles a double-headed arrow. Drag to the left to reduce the column so that the width is approximately 1", better accommodating the contents of the column.

Numbers are usually right aligned, so you right align numbers in Table 1.

c. Select the **second row** in Table 2, containing column headings. Click **Align Center** in the Alignment group. With the column headings selected, click the **Home tab** and click **Bold** in the Font group. Bold the contents of row 1 in Table 2. Bold the contents of the first two rows in Table 1.

d. Click anywhere in **Table 1**. Click the **Table Tools Design tab** and click **More** in the Table Styles group. Scroll through the gallery and select **List Table 3 - Accent 1** (third row, second column under List Tables). You must scroll through the list of styles to locate the List Tables area.

The table style removed some of the formatting from Step c, applying color-coordinated font color, shading, and a colored border. The style also removed the inside vertical borders.

e. Click the **First Column check box** in the Table Style Options group to deselect it. Click the **Table Tools Layout tab**. Select the **second row** in Table 1 (containing column headings) and click **Align Center** in the Alignment group.

f. Click the **View tab** and click **One Page** in the Zoom group to view the current page. Note that the tables are not centered on the page horizontally. Click **100%** in the Zoom group.

g. Right-click anywhere in **Table 1** and select **Table Properties**. Click **Center** in the Alignment group of the Table tab in the Table Properties dialog box to center the table horizontally. Click **OK**. Repeat this technique to center Table 2 horizontally. Click **One Page** in the Zoom group to view the effects of the realignment. Click **100%**.

h. Save the document. Keep the document open if you plan to continue with the next Hands-On Exercise. If not, close the document, and exit Word.

Advanced Table Features

Developing a basic Word table to organize data in columns is a fairly simple task. With a bit more effort, you can enhance a table using features that improve its readability and summarize table data. Many of the tasks typically associated with an Excel spreadsheet can be accomplished in a Word table, such as summing or averaging a numeric column or row. By using advanced table features in Word, you can create tables that not only organize data, but also present table contents in an attractive, easy-to-read format.

In this section, you will use Word to enhance tables with borders and shading of your choice. In addition, you will sort table data and learn to total and average numbers in a table. You will learn to include captions with tables, so that tables are correctly identified. By indicating that a heading row should recur on each printed page in which a table displays, you will ensure that table contents are easily identified, even if table rows are carried over to another page. Finally, you will simplify the task of creating a table by converting plain text into a table, and you will learn to convert a table to plain text.

Managing Table Data

A table is often used to summarize numeric data. For example, the table shown in Figure 3.11 organizes a list of students receiving a particular college scholarship. Scholarship amounts vary, so there is no standard amount awarded. The last row of the table shows a total scholarship amount, although for illustration, the formula that produces the total is shown in Figure 3.11. The table is sorted by student last name. Because the company awards many individual scholarships, there is a likelihood that the table could extend beyond one page. In that case, the first row (containing table headings) should be set to recur across all pages so that table data is identified by column headings, regardless of the page on which the table is continued. Using Word, you can manage table data to include calculations, sort table contents, and cause heading rows to recur across pages. Planning a table ahead of time is always preferable to recognizing the need for a table after text has already been typed. However, in some cases, you can convert plain text into a table. Conversely, after a table has been created, you can convert table text back to plain text.

Recipient Name	Major	Date Awarded	Amount Awarded	Amount Spent	Amount Left
Alim, Nisheeth	Accounting	5/15/2018	1,850	1,200	
Blair, Walter	Finance	4/23/2018	1,200	1,200	
Diminsha, Ahmed	Management	2/1/2018	1,350	728	
Don, Clarke	Finance	6/4/2018	2,550	1,014	
Edge, Latisha	Accounting	3/16/2018	1,500	0	
Gonzalez, Patricia	Entrepreneurship	3/12/2018	1,225	1,225	
Green, Amber	CIS	5/10/2018	2,850	856	
James, Greg	Marketing	4/23/2018	2,335	2,010	
McDonald, June	Accounting	5/15/2018	1,675	981	
Marish, Tia	CIS	2/10/2018	1,895	1,400	
Pintlala, Sarah	Management	8/1/2018	3,950	2,100	
Tellez, Anthony	Finance	6/2/2018	2,350	2,482	
Wallace, April	Marketing	2/28/2018	1,100	250	
		TOTAL	=SUM(ABOVE)		

Function to show total scholarship amount

FIGURE 3.11 Managing Table Data

Calculate Using Table Formulas and Functions

Organizing numbers in columns and rows within a Word table not only creates an attractive and easy-to-read display, but also simplifies the task of totaling, averaging, or otherwise summarizing those numbers. A *formula* is a calculation that can add, subtract, divide, or multiply cell contents. Although Word is not designed to perform heavy-duty statistical calculations, it is possible to determine basic solutions, such as a sum, an average, or a count, of items in cells. Word provides *functions*, which are built-in formulas, to simplify the task of performing basic calculations. A function uses values in a table to produce a result. For example, the SUM function totals values in a series of cells, whereas the COUNT function identifies the number of entries in a series of cells. The total scholarship amount shown in Figure 3.11 was calculated with a SUM function. In most cases, a function provides an alternative to what would otherwise be a much lengthier calculation.

Use a Formula

STEP 1 ▶▶ To use formulas, you must understand the concept of cell addresses. A Word table is very similar to an Excel worksheet, so if you are familiar with Excel, you will understand how Word addresses cells and develops formulas. Each cell in a Word table has a unique address. Columns are designated with letters (although such labeling is understood—letters do not actually display above each column) and rows with numbers. For example, Nisheeth Alim's award amount, shown in Figure 3.11, is in cell D2 (second row, fourth column). The amount he has spent is in cell E2, and the amount left is to be calculated in cell F2. The formula to calculate the amount left is =D2-E2, which subtracts the amount spent from the award amount. When indicating a cell reference, you do not have to capitalize the address. For example, =A10+A11 is evaluated identically to =a10+a11.

Unlike the way you would manage formulas in an Excel worksheet, you do not actually type a formula or function in a cell. Instead, you use the Formula dialog box to build a formula or use a function.

> **To create a formula in a Word table, complete the following steps:**
>
> 1. Click in the cell that is to contain the result of the calculation. For example, click in cell F2 to begin the formula to determine the amount of scholarship award left.
> 2. Click Formula in the Data group on the Table Tools Layout tab.
> 3. Accept the function shown in the Formula dialog box (see Figure 3.12), or type another to replace it.
> 4. Click the Number format arrow, if you plan to select a format, and select from several options. Click OK.

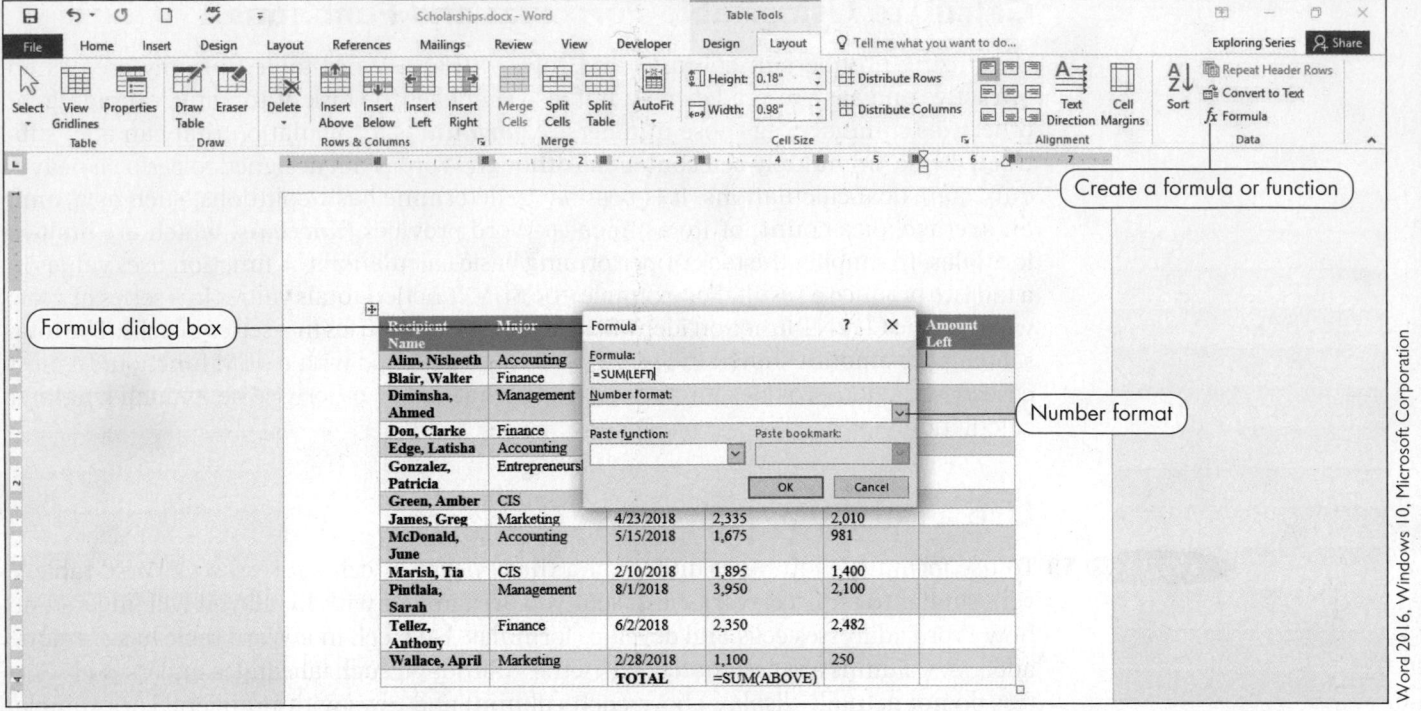

FIGURE 3.12 Using the Formula Dialog Box

> **TIP: NUMBER FORMAT**
> When identifying a number format, you have several options to select from when you click Number Format in the Formula dialog box. A # in a format indicates that leading zeroes will be suppressed. A 0 in a format indicates that leading zeroes will be displayed. Other format options enable you to display dollar signs or percent signs in the formula result.

A formula can contain more than one mathematical operator. The minus sign in the formula described in the preceding steps is considered an operator. Mathematical operators that you can use in creating formulas are described below:

- Exponentiation: ^
- Multiplication: *
- Division: /
- Addition: +
- Subtraction: −

When more than one operator is included in a formula, evaluation of the formula follows a set procedure, called the **_order of operations_**. The order of operations requires that the following operations be evaluated in order from highest to lowest:

1. Parenthetical information (anything in parentheses)
2. Exponentiation
3. Multiplication and Division—evaluated from left to right if both operators are present in a formula
4. Addition and Subtraction—evaluated from left to right if both operators are present in a formula

As an example, the expression =C12+C15*1.8 is evaluated as follows: Multiply cell C15 by 1.8 and add the result to cell C12.

> **TIP: UPDATING A FORMULA**
>
> Unlike Microsoft Excel, a formula in a table is not automatically updated when the contents of cells referenced by the formula change. However, you can manually update a formula. Simply right-click the cell containing the formula and select Update Field.

On occasion, you might develop a formula with multiple operators, but want to force one operation to be evaluated before another, even if it violates the order of operations. For example, the formula =B3+B4/2 is intended to calculate the average of the numbers in cells B3 and B4, except that the order of operations indicates that the division will occur first. That would divide B4 by 2 before adding it to B3, obviously resulting in an incorrect average. To force the addition to occur first, use parentheses around the terms that should be calculated first, for example, =(B3+B4)/2. By enclosing the addition operation in parentheses, it is evaluated first, with the division occurring second.

Occasionally, you might find it necessary to include a formula, or complicated equation, in a document, even outside a table. Most math symbols and operators are not located on the keyboard; however, you can create a formula so that it seamlessly integrates with surrounding text by making selections from the Symbols group on the Insert tab. Word even makes common equations, such as the area of a circle, available with a single click.

To use Word's equation tools to assist in developing a formula in a document (or to insert a common equation), complete the following steps:

1. Click the Insert tab and click Equation in the Symbols group.
2. Select from options on the Equation Tools Design tab to create a formula. The formula is created in a placeholder, so you can manage it independently of surrounding text.

Use a Function

To determine a final scholarship amount in the Total row of the table shown in Figure 3.11, you could click in the cell underneath the last scholarship award amount and add all cells in the fourth column, as in =D2+D3+D4+D5+D6. . . , continuing to list cells in the range through D14. A *range* is a series of adjacent cells. Although the formula would produce a final total, the formula would be extremely lengthy. Imagine the formula length in a more realistic situation in which hundreds of students received a scholarship! A much more efficient approach would be to include a SUM function, in which you indicate, by position, the series of cells to total. For example, the function to produce a total scholarship amount is =SUM(ABOVE). Similarly, a function to produce an average scholarship amount is =AVERAGE(ABOVE). In fact, you can select from various table functions, as shown in Table 3.1. The positional information within parentheses is referred to as an *argument*. Positional information refers to the position of the data being calculated. You can use positional notation of ABOVE, BELOW, LEFT, or RIGHT as arguments. An argument of ABOVE indicates that data to be summarized is located above the cell containing the function. Although not a comprehensive list, the functions shown in Table 3.1 are commonly used. Note that an argument will be included within parentheses in each function.

TABLE 3.1 Table Functions

Function	Action
=SUM(argument)	Totals a series of cells
=AVERAGE(argument)	Averages a series of cells
=COUNT(argument)	Counts the number of entries in a series of cells
=MAX(argument)	Displays the largest number in a series of cells
=MIN(argument)	Displays the smallest number in a series of cells

Pearson Education, Inc.

To place a function in a table cell, complete the following steps:

1. Click in the cell that is to contain the result of the calculation. For example, click in cell D15 of the table shown in Figure 3.11 to include a function totaling all scholarship amounts.
2. Click Formula in the Data group on the Table Tools Layout tab.
3. Edit the existing function or click Paste function (then select a function and type an argument. Click OK.

TIP: COMBINING ARGUMENTS

Combine arguments in a function to indicate cells to include. For example, =SUM(ABOVE,BELOW) totals numeric cells above and below the current cell. =SUM(LEFT,ABOVE) totals numeric cells to the left and above the current cell, whereas =SUM(RIGHT,BELOW) totals numeric cells to the right and below the current cell. Combine any two arguments, separated by a comma, to indicate cells to include.

Sort Data in a Table

STEP 2 ❯❯ Columns of text, dates, or numbers in a Word table can be sorted alphabetically, chronologically, or numerically. The table shown in Figure 3.11 is sorted alphabetically in ascending order by student name. It might be beneficial to sort the data in Figure 3.11 by date, so that scholarship awards are shown in chronological order. Or you could sort table rows numerically by award amount, with highest awards shown first, followed in descending order by lesser award amounts. You might even want to sort awards alphabetically by major, with scholarship award amounts within programs of study shown in order from low to high. Such a sort uses a primary category (major, in this case) and a secondary category (award amount). You can sort a Word table by up to three categories.

To sort table rows, complete the following steps:

1. Click anywhere in the table (or click in the column to sort by).
2. Click Sort in the Data group on the Table Tools Layout tab.
3. Indicate or confirm the primary category, or column, to sort by (along with the sort order, either ascending or descending), as shown in Figure 3.13.
4. Select any other sort columns, and indicate or confirm the sort order.
5. Specify whether the table includes a header row and click OK.

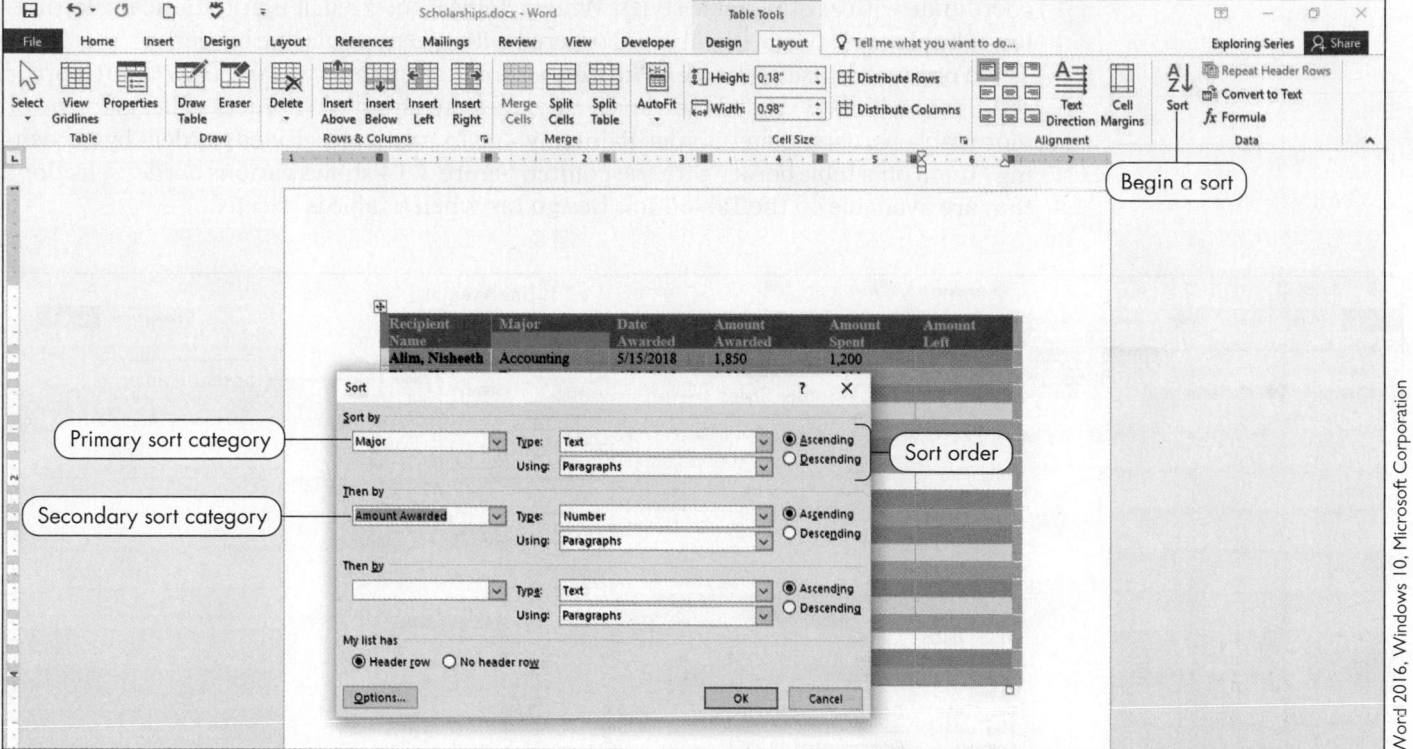

FIGURE 3.13 Sorting a Table

Include a Recurring Table Header

A table is typically comprised of a heading row followed by several rows of data. The heading row in Figure 3.11 includes text identifying the first column as Recipient Name, the second as Major, and so forth. With a large number of students receiving scholarships, the table could easily extend beyond one page. In that case, table rows on the additional pages would have no identifying heading row. To remedy that situation, you can cause one or more rows of headings to repeat at the top of every page on which a table extends. Repeated table heading rows are visible only in Print Layout view.

> **To cause one or more header rows to repeat, complete the following steps:**
> 1. Select the heading row(s).
> 2. Click Repeat Header Rows in the Data group on the Table Tools Layout tab.

Enhancing Table Data

You include data in a table to organize it in a way that makes it easy for a reader to comprehend. Using table styles and table formulas, you have learned to configure a table so it is attractive and so that it provides any necessary summary information. To further enhance table data, you can select custom shading and borders. Certain writing styles require the use of captions to identify tables included in reports; you will learn to work with captions in this section.

Include Borders and Shading

STEP 3 Enhancing a table with custom borders and shading is a simple task when you use Word's Border tools. A **border** is a line style you can apply to individual cells, to an entire table, or to individual areas within a table. You can design your own border, selecting a pen color, line style, and line weight, or you can select from a gallery of predesigned borders that coordinate with existing table styles. When a table is inserted, it is automatically formatted in Table Grid style, with all cells bordered with a ½ pt single line border.

Word makes use of **Border Painter**, a tool that enables you to easily apply border settings you have identified (or a border style selected from the Borders gallery) to one or more table borders. Using Border Painter, you can apply preselected borders by "brushing" them on a table border with the pointer. Figure 3.14 shows various border selections that are available on the Table Tools Design tab when a table is selected.

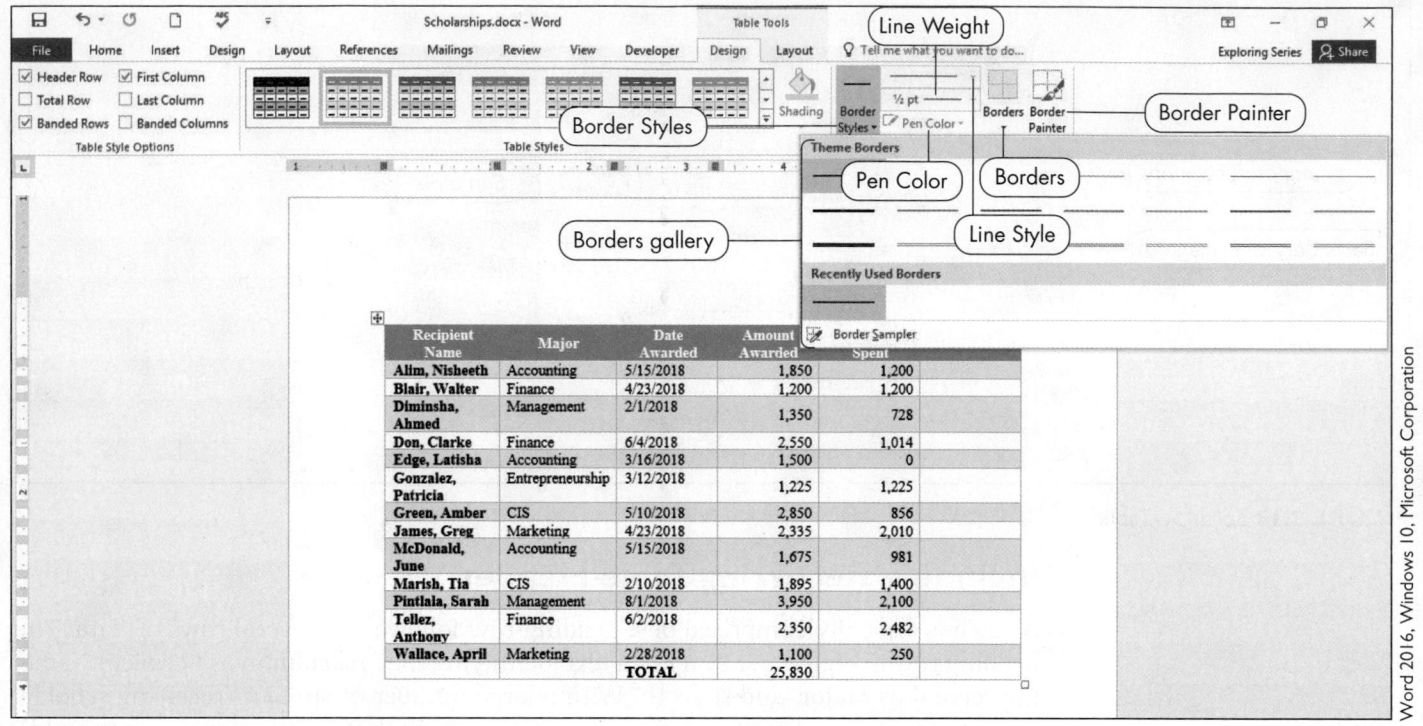

FIGURE 3.14 Working with Borders

In most cases, using the Borders and Shading dialog box is the simplest approach to changing borders and shading within a table. Options include border style, color, line weight, and shading (background) color.

To use the Borders and Shading dialog box to change borders in a table, complete the following steps:

1. Select the cells to modify (or click the Table Move handle to select the entire table).
2. Click the Borders arrow in the Table Styles group on the Table Tools Design tab. Click Borders and Shading to display the Borders and Shading dialog box (see Figure 3.15).
3. Select from options in the dialog box to add, remove, or modify table and cell borders. In addition, you can select shading when you click the Shading tab in the dialog box.

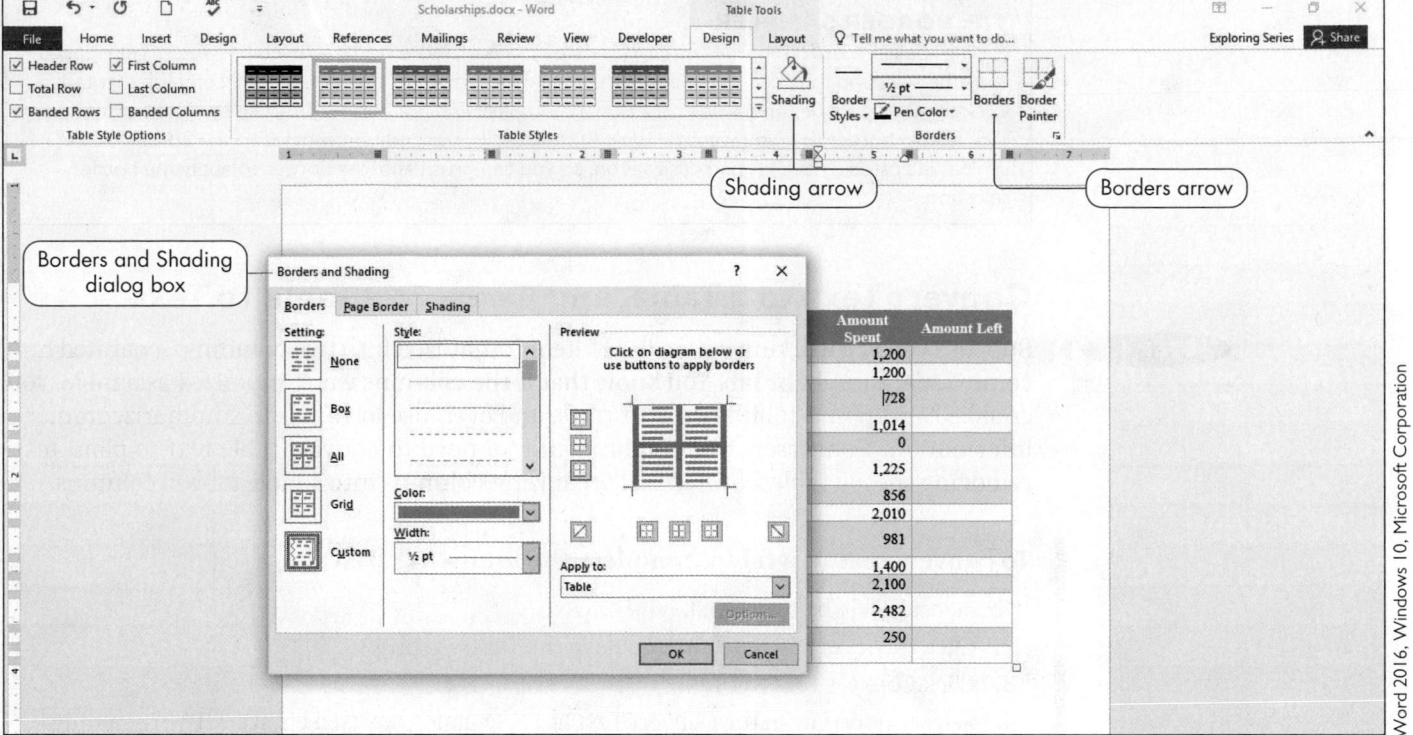

FIGURE 3.15 Using Borders and Shading

For more specificity than what might be found in the Borders and Shading dialog box, you can design a custom border. You can create a custom border by selecting a pen color, line style, and line weight (or selecting a predesigned border style) and then apply it to table borders, or you can select from a gallery of predesigned border styles. Regardless of whether you are applying a custom border or a predesigned style, you can select the borders to which to apply the selection when you click the Borders arrow (refer to Figure 3.15) and select a type (Outside Borders, Right Border, Left Border, etc.).

> **To design and apply custom borders, select a table and complete the following steps:**
>
> 1. Choose a pen color, line style, and line weight (refer to Figure 3.14). The pointer displays as a pen. Alternatively, click Border Styles and select a border style. Each border style combines border width, color, and size. If you change the document theme later, the border style will change to match the theme. The pointer displays as a pen.
> 2. Click the Borders arrow and select a border to which to apply the border selections. Alternatively, drag a border to apply the selected border design.
> 3. Click Border Painter to toggle off the border application, or press Esc.

As shown in Figure 3.15, the Design tab also includes options for selecting shading. **Shading** applies color or a pattern to the background of a cell or group of cells. You might want to apply shading to a heading row to emphasize it, setting it apart from the rows beneath. Click the Borders arrow in the Table Styles group and select a border position, or click Borders and Shading to display the Borders and Shading dialog box, which includes additional options related to border and shading design.

Convert Text to a Table, and Convert a Table to Text

STEP 4 ❯❯ Suppose you are working with a list of items organized into two columns, separated by a comma, paragraph, or tab. You know that if the columns were organized as a table, you could easily apply a table style, sort rows, and even use formulas to summarize numeric information. Conversely, you might identify a need to convert table text to plain text, removing special table features and organizing columns into simple tabbed columns.

To convert text to a table, complete the following steps:

1. Select text to be converted.
2. Click the Insert tab and click Table in the Tables group.
3. Click Convert Text to Table.
4. Select options from the Convert Text to Table dialog box (see Figure 3.16), including the number of columns and rows to include.
5. Click OK.

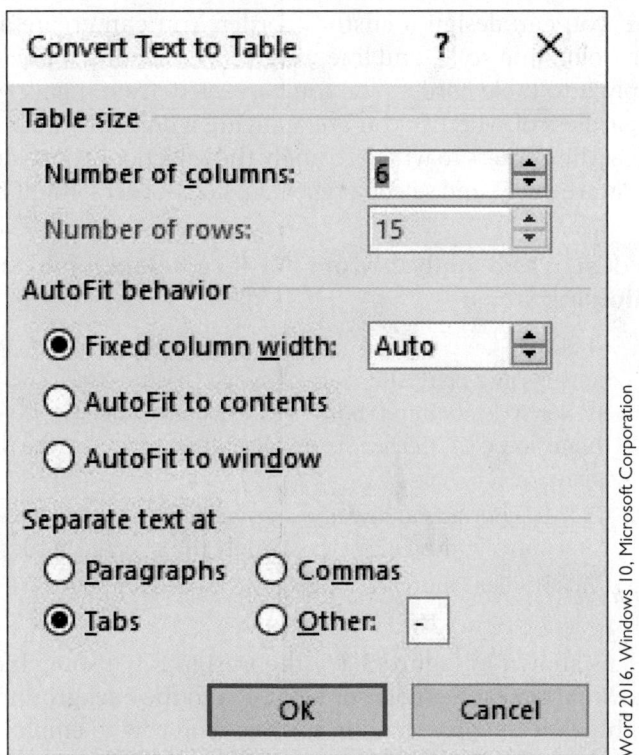

FIGURE 3.16 Converting Text to a Table

CHAPTER 3 • Document Productivity

To convert a table to text, complete the following steps:

1. Click anywhere in the table.
2. Click Convert to Text in the Data group on the Table Tools Layout tab.
3. Indicate how table text is to be divided in the Convert Table to Text dialog box (see Figure 3.17).
4. Click OK.

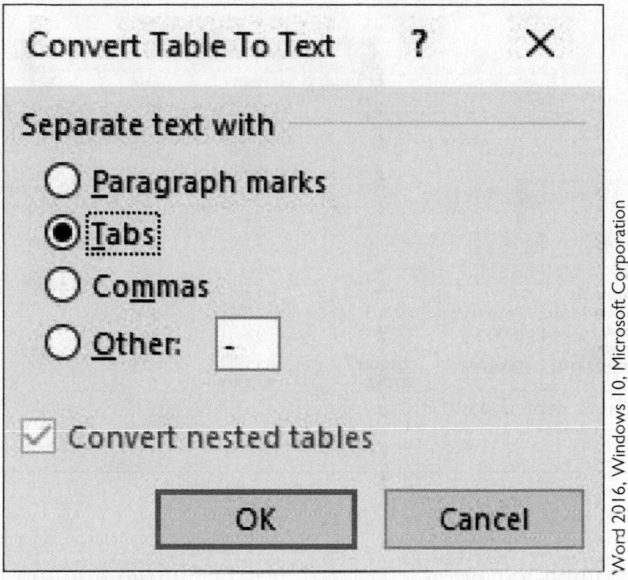

FIGURE 3.17 Converting a Table to Text

Include a Table Caption

A **caption**, such as *Table 1*, is a numbered item of text that identifies a table, figure, or other object in a Word document. A caption typically includes a label, such as the word *Figure* or *Table*, followed by a sequential number that can be automatically updated with the addition of new tables or captioned objects.

To include a table caption, complete the following steps:

1. Click a cell in the table.
2. Click the References tab and click Insert Caption in the Captions group. The Caption dialog box displays, as shown in Figure 3.18.
3. Click the Label arrow and select a type (Table, Figure, or Equation), or click New Label and type a new label.
4. Click the Position arrow and indicate a caption position—above or below the table.
5. Select *Exclude label from caption* if you prefer that the label is excluded from display.
6. Click Numbering to select a numbering style (1, 2, 3, or A, B, C, for example).
7. Click OK to close the dialog box.

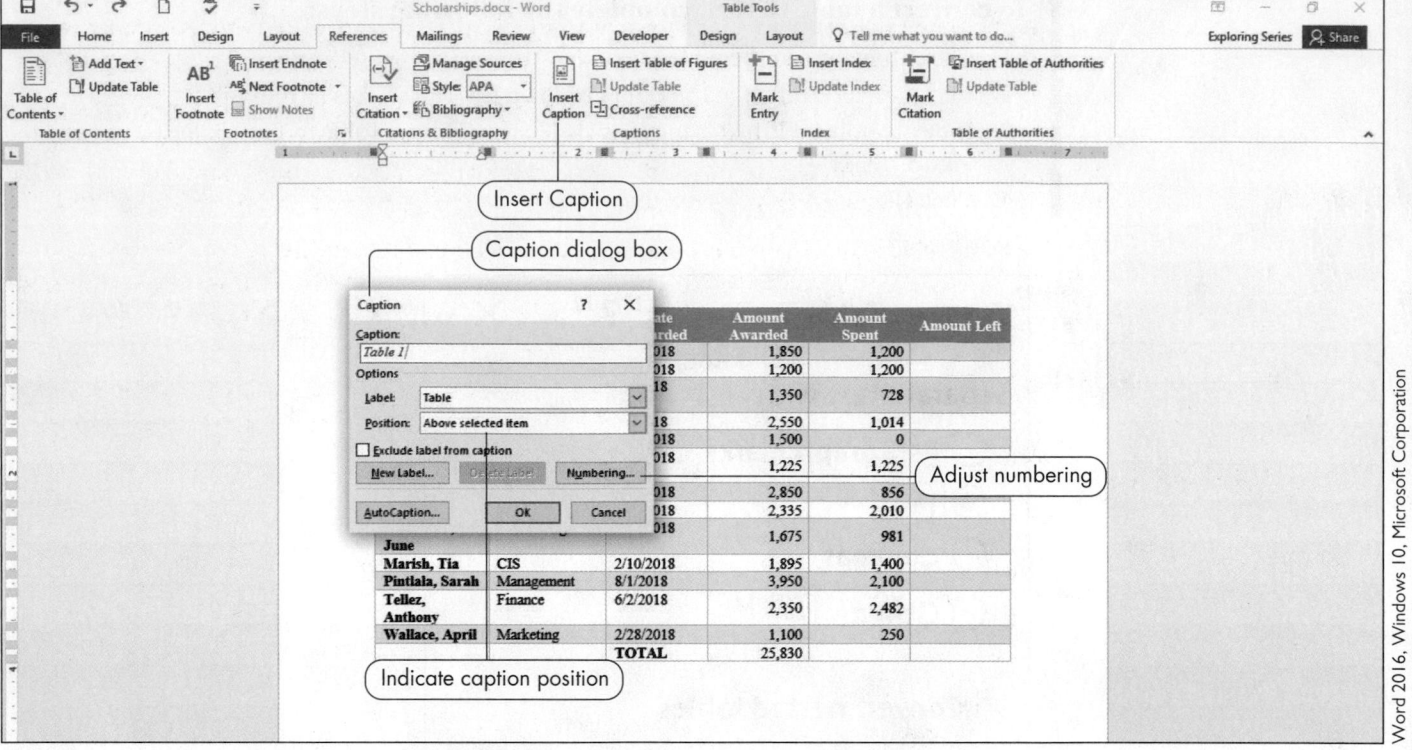

FIGURE 3.18 Inserting a Caption

When a caption is created, it is formatted in Caption style. You can use the Styles pane to modify the Caption style applied to all captions in the document.

To modify the caption style, complete the following steps:

1. Click the Styles Dialog Box Launcher in the Styles group on the Home tab.
2. Point to the Caption style in the Styles pane and click the Caption arrow.
3. Click Modify. Adjust the style format by making selections in the Modify Style dialog box, and click OK to close the dialog box.

As you continue to add captions to tables in a document, each caption is shown in sequence. For example, if the first caption is Table 1, then the second caption you add will automatically be labeled Table 2. If you should insert a table between existing tables, the caption you add to the table will automatically be shown in sequence, with captions on following tables updated accordingly. However, if you delete a table from a document, remaining captions are not automatically renumbered.

To update captions in a document, complete one of the following steps:

1. Press CTRL+A to select all document text, right-click anywhere in the selection, and then select Update Field (to update all captions in a document).
2. Right-click the caption number and click Update Field (to update only one caption).

4. When summing a long column of values in a Word table, would you use a function or a formula? In general terms, how would the function or formula be developed? ***p. 287***

5. A table contains several columns; among them is one containing employee last name and another containing department. You want to sort the table so that departments are shown in alphabetical order, with employee last names sorted alphabetically within departments. What steps would you follow to complete that sort operation? ***p. 290***

6. A table is split between two pages, with a heading row identifying columns on the first page. However, the heading row does not display above the table rows that continue on the second page, so it is difficult to determine what each column represents. How would you remedy that situation? ***p. 291***

7. What steps would you take to convert a list of names and addresses into a table? ***p. 294***

Hands-On Exercises

Watch the Video for this Hands-On Exercise!

MyITLab® HOE2 Training

Skills covered: Calculate Using Table Formulas and Functions • Sort Data in a Table • Include a Recurring Table Header • Include Borders and Shading • Include a Table Caption • Convert Text to a Table

2 Advanced Table Features

As you continue to work with the Key Findings section of the executive summary, you modify the two tables you previously created. The first table, showing major areas in which the university contributed to the economy, is modified to include a total row and to indicate the percentage represented by each category. You also explore Word's Borders gallery and design options as you customize the tables to reflect the color scheme of the university. Adding a caption to each table serves to identify the table and will be useful for your assistant when she prepares a Table of Figures later. You also apply a sort order to each table to organize each in a more understandable manner.

STEP 1 » CALCULATE USING TABLE FORMULAS AND FUNCTIONS

Table 1 includes a numeric column showing Traylor University's economic impact in several sectors. You add a row showing the total for all of the sectors. You also insert a column showing the percentage of the total represented by each sector's value. Refer to Figure 3.19 as you complete Step 1.

Key Findings

Table 1 shows the top industry sectors in which Traylor University makes a difference in terms of economic impact.

Table 1 – Industry Sectors

Sector and Division		Description	Economic Impact	Percentage of Total
487	22	Colleges and universities	1,770,281,355	41.83%
354	10	Private hospitals	544,871,166	12.88%
215	28	Retail interests	1,256,390,688	29.69%
589	18	Food services and drinking establishments	321,381,992	7.59%
501	11	Real estate companies	338,999,342	8.01%
		Total	4,231,924,543	

Step h: Updated total and percentages

Word 2016, Windows 10, Microsoft Corporation

FIGURE 3.19 Working with Table Formulas

a. Open *w03h1Traylor_LastFirst* if you closed it after Hands-On Exercise 1 and save it as **w03h2Traylor_LastFirst**, changing h1 to h2.

b. Ensure that page 5 is shown, displaying Table 1 and Table 2. Click in the **last row** of Table 1. Click **Insert Below** in the Rows & Columns group on the Table Tools Layout tab. Click in the **third column** of the new row (the Description column) and type **Total**, then apply bold formatting to the word Total. With the word still selected, click **Align Top Right** in the Alignment group.

You add a row in which to place a total economic impact figure.

c. Click in the **cell** immediately below the last economic impact number. Click **Formula** in the Data group. Accept the suggested function, **=SUM(ABOVE)**. Click the **Number format arrow** and select **(#,##0)**. Click **OK**.

The total economic impact is 4,241,924,543.

> **TROUBLESHOOTING:** If the total is incorrect, you most likely typed a number incorrectly in the column above. Refer to Figure 3.9 in the previous Hands-On Exercise for the correct numbers. Make any necessary corrections in Table 1. The total will not show the correct number until you complete Step h to update the field.

d. Click **Insert Right** in the Rows & Columns group. Click the **last cell** in the second row of the new column and type **Percentage of Total**.

Text will wrap in the cell. You add a new column that will show the percentage each sector's value represents of the total economic impact.

e. Click in the **last column** of the third row (in the Colleges and universities row). Click **Formula** in the Data group. Drag to select the suggested function in the Formula box. Type **=D3/D8*100**. Click the **Number format arrow**, scroll through the options, and then select **0.00%**. Click **OK**.

You create a formula to obtain the result. The formula divides the value in the cell to the left (cell D3) by the total value of economic impact in the last row of the table (cell D8). The result is multiplied by 100 to convert it to a percentage. The format you chose displays the result with a percent sign and two places to the right of the decimal. The percentage represented by Colleges and universities is 41.73%.

> **TROUBLESHOOTING:** If an error message displays in the cell instead of a percentage, or if the percentage is incorrect, click Undo and repeat Step e.

f. Click in the **last column** of the Private hospitals row. Click **Formula** in the Data group. Press **Backspace** to remove the suggested function from the Formula box. Type **=D4/D8*100**. Click **OK**.

The number format remains at 0.00%, so there is no need to change it.

g. Click in the **last column** of the Retail interests row and repeat Step f, changing *D4* in the formula to **D5** (because you are working with a value on the fifth row). Create a formula for Food services and drinking establishments and Real estate companies, adjusting the row reference in each formula.

h. Change the number in Economic Impact for Real estate companies in the second to last row in the table from 348,999,342 to **338,999,342**. Right-click the **total** in the next row, 4,241,924,543, and click **Update Field** to update the total. Right-click the **percentage of total** for Real estate companies in the last column of the second to last row. Click **Update Field**. Right-click each **remaining percentage figure** in the last column, updating each field.

i. Save the document.

You sort Table 1 so that the dollar amounts in Table 1 are arranged in descending order. That way, it is very clear in which sectors the university had the most impact. You also sort Table 2 in alphabetical order by Source. The resulting table appears well organized. After inserting text from another file, Table 2 is split between two pages. You repeat Table 2 heading rows to better identify table rows that are carried over to another page. Refer to Figure 3.20 as you complete Step 2.

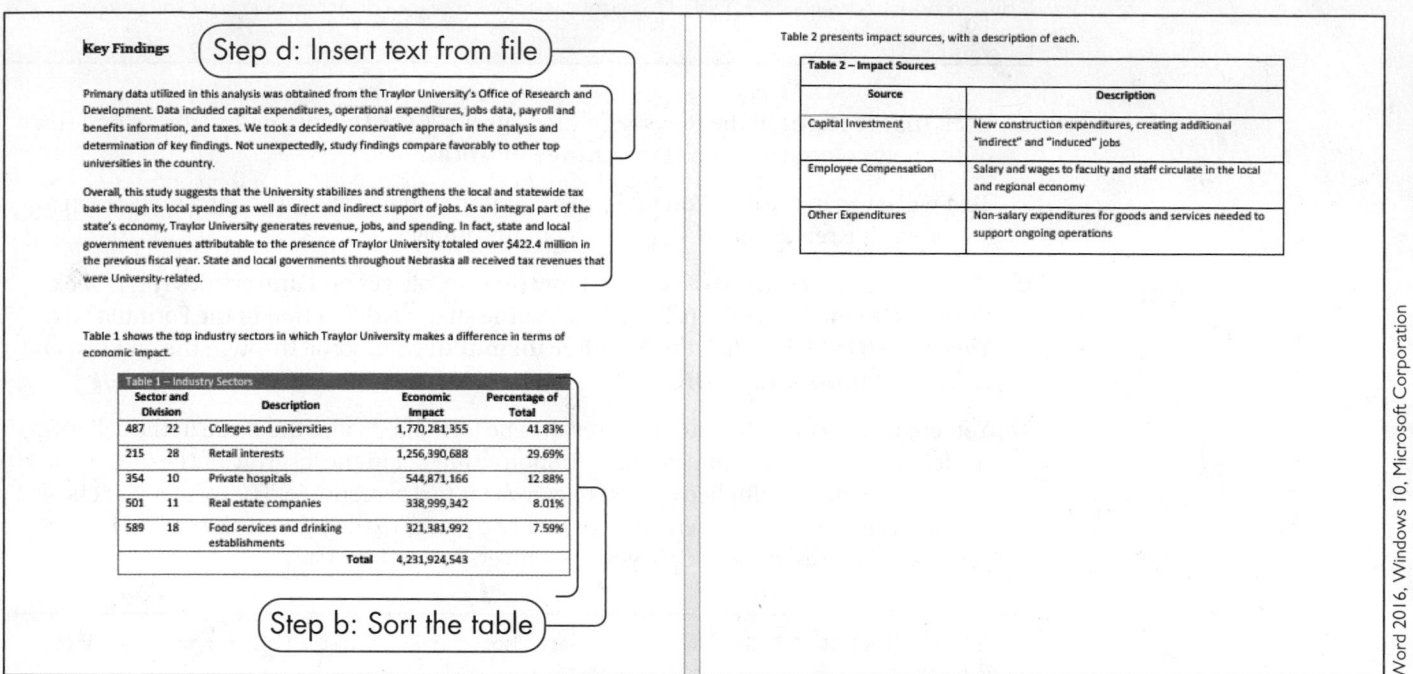

FIGURE 3.20 Sorted Tables

a. Show nonprinting characters if they are not already displayed. Position the pointer just outside the left edge of the third row of Table 1 (beginning with 487). The pointer should be a right-oriented white arrow. Drag down to select the five rows containing a description. Do not include the final total row.

You select the table rows that are to be sorted. You do not want to include the first two rows or the final total row in the sort because they do not contain individual values to sort.

b. Click **Sort** in the Data group on the Table Tools Layout tab. Click the **Sort by arrow** and select **Column 4**. Click **Descending** (in the Column 4 section). Click **OK**.

You sort the five rows containing a sector name (Colleges and universities, Retail interests, etc.) in descending order by the value in the fourth column (Economic Impact). It is clear that the sector most affected is Colleges and universities.

c. Position the pointer just outside the left edge of the third row of Table 2. Drag to select the remaining rows. Click **Sort** in the Data group. Make sure Column 1 displays in the **Sort by box**. Click **Ascending** and click **OK**.

You sort the three rows containing a source (Capital Investment, etc.) in ascending order alphabetically.

d. Click before the words *Table 1* in the first multi-line paragraph (outside the table) on page 5. Press **Enter**. Click before the second blank paragraph under Key Findings. Click the **Insert tab**, click the **Object arrow** in the Text group, and then select **Text from File**. Navigate to your student data files and double-click *w03h2KeyFindings*.

e. Scroll to the bottom of page 5 and note that Table 2 is now split between pages, with several rows on page 6. Those rows are not identified by column headings (Source and Description). Select the first two rows of Table 2 (on page 5). Click the **Table Tools Layout tab**. Click **Repeat Header Rows** in the Data group.

The first two rows of Table 2 repeat above the remaining rows of Table 2 shown on page 6.

f. Click **Undo**. Click before the words *Table 2 presents impact sources* on page 5. Press **Ctrl+Enter** to insert a manual page break.

You determine that the way Table 2 is divided between pages 5 and 6 is very unattractive, even with repeating heading rows, so you remove the repeating rows and insert a manual page break to force the entire table onto another page.

g. Save the document.

STEP 3 ›› INCLUDE BORDERS AND SHADING AND A TABLE CAPTION

You expect to add more tables later, but decide to format Tables 1 and 2 so they are more attractive and color-coordinated. You explore border and shading options, learning to "paint" borders and considering border selections from the Borders gallery. Because you expect to include numerous figures throughout the report, you insert captions to identify those tables. Refer to Figure 3.21 as you complete Step 3.

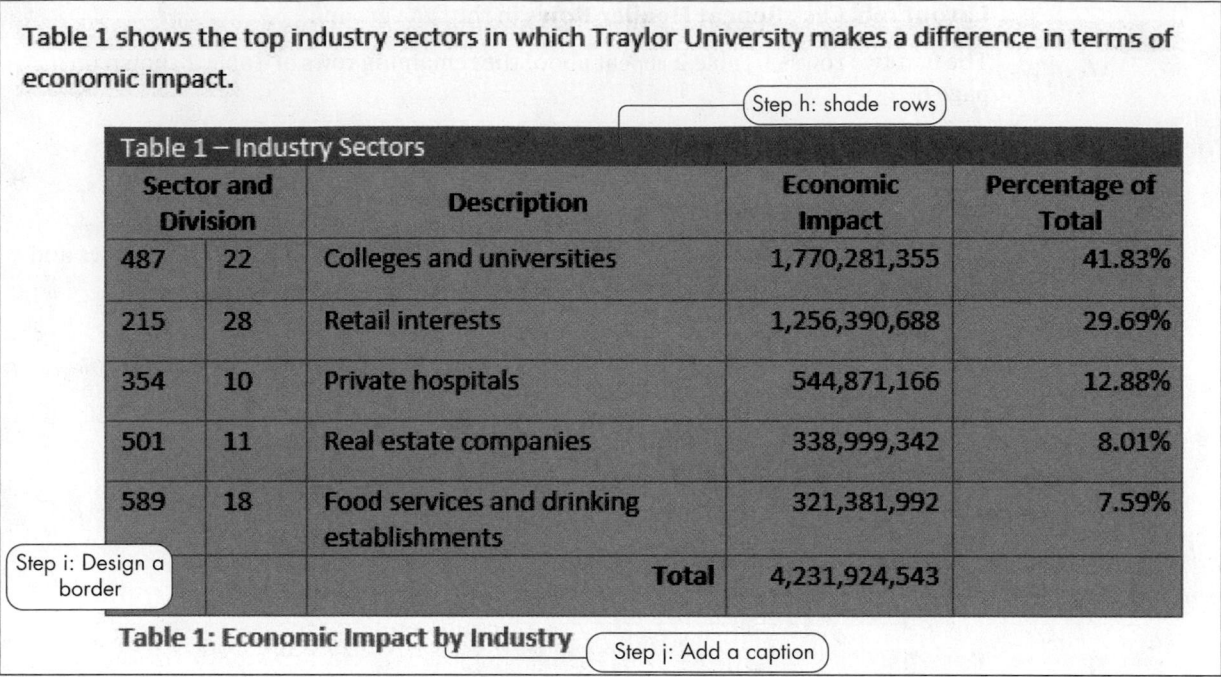

Table 1 shows the top industry sectors in which Traylor University makes a difference in terms of economic impact.

Step h: shade rows

Table 1 – Industry Sectors				
Sector and Division		**Description**	**Economic Impact**	**Percentage of Total**
487	22	Colleges and universities	1,770,281,355	41.83%
215	28	Retail interests	1,256,390,688	29.69%
354	10	Private hospitals	544,871,166	12.88%
501	11	Real estate companies	338,999,342	8.01%
589	18	Food services and drinking establishments	321,381,992	7.59%
		Total	4,231,924,543	

Step i: Design a border

Table 1: Economic Impact by Industry

Step j: Add a caption

Table 2 presents impact sources, with a description of each.

Table 2 – Impact Sources	
Source	**Description**
Capital Investment	New construction expenditures, creating additional "indirect" and "induced" jobs
Employee Compensation	Salary and wages to faculty and staff circulate in the local and regional economy
Other Expenditures	Non-salary expenditures for goods and services needed to support ongoing operations

Step b: Apply custom color

Step d: Design borders

Step c: Apply shading

Table 2: Sources of Economic Impact

Word 2016, Windows 10, Microsoft Corporation

FIGURE 3.21 Including Borders, Shading, and Captions

    a. Click the **Table Move handle** to select Table 2. Click the **Table Tools Design tab** and click **Border Styles** in the Borders group. Click **Double solid lines, ½ pt, Accent 4** (third row, fifth column under Theme Borders). Click the **Borders arrow** in the Borders group and click **All Borders**.

b. Select **row 1** in Table 2. Click the **Shading arrow** in the Table Styles group on the Table Tools Design tab and select **More Colors**. Click the **Custom tab** and adjust Red to **240**, Green to **239**, and Blue to **29**. Click **OK**.

c. Select **rows 2, 3, 4,** and **5** in Table 2. Click the **Shading arrow** and click **Purple, Accent 4, Lighter 40%** (fourth row, eighth column).

Traylor University's school colors are purple and gold, so you design tables with that color combination.

d. Click **Pen Color** in the Borders group. Click the **Yellow color** shown under Recent Colors. The pointer displays as an ink pen, indicating that Border Painter is active. The line style and line weight retain the earlier settings (double line at ½ pt). Drag the pen along the horizontal border dividing row 1 from row 2 in Table 2. Next, drag the pen along the horizontal border dividing row 2 from row 3. Do the same for the next two horizontal borders dividing row 3 from row 4, and row 4 from row 5. Drag the pen along the vertical border dividing the first column from the second (in the purple shaded area). Press **Esc** to turn off Border Painter.

e. Select the **first two rows** in Table 2. Click the **Table Tools Layout tab** and increase the row height in the Cell Size group to **0.4"**.

The first two rows in Table 2 are resized slightly.

f. Click the **Table Tools Design tab**. Click **Border Painter** in the Borders group. Scroll to page 5 and drag the pen along the horizontal border dividing row 2 from row 3 in Table 1. Do the same for the horizontal borders dividing all other rows, but do not drag the bottom border of the table or the horizontal border dividing row 1 from row 2. Drag the pen along the vertical gridlines dividing all columns, but do not drag the outside borders of the table. Press **Esc**.

You use Border Painter to "paint" the currently selected yellow border on the gridlines dividing rows and columns in Table 1.

g. Click anywhere in **Table 1** and click the **Table Move handle** to select Table 1. Click the **Border Styles arrow**. Select **Double solid lines, ½ pt, Accent 4** (third row, fifth column). Click the **Borders arrow** and click **Outside Borders**.

You select a border style and apply it to the outside borders of the selected table.

h. Select **row 1** in Table 1. Click the **Shading arrow** in the Table Styles group and click **Purple Accent 4** (first row, eighth column). Select **rows 2 through 8** in Table 1. Click the **Shading arrow** and click **Purple, Accent 4, Lighter 40%** (fourth row, eighth column under Theme Colors).

i. Click the **Table Move handle** to select Table 1. Click the **Borders arrow** and click **Borders and Shading**. Click **All** in the Setting area, then scroll up and click the **first selection** in the Style box (single purple line). Click **Width** and select **1 pt**. Click **OK**.

You decide a more conservative format would be attractive, so you use the Borders and Shading dialog box to apply a purple border between all cells.

j. Click anywhere in **Table 1**. Click the **References tab**. Click **Insert Caption** in the Captions group. With the insertion point immediately after the phrase *Table 1* in the Caption box, type **:** and press **Spacebar**. Type **Economic Impact by Industry**. (Do not type the period.) Ensure that Below selected item is shown as the caption position. Click **OK**. Click the **Home tab** and click **Increase Indent** in the Paragraph group. Click anywhere in **Table 2** and insert a caption below the selected item. The caption should read **Table 2: Sources of Economic Impact**. (Do not type the period.)

k. Click the **Home tab**. Click the **Styles Dialog Box Launcher**. Scroll down and point to Caption in the Styles pane. Change the font size to 11 and the font color to Purple, Accent 4. Click OK. Close the Styles pane.

You modify the Caption style to include purple font so the caption text coordinates with the table color scheme.

l. Save the document.

One additional table is necessary to complete the executive summary, but the necessary data are arranged in a tabbed format instead of a table. You convert the columns of data into a table. Refer to Figure 3.22 as you complete Step 4.

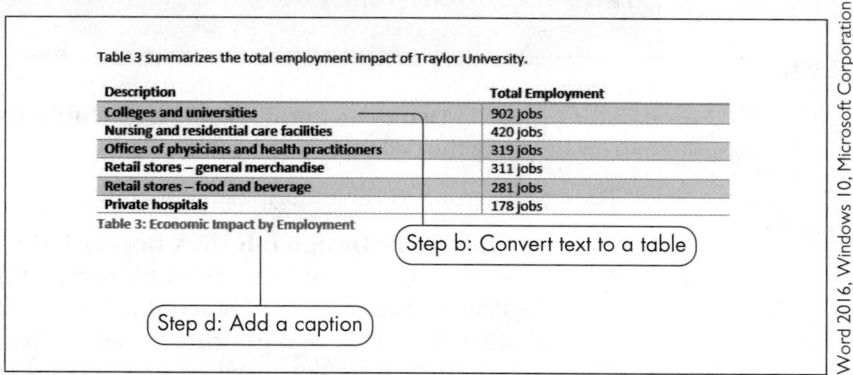

FIGURE 3.22 Working with Tables and Captions

a. Press **Ctrl+End** to move to the end of the document. Press **Enter** twice. Click the **Insert tab**, click the **Object arrow**, and then select **Text from File**. Navigate to the location of your student data files and double-click *w03h2Text*.

Columned text is inserted in the document, with each column separated by a tab.

b. Select the newly inserted text, beginning with *Description* and ending with *178 jobs*. Click **Table** in the Tables group and click **Convert Text to Table**. Click **OK** to accept the default settings of 2 columns and 7 rows.

> **TROUBLESHOOTING:** If the Convert Text to Table dialog box suggests another setting, such as 1 column and 9 rows, you selected the blank paragraphs below the tabbed text in addition to the text. Click Cancel and repeat Step b, selecting only the tabbed text.

c. Click **More** in the Table Styles group. Click **Grid Table 2 - Accent 4** (second row, fifth column in the Grid Tables section).

d. Click in the newly created table, click the **References tab**, and then click **Insert Caption** in the Captions group. Add the caption **Table 3: Economic Impact by Employment**. (Do not type the period.) Ensure that the position is *Below selected item*. Click **OK**.

Note that the caption is formatted with the purple font that you indicated earlier.

e. Click before the blank paragraph preceding Table 3, press **Enter**, and type **Table 3 summarizes the total employment impact of Traylor University.**

f. Check the document for spelling errors, correcting any that are identified.

g. Save and close the document. You will submit this file to your instructor at the end of the last Hands-On Exercise.

Mail Merge

At some point in your personal or professional life, you will need to send the same document to a number of different people. The document might be an invitation, a letter, or a memo. For the most part, document text will be the same, regardless of how many people receive it. However, certain parts of the document are likely to be unique to the recipient, such as the inside address included in a letter. Consider the task of conducting a job search. Having prepared a cover letter to accompany your résumé for a job search, you will want to include the recipient's name and address in the letter so that the document appears to have been prepared especially for the company to which you are applying. Word's *Mail Merge* feature enables you to easily generate those types of documents. Mail Merge is a process that combines content from a *main document* and a *data source*, with the option of creating a new document. A data source is a list of variable data to include in the document, effectively personalizing it, such as recipient name and address.

Mail merge is often used to send personalized email messages to multiple recipients. Unlike sending email to a group of recipients or listing recipients as blind carbon copies, creating a mail-merged email makes it appear as if each recipient is the sole addressee. You can also use mail merge to send an email in which the message is personalized for each recipient, perhaps referring to the recipient by name within the body of the message.

You might use mail merge to create a set of form letters, personalizing or modifying each one for the recipient. A *form letter* is a document that is often mass produced and sent to multiple recipients. The small amount of personal information included in the form letter—perhaps the salutation or the recipient's address—can be inserted during the mail merge procedure.

In this section, you will learn to use Mail Merge to create a main document and select a recipient list. You will then combine, or merge, the main document and data source to produce a document that is personalized for each recipient.

Creating a Mail Merge Document

The mail merge process begins with a main document that contains wording that remains the same for all recipients. In the case of the cover letter used in your job search, the main document would include paragraphs that are intended for all recipients to read—perhaps those that describe your qualifications and professional goals. *Merge fields* are also included in the main document. A merge field is a placeholder for variable data, which might include a recipient's address or a salutation directed to a particular person. During the mail merge process, a data source that contains variable data is combined with the main document to produce personalized documents. You might merge a data source of employer addresses with a main document to produce a personalized letter for each potential employer. Mail merge also enables you to print labels or envelopes, obtaining addresses from a data source.

To begin a mail merge, open a main document, which you might have prepared earlier. The main document is likely to contain merge fields for combining with a data source. You will learn to create merge fields later in this chapter. The main document can also be blank, as would be the case when preparing mailing labels that you intend to merge with an address data source. Click the Mailings tab and click Start Mail Merge in the Start Mail Merge group. Although you can select from several document types, including letters, email messages, envelopes, labels, or a directory, you can click Start Mail Merge Wizard for a step-by-step approach to developing a merged document. A wizard guides you through a process one step at a time, asking questions and using the responses to direct the end result. In the case of the Mail Merge Wizard, step-by-step directions display in the Mail Merge pane on the right side of the main document. The self-explanatory options for the current step appear in the top portion of the pane, with a link to the next step shown at the bottom of the same pane. Figure 3.23 shows the first step in the Mail Merge process.

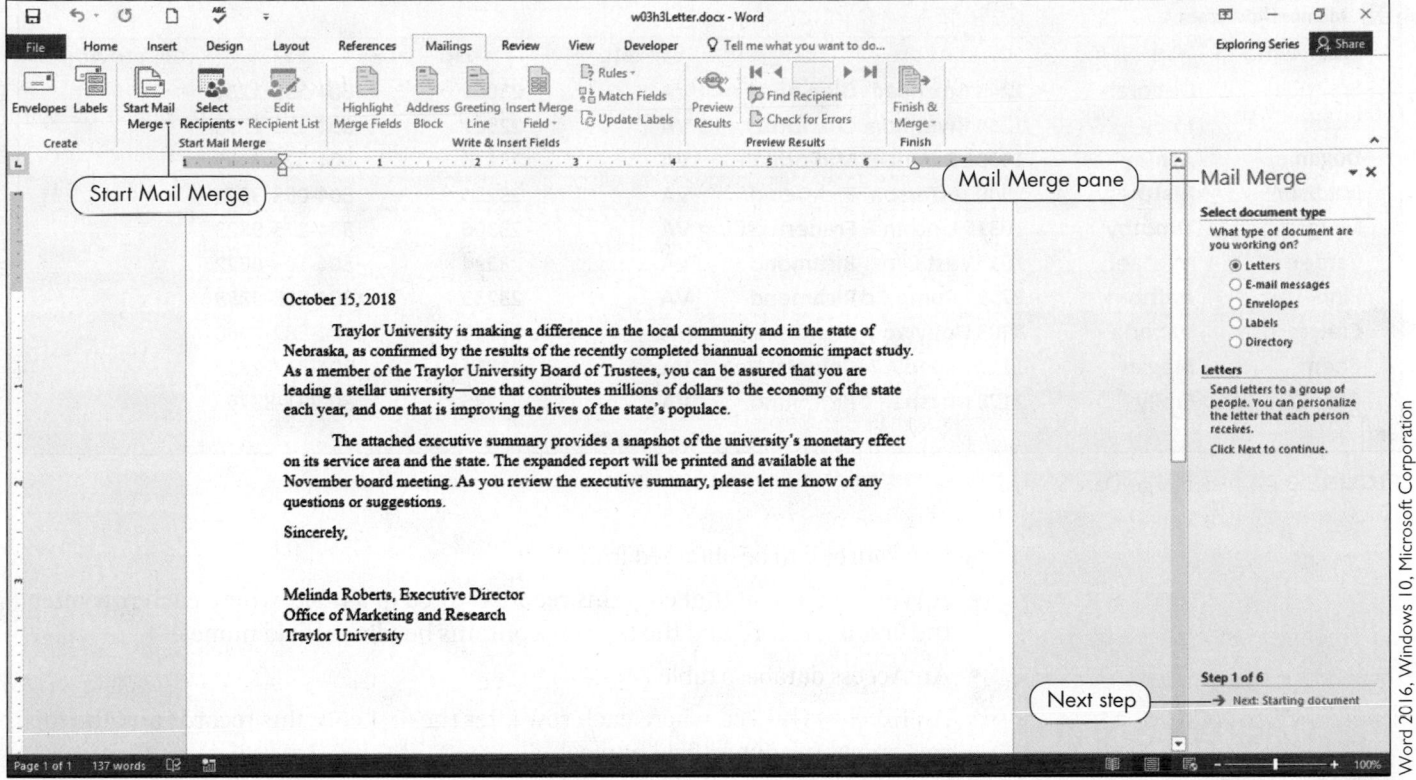

FIGURE 3.23 Beginning a Mail Merge

Click the link to the next step at the bottom of the pane to move forward in the mail merge process. In subsequent steps, you can click a link to the previous step to correct any mistakes you might have made. As is typical of wizards, the Mail Merge Wizard simplifies a task so you can follow obvious links to complete the process.

Select or Create a Recipient List

STEP 1 ⟩⟩ The first step in the mail merge process, shown in Figure 3.23, is to identify the type of document you are producing—letters, email messages, envelopes, labels, or directory. If creating a form letter in which certain variable data will be inserted, you can begin with the main document, or letter, open (if you have already included merge fields in the document). If you have not yet created the form letter, you will begin with a blank document. Similarly, you would begin with a blank document when creating envelopes or labels. After indicating the document type, click *Next: Starting document* at the bottom of the Mail Merge task pane (refer to Figure 3.23). To use the current document, which is the default selection, click *Next: Select recipients*. Otherwise, you can select *Start from existing document* to begin the mail merge with an existing mail merge document, making changes to the content or recipients. If a template is available, you can also begin with a template.

The data source provides variable data to include in the document, such as recipient name, address, phone number, and company information. Each item of information is referred to as a ***field***. For example, the data source might include a last name field, a first name field, a street address field, etc. A group of fields for a particular person or thing, presented as a row in the data source, is called a ***record***. Figure 3.24 illustrates a sample data source. Note that each record in the data source represents a person, with each record subdivided into fields. The data source shown in Figure 3.24 is an Access database table.

MemberAddresses							
LastName	FirstName	Street Addre	City	State	Zip	Fax	Click to Add
Smith	Deborah	1243 Cox Road	Glen Allen	VA	23060	804-555-1234	
Slater	Mary	1234 River Roa	Charlottesville	VA	22901	804-111-2233	
Dugan	Ashley	14301 Sonmaer	Midlothian	VA	23113	804-376-1135	
Madison	Matthew	9900 Jefferson	Richmond	VA	23234	804-098-3376	
Morgan	Timothy	10315 Lincoln F	Fredericksburg	VA	23306	804-175-9823	
Carden	Michael	101 West Cary I	Richmond	VA	23234	804-123-0072	
Finnegan	Anthony	27912 Pump Cc	Richmond	VA	23235	804-098-9888	
Crawford	Victoria	3903 Hollywoo	Midlothian	VA	23113	804-587-2000	
Chen	Megan	111 Second Av	Colonial Heigh	VA	23834	804-347-2812	
Pitts	Emily	2178 Marshall [	Richomnd	VA	23235	80-231-3876	

Word 2016, Windows 10, Microsoft Corporation

FIGURE 3.24 Mail Merge Data Source

A data source can be obtained from:

- A Word document that contains records stored in a table, where each row after the first is a record and the top row contains headings (field names)
- An Access database table
- An Excel worksheet, where each row after the first contains records and the top row shows headings (field names)
- A group of Outlook contacts

The first row in the data source is called the ***header row*** and identifies the fields in the remaining rows. Each row beneath the header row contains a record, and every record contains the same fields in the same order—for example, Title, FirstName, LastName, etc.

If you do not have a preexisting list to use as a data source, you can create one.

To create a new data source, complete the following steps:

1. Select *Type a new list* in the Mail Merge pane to create a data source.
2. Click Create in the *Type a new list* area. A New Address List dialog box displays with the most commonly used fields for a mail merge.
3. Type data or click Customize Columns to add, delete, or rename the fields to meet your particular needs. The data source is saved as an Access database file.

Use an Excel Worksheet as a Data Source

An Excel worksheet organizes data in columns and rows, and it can be used to develop a data source that can be merged with a main document during a mail merge. With only a bit of introduction, you can learn to enter data in an Excel worksheet, designing columns and rows of data so that a lengthy address list can be easily maintained. With millions of columns and rows available in a single worksheet, Excel can store a huge number of records, making them available as you create a mail merge document. Figure 3.25 shows an Excel worksheet that can be used as a data source. Note the header row, with records beneath.

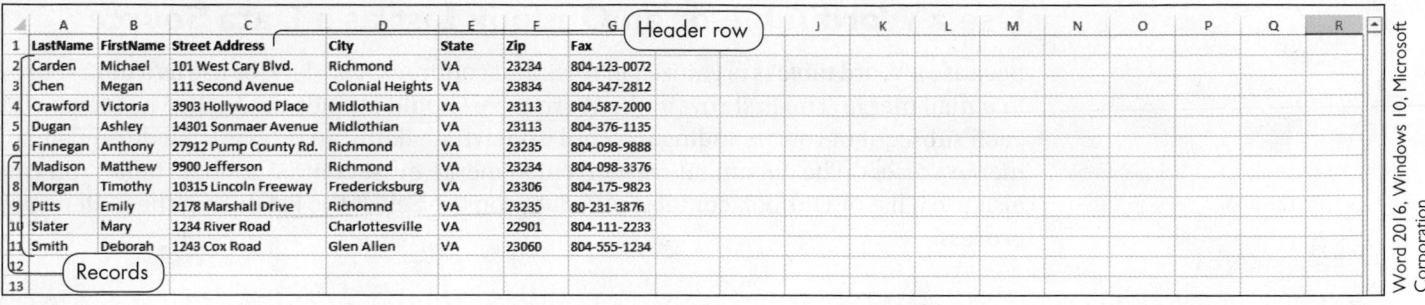

FIGURE 3.25 Excel Worksheet

To merge a Word document with an Excel data source, complete the following steps:

1. Select *Use an existing list* in Step 3 of the mail merge process (see Figure 3.26).
2. Click Browse. Navigate to the Excel workbook and double-click the file.
3. Select a sheet and click OK.

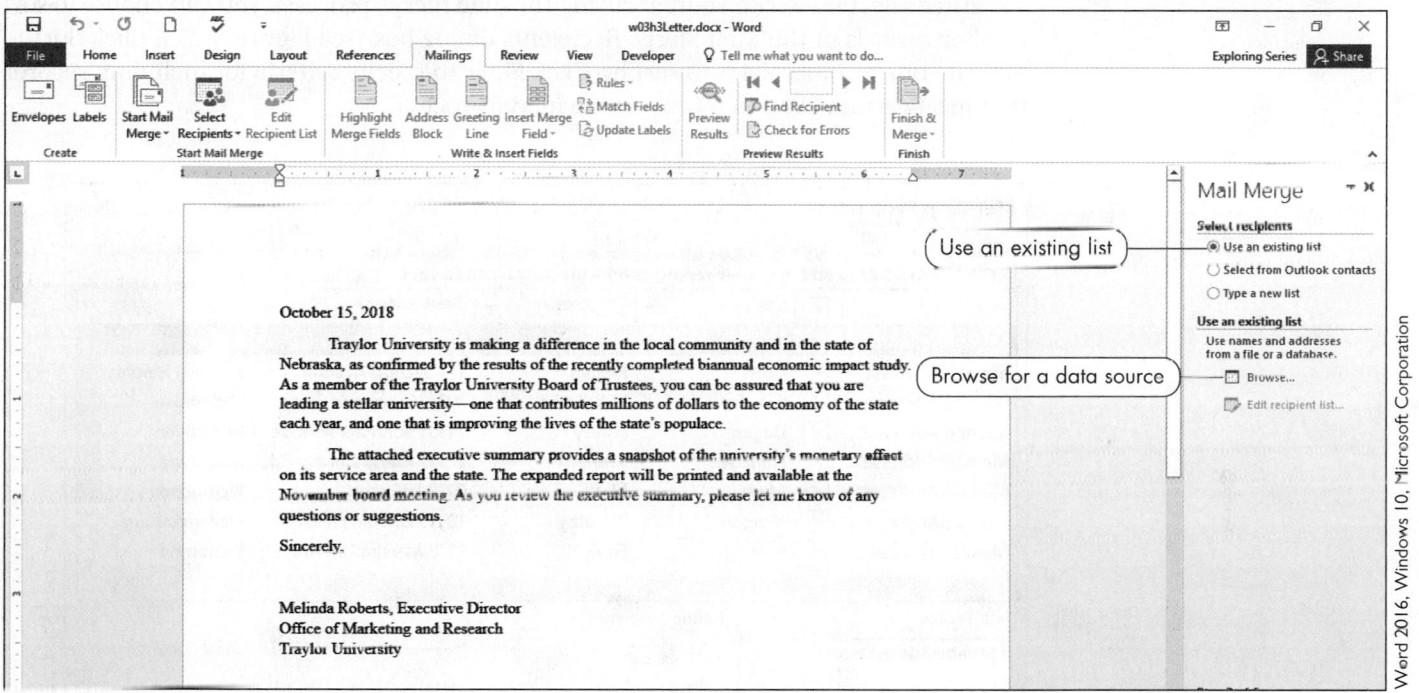

FIGURE 3.26 Selecting an Existing List

Use an Access Database as a Data Source

As a database program, Microsoft Access is designed to manage large amounts of data. An Access database typically contains one or more tables; each table is a collection of related records that contain fields of information. Access enables you to query a table, which is the process of filtering records to show only those that meet certain search criteria. For example, you might want to view only the records of employees who work in the Accounting department. If you want to send a personalized communication, such as a letter or email, to all employees in the Accounting department, you could use the query as a basis for a mail merge. An Access table is well suited for use as a mail merge data source, due to its datasheet design (approximating an Excel worksheet) and its propensity for filtering records. Figure 3.24 shows a sample Access table that could be used as a data source.

Use a Word Table or an Outlook List as a Data Source

Because a Word table is organized in rows and columns, it is ideal for use as a data source in a mail merge. The first row in the Word table should include descriptive headers, with each subsequent row including a record from which data can be extracted during a mail merge process. The document used in a mail merge must contain a single table. You can also use a list of Outlook contacts as a data source. Select the list during the mail merge process.

Sort and Filter Records in a Data Source

STEP 2 ▶▶ Before merging a data source with the main document, you might want to rearrange records in the data source so that output from a mail merge is arranged accordingly. For example, you might want to sort the data source in alphabetical order by last name so that letters are arranged alphabetically or so that mailing labels print in order by last name. In addition, you could consider filtering a data source to limit the mail merge output based on particular criteria. You might, for example, want to print letters to send to Alabama clients only. By filtering a data source by state, using a criterion of Alabama, you could ensure that letters are sent to Alabama clients only.

After selecting a data source (during the mail merge process), you can choose to sort or filter records in the Mail Merge Recipients dialog box (see Figure 3.27). Click Sort to indicate one or more fields to sort by. Click Filter to specify criteria for including records that meet certain conditions during the merge process.

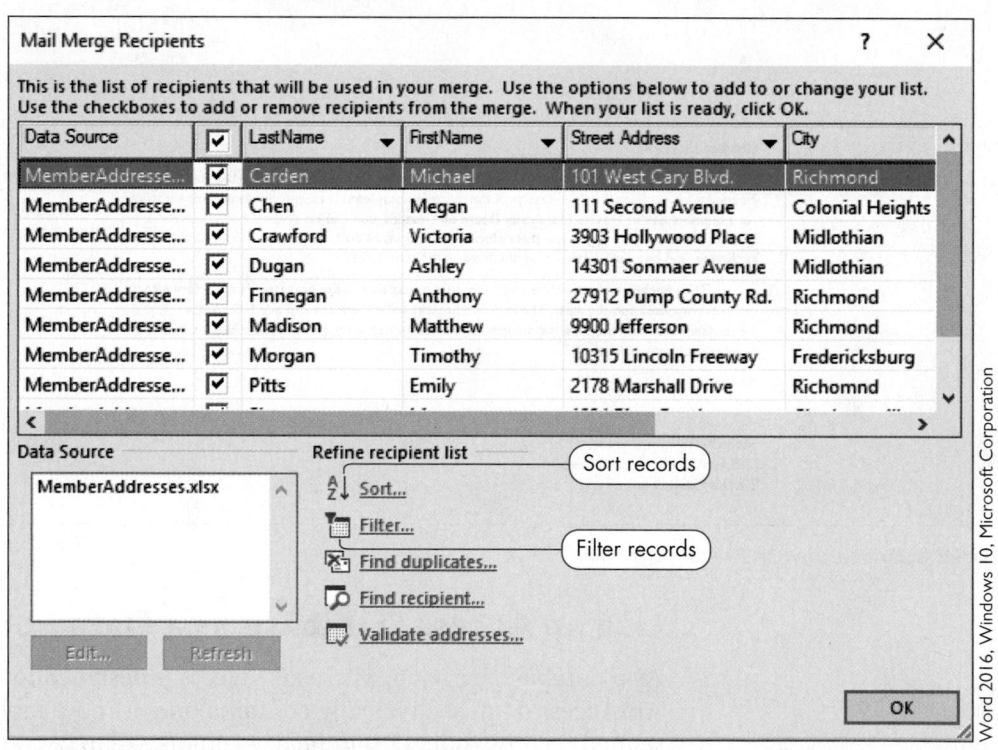

FIGURE 3.27 Sorting and Filtering a Data Source

Completing a Mail Merge

The goal of a mail merge is often to produce a personalized document or email that can be sent to multiple recipients. As the document is prepared, you will indicate locations of variable data, such as a mailing address or a personalized greeting. Such areas of information are called merge fields. After inserting merge fields, you will combine the main document with a data source, a process that results in a single document that includes items (say, letters or labels) that are personalized for each recipient. For example, if a data source contains 60 recipient addresses that are then merged with a main document (a letter with placeholders for variable data such as recipient name and address), the resulting merged document will contain 60 letters.

Insert Merge Fields

STEP 3 ▶▶ When you write a letter or create an email in preparation for a mail merge, you will insert one or more merge fields in the main document in the location(s) of variable data. As shown in Figure 3.28, the Mail Merge Wizard enables you to select an Address block, Greeting line, or other item that can be included as a placeholder in the main document. The data source must contain fields that are recognizably named. For example, a field containing last names should be given a field name that is likely to be recognized as containing a person's last name, such as LastName. Because a merge field corresponds with a field in the data source, matching the two fields guarantees that the right data will be inserted into the main document when you complete the merge.

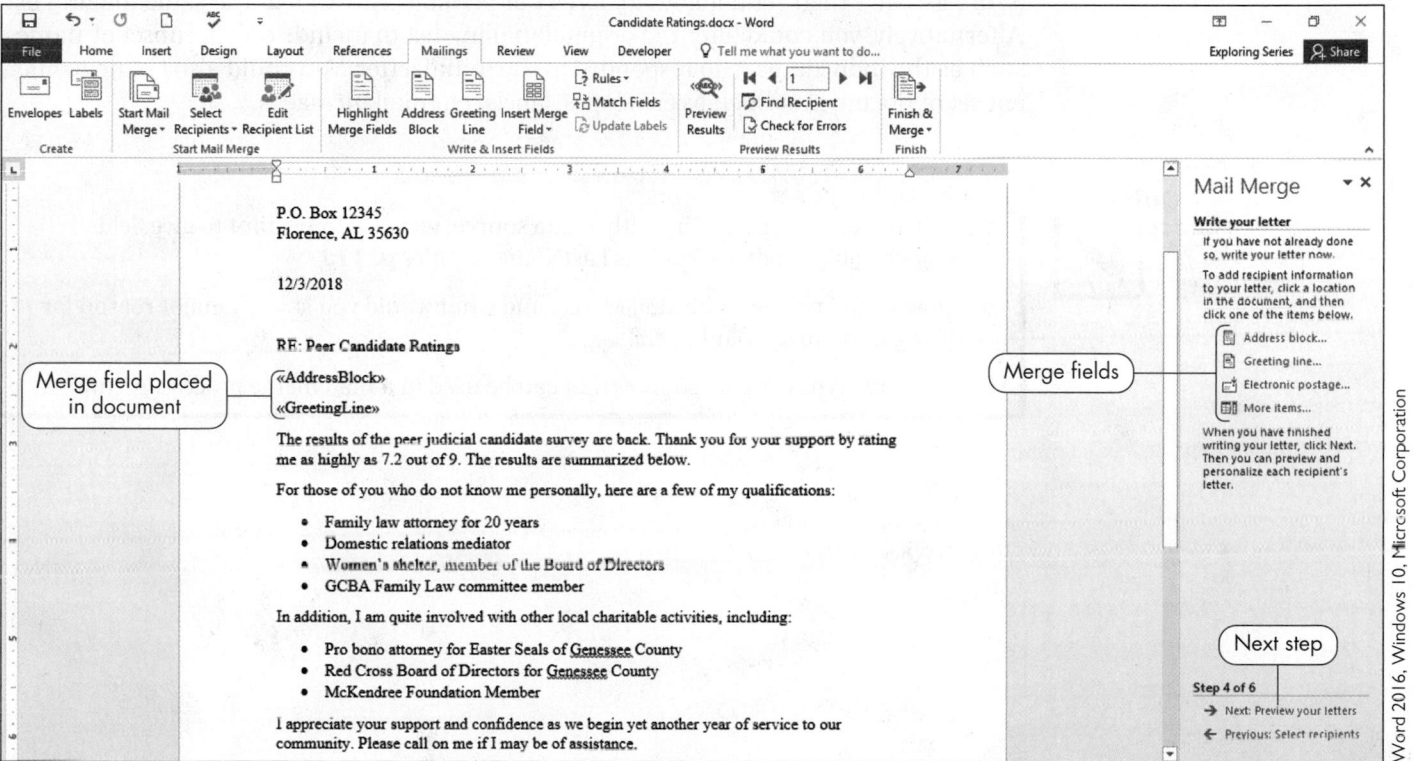

FIGURE 3.28 Merging Fields

Merge fields display in the main document within angle brackets, for example <<AddressBlock>>, <<FirstName>>, or <<Donation>>. Those entries are not typed explicitly but are entered automatically when you select one of the fields that displays in Step 4 of the Mail Merge Wizard (refer to Figure 3.28). As the document is merged with a data source, data from the data source will be placed in the position of the merge fields. Therefore, <<AddressBlock>> will not display in the merged document; instead a particular recipient's multiline mailing address will be shown, followed by the same letter addressed to another recipient in the data source.

Merge a Main Document and a Data Source

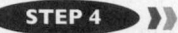 **STEP 4** ❯❯ After you create the main document and identify the source data, you are ready to begin the merge process. The merge process examines each record in the data source, and when a match is found, it replaces the merge field in the main document with the information from the data source. A copy of the main document is created for each record in the data source, creating individualized documents.

To complete the merge, click Next: Preview your letters (refer to Figure 3.28). You can view each merged document, making changes to the recipient list, if necessary. Click Next: Complete the merge. Two options display: Edit individual letters (or other document) and Print. To create a merged document, select Edit individual letters. This enables you to preview each page of the merged document prior to saving or printing. If you select Print, you will have the opportunity to specify which pages to print; however, you cannot preview the document prior to printing. To conserve paper, you should choose Edit individual letters and use Print only when you are ready to print.

The same data source can be used to create multiple sets of form documents. You could, for example, create a marketing campaign in which you send an initial letter to the entire list, and then send follow-up letters at periodic intervals to the same mailing list. Alternatively, you could filter the original mailing list to include only a subset of names, such as the individuals who responded to the initial letter. You could also create a different set of documents, such as envelopes, labels, or email messages.

Quick
Concepts

8. When creating or working with a data source, why is it important to give fields recognizable headings, such as LastName or Title? *p. 311*

9. How would you describe Mail Merge, and what would you say is a major reason for using it? *p. 306*

10. List three types of data sources that can be used in a mail merge process. *p. 308*

Hands-On Exercises

 Watch the Video
for this Hands-On
Exercise!

 MyITLab®
HOE3 Training

3 Mail Merge

The executive summary is ready for you to send to members of the board of trustees. You merge a form letter with a data source of addresses, merging fields in the process to personalize each letter.

STEP 1 ›› CREATE A RECIPIENT LIST

You use Word to create a recipient list, including the names and addresses of members of the board of trustees. Refer to Figure 3.29 as you complete Step 1.

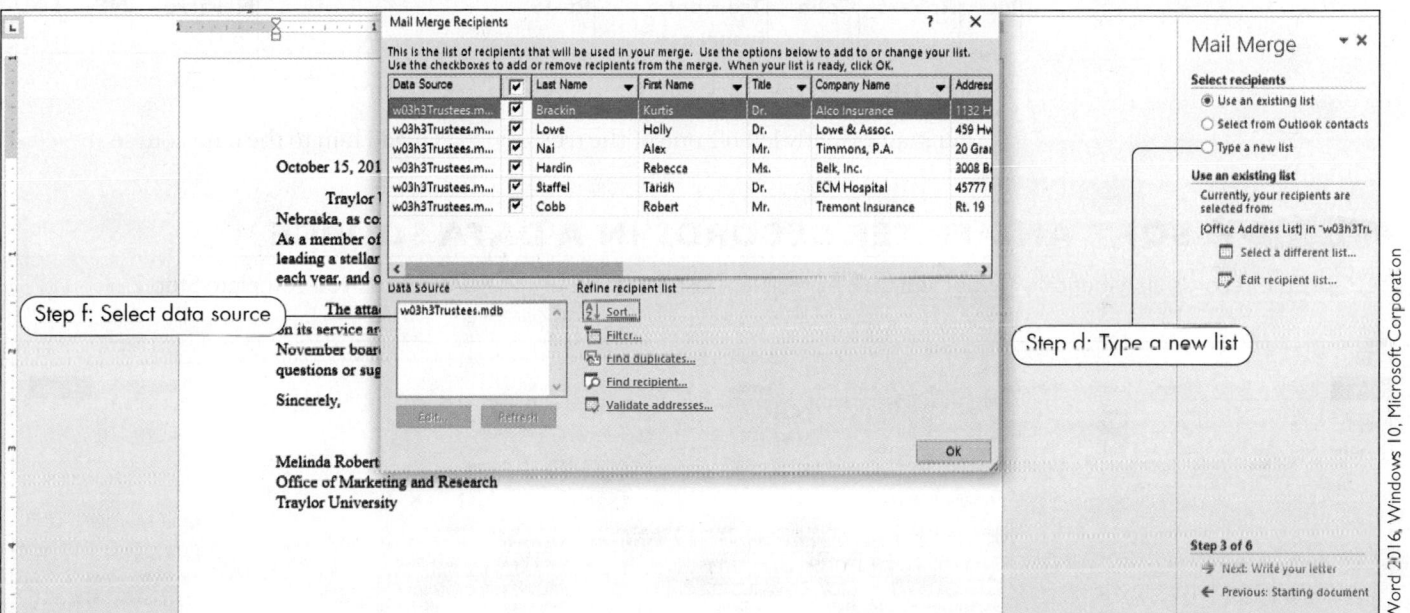

FIGURE 3.29 Creating a Recipient List

a. Open *w03h3Letter* and save it as **w03h3Letter_FirstLast**.

b. Click the **Mailings tab** and click **Start Mail Merge** in the Start Mail Merge group. Click **Step-by-Step Mail Merge Wizard**. Ensure that *Letters* is selected in the *Select document type* area of the Mail Merge pane and click **Next: Starting document** at the bottom of the Mail Merge pane.

c. Ensure that *Use the current document* is selected in the *Select starting document* area. Click **Next: Select recipients**.

d. Select **Type a new list** in the *Select recipients* area and click **Create**. Type the information in the table below, pressing **Tab** to move from one field (column) to another. You will not include data in the country, phone, or email fields. Tab through all fields and continue entering data on a new row for a new record (or click **New Entry** to begin a new record). After typing the last record, click **OK**.

Title	First Name	Last Name	Company	Address 1	Address 2	City	State	ZIP
Dr.	Kurtis	Brackin	Alco Insurance	1132 Hendrix Lane		Sim Creek	NE	68801
Dr.	Holly	Lowe	Lowe & Assoc.	459 Hwy. 34		Oglala	NE	68604
Mr.	Alex	Nai	Timmons, P.A.	20 Grant Street		Navarre	NE	68811
Ms.	Rebecca	Hardin	Belk, Inc.	3008 Beltline Hwy.	Suite 10	Dinsford	NE	68445
Dr.	Tarish	Staffel	ECM Hospital	45777 Riverbend Drive		Florence	NE	68803

e. Type **w03h3Trustees** in the File name box and click **Save** to save the data source with your student files.

The address list displays as shown in Figure 3.29, with all recipients checked. It is an Access database. Note that you can deselect any recipients to which you do not want to send the letter. In this case, you send the letter to all.

f. Click **w03h3Trustees.mdb** in the Data Source box. Click **Edit**. Click **New Entry** and add the following record, leaving the Address 2 field blank:

Mr.	Robert	Cobb	Tremont Insurance	Rt. 19		Navarre	NE	68811

Click **OK**. Click **Yes**. Click **OK**.

You inadvertently left off one of the trustees, so you add him to the data source.

STEP 2 ›› SORT AND FILTER RECORDS IN A DATA SOURCE

You sort the records alphabetically by city and then by recipient last name. Refer to Figure 3.30 as you complete Step 2.

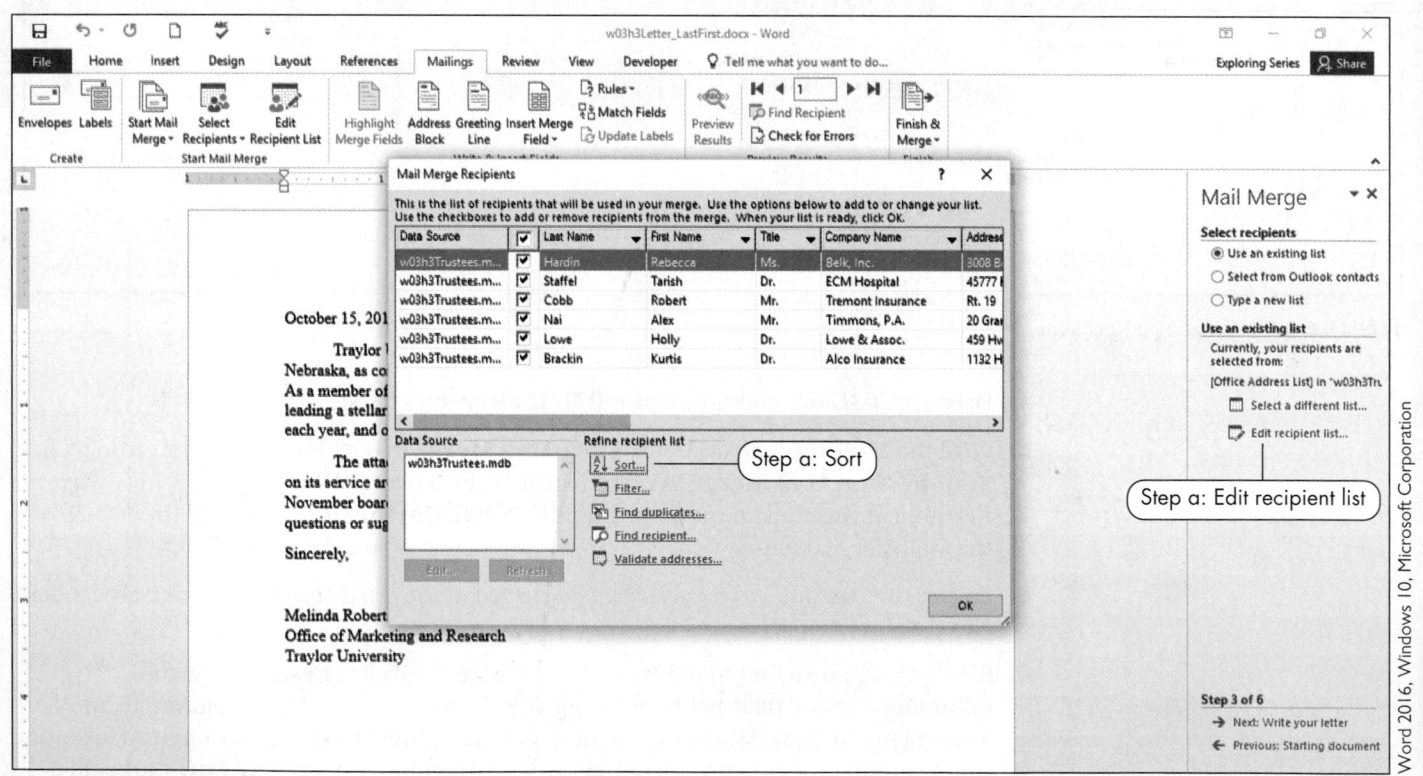

FIGURE 3.30 Sorting a Recipient List

a. Click **Edit recipient list** in the *Use an existing list* area on the Mail Merge pane. Click **Sort** in the *Refine recipient list* area of the Mail Merge Recipients dialog box.

You open the data source in order to sort it.

b. Click the **Sort by arrow**, scroll down, and then click **City**. Ensure that sort order is Ascending. Click the **Then by arrow** and click **Last Name**. Ensure that sort order is Ascending. Click **OK**.

c. Scroll to the right to confirm that records are sorted by City. Scroll back to the left and confirm that the two records with a city of Navarre (records 3 and 4) are also sorted by Last Name. Click **OK**.

Although the body of the letter will be the same for all recipients, you create merge fields to accommodate variable data, including each recipient's name and address. Refer to Figure 3.31 as you complete Step 3.

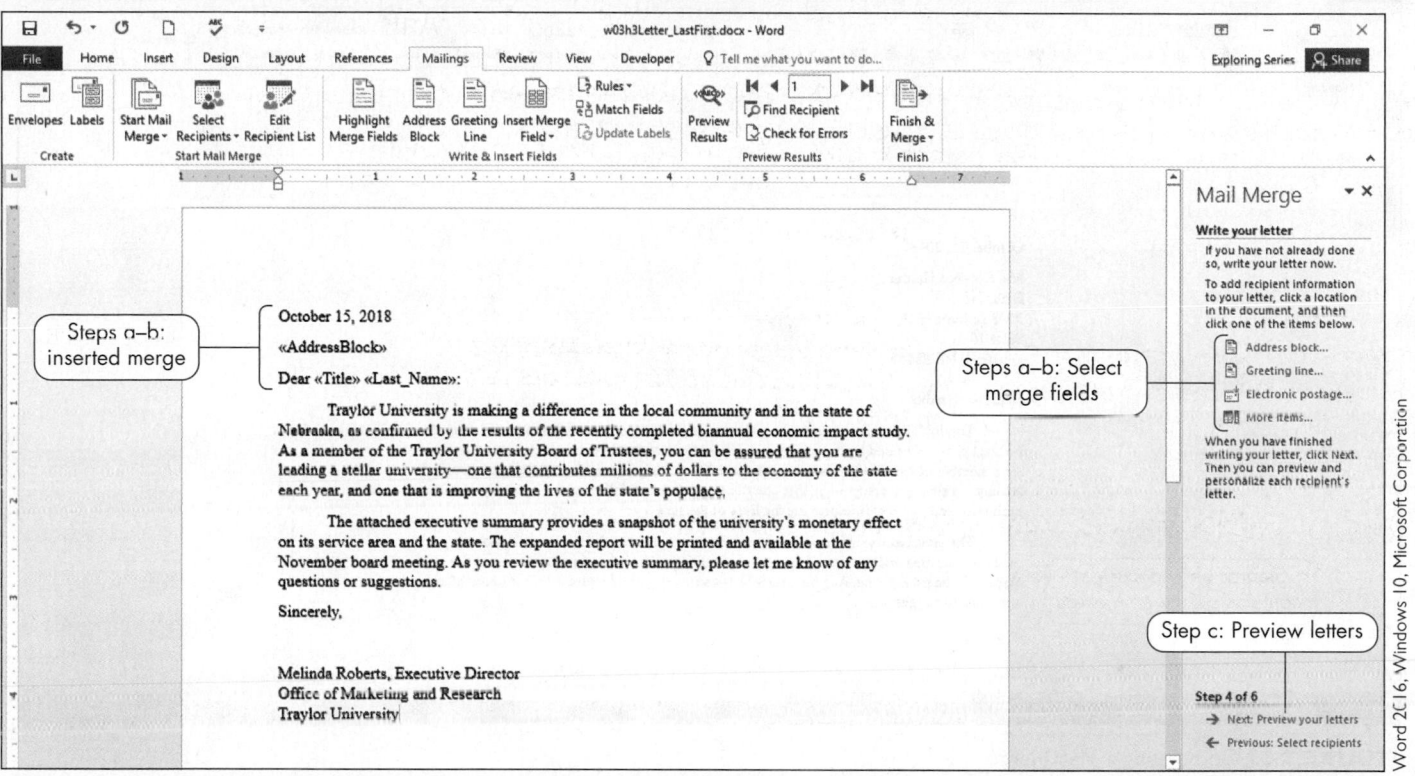

FIGURE 3.31 Inserting Merge Fields

a. Click after 2018 in the first line of the document. Press **Enter**. Click **Next: Write your letter** at the bottom of the Mail Merge pane. Click **Address block** in the Mail Merge pane. Note the address in the Preview area. Ensure that *Insert recipient's name in this format, Insert company name,* and *Insert postal address* are selected. Click **OK**.

The AddressBlock merge field is inserted, with double chevrons on each side, indicating its status.

b. Press **Enter**. Type **Dear** and press **Spacebar**. Click **More items** in the Mail Merge pane. With Title selected, click **Insert**. Click **Close**. Press **Spacebar**. Click **More items**, click **Last Name**, click **Insert**, and then click **Close**. Type **:**.

You add a salutation, including the title and last name, followed by a colon (:).

> **TROUBLESHOOTING:** If you make a mistake when entering merge fields, you can backspace or otherwise delete a field.

c. Click **Next: Preview your letters** in the Mail Merge pane.

d. Select the address block, from **Ms. Rebecca Hardin** through **Dinsford, NE 68445**. Click the **Layout tab** and remove any paragraph spacing shown in the Paragraph group. Click after the **zip code** and press **Enter**.

Having inserted merge fields into the form letter, the letter is complete. Now you merge the main document with the data source so that each letter is personally addressed and ready to be printed. Refer to Figure 3.32 as you complete Step 4.

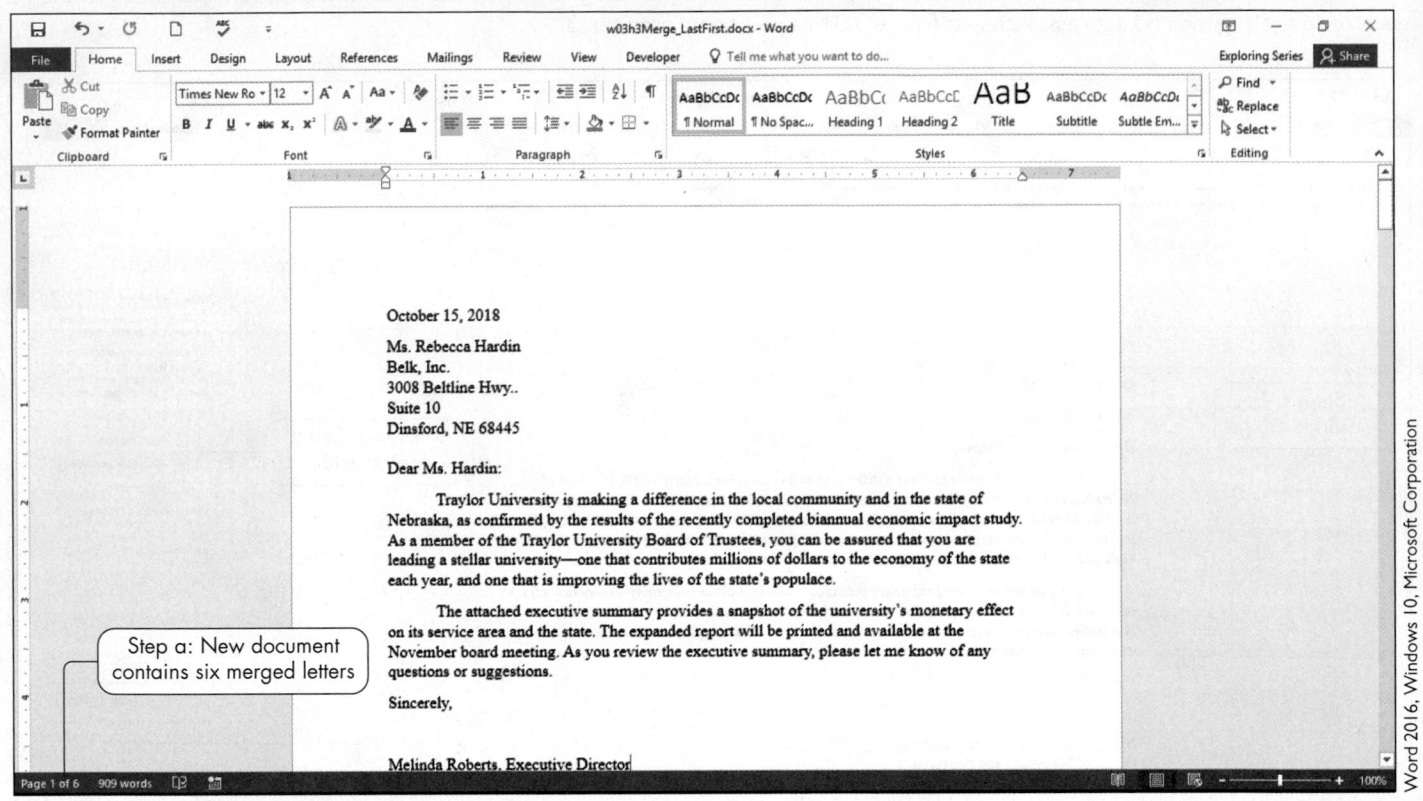

FIGURE 3.32 Completing a Mail Merge

a. Click **Next: Complete the merge** at the bottom of the Mail Merge pane. Click **Edit individual letters**. Ensure that *All* is selected in the *Merge to New Document* dialog box and click **OK**.

Scroll through the letters, noting that each address and salutation is unique to the recipient. The main document and data source were merged to create a new document titled Letters1. You will save the document.

b. Save the document as **w03h3Merge_LastFirst** and close the document. Save and close w03h3Letter_LastFirst. Based on your instructor's directions, submit the following:

w03h2Traylor_LastFirst

w03h3Merge_LastFirst

Chapter Objectives Review

1. Insert a table.

- Create or draw a table: You can include a table in a document by indicating the number of rows and columns, allowing Word to create the table, or you can draw the table, designing rows and columns of varying height and width.
- Insert and delete rows and columns: You will often find it necessary to insert or delete rows and columns in a table to accommodate additional data or to otherwise update a table.
- Merge and split cells: As you update a table, you can merge cells in a row or column, accommodating text that is to be aligned within the row or column, and you can split cells within an existing row or column as well.
- Change row height and column width: You can increase or decrease row height and column width in several ways—using selections on the Table Tools Layout tab, as well as manually dragging column or row borders.

2. Format a table.

- Apply table styles: Apply predesigned color, borders, and shading to a table by selecting a table style.
- Adjust table position and alignment: A table can be aligned horizontally on a page; in addition, you can align cell contents within each cell horizontally and vertically.
- Format table text: Format text included in a cell just as you would format text outside a table, with bold, italics, underlining, etc. You can also apply paragraph formatting, such as alignment, bullets, and numbering.

3. Manage table data.

- Calculate using table formulas or functions. Numeric data in a table can be summarized through the use of formulas or functions. Formulas refer to table cells as a column and row, such as cell A1.
- Use a formula: A formula includes table cells and mathematical operators to calculate data in a table.
- Use a function: A function is a simplified formula, such as SUM or AVERAGE, which can be included in a table cell.
- Sort data in a table: You can sort table columns in ascending or descending order, including up to three sort categories. For example, you can sort a table by department name, and then by employee name within department.
- Include a recurring table header: When table rows are divided between pages, you can repeat heading rows so that they display at the top of table rows on a new page.

4. Enhance table data.

- Include borders and shading: Use borders and shading to customize a table's design. You can use Word's Borders gallery, Border Painter, or the Borders and Shading dialog box to enhance a table with borders and shading.
- Convert text to a table, and convert a table to text: You can convert text that is arranged in columns, with tabs separating columns, to a table. Conversely, you can convert text arranged in a table into text that is tabbed or otherwise divided into columns.
- Include a table caption: A table caption identifies a table, numbering each table in a document sequentially. You can modify the caption style and update caption numbering when tables are deleted.

5. Create a Mail Merge document.

- Select or create a recipient list: To prepare a form letter or other document type so that it is personalized with variable data, such as recipient name and address, you select or create a recipient list that will be merged with the main document.
- Use an Excel worksheet as a data source: A worksheet, comprised of columns and rows, can be used as a data source containing records used in a mail merge.
- Use an Access database as a data source: An Access table or query, containing records with data that can be merged with a main document, is often used as a data source for a mail merge.
- Use a Word table or an Outlook list as a data source: A Word table is often used as a data source, with data merged into a main document. Similarly, Outlook contacts can be incorporated into a main document during a mail merge.
- Sort and filter records in a data source: Records in a data source can be sorted or filtered before they are merged with the main document.

6. Complete a Mail Merge.

- Insert merge fields: Merge fields are placeholders in a main document to accommodate variable data obtained from a data source.
- Merge a main document and a data source: As you complete a mail merge procedure, you update a main document with variable data from a data source, resulting in a new document that is a combination of the two.

Key Terms Matching

Match the key terms with their definitions. Write the key term letter by the appropriate numbered definition.

a. Argument
b. Border
c. Border Painter
d. Caption
e. Cell
f. Data source
g. Form letter
h. Formula
i. Function
j. Insert control

k. Mail Merge
l. Main document
m. Merge field
n. Order of operations
o. Record
p. Shading
q. Table
r. Table alignment
s. Table style

1. _____ The position of a table between the left and right document margins. **p. 276**

2. _____ A descriptive title for a table. **p. 295**

3. _____ A document used in a mail merge process with standard information that you personalize with recipient information. **p. 306**

4. _____ A line that surrounds a Word table, cell, row, or column. **p. 291**

5. _____ A named collection of color, font, and border design that can be applied to a table. **p. 275**

6. _____ A background color that displays behind text in a table, cell, row, or column. **p. 293**

7. _____ A combination of cell references, operators, and values used to perform a calculation. **p. 287**

8. _____ The intersection of a column and row in a table. **p. 270**

9. _____ A process that combines content from a main document and a data source. **p. 306**

10. _____ Contains the information that stays the same for all recipients in a mail merge. **p. 306**

11. _____ An indicator that displays between rows or columns in a table, enabling you to insert one or more rows or columns. **p. 272**

12. _____ Organizes information in a series of rows and columns. **p. 270**

13. _____ A list of information that is merged with a main document during a mail merge procedure. **p. 306**

14. _____ Determines the sequence by which operations are calculated in an expression. **p. 288**

15. _____ Serves as a placeholder for the variable data that will be inserted into the main document during a mail merge procedure. **p. 306**

16. _____ A pre-built formula that simplifies creating a complex calculation. **p. 287**

17. _____ Feature that enables you to choose border formatting and click on any table border to apply the formatting. **p. 292**

18. _____ A positional reference contained in parentheses within a function. **p. 289**

19. _____ A group of related fields representing one entity, such as a person, place, or event. **p. 307**

Multiple Choice

1. A mail merge procedure combines two items—a main document and a(n):

    (a) Merge field.

    (b) Data table.

    (c) Data source.

    (d) Address list.

2. When you use the Table command on the Insert tab, Word inserts a table in a document, automatically aligning it:

    (a) In the center of the page.

    (b) At the right margin.

    (c) At the left margin.

    (d) Evenly divided between the right and left margins.

3. When used in a table, an insert control enables you to insert a:

    (a) Blank row or column.

    (b) Table in a document.

    (c) Caption above or below a table.

    (d) Formula in a cell.

4. Why might you choose to draw a table instead of using the Table command on the Insert tab?

    (a) The Ribbon is temporarily hidden so the Insert tab is not available.

    (b) You know that rows and/or columns will have varying heights or widths.

    (c) The table will contain a minimal number of columns and/or rows so it is much quicker to draw it.

    (d) You know that it is easier to modify a table that is drawn (erasing gridlines or applying table styles).

5. You plan to place a function or formula in cell C4 of a Word table to total the cells in the column above. How would that function or formula appear?

    (a) =SUM(ABOVE)

    (b) -C1+C2+C3+C4

    (c) =TOTAL(ABOVE)

    (d) =SUM(C1-C3)

6. If a table with a heading row extends from one page to another, rows on the second page will not be identified by a heading row. How would you correct that situation?

    (a) Drag the heading row(s) to the top of the second page.

    (b) Insert a manual page break at the top of the second page.

    (c) Select the heading row(s) and cut and paste them to the top of the rows on the second page.

    (d) Select the heading row(s) and click Repeat Header Rows on the Table Tools Layout tab.

7. Enhancing the appearance of a table by applying colors, borders, shading, and other design elements (as a set) is made possible by which of the following features?

    (a) Table styles

    (b) Border styles

    (c) Caption style

    (d) Border Painter

8. During a mail merge process, what operation can you perform on a data source so only data that meet specific criteria, such as a particular city, are included in the merge?

    (a) Sort

    (b) Propagate

    (c) Delete

    (d) Filter

9. What happens when you press Tab from within the last cell of a table?

    (a) A Tab character is inserted just as it would be for ordinary text.

    (b) Word inserts a new row below the current row.

    (c) Word inserts a new column to the right of the current column.

    (d) The insertion point displays in the paragraph below the table.

10. Having applied custom borders to a table, what feature do you use to copy the border style to another table?

    (a) Borders gallery

    (b) Format Painter

    (c) Border Painter

    (d) Border style

Practice Exercises

1 Academics

As an executive assistant working in the Admissions Office at Carnes State University, you are involved with a research project that is exploring the relationship between student GPA and involvement in academic clubs and scholarly activities. Academic and extracurricular data from a random sample of students in the College of Business has been summarized in a Word table that will be included in a brief memo to others on campus. You edit and format the report, preparing it for final submission. Refer to Figure 3.33 as you complete this exercise.

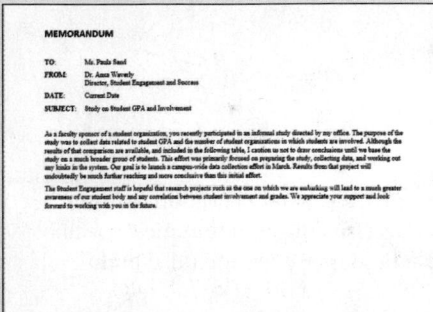 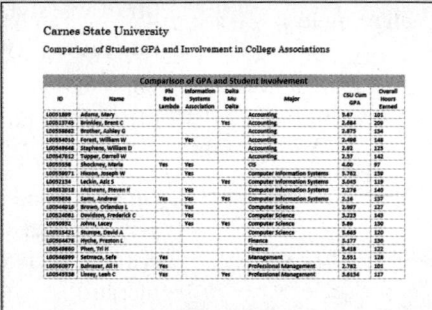 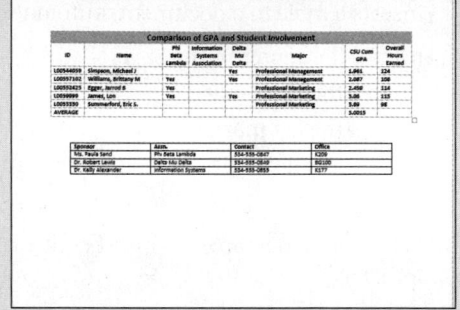

Word 2016, Windows 10, Microsoft Corporation

FIGURE 3.33 Academics Tables

a. Open *w03p1Academics* and save the document as **w03p1Academics_LastFirst**. Ensure that nonprinting characters are displayed.

b. Click before the blank paragraph mark at the top of page 2. Using Century Schoolbook font at 20-point size, type **Carnes State University** and press **Enter**. Change the font size to **16**. Type **Comparison of Student GPA and Involvement in College Associations**. Press **Enter**. Check the document for spelling and grammatical errors. All names in the table are correct.

c. Point to the outside left edge of the first row in the table and click to select the entire row. Click the **Table Tools Layout tab** and click **Align Center** in the Alignment group.

d. Click after the last entry in the last row, ending in *115*. Press **Tab**. Type the following data, tabbing between all entries except the last. Do not press Tab after the last item.

L0051899	Adams, Mary					Accounting	3.67	101
L0055558	Shockney, Maria	Yes	Yes			CIS	4.00	97

e. Right-click any name identified as misspelled and click **Ignore All**. Click **Sort** in the Data group. In the Sort dialog box, click the **Sort by arrow** and select **Major**. The sort should occur in ascending order. Click the **Then by arrow** and sort by **Name** in ascending order. Click **OK**.

f. Indicate that Michael Simpson and Andrew Sams are both active in Delta Mu Delta by typing **Yes** in the Delta Mu Delta column for each of those students.

g. Click anywhere in the first row. Click **Insert Above** in the Rows & Columns group. Click **Merge Cells** in the Merge group. Change the font size to **16**. Type **Comparison of GPA and Student Involvement**. (Do not type the period.)

h. Click the **Table Tools Design tab**, click the **Shading arrow**, and then click **Gold, Accent 4** (row 1, column 8). Select all text in the third row through the end of the table, beginning with *L0051899* and ending with *98* (on page 3). Bold the selection. Click any cell to deselect the area.

i. Click the **Table Move handle** to select the entire table. Click the **Table Tools Design tab**. Click the **Pen Color arrow** in the Borders group and select **Gold, Accent 4**. Click the **Line weight arrow** and click **1½ pt**. Ensure that a single line border is shown. Click the **Borders arrow** and click **All Borders**. Click any cell to deselect the area.

j. Click after **98** at the end of the last row. Press **Tab**. Type **AVERAGE**. Press **Tab** six times to reach the CSU Cum GPA column. Click the **Table Tools Layout tab**. Click **Formula** in the Data group. Click between **SUM** and **(ABOVE)** in the Formula dialog box. Press **Backspace** repeatedly to remove the word *SUM*, and type **AVERAGE**. Click **OK**.

k. Click the **View tab** and click **Multiple Pages** in the Zoom group. Note that the table is split between two pages. Click **100%** in the Zoom group. Select the first two rows of the table on page 2. Click the **Table Tools Layout tab** and click **Repeat Header Rows** in the Data group. View the document in multiple pages once more to see the change. Change the view back to **100%**.

l. Click anywhere in the table. Point to the outside left edge of the table between *Frederick Davidson* and *David Stumpe*. Click the **Insert indicator**. Click in the first cell of the new row and type the following record, tabbing between cells.

| L00500932 | Johns, Lacey | | Yes | Yes | Computer Science | 3.89 | 130 |

m. Move to page 3 and right-click the average (in the second to last column) in the last row. Click **Update Field**. Click the **References tab** and click **Insert Caption** in the Captions group. Ensure that the caption begins with Table. Type a colon (:) and then press **Spacebar**. Type **GPA and Student Involvement**. (Do not type the period.) Ensure that the caption will display below the table and click **OK**.

n. Press **Enter** twice. Click the **Insert tab** and click the **Object arrow** in the Text group. Click **Text from File**. Navigate to the location of the student data files and double-click *w03p1Sponsors*.

o. Select the newly inserted text, from *Sponsor* through *K177*. Do not select the blank paragraph on the next line. Click **Table** in the Tables group and click **Convert Text to Table**. Confirm that the new table will include four columns and four rows. Click **OK**.

p. Right-click anywhere in the selected table and click **Table Properties**. Click the **Column tab**. Ensure that the Preferred Width check box is selected, as indicated by a check mark in the box. Change the width to **2** and ensure that the measurement is in Inches. Click **OK**. Do not deselect the table. Click **More** in the Table Styles group and select **Grid Table 4 - Accent 4** (column 5, row 4 under Grid Tables).

q. Right-click anywhere in the selected table and click **Table Properties**. Click the **Table tab**. Click **Center**. Click **OK**. Insert a caption below the table that reads **Table 2: Faculty Sponsors**. (Do not type the period.) Click the **Home tab** and click **Increase Indent** in the Paragraph group to indent the caption.

r. Save the document. Press **Ctrl+Home**. Click the **Mailings tab** and click **Start Mail Merge** in the Start Mail Merge group. Click **Step-by-Step Mail Merge Wizard**.

s. Ensure that Letters is selected as the document type, and click **Next: Starting document**. Ensure that Use the current document is selected as the starting document and click **Next: Select recipients**.

t. Ensure that Use an existing list is selected, and click **Browse**. Navigate to the location of the data files and double-click *w03p1Faculty*. Click **OK** to select the worksheet. Click **OK**. Click **Next: Write your letter**.

u. Click before the paragraph mark following *TO:*. Click **More items** in the right pane. With **Title** selected, click **Insert**. Click **Close**. Press **Spacebar**. Click **More items**, select **First Name**, click **Insert**, and click **Close**. Press **Spacebar**. Click **More items** and insert **Last Name**, closing the dialog box afterward. Click before the paragraph mark following *DATE:* and type today's date.

v. Click **Next: Preview your letters**. Click **Next: Complete the merge**. Click **Edit individual letters**. Ensure that All is selected, and click **OK**. Scroll through the merged document to see that three recipients will receive the memo and tables. The document should include nine pages.

w. Save the document as **w03p1AcademicsMerge_LastFirst** and close the document. Save and close the file w03p1Academics_LastFirst. Based on your instructor's directions, submit w03p1AcademicsMerge_LastFirst.

As a health sciences graduate, you are coordinating a weight loss and fitness program for a local health club, Fitness Matters. Participants in the weight loss program have each set a weight loss goal that you have recorded in a spreadsheet, along with the actual amount lost at the end of the first six weeks. You want to recognize those who have lost at least 10 pounds by sending a congratulatory letter. Because you already have the participants' information stored in a database table, you decide to create a mail merge document that you can use to quickly create letters to send to each person who has lost at least 10 pounds. Refer to Figure 3.34 as you complete this exercise.

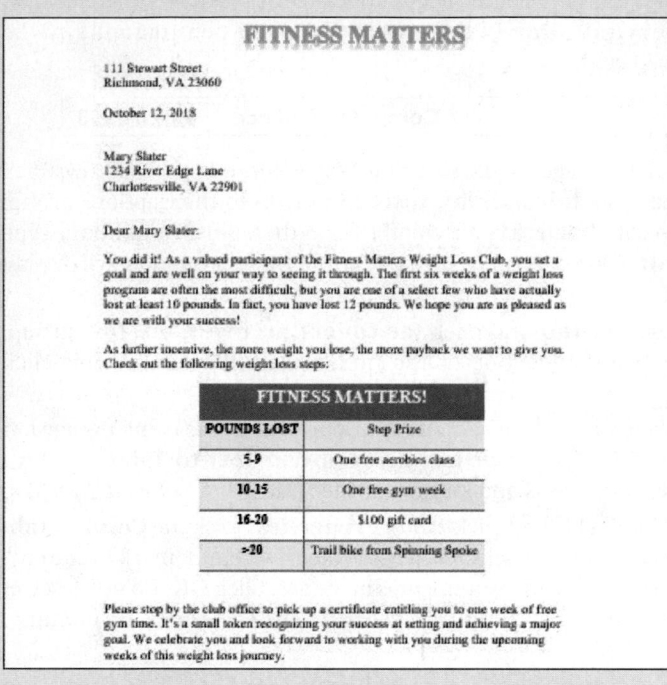
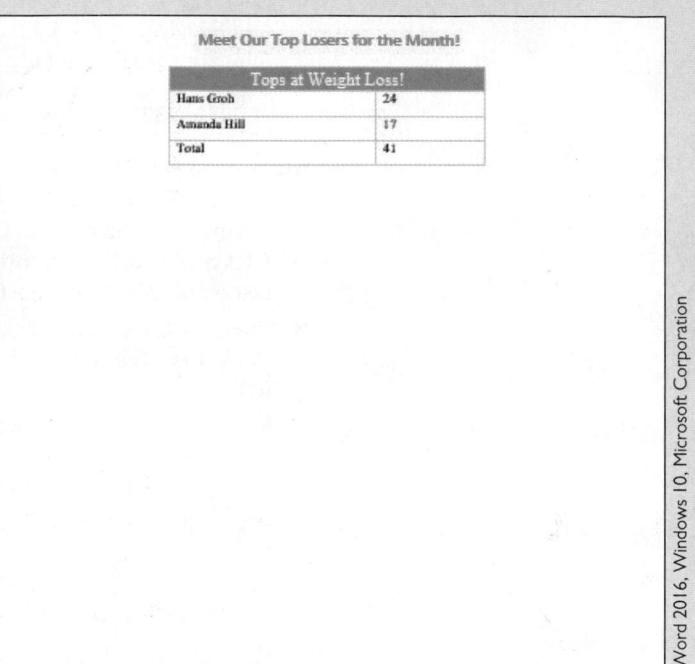

FIGURE 3.34 Fitness Matters Letter

a. Open *w03p2Letter* and save the document as **w03p2Letter_LastFirst**. Show nonprinting characters if they are not already displayed. Click before the blank paragraph mark after the second body paragraph. Click the **Insert tab**. Click **Table**. Drag to select 3 columns and 3 rows. Click in the bottom-right cell.

b. Type **Pounds Lost** in the first cell on the first row. Press **Tab**. Type **Level**. Press **Tab**. Type **Step Prize**. Press **Tab**. Complete the table as shown below.

10-15	Bronze	One free gym week
16-20	Silver	$100 gift card

c. Point to the top of the middle column so that the pointer is a downward arrow. Click to select the column. Right-click the selected column and click **Delete Columns**. Click in the first row. Click the **Table Tools Layout tab**. Click **Insert Above** in the Rows & Columns group. Click **Merge Cells**. Change the font size to **16**. Type **Fitness Matters!** Click the **Table Tools Layout tab** and click **Align Center** in the Alignment group.

d. Click anywhere in the fourth row. Click **Insert Below** in the Rows & Columns group. Complete the new row as shown below (contents of the last cell on the right will wrap).

>20	**Trail bike from Spinning Spoke**

e. Click **AutoFit** in the Cell Size group. Click **AutoFit Contents**. Click the **Table Tools Design tab**. Click **Plain Table 3** in the Table Styles group (fifth style from the left).

f. Right-click any cell in the table. Click **Table Properties**. Click **Center**. Click **OK**.

g. Click the **Pen Color arrow** and select **Green, Accent 6, Darker 25%** (row 5, column 10). Click **Line weight** and select **1 ½ pt**. Ensure that the line style option is a single line. Drag each horizontal gridline in the table, including the top and bottom of the table to paint each border. Press **Esc**.

h. Click the **Table Move handle**. Click the **Table Tools Layout tab** and click **Align Center** in the Alignment group.

i. Click any cell to deselect the area. Point to the outside left edge of the table between the second and third rows. Click the **Insert indicator**. Click in the first cell on row 3. Type **5-9** and press **Tab**. Type **One free aerobics class**. Select row 1. Click the **Table Tools Design tab**. Click the **Shading arrow** and select **Green, Accent 6, Darker 25%**. Change the font color of the text in row 1 to **White, Background 1**.

j. Press **Ctrl+End**. Click the **View tab** and ensure that Ruler is selected. Press **Ctrl+Enter** to insert a page break. Press **Enter** twice. Click the **Home tab** and click **Heading 1** in the Styles group. Type **Meet Our Top Losers for the Month!** Click **Center** in the Paragraph group. Select the heading line, bold the text, and change the font color to **Green, Accent 6**. Click after the heading line and press **Enter** twice.

k. Click the **Insert tab**. Click **Table** and select **Draw Table**. The pointer appears as a pencil. Positioning the insertion point below the heading line, drag a box approximately 4 inches wide and 1¼ inches tall, using the vertical and horizontal rulers as guides. Draw one vertical grid line about 2½ inches from the left side of the box. Draw two horizontal grid lines to divide the table into three approximately evenly spaced rows of about ½ inch each. Press **Esc**.

l. Select row 1 and click **Merge Cells** in the Merge group. Type **Tops at Weight Loss!** Complete the remaining table cells as following:

Amanda Hill	17
Hans Groh	24

m. Click the **Design tab** and apply the **Grid Table 1 Light - Accent 6** table style (row 1, column 7 under Grid Tables). With the insertion point positioned after **24** in the last cell on the last row press **Tab**. Type **Total**. Press **Tab**. Click the **Table Tools Layout tab** and click **Formula** in the Data group. Click **OK** to accept the suggested SUM function.

n. Select rows 2 and 3. Click **Sort** in the Data group. Click the **Sort by arrow** and select Column 2. Select descending order. Click **OK**. Right-click any cell in the table and select **Table Properties**. Click **Center** and click **OK**.

o. Select row 1. Click **Align Center** in the Alignment group. Change the font size to **16**. Click the **Table Tools Design tab**, click the **Shading arrow**, and click **Green, Accent 6**. Change the font color of the text in row 1 to **White, Background 1**. Click anywhere to deselect the area.

p. Click the **Table Move handle**. Right-click any selected cell and click **Table Properties**. Click the **Row tab**. Change the row height to **0.3**. Check spelling and save the document.

q. Click the **Mailings tab** and click **Start Mail Merge** in the Start Mail Merge group. Click **Step-by-Step Mail Merge Wizard**. Ensure that Letters is selected as the document type and click **Next: Starting document**. Ensure that Use the current document is selected and click **Next: Select recipients**.

r. Ensure that Use an existing list is selected and click **Browse**. Navigate to the location where data files are stored and double-click *w03p2Members*. Ensure that Sheet1 is selected and click OK.

s. Click **Sort** in the Mail Merge Recipients dialog box. Click the **Sort by arrow** and click **City**. Click the **Then by arrow** and select **Last Name**. Both selections should be sorted in ascending order. Click **OK**.

t. Click **Filter**. Click in the first **Field box**, scroll down, and click **Pounds Lost**. Click in the **Comparison box** and click **Greater than or equal**. Click in the **Compare to box** and type **10**. Click **OK.** Click **OK** again.

u. Click **Next: Write your letter**. Insert merge fields by completing the following steps:

- Click before the blank paragraph mark below the date on page 1. Click **Address block** in the Mail Merge pane and click **OK** to insert the default format of the member's address at the top of the letter.
- Place the insertion point at the left of the colon in the salutation line beginning with Dear. Press **Spacebar**. Click **More items** in the Mail Merge pane. Click **FirstName**, click **Insert**, and then click **Close**. Press **Spacebar** and click **More items**. With LastName selected, click **Insert** and click **Close**.
- Place the insertion point at the left of the word **pounds** in the second-to-last sentence in the first body paragraph (beginning with **In fact, you have lost**). Click **More items** and click **Pounds Lost**. Click **Insert** and click **Close**. Press **Spacebar**.

v. Click **Next: Preview your letters**. Click **Next: Complete the merge**. Click **Edit individual letters**. Ensure that All is selected and click OK. The letters are shown in a new document, titled *Letters1*.

w. Scroll through the pages to ensure that five two-page letters are included. Save the document as **w03p2LetterMerge_LastFirst** and close the document. Save and close the file w03p2Letter_LastFirst. Based on your instructor's directions, submit w03p2LetterMerge_LastFirst.

Mid-Level Exercises

1 Football Statistics

As a communication specialist for the Midwest Athletic Conference, you are preparing a summary of football statistics for inclusion in material published by the conference. Specifically, you highlight stats from the offensive units of leading teams in the conference. A Word table is an ideal way to summarize those statistics, so you prepare and populate several tables. Where appropriate, you include formulas to summarize table data. The tables must be attractively formatted, so you use Word's design and bordering tools as well.

a. Open *w03m1Football* and save it as **w03m1Football_LastFirst**.

b. Select text in the document from # (in the top-left corner) to 13.4 (in the bottom-right corner) and convert the text to a table. Change page orientation to **Landscape**. Change the font of the second and third lines (Midwest Athletic Conference and Season Statistics) to Cambria 16 pt.

c. Delete column 1. Change the font of all table data to **Cambria 10 pt**. AutoFit the contents of the table.

d. Ensure that no team names in column 1 are bold or underlined.

e. Insert a row above row 1 in the table. Complete the following steps to populate and format the new row:
- Type **Offensive Statistics** in the first cell on the new row.
- Type **Rushing Statistics** in the next cell on the first row.
- Select the second, third, fourth, fifth, and sixth cells on the first row. Merge the selected cells.
- Align Rushing Statistics in the center of the merged cell.
- Type **Passing Statistics** in the next cell on the first row.
- Select the cell containing Passing Statistics and the next three cells on the first row. Merge the cells.
- Align Passing Statistics in the center of the merged cell.
- Merge the remaining cells on row 1, type **Total** in the merged cell, and then center the word Total.

f. Insert a row between *HARKINSVILLE* and *DAKOTA STATE* and type the following data in the new row.

| JAMES COLLEGE | 38.2 | 41.0 | 220.5 | 4.2 | 19.7 | 32.7 | 0.601 | 199.2 | 7.6 | 57.9 | 449.3 | 5.9 | 12.7 |

g. Select a table style of **Grid Table 5 Dark - Accent 2** (row 5, column 3 under Grid Tables). Select all table text. Apply a Pen Color of **Orange, Accent 2, Darker 50%** (row 6, column 6 under Theme Colors) with a line weight of ½ pt and a line style of a single line to outside borders.

h. Select an orange double-line border style and apply it to the border along the horizontal line separating row 1 from row 2, and also along the vertical line separating the first column from the second.

i. Move to the end of the document, press **Enter** twice and insert a 3 × 5 table. Enter the following data in the table.

Calvin Spraggins	SPR	1428
Demaryius Schuster	DEN	1197
Brandon Marchant	CHI	1182
Wayne McAnalley	IND	1156
Sparky Hall	HOU	1114

j. Change the column width of all columns in the table to 1.5". Center all entries in the last two columns.

k. Insert a new blank row at the top of the table and complete the following steps:
- Type **Receiving Yards** in the first cell on row 1.
- Change the font size of the entry on row 1 to **14 pt**.
- Merge all cells on row 1.
- Ensure that Receiving Yards is centered.

l. Shade the first row with **Orange, Accent 2, Lighter 60%** (row 3, column 6 under Theme Colors).

m. Add a new blank row at the end of the table and type **Average** in the first cell of the new row. Enter a formula in the last cell of the new row to average all entries in the column above. You do not need to select a number format.

n. Align both tables horizontally in the center of the page. Check for spelling and grammatical errors. All names in both tables are correct.

o. Change the receiving yards for Calvin Spraggins to **1451**. Update the average to reflect the change.

DISCOVER

p. Use Border Painter to sample the double-line border that divides the first and second rows of the first table (Offensive Statistics) and paint it on the border dividing the first and second rows in the second table.

q. Add a caption below the bottom of the first table with the following text: **Figure 1: Midwest Athletic Conference Offensive Statistics**. Add a caption below the bottom of the second table that reads **Figure 2: Total Receiving Yards**. Modify the Caption style to include a font color of **Orange, Accent 2, Darker 50%**. Caption style font should be bold (not italicized) and centered. Save the document.

r. Begin a step-by-step mail merge. The document type is Letters and you will use the current document. Recipients are located in Sheet1 of *w03m1Universities*.

s. Sort the data source by University in ascending order. Merge the University field with the source document so that the university name displays after the text *Draft Prepared for:* on page 1.

t. Save the merged document as **w03m1FootballMerge_LastFirst** and close the file. Save and close w03m1Football_LastFirst. Based on your instructor's directions, submit w03m1FootballMerge_LastFirst.

2 Travel

You work with an accounting firm that employs a large number of private consultants, specializing in auditing. Those consultants often must travel and occasionally are due reimbursements for travel costs. You are assisting in the design of a travel reimbursement form and are considering using Word for that task. You know that Word's table features, including the use of formulas, might simplify the task of generating a form to summarize reimbursements that are due. In this exercise, you develop a professional-looking reimbursement form and use formulas to calculate totals within the table. You also create a mail merge document generating a memo to accounting firm partners seeking approval of the form design.

a. Begin a blank document and save it as **w03m2Form_LastFirst**. Show nonprinting characters if they are not already displayed. Change the font to **Garamond 18-pt** with **Bold** format. Type **Travel Reimbursement Form**. Press **Enter** twice. Change the font size to **12**.

b. Insert a 2 × 4 table. Complete the table as follows:

Consultant/Employee Name	
Account #	
Job #	

c. Delete the fourth row of the table. Change the orientation to landscape. Change the column width of the first column to **2.7"**. Change the width of the second column to **5.5"**. Change the height of all rows to **0.5"**.

d. Ensure that all text in the first column is Bold and change the font size to **14**. Change the alignment of all text in the first column to **Align Center Left**.

e. Select the table. Change the Pen Color to **Gold, Accent 4, Darker 25%**. Change the Line Style to the first double line shown. Line weight should be ½ pt. Apply the selected settings to all inside gridlines.

f. Change the Pen Color to **Gold, Accent 4, Darker 50%**. Change the Line Style to the ninth line style shown (a thick top border and a thinner bottom). Apply the border setting to all outside borders.

g. Select the first column and change the shading to **Gold, Accent 4, Lighter 60%**. Move to the end of the document. Press **Enter**.

h. Insert a 5 × 5 table. Complete the first row of the table as follows, allowing text wrapping to occur within cells:

Date	Departure Address	Arrival Address	Airfare (if applicable)	Taxi/Transport (if applicable)

i. Select the second row and change the font color to red. Complete the row as follows, allowing text wrapping to occur within cells. Do not press Enter in any cell.

e.g. 1/15/2017	601 Walnut St., Amherst NJ	1132 Anderson Ct., Lexington KY

j. AutoFit the table contents. Change the column width of the last column to **1.5"**. Add a column after the last column. Type **Hotel (if applicable)** in the first cell of the new column.

k. Add two blank rows at the end of the table. Type **Total** in the first cell on the last row. Include a formula in the fourth, fifth, and sixth cells on the last row to sum the contents of each respective column. Format each total as **Currency**. Because there are no amounts in the monetary columns, each total will display 0.

l. Apply the table style **Grid Table 1 Light - Accent 4** to the table (row 1, column 5 under Grid Tables). Select row 1 and change the shading to **Gold, Accent 4, Lighter 60%**. Center align all entries in row 1. Deselect the First Column option (on the Table Tools Design tab) to toggle bold formatting in the first column.

m. Complete row 3 of the table as follows:

5/16/2017	2795 Hwy. 55, Birmingham AL	1801 Arlington St., Boston MA	452.97	69.00	352.77

n. Update each value in the last row to show the current sum. Add another row of fictional travel information in row 4 and update the totals row. The data you enter can be for any destination with a reasonable cost. Update the totals row.

o. Apply a diagonal Draft watermark to the page containing the two tables. Insert a blank page at the beginning of the document and move to the top of the new page. Insert text from *w03m2Memo*. Double-click in the header area and deselect Different First Page to remove the watermark from the first page

DISCOVER

p. Select the second table on page 2 and distribute the rows.

q. Type your first and last names after the word From on the first page. Your name should not be bold. Include the current date on the appropriate line. The date should not be bold.

r. Check spelling and correct any mistakes. Begin a step-by-step mail merge process and ensure that Letters is selected. You should use the current document. Use an existing list for recipients. Browse the location of your student data files for *w03m2Partners*. Include all source records from Sheet1, but sort the results in ascending order by LastName.

s. Merge fields so that each recipient's first name and last name is shown as the recipient. The first and last names should not be bold. Complete the merge, editing individual letters to merge all.

t. Save the merged document as **w03m2FormMerge_LastFirst** and close the file. Save and close w03m2Form_LastFirst. Based on your instructor's directions, submit w03m2FormMerge_LastFirst.

3 Remodeling

 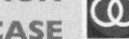

As a general contractor, you are often called upon to help plan remodeling projects. A local shelter for women and children is considering updating a bathroom and asked for your help in identifying necessary construction materials and an estimated cost for the equipment. The shelter is run by a board of directors to whom you will send a letter of introduction that includes a table of materials. This project is designed to be completed by a group of three students. The project is completed as follows:

a. The team will decide on a shared location in which to place files, such as OneDrive, Dropbox, or server space allotted by the college or university. All team members should become familiar with the shared space and any login requirements.

b. Determine a group name to be used throughout this project, or use one assigned by your instructor. Allocate one of three major tasks to each team member. One student will develop a main document to be used in a mail merge, one student will develop a data source to merge with the main document, and one student will develop a table of building materials to include in the main document before it is merged.

Student 1:

c. Develop an introduction letter to the members of the board of trustees. The letter will be designed as the main document in a mail merge; as such it will include fields for variable data such as each board member's name and mailing address. Indicate in the letter that the included table of materials outlines an estimated cost for each item as well as a total estimate for the remodeling project. The letter should be worded so that another student can easily insert the table of materials.

d. Format the letter attractively, using appropriate alignment, line spacing, and paragraph spacing. The letter should be error-free and grammatically correct. When complete (although without the table that will be inserted later), save the letter as **w03m3Introduction_GroupName**. Upload the letter to the shared location and contact the next student.

Student 2:

e. Develop a data source containing the names and addresses of all six board members. The data source can be a Word table, an Access database table or query, or an Excel worksheet.

f. Use descriptive field names and design the data source so it can be merged with a Word document. Include six records. Save the data source as **w03m3Trustees_GroupName** and upload the document to the shared location. Contact Student 3.

Student 3:

g. Convert the text found in *w03m3Construction* into a Word table and format the table so it is attractive, well structured, and descriptive. The table initially contains three columns, including description, quantity, and unit cost. A fourth column should be added to include a formula for each item (multiplying the quantity by the unit cost). Save the table as **w03m3Construction_GroupName** and upload the document to the shared location. Contact Student 2.

Student 2:

h. From the shared location, access or download *w03m3Introduction_GroupName* and *w03m3Construction_GroupName*. Insert text from (or copy and paste) the table into *w03m3Introduction_GroupName*, adjusting wording within the letter, if necessary, to assimilate the table. Save the revised letter as **w03m3Introduction_GroupName** and upload the file to the shared location, replacing the previous version with the new. Contact Student 1.

Student 1:

i. Download *w03m3Introduction_GroupName* and *w03m3Trustees_GroupName*. Merge the two documents through Word's mail merge process, incorporating variable data where indicated in the letter. Save the merged document as **w03m3ConstructionLetter_GroupName**.

j. Based on your instructor's directions, submit w03m3ConstructionLetter_GroupName.

Beyond the Classroom

Personal Budget Report

GENERAL CASE

FROM SCRATCH

You are taking a personal finance class this semester, and one of the assignments is to provide a report about your income, expenses, and spending habits for a 12-month period. Begin a new document and type two paragraphs that describe your spending habits. Be as general as you like, and feel free to create a fictional account of your spending, if you prefer. In the first paragraph, include your primary sources of income and how you allocate your income to different sources such as savings accounts and expenses. In the second paragraph, describe your major expenses. Create a Word table that details your budget under various major categories such as **Income**, **Expenses**, and **Savings**. Include subcategories such as **Fixed Expenses** and **Variable Expenses**. Examples of fixed expenses include tuition, rent, auto insurance, cable, and cell phone charges. Variable expenses include food, books, school supplies, and utilities. Create multiple columns that enable you to break down your income and costs by category and by month, and then add formulas to show subtotals for each month and the grand total for the 12-month period. Save your report as **w03b1Budget_LastFirst** and close the document. Based on your instructor's directions, submit w03b1Budget_LastFirst.

Assignment Planner

DISASTER RECOVERY

Your computer applications instructor assigned the task of using your Word skills to design an assignment planner. She challenged you to use what you have learned about Word tables to design an attractive document, with a table grid set up so you can enter class assignments for each week. The assignment is a group project, so you and your classmates decide to pattern the assignment planner table after a notebook you already use to record assignments. The first attempt at table design did not go so well, and the classmate who began the project needs help. Open *w03b2Planner* and redesign the document to produce an attractive planner that you could actually use. Do not settle for a mundane table. Use what you have learned about table styles, creating borders, and adjusting row height, column width, and alignment to create a stunning table. Make sure your table has enough space for a five-day week and six subjects. Complete the table with a sample week of assignments in classes in which you are enrolled. Save the completed document as **w03b2Planner_LastFirst** and close the document. Based on your instructor's directions, submit w03b2Planner_LastFirst.

Capstone Exercise

Your family owns Baker Home Store, a local home improvement business. As the general manager, you are involved in all facets of the business, from working with suppliers to ensuring customer satisfaction. Often, customers are interested in making improvements to homes that are being sold. You are currently preparing a brief guide providing tips on improving a house or getting it ready to sell. The basic outline of the document is ready. You review the document and add a couple of informative tables before the item is ready to send to your valued customers. Upon completing your edits, you use mail merge to distribute the document.

Create and Enhance Tables

You know that information presented in a tabular format is often more easily understood, especially where numeric data is involved. As you review the document draft, you see a couple of places where a table might be useful. You create and format two tables related to home improvement.

a. Open *w03c1Home* and save it as **w03c1Home_LastFirst**.

b. Move to the end of the document and convert the text beginning with *Under $100* and ending with *Update maintenance* to a table.

c. Insert a row above row 1. Type **Home Improvement Tips** in the first cell of the new row. Merge all cells in the row. Bold and center the text in row 1. Change the font size of the text in row 1 to 18 pt. Bold and center the text in row 2.

d. AutoFit the table contents. Center the table horizontally on the page.

e. Shade row 1 with Blue, Accent 1, Lighter 40%. Shade row 2 with Blue, Accent 1, Lighter 80%. Apply a Blue, Accent 1, Darker 25%, ½ pt size, double line border around the outside of the table.

f. Add a hard return after the first complete sentence at the top of page 2 (An energy efficient home is more valuable and is much more marketable in the long run.). Insert a 7 × 6 table. Complete the table as follows.

Months	Modification	ROI	Kwh savings	Cost per kwh	Annual savings	Cost per unit
3	High efficiency showerhead	400%	400	$0.08	$32	$8
13	Fireplace pillow stops	91%	400	$0.10	$32	$35
17	Attic insulation	69%	5.6	$0.08	$45	$0.65
44	Duct sealing	27%	12	$0.08	$96	$3.50
88	Floor insulation	14%	1.7	$0.08	$14	$1

g. Delete the first column (Months). Insert a row above row 1, merge cells in the row, and type **Return on investment estimates for household energy efficiency improvements**. (Do not type the period.) Change the table style to Grid Table 2 - Accent 3 (row 2, column 4 under Grid Tables).

h. Insert a row between rows 5 and 6 (Attic insulation and Duct sealing). Type the following data in the new row.

Wrap water pipes	48%	60	$0.15	$4.80	$10

i. Remove bold formatting from rows 3 through 8 in column 1. Ensure that text in rows 1 and 2 is bold. Center the table horizontally on the page. Insert a row after the last row and type **Total** in the first cell of the new row. In the fifth column on the last row, enter a formula to sum the annual savings. The total should be formatted as currency. Change the annual savings for the high efficiency showerhead to $35. Update the total to reflect the new value.

j. Insert a column at the right of the Cost per unit column. Type **Estimated cost increase** as the new column heading. In rows 3–8 of the new column, include a formula that increases the cost per unit by 3%. The formula should multiply the cost per unit by .03 and then add the result back to cost per unit. For example, the Estimated cost increase formula for the High efficiency showerhead is =F3*.03+F3. All results should be formatted at currency.

k. Check spelling and correct any mistakes. Create a caption to be shown below the table. The caption should be **Table 1: Return on investment for energy improvements.**

l. Modify the Caption style to include centered, bold and italicized font with a font color of Blue, Accent 1, Darker 50%. Save the document.

Use Mail Merge to Create Personalized Letters

You prepare a letter to current customers, thanking them for their business and including the collection of home improvement tips. You use Mail Merge to create personalized letters.

m. Move to the top of the document and insert a page break. Place the insertion point at the top of the new page. Insert text from *w03c1Thanks*. Show nonprinting characters if they are not already displayed.

n. Conduct a mail merge, using Sheet1 of *w03c1Customers* as the data source for addresses. Filter the data source so that only records with a zip of 65757 are included.

o. Insert an address block below the date, using default settings. Following the space after the word Dear (immediately before the colon), insert the title, followed by a space and the last name. Include your name in the closing instead of *Student Name*. Preview the letters and adjust the spacing of the address so that it displays as a single-spaced unit with no paragraph spacing.

p. Complete the merge of all records, producing a document containing two letters (four pages each).

q. Save the merged document as **w03c1HomeMerge_LastFirst** and close the file. Save and close w03c1Home_LastFirst. Based on your instructor's directions, submit w03c1Home_Merge_LastFirst.

LEARNING OUTCOME | You will model professional use of collaboration and research tools.

OBJECTIVES & SKILLS: After you read this chapter, you will be able to:

CASE STUDY | Literature Analysis

You are a college student enrolled in several classes in which you are required to write papers. One is a literature class, and the other is a business management class. Each class requires that you adhere to a specific writing style; each style differs with respect to writing guidelines and the use of citations. As a requirement for the literature class in which you are enrolled, you will prepare an analysis of *The White Heron*, a short story by Sarah Orne Jewett. The analysis is a group effort, completed by five students, including you. You are required to develop the paper based on a particular writing style, and you will include citations and a bibliography. Your instructor will provide feedback in the form of comments that the group will then incorporate into the paper. Because you are a commuting student with a part-time job, you are not always on campus and your time is very limited. As is typical of many college students, even those in your literature group, time and availability are in short supply. The group is quick to realize that much of the coordination on the project must be done from a distance. You will share the project in such a way that each student can contribute, although not in a group setting. Instead, the document will be available online, with each student reviewing, contributing, and reposting the project. Another project involves a short paper for your business management class in which you will include a cover page as well as footnotes.

Communicating and Producing Professional Papers

CHAPTER 4

Mimagephotography/
Fotolia

FIGURE 4.1 Literature Analysis Document

Word 2016, Windows 10, Microsoft Corporation

CASE STUDY | Literature Analysis

Starting Files	Files to be Submitted
w04h1Analysis	w04h1Analysis_LastFirst
w04h1Airlines	w04h1Airlines_LastFirst
w04h2WhiteHeron	w04h2WhiteHeron_LastFirst
w04h2Entry.pdf	w04h2Entry_LastFirst.pdf
Blank document	w04h3OneDrive_LastFirst
w04h3Analysis	w04h3Analysis_GroupName_LastFirst
	w04h3Analysis_LastFirst

Research Paper Basics

Researching a topic and preparing a research paper are common components of most college degrees. The task of writing a research paper is often met with dread by many college students, and although Word cannot replace the researcher, it can provide a great deal of support for properly citing sources and adhering to specific style manuals. A **style manual**, or style guide, is a set of standards for designing documents. In addition, Word assists with preparing footnotes and endnotes and preparing a bibliography. Although the research and wording of a research paper are up to you, Word is an excellent tool in the production of an attractive, well-supported document.

In this section, you will explore the use of Word features that support the preparation of a research paper. Specifically, you will learn the use of style manuals, create source references and insert citations, develop a bibliography, and work with footnotes and endnotes.

Using a Writing Style and Acknowledging Sources

As you write a research paper, you will develop content that supports your topic. The wording you use and the way you present your argument are up to you; however, you will be expected to adhere to a prescribed set of rules regarding page design and the citing of sources. Those rules are spelled out in a style guide that you can refer to as you develop a research paper. A style guide prescribes such settings as margins, line and paragraph spacing, the use of footnotes and endnotes, the way sources are cited, and the preparation of a bibliography.

It is common practice to use a variety of **sources** to supplement your own thoughts when writing a paper, report, legal brief, or other type of research-based document. In fact, the word research implies that you are seeking information from other sources to support or explore your topic when writing a research paper. Properly citing or giving credit to your sources of information ensures that you avoid plagiarizing. Merriam-Webster's Collegiate Dictionary's[1] definition of **plagiarizing** is "to steal and pass off (the ideas or words of another) as one's own." Not limited to failure to cite sources, plagiarism includes buying a paper that is already written or asking (or paying) someone else to write a paper for you. In addition to written words, plagiarism applies to spoken words, multimedia works, or graphics. Plagiarism has serious moral and ethical implications and is typically considered academic dishonesty in a college or university.

Select a Writing Style

When assigning a research paper, your instructor will identify the preferred **writing style**. Various writing styles are available and described in style manuals that are available both in print and online; however, the choice of writing style is often a matter of the academic discipline in which the research is conducted. For example, MLA style is often used in the humanities, while the field of social science typically prefers APA style. Those styles and others are described in this section.

A style manual does not require specific wording within a research paper. It will not assist with developing your topic or conducting research. However, it does provide a set of rules that results in standardized documents that present citations in the same manner and that include the same general page characteristics. In that way, research documents

---

[1]By permission. From Merriam-Webster's Collegiate® Dictionary, 11th edition © 2012 by Merriam-Webster, Inc. (www.Merriam-Webster.com).

contain similar page features and settings so a reader can focus on the content of a paper without the distraction of varying page setups. Among the most commonly used style manuals are **MLA (Modern Language Association)**, **APA (American Psychological Association)**, and **Chicago Manual of Style**.

If you have recently been assigned the task of writing a research paper as a requirement for an English class, you most likely were instructed to use MLA writing style. The humanities disciplines, including English, foreign languages, philosophy, religion, art, architecture, and literature, favor the MLA style, which has been in existence for more than 50 years. Brief parenthetical citations throughout a paper identify sources of information, with those sources arranged alphabetically in a works cited page. MLA style is used in many countries around the world, including the United States, Brazil, China, India, and Japan. Current MLA guidelines are published in *MLA Handbook for Writers of Research Papers* and *MLA Style Manual and Guide to Scholarly Publishing*.

Such disciplines as business, economics, communication, and social sciences promote the use of APA writing style. Developed in 1929, APA attempts to simplify the expression of scientific ideas and experiment reports in a consistent manner. Its focus is on the communication of experiments, literature reviews, and statistics. The *Publication Manual of the American Psychological Association* provides current rules and guidelines associated with the writing style.

Chicago writing style is an excellent choice for those who are preparing papers and books for publication. In fact, it is one of the most trusted resources within the book publishing industry. True to its name, the Chicago writing style was developed at the University of Chicago in 1906. It is described in *The Chicago Manual of Style*, currently in its 16th edition. The style is often referred to as CMS or CMOS. Often associated with the Chicago writing style, the Turabian writing style originated as a subset of Chicago. The dissertation secretary at the University of Chicago, Kate Turabian, narrowed the Chicago writing style to focus on writing papers. To do so, she omitted much of the information that is relevant for publishing. Currently, Turabian style is used mainly for the development of papers in the field of history.

Regardless of the writing style used, most research papers share common formatting features, as described below. With minor tweaks, a research paper generated according to these suggestions will be well on the way to completion:

- Align text at the left.
- Double-space lines.
- Include no paragraph spacing before or after.
- Set all margins (top, bottom, left, and right) at 1".
- Indent the first line of all body paragraphs by 1/2".
- Separate sentences by only one space.
- Use a serif font, such as Times New Roman, at 12 pt size.
- Create a right-aligned header, including the page number, positioned 1/2" from the top of the page.

Create a Source and Include a Citation

STEP 1 ›› By its very nature, a research paper is a collection of ideas and statements related to a topic. Many of those ideas are your own, summarizing your knowledge and conclusions. However, you will often include facts and results obtained from other sources. When you quote another person, glean ideas from others, or include information from another publication, you must give credit to the source by citing it in the body of your paper and/or including it in a bibliography. A *citation* is a brief, parenthetical reference placed at the end of a sentence or paragraph. Word enables you to select a writing style upon which all citations, sources, and bibliographic entries will be based.

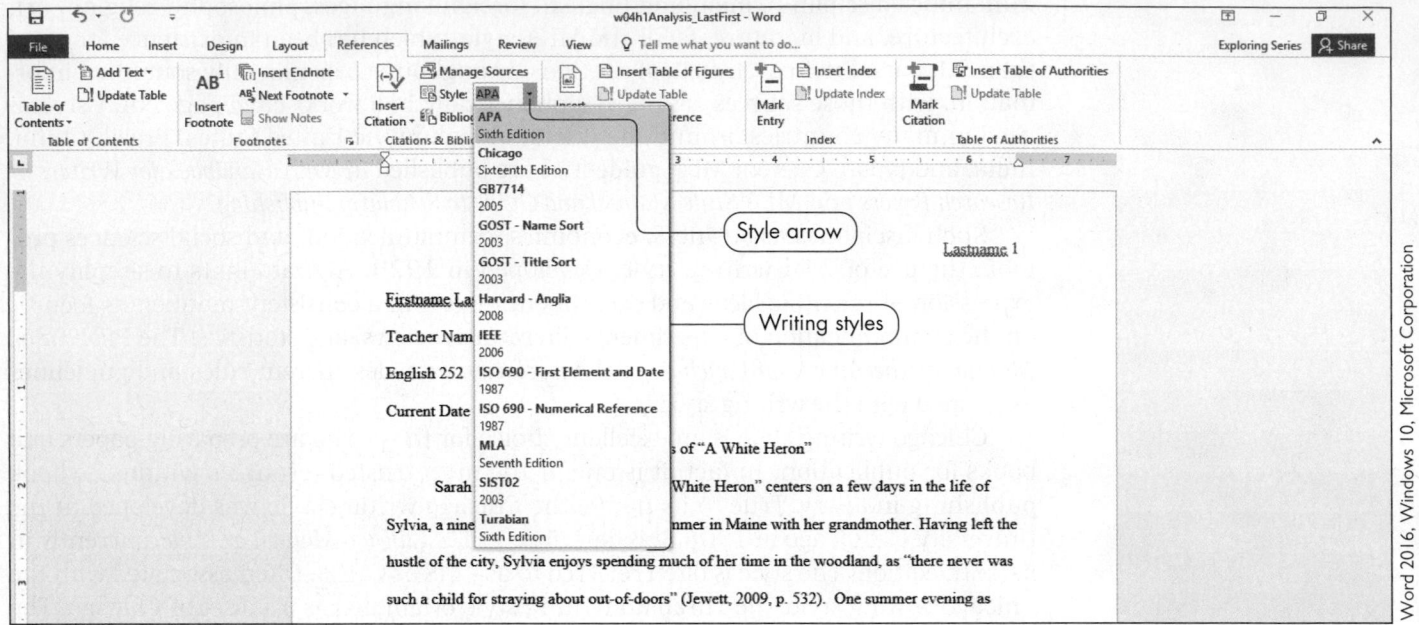

FIGURE 4.2 Select a Writing Style

Whenever you quote or paraphrase another person or publication, you should reference the source with a citation. Typically, a citation includes an author or publication name, with an optional page number. A citation directs a reader to a source of information you used. For more information, the reader can check the source on your bibliography or works cited page. Word formats sources and citations according to the writing style you specify, freeing you from the task of constantly checking a writing style for guidance. Even so, you should always compare citations and bibliographic entries created by Word with the most current writing style guidelines to ensure accuracy.

Proper placement of a citation within a research paper is critical. A citation should appear near a source of reference without interrupting the flow of a sentence. Use your judgment in placing a citation. For example, a long section of text that comes from one source should be cited at the end of the section—not after every sentence within the section. In other cases, a sentence that includes a quote or a direct reference to a particular source should be cited at the end of the sentence. Check a writing style manual for assistance with determining where to place a citation. Citations are typically placed before a punctuation mark that ends a sentence. As you create a citation, you add a reference source. A cited reference includes the type of source (book, journal article, report, website, etc.), title, publisher, page number(s), and other items specific to the type of source. At the conclusion of a report, you can use Word to create a bibliography, listing all of the sources you have cited.

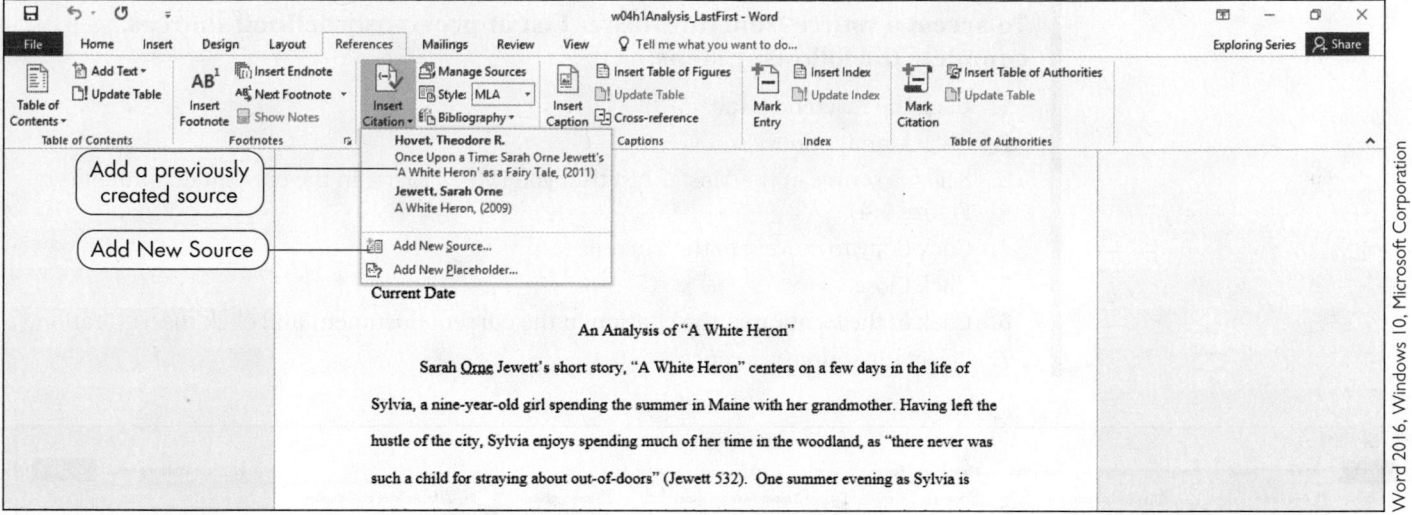

FIGURE 4.3 Add a Source

Depending on the writing style in use, the way a citation is worded may vary. Although Word automatically formats citations in parentheses with the author's last name and some other information, you might need to modify the wording or placement of items to accommodate the writing style. For example, if a sentence you are citing includes the author's name, most writing styles require only the page number in the citation, not the author's name. However, Word will place the author's name in the citation, so you must edit the citation to remove the name. A parenthetical citation is considered a field, which can be selected as a unit within a paper, with actions that can be taken after selecting (such as editing or removing). As such, you can simply click the citation to select it.

To edit a citation, complete the following steps:

1. Click the parenthetical citation.
2. Click the Citation Options arrow.
3. Click Edit Citation.
4. Add a page reference and/or suppress the Author, Year, or Title by selecting the appropriate boxes.
5. Click OK.

> **TIP: EDITING A CITATION AND SOURCE**
> When you click a parenthetical citation and click the Citation Options arrow, you can do more than simply edit the citation. You can also choose Edit Source (updating the source citation wherever it appears in the document) or Convert citation to static text (removing the field designation from the citation so that you can treat it like normal text). When you convert the citation to text, however, it is no longer included in a bibliography generated by Word unless it also appears elsewhere in the paper.

Share and Search for a Source

When you create a source, it is available for use in the current document, saved in the document's **Current List**. It is also placed in a **Master List**, which is a database of all sources created in Word on a particular computer. Sources saved in the Master List can be shared in any Word document. This feature is helpful to those who use the same sources on multiple occasions. Suppose you are working with a research paper that addresses a topic similar to that of another paper you created on the same computer.

To access a source from the Master List of previously defined sources, complete the following steps:

1. Click the References tab.
2. Click Manage Sources.
3. Select a source in the Master List that you intend to use in the current document (see Figure 4.4).
4. Click Copy to move it to the Current List.
5. Click Close.
6. Click in the location of the citation in the current document and click Insert Citation.
7. Select the source reference.

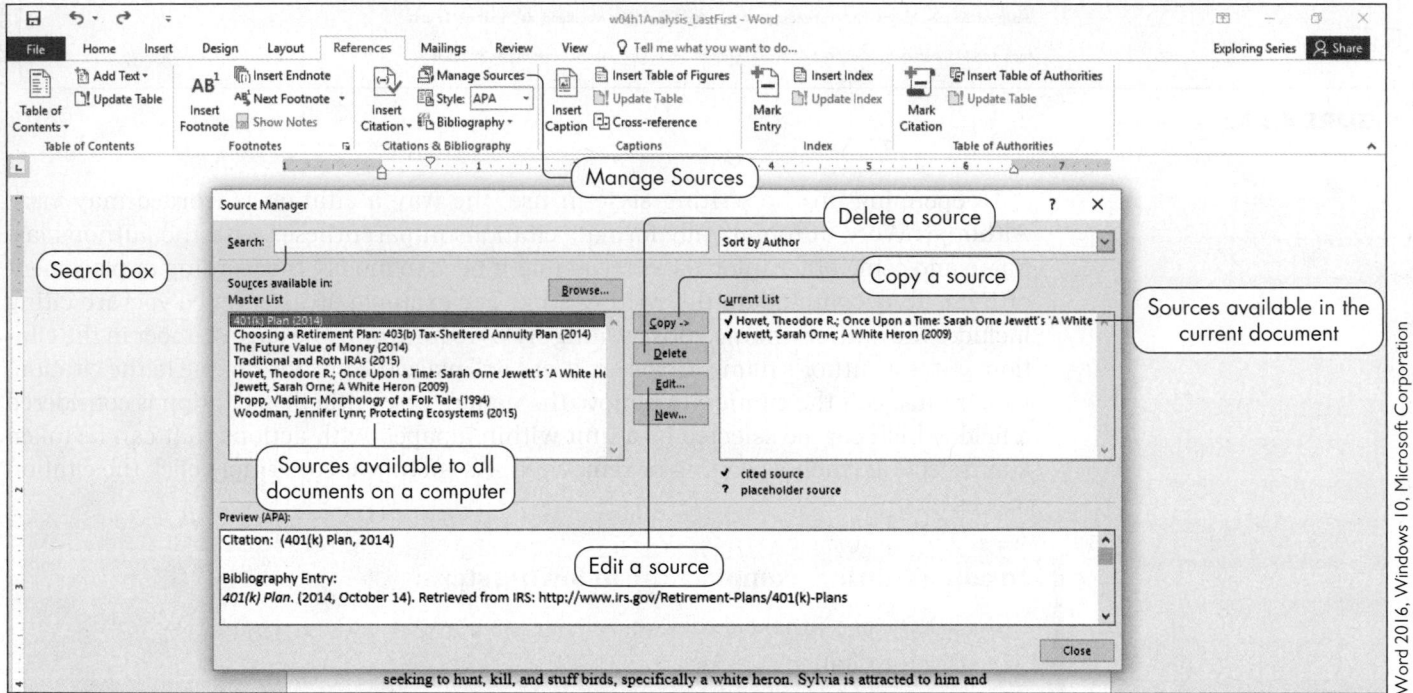

FIGURE 4.4 Manage a Source

The Source Manager not only enables you to share sources among several documents, but it also makes it easy to delete and edit sources. Click Manage Sources on the References tab, select a source from either the Master or Current List, and then click Delete or Edit (refer to Figure 4.4).

Especially if sources are numerous, you might appreciate a quick way to search for a particular source. You can search by author, title, or year. Type a search term in the Search box of the Source Manager dialog box (refer to Figure 4.4). As you type, Word narrows the results so you can more easily determine if a source exists that meets your search criteria.

Create a Bibliography

STEP 2 ❯❯ A **bibliography** is a list of documents or sources consulted by an author during research for a paper. It not only guides a reader to sources of your research for additional study, but it also provides a reader with an opportunity to validate your references for accuracy. In theory, a bibliography lists not only those references that were cited in parenthetical terms throughout the paper, but also those that were not cited but were helpful as you prepared the paper. However, Word includes in a bibliography (or **works cited** page) only those sources that were cited in the paper, which is the way most research documents are expected to be prepared. Therefore, a bibliography and a works cited page (which is designed to contain only cited references) are considered synonymous terms when working with Word. After a bibliography is prepared, you can always edit it to add additional references if required. Figure 4.5 shows a bibliography developed in Word. The bibliography is formatted according to the MLA writing style, which requires the use of Works Cited as a title. Note that all sources include a hanging indent, which is typical of all writing style requirements. In addition, entries are listed in alphabetical order by last names of authors or editors, or by first words of titles.

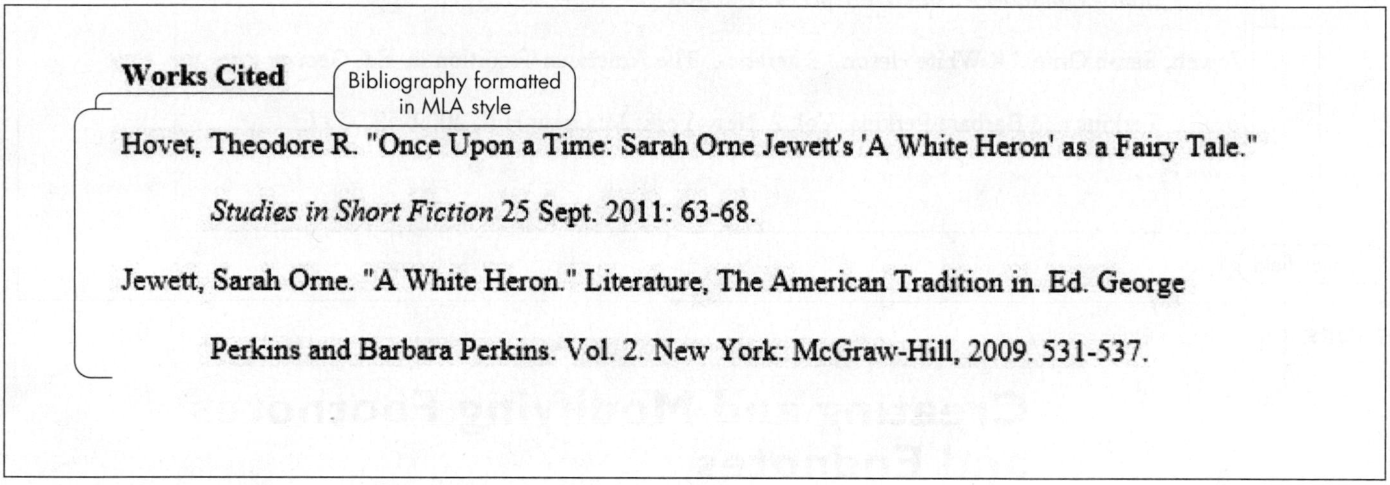

Works Cited

Bibliography formatted in MLA style

Hovet, Theodore R. "Once Upon a Time: Sarah Orne Jewett's 'A White Heron' as a Fairy Tale."

Studies in Short Fiction 25 Sept. 2011: 63-68.

Jewett, Sarah Orne. "A White Heron." Literature, The American Tradition in. Ed. George

Perkins and Barbara Perkins. Vol. 2. New York: McGraw-Hill, 2009. 531-537.

Word 2016, Windows 10, Microsoft Corporation

FIGURE 4.5 Bibliography

Depending on the writing style you are following, the term used for the list of references varies. MLA uses the term Works Cited, whereas APA requires References. Still others prefer Bibliography. You should be familiar with the preferred term and organization before using Word to develop the list of references.

To simplify the addition of the reference page, complete the following steps:

1. Insert a page break at the end of the research paper.
2. Click the References tab.
3. Click Bibliography.
4. Select Bibliography, References, or Works Cited (depending on the particular writing style requirement). If you want no heading but simply the formatted references, click Insert Bibliography.

Regardless of which approach you take, you should always confirm that the resulting page meets all requirements of the particular style to which you are writing. Just as you would proofread a document instead of relying solely on Word's spelling checker, you should also consult a writing style manual to make sure your bibliography is correct.

When Word creates a bibliography page, it places all citations in a single field. As shown in Figure 4.6, when you click a bibliography list that Word has prepared, the entire list is shown as a unit, called a Citation field. The field can be updated; for example, if at a later time you include additional sources within the paper, click Update Citations and Bibliography (see Figure 4.6) to include the new sources in the bibliography. You can also choose to format the existing bibliography with a different title (perhaps changing from Works Cited to References), and you can convert the bibliography to static text, removing the field designation from the bibliography so that you can edit and delete references as you like. At that point, however, you cannot update the bibliography with additional sources.

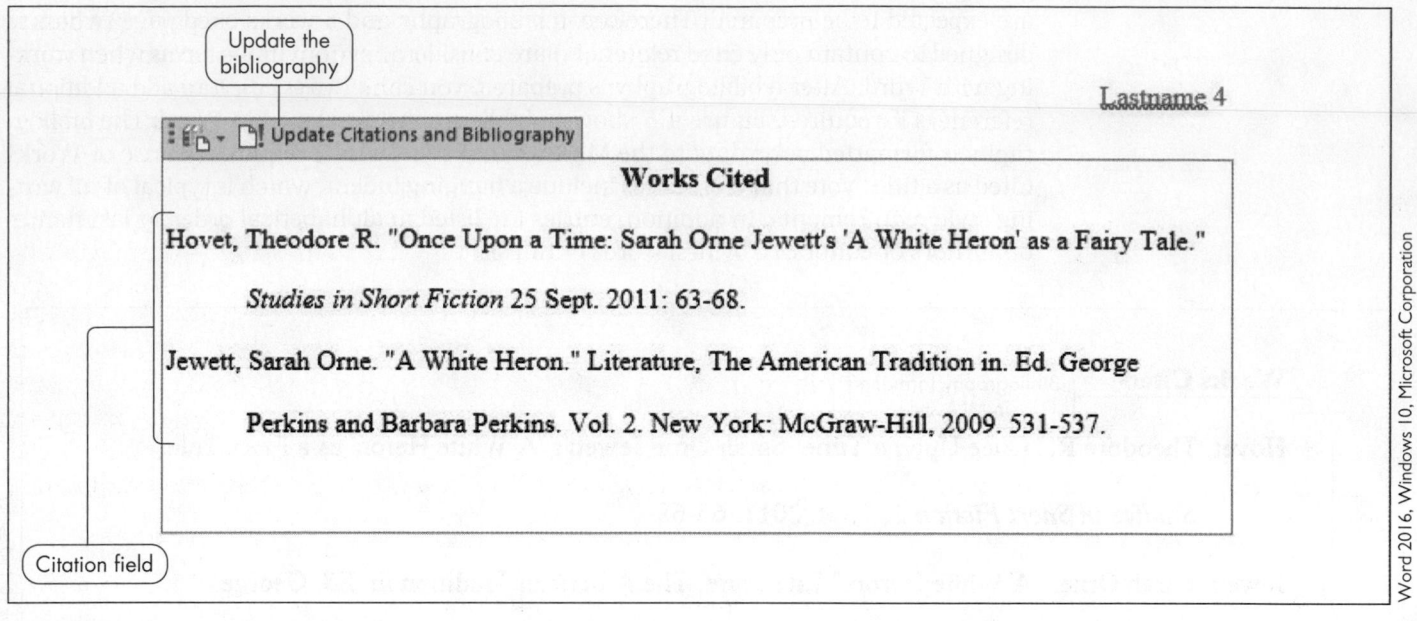

FIGURE 4.6 Update a Bibliography

Creating and Modifying Footnotes and Endnotes

A ***footnote*** is a citation or note that appears at the bottom of a page, while an ***endnote*** serves the same purpose but appears at the end of a document. Like parenthetical citations, the purpose of a footnote and endnote is to draw a reader's attention to a specific source of information. In addition, footnotes and endnotes are often used to further describe a statistic or statement used in the report without including additional detail in the text. A footnote, providing clarification of a statistic, is shown in Figure 4.7. Note that the footnote is linked by superscript (elevated number) to the corresponding reference in the paper.

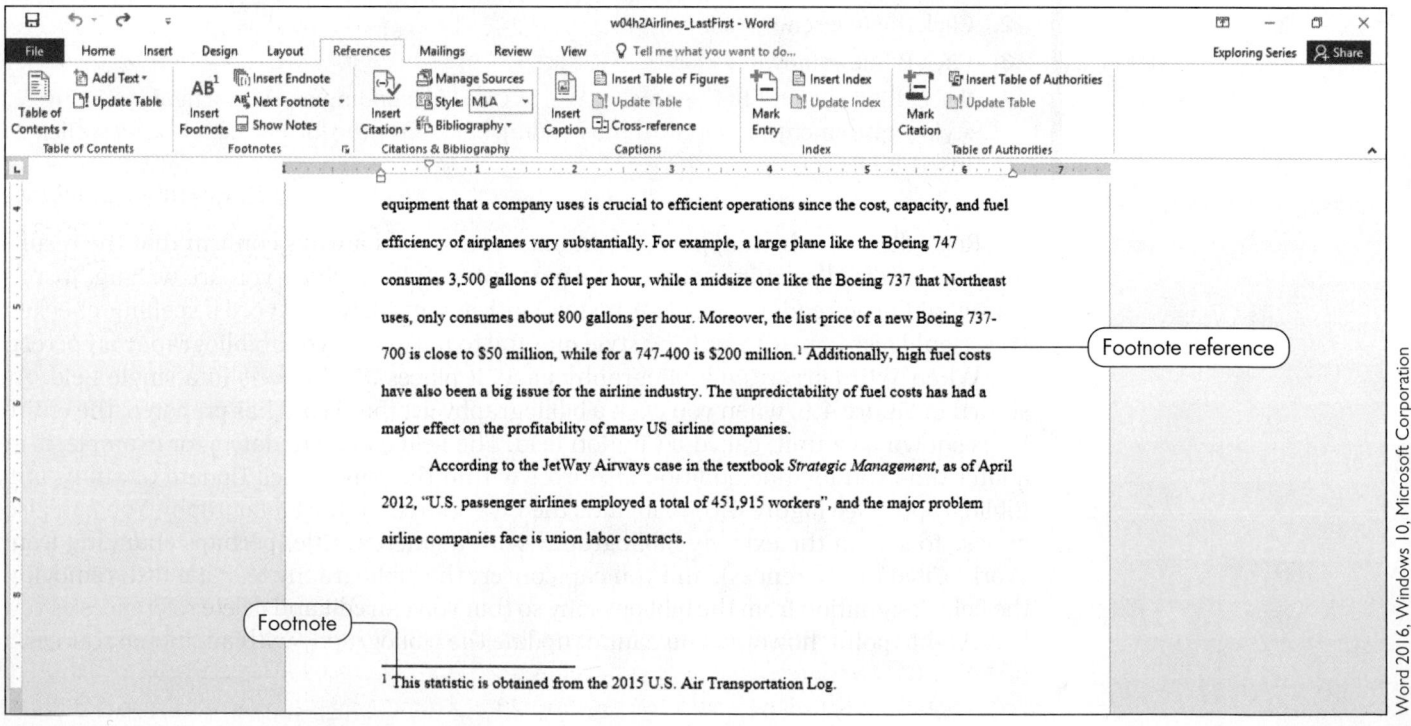

FIGURE 4.7 Include a Footnote

You should never use both footnotes and endnotes in the same paper. Choosing whether to use footnotes or endnotes, if at all, depends in part on the number of citations included and the way you want your reader to process the report's information. Because endnotes are included as a list at the end of the document, they do not add clutter to the end of pages. In addition, they might make the report easier to read because a reader's gaze is not constantly shifting back and forth from the bottom of a page to the text. Conversely, a footnote provides immediate clarification of a source and enables the writer to make additional comments related to a statement on the same page as the footnote.

Although you might choose to include footnotes to provide additional information related to a statement on the same page, you will most likely use a bibliography or works cited page to provide a complete list of referenced sources in a paper. An advantage to using a bibliography for that task is that each source is listed only once. In contrast, a footnote or endnote appears each time a source is referenced, regardless of how many times the same source is cited in a paper. Although subsequent footnotes and endnotes referencing the same source are abbreviated, they are still listed, often resulting in a cluttered, possibly distracting, arrangement of repetitive information.

TIP: FOOTNOTES VERSUS IN-TEXT CITATIONS
The choice of whether to use a footnote or an in-text citation to reference a source depends somewhat on the writing style you are following. Always refer to the writing style guide when considering which to use, as each style tends to prefer one to the other. The choice is also related to the type of document. For example, legal documents almost always rely heavily on footnotes instead of parenthetical citations.

Including a bibliography does not mean that you cannot use footnotes to provide more detailed descriptions of statements or facts in the paper. You might use a footnote to provide an explanation of statistics. For example, a statistic on the number of victims in a natural disaster or the amount of money given through a government program could be further detailed in a footnote. You might also define or illustrate a concept included in the report, providing a personal comment. Much of business writing is actually persuasive text, in which you explain a situation or encourage others to take some action. Using a footnote is a great way to further describe a statistic used in your text without having to incorporate it into the written paragraph. That way, you do not risk cluttering the manuscript with overly explanatory text, perhaps losing or diverting the attention of the reader. You should be aware, however, that most writing styles limit a footnote to only one sentence. Therefore, any planned explanation of a report statement must be condensed to just one sentence.

Create Footnotes and Endnotes

STEP 3 ▶▶ Source information in a document that you reference with a footnote or endnote includes a number or symbol in superscript. The reference is then keyed to the same number or symbol at the end of the page (footnote) or at the end of the document (endnote). The References tab includes the Insert Footnote and Insert Endnote options.

To insert a footnote or endnote, complete the following steps:

1. Click beside the text to reference (or after ending punctuation, if referencing a sentence).
2. Click the References tab.
3. Click Insert Footnote (or Insert Endnote) in the Footnotes group.
4. Type footnote/endnote text.

A footnote is automatically positioned at the end of the page, with the same superscript as that assigned to the in-text reference. An endnote is automatically positioned sequentially with other endnotes on a page at the end of the document. By default, Word sequentially numbers footnotes with Arabic numerals (1, 2, and 3). Endnotes are numbered with lowercase Roman numerals (i, ii, and iii). If you add or delete footnotes or endnotes, Word renumbers remaining notes automatically.

Modify Footnotes and Endnotes

Occasionally, you will determine that different wording better suits a particular footnote or endnote. Or perhaps you want to remove a footnote or endnote completely. You can even change the format of a footnote or endnote, changing the font, font size, or character formatting. To modify a footnote or endnote, double-click the numeric reference in the body of the document. The insertion point will be placed to the left of the corresponding footnote or endnote text.

To insert a footnote or endnote while specifying settings other than those selected by default, use the Footnote and Endnote dialog box. Click the Footnotes Dialog Box Launcher in the Footnotes group on the References tab to open the dialog box. As shown in Figure 4.8, you can modify the placement, number format, symbol, and initial number before you insert a new footnote or endnote.

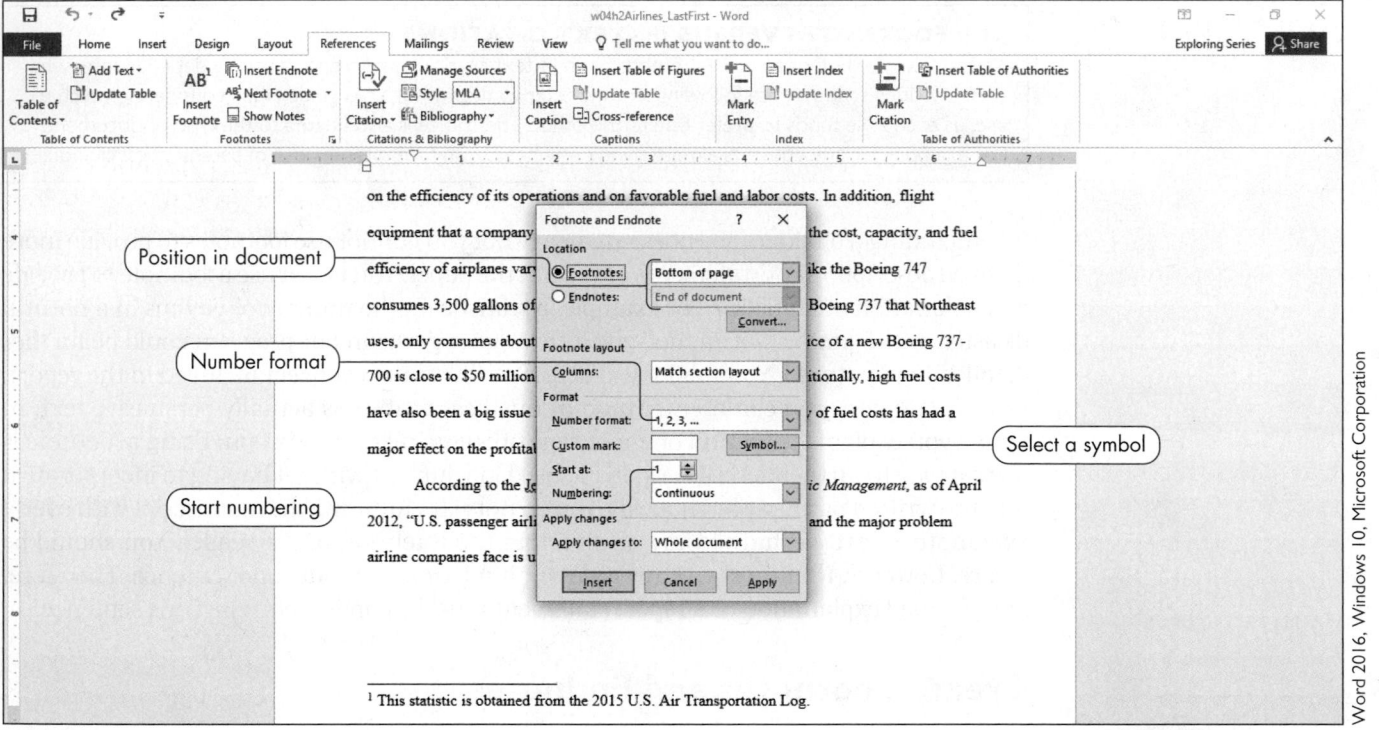

FIGURE 4.8 Footnote and Endnote Dialog Box

You can remove note text and replace it with alternate wording, just as you would adjust wording in a document. If you plan to change the format of a single note, instead of affecting all footnotes or endnotes in a document, you can select text and apply different formatting—perhaps italicizing or bolding words.

More often, you might want to adjust the format of every footnote or endnote in a document. Footnotes are formatted in Footnote Text style, and endnotes are formatted in Endnote Text style. Those styles include a specific font and font size.

> **To modify the style of either a footnote or endnote so that the formatting changes you make are applied to all notes in a document, complete the following steps:**
>
> 1. Right-click a footnote or endnote and click Style.
> 2. Click Modify (in the Style dialog box).
> 3. Adjust font and alignment settings or click Format for more selections.
> 4. Click OK repeatedly to accept settings and return to the document.

Exploring Special Features

Although writing a research paper is a typical requirement of a college class, it is not the only type of paper you are likely to write. In the workplace, you might be asked to contribute to technical reports, grant proposals, and other types of business documents. Those reports are not likely to be as strictly bound to writing style rules as are reports written for academic purposes. In fact, you might find it necessary to include special features such as a table of contents, an index, and even a cover page to properly document a paper and make it easier to navigate. Such features are not usually included in a college research report or required by academic writing style guides, but they are common components of papers, chapters, and articles to be published or distributed.

Create a Table of Contents

STEP 4 ▶▶ A *table of contents* lists headings in the order they appear in a document, along with the page numbers on which the entries begin. The key to enabling Word to create a table of contents is to apply heading styles to headings in the document at appropriate levels. You can apply built-in styles, Heading 1 through Heading 9, or identify your own custom styles to use when generating the table of contents. For example, if you apply Heading 1 style to major headings, Heading 2 style to subordinate headings, and lesser numbered heading styles to remaining headings as appropriate, Word can create an accurate table of contents. At your request, Word will update the table of contents when you change heading text, sequence, or level.

> **To insert a predefined table of contents, complete the following steps:**
>
> 1. Ensure that headings in the document are formatted with heading styles according to level.
> 2. Click the References tab.
> 3. Click Table of Contents in the Table of Contents group.
> 4. Select an Automatic table style to create a formatted table of contents that can be updated when heading text or positioning changes (or select Manual Table to create a table of contents that is not updated when changes occur).

For more flexibility as you design a table of contents, you can click Table of Contents (on the References tab) and then select Custom Table of Contents. From the Table of Contents dialog box, select options related to page numbering and alignment, general format, level of headings to show, and leader style (the characters that lead the reader's eye from a heading to its page number). The subsequent table of contents can be updated when changes occur in headings within the document.

A table of contents created by Word is inserted as a field. When you click a table of contents, the entire table is shown as an entity that you can update or remove. As shown in Figure 4.9, controls at the top of the selection enable you to update, modify, or remove a table of contents. As you make changes to a document, especially if those changes affect the number, positioning, or sequencing of headings, you will want to update any associated table of contents. You will indicate whether you want to update page numbers only or the entire table.

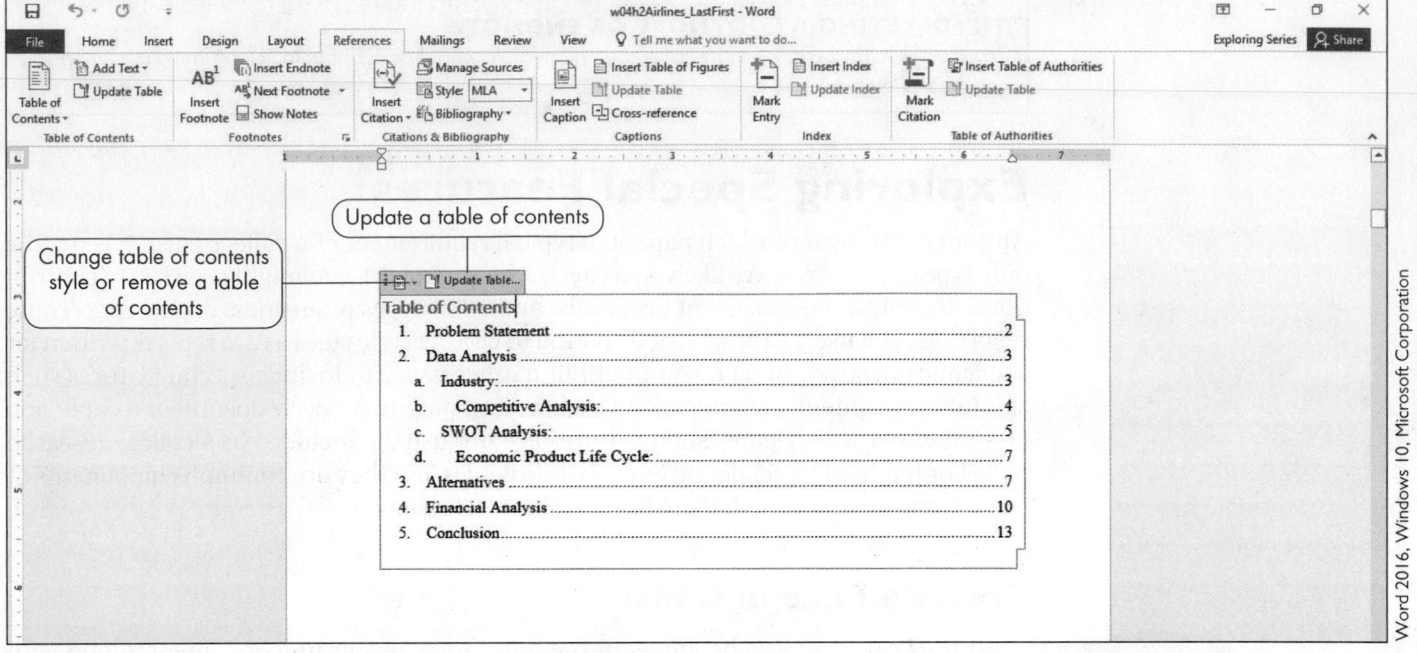

FIGURE 4.9 Update a Table of Contents

Create an Index

No doubt you have used an *index* to locate a topic of interest in a book. In doing so, you were able to move quickly to the topic. Most books and many lengthy papers include an index. Typically located at the end of a book or document, an index provides an alphabetical listing of topics included in a document, along with related page numbers. Using Word, you can mark items to include and then have them automatically formatted as an index.

To mark items to include in an index, complete the following steps:

1. Select a word or phrase to include in an index.
2. Click the References tab and click Mark Entry in the Index group.
3. Select or confirm settings in the Mark Index Entry dialog box as follows:
   - Ensure that text in the Main entry box is stated exactly as it should appear in the index.
   - Click Mark, if only one occurrence of the selected text is to be noted in the index. Otherwise, click Mark All to include all occurrences of the selected text.
   - Include a cross reference, if needed. For example, an index entry for appetizers could be cross-referenced with hors d'oeuvres. Click Mark.
4. Repeat Steps 1 and 3 for any additional terms to mark as index entries. Close the dialog box when all items have been marked.

As you mark entries for inclusion in the index, they will be coded in the document with a tag. After marking entries to include in an index, you are ready to create the index, typically among the last pages of a document. Word arranges the index entries in alphabetical order and supplies appropriate page references.

To create an index, complete the following steps:

1. Insert a blank page at the end of the document or at a location where the index is to display. Position the insertion point on the blank page.
2. Click the References tab and click Insert Index in the Index group.
3. Adjust settings in the Index dialog box, including the format style, number of columns, language, and alignment.
4. Click OK.

Creating an index is usually among the last tasks related to preparing a paper, chapter, or book. However, even if an index has been created, you can still update the index with new entries. New entries are alphabetized along with the original entries in the index.

To update an index so that newly marked entries are included, complete the following steps:

1. Click in the index to select it.
2. Click the References tab.
3. Click Update Index in the Index group.

Create a Cover Page

STEP 5 ▶▶ A *cover page*, sometimes called a *title page*, is placed at the beginning of a report. Some writing styles do not require a cover page for a research report, whereas others do. APA writing style requires a cover page for a research report, formatted in a certain way. When writing a research paper, consult the writing guide of the style you are following for information related to the format of a cover page (if a cover page is required). You can use Word to create a cover page in any of a variety of styles.

To insert a cover page, complete the following steps:

1. Click the Insert tab.
2. Click Cover Page in the Pages group.
3. Select from a number of designs, or click More Cover Pages from Office.com for more choices.
4. Personalize the cover page with your name, report title, and any other variable data.

While templates are available, some situations merit a plain cover page that you create yourself. For instance, if you want a cover page to be formatted in the same way as the remainder of the report, you might consider creating and customizing a cover page in its own section.

To create a customized cover page from scratch, complete the following steps:

1. Click the Layout tab.
2. Click Breaks, and click Next Page in the Section Breaks group.
3. Type the content of your cover page to include information such as your name, date, and title of the document.
4. Select Different First Page on the Header and Footer Tools Design tab if you create a page number header or footer. You do not want the cover page to include a page number.

Quick Concepts

1. What type of writing style would you expect to be required to use for a writing assignment in a business class, and why? *p. 335*
2. How would you edit a citation to remove an author name and add a page number? *p. 337*
3. You find that some of the same sources in the research paper you are currently working on were used in your previous research paper. How can you pull sources from the previous paper so that you do not have to recreate them? *p. 337*
4. How can you make sure a table of contents is updated to reflect the current content of a document, especially if content has changed? *p. 343*

Hands-On Exercises

Watch the Video
for this Hands-On
Exercise!

MyITLab®
HOE1 Training

Skills covered: Select a Writing Style • Create a Source and Include a Citation • Share and Search for a Source • Create a Bibliography • Create Footnotes • Modify Footnotes • Create a Table of Contents • Create an Index • Create a Cover Page

1 Research Paper Basics

You have completed a draft of an analysis of the short story *A White Heron*. As a requirement for the literature class in which you are enrolled, you must format the paper according to MLA style, including citations and a bibliography. In addition to the literature analysis, you have also completed a marketing plan for a fictional company, required for a business management class. The instructor of that class has asked that you consider submitting the paper for inclusion in a collection of sample papers produced by the School of Business at your university. For that project, you will include a cover page, a table of contents, and an index.

STEP 1 >> SELECT A WRITING STYLE AND CREATE A SOURCE

You will format the analysis of *A White Heron* in MLA style and include citations where appropriate. Refer to Figure 4.10 as you complete Step 1.

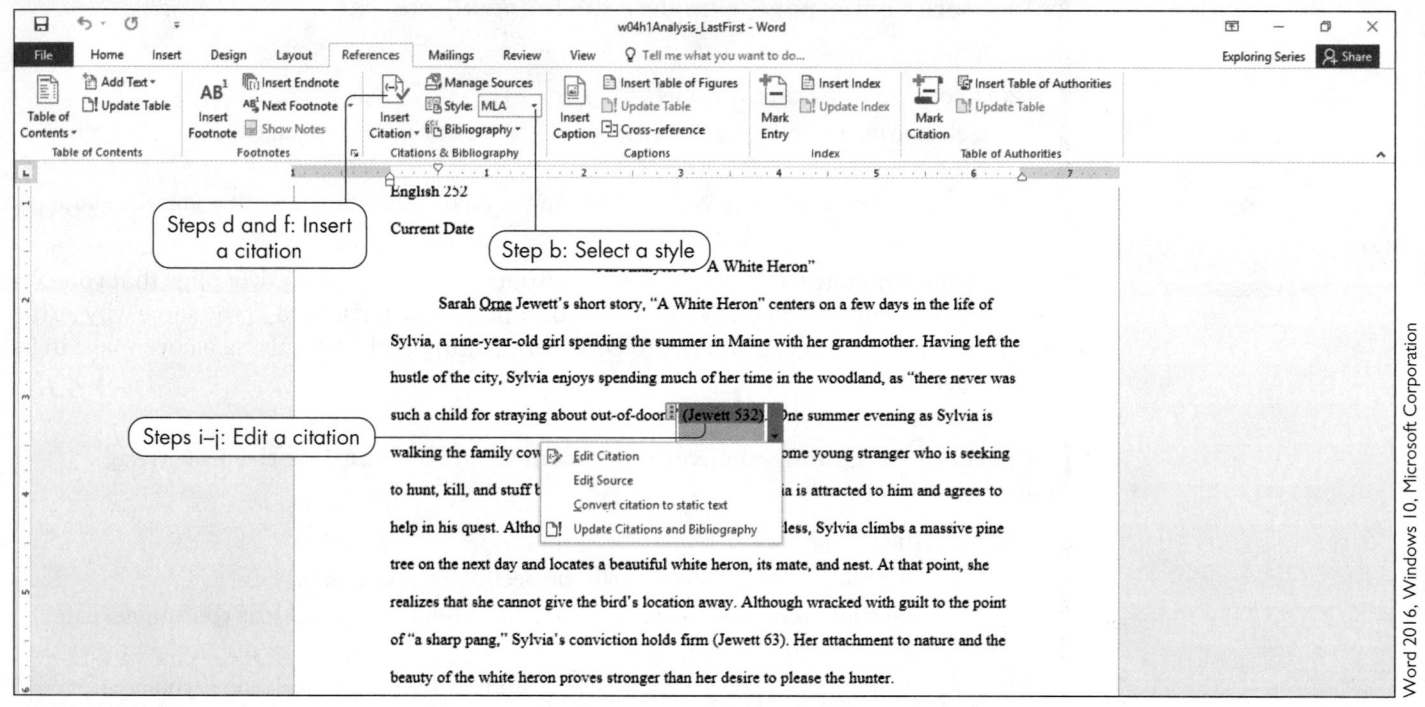

FIGURE 4.10 Add Sources and Insert Citations

a. Open *w04h1Analysis* and save it as **w04h1Analysis_LastFirst**.

> **TROUBLESHOOTING:** If you make any major mistakes in this exercise, you can close the file, open *w04h1Analysis* again, and then start this exercise over.

b. Click the **References tab** and click the **Style arrow** in the Citations & Bibliography group. Select **MLA Seventh Edition**. Ensure that the following settings, required by the MLA writing style, are in place, adjusting any that may be missing or incorrect:

- Document is double-spaced.
- The font is Times New Roman 12 pt.

Word 2016, Windows 10, Microsoft Corporation

- There is no paragraph spacing before or after any paragraph.
- Margins are 1" at the top, bottom, left, and right.
- All body paragraphs are indented .5".
- The report title is centered.

c. Insert a right-aligned header that includes your last name, followed by a space and a plain page number. Make sure the page number is inserted as a field, not simply typed. The header should be formatted as **Times New Roman 12 pt**.

d. Place the insertion point after the ending quotation mark and before the ending period in Jewett's notation in the first body paragraph (ending in *straying about out-of-doors*). Click the **References tab** and then click **Insert Citation** in the Citations & Bibliography group. Click **Add New Source**. Click the **Type of Source arrow** and click **Book Section**. Complete the citation as follows, but do not click OK after completing the source.

Author: **Jewett, Sarah Orne**

Title: **A White Heron**

Book Title: **The American Tradition in Literature**

Year: **2009**

Pages: **531–537**

City: **New York**

Publisher: **McGraw-Hill**

e. Click to select **Show All Bibliography Fields**. Click in the **Editor box** and type **Perkins, George**. Click **Edit** beside Editor. Type **Perkins** in the Last box. Click in the **First box** and type **Barbara**. Click **Add** and click **OK**. Click in the **Volume box** and type **2**. Click **OK**.

You have added a source related to a section of a book in which the short story is printed.

f. Click after the word *firm* and before the ending period in Jewett's notation (that ends in *Sylvia's conviction holds firm*) in the first paragraph. Click **Insert Citation** in the Citations & Bibliography group and click **Jewett, Sarah Orne** to insert a citation to the same source as that created earlier.

g. Place the insertion point after the ending quotation mark and before the ending period in Hovet's notation in the second body paragraph (ending in *functions that are also present in "A White Heron"*). Add a new source, selecting **Article in a Periodical** as the source type:

Author: **Hovet, Theodore R.**

Title: **Once Upon a Time: Sarah Orne Jewett's 'A White Heron' as a Fairy Tale**

Periodical Title: **Studies in Short Fiction**

Year: **2011**

Month: **Sept.**

Day: **25**

Pages: **63–68**

h. Click to select **Show All Bibliography Fields**, set the Volume to **15** and the Issue to **1**, and then click **OK**.

i. Click Jewett's parenthetical citation in the first body paragraph beside the words *straying about out-of-doors*. Click the **Citation Options arrow** and click **Edit Citation**. Type **532** in the Pages box. Click **OK**.

You have added a page number to identify the source as required by MLA writing style.

j. Edit the next citation in the first body paragraph (following the sentence that ends in *Sylvia's conviction holds firm*) to include page number **537**. Click the only Hovet citation in the second body paragraph. Click the **Citation Options arrow** and click **Edit Citation**. Suppress the display of Author, Year, and Title, but include a Page Number of **63**. Click **OK**.

k. Save the document.

STEP 2 ›› **SHARE AND SEARCH FOR A SOURCE AND CREATE A BIBLIOGRAPHY**

Now that sources are cited and stored in the document, you can quickly insert the bibliography at the end. You will also explore the sharing of sources. Refer to Figure 4.11 as you complete Step 2.

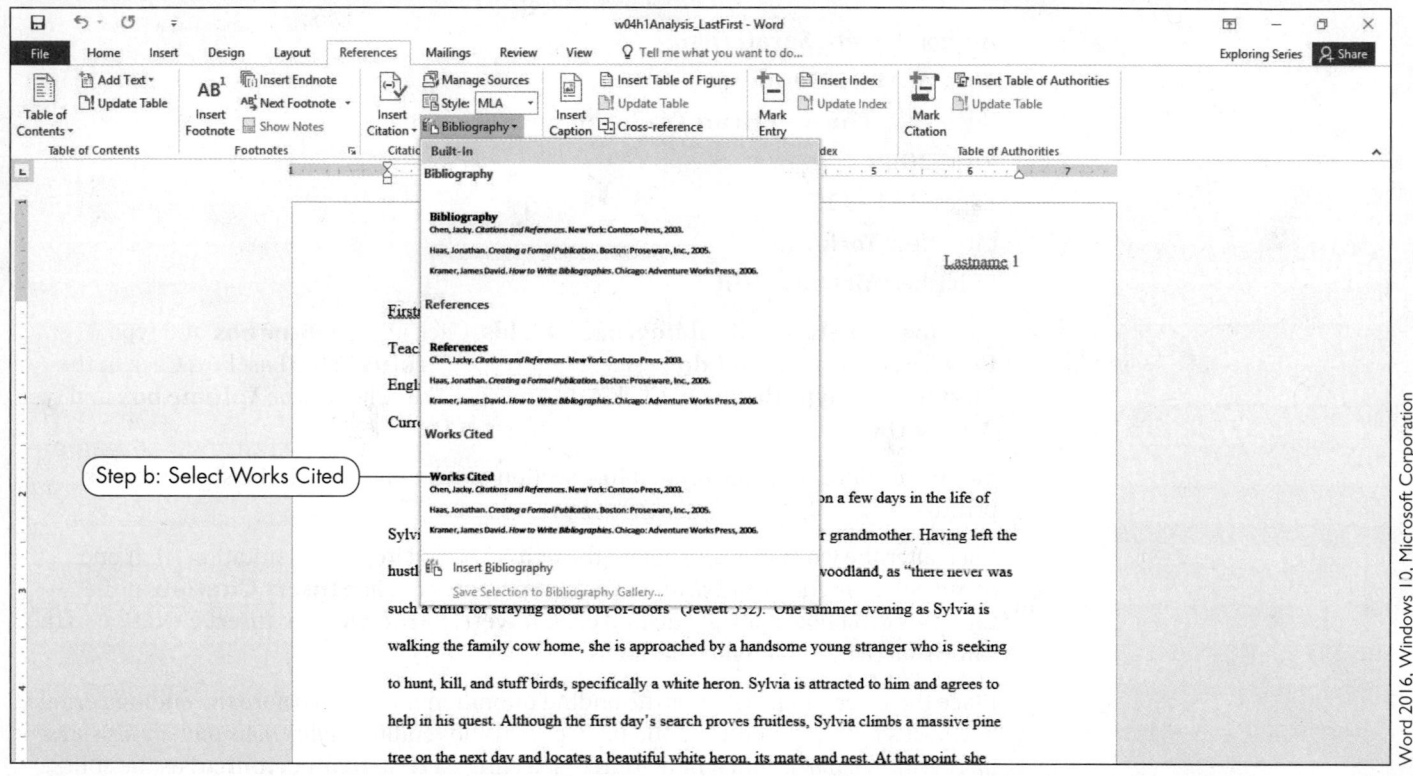

FIGURE 4.11 Create a Bibliography

a. Click **Manage Sources**.

Note that the sources you created in the previous step are shown in the Master List and the Current List. They are available for use in other documents, as well as in the current document.

> **TROUBLESHOOTING:** It is possible that sources other than those you just added are also shown in the Master List. The list includes all sources you have included in other documents as well as those in the current document.

b. Click **Close**. Press **Ctrl+End** to move to the end of the document. Press **Ctrl+Enter** to insert a page break. Click **Bibliography** in the Citations & Bibliography group and click **Works Cited**.

A bibliography is always included as a separate page at the end of the document. Therefore, you insert a page break before adding the bibliography. The bibliography includes the heading Works Cited. The two sources you used in your analysis are listed, although you may have to scroll up to see them.

c. Drag to select all text on the Works Cited page, including the heading Works Cited and all sources. Change the line spacing to **2.0** (or double), the paragraph spacing Before and After to **0**, and the font to **Times New Roman 12 pt**. Select the Works Cited heading, remove the bold format, and center the line.

The Works Cited page adheres to MLA writing style guidelines.

d. Save and close the document. Leave Word open for the next step. You will submit this file to your instructor at the end of the last Hands-On Exercise.

STEP 3 ›› CREATE AND MODIFY FOOTNOTES

You are a business major enrolled in a business management class. As a final project, you have prepared a case analysis of a fictional airline. Due to the large amount of statistical data included, you expect to use footnotes to provide additional clarification. Because footnotes and endnotes are mutually exclusive—you only use one or the other in a single paper—you will not use endnotes. However, you know that the way in which endnotes and footnotes are added is very similar. Refer to Figure 4.12 as you complete Step 3.

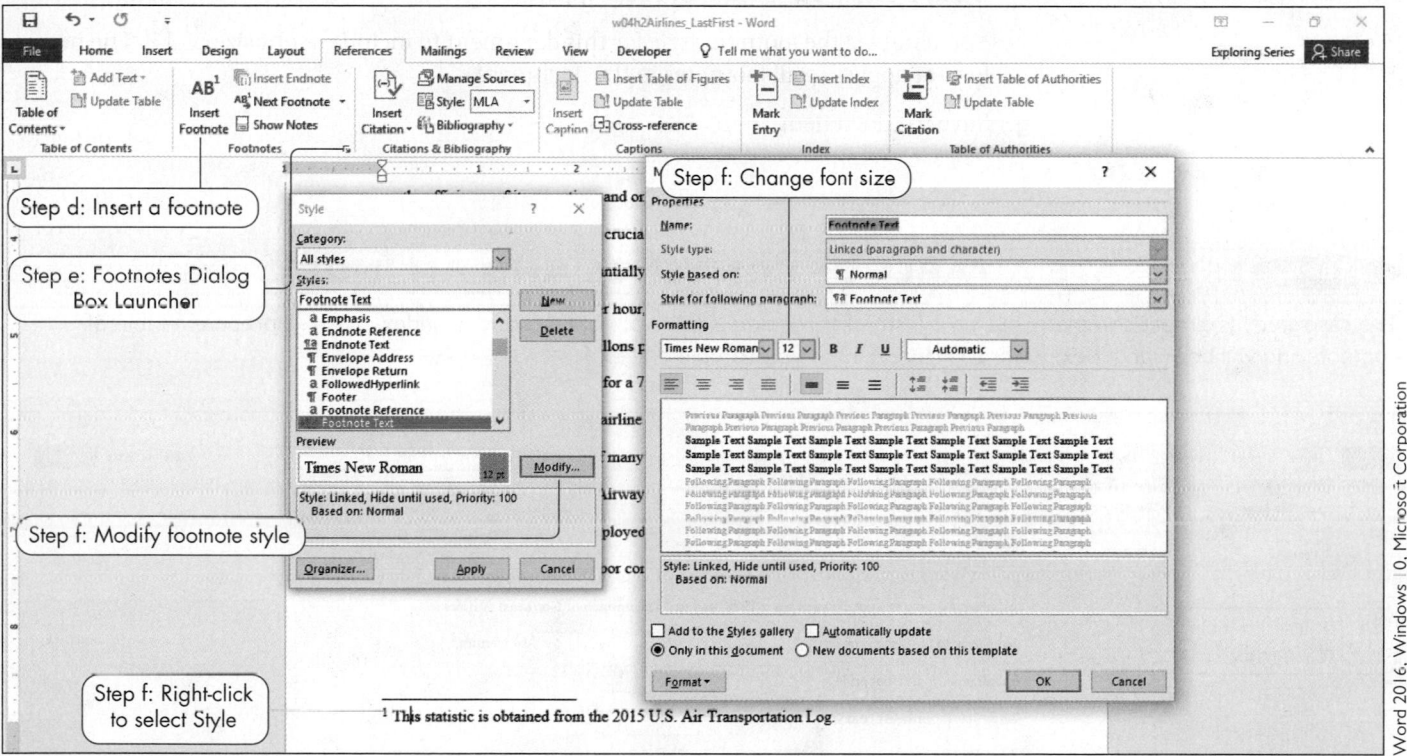

FIGURE 4.12 Modify Footnotes

a. Open *w04h1Airlines* and save it as **w04h1Airlines_LastFirst**.

b. Click the **Select arrow** in the Editing group on the Home tab, click **Select All**, and then apply the following formatting:

- Font is **Times New Roman** at **12** pt size.
- Line spacing is **2.0** (or double).
- Paragraph spacing Before and After is **0**.
- Alignment is **left** aligned.

c. Deselect the text.

d. Click **Find** in the Editing group. The Navigation Pane opens on the left. Type **200 million** in the Search box and press **Enter**. Click after the period (ending the sentence in *$200 million*), which is shown highlighted. Close the Navigation Pane. Click the **References tab** and click **Insert Footnote** in the Footnotes group. Type **This statistic is obtained from the 2015 U.S. Air Transportation Log.** (include the period).

You insert a footnote, numbered with a superscript, further clarifying the information stated.

e. Scroll to page 4 and place the insertion point after the period ending the first paragraph (ending in *for over 34 years*). Click the **Footnotes Dialog Box Launcher** and click **Insert**. Type **Competitors to Northeast have proven slightly less profitable.** (include the period).

You insert another footnote, numbered sequentially after the first footnote. Using the Footnote and Endnote dialog box, you have options to specify various choices, including numbering and formatting.

f. Right-click the footnote at the bottom of page 4 and click **Style**. Click **Modify**. Change the font size to **12**. Click **OK**. Click **Apply**.

You changed the footnote style for this document to include a font size of 12. The new format applies to all footnotes in the document.

g. Save the document.

STEP 4 ›› **CREATE A TABLE OF CONTENTS AND AN INDEX**

The case study is almost complete, but your instructor requires a table of contents and an index. You will prepare a table of contents and will begin an index. Refer to Figure 4.13 as you complete Step 4.

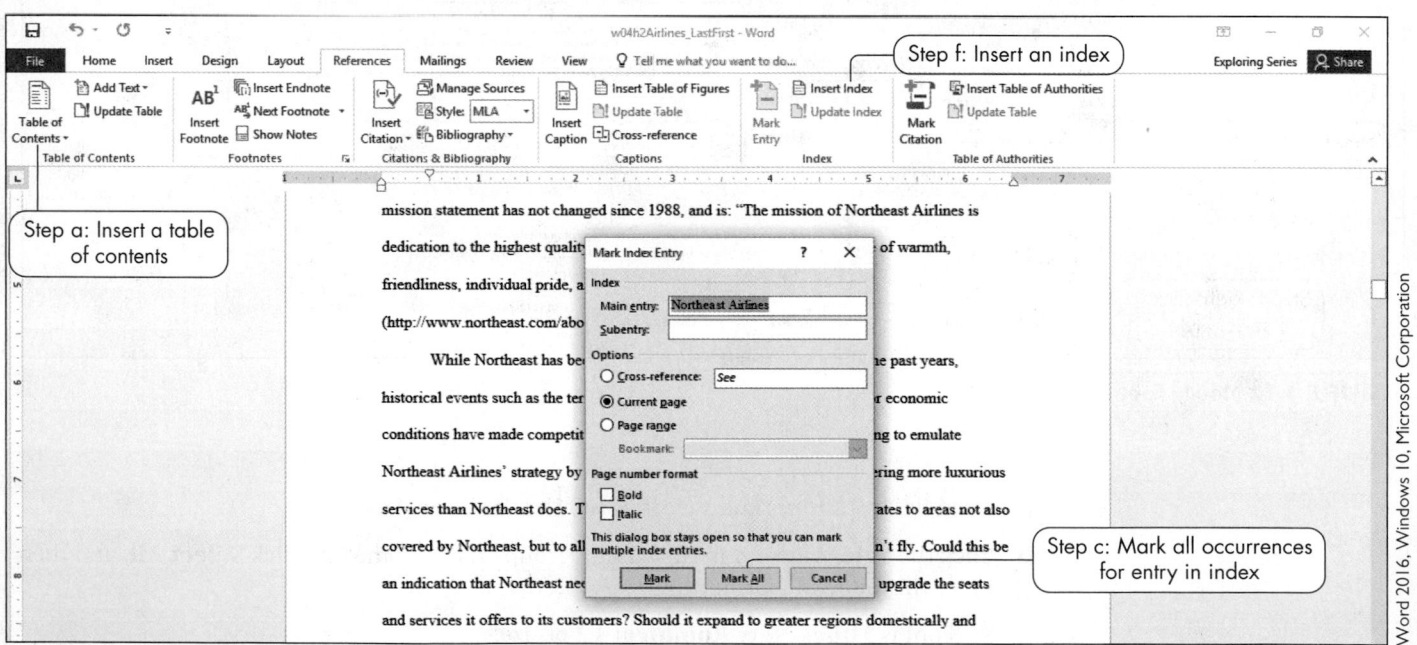

FIGURE 4.13 Create a Table of Contents and Index

a. Press **Ctrl+Home** to move to the beginning of the document. Press **Ctrl+Enter** to insert a page break. Move the insertion point to the beginning of the new page and press **Enter** twice. Click the **References tab**, and click **Table of Contents** in the Table of Contents group. Select **Automatic Table 2**.

You inserted a table of contents comprising headings and page numbers from the report.

b. Point to the **Situational Analysis link** in the Table of Contents, and press **Ctrl+Click** to move to that section of the document. Change the Situational Analysis heading to **Data Analysis**. Press **Ctrl+Home** to move to the beginning of the document and ensure that the table of contents is selected. Click **Update Table** at the top-left corner of the table. Click **Update entire table**. Click **OK**.

You changed the wording of a heading in the report. After updating the table of contents, the new wording is also included there.

c. Point to the **Problem Statement link** in the Table of Contents, and press **Ctrl+Click** to move to that section of the document. Select **Northeast Airlines** in the first sentence of the first body paragraph. Click **Mark Entry** in the Index group, click **Mark All** in the Mark Index Entry dialog box, and then click **Close**.

You have marked the phrase Northeast Airlines for inclusion in the index. By selecting Mark All, you have instructed Word to include a page reference to the phrase wherever it occurs in the document.

d. Select the word **Northeast** in the sentence that begins *Northeast operates solely Boeing 737s* in the same paragraph. Click **Mark Entry** in the Index group. Select **Cross-reference** and type **Northeast Airlines** beside the word *See*. Click **Mark**. Click **Close**.

Because you refer to Northeast Airlines throughout the document as either Northeast Airlines or Northeast, you will cross-reference the term so that it appears appropriately in the index.

e. Scroll to page 4 and mark the first word on the page, **Code-sharing**, as an index entry, making sure to mark all occurrences.

f. Press **Ctrl+End** to go to the end of the document and insert a page break. Ensure the insertion point is at the top of the new blank page.

g. Click **Insert Index** in the Index group. Click **OK** to accept all default settings and insert the index.

You inserted an index comprising the three terms you marked earlier. A complete index would most likely consist of many more terms, with all terms referenced to pages in the document.

h. Save the document.

As a final touch, you create a cover page with information related to the report title, your name, the course number, and the current date. Refer to Figure 4.14 as you complete Step 5.

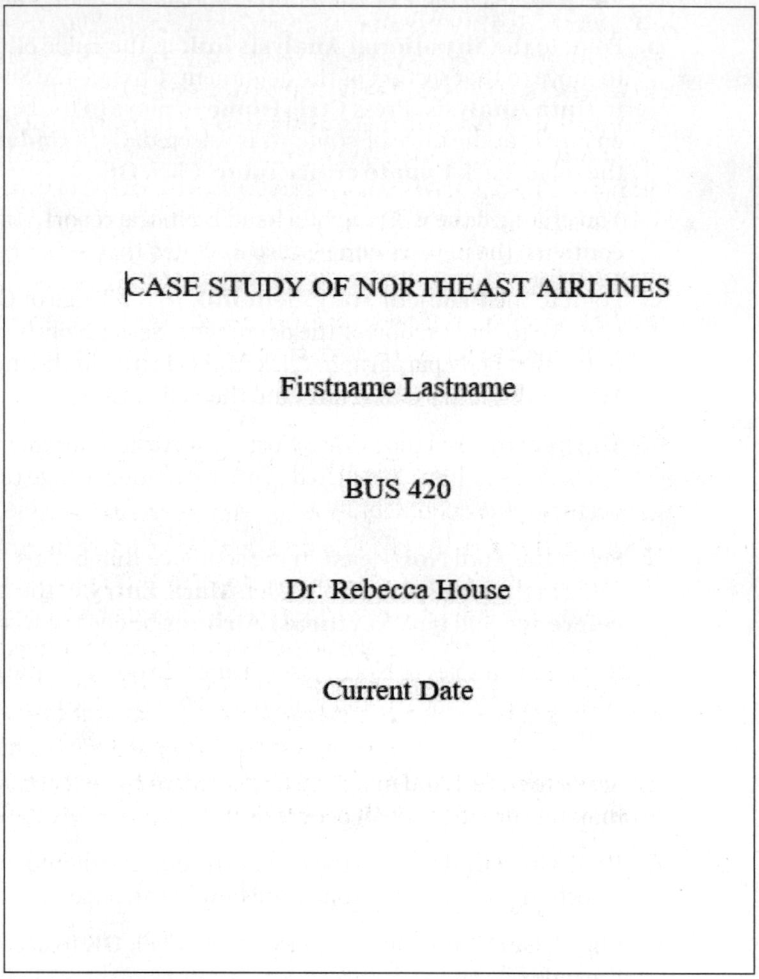

CASE STUDY OF NORTHEAST AIRLINES

Firstname Lastname

BUS 420

Dr. Rebecca House

Current Date

Word 2016, Windows 10, Microsoft Corporation

FIGURE 4.14 Create a Cover Page

a. Insert a page break at the beginning of the document and place the insertion point at the top of the new blank page. Click the **Home tab** and click **Center alignment** in the Paragraph group. Change the font size to **16 pt** and font color to **Black, Text 1**.

b. Type **CASE STUDY OF NORTHEAST AIRLINES**, and click **Numbering** to remove the numbered list. Press **Enter** three times. Click **Numbering**. Type your first and last names. Press **Enter** three times. Type **BUS 420**. Press **Enter** three times. Type **Dr. Rebecca House**. Press **Enter** three times. Type the current date. Ensure that text on the cover page is neither bold nor italicized.

Although Word provides many more colorful choices of cover pages, you design a more conservative cover page to accompany this business report.

c. Click the **Layout tab** and click the **Page Setup Dialog Box Launcher**. Click the **Layout tab**. Click the **Vertical Alignment arrow** and click **Center**. Click **OK**.

You centered the cover page vertically.

d. Click the **View tab** and click **One Page**.

The cover page is centered vertically on the page.

e. Save and close the file. You will submit this file to your instructor at the end of the last Hands-On Exercise.

Document Tracking

Whether in a college class or in the workplace, it is likely that you will seek feedback from others or that you will collaborate with others on the completion of a project. Word has a feature called *Markup* to help you customize how tracked changes are displayed in a document. Word's approach to group editing makes it easy to track changes and review any comments that have been made. Documents are often saved in PDF format to share with others. *PDF (Portable Document Format)* is a file format that captures all of the elements of a page and stores them electronically. Especially useful for documents like magazine articles, brochures, and flyers, PDF format accurately represents all page elements, including graphics and text effects. Using Microsoft Word, you can now convert a PDF document into a Word document and edit the content.

In this section, you will explore reviewing documents, adding and replying to comments in the process. As you track changes in a document, you will learn to control the level of detail that shows, and you can accept or reject changes made by others. Finally, you will explore ways that Word enables you to work with PDF documents.

Reviewing a Document

In today's organizational environment, teams of people with diverse backgrounds, skills, and knowledge prepare documents. Team members work together while planning, developing, writing, and editing important documents. A large part of that process is reviewing work begun or submitted by others. No doubt you have focused on a document so completely that you easily overlooked obvious mistakes or alternative wording. A reviewer, bringing a fresh perspective, can often catch mistakes, perhaps even suggest ways to improve readability. In reviewing a document, you will most often find ways to change wording or otherwise edit the format, and you might find an opportunity to provide *comments* related to the content. Although comments are most often directed to the attention of another author or editor, you can even include comments to remind yourself of a necessary action.

Use Markup

There are four markup views: Simple Markup, All Markup, No Markup, and Original. Word provides a clutter-free way to make comments, reply to comments, and track changes that might have been made to a document by others during a review process. Using *Simple Markup* (see Figure 4.15), you can minimize the clutter of multiple comments, viewing only those that you choose. The same document with the same comments, shown in Simple Markup, is much less cluttered. A small balloon, called the *comment balloon*, displays on the right side of a paragraph in which a comment has been made and provides access to the comment. To see a comment in Simple Markup, click the Show Comments toggle button in the Comments group or click the comment balloon. Also, you will not see changes in Simple Markup, even with Track Changes toggled on. Instead, a red vertical bar on the left side of a modified paragraph in which edits have been made alerts a reader to the existence of edits. Click the red bar (refer to Figure 4.16) to show the changes. Click the bar again to remove them from view.

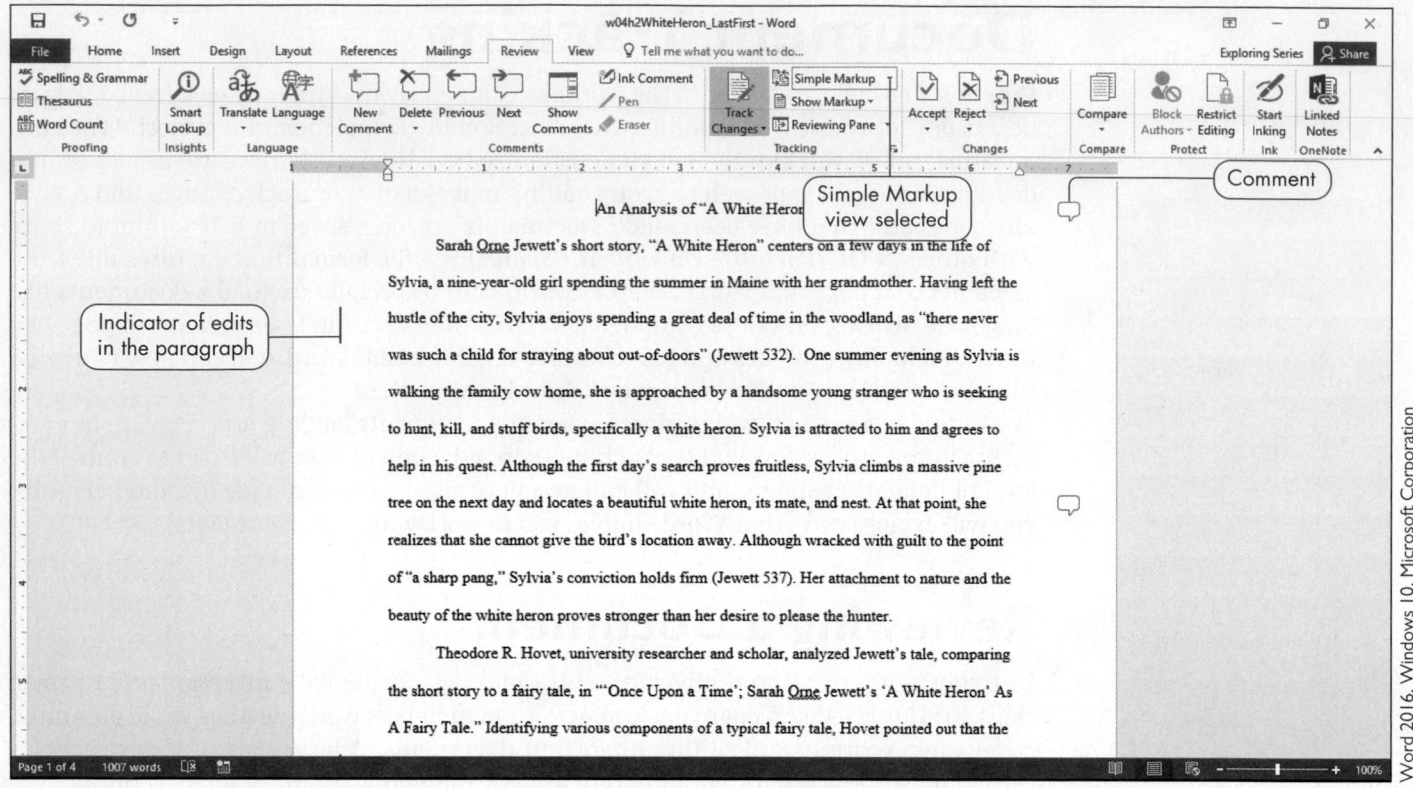

FIGURE 4.15 Simple Markup View

The document in Figure 4.16 is shown with All Markup in the Tracking group selected. This view shows the final version of the document with all the markups and comments. Other options for markup views are No Markup and Original. The No Markup option displays the final version of the document and does not show any of the markups or comments. It enables you to preview the final version of the document before accepting the changes. For a completely clean view of a document, temporarily hiding all comments and revisions, click the Markup arrow in the Tracking group on the Review tab and click No Markup. Although no revisions or comments show, keep in mind that they are only hidden. To remove them permanently, you have to accept or reject all changes. The Original view shows the original version of the document and hides all markups.

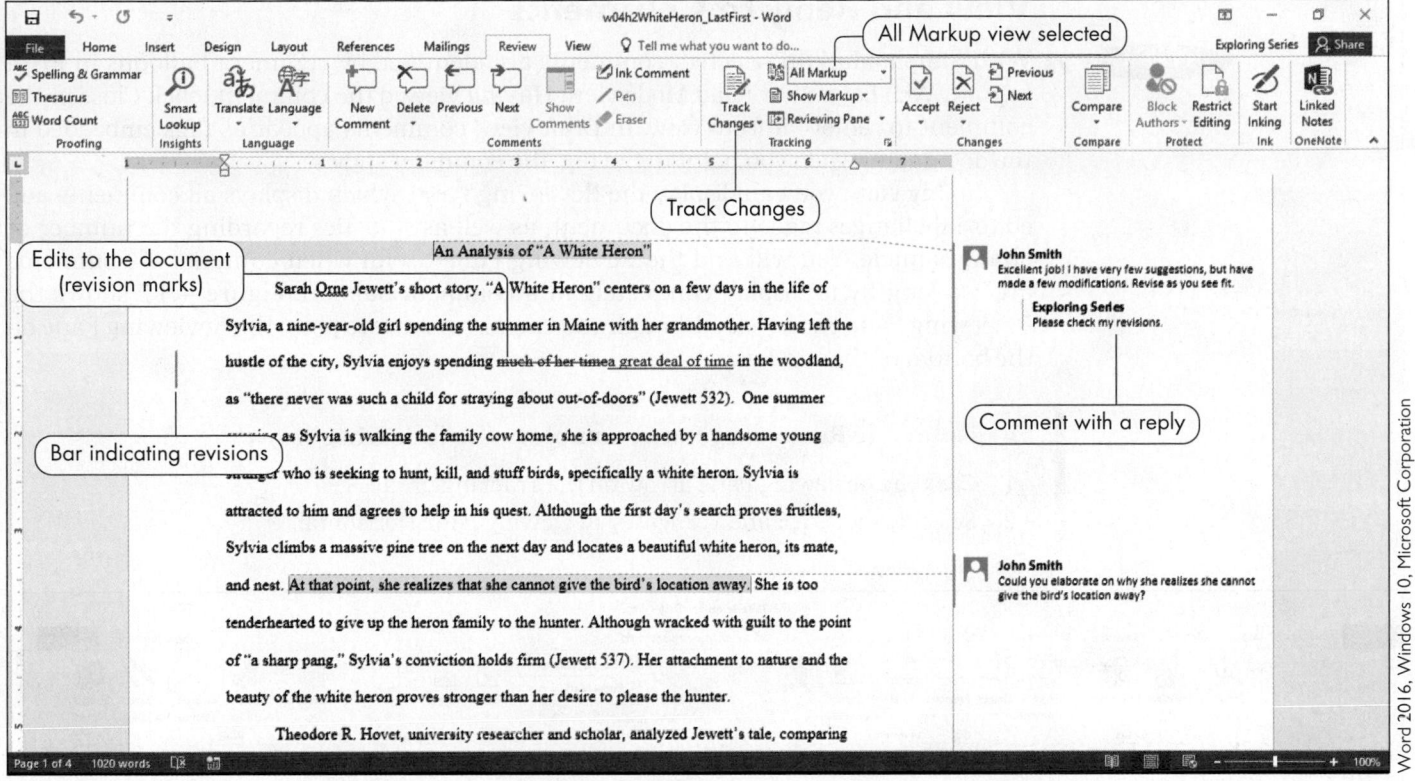

FIGURE 4.16 All Markup View

> **To use any of the Markup options, complete the following steps:**
>
> 1. Click the Review tab.
> 2. Click the Display for Review arrow in the Tracking group.
> 3. Point to one of the four options and click it.

Add a Comment

Besides changing the markup view and tracking changes, the Review tab includes options related to adding and replying to comments. You might choose to add a comment in Simple Markup view, which is much less cluttered.

> **To add a comment, complete the following steps:**
>
> 1. Click in the document or select a word or phrase you want to comment.
> 2. Click New Comment in the Comments group on the Review tab.
> 3. Type a comment in the subsequent comment balloons. You will be identified as the author in the comment balloon, with the date and time of the comment.

If you do not select anything prior to clicking New Comment, Word assigns the comment to the word or object closest to the insertion point.

TIP: CONFIRMING THE USER NAME

Before you use the Comments feature, make sure your name appears as you want it to display in any comments. To do so, click the File tab and click Options. In the General section, confirm that your name and initials display as the user. Word uses that information to identify the person who uses collaboration tools, such as Comments. If you are in a lab environment, you might not have permission to modify settings or change the user name; however, you should be able to change those settings on a home computer.

View and Reply to Comments

STEP 1 With Simple Markup selected, comments are identified by comment balloons in Print Layout, Web Layout, or Read Mode view. Having viewed the comment, click Close in the comment to remove it from view. In Draft view, comments appear as tags embedded in the document; when you point to the tag, the comment shows.

In any view, you can display the Reviewing Pane, which displays all comments and editorial changes made to the document, as well as statistics regarding the number of changes made. You will find the Reviewing Pane useful when contents of comments are too lengthy to display completely in a comment balloon. Figure 4.17 shows the Reviewing Pane on the left, although you can also choose to place the Reviewing Pane on the bottom of the window.

> **To display the Reviewing Pane, complete the following steps:**
>
> 1. Click the Reviewing Pane arrow on the Tracking group.
> 2. Select Reviewing Pane Vertical or Reviewing Pane Horizontal.

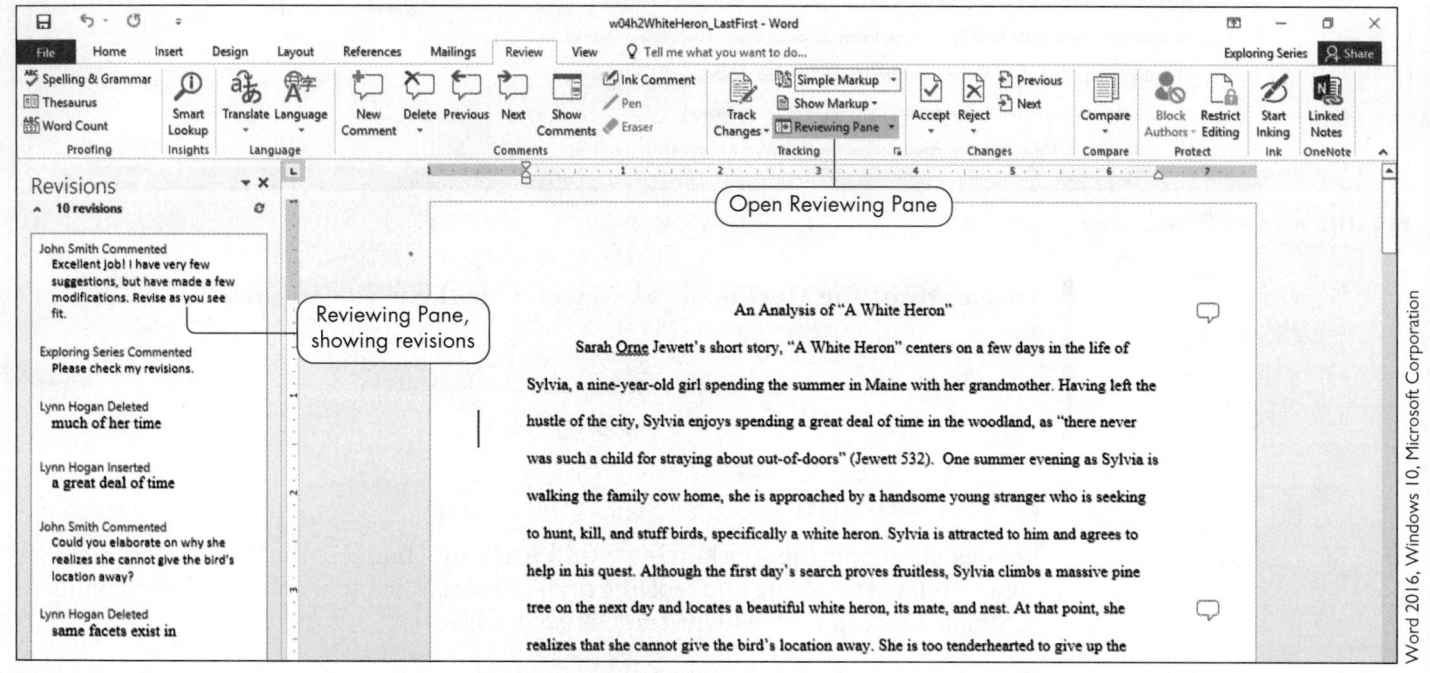

FIGURE 4.17 Reviewing Pane

Managing a large number of comments in a document could become overwhelming. If you have to create another comment to reply to a comment, you will complicate the display even more. Word addresses that problem with a feature that enables you to reply to a comment within the original comment. Click a balloon to view a comment, and click Reply 🔄 (see Figure 4.18) to type a response. The response will be placed in the original comment's comment balloon. All replies to original comments are indented beneath the original, with the commenter identified by name, which makes it easy to follow the progression of a comment through its replies, if any.

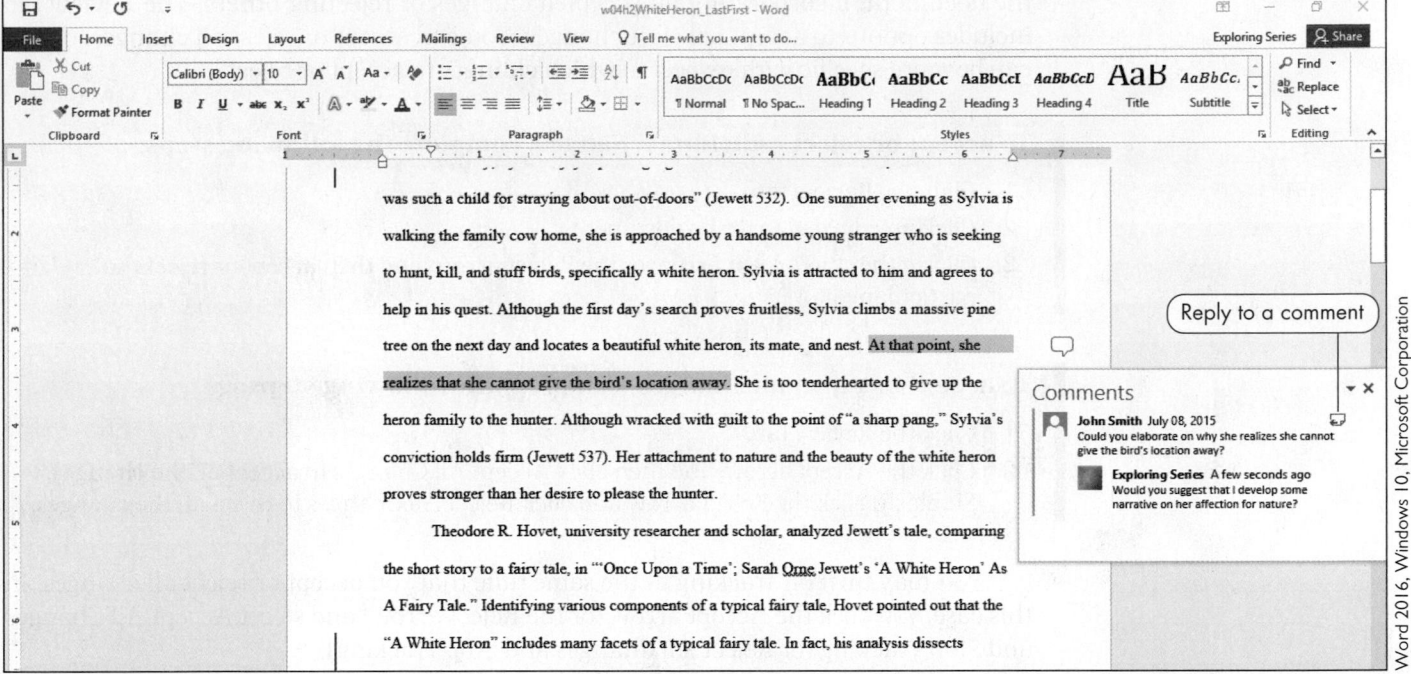

was such a child for straying about out-of-doors" (Jewett 532). One summer evening as Sylvia is walking the family cow home, she is approached by a handsome young stranger who is seeking to hunt, kill, and stuff birds, specifically a white heron. Sylvia is attracted to him and agrees to help in his quest. Although the first day's search proves fruitless, Sylvia climbs a massive pine tree on the next day and locates a beautiful white heron, its mate, and nest. At that point, she realizes that she cannot give the bird's location away. She is too tenderhearted to give up the heron family to the hunter. Although wracked with guilt to the point of "a sharp pang," Sylvia's conviction holds firm (Jewett 537). Her attachment to nature and the beauty of the white heron proves stronger than her desire to please the hunter.

Theodore R. Hovet, university researcher and scholar, analyzed Jewett's tale, comparing the short story to a fairy tale, in "'Once Upon a Time'; Sarah Orne Jewett's 'A White Heron' As A Fairy Tale." Identifying various components of a typical fairy tale, Hovet pointed out that the "A White Heron" includes many facets of a typical fairy tale. In fact, his analysis dissects

FIGURE 4.18 Reply to a Comment

When a comment has been addressed, it may no longer be relevant to the review process, and you might want to prohibit any further replies to the original comment. To deactivate a comment, right-click the open comment and select Mark Comment Done. Although the balloon remains in Simple Markup, the comment is grayed out when you click the balloon, so it is evident that it has been addressed. Further replies to the original comment are prohibited.

Tracking Changes

STEP 3 ▶▶ Whether you work individually or with a group, you can monitor any revisions you make to a document. The *Track Changes* feature keeps track of all additions, deletions, and formatting changes made to the document. Click Track Changes (refer to Figure 4.15) to track all changes made to a document. Click it again to toggle the feature off so that changes are no longer tracked. Track Changes is particularly useful in situations in which a document must be reviewed by several people—each of whom can offer suggestions or change parts of the document—and then returned to one person who will finalize the document.

Use Track Changes

When Track Changes is not active, any change you make to a document is untraceable, and no one will know what you change unless he or she compares your revised document with the previous version. When Track Changes is active, it applies *revision marks*, which indicate where a person added, deleted, or formatted text. In addition, a bar displays on the left side of any paragraph in which edits have occurred (refer to Figure 4.15).

Accept and Reject Changes

As you complete revision on a document, you will review all comments and act on them or otherwise reply to the reviewer. You also have the opportunity to view all edits, including changes in wording and formatting. At that point, you will produce a clean copy of the document, incorporating all accepted changes or rejecting others. The Review tab includes options to accept or reject changes. You can accept or reject all changes, or you can be more specific with respect to which changes to accept or reject.

To accept or reject individual changes, complete the following steps:

1. Click the Review tab.
2. Click an edited area in the document.
3. Click either the Accept arrow or the Reject arrow, and then accept or reject that particular edit.

To accept or reject all changes, complete the following steps:

1. Click the Review tab.
2. Click the Accept arrow, and then click Accept All Changes to accept all the changes. Similarly, click the Reject arrow and click Reject All Changes to reject all the changes.

You may turn off tracking at the same time that you accept or reject all changes. In this case, you click the Accept arrow (or the Reject arrow) and select Accept All Changes and Stop Tracking (or Reject All Changes and Stop Tracking).

> **TIP: USING SHOW MARKUP**
> Click Show Markup in the Tracking group on the Review tab to view document revisions organized by the type of revision (such as comments, formatting, insertions, and deletions) as well as by reviewer. You can toggle each selection on or off, so you can view the types of markups that you want to see.

Work with PDF Documents

STEP 2 ›› *PDF Reflow* is a feature that produces editable Word documents from PDF files— documents that retain the intended formatting and page flow of the original PDF document. PDF Reflow seeks to convert recognizable features of a PDF document into items that are native to Word. For example, a table in a PDF document is converted into a table in a Word document so you can use Word's table feature to modify and update the item. Similarly, bulleted lines in a PDF file become bulleted paragraphs in a Word document. Although using PDF Reflow does not always convert every feature flawlessly, the result is usually a close imitation of the original. PDF Reflow is more attuned to converting text than graphics.

To convert a PDF document to Word, complete the following steps:

1. Start Word.
2. Click Open Other Documents, and browse to the folder for the PDF document to open.
3. Click OK if warned that the conversion might take a while.
4. Click OK if warned that your PDF document contains interactive features that are not supported by PDF Reflow.

Within a few seconds, the PDF file opens as a Word document. At that point, you can edit it as you would any Word document.

To save a Word document as a PDF file, complete the following steps:

1. Open a document in Word.
2. Click the File tab, and click Export.
3. Click Create PDF/XPS Document, and click Create PDF/XPS.
4. Navigate to the location where you save your files, rename the file, and ensure that *Open file after publishing* is checked.
5. Click Publish.

The newly created PDF/XPS document will preserve the layout, format fonts, and images of the original Word document. The content of the document can't be changed easily, but you can download free viewers from the Web to view it.

Quick
 Concepts

5. When you reply to a comment, where is your reply placed? *p. 356*

6. In Simple Markup, how can you tell that edits have been made to a paragraph? How can you see the changes that have been made? *p. 353*

7. As you complete a research paper that has been marked up by several reviewers (with Track Changes on), you now want to provide a clean copy. What steps might you follow to do that? *p. 357*

8. Briefly describe the Word feature that converts a PDF file into a Word document so that you can edit the document. *p. 358*

Hands-On Exercises

Watch the Video
for this Hands-On
Exercise!

MyITLab®
HOE2 Training

Skills covered: Use Markup • Add a Comment • View and Reply to Comments • Work with a PDF Document • Use Track Changes • Accept and Reject Changes

2 Document Tracking

Your literature group submitted a draft copy of the analysis of *A White Heron*. Your literature instructor, Mr. Smith, made comments and suggested some additional editing before the paper is considered complete. Even at this early stage, however, your instructor is very pleased with your group's initial analysis. In fact, he suggested that you prepare to submit the paper to the campus Phi Kappa Phi Honor Society for judging in a writing contest. He will provide a copy of the entry form in PDF format so you can have it on hand when you submit the paper. At this point, you will review his comments and changes and act on his suggestions.

STEP 1 ❯❯ USE MARKUP AND ADD, VIEW, AND REPLY TO COMMENTS

Your instructor returned to you an electronic copy of the analysis with a few comments and edits. You will review the suggestions, make a few changes, and save the document for final review and group collaboration later. Refer to Figure 4.19 as you complete Step 1.

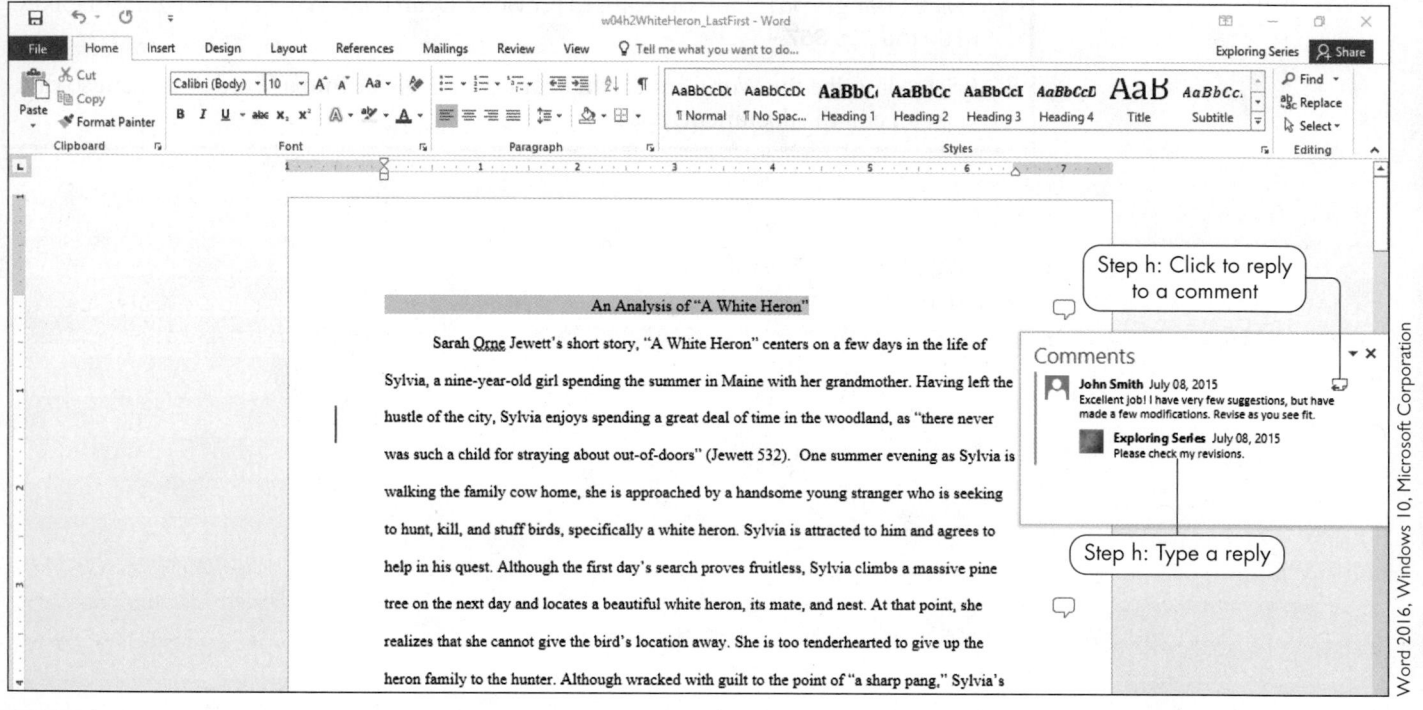

FIGURE 4.19 Work with Comments

a. Open *w04h2WhiteHeron* and save it as **w04h2WhiteHeron_LastFirst**.

b. Click the **Review tab**, click the **Simple Markup arrow** in the Tracking group, and then click **All Markup**. Review the comments made by your instructor, as well as the tracked edits in the document. Click the **All Markup arrow** in the Tracking group and click **Simple Markup** to return to an uncluttered view.

> **TROUBLESHOOTING:** It is possible that All Markup is selected as the markup view before you begin this exercise. In that case, review the comments and edits, click the All Markup arrow, and then click Simple Markup. Continue to Step c.

c. Click the **Reviewing Pane arrow** in the Tracking group and click **Reviewing Pane Vertical**. Scroll through the comments and edits shown in the Reviewing Pane. Close the Reviewing Pane (titled Revisions).

d. Click the **vertical red bar** on the left side of the first body paragraph to view all edits and comments to be displayed in All Markup view. Click the bar again to hide the tracked changes and return to Simple Markup view. Point to the **first comment balloon** on the right of the report title and note the highlighted text *See Comments*. Click the **comment balloon** to view the comment. Click the **comment balloon** again to close the comment.

e. Click the **third comment balloon** on the first page and note that you need to add a citation. Click **Close** in the markup balloon to close it. Click after the quotation mark and before the period in the sentence in the last paragraph on the first page (ending with *for the course of action*). Add a new source for the following book:

Type of Source: **Book Section**
Author: **Propp, Vladimir**
Title: **Morphology of a Folk Tale**
Year: **1994**
City: **New York**
Publisher: **Anniston**

f. Scroll to the end of the document and click to select the **Works Cited field**. Click **Update Citations and Bibliography**.

You added a new source and updated the Works Cited page to include the newly added source.

g. Scroll to page 1 and click the **second comment balloon** to view the comment. Close the markup balloon. Click before the word *Although* in the sentence in the first body paragraph (that begins with *Although wracked with guilt*). Type **She is too tenderhearted to give up the heron family to the hunter.** (include the period). Press **Spacebar**.

h. Click the **first comment** on page 1, point to the comment text, and click **Reply** (see Figure 4.18) at the right side of the instructor name. Type **Please check my revisions.** (include the period). Close the comment.

i. Save and close the document. Keep Word open for the next step.

STEP 2 ›› **WORK WITH A PDF DOCUMENT**

You are ready to finalize the paper, and your instructor has let you know that you must include an entry form with the submission. You are not on campus, so your instructor has emailed the entry form as a PDF document. You will convert the form to Word and then complete it with your name and report information. You will then save it as a PDF document for later submission. Refer to Figure 4.20 as you complete Step 2.

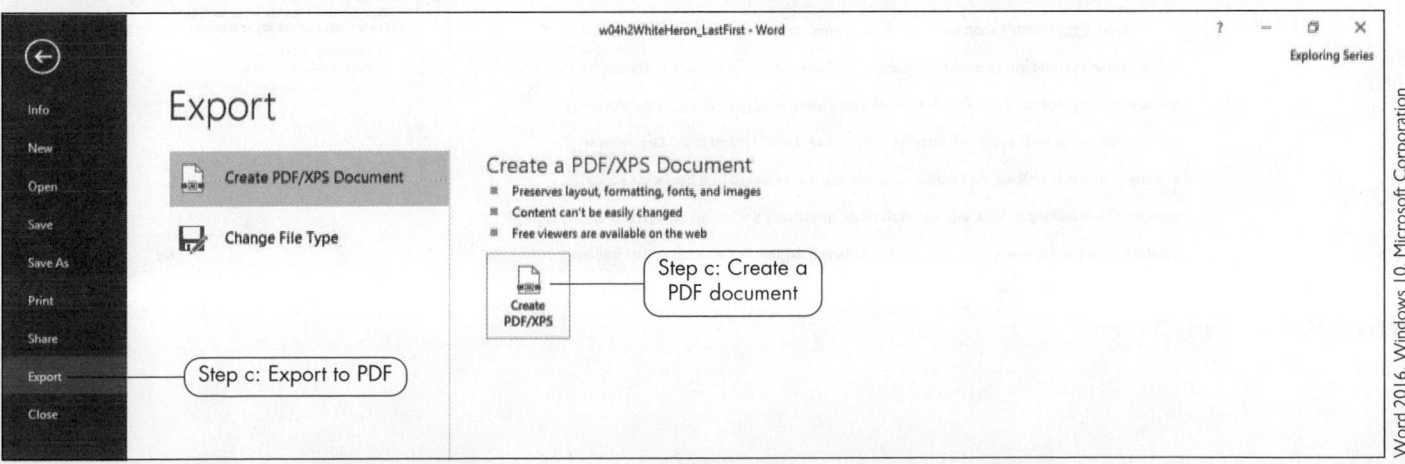

FIGURE 4.20 Work with a PDF Document

a. Click the **File tab** and click **Open**. Change the type of files to **PDF Files (*.PDF)**. Open *w04h2Entry* from your student files. Click **OK** if warned that the conversion might take a while.

b. Click after **Date** and type today's date. Complete the remaining information, including your name, instructor's name, college class, email, and report title, **An Analysis of "A White Heron"**.

PDF Reflow has converted the original PDF version of the entry form and opened it in Word so you can modify it.

> **TROUBLESHOOTING:** If the document opened as an Adobe PDF file instead of as a Word document, you opened the file from File Explorer. Instead, you should open the document from within Word when you click the File tab and click Open.

c. Click the **File tab** and click **Export**. Click **Create PDF/XPS Document**, and click **Create PDF/XPS**. Navigate to the location where you save your assignments, rename the file as **w04h2Entry_LastFirst**, and ensure that *Open file after publishing* is checked. Click **Publish**.

You saved the entry form you completed in Word as a PDF file for later submission with the entry.

d. Close the document after the PDF version of the completed entry form is displayed. Close the Word version of the entry form without saving it. You will submit the w04h2Entry_LastFirst.pdf file to your instructor at the end of the last Hands-On Exercise.

STEP 3 ❱❱ **USE TRACK CHANGES AND ACCEPT AND REJECT CHANGES**

You are ready to submit the paper, but you must first accept or reject changes and remove all comments. Refer to Figure 4.21 as you complete Step 3.

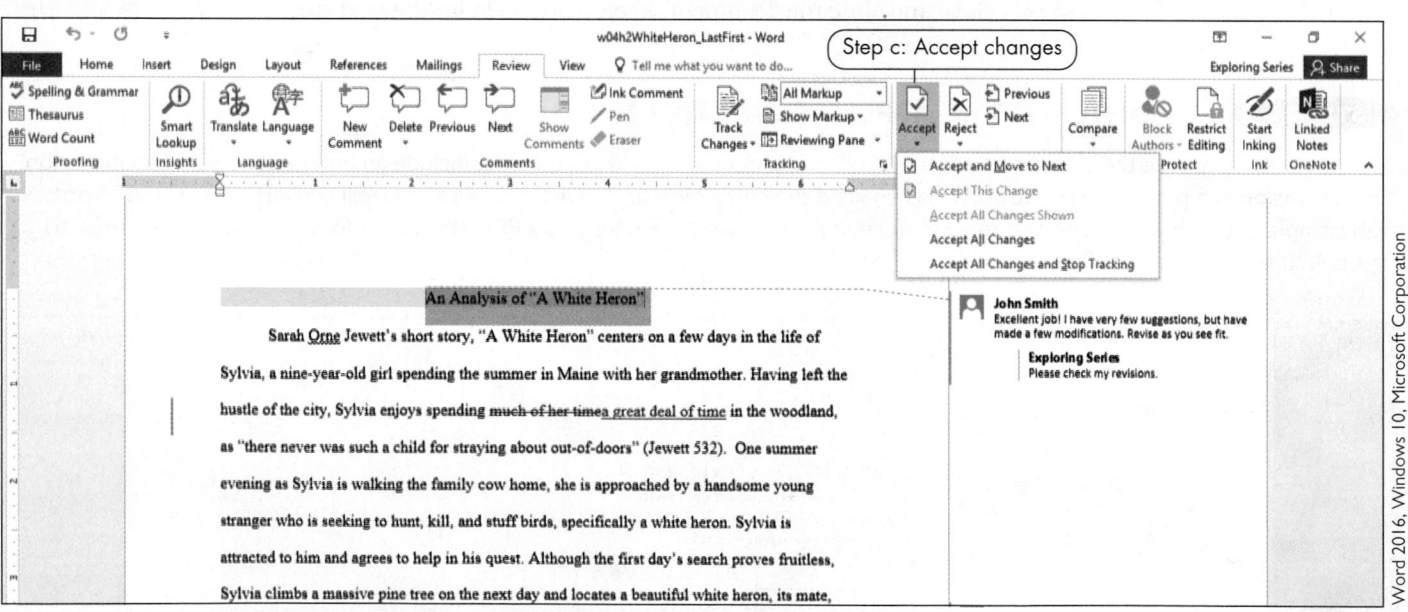

FIGURE 4.21 Track Changes

a. Open *w04h2WhiteHeron_LastFirst*. Click the **Review tab** and click **All Markup**.

b. Click anywhere in the sentence you added on the first page (*She is too tenderhearted to give up the heron family to the hunter*). Click the **Reject arrow** in the Changes group and click **Reject Change**.

You decide the additional sentence is not necessary, so you reject the change you made earlier.

c. Click the **Accept arrow** and click **Accept All Changes and Stop Tracking**. Delete all comments.

You have accepted all remaining changes and deleted all comments. The document is now ready for the group to finalize.

d. Save and close the file. You will submit this file to your instructor at the end of the last Hands-On Exercise.

Online Document Collaboration

With its continuing commitment to incorporate collaboration features, Microsoft is simplifying how individuals in any location can work together in groups to complete projects. The global marketplace and Web 2.0 technologies create a dynamic in which collaboration on projects is the norm, rather than the exception. Marketing proposals, company reports, and all sorts of other documents are often prepared by a group of people working with a shared documents folder, in which all can contribute to the shared documents at any time. Similarly, group projects that are assigned as part of a class requirement can often be completed by sharing documents online for review and completion. Recognizing the proliferation of devices that students and professionals use to collaborate on projects, including personal computers and mobile devices such as smartphones and tablets, the Office 2016 suite has become a complete, cross-platform, cross-device solution for getting work done. Individuals can work from anywhere and on almost any device. The key to such sharing is online accessibility.

In this section, you will learn how to use OneDrive and incorporate OneDrive into File Explorer. You will also learn how to use Word Online. Further, you will explore the various options of sharing your documents and collaborating with your peers using Word 2016 and Word Online. In addition, you will learn to present a document online to an audience.

Using OneDrive and Word Online

By default, Word facilitates document sharing by saving documents to **OneDrive**, which is a Web-based storage site and sharing utility. Saving to OneDrive is sometimes referred to as "saving to the cloud," because a document saved in that way is available online (in the cloud).

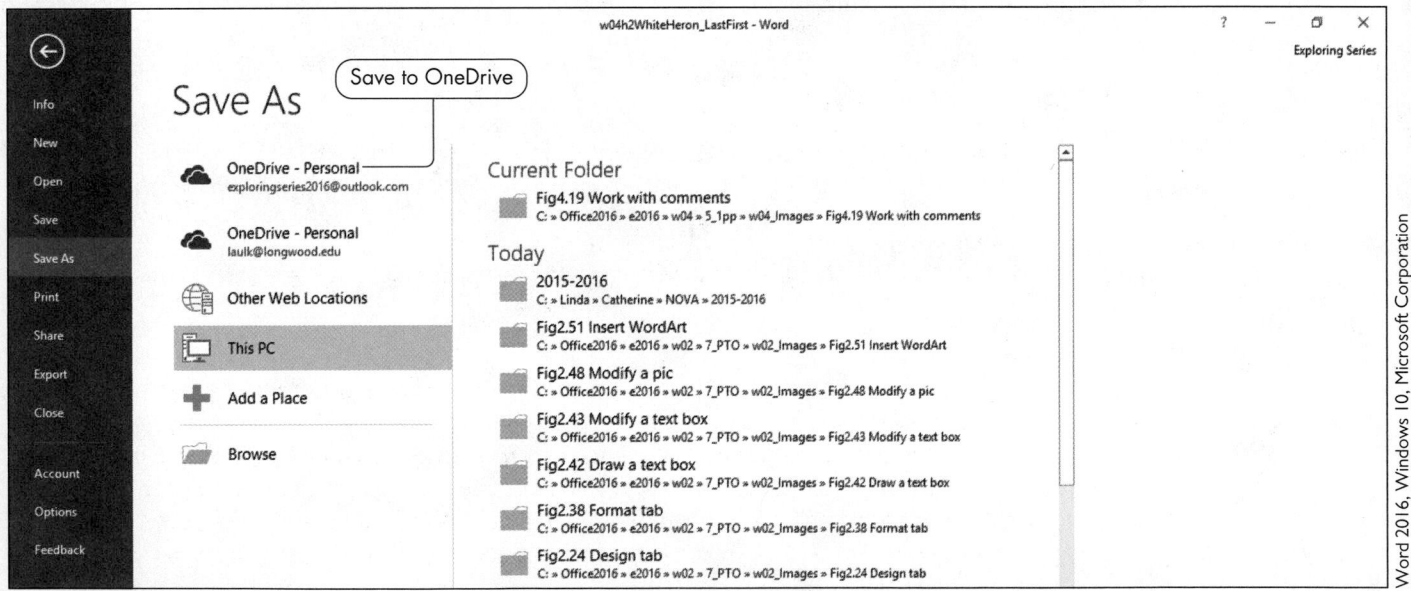

FIGURE 4.22 Save to OneDrive

You can use OneDrive to share documents with others, facilitating online collaboration in the production of documents and the completion of projects, or as a repository for backup copies of files. With lots of free storage made available to users, OneDrive is a viable storage alternative to a local drive. In fact, it is often used in lieu of a flash drive because it makes files available from any Internet-connected location.

Use OneDrive

STEP 1 ›› It would be good practice to use OneDrive as a storage location so that you can retrieve documents from any Internet-connected device and share documents with others. You may also want to use OneDrive as a location for backing up documents. For example, you might save an important document on your hard drive and upload it to OneDrive, or save it to OneDrive directly as a backup. If you grant access, others can view and edit the document. As you edit the local copy of the document or as co-authors edit the OneDrive copy, both copies of the same document are synchronized so that they are identical.

To save a Word document to OneDrive, complete the following steps:

1. Click the File tab and click Save As.
2. Click the OneDrive folder.
3. Create a new folder or navigate to the subfolder in the OneDrive folder.
4. Click Save.

To upload a file to OneDrive, complete the following steps:

1. Go to OneDrive.com.
2. Sign in using your Microsoft login information (or click Sign up now to create a new account).
3. Follow all prompts to upload the file, creating a new OneDrive folder if desired.

Use OneDrive with File Explorer

Windows 10 incorporates OneDrive into File Explorer to simplify the process of organizing and managing OneDrive folders (and contents), as well as ensuring that files are synchronized. Because OneDrive is a folder in File Explorer, files and folders can be moved and copied between OneDrive and other storage locations on your computer. In the File Explorer interface, shown in Figure 4.23, you can drag and drop files between folders, including OneDrive. You can also delete and save files to OneDrive as easily as you can from any other folder in File Explorer.

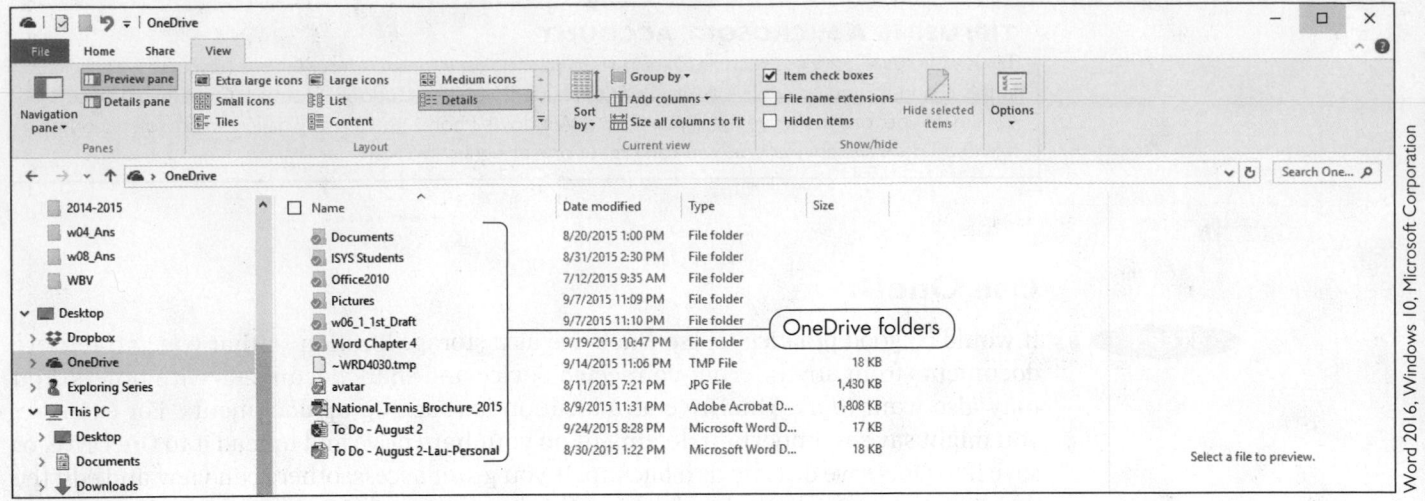

FIGURE 4.23 OneDrive in File Explorer

Everything placed in the OneDrive folder in File Explorer is also made available in OneDrive, with files synchronized whenever changes are made either locally or online. Whenever you add, change, or delete files in one location, files in another location are updated. When co-authors collaborate on a shared OneDrive document, those edits are incorporated into the local copy of the document. With the latest version of OneDrive, you can also select which folders to sync between the online storage and your computer, and which folders to be available online. Using this feature can help manage storage space on your computing device, and save time by only syncing those files that you modify and use most often.

To choose and sync files and folders between OneDrive and File Explorer, complete the following steps:

1. Open File Explorer.
2. Click the OneDrive icon.
3. Right-click any of the folders in OneDrive.
4. Click Choose OneDrive folders to sync.
5. Deselect those folders you do not want to sync and display in File Explorer in the *Sync your OneDrive files to this PC* dialog box. Only checked folders will sync (see Figure 4.24).
6. Click OK to sync the files and folders.

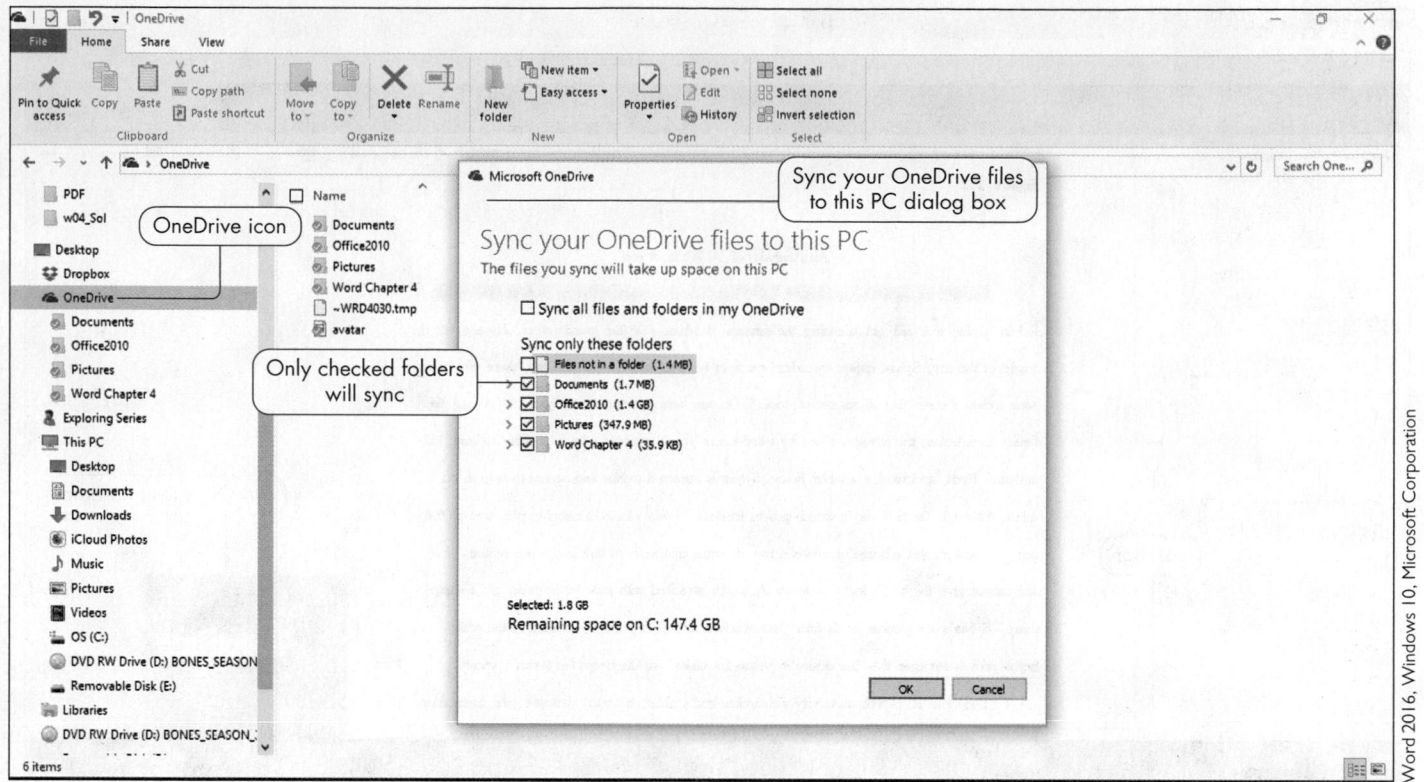

FIGURE 4.24 Choose and Sync Folders between OneDrive and File Explorer

Although you can navigate to the OneDrive folder through File Explorer, Windows provides easy access to the OneDrive folder in the Notification area on the taskbar, as shown in Figure 4.25.

To access OneDrive via the taskbar, complete the following steps:

1. Click the Show hidden icons arrow on the taskbar.
2. Click OneDrive to confirm that it is up to date.
3. Click *Open your OneDrive folder* for immediate access to files saved in OneDrive via the File Explorer.
4. Right-click any of the folders in OneDrive to sync your files and folders locally since they are also available on your computer.
5. Click *Choose OneDrive folders to sync.*
6. Deselect those folders you do not want to sync and display in File Explorer in the *Sync your OneDrive files to this PC* dialog box. Only checked folders will sync (see Figure 4.24).
7. Click OK to sync the files and folders.

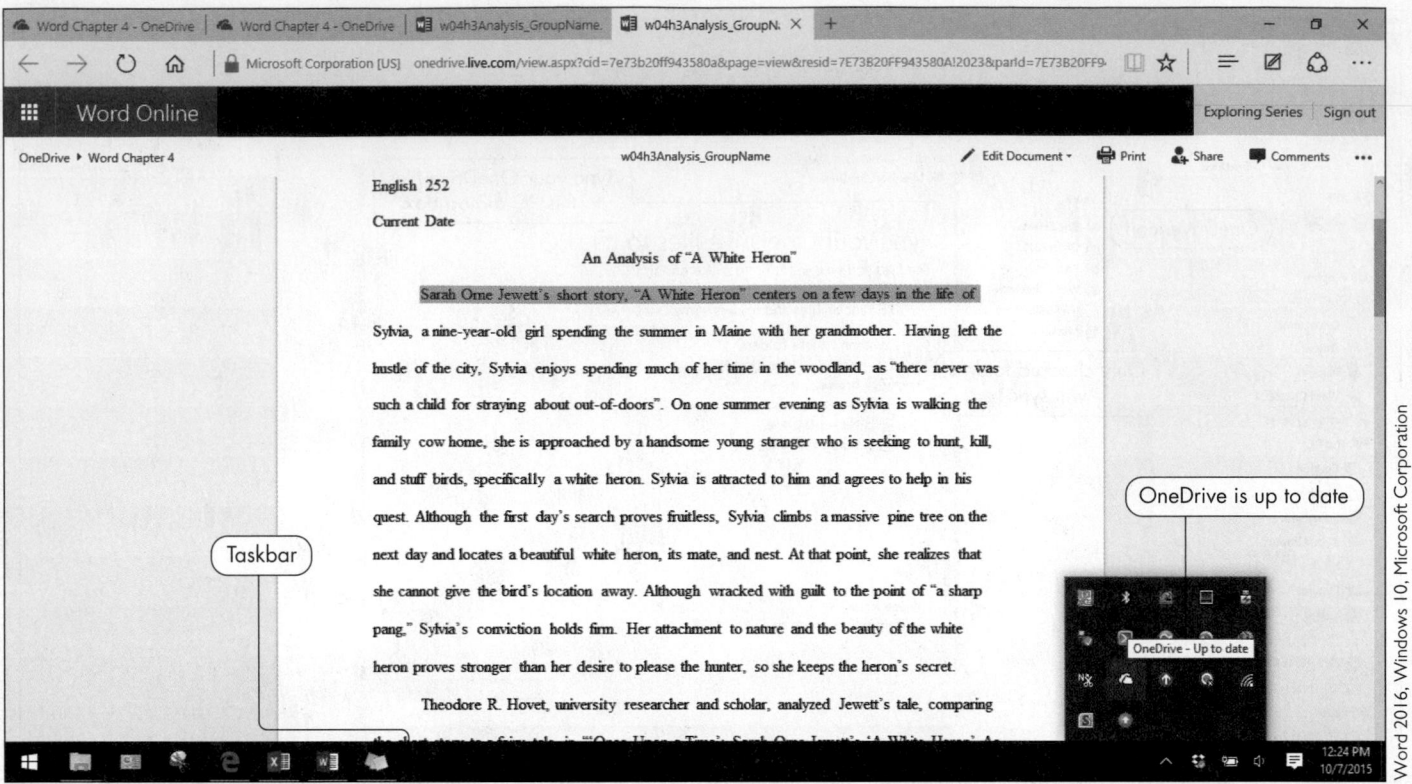

FIGURE 4.25 Access OneDrive via the Taskbar

Use Word Online

Word Online is a Web-based version of Word with sufficient capabilities to enable you to edit and format a document online. As a component of Office Online, which also includes Excel Online, PowerPoint Online, and OneNote Online, Word Online is free and is available to you when you sign in to OneDrive.com to begin a new document or open a document previously saved in OneDrive. The document opens in a browser window with a limited selection of commands. Because it is Web-based, you are not required to install software on your computer to use Word Online. Neither are you required to have purchased a copy of Word 2016. Using Word Online, you can create and edit Word documents from any Internet-connected computer, and across any platform. Word Online enables you to create basic documents and share them with others through a link or email.

> **To create a new document in Word Online, complete the following steps:**
>
> 1. Log in to your Microsoft account at OneDrive.com.
> 2. Click the arrow next to New (see Figure 4.26).
> 3. Click and select Word document.
> 4. Click the default file name, *Document1*, on the title bar and type a file name.
> 5. Type content in the document, and it is automatically saved to OneDrive

When you click the View tab, you will notice that there are two views: Editing and Reading. Editing view enables you to make changes to a document, while Reading view shows the document as it will print and enables the addition of comments. By default, all new documents open in Editing view. At any point, you can click OPEN IN WORD to take advantage of the more full-featured Word version if it is installed on your computer.

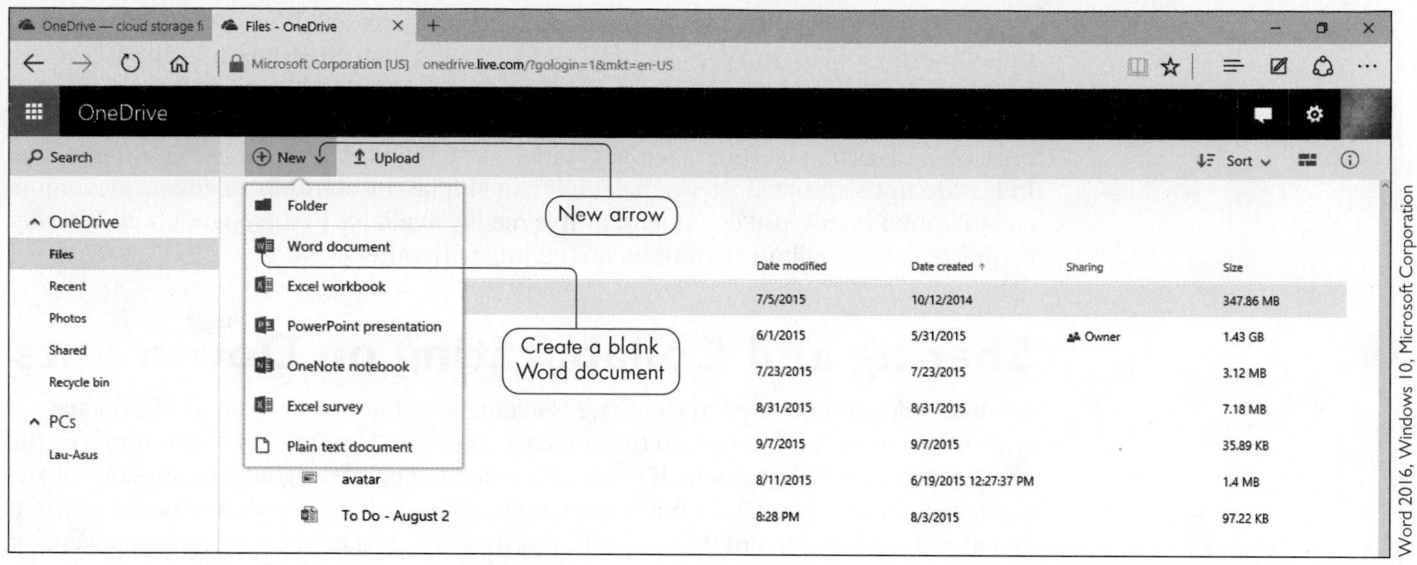

FIGURE 4.26 Create a New Document in Word Online

> ## To edit a newly created document in Word Online, complete the following steps:
>
> 1. Click the View tab in the newly created document, and click Reading view.
> 2. Select Edit in Word on the Edit Document tab (to open the document in a full Word version if installed on your computer) or Edit in Word Online (to open the document for editing in Word Online) (as shown in Figure 4.27).
> 3. Type content in the document, and it is automatically saved to OneDrive.

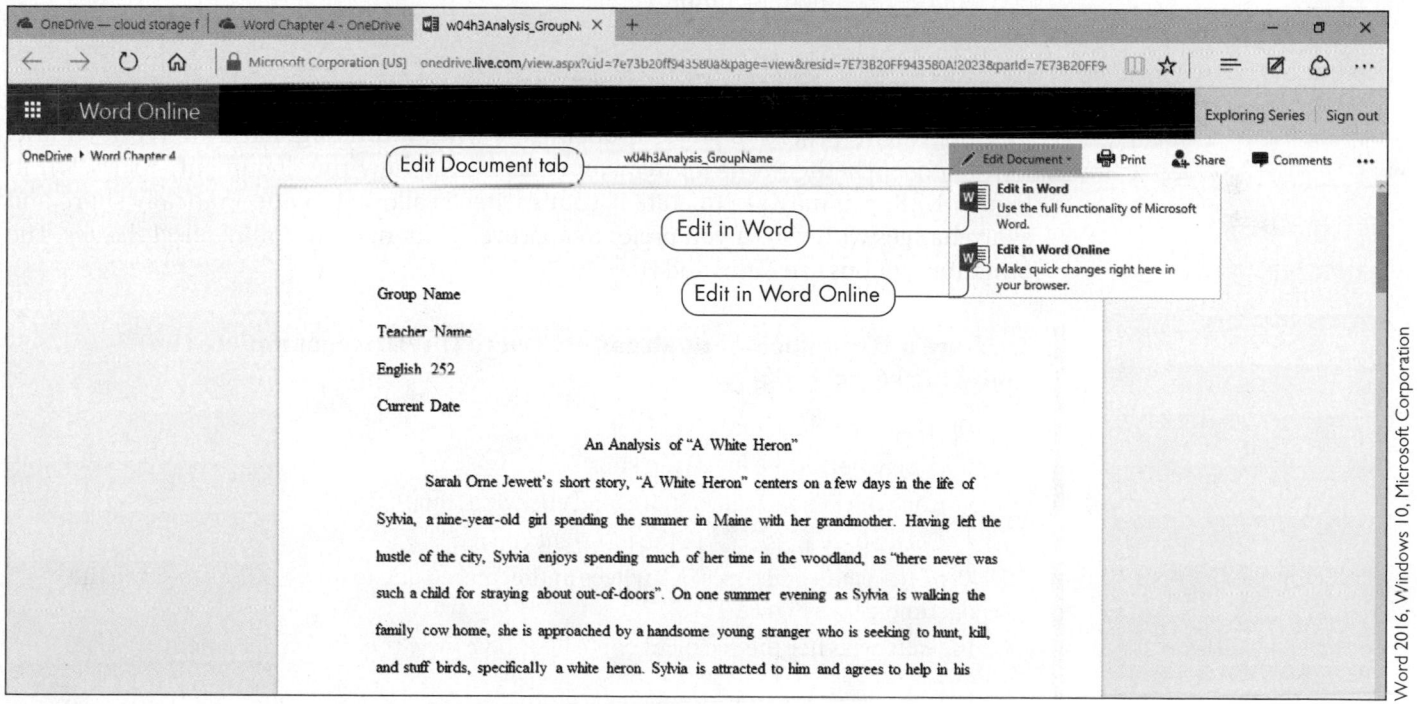

FIGURE 4.27 Use Word Online

Word Online has the familiar look and feel of Microsoft Word; however, you will note that the Ribbon in Word Online has fewer tabs than the Ribbon in the Word version installed on your computer. As you work with Word Online, you will find some differences and limitations. For example, dialog box launchers and track changes are not present, and certain features such as Citations and Bibliography, Table of Contents, and Index are not supported. Nevertheless, it can still be the solution to encourage online collaboration on a Word document, as it is readily available to anyone with an Internet connection and facilitates simultaneous editing with others.

Sharing and Collaborating on Documents

Because a document saved in OneDrive is available online, you can share the document with others who have access to the Internet. Also, sharing via OneDrive removes the hassles of version control, which is a problem created by passing around versions of the same document via email. Although you are likely to use Word to share documents, you can also share a document that opens in Word Online. You might even find it convenient to share a file other than one created with a Microsoft Office application, such as a picture or a PDF file, through OneDrive.com.

Share Documents

STEP 3 ⟫⟫ After saving a document to OneDrive or if you are working with Word Online, you can share your document with others in several ways and with varying levels of permission. You may share a file for informational purposes only if you do not intend to ask others to edit or collaborate on the document. Other times, you will invite collaboration. You can share a document through a link, through email, as a blog post, or even as an online presentation. As you share a document, you can indicate whether those you share with can edit the document or simply view it.

Invite Others to Share a Document

You can invite others to share a document with you using Word or Word Online. You choose whether your invitee can edit or only view the document. As shown in Figure 4.28, you may also dictate if your invitee is allowed to automatically share and sync changes with you. If you prefer to approve all changes, you may select *Ask me*. The other two options are *Never* and *Always*.

To share a Word document already saved to OneDrive, complete the following steps:

1. Open the saved document in Word.
2. Complete one of the following substeps:
   - Click the File tab, click Share, and click Share with people.
   - Click Share ⟨ 🔒 Share ⟩ at the top-right corner.
3. Type the email addresses of invitees in the Share pane to invite others to share the document (see Figure 4.28).
4. Indicate whether the recipient can edit or only view the shared document.
5. Type a message.
6. Select one of the three options for *Automatically share changes*: Ask me, Always, or Never
7. Click Share.

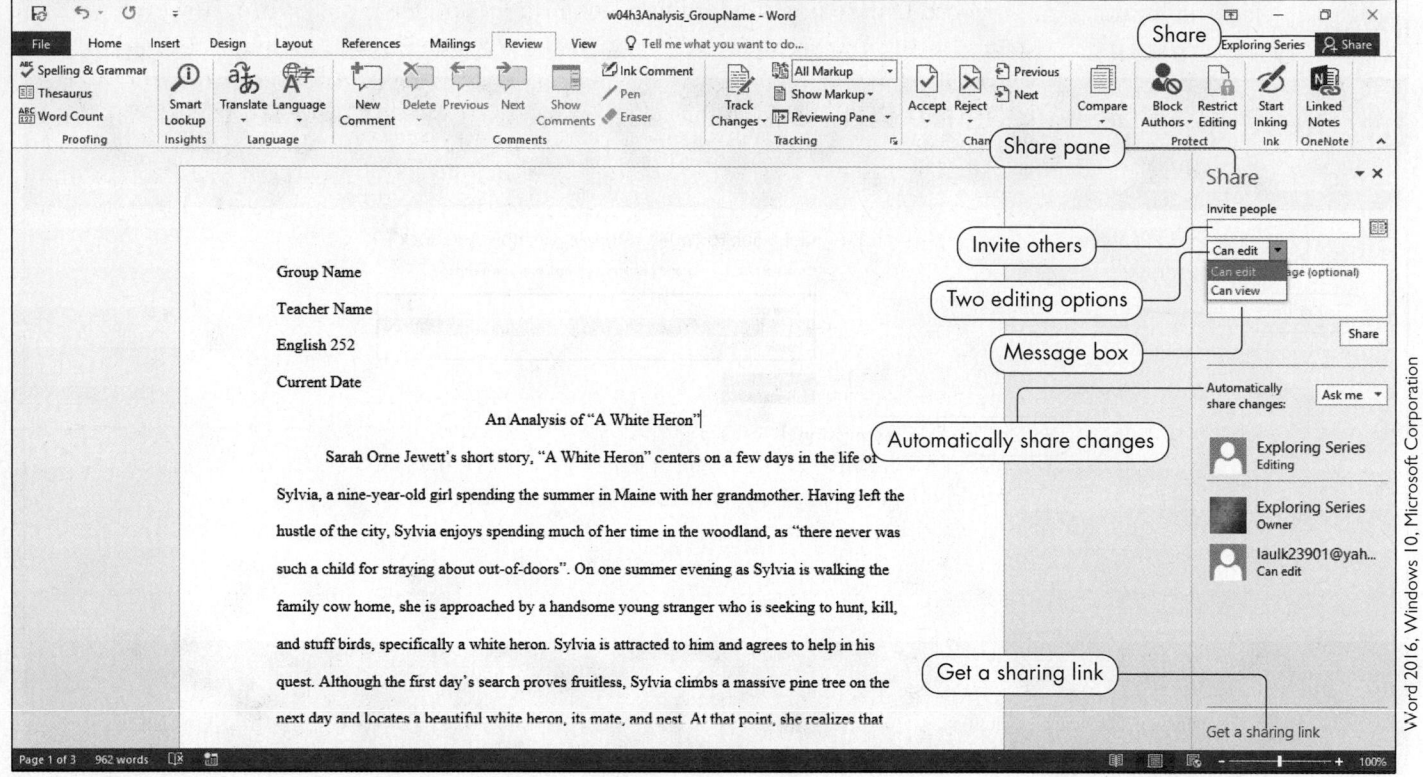

FIGURE 4.28 Invite Others

> Word 2016, Windows 10, Microsoft Corporation

TIP: SHARE A FILE IN ONEDRIVE

When viewing a list of files in OneDrive at OneDrive.com, you can right-click a file and click Share to open a Share dialog box from which you can select a method of sharing. If you have already opened the document in Word Online and clicked Edit in Word or Edit in Word Online, you click the File tab and then click Share.

To use Word Online to create a link to a shared document, complete the following steps:

1. Open the document in Word Online by clicking the document in your OneDrive account.
2. Click Share.
3. Click Get a link (see Figure 4.29).
4. Select a level of permission.
5. Click Create. Click Shorten link, if desired, to generate a shortened version of the link.
6. Copy the generated link for distribution to intended recipients.
7. Click Done.

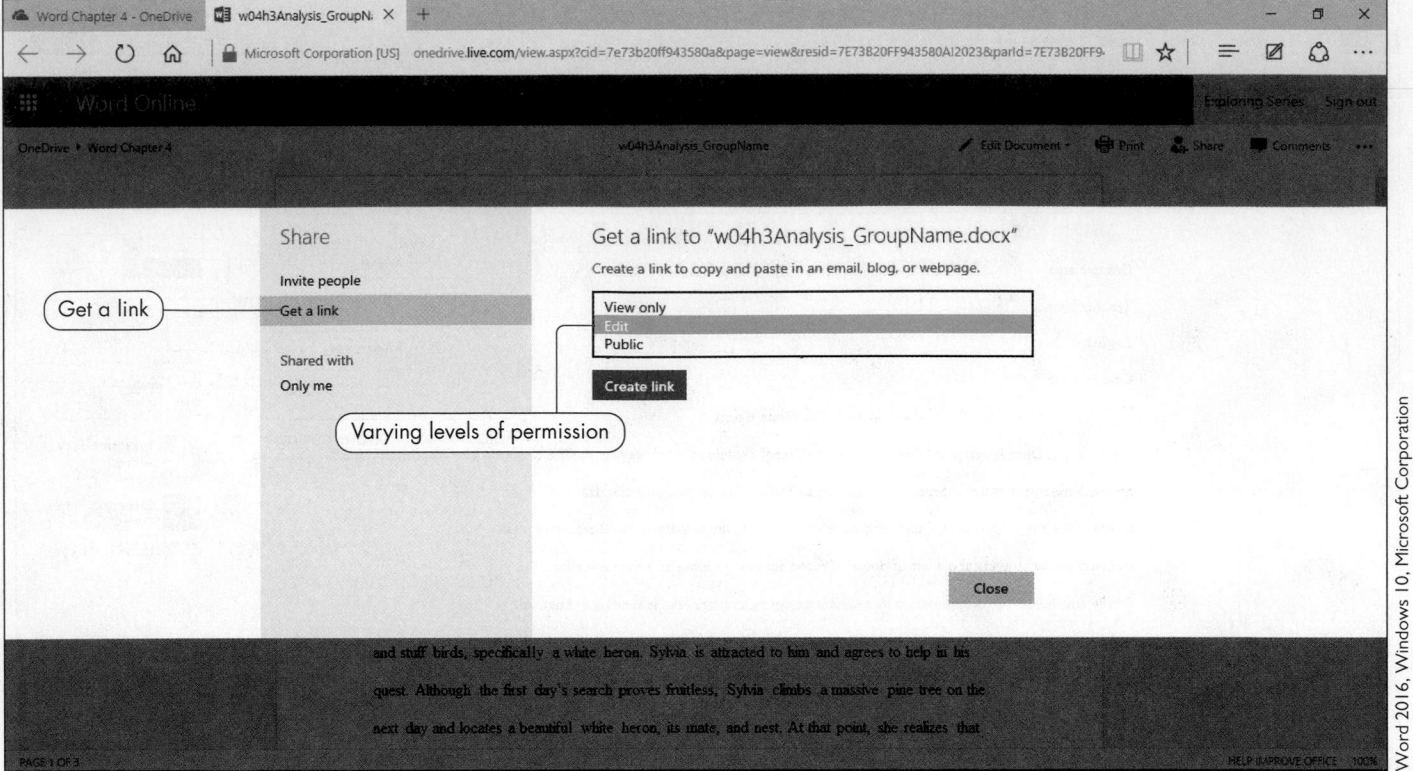

FIGURE 4.29 Share a Link

To use Word to create and share a link to a document already saved in OneDrive, complete the following steps:

1. Open the saved document in Word.
2. Click File, click Share, and click Share with People.
3. Click Get a sharing link at the bottom of the Share pane (see Figure 4.28).
4. Click Edit link if you want anyone with the link to edit the shared document.
5. Click View-only link if you want anyone with the link to view but not edit the shared document.
6. Click Copy and distribute the generated link to intended recipients.

Share a Document Through Email

With Word, you can also email a document to others if you know their email addresses. You can use email to distribute and share documents, but with little focus on collaborative efforts. When you share a document via email, you may choose one of the following five levels of sharing:

- Send as Attachment: In this option, everyone gets a copy of the original Word document to review. This could be a problem for large files with photos and images, or database files.

- Send a Link: Everyone receives a URL link to work on the same copy that was saved in a shared location, for example, OneDrive. This option has the highest level of collaboration, where everyone sees the latest changes. Since the document is stored on another location, the size of the email will be relatively small.

- Send as PDF: Everyone gets a PDF attachment of the original Word document. The PDF file preserves all layout, formatting, fonts, and images. This is a recommended option if email recipients are using different versions of Word.
- Send as XPS: Everyone gets an XPS attachment. The XPS (XML Paper Specification) format preserves all layout, formatting, fonts, and images in the document, and the content cannot be easily changed.
- Send as Internet Fax: With this method, no fax machine is needed. However, you will need a fax service provider to send the document.

Email recipients will receive a copy of the attached document. If they want to make changes, the changes must be saved and the document emailed back to the primary author. Unfortunately, co-authors might be using different versions of Word, sometimes resulting in incompatibility issues. Further, the primary author needs to consolidate all the changes onto one document, which can be a daunting task when there are many returned documents and changes. Therefore, sharing documents via email is the least collaborative, most non-interactive, method of working together. Consequently, sharing a document via email is best as a way to distribute copies of a document that requires little or no intention of collaboration among email recipients.

To share a document through email, complete the following steps:

1. Click the File tab and click Share.
2. Click Email (see Figure 4.30).
3. Select one of the five methods of including the document.
4. Respond to any prompts presented.

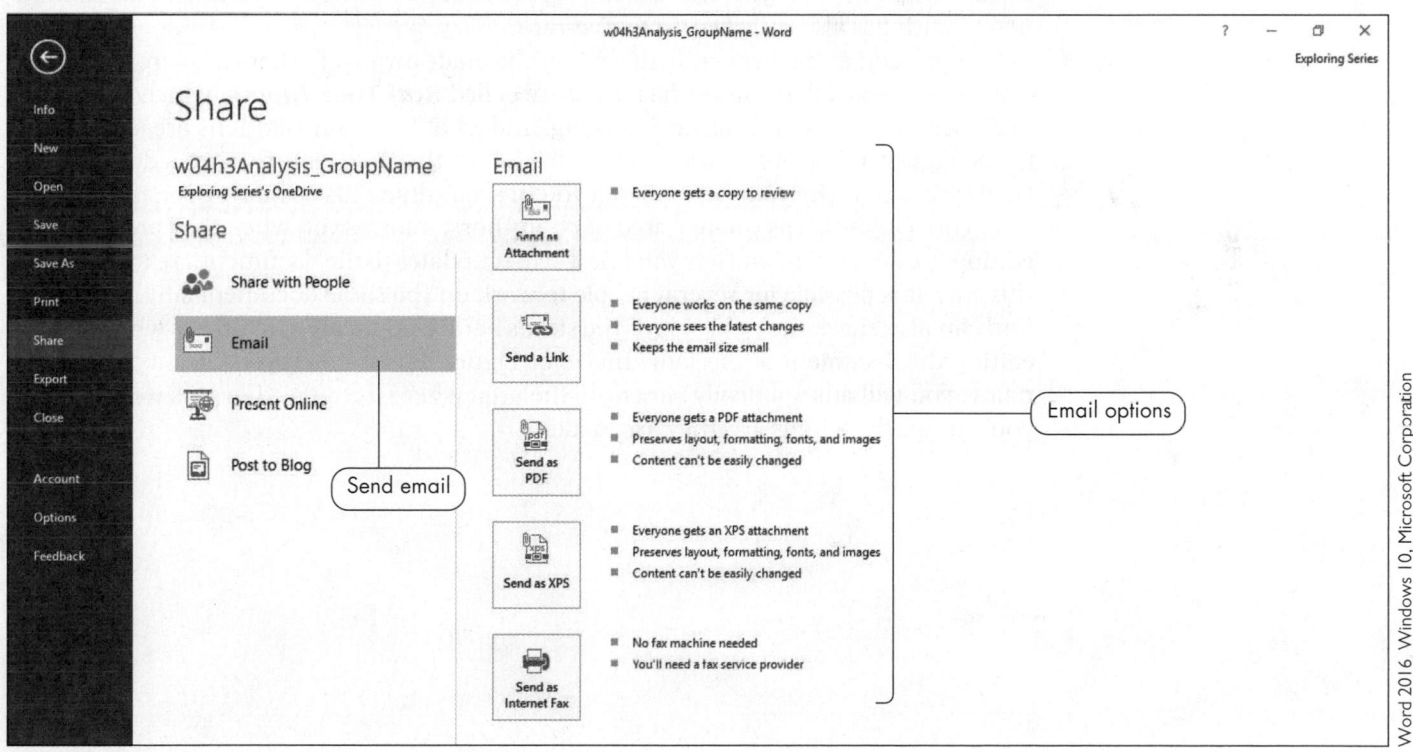

FIGURE 4.30 Share a Document Through Email

Post a Document to a Blog

Everyone can post any information to the Web for personal, social, or professional reasons. This information can be personal thoughts, opinions, interests, or simply whatever an individual wants to share with others or make public. This chronological publication of personal thoughts and Web links is called a ***blog***. The term *blog* is derived from the phrase *Web log*, which refers to publishing personal information on the Web. Blogs can provide a vehicle to display the works of current or future journalists and authors, or they can simply reflect the emotions and ideas of an individual at a particular point in time. Word makes it very easy for a group of people to share their opinions and thoughts on a group project by posting a document to a blog. The Post to Blog feature is available by clicking the File tab and then clicking Share.

Collaborate on a Document

STEP 4 ▶▶ Co-authoring a document is simple, with no specific commands required to begin editing. Simply open a shared document from OneDrive and use either Word or Word Online to modify the document. Of course, the document must be shared in such a way that editing by other authors is permitted. When you save or upload a Word document to OneDrive, anyone with whom you share the document (with editing privileges) can access and edit the document, even if you are also editing the document at the same time. This simultaneous editing is also called ***real-time co-authoring***.

As you edit a shared document, you will be made aware of others who are editing the same document. Word Online has a feature called ***Real Time Typing***, which allows you to see where your co-authors are working, and what their contributions are as they type it (see Figure 4.31). For a quick demonstration of this new feature, save a document to OneDrive, and invite your peers to join you in a simultaneous authoring session.

Word Online keeps you apprised of co-authors, informs you when they are no longer editing the document, and lets you know when updates to the document are available. In this way, it is possible for several people to work on the same document simultaneously. You can also check the right side of the status bar for notification of others who might be editing the document at the same time (see Figure 4.32). When you click a co-author's name, you will automatically be sent to the area where the co-author was working, and you can see the changes as they are made.

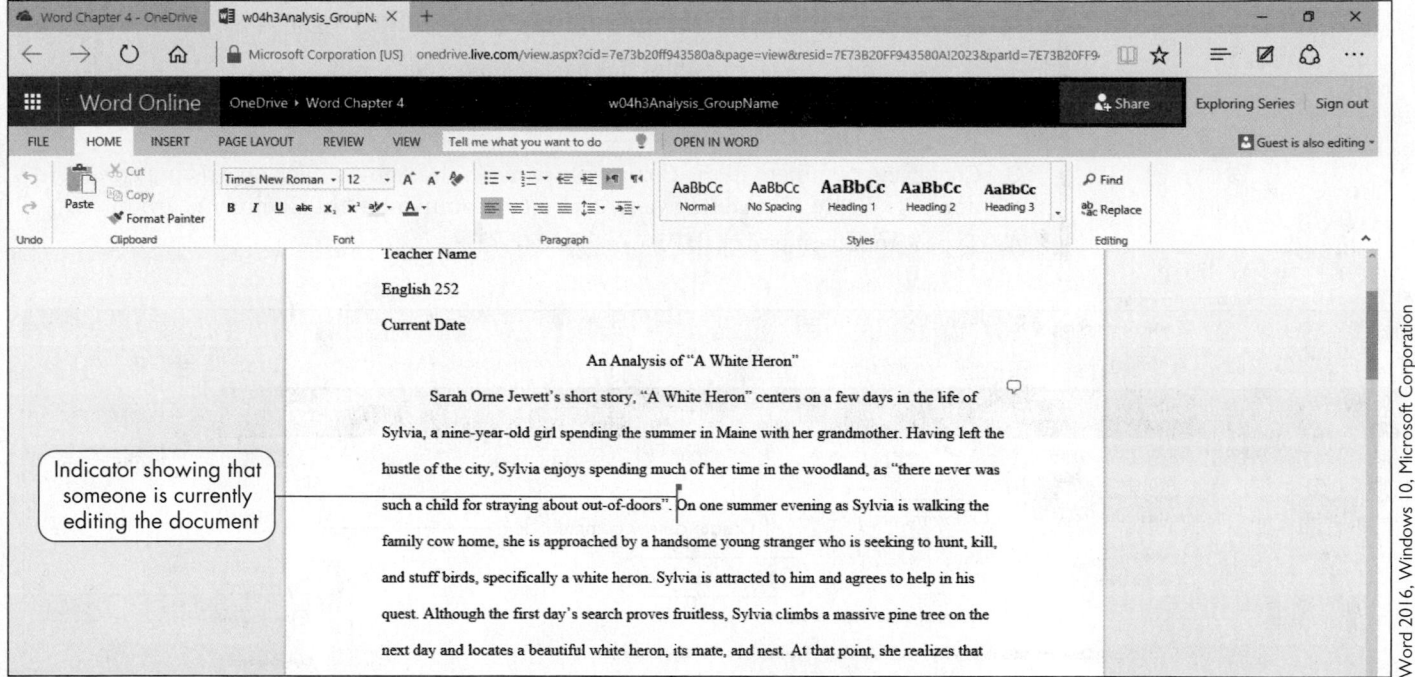

FIGURE 4.31 Notification of Co-Authors

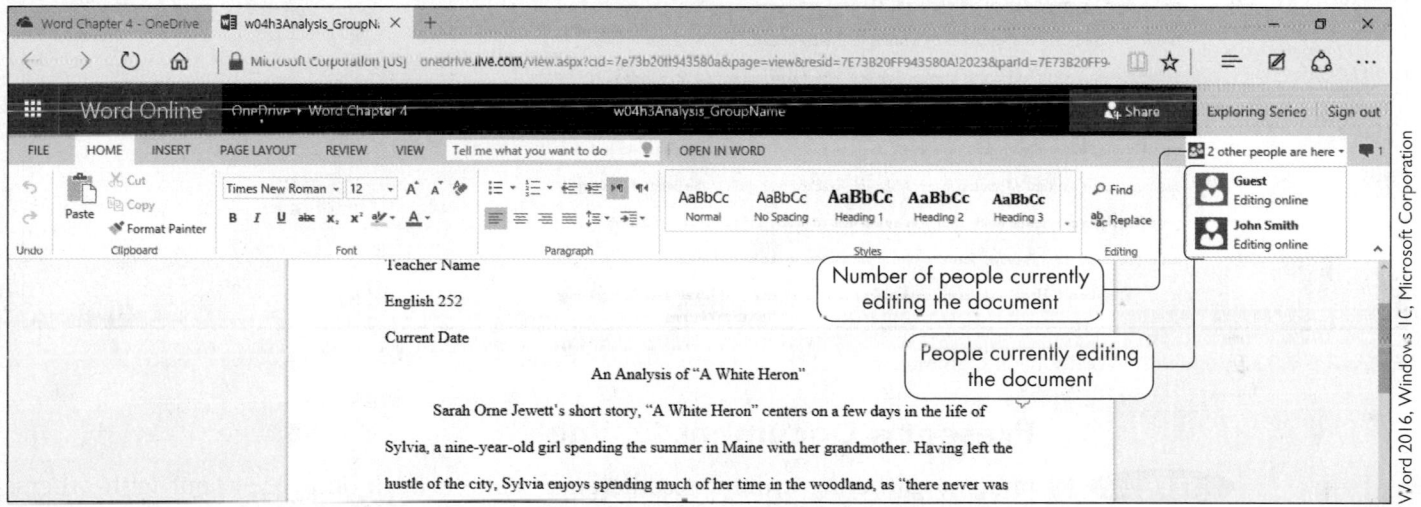

FIGURE 4.32 Identify Current Co Authors

At any point, you can switch to Word to continue working with a shared document. Because Word Online is somewhat limited, you might find that you need to edit a document in Word to access a feature not found in Word Online. For example, you might want to add a bibliography or check a document in Outline view. Even when working in Word, you will be apprised of other editors.

When you work with a shared document, you may want to make comments about the content or ask questions of co-authors. Often, the purpose of sharing a document is to seek feedback. Those with whom you share a document might not make any edits at all—they could simply comment on the document so that you can improve or validate the content. Using Word or Word Online, you can create comments as well as reply to comments others might include.

When using Word Online, you can create or respond to comments in either Editing view or Reading view. If you are in Editing view, click the Review tab and click Show Comments. If you are in Reading view, click Comments on the tab.

To create or reply to a comment, complete the following steps:

1. Select a line of text (or double-click to select a paragraph).
2. Click Comments if you are in Reading view (see Figure 4.33). Click the Review tab if you are in Editing view.
3. Click New Comment in the Comments pane on the right or click an existing comment and click Reply. If in Editing view, click New Comment in the Comments group.
4. Type a comment and click Post.

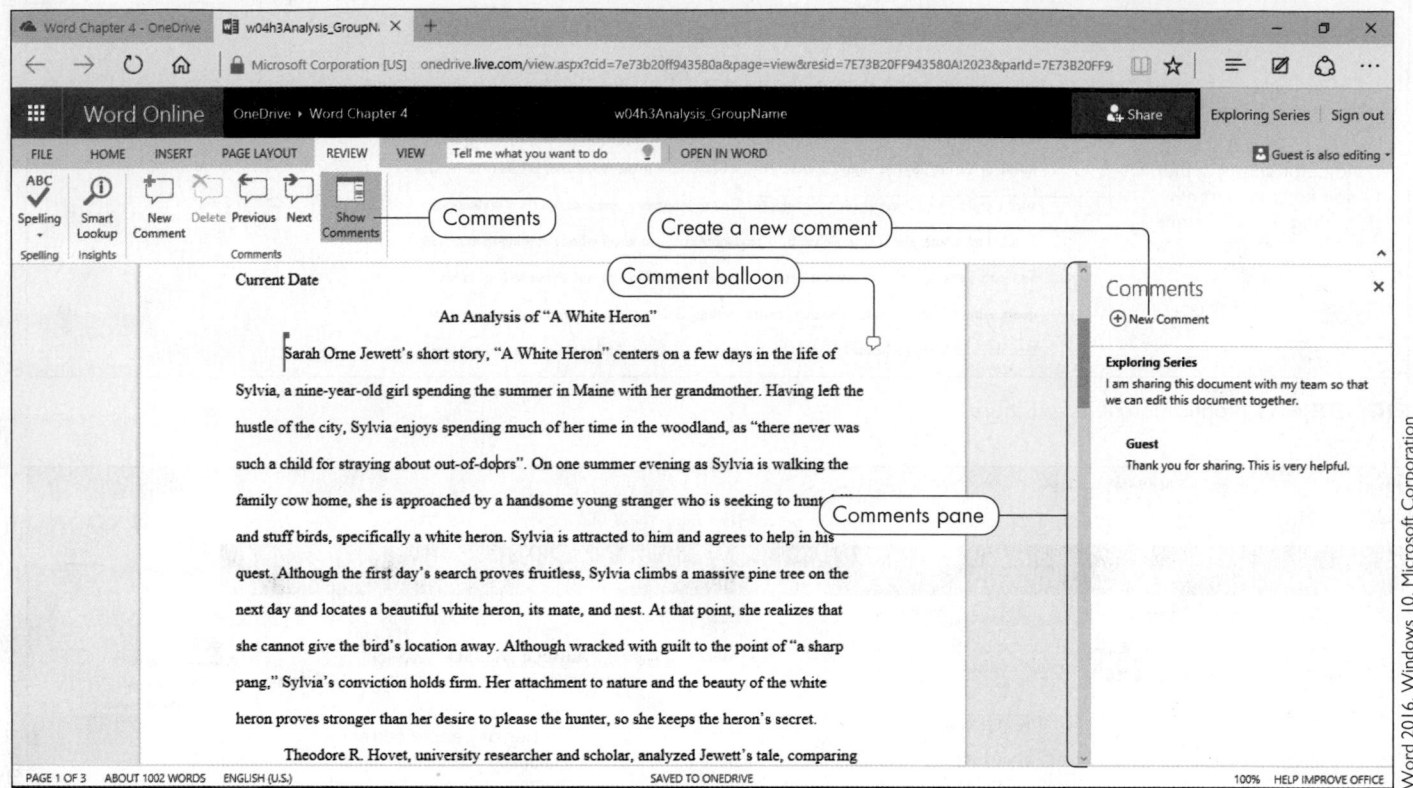

FIGURE 4.33 Work with Word Online Comments

Present a Document Online

 Imagine gathering around a conference table to work on a document with others. Sharing ideas and commenting on content, the group works to produce a collaborative document that is representative of the group's best effort. Now expand that view to include co-authors who are widespread geographically instead of gathered in a conference room. Online at the same time, the far-flung group can view a document and collaborate on content, although not simultaneously, ultimately producing a document to which all attendees have had the opportunity to contribute. After a document presentation, conference attendees can download a copy of the document for additional editing. Word enables you to invite attendees and present a document online. Whether your goal is to present a document for discussion (but no editing) or to seek input from a group after the conference, you will appreciate the ease with which Word facilitates that task.

Begin an Online Presentation

During an online presentation, a conference leader will present a document. Although attendees can navigate the document independently during the presentation, they cannot edit the document. If an attendee independently navigates the document during the presentation, he or she will stop following the presenter but can rejoin the presentation at any time. As the conference leader, you can make a document available for download, and invite an audience to view the document as you work with it.

To present a document online, the conference leader will complete the following steps:

1. Open the document to share in Word.
2. Click File, click Share, select Present Online, and then click Present Online (see Figure 4.34).
3. Check the *Enable remote viewers to download the document* box to select it if you want to share the document with the attendees.
4. Click Copy Link (to copy and paste the meeting hyperlink, perhaps in a Skype chat window or a Web browser) or *Send in Email* (to email the hyperlink in your Outlook email account).
5. Click Start Presentation. Your attendees can click the hyperlink or paste it in a browser window to view the document. Attendees can view the document even if they do not have a copy of Word installed on their computers.

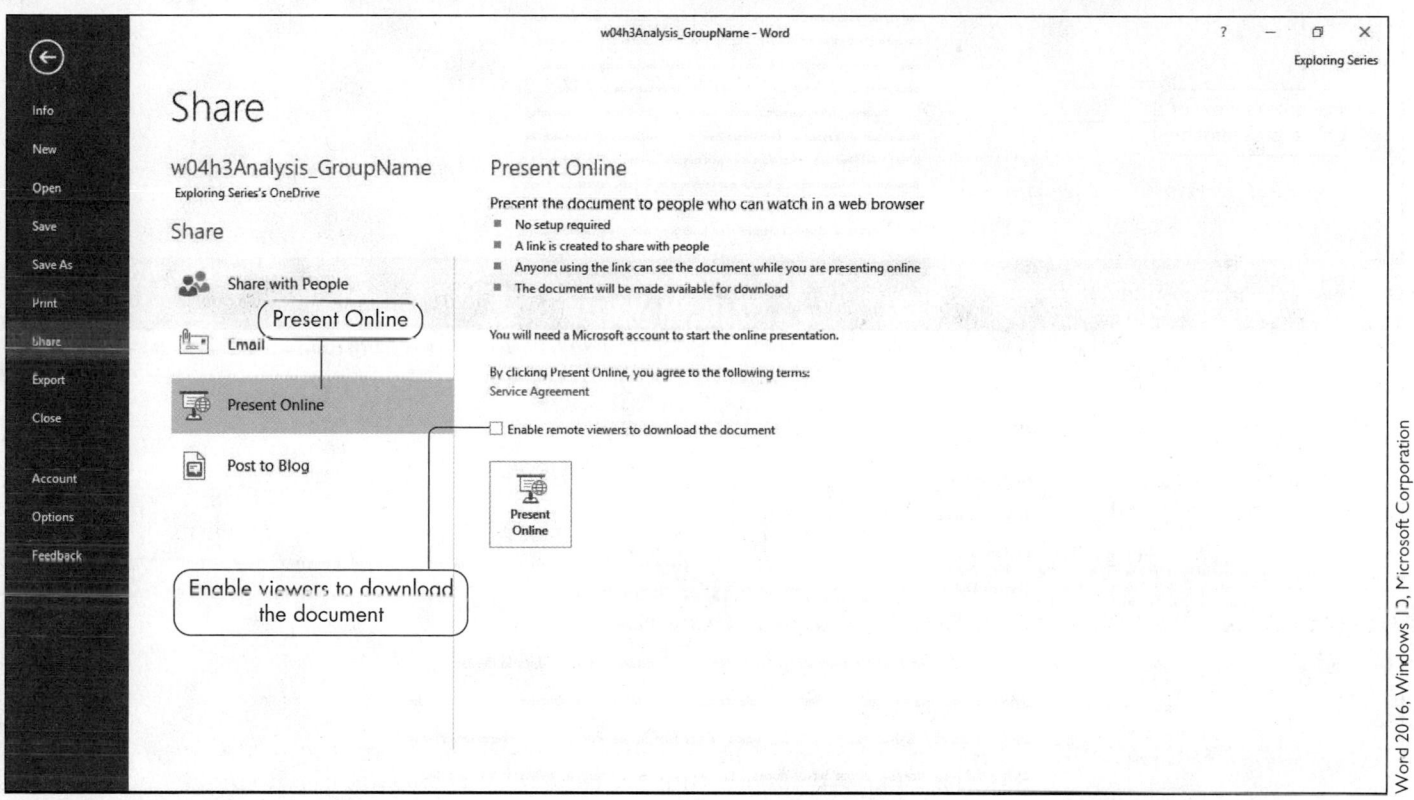

FIGURE 4.34 Present a Document Online

Figure 4.35 shows a presenter's view as well as an attendee's. If the presenter's goal is to inform an audience without inviting participation, he or she can simply navigate through the document as the audience follows along online. When the presentation is complete, the presenter will click End Online Presentation to disconnect from the audience.

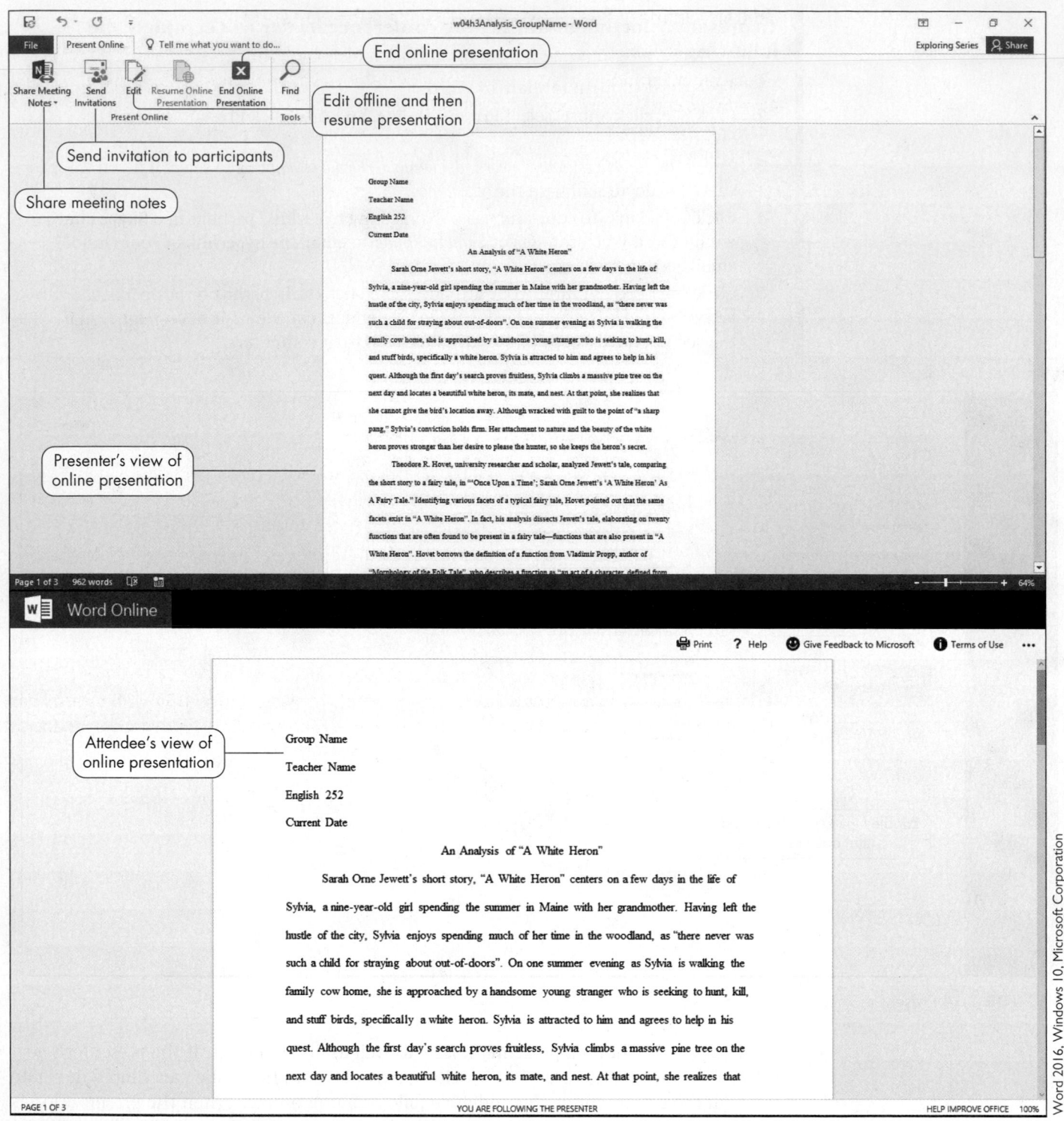

FIGURE 4.35 Present and View an Online Document

Edit an Online Word Document During a Presentation

While presenting a document online, you might identify errors that you want to correct or notice modifications that you want to make. Perhaps a name is misspelled, or you see that a sentence could be reworded for better readability. Click Edit to temporarily move offline. After editing the document, click Resume, as shown in Figure 4.36, to return to the online presentation. Attendees will be informed that the presenter has made changes to the file.

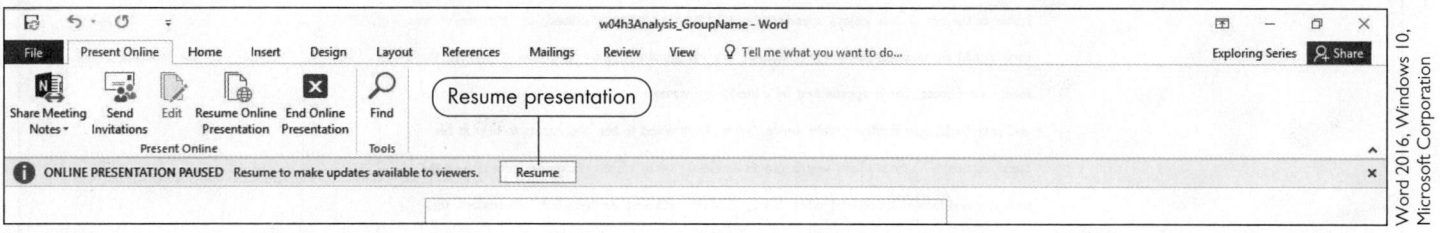

FIGURE 4.36 Edit a Document During a Presentation

Navigate a Document During a Presentation

As the presenter, you will work with a document that displays on each attendee's screen. As your screen displays changes, so do the displays of those watching the presentation. On occasion, you might move to a page before someone in your audience has had time to read all of the content previously presented. In that case, an attendee can independently navigate a document, although doing so causes him or her to temporarily leave the presentation. It does not, however, interrupt your presentation or change anyone else's display. An audience member can independently navigate a document being presented online but cannot make changes to the document during the presentation.

When you leave a presentation as an attendee, you will see a temporary alert informing you that you are no longer following the presenter (see Figure 4.37). The status bar also lets you know you are no longer following along. Click Follow Presenter to return to the online presentation.

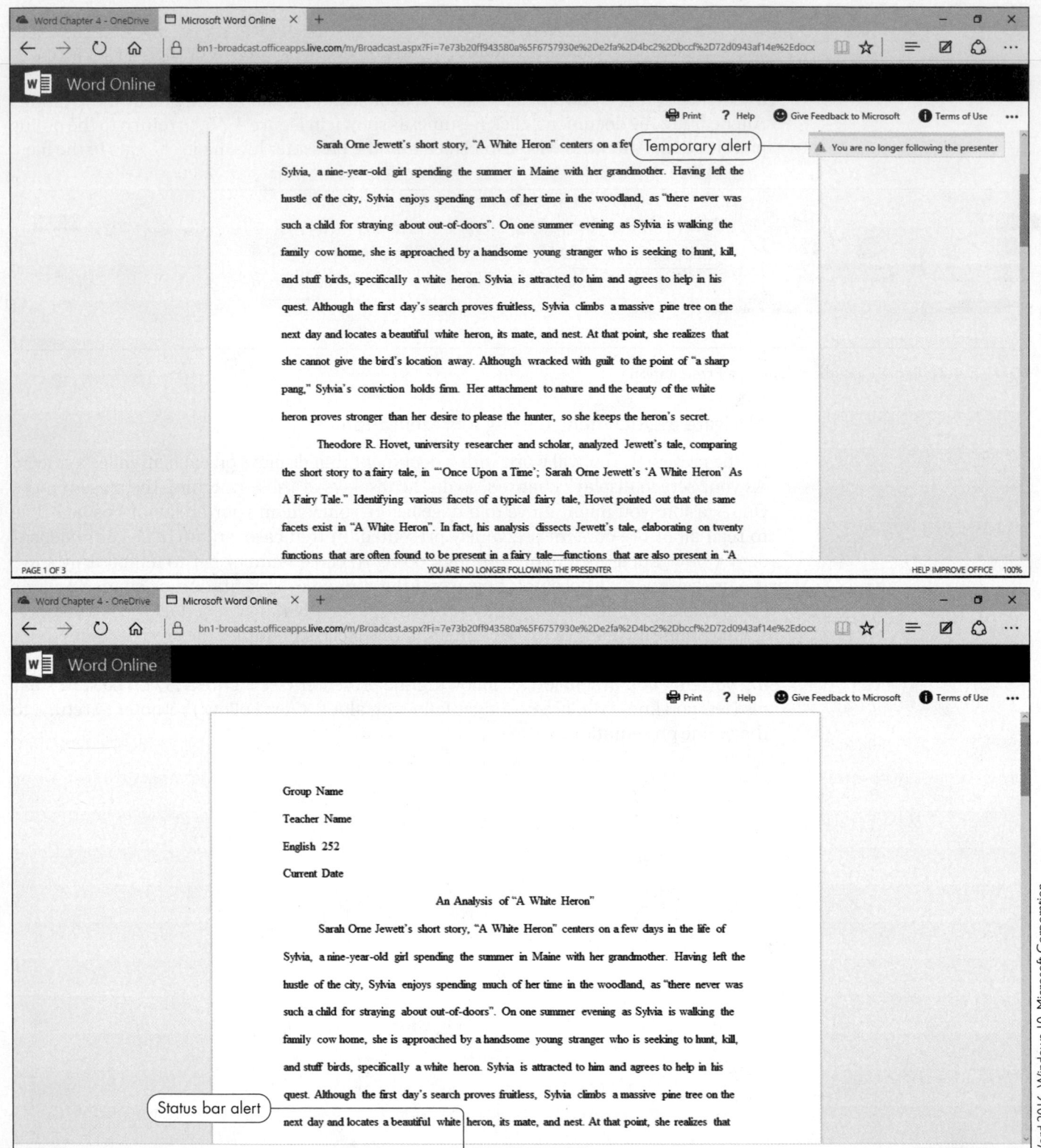

FIGURE 4.37 Attendee Independent Navigation

Word 2016, Windows 10, Microsoft Corporation

9. As you save a document to OneDrive, you will most likely also want to have a copy on your computer for backup purposes. How can you make sure that as you modify one copy, the other is also updated? *p. 365*

10. Both Word 2016 and Word Online enable you to create and edit a document. When might one be preferred over the other? *p. 368*

11. After editing a shared document online, you want to make your edits available to co-authors who might be editing the same file. How would you do that? *p. 374*

12. Editing view and Reading view of Word Online serve different purposes. What are some extra features that Editing view has? *p. 368*

Hands-On Exercises

 Watch the Video for this Hands-On Exercise!

 MyITLab® HOE3 Training

Skills covered: Use OneDrive with File Explorer • Present a Document Online • Use Word Online • Share Documents • Collaborate on a Document

3 Online Document Collaboration

Your literature group will finalize the analysis of *A White Heron* by collaborating on a few last-minute edits online. Your instructor will assign you to work in a group of four students to complete this Hands-On Exercise. The group will select a chairperson who will assume the task of posting and sharing the document. You must also have a group name that you will include in the filename. You will work with a draft of the analysis of the short story, co-authoring the document online with classmates in your group.

STEP 1 ›› USE ONEDRIVE WITH FILE EXPLORER

You plan to use OneDrive to share the analysis of *A White Heron* so that classmates can collaborate on the project. You know that OneDrive provides storage space that can be accessed by others, and as a backup, the chairperson of your group will save a copy of the analysis on a hard drive. In doing so, you will want to make sure that edits made to the paper at either location are synchronized with the other location so that both copies remain current. You can use OneDrive to accomplish the goal, but first you will learn a bit more about OneDrive. Before beginning this exercise, you should have a Microsoft account. If you do not have a Microsoft account, create one at signup.live.com. Refer to Figure 4.38 as you complete Step 1.

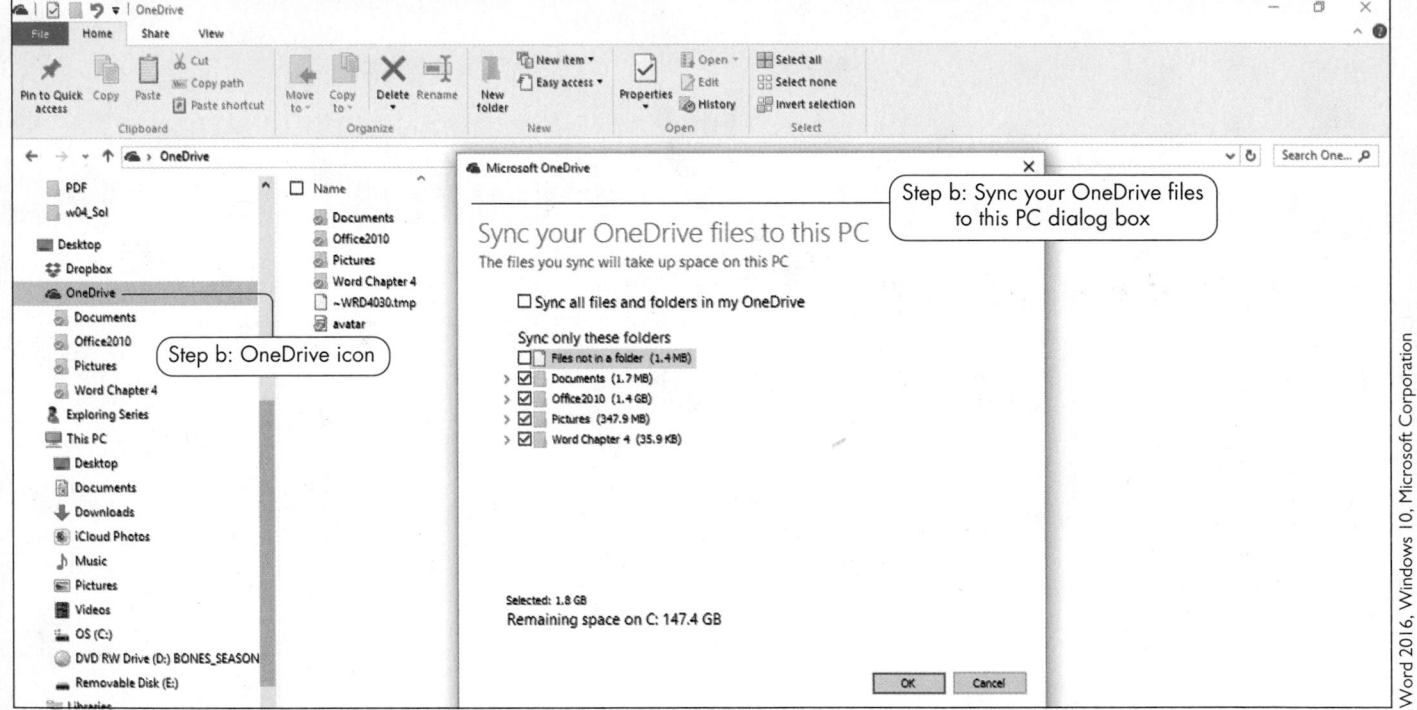

FIGURE 4.38 OneDrive and File Explorer

a. Open a new blank Word document. Open an Internet browser window, and go to https://onedrive.live.com/about/en-us/. Scroll through the webpage, and learn more about OneDrive. You will now begin to summarize what you have learned.

b. Type **OneDrive** on the blank Word document. Press **Enter**. Type your first name and last name. Press **Enter**. Provide an example of when you might use OneDrive, and explain how you use File Explorer to coordinate and sync your files and folders to OneDrive. In your description, include a screen capture of the Sync your OneDrive files to this PC dialog box.

c. Save the document as **w04h3OneDrive_LastFirst** and close the file. You will submit this file to your instructor at the end of the last Hands-On Exercise.

d. Close the browser window.

Before collaborating on the analysis that is to be shared and edited by the group, the chairperson will present the document online to group members, highlighting areas to be edited in a later step. The group chairperson will make the presentation, sharing it with group members who will watch the presentation from their own Internet-connected computers. The group chairperson will use Word to prepare the online presentation, providing a link to attendees so they can watch the presentation on their own computers. All group members must have a Microsoft account before beginning this exercise. Your instructor should assign your group a name. Refer to Figure 4.39 as you complete Step 2.

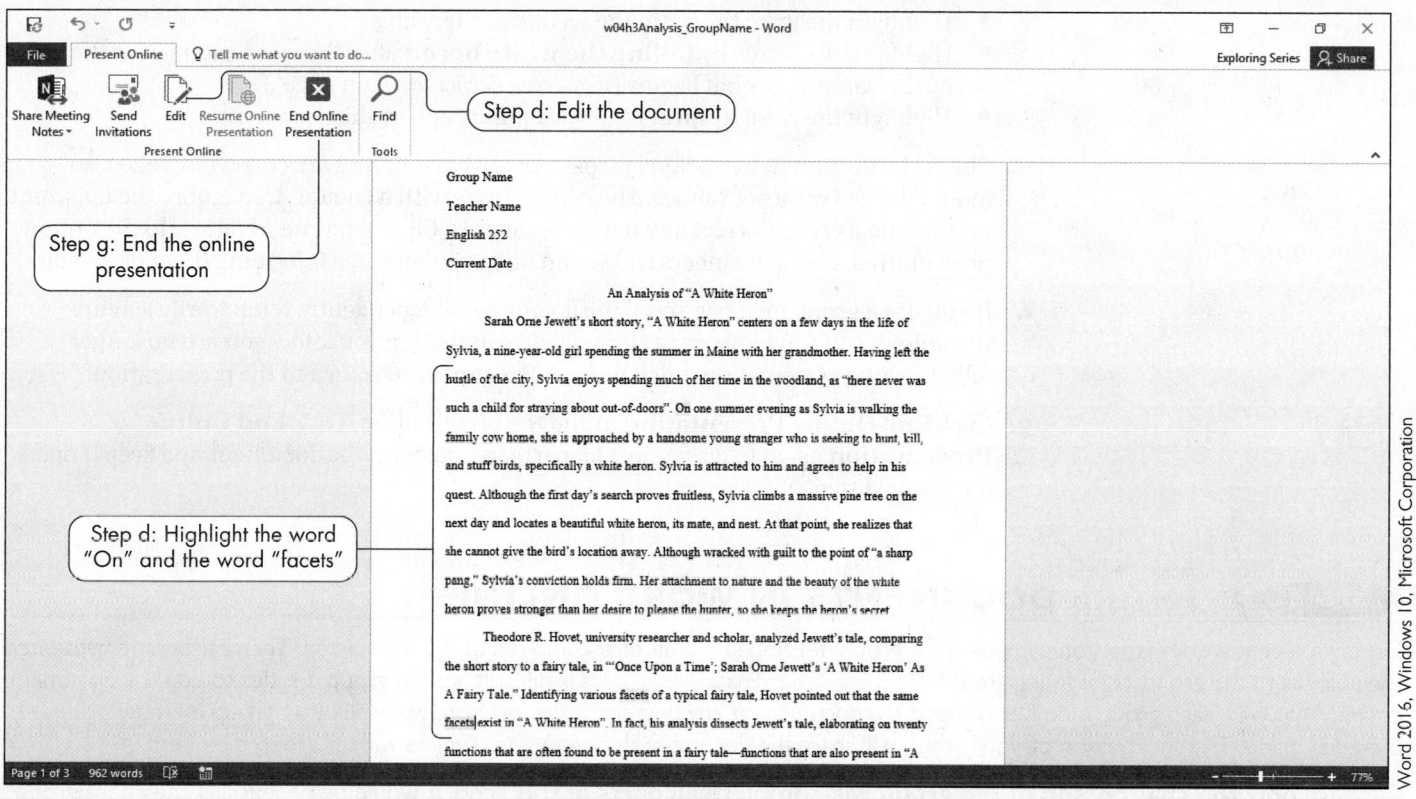

FIGURE 4.39 Present an Online Document

The chairperson performs Steps a–e and g, and group member performs Steps b (last part) and f:

a. Open *w04h3Analysis* and save it as **w04h3Analysis_GroupName**, replacing *GroupName* with the name assigned to the group by your instructor. Keep the document open.

> **TROUBLESHOOTING:** To complete all steps of this exercise, every group member must have a Microsoft account. If you do not have a Microsoft account, create one at signup.live.com.

b. Click the **File tab** and click **Share**. Click **Present Online** and click **Present Online** again. Log in to the Microsoft account and provide a copy of the link to all group members. Group members will click the link to open the presentation on their computers.

> **TROUBLESHOOTING:** If you are unable to connect, proceed directly to Step 3, skipping all of the following parts of Step 2. However, you should check spelling first, correcting all mistakes (note that author names are not misspelled).

c. Click **START PRESENTATION**, scroll through the document, and present it to the group. Each group member should see the document on individual computers as it is being presented.

d. Click **Edit** to temporarily pause the presentation to make edits. Click the **Home tab**, click **Text Highlight Color**, and highlight the following areas in the document, indicating that they are to be edited later (toggle off Text Highlight Color when highlighting is complete):

- Highlight the word **On** in the fourth sentence of the first paragraph.
- Highlight the word **facets** in the second paragraph.
- Highlight the words **by killing the white heron** after the word *nature* near the end of the paragraph (that begins *On an even deeper level*) on page 3.
- Highlight the word **helpful** in the last paragraph of the document.

e. Check the document for spelling errors. All authors' names are correctly spelled, so ignore flagged errors of names. The essay begins with a capital *A*, so ignore the apparent grammatical error. Correct any misspelled words. Click **Resume** to return to the online presentation. Group members will see an onscreen message informing them of an edit.

f. If you are a group member, scroll the document independently, temporarily leaving the presentation. A temporary alert will display, letting you know you are no longer following the presentation. Click **Follow Presenter** to return to the presentation.

g. Click **End Online Presentation** to end the presentation. Click **End Online Presentation** again to disconnect all participants. Save the document and keep it open for the next step.

STEP 3 ⟩⟩ SHARE DOCUMENTS IN WORD ONLINE

During a recent work session on campus, your group developed a draft of the analysis of *A White Heron*. The chairperson presented the analysis to the group, highlighting areas for editing. Coordinating schedules is difficult, so the group decides to edit the document online. That way, each group member can edit the document at any time from any location, while all other group members can see the edits made. The chairperson of your group will share the document through Word Online with all group members.

Although **only the chairperson of the group will complete all parts of this step**, it would be beneficial if the entire group were together to watch or participate in that process. If it is not possible for the entire group to be together, each group member will begin with Step 4, after the chairperson has shared a link to the shared document. Refer to Figure 4.40 as Step 3 is completed.

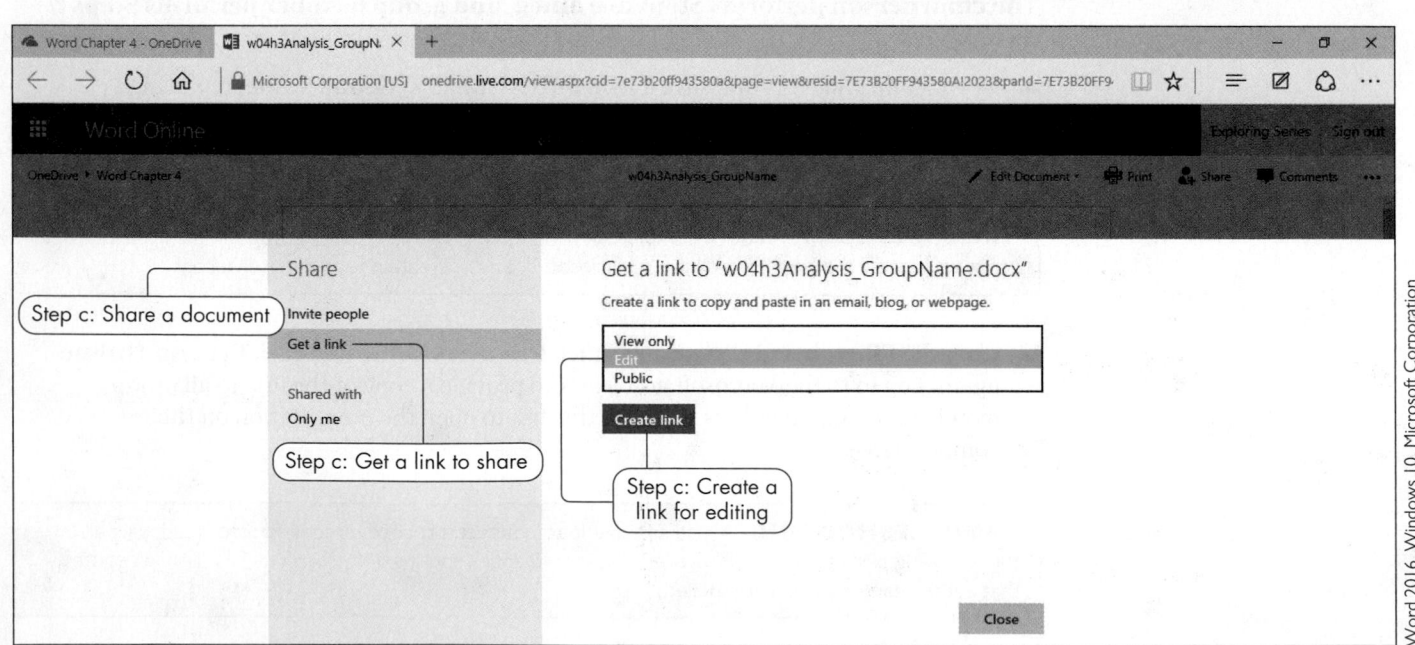

FIGURE 4.40 Share a Document in Word Online

The chairperson performs all the following steps:

a. Open the document if it is not already open, and save the document as *w04h3Analysis_ GroupName* in a new folder in OneDrive by clicking the **File tab** and then **Save As**. Click **Browse**, and select **OneDrive**. Click **New Folder**, type **Word Chapter 4**, and then press **Enter**. Click **Word Chapter 4** and click **Save**. Close the document.

> **TROUBLESHOOTING:** If you have difficulty saving the file to OneDrive, make sure the file is saved to a local drive first. To save the file to OneDrive.com directly, complete the following steps:
>
> **Go to OneDrive.com in your browser and log in.**
> 1. Click Create, click Folder, type Word Chapter 4, and then press Enter. Click the new folder.
> 2. Click Upload and click Files. Navigate to the *w04h3Analysis_GroupName* file on your computer and double-click the file. After the file is uploaded, close the OneDrive information window at the bottom-right corner of the browser.
> 3. Click *w04h3Analysis_GroupName* in OneDrive to open it.
> 4. Proceed to Step b.

b. Go to OneDrive.com and sign in. Navigate to the **Word Chapter 4** folder, and right-click **w04h3Analysis_GroupName** to open a shortcut menu.

> **TROUBLESHOOTING:** If you cannot find the document in OneDrive, click in the Search box at the top-left corner of the screen. Type w04h3Analysis_GroupName (replacing *GroupName* with your group's name, as you saved it in Step a). Press Enter. Click the file name, if found, to open the document in Word Online.

c. Click **Share** and click **Get a link**. Ensure that Edit is the chosen option. Click **Shorten link** to display a shorter version of the link. Copy the link for distribution to team members, or have each team member (including the chairperson) make note of the link for later reference. You might include the link in an email to group members or otherwise post it where group members can access it. Click **Close**.

d. Close the browser.

Each team member has a link to a shared document—w04h3Analysis_GroupName. Each person will access w04h3Analysis_GroupName, reviewing and editing the report individually on his/her own computer. You do not have to access the report simultaneously, although that is an option. All team members will complete all parts of this step (with the exception of the last sentence of part b and all of part c). Refer to Figure 4.41 as you complete Step 4.

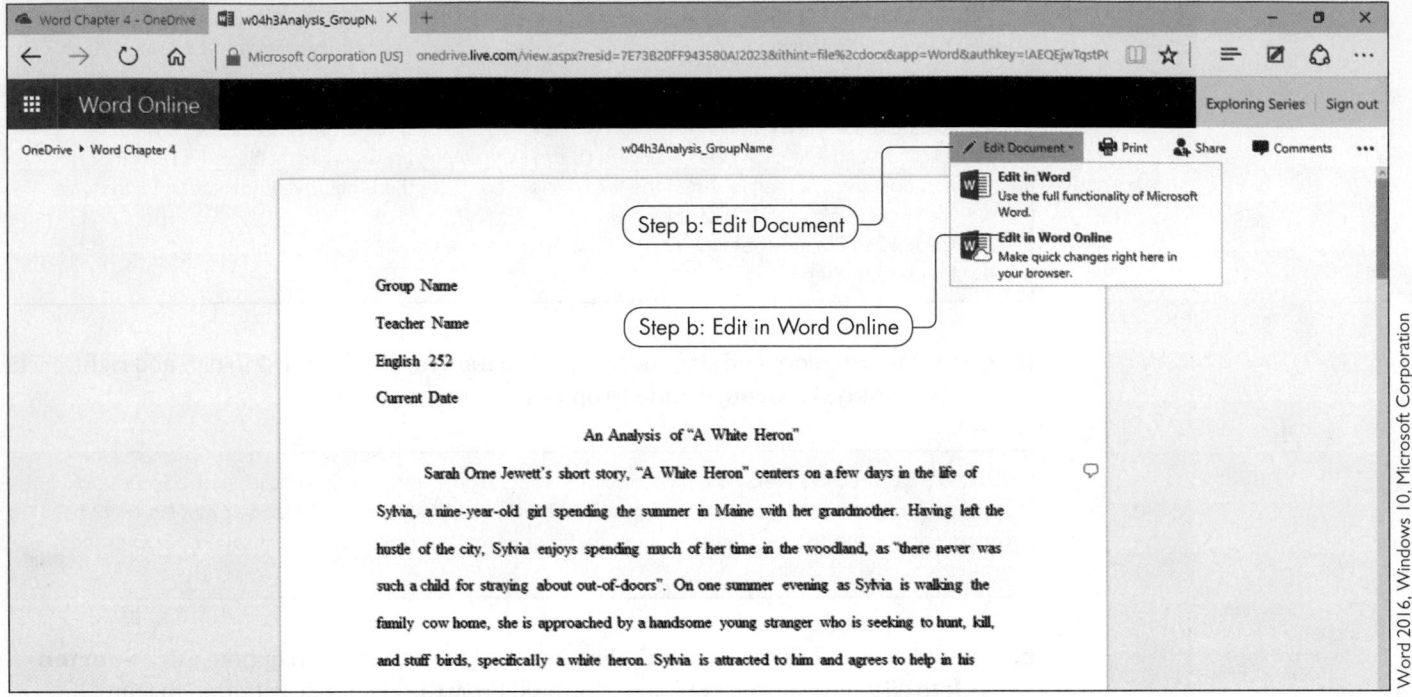

FIGURE 4.41 Collaborate on a Shared Document

a. Open a browser window and type or paste the link provided in part c of the previous step. Press **Enter**.

> **TROUBLESHOOTING:** If the link you use does not display the shared document, the chairperson can repeat Step 3 to produce another link.

b. Click **Edit in Word Online** to start editing the shared document. Provide login information related to your Windows account if required. The chairperson will change the words Group Name in the first line of the document to the actual group name assigned by the instructor in Step 2 of this Hands-On Exercise.

c. Divide the following tasks among group members, excluding the chairperson, with each task completed by only one team member (unless there are fewer team members than tasks; in that case, assign the tasks as appropriate). As each group member completes a task, it is automatically saved. These tasks can be done simultaneously, and you will see indicators showing that someone is currently editing the document too.

Task 1: Remove the word *On* from the fourth sentence of the first paragraph. The sentence should begin with the word *One*.

Task 2: Change the word *facets* in the second paragraph to **components**. Remove the text highlight if present.

Task 3: Change the words *by killing the white heron* to **by revealing the white heron** after the word *nature* (near the end of the paragraph that begins *On an even deeper level*). Remove the text highlight if present.

Task 4: Change the word *helpful* to **interesting** in the last paragraph of the document. Remove the text highlight if present.

d. When all edits are complete, click the **File tab**. Click **Save As**, and click **Download a Copy**. Click **Click here to download your document** in the Microsoft Word Online dialog box, and click **Open** in the new browser window. Close the browser.

The document opens in Word on your computer. You may also Click View downloads in the new browser window, and the Downloads pane displaying the downloaded file opens on the right.

e. Click **Enable Editing**, and save the document as **w04h3Analysis_LastFirst**, replacing LastFirst with your name. Change the group name on the first page to your own first and last names and include a real or fictitious instructor name. Ensure the current date shows today's date.

f. Save and close the file. Based on your instructor's directions, submit the following:

w04h1Analysis_LastFirst

w04h1Airlines_LastFirst

w04h2Entry_LastFirst.pdf

w04h2WhiteHeron_LastFirst

w04h3OneDrive_LastFirst

w04h3Analysis_GroupName_LastFirst

w04h3Analysis_LastFirst

Chapter Objectives Review

After reading this chapter, you have accomplished the following objectives:

1. Use a writing style and acknowledge sources.

- Select a writing style: A research paper is typically written to adhere to a particular writing style, often dictated by the academic discipline.
- Create a source and include a citation: Each source consulted for a paper must be cited, according to the rules of a writing style.
- Share and search for a source: Sources are included in a Master List, available to all documents created on the same computer, and a Current List, available to the current document.
- Create a bibliography: A bibliography, also known as works cited or references, lists all sources used in the preparation of a paper.

2. Create and modify footnotes and endnotes.

- Create footnotes and endnotes: Footnotes (located at the bottom of a page) and endnotes (located at the end of a paper) enable you to expand on a statement or provide a citation.
- Modify footnotes and endnotes: You can change the format or style of footnotes and endnotes, or delete them.

3. Explore special features.

- Create a table of contents: If headings are formatted in a heading style, Word can prepare a table of contents, listing headings and associated page numbers.
- Create an index: Mark entries for inclusion in an index, which is an alphabetical listing of marked topics and associated page numbers.
- Create a cover page: Some writing styles require a cover page, which you can create as the first page, listing a report title and other identifying information.

4. Review a document.

- Use markup: This feature can help you customize how tracked changes are displayed in a document. There are four markup views: Simple Markup, All Markup, No Markup, and Original.
- Add a comment: A comment is located in a comment balloon in the margin of a report, providing a note to the author.
- View and reply to comments: Simple Markup enables you to view comments and reply to them in an unobtrusive manner.

5. Track changes.

- Use Track Changes: With Track Changes active, all edits in a document are traceable so you can see what has been changed.
- Accept and reject changes: With Track Changes active, you can evaluate each edit made, accepting or rejecting it.
- Work with PDF documents: PDF Reflow is a Word feature that converts a PDF document into an editable Word document.

6. Use OneDrive and Word Online.

- Use OneDrive: The Windows 10 OneDrive app and OneDrive for Windows app simplify the use of OneDrive for saving documents. OneDrive is used to share documents with others, to facilitate online collaboration, or as a repository for backup files.
- Use OneDrive with File Explorer: Windows 10 incorporates OneDrive into File Explorer to simplify the process of organizing and managing OneDrive folders (and contents), as well as ensuring that files are synchronized.
- Use Word Online: Word Online is a Web-based version of Word that enables you to create, edit, and format a document online without having to install Word on your computer.

7. Share and collaborate on documents.

- Share documents: Use Word and Word Online to share documents through links, emails, or blog posts, with varying levels of permission.
- Collaborate on a document: With an online document, multiple authors can collaborate on the shared document, editing it simultaneously.
- Present a document online: Word enables you to present a document online, although those viewing the presentation cannot edit it at the same time as the presentation.

Key Terms Matching

Match the key terms with their definitions. Write the key term letter by the appropriate numbered definition.

a. Bibliography
b. Citation
c. Comment
d. Comment balloon
e. Cover page
f. Endnote
g. Footnote
h. Index
i. MLA
j. OneDrive

k. PDF Reflow
l. Plagiarizing
m. Real-time co-authoring
n. Revision mark
o. Simple Markup
p. Source
q. Style manual
r. Table of contents
s. Track Changes
t. Works Cited

1. _____ Word feature that converts a PDF document into an editable Word document. **p. 358**

2. _____ A list of sources consulted by an author in his or her work; the listing preferred by MLA. **p. 338**

3. _____ A note recognizing a source of information or a quoted passage. **p. 335**

4. _____ A Web-based storage site and sharing utility. **p. 364**

5. _____ An alphabetical listing of topics covered in a document along with the page numbers where the topic is discussed. **p. 344**

6. _____ Word feature that monitors all additions, deletions, and formatting changes you make in a document. **p. 357**

7. _____ A citation that appears at the end of a document. **p. 340**

8. _____ Word feature that simplifies the display of comments and revision marks, resulting in a clean, uncluttered look. **p. 353**

9. _____ Page that lists headings in the order they appear in a document and the page numbers where the entries begin. **p. 343**

10. _____ A note, annotation, or additional information to the author or another reader about the content of a document. **p. 353**

11. _____ A list of sources consulted by an author in his or her work. **p. 338**

12. _____ A shapte that displays on the right side of a paragraph in which a comment has been made and provides access to the comment. **p. 353**

13. _____ A guide to a particular writing style outlining required rules and conventions related to the preparation of papers. **p. 334**

14. _____ The act of using and documenting the works of another as one's own. **p. 334**

15. _____ A citation that appears at the bottom of a page. **p. 340**

16. _____ A writing style established by the Modern Language Association with rules and conventions for preparing research papers (used primarily in the area of humanities). **p. 335**

17. _____ A Word feature that shows several authors simultaneously editing the document in Word or Word Online. **p. 374**

18. _____ Indicates where text is added, deleted, or formatted while the feature is active. **p. 357**

19. _____ The first page of a report, including the report title, author or student, and other identifying information. **p. 345**

20. _____ A publication, person, or media item that is consulted in the preparation of a paper and given credit. **p. 334**

Multiple Choice

1. When you are working on a group paper with your classmates, members can take turns to write and edit the content of the paper. Which feature must the group use so that members can see the changes made to the same document?

   (a) Mark Index Entries
   (b) Track Changes
   (c) Accept Changes
   (d) Create Cross-References

2. What Word Online view is required when you want to access commands on the tab?

   (a) Editing
   (b) Web Layout
   (c) Print Layout
   (d) Reading

3. Which of the following statements is *true* about sharing a document through Word Online?

   (a) It cannot be simultaneously edited by more than one person.
   (b) It must be a Word document.
   (c) It is available for viewing only, not editing.
   (d) It is available for simultaneous editing and collaboration.

4. The choice of whether to title a list of sources Bibliography, Works Cited, or References is dependent upon:

   (a) The writing style in use.
   (b) The version of Word you are using.
   (c) Whether the sources are from academic publications or professional journals.
   (d) Your own preference.

5. When working with Word Online, how can you tell that someone is editing a shared document at the same time that you are?

   (a) The Reviewing Pane displays, providing the names of others who are editing the document.
   (b) A comment balloon displays in the left margin.
   (c) A note displays on the right side of the status bar.
   (d) There is no way to tell who is editing at the same time.

6. Which of the following is *not* an option on Word's References tab?

   (a) Insert a New Comment
   (b) Update a Table of Contents
   (c) Insert a Footnote
   (d) Manage Sources

7. The writing style you are most likely to use in a business class is:

   (a) APA
   (b) Chicago
   (c) Turabian
   (d) MLA

8. To ensure that documents you save in OneDrive are synchronized with copies of the same documents saved on your hard drive, you could use:

   (a) the Backup setting in Word Options.
   (b) the Windows 10 Startup screen.
   (c) File Explorer.
   (d) the AutoRecover option.

9. Which feature provides a simple, uncluttered, view of comments and tracked changes made to a document?

   (a) Track All
   (b) Show Markup
   (c) Simple Markup
   (d) All Markup

10. After you create and insert a table of contents into a document:

    (a) Any subsequent page changes arising from the insertion or deletion of text to existing paragraphs must be entered manually.
    (b) Any additions to the entries in the table arising due to the insertion of new paragraphs defined by a heading style must be entered manually.
    (c) An index cannot be added to the document.
    (d) You can select a table of contents and click Update Table to bring the table of contents up to date.

Practice Exercises

1 Live. Work. Dine. Shop.

You are the assistant publicity manager of a construction company building a community where residents can live, work, dine, and shop within the community without having to get into a car. You and a team of colleagues are designing promotional materials for this project. You conducted your research online for such communities in other states, and wrote a promotional article. You will share your research with your team members online so that they can contribute, comment, and collaborate with you before submitting it to your manager for final approval. Refer to Figure 4.42 as you complete this exercise.

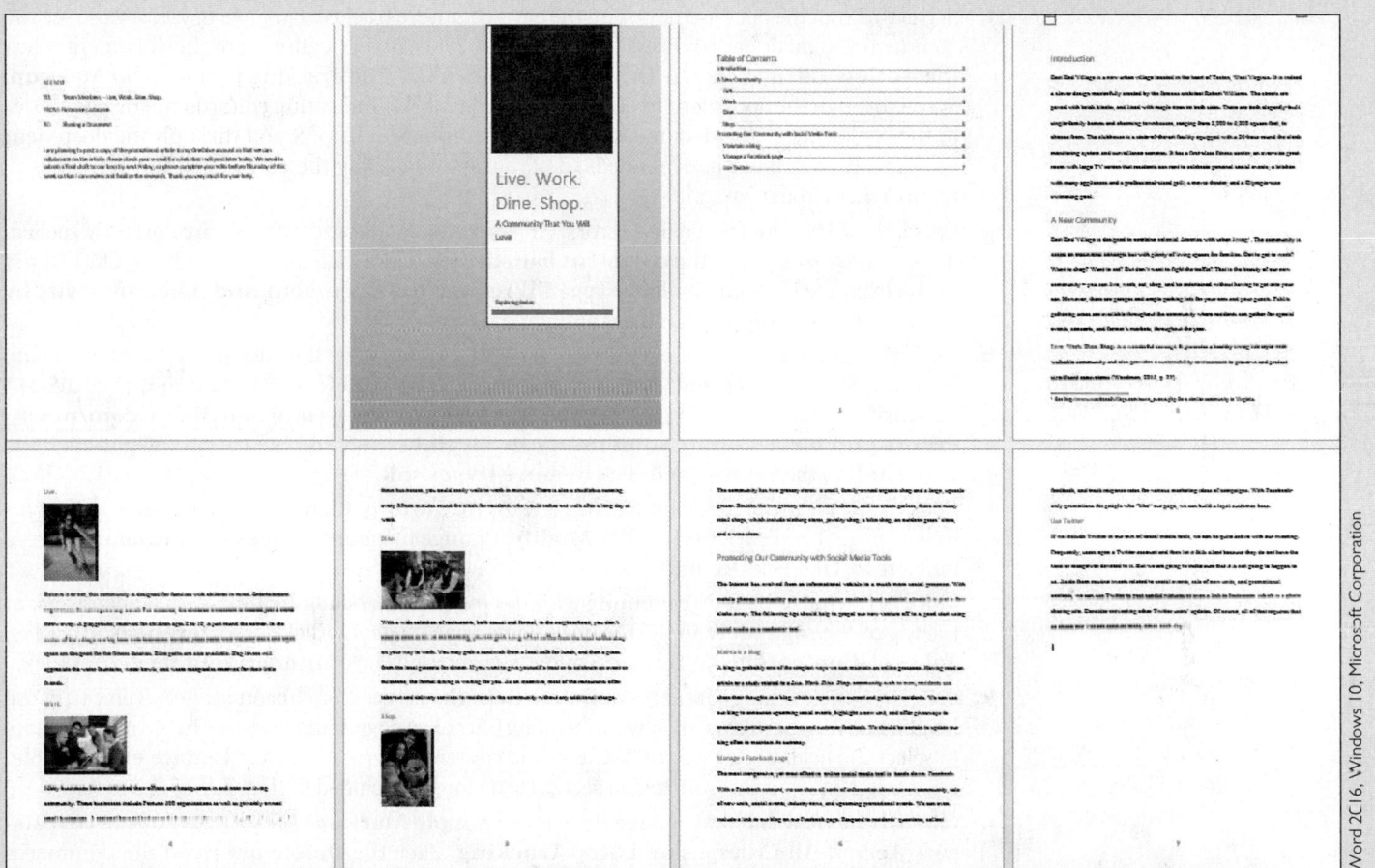

FIGURE 4.42 Design a Promotional Article

Word 2C16, Windows 10, Microsoft Corporation

a. Open *w04p1Live* and save it as **w04p1Live_LastFirst**.

b. Press **Ctrl+Home**. Click the **Insert tab**, click **Cover Page**, and then select **Austin**. Complete the cover page by completing the following:

- Click **Document title** and type **Live. Work. Dine. Shop.** (include the periods).
- Click **Document subtitle** and type **A Community That You Will Love**.
- Remove the current author (unless the current author shows your first and last names) and type your first and last names.
- Right-click the **Abstract paragraph** at the top of the page and click **Remove Content Control**.

c. Click the **Review tab**. Click the **Track Changes arrow** and click **Track Changes**. All of your edits will be marked as you work. Change the view to **All Markup**.

d. Make the following changes to the document:
- Change the Promotion heading on page 4 to **Promoting Our Community with Social Media Tools**.
- Select all text except the cover page. Change line spacing to **Double** (or **2.0**).
- Click the **Layout tab** and ensure that paragraph spacing Before and After is **0**.
- Scroll to page 5 and select the heading **Maintain a blog**. Click the **Review tab** and click **New Comment**. Type **Mary, what do you think about this idea?**

e. Insert a page break at the beginning of the cover page, and move to the beginning of the new page. Insert text from the PDF file *w04p1Invite*. Replace Firstname Lastname with your first and last names. Because Track Changes is on, the text you inserted is colored to indicate it is a new edit.

f. Scroll through the document, noting the edits that were tracked. On page 6, you should see the comment you made earlier. Press **Ctrl+Home** to move to the beginning of the document. Click the **Review tab** and change the Display for Review in the Tracking group to **No Markup**. Scroll through the document to note that revision marks (indicating edits) do not display. Move to the beginning of the document and select **Simple Markup**. Scroll through the document once more. Click a bar beside an edited paragraph to display the edits. Click the bar again to remove them from view.

g. Check the document for spelling errors. All names of people and websites are correctly spelled. Scroll to page 6 and click the **comment balloon** beside the *Maintain a blog* section. Click **Reply** in the expanded markup balloon. Type **I'll review the document and make my edits by Wednesday morning**. Close the comment balloon.

h. Click after the period at the end of the first sentence on page 3, under the *A New Community* heading. The sentence ends with *urban living*. Click the **References tab** and click **Insert Footnote** in the Footnotes group. Type **See http://www.westbroadvillage.com/news_events.php for a similar community in Virginia.** (include the period). Right-click the **hyperlink** in the footnote and click **Remove Hyperlink**.

i. Click the **Review tab**, and change the view to **No Markup**. Right-click the footnote at the bottom of page 3 and click **Style**. Click **Modify**. Change the font to **Times New Roman** and the font size to **10**. Click **OK** and click **Close**.

j. Move to the top of page 3 (beginning with the *Introduction* heading) and insert a page break at the top of the page. Move to the top of the new page (page 3). Click the **References tab**. Click **Table of Contents** in the Table of Contents group and click **Automatic Table 2**.

k. Point to Conclusion link and press **Ctrl+Click**. Delete the Conclusion section (removing the heading and the paragraph below the heading). Scroll to page 3 and click the **Table of Contents** to select the field. Click **Update Table** in the content control and select **Update entire table**. Click **OK**. Note that the Conclusion section is no longer included in the table of contents.

l. Click the **Review tab** and change the view to **Simple Markup**. Click the **Accept arrow** and click **Accept All Changes and Stop Tracking**. Click the **Delete arrow** in the Comments group and click **Delete All Comments in Document**. Scroll through the document and note that edits are no longer marked.

m. Click before the period in the last sentence in the second paragraph in the *A New Community* section that ends *protect significant ecosystems*. Click the **References tab** and click the **Style arrow** in the Citations & Bibliography group. Select **APA Sixth Edition**. Click **Insert Citation** in the Citations & Bibliography group and click **Add New Source**. Add the following source from a Journal Article and click **OK**:

Author: **Woodman, Jennifer Lynn**

Title: **Protecting Ecosystems**

Journal Name: **Journal of Ecosystems Studies**

Year: **2015**

Pages: **23–30**

Volume: **6**

Issue: **4**

(Hint: Click **Show All Bibliography Fields** to enter the volume and issue.)

n. Click the **citation** you just created, click the **Citation Options arrow**, and then click **Edit Citation**. Type **23** in the Pages box. Click **OK**.

o. Save the document. Click the **File tab** and click **Export**. Ensure that Create PDF/XPS Document is selected and click **Create PDF/XPS**. Leave the file name as w04p1Live_LastFirst and ensure that the type is PDF. Click **Publish** to save the document as a PDF file.

p. Close all open files, saving a file if prompted to do so. Based on your instructor's directions, submit the following:

w04p1Live_LastFirst.docx

w04p1Live_LastFirst.pdf

2 DREAM Act Letter

You are a partner in a law firm that deals with a large number of potential DREAM Act beneficiaries. The DREAM Act (Development, Relief, and Education for Alien Minors) provides conditional permanent residency to undocumented residents under certain conditions (good moral character, completion of U.S. high school degree, arrival in the United States as minors, etc.). Supporters of the Act contend that it provides social and economic benefits, whereas opponents label it as an amnesty program that rewards illegal immigration. Your law firm has partnered with leading law professors across the country to encourage the U.S. Executive Branch (Office of the President) to explore various options related to wise administration of the DREAM Act. In a letter to the president, you outline your position. Because it is of a legal nature, the letter makes broad use of footnotes and in-text references. Because the letter is to be signed and supported by law professors across the country, you will share the letter online, making it possible for others to edit and approve of the wording. Refer to Figure 4.43 as you complete this exercise.

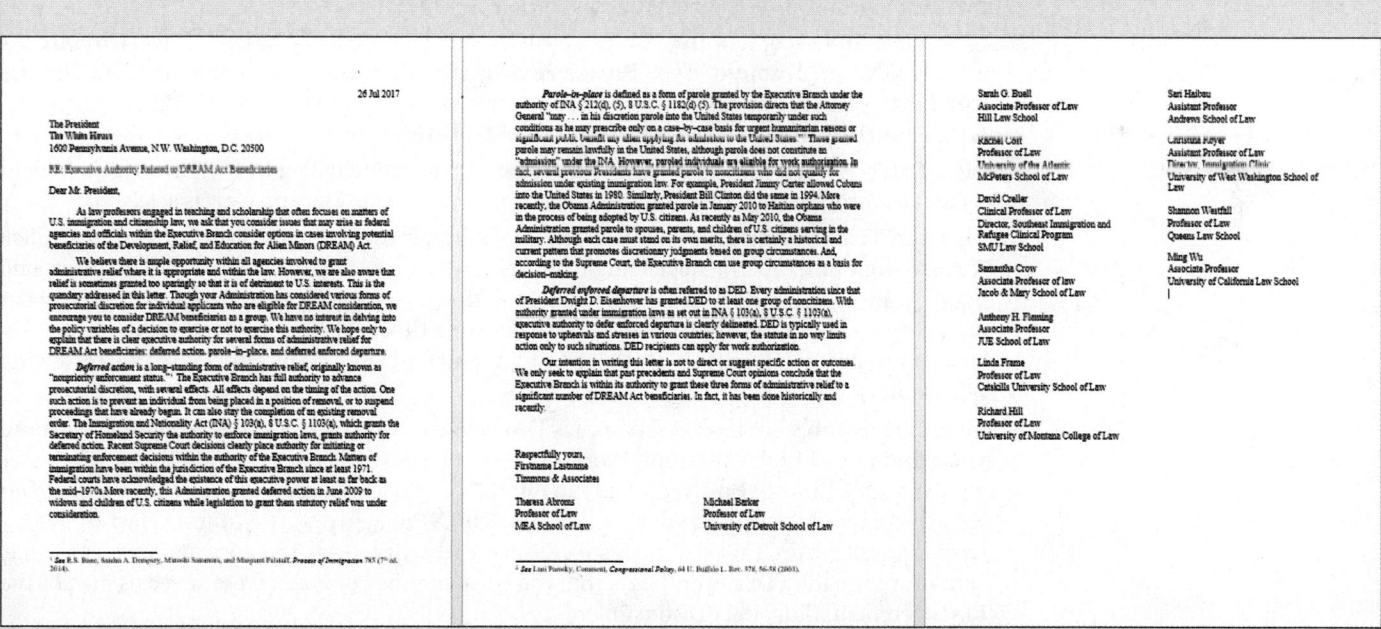

FIGURE 4.43 Format the DREAM Act Letter

a. Open a blank document. Click the **File tab** and click **Open**. Navigate to your data files and double-click the PDF file *w04p2Law.pdf*. Click **OK** when advised that Word will convert the document into an editable Word document. Save it as a Word document with the file name **w04p2Law_LastFirst**.

b. Scroll through the document and change Firstname Lastname in the closing to your first and last names. Check the document for spelling errors. All names are spelled correctly. The word *parol* should be spelled parole. The word *nonpriority* is not misspelled. Select text in the document from *As law professors engaged in teaching and scholarship* through *historically and recently*. Make sure paragraph spacing After is **6 pt**. Deselect the text. Change the margin setting to **Normal**.

c. Scroll down and select text from *Theresa Abroms* through the end of the document. Format the selected text in two columns. Deselect the text. Ensure that *Rachel Cost* and her information are in the same column by adding a **hard return** in front of her name. Scroll to the last page and place the insertion point to the left of *Sari Haibau*. Click **Breaks** in the Page Setup group on the Layout tab. Click **Column**.

d. Place the insertion point after the ending quotation mark that ends the first sentence in the third body paragraph on page 1. Click the **References tab** and click **Insert Footnote** in the Footnotes group. Type *See* **R.S. Bane, Sandra A. Dempsey, Minoshi Satomura, and Margaret Falstaff,** *Process of Immigration* **785 (7th ed. 2014).** (include the period). [Note: the word *See* is italicized in the footnote.]

e. Scroll to page 2 and place the insertion point after the quotation mark that ends the second sentence in the paragraph that begins *Parole-in-place is defined.* Click the **Footnotes Dialog Box Launcher** in the Footnotes group and click **Insert**. Type *See* **Lani Parosky, Comment,** *Congressional Policy,* **64 U. Buffalo L. Rev. 578, 56–58 (2003).** (include the period). [Note: the word *See* is italicized in the footnote.]

f. Save the document. Save the document to a OneDrive account in a new folder named **Word Practice Exercises**. After saving the file to OneDrive, close the document and exit Word.

g. Go to OneDrive.com and sign in to your Microsoft account. Navigate to the Word Practice Exercises folder and click **w04p2Law_LastFirst**. Click **Edit Document** and click **Edit in Word Online**. Scroll through the document and note that Word Online shows a placeholder for the footnotes you created. However, you cannot edit or work with footnotes in Word Online because it is limited in features. Point to a footnote placeholder to read a comment to the effect that you must open Word to work with footnotes.

h. Click **View** and select **Reading View**. Select the date at the top of the letter. Click **Comments** and click **New Comment**. Type **Please review this document in its entirety and make any edits you feel necessary.** (include the period). Click **Post**. Close the Comments pane. Click **Edit Document** and click **Edit in Word Online**.

i. Click **OPEN IN WORD** at the top. Click **Yes** in the warning dialog box. When the document opens in Word, click the **Review tab** and ensure that Simple Markup view is selected.

j. Click the **Track Changes arrow** in the Tracking group and click **Track Changes**. Click **Reviewing Pane** (not the Reviewing Pane arrow). Reverse the words *to* and *not* in the second body paragraph on page 1. Note the changes in the Reviewing Pane as well as the vertical bar on the right side of the affected paragraph indicating that edits have been made. Click the **vertical bar** to view the changes. Click it again to return to Simple Markup. Close the Reviewing (Revisions) Pane.

k. Click the **File tab**, click **Save As**, and click **Download a Copy**. Click **Click here to download your document** in the Microsoft Word Online dialog box, and click Open in the new browser window. Click **Enable Editing**. Click the **File tab** and click **Export**. Ensure that Create PDF/XPS Document is selected and click **Create PDF/XPS**. Leave the file name as w04p2Law_LastFirst and ensure that the type is PDF. Click **Publish** to save the document as a PDF file. Scroll through the PDF file and note that the edits and the comment were saved as part of the PDF document. Close the PDF document.

l. Ensure that w04p2Law_LastFirst.docx is displayed, click the **Review tab**, click the **Accept arrow** in the Changes group, and then click **Accept All Changes and Stop Tracking**. Right-click the **comment** and click **Delete Comment**.

m. Save the document. Close all open files. Based on your instructor's directions, submit the following:

w04p2Law_LastFirst.docx

w04p2Law_LastFirst.pdf

Mid-Level Exercises

1 WWW Web Services Agency

You work as a Web designer at WWW Web Services Agency and have been asked to provide some basic information to be used in a senior citizens' workshop. You want to provide the basic elements of good Web design and format the document professionally. Use the basic information you have already prepared in a Word document and revise it to include elements appropriate for a research-oriented paper.

a. Create a new blank document in Word. Open the PDF file *w04m1Web*, agreeing that Word will enable the document as a Word document. Save the subsequent Word document as **w04m1Web_LastFirst**.

b. Change the author name to **Shannon Lee**.

c. Place the insertion point at the end of the Proximity paragraph (after the period) on the second page of the document. The paragraph ends with *indicates less proximity*. Insert the following footnote: **Max Rebaza, Effective Websites, Chicago: Windy City Publishing, Inc. (2014)**. Do not include the period.

d. Insert a table of contents on a new page after the cover page. Use a style of your choice.

e. Add a bibliography to the document by inserting citation sources from the footnotes already in place. Because you will not use in-text citations, you will use the Source Manager to create the sources. To add new sources, complete the following steps:

  • Click the **References tab** and click **Manage Sources** in the Citations & Bibliography group.
  • Add a source for the footnote you created in Step c (a Book). Click **New** in the Source Manager dialog box and add the source to both the Current List and the Master List.
  • Create citation sources for the two additional sources identified in the document footnotes. The footnote on the fourth page is from an article in a periodical (issue 7), and the footnote on the fifth page cites a journal article.

f. Insert a bibliography at the end of the document on a separate page using the **Chicago** style. Select **Bibliography**. Apply **Heading 2 style** to the Bibliography heading and center the heading. Double space the bibliography and ensure that there is no paragraph spacing before or after.

g. Mark all occurrences of **Web, content,** and **site** as index entries. Create an index on a separate page after the bibliography using the **Formal** format.

h. Click the **File tab** and share the document, saving it to a folder of your choice in OneDrive in the process. After the document has been saved, click the **File tab** and get a shortened sharing link that can be edited by anyone with whom you share the link. Copy the link and paste it as a footer in w04m1Web_LastFirst.

i. Begin to track changes. Select the heading **Proximity and Balance** on the third page. Add a new comment, typing **This section seems incomplete. Please check and add content.**

j. Add the following sentence as the second sentence in the Contrast and Focus section: **You are most likely familiar with the concept of contrast when working with pictures in an image editor.**

k. Save the document in the location of your student files (not OneDrive), replacing the existing file and close the file. Based on your instructor's directions, submit w04m1Web_LastFirst.

2 Study Abroad

You want to study for a semester in a foreign country. For the application process, you need to write a proposal describing the program that you are interested in. You conducted online research, found a foreign university that appealed to you, and developed a list of activities that you will participate in while away. Now you want to format the Word document to enhance the readability and to include a cover page, table of contents, and index, before submitting it to your academic advisor for discussion.

a. Open *w04m2StudyAbroad* and save it as **w04m2StudyAbroad_LastFirst**.

b. Accept all formatting changes in the document. Turn on **Track Changes** so any further changes will be flagged.

c. Apply **Heading 1 style** to section headings that display in all capital letters. Apply **Heading 2 style** (scroll to locate the style) to section headings that display alone on a line in title case (the first letter of each word is capitalized).

d. Check all comments in the report, acting on them. Reply to each comment after you have read and/or taken action on the item.

e. Insert a footnote on page 1 at the end of the first sentence in the first paragraph (after the period), which ends with *Strasbourg, France*. Type the following for the footnote: **EU Studies Program in Strasbourg, France. http://www.eustudiesprogram.eu/resources/eustudies-web .pdf**. Change the number format for footnotes to **a, b, c** in the Footnotes dialog box. (Click **Apply**, not Insert.) Locate the endnote at the end of the page and convert it to a footnote.

f. Create a footer for the document consisting of the title **Study Abroad**, followed by a space and a page number. If the page number already appears as a footer, adjust it so that it follows Study Abroad. Left align the footer in the footer area. Do not display the footer on the first page.

g. Create a cover page of your choosing. Delete any placeholders that you are not using.

h. Create a page specifically for the table of contents right after the cover page, and generate a table of contents.

i. Mark all occurrences of the following text for inclusion in the index: Alsace, Black Forest, classes, EU, France, Grand Île, and Rhine valley. Cross-reference Strasbourg with France and European Union with EU. On a separate page at the end of the document, create the index in **Classic format**.

j. Share the document with your instructor, saving it to a folder of your choice in OneDrive in the process. After the document has been saved, get a sharing link that can be edited by anyone with whom you share the link. Copy the link and paste it as a footer (on a separate line below the page number) in w04m2StudyAbroad_LastFirst.

k. Save the document in the location of your student files (not OneDrive), replacing the existing file.

l. Save the document as a PDF file with the same filename. Save and close both files. Based on your instructor's directions, submit the following:

w04m2StudyAbroad_LastFirst.docx

w04m2StudyAbroad_LastFirst.pdf

3 American History

COLLABORATION CASE

FROM SCRATCH

You are working on a group project in an American history class. You and two other students will conduct online research and prepare a paper on favorite first ladies, including a brief history of the United States and a summary of American government.

a. Determine a group name to be used throughout this project, or use one assigned by your instructor. Also, select a writing style for the paper because you need to create and cite sources of your research and include a bibliography at the end of the paper.

b. Allocate one of three tasks to each team member. One student will develop a paragraph describing a favorite first lady (along with a photo), another will compose a paragraph giving a very brief history of the United States, and a third will describe our system of government. All paragraphs will be included in one shared document that will be submitted to your instructor.

Student 1:

c. Begin a blank document, turn on Track Changes, and include three headings, formatted in Heading 1 style: **Favorite First Lady**, **History**, and **American Government**. Save the document as **w04m3History_GroupName**, replacing Group Name with the name assigned by your instructor. In a paragraph beneath the Favorite First Lady heading, format text as **Times New Roman 12 pt**. Type a paragraph about your favorite first lady; include a photo of the first lady and at least two citations. On a separate page, create a Works Cited section. Type your name in the footer, save the document, and share it with the next student.

Student 2:

d. Open the shared document w04m3History_GroupName. In a paragraph beneath the History heading, format text as Times New Roman 12 pt. Write a paragraph about a brief description of American history and include at least **two citations**. Type your name in the footer, save the document, and share it with the next student.

Student 3:

e. Open the shared document w04m3History_GroupName. In a paragraph beneath the American Government heading, format text as **Times New Roman 12 pt**. Write a paragraph about the American government and include at least two citations. Update the Works Cited section. Type your name in the footer and save the document. Select the Favorite First Lady heading and insert a new comment. In the comment, provide the names of group members and the date of submission. Turn Track Changes off, save the document, and then save it as a PDF. Close both files. Share the PDF document with your teammates through an email link. The group will prepare and conduct an online presentation of the paper to the instructor. Based on your instructor's directions, submit the following:

w04m3History_GroupName.docx

w04m3History_GroupName.pdf

Beyond the Classroom

An Ethics Paper on Cheating

GENERAL CASE

FROM SCRATCH

Cheating and the violation of schools' honor codes have become major problems in many school systems. We often hear stories of how high school and college students can easily cheat on tests or written papers without being caught. You will use the Internet to research the topic of plagiarism, honor codes, and the honor and judicial program at your university and several other universities in your state. You should use more than five sources, with at least one each from the Internet, a book, and a journal. After your research is complete, you will write a three-page, double-spaced report describing your findings. Include the definition of plagiarism, the penalty for violating the honor code at your school, and the statistics for cheating in high schools and colleges. Cite all the sources in your paper, insert at least one footnote, and develop a bibliography for your paper based on the APA Sixth Edition writing style. Save the report as **w04b1Cheating_LastFirst**. Also save the report on OneDrive and create a sharing link. Include the link as a footnote in the paper you will submit. Save and close the file. Based on your instructor's directions, submit w04b1Cheating_LastFirst.

Computer History

DISASTER RECOVERY ✚

You are preparing a brief history of computers for inclusion in a group project. Another student began the project, but ran completely out of time and needs your help. Open *w04b2Computers* and save it as **w04b2Computers_LastFirst**. Turn on Track Changes and respond to all comments left for you by the previous student. Save and close the file. Based on your instructor's directions, submit w04b2Computers_LastFirst.

Capstone Exercise

You are enrolled in a personal finance course at your local university. One of the assignments is to write a group paper with another student about the different types of retirement plans. You and your partner conducted research on the topic and wrote a final draft of the report. You have the research paper and want to format it to enhance readability and address your partner's comments.

Track Revisions

The document you receive has a few comments and shows the last few changes by your partner. You will accept or reject the changes and then make a few of your own.

a. Open *w04c1Retirement* and save it as **w04c1Retirement_LastFirst**.

b. Ensure that the markup view is All Markup. Review the comments. On the first page, reject the replacement of the two words "NOW" in lowercase.

c. Accept all other tracked changes in the document and stop tracking. Keep all comments.

d. Change all headings to the correct heading styles as per the comments left by your partner.

e. Click the first comment balloon and reply to the comment by typing **I have made the style replacement.**

f. Select the table on page 2, click the **References tab**, and then click **Insert Caption** in the Captions group. Modify the caption text to read **Table 1: The Future Value of Money**. Make sure the caption displays above the selected item. Assign the caption **Table 2: Comparisons between a Traditional and a Roth IRA** for the next table, as instructed in the comments. Format both captions as normal and centered.

Credit Sources

You are now ready to add the citations for resources that your partner used when assembling this report.

a. Select **APA Sixth Edition style**. Click before the period ending in the first sentence of the *403(b) Plans* section. The sentence ends in *(TSA) plan*. Insert the following website citation:

Name of Webpage: **Choosing a Retirement Plan: 403(b) Tax-Sheltered Annuity Plan**
Name of Website: **IRS**
Year: **2014**
Month: **October**
Day: **08**
URL: **http://www.irs.gov/Retirement-Plans/ Choosing-a-Retirement-Plan:-403(b)-Tax-Sheltered-Annuity-Plan**

b. Click before the period ending the first sentence of the *401(K)* section. The sentence ends with *at their workplace*. Insert the following website citation:

Name of Webpage: **401(k) Plans**
Name of Website: **IRS**
Year: **2014**
Month: **October**
Day: **14**
URL: **http://www.irs.gov/Retirement-Plans/401(k)-Plans**

c. Add the source for the first table to the citation. You can follow the example as shown in the second table. The name of the webpage is the same as the table caption, and use **14** for Day.

d. Insert a footnote on page 2 at the end of the table heading in the *Introduction* section (the first line of the table), which ends with *6% annual return*. Type the following for the footnote: **The calculation did not take into consideration the cost of living adjustment (COLA)**. (Do not include the period.) Change the number format for footnotes to **a, b, c** in the Footnotes dialog box. (Click **Apply**, not Insert.)

e. Insert a **blank page** at the end of the report and insert a **bibliography** in APA style on the blank page with the title **Works Cited**. The bibliography should be **double spaced**, with no paragraph spacing and a font of **Times New Roman 12 pt**. The title Works Cited should be **centered**, **12 pt**, and not bold. All text in the bibliography should be **Black, Text 1 font color**.

Change the Cover Page, and Insert a Table of Contents and Index

You did not like the cover page, so you change it to another design. Also, to put the finishing touches on your document, you add a table of contents and an index.

a. Change the Facet cover page to **Integral**. Delete the Document subtitle and Course title placeholders.

b. Automatically generate a table of contents and display it on a page between the cover page and page 2. The style is **Automatic Table 1**.

c. Mark the following words as index entries, selecting **Mark All** for each: **Contribution, Roth IRA, Traditional IRA, 403(b),** and **401(k)**. Cross-reference **contribution with deduction**.

d. Add an index on a blank page at the end of the document. Use the **Classic format**. Use all other default settings.

e. Display a centered page number, using **Plain Number 2** format, in the footer of the document. Do not display the page number footer on the first page. Numbering begins with page 1 on the Table of Contents page.

f. Ensure that the second table is on one page, and update the Table of Contents.

g. Save the file, then save it again as a PDF document with the file name **w04c1Retirement_LastFirst.** Close both files and based on your instructor's directions, submit the following:

w04c1Retirement_LastFirst.docx
w04c1Retirement_LastFirst.pdf

Introduction to Excel

LEARNING OUTCOME

You will create and format a basic Excel worksheet.

OBJECTIVES & SKILLS: After you read this chapter, you will be able to:

Introduction to Spreadsheets

Mathematical Operations and Formulas

Worksheet Structure and Clipboard Tasks

Worksheet Formatting

Worksheets, Page Setup, and Printing

CASE STUDY | OK Office Systems

Alesha Bennett, the general manager at OK Office Systems (OKOS), asked you to calculate the retail price, sale price, and profit analysis for selected items on sale this month. Using markup rates provided by Alesha, you will calculate the retail price, the amount OKOS charges its customers for the products. You will calculate sale prices based on discount rates between 10% and 30%. Finally, you will calculate the profit margin to determine the percentage of the final sale price over the cost.

After you create the initial pricing spreadsheet, you will be able to change values and see that the formulas update the results automatically. In addition, you will insert data for additional sale items or delete an item based on the manager's decision. After inserting formulas, you will format the data in the worksheet to have a professional appearance.

Creating and Formatting a Worksheet

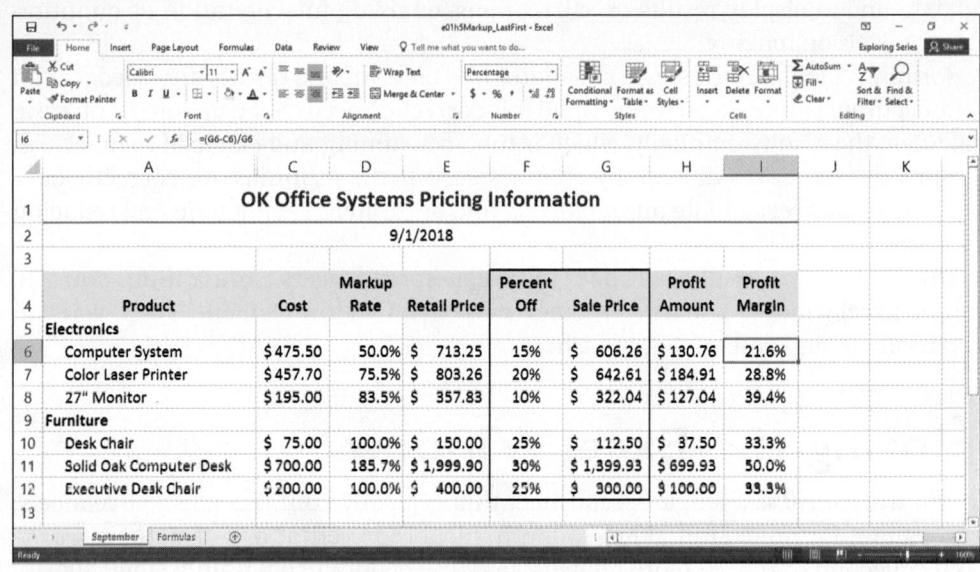

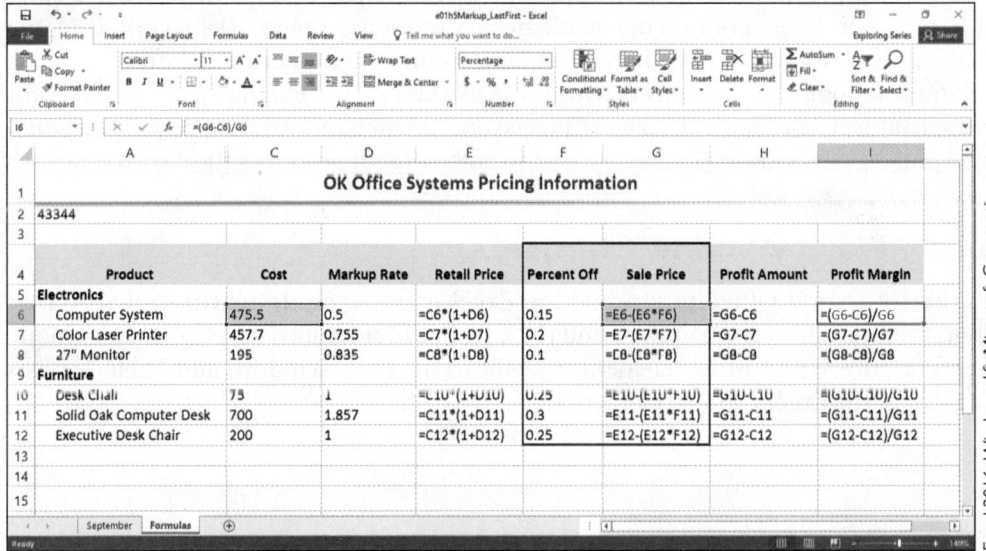

FIGURE 1.1 Completed OKOS Worksheet

CASE STUDY | OK Office Systems

Starting File	File to be Submitted
e01h1Markup	**e01h5Markup_LastFirst**

Introduction to Spreadsheets

Organizing, calculating, and evaluating quantitative data are important skills needed today for personal and managerial decision making. You track expenses for your household budget, maintain a savings plan, and determine what amount you can afford for a house or car payment. Retail managers create and analyze their organizations' annual budgets, sales projections, and inventory records. Charitable organizations track the donations they receive, the distribution of those donations, and overhead expenditures.

You should use a spreadsheet to maintain data and perform calculations. A *spreadsheet* is an electronic file that contains a grid of columns and rows used to organize related data and to display results of calculations, enabling interpretation of quantitative data for decision making.

Performing calculations using a calculator and entering the results into a ledger can lead to inaccurate values. If an input value is incorrect or needs to be updated, you have to recalculate the results manually, which is time-consuming and can lead to inaccuracies. A spreadsheet makes data entry changes easy. If the formulas are correctly constructed, the results recalculate automatically and accurately, saving time and reducing room for error.

In this section, you will learn how to design spreadsheets. In addition, you will explore the Excel window and learn the name of each window element. Then, you will enter text, values, and dates in a spreadsheet.

Exploring the Excel Window

In Excel, a *worksheet* is a single spreadsheet that typically contains descriptive labels, numeric values, formulas, functions, and graphical representations of data. A *workbook* is a collection of one or more related worksheets contained within a single file. By default, new workbooks contain one worksheet. Storing multiple worksheets within one workbook helps organize related data together in one file and enables you to perform calculations among the worksheets within the workbook. For example, you might want to create a budget workbook of 13 worksheets, one for each month to store your personal income and expenses and a final worksheet to calculate totals across the entire year.

Identify Excel Window Elements

Like other Microsoft Office programs, the Excel window contains the Quick Access Toolbar, the title bar, sizing buttons, and the Ribbon. In addition, Excel contains unique elements. Figure 1.2 identifies elements specific to the Excel window, and Table 1.1 lists and describes the Excel window elements.

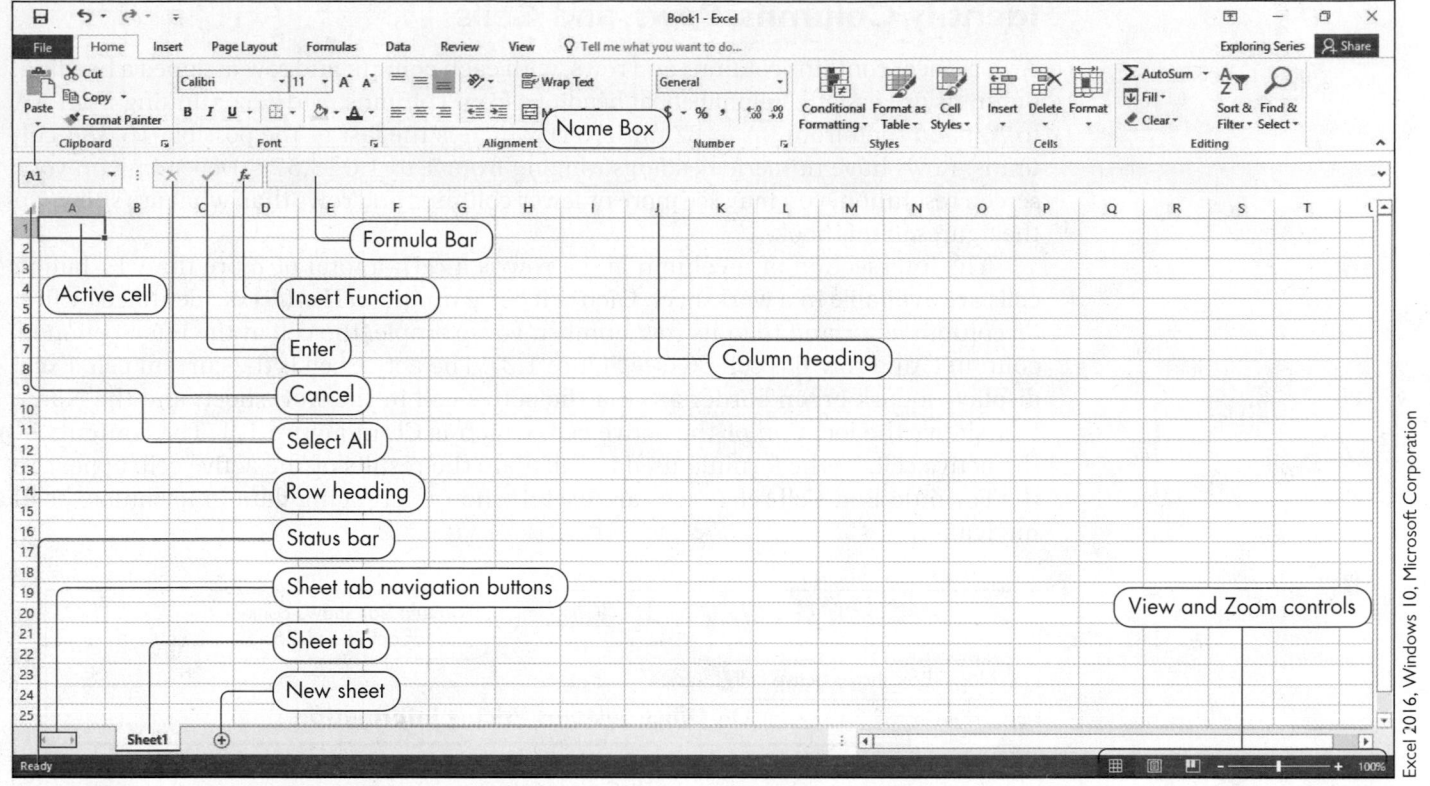

FIGURE 1.2 Excel Window

TABLE 1.1 Excel Elements

Element	Description
Name Box	An element located below the Ribbon and displays the address of the active cell. Use the Name Box to go to a cell, assign a name to one or more cells, or select a function.
Cancel ☒	When you enter or edit data, click Cancel to cancel the data entry or edit, and revert back to the previous data in the cell, if any. Cancel changes from gray to red when you position the pointer over it.
Enter ☑	When you enter or edit data, click Enter to accept data typed in the active cell and keep the current cell active. Enter changes from gray to blue when you position the pointer over it.
Insert Function *fx*	Click to display the Insert Function dialog box to search for and select a function to insert into the active cell. The Insert Function icon changes from gray to green when you position the pointer over it.
Formula Bar	An element located below the Ribbon and to the right of the Insert Function command. Shows the contents of the active cell. You enter or edit cell contents here or directly in the active cell. Drag the bottom border of the Formula Bar down to increase the height of the Formula Bar to display large amounts of data or a long formula contained in the active cell.
Select All ◻	The triangle at the intersection of the row and column headings in the top-left corner of the worksheet. Click it to select everything contained in the active worksheet.
Column headings	The letters above the columns. For example, B is the letter above the second column.
Row headings	The numbers to the left of the rows, such as 1, 2, 3, and so on. For example, 3 is the row heading for the third row.
Active cell	The current cell, which is indicated by a dark green border.
Sheet tab	A visual label that looks like a file folder tab. A sheet tab shows the name of a worksheet contained in the workbook. When you create a new Excel workbook, the default worksheet is named Sheet1.
New sheet ⊕	Click to insert a new worksheet to the right of the current worksheet.
Sheet tab navigation	If your workbook contains several worksheets, Excel may not show all the sheet tabs at the same time. Use the buttons to display the first, previous, next, or last worksheet.
Status bar	The row at the bottom of the Excel window. It displays information about a selected command or operation in progress. For example, it displays *Select destination and press ENTER or choose Paste* after you use the Copy command.
View controls	Icons on the right side of the status bar that control how the worksheet is displayed. Click a view control to display the worksheet in Normal, Page Layout, or Page Break Preview. ***Normal view*** displays the worksheet without showing margins, headers, footers, and page breaks. ***Page Layout view*** shows the margins, header and footer area, and a ruler. ***Page Break Preview*** indicates where the worksheet will be divided into pages.
Zoom control	Drag the zoom control to increase the size of the worksheet onscreen to see more or less of the worksheet data.

Identify Columns, Rows, and Cells

A worksheet contains columns and rows, with each column and row assigned a heading. Columns are assigned alphabetical headings from columns A to Z, continuing from AA to AZ, and then from BA to BZ until XFD, which is the last of the possible 16,384 columns. Rows have numeric headings ranging from 1 to 1,048,576. Depending on your screen resolution, you may see more or fewer columns and rows than what are shown in the figures in this book.

The intersection of a column and a row is a *cell*; a total of more than 17 billion cells are available in a worksheet. Each cell has a unique *cell address*, identified by first its column letter and then its row number. For example, the cell at the intersection of column C and row 6 is cell C6 (see Figure 1.3). The active cell is the current cell. Excel displays a dark green border around the active cell in the worksheet, and the Name Box shows the location of the active cell, which is C6 in Figure 1.3. The contents of the active cell, or the formula used to calculate the results of the active cell, appear in the Formula Bar. Cell references are useful when referencing data in formulas, or in navigation.

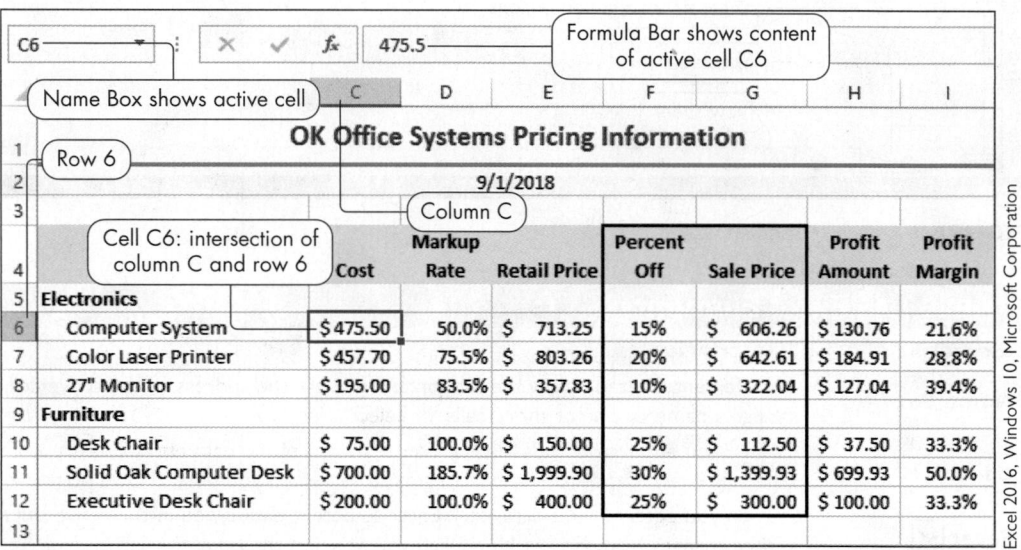

FIGURE 1.3 Columns, Rows, and Cells

Navigate in and Among Worksheets

To navigate to a new cell, click it or use the arrow keys on the keyboard. When you press Enter, the next cell down in the same column becomes the active cell. If you work in a large worksheet, use the vertical and horizontal scroll bars to display another area of the worksheet and click in the desired cell to make it the active cell. The keyboard contains several keys that can be used in isolation or in combination with other keys to navigate in a worksheet. Table 1.2 lists the keyboard navigation methods. The Go To command is helpful for navigating to a cell that is not visible onscreen.

Pearson Education, Inc.

TABLE 1.2 Keystrokes and Actions

Keystroke	Used to
↑	Move up one cell in the same column.
↓	Move down one cell in the same column.
←	Move left one cell in the same row.
→	Move right one cell in the same row.
Tab	Move right one cell in the same row.
Page Up	Move the active cell up one screen.
Page Down	Move the active cell down one screen.
Home	Move the active cell to column A of the current row.
Ctrl+Home	Make cell A1 the active cell.
Ctrl+End	Make the rightmost, lowermost active corner of the worksheet—the intersection of the last column and row that contains data—the active cell. Does not move to cell XFD1048576 unless that cell contains data.
F5 or Ctrl+G	Display the Go To dialog box to enter any cell address.

To display the contents of another worksheet within the workbook, click the sheet tab at the bottom of the workbook window, above the status bar. After you click a sheet tab, you can then navigate within that worksheet.

Entering and Editing Cell Data

You should plan the structure of a worksheet before you start entering data. Using the OKOS case presented at the beginning of the chapter as an example, use the following steps to plan the worksheet design, enter and format data, and complete the workbook. Refer to Figure 1.1 for the completed workbook.

Plan the Worksheet Design

1. **State the purpose of the worksheet.** The purpose of the OKOS worksheet is to store data about products on sale and to calculate important details, such as the retail price based on markup, the sales price based on a discount rate, and the profit margin.

2. **Decide what outputs are needed to achieve the purpose of the worksheet.** Outputs are the results you need to calculate. For the OKOS worksheet, the outputs include columns to calculate the retail price (i.e., the selling price to your customers), the sale price, and the profit margin. In some worksheets, you might want to create an *output area*, the region in the worksheet to contain formulas dependent on the values in the input area.

3. **Decide what input values are needed to achieve the desired output.** Input values are the initial values, such as variables and assumptions. You may change these values to see what type of effects different values have on the end results. For the OKOS worksheet, the input values include the costs OKOS pays the manufacturers, the markup rates, and the proposed discount rates for the sale. In some worksheets, you should create an *input area*, a specific region in the worksheet to store and change the variables used in calculations. For example, if you applied the same Markup Rate and same Percent Off for all products, it would be easier to create an input area at the top of the worksheet to change the values in one location rather than in several locations.

Enter and Format the Data

4. **Enter the labels, values, and formulas in Excel.** Use the design plan (steps 2–3) as you enter labels, input values, and formulas to calculate the output. In the OKOS worksheet, descriptive labels (the product names) appear in the first column to indicate that the values on a specific row pertain to a specific product. Descriptive labels appear at the top of each column, such as Cost and Retail Price, to describe the values in the respective column. Change the input values to test that your formulas produce correct results. If necessary, correct any errors in the formulas to produce correct results. For the OKOS worksheet, change some of the original costs and markup rates to ensure the calculated retail price, selling price, and profit margin percentage results update correctly.

5. **Format the numerical values in the worksheet.** Align decimal points in columns of numbers and add number formats and styles. In the OKOS worksheet, you will use Accounting Number Format and the Percent Style to format the numerical data. Adjust the number of decimal places as needed.

6. **Format the descriptive titles and labels.** Add bold and color to headings so that they stand out and are attractive. Apply other formatting to headings and descriptive labels. In the OKOS worksheet, you will center the main title over all the columns, bold and center column labels over the columns, and apply other formatting to the headings.

Complete the Workbook

7. **Document the workbook as thoroughly as possible.** Include the current date, your name as the workbook author, assumptions, and purpose of the workbook. Some people provide this documentation in a separate worksheet within the workbook. You can also add some documentation in the Properties section when you click the File tab.

8. **Save and share the completed workbook.** Preview and prepare printouts for distribution in meetings, send an electronic copy of the workbook to those who need it, or upload the workbook on a shared network drive or in the cloud.

Enter Text

STEP 1 ⟩⟩ *Text* is any combination of letters, numbers, symbols, and spaces not used in calculations. Excel treats phone numbers, such as 555-1234, and Social Security numbers, such as 123-45-6789, as text entries. You enter text for a worksheet title to describe the contents of the worksheet, as row and column labels to describe data, and as cell data. In Figure 1.4, the cells in column A contain text, such as Class. Text aligns at the left cell margin by default.

To enter text in a cell, complete the following steps:

1. Make sure the cell is active where you want to enter text.
2. Type the text. If you want to enter a numeric value as text, such as a class section number, type an apostrophe and the number, such as '002.
3. Make another cell the active cell after entering data by completing one of the following steps:

   • Press Enter on the keyboard.
   • Press an arrow key on the keyboard.
   • Press Tab on the keyboard.

   Keep the current cell active after entering data by completing one of the following steps:

   • Press Ctrl+Enter on the keyboard.
   • Click Enter (the check mark between the Name Box and the Formula Bar).

As soon as you begin typing a label into a cell, the ***AutoComplete*** feature searches for and automatically displays any other label in the same column that matches the letters you type. The top half of Figure 1.4 shows Spreadsheet Apps is typed in cell A3. When you start to type *Sp* in cell A4, AutoComplete displays Spreadsheet Apps because a text entry in the same column already starts with *Sp*. Press Enter to accept the repeated label, or continue typing to enter a different label, such as Spanish II. The bottom half of Figure 1.4 shows that '002 was entered in cell B4 to start the text with a 0. Otherwise, Excel would have eliminated the zeros in the class section number. Ignore the error message that displays when you intentionally use an apostrophe to enter a number which is not actually a value.

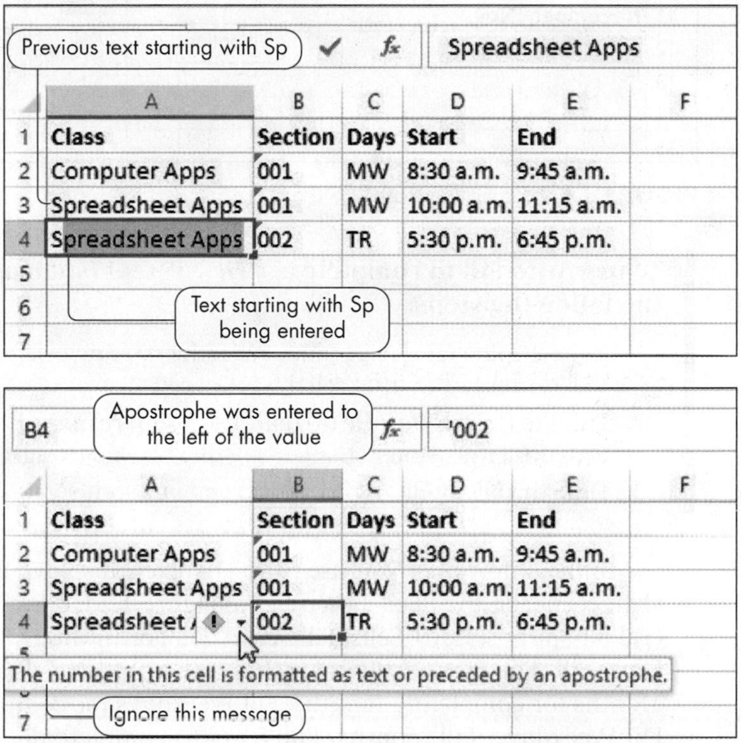

Excel 2016, Windows 10, Microsoft Corporation

FIGURE 1.4 Entering Text

Use Auto Fill to Complete a Sequence

STEP 2 »» While AutoComplete helps to complete a label that is identical to another label in the same column, ***Auto Fill*** is a feature that helps you complete a sequence of words or values. For example, if you enter January in a cell, use Auto Fill to fill in the rest of the months in adjacent cells so that you do not have to type the rest of the month names. Auto Fill can help you complete other sequences, such as quarters (Qtr 1, etc.), weekdays, and weekday abbreviations after you type the first item in the sequence. Figure 1.5 shows the results of filling in months, abbreviated months, quarters, weekdays, abbreviated weekdays, and increments of 5.

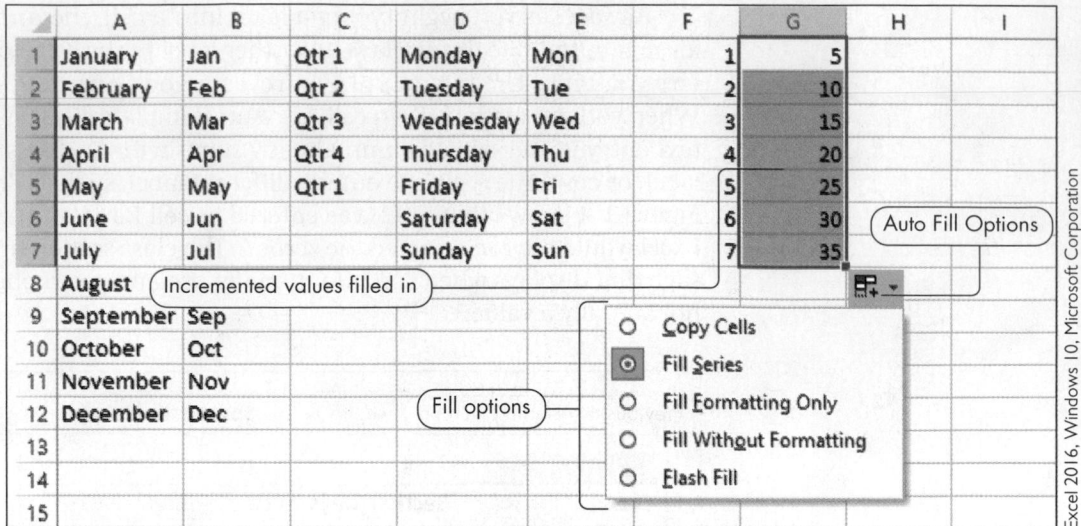

FIGURE 1.5 Auto Fill Examples

To use Auto Fill to complete a series of text (such as month names), complete the following steps:

1. Type the first label (e.g., January) in the starting cell (e.g., cell A1) and press Ctrl+Enter to keep that cell the active cell.

2. Point to the **fill handle** (a small green square in the bottom-right corner of the active cell) until the pointer changes to a thin black plus sign.

3. Drag the fill handle to repeat the content in other cells (e.g., through cell A12).

Immediately after you use Auto Fill, Excel displays Auto Fill Options in the bottom-right corner of the filled data (refer to Figure 1.5). Click Auto Fill Options to display several fill options: Copy Cells, Fill Series, Fill Formatting Only, Fill Without Formatting, or Flash Fill. The menu will also include other options, depending on the cell content: Fill Months for completing months; Fill Weekdays for completing weekdays; and Fill Days, Fill Weekdays, Fill Months, Fill Years to complete dates. Select Fill Formatting Only when you want to copy the formats but not complete a sequence. Select Fill Without Formatting when you want to complete the sequence but do not want to format the rest of the sequence.

To use Auto Fill to fill a sequence of consecutive numbers (such as 1, 2, 3, etc.), complete the following steps:

1. Type the first number in the starting cell (e.g., cell F1) and press Ctrl+Enter to keep that cell the active cell.

2. Drag the fill handle to fill the content in other cells. Excel will copy the same number for the rest of the cells.

3. Click Auto Fill Options and select Fill Series. Excel will change the numbers to be in sequential order, starting with the original value you typed.

For non-consecutive numeric sequences, you must specify the first two values in sequence. For example, if you want to fill in 5, 10, 15, and so on, you must enter 5 and 10 in two adjacent cells before using Auto Fill so that Excel knows to increment by 5.

> **To use Auto Fill to fill a sequence of number patterns (such as 5, 10, 15, 20 shown in the range G1:G7 in Figure 1.5), complete the following steps:**
>
> 1. Type the first two numbers of the sequence in adjoining cells.
> 2. Select those two cells containing the starting two values.
> 3. Drag the fill handle to fill in the rest of the sequence.

TIP: FLASH FILL

Flash Fill is a similar feature to Auto Fill in that it can quickly fill in data for you; however, *Flash Fill* uses data in previous columns as you type in a new label in an adjoining column to determine what to fill in. For example, assume that column A contains a list of first and last names (such as Penny Sumpter in cell A5), but you want to have a column of just first names. To do this, type Penny's name in cell B5, click Fill in the Editing group on the Home tab and select Flash Fill to fill in the rest of column B with people's first names based on the data entered in column A.

Enter Values

STEP 3 ▶▶ *Values* are numbers that represent a quantity or a measurable amount. Excel usually distinguishes between text and value data based on what you enter. The primary difference between text and value entries is that value entries can be the basis of calculations, whereas text cannot. In Figure 1.3, the data below the Cost, Markup Rates, and Percent Off labels are values. Values align at the right cell margin by default. After entering values, align decimal places and apply formatting by adding characters, such as $ or %. Entering values is the same process as entering text: Type the value in a cell and click Enter or press Enter.

TIP: ENTERING VALUES WITH TRAILING ZEROS OR PERCENTAGES

You do not need to type the last 0 in 475.50 shown in cell C6 in Figure 1.3. Excel will remove or add the trailing 0 depending on the decimal place formatting. Similarly, you do not have to type the leading 0 in a percentage before the decimal point. Type a percent in the decimal format, such as .5 for 50%. You will later format the value.

Enter Dates and Times

STEP 4 ▶▶ You can enter dates and times in a variety of formats. You should enter a static date to document when you create or modify a workbook or to document the specific point in time when the data were accurate, such as on a balance sheet or income statement. Later, you will learn how to use formulas to enter dates that update to the current date. In Figure 1.6, the data in column A contains the date 9/1/2018 but in different formats. Dates are values, so they align at the right side of a cell. The data in column C contains the time 2:30 PM but in different formats.

◢	A	B	C	D
1	9/1/2018		2:30:00 PM	
2	Saturday, September 1, 2018		14:30	
3	9/1		2:30 PM	
4	9/1/18		14:30:00	
5	09/01/18		2:30:00 PM	
6	1-Sep			
7	1-Sep-18			
8	September 1, 2018			
9				

Excel 2016, Windows 10, Microsoft Corporation

FIGURE 1.6 Date and Time Examples

Excel displays dates differently from the way it stores dates. For example, the displayed date 9/1/2018 represents the first day in September in the year 2018. Excel stores dates as serial numbers starting at 1 with January 1, 1900, so that you can create formulas, such as to calculate how many days exist between two dates. For example, 9/1/2018 is stored as 43344.

Edit and Clear Cell Contents

After entering data in a cell, you may need to change it. For example, you may want to edit a label to make it more descriptive, such as changing a label from OKC Office Systems Information to OKC Office Systems Pricing Information. Furthermore, you might realize a digit is missing from a value and need to change 500 to 5000.

To edit the contents of a cell, compete the following steps:

1. Click the cell.
2. Click in the Formula Bar or press F2 to put the cell in edit mode. The insertion point displays on the right side of the data in the cell when you press F2.
3. Make the changes to the content in the cell.
4. Click or press Enter.

You may want to clear or delete the contents in a cell if you no longer need data in a cell.

To clear the contents of a cell, complete the following steps:

1. Click the cell.
2. Press Delete or click the cell, click Clear in the Editing group on the Home tab, and select the desired option (see Figure 1.7).

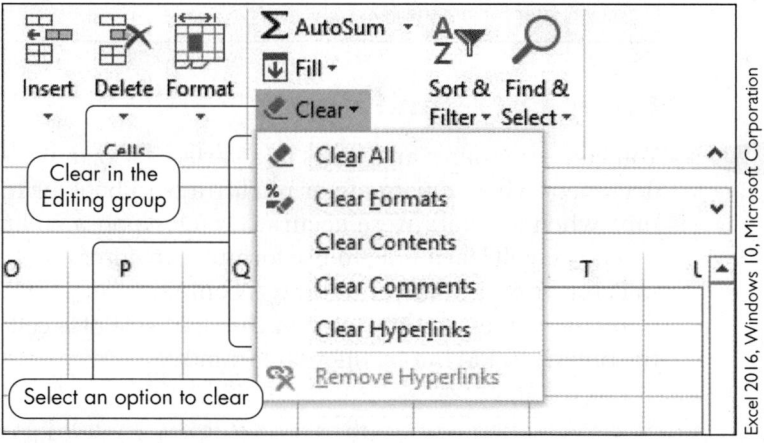

FIGURE 1.7 Clear Options

Quick Concepts

1. What are two major advantages of using an electronic spreadsheet instead of a paper-based ledger? *p. 404*

2. What are the visual indicators that a cell is the active cell? *p. 406*

3. What steps should you perform before entering data into a worksheet? *pp. 407-408*

4. What three types of content can you can enter into a cell? Give an example (different from those in the book) for each type. *pp. 408-411*

Skills covered: Enter Text
• Use Auto Fill to Complete a
Sequence • Enter Values • Enter a
Date • Clear Cell Contents

1 Introduction to Spreadsheets

As the assistant manager of OKOS, you will create a worksheet that shows the cost (the amount OKOS pays its suppliers), the markup percentage (the amount by which the cost is increased), and the retail selling price. You also will list the discount percentage (such as 25% off) for each product, the sale price, and the profit margin percentage.

STEP 1 ▶▶ ENTER TEXT

Now that you have planned the OKOS worksheet, you are ready to enter labels for the title, column labels, and row labels. You will type a title in cell A1, product labels in the first column, and row labels in the fourth row. Refer to Figure 1.8 as you complete Step 1.

	A	B	C	D	E	F	G	H	I
1	OK Office Sys... mation								
2									
3									
4	Product	Code	Cost	Markup Ra	Retail Pric	Percent O	Sale Price	Profit Margin	
5	Computer System					0.15			
6	Color Laser Printer					0.2			
7	Filing Cabinet					0.1			
8	Desk Chair					0.25			
9	Solid Oak Computer Desk					0.3			
10	27" Monitor					0.1			
11									
12									

Step b: Enter text for first product

Steps b and c: Labels extend into empty column B

Step c: Name of products

Excel 2016, Windows 10, Microsoft Corporation

FIGURE 1.8 Text Entered in Cells

a. Open *e01h1Markup* and save it as **e01h1Markup_LastFirst**.

When you save files, use your last and first names. For example, as the Excel author, I would save my workbook as *e01h1Markup_MulberyKeith*.

> **TROUBLESHOOTING:** If you make any major mistakes in this exercise, you can close the file, open *e01h1Markup* again, and then start this exercise over.

b. Click **cell A5**, type **Computer System**, and then press **Enter**.

When you press Enter, the next cell down—cell A6 in this case—becomes the active cell. The text does not completely fit in cell A5, and some of the text appears in cell B5. If you make cell B5 the active cell, the Formula Bar is empty, indicating that nothing is stored in that cell.

c. Type **Color Laser Printer** in **cell A6** and press **Enter**.

When you start typing C in cell A6, AutoComplete displays a ScreenTip suggesting a previous text entry starting with C—Computer System—but keep typing to enter Color Laser Printer instead.

d. Continue typing the rest of the text in **cells A7** through **A10** as shown in Figure 1.8. Text in column A appears to flow into column B.

You just entered the product labels to describe the data in each row.

TROUBLESHOOTING: If you make an error, click in the cell containing the error and retype the label, or press F2 to edit the cell contents, move the insertion point using the arrow keys, press Backspace or Delete to delete the incorrect characters, type the correct characters, and press Enter. If you type a label in an incorrect cell, click the cell and press Delete.

e. Click **Save** on the Quick Access Toolbar to save the changes you made to the workbook.

You should develop a habit of saving periodically. That way if your system unexpectedly shuts down, you will not lose everything you worked on.

STEP 2 ›› USE AUTO FILL TO COMPLETE A SEQUENCE

You want to assign a product code for each product on sale. You will assign consecutive numbers 101 to 106. After typing the first code number, you will use Auto Fill to complete the rest of the series. Refer to Figures 1.9 and 1.10 as you complete Step 2.

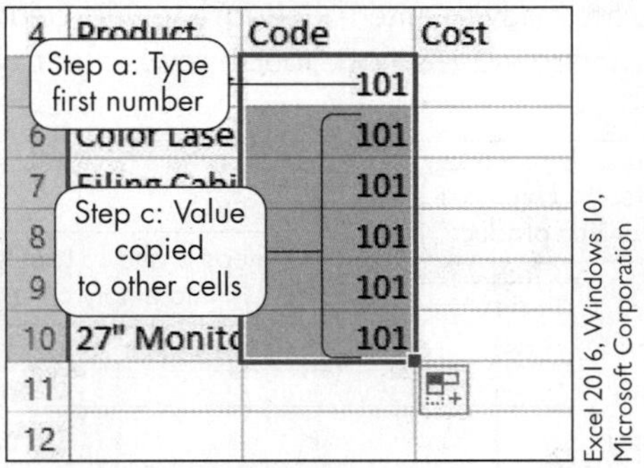

FIGURE 1.9 Auto Fill Copied Original Value

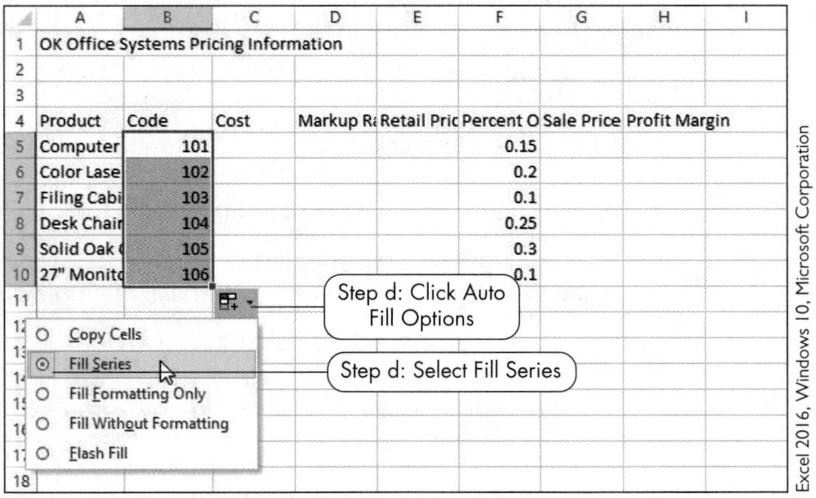

FIGURE 1.10 Auto Fill Sequence

a. Click **cell B5**, type **101**, and then press **Ctrl+Enter**.

The product name Computer System no longer overlaps into column B after you enter data into cell B5. The data in cell A5 is not deleted; the rest of the label is hidden until you increase the column width later.

b. Position the pointer on the fill handle in the bottom-right corner of **cell B5**.

The pointer looks like a black plus sign when you point to a fill handle.

c. Double-click the **cell B6 fill handle**.

Excel copies 101 as the item number for the rest of the products. Excel stops inserting item numbers in column B when it detects the last label in cell A10 (refer to Figure 1.9).

d. Click **Auto Fill Options** and select **Fill Series**. Save the workbook.

Excel changes the duplicate values to continue sequentially in a series of numbers.

Now that you have entered the descriptive labels and item numbers, you will enter the cost and markup rate for each product. Refer to Figure 1.11 as you complete Step 3.

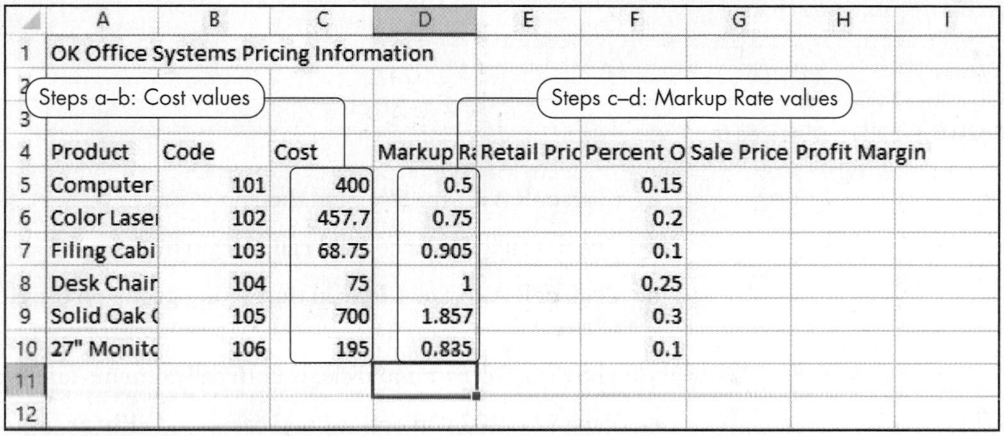

	A	B	C	D	E	F	G	H	I
1	OK Office Systems Pricing Information								
2	Steps a–b: Cost values				Steps c–d: Markup Rate values				
3									
4	Product	Code	Cost	Markup R;	Retail Pric	Percent O	Sale Price	Profit Margin	
5	Computer	101	400	0.5		0.15			
6	Color Laser	102	457.7	0.75		0.2			
7	Filing Cabi	103	68.75	0.905		0.1			
8	Desk Chair	104	75	1		0.25			
9	Solid Oak (	105	700	1.857		0.3			
10	27" Monitc	106	195	0.835		0.1			
11									
12									

FIGURE 1.11 Values Entered in Cells

a. Click **cell C5**, type **400**, and then press **Enter**.

b. Type the remaining costs in **cells C6** through **C10** shown in Figure 1.11.

To improve your productivity, use the number keypad (if available) on the right side of your keyboard. It is much faster to type values and press Enter on the number keypad rather than to use the numbers on the keyboard. Make sure Num Lock is active before using the number keypad to enter values.

c. Click **cell D5**, type **0.5**, and then press **Enter**.

You entered the markup rate as a decimal instead of a percentage. You will apply Percent Style later, but now you will concentrate on data entry.

d. Type the remaining values in **cells D6** through **D10** as shown in Figure 1.11. Save the workbook.

As you review the worksheet, you realize you need to provide a date to indicate when the sale starts. Refer to Figure 1.12 as you complete Step 4.

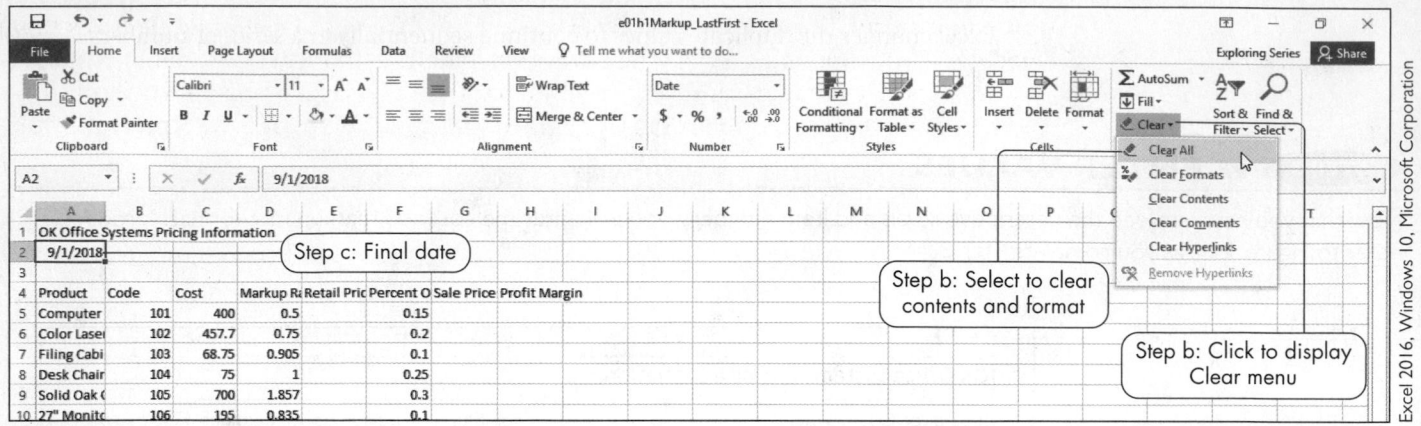

FIGURE 1.12 Date Entered in a Cell

a. Click **cell A2**, type **9/1**, and then press **Enter**.

The date aligns on the right cell margin by default. Excel displays 1-Sep instead of 9/1.

b. Click **cell A2**, click **Clear** in the Editing group on the Home tab, and then select **Clear All**.

The Clear All command clears both cell contents and formatting in the selected cell(s).

c. Type **9/1/2018** in **cell A2** and press **Ctrl+Enter**.

> **TROUBLESHOOTING:** If you did not use Clear All and typed 9/1/2018 in cell A2, Excel would have retained the previous date format and displayed 1-Sep again.

When you type the month, day, and year such as 9/1/2018, Excel enters the date in that format (unless it has a different date format applied).

d. Save the workbook. Keep the workbook open if you plan to continue with the next Hands-On Exercise. If not, close the workbook, and exit Excel.

Mathematical Operations and Formulas

A *formula* combines cell references, arithmetic operations, values, and/or functions used in a calculation. Formulas transform static numbers into meaningful results that update as values change. For example, a payroll manager can build formulas to calculate the gross pay, deductions, and net pay for an organization's employees, or a doctoral student can create formulas to perform various statistical calculations to interpret his or her research data.

In this section, you will learn how to use mathematical operations in Excel formulas. You will refresh your memory of the mathematical order of operations and learn how to construct formulas using cell addresses so that when the value of an input cell changes, the result of the formula changes without you having to modify the formula.

Creating Formulas

Use formulas to help you analyze how results will change as the input data changes. You can change the value of your assumptions or inputs and explore the results quickly and accurately. For example, if your rent increases, how does that affect your personal budget? Analyzing different input values in Excel is easy after you build formulas. Simply change an input value and observe the change in the formula results. In the OKOS product sales worksheet, the results for the Retail Price, Sale Price, and Profit Margin labels were calculated by using formulas (refer to Figure 1.1).

Use Cell References in Formulas

STEP 1 ▶▶ You should use cell references instead of values in formulas where possible. You may include values in an input area—such as dates, salary, or costs—that you will need to reference in formulas. Referencing these cells in your formulas, instead of typing the value of the cell to which you are referring, keeps your formulas accurate if you change values to perform a what-if analysis.

Figure 1.13 shows a worksheet containing input values and results of formulas. The figure also displays the actual formulas used to generate the calculated results. For example, cell E2 contains the formula =B2+B3. Excel uses the value stored in cell B2 (10) and adds it to the value stored in cell B3 (2). The result (12) appears in cell E2 instead of the actual formula. The Formula Bar displays the formula entered into the active cell.

| E2 | ▼ | ⋮ | ✕ ✓ *fx* | =B2+B3 | | |

◢	A	B	C	D	E	F
1	**Description**	**Values**		**Description**	**Results**	**Formulas in Column E**
2	First input value	10		Sum of 10 and 2	12	=B2+B3
3	Second input value	2		Difference between 10 and 2	8	=B2-B3
4				Product of 10 and 2	20	=B2*B3
5				Results of dividing 10 by 2	5	=B2/B3
6				Results of 10 to the 2nd power	100	=B2^B3

Excel 2016, Windows 10, Microsoft Corporation

FIGURE 1.13 Formula Results

To enter a formula, complete the following steps:

1. Click the cell.
2. Type an equal sign (=), followed by the arithmetic expression, using cell references instead of values. Do not include any spaces in the formula.
3. Click Enter or press Enter.

TIP: EQUAL SIGN NEEDED

If you type B2+B3 without the equal sign, Excel does not recognize that you entered a formula and stores the "formula" as text.

TIP: UPPER OR LOWERCASE

When you create a formula, type the cell references in uppercase, such as =B2+B3, or lowercase, such as =b2+b3. Excel changes cell references to uppercase automatically.

In Figure 1.13, cell B2 contains 10, and cell B3 contains 2. Cell E2 contains =B2+B3 but shows the result 12. If you change the value of cell B3 to 5, cell E2 displays the new result, which is 15. However, if you had typed actual values in the formula, =10+2, you would have to edit the formula to =10+5, even though the value in cell B3 was changed to 5. Using values in formulas can cause problems as you might forget to edit the formula or you might have a typographical error if you edit the formula. Always design worksheets in such a way as to be able to place those values that might need to change as input values. Referencing cells with input values in formulas instead of using the values themselves will avoid having to modify your formulas if an input value changes later.

TIP: WHEN TO USE A VALUE IN A FORMULA

Use cell references instead of actual values in formulas, unless the value will never change. For example, if you want to calculate how many total months are in a specified number of years, enter a formula such as =B5*12, where B5 contains the number of years. You might want to change the number of years, so you type that value in cell B5. However, every year always has 12 months, so you can use the value 12 in the formula.

Apply the Order of Operations

The **order of operations** (also called order of precedence) are rules that controls the sequence in which arithmetic operations are performed, which affects the result of the calculation. Excel performs mathematical calculations left to right in this order: **P**arentheses, **E**xponentiation, **M**ultiplication or **D**ivision, and finally **A**ddition or **S**ubtraction. Some people remember the order of operations with the phrase *Please Excuse My Dear Aunt Sally*.

Table 1.3 lists the primary order of operations. Use Help to learn about the complete order of precedence.

TABLE 1.3	Order of Operations	
Order	**Description**	**Symbols**
1	Parentheses	( )
2	Exponentiation	^
3	Multiplication and Division	* and / (respectively)
4	Addition and Subtraction	+ and − (respectively)

Pearson Education, Inc.

Figure 1.14 shows formulas, the sequence in which calculations occur, calculations, the description, and the results of each order of operations. The highlighted results are the final formula results. This figure illustrates the importance of symbols and use of parentheses.

	A	B	C	D	E	F
1	**Input**		**Formula**	**Sequence**	**Description**	**Result**
2	2		=A2+A3*A4+A5	1	3 (cell A3) * 4 (cell A4)	12
3	3			2	2 (cell A2) + 12 (order 1)	14
4	4			3	14 (order 2) + 5 (cell A5)	19
5	5					
6			=(A2+A3)*(A4+A5)	1	2 (cell A2) + 3 (cell A3)	5
7				2	4 (cell A4) + 5 (cell A5)	9
8				3	5 (order 1) * 9 (order 2)	45
9						
10			=A2/A3+A4*A5	1	2 (cell A2) / 3 (cell A3)	0.666667
11				2	4 (cell A4) * 5 (cell A5)	20
12				3	0.666667 (order 1) + 20 (order 2)	20.66667
13						
14			=A2/(A3+A4)*A5	1	3 (cell A3) + 4 (cell A4)	7
15				2	2 (cell A2) / 7 (order 1)	0.285714
16				3	0.285714 (order 2) * 5 (cell A5)	1.428571
17						
18			=A2^2+A3*A4%	1	4 (cell A4) is converted to percentage	0.04
19				2	2 (cell A2) to the power of 2	4
20				3	3 (cell A3) * 0.04 (order 1)	0.12
21				4	4 (order 2) + 0.12 (order 3)	4.12

Excel 2016, Windows 10, Microsoft Corporation

FIGURE 1.14 Formula Results Based on Order of Operations

Use Semi-Selection to Create a Formula

STEP 2 ›› To decrease typing time and ensure accuracy, use **semi-selection**, a process of selecting a cell or range of cells for entering cell references as you create formulas. Semi-selection is often called **pointing** because you use the pointer to select cells as you build the formula. Some people prefer using the semi-selection method instead of typing a formula so that they can make sure they use the correct cell references as they build the formula.

To use the semi-selection technique to create a formula, complete the following steps:

1. Click the cell where you want to create the formula.
2. Type an equal sign (=) to start a formula.
3. Click the cell that contains the value to use in the formula. A moving marquee appears around the cell or range you select, and Excel displays the cell or range reference in the formula.
4. Type a mathematical operator.
5. Continue clicking cells, selecting ranges, and typing operators to finish the formula. Use the scroll bars if the cell is in a remote location in the worksheet, or click a worksheet tab to see a cell in another worksheet.
6. Press Enter to complete the formula.

Copy Formulas

STEP 3 ⟫ After you enter a formula in a cell, you duplicate the formula without retyping the formula for other cells that need a similar formula. Previously, you learned about the Auto Fill feature that enables you to use the fill handle to fill in a series of values, months, quarters, and weekdays. You can also use the fill handle to copy the formula in the active cell to adjacent cells down a column or across a row, depending on how the data are organized. Cell references in copied formulas adjust based on their relative locations to the original formula.

To copy a formula to other cells using the fill handle, complete the following steps:

1. Click the cell with the content you want to copy to make it the active cell.
2. Point to the fill handle in the bottom-right corner of the cell until the pointer changes to the fill pointer (a thin black plus sign).
3. Drag the fill handle to copy the formula.

Displaying Cell Formulas

STEP 4 ⟫ Excel shows the result of the formula in the cell (see the top half of Figure 1.15); however, you might want to display the formulas instead of the calculated results in the cells (see the bottom half of Figure 1.15). Displaying the cell formulas may help you double-check all your formulas at one time or troubleshoot a problem with a formula instead of clicking in each cell containing a formula and looking at just the Formula Bar.

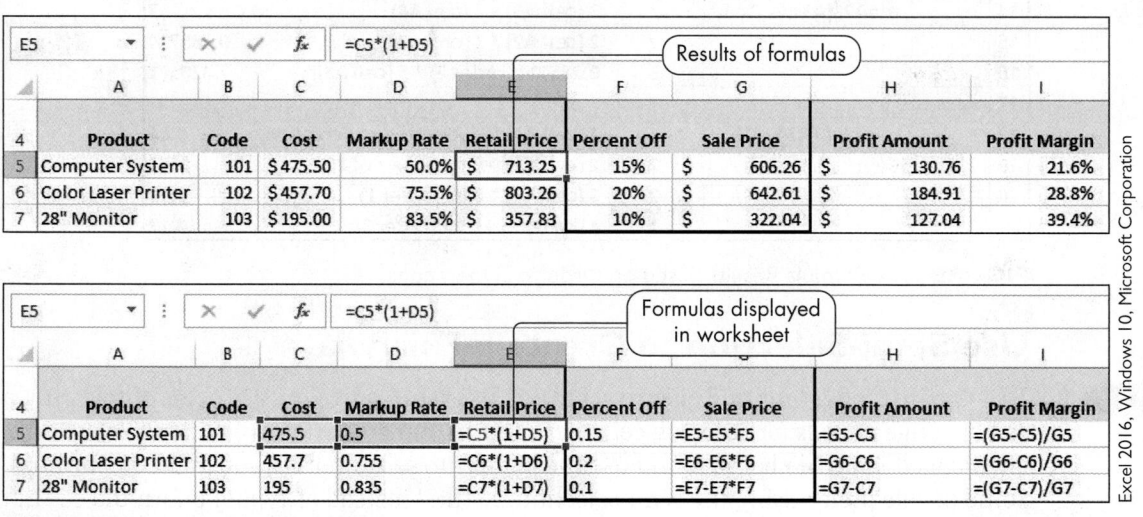

FIGURE 1.15 Formulas and Formula Results

To display cell formulas in the worksheet, complete one of the following steps:

- Press Ctrl and the grave accent (`) key, sometimes referred to as the tilde key, in the top-left corner of the keyboard, below the Esc key.
- Click Show Formulas in the Formula Auditing group on the Formulas tab.

To hide the formulas and display the formula results again, repeat the preceding process.

5. What is the order of operations? Provide and explain two examples that use four different operators: one with parentheses and one without. *p. 418*

6. Why should you use cell references instead of typing values in formulas? *p. 418*

7. When would it be useful to display formulas instead of formula results in a worksheet? *p. 420*

Hands-On Exercises

Watch the Video
for this Hands-On
Exercise!

MyITLab®
HOE2 Training

Skills covered: Use Cell
References in Formulas • Apply
the Order of Operations • Use
Semi-Selection to Create a Formula
• Copy Formulas • Display Cell
Formulas

2 Mathematical Operations and Formulas

In Hands-On Exercise 1, you created the basic worksheet for OKOS by entering text, values, and a date for items on sale. Now you will insert formulas to calculate the missing results—specifically, the retail (before sale) price, sale price, and profit margin. You will use cell addresses in your formulas, so when you change a referenced value, the formula results will update automatically.

STEP 1 ›› USE CELL REFERENCES IN A FORMULA AND APPLY THE ORDER OF OPERATIONS

The first formula you create will calculate the retail price. The retail price is the price you originally charge. It is based on a percentage of the original cost so that you earn a profit. Refer to Figure 1.16 as you complete Step 1.

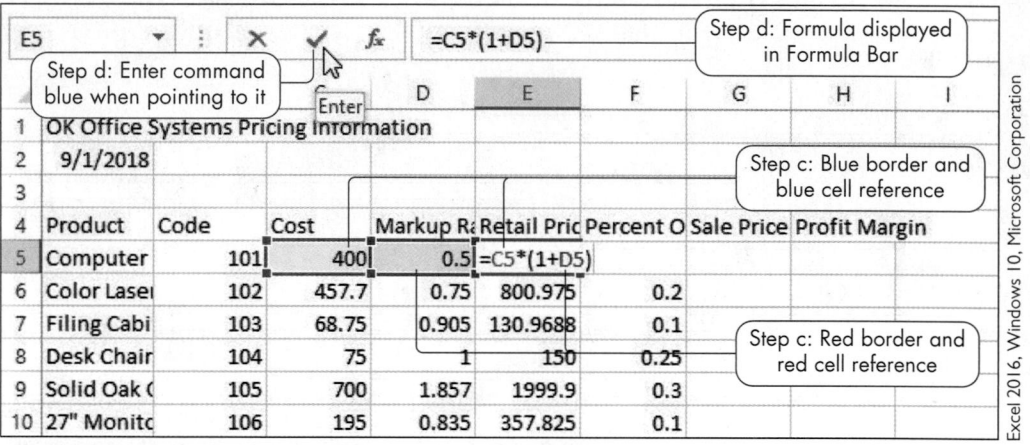

FIGURE 1.16 Retail Price Formula

a. Open *e01h1Markup_LastFirst* if you closed it at the end of Hands-On Exercise 1 and save it as **e01h2Markup_LastFirst**, changing h1 to h2.

b. Click **cell E5**.

Cell E5 is the cell where you will enter the formula to calculate the retail selling price of the first item.

c. Type **=C5*(1+D5)** and view the formula and the colored cells and borders on the screen.

As you build or edit a formula, each cell address in the formula displays in a specific color, and while you type or edit the formula, the cells referenced in the formula have a temporary colored border. For example, in the formula =C5*(1+D5), C5 appears in blue, and D5 appears in red. Cell C5 has a temporarily blue border and light blue shading, and cell D5 has a temporarily red border with light red shading to help you identify cells as you construct your formulas (refer to Figure 1.16).

You enclosed 1+D5 in parentheses to control the order of operations so that 1 is added to the value in cell D5 (0.5). The result is 1.5, which represents 150% of the cost. That result is then multiplied by the value in C5 (400). If you did not use the parentheses, Excel would multiply the value in C5 by 1 (which would be 400) and add that result to the value in D5 (0.5) for a final result of 400.5, which would have given you incorrect results.

An alternative formula also calculates the correct retail price: =C5*D5+C5 or =C5+C5*D5. In this formula, 400 (cell C5) is multiplied by 0.5 (cell D5); that result (200) represents the dollar value of the markup. Excel adds the value 200 to the original cost of 400 to obtain 600, the retail price. You were instructed to enter =C5*(1+D5) to demonstrate the order of operations.

d. Click **Enter** ☑ (between the Name Box and the Formula Bar) and view the formula in the Formula Bar to check it for accuracy.

The result of the formula, 600, appears in cell E5, and the formula displays in the Formula Bar. This formula first adds 1 (the decimal equivalent of 100%) to 0.5 (the value stored in cell D5). Excel multiplies that sum of 1.5 by 400 (the value stored in cell C5). This calculation reflects a retail price is 150% of the original cost.

> **TROUBLESHOOTING:** If the result is not correct, click the cell and look at the formula in the Formula Bar. Click in the Formula Bar, edit the formula to match the formula shown in Step c, and click Enter (the check mark between the Name Box and the Formula Bar). Make sure you start the formula with an equal sign.

e. Position the pointer on the **cell E5 fill handle**. When the pointer changes from a white plus sign to a thin black plus sign, double-click the **fill handle**.

Excel copies the retail price formula for the remaining products in your worksheet. Excel detects when to stop copying the formula when it detects the last label in the dataset.

f. Click **cell E6**, the cell containing the first copied retail price formula, look at the Formula Bar, and then save the workbook.

The formula in cell E6 is =C6*(1+D6). It was copied from the formula in cell E5, which is =C5*(1+D5). Excel adjusts the row references in this formula as you copied the formula down a column so that the results are based on each row's data.

> **TROUBLESHOOTING:** The result in cell E7 may show more decimal places than shown in Figure 1.16. Do not worry about this slight difference.

STEP 2 ›› USE SEMI-SELECTION AND APPLY THE ORDER OF OPERATIONS TO CREATE A FORMULA

Now that you have calculated the retail price, you will calculate a sale price. This week, the computer is on sale for 15% off the retail price. Refer to Figure 1.17 as you complete Step 2.

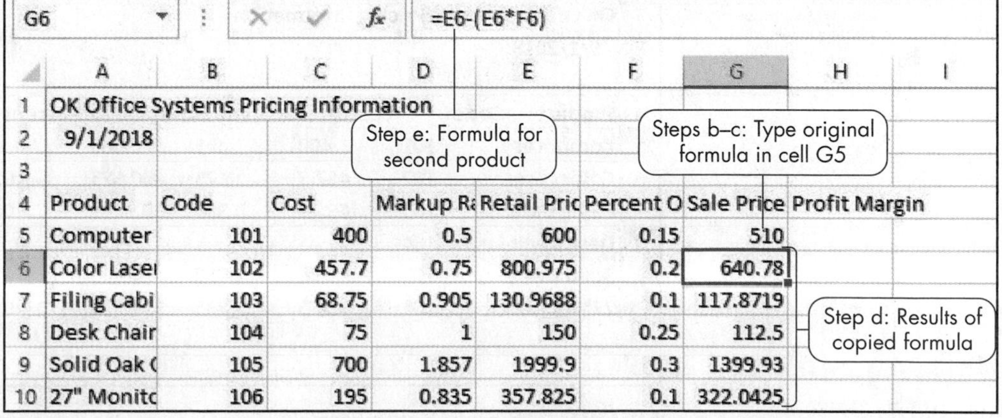

FIGURE 1.17 Sale Price Formula

a. Click **cell G5**, the cell where you will enter the formula to calculate the sale price.

b. Type **=**, click **cell E5**, type **-**, click **cell E5**, type *****, and then click **cell F5**. Notice the color-coding in the cell addresses. Press **Ctrl+Enter** to keep the current cell the active cell.

You used the semi-selection method to enter a formula. The result is 510. Looking at the formula, you might think E5–E5 equals zero; remember that because of the order of operations, multiplication is calculated before subtraction. The product of 600 (cell E5) and 0.15 (cell F5) equals 90, which is then subtracted from 600 (cell E5), so the sale price is 510.

> **TROUBLESHOOTING:** You should check the result for logic. Use a calculator to spot-check the accuracy of formulas. If you mark down merchandise by 15% of its regular price, you are charging 85% of the regular price. You should spot-check your formula to ensure that 85% of 600 is 510 by multiplying 600 by 0.85.

c. Click **cell G5**, type **=E5-(E5*F5)**, and then click **Enter**.

Although the parentheses are not needed because the multiplication occurs before the subtraction, it may be helpful to add parentheses to make the formula easier to interpret.

d. Double-click the **cell G5 fill handle** to copy the formula down column G.

e. Click **cell G6**, the cell containing the first copied sale price formula, view the Formula Bar, and save the workbook.

The original formula was =E5-(E5*F5). The copied formula in cell G6 is adjusted to =E6-(E6*F6) so that it calculates the sales price based on the data in row 6.

STEP 3 »» **USE CELL REFERENCES IN A FORMULA AND APPLY THE ORDER OF OPERATIONS**

After calculating the sale price, you want to know the profit margin OKOS will earn. OKOS paid $400 for the computer and will sell it for $510. The profit of $110 is then divided by the $400 cost, which gives OKOS a profit margin of 0.215686, which will be formatted later as a percent 21.6%. Refer to Figure 1.18 as you complete Step 3.

H5			fx	=(G5-C5)/G5			Step b: Formula in Formula Bar	
	A	B	C	D	E	F	G	H	I
1	OK Office Systems Pricing Information								
2	9/1/2018								
3									
4	Product	Code	Cost	Markup Ra	Retail Pric	Percent O	Sale Price	Profit Margin	
5	Computer	101	400	0.5	600	0.15	510	0.215686	
6	Color Laser	102	457.7	0.75	800.975	0.2	640.78	0.285714	
7	Filing Cabi	103	68.75	0.905	130.9688	0.1	117.8719	0.41674	
8	Desk Chair	104	75	1	150	0.25	112.5	0.333333	
9	Solid Oak (	105	700	1.857	1999.9	0.3	1399.93	0.499975	
10	27" Monitc	106	195	0.835	357.825	0.1	322.0425	0.39449	
11									
12									

Step c: Results after copying the formula

Excel 2016, Windows 10, Microsoft Corporation

FIGURE 1.18 Profit Margin Formula

a. Click **cell H5**, the cell where you will enter the formula to calculate the profit margin.

The profit margin is the profit (difference in sales price and cost) percentage of the sale price.

b. Type **=(G5-C5)/G5** and notice the color-coding in the cell addresses. Press **Ctrl+Enter**.

The formula must first calculate the profit, which is the difference between the sale price (510) and the original cost (400). The difference (110) is then divided by the sale price (510) to determine the profit margin of 0.215686, or 21.6%.

c. Double-click the **cell H5 fill handle** to copy the formula down the column.

d. Click **cell H6**, the cell containing the first copied profit margin formula, look at the Formula Bar, and then save the workbook.

The original formula was =(G5-C5)/G5, and the copied formula in cell H6 is =(G6-C6)/G6.

STEP 4 ›› DISPLAY CELL FORMULAS

You want to see how the prices and profit margins are affected when you change some of the original cost values. For example, the supplier might notify you that the cost to you will increase. In addition, you want to see the formulas displayed in the cells temporarily. Refer to Figures 1.19 and 1.20 as you complete Step 4.

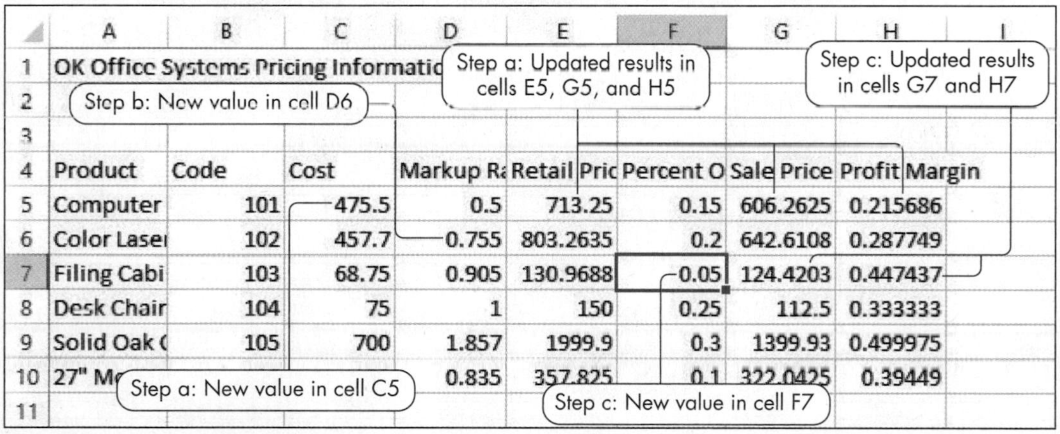

FIGURE 1.19 Results of Changed Values

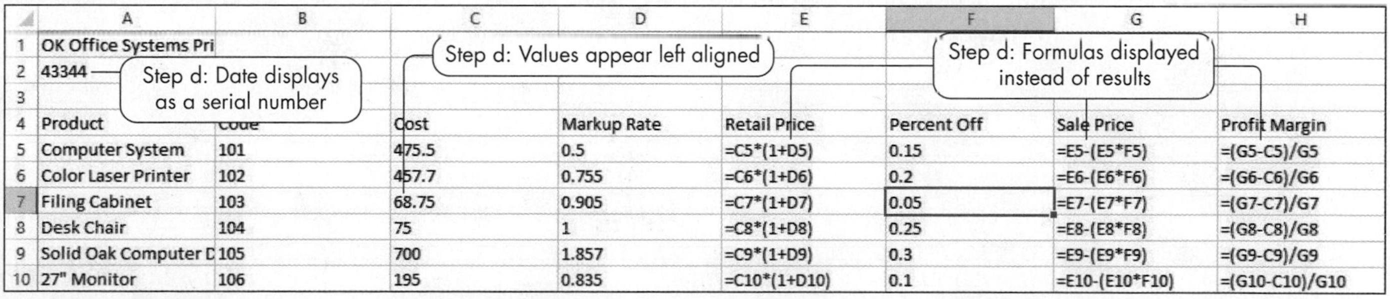

FIGURE 1.20 Formulas Displayed in the Worksheet

a. Click **cell C5**, type **475.5**, and then press **Enter**.

The results of the retail price, sale price, and profit margin formulas change based on the new cost.

b. Click **cell D6**, type **0.755**, and then press **Enter**.

The results of the retail price, sale price, and profit margin formulas change based on the new markup rate.

c. Click **cell F7**, type **0.05**, and then press **Ctrl+Enter**.

The results of the sale price and profit margin formulas change based on the new markdown rate. Note that the retail price did not change because that formula is not based on the markup rate.

d. Press **Ctrl+`** (the grave accent mark).

The workbook now displays the formulas rather than the formula results (refer to Figure 1.20). This is helpful when you want to review several formulas at one time. Numbers are left-aligned, and the date displays as a serial number when you display formulas.

e. Press **Ctrl+`** (the grave accent mark).

The workbook now displays the formula results in the cells again.

f. Save the workbook. Keep the workbook open if you plan to continue with the next Hands-On Exercise. If not, close the workbook, and exit Excel.

Worksheet Structure and Clipboard Tasks

Although you plan worksheets before entering data, you might need to insert a new row to accommodate new data, delete a column that you no longer need, hide a column of confidential data before printing worksheets for distribution, or adjust the size of columns and rows so that the data fit better. Furthermore, you may decide to move data to a different location in the same worksheet or even to a different worksheet. Instead of deleting the original data and typing it in the new location, select and move data from one cell to another. In some instances, you might want to create a copy of data entered so that you can explore different values and compare the results of the original data set and the copied and edited data set.

In this section, you will learn how to make changes to columns and rows. Furthermore, you will also learn how to select ranges, move data to another location, copy data to another range, and use the Paste Special feature.

Managing Columns and Rows

As you enter and edit worksheet data, you might need to adjust the row and column structure to accommodate new data or remove unnecessary data. You can add rows and columns to add new data and delete data, columns, and rows that you no longer need. Adjusting the height and width of rows and columns, respectively, can often present the data better.

Insert Cells, Columns, and Rows

STEP 1 ▶▶ After you construct a worksheet, you might need to insert cells, columns, or rows to accommodate new data. For example, you might want to insert a new column to perform calculations or insert a new row to list a new product.

> **To insert a new column or row, complete the following set of steps:**
>
> 1. Click in the column or row.
> 2. Click the Insert arrow in the Cells group on the Home tab (see Figure 1.21).
> 3. Select Insert Sheet Columns or Insert Sheet Rows.

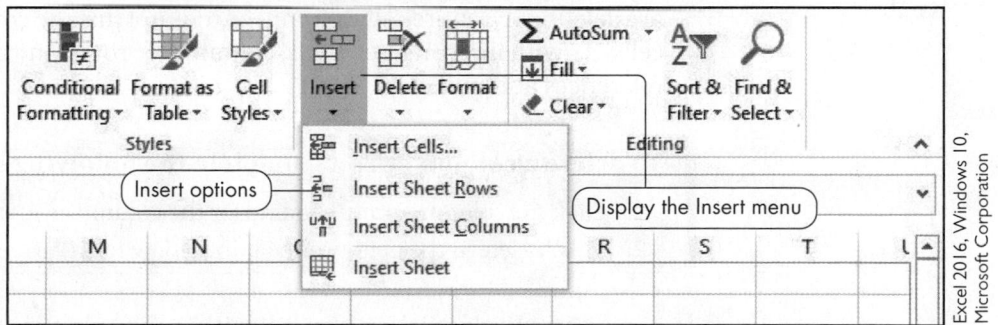

FIGURE 1.21 Insert Menu

Alternatively, you can use a shortcut menu. Right-click the column (letter) or row (number) heading. Then select Insert from the shortcut menu

Excel inserts new columns to the left of the current column and new rows above the active row. If the current column is column C and you insert a new column, the new column becomes column C, and the original column C data are now in column D. Likewise, if the current row is 5 and you insert a new row, the new row is row 5, and the original row 5 data are now in row 6. When you insert cells, rows, and columns, cell addresses in formulas adjust automatically.

Inserting a cell is helpful when you realize that you left out an entry after you have entered all of the data. Instead of inserting a new row or column, you just want to move the existing content down or over to enter the missing value. You can insert a single cell in a particular row or column.

To insert one or more cells, complete the following steps:

1. Click in the cell where you want the new cell.
2. Click the Insert arrow in the Cells group on the Home tab.
3. Select Insert Cells.
4. Select an option from the Insert dialog box (see Figure 1.22) to position the new cell and click OK.

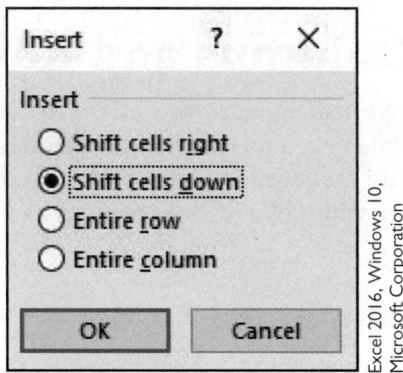

FIGURE 1.22 Insert Dialog Box

Alternatively, click Insert in the Cells group. The default action of clicking Insert is to insert a cell at the current location, which moves existing data down in that column only.

Delete Cells, Columns, and Rows

STEP 2 ⟩⟩ If you no longer need a cell, column, or row, you should delete it. For example, you might want to delete a row containing a product you no longer carry. In these situations, you are deleting the entire cell, column, or row, not just the contents of the cell to leave empty cells. As with inserting new cells, columns, or rows, any affected formulas adjust the cell references automatically.

To delete a column or row, complete the following sets of steps:

1. Click the column or row heading for the column or row you want to delete.
2. Click Delete in the Cells group on the Home tab.

Alternatively, click in any cell within the column or row you want to delete, click the Delete arrow in the Cells group on the Home tab (see Figure 1.23), and then select Select Delete Sheet Columns or Delete Sheet Rows. Another alternative is to right-click the column letter or row number for the column or row you want to delete and then select Delete from the shortcut menu.

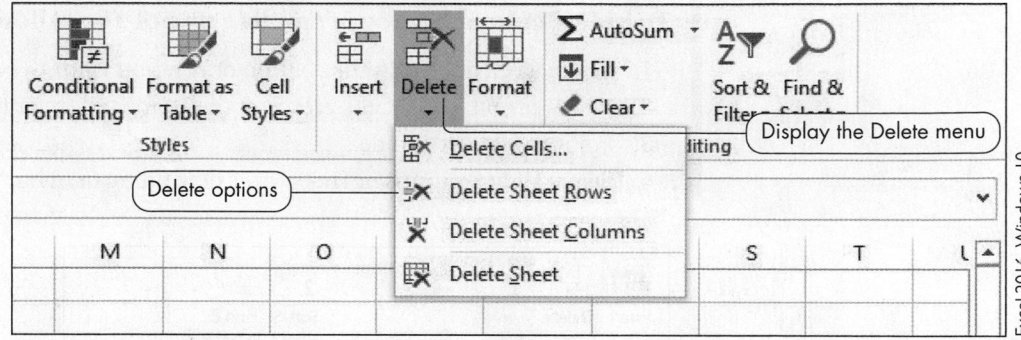

FIGURE 1.23 Delete Menu

To delete a cell or cells, complete the following steps:

1. Select the cell(s).
2. Click the Delete arrow in the Cells group.
3. Select Delete Cells to display the Delete dialog box (see Figure 1.24).
4. Click the appropriate option to shift cells left or up and click OK.

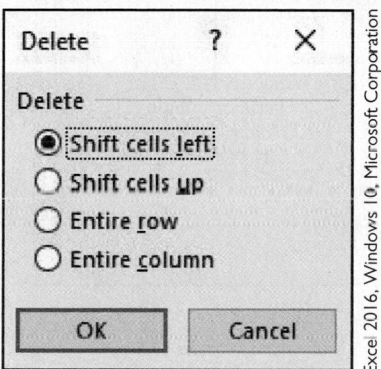

FIGURE 1.24 Delete Dialog Box

Alternatively, click Delete in the Cells group. The default action of clicking Delete is to delete the active cell, which moves existing data up in that column only.

Hide and Unhide Columns and Rows

If your worksheet contains information you do not want to display, hide some columns and/or rows before you print a copy for public distribution. However, the column or row is not deleted. If you hide column B, you will see columns A and C side by side. If you hide row 3, you will see rows 2 and 4 together. Figure 1.25 shows that column B and row 3 are hidden. Excel displays a double line between column headings (such as between A and C), indicating one or more columns are hidden, and a double line between row headings (such as between 2 and 4), indicating one or more rows are hidden.

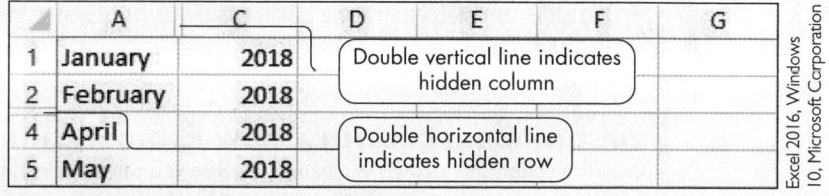

FIGURE 1.25 Hidden Columns and Rows

To hide a column or row, complete one of the following sets of steps:

1. Select a cell or cells in the column or row you want to hide.
2. Click Format in the Cells group on the Home tab (refer to Figure 1.26).
3. Point to Hide & Unhide.
4. Select Hide Columns or Hide Rows, depending on what you want to hide.

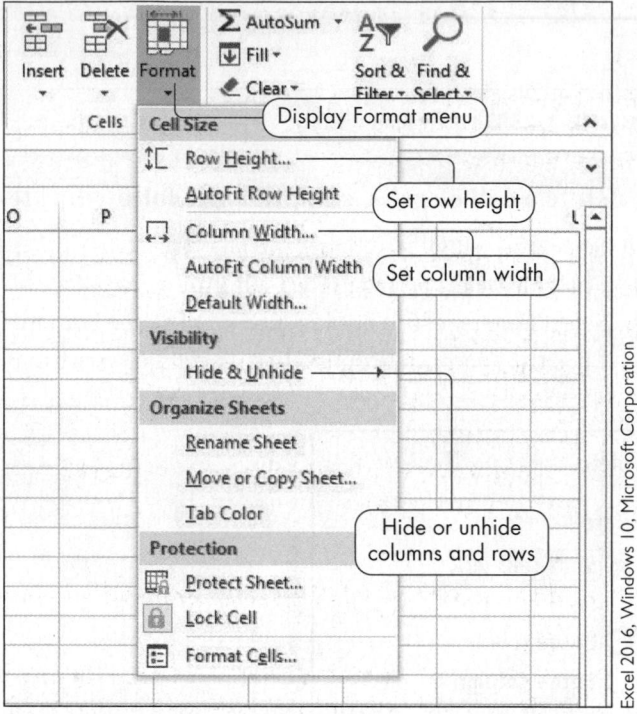

FIGURE 1.26 Format Menu

Alternatively, you can right-click the color or row heading(s) you want to hide. Then select Hide.

You can hide multiple columns and rows at the same time. To select adjacent columns (such as columns B through E) or adjacent rows (such as rows 2 through 4), drag across the adjacent column or row headings and use the Hide command.

To hide nonadjacent columns or rows, complete the following steps:

1. Press and hold Ctrl while you click the desired column or row headings.
2. Use any acceptable method to hide the selected columns or rows.

To unhide a column or row, complete the following steps:

1. Select the columns or rows on both sides of the hidden column or row. For example, if column B is hidden, drag across column letters A and C.
2. Click Format in the Cells group on the Home tab (refer to Figure 1.26), point to Hide & Unhide, and select Unhide Columns or Unhide Rows, depending on what you want to display again.

TIP: UNHIDING COLUMN A, ROW 1, AND ALL HIDDEN ROWS/COLUMNS
Unhiding column A or row 1 is different because you cannot select the row or column on either side. To unhide column A or row 1, type A1 in the Name Box and press Enter. Click Format in the Cells group on the Home tab, point to Hide & Unhide, and select Unhide Columns or Unhide Rows to display column A or row 1, respectively. If you want to unhide all columns and rows, click Select All (the triangle above the row 1 heading and to the left of the column A heading) and use the Hide & Unhide submenu.

Adjust Column Width

STEP 3 ›› After you enter data in a column, you often need to adjust the ***column width***—the horizontal measurement of a column in a table or a worksheet. In Excel, column width is measured by the number of characters or pixels. For example, in the worksheet you created in Hands-On Exercises 1 and 2, the labels in column A displayed into column B when those adjacent cells were empty. However, after you typed values in column B, the labels in column A appeared cut off. You will need to widen column A to show the full name of all of your products.

TIP: POUND SIGNS DISPLAYED

Numbers and dates appear as a series of pound signs (######) when the cell is too narrow to display the complete value, and text appears to be truncated.

To widen a column to accommodate the longest label or value in a column, complete one of the following sets of steps:

- Point to the right vertical border of the column heading. When the pointer displays as a two-headed arrow, double-click the border. For example, if column B is too narrow to display the content in that column, double-click the right vertical border of the column B heading.
- Click Format in the Cells group on the Home tab (refer to Figure 1.26) and select AutoFit Column Width.

To adjust the width of a column to an exact width, complete the following sets of steps:

- Drag the vertical border to the left to decrease the column width or to the right to increase the column width. As you drag the vertical border, Excel displays a ScreenTip specifying the width (see Figure 1.27) from 0 to 255 characters and in pixels.
- Click Format in the Cells group on the Home tab (refer to Figure 1.26), select Column Width, type a value that represents the maximum number of characters to display in the Column width box in the Column Width dialog box, and then click OK.

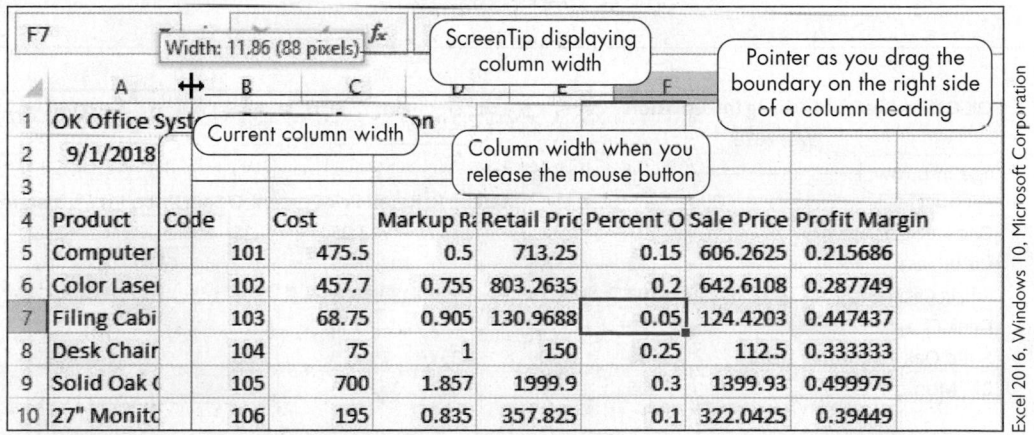

FIGURE 1.27 Increasing Column Width

Adjust Row Height

You can adjust the ***row height***—the vertical measurement of the row—in a way similar to how you change column width by double-clicking the border between row numbers or by selecting Row Height or AutoFit Row Height from the Format menu (refer to Figure 1.26). In Excel, row height is a value between 0 and 409 based on point size (abbreviated as pt) and pixels. Whether you are measuring font sizes or row heights, one point size is equal to 1/72 of an inch. Your row height should be taller than your font size. For example, with an 11-pt font size, the default row height is 15.

TIP: MULTIPLE COLUMN WIDTHS AND ROW HEIGHTS

You can set the size for more than one column or row at a time to make the selected columns or rows the same size. Drag across the column or row headings for the area you want to format, and set the size using any method.

Selecting, Moving, Copying, and Pasting Data

You may already know the basics of selecting, cutting, copying, and pasting data in other programs, such as Microsoft Word. These tasks are somewhat different when working in Excel.

Select a Range

STEP 4 ›› A ***range*** refers to a group of adjacent or contiguous cells in a worksheet. A range may be as small as a single cell or as large as the entire worksheet. It may consist of a row or part of a row, a column or part of a column, or multiple rows or columns, but will always be a rectangular shape, as you must select the same number of cells in each row or column for the entire range. A range is specified by indicating the top-left and bottom-right cells in the selection. For example, in Figure 1.28, the date is a single-cell range in cell A2, the Color Laser Printer data are stored in the range A6:H6, the cost values are stored in the range C5:C10, and the sales prices and profit margins are stored in range G5:H10. A ***nonadjacent range*** contains multiple ranges, such as D5:D10 and F5:F10. At times, you will select nonadjacent ranges so that you can apply the same formatting at the same time, such as formatting the nonadjacent range D5:D10 and F5:F10 with Percent Style.

	A	B	C	D	E	F	G	H	I
1	OK Office Systems Pricing Information								
2	9/1/2018			Rectangular range of cells					
4	Product	Code	Cost	Markup Ra	Retail Pric	Percent O	Sale Price	Profit Margin	
5	Computer System	101	475.5	0.5	713.25	0.15	606.2625	0.215686	
6	Color Laser Printer	102	457.7	0.755	803.2635	0.2	642.6108	0.287749	
7	Filing Cabinet	103	68.75	0.905	130.9688	0.05	124.4203	0.447437	
8	Desk Chair	104	75	1	150	0.25	112.5	0.333333	
9	Solid Oak Computer Desk	105	700	1.857	1999.9	0.3	1399.93	0.499975	
10	27" Monitor	106	195	0.835	357.825	0.1	322.0425	0.39449	
11									

Range in a row · Single-cell range · Range in a column

Excel 2016, Windows 10, Microsoft Corporation

FIGURE 1.28 Sample Ranges

Table 1.4 lists methods to select ranges, including nonadjacent ranges.

TABLE 1.4	Selecting Ranges
To Select:	**Do This:**
A range	Drag until you select the entire range. Alternatively, click the first cell in the range, press and hold Shift, and click the last cell in the range.
An entire column	Click the column heading.
An entire row	Click the row heading.
Current range containing data, including headings	Click in the range of data and press Ctrl+A.
All cells in a worksheet	Click Select All or press Ctrl+A twice.
Nonadjacent range	Select the first range, press and hold Ctrl, and select additional range(s).

A green border appears around a selected range. Any command you execute will affect the entire range. The range remains selected until you select another range or click in any cell in the worksheet.

> **TIP: NAME BOX**
> Use the Name Box to select a range by clicking in the Name Box, typing a range address such as B15:D25, and pressing Enter.

Move a Range

You can move cell contents from one range to another. For example, you might want to move an input area from the right side of the worksheet to above the output range. When you move a range containing text and values, the text and values do not change. However, any formulas that refer to cells in that range will update to reflect the new cell addresses.

To move a range, complete the following steps:

1. Select the range.
2. Click Cut in the Clipboard group to copy the range to the Clipboard (see Figure 1.29). Unlike cutting data in other Microsoft Office applications, the data you cut in Excel remain in their locations until you paste them elsewhere. A moving dashed green border surrounds the selected range and the status bar displays *Select destination and press ENTER or choose Paste.*
3. Ensure the destination range—the range where you want to move the data—is the same size or greater than the size of the cut range.
4. Click in the top-left corner of the destination range, and use the Paste command (see Figure 1.29). If any cells within the destination range contain data, Excel overwrites that data when you use the Paste command.

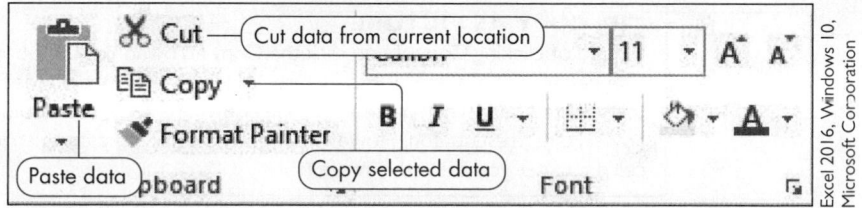

FIGURE 1.29 Cut, Copy, Paste

Copy and Paste a Range

STEP 5 ►► You may want to copy cell contents from one range to another. When you copy a range, the original data remain in their original locations. For example, you might copy your January budget to another worksheet to use as a model for creating your February budget. Cell references in copied formulas adjust based on their relative locations to the original data. Furthermore, you want to copy formulas from one range to another range. In this situation where you cannot use the fill handle, you will use the Copy and Paste functions to copy the formula.

> **To copy a range, complete the following steps:**
>
> 1. Select the range.
> 2. Click Copy in the Clipboard group (refer to Figure 1.29) to copy the contents of the selected range to the Clipboard. A moving dashed green border surrounds the selected range and the status bar displays *Select destination and press ENTER or choose Paste*.
> 3. Ensure the destination range—the range where you want to copy the data—is the same size or greater than the size of the copied range.
> 4. Click in the top-left corner of the destination range where you want the duplicate data, and click Paste (refer to Figure 1.29). If any cells within the destination range contain data, Excel overwrites that data when you use the Paste command. The original range still has the moving dashed green border, and the pasted copied range is selected with a solid green border. Figure 1.30 shows a selected range (A4:H10) and a copy of the range (J4:Q10). Immediately after you click Paste, the **Paste Options button** displays in the bottom-right corner of the pasted data. Click the arrow to select a different result for the pasted data.
> 5. Press Esc to turn off the moving dashed border around the originally selected range.

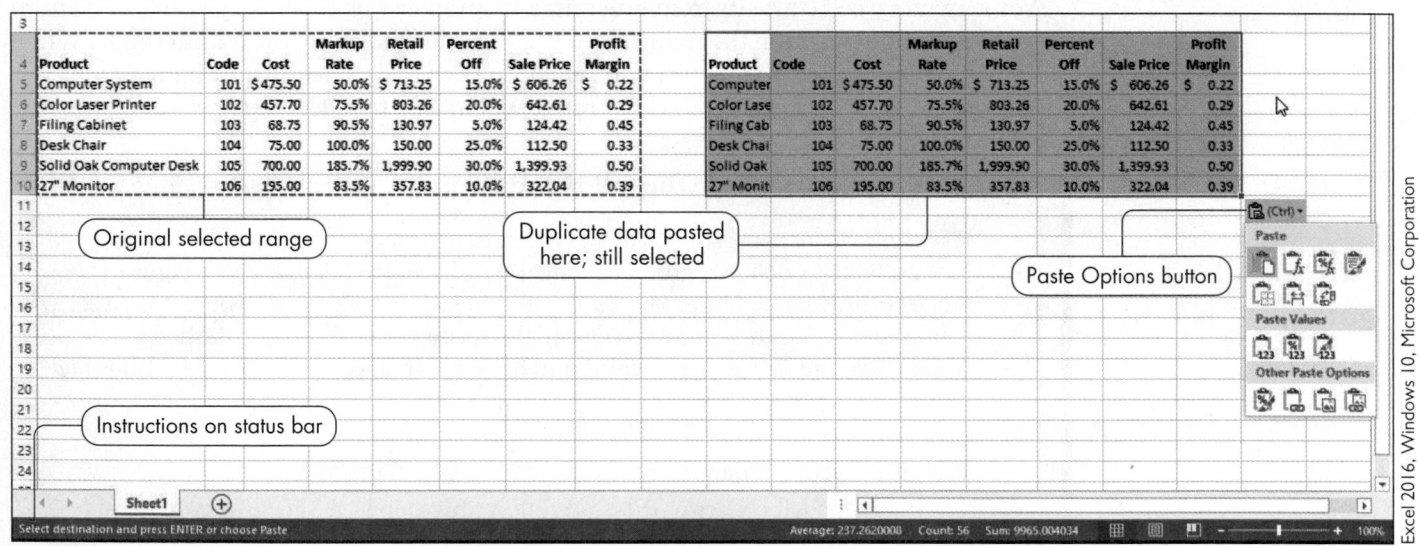

FIGURE 1.30 Copied and Pasted Range

> **TIP: COPY AS PICTURE**
> Instead of clicking Copy, if you click the Copy arrow in the Clipboard group, you can select Copy (the default option) or Copy as Picture. When you select Copy as Picture, you copy an image of the selected data. Then paste the image elsewhere in the workbook or in a Word document or PowerPoint presentation. However, when you copy the data as an image, you cannot edit individual cell data after you paste the image.

Use Paste Options and Paste Special

STEP 6 ›› Sometimes you might want to paste data in a different format than they are in the Clipboard. For example, you might want to preserve the results of calculations before changing the original data. To do this, you can paste the data as values. If you want to copy data from Excel and paste them into a Word document, you can paste the Excel data as a worksheet object, as unformatted text, or in another format.

> **To paste data from the Clipboard into a different format, complete the following steps:**
>
> 1. Click the Paste arrow in the Clipboard group (see Figure 1.31).
> 2. Point to command to see a ScreenTip and a preview of how the pasted data will look.
> 3. Click the option you want to apply.

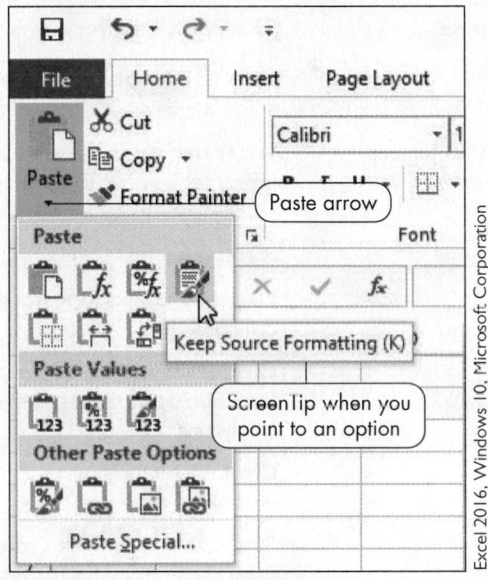

FIGURE 1.31 Paste Options

Table 1.5 lists and describes some of the options in the Paste gallery that opens when you click the Paste arrow in the Clipboard or the Paste Options button that displays immediately after you use Paste. Paste options enable you to paste content or attributes, such as a formula or format.

TABLE 1.5   Paste Options

Icon	Option Name	Paste Description
	Paste	Cell contents and all formatting from copied cells
	Formulas	Formulas, but no formatting, from copied cells
	Formulas & Number Formatting	Formulas and number formatting, such as Currency, but no font formatting, such as font color, fill color, or borders
	Keep Source Formatting	Cell contents and formatting from copied cells
	No Borders	Cell contents, number formatting, and text formatting except borders
	Keep Source Column Widths	Cell contents, number and text formatting, and the column width of the source data when pasting in another column
	Transpose	Transposes data from rows to columns and columns to rows
	Values	Unformatted values that are the results of formulas, not the actual formulas
	Values & Number Formatting	Values that are the results of formulas, not the actual formulas; preserves number formatting but not text formatting
	Values & Source Formatting	Values that are the results of formulas, not the actual formulas; preserves number and text formatting
	Formatting	Number and text formatting only from the copied cells; no cell contents
	Paste Link	Creates a reference to the source cells (such as =$G$15), not the cell contents; preserves number formatting but not text formatting
	Picture	Creates a picture image of the copied data; pasted data is not editable
	Linked Picture	Creates a picture with a reference to the copied cells; if the original cell content changes, so does the picture
	Paste Special	Opens the Paste Special dialog box (see Figure 1.32)

Pearson Education, Inc.

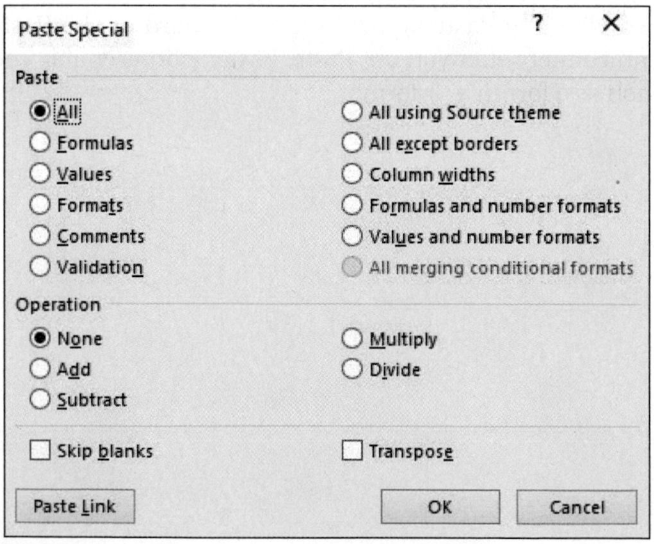

FIGURE 1.32 Paste Special Dialog Box

Excel 2016, Windows 10, Microsoft Corporation

⊿	A	B	C	D	E	F	G	H	I	J
1	Month	Gas	Electric	Water		Month	January	February	March	
2	January	$275	$120	$35		Gas	$275	$265	$200	
3	February	$265	$114	$35		Electric	$120	$114	$118	
4	March	$200	$118	$35		Water	$35	$35	$35	
5										(Ctrl) ▾
6										

Excel 2016, Windows 10, Microsoft Corporation

FIGURE 1.33 Transposed Data

Copy Excel Data to Other Programs

You can copy Excel data and use it in other applications, such as in a Word document or in a PowerPoint slide show. For example, you might perform statistical analyses in Excel and copy the data into a research paper in Word. Or, you might want to create a budget in Excel and copy the data into a PowerPoint slide show for a meeting.

After selecting and copying a range in Excel, you must decide how you want the data to appear in the destination application. Click the Paste arrow in the destination application to see a gallery of options or to select the Paste Special option.

Quick Concepts

8. Give an example of when you would delete a column versus when you would hide a column. *pp. 428-429*

9. When should you adjust column widths instead of using the default width? *p. 431*

10. Why would you use the Paste Special options in Excel? *p. 435*

Hands-On Exercises

Watch the Video
for this Hands-On
Exercise!

MyITLab®
HOE3 Training

Skills covered: Insert Columns
and Rows • Delete a Row • Hide a
Column • Adjust Column Width •
Adjust Row Height • Select a Range
• Move a Range • Copy and Paste a
Range • Use Paste Special

3 Worksheet Structure and Clipboard Tasks

You want to insert a column to calculate the amount of markup and delete a row containing data you no longer need. You also want to adjust column widths to display the labels in the columns. In addition, your supervisor asked you to enter data for a new product. Because it is almost identical to an existing product, you will copy the original data and edit the copied data to save time. You also want to experiment with the Paste Special option to see the results of using it in the OKOS workbook.

STEP 1 >> INSERT A COLUMN AND ROWS

You decide to add a column to display the amount of profit. Because profit is a dollar amount, you want to keep the profit column close to another column of dollar amounts. Therefore, you will insert the profit column before the profit margin (percentage) column. You will insert new rows for product information and category names. Refer to Figure 1.34 as you complete Step 1.

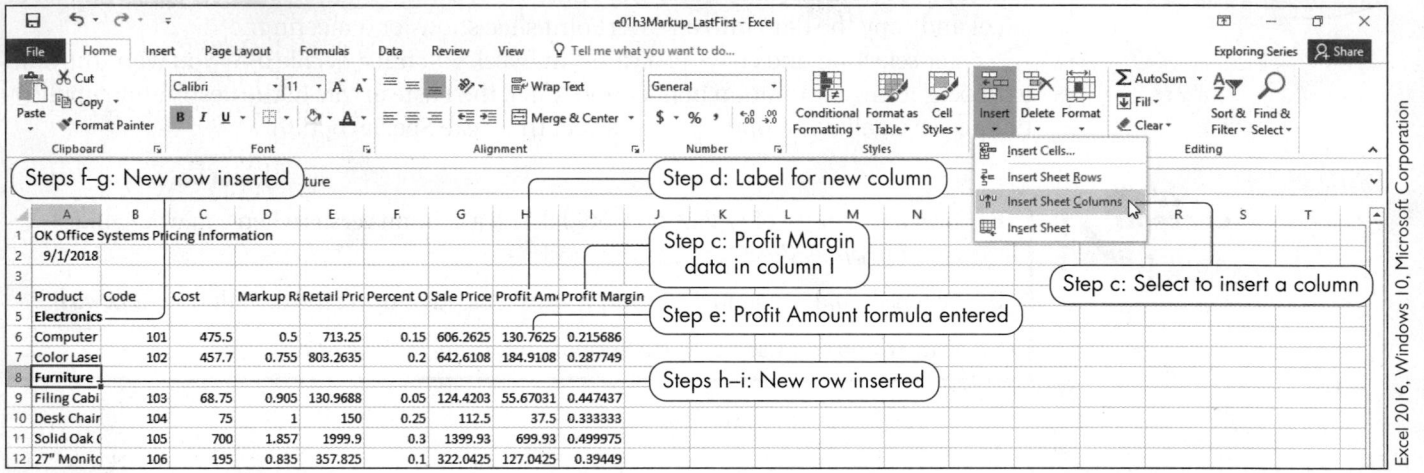

FIGURE 1.34 Column and Rows Inserted

a. Open *e01h2Markup_LastFirst* if you closed it at the end of Hands-On Exercise 2 and save it as **e01h3Markup_LastFirst**, changing h2 to h3.

b. Click **cell H5** (or any cell in column H).

   You want to insert a column between the Sale Price and Profit Margin columns so that you can calculate the profit amount in dollars.

c. Click the **Insert arrow** in the Cells group and select **Insert Sheet Columns**.

   You inserted a new blank column H. The data in the original column H are now in column I.

d. Click **cell H4**, type **Profit Amount**, and then press **Enter**.

e. Ensure the active cell is **cell H5**. Type **=G5-C5** and click **Enter**. Double-click the **cell H5 fill handle**.

   You calculated the profit amount by subtracting the original cost from the sale price and then copied the formula down the column.

f. Right-click the **row 5 heading** and select **Insert** from the shortcut menu.

   You inserted a new blank row 5, which is selected. The original rows of data move down a row each.

g. Click **cell A5**. Type **Electronics** and press **Ctrl+Enter**. Click **Bold** in the Font group on the Home tab.

You typed and applied bold formatting to the category name Electronics above the list of electronic products.

h. Right-click the **row 8 heading** and select **Insert** from the shortcut menu.

You inserted a new blank row 8. The data that was originally on row 8 is now on row 9.

i. Click **cell A8**. Type **Furniture** and press **Ctrl+Enter**. Click **Bold** in the Font group on the Home tab and save the workbook.

You typed and applied bold formatting to the category name Furniture above the list of furniture products.

STEP 2 ›› DELETE A ROW AND HIDE A COLUMN

You just realized that you do not have enough filing cabinets in stock to offer on sale, so you need to delete the Filing Cabinet row. The item numbers are meaningful to you, but the numbers are not necessary for the other employees. Before distributing the worksheet to the employees, you want to hide column B. Because you might need to see that data later, you will hide it rather than delete it. Refer to Figure 1.35 as you complete Step 2.

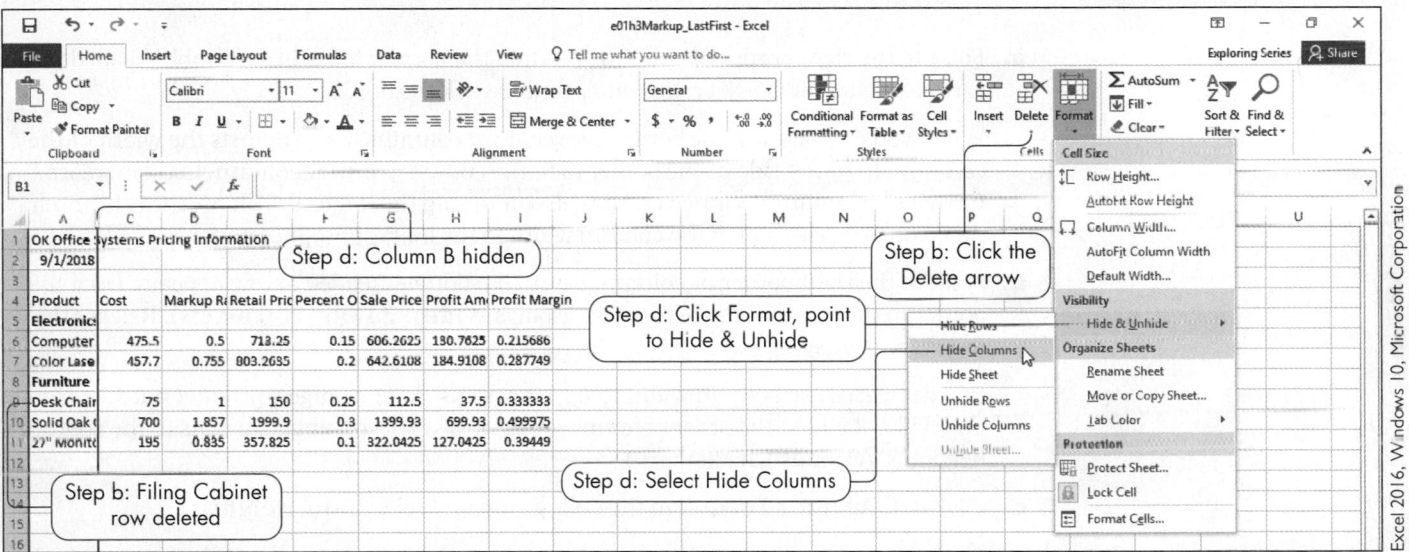

FIGURE 1.35 Row Deleted and Column Hidden

a. Click **cell A9** (or any cell on row 9), the row that contains the Filing Cabinet data.

b. Click the **Delete arrow** in the Cells group and select **Delete Sheet Rows**.

The Filing Cabinet row is deleted, and the remaining rows move up one row.

> **TROUBLESHOOTING:** If you accidentally delete the wrong row or accidentally selected Delete Sheet Columns instead of Delete Sheet Rows, click Undo on the Quick Access Toolbar to restore the deleted row or column.

c. Click the **column B heading**.

d. Click **Format** in the Cells group, point to **Hide & Unhide**, and then select **Hide Columns**.

Excel hides column B. You see a gap in column heading letters A and C, indicating column B is hidden instead of deleted.

e. Save the workbook.

As you review your worksheet, you notice that the labels in column A appear cut off. You will increase the width of that column to display the entire product names. In addition, you want to make row 1 taller. Refer to Figure 1.36 as you complete Step 3.

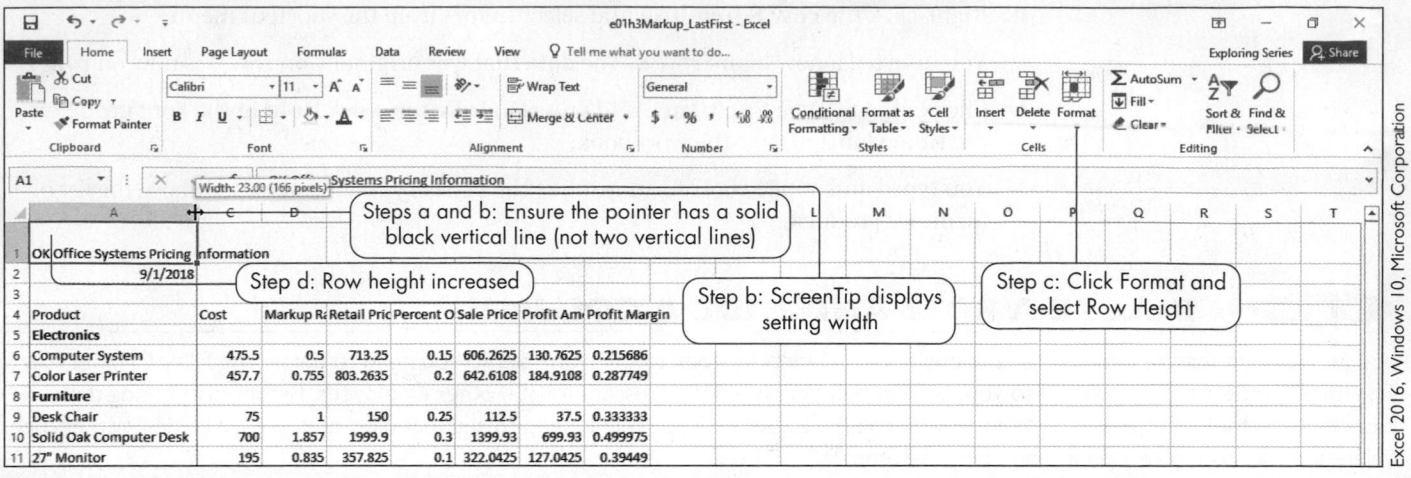

FIGURE 1.36 Column Width and Row Height Changed

a. Point to the right border of column A. When the pointer looks like a double-headed arrow with a solid black vertical line, double-click the border.

When you double-click the border between two columns, Excel adjusts the width of the column on the left side of the border to fit the contents of that column. Excel increased the width of column A based on the cell containing the longest content (the title in cell A1). You decide to adjust the column width to the longest product name instead.

b. Point to the right border of column A until the double-headed arrow appears. Drag the border to the left until the ScreenTip displays **Width: 23.00 (166 pixels)**. Release the mouse button.

You decreased the column width to 23 for column A. The longest product name is visible. You will not adjust the other column widths until after you apply formats to the column headings in Hands-On Exercise 4.

c. Click **cell A1**. Click **Format** in the Cells group and select **Row Height**.

The Row Height dialog box opens so that you can adjust the height of the current row.

d. Type **30** in the **Row height box** and click **OK**. Save the workbook.

You increased the height of the row that contains the worksheet title so that it is more prominent.

You want to move the 27" Monitor product to be immediately after the Color Laser Printer product. Before moving the 27" Monitor row, you will insert a blank row between the Color Laser Printer and Furniture rows. Refer to Figure 1.37 as you complete Step 4.

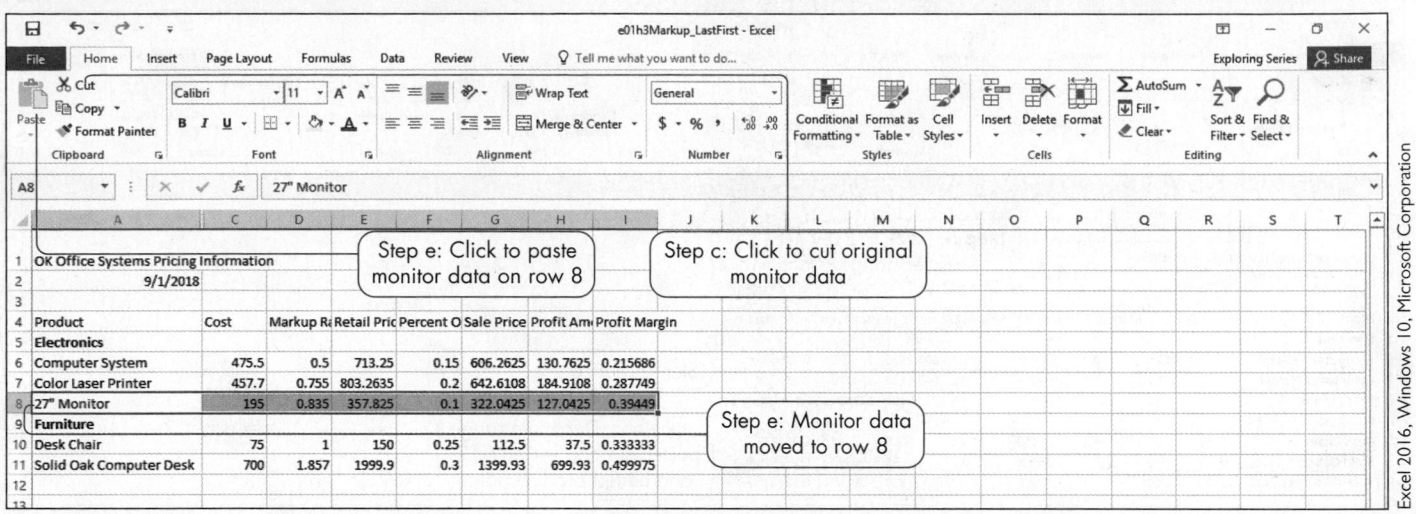

FIGURE 1.37 Row Moved to New Location

a. Right-click the **row 8 heading** and select **Insert** from the menu.

You will insert a blank row so that you can move the 27" Computer Monitor data to be between the Color Laser Printer and Furniture rows.

b. Select the **range A12:I12**.

You selected the range of cells containing the 27" Monitor data.

c. Click **Cut** in the Clipboard group.

A moving dashed green border outlines the selected range. The status bar displays the message *Select destination and press ENTER or choose Paste.*

d. Click **cell A8**.

This is the first cell in the destination range. If you cut and paste a row without inserting a new row first, Excel will overwrite the original row of data, which is why you inserted a new row in step a.

e. Click **Paste** in the Clipboard group and save the workbook.

The 27" Monitor product data is now located on row 8.

Alesha told you that a new chair is on its way. She asked you to enter the data for the Executive Desk Chair. Because most of the data is the same as the Desk Chair data, you will copy the original Desk Chair data, edit the product name, and change the cost to reflect the cost of the second chair. Refer to Figure 1.38 as you complete Step 5.

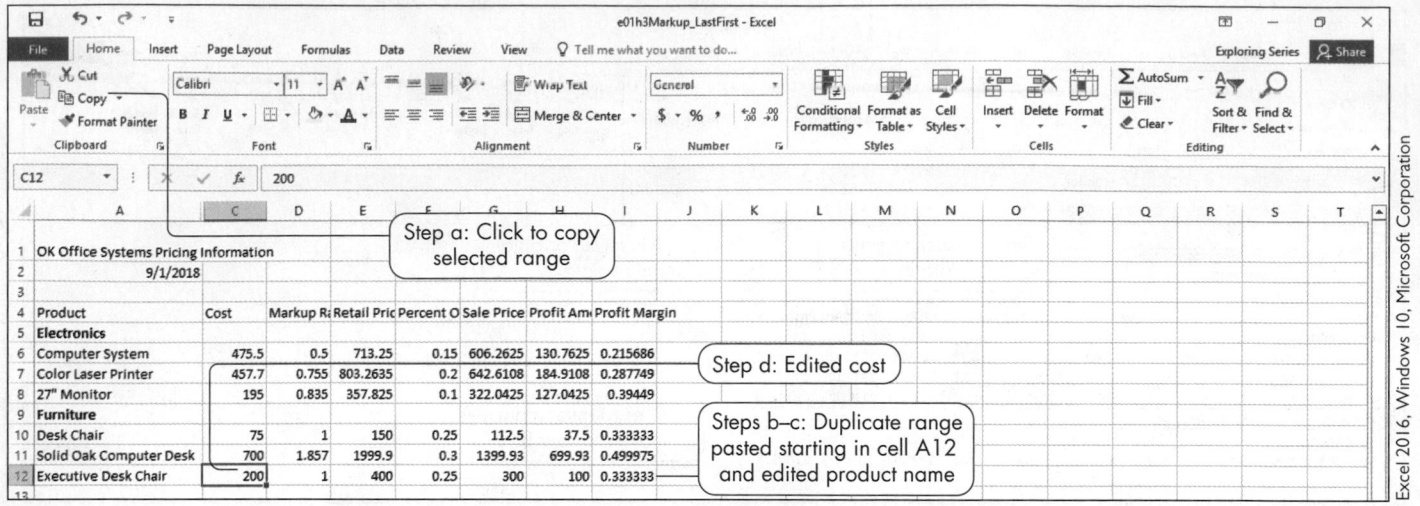

FIGURE 1.38 Data Copied and Edited

a. Select the **range A10:I10** and click **Copy** in the Clipboard group.

You copied the row containing the Desk Chair product data to the Clipboard.

b. Click **cell A12**, click **Paste** in the Clipboard group, and then press **Esc**.

The pasted range is selected in row 12.

c. Click **cell A12**, press **F2** to activate Edit Mode, press **Home**, type **Executive**, press **Spacebar**, and then press **Enter**.

You edited the product name to display Executive Desk Chair.

d. Change the value in **cell C12** to **200**. Save the workbook.

The formulas calculate the results based on the new cost of 200 for the Executive Desk Chair.

STEP 6 >> USE PASTE SPECIAL

During your lunch break, you want to experiment with some of the Paste Special options. Particularly, you are interested in pasting Formulas and Value & Source Formatting. First, you will apply bold and a font color to the title to help you test these Paste Special options. Refer to Figure 1.39 as you complete Step 6.

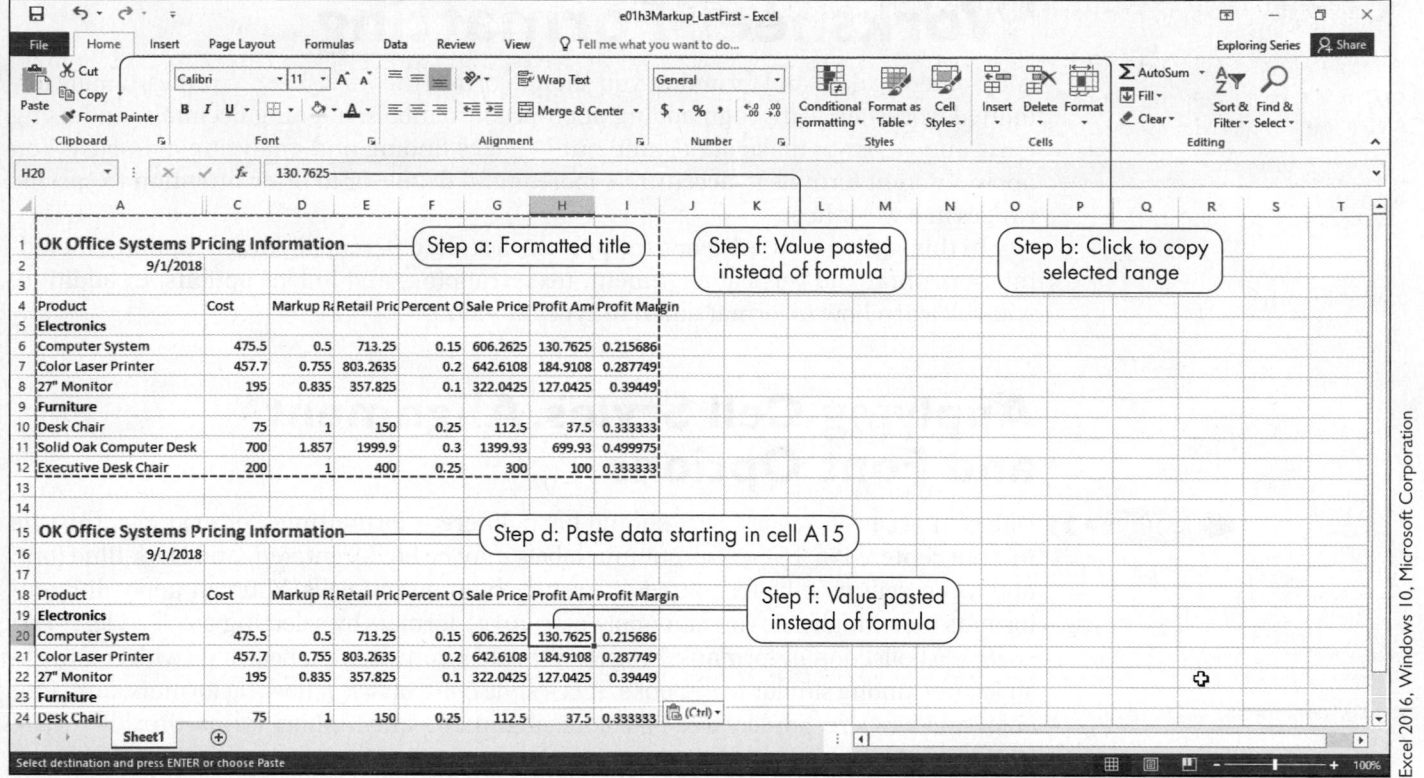

FIGURE 1.39 Paste Special Results

a. Click **cell A1**. Change the font size to **14**, click **Bold**, click the **Font Color arrow** in the Font group and then select **Gold, Accent 4, Darker 50%**.

You will format text to see the effects of using different Paste Special options.

b. Select the **range A1:I12** and click **Copy** in the Clipboard group.

c. Click **cell A15**, the top-left corner of the destination range.

d. Click the **Paste arrow** in the Clipboard group and point to **Formulas**, the second icon from the left in the Paste group.

Without clicking the command, Excel shows you a preview of what that option would do. The pasted copy would not contain the font formatting you applied to the title or the bold on the two category names. In addition, the pasted date would appear as a serial number. The formulas would be maintained.

e. Position the pointer over **Values & Source Formatting**, the first icon from the right in the Paste Values group.

This option would preserve the formatting, but it would convert the formulas into the current value results.

f. Click **Values & Source Formatting**, click **cell H6** to see a formula, and then click **cell H20**. Press **Esc** to turn off the border.

Cell H6 contains a formula, but in the pasted version, the equivalent cell H20 has converted the formula result into an actual value. If you were to change the original cost on row 20, the contents of cell H20 would not change. In a working environment, this is useful only if you want to capture the exact value in a point in time before making changes to the original data.

g. Save the workbook. Keep the workbook open if you plan to continue with the next Hands-On Exercise. If not, close the workbook and exit Excel.

Worksheet Formatting

After entering data and formulas, you should format the worksheet. A professionally formatted worksheet—through adding appropriate symbols, aligning decimals, and using fonts and colors to make data stand out—makes finding and analyzing data easy. You apply different formats to accentuate meaningful details or to draw attention to specific ranges in a worksheet.

In this section, you will learn to apply a cell style, different alignment options, including horizontal and vertical alignment, text wrapping, and indent options. In addition, you will learn how to format different types of values.

Applying Cell Styles, Alignment, and Font Options

STEP 1 ›› Different areas of a worksheet should have different formatting. For example, the title may be centered in 16-pt size; column labels may be bold, centered, and Dark Blue font; and input cells may be formatted differently from output cells. You can apply different formats individually, or you can apply a group of formats by selecting a cell style. A ***cell style*** is a collection of format settings to provide a consistent appearance within a worksheet and among similar workbooks. A cell style controls the following formats: font, font color and font size, borders and fill colors, alignment, and number formatting.

> **To apply a cell style to a cell or a range of cells, complete the following steps:**
>
> 1. Click Cell Styles in the Styles group on the Home tab to display the Cell Styles gallery (see Figure 1.40).
> 2. Position the pointer over a style name to see a Live Preview of how the style will affect the selected cell or range. The gallery provides a variety of built-in styles to apply to your worksheet data.
> 3. Click a style to apply it to the selected cell or range.

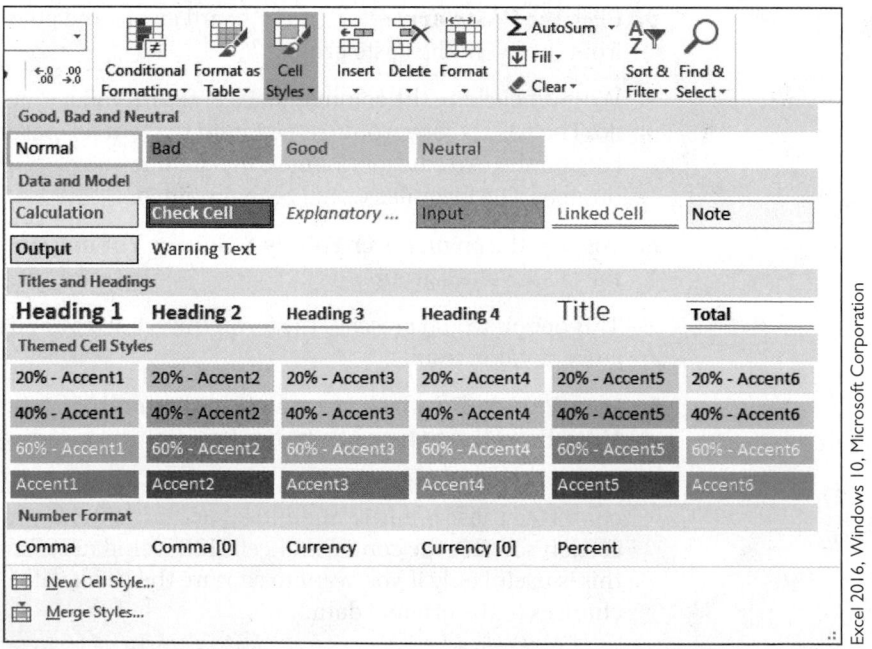

FIGURE 1.40 Cell Styles

Alignment refers to how data are positioned in the boundaries of a cell. Each type of data has a default alignment. Text aligns at the left cell margin, and dates and values align at the right cell margin. You should change the alignment of cell contents to improve the appearance of data within the cells. The Alignment group (see Figure 1.41) on the Home tab contains several commands to help you align and format data.

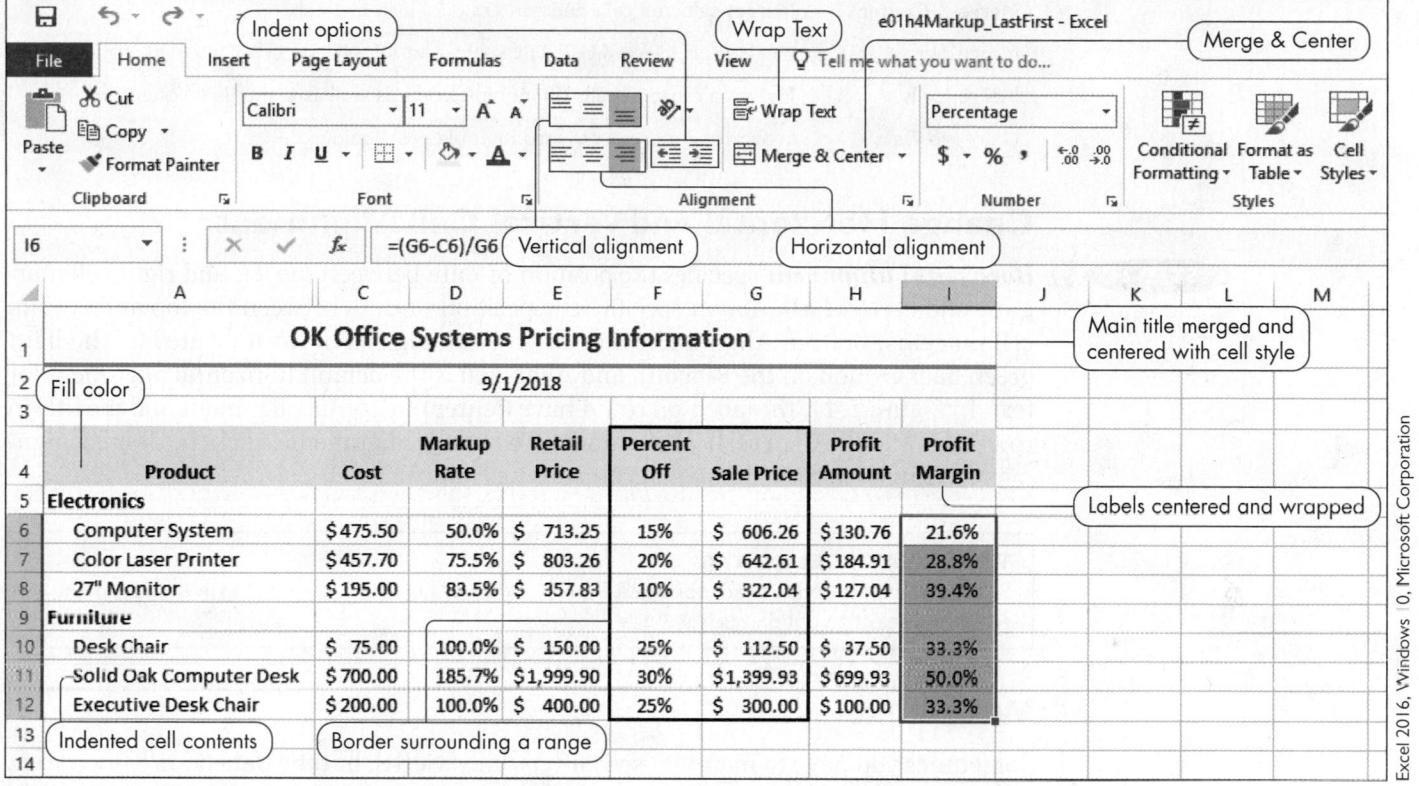

FIGURE 1.41 Alignment and Font Settings Applied

TIP: ALIGNMENT OPTIONS

The Format Cells dialog box contains additional alignment options. To open the Format Cells dialog box, click the Dialog Box Launcher in the Alignment group on the Home tab. The Alignment tab in the dialog box contains the options for aligning data.

Merge and Center Labels

STEP 1 You may want to place a title at the top of a worksheet and center it over the columns of data in the worksheet. You can center main titles over all columns in the worksheet, and you can center category titles over groups of related columns. You can also merge cells on adjacent rows.

To merge and center cells, complete the following steps:

1. Enter the text in the top left cell of the range.
2. Select the range of cells across which you want to center the label.
3. Click Merge & Center in the Alignment group on the Home tab.

Only data in the far left cell (or top-right cell) are merged. Any other data in the merged cells are deleted. Excel merges the selected cells together into one cell, and the merged cell address is that of the original cell on the left. The data are centered within the merged cell.

If you want to split a merged cell into multiple cells, click the merged cell and click Merge & Center. Unmerging places the data in the top-left cell.

For additional options, click the Merge & Center arrow. Table 1.6 lists the four merge options.

TABLE 1.6 Merge Options

Option	Results
Merge & Center	Merges selected cells and centers data into one cell.
Merge Across	Merges the selected cells but keeps text left aligned or values right aligned.
Merge Cells	Merges a range of cells on multiple rows as well as in multiple columns.
Unmerge Cells	Separates a merged cell into multiple cells again.

Pearson Education, Inc.

Change Horizontal and Vertical Cell Alignment

STEP 2 ⟩⟩ *Horizontal alignment* specifies the position of data between the left and right cell margins, and *vertical alignment* specifies the position of data between the top and bottom cell margins. Bottom Align is the default vertical alignment (as indicated by the light green background on the Ribbon), and Align Left is the default horizontal alignment for text. In Figure 1.41, the labels on row 4 have Center horizontal alignment and the title in row 1 has Middle Align vertical alignment. To change alignments, click the desired alignment setting(s) in the Alignment group on the Home tab.

> **TIP: ROTATE CELL DATA**
> People sometimes rotate headings in cells. To rotate data in a cell, click Orientation in the Alignment group and select an option, such as Angle Clockwise.

Wrap Text

Sometimes you have to maintain specific column widths, but the data do not fit entirely. Use *wrap text* to make data appear on multiple lines by adjusting the row height to fit the cell contents within the column width. Excel wraps the text on two or more lines within the cell. In Figure 1.41, the Markup Rate and Percent Off labels on row 4 are examples of wrapped text.

To wrap text within a cell, complete the following steps:

1. Click the cells or select the range of cells that contain labels that need to be wrapped.
2. Click Wrap Text in the Alignment group.

> **TIP: LINE BREAK IN A CELL**
> If a long text label does not fit well in a cell even after you have applied wrap text, you might want to insert a line break to display the text label on multiple lines within the cell. To insert a line break while you are typing a label, press Alt+Enter where you want to start the next line of text within the cell.

Increase and Decrease Indent

STEP 3 ⟩⟩ Cell content is left-aligned or right-aligned based on the default data type. However, you can *indent* the cell contents to offset the data from its current alignment. For example, text is left-aligned, but you can indent it to offset it from the left side. Indenting helps others see the hierarchical structure of data. Accountants often indent the word Totals in financial statements so that it stands out from a list of items above the total row. Values are right-aligned by default, but you can indent a value to offset it from the right side of the cell. In Figure 1.41, Computer System and Desk Chair are indented.

To increase or decrease the indent of data in a cell, complete the following steps:

1. Click the cell that contains data.
2. Click Increase Indent or Decrease Indent in the Alignment group.

TIP: INDENTING VALUES

Values are right aligned by default. You should align the decimal places in a column of values. If the column label is wide, the values below it appear too far on the right. To preserve the values aligning at the decimal places, use the Align Right horizontal alignment and click Increase Indent to shift the values over to the left a little for better placement.

Apply Borders and Fill Color

STEP 4 »» You can apply a border or fill color to accentuate data in a worksheet. A **border** is a line that surrounds a cell or a range of cells. Use borders to offset some data from the rest of the worksheet data. To apply a border, select the cell or range that you want to have a border, click the Borders arrow in the Font group, and select the desired border type. In Figure 1.41, a border surrounds the range F4:G12. To remove a border, select No Border from the Borders menu.

Add some color to your worksheets to emphasize data or headers by applying a fill color. **Fill color** is a background color that displays behind the data in a cell so that the data stand out. You should choose a fill color that contrasts with the font color. For example, if the font color is Black, Text 1, you might choose Yellow fill color. If the font color is White, Background 1, you might apply Blue or Dark Blue fill color. The color palette contains two sections: Theme Colors and Standard Colors. The Theme Colors section displays variations of colors that match the current theme applied in the worksheet. For example, it contains shades of blue, such as Blue, Accent 5, Lighter 80%. The Standard Colors section contains basic colors, such as Dark Red and Red.

To apply a fill color, complete the following steps:

1. Select the cell or range that you want to have a fill color.
2. Click the Fill Color arrow on the Home tab to display the color palette.
3. Select the color choice from the Fill Color palette. In Figure 1.41, the column labels in row 4 contain the Blue, Accent 1, Lighter 80% fill color. If you want to remove a fill color, select No Fill from the bottom of the palette. Select More Colors to open the Colors dialog box, click the Standard tab or Custom tab, and then click a color.

For additional border and fill color options, complete the following steps:

1. Click the Dialog Box Launcher in the Font group to display the Format Cells dialog box.
2. Click the Border tab to select border options, including the border line style and color.
3. Click the Fill tab to set the background color, fill effects, and patterns.

Applying Number Formats

Values have no special formatting when you enter data. However, you should apply **number formats**, settings that control how a value is displayed in a cell. For example, you might want to apply either the Accounting or Currency number format to monetary values. Changing the number format changes the way the number displays in a cell, but the format does not change the stored value. If, for example, you enter 123.456 into a cell and format the cell with the Currency number type, the value shows as $123.46 onscreen, but the actual value 123.456 is used for calculations. When you apply a number format, specify the number of decimal places to display onscreen.

Apply a Number Format

STEP 5 ⟩⟩ The default number format is General, which displays values as you originally enter them. General number format does not align decimal points in a column or include symbols, such as dollar signs, percent signs, or commas. Table 1.7 lists and describes the primary number formats in Excel.

TABLE 1.7 Number Formats

Format Style	Display
General	A number as it was originally entered. Numbers are shown as integers (e.g., 12345), decimal fractions (e.g., 1234.5), or in scientific notation (e.g., 1.23E+10) if the number exceeds 11 digits.
Number	A number with or without the 1,000 separator (e.g., a comma) and with any number of decimal places. Negative numbers can be displayed with parentheses and/or red.
Currency	A number with the 1,000 separator and an optional dollar sign (which is placed immediately to the left of the number). Negative values are preceded by a minus sign or are displayed with parentheses or in red. Two decimal places display by default.
Accounting Number Format	A number that contains the $ on the left side of the cell and formats the value with a comma for every three digits on the left side of the decimal point and displays two digits to the right of the decimal point. Negative values display in parentheses, and zero values display as hyphens.
Comma Style	A number is formatted with a comma for every three digits on the left side of the decimal point and displays two digits to the right of the decimal point. Used in conjunction with Accounting Number Format to align commas and decimal places.
Date	The date in different ways, such as Long Date (March 14, 2016) or Short Date (3/14/16 or 14-Mar-16).
Time	The time in different formats, such as 10:50 PM or 22:50 (military time).
Percent Style	The value as it would be multiplied by 100 (for display purpose), with the percent symbol. The default number of decimal places is zero if you click Percent Style in the Number group or two decimal places if you use the Format Cells dialog box. However, you should typically increase the number of decimal points to show greater accuracy.
Fraction	A number as a fraction; use when no exact decimal equivalent exists. A fraction is entered into a cell as a formula such as =1/3. If the cell is not formatted as a fraction, the formula results display.
Scientific	A number as a decimal fraction followed by a whole number exponent of 10; for example, the number 12345 would appear as 1.23E+04. The exponent, +04 in the example, is the number of places the decimal point is moved to the left (or right if the exponent is negative). Very small numbers have negative exponents.
Text	The data left aligned; is useful for numerical values that have leading zeros and should be treated as text, such as postal codes or phone numbers. Apply Text format before typing a leading zero so that the zero displays in the cell.
Special	A number with editing characters, such as hyphens in a Social Security number.
Custom	Predefined customized number formats or special symbols to create your own customized number format.

The Number group on the Home tab contains commands for applying **Accounting Number Format**, **Percent Style**, and **Comma Style** numbering formats. You can click the Accounting Number Format arrow and select other denominations, such as English pounds or euros. For other number formats, click the Number Format arrow and select the numbering format you want to use. For more specific numbering formats than those provided, select More Number Formats from the Number Format menu or click the Number Dialog Box Launcher to open the Format Cells dialog box with the Number tab options readily available. Figure 1.42 shows different number formats applied to values.

◢	A	B
1	General	1234.567
2	Number	1234.57
3	Currency	$1,234.57
4	Accounting	$ 1,234.57
5	Comma	1,234.57
6	Percent	12%
7	Short Date	3/1/2018
8	Long Date	Thursday, March 1, 2018

Excel 2016, Windows 10, Microsoft Corporation

FIGURE 1.42 Number Formats

Increase and Decrease Decimal Places

STEP 5 ▶▶ After applying a number format, you may need to adjust the number of decimal places that display. For example, if you have an entire column of monetary values formatted in Accounting Number Format, Excel displays two decimal places by default. If the entire column of values contains whole dollar values and no cents, displaying .00 down the column looks cluttered. Decrease the number of decimal places to show whole numbers only.

> **To change the number of decimal places displayed, complete the following steps:**
>
> 1. Click the cell or select a range of cells containing values that need to have fewer or more decimal places.
> 2. Click Increase Decimal in the Number group on the Home tab to display more decimal places for greater precision or Decrease Decimal to display fewer or no decimal places.

Quick Concepts

11. What is the importance of formatting a worksheet? *p. 444*

12. Describe five alignment and font formatting techniques used to format labels that are discussed in this section. *p. 444*

13. What are the main differences between Accounting Number Format and Currency format? Which format has its own command on the Ribbon? *p. 448*

Hands-On Exercises

Watch the Video
for this Hands-On
Exercise!

MyITLab®
HOE4 Training

Skills covered: Apply a Cell Style • Merge and Center Data • Change Cell Alignment • Wrap Text • Increase Indent • Apply a Border • Apply Fill Color • Apply Number Formats • Increase and Decrease Decimal Places

4 Worksheet Formatting

In the first three Hands-On Exercises, you entered data about products on sale, created formulas to calculate markup and profit, and inserted new rows and columns to accommodate the labels Electronics and Furniture to identify the specific products. You are ready to format the worksheet. Specifically, you will center the title, align text, format values, and apply other formatting to enhance the readability of the worksheet.

STEP 1 ➤➤ APPLY A CELL STYLE AND MERGE AND CENTER THE TITLE

To make the title stand out, you want to apply a cell style and center it over all the data columns. You will use the Merge & Center command to merge cells and center the title at the same time. Refer to Figure 1.43 as you complete Step 1.

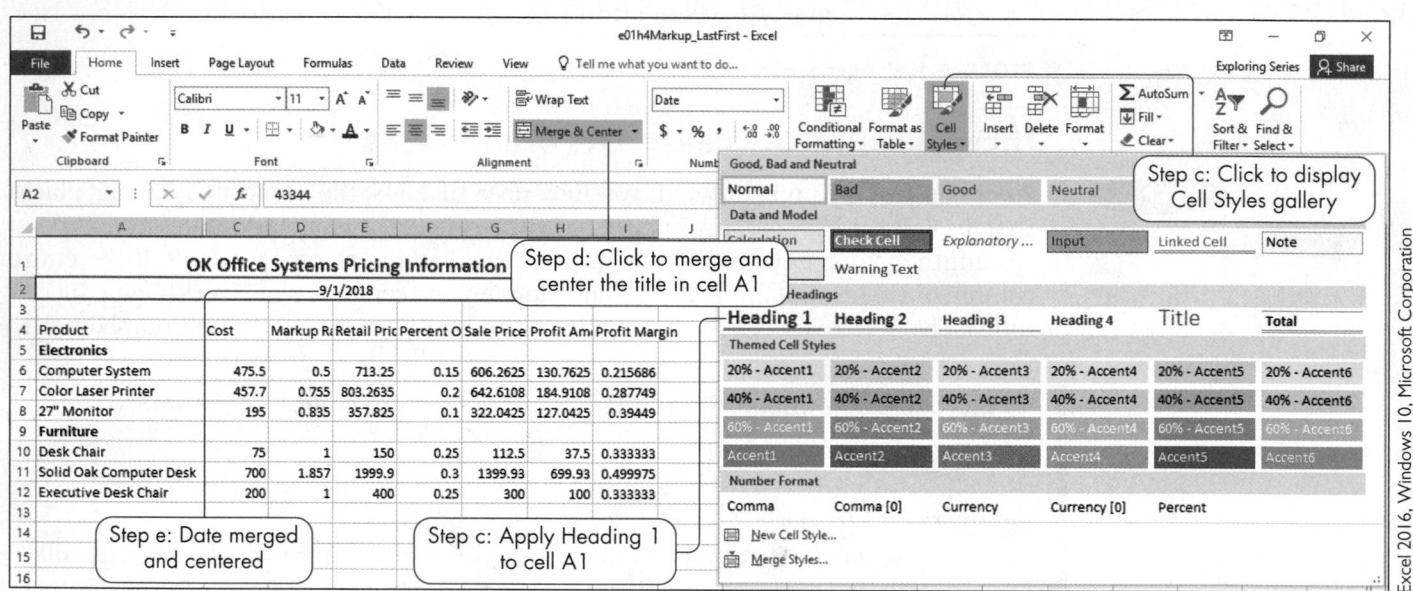

FIGURE 1.43 Cell Style Applied; Data Merged and Centered

a. Open *e01h3Markup_LastFirst* if you closed it at the end of Hands-On Exercise 3 and save it as **e01h4Markup_LastFirst**, changing h3 to h4.

b. Select the **range A15:I26** and press **Delete**.

You maintained a copy of your Paste Special results in the *e01h3Markup_LastFirst* workbook, but you do not need it to continue.

c. Select the **range A1:I1**, click **Cell Styles** in the Styles group on the Home tab, and then click **Heading 1**.

You applied the Heading 1 style to the range A1:I1. This style formats the contents with 15-pt font size, Blue-Gray, Text 2 font color, and a thick blue bottom border.

d. Click **Merge & Center** in the Alignment group.

Excel merges cells in the range A1:I1 into one cell and centers the title horizontally within the merged cell, which is cell A1.

> **TROUBLESHOOTING:** If you merge too many or not enough cells, unmerge the cells and start again. To unmerge cells, click in the merged cell. The Merge & Center command is shaded in green when the active cell is merged. Click Merge & Center to unmerge the cell. Then select the correct range to merge and use Merge & Center again.

e. Select the **range A2:I2**. Click **Merge & Center** in the Alignment group. Save the workbook.

> **TROUBLESHOOTING:** If you try to merge and center data in the range A1:I2, Excel will keep the top-left data only and delete the date. To merge separate data on separate rows, you must merge and center data separately.

STEP 2 » CHANGE CELL ALIGNMENT

You will wrap the text in the column headings to avoid columns that are too wide for the data, but which will display the entire text of the column labels. In addition, you will horizontally center column labels between the left and right cell margins. Refer to Figure 1.44 as you complete Step 2.

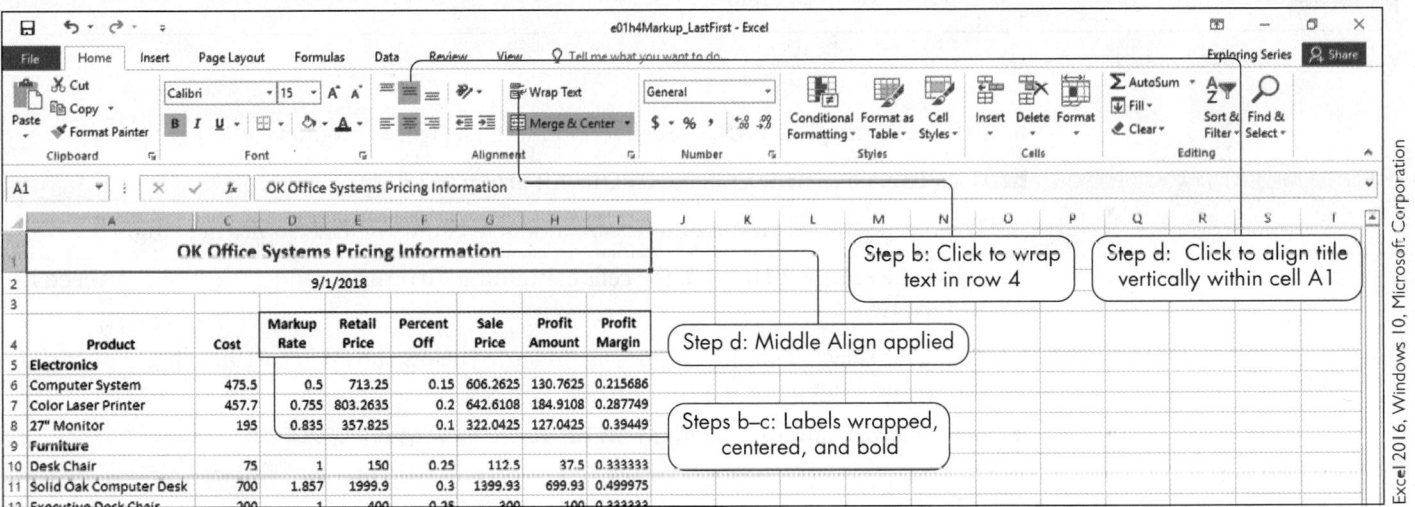

FIGURE 1.44 Formatted Column Labels

a. Select the **range A4:I4** to select the column labels.

b. Click **Wrap Text** in the Alignment group.

The multiple-word column headings are now visible on two lines within each cell.

c. Click **Center** in the Alignment group and click **Bold** in the Font group to format the selected column headings.

The column headings are centered horizontally between the left and right edges of each cell.

d. Click **cell A1**, which contains the title, click **Middle Align** in the Alignment group, and then save the workbook.

Middle Align vertically centers data between the top and bottom edges of the cell.

As you review the first column, you notice that the category names, Electronics and Furniture, do not stand out. You decide to indent the labels within each category to better display which products are in each category. Refer to Figure 1.45 as you complete Step 3.

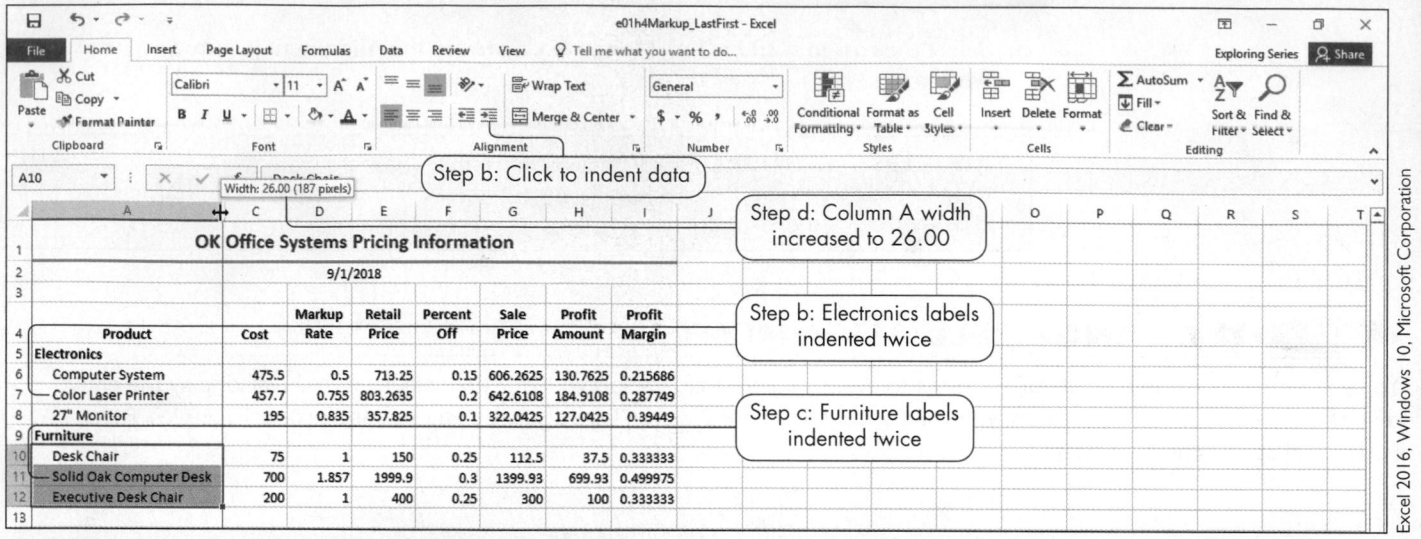

FIGURE 1.45 Indented Cell Contents

a. Select the **range A6:A8**, the cells containing Electronic products labels.

b. Click **Increase Indent** in the Alignment group twice.

The three selected product names are indented below the Electronics heading.

c. Select the **range A10:A12**, the cells containing furniture products, and click **Increase Indent** twice.

The three selected product names are indented below the Furniture heading. Notice that the one product name appears cut off.

d. Increase the column A width to **26.00**. Save the workbook.

You want to apply a light blue fill color to highlight the column headings. In addition, you want to emphasize the percent off and sale prices. You will do this by applying a border around that range. Refer to Figure 1.46 as you complete Step 4.

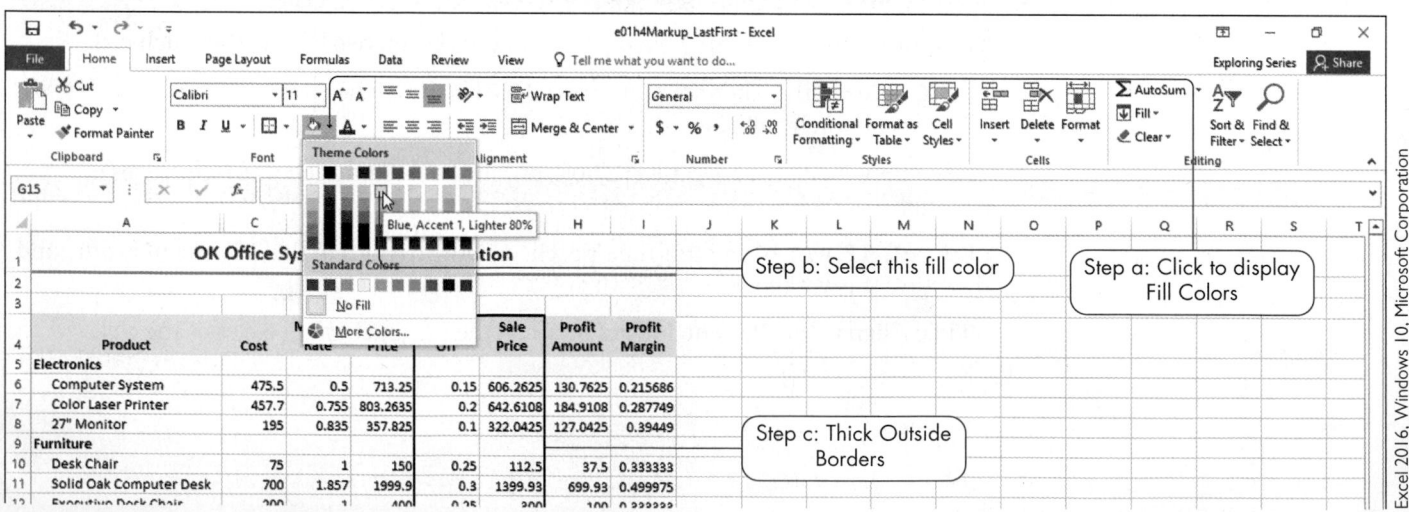

FIGURE 1.46 Border and Fill Color Applied

a. Select the **range A4:I4** and click the **Fill Color arrow** in the Font group.

b. Click **Blue, Accent 1, Lighter 80%** in the Theme Colors section (second row, fifth column).

You applied a fill color to the selected cells to draw attention to these cells.

c. Select the **range F4:G12**, click the **Border arrow** in the Font group, and then select **Thick Outside Borders**.

You applied a border around the selected cells.

d. Click in an empty cell below the columns of data to deselect the cells. Save the workbook.

STEP 5 » APPLY NUMBER FORMATS AND INCREASE AND DECREASE DECIMAL PLACES

You need to format the values to increase readability and look more professional. You will apply number formats and adjust the number of decimal points displayed. Refer to Figure 1.47 as you complete Step 5.

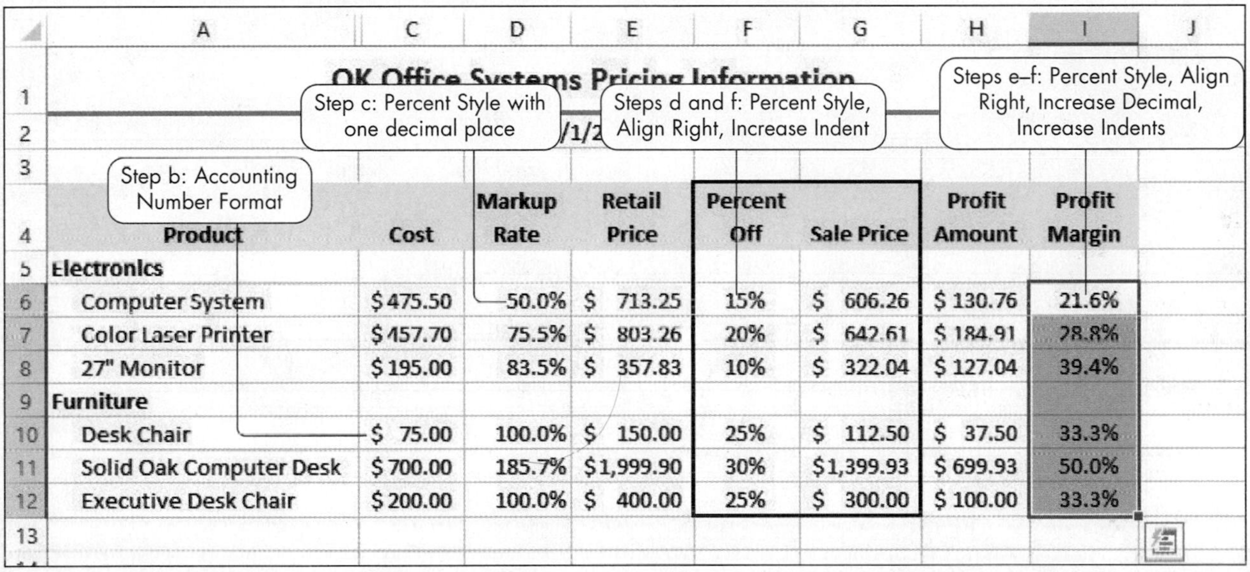

	A	C	D	E	F	G	H	I
1	OK Office Systems Pricing Information							
2								
3								
4	Product	Cost	Markup Rate	Retail Price	Percent Off	Sale Price	Profit Amount	Profit Margin
5	Electronics							
6	Computer System	$ 475.50	50.0%	$ 713.25	15%	$ 606.26	$ 130.76	21.6%
7	Color Laser Printer	$ 457.70	75.5%	$ 803.26	20%	$ 642.61	$ 184.91	28.8%
8	27" Monitor	$ 195.00	83.5%	$ 357.83	10%	$ 322.04	$ 127.04	39.4%
9	Furniture							
10	Desk Chair	$ 75.00	100.0%	$ 150.00	25%	$ 112.50	$ 37.50	33.3%
11	Solid Oak Computer Desk	$ 700.00	185.7%	$1,999.90	30%	$1,399.93	$ 699.93	50.0%
12	Executive Desk Chair	$ 200.00	100.0%	$ 400.00	25%	$ 300.00	$ 100.00	33.3%
13								

Exce 2016, Windows 10, Microsoft Corporation

FIGURE 1.47 Number Formats and Decimal Places

a. Select the **range C6:C12.** Press and hold **Ctrl** as you select the **ranges E6:E12** and **G6:H12.**

Because you want to apply the same format to nonadjacent ranges, you hold down Ctrl while selecting each range.

b. Click **Accounting Number Format** in the Number group. If some cells display pound signs, increase the column widths as needed.

You formatted the selected nonadjacent ranges with the Accounting Number Format. The dollar signs align on the left cell margins and the decimals align.

c. Select the **range D6:D12**, click **Percent Style** in the Number group, and then click **Increase Decimal** in the Number group.

You formatted the values in the selected range with Percent Style and increased the decimal to show one decimal place to avoid misleading your readers by displaying the values as whole percentages.

d. Apply **Percent Style** to the **range F6:F12**.

e. Select the **range I6:I12**, apply **Percent Style**, and then click **Increase Decimal**.

f. Select the **range F6:F12**, click **Align Right**, and then click **Increase Indent** twice. Select the **range I6:I12**, click **Align Right**, and then click **Increase Indent**.

With values, you want to keep the decimal points aligned, but you can then use Increase Indent to adjust the indent so that the values appear more centered below the column labels.

g. Save the workbook. Keep the workbook open if you plan to continue with the next Hands-On Exercise. If not, close the workbook and exit Excel.

Worksheets, Page Setup, and Printing

When you start a new blank workbook in Excel, the workbook contains one worksheet named Sheet1. However, you can add additional worksheets. The text, values, dates, and formulas you enter into the individual worksheets are saved under one workbook file name. Having multiple worksheets in one workbook is helpful to keep related items together.

Although you might distribute workbooks electronically as email attachments or you might upload workbooks to a corporate server, you should prepare the worksheets in case you need to print them or in case others who receive an electronic copy of your workbook want to print the worksheets.

In this section, you will copy, move, and rename worksheets. You will also select options on the Page Layout tab. Specifically, you will use the Page Setup, Scale to Fit, and Sheet Options groups. After selecting page setup options, you will learn how to print your worksheet.

Managing Worksheets

Creating a multiple-worksheet workbook takes some planning and maintenance. Worksheet tab names should reflect the contents of the respective worksheets. In addition, you can insert, copy, move, and delete worksheets within the workbook. You can even apply background color to the worksheet tabs so that they stand out onscreen. Figure 1.48 shows a workbook in which the sheet tabs have been renamed, colors have been applied to worksheet tabs, and a worksheet tab has been right-clicked so that the shortcut menu appears.

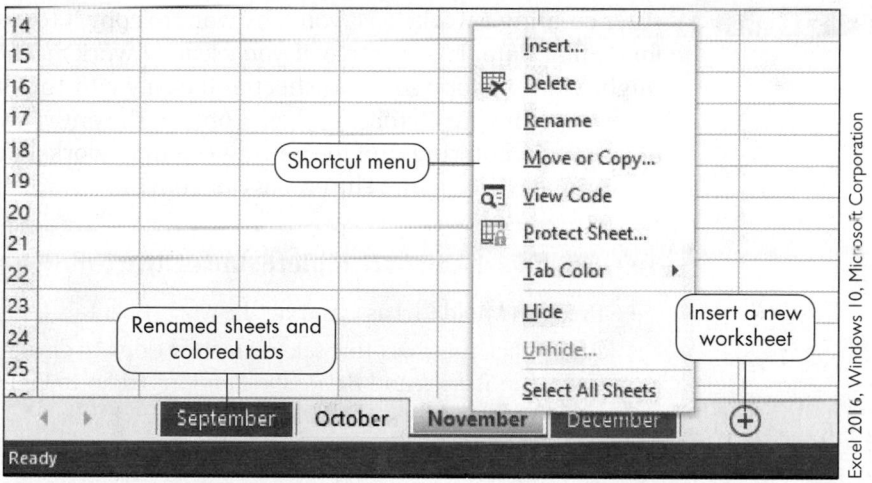

FIGURE 1.48 Worksheet Tabs

The active sheet tab has a green horizontal bar below the sheet name, and the sheet name is bold and green. If a color (such as Red) has been applied to the sheet tab, the tab shows in the full color when it is not active. When that sheet is active, the sheet tab color is a gradient of the selected color.

Insert and Delete a Worksheet

Sometimes you need more than one worksheet in the workbook. For example, you might want one worksheet for each month to track your monthly income and expenses for one year. When tax time comes around, you have all your data stored in one workbook file. You can insert additional, rename, copy, and move worksheets. Adding worksheets within one workbook enables to you save related sheets of data together.

> **To insert a new worksheet, complete one of the following sets of steps:**
>
> - Click New sheet to the right of the last worksheet tab.
> - Click the Insert arrow (either to the right or below Insert) in the Cells group on the Home tab and select Insert Sheet.
> - Right-click any sheet tab, select Insert from the shortcut menu (refer to Figure 1.48), click Worksheet in the Insert dialog box, and click OK.
> - Press Shift+F11.

If you no longer need the data in a worksheet, delete the worksheet. Doing so will eliminate extra data in a file and reduce file size.

> **To delete a worksheet in a workbook, complete one of the following sets of steps:**
>
> - Click the Delete arrow (either to the right or below Delete) in the Cells group on the Home tab and select Delete Sheet.
> - Right-click any sheet tab and select Delete from the shortcut menu (refer to Figure 1.48).

If the sheet you are trying to delete contains data, Excel will display a warning: *Microsoft Excel will permanently delete this sheet. Do you want to continue?* Click Delete to delete the worksheet, or click Cancel to keep the worksheet. If you try to delete a blank worksheet, Excel will not display a warning; it will immediately delete the sheet.

Copy or Move a Worksheet

STEP 1 ›› After creating a worksheet, you may want to copy it to use as a template or starting point for similar data. For example, if you create a worksheet for your September budget, you might want to copy the worksheet and easily edit the data on the copied worksheet to enter data for your October budget. Copying the entire worksheet saves you a lot of valuable time in entering and formatting the new worksheet, and it preserves the column widths and row heights. The process for copying a worksheet is similar to moving a sheet.

> **To copy a worksheet, complete one of the following sets of steps:**
>
> - Press and hold Ctrl as you drag the worksheet tab.
> - Right-click the sheet tab, select Move or Copy to display the Move or Copy dialog box, select the *To book* and *Before sheet* options (refer to Figure 1.49), click the *Create a copy* check box, and then click OK.

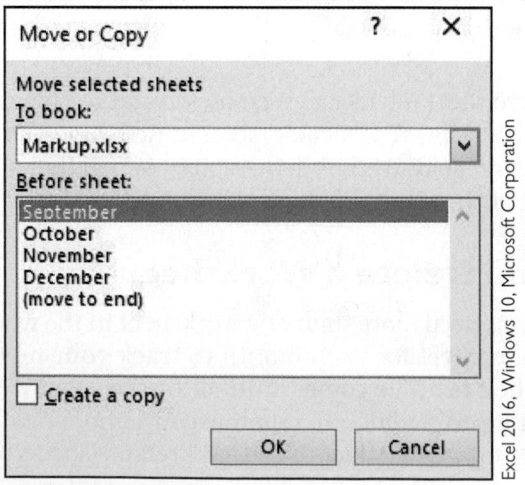

FIGURE 1.49 Move or Copy Dialog Box

You can arrange the worksheet tabs in a different sequence. For example, if the December worksheet is to the left of the October and November worksheets, move the December worksheet to be in chronological order.

To move a worksheet, complete one of the following sets of steps:

- Drag a worksheet tab to the desired location. As you drag a sheet tab, the pointer resembles a piece of paper. A down-pointing triangle appears between sheet tabs to indicate where the sheet will be placed when you release the mouse button.
- Click Format in the Cells group on the Home tab (refer to Figure 1.35) and select Move or Copy Sheet.
- Right-click the sheet tab you want to move and select Move or Copy to display the Move or Copy dialog box. You can move the worksheet within the current workbook or to a different workbook. In the *Before sheet* list, select the worksheet you want to come after the moved worksheet and click OK.

Rename a Worksheet

The default worksheet name Sheet1 does not describe the contents of the worksheet. You should rename worksheet tabs to reflect the sheet contents. For example, if your budget workbook contains monthly worksheets, name the worksheets September, October, etc. Although you can have spaces in worksheet names, keep worksheet names relatively short. The longer the worksheet names, the fewer sheet tabs you will see at the bottom of the workbook window without scrolling.

To rename a worksheet, complete one of the following sets of steps:

- Double-click a sheet tab, type the new name, and then press Enter.
- Click the sheet tab for the sheet you want to rename, click Format in the Cells group on the Home tab (refer to Figure 1.35), select Rename Sheet, type the new sheet name, and then press Enter.
- Right-click the sheet tab, select Rename from the shortcut menu (refer to Figure 1.48), type the new sheet name, and then press Enter.

> **TIP: CHANGE TAB COLOR**
> You can change the color of each worksheet tab to emphasize the difference among the sheets. For example, you might apply red to the September tab and yellow to the October tab. Right-click a sheet tab, select Tab Color, and select a color from the color palette.

Selecting Page Setup Options

The Page Setup group on the Page Layout tab contains options to set the margins, select orientation, specify page size, select the print area, and apply other options (see Figure 1.50). The Scale to Fit group contains options for adjusting the scaling of the spreadsheet on the printed page. When possible, use the commands in these groups to apply page settings. Table 1.8 lists and describes the commands in the Page Setup group.

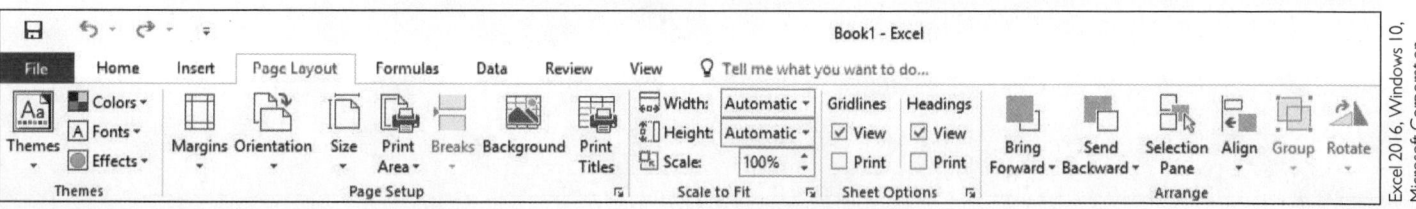

FIGURE 1.50 Page Layout Tab

TABLE 1.8	Page Setup Commands
Command	**Description**
Margins	Displays a menu to select predefined margin settings. The default margins are 0.75" top and bottom and 0.7" left and right. You will often change these margin settings to balance the worksheet data better on the printed page. If you need different margins, select Custom Margins.
Orientation	Displays orientation options. The default page orientation is portrait, which is appropriate for worksheets that contain more rows than columns. Select landscape orientation when worksheets contain more columns than can fit in portrait orientation. For example, the OKOS worksheet might appear better balanced in landscape orientation because it has eight columns.
Size	Displays a list of standard paper sizes. The default size is 8 ½" by 11". If you have a different paper size, such as legal paper, select it from the list.
Print Area	Displays a list to set or clear the print area. When you have very large worksheets, you might want to print only a portion of that worksheet. To do so, select the range you want to print, click Print Area in the Page Setup group, and select Set Print Area. When you use the Print commands, only the range you specified will be printed. To clear the print area, click Print Area and select Clear Print Area.
Breaks	Displays a menu to insert or remove page breaks.
Background	Enables you to select an image to appear as the background behind the worksheet data when viewed onscreen (backgrounds do not appear when the worksheet is printed).
Print Titles	Enables you to select column headings and row labels to repeat on multiple-page printouts.

> **TIP: APPLYING PAGE SETUP OPTIONS TO MULTIPLE WORKSHEETS**
> When you apply Page Setup Options, those settings apply to the current worksheet only. However, you can apply page setup options, such as margins or a header, to multiple worksheets at the same time. To select adjacent sheets, click the first sheet tab, press and hold Shift, and click the last sheet tab. To select nonadjacent sheets, press and hold Ctrl as you click each sheet tab. Then choose the Page Setup options to apply to the selected sheets. When you are done, right-click a sheet tab and select Ungroup Sheets.

Specify Page Options

 To apply several page setup options at once or to access options not found on the Ribbon, click the Page Setup Dialog Box Launcher. The Page Setup dialog box organizes options into four tabs: Page, Margins, Header/Footer, and Sheet. All tabs contain Print and Print Preview buttons. Figure 1.51 shows the Page tab.

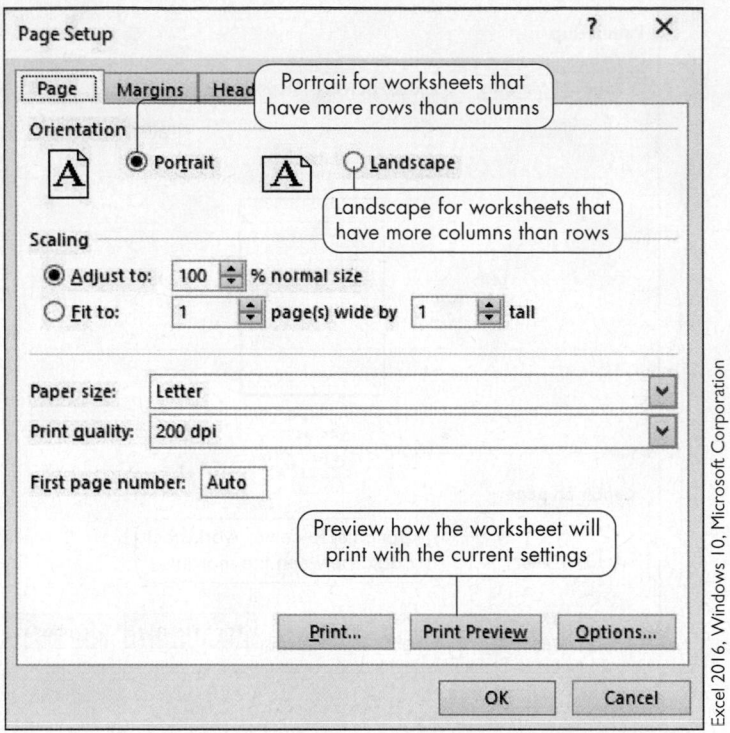

FIGURE 1.51 Page Setup Dialog Box: Page Tab

The Page tab contains options to select the orientation and paper size. In addition, it contains scaling options that are similar to the options in the Scale to Fit group on the Page Layout tab. You use scaling options to increase or decrease the size of characters on a printed page, similar to using a zoom setting on a photocopy machine. You might want to use the *Fit to* option to force the data to print on a specified number of pages.

Set Margin Options

The Margins tab (see Figure 1.52) contains options for setting the specific margins. In addition, it contains options to center the worksheet data horizontally or vertically on the page, which are used to balance worksheet data equally between the left and right margins or top and bottom margins, respectively.

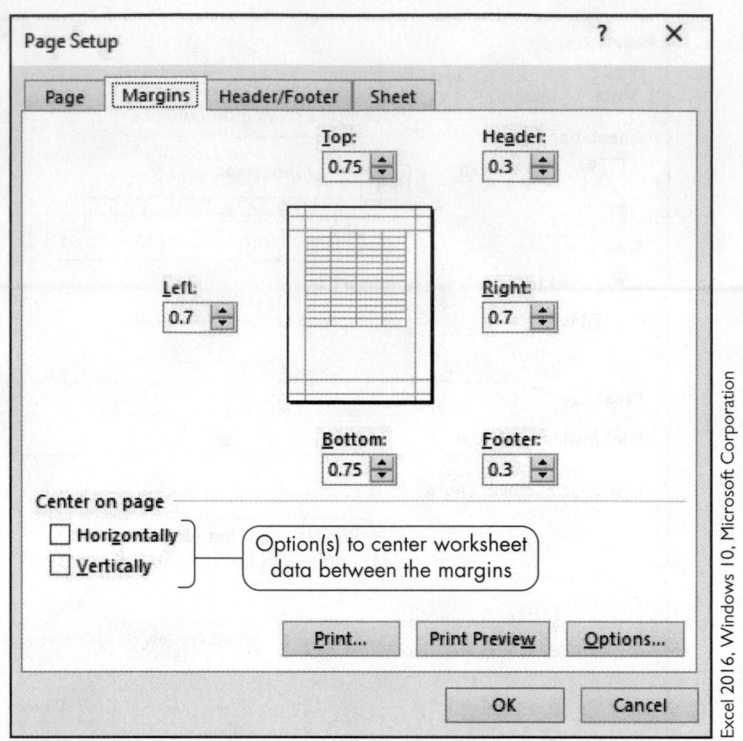

FIGURE 1.52 Page Setup Dialog Box: Margins Tab

Create Headers and Footers

STEP 3 ▶▶ The Header/Footer tab (see Figure 1.53) lets you create a header and/or footer that appears at the top and/or bottom of every printed page. Click the arrows to choose from several preformatted entries, or alternatively, click Custom Header or Custom Footer, insert text and other objects, and click the appropriate formatting button to customize the headers and footers. Use headers and footers to provide additional information about the worksheet. You can include your name, the date the worksheet was prepared, and page numbers, for example.

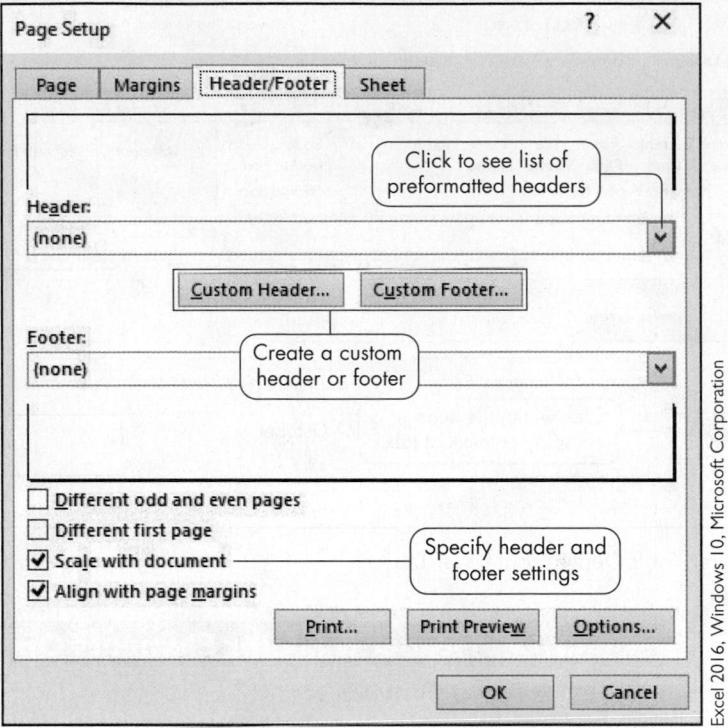

FIGURE 1.53 Page Setup Dialog Box: Header/Footer Tab

You can create different headers or footers on different pages, such as one header with the file name on odd-numbered pages and a header containing the date on even-numbered pages. Click the *Different odd and even pages* check box to select it in the Page Setup dialog box (see Figure 1.53).

You might want the first page to have a different header or footer from the rest of the printed pages, or you might not want a header or footer to show up on the first page but want the header or footer to display on the remaining pages. Click the *Different first page* check box to select it in the Page Setup dialog box to specify a different first page header or footer.

Instead of creating headers and footers using the Page Setup dialog box, you can click the Insert tab and click Header & Footer in the Text group. Excel displays the worksheet in Page Layout view with the insertion point in the center area of the header. Click inside the left, center, or right section of a header or footer. When you click inside a section within the header or footer, Excel displays the Header & Footer Tools Design contextual tab (see Figure 1.54). Enter text or insert data from the Header & Footer Elements group on the tab. Table 1.9 lists and describes the options in the Header & Footer Elements group. To get back to Normal view, click any cell in the worksheet and click Normal in the Workbook Views group on the View tab.

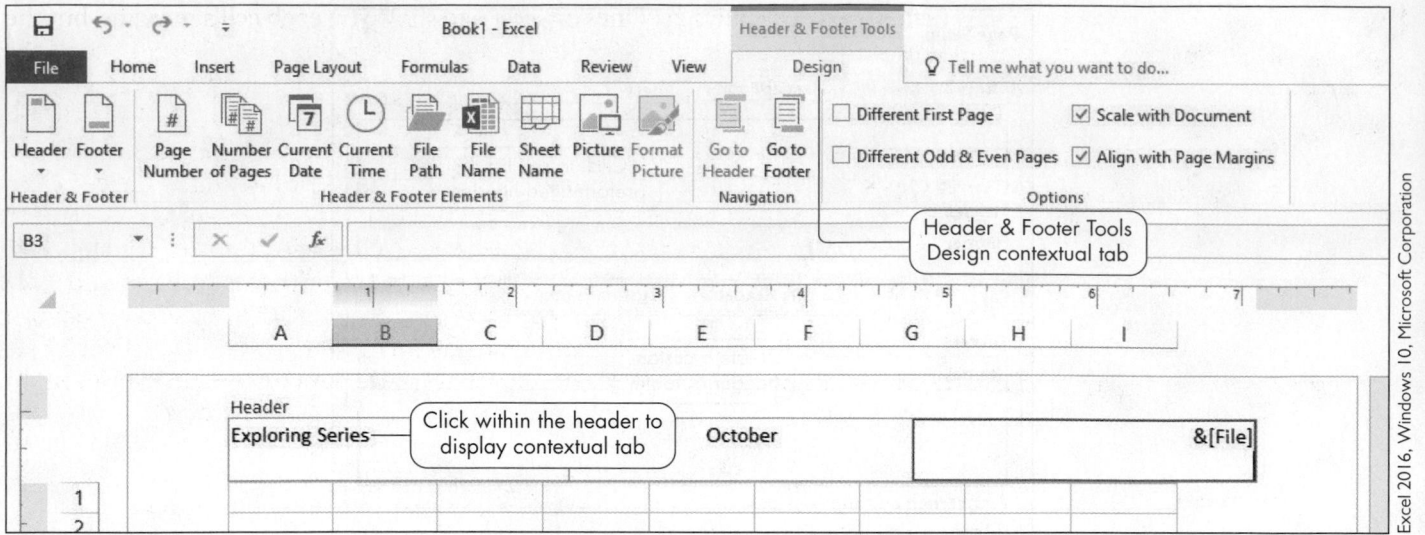

FIGURE 1.54 Headers & Footer Tools Design Contextual Tab

TABLE 1.9	Header & Footer Elements Options
Option Name	**Result**
Page Number	Inserts the code &[Page] to display the current page number.
Number of Pages	Inserts the code &[Pages] to display the total number of pages that will print.
Current Date	Inserts the code &[Date] to display the current date, such as 5/19/2018. The date is updated to the current date when you open or print the worksheet.
Current Time	Inserts the code &[Time] to display the current time, such as 5:15 PM. The time is updated to the current time when you open or print the worksheet.
File Path	Inserts the code &[Path]&[File] to display the path and file name, such as C:\Users\Keith\Documents\e01h4Markup. This information changes if you save the workbook with a different name or in a different location.
File Name	Inserts the code &[File] to display the file name, such as e01h4Markup. This information changes if you save the workbook with a different name.
Sheet Name	Inserts the code &[Tab] to display the worksheet name, such as September. This information changes if you rename the worksheet.
Picture	Inserts the code &[Picture] to display and print an image as a background behind the data, not just the worksheet.
Format Picture	Enables you to adjust the brightness, contrast, and size of an image after you use the Picture option.

> **TIP: VIEW TAB**
> If you click the View tab and click Page Layout, Excel displays an area *Click to add header* at the top of the worksheet.

Select Sheet Options

The Sheet tab (see Figure 1.55) contains options for setting the print area, print titles, print options, and page order. Some of these options are also located in the Sheet Options group on the Page Layout tab.

By default, Excel displays gridlines onscreen to show you each cell's margins, but the gridlines do not print unless you specifically select the Gridlines check box in the Page Setup dialog box or the Print Gridlines check box in the Sheet Options group on the Page Layout tab. In addition, Excel displays row (1, 2, 3, etc.) and column (A, B, C, etc.) headings onscreen. However, these headings do not print unless you click the *Row and column headings* check box in the Page Setup dialog box or click the Print Headings check box in the Sheet Options group on the Page Layout tab. For most worksheets, you do not need to print gridlines and row/column headings. However, when you want to display and print cell formulas instead of formula results, you might want to print the gridlines and row/column headings. Doing so will help you analyze your formulas. The gridlines help you see the cell boundaries, and the headings help you identify what data are in each cell. At times, you might want to display gridlines to separate data on a regular printout to increase readability.

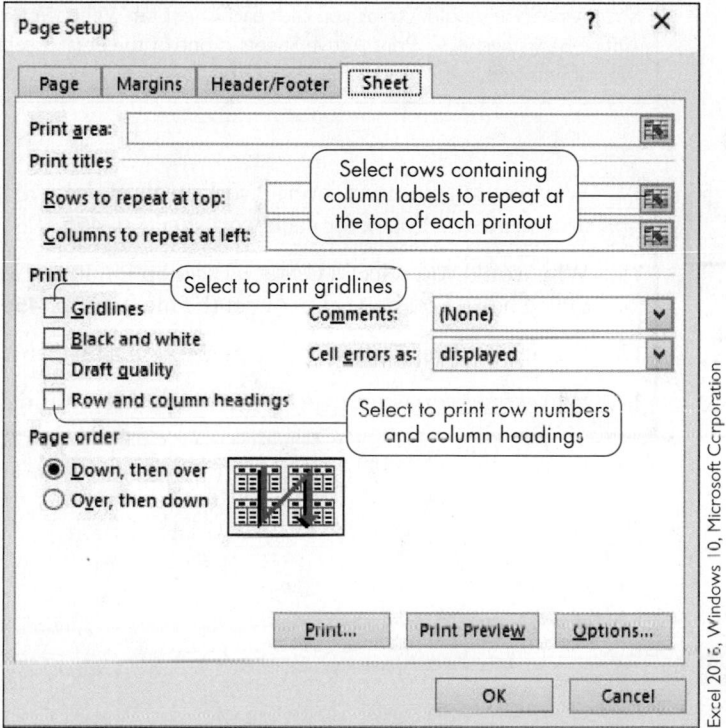

FIGURE 1.55 Page Setup Dialog Box: Sheet Tab

TIP: REPEATING ROWS AND COLUMNS
If you have spreadsheet data that would take more than one printed page, open the Page Setup dialog box, click the Sheet tab, click in the *Rows to repeat at top* box, and then select the row(s) containing column labels. That way, when the pages print, the rows containing the descriptive column labels will repeat at the top of each printed page so that you can easily know what data is in each column. Likewise, if the spreadsheet has too many columns to print on one page, you can click in the *Columns to repeat at left* box on the Sheet tab within the Page Setup dialog box and select the column(s) so that the row labels will display on the left side of each printed page.

Previewing and Printing a Worksheet

STEP 4 ➤➤ Microsoft Office Backstage view displays print options and displays the worksheet in print preview mode. Print preview helps you see before printing if the data are balanced on the page or if data will print on multiple pages.

You can specify the number of copies to print and which printer to use to print the worksheet. The first option in the Settings area specifies what to print. The default option is Print Active Sheets. You might want to choose other options, such as Print Entire Workbook or Print Selection, or specify which pages to print. If you are connected to a printer capable of duplex printing, you can print on only one side or print on both sides. You can also collate, change the orientation, specify the paper size, adjust the margins, and adjust the scaling.

The bottom of the Print window indicates how many pages will print. If you do not like how the worksheet will print, click Page Setup at the bottom of the print settings to open the Page Setup dialog box so that you can adjust margins, scaling, column widths, and so on until the worksheet data appear the way you want them to print.

TIP: PRINTING MULTIPLE WORKSHEETS

To print more than one worksheet at a time, select the sheets you want to print. To select adjacent sheets, click the first sheet tab, press and hold Shift, and click the last sheet tab. To select nonadjacent sheets, press and hold Ctrl as you click each sheet tab. When you display the Print options in Microsoft Office Backstage view, Print Active Sheets is one of the default settings. If you want to print all of the worksheets within the workbook, change the setting to Print Entire Workbook.

Quick Concepts

14. Why would you insert several worksheets of data in one workbook instead of creating a separate workbook for each worksheet? *p. 455*

15. Why would you select a *Center on page* option in the Margins tab within the Page Setup dialog box if you have already set the margins? *p. 459*

16. List at least five elements you can insert in a header or footer. *p. 462*

17. Why would you want to print gridlines and row and column headings? *p. 463*

Hands-On Exercises

 Watch the Video for this Hands-On Exercise!

5 Worksheets, Page Setup, and Printing

You are ready to complete the OKOS worksheet. You want to copy the existing worksheet so that you display the results on the original sheet and display formulas on the duplicate sheet. Before printing the worksheet for your supervisor, you want to make sure the data will appear professional when printed. You will adjust some page setup options to put the finishing touches on the worksheet.

STEP 1 ›› COPY, MOVE, AND RENAME A WORKSHEET

You want to copy the worksheet, move it to the right side of the original worksheet, and rename the duplicate worksheet so that you can show formulas on the duplicate sheet. Refer to Figure 1.56 as you complete Step 1.

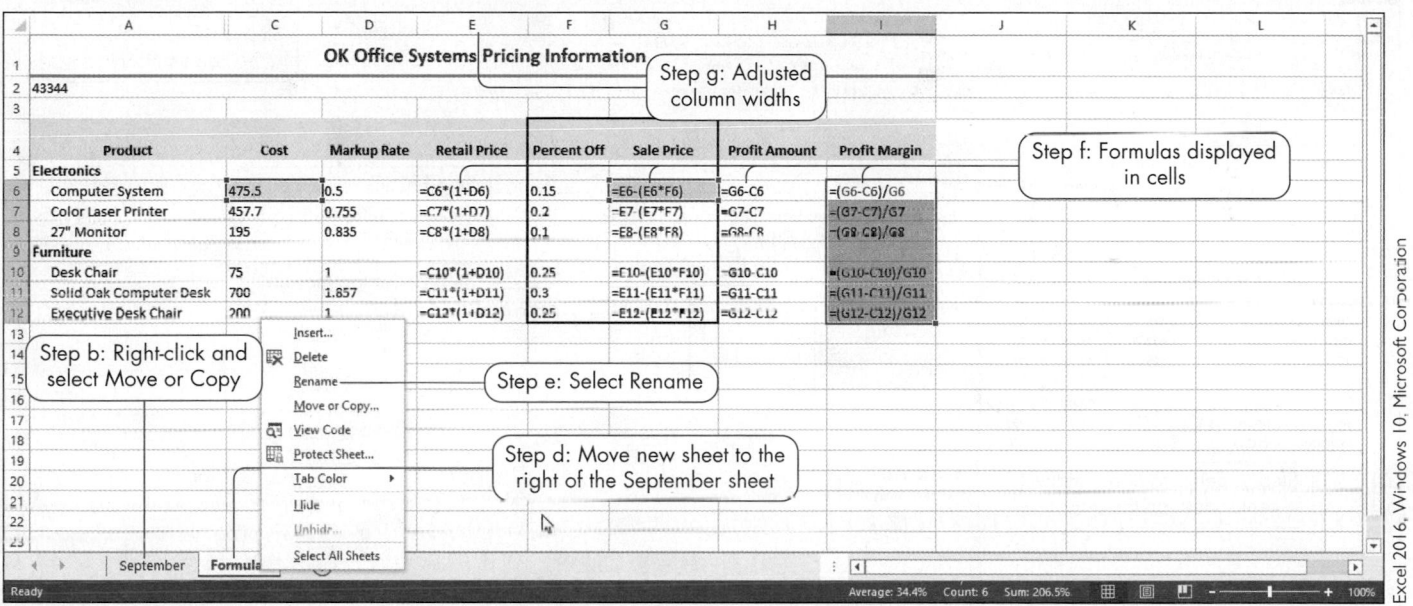

FIGURE 1.56 Worksheets

a. Open *e01h4Markup_LastFirst* if you closed it at the end of Hands-On Exercise 4 and save it as **e01h5Markup_LastFirst**, changing h4 to h5.

b. Right-click the **Sheet1 tab** at the bottom of the worksheet and select **Move or Copy**.

The Move or Copy dialog box opens so that you can move the existing worksheet or make a copy of it.

c. Click the **Create a copy check box** to select it and click **OK**.

The duplicate worksheet is named Sheet1 (2) and is placed to the left of the original worksheet.

d. Drag the **Sheet1 (2) worksheet tab** to the right of the Sheet1 worksheet tab.

The duplicate worksheet is now on the right side of the original worksheet.

e. Right-click the **Sheet1 sheet tab**, select **Rename**, type **September**, and then press **Enter**. Rename Sheet1 (2) as **Formulas**.

You renamed the original worksheet as September to reflect the September sales data, and you renamed the duplicate worksheet as Formulas to indicate that you will keep the formulas displayed on that sheet.

f. Press **Ctrl+`** to display the formulas in the Formulas worksheet.

g. Change these column widths in the Formulas sheet:

- Column A **(13.00)**
- Columns C and D **(6.00)**
- Columns E, G, H, and I **(7.00)**
- Column F **(5.00)**

You reduced the column widths so that the data will fit on a printout better.

h. Save the workbook.

STEP 2 ▶▶ **SET PAGE ORIENTATION, SCALING, AND MARGIN OPTIONS**

Because the worksheet has several columns, you decide to print it in landscape orientation. You want to set a 1" top margin and center the data between the left and right margins. Furthermore, you want to make sure the data fits on one page on each sheet. Currently, if you were to print the Formulas worksheet, the data would print on two pages. Refer to Figure 1.57 as you complete Step 2.

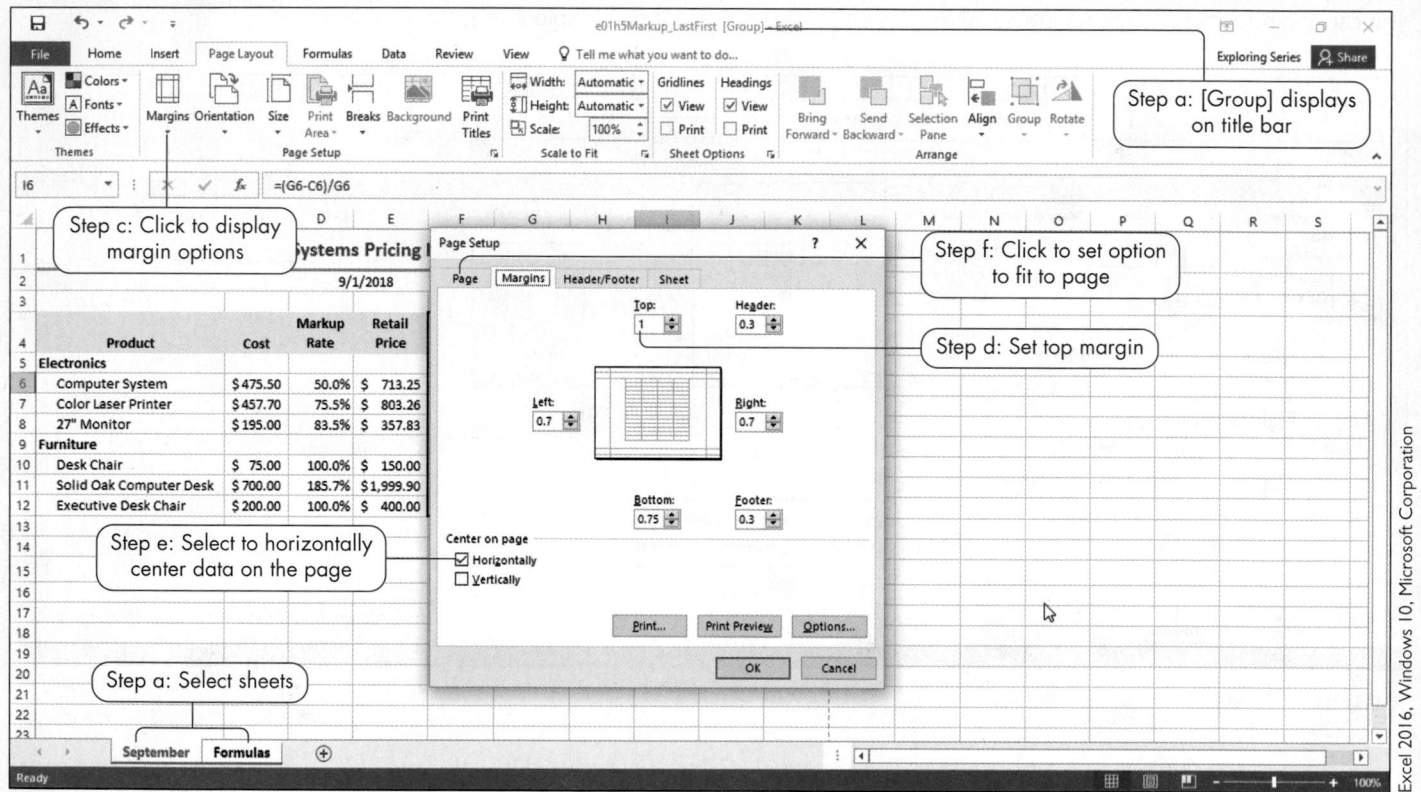

FIGURE 1.57 Page Setup Options Applied

a. Click the **September sheet tab**, press and hold down **Ctrl**, and then click the **Formulas sheet tab**.

Both worksheets are grouped together as indicated by [Group] after the file name on the title bar. Anything you do on one sheet affects both sheets.

b. Click the **Page Layout tab**, click **Orientation** in the Page Setup group, and then select **Landscape** from the list.

Because both worksheets are grouped, both worksheets are formatted in landscape orientation.

c. Click **Margins** in the Page Setup group on the Page Layout tab and select **Custom Margins**.

The Page Setup dialog box opens with the Margins tab options displayed.

d. Click the **Top spin arrow** to display **1**.

Because both worksheets are grouped, the 1" top margin is set for both worksheets.

e. Click the **Horizontally check box** to select it in the Center on page section.

Because both worksheets are grouped, the data on each worksheet are centered between the left and right margins.

f. Click the **Page tab** within the Page Setup dialog box, click **Fit to** in the Scaling section, and then click **OK**. Save the workbook.

The Fit to option ensures that each sheet fits on one page.

STEP 3 ›› CREATE A HEADER

To document the grouped worksheets, you want to include your name, the sheet name, and the file name in a header. Refer to Figure 1.58 as you complete Step 3.

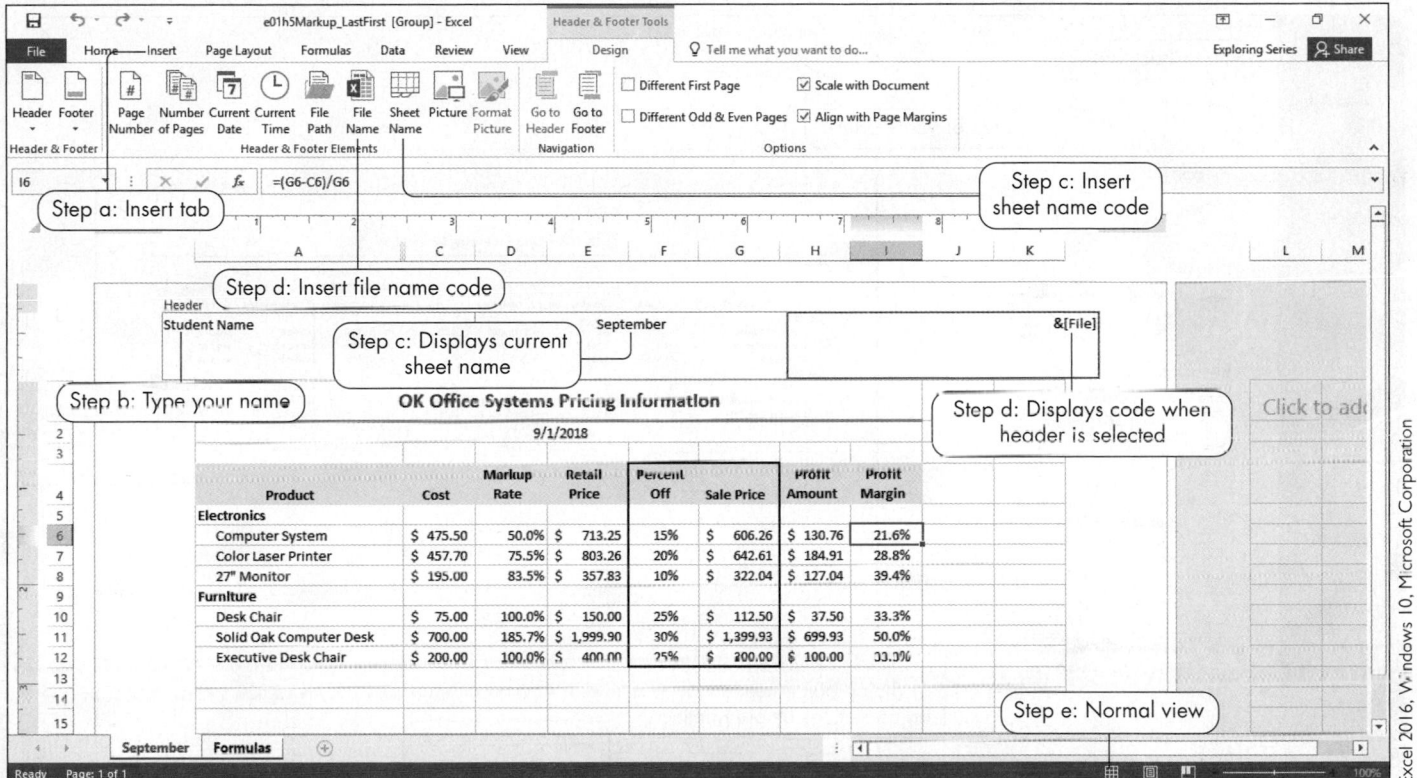

FIGURE 1.58 Header

a. Ensure the worksheets are still grouped, click the **Insert tab**, and then click **Header & Footer** in the Text group.

Excel displays the Header & Footer Tools Design contextual tab and the worksheet displays in Page Layout view, which displays the header area, margin space, and ruler. The insertion point blinks inside the center section of the header.

b. Click in the left section of the header and type your name.

c. Click in the center section of the header and click **Sheet Name** in the Header & Footer Elements group on the Design tab.

Excel inserts the code &[Tab]. This code displays the name of the worksheet. If you change the worksheet tab name, the header will reflect the new sheet name.

d. Click in the right section of the header and click **File Name** in the Header & Footer Elements group on the Design tab.

Excel inserts the code &[File]. This code displays the name of the file. Because the worksheets were grouped when you created the header, a header will appear on both worksheets. The file name will be the same; however, the sheet names will be different.

e. Click in any cell in the worksheet, click **Normal** on the status bar, and then save the workbook.

Normal view displays the worksheet, but does not display the header or margins.

f. Click the **Review tab** and click **Spelling** in the Proofing group. Correct all errors, if any, and click **OK** when prompted with the message, *Spell check complete. You're good to go!* Save the workbook.

You should always spell-check a workbook before publishing it.

STEP 4 ›› VIEW IN PRINT PREVIEW AND PRINT

Before printing the worksheets, you should preview it. Doing so helps you detect margin problems and other issues, such as a single row or column of data flowing onto a new page. Refer to Figure 1.59 as you complete Step 4.

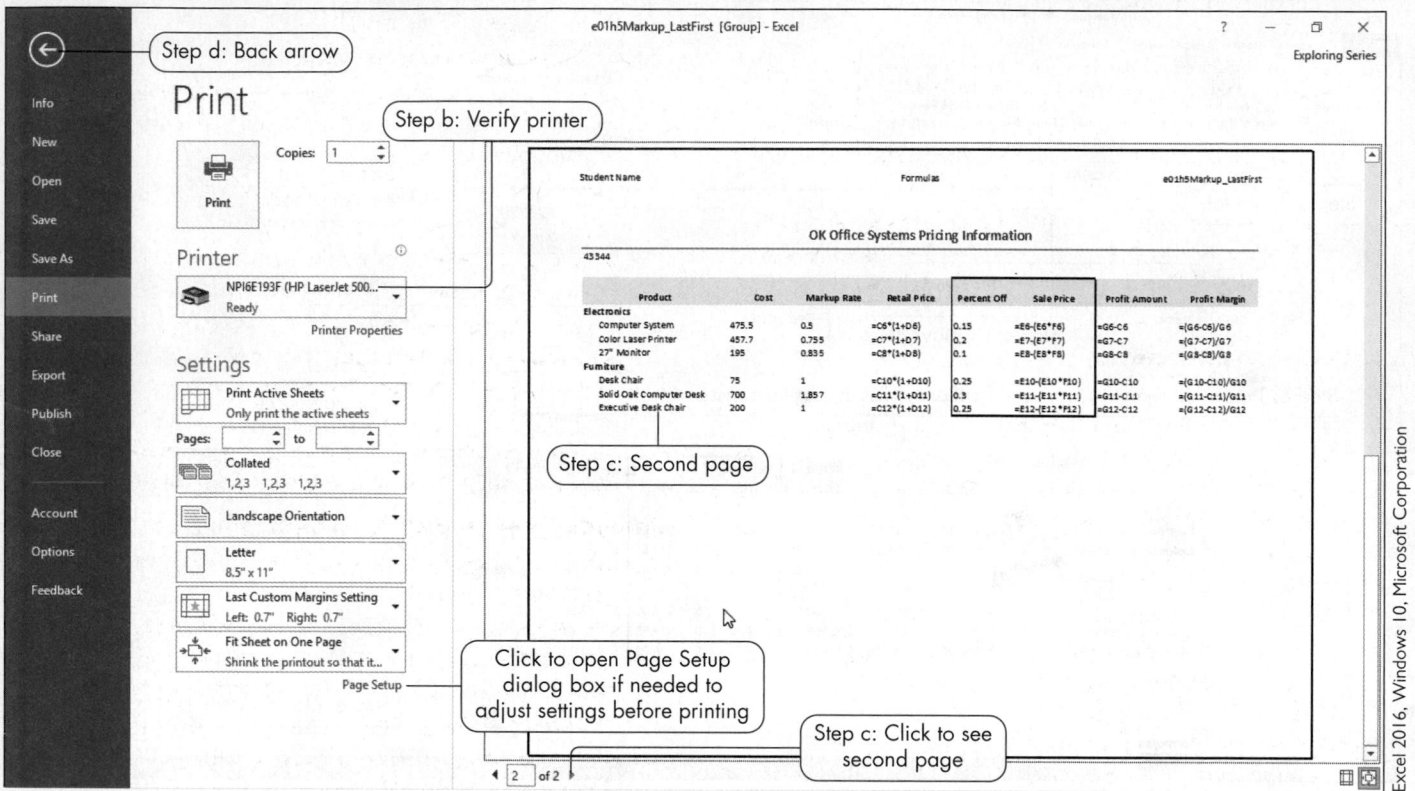

FIGURE 1.59 Worksheet in Print Preview

a. Click the **File tab** and click **Print**.

The Microsoft Office Backstage view displays print options and a preview of the worksheet.

b. Verify the Printer box displays the printer that you want to use to print your worksheet, and verify the last Settings option displays Fit Sheet on One Page.

The bottom of Backstage shows 1 of 2, indicating two pages will print.

c. Click **Next Page** to see the second page, which is the data on the Formulas worksheet, and verify the last Settings option displays Fit Sheet on One Page.

Check the Print Preview window to make sure the data are formatted correctly and would print correctly.

d. Click the **Back arrow** and save the workbook.

Although you did not print the worksheets, all the print options are saved.

e. Save and close the file. Based on your instructor's directions, submit e01h5Markup_LastFirst. Once the file is closed, the Formulas sheet may not display the formulas when you open the workbook again. If that happens, press **Ctrl+`** again.

Chapter Objectives Review

After reading this chapter, you have accomplished the following objectives:

I. Explore the Excel window.

- A worksheet is a single spreadsheet containing data. A workbook is a collection of one or more related worksheets contained in a single file.
- Identify Excel window elements: The Name Box displays the name of the current cell. The Formula Bar displays the contents of the current cell. The active cell is the current cell. A sheet tab shows the name of the worksheet.
- Identify columns, rows, and cells: Columns have alphabetical headings, such as A, B, C. Rows have numbers, such as 1, 2, 3. A cell is the intersection of a column and row and is indicated with a column letter and a row number.
- Navigate in and among worksheets: Use the arrow keys to navigate within a sheet, or use the Go To command to go to a specific cell. Click a sheet tab to display the contents on another worksheet.

2. Enter and edit cell data.

- You should plan the worksheet design by stating the purpose, deciding what output you need, and then identifying what input values are needed. Next, you enter and format data in a worksheet. Finally, you document, save, and then share a workbook.
- Enter text: Text may contain letters, numbers, symbols, and spaces. Text aligns at the left side of a cell.
- Use Auto Fill to complete a sequence. Auto Fill can automatically fill in sequences, such as month names or values, after you enter the first label or value. Double-click the fill handle to fill in the sequence.
- Enter values: Values are numbers that represent a quantity. Values align at the right side of a cell by default.
- Enter dates and times: Excel stores dates and times as serial numbers so that you can calculate the number of days between dates or times.
- Edit and clear contents: You might want to edit the contents of a cell to correct errors or to make labels more descriptive. Use the Clear option to clear the cell contents and/or formats.

3. Create formulas.

- A formula is used to perform a calculation. The formula results display in the cell.
- Use cell references in formulas: Use references, such as =B5+B6, instead of values within formulas.
- Apply the order of operations: The most commonly used operators are performed in this sequence: Parentheses, exponentiation, multiplication, division, addition, and subtraction.

- Use semi-selection to create a formula: When building a formula, click a cell containing a value to enter that cell reference in the formula.
- Copy formulas with the fill handle: Double-click the fill handle to copy a formula down a column.

4. Display cell formulas.

- By default, the results of formulas appear in cells.
- Display formulas by pressing Ctrl+`.

5. Manage columns and rows.

- Insert cells, columns, and rows: Insert a cell to move the remaining cells down or to the right. Insert a new column or row for data.
- Delete cells, columns, and rows: You should delete cells, columns, and rows you no longer need.
- Hide and unhide columns and rows: Hiding rows and columns protects confidential data from being displayed.
- Adjust column width: Double-click between the column headings to widen a column based on the longest item in that column, or drag the border between column headings to increase or decrease a column width.
- Adjust row height: Drag the border between row headings to increase or decrease the height of a row.

6. Select, move, copy, and paste data.

- Select a range: A range may be a single cell or a rectangular block of cells.
- Move a range to another location: After selecting a range, cut it from its location. Then select the top-left corner of the destination range to make it the active cell and paste the range there.
- Copy and paste a range: After selecting a range, click Copy, click the top-left corner of the destination range, and then click Paste to make a copy of the original range.
- Use Paste Options and Paste Special: The Paste Special option enables you to specify how the data are pasted into the worksheet.
- Copy Excel data to other programs: You can copy Excel data and paste it in other programs, such as in Word or PowerPoint.

7. Apply cell styles, alignment, and font options.

- Cell styles contain a collection of formatting, such as font, font color, font size, fill, and borders. You can apply an Excel cell style to save formatting time.
- Merge and center labels: Type a label in the left cell, select a range including the data you typed, and then click Merge & Center to merge cells and center the label within the newly merged cell.

- Change horizontal and vertical cell alignment: The default horizontal alignment depends on the data entered, and the default vertical alignment is Bottom Align.
- Wrap text: Use the Wrap Text option to present text on multiple lines in order to avoid having extra-wide columns.
- Increase and decrease indent: To indicate hierarchy of data or to offset a label, increase or decrease how much the data are indented in a cell.
- Apply borders and fill colors: Borders and fill colors help improve readability of worksheets.

8. Apply number formats.
- Apply a number format: The default number format is General, which does not apply any particular format to values. Apply appropriate formats to values to present the data with the correct symbols and decimal alignment. For example, Accounting Number Format is a common number format for monetary values.
- Increase and decrease decimal places: After applying a number format, you might want to increase or decrease the number of decimal places displayed.

9. Manage worksheets.
- Insert and delete a worksheet: You can insert new worksheets to include related data within one workbook, or you can delete extra worksheets you do not need.

- Copy or move a worksheet: Drag a sheet tab to rearrange the worksheets. You can copy a worksheet within a workbook or to another workbook.
- Rename a worksheet: The default worksheet tab name is Sheet1, but you should change the name to describe the contents of the worksheet.

10. Select page setup options.
- The Page Layout tab on the Ribbon contains options for setting margins, selecting orientation, specifying page size, selecting the print area, and applying other settings.
- Specify page options: Page options include orientation, paper size, and scaling.
- Set margin options: You can set the left, right, top, and bottom margins. In addition, you can center worksheet data horizontally and vertically on a page.
- Create headers and footers: Insert a header or footer to display documentation, such as your name, date, time, and worksheet tab name.
- Select sheet options: Sheet options control the print area, print titles, print options, and page order.

11. Preview and print a worksheet.
- Before printing a worksheet, you should display a preview to ensure the data will print correctly. The Print Preview helps you see if margins are correct or if isolated rows or columns will print on separate pages.
- After making appropriate adjustments, you can print the worksheet.

Key Terms Matching

Match the key terms with their definitions. Write the key term letter by the appropriate numbered definition.

a. Alignment
b. Auto Fill
c. Cell
d. Column width
e. Fill color
f. Fill handle
g. Formula
h. Formula Bar
i. Input area
j. Name Box

k. Order of operations
l. Output area
m. Range
n. Row height
o. Sheet tab
p. Text
q. Value
r. Workbook
s. Worksheet
t. Wrap text

1. _____ A spreadsheet that contains formulas, functions, values, text, and visual aids. **p. 404**

2. _____ A file containing related worksheets. **p. 404**

3. _____ A range of cells containing values for variables used in formulas. **p. 407**

4. _____ A range of cells containing results based on manipulating the variables. **p. 407**

5. _____ Identifies the address of the current cell. **p. 405**

6. _____ Displays the content (text, value, date, or formula) in the active cell. **p. 405**

7. _____ Displays the name of a worksheet within a workbook. **p. 405**

8. _____ The intersection of a column and row. **p. 406**

9. _____ Includes letters, numbers, symbols, and spaces. **p. 408**

10. _____ A number that represents a quantity or an amount. **p. 411**

11. _____ Rules that control the sequence in which Excel performs arithmetic operations. **p. 418**

12. _____ Enables you to copy the contents of a cell or cell range or to continue a sequence by dragging the fill handle over an adjacent cell or range of cells. **p. 409**

13. _____ A small green square at the bottom-right corner of a cell. **p. 410**

14. _____ The horizontal measurement of a column. **p. 431**

15. _____ The vertical measurement of a row. **p. 432**

16. _____ A rectangular group of cells. **p. 432**

17. _____ The position of data between the cell margins. **p. 445**

18. _____ Formatting that enables a label to appear on multiple lines within the current cell. **p. 446**

19. _____ The background color appearing behind data in a cell. **p. 447**

20. _____ A combination of cell references, operators, values, and/or functions used to perform a calculation. **p. 417**

Multiple Choice

1. Which step is *not* part of planning a worksheet design?

   (a) Decide what input values are needed.

   (b) State the purpose of the worksheet.

   (c) Decide what outputs are needed to achieve the purpose.

   (d) Enter labels, values, and formulas.

2. You just copied a range of data containing formulas. However, you want to preserve the formula results and the original number and text formatting in the pasted range. Which paste option would you select?

   (a) Formulas

   (b) Keep Source Formatting

   (c) Values & Source Formatting

   (d) Values & Number Formatting

3. Given the formula =B1*B2+B3/B4^2, what operation is calculated first?

   (a) B1*B2

   (b) B2+B3

   (c) B3/B4

   (d) B4^2

4. How can you display formulas within the cells instead of the cell results?

   (a) Press Ctrl+G.

   (b) Press Ctrl+`.

   (c) Click Cell References on the Home tab.

   (d) Press Ctrl+C.

5. What is a fast way to apply several formats at one time?

   (a) Click each one individually.

   (b) Apply a cell style.

   (c) Use Auto Fill.

   (d) Use Copy and Paste options.

6. Which of the following is *not* an alignment option?

   (a) Increase Indent

   (b) Merge & Center

   (c) Fill Color

   (d) Wrap Text

7. Which of the following characteristics is *not* applicable to the Accounting Number Format?

   (a) Dollar sign immediately on the left side of the value

   (b) Commas to separate thousands

   (c) Two decimal places

   (d) Zero values displayed as hyphens

8. You selected and copied worksheet data containing formulas. However, you want the pasted copy to contain the current formula results rather than formulas. What do you do?

   (a) Click Paste in the Clipboard group on the Home tab.

   (b) Click the Paste arrow in the Clipboard group and select Formulas.

   (c) Click the Paste arrow in the Clipboard group and select Values & Source Formatting.

   (d) Display the Paste Special dialog box and select Formulas & Number Formatting.

9. Assume that the data on a worksheet consume a whole printed page and a couple of columns on a second page. You can do all of the following *except* what to force the data to print all on one page?

   (a) Decrease the Scale value.

   (b) Increase the left and right margins.

   (c) Decrease column widths if possible.

   (d) Select a smaller range as the print area.

10. What should you do if you see pound signs (###) instead of values or results of formulas?

   (a) Increase the zoom percentage.

   (b) Delete the column.

   (c) Adjust the row height.

   (d) Increase the column width.

Practice Exercises

1 Mathematics Review

You want to brush up on your math skills to test your logic by creating formulas in Excel. You realize that you should avoid values in formulas most of the time. Therefore, you created an input area that contains values you will use in your formulas. To test your knowledge of formulas, you will create an output area that will contain a variety of formulas using cell references from the input area. You will include a formatted title, the date prepared, and your name. After creating and verifying formula results, you will change input values and observe changes in the formula results. You want to display cell formulas, so you will create a picture copy of the formulas view. Refer to Figure 1.60 as you complete this exercise.

	A	B	C	D	E
1				**Excel Formulas and Order of Precedence**	
2	Date Created:	42614		Student Name	
3					
4	**Input Area:**			**Output Area:**	
5	First Value	2		Sum of 1st and 2nd values	=B5+B6
6	Second Value	4		Difference between 4th and 1st values	=B8-B5
7	Third Value	6		Product of 2nd and 3rd values	=B6*B7
8	Fourth Value	8		Quotient of 3rd and 1st values	=B7/B5
9				2nd value to the power of 3rd value	=B6^B7
10				1st value added to product of 2nd and 4th values and difference between sum and 3rd value	=B5+B6*B8-B7
11				Product of sum of 1st and 2nd and difference between 4th and 3rd values	=(B5+B6)*(B8-B7)
12				Product of 1st and 2nd added to product of 3rd and 4th values	=(B5*B6)+(B7*B8)

Excel 2016, Windows 10, Microsoft Corporation

FIGURE 1.60 Formula Practice

a. Open *e01p1Math* and save it as **e01p1Math_LastFirst**.

b. Type the current date in **cell B2** in this format: 9/1/2018. Type your first and last names in **cell D2**.

c. Adjust the column widths by doing the following:
   - Click in any cell in column A and click **Format** in the Cells group.
   - Select **Column Width**, type **12.57** in the Column width box, and then click **OK**.
   - Click in any cell in column B and set the width to **11**.
   - Click in any cell in column D and set the width to **35.57**.

d. Select the **range A1:E1**, click **Merge & Center** in the Alignment group, click **Bold** in the Font group, and then change the font size to **14**.

e. Select the **range B5:B8** and click **Center** in the Alignment group.

f. Select the **range D10:D12** and click **Wrap Text** in the Alignment group.

g. Enter the following formulas in column E:
   - Click **cell E5**. Type **=B5+B6** and press **Enter**. Excel adds the value stored in cell B5 (1) to the value stored in cell B6 (2). The result (3) appears in cell E5, as described in cell D5.
   - Enter appropriate formulas in **cells E6:E8**, pressing **Enter** after entering each formula. Subtract to calculate a difference, multiply to calculate a product, and divide to calculate a quotient.
   - Type **=B6^B7** in **cell E9** and press **Enter**. Calculate the answer: 2*2*2 = 8.
   - Enter **=B5+B6*B8-B7** in **cell E10** and press **Enter**. Calculate the answer: 2*4 = 8; 1+8 = 9; 9-3 = 6. Multiplication occurs first, followed by addition, and finally subtraction.
   - Enter **=(B5+B6)*(B8-B7)** in **cell E11** and press **Enter**. Calculate the answer: 1+2 = 3; 4-3 = 1; 3*1 = 3. This formula is almost identical to the previous formula; however, calculations in parentheses occur before the multiplication.
   - Enter **=B5*B6+B7*B8** in **cell E12** and press **Enter**. Calculate the answer: 1*2 = 2; 3*4 = 12; 2+12 = 14.

h. Edit a formula and the input values:

- Click **cell E12** and click in the Formula Bar to edit the formula. Add parentheses as shown: **=(B5*B6)+(B7*B8)** and click **Enter** to the left side of the Formula Bar. The answer is still 14. The parentheses do not affect order of operations because multiplication occurred before the addition. The parentheses help improve the readability of the formula.
- Type **2** in **cell B5**, **4** in **cell B6**, **6** in **cell B7**, and **8** in **cell B8**.
- Double-check the results of the formulas using a calculator or your head. The new results in cells E5:E12 should be 6, 6, 24, 3, 4096, 28, 12, and 56, respectively.

i. Double-click the **Sheet1 tab**, type **Results**, and then press **Enter**. Right-click the **Results sheet tab**, select **Move or Copy**, click **(move to end)** in the *Before sheet* section, click the **Create a copy check box** to select it, and click **OK**. Double-click the **Results (2) sheet tab**, type **Formulas**, and then press **Enter**.

j. Ensure that the Formulas sheet tab is active, click the **Formulas sheet tab** and click **Show Formulas** in the Formula Auditing group. Double-click between the column A and column B headings to adjust the column A width. Double-click between the column B and column C headings to adjust the column B width. Set **24.00 width** for column D.

k. Ensure that the Formulas worksheet is active, click the **Page Layout tab**, and do the following:

- Click the **Gridlines Print check box** to select it in the Sheet Options group.
- Click the **Headings Print check box** to select it in the Sheet Options group.

l. Click the **Results sheet tab**, press and hold **Ctrl**, and click the **Formulas sheet tab** to select both worksheets. Do the following:

- Click **Orientation** in the Page Setup group and select **Landscape**.
- Click the **Insert tab**, click **Header & Footer** in the Text group. Click **Go to Footer** in the Navigation group.
- Type your name on the left side of the footer.
- Click in the center section of the footer and click **Sheet Name** in the Header & Footer Elements group.
- Click in the right section of the footer and click **File Name** in the Header & Footer elements group.

m. Click in the worksheet, press **Ctrl+Home**, and click **Normal View** on the status bar.

n. Click the **File tab** and click **Print**. Verify that each worksheet will print on one page. Press **Esc** to close the Print Preview, and right-click the worksheet tab and click **Ungroup Sheets**.

o. Save and close the file. Based on your instructor's directions, submit e01p1Math_LastFirst.

2 Calendar Formatting

You want to create a calendar for July 2018. The calendar will enable you to practice alignment settings, including center, merge and center, and indents. In addition, you will need to adjust column widths and increase row height to create cells large enough to enter important information, such as birthdays, in your calendar. You will create a formula and use Auto Fill to complete the days of the week and the days within each week. To improve the appearance of the calendar, you will add fill colors, font colors, and borders to create a red, white, and blue effect to celebrate Independence Day. Refer to Figure 1.61 as you complete this exercise.

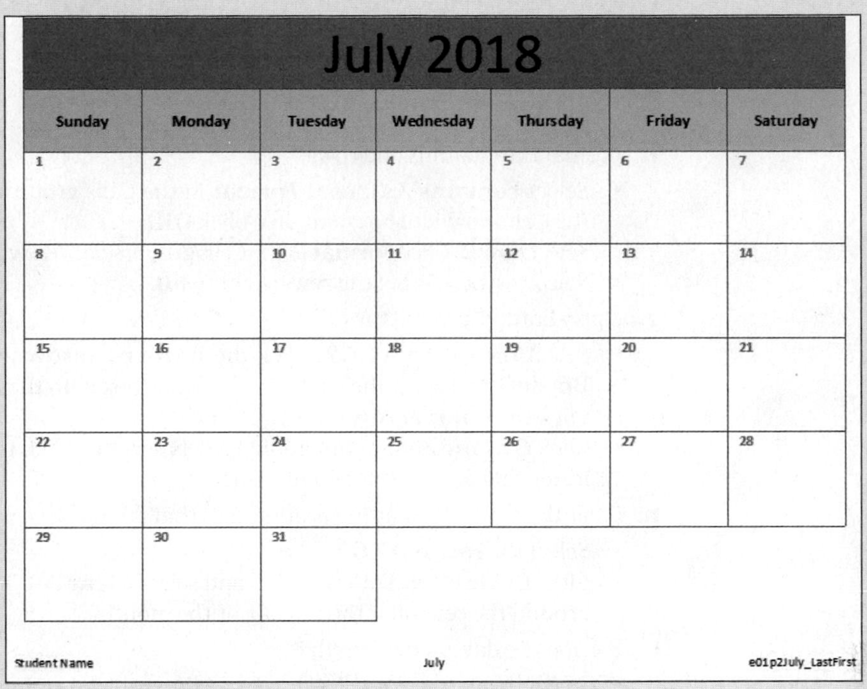

July 2018

Sunday	Monday	Tuesday	Wednesday	Thursday	Friday	Saturday
1	2	3	4	5	6	7
8	9	10	11	12	13	14
15	16	17	18	19	20	21
22	23	24	25	26	27	28
29	30	31				

Student Name   July   e01p2July_LastFirst

Excel 2016, Windows 10, Microsoft Corporation

FIGURE 1.61 Calendar

a. Click the **File tab**, select **New**, and click **Blank workbook**. Save the workbook as **e01p2July_LastFirst**.

b. Type **'July 2018** in **cell A1** and click **Enter** on the left side of the Formula Bar.

> **TROUBLESHOOTING:** If you do not type the apostrophe before July 2018, the cell will display July-18 instead of July 2018.

c. Format the title:
   - Select the **range A1:G1** and click **Merge & Center** in the Alignment group.
   - Change the font size to **48**.
   - Click the **Fill Color arrow** and click **Blue** in the Standard Colors section of the color palette.
   - Click **Middle Align** in the Alignment group.

d. Complete the days of the week:
   - Type **Sunday** in **cell A2** and click **Enter** to the left side of the Formula Bar.
   - Drag the **cell A2 fill handle** across the row through **cell G2** to use Auto Fill to complete the rest of the weekdays.
   - Ensure that the **range A2:G2** is selected. Click the **Fill Color arrow** and select **Blue, Accent 1, Lighter 40%** in the Theme Colors section of the color palette.
   - Apply bold and change the font size to **14 size** to the selected range.
   - Click **Middle Align** and click **Center** in the Alignment group to format the selected range.

e. Complete the days of the month:
   - Type **1** in **cell A3** and press **Ctrl+Enter**. Drag the **cell A3 fill handle** across the row through **cell G3**.
   - Click **Auto Fill Options** in the bottom-right corner of the copied data and select **Fill Series** to change the numbers to 1 through 7.
   - Type **=A3+7** in **cell A4** and press **Ctrl+Enter**. Usually you avoid numbers in formulas, but the number of days in a week is always 7. Drag the **cell A4 fill handle** down through **cell A7** to get the date for each Sunday in July.

- Keep the **range A4:A7** selected and drag the fill handle across through **cell G7**. This action copies the formulas to fill in the days in the month.
- Select the **range D7:G7** and press **Delete** to delete the extra days 32 through 35 because July has only 31 days.

f. Format the columns and rows:

- Select **columns A:G**. Click **Format** in the Cells group, select **Column Width**, type **16** in the Column width box, and then click **OK**.
- Select **row 2**. Click **Format** in the Cells group, select **Row Height**, type **54**, and then click **OK**.
- Select **rows 3:7**. Set the row height to **80**.

g. Apply borders around the cells:

- Select the **range A1:G7**. Click the **Borders arrow** in the Font group and select **More Borders** to display the Format Cells dialog box with the Border tab selected.
- Click the **Color arrow** and select **Red**.
- Click **Outline** and **Inside** in the Presets section. Click **OK**. This action applies a red border inside and outside the selected range.

h. Clear the border formatting around cells that do not have days:

- Select the **range D7:G7**.
- Click **Clear** in the Editing group and select **Clear All**. This action removes the red borders around the cells after the last day of the month.

i. Format the days in the month:

- Select the **range A3:G7**. Click **Top Align** and **Align Left** in the Alignment group.
- Click **Increase Indent** in the Alignment group to offset the days from the border.
- Click **Bold** in the Font group, click the **Font Color arrow** and select **Blue**, and click the **Font Size arrow**, and then select **12**.

j. Double-click the **Sheet1 tab**, type **July**, and then press **Enter**.

k. Deselect the range and click the **Page Layout tab** and do the following:

- Click **Orientation** in the Page Setup group and select **Landscape**.
- Click **Margins** in the Page Setup group and select **Custom Margins**. Click the **Horizontally check box** to select it in the *Center on page* section and click **OK**.

l. Click the **Insert tab** and click **Header & Footer** in the Text group and do the following:

- Click **Go to Footer** in the Navigation group.
- Click in the left side of the footer and type your name.
- Click in the center of the footer and click **Sheet Name** in the Header & Footer Elements group on the Design tab.
- Click in the right side of the footer and click **File Name** in the Header & Footer Elements group on the Design tab.
- Click in any cell in the workbook, press **Ctrl+Home**, and then click **Normal** on the status bar.

m. Save and close the file. Based on your instructor's directions, submit e01p2July_LastFirst.

3 Downtown Theatre

You are the assistant manager at Downtown Theatre, where touring Broadway plays and musicals are performed. You will analyze ticket sales by completing a worksheet that focuses on seating charts for each performance. The spreadsheet will identify the seating sections, total seats in each section, and the number of seats sold for a performance. You will then calculate the percentage of seats sold and unsold. Refer to Figure 1.62 as you complete this exercise.

	A	B	C	D	E	F
1	**Downtown Theatre**					
2	Ticket Sales by Seating Section					
3	3/31/2018					
4						
5	**Section**	**Available Seats**	**Seats Sold**	**Percentage Sold**	**Percentage Unsold**	
6	Box Seats	25	12	48.0%	52.0%	
7	Front Floor	120	114	95.0%	5.0%	
8	Back Floor	132	108	81.8%	18.2%	
9	Tier 1	40	40	100.0%	0.0%	
10	Mezzanine	144	138	95.8%	4.2%	
11	Balcony	106	84	79.2%	20.8%	

Excel 2016, Windows 10, Microsoft Corporation

FIGURE 1.62 Theatre Seating Data

a. Open *e01p3TicketSales* and save it as **e01p3TicketSales_LastFirst**.

b. Double-click the **Sheet1 sheet tab**, type **Seating**, and press **Enter**.

c. Type **3/31/2018** in **cell A3** and press **Enter**.

d. Format the title:
   - Select the **range A1:E1** and click **Merge & Center** in the Alignment group.
   - Click **Cell Styles** in the Styles group and select **Title** in the Titles and Headings section.
   - Click **Bold** in the Font group.

e. Format the subtitle and date:
   - Use the Merge & Center command to merge the **range A2:E2** and center the subtitle.
   - Use the Merge & Center command to merge the **range A3:E3** and center the date.

f. Select the **range A5:E5**, click **Wrap Text**, click **Center**, and click **Bold** to format the column labels.

g. Right-click the **row 9 heading** and select **Insert** from the shortcut menu to insert a new row. Type the following data in the new row: **Back Floor**, **132**, **108**.

h. Move the Balcony row to be the last row by doing the following:
   - Click the **row 6 heading** and click **Cut** in the Clipboard group on the Home tab.
   - Right-click the **row 12 heading** and select **Insert Cut Cells** from the menu.

i. Adjust column widths by doing the following:
   - Double-click between the column A and column B headings.
   - Select **columns B** and **C headings** to select the columns, click **Format** in the Cells group, select **Column Width**, type **9** in the **Column width box**, and then click **OK**. Because columns B and C contain similar data, you set the same width for these columns.
   - Set the width of columns D and E to **12**.

j. Select the **range B6:C11**, click **Align Right** in the Alignment group, and then click **Increase Indent** twice in the Alignment group.

k. Click **cell D6** and use semi-selection to calculate and format the percentage of sold and unsold seats by doing the following:

- Type **=**, click **cell C6**, type **/**, and then click **cell B6** to enter =C6/B6.
- Press **Tab** to enter the formula and make cell E6 the active cell. This formula divides the number of seats sold by the total number of Box Seats.
- Type **=(B6-C6)/B6** and click **Enter** on the left side of the Formula Bar to enter the formula and keep cell E6 the active cell. This formula must first subtract the number of sold seats from the available seats to calculate the number of unsold seats. The difference is divided by the total number of available seats to determine the percentage of unsold seats.
- Select the **range D6:E6**, click **Percent Style** in the Number group, and then click **Increase Decimal** in the Number group. Keep the range selected.
- Double-click the **cell E6 fill handle** to copy the selected formulas down their respective columns. Keep the range selected.
- Click **Align Right** in the Alignment group and click **Increase Indent** twice in the Alignment group. These actions will help center the data below the column labels. Do not click Center; doing so will center each value and cause the decimal points not to align. Deselect the range.

l. Display and preserve a screenshot of the formulas by doing the following:

- Click **New sheet**, double-click the **Sheet1 sheet tab**, type **Formulas**, and then press **Enter**.
- Click the **View tab** and click **Gridlines** in the Show group to hide the gridlines on the Formulas worksheet. This action will prevent the cell gridlines from bleeding through the screenshot you are about to embed.
- Click the **Seating sheet tab**, click the **Formulas tab** on the Ribbon, and then click **Show Formulas** in the Formula Auditing group to display cell formulas.
- Click **cell A1** and drag down to **cell E11** to select the range of data.
- Click the **Home tab**, click **Copy arrow** in the Clipboard group, select **Copy as Picture**, and then click **OK** in the Copy Picture dialog box.
- Click the **Formulas sheet tab**, click **cell A1**, and then click **Paste**.
- Click the **Page Layout tab**, click **Orientation** in the Page Setup group, and then select **Landscape** to change the orientation for the Formulas sheet.
- Click the **Seating sheet tab**, click the **Formulas tab**, and then click **Show Formulas** in the Formula Auditing group to hide the cell formulas.

m. Click the **Seating sheet tab**, press **Ctrl** and click the **Formulas sheet tab** to group the two sheets. Click the **Page Layout tab**, click **Margins** in the Page Setup group, and then select **Custom Margins**. Click the **Horizontally check box** to select it and click **Print Preview**. Excel centers the data horizontally based on the widest item in each worksheet. Verify that the worksheets each print on one page. If not, go back into the Page Setup dialog box for each worksheet and reapply settings if needed. Press **Esc** to leave the Print Preview mode.

n. Click the **Page Setup Dialog Box Launcher**, click the **Header/Footer tab** in the Page Setup dialog box, click **Custom Footer**, click in the left section of the header and type your name, click in the center section of the header, click **Insert Sheet Name**, click in the **right section of the header**, click **Insert File Name**, and then click **OK** to close the Footer dialog box. Click **OK** to close the Page Setup dialog box.

o. Right-click the **Seating sheet tab** and select **Ungroup Sheets**.

p. Save and close the file. Based on your instructor's directions, submit e01p3TicketSales_LastFirst.

Mid-Level Exercises

1 Guest House Rental Rates

ANALYSIS CASE

You manage a beach guest house in Ft. Lauderdale containing three types of rental units. Prices are based on peak and off-peak times of the year. You want to calculate the maximum daily revenue for each rental type, assuming all units are rented. In addition, you will calculate the discount rate for off-peak rental times. Finally, you will improve the appearance of the worksheet by applying font, alignment, and number formats.

a. Open *e01m1Rentals* and save it as **e01m1Rentals_LastFirst**.

b. Apply the **Heading 1** cell style to the **range A1:G1** and the **20% - Accent1** cell style to the **range A2:G2**.

c. Merge and center Peak Rentals in the **range C4:D4**, over the two columns of peak rental data. Apply **Dark Red fill color** and **White, Background 1 font color**.

d. Merge and center Off-Peak Rentals in the **range E4:G4** over the three columns of off-peak rental data. Apply **Blue fill color** and **White, Background 1 font color**.

e. Center and wrap the headings on row 5. Adjust the width of columns D and F, if needed. Center the data in the **range B6:B8**.

f. Create and copy the following formulas:
- Calculate the Peak Rentals Maximum Revenue by multiplying the number of units by the peak rental price per day.
- Calculate the Off-Peak Rentals Maximum Revenue by multiplying the number of units by the off-peak rental price per day.
- Calculate the Discount rate for the Off-Peak rental price per day. For example, using the peak and off-peak per day values, the studio apartment rents for 75% of its peak rental rate. However, you need to calculate and display the off-peak discount rate, which is .20 for the Studio Apartment. To calculate the discount rate, divide the off-peak per day rate by the peak per day rate. Subtract that result from 1, which represents 100%.

g. Format the monetary values with **Accounting Number Format**. Format the Discount Rate formula results in **Percent Style** with one decimal place. Adjust column widths if necessary to display the data.

DISCOVER

h. Apply **Blue, Accent 1, Lighter 80% fill color** to the **range E5:G8**.

i. Select the **range C5:D8** and apply a custom color with **Red 242**, **Green 220**, and **Blue 219**.

j. Answer the four questions below the worksheet data. If you change any values to answer the questions, change the values back to the original values.

k. Create a copy of the Rental Rates worksheet, place the new sheet to the right side of the original worksheet, and rename the new sheet **Formulas**. Display cell formulas on the Formulas sheet.

l. Group the worksheets and do the following:
- Select landscape orientation.
- Set **1"** top, bottom, left, and right margins. Center the data horizontally on the page.
- Insert a footer with your name on the left side, the sheet name code in the center, and the file name code on the right side.
- Apply the setting to fit to one page.

m. Click the **Formulas sheet tab** and set options to print gridlines and headings. Adjust column widths.

n. Save and close the file. Based on your instructor's directions, submit e01m1Rentals_LastFirst.

2 Real Estate Sales Report

You are a small real estate agent in Indianapolis. You track the real estate properties you list for clients. You want to analyze sales for selected properties. Yesterday, you prepared a workbook with a worksheet for recent sales data and another worksheet listing several properties you listed. You want to calculate the number of days that the houses were on the market and their sales percentage of the list price. In one situation, the house was involved in a bidding war between two families that really wanted the house. Therefore, the sale price exceeded the list price.

a. Open *e01m2Sales* and save it as **e01m2Sales_LastFirst**.

b. Delete the row that has incomplete sales data. The owners took their house off the market.

c. Type **2018-001** in **cell A5** and use Auto Fill to complete the series to assign a property ID to each property.

d. Calculate the number of days each house was on the market in column C. Copy the formula down that column.

e. Format list prices and sold prices with **Accounting Number Format** with zero decimal places.

f. Calculate the sales price percentage of the list price in cell H5. The second house was listed for $500,250, but it sold for only $400,125. Therefore, the sale percentage of the list price is 79.99%. Format the percentages with two decimal places.

g. Wrap the headings on row 4.

h. Insert a new column between the Date Sold and List Price columns. Do the following:
- Move the Days on Market range C4:C13 to the new column.
- Delete the empty column C.

i. Edit the list date of the 41 Chestnut Circle house to be **4/22/2018**. Edit the list price of the house on Amsterdam Drive to be **$355,000**.

j. Select the property rows and set a **25 row height** and apply **Middle Align**.

k. Apply the **All Borders** border style to the **range A4:H12**. Adjust column widths as necessary.

l. Apply **Align Right** and indent twice the values in the **range E5:E12**.

m. Apply **120% scaling**.

n. Delete the Properties worksheet.

o. Insert a new worksheet and name it **Formulas**.

p. Use the Select All feature to select all data on the Houses Sold worksheet and copy it to the Formulas worksheet.

q. Complete the following steps on the Formulas worksheet:
- Hide the Date Listed and Date Sold columns.
- Display cell formulas.
- Set options to print gridlines and row and column headings.
- Adjust column widths.

r. Group the worksheets and do the following:
- Set landscape orientation.
- Center the page horizontally and vertically between the margins.
- Insert a footer with your name on the left side, the sheet tab code in the center, and the file name code on the right side.

s. Save and close the file. Based on your instructor's directions, submit e01m2Sales_LastFirst.

3 Problem Solving with Classmates

COLLABORATION CASE

Your instructor wants all students in the class to practice their problem-solving skills. Pair up with a classmate so that you can create errors in a workbook and then see how many errors your classmate can find in your worksheet and how many errors you can find in your classmate's worksheet.

a. Create a folder named **Exploring** on your OneDrive and give access to that drive to a classmate and your instructor.

b. Open *e01h5Markup_LastFirst*, which you created in the Hands-On Exercises, and save it as **e01m3Markup_LastFirst**, changing h5 to m3.

c. Edit each main formula to have a deliberate error (such as a value or incorrect cell reference) in it and then copy the formulas down the columns.

d. Save the workbook to your shared folder on your OneDrive.

e. Open the workbook your classmate saved on his or her OneDrive and save the workbook with your name after theirs, such as *e01m3Markup_MulberyKeith_KrebsCynthia*.

f. Find the errors in your classmate's workbook, insert comments to describe the errors, and then correct the errors.

g. Save the workbook back to your classmate's OneDrive and close the file. Based on your instructor's dircctions, submit e01m3Markup_LastFirst_LastFirst.

Beyond the Classroom

Tip Distribution

You are a server at a restaurant in Portland. You must tip the bartender 13% of each customer's drink sales and the server assistant 1.75% of the food sales plus 2% of the drink sales. You want to complete a worksheet that shows the sales, tips, and your net tip. Open *e01b1Server* and save it as **e01b1Server_LastFirst**.

Insert a column between the Drinks and Tip Left columns. Type the label **Subtotal** in cell D6. Calculate the food and drinks subtotal for the first customer and copy the formula down the column. In column F, enter a formula to calculate the amount of the tip as a percentage of the subtotal for the first customer's sales. Format the results with Percent Style with one decimal place. Type **13%** in cell G7, type **1.75%** in cell H7, and type **2%** in cell I7. Copy these percentage values down these three columns. Horizontally center the data in the three percentage columns.

In cell J7, calculate the bartender's tip for the first customer, using the rule specified in the first paragraph. In cell K7, calculate the assistant's tip for the first customer, using the rule specified in the first paragraph. In cell L7, calculate your net tip after giving the bartender and server their share of the tips. Copy the formulas from the range J7:L7 down their respective columns. Merge and center **Customer Subtotal and Tip** in the range B5:E5, **Tip Rates** in the range F5:I5, and **Tip Amounts** in the range J5:L5. Apply Currency format to the monetary values. Apply borders around the Tip Rates and Tip Amounts sections similar to the existing border around the Customer Subtotal and Tip section. For the range A6:L6, apply **Orange, Accent 2, Lighter 40%** fill color, center horizontal alignment, and wrap text. Apply **Orange, Accent 2, Lighter 80%** fill color to the values in the Tip Left column and the My Net Tip column.

Set 0.2" left and right margins, select Landscape orientation, and set the scaling to fit to one page. Include a footer with your name on the left footer, the sheet name code in the center, and file name code on the right side. Copy the worksheet and place the copied worksheet on the right side of the original worksheet. Rename the copied worksheet as **Tip Formulas**. On the Tip Formulas worksheet, display cell formulas, print gridlines, print headings, and adjust the column widths. Change the Tips sheet tab color to **Orange, Accent 2**, and change the Tip Formulas sheet tab color to **Orange, Accent 2, Darker 25%**. Save and close the file. Based on your instructor's directions, submit e01b1Server_LastFirst.

Net Proceeds from House Sale

Daryl Patterson is a real estate agent. He wants his clients to have a realistic expectation of how much money they will receive when they sell their houses. Sellers know they have to pay a commission to the agent and pay off their existing mortgages; however, many sellers forget to consider they might have to pay some of the buyer's closing costs, title insurance, and prorated property taxes. The realtor commission and estimated closing costs are based on the selling price and the respective rates. The estimated property taxes are prorated based on the annual property taxes and percentage of the year. For example, if a house sells three months into the year, the seller pays 25% of the property taxes. Daryl created a worksheet to enter values in an input area to calculate the estimated deductions at closing and calculate the estimated net proceeds the seller will receive. However, the worksheet contains errors. Open *e01b2Proceeds* and save it as **e01b2Proceeds_LastFirst**. Review the font formatting and alignment for consistency.

Use Help to learn how to insert comments into cells. As you identify the errors, insert comments in the respective cells to explain the errors. Correct the errors, including formatting errors. Apply Landscape orientation, 115% scaling, 1.5" top margin, and center horizontally. Insert your name on the left side of the header, the sheet name code in the center, and the file name code on the right side. Save and close the file. Based on your instructor's directions, submit e01b2Proceeds_LastFirst.

Capstone Exercise

You are a division manager for a regional hearing-aid company in Cheyenne, Wyoming. Your sales managers travel frequently to some of the offices in the western region. You need to create a travel expense report for your managers to use to record their budgeted and actual expenses for their travel reports. The draft report contains a title, input areas, and a detailed expense area.

Format the Title and Complete the Input Areas

Your first tasks are to format the title and complete the input area. The input area contains two sections: Standard Inputs that are identical for all travelers and Traveler Inputs that the traveler enters based on his or her trip.

a. Open *e01c1Travel* and save it as **e01c1Travel_LastFirst**.

b. Merge and center the title over the **range A1:E1** and set the row height for the first row to **40**.

c. Apply the **Input cell style** to the **ranges B3:B6, E3:E4**, and **E6:E7**, and then apply the **Calculation cell style** to **cell E5**. Part of the borders are removed when you apply these styles.

d. Select the **ranges A3:B6** and **D3:E7**. Apply **Thick Outside Borders**.

e. Enter **6/1/2018** in **cell E3** for the departure date, **6/5/2018** in **cell E4** for the return date, **149** in **cell E6** for the hotel rate per night, and **18%** in **cell E7** for the hotel tax rate.

f. Enter a formula in **cell E5** to calculate the number of days between the return date and the departure date.

Insert Formulas

The Detailed Expenses section contains the amount budgeted for the trip, the actual expenses reported by the traveler, percentage of the budget spent on each item, and the amount the actual expense went over or under budget. You will insert formulas for this section. Some budgeted amounts are calculated based on the inputs. Other budgeted amounts, such as airfare, are estimates.

a. Enter the amount budgeted for Mileage to/from Airport in **cell B12**. The amount is based on the mileage rate and roundtrip to the airport from the Standard Inputs section.

b. Enter the amount budgeted for Airport Parking in **cell B13**. This amount is based on the airport parking daily rate and the number of total days traveling (the number of nights + 1) to include both the departure and return dates. For example, if a person departs on June 1 and returns on June 5, the total number of nights at a hotel is 4, but the total number of days the vehicle is parked at the airport is 5.

c. Enter the amount budgeted for Hotel Accommodations in **cell B16**. This amount is based on the number of nights, the hotel rate, and the hotel tax rate.

d. Enter the amount budgeted for Meals in **cell B17**. This amount is based on the daily meal allowance and the total travel days (# of hotel nights + 1).

e. Enter the % of Budget in **cell D12**. This percentage indicates the percentage of actual expenses to budgeted expenses. Copy the formula to the **range D13:D18**.

f. Enter the difference between the actual and budgeted expenses in **cell E12**. Copy the formula to the **range E13:E18**. If the actual expenses exceeded the budgeted expenses, the result should be positive. If the actual expenses were less than the budgeted expense, the result should be negative, indicating under budget.

Add Rows, Indent Labels, and Move Data

The Detailed Expenses section includes a heading Travel to/from Destination. You want to include two more headings to organize the expenses. Then you will indent the items within each category. Furthermore, you want the monetary columns together, so you will insert cells and move the Over or Under column to the right of the Actual column.

a. Insert a new row 15. Type **Destination Expenses** in **cell A15**. Bold the label.

b. Insert a new row 19. Type **Other** in **cell A19**. Bold the label.

c. Indent twice the labels in the **ranges A12:A14, A16:A18**, and **A20**.

d. Select the **range D10:D21** and insert cells to shift the selected cells to the right.

e. Cut the **range F10:F21** and paste it in the **range D10:D21** to move the Over or Under data in the new cells you inserted.

Format the Detailed Expenses Section

You are ready to format the values to improve readability. You will apply Accounting Number Format to the monetary values on the first and total rows, Comma Style to the monetary values in the middle rows, and Percent Style for the percentages.

a. Apply **Accounting Number Format** to the **ranges B12:D12** and **B21:D21**.

b. Apply **Comma Style** to the **range B13:D20**.

c. Apply **Percent Style** with one decimal place to the **range E12:E20**.

d. Underline the **range: B20:D20**. Do not use the border feature.

e. Apply the cell style **Bad** to **cell D21** because the traveler went over budget.

f. Select the **range A10:E21** and apply **Thick Outside Borders**.

g. Select the **range A10:E10**, apply **Blue-Gray, Text 2, Lighter 80% fill color**, apply **Center** alignment, and apply **Wrap Text**.

Manage the Workbook

You will apply page setup options, insert a footer, and, then duplicate the Expenses statement worksheet.

a. Spell-check the workbook and make appropriate corrections.

b. Set a **1.5"** top margin and select the margin setting to center the data horizontally on the page.

c. Insert a footer with your name on the left side, the sheet name code in the center, and the file name code on the right side.

d. Copy the Expenses worksheet, move the new worksheet to the end, and rename it **Formulas**.

e. Display the cell formulas on the Formulas worksheet, change to landscape orientation, and adjust column widths. Use the Page Setup dialog box or the Page Layout tab to print gridlines and row and column headings.

f. Save and close the file. Based on your instructor's directions, submit e01c1Travel_LastFirst.

Formulas and Functions

You will apply formulas and functions to calculate and analyze data.

OBJECTIVES & SKILLS: After you read this chapter, you will be able to:

CASE STUDY | Townsend Mortgage Company

You are an assistant to Erica Matheson, a mortgage broker at the Townsend Mortgage Company. Erica spends her days reviewing mortgage rates and trends, meeting with clients, and preparing paperwork. She relies on your expertise in using Excel to help analyze mortgage data.

Today, Erica provided you with sample mortgage data: loan number, house cost, down payment, mortgage rate, and the length of the loan in years. She asked you to perform some basic calculations so that she can check the output provided by her system to verify if it is calculating results correctly. She wants you to calculate the amount financed, the periodic interest rate, the total number of payment periods, the percent of the house cost that is financed, and the payoff year for each loan. In addition, you will calculate totals, averages, and other basic statistics.

Furthermore, she has asked you to complete another worksheet that uses functions to look up interest rates from a separate table, calculate the monthly payments, and determine how much (if any) the borrower will have to pay for private mortgage insurance (PMI).

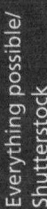

Performing Quantitative Analysis

CHAPTER 2

Townsend Mortgage Company

	A	B	C	D	E	F	G	H	I	J	K	L
1	**Townsend Mortgage Company**											
2												
3	**Input Area**											
4	Today's Date:	10/2/2018										
5	Pmts Per Year:	12										
6												
7	Loan #	House Cost	Down Payment	Amount Financed	Mortgage Rate	Rate Per Period	Years	# of Pmt Periods	% Financed	Date Financed	Payoff Year	
8	452786	$ 400,000	$ 80,000	$ 320,000	3.625%	0.302%	25	300	80.0%	5/1/2016	2041	
9	453000	$ 425,000	$ 60,000	$ 365,000	3.940%	0.328%	30	360	85.9%	11/3/2016	2046	
10	453025	$ 175,500	$ 30,000	$ 145,500	3.550%	0.296%	25	300	82.9%	4/10/2017	2042	
11	452600	$ 265,950	$ 58,000	$ 207,950	2.500%	0.208%	15	180	78.2%	10/14/2017	2032	
12	452638	$ 329,750	$ 65,000	$ 264,750	3.250%	0.271%	30	360	80.3%	2/4/2018	2048	
13												
14	**Summary Statistics**											
15	Statistics	House Cost	Down Payment	Amount Financed								
16	Total	$ 1,596,200	$ 293,000	$ 1,303,200								
17	Average	$ 319,240	$ 58,600	$ 260,640								
18	Median	$ 329,750	$ 60,000	$ 264,750								
19	Lowest	$ 175,500	$ 30,000	$ 145,500								
20	Highest	$ 425,000	$ 80,000	$ 365,000								
21	# of Mortgages	5	5	5								

Details | Payment Info | (+)

Ready

FIGURE 2.1 Townsend Mortgage Company Worksheet

CASE STUDY | Townsend Mortgage Company

Starting File	File to be Submitted
e02h1Loans	**e02h3Loans_LastFirst**

Formula Basics

When you increase your understanding of formulas, you can build robust workbooks that perform a variety of calculations for quantitative analysis. Your ability to build sophisticated workbooks and to interpret the results increases your value to any organization. By now, you should be able to build simple formulas using cell references and mathematical operators and use the order of operations to control the sequence of calculations in formulas.

In this section, you will create formulas in which cell addresses change or remain fixed when you copy them.

Using Relative, Absolute, and Mixed Cell References in Formulas

When you copy a formula, Excel either adjusts or preserves the cell references in the copied formula based on how the cell references appear in the original formula. Excel uses three different ways to reference a cell in a formula: relative, absolute, and mixed. Relative references change when a formula is copied. For example, if a formula containing the cell A1 is copied down one row in the column, the reference would become A2. In contrast, absolute references remain constant, no matter where they are copied. Mixed references are a combination of both absolute and relative, where part will change and part will remain constant.

When you create a formula that you will copy to other cells, ask yourself the following question: Do the cell references contain constant or variable values? In other words, should the cell references be adjusted or always refer to the same cell location, regardless of where the copied formula is located?

Use a Relative Cell Reference

STEP 1 ›› A *relative cell reference* is the default method of referencing in Excel. It indicates a cell's relative location, such as five rows up and one column to the left, from the original cell containing the formula. When you copy a formula containing a relative cell reference, the cells referenced in the copied formula change relative to the position of the copied formula. Regardless of where you paste the formula, the cell references in the copied formula maintain the same relative distance from the cell containing the copied formula, as the cell references the relative location to the original formula cell.

In Figure 2.2, the formulas in column F contain relative cell references. When you copy the original formula =D2-E2 from cell F2 down one row to cell F3, the copied formula changes to =D3-E3. Because you copy the formula *down* the column to cell F3, the column letters in the formula stay the same, but the row numbers change to reflect the row to which you copied the formula. Using relative referencing is an effective time saving tool. For example, using relative cell addresses to calculate the amount financed ensures that each borrower's down payment is subtracted from his or her respective house cost.

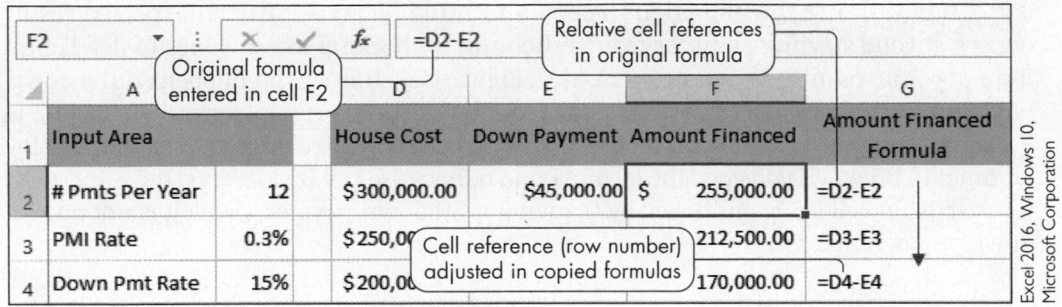

FIGURE 2.2 Relative Cell References

Use an Absolute Cell Reference

STEP 2 ⟩⟩ In many calculations there are times in which a value should remain constant, such as an interest rate or payoff date. In these situations absolute cell references are utilized. An ***absolute cell reference*** provides a constant reference to a specific cell. When you copy a formula containing an absolute cell reference, the cell reference in the copied formula does not change, regardless of where you copy the formula. An absolute cell reference appears with a dollar sign before both the column letter and row number, such as $B$4.

In Figure 2.3, the down payment is calculated by multiplying the house cost by the down payment rate (15%). Each down payment calculation uses a different purchase price and constant down payment rate, therefore an absolute reference is required. Cell E2 contains =D2*$B$4 ($300,000*15.0%) to calculate the first borrower's down payment ($45,000). When you copy the formula down to the next row, the copied formula in cell E3 is =D3*$B$4. The relative cell reference D2 changes to D3 (for the next house cost) and the absolute cell reference $B$4 remains the same to refer to the constant 15.0% down payment rate. This formula ensures that the cell reference to the house cost changes for each row but that the house cost is always multiplied by the rate in cell B4.

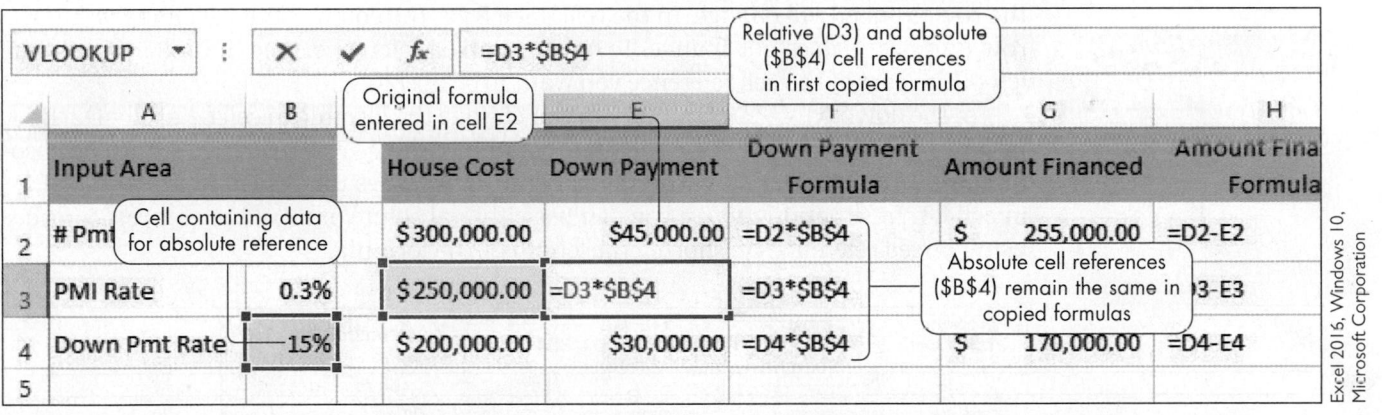

FIGURE 2.3 Relative and Absolute Cell References

TIP: INPUT AREA AND ABSOLUTE CELL REFERENCES

To illustrate the effect of modifying an assumption (e.g., the down payment rate changes from 15% to 20%), it is efficient to enter the new input value in only one cell (e.g., B4) rather than including the same value in a string of formulas. In Figure 2.3, values that can be modified, such as the down payment rate, are put in an input area. Generally, formulas use absolute references to the cells in the input area. For example, B4 is an absolute cell reference in all the down payment calculations. If the value in B4 is modified, Excel recalculates the amount of down payment for all the down payment formulas. By using cell references from an input area, you can perform what-if analyses very easily.

When utilizing the fill option to copy a formula, if an error or unexpected result occurs, a good starting point for troubleshooting is checking input values to determine if an absolute or mixed reference is needed. Figure 2.4 shows what happens if the down payment formula used a relative reference to cell B4. If the original formula in cell E2 is =D2*B4, the copied formula becomes =D3*B5 in cell E3. The relative cell reference to B4 changes to B5 when you copy the formula down. Because cell B5 is empty, the $350,000 house cost in cell D3 is multiplied by 0, giving a $0 down payment, which is not a valid down payment amount.

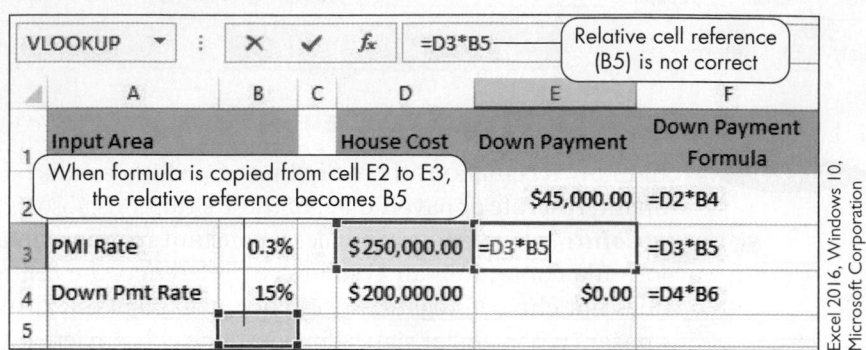

FIGURE 2.4 Error in Formula

Use a Mixed Cell Reference

STEP 3 ▶▶ A *mixed cell reference* combines an absolute cell reference with a relative cell reference. When you copy a formula containing a mixed cell reference, either the column letter or the row number that has the absolute reference remains fixed while the other part of the cell reference that is relative changes in the copied formula. $B4 and B$4 are examples of mixed cell references. In the reference $B4, the column B is absolute, and the row number is relative; when you copy the formula, the column letter B does not change, but the row number will change. In the reference B$4, the column letter B changes, but the row number, 4, does not change. To create a mixed reference, type the dollar sign to the left of the part of the cell reference you want to be absolute.

In the down payment formula, you can change the formula in cell E2 to be =D2*B$4. Because you are copying down the same column, only the row reference 4 must be absolute; the column letter stays the same. Figure 2.5 shows the copied formula =D3*B$4 in cell E3. In situations where you can use either absolute or mixed references, consider using mixed references to shorten the length of the formula.

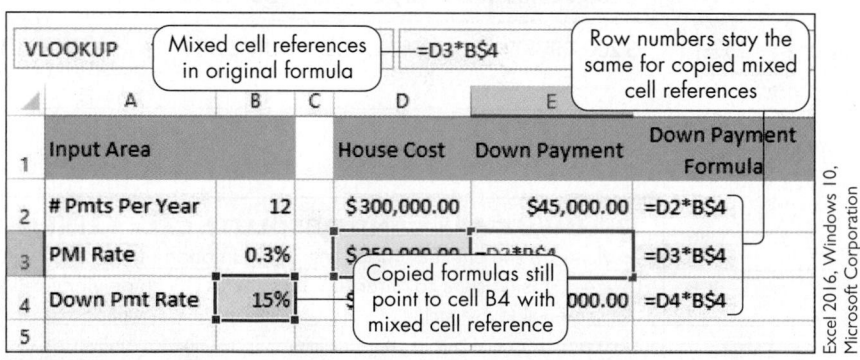

FIGURE 2.5 Relative and Mixed Cell References

Quick Concepts

1. What happens when you copy a formula containing a relative cell reference one column to the right? *p. 488*

2. Why would you use an absolute reference in a formula? *p. 489*

3. What is the benefit of using a mixed reference? *p. 490*

Hands-On Exercises

Watch the Video for this Hands-On Exercise!

MyITLab® HOE1 Training

Skills covered: Use a Relative Cell Reference • Use an Absolute Cell Reference • Use a Mixed Cell Reference

1 Formula Basics

Erica prepared a workbook containing data for five mortgages financed with the Townsend Mortgage Company. The data include house cost, down payment, mortgage rate, number of years to pay off the mortgage, and the financing date for each mortgage.

STEP 1 ›› USE A RELATIVE CELL REFERENCE

You will calculate the amount financed by each borrower by creating a formula with relative cell references that calculates the difference between the house cost and the down payment. After verifying the results of the amount financed by the first borrower, you will copy the formula down the Amount Financed column to calculate the other borrowers' amounts financed. Refer to Figure 2.6 as you complete Step 1.

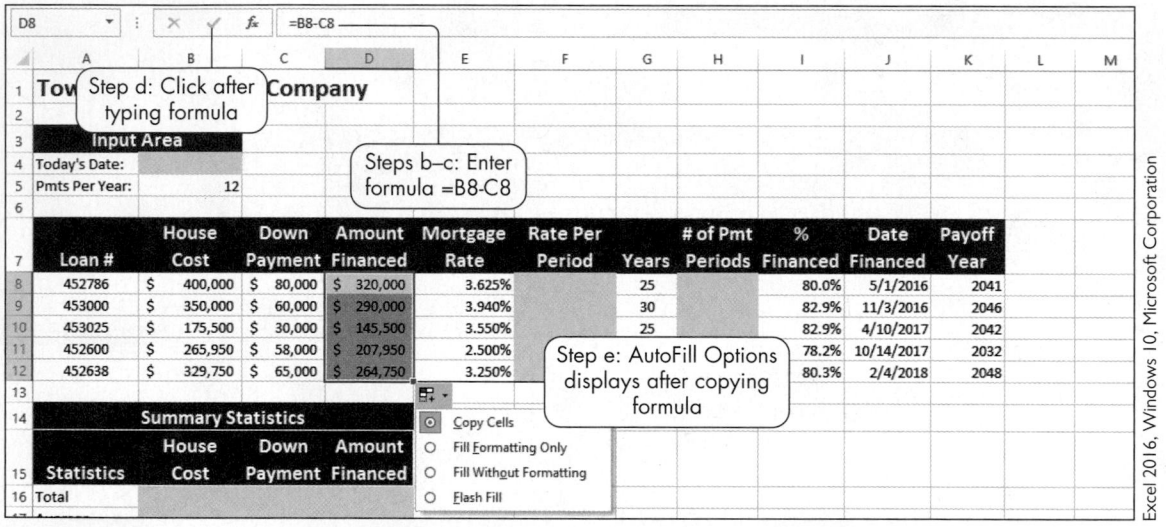

FIGURE 2.6 Formula Containing Relative Cell Reference Copied

a. Open *e02h1Loans* and save it as **e02h1Loans_LastFirst**.

> **TROUBLESHOOTING:** If you make any major mistakes in this exercise, you can close the file, open *e02h1Loans* again, and then start this exercise over.

The workbook contains two worksheets: Details (for Hands-On Exercises 1 and 2) and Payment Info (for Hands-On Exercise 3). You will enter formulas in the shaded cells.

b. Click **cell D8** in the Details sheet. Type **=** and click **cell B8**, the cell containing the first borrower's house cost.

c. Type **-** and click **cell C8**, the cell containing the down payment by the first borrower.

d. Click **Enter** ☑ (the check mark between the Name Box and Formula Bar) to complete the formula.

The first borrower financed (i.e., borrowed) $320,000, the difference between the cost ($400,000) and the down payment ($80,000).

e. Double-click the **cell D8 fill handle**.

You copied the formula down the Amount Financed column for each mortgage row.

f. Click **cell D9** and view the formula in the Formula Bar.

The formula in cell D8 is =B8-C8. The formula copied to cell D9 is =B9-C9. Because the original formula contained relative cell references, when you copy the formula down to the next row, the row numbers for the cell references change. Each result represents the amount financed for that particular borrower.

g. Press ⬇ and look at the cell references in the Formula Bar to see how the references change for each formula you copied. Save the workbook with the new formula you created.

Column E contains the mortgage rate for each loan. Because the borrowers will make monthly payments, you will modify the given annual interest rate (APR) to a monthly rate by dividing it by 12 (the number of payments in one year) for each borrower. Refer to Figure 2.7 as you complete Step 2.

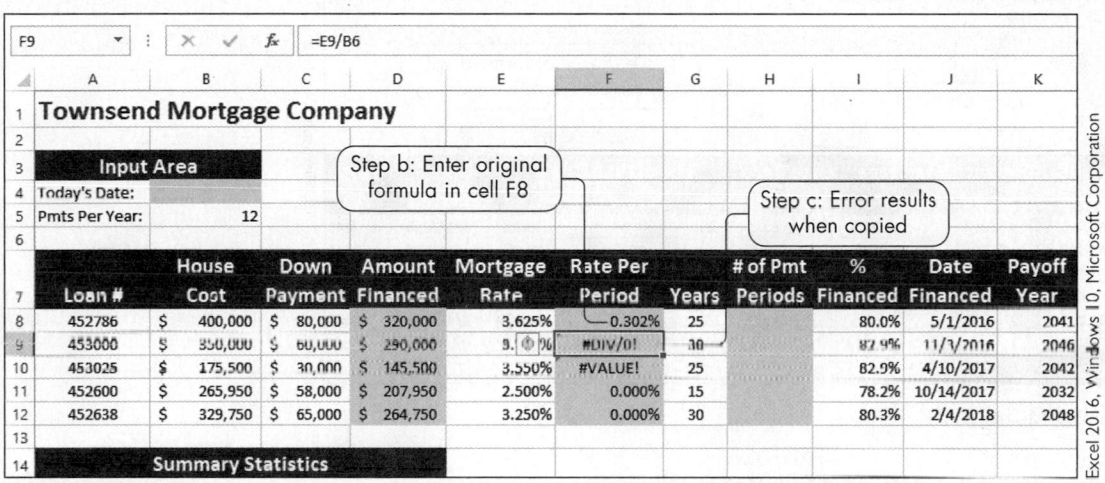

FIGURE 2.7 Formula Containing Incorrect Relative Cell Reference Copied

a. Click **cell F8**.

You will create a formula to calculate the monthly interest rate for the first borrower.

b. Type **=E8/B5** and click **Enter** (the check mark between the Name Box and the Formula Bar).

Typically, you should avoid typing values directly in formulas. Therefore, you use a reference to cell B5, where the number of payments per year is placed in the input area, so that the company can change the payment period to bimonthly (24 payments per year) or quarterly (four payments per year) without adjusting the formula.

c. Double-click the **cell F8 fill handle**, click **cell F9**, and then view the results (see Figure 2.7).

An error icon displays to the left of cell F9, which displays #DIV/0!, and cell F10 displays #VALUE!. The original formula was =E8/B5. Because you copied the formula =E8/B5 down the column, the first copied formula is =E9/B6, and the second copied formula is =E10/B7. Although you want the mortgage rate cell reference (E8) to change (E9, E10, etc.) from row to row, you do not want the divisor (cell B5) to change. You need all formulas to divide by the value stored in cell B5, so you will edit the formula to make B5 an absolute reference.

d. Click **Undo** in the Quick Access Toolbar to undo the AutoFill process. With F8 as the active cell, click to the right of **B5** in the Formula Bar.

e. Press **F4** and click **Enter** (the check mark between the Name Box and the Formula Bar).

Excel changes the cell reference from B5 to $B$5, making it an absolute cell reference.

f. Double-click the fill handle to copy the formula down the Rate Per Period column. Click **cell F9** and view the formula in the Formula Bar.

The formula in cell F9 is =E9/$B$5. The reference to E9 is relative and the reference to B5 is absolute. The results of all the calculations in the Rate Per Period column are now correct.

g. Save the workbook.

STEP 3 ›› USE A MIXED CELL REFERENCE

The next formula you create will calculate the total number of payment periods for each loan. Refer to Figure 2.8 as you complete Step 3.

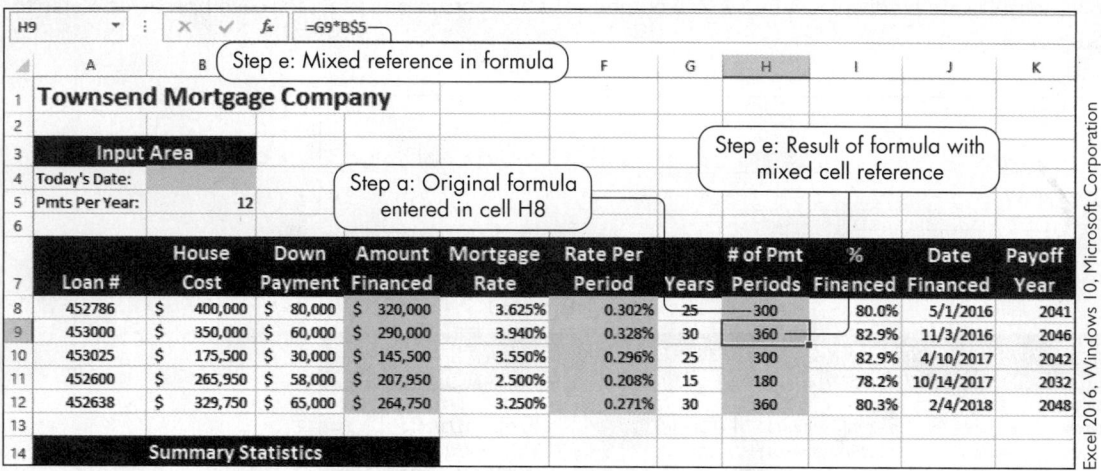

FIGURE 2.8 Formula Containing Mixed Cell Reference Copied

a. Click **cell H8** and type **=G8*B5**.

You will multiply the number of years (25) by the number of payment periods in one year (12) using cell references.

b. Press **F4** to make the B5 cell reference absolute and click **Enter**.

You want B5 to be absolute so that the cell reference remains B5 when you copy the formula. The product of 25 years and 12 months is 300 months or payment periods.

c. Copy the formula down the # of Pmt Periods column.

The first copied formula is =G9*$B$5, and the result is 360. You want to see what happens if you change the absolute reference to a mixed reference and copy the formula again. Because you are copying down a column, the column letter B can be relative because it will not change either way, but the row number 5 must be absolute.

d. Ensure that cell H8 is the active cell and click **Undo** on the Quick Access Toolbar to undo the copied formulas.

e. Click within the **$B$5 cell reference** in the Formula Bar. Press **F4** to change the cell reference to a mixed cell reference: B$5. Press **Ctrl+Enter** and copy the formula down the # of Pmt Periods column. Click **cell H9**.

The first copied formula is =G9*B$5 and the result is still 360. In this situation, using either an absolute reference or a mixed reference provides the same results.

f. Save the workbook. Keep the workbook open if you plan to continue with the next Hands-On Exercise. If not, close the workbook and exit Excel.

Function Basics

An Excel *function* is a predefined computation that simplifies creating a formula that performs a complex calculation. Excel contains more than 400 functions, which are organized into 14 categories. Table 2.1 lists and describes the primary function categories used in this chapter.

TABLE 2.1 Function Categories and Descriptions

Category	Description
Date & Time	Provides methods for manipulating date and time values.
Financial	Performs financial calculations, such as payments, rates, present value, and future value.
Logical	Performs logical tests and returns the value of the tests. Includes logical operators for combined tests, such as AND, OR, and NOT.
Lookup & Reference	Looks up values, creates links to cells, or provides references to cells in a worksheet.
Math & Trig	Performs standard math and trigonometry calculations.
Statistical	Performs common statistical calculations, such as averages and standard deviations.

Pearson Education, Inc.

When using functions, you must adhere to correct *syntax*, the rules that dictate the structure and components required to perform the necessary calculations. Start a function with an equal sign, followed by the function name, and then its arguments enclosed in parentheses.

- The function name describes the purpose of the function. For example, the function name SUM indicates that the function sums, or adds, values.

- A function's *arguments* specify the inputs—such as cells, values, or arithmetic expressions—that are required to complete the operation. In some cases, a function requires multiple arguments separated by commas.

In this section, you will learn how to insert common functions using the keyboard and the Insert Function and Function Arguments dialog boxes.

Inserting a Function

To insert a function by typing, first type an equal sign, and then begin typing the function name. *Formula AutoComplete* displays a list of functions and defined names that match letters as you type a formula. For example, if you type =SU, Formula AutoComplete displays a list of functions and names that start with *SU* (see Figure 2.9). You can double-click the function name from the list or continue typing the function name. You can even point to a list item and see the ScreenTip describing the function.

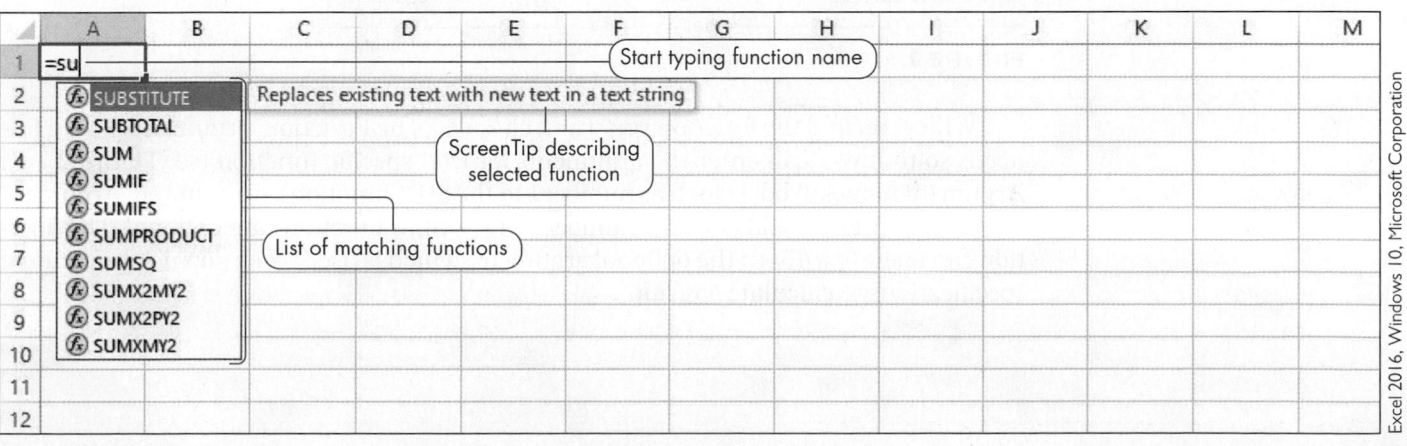

FIGURE 2.9 Formula AutoComplete

Excel 2016, Windows 10, Microsoft Corporation

After you type the function name and opening parenthesis, Excel displays the **func-tion ScreenTip**, a small pop-up description that displays the function's arguments. The argument you are currently entering is bold in the function ScreenTip (see Figure 2.10). Square brackets indicate optional arguments. For example, the SUM function requires the number1 argument, but the number2 argument is optional. Click the argument name in the function ScreenTip to select the actual argument in the formula you are creating if you want to make changes to the argument.

	A	B	C	D	E	F	G	H	I	J
1	=SUM(									
2	SUM(**number1**, [number2], ...)									
3										

FIGURE 2.10 Function ScreenTip

You can also use the Insert Function dialog box to search for a function, select a function category, and select a function from the list (see Figure 2.11). The dialog box is helpful if you want to browse a list of functions, especially if you are not sure of the function you need and want to see descriptions.

To display the Insert Function dialog box, click Insert Function f_x (located between the Name Box and the Formula Bar) or click Insert Function in the Function Library group on the Formulas tab. From within the dialog box, select a function category, such as Most Recently Used, and select a function to display the syntax and a brief description of that function. Click *Help on this function* to display details about the selected function.

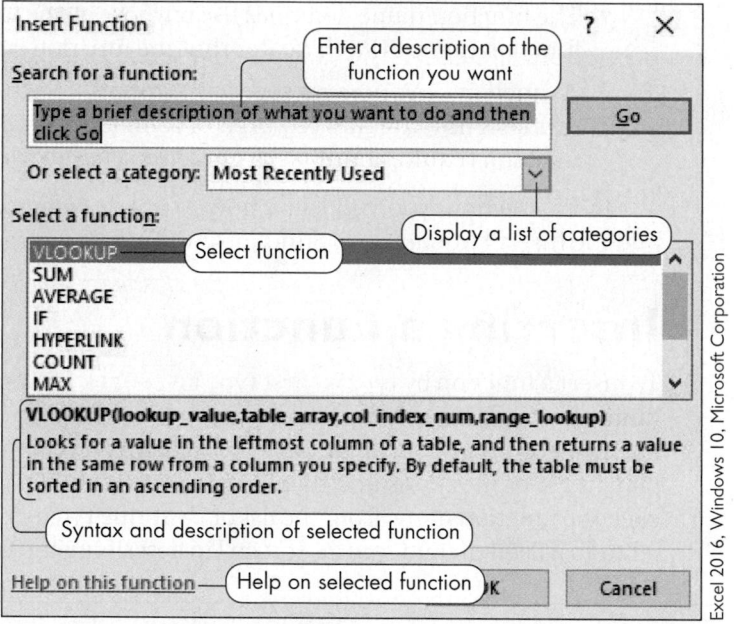

FIGURE 2.11 Insert Function Dialog Box

When you find the function you want, click OK. The Function Arguments dialog box opens so that you can enter the arguments for that specific function (see Figure 2.12). Argument names in bold (such as number1 in the SUM function) are required. Argument names that are not bold (such as number2 in the SUM function) are optional. The function can operate without the optional argument, which is used when you need additional specifications to calculate a result.

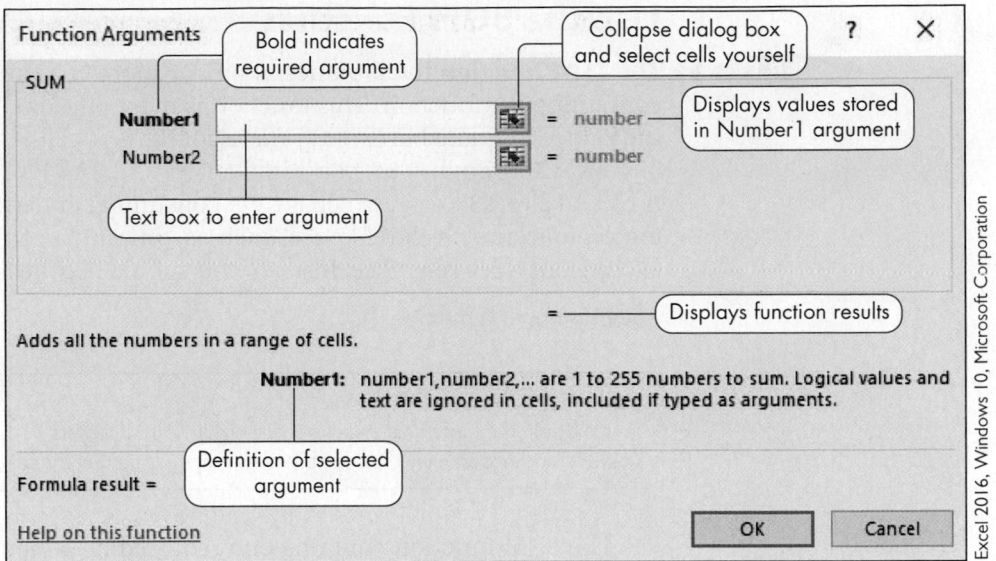

FIGURE 2.12 Function Arguments Dialog Box

Type the cell references in the argument boxes, or click a collapse button to the right side of an argument box to collapse the dialog box and select the cell or range of cells in the worksheet to designate as that argument. If you click the collapse button to select a range, you need to click the expand button to expand the dialog box again. You also have the ability to manually select the cells for the argument without clicking the collapse button. The collapse button is best used if the desired cells for the arguments view is obstructed. The value, or results, of a formula contained in the argument cell displays on the right side of the argument box (such as 5; 10; 15; 20; 25—the values stored in the range A1:A5 used for the number1 argument). If the argument is not valid, Excel displays an error description on the right side of the argument box.

The bottom of the Function Arguments dialog box displays a description of the function and a description of the argument containing the insertion point. As you enter arguments, the bottom of the dialog box also displays the results of the function, such as 75.

TIP: #NAME?

If you enter a function and #NAME? displays in the cell, you might have mistyped the function name. To avoid this problem, select the function name from the Formula AutoComplete list as you type the function name, or use the Insert Function dialog box. You can type a function name in lowercase letters. If you type the name correctly, Excel converts the name to all capital letters when you press Enter, indicating that you spelled the function name correctly.

Inserting Basic Math and Statistics Functions

Excel includes commonly used math and statistical functions that you can use for a variety of calculations. For example, you can insert functions to calculate the total amount you spend on dining out in a month, the average amount you spend per month purchasing music online, your highest electric bill, and your lowest time to run a mile this week. When using these functions, a change in the values within the ranges referenced will change the results of the function.

Use the SUM Function

STEP 1 ›› The **SUM function** totals values in one or more cells and displays the result in the cell containing the function. This function is more efficient to create when you need to add the values contained in three or more contiguous cells. For example, to add the contents of cells A2 through A14, you could enter =A2+A3+A4+A5+A6+A7+A8+A9+A10+A11+A12+A13+A14, which is time-consuming and increases the probability of entering an inaccurate cell reference, such as entering a cell reference twice or accidentally leaving out a cell reference. Instead, you should use the SUM function, =SUM(A2:A14).

=SUM(number1, [number2],…)

> **TIP: FUNCTION SYNTAX**
> In this book, the function syntax lines are highlighted. Brackets [ ] indicate optional arguments; however, do not actually type the brackets when you enter the argument.

The SUM function contains one required argument (number1) that represents a range of cells to add. The range, such as A2:A14, specifies the first and last of an adjacent group of cells containing values to SUM. Excel will sum all cells within that range. The number2 optional argument is used when you want to sum values stored in nonadjacent cells or ranges, such as =SUM(A2:A14,F2:F14). The ellipsis in the function syntax indicates that you can add as many additional ranges as desired, separated by commas.

> **TIP: AVOIDING FUNCTIONS FOR BASIC FORMULAS**
> Do not use a function for a basic mathematical expression. For example, although =SUM(B4/C4) produces the same result as =B4/C4, the SUM function is not needed to perform the basic arithmetic division. Furthermore, someone taking a quick look at that formula might assume it performs addition instead of division. Use the most appropriate, clear-cut formula, =B4/C4.

> **To insert the SUM function (for example, to sum the values of a range), complete one of the following steps:**
>
> - Type =SUM(type the range), and press Enter.
> - Type =SUM(drag to select the range, then type the closing) and press Enter.
> - Click a cell, click Sum [Σ AutoSum ▾] in the Editing group on the Home tab, press Enter to select the suggested range (or drag to select a range), and then press Enter.
> - Click in a cell, click AutoSum in the Function Library group on the Formulas tab, either press Enter to select the suggested range or type the range, and then press Enter.
> - Click the cell directly underneath the range you would like to SUM and press Alt=.

Figure 2.13 shows the result of using the SUM function in cell D2 to total scores (898).

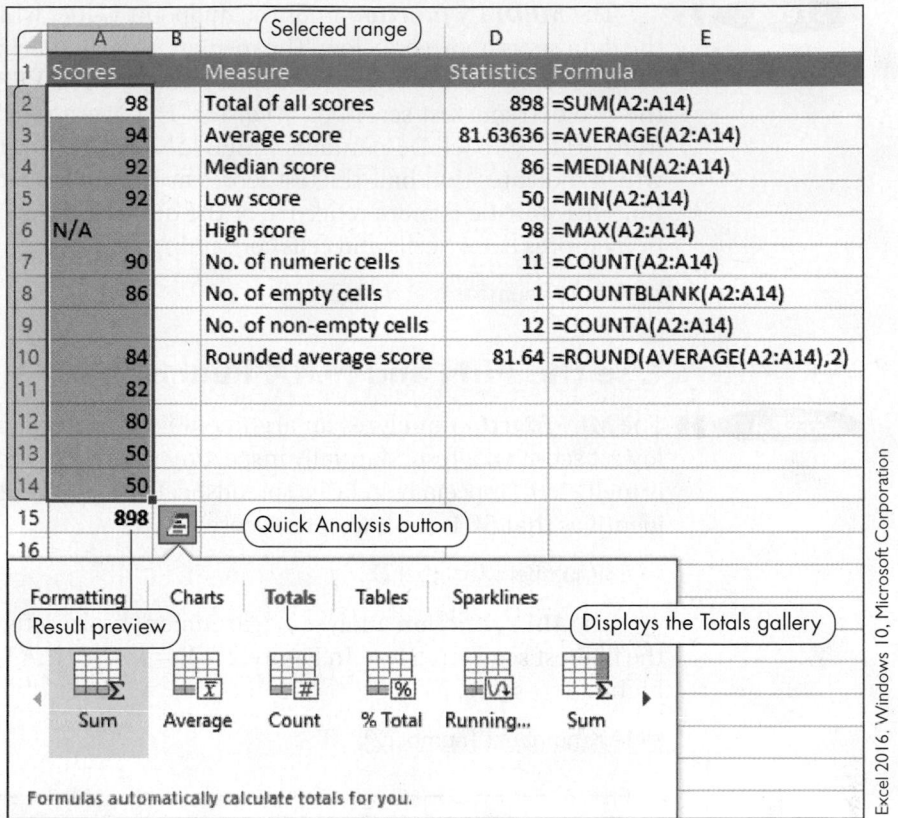

	A	B		D	E
1	Scores		Measure	Statistics	Formula
2	98		Total of all scores	898	=SUM(A2:A14)
3	94		Average score	81.63636	=AVERAGE(A2:A14)
4	92		Median score	86	=MEDIAN(A2:A14)
5	92		Low score	50	=MIN(A2:A14)
6	N/A		High score	98	=MAX(A2:A14)
7	90		No. of numeric cells	11	=COUNT(A2:A14)
8	86		No. of empty cells	1	=COUNTBLANK(A2:A14)
9			No. of non-empty cells	12	=COUNTA(A2:A14)
10	84		Rounded average score	81.64	=ROUND(AVERAGE(A2:A14),2)
11	82				
12	80				
13	50				
14	50				
15	898				
16					

Selected range · Quick Analysis button · Displays the Totals gallery · Result preview

Formatting Charts Totals Tables Sparklines

Sum Average Count % Total Running... Sum

Formulas automatically calculate totals for you.

FIGURE 2.13 Function Results

Excel 2016, Windows 10, Microsoft Corporation

TIP: SUM ARROW

If you click Sum in the Editing group on the Home tab or in the Function Library group on the Formulas tab, Excel inserts the SUM function. However, if you click the Sum arrow, Excel displays a list of basic functions to select: Sum, Average, Count Numbers, Max, and Min. If you want to insert another function, select More Functions from the list.

TIP: NEST FUNCTIONS AS ARGUMENTS

A *nested function* occurs when one function is embedded as an argument within another function. Each function has its own set of arguments that must be included. For example, cell D10 in Figure 2.13 contains =ROUND(AVERAGE(A2:A14),2). The ROUND function requires two arguments: number (the number to be rounded) and num_digits (the number of decimals to which the number is to be rounded).

The AVERAGE function is used to create the number to be rounded, and is nested in the number argument of the ROUND function. AVERAGE(A2:A14) returns 81.63636. That value is then rounded to two decimal places, indicated by 2 in the num_digits argument. The result is 81.64. If you change the second argument from 2 to 0, such as =ROUND(AVERAGE (A2:A14),0), the result would be 82.

Use the AVERAGE and MEDIAN Functions

STEP 2 ▶▶ People often describe data based on central tendency, which means that values tend to cluster around a central value. Excel provides two functions to calculate central tendency: AVERAGE and MEDIAN. The *AVERAGE function* calculates the arithmetic mean, or average, for the values in a range of cells. You can use this function to calculate the class average on a biology test or the average number of points scored per game by a basketball player. In Figure 2.13, =AVERAGE(A2:A14) in cell D3 returns 81.63636 as the average test score. The AVERAGE function ignores empty cells and cells containing N/A or text.

=AVERAGE (number1,[number2],...)

The **MEDIAN function** finds the midpoint value, which is the value that one half of the data set is above or below. The median is particularly useful because extreme values often influence arithmetic mean calculated by the AVERAGE function. In Figure 2.13, the two extreme test scores of 50 distort the average. The rest of the test scores range from 80 to 98. Cell D4 contains =MEDIAN(A2:A14). The median for test scores is 86, which indicates that half the test scores are above 86 and half the test scores are below 86. This statistic is more reflective of the data set than the average. The MEDIAN function ignores empty cells and cells containing N/A or text.

=MEDIAN(number1,[number2],…)

Use the MIN and MAX Functions

The **MIN function** analyzes an argument list to determine the lowest value, such as the lowest score on a test. Manually inspecting a range of values to identify the lowest value is inefficient, especially in large spreadsheets. In Figure 2.13, =MIN(A2:A14) in cell D5 identifies that 50 is the lowest test score.

=MIN(number1,[number2],…)

The **MAX function** analyzes an argument list to determine the highest value, such as the highest score on a test. In Figure 2.13, =MAX(A2:A14) in cell D6 identifies 98 as the highest test score.

=MAX(number1,[number2],…)

TIP: NONADJACENT RANGES

In most basic aggregate functions such as SUM, MIN, MAX, and AVERAGE, you can use multiple ranges as arguments, such as finding the largest number within two nonadjacent (nonconsecutive) ranges. For example, you can find the highest test score where some scores are stored in cells A2:A14 and others are stored in cells K2:K14. Separate each range with a comma in the argument list, so that the formula is =MAX(A2:A14,K2:K14).

Use the COUNT Functions

Excel provides three basic count functions—COUNT, COUNTBLANK, and COUNTA—to count the cells in a range that meet a particular criterion. The **COUNT function** tallies the number of cells in a range that contain values you can use in calculations, such as numerical and date data, but excludes blank cells or text entries from the tally. In Figure 2.13, the selected range spans 13 cells; however, =COUNT(A2:A14) in cell D7 returns 11, the number of cells that contain numerical data. It does not count the cell containing the text *N/A* or the blank cell.

The **COUNTBLANK function** tallies the number of cells in a range that are blank. In Figure 2.13, =COUNTBLANK(A2:A14) in cell D8 identifies that one cell in the range A2:A14 is blank. The **COUNTA function** tallies the number of cells in a range that are not blank, that is, cells that contain data, whether a value, text, or a formula. In Figure 2.13, =COUNTA(A2:A14) in cell D9 returns 12, indicating that the range A2:A14 contains 12 cells that contain some form of data. It does not count the blank cell; however, it will count cells that contain text such as cell A6.

=COUNT(value1,[value2],…)

=COUNTBLANK(range)

=COUNTA(value1,[value2],…)

Perform Calculations with Quick Analysis Tools

Quick Analysis is a set of analytical tools you can use to apply formatting, create charts or tables, and insert basic functions. When you select a range of data, the Quick Analysis button displays adjacent to the bottom-right corner of the selected range. Click the Quick Analysis button to display the Quick Analysis gallery and select the analytical tool to meet your needs.

Figure 2.13 shows the Totals gallery options so that you can sum, average, or count the values in the selected range. Select % Total to display the percentage of the grand total of two or more columns. Select Running Total to provide a cumulative total at the bottom of multiple columns. Additional options can be seen by clicking the right expansion arrow.

Using Date Functions

In order to maximize the use of dates and date functions in Excel, it is important to understand how they are handled in the program. Excel assigns serial numbers to dates. The date January 1, 1900 is the equivalent to the number 1. The number 2 is the equivalent of January 2, 1900 and so on. Basically, Excel adds 1 to every serial number as each day passes. Therefore the newer the date, the bigger the equivalent serial number. For example, assume today is January 1, 2018, and you graduate on May 6, 2018. To determine how many days until graduation, subtract today's date from the graduation date. Excel uses the serial numbers for these dates (43101 and 43226) to calculate the difference of 125 days.

Insert the TODAY Function

STEP 5 ▶▶ The *TODAY function* displays the current date in a cell. Excel updates the TODAY function results when you open or print the workbook. The TODAY() function does not require arguments, but you must include the parentheses. If you omit the parentheses, Excel displays #NAME? in the cell with a green triangle in the top-left corner of the cell. When you click the cell, an error icon appears that you can click for more information.

`=TODAY()`

Insert the NOW Function

The *NOW function* uses the computer's clock to display the current date and military time that you last opened the workbook. (Military time expresses time on a 24 hour period where 1:00 is 1 a.m. and 13:00 is 1 p.m.) The date and time will change every time the workbook is opened. Like the TODAY function, the NOW function does not require arguments, but you must include the parentheses. Omitting the parentheses creates a #NAME? error.

`=NOW()`

TIP: UPDATE THE DATE AND TIME
Both the TODAY and NOW functions display the date/time the workbook was last opened or last calculated. These functions do not continuously update the date and time while the workbook is open. To update the date and time, press F9 or click the Formulas tab and click *Calculate Now* in the Calculation group.

Quick Concepts

4. What visual features help guide you through typing a function directly in a cell? *p. 496*

5. What type of data do you enter in a Function Arguments dialog box, and what are four things the dialog box tells you? *p. 497*

6. What is the difference between the AVERAGE and MEDIAN functions? *pp. 499–500*

7. What is a nested function, and why would you create one? *p. 499*

Hands-On Exercises

Watch the Video for this Hands-On Exercise!

MyITLab®
HOE2 Training

2 Function Basics

The Townsend Mortgage Company worksheet contains an area in which you will enter summary statistics. In addition, you will include the current date.

STEP 1 ›› USE THE SUM FUNCTION

The first summary statistic you calculate is the total value of the houses bought by the borrowers. You will use the SUM function. Refer to Figure 2.14 as you complete Step 1.

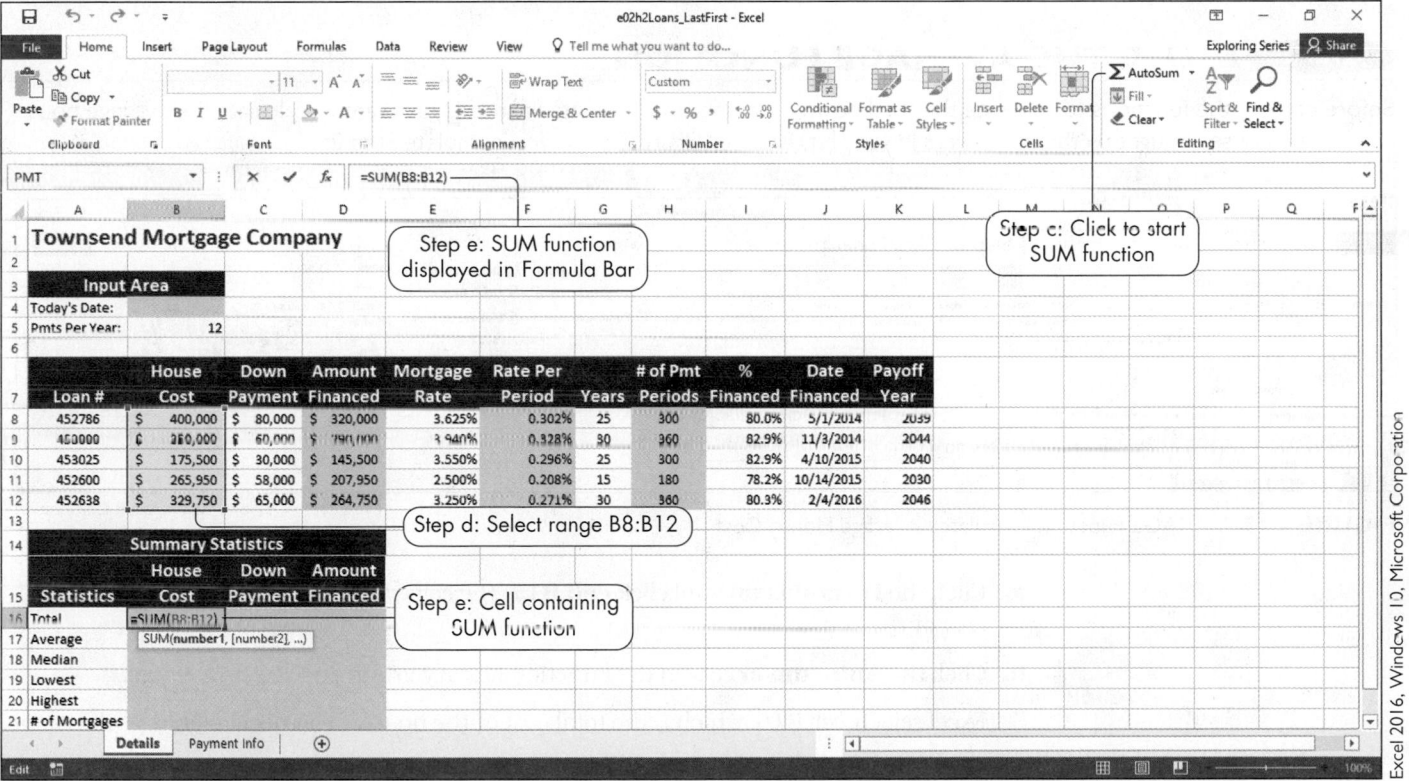

FIGURE 2.14 SUM Function Calculates Total House Cost

a. Open *e02h1Loans_LastFirst* if you closed it at the end of Hands-On Exercise 1 and save it as **e02h2Loans_LastFirst**, changing h1 to h2.

b. Ensure that the Details worksheet is active and click **cell B16**, the cell where you will enter a formula for the total house cost.

c. Click **AutoSum** Σ AutoSum in the Editing group on the Home tab.

Excel anticipates the range of cells containing values you want to sum based on where you enter the formula—in this case, A8:D15. This is not the correct range, so you must enter the correct range.

> **TROUBLESHOOTING:** AutoSum, like some other commands in Excel, contains two parts: the main command button and an arrow. Click the main command button when instructed to click Sum to perform the default action. Click the arrow when instructed to click the Sum arrow for additional options. If you accidentally clicked the arrow instead of Sum, press Esc to cancel the SUM function from being completed and try Step c again.

d. Select the **range B8:B12**, the cells containing house costs.

As you use the semi-selection process, Excel enters the range in the SUM function.

> **TROUBLESHOOTING:** If you entered the function without changing the arguments, repeat Steps b–d or edit the arguments in the Formula Bar by deleting the default range, typing B8:B12 between the parentheses and pressing Enter.

e. Click **Enter**.

Cell B16 contains the function = SUM(B8:B12), and the result is $1,521,200.

f. Save the workbook.

STEP 2 ›› USE THE AVERAGE FUNCTION

Before copying the functions to calculate the total down payments and amounts financed, you want to calculate the average house cost of the houses bought by the borrowers in your list. Refer to Figure 2.15 as you complete Step 2.

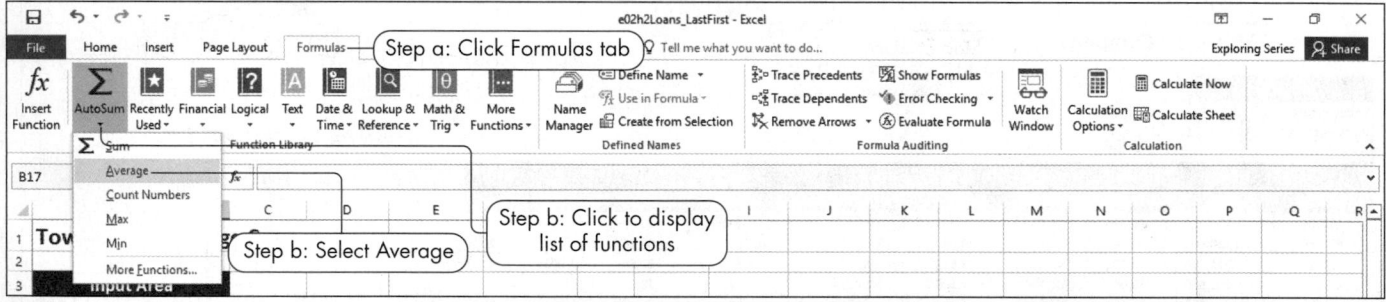

Excel 2016, Windows 10, Microsoft Corporation

FIGURE 2.15 AVERAGE Function Calculates Average House Cost

a. Click the **Formulas tab** and click **cell B17**, the cell where you will display the average cost of the houses.

b. Click the **AutoSum arrow** in the Function Library group and select **Average**.

Excel selects cell B16, which is the total cost of the houses. You need to change the range.

c. Select the **range B8:B12**, the cells containing the house costs.

The function is =AVERAGE(B8:B12).

d. Press **Enter**, making cell B18 the active cell.

The average house cost is $304,240.

e. Save the workbook.

STEP 3 ›› USE THE MEDIAN FUNCTION

You realize that extreme house costs may distort the average. Therefore, you decide to identify the median house cost to compare it to the average house cost. Refer to Figure 2.16 as you complete Step 3.

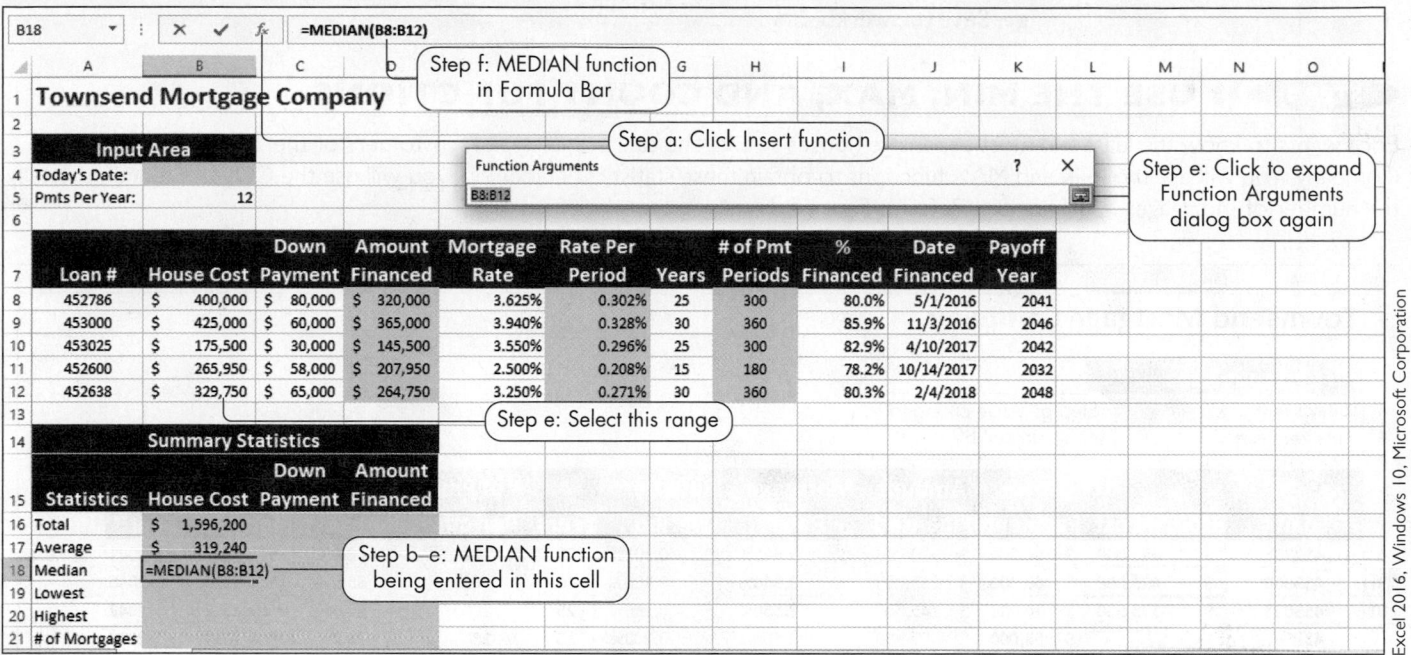

FIGURE 2.16 MEDIAN Function Calculates the Median House Cost

a. Ensure that cell B18 is the active cell. Click **Insert Function** f_x between the Name Box and the Formula Bar, or in the Function Library group on the Formulas tab.

   The Insert Function dialog box opens. Use this dialog box to select the MEDIAN function because it is not available on the Ribbon.

b. Type **median** in the *Search for a function box* and click **Go**.

   Excel displays a list of functions in the *Select a function* list. The MEDIAN function is selected at the top of the list; the bottom of the dialog box displays the syntax and the description.

c. Read the MEDIAN function description and click **OK**.

   The Function Arguments dialog box opens. It contains one required argument, Number1, representing a range of cells containing values. It has an optional argument, Number2, which you can use if you have nonadjacent ranges that contain values.

d. Click **Collapse Dialog Box** 🔡 to the right of the Number1 box.

   You collapsed the Function Arguments dialog box so that you can select the range.

e. Select the **range B8:B12** and click **Expand Dialog Box** 🔡 in the Function Arguments dialog box.

   The Function Arguments dialog box expands, displaying B8:B12 in the Number1 box.

f. Click **OK** to accept the function arguments and close the dialog box.

Half of the houses purchased cost more than the median, $329,750, and half of the houses cost less than this value. Notice the difference between the median and the average: The average is lower because it is affected by the lowest-priced house, $175,500.

g. Save the workbook.

STEP 4 » USE THE MIN, MAX, AND COUNT FUNCTIONS

Erica wants to know the least and most expensive houses so that she can analyze typical customers of the Townsend Mortgage Company. You will use the MIN and MAX functions to obtain these statistics. In addition, you will use the COUNT function to tally the number of mortgages in the sample. Refer to Figure 2.17 as you complete Step 4.

	A	B	C	D	E	F	G	H	I	J	K	L
1	**Townsend Mortgage Company**											
2												
3	**Input Area**											
4	Today's Date:											
5	Pmts Per Year:											
6												
7	Loan #	House Cost	Down Payment	Amount Financed	Mortgage Rate	Rate Per Period	Years	# of Pmt Periods	% Financed	Date Financed	Payoff Year	
8	452786	$ 400,000	$ 80,000	$ 320,000	3.625%	0.302%	25	300	80.0%	5/1/2016	2041	
9	453000	$ 425,000	$ 60,000	$ 365,000	3.940%	0.328%	30	360	85.9%	11/3/2016	2046	
10	453025	$ 175,500	$ 30,000	$ 145,500	3.550%	0.296%	25	300	82.9%	4/10/2017	2042	
11	452	$ 58,000	$ 207,950		2.500%	0.208%	15	180	78.2%	10/14/2017	2032	
12	452	$ 65,000	$ 264,750		3.250%	0.271%	30	360	80.3%	2/4/2018	2048	
13												
14	**Summary Statistics**											
15	Statistics	House Cost	Down Payment	Amount Financed								
16	Total	$ 1,596,200	$ 293,000	$ 1,303,200								
17	Average	$ 319,240	$ 58,600	$ 260,640								
18	Median	$ 329,750	$ 60,000	$ 264,750								
19	Lowest	$ 175,500	$ 30,000	$ 145,500								
20	Highest	$ 425,000	$ 80,000	$ 365,000								
21	# of Mortgages	5	5	5								

Callouts in figure:
- Step g: Value changed in cell B9
- Step b: Cell contains MIN function
- Step f: Formulas copied to these columns
- Step c: Cell contains MAX function
- Step d: Cell contains COUNT function

FIGURE 2.17 MIN, MAX, and COUNT Function Results

a. Click **cell B19**, the cell to display the cost of the lowest-costing house.

b. Click the **AutoSum arrow** in the Function Library group, select **MIN**, select the **range B8:B12**, and then press **Enter**.

The MIN function identifies that the lowest-costing house is $175,500.

c. Click **cell B20**. Click the **AutoSum arrow** in the Function Library group, select **MAX**, select the **range B8:B12**, and then press **Enter**.

The MAX function identifies that the highest-costing house is $400,000.

d. Click **cell B21**. Type **=COUNT(B8:B12)** and press **Enter**.

As you type the letter C, Formula AutoComplete suggests functions starting with C. As you continue typing, the list of functions narrows. After you type the beginning parenthesis, Excel displays the function ScreenTip, indicating the arguments for the function. The range B8:B12 contains five cells.

e. Select the **range B16:B21**.

You want to select the range of original statistics to copy the cells all at one time to the next two columns.

f. Drag the fill handle to the right by two columns to copy to the range C16:D21. Click **cell D21**.

Because you used relative cell references in the functions, the range in the function changes from =COUNT(B8:B12) to =COUNT(D8:D12).

g. Click **cell B9** and, change the cell value to **425000**, and click **Enter**.

The results of all formulas and functions change, including the total, average, and max house costs.

h. Save the workbook.

STEP 5 ›› USE THE TODAY FUNCTION

Before finalizing the worksheet you will insert the current date. You will use the TODAY function to display the current date. Refer to Figure 2.18 as you complete Step 5.

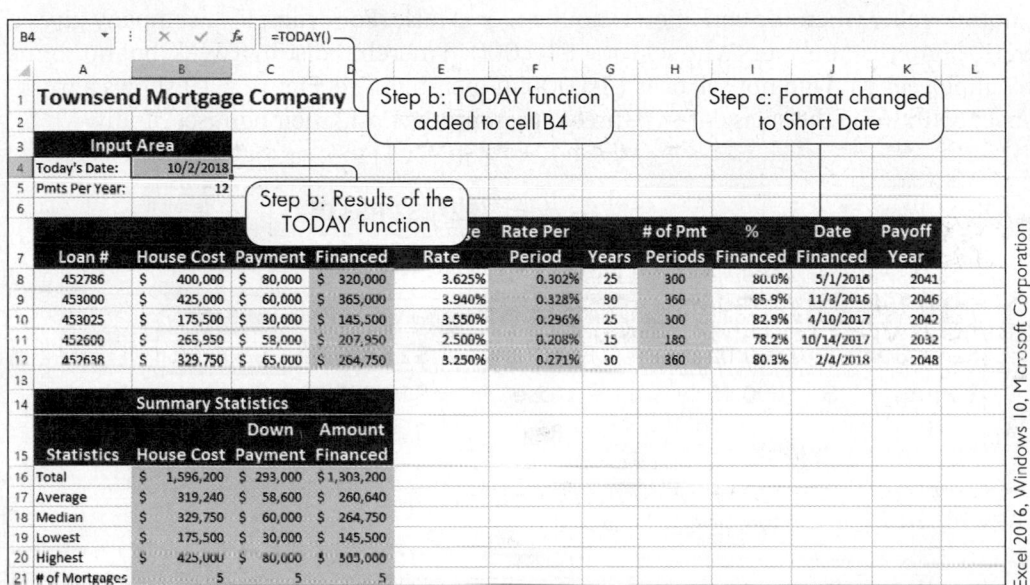

FIGURE 2.18 Insert the Current Date with the TODAY Function

a. Click **cell B4**, the cell to contain the current date.

b. Click **Date & Time** in the Function Library group, select **TODAY** to display the Function Arguments dialog box, and then click **OK** to close the dialog box.

The Function Arguments dialog box opens, although no arguments are necessary for this function. Excel displays TODAY() in the Edit formula bar, and inserts the current date in Short Date format, such as 6/1/2018, based on the computer system's date.

c. Click the **Format arrow** from the Cells group and select **AutoFit Column Width**.

d. Save the workbook. Keep the workbook open if you plan to continue with the next Hands-On Exercise. If not, close the workbook and exit Excel.

Logical, Lookup, and Financial Functions

As you prepare complex spreadsheets using functions, you will frequently use three function categories: logical, lookup and reference, and finance. Logical functions test the logic of a situation and return a particular result. Lookup and reference functions are useful when you need to look up a value in a list to identify the applicable value. Financial functions are useful to anyone who plans to take out a loan or invest money.

In this section, you will learn how to use the logical, lookup, and financial functions.

Determining Results with the IF Function

STEP 3 ›› The most common logical function is the *IF function*, which tests specified criteria to see if it is true or false, then returns one value when a condition is met, or is true, and returns another value when the condition is not met, or is false. For example, a company gives a $500 bonus to employees who sold *over* $10,000 in merchandise in a week, but no bonus to employees who did not sell over $10,000 in merchandise. Figure 2.19 shows a worksheet containing the sales data for three representatives and their bonuses, if any.

F2	▼	⋮	✕ ✓	*fx*	=IF(E2>B$2,B$3,0)		Result if condition is false

	A	B	C	D	E	F	G
1	**Input Are** Condition to be tested			**Sales Rep**	**Sales**	**Bonus**	
2	Sales Goal	$10,000.00		Tiffany	$11,000.00	$500.00	
3	Bonus	$ 500.00		Jose	$10,000.00	$ -	
4				Rex	$ 9,000.00	$ -	
5			Result if condition is true				

Excel 2016, Windows 10, Microsoft Corporation

FIGURE 2.19 Function to Calculate Bonus

The IF function has three arguments: (1) a condition that is tested to determine if it is either true or false, (2) the resulting value if the condition is true, and (3) the resulting value if the condition is false.

`=IF(logical_test,[value_if_true],[value_if_false])`

You might find it helpful to create two flowcharts to illustrate an IF function. First, construct a flowchart that uses words and numbers to illustrate the condition and results. For example, the left flowchart in Figure 2.20 illustrates the condition to see if sales are greater than $10,000, and the $500 bonus if the condition is true or $0 if the condition is false. Then, create a second flowchart—similar to the one on the right side of Figure 2.20—that replaces the words and values with actual cell references. Creating these flowcharts can help you construct the IF function that is used in cell F2 in Figure 2.19.

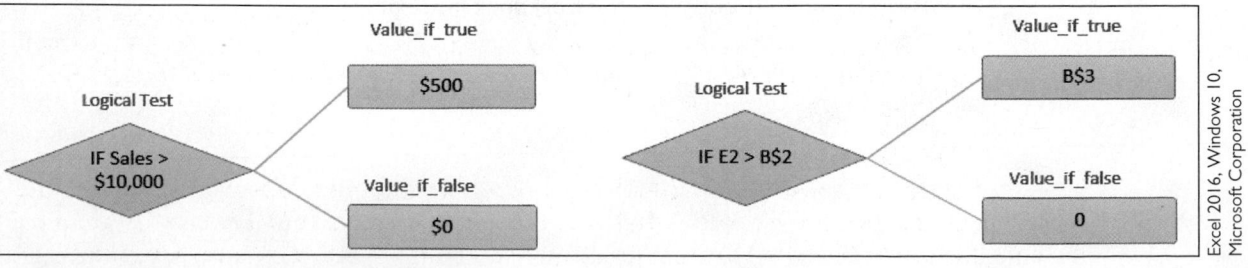

FIGURE 2.20 Flowcharts Illustrating IF Function

Design the Logical Test

The first argument for the IF function is the logical test. The *logical test* contains either a value or an expression that evaluates to true or false. The logical test requires a comparison between at least two variables, such as the values stored in cells E2 and B2. In this example a salesperson receives a bonus IF he or she sells more than the $10,000 quota. The variable of total sales is in cell E2 and the constant of the sales quota is in cell B2. Therefore the logical test IF E2 > B2 translates into the following: if the amount of sales generated is greater than $10,000. Table 2.2 lists and describes in more detail the logical operators to make the comparison in the logical test.

In Figure 2.19, cell F2 contains an IF function where the logical test is E2>$B$2 to determine if Tiffany's sales in cell E2 are greater than the sales goal in cell B2. Copying the function down the column will compare each sales representative's sales with the $10,000 value in cell B2.

TABLE 2.2	Logical Operators
Operator	**Description**
=	Equal to
<>	Not equal to
<	Less than
>	Greater than
<=	Less than or equal to
>=	Greater than or equal to

Pearson Education, Inc.

Design the Value_If_True and Value_If_False Arguments

The second and third arguments of an IF function are value_if_true and value_if_false. When Excel evaluates the logical test, the result is either true or false. If the logical test is true, the value_if_true argument executes. If the logical test is false, the value_if_false argument executes. Only one of the last two arguments is executed; both arguments cannot be executed, because the logical test is either true or false but not both.

The value_if_true and value_if_false arguments can contain text, cell references, formulas, or constants. In Figure 2.19, cell F2 contains an IF function in which the value_if_true argument is B$3 and the value_if_false argument is 0. Because the logical test (E2>B$2) is true—that is, Tiffany's sales of $11,000 are greater than the $10,000 goal—the value_if_true argument is executed, and the result displays $500, the value that is stored in cell B3.

Jose's sales of $10,000 are *not* greater than $10,000, and Rex's sales of $9,000 are *not* greater than $10,000. Therefore, the value_if_false argument is executed and returns no bonus in cells F3 and F4.

> **TIP: AT LEAST TWO POSSIBLE RIGHT ANSWERS**
> Every IF function can have at least two right solutions to produce the same results. Since the logical test is a comparative expression, it can be written two ways. For example, comparing whether E2 is greater than B2 can be written using greater than (E2>B2) or the reverse can also be compared to see if B2 is less than E2 (B2<E2). Depending on the logical test, the value if true and value if false arguments will switch.

Figure 2.21 illustrates several IF functions, how they are evaluated, and their results. The input area contains values that are used in the logical tests and results. You can create this worksheet with the input area and IF functions to develop your understanding of how IF functions work.

⬜	A	B	C
1	Input Values		
2	$ 1,000.00		
3	$ 2,000.00		
4	10%		
5	5%		
6	$ 250.00		
7			
8	IF Function	Evaluation	Result
9	=IF(A2=A3,A4,A5)	$1,000 is equal to $2,000: FALSE	5%
10	=IF(A2<A3,A4,A5)	$1,000 is less than $2,000: TRUE	10%
11	=IF(A2<>A3,"Not Equal","Equal")	$1,000 and $2,000 are not equal: TRUE	Not Equal
12	=IF(A2>A3,A2*A4,A2*A5)	$1,000 is greater than $2,000: FALSE	$ 50.00
13	=IF(A2>A3,A2*A4,MAX(A2*A5,A6))	$1,000 is greater than $2,000: FALSE	$ 250.00
14	=IF(A2*A4=A3*A5,A6,0)	$100 (A2*A4) is equal to $100 (A3*A5): TRUE	$ 250.00

Excel 2016, Windows 10, Microsoft Corporation

FIGURE 2.21 Sample IF Functions

- **Cell A9.** The logical test A2=A3 compares the values in cells A2 and A3 to see if they are equal. Because $1,000 is not equal to $2,000, the logical test is false. The value_if_false argument is executed, which displays 5%, the value stored in cell A5.

- **Cell A10.** The logical test A2<A3 determines if the value in cell A2 is less than the value in A3. Because $1,000 is less than $2,000, the logical test is true. The value_if_true argument is executed, which displays the value stored in cell A4, which is 10%.

- **Cell A11.** The logical test A2<>A3 determines if the values in cells A2 and A3 are not equal. Because $1,000 and $2,000 are not equal, the logical test is true. The value_if_true argument is executed, which displays the text Not Equal.

- **Cell A12.** The logical test A2>A3 is false. The value_if_false argument is executed, which multiplies the value in cell A2 ($1,000) by the value in cell A5 (5%) and displays $50. The parentheses in the value_if_true (A2*A4) and value_if_false (A2*A5) arguments are optional. They are not required but may help you read the function arguments better.

- **Cell A13.** The logical test A2>A3 is false. The value_if_false argument, which contains a nested MAX function, is executed. The MAX function, MAX(A2*A5,A6), multiplies the values in cells A2 ($1,000) and A5 (5%) and returns the higher of the product ($50) and the value stored in cell A6 ($250).

- **Cell A14.** The logical test A2*A4=A3*A5 is true. The contents of cell A2 ($1,000) are multiplied by the contents of cell A4 (10%) for a result of $100. That result is then compared to the result of A3*A5, which is also $100. Because the logical test is true, the function returns the value of cell A6 ($250).

TIP: TEXT AND NESTED FUNCTIONS IN IF FUNCTIONS

You can use text within a formula. For example, you can build a logical test comparing the contents of cell A1 to specific text, such as A1="Input Values". The IF function in cell A11 in Figure 2.21 uses "Not Equal" and "Equal" in the value_if_true and value_if_false arguments. When you use text in a formula or function, you must enclose the text in quotation marks. However, do not use quotation marks around formulas, cell references, or values. You can also nest functions in the logical test, value_if_true, and value_if_false arguments of the IF function. When you nest functions as arguments, make sure the nested function contains the required arguments for it to work and that you nest the function in the correct argument to calculate accurate results. For example, cell C13 in Figure 2.21 contains a nested MAX function in the value_if_false argument.

Using Lookup Functions

You can use lookup and reference functions to quickly find data associated with a specified value. For example, when you order merchandise on a website, the webserver looks up the shipping costs based on weight and distance; or at the end of a semester, your professor uses your average, such as 88%, to look up the letter grade to assign, such as B+. There are numerous lookup functions in Excel, including HLOOKUP, INDEX, LOOKUP, MATCH, and VLOOKUP. Each lookup function can be used to identify and return information based, in part, on how the data is organized.

Use the VLOOKUP function

STEP 1 ⟩⟩ The **VLOOKUP function** accepts a value and looks for the value in the left column of a specified table array and returns another value located in the same row from a specified column. Use VLOOKUP to search for exact matches or for the nearest value that is less than or equal to the search value, such as assigning a B grade for a class average between 80% and 89%. The VLOOKUP function has the following three required arguments and one optional argument: (1) lookup_value, (2) table_array, (3) col_index_num, and (4) range_lookup.

=VLOOKUP(lookup_value,table_array,col_index_num,[range_lookup])

Figure 2.22 shows a partial grade book that contains a vertical lookup table, as well as the final scores and letter grades. The function in cell F3 is =VLOOKUP(E3,$A$3:$B$7,2).

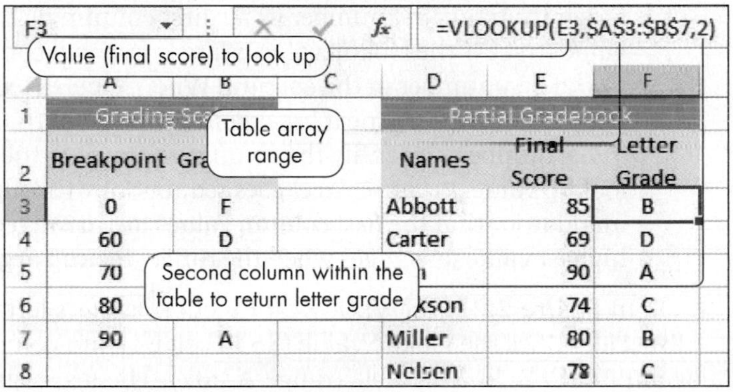

FIGURE 2.22 VLOOKUP Function for Grade Book

The **lookup value** is the cell reference of the cell that contains the value to look up. The lookup value for the first student is cell E3, which contains 85. The **table array** is the range that contains the lookup table: $A$3:$B$7. The table array range must be absolute, the value you want to look up must be located in the first column, and cannot include column labels for the lookup table. The **column index number** is the column number in the lookup table that contains the return values. In this example, the column index number is 2, which corresponds to the letter grades in column B.

> **TIP: USING VALUES IN FORMULAS**
> You know to avoid using values in formulas because the input values in a worksheet cell might change. However, as shown in Figure 2.22, the value 2 is used in the col_index_number argument of the VLOOKUP function. The 2 refers to a particular column within the lookup table and is an acceptable use of a number within a formula.

The last argument in the VLOOKUP function is the optional *range_lookup*. This argument determines how the VLOOKUP function handles lookup values that are not an exact match for the data in the lookup table. By default, the range_lookup is set to TRUE, which is appropriate to look up values in a range. Omitting the optional argument or typing TRUE in it enables the VLOOKUP function to find the nearest value that is less than or equal in the table to the lookup value. For this reason, the first column in a VLOOKUP table array should be sorted from smallest to largest (or A to Z alphabetically) when defaulting to TRUE.

To look up an exact match, enter FALSE in the range_lookup argument. For example, if you are looking up product numbers, you must find an exact match to display the price. The function would look like this: =VLOOKUP(D15,$A$1:$B$50,2,FALSE). The function returns a value for the first lookup value that matches the first column of the lookup table. If no exact match is found, the function returns #N/A.

Here is how the VLOOKUP function works:

1. The first argument of the function evaluates the value to be located in the left column of lookup table.

2. Excel searches the first column of the lookup table until it (a) finds an exact match (if possible) or (b) identifies the correct range if an exact match is not required.

3. If Excel finds an exact match, it moves across the table to the column designated by the column index number on that same row, and returns the value stored in that cell. If the last argument is TRUE or omitted, then Excel is looking for an approximate value (NOT an exact value). In this example, if the lookup value is larger than the first number in the first column of the table, it looks to the next value to see if the lookup value is larger and will continue to do so until reaching the largest number in the column. When Excel detects that the lookup value is not greater than the next breakpoint, it stays on that row. It then uses the column index number to identify the column containing the value to return for the lookup value. Because Excel goes sequentially through the breakpoint values, it is mandatory that the first column values are arranged from the lowest value to the highest value for ranges when the range_lookup argument is TRUE or omitted.

In Figure 2.22, the VLOOKUP function assigns letter grades based on final scores. Excel identifies the lookup value (85 in cell E3) and compares it to the values in the first column of the lookup table (range A3:B7). The last argument is omitted, so Excel tries to find an exact match of 85 or an approximate match; and because the table contains breakpoints rather than every conceivable score and the first column of the lookup table is arranged from the lowest to the highest breakpoints, Excel detects that 85 is greater than 80 but is not greater than 90. Therefore, it stays on the 80 row. Excel looks at the second column (column index number of 2) and returns the letter grade of B. The B grade is then displayed in cell F3.

Create the Lookup Table

A *lookup table* is a range containing a table of values and text from which data can be retrieved. The table should contain at least two rows and two columns, not including headings. Figure 2.23 illustrates a college directory with three columns. The first column contains professors' names. You look up a professor's name in the first column to see his or her office (second column) and phone extension (third column).

Name	Office	Extension
Brazil, Estivan	GT 218b	7243
Fiedler, Zazilia	CS 417	7860
Lam, Kaitlyn	SC 124a	7031
Rodriquez, Lisa	GT 304	7592
Yeung, Braden	CS 414	7314

Excel 2016, Windows 10, Microsoft Corporation

FIGURE 2.23 College Directory Lookup Table Analogy

It is important to plan the table so that it conforms to the way in which Excel can utilize the data in it. Excel cannot interpret the structure of Table 2.3. If the values you look up are exact values, you can arrange the first column in any logical order. However, to look up an approximate value in a range (such as the range 80–89), you must arrange data from the lowest to the highest value and include only the lowest value in the range (such as 80) instead of the complete range (as demonstrated in Table 2.3). The lowest value for a category or in a series is the ***breakpoint***. Table 2.4 shows how to construct the lookup table in Excel. The first column contains the breakpoints—such as 60, 70, 80, and 90—or the lowest values to achieve a particular grade. The lookup table contains one or more additional columns of related data to retrieve.

TABLE 2.3 Grading Scale

Range	Grade
90–100	A
80–89	B
70–79	C
60–69	D
Below 60	F

Pearson Education Inc

TABLE 2.4 Grades Lookup Table

Range	Grade
0	F
60	D
70	C
80	B
90	A

Pearson Education, Inc.

You can nest functions as arguments inside the VLOOKUP function. For example, Figure 2.24 illustrates shipping amounts that are based on weight and location (Boston or Chicago). In the VLOOKUP function in cell C3, the lookup_value argument looks up the weight of a package in cell A3. That weight (14 pounds) is compared to the data in the table array argument, which is $E$3:$G$5. To determine which column of the lookup table to use, an IF function is nested as the column_index_number argument. The nested IF function compares the city stored in cell B3 to the text Boston. If cell B3 contains Boston, it returns 2 to use as the column_index_number to identify the shipping value for a package that is going to Boston. If cell B3 does not contain Boston (i.e., the only other city in this example is Chicago), the column_index_number is 3.

C3 =VLOOKUP(A3,$E$3:$G$5,IF(B3="Boston",2,3))

	A	B	C	D	E	F	G	H
1	Customer Data				Lookup Data			
2	Weight	Location	Shipping		Weight	Boston	Chicago	
3	14	Boston	$ 19.95		0	$ 9.95	$ 12.95	
4	4	Chicago	$ 12.95		5	$ 14.95	$ 16.95	
5	8	Boston	$ 14.95		10	$ 19.95	$ 22.95	

Excel 2016, Windows 10, Microsoft Corporation

FIGURE 2.24 IF Function Nested in VLOOKUP Function

Use the HLOOKUP Function

Lookup functions are not limited to only vertical tables. In situations in which data is better organized horizontally, you can design a lookup table where the first row contains the values for the basis of the lookup or the breakpoints, and additional rows contain data to be retrieved. With a horizontal lookup table, use the ***HLOOKUP function***. Table 2.5 shows how quarterly sales data would look in a horizontal lookup table.

TABLE 2.5 Horizontal Lookup Table

Region	Qtr1	Qtr2	Qtr3	Qtr4
North	3495	4665	4982	5010
South	8044	7692	7812	6252
East	5081	6089	5982	6500
West	4278	4350	4387	7857

Pearson Education, Inc.

The syntax is almost the same as the syntax for the VLOOKUP function, except the third argument is row_index_num instead of col_index_num.

=HLOOKUP(lookup_value,table_array,row_index_num,[range_lookup])

Calculating Payments with the PMT Function

STEP 2 Excel contains several financial functions to help you perform calculations with monetary values. If you take out a loan to purchase a car, you need to know the monthly payment, which depends on the price of the car, the down payment, and the terms of the loan, in order to determine if you can afford the car. The decision is made easier by developing the worksheet in Figure 2.25 and by changing the various input values as indicated.

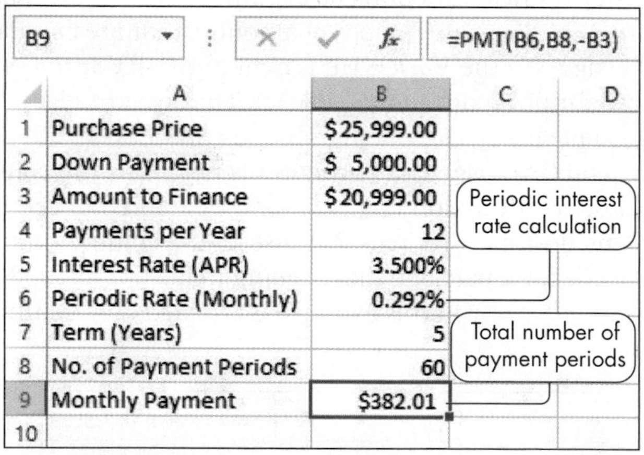

Excel 2016, Windows 10, Microsoft Corporation

FIGURE 2.25 Car Loan Worksheet

Creating a loan model helps you evaluate options. You realize that the purchase of a $25,999 car is prohibitive because the monthly payment is $382.01. Purchasing a less expensive car, coming up with a substantial down payment, taking out a longer-term loan, or finding a better interest rate can decrease your monthly payments.

The **PMT function** calculates payments for a loan with a fixed amount at a fixed periodic rate for a fixed time period. The PMT function uses three required arguments and up to two optional arguments: (1) rate, (2) nper, (3) pv, (4) fv, and (5) type.

=PMT(rate,nper,pv,[fv],[type])

The **rate** is the interest rate per payment period. If the annual percentage rate (APR) is 12% and you make monthly payments, the periodic rate is 1% (12%/12 months). With the same APR and quarterly payments, the periodic rate is 3% (12%/4 quarters). Divide the APR by the number of payment periods in one year. However, instead of calculating the periodic interest rate within the PMT function, you can calculate it in a separate cell and refer to that cell in the PMT function, as is done in cell B6 of Figure 2.25.

The **nper** is the total number of payment periods. The term of a loan is usually stated in years; however, you make several payments per year. For monthly payments, you make 12 payments per year. To calculate the nper, multiply the number of years by the number of payments in one year. You can either calculate the number of payment periods in the PMT function, or calculate the number of payment periods in cell B8 and use that calculated value in the PMT function.

The **pv** is the present value of the loan. The result of the PMT function is a negative value because it represents your debt. However, you can display the result as a positive value by typing a minus sign in front of the present value cell reference in the PMT function.

TIP: FINANCIAL FUNCTIONS AND NEGATIVE VALUES

When utilizing the PMT and other financial functions in Excel, you will often receive negative numbers. This happens because Excel understands accounting cash flow and the negative value represents a debt or outgoing monetary stream. It is important to understand why this happens and also to understand in some situations this should be a positive number, for example, if you are the company that granted the loan. In this situation you would receive an incoming cash flow, which should be a positive number. In contrast, if you are the requester of a loan, the payment should be negative as you will have a cash outflow each payment period. This can be manipulated by changing the pv argument of the PMT function between positive and negative values or by adding—in front of the PMT function.

Quick Concepts ✔

8. Describe the three arguments for an IF function. **p. 509**

9. How should you structure a vertical lookup table if you need to look up values in a range? **pp. 512–513**

10. What are the first three arguments of a PMT function? Why would you divide by or multiply an argument by 12? **p. 515**

Hands-On Exercises

Watch the Video
for this Hands-On
Exercise!

MyITLab®
HOE3 Training

Skills covered: Use the
VLOOKUP Function • Use the PMT
Function • Use the IF Function

3 Logical, Lookup, and Financial Functions

Erica wants you to complete another model that she might use for future mortgage data analysis. As you study the model, you realize you need to incorporate logical, lookup, and financial functions.

STEP 1 ›› USE THE VLOOKUP FUNCTION

Rates vary based on the number of years to pay off the loan. Erica created a lookup table for three common mortgage years, and she entered the current APR. The lookup table will provide efficiency later when the rates change. You will use the VLOOKUP function to display the correct rate for each customer based on the number of years of the respective loans. Refer to Figure 2.26 as you complete Step 1.

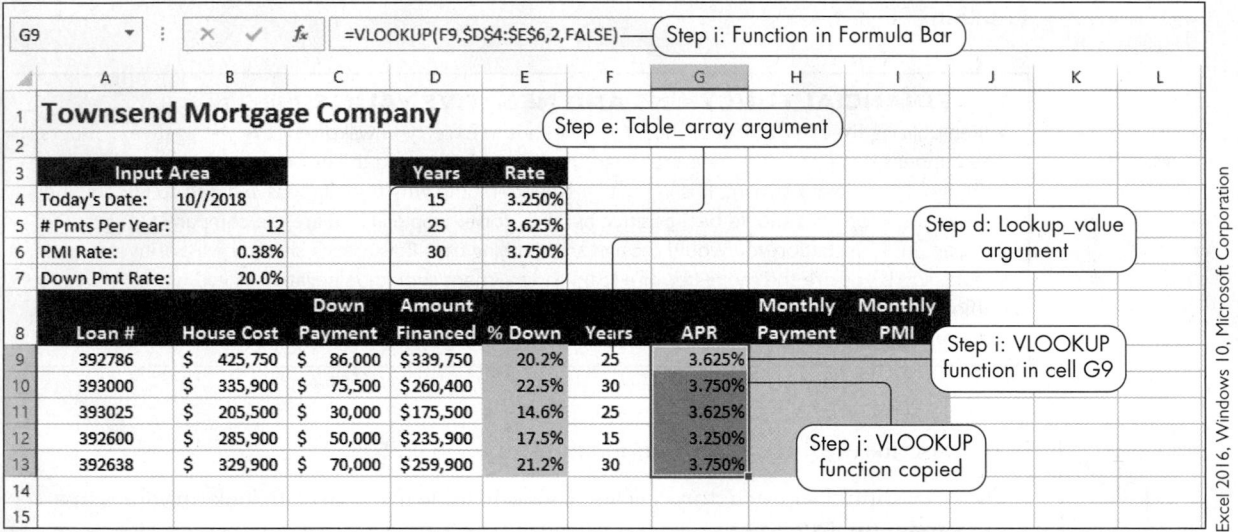

FIGURE 2.26 VLOOKUP Function to Determine APR

a. Open *e02h2Loans_LastFirst* if you closed it at the end of Hands-On Exercise 2 and save it as **e02h3Loans_LastFirst**, changing h2 to h3.

b. Click the **Payment Info worksheet tab** to display the worksheet containing the data to complete. Click **cell G9**, the cell that will store the APR for the first customer.

c. Click the **Formulas tab**, click **Lookup & Reference** in the Function Library group, and then select **VLOOKUP**.

The Function Arguments dialog box opens.

d. Ensure that the insertion point is in the Lookup_value box, click the **Collapse Dialog Box**, click **cell F9** to enter F9 in the Lookup_value box, and then click the **Expand Dialog Box** to return to Function Arguments dialog box.

Cell F9 contains the value you need to look up from the table: 25 years.

e. Press **Tab**, click **Collapse Dialog Box** to the right of the Table_array box, select the **range D4:E6**, and then click **Expand Dialog Box** to return to the Function Arguments dialog box.

This is the range that contains that data for the lookup table. The Years values in the table are arranged from lowest to highest. Do *not* select the column labels for the range.

Anticipate what will happen if you copy the formula down the column. What do you need to do to ensure that the cell references always point to the exact location of the table? If your answer is to make the table array cell references absolute, then you answered correctly.

f. Press **F4** to make the range references absolute.

The Table_array box now contains $D$4:$E$6.

g. Press **Tab** and type **2** in the Col_index_num box.

The second column of the lookup table contains the Rates that you want to return and display in the cells containing the formulas.

h. Press **Tab** and type **False** in the Range_lookup box.

To ensure an exact match to look up in the table, you enter *False* in the optional argument.

i. Click **OK**.

The VLOOKUP function uses the first loan's term in years (25) to find an exact match in the first column of the lookup table, and then returns the corresponding rate from the second column, which is 3.625%.

j. Copy the formula down the column.

Spot-check the results to make sure the function returned the correct APR based on the number of years.

k. Save the workbook.

STEP 2 » USE THE PMT FUNCTION

The worksheet now has all the necessary data for you to calculate the monthly payment for each loan: the APR, the number of years for the loan, the number of payment periods in one year, and the initial loan amount. You will use the PMT function to calculate the monthly payment, which includes paying back the principal amount with interest. This calculation does not include escrow amounts, such as property taxes or insurance. Refer to Figure 2.27 as you complete Step 2.

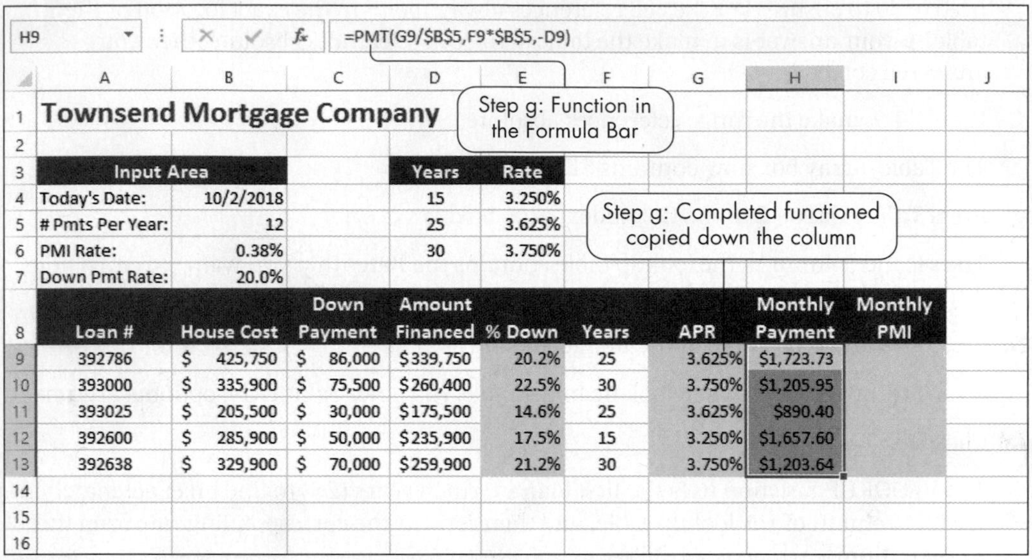

Excel 2016, Windows 10, Microsoft Corporation

FIGURE 2.27 PMT Function to Calculate Monthly Payment

a. Click **cell H9**, the cell that will store the payment for the first customer.

b. Click **Financial** in the Function Library group, scroll through the list, and then select **PMT**.

The Function Arguments dialog box opens.

> **TROUBLESHOOTING:** Make sure you select PMT, not PPMT. The PPMT function calculates the principal portion of a particular monthly payment, not the total monthly payment itself.

c. Type **G9/B5** in the Rate box.

Think about what will happen if you copy the formula. The argument will be G10/B6 for the next customer. Are those cell references correct? G10 does contain the APR for the next customer, but B6 does not contain the correct number of payments in one year. Therefore, you need to make B5 an absolute cell reference because the number of payments per year does not vary.

d. Press **F4** to make the reference to cell B5 absolute.

e. Press **Tab** and type **F9*$B$5** in the Nper box.

You calculate the nper by multiplying the number of years by the number of payments in one year. You must make B5 an absolute cell reference so that it does not change when you copy the formula down the column.

f. Press **Tab** and type **-D9** in the Pv box.

The bottom of the dialog box indicates that the monthly payment is 1723.73008 or $1,723.73.

> **TROUBLESHOOTING:** If the payment displays as a negative value, you probably forgot to type the minus sign in front of the D9 reference in the Pv box. Edit the function and type the minus sign in the correct place.

g. Click **OK**. Copy the formula down the column.

h. Save the workbook.

STEP 3 **》 USE THE IF FUNCTION**

Lenders often want borrowers to have a 20% down payment. If borrowers do not put in 20% of the cost of the house as a down payment, they pay a private mortgage insurance (PMI) fee. PMI serves to protect lenders from absorbing loss if the borrower defaults on the loan, and it enables borrowers with less cash to secure a loan. The PMI fee is about 0.38% of the amount financed. Some borrowers have to pay PMI for a few months or years until the balance owed is less than 80% of the appraised value. The worksheet contains the necessary values in the input area. You use the IF function to determine which borrowers must pay PMI and how much they will pay. Refer to Figure 2.28 as you complete Step 3.

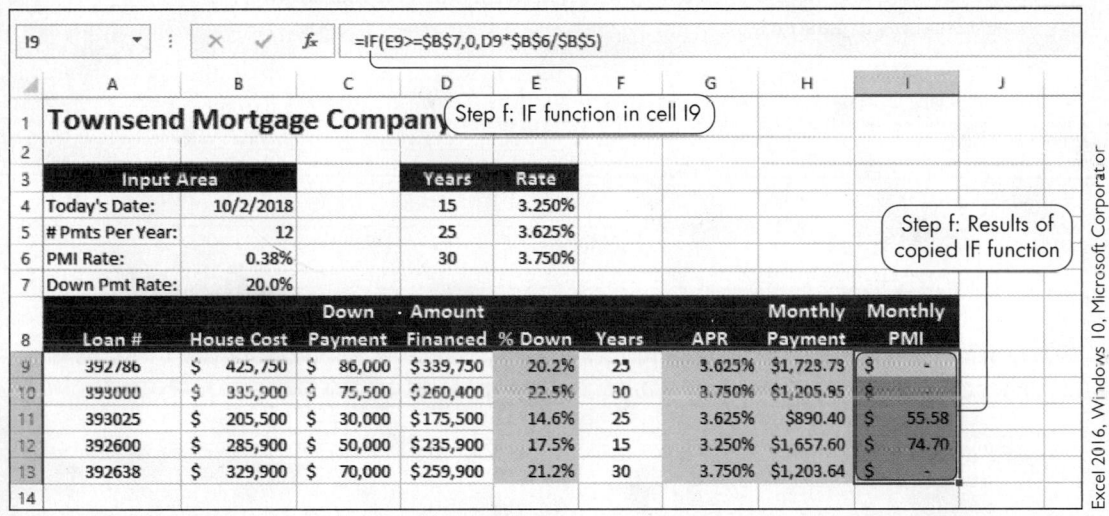

FIGURE 2.28 IF Function to Calculate Monthly PMI

a. Click **cell I9**, the cell that will store the PMI, if any, for the first customer.

b. Click **Logical** in the Function Library group and select **IF**.

The Function Arguments dialog box opens. You will enter the three arguments.

c. Type **E9>=$B$7** in the Logical_test box.

The logical test compares the down payment percentage to see if the customer's down payment is at least 20%, the threshold stored in B7, of the amount financed. The customer's percentage cell reference is relative so that it will change when you copy it down the column; however, cell B7 must be absolute because it contains a value that should remain constant when the formula is copied to other cells.

d. Press **Tab** and type **0** in the Value_if_true box.

If the customer makes a down payment that is at least 20% of the purchase price, the customer does not pay PMI, so a value of 0 will display whenever the logical test is true. The first customer paid 20% of the purchase price, so he or she does not have to pay PMI.

e. Press **Tab** and type **D9*$B$6/$B$5** in the Value_if_false box.

If the logical test is false, the customer must pay PMI, which is calculated by multiplying the amount financed (D9) by the periodic PMI rate (the result of dividing the yearly PMI (B6) by the number of payments per year (B5)).

f. Click **OK** and copy the formula down the column.

The first, second, and fifth customers paid 20% of the purchase price, so they do not have to pay PMI. The third and fourth customers must pay PMI because their respective down payments were less than 20% of the purchase price.

TROUBLESHOOTING: If the results are not as you expected, check the logical operators. People often mistype < and > or forget to type = for >= situations. Correct any errors in the original formula and copy the formula again.

---

g. Set the worksheets to print on one page. Add a footer with your name on the left, sheet code in the middle, and the file name code on the right.

h. Save and close the file. Based on your instructor's directions, submit e02h3Loans_LastFirst.

Chapter Objectives Review

After reading this chapter, you have accomplished the following objectives:

1. Use relative, absolute, and mixed cell references in formulas.

- Use a relative cell address: A relative reference indicates a cell's location relative to the formula cell. When you copy the formula, the relative cell reference changes.
- Use an absolute cell reference: An absolute reference is a permanent pointer to a particular cell, indicated with $ before the column letter and the row number, such as $B$5. When you copy the formula, the absolute cell reference does not change.
- Use a mixed cell reference: A mixed reference contains part absolute and part relative reference, such as $B5 or B$5. Either the column or the row reference changes, while the other remains constant when you copy the formula.

2. Insert a function.

- A function is a predefined formula that performs a calculation. It contains the function name and arguments. Formula AutoComplete, function ScreenTips, and the Insert Function dialog box help you select and create functions. The Function Arguments dialog box guides you through the entering requirements for each argument.

3. Insert basic math and statistics functions.

- Use the SUM function: The SUM function calculates the total of a range of values. The syntax is =SUM(number1,[number2],...).
- Use the AVERAGE and MEDIAN functions: The AVERAGE function calculates the arithmetic mean of values in a range. The MEDIAN function identifies the midpoint value in a set of values.
- Use the MIN and MAX functions: The MIN function identifies the lowest value in a range, whereas the MAX function identifies the highest value in a range.
- Use the COUNT functions: The COUNT function tallies the number of cells in a range, that contain values, whereas the COUNTBLANK function tallies the number of blank cells in a range, and COUNTA tallies the number of cells that are not empty.

- Perform calculations with Quick Analysis tools: With the Quick Analysis tools you can apply formatting, create charts or tables, and insert basic functions.

4. Use date functions.

- Insert the TODAY function: The TODAY function displays the current date.
- Insert the NOW function: The NOW function displays the current date and time.

5. Determine results with the IF function.

- Design the logical test: The IF function is a logical function that evaluates a logical test using logical operators, such as <, >, and =, and returns one value if the condition is true and another value if the condition is false.
- Design the value_if_true and value_if_false arguments: The arguments can contain cell references, text, or calculations. If a logical test is true, Excel executes the value_if_true argument. If a logical test is false, Excel executes the value_if_false argument.
- You can nest or embed other functions inside one or more of the arguments of an IF function to create more complex formulas.

6. Use lookup functions.

- Use the VLOOKUP function: The VLOOKUP function contains the required arguments lookup_value, table_array, and col_index_num and one optional argument, range_lookup.
- Create the lookup table: Design the lookup table using exact values or the breakpoints for ranges. If using breakpoints, the breakpoints must be in ascending order.
- Use the HLOOKUP function: The HLOOKUP function looks up values by row (horizontally) rather than by column (vertically).

7. Calculate payments with the PMT function.

- The PMT function calculates periodic payments for a loan with a fixed interest rate and a fixed term. The PMT function requires the periodic interest rate, the total number of payment periods, and the original value of the loan.

Key Terms Matching

Match the key terms with their definitions. Write the key term letter by the appropriate numbered definition.

a. Absolute cell reference
b. Argument
c. AVERAGE function
d. COUNT function
e. IF function
f. Logical test
g. Lookup table
h. MAX function
i. MEDIAN function
j. MIN function

k. Mixed cell reference
l. NOW function
m. PMT function
n. Relative cell reference
o. SUM function
p. Syntax
q. TODAY function
r. VLOOKUP function

1. _____ A set of rules that governs the structure and components for properly entering a function. **p. 495**

2. _____ Displays the current date. **p. 501**

3. _____ Indicates a cell's specific location; the cell reference does not change when you copy the formula. **p. 489**

4. _____ An input, such as a cell reference or value, needed to complete a function. **p. 495**

5. _____ Identifies the highest value in a range. **p. 500**

6. _____ Tallies the number of cells in a range that contain values. **p. 500**

7. _____ Looks up a value in a vertical lookup table and returns a related result from the lookup table. **p. 511**

8. _____ A range that contains data for the basis of the lookup and data to be retrieved. **p. 511**

9. _____ Calculates the arithmetic mean, or average, of values in a range. **p. 499**

10. _____ Identifies the midpoint value in a set of values. **p. 500**

11. _____ Displays the current date and time. **p. 501**

12. _____ Evaluates a condition and returns one value if the condition is true and a different value if the condition is false. **p. 508**

13. _____ Calculates the total of values contained in two or more cells. **p. 498**

14. _____ Calculates the periodic payment for a loan with a fixed interest rate and fixed term. **p. 515**

15. _____ Indicates a cell's location from the cell containing the formula; the cell reference changes when the formula is copied. **p. 488**

16. _____ Contains both an absolute and a relative cell reference in a formula; the absolute part does not change but the relative part does when you copy the formula. **p. 490**

17. _____ An expression that evaluates to true or false. **p. 509**

18. _____ Displays the lowest value in a range. **p. 500**

Multiple Choice

1. If cell E15 contains the formula =$C$5*J$15, what type of cell reference is the J$15 in the formula?

   (a) Relative reference
   (b) Absolute reference
   (c) Mixed reference
   (d) Syntax

2. What function would most efficiently accomplish the same thing as =(B5+C5+D5+E5+F5)/5?

   (a) =SUM(B5:F5)/5
   (b) =AVERAGE(B5:F5)
   (c) =MEDIAN(B5:F5)
   (d) =COUNT(B5:F5)

3. When you start to type =AV, what feature displays a list of functions and defined names?

   (a) Function ScreenTip
   (b) Formula AutoComplete
   (c) Insert Function dialog box
   (d) Function Arguments dialog box

4. A formula containing the entry =$B3 is copied to a cell one column to the right and two rows down. How will the entry appear in its new location?

   (a) =$B3
   (b) =B3
   (c) =$C5
   (d) =$B5

5. Which of the following functions should be used to insert the current date and time in a cell?

   (a) =TODAY()
   (b) =CURRENT()
   (c) =NOW()
   (d) =DATE

6. Which of the following is not an argument of the IF function?

   (a) value_if_true
   (b) value_if_false
   (c) logical_test
   (d) lookup_value

7. Which of the following is *not* true about the VLOOKUP function?

   (a) The lookup table must be in ascending order.
   (b) The lookup table must be in descending order.
   (c) The default match type is approximate.
   (d) The match type must be false when completing an exact match.

8. The function =PMT(C5,C7,-C3) is stored in cell C15. What must be stored in cell C5?

   (a) APR
   (b) Periodic interest rate
   (c) Loan amount
   (d) Number of payment periods

9. Which of the following is *not* an appropriate use of the SUM function?

   (a) =SUM(B3:B45)
   (b) =SUM(F1:G10)
   (c) =SUM(A8:A15,D8:D15)
   (d) =SUM(D15-C15)

10. What is the keyboard shortcut to create an absolute reference?

   (a) F2
   (b) F3
   (c) F4
   (d) Alt

Practice Exercises

1 Hamilton Heights Auto Sales

You are the primary loan manager for Hamilton Heights Auto Sales, an auto sales company located in Missouri. In order to most efficiently manage the auto loans your company finances, you have decided to create a spreadsheet to perform several calculations. You will insert the current date, calculate down payment and interest rates based on credit score, calculate periodic payment amounts, and complete the project with basic summary information. Refer to Figure 2.29 as you complete this exercise.

A2	▼ : × ✓ fx	Date						
	A	B	C	D	E	F	G	H
1	Hamilton Heights Auto Sales							
2	Date	10/2/2018						
3	Auto Finance Worksheet							
4	Vin #	Purchase Price	Credit Rating	Down Payment		Amount Financed		Rate	Payment
5	619600647	$ 23,417.00	579	$ 2,341.70	$ 21,075.30	4.00%	$388.13
6	464119439	$ 23,732.00	763	$ -	$ 23,732.00	3.00%	$426.43
7	122140305	$ 44,176.00	657	$ 4,417.60	$ 39,758.40	3.50%	$723.27
8	276772526	$ 42,556.00	827	$ -	$ 42,556.00	2.75%	$759.96
9	335963723	$ 24,305.00	652	$ 2,430.50	$ 21,874.50	3.50%	$397.94
10	401292230	$ 27,847.00	676	$ 2,784.70	$ 25,062.30	3.50%	$455.93
11		$ 186,033.00			$ 29,009.75		
12							
13	Credit Score	APR		Down Payment	Credit Score Threshold		
14	500	4.00%		10%	750		
15	650	3.50%					
16	700	3.25%		Payments Per Year	Total # of Payments		
17	750	3.00%		12	60		
18	800	2.75%					
19	850	2.25%					

FIGURE 2.29 Hamilton Heights Auto Sales

a. Open *e02p1AutoSales* and save it as **e02p1AutoSales_LastFirst**.

b. Click **cell B2**, click the **Formulas tab**, click **Date & Time** in the Function Library group, select **NOW**, and then click **OK** to enter today's date in the cell.

c. Click **cell D5** on the Formulas tab, click **Logical** in the Function Library group, and select **IF**.

d. Type **C5<=$E$14** in the Logical_test box, type **$D$14*B5** in the Value_if_true box, type **0** in the Value_if_false box, and then click **OK**.

This uses the IF function to calculate the required down payment based on credit score. If the customer has a credit score higher than 750 a down payment is not required. All clients with credits scores lower than 750 must pay a required 10% down payment in advance.

e. Use the fill handle to copy the contents of **cell D5** down the column, click **Auto Fill Options** to the lower-right of the copied cells, and then click **Fill Without Formatting** to ensure that the **Bottom Double border** remains applied to cell D10.

f. Calculate the Amount Financed by doing the following:
- Click **cell E5** and type **=B5-D5**.
- Use **cell E5's fill handle** to copy the function down the column.
- Apply **Bottom Double border** to cell E10.

g. Calculate the Rate by doing the following:
- Click **cell F5**. Click **Lookup & Reference** in the Function Library group and select **VLOOKUP**.
- Type **C5** in the Lookup_value box, type **$A$14:$B$19** in the Table_array box, type **2** in the Col_index_num box, and then click **OK**.
- Double-click **cell F5's fill handle** to copy the function down the column.
- Click **Auto Fill Options**, and click **Fill Without Formatting**.

h. Calculate the required periodic payment by doing the following:

- Click **cell G5**, click **Financial** in the Function Library Group, and then click **PMT**.
- Type **F5/$D$17** in the Rate box, type **$E$17** in the Nper box, type **–E5** in the Pv box, and then click **OK**.
- Double-click **cell G5's** fill handle to copy the function down the column.
- Click the **Auto Fill Options** button, and click **Fill Without Formatting**.

i. Select the **range B5:B10**, click the **Quick Analysis button**, click **TOTALS**, and select **Sum** from the Quick Analysis Gallery.

j. Click **cell E11** and type **=AVERAGE(E5:E10)** to calculate the average amount financed.

k. Create a footer with your name on the left side, the sheet name code in the center, and the file name on the right side.

l. Save and close the workbook. Based on your instructor's directions, submit e02p1AutoSales_LastFirst.

2 Lockridge Marketing Analytics

As a business analyst for Lockridge Marketing Analytics, you have been tasked with awarding performance bonuses. You prepare a model to calculate employee bonuses based on average customer satisfaction survey results. The survey is based on a scale of 1 to 5 with 5 being the highest rating. Employees with survey results where ratings are between 1 and 2.9 do not receive bonuses, scores between 3 and 3.9 earn a 2% one-time bonus on their monthly salary, and scores of 4 or higher receive a 5% bonus. In addition, you calculate basic summary data for reporting purposes. Refer to Figure 2.30 as you complete this exercise.

J10

	A	B	C	D	E	F
1	Lockridge Marketing Analytics					
2						
3	**Inputs and Constants**				**Bonus Data**	
4	Today:	10/2/2018		**Rating**	1	3
5	Employees Surveyed	6		**Bonus**	0%	2%
6						
7						
8						
9	**Survey Code**	**Current Salary**	**Monthly Salary**	**Survey Score**	**Rating Bonus**	**Monthly Take Home**
10	38078	$ 50,000	$ 4,166.67	5	$ 208.33	$ 4,375.00
11	41105	$ 75,250	$ 6,270.83	3.5	$ 125.42	$ 6,396.25
12	39752	$ 67,250	$ 5,604.17	4.2	$ 280.21	$ 5,884.38
13	37872	$ 45,980	$ 3,831.67	3	$ 76.63	$ 3,908.30
14	40616	$ 58,750	$ 4,895.83	4.2	$ 244.79	$ 5,140.63
15	40347	$ 61,000	$ 5,083.33	4.5	$ 254.17	$ 5,337.50
16						
17						
18	**Statistics**					
19	Lowest Bonus	$ 76.63				
20	Average Bonus	$ 198.26				
21	Highest Bonus	$ 280.21				

FIGURE 2.30 Lockridge Marketing Analytics

a. Open *e02p2Bonus* and save it as **e02p2Bonus_LastFirst**.

b. Click **cell B4**, click the **Formulas tab**, click **Date & Time** in the Function Library group, select **TODAY**, and then click **OK** to enter today's date in the cell.

c. Click **cell B5**, click the **AutoSum arrow** in the Function Library group, and then select **Count Numbers**. Select the **range A10:A15** and press **Enter**.

d. Click **cell C10**, type **=B10/12**, press **Ctrl+Enter**, and double-click the **fill handle**.

e. Enter the Rating Bonus based on survey average by doing the following:
  - Click **cell E10** and type **=C10***.
  - Click **Lookup & Reference** in the Function Library group and select **HLOOKUP**.
  - Type **D10** in the Lookup_value box, type **E$4:G$5** in the Table_array box, type **2** in the Col_index_num box, and then click **OK**.
  - Double-click the **cell E10 fill handle** to copy the formula down the Rating Bonus column.

f. Calculate each employee's monthly take-home by doing the following:
  - Click **cell F10** and type **=C10+E10**.
  - Double-click the **cell F10 fill handle**.

g. Calculate basic summary statistics by doing the following:
  - Click **cell B19**, click the **Formulas tab**, click the **AutoSum arrow**, and then select **MIN**.
  - Select the **range E10:E15** and then press **Enter**.
  - In **cell B20**, click the **AutoSum arrow**, select **AVERAGE**, select the **range E10:E15**, and then press **Enter**.
  - In **cell B21**, click the **AutoSum arrow**, select **MAX**, select the **range E10:E15**, and then press **Enter**.

h. Create a footer with your name on the left side, the sheet name in the center, and the file name code on the right side.

i. Save and close the workbook. Based on your instructor's directions, submit e02p2Bonus_LastFirst.

Mid-Level Exercises

1 Metropolitan Zoo Gift Shop Weekly Payroll

ANALYSIS CASE

As manager of the gift shop at the Metropolitan Zoo, you are responsible for managing the weekly payroll. Your assistant developed a partial worksheet, but you need to enter the formulas to calculate the regular pay, overtime pay, gross pay, taxable pay, withholding tax, FICA, and net pay. In addition, you want to include total pay columns and calculate some basic statistics. As you construct formulas, make sure you use absolute and relative cell references correctly in formulas.

a. Open the *e02m1Payroll* workbook and save it as **e02m1Payroll_LastFirst**.

b. Study the worksheet structure and read the business rules in the Notes section.

c. Use IF functions to calculate the regular pay and overtime pay based on a regular 40-hour workweek in **cells E5** and **F5**. Pay overtime only for overtime hours. Calculate the gross pay based on the regular and overtime pay. Abram's regular pay is $398. With 8 overtime hours, Abram's overtime pay is $119.40.

d. Create a formula in **cell H5** to calculate the taxable pay. Multiply the number of dependents by the deduction per dependent and subtract that from the gross pay. With two dependents, Abram's taxable pay is $417.40.

e. Use a VLOOKUP function in **cell I5** to identify and calculate the federal withholding tax. With a taxable pay of $417.40, Abram's tax rate is 25% and the withholding tax is $104.35. The VLOOKUP function returns the applicable tax rate, which you must then multiply by the taxable pay.

f. Calculate FICA in **cell J5** based on gross pay and the FICA rate, and calculate the net pay in cell K5.

g. Copy all formulas down their respective columns.

h. Use Quick Analysis tools to calculate the total regular pay, overtime pay, gross pay, taxable pay, withholding tax, FICA, and net pay on **row 17**.

i. Apply **Accounting Number Format** to the **range C5:C16**. Apply **Accounting Number Format** to the first row of monetary data and to the total row. Apply the **Comma style** to the monetary values for the other employees. Underline the last employee's monetary values and use the Format Cells dialog box to apply Top and Double Bottom borders for the totals.

j. Insert appropriate functions to calculate the average, highest, and lowest values in the Summary Statistics area (the **range I21:K23**) of the worksheet. Format the # of hours calculations as **Number format** with one decimal and the remaining calculations with **Accounting Number Format**.

k. Insert a new sheet named **Overtime**. List the number of overtime hours for the week. Calculate the yearly gross amount spent on overtime assuming the same number of overtime hours per week. Add another row with only half the overtime hours (using a formula). What is your conclusion and recommendation on overtime? Format this worksheet.

l. Insert a footer with your name on the left side, the sheet name in the center, and the file name code on the right side of both worksheets.

m. Save and close the workbook. Based on your instructor's directions, submit e02m1Payroll_LastFirst.

2 Mortgage Calculator

FROM SCRATCH

As a financial consultant, you work with a family who plans to purchase a $35,000 car. You want to create a worksheet containing variable data (the price of the car, down payment, date of the first payment, and borrower's credit rating) and constants (sales tax rate, years, and number of payments in one year). Borrowers pay 0.5% sales tax on the purchase price of the vehicle and their credit rating determines the required down payment percentage and APR. Your worksheet needs to perform various calculations.

a. Start a new Excel workbook, save it as **e02m2Loan_LastFirst**, and then rename Sheet1 **Payment**.

b. Type **Auto Loan Calculator** in cell A1, and then merge and center the title on the first row in the **range A1:F1**. Apply **bold, 18 pt** font size, and **Gold, Accent 4, Darker 25%** font color.

c. Type the labels in the **range A3:A12**. For each label, such as *Negotiated Cost of Vehicle*, merge the cells, such as the **range A4:B4**. Use the Format Painter to copy the formatting to the remaining nine labels. Next type and format the Inputs and Constants values in **column C**.

d. Type **Credit**, **Down Payment**, and **APR** in the **range A14:C14**, type the four credit ratings in the first column, the required down payment percentages in the second column, and the respective APRs in the third column. Next format the percentages, and then indent the percentages in the cells as needed.

e. Type labels in the Intermediate Calculations *and* Outputs sections in **column E**.

f. Enter formulas in the Intermediate Calculations and Outputs sections to calculate the following:
- **APR** based on credit rating: Use a Lookup function that references the borrower's credit rating and the table array in range. Include the range_lookup argument to ensure an exact match.

DISCOVER

- **Minimum down payment required**: Use a lookup function and calculation. Use the credit rating as the lookup value, and the **table array A15:C18**. Include the range_lookup argument to ensure an exact match. Multiply the function results by the negotiated cost of the house.
- **Sales tax**: Multiply the negotiated cost of the vehicle by the sales tax rate.
- **Total down payment**: The sum of the minimum down payment required and any additional down payment made.
- **Amount of the loan**: The difference between the negotiated cost of the house and the total down payment.
- **Monthly payment**: Principal and interest using the PMT function.

g. Format each section with fill color, bold, underline, number formats, borders, and column widths as needed.

h. Insert a footer with your name on the left side, the sheet name in the center, and the file name code on the right side of both sheets.

i. Save and close the workbook. Based on your instructor's directions, submit e02m2Loan_LastFirst.

3 Facebook and Blackboard

COLLABORATION CASE

FROM SCRATCH

Social media extends past friendships to organizational and product "fan" pages. Organizations such as Lexus, Pepsi, and universities create pages to provide information about their organizations. Some organizations even provide product details, such as for the Lexus ES350. Facebook includes a wealth of information about Microsoft Office products. People share information, pose questions, and reply with their experiences.

a. Log in to your Facebook account. If you do not have a Facebook account, sign up for one and add at least two classmates as friends. Search for Microsoft Excel 2016 and click **Like**.

b. Review postings on the Microsoft Excel wall. Notice that some people post what they like most about Excel or how much it has improved their productivity. Post a note about one of your favorite features about Excel that you have learned so far or how you have used Excel in other classes or on the job.

c. Click the **Discussions link** on the Microsoft Excel Facebook page and find topics that relate to IF or HLOOKUP functions. Post a response to one of the discussions. Take a screenshot of your posting and insert it into a Word document. Save the Word document **as e02m3_LastFirst**.

d. Create a team of three students. Create one discussion that asks people to describe their favorite use of any of the nested functions used in this chapter. Each team member should respond to the posting. Monitor the discussion and, when you have a few responses, capture a screenshot of the dialogue and insert it into your Word document.

e. Go to www.youtube.com and search for one of these Excel topics: absolute references, mixed references, semi-selection, IF function, VLOOKUP function, or PMT function.

f. Watch several video clips and find one of particular interest to you.

g. Post the URL on your Facebook wall. Specify the topic and describe why you like this particular video.

h. Watch videos from the links posted by other students on their Facebook walls. Comment on at least two submissions. Point out what you like about the video or any suggestions you have for improvement.

i. Insert screenshots of your postings in a Word document, if required by your instructor. Save and close the file. Based on your instructor's directions submit e02m3_LastFirst.

Beyond the Classroom

Auto Finance

After graduating from college and obtaining your first job, you have decided to purchase a new vehicle. Before purchasing the car, you want to create a worksheet to estimate the monthly payment based on the purchase price, APR, down payment, and years. Your monthly budget is $500 and you will use conditional logic to automatically determine if you can afford the cars you are evaluating. Open the workbook *e02b1CarLoan* and save it as **e02b1CarLoan_LastFirst**.

Insert a function to automatically enter the current date in cell A4. Starting in cell B12 enter a formula to calculate the down payment for each vehicle price range based on the down payment percentage listed in cell D4. Be sure to use the appropriate absolute or mixed reference and copy the formula to complete range B13:B16. Before calculating the periodic payment for each vehicle, you will need to research the current vehicle interest rates. Conduct an Internet search to determine the current interest rate for a five-year auto loan and enter the value in cell D5. In cell C12 type a function that calculates the periodic payment for the first vehicle based on the input information in range D4:D7. Be sure to use the appropriate absolute or mixed reference and copy the formula to complete range C12:C16. In column D, use an IF function to determine if the first vehicle is financially viable; display either Test Drive or NA based on the criteria in cell D8. Be sure to use the appropriate absolute or mixed reference and copy the formula to complete range D12:D16.

Include a footer with your name on the left side, the date in the center, and the file name on the right side. Save and close the workbook. Based on your instructor's directions, submit e02b1CarLoan_LastFirst.

Park City Condo Rental

You and some friends are planning a Labor Day vacation to Park City, Utah. You have secured a four-day condominium that costs $1,200. Some people will stay all four days; others will stay part of the weekend. One of your friends constructed a worksheet to help calculate each person's cost of the rental. The people who stay Thursday night will split the nightly cost evenly. To keep the costs down, everyone agreed to pay $30 per night per person for Friday, Saturday, and/or Sunday nights. Depending on the number of people who stay each night, the group may owe more money. Kyle, Ian, Isaac, and Daryl agreed to split the difference in the total rental cost and the amount the group members paid. Open the workbook *e02b2ParkCity*, and save it as **e02b2ParkCity_LastFirst**.

Review the worksheet structure, including the assumptions and calculation notes at the bottom of the worksheet. Check the formulas and functions, making necessary corrections. With the existing data, the number of people staying each night is 5, 8, 10, and 7, respectively. The total paid given the above assumptions is $1,110, giving a difference of $90 to be divided evenly among the first four people. Kyle's share should be $172.50. In the cells containing errors, insert comments to describe the error and fix the formulas. Verify the accuracy of formulas by entering an IF function in cell I1 to ensure that the totals match. Nick, James, and Body inform you they cannot stay Sunday night, and Rob wants to stay Friday night. Change the input accordingly. The updated total paid is now $1,200, and the difference is $150. Include a footer with your name on the left side, the date in the center, and the file name on the right side. Save and close the workbook. Based on your instructor's directions, submit e02b2ParkCity_LastFirst.

Capstone Exercise

You are an account manager for Inland Jewelers, a regional company that makes custom class rings for graduating seniors. Your supervisor requested a workbook to report on new accounts created on payment plans. The report should provide details on total costs to the student as well as payment information. Each ring financed has a base price that can fluctuate based on ring personalization.

Insert Current Date

You open the starting workbook you previously created, and insert the current date and time.

- **a.** Open the *e02c1ClassRing* workbook, and then save it as **e02c1ClassRing_LastFirst**.

- **b.** Insert a function in **cell B2** to display the current date and format as a **Long Date**.

- **c.** Set column B's width to **Autofit**.

Calculate Cost

You are ready to calculate the cost of each class ring ordered. The rings are priced based on their base metal as displayed in the range A15:B19.

- **a.** Insert a lookup function in **cell C5** to display the ring cost for the first student.

- **b.** Copy the function from **cell C5** down through **C11** to complete column C.

- **c.** Apply **Accounting Number Format** to **column C**.

Determine the Total Due

You will calculate the total due for each student's order. The total is the base price of the ring plus an additional charge for personalization if applicable.

- **a.** Insert an IF function in **cell E5** to calculate the total due. If the student has chosen to personalize the ring,

there is an additional charge of 5% located in **cell B21** that must be applied; if not, the student pays only the base price. Use appropriate relative and absolute cell references.

- **b.** Copy the function from **cell E5** down through **E11** to complete column E.

- **c.** Apply **Accounting Number Format** to **column E**.

Calculate the Monthly Payment

Your next step is to calculate the periodic payment for each student's account. The payments are based on the years financed in column F and the annual interest rate in cell B22. All accounts are paid on a monthly basis.

- **a.** Insert the function in **cell G5** to calculate the first student's monthly payment, using appropriate relative and absolute cell references.

- **b.** Copy the formula down the column.

- **c.** Apply **Accounting Number Format** to **column G**.

Finalize the Workbook

You perform some basic statistical calculations and finalize the workbook with formatting and page setup options.

- **a.** Calculate totals in **cells C12, E12,** and **G12**.

- **b.** Apply **Accounting Number Format** to the **cells C12, E12,** and **G12**.

- **c.** Set **0.3"** left and right margins and ensure that the page prints on only one page.

- **d.** Insert a footer with your name on the left side, the sheet name in the center, and the file name on the right side.

- **e.** Save and close the workbook. Based on your instructor's directions, submit e02c1ClassRing_LastFirst.

Charts

LEARNING OUTCOME **You will create charts and insert sparklines to represent data visually.**

OBJECTIVES & SKILLS: After you read this chapter, you will be able to:

CASE STUDY | Computer Job Outlook

You are an academic advisor for the School of Computing at a private university in Seattle, Washington. You will visit high schools over the next few weeks to discuss the computing programs at the university and to inform students about the job outlook in the computing industry. Your assistant, Doug Demers, researched growing computer-related jobs in the *Occupational Outlook Handbook* published by the Bureau of Labor Statistics on the U.S. Department of Labor's website. In particular, Doug listed seven jobs, the number of those jobs in 2010, the projected number of jobs by 2020, the growth in percentage increase and number of jobs, and the 2010 median pay. This dataset shows an 18%–31% increase in computer-related jobs in that 10-year time period.

To prepare for your presentation to encourage students to enroll in your School of Computing, you will create several charts that depict the job growth in the computer industry. You know that different charts provide different perspectives on the data. After you complete the charts, you will be able to use them in a variety of formats, such as presentations, fliers, and brochures.

Everything possible/ Shutterstock

Depicting Data Visually

CHAPTER 3

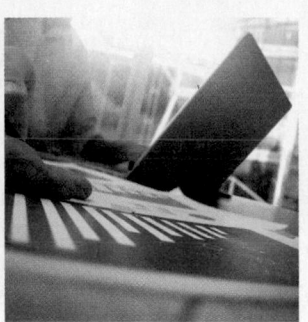

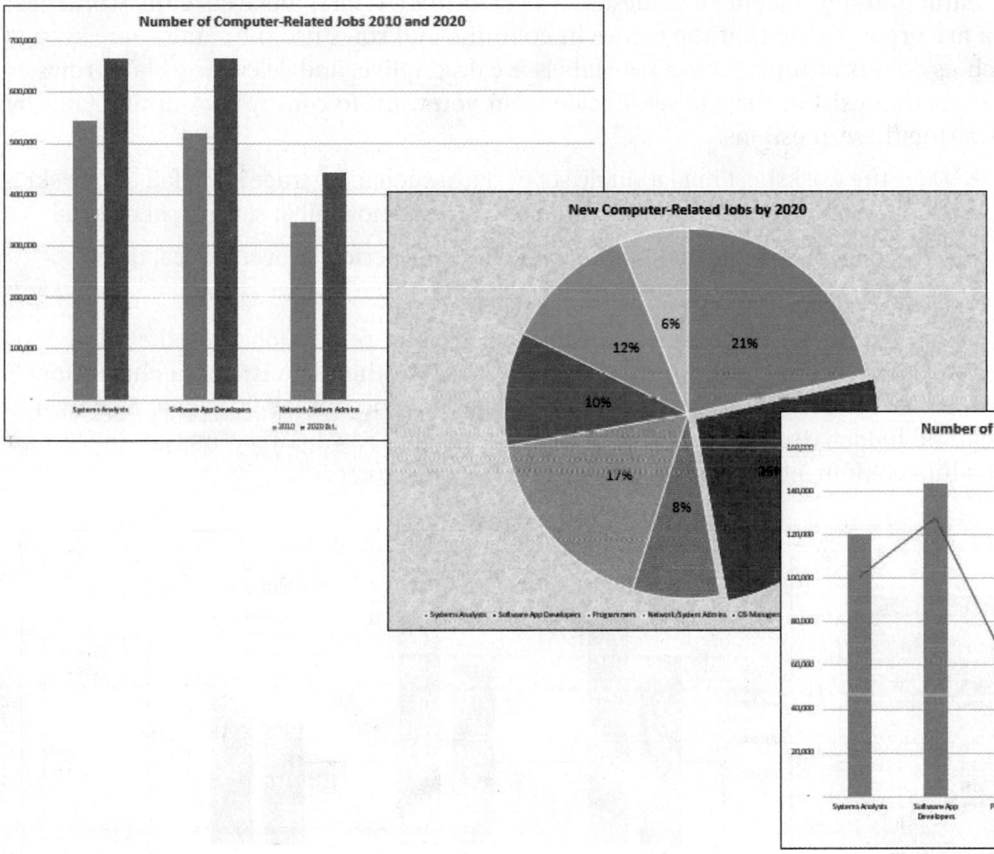

Excel 2016, Windows 10, Microsoft Corporation

FIGURE 3.1 Computer Job Outlook Charts

CASE STUDY | Computer Job Outlook

Starting File	File to be Submitted
e03h1Jobs	e03h3Jobs_LastFirst

Chart Basics

A *chart* is a visual representation of numerical data that compares data and reveals trends or patterns to help people make informed decisions. An effective chart depicts data in a clear, easy-to-interpret manner and contains enough data to be useful without overwhelming your audience.

In this section, you will select the data source, choose the best chart type to represent numerical data, and designate the chart's location.

Selecting the Data Source

Look at the structure of the worksheet—the column labels, the row labels, the quantitative data, and the calculated values. Before creating a chart, make sure the worksheet data are organized so that the values in columns and rows use the same value system (such as dollars or units), make sure labels are descriptive, and delete any blank rows or columns that exist in the dataset. Decide what you want to convey to your audience by answering these questions:

- Does the worksheet hold a single set of data, such as average snowfall at one ski resort, or multiple sets of data, such as average snowfall at several ski resorts?

- Do you want to depict data for one specific time period or over several time periods, such as several years or decades?

Figure 3.2 shows a worksheet containing computer-related job titles, the number of jobs in 2010, the projected number of jobs by 2020, other details, and a chart. Row 3 contains labels merged and centered over individual column labels in row 5. Row 4 is blank and hidden. It is a good practice to insert a blank row between merged labels and individual column labels to enable you to sort the data correctly.

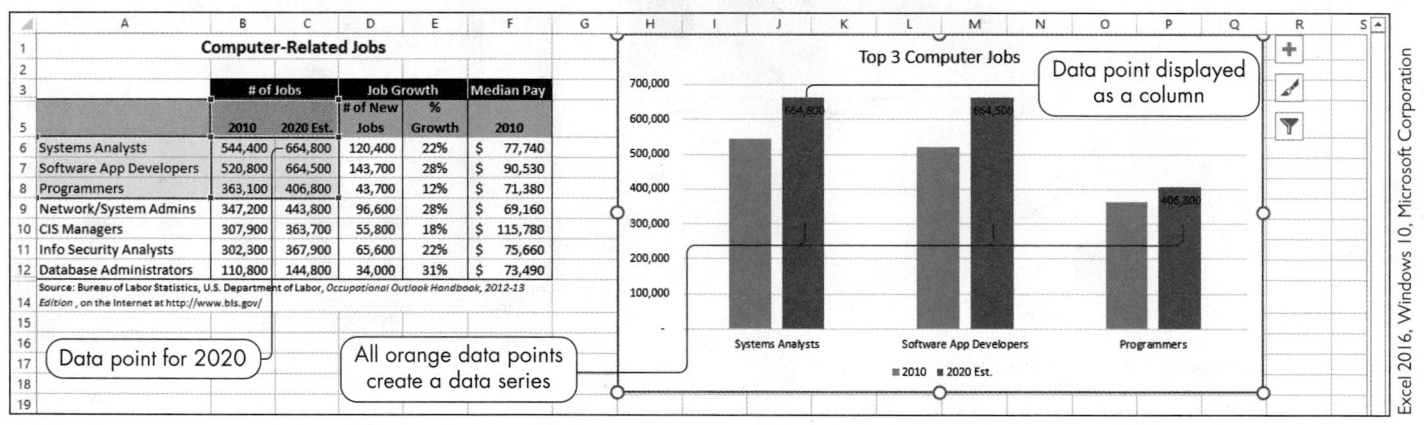

FIGURE 3.2 Dataset and Chart

Each cell containing a value is a *data point*. For example, the value 664,800 in cell C6 is a data point for the estimated number of Systems Analysts in 2020. Each data point in the worksheet creates an individual data point in the chart. A group of related data points that display in row(s) or column(s) in the worksheet create a *data series*. For example, the values 664,800, 664,500, and 406,800 comprise the number of estimated jobs by 2020 data series, which is indicated by the orange columns in the chart.

Identify the data range by selecting values and labels that you want to include in the chart. If the values and labels are not stored in adjacent cells, hold Ctrl while selecting the nonadjacent ranges. Do not select worksheet titles or subtitles; doing so would add unnecessary data to the chart. To create the chart in Figure 3.2, select the range A5:C8. It is important to select parallel ranges. A parallel range is one that consists of the same starting and end point as another similar range. For example, the range C5:C12 is a parallel range to A5:A12. Including the column headings on row 5 (even though cell A5 is blank) is necessary to include the years in the legend at the bottom of the chart area.

Excel transforms the selected data into a chart. A chart may include several chart elements or components. Table 3.1 lists and describes some of these elements. Figure 3.3 shows a chart area that contains these elements.

TABLE 3.1	Chart Elements
Chart Element	**Description**
Chart area	The container for the entire chart and all of its elements.
Plot area	Region containing the graphical representation of the values in the data series. Two axes form a border around the plot area.
X-axis	The horizontal border that provides a frame of reference for measuring data left to right.
Y-axis	The vertical border that provides a frame of reference for measuring data up and down.
Legend	A key that identifies the color, gradient, picture, texture, or pattern assigned to each data series in a chart. For example, blue might represent values for 2010, and orange might represent values for 2020.

Pearson Education, Inc.

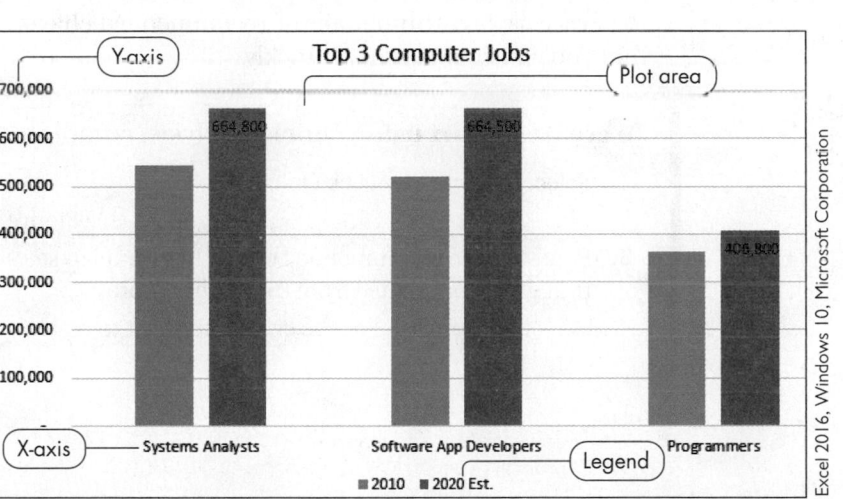

FIGURE 3.3 Chart Elements

Excel refers to the axes as the category axis and value axis. The ***category axis*** is the axis that displays descriptive labels for the data points plotted in a chart. The category axis labels are typically text contained in the first column of worksheet data (such as job titles) used to create the chart. The ***value axis*** is the axis that displays incremental numbers to identify the approximate values (such as number of jobs or revenue) of data points in a chart.

Choosing a Chart Type

You can create different charts from the same dataset; each chart type tells a different story. Select a chart type that appropriately represents the data and tells a story. For example, one chart might compare the number of computer-related jobs between 2010 and 2020, and another chart might indicate the percentage of new jobs by job title. The most commonly used chart types are column, bar, line, pie, and combo (see Table 3.2). Each chart type is designed to provide a unique perspective to the selected data.

TABLE 3.2 Common Chart Types

Chart	Chart Type	Description
	Column	Displays values in vertical columns where the height represents the value; the taller the column, the larger the value. Categories display along the horizontal (category) axis.
	Bar	Displays values in horizontal bars where the length represents the value; the longer the bar, the larger the value. Categories display along the vertical (category) axis.
	Line	Displays category data on the horizontal axis and value data on the vertical axis. Appropriate to show continuous data to depict trends over time, such as months, years, or decades.
	Pie	Shows proportion of individual data points to the total or whole of all those data points.
	Combo	Combines two chart types (such as column and line) to plot different data types (such as values and percentages)

Pearson Education, Inc.

Quick Analysis. When you select a range of adjacent cells (such as the range A5:C12) and position the pointer over that selected range, Excel displays Quick Analysis in the bottom-right corner of the selected area. However, Quick Analysis does not display when you select nonadjacent ranges, such as ranges A6:A12 and D6:D12. Quick Analysis displays thumbnails of recommended charts based on the data you selected so that you can create a chart quickly.

> **To create a chart using Quick Analysis, complete the following steps:**
>
> 1. Select the data and click Quick Analysis.
> 2. Click Charts in the Quick Analysis gallery (see Figure 3.4).
> 3. Point to each recommended chart thumbnail to see a preview of the type of chart that would be created from the selected data.
> 4. Click the thumbnail of the chart you want to create.

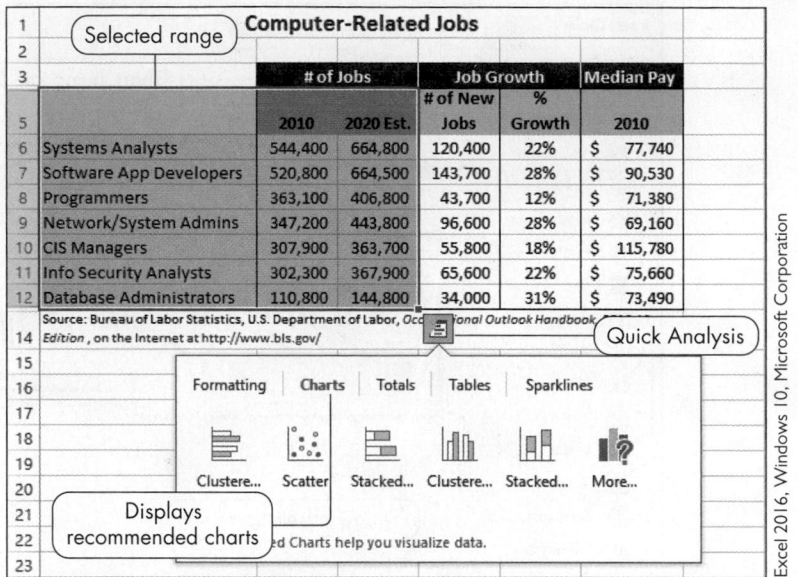

FIGURE 3.4 Quick Analysis Tool

Insert Tab. The Insert tab contains commands for creating a variety of charts. You must use the Insert tab to create a chart when you select nonadjacent ranges, but you can also use the Insert tab to create a chart when you select adjacent ranges. Clicking a particular chart on the Insert tab displays a gallery of icons representing more specific types of charts.

To create a chart using the Insert tab, complete the following steps:

1. Select the data and click the Insert tab.
2. Complete one of the following steps to select the chart type:
   - Click the chart type (such as Column) in the Charts group and click a chart subtype (such as Clustered Column) from the chart gallery (see Figure 3.5).
   - Click Recommended Charts in the Charts group to open the Insert Chart dialog box, click a thumbnail of the chart you want in the Recommended Charts tab or click the All Charts tab (see Figure 3.6) and click a thumbnail, and then click OK.

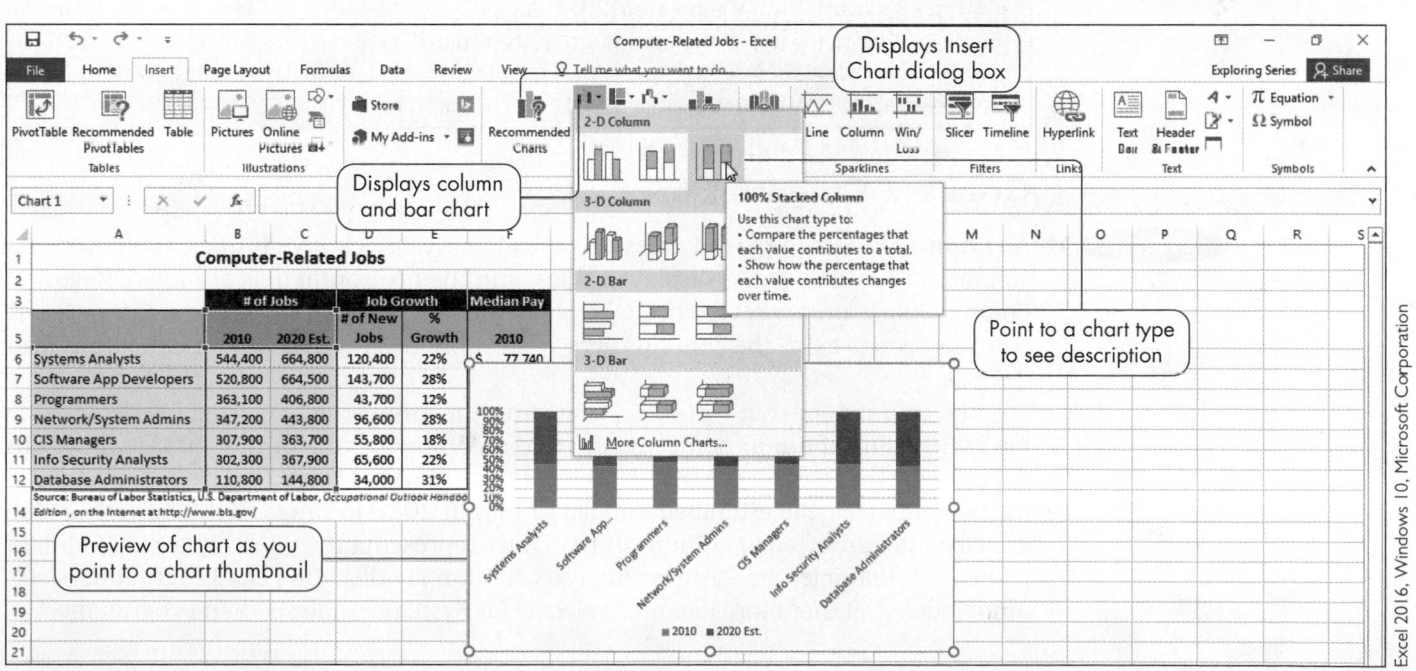

FIGURE 3.5 Chart Gallery

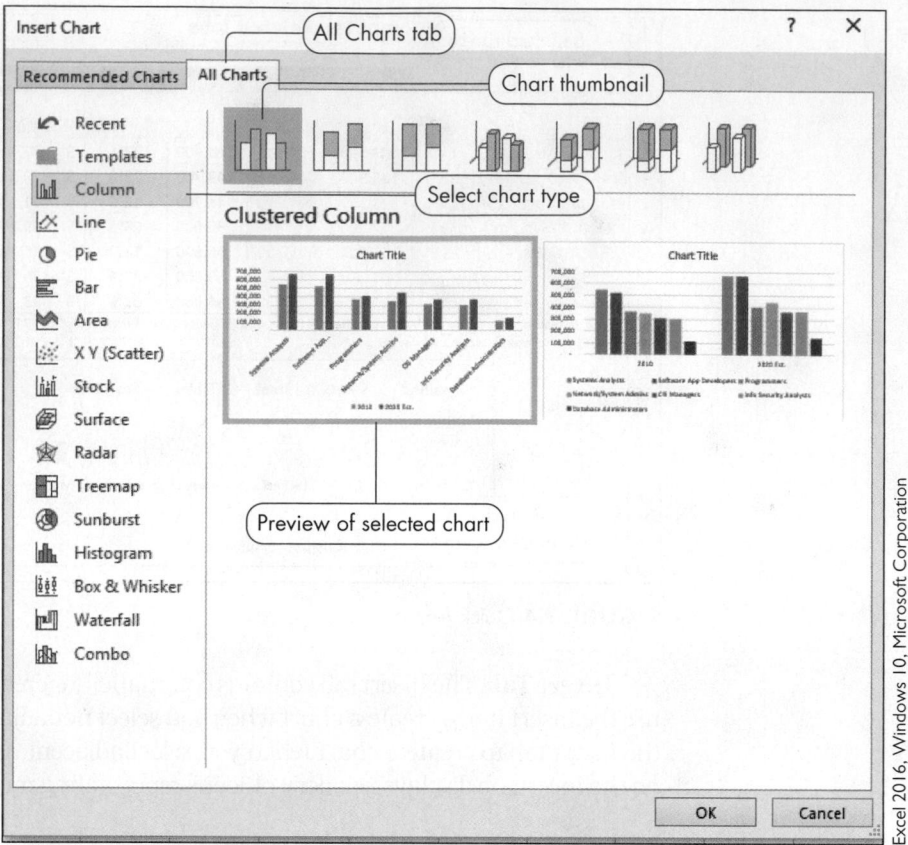

FIGURE 3.6 Insert Chart Dialog Box

TIP: RECOMMENDED VS. LIST OF ALL CHARTS

If you are unsure which type of chart would be a good choice for the selected data, click Recommended Charts in the Chart group. Excel will analyze the selected data and display thumbnails of recommended charts in the Insert Chart dialog box. Click a thumbnail to see a larger visualization of how your selected data would look in that chart type. The dialog box displays a message indicating the purpose of the selected chart, such as *A clustered bar chart is used to compare values across a few categories. Use it when the chart shows duration or when the category text is long.*

Click the All Charts tab in the Insert Chart dialog box to display a list of all chart types. After you click a type on the left side of the dialog box, the top of the right side displays specific subtypes, such as Clustered Column. When you click a subtype, the dialog box displays an image of that subtype using the selected data.

Create a Column Chart

STEP 1 ❯❯ A ***column chart*** compares values across categories, such as job titles, using vertical columns. The vertical axis displays values, and the horizontal axis displays categories. Column charts are most effective when they are limited to seven or fewer categories. If more categories exist, the columns appear too close together, making it difficult to read the labels.

The column chart in Figure 3.7 compares the number of projected jobs by job title for 2020 using the non-adjacent ranges A5:A9 and C5:C9 in the dataset shown in Figure 3.5. The first four job titles stored in the range A6:A9 form the category axis, and the increments of the estimated number of jobs in 2020 in range C6:C9 form the value axis. The height of each column in the chart represents the value of individual data points. For example, the Systems Analysts column is taller than the Programmers column, indicating that more jobs are projected for Systems Analysts than Programmers.

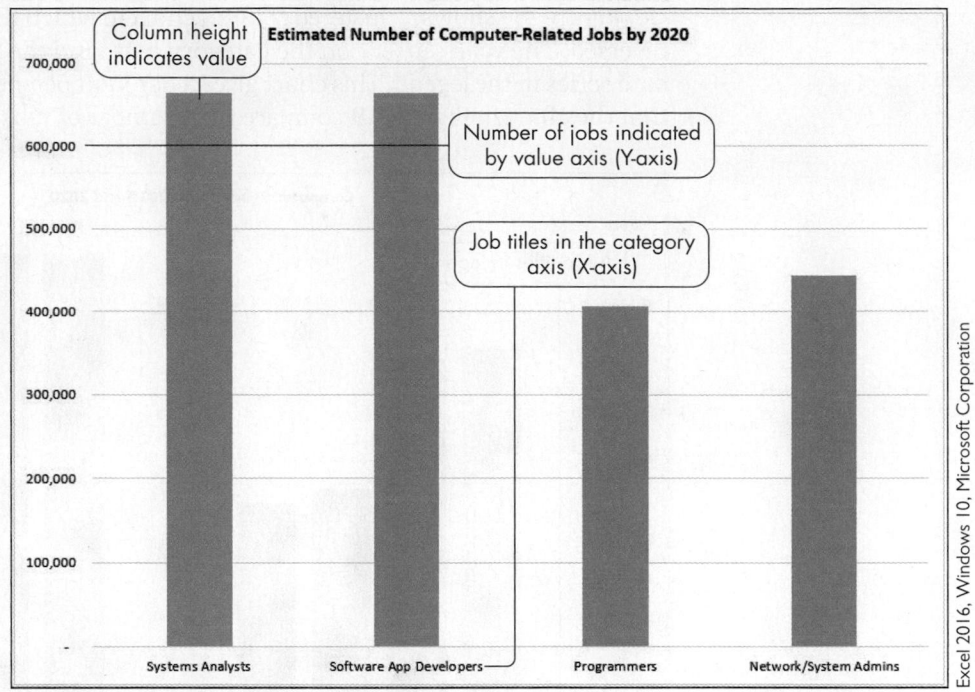

FIGURE 3.7 Column Chart

A ***clustered column chart*** compares groups—or clusters—of columns set side by side. The clustered column chart facilitates quick comparisons across data series, and it is effective for comparing several data points among categories. Figure 3.8 shows a clustered column chart created from the adjacent range A5:C9 in the dataset shown in Figure 3.5. By default, the job titles in the range A6:A9 appear on the category axis, and the yearly data points appear as columns with the value axis showing incremental numbers. Excel assigns a different color to each yearly data series and includes a legend so that you know what color represents which data series. The 2010 data series is light blue, and the 2020 data series is dark blue. This chart makes it easy to compare the predicted job growth from 2010 to 2020 for each job title and then to compare the trends among job titles.

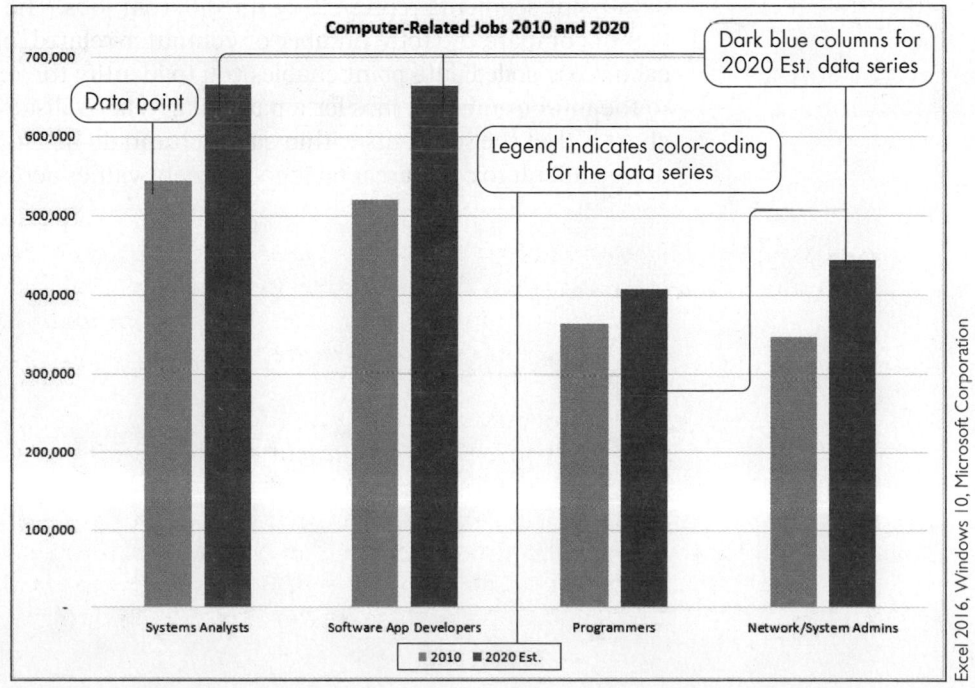

FIGURE 3.8 Clustered Column Chart

Figure 3.9 shows a clustered column chart in which the categories and data series are reversed. The years appear on the category axis, and the job titles appear as color-coded data series in the legend. This chart gives a different perspective from that in Figure 3.8 in that the chart in Figure 3.9 compares the number of jobs within a given year.

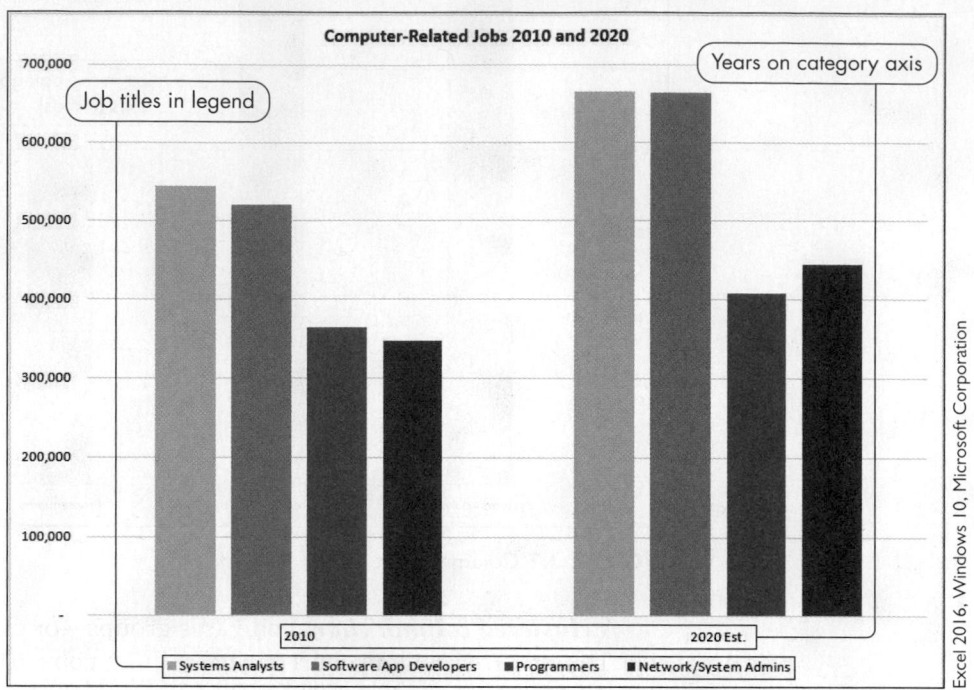

FIGURE 3.9 Clustered Column Chart: Category Axis and Legend Reversed

A **stacked column chart** shows the relationship of individual data points to the whole category. A stacked column chart displays only one column for each category. Each category within the stacked column is color-coded for one data series. Use the stacked column chart when you want to compare total values across categories, as well as to display the individual category values. Figure 3.10 shows a stacked column chart in which a single column represents each categorical year, and each column stacks color-coded data-point segments representing the different jobs. The stacked column chart enables you to compare the total number of computer-related jobs for each year. The height of each color-coded data point enables you to identify the relative contribution of each job to the total number of jobs for a particular year. A disadvantage of the stacked column chart is that the segments within each column do not start at the same point, making it more difficult to compare individual segment values across categories.

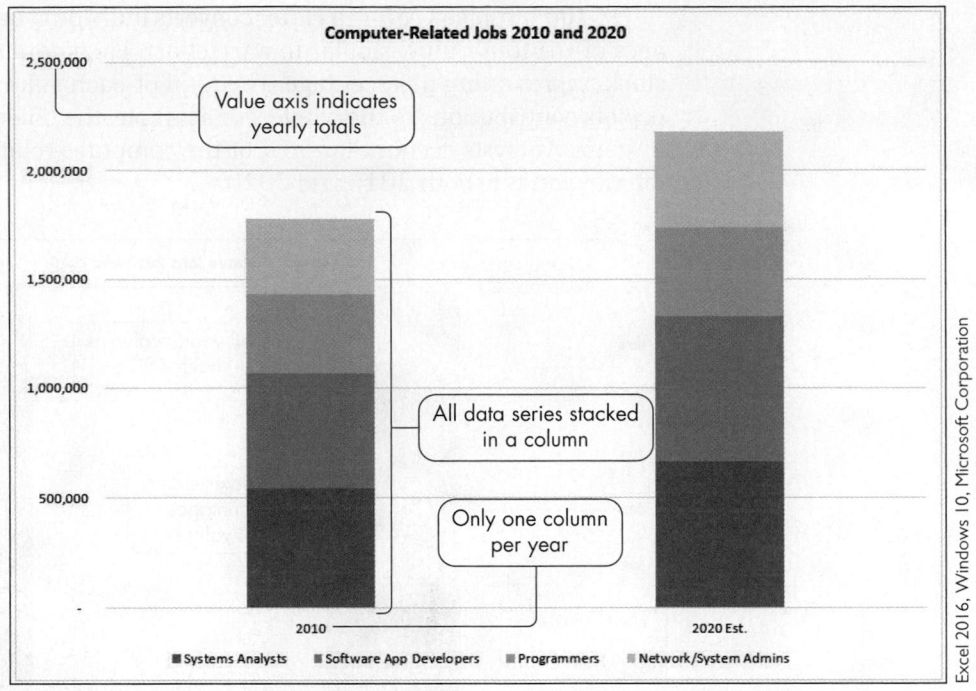

FIGURE 3.10 Stacked Column Chart

When you create a stacked column chart, make sure data are additive: Each column represents a sum of the data for each segment. Figure 3.10 correctly uses years as the category axis and the jobs as data series. For each year, Excel adds the number of jobs, and the columns display the total number of jobs. For example, the estimated total number of the four computer-related jobs in 2020 is about 2,180,000. Figure 3.11 shows a meaningless stacked column chart because the yearly number of jobs by job title is *not* additive. Adding the number of current actual jobs to the number of estimated jobs in the future does not make sense. It is incorrect to state that about 1,200,000 Systems Analysts jobs exist. Be careful when constructing stacked column charts to ensure that they lead to logical interpretation of data.

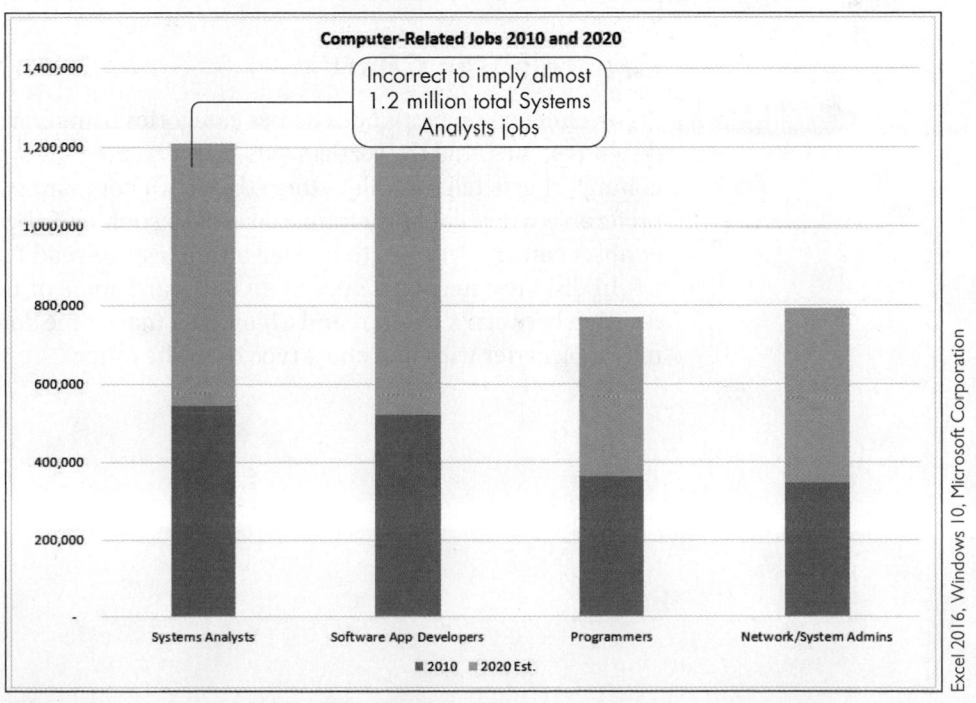

FIGURE 3.11 Incorrectly Constructed Stacked Column Chart

A **100% stacked column chart** converts individual data points (values) into percentages of the total value, similar to a pie chart. Each data series is a different color of the stack, representing a percentage. The total of each column is 100%. This type of chart depicts contributions to the whole. For example, the chart in Figure 3.12 illustrates that Systems Analysts account for 30% of the computer-related jobs represented by the four job categories in both 2010 and 2020.

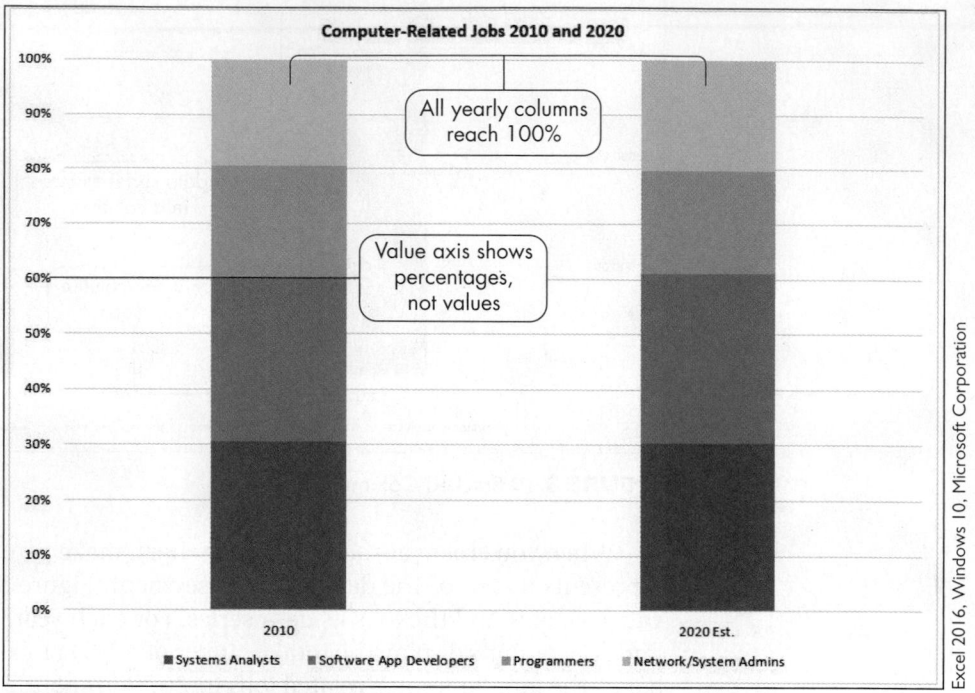

FIGURE 3.12 100% Stacked Column Chart

TIP: AVOID 3-D CHARTS

Avoid creating 3-D charts, because the third dimension is a superficial enhancement that usually distorts the charted data. For example, some columns appear taller or shorter than they actually are because of the angle of the 3-D effect, or some columns might be hidden by taller columns in front of them.

Create a Bar Chart

STEP 2 ⟩⟩ A **bar chart** compares values across categories using horizontal bars. The horizontal axis displays values, and the vertical axis displays categories (see Figure 3.13). Bar charts and column charts tell a similar story: they both compare categories of data. A bar chart is preferable when category names are long, such as *Software App Developers*. A bar chart enables category names to appear in an easy-to-read format, whereas a column chart might display category names at an awkward angle or in a smaller font size. The overall decision between a column and a bar chart may come down to the fact that different data may look better with one chart type than the other.

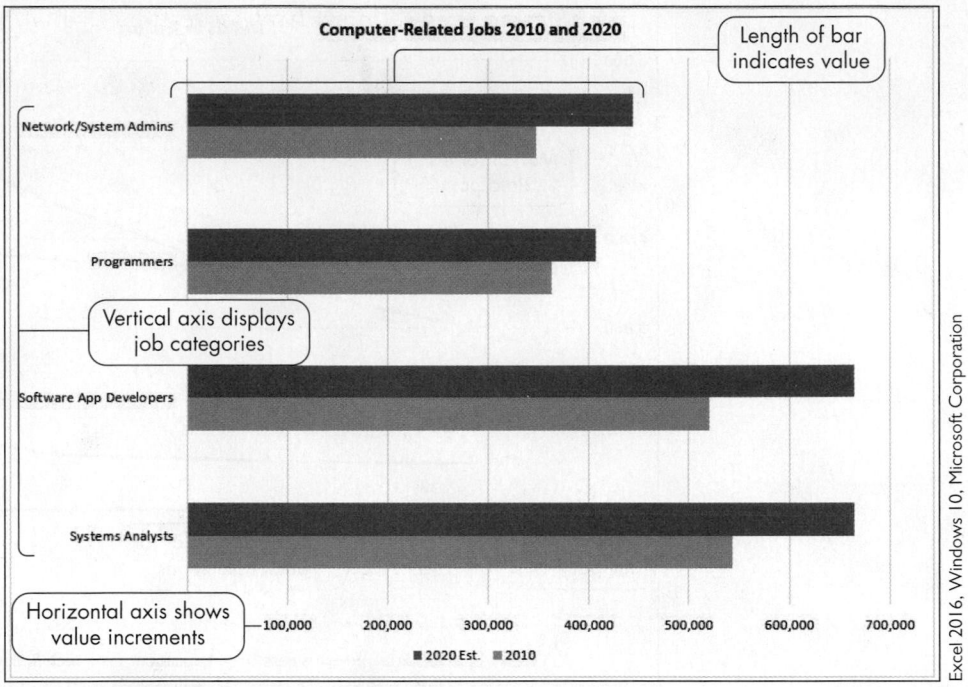

FIGURE 3.13 Clustered Bar Chart

Change the Chart Type

After you create a chart, you may decide that the data would be better represented by a different type of chart. For example, you might decide a bar chart would display the labels better than a column chart, or you might want to change a clustered bar chart to a stacked bar chart to provide a different perspective for the data. Use the Change Chart Type feature to change a chart to a different type of chart.

To change the type of an existing chart, complete the following steps:

1. Select the chart and click the Design tab.
2. Click Change Chart Type in the Type group to open the Change Chart Type dialog box (which is similar to the Insert Chart dialog box).
3. Click the All Charts tab within the dialog box.
4. Click a chart type on the left side of the dialog box.
5. Click a chart subtype on the right side of the dialog box and click OK.

Create a Line Chart

A *line chart* displays lines connecting data points to show trends over equal time periods. Excel displays each data series with a different line color. The category axis (X-axis) represents time, such as 10-year increments, whereas the value axis (Y-axis) represents a value, such as money or quantity. A line chart enables you to detect trends because the line continues to the next data point. To show each data point, choose the Line with Markers chart type. Figure 3.14 shows a line chart indicating the number of majors from 2005 to 2020 (estimated) at five-year increments. The number of Arts majors remains relatively constant, but the number of Tech & Computing majors increases significantly over time, especially between the years 2010 and 2020.

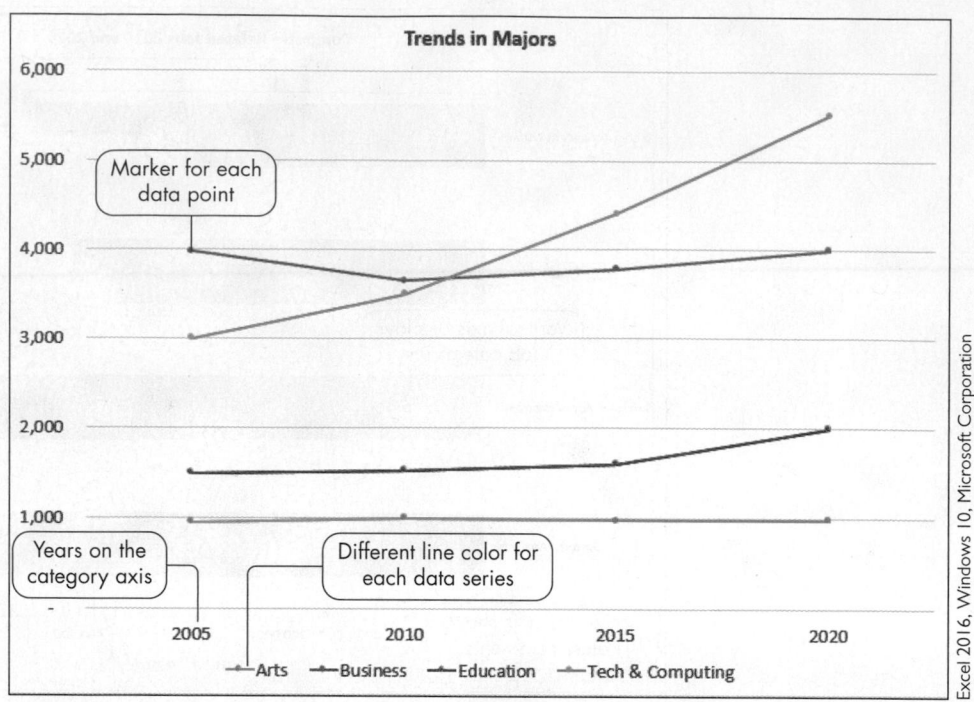

FIGURE 3.14 Line Chart

Create a Pie Chart

STEP 4 »» A *pie chart* shows each data point as a proportion to the whole data series. The pie chart displays as a circle, or "pie," where the entire pie represents the total value of the data series. Each slice represents a single data point. The larger the slice, the larger percentage that data point contributes to the whole. Use a pie chart when you want to convey percentage. Unlike column, bar, and line charts that typically chart multiple data series, pie charts represent a single data series only.

The pie chart in Figure 3.15 divides the pie representing the estimated number of new jobs into seven slices, one for each job title. The size of each slice is proportional to the percentage of total computer-related jobs depicted in the worksheet for that year. For example, Systems Analysts account for 21% of the estimated total number of new computer-related jobs in 2020. Excel creates a legend to indicate which color represents which pie slice. When you create a pie chart, limit it to about seven data points. Pie charts with too many slices appear too busy to interpret, or shades of the same color scheme become too difficult to distinguish.

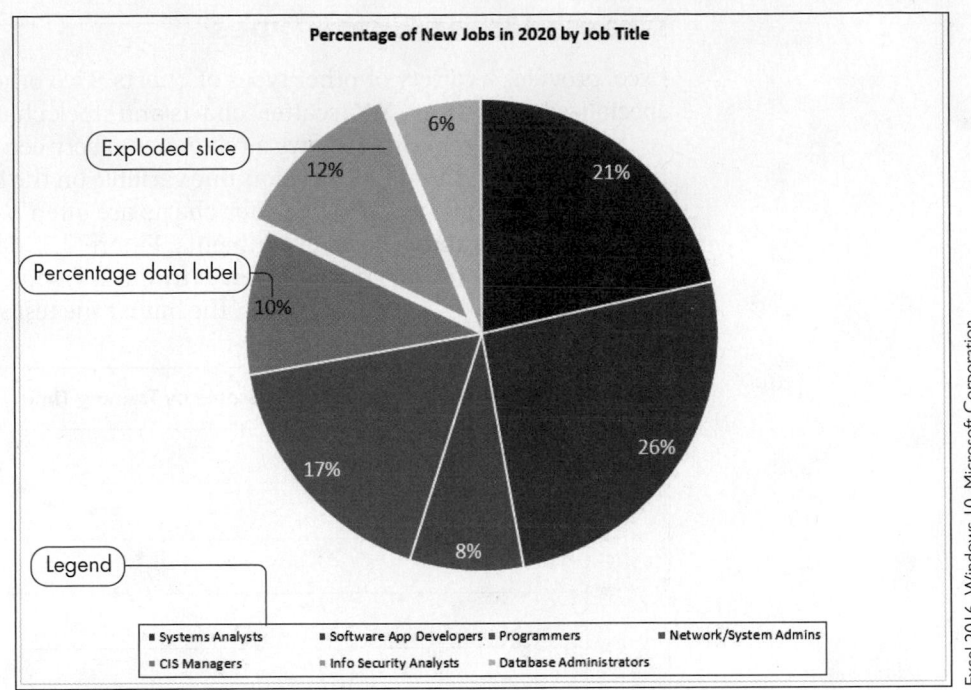

FIGURE 3.15 Pie Chart

Create a Combo Chart

STEP 5 ▶▶ A *combo chart* is a chart that combines two chart types, such as column and line charts. This type of chart is useful to show two different but related data types. For example, you might want to show the number of new jobs in columns and the percentage growth of new jobs in a line within the same chart (see Figure 3.16). A combo chart has a primary and a secondary axis. The primary axis displays on the left side of the chart. In this case, the primary axis indicates the number of jobs represented in the columns. The secondary axis displays on the right side of the chart. In this case, the secondary axis indicates the percentage of new jobs created as represented by the line.

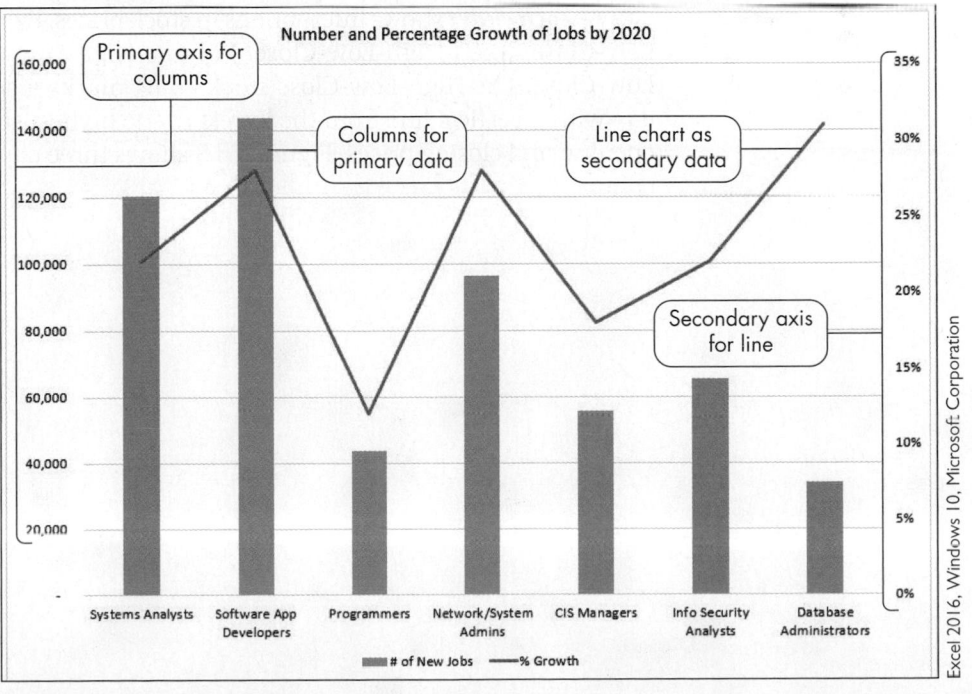

FIGURE 3.16 Combo Chart

Create Other Chart Types

Excel provides a variety of other types of charts. Two other chart types that are used for specialized analysis are X Y (scatter) charts and stock charts.

An **X Y (scatter) chart** shows a relationship between two numerical variables using their X and Y coordinates. Excel plots one variable on the horizontal X-axis and the other variable on the vertical Y-axis. Scatter charts are often used to represent data in educational, scientific, and medical experiments. Figure 3.17 shows the relationship between the number of minutes students view a training video and their test scores. The more minutes of a video a student watches, the higher the test score.

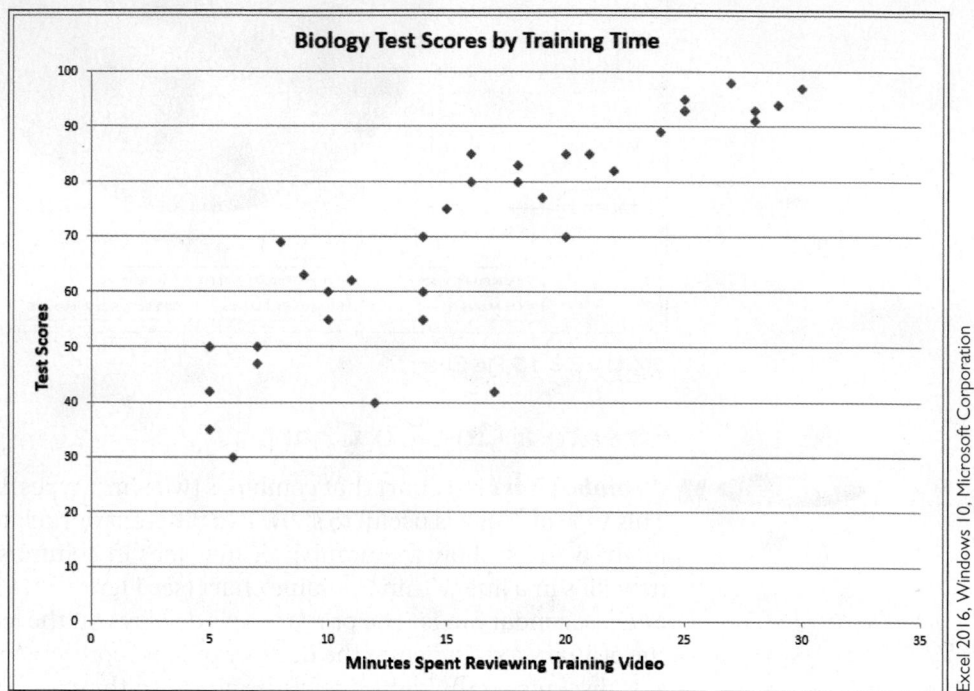

FIGURE 3.17 X Y (Scatter) Chart

A **stock chart** shows fluctuations in stock prices. Excel has four stock subtypes: High-Low-Close, Open-High-Low-Close, Volume-High-Low-Close, and Volume-Open-High-Low-Close. The High-Low-Close stock chart marks a stock's trading range on a given day with a vertical line from the lowest to the highest stock prices. Rectangles mark the opening and closing prices. Figure 3.18 shows three days of stock prices for a particular company.

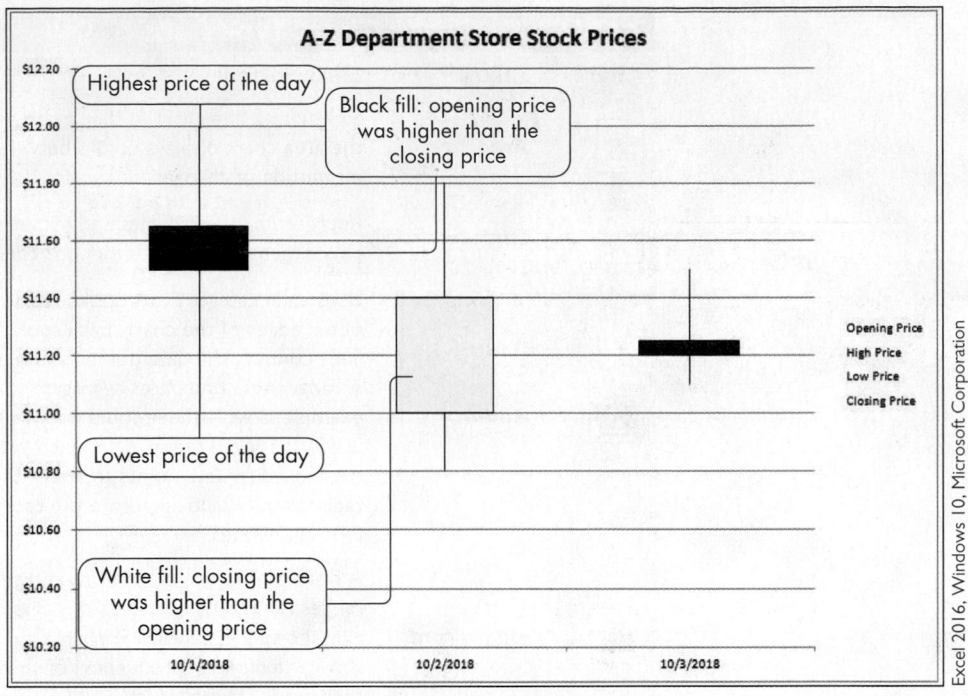

FIGURE 3.18 Stock Chart

The rectangle represents the difference in the opening and closing prices. If the rectangle has a white fill, the closing price is higher than the opening price. If the rectangle has a black fill, the opening price is higher than the closing price. In Figure 3.18, on October 1, the opening price was $11.65, and the closing price was $11.50, indicated by the top and bottom of the black rectangle. A line below the rectangle indicates that the lowest trading price is lower than the opening and closing prices. The lowest price was $11.00 on October 1. A line above the rectangle indicates that the highest trading price is higher than the opening and closing prices. The highest price was $12.00 on October 1. If no line exists below the rectangle, the lowest price equals either the opening or closing price, and if no line exists above the rectangle, the highest price equals either the opening or closing price.

> **TIP: ARRANGE DATA FOR A STOCK CHART**
> To create an Open-High-Low-Close stock chart, you must arrange data with Opening Price, High Price, Low Price, and Closing Price as column labels in that sequence. If you want to create other variations of stock charts, you must arrange data in a structured sequence required by Excel.

Table 3.3 lists and describes some of the other types of charts you can create in Excel.

TABLE 3.3 Other Chart Types

Chart	Chart Type	Description
▲	**Area**	Similar to a line chart in that it shows trends over time; however, the area chart displays colors between the lines to help illustrate the magnitude of changes.
◆	**Surface**	Represents numeric data and numeric categories. Displays trends using two dimensions on a continuous curve.
⬠	**Radar**	Uses each category as a spoke radiating from the center point to the outer edges of the chart. Each spoke represents each data series, and lines connect the data points between spokes, similar to a spider web. A radar chart compares aggregate values for several data series. For example, a worksheet could contain the number of specific jobs for 2015, 2016, 2017, and 2018. Each year would be a data series containing the individual data points (number of specific jobs) for that year. The radar chart would aggregate the total number of jobs per year for all four data series.
▮	**Histogram**	A histogram is similar to a column chart. The category axis shows bin ranges (intervals) where data is aggregated into bins, and the vertical axis shows frequencies. For example, your professor might want to show the number (frequency) of students who earned a score within each grade interval, such as 60-69, 70-79, 80-89, and 90-100.

Pearson Education, Inc.

Moving, Sizing, and Printing a Chart

STEP 3 ▶▶ Excel inserts the chart as an embedded object in the current worksheet, often to the right of, but sometimes on top of and covering up, the data area. After you insert a chart, you usually need to move it to a different location and adjust its size. If you need to print a chart, decide whether to print the chart only or the chart and its data source.

Move a Chart

When you create a chart, Excel displays the chart in the worksheet, often on top of existing worksheet data. Therefore, you should move the chart so that it does not cover up data. If you leave the chart in the same worksheet, you can print the data and chart on the same page.

To move a chart on an active worksheet, complete the following steps:

1. Point to the chart area to display the Chart Area ScreenTip and the pointer includes the white arrowhead and a four-headed arrow.
2. Drag the chart to the desired location.

You might want to place the chart in a separate worksheet, called a *chart sheet*. A chart sheet contains a single chart only; you cannot enter data and formulas on a chart sheet. If you want to print or view a full-sized chart, move the chart to its own chart sheet.

To move a chart to another sheet or a chart sheet, complete the following steps:

1. Select the chart.
2. Click the Design tab and click Move Chart in the Location group (or right-click the chart and select Move Chart) to open the Move Chart dialog box (see Figure 3.19).
3. Select one of these options to indicate where you want to move the chart:
   - Click *New sheet* to move the chart to its own sheet. The default chart sheet for the first chart is Chart1, but you can rename it in the Move Chart dialog box or similarly to the way you rename other sheet tabs.
   - Click *Object in*, click the *Object in* arrow, and select the worksheet to which you want to move the chart.
4. Click OK.

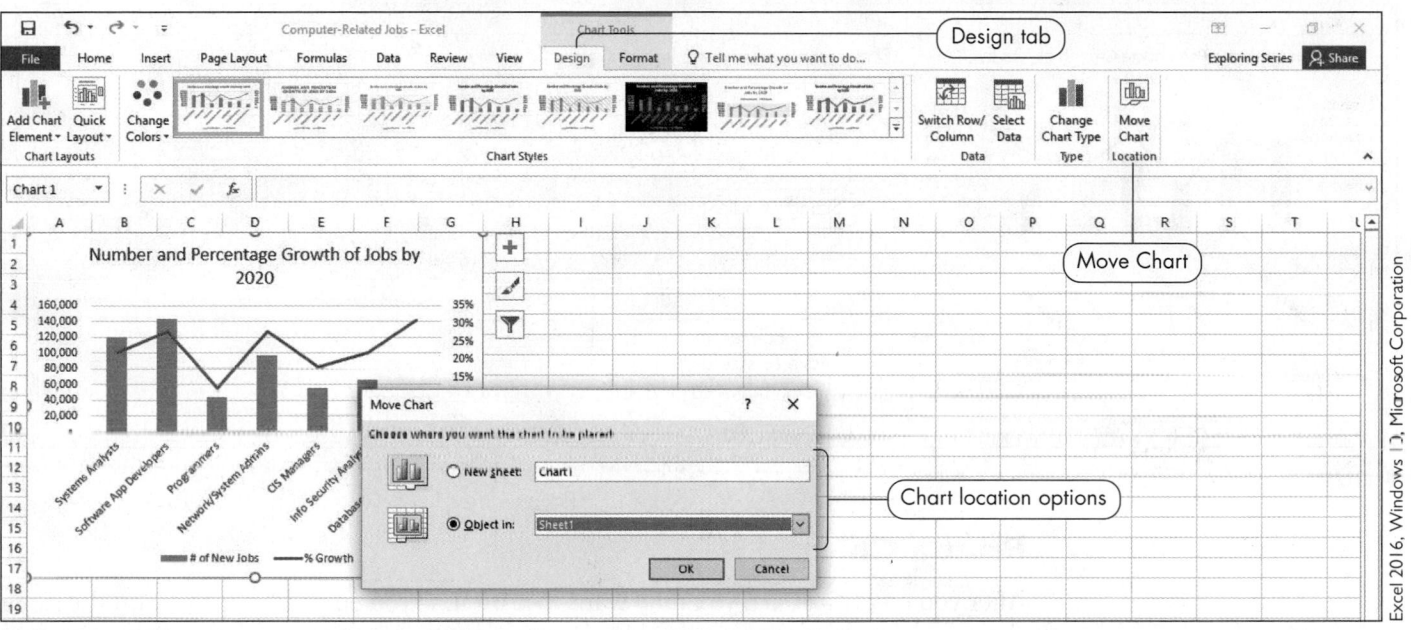

FIGURE 3.19 Design Tab and Move Chart Dialog Box

Size a Chart

If you move a chart to a chart sheet, the chart is enlarged to fill the entire sheet. If you keep a chart embedded within a worksheet, you might want to size the chart to fit in a particular range or to ensure the chart elements are proportional. Use the sizing handles or the Format tab on the Ribbon to change the size of the chart.

To change the chart size with sizing handles, complete the following steps:

1. Select the chart. Excel displays a line border and sizing handles around the chart when you select it. **Sizing handles** are eight circles that display around the four corners and outside middle sections of a chart when you select it.
2. Point to the outer edge of the chart where the sizing handles are located until the pointer changes to a two-headed arrow.
3. Drag the border to adjust the chart's height or width. Drag a corner sizing handle to increase or decrease the height and width of the chart at the same time. Press and hold Shift as you drag a corner sizing handle to change the height and width proportionately.

1. Select the chart.
2. Click the Format tab.
3. Change the value in the Height and Width boxes in the Size group (see Figure 3.20).

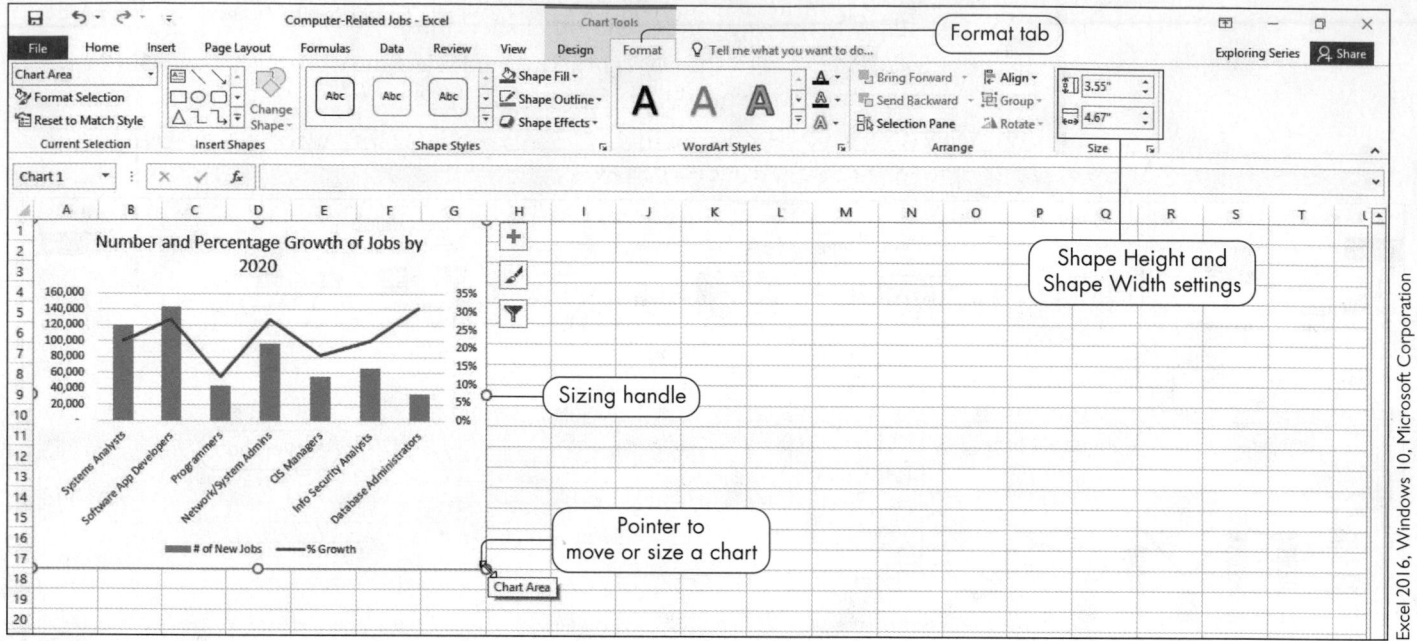

FIGURE 3.20 Sizing a Chart

Print a Chart

After you create a chart, you may want to print it. If you embedded a chart on the same sheet as the data source, you need to decide if you want to print the data only, the data and the chart, or the chart only.

To print the data only, complete the following steps:

1. Select the data.
2. Click the File tab and click Print.
3. Click the first arrow in the Settings section and select Print Selection.
4. Click Print.

To print only the chart as a full page, complete the following steps:

1. Select the chart if it is on a worksheet that also contains data.
2. Click the File tab and click Print.
3. Make sure the default setting is Print Selected Chart.
4. Click Print.

If the data and chart are on the same worksheet, print the worksheet contents to print both, but do not select either the chart or the data before displaying the Print options. The preview shows you what will print. Make sure it displays what you want to print before clicking Print.

If you moved the chart to a chart sheet, the chart is the only item on that worksheet. When you display the print options, the default is Print Active Sheets, and the chart will print as a full-page chart.

Quick Concepts

1. Why should you not include aggregates, such as totals or averages, along with individual data points in a chart? *p. 535*

2. Describe the purpose of each of these chart types: (a) column, (b) bar, (c) line, (d) pie, and (e) combo. *p. 536*

3. How can you use Quick Analysis to create a chart? *p. 536*

4. How do you decide whether to move a chart within the worksheet where you created it or move it to a chart sheet? *p. 548*

1 Chart Basics

Doug Demers, your assistant, gathered data about seven computer-related jobs from the *Occupational Outlook Handbook* online. He organized the data into a structured worksheet that contains the job titles, the number of jobs in 2010, the projected number of jobs by 2020, and other data. Now you are ready to transform the data into visually appealing charts.

STEP 1 ›› CREATE A CLUSTERED COLUMN CHART

You want to compare the number of jobs in 2010 to the projected number of jobs in 2020 for all seven computer-related professions that Doug entered into the worksheet. You decide to create a clustered column chart to depict this data. After you create this chart, you will move it to its own chart sheet. You will format the charts in Hands-On Exercise 2. Refer to Figure 3.21 as you complete Step 1.

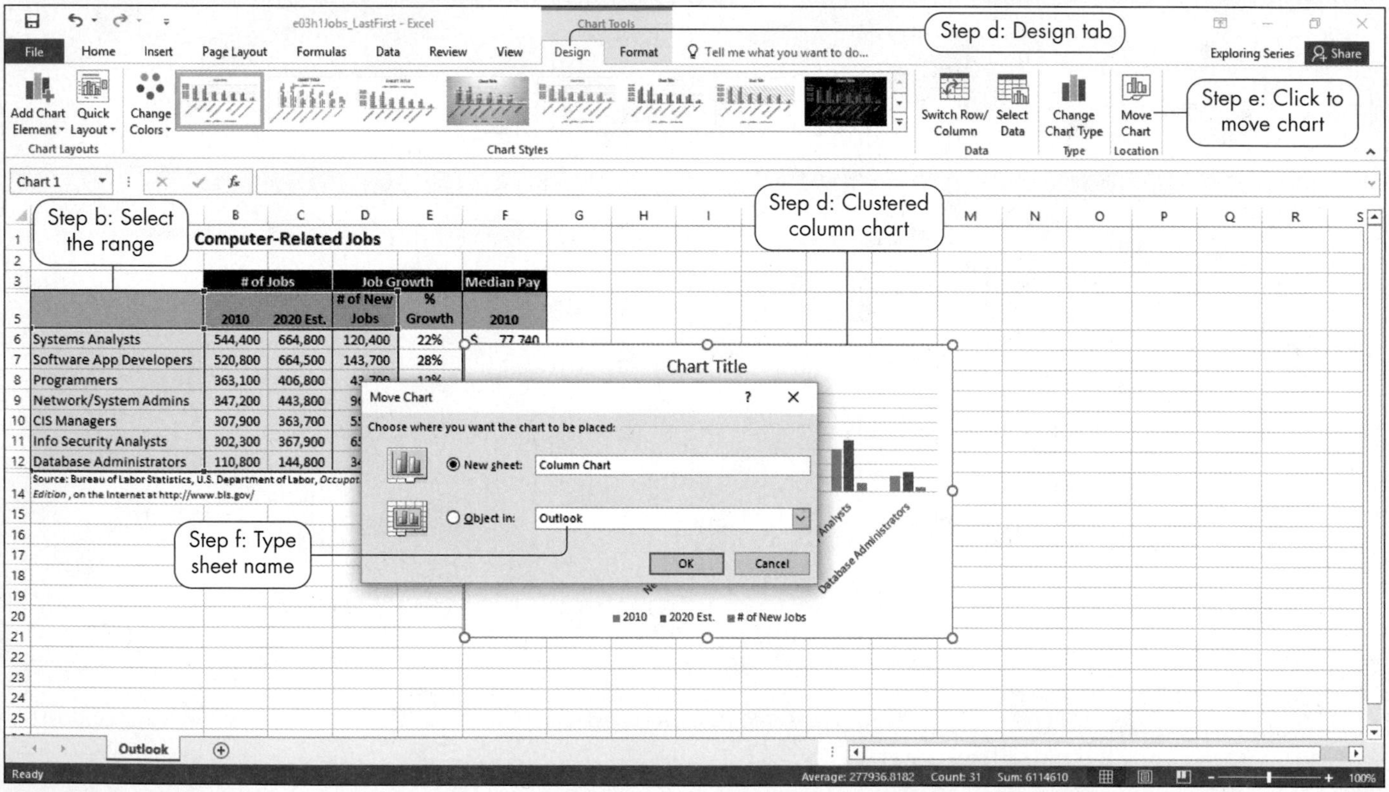

FIGURE 3.21 Clustered Column Chart

    a. Open *e03h1Jobs* and save it as **e03h1Jobs_LastFirst**.

> **TROUBLESHOOTING:** If you make any major mistakes in this exercise, you can close the file, open *e03h1Jobs* again, and then start this exercise over.

b. Select the **range A5:D12**.

You selected the job titles, the number of jobs in 2010, the projected number of jobs in 2020, and the number of new jobs. Because you are selecting three data series (three columns of numerical data), you must also select the column headings on row 5.

c. Click **Quick Analysis** at the bottom-right corner of the selected range and click **Charts**.

The Quick Analysis gallery displays recommended charts based on the selected range.

d. Point to **Clustered Column** (the third thumbnail in the Charts gallery) to see a preview of what the chart would look like and click **Clustered Column**.

Excel inserts a clustered column chart based on the selected data. The Design tab displays on the Ribbon while the chart is selected.

e. Click **Move Chart** in the Location group.

The Move Chart dialog box opens for you to specify where to move the chart.

f. Click **New sheet**, type **Column Chart**, and then click **OK**. Save the workbook.

Excel moves the clustered column chart to a new sheet called Column Chart.

STEP 2 ›› CREATE A BAR CHART

You want to create a bar chart to depict the number of jobs in 2010 and the number of new jobs that will be created by 2020. Finally, you want to change the chart to a stacked bar chart to show the total jobs in 2020 based on the number of jobs in 2010 and the number of new jobs. Refer to Figure 3.22 as you complete Step 2.

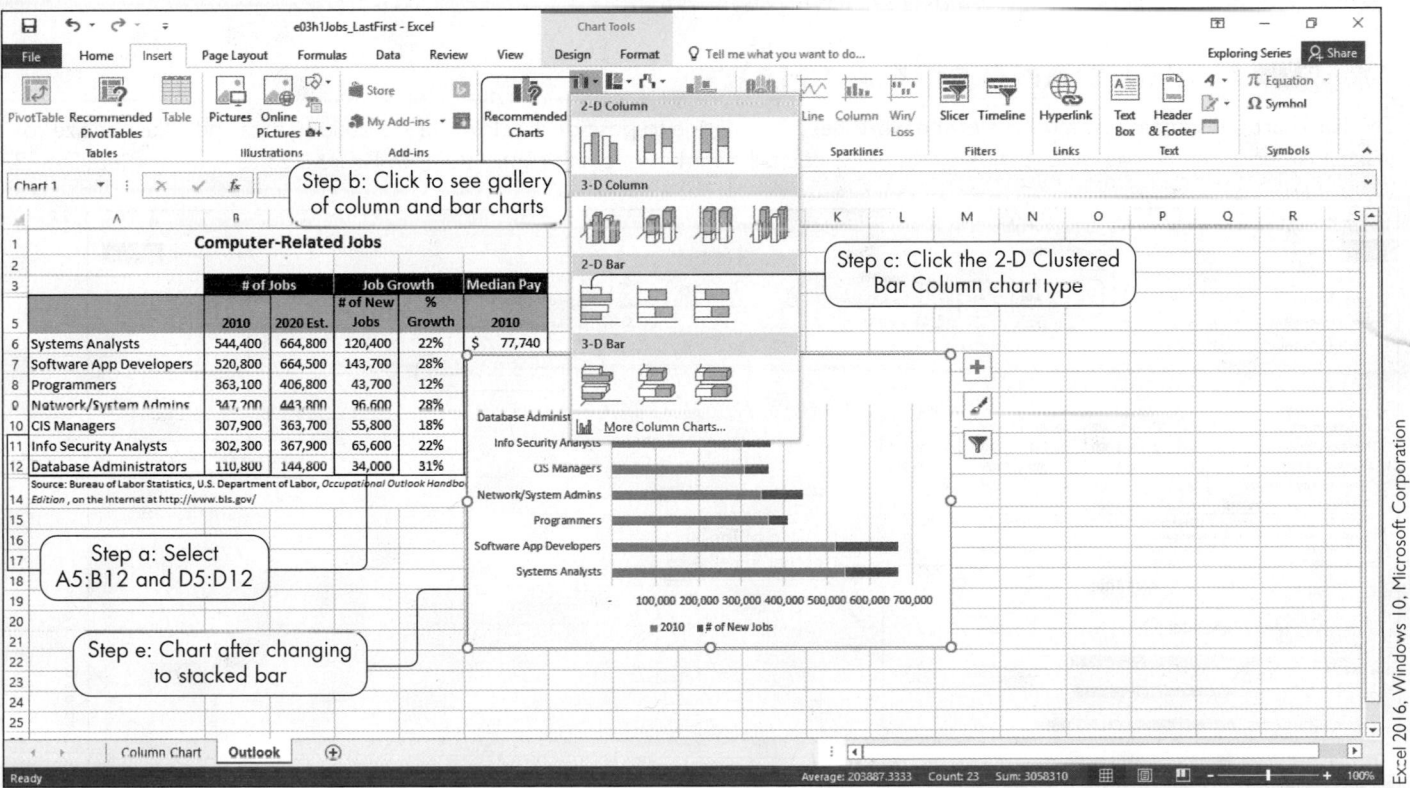

FIGURE 3.22 Bar Chart

a. Click the **Outlook sheet tab**, select the **range A5:B12**, press and hold **Ctrl**, and then select the **range D5:D12**.

You used Ctrl to select nonadjacent ranges: the job title labels, the number of jobs in 2010, and the number of new jobs.

> **TIP: PARALLEL RANGES**
>
> Nonadjacent ranges should be parallel so that the legend will correctly reflect the data series. This means that each range should contain the same number of related cells. For example, A5:A12, B5:B12, and D5:D12 are parallel ranges. Even though cell A5 is blank, you must select it to have a parallel range with the other two selected ranges that include cells on row 5.

b. Click the **Insert tab** and click **Insert Column or Bar Chart** in the Charts group.

The gallery shows both column and bar chart thumbnails.

c. Click **Clustered Bar** in the 2-D Bar section to create a clustered bar chart.

Excel inserts the clustered bar chart in the worksheet.

d. Click **Change Chart Type** in the Type group on the Design tab.

The Change Chart Type dialog box opens. The left side of the dialog box lists all chart types. The top-right side displays thumbnails of various bar charts, and the lower section displays a sample of the selected chart.

e. Click **Stacked Bar** in the top center of the dialog box and click **OK**. Save the workbook.

Excel displays the number of jobs in 2010 in blue and stacks the number of new jobs in orange into one bar per job title. This chart tells the story of how the total projected number of jobs in 2020 is calculated: the number of existing jobs in 2010 (blue) and the number of new jobs (orange).

STEP 3 ❯❯ MOVE AND SIZE A CHART

The bar chart is displayed in the middle of the worksheet. You decide to position it below the job outlook data and adjust its size to make it larger so that it is as wide as the dataset and a little taller for better proportions. Refer to Figure 3.23 as you complete Step 3.

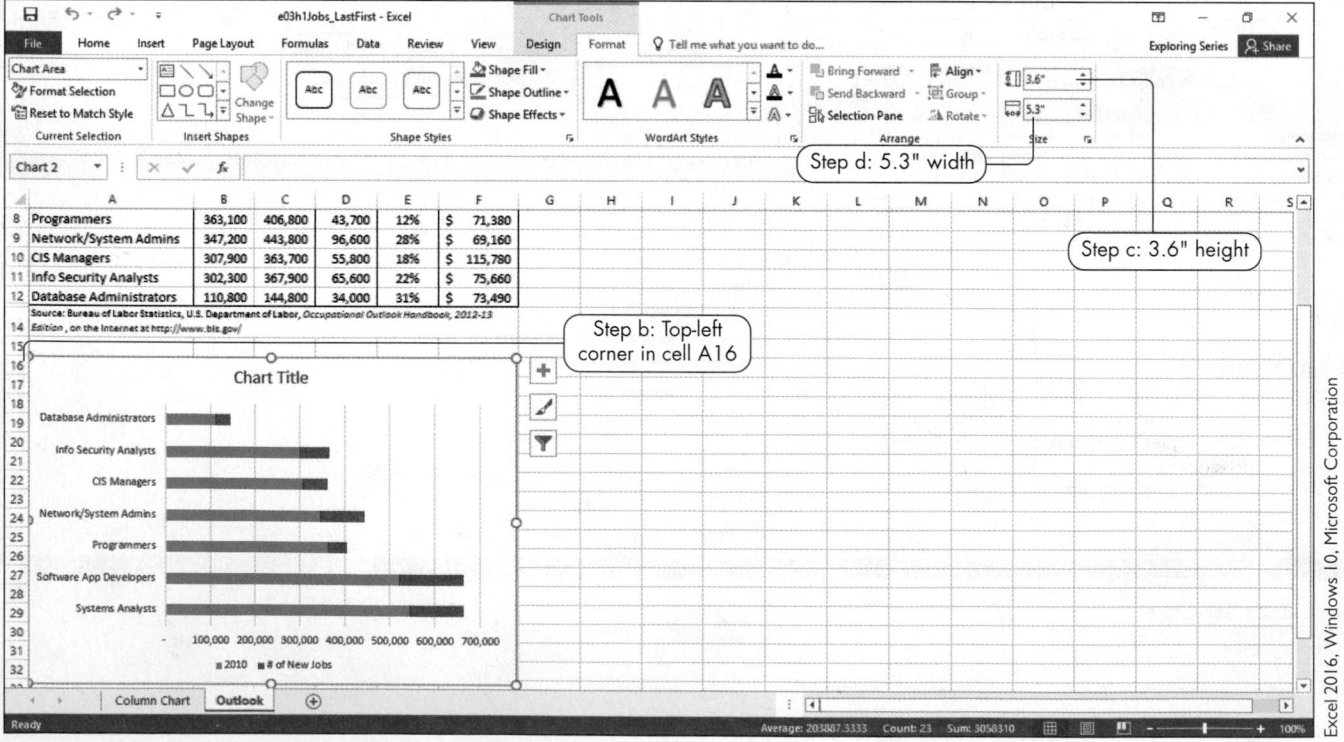

FIGURE 3.23 Stacked Bar Chart Moved and Sized

a. Point to an empty part of the chart area.

The pointer displays a four-headed arrow with the regular white arrowhead, and the Chart Area ScreenTip displays.

> **TROUBLESHOOTING:** Make sure you see the Chart Area ScreenTip as you perform Step b. If you move the pointer to another chart element—such as the legend—you will move or size that element instead of moving the entire chart.

b. Drag the chart so that the top-left corner of the chart appears in **cell A16**.

You positioned the chart below the worksheet data.

c. Click the **Format tab**, select the value in the **Shape Height box**, type **3.6**, and then press **Enter**.

The chart is now 3.6" tall.

d. Select the value in the **Shape Width box**, type **5.3**, and then press **Enter**. Save the workbook.

The chart is now 5.3" wide.

STEP 4 ›› CREATE A PIE CHART

You decide to create a pie chart that depicts the percentage of new jobs by job title calculated from the total number of new jobs created for the seven job titles Doug researched. After creating the pie chart, you will move it to its own sheet. Refer to Figure 3.24 as you complete Step 4.

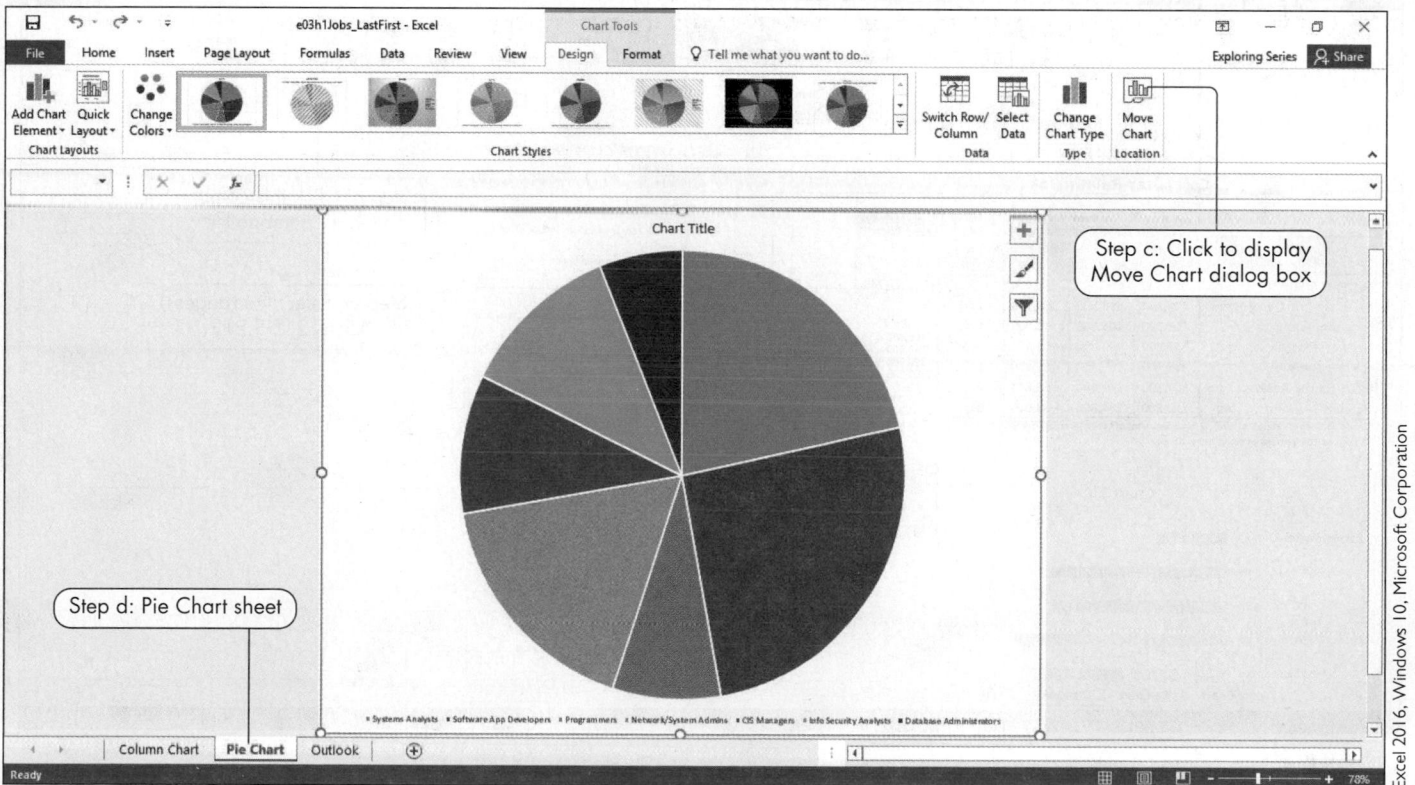

FIGURE 3.24 Pie Chart

a. Select the **range A6:A12**, press and hold **Ctrl**, then select the **range D6:D12**.

> **TROUBLESHOOTING:** Do not select cells A5 and D5 this time because you are creating a pie chart. When creating a chart from a single data series (e.g., # of New Jobs), you do not need to select the column headings.

b. Click the **Insert tab**, click **Insert Pie or Doughnut Chart** in the Charts group, and then select **Pie** in the 2-D Pie group on the gallery.

The pie chart displays in the worksheet.

c. Click **Move Chart** in the Location group on the Design tab.

The Move Chart dialog box opens.

d. Click **New sheet**, type **Pie Chart**, and then click **OK**. Save the workbook.

Excel creates a new sheet called Pie Chart. The pie chart is the only object on that sheet.

STEP 5 ›› CREATE A COMBO CHART

You want to create a combo chart that shows the number of new jobs in columns and the percentage of new jobs created in a line on the secondary axis. Although the number of new jobs may appear low as represented by the smallest column (such as 34,000 new database administrators), the actual percentage of new jobs created between 2010 and 2020 may be significant as represented by the steep incline of the orange line (such as 31% growth for database administrators). Refer to Figure 3.25 as you complete Step 5.

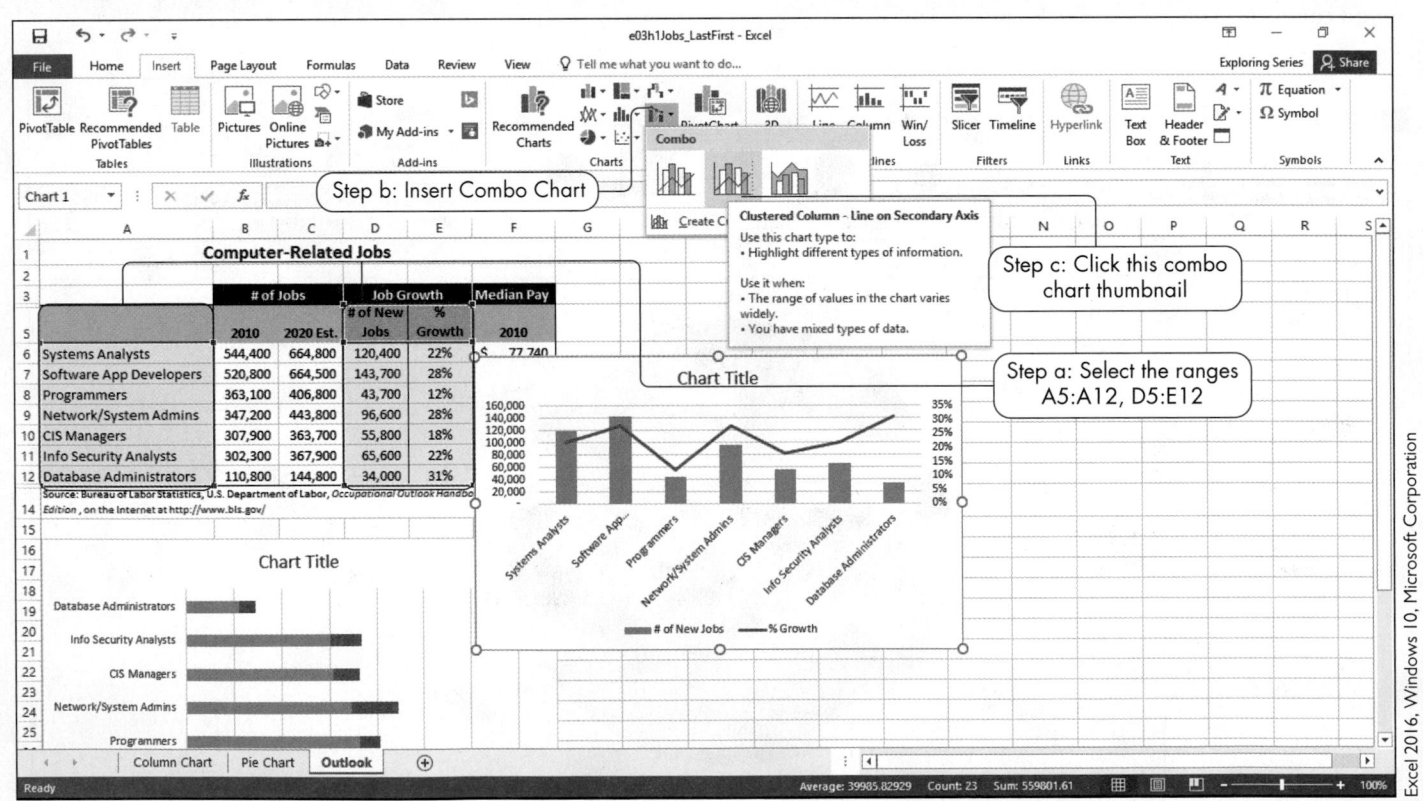

FIGURE 3.25 Combo Chart

a. Click the **Outlook sheet tab**, select the **range A5:A12**, press and hold **Ctrl**, then select the **range D5:E12**.

b. Click the **Insert tab** and click **Insert Combo Chart** in the Charts group.

The Combo Chart gallery of thumbnails displays.

c. Click the **Clustered Column – Line on Secondary Axis thumbnail**, which is the middle thumbnail.

Excel creates a combo chart based on the thumbnail you selected. The number of new jobs displays in blue columns, and the percentage growth displays as an orange line.

d. Click **Move Chart** in the Location group on the Design tab, click **New sheet**, type **Combo Chart**, and then click **OK**.

e. Save the workbook. Keep the workbook open if you plan to continue with the next Hands-On Exercise. If not, close the workbook, and exit Excel.

Chart Elements

After creating a chart, you should add appropriate chart elements. A ***chart element*** is a component that completes or helps clarify the chart. Some chart elements, such as chart titles, should be included in every chart. Other elements are optional. Table 3.4 describes the chart elements, and Figure 3.26 illustrates several chart elements.

TABLE 3.4	Chart Elements
Element	**Description**
Axis title	Label that describes the category or value axes. Display axis titles, such as In Millions of Dollars or Top 7 Computer Job Titles, to clarify the axes. Axis titles are not displayed by default.
Chart title	Label that describes the entire chart. It should reflect the purpose of the chart. For example, Houses Sold is too generic, but Houses Sold in Seattle in 2018 indicates the what (Houses), the where (Seattle), and the when (2018). The default text is Chart Title.
Data label	Descriptive label that shows the exact value or name of a data point. Data labels are not displayed by default.
Data table	A grid that contains the data source values and labels. If you embed a chart on the same worksheet as the data source, you might not need to include a data table. Only add a data table with a chart that is on a chart sheet.
Error bars	Visuals that indicate the standard error amount, a percentage, or a standard deviation for a data point or marker. Error bars are not displayed by default.
Gridlines	Horizontal or vertical lines that display in the plot area, designed to help people identify the values plotted by the visual elements, such as a column.
Legend	A key that identifies the color, gradient, picture, texture, or pattern assigned to each data series. The legend is displayed by default for some chart types.
Trendline	A line that depicts trends or helps forecast future data, such as estimating future sales or number of births in a region. Add a trendline to column, bar, line, stock, scatter, and bubble charts. Excel will analyze the current trends and display a line indicating future values based on those trends.

Pearson Education, Inc.

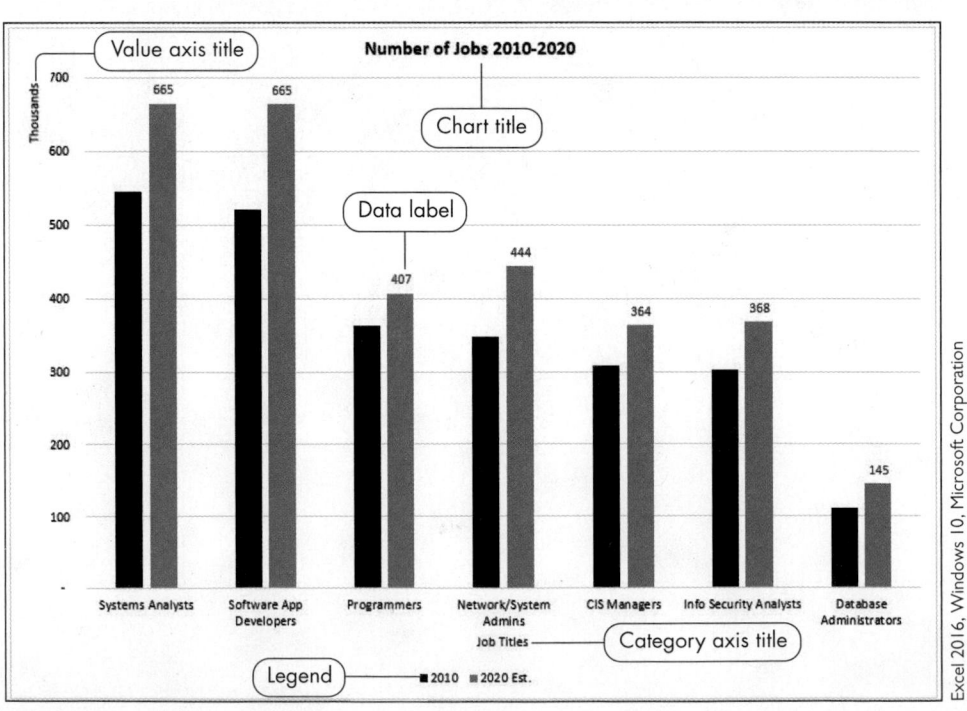

FIGURE 3.26 Chart Elements

Excel 2016, Windows 10, Microsoft Corporation

In this section, you will learn how to add, edit, and format chart elements. Specifically, you will learn how to type a chart title, add axis titles, add data labels, and position the legend. Furthermore, you will learn how to format these elements as well as format axes, position the legend, and add gridlines. Finally, you will learn how to format the chart area, plot area, data series, and a data point.

Adding, Editing, and Formatting Chart Elements

After you create a chart, you usually need to add elements to provide labels to describe the chart. Adding descriptive text for labels provides information for the reader to comprehend the chart without knowing or seeing the underlying data. When you create a chart, one or more elements may display by default. For example, when you created the charts in Hands-On Exercise 1, Excel displayed a placeholder for the chart title and displayed a legend so that you know which color represents each data series.

When a chart is selected, three icons display to the right of the chart: Chart Elements, Chart Styles, and Chart Filters. In addition, the Design tab contains the Chart Layouts group that allows you to add and customize chart elements and change the layout of the chart.

When you point to a chart element, Excel displays a ScreenTip with the name of that element. To select a chart element, click it when you see the ScreenTip, or click the Format tab, click the Chart Elements arrow in the Current Selection group, and select the element from the list.

Edit, Format, and Position the Chart Title

STEP 1 ❯❯ Excel includes the placeholder text *Chart Title* above the chart. You should replace that text with a descriptive title. In addition, you might want to format the chart title by applying bold and changing the font, font size, font color, and fill color.

To edit and format the chart title, complete the following steps:

1. Select the chart title.
2. Type the text you want to appear in the title and press Enter.
3. Click the Home tab.
4. Apply the desired font formatting, such as increasing the font size and applying bold.
5. Click the chart to deselect the chart title.

TIP: FONT COLOR
The default font color for the chart title, axes, axes titles, and legend is Black, Text 1, Lighter 35%. If you want these elements to stand out, change the color to Black, Text 1 or another solid color.

By default, the chart title displays centered above the plot area. Although this is a standard location for the chart, you might want to position it elsewhere.

To change the position of the chart title, complete the following steps:

1. Select the chart title and click Chart Elements to the right of the chart.
2. Point to the Chart Title and click the triangle on the right side of the menu option, Chart Title (see Figure 3.27).
3. Select one of the options:
   - Above Chart: Centers the title above the plot area, decreasing the plot area size to make room for the chart title.
   - Centered Overlay: Centers the chart title horizontally without resizing the plot area; the title displays over the top of the plot area.
   - More Options: Opens the Format Chart Title task pane to apply fill, border, and alignment settings. A **task pane** is a window of options to format and customize chart elements. The task pane name and options change based on the selected chart element. For example, when you double-click the chart title, the Format Chart Title task pane displays.
4. Click Chart Elements to close the menu.

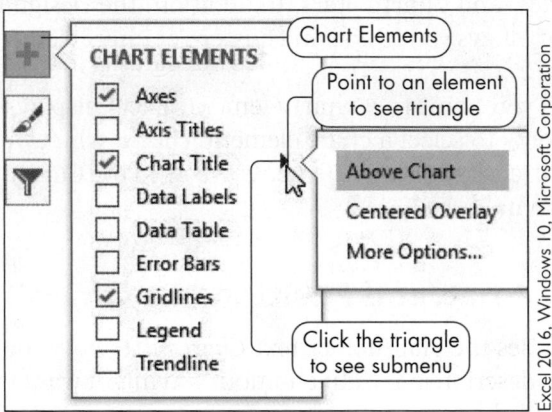

FIGURE 3.27 Chart Elements List

TIP: LINKING A CHART TITLE OR AN AXIS TITLE TO A CELL
Instead of typing text directly in the Chart Title or Axis Title placeholder, you can link the title to a label in a cell. Click the Chart Title or Axis Title placeholder, type = in the Formula Bar, click the cell containing the label you want for the title, and then press Enter. Excel will enter the sheet name and cell reference, such as =Outlook!$A$1, in the Formula Bar. If you change the worksheet label, Excel will also change the title in the chart.

Add, Format, and Position Axis Titles

STEP 2 ›› Axis titles are helpful to provide more clarity about the value or category axis. Axis titles also help you conform to ADA compliance requirements. For example, if the values are abbreviated as 7 instead of 7,000,000 you should indicate the unit of measurement on the value axis as In Millions. You might want to further clarify the labels on the category axis by providing a category axis title, such as Job Titles.

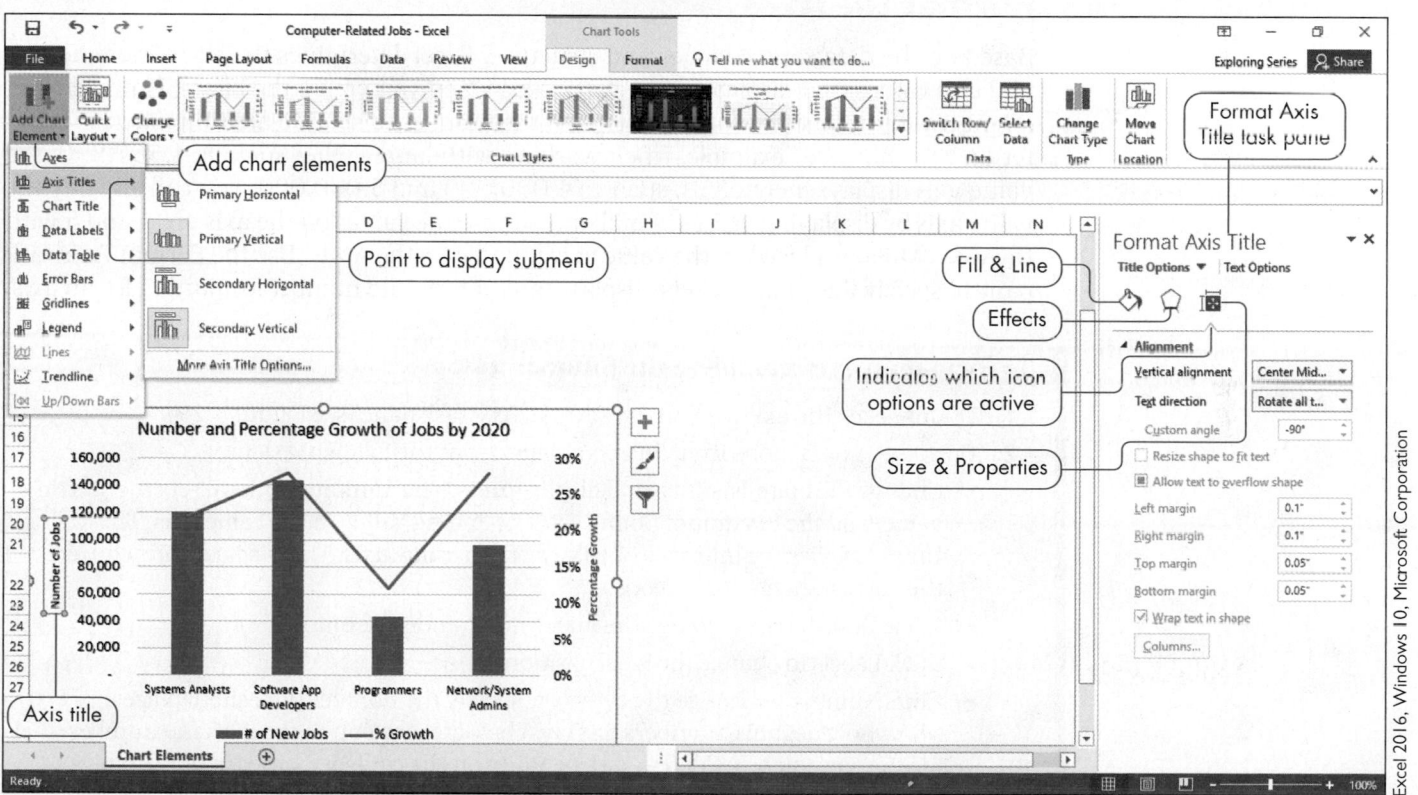

FIGURE 3.28 Chart Elements Menu and Format Axis Title Task Pane

The horizontal axis title displays below the category labels, and the rotated vertical axis title displays on the left side of the value axis. After including an axis title, click the title, type the text for the title, and then press Enter similarly to editing text for a chart title. You might want to apply font formatting (such as font size and color) to the axis titles similarly to formatting a chart title. Use the Format Axis Title task pane to customize and format the axis title.

To position and format the axis title, complete the following:

1. Double-click the axis title to open the Format Axis Title task pane (refer to Figure 3.28). Each task pane has categories, such as Title Options and Text Options. Below these categories are icons, such as Fill & Line, Effects, and Size & Properties.

2. Click Title Options and click the Size & Properties icon. The options in the task pane change to display options related to the icon you click. A thin horizontal gray line separates the icons from the options. The line contains a partial triangle that points to the icon that is active to indicate which options are displayed. Figure 3.28 shows the triangle is pointing to Size & Properties.

3. Change the *Vertical alignment* or *Horizontal alignment* option to the desired position.

4. Click other icons, such as Fill & Line, and select the desired options.

5. Close the Format Axis Title task pane.

6. Click the Home tab and apply font formatting, such as Font Color.

TIP: REMOVE AN ELEMENT

To remove an element, click Chart Elements and click a check box to deselect the check box. Alternatively, click Add Chart Element in the Chart Layouts group on the Chart Tools Design tab, point to the element name, and then select None. You can also select a chart element and press Delete to remove it.

Format the Axes

Based on the data source values and structure, Excel determines the start, incremental, and end values that display on the value axis when you create the chart. However, you might want to adjust the value axis so that the numbers displayed are simplified or fit better on the chart. For example, when working with large values such as 4,567,890, the value axis displays increments, such as 4,000,000 and 5,000,000. You can simplify the value axis by displaying values in millions, so that the values on the axis are 4 and 5 with the word Millions placed by the value axis to indicate the units. Use the Format Axis task pane to specify the bounds, units, display units, labels, and number formatting for an axis.

To format an axis, complete the following steps:

1. Double-click the axis to open the Format Axis task pane (see Figure 3.29).

2. Click the Axis Options icon, and complete any of the following steps:

   • Change the bounds, units, and display units. The Minimum Bound sets the starting value, and the Maximum Bound sets the ending value on the value axis. The Major Units specifies the intervals of values on the value axis. The Display units converts the values, such as to Millions.

   • Click Tick Marks to change the major and minor tick marks.

   • Click Labels to change the label position.

   • Click Number to change the category, specify the number of decimal places, select how negative numbers display. The Category option specifies the number formatting, such as Currency. Depending on the category, other options may display, such as Decimal places so that you can control the number of decimal places on the value axis.

3. Close the Format Axis task pane.

4. Click the Home tab and apply font formatting, such as Font Color.

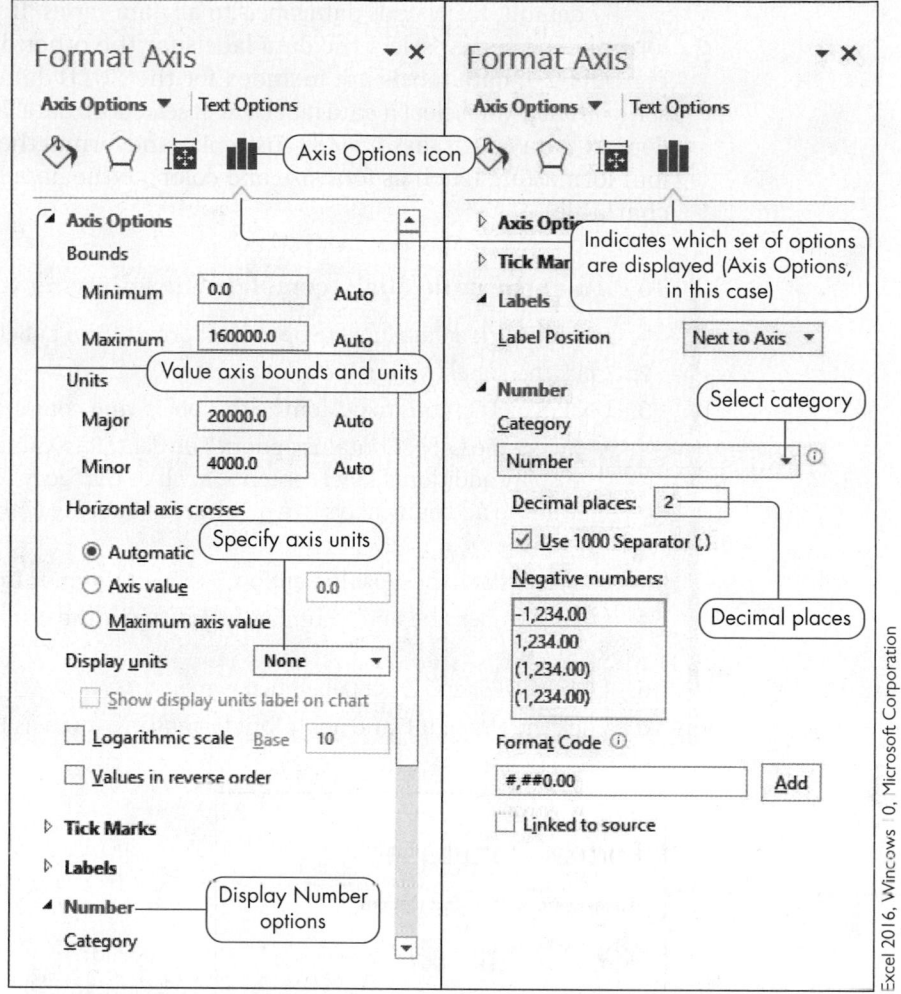

FIGURE 3.29 Format Axis Task Pane

TIP: DISPLAYING OPTIONS WITHIN TASK PANES

A diagonal black triangle next to a category, such as Axis Options, indicates that all of a category's options are displayed (expanded). A triangle with a white fill, such as the one next to Tick Marks, indicates that the category options are not displayed (collapsed).

Add, Position, and Format Data Labels

STEP 3 ▶▶ A data label is descriptive text that shows the exact value or name of a data point. Data labels are useful to indicate specific values for data points you want to emphasize. Typically, you would add data labels only to specific data points, and not all data points. Use either Chart Elements or the Design tab to display data labels.

To add and position data labels, complete the following steps:

1. Select the chart and click Chart Elements to the right of the chart.
2. Click the Data Labels check box to display data labels.
3. Click the arrow to the right of the Data Labels item to select the position, such as Center or Outside End.
4. Click Chart Elements to close the menu.

By default, Excel adds data labels to all data series. If you want to display data labels for only one series, select the data labels for the other data series and press Delete. In Figure 3.26, data labels are included for the 2020 data series but not the 2010 data series. When you select a data label, Excel selects all data labels in that data series. Use the Format Data Labels task pane to customize and format the data labels. You can also apply font formatting (such as font size and color) to the data labels similarly to formatting a chart title.

To format the data labels, complete the following steps:

1. Double-click a data label to open the Format Data Labels task pane (see Figure 3.30).
2. Click the Label Options icon.
3. Click Label Options to customize the labels, and complete any of the following steps:
   - Select the Label Contains option. The default is Value, but you might want to display additional label contents, such as Category Name. For example, you might want to add data labels to a pie chart to indicate both Percentage and Category Names.
   - Select the Label Position option, such as Center or Inside End.
4. Click Number and apply number formatting if the numeric data labels are not formatted.
5. Close the Format Data Labels task pane.
6. Click the Home tab and apply font formatting, such as Font Color.

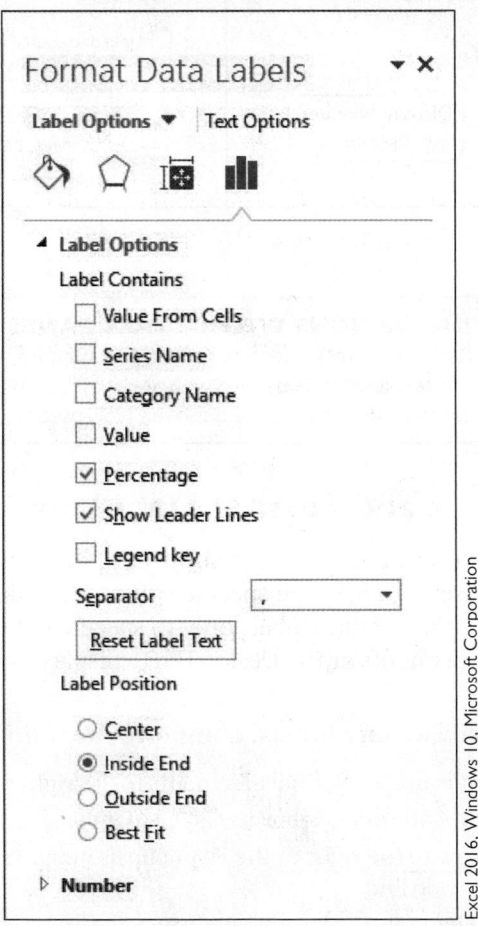

FIGURE 3.30 Format Data Labels Task Pane

Position and Format the Legend

When you create a multiple series chart, the legend displays, providing a key to the color-coded data series. Position the legend to the right, top, bottom, or left of the plot area, similarly to choosing the position for a chart title using Chart Elements. Make sure that the columns, bars, or lines appear proportionate and well balanced after you position the legend. Use the Format Legend task pane to customize and format the legend.

To format the legend, complete the following steps:

1. Double-click the legend to open the Format Legend task pane.
2. Click the Legend Options icon.
3. Select the position of the legend: Top, Bottom, Left, Right, or Top Right.
4. Click the Fill & Line icon, click Border, and set border options if you want to change the border settings for the legend.
5. Close the Format Legend task pane.
6. Click the Home tab and apply font formatting, such as Font Color.

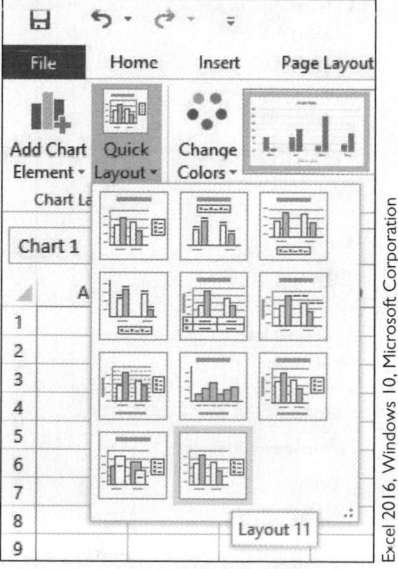

FIGURE 3.31 Quick Layout Gallery

Add and Format Gridlines

Gridlines are horizontal or vertical lines that span across the plot area of the chart to help people identify the values plotted by the visual elements, such as a column. Excel displays horizontal gridlines for column, line, scatter, stock, surface, and bubble charts and vertical gridlines for bar charts. Click either Chart Elements or Add Chart Elements in the Chart Layouts group on the Design tab to add gridlines.

Format gridlines by double-clicking a gridline to open the Format Major Gridlines task pane. You can change the line type, color, and width of the gridlines.

> **TIP: ALTERNATIVE FOR OPENING FORMAT TASK PANES**
> Another way to display a task pane is to right-click the chart element and choose Format <element>, where <element> is the specific chart element. If you do not close a task pane after formatting a particular element, such as gridlines, and then click another chart element, the task pane will change so that you can format that particular chart element.

Format the Chart Area, Plot Area, and Data Series

STEP 4 ›› Apply multiple settings, such as fill colors and borders, at once using the Format task pane for an element. To open a chart element's task pane, double-click the chart element. Figure 3.32 displays the Format Chart Area, Format Plot Area, and Format Data Series task panes with different fill options selected to display the different options that result. All three task panes include the same fill and border elements. For example, you might want to change the fill color of a data series from blue to green. After you select a fill option, such as *Gradient fill*, the remaining options change in the task pane.

FIGURE 3.32 Format Task Panes

Excel 2016, Windows 10, Microsoft Corporation

Format a Data Point

STEP 4 ▶▶ Earlier in this chapter, you learned that a data point reflects a value in a single cell in a worksheet. You can select that single data point in a chart and format it differently from the rest of the data series. Select the data point you want to format, display the Format Data Point task pane, and make the changes you want. For example, you might want to focus a person's attention on a particular slice by separating one or more slices from the rest of the chart in an ***exploded pie chart*** (refer to Figure 3.15).

To format a pie slice data point, complete the following steps:

1. Click within the pie chart, pause, and then click the particular slice you want to format.
2. Right-click the selected pie slice and select Format Data Point to open the Format Data Point task pane.
3. Click the Fill & Line icon and click the desired option (such as Solid fill) in the Fill category.
4. Click the Color arrow and select a color for a solid fill; select a *Preset gradient*, type, color, and other options for a gradient fill; or insert a picture or select a texture for a picture or texture fill.
5. Click the Series Options icon and drag the Point Explosion to the right to explode the selected pie slice, such as to 12% (see Figure 3.33).
6. Close the Format Data Point task pane.

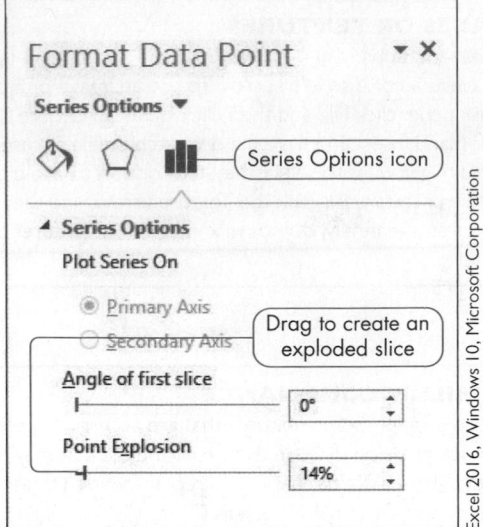

FIGURE 3.33 Format Data Point Task Pane

TIP: DRAG TO EXPLODE A PIE SLICE

Another way to explode a pie slice is to select the specific slice and then drag it away from the pie.

Use the Chart Tools Format Tab

The Format tab contains options to select a chart element, insert shapes, apply shape styles, apply WordArt styles, arrange objects, and specify the size of an object. Table 3.5 lists and describes the groups on the Format tab.

TABLE 3.5	Chart Tools Format Tab
Group	**Description**
Current Selection	Selects a chart element, displays the task pane to format the selected element, and clears custom formatting of the selected element.
Insert Shapes	Inserts a variety of shapes in a chart.
Shape Styles	Specifies a shape style, fill color, outline color, and shape effect.
WordArt Styles	Adds artistic style, text fill, and text effects to an object.
Arrange	Brings an object forward or backward to layer multiple objects; aligns, groups, and rotates objects.
Size	Adjusts the height and width of the selected object.

Quick Concepts

5. List at least four types of appropriate labels that describe chart elements. What types of things can you do to customize these labels? ***p. 558***

6. What is the purpose of exploding a slice on a pie chart? ***p. 567***

7. What are some of the fill options you can apply to a chart area or a plot area? ***p. 566***

Hands-On Exercises

Skills covered: Edit and Format Chart Titles • Add and Format Axes Titles • Format Axes • Add, Position, and Format Data Labels • Format the Chart Area • Format a Data Point

2 Chart Elements

You want to enhance the computer job column, bar, and pie charts by adding some chart elements. In particular, you will enter a descriptive chart title for each chart, add and format axis titles for the bar chart, add and format data labels for the pie chart, and change fill colors in the pie chart.

STEP 1 ›› EDIT AND FORMAT CHART TITLES

When you created the column, bar, and pie charts in Hands-On Exercise 1, Excel displayed *Chart Title* at the top of each chart. You will add a title that appropriately describes each chart. In addition, you want to format the chart titles by applying bold and enlarging the font sizes. Refer to Figure 3.34 as you complete Step 1.

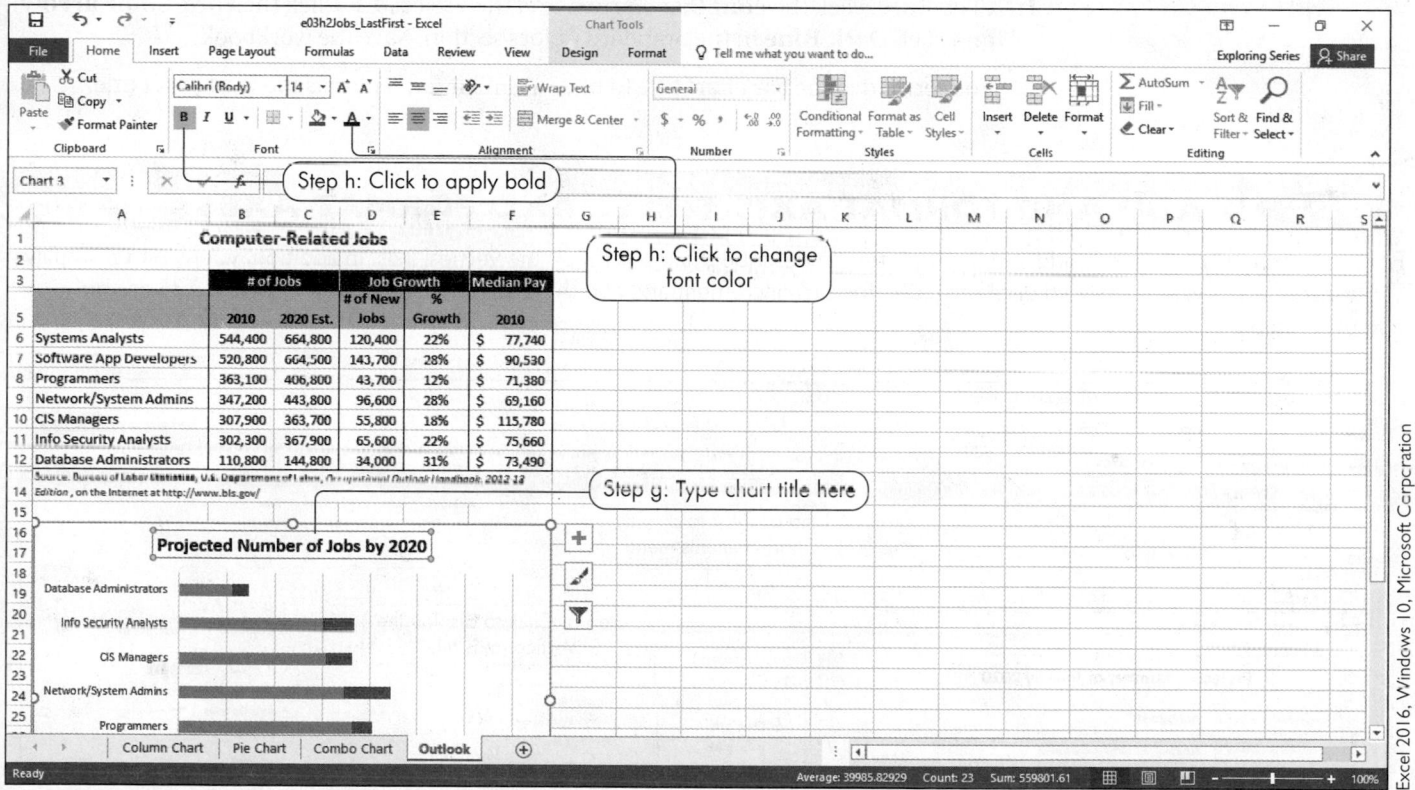

FIGURE 3.34 Formatted Chart Title

a. Open *e03h1Jobs_LastFirst* if you closed it at the end of the Hands-On Exercise 1, and save it as **e03h2Jobs_LastFirst**, changing h1 to h2.

b. Make sure the Combo Chart sheet is the active sheet, select the **Chart Title** placeholder, type **Number of New Computer-Related Jobs by 2020**, and then press **Enter**.

As you type a chart title, Excel displays the text in the Formula Bar. The text does not appear in the chart title until after you press Enter.

> **TROUBLESHOOTING:** If you double-click a title and type directly into the title placeholder, do not press Enter after typing the new title. Doing so will add a blank line.

c. Click the **Home tab**, click **Bold**, click the **Font Color arrow**, and then select **Black, Text 1**.

You applied font formats so that the chart title stands out.

d. Click the **Pie Chart sheet tab**, select the **Chart Title** placeholder, type **New Computer-Related Jobs by 2020**, and then press **Enter**.

Excel displays the text you typed for the chart title.

e. Click the **Home tab**, click **Bold**, click the **Font Size arrow** and select **18**, and then click the **Font Color arrow** and select **Black, Text 1**.

You formatted the pie chart title so that it stands out.

f. Click the **Column Chart sheet tab**, select the **Chart Title** placeholder, type **Number of Computer-Related Jobs 2010 and 2020**, and then press **Enter**. Click **Bold**, click the **Font Size arrow**, and then select **18**. Click the **Font Color arrow** and click **Black, Text 1** font color to the chart title.

g. Click the **Outlook sheet tab**, select the **Chart Title** placeholder, type **Projected Number of Jobs by 2020**, and then press **Enter**.

h. Click **Bold**, click the **Font Size arrow**, and then select **14**. Click the **Font Color arrow** and click **Dark Blue** in the Standard Colors section. Save the workbook.

You formatted the bar chart title to have a similar font color as the worksheet title.

STEP 2 》》 ADD AND FORMAT AXIS TITLES AND FORMAT AXES

For the bar chart, you want to add and format a title to describe the job titles on the vertical axis. In addition, you want to simplify the horizontal axis values to avoid displaying ,000 for each increment and add the title *Thousands*. Refer to Figure 3.35 as you complete Step 2.

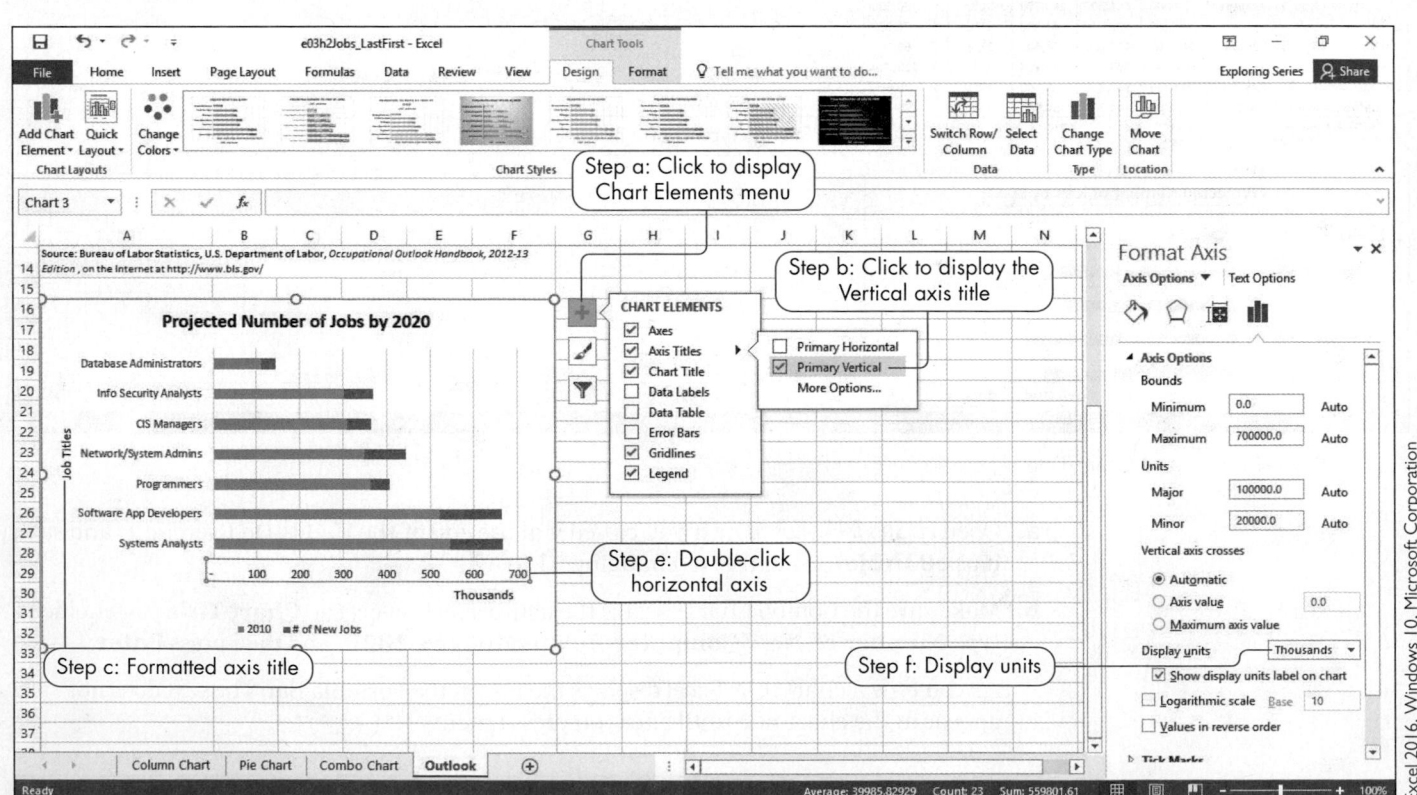

FIGURE 3.35 Formatted Axis Titles and Axes

a. Ensure that the bar chart is selected in the Outlook worksheet and click **Chart Elements** to the right of the chart.

Excel displays the Chart Elements menu.

b. Point to **Axis Titles**, click the **Axis Titles arrow**, and then click the **Primary Vertical check box** to select it. Close the menu.

Excel displays Axis Title on the left side of the vertical axis.

c. Ensure that the Axis Title placeholder is selected, type **Job Titles**, and then press **Enter**.

d. Click **Font Color** to apply the default Dark Blue font color to the selected axis title.

e. Point to the **horizontal axis**. When you see the ScreenTip, Horizontal (Value) Axis, double-click the values on the horizontal axis.

The Format Axis task pane opens for you to format the value axis.

f. Click the **Display units arrow** and select **Thousands**.

> **TROUBLESHOOTING:** If the Display units is not shown, click the Axis Options icon, and click Axis Options to display the options.

The axis now displays values such as 700 instead of 700,000. The title Thousands displays in the bottom-right corner of the horizontal axis.

g. Click the **Home tab**, select the title **Thousands**, and then apply **Dark Blue font color** in the Font group. Close the Format Axis task pane. Save the workbook.

STEP 3 ›› ADD AND FORMAT DATA LABELS

The pie chart includes a legend to identify which color represents each computer-related job; however, it does not include numerical labels to help you interpret what percentage of all computer-related jobs will be hired for each position. You want to insert and format percentage value labels. Refer to Figure 3.36 as you complete Step 3.

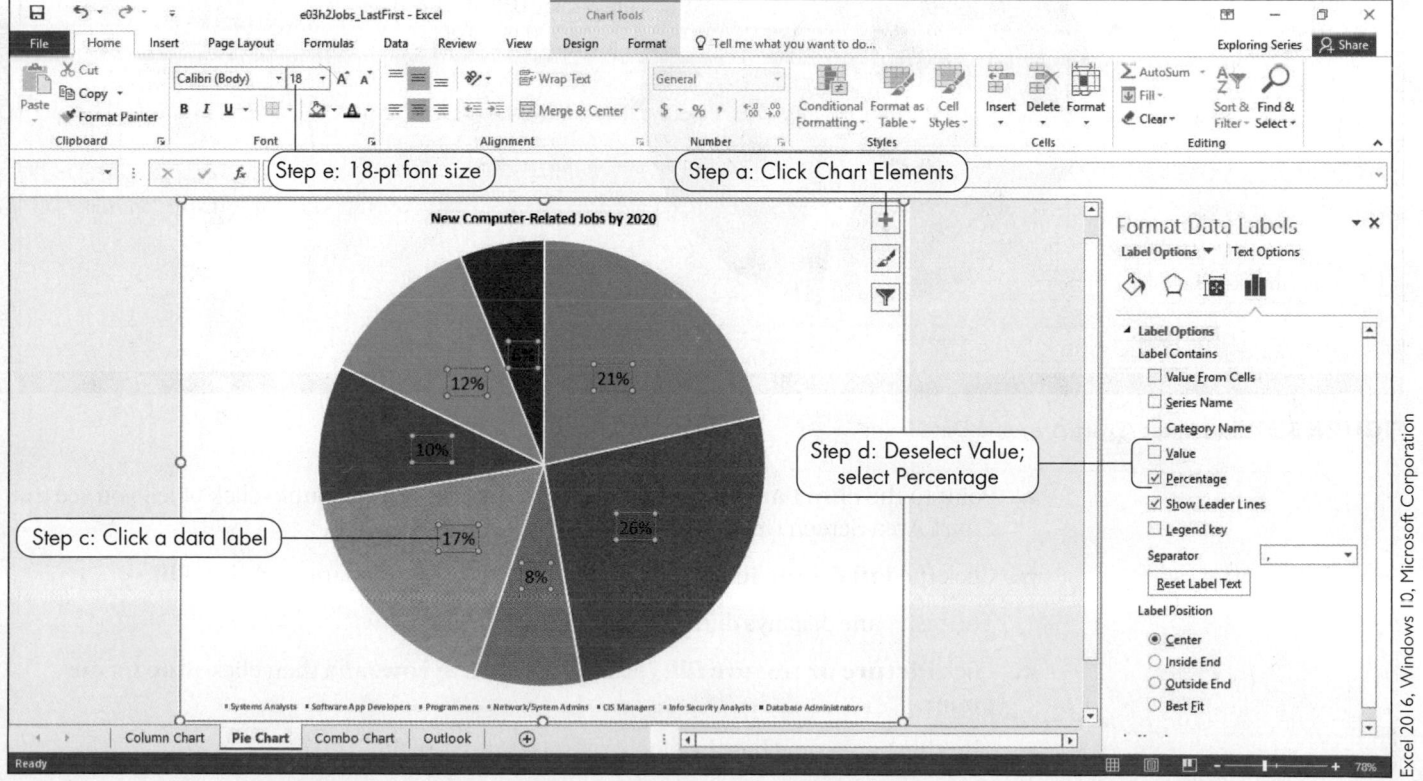

FIGURE 3.36 Formatted Data Labels

a. Click the **Pie Chart sheet tab** and click **Chart Elements**.

b. Click the **Data Labels arrow** and select **Center**. Close the Chart Elements menu.

You added data labels to the pie slices. The default data labels show the number of new jobs in the pie slices.

c. Right-click one of the data labels and select **Format Data Labels** to open the Format Data Label task pane.

d. Click **Label Options**, click the **Percentage check box** to select it, and then click the **Value check box** to deselect it. Close the Format Data Labels task pane.

Typically, pie chart data labels show percentages instead of values.

e. Change the font size to **18** to make the data labels larger. Save the workbook.

STEP 4 ›› **FORMAT THE CHART AREA AND A DATA POINT**

You want to apply a texture fill to the chart area and change the fill colors for the Software Apps Developers and the Database Administrators slices. Refer to Figure 3.37 as you complete Step 4.

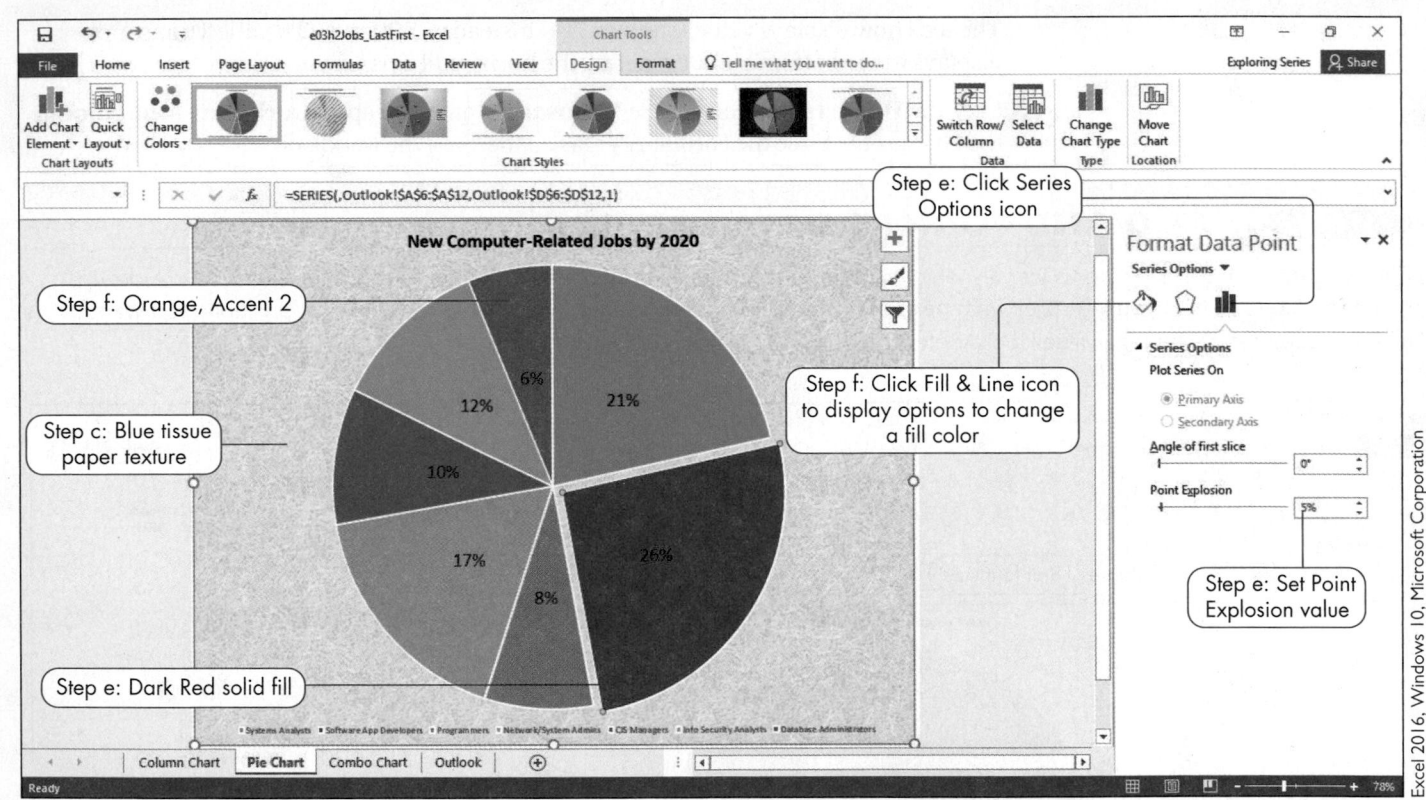

FIGURE 3.37 Formatted Chart Area and Data Point

a. Point to the **chart area** (the white space in the chart) and double-click when you see the Chart Area ScreenTip.

b. Click the **Fill & Line icon** in the Format Chart Area task pane and click **Fill**.

The task pane displays different fill options.

c. Click **Picture or texture fill**, click the **Texture arrow**, and then click **Blue tissue paper**.

The chart area now has the blue tissue paper texture fill.

d. Click the **26% Orange, Accent 2 slice**, pause, and then click the **26% Orange, Accent 2 slice** again to select just that data point (slice).

The first click selects all slices of the pie. The second click selects only the Software App Developers slice so that you can format that data point. Because you did not close the Format Chart Area task pane after Step c, Excel changes to the Format Data Point task pane when you select a data point.

e. Complete the following steps to format the selected data point:

- Click the **Fill & Line icon**, click **Solid fill**, click the **Color arrow**, and then click **Dark Red** in the Standard Colors section.
- Click the **Series Options icon** in the Format Data Point task pane and click the **Point Explosion increment** to **5%**.

You changed the fill color and exploded the slice for the selected data point.

f. Click the **6% Database Administrators slice**, click the **Fill & Line icon** in the Format Data Point task pane, click **Solid fill**, click the **Color arrow**, and then click **Orange, Accent 2**. Close the Format Data Point task pane.

The new color for the Database Administrators slice makes it easier to read the percentage data label.

g. Save the workbook. Keep the workbook open if you plan to continue with the next Hands-On Exercise. If not, close the workbook and exit Excel.

Chart Design and Sparklines

After you add and format chart elements, you might want to experiment with other features to enhance a chart. The Chart Tools Design tab contains two other groups: Chart Styles and Data. These groups enable you to apply a different style or color scheme to a chart or manipulate the data that are used to build a chart. You can also click Chart Styles and Chart Filters to the right of a chart to change the design of a chart.

At times, you might want to insert small visual chart-like images within worksheet cells to illustrate smaller data series rather than a large chart to illustrate several data points. Excel enables you to create small chart-like images in close proximity to individual data points to help you visualize the data.

In this section, you will learn how to apply chart styles and colors, filter chart data, and insert and customize miniature charts (sparklines) within individual cells.

Applying a Chart Style and Colors

STEP 1 ❯❯ A *chart style* is a collection of formatting that controls the color of the chart area, plot area, and data series. Styles, such as flat, 3-D, or beveled, also affect the look of the data series. Figure 3.38 shows the options when you click Chart Styles to the right of the chart, and Figure 3.39 shows the Chart Styles gallery that displays when you click Chart Styles on the Design tab. The styles in the Chart Styles gallery reflect what is available for the currently selected chart, such as a pie chart. If you select a different type of chart, the gallery will display styles for that particular type of chart.

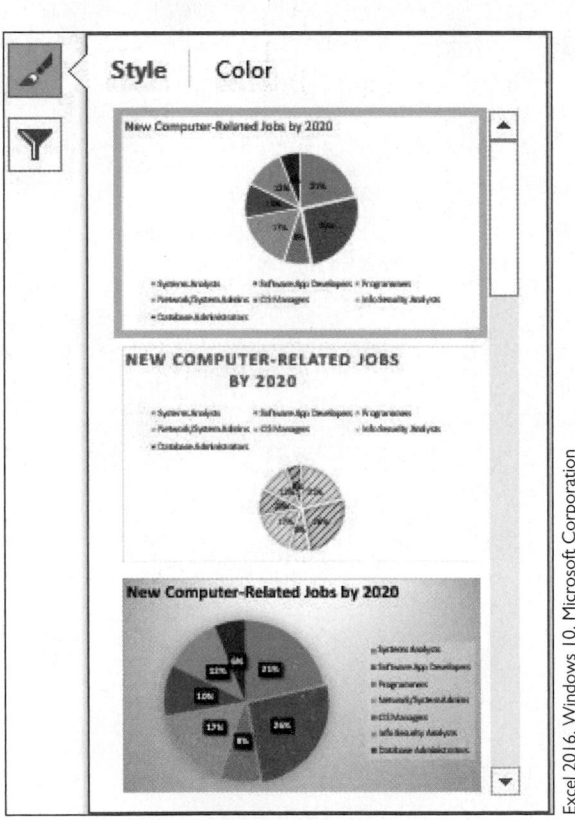

FIGURE 3.38 Chart Styles

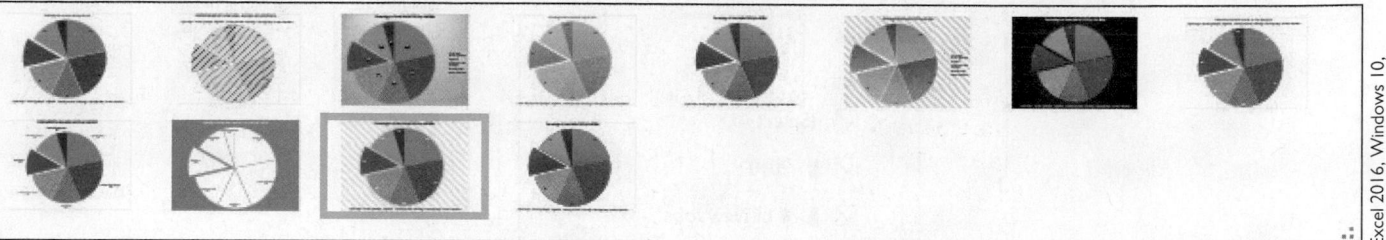

Excel 2016, Windows 10, Microsoft Corporation

FIGURE 3.39 Chart Styles Gallery

> **TIP: CHOOSING APPROPRIATE CHART STYLES**
> When choosing a chart style, make sure the style complements the chart data and is easy to read. Also, consider whether you will display the chart onscreen in a presentation or print the chart. If you will display the chart in a presentation, consider selecting a style with a black background.

To change the color scheme of the chart, complete the following steps:

1. Click Chart Styles to the right of the chart.
2. Click Color or click Change Colors in the Chart Styles group on the Design tab.
3. Select from the Colorful and Monochromatic sections.

Modifying the Data Source

The data source is the range of worksheet cells that are used to construct a chart. Although you should select the data source carefully before creating a chart, you may decide to alter that data source after you create and format the chart. The Data group on the Design tab is useful for adjusting the data source. Furthermore, you can apply filters to display or hide a data series without adjusting the entire data source.

Apply Chart Filters

 A ***chart filter*** controls which data series and categories are visible in a chart. By default, all the data you selected to create the chart are used to construct the data series and categories. However, you can apply a chart filter to focus on particular data. For example, you might want to focus on just one job title at a time. Click Chart Filters to the right of the chart to display the options (see Figure 3.40). A check mark indicates the data series or categories currently displayed in the chart. Click a check box to deselect or hide a data series or a category.

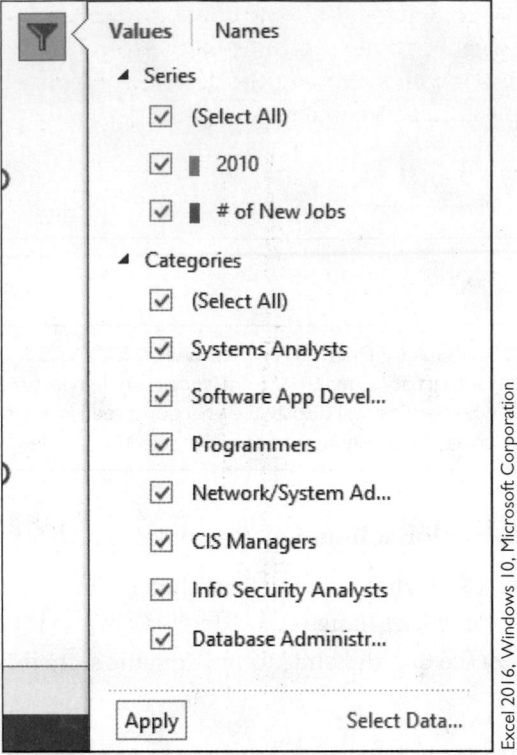

FIGURE 3.40 Chart Filter Options

Click Select Data in the Data group on the Design tab to open the Select Data Source dialog box (see Figure 3.41). This dialog box is another way to filter which categories and data series are visible in your chart. Furthermore, this dialog box enables you to change the chart data range, as well as add, edit, or remove data that is being used to create the chart. For example, you might want to add another data series or remove an existing data series from the chart.

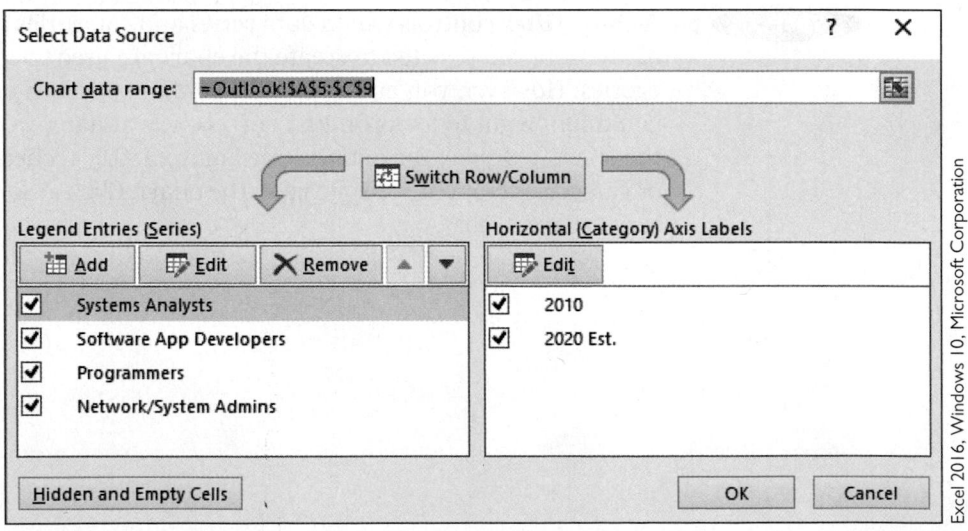

FIGURE 3.41 Select Data Source Dialog Box

Switch Row and Column Data

You might want to switch data used to create the horizontal axis and the legend to give a different perspective and to change the focus on the data. For example, you might want to display years as data series to compare different years for categories, and then you might want to switch the data to show years on the category axis to compare job titles within the same year. In Figure 3.42, the chart on the left uses the job titles to build the data series and legend, and the years display on the horizontal axis. The chart on the right shows the results after switching the data: the job titles build the horizontal axis, and the years build the data series and legend.

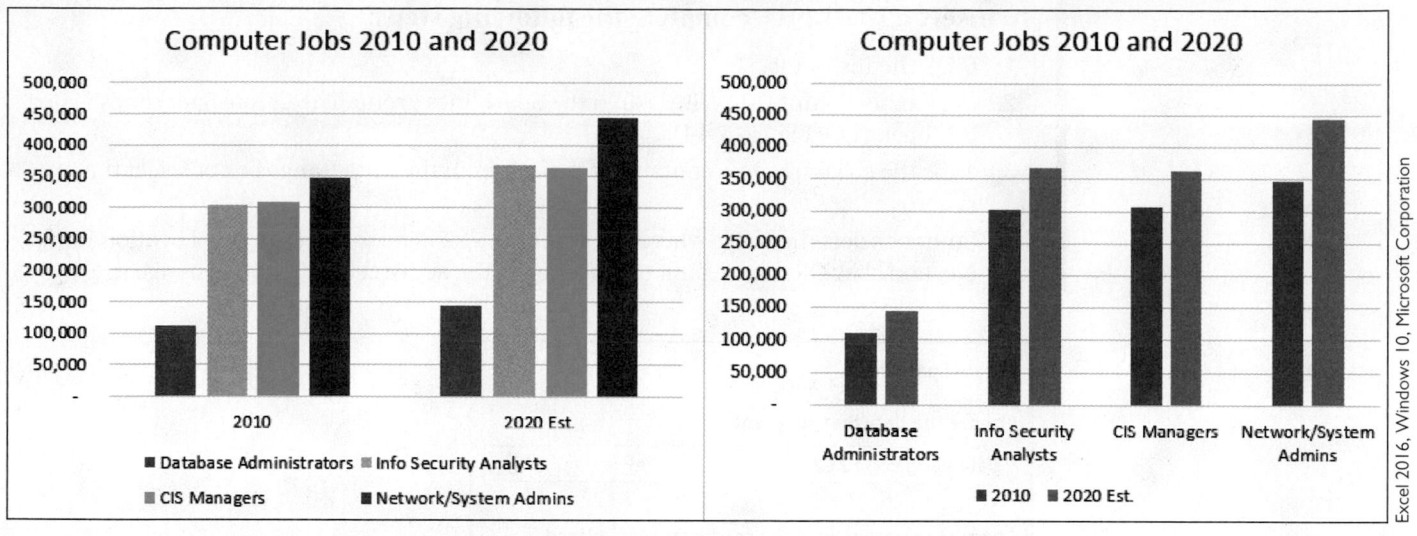

FIGURE 3.42 Original Chart and Chart with Switched Rows/Columns

> **To switch the row and column data, complete the following steps:**
> 1. Select the chart.
> 2. Click Switch Row/Column in the Data group on the Design tab.

Creating and Customizing Sparklines

A *sparkline* is a small line, column, or win/loss chart contained in a single cell. The purpose of a sparkline is to present a condensed, simple, succinct visual illustration of data. Unlike a regular chart, a sparkline does not include any of the standard chart labels, such as a chart title, axis label, axis titles, legend, or data labels. Inserting sparklines next to data helps to create a visual "dashboard" to help you understand the data quickly without having to look at a full-scale chart.

Figure 3.43 shows three sample sparklines: line, column, and win/loss. The line sparkline shows trends over time, such as each student's trends in test scores. The column sparkline compares test averages. The win/loss sparkline depicts how many points a team won or lost each game.

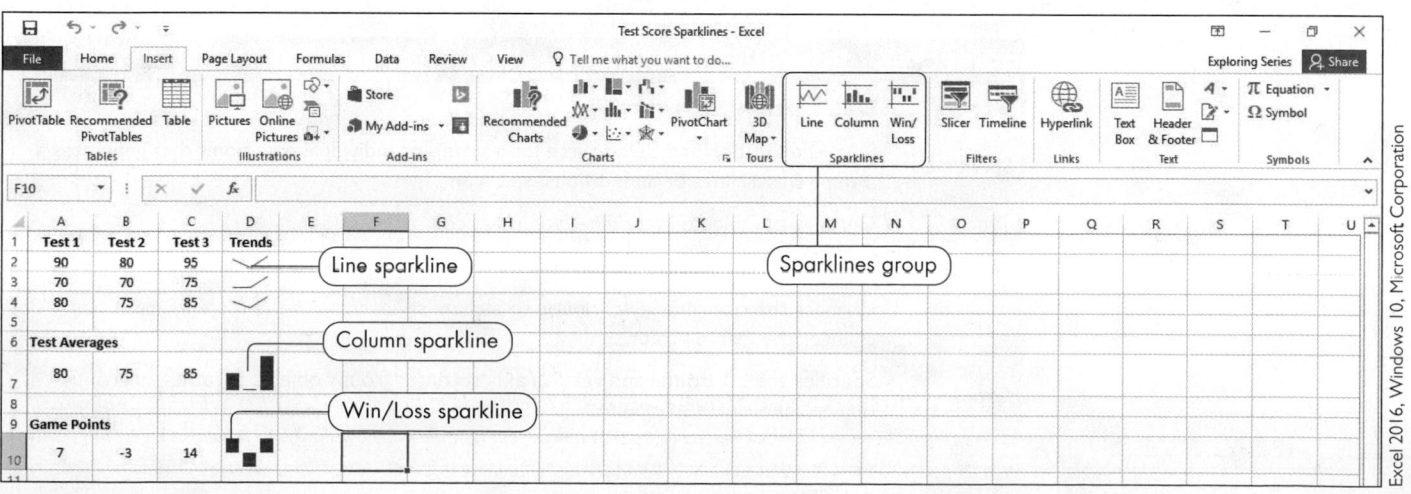

FIGURE 3.43 Sample Sparklines

Insert a Sparkline

STEP 3 ❯❯ Before creating a sparkline, identify the data range you want to depict (such as A2:C2 for the first person's test score) and where you want to place the sparkline (such as cell D2).

To insert a sparkline, complete the following steps:

1. Click the Insert tab.
2. Click Line, Column, or Win/Loss in the Sparklines group. The Create Sparklines dialog box opens (see Figure 3.44).
3. Type the cell references containing the values in the Data Range box or select the range.
4. Enter or select the range where you want the sparkline to display in the Location Range box and click OK. The default cell location is the active cell unless you change it.

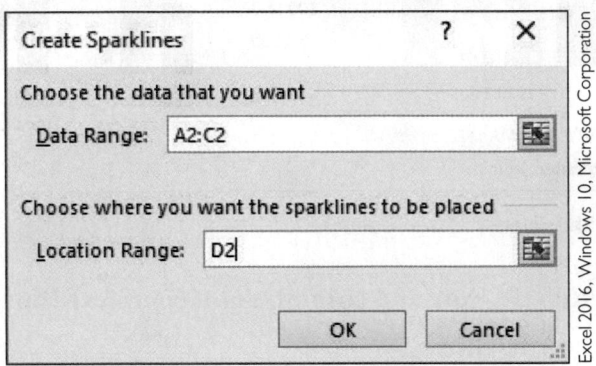

FIGURE 3.44 Create Sparklines Dialog Box

Customize a Sparkline

After you insert a sparkline, the Sparkline Tools Design tab displays (see Figure 3.45), with options to customize the sparkline. Table 3.6 lists and describes the groups on the Sparkline Tools Design tab.

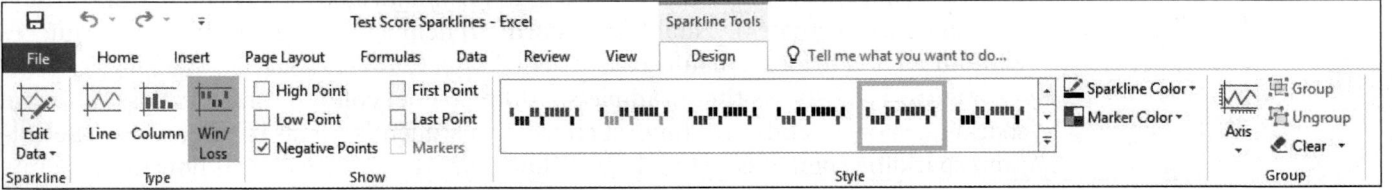

Excel 2016, Windows 10, Microsoft Corporation

FIGURE 3.45 Sparkline Tools Design Tab

TABLE 3.6	Sparkline Tools Design Tab
Group	**Description**
Sparkline	Edits the location and data source for a group or individual data point that generates a group of sparklines or an individual sparkline.
Type	Changes the selected sparkline type (line, column, win/loss).
Show	Displays points, such as the high points, or markers within a sparkline.
Style	Changes the sparkline style, similar to a chart style, changes the sparkline color, or changes the marker color.
Group	Specifies the horizontal and vertical axis settings, groups objects together, ungroups objects, and clears sparklines.

Pearson Education, Inc.

8. What are two ways to change the color scheme of a chart? *p. 575*

9. How can you change a chart so that the data in the legend are on the X-axis and the data on the X-axis are in the legend? *pp. 576–577*

10. What is a sparkline, and why would you insert one? *p. 577*

Hands-On Exercises

Watch the Video
for this Hands-On
Exercise!

MyITLab®
HOE3 Training

Skills covered: Apply a Chart Style • Apply Chart Filters • Insert a Sparkline • Customize Sparklines

3 Chart Design and Sparklines

Now that you have completed the pie chart, you want to focus again on the bar chart. You are not satisfied with the overall design and want to try a different chart style. In addition, you would like to include sparklines to show trends for all jobs between 2010 and 2020.

STEP 1 ›› APPLY A CHART STYLE

You want to give more contrast to the bar chart. Therefore, you will apply the Style 2 chart style. That style changes the category axis labels to all capital letters and displays data labels inside each segment of each bar. Refer to Figure 3.46 as you complete Step 1.

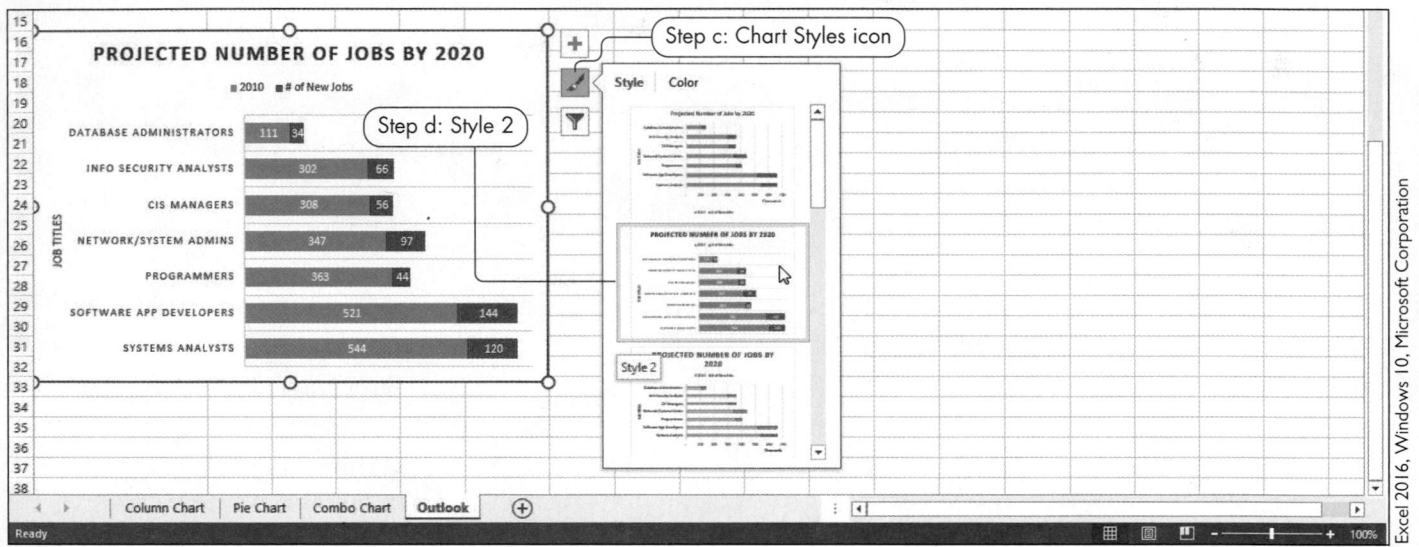

FIGURE 3.46 Chart Style Applied

a. Open *e03h2Jobs_LastFirst* if you closed it at the end of the Hands-On Exercise 2, and save it as **e03h3Jobs_LastFirst**, changing h2 to h3.

b. Click the **Outlook sheet tab** and click the bar chart to select it.

c. Click **Chart Styles** to the right of the chart.

The gallery of chart styles opens.

d. Point to **Style 2**. When you see the ScreenTip that identifies Style 2, click **Style 2**. Click **Chart Styles** to close the gallery. Save the workbook.

Excel applies the Style 2 chart style to the chart, which displays value data labels in white font color within each stack of the bar chart. The chart title and the category labels display in all capital letters. The legend displays above the plot area.

When you first created the clustered column chart, you included the number of new jobs as well as the number of 2010 jobs and the projected number of 2020 jobs. However, you decide that the number of new jobs is implied by comparing the 2010 to the 2020 jobs. Therefore, you want to set a chart filter to exclude the number of new jobs. Refer to Figure 3.47 as you complete Step 2.

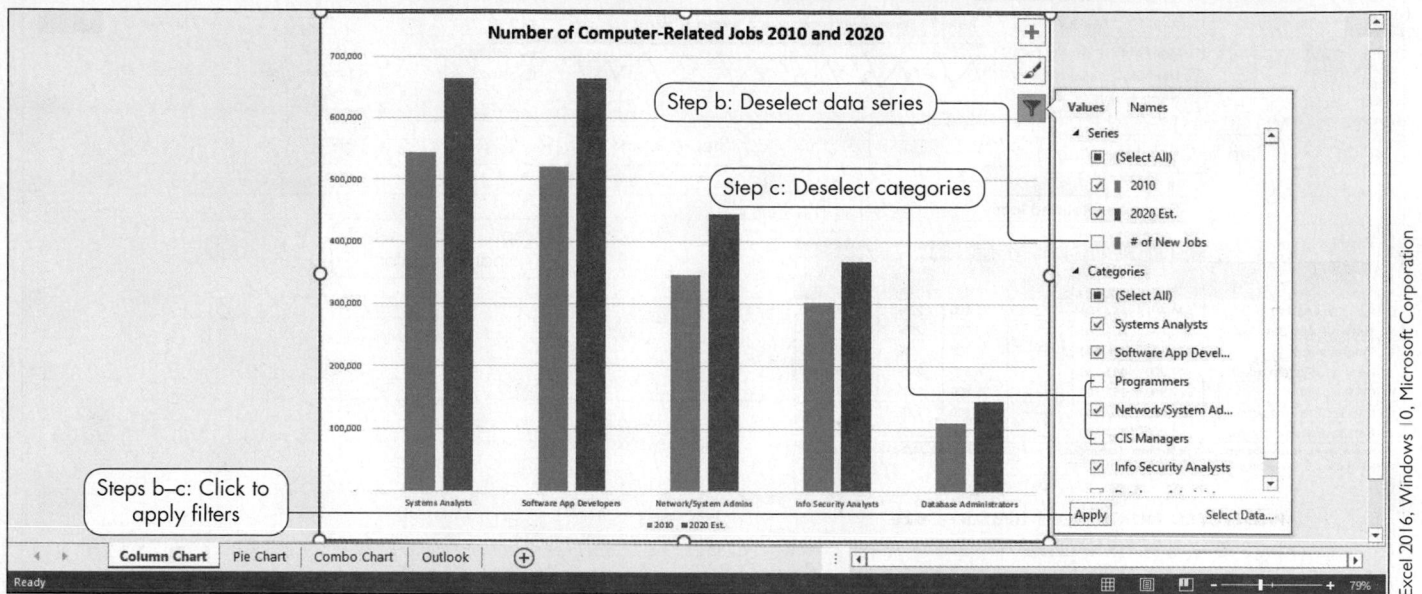

FIGURE 3.47 Chart Filters

a. Click the **Column Chart sheet tab** and click **Chart Filters** on the right of the chart area.

b. Point to the various filter options to see a preview of the filtered data. Click the **# of New Jobs check box** in the Series group to deselect it and click **Apply** at the bottom of the filter window.

The number of new jobs (gray) data series no longer displays in the clustered column chart.

c. Click the **Programmers check box** to deselect the category, click the **CIS Managers check box** to deselect it, and then click **Apply**. Click **Chart Filters** to close the menu. Save the workbook.

The Programmers and CIS Managers categories no longer display in the clustered column chart.

You want to insert sparklines to show the trends between 2010 and 2020. After inserting the sparklines, you want to display the high points to show that all jobs will have major increases by 2020. Refer to Figure 3.48 as you complete Step 3.

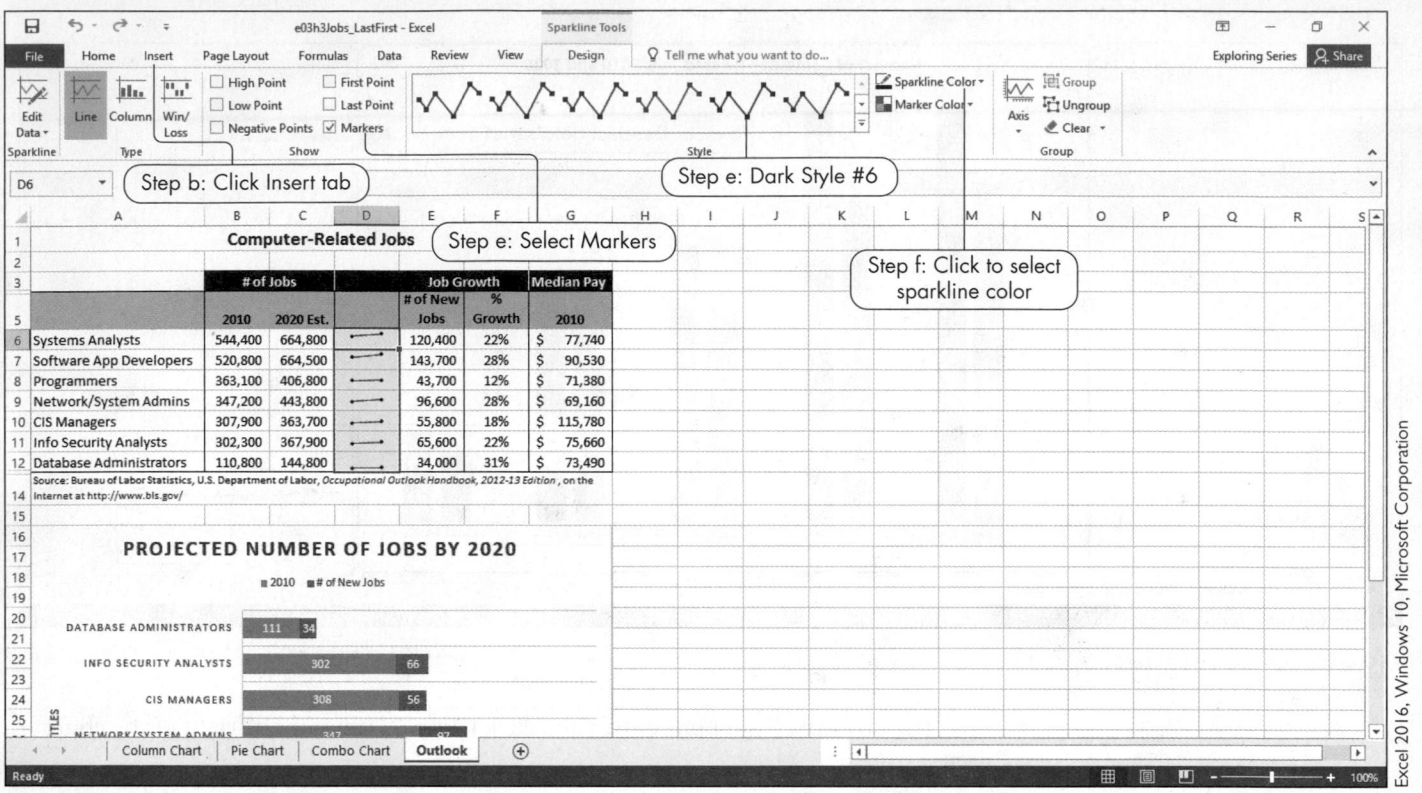

FIGURE 3.48 Sparkline Tools Design Tab

a. Click the **Outlook sheet tab**, select **cell D6**, click the **Insert arrow** in the Cells group, and then select **Insert Sheet Columns**.

   You inserted a new column so that you can place the sparklines close to the data you want to visualize.

b. Click the **Insert tab** and click **Line** in the Sparklines group.

c. Select the **range B6:C12** to enter that range in the Data Range box.

   You selected multiple rows at one time to create a group of sparklines.

d. Press **Tab** and select the **range D6:D12** to enter that range in the Location Range box. Click **OK**.

   Excel inserts sparklines in the range D6:D12 with each sparkline representing data on its respective row. The Sparkline Tools Design tab displays.

e. Click the **Markers check box** in the Show group to select it and click **Sparkline Style Dark #6** in the Style group.

f. Click **Sparkline Color** in the Style group and click **Red** in the Standard Colors section.

g. Click **Axis** in the Group group and click **Same for All Sparklines** in the Vertical Axis Minimum Value Options section. Click **Axis** again and click **Same for All Sparklines** in the Vertical Axis Maximum Value Options section.

   Because the sparklines look identical in trends, you changed the axis settings to set the minimum and maximum values as relative to the sparkline values in the entire selected range of rows rather than the default setting that bases the minimum and maximum for each row.

h. Save and close the file. Based on your instructor's directions, submit e03h3Jobs_LastFirst.

Chapter Objectives Review

After reading this chapter, you have accomplished the following objectives:

I. Select the data source.

- Decide which data you want to include in a chart. Each value is a data point, and several related data points create a data series in a chart.
- Select the range of data, including appropriate labels. The labels become the legend and the category axis.

2. Choose a chart type.

- After selecting a range, click Quick Analysis and click Charts to display a gallery of recommended chart types.
- Create a column chart: A clustered column chart compares groups of side-by-side columns where the height of the column indicates its value. The taller the column, the larger the value. A stacked column chart shows relationships of individual data points to the whole.
- Create a bar chart: A bar chart compares values across categories using horizontal bars where the width of the bar indicates its value. The wider the bar, the larger the value. A stacked bar chart shows relationships of individual data points to the whole.
- Change the chart type: After creating a chart, you might want to change it to a different type by clicking Change Chart Type in the Type group on the Design tab.
- Create a line chart: A line chart compares trends over time. Values are displayed on the value axis, and time periods are displayed on the category axis.
- Create a pie chart: A pie chart indicates the proportion to the whole for one data series. The size of the slice indicates the size of the value. The larger the pie slice, the larger the value.
- Create a combo chart: A combo chart combines elements of two chart types, such as column and line, to depict different data, such as individual data points compared to averages or percentages.
- Create other chart types: An X Y (scatter) chart shows a relationship between two numerical variables. A stock chart shows fluctuations in prices of stock, such as between the opening and closing prices on a particular day.

3. Move, size, and print a chart.

- Move a chart: The Move Chart dialog box enables you to select a new sheet and name the new chart sheet. To move a chart within a worksheet, click and drag the chart to the desired area.
- Size a chart: Adjust the chart size by dragging a sizing handle or specifying exact measurements in the Size group on the Format tab.

- Print a chart: To print a chart with its data series, the chart needs to be on the same worksheet as the data source. To ensure both the data and the chart print, make sure the chart is not selected. If the chart is on its own sheet or if you select the chart on a worksheet containing other data, the chart will print as a full-sized chart.

4. Add, edit, and format chart elements.

- Click Chart Elements to add elements. Chart elements include a chart title, axis titles, data labels, legend, gridlines, chart area, plot area, data series, and data point.
- Edit, format, and position the chart title: The default chart title is Chart Title, but you should edit it to provide a descriptive title for the chart. Apply font formats, such as bold and font size, to the chart title. Position the chart title above the chart, centered and overlaid, or in other locations.
- Add, format, and position axis titles: Display titles for the value and category axes to help describe the axes better. Apply font formats, such as bold and font size, to the axis titles.
- Format the axes: Change the unit of display for the value axis, such as converting values to In Millions.
- Add, position, and format data labels: Data labels provide exact values for a data series. Select the position of the data labels and the content of the data labels. Apply font formats, such as bold and font size, to the data labels.
- Position and format the legend: Position the legend to the right, top, bottom, or left of the plot area. Change the font size to adjust the label sizes within the legend.
- Add and format gridlines: Gridlines help the reader read across a column chart. Adjust the format of the major and minor gridlines.
- Format the chart area, plot area, and data series: The Format task panes enable you to apply fill colors, select border colors, and apply other settings.
- Format a data point: Format a single data point, such as changing the fill color for a single pie slice or specifying the percentage to explode a slice in a pie chart. Apply font formats, such as bold and font size, to the data points.
- Use the Chart Tools Format tab: Use this tab to select a chart element and insert and format shapes.

5. Apply a chart style and colors.

- Apply a chart style: This feature applies predetermined formatting, such as the background color and the data series color.

6. Modify the data source.

- Add or remove data from the data source to change the data in the chart.
- Apply chart filters: The Select Data Source dialog box enables you to modify the ranges used for the data series. When you deselect a series, Excel removes that series from the chart.
- Switch row and column data: You can switch the way data is used to create a chart by switching data series and categories.

7. Create and customize sparklines.

- Create a sparkline: A sparkline is a miniature chart in a cell representing a single data series.
- Customize a sparkline: Change the data source, location, and style. Display markers and change line or marker colors.

Key Terms Matching

Match the key terms with their definitions. Write the key term letter by the appropriate numbered definition.

a. Axis title
b. Bar chart
c. Category axis
d. Chart area
e. Chart title
f. Clustered column chart
g. Combo chart
h. Data label
i. Data point
j. Data series

k. Gridline
l. Legend
m. Line chart
n. Pie chart
o. Plot area
p. Sizing handle
q. Sparkline
r. Task pane
s. Value axis
t. X Y (scatter) chart

1. _____ Chart that groups columns side by side to compare data points among categories. **p. 539**

2. _____ Miniature chart contained in a single cell. **p. 577**

3. _____ Chart type that shows trends over time in which the value axis indicates quantities and the horizontal axis indicates time. **p. 543**

4. _____ Label that describes the entire chart. **p. 558**

5. _____ Label that describes either the category axis or the value axis. **p. 558**

6. _____ Key that identifies the color, gradient, picture, texture, or pattern fill assigned to each data series in a chart. **p. 535**

7. _____ Chart type that compares categories of data horizontally. **p. 542**

8. _____ Chart that shows each data point in proportion to the whole data series. **p. 544**

9. _____ Numeric value that describes a single value on a chart. **p. 534**

10. _____ Chart that contains two chart types, such as column and line, to depict two types of data, such as individual data points and percentages. **p. 545**

11. _____ A circle that enables you to adjust the height or width of a selected chart. **p. 549**

12. _____ Horizontal or vertical line that extends from the horizontal or vertical axis through the plot area. **p. 566**

13. _____ Chart type that shows the relationship between two variables. **p. 546**

14. _____ Group of related data points that display in row(s) or column(s) in a worksheet. **p. 534**

15. _____ Window of options to format and customize chart elements. **p. 560**

16. _____ Provides descriptive labels for the data points plotted in a chart. **p. 535**

17. _____ Section of a chart that contains graphical representation of the values in a data series. **p. 535**

18. _____ A container for the entire chart and all of its elements. **p. 535**

19. _____ An identifier that shows the exact value of a data point in a chart. **p. 558**

20. _____ Displays incremental numbers to identify approximate values, such as dollars or units, of data points in a chart. **p. 535**

Multiple Choice

1. Which type of chart is the *least* appropriate for depicting yearly rainfall totals for five cities for four years?

   (a) Pie chart
   (b) Line chart
   (c) Column chart
   (d) Bar chart

2. Look at the stacked bar chart in Figure 3.35. Which of the following is a category on the category axis?

   (a) Thousands
   (b) Job Titles
   (c) CIS Managers
   (d) 700

3. Which of the following is not a type of sparkline?

   (a) Line
   (b) Bar
   (c) Column
   (d) Win-Loss

4. If you want to show exact values for a data series in a bar chart, which chart element should you display?

   (a) Chart title
   (b) Legend
   (c) Value axis title
   (d) Data labels

5. The value axis currently shows increments such as 50,000 and 100,000. What option would you select to display the values in increments of 50 and 100?

   (a) More Primary Vertical Axis Title Options
   (b) Show Axis in Thousands
   (c) Show Axis in Millions
   (d) Show Right to Left Axis

6. You want to create a single chart that shows the proportion of yearly sales for five divisions for each year for five years. Which type of chart can accommodate your needs?

   (a) Pie chart
   (b) Surface chart
   (c) Clustered bar chart
   (d) 100% stacked column chart

7. Currently, a column chart shows values on the value axis, years on the category axis, and state names in the legend. What should you do if you want to organize data with the states on the category axis and the years shown in the legend?

   (a) Change the chart type to a clustered column chart.
   (b) Click Switch Row/Column in the Data group on the Design tab.
   (c) Click Layout 2 in the Chart Layouts group on the Design tab and apply a different chart style.
   (d) Click Legend in the Labels group on the Layout tab and select Show Legend at Bottom.

8. What do you click to remove a data series from a chart so that you can focus on other data series?

   (a) Chart Elements
   (b) Chart Series
   (c) Chart Filters
   (d) Chart Styles

9. Which of the following does not display automatically when you create a clustered column chart?

   (a) Data labels
   (b) Chart title placeholder
   (c) Gridlines
   (d) Legend

10. After you create a line type sparkline, what option should you select to display dots for each data point?

    (a) High Point
    (b) Negative Point
    (c) Sparkline Color
    (d) Markers

Practice Exercises

1 Hulett Family Utility Expenses

Your cousin, Alex Hulett, wants to analyze his family's utility expenses for 2018. He gave you his files for the electric, gas, and water bills for the year. You created a worksheet that lists the individual expenses per month, along with yearly totals per utility type and monthly totals. You will create some charts to depict the data. Refer to Figure 3.49 as you complete this exercise.

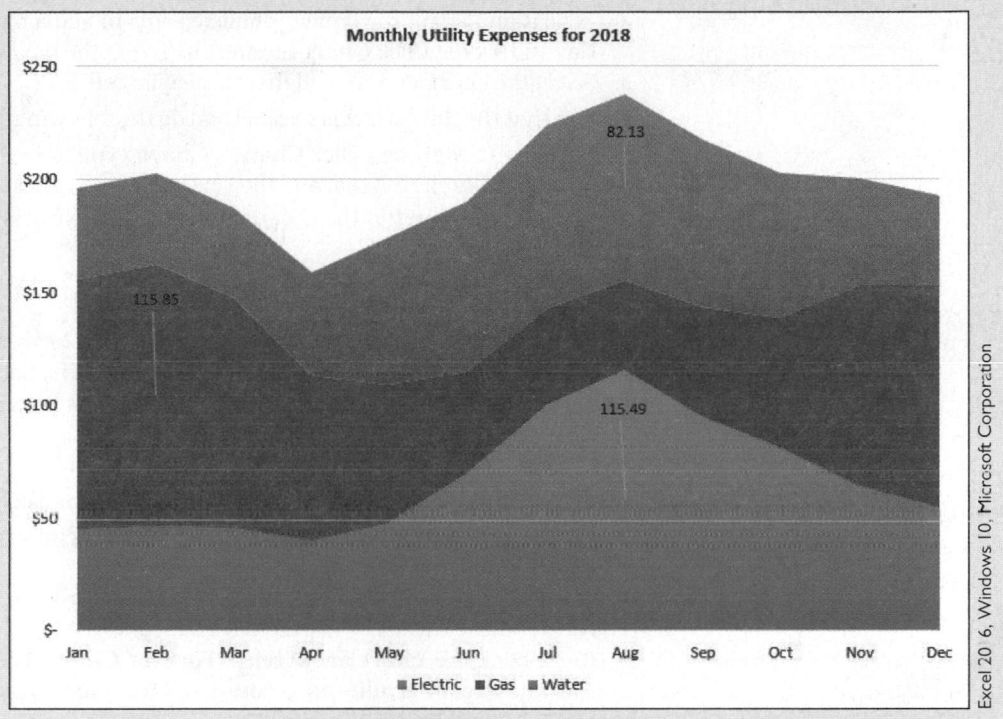

FIGURE 3.49 Hulett Family Utility Expenses

a. Open *e03p1Utilities* and save it as **e03p1Utilities_LastFirst**.

b. Select the **range A4:E17**, click **Quick Analysis**, click **Charts**, and then click **Clustered Column**.

c. Click **Chart Filters** to the right of the chart and do the following:
   • Deselect the **Monthly Totals check box** in the Series group.
   • Scroll through the Categories group and deselect the **Yearly Totals check box**.
   • Click **Apply** to remove totals from the chart. Click **Chart Filters** to close the menu.

d. Point to the **chart area**. When you see the Chart Area ScreenTip, drag the chart so that the top-left corner of the chart is in **cell A21**.

e. Click the **Format tab** and change the size by doing the following:
   • Click in the **Shape Width box** in the Size group, type **6"**, and then press **Enter**.
   • Click in the **Shape Height box** in the Size group, type **3.5"**, and then press **Enter**.

f. Click the **Design tab**, click **Quick Layout** in the Chart Layouts group, and then click **Layout 3**.

g. Select the **Chart Title placeholder**, type **Monthly Utility Expenses for 2018**, and then press **Enter**.

h. Click the chart, click the **More button** in the Chart Styles group, and then click **Style 6**.

i. Click **Copy** on the Home tab, click **cell A39**, and then click **Paste**. With the second chart selected, do the following:

- Click the **Design tab**, click **Change Chart Type** in the Type group, click **Line** on the left side of the dialog box, select **Line with Markers** in the top-center section, and then click **OK**.
- Click the **Electric data series line** to select it and click the highest marker to select only that marker. Click **Chart Elements** and click **Data Labels**.
- Repeat and adapt the previous bulleted step to add a data label to the highest markers for Gas and Water. Click **Chart Elements** to close the menu.
- Select the chart, copy it, and then paste it in **cell A57**.

j. Ensure that the third chart is selected and do the following:

- Click the **Design tab**, click **Change Chart Type** in the Type group, select **Area** on the left side, click **Stacked Area**, and then click **OK**.
- Click **Move Chart** in the Location group, click **New sheet**, type **Area Chart**, and then click **OK**.
- Select each data label and change the font size to **12**. Move each data label up closer to the top of the respective shaded area.
- Select the value axis and change the font size to **12**.
- Right-click the value axis and select **Format Axis**. Scroll down in the Format Axis task pane, click **Number**, click in the **Decimal places box**, and then type **0** . Close the Format Axis task pane.
- Change the font size to **12** for the category axis and the legend.

k. Click the **Expenses sheet tab**, select the line chart, and do the following:

- Click the **Design tab**, click **Move Chart** in the Location group, click **New sheet**, type **Line Chart**, and then click **OK**.
- Change the font size to **12** for the value axis, category axis, data labels, and legend.
- Format the vertical axis with zero decimal places.
- Right-click the **chart area**, select **Format Chart Area**, click **Fill**, click **Gradient fill**, click the **Preset gradients arrow**, and then select **Light Gradient – Accent 1**. Close the Format Chart Area task pane.

l. Click the **Expenses sheet**, select the **range B5:D16** and do the following:

- Click the **Insert tab**, click **Line** in the Sparkline group, click in the **Location Range box**, type **B18:D18**, and then click **OK**.
- Click the **High Point check box** to select it and click the **Low Point check box** to select it in the Show group with all three sparklines selected.

m. Create a footer with your name on the left side, the sheet name code in the center, and the file name code on the right of each sheet.

n. Save and close the file. Based on your instructor's directions, submit e03p1Utilities_LastFirst.

2 Trends in Market Value of Houses on Pine Circle

You live in a house on Pine Circle, a quiet cul-de-sac in a suburban area. Recently, you researched the market value and square footage of the five houses on Pine Circle. Now, you want to create charts to visually depict the data to compare values for the houses in the cul-de-sac. Refer to Figure 3.50 as you complete this exercise.

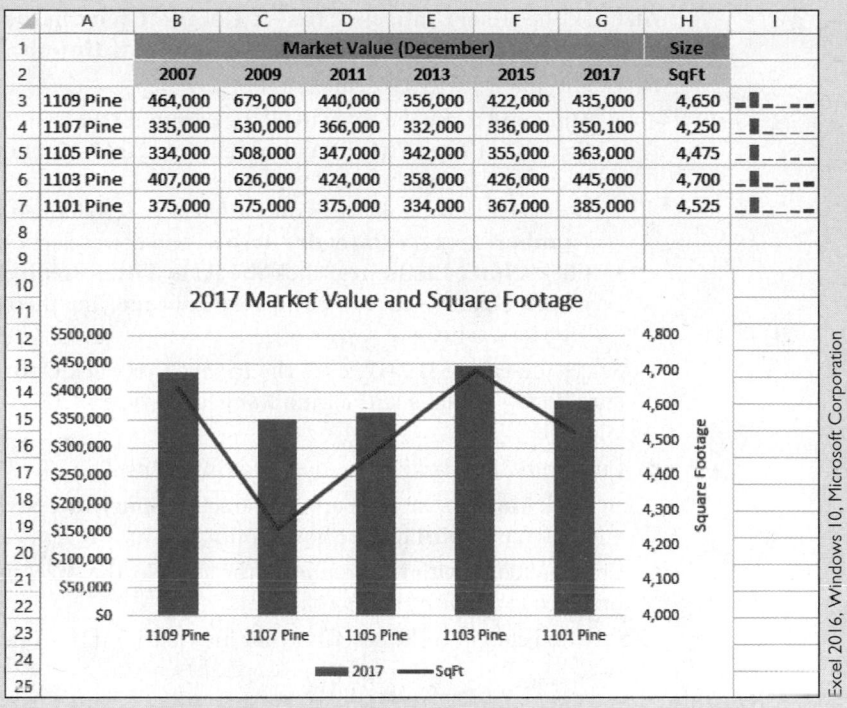

	A	B	C	D	E	F	G	H	I
1				Market Value (December)				Size	
2		2007	2009	2011	2013	2015	2017	SqFt	
3	1109 Pine	464,000	679,000	440,000	356,000	422,000	435,000	4,650	
4	1107 Pine	335,000	530,000	366,000	332,000	336,000	350,100	4,250	
5	1105 Pine	334,000	508,000	347,000	342,000	355,000	363,000	4,475	
6	1103 Pine	407,000	626,000	424,000	358,000	426,000	445,000	4,700	
7	1101 Pine	375,000	575,000	375,000	334,000	367,000	385,000	4,525	

FIGURE 3.50 Market Values

a. Open *e03p2Pine* and save it as **e03p2Pine_LastFirst**.

b. Select the **range A2:G7**, click **Quick Analysis**, click **Charts**, and then click **Line**.

c. Click **Move Chart** in the Location group, click **New sheet**, type **Line**, and then click **OK**.

d. Select the **Chart Title placeholder** and do the following:
   - Type **Market Value of Pine Circle Houses** and press **Enter**.
   - Apply bold to the chart title, change the font size to **20**, and then select **Olive Green, Accent 3, Darker 50% font color**.

e. Click the **value axis** on the left side of the chart and do the following:
   - Change the font size to 12 and select **Olive Green, Accent 3, Darker 50% font color**.
   - Double-click the value axis to open the Format Axis task pane.
   - Type **300000** in the Minimum Bounds box and press **Enter**. The Maximum Bounds box should change to 700000 automatically.
   - Scroll down in the Format Axis task pane and click **Number** to display those options.
   - Click the **Category arrow** and select **Currency**.
   - Close the Format Axis task pane.

f. Click **Chart Elements**, click the **Axis Titles triangle**, and then click the **Primary Vertical check box** to select it. Type **December Market Values** in the **Axis Title placeholder** and press **Enter**.

g. Make sure the Chart Elements menu is showing, click the **Gridlines triangle**, and then click the **Primary Minor Horizontal check box** to select it.

h. Click the blue **1109 Pine data series line**, click the **Data Labels check box** to select it, and then click **Chart Elements** to close the menu.

i. Click the data labels you just created, click the **Home tab**, click the **Font Color arrow**, and then select **Blue** in the Standard Colors section.

j. Select the category axis, change the font size to **12**, and select **Olive Green, Accent 3, Darker 50% font color**.

k. Right-click the legend and select **Format Legend**. Click **Top** in the Legend Position section of the Format Legend task pane and close the task pane.

l. Click the **Pine Circle sheet tab** and select the **ranges A2:A7** and **G2:H7**.

m. Click the **Insert tab**, click **Insert Combo Chart** in the Charts group, and then click the **Clustered Column – Line on Secondary Axis thumbnail**.

n. Do the following to the chart:
- Move and resize the chart to fill the **range A10:H25**.
- Select the **Chart Title placeholder**, type **2017 Market Value and Square Footage**, and then press **Enter**.
- Double-click the value axis on the left side, scroll down in the Format Axis task pane, click **Number**, click the **Category arrow**, and then select **Currency**.
- Click **Chart Elements**, click the **Axis Titles triangle**, click the **Secondary Vertical check box** to select it, type **Square Footage**, and then press **Enter**. Close the Format Axis Title task pane.

o. Select the **range B3:G7**, click the **Insert tab**, click **Column** in the Sparklines group, make sure B3:G7 displays in the Data Range box, type **I3:I7** in the Location Range box, and then click **OK**.

p. Customize the sparklines by doing the following:
- Click **More** in the Style group and select **Sparkline Style Accent 6, Darker 25%**.
- Click **Last Point** in the Show group.

q. Create a footer with your name on the left side, the sheet name code in the center, and the file name code on the right of both sheets.

r. Save and close the file. Based on your instructor's directions, submit e03p2Pine_LastFirst.

Mid-Level Exercises

1 Airport Passenger Counts

As an analyst for the airline industry, you track the number of passengers at the top five major U.S. airports: Atlanta, Chicago, Los Angeles, Dallas/Fort Worth, and Denver. You researched passenger data at http://www.aci-na.org. One worksheet you created lists the number of total yearly passengers at the top five airports for a six-year period. To prepare for an upcoming meeting, you need to create a clustered column chart to compare the number of passengers at each airport. Next, you will create a bar chart to compare the passenger count for the latest year of data available and then emphasize the airport with the largest number of passenger traffic. Finally, you want to insert sparklines to visually represent trends in passengers at each airport over the six-year period. You can then refer to the sparklines and clustered column chart to write a paragraph analyzing the trends to detect.

a. Open *e03m1Airports* and save it as **e03m1Airports_LastFirst**.

b. Create a clustered column chart for the **range A4:G9**. Position and resize the chart to fit in the **range A15:G34**.

c. Customize the chart by doing the following:
   - Swap the data on the category axis and in the legend.
   - Apply the **Style 6 chart style**.
   - Select **Color 12** in the Monochromatic section of the Change Colors gallery.
   - Apply the **Light Gradient – Accent 1** preset gradient fill to the chart area.
   - Change the fill color of the 2013 data series to **Dark Blue** and change the fill color of the 2008 data series to **Blue, Accent 5, Lighter 60%**.

   - Use Help and add a solid **Blue border** around the legend.

d. Type **Passengers by Top U.S. Airports** as the chart title. Change the font color to **Blue**.

e. Adjust the value axis by doing the following:
   - Change the display units to **Millions** for the value axis.
   - Edit the axis title to display **Millions of Passengers**.

f. Display data labels above the columns for the 2013 data series only.

g. Create a clustered bar chart for the **range A5:A9** and **G5:G9** and then do the following:
   - Move the bar chart to a chart sheet named **Bar Chart**.
   - Enter **Passengers at Top 5 U.S. Airports in 2013** as the chart title.
   - Apply the **Style 3 chart style.**
   - Change the font color to **Dark Blue** on the chart title, category axis, and the value axis.
   - Format the Atlanta data point with **Dark Blue fill color**.

h. Display the Passenger worksheet and insert **Line sparklines** in the **range H5:H9** to illustrate the data in the **range B5:G9**. This should insert a sparkline to represent yearly data for each airport.

i. Customize the sparklines by doing the following:
   - Show the high and low points in each sparkline.
   - Apply **Black, Text 1 color** to the high point marker in each sparkline.
   - Apply **Dark Red color** to the low point marker in each sparkline.

j. Click **cell A36** and compose a paragraph that analyzes the trends depicted by the airport sparklines. Notice the overall trends in decreased and increased number of passengers and any unusual activity for an airport. Spell-check the worksheet and correct any errors.

k. Set **0.2"** left and right margins and scale to fit to 1 page for the Passenger worksheet.

l. Insert a footer with your name on the left side, the sheet name code in the center, and the file name code on the right on all worksheets.

m. Save and close the file. Based on your instructor's directions, submit e03m1Airports_LastFirst.

2 Grade Analysis

You are a teaching assistant for Dr. Monica Unice's introductory psychology class. You have maintained her grade book all semester, entering three test scores for each student and calculating the final average. You created a section called Final Grade Distribution that contains calculations to identify the number of students who earned an A, B, C, D, or F. Dr. Unice wants you to create a chart that shows the percentage of students who earn each letter grade. Therefore, you decide to create and format a pie chart. You will also create a bar chart to show a sample of the students' test scores. Furthermore, Dr. Unice wants to see if a correlation exists between attendance and students' final grades; therefore, you will create a scatter chart depicting each student's percentage of attendance with his or her respective final grade average.

a. Open *e03m2Psych* and save it as **e03m2Psych_LastFirst**.

b. Create a pie chart from the Final Grade Distribution data located below the student data in the **range F38:G42** and move the pie chart to its own sheet named **Grades Pie**.

c. Customize the pie chart with these specifications:
- Apply the **Style 7 chart style.**
- Type **PSY 2030 Final Grade Distribution - Fall 2018** for the chart title.
- Explode the B grade slice by **10%**.
- Remove the legend.

d. Add centered data labels and customize the labels with these specifications:
- Display these data labels: **Percentage** and **Category Name**. Remove other data labels.
- Change the font size to **20** and apply **Black, Text 1** font color.

e. Create a clustered bar chart using the **range A7:D12** and move the bar chart to its own sheet named **Students Bar Chart**.

f. Customize the bar chart with these specifications:
- Apply the **Style 5 chart style**.
- Type **Sample Student Test Scores** for the chart title.
- Position the legend on the right side.
- Add data labels in the Outside End position for the Final Exam data series.
DISCOVER
- Arrange the categories in reverse order so that Atkin is listed at the top and Ethington is listed at the bottom of the bar chart.

DISCOVER
g. Create a scatter chart using the **range E7:F33**, the attendance record and final averages from the Grades worksheet. Move the scatter chart to its own sheet named **Scatter Chart**.

h. Apply these label settings to the scatter chart:
- Remove the legend.
- Type **Attendance-Final Average Relationship** for the chart title.
- Add the following primary horizontal axis title: **Percentage of Attendance**.
- Add the following primary vertical axis title: **Student Final Averages**.

DISCOVER
i. Use Help to learn how to apply the following axis settings:
- Vertical axis: 40 minimum bound, 100 maximum bound, 10 major units, and a number format with zero decimal places
- Horizontal axis: 40 minimum bound, 100 maximum bound, automatic units

j. Change the font size to **12** on the vertical axis title, vertical axis, horizontal axis title, and horizontal axis. Bold the chart title and the two axes titles.

k. Add the **Parchment texture fill** to the plot area.

l. Insert a linear trendline.

m. Insert Line sparklines in the **range H8:H33** using the three tests score columns. Change the sparkline color to **Purple** and show the low points.

n. Insert a footer with your name on the left, the sheet name code in the center, and the file name code on the right on all the sheets.

o. Save and close the file. Based on your instructor's directions, submit e03m2Psych_LastFirst.

3 Box Office Movies

COLLABORATION CASE

FROM SCRATCH

You and two of your friends like to follow the popularity of new movies at the theater. You will research current movies that have been showing for four weeks and decide which movies on which to report. Work in teams of three for this activity. After obtaining the data, your team will create applicable charts to illustrate the revenue data. Team members will critique each other's charts.

a. Have all three team members log in to a chat client and engage in a dialogue about which movies are currently playing. Each member should research a different theater to see what is playing at that theater. Decide on six movies that have been in theaters for at least four weeks to research. Save a copy of your instant message dialogue and submit based on your instructor's directions.

b. Divide the six movies among the three team members. Each member should research the revenue reported for two movies for the past four weeks. Make sure your team members use the same source to find the data.

Student 1:

c. Create a new Excel workbook and enter appropriate column labels and the four-week data for all six movies. Name Sheet1 **Data**.

d. Format the data appropriately. Save the workbook as **e03m3Movies_GroupName**. Upload the workbook to a shared location, such as OneDrive, invite the other students to share this location, and send a text message to the next student.

Student 2:

e. Create a line chart to show the trends in revenue for the movies for the four-week period.

f. Add a chart title, format the axes appropriately, select a chart style, and then apply other formatting.

g. Move the chart to its own sheet named **Trends**. Save the workbook, upload it to the shared location, and send a text message to the next student.

Student 3:

h. Add a column to the right of the four-week data and total each movie's four-week revenue.

i. Create a pie chart depicting each movie's percentage of the total revenue for your selected movies.

j. Add a chart title, explode one pie slice, add data labels showing percentages and movie names, and then apply other formatting.

k. Move the chart to its own sheet named **Revenue Chart**. Save the workbook, upload it to the shared location, and send a text message to the next student.

Student 1:

l. Critique the charts. Insert a new worksheet named **Chart Critique** that provides an organized critique of each chart. Type notes that list each team member's name and specify what each student's role was in completing this exercise.

m. Save the workbook, upload it to the shared location, and send a text message to the next student.

Student 2:

n. Read the critique of the line chart and make any appropriate changes for the line chart. On the critique worksheet, provide a response to each critique and why you made or did not make the suggested change.

o. Save the workbook, upload it to the shared location, and send a text message to the next student.

Student 3:

p. Read the critique of the pie chart and make any appropriate changes for the pie chart. On the critique worksheet, provide a response to each critique and why you made or did not make the suggested change.

q. Save and close the file. Based on your instructor's directions, submit e03m3Movies_GroupName.

Beyond the Classroom

Historical Stock Prices

You are interested in investing in the stock market. First, you need to research the historical prices for a particular stock. Launch a Web browser, go to finance.yahoo.com, type a company name, such as Apple, and then select the company name from a list of suggested companies. Click the Historical Prices link. Copy the stock data (date, high, low, open, close, volume) for a six-month period and paste it in a new workbook, adjusting the column widths to fit the data. Save the workbook as **e03b1StockData_LastFirst**. Rename Sheet1 **Data**. Display data for only the first date listed for each month; delete rows containing data for other dates. Sort the list from the oldest date to the newest date. Use Help if needed to learn how to sort data and how to create a Volume-Open-High-Low-Close chart. Then rearrange the data columns in the correct sequence. Format the data and column labels.

Insert a row to enter the company name and insert another row to list the company's stock symbol, such as AAPL. Copy the URL from the Web browser and paste it as a source below the list of data and the date you obtained the data. Merge the cells containing the company name and stock symbol through the last column of data and word-wrap the URL.

Create a Volume-Open-High-Low-Close chart on a new chart sheet named **Stock Chart**. Type an appropriate chart title. Set the primary vertical axis (left side) unit measurement to millions and include an axis title **Volume in Millions**. Include a secondary vertical axis (right side) title **Stock Prices**. Apply the Currency number style with 0 decimal places for the secondary axis values. Change the font size to 11 and the font color to Black, Text 1 on the vertical axes and category axis. Hide the legend.

Use Help to research how to insert text boxes. Insert a text box that describes the stock chart: white fill rectangles indicate the closing price was higher than the opening price; black fill rectangles indicate the closing price was lower than the opening price; etc. Create a footer with your name, the sheet name code, and the file name code on both worksheets. Save and close the file. Based on your instructor's directions, submit e03b1StockData_LastFirst.

Harper County Houses Sold

You want to analyze the number of houses sold by type (e.g., rambler, two story, etc.) in each quarter in Harper County. You entered quarterly data for 2018, calculated yearly total number of houses sold by each type, and quarterly total number of houses sold. You asked an intern to create a stacked column chart for the data, but the chart contains a lot of errors.

Open *e03b2Houses* and save it as **e03b2Houses_LastFirst**. Identify the errors and poor design for the chart. Below the chart, list the errors and your corrections in a two-column format. Then correct the problems in the chart. Link the chart title to the cell containing the most appropriate label in the worksheet. Create a footer with your name, the sheet name code, and the file name code. Adjust the margins and scaling to print the worksheet data, including the error list, and the chart on one page. Save and close the file. Based on your instructor's directions, submit e03b2Houses_LastFirst.

Capstone Exercise

You are an analyst for the airline industry. You created a workbook that lists overall airline arrival statistics for several years. In particular, you listed the percentage and number of on-time arrivals, late arrivals, canceled flights, and diverted flights based on information provided by the Bureau of Transportation Statistics. You want to create charts and insert sparklines that show the trends to discuss with airline and airport managers.

Insert and Format Sparklines

The first dataset shows the percentages. You want to insert sparklines that show the trends in the five-year data. The sparklines will help show any trends in on-time arrivals compared to late arrivals, canceled flights, and diverted flights.

a. Open the *e03c1Arrivals* workbook and save it as **e03c1Arrivals_LastFirst**.

b. Insert Line sparklines in the **range G4:G7**, using the data for the five years.

c. Display the high and low points for the sparklines.

d. Change the high point marker color to **Green**.

Create a Pie Chart

You want to focus on the arrival percentages for 2014. Creating a pie chart will help people visualize the breakdown of all operations for that year. After you create the chart, you will move it to its own chart sheet and edit the chart title to reflect 2014 flight arrivals.

a. Select the **range A4:A7** and the **range F4:F7**.

b. Create a pie chart and move it to a chart sheet named **Pie Chart**.

c. Change the chart title to **2014 Flight Arrivals**.

Add and Format Chart Elements

You want to format the chart by applying a different chart style and positioning the legend above the plot area. Furthermore, you need to add data labels so that you will know the percentages for the arrival categories. Finally, you want to emphasize the canceled flights in Dark Red and explode the late arrival pie slice.

a. Apply the **Style 12 chart style** to the pie chart.

b. Format the chart title with **Blue font color**.

c. Position the legend between the chart title and the plot area.

d. Add data labels to the Best Fit position and display.

e. Apply bold to the data labels and change the font size to **12**.

f. Format the Canceled data point with **Dark Red fill color** and format the Late Arrival data point in **Green**.

g. Explode the Late Arrival data point by **5%**.

Create and Size a Column Chart

To provide a different perspective, you will create a clustered column chart using the actual number of flights. The Total Operations row indicates the total number of reported (scheduled) flights. After creating the chart, you will position and size the chart below the source rows.

a. Create a clustered column chart using the **range A10:F15** in the Arrivals sheet.

b. Edit the chart title: **On-Time and Late Flight Arrivals**.

c. Position the clustered column chart so that the top-left corner is in **cell A20**.

d. Change the width to **5.75"** and the height to **3.5"**.

Format the Column Chart

Now that you have created the column chart, you realize that some data seems irrelevant. You will filter out the unneeded data, format the value axis to remove digits, insert a vertical axis title, apply a color change, and format the chart area.

a. Apply chart filters to remove the canceled, diverted, and total operations data.

b. Select the value axis, set **500000** for the Major unit, display the axis units **in Millions**, select category **Number** format with **1** decimal place.

c. Add a primary vertical axis title **Number of Flights**.

d. Apply the **Color 2 chart color** to the chart.

e. Apply the **Light Gradient – Accent 3** fill to the chart area.

Finalizing the Workbook

You want to prepare the workbook in case someone wants to print the data and charts. The margins and scaling have already been set. You just need to insert a footer.

a. Create a footer on each worksheet with your name, the sheet name code, and the file name code.

b. Save and close the file. Based on your instructor's direction, submit e03c1Arrivals_LastFirst.

Excel

Datasets and Tables

LEARNING OUTCOME — You will demonstrate how to manage and analyze large sets of data.

OBJECTIVES & SKILLS: After you read this chapter, you will be able to:

CASE STUDY | Reid Furniture Store

Vicki Reid owns Reid Furniture Store in Portland, Oregon. She divided her store into four departments: Living Room, Bedroom, Dining Room, and Appliances. All merchandise is categorized into one of these four departments for inventory records and sales. Vicki has four sales representatives: Chantalle Desmarais, Jade Gallagher, Sebastian Gruenewald, and Ambrose Sardelis. The sales system tracks which sales representative processed each transaction.

The business has grown rapidly, and Vicki hired you to analyze the sales data in order to increase future profits. For example, which department generates the most sales? Who is the leading salesperson? Do most customers purchase or finance? Are sales promotions necessary to promote business, or will customers pay the full price?

You downloaded March 2018 data from the sales system into an Excel workbook. To avoid extraneous data that is not needed in the analysis, you did not include customer names, accounts, or specific product numbers. The downloaded file contains transaction numbers, dates, sales representative names, departments, general merchandise descriptions, payment types, transaction types, and the total price.

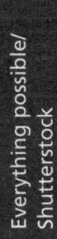

CHAPTER 4

Managing Large Volumes of Data

Reid Furniture Store — March Totals

	A	B	C	D	E	F	G	H	I	J
1	Reid Furniture Store									
2	Monthly Transactions:			March 2018						
3	Down Payment Requirement:			25%						
4										
5	Trans_No	Operator	Sales_First	Sales_Last	Date	Department	Furniture	Pay_Type	Trans_Type	Amount
6	2018-001	KRM	Sebastian	Gruenewald	3/1/2018	Bedroom	Mattress	Finance	Promotion	2,788
7	2018-002	RKM	Sebastian	Gruenewald	3/1/2018	Bedroom	Mattress	Finance	Promotion	3,245
8	2018-003	MAP	Jade	Gallagher	3/1/2018	Living Room	Sofa, Loveseat, Chair Package	Finance	Promotion	10,000
9	2018-004	MAP	Jade	Gallagher	3/1/2018	Living Room	End Tables	Finance	Promotion	1,000
10	2018-005	MAP	Jade	Gallagher	3/1/2018	Appliances	Washer and Dryer	Finance	Promotion	2,750
11	2018-006	COK	Ambrose	Sardelis	3/1/2018	Living Room	Sofa, Loveseat, Chair Package	Finance	Promotion	12,000
12	2018-006	COK	Ambrose	Sardelis	3/1/2018	Living Room	Sofa, Loveseat, Chair Package	Finance	Promotion	12,000
13	2018-007	MAP	Jade	Gallagher	3/1/2018	Dining Room	Dining Room Table	Finance	Promotion	3,240
14	2018-008	COK	Chantalle	Desmarais	3/1/2018	Dining Room	Dining Room Table	Finance	Promotion	4,080
15	2018-009	KRM	Sebastian	Gruenewald	3/1/2018	Appliances	Washer and Dryer	Finance	Promotion	2,750
16	2018-010	MAP	Jade	Gallagher	3/2/2018	Dining Room	Dining Room Table and Chairs	Finance	Standard	6,780
17	2018-011	COK	Chantalle	Desmarais	3/2/2018	Dining Room	Dining Room Table and Chairs	Finance	Standard	10,000
18	2018-012	KRM	Ambrose	Sardelis	3/2/2018	Appliances	Washer	Paid in Full	Promotion	1,100
19	2018-013	COK	Chantalle	Desmarais	3/3/2018	Living Room	Recliners	Finance	Standard	2,430
20	2018-014	COK	Jade	Gallagher	3/3/2018	Dining Room	Dining Room Table and Chairs	Paid in Full	Standard	4,550
21	2018-015	MAP	Chantalle	Desmarais	3/3/2018	Living Room	Sofa, Loveseat, Chair Package	Finance	Standard	6,784
22	2018-016	MAP	Jade	Gallagher	3/4/2018	Appliances	Dishwasher	Paid in Full	Standard	640
23	2018-017	MAP	Jade	Gallagher	3/4/2018	Appliances	Refrigerator, Oven, Microwave Combo	Finance	Promotion	8,490
24	2018-018	KRM	Sebastian	Gruenewald	3/4/2018	Appliances	Refrigerator, Oven, Microwave Combo	Finance	Promotion	6,780

Sheet tabs: March Totals | March Individual

Reid Furniture — March Individual

	A	B	C	D	E	F	G	H	I	J	K
1	Reid Furniture										
2	Monthly Transactions:		March 2018								
3	Down Payment Requirement:		25%								
4											
5	Trans_No	Date	Sales_First	Sales_Last	Department	Furniture	Pay_Type	Trans_Type	Amou	Down_P	Owe
6	2018-001	3/1/2018	Sebastian	Gruenewald	Bedroom	Mattress	Finance	Promotion	2,788	697.00	2,091.00
7	2018-002	3/1/2018	Sebastian	Gruenewald	Bedroom	Mattress	Finance	Promotion	3,245	811.25	2,433.75
8	2018-003	3/1/2018	Jade	Gallagher	Living Room	Sofa, Loveseat, Chair Package	Finance	Promotion	10,000	2,500.00	7,500.00
9	2018-004	3/1/2018	Jade	Gallagher	Living Room	End Tables	Finance	Promotion	1,000	250.00	750.00
10	2018-005	3/1/2018	Jade	Gallagher	Appliances	Washer and Dryer	Finance	Promotion	2,750	687.50	2,062.50
11	2018-006	3/1/2018	Ambrose	Sardelis	Living Room	Sofa, Loveseat, Chair Package	Finance	Promotion	12,000	3,000.00	9,000.00
12	2018-007	3/1/2018	Jade	Gallagher	Dining Room	Dining Room Table	Finance	Promotion	3,240	810.00	2,430.00
13	2018-008	3/1/2018	Chantalle	Desmarais	Dining Room	Dining Room Table	Finance	Promotion	4,080	1,020.00	3,060.00
14	2018-009	3/1/2018	Sebastian	Gruenewald	Appliances	Washer and Dryer	Finance	Promotion	2,750	687.50	2,062.50
15	2018-010	3/2/2018	Jade	Gallagher	Dining Room	Dining Room Table and Chairs	Finance	Standard	6,780	1,695.00	5,085.00
16	2018-011	3/2/2018	Chantalle	Desmarais	Dining Room	Dining Room Table and Chairs	Finance	Standard	10,000	2,500.00	7,500.00
17	2018-012	3/2/2018	Ambrose	Sardelis	Appliances	Washer	Paid in Full	Promotion	1,100	1,100.00	-
18	2018-013	3/3/2018	Chantalle	Desmarais	Living Room	Recliners	Finance	Standard	2,430	607.50	1,822.50
19	2018-014	3/3/2018	Jade	Gallagher	Dining Room	Dining Room Table and Chairs	Paid in Full	Standard	4,550	4,550.00	-
20	2018-015	3/3/2018	Chantalle	Desmarais	Living Room	Sofa, Loveseat, Chair Package	Finance	Standard	6,784	1,696.00	5,088.00
21	2018-016	3/4/2018	Jade	Gallagher	Appliances	Dishwasher	Paid in Full	Standard	640	640.00	-
22	2018-017	3/4/2018	Jade	Gallagher	Appliances	Refrigerator, Oven, Microwave Combo	Finance	Promotion	8,490	2,122.50	6,367.50
23	2018-018	3/4/2018	Sebastian	Gruenewald	Appliances	Refrigerator, Oven, Microwave Combo	Finance	Promotion	6,780	1,695.00	5,085.00
24	2018-019	3/5/2018	Gallagher		Living Room	Sofa	Paid in Full	Standard	2,500	2,500.00	-

Sheet tabs: March Totals | March Individual

FIGURE 4.1 Reid Furniture Store Datasets

CASE STUDY | Reid Furniture Store

Starting File	File to be Submitted
e04h1Reid	**e04h4Reid_LastFirst**

Large Datasets

So far you have worked with worksheets that contain small datasets, a collection of structured, related data in a limited number of columns and rows. In reality, you will probably work with large datasets consisting of hundreds or thousands of rows and columns of data. When you work with small datasets, you can usually view most or all of the data without scrolling. When you work with large datasets, you probably will not be able to see the entire dataset onscreen even on a large, widescreen monitor set at high resolution. You might want to keep the column and row labels always in view, even as you scroll throughout the dataset. Figure 4.2 shows Reid Furniture Store's March 2018 sales transactions. Because it contains a lot of transactions, the entire dataset is not visible. You could decrease the zoom level to display more transactions; however, doing so decreases the text size onscreen, making it hard to read the data.

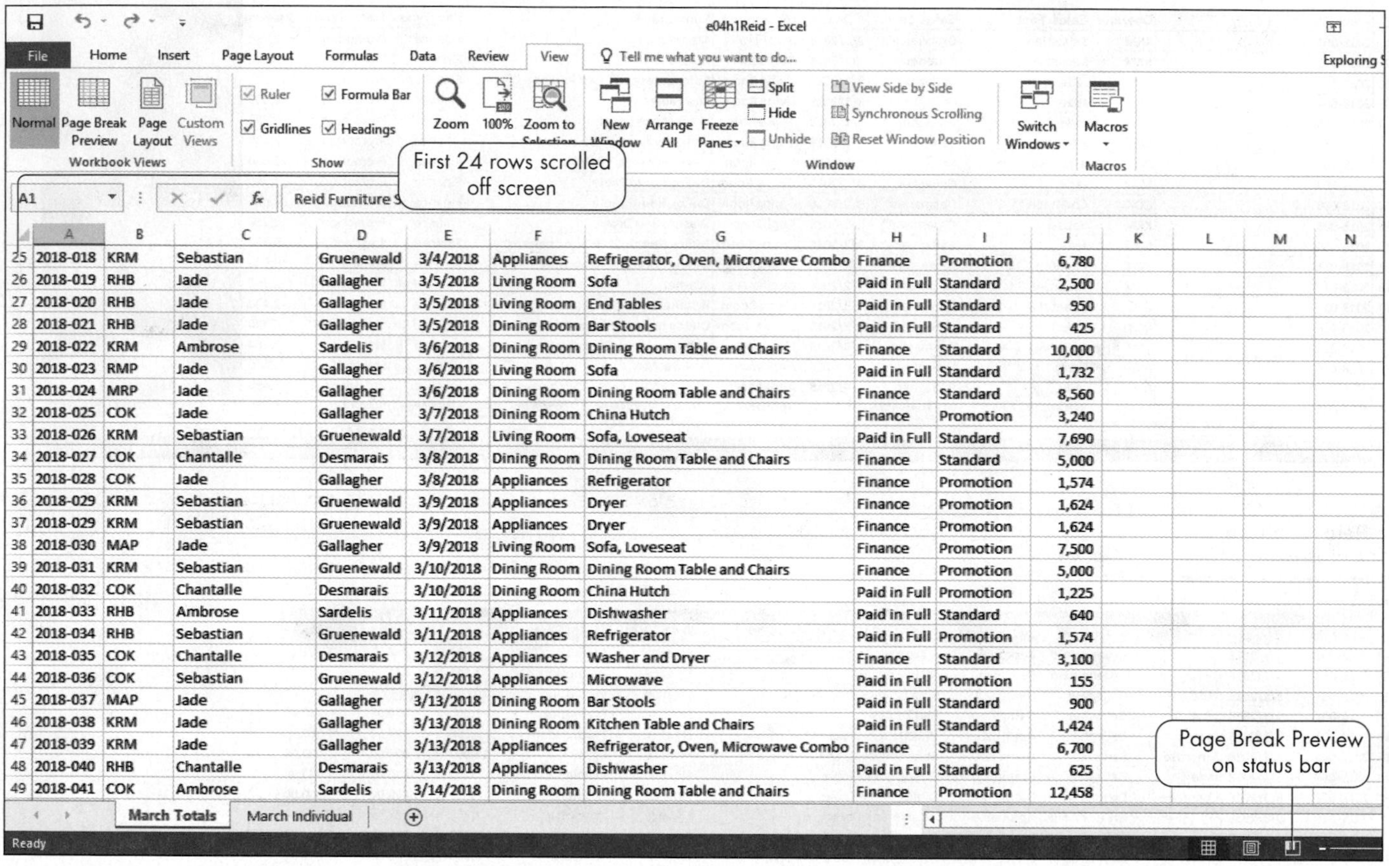

Excel 2016, Windows 10, Microsoft Corporation

FIGURE 4.2 Large Dataset

As you work with larger datasets, realize that the data will not always fit on one page when it is printed. You will need to preview the automatic page breaks and probably insert some manual page breaks in more desirable locations, or you might want to print only a selected range within the large dataset to distribute to others.

In this section, you will learn how to keep labels onscreen as you scroll through a large dataset. In addition, you will learn how to manage page breaks, print only a range instead of an entire worksheet, and print column labels at the top of each page of a large dataset.

Freezing Rows and Columns

STEP 1 ›› When you scroll to parts of a dataset not initially visible, some rows and columns, such as headings, disappear from view. When the row and column labels scroll off the screen, you may not remember what each column or row represents. You can keep labels onscreen by freezing them. *Freezing* is the process of keeping rows and/or columns visible onscreen at all times even when you scroll through a large dataset. Table 4.1 describes the three freeze options.

TABLE 4.1 Freeze Options	
Option	**Description**
Freeze Panes	Keeps both rows and columns above and to the left of the active cell visible as you scroll through a worksheet.
Freeze Top Row	Keeps only the top row visible as you scroll through a worksheet.
Freeze First Column	Keeps only the first column visible as you scroll through a worksheet.

Pearson Education, Inc.

To freeze one or more rows and columns, use the Freeze Panes option. Before selecting this option, make the active cell one row below and one column to the right of the rows and columns you want to freeze. For example, to freeze the first five rows and the first column, make cell B6 the active cell before clicking the Freeze Panes option. As Figure 4.3 shows, Excel displays a horizontal line below the last frozen row (row 5) and a vertical line to the right of the last frozen column (column F). Unfrozen rows (such as rows 6–14) and unfrozen columns (such as columns G and H) are no longer visible as you scroll down and to the right, respectively.

	A	B	C	D	E	F	G	H	I	J	K
1	**Reid Furniture Store**						Vertical line to the right of last frozen column				
2	Monthly Transactions:			March 2018							
3	Down Payment Requirement:			25%				Horizontal line below last frozen row			
4	Rows 1–5 and columns A–F frozen										
5	Trans_No	Operator	Sales_First	Sales_Last	Date	Department	Furniture	Pay_Type	Trans_Type	Amount	
21	2018-015	MAP	Chantalle	Desmarais	3/3/2018	Living Room	Sofa, Loveseat, Chair Package	Finance	Standard	6,784	
22	2018-016	MAP	Jade	Gallagher	3/4/2018	Appliances	Dishwasher	Paid in Full	Standard	640	
23	2018-017	MAP	Jade	Gallagher	3/4/2018	Appliances	Refrigerator, Oven, Microwave Combo	Finance	Promotion	8,490	
24	2018-018	KRM	Sebastian	Gruenewald	3/4/2018	Appliances	Refrigerator, Oven, Microwave Combo	Finance	Promotion	6,780	
25	2018-018	KRM	Sebastian	Gruenewald	3/4/2018	Appliances	Refrigerator, Oven, Microwave Combo	Finance	Promotion	6,780	
26	2018-019	RHB	Jade	Gallagher	3/5/2018	Living Room	Sofa	Paid in Full	Standard	2,500	
27	2018-020	RHB	Jade	Gallagher	3/5/2018	Living Room	End Tables	Paid in Full	Standard	950	
28	2018-021	RHB	Jade	Gallagher	3/5/2018	Dining Room	Bar Stools	Paid in Full	Standard	425	
29	2018-022	KRM	Ambrose	Sardelis	3/6/2018	Dining Room	Dining Room Table and Chairs	Finance	Standard	10,000	
30	2018-023	RMP	Jade	Gallagher	3/6/2018	Living Room	Sofa	Paid in Full	Standard	1,732	
31	2018-024	MRP	Jade	Gallagher	3/6/2018	Dining Room	Dining Room Table and Chairs	Finance	Standard	8,560	
32	2018-025	COK	Jade	Gallagher	3/7/2018	Dining Room	China Hutch	Finance	Promotion	3,240	
33	2018-026	KRM	Sebastian	Gruenewald	3/7/2018	Living Room	Sofa, Loveseat	Paid in Full	Standard	7,690	
34	2018-027	COK	Chantalle	Desmarais	3/8/2018	Dining Room	Dining Room Table and Chairs	Finance	Standard	5,000	
35	2018-028	COK	Jade	Gallagher	3/8/2018	Appliances	Refrigerator	Finance	Promotion	1,574	
36	2018-029	KRM	Sebastian	Gruenewald	3/9/2018	Appliances	Dryer	Finance	Promotion	1,624	
37	2018-029	KRM	Sebastian	Gruenewald	3/9/2018	Appliances	Dryer	Finance	Promotion	1,624	
38	2018-030	MAP	Jade	Gallagher	3/9/2018	Living Room	Sofa, Loveseat	Finance	Promotion	7,500	
39	2018-031	KRM	Sebastian	Gruenewald	3/10/2018	Dining Room	Dining Room Table and Chairs	Finance	Promotion	5,000	

‹ › | **March Totals** | March Individual | ⊕

Excel 2016, Windows 10, Microsoft Corporation

FIGURE 4.3 Freeze Panes Set

To unlock the rows and columns from remaining onscreen as you scroll, click Freeze Panes in the Window group and select Unfreeze Panes, which only appears on the menu when you have frozen rows and/or columns. After you unfreeze the panes, the Freeze Panes option appears instead of Unfreeze Panes on the menu again.

When you freeze panes and press Ctrl+Home, the first unfrozen cell is the active cell instead of cell A1. For example, with column F and rows 1 through 5 frozen in Figure 4.3, pressing Ctrl+Home makes cell G6 the active cell. If you want to edit a cell in the frozen area, click the particular cell to make it active and edit the data.

Printing Large Datasets

For a large dataset, some columns and rows may print on several pages. Analyzing the data on individual printed pages is difficult when each page does not contain column and row labels. To prevent wasting paper, always use Print Preview. Doing so enables you to adjust page settings until you are satisfied with how the data will print.

The Page Layout tab (see Figure 4.4) contains options to help you prepare large datasets to print. Previously, you changed the page orientation, set different margins, and adjusted the scaling. In addition, you can manage page breaks, set the print area, and print titles.

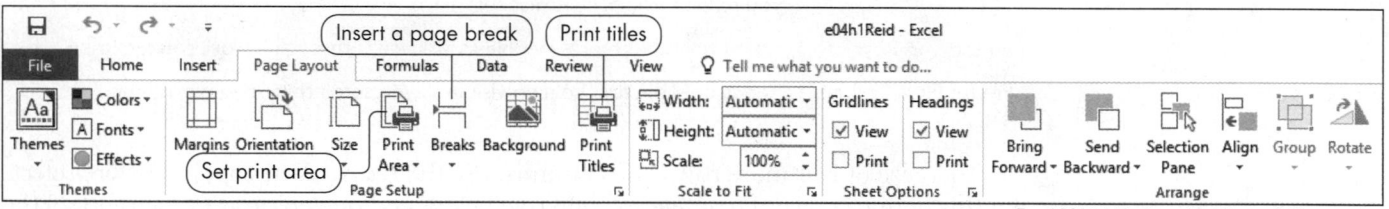

FIGURE 4.4 Page Setup Options

Excel 2016, Windows 10, Microsoft Corporation

Display and Change Page Breaks

STEP 2 ❯❯ Based on the paper size, orientation, margins, and other settings, Excel identifies how much data can print on a page. Then it displays a ***page break***, indicating where data will start on another printed page. To identify where these automatic page breaks will occur, click Page Break Preview on the status bar or in the Workbook Views group on the View tab. In Page Break Preview, Excel displays watermarks, such as Page 1, indicating the area that will print on a specific page. Blue dashed lines indicate where the automatic page breaks occur, and solid blue lines indicate manual page breaks.

If the automatic page breaks occur in an undesirable location, you can insert a manual page break. For example, if you have a worksheet listing sales data by date, the automatic page break might occur within a group of rows for one date, such as between two rows of data for 3/1/2018. To make all rows for that date appear together, you can either insert a page break above the first data row for that date or decrease the margins so that all 3/1/2018 transactions fit at the bottom of the page.

> **To set a manual break at a specific location, complete the following steps:**
>
> 1. Click the cell that you want to be the first row and column on a new printed page. For example, if you click cell D50, you create a page for columns A through C, and then column D starts a new page.
> 2. Click the Page Layout tab.
> 3. Click Breaks in the Page Setup group and select Insert Page Break. Excel displays a solid blue line in Page Break Preview or a dashed line in Normal view to indicate the manual page breaks you set. Figure 4.5 shows a worksheet with both automatic and manual page breaks.

To remove a manual page break, complete the following steps:

1. Click a cell below a horizontal page break or a cell to the right of a vertical page break.
2. Click Breaks in the Page Setup group and select Remove Page Break.

To reset all page breaks back to the automatic page breaks, complete the following steps:

1. Click Breaks in the Page Setup group.
2. Select Reset All Page Breaks.

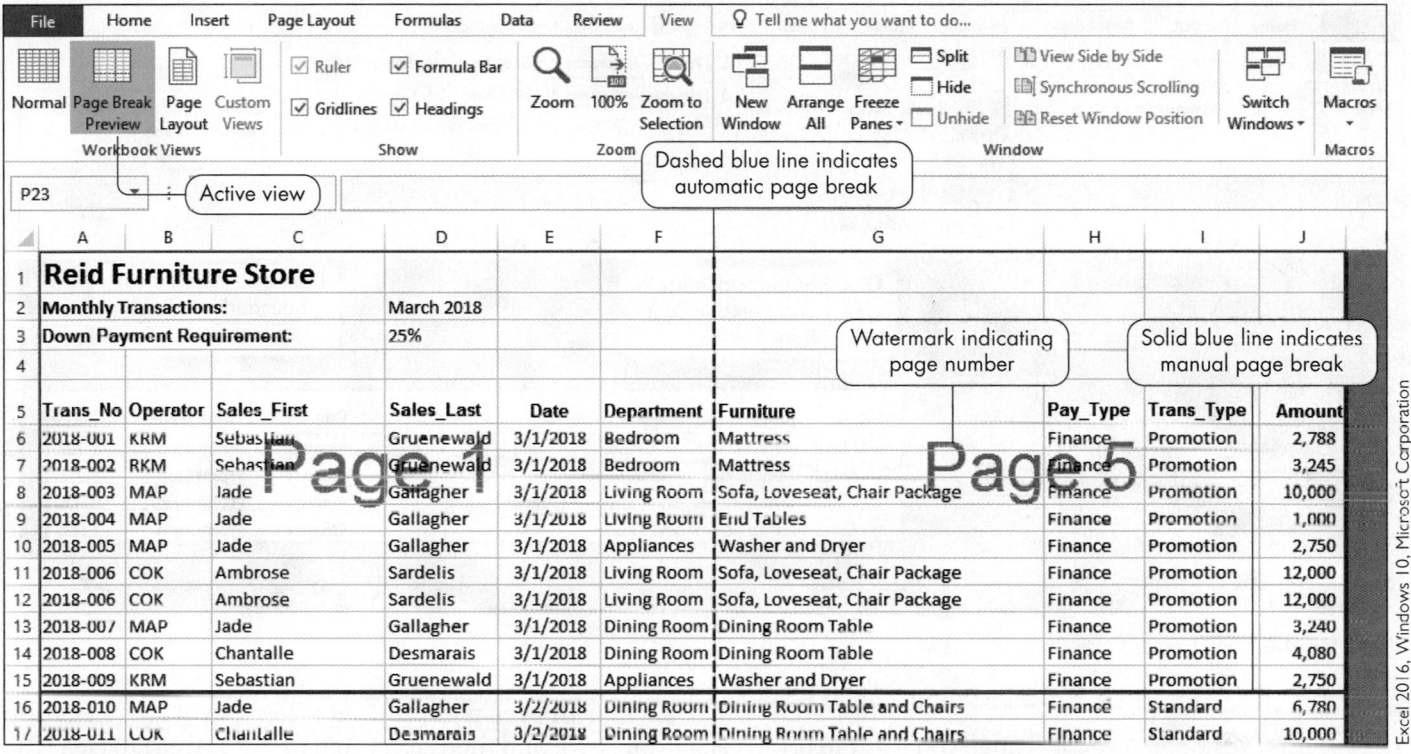

FIGURE 4.5 Page Breaks in Page Break Preview

TIP: USING THE POINTER TO MOVE PAGE BREAKS
To use the pointer to adjust a page break, point to the page break line to see the two-headed arrow and drag the line to the location where you want the page break to occur.

Set and Clear a Print Area

STEP 3 ❱❱ The default Print settings send an entire dataset on the active worksheet to the printer. However, you might want to print only part of the worksheet data. If you display the worksheet in Page Break view, you can identify which page(s) you want to print. Then click the File tab and select Print. Under Settings, type the number(s) of the page(s) you want to print. For example, to print page 2 only, type 2 in the Pages text box and in the *to* text box.

You can further restrict what is printed by setting the ***print area***, which is the range of cells that will print. For example, you might want to print only an input area or just the transactions that occurred on a particular date.

In Page Break Preview, the print area has a white background and solid blue border; the rest of the worksheet has a gray background (see Figure 4.6). In Normal view or Page Layout view, the print area is surrounded by thin gray lines.

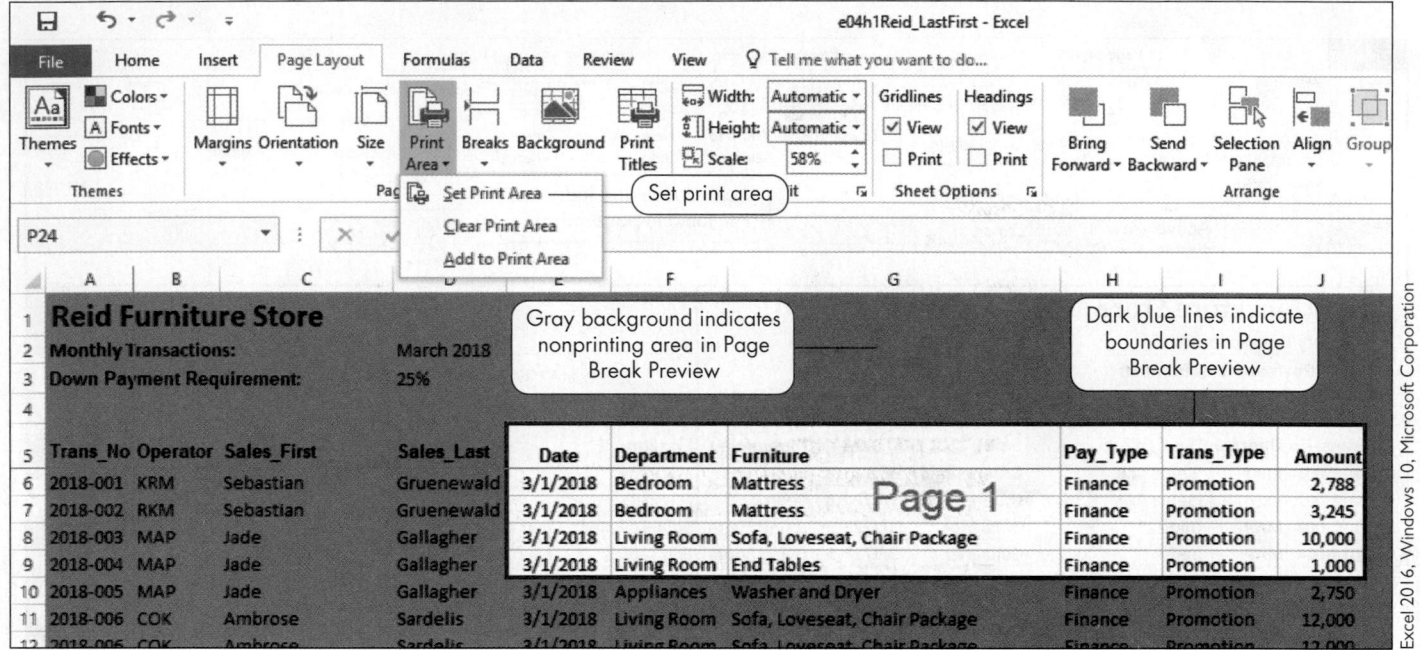

FIGURE 4.6 Print Area in Page Break Preview

To add print areas where each print area will print on a separate page, select the range you want to print, click Print Area, and then select Add to Print Area. To clear the print area, click Print Area in the Page Setup group and select Clear Print Area.

TIP: PRINT A SELECTION

Another way to print part of a worksheet is to select the range you want to print. Click the File tab and click Print. Click the first arrow in the Settings section and select Print Selection. This provides additional flexibility compared to using a defined print area in situations in which you may be required to print materials outside a consistent range of cells.

Print Titles

STEP 4 ▶▶ When you print large datasets, it is helpful if every page contains descriptive column and row labels. When you click Print Titles in the Page Setup group on the Page Layout tab, Excel opens the Page Setup dialog box with the Sheet tab active so that you can select which row(s) and/or column(s) to repeat on each page of a printout (see Figure 4.7).

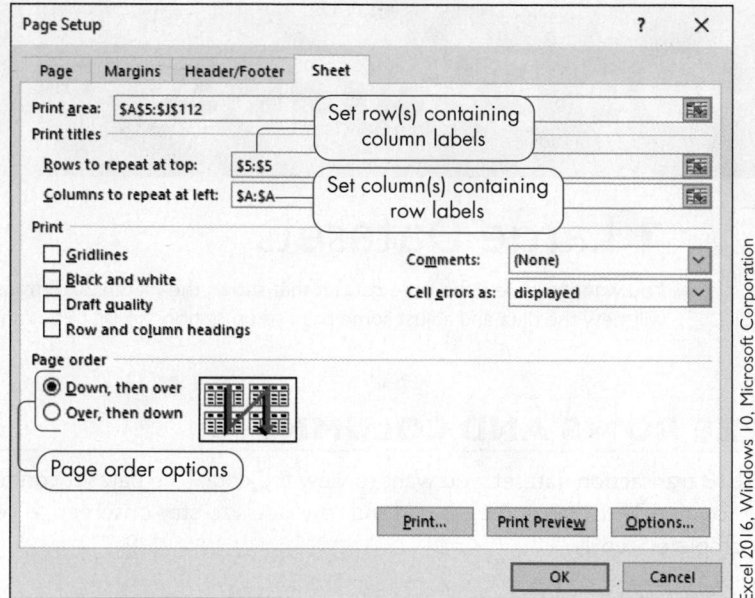

FIGURE 4.7 Sheet Tab Options

To repeat rows or columns at the top or left of each page when printed, select the row(s) that contain the labels or titles (such as row 5) in the *Rows to repeat at top* box to display $5:$5. To print the row labels at the left side of each page, select the column(s) that contain the labels or titles (such as column A) in the *Columns to repeat at left* box to display AA.

Control Print Page Order

Print order is the sequence in which the pages are printed. By default, the pages print in this order: top-left section, bottom-left section, top-right section, and bottom-right section. However, you might want to print the entire top portion of the worksheet before printing the bottom portion. To change the print order, open the Page Setup dialog box, click the Sheet tab, and then select the desired Page order option (refer to Figure 4.7).

Quick Concepts

1. What is the purpose of freezing panes in a worksheet? *p. 599*

2. Why would you want to insert page breaks instead of using the automatic page breaks? *p. 600*

3. What steps should you take to ensure that column labels display on each printed page of a large dataset? *pp. 602–603*

Hands-On Exercises

Watch the Video
for this Hands-On
Exercise!

MyITLab®
HOE1 Training

Skills covered: Freeze Rows and Columns • Display and Change Page Breaks • Set and Clear a Print Area • Print Titles

1 Large Datasets

You want to review the large dataset that shows the March 2018 transactions for Reid Furniture Store. You will view the data and adjust some page setup options so that you can print necessary labels on each page.

STEP 1 » FREEZE ROWS AND COLUMNS

Before printing the March 2018 transaction dataset, you want to view the data. The dataset contains more rows than will display onscreen at the same time. You decide to freeze the column and row labels to stay onscreen as you scroll through the transactions. Refer to Figure 4.8 as you complete Step 1.

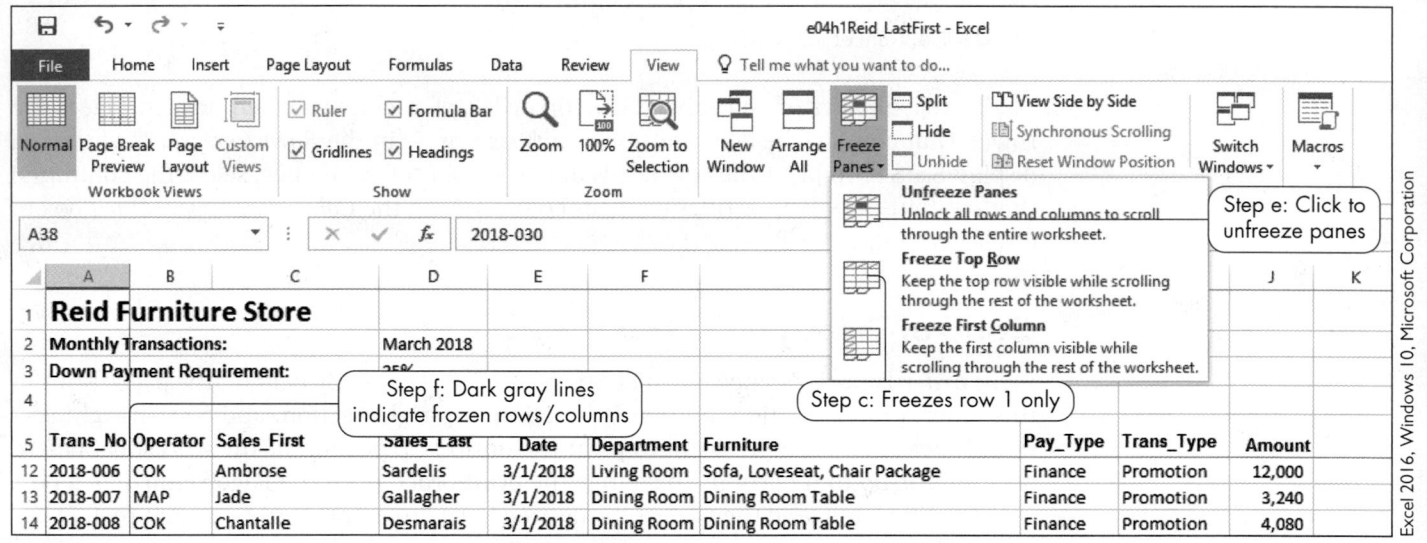

FIGURE 4.8 Freeze Panes Activated

a. Open *e04h1Reid* and save it as **e04h1Reid_LastFirst**.

> **TROUBLESHOOTING:** If you make any major mistakes in this exercise, you can close the file, open *e04h1Reid* again, and then start this exercise over.

The workbook contains two worksheets: March Totals (for Hands-On Exercises 1–3) and March Individual (for Hands-On Exercise 4).

b. Press **Page Down** four times to scroll through the dataset. Then press **Ctrl+Home** to go back to the top of the worksheet.

After you press Page Down, the column labels in row 5 scroll off the screen, making it challenging to remember what type of data are in some columns.

c. Click the **View tab**, click **Freeze Panes** in the Window group, and then select **Freeze Top Row**.

A dark gray horizontal line displays between rows 1 and 2.

d. Press **Page Down** to scroll down through the worksheet.

As rows scroll off the top of the Excel window, the first row remains frozen onscreen. The title by itself is not helpful; you need to freeze the column labels as well.

TROUBLESHOOTING: Your screen may differ from Figure 4.8 due to different Windows resolution settings. If necessary, continue scrolling right and down until you see columns and rows scrolling offscreen.

---

e. Click **Freeze Panes** in the Window group and select **Unfreeze Panes**.

f. Click **cell B6**, the cell below the row and one column to the right of what you want to freeze. Click **Freeze Panes** in the Window group and select **Freeze Panes**.

Excel displays a vertical line between columns A and B, indicating that column A is frozen, and a horizontal line between rows 5 and 6, indicating the first five rows are frozen.

g. Press **Ctrl+G**, type **Q112** in the Reference box of the Go To dialog box, and then click **OK** to make cell Q112 the active cell.

Rows 6 through 96 and columns B and C are not visible because they scrolled off the screen. Note that the results will vary slightly based on screen resolution.

h. Save the workbook.

You plan to print the dataset so that you and Vicki Reid can discuss the transactions in your weekly meeting. Because the large dataset will not fit on one page, you want to see where the automatic page breaks are and then insert a manual page break. Refer to Figure 4.9 as you complete Step 2.

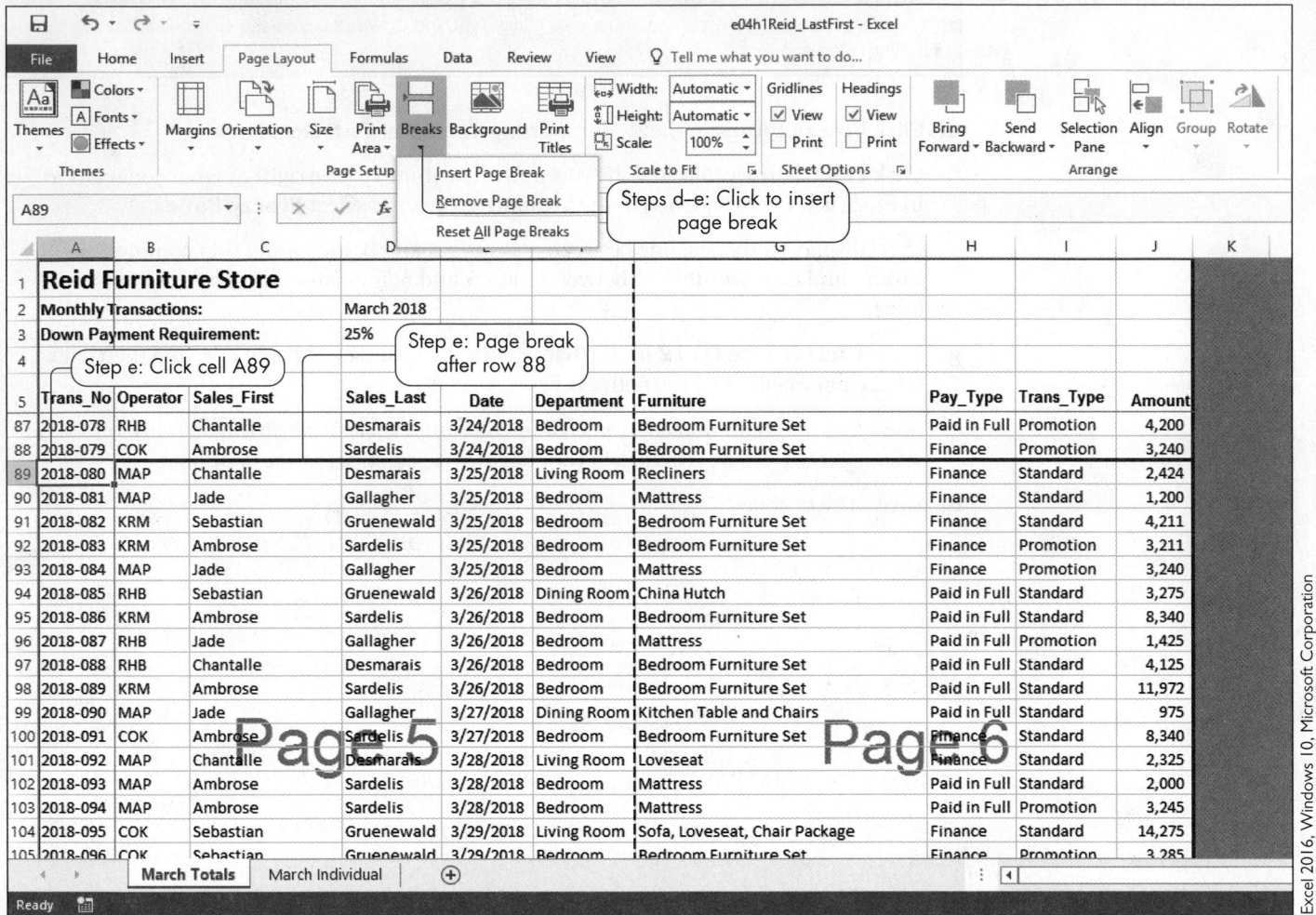

FIGURE 4.9 Page Breaks

a. Press **Ctrl+Home** to move to **cell B6**, the first cell in the unfrozen area. Click the **View tab** and click **Page Break Preview** in the Workbook Views group or on the status bar.

Excel displays blue dashed lines to indicate the automatic page breaks.

b. Scroll down until you see row 44 below the frozen column labels.

The automatic horizontal page break is between rows 46 and 47 (or between rows 45 and 46). You do not want transactions for a particular day to span between printed pages, so you need to move the page break up to keep all 3/13/2018 transactions together.

c. Click **cell A45**, the first cell containing 3/13/2018 data and the cell to start the top of the second page.

d. Click the **Page Layout tab**, click **Breaks** in the Page Setup group, and then select **Insert Page Break**.

You inserted a page break between rows 44 and 45 so that the 3/13/2018 transactions will be on one page.

e. Click **cell A89**, click **Breaks** in the Page Setup group, and then select **Insert Page Break**.

You inserted a page break between rows 88 and 89 to keep the 3/25/2018 transactions on the same page.

f. Save the workbook.

STEP 3 ›› SET AND CLEAR A PRINT AREA

You want to focus on the transactions for only March 1, 2018. To avoid printing more data than you need, you will set the print area to print transactions for only that day. Refer to Figure 4.10 as you complete Step 3.

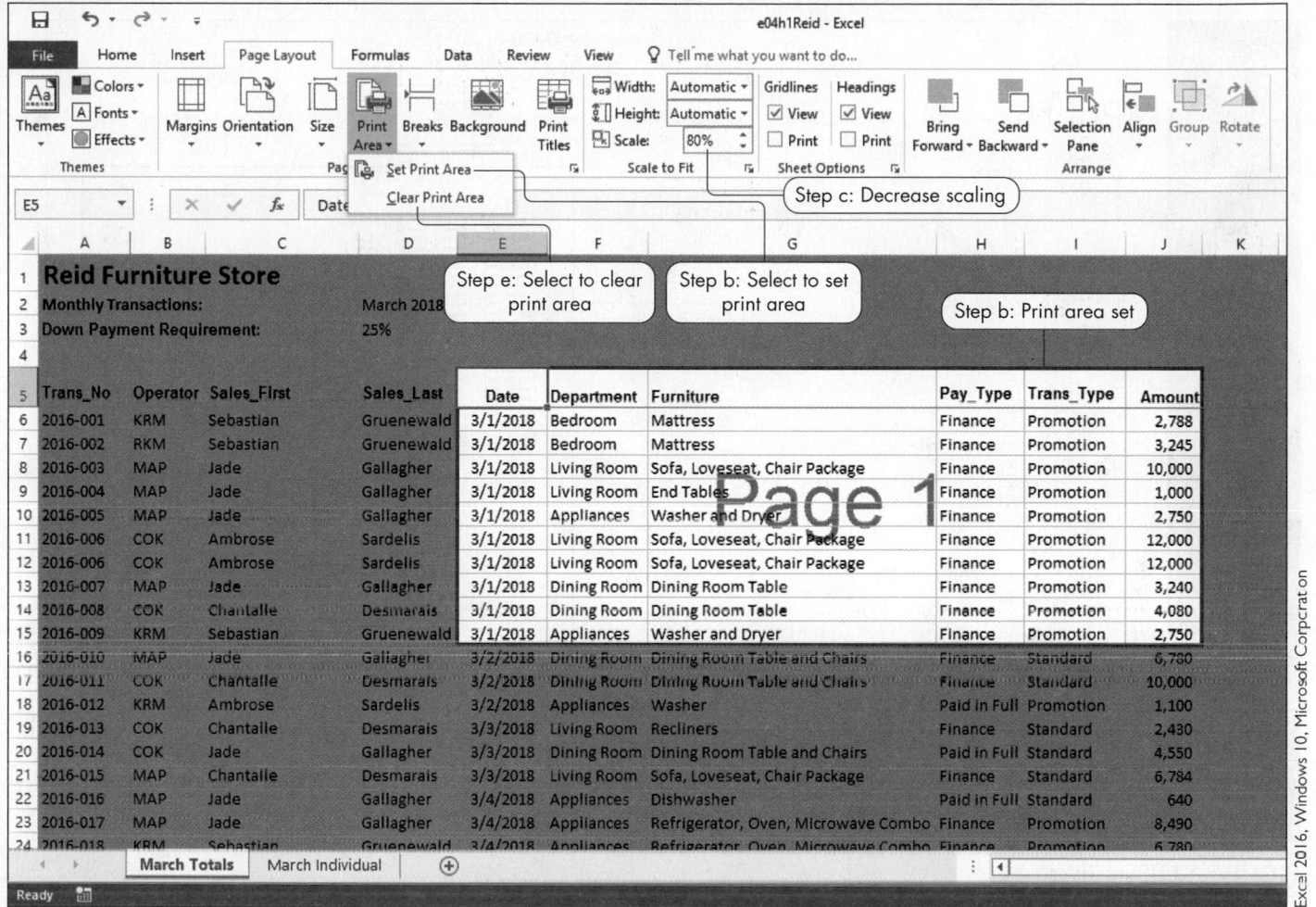

FIGURE 4.10 Print Area Set

a. Select the **range E5:J15**, the range of data for March 1, 2018.

b. Click the **Page Layout tab**, click **Print Area** in the Page Setup group, and then select **Set Print Area**.

Excel displays the print area with a border. The rest of the worksheet displays with a gray background.

c. Click **cell E5** and click the **Scale arrow** down four times to display 80% in the Scale to Fit group.

The selected print area will print on one page.

d. Press **Ctrl+P** to see that only the print area will print. Press **Esc**.

e. Click **Print Area** in the Page Setup group and select **Clear Print Area**.

f. Save the workbook.

Hands-On Exercise 1   **607**

Only the first page will print both row and column labels. Pages 2 and 3 will print the remaining row labels, page 4 will print the remaining column labels, and pages 5 and 6 will not print either label. You want to make sure the column and row labels print on all pages. To do this, you will print titles. Refer to Figure 4.11 as you complete Step 4.

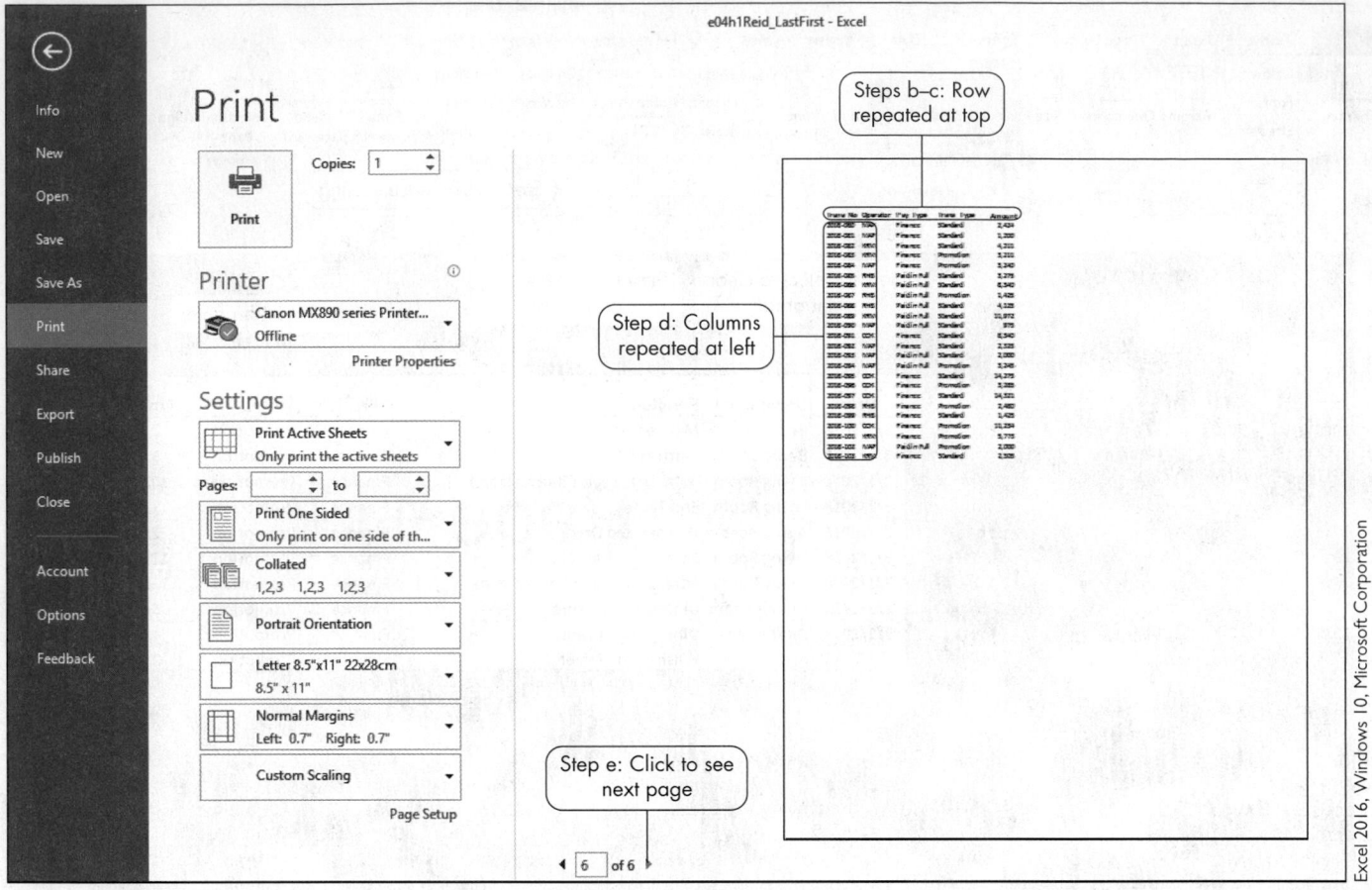

FIGURE 4.11 Print Titles

a. Click **Print Titles** in the Page Setup group.

The Page Setup dialog box opens, displaying the Sheet tab.

b. Click **Collapse Dialog Box** on the right side of the *Rows to repeat at top* box.

Clicking Collapse Dialog Box reduces the dialog box so that you can select a range in the worksheet easily.

c. Click the **row 5 heading** and click **Expand Dialog Box** within the *Page Setup: Rows to repeat at top* dialog box.

You selected the fifth row, which contains the column labels, and expanded the Page Setup dialog box back to its full size.

d. Click in the **Columns to repeat at left box**, type **A:B**, click the **Over, then down** Page order, and then click **Print Preview**.

You have manually entered the columns that contain the heading you want to repeat.

e. Click **Next Page** at the bottom of the Print Preview. Click **Next Page** until the sixth page displays.

Figure 4.11 shows a preview of the sixth page. The column labels and the first two columns appear on all pages.

f. Click the **Back arrow**.

g. Save the workbook. Keep the workbook open if you plan to continue with the next Hands-On Exercise. If not, close the workbook, and exit Excel.

Excel Tables

All organizations maintain lists of data. Businesses maintain inventory lists, educational institutions maintain lists of students and faculty, and governmental entities maintain lists of contracts. Although more complicated related data should be stored in a database management program, such as Access, you can manage basic data structure in Excel tables. A *table* is a structured range that contains related data organized in a method that increases the capability to manage and analyze information.

In this section, you will learn table terminology and rules for structuring data. You will create a table from existing data, manage records and fields, and remove duplicates. You will then apply a table style to format the table.

Understanding the Benefits of Data Tables

When dealing with large datasets it is imperative that documents are strategically organized to maintain data integrity and ease of use. Thus far you have worked with the manipulation of data ranges, and while you can use many tools in Excel to analyze simple data ranges, tables provide many additional analytical and time saving benefits. Using tables in Excel can help create and maintain data structure. *Data structure* is the organization method used to manage multiple data points within a dataset. For example, a dataset of students may include names, grades, contact information, and intended majors of study. The data structure of this dataset would define how the information is stored, organized, and accessed. Although you can manage and analyze data structure as a range in Excel, a table provides many advantages:

- Column headings remain onscreen without having to use Freeze Panes.
- Filter arrows let you sort and filter efficiently.
- Table styles easily format table rows and columns with complementary fill colors.
- Calculated columns let you create and edit formulas that copy down the columns automatically.
- A calculated total row lets you implement a variety of summary functions.
- You can use structured references instead of cell references in formulas.
- You can export table data to a SharePoint list.

Designing and Creating Tables

A table is a group of related data organized in a series of rows and columns that is managed independently from any other data on the worksheet. Once a data range is converted into a table, each column represents a *field*, which is an individual piece of data, such as last names or quantities sold. Each field should represent the smallest possible unit of data. For example, instead of a Name field, separate name data into First Name and Last Name fields. Instead of one large address field, separate address data into Street Address, City, State, and ZIP Code fields. Separating data into the smallest units possible enables you to manipulate the data in a variety of ways for output. Each row in a table represents a *record*, which is a collection of related data about one entity. For example, all data related to one particular transaction form a record in the Reid Furniture Store worksheet.

You should plan the structure before creating a table. The more thoroughly you plan, the fewer changes you will have to make to gain information from the data in the table after you create it. To help plan your table, follow these guidelines:

- Enter field (column) names on the top row of the table.
- Keep field names short, descriptive, and unique. No two field names should be identical.

- Format the field names so that they stand out from the data.
- Enter data for each record on a row below the field names.
- Do not leave blank rows between records or between the field names and the first record.
- Delete any blank columns between fields in the dataset.
- Make sure each record has something unique, such as a transaction number or ID.
- Insert at least one blank row and one blank column between the table and other data, such as the main titles. When you need multiple tables in one workbook, a best practice is to place each table on a separate worksheet.

Create a Table

STEP 1 ›› While it is possible to create a table from random unorganized data, it is a best practice first to plan the data structure. When your worksheet data is structured correctly, you can easily create a table. Furthermore, by taking the time to create an organized data structure you will ensure that the data can be used to identify specific information easily, is easy to manage, and is scalable.

To create a table from existing data, complete the following steps:

1. Click within the existing range of data.
2. Click the Insert tab and click Table in the Tables group. The Create Table dialog box opens (see Figure 4.12), prompting you to enter the range of data.
   - Select the range for the *Where is the data for your table* box if Excel does not correctly predict the range.
   - Select the *My table has headers* check box if the existing range contains column labels.
3. Click OK to create the table.

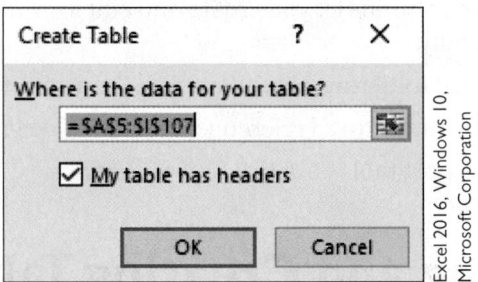

FIGURE 4.12 Create Table Dialog Box

TIP: QUICK ANALYSIS TABLE CREATION
You can also create a table by selecting a range, clicking the Quick Analysis button, clicking Tables (see Figure 4.13) in the Quick Analysis gallery, and then clicking Table. While Quick Analysis is efficient for tasks such as creating a chart, it may take more time to create a table because you have to select the entire range first. Some people find that it is faster to create a table on the Insert tab.

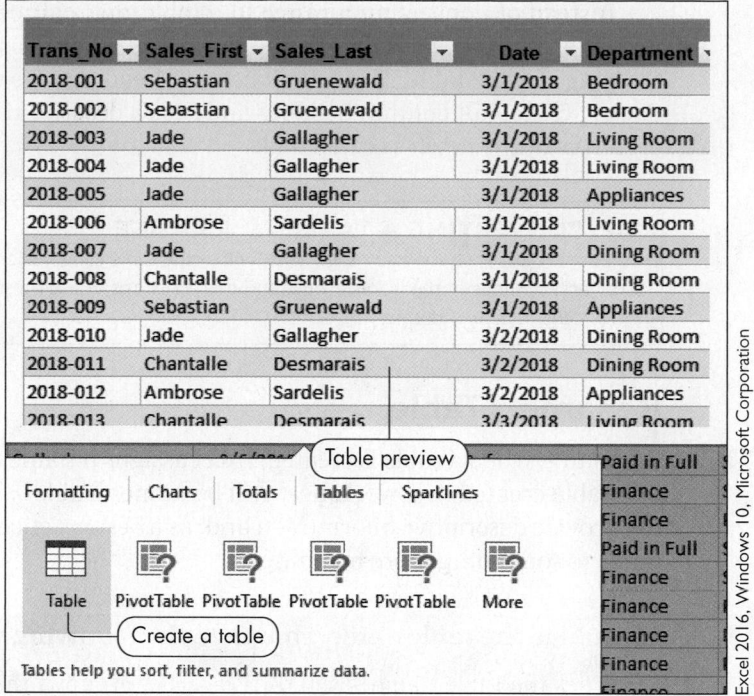

FIGURE 4.13 Quick Analysis Gallery

After you create a table, the Table Tools Design tab displays. Excel applies the default Table Style Medium 2 style to the table, and each cell in the header row has filter arrows (see Figure 4.14). This book uses the term *filter arrows* for consistency.

> **TIP: FILTER ARROWS**
> Click the Filter Button check box in the Table Style Options group on the Design tab to display or hide the filter arrows (see Figure 4.14). For a range of data instead of a table, click Filter in the Sort & Filter group on the Data tab to display or hide the filter arrows.

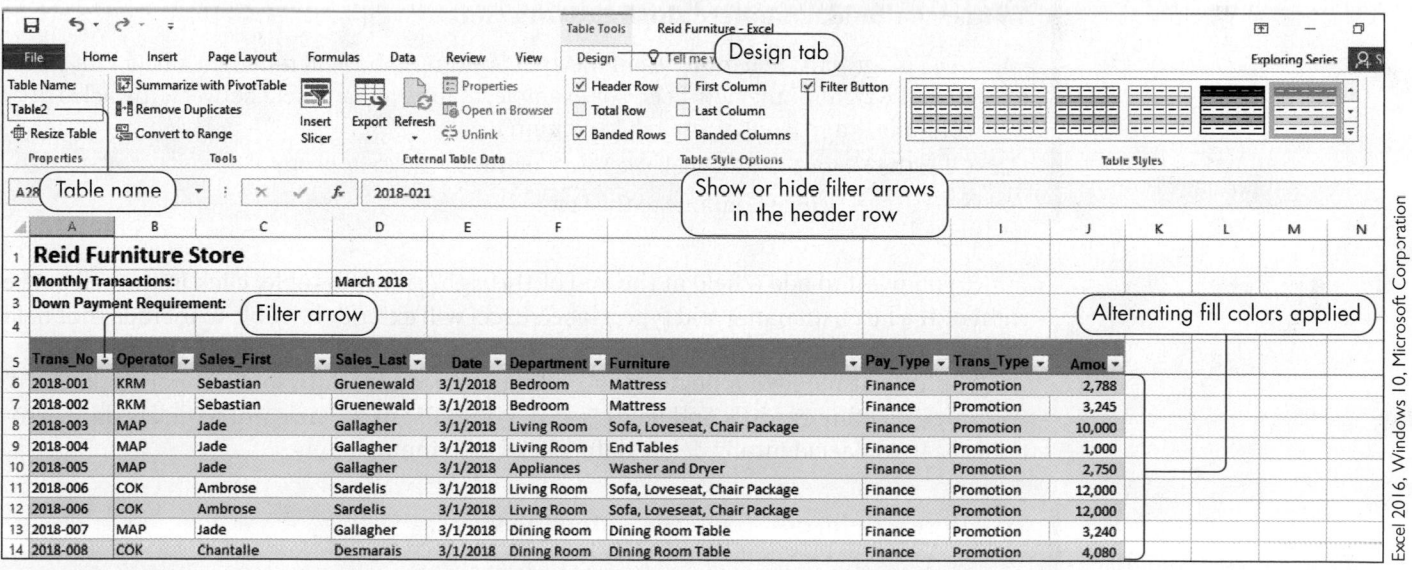

FIGURE 4.14 Excel Table in Default Format

Instead of converting a range to a table, you can create a table structure first and add data to it later. Select an empty range and follow the previously listed steps to create the range for the table. The default column headings are Column1, Column2, and so on. Click each default column heading and type a descriptive label. Then enter the data into each row of the newly created table.

TIP: CONVERTING A TABLE TO A RANGE
To convert a table back to a range, click within the table range, click the Table Tools Design tab, click Convert to Range in the Tools group, and then click Yes in the message box asking, *Do you want to convert the table to a normal range?*

Rename a Table

 By default, when a table is created, Excel assigns a name automatically. For example, the first table created in a worksheet will be named Table1. The default nomenclature does not provide descriptive information and, as a best practice, you should change the default name to something more meaningful.

To change the table name, complete the following steps:

1. Click the Table Name box in the Properties group of the Table Tools Design tab.
2. Type a new name using the same rules you applied when assigning range names, and press Enter.

Once a name has been assigned to a table, it can be used when building functions in place of the traditional absolute reference.

Add and Delete Fields

After creating a table, you may need to insert a new field. For example, you might want to add a field for product numbers to the Reid Furniture Store transaction table.

To insert a field, complete the following steps:

1. Click in any data cell (other than the cell containing the field name) in a field that will be to the right of the new field. For example, to insert a new field between the fields in columns A and B, click any cell in column B.
2. Click the Home tab and click the Insert arrow in the Cells group.
3. Select Insert Table Columns to the Left.

If you want to add a field at the end of the right side of a table, click in the cell to the right of the last field name and type a label. Excel will extend the table to include that field and will format the cell as a field name.

You can also delete a field if you no longer need any data for that particular field. Although deleting records and fields is easy, you must make sure not to delete data erroneously. If you accidentally delete data, click Undo immediately.

To delete a field, complete the following steps:

1. Click a cell in the field that you want to delete.
2. Click the Delete arrow in the Cells group on the Home tab.
3. Select Delete Table Columns.

Add, Edit, and Delete Records

**STEP 4** ❱❱ After you begin storing data in your newly created table, you might want to add new records, such as adding a new client or a new item to an inventory table. One of the advantages to using tables in Excel is the ability to easily add, edit, or delete records within the dataset.

> **To add a record to a table, complete the following steps:**
>
> 1. Click a cell in the record below which you want the new record inserted. If you want to add a new record below the last record, click the row containing the last record.
> 2. Click the Home tab and click the Insert arrow in the Cells group.
> 3. Select Insert Table Rows Above to insert a row above the current row, or select Insert Table Row Below if the current row is the last one and you want a row below it.

You can also add a record to the end of a table by clicking in the row immediately below the table and typing. Excel will extend the table to include that row as a record in the table and will apply consistent formatting.

You might need to change data for a record. For example, when a client moves, you need to change the client's address. You edit data in a table the same way you edit data in a regular worksheet cell.

Finally, you can delete records. For example, if you maintain an inventory of artwork in your house and sell a piece of art, delete that record from the table.

> **To delete a record from the table, complete the following steps:**
>
> 1. Click a cell in the record that you want to delete.
> 2. Click the Home tab and click the Delete arrow in the Cells group.
> 3. Select Delete Table Rows.

Remove Duplicate Rows

STEP 5 ❱❱ A table might contain duplicate records, which can give false results when totaling or performing other calculations on the dataset. For a small table, you might be able to detect duplicate records by scanning the data. For large tables, it is more difficult to identify duplicate records by simply scanning the table with the eye.

> **To remove duplicate records, complete the following steps:**
>
> 1. Click within the table and click the Design tab.
> 2. Click Remove Duplicates in the Tools group to display the Remove Duplicates dialog box (see Figure 4.15). As an alternate method, you can also click the Data tab and click Remove Duplicates in the Data Tools group to open the Remove Duplicates dialog box.
> 3. Click Select All to set the criteria to find a duplicate for every field in the record and click OK. If you select individual column(s), Excel looks for duplicates in the specific column(s) only and deletes all but one record of the duplicated data. Excel will display a message box informing you of how many duplicate rows it removed.

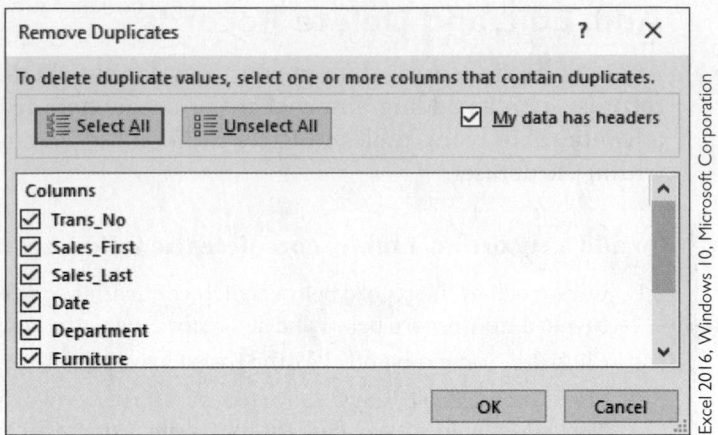

FIGURE 4.15 Remove Duplicates Dialog Box

Applying a Table Style

When you create a table, it is automatically formatted with a table style of alternating colored rows and a bold style for the header row. *Table styles* control the fill color of the header row (the row containing field names) and rows of records. In addition, table styles specify bold and border lines. You can change the table style to a color scheme that complements your organization's color scheme or to emphasize data in the header rows or columns. Click the More button in the Table Styles group to display the Table Styles gallery (see Figure 4.16). To see how a table style will format your table using Live Preview, point to a style in the Table Styles gallery. After you identify a style you want, click it to apply it to the table.

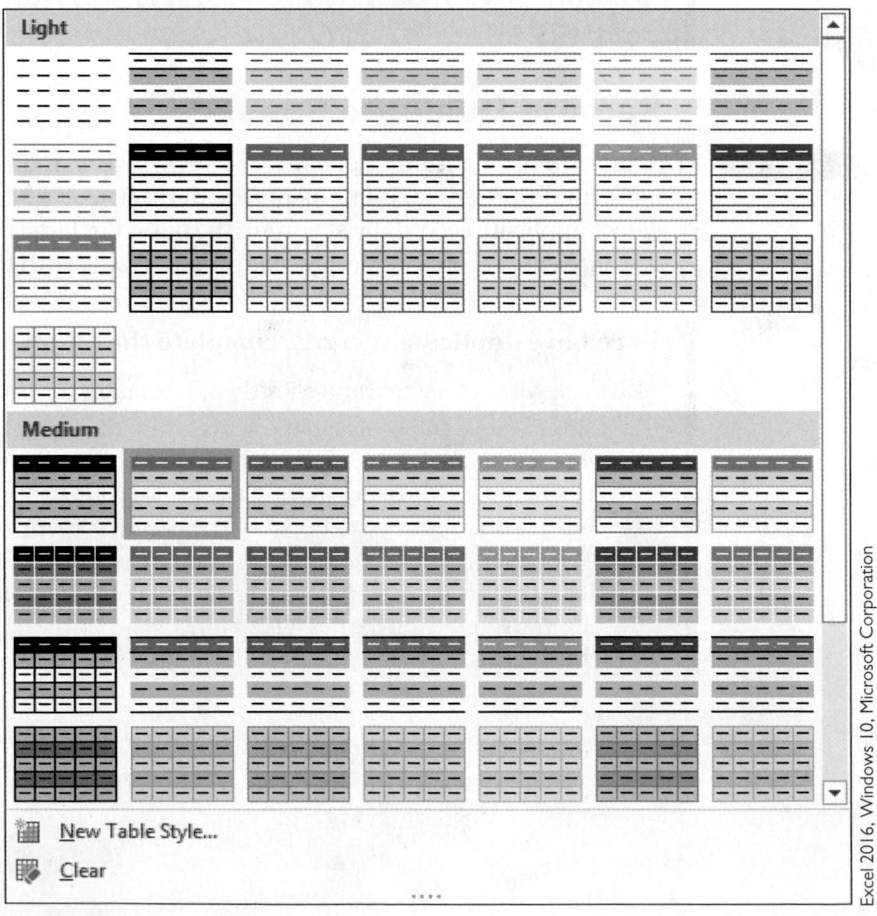

FIGURE 4.16 Table Styles Gallery

After you select a table style, you can control what the style formats. The Table Style Options group contains check boxes to select specific format actions in a table. Table 4.2 lists the options and the effect of each check box. Avoid overformatting the table. Applying too many formatting effects may obscure the message you want to present with the data.

TABLE 4.2	Table Style Options
Check Box	**Action**
Header Row	Displays the header row (field names) when checked; removes field names when not checked. Header Row formatting takes priority over column formats.
Total Row	Displays a total row when selected. Total Row formatting takes priority over column formats.
First Column	Applies a different format to the first column so that the row headings stand out. First Column formatting takes priority over Banded Rows formatting.
Last Column	Applies a different format to the last column so that the last column of data stands out; effective for aggregated data, such as grand totals per row. Last Column formatting takes priority over Banded Rows formatting.
Banded Rows	Displays alternate fill colors for even and odd rows to help distinguish records.
Banded Columns	Displays alternate fill colors for even and odd columns to help distinguish fields.
Filter Button	Displays a filter button on the right side of each heading in the header row.

Pearson Education, Inc.

Quick Concepts

4. List at least four guidelines for planning a table in Excel. **pp. 609–610**

5. Why would you convert a range of data into an Excel table? **p. 610**

6. What are six options you can control after selecting a table style? **p. 615**

Skills covered: Create a Table • Rename a Table • Add and Delete Fields • Add, Edit, and Delete Records • Remove Duplicate Rows • Apply a Table Style

2 Excel Tables

You want to convert the March Totals data to a table. As you review the table, you will delete the unnecessary Operator field, add two new fields, insert a missing furniture sale transaction, and remove duplicate transactions. Finally, you will enhance the table appearance by applying a table style.

STEP 1 ▶▶ CREATE A TABLE

Although Reid Furniture Store's March transaction data are organized in an Excel worksheet, you know that you will have additional functionality if you convert the range to a table. Refer to Figure 4.17 as you complete Step 1.

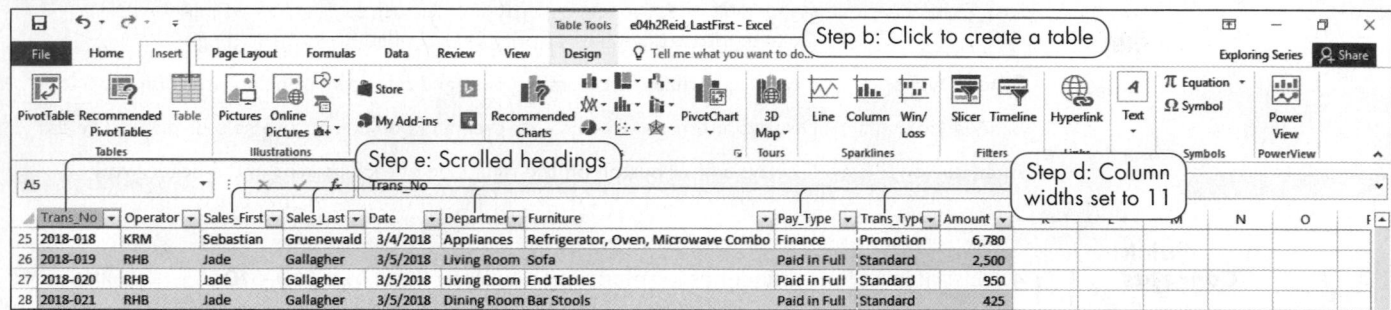

FIGURE 4.17 Range Converted to a Table

Excel 2016, Windows 10, Microsoft Corporation

a. Open *e04h1Reid_LastFirst* if you closed it at the end of Hands-On Exercise 1, and save it as **e04h2Reid_LastFirst**, changing h1 to h2. Click **Normal** on the status bar.

b. Click in any cell within the transactional data, click the **Insert tab**, and then click **Table** in the Tables group.

The Create Table dialog box opens. The *Where is the data for your table?* box displays =$A$5:$J$112. Keep the *My table has headers* check box selected so that the headings on the fifth row become the field names for the table.

c. Click **OK** and click **cell A5**.

Excel creates a table from the data range and displays the Design tab, filter arrows, and alternating fill colors for the records. The columns widen to fit the field names, although the wrap text option is still applied to those cells.

d. Set the column width to **11** for the Sales_First, Sales_Last, Department, Pay_Type, and Trans_Type fields.

e. Unfreeze the panes and scroll through the table.

With a regular range of data, column labels scroll off the top of the screen if you do not freeze panes. When you scroll within a table, the table's header row remains onscreen by moving up to where the Excel column (letter) headings usually display (see Figure 4.17). Note that it will not retain the bold formatting when scrolling.

f. Save the workbook.

After creating the table, you will change the name from the default "Table1" to a more descriptive title that meets your business standards. Refer to Figure 4.18 as you complete Step 2.

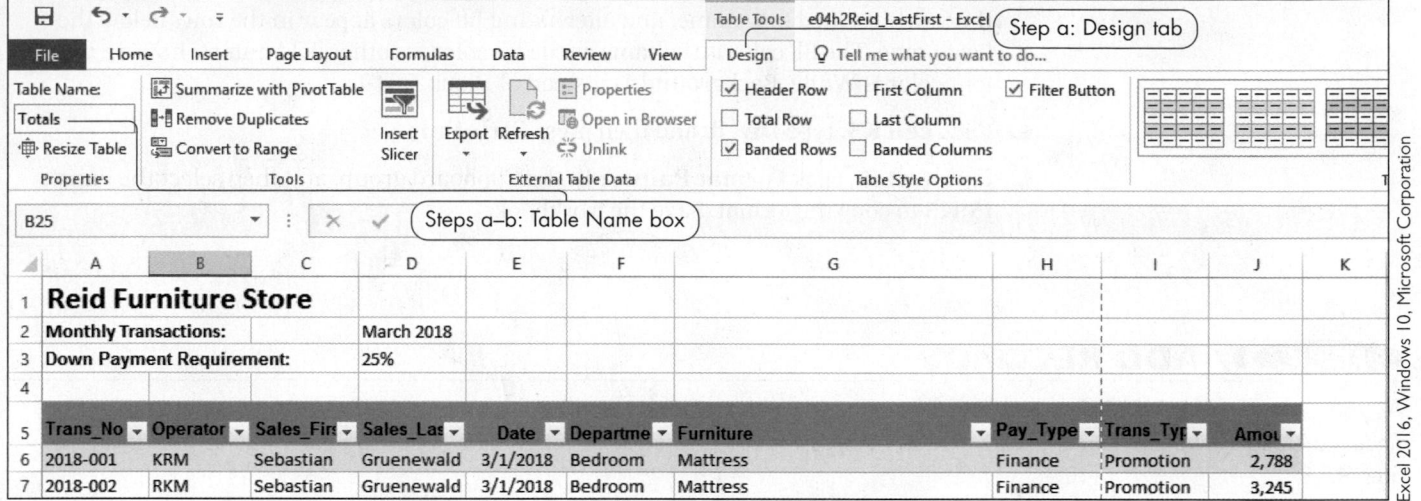

FIGURE 4.18 Rename the Table

a. Click the **Design tab**, and click the **Table Name box** in the Properties group.

b. Type **Totals** in the Table Name box and press **Enter**.

When a table is created, Excel assigns the default name "table" and a sequential number based on the number of tables in the document. For example, if there were two tables in the document the default name for the second table would be "Table2." In this step you have added a custom name that will be used throughout the rest of the project.

STEP 3 》》 **ADD AND DELETE FIELDS**

The original range included a column for the data entry operators' initials. You will delete this column because you do not need it for your analysis. In addition, you want to add a field to display down payment amounts in the future. Refer to Figure 4.19 as you complete Step 3.

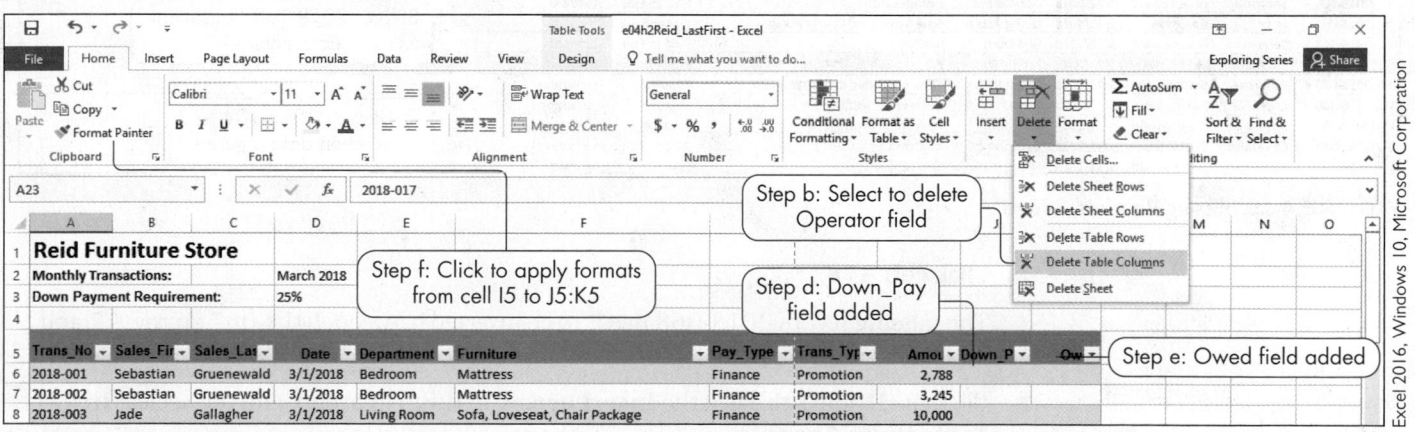

FIGURE 4.19 Newly Created Fields

a. Click any cell containing a value in the Operator column.

You need to make a cell active in the field you want to remove.

b. Click the **Home tab**, click the **Delete arrow** in the Cells group, and then select **Delete Table Columns**.

Excel deletes the Operator column and may adjust the width of other columns.

c. Set the widths of columns E, F, and G to AutoFit. Click **cell J5**, the first blank cell on the right side of the field names.

d. Type **Down_Pay** and press **Ctrl+Enter**.

Excel extends the table formatting to column J automatically. A filter arrow appears for the newly created field name, and alternating fill colors appear in the rows below the field name. The fill color is the same as the fill color for other field names; however, the font color is White, Background 1, instead of Black Text 1.

e. Click **cell K5**, type **Owed**, and then press **Ctrl+Enter**.

f. Click **cell I5**, click **Format Painter** in the Clipboard group, and then select the **range J5:K5** to copy the format. Save the workbook.

STEP 4 ▶▶ ADD RECORDS

As you review the March 2018 transaction table, you notice that two transactions are missing: 2018-068 and 2018-104. After finding the paper invoices, you are ready to add records with the missing transaction data. Refer to Figure 4.20 as you complete Step 4.

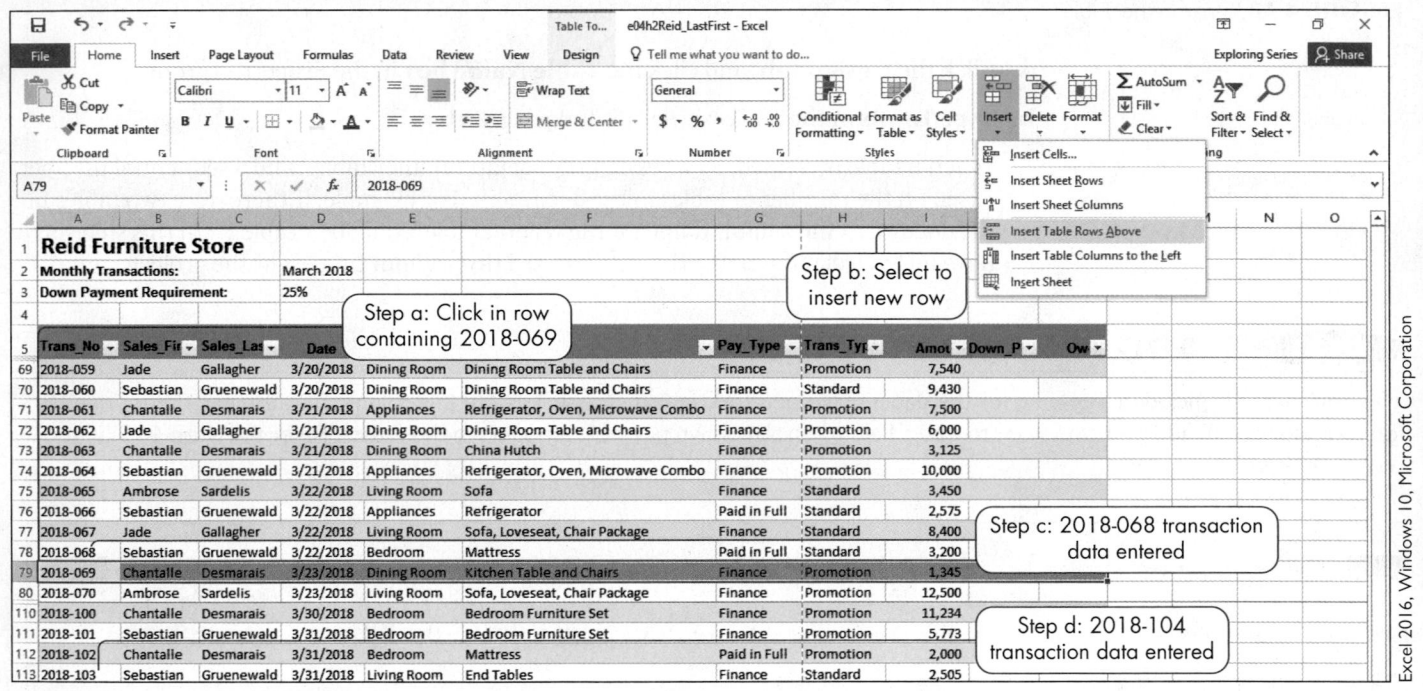

FIGURE 4.20 Missing Records Added

a. Click **cell A78**.

The missing record 2018-068 needs to be inserted between 2018-067 on row 77 and 2018-069 on row 78.

b. Click the **Home tab**, click the **Insert arrow** in the Cells group, and then select **Insert Table Rows Above**.

Excel inserts a new table row on row 78, between the 2018-067 and 2018-069 transactions.

c. Enter the following data in the respective fields on the newly created row:

2018-068, Sebastian, Gruenewald, 3/22/2018, Bedroom, Mattress, Paid in Full, Standard, 3200

d. Click **cell A114** and enter the following data in the respective fields:

2018-104, **Ambrose**, **Sardelis**, **3/31/2018**, **Appliances**, **Refrigerator**, **Paid in Full**, **Standard**, **1500**

When you start typing 2018-104 in the row below the last record, Excel immediately includes and formats row 114 as part of the table. Review Figure 4.20 to ensure that you inserted the records in the correct locations. In the figure, rows 81–109 are hidden to display both new records in one screenshot.

e. Save the workbook.

STEP 5 ›› REMOVE DUPLICATE ROWS

You noticed that the 2018-006 transaction is duplicated on rows 11 and 12 and that the 2018-018 transaction is duplicated on rows 24 and 25. You think the table may contain other duplicate rows. To avoid having to look at the entire table row by row, you will have Excel find and remove the duplicate rows for you. Refer to Figure 4.21 as you complete Step 5.

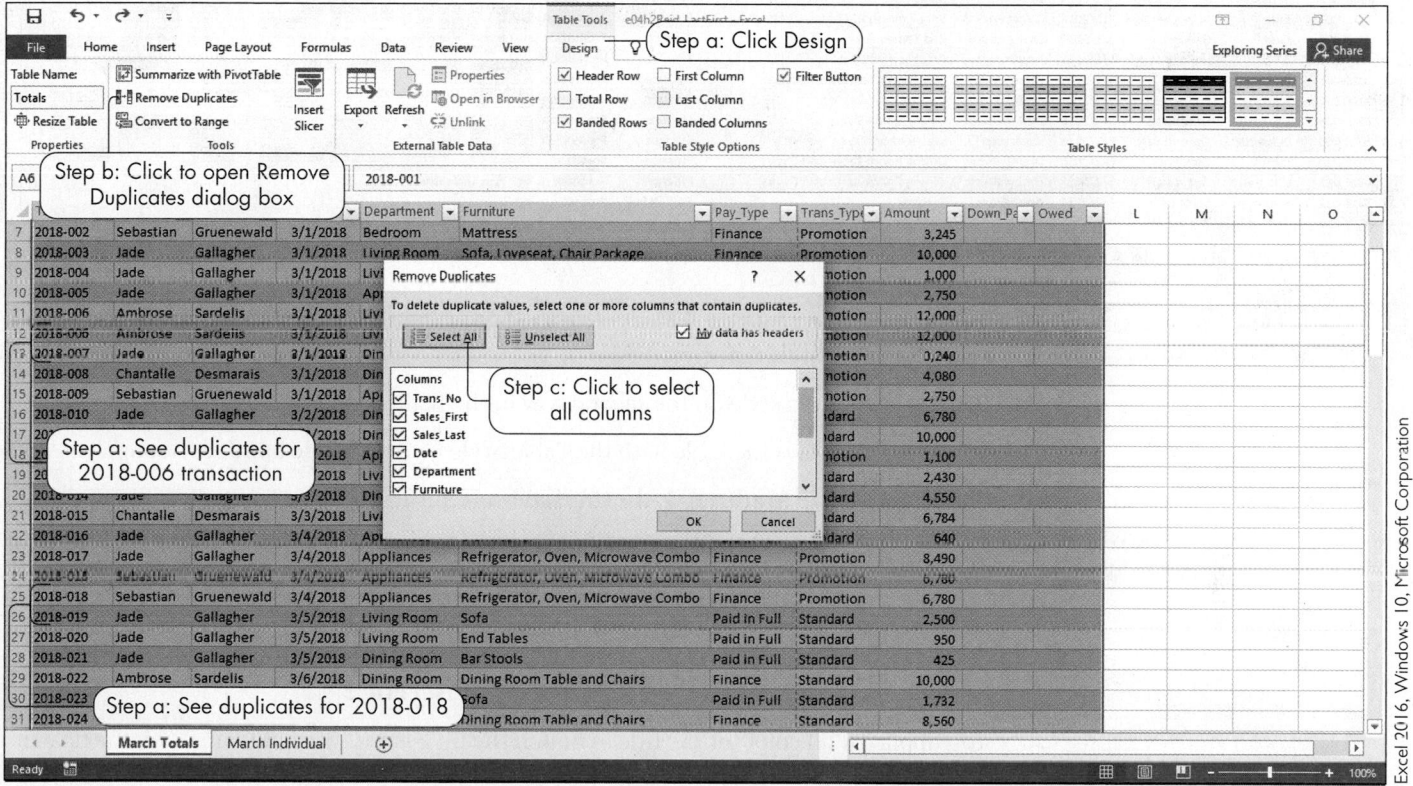

FIGURE 4.21 Remove Duplicate Records

a. Click a cell in the table. Scroll to see rows 11 and 12. Click the **Design tab**.

The records on rows 11 and 12 are identical. Rows 24 and 25 are also duplicates. You need to remove the extra rows.

b. Click **Remove Duplicates** in the Tools group.

The Remove Duplicates dialog box opens.

c. Click **Select All**, make sure the *My data has headers* check box is selected, and then click **OK**.

Excel displays a message box indicating 5 *duplicate records found and removed; 104 unique values remain*.

d. Click **OK** in the message box. Click **cell A109** to view the last record in the table. Save the workbook.

Transaction 2018-104 is located on row 109 after the duplicate records are removed.

Now that you have finalized the fields and added missing records to the March 2018 transaction table, you want to apply a table style to format the table. Refer to Figure 4.22 as you complete Step 6.

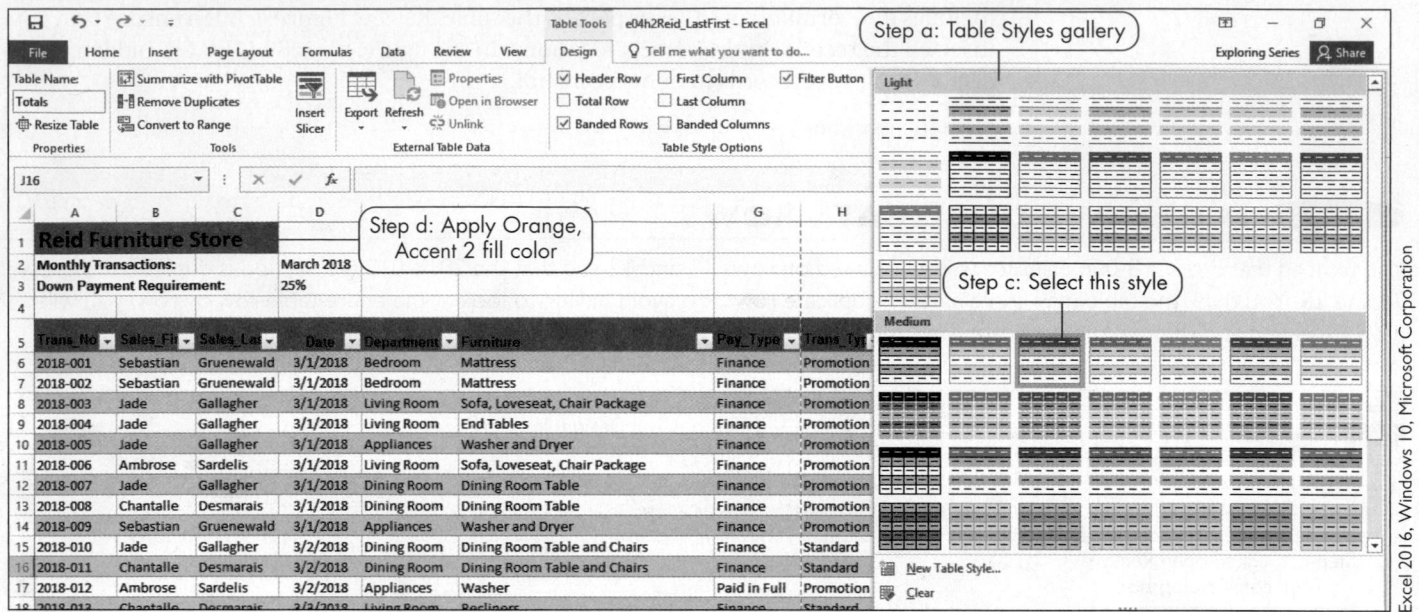

FIGURE 4.22 Table Style Applied

a. Click a cell in the table. Click the **Design tab** and click **More** in the Table Styles group to open the Table Styles gallery.

b. Point to the fourth style on the second row in the Light section.

   Live Preview shows the table with the Table Style Light 10 style but does not apply it.

c. Click **Table Style Medium 3**, the third style on the first row in the Medium section.

   Excel formats the table with the Medium 3 table style, which applies Orange, Accent 2 fill color to the table header row and Orange, Accent 2, Lighter 80% fill color to every other record.

d. Press **Ctrl+Home**. Select the **range A1:C1**, click the **Fill Color arrow** in the Font group on the Home tab, and then click **Orange, Accent 2**.

   You applied a fill color for the title to match the fill color of the field names on the header row in the table.

e. Save the workbook. Keep the workbook open if you plan to continue with the next Hands-On Exercise. If not, close the workbook, and exit Excel.

Table Manipulation

Along with maintaining data structure, tables have a variety of options to enhance and manipulate data, in addition to managing fields, adding records, and applying table styles. You can build formulas and functions, arrange records in different sequences to get different perspectives on the data, and restrict the onscreen appearance of data using filtering. For example, you can arrange the transactions by sales representative. Furthermore, you can display only particular records instead of the entire dataset to focus on a subset of the data. For example, you might want to focus on the financed transactions.

In this section, you will learn how to create structured references, and how to sort records by text, numbers, and dates in a table. In addition, you will learn how to filter data based on conditions you set.

Creating Structured References in Formulas

STEP 1 ▶▶ Your experience in building formulas involves using cell references, such as =SUM(B1:B15) or =H6*$B$3. Cell references in formulas help to identify where the content is on a worksheet, but does not tell the user what the content represents. An advantage to Excel tables is that they use structured references to clearly indicate which type of data is used in the calculations. A *structured reference* is a tag or use of a table element, such as a field heading, as a reference in a formula. As shown in Figure 4.23, structured references in formulas clearly indicate which type of data is used in the calculations.

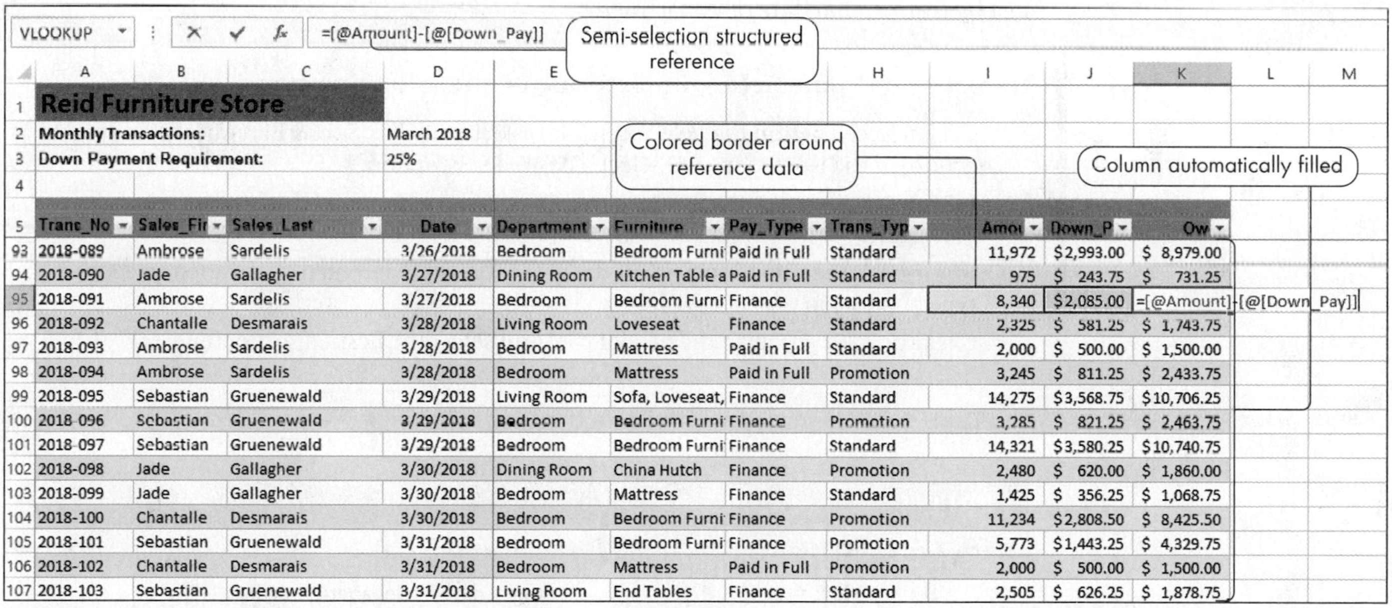

FIGURE 4.23 Structured Reference

When creating a formula in a table using structured references, field headings are set off by brackets around column headings or field names, such as =[Amount]–[Down_Pay]. The use of field headings without row references in a structured formula is called an *unqualified reference*. After you type the equal sign to begin your formula, type an opening bracket, and then Formula AutoComplete displays a list of field headings. Type or double-click the column name from the list and type the closing bracket. Excel displays a colored border around the referenced column that coordinates with the structured reference in the formula, similar to Excel identifying cell references and their worksheet placement. When you enter a formula using structured references, Excel copies the formula down the rest of the table column automatically, compared to typing references in formulas and using the fill handle to copy the formula down a column.

You can also use the semi-selection process to create a formula. As you click cells to enter a formula in a table, Excel builds a formula like this: =[@Amount]–[@Down_Pay], where the @ indicates the current row. If you use the semi-selection process to create a formula outside the table, the formula includes the table and field names, such as =Table1[@Amount]–Table1[@Down_Pay]. Table1 is the name of the table; Amount and Down_Pay are field names. This structured formula that includes references, such as table name, is called a *fully qualified structured reference*. When you build formulas *within* a table, you can use either unqualified or fully qualified structured references. If you need to use table data in a formula *outside* the table boundaries, you must use fully qualified structured references.

Sorting Data

Sometimes if you rearrange the order of records, new perspective is gained making the information easier to understand. In Figure 4.2, the March 2018 data are arranged by transaction number. You might want to arrange the transactions so that all of the transactions for a particular sales representative are together. **Sorting** is the process of arranging records by the value of one or more fields within a table. Sorting is not limited to data within tables; normal data ranges can be sorted as well.

Sort One Field

STEP 2 ▶▶ You can sort data in a table or a regular range in a worksheet. For example, you could sort by transaction date or department.

> **To sort by only one field, complete one of the following steps:**
>
> - Click in a cell within the field you want to sort and click Sort & Filter in the Editing group on the Home tab, and select a desired sort option.
> - Click in a cell within the field you want to sort and click Sort A to Z, Sort Z to A, or Sort in the Sort & Filter group on the Data tab.
> - Right-click the field to sort, point to Sort on the shortcut menu, and then select the type of sort you want.
> - Click the filter arrow in the header row and select the desired sort option.

Table 4.3 lists sort options by data type.

TABLE 4.3	Sort Options	
Data Type	**Options**	**Explanation**
Text	Sort A to Z	Arranges data in alphabetical order.
	Sort Z to A	Arranges data in reverse alphabetical order.
Dates	Sort Oldest to Newest	Displays data in chronological order, from oldest to newest.
	Sort Newest to Oldest	Displays data in reverse chronological order, from newest to oldest.
Values	Sort Smallest to Largest	Arranges values from the smallest value to the largest.
	Sort Largest to Smallest	Arranges values from the largest value to the smallest.
Color	Sort by Cell Color	Arranges data together for cells containing a particular fill color.
	Sort by Font Color	Arranges data together for cells containing a particular font color.

Pearson Education, Inc.

Sort Multiple Fields

STEP 3 ›› After sorting, if a second sort is applied the original sort will be removed. However, at times, sorting by only one field does not yield the desired outcome. Using multiple level sorts enables like records in the primary sort to be further organized by additional sort levels. For example, you could sort by date of transaction and then by last name. Excel enables you to sort data on 64 different levels.

To perform a multiple level sort, complete the following steps:

1. Click in any cell in the table.
2. Click Sort in the Sort & Filter group on the Data tab to display the Sort dialog box.
3. Select the primary sort level by clicking the Sort by arrow, selecting the field to sort by, and then clicking the Order arrow and selecting the sort order from the list.
4. Click Add Level, select the second sort level by clicking the Then by arrow, select the column to sort by, click the Order arrow, and then select the sort order from the list.
5. Continue to click Add Level and add sort levels until you have entered all sort levels (see Figure 4.24). Click OK.

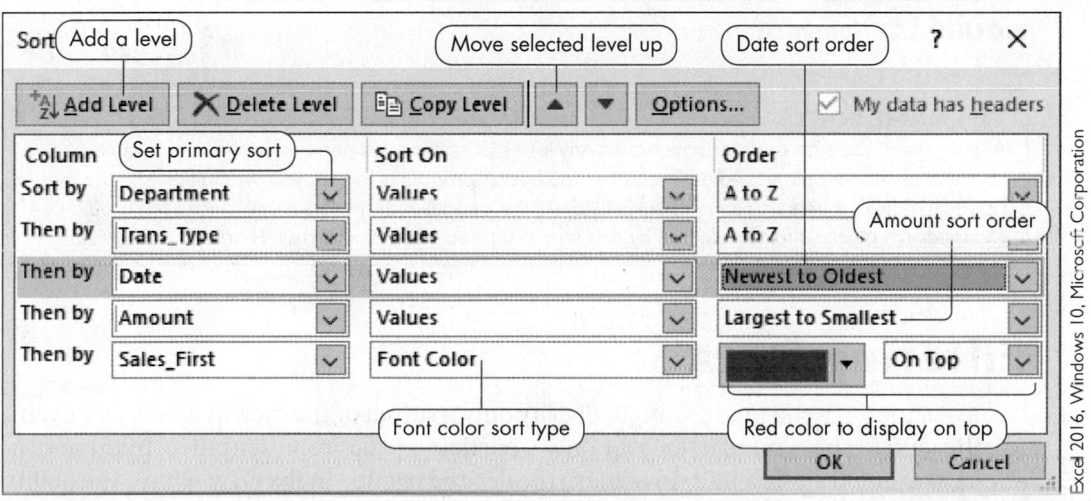

FIGURE 4.24 Sort Dialog Box

Create a Custom Sort

STEP 4 ›› Excel arranges data in alphabetical or numerical order. For example, days of the week are sorted alphabetically: Friday, Monday, Saturday, Sunday, Thursday, Tuesday, and Wednesday. However, you might want to create a custom sort sequence. For example, you can create a custom sort to arrange days of the week in order from Sunday to Saturday.

To create a custom sort sequence, complete the following steps:

1. Click Sort in the Sort & Filter group on the Data tab.
2. Click the Order arrow and select Custom List to display the Custom Lists dialog box (see Figure 4.25).
3. Select an existing sort sequence in the Custom lists box, or select NEW LIST.
4. Type the entries in the desired sort sequence in the List entries box, pressing Enter between entries.
5. Click Add and click OK.

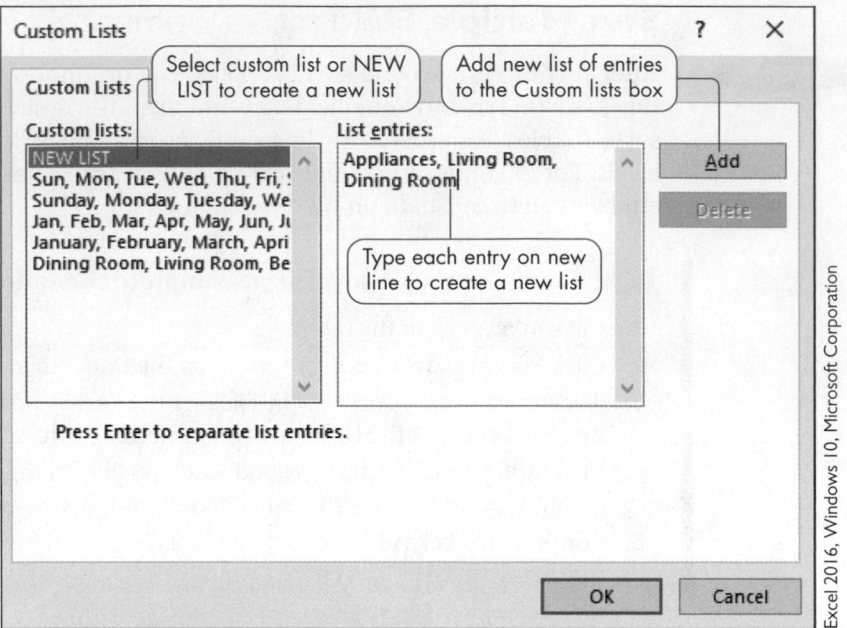

FIGURE 4.25 Custom Lists Dialog Box

> **TIP: NAME SORTS**
> Always check the data to determine how many levels of sorting you need to apply. If your table contains several people with the same last name but different first names, you would first sort by the Last Name field, then sort by First Name field. All the people with the last name Desmarais would be grouped together and further sorted by first name, such as Amanda and then Bradley.

Filtering Data

In some situations you might want to display only a subset of the data available, for example, the data to show transactions for only a particular sales representative. In these situations, you could apply a filter to achieve the desired results. In Excel, you have the ability to filter using various criteria such as date, value, text, and color. **Filtering** is the process of specifying conditions to display only those records that meet certain conditions.

> **TIP: COPYING BEFORE FILTERING DATA**
> Often, you need to show different filters applied to the same dataset. You can copy the worksheet and filter the data on the copied worksheet to preserve the original dataset.

Apply Text Filters

STEP 5 ›› When you apply a filter to a text field, the filter menu displays each unique text item. You can select one or more text items from the list to be filtered. Once completed only the selected text will be displayed.

> **To apply a text filter, complete the following steps:**
> 1. Click any cell in the range of data to be filtered.
> 2. Click the Data tab and click Filter in the Sort & Filter group to display the filter arrows.
> 3. Click the filter arrow for the column you will filter.
> 4. Deselect the (Select All) check mark and click the check boxes for the text you would like to remain visible in the dataset. Click OK.

You can also select Text Filters to see a submenu of additional options, such as Begins With, to select all records for which the name begins with the letter G, for example.

Figure 4.26 shows the Sales_Last filter menu with two names selected. Excel displays records for these two reps only. The records for the other sales reps are hidden but not deleted. The filter arrow displays a filter icon, indicating which field is filtered. Excel displays the row numbers in blue, indicating that you applied a filter. The missing row numbers indicate hidden rows of data. When you remove the filter, all the records display again.

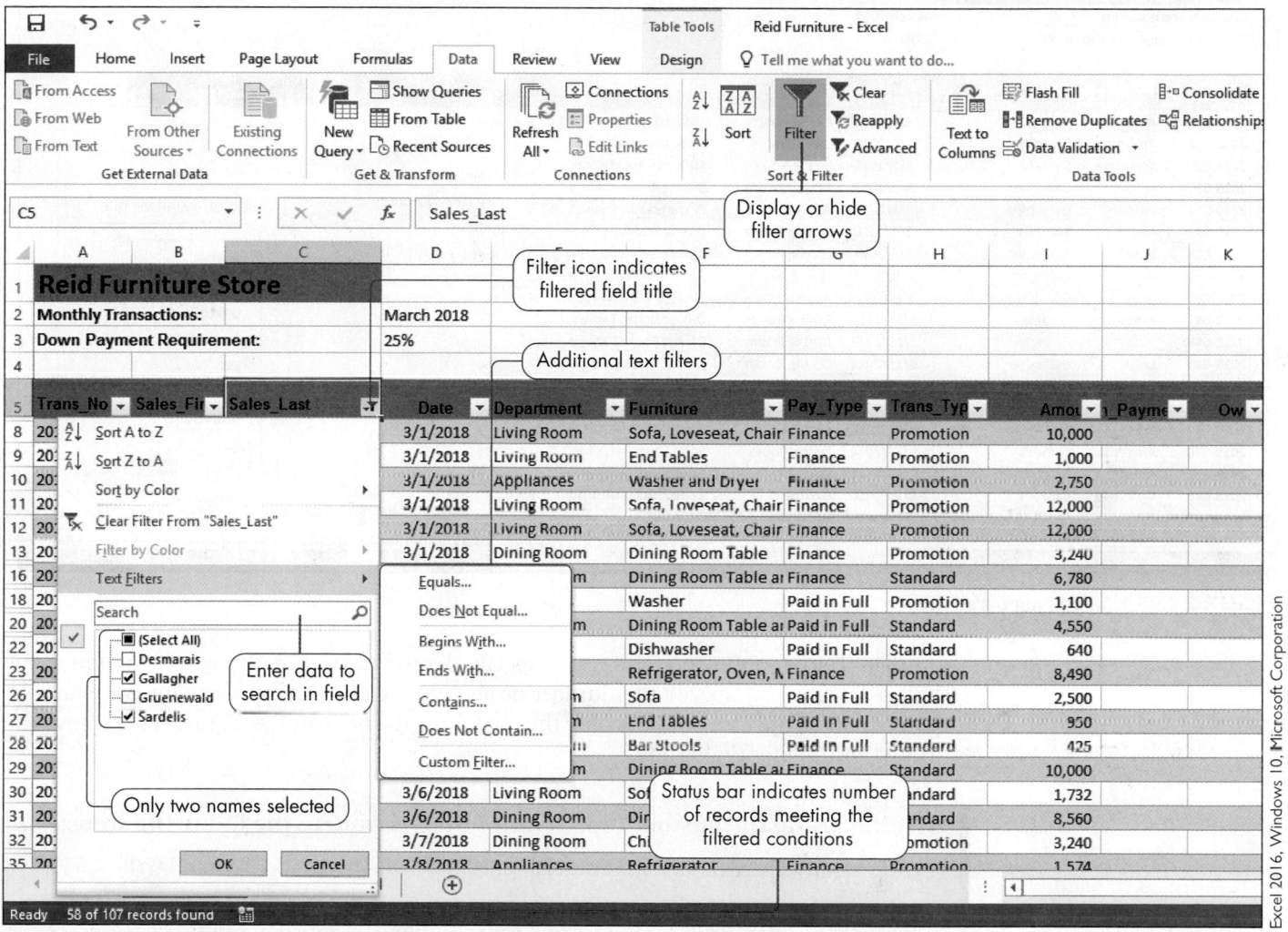

FIGURE 4.26 Filtered Text

Apply Number Filters

STEP 6 ▶▶ Excel contains a variety of number filters that enable you to display specific numbers, or a range of numbers such as above average or top 10 values. When you filter a field of numbers, you can select specific numbers. Or, you might want to filter numbers by a range, such as numbers greater than $5,000 or numbers between $4,000 and $5,000. If the field contains a large number of unique entries, you can click in the Search box and enter a value to display all matching records. For example, if you enter $7, the list will display only values that start with $7. The filter submenu enables you to set a variety of number filters. In Figure 4.27, the amounts are filtered to show only those that are above the average amount. In this situation, Excel calculates the average amount as $4,512. Only records above that amount display.

Excel 2016, Windows 10, Microsoft Corporation

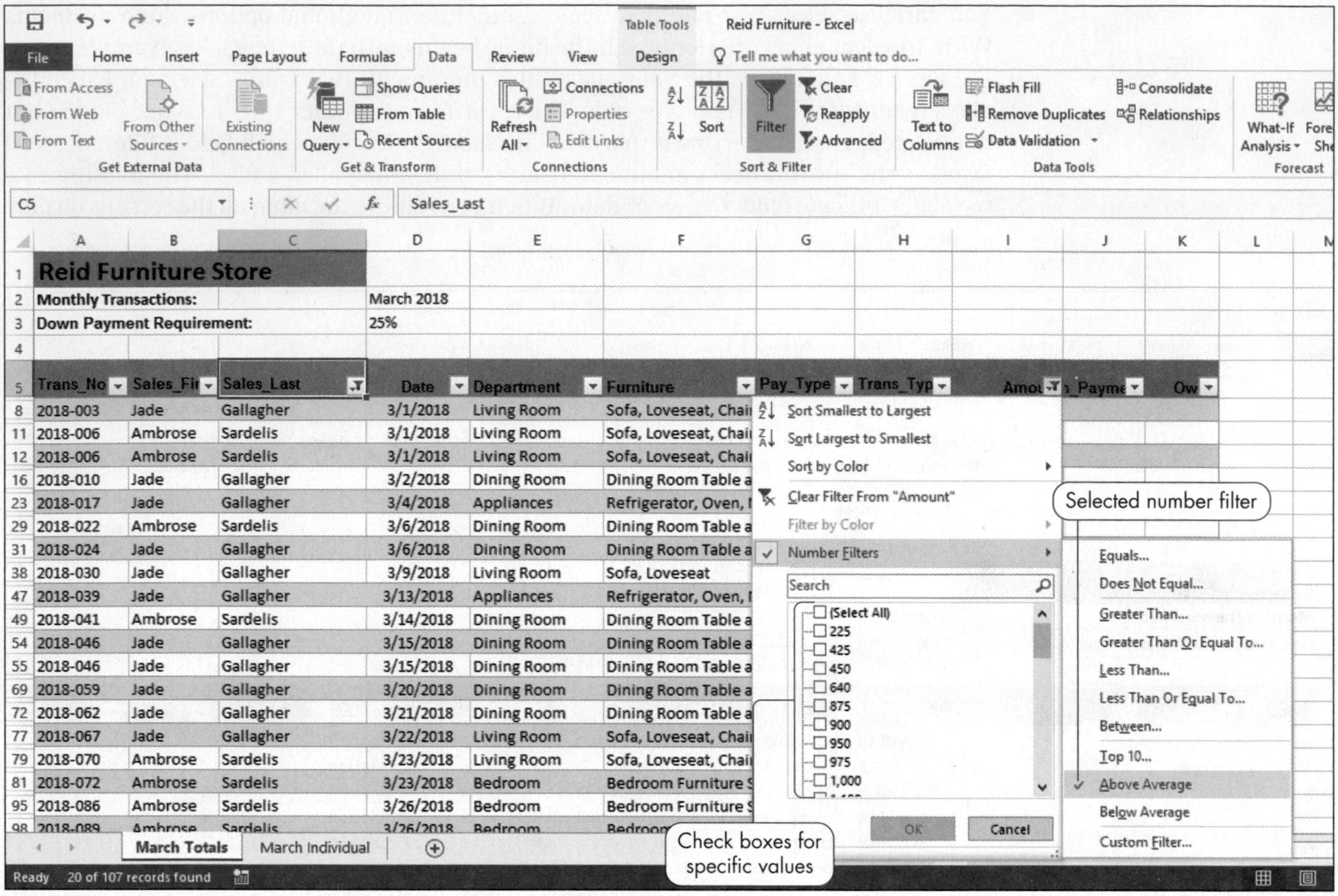

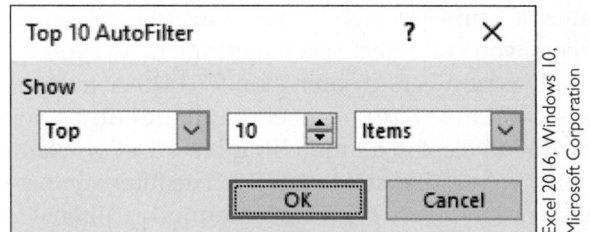

FIGURE 4.27 Filtered Numbers

The Top 10 option enables you to specify the top records. Although the option name is Top 10, you can specify the number or percentage of records to display. For example, you can filter the list to display only the top five or the bottom 7%. Figure 4.28 shows the Top 10 AutoFilter dialog box.

To filter using the custom Top 10 AutoFilter, complete the following steps:

1. Click anywhere in the range or table, click the Data tab, and click Filter in the Sort & Filter group.
2. Click the filter arrow for the column that contains the data you would like to manipulate, point to Number Filters, and select Top 10.
3. Choose Top or Bottom value, click the last arrow to select either Items or Percent, and click OK.

Excel 2016, Windows 10, Microsoft Corporation

FIGURE 4.28 Top 10 AutoFilter Dialog Box

Apply Date Filters

STEP 7 When you filter a field of dates, you can select specific dates or a date range, such as dates after 3/15/2018 or dates between 3/1/2018 and 3/7/2018. The submenu enables you to set a variety of date filters. For more specific date options, point to Date Filters, point to *All Dates in the Period*, and then select a period, such as Quarter 2 or October. Figure 4.29 shows the Date Filters menu.

Excel 2016, Windows 10, Microsoft Corporation

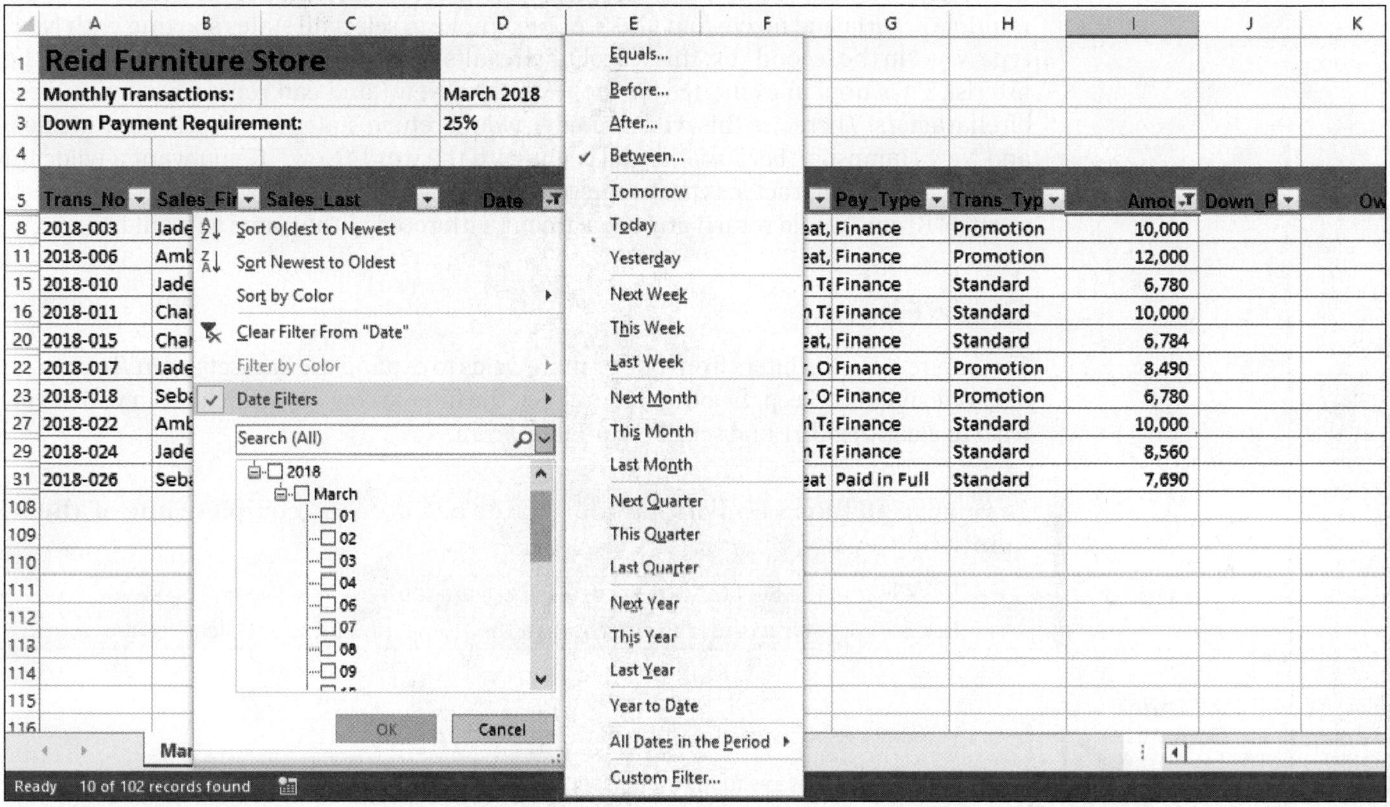

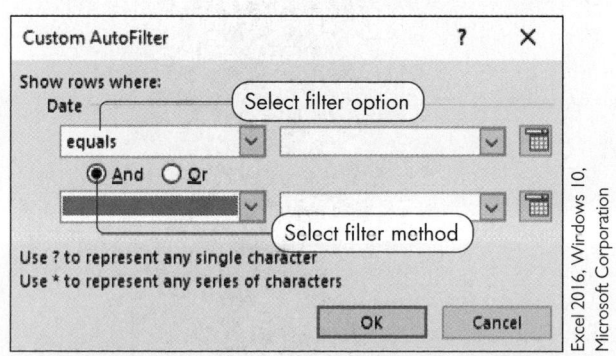

FIGURE 4.29 Filtered Dates

Apply a Custom Filter

Suppose as the manager of a furniture store, you are only interested in marketing directly to people who spent between $500 and $1,000 in the last month. To quickly identify the required data, you could use a custom AutoFilter. If you select options such as Greater Than or Between, Excel displays the Custom AutoFilter dialog box (see Figure 4.30). You can also select Custom Filter from the menu to display this dialog box, which is designed for more complex filtering requirements.

Excel 2016, Windows 10, Microsoft Corporation

FIGURE 4.30 Custom AutoFilter Dialog Box

The dialog box indicates the column being filtered. To set the filters, click the arrows to select the comparison type, such as equals or contains. Click the arrow on the right to select a specific text, value, or date entry, or type the data yourself. For ranges of dates or values, click And, and then specify the comparison operator and value or date for the next condition row. For text, click Or. For example, if you want both Gallagher and Desmarais, you must select Or because each data entry contains either Gallagher or Desmarais but not both at the same time.

When filtering, you can use wildcards to help locate information in which there are multiple criteria and no custom filters. For example, to select all states starting with New, type *New** in the second box; this will obtain results such as New York or New Mexico. The asterisk (*) is used in exchange for the text after "New" and can represent any number of characters. Therefore this wildcard filter would return states New York, New Mexico, and New Hampshire because they all begin with the word "New." If you want a wildcard for only a single character, type the question mark (?). For example when filtering departments, "R?om" would return any department with room in the name as would "Room*."

Clear Filters

You can remove the filters from one or more fields to expand the dataset again. To remove only one filter and keep the other filters, click the filter arrow for the field from which you wish to clear the filter and select Clear Filter From.

> **To remove all filters and display all records in a dataset, complete one of the following steps:**
>
> - Click Clear in the Sort & Filter group on the Data tab.
> - Click Sort & Filter in the Editing group on the Home tab and select Clear.

Quick Concepts

7. What is the purpose of sorting data in a table? *p. 622*

8. What are two ways to arrange (sort) dates? *p. 622*

9. List at least five ways you can filter numbers. *p. 625*

10. Assume you are filtering a list and want to display records for people who live in Boston or New York. What settings do you enter in the Custom AutoFilter dialog box for that field? *p. 624*

Hands-On Exercises

Watch the Video
for this Hands-On
Exercise!

MyITLab®
HOE3 Training

Skills covered: Create a
Structured Reference in a Formula •
Sort One Field • Sort Multiple Fields
• Create a Custom Sort • Apply
Text Filters • Apply a Number Filter
• Apply a Date Filter

3 Table Manipulation

You want to start analyzing the March 2018 transactions for Reid Furniture Store by calculating the totals owed, then sorting and filtering data in a variety of ways to help you understand the transactions better.

STEP 1 ›› CREATE A STRUCTURED REFERENCE IN A FORMULA

First, you want to calculate the down payment owed by each customer. You will then calculate the total amount owed by subtracting the down payment from the total down payment. You will use structured references to complete these tasks. Refer to Figure 4.31 as you complete Step 1.

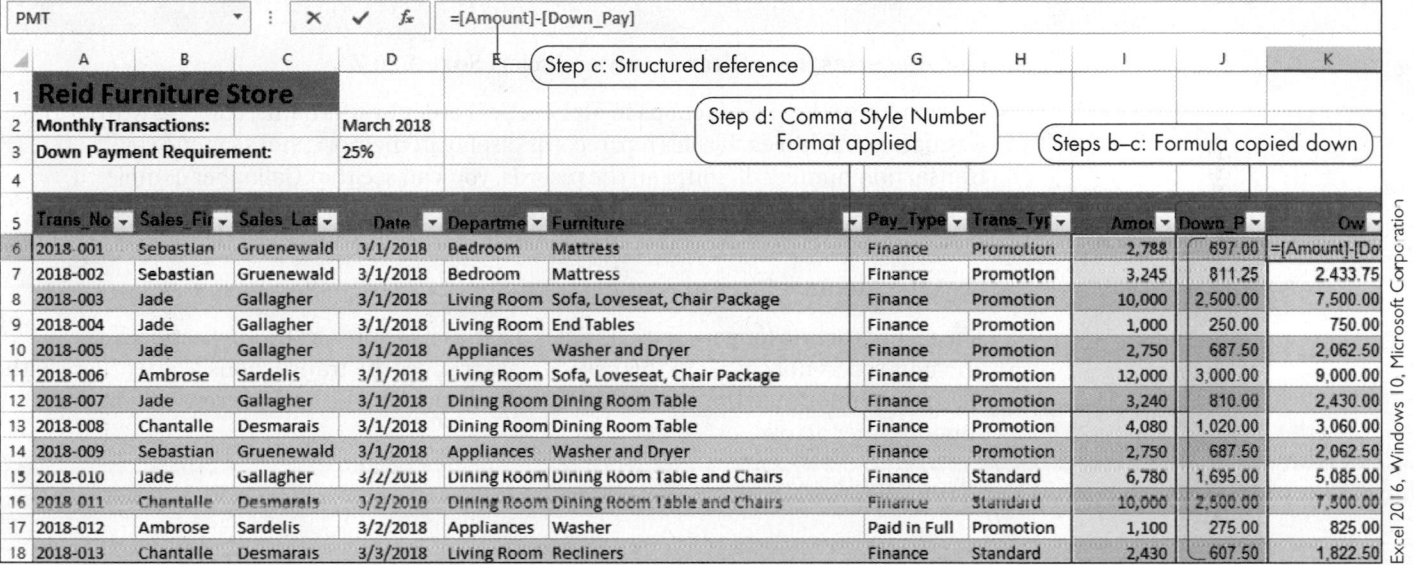

FIGURE 4.31 Create a Structured Reference

a. Open *e04h2Reid_LastFirst* if you closed it at the end of Hands-On Exercise 2. Save it as **e04h3Reid_LastFirst**, changing h2 to h3.

b. Click **cell J6**. Type the formula **=[Amount]*$D$3** and press **Enter**.

The down payment required is 25% of the total purchase price. Structured reference format is used for Amount to create the formula that calculates the customer's down payment. Excel copies the formula down the column.

c. Click **cell K6**. Type the formula **=[Amount]-[Down_Pay]** and press **Enter**.

The formula calculates the total value owed to the sales rep and copies the formula down the column.

d. Select the **range J6:K109** and apply the **Comma Style Number Format**.

e. Save the workbook.

You want to compare the number of transactions by sales rep, so you will sort the data by the Sales_Last field. After reviewing the transactions by sales reps, you then want to arrange the transactions to show the one with the largest purchase first and the smallest purchase last. Refer to Figure 4.32 as you complete Step 2.

FIGURE 4.32 Sorted Data

a. Click the **Sales_Last filter arrow** and select **Sort A to Z**.

Excel arranges the transactions in alphabetical order by last name, starting with Desmarais. Within each sales rep, records display in their original sequence by transaction number. If you scan the records, you can see that Gallagher completed the most sales transactions in March. The up arrow icon on the Sales_Last filter arrow indicates that records are sorted in alphabetical order by that field.

b. Click the **Amount filter arrow** and select **Sort Largest to Smallest**.

The records are no longer sorted by Sales_Last. When you sort by another field, the previous sort is not saved. In this case, Excel arranges the transactions from the one with the largest amount to the smallest amount, indicated by the down arrow icon in the Amount filter arrow.

c. Save the workbook.

You want to review the transactions by payment type (financed or paid in full). Within each payment type, you further want to compare the transaction type (promotion or standard). Finally, you want to compare costs within the sorted records by displaying the highest costs first. You will use the Sort dialog box to perform a three-level sort. Refer to Figure 4.33 as you complete Step 3.

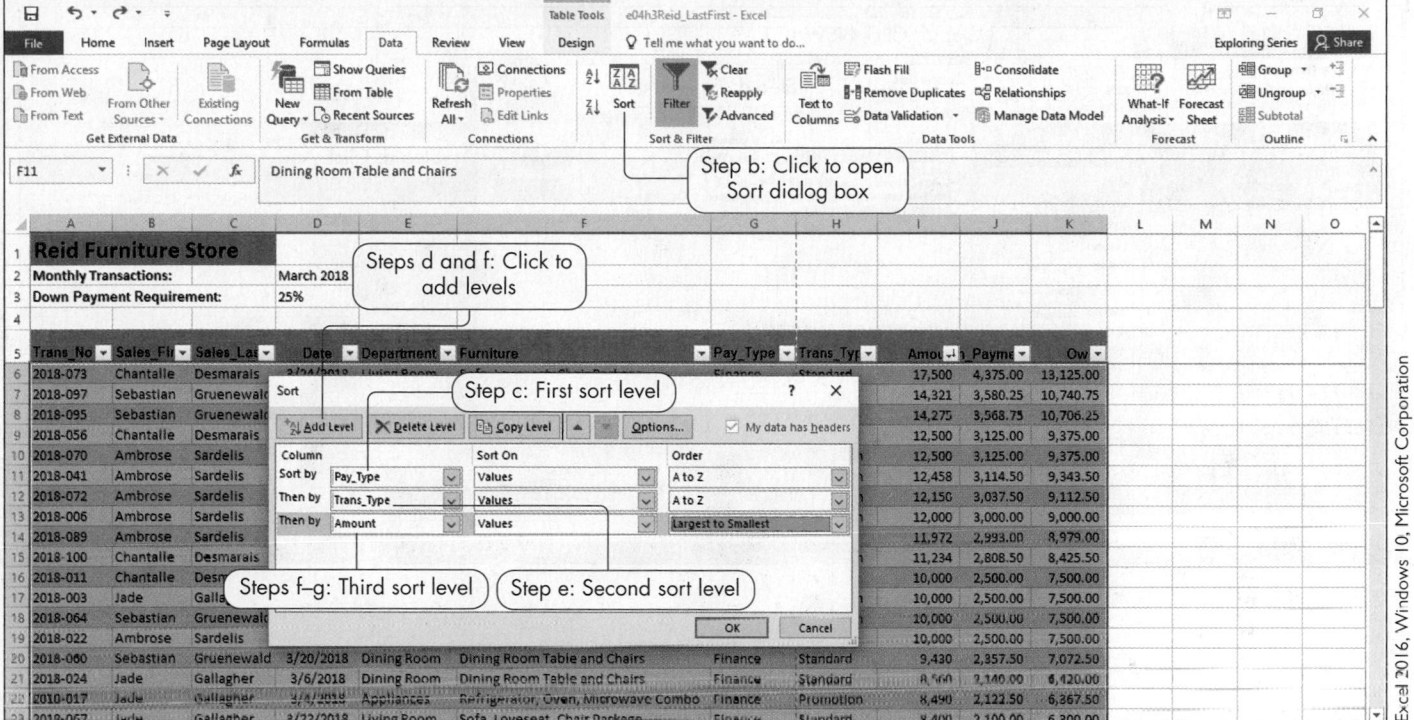

FIGURE 4.33 Three-Level Sort

a. Click inside the table and click the **Data tab**.

Both the Data and Home tabs contain commands to open the Sort dialog box.

b. Click **Sort** in the Sort & Filter group to open the Sort dialog box.

c. Click the **Sort by arrow** and select **Pay_Type**. Click the **Order arrow** and select **A to Z**.

You start by specifying the column for the primary sort. In this case, you want to sort the records first by the Payment Type column.

d. Click **Add Level**.

The Sort dialog box adds the Then by row, which adds a secondary sort.

e. Click the **Then by arrow** and select **Trans_Type**.

The default order is A to Z, which will sort in alphabetical order by Trans_Type. Excel will first sort the records by the Pay_Type (Finance or Paid in Full). Within each Pay_Type, Excel will further sort records by Trans_Type (Promotion or Standard).

f. Click **Add Level** to add another Then by row. Click the second **Then by arrow** and select **Amount**.

g. Click the **Order arrow** for the Amount sort and select **Largest to Smallest**.

Within the Pay_Type and Trans_Type sorts, this will arrange the records with the largest amount first in descending order to the smallest amount.

h. Click **OK** and scroll through the records. Save the workbook.

Most customers finance their purchases instead of paying in full. For the financed transactions, more than half were promotional sales. For merchandise paid in full, a majority of the transactions were standard sales, indicating that people with money do not necessarily wait for a promotional sale to purchase merchandise.

For the month of March you want to closely monitor sales of the Dining Room and Living Room departments. After completing the prior sort, you will add an additional level to create a custom sort of the department's data. Refer to Figure 4.34 as you complete Step 4.

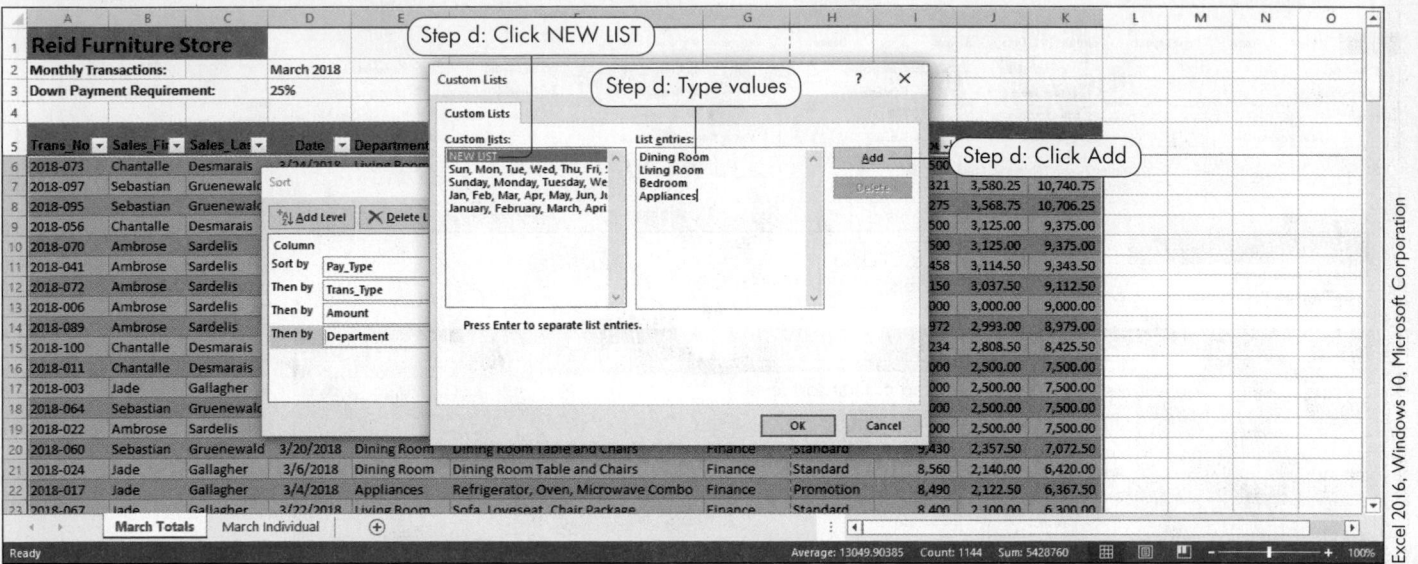

FIGURE 4.34 Custom Sort

a. Click inside the table and click **Sort** in the Sort & Filter group to open the Sort dialog box.

   The Sort dialog box will open with the prior sort criteria displayed.

b. Click the **last level added** in the prior step and click **Add Level**.

c. Select **Department**. Click the **Order arrow** and select **Custom List**.

   This will open the Custom Lists dialog box, enabling you to manually specify the sort order.

d. Click **NEW LIST** in the Custom lists box, click the **List entries box** and type **Dining Room, Living Room, Bedroom, Appliances**. Click **Add**, click **OK**, and click **OK** again to complete to return to the worksheet..

   After completing the custom list, the data in column E will be sorted by Dining Room, Living Room, Bedroom, and Appliances as the last step within the custom sort.

e. Save the workbook.

Now that you know Jade Gallagher had the most transactions for March, you will filter the table to focus on her sales. You notice that she sells more merchandise from the Dining Room department, so you will filter out the other departments. Refer to Figure 4.35 as you complete Step 5.

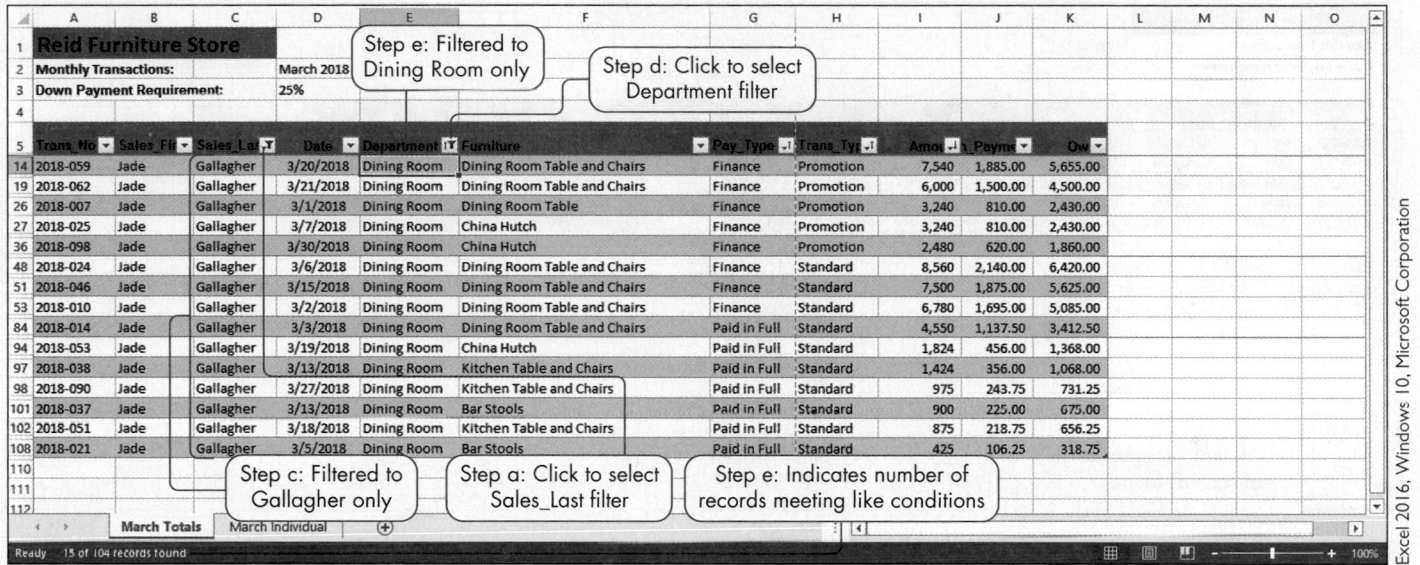

FIGURE 4.35 Apply Text Filters

a. Click the **Sales_Last filter arrow**.

The (Select All) check box is selected.

b. Click the **(Select All) check box** to deselect all last names.

c. Click the **Gallagher check box** to select it and click **OK**.

The status bar indicates that 33 out of 104 records meet the filtering condition. The Sales_Last filter arrow includes a funnel icon, indicating that this column is filtered.

d. Click the **Department filter arrow**.

e. Click the **(Select All) check box** to deselect all departments, click the **Dining Room check box** to focus on that department, and then click **OK**. Save the workbook.

The remaining 15 records show Gallagher's dining room sales for the month. The Department filter arrow includes a funnel icon, indicating that this column is also filtered.

Vicki is considering giving a bonus to employees who sold high-end dining room furniture during a specific time period (3/16/2018 to 3/31/2018). You want to determine if Jade Gallagher qualifies for this bonus. In particular, you are interested in how much gross revenue she generated for dining room furniture that cost at least $5,000 or more. Refer to Figure 4.36 as you complete Step 6.

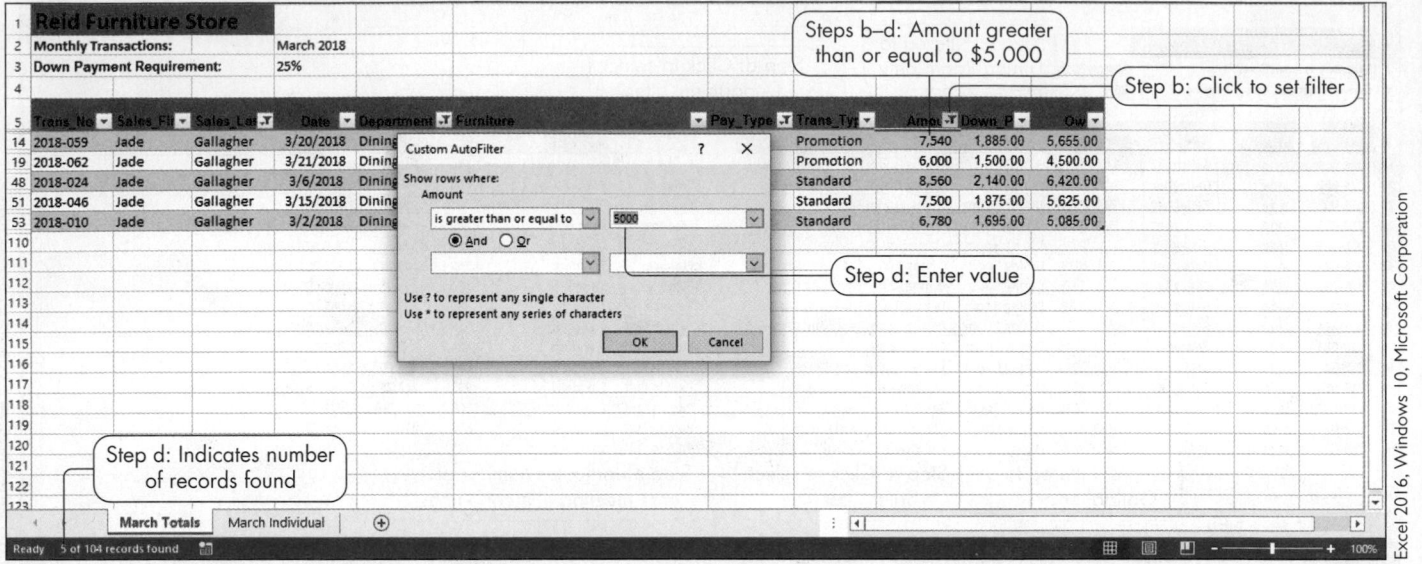

FIGURE 4.36 Filtered to Amounts Greater Than or Equal to $5,000

a. Select the **range I14:I108** of the filtered list and then view the status bar.

   The average transaction amount is $3,754 with 15 transactions (i.e., 15 filtered records).

b. Click the **Amount filter arrow**.

c. Point to **Number Filters** and select **Greater Than Or Equal To**.

   The Custom AutoFilter dialog box opens.

d. Type **5000** in the box to the right of *is greater than or equal to* and click **OK**. Save the workbook.

   When typing numbers, you can type raw numbers such as 5000 or formatted numbers such as $5,000. Out of Gallagher's original 15 dining room transactions, only 5 transactions (one-third of her sales) were valued at $5,000 or more.

Finally, you want to study Jade Gallagher's sales records for the last half of the month. You will add a date filter to identify those sales records. Refer to Figure 4.37 as you complete Step 7.

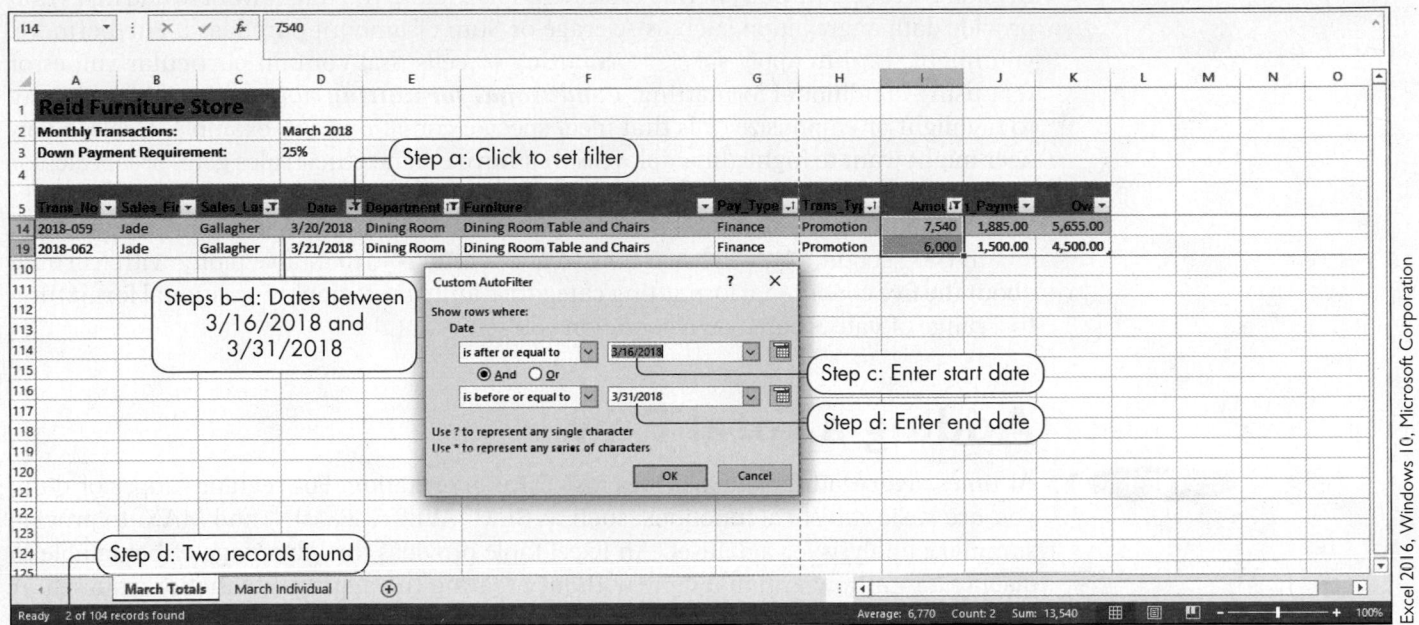

FIGURE 4.37 Filtered by Dates Between 3/16/2018 and 3/31/2018

a. Click the **Date filter arrow**.

b. Point to **Date Filters** and select **Between**.

The Custom AutoFilter dialog box opens. The default comparisons are *is after or equal to* and *is before or equal to*, ready for you to enter the date specifications.

c. Type **3/16/2018** in the box on the right side of *is after or equal to*.

You specified the starting date of the range of dates to include. You will keep the *And* option selected.

d. Type **3/31/2018** in the box on the right side of *is before or equal to*. Click **OK**.

Gallagher had only two dining room sales greater than $5,000 during the last half of March.

e. Save the workbook. Keep the workbook open if you plan to continue with the next Hands-On Exercise. If not, close the workbook, and exit Excel.

Table Aggregation and Conditional Formatting

In addition to sorting and filtering tables to analyze data, you might want to add fields that provide data aggregation such as Average or Sum of amount purchased. Furthermore, you might want to apply special formatting to cells that contain particular values or text using conditional formatting. ***Conditional formatting*** applies special formatting to highlight or emphasize cells that meet specific conditions. For example, a sales manager might want to highlight employees that have reached their sales goal, or a professor might want to highlight test scores that fall below the average. You can also apply conditional formatting to point out data for a specific date or duplicate values in a range.

In this section, you will learn how to add a total row to a table along with learning about the five conditional formatting categories and how to apply conditional formatting to a range of values based on a condition you set.

Adding a Total Row

STEP 1 ⟫ At times, aggregating data provides insightful information. For regular ranges of data, you use basic statistical functions, such as SUM, AVERAGE, MIN, and MAX, to provide summary analysis for a dataset. An Excel table provides the advantage of being able to display a total row automatically without creating the aggregate function yourself. A ***total row*** displays below the last row of records in an Excel table and enables you to display summary statistics, such as a sum of values displayed in a column.

> **To display and use the total row, complete the following steps:**
>
> 1. Click any cell in the table.
> 2. Click the Design tab.
> 3. Click Total Row in the Table Style Options group. Excel displays the total row below the last record in the table. Excel displays Total in the first column of the total row.
> 4. Click a cell in the total row, click that cell's total row arrow, and then select the function result that you desire. Excel calculates the summary statistics for values, but if the field is text, the only summary statistic that can be calculated is Count.
> 5. Add a summary statistic to another column click in the empty cell for that field in the total row and click the arrow to select the desired function. Select None to remove the function.

Figure 4.38 shows the active total row with totals applied to the Amount, Down_Pay, and Owed fields. A list of functions displays to change the function for the last field.

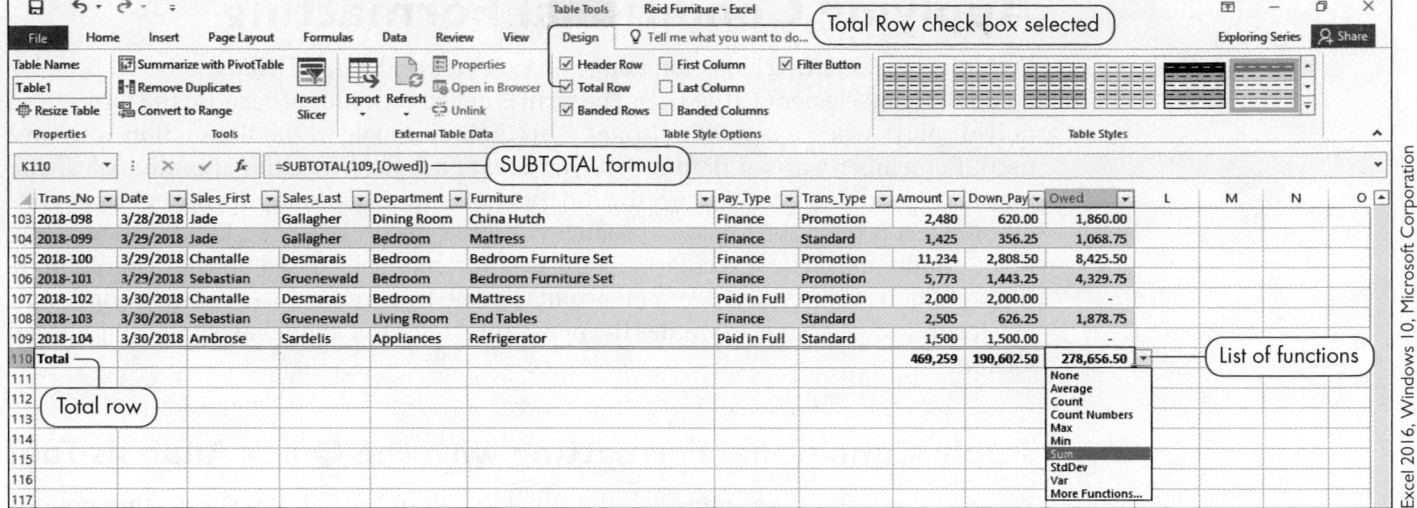

FIGURE 4.38 Total Row

The calculations on the total row use the SUBTOTAL function. The **SUBTOTAL function** calculates an aggregate value, such as totals or averages, for displayed values in a range, table, or database. If you click in a calculated total row cell, the SUBTOTAL function displays in the Formula Bar. The function for the total row looks like this: =SUBTOTAL(function_num,ref1). The function_num argument is a number that represents a function (see Table 4.4). The ref1 argument indicates the range of values to calculate. The SUBTOTAL function used to total the values in the Owed field would be =SUBTOTAL(109,[Owed]), where the number 109 represents the SUM function, and [Owed] represents the Owed field. A benefit of the SUBTOTAL function is that it subtotals data for filtered records, so you have an accurate total for the visible records.

=SUBTOTAL(function_num,ref1,…)

Function	Function Number	Table Number
TABLE 4.4 Subtotal Function Numbers		
AVERAGE	1	101
COUNT	2	102
COUNTA	3	103
MAX	4	104
MIN	5	105
PRODUCT	6	106
STDEV.S	7	107
STDEV.P	8	108
SUM	9	109
VAR.S	10	110
VAR.P	11	111

TIP: FILTERING DATA AND SUBTOTALS

If you filter the data and display the total row, the SUBTOTAL function's 109 argument ensures that only the displayed data are summed; data for hidden rows are not calculated in the aggregate function.

Applying Conditional Formatting

Conditional formatting helps you and your audience understand a dataset better because it adds a visual element to the cells. The term is called conditional because the formatting only displays when a condition is met. This is similar logic to the IF function you have used. Remember with an IF function, you create a logical test that is evaluated. If the logical or conditional test is true, the function produces one result. If the logical or conditional test is false, the function produces another result. With conditional formatting, if the condition is true, Excel formats the cell automatically based on that condition. If the condition is false, Excel does not format the cell. If you change a value in a conditionally formatted cell, Excel examines the new value to see if it should apply the conditional format.

Apply Conditional Formatting with the Quick Analysis Tool

When you select a range and click the Quick Analysis button, the Formatting options display in the Quick Analysis gallery. Point to a thumbnail to see how it will affect the selected range (see Figure 4.39). You can also apply conditional formatting by clicking Conditional Formatting in the Styles group on the Home tab.

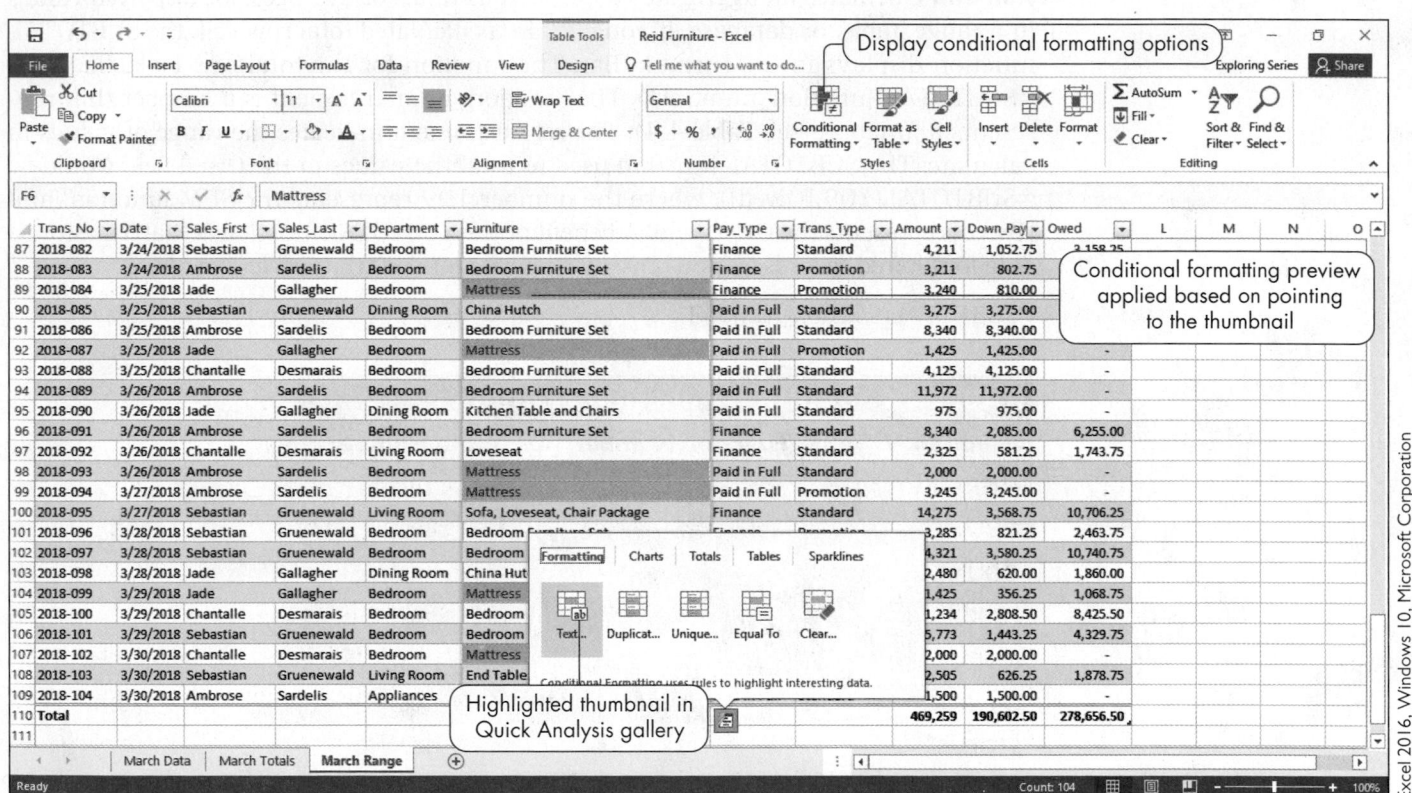

FIGURE 4.39 Quick Analysis Gallery to Apply Conditional Formatting

Table 4.5 describes the conditional formatting options in the Quick Analysis gallery.

TABLE 4.5	Conditional Formatting Options in Quick Analysis Gallery
Options	Description
Text Contains	Formats cells that contain the text in the first selected cell. In Figure 4.39, the first selected cell contains Mattress. If a cell contains Mattress and Springs, Excel would format that cell also because it contains Mattress.
Duplicate Values	Formats cells that are duplicated in the selected range.
Unique Values	Formats cells that are unique; that is, no other cell in the selected range contains the same data.
Equal To	Formats cells that are exactly like the data contained in the first selected cell.
Clear Format	Removes the conditional formatting from the selected range.

Pearson Education, Inc.

Table 4.6 lists and describes a number of different conditional formats that you can apply if you want more specific rules.

TABLE 4.6	Conditional Formatting Options
Options	Description
Highlight Cells Rules	Highlights cells with a fill color, font color, or border (such as Light Red Fill with Dark Red Text) if values are greater than, less than, between two values, equal to a value, or duplicate values; text that contains particular characters; or dates when a date meets a particular condition, such as *In the last 7 days*.
Top/Bottom Rules	Formats cells with values in the top 10 items, top 10%, bottom 10 items, bottom 10%, above average, or below average. You can change the exact values to format the top or bottom items or percentages, such as top 5 or bottom 15%.
Data Bars	Applies a gradient or solid fill bar in which the width of the bar represents the current cell's value compared relatively to other cells' values.
Color Scales	Formats different cells with different colors, assigning one color to the lowest group of values and another color to the highest group of values, with gradient colors to other values.
Icon Sets	Inserts an icon from an icon palette in each cell to indicate values compared to each other.

Pearson Education, Inc.

To apply a conditional format, complete the following steps:

1. Select the cells for which you want to apply a conditional format, click the Home tab, and click Conditional Formatting in the Styles group.
2. Select the conditional formatting category you want to apply.

Apply Highlight Cells Rules

STEP 2 ⟩⟩ The Highlight Cells Rules category enables you to apply a highlight to cells that meet a condition, such as cells containing values greater than a particular value. This option contains predefined combinations of fill colors, font colors, and/or borders. For example, suppose you are a sales manager who developed a worksheet containing the sales for each day of a month. You are interested in sales between $5000 and $10,000. You might want to apply a conditional format to cells that contain values within the desired range. To apply this conditional formatting, you would select Highlight Cells Rules and then select Between. In the Between dialog box (see Figure 4.40), type 5000 in the first value box and 10000 in the second value box, select the type of conditional formatting, such as Light Red Fill with Dark Red Text, and then click OK to apply the formats.

Excel 2016, Windows 10, Microsoft Corporation

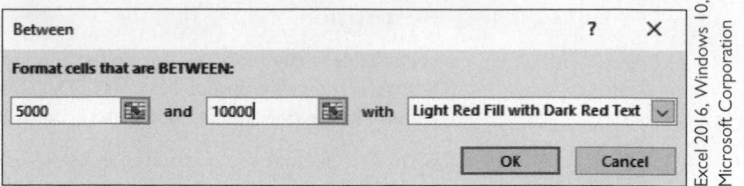

FIGURE 4.40 Between Dialog Box

Figure 4.41 shows two columns of data that contain conditional formats. The Department column is conditionally formatted to highlight text with a Light Red Fill with Dark Red Text for cells that contain Living Room, and the Amount column is conditionally formatted to highlight values between $5,000 and $10,000 with a Dark Red Border.

Excel 2016, Windows 10, Microsoft Corporation

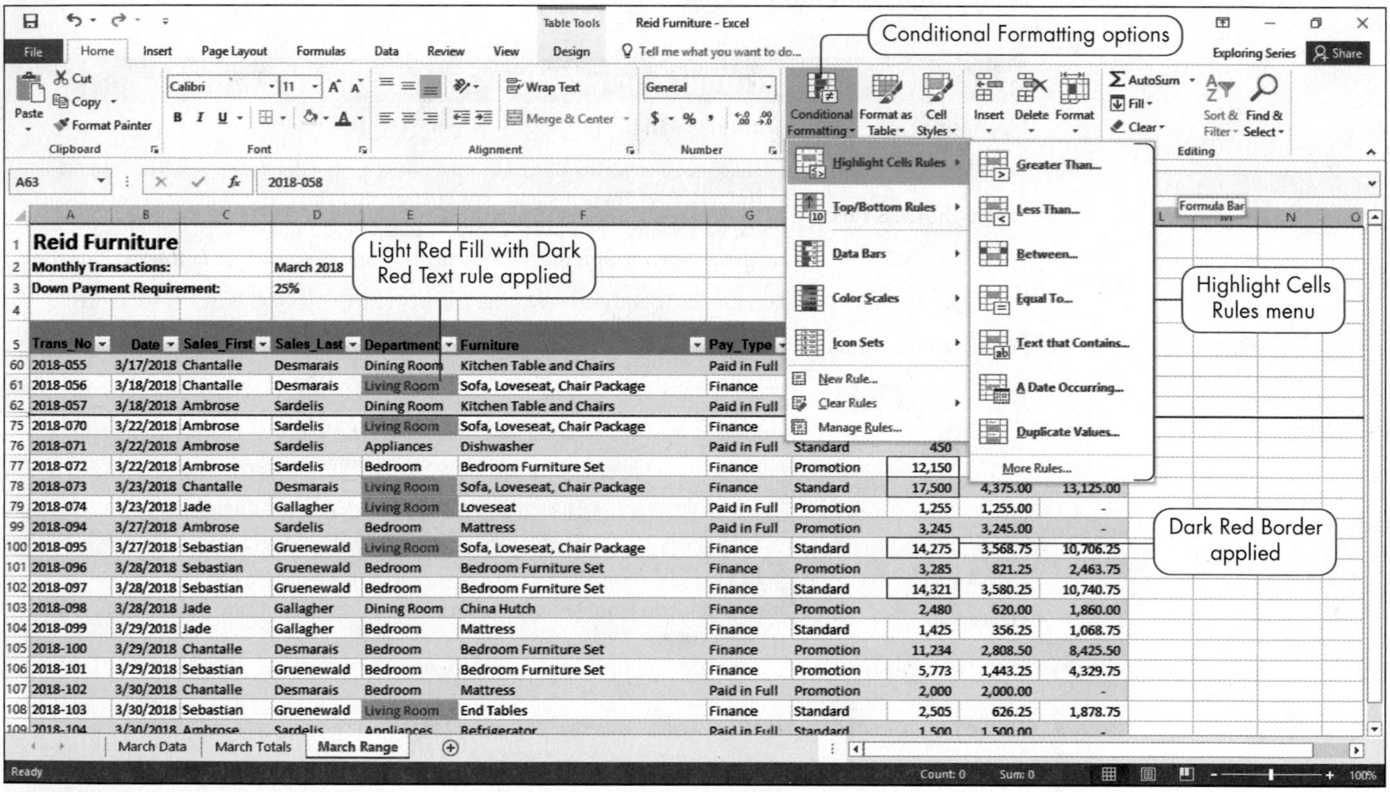

FIGURE 4.41 Highlight Cells Rules Conditional Formatting

Specify Top/Bottom Rules

STEP 3 You might be interested in identifying the top five sales to reward the sales associates, or want to identify the bottom 15% of of sales for more focused marketing. The Top/Bottom Rules category enables you to specify the top or bottom number, top or bottom percentage, or values that are above or below the average value in a specified range. In Figure 4.42, the Amount column is conditionally formatted to highlight the top five amounts. (Some rows are hidden so that all top five values display in the figure.) Although the menu option is Top 10 Items, you can specify the exact number of items to format.

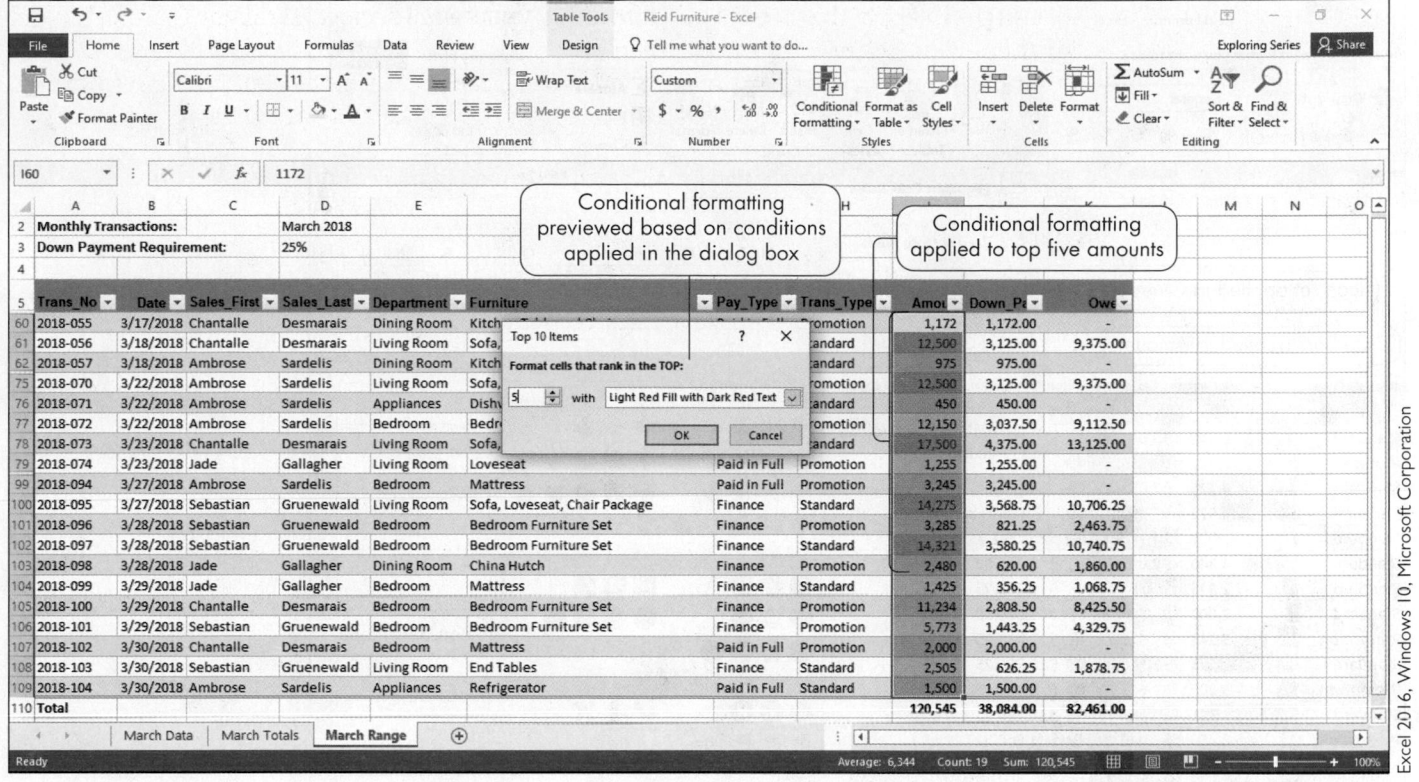

FIGURE 4.42 Top 10 Items Dialog Box

Display Data Bars, Color Scales, and Icon Sets

STEP 4 »» *Data bars* apply a gradient or solid fill bar in which the width of the bar represents the current cell's value compared relatively to other cells' values (see Figure 4.43). The width of the data bar represents the value in a cell, with a wider bar representing a higher value and a narrower bar a lower value. Excel locates the largest value and displays the widest data bar in that cell. Excel then finds the smallest value and displays the smallest data bar in that cell. Excel sizes the data bars for the remaining cells based on their values relative to the high and low values in the column. If you change the values, Excel updates the data bar widths. Excel uses the same color for each data bar, but each bar differs in size based on the value in the respective cells.

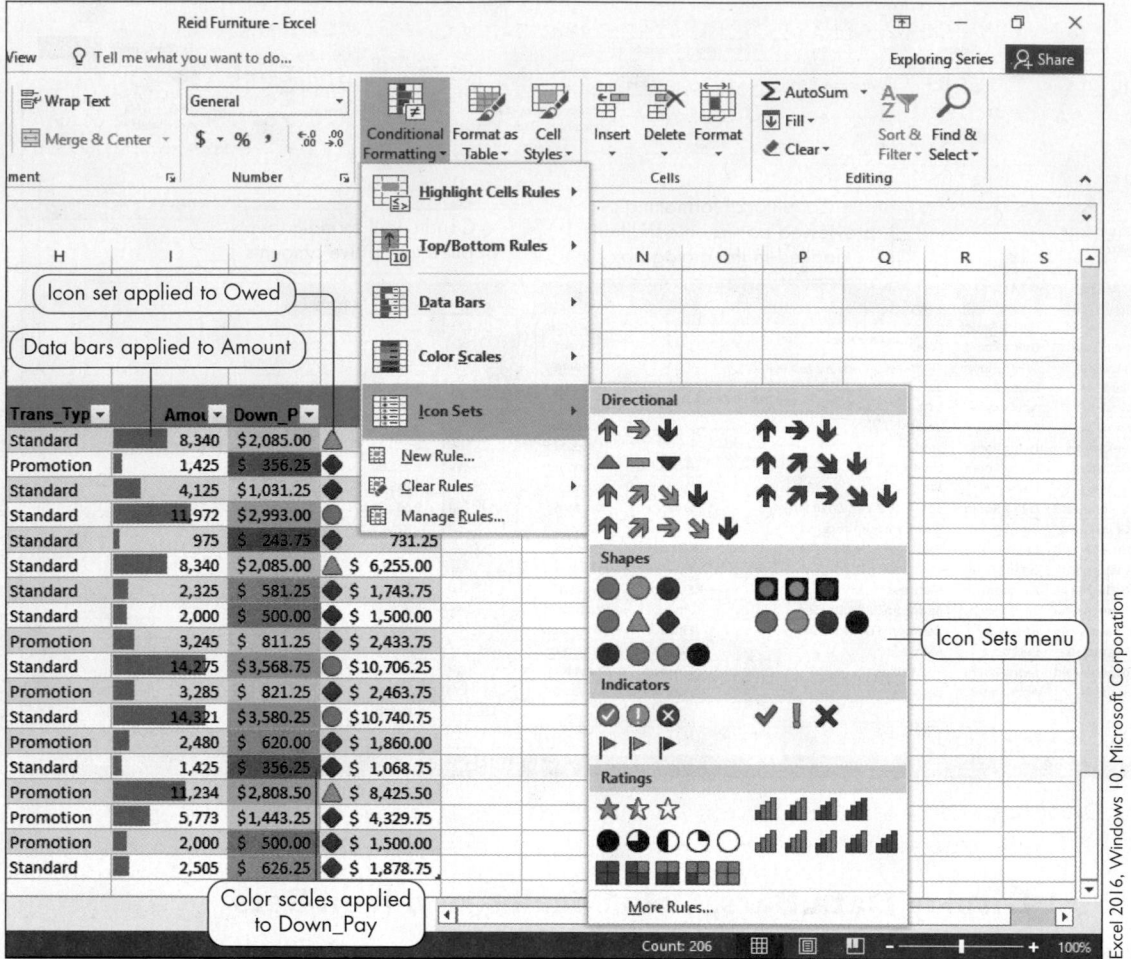

FIGURE 4.43 Data Bars, Color Scales, and Icon Sets

Color scales format cells with different colors based on the relative value of a cell compared to other selected cells. You can apply a two- or three-color scale. This scale assists in comparing a range of cells using gradations of those colors. The shade of the color represents higher or lower values. In Figure 4.43, for example, the red color scales display for the lowest values, the green color displays for the highest values, and gradients of yellow and orange represent the middle range of values in the Down_Pay column. Use color scales to understand variation in the data to identify trends, for example, to view good stock returns and weak stock returns.

Icon sets are symbols or signs that classify data into three, four, or five categories, based on the values in a range. Excel determines categories of value ranges and assigns an icon to each range. In Figure 4.43, a three-icon set was applied to the Owed column. Excel divided the range of values between the lowest value of $0 and the highest value of $13,125 into thirds. The red diamond icon displays for the cells containing values in the lowest third ($0 to $4,375), the yellow triangle icon displays for cells containing the values in the middle third ($4,376 to $8,750), and the green circle icon displays for cells containing values in the top third ($8,751 to $13,125). Most purchases fall into the lowest third.

> **TIP: DON'T OVERDO IT!**
> Although conditional formatting helps identify trends, you should use this feature wisely and sparingly. Apply conditional formatting only when you want to emphasize important data. When you decide to apply conditional formatting, think about which category is best to highlight the data.

Creating a New Rule

The default conditional formatting categories provide a variety of options. Excel also enables you to create your own rules to specify different fill colors, borders, or other formatting if you do not want the default settings. Excel provides three ways to create a new rule.

To create a new Conditional Formatting rule, complete one of the following steps:

- Click Conditional Formatting in the Styles group and select New Rule.
- Click Conditional Formatting in the Styles group, select Manage Rules to open the Conditional Formatting Rules Manager dialog box, and then click New Rule.
- Click Conditional Formatting in the Styles group, select a rule category such as Highlight Cells Rules, and then select More Rules.

When creating a new rule, the New Formatting Rule dialog box opens (see Figure 4.44) so that you can define the conditional formatting rule. First, select a rule type, such as *Format all cells based on their values*. The *Edit the Rule Description* section changes, based on the rule type you select. With the default rule type selected, you can specify the format style (2-Color Scale, 3-Color Scale, Data Bar, or Icon Sets). You can then specify the minimum and maximum values, the fill colors for color sets or data bars, or the icons for icon sets. After you edit the rule description, click OK to save your new conditional format.

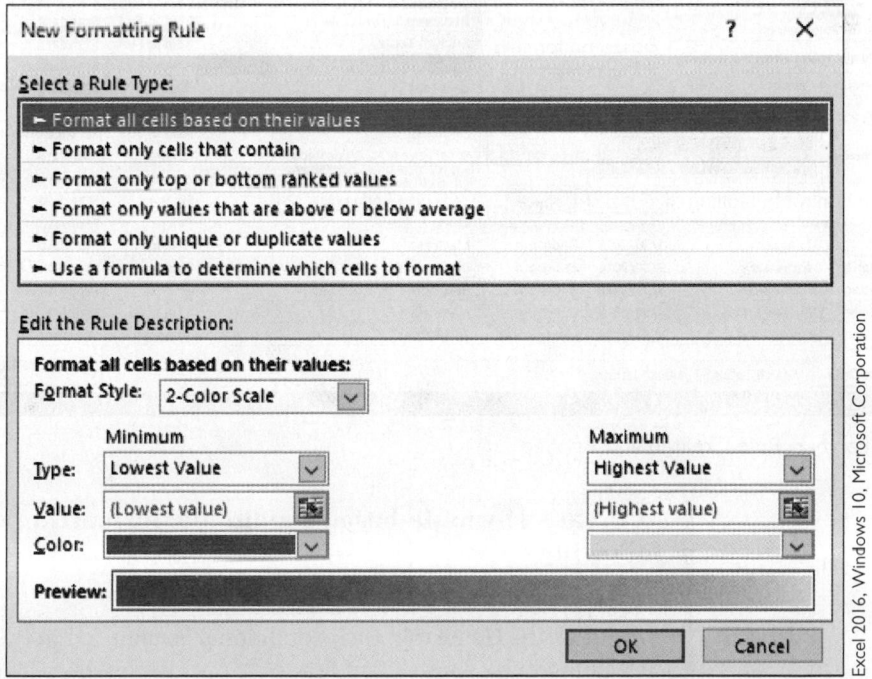

FIGURE 4.44 New Formatting Rule Dialog Box

If you select any rule type except the *Format all cells based on their values* rule, the dialog box contains a Format button. When you click Format, the Format Cells dialog box opens so that you can specify number, font, border, and fill formats to apply to your rule.

> **TIP: FORMAT ONLY CELLS THAT CONTAIN**
>
> When creating new Conditional Formatting rules, you have the option to format only cells that contain a specific value. This option provides a wide array of things you can format: values, text, dates, blanks, no blanks, errors, or no errors. Formatting blanks is helpful to see where you are missing data, and formatting cells containing errors helps you find those errors quickly. These options can be accessed from the Select a Rule Type box in the New Formatting Rule dialog box when creating a Conditional Formatting rule.

Use Formulas in Conditional Formatting

STEP 5 ▶▶ Suppose you want to format merchandise amounts of financed items *and* amounts that are $10,000 or more. You can use a formula to create a conditional formatting rule to complete the task. Figure 4.45 shows the Edit Formatting Rule dialog box and the corresponding conditional formatting applied to cells.

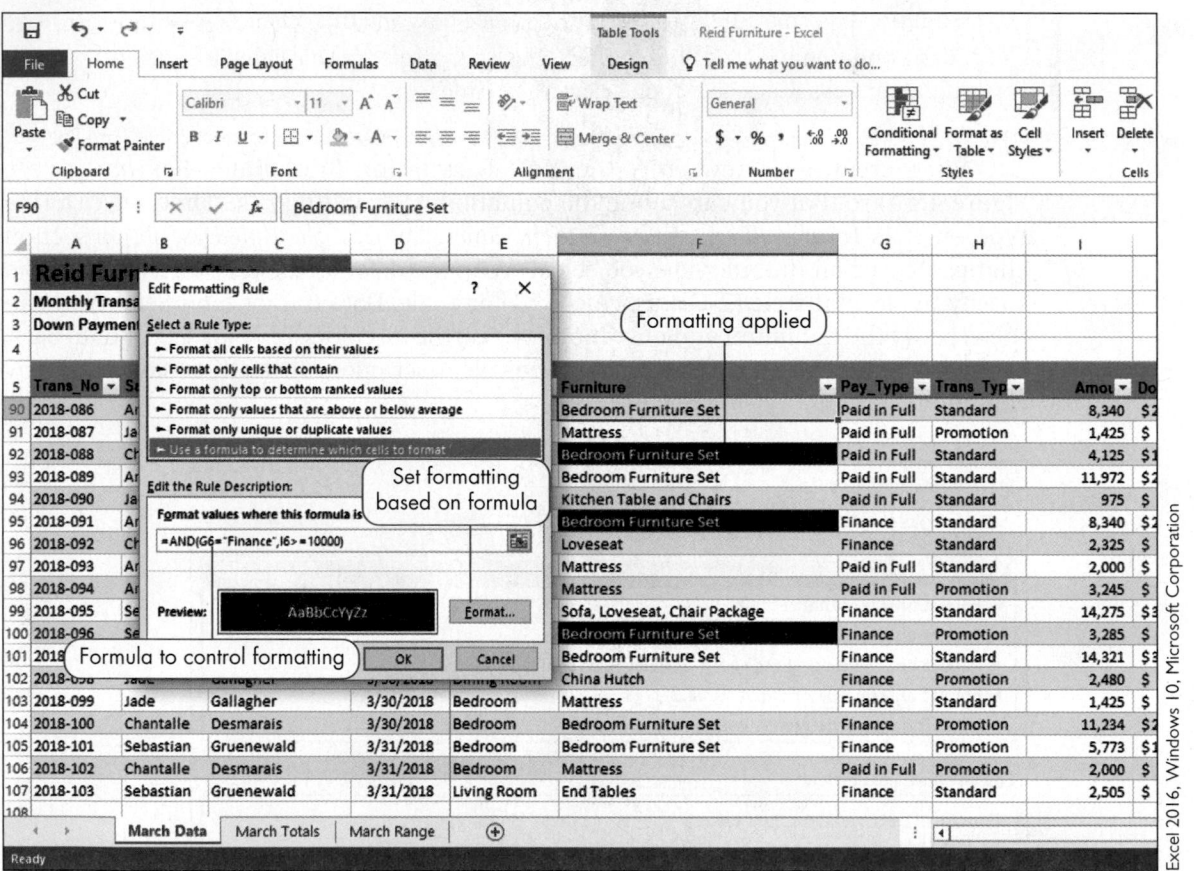

FIGURE 4.45 Formula Rule Created and Applied

> **To create a formula-based conditional formatting rule, complete the following steps:**
>
> 1. Select the desired data range.
> 2. Click the Home tab, click Conditional Formatting in the Styles group, and click New Rule.
> 3. Select *Use a formula to determine which cells to format* and type the formula, using cell references in the first row, in the *Format values where this formula is true* box.

Once complete, Excel applies the general formula to the selected range, substituting the appropriate cell reference as it makes the comparisons. In the Figure 4.45 example, =AND(G6="Finance",I6>=10000) requires that the text in the Pay_Type column (column G) contain Finance and the Amount column (column I) contain a value that is greater than or equal to $10,000. The AND function requires that both logical tests be met to apply the conditional formatting. A minimum of two logical tests are required; however, you can include additional logical tests. Note that *all* logical tests must be true to apply the conditional formatting.

= AND(logical1,logical2,…)

Manage Rules

Periodically conditional formatting rules may need to be updated, moved, or completely deleted.

To edit or delete conditional formatting rules you create, click Conditional Formatting in the Styles group and select Manage Rules. The Conditional Formatting Rules Manager dialog box opens (see Figure 4.46). Click the *Show formatting rules for* arrow and select from *current selection, the entire worksheet,* or *this table.* Select the rule, click Edit Rule or Delete Rule, and click OK after making the desired changes. To remove conditional formatting from a range of cells, select the cells. Then click Conditional Formatting, point to Clear Rules, and select Clear Rules from Selected Cells.

To clear all conditional formatting from the entire worksheet, complete the following steps:

1. Click Conditional Formatting in the Styles group on the Home tab.
2. Point to Clear Rules, and then select Clear Rules from Entire Sheet.

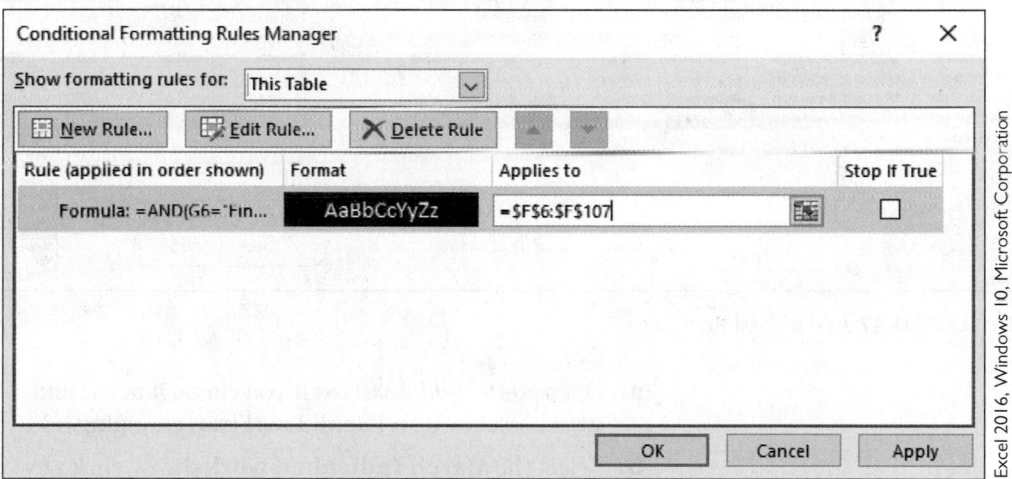

FIGURE 4.46 Conditional Formatting Rules Manager Dialog Box

Quick Concepts

11. How is conditional formatting similar to an IF function? *p. 638*

12. What conditional formatting would be helpful to identify the three movies with the highest revenue playing at theaters? *pp. 640–641*

13. How is data bar conditional formatting helpful when reviewing a column of data? *p. 641*

Hands-On Exercises

Skills covered: Add a Total Row • Apply Highlight Cells Rules • Specify Top/Bottom Rules • Display Data Bars • Use a Formula in Conditional Formatting

4 Table Aggregation and Conditional Formatting

Vicki Reid wants to review the transactions with you. She is interested in Sebastian Gruenewald's sales record and the three highest transaction amounts. In addition, she wants to compare the down payment amounts visually. Finally, she wants you to analyze the amounts owed for sales completed by Sebastian.

STEP 1 ›› ADD A TOTAL ROW

You want to see the monthly totals for the Amount, Down_Pay, and Owed columns. You will add a total row to calculate the values. Refer to Figure 4.47 as you complete Step 1.

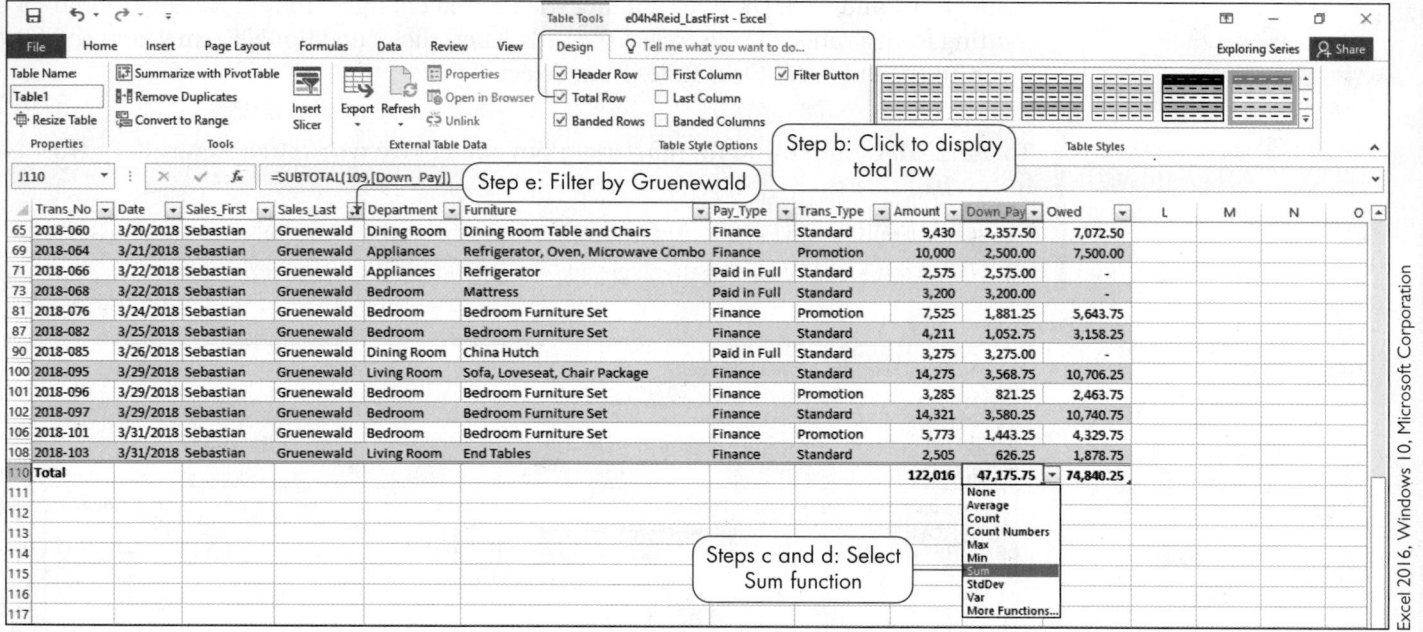

FIGURE 4.47 Add a Total Row

a. Open *e04h3Reid_LastFirst* if you closed it at the end of Hands-On Exercise 3. Save the workbook as **e04h4Reid_LastFirst**, changing h3 to h4.

b. Select the **March Individual worksheet**, click any cell inside the table, click the **Design tab**, and then click **Total Row** in the Table Style Options group.

Excel displays the total row after the last record. It sums the last field of values automatically. The total amount customers owe is $278,656.50.

c. Click the **Down_Pay cell** in row 110, click the **total arrow**, and then select **Sum**.

You added a total to the Down_Pay field. The total amount of down payment collected is $190,602.50. The formula displays as =SUBTOTAL(109,[Down_Pay]) in the Formula Bar.

d. Click the **Amount cell** in row 110, click the **total arrow**, and then select **Sum**.

You added a total to the Amount column. The total amount of merchandise sales is $469,259. The formula displays as =SUBTOTAL(109,[Amount]) in the Formula Bar.

e. Click the **Sales_Last filter arrow**, click the **(Select All) check box**, click the **Gruenewald check box** to select it, and then click **OK**.

The total row values change to display the totals for only Gruenewald: $122,016 (Amount), 47,175.75 (Down_Pay), and 74,840.25 (Owed). This is an advantage of using the total row, which uses the SUBTOTAL function, as opposed to if you had inserted the SUM function manually. The SUM function would provide a total for all data in the column, not just the filtered data.

f. Click the **Data tab** and click **Clear** in the Sort & Filter group to remove all filters.

g. Save the workbook.

STEP 2 ›› **APPLY HIGHLIGHT CELLS RULES**

You want to identify Sebastian's sales for March 2018 without filtering the data. You will set a conditional format to apply a fill and font color so cells that document appliance sales stand out. Refer to Figure 4.48 as you complete Step 2.

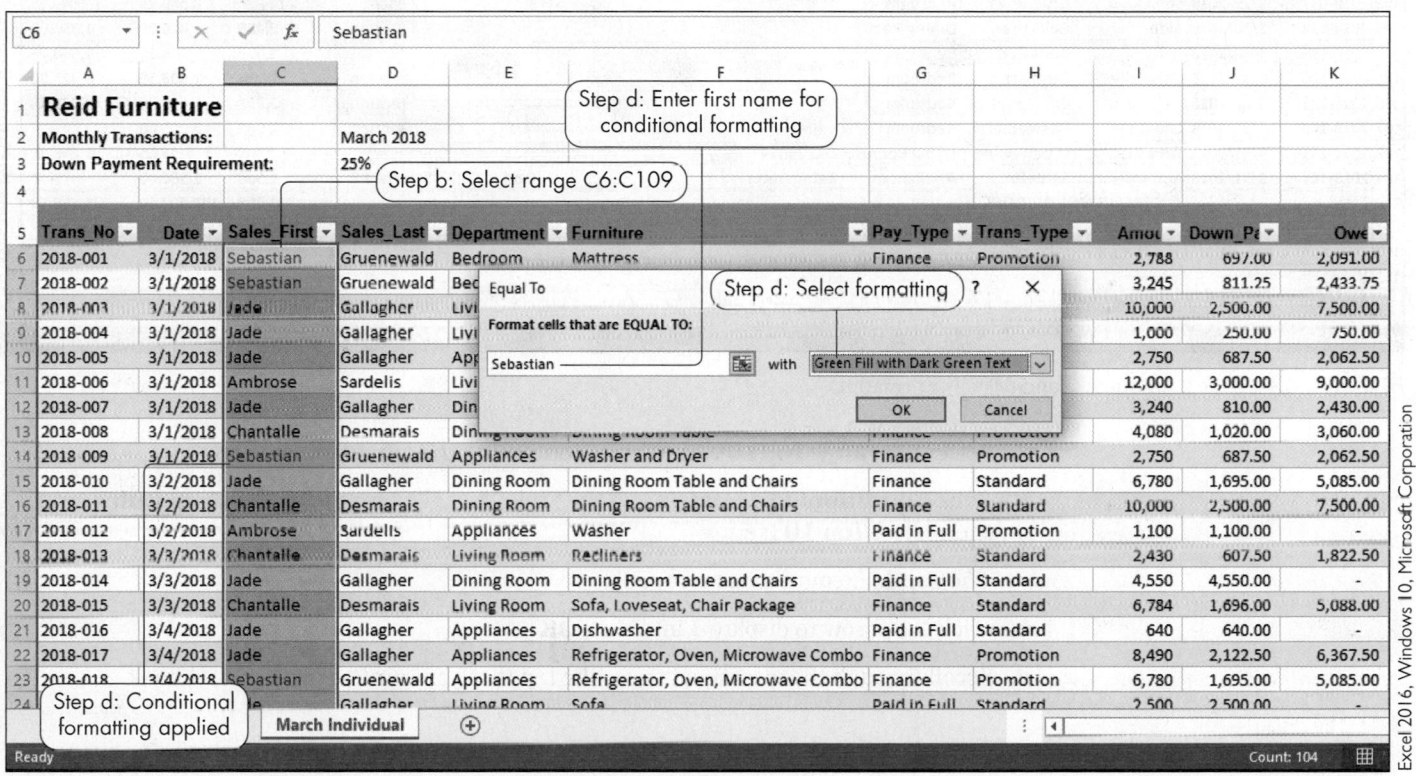

FIGURE 4.48 Conditional Formatting Rules Manager Dialog Box

a. Select **row headings 6 through 109** in the March Individual worksheet. Click the **Home tab**, click the **Fill Color arrow**, and then select **No Fill**.

You removed the previous table style. This will avoid having too many fill colors when you apply conditional formatting rules.

b. Select the **range C6:C109**.

c. Click **Conditional Formatting** in the Styles group, point to **Highlight Cells Rules**, and then select **Text that Contains**.

The Text that Contains dialog box opens.

d. Type **Sebastian** in the box, click the **with arrow**, and then select **Green Fill with Dark Green Text**. Click **OK**. Deselect the range and save the workbook.

Excel formats only cells that contain Sebastian with the fill and font color.

Vicki is now interested in identifying the highest three sales transactions in March. Instead of sorting the records, you will use the Top/Bottom Rules conditional formatting. Refer to Figure 4.49 as you complete Step 3.

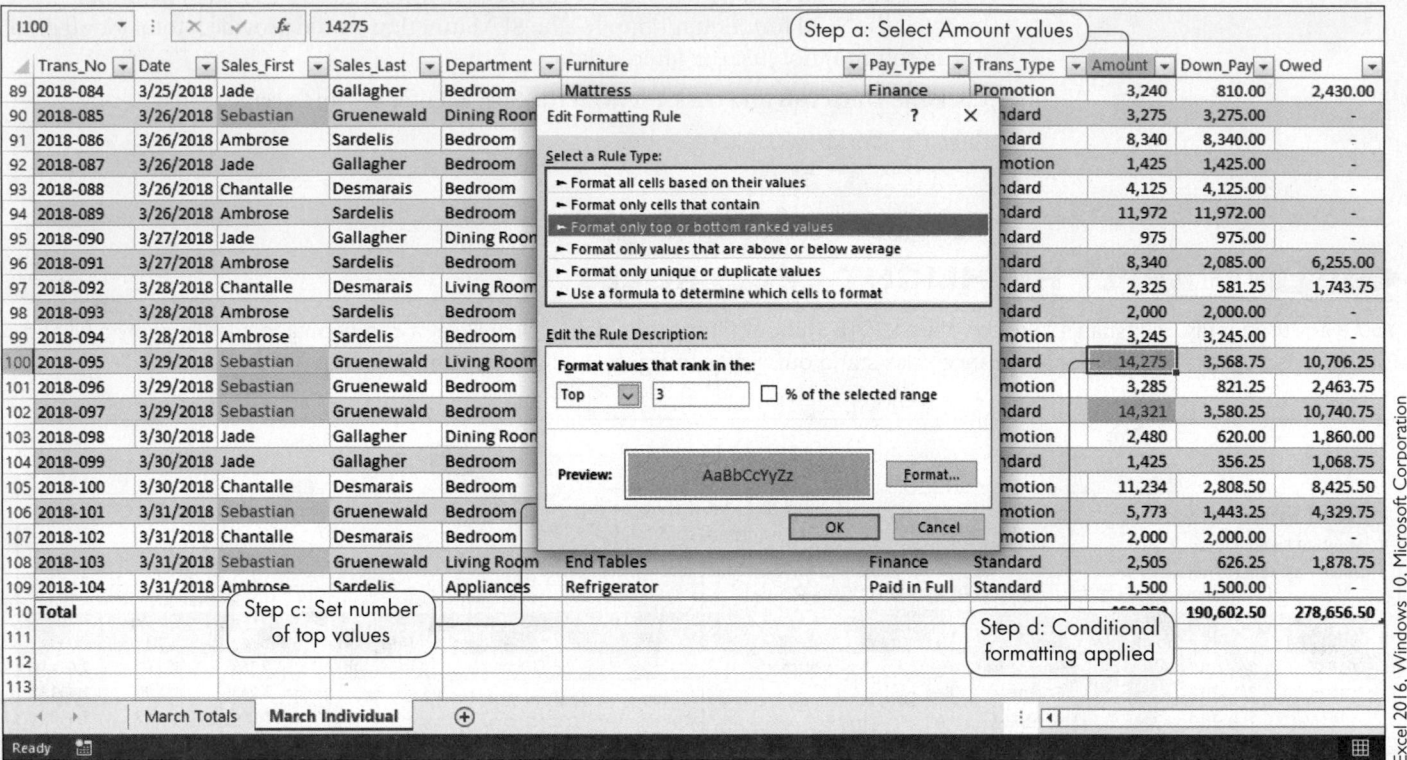

FIGURE 4.49 Top 3 Amounts Conditionally Formatted

a. Select the **range I6:I109**, the range containing the amounts.

b. Click **Conditional Formatting** in the Styles group, point to **Top/Bottom Rules**, and then select **Top 10 Items**.

The Top 10 Items dialog box opens.

c. Click the arrow to display **3** and click **OK**.

d. Scroll through the worksheet to see the top three amounts. Save the workbook.

Vicki wants to compare all of the down payments. Data bars would add a nice visual element as she compares down payment amounts. Refer to Figure 4.50 as you complete Step 4.

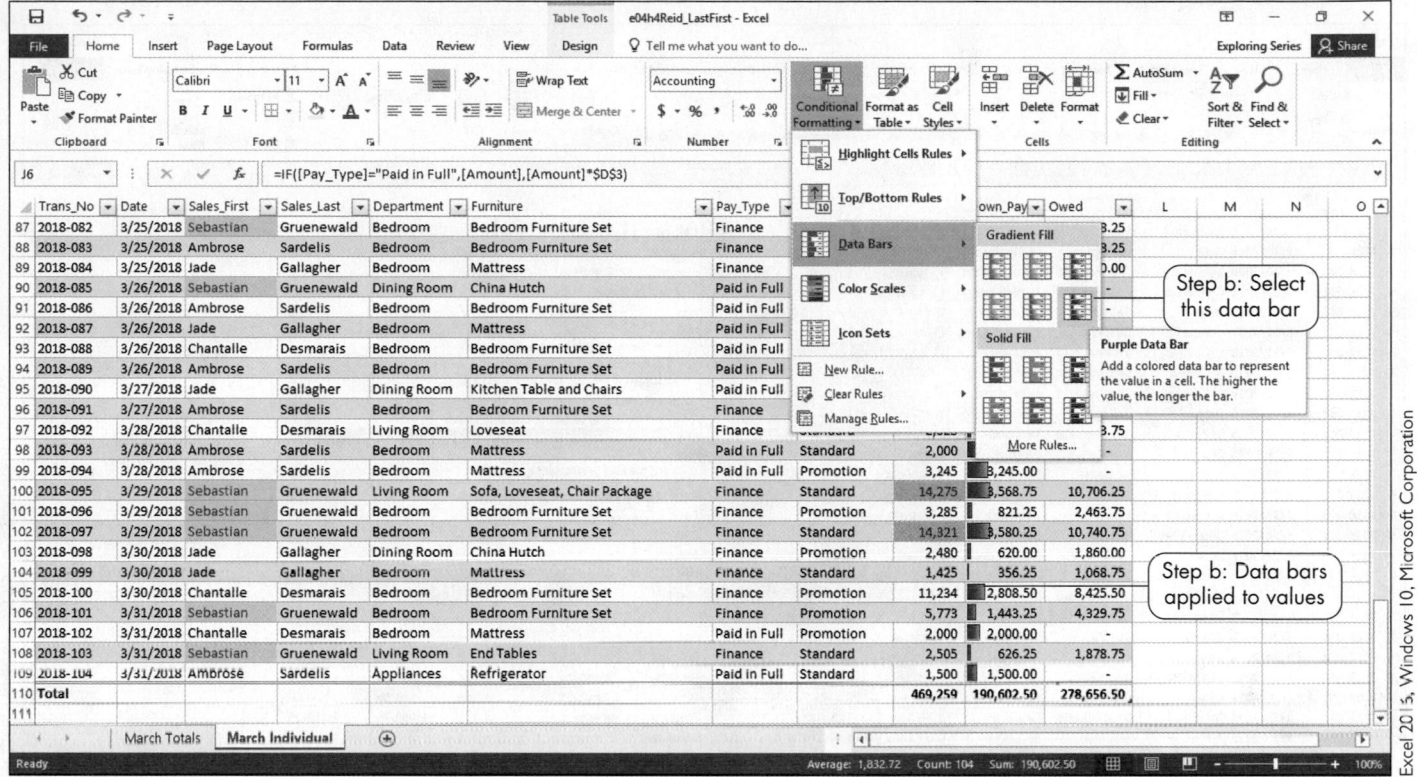

FIGURE 4.50 Data Bars Conditional Formatting

a. Select the **range J6:J109**, which contains the down payment amounts.

b. Click **Conditional Formatting** in the Styles group, point to **Data Bars**, and then select **Purple Data Bar** in the Gradient Fill section. Scroll through the list and save the workbook.

Excel displays data bars in each cell. The larger bar widths help Vicki quickly identify the largest down payments. However, the largest down payments are identical to the original amounts when the customers pay in full. This result illustrates that you should not accept the results at face value. Doing so would provide you with an inaccurate analysis.

Vicki's next request is to analyze the amounts owed by Sebastian's customers. In particular, she wants to highlight the merchandise for which more than $5,000 is owed. To do this, you realize you need to create a custom rule that evaluates both the Sales_First column and the Owed column. Refer to Figure 4.51 as you complete Step 5.

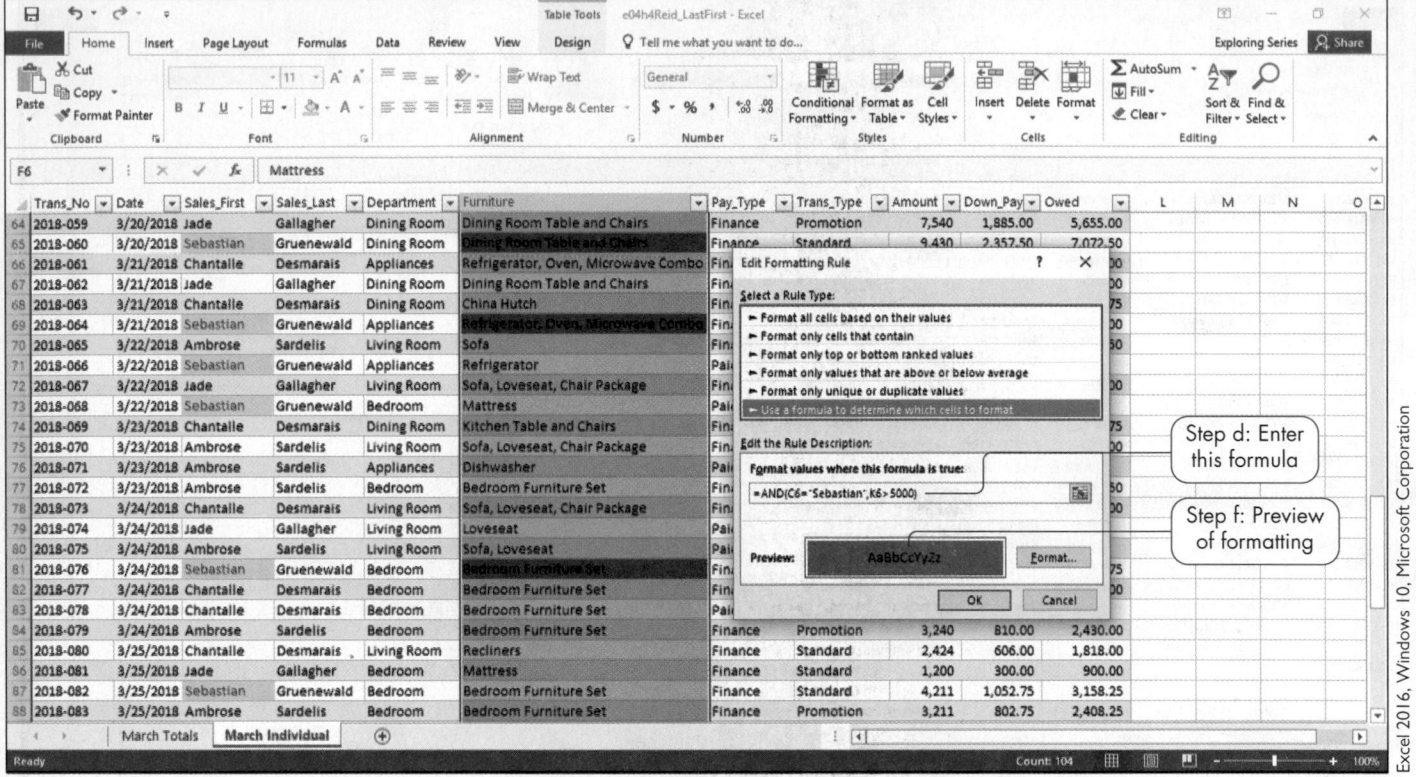

FIGURE 4.51 Custom Rule Created

a. Select the **range F6:F109**, which contains the furniture merchandise.

b. Click **Conditional Formatting** in the Styles group and select **New Rule**.

   The New Formatting Rule dialog box opens.

c. Select **Use a formula to determine which cells to format**.

d. Type **=AND(C6="Sebastian",K6>5000)** in the *Format values where this formula is true* box.

   Because you are comparing the contents of cell C6 to text, you must enclose the text within quotation marks.

e. Click **Format** to open the Format Cells dialog box.

f. Click the **Font tab**, and click **Bold** in the Font style list. Click the **Border tab**, click the **Color arrow**, select **Blue, Accent 5**, and then click **Outline**. Click the **Fill tab**, click **Blue, Accent 5 background color** (the second color from the right on the first row), and then click **OK**.

   Figure 4.51 shows the Edit Formatting Rule dialog box, but the options are similar to the New Formatting Rule dialog box.

g. Click **OK** in the New Formatting Rule dialog box and scroll through the list to see which amounts owed are greater than $5,000 for Sebastian only.

> **TROUBLESHOOTING:** If the results seem incorrect, click Conditional Formatting and select Manage Rules. Edit the rule you just created and make any corrections to the formula.

h. Save and close the file. Based on your instructor's directions, submit the file e04h4Reid_LastFirst.

Chapter Objectives Review

After reading this chapter, you have accomplished the following objectives:

1. Freeze rows and columns.

- The Freeze Panes setting freezes the row(s) above and the column(s) to the left of the active cell. When you scroll, those rows and columns remain onscreen.
- Use Unfreeze Panes to clear the frozen rows and columns.

2. Print large datasets.

- Display and change page breaks: Display the data in Page Break Preview to see the automatic page breaks. Dashed blue lines indicate automatic page breaks. You can insert manual page breaks, indicated by solid blue lines.
- Set and clear a print area: If you do not want to print an entire worksheet, select a range and set a print area.
- Print titles: Select rows to repeat at top and/or columns to repeat at left to print the column and row labels on every page of a printout of a large dataset.
- Control print page order: You can control the sequence in which the pages will print.

3. Understand the benefits of data tables.

- A table is a structured range that contains related data. Tables have several benefits over regular ranges. The column labels, called field names, display on the first row of a table. Each row is a complete set of data for one record.

4. Design and create tables.

- Plan a table before you create it. Create unique field names on the first row of the table and enter data below the field names, avoiding blank rows.
- Create a table: You can create a table from existing data. Excel applies the Table Style Medium 2 format and assigns a name, such as Table1, to the table. When the active cell is within a table, the Table Tools Design tab displays.
- Rename a table: When a table is created, Excel assigns a generic name and enables you to edit the default to a more suitable name.
- Add and delete fields: You can insert and delete table rows and columns to adjust the structure of a table.
- Add, edit, and delete records: You can add table rows, edit records, and delete table rows.
- Remove duplicate rows: Use the Remove Duplicates dialog box to remove duplicate records in a table. Excel will display a dialog box telling you how many records are deleted.

5. Apply a table style.

- Table styles control the fill color of the header row and records within the table.

6. Create structured references in formulas.

- Structured references use tags as field headings that can be used in formulas in place of cell references.

7. Sort data.

- Sort one field: You can sort text in alphabetical or reverse alphabetical order, values from smallest to largest or largest to smallest, and dates from oldest to newest or newest to oldest. Click the filter arrow and select the sort method from the list.
- Sort multiple fields: Open the Sort dialog box and add column levels and sort orders.
- Create a custom sort: You can create a custom sort for unique data, such as ensuring that the months sort in sequential order rather than alphabetical order.

8. Filter data.

- Filtering is the process of specifying conditions for displaying records in a table. Only records that meet those conditions display; the other records are hidden.
- Apply text filters: A text filter can find exact text, text that does not equal a condition, text that begins with a particular letter, and so forth.
- Apply number filters: A number filter can find exact values, values that do not equal a particular value, values greater than or equal to a value, and so on.
- Apply date filters: You can set filters to find dates before or after a certain date, between two dates, yesterday, next month, and so forth.
- Apply a custom filter: You can create a custom AutoFilter to filter values by options such as Greater Than, Less Than, or Before.
- Clear filters: If you do not need filters, you can clear the filters.

9. Add a total row.

- You can display a total row after the last record. You can add totals or select a different function, such as Average.

10. Apply conditional formatting.

- Apply conditional formatting with the Quick Analysis Tool: After selecting text, click Formatting in the Quick Analysis gallery to apply a conditional format.
- Apply a highlight cells rule: This rule highlights cell contents with a fill color, font color, and/or border color where the contents match a particular condition.
- Specify a top/bottom rule: This rule enables you to highlight the top or bottom x number of items or percentage of items.
- Display data bars, color scales, and icon sets: Data bars compare values within the selected range. Color scales indicate values that occur within particular ranges. Icon sets display icons representing a number's relative value compared to other numbers in the range.

11. Create a new rule.

- You can create conditional format rules. The New Formatting Rule dialog box enables you to select a rule type.
- Use formulas in conditional formatting: You can create rules based on content in multiple columns.
- Manage rules: Use the Conditional Formatting Rules Manager dialog box to edit and delete rules.

Key Terms Matching

Match the key terms with their definitions. Write the key term letter by the appropriate numbered definition.

a. Color scale
b. Conditional formatting
c. Data bar
d. Field
e. Filtering
f. Freezing
g. Icon set
h. Page break
i. Print area

j. Print order
k. Record
l. Sorting
m. Structured reference
n. SUBTOTAL function
o. Table
p. Table style
q. Total row

1. _____ A conditional format that displays a horizontal gradient or solid fill indicating the cell's relative value compared to other selected cells. **p. 640**

2. _____ The process of listing records or text in a specific sequence, such as alphabetically by last name. **p. 622**

3. _____ The process of specifying conditions to display only those records that meet those conditions. **p. 624**

4. _____ A set of rules that applies specific formatting to highlight or emphasize cells that meet specifications. **p. 636**

5. _____ A group of related fields representing one entity, such as data for one person, place, event, or concept. **p. 609**

6. _____ The rules that control the fill color of the header row, columns, and records in a table. **p. 614**

7. _____ An indication of where data will start on another printed page. **p. 600**

8. _____ A table row that appears below the last row of records in an Excel table and displays summary or aggregate statistics, such as a sum or an average. **p. 636**

9. _____ A conditional format that displays a particular color based on the relative value of the cell contents to the other selected cells. **p. 642**

10. _____ The sequence in which the pages are printed. **p. 603**

11. _____ A tag or use of a table element, such as a field label, as a reference in a formula. **p. 621**

12. _____ Symbols or signs that classify data into three, four, or five categories, based on the values in a range. **p. 642**

13. _____ The range of cells within a worksheet that will print. **p. 601**

14. _____ A predefined formula that calculates an aggregate value, such as totals, for values in a range, a table, or a database. **p. 637**

15. _____ The smallest data element contained in a table, such as first name, last name, address, and phone number. **p. 609**

16. _____ A structure that organizes data in a series of records (rows), with each record made up of a number of fields (columns). **p. 609**

17. _____ The process of keeping rows and/or columns visible onscreen at all times even when you scroll through a large dataset. **p. 599**

Multiple Choice

1. You have a large dataset that will print on several pages. You want to ensure that related records print on the same page with column and row labels visible and that confidential information is not printed. You should apply all of the following page setup options *except* which one to accomplish this task?

   (a) Set a print area.
   (b) Print titles.
   (c) Adjust page breaks.
   (d) Change the print page order.

2. You are working with a large worksheet. Your row headings are in column A. Which command(s) should be used to see the row headings and the distant information in columns X, Y, and Z?

   (a) Freeze Panes command
   (b) Hide Rows command
   (c) New Window command and cascade the windows
   (d) Split Rows command

3. Which statement is *not* a recommended guideline for designing and creating an Excel table?

   (a) Avoid naming two fields with the same name.
   (b) Ensure that no blank columns separate data columns within the table.
   (c) Leave one blank row between records in the table.
   (d) Include field names on the first row of the table.

4. Which of the following characters are wildcards in Excel? (Check all that apply.)

   (a) *
   (b) #
   (c) ?
   (d) $

5. What should you do to ensure that records in a table are unique?

   (a) Do nothing; a logical reason probably exists to keep identical records.
   (b) Use the Remove Duplicates command.
   (c) Look at each row yourself and manually delete duplicate records.
   (d) Find the duplicate records and change some of the data to be different.

6. Which Conditional Formatting rule is best suited to apply formatting to the top five values in a range of values?

   (a) Above Average
   (b) Greater Than
   (c) Top 10 Items
   (d) Between

7. Which date filter option enables you to restrict the view to only dates that occur in March of 2018?

   (a) Equals
   (b) Before
   (c) After
   (d) Between

8. Which of the following is an unqualified structured reference?

   (a) =[Purchase_Price]-[Down_Payment]
   (b) =Sales[Purchase_Price]-Sales[Down_Payment]
   (c) =Purchase_Price-Down_Payment
   (d) =[Sales]Purchase_Price-[Sales]Down_Payment

9. Which of the following is not an aggregate function that can be applied in a total row?

   (a) MAX
   (b) AVERAGE
   (c) COUNT
   (d) VLOOKUP

10. If you would like to set a conditional formatting rule based on the function =AND(G6="Finance", H7<7000), which formatting rule type is needed?

    (a) Format all cells based on their values
    (b) Format only cells that contain
    (c) Use a formula to determine which cells to format
    (d) Format only values that are above or below average

Practice Exercises

1 Collectables and Replacement Values

Marie Maier has collected dinnerware, from a fine china company, since 1986. Between 1986 and 2012, the company produced 30 colors, each with a unique name. Marie created a table in Word that lists the name, number, year introduced, and year retired (if applicable) for each color. She created another table in Word that lists the item number, item, replacement value, and source of information for each item in her collection. Her main sources for replacement values are Homer Laughlin (www.fiestafactorydirect.com), Replacements, Ltd. (www.replacements.com), eBay (www.ebay.com), and two local antique stores. She needs your help to convert the data to Excel tables, apply table formatting, delete duplicate records, insert functions, and sort and filter the data. Refer to Figure 4.52 as you complete this exercise.

	A	B	C	D	E	F	G	H	
1	Color Number	Year Introduced	Year Retired	Status	Color	Item Number	Item	Replacement Value	
31	102	2000	2010	Retired	Cinnabar	571	Canister Small	49.99	Dc
32	102	2000	2010	Retired	Cinnabar	830	5 Piece Place Setting	35.99	Dc
33	102	2000	2010	Retired	Cinnabar	484	Pitcher Large Disc	34.99	Ke
34	102	2000	2010	Retired	Cinnabar	467	Chop Plate	25.00	Dc
35	102	2000	2010	Retired	Cinnabar	497	Salt and Pepper Set	20.00	Dc
36	102	2000	2010	Retired	Cinnabar	465	Luncheon Plate	12.50	Dc
37	102	2000	2010	Retired	Cinnabar	439	Spoon Rest	11.99	Th
38	102	2000	2010	Retired	Cinnabar	570	Java Mug	9.99	Re
39	102	2000	2010	Retired	Cinnabar	453	Mug	8.49	Th
40	102	2000	2010	Retired	Cinnabar	446	Tumbler	6.99	Th
41	103	1986	2005	Retired	Rose	494	Covered Coffee Server	75.00	Ke
42	103	1986	2005	Retired	Rose	495	Covered Casserole	65.00	Dc
43	103	1986	2005	Retired	Rose	489	Pyramid Candleholders	59.99	Dc
44	103	1986	2005	Retired	Rose	486	Sauceboat	39.99	Eb
45	103	1986	2005	Retired	Rose	830	5 Piece Place Setting	35.00	Eb
46	103	1986	2005	Retired	Rose	821	Sugar/Cream Tray Set	29.99	Eb
47	103	1986	2005	Retired	Rose	484	Pitcher Large Disc	24.99	Eb
48	103	1986	2005	Retired	Rose	478	AD Cup and Saucer	19.99	Eb
49	103	1986	2005	Retired	Rose	471	Bowl Large 1 qt	19.99	Dc
50	103	1986	2005	Retired	Rose	497	Salt and Pepper Set	18.00	Eb
51	103	1986	2005	Retired	Rose	467	Chop Plate	16.95	Eb
52	103	1986	2005	Retired	Rose	451	Rim Soup	12.50	Eb

FIGURE 4.52 Fiesta® Collection

Excel 2016, Windows 10, Microsoft Corporation

a. Open *e04p1Collectables* and save it as **e04p1Collectables_LastFirst**.

b. Select the **range A2:D31** on the Colors Data sheet, click in the **Name Box**, type **Colors**, and then press **Enter** to assign the name *Colors* to the selected range.

c. Click **cell A2** on the Items sheet, click the **View tab**, click **Freeze Panes** in the Window group, and then select **Freeze Top Row**.

d. Click the **Insert tab**, click **Table** in the Tables group, and then click **OK** in the Create Table dialog box.

e. Click **More Styles** in the Table Styles group and click **Table Style Medium 5**.

f. Click the **Data tab**, click **Remove Duplicates** in the Data Tools group, and then click **OK** in the Remove Duplicates dialog box. Click **OK** in the message box that informs you that 6 duplicate values were found and removed; 356 unique values remain.

g. Click **cell A2**, click the **Home tab**, click **Sort & Filter** in the Editing group, and then select **Sort Smallest to Largest**.

h. Click **cell B2**, click the **Insert arrow** in the Cells group, and then select **Insert Table Columns to the Left**. Insert two more columns to the left. Do the following to insert functions and customize the results in the three new table columns:

- Type **Year Introduced** in **cell B1**, **Year Retired** in **cell C1**, and **Color** in **cell D1**.
- Click **cell B2**, type **=VLOOKUP([Color Number],colors,3,False)**, and then press **Enter**. Excel copies the function down the Year Introduced column. This function looks up each item's color number using the structured reference *[Color Number]*, looks up that value in the colors table, and then returns the year that color was introduced, which is in the third column of that table.
- Click **cell B2**, click **Copy**, click **cell C2**, and then click **Paste**. Change the *3* to **4** in the col_index_num argument of the pasted function and press **Enter**. Excel copies the function down the Year Retired column. This function looks up each item's color number using the structured reference *[Color Number]*, looks up that value in the colors table, and then returns the year that color was retired, if applicable, which is in the fourth column of that table. The function returns 0 if the retired cell in the lookup table is blank.

DISCOVER

- Click the **File tab**, click **Options**, click **Advanced**, scroll down to the Display options for this worksheet section, click the **Show a zero in cells that have zero value check box** to deselect it, and then click **OK**. The zeros disappear. (This option hides zeros in the active worksheet. While this is not desirable if you need to show legitimate zeros, this worksheet is designed to avoid that issue.)
- Click **cell C2**, click **Copy**, click **cell D2**, and then click **Paste**. Change the *4* to **2** in the col_index_num argument of the pasted function and press **Enter**. Excel copies the function down the Color column. This function looks up each item's color number using the structured reference *[Color Number]* to look up that value in the colors table and returns the color name, which is in the second column of that table.

i. Apply wrap text, horizontal centering, and **30.50 row height** to the column labels row. Adjust column widths to AutoFit. Center data horizontally in the Color Number, Year Introduced, Year Retired, and Item Number columns. Apply **Comma Style** to the Replacement Values. Deselect the data.

j. Click **Sort & Filter** in the Editing group and select **Custom Sort** to display the Sort dialog box. Do the following in the Sort dialog box:

- Click the **Sort by arrow** and select **Color**.
- Click **Add Level**, click the **Then by arrow**, and then select **Replacement Value**.
- Click the **Order arrow** and select **Largest to Smallest**.
- Click **Add Level**, click the **Then by arrow**, and select **Source**.
- Click the **Order arrow**, select **Custom List**, and type the following entries: **Ebay Auction, Downtown Antique Store, The Homer Laughlin China Co., Replacements LTD., Keith's Antique Store**. Click **Add** and click **OK**. Click **OK**.

k. Right-click the **Items sheet tab**, select **Move or Copy**, click **(move to end)**, click the **Create a copy check box** to select the option, and then click **OK**. Rename the copied sheet **Retired**.

l. Ensure that Retired is the active sheet. Insert a table column between the Year Retired and Color columns.

- Type **Status** in **cell D1** as the column label.
- Click **cell D2**, type **=IF([Year Retired]=0, "Current","Retired")**, and then press **Enter**. This function determines that if the cell contains a 0 (which is hidden), it will display the word *Current*. Otherwise, it will display *Retired*.

m. Click the **Status filter arrow**, deselect the **Current check box**, and then click **OK** to filter out the current colors and display only retired colors.

n. Click the **Design tab** and click **Total Row** in the Table Style Options group. Click **cell I358**, click the **Source total cell** (which contains a count of visible items), click the **Source total arrow**, and then select **None**. Click **cell H358**, the Replacement Value total cell, click the **Replacement Value total arrow**, and then select **Sum**.

o. Prepare the Retired worksheet for printing by doing the following:
- Set **0.2"** left and right page margins.
- Select the **range E1:I358**, click the **Page Layout tab**, click **Print Area** in the Page Setup group, and then select **Set Print Area**.
- Click **Print Titles** in the Page Setup group, click the **Rows to repeat at top Collapse Dialog Box**, click the **row 1 header**, and then click **Expand Dialog Box**. Click **OK**.
- Click the **View tab** and click **Page Break Preview** in the Workbook Views group. Decrease the top margin to avoid having only one or two records print on the last page.

p. Create a footer with your name on the left side, the sheet name code in the center, and the file name code on the right side of each worksheet.

q. Save and close the file. Based on your instructor's directions, submit e04p1Collectables_LastFirst.

2 Sunny Popcorn, Inc.

You are a financial analyst for Sunny Popcorn, Inc. and have been given the task of compiling a workbook to detail weekly sales information. The current information provided detailed sales rep information, flavors ordered, account type, and volume ordered. The owners are specifically interested in local sales that are generating at least $150.00 a week. To complete the document you will sort, filter, use table tools, and apply conditional formatting. Refer to Figure 4.53 as you complete this exercise.

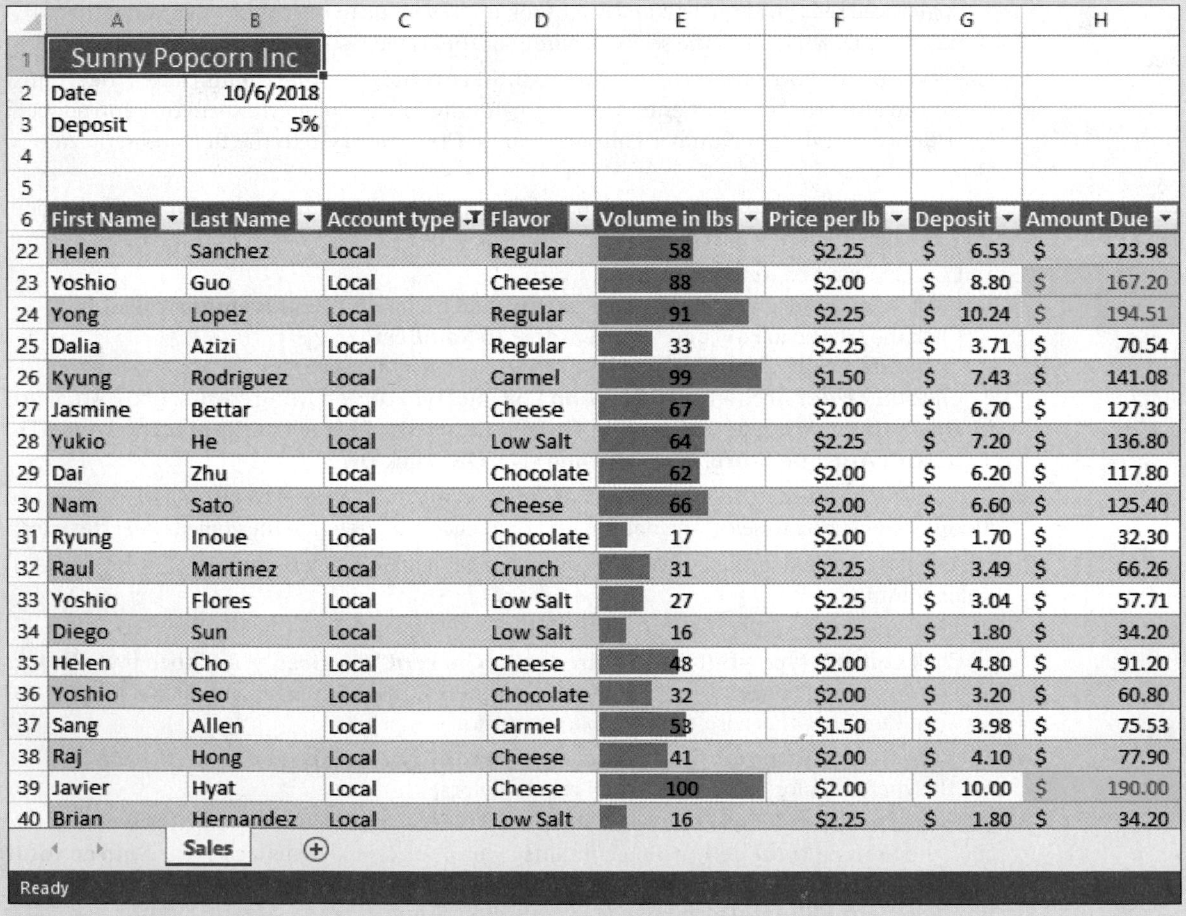

	First Name	Last Name	Account type	Flavor	Volume in lbs	Price per lb	Deposit	Amount Due
1	Sunny Popcorn Inc							
2	Date	10/6/2018						
3	Deposit	5%						
4								
5								
22	Helen	Sanchez	Local	Regular	58	$2.25	$ 6.53	$ 123.98
23	Yoshio	Guo	Local	Cheese	88	$2.00	$ 8.80	$ 167.20
24	Yong	Lopez	Local	Regular	91	$2.25	$ 10.24	$ 194.51
25	Dalia	Azizi	Local	Regular	33	$2.25	$ 3.71	$ 70.54
26	Kyung	Rodriguez	Local	Carmel	99	$1.50	$ 7.43	$ 141.08
27	Jasmine	Bettar	Local	Cheese	67	$2.00	$ 6.70	$ 127.30
28	Yukio	He	Local	Low Salt	64	$2.25	$ 7.20	$ 136.80
29	Dai	Zhu	Local	Chocolate	62	$2.00	$ 6.20	$ 117.80
30	Nam	Sato	Local	Cheese	66	$2.00	$ 6.60	$ 125.40
31	Ryung	Inoue	Local	Chocolate	17	$2.00	$ 1.70	$ 32.30
32	Raul	Martinez	Local	Crunch	31	$2.25	$ 3.49	$ 66.26
33	Yoshio	Flores	Local	Low Salt	27	$2.25	$ 3.04	$ 57.71
34	Diego	Sun	Local	Low Salt	16	$2.25	$ 1.80	$ 34.20
35	Helen	Cho	Local	Cheese	48	$2.00	$ 4.80	$ 91.20
36	Yoshio	Seo	Local	Chocolate	32	$2.00	$ 3.20	$ 60.80
37	Sang	Allen	Local	Carmel	53	$1.50	$ 3.98	$ 75.53
38	Raj	Hong	Local	Cheese	41	$2.00	$ 4.10	$ 77.90
39	Javier	Hyat	Local	Cheese	100	$2.00	$ 10.00	$ 190.00
40	Brian	Hernandez	Local	Low Salt	16	$2.25	$ 1.80	$ 34.20

Sales

Ready

FIGURE 4.53 Sunny Popcorn Inc

a. Open *e04p2Popcorn* and save it as **e04p2Popcorn_LastFirst**.

b. Click **cell C7**, click the **Home tab**, click the **Sort & Filter arrow** in the Editing group, and select **Sort A to Z**. This sorts the data by account type in Column C.

c. Click the **Insert tab**, click **Table** in the Tables group, and click **OK** in the Create Table dialog box.

d. Click **Table Style Medium 3** in the Table Styles group on the Design tab.

e. Click cell **G7** and type **=[Price per lb]*[Volume in lbs]*$B$3** and press **Enter**.

f. Click cell **H7** and type **=[Price per lb]*[Volume in lbs]-[Deposit]** and press **Enter**

g. Select the **range G7:H106**, click the **Home tab**, and click **Accounting Number Format** in the Number group.

h. Click the **Design tab** and click **Total Row** in the Table Style Options group.

i. Click the **Deposit Total Row arrow**, and select **Sum**, click the **Volume in lbs Total Row arrow**, and then select **Average**. Apply **Number Style Format** to the results in **cell E107**.

j. Click the **filter arrow** of the Account type column, click the **Select All check box** to deselect it, click **Local**, and click **OK**.

k. Select the **range H22:H51**, click **Quick Analysis**, and then select **Greater Than**. Type **150.00** in the Format cells that are GREATER THAN box, select **Green Fill with Dark Green Text**, and click **OK**.

l. Select the **range E22:E51**, click **Quick Analysis**, and then select **Data Bars**.

m. Click the **Page Layout tab**, click the **Scale box** in the Scale to Fit group, and then type **85%**.

n. Create a footer with your name on the left side, the sheet name code in the center, and the file name code on the right side of each worksheet.

o. Save and close the file. Based on your instructor's directions, submit e04p2Popcorn_LastFirst.

Mid-Level Exercises

1 Crafton's Pet Supplies

You are the inventory manager for Crafton's Pet Supplies. You are currently preforming analysis to determine inventory levels, as well as the total value of inventory on hand. Your last steps will be to check the report for duplicate entries and format for printing.

a. Open *e04m1Inventory* and save it as **e04m1Inventory_LastFirst**.

b. Freeze the panes so that the column labels do not scroll offscreen.

c. Convert the data to a table and name the table **Inventory2018**.

d. Apply **Table Style Medium 3** to the table.

e. Sort the table by Warehouse (A to Z), then Department, and then by Unit Price (smallest to largest). Create a custom sort order for Department so that it appears in this sequence: Food & Health, Collars & Leashes, Toys, Clothes, Training, and Grooming.

f. Remove duplicate records from the table. Excel should find and remove one duplicate record.

g. Create an unqualified structured reference in column G to determine the value of the inventory on hand and apply **Accounting Number Format**. To calculate the inventory on hand multiply the **Unit Price** and the **Amount on Hand.**

h. Apply a **Total Row** to the Inventory2018 table, set the Inventory Value to Sum, and the Amount on Hand to Average. Format the results to display with two decimal points.

i. Create a new conditional formatting rule that displays any Inventory Value for the **Food & Health** department with a value of $30,000 or more as **Red Accent 2 fill color**. There will be two qualifying entries.

j. Ensure the warehouse information is not broken up between pages when printed. Add a page break to make sure that each warehouse prints on its own consecutive page.

k. Set the worksheet to **Landscape orientation**, and repeat row 1 labels on all pages.

l. Display the Inventory sheet in Page Break Preview.

m. Insert a footer with your name on the left side, the sheet name code in the center, and the file name code on the right side of all four sheets.

n. Save and close the file. Based on your instructor's directions, submit e04m1Inventory_LastFirst.

2 Artwork

ANALYSIS CASE

You work for a gallery that is an authorized Greenwich Workshop fine art dealer (www.greenwichworkshop.com). Customers in your area are especially fond of James C. Christensen's art. Although customers can visit the website to see images and details about his work, they have requested a list of all his artwork. Your assistant prepared a list of artwork: art, type, edition size, release date, and issue price. In addition, you included a column to identify which pieces are sold out at the publisher, indicating the rare, hard-to-obtain artwork that is available on the secondary market. You now want to convert the data to a table so that you can provide information to your customers.

a. Open *e04m2FineArt* and save it as **e04m2FineArt_LastFirst**.

b. Convert the data to a table and apply **Table Style Medium 5**.

c. Add a row (below the record for *The Yellow Rose*) for this missing piece of art: **The Yellow Rose**, **Masterwork Canvas Edition**, **50** edition size, **May 2009** release date, **$895** issue price. Enter **Yes** to indicate the piece is sold out.

d. Sort the table by Type in alphabetical order and then by Release Date from newest to oldest.

e. Add a total row that shows the largest edition size and the most expensive issue price. Delete the Total label in **cell A205** and **cell H205**. Add a descriptive label in **cell C205** to reflect the content on the total row.

DISCOVER

f. Create a custom conditional format for the Issue Price column with these specifications:
  - **4 Traffic Lights** icon set (Black, Red, Yellow, Green)
  - **Red icon** when the number is greater than 1000
  - **Yellow icon** when the number is less than or equal to 1000 and greater than 500
  - **Green icon** when the number is less than or equal to 500 and greater than 250
  - **Black icon** when the number is less than or equal to 250.

DISCOVER

g. Filter the table by the **Red Traffic Light** conditional formatting icon.

h. Answer the questions in the range D213:D217 based on the filtered data.

i. Set the print area to print the **range C1:H205**, select the **first row to repeat at the top of each printout**, set **1"** top and bottom margins, set **0.3"** left and right margins, and then select **Landscape orientation**. Set the option to fit the data to 1 page.

j. Wrap text, and horizontally center column labels and adjust column widths and row heights as needed.

k. Create a footer with your name on the left side, the sheet name code in the center, and the file name code on the right side.

l. Save and close the file. Based on your instructor's directions, submit e04m2FineArt_LastFirst.

3 Party Music

COLLABORATION CASE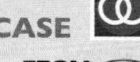

FROM SCRATCH

You are planning a weekend party and want to create a mix of music so that most people will appreciate some of the music you will play at the party. To help you decide what music to play, you have asked five classmates to help you create a song list. The entire class should decide on the general format, capitalization style, and the sequence: Song, Artist, Genre, Released, and approximate song length.

a. Conduct online research to collect data for your favorite 25 songs.

b. Enter the data into a new workbook in the format, capitalization style, and sequence that was decided by the class.

c. Save the workbook as **e04m3PlayList_LastFirst**.

d. Upload the file to a shared folder on OneDrive or Dropbox that everyone in the class can access.

e. Download four workbooks from friends and copy and paste data from their workbooks into yours.

f. Convert the data to a table and apply a table style of your choice.

g. Detect and delete duplicate records. Make a note of the number of duplicate records found and deleted.

h. Sort the data by genre using the custom list: Pop, Rock, R&B, and Jazz, then by artist in alphabetical order, and then by release date with the oldest year first.

i. Set a filter to display songs that were released before 2018.

j. Display the total row and select the function to count the number of songs displayed.

k. Insert comments in the workbook to indicate which student's workbooks you used, the number of duplicate records deleted, and the number of filtered records.

l. Save and close the file. Based on your instructor's directions, submit e04m3PlayList_LastFirst.

Beyond the Classroom

Flight Arrival Status

As an analyst for an airport, you want to study the flight arrivals for a particular day. Select an airport and find its list of flight arrival data. Some airport websites do not list complete details, so search for an airport that does, such as Will Rogers World Airport or San Diego International Airport. Copy the column labels and arrival data (airline, flight number, city, gate, scheduled time, status, etc.) for one day and paste them in a new workbook. The columns may be in a different sequence from what is listed here. However, you should format the data as needed. Leave two blank rows below the last row of data and enter the URL of the webpage from which you got the data, the date, and the time. Save the workbook as **e04b1Flights_LastFirst**. Convert the list to a table and apply a table style.

Sort the table by scheduled time and then by gate number. Apply conditional formatting to the Status column to highlight cells that contain the text Delayed (or similar text). Add a total row to calculate the MODE for the gate number and arrival time. The MODE is the number that appears the most frequently in the dataset. You must select **More Functions** from the list of functions in the total row and search for and select **MODE**. Change the total row label in the first column from Total to **Most Frequent**. Use Help to refresh your memory on how to nest an IF function inside another IF function. Add a calculated column on the right side of the table using a nested IF function and structured references to display **Late** if the actual time was later than the scheduled time, **On Time or Early** if the actual time was earlier than or equal to the scheduled time, or **Incomplete** if the flight has not landed yet.

Name the worksheet **Arrival Time**. Copy the worksheet and name the copied worksheet **Delayed**. Filter the list by delayed flights. Include a footer with your name on the left side, the sheet name code in the center, and the file name code on the right side of both worksheets. Adjust the margins on both worksheets as necessary. Save and close the file. Based on your instructor's directions, submit e04b1Flights_LastFirst.

Dairy Farm

You are the product manager for Schaefer Dairy farm, a local organic farm that produces dairy products. Each month you must run an inventory report to identify and discard expired products before they are sold. Open *e04b2Dairy* and save it as **e04b2Dairy_LastFirst**. Convert the **range A5:E105** to a table, give the table a name, and apply a table style.

Freeze all data above row 6 and create a conditional formatting rule that highlights any package date that is 30 days or older than the manufacture date in B4. Sort the table first by the newly created highlight color then by department. Next, in column E create an IF function using structured referencing to determine the course of action for expired products. The function should display **discard** if the product is expired and nothing if the product is still sellable. Filter the table to display only items that should be discarded, then add a total row that counts the number of items to discard. Format the table so the column headings print at the top of each page and create a footer with your name, the sheet name code, and the file name code. Save and close the file. Based on your instructor's directions, submit e04b2Dairy_LastFirst.

Capstone Exercise

You work for Rockville Auto Sales and have been asked to aid in the development of a spreadsheet to manage sales and inventory information. You will start the task with a prior worksheet that contains vehicle information and sales data for 2018. You need to convert the data to a table. You will manage the large worksheet, prepare the worksheet for printing, sort and filter the table, include calculations, and then format the table.

Prepare the Large Worksheet as a Table

You will freeze the panes so that labels remain onscreen. You also want to convert the data to a table so that you can apply table options.

a. Open the *e04c1AutoSales* workbook and save it as **e04c1AutoSales_LastFirst**.

b. Freeze the first row on the Fleet Information worksheet.

c. Convert the data to a table, name the table **Inventory**, and apply the **Table Style Medium 19**.

d. Remove duplicate records.

Sort and Print the Table

To help the sales agents manage vehicle inventory, you will sort the data. Then you will prepare the large table to print.

a. Sort the table by Make in alphabetical order, add a second level to sort by Year, and a third level to sort by Sticker Price smallest to largest.

b. Repeat the field names on all pages.

c. Change page breaks so each vehicle make is printed on a separate page.

d. Add a footer with your name on the left side, the sheet name code in the center, and the file name code on the right side.

Add Calculated Fields and a Total Row

For tax purposes, the accounting department needs you to calculate the number of vehicles sold, the total value of sticker prices, and actual sales price for vehicles sold in the first quarter.

a. Click the Sales Information worksheet and convert the data to a table, name the table Sales, and apply the **Table Style Dark 11**.

b. Create a formula with structured references to calculate the percentage of the Sticker Price in column E.

c. Format the **range E2:E30** with **Percentage Style** Number Format.

d. Add a total row to display the Average of % of Sticker Price and Sum of Sticker Price and Sale Price.

e. Adjust the width of **columns B:E** to show the total values.

Apply Conditional Formatting

You want to help the office manager visualize the differences among the sales. To highlight sales trends, you will apply data bar conditional formatting to the % of Value column.

a. Apply **Data Bars conditional formatting** to the % of Sticker Price data.

b. Create a new conditional format that applies yellow fill and bold font to values that sold for less than 60% of the list price.

c. Edit the conditional format you created so that it formats values 70% or less.

Copy and Filter the Data

In order to isolate first quarter sales, you will filter the data. To keep the original data intact for the sales agents, you will copy the table data to a new sheet and use that sheet to display the filtered data.

a. Copy the Sales Information sheet and place the duplicate sheet to the right of the original sheet tab.

b. Rename the duplicate worksheet **First Quarter Sales**.

c. Rename the table **FirstQuarter**.

d. Display the filter arrows for the data.

e. Filter the data to display January, February, and March sales.

Finalize the Workbook

You are ready to finalize the workbook by adding a footer to the new worksheet and saving the final workbook.

a. Add a footer with your name on the left side, the sheet name code in the center, and the file name code on the right side.

b. Select **Landscape orientation** for all sheets and set appropriate margins so that the data will print on one page.

c. Save and close the file. Based on your instructor's directions, submit e04c1AutoSales_LastFirst.

Introduction to Access

LEARNING OUTCOME You will demonstrate understanding of relational database concepts.

OBJECTIVES & SKILLS: After you read this chapter, you will be able to:

CASE STUDY | Managing a Business in the Global Economy

Northwind Traders is an international gourmet food distributor that imports and exports specialty foods from around the world. Keeping track of customers, vendors, orders, and inventory is a critical task. The owners of Northwind have just purchased an order-processing database created with Microsoft Access 2016 to help manage their customers, suppliers, products, and orders.

You have been hired to learn, use, and manage the database. Northwind's owners are willing to provide training about their business and Access. They expect the learning process to take about three months. After three months, your job will be to support the order-processing team as well as to provide detail and summary reports to the sales force as needed. Your new job at Northwind Traders will be a challenge, but it is also a good opportunity to make a great contribution to a global company. Are you up to the task?

CHAPTER 1

Finding Your Way Through an Access Database

Syda Productions/
Shutterstock

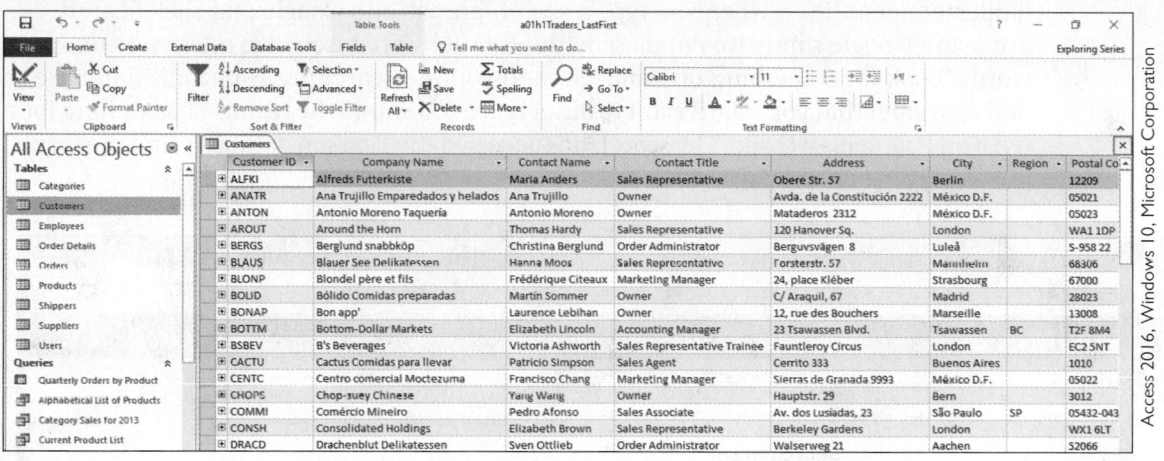

FIGURE 1.1 Northwind Traders Database

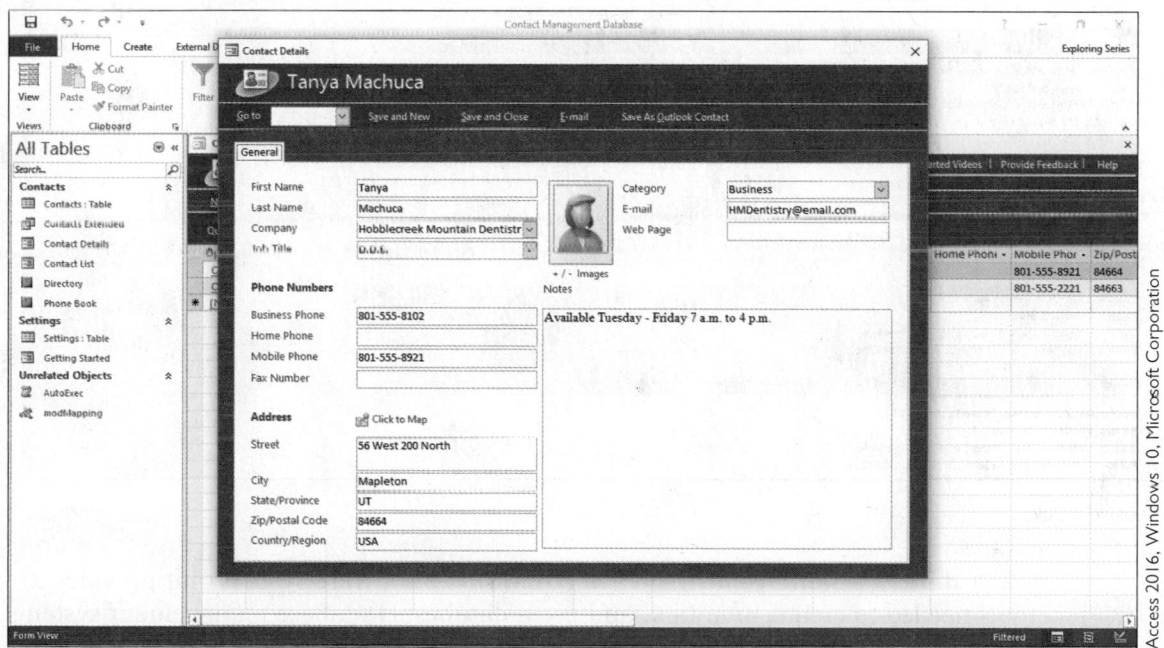

FIGURE 1.2 Northwind Traders Contacts Database

CASE STUDY | Managing a Business in the Global Economy

Starting File	Files to be Submitted
a01h1Traders	a01h1Traders_LastFirst_*CurrentDate*
	a01h2Traders_LastFirst
	a01h3Contacts_LastFirst

Databases Are Everywhere!

A *database* is a collection of data organized as meaningful information that can be accessed, managed, stored, queried, sorted, and reported. You probably participate in data collection and are exposed to databases on a regular basis. Your college or university stores your personal and registration data. When you registered for this course, your data was entered into a database. If you have a bank account, have a Social Security card, have a medical history, or have booked a flight with an airline, your information is stored in a database.

You use databases online without realizing it, such as when you shop or check your bank statement. Even when you type a search phrase into Google and click Search, you are using Google's massive database with all of its stored webpage references and keywords. Look for something on Amazon, and you are searching Amazon's database to find a product that you might want to buy. Figure 1.3 shows the results of searching for a term on Pearson's website. The search has accessed the Pearson database, and the results are displayed in a webpage.

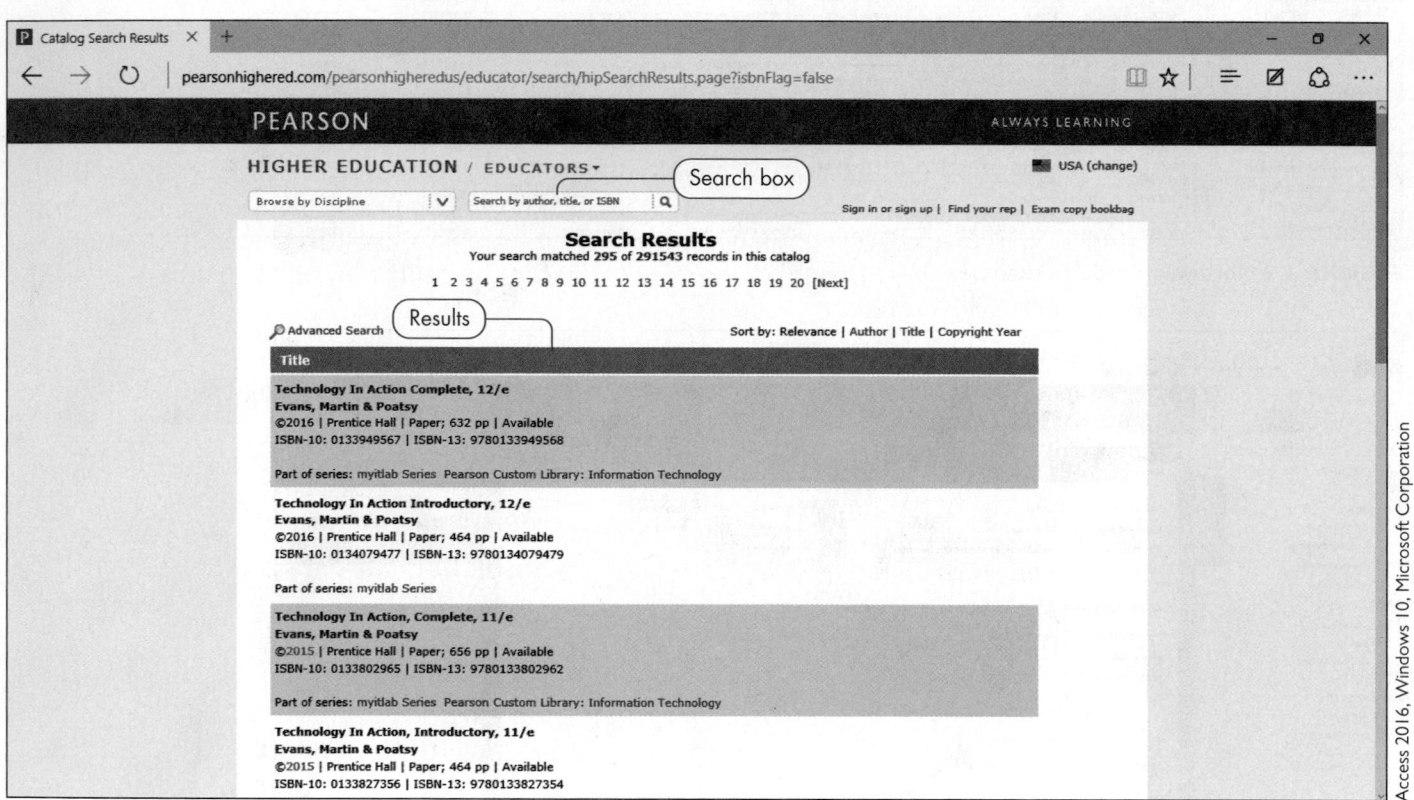

FIGURE 1.3 Pearson Website Search

A *database management system (DBMS)* is a software system that provides the tools needed to create, maintain, and use a database. Database management systems make it possible to access and control data and display the information in a variety of formats. *Access* is the database management system included in professional editions of the Office 2016 suite. Access is a valuable decision-making tool used by many organizations. More advanced DBMS packages include Microsoft SQL Server, MySQL, and Oracle.

Organizations from all industries rely on data to conduct daily operations. Businesses maintain and analyze data about their students, customers, employees, orders, volunteers, activities, and facilities. Data and information are two terms that are often used interchangeably. However, when it comes to databases, the two terms mean different things. Data is what is entered into a database. Information is the finished product that is produced by the database. Data is converted to information by selecting, performing calculations, and sorting. Decisions in an organization are usually based on information produced by a database, rather than raw data. For example, the number 55 is just data, because it could mean anything. Only when a label is attached to it (for example, as someone's age) does it take on meaning and become information.

In this section, you will learn the fundamentals of organizing data in a database, explore Access database objects and the purpose of each object, and examine the Access interface.

Opening, Saving, and Enabling Content in a Database

STEP 1 ⟩⟩ As you work through the material in this book, you will frequently be asked to open a database, save it with a new name, and enable content. You can also start by creating a new database if appropriate.

If you have been provided a database, open the file to get started. When you open any database for the first time, you will be presented with a warning that it might contain harmful code. By enabling the content, the database file will be trusted on the computer you are working on. All content from this publisher and associated with this book can be trusted.

To open an existing Access database and enable content, complete the following steps:

1. Start Access 2016. Backstage view displays. (Note: If Access is already open, click the File tab to display Backstage view).
2. Click Open Other Files.
3. Click Browse ▦ to open the Open dialog box.
4. Locate and select the database and click Open.
5. Click Enable Content on the message bar (see Figure 1.4). Access will close and reopen the database, and the security warning disappears and will not appear again for this database.

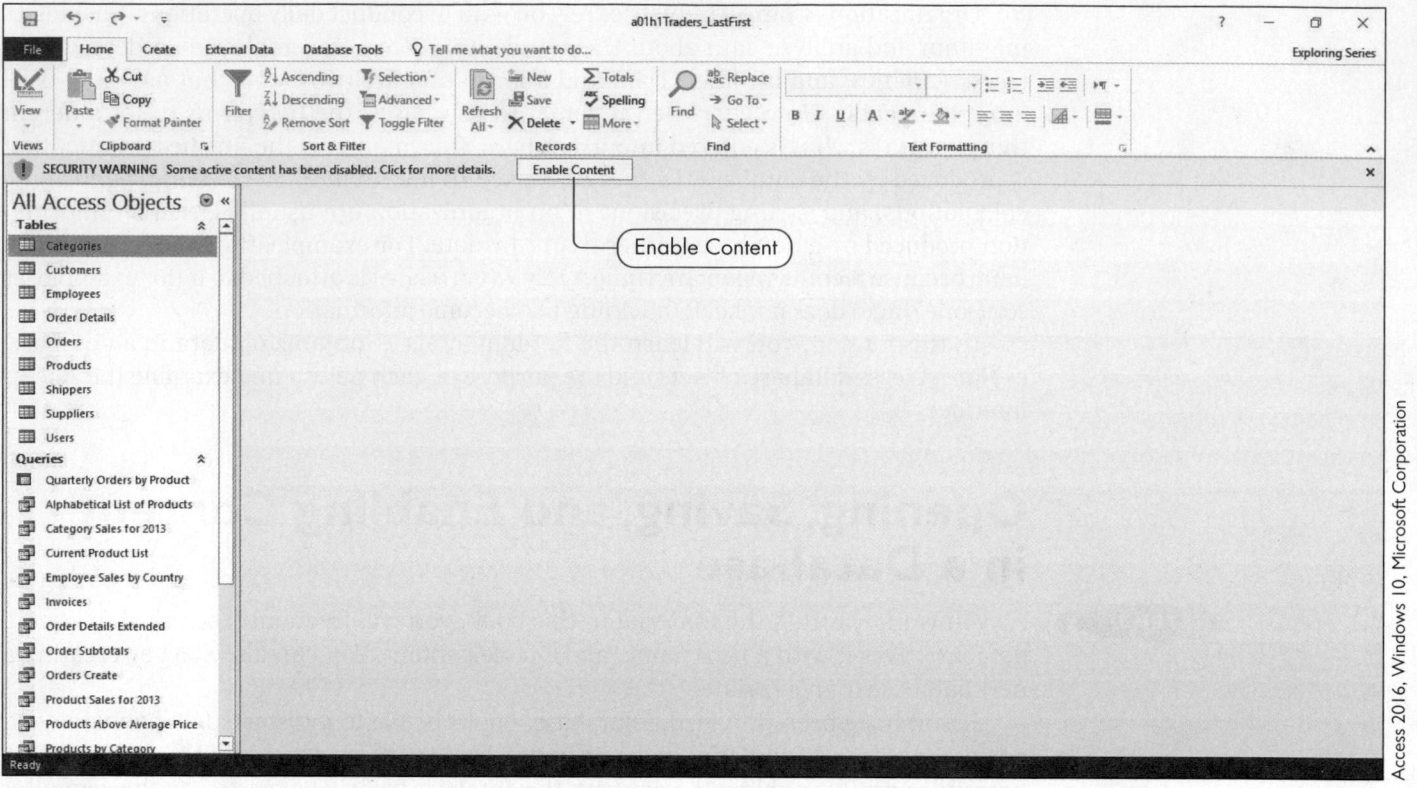

FIGURE 1.4 Access Security Warning

Backstage view gives you access to the Save As command. Most assignments will have you save the starting database file with a new name.

> **To save the database with a new name, complete the following steps:**
>
> 1. Click the File tab.
> 2. Select Save As.
> 3. Ensure Save Database As is selected (see Figure 1.5).
> 4. Click Save As.
> 5. Type the new name for your database, and click Save.

Access 2016, Windows 10, Microsoft Corporation

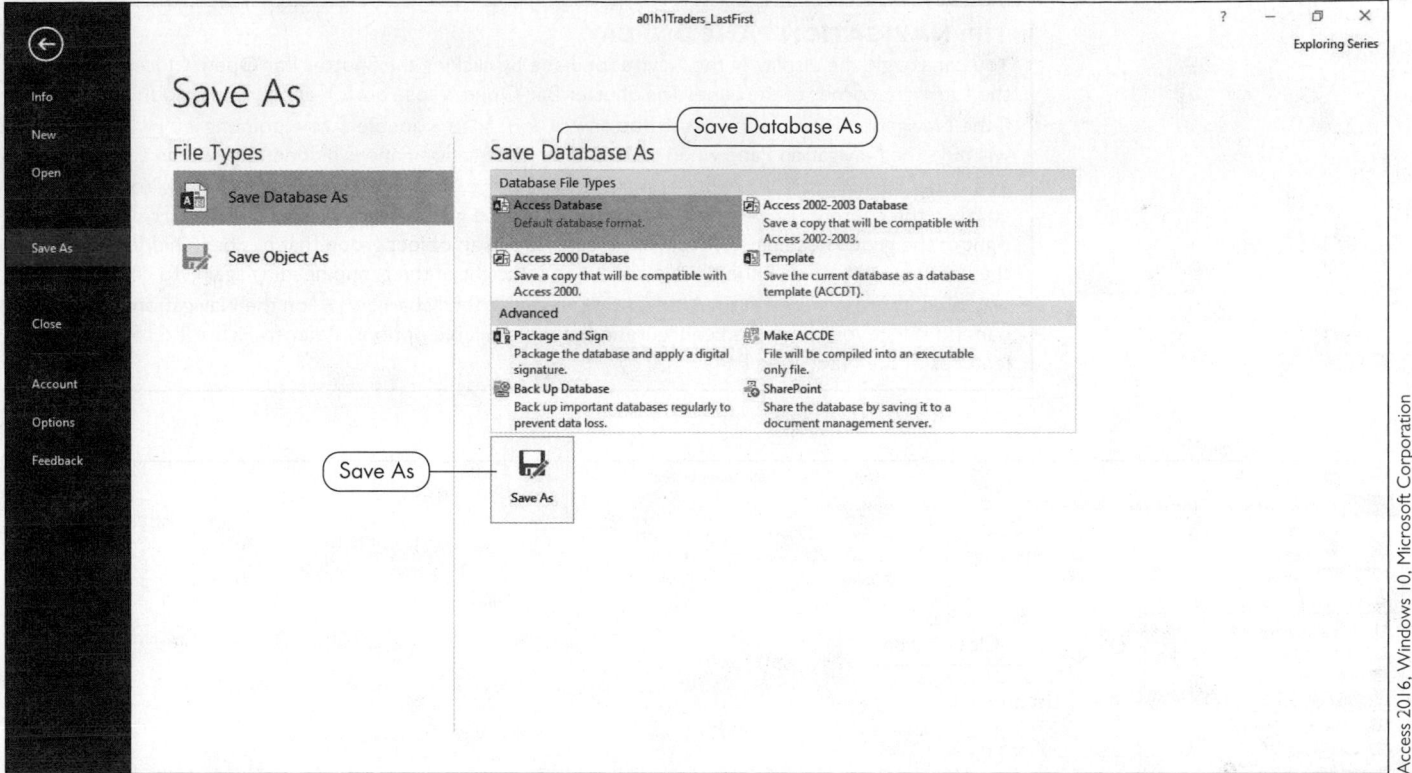

FIGURE 1.5 Access Save As Options

TIP: ALTERNATIVE SAVE FORMAT: ACCESS DATABASE EXECUTABLE

Creating an Access Database Executable (ACCDE) file allows users to enter data, but not add, modify, or delete objects. In other words, the only task they can do is data entry. This file format protects against users changing designs or deleting objects.

To create an Access Database Executable, click the File tab, click Save As, and double-click Make ACCDE. Click Save to save as an Access Database Executable.

Recognizing Database Object Types

STEP 2 ❱❱ Databases must be carefully managed to keep information accurate. Data need to be changed, added, and deleted. Managing a database also requires that you understand when data is saved and when you need to use the Save commands.

In Access, each component created and used to make the database function is known as an *object*. Objects include tables, queries, forms, and reports, and can be found in the *Navigation Pane*. The Navigation Pane is an Access interface element that organizes and lists the objects in an Access database. The Navigation Pane appears on the left side of the screen, and displays all objects. You can open any object by double-clicking the object's name in the list.

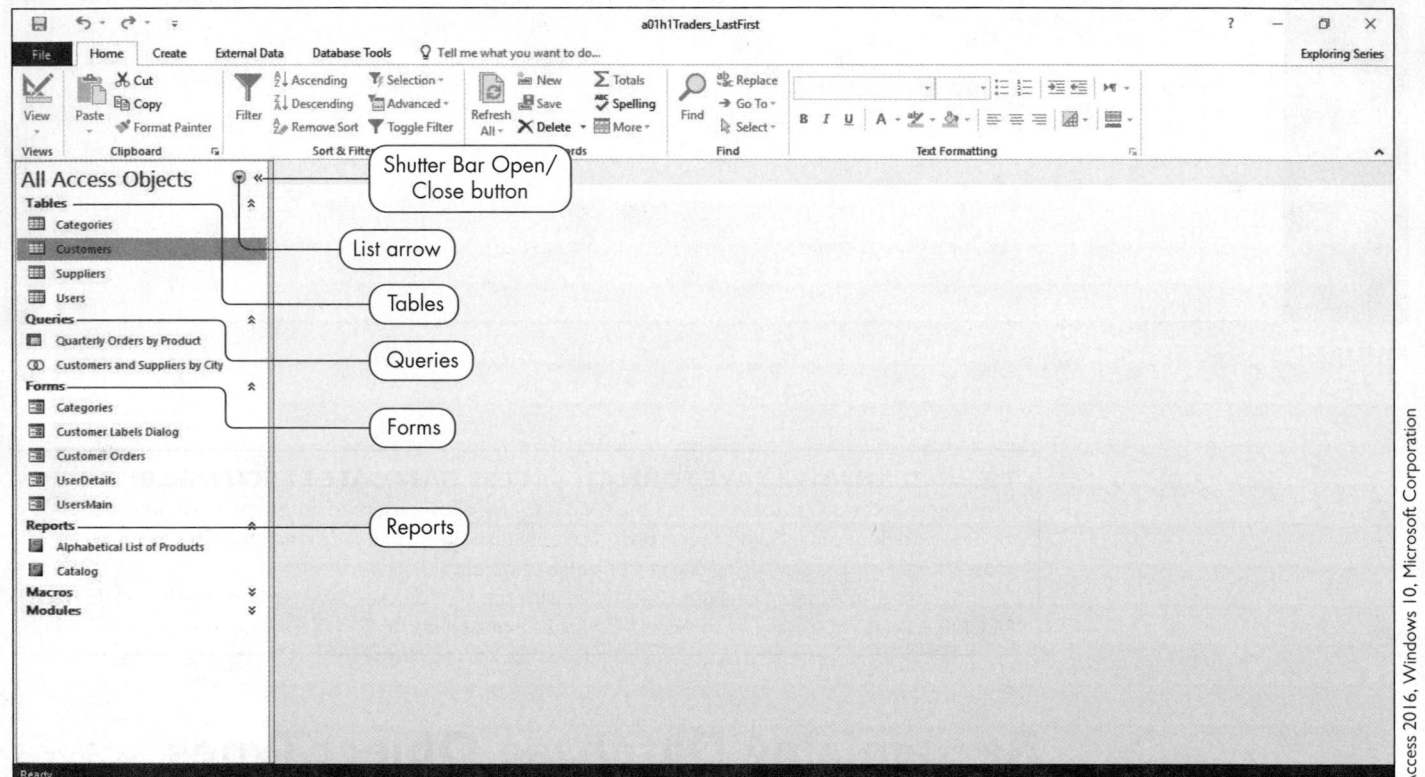

FIGURE 1.6 Navigation Pane Features

Most databases contain multiple tables. By default, the objects display in groups by object type in the Navigation Pane. In other words, you will see a list of tables, followed by queries, followed by forms, followed by reports. The purpose of each of these objects is described below.

- A **table** is where all data is stored in your database, and thus can be said to be the foundation of each database. Tables organize data into columns and rows. Each column represents a **field**, a category of information we store in a table. For example, in the Northwind database, a table containing customer information would include fields such as Customer ID, Company Name, and City. Each row in a table contains a **record**, a complete set of all the fields about one person, place, event, or concept. A customer record, for example, would contain all of the fields about a single customer, including the Customer ID, the Company Name, Contact Name, Contact Title, Address, City, etc. Figure 1.7 shows both fields and records. The **primary key** is a field (or combination of fields) that uniquely identifies each record in a table. Common primary keys are driver's license number, government

ID number (such as a Social Security number), passport number, and student ID. Many of these primary keys are generated by a database. Your college or university's database likely assigns a unique identifier to a student as soon as they apply, for example.

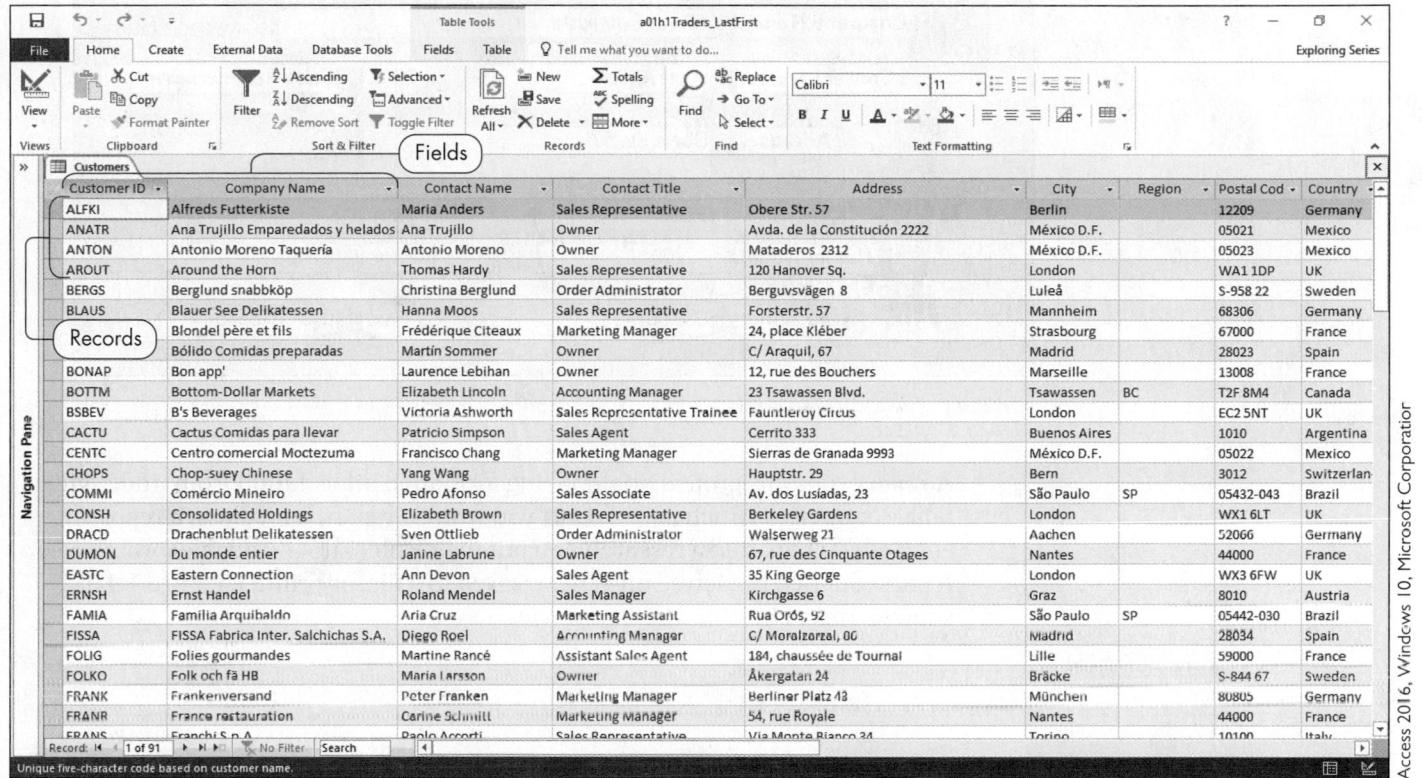

FIGURE 1.7 An Access Table

- A ***query*** (or queries, plural) is a question you ask about the data in your database. Notice the word query is similar to the word inquiry, which means question. It produces a subset of data that provides information about the question you have asked. For example, a query may display a list of which customers live in a specific town, or a list of children registered for a specific after-school program. You can double-click a query in the Navigation Pane and you will notice the interface is similar to that of a table, as shown in Figure 1.8.

Company Name	Contact Name	Country	City	Region	Phone
Bólido Comidas preparadas	Martín Sommer	Spain	Madrid		(91) 555 22 82
FISSA Fabrica Inter. Salchichas S.A.	Diego Roel	Spain	Madrid		(91) 555 94 44
Romero y tomillo	Alejandra Camino	Spain	Madrid		(91) 745 6200

Customers in Madrid

FIGURE 1.8 An Access Query

- A ***form*** allows simplified entry and modification of data. Much like entering data on a paper form, a database form enables you to add, modify, and delete table data. Most forms display one record at a time, which helps prevent data entry errors. Forms are typically utilized by the users of the database, while the database designer creates and edits the form structure. Figure 1.9 shows a form. Notice a single record is displayed.

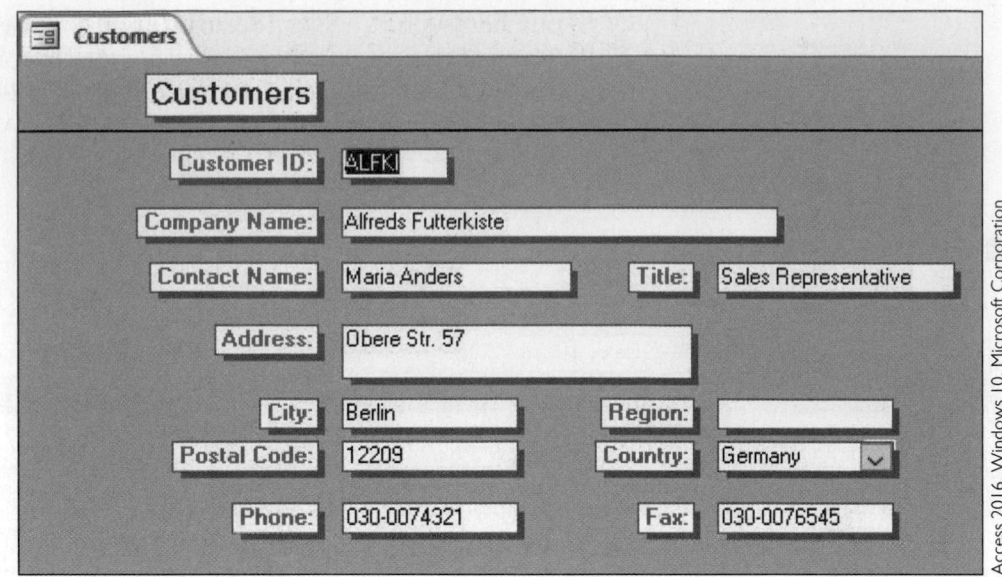

FIGURE 1.9 An Access Form

- A ***report*** contains professional-looking formatted information from underlying tables or queries. Much like a report you would prepare for a class, a report enables you to perform research and put the results into a readable format. The report can then be viewed on-screen, saved to a file, or printed. Figure 1.10 shows a report in Print Preview mode.

	Customer Contacts						

Customer Contacts

Contact Name	Company Name	Contact Title	Phone	City	Region	Country
Alejandra Camino	Romero y tomillo	Accounting Manager	(91) 745 6200	Madrid		Spain
Alexander Feuer	Morgenstern Gesundkost	Marketing Assistant	0342-023176	Leipzig		Germany
Ana Trujillo	Ana Trujillo Emparedados y helados	Owner	(5) 555-4729	México D.F.		Mexico
Anabela Domingues	Tradição Hipermercados	Sales Representative	(11) 555-2167	São Paulo	SP	Brazil
André Fonseca	Gourmet Lanchonetes	Sales Associate	(11) 555-9482	Campinas	SP	Brazil
Ann Devon	Eastern Connection	Sales Agent	(171) 555-0297	London		UK
Annette Roulet	La maison d'Asie	Sales Manager	61.77.61.10	Toulouse		France
Antonio Moreno	Antonio Moreno Taquería	Owner	(5) 555-3932	México D.F.		Mexico
Aria Cruz	Familia Arquibaldo	Marketing Assistant	(11) 555-9857	São Paulo	SP	Brazil
Art Braunschweiger	Split Rail Beer & Ale	Sales Manager	(307) 555-4680	Lander	WY	USA
Bernardo Batista	Que Delícia	Accounting Manager	(21) 555-4252	Rio de Janeiro	RJ	Brazil
Carine Schmitt	France restauration	Marketing Manager	40.32.21.21	Nantes		France
Carlos González	LILA-Supermercado	Accounting Manager	(9) 331-6954	Barquisimeto	Lara	Venezuela
Carlos Hernández	HILARIÓN-Abastos	Sales Representative	(5) 555-1340	San Cristóbal	Táchira	Venezuela
Catherine Dewey	Maison Dewey	Sales Agent	(02) 201 24 67	Bruxelles		Belgium
Christina Berglund	Berglund snabbköp	Order Administrator	0921-12 34 65	Luleå		Sweden
Daniel Tonini	La corne d'abondance	Sales Representative	30.59.84.10	Versailles		France

Page: |◄ ◄ 1 ► ►| 🏷 No Filter ◄

FIGURE 1.10 An Access Report

Figure 1.11 displays the different object types in Access with the foundation object—the table—in the center of the illustration. The purpose each object serves is explained underneath the object name. The flow of information between objects is indicated by single-arrowhead arrows if the flow is one direction only. Two-arrowhead arrows indicate that the flow goes both directions. For example, you can use forms to view, add, delete, or modify data from tables.

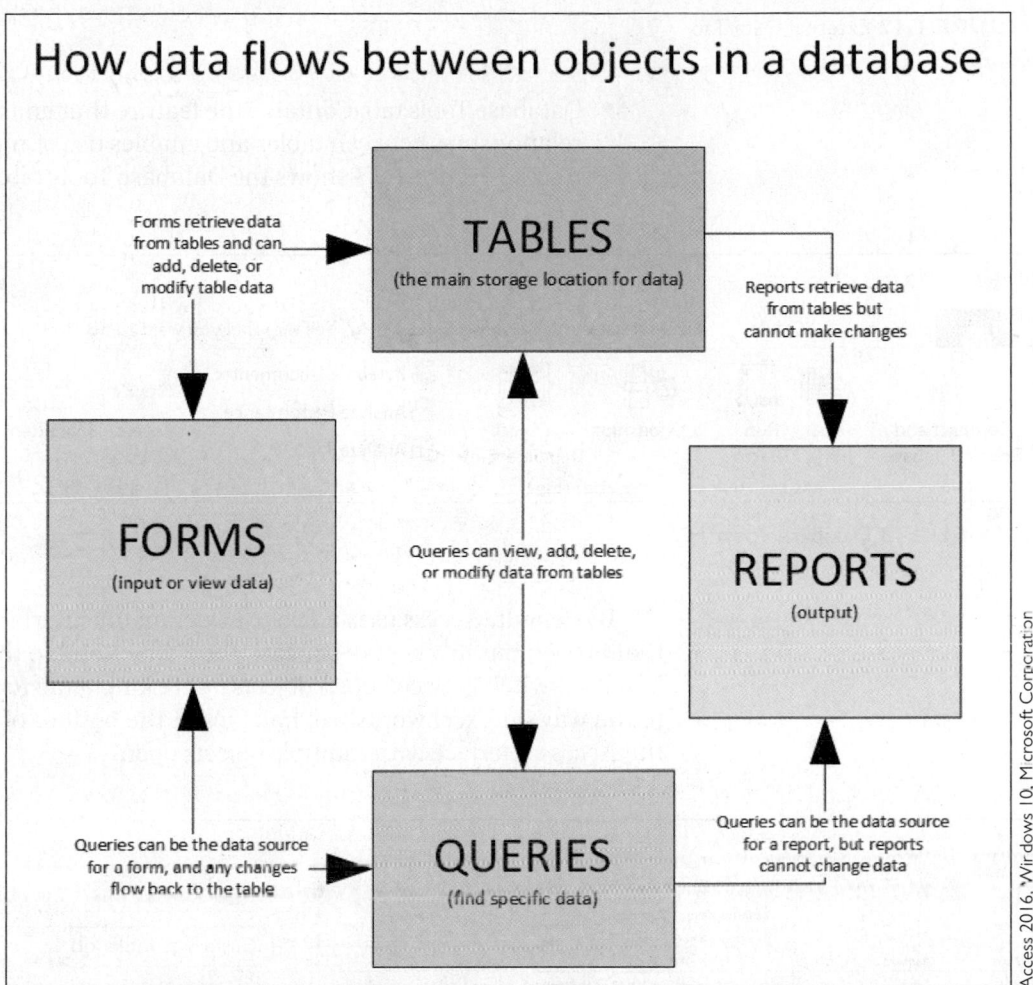

How data flows between objects in a database

Forms retrieve data from tables and can add, delete, or modify table data

TABLES
(the main storage location for data)

Reports retrieve data from tables but cannot make changes

FORMS
(input or view data)

Queries can view, add, delete, or modify data from tables

REPORTS
(output)

Queries can be the data source for a form, and any changes flow back to the table

QUERIES
(find specific data)

Queries can be the data source for a report, but reports cannot change data

Access 2016, Windows 10, Microsoft Corporation

FIGURE 1.11 Flow of Information Between Object Types

Two other object types, macros and modules, are rarely used by beginning Access users. A *macro* object is a stored series of commands that carry out an action. Macros are often used to automate tasks. A *module* is an advanced object written using the VBA (Visual Basic® for Applications) programming language. Modules provide more functionality than macros, but are not generally required for even intermediate users.

Examine the Access Interface

While Access includes the standard elements of the Microsoft Office applications interface such as the title bar, the Ribbon, the Home tab, Backstage view, and scroll bars, it also includes elements unique to Access.

The Access Ribbon has five tabs that always display, as well as tabs that appear only when particular objects are open. The two tabs that are unique to Access are:

- External Data tab: Contains all of the operations used to facilitate data import and export. See Figure 1.12.

FIGURE 1.12 External Data Tab

Access 2016, Windows 10, Microsoft Corporation

- Database Tools tab: Contains the feature that enables users to create relationships between tables and enables use of more advanced features of Access. Figure 1.13 shows the Database Tools tab.

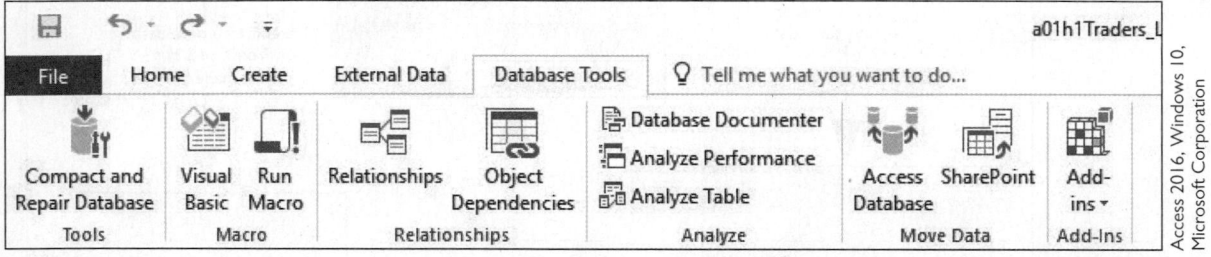

FIGURE 1.13 Database Tools Tab

By default, Access uses a Tabbed Documents interface. That means that each object that is open has its own tab beneath the Ribbon and to the right of the Navigation Pane. You can switch between open objects by clicking a tab to make that object active, similar to the way an Excel worksheet has tabs at the bottom of the screen. Figure 1.14 shows the Access interface with multiple objects open.

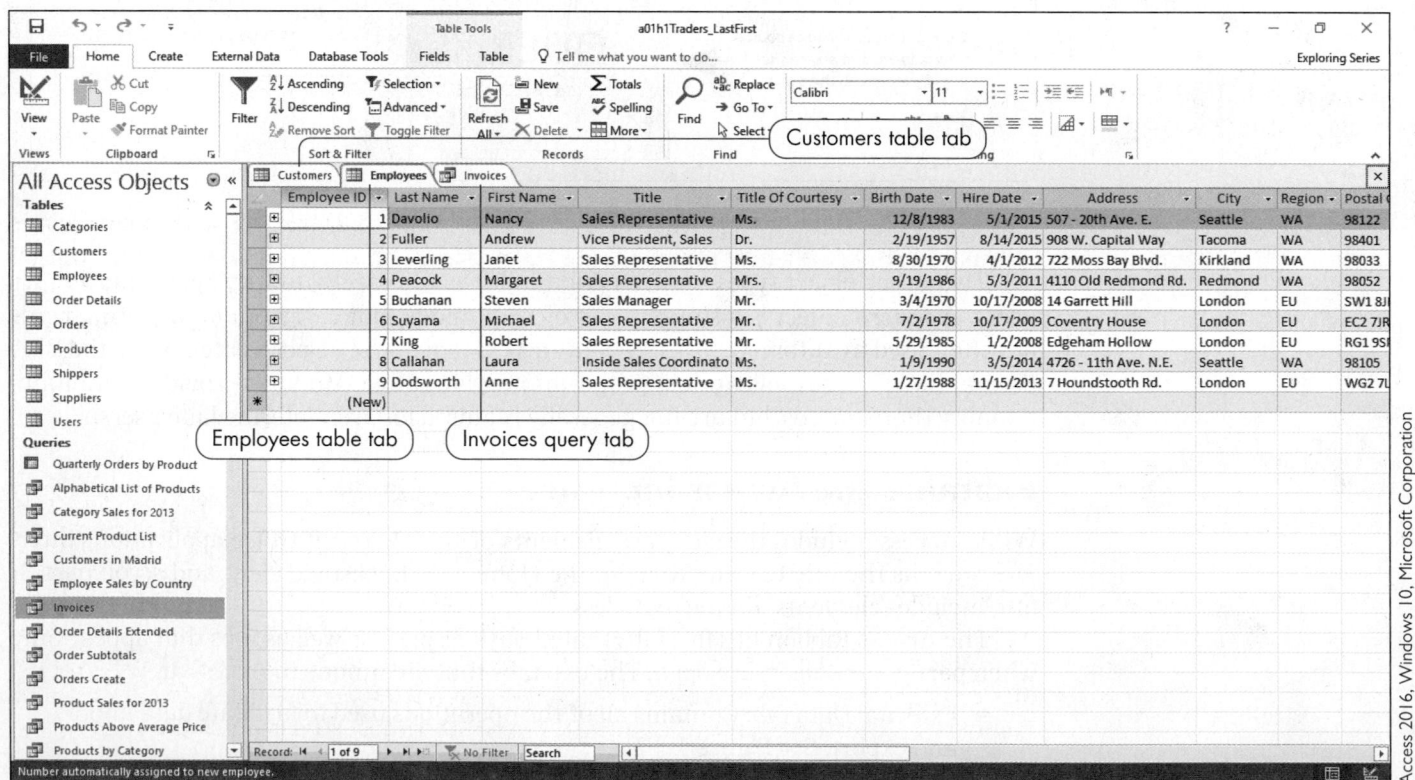

FIGURE 1.14 Access Database with Multiple Objects Open

Explore Table Datasheet View

Access provides two different ways to view a table: Datasheet view and Design view. When you double-click a table, Datasheet view displays by default. **Datasheet view** is a grid containing fields (columns) and records (rows). You can view, add, edit, and delete records in Datasheet view. Figure 1.15 shows the Customers table in Datasheet view. Each row contains a record for a specific customer. Click the record selector, or row heading, at the beginning of a row to select the record. Each column represents a field, or one attribute about a customer. Click the field selector, or column heading, to select a field.

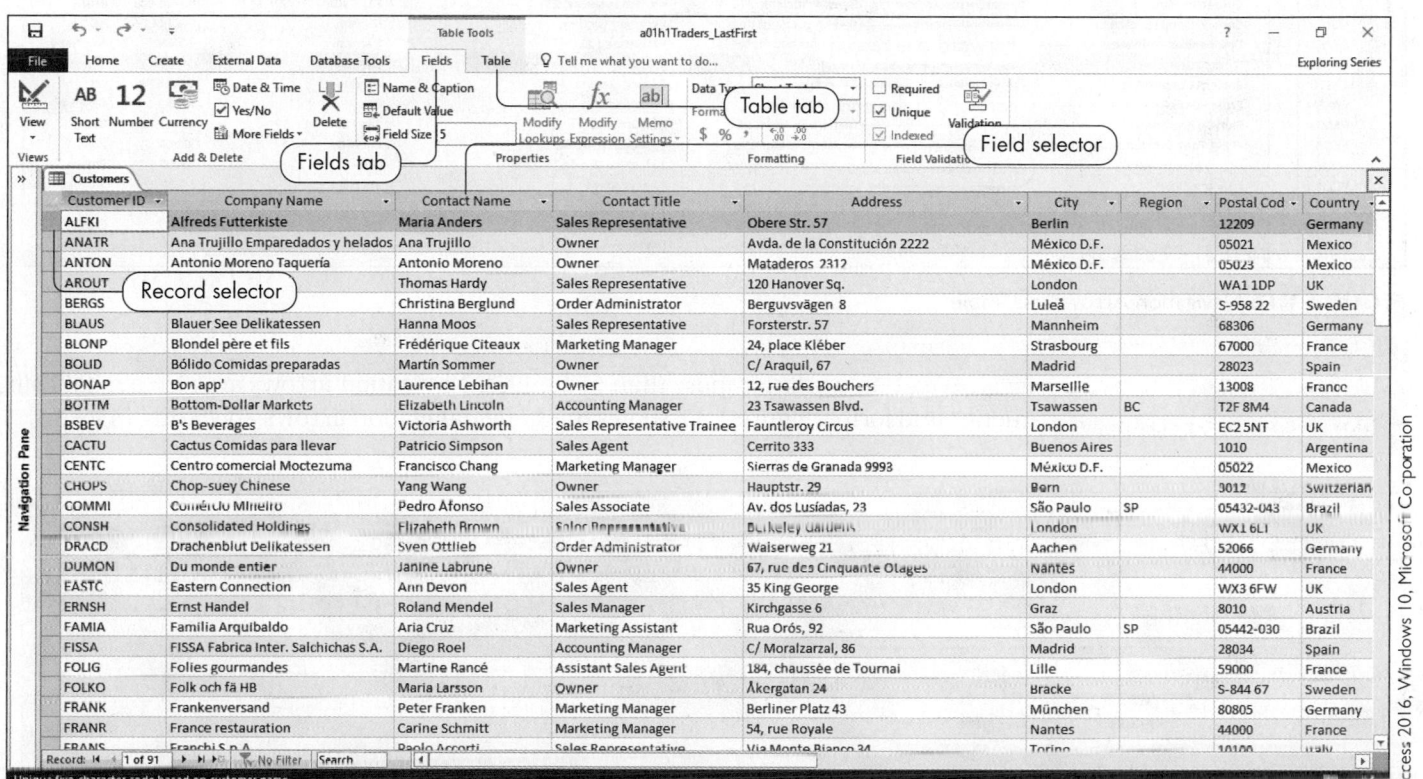

FIGURE 1.15 Datasheet View for Customers Table

Notice the Customers table shows records for 91 employees. The customer records contain multiple fields about each customer, including the Company Name, Contact Name, and so on. Occasionally a field does not contain a value for a particular record. For example, many customers do not have a Region assigned. Access shows a blank cell when data is missing.

Navigate Through Records

The navigation bar at the bottom of Figure 1.16 shows that the Customers table has 91 records and that record number 18 is the current record. The pencil symbol to the left of record 18 indicates that the data in that record is being edited and that changes have not yet been saved. The pencil icon disappears when you move to another record. Access saves data automatically as soon as you move from one record to another. This may seem counterintuitive at first because other Office applications, such as Word and Excel, do not save changes and additions automatically. The navigation arrows enable you to go to the first record, the previous record, the next record, or the last record. Click the right arrow with a yellow asterisk to add a new (blank) record.

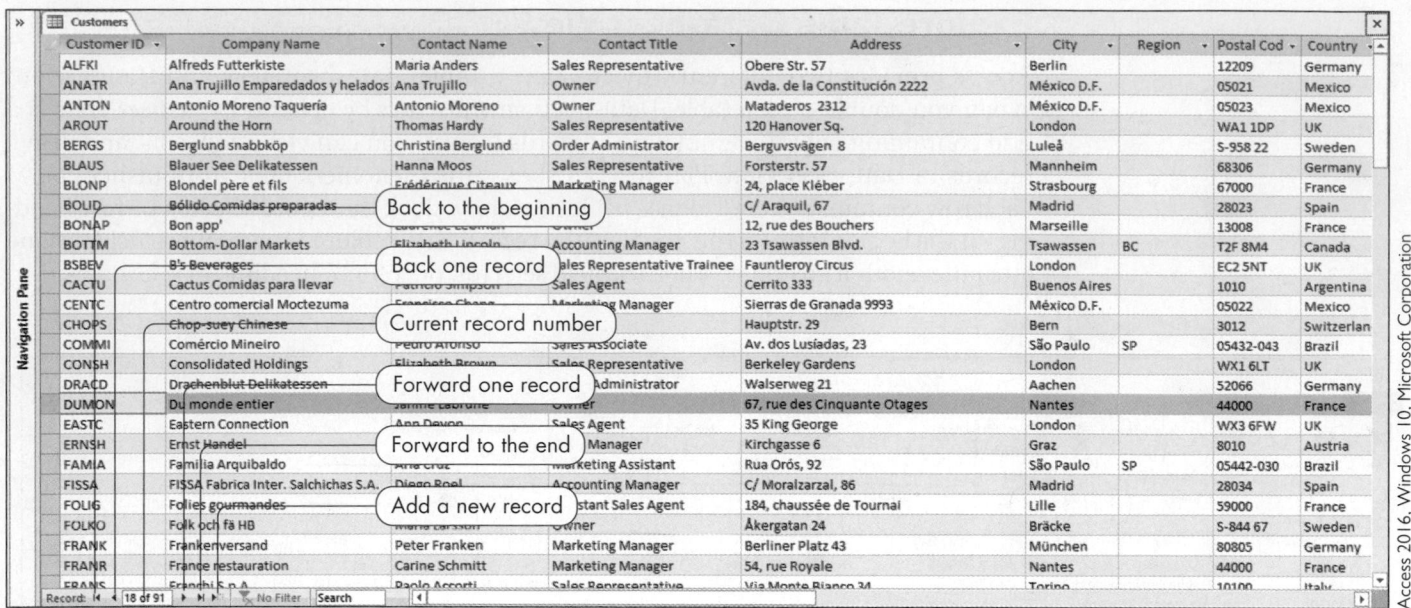

FIGURE 1.16 Navigation Arrows in a Table

Navigation works for more than just tables. Navigation arrows are also available in queries and forms. Figure 1.17 shows the same navigation arrows appearing in forms.

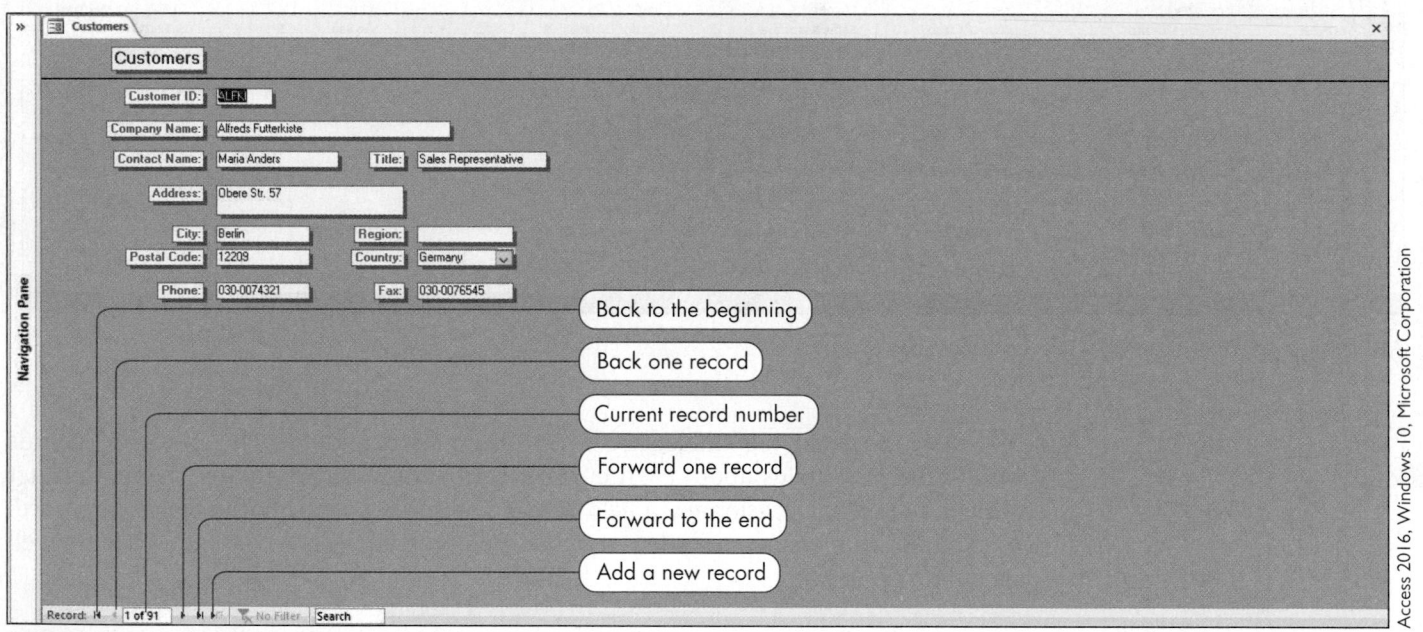

FIGURE 1.17 Navigation Arrows in a Form

In addition to navigating, you also have access to the Find command. The Find command is located in the Find group on the Home tab, and can be used to locate specific records. You can search for a single field or the entire record, match all or part of the selected field(s), move forward or back in a table, or specify a case-sensitive search.

To find a record using the Find command, complete the following steps:

1. Open the table that contains the data you are searching for. Note that if you want to search a query, form, or report, you can follow the same steps, except open the appropriate object instead of the table.
2. Click any cell within the field you want to search. For example, if you want to search the City field in the Customers table, as shown in Figure 1.18, click any City value.
3. Ensure the Home tab is selected.
4. Click Find in the Find group.
5. Type the value you are searching for in the Find What box. Note that the entry is not case sensitive.
6. Click Find Next to find the next matching value.

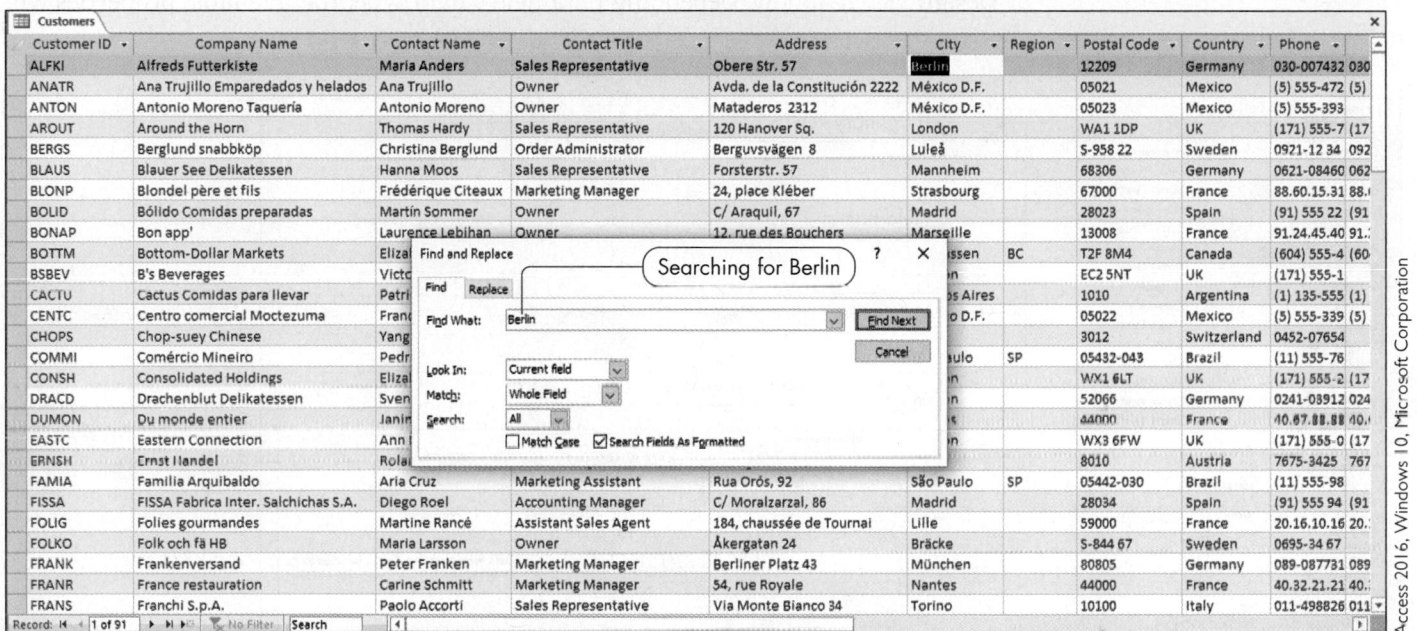

FIGURE 1.18 Find Command

Explore Table Design View

Design view gives you a detailed view of the table's structure and is used to create and modify a table's design by specifying the fields it will contain, the fields' data types, and their associated properties. When you double-click a table in the Navigation Pane, it will open in Datasheet view, as the design of a table typically does not change frequently.

To switch between Datasheet and Design view, complete the following steps:

1. Click the Home tab.
2. Click View in the Views group to toggle between the current view and the previous view. See Figure 1.19.

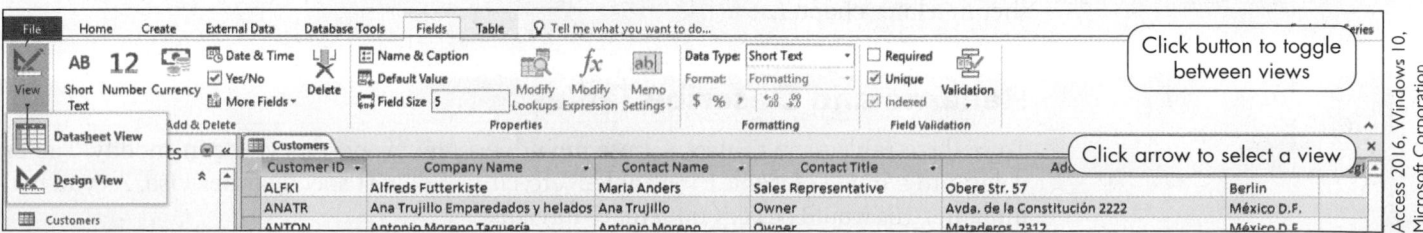

FIGURE 1.19 View Button

Also notice the arrow that allows you to select either Design or Datasheet view. Either way of performing this task is correct.

Data types define the type of data that will be stored in a field, such as short text, numeric, currency, date/time, etc. For example, if you need to store the hire date of an employee, you would input a field name and select the Date/Time data type. A ***field property*** defines the characteristics of a field in more detail. For example, for the field OrderDate, you could set add validation (the OrderDate must be today's date or later), or choose whether the field is required or not. Though some changes can be made to the field properties in Datasheet view, Design view gives you access to more properties.

Figure 1.20 shows Design view for the Orders table. In the top portion, each row contains the field name the data type, and an optional description for each field in the table. In the bottom portion, the Field Properties pane contains the properties (details) for a field. Click a field, and the properties for that field display in the Field Properties section of Design view window. Depending on a field's data type, the available properties will change.

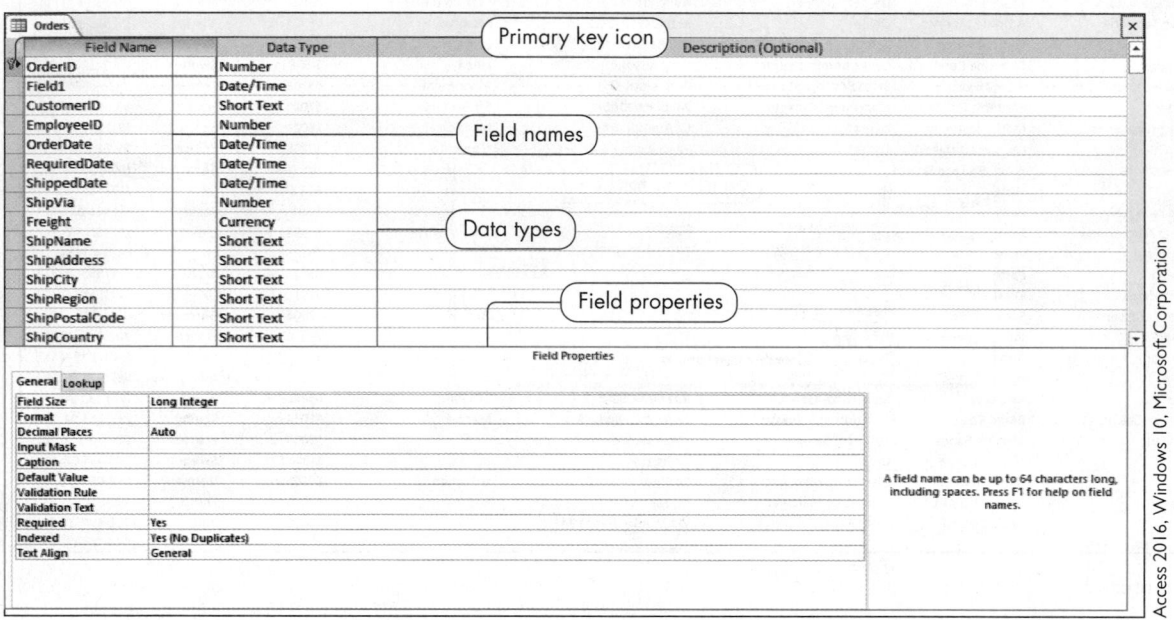

FIGURE 1.20 Orders Table Design View

Notice the key icon next to the OrderID field; this denotes this field is the primary key in the Orders table; it ensures that each record in the table is unique and can be distinguished from every other record. You may have multiple orders from the same customer, but you can tell they are different because there are two separate OrderIDs. This is why many companies ask for you to include your account number when you pay a bill. The account number, similar to an OrderID, uniquely identifies you and helps ensure that the payment is not applied to the wrong customer.

In Figure 1.20, the OrderID field has an AutoNumber data type—a number that is generated by Access and is automatically incremented each time a record is added. Each field's data type determines the type of input accepted. Data types will be discussed further in a later chapter.

Rename and Describe Tables

To make a table easy to use, Access includes a few properties you can modify. Tables default to a name of Table1 (or Table2, etc.) if you do not specify otherwise. As you can imagine, this would be very difficult to navigate.

To rename a table, complete the following steps:

1. Verify that the table is closed. If it is not closed, right-click the table tab and select Close. A table cannot be renamed while it is open.
2. Right-click the table name in the Navigation Pane.
3. Select Rename on the shortcut menu.
4. Type the new name over the selected text and press Enter.

Tables also include a description, which can be useful to provide documentation about the contents of a table. For example, most tables in the Northwind database are straightforward. However, just in case, the database comes with predefined descriptions for most tables. This can provide a user with additional clarification regarding the purpose of a table if they know where to look. By default, descriptions are not shown unless you right-click the table and select Table Properties. If you are working with a complex database, adding descriptions can be extremely helpful for new users. Figure 1.21 shows a table description.

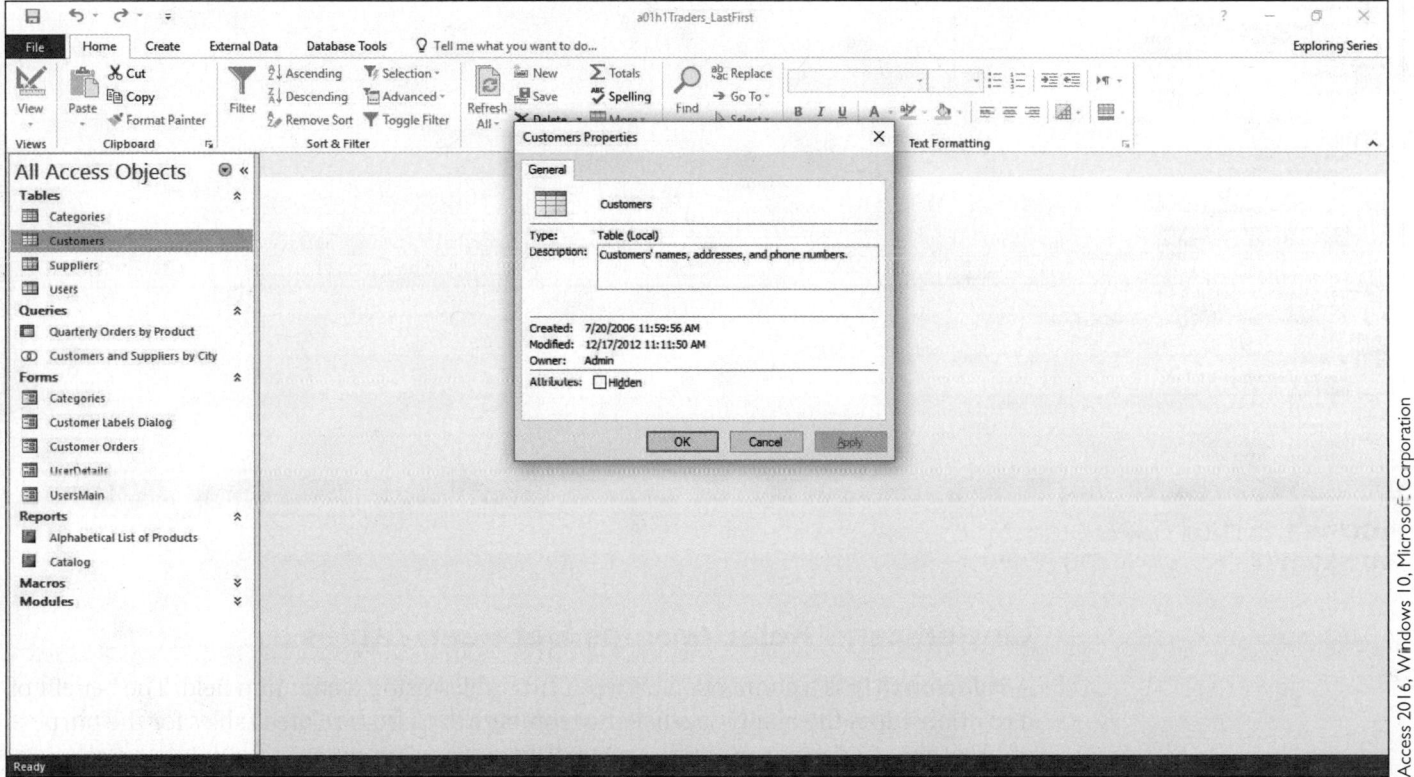

FIGURE 1.21 Previewing a Table Description

To enter a table description, complete the following steps:

1. Right-click the table name in the Navigation Pane.
2. Select Table Properties on the shortcut menu.
3. Type the description in the Table Properties dialog box and click OK.

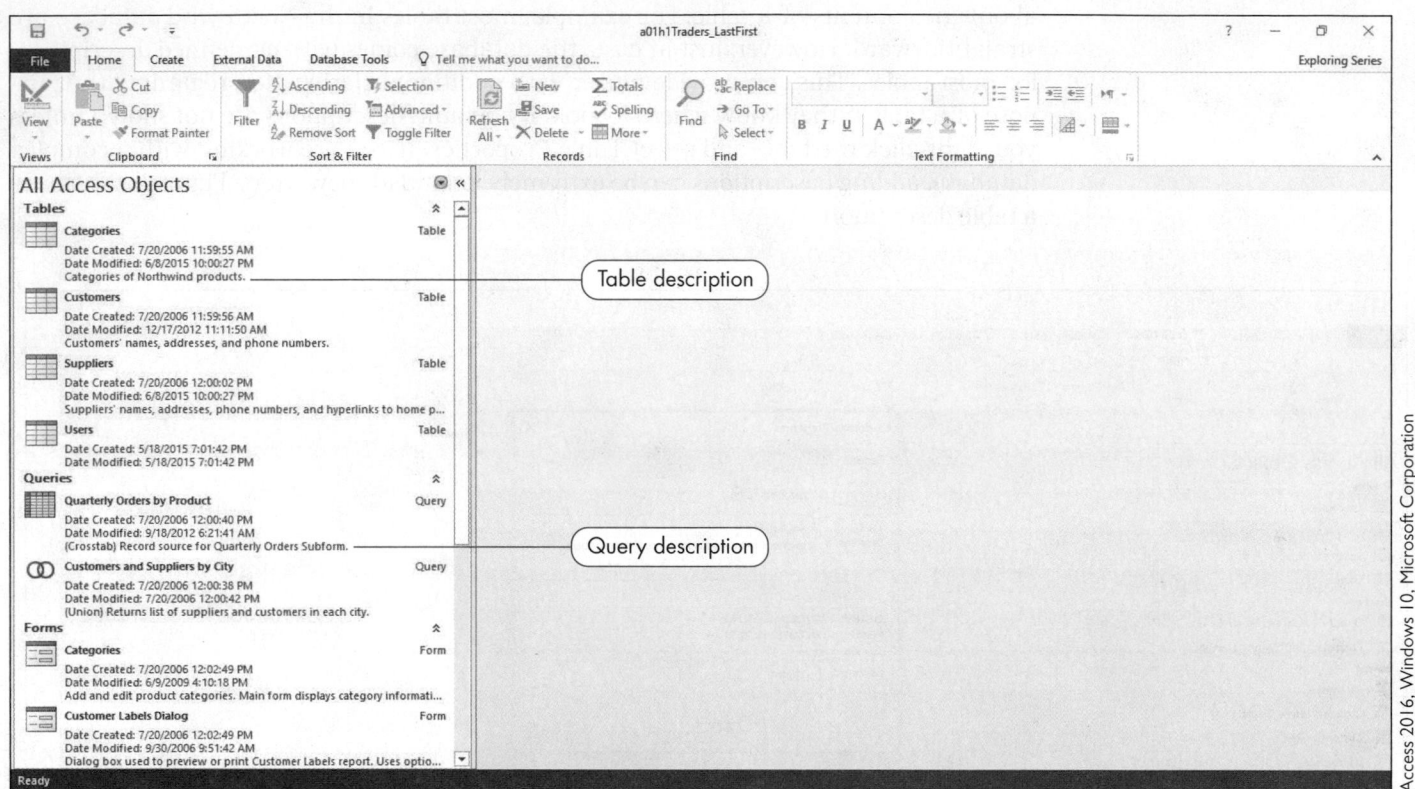

FIGURE 1.22 Detail View of Objects

Understand Relationships Between Tables

A **relationship** is a connection between two tables using a common field. The benefit of a relationship is the ability to efficiently combine data from related tables for the purpose of creating queries, forms, and reports. If you are using an existing database, relationships are likely created already. The design of the Northwind database, which contains multiple tables, is illustrated in Figure 1.23. The tables have been created, the field names have been added, and the data types have been set. The diagram shows the relationships that were created between tables using join lines. Join lines enable you to create a relationship between two tables using a common field. For example, the Suppliers table is joined to the Products table using the common field SupplierID. These table connections enable you to query the database for information stored in multiple tables. This feature gives the manager the ability to ask questions like "What products are produced by the supplier Exotic Liquids?" In this case, the name of the supplier (Exotic Liquids) is stored in the Supplier table, but the products are stored in the Products table. Notice in Figure 1.24, you can tell there is a table related to the Supplier table, because a plus sign ⊞ appears to the left of each Supplier. If you click the plus sign, you will see a list of products produced by this company.

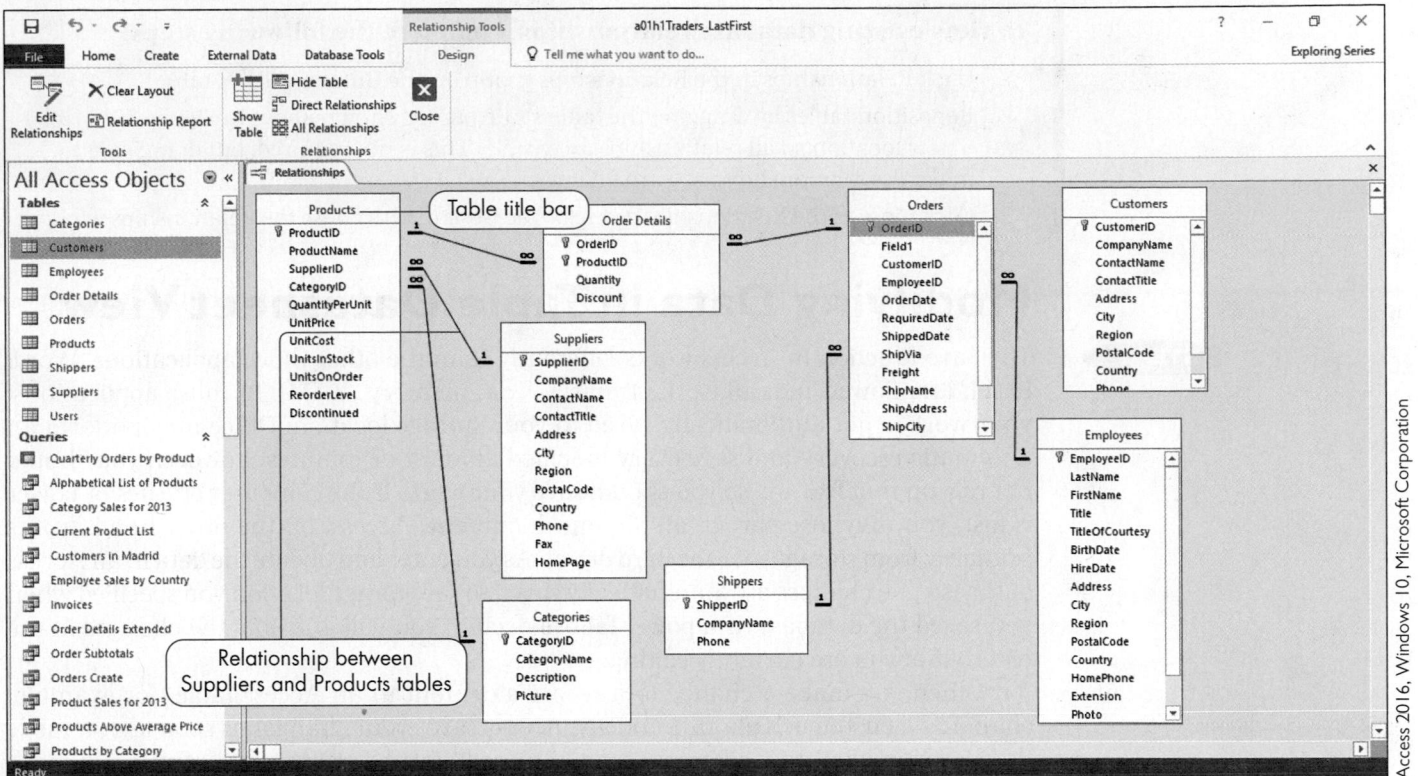

FIGURE 1.23 Northwind Database Relationships

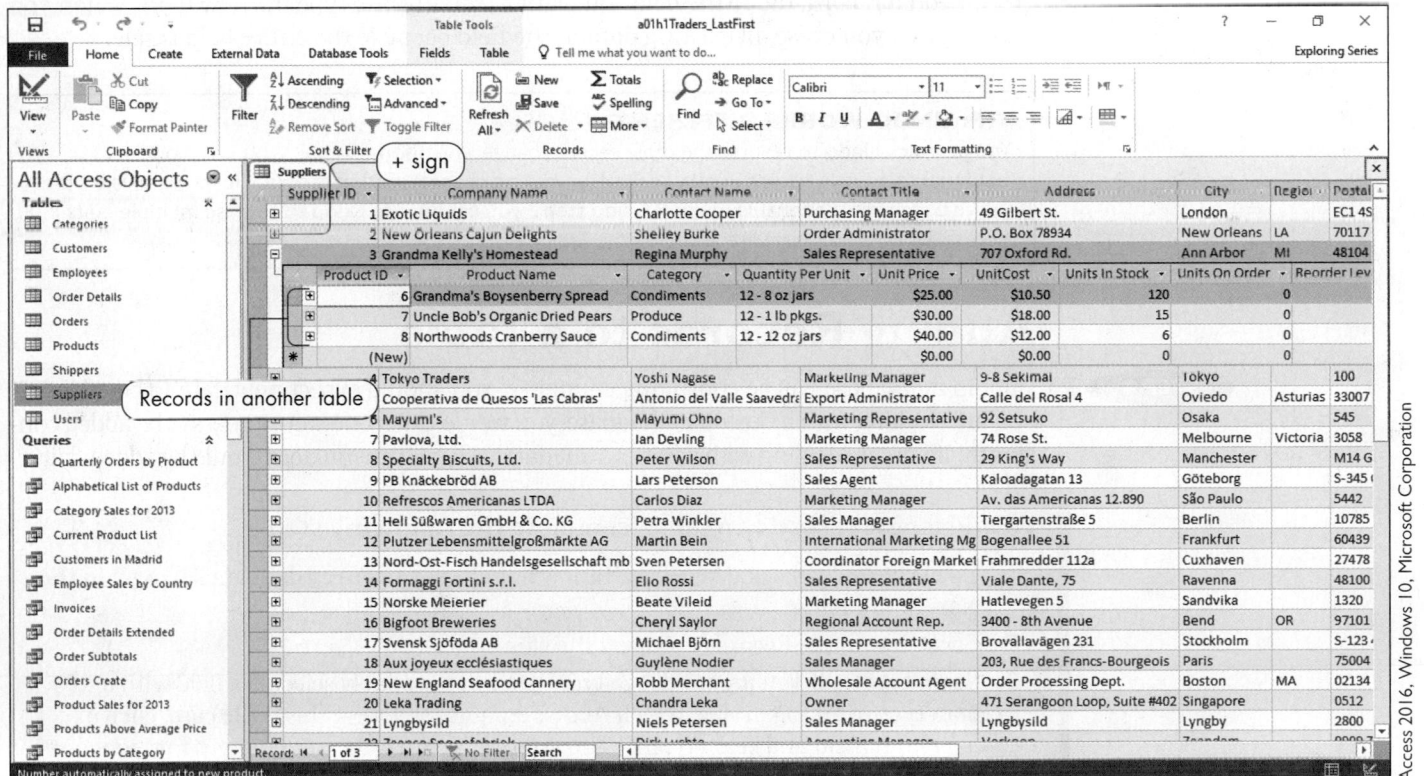

FIGURE 1.24 Related Tables

Relationships will be discussed further in a later chapter. However, you can view the existing relationships in any database to familiarize yourself with the way tables work together.

> **To view existing database relationships, complete the following steps:**
>
> 1. Click Relationships in the Relationships group on the Database Tools tab.
> 2. Reposition tables by dragging the table's title bar (as shown above in Figure 1.23) to a new location so all relationships are visible. This is not required, but doing so may make the relationships easier to follow.
> 3. Click Close in the Relationships group of the Design tab to close the Relationships window.

Modifying Data in Table Datasheet View

 The Save function in Access works differently than the other Office applications. Word, Excel, and PowerPoint all work primarily from memory (RAM). In those applications, your work is not automatically saved to your storage location. Office may perform an automatic recovery and save every specified amount of minutes; however, you should not rely on that feature, so you should save your work. If the computer crashes or power is lost, you may lose part or all of your document. Access, on the other hand, works primarily from storage (i.e., the hard drive). As you enter and update the data in an Access database, the changes are automatically saved to the storage location you specified when you saved the database. If a power failure occurs, you will lose only the changes to the record that you are currently editing.

When you make a change to a record's content in an Access table (for example, changing a customer's phone number), Access saves your changes as soon as you move the insertion point to a different record. You will only be prompted to save if you make changes to the design of the table (such as changing the font or background color). Editing data is done similarly in queries and forms. Recall that reports cannot change data, so changes to data cannot be done there.

To edit a record, tab to the field you want to modify and type the new data. When you start typing, you erase all existing data in the field because the entire field is selected.

TIP: UNDO WORKS DIFFERENTLY
You can click Undo to reverse the most recent change (the phone number you just modified, for example) to a single record immediately after making changes to that record. However, unlike other Office programs that enable multiple Undo steps, you cannot use Undo to reverse multiple edits in Access. Undo (and Redo) are found on the Quick Access Toolbar.

Adding Records to a Table

 Data in a database will be constantly changing. You should expect new data to be added. If you are working with a Customer database, you would expect new customers to be added constantly. If you are dealing with a Restaurant database, new menu items could be added daily.

> **To add a new record to a table, complete the following steps:**
>
> 1. Open the table in Datasheet view (if it is not already open) by double-clicking it in the Navigation Pane.
> 2. Click New in the Records group on the Home tab.
> 3. Begin typing. If you are unable to type, you have probably selected a field with a data type of AutoNumber, which Access assigns for you. If this is the case, click in a different field and begin typing. The asterisk record indicator changes to a pencil symbol to show that you are in editing mode (see Figure 1.25). Note: you can follow the same process to add a record in a form (shown in Figure 1.26) or query.
> 4. Press Tab to move to the following field and enter data, and repeat this step until you have input all required data for this record.
> 5. Move to another record by clicking elsewhere or pressing Tab in the last field in a record. As soon as you move to another record, Access automatically saves the changes to the record you created or changed.

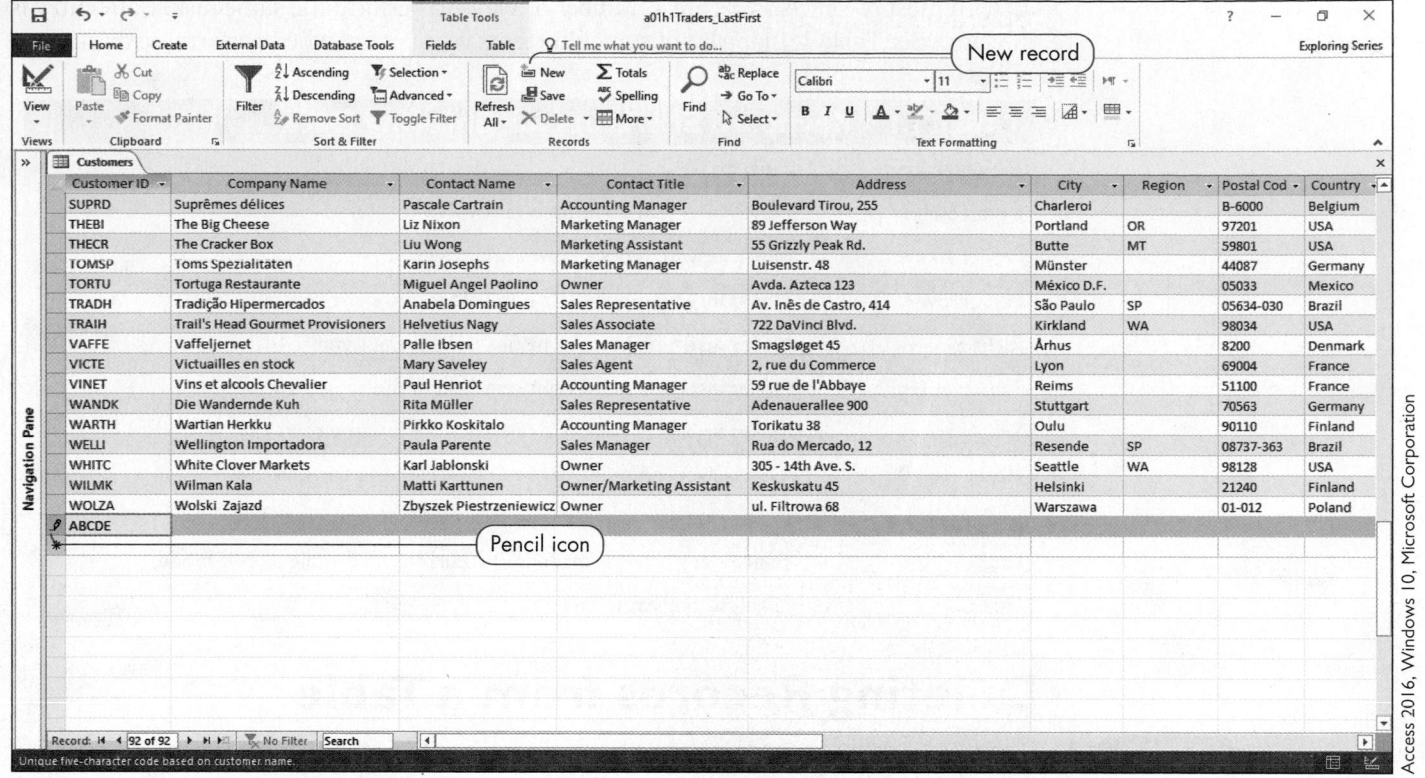

FIGURE 1.25 Adding a Record Using a Table

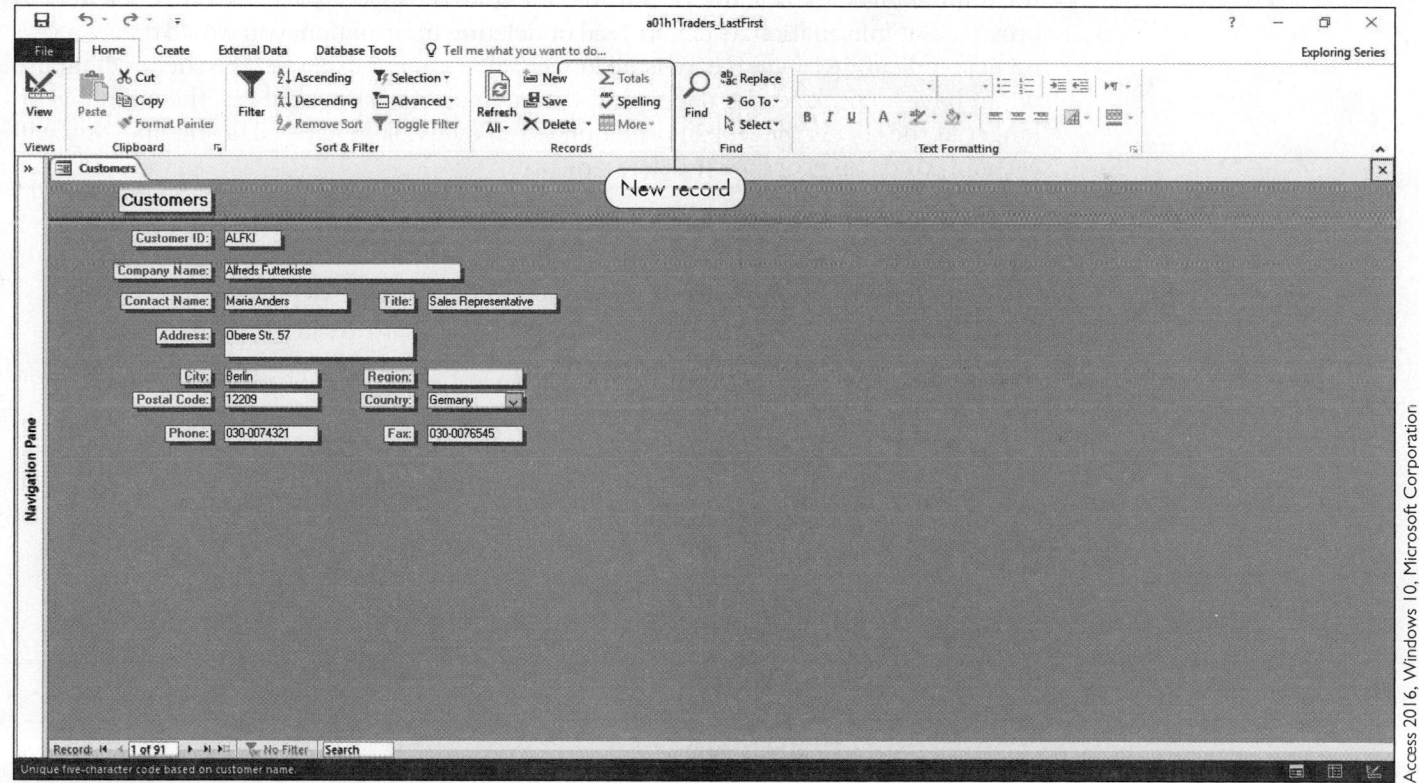

FIGURE 1.26 Adding a Record Using a Form

As with most of Office, there are a number of ways to perform the same task. Data entry is the same. See Table 1.1 for a list of some shortcuts you can use when performing data entry.

TABLE 1.1	**Keyboard Shortcuts for Entering Data**
Keystroke	**Result**
Up arrow (↑)	Moves insertion point up one row.
Down arrow (↓)	Moves insertion point down one row.
Left arrow (←)	Moves insertion point left one field in the same row.
Right arrow (→)	Moves insertion point right one field in the same row.
Tab or Enter	Moves insertion point right one field in the same row.
Shift+Tab	Moves insertion point left one field in the same row.
Home	Moves insertion point to the first field in the current row.
End	Moves insertion point to the last field in the current row.
Esc	Cancels any changes made in the current field while in Edit mode.
Ctrl+Z	Reverses the last unsaved edit.

Deleting Records from a Table

STEP 5 ▶▶ Deciding to delete records is not a simple decision. Many times, deleting records is a bad idea. Say you are working in the database for an animal shelter. Once an animal has been adopted, you may be tempted to delete the animal from the database. However, you would then lose any record of the animal ever existing, and if the owner calls asking if the animal has had its shots, or how old the animal is, you would no longer be able to provide that information. Often, instead of deleting information, you would create a yes/no field indicating that a record is no longer relevant. For example, the shelter database might have a check box for adopted. If the adopted box is checked yes, the animal is no longer at the shelter, but the information is still available. That said, sometimes you will certainly find it appropriate to delete a record.

> **To delete a record from a table, complete the following steps:**
>
> 1. Click the record selector for the record you want to delete (see Figure 1.27).
> 2. Click Delete in the Records group on the Home tab. Click Yes in the warning dialog box. Note that you can take similar steps in queries and forms.

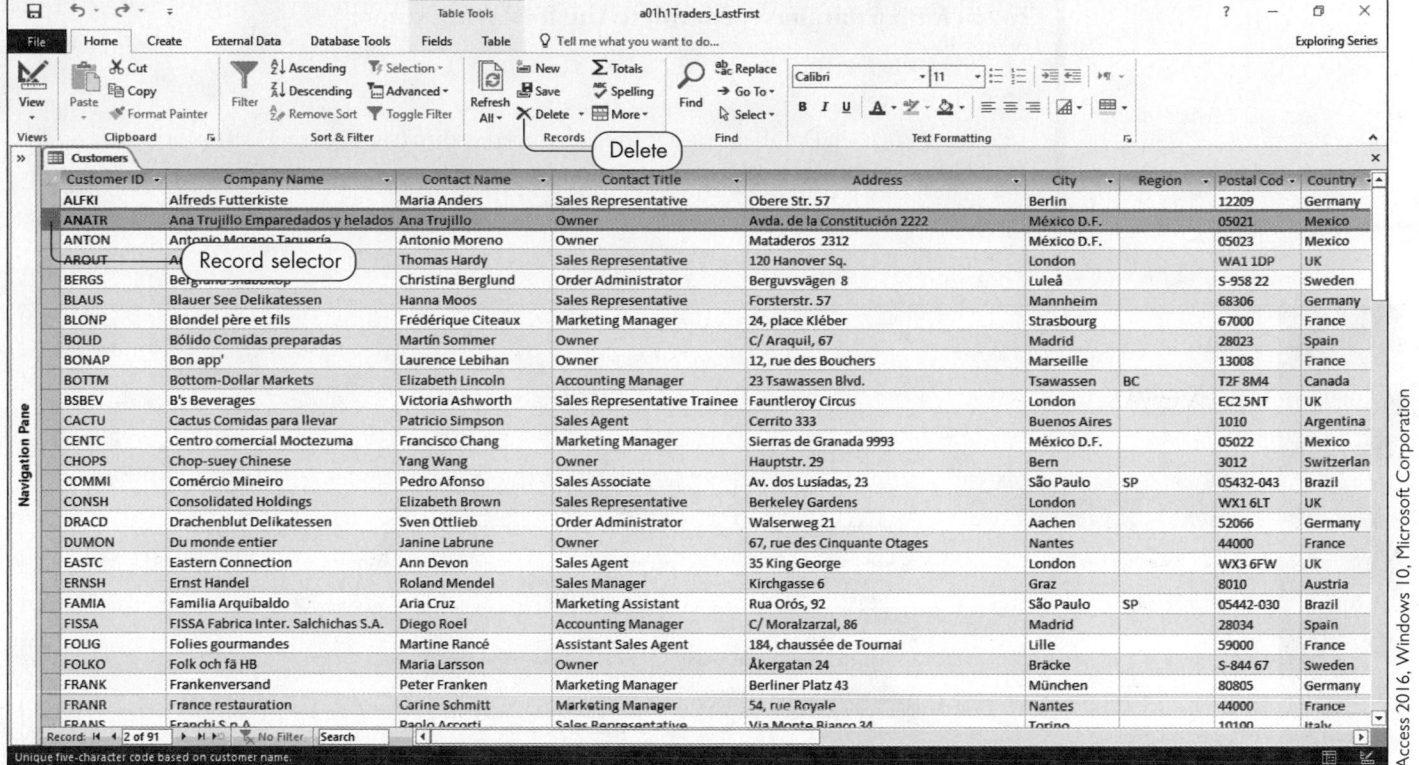

FIGURE 1.27 Deleting a Record

If you attempt to delete a record, you may get an error message. For example, if you try to delete a customer who has adopted pets, you may get a message stating *You cannot delete this record because another table has related records*. Even though the customer may have moved, they cannot be deleted because related records exist in another table, in this case, animals the customer has adopted.

Using Database Utilities

Database administrators spend a lot of time maintaining databases. Software utility programs make this process simpler. As Access is a database management utility, there are a number of tools that can be used to protect, maintain, and improve performance of a database.

Back Up a Database

STEP 6 ›› *Back Up Database* is a utility that creates a duplicate copy of the entire database to protect from loss or damage. Imagine what would happen to a firm that loses track of orders placed, a charity that loses the list of donor contributions, or a hospital that loses the digital records of its patients. Making backups is especially important when you have multiple users working with the database. When you use the Back Up Database utility, Access provides a file name for the backup that uses the same file name as the database you are backing up, an underscore, and the current date. This makes it easy for you to keep track of databases by the date they were created.

Keep in mind, backing up a database on the same storage device as the original database can leave you with no protection in the event of hardware failure. Backups are typically stored on a separate device, such as an external hard drive or network drive.

> **To back up a database, complete the following steps:**
>
> 1. Click the File tab.
> 2. Click Save As.
> 3. Click Back Up Database under the Advanced group (see Figure 1.28).
> 4. Click Save As. Revise the location and file name if you want to change either and click Save.

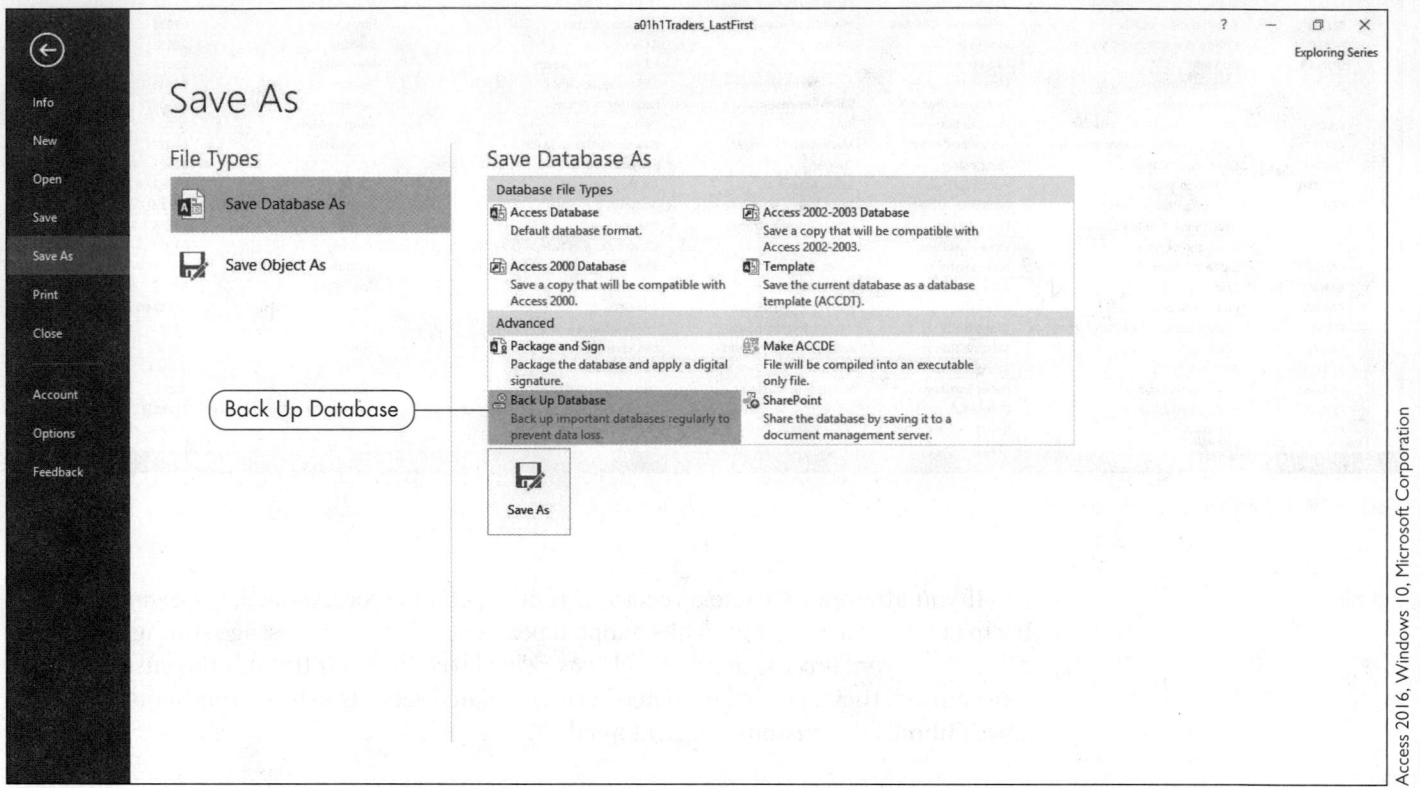

FIGURE 1.28 Back Up Database Option

Compact and Repair a Database

Databases have a tendency to expand with everyday use and may become corrupt, so Access provides the ***Compact and Repair Database*** utility. Compact and Repair Database reduces the size of a database and fixes any errors that may exist in the file.

> **To compact and repair an open database, complete the following steps:**
>
> 1. Click the File tab.
> 2. Click Compact and Repair Database in the Info options. If you have any unsaved design changes, you will be prompted to save before the compact and repair can complete.

Alternately, you can have Access perform a Compact and Repair automatically.

To have Access compact and repair a database each time you close the database, complete the following steps:

1. Click the File tab.
2. Click Options.
3. Click Current Database.
4. Click the Compact on Close check box under Application Options in the Options for the current database pane.
5. Click OK.

TIP: SPLIT DATABASES

Another utility built into Access is the *Database Splitter* tool, which puts the tables in one file (the back-end database), and the queries, forms, and reports in a second file (the front-end database). This way, each user can create their own queries, forms, and reports without potentially changing an object someone else needs.

To split a database, click the Database Tools tab and click Access Database in the Move Data group. Click Split Database and click OK.

Encrypt a Database

To protect a database from unauthorized access, you can encrypt the database, which enables you to password-protect the stored information. Adding a password requires that the database be opened in exclusive mode. Open Exclusive mode guarantees that you are the only one currently using the database.

To open a database in exclusive mode, complete the following steps:

1. Ensure that the database is closed. You cannot open a database with exclusive access unless it is currently closed.
2. Click the File tab.
3. Click Open.
4. Click Browse to display the Open dialog box.
5. Locate and click the database you want to open, and click the Open arrow at the bottom of the dialog box. Make sure you click the arrow next to the word Open, and not the Open button.
6. Select Open Exclusive from the list. The database opens in exclusive mode.

To add a password once the database has been opened in exclusive mode, complete the following steps:

1. Click the File tab.
2. Click Encrypt with Password. The Set Database Password dialog box opens.
3. Type a password, and re-enter the password in the Verify box. Click OK.

Print Information

Though Access is primarily designed to store data electronically, you may want to produce a print copy of your data.

To print information from any object (table, query, form, report) in your database, complete the following steps:

1. Click the File tab.
2. Click Print. The right panel display changes to enable you to choose a print option.
3. Click Print.
4. Change any settings that may need changing (for example, the print range or number of copies).
5. Click OK.

It is good practice to preview your work before printing a document. This way, if you notice an error, you can fix it and not waste paper.

To preview your work before printing, complete the following steps:

1. Click the File tab.
2. Click Print.
3. Click Print Preview.
4. Click Close Print Preview on the Print Preview tab to exit without printing, or click Print to open the Print dialog box (see Figure 1.29).

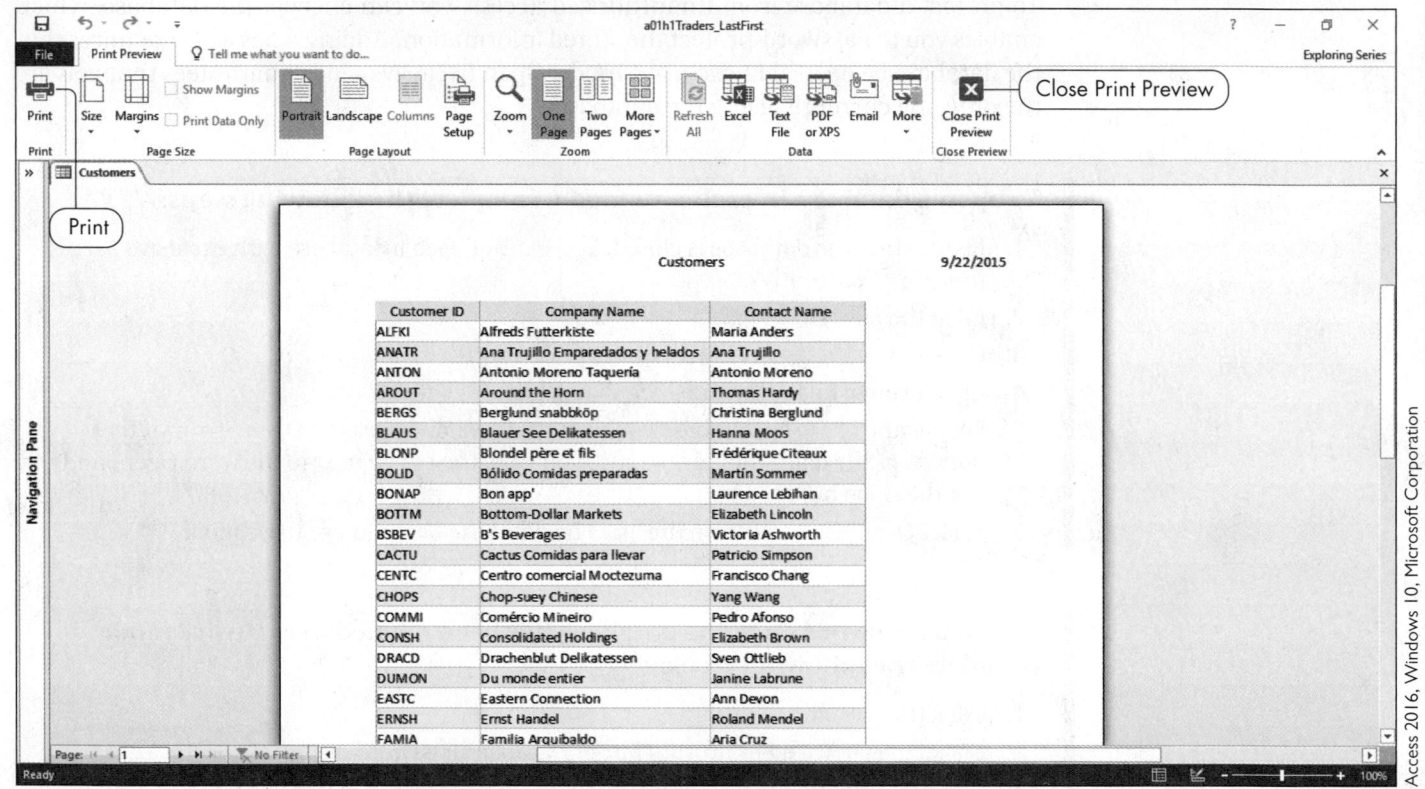

FIGURE 1.29 Table Print Preview

Quick Concepts

1. Name the four main types of objects in an Access database and briefly describe the purpose of each. *pp. 668–670*

2. What is the difference between Datasheet view and Design view in a table? *pp. 673, 675*

3. How does Access handle saving differently than other Office programs such as Excel? *p. 680*

4. How do relationships benefit a database user? *p. 678*

Hands-On Exercises

Watch the Video
for this Hands-On
Exercise!

MyITLab®
HOE1 Training

Skills covered: Open a Database • Save a Database with a New Name • Enable Content in a Database • Examine the Access Interface • Explore Table Datasheet View • Navigate Through Records • Explore Table Design View • Rename and Describe Tables • Understand Relationships Between Tables • Understand the Difference Between Working in Storage And Memory • Change Data in Table Datasheet View • Add Records to a Table • Delete Records from A Table • Back Up a Database • Compact and Repair a Database • Encrypt a Database • Print Information

1 Databases Are Everywhere!

Northwind purchases food items from suppliers around the world and sells them to restaurants and specialty food shops. Northwind depends on the data stored in its Access database to process orders and make daily decisions. You will open the Northwind database, examine the Access interface, review the existing objects in the database, and explore Access views. You will add, edit, and delete records using both tables and forms. Finally, you will back up the database.

STEP 1 ➤➤ **OPEN, SAVE, AND ENABLE CONTENT IN A DATABASE**

As you begin your job, you first will become familiar with the Northwind database. This database will help you learn the fundamentals of working with database files. Refer to Figure 1.30 as you complete Step 1.

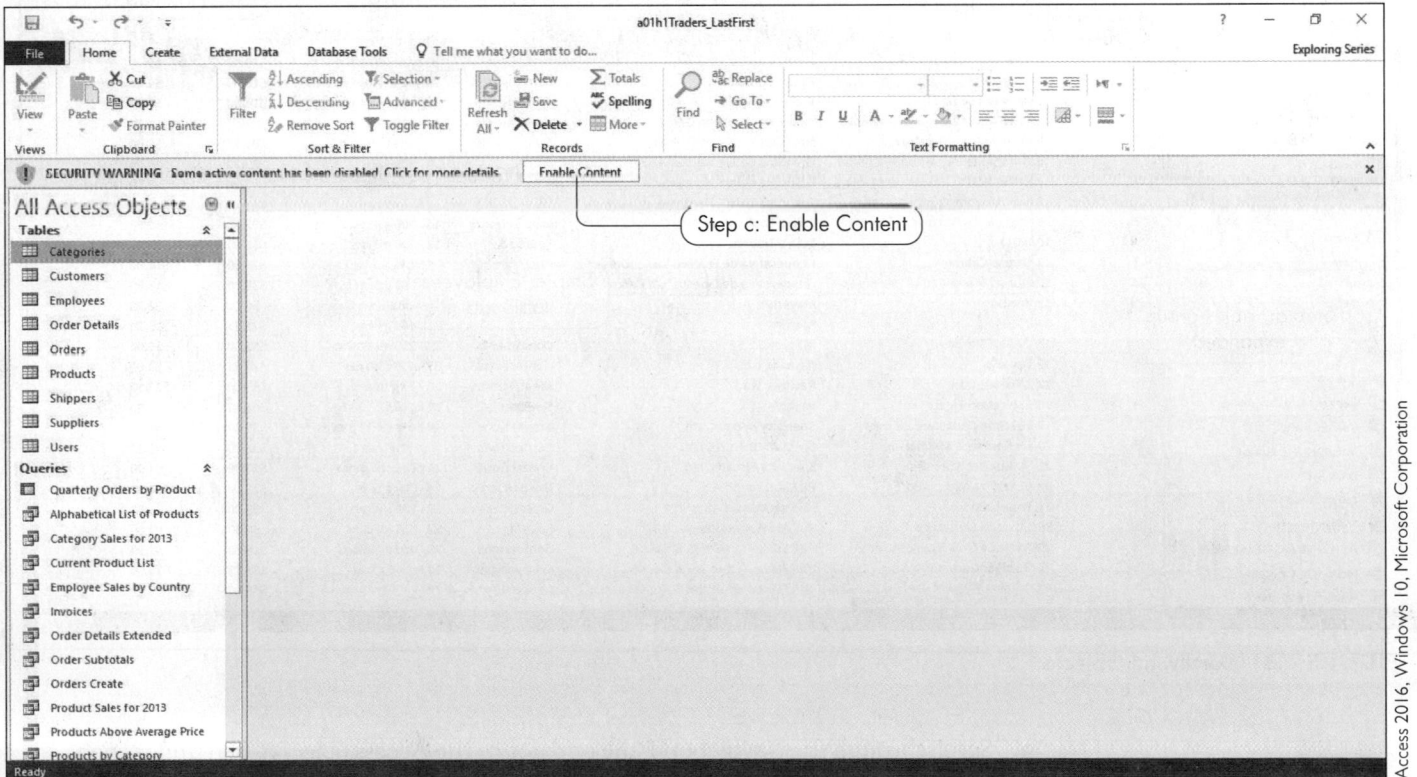

FIGURE 1.30 Northwind Database

a. Open Access, click **Open Other Files**, and click **Browse** ▣. Navigate to the folder location designated by your instructor. Click *a01h1Traders* and click **Open**.

> **TROUBLESHOOTING:** If you make any major mistakes in this exercise, you can close the file, open *a01h1Traders* again, and then start this exercise over.

b. Click the **File tab** and click **Save As**. Click **Save As** and save the file as **a01h1Traders_LastFirst**.

When you save files, use your last and first names. For example, as the Access author, I would save my database as "a01h1Traders_CameronEric."

The Security Warning message bar appears below the Ribbon, indicating that some database content is disabled.

c. Click **Enable Content** on the Security Warning message bar.

When you open an Access file, you should enable the content.

STEP 2 ›› RECOGNIZE DATABASE OBJECT TYPES

Now that you have opened the Northwind database, you examine the Navigation Pane, objects, and views to become familiar with these fundamental Access features. Refer to Figure 1.31 as you complete Step 2.

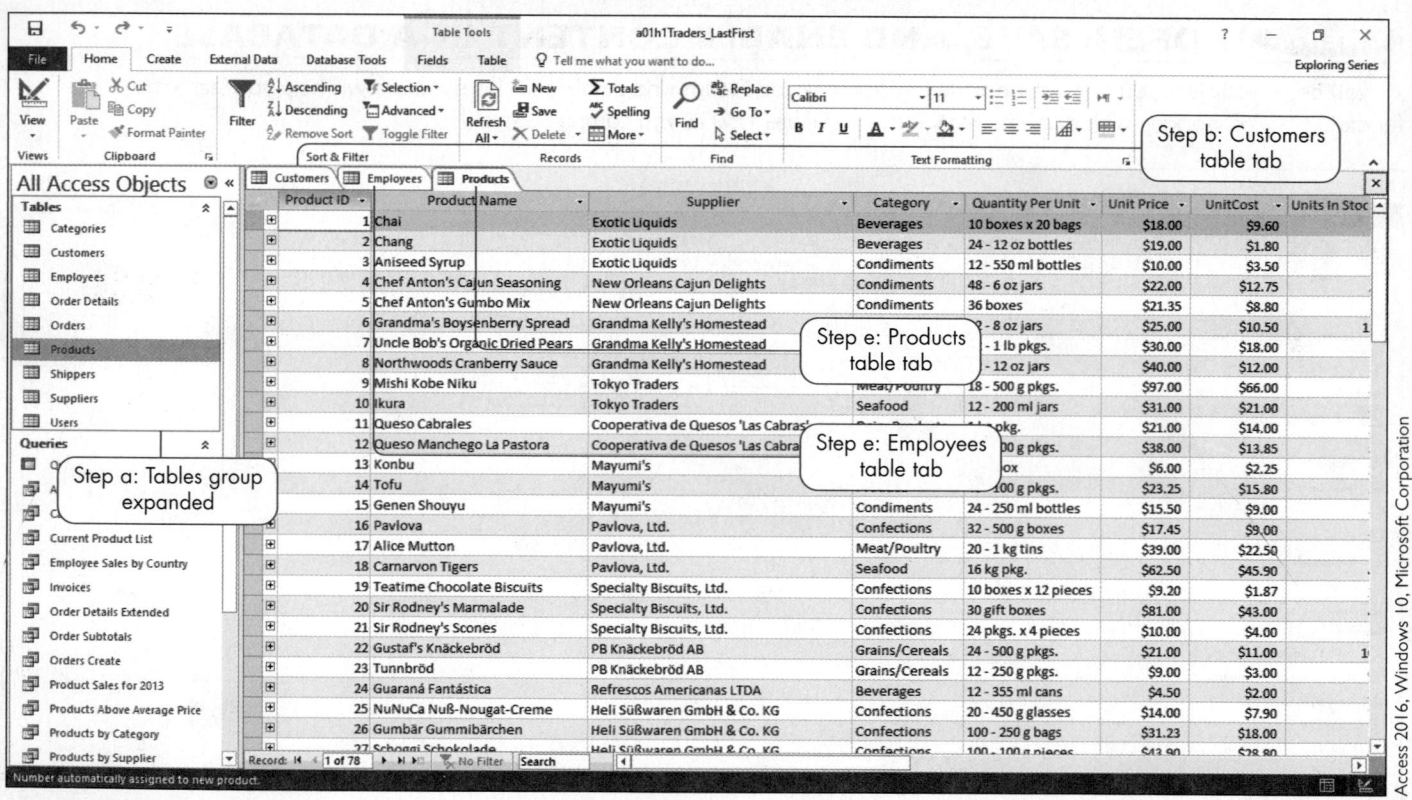

FIGURE 1.31 Northwind Objects

a. Scroll through the Navigation Pane and notice the Access objects listed under each expanded group.

The Tables group and the Forms group are expanded, displaying all of the table and form objects. The Queries, Reports, Macros, and Modules groups are collapsed so that the objects in those groups are not displayed.

b. Double-click the **Customers table** in the Navigation Pane.

The Customers table opens in Datasheet view, showing the data contained in the table. The Customers tab displays below the Ribbon indicating the table object is open. Each customer's record displays on a table row. The columns of the table display the fields that comprise the records.

c. Click **View** in the Views group on the Home tab.

The view of the Customers table switches to Design view. The top portion of Design view displays each field that comprises a customer record, the field's data type, and an optional description of what the field should contain. The bottom portion of Design view displays the field properties (details) for the selected field.

d. Click **View** in the Views group on the Home tab again.

Because the View button is a toggle, your view returns to Datasheet view, which shows the data stored in the table.

e. Double-click **Employees** in the Tables group of the Navigation Pane. Double-click **Products** in the same location.

The Employees and Products tables open. The tabs for three table objects display below the Ribbon: Customers, Employees, and Products.

f. Click **Shutter Bar Open/Close** ⟨«⟩ on the title bar of the Navigation Pane to hide the Navigation Pane. Click again to ⟨»⟩ show the Navigation Pane.

Shutter Bar Open/Close toggles to allow you to view more in the open object window, or to enable you to view your database objects.

g. Scroll down in the Navigation Pane and click **Reports**.

The Reports group expands, and all report objects display.

h. Scroll up until you can see Forms. Click **Forms** in the Navigation Pane.

The Forms group collapses and individual form objects no longer display.

You want to learn to edit the data in the Northwind database, because data can change. For example, employees will change their address and phone numbers when they move, and customers will change their order data from time to time. Refer to Figure 1.32 as you complete Step 3.

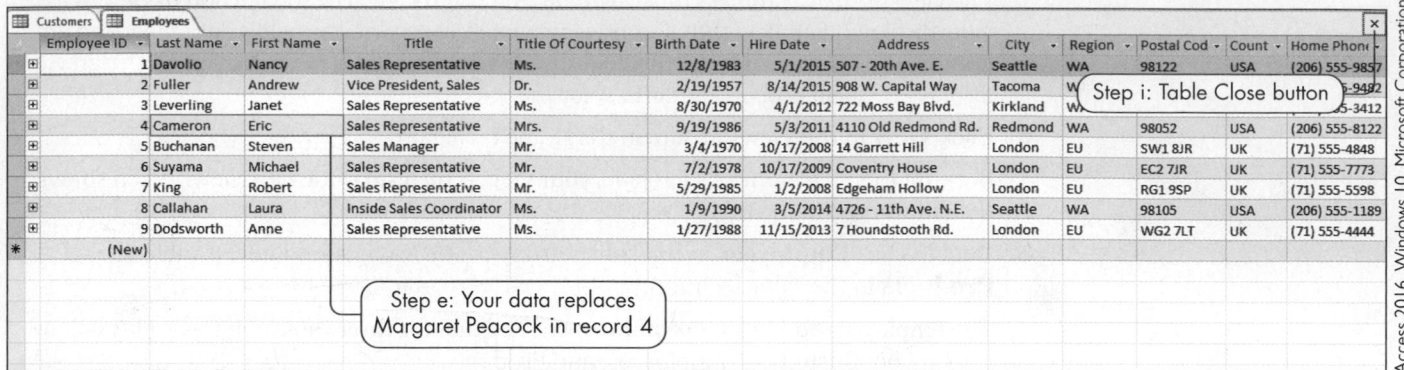

FIGURE 1.32 Northwind Employees Table

a. Click the **Employees tab** to view the Employees table.

b. Double-click **Peacock** (the value of the Last Name field in the fourth row); the entire name highlights. Type your last name to replace Peacock.

   The pencil symbol in the record selector box indicates that the record is being edited but has not yet been saved.

c. Press **Tab** to move to the next field in the fourth row. Replace Margaret with your first name and press **Tab**.

   You have made changes to two fields in the same record.

d. Click **Undo** on the Quick Access Toolbar.

   Your first and last names revert back to Margaret Peacock because you have not yet left the record.

e. Type your first and last names again to replace Margaret Peacock. Press **Tab**.

   You should now be in the title field and the title, Sales Representative, is selected. The record has not been saved, as indicated by the pencil symbol in the record selector box.

f. Click anywhere in the third row where Janet Leverling's data is stored.

   The pencil symbol disappears, indicating that your changes have been saved.

g. Click the **Address field** in the first row, Nancy Davolio's record. Select the entire address and then type **4004 East Morningside Dr.** Click anywhere on the second record, Andrew Fuller's record.

h. Click **Undo**.

   Nancy Davolio's address reverts back to 507 - 20th Ave. E. However, the Undo command is now faded. You can no longer undo the change that you made replacing Margaret Peacock's name with your own.

i. Click **Close** ⊠ at the top of the table to close the Employees table.

   The Employees table closes. You are not prompted to save your changes; they have already been saved for you because Access works in storage, not memory. If you reopen the Employees table, you will see your name in place of Margaret Peacock's name.

You have been asked to add new information about a new line of products to the Northwind database. Refer to Figure 1.33 as you complete Step 4.

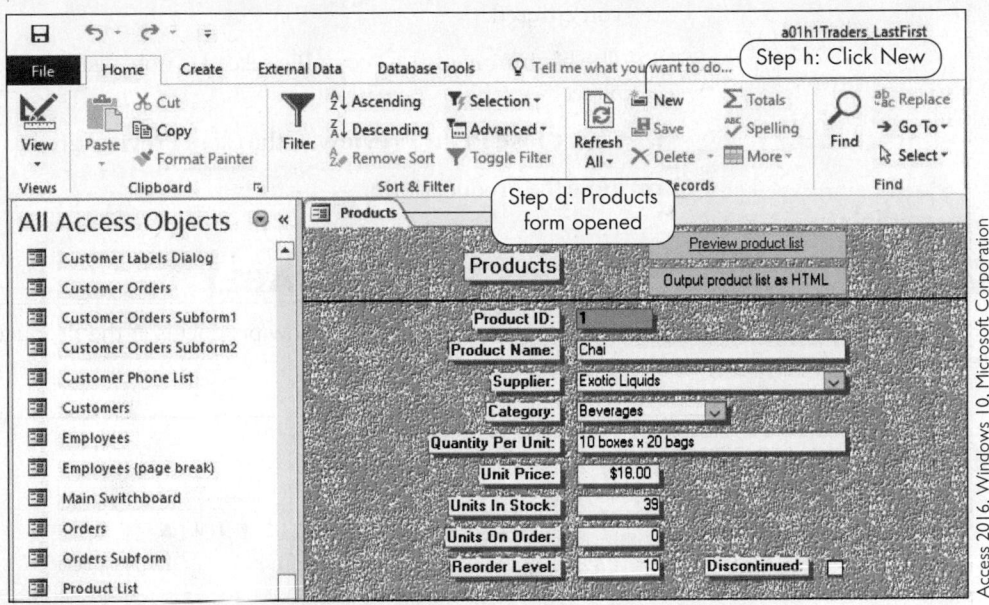

FIGURE 1.33 Adding Data Using Products Form

a. Right-click the **Customers tab** and click **Close All**.

b. Click the **Tables group** in the Navigation Pane to collapse it. Click the **Reports group** in the Navigation Pane to collapse it as well.

c. Click the **Forms group** in the Navigation Pane to expand the list of available forms.

d. Double-click the **Products form** to open it.

e. Click the **Next record** arrow. Click **Last record**, click **Previous record**, and then click **First record**.

f. Click **Find** in the Find group on the Home tab, type **Grandma** in the **Find box**, click the **Match arrow**, and then select **Any Part of Field**. Click **Find Next**.

> You should see the data for Grandma's Boysenberry Spread. Selecting the Any Part of Field option will return a match even if it is contained in the middle of a word.

g. Close the Find dialog box.

h. Click **New** in the Records group of the Home tab.

i. Type the following information for a new product. Click, or press **Tab**, to move into the next cell. Notice as soon as you begin typing, Access will assign a ProductID to this product.

Field Name	Value to Type
Product Name	*Your names* **Pecan Pie** (replacing Your name with your last name)
Supplier	**Grandma Kelly's Homestead** (click the arrow to select from the list of Suppliers)
Category	**Confections** (click the arrow to select from the list of Categories)
Quantity Per Unit	**1**
Unit Price	**15.00**
Units in Stock	**18**
Units on Order	**50**
Reorder Level	**20**
Discontinued	**No** (leave the check box unchecked)

j. Click anywhere on the Pecan Pie record you just typed. Click the **File tab**, click **Print**, and then click **Print Preview**.

The first four records display in the Print Preview.

k. Click **Last Page** in the navigation bar and click **Previous Page** to show the new record you entered.

The beginning of the Pecan Pie record is now visible. The record continues on the next page.

l. Click **Close Print Preview** in the Close Preview group.

m. Close the Products form.

STEP 5 ›› **DELETE RECORDS FROM A TABLE**

To help you understand how Access stores data, you verify that the new product is in the Products table. You also attempt to delete a record. Refer to Figure 1.34 as you complete Step 5.

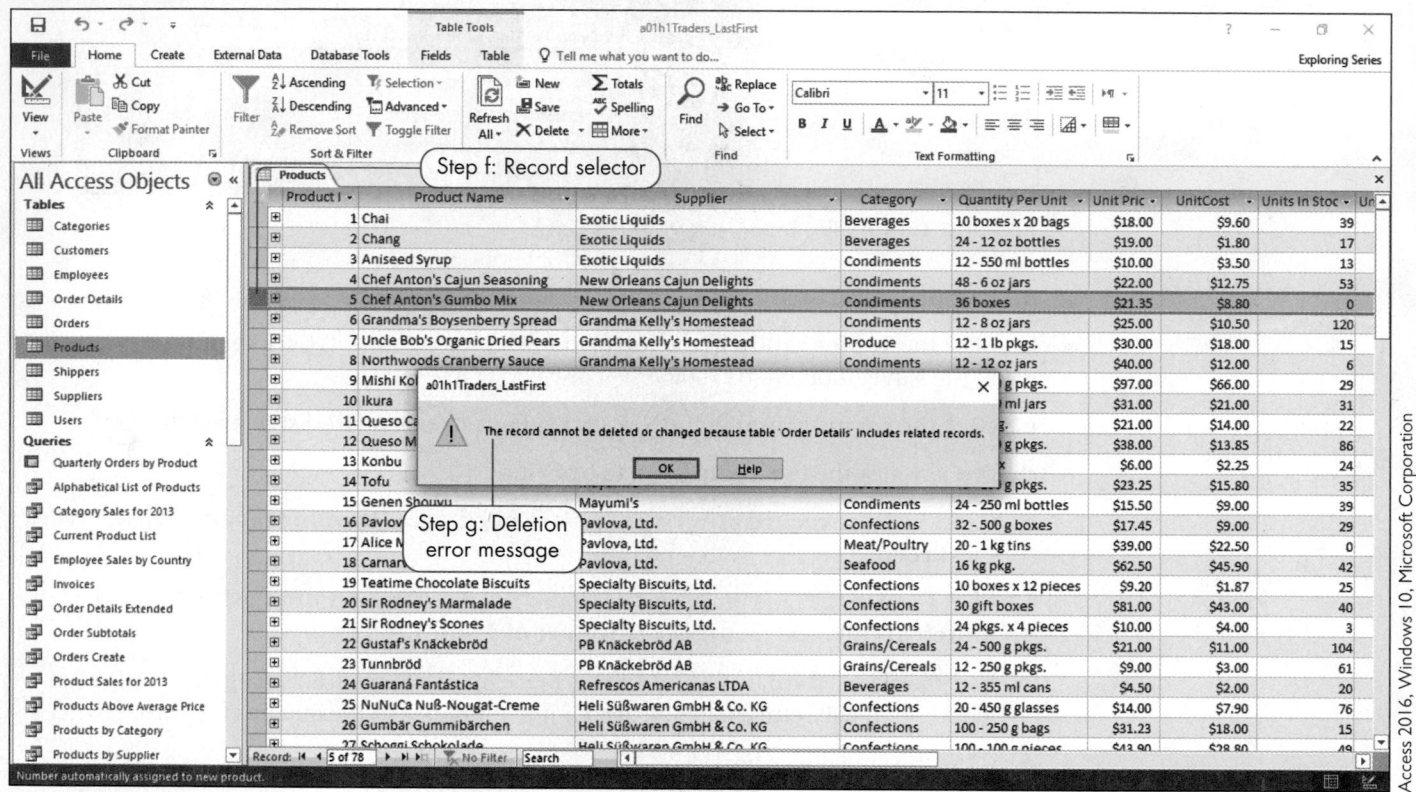

FIGURE 1.34 Deleting Data

a. Click the **Forms group** in the Navigation Pane to collapse it. Expand the **Tables group**.

b. Double-click the **Products table** to open it.

c. Click **Last record** in the navigation bar.

The Pecan Pie record you entered in the Products form is listed as the last record in the Products table. The Products form was created from the Products table. Your newly created record, Pecan Pie, is stored in the Products table even though you added it using the form.

d. Navigate to the fifth record in the table, Chef Anton's Gumbo Mix.

e. Use the horizontal scroll bar to scroll right until you see the Discontinued field.

The check mark in the Discontinued check box tells you that this product has been discontinued.

f. Click the **record selector** to the left of the fifth record.

A border surrounds the record and the record is shaded, indicating it is selected.

g. Click **Delete** in the Records group and read the error message.

The error message that displays tells you that you cannot delete this record because the table 'Order Details' has related records. (Customers ordered this product in the past.) Even though the product is now discontinued and no stock remains, it cannot be deleted from the Products table because related records exist in the Order Details table.

h. Click **OK**.

i. Navigate to the last record and click the **record selector** to highlight the entire row.

The Pecan Pie record you added earlier is displayed.

j. Click **Delete** in the Records group. Read the warning.

The warning box that displays tells you that this action cannot be undone. Although this product can be deleted because it was just entered and no orders were created for it, you do not want to delete the record.

k. Click **No**. You do not want to delete this record. Close the Products table.

> **TROUBLESHOOTING:** If you clicked Yes and deleted the record, return to Step 4d. Re-open the form and re-enter the information for this record. This will be important later in this lesson.

STEP 6 ›› USE DATABASE UTILITIES

You will protect the Northwind database by using the Back Up Database utility. Refer to Figure 1.35 as you complete Step 6.

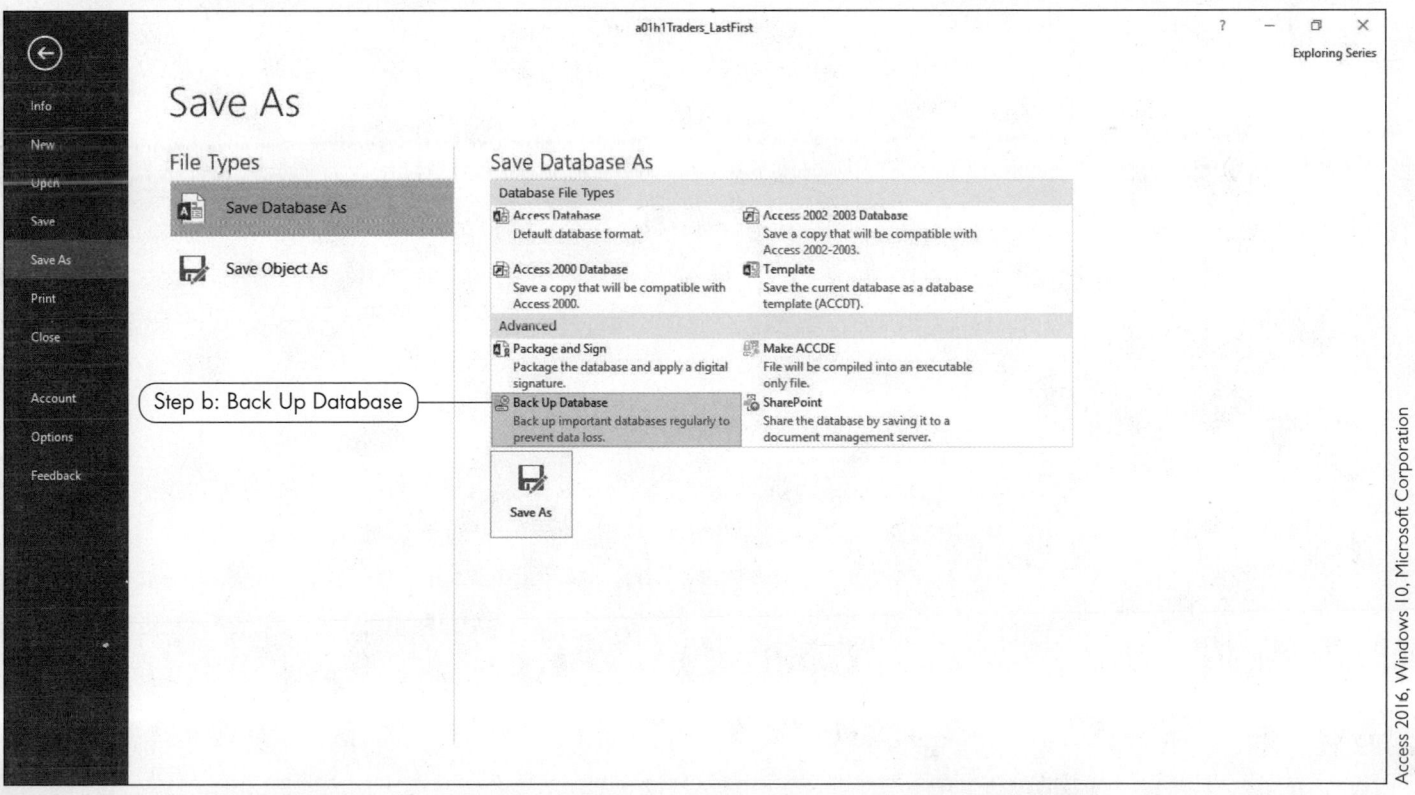

FIGURE 1.35 Backing Up a Database

a. Click the **File tab** and click **Save As**.

b. Double-click **Back Up Database** under the Advanced section to open the Save As dialog box.

 The backup utility assigns the default name by adding a date to your file name.

c. Verify that the Save in folder displays the location where you want your file saved and click **Save**.

 You just created a backup of the database after completing Hands-On Exercise 1. The original database file remains onscreen.

d. Keep the database open if you plan to continue with Hands-On Exercise 2. If not, close the database and exit Access.

Filters and Sorts

Access provides you with many tools that you can use to change the order of information and to identify and extract only the data needed at the moment. You may want to find specific information, such as which suppliers are located in Denton, TX, or which customers have placed orders in the last seven days. There may be other times you simply want to sort information rather than extract information.

In this section, you will learn how to sort information and to isolate records in a table based on criteria.

Working with Filters

Suppose you wanted to see a list of the products in the Confections category in the Northwind database. To obtain this list, you would open the Products table in Datasheet view and create a filter. A *filter* allows you to specify conditions to display only those records that meet those conditions. These conditions are known as criteria (or criterion, singular), and are a number, a text phrase, or an expression (such as >50) used to select records from a table. Therefore, to view a list of all Confections, you would filter the Products table, displaying only records with a Category value of Confections. In this case, Category being equal to Confections is the criterion.

You can use filters to analyze data quickly. Applying a filter does not delete any records; filters only hide records that do not match the criteria. Two types of filters are discussed in this section: Selection filter and Filter By Form.

Use a Selection Filter to Find Exact Matches

STEP 1 ➤➤ A *Selection filter* displays only the records that match a criterion you select. You can use a Selection filter to find records that equal a criterion. For example, if you filter a name field and you select "equals Eric", you would only find customers who have a name of Eric (but not any other variation). Selection filters are not case sensitive, so any variation of capitalization (ERIC, eric) would also appear in the search results.

> **To use a Selection filter to find an exact match, complete the following steps:**
>
> 1. Click in any field that contains the criterion on which you want to filter.
> 2. Click Selection in the Sort & Filter group on the Home tab.
> 3. Select Equals "criterion" from the list of options (*criterion* will be replaced by the value of the field).

Figure 1.36 displays a Customers table with 91 records. The records in the table are displayed in sequence according to the CustomerID. The navigation bar at the bottom indicates that the active record is the second row in the table. Owner in the Job Title field is selected.

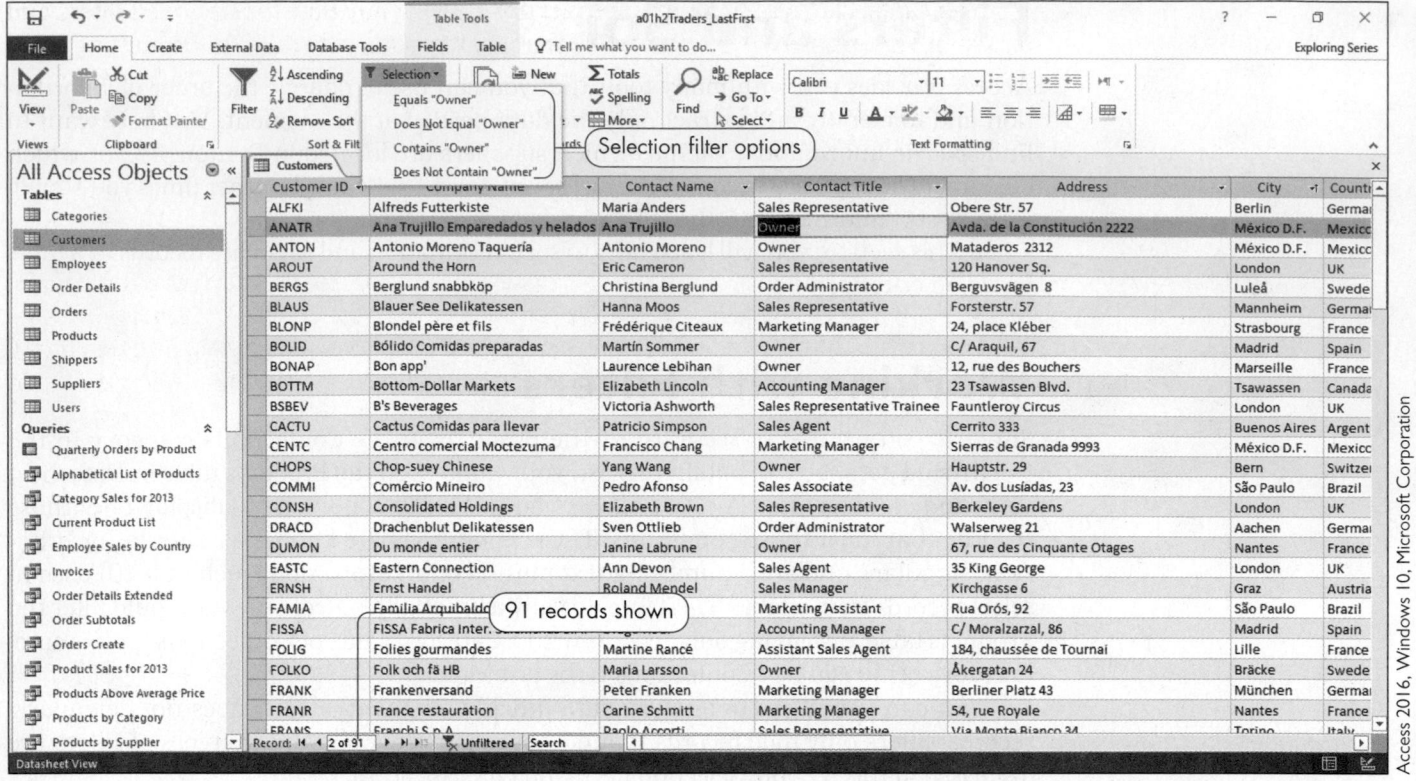

FIGURE 1.36 Unfiltered Customers Table

Figure 1.37 displays a filtered view of the Customers table, showing records with the job title Owner. The navigation bar shows that this is a filtered list containing 17 records matching the criterion. The Customers table still contains the original 91 records, but only 17 records are visible with the filter applied.

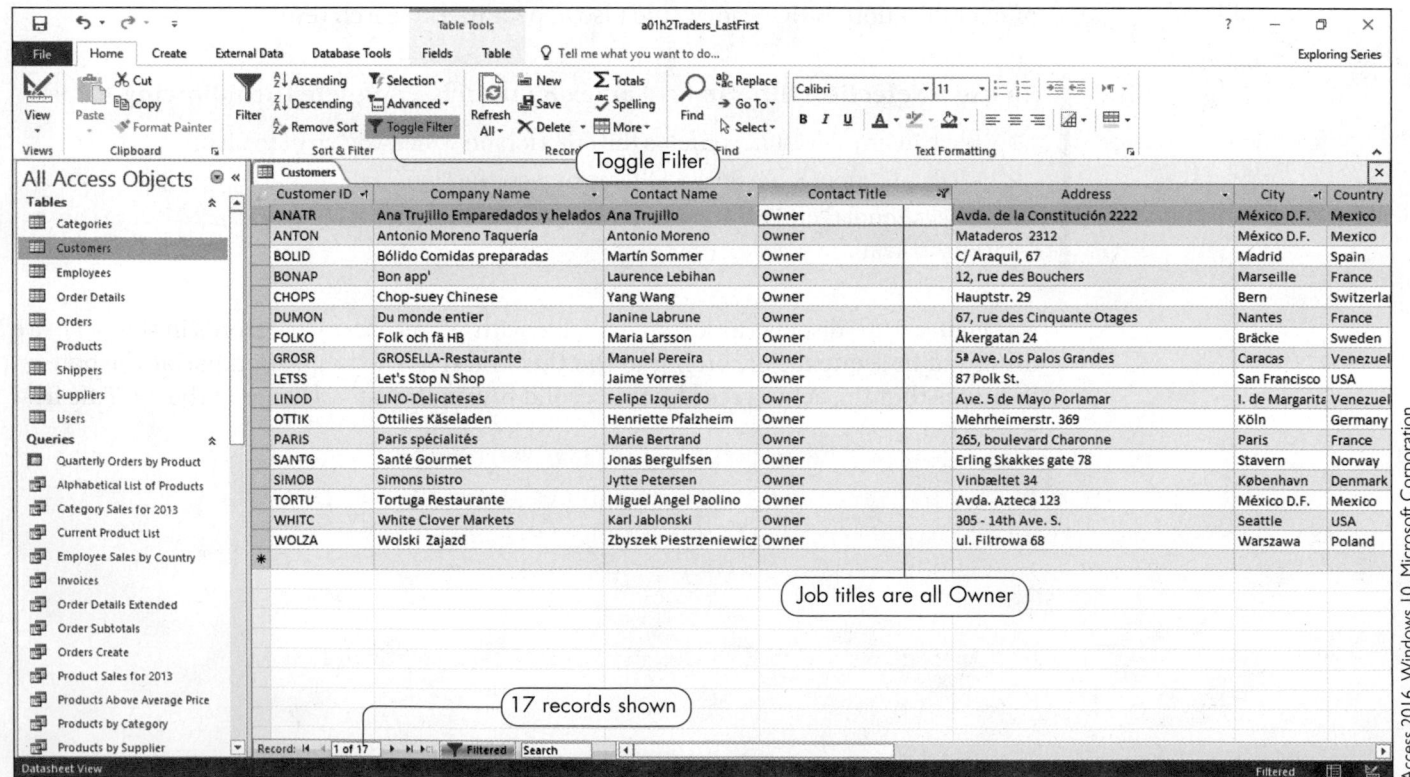

FIGURE 1.37 Filtered Customers Table

You can click Toggle Filter (refer to Figure 1.37) at any time to remove all filters and display all the records in the table. Filters are a temporary method for examining table data. If you close the filtered table and reopen it, the filter will be removed and all of the records will be visible again. You can at any point click Toggle Filter to display the results of the last saved filter.

Use a Selection Filter to Find Records Containing a Value

STEP 2 ≫ You can also use a Selection filter to find records that contain a criterion. For example, if you filter a name field and you select "contains Eric", it would find Eric, as well as names containing Eric (such as Erica, Erich, Erick, and even Broderick, Frederick, and Frederica). As with the exact match, this is not case sensitive, as shown in the results in Figure 1.38.

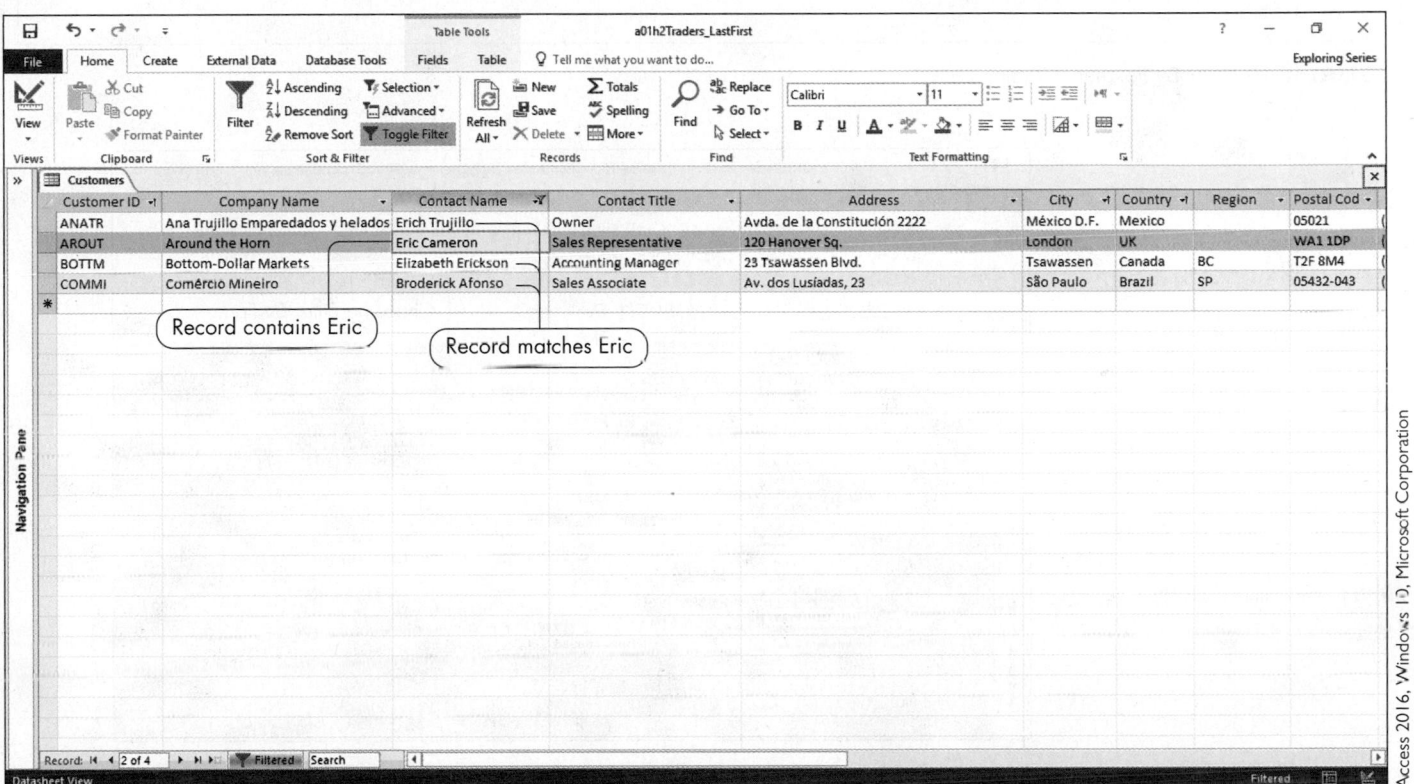

FIGURE 1.38 Finding Records Containing a Value

> **To use a Selection filter to find all values containing certain text, complete the following steps:**
>
> 1. Click in any field that contains the criterion on which you want to filter.
> 2. Click Selection in the Sort & Filter group on the Home tab.
> 3. Select Contains "criterion" from the list of options (*criterion* will be replaced by the value of the field).

Your results will show all records containing a partial or full match.

Use Filter By Form

STEP 3 ≫ *Filter By Form* is a more versatile method of selecting data because it enables you to display records based on multiple criteria. When you use Filter By Form, all of the records are hidden and Access creates a blank form in a design grid. You see only field names with an arrow in the first field. Figure 1.39 shows Filter By Form in Datasheet view, and Figure 1.40 shows Filter By Form in a form view.

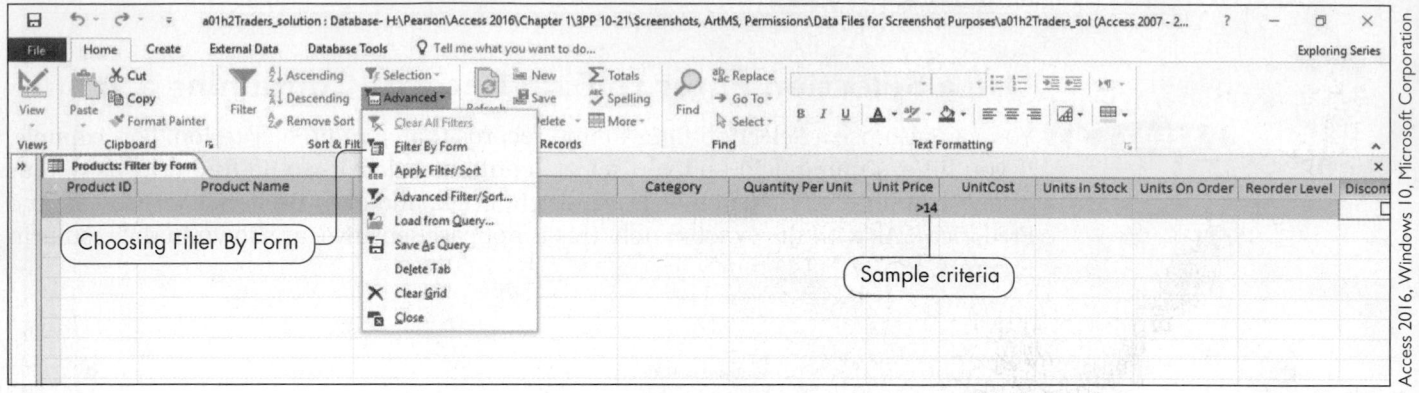

FIGURE 1.39 Filter By Form in a Table

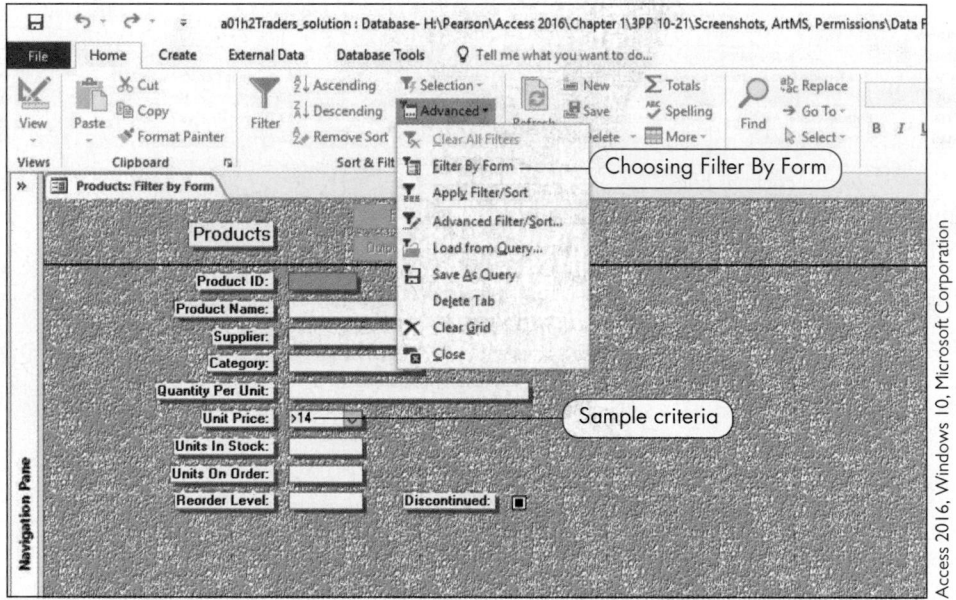

FIGURE 1.40 Filter By Form in a Form

An advantage of using this filter method is that you can specify AND and OR logical operators. If you use the AND operator, a record is included in the results if all the criteria are true. If you use the OR operator, a record is included if at least one criterion is true. Another advantage of Filter By Form is that you can use a comparison operator such as equal (=), not equal (<>), greater than (>), less than (<), greater than or equal to (>=), and less than or equal to (<=).

To use Filter By Form, complete the following steps:

1. Click Advanced in the Sort & Filter group on the Home tab.
2. Click Filter By Form.
3. Click in the field you want to use as a criterion. Click the arrow to select the criterion from existing data.
4. Add additional criterion and comparison operators as required.
5. Click Toggle Filter in the Sort & Filter group on the Home tab to apply the filter.

Performing Sorts

You can change the order of information by sorting one or more fields. A *sort* lists records in a specific sequence, such as alphabetically by last name or by ascending EmployeeID.

Sort Table Data

STEP 4 ➤➤ Ascending sorts a list of text data in alphabetical order or a numeric list in lowest to highest order. Descending sorts a list of text data in reverse alphabetical order or a numeric list in highest to lowest order. You can equate this to these terms outside of a database. When you are coming down from a high place (such as the top of a ladder), you are said to be descending, and when you are climbing a ladder, you are ascending. Figure 1.41 shows the Customers table sorted in ascending order by city name.

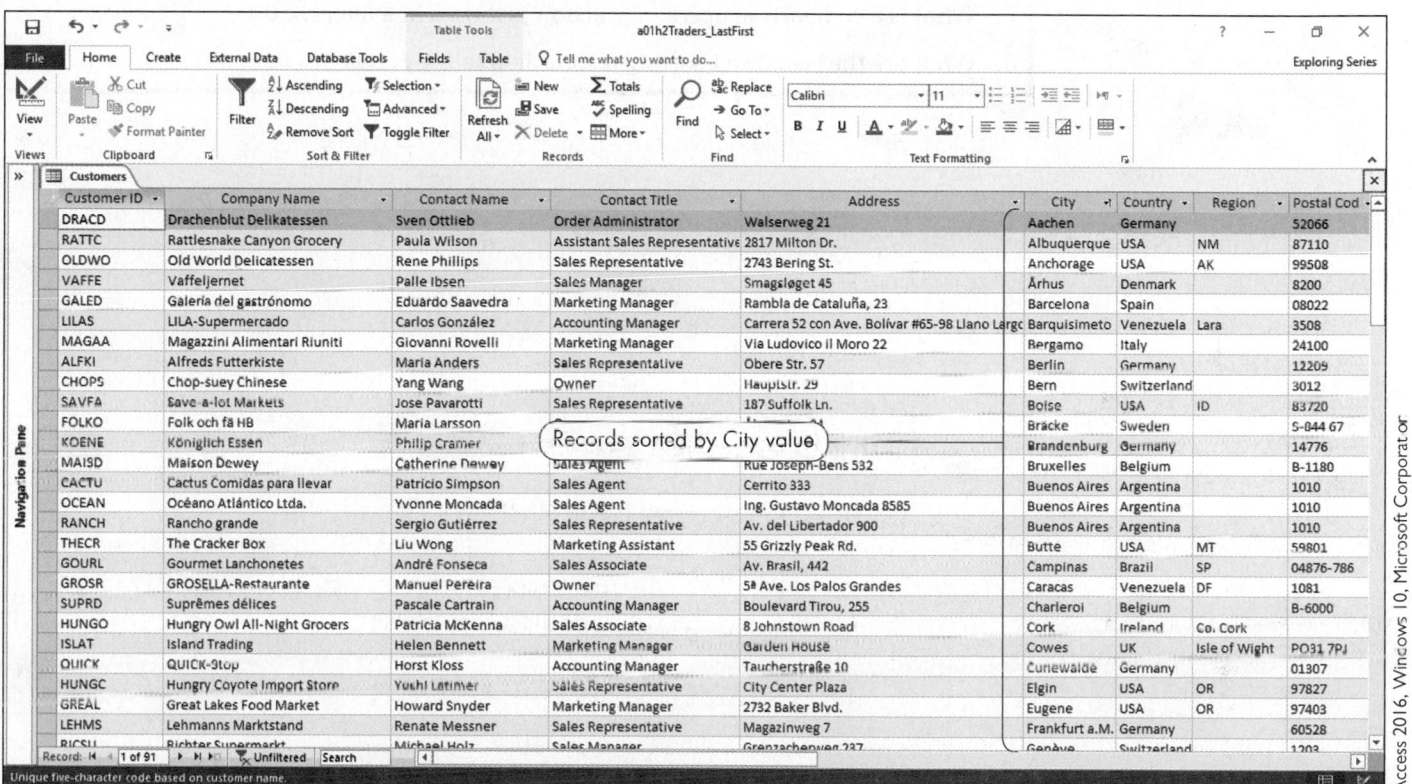

FIGURE 1.41 Sorted Customers Table

> **To sort a table on one criterion, complete the following steps:**
> 1. Click in the field that you want to use to sort the records.
> 2. Click Ascending or Descending in the Sort & Filter group on the Home tab.

Access can sort records by more than one field. When sorting by multiple criteria, Access first sorts by the field located on the left. It is important to understand that in order to sort by multiple fields, you must arrange your columns in this order. This may lead to moving a field to the left so it is sorted first.

> **To move a field, complete the following steps:**
>
> 1. Click the column heading and hold down the left mouse button. A thick line appears to the left of the column.
> 2. Drag the field to the appropriate position.

Once the column has been moved, you can perform a sort by selecting the field to the left, sorting, and then doing the same for the secondary sort column.

Quick Concepts

5. What is the purpose of creating a filter? *p. 695*

6. What is the difference between a Selection filter and a Filter By Form? *pp. 695, 697*

7. What is a comparison operator and how is it used in a filter? *p. 698*

8. What are the benefits of sorting records in a table? *p. 699*

Hands-On Exercises

Watch the Video for this Hands-On Exercise!

MyITLab®
HOE2 Training

Skills covered: Use a Selection Filter to Find Exact Matches • Use a Selection Filter to Find Records Containing a Value • Use Filter By Form • Sort Table Data

2 Filters and Sorts

The sales manager at Northwind Traders wants quick answers to her questions about customer orders. You use the Access database to filter tables to answer these questions, then sort the records based on the manager's requirements.

STEP I ›› USE A SELECTION FILTER TO FIND EXACT MATCHES

The sales manager asks for a list of customers who live in London. You use a Selection filter with an equal condition to locate these customers. Refer to Figure 1.42 as you complete Step 1.

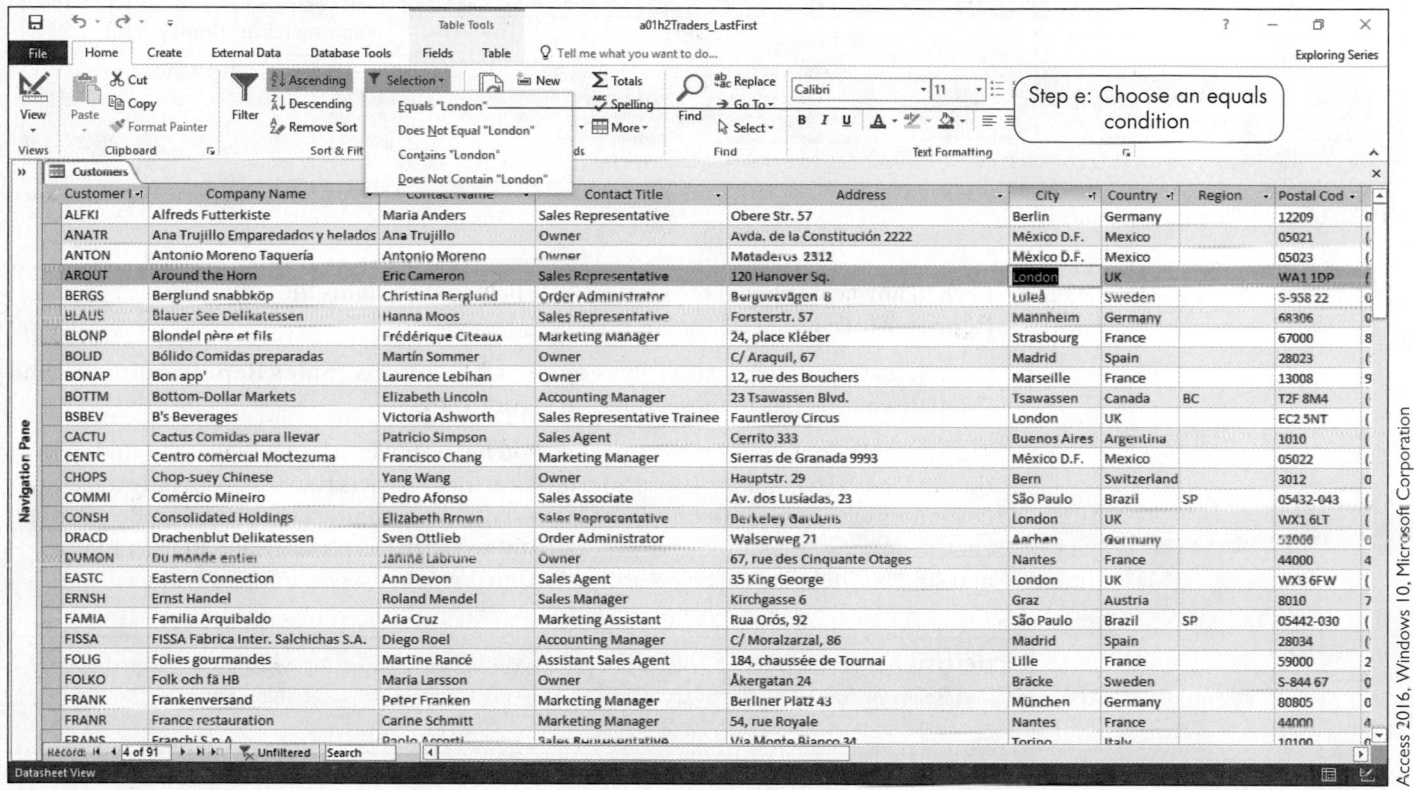

FIGURE 1.42 Filtering the Customers Table

a. Open the *a01h1Traders_LastFirst* database if you closed it after the last Hands-On Exercise and save it as **a01h2Traders_LastFirst**, changing h1 to h2. Click **Enable Content**.

b. Double-click the **Customers table** in the Navigation Pane, navigate to record 4, and then replace Thomas Hardy with your name in the Contact Name field.

c. Scroll right until the City field is visible. The fourth record has a value of London in the City field. Click the field to select it.

d. Click **Selection** in the Sort & Filter group on the Home tab.

e. Select **Equals "London"** from the menu. Six records are displayed.

The navigation bar display shows that six records that meet the London criterion are available. The other records in the Customers table are hidden. The Filtered icon also displays on the navigation bar and column heading, indicating that the Customers table has been filtered.

f. Click **Toggle Filter** in the Sort & Filter group to remove the filter.

g. Click **Toggle Filter** again to reset the filter.

STEP 2 » **USE A SELECTION FILTER TO FIND RECORDS CONTAINING A VALUE**

The sales manager asks you to narrow the list of London customers so that it displays only Sales Representatives. To accomplish this task, you add a second layer of filtering using a Selection filter. Refer to Figure 1.43 as you complete Step 2.

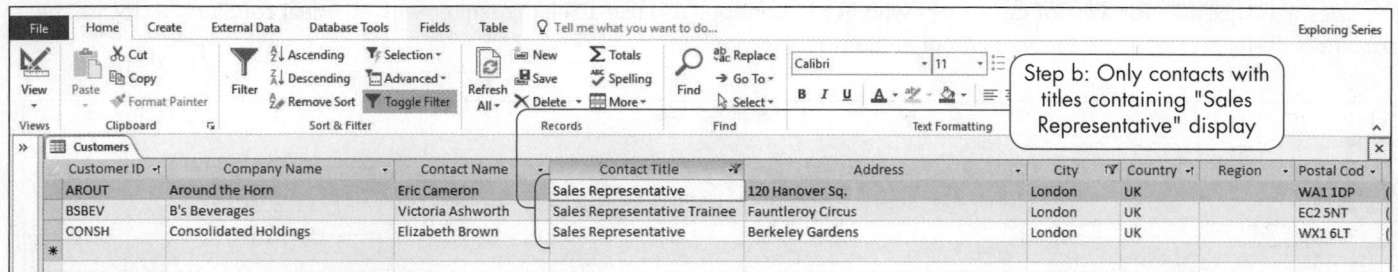

Access 2016, Windows 10, Microsoft Corporation

FIGURE 1.43 Filtered Customers

a. Click in any field value in the Contact Title field that contains the value **Sales Representative**.

b. Click **Selection** in the Sort & Filter group, click **Contains "Sales Representative"**, and compare your results to those shown in Figure 1.43.

Three records match the criteria you set. You have applied a second layer of filtering to the customers in London. The second layer further restricts the display to only those customers who have the words Sales Representative contained in their titles. Because you chose Contains as your filter, any representatives with the phrase Sales Representative appear. This includes Victoria Ashworth, who is a Sales Representative Trainee.

> **TROUBLESHOOTING:** If you do not see the record for Victoria Ashworth, you selected Equals "Sales Representative" instead of Contains "Sales Representative". Repeat Steps a and b, making sure you select Contains "Sales Representative".

c. Close the Customers table. Click **Yes** when prompted to save the design changes to the Customers table.

You are asked to provide a list of records that do not match just one set of criteria. You will provide a list of all extended prices less than $50 for a specific sales representative. Use Filter By Form to provide the information when two or more criteria are necessary. You also preview the results in Print Preview to see how the list would print. Refer to Figure 1.44 as you complete Step 3.

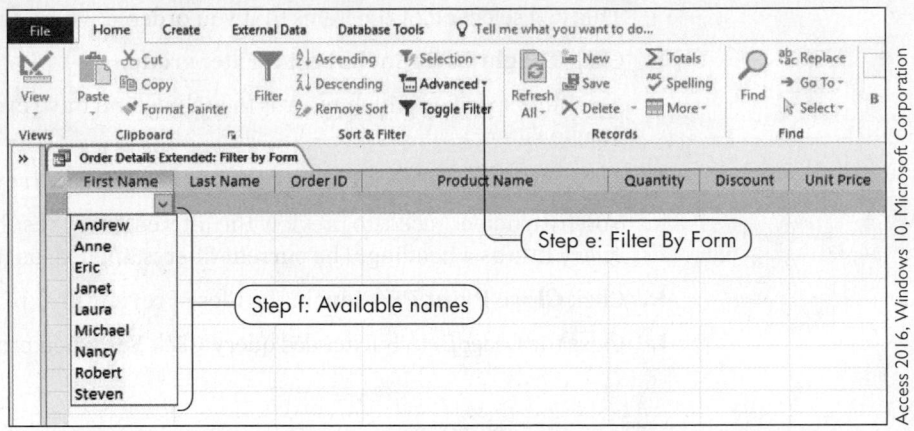

FIGURE 1.44 Using Filter By Form

a. Click the **Tables group** in the Navigation Pane to collapse the listed tables.

b. Click the **Queries group** in the Navigation Pane to expand the list of available queries.

c. Locate and double-click **Order Details Extended** to open it.

This query contains information about orders. It has fields containing information about the sales person, the Order ID, the product name, the unit price, quantity ordered, the discount given, and an extended price. The extended price is a field used to total order information.

d. Click **Advanced** in the Sort & Filter group and select **Filter By Form** from the list. The first field, First Name, is active by default.

All of the records are now hidden, and you see only field names and an arrow in the first field. Although you are applying Filter By Form to a query, you can use the same process as applying Filter By Form to a table. You are able to input more than one criterion using Filter By Form.

e. Click the **First Name arrow**.

A list of all available first names appears. Your name should be on the list. Figure 1.44 shows *Eric Cameron*, which replaced Margaret Peacock in Hands-On Exercise 1.

TROUBLESHOOTING: If you do not see your name and you do see Margaret on the list, you probably skipped steps in Hands-On Exercise 1. Close the query without saving changes, return to the first Hands-On Exercise, and then rework it, making sure not to omit any steps. Then you can return to this location and work the remainder of this Hands-On Exercise.

f. Select your first name from the list.

g. Click in the first row under the Last Name field to reveal the arrow. Locate and select your last name by clicking it.

h. Scroll right until you see the Extended Price field. Click in the first row under the Extended Price field and type **<50**.

This will select all of the items that you ordered where the total was less than 50.

i. Click **Toggle Filter** in the Sort & Filter group.

You have specified which records to include and have executed the filtering by clicking Toggle Filter.

j. Click the **File tab**, click **Print**, and then click **Print Preview**.

You instructed Access to preview the filtered query results. The preview displays the query title as a heading. The current filter is applied, as well as page numbers.

k. Click **Close Print Preview** in the Close Preview group.

l. Close the Order Details Extended query. Click **Yes** when prompted to save your changes.

STEP 4 ›› SORT TABLE DATA

The Sales Manager is pleased with your work; however, she would like some of the information to appear in a different order. You will now sort the records in the Customers table using the manager's new criteria. Refer to Figure 1.45 as you complete Step 4.

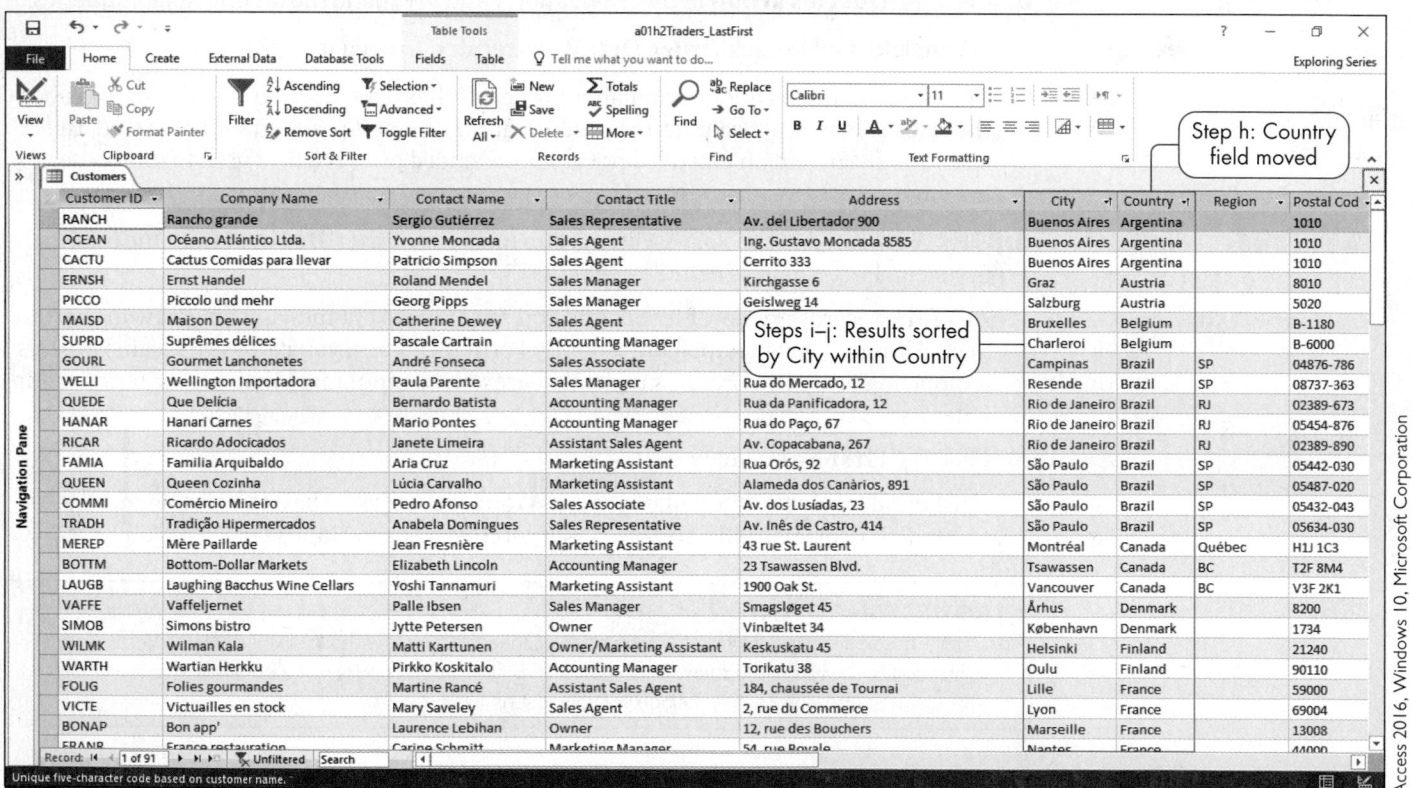

FIGURE 1.45 Updated Customers Table

a. Click the **Queries group** in the Navigation Pane to collapse the listed queries.

b. Click the **Tables group** in the Navigation Pane to expand the list of available tables and double-click the **Customers table** to open it.

This table contains information about customers. The table is sorted in alphabetical order by Company Name.

c. Click **Shutter Bar Open/Close** in the Navigation Pane to hide the Navigation Pane.

It will be easier to locate fields in the Customer table if the Navigation Pane is hidden.

d. Click any entry in the Customer ID field. Click **Descending** in the Sort & Filter group on the Home tab.

Sorting in descending order on a text field produces a reverse alphabetical order.

e. Scroll right until you can see both the Country and City fields.

f. Click the **Country column heading**.

The entire field is selected.

g. Click the **Country column heading** again and hold down the **left mouse button**.

A thick line displays on the left edge of the Country field.

h. Check to make sure that you see the thick line. Drag the **Country field** to the left until the thick line moves between the City and Region fields. Release the mouse button and the Country field position moves to the right of the City field.

You moved the Country field next to the City field so that you can easily sort the table based on both fields.

i. Click any city name in the City field and click **Ascending** in the Sort & Filter group.

The City field displays the cities in alphabetical order.

(j.) Click any country name in the Country field and click **Ascending**.

The countries are sorted in alphabetical order. The cities within each country also are sorted alphabetically. For example, the customer in Graz, Austria, is listed before the customer in Salzburg, Austria.

k. Close the Customers table. Click **Yes** to save the changes to the design of the table.

l. Click **Shutter Bar Open/Close** in the Navigation Pane to show the Navigation Pane.

STEP 5 ▶▶ **VIEW RELATIONSHIPS**

To further familiarize yourself with the database, you examine the connections between the tables in the Northwind database. Refer to Figure 1.46 as you complete Step 5.

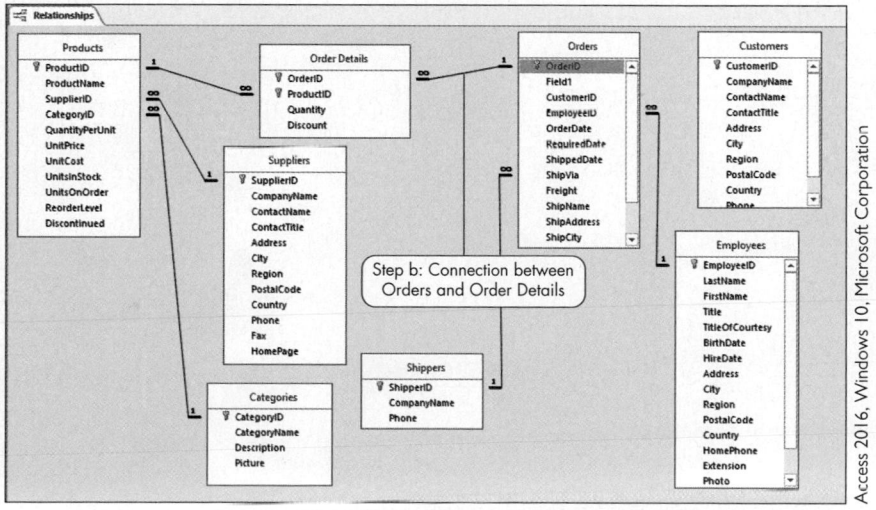

FIGURE 1.46 Northwind Relationships

a. Click the **Database Tools tab** and click **Relationships** in the Relationships group.

b. Examine the join lines showing the relationships that connect the various tables. For example, the Orders table is connected to the Order Details table using the OrderID field as the common field.

c. Close the Relationships.

d. Close the database. You will submit this file to your instructor at the end of the last Hands-On Exercise.

Access Database Creation

Now that you have examined the fundamentals of an Access database and explored the power of databases, it is time to create one! In this section, you explore the benefits of creating a database using each of the methods discussed in the next section.

Creating a Database

When you first start Access, Backstage view opens and provides you with three methods for creating a new database. These methods are:

- Create a blank desktop database
- Create a database from a template (note: there will be many templates shown)
- Create a custom web app

Creating a blank desktop database lets you create a database specific to your requirements. Rather than starting from scratch by creating a blank desktop database, you may want to use a template to create a new database. An Access **template** is a predefined database that includes professionally designed tables, forms, reports, and other objects that you can use to jumpstart the creation of your database. Creating a **custom web app** enables you to create a database that you can build and then use and share with others through the Web.

Figure 1.47 shows the options for creating a custom web app, a blank desktop database, and multiple templates from which you can select the method for which you want to create a database.

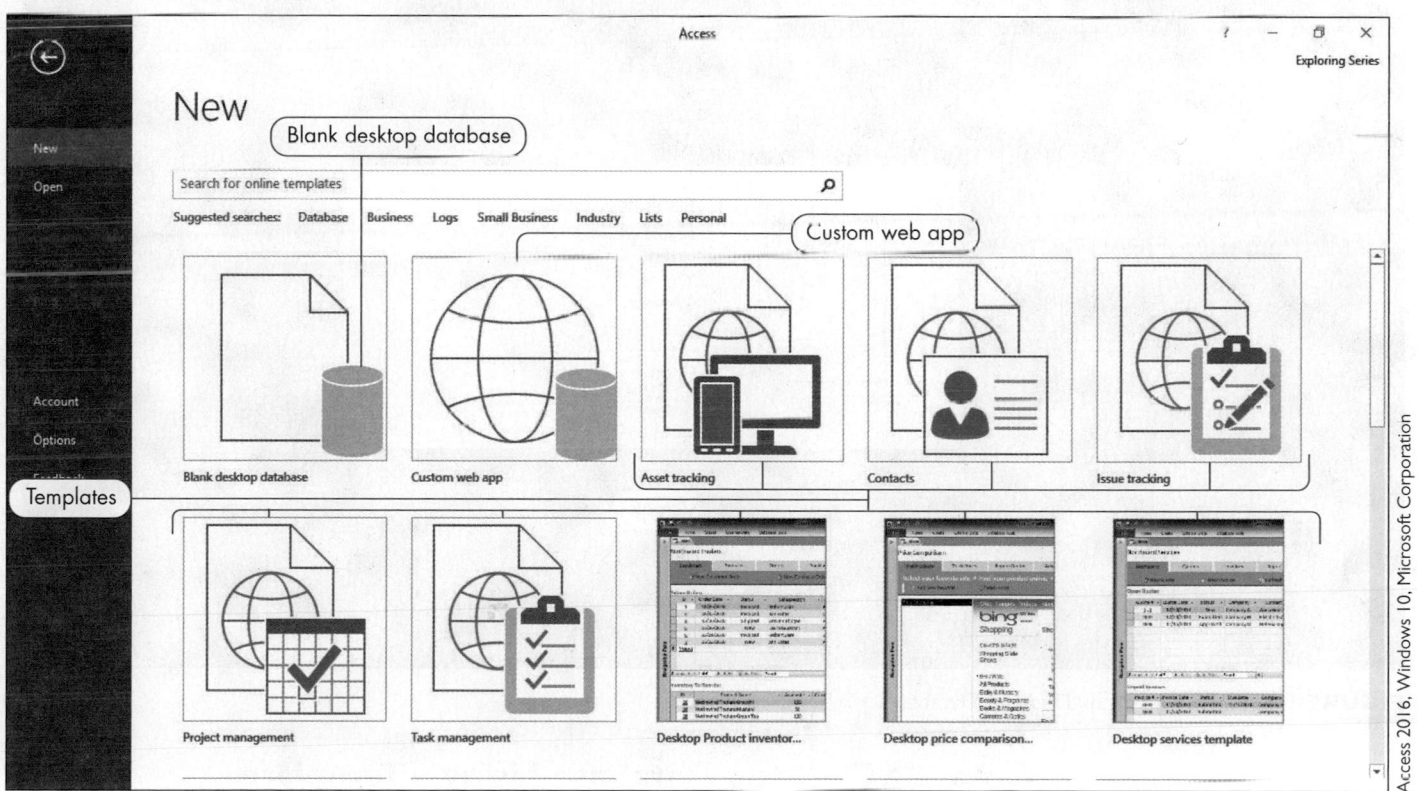

FIGURE 1.47 Options for Creating a New Database

Create a Blank Desktop Database

Often, if you are migrating from Excel to Access, you would start by creating a blank desktop database. At that point, you could import your existing structure and data into a new table. Another time you might use a blank desktop database is when you are starting a project and want to design your own tables.

When you create a blank desktop database, Access opens to a blank table in Datasheet view where you can add fields or data. You can also refine the table in Design view. You would then create additional tables and objects as necessary. Obviously, this task requires some level of Access knowledge, so unless you have requirements to follow, you may be better served using a template.

To create a blank desktop database, complete the following steps:

1. Open Access. (If Access is already open, click the File tab to open Backstage view and click New.)
2. Click the Blank desktop database tile.
3. Type the file name for the file in the text box, click Browse to navigate to the folder where you want to store the database file, and then click OK.
4. Click Create (see Figure 1.48).
5. Type data in the empty table that displays.

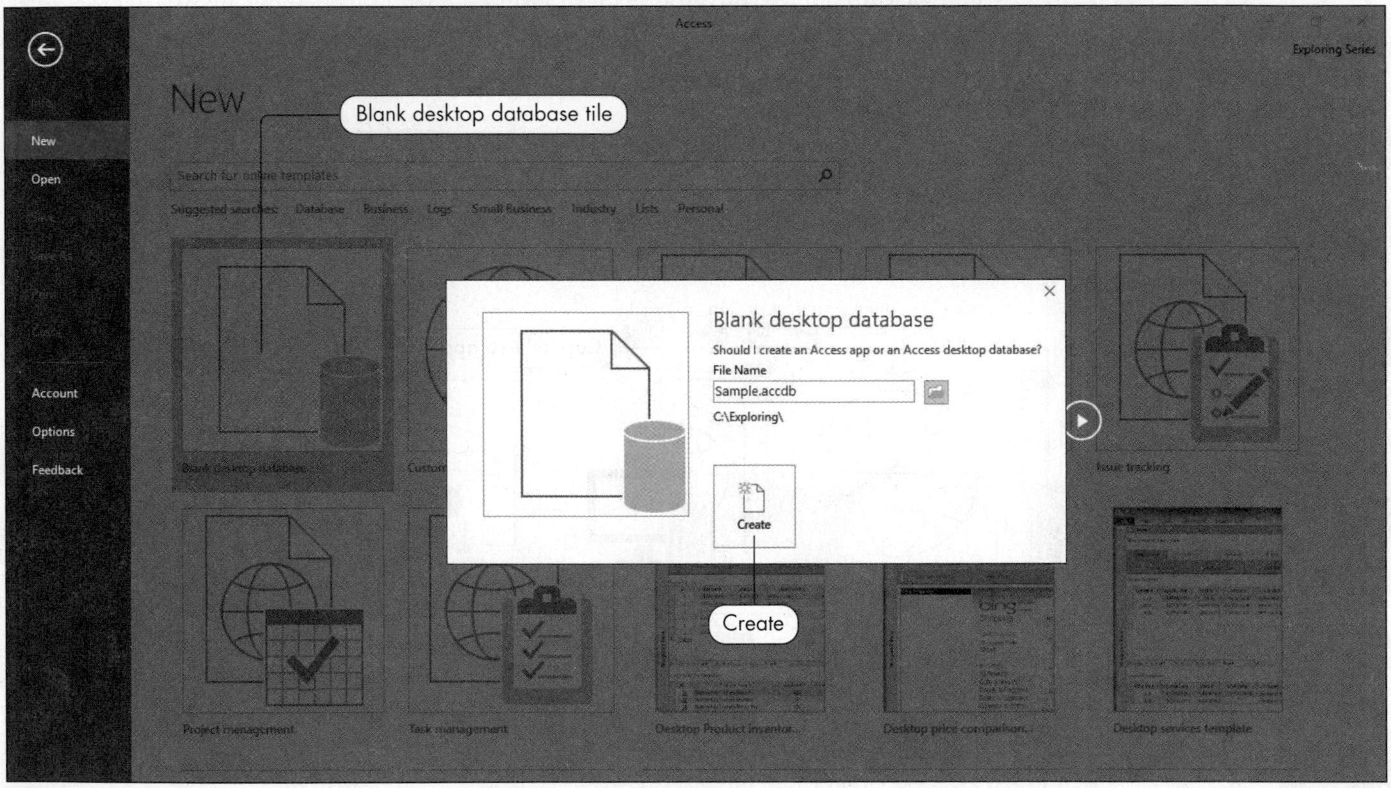

Access 2016, Windows 10, Microsoft Corporation

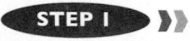

FIGURE 1.48 Creating a Blank Desktop Database

Create a Desktop Database Using a Template

STEP 1 »» Using a template to start a database saves you a great deal of creation time. Working with a template can also help a new Access user become familiar with database design. Templates are available from Backstage view, where you can select from a variety of templates or search online for more templates.

Access also provides templates for desktop use.

> **To create a desktop database from a template, complete the following steps:**
>
> 1. Open Access. (If Access is already open, click the File tab to open Backstage view and click New.)
> 2. Click the desktop database template you want to use, or use the search box at the top of the page. Figure 1.49 shows some examples of templates.
> 3. Type the file name for the file in the text box, click Browse to navigate to the folder where you want to store the database file, and then click OK.
> 4. Click Create to download the template.
>
>   The database will be created and will open.
>
> 5. Click Enable Content in the Security Warning message bar.

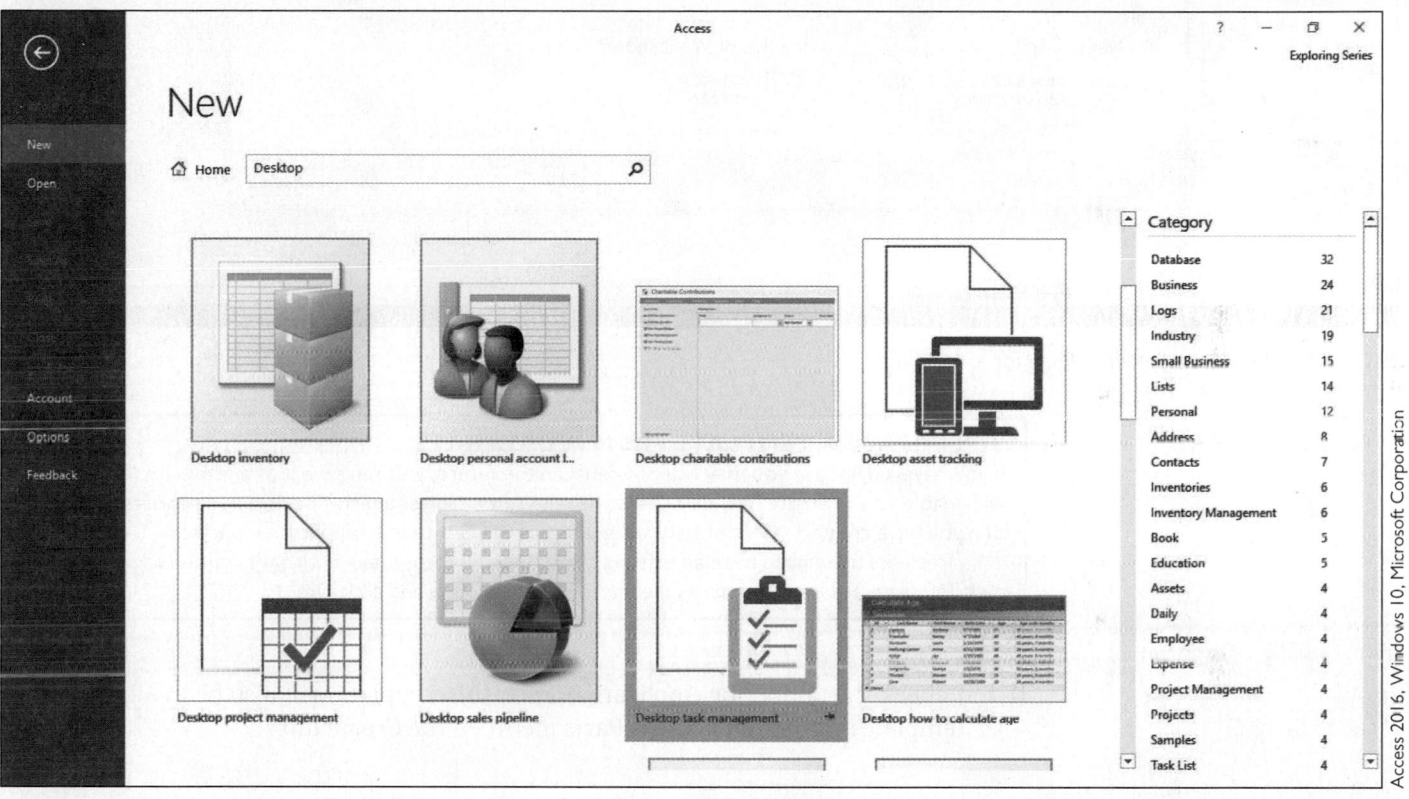

FIGURE 1.49 Database Templates

Once the database is open, you may see a Getting Started page that includes links you can use to learn more about the database. When finished reviewing the learning materials, close the Getting Started page to view the database. Figure 1.50 displays the Getting Started page included with the Desktop task management template. Notice the hyperlink to import contacts from Microsoft Outlook. If you use Outlook, this is a nice feature. Close the Getting Started page to return to the database. Because you downloaded a template, some objects will have already been created. You can work with these objects just as you did in the first three sections of this chapter. Edit any object to meet your requirements.

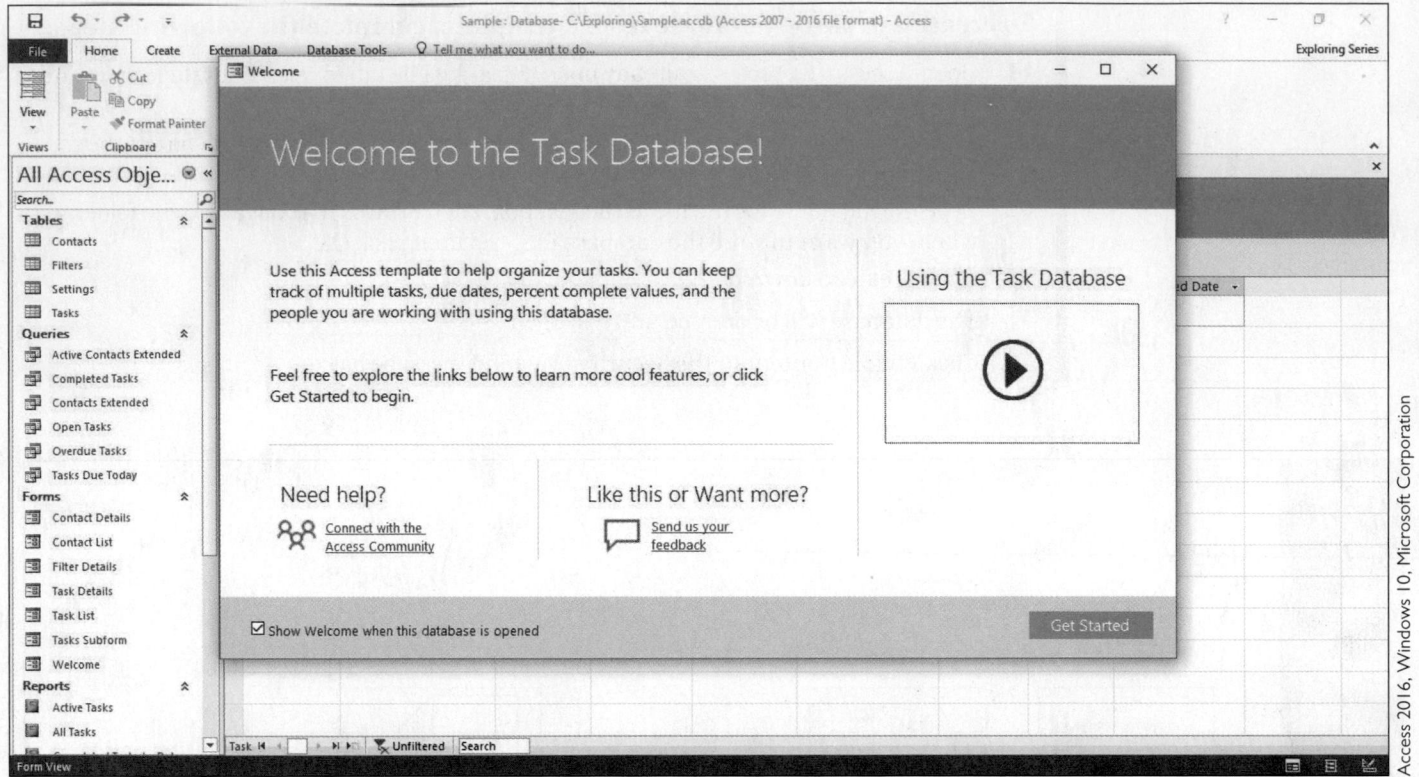

FIGURE 1.50 Getting Started Page for a Template

TIP: CREATE A TEMPLATE FROM A DATABASE

If you have a database you may want to reuse in the future, you can save it as a template. Doing so will enable you to create new databases with the same tables, queries, forms, and reports as the one you have created. You can also reuse parts of the database as application parts.

To create a template from an existing database, click the File tab, click Save As, and then double-click Template. Set options such as the name and description and click OK.

If you check the option for Application Part, this template will also be available under User Templates on the Application Parts menu on the Create tab.

Add Records to a Downloaded Desktop Database

STEP 2 ❯❯ Once a desktop database template has been downloaded, you can use it as you would use any Access database. Figure 1.51 shows the Desktop Task Management template. Review the objects listed in the Navigation Pane. Once you are familiar with the database design, you can enter your data using a table or form.

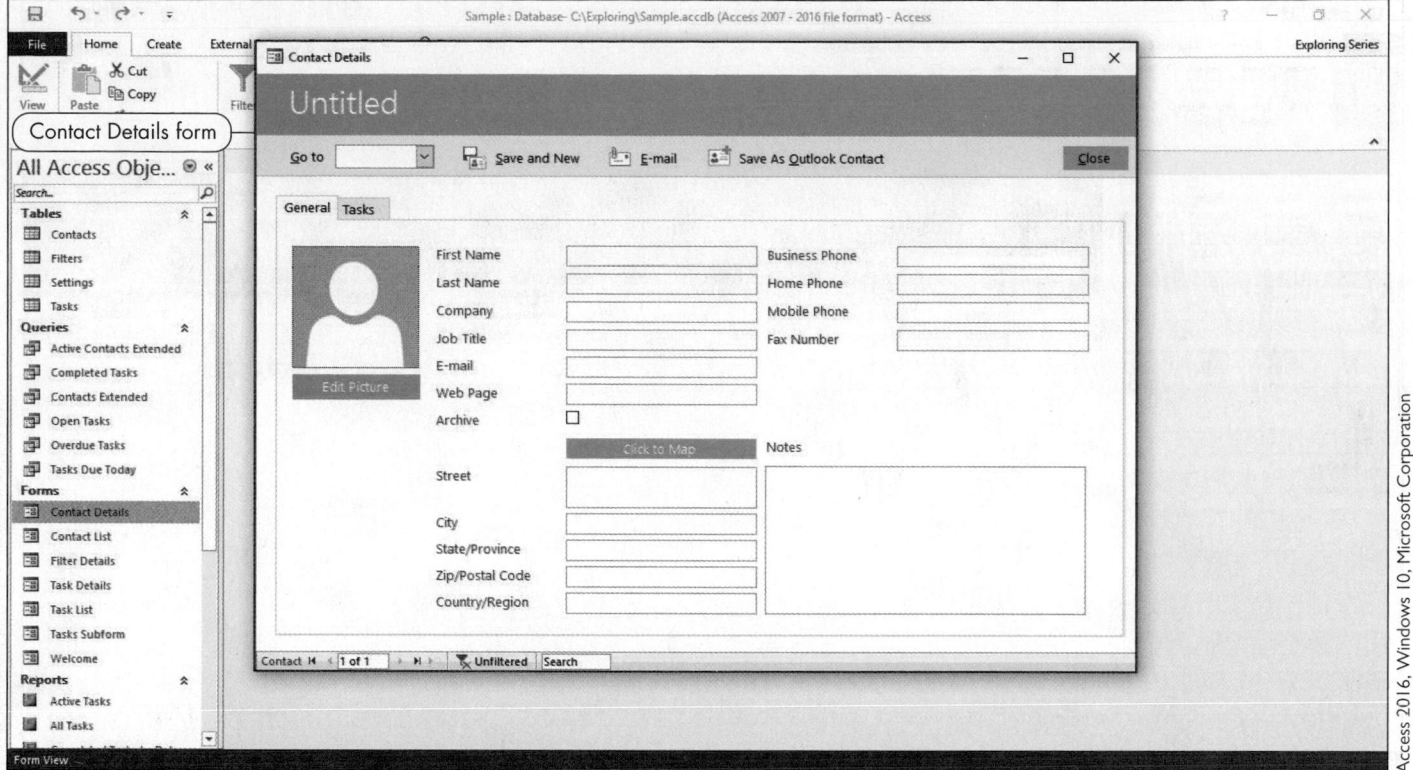

FIGURE 1.51 Desktop Task Management Database

Explore the Database Objects in a Downloaded Desktop Database Template

One of the reasons to use a template is so you do not have to create any of the objects. Therefore, you will notice each template comes with a varying amount of predefined queries, forms, and reports. Familiarize yourself with the unique features of a template; as they are professionally designed, they are typically well thought out.

Create a Table Using an Application Part

An *application part* enables you to add a set of common Access components to an existing database, such as a table, a form, and a report for a related task. These are provided by Microsoft and offer components (for example, a Contacts table) you can add to an existing database, rather than creating an entirely new database, as shown in Figure 1.52.

To add an application part to a database, complete the following steps:

1. Click Application Parts in the Templates group on the Create tab.
2. Select one of the options from the list.
3. Respond to the dialog boxes. For example, if you insert an Issues application part, you may be prompted to create a relationship between Issues and an existing table (such as Customers). Setting up a relationship is not required, but may be appropriate.
4. Check the Navigation Pane to verify that the new components were created.

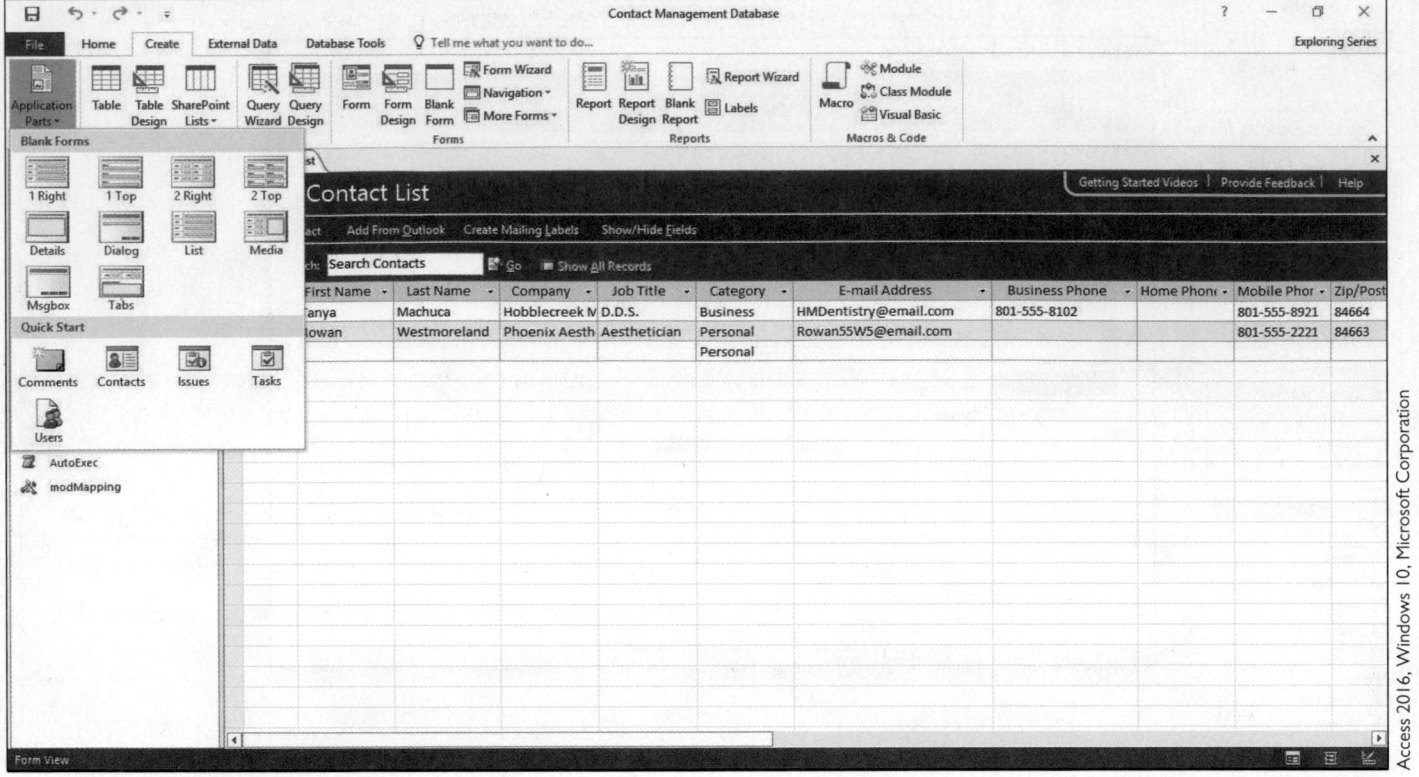

FIGURE 1.52 Adding an Application Part

Create a Web App Using a Template

An Access Web app (or application) is a type of database that lets you build a browser-based database app. You can create a database in the cloud that you and others can access and use simultaneously. This requires that you use a host server such as SharePoint (a Web app platform developed by Microsoft) or Office 365 (a cloud service edition of SharePoint).

Before creating a Web app, ensure that you have access to a host server. In a business environment, this would likely be set up and maintained by your Information Technology department. Your college or university may not give students access to this server. If they do, your professor can give you the information you will need.

To create a Web app using SharePoint, complete the following steps:

1. Click the File tab.
2. Click New.
3. Click Custom web app.
4. Type an App Name.
5. Input the web location (which will be provided by your company's technology professionals or by your professor, if available).
6. Click Create.
7. Create tables. This can be done manually, from a template, or from an existing data source.

In a business environment (and on the Microsoft Office Specialist examination for Access) you may need to migrate the database you have created to a SharePoint server. Doing so is similar to the Save operation covered earlier in the chapter.

> **To migrate an existing database to a SharePoint server, complete the following steps:**
>
> 1. Click the File tab.
> 2. Click Save As.
> 3. Click SharePoint.
> 4. Click Save As.
> 5. Select the location on the SharePoint server where you wish to save your database, and click Save.

As mentioned earlier, SharePoint is typically used more in a corporate environment, so you may not have a SharePoint server available at your college or university.

Quick Concepts

9. What is a custom web app, and what is required to build a custom web app? *p. 707*

10. What are two benefits of using a template to create a database? *p. 708*

11. If you want to add a component to an existing database (such as a Contacts table), what would you use? *p. 711*

Watch the Video for this Hands-On Exercise!

MyITLab®
HOE3 Training

Skills covered: Create a Database Using a Template • Add Records to a Downloaded Desktop Database • Explore the Database Objects in a Downloaded Desktop Database Template

3 Access Database Creation

After working with the Northwind database on the job, you decide to use Access to create a personal contact database. Rather than start from a blank table, you use an Access Contact Manager desktop template to make your database creation simpler.

STEP 1 ⟩⟩ CREATE A DATABASE USING A TEMPLATE

You locate an Access desktop template that you can use to create your personal contact database. This template not only allows you to store names, addresses, telephone numbers, and other information, but also lets you categorize your contacts, send email messages, and create maps of addresses. You download and save the template. Refer to Figure 1.53 as you complete Step 1.

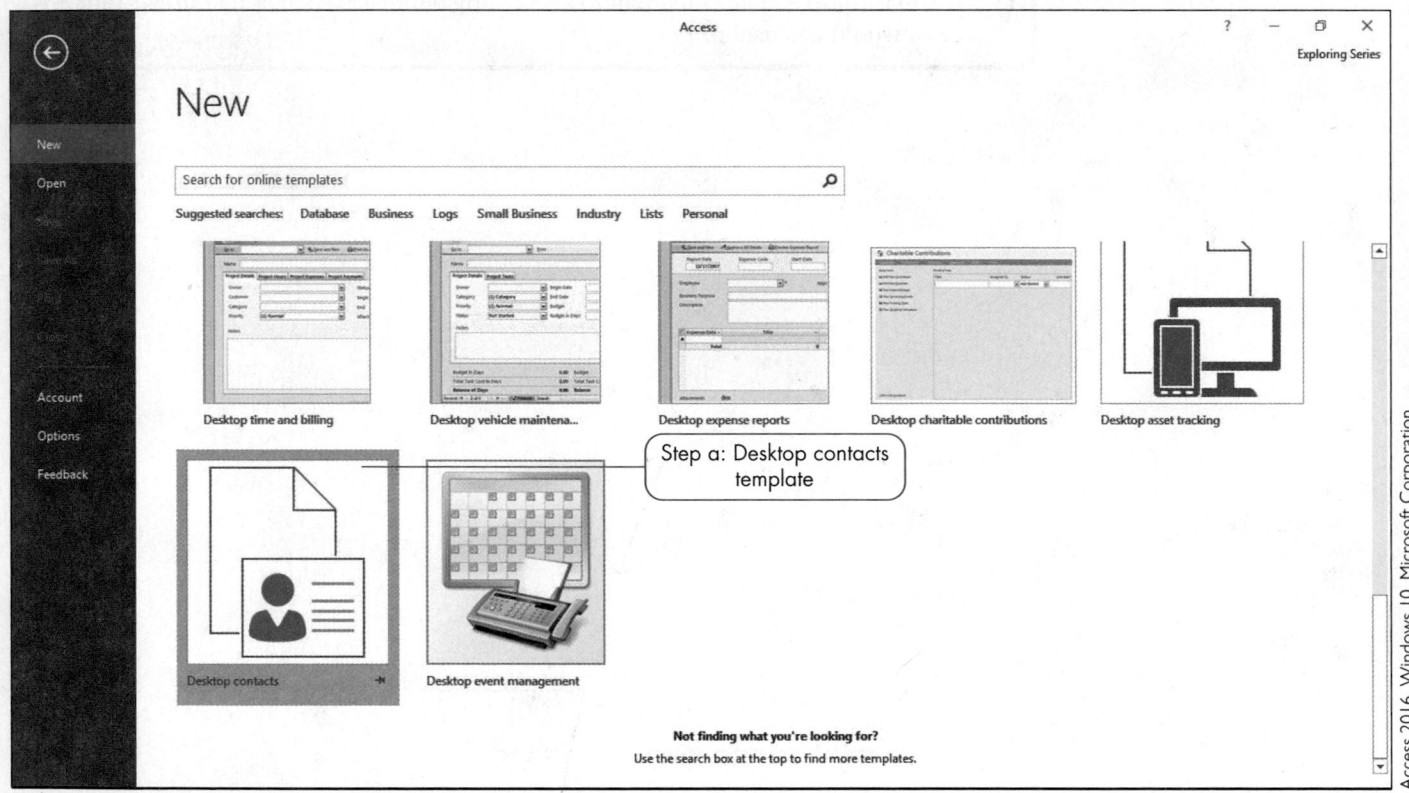

FIGURE 1.53 Database Templates

a. Open Access. Scroll down and click the **Desktop contacts** template tile.

> **TROUBLESHOOTING:** If the Desktop contacts template is not visible, you can use the search box at the top of the screen.

b. Click **Browse** to navigate to the folder where you are saving your files, type **a01h3Contacts_LastFirst** as the file name, and then click **OK**.

c. Click **Create** to download the template.

d. Click the *Show Getting Started when this database is opened* check box to deselect it, and close the Getting Started with Contacts page.

The database displays the Contact List form.

e. Click **Enable Content** on the Security Warning message bar.

Because the database opens in the Contact List form, you decide to begin by entering a contact in the form. Refer to Figure 1.54 as you complete Step 2.

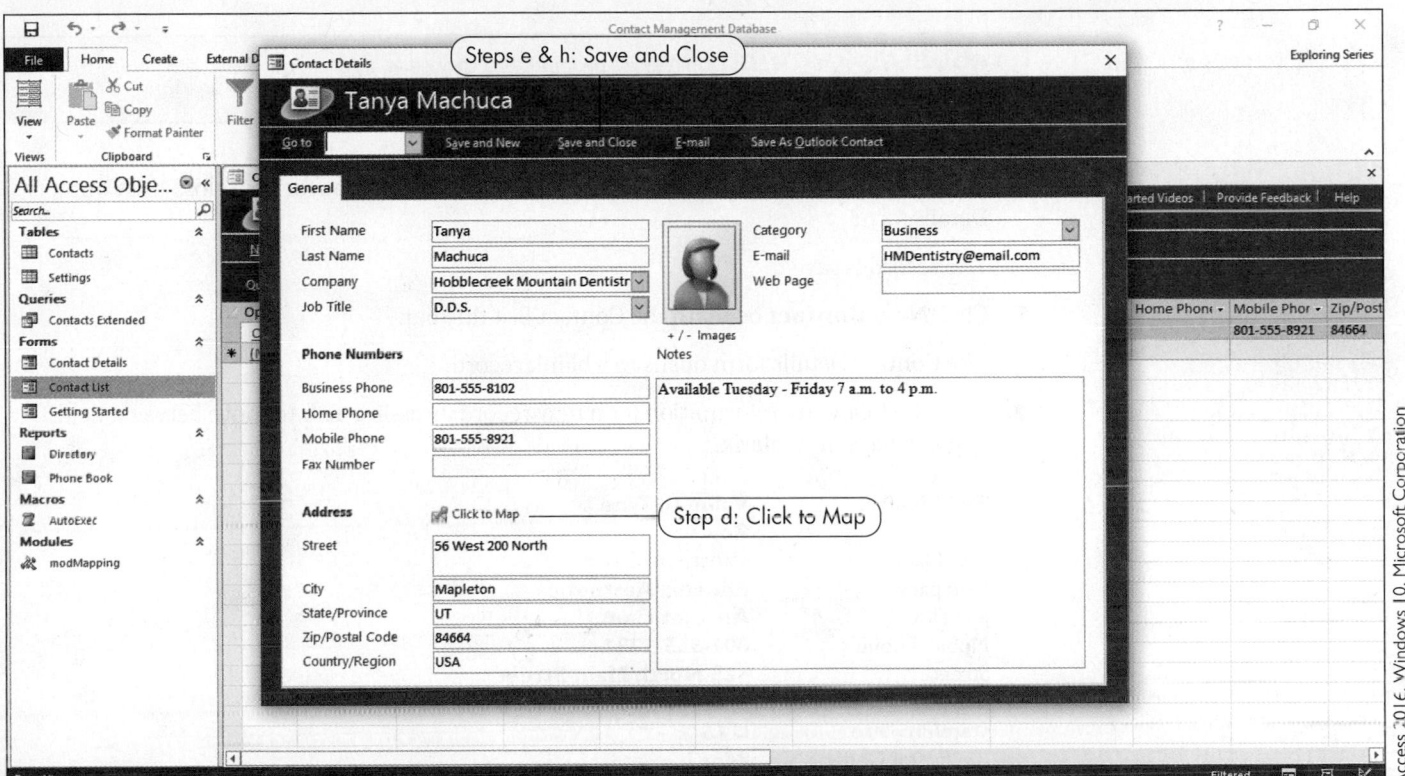

FIGURE 1.54 Contact Details for Tanya Machuca

a. Click in the First Name field of the first record. Type the following information, pressing **Tab** between each entry. Do not press Tab after entering the ZIP/Postal Code.

Field Name	Value to Type
First Name	**Tanya**
Last Name	**Machuca**
Company	**Hobblecreek Mountain Dentistry**
Job Title	**D.D.S.**
Category	**Business** (select from list)
E-mail	**HMDentistry@email.com**
Business Phone	**801-555-8102**
Home Phone	(leave blank)
Mobile Phone	**801-555-8921**
Zip/Postal Code	**84664**

b. Click **Open** in the first field of Dr. Machuca's record.

Open is a hyperlink to a different form in the database. The Contact Details form opens, displaying Dr. Machuca's information. More fields are available for you to use to store information. (Note that this form could also be opened from the Navigation Pane.)

c. Type the following additional information to the record:

Field Name	Value to Type
Street	56 West 200 North
City	Mapleton
State/Province	UT
Country/Region	USA
Notes	Available Tuesday - Friday 7 a.m. to 4 p.m.

d. Click the **Click to Map** hyperlink to view a map to Dr. Machuca's office.

Bing displays a map to the address in the record. You can get directions, locate nearby businesses, and use many other options.

TROUBLESHOOTING: You may be prompted to choose an application. Select any Web browser such as Microsoft Edge from the list.

e. Close the map. Click **Save and Close** in the top center of the form to close the Contact Details form.

The record is saved.

f. Click **New Contact** beneath the Contact List title bar.

The Contact Details form opens to a blank record.

g. Type the following information for a new record, pressing **Tab** to move between fields. Some fields will be blank.

Field Name	Value to Type
First Name	Rowan
Last Name	Westmoreland
Company	Phoenix Aesthetics
Job Title	Aesthetician
Mobile Phone	801-555-2221
Street	425 North Main Street
City	Springville
State/Province	UT
Zip/Postal Code	84663
Category	Personal
E-mail	Rowan55W5@email.com
Notes	Recommended by Michelle

h. Click **Save and Close**.

You explore the objects created by the template so that you understand the organization of the database. Refer to Figure 1.55 as you complete Step 3.

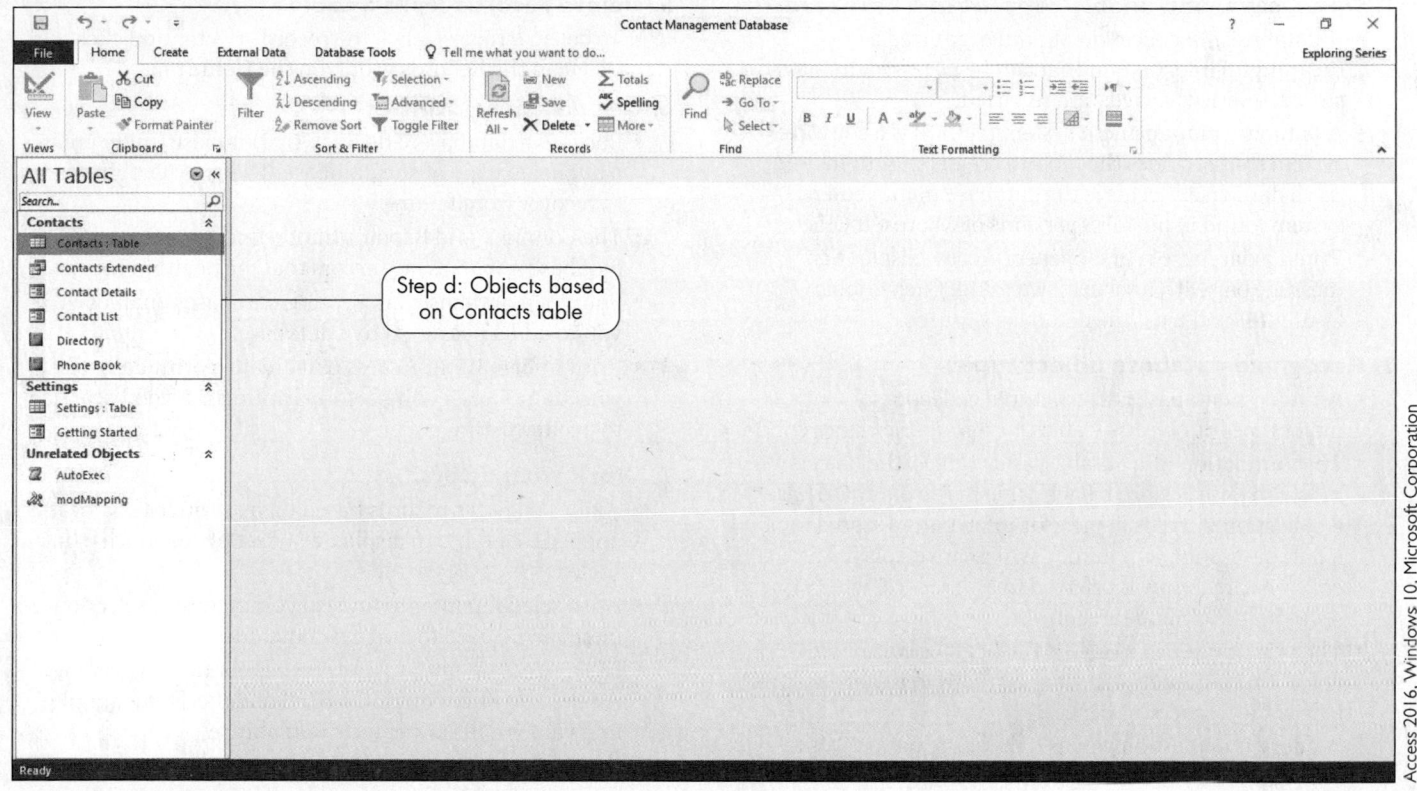

FIGURE 1.55 Tables and Related Views

a. Double-click the **Contacts table** in the Navigation Pane.

The information you entered using the Contact List form and the Contact Details form displays in the Contacts table.

b. Double-click the **Phone Book report** in the Navigation Pane.

The Phone Book report opens displaying the contact name and phone information organized by category.

c. Double-click the **Directory report** in the Navigation Pane.

The Directory report opens, displaying a full alphabetical contact list. The Directory report was designed to display more fields than the Phone Book, but it is not organized by category.

d. Click **All Access Objects** on the Navigation Pane and select **Tables and Related Views**.

You can now see the objects that are based on the Contacts table.

e. Right-click the **Directory report tab** and select **Close All**.

f. Close the database and exit Access. Based on your instructor's directions, submit the following:

a01h1Traders_LastFirst_*CurrentDate*

a01h2Traders_LastFirst

a01h3Contacts_LastFirst

Chapter Objectives Review

After reading this chapter, you have accomplished the following objectives:

1. Open, save, and enable content in a database.

- A database is a collection of data organized as meaningful information that can be accessed, managed, stored, queried, sorted, and reported.
- A database management system (DBMS) is a software system that provides the tools to create, maintain, and use a database. Access is the database management system found in business versions of Microsoft Office.
- When a database is first opened, Access displays a message bar with a security warning. Click Enable Content if you trust the database's source.

2. Recognize database object types.

- An Access database is a structured collection of four major types of objects—tables, forms, queries, and reports.
- The foundation of a database is its tables, the objects in which data is stored. Each table in the database has a collection of fields (a piece of information stored in a database, such as a name), which are displayed as columns. Each row is referred to as a record, which is a set of all fields about an entry in the table.
- The primary key in a table is the field (or combination of fields) that uniquely identifies a record in a table (such as a driver's license number).
- A query is a question you ask about the data in your database.
- A form enables simplified entry and modification of data.
- A report contains professional-looking formatted information from underlying tables or queries.
- Examine the Access interface: Objects are organized and listed in the Navigation Pane. Access also uses a Tabbed Documents interface in which each object that is open has its own tab.
- Explore table Datasheet view: Datasheet view is a grid containing fields (columns) and records (rows).
- Navigate through records: Navigation arrows enable you to move through records, with arrows for the first, previous, next, and last records, as well as one to add a new record.
- Explore table Design view: Design view gives you a detailed view of the table's structure and is used to create and modify a table's design by specifying the fields it will contain, the fields' data types, and their associated properties.
- Rename and describe tables: Tables can be renamed as necessary and a description can be added. The description gives the user more information about what an object does.

3. Modify data in table Datasheet view.

- Access works primarily from storage. Records can be added, modified, or deleted in the database, and as the information is entered, it is automatically saved. Undo cannot reverse edits made to multiple records.

4. Add records to a table.

- A pencil symbol displays in the record selector box to indicate when you are in editing mode. Moving to another record saves the changes.

5. Delete records from a table.

- To delete a record, click the record selector and click Delete in the Records group on the Home tab.

6. Use database utilities.

- Back up a database: The Back Up Database utility creates a duplicate copy of the database. This may enable users to recover from failure.
- The Compact and Repair utility reduces the size of a database and fixes any errors that may exist in the file.
- Encrypt a database: Encrypting databases enables you to add a password to a database.
- Print information: Access can create a print copy of your data. Previewing before printing is a good practice to avoid wasting paper.

7. Work with filters.

- A filter displays records based on a set of criteria that is applied to a table to display a subset of records in that table.
- Use a selection filter to find exact matches: A selection filter can be used to find exact matches.
- Use a selection filter to find records containing a value: A selection filter can find partial matches, for example, find values containing a certain phrase.
- Use filter by form: Filter By Form displays records based on multiple criteria and enables the user to apply logical operators and use comparison operators.

8. Perform sorts.

- Sort table data: Sorting changes the order of information, and information may be sorted by one or more fields.
- Data can be sorted ascending (low to high) or descending (high to low).

9. Create a database.

- Creating a blank desktop database: Creating a blank desktop database enables you to create a database specific to your requirements.
- Create a desktop database using a template: A template is a predefined database that includes professionally designed tables, forms, reports, and other objects that you can use to jumpstart the creation of your database.
- Add records to a downloaded desktop database: Once a database has been created, it can be used as any other database is.
- Explore the database objects in a downloaded database template: Once you create a database using a template, explore it and become familiar with the contents.
- Create a table using an application part: If you require a certain type of table (such as Contacts) you can add them using an application part.
- Create a Web app using a template: Creating a custom web app enables you to create a database that you can build and use and share with others through the Web.

Key Terms Matching

Match the key terms with their definitions. Write the key term letter by the appropriate numbered definition.

a. Application part
b. Database
c. Database Management System (DBMS)
d. Datasheet view
e. Design view
f. Field
g. Filter
h. Filter By Form
i. Form
j. Navigation Pane

k. Object
l. Primary key
m. Query
n. Record
o. Relationship
p. Report
q. Selection filter
r. Sort
s. Table
t. Template

1. _____ A filtering method that displays only records that match selected criteria. **p. 695**

2. _____ A filtering method that displays records based on multiple criteria. **p. 697**

3. _____ A main component that is created and used to make a database function, such as a table or form. **p. 667**

4. _____ A method of listing records in a specific sequence (such as alphabetically). **p. 699**

5. _____ A predefined database that includes professionally designed tables, forms, reports, and other objects. **p. 707**

6. _____ A question you ask about the data in your database. **p. 669**

7. _____ An Access interface element that organizes and lists database objects in a database. **p. 667**

8. _____ An Access object that simplifies entering, modifying, and deleting table data. **p. 669**

9. _____ A set of common Access components that can be added to an existing database. **p. 711**

10. _____ An object that contains professional-looking formatted information from underlying tables or queries. **p. 670**

11. _____ An object used to store data, organizing data into columns and rows. **p. 668**

12. _____ Complete set of all the fields about one person, place, event, or concept. **p. 668**

13. _____ The field (or combination of fields) that uniquely identifies each record in a table. **p. 668**

14. _____ View that enables you to create and modify a table design. **p. 675**

15. _____ A collection of data organized as meaningful information that can be accessed, managed, stored, queried, sorted, and reported. **p. 664**

16. _____ A connection between two tables using a common field. **p. 678**

17. _____ A grid that enables you to add, edit, and delete the records of a table. **p. 673**

18. _____ A piece of information stored in a table, such as a company name or city. **p. 668**

19. _____ A software system that provides the tools needed to create, maintain, and use a database. **p. 664**

20. _____ Enables you to specify conditions to display only those records that meet certain conditions. **p. 695**

Multiple Choice

1. Which of the following is an example of an Access object?

   (a) Database
   (b) Field
   (c) Form
   (d) Record

2. Where is data in a database stored?

   (a) Form
   (b) Query
   (c) Report
   (d) Table

3. You edit several records in an Access table. When should you execute the Save command?

   (a) Immediately after you edit a record
   (b) Once at the end of the session
   (c) Records are saved automatically; the save command is not required
   (d) When you close the table

4. Which of the following is *not* true of an Access database?

   (a) Each field has a data type that establishes the kind of data that can be entered.
   (b) Every record in a table has the same fields as every other record.
   (c) Every table in a database contains the same number of records as every other table.
   (d) A primary key uniquely identifies a record.

5. Which of the following is true regarding table views?

   (a) You can add, edit, and delete records using Design view.
   (b) Datasheet view shows a detailed view of the table design.
   (c) Datasheet view provides access to more field properties than Design view.
   (d) Changes made in Datasheet view are automatically saved when you move the insertion point to a different record.

6. Which of the following utilities is used to recover in the event of loss or damage?

   (a) Back Up Database
   (b) Compact and Repair Database
   (c) Database Splitter
   (d) Encrypt Database

7. Which of the following would be matched if you use a Selection filter's exact match option for the name Ann?

   (a) Ann, ANN, and ann
   (b) Danny, Ann, and Anny
   (c) Ann (but not ANN)
   (d) Both a and b

8. Which of the following conditions is available through a Selection filter?

   (a) Equal condition
   (b) Delete condition
   (c) AND condition
   (d) OR condition

9. All of the following statements are true about creating a database *except*:

   (a) Creating a custom web app requires that you use a server (such as SharePoint).
   (b) When creating a blank desktop database, Access opens to a blank table in Datasheet view.
   (c) Using a template to create a database saves time because it includes predefined objects.
   (d) The objects provided in a template cannot be modified.

10. To add a predefined table to an existing database, you should use which of the following?

    (a) Application part
    (b) Blank desktop database
    (c) Custom web app
    (d) Database template

Practice Exercises

1 Replacement Parts

As a recent hire at Replacement Parts, you are tasked with performing updates to the customer database. You have been asked to open the company's database, save it with a new name, and then modify, add, and delete records. You will then back up the database, apply filters and sorts, and use an application part to add a new table that will be used to track customer shipping and receiving complaints. Refer to Figure 1.56 as you complete the exercise.

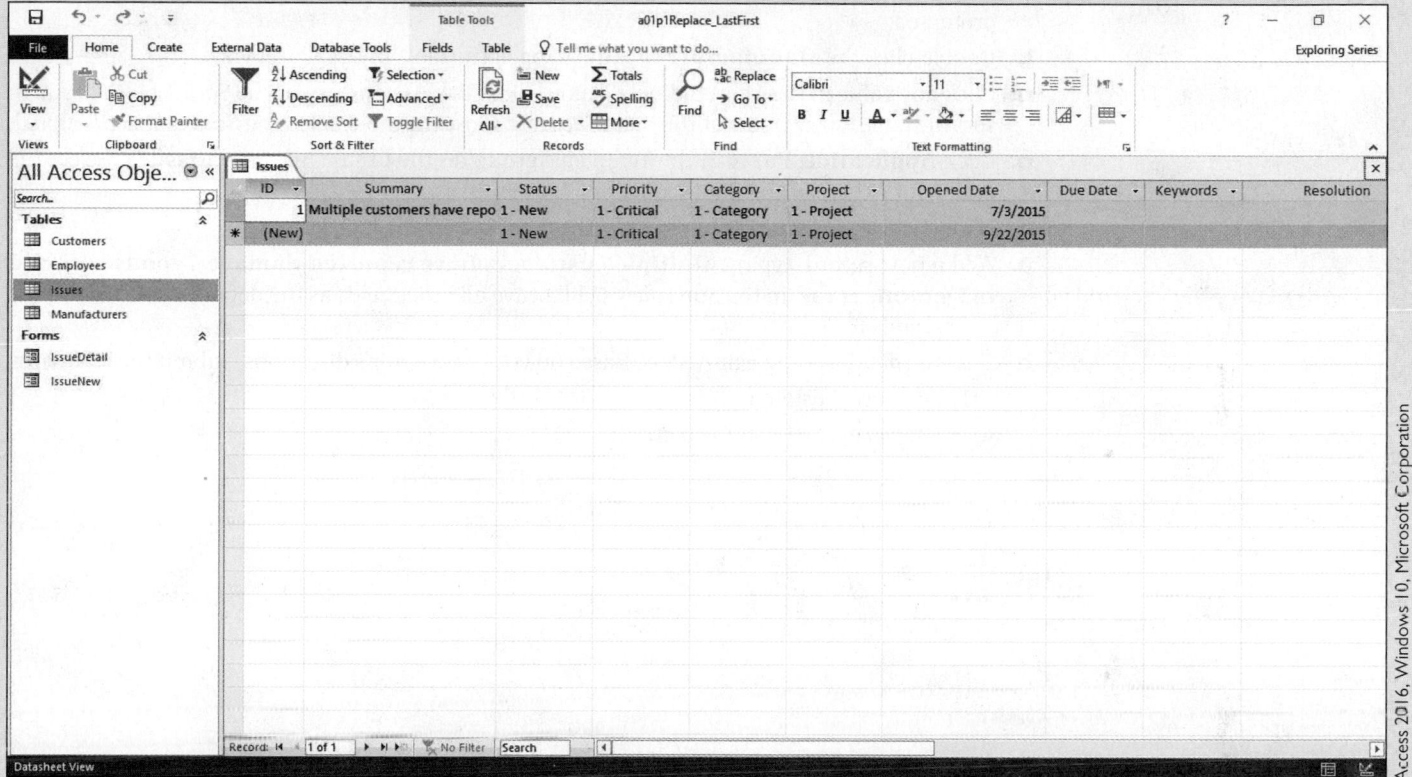

FIGURE 1.56 Issues Table Added to Replacement Parts Database

a. Open the *a01p1Replace* file. Save the database as **a01p1Replace_LastFirst**. Click **Enable Content** on the message bar.

b. Double-click the **Manufacturers table** to open the table in Datasheet view. Locate record 800552 (Haas). Change the name to **Haas International** and the CountyOfOrigin to **Austria**.

c. Type the following new records:

MfgID	ManufacturerName	CountryOfOrigin	EmployeeID
801411	Bolshoy Fine China	Russia	817080
801422	Tejada and Sons	Dominican Republic	816680
801433	Lubitz UK	England	817580

d. Delete record **800661** (John Bradshaw).

e. Close the Manufacturers table.

f. Click the **File tab**, click **Save As**, and then double-click **Back Up Database**. Accept the default backup file name and click **Save**.

g. Double-click the **Customers table** to open the table in Datasheet view.

h. Click the **State field** for the first record (Diego Martinez). Click **Selection** in the Sort & Filter group, and then click **Equals "OR"** to display the two customers in Oregon. Close the table, selecting **Save** when prompted.

i. Double-click the **Employees table** to open the table in Datasheet view.

j. Click the **plus sign** ⊞ next to Alfonso Torres. Notice he is assigned as the representative for the manufacturer Antarah.

This information is available due to the relationship already created in the database between Employees and Manufacturers.

k. Click **Advanced** in the Sort & Filter group on the Home tab, and select **Filter By Form.** Click in the Salary field. Type **>60000** and click **Toggle Filter** in the Sort & Filter group on the Home tab to apply the filter. Six employees are displayed. Close the table, selecting **Save** when prompted.

l. Double-click the **Manufacturers table** to open the table in Datasheet view.

m. Click any value in the Manufacturer Name field. Click **Ascending** in the Sort & Filter group to sort the table by the name of the manufacturer. Close the table, selecting **Save** when prompted.

n. Click **Application Parts** in the Templates group on the Create tab. Select **Issues.** Select the option for "There is no relationship." Click **Create.**

o. Double-click the **Issues table** to open the table in Datasheet view.

p. Add a new record, typing **Multiple customers have reported damaged goods received in Denton, Texas.** in the Summary field. Leave all other fields as the default values. Compare your results to Figure 1.56.

q. Close the database and exit Access. Based on your instructor's directions, submit the following:

a01p1Replace_LastFirst

a01p1Replace_LastFirst_*CurrentDate*

2 Custom Coffee

The Custom Coffee Company provides coffee, tea, and snacks to offices in Miami. Custom Coffee also provides and maintains the equipment for brewing the beverages. To improve customer service, the owner recently had an Access database created to keep track of customers, orders, and products. This database will replace the Excel spreadsheets currently maintained by the office manager. The company hired you to verify and input all the Excel data into the Access database. Refer to Figure 1.57 as you complete the exercise.

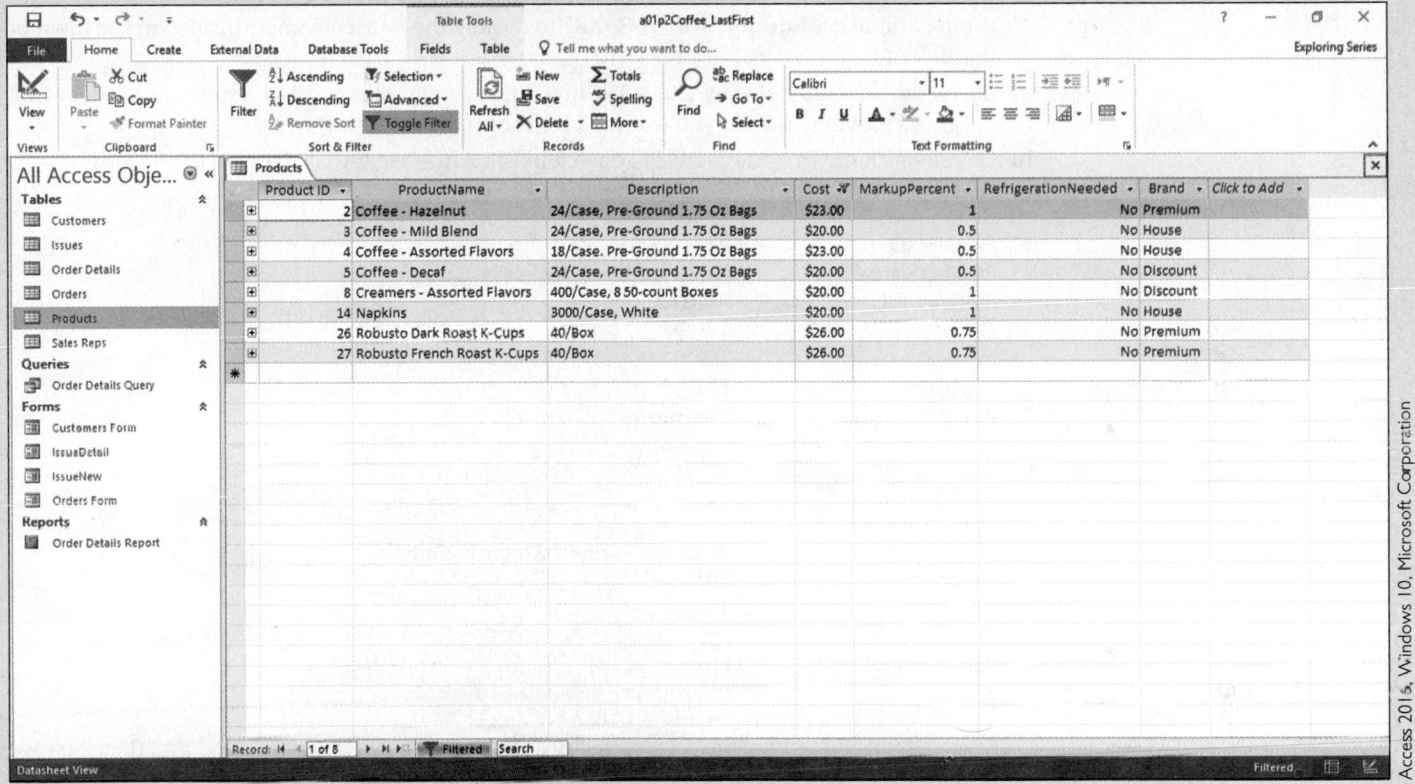

FIGURE 1.57 Filtered Products Table

a. Open the *a01p2Coffee* file and save the database as **a01p2Coffee_LastFirst**. Click **Enable Content** on the message bar.

b. Click the **Database Tools tab** and click **Relationships** in the Relationships group. Review the table relationships. Notice the join line between the Customers and Orders tables.

c. Click **Close** in the Relationships group.

d. Double-click the **Sales Reps table** to open it in Datasheet view. For rep number 2, replace **YourFirstName** and **YourLastName** with your first and last names. For example, as the Access author, I would type *Eric* in place of YourFirstName and *Cameron* in place of YourLastName. Close the table by clicking **Close** on the right side of the Sales Reps window.

e. Double-click the **Customers table** to open it in Datasheet view. Click **New** in the Records group. Add a new record by typing the following information; press **Tab** after each field:

Customer Name:	**Bavaro Driving School**
Contact:	**Ricky Watters**
Address1:	**1 Clausen Way**
Address2:	**Floor 2**
City:	**South Bend**

State:	**IN**
Zip Code:	**46614**
Phone:	**(857) 519-6661**
Credit Rating:	**A**
Sales Rep ID:	**2**

Notice the pencil symbol in the record selector for the new row. This symbol indicates the new record has not been saved. Press **Tab**. The pencil symbol disappears, and the new customer is automatically saved to the table.

f. Click the **City field** for the second record (South Bend). Click **Selection** in the Sort & Filter group, and select **Equals "South Bend"** to display the four customers located in the town of South Bend.

g. Save and close the table by clicking **Close** on the right side of the Customers window, and clicking **Yes** when asked if you want to save the changes.

h. Double-click the **Products** table to open it in Datasheet view. Click **New** in the Records group. Add a new record by typing the following information:

Product ID:	**26**
ProductName:	**Robusto Dark Roast K-Cups**
Description:	**40/Box**
Cost:	**26**
MarkupPercent:	**.75**
RefrigerationNeeded	**No**
Brand	**Premium**

i. Add a second product using the following information:

Product ID:	**27**
ProductName:	**Robusto French Roast K-Cups**
Description:	**40/Box**
Cost:	**26**
MarkupPercent:	**.75**
RefrigerationNeeded	**No**
Brand	**Premium**

j. Click **Advanced** in the Sort & Filter group and select **Filter By Form**. Type **>=20** in the Cost field and click **Toggle Filter** in the Sort & Filter group.

All products costing $20 or more (there will be 8) display. See Figure 1.57.

k. Save and close the table by clicking **Close** on the right side of the Products window, and clicking Yes when asked if you want to save the changes.

l. Click the **File tab**, click **Save As**, and then double-click **Back Up Database**. Accept the default backup file name and click **Save.**

m. Click **Application Parts** in the Templates group of the Create tab. Select **Issues**. Click **Next** to accept the default relationship. Select **CustomerName** as the Field from 'Customers', select **Sort Ascending** from Sort this field, and then type **Customer** as the name for the lookup column. Click Create.

n. Double-click the **Issues table** to open it in Datasheet view.

o. Select **Advantage Sales** for the Customer and type **Customer reports hazelnut coffee delivered instead of decaf.** in the Summary field. Leave all other fields as the default values.

p. Close the database and exit Access. Based on your instructor's directions, submit the following:

a01p2Coffee_LastFirst

a01p2Coffee_LastFirst_*CurrentDate*

FROM SCRATCH You and two friends from your gym have decided to use Access to help you reach your weight goals. You decide to use the Access Nutrition template to help you get organized. Refer to Figure 1.58 as you complete this exercise.

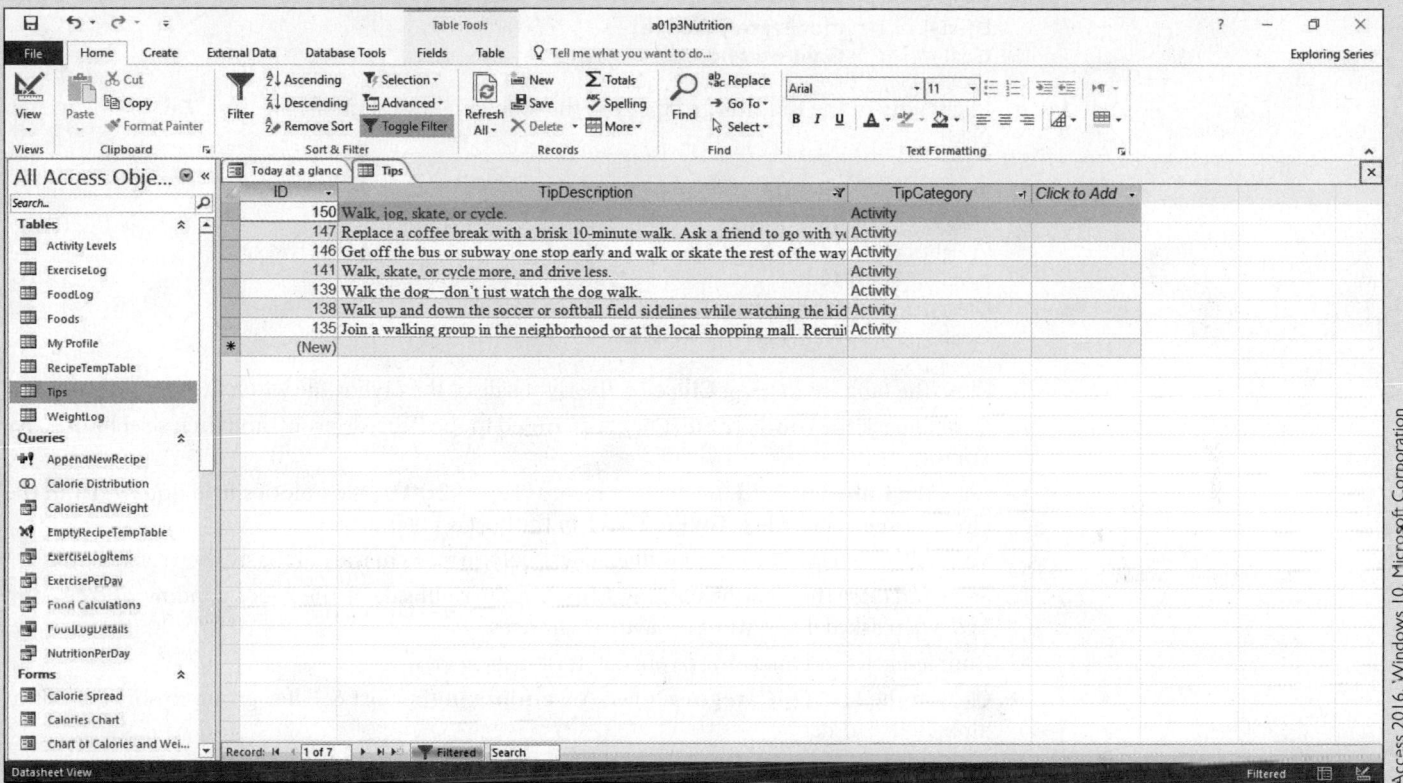

FIGURE 1.58 Filtered Tips Table

a. Open Access and click the **Desktop Nutrition tracking** template in Backstage view.

b. Type **a01p3Nutrition_LastFirst** in the File name box. Click **Browse**. Navigate to the location where you are saving your files in the File New Database dialog box, click **OK** to close the dialog box, and then click **Create** to create the new database.

c. Click **Enable Content** on the message bar. Double-click the **My Profile** table in the Navigation Pane to open it in Datasheet view.

d. Delete the existing record.

e. Type the following information in as a new record, pressing **Tab** between each field:

Sex:	**Male**
Height:	**64**
Weight:	**190**
Age:	**48**
Lifestyle:	**Lightly Active**
Goal:	**Lose weight**

f. Click **New** in the Records group. Type the following information, pressing **Tab** between each field:

Sex:	**Male**
Height:	**69**
Weight:	**140**
Age:	**45**
Lifestyle:	**Moderately Active**
Goal:	**Gain weight**

g. Click **New** in the Records group. Type the following information, pressing **Tab** between each field:

Sex:	**Female**
Height:	**66**
Weight:	**140**
Age:	**40**
Lifestyle:	**Moderately Active**
Goal:	**Maintain my weight**

h. Close the table by clicking **Close** on the right side of the My Profile window.

i. Double-click the **Foods table**. Click **Advanced** in the Records group and then select **Filter By Form**.

j. Click the **Calories field** for the first record. Type **<200** in the Calories field and **>=15** in the Fiber [grams] field. Click **Toggle Filter** in the Sort & Filter group.

You will have a list of all high = fiber, low = calorie foods in the database (there are three).

k. Save and close the table by clicking **Close** on the right side of the Foods window, and clicking **Yes** when asked if you want to save the changes.

l. Double-click the **Tips table** to open it in Datasheet view.

m. Click in the first **TipCategory**. Click **Ascending** in the Sort & Filter group to sort the tips in alphabetical order.

n. Highlight the word **Walk** in the fifth record (ID #138). Make sure you do not highlight the space after the word Walk when you highlight. Click **Selection** in the Sort & Filter group, and select **Contains "Walk"**.

Seven tips appear that contain the word walk. See Figure 1.58.

o. Save and close the table by clicking **Close** on the right side of the Tips window, and clicking **Yes** when asked if you want to save the changes.

p. Click the **File tab**, click **Save As**, and then double-click **Back Up Database**. Use the default backup file name.

q. Close the database and exit Access. Based on your instructor's directions, submit the following:

a01p3Nutrition_LastFirst

a01p3Nutrition _LastFirst_*CurrentDate*

Mid-Level Exercises

1 Sunshine Mental Health Services

Sunshine Mental Health Services provides counseling and medication services. They have recently expanded their database to include patients in addition to the staff. You were hired to replace their former Information Technology support staff member. You will work to update the data in the database, familiarize yourself with the table relationships, filter and sort a table, and add a table to keep track of user accounts.

a. Open the *a01m1Sunshine* file and save the database as **a01m1Sunshine_LastFirst**. Click **Enable Content** on the Security Warning message bar.

b. Open the **Staff table** in Datasheet view.

c. Locate the record for Kovit Ang (StaffID 80073). Replace his Address with **11 Market Street**, replace his City with **Harrison**, and his ZIPCode with **04040**. Leave all other fields with their current values.

d. Add yourself as a new staff member. Type a StaffID of **99999** and type your name in the FullName field. Type **1 Clinton Terrace** for your Address, **Harrison** as your City, **ME** as your State, and **04040** as your ZIP. Type a JobCode of **300**, a Salary of **48500**, and a 401k contribution of **0.02**. Click the box in the Active field so a check box appears in the box.

e. Delete record **80399** (Stan Marsh).

f. Sort the table by Salary in descending order. Save and close the table.

g. Click **Relationships** in the Relationships group on the Database Tools tab and notice the relationship between the Position table and the Staff table, and the relationship between the Staff table and Patients table. Each position has staff associated with it, and staff members have patients associated with them. Close the Relationships window.

h. Rename the **Pos table** to **Position**. Add a description to the table stating **This table contains a list of all available job titles at the company**. Click **OK**.

i. Open the **Position table** in Datasheet view. Click the **plus sign** next to JobCode 100 (Social Worker). Notice seven social workers are employed by the company. Click the **plus sign** next to JobCode 300 (IT Support). Only your name should appear. Close the table.

j. Open the **Patients table** in Datasheet view. Use a Selection filter to show all patients associated with StaffID **80073**. Save and close the table.

k. Open the **Staff table** in Datasheet view. Use Filter By Form to display all staff members who earn a salary of more than **80000**. Toggle the filter to verify the results. Save and close the table.

l. Back up the database. Accept the default file name.

m. Add a **Users application part** to the database. Change the relationship so there is One 'Staff' to many 'Users' by clicking the arrow next to Patients and selecting **Staff**. Click **Next**. Select the **FullName** field from 'Staff', choose the **Sort Ascending** option, and name the lookup column **User**. Click **Create**.

n. Open the **Users table** in Datasheet view.

o. Select **Adolfo Ortiz** in the User field. Type **aortiz@sunshinementalhealth.org** for Email and **aortiz** for Login. Leave the FullName blank. Close the table.

DISCOVER

p. Create a form based on the Patients table using the Form button in the Forms group of the Create tab. Save the form as **Patient Data Entry**.

q. Switch to Form view of the form. Delete the phone number for PatientID **1** (Minoru Kobayashi). Close the form.

r. Close the database and exit Access. Based on your instructor's directions, submit the following:
a01m1Sunshine_LastFirst
a01m1Sunshine_LastFirst_*CurrentDate*

2 National Conference

ANALYSIS CASE

The Association of Higher Education will host its National Conference on your campus next year. To facilitate the conference, the Information Technology department has replaced last year's Excel spreadsheets with an Access database containing information on the rooms, speakers, and sessions. Your assignment is to create a room itinerary that will list all of the sessions, dates, and times for each room. The list will be posted on the door of each room for the duration of the conference.

a. Open the *a01m2NatConf* file and save the database as **a01m2NatConf_LastFirst**. Click **Enable Content** on the Security Warning message bar.

b. Open **Relationships**.

c. Review the objects and relationships in the database. Notice that there is a relationship between Speakers and SessionSpeaker. Close the relationships.

d. Open the **SessionSpeaker table**. Scroll to the first blank record at the bottom of the table and type a new record using SpeakerID **99** and SessionID **09**. (Note: Speaker 99 does not exist.) How does Access respond? Press **Escape** twice to cancel your change.

e. Open the **Speakers table**. Replace *YourFirstName* with your first name and *YourLastName* with your last name. Close the Speakers table.

f. Open the **Sessions table** and use a Selection filter to identify the sessions that take place in room 101.

g. Sort the filtered results in ascending order by the **SessionTitle** field. Save and close the table.

h. Open the **Master List - Sessions and Speakers** report. Right-click the **Master List - Sessions and Speakers** tab and select **Report View**.

DISCOVER

i. Apply a filter that limits the report to sessions in **Room 101** only. The process will be similar to applying a filter to a table.

j. View the report in Print Preview. Close Print Preview and close the report.

k. Back up the database. Use the default backup file name.

 l. Open the *a01m2Analysis* document in Word and save as **a01m2Analysis_LastFirst**. Use the database objects you created to answer the questions. Save and close the document.

m. Close the database and exit Access. Based on your instructor's directions, submit the following:

   a01m2NatConf_LastFirst
   a01m2NatConf_LastFirst_*CurrentDate*
   a01m2Analysis_LastFirst

3 New Castle County Technical Services

RUNNING CASE

New Castle County Technical Services (NCCTS) provides technical support for a number of companies in the greater New Castle County, Delaware, area. They are working to move their record keeping to an Access database. You will add, update, and delete some records, add filters, and create a backup.

This project is a running case. You will use the same database file across Chapters 1 through 4.

a. Open the database *a01m3NCCTS* and save the database as **a01m3NCCTS_LastFirst**. Click **Enable Content** on the Security Warning message bar.

b. Open the **Call Types table** in Datasheet view. Type the following rates for the HourlyRate field and then close the table:

Description	HourlyRate
Hardware Support	30
Software Support	25
Network Troubleshooting	40
Network Installation	40
Training	50

Description	HourlyRate
Security Camera Maintenance	40
Virus Removal	25
Disaster Recovery	60
VoIP Service	45
Other	35

c. Open the **Reps table** in Datasheet view. Add a new record, filling in the value **8** for the RepID field, your last name as the rep's last name, and your first name as the rep's first name.

d. Sort the Reps table by **LastName** in ascending order. Close the table.

e. Open the **Customers table** in Datasheet view. Locate the record for **Edwin VanCleef** (PC030). Delete the entire record.

f. Click in the **City field** for SVC Pharmacy. Use the Selection filter to only show customers who are located in the city of **Newark**. Save and close the table.

g. Open the **Calls table** in Datasheet view. Use **Filter By Form** to filter the HoursLogged field so only calls with 10 or more hours logged on the call (**>=10**) are displayed. Save and close the table.

h. Back up the database, using the default name.

i. Close the database and exit Access. Based on your instructor's directions, submit the following:
a01m3NCCTS_LastFirst
a01m3NCCTS_LastFirst_*CurrentDate*

Beyond the Classroom

Creating a Student Database

GENERAL CASE ✓

FROM SCRATCH

Create a new blank desktop database, name the file **a01b1Students_LastFirst**, and then save the database in the location where you are saving your files. Create a new table using the Contacts application part. Delete the Company, JobTitle, BusinessPhone, HomePhone, FaxNumber, Country/Region, WebPage, Attachments, ContactName, and FileAs fields from the Company table. Save the table, then switch to Datasheet view. Enter the information about at least five students, fictional or real, including your own information. Enter their major in the Notes field. Sort the table by last name in ascending order. Create a filter to display students with your major. Delete all queries, forms, and reports. Close the database and exit Access. Based on your instructor's directions, submit a01b1Students_LastFirst.

Lugo Web Hosting

DISASTER RECOVERY ✚

Your Access database has become corrupted and you are in the process of restoring it from a backup from two weeks ago. In the last two weeks, there have been only a few changes. All users who previously had a 900 GB quota have had their quotas increased to 1 TB. In addition, all users who were previously on the server named Aerelon have been moved to another server, Caprica. You have determined you can use filters to help fix the data in the Users table. Open the *a01b2Lugo_Backup* file and save the database as **a01b2Lugo_LastFirst**. Apply filters to show users who meet the conditions above and then manually change the data for each user. Sort the table by the server in ascending order. Close the database and exit Access. Based on your instructor's directions, submit a01b2Lugo_LastFirst.

Capstone Exercise

You are employed as a technical supervisor at a chain of bookstores. One of the store managers has expressed confusion about Access. You have offered to train her on the basics of Access. To avoid mistakes in the main database, you will save the file with a new name. You will then train her on the basics of the database system, including making data modifications, sorting and filtering, adding a table using an application part, and creating a backup.

Modify Data in a Table

You will open an original database file and save the database with a new name. You will then demonstrate adding, updating, and deleting information.

a. Open the *a01c1Books* file and save the database as **a01c1Books_LastFirst**.

b. Open the **Publishers table** in Datasheet view. Notice that some of the publisher city and state information is missing. Update the database with the information below and close the table.

PubID	PubName	PubCity	PubState
DC	DC Comics	New York	NY
SM	St. Martin	Boston	MA
TB	Triumph Books	Chicago	IL
TL	Time Life	Pueblo	CO

c. Change the PubCity for Pearson to **Hoboken**.

d. Close the Publishers table.

e. Open the **Author table** in Datasheet view.

f. Navigate to the last record (Author ID of XXXX01) and replace **YourFirstName** with your first name and **YourLastName** with your last name. Close the table.

g. Open the **Author table** again and notice the changes you made have been stored.

h. Click the **plus sign** next to your name. Notice the book Social Media: A Student's View is listed. Close the table again.

i. Open the **Books table** in Datasheet view. Notice the book with ISBN 9780809400775 (American Cooking: The Northwest) has no items in stock. Delete this record.

j. Close the table.

Sort a Table and Apply a Selection Filter

You will sort the publisher's table by name and then apply a filter to display only publishers located in New York.

a. Open the **Publishers table** in Datasheet view. Notice Time Life appears after Triumph Books. This is because the table is sorted by the PubID field.

b. Click in any record in the PubName field and sort the field in ascending order.

c. Apply a Selection filter to display only publishers with a PubCity equal to **New York**.

d. Close the table and save the changes.

Use Filter By Form

You will obtain a list of all books with more than 50 units in stock. This will help the management decide on what books to put on sale. You will use Filter By Form to accomplish this. You will also demonstrate how filters are saved.

a. Open the **Books table** in Datasheet view.

b. Use Filter By Form to display books with more than **50** units in stock. Save and close the table.

c. Open the **Books table** in Datasheet view. Click **Toggle Filter** in the Sort & Filter group to demonstrate that the filter is saved.

Back Up a Database and Add an Application Part

You will demonstrate adding an application part to the manager to show how tables are created. You will first back the database up to reinforce the importance of backing up the data.

a. Create a backup copy of your database, accepting the default file name.

b. Add a Comments application part, selecting the option **One 'Books' to many 'Comments'**. Select the **Title field** for the Field from Books and **Sort Ascending** for Sort this field. Name the lookup column **Book**.

c. Open the **Comments table** in Datasheet view. Add a new comment. Select **Social Media: A Student's View** for the Book. Use the current date and add **A fun and insightful book!** for the Comment field.

d. Close the database and exit Access. Based on your instructor's directions, submit the following:

a01c1Books_LastFirst

a01c1Books_LastFirst_*CurrentDate*

Tables and Queries in Relational Databases

CASE STUDY | Bank Audit

During a year-end review, a bank auditor uncovers mishandled funds at Commonwealth Federal Bank in Wilmington, Delaware. In order to analyze the data in more detail, the auditor asks you to create an Access database so he can review the affected customers, the compromised accounts, and the branches involved.

As you begin, you realize that some of the data are contained in external Excel and Access files that you decide to import directly into the new database. Importing from Excel and Access is fairly common, and will help to avoid errors that are associated with data entry. Once the data have been imported, you will use queries to determine exactly which records are relevant to the investigation.

This chapter introduces the Bank database case study to present the basic principles of table and query design. Once the new database is created and all the data are entered, you will help the auditor answer questions by creating and running queries. The value of that information depends entirely on the quality of the underlying data—the tables.

CHAPTER 2

Designing Databases and Extracting Data

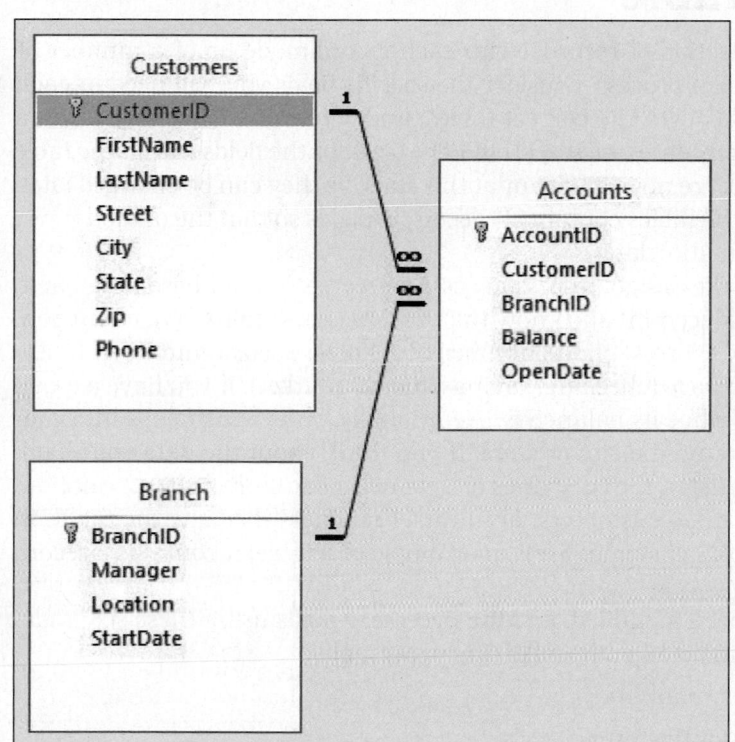

FIGURE 2.1 Bank Audit Database

The "Number of Customer Accounts" table shows:

Customer ID	Number of Accounts
30001	5
30002	1
30003	4
30004	4
30005	4
30006	1
30007	2
30009	2
30010	2
30011	3

CASE STUDY | Bank Audit

Starting Files	File to be Submitted
Blank desktop database a02h2Accounts a02h2Customers	a02h4Bank_LastFirst

Table Design, Creation, and Modification

Good database design begins with the tables. Tables provide the framework for all of the activities you perform in a database. If the framework is poorly designed, the database will not function as expected. Whether you are experienced in designing tables or are a new database designer, the process should not be done haphazardly. You should follow a systematic approach when creating tables for a database.

In this section, you will learn the essentials of good table design. After developing and analyzing the table design on paper, you will implement that design in Access. While you learned to create tables in the previous chapter, in this chapter you will learn to refine them by changing the properties of various fields.

Designing a Table

Recall that a table is a collection of records, with each record made up of a number of fields. During the table design process, consider the specific fields you will need in each table; list the proposed fields with the correct tables, and determine what type of data each field will store (numbers, dates, pictures, etc.) The order of the fields within the table and the specific field names are not significant at this stage as they can be changed later. What is important is that the tables contain all necessary fields so that the database can produce the required information later.

For example, consider the design process necessary to create a database for a bank. Most likely you have a bank account and know that the bank maintains data about you. Your bank has your name, address, phone number, and Social Security number. It also knows which accounts you have (checking, savings, money market), if you have a credit card with that bank, and what its balance is. Additionally, your bank keeps information about its branches around the city or state. If you think about the data your bank maintains, you can make a list of the categories of data needed to store that information. These categories for the bank—customers, accounts, branches—become the tables in the bank's database. A bank's customer list is an example of a table; it contains a record for each bank customer.

After the tables have been identified, add the necessary fields using these six guidelines, which are discussed in detail in the following paragraphs:

- Include the necessary data.
- Design for now and for the future.
- Store data in their smallest parts.
- Determine primary keys.
- Link tables using common fields.
- Design to accommodate calculations.

Figure 2.2 shows a customer table and two other tables found in a sample Bank database. It also lists fields that would be needed in each table.

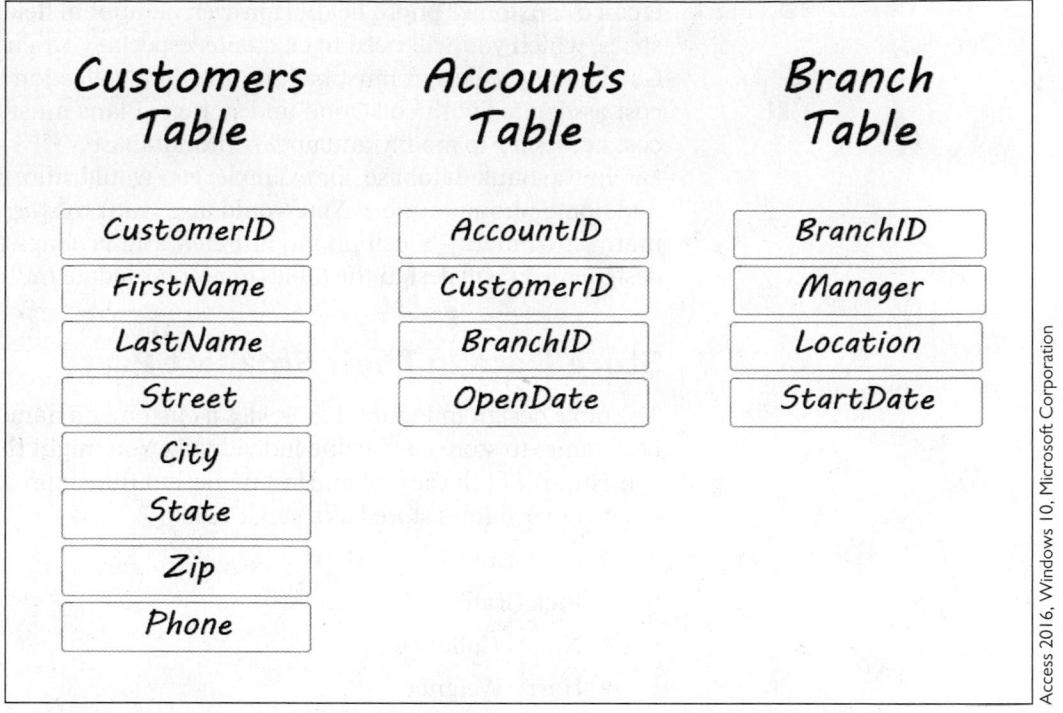

FIGURE 2.2 Rough Draft of Tables and Fields in a Sample Bank Database

Include Necessary Data

A good way to determine what data are necessary in tables is to consider the output you will need from your database. You will probably need to create professional-looking reports for others, so begin by creating a rough draft of the reports you will need. Then design tables that contain the fields necessary to create those reports. In other words, ask yourself what information will be expected from the database (output) and determine the data required (input) to produce that information. Consider, for example, the tables and fields in Figure 2.2. Is there required information that could not be generated from those tables?

- You will be able to determine how long a customer has banked with the branch because the date he or she opened the account is stored in the Accounts table, which will connect to the Customers and Branch tables.

- You will be able to determine which branch a customer uses because the Accounts table includes both the CustomerID and the BranchID. The Accounts table will eventually connect to both the Customers and Branch tables, making it possible to gather this information.

- You will not be able to generate the monthly bank statement. In order to generate a customer bank statement (showing all deposits and withdrawals for the month), you would need to add an additional table—to track activity for each account.

- You will not be able to email a customer because the Customers table does not contain an email field at this time.

If you discover a missing field, such as the email field, you can add it during the initial design process or later.

Design for Now and for the Future

As the information requirements of an organization evolve over time, the database systems that hold the data must change as well. When designing a database, try to anticipate the future needs of the system and build in the flexibility to satisfy those demands. For example, you may also decide to create additional fields for future use (such as an email or customer photo field). However, additional fields will also require more storage space, which you will need to calculate, especially when working with larger databases. Good database design must balance the data collection needs of the company with the cost associated with collection and storage. Plans must also include the frequency and cost necessary to modify and update the database.

In the Bank database, for example, you would store each customer's name, address, and home phone number. You would also want to store additional phone numbers for many customers—a cell phone number, and perhaps a work number. As a database designer, you will design the tables to accommodate multiple entries for similar data.

Store Data in Their Smallest Parts

The table design in Figure 2.2 divides a customer's name into two fields (FirstName and LastName) to store each value individually. You might think it easier to use a single field consisting of both the first and last name, but that approach is too limiting. Consider a list of customer names stored as a single field:

- Sue Grater
- Rick Grater
- Nancy Gallagher
- Harry Weigner
- Barb Shank
- Pete Shank

The first problem in this approach is the lack of flexibility: You could not easily create a salutation for a letter using the form *Dear Sue* or *Dear Ms. Gallagher* because the first and last names are not accessible individually.

A second difficulty is that the list of customers cannot be easily displayed in alphabetical order by last name because the last name begins in the middle of the field. The most common way to sort names is by the last name, which you can do more efficiently if the last name is stored as a separate field.

Think of how an address might be used. The city, state, and postal code should always be stored as separate fields. You may need to select records from a particular state or postal code, which will be easier if you store the data as separate fields.

Determine Primary Keys

When designing your database tables, it is important to determine the primary key, the field that will uniquely identify each record in a table. For example, in Figure 2.2, the CustomerID field will uniquely identify each customer in the database.

Plan for Common Fields Between Tables

As you create the tables and fields for the database, keep in mind that some tables will be joined in relationships using common fields. Creating relationships will help you to extract data from more than one table when creating queries, forms, and reports. For example, you will be able to determine which customers have which accounts by joining the Customers and Accounts tables. For now, you should name the common fields the same (although that is not a firm requirement in Access). For example, CustomerID in the Customers table will join to the CustomerID field in the Accounts table. Draw a line between common fields to indicate the joins, as shown in Figure 2.3. These join lines will be created in Access when you learn to create table relationships later in the chapter.

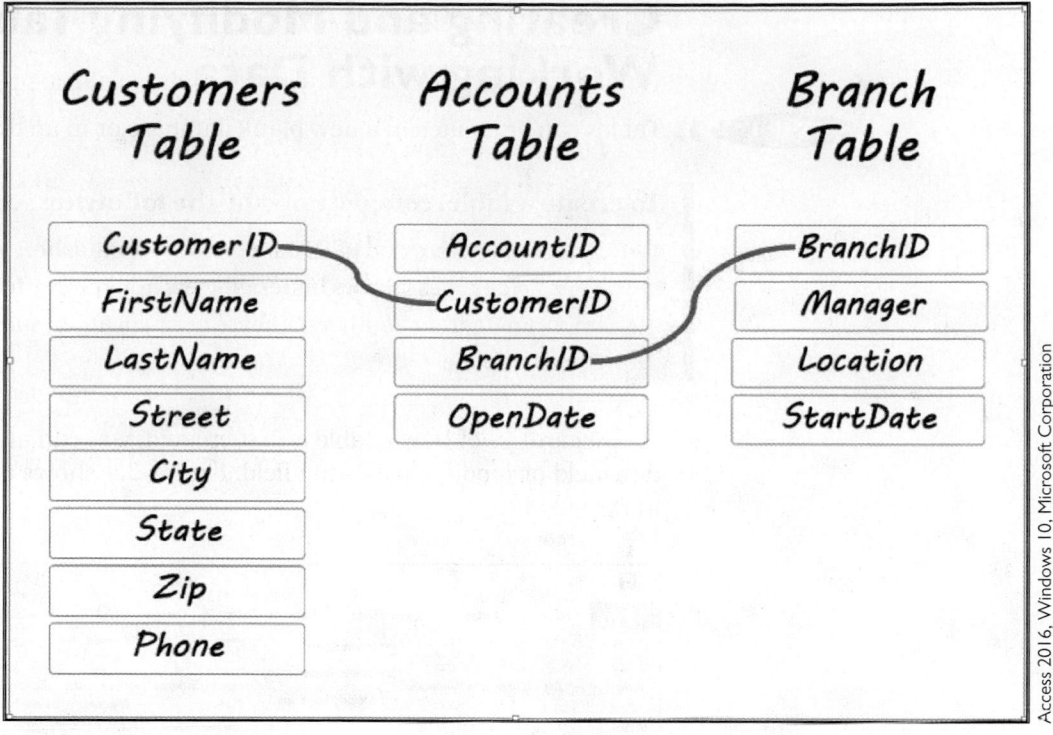

FIGURE 2.3 Determine Relationships Using Common Fields

Avoid **data redundancy**, which is the unnecessary storing of duplicate data in two or more tables. Having redundant or duplicate data in multiple tables can lead to serious errors. Suppose the customer address data were stored in both the Customers and Accounts tables. If a customer moved to a new address, it is possible that the address would be updated in only one of the two tables. The result would be inconsistent and unreliable information. Depending on which table you would use to check an address, either the new or the old one might be given to someone requesting the information. Storing the address in only one table is more reliable; if it changes, it only needs to be updated one time (in the Customers table) and can be referenced again and again from that table.

TIP: ADD CALCULATED FIELDS TO A TABLE

A calculated field produces a value from an expression or function that references one or more existing fields. Access enables you to store calculated fields in a table using the calculated data type, and to include those fields in queries, forms, and reports. However, many Access users prefer to create calculated fields in their query designs rather than in the tables themselves.

Design to Accommodate Calculations

Calculated fields are frequently created in database objects with numeric data, such as a monthly interest field that multiplies the balance in a customer's account by 1% each month (Balance*.01). You can also create calculated fields using date/time data. For example, if you want to store the length of time a customer has had an account, you can create a calculated field that subtracts the opening date from today's date. The result will be the number of days each customer has been an account holder.

A person's age is another example of a calculated field using date arithmetic—the date of birth is subtracted from today's date and the result is divided by 365 (or 365.25 to account for leap years). It might seem easier to store a person's age as a number rather than the birth date and avoid the calculated field, but that would be a mistake because age changes over time and the field would need to be updated each time it changes. You can use date arithmetic to subtract one date from another to find out the number of days, months, or years that have elapsed between them.

Creating and Modifying Tables and Working with Data

STEP 1 ›› Tables can be created in a new blank database or in an existing database.

> **To create a table, complete one of the following steps:**
> - Enter field names and table data directly in Datasheet view.
> - Type field names in rows in Design view and then enter the data in Datasheet view.
> - Import data from another database or application, such as Excel.
> - Use a template.

Regardless of how a table is first created, you can always modify it later to include a new field or modify an existing field. Figure 2.4 shows a table created by entering fields in Design view.

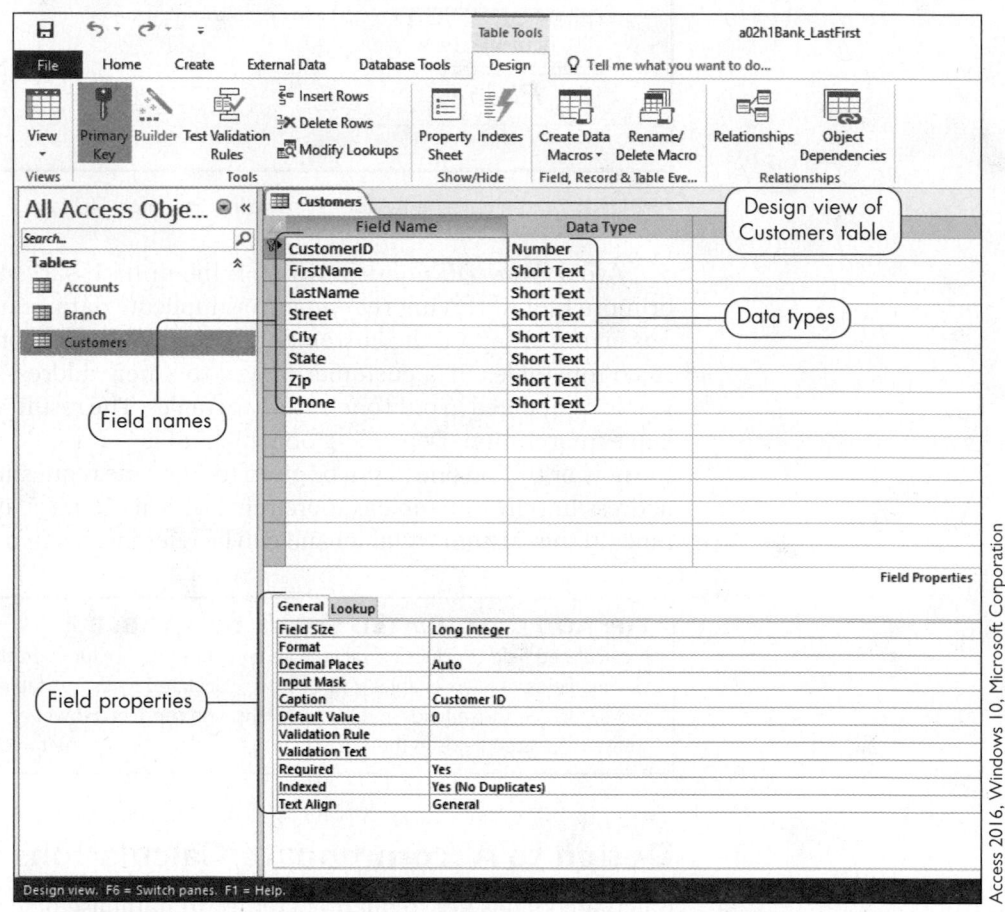

FIGURE 2.4 Customers Table Created in Design View

When you add a new field to a table, the field must be given an appropriate name to identify the data it holds. The field name should be descriptive of the data and can be up to 64 characters in length, including letters, numbers, and spaces. Field names cannot begin with a leading blank space. Database developers sometimes use Pascal Case notation for field names. Instead of spaces in multiword field names, you can use uppercase letters to distinguish the first letter of each new word, for example, ProductCost or LastName (sometimes developers use Camel Case, which is similar to Pascal Case, where the first letter of the first word is lowercase). It is sometimes preferable to avoid spaces in field names, because spaces can cause naming conflicts with other applications that may use these fields, such as Microsoft Visual Basic for Applications.

Fields can be added, deleted, or renamed either in Design view or Datasheet view. To delete a field in Datasheet view, select the field and press Delete. Click Yes in the message box.

> **To delete a field in Design view, complete the following steps:**
>
> 1. Click the record selector of the field you want to delete to select it.
> 2. Click Delete Rows in the Tools group on the Design tab.
> 3. Click Yes in the message box that displays to confirm that you want to permanently delete the field and the data in it. Click No if you do not want to delete the field.
> 4. Click Yes in the second message box that displays if the selected field you are deleting is a primary key. Click No if you do not want to delete the primary key.

To rename a field, double-click the field name you want to change, type the new field name, press Enter, and then save the table.

TIP: HIDE FIELDS IN AN ACCESS DATASHEET

To hide a field in a datasheet, right-click the column selector that displays the field name and from the shortcut menu, select Hide Fields. To make the field visible again, right-click any column selector, select Unhide Fields, and select the appropriate column's check box.

Determine Data Type

Every field has an assigned *data type* that determines the type of data that can be entered and the operations that can be performed on that data. Access recognizes 12 data types. Table 2.1 lists these data types, their uses, and examples of each. You can change a data type after you have entered data into your table, but do so with caution. Be aware of messages from Access indicating that you may lose data when you save your changes. In some cases, changing data types is inconsequential; for example, you may want to convert a number to a currency value. This type of change would only affect the formatting displayed with the values, but not the underlying values themselves. In any case, when designing tables, choose the initial data type carefully, and be sure to back up your database before changing data types.

TABLE 2.1   Data Types and Uses

Data Type	Description	Example
Short Text	Stores alphanumeric data, such as a customer's name or address. It can contain alphabetic characters, numbers, and/or special characters (e.g., an apostrophe in O'Malley). Social Security numbers, telephone numbers, and postal codes should be designated as text fields because they are not used in calculations and often contain special characters such as hyphens and parentheses. A short text field can hold up to 255 characters.	2184 Walnut Street
Long Text	Lengthy text or combinations of text and numbers, such as several sentences or paragraphs; used to hold descriptive data. Long text controls can display up to 64,000 characters.	A description of product packaging
Number	Contains a value that can be used in a calculation, such as the number of credits a course is worth. The contents are restricted to numbers, a decimal point, and a plus or minus sign.	12
Date/Time	Stores dates or times that can be used in date or time arithmetic.	10/31/2018 1:30:00 AM
Currency	Used for fields that contain monetary values.	$1,200

TABLE 2.1 Continued

Data Type	Description	Example
AutoNumber	A special data type used to assign the next consecutive number each time you add a record. The value of an AutoNumber field is unique for each record in the table.	1, 2, 3
Yes/No	Only one of two values can be stored, such as Yes or No, True or False, or On or Off (also known as a Boolean). For example, is a student on the Dean's list: Yes or No.	Yes
OLE Object	Contains an object created by another application. OLE objects include pictures and sounds.	JPG image
Hyperlink	Stores a Web address (URL) or the path to a folder or file. Hyperlink fields can be clicked to retrieve a webpage or to launch a file stored locally.	http://www.irs.gov
Attachment	Used to store multiple images, spreadsheet files, Word documents, and other types of supported files.	An Excel workbook
Calculated	The results of an expression that references one or more existing fields.	[Price]*.05
Lookup Wizard	Creates a field that enables you to choose a value from another table or from a list of values by using a list box or a combo box.	Accounts table with a CustomerID field that looks up the customer from the records in the Customers table

Pearson Education, Inc.

Set a Table's Primary Key

STEP 2 ➤➤ The primary key is the field (or possibly a combination of fields) that uniquely identifies each record in a table. Access does not require that each table have a primary key. However, a good database design usually includes a primary key in each table. You should select unique and infrequently changing data for the primary key. For example, a credit card number may seem to be unique, but would not make a good primary key because it is subject to change when a new card is issued due to fraudulent activity.

You probably would not use a person's name as the primary key, because several people could have the same name. A value like CustomerID, as shown in the Customers table in Figure 2.5, is unique and is a better choice for the primary key. When no field seems to stand out as a primary key naturally, you can create a primary key field with the AutoNumber data type. The **AutoNumber** data type is a number that automatically increments each time a record is added.

Figure 2.6 depicts a Speakers table, where no unique field can be identified from the data itself. In this case, you can identify the SpeakerID field with an AutoNumber data type. Access automatically numbers each speaker record sequentially with a unique ID as each record is added.

Customer ID	FirstName	LastName	Street	City	State	Zip	Phone	Click to Add
30001	Allison	Millward	2732 Baker Blvd.	Greensboro	NC	27492	(555) 334-5678	
30002	Bernett	Fox	12 Orchestra Terrace	High Point	NC	27494	(555) 358-5554	
30003	Clay	Hayes	P.O. Box 555	Greensboro	NC	27492	(555) 998-4457	
30004	Cordle	Collins	2743 Bering St.	Winston-Salem	NC	27492	(555) 447-2283	
30005	Eaton	Wagner	2743 Bering St.	Greensboro	NC	27492	(555) 988-3346	
30006	Kwasi	Williams	89 Jefferson Way	High Point	NC	27494	(555) 447-5565	
30007	Natasha	Simpson	187 Suffolk Ln.	Greensboro	NC	27493	(555) 775-3389	
30008	Joy	Jones	305 - 14th Ave. S.	Winston-Salem	NC	27493	(555) 258-7655	
30009	John	Nunn	89 Chiaroscuro Rd.	Greensboro	NC	27494	(555) 998-5557	
30010	Laura	Peterson	120 Hanover Sq.	Winston-Salem	NC	27492	(555) 334-6654	
30011	YourName	YourName	800 University Ave.	High Point	NC	27494	(555) 447-1235	
0								

Access 2016, Windows 10, Microsoft Corporation

FIGURE 2.5 Customers Table with a Natural Primary Key

SpeakerID	First Name	Last Name	Address	City	State	Zip Code	Phone Number	Email	AreaOfExpertise	Click to Add
1	Jerri	Williams	10000 SW 59 Court	Miami	FL	33146	(305) 777-8888	cahsley@um.edu	Student Life	
2	Warren	Brasington	9470 SW 25 Street	Philadelphia	PA	19104	(215) 888-7654	wbrasington@up.edu	Residence Halls	
3	James	Shindell	14088 Malaga Avenue	Miami	FL	33146	(305) 773-4343	jshindell@um.edu	Administration	
		...ood	400 Roderigo Avenue	Gainesville	FL	32611	(352) 555-5555	ewood@uf.edu	Student Life	
			9290 NW 59 Steet	Athens	GA	30602	(706) 777-1111	kpark@ug.edu	Student Life	
		...amson	108 Los Pinos Place	Tuscaloosa	AL	35487	(205) 888-4554	wwilliamson@ua.edu	Deans' Office	
7	Holly	Davis	8009 Riviera Drive	Gainesville	FL	32611	(352) 388-7676	hdavis.uf.edu	Residence Halls	
8	David	Tannen	50 Main Street	Philadelphia	PA	19104	(215) 777-2211	dtannen@up.edu	Student Life	
9	Jeffrey	Jacobsen	490 Bell Drive	Athens	GA	30602	(706) 388-9999	jjacobsen@ug.edu	Wellness	
10	Jerry	Masters	2000 Main Highway	Miami	FL	33146	(305) 777-8998	jmasters@um.edy	Wellness	
11	Kevin	Kline	2980 SW 89 Street	Gainesville	FL	32611	(352) 877-8900	kkline@uf.edu	Student Life	
			110 Center Highway	Athens	GA	30602	(706) 893-8872	jwithers@ug.edu	Wellness	
			2987 SW 14 Avenue	Philadelphia	PA	19104	(215) 558-7748	ballman@up.edu	Counseling Center	
			1008 West Marine Road	Miami	FL	33146	(305) 877-4993	mmiller@um.edu	Student Life	
15	Nancy	Vance	1878 W. 6 Street	Gainesville	FL	32611	(352) 885-4330	nvance@uf.edu	Counseling Center	
16	George	Jensen	42-15 81 Street	Elmhurst	NY	11373	(718) 555-6666	gjensen@school.edu	Residence Halls	
(New)										

(Callout: SpeakerID (AutoNumber data type) is the primary key)
(Callout: Next record will be assigned SpeakerID 17)

FIGURE 2.6 Speakers Table with an AutoNumber Primary Key

Explore a Foreign Key

In order to share data between two tables, the tables must share a common field. The common field will generally be the primary key in one table; the same field in the adjoining table is denoted as the *foreign key*. The CustomerID is the primary key (identified with a primary key icon) in the Customers table and uniquely identifies each customer in the database. It also displays as a foreign key in the related Accounts table. The Accounts table contains the CustomerID field to establish which customer owns the account. A CustomerID can be entered only one time in the Customers table, but it may be entered multiple times in the Accounts table because one customer may own several accounts (checking, savings, credit card, etc.). Therefore, the CustomerID is the primary key in the Customers table and a foreign key in the Accounts table, as shown in Figure 2.7.

Customers

Customer ID	FirstName	LastName	Street	City	State	Zip	Phone	Click to Add
30001	Allison	Millward	2732 Baker Blvd.	Greensboro	NC	27492	(555) 334-5678	
30002	Bernett	Fox	12 Orchestra Terrace	High Point	NC	27494	(555) 358-5554	
30003	Clay	Hayes	P.O. Box 555	Greensboro	NC	27492	(555) 998-4457	
30004	Cordie	Collins	2743 Bering St.	Winston-Salem	NC	27492	(555) 447-2283	
		Wagner	2743 Bering St.	Greensboro	NC	27492	(555) 988-3346	
		Williams	89 Jefferson Way	High Point	NC	27494	(555) 447-1565	
		Simpson	187 Suffolk Ln.	Greensboro	NC	27493	(555) 775-3389	
30008	Joy	Jones	305 - 14th Ave. S.	Winston-Salem	NC	27493	(555) 258-7655	
30009	John	Nunn	89 Chiaroscuro Rd.	Greensboro	NC	27494	(555) 998 5557	
30010	Laura	Peterson	120 Hanover Sq.	Winston-Salem	NC	27492	(555) 334-6654	
30011	YourName	YourName	800 University Ave.	High Point	NC	27494	(555) 447-1235	
0								

(Callout: Primary Key in Customers table)

Accounts

Account ID	Customer ID	Branch ID	Balance	Open Date	Click to Add
1001	30010	B50	$5,600.00	4/28/2012	
1002	30001	B10	$1,200.00	4/13/2010	
1003	30004	B20	$15,490.00	5/28/2009	
			$620.00	9/21/2008	
			$1,300.00	7/22/2010	
			$330.00	1/3/2008	
			$1,620.00	6/7/2011	
1008	30004	B40	$2,100.00	9/30/2012	
1009	30005	B50	$1,500.00	2/7/2011	
1010	30001	B20	$3,000.00	3/18/2015	
1011	30005	B10	$290.00	10/16/2016	
1012	30002	B30	$1,900.00	3/14/2012	

(Callout: Foreign Key in Accounts table)

FIGURE 2.7 Two Tables Illustrating Primary and Foreign Keys

TIP: BEST FIT COLUMNS

If a field name is cut off in Datasheet view, you can adjust the column width by positioning the pointer on the vertical border on the right side of the column. When the pointer displays as a two-headed arrow, double-click the border. You can also click More in the Records group on the Home tab, select Field Width, and then click Best Fit in the Column Width dialog box.

Work with Field Properties

STEP 3 ›› While a field's data type determines the type of data that can be entered and the operations that can be performed on that data, its *field properties* determine how the field looks and behaves. The field properties are set to default values according to the data type, but you can modify them if necessary. Field properties are commonly set in Design view, as shown in Figure 2.4; however, certain properties can be set in Datasheet view, on the Table Tools Fields tab. Common property types are defined in Table 2.2.

Field Size is a commonly changed field property. The field size determines the amount of space a field uses in the database. A field with a Short Text data type can store up to 255 characters; however, you can limit the characters by reducing the field size property. For example, you might limit the State field to only two characters because all state abbreviations are two letters. When setting field sizes, you may want to anticipate any future requirements of the database that might necessitate larger values to be stored.

You can set the **Caption property** to create a label that is more understandable than a field name. While Pascal Case is often preferred for field names, adding a space between words is often more readable. When a caption is set, it displays at the top of a table or query column in Datasheet view (instead of the field name), and when the field is used in a report or form. For example, a field named CustomerID could have the caption *Customer Number*.

Set the Validation Rule property to restrict data entry in a field to ensure that correct data are entered. The validation rule checks the data entered when the user exits the field. If the data entered violate the validation rule, an error message displays and prevents the invalid data from being entered into the field. For example, if you have set a rule on a date field that the date entered must be on or after today, and a date in the past is entered in the field, an error message will display. You can customize the error message (validation text) when you set the validation rule.

The Input Mask property simplifies data entry by providing literal characters that are typed for every entry, such as hyphens in a Social Security number (- -), or dashes in a phone number. Input masks ensure that data in fields such as these are consistently entered and formatted.

TABLE 2.2	Common Access Table Property Types and Descriptions
Property Type	**Description**
Field Size	Determines the maximum number of characters of a text field or the format of a number field.
Format	Changes the way a field is displayed or printed but does not affect the stored value.
Input Mask	Simplifies data entry by providing literal characters that are typed for every entry, such as hyphens in a Social Security number (- -) or slashes in a date. It also imposes data validation by ensuring that data entered conform to the mask.
Caption	Enables an alternate (or more readable) name to be displayed other than the field name; alternate name displays in datasheets, forms, and reports.
Default Value	Enters automatically a predetermined value for a field each time a new record is added to the table. For example, if most customers live in Los Angeles, the default value for the City field could be set to Los Angeles to save data entry time and promote accurate data entry.
Validation Rule	Requires data entered to conform to a specified rule.
Validation Text	Specifies the error message that is displayed when the validation rule is violated.
Required	Indicates that a value for this field must be entered. Primary key fields always require data entry.
Allow Zero Length	Allows entry of zero length text strings ("") in a Hyperlink, or Short or Long Text fields.
Indexed	Increases the efficiency of a search on the designated field.
Expression	Used for calculated fields only. Specifies the expression you want Access to evaluate and store.
Result Type	Used for calculated fields only. Specifies the format for the calculated field results.

> **TIP: FREEZE FIELDS IN AN ACCESS DATABASE**
> To keep a field viewable while you are scrolling through a table, select the field or fields you want to freeze, right-click, and then select Freeze Fields. If you want the field(s) to remain frozen when you are finished working, save the changes when you close the table. To unfreeze all fields, right-click the field(s) and select Unfreeze All Fields.

Create a New Field in Design View

STEP 4 ⟩⟩ At times, it may be necessary to add table fields that were not included in the original design process. While it is possible to add fields in Datasheet view (using the Click to Add arrow at the top of an empty column), Design view, as shown in Figure 2.4, offers more flexibility in setting field properties.

To add a new field in Design view, complete the following steps:

1. Click in the first empty field row in the top pane of the table's Design view.
2. Enter the Field Name, Data Type, and Description (optional), and then set the Field Properties.
3. Click the row selector, and then click and drag the new field to place it in a different position in the table.
4. Click Save on the Quick Access Toolbar, and then switch to Datasheet view to enter or modify data.

Modify the Table in Datasheet View

STEP 5 ⟩⟩ Whereas Design view is commonly used to create and modify the table structure by enabling you to add and edit fields and set field properties, Datasheet view is used to add, edit, and delete records. Datasheet view of an Access table displays data in a grid format—rows represent records and columns represent fields. You can select a record by clicking the record selector on the left side of each record. Use the new blank record (marked with an asterisk) at the end of the table to add a new record, or click the New (blank) record button on the navigation bar at the bottom of the table.

Quick Concepts

1. What is meant by "Store data in its smallest parts" when designing database tables? *p. 736*
2. What is the difference between a primary key and a foreign key? *p. 741*
3. Which field property creates a more readable label that displays in the top row in Datasheet view and in forms and reports? *p. 742*

Hands-On Exercises

Watch the Video
for this Hands-On
Exercise!

MyITLab®
HOE1 Training

Skills covered: Create a Table in Datasheet View • Delete a Field • Set a Table's Primary Key • Work with Field Properties • Create a New Field in Design View • Modify the Table in Datasheet View

1 Table Design, Creation, and Modification

Creating a database for the bank auditor at Commonwealth Federal Bank as he investigates the mishandled funds will be a great opportunity for you to showcase your database design and Access skills.

STEP 1 ➤➤ CREATE A TABLE IN DATASHEET VIEW

You create a new desktop database to store information about the mishandled funds. You enter the data for the first record (BranchID, Manager, and Location). Refer to Figure 2.8 as you complete Step 1.

ID	BranchID	Manager	Location	Click to Add
1	B10	Krebs	Uptown	
2	B20	Esposito	Eastern	
3	B30	Amoako	Western	
4	B40	Singh	Southern	
5	B50	YourLastName	Campus	
* (New)				

Step i: Save the table as Branch

Step h: Type the data directly into the datasheet

Access 2016, Windows 10, Microsoft Corporation

FIGURE 2.8 Create the Branch Table in Datasheet View

a. Start Microsoft Office Access 2016 and click **Blank desktop database**.

b. Type **a02h1Bank_LastFirst** into the File Name box.

c. Click **Browse** to find the folder location where you will store the database and click **OK**. Click **Create** to create the new database.

Access will create the new database named a02h1Bank_LastFirst and a new table will automatically open in Datasheet view. There is already an ID field in the table by default.

d. Click **Click to Add** and select **Short Text** as the Data type.

Click to Add changes to Field1. Field1 is selected to make it easier to change the field name.

e. Type **BranchID** and press **Tab**.

A list of data types for the third column opens so that you can select the data type for the third column.

f. Select Short Text in the Click to Add window, type **Manager**, and then press **Tab**.

g. Select Short Text in the Click to Add window, and then type **Location**.

h. Click in the first column (the ID field) next to the New Record asterisk, press **Tab**, and then type the data for the new table as shown in Figure 2.8, letting Access assign the ID field for each new record (using the AutoNumber data type). Replace *YourLastName* with your own last name.

i. Click **Save** on the Quick Access Toolbar. Type **Branch** in the Save As dialog box and click **OK**.

Entering field names, data types, and data directly in Datasheet view provides a simplified way to create the table initially.

744 CHAPTER 2 • Hands-On Exercise 1

It is possible to modify tables even after data have been entered; however, be alert to potential messages from Access after you make design changes that may affect your data. In this step, you will modify the Branch table. You examine the design of the table and realize that the BranchID field is a unique identifier, making the ID field redundant. You delete the ID field and make the BranchID field the primary key field. Refer to Figure 2.9 as you complete Step 2.

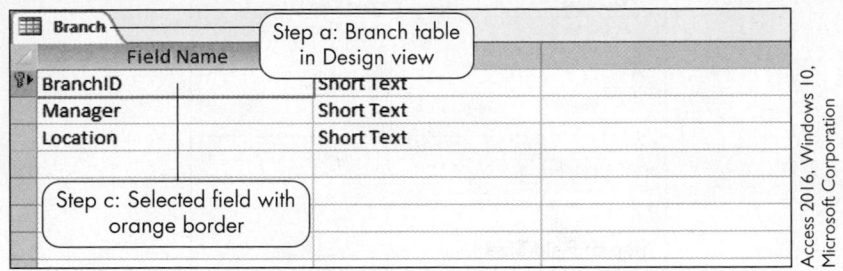

FIGURE 2.9 Branch Table in Design View

a. Click **View** in the Views group on the Home tab to switch to Design view of the Branch table.

The field name for each of the four fields displays along with the data type.

b. Ensure that the ID field selected, click **Delete Rows** in the Tools group on the Design tab. Click **Yes** to both warning messages.

Access responds with a warning that you are about to permanently delete a field and a second warning that the field is the primary key. You delete the field because you will set the BranchID field as the primary key.

c. Ensure that the BranchID field is selected, as shown in Figure 2.9.

d. Click **Primary Key** in the Tools group on the Design tab.

You set BranchID as the primary key. The Indexed property in the Field Properties section at the bottom of the design window displays Yes (No Duplicates).

e. Click **Save** on the Quick Access Toolbar to save the table.

TIP: SHORTCUT MENU
You can right-click a row selector to display a shortcut menu to copy a field, set the primary key, insert or delete rows, or access table properties. Use the shortcut menu to make these specific changes to the design of a table.

You will modify the table design further to comply with the bank auditor's specifications. Refer to Figure 2.10 as you complete Step 3.

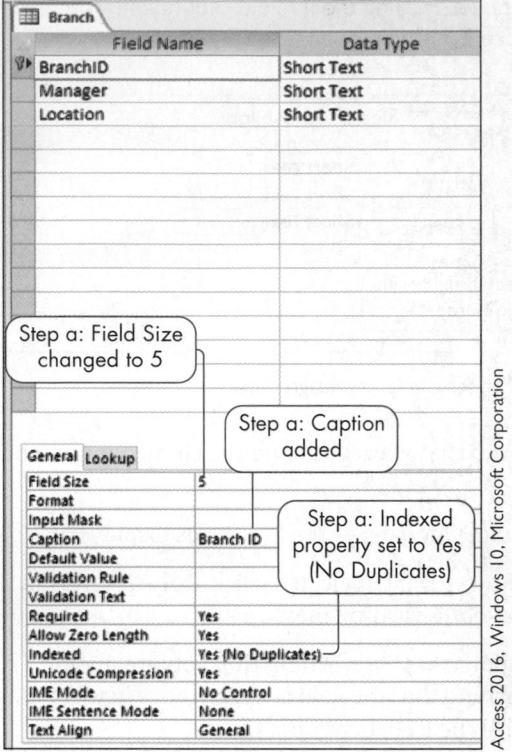

FIGURE 2.10 Changes to the Field Properties of the Branch Table in Design View

a. Click in the **BranchID field name**; modify the BranchID field properties by completing the following steps:

- Click in the **Field Size box** and change 255 to **5**.
- Click in the **Caption box** and type **Branch ID**. Make sure Branch and ID have a space between them.

    A caption provides a more descriptive field name. It will display as the column heading in Datasheet view.
- Check the Indexed property; confirm it is Yes (No Duplicates).

b. Click the **Manager field name**; modify the Manager field properties by completing the following steps:

- Click in the **Field Size box** in the Field Properties pane, and change 255 to **30**.
- Click in the **Caption box** in the Field Properties pane, and type **Manager's Name**.

c. Click the **Location field name** and modify the following Location field properties by completing the following steps:

- Click in the **Field Size box** and change 255 to **30**.
- Click in the **Caption box** and type **Branch Location**.

TIP: F6 FUNCTION KEY TO SWITCH TO FIELD PROPERTIES
With a field name selected in the top pane of the Design window, you can press the F6 function key to toggle to the field properties for the selected field. Continue to press F6 to cycle through the additional elements of the Access screen.

You notify the auditor that a date field is missing in your new table. Modify the table to add the new field. Refer to Figure 2.11 as you complete Step 4.

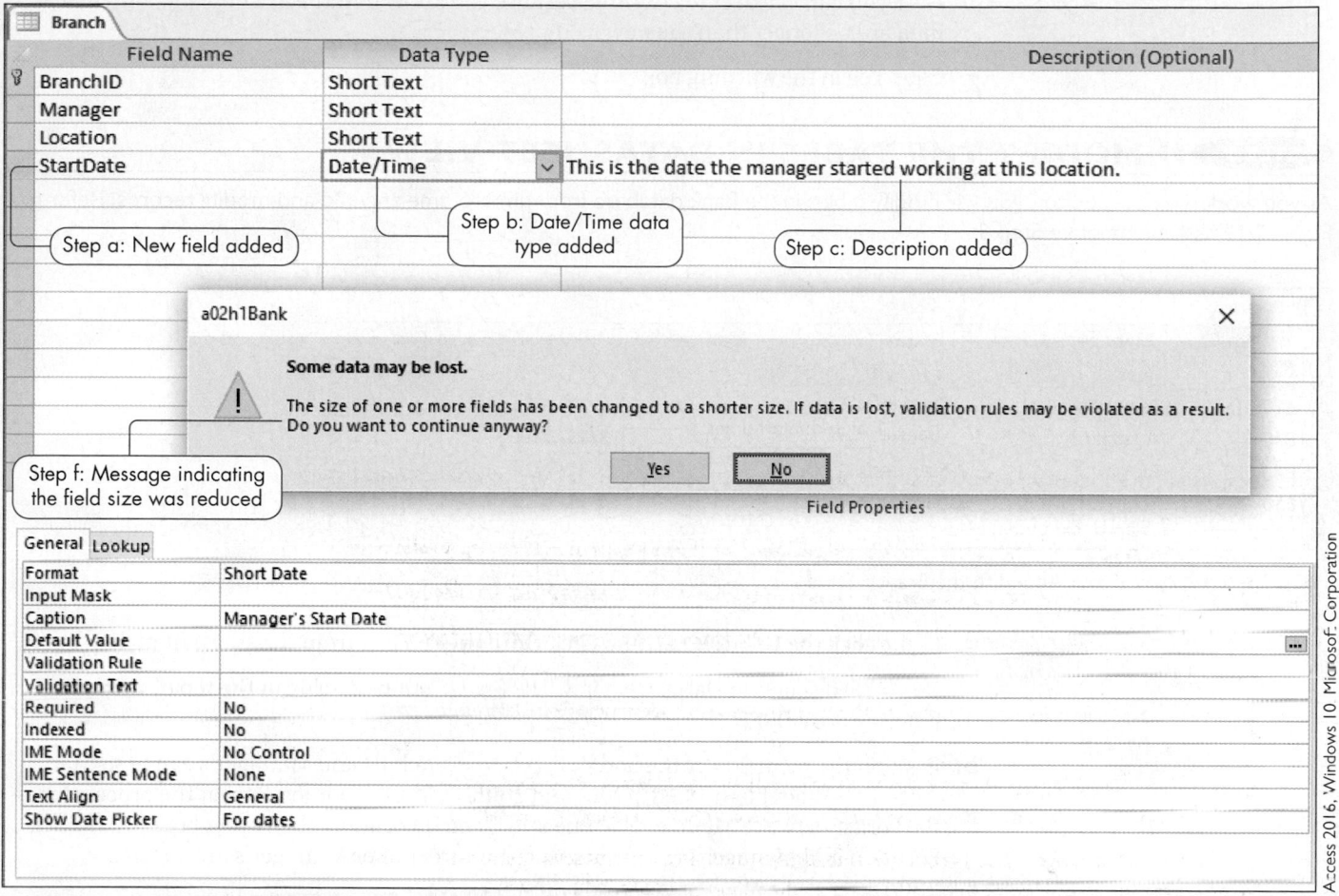

FIGURE 2.11 Adding a New Field to the Branch Table in Design View

a. Click in the first blank field row below the Location field name and type **StartDate**.

   You added a new field to the table.

b. Press **Tab** to move to the Data Type column. Click the **Data Type arrow** and select **Date/Time**.

> **TIP: KEYBOARD SHORTCUT FOR DATA TYPES**
> You also can type the first letter of the data type, such as d for Date/Time, s for Short Text, or n for Number. To use the keyboard shortcut, click in the field name and press Tab to advance to the Data Type column. Next, type the first letter of the data type.

c. Press **Tab** to move to the Description column and type **This is the date the manager started working at this location.**

d. Click in the **Format box** in the Field properties pane, click the **arrow**, and then select **Short Date** from the list of date formats.

e. Click in the **Caption box** and type **Manager's Start Date**.

f. Click **Save** on the Quick Access Toolbar.

A warning dialog box opens to indicate that "Some data may be lost" because the size of the BranchID, Manager, and Location field properties were shortened (in the previous step). It asks if you want to continue anyway. Always read the Access warning! In this case, you can click Yes to continue because you know that the existing and anticipated data are no longer than the new field sizes.

g. Click **Yes** in the warning box.

STEP 5 ›› **MODIFY THE TABLE IN DATASHEET VIEW**

As you work with the auditor, you will modify tables in the Bank database from time to time and add and modify records. Refer to Figure 2.12 as you complete Step 5.

Branch ID ▾	Manager's Name ▾	Branch Location ▾	Manager's Start Date ▾	Click to Add ▾
B10	Krebs	Uptown	12/3/2014	
B20	Esposito	Eastern	6/18/2013	
B30	Amoako	Western	3/13/2011	
B40	Singh	Southern	9/15/2014	
B50	YourLastName	Campus	10/11/2016	

Step d: Start dates

Step b: Expanded fields

Access 2016, Windows 10, Microsoft Corporation

FIGURE 2.12 Start Dates Added to the Branch Table

a. Right-click the **Branch tab** and click **Datasheet View** from the shortcut menu.

The table displays in Datasheet view. The field captions display at the top of the columns, but they are cut off.

b. Position the pointer over the border between Branch ID and Manager's Name so that it becomes a double-headed arrow, and double-click the border. Repeat the process for the border between Manager's Name and Branch Location, the border between Branch Location and Manager's Start Date, and the border after Manager's Start Date.

The columns contract or expand to display the best fit for each field name.

c. Click inside the **Manager's Start Date** in the first record and click the **Date Picker** 🗓 next to the date field. Use the navigation arrows to find and select **December 3, 2014** from the calendar.

You can also enter the dates by typing them directly into the StartDate field.

d. Type the start date directly in each field for the rest of the managers, as shown in Figure 2.12.

e. Click the **Close** ⊠ at the top-right corner of the datasheet, below the Ribbon. Click **Yes** to save the changes.

> **TROUBLESHOOTING:** If you accidentally click Close on top of the Ribbon, you will exit Access completely. To start again, launch Access and click the first file in the Recent list.

f. Double-click the **Branch table** in the Navigation Pane to open the table. Check the start dates.

g. Click the **File tab**, click **Print**, and then click **Print Preview**.

Occasionally, users will print an Access table. However, database developers usually create reports to print table data.

h. Click **Close Print Preview** and close the Branch table.

i. Keep the database open if you plan to continue with the Hands-On Exercise. If not, close the database and exit Access.

Multiple-Table Databases

In Figure 2.2, the sample Bank database contains three tables—Customers, Accounts, and Branch. You created one table, the Branch table, in the previous section using Datasheet view and modified the table fields in Design view. You will create the two remaining tables using different methods—by importing data from external sources.

In this section, you will learn how to import data from Excel and Access, modify tables, create indexes, create relationships between tables, and enforce referential integrity.

Sharing Data

Most companies and organizations store some type of data in Excel spreadsheets. Often, the data stored in those spreadsheets can be more efficiently managed in an Access database. At other times, importing data from Excel and other applications can reduce the data entry effort for your database.

Import Excel Data

STEP 1 ›› Access provides you with a wizard that guides you through the process of importing data from Excel.

> **To import an Excel spreadsheet to Access, complete the following steps:**
>
> 1. Click the External Data tab.
> 2. Click Excel in the Import & Link group. The Get External Data – Excel Spreadsheet dialog box opens, as shown in Figure 2.13.

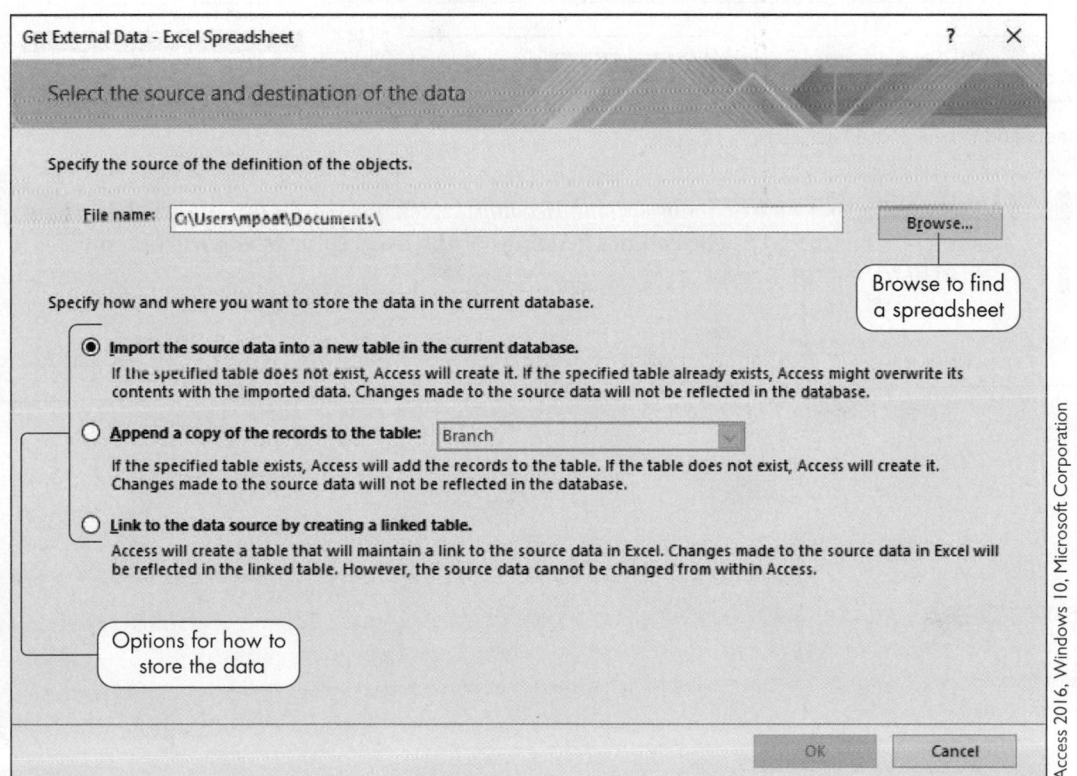

FIGURE 2.13 Import Excel Data

3. Click Browse to locate the Excel file you want to import, click the file to select it, and then click Open to specify this file as the source of the data.

4. Ensure the *Import the source data* option is selected, and click OK. The Import Spreadsheet Wizard launches.

5. Select the worksheet from the list of worksheets shown at the top of the dialog box, as shown in Figure 2.14 and then click Next.

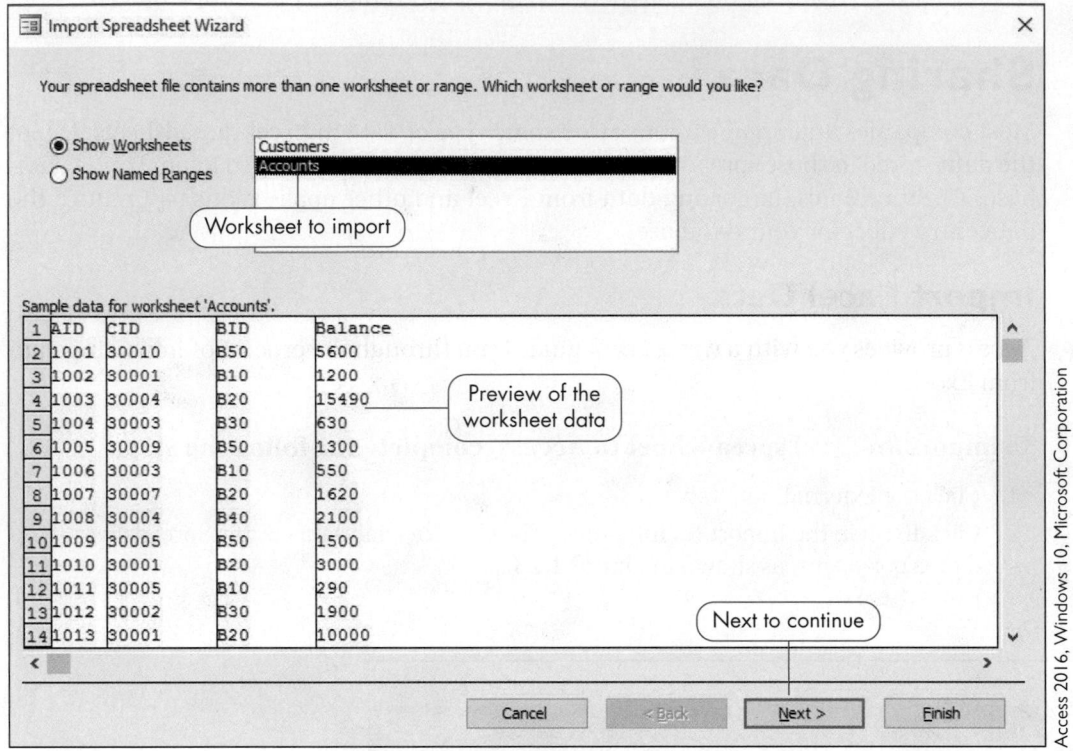

FIGURE 2.14 Available Worksheets and Preview of Data

6. Ensure the *First Row Contains Column Headings* check box is selected, and click Next, as shown in Figure 2.15. The column headings of the Excel spreadsheet will become the field names in the Access table.

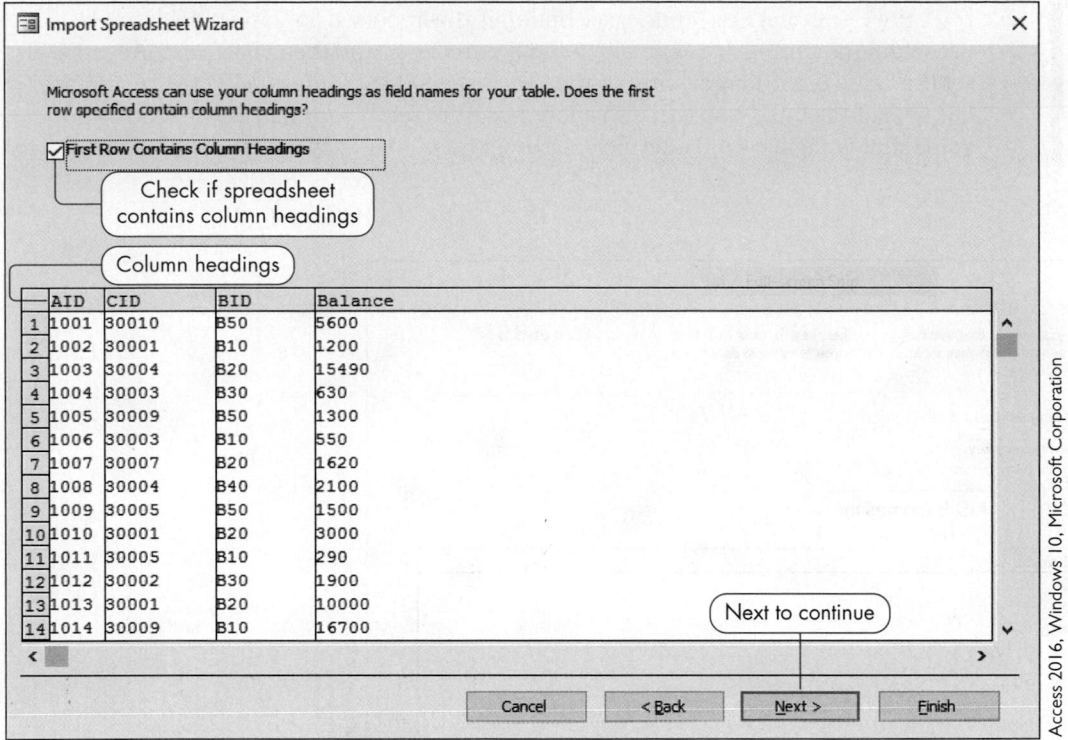

FIGURE 2.15 Excel Column Headings Become Access Field Names

7. Change the field options for the imported data, as shown in Figure 2.16, and then click Next.

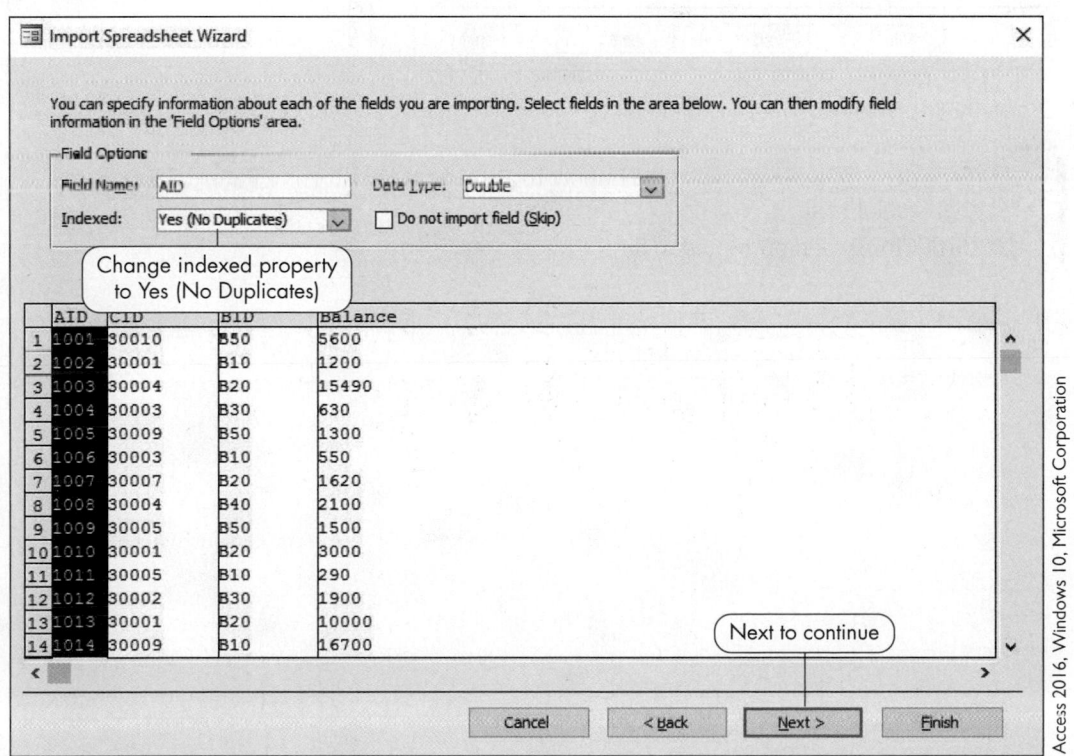

FIGURE 2.16 Change Field Options for Imported Data

8. Click the *Choose my own primary key* option if the imported data has a field that is acceptable as a primary key, as shown in Figure 2.17, and then click Next. Access will set the value in the first column of the spreadsheet (for example, AID) as the primary key field of the table. You can also allow Access to set the primary key if there is no value that is eligible to be a key field, or to set no primary key at all.

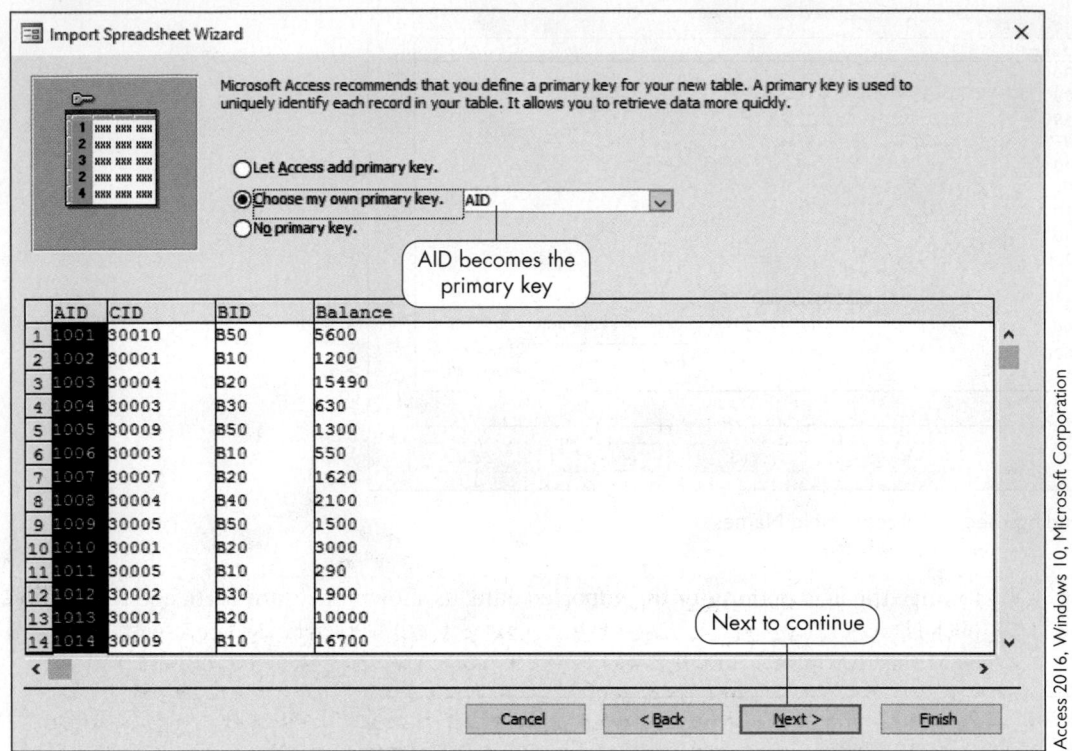

FIGURE 2.17 Set the Primary Key

9. Type the new table name in the Import to Table box, as shown in Figure 2.18, and then click Finish.

10. Click Close when prompted to Save Import Steps.

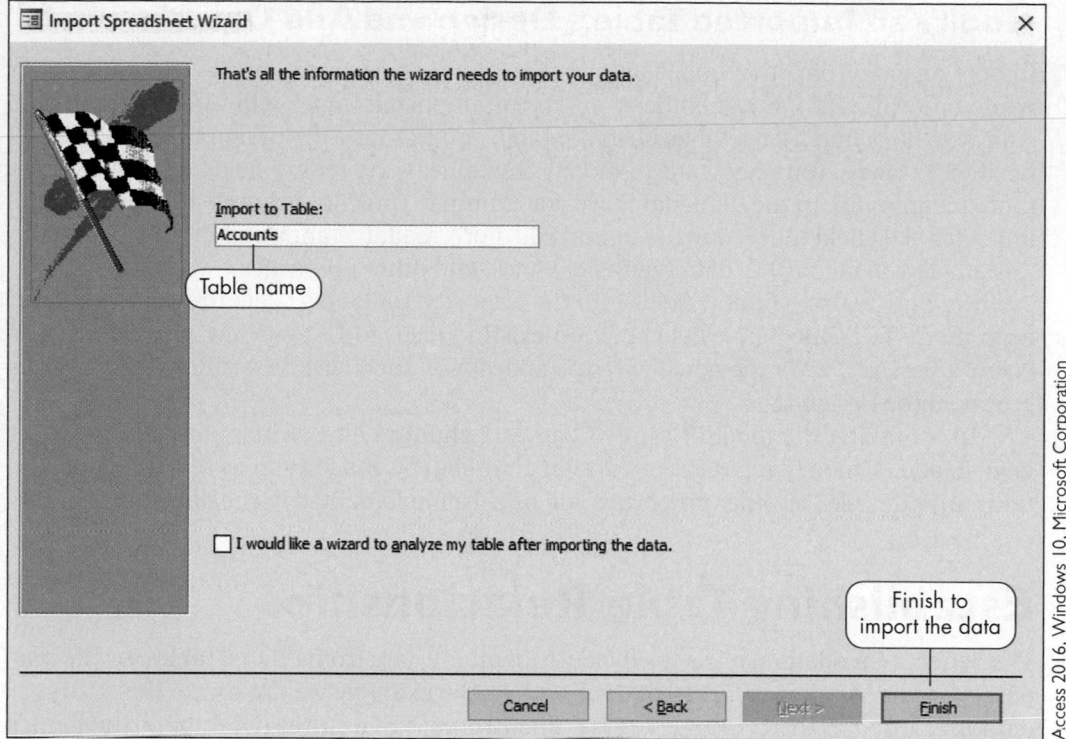

That's all the information the wizard needs to import your data.

Import to Table:

Accounts

Table name

☐ I would like a wizard to analyze my table after importing the data.

Finish to import the data

Cancel   < Back   Next >   Finish

Access 2016, Windows 10, Microsoft Corporation

FIGURE 2.18 Enter a Table Name

TIP: LINKING TO EXTERNAL DATA
At times you might need to include a table in your database that already exists in another database. Instead of importing the data from this external source, you can create a link to it from within your database, and the table remains in the original database. You will be able to use the linked data as usual, without being able to modify the original table's design. You can also link to existing spreadsheets from your database without having to copy a large amount of data into your file.

Import Access Data

 **STEP 2** ⟫ A wizard can also guide you as you import data from Access databases. You can import tables, queries, forms, reports, pages, macros, and modules from other databases. You can also modify the design of objects that are imported into your database.

> **To import an Access table into an existing database, complete the following steps:**
>
> 1. Click the External Data tab.
> 2. Click Access in the Import & Link group. The Get External Data – Access Database dialog box opens.
> 3. Ensure that the *Import tables, queries, forms, reports, macros, and modules into the current database* option is selected.
> 4. Click Browse to locate the Access database you want to import.
> 5. Click the file to select it, and then click Open to specify this file as the source of the data.
> 6. Select the table you want to import, and then click OK. (Click Select All if the database contains multiple tables and you want to import all of them, and then click OK.)

Modify an Imported Table's Design and Add Data

STEP 3 ⟩⟩ Importing data from other applications saves typing and prevents errors that may occur while entering data, but modifications to the imported tables will often be required. After you have imported a table, open the table and examine the design to see if changes need to be made. You may want to modify the table by renaming fields so that they are more meaningful. In the Bank database, for example, you could change the name of the imported AID field to AccountID to make it more readable and meaningful. Switch to Design view to modify the data types, field sizes, and other properties.

You may want to fit new fields into the imported tables or delete unnecessary fields from them. To create a new field between existing fields in Design view, click in the row below where you want the new field to be added, and then click Insert Rows in the Tools group on the Design tab.

STEP 4 ⟩⟩ After making the modifications, save your changes and switch back to Datasheet view to add or modify records. Any design changes you made such as to field sizes, captions, input masks, or other properties will now be implemented in the datasheet.

Establishing Table Relationships

STEP 5 ⟩⟩ The benefit of a relationship is to efficiently combine data from related tables for the purpose of creating queries, forms, and reports. In the example we are using, the customer data are stored in the Customers table. The Branch table stores data about the bank's branches, management, and locations. The Accounts table stores data about account ownership and balances.

The common fields that were determined in the design phase of the tables can now be used to establish relationships between them.

> **To create the relationship between the common fields of two tables, complete the following steps:**
>
> 1. Click the Database Tools tab.
> 2. Click Relationships in the Relationships group.
> 3. Drag the primary key field name from one table to the foreign key field name of the related table (for example, CustomerID in the Customers table to CustomerID in the Accounts table).
> 4. Set the desired options in the Edit Relationships dialog box, and click OK. Figure 2.19 shows the Bank database with relationships created by joining common fields.

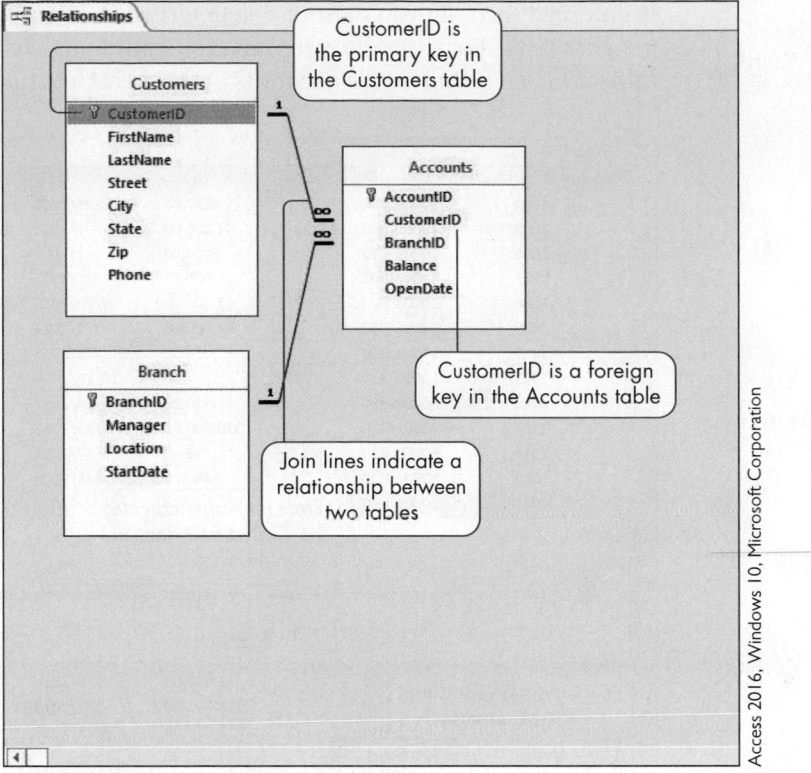

FIGURE 2.19 Relationships in the Bank Database

> **TiP: RETRIEVE DATA QUICKLY WITH INDEXING**
> When you set the primary key in Access, the Indexed property is automatically set to Yes (No Duplicates). The indexed property setting enables quick sorting in primary key order and quick retrieval based on the primary key. For non-primary key fields, it may be beneficial to set the Indexed property to Yes (Duplicates OK). Again, Access uses indexing to sort and retrieve data quickly based on the indexed field.

The primary key of a table plays a significant role when setting relationships. You cannot join two tables unless a primary key has been set in the primary table, which is one side of the relationship's join line. The other side of the relationship join line is most often the foreign key of the related table. A foreign key is a field in one table that is also the primary key and common field of another table. In the Bank database, CustomerID has been set as the primary key in the Customers table and also exists in the Accounts table. Therefore, a relationship can be set between the Customers table and the Accounts table, where CustomerID is the foreign key. Similarly, the Branch table can be joined to the Accounts table because BranchID has been set as the primary key in the Branch table, and BranchID is the foreign key in the Accounts table.

Enforce Referential Integrity

STEP 6 ›› When you begin to create a relationship in Access, the Edit Relationships dialog box displays. The first check box, Enforce Referential Integrity, should be checked in most cases. **Referential integrity** enforces rules in a database that are used to preserve relationships between tables when records are changed.

When referential integrity is enforced, you cannot enter a foreign key value in a related table unless the primary key value exists in the primary table. In the case of the Bank database, the customer information is first entered into the Customers table before a customer's account information (which also includes CustomerID) can be entered into the Accounts table. If you attempt to enter an account prior to entering the customer information, an error will display, as shown in Figure 2.20. When referential integrity is enforced, usually you cannot delete a record in one table if it has related records in another table. For example, you may not want to delete a customer from the Customers table if he or she has active accounts in the Accounts table.

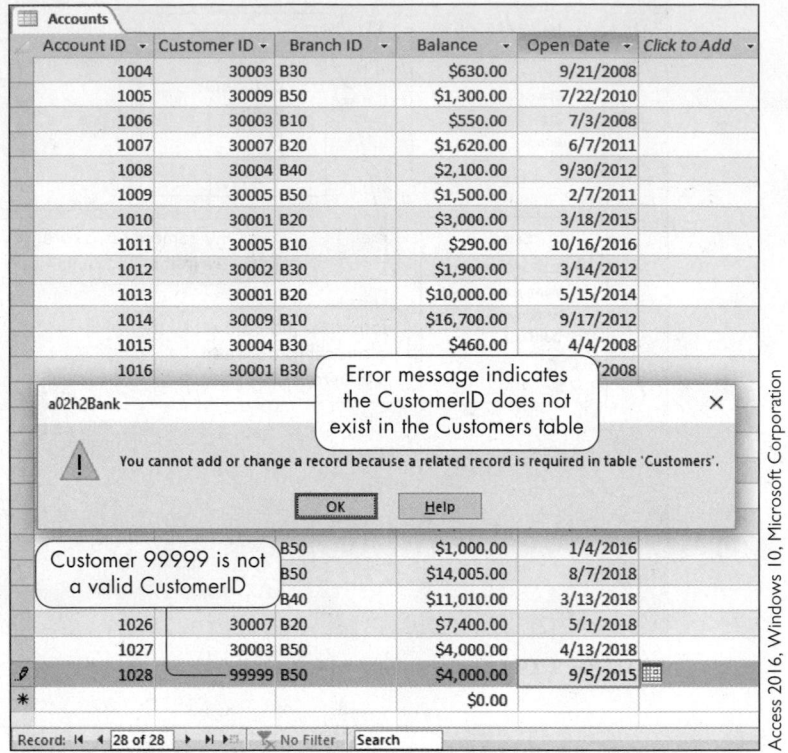

FIGURE 2.20 Error Message for Referential Integrity Violation

Set Cascade Options

When you create a relationship in Access and click the Enforce Referential Integrity check box, Access presents two additional options: Cascade Update Related Fields and Cascade Delete Related Records (see Figure 2.21). Check the **Cascade Update Related Fields** option so that when the primary key value is modified in a primary table, Access will automatically update all foreign key values in a related table. If a CustomerID is updated for some reason, all of the matching CustomerID values in the Accounts table will update automatically.

Check the **Cascade Delete Related Records** option so that when a record containing a primary key value is deleted in a primary table, Access will automatically delete all records in related tables that match the primary key. If one branch of a bank closes and its record is deleted from the Branch table, any account that is associated with this branch would then be deleted. Access will give a warning first to enable you to avoid the action of deleting records inadvertently.

Setting the Cascade Update and Cascade Delete options really depends on the business rules of an organization, and they should be set with caution. For example, if a branch of a bank closes, do you really want the accounts at that branch to be deleted? Another option might be to assign them to a different branch of the bank.

Establish a One-to-Many Relationship

Figure 2.21 also shows that the relationship that will be created will be a one-to-many relationship. Access provides three different relationships for joining tables: one-to-one, one-to-many, and many-to-many. The most common type by far is the one-to-many relationship. A **one-to-many relationship** is established when the primary key value in the primary table can match many of the foreign key values in the related table.

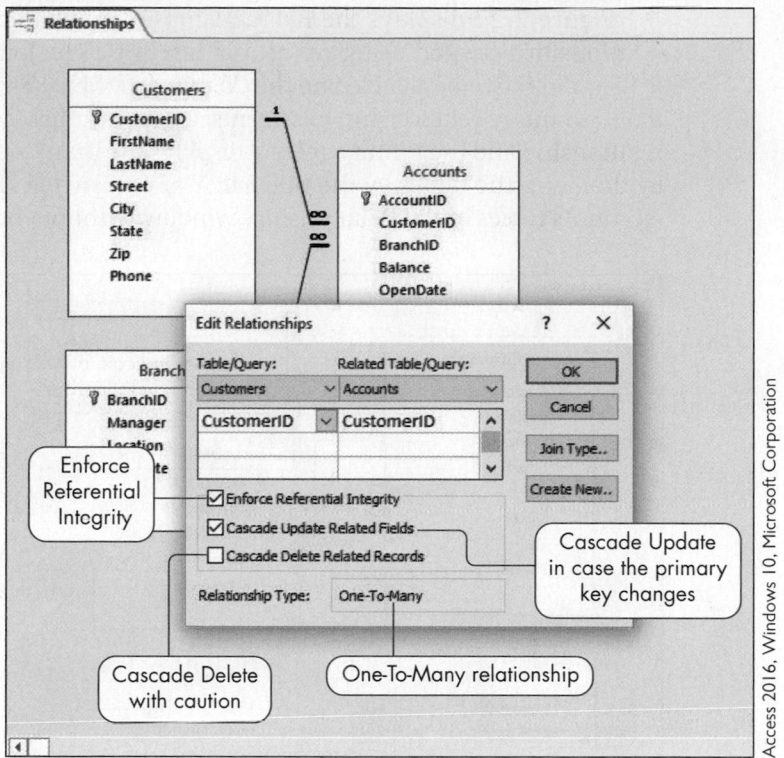

FIGURE 2.21 Cascade Update and Delete Options

For example, a bank customer will be entered into the Customers table one time only. The primary key value, which is the CustomerID number, might be 1585. That same customer could set up a checking, savings, and credit card account. With each account, the CustomerID (1585) is required and therefore will occur three times in the Accounts table. The value is entered one time in the Customers table and three times in the Accounts table. Therefore, the relationship between Customers and Accounts is described as one-to-many. Table 2.3 lists and describes all three types of relationships you can create between Access tables.

TABLE 2.3	Relationship Types
Relationship Type	**Description**
One-to-Many	The primary key table must have only one occurrence of each value. For example, each customer must have a unique identification number in the Customers table. The foreign key field in the related table may have repeating values. For example, one customer may have many different account numbers.
One-to-One	Two different tables use the same primary key. Exactly one record exists in the second table for each record in the first table. Sometimes security issues require a single table to be split into two related tables. For example, in an organization's database anyone in the company might be able to access the Employee table and find the employee's office number, department assignment, or telephone extension. However, only a few people need to have access to the employee's network login password, salary, Social Security number, performance review, or marital status, which would be stored in a second table. Tables containing this information would use the same unique identifier to identify each employee.
Many-to-Many	This is an artificially constructed relationship allowing many matching records in each direction between tables. It requires construction of a third table called a junction table. For example, a database might have a table for employees and one for projects. Several employees might be assigned to one project, but one employee might also be assigned to many different projects.

Figure 2.22 displays the Relationships window for the Bank database and all the relationships created using referential integrity. The join line between the CustomerID field in the Customers table and the CustomerID field in the Accounts table indicates that a one-to-many relationship has been set. The number 1 displays on the one side of the relationship and the infinity symbol displays the many side. You can rearrange the tables by dragging the tables by the title bar. You can switch the positions of the Branch and Accounts tables in the Relationships window without changing the relationship itself.

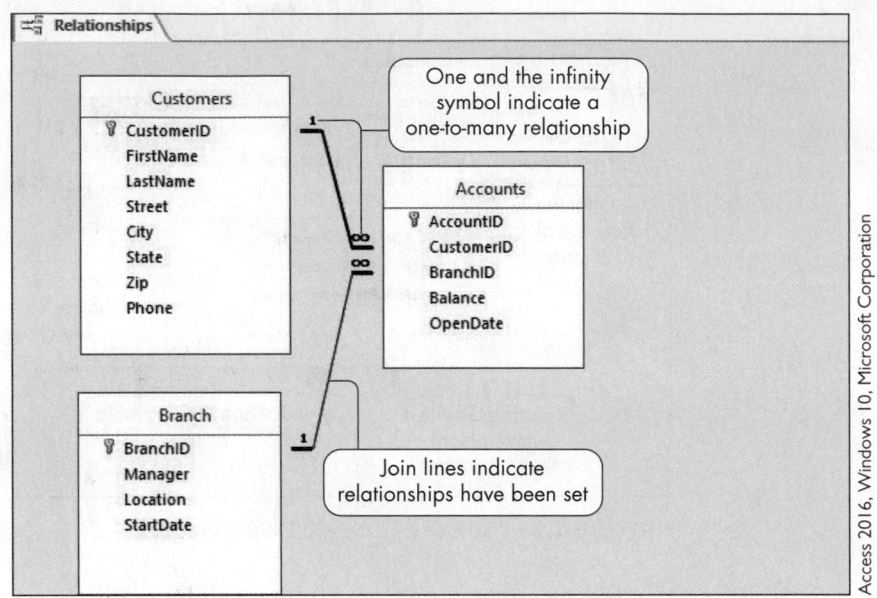

FIGURE 2.22 Relationships Window Displaying One-to-Many Relationships

---

TIP: NAVIGATING BETWEEN THE RELATIONSHIPS WINDOW AND A TABLE'S DESIGN

When you right-click a table's title bar in the Relationships window, the shortcut menu offers you the option to open the table in Design view. This is a convenient feature because if you want to link one table to another table, the joined fields must have the same data type. This shortcut enables you to check the fields and revise them if a table contains a field with the wrong data type.

Quick Concepts

4. Describe a scenario that may require you to import Excel data into Access. **p. 749**

5. What is the purpose of setting a relationship between two tables? **p. 754**

6. Why would you decide to use the Cascade Delete option (or not) when setting a relationship? **p. 756**

7. Specify two database tables that you might design that would contain a one-to-many relationship. Describe the relationship. **p. 756**

Hands-On Exercises

Watch the Video for this Hands-On Exercise!

MyITLab®
HOE2 Training

Skills covered: Import Excel Data • Import Data from an Access Database • Modify an Imported Table's Design • Add Data to an Imported Table • Establish Table Relationships • Enforce Referential Integrity

2 Multiple-Table Databases

You created a new Bank database, and a new Branch table. Now you are ready to import additional tables—one from an Excel spreadsheet and one from an Access database. Assume that the data are formatted correctly and are structured properly so that you can begin the import process.

STEP 1 ›› IMPORT EXCEL DATA

You and the auditor have discovered several of Commonwealth's files that contain customer data. These files need to be analyzed, so you decide to import the data into Access. In this step, you import an Excel spreadsheet into the Bank database. Refer to Figure 2.23 as you complete Step 1.

All Access Obje... ⊙ «

Search...

Tables ⊗
- Branch
- Customers

Step e: Imported column headings

Customers

CID	FirstName	LastName	Street	City	State	Zip	Phone	Click to Add
30001	Allison	Millward	2732 Baker Blvd.	Greensboro	NC	27492	5553345678	
30002	Bernett	Fox	12 Orchestra Terrace	High Point	NC	27494	5553585554	
30003	Clay	Hayes	P.O. Box 555	Greensboro	NC	27492	5559984457	
30004	Cordie	Collins	2743 Bering St.	Winston-Salem	NC	27492	5554472283	
30005	Eaton	Wagner	2743 Bering St.	Greensboro	NC	27492	5559883346	
30006	Kwasi	Williams	89 Jefferson Way	High Point	NC	27494	5554475565	
30007	Natasha	Simpson	187 Suffolk Ln.	Greensboro	NC	27493	5557753389	
30008	Joy	Jones	305 - 14th Ave. S.	Winston-Salem	NC	27493	5552587655	
30009	John	Nunn	89 Chiaroscuro Rd.	Greensboro	NC	27494	5559985557	
30010	Laura	Peterson	120 Hanover Sq.	Winston-Salem	NC	27492	5553346654	

Access 2016, Windows 10, Microsoft Corporation

FIGURE 2.23 Imported Customers Table

a. Open *a02h1Bank_LastFirst* if you closed it at the end of Hands-On Exercise 1, and save it as **a02h2Bank_LastFirst**, changing h1 to h2.

b. Click **Enable Content** below the Ribbon to indicate that you trust the contents of the database.

c. Click the **External Data tab** and click **Excel** in the Import & Link group to launch the Get External Data – Excel Spreadsheet feature. Ensure that the *Import the source data into a new table in the current database* option is selected.

> **TROUBLESHOOTING:** Ensure that you click Excel in the Import & Link group to import the spreadsheet and not the Excel command in the Export group.

d. Click **Browse** and navigate to your student data files. Select the *a02h2Customers* workbook. Click **Open** and click **OK** to open the Import Spreadsheet Wizard.

e. Ensure that the *First Row Contains Column Headings* check box is checked to indicate to Access that column headings exist in the Excel file.

The field names CID, FirstName, LastName, Street, City, State, ZIP, and Phone will import from Excel along with the data stored in the rows in the worksheet. You will modify the field names later in Access.

f. Click **Next**.

g. Ensure that CID is displayed in the Field Name box in Field Options. Click the **Indexed arrow** and select **Yes (No Duplicates)**. Click **Next**.

The CID (CustomerID) will become the primary key in this table. It needs to be a unique identifier, so you must change the property to No Duplicates.

Hands-On Exercise 2

759

h. Click the **Choose my own primary key option**. Make sure that the CID field is selected. Click **Next**.

The final screen of the Import Spreadsheet Wizard asks you to name your table. The name of the Excel worksheet is Customers, and Access defaults to the worksheet name. It is an acceptable name.

i. Click **Finish** to accept Customers as the table name.

A dialog box opens prompting you to save the steps of this import to use again. If this is data that is to be collected in Excel and updated to the database on a regular basis, saving the import steps would save time. You do not need to save the import steps in this example.

j. Click **Close**.

The new table displays in the Navigation Pane of the Bank database.

k. Open the imported Customers table in Datasheet view and double-click the border between each of the field names to adjust the columns to Best Fit. Compare your table to Figure 2.23.

l. Save and close the table.

STEP 2 ›› IMPORT DATA FROM AN ACCESS DATABASE

The auditor asks you to import an Access database table that contains account information related to the accounts you are analyzing. You use the Import Wizard to import the database table. Refer to Figure 2.24 as you complete Step 2.

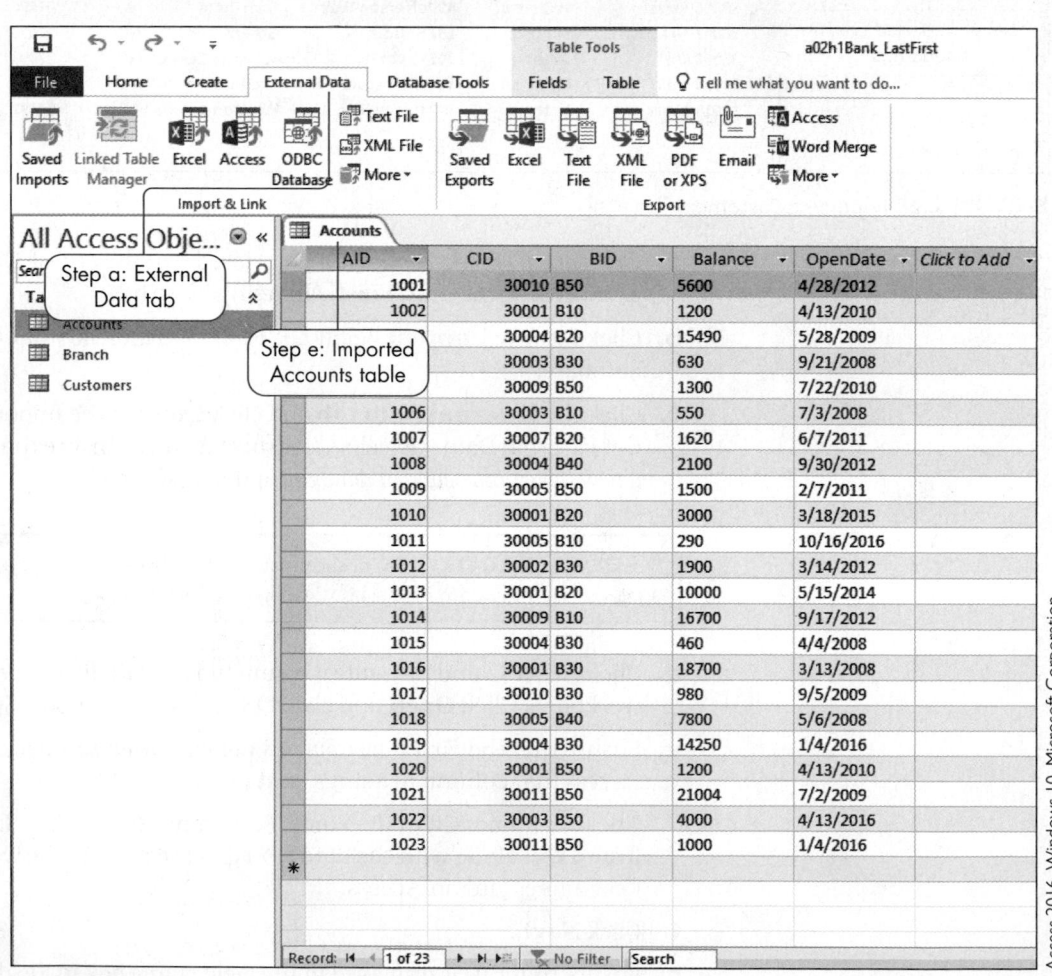

FIGURE 2.24 Imported Accounts Table

a. Click the **External Data tab** and click **Access** in the Import & Link group to launch the Get External Data – Access Database feature. Ensure that the *Import tables, queries, forms, reports, macros, and modules into the current database* option is selected.

b. Click **Browse** and navigate to your student data files. Select the *a02h2Accounts* database. Click **Open** and click **OK** to open the Import Objects dialog box.

c. Click the **Accounts table** for importing and click **OK**.

d. Click **Close** in the Save Import Steps dialog box.

The Navigation Pane now contains three tables: Accounts, Branch, and Customers.

e. Open the imported Accounts table in Datasheet view and compare it to Figure 2.24.

f. Close the table.

STEP 3 ›› MODIFY AN IMPORTED TABLE'S DESIGN

When importing tables from either Excel or Access, the fields may have different data types and property settings than required to create table relationships. You will modify the tables so that each field has the correct data type and field size. Refer to Figure 2.25 as you complete Step 3.

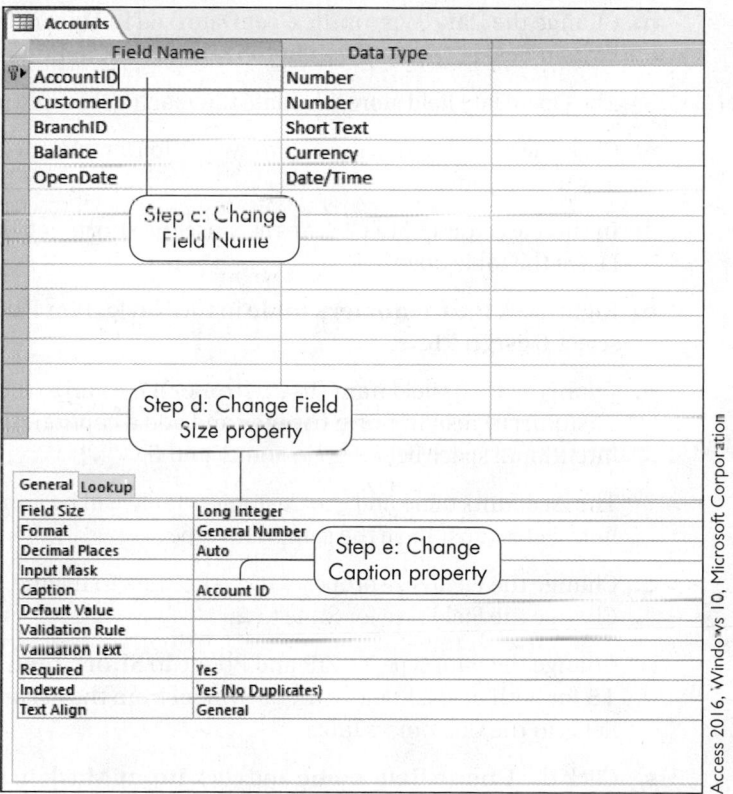

FIGURE 2.25 Modified Accounts Table Design

a. Right-click the **Accounts table** in the Navigation Pane.

b. Select Design view from the shortcut menu to open the table in Design view.

The Accounts table displays with the primary key AID selected.

c. Change the AID field name to **AccountID**.

d. Change the Field Size property to **Long Integer**.

Long Integer ensures that there will be enough numbers as the number of customers grows over time and may exceed 32,768 (the upper limit for Integer values).

e. Type **Account ID** in the Caption box for the AccountID field. The caption contains a space between Account and ID.

f. Click the **CID** field. Change the CID field name to **CustomerID**.

g. Change the Field Size property to **Long Integer**.

You can select the Field Size option using the arrow, or you can type the first letter of the option you want. For example, type l for Long Integer or s for Single. Make sure the current option is completely selected before you type the letter.

h. Type **Customer ID** in the Caption box for the CustomerID field. The caption contains a space between Customer and ID.

i. Click the **BID field**. Change the BID field name to **BranchID**.

j. Type **5** in the Field Size property box in the Field Properties.

k. Type **Branch ID** in the Caption property box for the Branch ID field.

l. Change the Data Type of the Balance field to **Currency**.

The Currency data type is used for fields that contain monetary values. In this case, changing the data type is not consequential; formatting the imported Balance field as Currency will not change the original data values.

m. Change the Data Type of the OpenDate field to **Date/Time** and set **Short Date** in the Format field property. Type **Open Date** in the Caption property box.

The OpenDate field stores the date that each account was opened.

n. Click **View** in the Views group to switch to Datasheet view. Read the messages and click **Yes** to each one.

In this case, it is OK to click Yes because the shortened fields will not cut off any data. Leave the table open.

o. Right-click the **Customers table** in the Navigation Pane and from the shortcut menu, select **Design View**.

p. Change the CID field name to **CustomerID**. Change the Field Size property of the CustomerID field to **Long Integer** and add a caption, **Customer ID**. Take note of the intentional space between Customer and ID.

The Accounts table and the Customers table will be joined using the CustomerID field. Both fields must have the same data type.

q. Change the Field Size property to **20** for the FirstName, LastName, Street, and City fields. Change the Field Size for State to **2**.

r. Change the data type for ZIP and Phone to **Short Text**. Change the Field Size property to **15** for both fields. Remove the @ symbol from the Format property where it exists for all fields in the Customers table.

s. Click the **Phone field name** and click **Input Mask** in Field Properties. Click the **ellipsis** on the right side to launch the Input Mask Wizard. Click **Yes** to save the table and click **Yes** to the *Some data may be lost* warning. Click **Finish** to apply the default phone number input mask.

The phone number input mask enables users to enter 6105551212 in the datasheet, and Access will display it as (610) 555-1212.

t. Click **Save** to save the design changes to the Customers table.

Now that you have created the Access tables, you discover that you need to add another customer and his account records to them. Refer to Figure 2.26 as you complete Step 4.

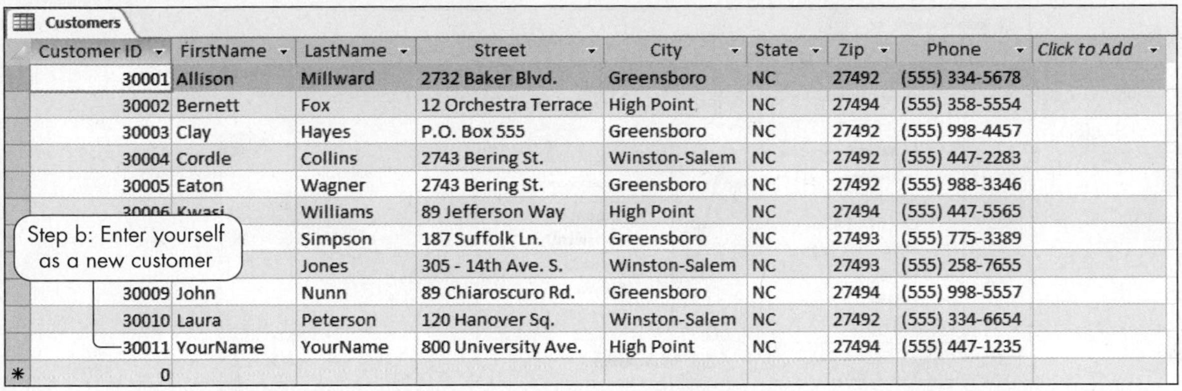

Customer ID	FirstName	LastName	Street	City	State	Zip	Phone	Click to Add
30001	Allison	Millward	2732 Baker Blvd.	Greensboro	NC	27492	(555) 334-5678	
30002	Bernett	Fox	12 Orchestra Terrace	High Point	NC	27494	(555) 358-5554	
30003	Clay	Hayes	P.O. Box 555	Greensboro	NC	27492	(555) 998-4457	
30004	Cordle	Collins	2743 Bering St.	Winston-Salem	NC	27492	(555) 447-2283	
30005	Eaton	Wagner	2743 Bering St.	Greensboro	NC	27492	(555) 988-3346	
30006	Kwasi	Williams	89 Jefferson Way	High Point	NC	27494	(555) 447-5565	
		Simpson	187 Suffolk Ln.	Greensboro	NC	27493	(555) 775-3389	
		Jones	305 - 14th Ave. S.	Winston-Salem	NC	27493	(555) 258-7655	
30009	John	Nunn	89 Chiaroscuro Rd.	Greensboro	NC	27494	(555) 998-5557	
30010	Laura	Peterson	120 Hanover Sq.	Winston-Salem	NC	27492	(555) 334-6654	
30011	YourName	YourName	800 University Ave.	High Point	NC	27494	(555) 447-1235	
0								

Step b: Enter yourself as a new customer

Access 2016, Windows 10, Microsoft Corporation

FIGURE 2.26 Customers Table Displaying the Added Customer ID 30011

a. Click **View** in the Views group to display the Customers table in Datasheet view.

The asterisk at the bottom of the table data in the row selector area is the indicator of a place to enter a new record.

b. Click next to the * in the **Customer ID field** in the new record row below 30010. Type **30011**. Fill in the rest of the data using your personal information as the customer. You may use a fictitious address and phone number.

Note the phone number format. The input mask you set formats the phone number.

c. Close the Customers table. The Accounts table tab is open.

> **TROUBLESHOOTING:** If the Accounts table is not open, double-click Accounts in the Navigation Pane.

d. Click next to the * in the **Account ID field** in the new record row. Type **1024**. Type **30011** as the Customer ID and **B50** as the Branch ID. Type **14005** for the Balance field value. Type **8/7/2018** for the Open Date.

e. Add the following records to the Accounts table:

Account ID	Customer ID	Branch ID	Balance	Open Date
1025	30006	B40	$11,010	3/13/2018
1026	30007	B20	$7,400	5/1/2018

f. Close the Accounts table, but keep the database open.

The tables for the bank investigation have been designed and populated. Now you will establish connections between the tables. Look at the primary and foreign keys as a guide. Refer to Figure 2.27 as you complete Step 5.

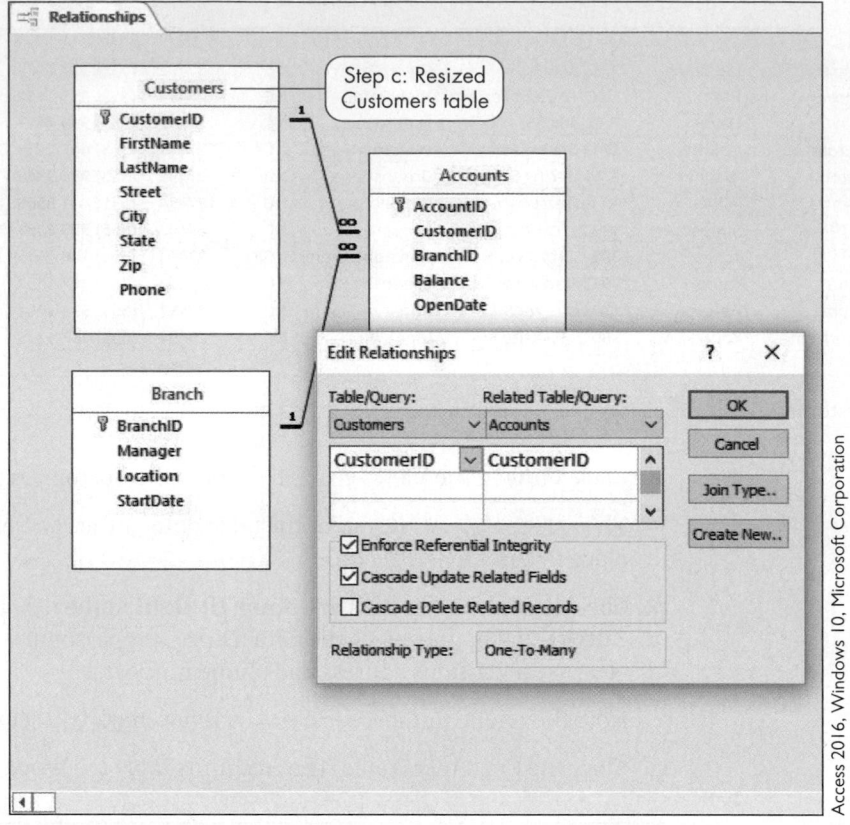

FIGURE 2.27 Relationships Between Tables

a. Click the **Database Tools tab** and click **Relationships** in the Relationships group.

The Relationships window opens and the Show Table dialog box displays.

> **TROUBLESHOOTING:** If the Show Table dialog box does not open, click Show Table in the Relationships group on the Relationship Tools Design tab.

b. Double-click each of the three tables displayed in the Show Table dialog box to add them to the Relationships window. Click **Close** in the Show Table dialog box.

> **TROUBLESHOOTING:** If you have a duplicate table, click the title bar of the duplicated table and press Delete.

c. Click and drag the border of the Customers table field list to resize it so that all of the fields are visible. Arrange the tables as shown in Figure 2.27.

d. Drag the **BranchID field** (the primary key) in the Branch table onto the BranchID field (the foreign key) in the Accounts table. The Edit Relationships dialog box opens. Click the **Enforce Referential Integrity** and **Cascade Update Related Fields check boxes** to select them. Click **Create**.

A black line displays, joining the two tables. It has a 1 at the end near the Branch table and an infinity symbol on the end next to the Accounts table. You have established a one-to-many relationship between the Branch and Accounts tables. Each single branch is connected with many accounts.

e. Drag the **CustomerID field** (the primary key) in the Customers table onto the CustomerID field (the foreign key) in the Accounts table. The Edit Relationships dialog box opens. Click the **Enforce Referential Integrity** and **Cascade Update Related Fields check boxes** to select them. Click **Create**.

You have established a one-to-many relationship between the Customers and Accounts tables. A customer will have only a single CustomerID number. The same customer may have many different accounts: Savings, Checking, Credit Card, and so forth.

> **TROUBLESHOOTING:** If you get an error message when you click Create, verify that the data types of the joined fields are the same. To check the data types from the Relationships window, right-click the title bar of a table and select Table Design from the shortcut menu. Modify the data type of the join fields, if necessary. Customer ID should be Number and Branch ID should be Short Text in both tables.

f. Click **Save** on the Quick Access Toolbar to save the changes to the relationships. Close the Relationships window.

STEP 6 ›› ENFORCE REFERENTIAL INTEGRITY

The design of the Bank database must be 100% correct; otherwise, data entry may be compromised. Even though you are confident that the table relationships are set correctly, you decide to test them by entering some invalid data. If referential integrity is enforced, the invalid data will be rejected by Access. Refer to Figure 2.28 as you complete Step 6.

Account ID	Customer ID	Branch ID	Balance	Open Date	Click to Add
1003	30004	B20	$15,490.00	5/28/2009	
1004	30003	B30	$630.00	9/21/2008	
1005	30009	B50	$1,300.00	7/22/2010	
1006	30003	B10	$550.00	7/3/2008	
1007	30007	B20	$1,620.00	6/7/2011	
1008	30004	B40	$2,100.00	9/30/2012	
1009	30005	B50	$1,500.00	2/7/2011	
1010	30001	B20	$3,000.00	3/18/2015	
1011	30005				
1012	30002				
1013	30001				
1014	30009				
1015	30004				
1016	30001				
1017	30010	B30	$980.00	9/5/2009	
1018	30005	B40	$7,800.00	5/6/2008	
1019	30004	B30	$14,250.00	1/4/2016	
1020	30001	B50	$1,200.00	4/13/2010	
1021	30011	B50	$21,004.00	7/2/2009	
1022	30003	B50	$4,000.00	4/13/2016	
1023			$1,000.00	1/4/2016	
1024			$14,005.00	8/7/2018	
1025	30006	B40	$11,010.00	3/13/2018	
1026	30007	B20	$7,400.00	5/1/2018	
1027	30003	B60	$4,000.00	4/13/2018	
*			$0.00		

a02h2Bank

Step b: Access warns you that B60 is invalid

⚠ You cannot add or change a record because a related record is required in table 'Branch'.

OK   Help

Step b: B60 is not a valid branch

Record: ⏮ ◀ 27 of 27 ▶ ⏭ ▷▣ No Filter Search

FIGURE 2.28 Referential Integrity Enforces Accurate Data Entry

a. Double-click the **Accounts table** to open it in Datasheet view.

b. Add a new record, pressing **Tab** after each field: Account ID: **1027**, Customer ID: **30003**, Branch: **B60**, Balance: **4000**, Open Date: **4/13/2018**. Press **Enter**.

You attempted to enter a nonexistent BranchID (B60) and were not allowed to make that error. A warning message is telling you that a related record in the Branch table is required, because the Accounts table and the Branch table are connected by a relationship with Enforce Referential Integrity checked.

c. Click **OK**. Double-click the **Branch table** in the Navigation Pane and examine the data in the BranchID field. Notice the Branch table has no B60 record. Close the Branch table.

d. Replace B60 with **B50** in the new Accounts record and press **Tab** three times. As soon as the focus moves to the next record, the pencil symbol disappears and your data are saved.

You successfully identified a BranchID that Access recognizes. Because referential integrity between the Accounts and Branch tables has been enforced, Access looks at each data entry item in a foreign key and matches it to a corresponding value in the table where it is the primary key. In Step b, you attempted to enter a nonexistent BranchID and were not allowed to make that error. In Step d, you entered a valid BranchID. Access examined the index for the BranchID in the Branch table and found a corresponding value for B50.

e. Close the Accounts table.

f. Close any open tables.

g. Keep the database open if you plan to continue with the Hands-On Exercise. If not, close the database and exit Access.

Single-Table Queries

A *query* enables you to ask questions about the data stored in a database and then provides the answers to the questions by creating subsets or summaries of data in a datasheet. If you wanted to see which customers currently have an account with a balance over $5,000, you could find the answer by creating an Access query.

In this section, you will use the Simple Query Wizard and Query Design view to create single-table queries that display only data that you select. Multitable queries will be covered in the next section.

Creating a Single-Table Query

Because data are stored in tables in a database, you always begin a query by determining which table (or tables) contain the data that you need. For the question about account balances over $5,000, you would use the Accounts table. You can create a single-table query in two ways—by using the Simple Query Wizard or the Query Design tool in the Queries group on the Create tab. While the Simple Query Wizard offers a step-by-step guide to creating a query, the Query Design tool allows for more flexibility and customization, and is often the preferred method for creating queries.

After you design a query, you run it to display the results in a datasheet. A query's datasheet looks like a table's datasheet, except that it is usually a subset of the fields and records found in the table on which it is based. The subset shows only the records that match the criteria that were added in the query design. The subset may contain different sorting of the records than the sorting in the underlying table. You can enter new records in a query, modify existing records, or delete records in Datasheet view. Any changes made in Datasheet view are reflected in the underlying table on which the query is based.

Create a Single-Table Select Query

Select queries are a type of query that displays only the fields and records that match criteria entered in the query design process.

To create a select query using the Query Design tool, complete the following steps:

1. Click the Create tab.
2. Click Query Design in the Queries group on the Design tab.
3. Select the table you want for your query from the Show Table dialog box.
4. Click Add to add the table to the top pane of the query design and close the Show Table dialog box.
5. Drag the fields needed from the table's field list to the query design grid (or alternatively, double-click the field names); then add criteria and sorting options.
6. Click Run in the Results group on the Design tab to show the results in Datasheet view.

Use Query Design View

Query Design view is divided into two sections: The top pane displays the tables from which the data will be retrieved, and the bottom pane (known as the query design grid) displays the fields and the criteria that you set. In the query design grid, you select only the fields that contain the data you want in the query and arrange them in the order that you want them displayed in the query results. You add criteria to further limit (or filter) the records to display only those that you require in the results. The design grid also enables you to sort the records based on one or more fields. You can create calculated fields to display data based on expressions that use the fields in the underlying table. For example, you could calculate the monthly interest earned on each bank account by multiplying the Balance by an interest rate. If a query contains more than one table, the join lines between tables display as they were created in the Relationships window.

The query design grid (the bottom pane) contains columns and rows. Each field in the query has its own column and contains multiple rows. The rows allow you to control the query results.

- The Field row displays the field name.
- The Table row displays the data source (in some cases, a field occurs in more than one table, for example, when it is a join field; therefore, it is often beneficial to display the table name in the query design grid).
- The Sort row enables you to sort in ascending or descending order (or neither).
- The Show row controls whether the field will be displayed or hidden in the query results.
- The *Criteria row* is used to set the rules that determine which records will be selected, such as customers with account balances greater than $5,000.

Figure 2.29 displays the query design grid with the Show Table dialog box open. The Accounts table has been added from the Show Table dialog box. Figure 2.30 shows Design view of a sample query with four fields, with a criterion set for one field and sorting set on another. The results of the query display in Datasheet view, as shown in Figure 2.31.

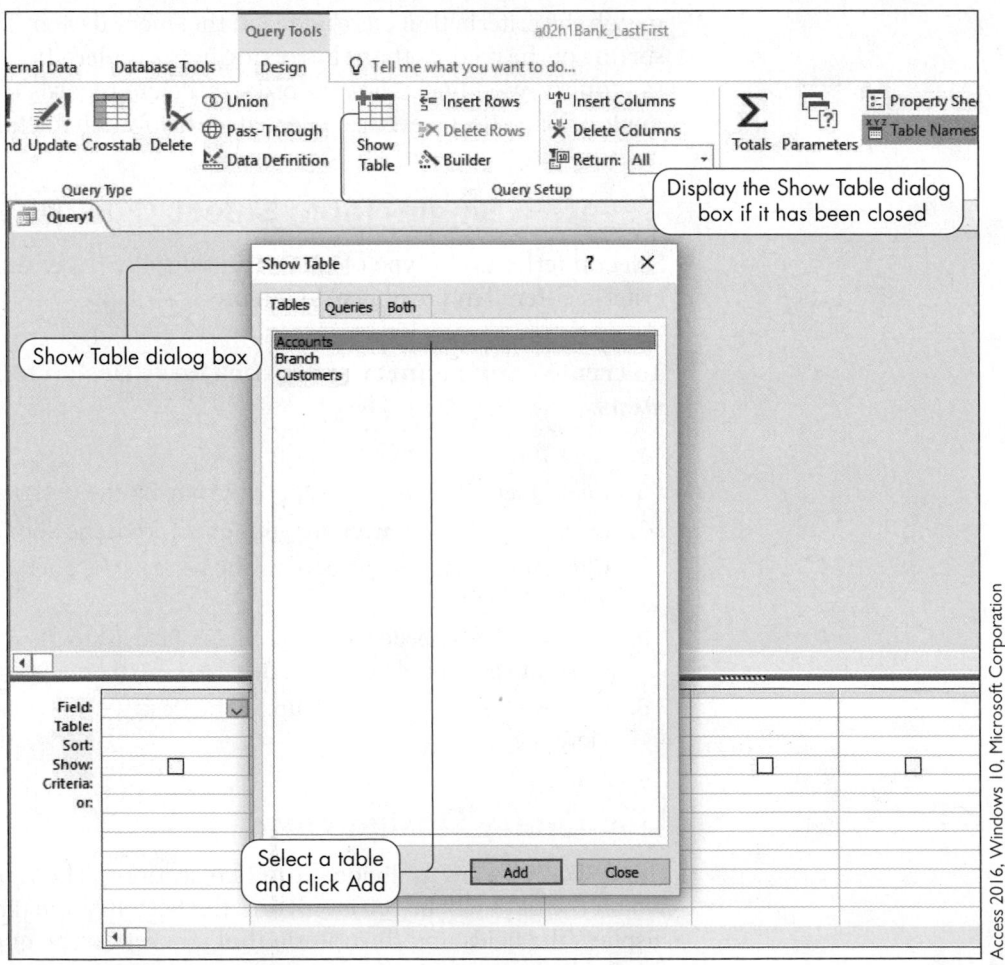

FIGURE 2.29 Query Design View with Show Table Dialog Box

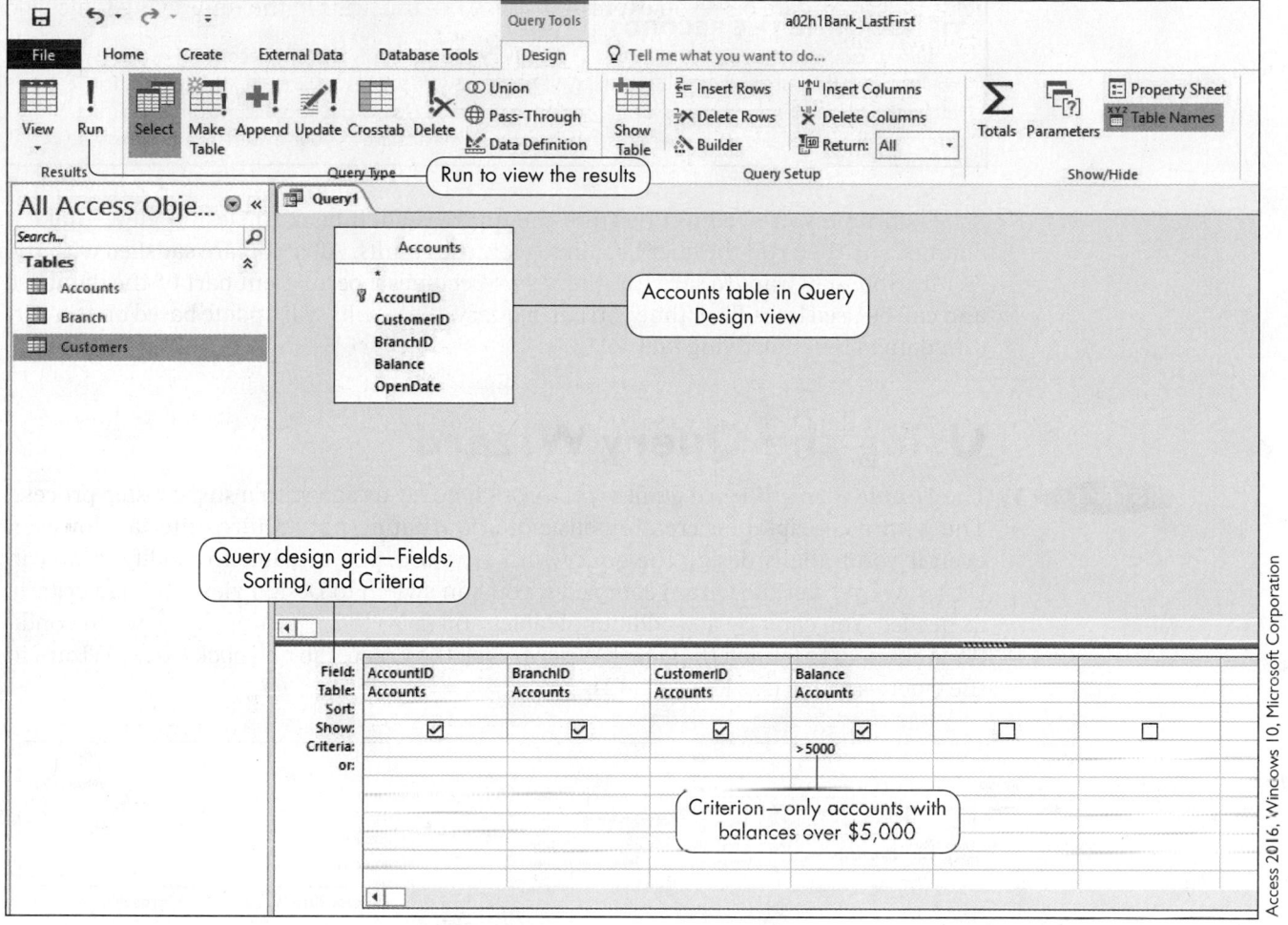

FIGURE 2.30 Query Design View with Sample Criterion

FIGURE 2.31 Query Results in Datasheet View

Each time you need to fine-tune the query, switch back to Design view, make a change, and then run the query again to view the results. After you are satisfied with the results, you may want to save the query so it becomes a permanent part of the database and can be used later. Each time you run a query, the results will update based on the current data in the underlying table(s).

Using the Query Wizard

STEP 1 ❯❯ The **Simple Query Wizard** guides you through query design with a step-by-step process. The wizard is helpful for creating basic queries that do not require criteria. However, even if you initially design the query with a wizard, you are able to modify it later in Design view. After the wizard completes, you can switch to Design view and add criteria as needed. You can also add additional tables and fields to an existing query when conditions change. To launch the Query Wizard, click the Create tab and click Query Wizard in the Queries group (see Figure 2.32).

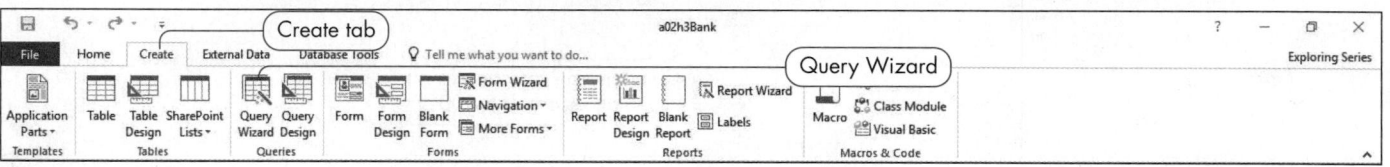

FIGURE 2.32 Launching the Query Wizard

Access 2016, Windows 10, Microsoft Corporation

Select Simple Query Wizard in the New Query dialog box, as shown in Figure 2.33.

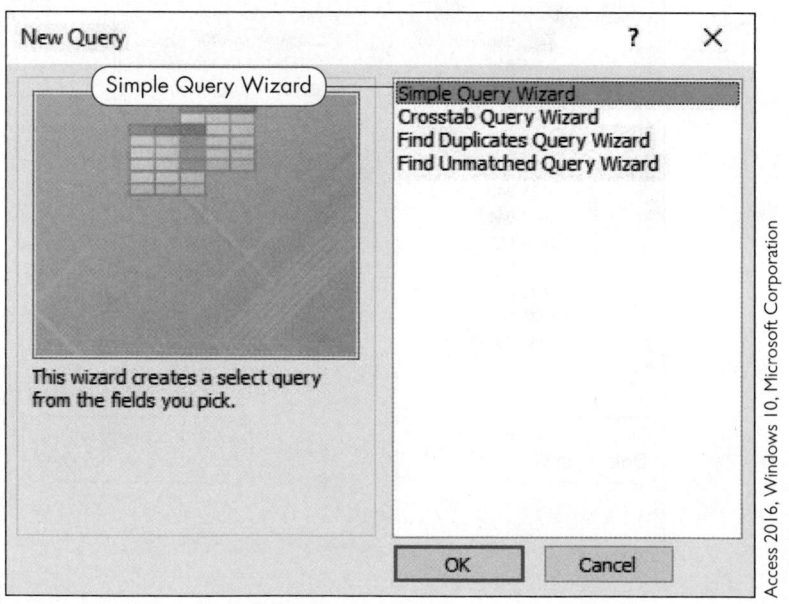

Access 2016, Windows 10, Microsoft Corporation

FIGURE 2.33 Simple Query Wizard

In the first step of the Simple Query Wizard dialog box, you specify the tables or queries and fields required in your query. When you select a table from the Tables/Queries arrow (queries can also be based on other queries), a list of the table's fields displays in the Available Fields list box (see Figures 2.34 and 2.35).

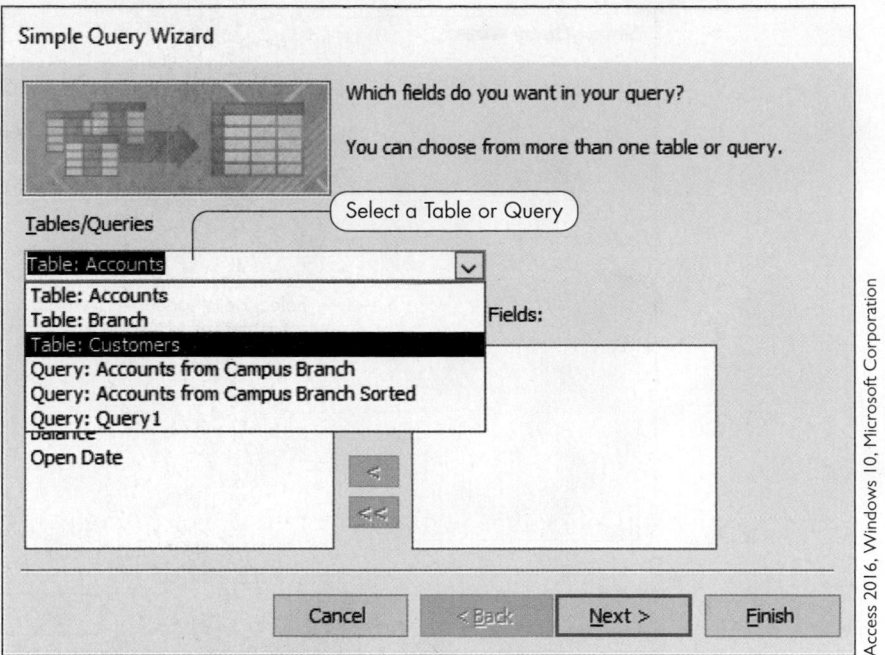

FIGURE 2.34 Specify Which Tables or Queries to Use

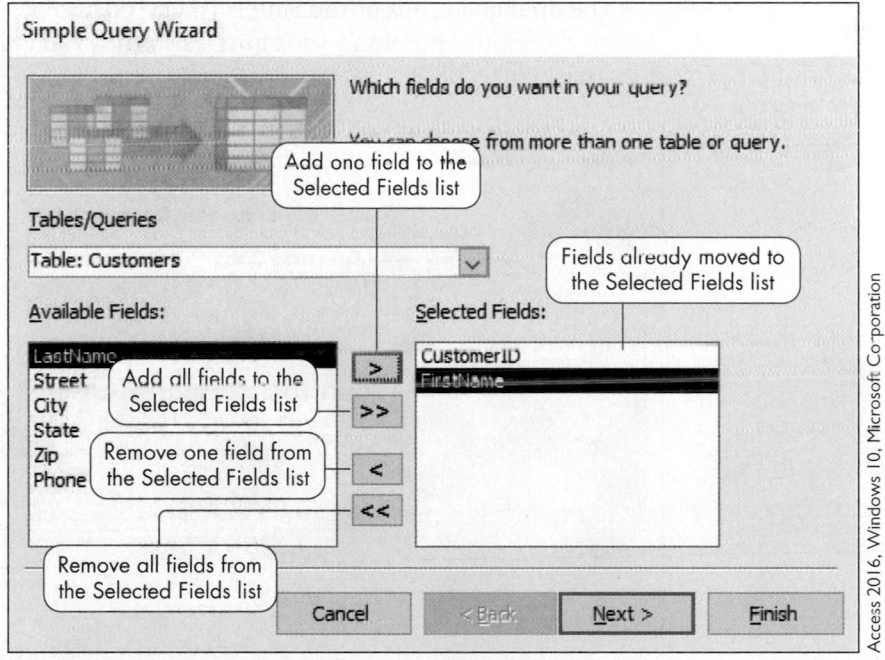

FIGURE 2.35 Specify the Fields for the Query

Select the necessary fields and add them to the Selected Fields list box using the directional arrows shown in Figure 2.35. In the next screen (shown in Figure 2.36), you choose between a detail and a summary query. The detail query shows every field of every record in the result. The summary query enables you to group data and view only summary records. For example, if you were interested in the total funds deposited at each of the bank branches, you would set the query to Summary, click Summary Options, and then click Sum on the Balance field. Access would then sum the balances of all accounts for each branch.

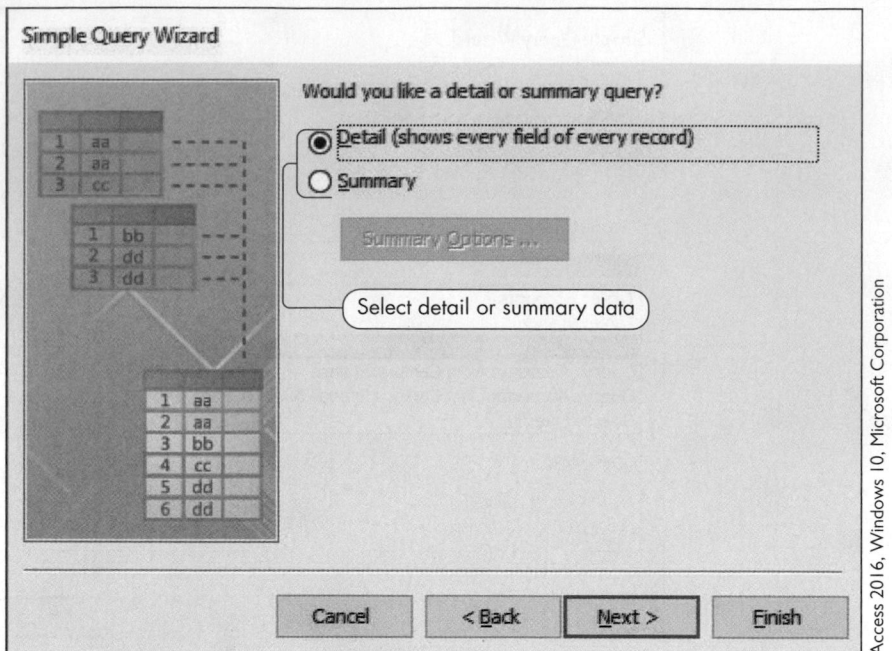

FIGURE 2.36 Choose Detail or Summary Data

The final dialog box of the Simple Query Wizard prompts for the name of the query. Assign descriptive names to your queries so that you can easily identify what each one does (see Figure 2.37).

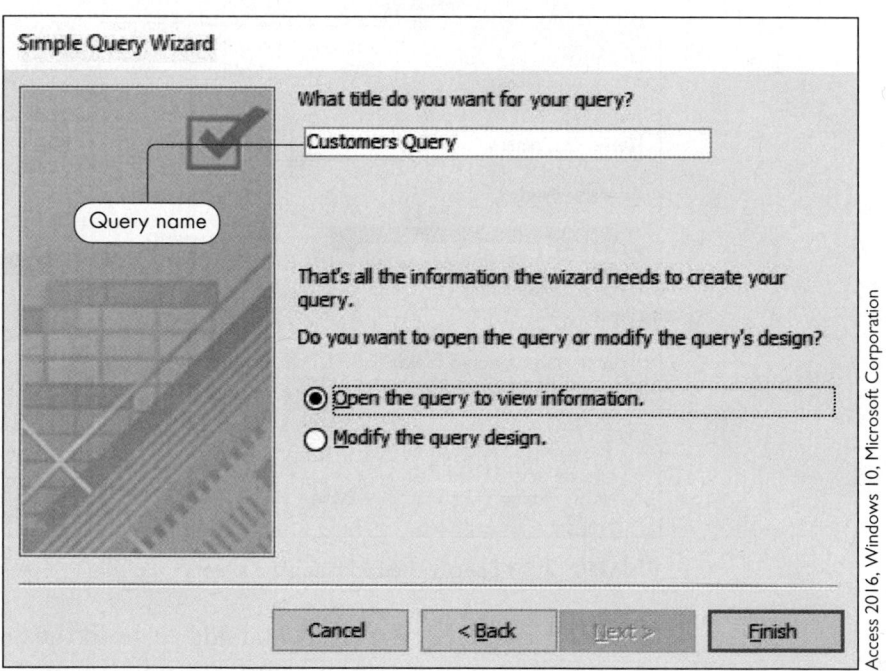

FIGURE 2.37 Name the Query

Specifying Query Criteria for Different Data Types

STEP 2 You set criteria to limit the records to display only those that you require in the query results. When specifying a criterion for a query, you may need to include a delimiter—a special character that surrounds a criterion's value. The delimiter required is determined by the field data type. Text fields require quotation marks before and after the text; for example, "Campus" could be used to display customers from the Campus branch in the Bank database. Access automatically adds the quotation marks around text, but to ensure that the correct delimiter is used, you may want to include the delimiters yourself.

When the criterion is in a date field, you enclose the criterion in pound signs, such as #10/14/2018#. Access automatically adds the pound signs around dates, but to ensure that the correct delimiter is used, you may want to include the delimiters yourself. A date value can be entered using any allowed format, such as February 2, 2018, 2/2/2018, or 2-Feb-18. Use plain digits (no delimiter) for the criteria of a numeric field, currency, or AutoNumber. You can enter numeric criteria with or without a decimal point and with or without a minus sign. Commas and dollar signs are not allowed. You enter criteria for a Yes/No field as Yes or No. See Table 2.4 for query criteria and examples.

TABLE 2.4 Query Criteria

Data Type	Criteria	Example
Text	"Harry"	For a FirstName field, displays only text that matches Harry exactly. The quotation marks can be typed, or Access will add them automatically.
Numeric	5000	For a Quantity field, displays only numbers that match 5000 exactly (do not specify commas, currency symbols, etc.).
Date	#2/2/2018#	For a ShippedDate field, shows orders shipped on February 2, 2018.
Yes/No	Yes	For a Discontinued field, returns records where the check box is selected, denoting Yes.

Pearson Education, Inc.

Use Wildcards

Wildcards are special characters that can represent one or more characters in a text value. Suppose you want to use a criterion to search for the last name of a customer, but you are not sure how to spell the name; however, you know that the name starts with the letters *Sm*. You can use a wildcard with a text value (such as Sm*) to search for the name.

You enter wildcard characters in text values in the Criteria row of a query. Therefore, if you want to search for names that start with the letters *Sm*, specify the criterion in the LastName field as *Sm**. All last names that begin with *Sm* would display in the results. Wildcard characters can be placed in the beginning, middle, or end of a text string. Table 2.5 shows more query criterion examples that use wildcards.

TABLE 2.5 Query Criteria Using Wildcards

Character	Description	Example	Result
*	Matches any number of characters in the same position as the asterisk	Sm*	Small, Smiley, Smith, Smithson
?	Matches a single character in the same position as the question mark	H?ll	Hall, Hill, Hull
[ ]	Matches any single character within the brackets	F[ae]ll	Fall and Fell, but not Fill or Full
[!]	Matches any character not in the brackets	F[!ae]ll	Fill and Full, but not Fall or Fell

Pearson Education, Inc.

Use Comparison Operators in Queries

Comparison operators, such as equal (=), not equal (<>), greater than (>), less than (<), greater than or equal to (>=), and less than or equal to (<=), can be used in query criteria. Comparison operators enable you to limit the query results to only those records that meet the criteria. For example, if you only want to see accounts that have a balance greater than $5,000, you would type >5000 in the Criteria row of the Balance field. Table 2.6 shows more comparison operator examples.

TABLE 2.6 Comparison Operators in Queries	
Expression	**Example**
=10	Equals 10
<>10	Not equal to 10
>10	Greater than 10
>=10	Greater than or equal to 10
<10	Less than 10
<=10	Less than or equal to 10

Pearson Education, Inc.

Work with Null

Sometimes finding null values is an important part of making a decision. For example, if you need to know which orders have been completed but not shipped, you would create a query to find the orders with a null (missing) ShipDate. The term that Access uses for a blank field is **null**. Table 2.7 provides two examples of when to use the null criterion in a query.

TABLE 2.7 Establishing Null Criteria Expressions		
Expression	**Description**	**Example**
Is Null	Use to find blank fields	For a SalesRepID field in the Customers table when the customer has not been assigned to a sales representative.
Is Not Null	Used to find fields with data	For a ShipDate field; a value has been entered to indicate that the order was shipped to the customer.

Pearson Education, Inc.

Establish AND, OR, and NOT Criteria

Remember the earlier question, "Which customers currently have an account with a balance over $5,000?" This question was answered by creating a query with a single criterion. At times, questions are more focused and require queries with multiple criteria. For example, you may need to know "Which customers from the Eastern branch currently have an account with a balance over $5,000?" To answer this question, you specify two criteria in different fields using the **AND condition**. This means that the query results will display only records that match *all* criteria. When the criteria are in the same row of the query design grid, Access interprets this as an AND condition. You can also use the AND logical operator to test two criteria in the same field, as shown in Table 2.8.

When you have multiple criteria and you need to satisfy only one, not all of the criteria, use the **OR condition**. The query results will display records that match any of the specified criteria. You can use the OR logical operator, and type the expression into the Criteria row, separating the criteria with the OR keyword. Table 2.8 shows an example of an OR condition created using this method. You can also type the first criterion into the Criteria row and then type the next criterion by using the Or row in the same field or a different field in the design grid (see Figure 2.38).

The NOT logical operator returns all records except the specified criteria. For example, "Not Eastern" would return all accounts except those opened at the Eastern branch.

TABLE 2.8 AND, OR, and NOT Queries

Logical Operator	Example	Result
AND	>5000 AND <10000	For a Balance field, returns all accounts with a balance greater than $5,000 and less than $10,000.
OR	"Eastern" OR "Campus"	For a Location field, returns all accounts that are at the Eastern or the Campus branch.
NOT	Not "Campus"	For a Location field, returns all records except those in the Campus branch.

FIGURE 2.38 Query Design Views Showing the AND, OR, and NOT Operators

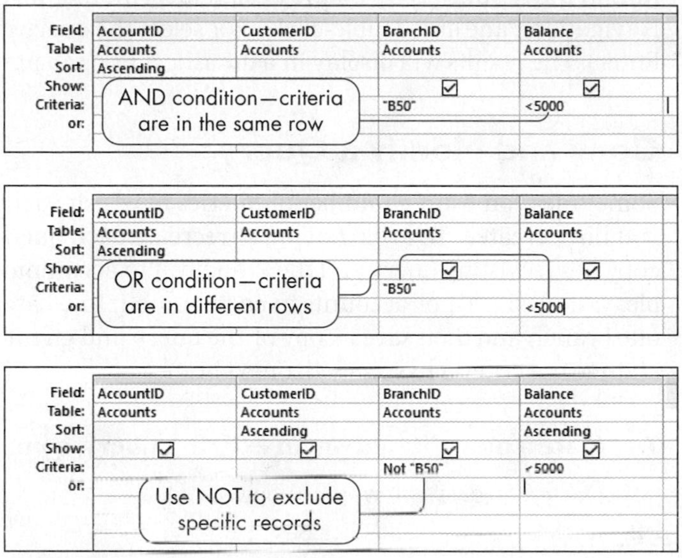

TIP: FINDING VALUES IN A DATE RANGE

To find the values contained within a date range, use the greater than (>) and less than (<) operators. For example, to find the values of dates on or after January 1, 2018, and on or before December 31, 2018, use the criterion >=1/1/2018 and <=12/31/2018. You can also use the BETWEEN operator to find the same inclusive dates, for example, BETWEEN 1/1/2018 and 12/31/2018.

Understanding Query Sort Order

The query sort order determines the order of records in a query's Datasheet view. You can change the order of records by specifying the sort order in Design view. When you want to sort using more than one field, the sort order is determined from left to right. The order of columns should be considered when first creating the query. For example, a query sorted by LastName and then by FirstName must have those two fields in the correct order in the design grid. When modifying sort order, it is sometimes necessary to rearrange fields, or add and delete columns in the query design grid.

To change order, add, or delete fields in the query design grid, complete one of the following steps:

- Change the order of a field: select the column you want to move by clicking the column selector. Click again and drag the selected field to its new location.

- Insert an additional column in the design grid: select a column and click Insert Columns in the Query Setup group on the Design tab. The additional column will insert to the left of the selected column.

- Delete a column: click the column selector to select the column and click Delete Columns in the Query Setup group, or press Delete on the keyboard.

Running, Copying, and Modifying a Query

Once your query is designed and saved, you run it to view the results. After you create a query, you may want to create a duplicate copy to use as the basis for creating a similar query. Duplicating a query saves time when you need the same tables and fields but with slightly different criteria.

Run a Query

There are several ways to run a query. One method is from within Design view; click Run in the Results group on the Design tab. Another method is to locate the query in the Navigation Pane and double-click it (or select the query in the Navigation Pane and press Enter). The results will display in a datasheet as a tab in the main window.

Copy and Modify a Query

Sometimes you want a number of queries in which each query is similar to another that you have created. To avoid having to recreate each query from scratch, you can create a copy of an existing query and then modify it to accommodate the new criteria. For example, you need a list of accounts in each branch. In a case like this, you create a query for one branch and then save a copy of the query and give it a new name. Finally, you would change the criteria to specify the next branch.

To create a query based on an existing query, complete the following steps:

1. Open the query you want to copy.
2. Click the File tab and click Save As.
3. Click Save Object As in the File Types section.
4. Ensure that Save Object As is selected in the Database File Types section and click Save As.
5. Type the name you want to use for the new query in the Save As dialog box and click OK (see Figure 2.39).
6. Switch to Design view of the copied query and modify the query criteria, as necessary.
7. Save and run the modified query.

TIP: COPYING THE QUERY IN THE NAVIGATION PANE
You can also right-click the original query in the Navigation Pane and from the shortcut menu, select Copy. Right-click in the empty space of the Navigation Pane again and then select Paste. Type a name for the new query in the Paste As dialog box and click OK.

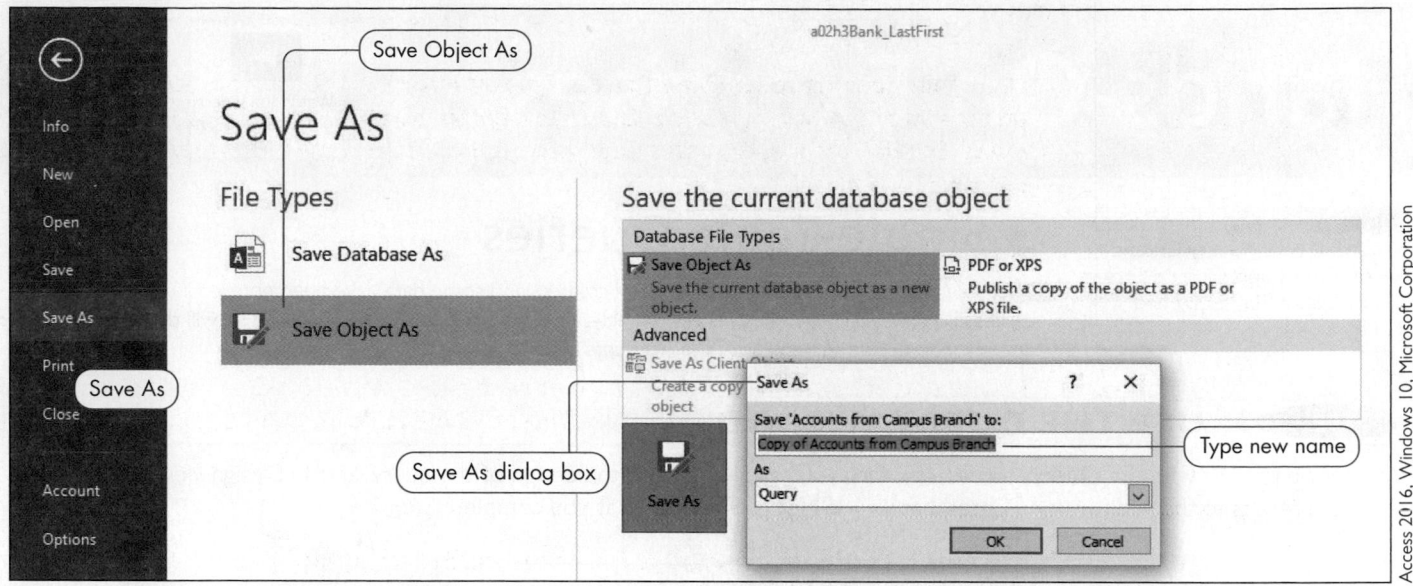

FIGURE 2.39 Using Save Object As to Save a Copy of a Query

Change Query Data

 **STEP 3** ❱❱ Be aware that query results in the datasheet display the actual records that are stored in the underlying table(s). Being able to correct an error immediately while it is displayed in the query datasheet is an advantage. You can save time by not having to close the query, open the table, find the error, fix it, and then run the query again. However, use caution when editing records in query results since you will be changing the original table data.

Quick Concepts

8. Define a single-table query. Give an example. **p. 766**

9. Give an example of how to use the Criteria row to find certain records in a table. **p. 768**

10. Why would you use an OR condition in a query? **p. 774**

11. Why would you want to copy an existing query? **p. 776**

Hands-On Exercises

Watch the Video
for this Hands-On
Exercise!

MyITLab®
HOE3 Training

Skills covered: Use the Query Wizard • Specify Query Criteria • Specify Query Sort Order • Change Query Data • Run, Copy, and Modify a Query

3 Single-Table Queries

The tables and table relationships have been created, and some data have been entered in the Bank database. Now, you begin the process of analyzing the bank data for the auditor. You will do so using queries. You decide to begin with the Accounts table.

STEP 1 ›› USE THE QUERY WIZARD

You decide to start with the Query Wizard, knowing you can always alter the design of the query later in Design view. You will show the results to the auditor using Datasheet view. Refer to Figure 2.40 as you complete Step 1.

Account ID ▾	Customer ID ▾	Branch ID ▾	Balance ▾
1001	30010	B50	$5,600.00
1002	30001	B10	$1,200.00
Step e: Fields added to query			$15,490.00
1004	30003	B30	$630.00
1005	30009	B50	$1,300.00
1006	30003	B10	$550.00
1007	30007	B20	$1,620.00
1008	30004	B40	$2,100.00
1009	30005	B50	$1,500.00
1010	30001	B20	$3,000.00
1011	30005	B10	$290.00
1012	30002	B30	$1,900.00
1013	30001	B20	$10,000.00
1014	30009	B10	$16,700.00
1015	30004	B30	$460.00
1016	30001	B30	$18,700.00
1017	30010	B30	$980.00
1018	30005	B40	$7,800.00
1019	30004	B30	$14,250.00
1020	30001	B50	$1,200.00
1021	30011	B50	$21,004.00
1022	30003	B50	$4,000.00
1023	30011	B50	$1,000.00
1024	30011	B50	$14,005.00
Step h: 27 records displayed		B40	$11,010.00
1026	30007	B20	$7,400.00
1027	30003	B50	$4,000.00

Accounts from Campus Branch

Record: I◄ ◄ 1 of 27 ► ►I ►▪ ▾ No Filter Search

Access 2016, Windows 10, Microsoft Corporation

FIGURE 2.40 Query Results Before Criteria Are Applied

a. Open *a02h2Bank_LastFirst* if you closed it at the end of Hands-On Exercise 2, and save it as **a02h3Bank_LastFirst**, changing h2 to h3.

b. Click the **Create tab** and click **Query Wizard** in the Queries group.

The New Query dialog box opens. Simple Query Wizard is selected by default.

c. Click **OK**.

d. Verify that Table: Accounts is selected in the Tables/Queries box.

e. Click **AccountID** in the Available Fields list, then click **Add One Field** ⟩ to move it to the Selected Fields list. Repeat the process with **CustomerID**, **BranchID**, and **Balance**.

The four fields should now display in the Selected Fields list box.

f. Click **Next**.

g. Confirm that Detail (shows every field of every record) is selected and click **Next**.

h. Name the query **Accounts from Campus Branch**. Click **Finish**.

This query name describes the data in the query results. Your query should have four fields: AccountID, CustomerID, BranchID, and Balance. The Navigation bar indicates that 27 records meet the query criteria.

The auditor indicated that the problem seems to be confined to the Campus branch. You use this knowledge to revise the query to display only Campus accounts. Refer to Figure 2.41 as you complete Step 2.

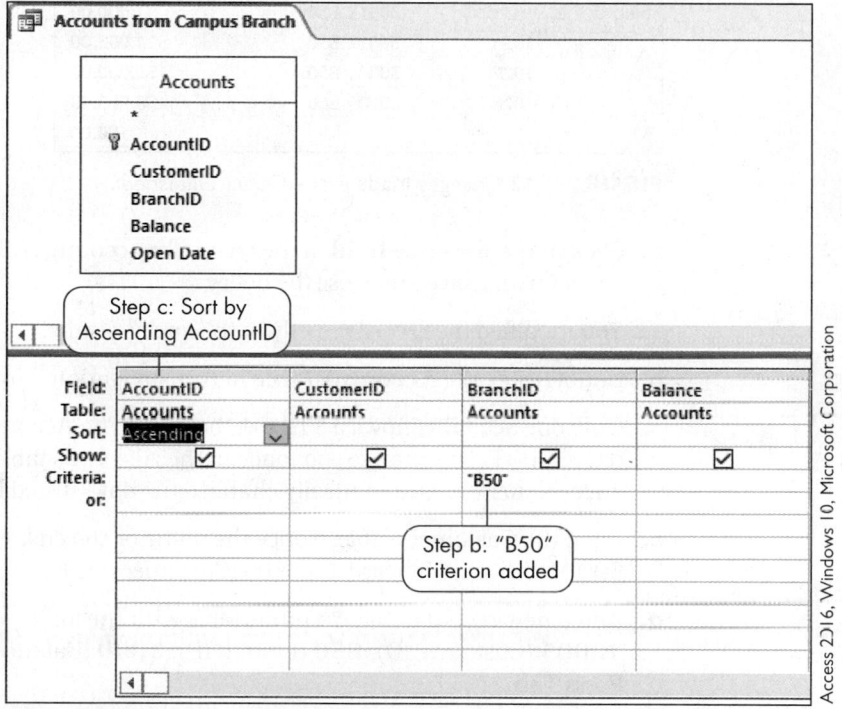

FIGURE 2.41 Enter Criteria and Add Sort Order

a. Click the **Home tab** and click **View** in the Views group.

The Accounts from Campus Branch query opens in Design view. You have created this query to view only those accounts at the Campus branch. However, other branches' accounts also display. You need to limit the query results to only the records of interest.

b. Click in the **Criteria row** (fifth row) in the BranchID column, type **B50**, and press **Enter**.

B50 is the BranchID for the Campus branch. Access queries are not case sensitive; therefore, b50 and B50 will produce the same results. Access adds quotation marks around text criteria after you press Enter, or you can type them yourself.

c. Click in the **Sort row** (third row) in the AccountID column and select **Ascending**.

d. Click **Run** in the Results group.

You should see nine records in the query results, all from Branch B50, sorted in ascending order by Account ID.

STEP 3 ›› CHANGE QUERY DATA AND RUN, COPY, AND MODIFY A QUERY

When the query results are on the screen, the auditor notices that some of the data are incorrect, and one of the accounts is missing. From your experience with Access, you explain to the auditor that the data can be changed directly in a query rather than switching back to the table. Refer to Figure 2.42 as you complete Step 3.

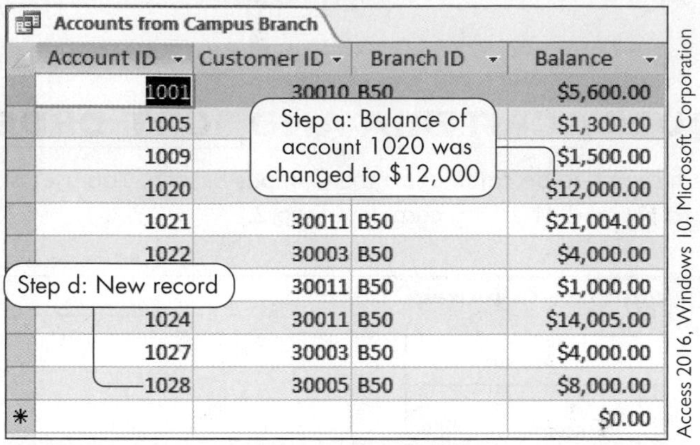

FIGURE 2.42 Changes Made in the Query Datasheet

a. Click in the **Balance field** in the record for account 1020. Change $1,200 to **$12,000**. Press **Enter**. Save and close the query.

You modified the record directly in the query results.

b. Double-click the **Accounts table** in the Navigation Pane

Only one account shows a $12,000 balance. The Account ID is 1020 and the Customer ID is 30001. The change you made in the Accounts table from the Campus Branch query datasheet automatically changed the data stored in the underlying table.

c. Open the Customers table. Notice the name of the customer whose CustomerID is 30001, Allison Millward. Close the Customers table.

d. Add a new record to the Accounts table with the following data: **1028** (Account ID), **30005** (Customer ID), **B50** (Branch ID), **8000** (Balance), and **8/4/2018** (Open Date). Press **Tab**.

> **TROUBLESHOOTING:** If the Accounts table is not open, double-click Accounts in the Navigation Pane.

The new record is added to the Accounts table.

e. Double-click the **Accounts from Campus Branch query** in the Navigation Pane.

Customer 30005 now shows two accounts: one with a balance of $1,500 and one with a balance of $8,000.

f. Click the **File tab**, click **Save As**, click **Save Object As**, and then click **Save As**. Type **Accounts from Campus Branch Sorted** as the query name. Click **OK**.

g. Click **View** in the Views group to return to Design view of the copied query.

h. Click in the **Sort row** of the AccountID field and select **(not sorted)**. Click in the **Sort row** of the CustomerID field and select **Ascending**. Click in the **Sort row** of the BalanceID field and select **Ascending**.

i. Click **Run** in the Results group.

Customer 30005 now shows two accounts with the two balances sorted in ascending order. Likewise, all other customers with more than one account are listed in ascending order by balance.

j. Save the query. Close the Accounts from Campus Branch Sorted query and close the Accounts table.

k. Keep the database open if you plan to continue with the Hands-On Exercise. If not, close the database and exit Access.

Multitable Queries

Multitable queries contain two or more tables, and enable you to take advantage of the relationships that have been set in your database. When you extract information from a database with a query, often you will need to pull data from multiple tables. One table may contain the core information that you want, while another table may contain the related data that make the query provide the complete results.

For example, the sample Bank database contains three tables: Customers, Accounts, and Branch. You connected the tables through relationships in order to store data efficiently and to enforce consistent data entry between them. The Customers table provides the information for the owners of the accounts. However, the Accounts table includes the balances of each account—the key financial information. Therefore, both the Customers and Accounts tables are needed to provide the information that you want: which Customers own which Accounts.

Creating a Multitable Query

There are several ways to create multitable queries. The simplistic method is to add tables to an existing query, or to copy an existing query and then add to it. You can also create a multitable query from scratch either using the Query Wizard or the Query Design tool.

Add Additional Tables to a Query

STEP 1 ⟫ One way to create a multitable query is to add tables and fields to an existing query, for example to add branch or customer data to a query that includes account information.

To add tables to a saved query, complete the following steps:

1. Open the existing query in Design view.
2. Add additional tables to a query by dragging tables from the Navigation Pane directly into the top pane of the query design window.
3. Add fields, criteria, and sorting options in the query design grid.
4. Run and save the query.

For example, the Branch and Customers tables were added to the query, as shown in Figure 2.43. The join lines between tables indicate that relationships were previously set in the Relationships window. With the additional tables and fields available, you can now add the customer's name (from Customers) and the branch location name (from Branch) rather than using CustomerID and BranchID in your results. The datasheet will contain more readily identifiable information than ID numbers for customers and locations.

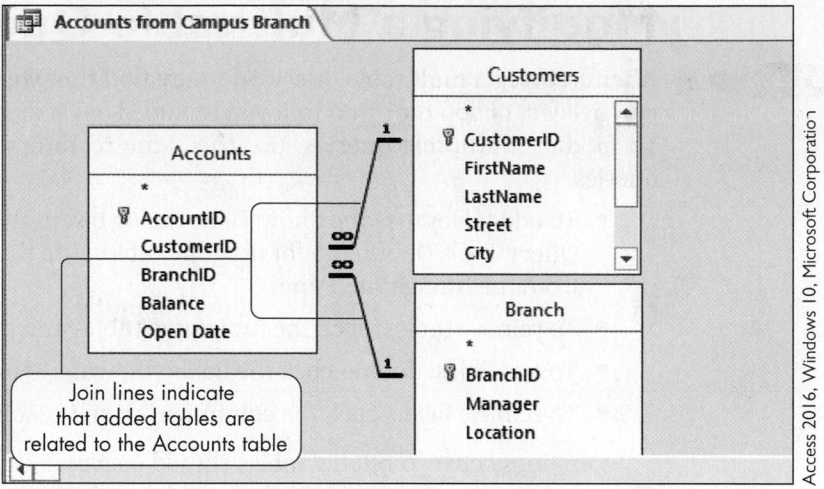

FIGURE 2.43 Two Additional Tables Added to a Query

Create a Multitable Query

STEP 2 ▶▶ Creating a multitable query from scratch is similar to creating a single-table query; however, choosing the right tables and managing the relationships in the query might require some additional skills. First, you should only use related tables in a multitable query. Related tables are tables that are joined in a relationship using a common field. Generally, related tables should already be joined in the Relationships window when you begin to create a multitable query. Using Figure 2.43 as a guide, creating a query with the Accounts and Branch tables would be acceptable, as would using Accounts and Customers tables, or Accounts, Branch, and Customers tables. All three scenarios include related tables. However, creating a query with only the Branch and Customers tables would not be acceptable because these tables are not directly related to one another (in other words, they do not have a common field).

To create a multitable query, complete the following steps:

1. Click the Create tab.
2. Click Query Design in the Queries group.
3. Add the tables you want in your query from the Show Table dialog box. Close the Show Table dialog box.
4. Drag the fields you want to display from the tables to the query design grid (or alternatively, double-click the field names); then add criteria and sorting options.
5. Click Run in the Results group on the Design tab to show the results in Datasheet view.

TIP: PRINT THE RELATIONSHIP REPORT TO HELP CREATE A MULTITABLE QUERY
When you create a multitable query, you only include related tables. As a guide, when the Relationships window is open, you can print the Relationship Report. Click the Database Tools tab, then click Relationship Report in the Tools group on the Relationship Tools Design tab. This report will provide a diagram that displays the tables, fields, and relationships in your database. The report is exportable to other formats such as Word if you want to share it with colleagues.

Modifying a Multitable Query

STEP 3 》》 After creating a multitable query, you may find that you did not include all of the fields you needed, or you may find that you included fields that are unnecessary to the results. To modify multitable queries, use the same techniques you learned for single-table queries.

- To add tables, use the Show Table dialog box in the Query Setup group on the Query Tools Design tab (or drag the tables into the top pane of the query design from the Navigation Pane).
- To remove tables, click the unwanted tables and press Delete.
- To add fields, double-click the fields you want to include.
- To remove fields, click the column selector of each field and press Delete.

Join lines between related tables should display automatically in a query if the relationships were previously established, as shown in Figure 2.43.

> **TIP: MULTITABLE QUERIES INHERIT RELATIONSHIPS**
>
> When you add two or more related tables to a query, join lines display automatically. You can delete a join line in a query with no impact on the relationship set in the database. Deleting a join line only affects the relationship in the individual query. The next time you create a query with the same tables, the relationships will be inherited from the database. And, if you open the Relationships window, you will find the join lines intact.

Add and Delete Fields in a Multitable Query

In Figure 2.44, three tables, as well as the join lines between the tables, display in the top pane of Design view. All the fields from each of the tables are now available for use in the query design grid. Figure 2.44 shows that Location (from the Branch table) replaced BranchID and LastName (from the Customers table) replaced CustomerID to make the results more useful. BranchID was deleted from the query; therefore, the "B50" criterion was removed as well. "Campus" was added to the Location field's Criteria row in order to extract the names of the branches rather than their BranchID numbers. Because criteria values are not case sensitive, typing "campus" is the same as typing "Campus" and both will return the same results. The results of the revised query are shown in Figure 2.45.

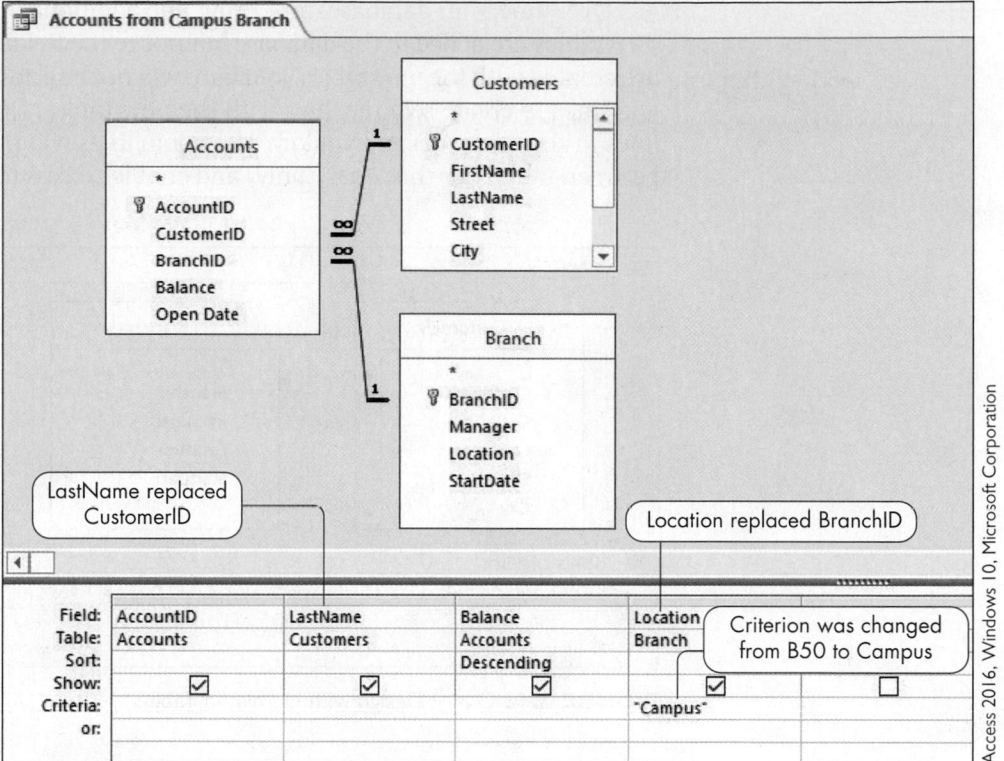

FIGURE 2.44 Modify the Query Design

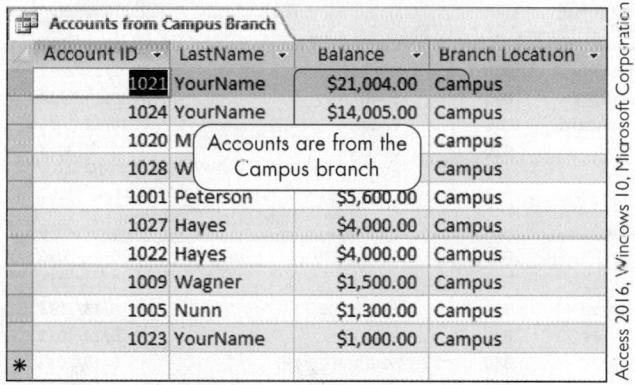

FIGURE 2.45 Datasheet View of a Multitable Query

Add Join Lines in a Multitable Query

In Figure 2.46, two tables are added to the query design, but no join line connects them. The results of the query will be unpredictable and will display more records than expected. The Customers table contains 11 records, and the Branch table contains 5 records. Because Access does not know how to interpret the unrelated tables, the results will show 55 records—every possible combination of customer and branch (11 × 5). See Figure 2.47.

To fix this problem, you can create join lines using existing tables if the tables contain a common field with the same data type. In this example, in which there is no common field, you can add an additional table that provides join lines between all three tables. You can add the Accounts table, which provides join lines between the two existing tables, Customers and Branch, and the added Accounts table. As soon as the third table is added to the query design, the join lines display automatically.

Over time, your databases may grow, and additional tables will be added. Occasionally, new tables are added to the database but not to the Relationships window. When queries are created with the new tables, join lines will not be established. When this happens, add join lines to create relationships with the new tables. Or you can create temporary join lines in the query design window. These join lines will provide a temporary relationship between tables (for that query only) and enable Access to interpret the query properly.

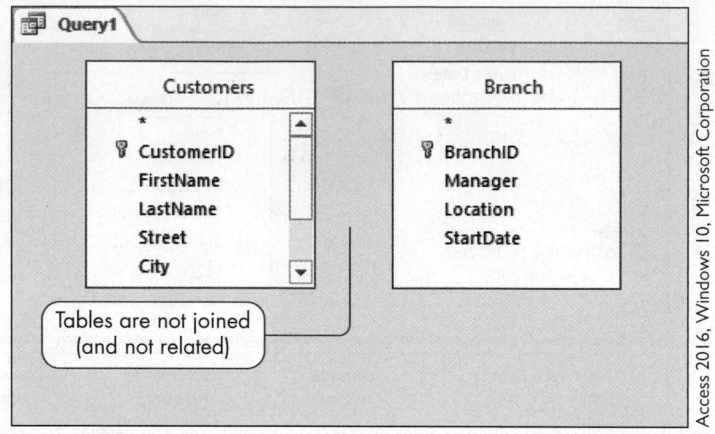

FIGURE 2.46 Query Design with Unrelated Tables

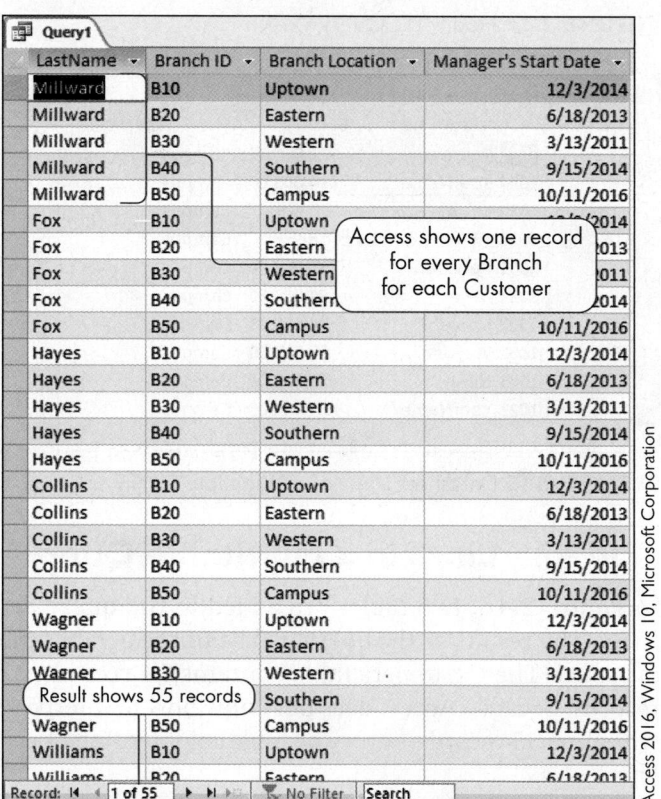

FIGURE 2.47 Query Results Using Unrelated Tables

Summarize Data Using a Multitable Query

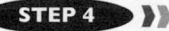**STEP 4** You can get valuable information from your database using a multitable query. For example, if you want to know how many accounts each customer has, you would create a new query and add both the Customers and Accounts tables to Design view. After you verify that the join lines are correct, you add the CustomerID field from the Customers table and the AccountID field from the Accounts table to the query design grid. When you initially run the query, the results show duplicates in the CustomerID column because some customers have multiple accounts.

To summarize this information (how many accounts each customer has), complete the following steps:

1. Switch to Design view and click Totals in the Show/Hide group on the Query Tools Design tab. The Total row displays. Both fields show the Group By option in the Total row. The Total row enables you to summarize records by using functions such as Sum, Average, Count, etc.

2. Click in the Total row of the AccountID field, select Count from the list of functions, and run the query again. This time the results show one row for each customer and the number of accounts for each customer.

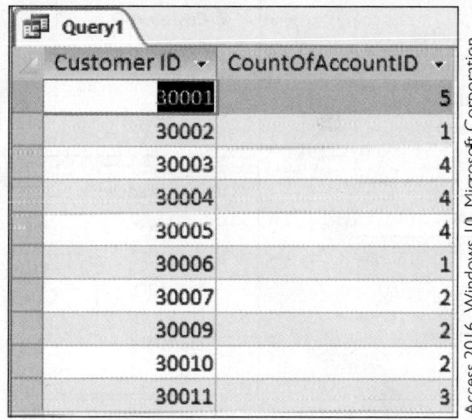

FIGURE 2.48 Datasheet Results with the Count of Accounts per Customer

Quick Concepts

12. What is the advantage of creating a multitable query? **p. 782**

13. What is the benefit of summarizing data in a multitable query? **p. 786**

14. What is the result of creating a query with two unrelated tables? **p. 785**

Hands-On Exercises

Watch the Video for this Hands-On Exercise!

MyITLab®
HOE4 Training

Skills covered: Add Additional Tables to a Query • Create a Multitable Query • Modify a Multitable Query • Summarize Data Using a Multitable Query

4 Multitable Queries

Based on the auditor's request, you will evaluate the data further. This requires creating queries that are based on multiple tables rather than on a single table. You decide to open an existing query, add additional tables, and then save the query with a new name.

STEP 1 ›› ADD ADDITIONAL TABLES TO A QUERY

The previous query was based on the Accounts table, but now you need to add information to the query from the Branch and Customers tables. You will add the Branch and Customers tables to the query. Refer to Figure 2.49 as you complete Step 1.

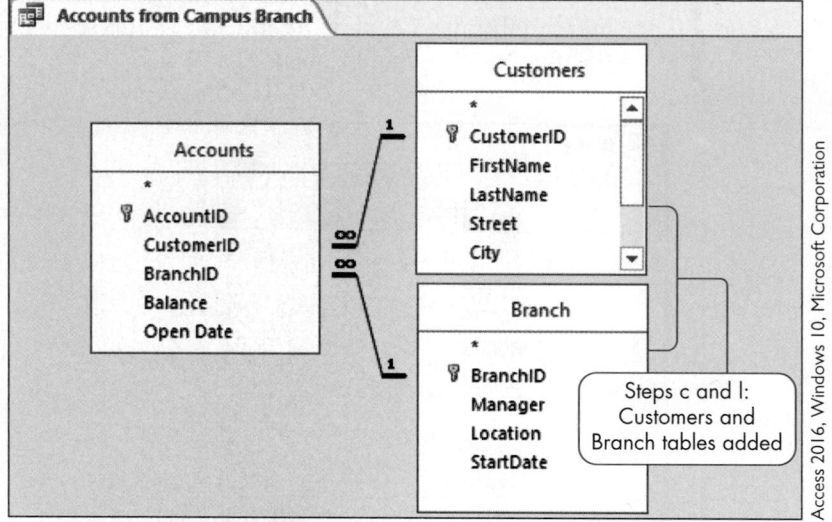

FIGURE 2.49 Add Tables to an Existing Query

a. Open *a02h3Bank_LastFirst* if you closed it at the end of Hands-On Exercise 3, and save it as **a02h4Bank_LastFirst**, changing h3 to h4.

b. Right-click the **Accounts from Campus Branch query** in the Navigation Pane and select **Design View** from the shortcut menu.

c. Drag the **Branch table** from the Navigation Pane to the top pane of the query design grid to the right of the Accounts table.

A join line connects the Branch table to the Accounts table. The tables in the query inherit the relationship created earlier in the Relationships window.

d. Drag the **Location field** from the Branch table to the first empty column in the design grid.

The Location field should be positioned to the right of the Balance field.

e. Click the **Show check box** below the BranchID field to clear the check box and hide this field from the results.

The BranchID field is no longer needed in the results because the Location field provides the branch name instead. Because you deselected the BranchID Show check box, the BranchID field will not display the next time the query is run.

f. Delete the B50 criterion in the BranchID field.

g. Type **Campus** as a criterion in the Location field and press **Enter**.

Access adds quotation marks around Campus for you because Campus is a text ⟨
You are substituting the Location criterion *(Campus)* in place of the BranchID cr
(B50).

h. Click in the AccountID field **Sort row**, click the arrow, and then click **(not sorted)**. Click
in the **Sort row** of the Balance field. Click the arrow and select **Descending**.

i. Click **Run** in the Results group.

The BranchID field does not display in Datasheet view because you hid the field in Step
e. Only Campus accounts display in the datasheet (10 records). Next, you will add the
Customers LastName field to and delete the CustomerID field from the query.

j. Save the changes to the query design.

k. Click **View** in the Views group to return to Design view. Point over the column selector
at the top of the BranchID field, and when a downward arrow displays, click to select it.
Press **Delete**.

The BranchID field has been removed from the grid.

l. Drag the **Customers table** from the Navigation Pane to the top pane of the query design
grid and reposition the tables so that the join lines are not blocked (see Figure 2.49).

The join lines automatically connect the Customers table to the Accounts table (similar
to Step c above).

m. Drag the **LastName field** in the Customers table to the second column in the design grid.

The LastName field should be positioned to the right of the AccountID field.

n. Click the **column selector** in the CustomerID field to select it. Press **Delete**.

The CustomerID field is no longer needed in the results because we added the LastName
field instead.

o. Click **Run** in the Results group.

The last names of the customers now display in the results.

p. Save and close the query.

STEP 2 ›› CREATE A MULTITABLE QUERY

After discussing the query results with the auditor, you realize that another query is needed to show those customers with account
balances of $1,000 or less. You create the query and view the results in Datasheet view. Refer to Figure 2.50 as you complete Step 2.

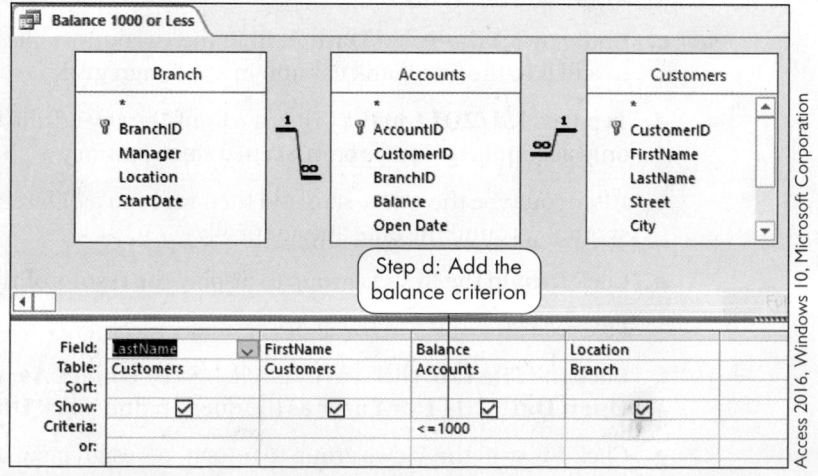

FIGURE 2.50 Create a Multitable Query

a. Click the **Create tab** and click **Query Design** in the Queries group.

b. Double-click the **Branch table name** in the Show Table dialog box. Double-click **Accounts** and **Customers** so that all three are added to Design view. Click **Close** in the Show Table dialog box.

Three tables are added to the query.

c. Double-click the following fields to add them to the query design grid: **LastName**, **FirstName**, **Balance**, and **Location**.

d. Type **<=1000** in the Criteria row of the Balance column.

e. Click **Run** in the Results group to see the query results.

Six records that have a balance of $1,000 or less display.

f. Click **Save** on the Quick Access Toolbar and type **Balance 1000 or Less** as the Query Name in the Save As dialog box. Click **OK**.

STEP 3 ⟩⟩ MODIFY A MULTITABLE QUERY

The auditor requests additional changes to the Balance 1000 or Less query you just created. You will modify the criteria to display the accounts that were opened on or after January 1, 2011, with balances of $2,000 or less. Refer to Figure 2.51 as you complete Step 3.

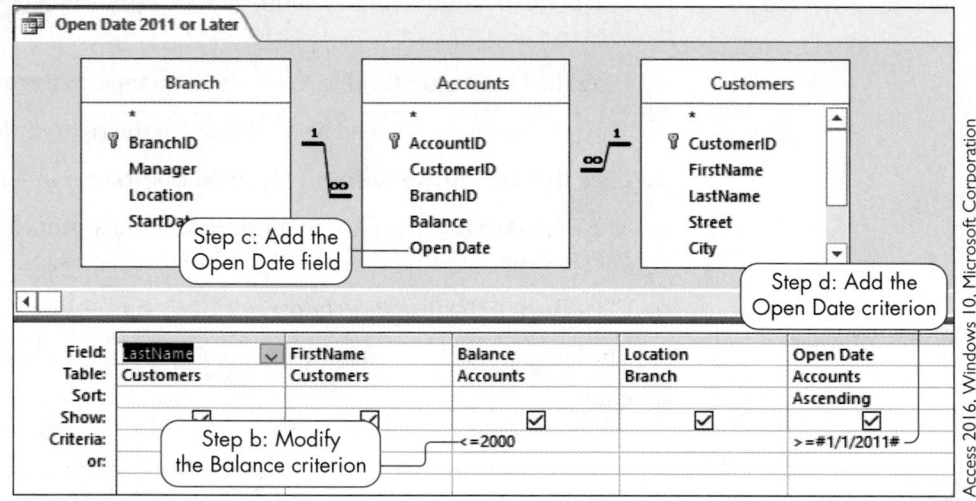

FIGURE 2.51 Query Using the And Condition

a. Click **View** in the Views group to switch the Balance 1000 or Less query to Design view.

b. Type **<=2000** in place of <=1000 in the Criteria row of the Balance field and press **Enter**.

c. Double-click the **Open Date field** in the Accounts table in the top pane of Design view to add it to the first blank column in the design grid.

d. Type **>=1/1/2011** in the Criteria row of the Open Date field and press **Enter** to extract only accounts that have been opened since January 1, 2011.

After you type the expression and then move to a different column, Access will add the # symbols around the date automatically.

e. Click **Run** in the Results group to display the results of the query.

Five records display in the query results.

f. Click the **File tab**, click **Save As**, click **Save Object As**, and then click **Save As**. Type **Open Date 2011 or Later** as the query name. Click **OK**.

g. Click **View** in the Views group to return to Design view of the copied query.

h. Click in the **Sort row** of the Open Date field and select **Ascending**.

i. Click **Run** in the Results group.

The records are sorted from the earliest open date on or after January 1, 2011, to the most recent open date.

j. Save and close the query.

STEP 4 ≫ SUMMARIZE DATA USING A MULTITABLE QUERY

The auditor wants to know the number of accounts each customer has opened. You create a query using a Total row to obtain these data. Refer to Figure 2.52 as you complete Step 4.

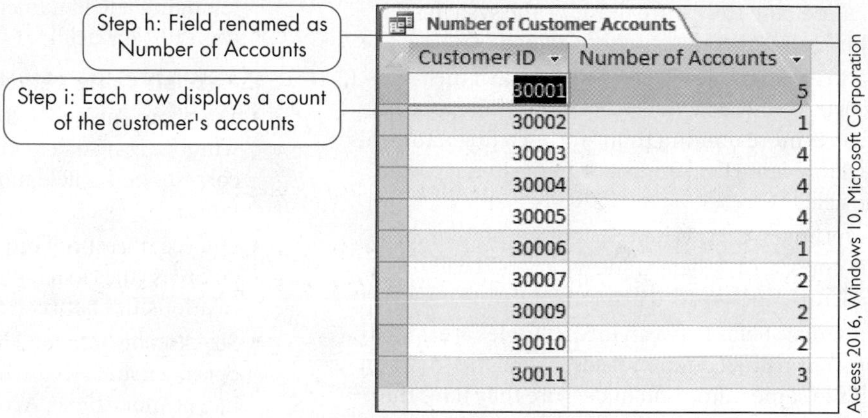

FIGURE 2.52 Number of Accounts per Customer

a. Click the **Create tab** and click **Query Design** in the Queries group.

b. Add the **Accounts table** and the **Customers table** to the top section of Design view. Click **Close** in the Show Table dialog box.

c. Double-click the **CustomerID** in the Customers table in the top section of Design view to add it to the first blank column in the design grid, and double-click the **AccountID** in the Accounts table to add it to the second column.

d. Click **Run** in the Results group.

The results show there are 28 records. Every account a customer has opened is displayed. The auditor wants only the total number of accounts a customer has, so you modify the query.

e. Click **View** in the Views group to return to Design view of the query.

f. Click **Totals** in the Show/Hide group.

Both columns show the Group By option in the Total row.

g. Click **Group By** in the Total row of the AccountID field and select **Count**.

h. Modify the AccountID field to read **Number of Accounts: AccountID**.

You typed a new field name followed by a colon that will display Number of Accounts in the datasheet when you run the query.

i. Click **Run** in the Results group. Resize the columns of the datasheet to fully display the results.

The results show one row for each customer and the number of accounts each customer has opened since the database was created.

j. Click **Save** on the Quick Access Toolbar and type **Number of Customer Accounts** as the query name. Close the query.

k. Close the database and exit Access. Based on your instructor's directions, submit a02h4Bank_LastFirst.

Chapter Objectives Review

After reading this chapter, you have accomplished the following objectives:

1. Design a table.

- Include necessary data: Consider the output requirements when creating table structure. Determine the data required to produce the expected information.
- Design for now and for the future: When designing a database, anticipate the future needs of the system and build in the flexibility to satisfy those demands.
- Store data in their smallest parts: Store data in their smallest parts for more flexibility. Storing a full name in a Name field is more limiting than storing a first name in a separate FirstName field and a last name in a separate LastName field.
- Determine primary keys: When designing your database tables, it is important to determine which field will uniquely identify each record in a table.
- Plan for common fields between tables: Tables are joined in relationships using common fields. Name the common fields with the same name and make sure they have the same data type.
- Design to accommodate calculations: Calculated fields are frequently created with numeric data. You can use date arithmetic to subtract one date from another to find the number of days, months, or years that have elapsed between them.

2. Create and modify tables and work with data.

- You can create tables in Datasheet view or Design view. Alternatively, you can import data from another database or an application such as Excel to create tables in an Access database.
- Determine data type: Data type properties determine the type of data that can be entered and the operations that can be performed on that data. Access recognizes 12 data types.
- Set a table's primary key: The primary key is the field that uniquely identifies each record in a table.
- Explore a foreign key: A foreign key is a field in one table that is also the primary key of another table.
- Work with field properties: Field properties determine how the field looks and behaves. Examples of field properties are the Field Size property and the Caption property.
- Create a new field in Design view: It may be necessary to add table fields that were not included in the original design process. While it is possible to add fields in Datasheet view, Design view offers more flexibility.
- Modify the table in Datasheet view: Datasheet view is used to add, edit, and delete records. Design view is used to create and modify the table structure by enabling you to add and edit fields and set field properties.

3. Share data.

- Import Excel data: You can import data from other applications such as an Excel spreadsheet.

- Import Access data: You can import data from another database by using the Import Wizard.
- Modify an imported table's design and add data: After importing a table, examine the design and make necessary modifications. Modifications may include changing a field name, adding new fields, or deleting unnecessary fields.

4. Establish table relationships.

- Use Show Table to add tables to the Relationships window. Drag a field name from one table to the corresponding field name in another table to join the tables.
- Enforce referential integrity: Referential integrity enforces rules in a database that are used to preserve relationships between tables when records are changed.
- Set cascade options: The Cascade Update Related Fields option ensures that when the primary key is modified in a primary table, Access will automatically update all foreign key values in a related table. The Cascade Delete Related Records option ensures that when the primary key is deleted in a primary table, Access will automatically delete all records in related tables that reference the primary key.
- Establish a one-to-many relationship: A one-to-many relationship is established when the primary key value in the primary table can match many of the foreign key values in the related table. One-to-one and many-to-many are also relationship possibilities, but one-to-many relationships are the most common.

5. Create a single-table query.

- Create a single-table select query: A single-table select query uses fields from one table to display only those records that match certain criteria.
- Use Query Design view: Use Query Design view to create and modify a query. The top portion of the view contains tables with their respective field names and displays the join lines between tables. The bottom portion, known as the query design grid, contains columns and rows that you use to control the query results.

6. Use the Query Wizard.

- The Query Wizard is an alternative method for creating queries. It enables you to select tables and fields from lists. The last step of the wizard prompts you to save the query.

7. Specify query criteria for different data types.

- Different data types require different syntax. Date fields are enclosed in pound signs (#) and text fields in quotations (" "). Numeric and currency fields require no delimiters.
- Use wildcards: Wildcards are special characters that can represent one or more characters in a text value. A question mark (?) is a wildcard that stands for a

single character in the same position as the question mark, while an asterisk (*) is a wildcard that stands for any number of characters in the same position as the asterisk.

- Use comparison operators in queries: Comparison operators such as equal (=), not equal (<>), greater than (>), less than (<), greater than or equal to (>=), and less than or equal to (<=) can be used in the criteria of a query to limit the query results to only those records that meet the criteria.
- Work with null: Access uses the term null for a blank field. Null criteria can be used to find missing information.
- Establish AND, OR, and NOT criteria: The AND, OR, and NOT conditions are used when queries require logical criteria. The AND condition returns only records that meet all criteria. The OR condition returns records meeting any of the specified criteria. The NOT logical operator returns all records except the specified criteria.

8. Understand query sort order.

- The query sort order determines the order of records in a query's Datasheet view. You can change the order of records by specifying the sort order in Design view.
- The sort order is determined from the order of the fields from left to right. Move the field columns to position them in left to right sort order.

9. Run, copy, and modify a query.

- Run a query: To obtain the results for a query, you must run the query. To run the query, click Run in the Results group in Design view. Another method is to locate the

query in the Navigation Pane and double-click it. A similar method is to select the query and press Enter.
- Copy and modify a query: To save time, after specifying tables, fields, and conditions for one query, copy the query, rename it, and then modify the fields and criteria in the second query.
- Change query data: You can correct an error immediately while data is displayed in the query datasheet. Use caution when editing records in query results because you will be changing the original table data.

10. Create a multitable query.

- Add additional tables to a query: Open the Navigation Pane and drag the tables from the Navigation Pane directly into the top section of Query Design view.
- Create a multitable query: Multitable queries contain two or more tables enabling you to take advantage of the relationships that have been set in your database.

11. Modify a multitable query.

- Add and delete fields in a multitable query: Multitable queries may need to be modified. Add fields by double-clicking the field name in the table you want; remove fields by clicking the column selector and pressing Delete.
- Add join lines in a multitable query: If the tables have a common field, create join lines by dragging the field name of one common field onto the field name of the other table. Or you can add an additional table that will provide a join between all three tables.
- Summarize data using a multitable query: Use the total row options of a field such as Count to get answers.

Key Terms Matching

Match the key terms with their definitions. Write the key term letter by the appropriate numbered definition.

a. AND condition
b. AutoNumber
c. Caption property
d. Cascade Delete Related Records
e. Cascade Update Related Fields
f. Comparison Operator
g. Criteria row
h. Data redundancy
i. Data type
j. Field property

k. Foreign key
l. Multitable query
m. Null
n. One-to-many relationship
o. OR condition
p. Query
q. Referential Integrity
r. Simple Query Wizard
s. Wildcard

1. _____ Special character that can represent one or more characters in the criterion of a query. **p. 773**

2. _____ Characteristic of a field that determines how it looks and behaves. **p. 742**

3. _____ Returns only records that meet all criteria. **p. 773**

4. _____ A row in the Query Design view that determines which records will be selected. **p. 768**

5. _____ Determines the type of data that can be entered and the operations that can be performed on that data. **p. 739**

6. _____ Used to create a more understandable label than a field name label that displays in the top row in Datasheet view and in forms and reports. **p. 742**

7. _____ Enables you to ask questions about the data stored in a database and provides answers to the questions in a datasheet. **p. 767**

8. _____ The term Access uses to describe a blank field. **p. 774**

9. _____ A number that automatically increments each time a record is added. **p. 739**

10. _____ The unnecessary storing of duplicate data in two or more tables. **p. 737**

11. _____ When the primary key value in the primary table can match many of the foreign key values in the related table. **p. 756**

12. _____ A field in one table that is also the primary key of another table. **p. 741**

13. _____ An option that directs Access to automatically update all foreign key values in a related table when the primary key value is modified in a primary table. **p. 756**

14. _____ Rules in a database that are used to preserve relationships between tables when records are changed. **p. 755**

15. _____ Contains two or more tables, enabling you to take advantage of the relationships that have been set in your database. **p. 782**

16. _____ Returns records meeting any of the specified criteria. **p. 774**

17. _____ Provides a step-by-step guide to help you through the query design process. **p. 770**

18. _____ When the primary key value is deleted in a primary table, Access will automatically delete all foreign key values in a related table. **p. 756**

19. _____ Uses greater than (>), less than (<), greater than or equal to (>=), and less than or equal to (<=), etc. to limit query results that meet these criteria. **p. 772**

Multiple Choice

1. All of the following are suggested guidelines for table design *except*:

   (a) Include all necessary data.

   (b) Store data in its smallest parts.

   (c) Avoid date arithmetic.

   (d) Link tables using common fields.

2. Which of the following determines how the field names can be made more readable in table and query datasheets?

   (a) Field size

   (b) Data type

   (c) Caption property

   (d) Normalization

3. When entering, deleting, or editing input masks:

   (a) The table must be in Design view.

   (b) The table must be in Datasheet view.

   (c) The table may be in either Datasheet or Design view.

   (d) Data may only be entered in a form.

4. With respect to importing data into Access, which of the following statements is *true*?

   (a) The Import Wizard works only for Excel files.

   (b) The Import Wizard is found on the Create tab.

   (c) You can assign a primary key while you are importing Excel data.

   (d) Imported table designs cannot be modified in Access.

5. The main reason to set a field size in Access is to:

   (a) Limit the length of values in a table.

   (b) Make it possible to delete records.

   (c) Keep your database safe from unauthorized users.

   (d) Keep misspelled data from being entered into a table.

6. An illustration of a one-to-many relationship would be:

   (a) An employee listed in the Employees table earns a raise so the Salaries table must be updated.

   (b) A customer may have more than one account in an accounts table.

   (c) Each employee in an Employees table has a matching entry in the Salaries table.

   (d) An employee leaves the company so that when he is deleted from the Employees table, his salary data will be deleted from the Salaries table.

7. A query's specifications as to which tables to include must be entered on the:

   (a) Table row of the query design grid.

   (b) Show row of the query design grid.

   (c) Sort row of the query design grid.

   (d) Criteria row of the query design grid.

8. When adding date criteria to the Query Design view, the dates you enter must be delimited by:

   (a) Parentheses ().

   (b) Pound signs (#).

   (c) Quotes (" ").

   (d) At signs (@).

9. It is more efficient to make a copy of an existing query rather than to create a new query when which of the following is *true*?

   (a) The existing query contains only one table.

   (b) The existing query and the new query use the same tables and fields.

   (c) The existing query and the new query have the exact same criteria.

   (d) The original query is no longer being used.

10. Which of the following is *true* for the Query Wizard?

    (a) No criteria can be added as you step through the Wizard.

    (b) You can only select related tables as a source.

    (c) Fields with different data types are not allowed.

    (d) You are required to summarize the data.

Practice Exercises

1 Philadelphia Bookstore

FROM SCRATCH

Tom and Erin Mullaney own and operate a bookstore in Philadelphia, Pennsylvania. Erin asked you to help her create an Access database to store the publishers and the books that they sell. The data for the publishers and books is currently stored in Excel worksheets that you decide to import into a new database. You determine that a third table—for authors—is also required. Your task is to create and populate the three tables, set the table relationships, and enforce referential integrity. You will then create queries to extract information from the tables. Refer to Figure 2.53 as you complete this exercise.

FIGURE 2.53 Books Relationships Window

a. Open Access and click **Blank desktop database**. Type **a02p1Books_LastFirst** in the **File Name box**. Click **Browse** to navigate to the location where you are saving your files in the File New Database dialog box, click **OK** to close the dialog box, and then click **Create** to create the new database.

b. Type **11** in the Click to Add column and click **Click to Add**. The field name becomes Field1, and *Click to Add* now displays as the third column. In the third column, type **Beschloss**, and then press **Tab**. Repeat the process for the fourth column; type **Michael R.** and press **Tab** two times. The insertion point returns to the first column where (New) is selected.

c. Press **Tab**. Type the rest of the data using the following table. These data will become the records of the Author table.

ID	Field1	Field2	Field3
1	11	Beschloss	Michael R.
(New)	12	Turow	Scott
	13	Rice	Anne
	14	King	Stephen
	15	Connelly	Michael
	16	Rice	Luanne
	17	*your last name*	*your first name*

d. Click **Save** on the Quick Access Toolbar. Type **Author** in the Save As dialog box and click **OK**.

e. Click **View** in the Views group to switch to Design view of the Author table.

f. Select **Field1**—in the second row—in the top portion of the table design and type **AuthorID** to rename the field. In the Field Properties section in the lower pane of the table design, type **Author ID** in the Caption box and verify that Long Integer displays for the Field Size property.

g. Select **Field2** and type **LastName** to rename the field. In the Field Properties section in the bottom portion of Design view, type **Author's Last Name** in the Caption box and type **20** as the field size.

h. Select **Field3** and type **FirstName** to rename the field. In the Field Properties section in the bottom portion of the table design, type **Author's First Name** as the caption and type **15** as the field size.

i. Click the **ID field row selector** (which displays the primary key) to select the row, and then click **Delete Rows** in the Tools group. Click **Yes** two times to confirm both messages.

j. Click the **AuthorID row selector**, and then click **Primary Key** in the Tools group to set the primary key.

k. Click **Save** on the Quick Access Toolbar to save the design changes. Click **Yes** to the *Some data may be lost* message. Close the table.

l. Click the **External Data tab** and click **Excel** in the Import & Link group to launch the Get External Data – Excel Spreadsheet feature. Verify that the *Import the source data into a new table in the current database* option is selected, click **Browse**, and then navigate to your student data folder. Select the *a02p1Books* workbook, click **Open**, and then click **OK**. This workbook contains two worksheets. Follow the steps below:

- Select the **Publishers worksheet** and click **Next**.
- Click the **First Row Contains Column Headings check box** to select it and click **Next**.
- Ensure that the PubID field is selected, click the **Indexed arrow**, select **Yes (No Duplicates)**, and then click **Next**.
- Click the **Choose my own primary key arrow**, ensure that PubID is selected, and then click **Next**.
- Accept the name Publishers for the table name, click **Finish**, and then click **Close** without saving the import steps.

m. Use the Import Wizard again to import the Books worksheet from the *a02p1Books* workbook into the Access database. Follow the steps below:

- Ensure that the Books worksheet is selected and click **Next**.
- Click the **First Row Contains Column Headings check box** to select it, and click **Next**.
- Click the **ISBN column**, click the down arrow, set the Indexed property box to **Yes (No Duplicates)**, and then click **Next**.
- Click the **Choose my own primary key arrow**, select **ISBN** as the primary key field, and then click **Next**.
- Accept the name Books as the table name. Click **Finish** and click **Close** without saving the import steps.

n. Right-click the **Books table** in the Navigation Pane and select **Design View**. Make the following changes:

- Click the **PubID field** and change the name to **PublisherID**.
- Set the caption property to **Publisher ID.**
- Change the PublisherID Field Size property to **2**.
- Click the **ISBN field** and change the Field Size property to **13**.
- Change the AuthorCode field name to **AuthorID**.
- Change the AuthorID Field Size property to **Long Integer**.
- Click the **ISBN field row selector** (which displays the primary key) to select the row. Click and drag to move the row up to the first position in the table design.
- Click **Save** on the Quick Access Toolbar to save the design changes to the Books table. Click **Yes** to the *Some data may be lost* warning.
- Close the table.

o. Right-click the **Publishers table** in the Navigation Pane and select **Design View**. Make the following changes:

- Click the **PubID field** and change the name to **PublisherID**.
- Change the PublisherID Field Size property to **2**.
- Change the Caption property to **Publisher's ID.**
- Change the Field Size property to **50** for the PubName and PubAddress fields.

- Change the Pub Address field name to **PubAddress** (remove the space).
- Change the PubCity Field Size property to **30**.
- Change the PubState Field Size property to **2**.
- Change the Pub ZIP field name to **PubZIP** (remove the space).
- Click **Save** on the Quick Access Toolbar to save the design changes to the Publishers table. Click **Yes** to the *Some data may be lost* warning. Close all open tables.

p. Click the **Database Tools tab** and click **Relationships** in the Relationships group. Click **Show Table**, if the Show Table dialog box does not open automatically. Follow the steps below:

- Double-click each table name in the Show Table dialog box to add it to the Relationships window and close the Show Table dialog box.
- Drag the **AuthorID field** from the Author table onto the AuthorID field in the Books table.
- Click the **Enforce Referential Integrity** and **Cascade Update Related Fields check boxes** in the Edit Relationships dialog box to select them. Click **Create** to create a one-to-many relationship between the Author and Books tables.
- Drag the **PublisherID field** from the Publishers table onto the PublisherID field in the Books table.
- Click the **Enforce Referential Integrity** and **Cascade Update Related Fields check boxes** in the Edit Relationships dialog box to select them. Click **Create** to create a one-to-many relationship between the Publishers and Books tables.
- Click **Save** on the Quick Access Toolbar to save the changes to the Relationships window, then in the Relationships group, click **Close**.

q. Click the **Create tab**, and then click **Query Wizard** in the Queries group. With Simple Query Wizard selected, click **OK**.

- Select the Publishers table, double-click to add **PubName**, **PubCity**, and **PubState** to the Selected Fields list. Click **Next**, and then click **Finish**. In Datasheet view, double-click the border to the right of each column to set the column widths to Best Fit. Click **Save** on the Quick Access Toolbar.

r. Click the **File tab**, click **Save As**, and then double-click **Save Object As**. Modify the copied query name to **New York Publishers Query**, and then click **OK**.

- Click **View** in the Views group on the Home tab to switch to Design view of the query. Click and drag the **Books table** from the Navigation Pane into the top pane of the query design window.
- Select the Books table, double-click **Title** and **PublDate** to add the fields to the query design grid.
- Click in the Criteria row of the PubState field, and type **NY**. Click the **Sort** cell of the PublDate field, click the arrow, and then click **Descending**.
- Click **Run** in the Results group (12 records display in the Datasheet sorted by PublDate in descending order). Double-click the border to the right of each column to set the column widths to Best Fit.
- Save and close the query.

s. Close the database and exit Access. Based on your instructor's directions, submit a02p1Books_LastFirst.

2 Employee Salary Analysis

The Morgan Insurance Company offers a full range of insurance services. They store all of the firm's employee data in an Access database. This file contains each employee's name and address, job performance, salary, and title, but needs to be imported into a different existing database. A database file containing two of the tables (Location and Titles) already exists; your job is to import the employee data from Access to create the third table. Once imported, you will modify field properties and set new relationships. The owner of the company, Victor Reed, is concerned that some of the Atlanta and Boston salaries may be below the guidelines published by the national office. He asks that you investigate the salaries of the two offices and create a separate query for each city. Refer to Figure 2.54 as you complete this exercise.

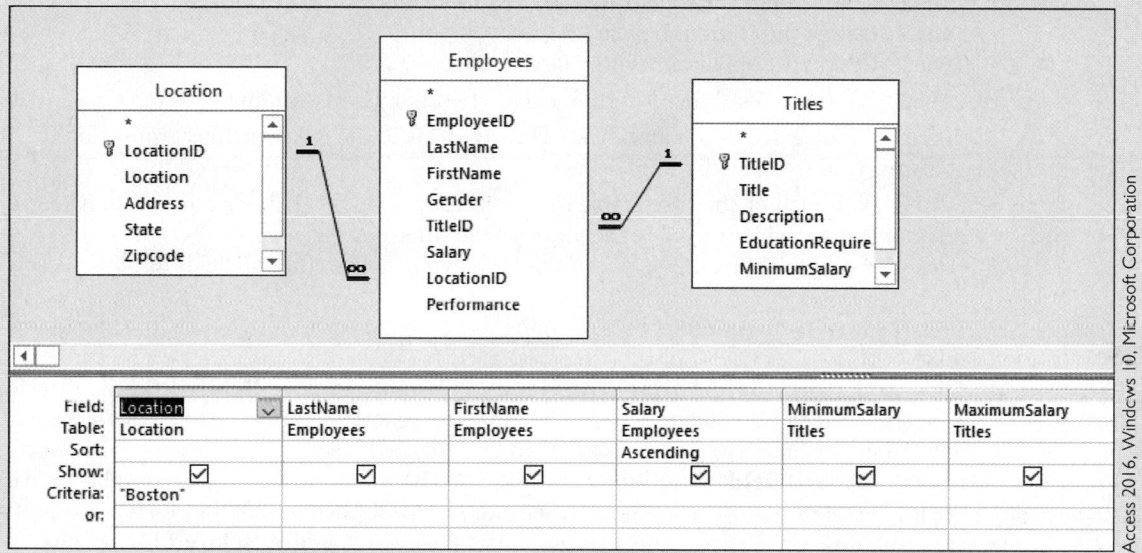

FIGURE 2.54 Boston Salaries Query Design

a. Open *a02p2Insurance* and save it as **a02p2Insurance_LastFirst**. Double-click the **Location table** and review the data to become familiar with the field names and the type of information stored in the table. Review the Titles table. Close both tables.

b. Click the **External Data tab**, click **Access** in the Import & Link group, and then complete the following steps:
   - Click **Browse** and navigate to the *a02p2Employees* database in the location of your student data files. Select the file, click **Open**.
   - Click **OK** in the Get External Data – Access Database dialog box.
   - Select the **Employees table**, and then click **OK**.
   - Click **Close** without saving the import steps.

c. Double-click the **Employees table** in the Navigation Pane, then click **View** in the Views group on the Home tab to switch to Design view of the Employees table. Make the following changes:
   - Ensure that the EmployeeID field is selected, and then click **Primary Key** in the Tools group.
   - Click the **LastName field** and change the Field Size property to **20**.
   - Change the Caption property to **Last Name**.
   - Click the **FirstName field** and change the Field Size property to **20**.
   - Change the Caption property to **First Name**.
   - Click the **LocationID field** and change the Field Size property to **3**.
   - Change the Caption property to **Location ID**.
   - Click the **TitleID field** and change the Field Size property to **3**.
   - Change the Caption property to **Title ID**.
   - Change the Salary field data type to **Currency** and change General Number in the Format property in field properties to **Currency**.
   - Save the design changes. Click **Yes** to the *Some data may be lost* warning.

d. Click **View** in the Views group to view the Employees table in Datasheet view and examine the data. Click any record in the Title ID and then click **Ascending** in the Sort & Filter group on the Home tab. Multiple employees are associated with the T01, T02, T03, and T04 titles.

e. Double-click the **Titles table** in the Navigation Pane to open it in Datasheet view. Notice that the T04 title is not in the list.

f. Add a new record in the first blank record at the bottom of the Titles table. Use the following data:

- Type **T04** in the TitleID field.
- Type **Senior Account Rep** in the Title field.
- Type **A marketing position requiring a technical background and at least three years of experience** in the Description field.
- Type **Four year degree** in the Education Requirements field.
- Type **45000** in the Minimum Salary field.
- Type **75000** in the Maximum Salary field.

g. Close all tables. Click **Yes** if you are prompted to save changes to the Employees table.

h. Click the **Database Tools tab** and click **Relationships** in the Relationships group, and then Click **Show Table**. Follow the steps below:

- Double-click each of the three table names in the Show Table dialog box to add it to the Relationships window and close the Show Table dialog box.
- Click and drag to adjust the height of the Employees table so that all fields display in each one.
- Drag the **LocationID field** in the Location table onto the LocationID field in the Employees table.
- Click the **Enforce Referential Integrity** and **Cascade Update Related Fields check boxes** in the Edit Relationships dialog box to select them. Click **Create** to create a one-to-many relationship between the Location and Employees tables.
- Drag the **TitleID field** in the Titles table onto the TitleID field in the Employees table (move the field lists by clicking and dragging their title bars as needed so that they do not overlap).
- Click the **Enforce Referential Integrity** and **Cascade Update Related Fields check boxes** in the Edit Relationships dialog box to select it. Click **Create** to create a one-to-many relationship between the Titles and Employees tables.
- Click **Save** on the Quick Access Toolbar to save the changes to the Relationships window and close the Relationships window.

i. Click the **Create tab** and click the **Query Wizard** in the Queries group. Follow the steps below:

- Select **Simple Query Wizard** and click **OK**.
- Select **Table: Employees** in the Tables/Queries box.
- Double-click **LastName** in the Available Fields list to move it to the Selected Fields list.
- Double-click **FirstName** in the Available Fields list to move it to the Selected Fields list.
- Double-click **LocationID** in the Available Fields list to move it to the Selected Fields list.
- Click **Next**.
- Type **Employees Location** as the query title and click **Finish**.
- Click **View** in the Views group on the Home tab to switch to Design view of the query. Click and drag the **Titles** table from the Navigation Pane into the top pane of the query design window.
- Double-click **Title** in the Titles table to add the field to the query design grid.
- Click the **Sort** cell of the LocationID field, click the arrow, and then click **Ascending**.
- Click **Run** in the Results group (311 records display in the Datasheet sorted by LocationID in ascending order). Double-click the border to the right of each column to set the column widths to Best Fit.
- Save and close the query.

j. Click the **Create tab** and click the **Query Wizard** in the Queries group. Follow the steps below:

- Select **Simple Query Wizard** and click **OK**.
- Select **Table: Location** in the Tables/Queries box.
- Double-click **Location** in the Available Fields list to move it to the Selected Fields list.
- Select **Table: Employees** in the Tables/Queries box.

- Double-click **LastName**, **FirstName**, and **Salary**.
- Select **Table: Titles** in the Tables/Queries box.
- Double-click **MinimumSalary** and **MaximumSalary**. Click **Next**.
- Ensure that the *Detail (shows every field of every record)* option is selected, and click **Next**.
- Type **Atlanta Salaries** as the query title and click **Finish**.

k. Click **View** in the Views group on the Home tab to switch to Design view of the Atlanta Salaries query.

- Click in the Criteria row of the Location field, and type **Atlanta**. Click the **Sort cell** of the Salary field, click the arrow, and then click **Ascending**.
- Click **Run** in the Results group. Review the data to determine if any of the Atlanta employees have a salary less than the minimum or greater than the maximum when compared to the published salary range. These salaries will be updated later.
- Save and close the query.

l. Right-click the **Atlanta Salaries query** in the Navigation Pane and from the shortcut menu, select **Copy**. Right-click a blank area in the Navigation Pane and select **Paste**. In the Paste As dialog box, type **Boston Salaries** for the query name. Click **OK**.

m. Right-click the **Boston Salaries query** in the Navigation Pane and select **Design View**. In the Criteria row of the Location field, replace Atlanta with **Boston**.

- Click **Run** in the Results group. Review the data to determine if any of the Boston employees have a salary less than the minimum or greater than the maximum when compared to the published salary range.
- Modify some data that have been incorrectly entered. In the query results, for the first employee, Frank Cusack, change the salary to **$48,700.00**; for Brian Beamer, **$45,900.00**; for Lorna Weber, **$45,700.00**; for Penny Pfleger, **$45,800.00**.
- Save and close the query.

n. Close the database and exit Access. Based on your instructor's directions, submit a02p2Insurance_LastFirst.

Mid-Level Exercises

1 My Game Collection

ANALYSIS CASE

Over the years, you have collected quite a few video games, so you have cataloged them in an Access database, in the Games table. After opening the database, you will create two more tables—one to identify the game system (System) that runs your game and the other to identify the category or genre of the game (Category). Then, you will join each table in a relationship so that you can query the database.

a. Open *a02m1Games* and save the database as **a02m1Games_LastFirst**. Open the Games table and review the fields containing the game information. Close the table.

b. Click the **Create tab** and click **Table Design** in the Tables group.

c. Type **SystemID** for the first Field Name and select **AutoNumber** as the Data Type.

d. Type **SystemName** for the second Field Name and accept **Short Text** as the Data Type.

e. Set **SystemID** as the primary key. Add the caption **System ID**.

f. Change the SystemName Field Size property to **15**. Add the caption **System Name**, making sure there is a space between System and Name. Save the table as **System**. Switch to Datasheet view.

g. Add the system names to the System table as shown below, letting Access use AutoNumber to create the SystemID values. Close the table when finished.

System ID	System Name
1	XBOX 360
2	PS3
3	Wii
4	NES
5	PC Game
6	Nintendo 3DS

h. Click the **Create tab** and click **Table Design** in the Tables group. Type **CategoryID** for the first Field Name and select **AutoNumber** as the Data Type. Set the CategoryID as the primary key.

i. Type **CategoryDescription** for the second Field Name and accept **Short Text** as the Data Type. Change the Field Size property to **25**. Add the caption **Category Description**, making sure there is a space between Category and Description. Save the table as **Category**, saving the changes to the table design. Switch to Datasheet view.

j. Add the category descriptions to the Category table as shown below, letting Access use AutoNumber to create the CategoryID values. Close the table when finished.

CategoryID	Category Description
1	Action
2	Adventure
3	Arcade
4	Racing
5	Rhythm
6	Role-playing
7	Simulation
8	Sports

k. Click the **Database Tools tab** and click **Relationships** in the Relationships group. Display all three tables in the Relationships window and close the Show Table dialog box. Create a one-to-many relationship between CategoryID in the Category table and CategoryID in the Games table. Enforce referential integrity and cascade update related fields.

l. Create a one-to-many relationship between SystemID in the System table and SystemID in the Games table. Enforce referential integrity and cascade update related fields. Close the Relationships window, saving the changes.

m. Use the Query Wizard to create a simple query using the Games table. Add the following fields in the query (in this order): GameName, Rating. Save the query as **Ratings Query**.

n. Switch to Design view. Sort the Rating field in ascending order and run the query. Close the query, saving the changes.

o. Create a multitable query in Design view using all three tables. Add the following fields (in this order): GameName, CategoryDescription, Rating, SystemName, and DateAcquired.

p. Sort the query in ascending order by GameName and run the query. Save the query as **Game List Query** and close the query.

q. Copy the **Game List Query** and paste it into the Navigation Pane using the name **PS3 Games**. Modify the query in Design view by using **PS3** as the criterion for SystemName. Remove the sort by GameName and sort in ascending order by Rating. The query results should include 7 records.

r. Close the PS3 Games query, saving the changes. Assume you are going home for Thanksgiving and you want to take your **Wii** gaming system and games home with you—but you only want to take home games with a rating of **Everyone**.

s. Create a query named **Thanksgiving Games** that shows the name of the game, its rating, the category description of the game, and the system name for each. Run the query. The results of the query will tell you which games to pack. Close the query.

t. Close the database and exit Access. Based on your instructor's directions, submit a02m1Games_LastFirst.

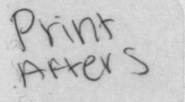

2 The Prestige Hotel

The Prestige Hotel chain caters to upscale business travelers and provides state-of-the-art conference, meeting, and reception facilities. It prides itself on its international, four-star cuisine. Last year, it began a member reward club to help the marketing department track the purchasing patterns of its most loyal customers. All of the hotel transactions are stored in the database. Your task is to help the managers of the Prestige Hotels in Denver and Chicago identify their customers who stayed in a room last year and who had three persons in their party.

a. Open *a02m2Hotel* and save the file as **a02m2Hotel_LastFirst**. Review the data contained in the three tables. Specifically, study the tables and fields containing the data you need to analyze: dates of stays in Denver and Chicago suites, the members' names, and the numbers in the parties.

b. Import the location data from the Excel file *a02m2Location* into your database as a new table. The first row of the worksheet contains column headings. Set the LocationID Indexed property to **Yes (No Duplicates)** and set the Data Type to **Long Integer**. Select the **LocationID field** as the primary key. Name the table **Location**. Do not save the import steps.

c. Open the Relationships window and create a relationship between the Location table and the Orders table using the LocationID field. Enforce referential integrity and cascade update related fields. Create a relationship between the Orders and Members tables using the MemNumber field, ensuring that you enforce referential integrity and cascade update related fields. Create a relationship between the Orders and Service tables using the ServiceID field, ensuring that you enforce referential integrity and cascade update related fields. Save and close the Relationships window.

d. Open the Members table and use the Find command to locate Bryan Gray's name. Replace his name with your own first and last names. Locate Nicole Lee's name and replace it with your name. Close the table.

e. Create a query using the following fields: ServiceDate (Orders table), City (Location table), NoInParty (Orders table), ServiceName (Service table), FirstName (Members table), and LastName (Members table). Set the criteria to limit the output to **Denver**. Use the Between operator to show services only from **7/1/2017** to **6/30/2018**. Set the NoInParty criterion to **3**. Sort the results in ascending order by the ServiceDate.

f. Run the query and examine the number of records in the status bar at the bottom of the query. It should display 155. If your number of records is different, examine the criteria and make corrections.

g. Change the order of the query fields so that they display as FirstName, LastName, ServiceDate, City, NoInParty, and ServiceName. Save the query as **Denver Rooms 3 Guests**. Close the query.

DISCOVER

h. Copy the **Denver Rooms 3 Guests** query and paste it, renaming the new query **Chicago Rooms 3 Guests**.

i. Open the Chicago Rooms 3 Guests query in Design view and change the criterion for City to **Chicago**. Run the query and save the changes. It should display 179 results. Close the query.

DISCOVER

j. Review the criteria of the two previous queries and then create a third query named **Denver and Chicago Rooms 3 Guests**. Use the criteria from the two individual queries as a basis to create a combination AND–OR condition. The results will display guests in **Denver** or **Chicago** with 3 guests and service dates between **7/1/2013** and **6/30/2018**. The records returned in the results should equal the sum of the records in the two individual queries (334 records). Run, save, and close the query.

k. Close the database and exit Access. Based on your instructor's directions, submit a02m2Hotel_LastFirst.

3 New Castle County Technical Services

RUNNING CASE

New Castle County Technical Services (NCCTS) provides technical support for a number of companies in the greater New Castle County, Delaware area. Once you have completed the changes to the database tables and set the appropriate relationships, you will be ready to extract information by creating queries.

a. Open the database *a01m3NCCTS_LastFirst* and save it as a02m3NCCTS_LastFirst changing 01 to 02.

> **TROUBLESHOOTING:** If you did not complete the Chapter 1 case, return to Chapter 1, complete the case to create the database, and then return to this exercise.

b. Open the Call Types table in Design view. Before you create your queries, you want to modify some of the table properties:
- Set the caption of the HourlyRate field to **Hourly Rate**.
- View the table in Datasheet view, and save the changes when prompted.

c. Close the table.

d. Make the following additional changes to the tables:
- Open the Calls table in Design view. Change the data type of the CallTypeID field to **Number**.
- Set the caption of the HoursLogged field to **Hours Logged**.
- Set the caption of the OpenedDate field to **Opened Date** and set the format to **Short Date**.
- Set the caption of the ClosedDate field to **Closed Date** and set the format to **Short Date**.
- Set the caption of the CustomerSatisfaction field to **Customer Satisfaction**.
- View the table in Datasheet view, and save the changes when prompted. You will not lose any data by making this change, so click **Yes** in the message box when prompted. Close the table.
- Open the Customers table in Design view. Set the field size of CompanyName to **50** and the caption to **Company Name**. View the table in Datasheet view, and save the changes when prompted. You will not lose any data by making this change, so click **Yes** in the message box when prompted. Close the table.
- Open the Reps table in Design view. Set the caption of the RepFirst field to **Rep First Name**. Set the caption of the RepLast field to **Rep Last Name**. View the table in Datasheet view, and save the changes when prompted. Close the table.

e. Open the Relationships window. Create a join line between the Call Types and Calls tables, ensuring that you enforce referential integrity and cascade update related fields. Set a relationship between Reps and Calls and between Customers and Calls using the same options. Save and close the Relationships window.

f. Create a multitable query, following the steps below:
- Add the following fields (in this order): **CallID** (from Calls), **Description** (from Call Types), **CompanyName** (from Customers), and **RepFirst** and **RepLast** (from Reps).
- Run the query, and then modify it to add **HoursLogged** (from Calls).
- Sort the query by HoursLogged in ascending order. Set the criteria of the HoursLogged field to **Is Not Null** and run the query again.
- Modify the criteria of the HoursLogged field to **>=5** and **<=10**, the description to **Disaster Recovery**, and the rep to **Barbara**.
- Save the query as **Complex Disaster Recovery Calls_Barbara**. Run and then close the query.

g. Create a copy of the **Complex Disaster Recovery Calls_Barbara** query, and modify it following the steps below:
- Save the copy of the query as **Complex Network Installation Calls_Barbara**.
- Modify the query so that the description displays Barbara's network installation calls that logged between 5 and 10 hours.
- Save, run, and then close the query.

h. Close the database and exit Access. Based on your instructor's directions, submit a02m3NCCTS_LastFirst.

Beyond the Classroom

Database Administrator Position

GENERAL CASE ✓

FROM SCRATCH

Create a database to keep track of candidates for open positions at Secure Systems, Inc., database management experts. Use the Internet to search for information about database management positions. One useful site is published by the federal government's Bureau of Labor Statistics. It compiles an Occupational Outlook Handbook describing various positions, the type of working environment, the education required, salary information, and the projected growth. The website is http://www.bls.gov/ooh. Research the necessary information in order to create the database using these requirements:

a. Create a new database named **a02b1Admin_LastFirst**.

b. Create three tables including the field names as follows, and in the specified orders:
   - **Candidates (CandidateID, FirstName, LastName, Phone, Email)**.
   - **JobOpenings (JobOpeningID, JobName, RequiredSkill, HourlyPayRate, DataPosted, Supervisor)**.
   - **Interviews (InterviewSequenceID, CandidateID, JobOpeningID, InterviewedBy, DateOfInterview, Rank)**.

c. Set the data types, field properties, and a primary key for each table.

d. Set table relationships, and be sure to enforce referential integrity between them. Cascade update related fields

e. Add 10 candidates to the Candidates table.

f. Add a **Database Administrator** job and four other sample jobs to the JobOpenings table.

g. Add eight sample interviews—four for the Database Administrator position and four others. Rank each candidate on a scale of 1 to 5 (with 5 as the highest).

h. Create a query that lists the LastName, FirstName, JobOpeningID, InterviewedBy, DateOfInterview, and Rank fields. Display only Database Administrator interviews with a ranking of 3 or lower. Sort by LastName and then by FirstName. Run and save the query as **Database Admin Low Rank**. Close the query

i. Close the database and exit Access. Based on your instructor's directions, submit a02b1Admin_LastFirst.

May Beverage Sales

DISASTER RECOVERY

A coworker explained that he was having difficulty with queries that were not returning correct results, and asked you to help diagnose the problem. Open *a02b2Traders* and save it as **a02b2Traders_LastFirst**. It contains two queries, *May 2018 Orders of Beverages and Confections* and *2018 Beverage Sales by Ship Country*. The May 2018 Orders of Beverages and Confections query is supposed to contain only information for orders shipped in May 2018. You find other shipped dates included in the results. Change the criteria to exclude the other dates. Run and save the query. Close the query.

The 2018 Beverage Sales by Ship Country query returns no results. Check the criteria in all fields and modify so that the correct results are returned. Run and save the query. Close the query.

Close the database and exit Access. Based on your instructor's directions, submit a02b2Traders_LastFirst.

Capstone Exercise

The Morris Arboretum in Chestnut Hill, Pennsylvania tracks donors in Excel. They also use Excel to store a list of plants in stock. As donors contribute funds to the Arboretum, they can elect to receive a plant gift from the Arboretum. These plants are both rare plants and hard-to-find old favorites, and they are part of the annual appeal and membership drive to benefit the Arboretum's programs. The organization has grown, and the files are too large and inefficient to handle in Excel. You will begin by importing the files from Excel into a new Access database. Then you will create a table to track donations, create a relationship between the two tables, and create some baseline queries.

Create a New Database

You will examine the data in the Excel worksheets to determine which fields will become the primary keys in each table and which fields will become the foreign keys.

a. Open the *a02c1Donors* Excel workbook, examine the data, and close the workbook.

b. Open the *a02c1Plants* Excel workbook, examine the data, and close the workbook.

c. Create a new, blank database named **a02c1Arbor_LastFirst**. Close the new blank table created automatically by Access without saving it.

Import Data from Excel

You will import two Excel workbooks into the database.

a. Click the **External Data tab** and click **Excel** in the Import & Link group.

b. Navigate to and select the *a02c1Donors* workbook to be imported.

c. Select the **First Row Contains Column Headings** option.

d. Set the DonorID field Indexed option to **Yes (No Duplicates)**.

e. Choose **DonorID** as the primary key when prompted and accept the table name Donors.

f. Import the *a02c1Plants* workbook, set the **ID field** as the primary key, and then change the indexing option to **Yes (No Duplicates)**.

g. Accept the table name Plants.

h. Change the ID field name in the Plants table to **PlantID**.

i. Open each table in Datasheet view to examine the data. Close the tables.

Create a New Table

You will create a new table to track the donations as they are received from the donors.

a. You will create a new table in Design view and save the table as **Donations**.

b. Add the following fields in Design view and set the properties as specified:
- Add the primary key field as **DonationID** with the **Number Data Type** and a field size of **Long Integer**.
- Add **DonorID** (a foreign key) with the **Number Data Type** and a field size of **Long Integer**.
- Add **PlantID** (a foreign key) as a **Number** and a field size of **Long Integer**.
- Add **DateOfDonation** as a **Date/Time** field.
- Add **AmountOfDonation** as a **Currency** field.

c. Switch to Datasheet view, and save the table when prompted. You will enter data into the table in a later step. Close the table.

Create Relationships

You will create the relationships between the tables using the Relationships window.

a. Open the Donors table in Design view and change the Field Size property for DonorID to **Long Integer** so it matches the Field Size property of DonorID in the Donations table. Save and close the table.

b. Open the Plants table in Design view and change the Field Size property for PlantID to **Long Integer** so it matches the Field Size property for PlantID in the Donations table. Save and close the table.

c. Identify the primary key fields in the Donors table and the Plants table and join them with their foreign key counterparts in the related Donations table. Enforce referential integrity and cascade and update related fields. Save and close the Relationships window.

Add Sample Data to the Donations Table

You will add 10 records to the Donations table.

a. Add the following records to the Donations table:

Donation ID	Donor ID	Plant ID	Date of Donation	Amount of Donation
10	8228	611	3/1/2018	$150
18	5448	190	3/1/2018	$ 55
6	4091	457	3/12/2018	$125
7	11976	205	3/14/2018	$100
1	1000	25	3/17/2018	$120
12	1444	38	3/19/2018	$ 50
2	1444	38	4/3/2018	$ 50
4	10520	49	4/12/2018	$ 60
5	3072	102	4/19/2018	$ 50
21	1204	25	4/22/2018	$120

b. Sort the Donations table by the AmountOfDonation field in descending order. Close the table.

Use the Query Wizard

You will create a query of all donations greater than $100 in the Donations table.

a. Add the DonorID and AmountOfDonation fields from Donations (in that order).

b. Save the query as **Donations Over 100**.

c. Add criteria to include only donations of more than $100.

d. Sort the query results in ascending order by AmountOfDonation.

e. Run the query.

f. Save and close the query.

Create a Query in Design View

You will create a query that identifies donors and donations.

a. Create a query that identifies the people who made a donation after April 1, 2018. This list will be given to the Arboretum staff so they can notify the donors that a plant is ready for pickup. The query should list the date of the donation, donor's full name (LastName, FirstName), phone number, the amount of the donation, and name of the plant they want (in that order). Add the tables and fields necessary to produce the query.

b. Sort the query by date of donation in descending order, then by donor last name in ascending order.

c. Run, close, and save the query as **Plant Pickup List**.

Copy and Modify a Query in Design View

You will copy a query and modify it to add and sort by a different field.

a. Copy the Plant Pickup List query and paste it using **ENewsletter** as the query name.

b. Open the ENewsletter query in Design view and delete the DateofDonation column.

c. Add the ENewsletter field to the first column of the design grid and set it to sort in ascending order, so that the query sorts first by ENewsletter and then by LastName.

d. Run, save, and close the query. Close the database and exit Access. Based on your instructor's directions, submit a02c1Arbor_LastFirst.

Using Queries to Make Decisions

LEARNING OUTCOME You will create queries to perform calculations and summarize data.

OBJECTIVES & SKILLS: After you read this chapter, you will be able to:

Calculations and Expressions

The Expression Builder and Functions

Aggregate Functions

CASE STUDY | Real Estate Investors

After completing their degrees in Business at Passaic County Community College (PCCC) and a weekend seminar in real estate investing, Donald Carter and Matthew Nevoso were ready to test their skills in the marketplace. Don and Matt had a simple strategy—buy distressed properties at a significant discount, then resell the properties for a profit. Based on their seminar, they knew to gather key information such as the asking price, the number of bedrooms, square feet, and days on the market. Because they are just starting out, they decided to consider less expensive houses.

Based on a tip from the real estate seminar, they decide to create a database using Access, using data from a variety of home listing services. They approached you to help them find houses that meet their criteria. This new database approach should hopefully help them acquire their first investment property.

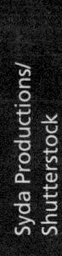

Perform Calculations and Summarize Data Using Queries

List Price Calculations	Mortgage Payments							
First Name ▾	Last Name ▾	List Price ▾	Square Feet ▾	Listing ▾	Sold ▾	Price Per Sq Ft ▾	Payment ▾	
Philip	DeFranco	$109,140.00	1133	10004	No	$96.33	$416.84	
Chardae	Myles	$129,780.00	1132	10028	No	$114.65	$495.67	
Makarem	Abdeljawad	$136,680.00	1375	10008	No	$99.40	$522.02	
Meera	Shah	$138,990.00	1276	10016	No	$108.93	$530.85	
StudentFirst	StudentLast	$140,693.00	1490	10069	No	$94.42	$537.35	
Makarem	Abdeljawad	$140,904.00	1301	10061	No	$108.30	$538.16	
Makarem	Abdeljawad	$142,380.00	1373	11028	No	$103.70	$543.80	
Chardae	Myles	$163,737.00	1476	10910	No	$110.93	$625.36	
Jaynish	Mody	$164,436.00	1850	10117	No	$88.88	$628.03	
Jaynish	Mody	$166,320.00	1437	10082	No	$115.74	$635.23	
Chardae	Myles	$166,552.00	1623	10851	No	$102.62	$636.12	
Chardae	Myles	$166,800.00	1598	10014	No	$104.38	$637.06	
Philip	DeFranco	$168,000.00	1680	10002	No	$100.00	$641.65	
Chardae	Myles	$168,354.00	1651	10885	No	$101.97	$643.00	
Philip	DeFranco	$174,230.00	1771	10104	No	$98.38	$665.44	
StudentFirst	StudentLast	$174,720.00	1610	10921	No	$108.52	$667.31	
Meera	Shah	$174,720.00	1694	11035	No	$103.14	$667.31	
Chardae	Myles	$175,336.00	1855	10868	No	$94.52	$669.66	
StudentFirst	StudentLast	$175,560.00	1562	11036	No	$112.39	$670.52	
Meera	Shah	$176,176.00	1761	10025	No	$100.04	$672.87	
Jaynish	Mody	$177,984.00	1707	10066	No	$104.27	$679.78	
Chardae	Myles	$179,088.00	1837	10010	No	$97.49	$683.99	
Chardae	Myles	$179,100.00	1946	11079	No	$92.03	$684.04	
Chardae	Myles	$179,712.00	1854	10102	No	$96.93	$686.38	
Chardae	Myles	$180,180.00	1896	10019	No	$95.03	$688.17	
Makarem	Abdeljawad	$180,810.00	1667	10044	No	$108.46	$690.57	
Total		**$167,100.47**		**32**		**$102.10**		

Record: 1 of 32 No Filter Search

FIGURE 3.1 Real Estate Investors Property Database – Mortgage Payments Query

Results by Realtor Revised			
NameOfList ▾	AvgOfSalePrice ▾	Number Sold ▾	DaysOnMarket ▾
Algernon Listings	$324,697.22	18	23.50
FastHouse	$288,314.50	6	22.33
Houses 4 Sale	$218,039.00	2	23.50
Local Listings	$341,085.67	9	23.56
Major Houses	$235,757.88	8	24.75
Trullo	$236,885.21	19	26.05
Wholesaler	$276,654.92	26	26.12
Total		**88**	

FIGURE 3.2 Real Estate Investors Property Database – Results by Realtor Revised Query

CASE STUDY | Real Estate Investors

Starting File	Files to be Submitted
a03h1Property	**a03h1PropertyCheck_LastFirst** **a03h3Property_LastFirst**

Calculations and Expressions

There are going to be times, when manipulating data in an Access database, that you will want to perform calculations. A field storing the number of hours worked multiplied by a field storing the hourly pay rate will calculate the gross pay, for example. Unfortunately, calculations may not always be that easy. If you have received a paycheck, you realize your gross pay is not the same as the amount as your paycheck. Your net pay will be lower, due to common deductions such as Social Security, Medicare, federal and state income taxes, unemployment insurance, and union dues. Some deductions may be a flat rate, and others may be calculated based on the paycheck amount, so even what appears to be a simple calculation can be complex.

At first glance, you may not see an obvious location for you to enter a calculation in Access. However, Access includes many built-in calculations and functions. Calculations appear commonly in queries, but can also be added to tables, forms, and reports.

In this section, you will learn how to create a calculated field in a query. You will also format the calculations to enhance readability.

Creating a Query with a Calculated Field

Rather than performing a calculation outside of the database and then inputting the result into your database, you should instead store the components of the calculation in the database. Calculating values rather than inputting values will reduce errors and inconsistencies. If your database stored the hours worked and paycheck amount, both fields would have to be updated if there was a change in the hours the employee worked. However, if you store only the hours worked and calculate the paycheck amount, you do not have to worry about updating multiple fields. The next time the paycheck is calculated, the results will be updated and corrected.

As another example, a table might contain the times when employees clock in and out of work. You could create a calculation in a query to determine how many hours each employee worked by subtracting the ClockIn field from the ClockOut field. A combination of elements that produce a value is known as an *expression*. A *calculated field* is a field that displays the result of an expression rather than data stored in a field.

You may find one or more of the following elements in a calculated field:

- Arithmetic operator (for example, *, /, +, or −)
- *Constant*, a value that does not change (such as −20 or 3.14)
- Function (built-in calculations like Pmt)
- Identifier (the names of fields, controls, or properties)

Understand the Order of Operations

The *order of operations* determines the sequence by which operations are calculated in a mathematical expression. Evaluate expressions in parentheses first, then exponents, then multiplication and division, and, finally, addition and subtraction. You may remember PEMDAS (or the mnemonic device "Please Excuse My Dear Aunt Sally") from a math class. Table 3.1 shows some examples of the order of operations. Access uses the following symbols:

- Parentheses ( )
- Exponentiation ^
- Multiplication *
- Division /
- Addition +
- Subtraction −

TABLE 3.1 Examples of Order of Operations

Expression	Order to Perform Calculations	Output
=2+3*3	Multiply first and then add.	11
=(2+3)*3	Add the values inside the parentheses first and then multiply.	15
=2+2^3	Evaluate the exponent first, $2^3=2*2*2$ (or 8). Then add.	10
=10/2+3	Divide first and then add.	8
=10/(2+3)	Add first to simplify the parenthetical expression and then divide.	2
=10*2–3*2	Multiply first and then subtract.	14

Pearson Education, Inc.

Build Expressions

STEP 1 >> As mentioned earlier, expressions can contain a number of different elements. Expressions can be typed manually or inserted using Access tools.

The challenging part is typically creating the expression. Consider the following scenario. Your company plans on allowing customers to pay off their balance in 12 monthly payments. The balance is stored in your Access database in a field named Balance. To divide this into equal payments, you would type Balance/12 in the Field row of a blank column. For example, if the Balance field was $1,200, you divide by 12. You are left with a monthly payment of $100. See Figure 3.3 for an example of the Balance field added to a query.

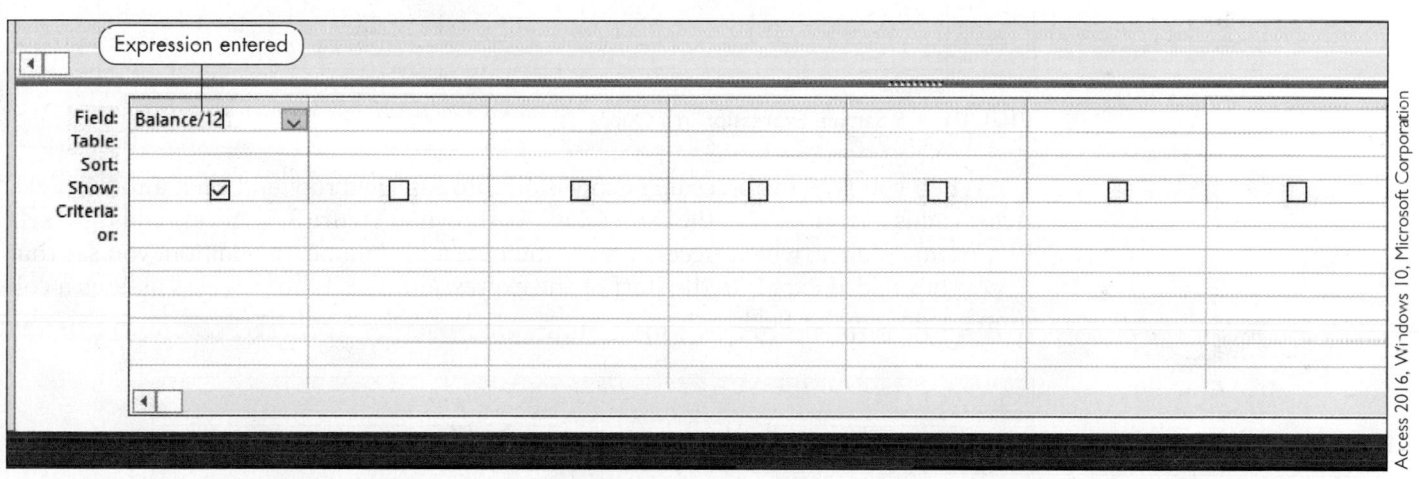

FIGURE 3.3 Balance Field in a Query

However, many companies will apply some sort of surcharge or add interest when customers pay balances off in installments. From your perspective as someone creating a query, this makes the calculation more complex. Your company may decide to add a surcharge of 20% (or, .20) of the balance. In this case, you will need to include a multiplication step in the above calculation. You will multiply the results by 1.20. Why multiply by 1.20 rather than .20? If you multiplied by .20 and divided by 12, you would only see the surcharge amount and not the total amount due for each payment. If the Balance field was $1,200, the monthly payment needs to be more than the $100 in the previous example.

If you multiply $1,200 by .20, you get a result of $20. The $20 does not represent the amount due, it represents the surcharge. Therefore, multiplying by 1.20 will give you the balance plus the surcharge. Dividing that by 12 gives you a monthly payment of $120. Note that there are multiple ways to implement this calculation, so this is not the only solution.

To create a calculated field within a query, complete the following steps:

1. Open the query in Design view.
2. Click the Field row (top row) of a blank column. Recall that the Field row is found in the bottom pane of the design.
3. Type the desired expression. See Figure 3.4 for an example of a query with an expression.
4. Click Run in the Results group to display the results in Datasheet view.

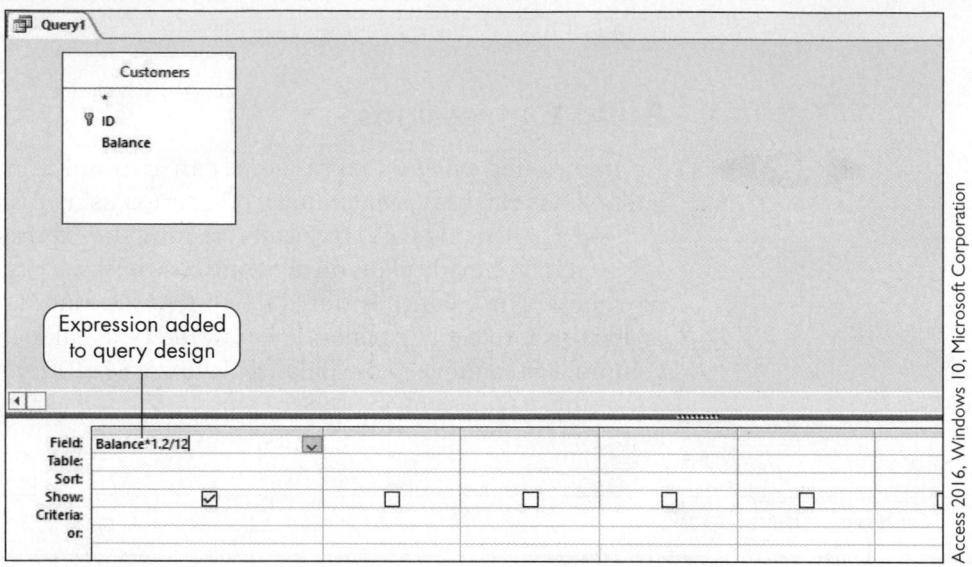

FIGURE 3.4 Sample Expression in a Query

When you type the preceding expression into the Field row and click another field, Access adds a few things to the expression. As shown in Figure 3.5, Access adds brackets [ ] around Balance, which Access uses to indicate a field name. In addition, you see that Access has added Expr1: to the start of the expression. This is how Access assigns a column heading to this field.

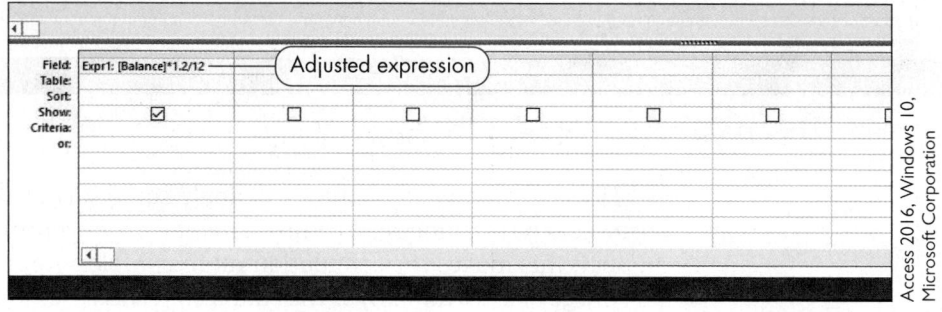

FIGURE 3.5 Modified Expression

If you were to run the query, the column heading would be *Expr1*. If you wanted to name this column MonthlySurcharge, you would start the expression with the name, followed by a colon, followed by the expression (or, if Expr1: already appears, replace Expr1 with the name and leave the colon in place). The column is renamed MonthlySurcharge in Figure 3.6.

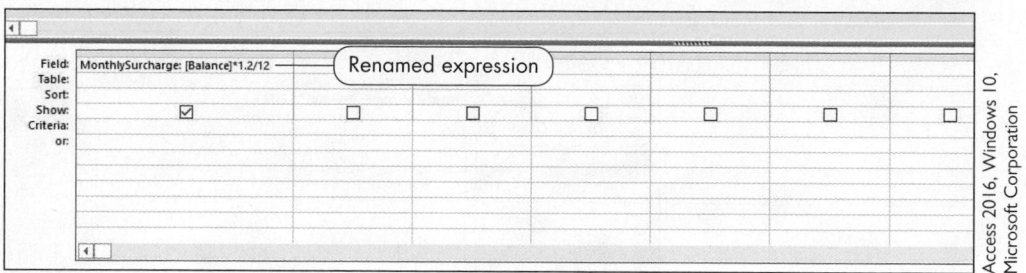

FIGURE 3.6 Expression Renamed

The query results, as shown in Figure 3.7, display a decimal number in the MonthlySurcharge column. Notice that the results are not easy to read and should be formatted.

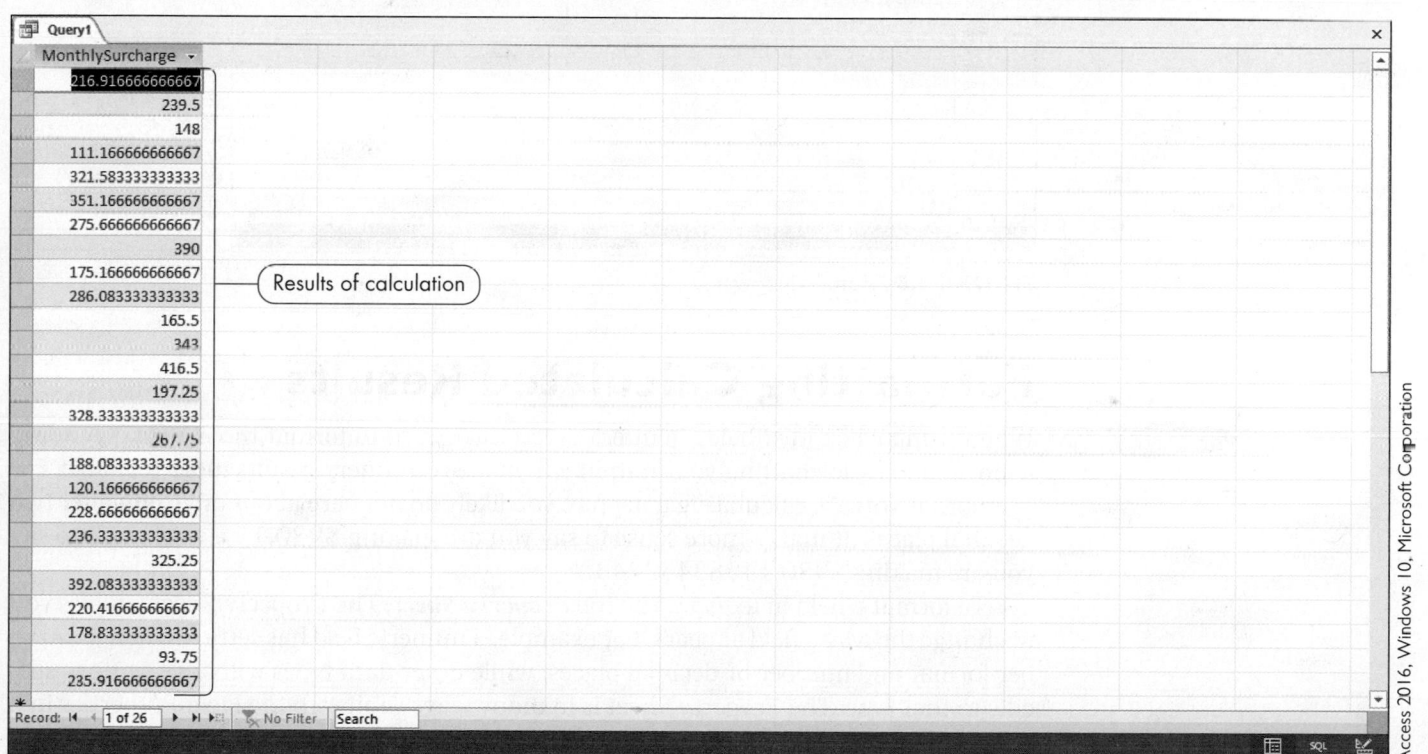

FIGURE 3.7 Unformatted Results

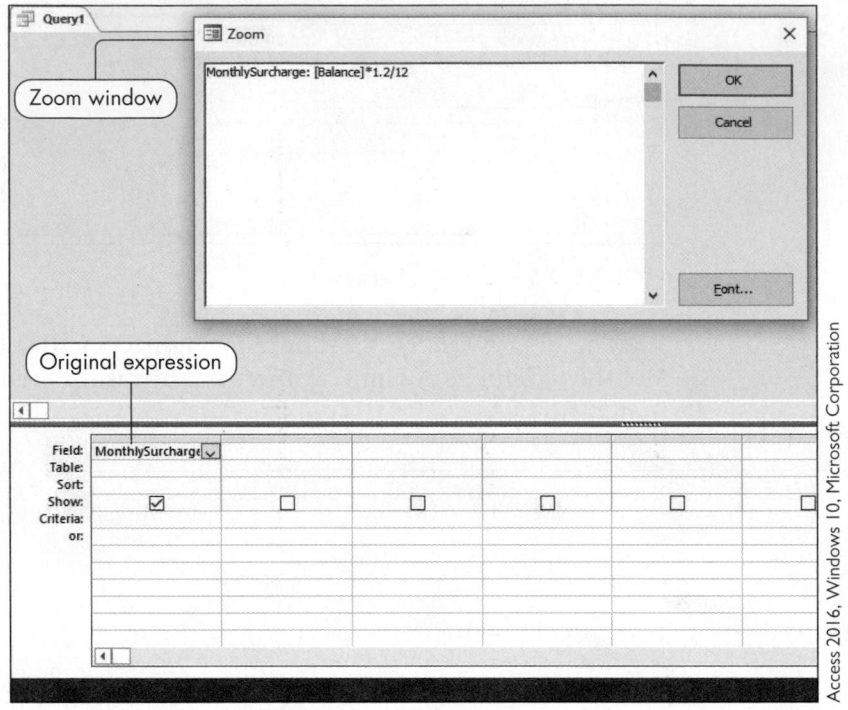

FIGURE 3.8 Zoom Window

Formatting Calculated Results

STEP 2 ›› When using calculated fields in queries, you may want to format the results. Spending a few moments formatting your output will make your query results more readable. For example, if you are calculating a net pay, you likely do not care about anything after two decimal places. It makes more sense to say you are making $980.15 a week than to say you are making $980.14983432743.

To format a field in a query, use the ***Property Sheet***. The Property Sheet enables you to change the way a field appears. For example, a numeric field has settings such as number format and number of decimal places, while other data types will have settings specific to that type. The Property Sheet is in many ways similar to the Field Properties in a table.

To format a field, complete the following steps:

1. Open the query in Design view.

2. Click the Field row of the field you want to format.

3. Click Property Sheet in the Show/Hide group on the Design tab.

4. Click the appropriate option and choose the setting desired. You can change the format by clicking the Format property arrow and selecting your desired format (such as Currency for numeric fields). For numeric fields, the Decimal Places property will allow you to choose the number of decimal places that display. To change the caption (which appears as the name of the column), click the text box next to the Caption property and type your desired column heading. Figure 3.9 shows the Property Sheet options related to a numeric field.

5. Close the Property Sheet, if desired, by clicking Close as shown in Figure 3.9. After using the Property Sheet, it will be displayed in the future when the query is opened in Design view, unless you close it. However, as most of your users will not be viewing the query in Design view, it should not matter either way if the Property Sheet is closed or not.

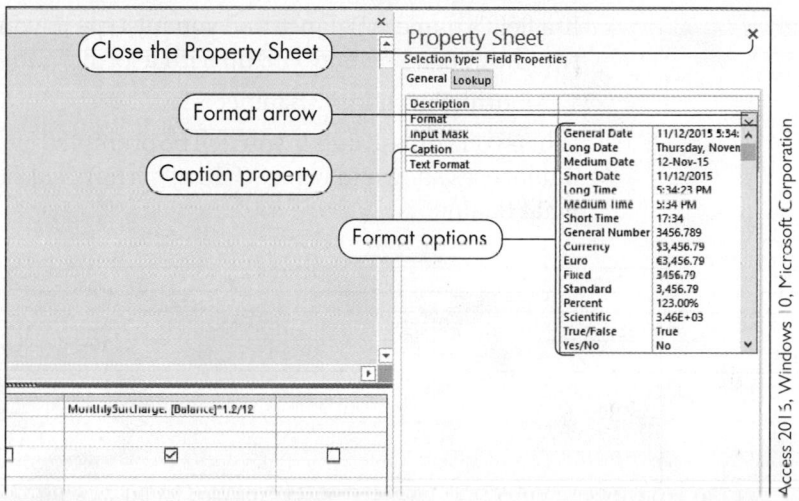

FIGURE 3.9 Property Sheet Options

Recovering from Common Errors

STEP 3 ❯❯ When creating calculated fields, there are a number of common errors that can occur. Learning how to recognize errors and recover from issues is important. Some common types of errors are shown below:

- Forgetting the colon between the column title and the formula

   A correct formula would look like this:

   MonthlySurcharge: [Balance]*1.2/12

   If you forget the colon, the formula looks like this instead:

   MonthlySurcharge [Balance]*1.2/12

   and you will get an invalid syntax error, indicating something is wrong with the way the formula is written, as shown in Figure 3.10.

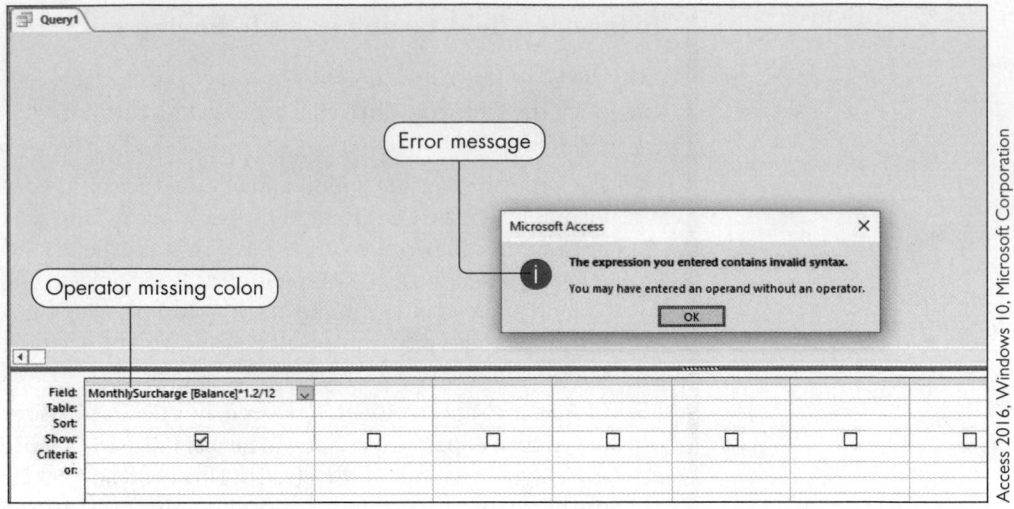

FIGURE 3.10 Syntax Error Warning

- Spelling a field name incorrectly

    If a field's name is Balance and you mistype it, you will get an error when you run the query. You may end up with a formula that looks like this:

    MonthlySurcharge: [Baalnce]*1.2/12

    When you run the query, you will be prompted by Access to give a value for Baalnce, as shown in Figure 3.11. This happens because Access does not know what Baalnce is.

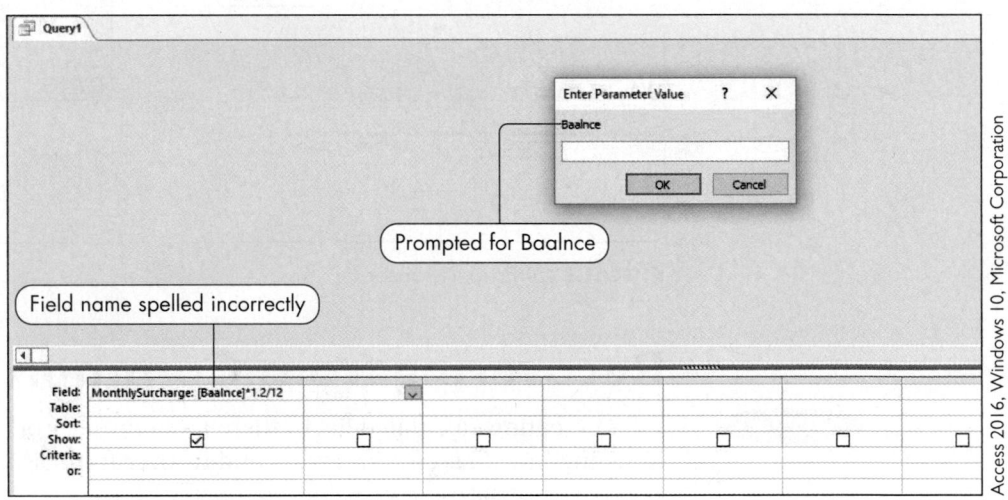

FIGURE 3.11 Result of Spelling Error in Field Name

- Forgetting the order of operations

    If you do not check your formulas, you may get bad values. For example, the following would not produce the expected output:

    NewMonthlyBalance: [Balance] + 100/12

    If you want addition to be done before division, you must remember the parentheses:

    NewMonthlyBalance: ([Balance] + 100)/12

Verifying Calculated Results

STEP 4 ▶▶ After your query runs, look at the field values in Datasheet view and look at the calculated values. You may find that the results do not make sense. In a real-world scenario, you will not be given step-by-step directions, and instead will apply critical thinking skills to your work. Access will calculate exactly what you tell it to calculate, even if you make logical errors in the calculation.

When you run a query, you need to analyze the results and ask yourself if the results make sense. Assume you are calculating a car payment for a $10,000 car, with monthly payments for 5 years. If your formula is incorrect, you may end up with a monthly payment result like $1,000. If you look at your results, you should say to yourself, "Does it make sense for me to pay $1,000 every month for five years to finance a $10,000 car?"

You can verify results with a calculator or by copying and pasting data into Excel. Recreate the calculations in Excel and compare the answers to the query results in Access. The Access calculated field, the calculator, and the Excel calculations should all return identical results.

Quick Concepts

1. What are the four types of elements that can appear as part of an expression in Access? **p. 812**

2. Briefly describe the order of operations. Give an example of how the order of operations makes a difference in a calculation. **p. 812**

3. How does Access respond when you spell a field name incorrectly in a query? **p. 818**

4. How can the Property Sheet make query results more readable? **p. 817**

Hands-On Exercises

Watch the Video for this Hands-On Exercise!

MyITLab® HOE1 Training

Skills covered: Build Expressions • Format Fields • Recognize and Correct Common Errors • Evaluate Results

1 Calculations and Expressions

Using the data from the homes for sale lists that Don and Matt acquired, you are able to help them target properties that meet their criteria. As you examine the data, you discover other ways to analyze the properties. You create several queries and present your results to the two investors for their comments.

STEP 1 ›› BUILD EXPRESSIONS

You begin your analysis by creating a query using the Properties and Agents tables from the Property database. The Properties table contains all the properties the investors will evaluate; the Agents table contains a list of real estate agents who represent the properties' sellers. In this exercise, you will add requested fields and only show properties that have not been sold. You will then build an expression to calculate the price per square foot for each property. Refer to Figure 3.12 as you complete Step 1.

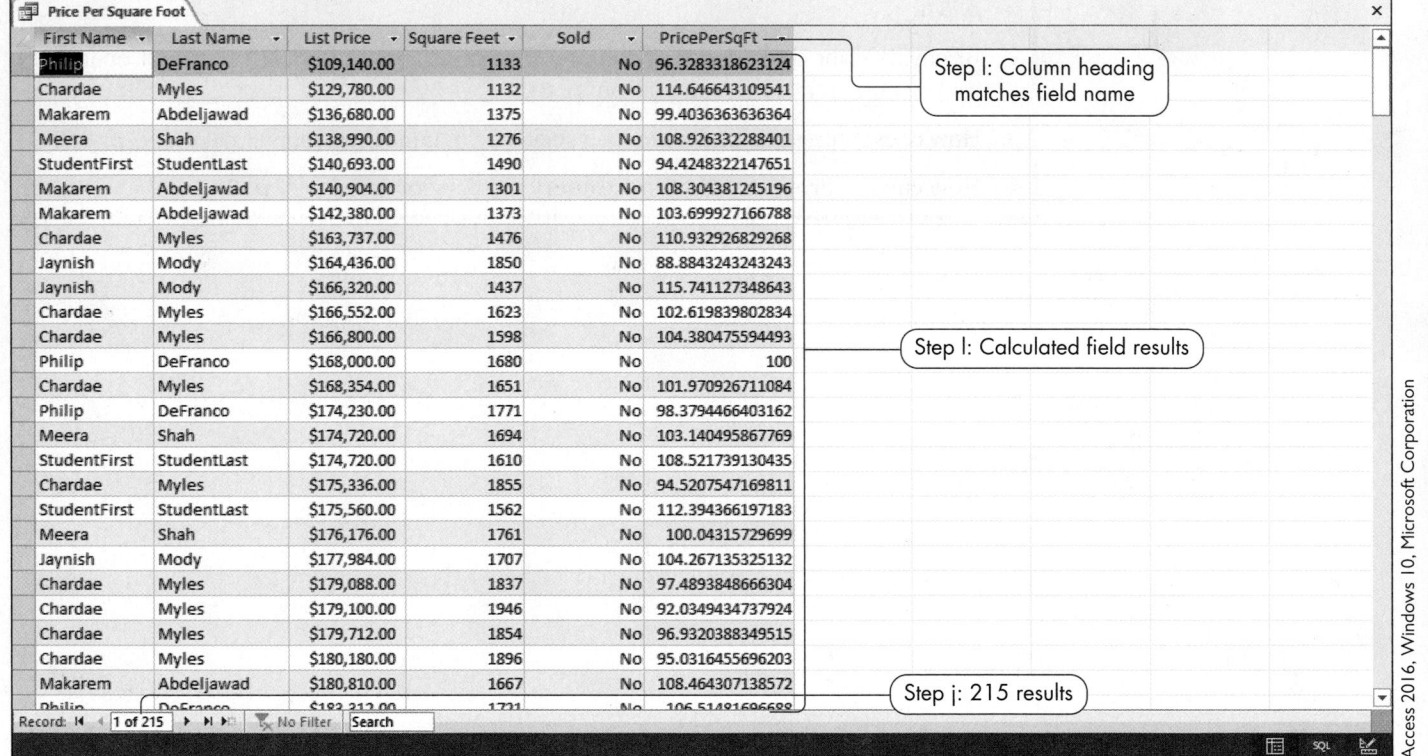

FIGURE 3.12 Modified Expression

a. Open *a03h1Property*. Save the database as **a03h1Property_LastFirst**.

> **TROUBLESHOOTING:** Throughout the remainder of this chapter and textbook, click Enable Content whenever you are working with student files.

> **TROUBLESHOOTING:** If you make any major mistakes in this exercise, you can close the file, open *a03h1Property* again, and then start this exercise over.

b. Open the Agents table and replace the name *Dilson Herrera* with your name. Close the table.

c. Click the **Create tab** and click **Query Design** in the Queries group to create a new query.

The Show Table dialog box opens so you can specify the table(s) and/or queries to include in the query design.

d. Select the **Agents table** and click **Add**. Select the **Properties table** and click **Add**. Click **Close** to close the Show Table dialog box.

e. Double-click the **FirstName** and **LastName fields** in the Agents table to add them to the query.

f. Double-click the **ListPrice**, **SqFeet**, and **Sold fields** in the Properties table to add them to the query.

g. Click **Run** in the Results group to display the results in Datasheet view.

A total of 303 properties appear in the results.

h. Switch to Design view. Type **No** in the Criteria row of the Sold field.

i. Click the **Sort row** in the ListPrice field. Click the **arrow** and select **Ascending**.

j. Click **Run** to see the results.

The 215 unsold properties appear in the datasheet, with the least expensive houses displayed first.

k. Click **Save** on the Quick Access Toolbar and type **Price Per Square Foot** as the Query Name in the Save As dialog box. Click **OK**.

l. Switch to Design view. Click the **Field row** of the first blank column of the query design grid. Right-click and select **Zoom** to show the Zoom window. Type **PricePerSqFt: ListPrice/SqFeet** and click **OK**.

Access inserts square brackets around the fields for you. The new field divides the values in the ListPrice field by the values in the SqFeet field.

m. Click **Run** in the Results group to view the results. Adjust column widths as necessary.

The new calculated field, PricePerSqFt, is displayed. Compare your results to those shown in Figure 3.12.

> **TROUBLESHOOTING:** If you see pound signs (#####) in an Access column, double-click the vertical line between column headings to increase the width.

> **TROUBLESHOOTING:** If, when you run the query, you are prompted for a value, cancel and return to Design view. Ensure that you have entered the formula from Step l in the first row of a blank column, not the criteria line.

n. Save the changes to the query and close the query.

Don and Matt would like the field formatted with two decimal places. You will change the format to Currency and add a caption to the calculated field. Refer to Figure 3.13 as you complete Step 2.

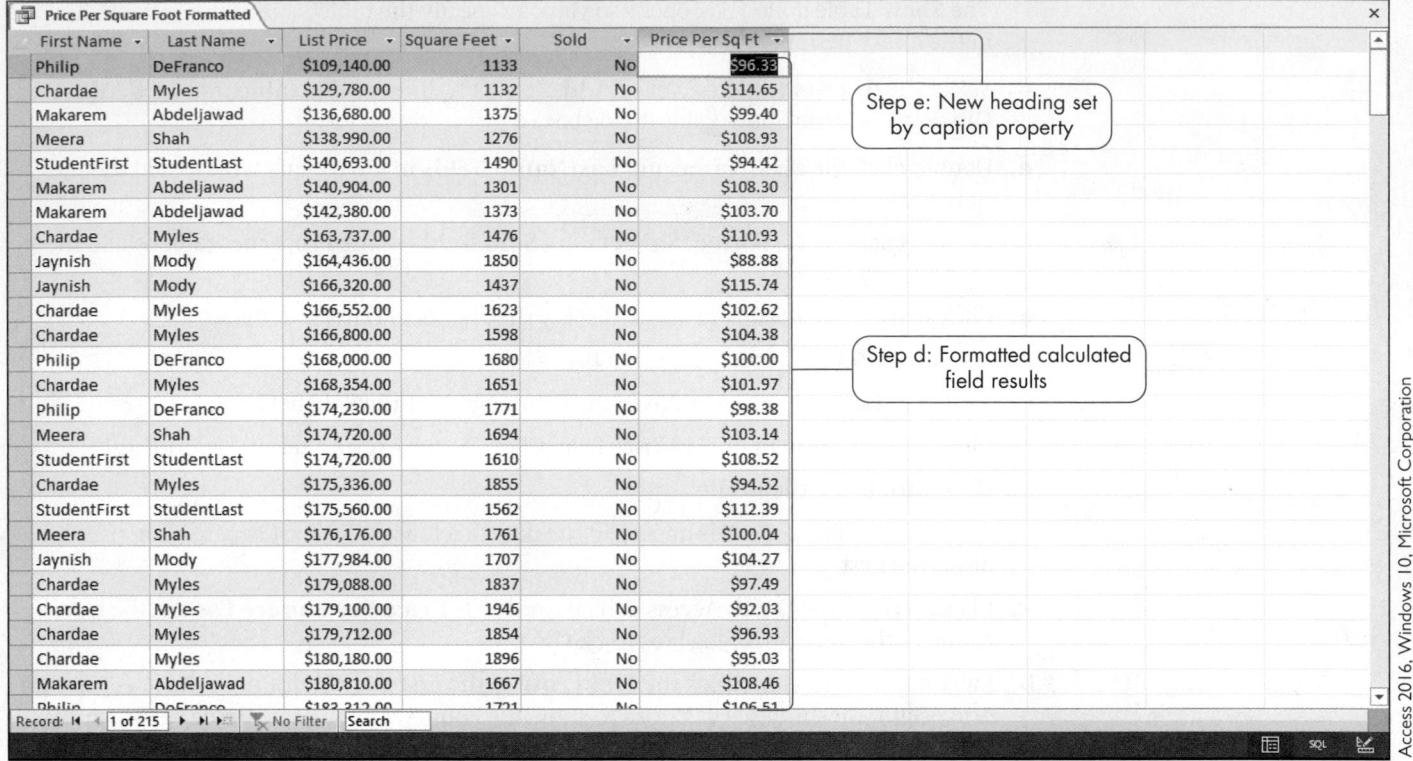

FIGURE 3.13 Modified Expression

a. Right-click the **Price Per Square Foot query** in the Navigation Pane and click **Copy**. Right-click in the Navigation Pane again and click **Paste**. Type **Price Per Square Foot Formatted** in the Paste As dialog box and click **OK**.

b. Open the Price Per Square Foot Formatted query in Design view.

c. Click the **PricePerSqFt calculated field cell**. Click **Property Sheet** in the Show/Hide group on the Design tab.

   The Property Sheet displays.

d. Click the **Format property**. Click the **Format property arrow** and select **Currency**.

e. Click the **Caption property** and type **Price Per Sq Ft**. Press **Enter**. Close the Property Sheet.

f. Click **Run** to view your changes.

   The calculated field values are formatted as Currency, and the column heading displays Price Per Sq Ft instead of PricePerSqFt.

g. Compare your result to Figure 3.13. Save the changes to the query.

A few errors arise as you test the new calculated fields. You check the spelling of the field names in the calculated fields because that is a common mistake. Refer to Figure 3.14 as you complete Step 3.

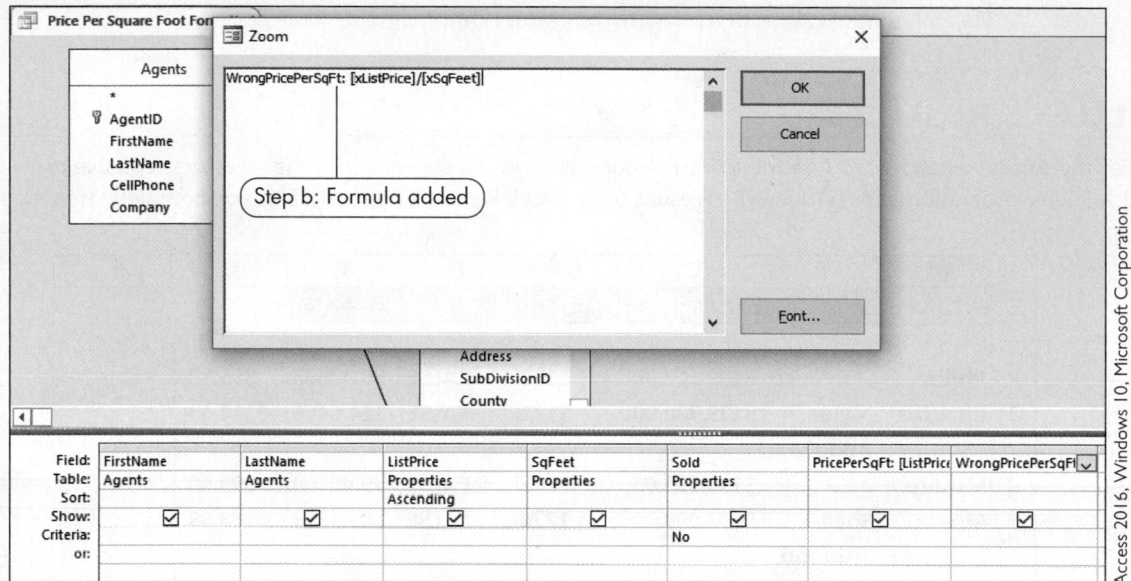

FIGURE 3.14 Incorrect Expression

a. Switch to Design view of the Price Per Square Foot Formatted query. Scroll to the first blank column of the query design grid and click the Field row.

b. Right-click and select **Zoom** to display the Zoom window. Type **WrongPricePerSqFt: xListPrice/xSqFeet**. Your formula should match Figure 3.14. Click OK in the Zoom window.

Be sure that you added the extra *x*'s to the field names. You are intentionally misspelling the field names to see how Access will respond.

c. Click **Property Sheet** in the Show/Hide group of the Design tab. Click the **Format property**. From the menu, select **Currency**. Click the **Caption box** and type **Wrong Price Per Sq Ft**. Close the Property Sheet.

d. Click **Run** in the Results group.

You should see the Enter Parameter Value dialog box. Access does not recognize xListPrice in the tables defined for this query in the first record. When Access does not recognize a field name, it will ask you to supply a value.

e. Type **100000** in the first parameter box. Press **Enter** or click **OK**.

Another Enter Parameter Value dialog box displays, asking that you supply a value for xSqFeet. Again, this error occurs because the tables defined for this query do not contain an xSqFeet field.

f. Type **1000** in the second parameter box and press **Enter**.

The query has the necessary information to run and returns the results in Datasheet view.

g. Examine the results of the calculation for Wrong Price Per Sq Ft.

All of the records show 100 because you entered the values 100000 and 1000, respectively, into the parameter boxes. The two values are treated as constants and give the same results for all records.

h. Return to Design view. Display the Zoom window. Correct the errors in the WrongPricePerSqFt field by changing the formula to **WrongPricePerSqFt: [ListPrice]/[SqFeet]**. Click **OK**.

i. Run and save the query. Close the query.

The calculated values in the last two columns should be the same.

STEP 4 ›› EVALUATE RESULTS

Because you are in charge of the Access database, you decide to verify your data prior to showing it to the investors. You use two methods to check your calculations: estimation and checking your results using Excel. Refer to Figure 3.15 as you complete Step 4.

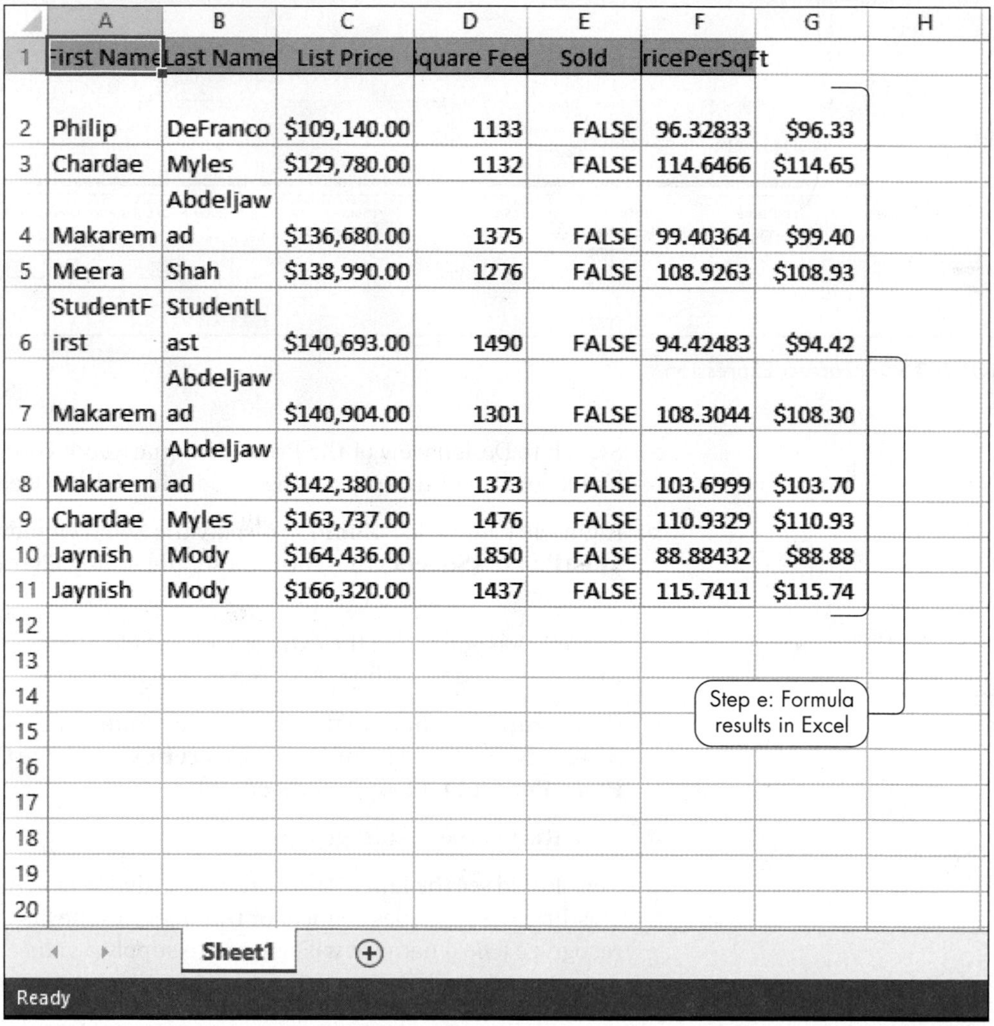

	A	B	C	D	E	F	G	H
1	First Name	Last Name	List Price	Square Fee	Sold	ricePerSqFt		
2	Philip	DeFranco	$109,140.00	1133	FALSE	96.32833	$96.33	
3	Chardae	Myles	$129,780.00	1132	FALSE	114.6466	$114.65	
4	Makarem	Abdeljawad	$136,680.00	1375	FALSE	99.40364	$99.40	
5	Meera	Shah	$138,990.00	1276	FALSE	108.9263	$108.93	
6	StudentFirst	StudentLast	$140,693.00	1490	FALSE	94.42483	$94.42	
7	Makarem	Abdeljawad	$140,904.00	1301	FALSE	108.3044	$108.30	
8	Makarem	Abdeljawad	$142,380.00	1373	FALSE	103.6999	$103.70	
9	Chardae	Myles	$163,737.00	1476	FALSE	110.9329	$110.93	
10	Jaynish	Mody	$164,436.00	1850	FALSE	88.88432	$88.88	
11	Jaynish	Mody	$166,320.00	1437	FALSE	115.7411	$115.74	
12								
13								
14								
15								
16								
17								
18								
19								
20								

Step e: Formula results in Excel

Sheet1   Ready

Access 2016, Windows 10, Microsoft Corporation

FIGURE 3.15 Calculation Copied to Excel

a. Open the Price Per Square Foot query in Datasheet view. Examine the PricePerSqFt field.

One of the ways to verify the accuracy of the calculated data is to ask yourself if the numbers make sense.

b. Locate the 13th record with Philip DeFranco as the listing agent, an asking price of $168,000, and square footage of 1680. The result ($100.00) makes sense, since 168,000/1680 = 100.

TROUBLESHOOTING: If the 13th record is not the one listed above, ensure that you have sorted the query by the List Price in ascending order, as specified in Step 1i.

c. Open a new, blank workbook in Excel and then switch to Access. Select the first 10 records. Click **Copy** in the Clipboard group on the Home tab.

You will verify the calculation in the first 10 records by pasting the results in Excel.

d. Switch to Excel and click the **Paste** button in the Clipboard group on the Home tab.

The field names display in the first row, and the 10 records display in the next 10 rows. The fields are located in columns A–F. The calculated field results are pasted in column F as values rather than as a formula.

> **TROUBLESHOOTING:** If you see pound signs (#####) in an Excel column, double-click the vertical line between column headings to increase the width.

e. Click **cell G2**. Type **=C2/D2** and press **Enter**. Click **cell G2**, and click **Copy** in the Clipboard group. Select the **range G3:G11** and click **Paste** in the Clipboard group. Compare your results to Figure 3.15.

The formula divides the list price by the square feet. Compare the results in columns F and G. The numbers should be the same, except for the number of decimal places.

f. Save the Excel workbook as **a03h1PropertyCheck_LastFirst**. Close the file, and exit Excel. You will submit this file to your instructor at the end of the last Hands-On Exercise.

g. Keep the database open if you plan to continue with the next Hands-On Exercise. If not, close the database and exit Access.

The Expression Builder and Functions

In the last Hands-On Exercise, you calculated the price per square foot for real estate properties to help evaluate properties on the investment list. You were able to type the expression manually.

When you encounter more complex expressions, the ***Expression Builder*** tool can help you create more complicated expressions. The Expression Builder's size enables you to easily see complex formulas and functions in their entirety. In addition, it provides easy access to objects, operators, and functions.

In this section, you will learn how to create expressions with the Expression Builder. You also will learn how to use built-in functions.

Creating Expressions Using the Expression Builder

STEP 1 ▶▶ The Expression Builder helps you create expressions by supplying you with access to fields, operators, and functions. When you use the Expression Builder to help create expressions, you can eliminate spelling errors in field names. Another advantage is that when you insert a function, placeholders tell you which values belong where. Experienced users may have functions memorized, but new users have the Expression Builder to provide support.

Once you open the Expression Builder, the Expression Builder dialog box displays. The top portion is an empty rectangular box known as the expression box. The left column of the Expression Builder dialog box contains Expression Elements (see Figure 3.16), which include the built-in functions, objects from the current database (including tables), and common expressions.

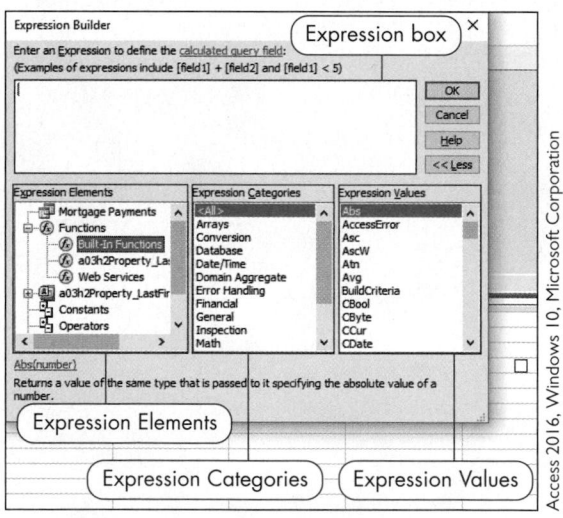

FIGURE 3.16 Expression Builder

The middle column displays the Expression Categories based on the item selected in the Expression Elements box (see Figure 3.16 above). For example, when the Built-In Functions item is selected in the Expression Elements box, the available built-in function categories, such as the Math category, are displayed in the Expression Categories box.

The right column displays the Expression Values, if any, for the categories that you selected in the Expression Categories box (see Figure 3.16 above). For example, if you click Built-In Functions in the Expression Elements box and click Date/Time in the Expression Categories box, the Expression Values box lists all of the built-in functions in the Date/Time category.

You can create an expression by manually typing text in the expression box or by double-clicking the elements from the bottom section in the Expression Builder dialog box.

To create an expression with the Expression Builder, complete the following steps:

1. Open a query in Design view (or create a new query).
2. Click the Field row of a blank column.
3. Click Builder in the Query Setup group of the Design tab to launch the Expression Builder.
4. Type the calculated field name and type a colon if you want to name the column. Although this is not required, as mentioned earlier in this chapter, this will change the title of the column in Datasheet view.
5. Type the name of a field (surrounded in [ ] brackets). Alternately, you can click the source table or query listed in the Expression Elements section and double-click the field you want. Using the second method will insert a field in a format resembling [Properties]![Beds] as shown in Figure 3.17. In this example, the table name Properties appears in brackets, followed by an exclamation point, followed by the field name Beds in brackets. As long as you do not have multiple fields with the same name, you can safely delete the table name and exclamation point (leaving you with [Beds] in this example). If you want to use operators (such as +) you can type those manually.
6. Repeat the previous step for each field you want to add to the calculation, remembering to take the order of operations into account. See Figure 3.17 as an example formula created in the Expression Builder.
7. Click OK to close the Expression Builder window.
8. Click Run in the Results group to view the results in Datasheet view.

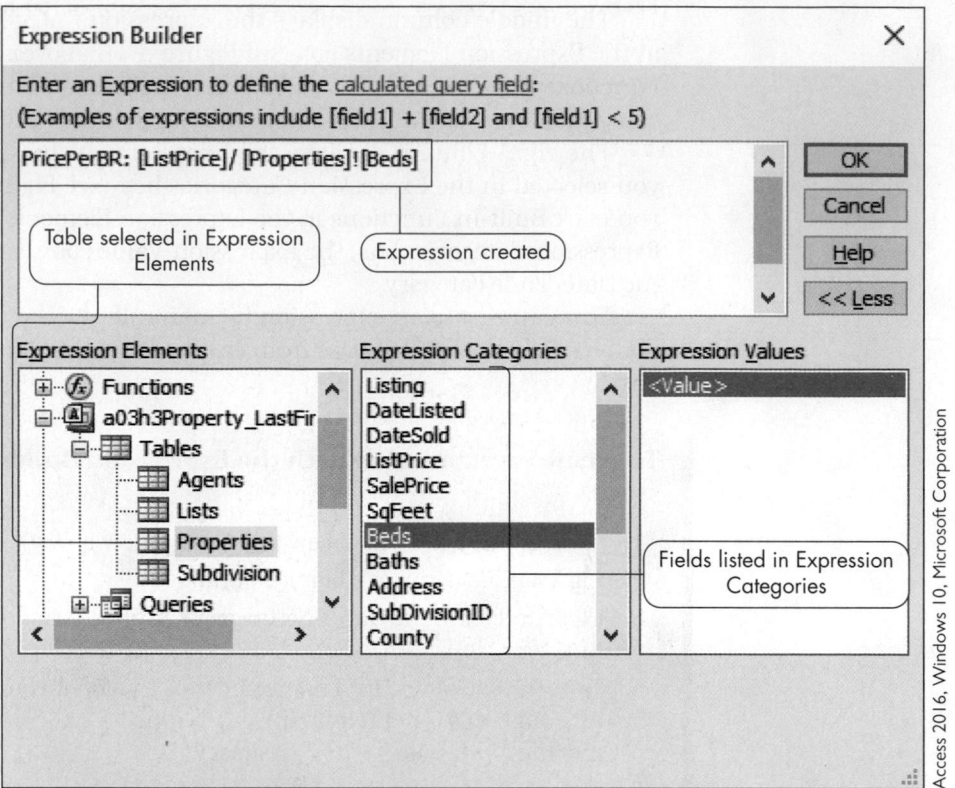

FIGURE 3.17 Expression Created in Expression Builder

Using Built-In Functions

A *function* is a predefined computation that performs a complex calculation. There are around 150 functions built into Access. If you are familiar with Excel, many of these will be familiar to you. Functions produce results based on inputs. Each input (such as a field name or a number) used to produce output for a function is known as an *argument*. Some functions have optional arguments, which are not required but may be necessary for your task.

Many of the tasks that are built-in would otherwise be difficult to perform. Figuring out the payment of a loan or determining the year portion of a date without functions would not be easy.

Once you identify what functionality is required, you can check the Built-In Functions in the Expression Builder to see if the function exists, or use search engines or Access Help. If the function exists, add the function to the expression box and replace «placeholder text» with the argument values. See Figure 3.18 for an example function inserted using the Expression Builder.

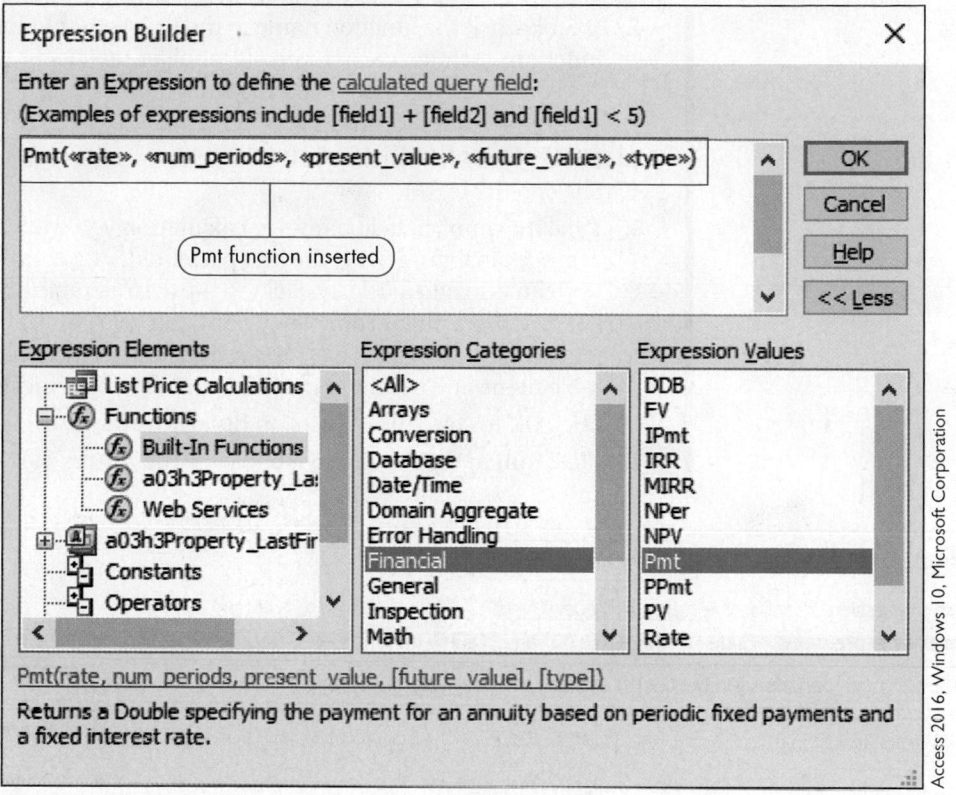

FIGURE 3.18 Function Inserted Using the Expression Builder

Functions work the same in Access, Excel, and programming languages (such as C#, Java, or Python). This chapter will demonstrate one function.

> **To create an expression containing a function with the Expression Builder, complete the following steps:**
>
> 1. Open a query in Design view (or create a new query).
> 2. Click the Field row of a blank column.
> 3. Click Builder in the Query Setup group of the Design tab to launch the Expression Builder.
> 4. Type the calculated field name and type a colon if you want to name the column. Although this is not required, as mentioned earlier in this chapter, this will change the title of the column in Datasheet view.
> 5. Double-click Functions in the Expression Elements section of the window (see Figure 3.19). Click Built-In Functions. The list of available functions will appear in the Expression Categories box.
> 6. Locate and click the function category in the Expression Categories section, as shown in Figure 3.19. If you are unsure of the category, you can use Help or search through the category labeled <All>.

7. Double-click the function name in the Expression Values section to add it. Most functions include one or more placeholder text fields, text surrounded by «» symbols. These provide you guidance as to what data should be entered in each location. Notice an example of placeholder text in Figure 3.19.

8. Click a placeholder text element to select it, unless your function does not have placeholder text.

9. Type the number, field name, or calculation you want to replace the placeholder (for example, in Figure 3.19, the first placeholder text was replaced by .05/12). Note that you can also add a field by clicking the desired table or query listed in the Expression Elements section and double-clicking the field you want. In Figure 3.19, notice that [Properties]![ListPrice] has replaced the third placeholder. As discussed earlier, the table name and exclamation point can often be removed safely.

10. Click OK to close the Expression Builder window.

11. Click Run in the Results group to view the results in Datasheet view.

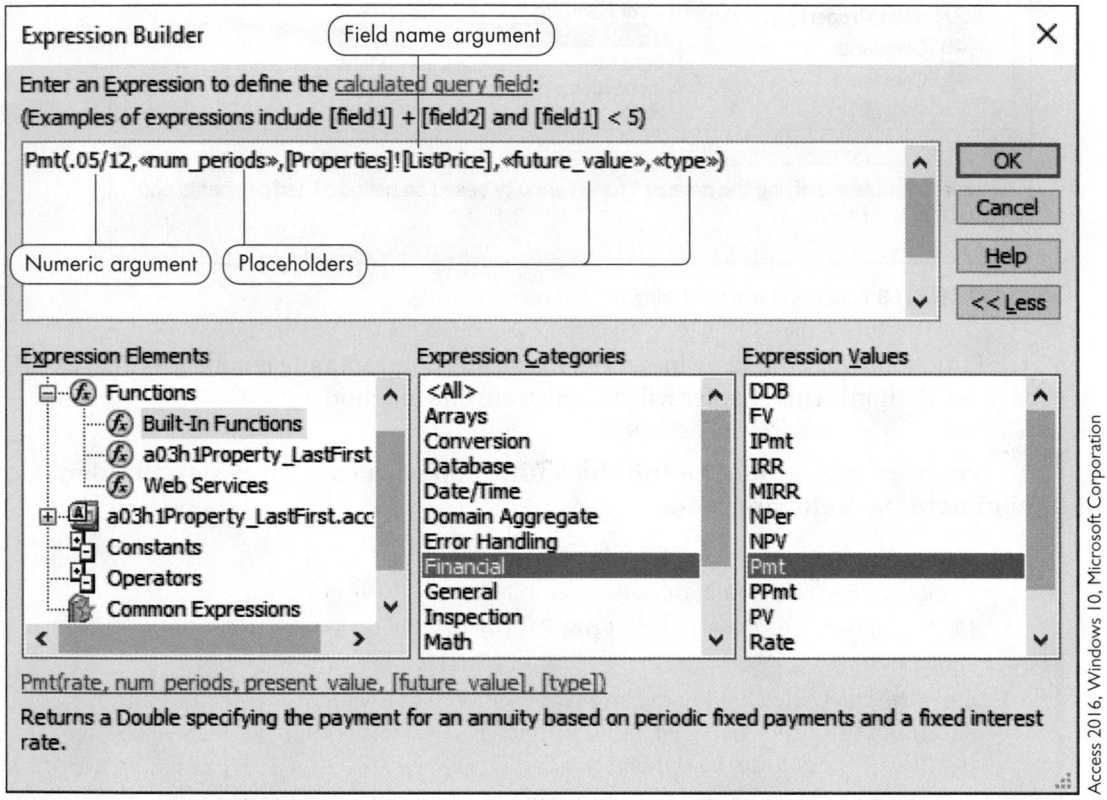

FIGURE 3.19 Expression with Some Arguments Filled In

Calculate a Loan Payment with the Pmt Function

 **STEP 2** ›› The **Pmt function** calculates the loan payment given the rate, number of periods (also known as term), and the present value of the loan (the principal). If necessary, two other arguments (future value and type) can be used, but they are not necessary for many calculations. The Pmt function uses the following syntax:

Pmt(rate, num_periods, present_value, future_value, type)

After inserting the function using the Expression Builder, you will supply at least the rate, num_periods, and present_value arguments. The arguments are as follows:

- **rate:** Interest rates are usually stated as yearly rates, so the rate must be converted to the rate per period. If a loan is paid monthly, divide the yearly rate by 12. Typically this is entered as a decimal followed by the division (for example, .05/12). It is also acceptable to enter this as a percentage (5%/12).

- **num_periods:** Multiply the number of years of the loan by the number of payments per year. The total number of payments for a monthly payment would be calculated as the number of years multiplied by 12.
- **present_value:** The amount of the loan.
- **future_value** and **type:** The last two arguments—future value and type—are both optional, so they are usually left blank or filled in with zero.

The following example shows how to use the Pmt function to calculate the payment for a loan with a 5% interest rate, paid 12 times a year. This loan will be paid for four years and has a present value of $12,500. Figure 3.20 shows how it appears in the Expression Builder.

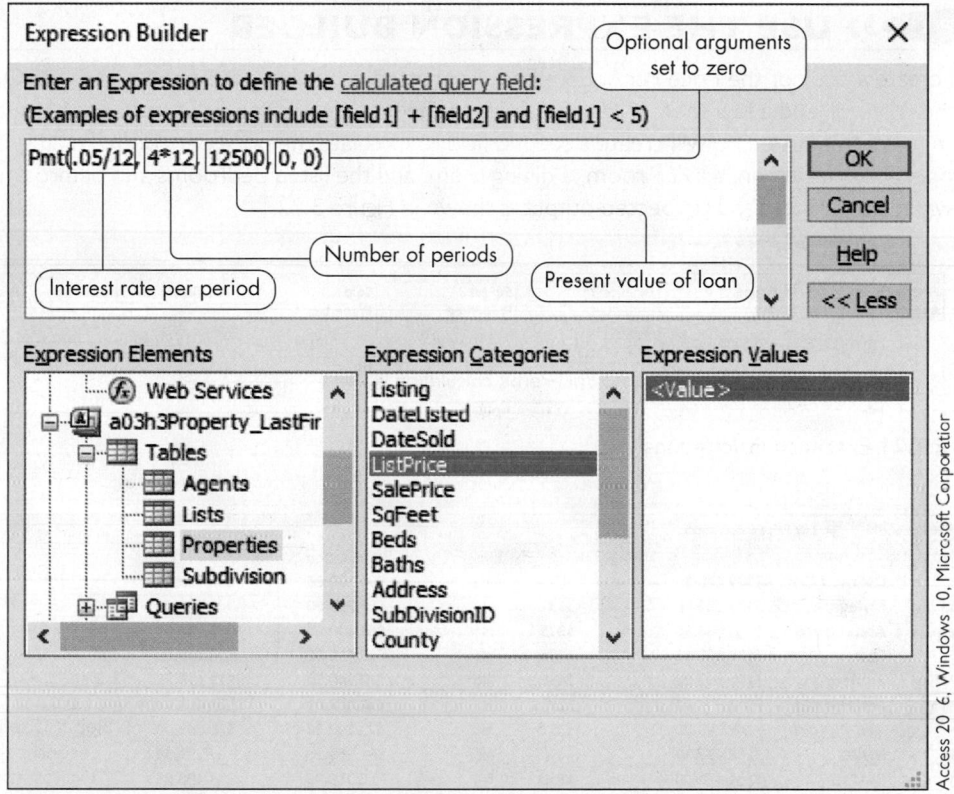

FIGURE 3.20 Pmt Function with Arguments Filled In

The Pmt function will return a negative value, as a loan payment is considered a debit. In this case, it returns −287.87. If you would like to display this as a positive number, place a negative sign in front of the loan amount.

Pmt(.05/12, 4*12, −12500, 0, 0)

By default, the column heading will display Expr1 for any calculated field, as shown in the first Hands-On Exercise. To change this, you can replace Expr1 with the desired column heading, followed by a colon (:), to the left of the calculation.

MonthlyPmt: Pmt(.05/12, 4*12, −12500, 0, 0)

Quick Concepts

5. List two benefits of using the Expression Builder to create expressions. **p. 826**

6. What is an example argument in the Pmt function? What does this argument do? **p. 830**

7. Given the following function: Pmt(.05/12, 5*12, 50000, 0, 0), how many years is the loan for and how much is the initial amount of the loan? **p. 831**

Hands-On Exercises

Skills covered: Use the Expression Builder • Calculate a Loan Payment with the Pmt Function

2 The Expression Builder and Functions

When Don and Matt ask you to calculate the price per bedroom and the price per room for each property, you use the Expression Builder to make the task easier. You also create an additional calculated field showing the estimated mortgage for each property.

STEP I ›› USE THE EXPRESSION BUILDER

You will create a copy of the Price Per Square Foot Formatted query from the previous Hands-On Exercise and paste it using a new name. You will add a few more calculated fields to the new query. You will create one calculation to determine the price per bedroom for each house. You will create a second field to calculate the price per room. For this calculation, you will assume that each property has a kitchen, a living room, a dining room, and the listed bedrooms and bathrooms. The calculations you will create are shown in Figure 3.21. Your expected output is shown in Figure 3.22.

Field:	FirstName	LastName	ListPrice	SqFeet	Sold		PricePerBR: [ListPrice]/[Beds]	PricePerRoom: [ListPrice]/[[Beds]+[Baths]+3]	
Table:	Agents	Agents	Properties	Properties	Properties				
Sort:			Ascending						
Show:	☑	☑	☑	☑	☑		☑	☑	
Criteria:					No				
or:									

Step i: PricePerBR calculation

Step s: PricePerRoom calculation

FIGURE 3.21 Expanded Calculations

First Name	Last Name	List Price	Square Feet	Sold	Price Per Bedroom	Price Per Room
Philip	DeFranco	$109,140.00	1133	No	$54,570.00	$18,190.00
Chardae	Myles	$129,780.00	1132	No	$64,890.00	$21,630.00
Makarem	Abdeljawad	$136,680.00	1375	No	$68,340.00	$22,780.00
Meera	Shah	$138,990.00	1276	No	$69,495.00	$23,165.00
StudentFirst	StudentLast	$140,693.00	1490	No	$70,346.50	$23,448.83
Makarem	Abdeljawad	$140,904.00	1301	No	$70,452.00	$23,484.00
Makarem	Abdeljawad	$142,380.00	1373	No	$71,190.00	$20,340.00
Chardae	Myles	$163,737.00	1476	No	$81,868.50	$27,289.50
Jaynish	Mody	$164,436.00	1850	No	$82,218.00	$23,490.86
Jaynish	Mody	$166,320.00	1437	No	$83,160.00	$27,720.00
Chardae	Myles	$166,552.00	1623	No	$83,276.00	$23,793.14
Chardae	Myles	$166,800.00	1598	No	$83,400.00	$27,800.00
Philip	DeFranco	$168,000.00	1680	No	$84,000.00	$25,846.15
Chardae	Myles	$168,354.00	1651	No	$84,177.00	$28,059.00
Philip	DeFranco	$174,230.00	1771	No	$87,115.00	$29,038.33
Meera	Shah	$174,720.00	1694	No	$87,360.00	$29,120.00
StudentFirst	StudentLast	$174,720.00	1610	No	$87,360.00	$26,880.00
Chardae	Myles	$175,336.00	1855	No	$87,668.00	$29,222.67
StudentFirst	StudentLast	$175,560.00	1562	No	$87,780.00	$29,260.00
Meera	Shah	$176,176.00	1761	No	$88,088.00	$25,168.00
Jaynish	Mody	$177,984.00	1707	No	$88,992.00	$27,382.15
Chardae	Myles	$179,088.00	1837	No	$89,544.00	$29,848.00
Chardae	Myles	$179,100.00	1946	No	$89,550.00	$25,585.71
Chardae	Myles	$179,712.00	1854	No	$89,856.00	$27,648.00
Chardae	Myles	$180,180.00	1896	No	$90,090.00	$30,030.00
Makarem	Abdeljawad	$180,810.00	1667	No	$90,405.00	$30,135.00
Philip	DeFranco	$182,312.00	1721	No	$91,656.00	$30,552.00

Tabs: Mortgage Payments | List Price Calculations

Step k: Caption set for first calculation

Step t: Caption set for second calculation

Record: 2 of 215 — No Filter — Search

FIGURE 3.22 Payment Calculation

a. Open *a03h1Property_LastFirst* if you closed it at the end of Hands-On Exercise 1, and save it as **a03h2Property_LastFirst**, changing h1 to h2.

b. Create a copy of the Price Per Square Foot Formatted query with the name **List Price Calculations**.

c. Open the List Price Calculations query in Design view. Click the **WrongPricePerSqFt field**. Click **Delete Columns** in the Query Setup group on the Design tab.

d. Click the **Field row** in the PricePerSqFt column and click **Builder** in the Query Setup group.

The Expression Builder dialog box opens, displaying the current formula.

e. Double-click the **PricePerSqFt field name** and type **PricePerBR**.

f. Double-click the **[SqFeet] field** in the expression and press **Delete**.

g. Click the **plus sign** ⊞ next to the a03h2Property_LastFirst database in the Expression Elements box to expand the list. Click the **plus sign** next to Tables and select the **Properties table**.

The fields from the Properties table are now listed in the middle column (Expression Categories).

h. Double-click the **Beds field** to add it to the expression box.

The expression now reads PricePerBR: [ListPrice]/[Properties]![Beds].

i. Highlight the **[Properties]! prefix** in front of *Beds* and press **Delete**.

The expression now reads PricePerBR: [ListPrice]/[Beds]. As the Beds field name is unique within our query, the table name is not necessary. Removing this makes the query easier to read. If a field named Beds appeared in more than one table in our query, removing the table name would cause problems.

j. Click **OK** and click **Run** to view the query results.

Notice that the column heading still reads Price Per Sq Ft. Also notice that the column's contents are formatted as Currency. These settings were copied when the query was copied.

k. Switch to Design view and ensure that the PricePerBR field is selected. Click **Property Sheet** in the Show/Hide group and change the **Caption** to **Price Per Bedroom**. Close the Property Sheet. Run the query and examine the changes.

The PricePerBR column now has an appropriate caption.

l. Switch to Design view. Select the entire **PricePerBR expression**, right-click the selected expression, and then select **Copy**. Right-click the **Field row** of the next blank column and select **Paste**.

You will edit the copied expression so that it reflects the price per room, assuming that the kitchen, living room, dining room, and the bedrooms and bathrooms will make up the number of rooms.

m. Click **Builder** in the Query Setup group.

n. Change the PricePerBR field name to **PricePerRoom**.

o. Add **an opening parenthesis** before the [Beds] portion of the formula. Type a **plus sign** after [Beds].

As you want the addition to be done first, enclose the addition in parentheses. The expression box should read PricePerRoom: [ListPrice]/([Beds]+

p. Click the **plus sign** next to the a03h2Property_LastFirst database in the Expression Elements box to expand the list. Click the **plus sign** next to Tables and select the **Properties table**.

The fields from the Properties table are now listed in the Expression Categories box.

q. Double-click the **Baths field** to add it to the expression box.

r. Type another plus sign after [Baths] and type **3** followed by a right parenthesis. In other words, you will type **+3)** in the expression box.

s. Delete the [Properties]! portion of the expression and click **OK** to close the Expression Builder.

The expression now reads PricePerRoom: [ListPrice]/([Beds]+[Baths]+3). Your final formula is the list price divided by the total number of rooms. The total number of rooms is the number of bedrooms (in the Beds field), plus the number of bathrooms (found in the Baths field), plus 3 (a constant representing the kitchen, living room, and dining room).

t. Click **Property Sheet** in the Show/Hide group. Type **Price Per Room** in the Caption box. Click the Format box, click the drop-down menu, and select **Currency**. Close the Property Sheet.

Compare your formulas to Figure 3.21. This figure has expanded the column widths for readability.

u. Run the query. Adjust column widths as necessary. Compare your results to Figure 3.22.

v. Save and close the query.

Don and Matt feel like they are close to making an offer on a house. They would like to restrict the query to houses that cost $190,000 or less. They would also like to calculate the estimated mortgage payment for each house. You create this calculation using the Pmt function. You make the following assumptions: 80% of the sale price to be financed, a 30-year term, monthly payments, and a fixed 4.0% annual interest rate. Refer to Figures 3.23 and 3.24 as you complete Step 2.

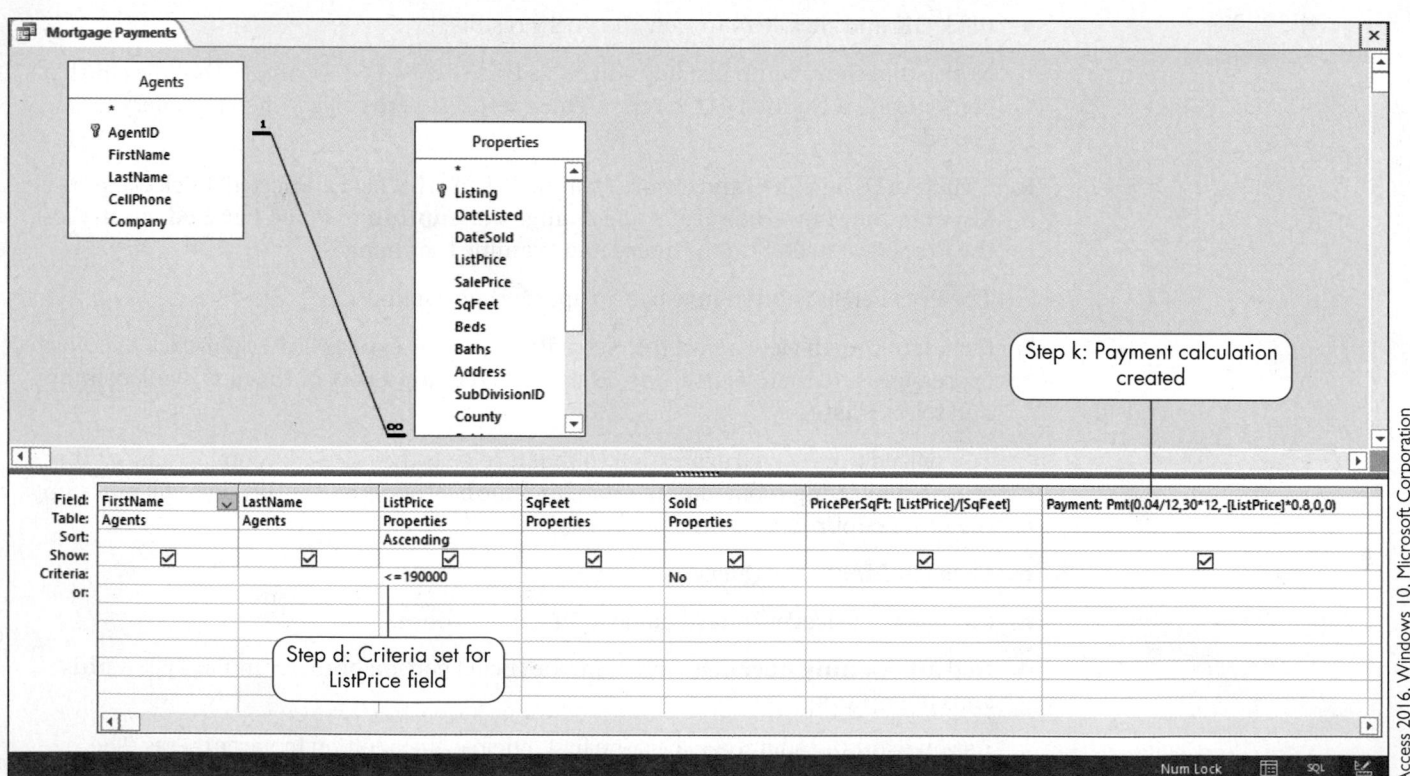

FIGURE 3.23 Mortgage Payments Design View

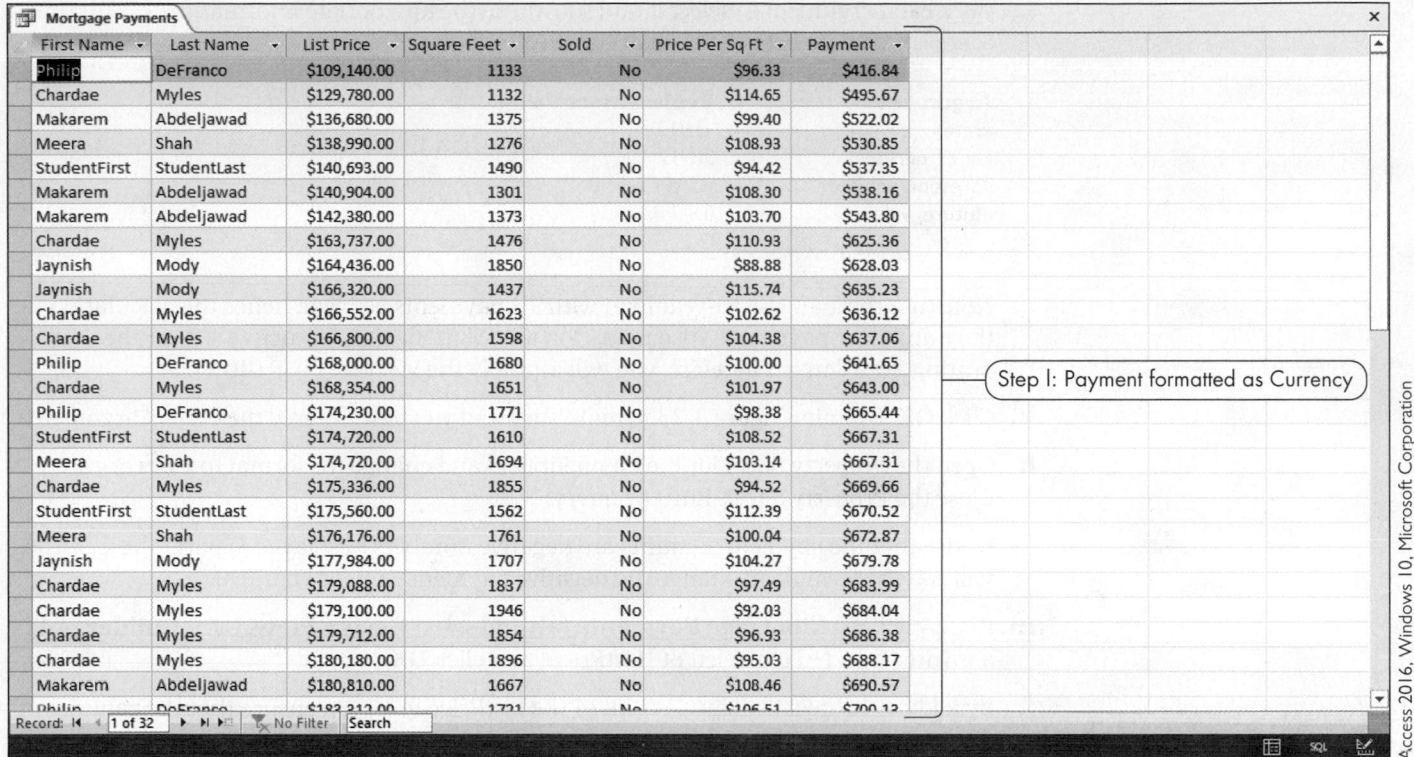

First Name	Last Name	List Price	Square Feet	Sold	Price Per Sq Ft	Payment
Philip	DeFranco	$109,140.00	1133	No	$96.33	$416.84
Chardae	Myles	$129,780.00	1132	No	$114.65	$495.67
Makarem	Abdeljawad	$136,680.00	1375	No	$99.40	$522.02
Meera	Shah	$138,990.00	1276	No	$108.93	$530.85
StudentFirst	StudentLast	$140,693.00	1490	No	$94.42	$537.35
Makarem	Abdeljawad	$140,904.00	1301	No	$108.30	$538.16
Makarem	Abdeljawad	$142,380.00	1373	No	$103.70	$543.80
Chardae	Myles	$163,737.00	1476	No	$110.93	$625.36
Jaynish	Mody	$164,436.00	1850	No	$88.88	$628.03
Jaynish	Mody	$166,320.00	1437	No	$115.74	$635.23
Chardae	Myles	$166,552.00	1623	No	$102.62	$636.12
Chardae	Myles	$166,800.00	1598	No	$104.38	$637.06
Philip	DeFranco	$168,000.00	1680	No	$100.00	$641.65
Chardae	Myles	$168,354.00	1651	No	$101.97	$643.00
Philip	DeFranco	$174,230.00	1771	No	$98.38	$665.44
StudentFirst	StudentLast	$174,720.00	1610	No	$108.52	$667.31
Meera	Shah	$174,720.00	1694	No	$103.14	$667.31
Chardae	Myles	$175,336.00	1855	No	$94.52	$669.66
StudentFirst	StudentLast	$175,560.00	1562	No	$112.39	$670.52
Meera	Shah	$176,176.00	1761	No	$100.04	$672.87
Jaynish	Mody	$177,984.00	1707	No	$104.27	$679.78
Chardae	Myles	$179,088.00	1837	No	$97.49	$683.99
Chardae	Myles	$179,100.00	1946	No	$92.03	$684.04
Chardae	Myles	$179,712.00	1854	No	$96.93	$686.38
Chardae	Myles	$180,180.00	1896	No	$95.03	$688.17
Makarem	Abdeljawad	$180,810.00	1667	No	$108.46	$690.57
Philip	DeFranco	$183,212.00	1721	No	$106.51	$700.13

Record: 1 of 32 — No Filter — Search

Step I: Payment formatted as Currency

FIGURE 3.24 Mortgage Payments Results

a. Create a copy of the Price Per Square Foot Formatted query named **Mortgage Payments**.

b. Right-click **Mortgage Payments** and select **Design View**.

c. Delete the WrongPricePerSqFt field.

> **TROUBLESHOOTING:** If you do not see the WrongPricePerSqFt field, ensure that you copied the correct query.

d. Type **<=190000** in the Criteria row of the ListPrice column. Press **Enter**.

The query, when it is run, will show only the houses that cost $190,000 or less.

e. Click the **Field row** of the first blank column. Click **Builder** in the Query Setup group to open the Expression Builder dialog box.

f. Double-click **Functions** in the Expression Elements box and select **Built-In Functions**.

g. Select **Financial** in the Expression Categories box.

h. Double-click **Pmt** in the Expression Values box.

The expression box displays:

Pmt(«rate», «num_periods», «present_value», «future_value», «type»)

i. Position the insertion point before the Pmt function. Type **Payment:** to the left of the Pmt function, with a space after the colon. The expression box now displays:

Payment: Pmt(«rate», «num_periods», «present_value», «future_value», «type»)

j. Click each argument to select it and substitute the appropriate information. Make sure there is a comma between each argument.

Argument	Replacement Value
«rate»	.04/12
«num_periods»	30*12
«present_value»	[ListPrice]*.8
«future_value»	0
«type»	0

Note that the loan is a 30-year loan with 12 payments per year, hence the calculation for the number of payments. Also note, Don and Matt plan on financing 80% of the cost, putting 20% down. Therefore, you will multiply the list price by .8 (80%).

k. Click **OK**. Examine Figure 3.23 to make sure that you have entered the correct arguments.

l. Open the Property Sheet for the Payment field and change the format to **Currency**. Close the Property Sheet. Run the query.

Notice that the payment amounts are negative numbers (displayed in parentheses). You will edit the formula to change the negative payment values to positive.

m. Right-click the **Mortgage Payments tab** and select **Design View**. Click **Builder**. Add a **minus sign (−)** to the left of [ListPrice] and click **OK**.

By adding the negative sign in front of the ListPrice field, you ensure that the value is displayed as a positive number. The expression now reads:

Payment: Pmt(.04/12,30*12, −[ListPrice]*.8,0,0)

n. Run the query and examine the results. Adjust column widths as necessary.

The query displays a column containing the calculated monthly mortgage payment, formatted as currency, as shown in Figure 3.24.

o. Save and close the query. Keep the database open if you plan to continue with the next Hands-On Exercise. If not, close the database and exit Access.

Aggregate Functions

An *aggregate function* performs a calculation on an entire column of data and returns a single value. One example of an aggregate function is Sum.

Access refers to aggregate functions as Totals. Totals can be added to Datasheet view of a query, or they can be added to a query's Design view. Based on the data type, different aggregate functions will be available. Numeric fields are eligible for all of the functions, whereas Short Text fields are not. A list of common aggregate functions is shown in Table 3.2.

In the Property database, the average home price per county could be presented in a query or a report. This would give prospective buyers a good idea of home prices in their target counties. Almost every company or organization that uses a database will require some type of aggregate data.

TABLE 3.2 Common Aggregate Functions

Function	Description
Avg (Average)	Calculates the average value for a column.
Count	Counts the number of values in a column.
Max (Maximum)	Returns the item with the highest value.
Min (Minimum)	Returns the item with the lowest value.
Sum	Totals the items in a column.

Pearson Education, Inc.

In this section, you will learn how to create and work with aggregate functions. Specifically, you will learn how to use the Total row and create a totals query.

Adding Aggregate Functions to Datasheets

STEP 1 ⟫ Aggregate data helps users evaluate the values in a single record to the aggregate of all the records. If you are considering buying a property in Story County, Iowa, for $150,000, and the average price of a property in that county is $450,000, you know you are getting a good deal (or buying a bad property).

Access provides two methods of adding aggregate functions—a *Total row*, which displays the results of the aggregate function as the last row in Datasheet view of a table or query, and a totals query created in Query Design view. The totals query will be defined shortly.

The Total row method is quick and easy and has the advantage of showing the totals while still showing the individual records. Adding a Total row to a query or table can be accomplished by most users, even those who are not familiar with designing a query. Figure 3.25 shows the Total row added to Datasheet view of a query. In this image, the average of the List Price is displayed. The available aggregate functions are shown in the Price Per Sq Ft column. You can choose any of the aggregate functions that apply to numeric fields.

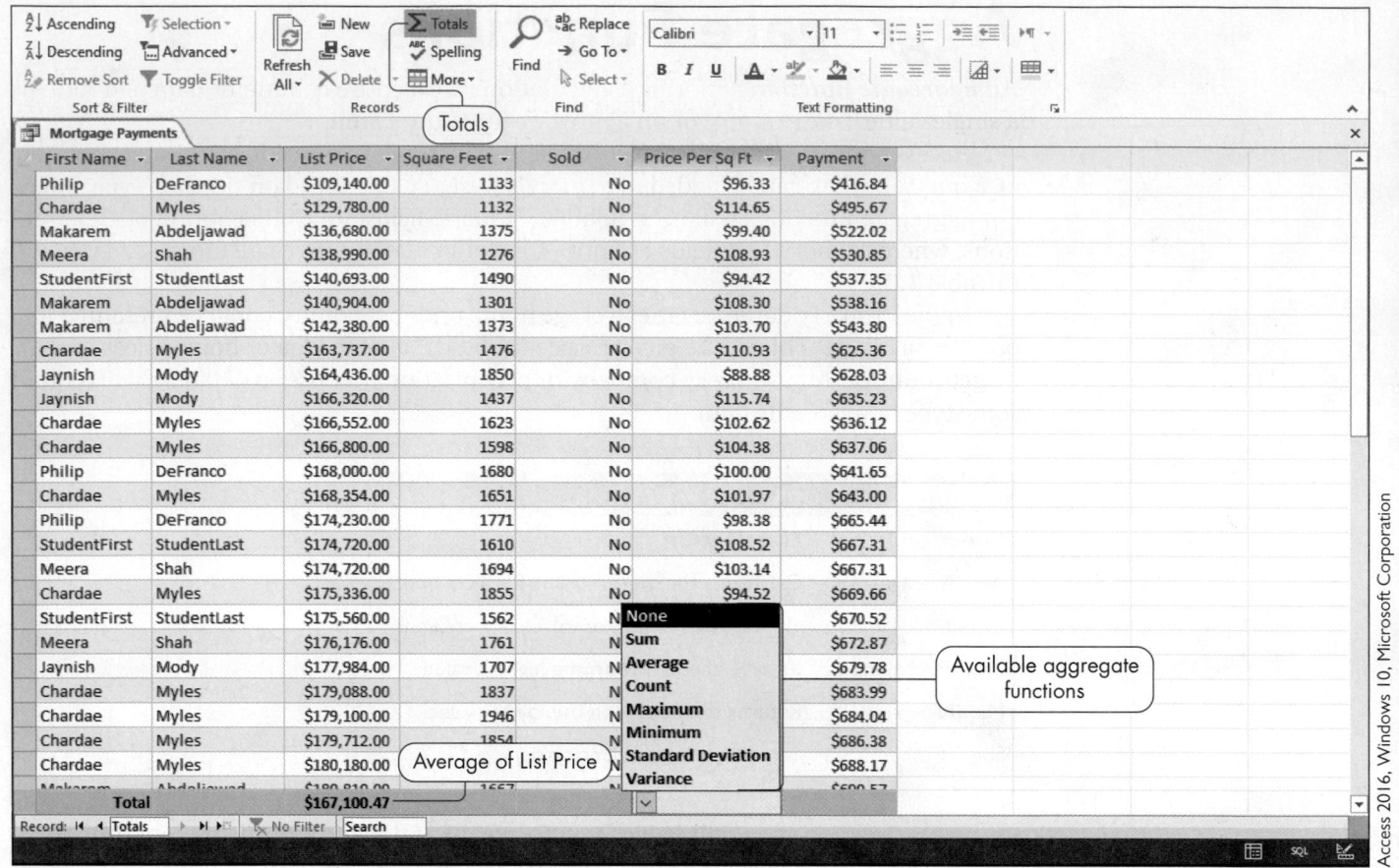

FIGURE 3.25 Total Row in Datasheet View

> **To add a Total row to the Datasheet view of a query or table, complete the following steps:**
>
> 1. View the query or table in Datasheet view.
> 2. Click Totals in the Records group on the Home tab. The Total row is added at the bottom of the datasheet, below the new record row.
> 3. Select one of the aggregate functions (such as Average, Count, or Sum) in the new Total row by clicking in the cell and clicking the arrow.

Creating Queries with Aggregate Functions

The total row, though useful, is limited. Many times, you may require in-depth statistics. Instead of wanting to see the average sale price for houses, you may want to see the average sale price by city. Instead of seeing the average price for every item your store sells, you may want to see the average price for each category. Using the total row in the previous example, this is not feasible. Another limitation of using the total row is that you might want to see the average sale price, minimum sale price, and maximum sale price. Using the previous method, this is difficult to do.

Another way to display aggregate functions requires changes to the query design. A **totals query** contains an additional row in the query design grid and is used to display aggregate data when the query is run. This provides two distinct advantages over the total row. The first allows you to show only the results of the aggregate functions (and not the detail), and the second enables you to see statistics by category.

Create a Totals Query

STEP 2 >> Instead of showing detail, the overall statistics for the entire table or query may be displayed using a totals query. For example, if you want to see the number of listings, average value, and the average size in square feet for all properties in your table, you can use a totals query to get that data and not see details. Instead of having hundreds of rows of data with a summary row at the bottom (which could be missed), a totals query can display only the aggregate function results. Figure 3.26 shows a totals query in Design view, and Figure 3.27 shows the results.

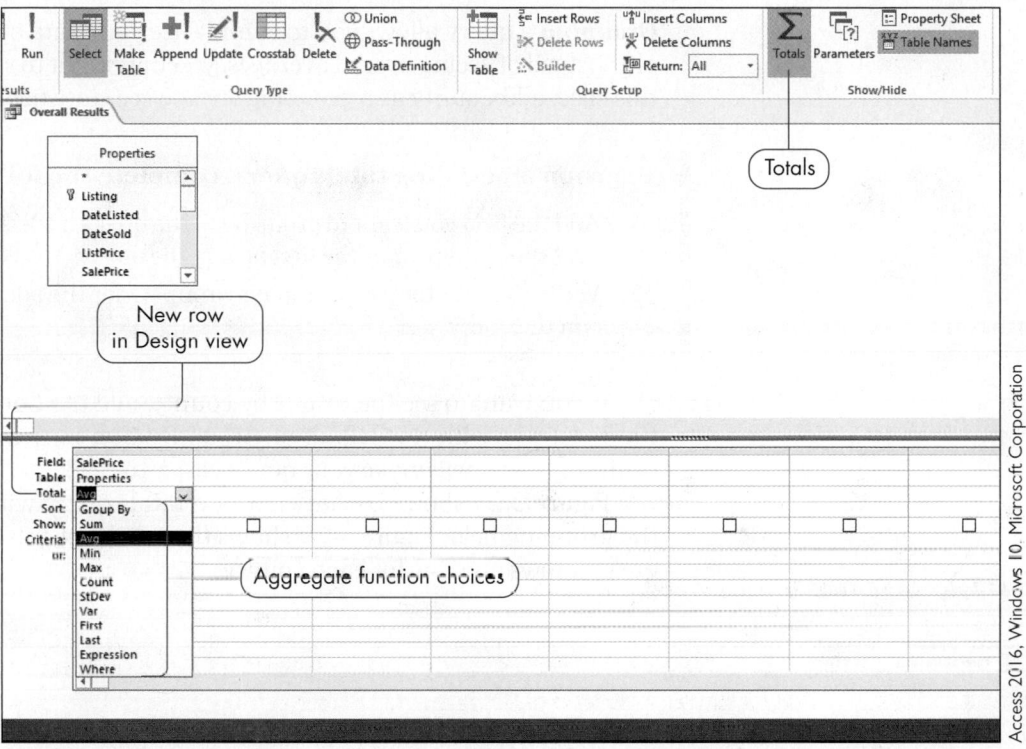

FIGURE 3.26 Totals Query Design View

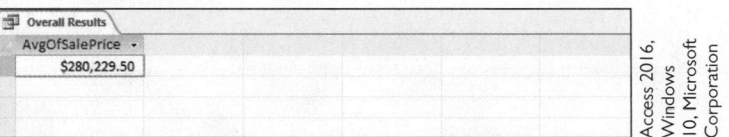

FIGURE 3.27 Totals Query Results

To create a totals query, complete the following steps:

1. Create a query in Design view and add the fields for which you want to get statistics.
2. Click Totals in the Show/Hide group on the Design tab. A new Total row displays in the query design grid between the Table and Sort rows. Notice that it defaults to Group By.
3. Click Group By and select the aggregate function you want applied for each field.
4. Display the Property Sheet (as done earlier in this chapter) and adjust settings to meet your requirements.
5. Click Run in the Results group to see the results.

Add Grouping to a Totals Query

Grouping a query allows you to summarize your data by the values of a field. For example, instead of seeing overall averages, you may want to see the results for each county. In this case, add County as a grouping level to see statistics by County.

To group an existing totals query, complete the following steps:

1. Add the field you want to group by to the query in Design view. For readability, the field should appear as the first field in the query.
2. Verify that the Total row displays Group By for the added field (see Figure 3.28), and run the query.

If you want to see the results by county, add the County field to the query and leave the Total row with the default of Group By. You may want to move this column to the beginning, as it will make your query easier to read.

Figure 3.28 shows Design view of a totals query with five columns, one of which is the grouping field. Figure 3.29 shows the results of this query. Notice that the resulting query shows one row for each county.

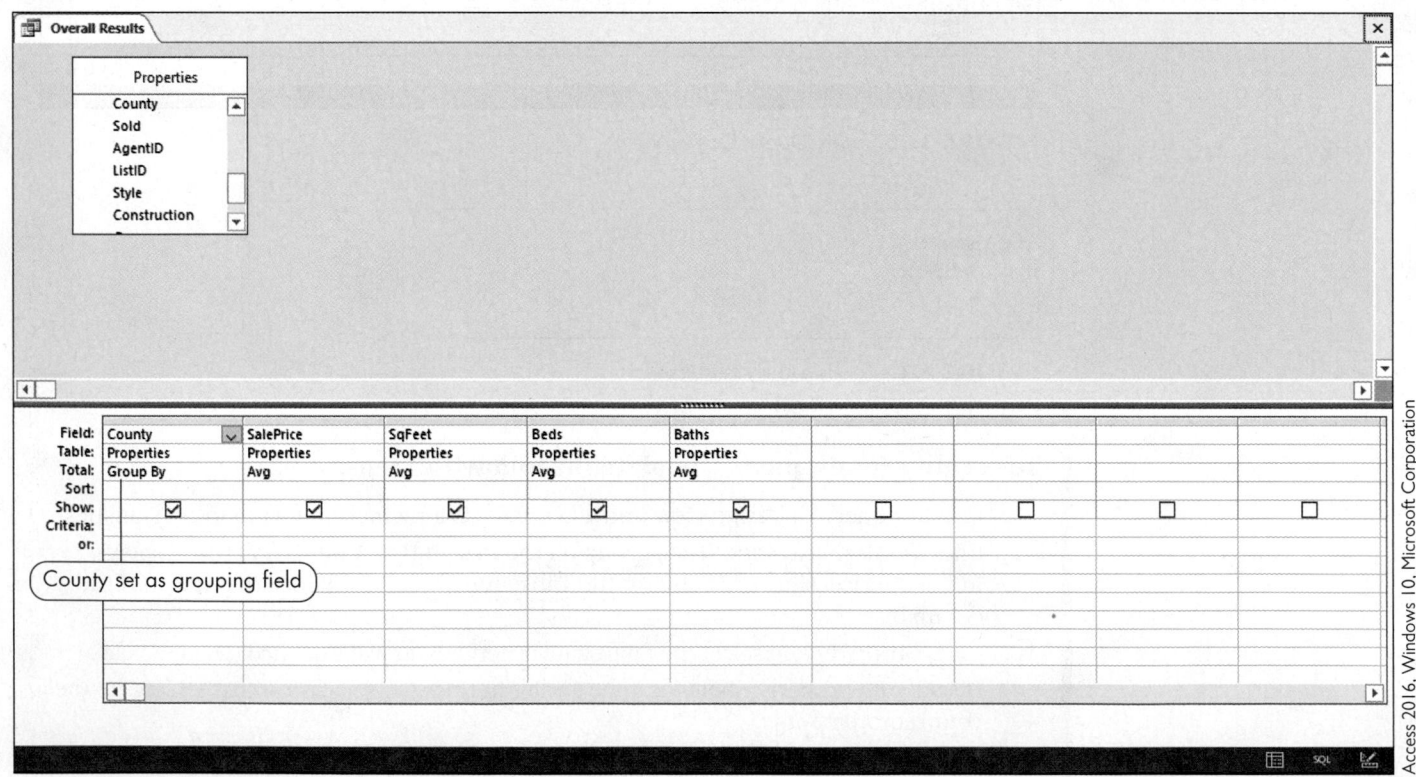

FIGURE 3.28 Grouped Totals Query Design View

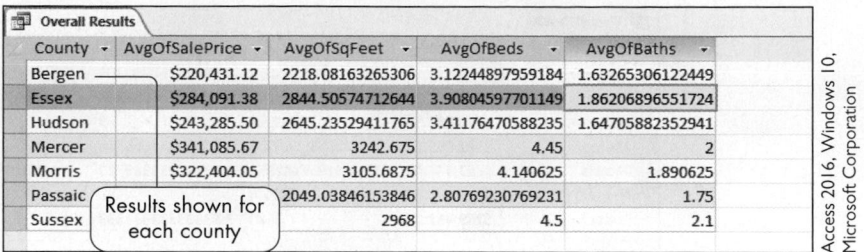

County ▾	AvgOfSalePrice ▾	AvgOfSqFeet ▾	AvgOfBeds ▾	AvgOfBaths ▾
Bergen	$220,431.12	2218.08163265306	3.12244897959184	1.63265306122449
Essex	$284,091.38	2844.50574712644	3.90804597701149	1.86206896551724
Hudson	$243,285.50	2645.23529411765	3.41176470588235	1.64705882352941
Mercer	$341,085.67	3242.675	4.45	2
Morris	$322,404.05	3105.6875	4.140625	1.890625
Passaic		2049.03846153846	2.80769230769231	1.75
Sussex		2968	4.5	2.1

Results shown for each county

FIGURE 3.29 Grouped Totals Query Results

Add Conditions to a Totals Query

Totals queries can provide even better information if you add criteria. For example, if you wanted to see the number of houses, average price, and average square feet for only the sold properties, grouped by county, you can add the Sold field to the query. Set the criteria to Yes to indicate that the Sold field is yes.

> **To add conditions to an existing totals query, complete the following steps:**
>
> 1. Double-click the field you want to limit by to add it to the design grid. The location of this field is not important, as it will not be displayed.
> 2. Select Where from the menu in the Total row.
> 3. Enter the condition.
> 4. Run the query.

Figure 3.30 shows a query with a condition added, and Figure 3.31 shows the results. Compare this to Figure 3.29 to see the change in results.

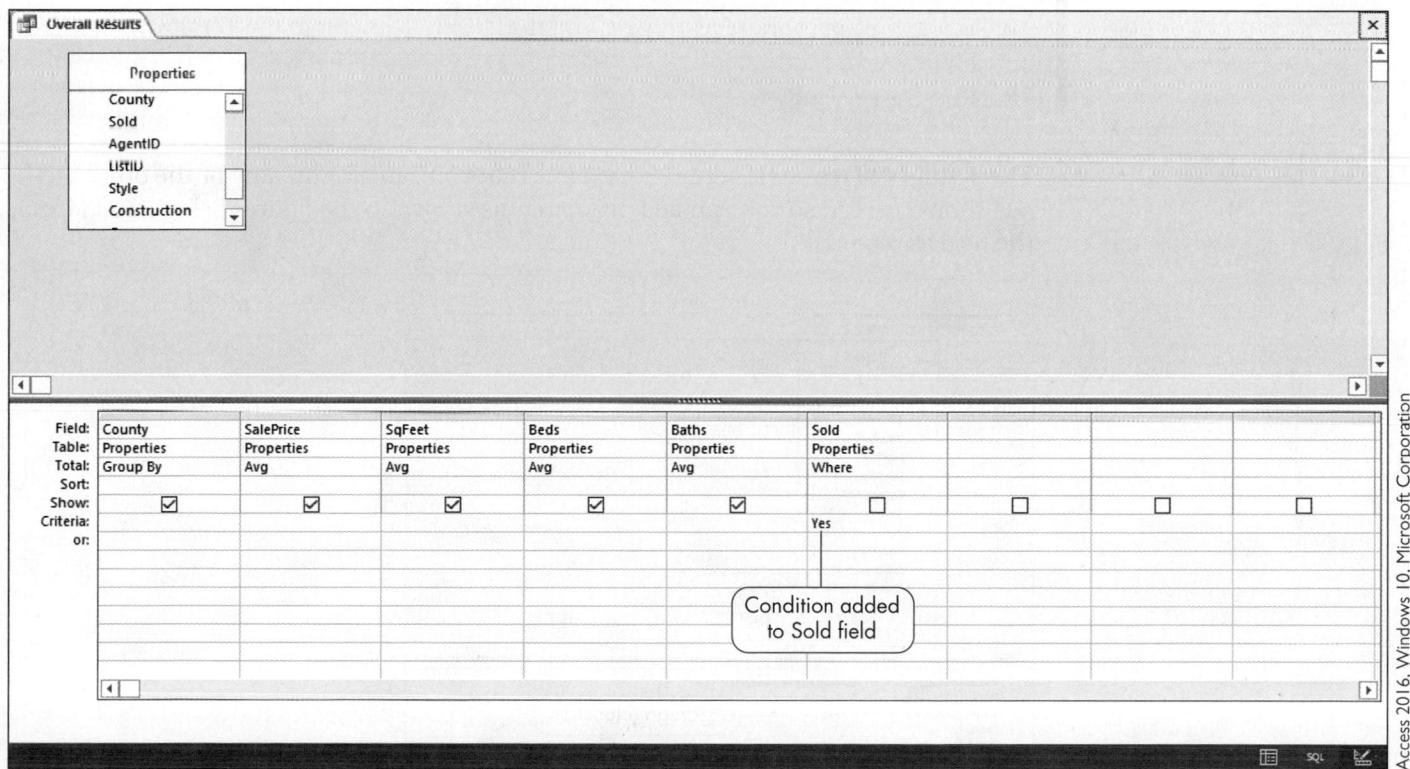

Condition added to Sold field

FIGURE 3.30 Totals Query with Condition Design View

Overall Results				
County	AvgOfSalePrice	AvgOfSqFeet	AvgOfBeds	AvgOfBaths
Bergen	$220,431.12	2223.11764705882	3.29411764705882	1.73529411764706
Essex	$284,091.38	2829.53846153846	3.96153846153846	1.94230769230769
Hudson	$243,285.50	2432.25	3	1.75
Mercer	$341,085.67	3440.55555555556	4.55555555555556	2
Morris	$322,404.05	3233.42857142857	4.33333333333333	1.9047619047619
Passaic	$219,325.20	2171.4	2.8	1.8
Sussex	$269,411.17	2610	3.83333333333333	2

Access 2016, Windows 10, Microsoft Corporation

FIGURE 3.31 Totals Query with Condition Results

> **TIP: MULTIPLE GROUPING LEVELS**
>
> At times, you may want to add multiple grouping fields. For example, instead of grouping by state, you might want to group by city. However, if you group by city, customers with the same city name in different states would be grouped together. For example, all 50 states have a location named Greenville. If you grouped by city, all customers with a city of Greenville, regardless of state, would appear as a group. This is probably not your intention. Instead, you probably would want to see results by city and state, and thus would want to add both fields to a query and select Group By.

Add a Calculated Field to a Totals Query

STEP 3 ➤➤ Calculated fields can also have aggregate functions applied to them. For example, you may want to calculate mortgage payments, and see the average of your calculation.

> **To apply an aggregate function to a totals query, complete the following steps:**
>
> 1. Create the calculation you want to summarize, using any of the methods discussed earlier this chapter.
> 2. Select the appropriate aggregate function from the menu in the Total row (see Figure 3.32).
> 3. Run the query.

The results will resemble Figure 3.33. Note that you can also use any of the other methods shown earlier, so you can add grouping (as shown in the figures below) and format the field as required.

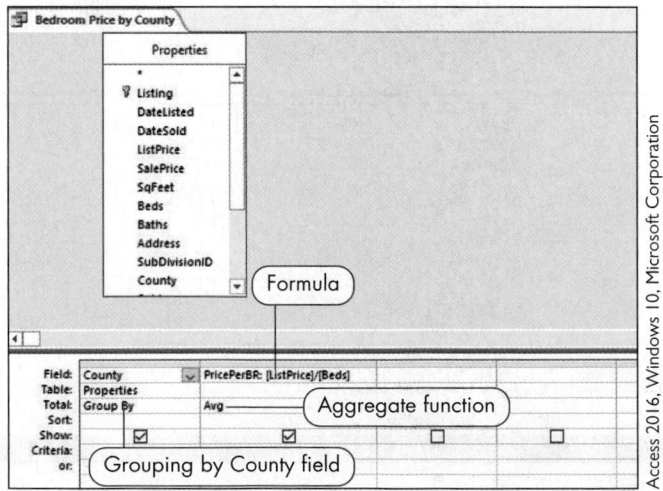

Access 2016, Windows 10, Microsoft Corporation

FIGURE 3.32 Adding Calculated Field to Totals Query

Bedroom Price by County	
County	PricePerBR
Bergen	$73,946.82
Essex	$76,025.00
Hudson	$81,793.61
Mercer	$74,941.35
Morris	$77,588.72
Passaic	$75,387.97
Sussex	$69,097.29

PricePerBR results for each County

Results grouped by County name

FIGURE 3.33 Calculated Field Results

Quick Concepts ✓

8. What are the benefits of aggregate functions? List three examples of aggregate functions. *p. 837*

9. How does a Total row change the display of the query's Datasheet view? *p. 837*

10. What is a totals query? *p. 838*

11. What would it mean if a query is "grouped by" state? *p. 840*

Skills covered: Display a Total Row for a Query • Create a Totals Query • Add Grouping to a Totals Query • Add Conditions to a Totals Query • Add a Calculated Field to a Totals Query

3 Aggregate Functions

The investors decide it would be helpful to analyze the property lists they purchased. Some of the lists do not have homes that match their target criteria. The investors will either purchase new lists or alter their criteria. You create several totals queries to evaluate the property lists.

STEP 1 ›› DISPLAY A TOTAL ROW FOR A QUERY

You begin your property list analysis by creating a total row in Datasheet view of the Mortgage Payments query. This will give you a variety of aggregate information for important columns. Refer to Figure 3.34 as you complete Step 1.

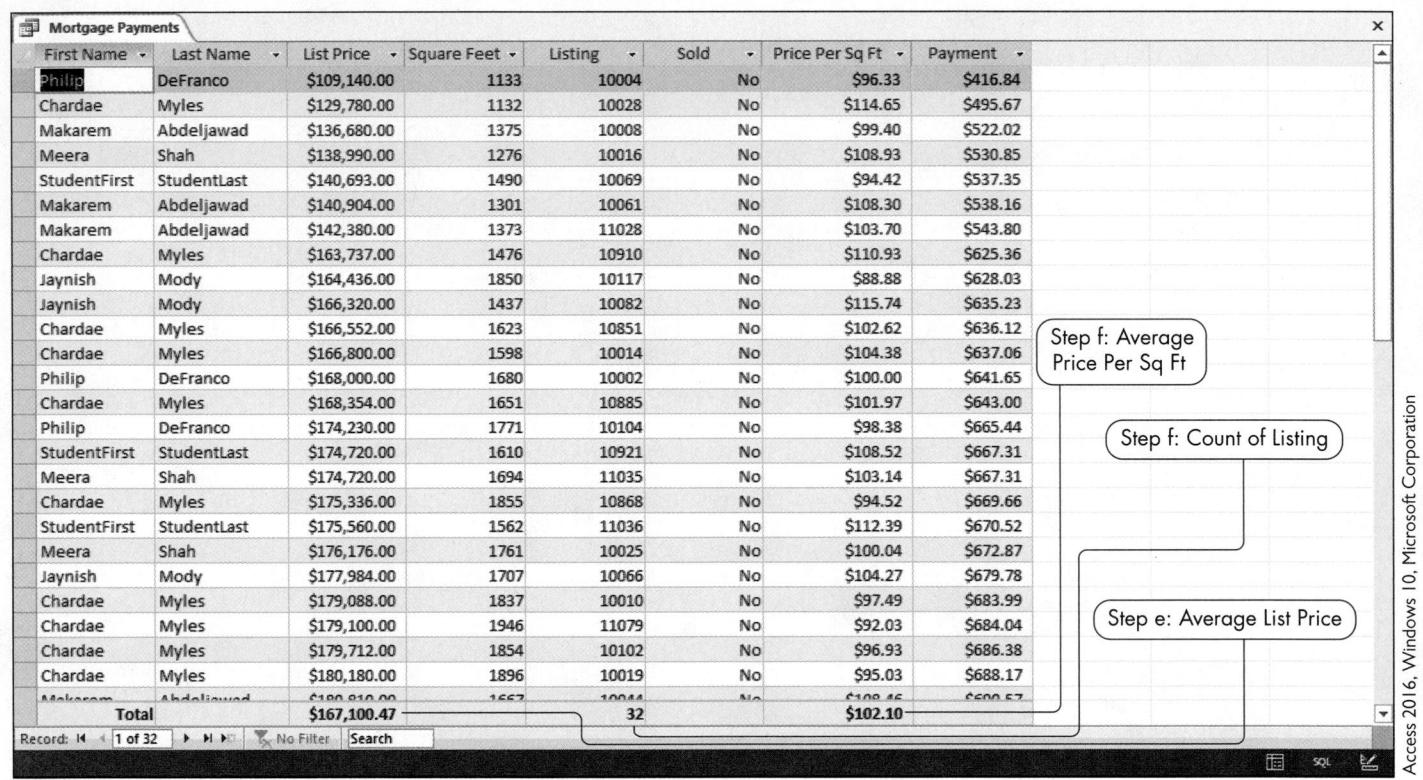

FIGURE 3.34 Totals Added to Datasheet View

a. Open *a03h2Property_LastFirst* if you closed it at the end of Hands-On Exercise 2 and save it as **a03h3Property_LastFirst**, changing h2 to h3.

b. Open the **Mortgage Payments query** in Design view. Drag the **Listing field** from the Properties table to the fifth column.

The Listing field is now in the fifth column, between the SqFeet and Sold fields. The other columns shift to the right.

> **TROUBLESHOOTING:** If you drag the Listing field to the wrong position, you can drag it again to the correct location.

c. Switch to Datasheet view. Click **Totals** in the Records group on the Home tab.

d. Click the **cell** that intersects the Total row and the List Price column.

e. Click the **arrow** and select **Average** to display the average value of all the properties that have not sold. Adjust column widths as necessary to ensure that all values are displayed.

The average list price of all properties is $167,100.47.

f. Click the **arrow** in the Total row in the Listing column and select **Count** from the list.

The count of properties in this datasheet is 32.

g. Click the **arrow** in the Total row in the Price Per Sq Ft column and select **Average** from the list.

The average price per square foot is $102.10.

h. Compare your results to Figure 3.34. Save and close the query.

STEP 2 ›› CREATE A TOTALS QUERY AND ADD GROUPING AND CONDITIONS

You create a totals query to help Don and Matt evaluate the properties in groups. Refer to Figure 3.35 and Figure 3.36 as you complete Step 2.

Access 2016, Windows 10, Microsoft Corporation

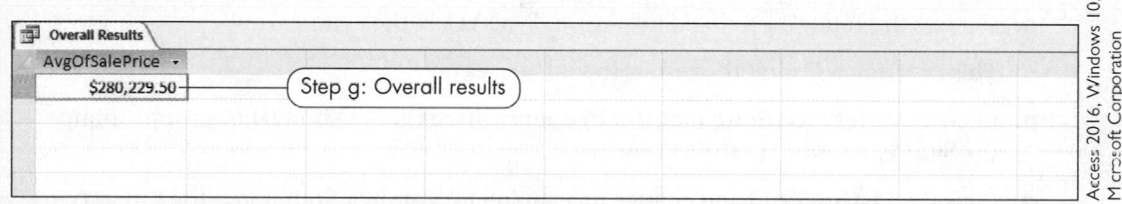

FIGURE 3.35 Overall Results Query Output

Access 2016, Windows 10, Microsoft Corporation

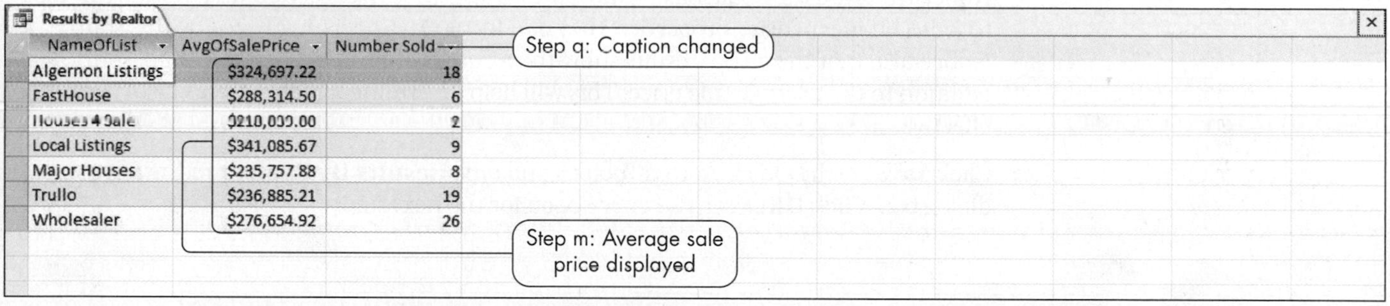

FIGURE 3.36 Results by Realtor Query Output

a. Click **Query Design** in the Queries group of the Create tab.

You create a new query in Query Design; the Show Table dialog box opens.

b. Click the **Properties table** in the Show Table dialog box and click **Add**. Close the Show Table dialog box.

c. Double-click the **SalePrice** and **Sold** fields to add them to the query.

d. Click **Totals** in the Show/Hide group of the Design tab to show the Total row.

A new row labeled Totals displays in the query design grid, between the Table and Sort rows. Each field has Group By listed in the new row by default.

e. Click the **Group By arrow** in the SalePrice column Total row and select **Avg**.

f. Click the **Group By arrow** in the Sold column Total row and select **Where**. Type **Yes** in the Criteria row.

This criterion will limit the results to sold houses only.

g. Click the **SalePrice field** and click **Property Sheet** in the Show/Hide group. Change the SalePrice format to **Currency**. Close the Property Sheet. Run the query and adjust the column width if necessary. Compare your results to Figure 3.35.

The results show an overall average of $280,229.50 for the sold properties in the database.

h. Click **Save** on the Quick Access Toolbar and type **Overall Results** in the Save As dialog box. Click **OK**. Close the query.

i. Click **Query Design** in the Query group of the Create tab to create a new query.

j. Add the Properties table and the Lists table from the Show Table dialog box. Close the Show Table dialog box.

k. Add the NameOfList field from the Lists table and the SalePrice, Listing, and Sold fields from the Properties table to the query.

l. Click **Totals** in the Show/Hide group to show the Total row.

A new row labeled Total appears between the Table and Sort rows.

m. Change the Total row for SalePrice to **Avg**.

n. Change the Total row for Listing to **Count**.

o. Change the Total row for Sold to **Where**. Type **Yes** in the Criteria row.

This criterion will limit the results to sold houses only.

p. Click the **SalePrice field** and click **Property Sheet** in the Show/Hide group. Change the SalePrice format to **Currency**.

q. Click the **Listing field** and change the caption to **Number Sold**. Close the Property Sheet. Run the query and widen the columns as shown in Figure 3.36.

Notice that Houses 4 Sale has the lowest average sale price. As Don and Matt are hoping to focus on inexpensive properties, they can focus on properties offered by this source. Notice also that the query results show the number of properties sold in each source, in addition to the average sale price. This will help determine which sources have been more effective.

r. Click **Save** on the Quick Access Toolbar and type **Results By Realtor** in the Save As dialog box. Click **OK**. Keep the query open for the next step.

The previous query shows the average value of the properties by realtor. However, Don and Matt learned at the seminar they attended that the longer a property has been on the market, the better your chances of negotiating a better price. You will revise the query to show, on average, how long each realtor takes to sell a house. Refer to Figure 3.37 as you complete Step 3.

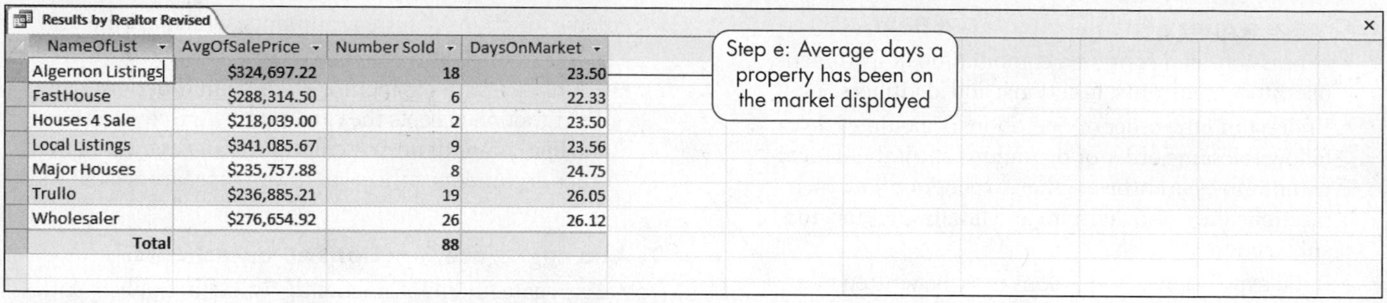

NameOfList	AvgOfSalePrice	Number Sold	DaysOnMarket
Algernon Listings	$324,697.22	18	23.50
FastHouse	$288,314.50	6	22.33
Houses 4 Sale	$218,039.00	2	23.50
Local Listings	$341,085.67	9	23.56
Major Houses	$235,757.88	8	24.75
Trullo	$236,885.21	19	26.05
Wholesaler	$276,654.92	26	26.12
Total		88	

Step e: Average days a property has been on the market displayed

Access 2016, Windows 10, Microsoft Corporation

FIGURE 3.37 Results by Realtor Revised Query Output

a. Click the **File tab**, select **Save As**, and click **Save Object As**. Click **Save As** and type **Results By Realtor Revised**. Click **OK**.

b. Click **Totals** in the Records group of the Home tab. Click in the Total row for the **NumberSold** column, click the arrow and select **Sum**.

The total number of houses sold (88) now displays at the bottom of the Number Sold column.

c. Switch to Design view. In the field row of the first blank column, type **DaysOnMarket: [DateSold]-[DateListed]** to create a new calculated field. Change the Total row from Group By to **Avg**.

The DaysOnMarket field will show the average number of days on the market for each sold listing.

d. Display the Property Sheet for the DaysOnMarket field and change the Format property to **Fixed**. Close the Property Sheet.

e. Run the query and examine the DaysOnMarket field. Adjust column widths as necessary. Compare your results to Figure 3.37.

Houses 4 Sale listings have an average of 23.50 days on the market. Since this is in-line with their competitors, it lets you know they are neither fast nor slow with sales.

f. Save and close the query.

g. Close the database and exit Access. Based on your instructor's directions, submit the following files:

a03h1PropertyCheck_LastFirst

a03h3Property_LastFirst

Chapter Objectives Review

After reading this chapter, you have accomplished the following objectives:

I. Create a query with a calculated field.

- Expressions can contain a combination of arithmetic operators, constants, functions, and identifiers.
- Understand the order of operations: Calculated fields follow the same order of operations as mathematical equations—parentheses, then exponentiation, then multiplication and division, and finally addition and subtraction.
- Build expressions: Expressions must be written in a certain way. Rules govern the way you give instructions to Access.

2. Format calculated results.

- Calculated results may not have the format you want; change the properties of a calculated field using the Property Sheet.

3. Recover from common errors.

- Common errors include forgetting the colon in the appropriate location, spelling errors, and misuse of the order of operations.

4. Verify calculated results.

- Always check the results of your equation; Access will check for errors in the way something is written, but not logic errors.

5. Create expressions using the Expression Builder.

- The Expression Builder will help you create complex expressions by enabling you to choose fields and built-in functions easily.
- Click the Builder icon to open the tool.

6. Use built-in functions.

- Access includes 150 built-in functions, or predefined computations that perform complex calculations.

- Some functions require arguments, which are inputs (often fields or constants) given to a function.
- Calculate a loan payment with the Pmt function: The Pmt function accepts the rate, number of payments, and loan amount and calculates a loan payment. Two other arguments, future value and type, are typically left as zero.

7. Add aggregate functions to datasheets.

- Aggregate functions, including functions such as Sum, Avg, and Count, perform calculations on an entire column of data and return a single value.
- The total row displays at the bottom of a query or table; it can perform any aggregate function on each column.

8. Create queries with aggregate functions.

- Create a totals query: Create a query as usual and click the Totals button in Design view.
- Add grouping to a totals query: Grouping enables you to summarize your data by the values of a field. For example, instead of showing overall averages, add County as a grouping field and see averages for each county.
- Add conditions to a totals query: Similar to other queries, conditions can be added to totals queries, such as only showing listings with the Sold field equal to No.
- Add a calculated field to a totals query: You can apply an aggregate function to the results of a calculation; for example, subtract one date from another, and calculate the overall average of the difference between those dates.

Key Terms Matching

Match the key terms with their definitions. Write the key term letter by the appropriate numbered definition.

a. Aggregate function
b. Argument
c. Calculated field
d. Constant
e. Expression
f. Expression Builder
g. Function

h. Grouping
i. Order of operations
j. Pmt function
k. Property Sheet
l. Total row
m. Totals query

1. _____ A combination of elements that produce a value. **p. 812**

2. _____ A field that displays the result of an expression rather than data stored in a field. **p. 812**

3. _____ A predefined computation that performs a complex calculation. **p. 828**

4. _____ A value that does not change. **p. 812**

5. _____ A method of summarizing data by the values of a field. **p. 840**

6. _____ An Access tool that helps you create more complicated expressions. **p. 826**

7. _____ Calculates the loan payment given the rate, number of periods (also known as term), and the present value of the loan (the principal). **p. 830**

8. _____ A way to display aggregate data when a query is run. **p. 837**

9. _____ The sequence by which operations are performed in a mathematical expression. **p. 812**

10. _____ A method to display aggregate function results as the last row in Datasheet view of a table or query. **p. 838**

11. _____ The location where you change settings such as number format and number of decimal places. **p. 817**

12. _____ The input used to produce output for a function. **p. 828**

13. _____ A calculation performed on an entire column of data that returns a single value. Includes functions such as Sum, Avg, and Count. **p. 837**

Multiple Choice

1. Which of the following *cannot* be used in a calculated field?

(a) The number 12

(b) An asterisk (*)

(c) [HoursWorked] (a field in the current database)

(d) All of these can be used in a calculated field

2. When creating a calculation, which of the following would be identified as an error by Access?

(a) A field name spelled wrong in a calculation.

(b) An incorrect formula (for example, adding two numbers instead of subtracting).

(c) An order of operations error (for example, [HourlyPay] + 2 * [HoursWorked]).

(d) A missing colon in the expression (for example: TotalHours [OTHours]+[RegHours]).

3. What is the result of the following expression?
2 * 5 + 8 - 6 / 2

(a) 6

(b) 15

(c) 20

(d) 23

4. Which of the following *cannot* be adjusted in the Property Sheet?

(a) Caption

(b) Mathematical expression

(c) Number format (for example, displaying numbers as Currency)

(d) Number of decimal places

5. Which of the following could *not* be done using an aggregate function?

(a) Averaging a series of numbers

(b) Calculating the payment amount of a loan

(c) Counting the number of values that exist

(d) Finding the smallest value

6. Which of the following can be added to a totals query?

(a) Conditions

(b) Grouping fields

(c) Aggregate functions

(d) All of the above can be added to a totals query.

7. Which statement about a totals query is true?

(a) A totals query is created in Datasheet view.

(b) A totals query may contain several grouping fields but only one aggregate field.

(c) A totals query is limited to only two fields, one grouping field and one aggregate field.

(d) A totals query may contain several grouping fields and several aggregate fields.

8. Which of the following statements is true?

(a) A total order cost is an example of a common field to group by.

(b) A last name is an example of a common field to group by.

(c) For best results, add as many "group by" fields as possible.

(d) None of the above statements is true.

9. If you want to calculate aggregate statistics about graduation rates for students in a college database, which of the following would provide the *least* useful information if you were to group by it?

(a) Gender

(b) High School

(c) Race

(d) Social Security Number

10. Which of the following about the Total row in Query design is *false*?

(a) The Total row enables you to apply aggregate functions to the fields.

(b) The Total row is hidden by default in all new queries.

(c) The Total row is located between the Table and Sort rows.

(d) The Total row applies only to non-numeric fields.

Practice Exercises

1 Conforto Insurance

The Conforto Insurance Agency is a mid-sized company with offices located across the country. Each employee receives an annual performance review. The review determines employee eligibility for salary increases and the annual performance bonus. The employee data is stored in an Access database, which is used to monitor and maintain employee records. Your task is to calculate the salary increase for each employee; you will also calculate the average salary for each position. Refer to Figure 3.38 as you complete this exercise.

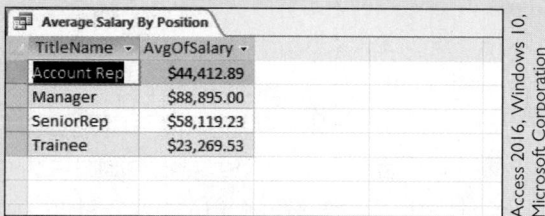

FIGURE 3.38 Average Salary by Position Results

a. Open *a03p1Insurance*. Save the database as **a03p1Insurance_LastFirst**.

b. Click the **Create tab** and click **Query Design** in the Queries group to create a new query. Select the **Employees table** and click **Add**. Select the **Titles table** and click **Add**. Click **Close** to close the Show Table dialog box.

c. Double-click the **LastName**, **FirstName**, **Performance**, and **Salary** fields from the Employees table to add them to the query. Double-click the **Increase** field from the Titles table to add it to the query.

d. Click the Field row of the first blank column in the query design grid and type **NewSalary: [Salary]+[Salary]*[Increase]** to create a calculated field that adds the existing salary to the increase.

e. Click **Run** in the Results group to run the query.

f. Switch to Design view. Ensure the NewSalary calculated field is selected. Click **Property Sheet** in the Show/Hide group to display the Property Sheet. Click the **Format property** in the Property Sheet. Click the **Format property arrow** and select **Currency**. Type **New Salary** in the Caption box.

g. Click **Run** in the Results group to view the results. Adjust column widths as necessary. Save the query as **Updated Salaries**. Close the query.

h. Click the **Create tab** and click **Query Design** in the Queries group to create a new query. Select the **Employees table** and click **Add**. Select the **Titles table** and click **Add**. Click **Close** to close the Show Table dialog box.

i. Double-click the **TitleName field** from the Titles table. Double-click the **Salary field** from the Employees table.

j. Click **Totals** in the Show/Hide group to display the Total row. Change the Total row for Salary to **Avg**. Leave the TitleName field set to Group By.

k. Click the **Salary field**. Click the **Format property** in the Property Sheet. Click the **Format property arrow** and select **Currency**.

l. Click **Run** in the Results group to view the results. Adjust column widths as necessary. Save the query as **Average Salary By Position** and compare your results to Figure 3.38. Close the query.

m. Close the database and exit Access. Based on your instructor's directions, submit a03p1Insurance_LastFirst.

South Bend Luxury Motor Yachts, a local boat seller, hired a new Chief Financial Officer (CFO). The new CFO, Rosta Marinova, asked the financing department to provide her with some summaries. She would like to determine how much financing the company is currently offering, offer financing with interest to customers, and see aggregate purchase statistics for local cities. Refer to Figure 3.39 as you complete this exercise.

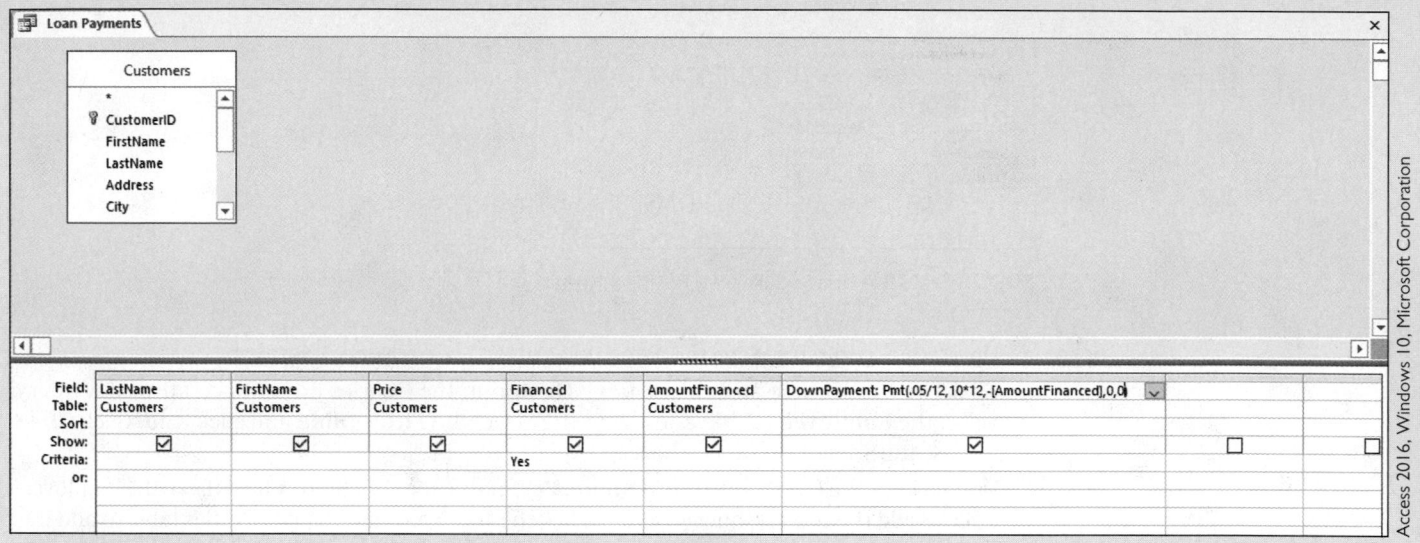

FIGURE 3.39 Loan Payments Design

a. Open *a03p2Boats* and save the database as **a03p2Boats_LastFirst**.

b. Click the **Create tab** and click **Query Design** in the Queries group to create a new query. Select the **Customers table** and click **Add**. Click **Close** to close the Show Table dialog box.

c. Double-click the **LastName**, **FirstName**, **Price**, **Financed**, and **AmountFinanced** fields.

d. Click the **Field row** of the first blank column and type **DownPayment: [Price]-[AmountFinanced]**.

e. Click **Run** in the Results group to run the query. Examine the results. Adjust column widths as necessary.

f. Click **Save** on the Quick Access Toolbar and type **Down Payment Amounts** as the Query Name in the Save As dialog box. Click **OK**.

g. Switch to Design view. Click the **Criteria row** for the Financed field and type **Yes**.

   This will limit the results to financed boats. Boats that were not financed were paid for in full when purchased.

h. Click the **checkbox** on the Show row of the Financed field so it does not display when the query is run.

i. Sort the query by DownPayment in descending order by clicking the **Sort row** for the DownPayment field and selecting **Descending**.

j. Click **Property Sheet** in the Show/Hide group. In the Caption box, type **Down Payment**.

k. Click **Run** in the Results group to view the results. Adjust column widths as necessary. Notice that the column heading for the DownPayment field appears with a space in the name.

l. Save and close the query.

m. Click the **Create tab** and click **Query Design** in the Queries group to create a new query. Select the **Customers table** and click **Add**. Click **Close** to close the Show Table dialog box.

n. Double-click the fields **LastName**, **FirstName**, **Price**, **Financed**, and **AmountFinanced** to add them to the query.

o. Click the Field row of the first blank column. Click **Builder** in the Query Setup group to open the Expression Builder. Double-click **Functions**, and select **Built-In Functions**. Select **Financial**, and double-click **Pmt** in the Expression Values box.

p. Position the insertion point before the Pmt function. Type **DownPayment:** to the left of the function (including the colon).

q. Click each argument to select it, and substitute the appropriate information below. Once you have entered the information, click **OK**.

- **.05/12** for rate (5% interest, paid monthly).
- **10*12** for num_periods (10 year loan, 12 payments per year).
- Use **[AmountFinanced]** for the present_value.
- Use **0** in place of future_value and type.

r. Click **Property Sheet** in the Show/Hide group. In the Caption box, type **Monthly Payment**. Select **Currency** as the format.

s. Click the **Criteria row** for the Financed field and type **Yes**.

t. Click **Run** in the Results group to examine the results.

u. Click **Totals** in the Show/Hide group on the Design tab. Click Group By in the Monthly Payment column, click the drop-down menu, and select **Avg**.

v. Switch to Design view. Add a **minus sign** in front of [AmountFinanced] in the DownPayment calculation to display the results as positive numbers. Compare your design to Figure 3.39.

w. Click **Run** in the Results group to examine the results. Adjust column widths as necessary. Save the query as **Loan Payments** and close the query.

x. Close the database and exit Access. Based on your instructor's directions, submit a03p2Boats_LastFirst.

Mid-Level Exercises

1 Small Business Loans

ANALYSIS CASE

FROM SCRATCH

You are the manager of a regional business loan department for the U.S. Small Business Administration office. You have decided to evaluate whether Access could be used in place of the Excel worksheet you are currently using. You will create a blank desktop database, add a table, add some sample customers, and import some recent data from an Excel spreadsheet. You will calculate the payments for the loans that are currently on the books by creating a query using the Pmt function. You will also summarize loans by the type of loan (M = Mortgage, C = Car, and O = Other).

a. Open Access and create a new blank desktop database named **a03m1Loans_LastFirst**.

b. Switch to Design view. Type **Customers** in the **Save As dialog box** and click **OK**.

c. Change the first Field Name to **CustomerID** and accept AutoNumber as the Data Type. Type **Company** in the second row and press **Tab**. Accept Short Text as the Data Type. Type **FirstName** in the third row and press **Tab**. Accept Short Text as the Data Type.

d. Type the remainder of the fields, selecting Short Text for the data type:

LastName	**Short Text**
City	**Short Text**
State	**Short Text**
Zip	**Short Text**

e. Verify that the first field is set as the primary key.

f. Switch to Datasheet view. Click **Yes** to save the table. Add the records as shown in the following table. Note that Access will assign an ID. Once you have typed the records, close the Customers table.

Company	FirstName	LastName	City	State	Zip
Jones and Co	**Robert**	**Paterson**	**Greensboro**	**NC**	**27401**
Elements, Inc.	**Merve**	**Kana**	**Paterson**	**NJ**	**07505**
Godshall Meats, LLC	**Francisco**	**De La Cruz**	**Beverly Hills**	**CA**	**90210**

DISCOVER

g. Click the **External Data tab** and click **Excel** in the Import & Link group. Click **Browse** to locate the *a03m1Loans* spreadsheet. Select the workbook and click **Open** at the bottom of the dialog box.

h. Ensure that *Import the source data into a new table in the current database.* is selected and click **OK**. Click **Next** three times, accepting the defaults, until you are asked to add a primary key. Click the *Choose my own Primary Key* option, and ensure **LoanID** is selected. Click **Next** once more and click **Finish**, accepting Loans as the table name. Click **Close** in the Get External Data dialog box.

i. Open the Loans table in Design view. Select the **InterestRate field** and change the format to **Percent**. Change the field size for the CustomerID field to **Long Integer**. Save and close the table, selecting **Yes** when prompted that some data may be lost.

j. Click the **Database Tools tab** and click **Relationships** in the Relationships group. Add both tables to the Relationships window and close the Show Table dialog box.

k. Drag the **CustomerID field** from the Customers table and drop it onto the **CustomerID field** in the Loans table. Check the **Enforce Referential Integrity** checkbox in the Edit Relationships dialog box and click **Create**. Save and close the Relationships window.

l. Create a query in Design view using the two tables. Add the **Company** field from the Customers table and the **LoanID**, **Amount**, **InterestRate**, **Term**, and **LoanClass fields** from the Loans table. Sort the query by LoanID in ascending order. Save the query as **Loan Payments**.

 m. Add a calculated field named **Payment** in the first blank column to calculate the loan payment for each loan, using the Expression Builder. Use the Pmt function. Insert the appropriate field names in place of the placeholder arguments. Assume that the loans have monthly payments (12 payments per year). Ensure that the payment displays as a positive number. Run the query. The first loan should have a value of 243.154499654298 (the extra decimal places will be removed shortly).

n. Switch to Design view and change the format for the Payment field to **Currency**. Run the query again to verify your change.

o. Click **Totals** in the Records group on the Home tab. Change the value for the Total row for the Amount column to **Sum** and the values for the InterestRate and Term to **Average**. Adjust column widths as necessary. Save and close the query.

p. Create a copy of Loan Payments. Save the new query as **Loan Payments Summary**.

q. Open the Loan Payments Summary query in Design view and rearrange the columns as follows: LoanClass, LoanID, Amount, and InterestRate. Delete columns Company, Term, and Payment. Click **Totals** in the Show/Hide group. Change the Total row for LoanID field to **Count**, for the Amount field to **Sum**, and for the InterestRate field to Avg. Run the query.

r. Switch to Design view and display the Property Sheet. For the LoanID field, change the caption to **Loans**. For the Amount field, change the caption to **Total Amount** and change the format to **Currency**. For the InterestRate field, change the caption to **Avg Interest Rate** and change the format to **Percent**. Run the query. Adjust column widths as necessary. Save and close the query.

s. Close the database and exit Access. Based on your instructor's directions, submit a03m1Loans_LastFirst.

2 Investment Properties

You are in charge of Dysan Investment's database, which contains all of the information on the properties your firm has listed and sold. Your task is to determine the length of time each property was on the market before it sold. You also have been tasked with calculating the sales commission from each property sold. Two agents will receive commission on each transaction: the listing agent and the selling agent. You also will summarize the sales data by employee and calculate the average number of days each employee's sales were on the market prior to selling and the total commission earned by the employees.

a. Open *a03m2Homes*. Save the database as **a03m2Homes_LastFirst**.

b. Create a new query, add the Agents, Properties, and SubDivision tables, and then add the following fields: from the Agents table, add the LastName field; from the Properties table, the DateListed, DateSold, SalePrice, SellingAgent, and ListingAgent fields; and from the SubDivision table, the Subdivision field.

DISCOVER

c. Add criteria to the table to ensure that the DateSold field is not empty (in other words, properties that have not been sold). You will need to use a function named IsNull to accomplish this. Format the SalePrice field as **Currency**. Save the query as **Sales Report**.

d. Create a calculated field using the Expression Builder named **DaysOnMarket** by subtracting DateListed from DateSold. This will calculate the number of days each sold property was on the market when it sold. Add a caption of **Days on Market**.

e. Calculate the commissions for the selling and listing agents using two calculated fields. The listing commission rate is 3.5% of the sale price, and the selling commission rate is 2.5% of the sale price. You can type these in directly or use the Expression Builder. Name the newly created fields **ListComm** and **SellComm**. Add captions of **Listing Commission** and **Selling Commission** and format the fields as **Currency**.

f. Run the query. Adjust column widths as necessary. Display the Total row. Calculate the average number of days on the market and the sum for the SalePrice and the two commission fields. Adjust column widths so all values are visible, and save and close the query.

g. Create a copy of the Sales Report query named **Sales Summary by Last Name**. Remove the DateListed, SellingAgent, ListingAgent, and Subdivision fields.

h. Display the Total row. Group by LastName and change the DateSold field Total row to **Where**, so the condition carries over. Show the sum of SalePrice, the average of DaysOnMarket, and the sum for both ListComm and SellComm. Change the caption for the SalePrice field to **Total Sales** and format the DaysOnMarket field as **Fixed**. Run the query. Adjust column widths as necessary.

i. Adjust the Total row in Datasheet view so it shows the sum of TotalSales. Adjust column widths as necessary. Save and close the query.

 DISCOVER

j. Create a copy of the Sales Summary by Last Name query named **Sales Summary by Subdivision** and open the query in Design view. Remove the LastName field. Add the Subdivision field to the query and ensure the Total row is set to Group By. Sort the query results on the DaysOnMarket field in Ascending order. Limit the results to only return the top five values (hint: look in the Query Setup group of the Design tab).

k. Run the query and ensure only the top 5 values display. Save and close the query.

l. Close the database and exit Access. Based on your instructor's directions, submit a03m2Homes_LastFirst.

3 New Castle County Technical Services

RUNNING CASE

New Castle County Technical Services (NCCTS) provides technical support for a number of local companies. Part of their customer service evaluation involves logging how calls are closed and a quick, one-question survey given to customers at the end of a call, asking them to rate their experience from 1 (poor) to 5 (excellent). To evaluate the effectiveness of their operation, they asked you to create some queries to help evaluate the performance of the company.

a. Open the database you finished last chapter *a02m3NCCTS_LastFirst* and save the database as **a03m3NCCTS_LastFirst**.

> **TROUBLESHOOTING:** If you did not complete the Chapter 2 case, return to Chapter 2, complete the case to create the database, and then return to this exercise.

b. Create a new query in Design view. Select the rep first and last names from the Reps table, and the CallID and CustomerSatisfaction fields from the Calls table.

c. Group by the RepFirst and RepLast fields. Display the count of the CallID field and average for the CustomerSatisfaction field.

d. Change the caption for the CallID field to **Num Calls**.

e. Format the CustomerSatisfaction average in Standard format and change the caption to **Avg Rating**.

f. Add a new calculated field named **AvgResponse**. Subtract the OpenedDate from the ClosedDate. Format the field as **Fixed**. Display the average for this field.

g. Run the query. Adjust column widths to ensure all data is displayed. Save the query as **Tech Ratings** and close the query.

h. Create a new query in Design view. Select the Description field from the Call Types table, and the CallID and CustomerSatisfaction field from the Calls table.

i. Group by the Description field. Display the count of the CallID field and average for the CustomerSatisfaction field.

j. Change the caption for the CallID field to **Num Calls**.

k. Format the CustomerSatisfaction average in Standard format and change the caption to **Avg Rating**.

l. Run the query. Adjust column widths as necessary. Save the query as **Call Type Effectiveness** and close the query.

m. Create a new query in Design view. Select the CompanyName field from the Customers table, and the CallID and CustomerSatisfaction field from the Calls table.

n. Group by the CompanyName field. Display the count of the CallID field and average for the CustomerSatisfaction field.

o. Format the CustomerSatisfaction average in Standard format and change the caption to **Avg Rating**.

p. Change the caption for the CallID field to **Num Calls**.

q. Run the query. Display the Total row. Show the sum of the Num Calls column. Adjust column widths as necessary.

r. Save the query as **Customer Happiness** and close the query.

s. Close the database and exit Access. Based on your instructor's directions, submit a03m3NCCTS_LastFirst.

Beyond the Classroom

Denton Credit Union

GENERAL CASE

Open *a03b1Denton*, which contains data from a local credit union. Save the database as **a03b1Denton_LastFirst**. Replace Your Name in the Branch table with your first and last name.

Create a query to calculate how long each manager has worked for the credit union: Display the manager and start date, and create a calculated field named **YearsWithCompany** to determine the number of years each manager has been in his or her position. Hint: Find a built-in Date/Time function to use the current date, subtract the start date, and divide the result by 365.25 (Note: the .25 at the end accounts for leap years). Display the calculated field in Fixed format, and add a caption to the field to display Years With Company as the column heading. Adjust column widths in Datasheet view as necessary. Save the query as Longevity.

Create a totals query to summarize each customer's account balances. List the customer's last name and first name from the Customer table, and the sum of all account balances (found in the Account table), grouping by both the last and first name. Format the total of the balances as Currency and add a caption of **Total Balance**. Display the sum of the total balances in Datasheet view ($141,074), adjust column widths as necessary, and save the query as **Customer Balances**.

Create a totals query to show each city (found in the Customer table) and total account balances for each city. For example, the total amount for customers in Denton is $61,510. Format the sum of the Balance field as currency with a caption of **Total Balance**. Adjust column widths as necessary in Datasheet view. Save the query as **Balances by City**.

Close the database and exit Access. Based on your instructor's directions, submit a03b1Denton_LastFirst.

Too Many Digits

DISASTER RECOVERY

This chapter introduced you to calculated fields. Open the database *a03b2Interest* and save the database as **a03b2Interest_LastFirst**. Open the Monthly Interest Payments query in Datasheet view. Notice the multiple digits to the right of the decimal in the MonthlyInterest column; there should only be two digits. Search the Internet or Access Help to find a function that will resolve this rounding problem. You only want to display two digits to the right of the decimal. Display the Total row in Datasheet view and display the total of the MonthlyInterest field. Adjust column widths as necessary. Save and close the query. Close the database and exit Access. Based on your instructor's directions, submit a03b2Interest_LastFirst.

Capstone Exercise

Northwind Traders, an international gourmet food distributor, hired a new CEO. She asked for your assistance in providing summaries of data that took place before she started with the company. To help her with her strategic planning, you will create queries to perform data analysis. Based on your meeting, you plan on creating four queries. One query will find orders with major delays. Another query will summarize the cost impact of customer discounts. A third query will be used to help evaluate financing. The final query will calculate the total sales by country.

Database File Setup

You will open the Northwind Traders food database, use Save As to make a copy of the database, and then use the new database to complete this capstone exercise. You will add yourself to the employee database.

a. Locate and open *a03c1Food* and save the database as **a03c1Food_LastFirst**.

b. Open the Employees table. Add yourself as an employee. Fill in all information, with the hire date as the current date. Set your Title to **Technical Aide**, extension to **1144**, and the Reports To field to **Buchanan, Steven**. Leave the Photo and Notes fields blank.

c. Close the Employees table.

Shipping Efficiency Query

You will create a query to calculate the number of days between the date an order was placed and the date the order was shipped for each order. The result of your work will be a list of orders that took more than 30 days to ship. The salespeople will be required to review the records and report the source of the delay for each order. The CEO feels there may be issues with one of the shipping companies, and would like data to back that up.

a. Create a query using Query Design. From the Customers table, include the fields CompanyName, ContactName, ContactTitle, and Phone. From the Orders table, include the fields OrderID, OrderDate, and ShippedDate.

b. Run the query and examine the records. Save the query as **Shipping Efficiency**.

c. Add a calculated field named **DaysToShip** to calculate the number of days taken to fill each order. (Hint: The expression will include the OrderDate and the ShippedDate; the results will not contain negative numbers.)

d. Run the query and examine the results. Does the data in the DaysToShip field look accurate? Save the query.

e. Add criteria to limit the query results to include only orders that took more than 30 days to ship.

f. Add the Quantity field from the Order Details table and the ProductName field from the Products table to the query. Sort the query by ascending OrderID. When the sales reps contact these customers, these two fields will provide useful information about the orders.

g. Add the caption **Days to Ship** to the DaysToShip field. Switch to Datasheet view to view the results. Adjust column widths as necessary.

h. Save and close the query.

Order Summary Query

The CEO is considering the financial impact of discounts. She asked for a query showing the employee name, number of orders they have taken, and the total discount amount they have given customers. She hopes to see if there is a correlation between the discount offered and the number of sales.

a. Create a query using Query Design and add the Orders, Order Details, Products, and Customers tables. Add the fields OrderID and OrderDate from the Orders table. Set both fields' Total row to **Group By**.

b. Add a calculated field in the third column. Name the field **ExtendedAmount**. This field should multiply the quantity ordered (from the Order Details table) by the unit price for that item (from the Products table). This will calculate the total amount for each order. Format the calculated field as **Currency** and change the caption to **Total Dollars**. Change the Total row to **Sum**.

c. Add a calculated field in the fourth column. Name the field **DiscountAmount**. The field should multiply the quantity ordered, the unit price for that item, and the discount field (from the Customers table). This will calculate the total discount for each order. Format the calculated field as **Currency** and add a caption of **Discount Amt**. Change the Total row to **Sum**.

d. Run the query. Examine the results. Most customers should have a discount of 10% of the total dollars, but some customers will have no discount. Save the query as **Order Summary**. Return to Design view.

e. Add criteria to the OrderDate field so only orders made between 1/1/2016 and 12/31/2016 are displayed. Change the Total row to **Where**. This expression will display only orders that were placed in 2016.

f. Run the query and view the results. Adjust column widths as necessary. Save and close the query.

Order Financing Query

The CEO would like the salespeople to discuss financing with customers. In order to do so, she would like you to create a query showing the impact on price for prior orders. This way, the reps can give customers a comparison with an order they have already placed. For the moment, she is considering a 5% interest rate, paid over 12 months. She would like you to leave the results as negative numbers.

a. Create a copy of the Order Summary query named **Order Financing**.

b. Open the Order Financing query in Design view and remove the DiscountAmount field.

c. Add a new field using the Expression Builder named **SamplePayment**. Insert the Pmt function with the following parameters:

- Use **.05/12** for the rate argument (5% interest, paid monthly).
- Use the number **12** for the num_periods argument (12 months).
- Use the calculated field **[ExtendedAmount]** for the present_value.
- Use the value **0** for both future_value and type.

d. Change the Total row to **Expression** for the SamplePayment field.

e. Change the Format for the SamplePayment field to **Currency**.

f. Run the query and examine the results. Adjust column widths as necessary. The results appear as negative numbers, as requested. Save and close the query.

Order Summary by Country Query

The company is planning on opening up some shipping centers internationally. The previous CEO had been considering Brazil, Denmark, and Germany as potential shipping center locations, but he was working from older data. You will provide a list of total shipment value by country for the year before the current CEO started to best inform her decision making.

a. Create a copy of the Order Summary query named **Order Summary by Country**.

b. Open the query in Design view. Replace the OrderID field with the Country field from the Customers table.

c. Run the query and examine the summary records; there should be 21 countries listed.

d. Switch to Design view and change the sort order so that the country with the highest ExtendedAmount is first and the country with the lowest ExtendedAmount is last.

e. Run the query and verify the results. Note the ExtendedAmount field has a caption of Total Dollars, so this is the field the query will be sorted by.

f. Save and close the query.

g. Close the database and exit Access. Based on your instructor's directions, submit a03c1Food_LastFirst.

Creating and Using Professional Forms and Reports

LEARNING OUTCOMES

- You will develop and modify forms to input and manage data.
- You will create and modify reports to display and present information.

OBJECTIVES & SKILLS: After you read this chapter, you will be able to:

CASE STUDY | Coffee Shop Starts New Business

Coffee shop owner Ryung Park decided to use her knowledge of the coffee and retail industry to sell her specialty products to businesses around the country. She created an Access database to help track her customer, product, and order information.

Ryung created a database with tables to store data for customers, products, sales reps, and orders. She is currently using these tables to enter data and retrieve information. Ryung realizes that forms have an advantage over tables because they can be designed to display one record at a time—this can reduce potential data-entry errors. Ryung would like to create several reports so she can stay on top of her business by reviewing them each week. You have been hired to help Ryung create the new forms and reports that she needs.

Moving Beyond Tables and Queries

CHAPTER 4

Syda Productions/
Shutterstock

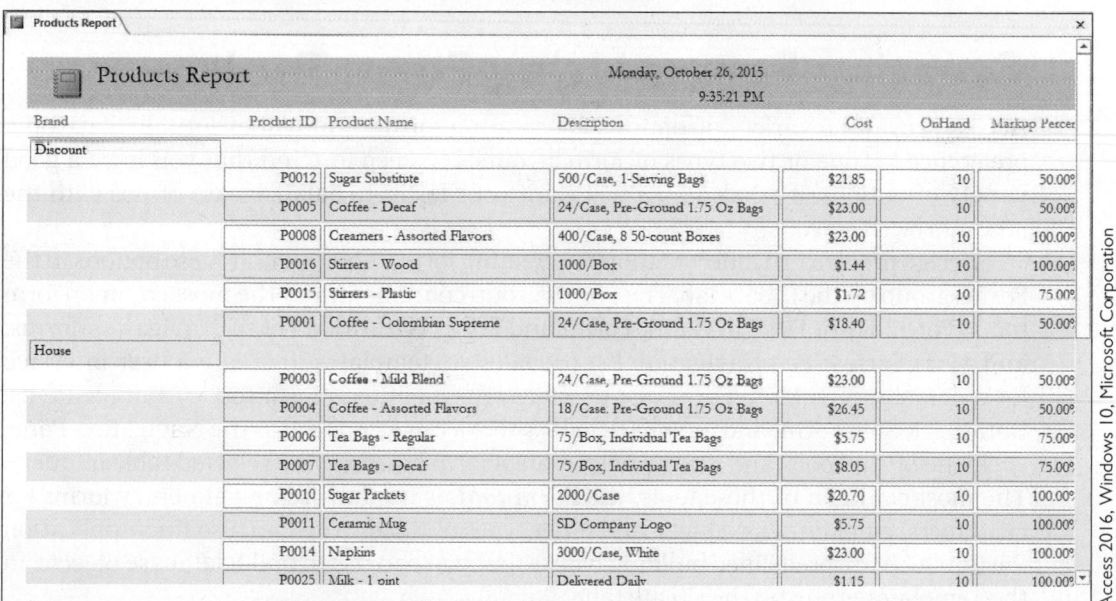

FIGURE 4.1 Coffee Shop Starts New Business Database

Access 2016, Windows 10, Microsoft Corporation

CASE STUDY | Coffee Shop Starts New Business

Starting File	Files to be Submitted
a04h1Coffee	a04h2Coffee_LastFirst a04h2Products_LastFirst

Form Basics

Most Access database applications use forms rather than tables for data entry and for finding information. A *form* is a database object used to add data to or edit data in a table. Three main reasons exist for using forms rather than tables for adding, updating, and deleting data:

- You are less likely to edit the wrong record by mistake.
- You can create a form that shows data from more than one table simultaneously.
- You can create Access forms to resemble the paper (or other types of) forms that users employ in their data entry processes.

When you are adding or editing data using a table with many records, you may navigate to the wrong record accidentally. A form is less likely to allow this type of error because most forms restrict entry to one record at a time.

Many forms require two tables as their record sources. For example, you may want to view a customer's details (name, address, email, phone, etc.) as well as all of the orders he or she has placed at the same time. This would require using data from both the Customers and the Orders tables in one form. Such a form enables a user to view two record sources at the same time and make changes—additions, edits, or deletions—to one or both sources of data. When a change is made in the form, the data in the underlying table (or tables) are affected. A form is really a mirror image of the data in the tables and simply presents a user-friendly interface for users of the database.

Access forms can be designed to emulate the paper documents already used by an organization. When paper forms are currently used to collect data, it is a good idea to design the electronic forms to resemble the paper forms. This will make the data entry process more efficient and ease the transition from paper form to electronic form

In this section, you will learn the basics of form design. You will discover multiple methods to create and modify Access forms.

Creating Forms Using Form Tools

Access provides a variety of options for creating forms. You will eventually develop a preference for one or two types of form layouts, but keep in mind that you have a good variety of options, if needed. You will want your forms to balance ease of use with the power to be effective.

Access provides 14 different tools for creating forms. You can find these options in the Forms group on the Create tab. The Forms group contains four of the most common form tools (Form, Form Design, Blank Form, and Form Wizard), a list of Navigation forms, and More Forms. The Navigation list provides six templates to create a user interface for a database; the More Forms list provides four additional form tools (Multiple Items, Datasheet, Split Form, and Modal Dialog). Select a table or query in the Navigation Pane, click one of the tools, and Access will create a form based on the selected table or query. The most common of these tools, the *Form tool*, is used to create data entry forms for customers, employees, products, and other types of tables. You can also find Application Parts, which are predefined building blocks that you can use to build database objects, in the Templates group on the Create tab.

A list of the Form tools available in Access is found in Table 4.1. Several of the tools will be covered in this chapter. Some tools will not be covered in detail, because they are not commonly used or because they are beyond the scope of this chapter (e.g., Form Design, Blank Form, Navigation forms, and Modal Dialog Form). Use Microsoft Access Help to find more information about Form tools not covered in this chapter.

TABLE 4.1 Form Tools in Access

Form Tool	Use
Form	Creates a form with a stacked layout that displays all of the fields in the record source.
Form Design	Creates a new blank form in Design view.
Blank Form	Creates a new blank form in Layout view.
Form Wizard	Creates a custom form based on your answers to a series of step-by-step questions.
Navigation	Creates user-interface forms that can also be used on the Internet. Six different Navigation form layouts are available from the list.
Split Form	Creates a two-part form with a stacked layout in one section and a tabular layout in the other.
Multiple Items	Creates a tabular layout form that includes all of the fields from the record source.
Datasheet	Creates a form that resembles the datasheet of a table or query.
Modal Dialog	Creates a custom dialog box that requires user input that is needed for a database object.

> **TIP: USABILITY TESTING**
> After a database object (such as a form) is finalized, it should be tested by both the database designer and the end users. The designer should be certain that the form meets any requirements the users have given him or her. The designer should also browse through the records to make sure the values in all records (and not just the first record) display correctly. After testing is completed by both designer and end users, the form should be modified and tested again before it is deployed with the database.

Ideally, a form should simplify data entry. Creating a form is a collaborative process between the database designer and the end users. This process continues throughout the life of the form, because the data needs of an organization may change over time. Forms designed long ago to collect data for a new customer account may not include an email or a website field; both the customer table and its associated form would have to be modified to include these fields. The designer needs to strike a balance between collecting the data required for use by the database and cluttering the form with extraneous fields. The database users generally offer good opinions about which fields should be on a form and how the form should behave. If you listen to their suggestions, your forms will function more effectively, the users' work will be easier, and the data will contain fewer data-entry errors.

After discussing the form with the users, it will help you to create the form in Access if you sketch the form first. After sketching the form, you will have a better idea of which form tool to use to create the form. After the form is created, use the sketch to determine which fields are required and what the order of the fields should be.

Identify a Record Source

Before you create a form, you must identify the record source. A *record source* (or data source) is the table or query that supplies the records for a form or report. Use a table if you want to include all the records from a single table. Create a query as the record source first if you need to filter the records in the source table, combine records from two or more related tables, or if you do not want to display all fields from the table(s) on your form. For example, if a sales rep wants to create a form that displays customers from a single state only—where his customers reside—he or she should base the form on a query.

Use the Form Tool

STEP 1 >> As noted earlier, the Form tool is the most common tool for creating forms. A usable form can be created with a single click.

> **To use the Form tool, complete the following steps:**
> 1. Select a table or query in the Navigation Pane.
> 2. Click Form in the Forms group on the Create tab.

Based on the table or query selected, Access automatically creates a new form. You may need to modify the form slightly, but you can create a stacked layout form with just one click. A *stacked layout* displays fields in a vertical column for one record at a time, as shown in Figure 4.2. The other type of layout you can use is a *tabular layout*, which displays data horizontally across the page.

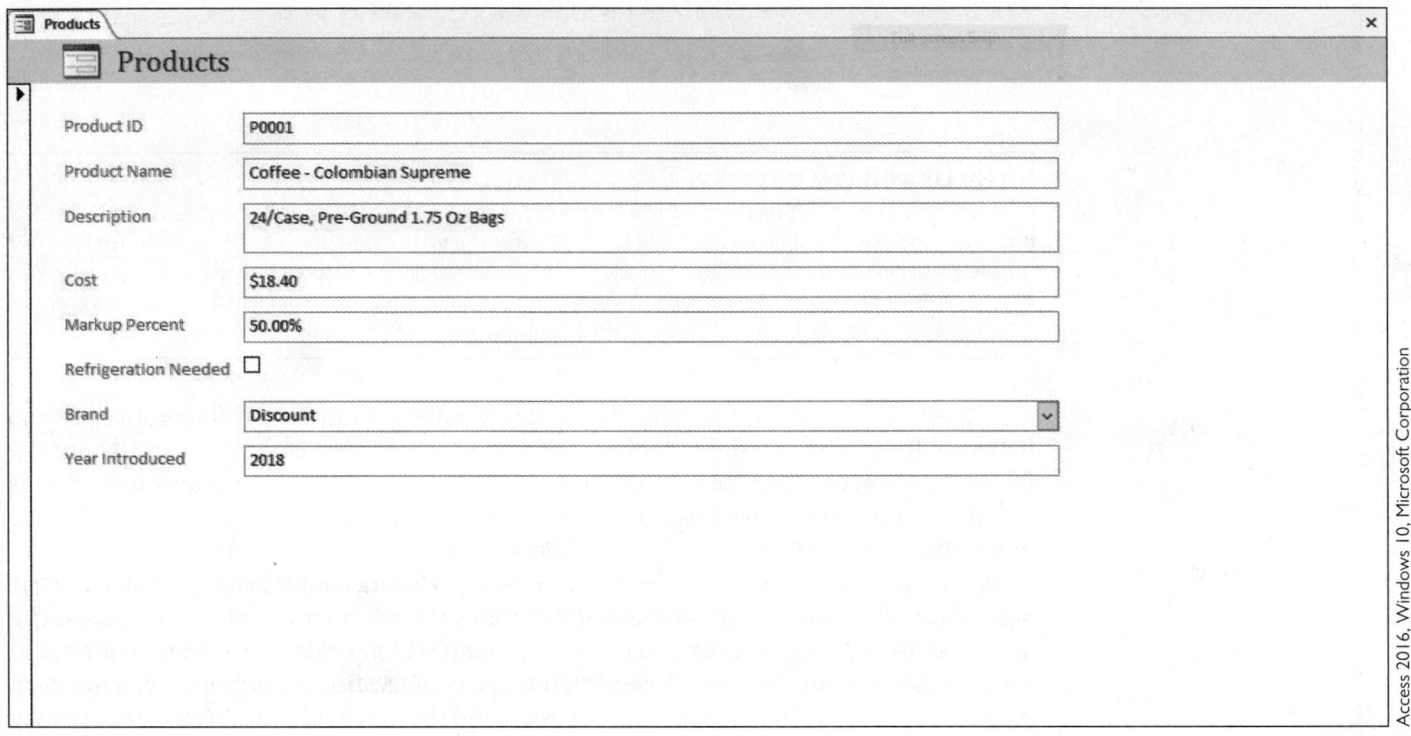

FIGURE 4.2 Form with a Stacked Layout

Understand Controls

Controls are the text boxes, buttons, labels, and other tools you use to add, edit, and display the data in a form or report. Notice in Figure 4.3 that each field has a label on the left and a text box on the right, both of which are referred to as controls. The form controls that display values are generally text box controls, and the boxes describing those values are label controls. In Figure 4.3, Product ID, Product Name, Description, etc. are label controls. The boxes containing the values for each field (P0001, Coffee–Colombian Supreme, etc.) are text box controls.

A *layout control* provides guides to help keep controls aligned horizontally and vertically and give your form a neat appearance, as shown in Figure 4.3.

There may be times when you will select controls in order to format, delete, or move them during your design process. To select an individual control, click the text box or the label as needed.

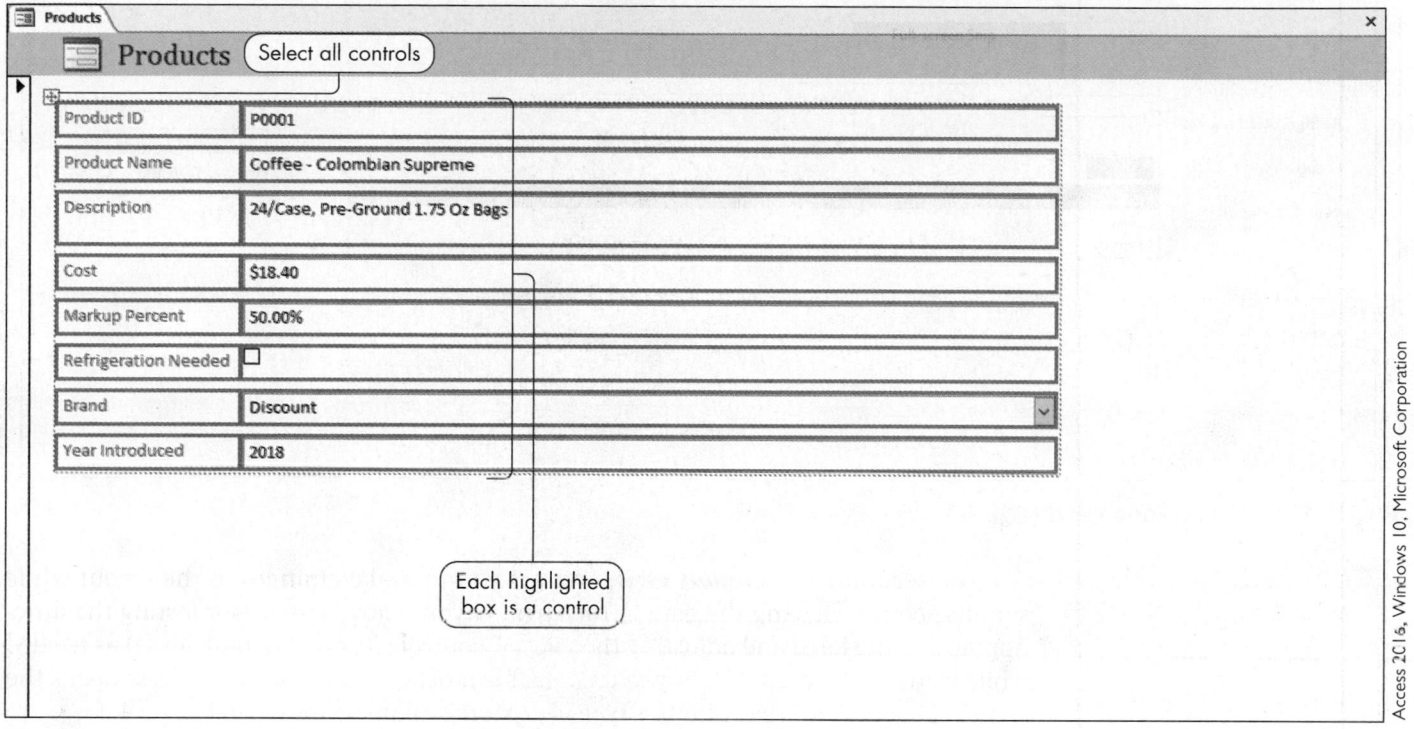

FIGURE 4.3 Form with Label and Text Box Controls

Work with Form Views

There are three different views of a form available. The first, **_Form view_**, is the user interface primarily used for data entry and modification. You cannot make changes to the form layout or design in Form view. Figure 4.4 shows a form in Form view. Notice that forms can be designed to include time-saving features such as drop-down lists and check boxes.

Access 2016, Windows 10, Microsoft Corporation

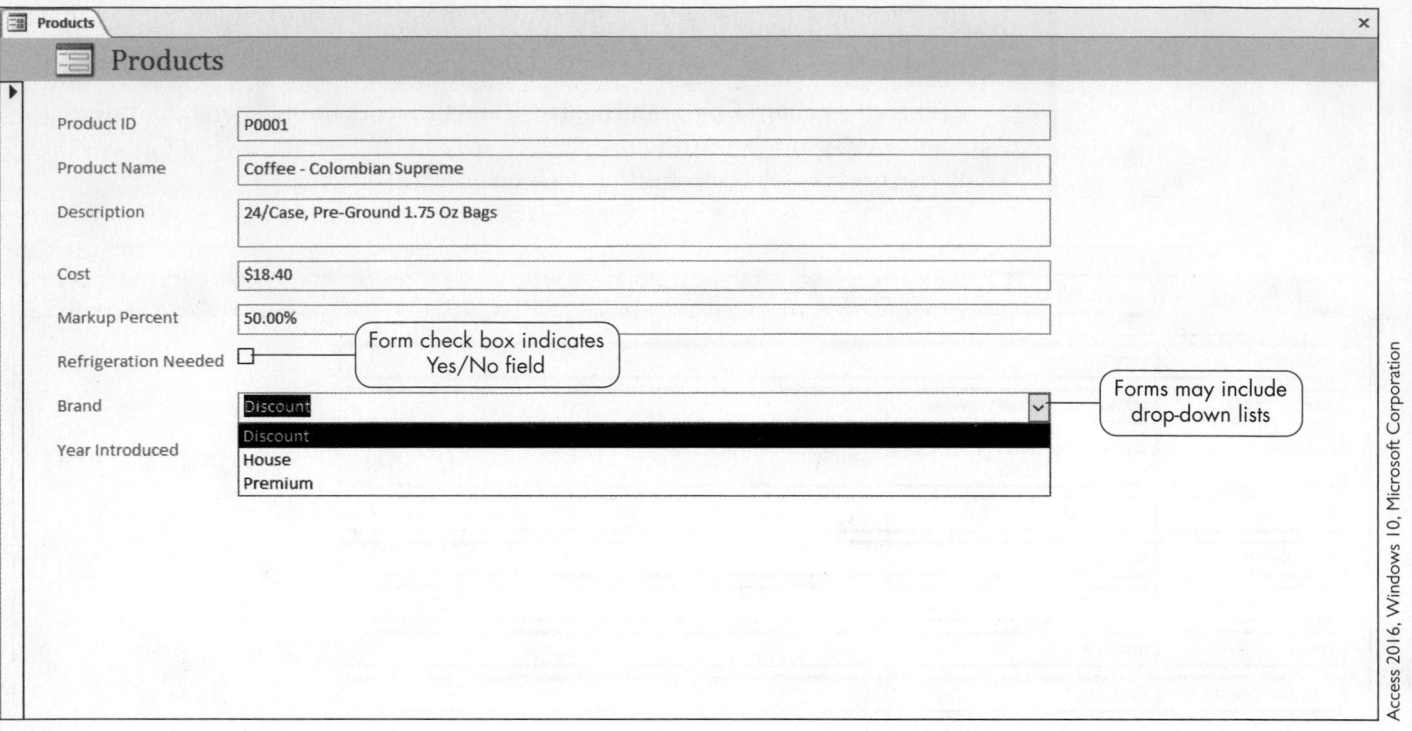

FIGURE 4.4 Form in Form View

The second view, ***Layout view***, enables you to make changes to the layout while simultaneously viewing the data in the form. Layout view is useful for testing the functionality of the form and adjusting the sizes of controls (text boxes and labels) as needed while viewing the data. When you create a form using the Form tool, Access opens the form in Layout view, ready for this type of customization, as shown in Figure 4.5.

Access 2016, Windows 10, Microsoft Corporation

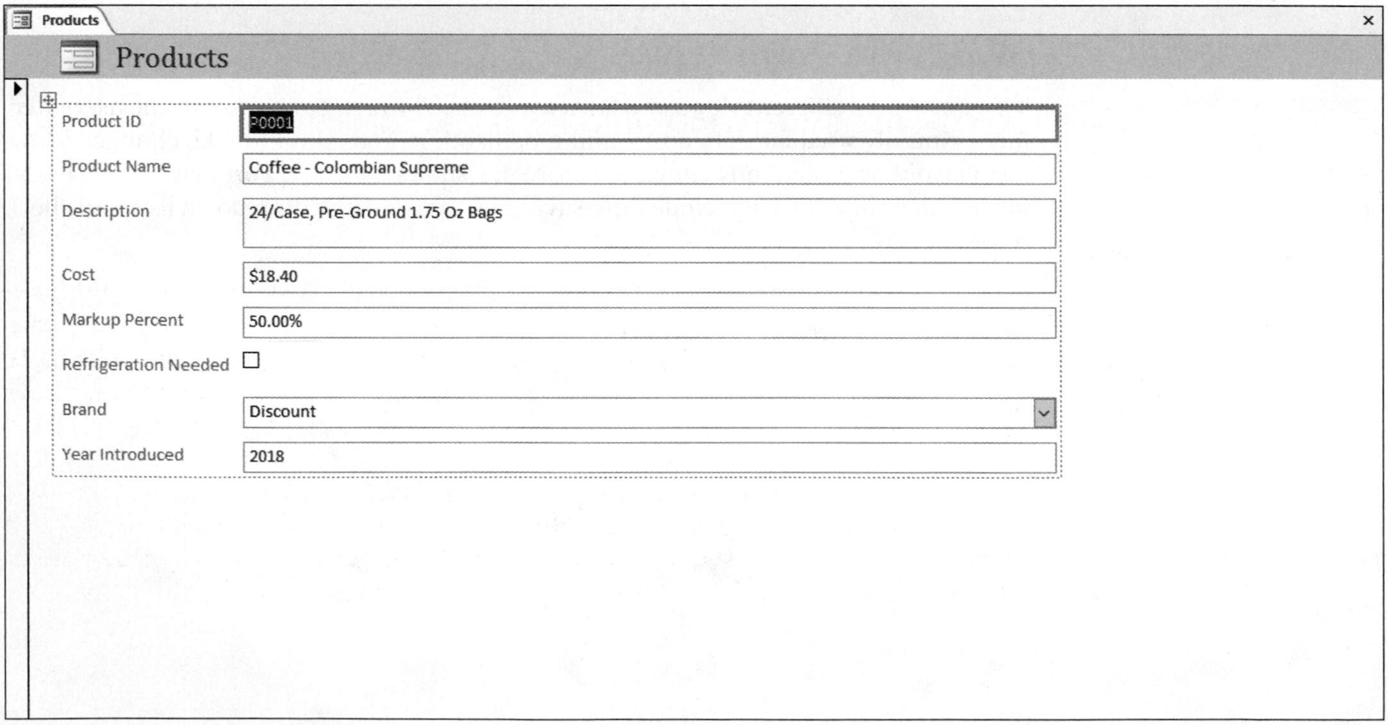

FIGURE 4.5 Form in Layout View

The third view, **Design view**, enables you to change advanced design settings that are not available in Layout view, such as removing a layout control, and gives you even more control over form design. Many forms can be made by toggling back and forth between Layout view for modifications and Form view for usability testing; however, Design view offers possibilities for more advanced adjustments. Figure 4.6 shows a form in Design view. Form views will be described in more detail later in this chapter.

To switch between the Form views, with the form open, click the View arrow in the Views group on the Home tab, and then select Form View, Layout View, or Design View. Alternatively, click the View buttons on the status bar at the bottom of the Access window, or right-click the form's window tab and select an option from the shortcut menu.

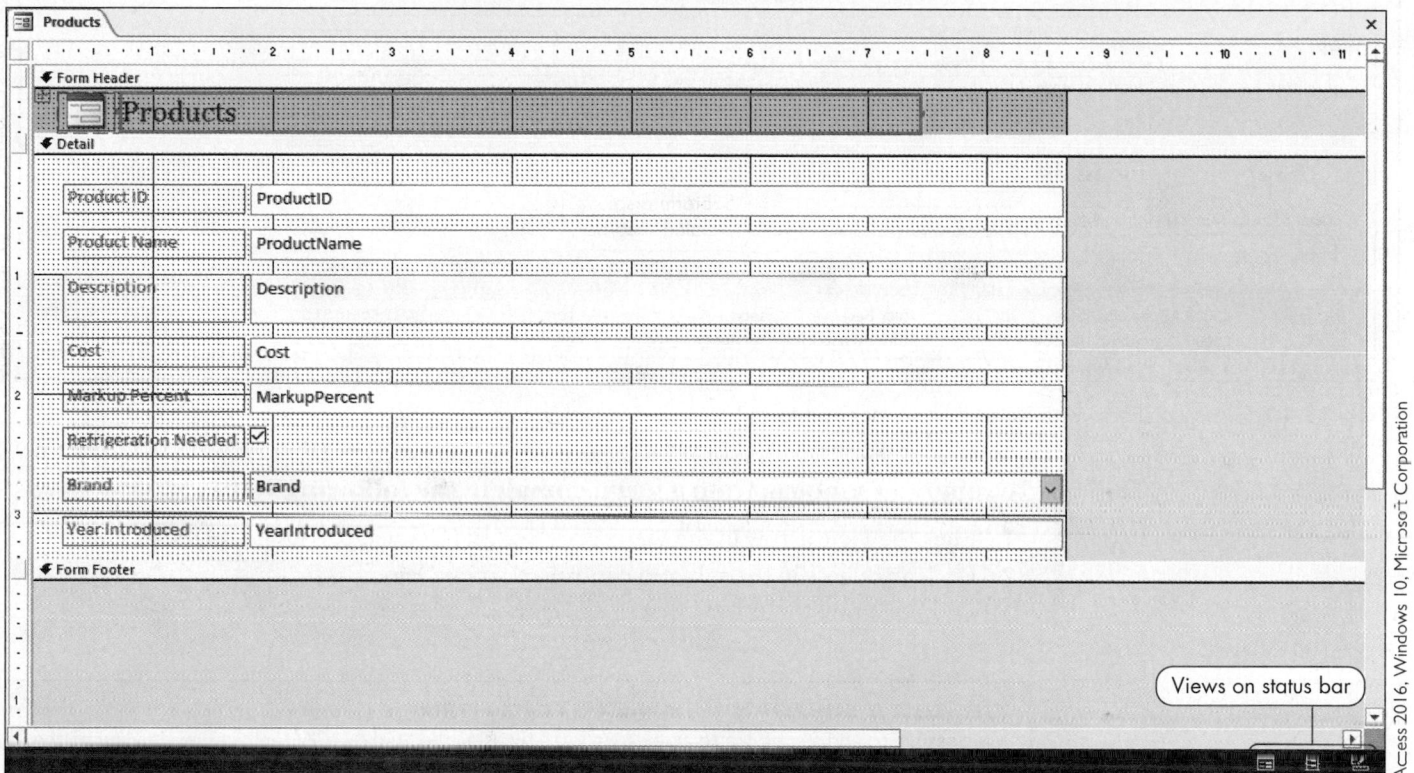

FIGURE 4.6 Form in Design View

Work with a Subform

When you use the Form tool to create a form, Access analyzes the table relationships in the database. If the table that the main form is based upon is related to another table, Access automatically adds a subform to the main form. The subform displays records in the related table, generally laid out in a datasheet format. For example, assume you have sales representatives stored in a Sales Reps table and related customer information stored in a Customers table. In this example, if you create a new form based on the Sales Reps table using the Form tool, Access will add a Customers subform to the bottom of the main form, displaying all customers assigned to each sales representative (see Figure 4.7). At times, you may want the subform as part of your form; at other times, you may want to remove it if it is not relevant to the requirements of the form design.

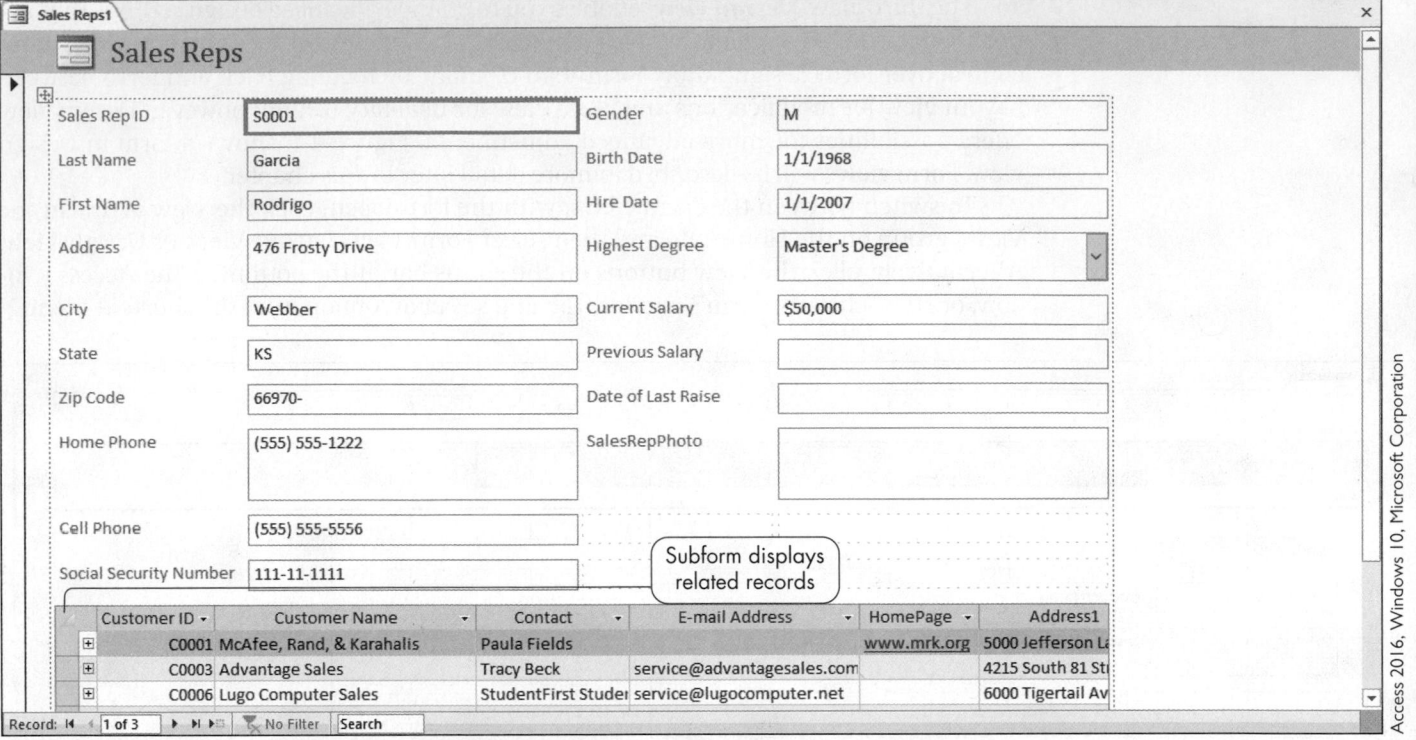

FIGURE 4.7 Sales Reps Form with Related Customers Subform

> **To remove a subform from a form, complete the following steps:**
>
> 1. Click the View arrow in the Views group on the Home tab, and select Design View.
> 2. Click anywhere in the subform control and press Delete.
> 3. Save the form.

> **TIP: ADD A SUBFORM TO AN EXISTING FORM**
> It is possible to add a subform to an existing form by using the SubForm Wizard. In Design view of the form, in the Controls group, click the Subform/Subreport tool, and then click in the form where you want the subform to display. The wizard will prompt you for the record source and through the steps for creating the subform.

Create a Split Form

A *split form* combines two views of the same record source—by default; the top section is displayed in a stacked layout (Form view) and the bottom section is displayed in a tabular layout (Datasheet view). If you select a record in the top section of the form, the same record will be selected in the bottom section of the form and vice versa. For example, if you create a split form based on an Orders table, you can select an Order in the bottom (datasheet) section and then enter or edit the order's information in the top (Form view) section (see Figure 4.8). This gives you the option to navigate between orders more quickly in the bottom section, and then when you locate the one you need, you can move to the top section to work with the record in Form view; however, you can add, edit, or delete records in either section. The splitter bar divides the form into two halves. You can adjust the splitter bar up or down (unless this option is disabled).

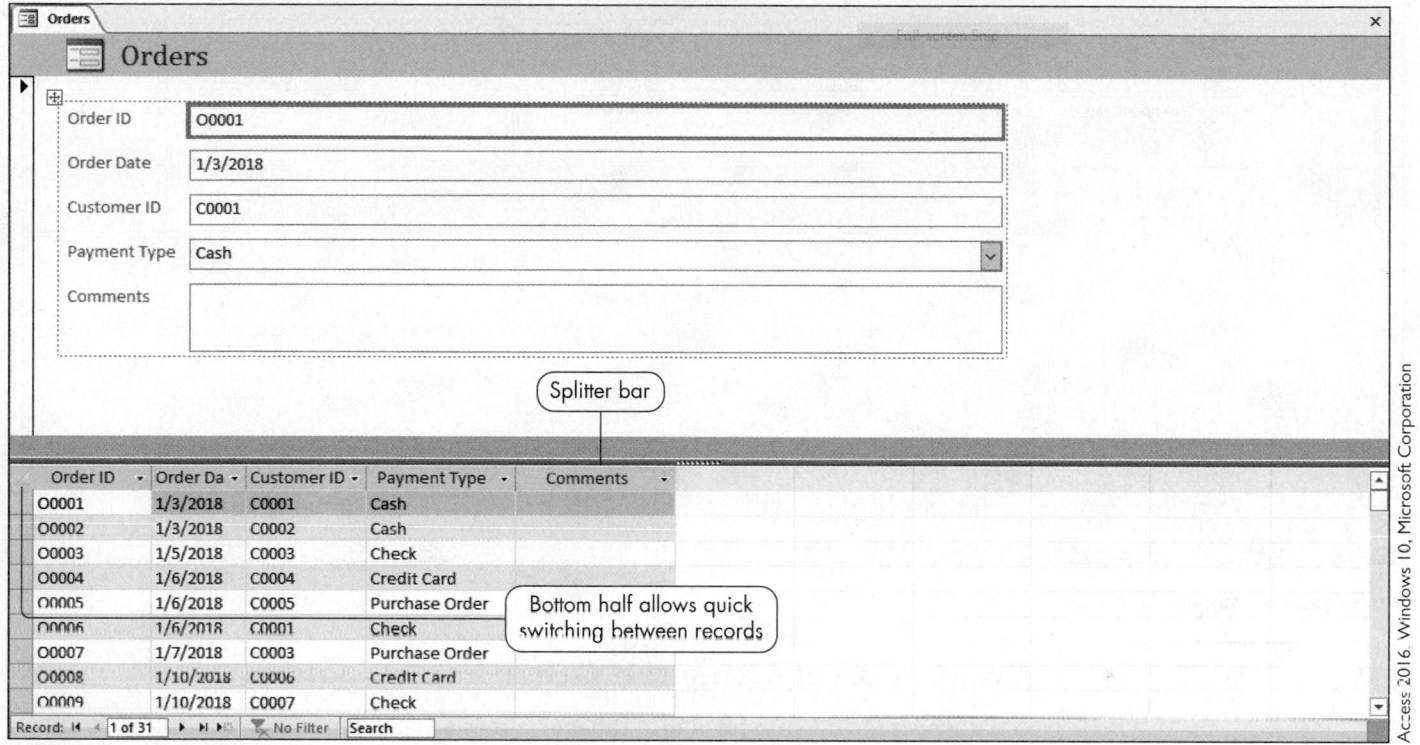

FIGURE 4.8 Split Form

Create a Multiple Items Form

A **multiple items form** displays multiple records in a tabular layout similar to a table's Datasheet view. However, a multiple items form provides you with more customization options than a datasheet, such as the ability to add graphical elements, buttons, and other controls. Figure 4.9 shows a multiple items form created from the Sales Rep table.

⊞ Sales Reps

Sales Rep ID	Last Name	First Name	Address	City	State	Zip Code	Home Phone
S0001	Garcia	Rodrigo	476 Frosty Drive	Webber	KS	66970-	(555) 555-1222
S0002	Xu	Huan	371 Rodeo Circle	Mine Hill	NJ	07803-	(555) 555-1222
S0003	Mukopadhyay	Priyanka	842 Purcell Road	Mount Vernon	NY	10557-	(555) 555-1222
* (New)							

Record: I◄ ◄ 1 of 3 ► ►I ►⊞ ▼ No Filter Search ◄

Access 2016, Windows 10, Microsoft Corporation

FIGURE 4.9 Multiple Items Form

Create Forms Using the Other Form Tools

A datasheet form is a replica of a table or query's Datasheet view except that it allows form properties to be set to control the behavior of the form. For example, you can create a datasheet form to display data in a table-like format but change the form's property so as not to allow a record to be deleted. This protects the data from accidental deletions while still providing users with the familiar Datasheet view.

> **TIP: FORM PROPERTIES**
> A form's Property Sheet enables you to control the behavior and formatting of controls in your forms. To access the Property Sheet, from Layout view or Design view, click Property Sheet in the Tools group on the Design tab. At the top of the Property Sheet, use the list arrow to select a control; you will see multiple tabs containing many individual attributes of the selected control that you can change. For example, the Format tab contains options for changing the styling of a control.

The Form Design tool and the Blank Form tools can be used to create forms manually from scratch in Design view or Layout view, respectively. Use these form types if you want to have complete control over your form's design. In either case, after opening a completely blank form, click Add Existing Fields in the Tools group on the Design tab, and then add the necessary fields by dragging and dropping them onto the blank form from the Field List pane.

The Navigation commands in the Forms group enable you to create user interfaces that have the look and feel of Web-based forms and enable users to open and close the objects of a database. For example, you can create a form that enables users to click buttons for the various forms, reports, and other objects that you want them to view in the database. This is an excellent way to simplify the database navigation for data-entry personnel who may not be that familiar with navigating in Access. These forms are also useful for setting up an Access database on the Internet.

The Modal Dialog Form tool can be used to create a dialog box. This feature is useful when you need to gather information from the user or provide information to the user, such as a message. Dialog boxes are common in all Microsoft Office applications.

...and Using Professional Forms and Reports

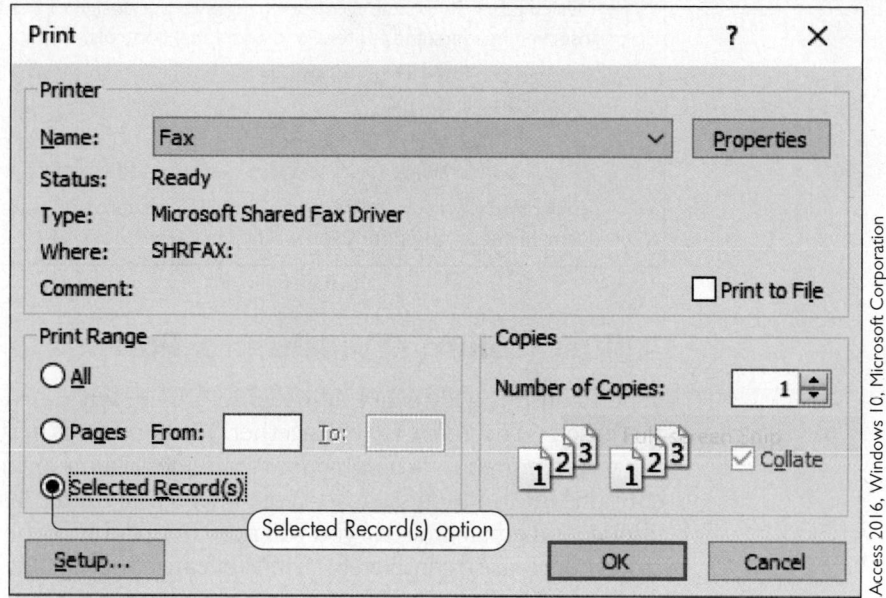

FIGURE 4.10 Print Selected Records Using a Form

Modifying Forms

As previously mentioned, Access provides different views for a form; most forms display Layout, Form, and Design views. As you work with the form tools to create and modify forms, you will need to switch between the three form views in Access. Much of your design work can be done in Layout view; sometimes, you will need to switch to Design view to use a more advanced feature, such as changing the order of the fields as you press Tab to move from one to the next, or to use an option that is otherwise unavailable. Users of the form will typically only work in Form view; there is little reason for a user to switch to Layout or Design view, and these views can be disabled by the database designer to protect the integrity of the form. Modifications to the form should ideally be done only by a designated designer.

Use Form View to Edit Data

STEP 2 ❯❯ Use Form view to add, edit, and delete data in a form; the layout and design of the form cannot be changed in this view. The Navigation bar at the bottom of the form provides buttons to move between records, and you can click the New (blank) record button to add a new record. You can move from one field to another field by pressing the Tab key or clicking the desired field with your mouse.

Use Layout View to Modify Form Design

Use Layout view to alter the form design while viewing the data. The data is not editable in this view. You use Layout view to add or delete fields in a form, change the order of fields, modify field or form properties (such as which views are available), change the control widths, and enhance a form by adding a theme or styling. Reviewing the data in

Layout view makes it easier to size controls, and to ensure that all data is visible in Form view. It is good practice to toggle back and forth between Layout view and Form view when making changes to the form's design.

TIP: USE THE FORM LAYOUT TOOLS TABS

Forms have a number of options that you can use in your design process. In Layout view, you have access to three contextual tabs on the Ribbon that provide a number of tools for modifying forms as follows:

- Design tab: Use this tab to make changes to the design of the form, such as applying themes, inserting headers and footers, and additional controls.
- Arrange tab: Use this tab to change the layout of a form, to move fields up or down, or to control margins.
- Format tab: Use this tab to work with fonts, font size, and colors, to add or remove bolding, italics, or underlining, adjust text alignment, or add a background image.

    Similarly, in Design view, the Form Design Tools tabs are available (Design, Arrange, and Format) with many of the same options you will find in Layout view.

Adjust Column Widths in a Form

When column widths are adjusted in a form with a stacked layout, all field sizes will increase and decrease in size together. Therefore, it is best to make sure that the columns are wide enough to accommodate the widest value in each field. For example, if a form contains information such as a customer's first name, last name, address, city, state, ZIP, phone, and email address, you will need to make sure the longest address and the longest email address are completely visible (because those fields are likely to contain the longest data values).

To increase or decrease column widths in a form with a stacked layout, complete the following steps:

1. Display the form in (Stacked) Layout view, and click the text box control of the first field to select it.
2. Point to the right border of the control until the pointer turns into a double-headed arrow. Drag the right edge of the control to the left or right until you arrive at the desired width.

You will notice that all field sizes change as you change the width of the first field. All fields that are included in the layout will have a standard width. If you want to resize one specific field, you will remove that field from the layout control. Select the field and the label to be removed, right-click, and then from the shortcut menu, click Layout, and select Remove Layout. If you remove a field from the layout control, it stays on the form but can be moved and resized more freely.

Add and Delete Form Fields

STEP 3 ⟩⟩ There will be instances when you will want to add or delete form fields. At times, new fields may be added to tables and then need to be incorporated into forms. At other times, you may decide that while a field is present in a table, it is not necessary to display it to users in a form.

To add a field to a form, complete the following steps:

1. Display the form in (Stacked) Layout view, and click Add Existing Fields in the Tools group on the Design tab.

   A Field List pane displays at the right of the form. For a single-table form, you will see a list of fields from the table (record source). For a multiple-table form, click the plus sign (+) to the left of the appropriate table to expand it, and locate the desired field(s).

2. Click and drag the desired field to the precise location on the form, using the shaded line as a guide for positioning the new field. Alternatively, you can double-click a field to add it to the form; the field will be added below the selected field. The other fields will automatically adjust to make room for the new field, as shown in Figure 4.11.

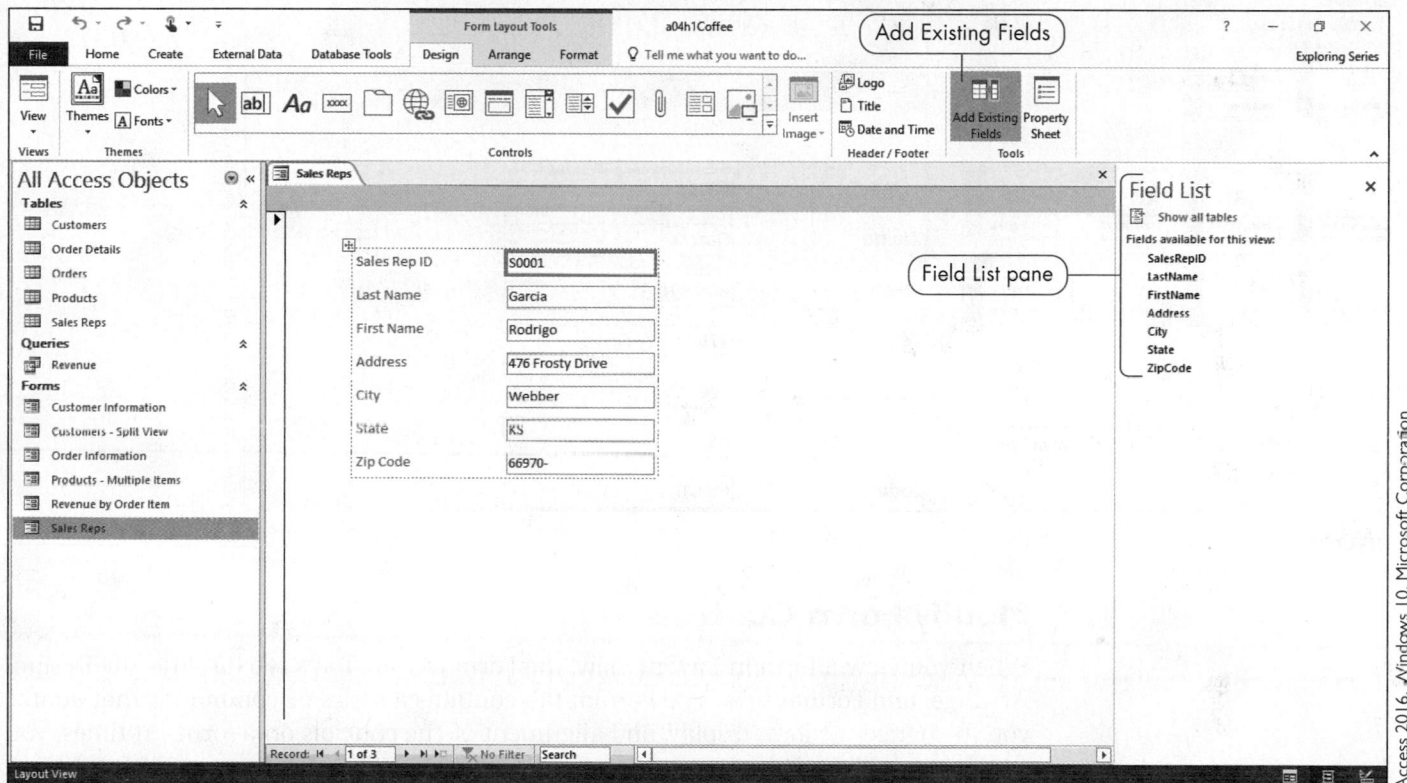

FIGURE 4.11 Add Fields to a Form

To delete a field from a form, complete the following steps:

1. Display the form in (Stacked) Layout view, and click the text box control of the field to be deleted (note the shaded border around the control).

2. Click Select Row in the Rows & Columns group on the Arrange tab in order to select the text box and its associated label. Alternatively, click the text box control, press and hold Ctrl, and then click the associated label control to select them both.

3. Press Delete.

The other fields will automatically adjust to close the gap around the deleted field.

Add a Theme to a Form

You can apply a theme to a form in order to give the form a more professional appearance. A *theme* is a defined set of colors, fonts, and graphics that can be applied to forms (or reports). In Layout or Design view, click Themes in the Themes group on the Design tab, point to a theme to see its name in the ScreenTip and a Live Preview of the theme in the form, and then click to select it. By default, the theme will be applied to all objects in your database.

Right-click a theme in the gallery to apply it to the current form only or to all the forms in your database that share a common theme. You can create customized themes and save them on your system so that they can be used again. Apply your custom settings, and then click the Save Current Theme command, as shown in Figure 4.12.

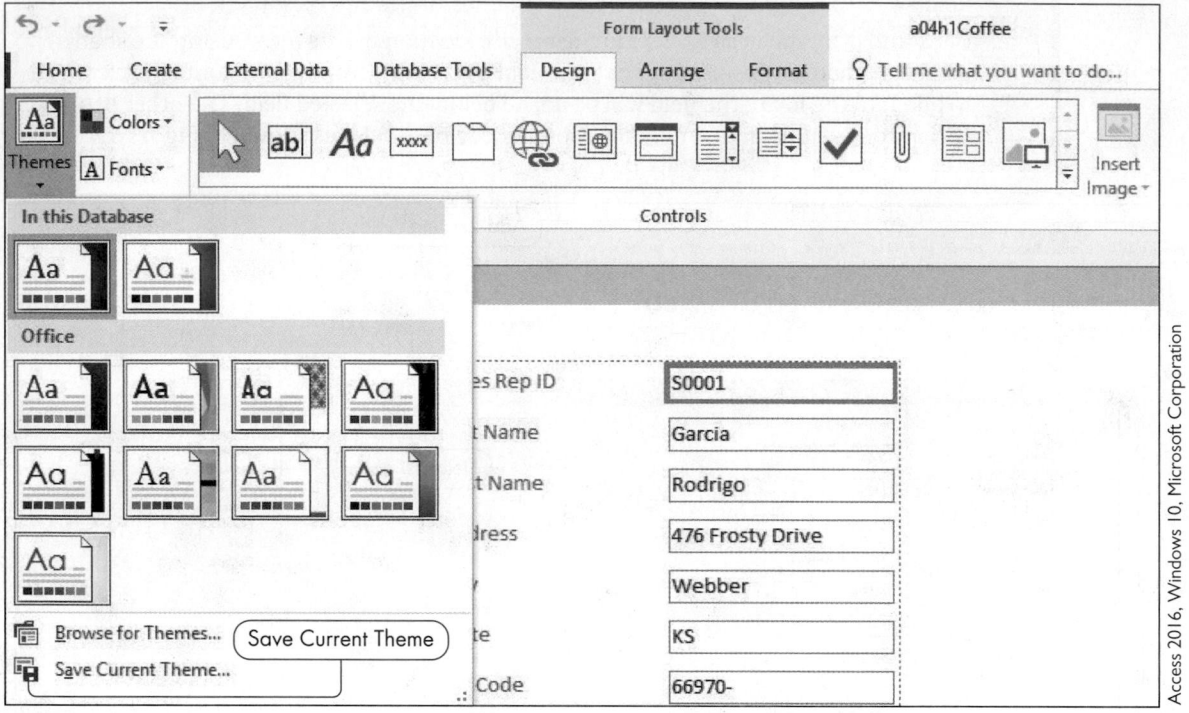

FIGURE 4.12 Add a Theme to a Form

Modify Form Controls

When you view a form in Layout view, the Form Layout Tools tab displays the Design, Arrange, and Format tabs. The Format tab contains a series of commands that enable you to change the font, display, and alignment of the controls on a form. At times, you may want to change the formatting of one or more controls. For example, if you have a form that shows the information about the sale of vehicles, you might want to emphasize the net profit of each transaction by changing the font or background color of the control.

From the Form Layout Tools Format tab, you can change a number of control attributes. Table 4.2 illustrates some of commands you would likely use.

TABLE 4.2 Common Formats for Form Controls

Font size	Click the Font Size arrow in the Font group.
Font emphasis	Click Bold, Italic, or Underline in the Font group.
Alignment	Click Align Left, Center, or Align Right in the Font group.
Background color	Click the Background Color arrow in the Font group.
Font color	Click the Font Color arrow in the Font group.
Number format	Use the tools in the Number group to select number formats such as Currency, Percent, Comma formatting, or to increase or decrease decimal places.

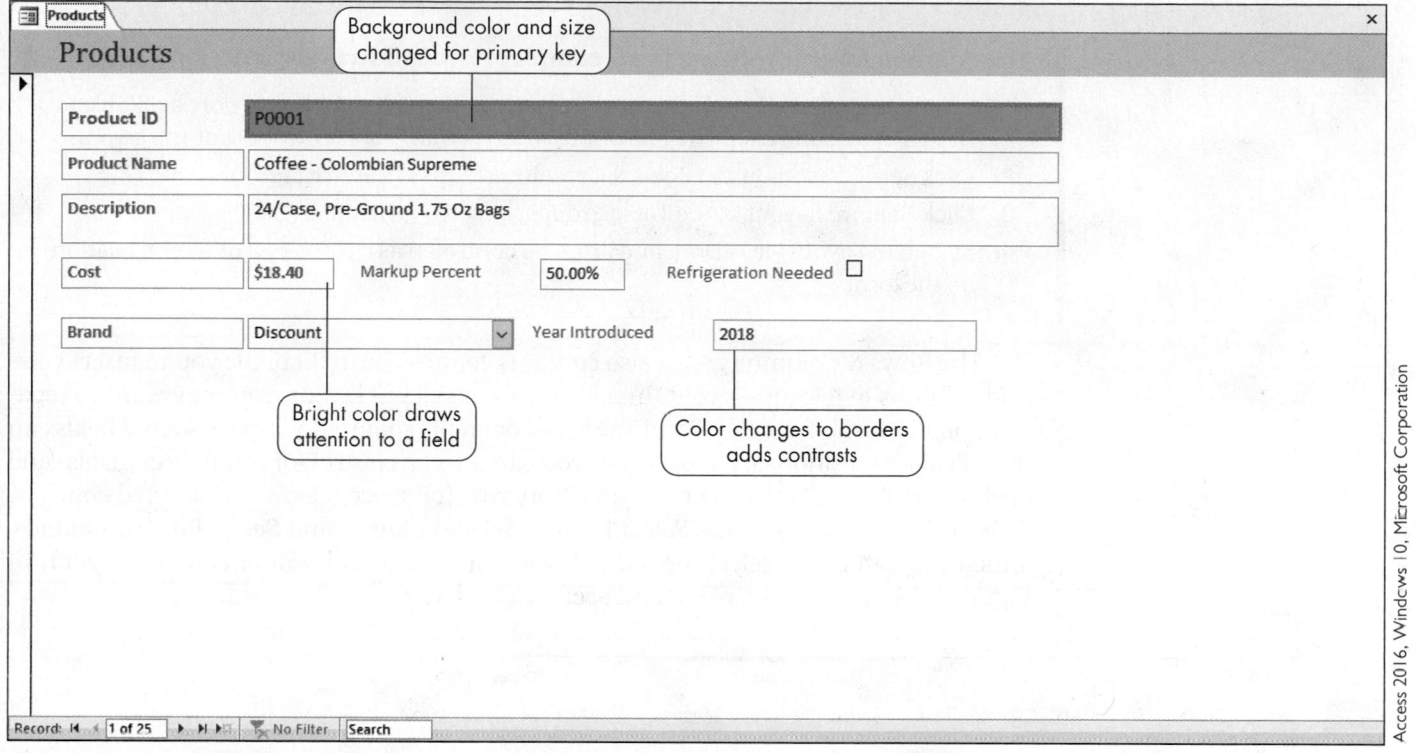

FIGURE 4.13 A Well-Designed Form with Styling

Working with a Form Layout

When you use one of the form tools to create a new form, Access adds a layout control to help align the fields. The layout control helps keep controls aligned in order to give your form a neat appearance. The layout control provides structure for the fields, but is somewhat restrictive. If you want to have more control over the location of your fields, you can remove the layout control and position the controls manually on the form.

To remove a control from a layout and reposition it, complete the following steps:

1. Select the field and the label to be removed, right-click, and from the shortcut menu, point to Layout and then select Remove Layout.
2. Drag and drop the control(s) as desired to a different location on the form.

Modify a Form Layout

STEP 4 ➤➤ You can use the tools on the Arrange tab to change the layout of a form, to move fields up and down, and to control margins. The Arrange tab displays in both Layout view and Design view.

The Table group of the Arrange tab contains commands that enable you to add gridlines to a form's layout, change the layout from stacked to tabular (and vice versa), or remove the layout (the Remove Layout command is available only in Design view).

To apply or change the layout of a form, complete the following steps:

1. Open the form in Layout or Design view.
2. Select multiple controls by clicking the first control, pressing and holding Ctrl, and then clicking the additional controls you want to include in the layout. To select all of the controls on a form, press Ctrl+A. If the controls already have a layout applied, click any control that is part of the layout, and click Select Layout in the Rows & Columns group on the Arrange tab.
3. Click Tabular or Stacked in the Table group on the Arrange tab.

To remove a form layout control, complete the following steps:

1. Switch to Design view (the Remove Layout option on the Ribbon is only available in Design view), and click any one of the controls that is currently part of the layout.
2. Click Select Layout in the Rows & Columns group on the Arrange tab.
3. Click Remove Layout in the Table group.
4. Switch to Layout view. Drag and drop the control(s) as desired to a different location on the form.

The Rows & Columns group also contains commands that enable you to insert rows and columns in a form's layout. In a form with a stacked layout, you may want to separate some controls from the rest of the fields, or create some empty space so that fields can be added or repositioned. For example, you can select a control (or multiple controls) and click Insert Below. This will create an empty row (or space) below the selected controls. This group also contains the Select Layout, Select Column, and Select Row commands, which you can use to select the entire layout, or a single column or row in a layout. In Figure 4.14, three empty rows have been inserted above the Cost field.

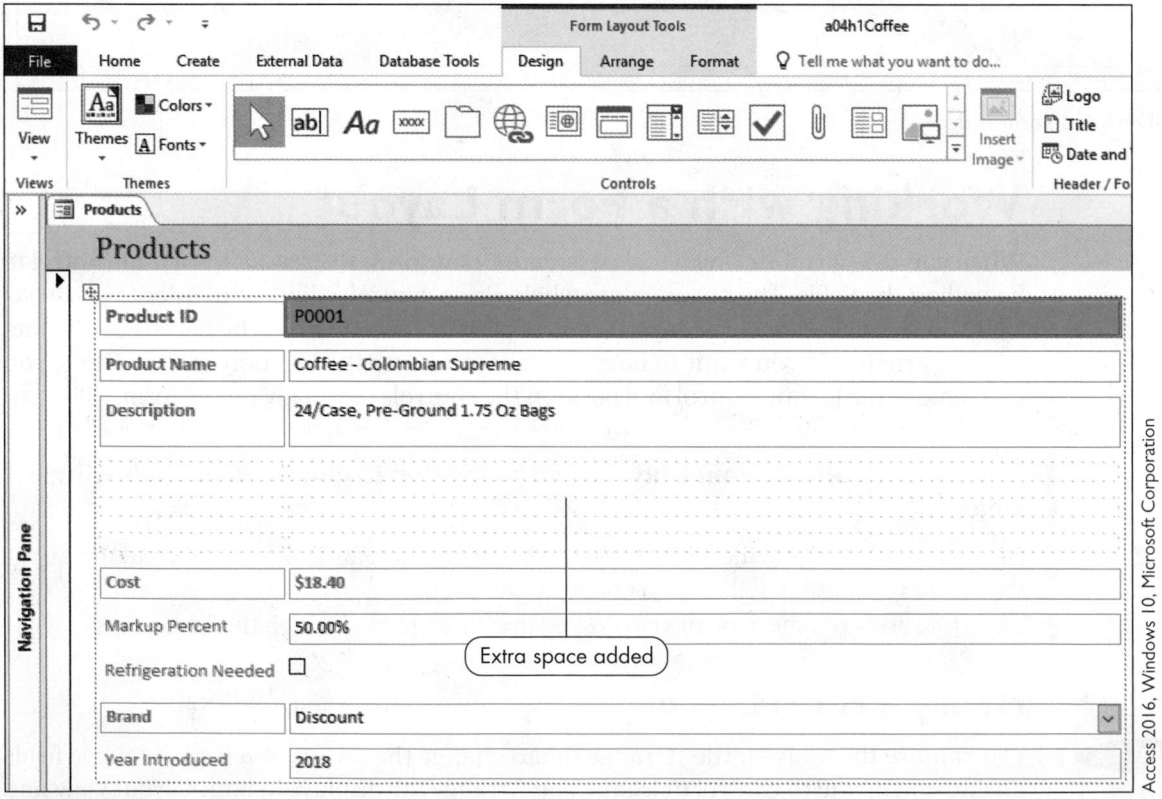

FIGURE 4.14 Rows Inserted in a Form Layout

TIP: APPLY A BACKGROUND IMAGE TO A FORM

To apply a background image to a form, open the form in Layout or Design view, and then click Background Image in the Background group on the Format tab. Next, click Browse to locate the image you want to apply to the form. Once the image has been applied to the form, you can change the properties of the image so that the image displays correctly. You can use the same tecÚique to add a background image to a report.

Sorting Records in a Form

When a form is created using a Form tool, the sort order of the records in the form is initially dependent on the sort order of the record source—the underlying table or query. Tables are usually sorted by the primary key, whereas queries are generally sorted in a variety of ways. No matter how the records are initially sorted, you can modify the sort order in a form. Adding and removing sorts are shown in Figure 4.15.

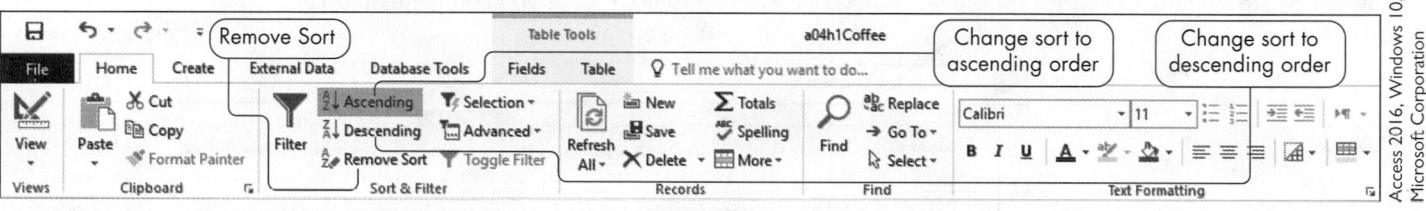

FIGURE 4.15 Adding and Removing Sort Order

Sort by a Single Field

You can easily sort on a single field, in ascending or descending order. The sort order in a form can be different from the sort order of an underlying table or query.

> **To sort by a single field, complete the following steps:**
>
> 1. Open the form in Form view, and select the field by which you want to sort.
> 2. Click Ascending or Descending in the Sort & Filter group on the Home tab.

If you want to sort on multiple fields, you can create a query with a more advanced sort order, and then base the form on the query. Open the query in Design view, add the sort settings you want, save the query, and then use the query as the record source of the form. To remove the sort order in a form, open the form in Form view, then click Remove Sort in the Sort & Filter group on the Home tab.

Quick Concepts

1. How does a form simplify data entry (when compared to entering data into a table)? **p. 864**

2. What is the record source of a form? **p. 865**

3. What is the advantage of creating a form with a subform? **p. 869**

4. Why is using a layout control to keep your form fields in a neat arrangement sometimes a disadvantage? **p. 866**

Hands-On Exercises

Watch the Video for this Hands-On Exercise!

MyITLab®
HOE1 Training

Skills covered: Create a Form Using the Form Tool • Create a Split Form • Create a Multiple Items Form • Edit Data in Form View • Delete a Field • Add a Field • Format Controls • Add a Theme • Modify a Form Layout • Sort Records in a Form

1 Form Basics

After talking with Ryung about her data-entry needs, you decide to create several sample forms using different formats. You will show each form to Ryung to get feedback and see if she has any preferences.

STEP 1 ›› CREATE FORMS USING FORM TOOLS

You will create a number of forms using different layouts. Refer to Figure 4.16 as you complete Step 1.

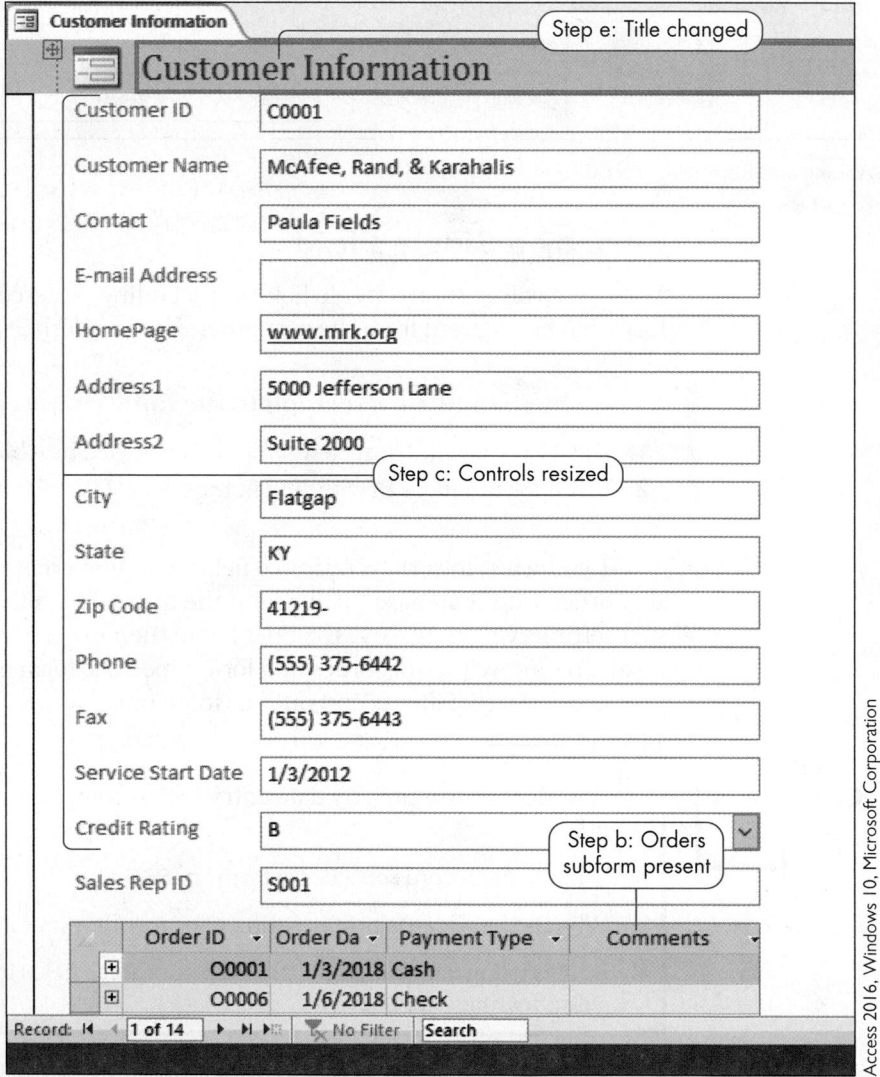

FIGURE 4.16 Customer Information Form

a. Open *a04h1Coffee* and save it as **a04h1Coffee_LastFirst**.

> **TROUBLESHOOTING:** Throughout the remainder of this chapter and textbook, click Enable Content whenever you are working with the student data files.

> **TROUBLESHOOTING:** If you make any major mistakes in this exercise, you can close the file, open *a04h1Coffee* again, and then start this exercise over.

b. Click the **Customers table** in the Navigation Pane to select the table but not to open it. Click the **Create tab**, and then click **Form** in the Forms group.

Access creates a new form with two record sources—Customers (with stacked layout, on top) and Orders (with datasheet layout, below). Access detected a one-to-many relationship between the Customers and Orders tables, and so it created a main form with its associated subform below it. The form opens in Layout view.

c. Ensure that the top text box containing *C0001* is selected. The text box is outlined with a shaded border. Move the pointer to the right edge of the shaded border until the pointer changes to a double-headed arrow. Drag the right edge to the left until the text box is approximately half of its original size.

All of the text boxes and the subform at the bottom adjust in size when you adjust the top text box. This is a characteristic of Layout view—enabling you to modify all controls at once.

> **TROUBLESHOOTING:** You may need to maximize the Access window or close the Navigation Pane if the right edge of the text box is not visible.

d. Ensure that the labels to the left of the text boxes display without being cut off. If they are cut off, adjust the size of the labels as you did in Step c.

e. Click **Save** on the Quick Access Toolbar, and then type **Customer Information** as the form name in the **Save As dialog box**. Click **OK**.

f. Click the **Customers title** at the top of the form to select it, click the title again, and then change the title to **Customer Information**. Press **Enter** to accept the change. Your form should now look like Figure 4.16. Save and close the form.

> **TROUBLESHOOTING:** If you make a mistake that you cannot easily recover from, consider deleting the form and creating it again. With the form closed, right-click the form name in the Navigation Pane, and from the shortcut menu, select Delete.

g. Verify that the Customers table is selected in the Navigation Pane. Click the **Create tab**, click **More Forms** in the Forms group, and then select **Split Form**.

Access creates a new form with a split view, one view in stacked layout and one view laid out like a datasheet.

h. Scroll down and click anywhere in the *Coulter Office Supplies* customer record in the bottom pane (datasheet) of the form (record 14).

The top pane shows all the information for this customer in a stacked layout view.

i. Click the **Customers title** at the top of the form to select it, click **Customers** again, and then change the title to **Customers - Split View**. Press **Enter** to accept the change.

j. Click **Save** on the Quick Access Toolbar and type **Customers - Split View** in the Form Name box Click **OK**. Close the form.

k. Click the **Products table** in the Navigation Pane. Click the **Create tab**, click **More Forms** in the Forms group, and then select **Multiple Items**.

Access creates a new multiple-item form based on the Products table. The form resembles a table's Datasheet view.

l. Click the **Products title** at the top of the form to select it, click **Products** again, and then change the title to **Products - Multiple Items**. Press **Enter** to accept the change.

m. Save the form as **Products - Multiple Items** and close the form.

n. Click the **Orders table** in the Navigation Pane. Click **Form** in the Forms group on the Create tab.

A form with a subform showing each line of the order is created.

o. Click the **Home tab**. Click the **View arrow** in the Views group, and select **Design View**. Click anywhere inside the subform and press **Delete**.

The subform is removed.

p. Switch to Form view to observe the change. Save the form as **Order Information**. Close all open objects.

STEP 2 » USE FORM VIEW TO EDIT DATA

Now that you have created several forms, you will show Ryung how to test the forms for usability Refer to Figure 4.17 as you complete Step 2.

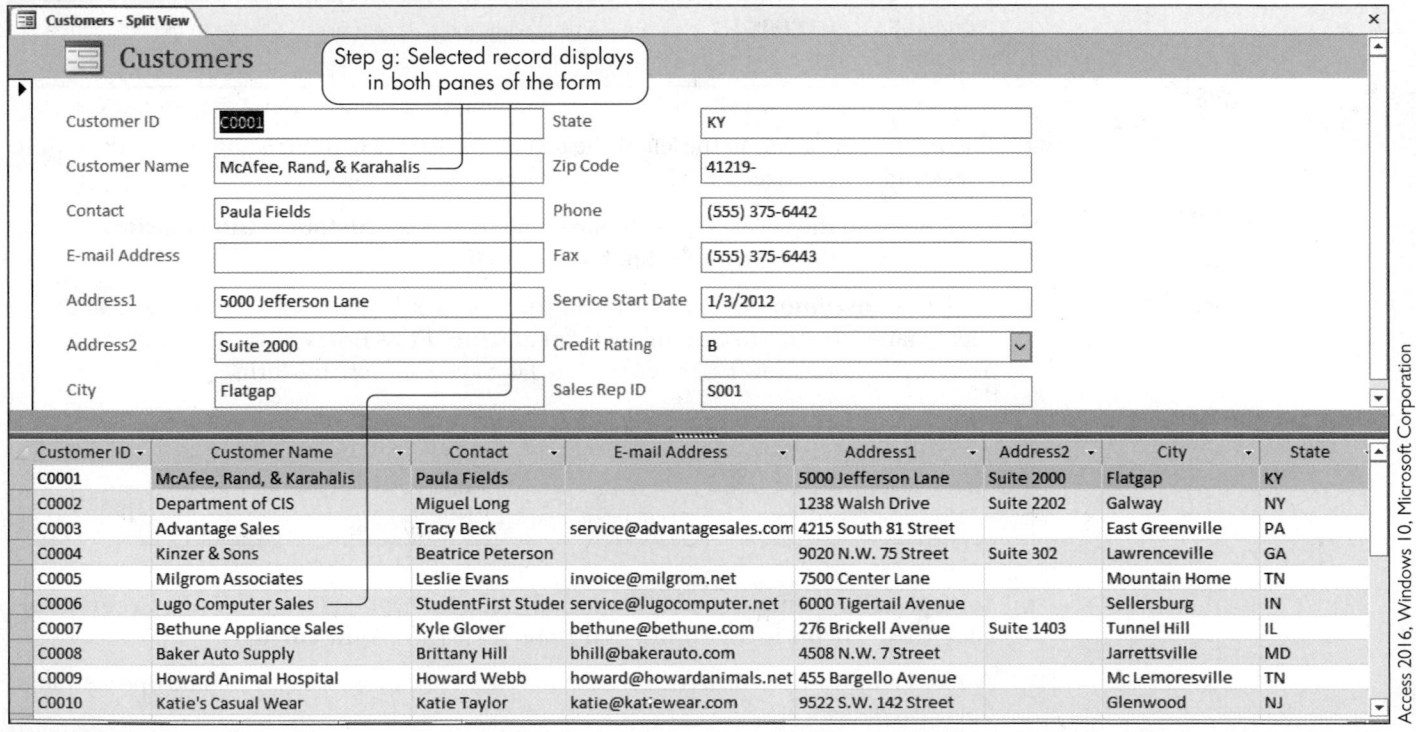

FIGURE 4.17

a. Right-click the **Customer Information form** in the Navigation Pane, and from the shortcut menu, select **Open**. Advance to the sixth customer, *Lugo Computer Sales*, using **Next record** on the Navigation bar at the bottom of the form.

> **TROUBLESHOOTING:** Two Navigation bars exist, the inside one for the subform and the bottom-most one for the main form. Make sure you use the bottom-most one that displays the record count of 14.

b. Double-click the **Customers table** in the Navigation Pane.

Two tabs now display in the main window. You will compare the table data and the form data while you make changes to both.

c. Verify that the sixth record of the Customers table is *Lugo Computer Sales*, which corresponds to the sixth record in the Customer Information form. Click the tabs to switch between the table and the form.

d. Click the **Customer Information tab** and replace *Adam Sanchez*, the contact for Lugo Computer Sales, with your name. Advance to the next record to save the changes. Click the **Customers tab** to see that the contact name changed in the table as well.

Changes to the Contact field and the other fields in the Customer Information form automatically change the data in the underlying table. Likewise, if you change data in the table, it will update automatically in the form.

> **TROUBLESHOOTING:** If the change from *Adam Sanchez* to your name does not display in the Customers table, check the Customer Information form to see if the pencil 🖉 displays in the left margin of the record. If it does, save the record by advancing to the next customer in the form and recheck to see if the name has changed in the underlying table.

e. Close the Customer Information form and the Customers table.

f. Open the Customers – Split View form. In the bottom pane of the split form, click **Lugo Computer Sales**, the sixth record. Notice that the top pane now displays the information for Lugo Computer Sales in a stacked layout. Notice also that there is an error in the email address—*service* is misspelled. In the top pane of the form, change the email address to **service@lugocomputer.net**.

g. Click another record in the bottom pane and then click back on **Lugo Computer Sales**, as shown in Figure 4.17.

The pencil disappears from the record selector box and the changes are saved to the table.

You will make some changes to the layouts based on feedback Ryung gave you after seeing the forms in action. You will also add a missing field to the main table and then add it to the form. Refer to Figure 4.18 as you complete Step 3.

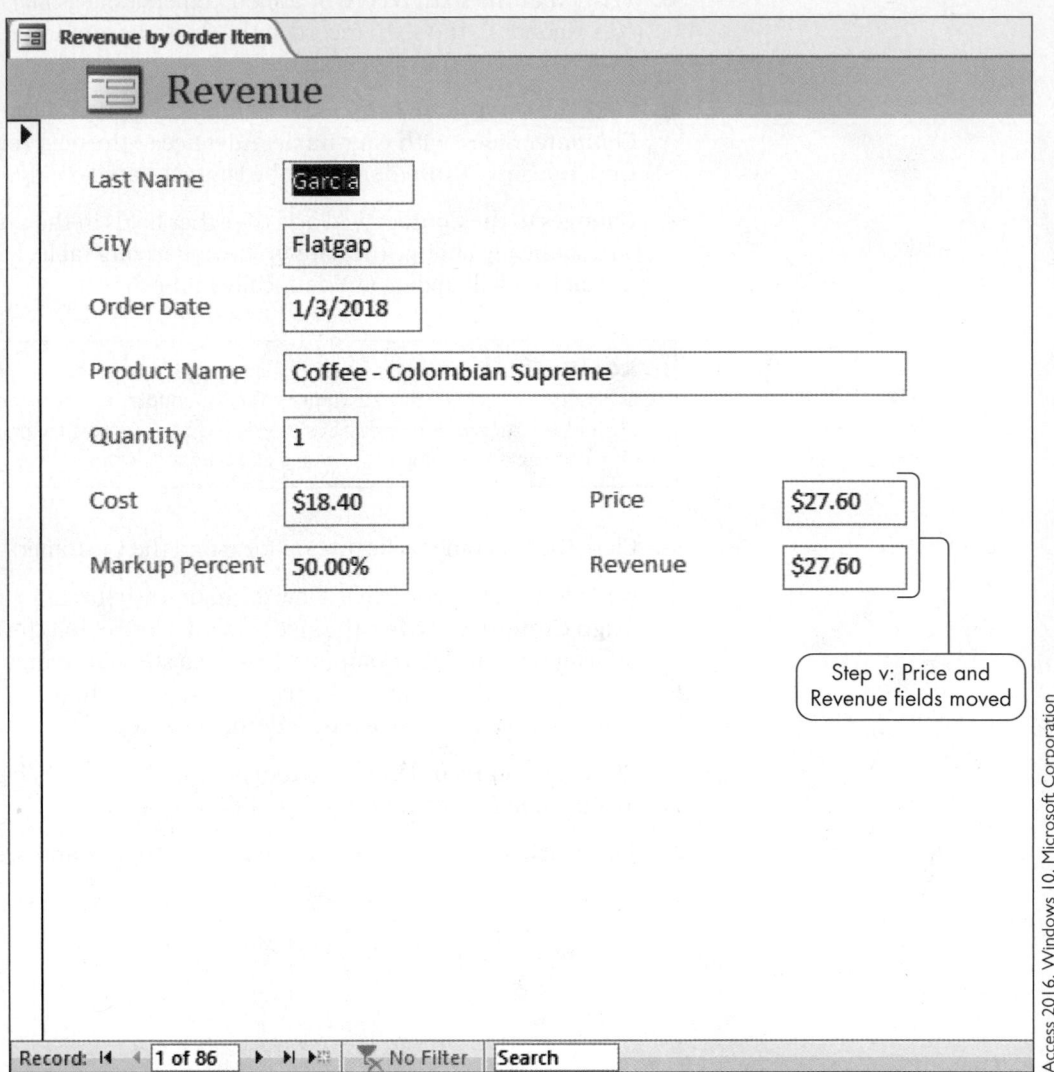

FIGURE 4.18 Completed Revenue by Order Item Form

a. Switch to Layout view with the Customers – Split View form open. Point to the **splitter bar**, the border between the top and bottom pane of the window. When the pointer shape changes to a double-headed arrow, drag the **splitter bar** until it almost touches the Sales Rep ID field. Save and close the form.

b. Open the Products – Multiple Items form in Layout view. Point to the bottom edge of **Product ID P0001** until the pointer shape changes to a double-headed arrow. Drag the bottom edge up to reduce the height of the rows so they are as tall as they need to be to accommodate the information.

   Changing the height of one row affects the height of all the rows in the form.

c. Click anywhere in the **Cost column** and click **Select Column** in the Rows & Columns group on the Arrange tab. Press **Delete** to remove the column (alternatively, right-click in the column, and from the shortcut menu, select **Delete Column**). Delete the **MarkupPercent** column.

d. Click the **Refrigeration Needed label** to select it. Change the label to the abbreviation **Refrig?** Resize the column so it is wide enough to display the label text. Save and close the form.

e. Open the Customer Information form in Layout view.

f. Click the **Design tab**. Click **Themes** in the Themes group. Right-click the **Slice theme** and select **Apply Theme to This Object Only**.

The fonts and color scheme that are built into the theme are applied.

> **TROUBLESHOOTING:** You can determine which theme is named Slice by pointing to a theme in the gallery and waiting for a ScreenTip to display. The Office theme is displayed first and the others are displayed in alphabetical order after it.

g. Click the **Format tab**. Click **Shape Fill** in the Control Formatting group. Select **Light Turquoise, Background 2** under Theme Colors.

The background color of the CustomerID field changes to light turquoise. The theme colors in the palette are those built into the Slice theme.

> **TROUBLESHOOTING:** If you do not see Light Turquoise, Background 2 in the theme colors, ensure that you have selected the Slice theme.

> **TROUBLESHOOTING:** If the entire form background changes to turquoise, click Undo and ensure that only the Customer ID text box containing *C0001* is selected.

h. Select the **Customer Name field** (which should be *McAfee, Rand, & Karahalis*). Change the font size to **16**.

The customer name appears in a larger font, setting it apart from the other fields.

i. Save and close the form.

j. Right-click the **Customers table** in the Navigation Pane, and select **Design View**.

You will add the HomePage hyperlink field to the Customers table.

k. Click the **Address1 field** and click **Insert Rows** in the Tools group on the Design tab.

A new row is inserted above the Address1 field.

l. Type **HomePage** in the blank **Field Name box** and select **Hyperlink** as the Data Type.

m. Save and close the Customers table.

n. Right-click the **Customer Information form** in the Navigation Pane, and select **Layout View**.

You will add the HomePage field to the Customer Information form.

o. Click **Add Existing Fields** in the Tools group on the Design tab to display the Field List pane.

p. Click the **HomePage field**. Drag the field from the Field List pane to the form, below the E-mail Address field, until a shaded line displays between *E-mail Address* and *Address1* and then drop it. Close the Field List pane.

Access displays a shaded line to help you place the field in the correct location.

> **TROUBLESHOOTING:** If the placement of the field is incorrect, you can click Undo and try again. Alternatively, select the label and text box controls and use the Move Up or Move Down commands in the Arrange group.

q. Switch to Form view. Press **Tab** until you reach the HomePage field, type **www.mrk.org**, and then press **Tab**.

Because HomePage is a hyperlink field, Access formats it automatically in the form.

Save and close the form.

r. Click the **Revenue query** in the Navigation Pane. Click **Form** in the Forms group on the Create tab to create a new form based on this query.

The Revenue query is the record source for the form.

s. Switch to Design view. Click the first label, **Last Name**, press and hold **Ctrl**, and then click each of the other controls (alternatively, press Ctrl+A).

You have selected all label and text box field controls (from *Last Name* down to *Revenue*).

t. Click **Remove Layout** in the Table group on the Arrange tab. Switch back to Layout view.

> **TROUBLESHOOTING:** Recall that the Remove Layout option only displays on the Ribbon in Design view, so if you do not see the button, ensure that you are in Design view.

u. Resize the controls individually so they are approximately the same sizes as shown in Figure 4.18.

v. Click the **Price control**. Press and hold **Ctrl** and click the **Revenue control**, the **Price label**, and the **Revenue label**. Drag the fields to the locations shown in Figure 4.18. Switch to Form view.

w. Save the form as **Revenue by Order Item**. Close the form.

Ryung has an old Sales Reps form that she hopes you can make easier to read but keep in the vertical format. She tested the Customer Information form and likes the way it is working; however, she asks you to change the sort order to make it easier to find customers alphabetically by their names Refer to Figure 4.19 as you complete Step 4.

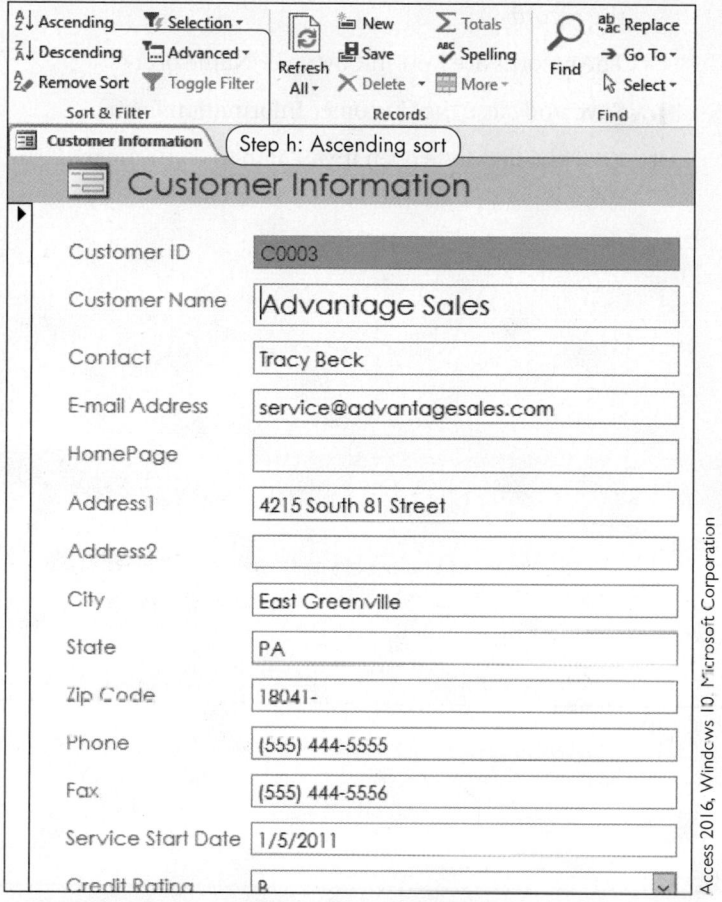

FIGURE 4.19

a. Open the Sales Reps form in Layout view. Notice that the form is not attractively laid out.

b. Click **Select All** in the Selection group on the Format tab.

All 14 controls are selected in the form.

c. Click **Tabular** in the Table group on the Arrange tab.

The controls are lined up horizontally across the top of the form.

d. Click **Stacked** in the Table group on the Arrange tab. Switch to Form view.

The controls are lined up vertically and the form is much easier to read.

e. Save and close the form.

f. Open the Customer Information form in Form view. Click **Next record** in the Navigation bar at the bottom several times to advance through the records.

Note that the customers are in Customer ID order.

g. Click **First record** in the Navigation bar to return to customer *McAfee, Rand, & Karahalis.*

h. Click in the **Customer Name text box**, and click **Ascending** in the Sort & Filter group on the Home tab.

Advantage Sales displays (Customer ID C0003), as it is the first customer name in alphabetical order, as shown in Figure 4.19.

i. Click **Next record** in the Navigation bar at the bottom of the form to advance through the records.

The records are now in Customer Name order.

j. Save and close the Customer Information form.

k. Keep the database open if you plan to continue with the Hands-On Exercise. If not, close the database, and exit Access.

Report Basics

By now, you know how to plan a database, create tables, establish relationships between tables, enter data into tables, and extract data using queries. In the previous section of this chapter, you learned how to create and modify several types of data-entry forms. In this section, you will learn how to create professional reports using the report-generating tools in Access.

A *report* is a document that displays information from a database in a format that outputs meaningful information to its readers. Access reports can be printed, viewed onscreen, or even saved as files, such as Word documents. You cannot use reports to change data in your database; a report is designed for output of information only based on data from tables or queries in your database (record sources).

The following are all examples of reports that might be created in Access:

- A telephone directory sorted by last name
- A customer report grouped by orders pending for each customer
- An employee list grouped by department
- A monthly statement from a bank
- A bill or invoice
- A set of mailing labels

Reports are used to help the reader understand and analyze information. For example, in a report you can group the customers together for each sales rep and highlight the customers who have not placed an order in six months. This is an example of using a list of customers from the Customers table together with other data in the database as an effective business analysis tool. To increase business, the sales reps could contact their customers who have not ordered in the past six months and review the findings with the sales manager. A sales report could then be run each month to see if the strategy has helped to produce any new business.

In this section, you will create reports in Access by first identifying a record source, then designing the report, and finally choosing a Report tool. You will learn how to modify a report by adding and deleting fields, resizing columns, and adding a theme. You will also learn about the report sections, the report views, and controls on reports.

Creating Reports Using Report Tools

Access provides five different report tools for creating reports. The report tools are located on the Create tab in the Reports group, as shown in Figure 4.20. The most common of the tools, the Report tool, is used to instantly create a tabular report based on a selected table or query. The Report Design tool is used to create a new blank report in Design view. This tool is used by advanced users who want to create a report from scratch with no help from Access. The Blank Report tool is used to create a new report in Layout view by inserting fields and controls manually to design the report. The Report Wizard tool will prompt you through a series of step-by-step screens and help you create a report based on your selections. The Labels tool is used to create printable labels using one of the preformatted templates provided by Access. Table 4.3 provides a summary of the five report tools and their usages. Once you create a report using one of the report tools, you can perform modifications in either Layout view or Design view.

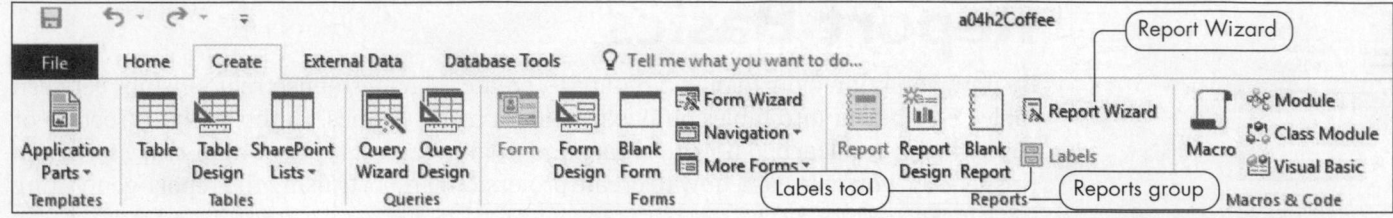

FIGURE 4.20 Reports Group on the Create Tab

Access 2016, Windows 10, Microsoft Corporation

TABLE 4.3	Report Tools and Their Usages
Report Tool	**Usage**
Report	Create a tabular report showing all of the fields in the record source.
Report Design	Create a new blank report in Design view. Add fields and controls manually.
Blank Report	Create a new blank report in Layout view. Drag and drop to add fields and controls manually.
Report Wizard	Answer a series of step-by-step questions and Access will design a custom report for you.
Labels	Select a preformatted label template and create printable labels.

Pearson Education, Inc.

Before you create a report in Access, you should consider the following questions:

- What is the purpose of the report?
- Who will use the report?
- Which tables, queries, and fields are needed for the report?
- How will the report be distributed? Will users view the report directly from the Access database, or will they receive it through email, fax, or the Internet?
- Will the results be converted to Word, Excel, HTML, or another format?

In the Forms section of this chapter, you learned that it is helpful to talk to users and design a form before you launch Access. The same applies to creating an Access report. Users can give you solid input, and creating a design will help you determine which report tool to use to create the report.

The first step in planning your report is to identify the record source. You may use one or more tables, queries, or a combination of tables and queries as the report's record source. Sometimes, a single table contains all of the records you need for the report. Other times, you will incorporate several tables. When data from multiple related tables are needed to create a report, you can first create a single query (with criteria, if necessary) and then base the report on that query. Multiple tables used in a query must be related, as indicated with join lines.

Reports can contain text and numeric data as well as formatting, calculated fields, graphics, and so forth. For example, you can add a company logo to the report header. Be sure that you have appropriate permission to use any company logo, graphic, or photo in your reports in order to avoid inappropriate or illegal use of an asset.

Use the Report Tool

 The easiest way to create a report is with the Report tool. The **Report tool** is used to create a tabular report based on the selected table or query.

To create a report using the Report tool, complete the following steps:

1. Select a table or query in the Navigation Pane.
2. Click Report in the Reports group on the Create tab.

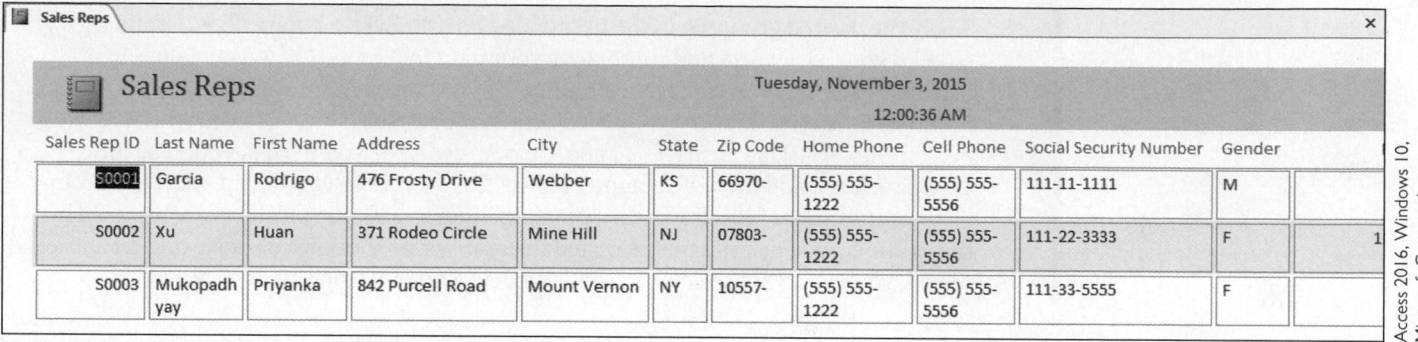

FIGURE 4.21 Tabular Report Created with the Report Tool

Access creates a tabular layout report instantly. Notice that this type of report displays data horizontally in columns across the page, as shown in Figure 4.21.

If you prefer, you can display a report using a stacked layout, which displays fields in a vertical column. This type of report is less common, as it would result in longer printouts. The number of pages depends on the number of records in the record source.

Use the Report Wizard

The **Report Wizard** prompts you for input in a series of steps to generate a customized report. The wizard enables you to make certain customizations quickly and easily without having to be an expert in report design.

> **To create a report using the Report Wizard, complete the following steps:**
>
> 1. Select the report's record source (table or query) in the Navigation Pane, and click Report Wizard in the Reports group on the Create tab. The wizard opens with the selected table or query (the record source) displayed in the first dialog box. Although you chose the record source before you started, the first dialog box enables you to select fields from the selected source or additional tables or queries.
>
> 2. Click the Tables/Queries list arrow to display a list of available tables or queries, if you want to choose a different record source. Select the fields you want to include in the report. You can select an available field and then click > to add a single field to the Selected Fields list, >> to select all fields, < to remove a field, << and to remove all fields from the report. See Figure 4.22. Set the desired fields and click Next.

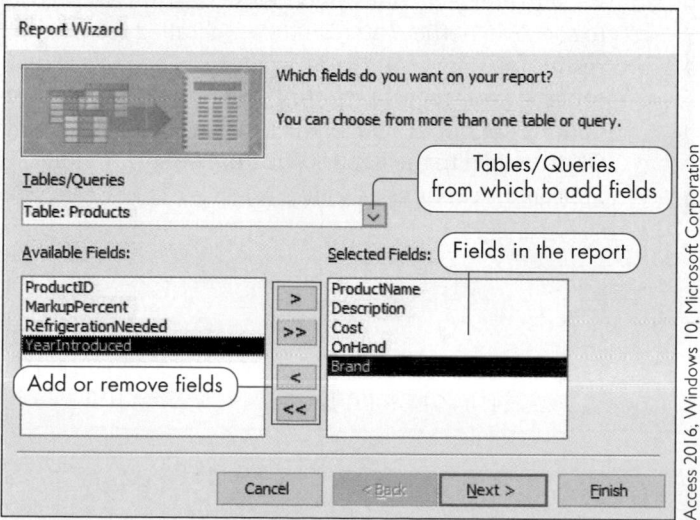

FIGURE 4.22 Selecting Fields in the Report Wizard

3. Apply the desired grouping in the next dialog box, shown in Figure 4.23. Grouping enables you to organize and summarize your data in a report, based on values in a field. For example, you can group products by their brand name and average the cost of products in each group. To group records in a report, select the field you want to group by and click Add One Field ⟩ to add the new group. If you need a second or third grouping level, add those field names in order. The order in which you select the groups dictates the order of display in the report. In Figure 4.23, the products are grouped by the Brand field. Once you have selected the appropriate options, click Next. For a basic report, you would not select any grouping fields, and instead just click Next.

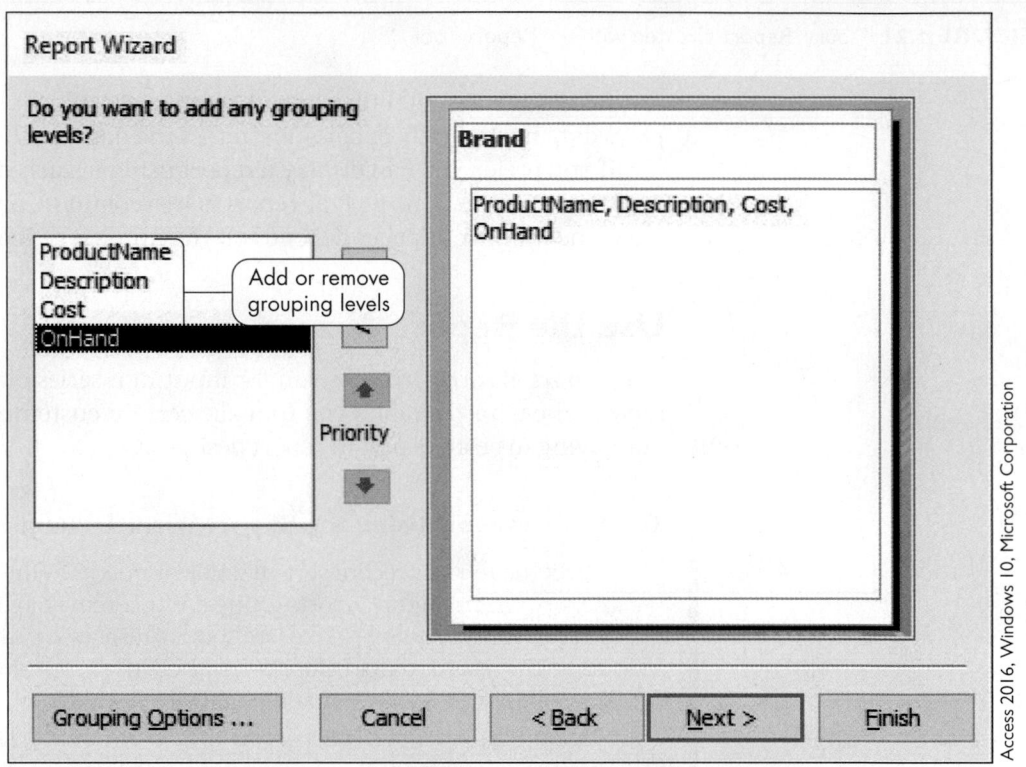

FIGURE 4.23 Grouping Options in the Report Wizard

4. Apply the desired sorting and summary options in the next dialog box. Figure 4.24 displays the sort options for a grouped report. You can click Summary Options if you want to add aggregate functions (e.g., sum, average, minimum, and maximum) and to specify whether you want to see detailed records on the report or only the aggregate results (see Figure 4.25). You can also choose to calculate values as percentages of totals in your report results. If no grouping is specified in your report, the summary options are not available. In Figure 4.25, no summary options are selected. Click OK to return to the Report Wizard. The sort options are the same as before. Set the appropriate options and click Next.

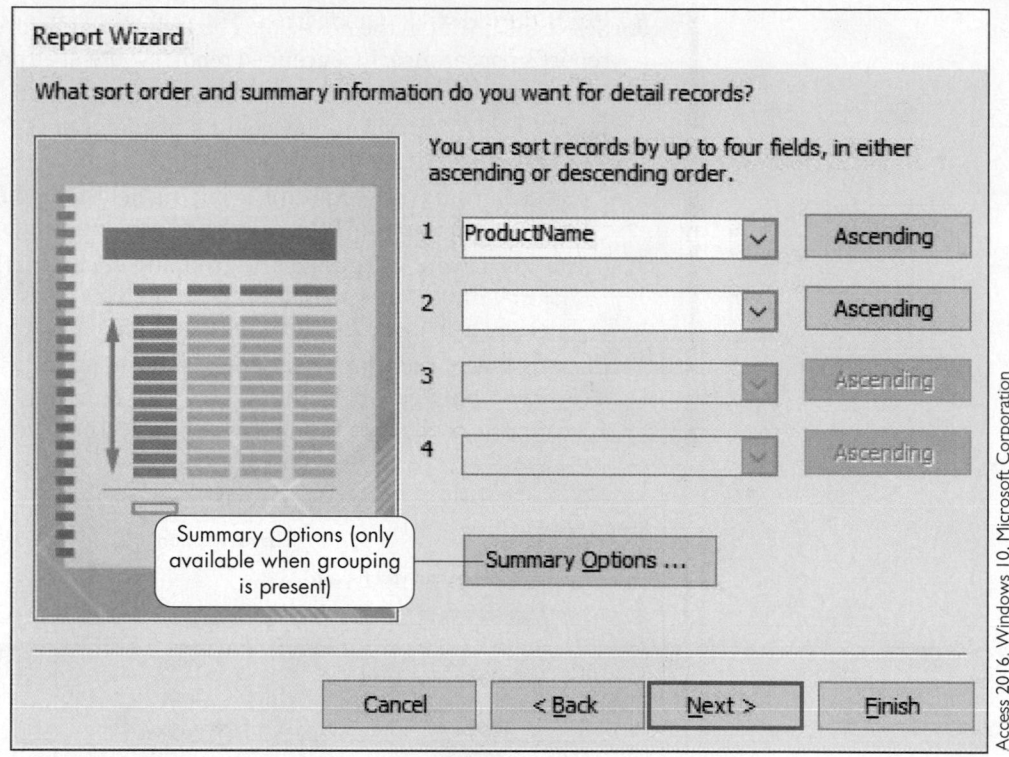

FIGURE 4.24 Sort and Summarize Grouped Data in the Report Wizard

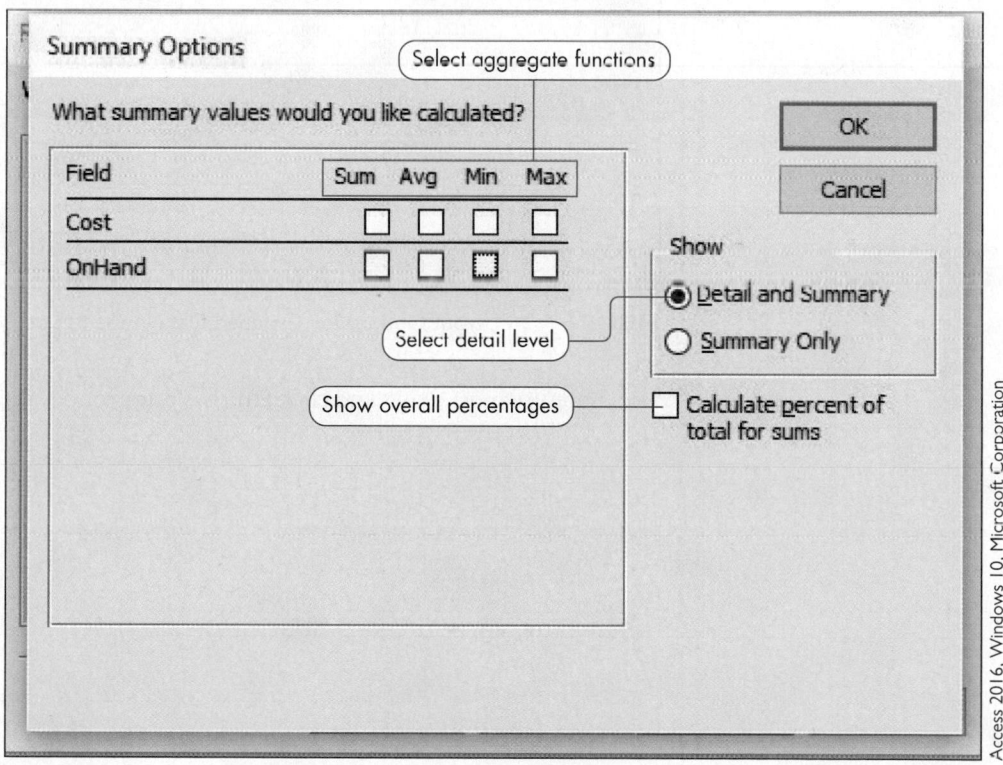

FIGURE 4.25 Summary Options Dialog Box

5. Select the layout in the next dialog box, shown in Figure 4.26, to determine the report's appearance. In a grouped report, you will be prompted to select the layout from three options:
   - Stepped Layout will display column headings at the top of the page and keep the grouping field(s) in their own row.
   - Block Layout will include the grouping field(s) in line with the data, saving some space when printing. It has one set of column headings at the top of each page.
   - Outline Layout will display the grouping field(s) on their own separate rows and has column headings inside each group. This leads to a longer report when printing but may help make the report easier to read.

   Clicking any of these layouts will give you a general preview in the preview area. In a report without grouping, the layouts are Columnar, Tabular, and Justified. You can determine how the data fits on a page by selecting Portrait or Landscape. Click Next.

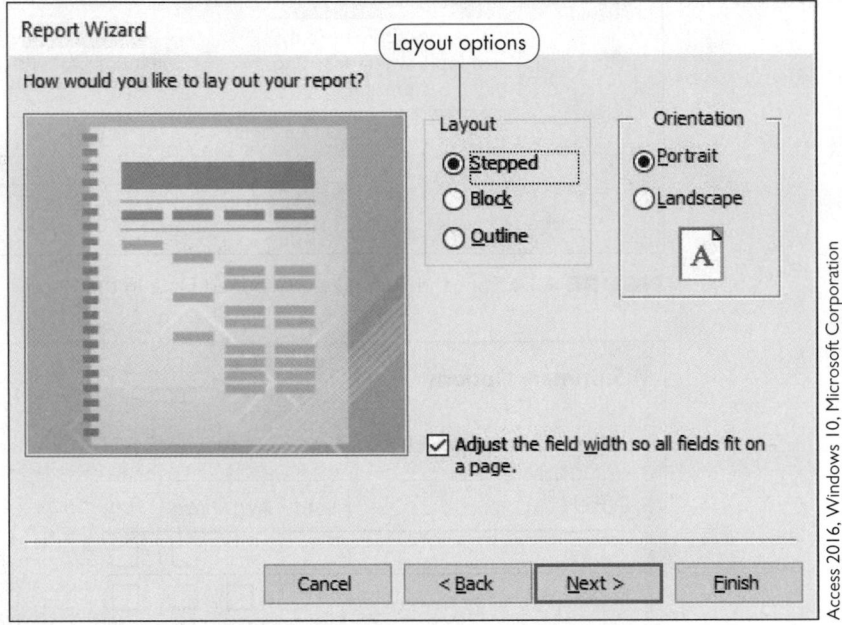

FIGURE 4.26 Layout Options for Grouped Data in the Report Wizard

6. Enter a report name and click Finish. Your grouped report will resemble Figure 4.27.

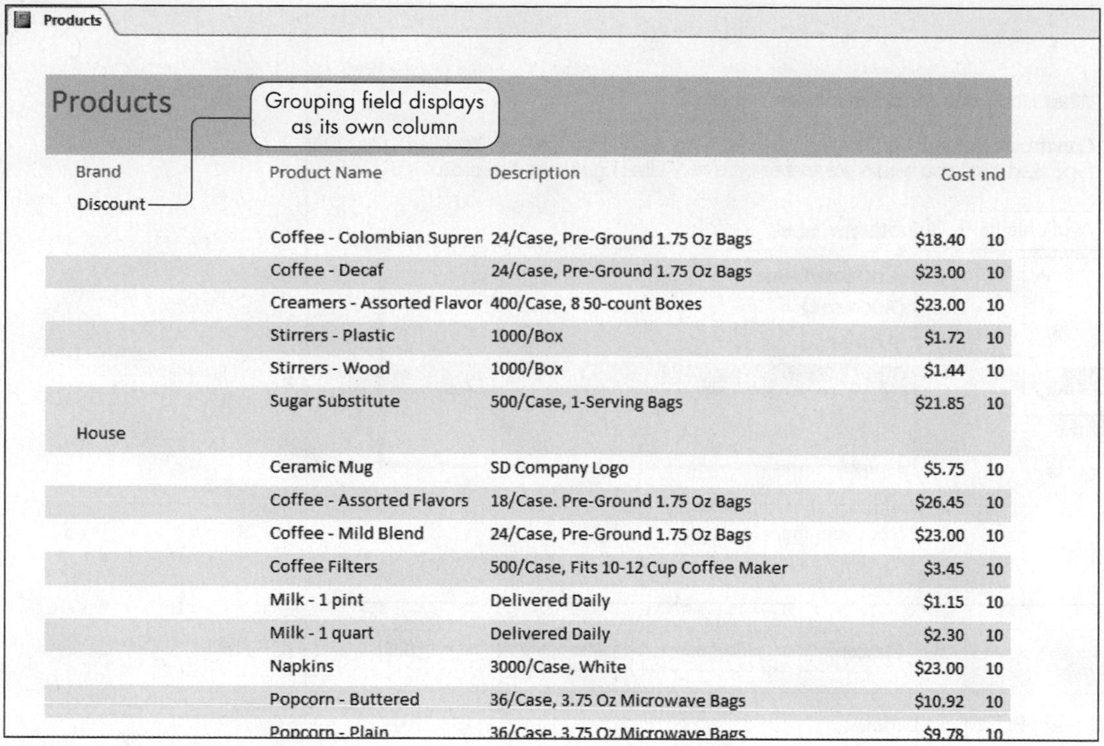

Brand	Product Name	Description	Cost	ınd
Discount				
	Coffee - Colombian Supren	24/Case, Pre-Ground 1.75 Oz Bags	$18.40	10
	Coffee - Decaf	24/Case, Pre-Ground 1.75 Oz Bags	$23.00	10
	Creamers - Assorted Flavor	400/Case, 8 50-count Boxes	$23.00	10
	Stirrers - Plastic	1000/Box	$1.72	10
	Stirrers - Wood	1000/Box	$1.44	10
	Sugar Substitute	500/Case, 1-Serving Bags	$21.85	10
House				
	Ceramic Mug	SD Company Logo	$5.75	10
	Coffee - Assorted Flavors	18/Case. Pre-Ground 1.75 Oz Bags	$26.45	10
	Coffee - Mild Blend	24/Case, Pre-Ground 1.75 Oz Bags	$23.00	10
	Coffee Filters	500/Case, Fits 10-12 Cup Coffee Maker	$3.45	10
	Milk - 1 pint	Delivered Daily	$1.15	10
	Milk - 1 quart	Delivered Daily	$2.30	10
	Napkins	3000/Case, White	$23.00	10
	Popcorn - Buttered	36/Case, 3.75 Oz Microwave Bags	$10.92	10
	Popcorn - Plain	36/Case, 3.75 Oz Microwave Bags	$9.78	10

FIGURE 4.27 Grouped Report

Use the Label Wizard

The ***Label Wizard*** enables you to easily create mailing labels, name tags, and other specialized tags. A mailing label report is a specialized report that you can create and print with name-brand labels, such as Avery and many others. If you purchase a store brand label from an office supply store, it will generally state the comparable manufacturer and product number; the wizard provides a long list of both manufacturers and label sizes.

To use the Label Wizard, complete the following steps:

1. Select the table or query that you will use as the record source for the report.
2. Click Labels in the Reports group on the Create tab.
3. Select the manufacturer, product number, unit of measure, label type, and then click Next.
4. Select the font and color options, and then click Next.
5. Add the fields to the prototype label, as shown in Figure 4.28. You add the fields exactly as you would like them to display, including adding commas, spacing, and pressing Enter to move to the next line, where applicable.

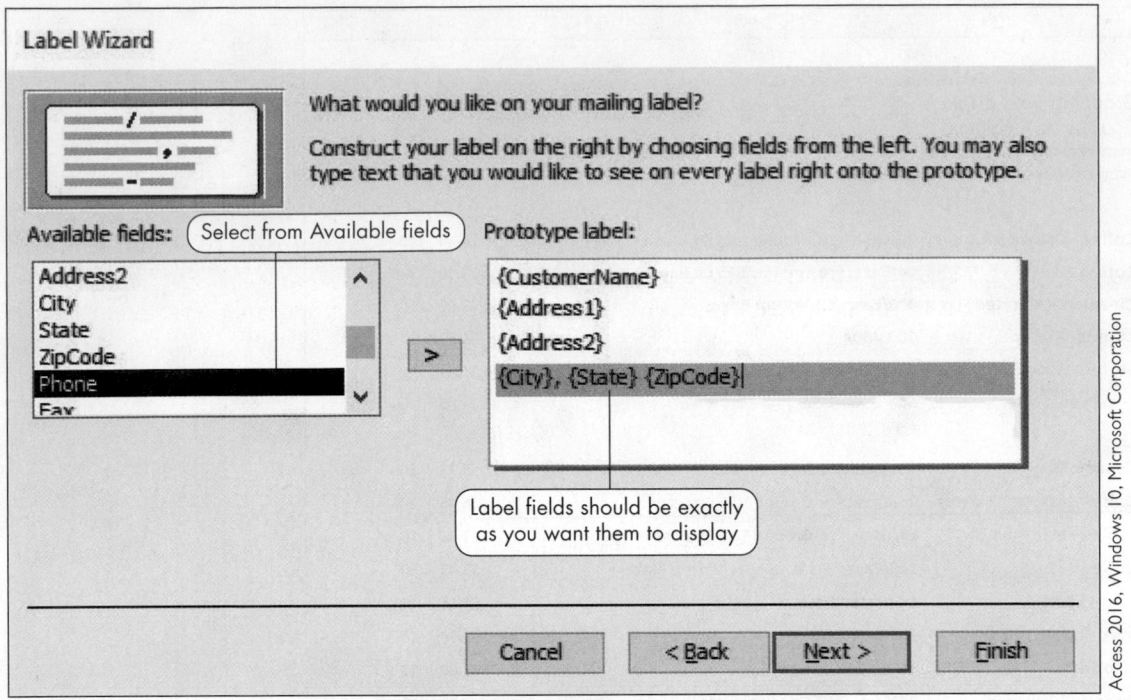

FIGURE 4.28 Create a Customers Prototype Label

6. Add sort fields; for example, you may want to sort by state or zip code, and then click Next.

7. Name the report and then click Finish to generate your label report. The results using the Customers table are shown in Figure 4.29.

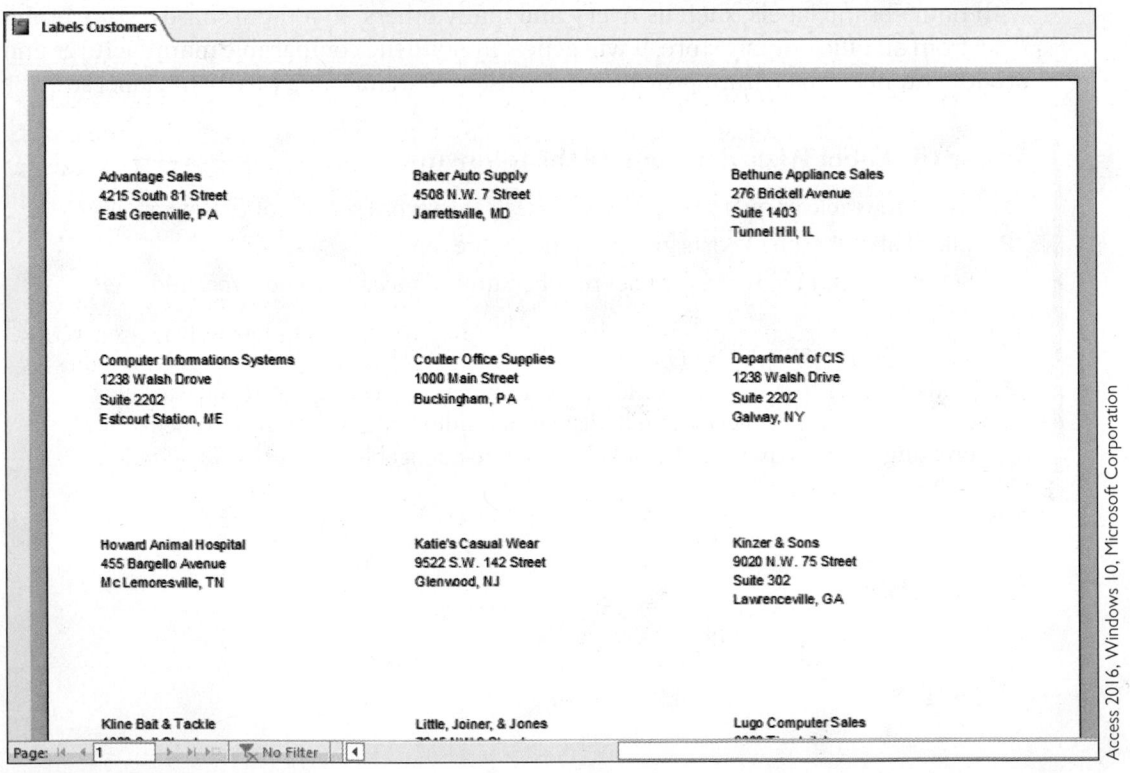

FIGURE 4.29 Customer Mailing Labels Created by Label Wizard

Using Report Views

As you work with the report tools to create and modify reports, you might need to switch between the four report views in Access—Report, Layout, Design, and Print Preview. Report view and Print Preview are generally used only for viewing or printing the report. To make modifications to a report, use Layout view and Design view. Most of the design work can be done in Layout view, but sometimes Design view is necessary to apply a more advanced feature, such as setting the tab order of the controls. To switch between the four views, click the View arrow in the Views group, and then select the desired view (alternatively, right-click the report tab, and from the shortcut menu, select the desired view).

View a Report in Report View

Report view enables you to view a report onscreen in a continuous page layout. However, because the data cannot be changed in Report view, it is simply a way of viewing the information without having to worry about accidentally moving a control. You can also use Report view to filter data, if necessary.

Print or Save a Report in Print Preview

STEP 2 ▶▶ *Print Preview* enables you to see exactly what the report will look like when it is printed. You cannot modify the design of the report or the data in Print Preview. By default, Print Preview will display all the pages in the report. Figure 4.29 displays the mailing labels report in Print Preview.

From Print Preview, you have the option to export and save the report to a different file type, such as Word. This is a useful option if you plan to share a report electronically but do not want to distribute the entire database. In the Data group, on the Print Preview tab, you will find a number of eligible file types, as shown in Figure 4.30. Select the option in the Data group, and then follow the onscreen prompts to export your report. Commonly used formats include Excel, Word, and Portable Document Format (PDF).

Portable Document Format (PDF) is a file type that was created for exchanging documents independently of software applications and operating system environments. In other words, you can email a report in PDF format to users running various operating systems, and they can open it even if they do not have Microsoft Access installed. PDF files open in Adobe Reader, a free downloadable program; recent versions of Windows have a built-in Reader program that displays PDF files as well.

Because databases contain a great deal of information, Access reports can become very long, requiring many pages to print. At times, reports can be formatted incorrectly, or blank pages might print in between each page of information. Be sure to troubleshoot your reports before sending them to the printer, or to recipients via email.

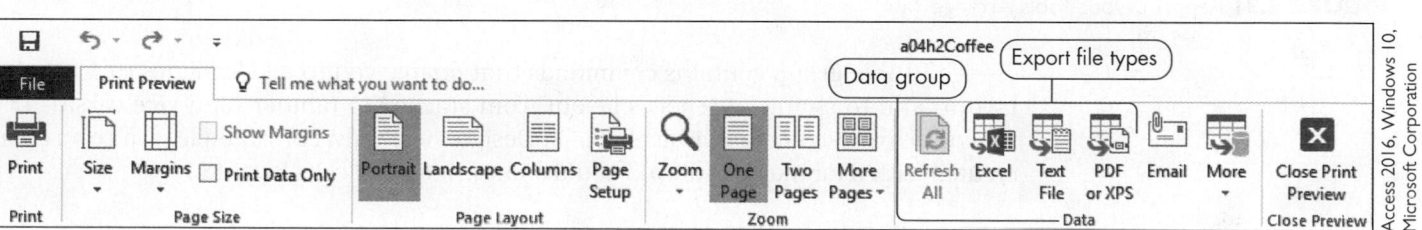

FIGURE 4.30 Data Group on Print Preview Tab

Alter a Report in Layout View

Use Layout view to alter the report design while still viewing the data. You should use Layout view to add or delete fields in the report, modify field properties, change the column widths, group, sort, and summarize data. The Page Setup tab presents options for setting the page size, orientation, and margins. Although you will be able to view your modifications along with the data in Layout view, you will still need to check the report in Print Preview to evaluate all the changes before printing it.

Modifying a Report

After you create a report by using one of the report tools, you may want to modify it. Some of the common changes you make in reports are adding and deleting controls, changing the arrangement, widths, and formatting of controls, and modifying the title. From either Layout or Design view, there are four tabs available for report modification:

- Design: Use this tab to make changes to the design of the report, such as adding fields, grouping and sorting records, changing themes, and inserting additional controls.
- Arrange: Use this tab to change the layout of a report, to move fields up and down, and to control margins and spacing.
- Format: Use this tab to work with fonts, font size, and colors, add or remove bolding, italics, or underlining, adjust text alignment, or add a background image or color.
- Page Setup: Use this tab to change paper size, margins, or page orientation, or to format reports into multiple columns.

Modify the Layout of a Report

STEP 3 ▶▶ The Arrange tab displays in both Layout view and Design view. Some key commands on the Arrange tab from Layout view are highlighted in Figure 4.31.

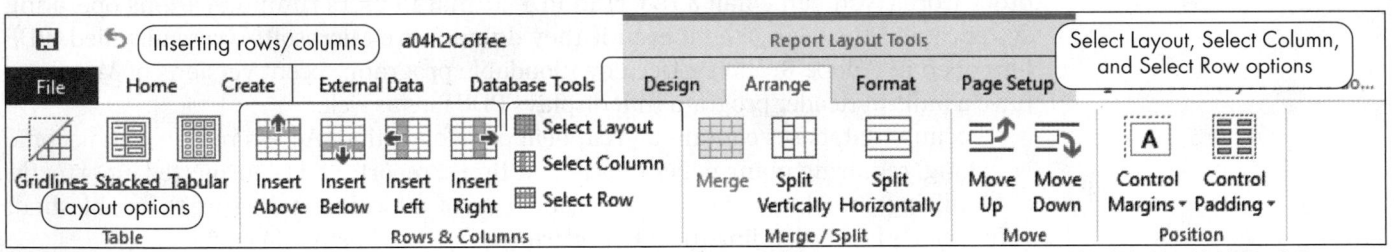

FIGURE 4.31 Report Layout Tools Arrange Tab

Access 2016, Windows 10, Microsoft Corporation

The Table group contains commands that enable you to add gridlines to a report's layout, and to change a report's layout from stacked to tabular (and vice versa). The Remove Layout command is available in Design view only. For example, if a report was created with a tabular layout, you could change it to a stacked layout.

> **To change a report's layout from tabular to stacked, complete the following steps:**
>
> 1. Open the report in Layout view and click the Arrange tab.
> 2. Click any text box in the Detail section of the report.
> 3. Click Select Layout in the Rows & Columns group.
> 4. Click Stacked in the Table group.

The Rows & Columns group contains commands that enable you to insert rows and columns inside a report's layout. In a report with a stacked layout, you may want to separate some controls from the rest of the fields, or create some empty space so that fields can be added or repositioned. For example, you can select a control (or multiple controls) and click Insert Below. This will create an empty row (or space) below the selected controls. This group also contains the Select Layout, Select Column, and Select Row commands, which you can use to select the entire layout, or a single column or row in a layout.

The Merge/Split group contains commands that enable you to merge and split the controls on a report. There are times when you might want to deviate from the basic row and column formats that the report tools create. For example, you can make a label such as *Product Name* display in two controls (Product and Name), with one positioned below the other, rather than in one single control.

The Move group contains commands to move a field up or down in a stacked layout. Moving controls up or down in a report may cause unexpected results; you can always click Undo if you need to reverse your changes.

The Position group contains commands to control the margins and the padding (the spacing between controls) in a report. The preset margin settings are convenient to use; ensure that if you change the margins, you preview the report to view the result.

Modify Report Controls

The Format tab contains a series of commands that enable you to change the font, display, and alignment of the controls on a report, as shown in Figure 4.32. The formatting tools in Access are similar to those in other Microsoft Office applications.

To format report controls, complete the following steps:

1. Open the report in Layout view (or Design view), then select the control(s) you want to format.
2. Click the Format tab, and click the formatting tools as desired.

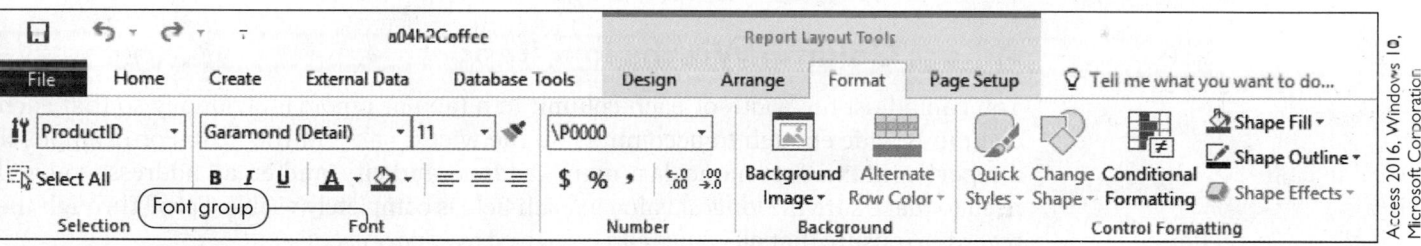

FIGURE 4.32 Report Layout Tools Format Tab

TIP: INSERT A LOGO IN A REPORT
To insert a logo in a report, open the report in Layout (or Design) view, and then click Logo in the Header / Footer group on the Design tab. In the Insert Picture dialog box, locate the image, click the file, and then click Open. The picture will display in the Report Header section; use the Property Sheet to modify the size and other attributes, if necessary.

Add a Field to a Report

At times, new fields may be added to tables and then need to be incorporated into reports. Alternatively, you might be creating a customized report and want to add fields individually. Adding a field to a report with a stacked or tabular layout is similar to adding a field to a form.

> **To add a field to a report, complete the following steps:**
>
> 1. Open the report in Layout view, then click Add Existing Fields in the Tools group on the Design tab.
>
>   The Field List pane displays at the right of the report. For a single-table report, you will be presented with a list of fields from the table (record source). For a multiple-table report, click the + (plus sign) to the left of the appropriate table to expand it, and locate the desired field(s).
>
> 2. Click and drag the desired field to the precise location on the report, using the shaded line as a guide for positioning the new field. Alternatively, you can double-click a field to add it to the report; the field will be added below the selected field. The other fields will automatically adjust to make room for the new field.

Delete a Field from a Report

You may decide that even though a field was available in a table or in a query that was used as the record source, it is not necessary to display it to users in a report. Not all fields in a database are necessarily relevant to reports that you create.

> **To delete a field from the Detail section of a report, complete the following steps:**
>
> 1. Open the report in Layout view, and click the text box control of the field to be deleted (note the shaded border around the control).
> 2. Click Select Row in the Rows & Columns group on the Arrange tab in order to select the text box and its associated label. Alternatively, click the text box control, press and hold Ctrl, and then click the associated label control to select them both.
> 3. Press Delete.

The other fields will automatically adjust to close the gap around the deleted field.

Adjust Column Widths in a Report

You can adjust the width of each column in a tabular report individually so that each column is wide enough to accommodate the widest value in the field. For example, if a report contains first name, last name, address and city, and email address, you will need to make sure the longest value in each field is completely visible. Scroll through the records to ensure that all values can be viewed by report users.

> **To modify column widths in a tabular report, complete the following steps:**
>
> 1. Open the report in Layout view, and click the text box control of the field you want to resize.
> 2. Point to the right border of the control until the pointer turns into a double-headed arrow. Drag the right edge of the control to the left or right until you arrive at the desired width.

Change Margins and Orientation

At times, you will want to print a report in Landscape orientation as opposed to Portrait; that decision will depend upon how many columns you want to display across the page, the widths of the fields, and other formatting considerations. The Page Setup tab presents options similar to those you may have used in Word. In the Page Size group, you can change the margins, and in the Page Layout group, you can work with Page Setup options, including setting the orientation of your report, as shown in Figure 4.33.

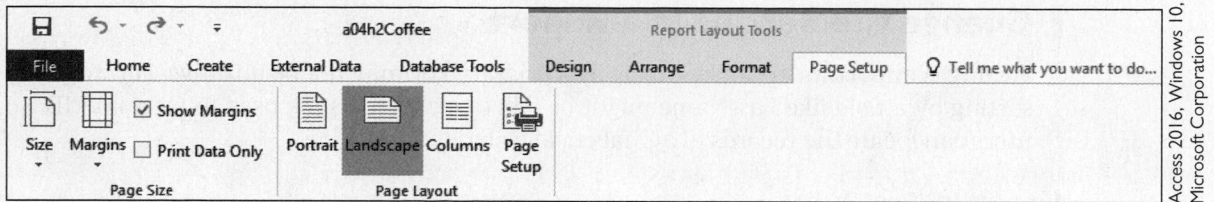

FIGURE 4.33 Report Layout Tools Page Setup Tab

Add a Theme to the Report

You can enhance the report's appearance by applying one of the built-in Access themes.

> **To apply a theme, complete the following steps:**
>
> 1. Open the report in Layout or Design view, and select Themes in the Themes group on the Design tab.
> 2. Point to a theme to see its name in the ScreenTip and a Live Preview of the theme in the report, and click to select it. By default, the theme will be applied to all objects in your database. Right-click a theme in the gallery to apply it to the current report only, or to all the reports in your database that share a common theme.

Work with a Report Layout Control

When you use one of the report tools to create a new report, Access will add a layout control to help align the fields. Layout controls in reports work similarly to layout controls in forms. The layout control provides guides to help keep controls aligned horizontally and vertically, and give your report a neat appearance. If you want to have more control over the location of your fields, you can remove the layout control and position the controls manually on the report.

> **To remove the layout control from a report, complete the following steps:**
>
> 1. Open the report in Design view (the option is not available on the Ribbon in Layout view), and click anywhere in the layout control you want to remove.
> 2. Click Select Layout in the Rows & Columns group on the Arrange tab.
> 3. Click Remove Layout in the Table group. All of the controls are still available in the report, but can now be managed individually.

You can add a layout control to a report by first selecting all the controls you want to include in the layout. To select multiple controls, click the first control, press and hold Ctrl, and then click the additional controls you want to include. To select all of the controls on a form, press Ctrl+A. Click Tabular or Stacked in the Table group.

Sorting Records in a Report

 When a report is created using the Report tool, the sort order of the records in the report is initially dependent on the sort order of the record source—similar to the way records are sorted in a form. The primary key of the record source usually controls the sort order. However, a report has an additional feature for sorting. While in Layout view or Design view, click Group & Sort in the Grouping & Totals group on the Design tab. The Group, Sort, and Total pane displays at the bottom of the report. This pane enables you to group records together and to override the sort order in the report's record source. Note that if you do not use the Report Wizard, this is generally how you would add grouping and totals to a report.

Change the Sorting in a Report

Sorting is important because sorting by a primary key may not be intuitive. For example, sorting by a field like LastName might be a better choice as opposed to CustomerID, so users can locate the records in alphabetical order by LastName.

> **To change the sorting in a report, complete the following steps:**
>
> 1. Open the report in Layout or Design view, and click Group & Sort in the Grouping & Totals group on the Design tab.
> 2. Click *Add a sort* and select the field by which you want to sort. The default sort order is ascending.
> 3. Add another sort by clicking *Add a sort* again. For example, you could sort first by Brand and then by ProductName, as shown in Figure 4.34.

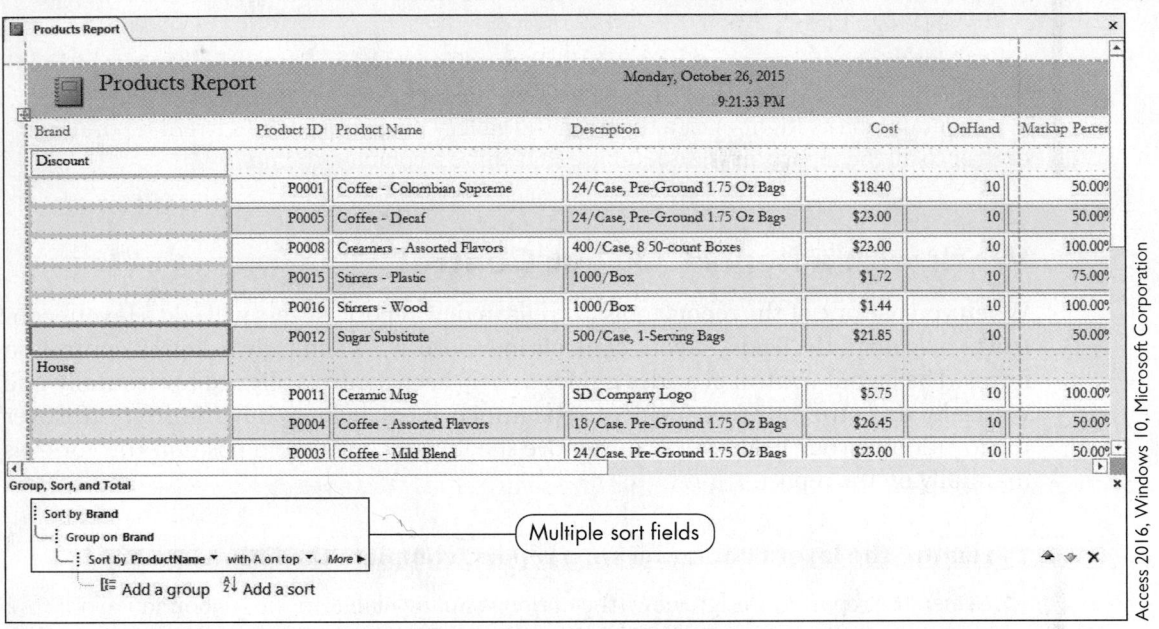

FIGURE 4.34 Report in Layout View with Two Sort Fields

 *Quick Concepts*

5. What is the difference between Report view and Layout view? *p. 897*

6. What is the benefit of saving a report as another type of file? *p. 897*

7. Why is it important to view your reports in Print Preview? *p. 897*

8. Why would you decide to remove a report layout control when modifying a report? *p. 901*

9. Why is sorting the records in a report important? *p. 901*

Skills covered: Use the Report Tool • Use the Report Wizard • Use Print Preview • Publish to PDF • Add a Field • Remove a Field • Change Orientation • Apply a Theme • Sort Records in a Report

2 Report Basics

You create a products report using the Access Report tool to help Ryung stay on top of the key information for her business. You will modify the column widths so that they all fit across one page. You will also use the Report Wizard to create additional reports that Ryung requires.

STEP 1 ›› CREATING REPORTS USING REPORT TOOLS

You use the Report tool to create an Access report to help Ryung manage her product information. This report is especially useful for determining which products she needs to order to fill upcoming orders. You also use the Report Wizard to determine sales by city. Refer to Figure 4.35 as you complete Step 1.

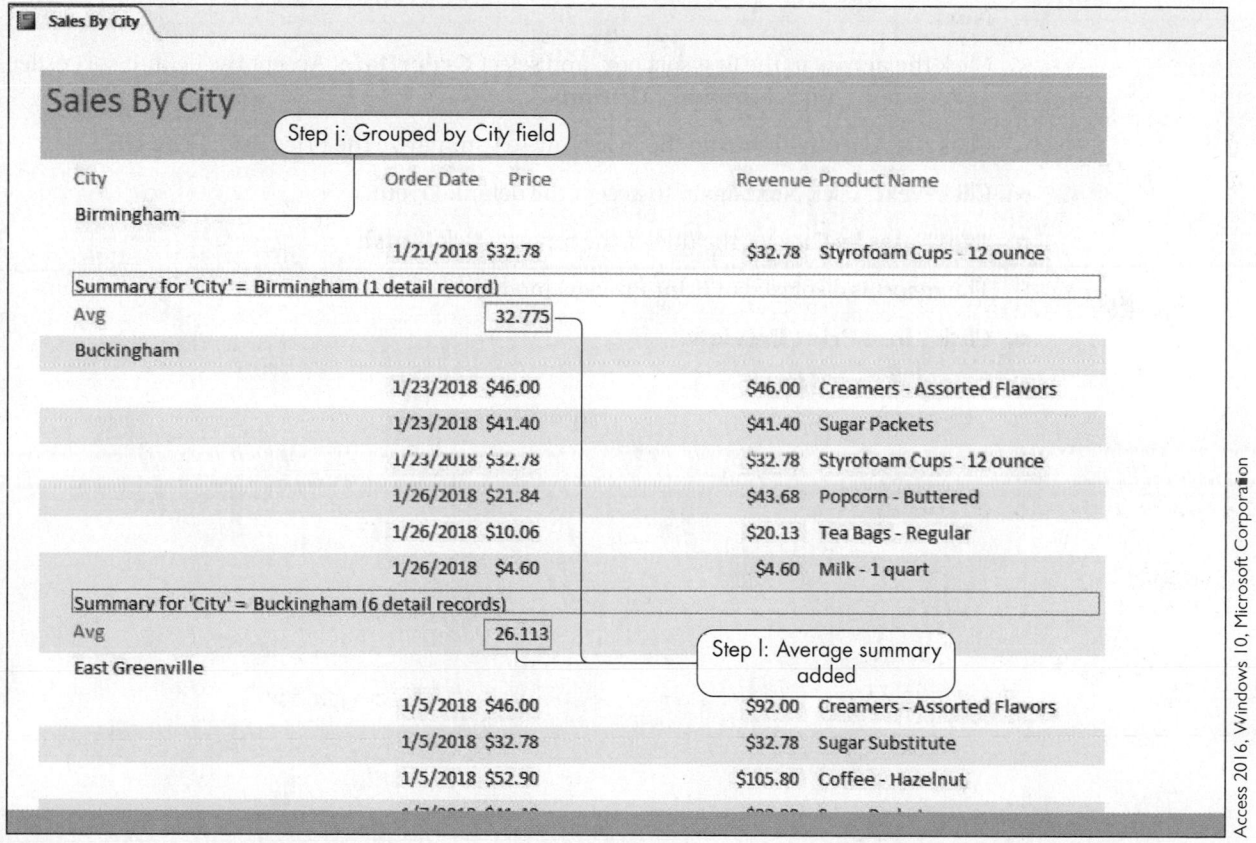

FIGURE 4.35 Sales by City Report

a. Open *a04h1Coffee_LastFirst* if you closed it at the end of Hands-On Exercise 1 and save it as **a04h2Coffee_LastFirst**, changing h1 to h2.

b. Select the **Products table** in the Navigation Pane. Click the **Create tab** and click **Report** in the Reports group.

Access creates a new tabular layout report based on the Products table. The report opens in Layout view ready for editing.

c. Click the **Products title** at the top of the report to select it, click again on **Products**, and then change the title to **Products Report**. Press **Enter** to accept the change.

d. Right-click the **Products report tab** and select **Print Preview**.

The report is too wide for the page; you will close Print Preview and change the orientation to Landscape.

e. Click **Close Print Preview** in the Close Preview group to return to Layout view.

f. Click the **Page Setup tab** and click **Landscape** in the Page Layout group.

The report changes to Landscape orientation. Most of the columns now fit across one page. You will make further revisions to the report later so that it fits on one page.

g. Save the report as **Products Report**. Close the report.

h. Select the **Revenue query** in the Navigation Pane. Click the **Create tab** and click **Report Wizard** in the Reports group.

The Report Wizard launches.

i. Click the **City field** and click **Add One Field** `>` to add the City field to the report. Repeat the same process for the **OrderDate**, **Price**, **Revenue**, and **ProductName fields**. Click **Next**.

j. Ensure that **City** is selected, click **Add One Field** `>` to add grouping by city. Click **Next**.

k. Click the **arrow** in the first sort box, and select **OrderDate**. Accept the default sort order as Ascending. Click **Summary Options**.

l. Click the **Avg check box** in the Price row to summarize the Price field. Click **OK**.

m. Click **Next**. Click **Next** again to accept the default layout.

n. Type **Sales by City** for the title of the report. Click **Finish**.

The report is displayed in Print Preview mode.

o. Click **Close Print Preview**.

p. Save and close the report.

The Products Report you created looks good, according to Ryung. However, she does not have Access installed on her home computer, and would like to have a copy of the report saved in PDF format so she can review it outside of the office. You will save a copy of the report for her Refer to Figure 4.36 as you complete Step 2.

Step a: Report in PDF format

Products Report

Sunday, November 4, 2015
9:24:45 PM

Product ID	Product Name	Description	Cost	Markup Percent	Refrigeration Needed	Brand
P0001	Coffee - Colombian Supreme	24/Case, Pre-Ground 1.75 Oz Bags	$18.40	50.00%	☐	Discount
P0002	Coffee - Hazelnut	24/Case, Pre-Ground 1.75 Oz Bags	$26.45	100.00%	☐	Premium
P0003	Coffee - Mild Blend	24/Case, Pre-Ground 1.75 Oz Bags	$23.00	50.00%	☐	House
P0004	Coffee - Assorted Flavors	18/Case. Pre-Ground 1.75 Oz Bags	$26.45	50.00%	☐	House
P0005	Coffee - Decaf	24/Case, Pre-Ground 1.75 Oz Bags	$23.00	50.00%	☐	Discount
P0006	Tea Bags - Regular	75/Box, Individual Tea Bags	$5.75	75.00%	☐	House
P0007	Tea Bags - Decaf	75/Box, Individual Tea Bags	$8.05	75.00%	☐	House
P0008	Creamers - Assorted Flavors	400/Case, 8 50-count Boxes	$23.00	100.00%	☐	Discount
P0009	Creamers - Liquid	200/Case, Individual Creamers	$17.25	100.00%	☑	Premium
P0010	Sugar Packets	2000/Case	$20.70	100.00%	☐	House
P0011	Ceramic Mug	SD Company Logo	$5.75	100.00%	☐	House
P0012	Sugar Substitute	500/Case, 1-Serving Bags	$21.85	50.00%	☐	Discount
P0013	Coffee Filters	500/Case, Fits 10-12 Cup Coffee Maker	$3.45	50.00%	☐	House
P0014	Napkins	3000/Case, White	$23.00	100.00%	☐	House
P0015	Stirrers - Plastic	1000/Box	$1.72	75.00%	☐	Discount
P0016	Stirrers - Wood	1000/Box	$1.44	100.00%	☐	Discount
P0017	Spoons	500/Box, White Plastic	$17.25	100.00%	☐	House
P0018	Popcorn - Plain	36/Case, 3.75 Oz Microwave Bags	$9.78	100.00%	☐	House
P0019	Popcorn - Buttered	36/Case, 3.75 Oz Microwave Bags	$10.92	100.00%	☐	House
P0020	Soup - Chicken	50 Envelopes	$11.50	100.00%	☐	Premium
P0021	Soup - Variety Pak	50 Envelopes	$13.80	100.00%	☐	Premium
P0022	Styrofoam Cups - 10 ounce	1000/Case	$19.55	50.00%	☐	House

Access 2016, Windows 0, Microsoft Corporation

FIGURE 4.36 Products Report Saved in PDF Format

a. Open the Products Report and on the **File** tab, click **Print**, and select **Print Preview**. Click **PDF or XPS** in the Data group on the Print Preview tab. Navigate to where you are saving your files, type the file name **a04h2Products_LastFirst**, ensure that *Open file after publishing* is selected, and then click **Publish**.

Windows will open the report in your system's default PDF viewer, which may be Adobe Reader or the Windows Reader app. Close the reader window. You will submit this file to your instructor at the end of the last hands-on exercise.

b. Ensure that you return to the Access window, and in the Export – PDF dialog box, click **Close** when prompted to save the export steps.

c. Click **Close Print Preview** and close the report.

Ryung realized the Products table is missing a field that she requires for her reports. She would like you to add the field to the table and update the report to include the new field. She would also like to make sure the report fits nicely across one landscape page. She also asked you to show her some sample color schemes Refer to Figure 4.37 as you complete Step 3.

Products Retrospect	Step t: Retrospect theme applied

Products Report   Tuesday, November 3, 2015   9:32:32 AM

Product ID	Product Name	Description	Cost	OnHand	Markup Percent	Refrig?	Brand
P0001	Coffee - Colombian Supreme	24/Case, Pre-Ground 1.75 Oz Bags	$18.40	10	50.00%	☐	Discount
P0002	Coffee - Hazelnut	24/Case, Pre-Ground 1.75 Oz Bags	$26.45	10	100.00%	☐	Premium
P0003	Coffee - Mild Blend	24/Case, Pre-Ground 1.75 Oz Bags	$23.00	10	50.00%	☐	House
P0004	Coffee - Assorted Flavors	18/Case. Pre-Ground 1.75 Oz Bags	$26.45	10	50.00%	☐	House
P0005	Coffee - Decaf	24/Case, Pre-Ground 1.75 Oz Bags	$23.00	10	50.00%	☐	Discount
P0006	Tea Bags - Regular	75/Box, Individual Tea Bags	$5.75	10	75.00%	☐	House
P0007	Tea Bags - Decaf	75/Box, Individual Tea Bags	$8.05	10	75.00%	☐	House
P0008	Creamers - Assorted Flavors	400/Case, 8 50-count Boxes	$23.00	10	100.00%	☐	Discount
P0009	Creamers - Liquid	200/Case, Individual Creamers	$17.25	10	100.00%	☑	Premium
P0010	Sugar Packets	2000/Case	$20.70	10	100.00%	☐	House
P0011	Ceramic Mug	SD Company Logo	$5.75	10	100.00%	☐	House
P0012	Sugar Substitute	500/Case, 1-Serving Bags	$21.85	10	50.00%	☐	Discount
P0013	Coffee Filters	500/Case, Fits 10-12 Cup Coffee Maker	$3.45	10	50.00%	☐	House
P0014	Napkins	3000/Case, White	$23.00	10	100.00%	☐	House
P0015	Stirrers - Plastic	1000/Box	$1.72	10	75.00%	☐	Discount

FIGURE 4.37 Products Retrospect Report

a. Right-click the **Products table** and select **Design View**.

   You need to add the OnHand field to the Products table.

b. Click in the **MarkupPercent field**, and then click **Insert Rows** in the Tools group on the Design tab.

   A new blank row displays above the MarkupPercent field.

c. Type **OnHand** in the Field Name box and select **Number** as the Data Type.

d. Save the table. Click **View** in the Views group to switch to Datasheet view.

   The new OnHand column contains no data. Next, you will add some sample data to the new field for testing purposes only.

e. Type the number **10** for each item's OnHand value.

f. Close the Products table.

g. Right-click **Products Report** in the Navigation Pane, and select **Layout View**.

h. Click **Add Existing Fields** in the Tools group on the Design tab to open the Field List pane.

i. Drag the **OnHand field** from the Field List pane between the Cost and MarkupPercent fields. Close the Field List pane.

   Because of the tabular layout control, Access adjusts all the columns to make room for the new OnHand field.

j. Display the report in Print Preview.

The report is still too wide for a single page.

k. Click **Close Print Preview**. Ensure that you are in Layout view.

l. Scroll to and then click anywhere in the **Year Introduced column**. Click the **Arrange tab** and click **Select Column** in the Rows & Columns group. Press **Delete** to remove the column.

The Year Introduced column is removed from the report.

m. Scroll to and then click the **ProductID column heading** and drag the right border to the left until the Product ID heading still fits, but any extra white space is removed.

n. Scroll to and then click the **Refrigeration Needed column heading** and rename the column **Refrig?**. Adjust the width of the *Refrig?* column heading so that any extra white space is removed.

o. Click **Themes** in the Themes group on the Design tab.

The available predefined themes display.

p. Right-click the **Organic theme** and select **Apply Theme to This Object Only**. Display the report in Print Preview.

Access reformats the report using the Organic theme. The report is still too wide for a single page. You will make further adjustments in the next steps.

q. Click **Close Print Preview** and save the report. Click the **File tab**, select **Save As**, select **Save Object As**, and then click **Save As**. Type **Products Organic** as the report name and click **OK**.

You saved the report with one theme. Now, you will apply a second theme to the report and save it with a different name.

r. Ensure that the report is in Layout view. You notice that the Brand column is extending over the dashed page break to its right and needs to be resized to fit on the page. Drag the right border of the Brand column to the left so that it fits inside the page break. Scroll down the report to ensure that all of the values in the column are visible. Narrow columns as required to ensure that all columns are fitting inside the dashed page break. Save the report.

s. Click **Themes** in the Themes group to apply a different theme. Right-click the **Retrospect theme** and select **Apply Theme to This Object Only**. Display the report in Print Preview.

If you do not apply the theme to this object only, all database objects will adopt the Retrospect theme.

t. Click **Close Print Preview**. Click the **File tab**, select **Save As**, select **Save Object As**, and then click **Save As**. Type **Products Retrospect** as the report name and click **OK**. Close the report.

You will be able to show Ryung two product reports with different themes applied.

Ryung would like the Products Report records to be sorted and grouped by Brand. You will change the sort order, group the records, and preview the report to see the results Refer to Figure 4.38 as you complete Step 4.

Products Report Step f: Report grouped by Brand

Brand	Product ID	Product Name	Description	Cost	OnHand	Markup Percer
Discount						
	P0012	Sugar Substitute	500/Case, 1-Serving Bags	$21.85	10	50.00%
	P0005	Coffee - Decaf	24/Case, Pre-Ground 1.75 Oz Bags	$23.00	10	50.00%
	P0008	Creamers - Assorted Flavors	400/Case, 8 50-count Boxes	$23.00	10	100.00%
	P0016	Stirrers - Wood	1000/Box	$1.44	10	100.00%
	P0015	Stirrers - Plastic	1000/Box	$1.72	10	75.00%
	P0001	Coffee - Colombian Supreme	24/Case, Pre-Ground 1.75 Oz Bags	$18.40	10	50.00%
House						
	P0003	Coffee - Mild Blend	24/Case, Pre-Ground 1.75 Oz Bags	$23.00	10	50.00%
	P0004	Coffee - Assorted Flavors	18/Case. Pre-Ground 1.75 Oz Bags	$26.45	10	50.00%
	P0006	Tea Bags - Regular	75/Box, Individual Tea Bags	$5.75	10	75.00%
	P0007	Tea Bags - Decaf	75/Box, Individual Tea Bags	$8.05	10	75.00%
	P0010	Sugar Packets	2000/Case	$20.70	10	100.00%
	P0011	Ceramic Mug	SD Company Logo	$5.75	10	100.00%
	P0014	Napkins	3000/Case, White	$23.00	10	100.00%
	P0025	Milk - 1 pint	Delivered Daily	$1.15	10	100.00%

Products Report — Monday, October 26, 2015 9:35:21 PM

Access 2016, Windows 10, Microsoft Corporation

FIGURE 4.38 Products Report Grouped by Brand

a. Open **Products Report** in Layout view.

b. Click **Group & Sort** in the Grouping & Totals group on the Design tab.

   The *Add a group* and *Add a sort* options display at the bottom of the report.

> **TROUBLESHOOTING:** If the options do not display, the Group, Sort, and Total pane may have been open. If the pane is closed after selecting the command, try clicking Group & Sort again.

c. Click **Add a sort**.

   A new Sort bar displays at the bottom of the report.

d. Select **Brand** from the list.

   The report is now sorted by Brand in ascending order (with Discount at the top).

e. Click **Add a group**.

f. Select **Brand** from the list.

   The report is now grouped by Brand.

g. View the report in Report view. Save and close the report.

h. Close the database and exit Access. Based on your instructor's directions, submit the following:

   a04h2Coffee_LastFirst
   a04h2Products_LastFirst

Chapter Objectives Review

After reading this chapter, you have accomplished the following objectives:

1. Create forms using form tools.

- Identify a record source: A record source is the table or query that supplies the records for the form.
- Use the Form tool: The Form tool creates a basic form that opens in Layout view.
- Understand controls: Controls are the text boxes, buttons, labels, and other tools you use to add, edit, and display data in a form or report.
- Work with form views: Form view is a simplified interface used for data entry, but it allows no design changes. Layout view enables users to make changes to the layout while viewing the data in the form. Design view enables you to change advanced design settings that are not available in Layout view.
- Work with a subform: A subform displays data from a related table for each record in the main table.
- Create a split form: A split form combines two views of the same record source—one section is displayed in a stacked layout and the other section is displayed in a tabular layout.
- Create a multiple items form: This form displays multiple records in a tabular layout similar to a table's Datasheet view, with more customization options.
- Create forms using the other form tools: A datasheet form is a replica of a table or query's Datasheet view except that it still retains form properties. The Form Design tool and the Blank Form tools can be used to create a form manually. The Navigation option in the Forms group enables you to create user interface forms that have the look and feel of Web-based forms and enable users to open and close the objects of a database. The Modal Dialog Form tool can be used to create a dialog box.

2. Modify forms.

- Use Form view to edit data: Most users will work in Form view. This enables changes to data but not to design elements.
- Use Layout view to modify form design: Layout view enables you to change the design of a form while viewing data.
- Adjust column widths in a form: Column widths often need to be adjusted. Size the columns to accommodate the widest entry in a field.
- Add and delete form fields: Fields can be added to an existing form using the Field List. Fields can be removed by selecting the text box and the label controls and pressing Delete.
- Add a theme to a form: Themes can be applied to a single form or to all objects in the database.
- Modify form controls: The Format tab enables changes to the font, including bold, italic, underlining, font size, font color, font background, and alignment.

3. Work with a form layout.

- Modify a form layout: The Arrange tab displays in both Layout view and Design view, and enables you to change form layout, field order, and spacing options.

4. Sort records in form.

- Sort by a single field: Forms can be sorted by a single field in either ascending or descending order.

5. Create reports using report tools.

- Use the Report tool: Access has five report tools. The Report tool instantly creates a tabular report based on a table or query. The Report Design tool creates a new blank report in Design view. The Blank Report tool creates a new blank report so that you can insert controls and design the report manually in Layout view. The Report Wizard tool steps you through the process to create a report. The Labels tool creates a page of mailing labels using a template.
- Use the Report Wizard to create a report: The Report Wizard will guide you step by step through creating a report, prompting you for input and generating output. The wizard enables you to group records of a common type and summarize data in your reports.
- Use the Label Wizard: The Label Wizard can produce printable labels. Access includes predefined standard formats for common labels.

6. Use report views.

- View a report in Report view: Report view is ideal for viewing data onscreen. Neither data nor the design can be changed in this view.
- Print or save a report in Print Preview: Print Preview shows how the report will display when printed. It also enables you to save the report as a file in a number of formats, such as Word and PDF.
- Alter a report in Layout view: Layout view enables you to change the design of a report while viewing data.

7. Modify a report.

- Modify the layout of a report: The Arrange tab displays in both Layout view and Design view. The tools on the Arrange tab enable you to work with the layout of a report to give it a more uniform appearance.
- Modify report controls: The Format tab enables changes to the font, including bold, italic, underlining, font size, font color, font background, and alignment.
- Add a field to a report: Fields can be added to an existing report using the Field List.
- Delete a field from a report: Fields can be deleted either in Layout or Design view.
- Adjust column widths in a report: Column widths often need to be adjusted. Be sure to make the column wide enough to display the widest value in a field.

- Change margins and orientation: You can display the report in portrait or landscape mode and increase or decrease margin sizes.
- Add a theme to the report: Themes can be applied to a single report or to all objects in the database.
- Work with a Report Layout control: The Layout control keeps the fields neatly spaced, making it harder to move fields independently but keeping a standard format.

8. Sort records in a report.
- Change the sorting in a report: You can sort report records by a single or multiple fields.

Key Terms Matching

Match the key terms with their definitions. Write the key term letter by the appropriate numbered definition.

a. Control
b. Design view
c. Form
d. Form tool
e. Form view
f. Label Wizard
g. Layout control
h. Layout view
i. Multiple Items form
j. Portable Document Format (PDF)

k. Print Preview
l. Record source
m. Report
n. Report tool
o. Report view
p. Report Wizard
q. Split form
r. Stacked layout
s. Tabular layout
t. Theme

1. _____ A database object that is used to add data into or edit data in a table. **p. 864**

2. _____ Used to create data entry forms for customers, employees, products, and other tables. **p. 864**

3. _____ The table or query that supplies the records for a form or report. **p. 865**

4. _____ Displays fields in a vertical column. **p. 866**

5. _____ Displays fields horizontally. **p. 866**

6. _____ A text box, button, label, or other tool you use to add, edit, and display the data in a form or report. **p. 866**

7. _____ Provides guides to help keep controls aligned horizontally and vertically and give your form a uniform appearance. **p. 866**

8. _____ A simplified user interface primarily used for data entry; does not allow you to make changes to the layout. **p. 867**

9. _____ Enables users to make changes to a layout while viewing the data in the form or report. **p. 868**

10. _____ Enables you to change advanced design settings you cannot see in Layout view, such as removing a layout control. **p. 869**

11. _____ Combines two views of the same record source—one section is displayed in a stacked layout and the other section is displayed in a tabular layout. **p. 870**

12. _____ Displays multiple records in a tabular layout similar to a table's Datasheet view, with more customization options. **p. 871**

13. _____ A defined set of colors, fonts, and graphics that can be applied to a form or report. **p. 875**

14. _____ A database document that outputs meaningful information to its readers. **p. 889**

15. _____ Used to instantly create a tabular report based on the table or query currently selected. **p. 890**

16. _____ Prompts you for input and then uses your answers to generate a customized report. **p. 891**

17. _____ Enables you to easily create mailing labels, name tags, and other specialized tags. **p. 895**

18. _____ Enables you to determine what a printed report will look like in a continuous page layout. **p. 897**

19. _____ Enables you to see exactly what the report will look like when it is printed. **p. 897**

20. _____ A file type that was created for exchanging documents independent of software applications and operating system environment. **p. 897**

Multiple Choice

1. A report can be made from one or more tables or a query. The object(s) that a report is based on is known as the:

   (a) Control.

   (b) Record Source.

   (c) Theme.

   (d) Tabular Layout.

2. Which of the following statements is *false*?

   (a) Both forms and reports can use tabular and stacked layouts.

   (b) A stacked layout displays data in a vertical column.

   (c) A tabular layout displays data horizontally.

   (d) Stacked layouts are more common for reports because they use less paper when printed.

3. In order to summarize data in a report and override the sort order of the record source you would use:

   (a) A text box.

   (b) A button on a report.

   (c) The Group, Sort, and Total Pane.

   (d) A label on a report.

4. The simplest view you can use to modify control widths in a form is:

   (a) Layout view.

   (b) Form view.

   (c) Design view.

   (d) Print Preview.

5. Which of the following views provides you with the most flexibility in modifying forms and reports?

   (a) Design view

   (b) Layout view

   (c) Form view/Report view

   (d) Print Preview

6. Which of the following statements about reports is *false*?

   (a) Reports can be saved to a file (such as a Word document) on your computer.

   (b) Reports are primarily used to modify data.

   (c) Reports can produce output in a number of ways, including mailing labels.

   (d) Reports can be created simply by using the Report tool.

7. Use the _____ to see exactly what the printed report will look like before printing.

   (a) Report tool

   (b) Report Wizard

   (c) Report view

   (d) Print Preview

8. If you need to send a report to a user who does not have Microsoft Office available, which of the following file formats would be the best choice to ensure it can be opened?

   (a) Word

   (b) Excel

   (c) Reader

   (d) Portable Document Format (PDF)

9. Which of the following statements is *false*?

   (a) Reports are generally used for printing, emailing, or viewing data on the screen.

   (b) Layouts for forms and reports are the predefined sets of colors, fonts, and graphics.

   (c) Forms are often used for inputting data.

   (d) Forms and reports both include controls, such as text boxes, that can be resized.

10. Which of the following statements is *true*?

    (a) You can group records to show a list of properties by state.

    (b) You can sort records in reports but not in forms.

    (c) A sort can only be set on one field at a time.

    (d) You can either group or sort records (but not both).

Practice Exercises

1 Financial Management Prospects

You are working as a customer service representative for a financial management firm. Your task is to contact a list of prospective customers and introduce yourself and the services of your company. You will create a form to view, add, and update data for one customer at a time. After creating the form, you will customize it and add sorting. You will also create a report to display all of the information on one screen, for viewing purposes. Refer to Figure 4.39 as you complete this exercise.

State	First	Last	Zip	Phone	Email	Birth	NetWorth
AR							
	Akira	Hayashi	71638	998-628-2984	AkiHayashi11452@live.com	10/3/1970	$74,000.00
	Yon	Seo	72578	424-632-3415	YoSeo18257@comcast.net	6/11/1956	$70,000.00
AZ							
	Majida	Hayek	86405	555-543-3972	MHayek20676@live.com	11/16/1971	$106,000.00
	Jiao	Hu	85279	958-317-4881	JiaHu17572@mail.com	5/4/1968	$58,000.00
	Betty	Thomas	85346	424-860-7223	BetThomas14786@hotmail.com	1/22/1962	$156,000.00
CA							
	Ashwin	Jayaraman	95653	224-746-8969	AsJayaraman15071@gmail.com	12/28/1950	$55,000.00
	Kenji	Matsumoto	93458	958-230-7462	KenMatsumoto10685@zohomail.com	10/17/1946	$212,000.00
CT							
	Dario	Gonzalez	06029	830-448-4777	DaGonzalez17243@aol.com	5/22/1962	$169,000.00
DC							
	Hiroshi	Kobayashi	20393	351-251-8794	HiKobayashi12104@yahoo.com	7/1/1951	$190,000.00
FL							

Leads — Monday, October 26, 2015 — 9:40:18 PM

FIGURE 4.39 Grouped and Sorted Leads Report

a. Open *a04p1Prospects*. Save the database as **a04p1Prospects_LastFirst**.

b. Click the **Leads table** in the Navigation Pane. Click the **Create tab**, and click **Form** in the Forms group.

A new form based on the Leads table opens in Layout view.

c. Select the **ID text box** of record 1 and drag the right border to the left to resize the column to approximately half of its original width.

The other text boxes will resize as well.

d. Change the title of the form to **New Leads**.

e. Click **Themes** in the Themes group of the Design tab. Apply the **Integral theme** to this form only.

f. Change the font size of the NetWorth text box control to **14** and change the Background Color to **Turquoise, Accent 3**.

g. Click **Select Row** in the Rows & Columns group on the Arrange tab. Click **Move Up** in the Move group until NetWorth displays above First.

> **TROUBLESHOOTING:** If the text box and the label do not move together, click Undo, ensure that both controls are selected, and then follow the instructions in Step g.

h. Save the form as **Leads Form**. Switch to Form view.

i. Navigate to Record 63. Enter your first and last names in the appropriate fields. Leave the Email field blank.

j. Click in the **Last field** and then click **Ascending** in the Sort & Filter group of the Home tab. Farrah Aaron should be the first record displayed unless your last name appears before hers alphabetically.

k. Save and close the form.

l. Click the **Leads table** in the Navigation Pane. Click the **Create tab**, click **More Forms** in the Forms group, and then select **Split Form**.

m. Modify the form title to read **Leads-Split Form**. Save the form as **Leads-Split Form** and close the form.

n. Click the **Leads table**. Click **Report** in the Reports group on the Create tab.

A new report is created based on the Leads table.

o. Make the fields as narrow as possible to remove extra white space. Change the report's orientation to **Landscape**.

p. Delete the **ID**, **Address**, and **City** columns from the report.

q. Ensure that **Group & Sort** is selected in the Grouping & Totals group on the Design tab. Group the records by **State** and sort them by **LastName** in ascending order. Close the Group, Sort, and Total pane.

r. Save the report as **Leads Report**. Close the report.

s. Close the database and exit Access. Based on your instructor's directions, submit a04p1Prospects_LastFirst.

2 Salary Analysis

The Human Resources department of the Comfort Insurance Agency has initiated its annual employee performance reviews. You will create a form for them to perform data entry using the Form tool and a multiple items form. You will create a report to display locations, and a report displaying employee salary increases by location. Additionally, you will save the salary increases report as a PDF file. Refer to Figure 4.40 as you complete this exercise.

Employee Compensation

Location	YearHired	LastName	FirstName	Salary	2018Increase	2018Raise
L01						
	2012	Abrams	Wendy	$47,500.00	3.00%	1425
	2008	Anderson	Vicki	$47,900.00	4.00%	1916
	2012	Bichette	Susan	$61,500.00	4.00%	2460
	2010	Block	Leonard	$26,200.00	3.00%	786
	2011	Brown	Patricia	$20,100.00	5.00%	1005
	2009	Brumbaugh	Paige	$49,300.00	3.00%	1479
	2011	Daniels	Phil	$42,600.00	3.00%	1278
	2010	Davis	Martha	$51,900.00	4.00%	2076
	2009	Drubin	Lolly	$37,000.00	3.00%	1110
	2011	Fantis	Laurie	$28,000.00	3.00%	840
	2009	Fleming	Karen	$41,100.00	3.00%	1233
	2008	Gander	John	$38,400.00	3.00%	1152
	2010	Grippando	Joan	$26,100.00	3.00%	783
	2012	Harrison	Jenifer	$44,800.00	3.00%	1344
	2011	Imber	Elise	$63,700.00	4.00%	2548
	2012	Johnshon	Billy	$21,800.00	5.00%	1090
	2012	Johnson	Debbie	$39,700.00	3.00%	1191

FIGURE 4.40 Employee Compensation Report

a. Open *a04p2Insurance*. Save the database as **a04p2Insurance_LastFirst**.

b. Click the **Locations table** in the Navigation Pane. Click the **Create tab**, and click **Form** in the Forms group.

c. Click the **View arrow** in the Views group on the Home tab, and select **Design View**. Click anywhere in the subform control, and press **Delete**. Switch to Layout view.

d. Ensure that the **LocationID text box** containing *LO1* in Record 1 is selected. Drag the right border to the left to resize the column to approximately half of its original width. The other text boxes will resize as well.

e. Click **Themes** in the Themes group on the Design tab. Right-click the **Wisp theme**, and select **Apply Theme to This Object Only**.

f. Change the font size of the Location text box control (containing *Atlanta*) to **14**, and change the Background Color to **Green, Accent 6, Lighter 60%**.

g. Click **Select Row** in the Rows & Columns group on the Arrange tab. Click **Move Up** in the Move group until Location displays above LocationID.

h. Save the form as **Locations Data Entry**.

i. Click **Layout view**, and delete the **LocationID field**. Delete the **Office Phone label**. Move the **Office Phone field** to the row immediately below the Location field.

j. Add **LocationID** back to the form from the Field List, immediately below the Address field. Close the Field List pane.

k. Switch to Form view, and then save and close the form.

l. Click the **Locations table** in the Navigation Pane. Click the **Create tab**, and click **Report** in the Reports group.

m. Click the **LocationID label**, and drag the right border of the label to the left to reduce the size of the control to approximately half of its original size.

n. Repeat the sizing process with the **Zipcode label** and the **OfficePhone label**. Adjust the other column widths until there are no controls on the right side of the vertical dashed line (page break). Drag the control containing the page number to the left so that it is inside the page break.

o. Display the report in Report view. Verify that the report is only one page wide in Report view. Save the report as **Locations** and close the report.

p. Click the **Employees Query** in the Navigation Pane. Click the **Create tab**, and click **Report Wizard** in the Reports group. Respond to the prompts as follows:
  • Add all the fields to the Selected Fields list. Click **HireDate,** and remove the field from the Selected Fields. Remove **YearHired** from the Selected Fields. Click **Next**.
  • Accept grouping by Location. Click **Next**.
  • Select **LastName** for the first sort order, and **FirstName** for the second (ascending order for both). Click **Summary Options**.
  • Click **Sum** for Salary, **Avg** for 2018Increase, and **Avg** for YearsWorked. Click **OK**. Click **Next**.
  • Accept the Stepped layout. Change Orientation to **Landscape**. Click **Next**.
  • Type **Employee Compensation** for the title of the report. Click **Finish**.

q. Click **Close Print Preview**. Switch to Layout view.

r. Adjust the column widths so that all of the data values are visible and the columns all fit within the vertical dashed border (page break). Some of the text boxes and labels will need to be relocated; select the control to be moved and click and drag it to a new location.

s. Click **Themes** in the Themes group on the Design tab. Right-click the **Slice theme** and select **Apply Theme to This Object Only**. Adjust the label widths and report title so that they are fully visible. Scroll to the bottom of the report and move any text boxes, such as the page number control, so that they are inside the page break. Resize all text boxes and labels so that their values are fully visible.

t. Delete the **YearsWorked field** and **label**.

u. Click and drag **YearHired** from the Field List into the report layout. Drag and drop the column into the space immediately to the right of the Location column. Close the Field List. Display the report in Print Preview. Compare your report to Figure 4.40. Make adjustments as required.

v. Save the report as a PDF file named **a04p2Employee_Compensation_LastFirst**. Close the reader program.

w. Save and close the Employee Compensation report.

x. Create a Multiple Items form based on the Titles table. Resize the fields so that they are all visible onscreen without scrolling. Save the form as **Job Titles**. Close the form.

y. Close the database and exit Access. Based on your instructor's directions, submit the following:

a04p2Insurance_LastFirst

a04p2Employee Compensation_LastFirst

Mid-Level Exercises

Hotel Chain

ANALYSIS CASE

You are the general manager of a large hotel chain. You track revenue by categories, such as conference room rentals and weddings. You want to create a report that shows which locations are earning the most revenue in each category. You will also create a report to show you details of your three newest areas: St. Paul, St. Louis, and Seattle.

a. Open *a04m1Rewards*. Save the database as **a04m1Rewards_LastFirst**.

b. Select the **Members table,** and create a Multiple Items form. Save the form as **Maintain Members**.

c. Modify the form in Layout view as follows:
- Change the MemNumber label to **MemID,** and reduce the MemNumber column width.
- Adjust the column widths to eliminate extra white space.
- Delete the form icon (the picture next to the title of the form) in the Form Header.

d. Change the sorting on the MemberSince control so that the members who joined most recently are displayed first.

DISCOVER

e. Click the **LastName field**. Change the Control Padding to **Wide**. (Hint: Search **Control Padding** in the *Tell me what you want to do...* box).

f. Save and close the form.

g. Select the **Revenue query,** and create a report using the Report Wizard. Answer the wizard prompts as follows:
- Include all fields in the report.
- Add grouping first by **City** and then by **ServiceName**.
- Add a Sum to the Revenue field, and click the **Summary Only option**.
- Select **Outline Layout**.
- Name the report **Revenue by City and Service**.

h. Scroll through all the pages to check the layout of the report while in Print Preview mode.

i. Close Print Preview. Switch to Layout view, and delete the **NumInParty** and **PerPersonCharge** controls.

j. Change the font size, font color, and background color of the Sum control (found at the bottom of the report) so the control stands out from the other controls.

k. Change the font size, font color, and background color of the Grand Total control (found at the end of the report) so the control stands out as well.

l. Change the sort on the report, so that it sorts by city in descending order—that is, so that the last city alphabetically (St. Paul) is displayed first.

m. Examine the data in the report to determine and note which city (St. Paul, St. Louis, or Seattle) has the highest Sum of event revenue. You will use this information to modify a query. Save and close the report.

n. Modify the Totals by Service query so that the criteria for the City field is the city you determined had the highest sum of event revenue (St. Paul, St. Louis, or Seattle). Run, save, and close the query.

o. Create a report using the Report tool based on the Totals by Service query. Name the report **Targeted City**.

p. Close the report.

q. Close the database and exit Access. Based on your instructor's directions, submit a04m1Rewards_LastFirst.

2 Benefit Auction

FROM SCRATCH

You are helping to organize a benefit auction to raise money for families who lost their homes in a natural disaster. The information for the auction is currently stored in an Excel spreadsheet, but you have volunteered to import it into Access. You will create a database that will store the data from Excel in Access. You will create a form to manage the data-entry process. You also create two reports: one that lists the items collected in each category and one for labels so you can send the donors a thank-you letter after the auction.

a. Open Access, and create a new database named **a04m2Auction_LastFirst**.
   A new table displays with an ID column.

b. Switch to Design view. Type **Items** in the **Save As dialog box**, and click **OK**.

c. Change the ID Field Name to **ItemID**. Type **Description** in the second row, and press **Tab**. Set **Short Text** as the Data Type. Type **50** in the **Field Size property** in Field Properties.

d. Type the remainder of the fields and adjust the data types as shown:

Field Name	Data Type
DateOfDonation	**Date/Time**
Category	**Short Text**
Price	**Currency**
DonorName	**Short Text**
DonorAddress1	**Short Text**
DonorAddress2	**Short Text**

e. Open Excel. Open the *a04m2Items* file. Examine the length of the Category, Donor Name, Donor Address 1, and Donor Address 2 columns. Determine how many characters are needed for each field based on the longest value in each column, and round that value up to the nearest 5. For example, if a field needs 23 characters, you would round up to 25. You will use this to change field sizes in the table.

f. Change the field sizes for Category, DonorName, DonorAddress1, and DonorAddress2 to the sizes you chose in Step e. Save the table.

g. Copy and paste the 26 rows from the Excel spreadsheet into the Items table. To paste the rows, locate the * to the left of the first blank row, click the Record Selector, right-click the Record Selector, and then from the shortcut menu, select Paste. Resize the columns so all data is visible. Close the table.

> **TROUBLESHOOTING:** Once you have pasted the data, ensure that your chosen field sizes did not cause you to lose data. If so, update the field sizes, delete the records you pasted to the table, and then repeat Step g.

h. Verify that the Items table is selected in the Navigation Pane. Create a new form using the **Form** tool.

i. Change the layout of the form to **Tabular Layout**. Resize field widths to reduce extra space. It is acceptable for field values in the text boxes to display on two lines.

j. Change the title of the form to **Items for Auction**.

k. Add conditional formatting so that each Price that is greater than 90 has a text color of **Green** (seventh column, first row below Standard Colors).

l. Save the form as **Auction Items Form**.

m. Switch to Form view. Create a new record with the following data. Note that the form will automatically assign an ItemID for you.

Description	DateOfDonation	Category	Price	DonorName	DonorAddress1	DonorAddress2
iPad	12/31/2018	House	$400	Staples	500 Market St.	Brick, NJ 087?

n. Add a sort to the form, so that the lowest priced items display first. Save and close the form.

o. Select the **Items table** in the Navigation Pane, and create a report using the Report Wizard. Include all fields except the two donor address fields, group by Category, include the Sum of Price as a Summary Option, accept the default layout, and then save the report as **Auction Items by Category**.

p. Switch to Layout view, and adjust the controls so that all data is visible. Adjust the widths of the controls until there are no controls extending over the right side of the vertical dashed line (page break). Preview the report to verify that the column widths are correct.

q. Sort the report so the least expensive item is displayed first in each group. Save and close the report.

r. Create mailing labels based on the Avery 5660 template. Place the donor name on the first line, address (**DonorAddress1**) on the second, and city, state, and ZIP (**DonorAddress2**) on the third line. Sort the labels by **DonorName**. Name the report **Donor Labels**. After you create the labels, display them in Print Preview mode to verify that all values will fit onto the label template. Close the label report.

s. Close the database and exit Access. Based on your instructor's directions, submit a04m2Auction_LastFirst.

3 New Castle County Technical Services

RUNNING CASE

New Castle County Technical Services (NCCTS) provides technical support for a number of companies in the greater New Castle County, Delaware, area. Now that you have completed the database tables, set the appropriate relationships, and created queries, you are ready to create a form and a report.

a. Open the database *a03m3NCCTS_LastFirst* and save it as **a04m3NCCTS_LastFirst**.

> **TROUBLESHOOTING:** If you did not complete the Chapter 3 case, return to Chapter 3, complete the case, and then return to this exercise.

b. Create a split form based on the Calls table.

c. Apply the **Integral theme** to this form only.

d. Add the **Description field** by dragging and dropping it immediately below the CallTypeID (Hint: Click **Show all tables** in the Field List pane, and locate the field by expanding the **Call Types table**). Close the Field List pane. Switch to Form view and ensure that the records are sorted by CallID in ascending order.

e. Save the form as **Calls Data Entry**, and close the form.

f. Use the Report tool to create a basic report based on the Customer Happiness query.

g. Sort the records by the **Avg Rating field** in ascending order.

h. Apply the **Integral theme** to this report only.

i. Change the title of the report to **Customer Satisfaction Ratings**, and format the background color of the control to **Medium Gray** (under Standard Colors).

j. Set the font color of the title control to **Blue, Accent 2**, the font size to **20**, and the alignment to **Center**. Click the default logo in the report header and press **Delete**.

k. Switch to Report view. Save the report as **Customer Satisfaction Survey**, and close the report.

l. Close the database and exit Access. Based on your instructor's directions, submit a04m3NCCTS_LastFirst.

Beyond the Classroom

Create a Split Form
GENERAL CASE ✓
FROM SCRATCH

This chapter introduced you to Access forms, including the split form. It is possible to convert an existing form into a split form if you know how to modify form properties. First, create a new database and name the file **a04b1Split_LastFirst**. Next, import only the Books table and Books form from the *a04b1BooksImport* database. To import the objects, click the **External Data tab** and click **Access** in the Import & Link group. Perform an Internet search to find the steps to convert a form to a split form. Use the information from the Internet to convert the Books form into a split form. Make sure the datasheet is in the bottom pane of the form. Delete the AuthorCode text box and label from the top pane of the form. Change the form so that it sorts by Title in ascending order. Increase the font size of the Title control to **14**, and change its background color to **Medium Gray** (under Standard Colors). Apply the **Integral** theme to this form only. Save the form as **Split Form Books**. Switch to Form view, and then close the form. Close the database and exit Access. Based on your instructor's directions, submit a04b1Split_LastFirst.

Properties by City
DISASTER RECOVERY ✚

A co-worker is having difficulty with an Access report and asked you for your assistance. He was trying to fix the report and seems to have made things worse. Open the *a04b2Sales* database and save the file as **a04b2Sales_LastFirst**. Open the Properties Report in Report view. The report columns do not fit across one page. In addition, there is a big gap between two fields, and he moved the Beds and Baths fields so they are basically on top of one another. Add all of the fields to a tabular layout. Group the records first by City, and then by Beds in descending order. Within each group, sort the report by ListPrice in descending order. Change the report to Landscape orientation and adjust the column widths so they all fit across one page (inside the dashed vertical page break). Apply the Organic theme to this report only, and switch to Report view. Save the new report as **Properties by City**, close the report, and then delete the original **Properties Report** from the database (right-click the report in the Navigation Pane, and from the shortcut menu, select **Delete**). Close the database and exit Access. Based on your instructor's directions, submit a04b2Sales_LastFirst.

Capstone Exercise

Your boss asked you to prepare a schedule for each speaker for the national conference being hosted next year on your campus. She wants to mail the schedules to the speakers so that they can provide feedback on the schedule prior to its publication. You assure her that you can accomplish this task with Access.

Database File Setup

You need to copy an original database file, rename the copied file, and then open the copied database to complete this Capstone exercise. After you open the copied database, you replace an existing employee's name with your name.

a. Open the *a04c1_NatConf* database, and save it as **a04c1NatConf_LastFirst**.

b. Open the Speakers table.

c. Find and replace *YourName* with your own first and last name. Close the table.

Create and Customize a Form

You want to create a form to add and update the Speakers table. Use the Form tool to create the form and modify the form as required. You will also add a layout to an existing form.

a. Select the **Speakers table** in the Navigation Pane as the record source for the form.

b. Use the **Form tool** to create a new form with a stacked layout.

c. Change the form's title to **Enter/Edit Speakers**.

d. Reduce the width of the text box controls to approximately half of their original size.

e. Delete the **Sessions subform** control from the form.

f. View the form and the data in Form view. Sort the records by **LastName** in ascending order.

g. Save the form as **Edit Speakers**. Close the form.

h. Open the Room Information form in Layout view. Select all controls in the form, and apply the **Stacked Layout**.

i. Switch to Form view, and then save and close the form.

Create a Report

You will create a report based on the Speaker and Room Schedule query. You decide to use the Report Wizard to accomplish this task. You will also email the schedule to the presenters, so you will save the report as a PDF file.

a. Select the **Speaker and Room Schedule query** in the Navigation Pane as the record source for the report.

b. Activate the **Report Wizard**, and use the following options as you proceed through the wizard steps:
- Select all of the available fields for the report.
- View the data by Speakers.
- Accept LastName and FirstName as the grouping levels.
- Use **Date** as the primary sort field in ascending order.
- Accept the Stepped and Portrait options.
- Save the report as **Speaker Schedule**.
- Switch to Layout view, and apply the **Organic theme** to this report only.

c. Switch to Report view to determine whether all of the columns fit across the page. Switch to Layout view, and ensure that the column widths are adjusted accordingly.

d. Switch to Print Preview, and save the report as a PDF named **a04c1Speaker_LastFirst**.

e. Close the reader program that displays the PDF report, and return to Access. Close Print Preview. Save and close the report.

Add an Additional Field to the Query and the Report

You realize that the session start times were not included in the query. You add the field to the query and then create a new report with the Report Wizard to include the missing field.

a. Open the Speaker and Room Schedule query in Design view.

b. Add the **StartingTime field** from the Sessions table to the design grid, after the Date field. Run the query.

c. Save and close the query.

d. Click the **Speaker and Room Schedule query**. Activate the Report Wizard again and use the following options:
- Select all of the available fields for the report.
- View the data by Speakers.
- Use the LastName and FirstName fields as the grouping levels.
- Use **Date** as the primary sort field in ascending order.
- Use **StartingTime** as the secondary sort field in ascending order.
- Select the **Stepped** and **Portrait options**.
- Name the report **Speaker Schedule Revised**.
- Switch to Layout view and apply the **Facet theme** to this report only.

e. Adjust the widths of the columns and other controls so that all the data is visible and fits across the page. Switch to Report view to ensure that the adjustments were appropriate. Return to Layout view, and make any required changes.

f. Add spaces to the column heading labels so that all values display as two words where appropriate, for example, the label *LastName* should read **Last Name**, *RoomID* as **Room ID**, etc.

g. Save and close the report.

h. Close the database and exit Access. Based on your instructor's directions, submit the following:

a04c1NatConf_LastFirst
a04c1Speaker_LastFirst

PowerPoint

Introduction to PowerPoint

LEARNING OUTCOME **You will plan, create, navigate, and print a basic presentation.**

OBJECTIVES & SKILLS: After you read this chapter, you will be able to:

CASE STUDY | Be a Trainer

You teach employee training courses for the Training and Development department of your State Department of Human Resources. You begin each course by presenting your objectives for the course using a Microsoft Office PowerPoint 2016 presentation. You create a slide show to help you organize your content and to help your audience retain the information.

Because of the exceptional quality of your presentations, the director of the State Department of Human Resources has asked you to prepare a new course on presentation skills. In the Hands-On Exercises for this chapter, you will work with two presentations for this course. One presentation will focus on the benefits of using PowerPoint, and the other will focus on the preparation for a slide show, including planning, organizing, and delivering.

Creating a Basic Presentation

The Essence of PowerPoint

▶ **You**

    ▶ Focus on content and enter your information

    ▶ Add additional elements to create interest

    ▶ Motivate your audience while presenting

▶ **PowerPoint**

    ▶ Helps you organize your thoughts

    ▶ Provides tools to make slide show creation easy

    ▶ Allows flexibility in delivery and presentation

PowerPoint 2016, Windows 10, Microsoft Corporation

FIGURE 1.1 Be a Trainer Slide

CASE STUDY | Be A Trainer

Starting File	Files to be Submitted
p01h1Intro	**p01h1Intro_LastFirst** **p01h1Intro_LastFirst.ppsx** **p01h4Content_LastFirst**

Work with PowerPoint

You can use Microsoft Office PowerPoint 2016 to create an electronic slide show or other materials for use in a professional presentation. A *slide* is the most basic element of PowerPoint (similar to a page being the most basic element of Microsoft Word). A collection of slides is referred to as a *deck* of slides. The slides may be easily arranged just as cards can be easily shuffled in a deck of cards. The arranged slides displayed onscreen for an audience is a *slide show*, often referred to as a presentation. A *PowerPoint presentation* is an electronic slide show that can be edited or delivered in a variety of ways: you can project the slide show on a screen as part of a presentation, run it automatically at a kiosk or from a DVD, display it on the World Wide Web, email it, or create printed handouts.

Figure 1.2 shows the first four slides of a PowerPoint presentation. The slides contain different types of content, such as text, an online picture, and a table. The presentation has a consistent color scheme. It is easy to create presentations with consistent and attractive designs using PowerPoint.

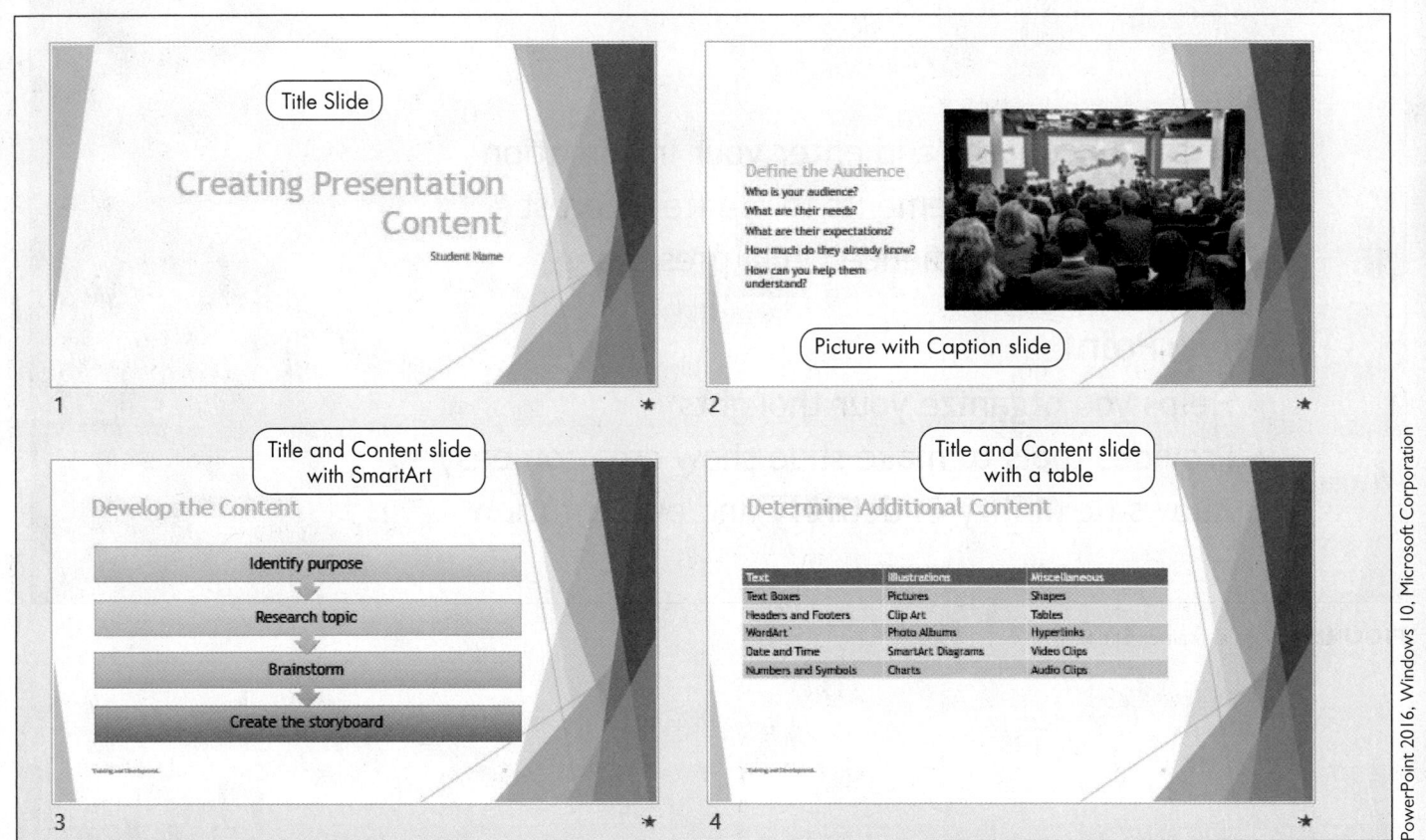

FIGURE 1.2 Various PowerPoint Slide Layouts

In this section, you will start your exploration of PowerPoint by opening and viewing a previously completed presentation. You will modify the presentation by adding identifying information, examining different PowerPoint views to discover the advantages of each, and saving the presentation.

Opening and Viewing a PowerPoint Presentation

STEP 1 ❯❯ When you open a new presentation or a previously created presentation, you see the default PowerPoint workspace, *Normal view*. Figure 1.3 shows Normal view, which displays the Ribbon and other common interface components as well as two panes that provide maximum flexibility in working with the presentation. The pane on the left side of the screen, the **Slides pane**, shows the slide deck with **thumbnails** (slide miniatures) representing the location of the slides. The slides are numbered to help you select the slide you want to edit. The large pane on the right side of the screen, the **Slide pane**, is the main workspace and displays the currently selected slide.

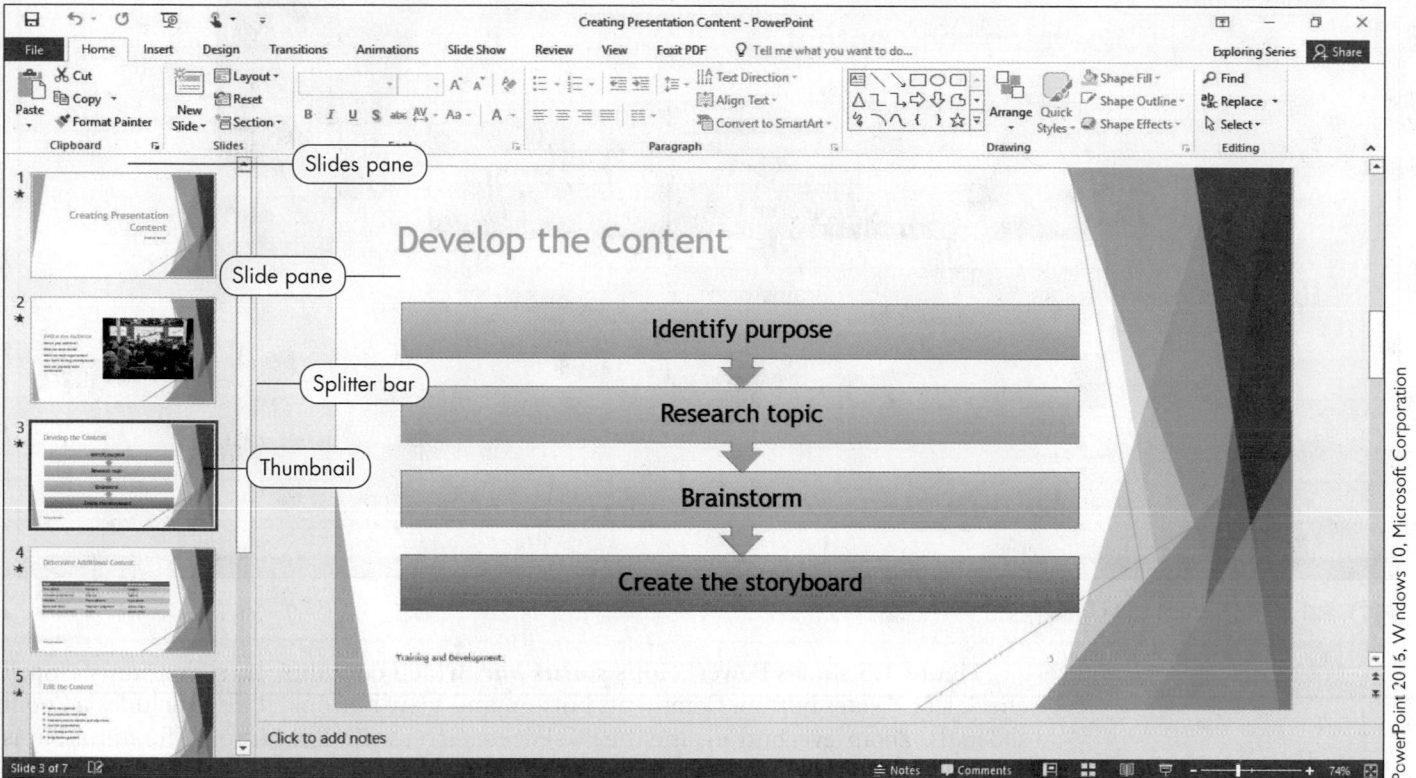

FIGURE 1.3 Normal View (Default PowerPoint View)

TIP: ADD-INS TAB
You may see an Add-Ins tab on the Ribbon. This tab indicates that additional functionality, such as an updated Office feature or an Office-compatible program, has been added to your system. Add-Ins are designed to increase your productivity.

While in Normal view, you can hide the left pane that displays the thumbnails. Doing so will expand the workspace so you can see more detail while editing slide content. To hide the pane with the thumbnails, drag the border that separates the panes one from another to the left until you see the word Thumbnails appear on the left side. Figure 1.4 shows an individual slide in Normal view with the Slides pane closed. You can quickly restore the view by clicking the arrow above Thumbnails or you can click the View tab and click Normal in the Presentation Views group. You can also widen the Slides pane to show more detail by dragging the splitter bar to the right.

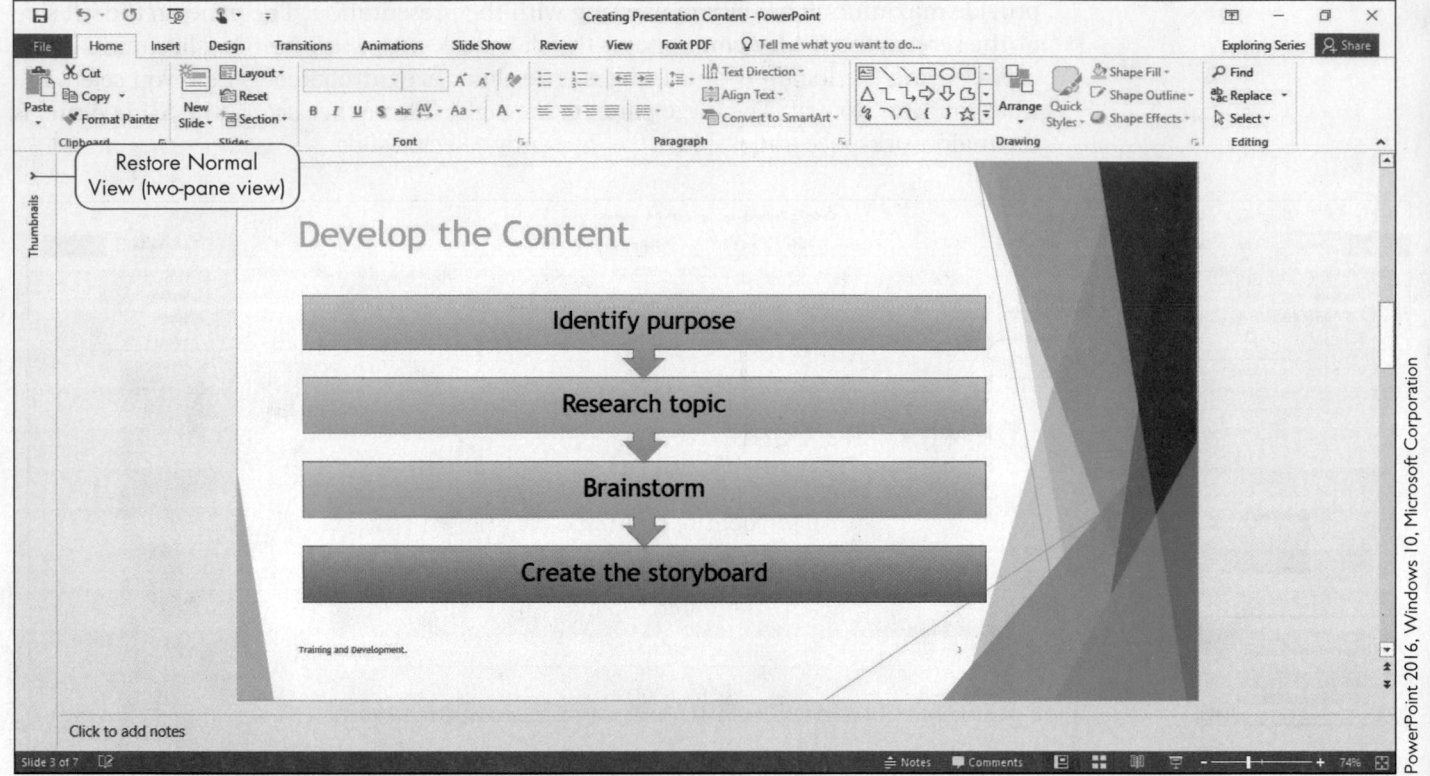

FIGURE 1.4 Individual Slide View

Figure 1.5 shows PowerPoint's *status bar*, which contains the slide number, Spell check icon, Notes button, Comments button, and View buttons. It also includes a Zoom slider, the Zoom level button, and the Fit slide to current window button. The status bar is located at the bottom of your screen and can be customized.

To customize the status bar, complete the following steps:

1. Right-click the status bar.
2. Select the options to display from the Customize Status Bar list.
3. Click off the Customize Status Bar list to return to editing.

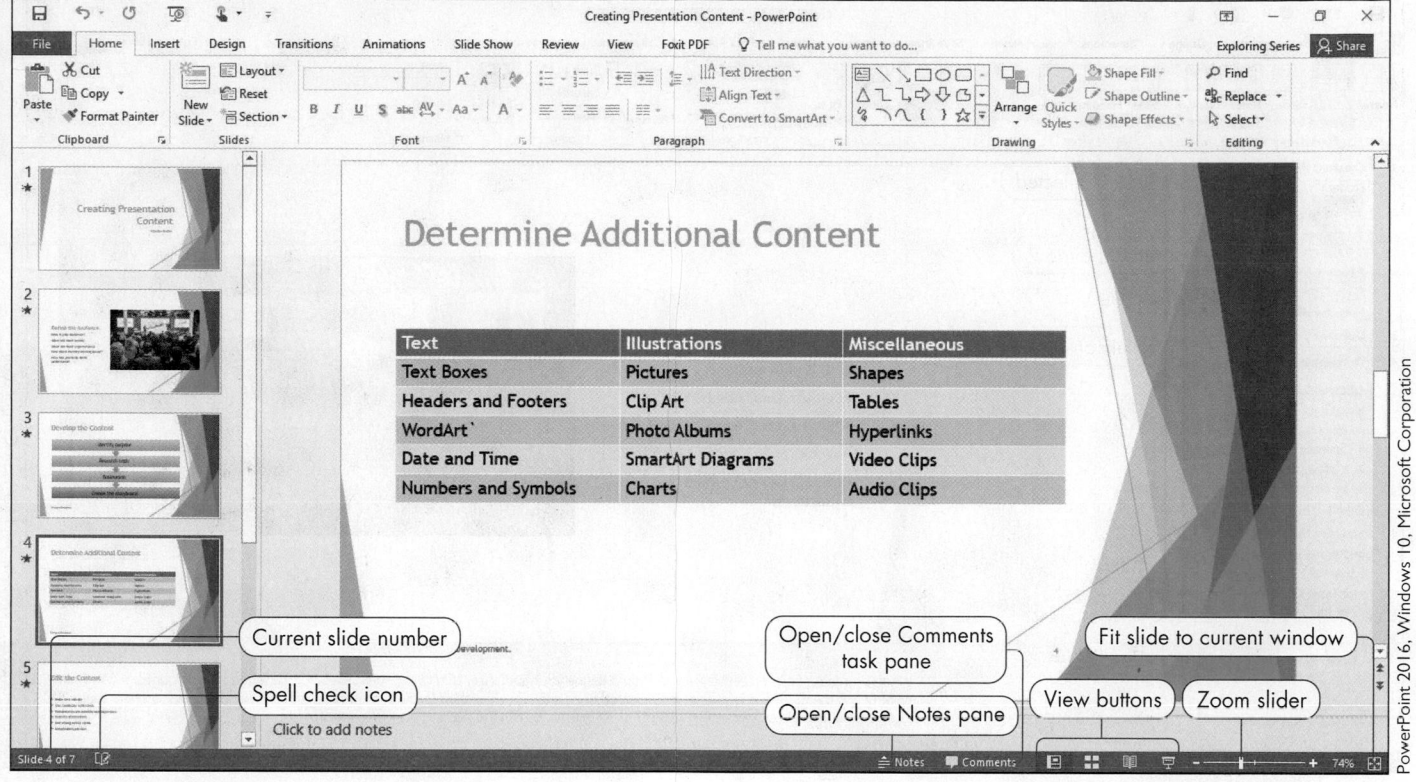

FIGURE 1.5 PowerPoint Status Bar

Use PowerPoint Views Effectively

In addition to Normal view, PowerPoint offers specialty views to enable you to work effectively and efficiently with your slides. The Presentation Views group on the View tab enables you to access these views:

- Normal
- Outline View
- Slide Sorter
- Notes Page
- Reading View

Use *Outline View* when you would like to enter text into your presentation using an outline. In other words, rather than having to enter the text into each placeholder on each slide separately, you can type the text directly into an outline. Figure 1.6 shows an example of Outline View.

PowerPoint 2016, Windows 10, Microsoft Corporation

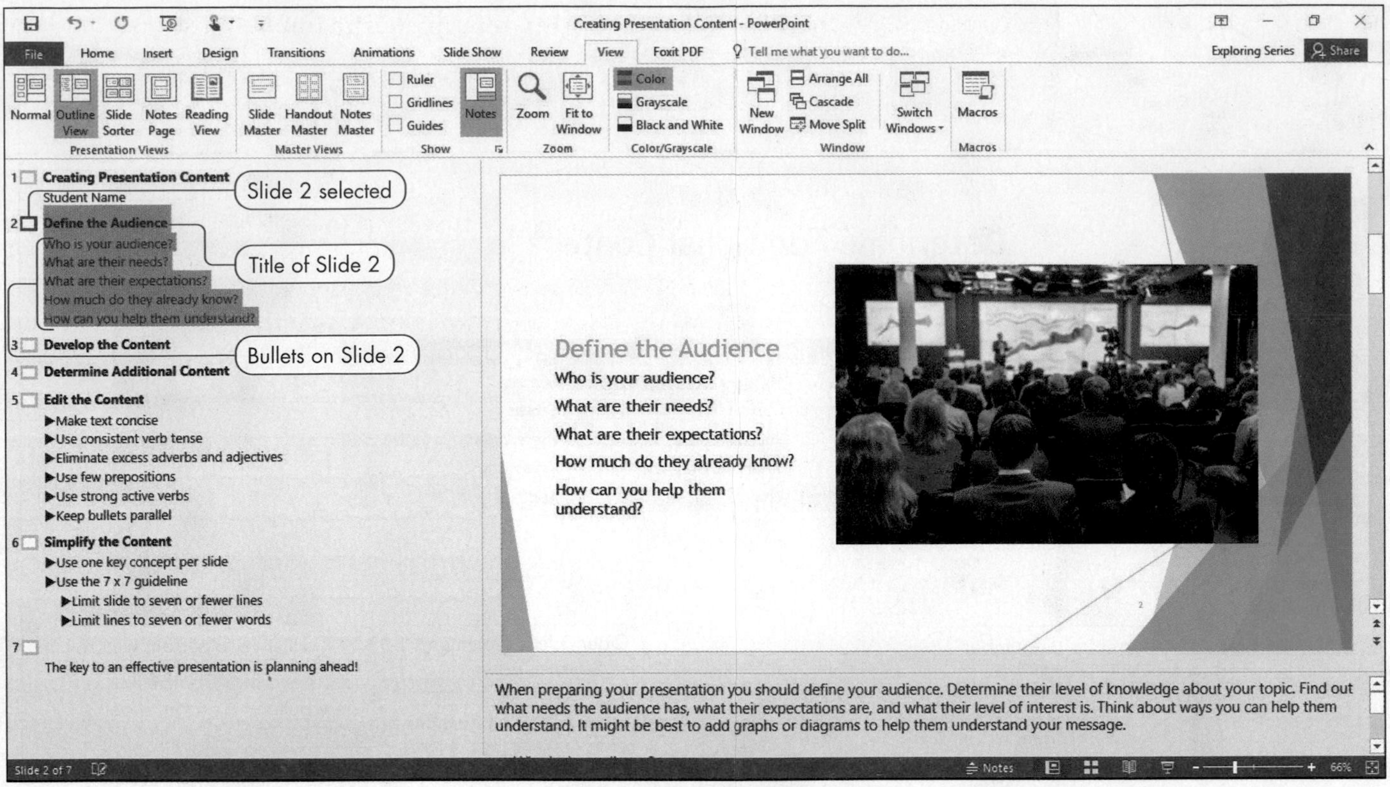

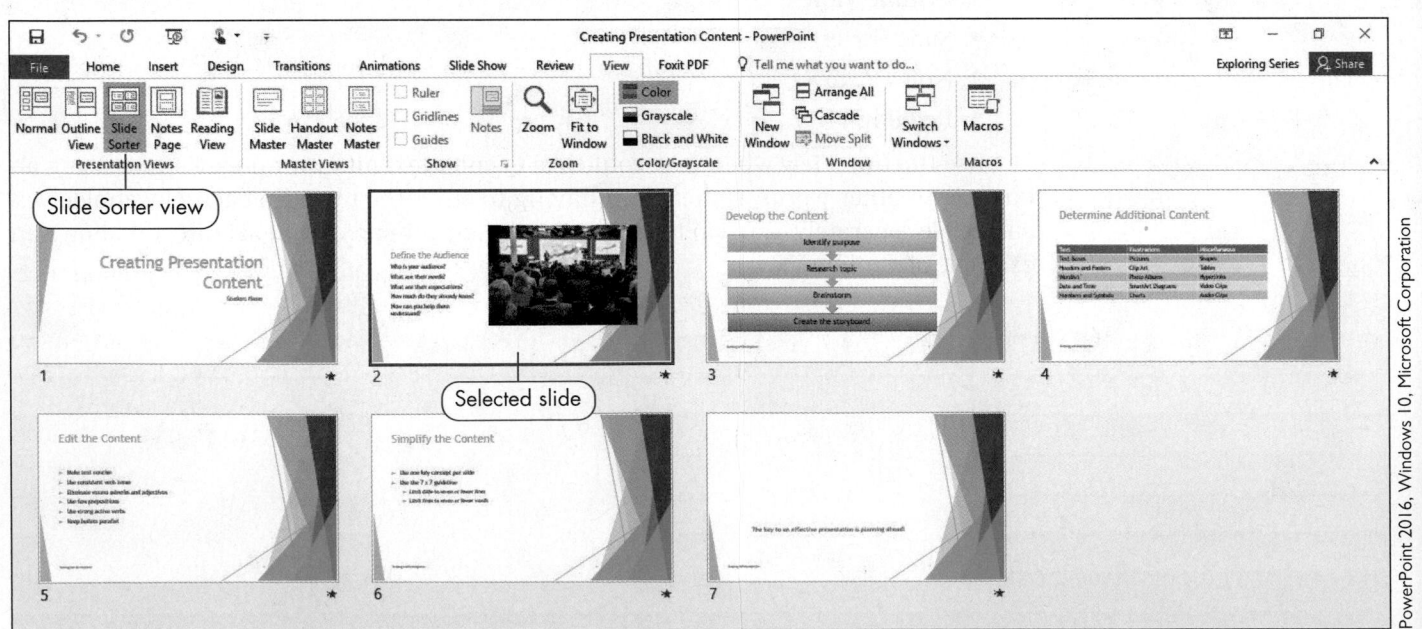

FIGURE 1.6 Outline View

Slide Sorter view displays thumbnails of your presentation slides, which enables you to view multiple slides simultaneously (see Figure 1.7). This view is helpful when you want to change the order of the slides, or to delete one or more slides. You can set transition effects (the way the slides transition from one to another) for multiple slides in Slide Sorter view. If you are in Slide Sorter view and double-click a slide thumbnail, PowerPoint displays the selected slide in Normal view.

PowerPoint 2016, Windows 10, Microsoft Corporation

FIGURE 1.7 Slide Sorter View

> **To rearrange slides in Slide Sorter view, complete the following steps:**
>
> 1. Move the pointer over the slide thumbnail of the slide you want to move.
> 2. Drag the slide to the new location.

Use **_Notes Page view_** when you need to enter and edit large amounts of text that you can refer to when presenting. Slides should contain just key points and you should elaborate on the key points verbally as you deliver the presentation. Consequently, speaker notes can be a most useful tool when giving a presentation. Notes do not display when the presentation is shown (except when Presenter view is used), but are intended to help the speaker remember the key points or additional information about each slide. Figure 1.8 shows an example of Notes Page view.

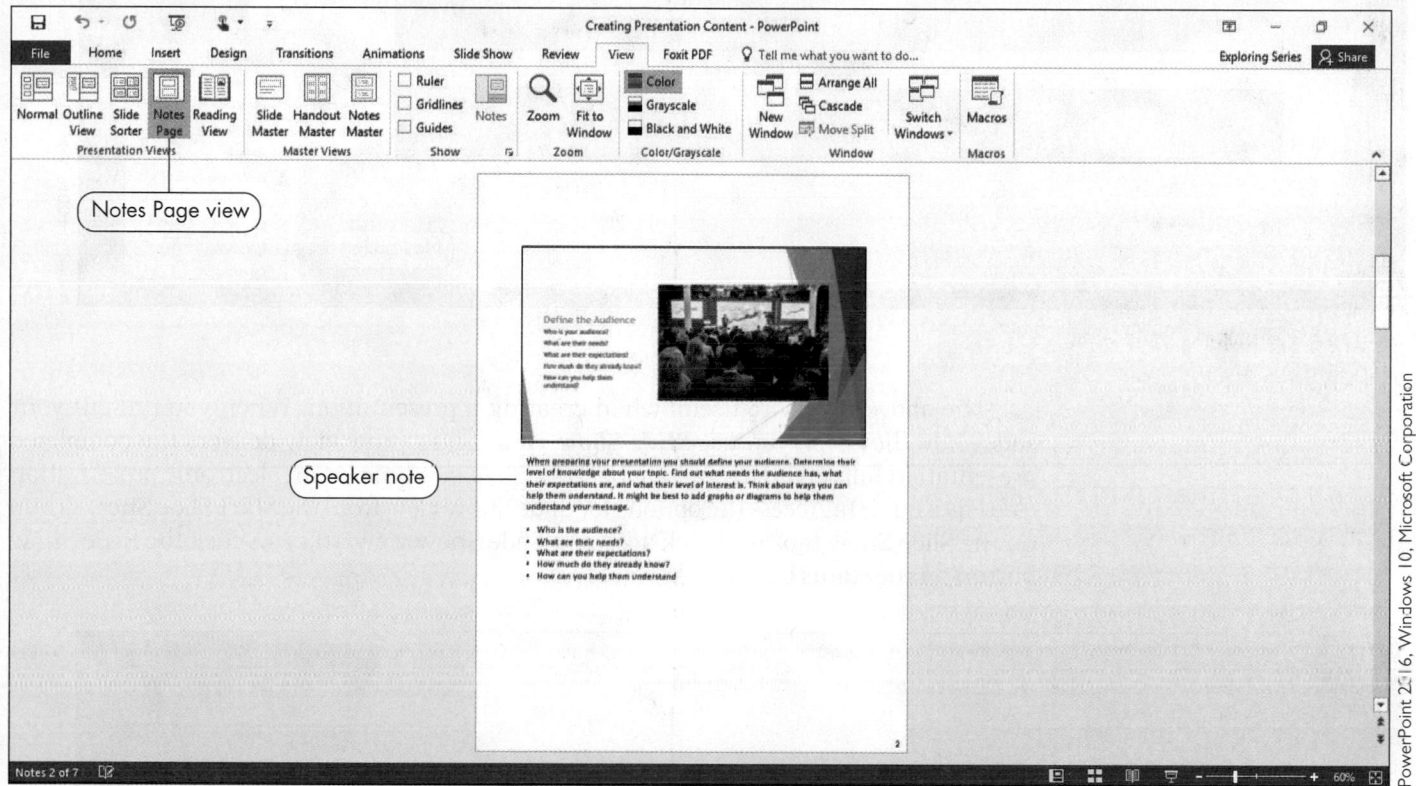

FIGURE 1.8 Notes Page View

Use **_Reading View_** to view the slide show full screen, one slide at a time. Animations and transitions are active in Reading View. A title bar, including the Minimize, Maximize/Restore Down (which changes its name and appearance depending on whether the window is maximized or at a smaller size), and Close buttons, is visible, as well as a modified status bar (see Figure 1.9). In addition to View buttons, the status bar includes navigation buttons for moving to the next or previous slide, as well as a menu for accomplishing common tasks such as printing. Press Esc to return quickly to the previous view.

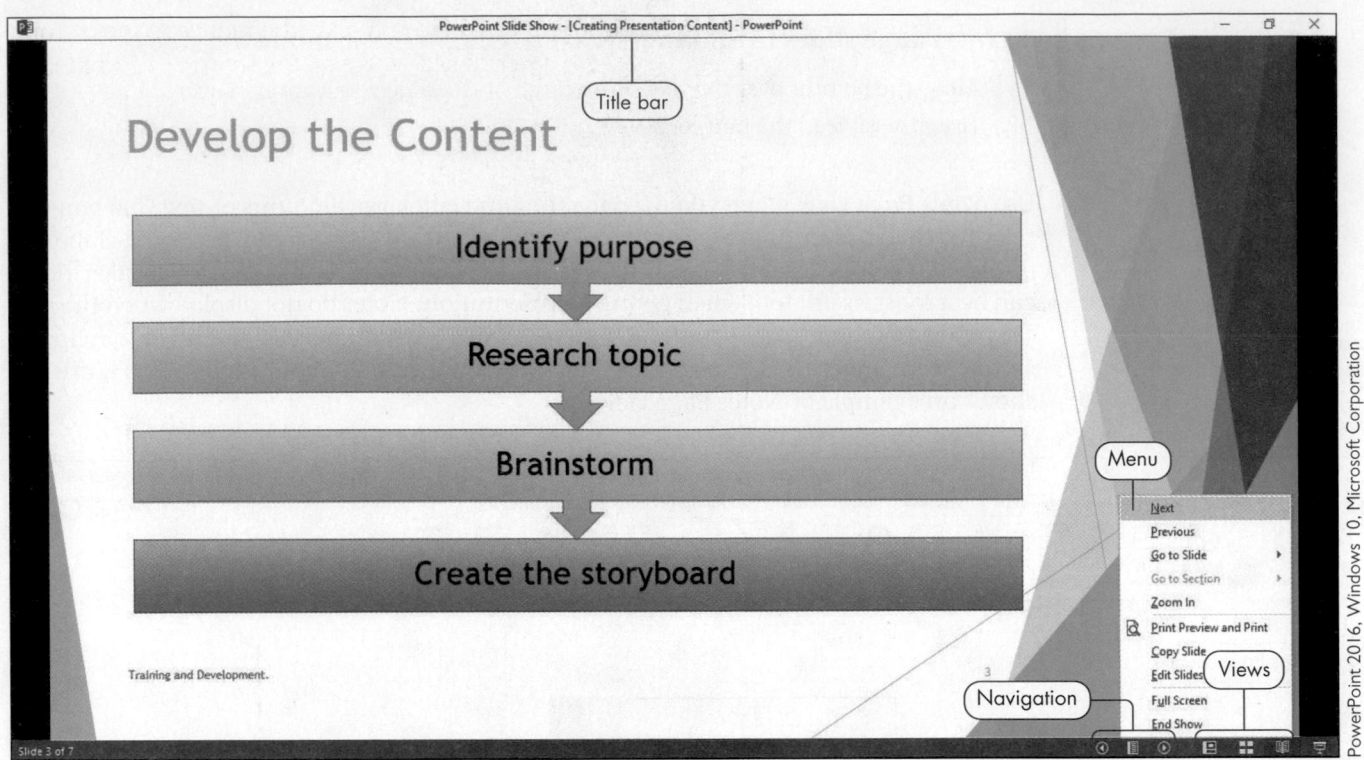

FIGURE 1.9 Reading View

The above views are useful when creating a presentation. When you present your slide show, however, you use ***Slide Show view***. Slide Show view delivers the completed presentation full screen to an audience, one slide at a time, as an electronic presentation (see Figure 1.10). Access the options for Slide Show view from the Start Slide Show group on the Slide Show tab. For quick access to Slide Show view, you can click the Slide Show button on the status bar.

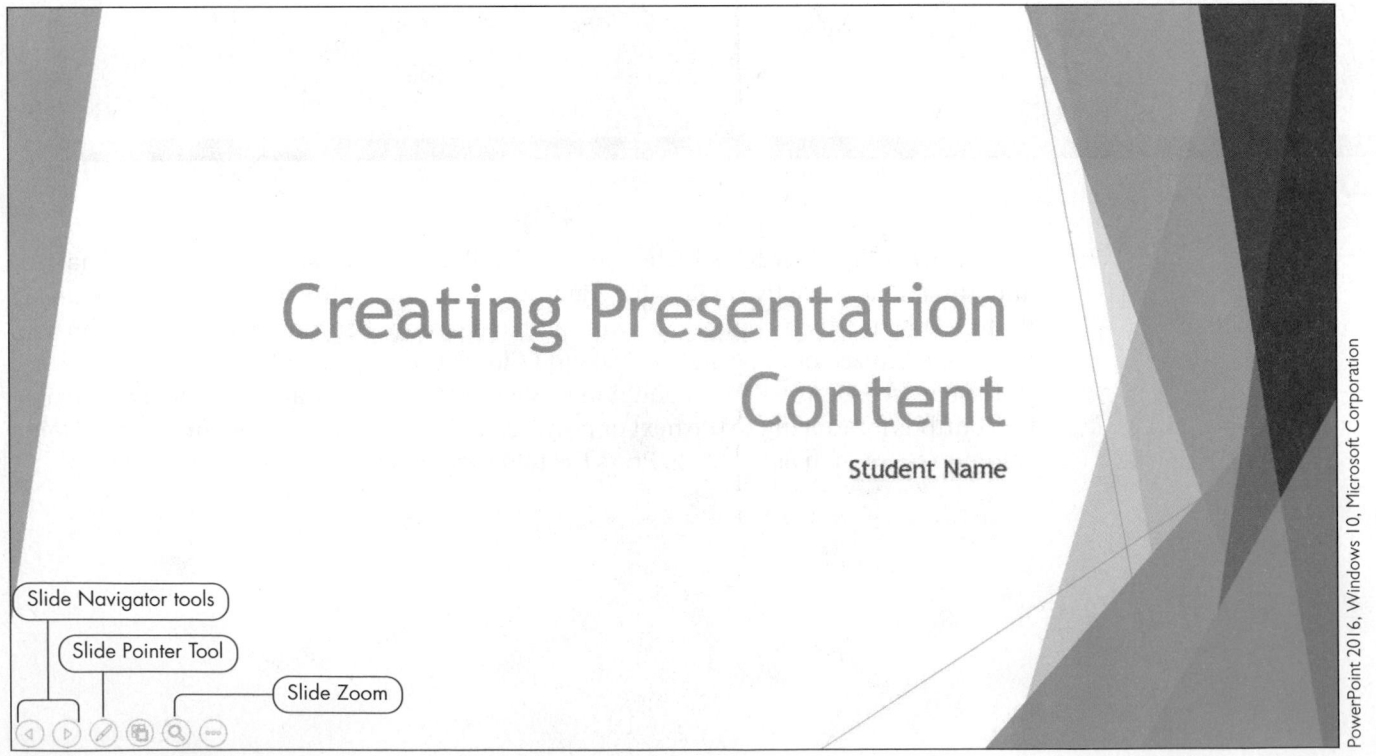

FIGURE 1.10 Slide Show View

The slide show can be presented manually, where you click the mouse to move from one slide to the next, or automatically, where each slide stays on the screen for a predetermined amount of time, after which the next slide appears. A slide show can contain a combination of both methods. To end the slide show, press Esc. This view also includes pointer tools, Slide Navigator that enables you to move between slides as needed without leaving Slide Show view, and Slide Zoom that you can use to focus your audience on your ideas.

Presenter view, accessed from the Monitors group on the Slide Show tab, is an especially valuable view that lets you deliver a presentation using two monitors simultaneously. Typically, one monitor is a projector that delivers the full-screen presentation to the audience; the other monitor is a laptop or computer that displays the presentation in Presenter view. Presenter view includes a slide, a thumbnail image of the next slide, and any speaker notes you have created. The view options are displayed on the second monitor so the presenter can control them. This view includes a timer that displays the time elapsed since the presentation began so you can keep track of the presentation length. Figure 1.11 shows the audience view on the right side of the figure and the Presenter view on the left side.

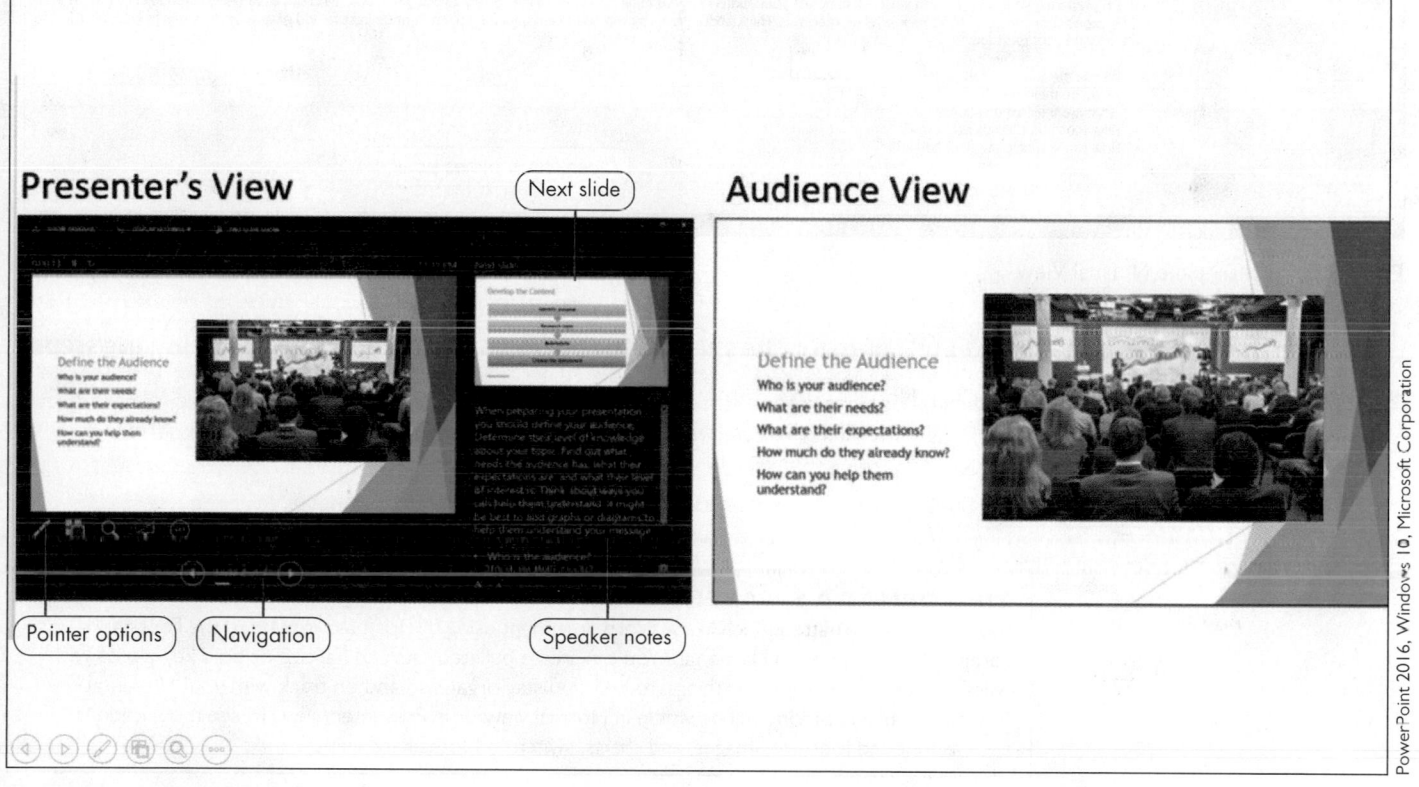

FIGURE 1.11 Presenter View

Typing a Speaker Note

STEP 2 » Rather than change your view to Notes Page view to type speaker notes, you can change Normal view from a two-paned view to a three-paned view as shown in Figure 1.12. To display the Notes pane, click Notes on the status bar. The Notes pane will display below the Slide Pane, the main working area.

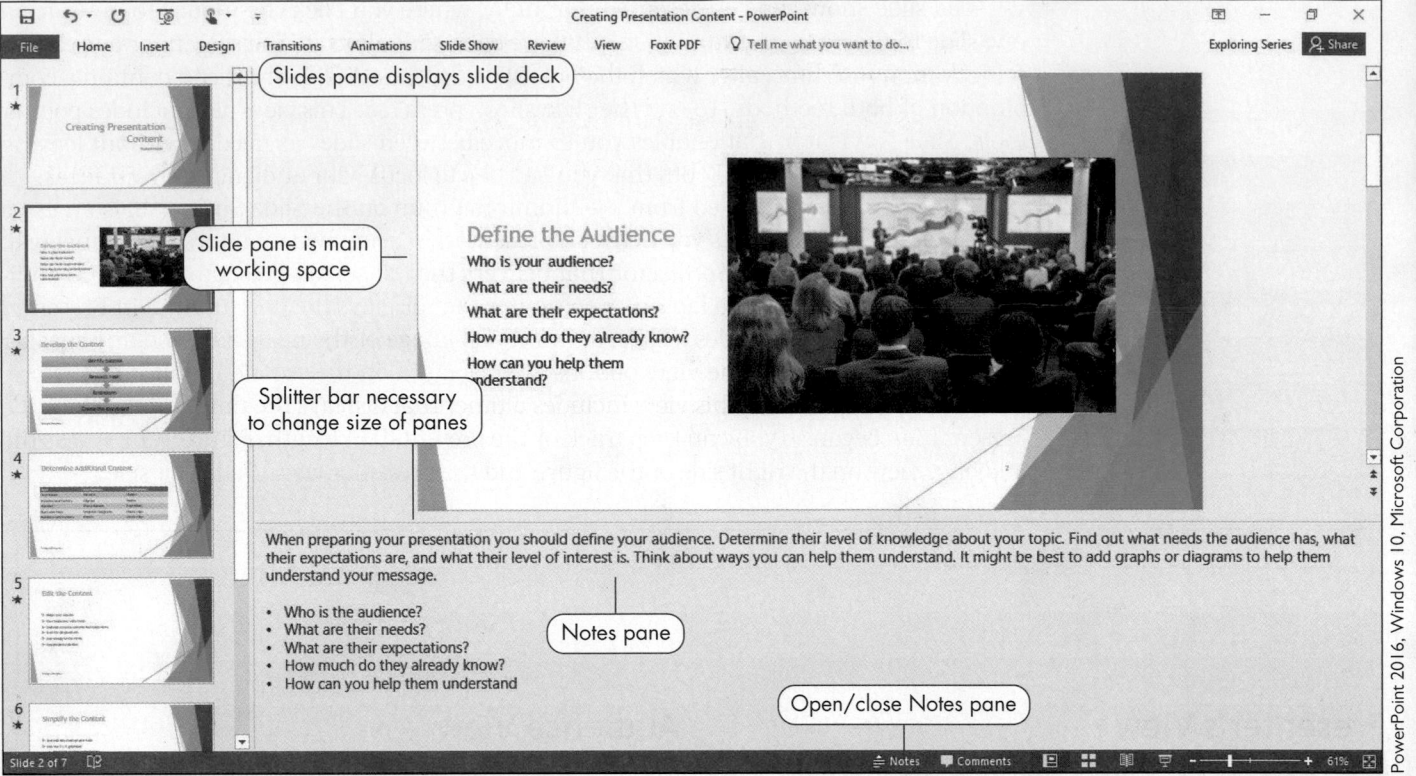

FIGURE 1.12 Tri-pane Normal View

To create a note for the speaker in the Notes pane, complete the following steps:

1. Click Notes on the status bar if the Notes pane is not visible.
2. Drag the splitter bar between the Slide pane and the Notes pane up to expand the Notes pane.
3. Click in the Notes pane and begin typing.

> **TIP: FORMAT A SPEAKER NOTE**
> Notes can be formatted much like a Word document using the formatting tools in the Font and Paragraph groups on the Home tab. You can create bulleted lists and italicize or bold key words you want to feature, among other things, to help you stay organized and on track with your presentation. Not all text modifications will be visible in Normal view or in Presenter view. To see modifications such as font and font size, images, and charts, switch to Notes Page view.

Saving as a PowerPoint Show

STEP 3 ▶▶ When you save a ***PowerPoint presentation***, by default it is saved with a .pptx file extension. Then, when you open the file, it opens to Normal view, or edit mode, so that you can make changes to the presentation. If you use Save As and save the presentation as a ***PowerPoint show*** with a .ppsx extension, the presentation opens in Slide Show view. You will not see the PowerPoint interface; the presentation is in play mode. This is valuable when you are ready to present and do not want your audience to see the PowerPoint interface. You double-click the PowerPoint show file with a .ppsx extension in File Explorer to open the presentation in Slide Show view. PowerPoint presentations are often saved as .ppsx files for distributing to others, too. Although a .ppsx file cannot be changed while viewing, you can open the file in PowerPoint and edit it.

1. Describe the main advantage for using each of the following views: Normal view, Notes Page view, Slide Sorter view, and Slide Show view. *pp. 929–933*

2. Discuss the purpose of a speaker note. *p. 931*

3. Explain the difference between a PowerPoint presentation (.pptx) and a PowerPoint show (.ppsx). *p. 934*

Hands-On Exercises

Skills covered: View a Presentation in Normal View • Use the Notes Pane • Save a Presentation in PowerPoint Show Mode

1 Work with PowerPoint

You have been asked to create a presentation on the benefits of PowerPoint for the Training and Development department. You decide to view an existing presentation to determine if it contains material you can adapt for your presentation. You view the presentation, add a speaker note, and then save the presentation as a PowerPoint presentation and as a PowerPoint show.

STEP 1 ›› OPEN AND VIEW A POWERPOINT PRESENTATION

You open a presentation created by your colleague. You experiment with various methods of advancing to the next slide and then return to Normal view. As you use the various methods of advancing to the next slide, you find the one that is most comfortable to you and then use that method as you view slide shows in the future. An audio clip of audience applause will play when you view Slide 4: The Essence of PowerPoint. You will want to wear a headset if you are in a classroom lab so that you do not disturb classmates. Refer to Figure 1.13 as you complete Step 1.

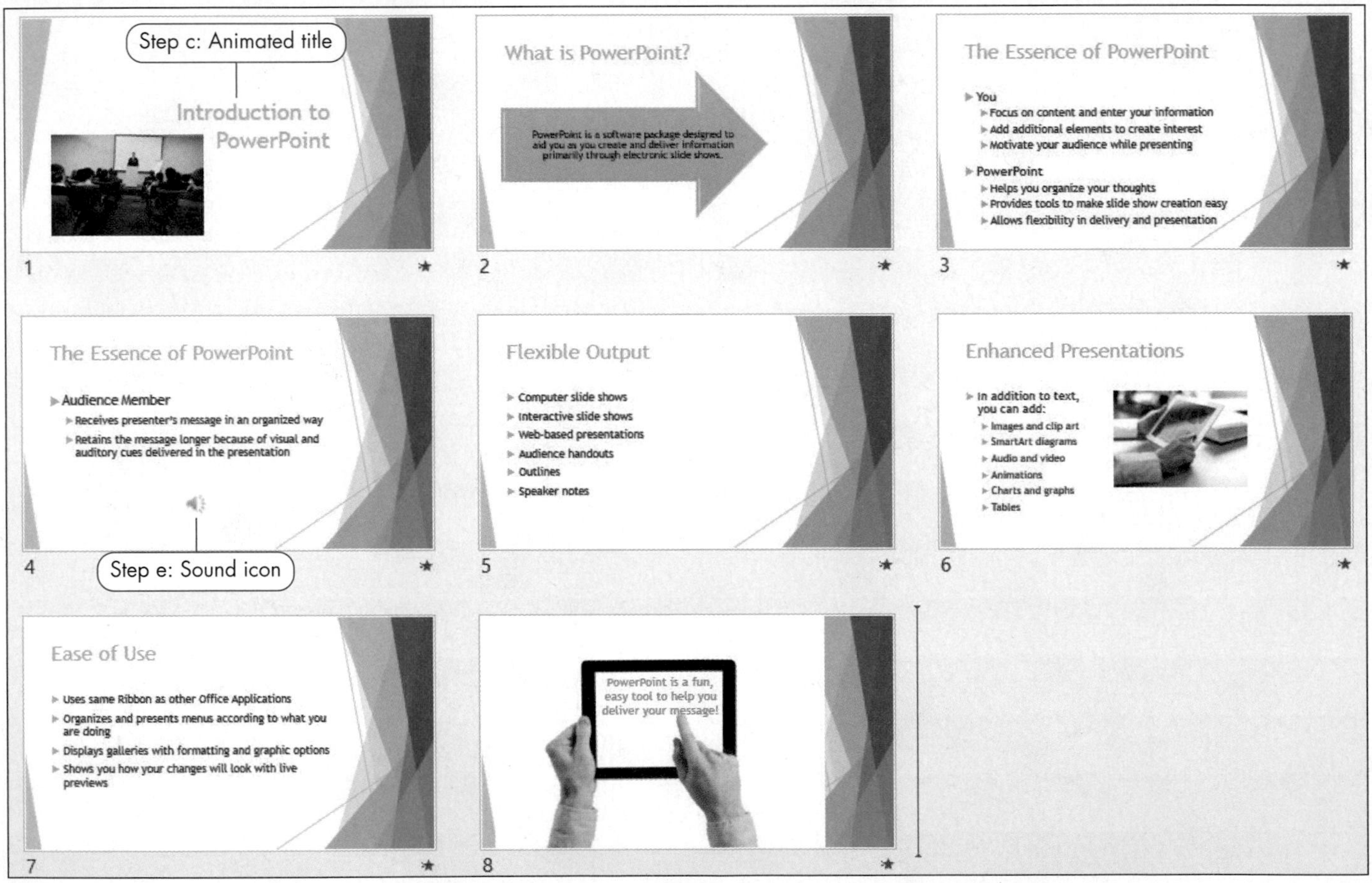

FIGURE 1.13 Introduction to PowerPoint Presentation

> **a.** Start PowerPoint and open the *p01h1Intro* file. Save the file as **p01h1Intro_LastFirst**. When you save files, use your last and first names. For example, as the PowerPoint author, I would name my presentation "p01h1Intro_KrebsCynthia".

> **TROUBLESHOOTING:** If you make any major mistakes in this exercise, you can close the file, open *p01h1Intro* again, and then start this exercise over.

b. Click **Slide Show** on the status bar.

The presentation begins with the title slide, the first slide in all slide shows. The title has an animation assigned, so it displays automatically.

c. Press **Spacebar** to advance to the second slide and read the slide.

The title animation on the second slide automatically wipes down, and the arrow wipes to the right.

d. Position the pointer in the lower-left corner side of the slide, and click the **right arrow** in the Navigation bar to advance to the next slide. Click to read the animated slide content.

The text on the third slide, and all following slides, has the same animation applied to create consistency in the presentation.

e. Press the **left mouse button** to advance to the fourth slide, which has a sound icon displayed on the slide.

The sound icon on the slide indicates sound has been added. The sound has been set to start automatically so you do not need to click anything for the sound to play.

> **TROUBLESHOOTING:** If you do not hear the sound, your computer may not have a sound card or your sound may be muted.

f. Continue to navigate through the slides until you come to the end of the presentation (a black screen).

g. Press **Esc** to return to Normal view.

STEP 2 ›› TYPE A SPEAKER NOTE

You add a speaker note to a slide to help you remember to mention some of the many objects that can be added to a slide. You also view the note in Notes view to see how it will print. Refer to Figure 1.14 as you complete Step 2.

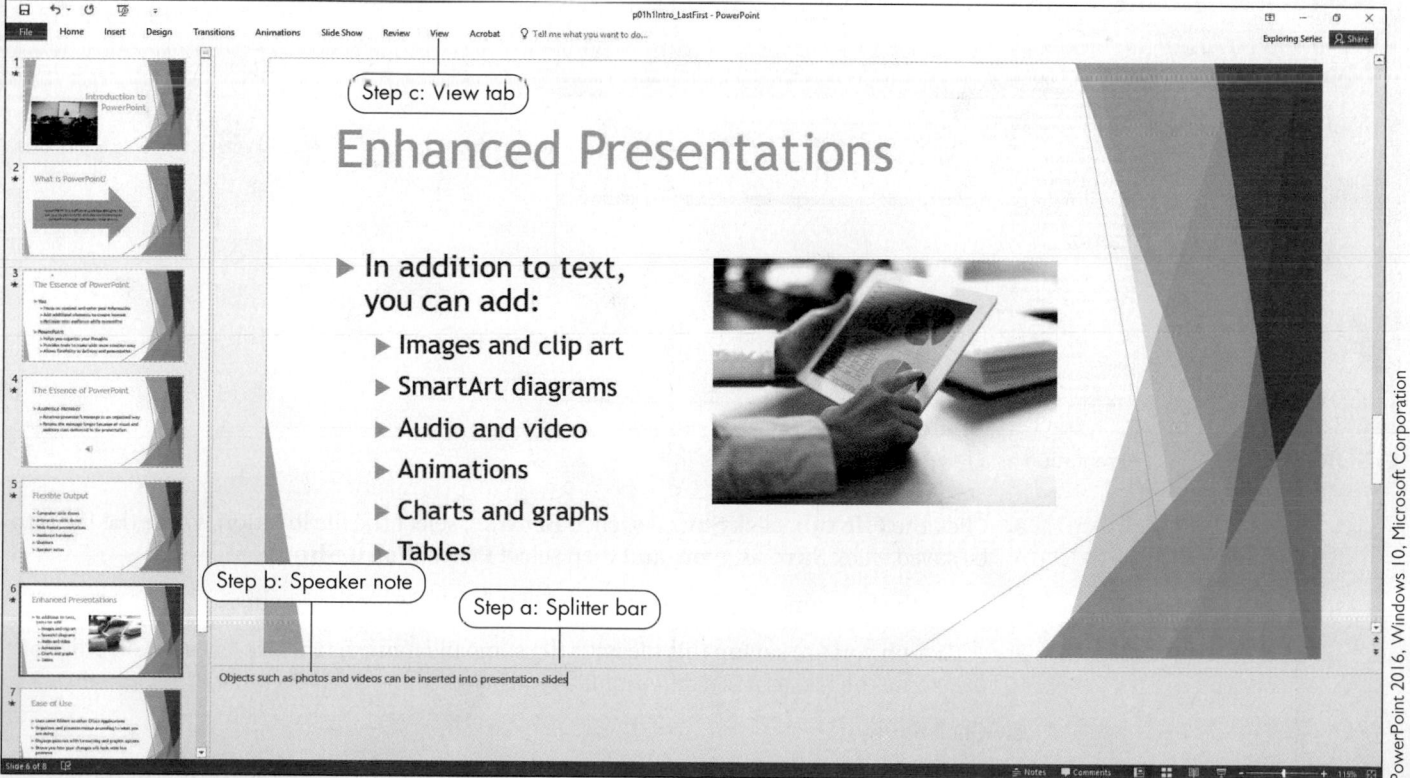

FIGURE 1.14 Speaker Note in Notes Pane of Normal View

a. Click the **Slide 6 thumbnail** and then drag the border between the Slide pane and the Notes pane up to expand the Notes pane.

Slide 6 is selected, and the slide displays in the Slide pane.

> **TROUBLESHOOTING:** If the Notes pane is not visible, click Notes on the status bar.

b. Type **Objects such as pictures and videos can be inserted into presentation slides.** in the Notes pane.

c. Click the **View tab** and click **Notes Page** in the Presentation Views group.

The slide is shown at a reduced size and the speaker note is shown below the slide.

d. Click **Normal** in the Presentation Views group.

This displays the presentation in Normal view.

e. Save the presentation.

STEP 3)) SAVE AS A POWERPOINT SHOW

You want to save the slide show as a PowerPoint show so that it opens automatically in Slide Show view rather than Normal view. Refer to Figure 1.15 as you complete Step 3.

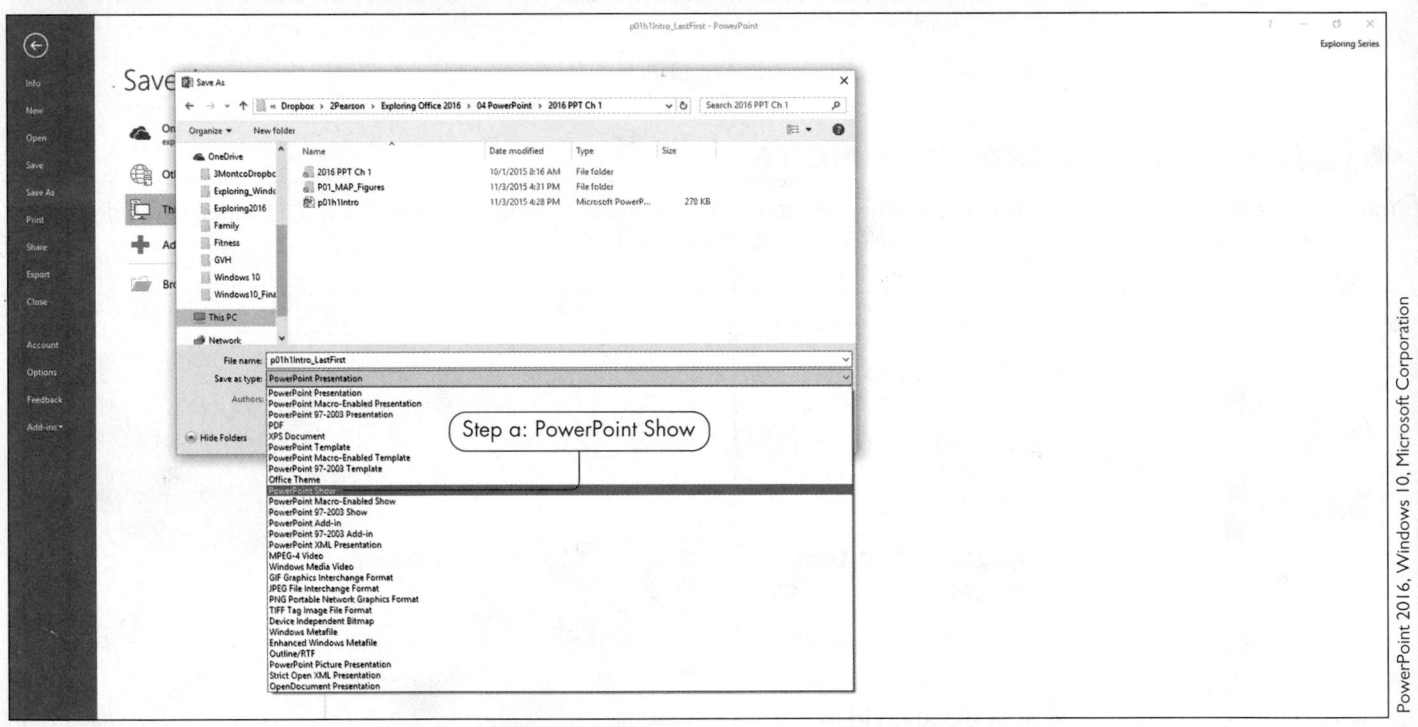

FIGURE 1.15 Saving a Presentation as a PowerPoint Show

a. Click the **File tab**, click **Save As**, click **Browse**, select the file location where the file is to be saved, click **Save as type**, and then select **PowerPoint Show**.

b. Leave the file name **p01h1Intro_LastFirst** for the PowerPoint show.

Although you are saving this file with the same file name as the presentation, it will not overwrite the file, as it is a different file type.

c. Click **Save**.

d. Close the presentation. You will submit these files to your instructor at the end of the last Hands-On Exercise.

Presentation Creation

You are ready to create your own presentation by choosing a theme, adding content, and applying formatting. You create the presentation by adding the content first and then applying formatting so that you can concentrate on your message and its structure without getting distracted by the formatting of the presentation.

In this section, you will create a visual plan called a storyboard. You will also learn to polish your presentation by using layouts, applying design themes, and reviewing your presentation for errors.

Planning and Preparing a Presentation

Creating an effective presentation requires advance planning. First, determine the purpose of your presentation. An informative presentation could notify the audience about a change in policy or procedure. An educational presentation could teach an audience about a subject or a skill. Sales presentations are often persuasive calls to action to encourage the purchase of a product, but they can also be used to sell an idea or process. A goodwill presentation could be used to recognize an employee or acknowledge an organization. You could even create a certificate of appreciation using PowerPoint.

Next, research your audience—determine their level of knowledge about your topic. Find out what needs the audience has, what their expectations are, and what their level of interest is.

After determining your purpose and researching your audience, brainstorm how to deliver your message. Before using your computer, you may want to sketch out your thoughts on paper to help you organize them. After organizing your key points, add them as content to the slide show, and then format the presentation.

Use a Storyboard

A *storyboard* is a visual plan for your presentation that helps you map out the direction of your presentation. It can be a very rough draft that you sketch out while brainstorming, or it can be an elaborate plan that includes the text and objects drawn as they would appear on a slide.

A simple PowerPoint storyboard is divided into sections representing individual slides. The first block in the storyboard is used for the title slide. Subsequent blocks are used to introduce the topics, develop the topics, and then summarize the information. Figure 1.16 shows a working copy of a storyboard for planning presentation content. The storyboard is in rough-draft form and shows changes made during the review process. A blank copy of the document in Figure 1.16 has been included with your student files should you want to use this for presentation planning. The PowerPoint presentation shown in Figure 1.17 incorporates the changes to the storyboard made during the review process.

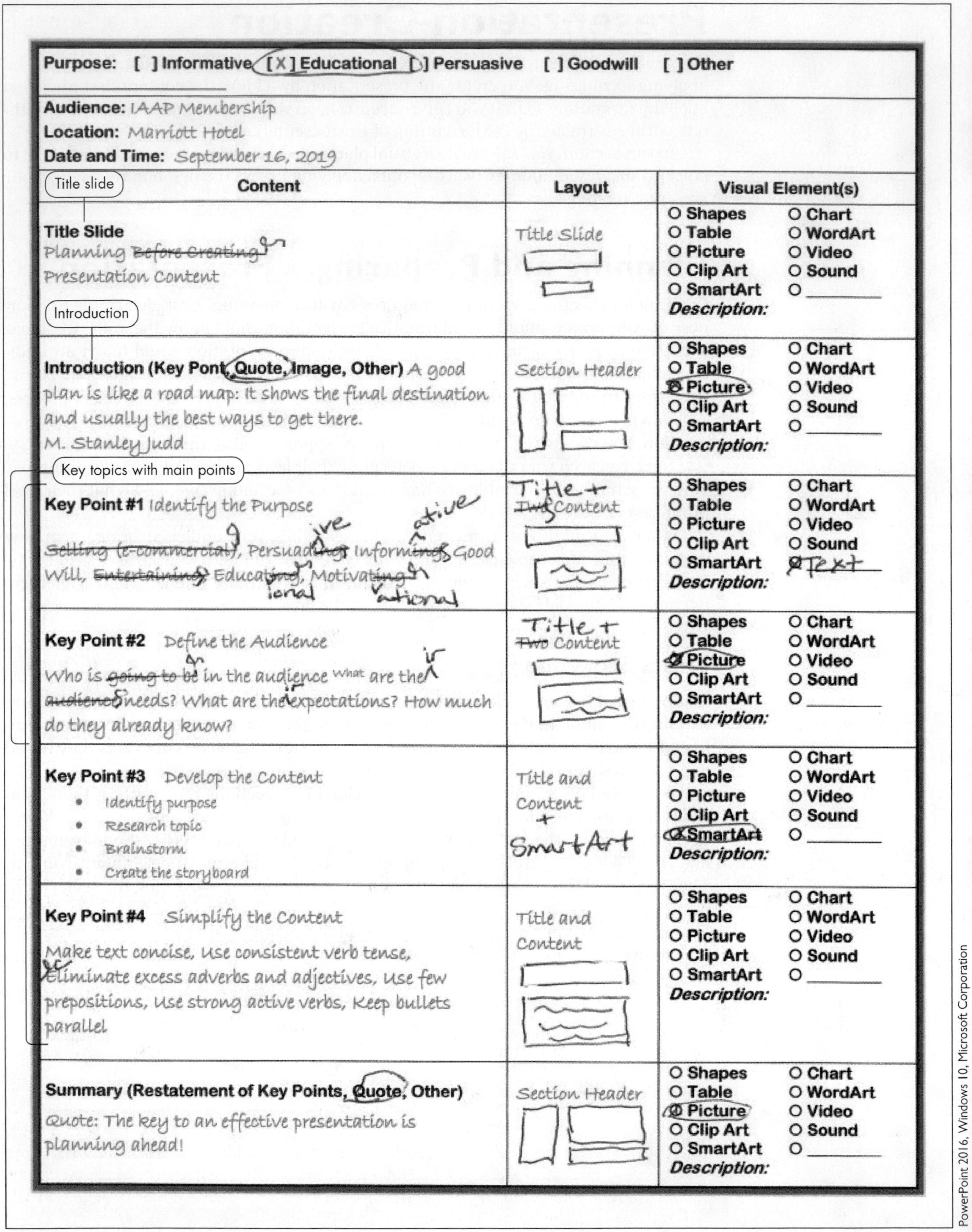

Purpose: [ ] Informative   (X) Educational   [ ] Persuasive   [ ] Goodwill   [ ] Other

Audience: IAAP Membership
Location: Marriott Hotel
Date and Time: September 16, 2019

(Title slide)

Content	Layout	Visual Element(s)
Title Slide *(Title slide)* Planning ~~Before Creating~~ Presentation Content *(Introduction)*	Title Slide	○ Shapes ○ Chart ○ Table ○ WordArt ○ Picture ○ Video ○ Clip Art ○ Sound ○ SmartArt ○ _____ *Description:*
Introduction (Key Point, (Quote), Image, Other) *A good plan is like a road map: It shows the final destination and usually the best ways to get there.* *M. Stanley Judd*	Section Header	○ Shapes ○ Chart ○ Table ○ WordArt ⊗ Picture ○ Video ○ Clip Art ○ Sound ○ SmartArt ○ _____ *Description:*
(Key topics with main points) **Key Point #1** Identify the Purpose ~~Selling (e-commercial)~~, Persuad~~ing~~ive, Informing Good Will, ~~Entertaining~~ Educational, Motivating	Title + ~~Two~~ Content	○ Shapes ○ Chart ○ Table ○ WordArt ○ Picture ○ Video ○ Clip Art ○ Sound ○ SmartArt ⊗ Text *Description:*
Key Point #2 Define the Audience Who is ~~going to be~~ in the audience? What are their ~~audience's~~ needs? What are their expectations? How much do they already know?	Title + ~~Two~~ Content	○ Shapes ○ Chart ○ Table ○ WordArt ⊗ Picture ○ Video ○ Clip Art ○ Sound ○ SmartArt ○ _____ *Description:*

Key Point #3 Develop the Content
  • Identify purpose
  • Research topic
  • Brainstorm
  • Create the storyboard
	Title and Content + SmartArt	○ Shapes ○ Chart
		○ Table ○ WordArt
		○ Picture ○ Video
		○ Clip Art ○ Sound
		(X) SmartArt ○ _____
		Description:

Key Point #4 Simplify the Content Make text concise, Use consistent verb tense, Eliminate excess adverbs and adjectives, Use few prepositions, Use strong active verbs, Keep bullets parallel	Title and Content	○ Shapes ○ Chart ○ Table ○ WordArt ○ Picture ○ Video ○ Clip Art ○ Sound ○ SmartArt ○ _____ *Description:*
Summary (Restatement of Key Points, (Quote), Other) Quote: The key to an effective presentation is planning ahead!	Section Header	○ Shapes ○ Chart ○ Table ○ WordArt ⊗ Picture ○ Video ○ Clip Art ○ Sound ○ SmartArt ○ _____ *Description:*

FIGURE 1.16 Rough-Draft Storyboard

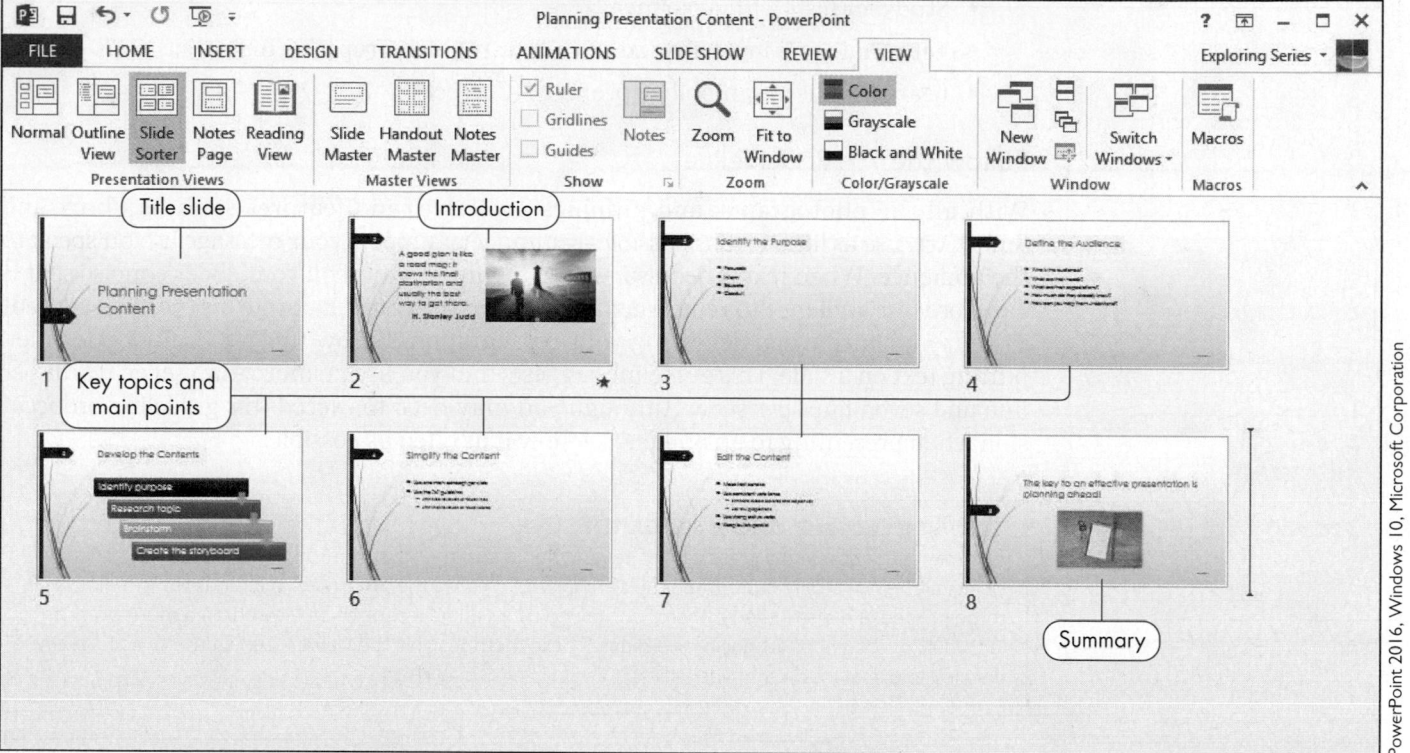

FIGURE 1.17 Slide Show Based on Storyboard

After you create the storyboard, review what you wrote.

Use Short Phrases

Shorten complete sentences to phrases that you can use as bulleted points by eliminating excess adverbs and adjectives and using only a few prepositions. Think like a newspaper editor writing a headline and distill the content into the most important words. For example, "Good computer skills are required of each student attending the CIS 150 course" could be shortened to "CIS 150 course requires good computer skills."

Use Active Voice

Edit the phrases so they begin with active voice when possible to involve the viewer. When using active voice, the subject of the phrase performs the action expressed in the verb. In phrases using passive voice, the subject is acted upon. Passive voice needs more words to communicate your ideas and can make your presentation seem flat. The following is an example of the same thought written in active voice and passive voice:

- Active Voice: Students need good computer skills.
- Passive Voice: Good computer skills are needed by students.

Use Parallel Construction

Use parallel construction so that your bullets are in the same grammatical form to help your audience see the connection between your phrases. If you start your first bullet with a noun, start each successive bullet with a noun; if you start your first bullet with a verb, continue starting your bullets with verbs. Parallel construction also gives each bullet an equal level of importance and promotes balance in your message. In the following example, the fourth bullet is not parallel to the first three bullets because it does not begin with a verb. The fifth bullet shows the bullet in parallel construction.

- Find a good place to study.
- Organize your study time.

- Study for tests with a partner.
- Terminology is important so learn how to use it properly. (Incorrect)
- Learn and use terminology properly. (Correct)

Follow the 7 × 7 Guideline

With all the photographs and graphics available, and features such as Chart and SmartArt, use as little text as possible. Let imagery support your message as you speak to the audience. When text is necessary, keep the information on your slides concise so it is easy for your audience to remember. You can explain and elaborate on the slide content to your audience when delivering your presentation. Follow the 7 × 7 guideline when putting text on a slide. This guideline suggests that you use no more than seven words per line and seven lines per slide. Although you may need to exceed this guideline on occasion when presenting to an audience, follow it as often as possible.

> **TIP: EXCEEDING THE 7 × 7 GUIDELINE**
> You may see slides with a great deal of text, multiple charts and graphs, or a combination of multiple objects. This is typically done when the person who created the presentation intends for the slide deck to be printed and distributed rather than viewed by an audience, or to be viewed on a monitor by an individual in control of advancing the slides. These methods give the viewer ample time to absorb any detailed information on the slide.

After you complete the planning and review process, you are ready to select the "look" of your presentation.

Choose a Theme

STEP 1 ⟫ When you first open PowerPoint you are provided the opportunity to choose from various design themes. A **theme** is a designer-quality look that includes coordinating colors, matching fonts, and effects such as shadows. The Blank Presentation uses the Office theme.

> **To create a new presentation, complete the following steps:**
> 1. Click File, and then click New.
> 2. Click the design theme you want to use.
> 3. Click Create and a new file will open with the design theme you selected.

You can always change the theme from the one that you initially choose. You can even select a variant for the theme. A **variant** is a variation of the theme design you have chosen. Each variant uses different color palettes and font families. Figure 1.18 shows the Ion theme with four variant options for this theme.

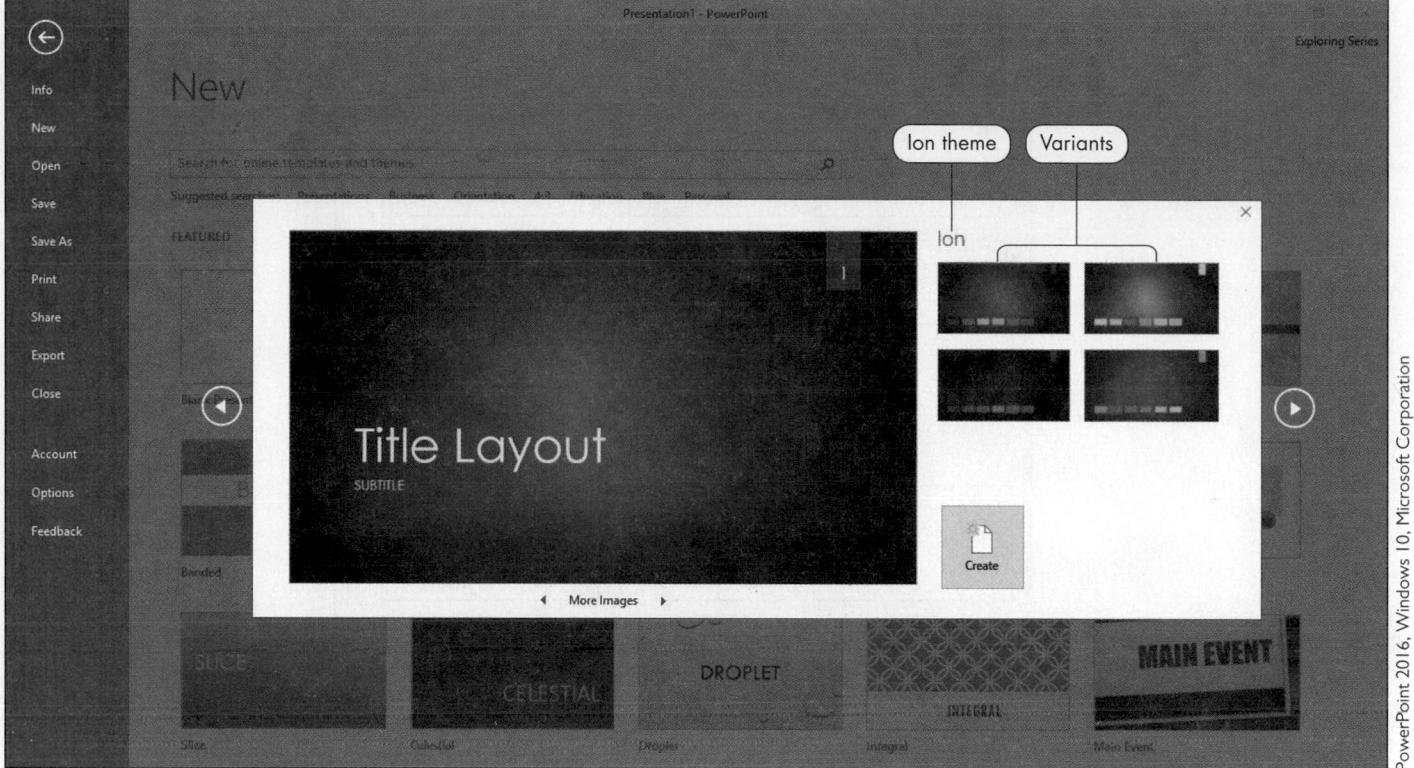

FIGURE 1.18 Ion Theme with Variant Options

To change a theme or apply a theme variant, complete the following steps:

1. Click the Design tab to display thumbnail previews in the Themes and Variants groups.
2. Click More to see all of the available themes.
3. Point to different themes to see a Live Preview of the theme applied to your presentation.
4. Click a theme to apply it to your presentation.
5. Click a variant in the Variants group to apply it to your presentation.

Adding Presentation Content

After you complete the planning and review process, you are ready to prepare the slide deck you will use during your presentation. To prepare the slide deck, you need to understand PowerPoint's use of slide layouts.

Use Slide Layouts

PowerPoint provides a set of predefined slide **layouts** that determine the position of placeholders in various locations. **Placeholders** are objects that hold specific content, such as titles, subtitles, or images. Placeholders determine the position of the objects on the slide. Some layouts also include a small palette of icons that you can use to insert a variety of objects.

When you click the New Slide arrow on the Home tab, a gallery from which you can choose a layout displays. Figure 1.19 shows the Layout Gallery available for you to use when you have selected Blank presentation with the Office theme. Table 1.1 describes some of the most common slide layouts.

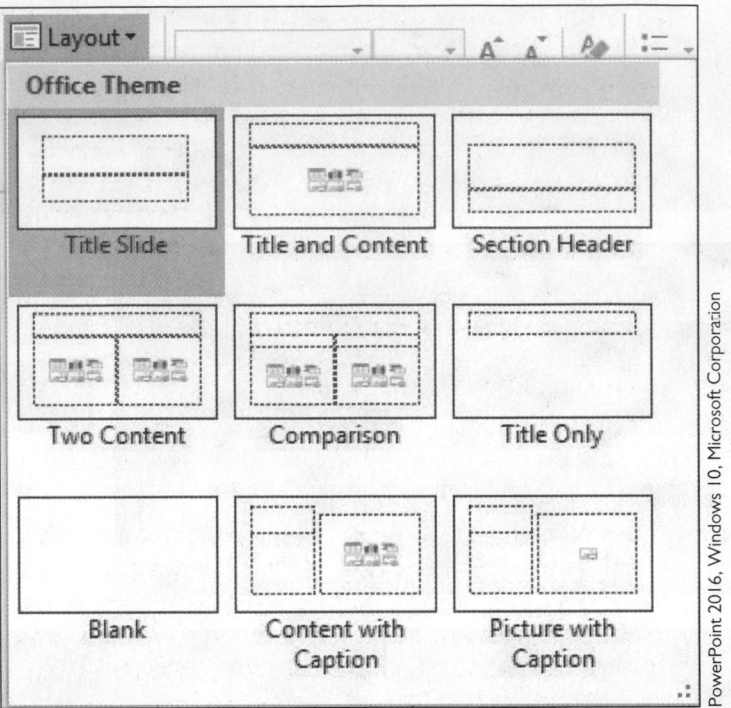

FIGURE 1.19 Layout Gallery for Office Theme

TABLE 1.1	**Common Layout Options**
Slide Layout	**Description**
Title Slide	A new, blank presentation opens to a title slide layout. This slide includes a placeholder for a title and a placeholder for a subtitle.
Title and Content	In addition to a placeholder for the title, this layout includes a content placeholder. Click and type in the content placeholder and you create a bulleted list. Or, click one of the icons on the palette in the center of the placeholder to insert objects such as a table, chart, SmartArt graphic, picture, online picture, or video.
Section Header	The Section Header layout enables you to separate different sections or main topics similar to how a tabbed page separates sections in a notebook.
Two Content	This layout includes two content placeholders which you can use to create two columns on the slide. Often this layout is used to put text on one side of the slide and graphic content on the other side. A title placeholder is also included.
Comparison	Use this layout to make a comparison between two points by listing supporting detail in columns. In addition to having two content placeholders, this layout also includes a heading placeholder over each content placeholder and a title placeholder.
Title Only	Only a title placeholder is included on the slide which gives you a lot of empty area you can use to insert any type of object such as shapes, WordArt, pictures, charts, etc.
Blank	The blank layout contains no placeholders making it ideal for content that will cover the entire slide, such as a picture.
Content with Caption	The left side of this layout includes a placeholder for a title and a placeholder for text. The right side includes a placeholder for content such as a chart or picture.
Picture with Caption	The top of the slide includes a large placeholder for a picture. Beneath the picture placeholder is a placeholder for a caption and a placeholder for descriptive text.

After you select a layout, click a placeholder. The border of the placeholder becomes a dashed line and you are able to enter content. If you click the dashed line placeholder border, the placeholder and all of its content are selected. The border changes to a solid line. Once selected, you can drag the placeholder to a new position, resize it, format the contents of the placeholder, or delete the placeholder. To format the contents of the placeholder, click the placeholder border and use the controls on the Home tab to format the text. If you only want to change a portion of the text, select the text and then use the controls on the Home tab to format the text.

TIP: UNUSED PLACEHOLDERS

It is not necessary to delete unused placeholders on a slide. Unused placeholders in a slide layout do not show when you display a slide show.

Create a Title Slide and an Introduction

STEP 2)) The title placeholder should be used for a short title that indicates the purpose of the presentation. Try to capture the title in two to five words. The subtitle placeholder should be used for information such as the speaker's name and title, the speaker's organization, the organization's logo, and the date of the presentation. To add this information to the placeholders, click in the placeholder and begin typing.

After the title slide, you should include an introduction slide that will get the audience's attention. The introduction could be a list of topics covered in the presentation, a thought-provoking quotation or question, or an image that relates to the topic. Introduction slides can also be used to distinguish between topics or sections of the presentation.

Create Key Point Slides

After you create the title slide and introduction, you should create a slide for each of the key points you outlined in your storyboard.

To add a slide, complete the following steps:

1. Click the New Slide arrow on the Home tab.
2. Click the layout that you want for your new slide in the gallery of layouts.

The New Slide button has two parts, the New Slide button and the New Slide arrow. Click the New Slide arrow when you want to choose a layout from the gallery. Click New Slide, which appears above the New Slide arrow, to quickly insert a new slide. If you click New Slide when the title slide is selected, the new slide uses the Title and Content layout. If the current slide uses any layout other than Title Slide, the subsequent new slide uses the same layout.

Each key point should be on a separate slide with the details needed to support it. The Title and Content layout is a very common layout used for presenting a key point and its supporting details. List the key point in the title placeholder, and then create a bulleted list in the content placeholder. To increase or decrease levels, or indents, for bulleted items, click Increase List Level or Decrease List Level in the Paragraph group on the Home tab. You can press Tab as a shortcut to increase a level, or Shift+Tab as a shortcut to decrease a level.

End with a Summary or Conclusion Slide

To give closure to your presentation, end with a summary slide that reiterates your presentation's key points. Or, create a conclusion slide that restates the purpose of the presentation or invokes a call to action. You may also want to repeat your contact information at the end of the presentation so the audience knows how to follow-up with any questions or needs.

Reviewing the Presentation

After you create the presentation, check for spelling errors, incorrect word usage, and inconsistent capitalization. Nothing is more embarrassing or can make you appear more unprofessional than a misspelled word enlarged on a big screen. Also view the slide show to ensure that the content is presented in the proper order, that the layouts provide the content in an effective manner, and that all transitions and animations work.

Check Spelling

 Use a five-step method for checking spelling in PowerPoint. Although proofreading five times may seem excessive, it will help ensure your presentation is professional.

> **To check spelling, complete the following steps:**
>
> 1. Read the slide content as you type it looking for wavy red underlines that indicate a potential typographical error or a repeated word. Read each slide after typing its information.
> 2. Use the Spelling feature located on the Review tab to check the entire presentation.
> 3. Ask a friend or colleague to review the presentation.
> 4. Display the presentation in Reading View and read each word out loud.
> 5. Correct all spelling or word usage errors found.

> **TIP: PROOFING OPTIONS**
> The Spelling feature, by default, does not catch contextual errors like *to*, *too*, and *two*, but you can set the proofing options to help you find and fix this type of error. To modify the proofing options, click File and click Options. Click Proofing in the PowerPoint Options window and click Check Grammar with Spelling. With this option selected, the spelling checker will flag contextual mistakes with a red wavy underline. To correct the error, right-click the flagged word and select the proper word choice.

Use the Thesaurus

As you create and edit your presentation, you may notice that you are using one word too often, especially at the beginning of bullets. Use the Thesaurus to help you make varied word choices. Access the Thesaurus from the Proofing group on the Review tab.

Check Slide Show Elements

 After checking the wording on the individual slides, it is helpful to view the presentation in Slide Show view to see if the elements you have incorporated are effective. Check the order of the information to make sure the content is presented in a logical order and that the layout showcases the information effectively. Make sure that the transitions and animations are working. Examine any media to make sure it supports the message.

> **To check the slide show elements, complete the following steps:**
>
> 1. Click the Slide Show tab.
> 2. Click From Beginning in the Start Slide Show group.
> 3. Advance through each slide checking layouts, transitions, and animations.
> 4. End the slide show and return to Normal view.
> 5. Change any layouts, placeholder locations, transitions, and animations as needed.

Reorder Slides

 STEP 5 As you review your presentation, you may realize that you need to reorder your slides. This can easily be done using Slide Sorter view.

To reorder slides, complete the following steps:

1. Click the View tab.
2. Click Slide Sorter in the Presentation Views group.
3. Select the slide you want to move and drag the slide to the new location.
4. Double-click any slide to return to Normal view.

Quick Concepts

4. Identify the three advanced planning steps you should follow before adding content to a slide show. *p. 939*

5. Define storyboard and describe how a storyboard aids you in creating a slide show. *p. 939*

6. Describe two guidelines you should follow when assessing your slide content. *pp. 941–942*

7. Explain the purpose of using a presentation theme. *p. 942*

Skills covered: Choose a Theme • Add Presentation Content • Check Spelling • Use the Thesaurus • Check Slide Show Elements • Reorder Slides

2 Presentation Creation

To help state employees learn the process for presentation creation, you decide to give them guidelines for determining content, structuring a slide show, and assessing content. You have previously created a storyboard, and now you create the slide show to deliver these guidelines.

STEP 1 ›› PLAN AND PREPARE A PRESENTATION

You are creating a Training and Development presentation for the employees from a previously created storyboard. You begin by selecting a theme, and as you progress through the steps you will add and edit several slides. You begin by choosing the Retrospect theme with a specific variation color and creating the Title Slide content. Figure 1.20 displays the storyboard used to plan the presentation.

Storyboard

Step a: Purpose

Purpose:	[X] Informative [ ] Educational [ ] Persuasive [ ] Goodwill [ ] Other

Audience: Training and Development
Location: CS 601a
Date and Time: July 1, 2019

Content	Layout	Visual Element(s)
Title Slide Creating Presentation Content Step a: Introduction slide	Title Slide	○ Shapes ○ Chart ○ Table ○ WordArt ○ Picture ○ Video ○ Clip Art ○ Sound ○ SmartArt ○ _____ *Description:*
Key Point #1 Define the Audience Who is the audience? What are their needs? What are their expectations? How much do they already know? How can you help them understand?	Two Content	○ Shapes ○ Chart ○ Table ○ WordArt X Picture ○ Video ○ Clip Art ○ Sound ○ SmartArt ○ _____ *Description:* People at presentation
Key Point #2 Develop the Content • Identify purpose • Research topic • Brainstorm • Create the storyboard	Title and Content	○ Shapes ○ Chart ○ Table ○ WordArt ○ Picture ○ Video ○ Clip Art ○ Sound ○ SmartArt ○ _____ *Description:*
Key Point #3 Determine Additional Content List types of text, illustrations, and other content	Title and Content	○ Shapes ○ Chart X Table ○ WordArt ○ Picture ○ Video ○ Clip Art ○ Sound ○ SmartArt ○ _____ *Description:*
Key Point #4 Edit the Content Make text concise. Use consistent verb tense. Eliminate excess adverbs and adjectives. Use few prepositions. Use strong active verbs. Keep bullets parallel.	Title and Content	○ Shapes ○ Chart ○ Table ○ WordArt ○ Picture ○ Video ○ Clip Art ○ Sound ○ SmartArt ○ _____ *Description:*
Key Point #5 Simplify the Content Make text concise. Use consistent verb tense. Eliminate excess adverbs and adjectives. Use few prepositions. Use strong active verbs. Keep bullets parallel.	Title and Content	○ Shapes ○ Chart ○ Table ○ WordArt ○ Picture ○ Video ○ Clip Art ○ Sound ○ SmartArt ○ _____ *Description:*
Step a: Summary slide **Summary (Restatement of Key Points, Quote, Other)** Quote: The key to an effective presentation is planning ahead!	Section Header	○ Shapes ○ Chart ○ Table ○ WordArt ○ Picture ○ Video ○ Clip Art ○ Sound ○ SmartArt ○ _____ *Description:*

Step a: Introduction slide

Step a: Key point slides

PowerPoint 2016, Windows 10, Microsoft Corporation

FIGURE 1.20 Storyboard for Creating Presentation Content Slide Show

a. Review the storyboard displayed in Figure 1.20. Note the purpose, introduction, key points, and summary.

b. Open PowerPoint. Select the **Retrospect theme**. Select the first theme variant, the **Orange variant**, and click **Create**.

c. Save the presentation as **p01h2Content_LastFirst**.

d. Click in the **title placeholder** on the Title Slide and type **Creating Presentation Content**.

e. Type your name in the **subtitle placeholder**.

f. Click **Notes** on the status bar. Type **Training and Development** in the Notes pane.

g. Save the presentation.

STEP 2 ›› ADD PRESENTATION CONTENT

You continue creating your presentation by adding a second slide with the Title and Content layout. After adding a title to the slide, you create a bulleted list to develop your topic. After adding the presentation content, you proofread the presentation to ensure no errors exist. Refer to Figure 1.21 as you complete Step 2.

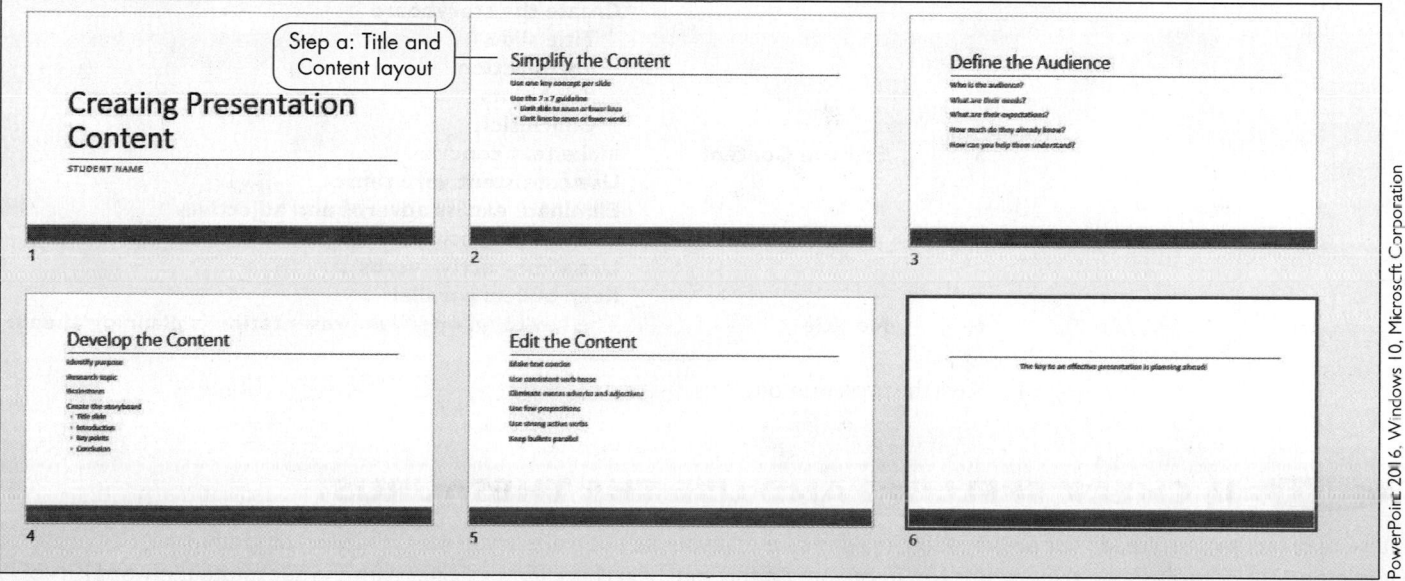

PowerPoint 2016, Windows 10, Microsoft Corporation

FIGURE 1.21 New Slides with Content in Slide Sorter View

a. Click **New Slide** in the Slides group on the Home tab.

Because you clicked the top half of New Slide, the new slide uses the Title and Content layout which is the default slide layout after a Title Slide layout. The new Slide 2 contains two placeholders: one for the title and one for body content.

b. Type **Simplify the Content** in the title placeholder.

c. Click in the **content placeholder** below the title placeholder, type **Use one main concept per slide**, and then press **Enter**.

By default, the list level is the same as the previous level. Note that the Retrospect theme does not automatically place bullets into the body of the presentation.

d. Type **Use the 7 × 7 guideline** and press **Enter**.

e. Click **Increase List Level** in the Paragraph group.

The list level indents and the font size is reduced indicating this is a subset of the main level.

f. Type **Limit slide to seven or fewer lines** and press **Enter**.

g. Type **Limit lines to seven or fewer words**. (Do not include the period.)

By default, the list level is the same as the previous level.

h. Click **New Slide** in the Slides group four times to create four more slides with the Title and Content layout.

To move between slides in the slide deck, click the thumbnail of the slide you want to edit in the Slide pane.

i. Type the following text in the appropriate slide. Use Increase List Level ⊞ and Decrease List Level ⊟ in the Paragraph group to change levels.

Slide	Slide Title	Content Data
3	Define the Audience	Who is the audience?
		What are their needs?
		What are their expectations?
		How much do they already know?
		How can you help them understand?
4	Develop the Content	Identify purpose
		Research topic
		Brainstorm
		Create the storyboard
		Title slide
		Introduction
		Key points
		Conclusion
5	Edit the Content	Make text concise
		Use consistent verb tense
		Eliminate excess adverbs and adjectives
		Use few prepositions
		Use strong active verbs
		Keep bullets parallel
6	No title	The key to an effective presentation is planning ahead!

j. Save the presentation.

STEP 3 ⟩⟩ CHECK SPELLING AND USE THE THESAURUS

It is important to proofread your presentation, making sure that you did not make any errors in spelling or grammar. Additionally, it is important not to use the same words too frequently. In this step, you check for spelling errors and substitute the word *key* for the word *main*.

a. Click **Spelling** in the Proofing group on the Review tab and correct any errors. Carefully proofread each slide.

The result of the spelling check depends on how accurately you entered the text of the presentation.

b. Click **Slide 2**, use the Thesaurus to change *main* in the first bulleted point to **key** and click **Close (X)** on the Thesaurus.

c. Save the presentation.

You view the slide show and decide that the concluding statement emphasizing the importance of planning can be improved by modifying the layout of the slide. Refer to Figure 1.22 as you complete Step 4.

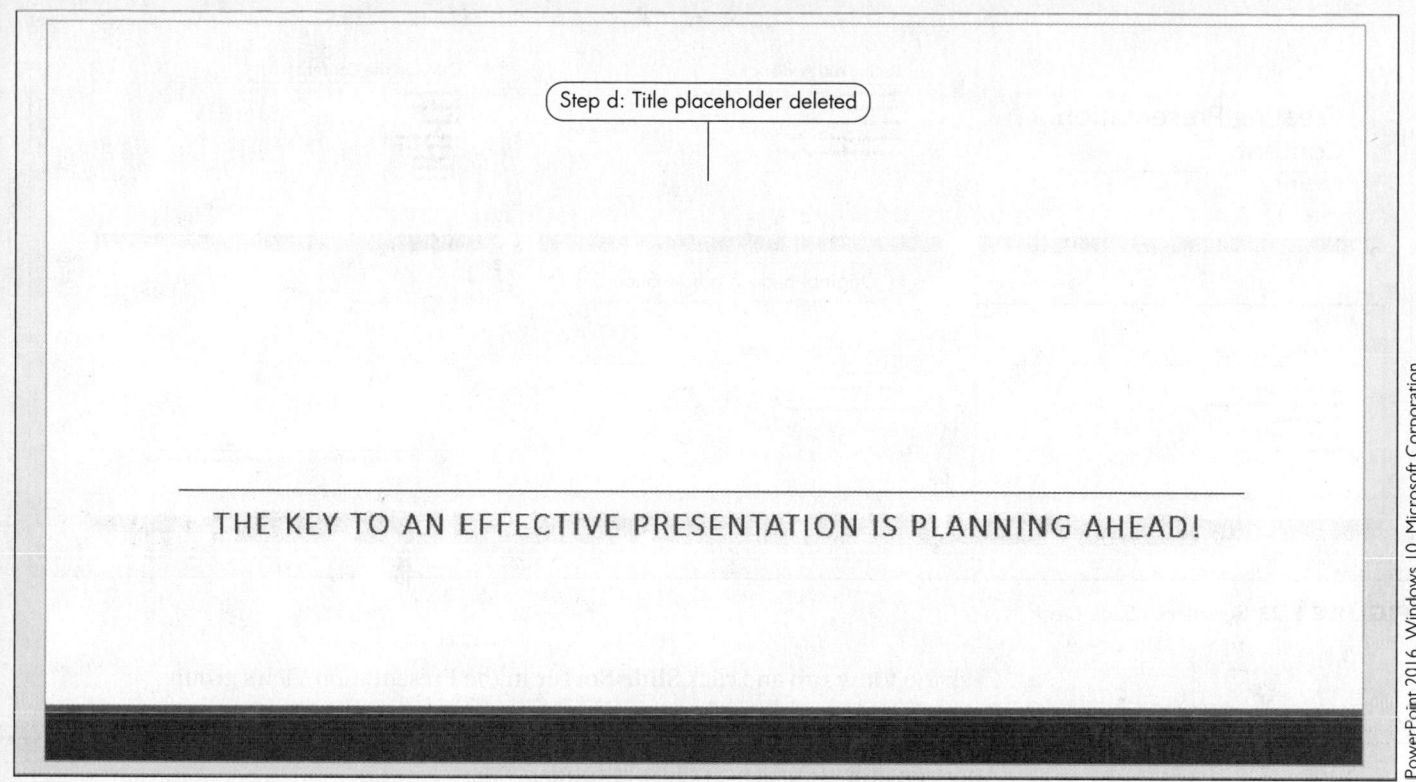

Step d: Title placeholder deleted

THE KEY TO AN EFFECTIVE PRESENTATION IS PLANNING AHEAD!

PowerPoint 2016, Windows 10, Microsoft Corporation

FIGURE 2.22 Slide with Modified Layout

a. View the presentation in Slide Show view and then return to Normal view.

b. Click the **Slide 6 thumbnail** in the Slides pane. Click the **Home tab** and click **Layout** in the Slides group.

c. Click **Section Header** from the Layout gallery.

The layout for Slide 6 changes to the Section Header layout. The Section Header layout adds emphasis to the statement on Slide 6.

d. Click the border of the title placeholder and press **Delete**.

The dotted line border becomes a solid line, which indicates the placeholder is selected. Pressing Delete removes the placeholder and the content of that placeholder. It is not necessary to delete the placeholder because empty placeholders do not display in Slide Show view, but deleting the placeholder gives you a cleaner look in Normal view.

e. Click the **subtitle placeholder** and click **Center** in the Paragraph group on the Home tab.

The layout of Slide 6 has now been modified.

f. Save the presentation.

You notice that the slides do not follow a logical order. You change the slide positions in Slide Sorter view. Refer to Figure 1.23 as you complete Step 5.

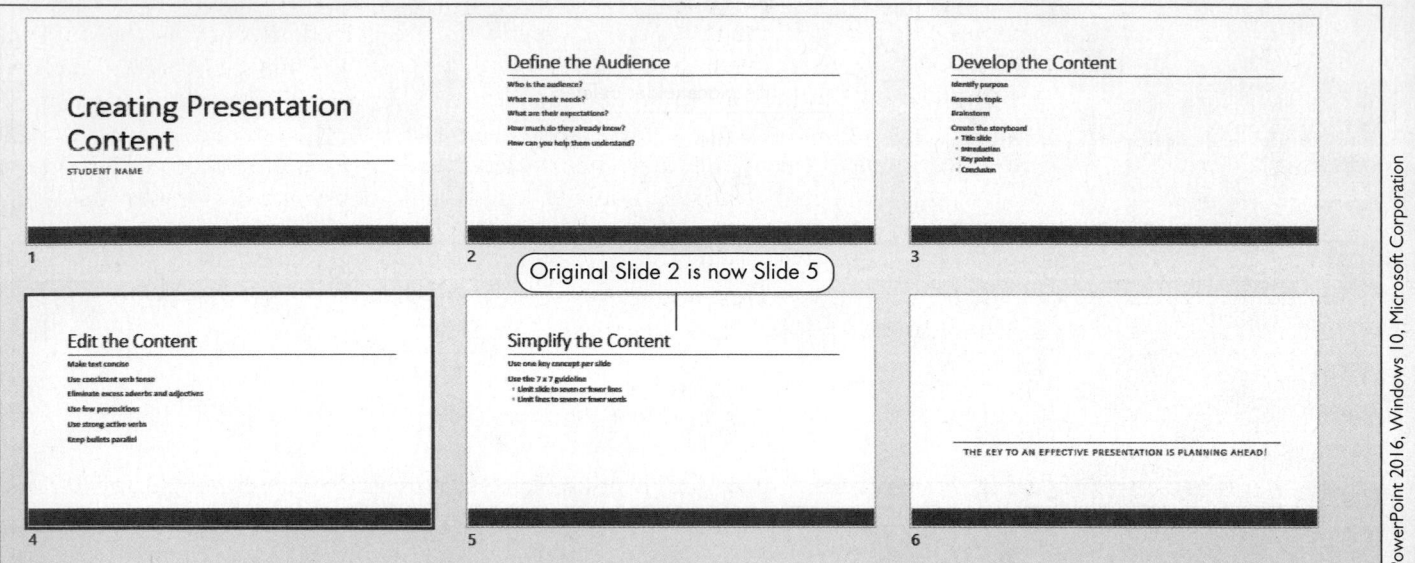

FIGURE 1.23 Reordered Slide Deck

a. Click the **View tab** and click **Slide Sorter** in the Presentation Views group.

b. Select **Slide 2** and drag it before the conclusion (last) slide so that it becomes Slide 5.

After you drop the slide, all slides renumber.

c. Double-click **Slide 6**.

Your presentation returns to Normal view.

d. Save the presentation. Keep the presentation open if you plan to continue with the next Hands-On Exercise. If not, close the presentation and exit PowerPoint.

Presentation Enhancement

You can strengthen your slide show by adding objects that support the message. PowerPoint enables you to include a variety of visual objects to add impact to your presentation. You can add tables, charts, and SmartArt diagrams created in PowerPoint, or you can insert objects that were created in other applications, such as a chart from Microsoft Excel or a table from Microsoft Word. You can add images, WordArt (stylized letters), sound, animated clips, and video clips to increase your presentation's impact. You can add animations and transitions to catch the audience's attention. You can also add identifying information to slides or audience handouts by adding headers and footers.

In this section, you will add a table to a slide to organize data in columns and rows. You will insert an online picture that relates to your topic and then you will move and resize the picture. You will apply transitions to control how one slide changes to another and add animations to text and pictures to add visual interest. You will finish by adding identifying information in a header and footer.

Adding a Table

STEP 1 ▶▶ A *table* organizes information in columns and rows. Tables can be simple and include just a few words or images, or they can be more complex and include structured numerical data.

> **To create a table on a new slide, complete the following steps:**
> 1. Create a new slide using any layout.
> 2. Click the Insert tab, and then click Table in the Tables group.
> 3. Drag over the grid to highlight the number of rows and columns that you need, and then click.
> 4. Type your information into the table cells.

You can also click the Insert Table icon on any slide layout that includes the icon. Figure 1.24 shows a table added to a slide. Once a table is created, you can resize a column or a row by positioning the pointer over the border you wish to resize and then dragging the border to the desired position.

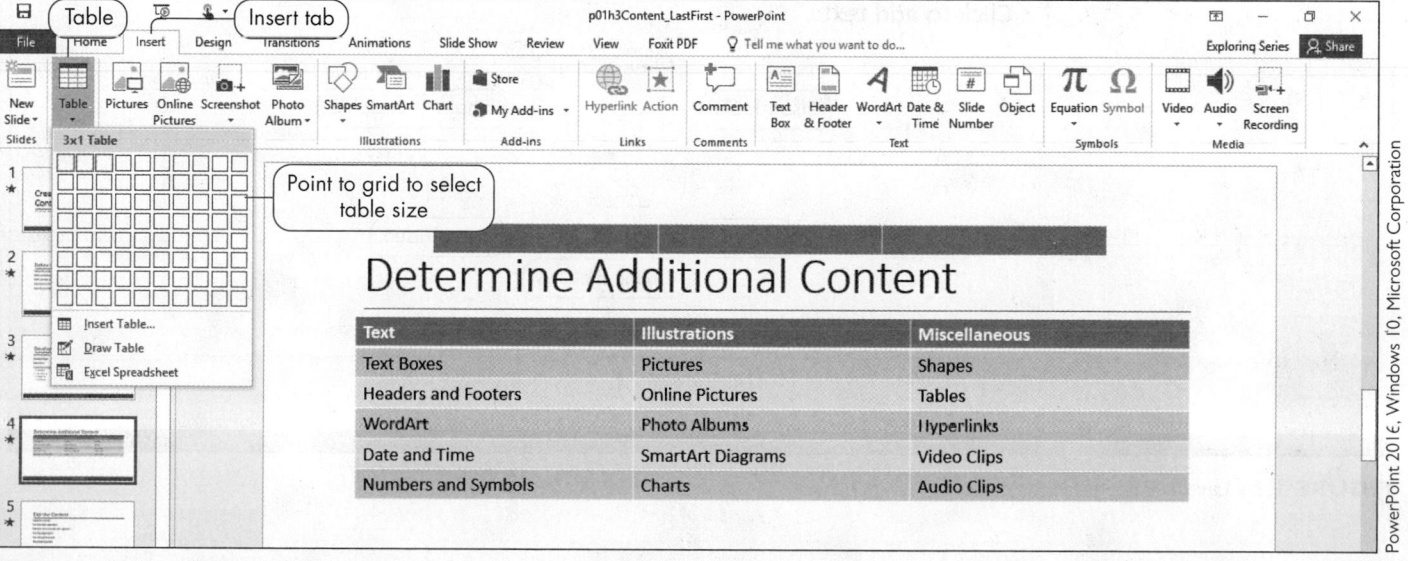

FIGURE 1.24 Slide with Table

Inserting Media Objects

STEP 2 ›› Adding media objects such as pictures, online pictures, audio, and/or video is especially important in PowerPoint, as PowerPoint is a visual medium. Use the Insert tab to insert media objects in any layout. The following layouts include a palette of icons you can use to quickly insert objects:

- Title and Content
- Two Content
- Comparison
- Content with Caption
- Picture with Caption

Clicking the Pictures icon in the content placeholder (or Pictures on the Insert tab) opens a dialog box you can use to browse for picture files on any computer or device to which you are connected. Clicking Online Pictures opens the Insert Pictures dialog box that enables you to search Bing images or your OneDrive account. Figure 1.25 displays the icons for inserting objects on the slide.

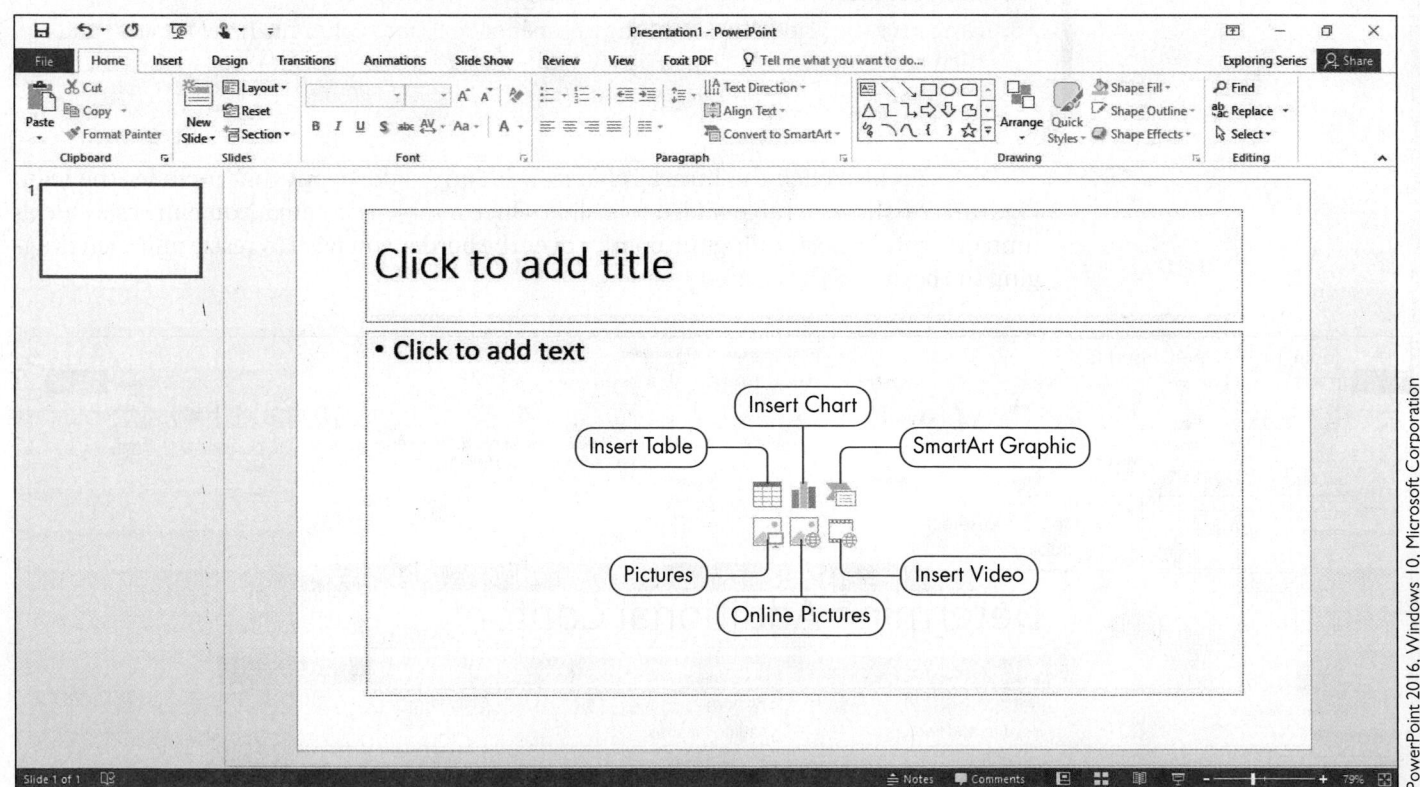

FIGURE 1.25 Layout Palette Icons

Applying Transitions and Animations

A ***transition*** is a visual effect that takes place when one slide is replaced by another slide while the presentation is displayed in Slide Show view or Reading View. An ***animation*** is motion that you can apply to text and objects. Animating text and objects can help focus attention on an important point, control the flow of information on a slide, and help you keep the audience's attention.

Apply Transitions

STEP 3 ❯❯ A transition is a specific type of animation that is used to provide visual interest as a slide is replaced by another slide. You can select from the basic transitions displayed on the Ribbon, or from the Transition gallery available in the Transition to This Slide group on the Transitions tab. You can control whether the transition applies to all the slides or just the current slide. Figure 1.26 displays the Transition gallery.

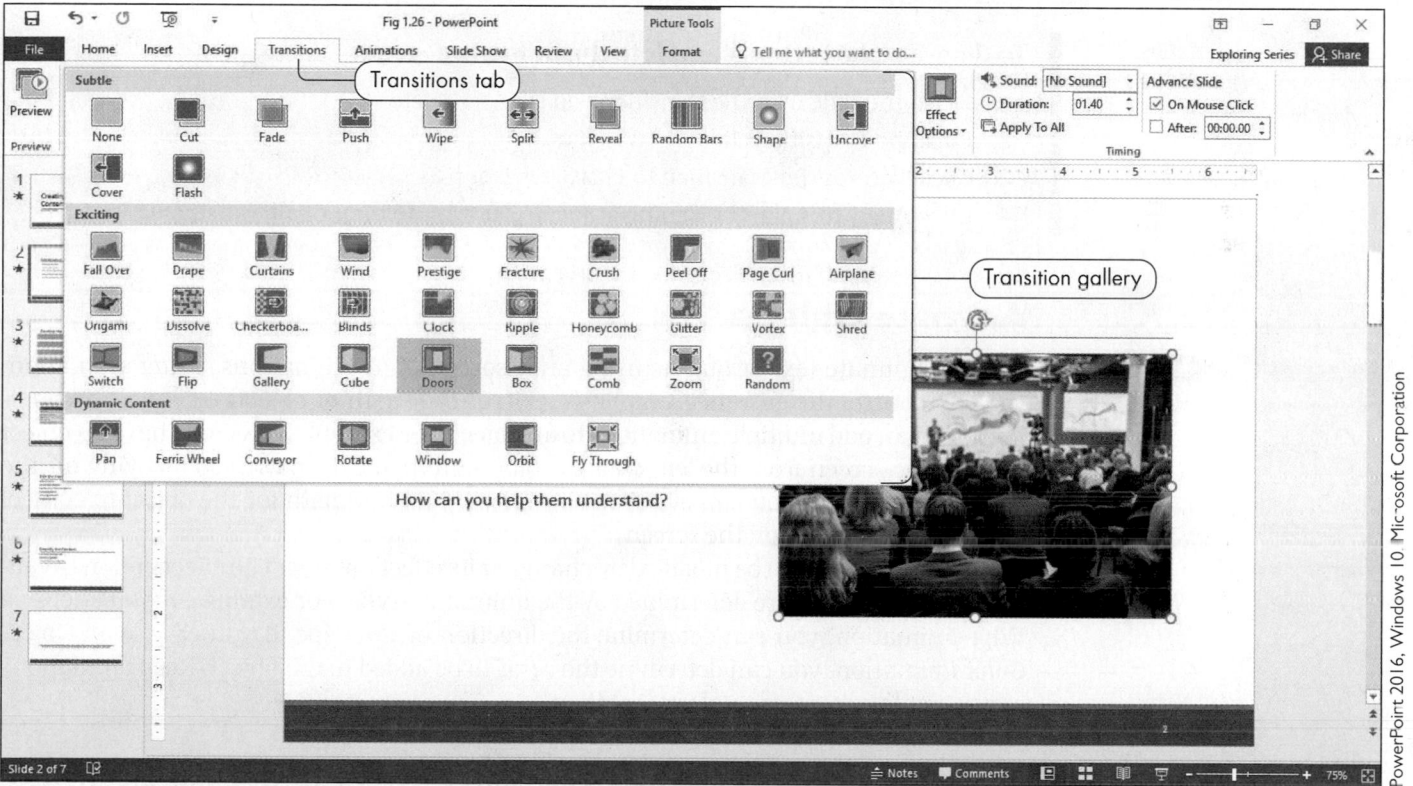

FIGURE 1.26 Transition Gallery

To apply a transition to a slide, complete the following steps:

1. Select the slide to which you want to add a transition.
2. Click the Transitions tab.
3. Click the More button in the Transition to This Slide group.
4. Select a transition from one of the following groups: Subtle, Exciting, and Dynamic Content.
5. Click Preview to see the transition applied to the slide.

After you choose a transition effect, you can select a sound to play when the transition occurs. You can choose the duration of the transition in seconds, which controls how quickly the transition takes place. The sound can be added by choosing an option in the Sound menu found in the Timing group on the Transitions tab.

Another determination you must make is how you want to start the transition process. Use the Advance Slide options in the Timing group to determine whether you want to manually click or press a key to advance to the next slide, or you want the slide to automatically advance after a specified number of seconds. You can set the number of seconds for the slide to display in the same area.

To delete a transition, complete the following steps:

1. Select the slide with the transition you want to delete.
2. Click the Transitions tab.
3. Click None in the Transition to This Slide group.
4. Click Apply to All in the Timing group if you want to remove all transitions.

Animate Objects

 You can animate text or objects using an assortment of animations. Using animation, you can control the entrance, emphasis, exit, and/or path of objects on a slide. In addition, you can add multiple animations to an object. For example, you could have an object fly onto the screen from the left, change color, and then exit the screen by flying off the screen to the right. You can even create your own motion path for the object to control the pattern it follows on the screen.

An animation can be modified by changing its effect options. The effect options available for animations are determined by the animation type. For example, if you choose a Wipe animation, you can determine the direction of the wipe. If you choose an Object Color animation, you can determine the color to be added to the object. Keep animations consistent for a professional presentation.

To apply an animation to text or other objects, complete the following steps:

1. Select the object you want to animate.
2. Click the Animations tab.
3. Click More in the Animation group to display the Animation gallery.
4. Select the animation type.
5. Click Effect Options to display any available options related to the selected animation type.

The slide in Figure 1.27 shows an animation effect added to a quote and an attribution. A tag with the number 1 is attached to the quote to show that it will run first. The attribution has a number 2 to show that it will play after the first animation. The Fly In animation in the gallery is shaded pink to show that it is the selected animation. Click Preview in the Preview group to see all animations on the slide play. You can also see the animations play in Reading View and in Slide Show view. Slides that include an animation display a star icon beneath the slide when viewed in Slide Sorter view or the Slides tab in Normal view.

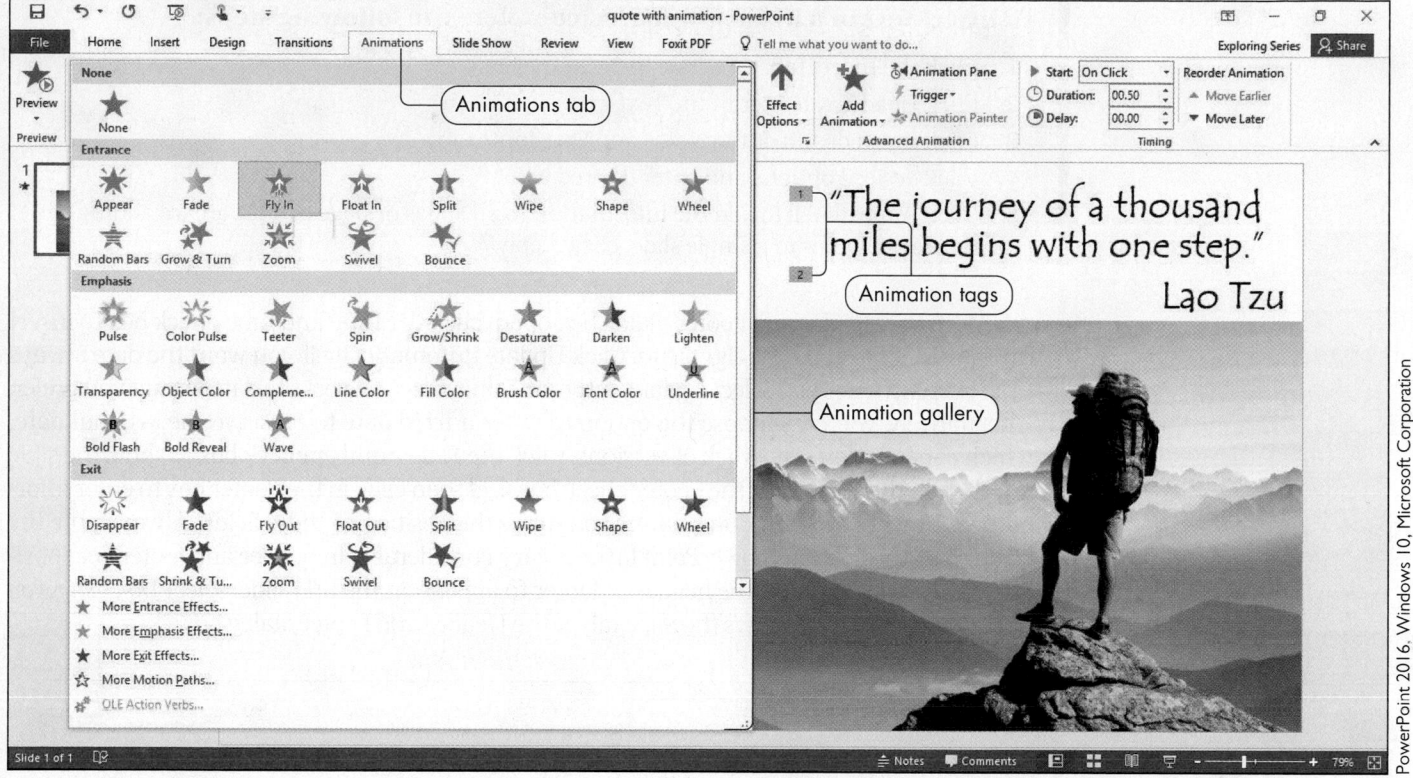

FIGURE 1.27 Animation Gallery

PowerPoint's Animation Painter feature enables you to copy an animation from one object to another. Animation Painter picks up the animation from the first object and applies it to the second on the same slide or a different slide.

> **To apply an animation to text or other objects, complete the following steps:**
>
> 1. Select the object that has the animation effect you want to copy to another object.
> 2. Click Animation Painter in the Advanced Animation group on the Animations tab.
> 3. Click the text or object to which you want to apply the animation.

TIP: EFFECTIVELY ADDING TRANSITIONS, ANIMATIONS, AND SOUND

When you select transitions, sounds, and animations, remember that too many sounds, transitions, and animations can be distracting. The audience will be wondering what is coming next rather than paying attention to your message. The speed of the transition is important, too—very slow transitions will lose the interest of your audience. Too many sound clips can be annoying. Consider whether you need to have the sound of applause with the transition of every slide. Is a typewriter sound necessary to keep your audience's attention, or will it grate on their nerves if it is used on every word? Ask someone to review your presentation and let you know of any annoying or jarring elements.

Inserting a Header or Footer

STEP 5 ⟫ The date of the presentation, the presentation audience, a logo, a company name, and other identifying information are very valuable, and you may want such information to appear on every slide, handout, or notes page. Use the Header and Footer feature to do this. The header generally appears at the top of pages in a handout or on a notes page, while a footer generally appears at the bottom of slides in a presentation or at the bottom of pages in a handout or on a notes page. Because the theme controls the placement of the header/footer elements, you may find headers and footers in various locations on the slide.

To insert text in a header or footer, complete the following steps:

1. Click the Insert tab.
2. Click Header & Footer in the Text group.
3. Click the Slide tab or the Notes and Handouts tab.
4. Click desired options and enter desired text.
5. Click Apply to All to add the information to all slides or pages, or if you are adding the header or footer to a single slide, click Apply.

With the Header and Footer dialog box open, click the Date and time check box to insert the current date and time signature. Click Update automatically if you want the date always to be current. Once you select Update automatically, you can select the date format you prefer. Alternatively, you can choose the option to enter a fixed date to preserve the original date, which can help you keep track of versions. Click the Slide number check box to show the slide number on the slide. Click the Footer check box and then click in the Footer box to enter information. The Preview window enables you to see the position of these fields. Always note the position of the fields, as PowerPoint layouts vary considerably in header and footer field positions. If you do not want the header or footer to appear on the title slide, select *Don't show on title slide.* Figure 1.28 shows the Slide tab of the Header and Footer dialog box.

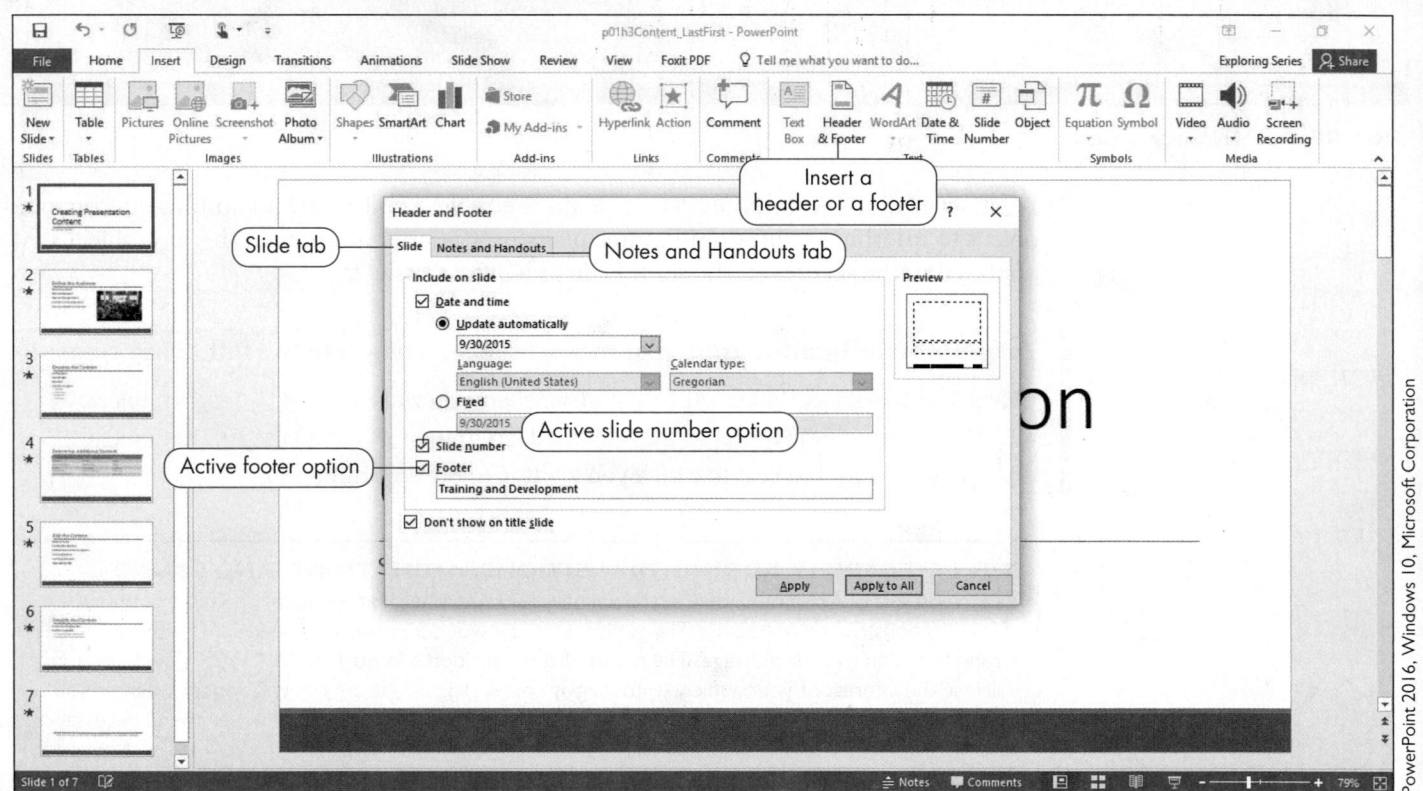

FIGURE 1.28 Header and Footer Dialog Box

The Notes and Handouts tab contains the same date/time options as the Slide tab, but it also gives you an option for a header. As you activate the fields, the Preview window shows the location of the fields. The header field is located in the upper-left corner of the printout. The date and time are located on the upper-right. The footer field is on the lower-left and the page number is located on the lower-right.

Quick Concepts

8. Explain why adding media objects to a PowerPoint slide show is important. *p. 954*

9. How does a table organize information? *p. 953*

10. Describe three benefits that can occur when objects are animated in a slide show. *p. 956*

11. Give an example of when you would use the Update automatically option in the Header and Footer feature. When would you use the Fixed date option? *p. 958*

Hands-On Exercises

Watch the Video for this Hands-On Exercise!

MyITLab® HOE3 Training

Skills covered: Add a Table • Insert Media Objects • Apply Transitions • Animate Objects • Insert a Footer

3 Presentation Enhancement

You decide to strengthen the slide show by adding a table and an online picture that will help state employees stay interested in the presentation and retain the information longer. You insert a table, add a picture, apply a transition, and animate the picture you have included. Finally, you create a slide footer and a Notes and Handouts header and footer.

STEP 1 » ADD A TABLE

To organize the list of objects that can be added to a PowerPoint slide, you create a table on a new slide. Listing these objects as bullets would take far more space than a table takes. Refer to Figure 1.29 as you complete Step 1.

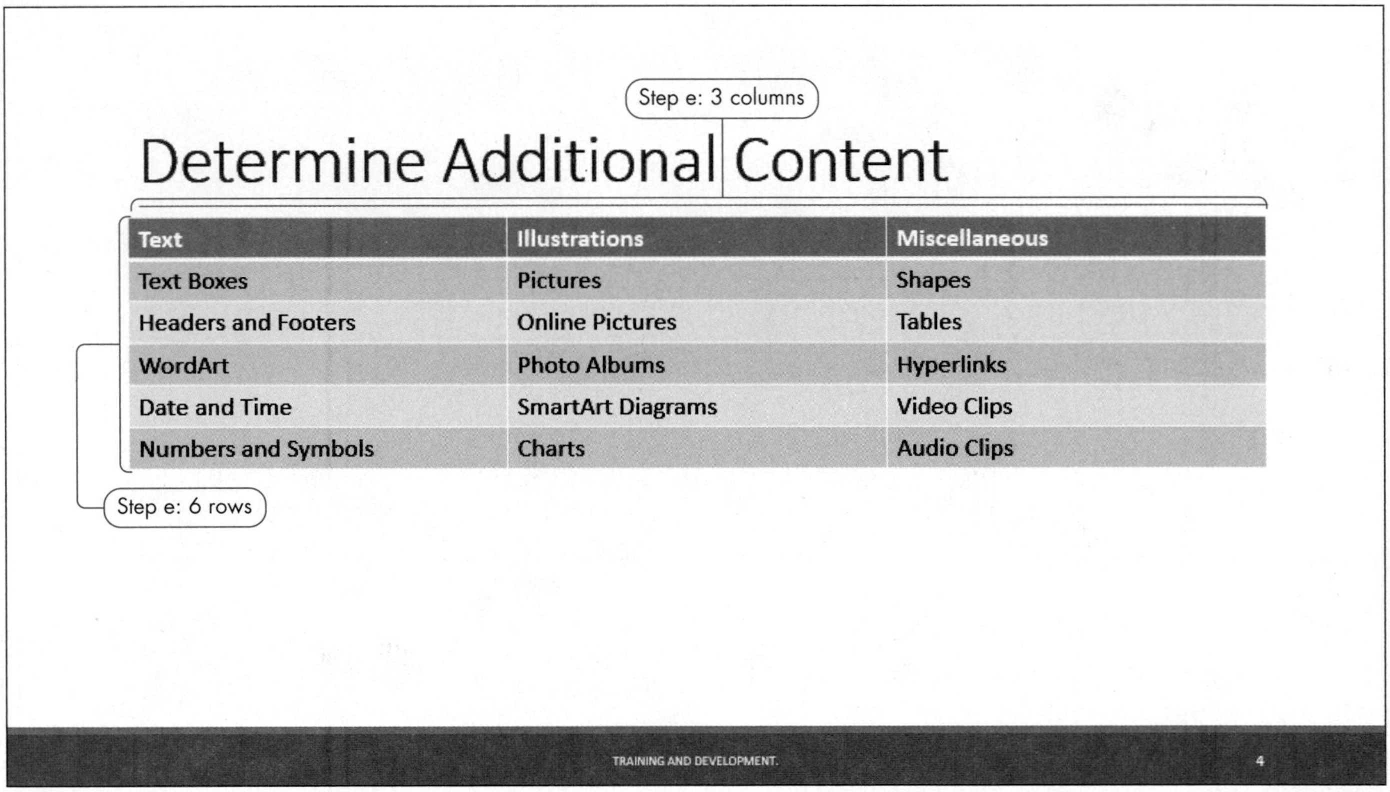

PowerPoint 2016, Windows 10, Microsoft Corporation

FIGURE 1.29 PowerPoint Table

a. Open *p01h2Content_LastFirst* if you closed it after the last Hands-On Exercise and save it as **p01h3Content_LastFirst**, changing h2 to h3.

b. Click **Slide 5** and click **New Slide** in the Slides group.

A new slide with the Title and Content layout is inserted after Slide 5.

c. Click the **title placeholder** and type **Determine Additional Content**.

d. Click **Insert Table** in the content placeholder in the center of the slide.

The Insert Table dialog box opens.

e. Set the number of columns to **3** and the number of rows to **6** and click **OK**.

PowerPoint creates the table and positions it on the slide. The first row is formatted differently from the other rows so that it can be used for column headings.

f. Type **Text** in the upper-left cell of the table. Press **Tab** to move to the next cell and type **Illustrations**. Press **Tab**, type **Miscellaneous**, and then press **Tab** to move to the next row.

g. Type the following text in the remaining table cells, pressing **Tab** after each entry.

Text Boxes	**Pictures**	**Shapes**
Headers and Footers	**Online Pictures**	**Tables**
WordArt	**Photo Albums**	**Hyperlinks**
Date and Time	**SmartArt Diagrams**	**Video Clips**
Numbers and Symbols	**Charts**	**Audio Clips**

h. Save the presentation.

STEP 2 ›› INSERT MEDIA OBJECTS

In this step, you insert a picture and then resize it to better fit the slide. The picture you insert relates to the topic and adds visual interest. Refer to Figure 1.30 as you complete Step 2.

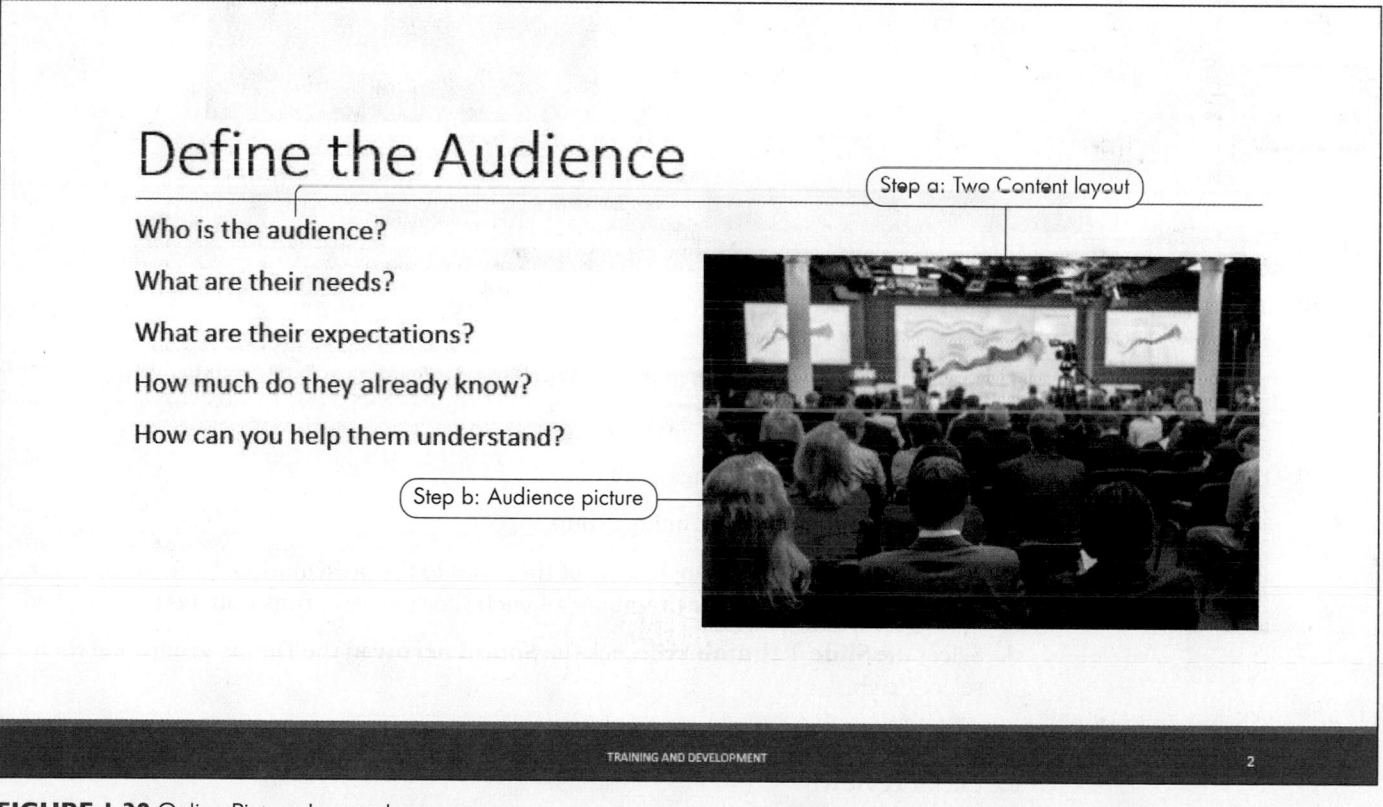

FIGURE 1.30 Online Picture Inserted

a. Display **Slide 2**, click **Layout** in the Slides group on the Home tab, and then click the **Two Content layout**.

Changing the layout for this slide will better accommodate the photo you will add in the next step.

b. Click the **Pictures icon** in the right content placeholder, navigate to the folder containing your student data files, and then select *p01h3Audience*. Refer to Figure 1.30 for a sample image. Click **Insert**.

c. Save the presentation.

To add motion when one slide changes into another, you apply a transition to all slides in the presentation. You select a transition that is not distracting but that adds emphasis to the slide show. You will also include a sound as the transition occurs. Refer to Figure 1.31 as you complete Step 3.

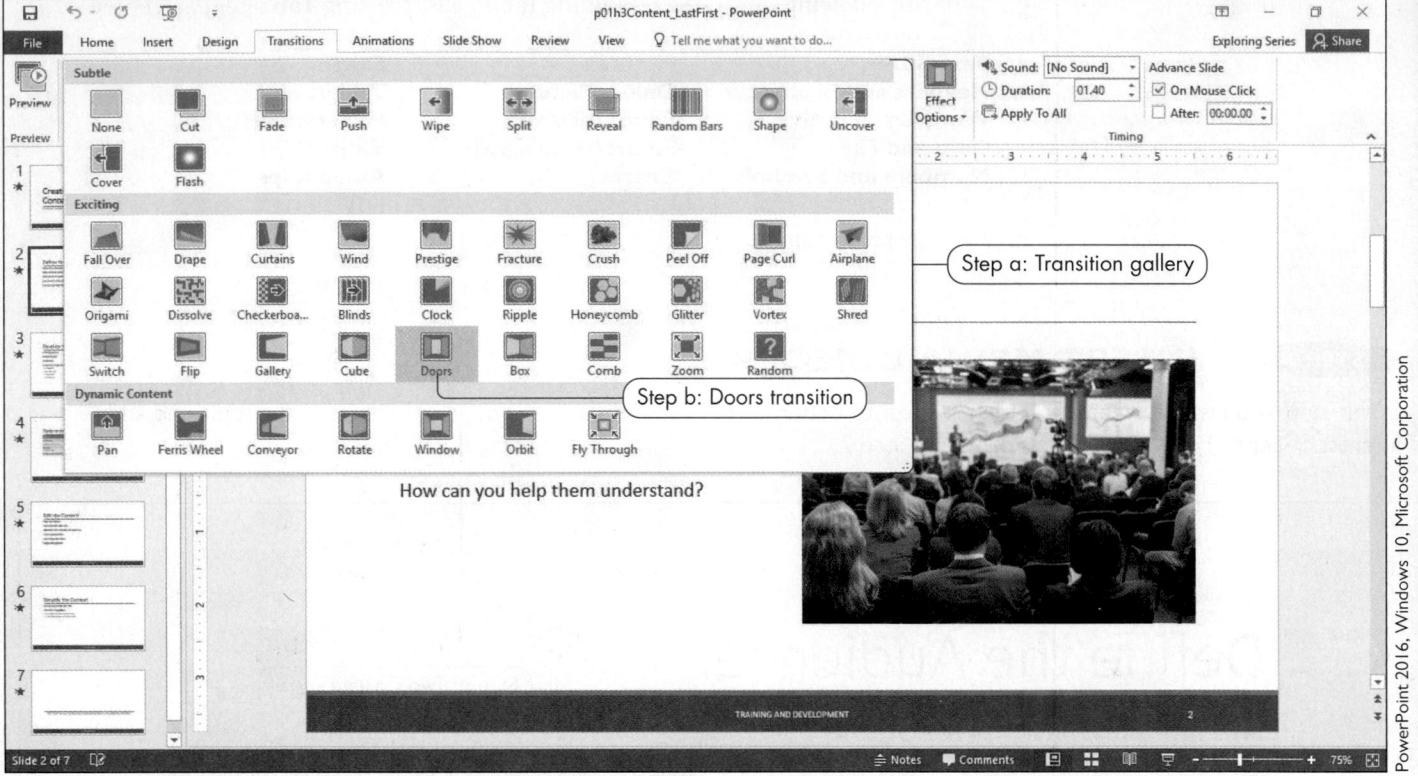

FIGURE 1.31 Transition Gallery

a. Click the **Transitions tab** and click **More** in the Transition to This Slide group.

    The Transition gallery displays.

b. Click **Doors** under Exciting.

c. Click **Apply to All** in the Timing group.

    The transition effect will apply to all of the slides in the presentation. Notice that a star has been added next to the thumbnail of each slide where a transition has been applied.

d. Select the **Slide 1 thumbnail**, click the **Sound arrow** in the Timing group, and then select **Push**.

    The Push sound will play as Slide 1 enters when in Slide Show view.

e. Click **Preview**.

    The Transition effect will play along with the sound for the first slide.

> **TROUBLESHOOTING:** If you are completing this activity in a classroom lab, you may need to plug in headphones or turn on speakers to hear the sound.

f. Save the presentation.

STEP 4 ›› ANIMATE AN OBJECT

You add animation to your slide show by controlling how individual objects such as lines of text or images enter or exit the slides. Refer to Figure 1.32 as you complete Step 4.

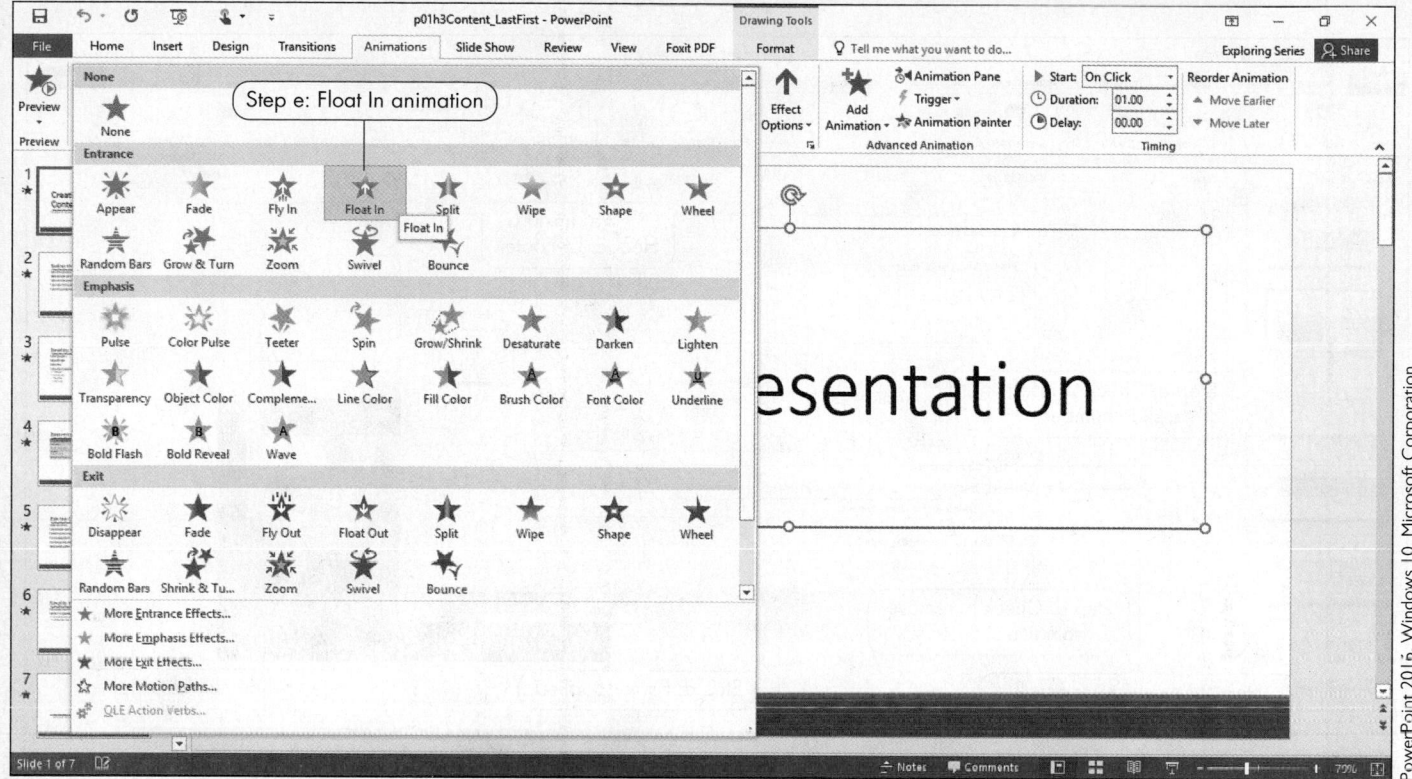

FIGURE 1.32 Title Placeholder with Animation

a. Select the **title placeholder** on Slide 1.

b. Click the **Animations tab** and click **More** in the Animation group.

c. Click **Float In** (under Entrance).

   The Float In animation is applied to the title placeholder.

d. Select the **picture** on Slide 2.

   You decide to apply and modify the Zoom animation and change the animation speed.

e. Click **More** in the Animation group and click **Zoom** (under Entrance).

f. Click **Effect Options** in the Animation group and select **Slide Center**.

   The picture now grows and zooms from the center of the slide.

g. Save the presentation.

›› CREATE A HANDOUT FOOTER

...use you are creating this presentation for the Training and Development department, you include this identifying information ... a slide footer. You also decide to include your personal information in a Notes and Handouts header and footer. Refer to Figure 1.33 as you complete Step 5.

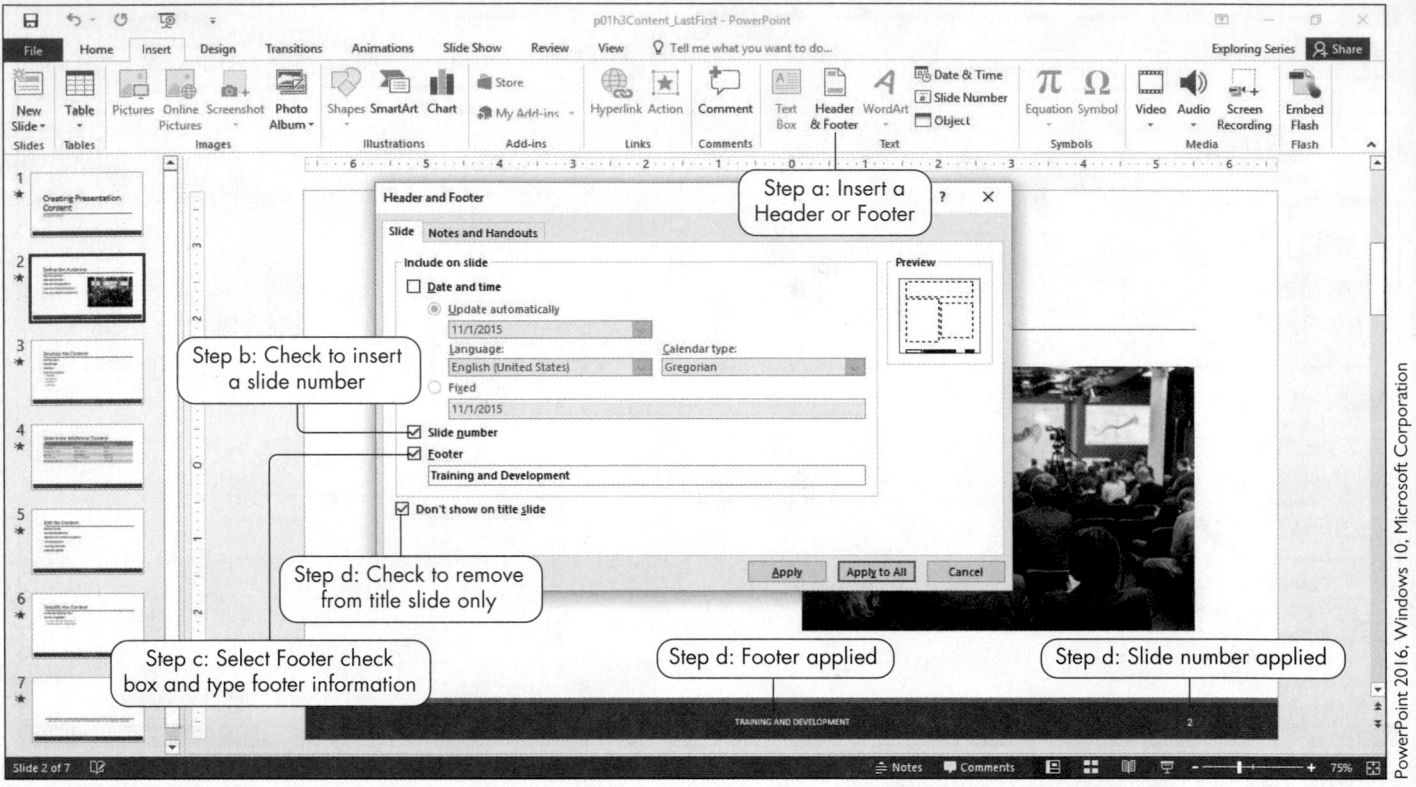

FIGURE 1.33 Slide Footer

a. Click the **Insert tab** and click **Header & Footer** in the Text group.

The Header and Footer dialog box opens, with the Slide tab active.

b. Click **Slide number check box** to select it.

The slide number will now appear on each slide. Note the position of the slide number in the Preview window: lower-right corner of the slide. The theme determined the position of the slide number.

c. Click the **Footer check box** to select it and type **Training and Development**.

Training and Development will appear on each slide. Note the position of the footer in the Preview window: bottom center of the slide.

d. Click the **Don't show on title slide** check box to select it and click **Apply to All**.

The slide footer and page number appear on all slides except the title slide.

e. Save the presentation. Keep the presentation open if you plan to continue with the next Hands-On Exercise. If not, close the presentation and exit PowerPoint.

Navigation and Printing

In the beginning of this chapter, you opened a slide show and advanced one by one through the slides by clicking the mouse. Audiences may ask questions that can be answered by going to another slide in the presentation. As you respond to the questions, you may find yourself jumping back to a previous slide or moving forward to a future slide. You may even find that during your presentation you wish to direct your audience's attention to a single area of a slide. PowerPoint's navigation options enable you to maneuver through a presentation easily.

To help your audience follow your presentation, you can choose to provide them with a handout. Various options are available for audience handouts. Be aware of the options, and choose the one that best suits your audience's needs. You may distribute handouts at the beginning of your presentation for note taking or provide your audience with the notes afterward.

In this section, you will run a slide show and navigate within the show. You will practice a variety of methods for advancing to new slides or returning to previously viewed slides. You will annotate a slide during a presentation and will change from screen view to black-screen view. Finally, you will print handouts of the slide show.

Navigating a Slide Show

STEP 1 ❯❯ PowerPoint provides multiple methods to advance through the slide show. You can also go back to a previous slide or jump to a specific slide, if needed. Use Table 1.2 to identify navigation options, and then experiment with each navigation method. Find the method that you are most comfortable using and stay with that method.

TABLE 1.2 Navigation Options

Navigation Option	Mouse	Keyboard	On-Screen
Advance to next slide or animation	Left-click	Press spacebar Press Page Down Press N Press down or right arrow Press Enter	Click right arrow
Return to previous slide or animation	Right-click, choose Previous	Press Backspace Press Page Up Press P Press up or left arrow	Click left arrow
End slide show	Right-click, choose End Show	Press Esc Press Ctrl+Break	Click ... , choose End Show
Go to specific slide	Right-click, click See All Slides, click slide	Type slide number, press Enter	Click <art> select slide.
Zoom in	Right-click, click Zoom In, move pointer to highlight area, click	+ or Ctrl ++	Click Magnifying glass icon, move pointer to highlight area, click
Zoom out	Right-click	Press Esc	

The See All Slides command displays all of your slides so you can easily identify and select the slide to which you want to go. You can access the See All Slides command in the navigation controls on the lower-left corner of the screen. Once you see all of the slides, you can click the slide of your choice.

To move to a specific slide on the screen using the See All Slides command, complete the following steps:

1. Right-click a slide while in Slide Show view.
2. Click See All Slides.
3. Click the slide you want to display.

If an audience member asks you a question that is best explained by a chart or diagram you have on a slide in your presentation, you can zoom in on a single section of the slide to answer the question. Figure 1.34 displays a slide in Slide Show view with an area highlighted for zooming on the left and a slide with the zoomed area on the right.

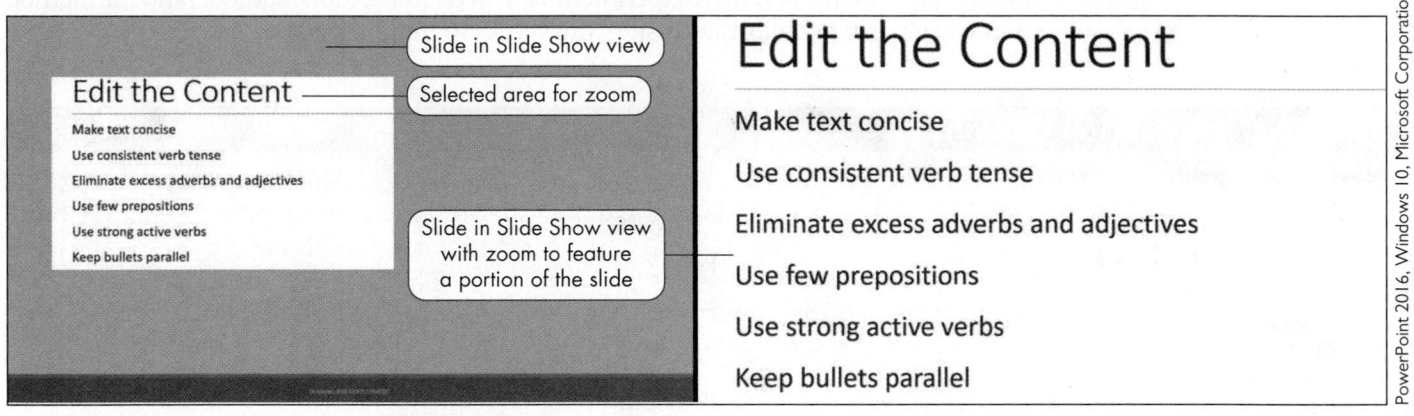

FIGURE 1.34 Zoom to Emphasize Part of a Slide

To enlarge a section of a slide on the screen, complete the following steps:

1. Navigate to the slide.
2. Point to the lower-left side of the screen to display the navigation controls.
3. Click the magnifying glass icon in the navigation controls on the lower-left corner. This will display a highlighted rectangular area on your slide.
4. Move the rectangular box over the area of the slide you want to emphasize. (Figure 1.34 shows the rectangular box.)
5. Click Esc to return to Normal view.

After the last slide in your slide show displays, the audience sees a black slide. This slide has two purposes: It enables you to end your show without having your audience see the PowerPoint design screen, and it cues the audience to expect the room lights to brighten. If you need to blacken the screen at any time during your presentation, you can press B. (If you blacken the screen in a darkened room, you must be prepared to quickly brighten some lights.) When you are ready to start your slide show again, simply press B again.

If you prefer bringing up a white screen, press W. White is much harsher on your audience's eyes, however. Only use white if you are in an extremely bright room. Whether using black or white, you are enabling the audience to concentrate on you, the speaker, without the slide show interfering.

Annotate the Slide Show

STEP 2 »» You may find it helpful to add *annotations* (notes or drawings) to your slides during a presentation. You can draw directly on your slide using the Pen tool. You can underline or circle words to call attention to them, draw an arrow to an object, or draw a simple illustration.

To add annotations, complete the following steps:

1. Point to the lower-left side of the slide to display the slide show controls.
2. Click the Pen tool to display the options for annotating a slide, or right-click a slide in Slide Show view.
3. Point to Pointer Options.
4. Click Pen or Highlighter.
5. Press and hold the left mouse button and write or draw on the screen.

To change the ink color for the Pen or Highlighter, complete the following steps:

1. Right-click on a slide to display the shortcut menu.
2. Point to Pointer Options.
3. Click Ink Color.
4. Click the color of your choice.

To erase what you have drawn, press E. With each slide, you must again activate the drawing pointer, in order to avoid accidentally drawing on your slides. The annotations you create are not permanent unless you save the annotations when exiting the slide show and then save the changes upon exiting the file. You may want to save the annotated file with a different file name from the original presentation so that you have both versions of the presentation.

Rather than annotate a slide, you may simply want to point to a specific section of the screen. The laser pointer feature enables you to do this.

To use the laser pointer, complete the following steps:

1. Right-click a slide in Slide Show view.
2. Point to Pointer Options.
3. Click Laser Pointer.
4. Move the pointer to the desired position.
5. Press Esc to end the laser pointer.

TIP: ANNOTATING SHORTCUTS

Press Ctrl+P to change the pointer to a drawing pointer while presenting, and click and draw on the slide, much the same way your favorite football announcer diagrams a play. Use Page Down and Page Up to move forward and backward in the presentation while the annotation is in effect. Press Ctrl+A to return the pointer to an arrow.

Printing in PowerPoint

A printed copy of a PowerPoint slide show can be used to display speaker notes for reference during the presentation, for audience handouts or a study guide, or as a means to deliver the presentation if there were an equipment failure. A printout of a single slide with text on it can be used as a poster or banner. Figure 1.35 shows the print options. Depending on your printer and printer settings, the names may vary.

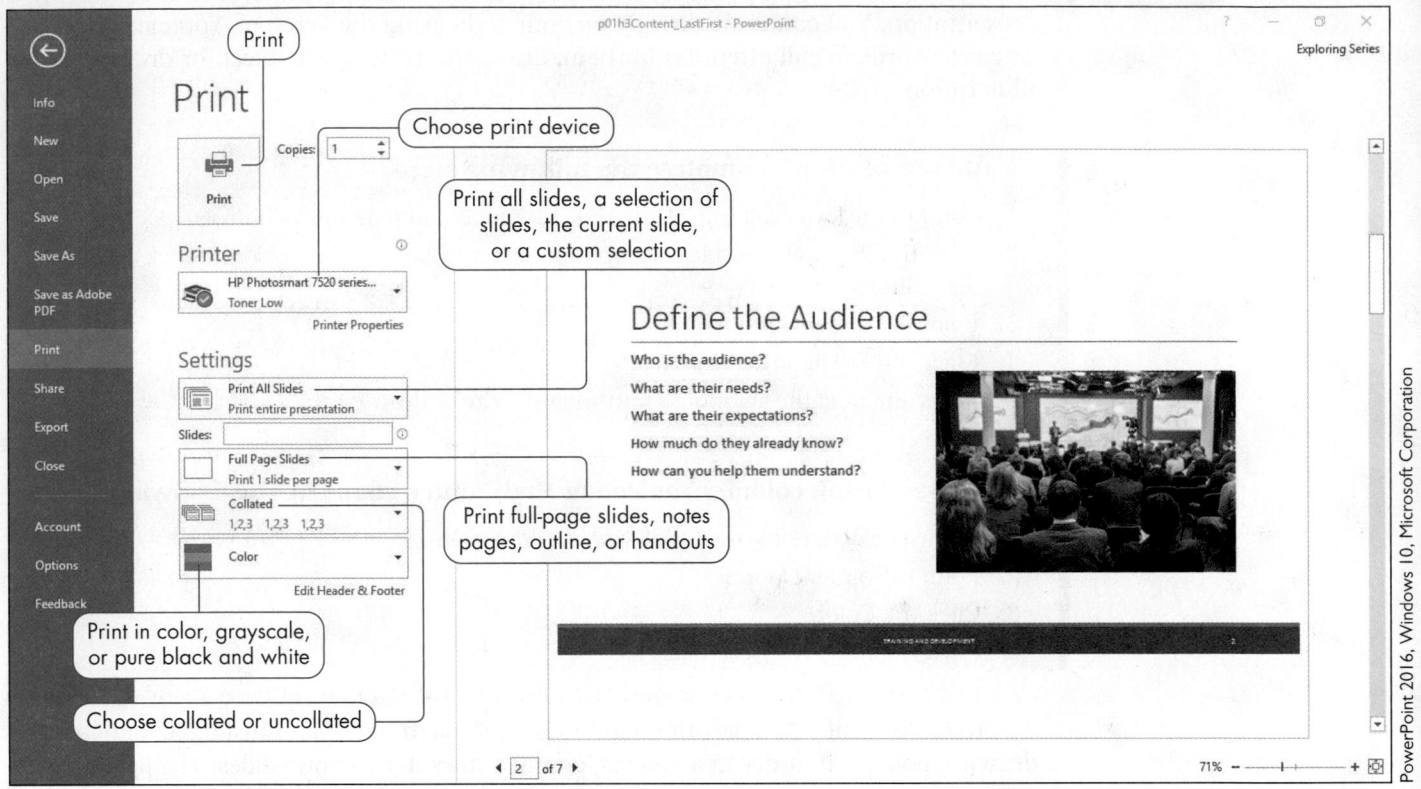

FIGURE 1.35 Print Options

To print a copy of the slide show using the default PowerPoint settings, complete the following steps:

1. Click the File tab and click Print.
2. Click the currently displayed printer to choose the print device you want to use.
3. Click Print All Slides and then select one of the options for the print area or for a custom range.
4. Click Full Page Slides to select the layout of the printout.
5. Click to select Collated or Uncollated.
6. Click Color to select Color, Grayscale, or Pure Black and White.
7. Click Print.

Print Full Page Slides

Use the Full Page Slides option to print the slides for use as a backup or when the slides contain a great deal of detail the audience needs to examine. You will be grateful for the backup if your projector bulb blows out or if your computer quits working during a presentation.

If you are printing the slides on paper smaller than the standard size, be sure to change the slide size and orientation before you print. By default, PowerPoint sets the slides for landscape orientation for printing so that the width is greater than the height (11" × 8 1/2"). If you are going to print a flyer or overhead transparency, however, you need to set PowerPoint to portrait orientation, to print so that the height is greater than the width (8 1/2" × 11").

To change your slide orientation, complete the following steps:

1. Click the Design tab.
2. Click Slide Size in the Customize group.
3. Click Customize Slide Size.
4. Click Portrait or Landscape in the Slides sized for section. You can also change the size of the slide as well as the orientation in this dialog box. If you want to create a custom size of paper to print, enter the height and width.

When you click Full Page Slides, several print options become available:

- Frame Slides: puts a black border around the slides in the printout, giving the printout a more polished appearance.

- Scale to Fit Paper: ensures that each slide prints on one page even if you have selected a custom size for your slide show, or if you have set up the slide show so that it is larger than the paper on which you are printing.

- High Quality: ensures that the shadows print if you have applied shadows to text or objects.

- Print Comments and Ink Markup: prints any comments or annotations; this option is active only if you have used added annotations to the slides.

After you click the File tab and click Print, you can determine the color option with which to print.

- Color: prints your presentation in color if you have a color printer or grayscale if you are printing on a black-and-white printer.

- Grayscale: prints in shades of gray, but be aware that backgrounds do not print when using the Grayscale option. By not printing the background, you make the text in the printout easier to read and you save ink or toner.

- Pure Black and White: prints in black and white only, with no gray color.

Print Handouts

STEP 3 The principal purpose for printing handouts is to give your audience something they can use to follow and take notes on during the presentation. With your handout and their notes, the audience has an excellent resource for the future. Handouts can be printed with one, two, three, four, six, or nine slides per page. Printing three slides per page is a popular option because it places thumbnails of the slides on the left side of the printout and lines on which the audience can write on the right side of the printout. Figure 1.36 shows the option set to Handouts and the Slides per page option set to 6.

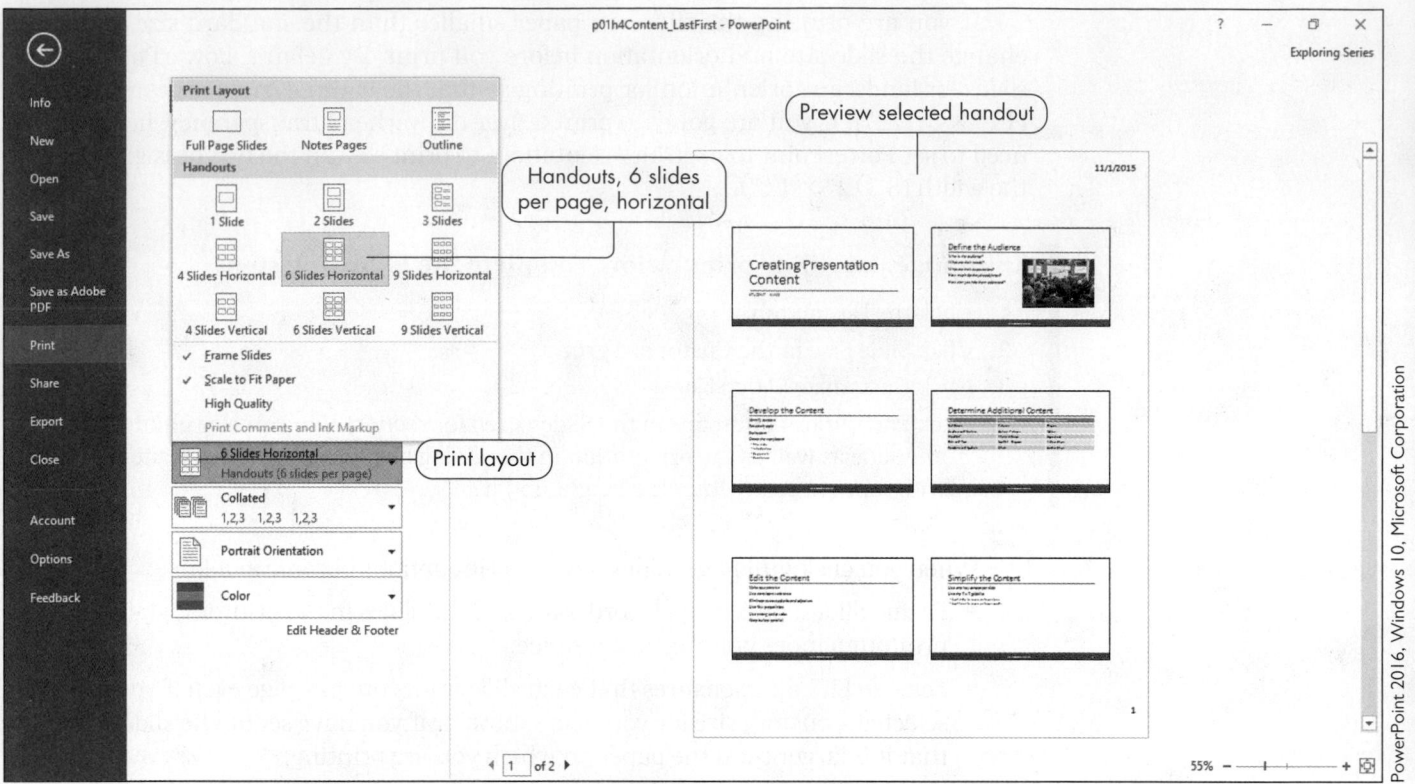

FIGURE 1.36 Setting Print Options

Print Notes Pages

If you include charts, technical information, or references in a speaker note, print a Notes Page if you want the audience to have a copy. To print a specific notes page, change the print layout to Notes Pages and click the Print All Slides arrow. Click Custom Range and enter the specific slide numbers to print.

Print Outlines

You may print your presentation as an outline made up of the slide titles and main text from each of your slides if you only want to deal with a few pages while presenting. The outline generally gives you enough detail to keep you on track with your presentation, but does not display speaker notes.

Remember, you, the speaker, are the most important part of any presentation. Do not rely on slides or handouts to get your message to the audience. These are supplemental materials for your presentation. The audience is there to hear YOU! Poor delivery will ruin even the best presentation. Speak slowly and clearly, maintain eye contact with your audience, and only use the information on the slides to guide you. Refer to the delivery tips in Table 1.3 before presenting.

TABLE 1.3 Practice the following delivery tips to gain confidence and polish your delivery

Before the presentation:

- Practice or rehearse your PowerPoint presentation until you are comfortable with the material and its corresponding slides.

- Know your material thoroughly. Glance at your notes infrequently.

- Arrive early to set up so you do not keep the audience waiting while you manage equipment.

- Have a backup in case the equipment does not work: Handouts work well.

- If appropriate, prepare handouts for your audience so they can relax and participate in your presentation rather than scramble taking notes.

- Make sure your notes pages acknowledge quotes, notes, data, and sources.

During the presentation:

- Speak naturally. Do not read from a prepared script or your PowerPoint Notes.

- Never post a screen full of small text and then torture your audience by saying, "I know you can't read this, so I will …"

- Speak to the person farthest away from you to be sure the people in the last row can hear you. Speak slowly and clearly.

- Vary your delivery. Show emotion or enthusiasm for your topic. If you do not care about your topic, why should the audience?

- Pause to emphasize key points when speaking.

- Look at the audience, not at the screen, as you speak to open communication and gain credibility.

- Use the three-second guide: Look into the eyes of a member of the audience for three seconds and then scan the entire audience. Continue doing this throughout your presentation. Use your eye contact to keep members of the audience involved.

- Blank the screen by pressing B or W at any time during your presentation when you want to solicit questions, comments, or discussion.

- Be judicious. Do not overwhelm your audience with your PowerPoint animations, sounds, and special effects. These features should enhance your message.

After the presentation:

- Thank the audience for their attention and participation. Leave on a positive note.

Quick Concepts ✓

12. How do you go to a specific slide when displaying a slide show? **p. 965**

13. Describe at least three uses for a printed copy of a PowerPoint slide show. **p. 969**

14. Discuss three things you should do while delivering a presentation and why you think doing these things strengthens your presentation. **p. 971**

Hands-On Exercises

Watch the Video
for this Hands-On
Exercise!

MyITLab®
HOE4 Training

Skills covered: Navigate a Slide Show • Annotate a Slide Show • Print Handouts

4 Navigation and Printing

To prepare for your presentation to Training and Development department employees, you practice displaying the slide show and navigating to specific slides. You also annotate a slide and print audience handouts.

STEP 1 ›› **NAVIGATE A SLIDE SHOW**

In this step, you practice various slide navigation techniques to become comfortable with their use. You also review the Slide Show Help feature to become familiar with navigation shortcuts. Refer to Figure 1.37 as you complete Step 1.

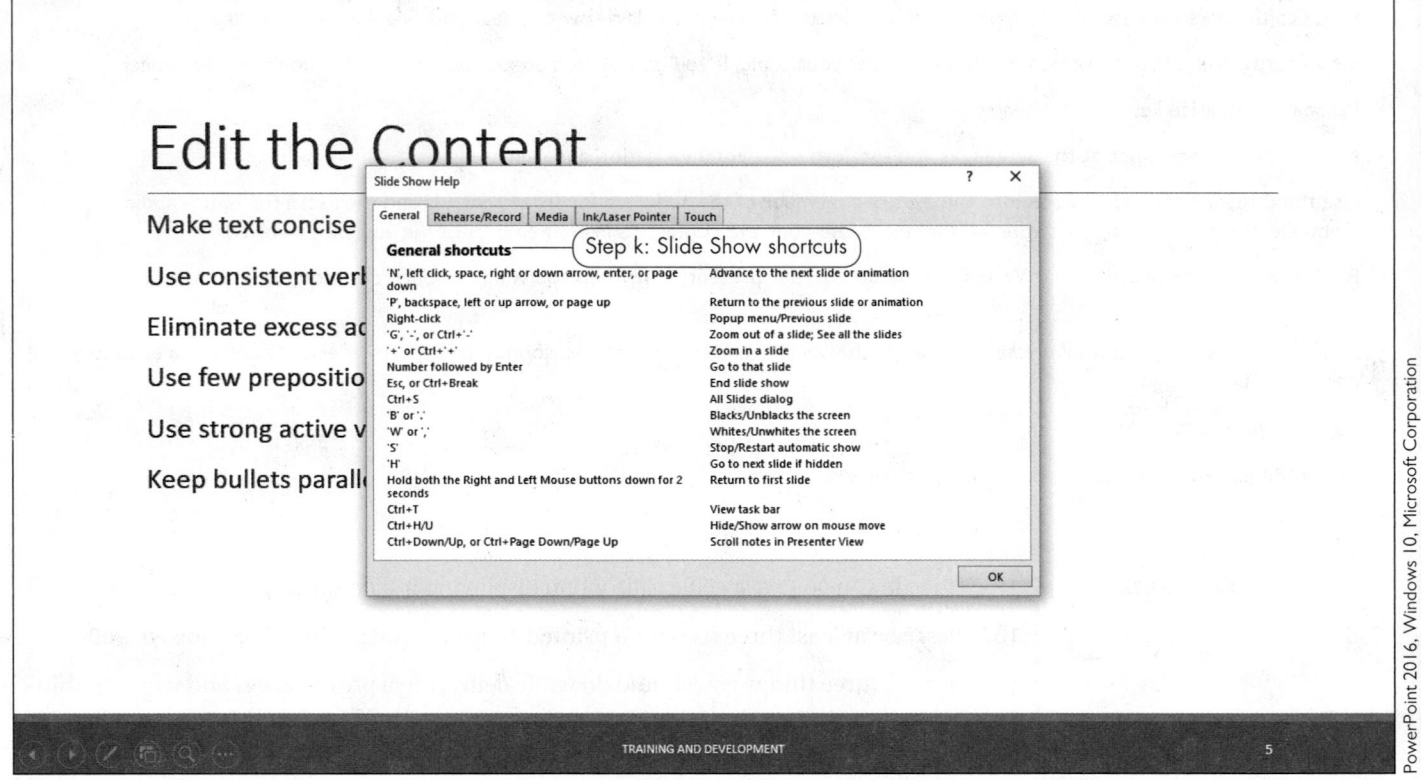

FIGURE 1.37 Slide Show Help

a. Open *p01h3Content_LastFirst* if you closed it at the end of Hands-On Exercise 3 and save it as **p01h4Content_LastFirst**, changing h3 to h4.

b. Click the **Slide Show tab** and click **From Beginning** in the Start Slide Show group.

Note the transition effect and sound you applied in Hands-On Exercise 3.

c. Press **Spacebar** to display the animated title.

d. Press the **left mouse button** to advance to Slide 2.

e. Press **Spacebar** to play the animation.

Note that the picture animation plays on click.

f. Click the **Magnifying glass icon** and zoom in only on the text for Slide 2.

g. Press **Enter** to advance to Slide 3.

h. Press **N** to advance to Slide 4.

i. Press **Backspace** to return to Slide 3.

j. Press the number **5** and press **Enter**.

Slide 5 displays.

k. Press **F1** and read the Slide Show Help window showing the shortcut tips that are available during the display of a slide show.

> **TROUBLESHOOTING:** If you are using a laptop, press FN+F1.

l. Close the Help window. Practice moving between slides using the shortcuts shown in Help.

STEP 2 ›› **ANNOTATE A SLIDE**

You practice annotating a slide using a pen, and then you remove the annotations. You practice darkening the screen and returning to the presentation from the dark screen. Refer to Figure 1.38 as you complete Step 2.

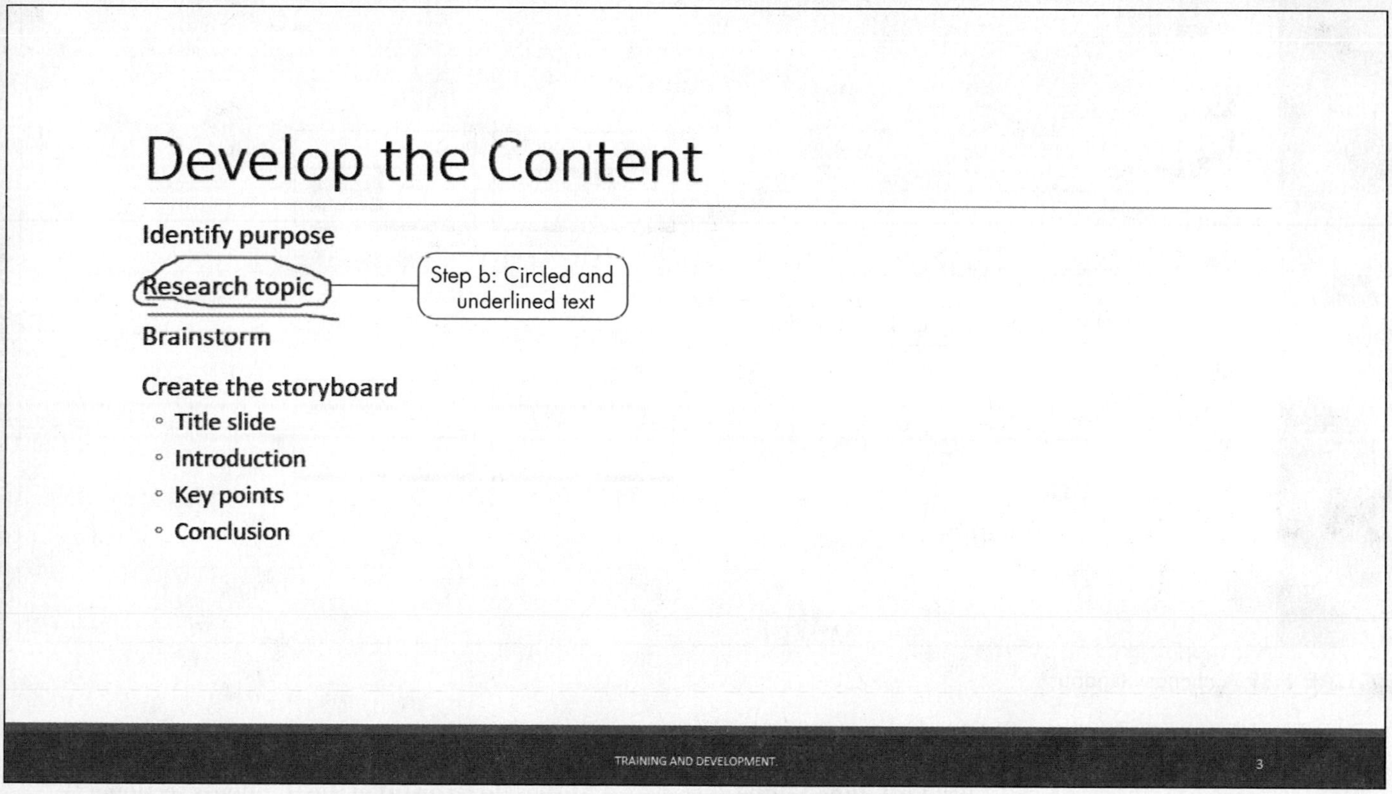

Develop the Content

Identify purpose

(Research topic) ──── Step b: Circled and underlined text

Brainstorm

Create the storyboard
- Title slide
- Introduction
- Key points
- Conclusion

TRAINING AND DEVELOPMENT.   3

PowerPoint 2016, Windows 10, Microsoft Corporation

FIGURE 1.38 Annotated Slide

a. Go to Slide 3 and then press **Ctrl+P**.

The pointer becomes a pen.

b. Circle and underline the words *Research topic* on the slide.

c. Press **E**.

The annotations erase.

d. Draw a box around *storyboard*.

e. Press **B**.

The screen blackens.

f. Press **B** again.

The slide show displays again.

g. Press **Esc** to end annotations.

h. Press **Esc** to end the slide show.

i. Save the presentation.

STEP 3 ⟩⟩ **PRINT HANDOUTS**

To enable your audience to follow along during your presentation, you print handouts of your presentation. You know that audience members may want to keep your handouts for future reference. Refer to Figure 1.39 as you complete Step 3.

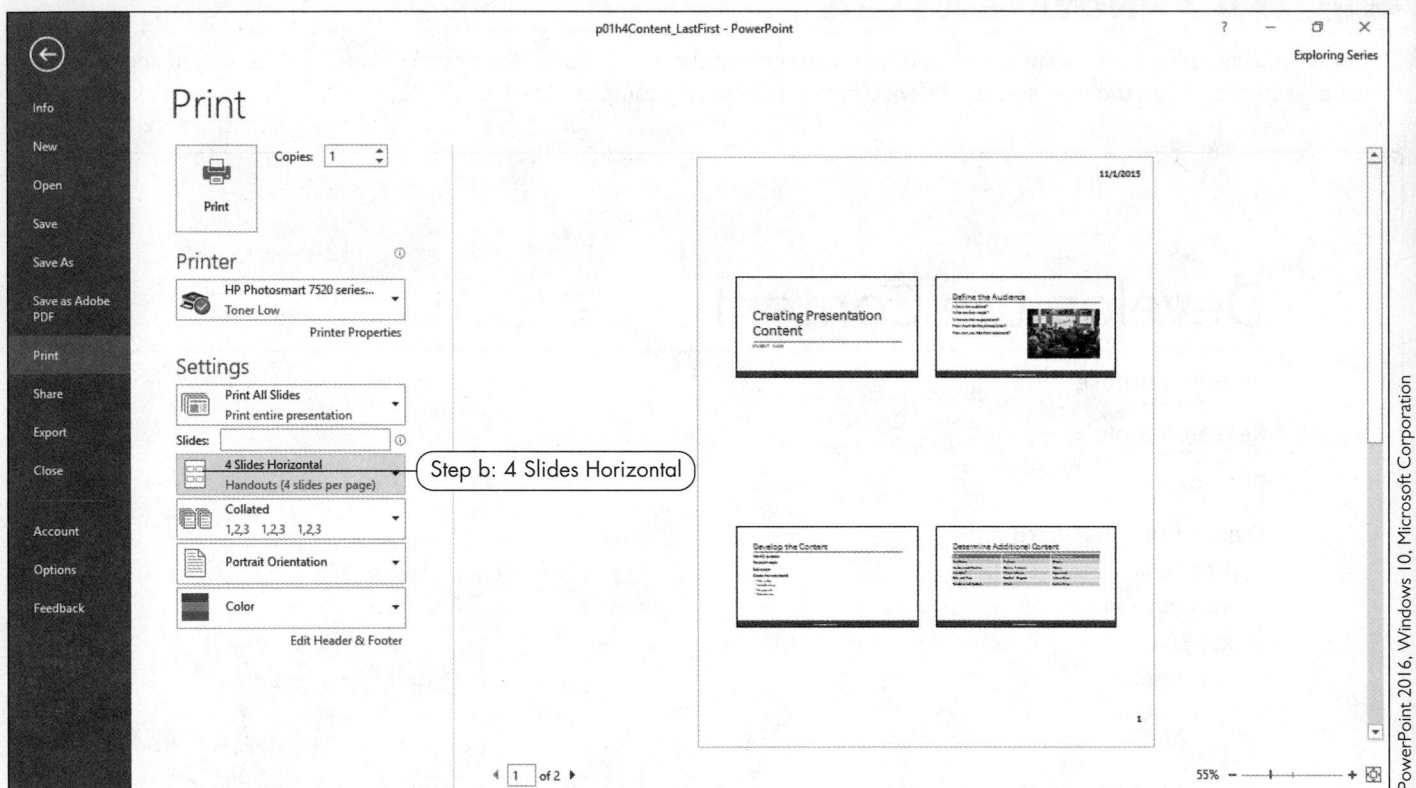

FIGURE 1.39 Audience Handout

a. Click **File** and then click **Print**.

b. Click **Full Page Slides** and select **4 Slides Horizontal** in the Handouts section.

> **TROUBLESHOOTING:** If you have previously selected a different print layout, Full Page Slides will be changed to that layout. Click the arrow next to the displayed layout option to select a different layout..

c. Click **Print** to print the presentation if requested by your instructor.

d. Save and close the file. Based on your instructor's directions, submit the following:

p01h1Intro_LastFirst

p01h1Intro_LastFirst.ppsx

p01h4Content_LastFirst

Chapter Objectives Review

After reading this chapter, you have accomplished the following objectives:

1. Open and view a PowerPoint presentation.

- Slide shows are electronic presentations that enable you to advance through slides containing content that will help your audience understand your message.
- Normal view, PowerPoint's default view, displays the slide deck in the Slides pane and the workspace in the Slide pane. A third pane, the Notes pane, may be displayed.
- Use PowerPoint views effectively: The Presentation Views group on the View tab enables you to access specialty views designed to help you work effectively and efficiently.
- Slide Sorter view displays thumbnails of slides to enable you to organize your presentation.
- Outline View enables you to easily create a presentation from an outline or view the outline of a presentation you have created.
- Notes Page view displays a thumbnail of the slide and any speaker notes that have been created.
- Slide Show view displays the slide show in full-screen view for an audience.
- Presenter view gives the presenter additional options while presenting, whereas the audience views the full-screen presentation.

2. Type a speaker note.

- Slides should contain only a minimum amount of information, and the speaker should deliver the majority of the information throughout the presentation.
- Speaker notes can be added to the PowerPoint presentation to provide the speaker with additional notes, data, or other comments to refer to during the presentation.

3. Save as a PowerPoint Show.

- By default, when you save a presentation it is saved with the file extension .pptx and, when opened, the presentation opens in Normal view for editing.
- You can save a presentation as a slide show, so that if you open it from a File Explorer winder, the file opens in Slide Show mode. Slide shows are saved with the file extension .ppsx.

4. Plan and prepare a presentation.

- Use a storyboard: Organize your ideas on a storyboard, and then create your presentation in PowerPoint.
- Review the storyboard to ensure that you use active voice, parallel construction, and follow the 7×7 guideline.
- Choose a theme: A theme applies coordinating colors, matching fonts, and effects to provide your presentation with a designer-quality look.

5. Add presentation content.

- Use slide layouts: When you add a slide, you can choose from a set of predefined slide layouts that determine the position of the objects or content on a slide.
- Placeholders hold content and determine the position of the objects on the slide.
- Create a title slide and introduction: The title slide should have a short title that indicates the purpose. An introduction slide will get the audience's attention.
- Create key point slides: The content of your presentation follows the title slide and the introduction. Create a slide for each of the key points in the storyboard.
- End with a summary or conclusion slide: The final slide of your presentation reviews the main points, restates the purpose, or invokes a call to action.

6. Review the presentation.

- Check spelling: Read each slide after typing its information, use the spelling feature, ask others to proofread the presentation, and display the presentation in Reading View then read each word out loud. Correct all spelling or word usage errors found for a professional presentation.
- Use the Thesaurus: The Thesaurus helps you make varied word choices.
- Check slide show elements: View the presentation in Slide Show view and check slide layouts, transitions, and animations to ensure that slides present information in a clear and orderly manner. Make changes as needed.
- Reorder slides: Change the order of the slides by dragging them to a new location in Slide Sorter view.

7. Add a table.

- Tables organize information in rows and columns to present structured data.

8. Insert media objects.

- Media objects such as online pictures, images, movies, and sound can be added to enhance the message of your slides and to add visual interest.

9. Apply animations and transitions.

- Apply transitions: Use transitions to control the movement of slides as one slide changes to another.
- Animate objects: Apply animation to objects to control the movement of an object on one slide.

10. Insert a header or footer.

- Headers and footers are used for identifying information on the slide or on handouts and notes pages. Header and footer locations vary depending on the theme applied.

11. Navigate a slide show.

- Various navigation methods advance the slide show, return to previously viewed slides, or go to specific slides.
- Annotate the slide show: Annotations are useful for adding comments to slides.

12. Print in PowerPoint.

- Print full page slides: Print full page slides for use as a backup or when the slides contain a great deal of detail the audience needs to examine.
- Print handouts: Handouts print miniatures of the slides using 1, 2, 3, 4, 6, or 9 slide thumbnails per page. Handouts are useful to an audience.
- Print notes pages: The Notes Page method prints a single thumbnail of a slide with its associated notes per page.
- Print outlines: Outline View prints the titles and main points of the presentation in outline format.

Key Terms Matching

Match the key terms with their definitions. Write the key term letter by the appropriate numbered definition.

a. Animation
b. Annotation
c. Layout
d. Normal view
e. Notes Page view
f. Placeholder
g. PowerPoint presentation
h. PowerPoint show
i. Presenter view
j. Reading View

k. Slide
l. Slide show
m. Slide Show view
n. Slide Sorter view
o. Status bar
p. Storyboard
q. Theme
r. Thumbnail
s. Transition
t. Variant

1. _____ Defines containers, positioning, and formatting for all of the content that appears on a slide. **p. 943**

2. _____ The default PowerPoint view, containing two panes that provide maximum flexibility in working with the presentation. **p. 926**

3. _____ A container that holds content. **p. 943**

4. _____ The movement applied to an object or objects on a slide. **p. 955**

5. _____ The most basic element of PowerPoint, analogous to a page in a Word document. **p. 926**

6. _____ A note or drawing added to a slide during a presentation. **p. 967**

7. _____ Located at the bottom of the screen in Normal view, this contains the slide number, spelling check, Notes, and Comments buttons, and options that control the view of your presentation. **p. 928**

8. _____ Used to view a slide show full screen, one slide at a time, for performing a thorough review of the slides without the full interface onscreen. **p. 931**

9. _____ A presentation saved with a .pptx extension. **p. 934**

10. _____ An electronic method to deliver your message using multiple slides. **p. 926**

11. _____ Used if the speaker needs to enter and edit large amounts of text for reference in the presentation. **p. 933**

12. _____ Uses a .ppsx extension. **p. 934**

13. _____ A specialty view that delivers a presentation on two monitors simultaneously. **p. 933**

14. _____ A variation of the theme you have chosen, using different color palettes and font families. **p. 942**

15. _____ The view used to deliver a completed presentation full screen to an audience, one slide at a time. **p. 932**

16. _____ A slide miniature. **p. 927**

17. _____ A specific animation that is applied when a previous slide is replaced by a new slide. **p. 955**

18. _____ Displays thumbnails of your presentation slides, allowing you to view multiple slides simultaneously. **p. 930**

19. _____ A visual design that helps you plan the direction of your presentation slides. **p. 939**

20. _____ A collection of formatting choices that includes colors, fonts, and special effects. **p. 942**

Multiple Choice

1. Which of the following features enable you to change the color of objects in your slide show without changing text?

   (a) Themes
   (b) Insert
   (c) Format Variants
   (d) Slide Color

2. Which of the following statements is *not* accurate about placeholders?

   (a) Placeholders may be resized.
   (b) All of the content contained in a placeholder is selected when the border of the placeholder is double-clicked.
   (c) Placeholder positions are determined by the slide layout and may not be changed.
   (d) Placeholders can contain text, pictures, tables, and more.

3. What is the term for theme alternatives using different color palettes and font families?

   (a) Palettes
   (b) Designs
   (c) Variants
   (d) Layouts

4. Which print method provides lined space for note taking by the audience?

   (a) Handout, 6 Slides Horizontal
   (b) Outline
   (c) Notes Pages
   (d) Handout, 3 Slides

5. Which of the following components are contained in Normal view?

   (a) Slide Sorter pane, Slides tab, and Reading pane
   (b) Slides pane and Slide pane
   (c) Slides tab, Slide pane, and Reading pane
   (d) Slide pane, Notes pane, and Slide Sorter pane

6. What view is the best choice if you want to reorder the slides in a presentation?

   (a) Slide Sorter view
   (b) Presenter view
   (c) Reading View
   (d) Slide Show view

7. Which of the following layouts is most commonly used when introducing the topic of the presentation and the speaker?

   (a) Blank
   (b) Title Slide
   (c) Comparison
   (d) 3 column

8. In reference to content development, which of the following points is *not* in active voice and is not parallel to the others?

   (a) Identify the purpose of the presentation.
   (b) Sketch out your thoughts on a storyboard.
   (c) Brainstorm your thoughts.
   (d) Your topic should be researched thoroughly.

9. Which feature will enable you to apply motion as one slide exits and another enters?

   (a) Transition
   (b) Timing
   (c) Animation
   (d) Advance

10. During a slideshow, which of the following would *not* focus audience attention on a specific object?

    (a) Put nothing on the slide but the object.
    (b) Apply an animation to the object.
    (c) Use the Pen tool to circle the object.
    (d) Apply a transition to the object.

Practice Exercises

1 Managing Your Stress

FROM SCRATCH

The slide show you create in this practice exercise covers concepts and skills that will help you manage your stress as a college student. You create a title slide, an introduction, four slides containing main points of the presentation, and a conclusion slide. Then, you review the presentation and edit a slide so that the text of the bulleted items is parallel. Finally, you print a title page to use as a cover and notes pages to staple together as a reference. Refer to Figure 1.40 as you complete the exercise.

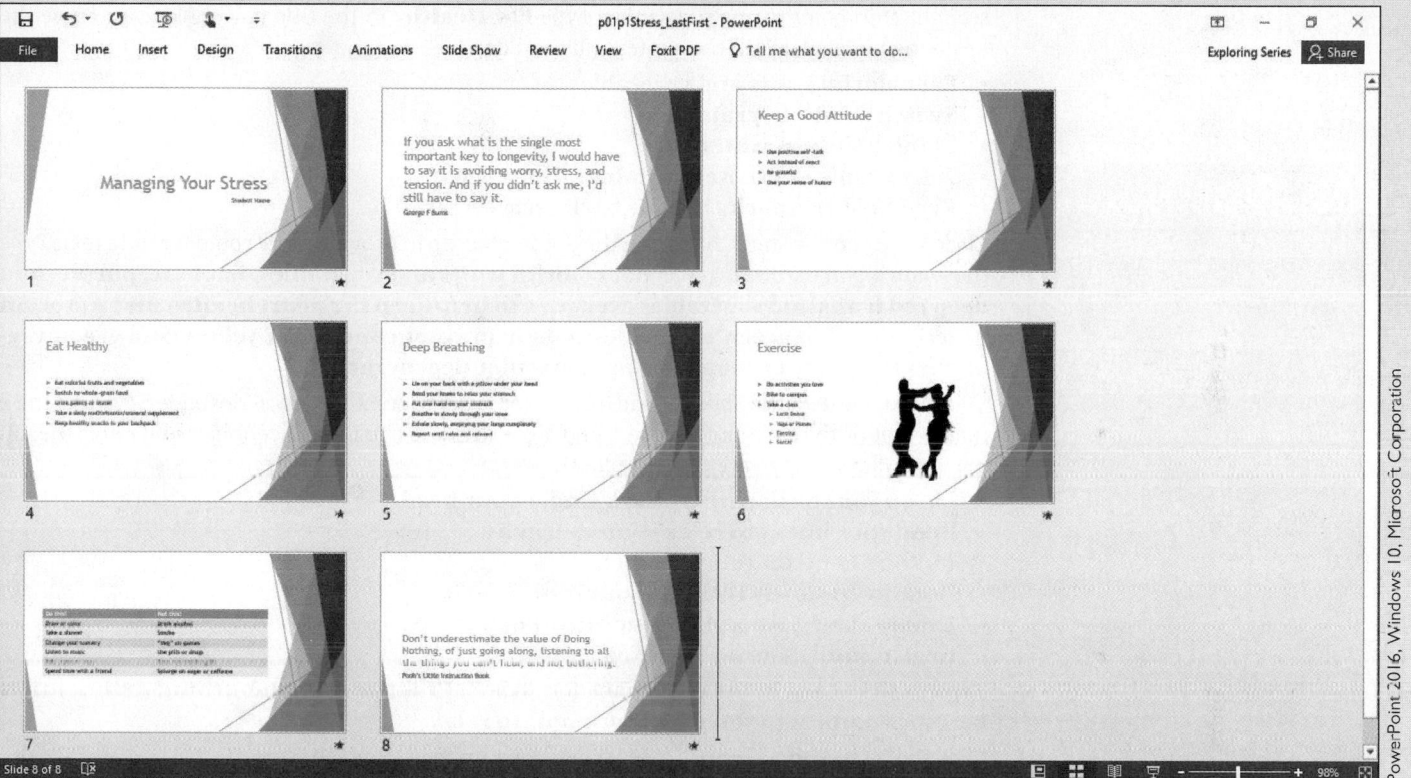

FIGURE 1.40 Managing Your Stress

a. Click **File** and click **New**.

b. Click the **Facet theme**. Click the variant with the blue color (upper-right corner) and click **Create**.

c. Save the presentation as **p01p1Stress_LastFirst**.

d. Click the **Insert tab**, click **Header & Footer** in the Text group, and then click the **Notes and Handouts tab** in the Header and Footer dialog box. Make the following changes:

- Select the **Date and time check box** and ensure that *Update automatically* is selected.
- Click to select the **Header check box** and type your name in the **Header box**.
- Click the **Footer check box** and type your instructor's name and your class name in the **Footer box**. Click **Apply to All**.

e. Click in the **title placeholder** and type **Managing Your Stress**. Click in the **subtitle placeholder** and type your name.

f. Click the **New Slide arrow** in the Slides group on the Home tab to create a new slide (Slide 2) using the **Section Header layout** for the introduction of the slide show. You use a quote for the introduction. Type **Don't underestimate the value of Doing Nothing, of just going along, listening to all the things you can't hear, and not bothering.** in the title placeholder. Type **Pooh's Little Instruction Book** in the subtitle placeholder.

g. Click the **New Slide arrow** in the Slides group on the Home tab to create a new slide (Slide 3) using the **Title and Content layout** for the first main point of the slide show. Type **Keep a Good Attitude** in the title placeholder and type the following bulleted text in the content placeholder:

- **Use positive self-talk**
- **Instead of reacting, act**
- **Be thankful**
- **Use your sense of humor**

h. Click **New Slide** in the Slides group on the Home tab to create a new slide (Slide 4) for the second main point of the slide show. Type **Eat Healthy** in the title placeholder and type the following bulleted text in the content placeholder:

- **Eat colorful fruits and vegetables**
- **Switch to whole-grain food**
- **Drink plenty of water**
- **Take a daily multivitamin/mineral supplement**
- **Keep healthy snacks in your backpack**

i. Click **Notes** on the status bar. Drag the Splitter bar up to provide more room for note text. Type the following in the Notes pane: **Eat colorful fruits and vegetables. Eat blue, purple, and deep red fruits and vegetables every day to help keep the heart healthy and the brain functioning. Eat green vegetables to help prevent cancer. Eat yellow and green vegetables to help prevent age-related macular degeneration.**

j. Click **New Slide** in the Slides group on the Home tab to create a new slide (Slide 5) for the third main point of the slide show. Type **Deep Breathing** in the title placeholder and enter the following bulleted text in the content placeholder:

- **Lie on your back with a pillow under your head**
- **Bend your knees to relax your stomach**
- **Put one hand on your stomach**
- **Breathe in slowly through your nose**
- **Exhale slowly, emptying your lungs completely**
- **Repeat until calm and relaxed**

k. Type the following in the Notes pane for Slide 5: **Practice deep breathing daily until it becomes natural to you when you want to relax.**

l. Click the **New Slide arrow** in the Slides group on the Home tab to create a new slide (Slide 6) using the **Two Content layout** for the fourth main point of the slide show. Type **Exercise** in the title placeholder and enter the following text in the content placeholder on the left side of the slide following the title:

- **Do activities you love**
- **Bike to campus**
- **Take a class**
  - **Latin Dance**
  - **Yoga or Pilates**
  - **Fencing**
  - **Soccer**

m. Click the **Online Pictures icon** in the content placeholder on the right side of the slide. Type **Latin dancing** in the search box for Bing images. Press **Enter**. Click an image of dancers and then click **Insert** to insert the image.

> **TROUBLESHOOTING:** If you cannot locate an image of dancers that you like, use one of the other suggested classes from Step l as your search string.

n. Type the following in the Notes pane: **Learning more about an activity you are interested in gets you moving and is a good stress reliever.**

o. Click the **New Slide arrow** in the Slides group on the Home tab. Click **Title and Content** to create a new slide (Slide 7) for the last main point of the slide show. Select the **title place-holder** and press **Delete**.

p. Click the **Insert Table icon** in the content placeholder. Set Number of columns to **2** and Number of rows to **7**. Click **OK**. Type the following text in the columns, pressing **Tab** after each entry except the last:

Do this!	Not this!
Draw or color	Drink alcohol
Take a shower	Smoke
Change your scenery	"Veg" on games
Listen to music	Use pills or drugs
Take a power nap	Zone out watching TV
Spend time with a friend	Splurge on sugar or caffeine

q. Type the following in the Notes pane for Slide 7: **Use healthy activities to relieve your stress. Many activities students use to relieve stress actually cause them a great deal more stress.**

r. Click the **New Slide arrow** in the Slides group on the Home tab and add a new slide (Slide 8) using the **Section Header layout**. You use a quote for the conclusion slide of the slide show. Type **If you ask what is the single most important key to longevity, I would have to say it is avoiding worry, stress, and tension. And if you didn't ask me, I'd still have to say it.** in the title placeholder and then type **George F Burns** in the subtitle placeholder.

s. Click Slide 3. Note that the slide bullets are not in parallel construction. The second bulleted point needs to be changed to active voice. Select *Instead of reacting, act* and type **Act instead of react**.

t. Click **thankful** in the third bullet. Click the **Review tab** and click **Thesaurus**. Click **grateful** in the Thesaurus. Click the **arrow** and then click **Insert**.

u. Click the **Transitions tab** and click **More** in the Transition to This Slide group. Click **Push** in the Transition gallery. Click **Apply to All** in the Timing Group.

v. Click the **View tab**, and click **Slide Sorter** in the Presentation Views group. Drag **Slide 8**, the George Burns quote, so that it becomes **Slide 2**. Drag the new **Slide 3**, the Pooh quote, so that it becomes **Slide 8**.

w. Click the **File tab**, click **Print**, and then click **Full Page Slides**. Click **Full Page Slides** and select **Notes Pages**, click **Frame Slides**, and click **Print**, if your instructor asks you to submit printed slides.

x. Click the **Review tab** and click **Spelling**. Correct any errors.

y. Click the **File tab** and click **Save** to save the presentation as a normal PowerPoint presentation type.

z. Click the **File tab** and click **Save As**. In the Save As dialog box, change the Save as type to **PowerPoint Show** and click **Save**. Close the file. Based on your instructor's directions, submit the following:

p01p1Stress_LastFirst.pptx

p01p1Stress_LastFirst.ppsx

2 Tips for a Successful Presentation

FROM SCRATCH Your employer is a successful business person who has been asked by the local Chamber of Commerce to give tips for presenting successfully using a PowerPoint presentation. She created a storyboard of her presentation and has asked you to create the presentation from the storyboard. Refer to Figure 1.41 as you complete this exercise.

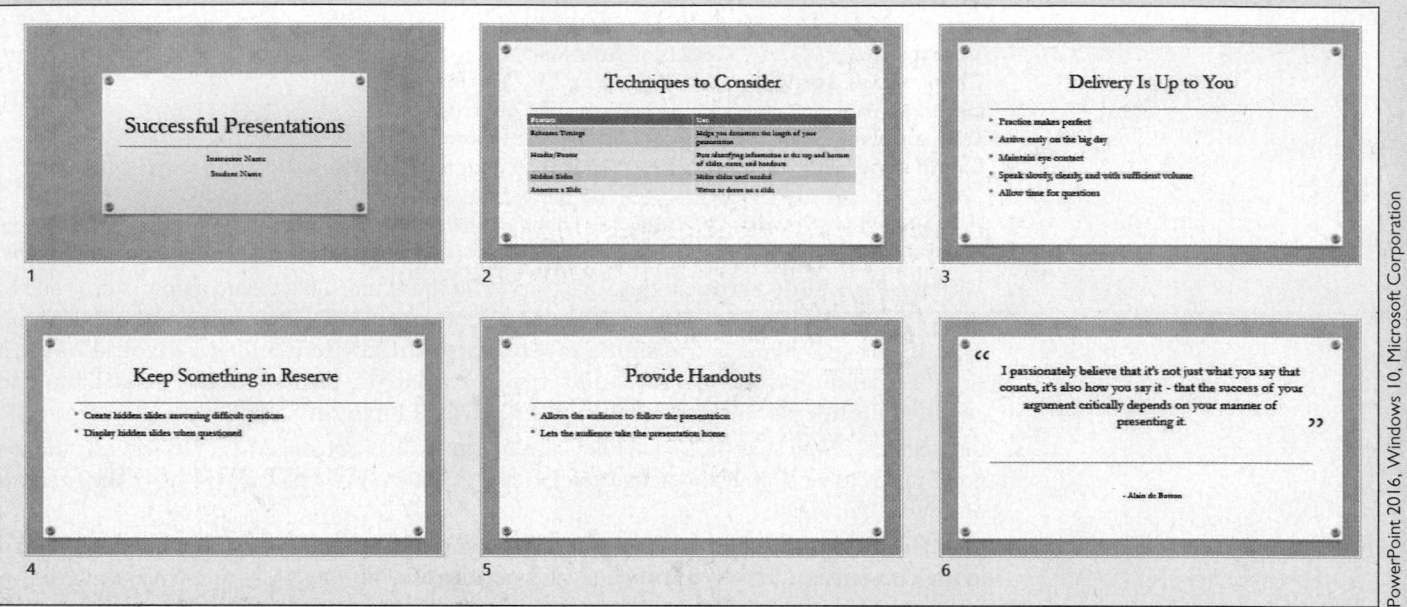

FIGURE 1.41 Successful Presentations

a. Click **File** and then click **New**.

b. Select **Organic**, select the variant in the lower-right corner, and then click **Create**.

c. Save the presentation as **p01p2Presenting_LastFirst**.

d. Click the **Insert tab**, click **Header & Footer**, and then click the **Notes and Handouts tab** in the Header and Footer dialog box.

   • Click to select the **Date and time check box** and click **Update automatically**.
   • Click to select the **Header check box** and type your name in the **Header box**.
   • Click to select the **Footer check box** and type your instructor's name and your class name. Click **Apply to All**.

e. Click in the **title placeholder** on Slide 1, and type **Successful Presentations**. Click in the **subtitle placeholder** and type your instructor's name. Press **Enter**. On the new line, type your name.

f. Click the **Home tab** and click **New Slide** in the Slides group.

g. Click in the **title placeholder** and type **Techniques to Consider**.

h. Click the **Insert Table icon** in the content placeholder and enter **2** columns and **5** rows.

i. Type the following information in the table cells, pressing **Tab** after each item except the last:

Feature	Use
Rehearse Timings	Helps you determine the length of your presentation
Header/Footer	Puts identifying information on the top and bottom of slides, notes, and handouts
Hidden Slides	Hides slides until needed
Annotate a Slide	Writes or draws on a slide

j. Click the **Home tab** and click **New Slide** in the Slides group. Type **Delivery Is Up to You** in the title placeholder.

k. Click in the **content placeholder** and type the following bulleted text:
- **Practice makes perfect**
- **Arrive early on the big day**
- **Maintain eye contact**
- **Speak slowly, clearly, and with sufficient volume**
- **Allow time for questions**

l. Click **New Slide** and type **Keep Something in Reserve** in the title placeholder.

m. Click in the **content placeholder** and type the following bulleted text:
- **Create hidden slides answering difficult questions**
- **Display hidden slides when questioned**

n. Click **New Slide** and type **Provide Handouts** in the title placeholder.

o. Click in the **content placeholder** and type the following bulleted text:
- **Allows the audience to follow the presentation**
- **Lets the audience take the presentation home**

p. Click the **New Slide arrow** and click **Quote with Caption**.

q. Type **I passionately believe that it's not just what you say that counts, it's also how you say it — that the success of your argument critically depends on your manner of presenting it.** in the title placeholder.

r. Click the **center placeholder** and press **Delete**.

s. Type **- Alain de Botton** in the bottom placeholder.

t. Select the **bottom placeholder** and then click the **Animations tab**. Click **Fly In** in the Animations group.

u. Click the **Review tab** and click **Spelling** in the Proofing group. Accept *Lets* in Slide 5. Review the presentation in Slide Show view to fix any spelling errors.

v. Click the **Slide Show tab** and click **From Beginning** in the Start Slide Show group. Press **Page Down** to advance through the slides. When you reach the last slide of the slide show, press the number **3** and press **Enter** to return to Slide 3.

w. Right-click, point to **Pointer Options**, and then click **Highlighter**. Highlight **Speak slowly, clearly, and with sufficient volume**.

x. Press **Page Down** to advance through the remainder of the presentation. Press **Esc** when you reach the black slide at the end of the slide show and click **Keep** to keep your slide annotations.

y. Click the **File tab**, click **Print**, and then click **Full Page Slides**. Click **Outline** and click **Print**, if your instructor asks you to submit printed slides.

z. Save and close the file. Based on your instructor's directions, submit p01p2Presenting_LastFirst.

Mid-Level Exercises

1 Planning Presentation Content

You received a high-definition mini action cam for Christmas and you have been using it to video your snowboarding, paddle boarding, and fishing trips. A friend who has seen your videos asked you to present a workshop on characteristics of HD mini action cams and why they are becoming commonly used, popular models, as well as tips for use. You create a slide show for your audience to view as you present.

a. Create a new presentation, applying the design theme of your choice to the presentation. Save the presentation as **p01m1Cam_LastFirst**.

b. Create a title slide that includes **Using a Mini Action Cam** as the title and your name and class in the subtitle placeholder.

c. Create a Title and Content slide using **Popular Models** as the title. Create the following two-column table in the content placeholder.

GoPros	Muvis
Garmins	Rolleis
Ghosts	iVues
Sonys	Panasonics
iONs	HTCs

d. Create a slide using the Content with Caption layout. Type **Characteristics** as the title, and list the following in the content placeholder on the left side of the slide: **Small, Lightweight, Tough, Attachable, POV video, Fish-eye perspective**. Insert an online picture of a mini action camera in the content placeholder on the right side of the slide.

e. Create a slide using the Two Content layout. Type **Popular Features** as the title. List the following in the content placeholder on the left side of the slide: **Slow motion, GPS tracking, Wrist remote, Waterproof casing**. List the following in the content placeholder on the right side of the slide: **Box cam style, Bullet cam style, Sunglasses mount, WiFi connectivity**.

f. Create a slide using the Title and Content layout. Type **Tips** as the title, and then type this list in the content placeholder:
- **Know your mount**
- **Practice running the camera by touch**
- **Get the light right**
- **Avoid water spots on the lens**

g. Create a slide using the Title and Content layout. Type **Sample Video** as the title. Use the Insert Video button on the palette of content options to insert the video *p01m1Video* located in your student files.

h. Change the view to Slide Sorter view, and then move Slide 3 (Characteristics) so that it becomes Slide 2. While in Slide Sorter view, assign the transition of your choice to all slides in the slide show. Note the star that appears under each slide that indicates the slide has a transition attached.

i. Double-click **Slide 2** to return to Normal view. Select the content placeholder that contains the list of characteristics. Apply the Wipe animation.

j. Change the view to Notes Page view. Add the notes for the speaker's reference as follows:

Slide	Note
2	Action cameras are small, lightweight cameras that are designed to attach to objects like helmets, surf or paddle boards, cars, sticks, and other objects to create point of view (POV) video.
4	When purchasing a mini action camera, determine how you are most likely to use the camera, then look at cameras that will provide those features.

5
- Check to see where the mount is steadiest so you don't get a choppy video while getting the shot you want.
- Practice until you can operate the camera by touch, as different mounts make it impossible to see the buttons.
- Use camera settings for different lighting conditions.
- Apply an anti-beading solution to the lens to prevent water spots from forming.

k. Add a slide number in the footer to all of the slides except the title slide. (Note: The slide number position on the slide will depend on the theme you selected.)

l. Review the slide show in Slide Show view to check spelling and word usage. Adjust layouts and placeholder location until all elements fit attractively and professionally on the slide.

m. Print notes pages.

n. Save and close the file. Based on your instructor's directions, submit p01m1Cam_LastFirst.

2 Wireless Network Safety

 **FROM SCRATCH**

You volunteer at the local community center. You have been asked to present to a group of young teens about staying safe when using wireless computer networks. You have researched the topic and using your notes you are ready to prepare your presentation.

a. Start a new presentation. Apply the Banded theme. Apply the black, blue, and green variant. Save the presentation as **p01m2Wifi_LastFirst**.

b. Add **Wi-Fi Safety** as a footer on all slides except the title slide. Also include an automatically updated date and time and a slide number.

c. Create a Notes and Handouts header with your name and a footer with your instructor's name and your class name. Apply to all.

d. Add the title **WiFi Safety** in the title placeholder. Type **Keeping Your Personal Information Safe** in the subtitle placeholder.

e. Insert a new slide using the Two Content layout. Type **Wireless Fidelity (WiFi)** as the title.

f. Type the following into the left content placeholder:
- **Uses radio waves to exchange data wirelessly via a computer network**
- **Commonly found at coffee shops and other public places**
- **Also called hotspots**

g. Add an online picture to the right content placeholder: Search for **WiFi photo** in the search box. Insert the photo of your choosing.

h. Insert a new slide using the **Title and Content layout** as the third slide in the presentation. Type **WiFi Hotspot Security** as the title.

i. Type the following into the content placeholder:
- **Avoid unsecured networks if possible**
- **Don't access confidential information**
- **Set network locations to "Public"**
- **Keep firewall and antivirus software up-to-date**

j. Click **Notes** on the status bar. Add the following text to the Notes pane:

Although a number of threats exist when using public WiFi hotspots, there are several ways you can protect yourself and your computer.

k. Insert a new slide using the Blank layout as the fourth slide in the presentation.

l. Click the **Insert tab**, click **Table**, and then insert a table with four rows and two columns. Type the following text in the table:

Threat	Explanation
Identity Theft	**Criminal act involving the use of your personal information for financial gain.**
Hacking	**Unauthorized access to a computer or network.**
Malware	**Software programs that are designed to be harmful. A virus is a type of malware.**

m. Position the table at the approximate center of the slide.

n. Apply the **Fade transition** from the Subtle category to all slides in the slide show.

o. Add the **Bounce animation** from the Entrance category to the content placeholder and then to the image on Slide 2. Start the animation for the image with the previous animation so they start at the same time.

DISCOVER

p. Move Slide 4 so that it becomes Slide 3.

q. Review the presentation and correct any errors you find.

r. Print the handouts, three per page, framed.

s. Save and close the file. Based on your instructor's directions, submit p01m2Wifi_LastFirst.

3 Creating a Free Website and Blog for Your PowerPoint Experiences

COLLABORATION CASE

FROM SCRATCH

Web 2.0 technologies make it easy for people to interact using the Internet. Web applications often combine functions to help us create our online identity, share information, collaborate on projects, and socialize. In this exercise, you will create an online identity for your use in your PowerPoint class, share information about your PowerPoint experience with others, and get to know a few of your classmates. You will create a website for use during your PowerPoint class, add information to the pages in your website, and then share the address of your site with others. You will also visit the websites of others in your class.

a. Open a Web browser and search for a site that enables you to create a free website or blog. For example: Google Sites, Web.com, Weebly, or any other free site.

b. Register for the site and then begin creating your site.

c. Enter a title for your website as follows: use your first name and last name followed by PPT to indicate this is your PowerPoint site.

d. Use whatever free design elements the site provides to create the look of your site.

e. Add a blog to your site. Add an entry to your blog that explains your previous experience with PowerPoint and why you have registered for this class. Search YouTube for a video about PowerPoint or presentation skills. Create a second blog entry about what you learned and include the link for others to view if interested.

f. Publish your website.

g. Exchange website addresses with at least three other students in your class. Visit your classmates' websites and leave a comment to indicate you have visited. Then, revisit your website to see what comments your classmates entered.

h. Email your instructor your website address so your instructor can visit your site.

Beyond the Classroom

Using Creative Commons

GENERAL CASE

FROM SCRATCH

Research copyright law as it applies in education, and then research the nonprofit organization Creative Commons (CC). Prepare a slide show to present to others that explains what Creative Commons is and how it enables you to legally use online media in your slide show. Create a storyboard on paper outlining your slide show. Then, create a PowerPoint presentation named **p01b1CC_LastFirst** based on your storyboard. Include a title slide and at least four slides related to this topic. Choose a theme, transitions, and animations. Insert at least one appropriate online picture with an attribution to its creator. Include speaker notes on most slides as necessary. Create a handout header with your name and the current date. Include a handout footer with your instructor's name and your class name. Review the presentation to ensure there are no errors and that your transition and animations work by viewing each slide in Slide Show view. Print as full page slides, or as directed by your instructor. Save and close the file. Based on your instructor's directions, submit p01b1CC_LastFirst.

Polishing a Business Presentation

DISASTER RECOVERY

A neighbor has created a slide show to present to a local business explaining his company's services. He has asked you to refine the slide show so it has a more professional appearance. Open *p01b2Green* and save the file as **p01b2Green_LastFirst**. View the slide show. Note that the text is difficult to read because of a lack of contrast with the background, there are capitalization errors and spelling errors, the bulleted points are not parallel, and images are positioned and sized poorly. Select and apply a design theme and a variant. Modify text following the guidelines presented throughout this chapter. Reposition placeholders as needed. Size and position the images in the presentation or replace them with your choice of images. Text may be included in speaker notes to emphasize visuals, if desired. Apply a transition to all slides. Add a minimum of two animations. Make other changes you choose. Create a handout header with your name and the current date. Include a handout footer with your instructor's name and your class name. Review the presentation to ensure there are no errors by viewing each slide in Slide Show view. Save your file and then save it again as a PowerPoint show. Close the file. Print notes pages if directed by your instructor. Based on your instructor's directions, submit the following:

p01b2Green_LastFirst
p01b2Green_LastFirst.ppsx

Capstone Exercise

Want'n Waffles is a small, successful mobile food business. The company was started by two culinary arts students and their families as a way to finance the students' college education. A year later they own three food trucks that sell breakfast waffles, waffle sandwiches, and dessert waffles. Street-food lovers line up around the block when the food trucks park in their neighborhood. The truck locations are advertised via Twitter and on Facebook so waffle lovers can follow the trucks from place to place. The business has increased its revenue and profits and the owners are looking to expand their operation by offering franchises in other college cities. They need to prepare a presentation for an important meeting with financiers.

Create a Title Slide

You add your name to the title slide, apply a theme, and create a slide for the Want'n Waffles mission statement.

a. Open *p01c1Waffles* and save it as **p01c1Waffles_LastFirst**.

b. Create a Notes and Handouts header with your name and a footer with your instructor's name and your class name. Include the date and time, updated automatically. Apply to all.

c. Replace YOUR NAME in the **subtitle placeholder** on Slide 1 with your name.

d. Apply the **Retrospect theme**.

Add Content

You add the information about your business as content slides.

a. Create a new slide after Slide 1 using the **Section Header layout**. Type the following in the title placeholder: **Want'n Waffles provides gourmet quality food prepared on the spot in a clean mobile truck.**

b. Double-click the border of the title placeholder, then change the font size to **60 pt** and apply **Italic**.

c. Add the following speaker note to Slide 3: **We can sell inexpensive breakfasts, lunches, and desserts because our overhead is low. We don't have to pay for a "brick and mortar" restaurant with all of the expenses of a building. Because we don't have to pay for servers, prices stay down while sales increase. Our trucks are a favorite with employees because they get quick service, excellent food, and the convenience of a location close to them. We are mobile so we can change location as needed to increase sales. Best of all, our food is FUN!**

Create Tables

You create a table to show the increase in sales from last year to this year and a table showing a few of your waffle specialties.

a. Create a table of four columns and seven rows in the content placeholder on Slide 4. Type the data from the table below in your table.

TABLE 1

Category	Last Year	This Year	Increase
Breakfast waffles	$125,915	$255,856	$129,941
Breakfast crepes	45,404	97,038	51,634
Waffle-wiches	61,510	138,555	77,045
Waffle cookies	22,100	43,200	21,100
Dessert waffles	151,012	246,065	95,053
Totals	$405,941	$780,714	$374,773

b. Apply the **Medium Style 2 – Accent 2** Table Style to the table.

c. Format the table text font to **18 pt**. Center align the column headings and right align all numbers.

d. Add a new slide after Slide 4 that uses the **Comparison layout**. Type **Want'n Waffle Specialties** as the title of the slide, use **Luncheon Waffles** as the heading for the left column, and type **Dessert Waffles** as the heading for the right column. Type the data from Table 2 below in your table and apply the same formatting to this table that you applied in Step c.

TABLE 2

Chicken and Waffle Grilled Cheese	Waffle Confetti Cake
PB&J Waffle Panini	Waffled Banana Bread
Zucchini-Parmesan Waffle	Chocolate Chip Waffle Cookies
Maple Bacon Waffle	Waffled Carrot Cake
Margherita Waffle Pizza	Waffle Sundae

e. View the slide show in Slide Sorter view.

f. Move Slide 5 (A Natural Franchise) so that it becomes Slide 3.

g. Note that Slide 2 includes the mission statement as the introduction slide, Slides 3 through 7 cover the key points of the presentation and include supporting data, and Slide 8 uses a plan for the future as the conclusion (summary) slide.

Add an Online Picture and Animate Content

You want to include a picture of a waffle creation to inspire interest in the franchise. To emphasize the profits the business has realized, you add animations. To help the audience absorb the next steps on the summary slide, you animate the text.

a. Display Slide 3. Use the content placeholder on the right side to open Online Pictures. Use **waffles** as your search keyword in the search box. Locate an image of a waffle and insert it in the placeholder.

b. Use the same online picture of a waffle on the last slide of your slide show. Position the image in the lower-right portion of your slide, and size it appropriately.

c. Select the **Our first year was profitable box** on Slide 5 and apply the **Fly In entrance animation**.

d. Select the **Our second year was significantly better box** and apply the **Fly In entrance animation**. Change the Start option to **After Previous**.

e. Apply the **Fly In entrance animation** to the text content placeholder on Slide 8.

f. Check the spelling in the slide show, and review the presentation for any other errors. Fix anything you think is necessary.

Navigate and Print

You proofread the presentation in Slide Show view and check the animations. You notice an error on a slide and correct it. When all errors have been corrected, you print a handout with four slides per page.

a. Start the slide show and navigate through the presentation, experimenting with various navigation methods.

b. Note the parallel construction error on Slide 4. The third bulleted point, *Profits are increasing*, does not start with an active verb as the other bulleted points do.

c. Annotate the conclusion slide, *The Next Steps*, by underlining **detailed financial proposal** and circling **two** and **ten** with a red pen.

d. Exit the presentation and keep the annotations.

e. Use the Slides pane in Normal view to navigate to Slide 4. Modify the third bulleted point as follows: **Increase profits.**

f. Print a handout with four slides, horizontal per page if directed to print by your instructor.

g. Save the file as a presentation and as a show. Close the file. Based on your instructor's directions, submit the following:

p01c1Waffles_LastFirst
p01c1Waffles_LastFirst.ppsx

Presentation Development

LEARNING OUTCOME You will apply tools to create and modify a presentation.

OBJECTIVES & SKILLS: After you read this chapter, you will be able to:

CASE STUDY | The Wellness Education Center

The Wellness Education Center at your school promotes overall good health to students and employees. The director of the Center asked you to create two slide shows that she can use to deliver presentations to the campus community.

You create a presentation to inform campus groups about the Center by downloading a template with a wellness theme from Microsoft Office Online. You modify several of the layouts the template provides to customize the template to your needs. To concentrate on the content of the slides, you use Outline view to enter slide text and edit the presentation outline.

You create a second presentation for the Center using an outline the director created in Microsoft Word. You import the outline, supplement it with slides you reuse from another presentation, and divide the presentation into sections. Using standard slide show design guidelines, polish the presentation by editing the content and the theme.

Dedicated to Promoting Healthy Lifestyles!

PowerPoint 2016, Windows 10, Microsoft Corporation

Wellness Education Center

FIGURE 2.1 Wellness Education Center Slide

CASE STUDY | The Wellness Education Center

Starting Files	Files to be Submitted
Blank presentation p02h3MedOutline p02h3Wellness p02h4Logo	p02h2Center_LastFirst p02h4Mission_LastFirst

Templates

One of the hardest things about creating a presentation is getting started. You may have a general idea of what you want to say but not how to organize your thoughts. Or you may know what you want to say but need help designing the look for the slides. PowerPoint's templates enable you to create professional-looking presentations and may even include content to help you decide what to say.

In this section, you will learn how to create a presentation using a template that you modify to fit your needs.

Creating a Presentation Using a Template

STEP 1 ❱❱ Templates and themes are not the same thing. A theme is a collection of design choices that includes colors, fonts, and special theme effects. A **template** is a file that includes the formatting elements like a background, a theme with a color scheme and font selections for titles and text boxes, and slide layouts that position content placeholders. Some templates include suggestions for how to modify the template, whereas others include ideas about what you could say to inform your audience about your topic. These suggestions can help you learn to use many of the features in PowerPoint.

PowerPoint offers templates online for you to use. You can quickly and easily download additional professional templates in a variety of categories. These templates were created by Microsoft, a Microsoft partner, or a member of the Microsoft community. You can select a suggested search term or type your own search term in the Search box. Then you can filter by category to narrow your search further. For example, you can download a template for a renewable energy presentation created by a Microsoft partner, an active listening presentation created by a Microsoft community member, or a business financial report created by Microsoft. Figure 2.2 shows four PowerPoint templates.

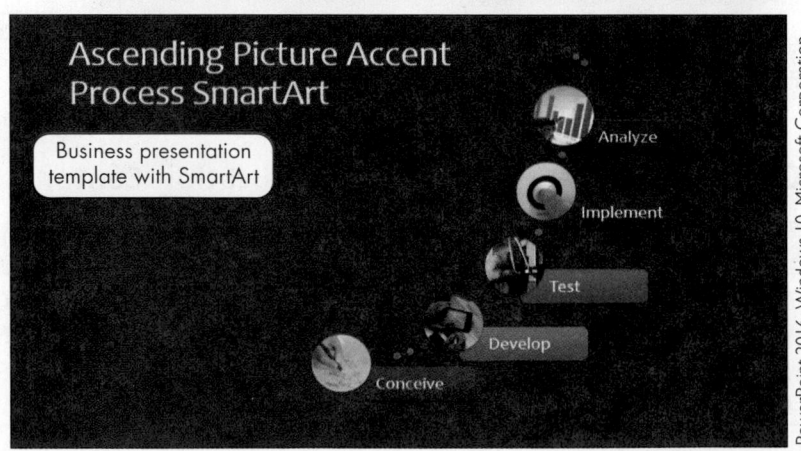

FIGURE 2.2 Templates

When you open PowerPoint you are presented with a variety of design themes from which to choose. If you want to use a template with suggested content or additional design themes, you need to search online.

To begin a presentation using a template, complete the following steps:

1. Start PowerPoint.
2. Click one of the suggested search terms, or click in the search box and type the text for which you would like to search. Press Enter. For example, you may want to search for Marketing templates, and thus you would type Marketing as your search term.
3. Click a template or theme to preview it in a new window.
4. Click Create to download the template. A new presentation file is created based on the template.

Figure 2.3 displays some of the templates available and where to search for templates and themes described in Step 2 above. Your view may show different template options, as Microsoft frequently updates the available templates.

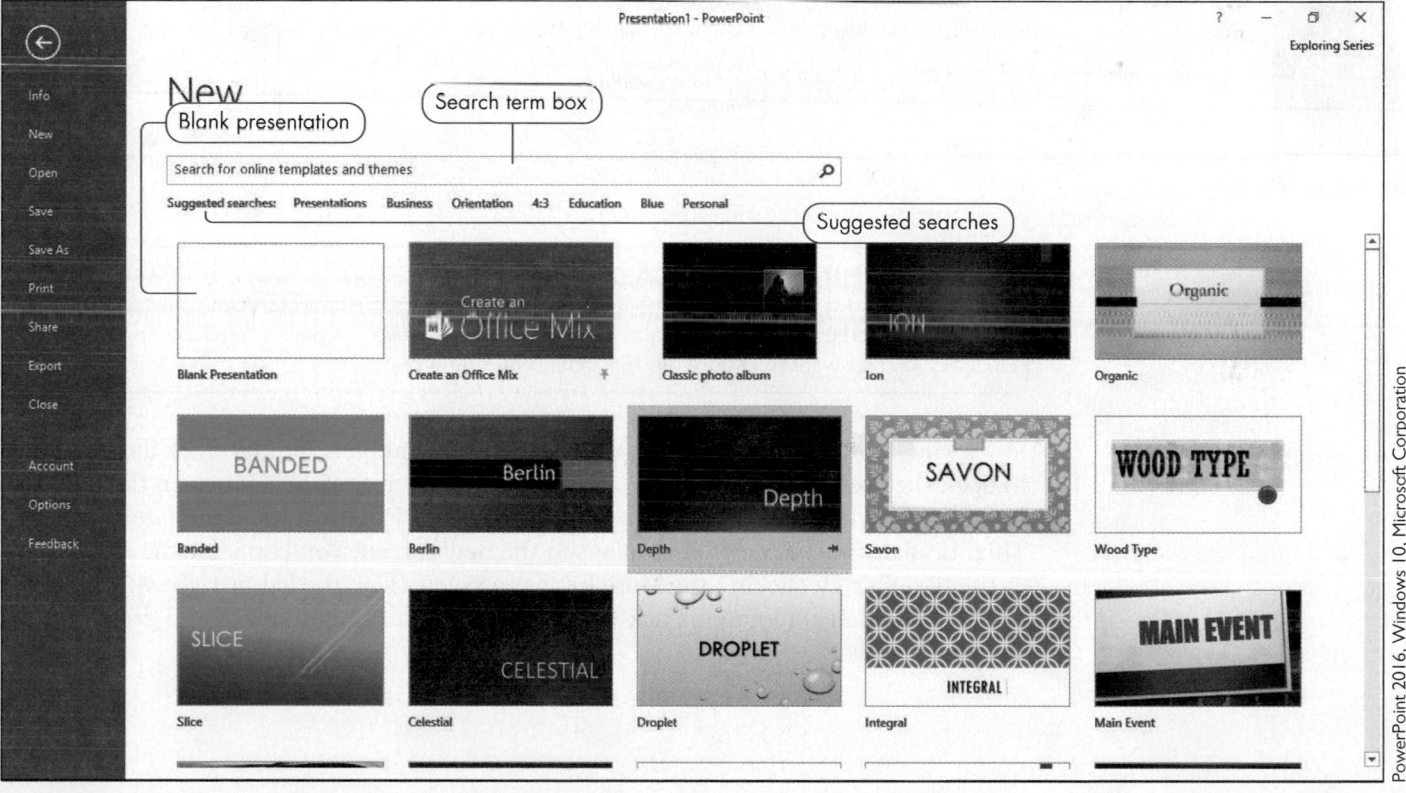

FIGURE 2.3 Templates and Themes

You can filter your results further by using one of the categories on the right side of the screen. For example, Figure 2.4 shows the search results for a search for Photo Albums. The column on the right shows several of the categories. Depending on your search criteria, you may also see non-PowerPoint templates in your search results.

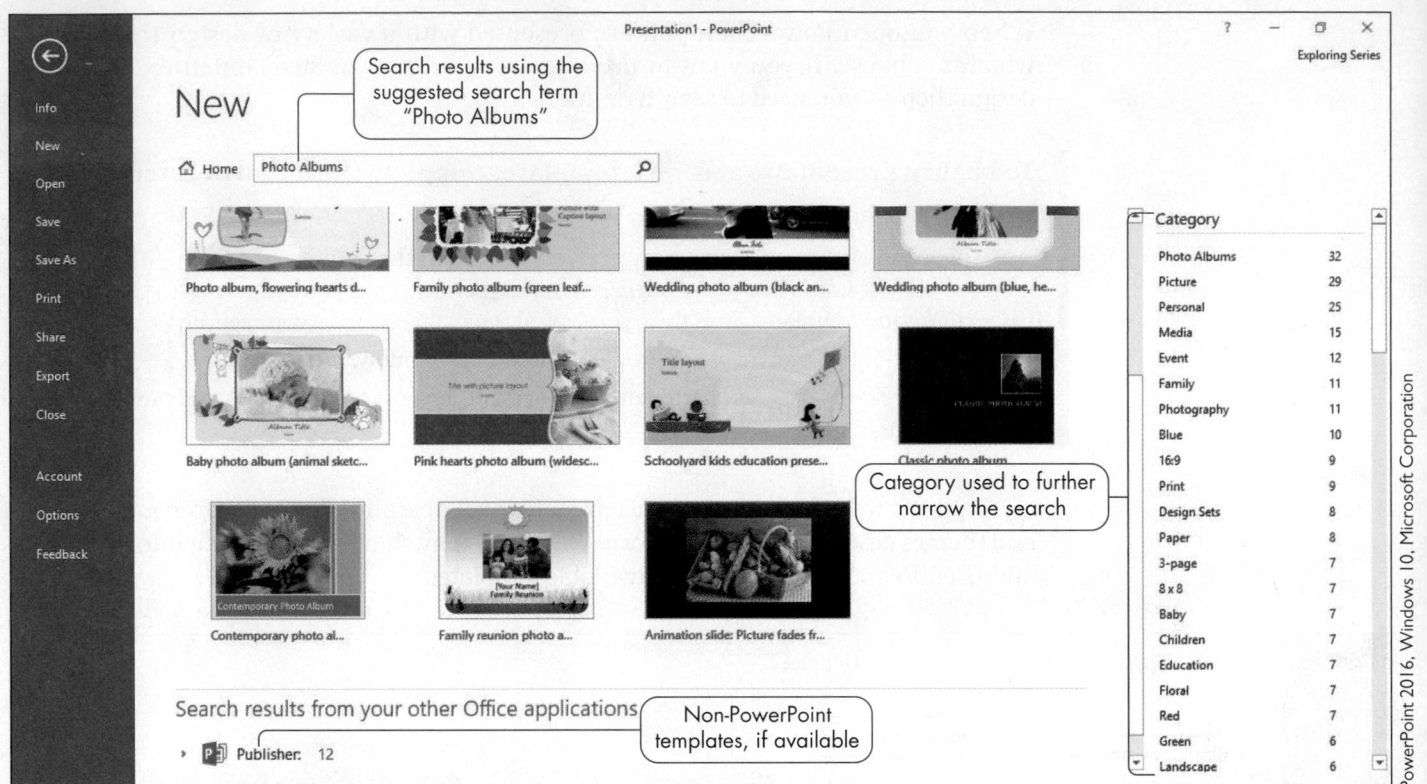

FIGURE 2.4 Template Categories

TIP: SEARCHING BY TEMPLATE DIMENSIONS
In the category list, you can search using 4:3 for templates with the typical screen dimensions or 16:9 for widescreen templates. Because most screens and televisions have moved to the widescreen format, you may want to choose the 16:9 dimension size.

If you know you want to work with a particular template, double-click its thumbnail to open the presentation. If you would like to preview it first, click once on the template to open a preview window. In Figure 2.5, the Classic Photo Album template is selected. The title slide for the template displays in the new screen. You can view the other slides in the template by clicking the More Images arrows. Click the left or right white arrows to preview other templates. Click Create to download the template and create a new presentation file.

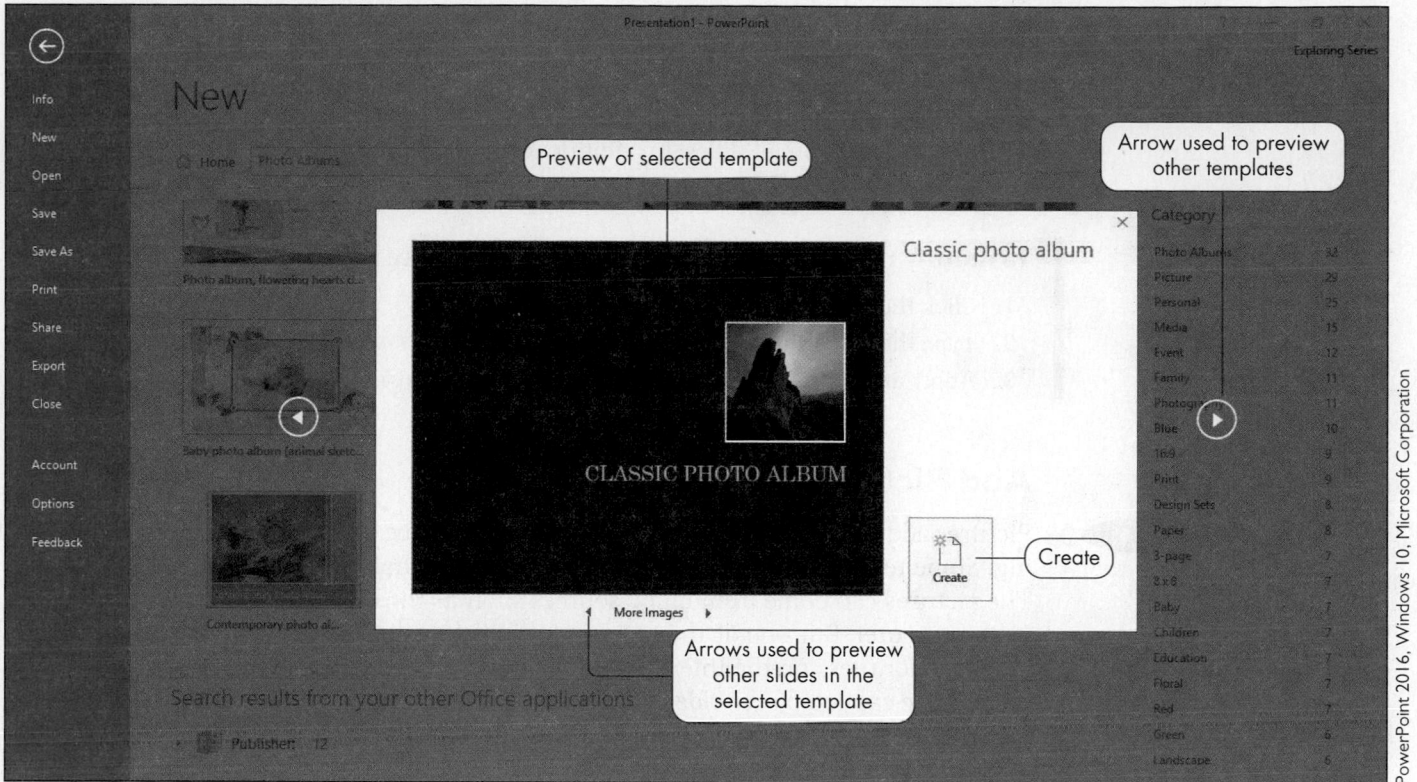

PowerPoint 2016, Windows 10, Microsoft Corporation

FIGURE 2.5 Template Preview

Modifying a Presentation Based on a Template

STEP 2 ›› The templates you download may have custom slide layouts unique to that particular template. After you download a template, you can modify it, perhaps by changing a font style or size, moving or deleting a placeholder, or moving an object on the slide. After you modify the presentation, you can save it and use it repeatedly. The ability to save these changes as a new template can save you a tremendous amount of time, because you will not have to redo your modifications the next time you use the presentation.

Modify a Placeholder and Layout

STEP 3 ›› A template may be customized in several ways. Slide layouts, also called layouts, are an obvious point at which to customize a template. You can change the layout by clicking the Layout arrow in the Slides group and selecting a new layout from those listed there. You can also change the layout by moving title, subtitle, or picture placeholders to a new position on individual slides. The placeholders can be resized or deleted.

> **To modify a layout by moving or resizing a placeholder, complete the following steps:**
>
> 1. Advance to the slide that you would like to modify.
> 2. Click the placeholder's border.
> 3. Drag the placeholder to a different part of the slide to change the position, or drag the border to resize the placeholder.

The colors and background fill for placeholders can be changed to visually carry out a theme. For example, the recruiters at your school may have a presentation developed that is used to explain to prospective students the types of support and academic services that are available at your school. The presentation's theme displays your school's colors in its placeholders on all slides. In addition, although the placeholders for a template may be assigned a default font type, size, or color, these characteristics are easily modified.

To modify the text within a placeholder, complete the following steps:

1. Click the placeholder text.
2. Type the text and then select it.
3. Apply any of the features available in the Font group on the Home tab.

Add Pictures and Captions

STEP 4 ❱❱ Pictures add visual interest to a presentation and can be used to effectively convey meaning. Some templates include slide layouts with placeholders for both pictures and text. The pictures can come from many sources such as those you have taken and stored on your computer. But one of the easiest methods to get pictures for your presentation is to search for them on the Internet and then add them to your slide in the picture placeholder. The caption placeholder can be used for additional information to explain or support the picture or idea. Note that some pictures located on the Internet may not be used without permission or license from the creator.

To locate pictures from the Internet to add to your template, complete the following steps:

1. Advance to a slide where you want to add a picture.
2. Select the picture placeholder.
3. Click Online Pictures in the Insert tab.
4. Type your search term into the Bing Image Search box.

Quick
Concepts

1. Are a template and a theme the same thing? Why or why not? ***p. 992***

2. Why might someone use a template rather than start from a blank presentation? ***p. 992***

3. What are some of the Suggested searches templates available in PowerPoint? What are some of the categories used to filter one of the Suggested searches? ***p. 994***

Hands-On Exercises

Watch the Video for this Hands-On Exercise!

MyITLab®
HOE1 Training

1 Templates

To promote the Wellness Education Center at your school, you decide to create a presentation that can be shown to campus groups and other organizations to inform them about the Center and its mission.

STEP I »» CREATE A NEW PRESENTATION BASED ON A TEMPLATE

You begin the Wellness Education Center presentation by looking for a template that is upbeat and that represents the idea that being healthy makes you feel good. You locate the perfect template (a photo album with warm sunflowers on the cover) from the Photo Albums Suggested search that you conduct. You open a new presentation based on the template and save the presentation. Refer to Figure 2.6 as you complete Step 1.

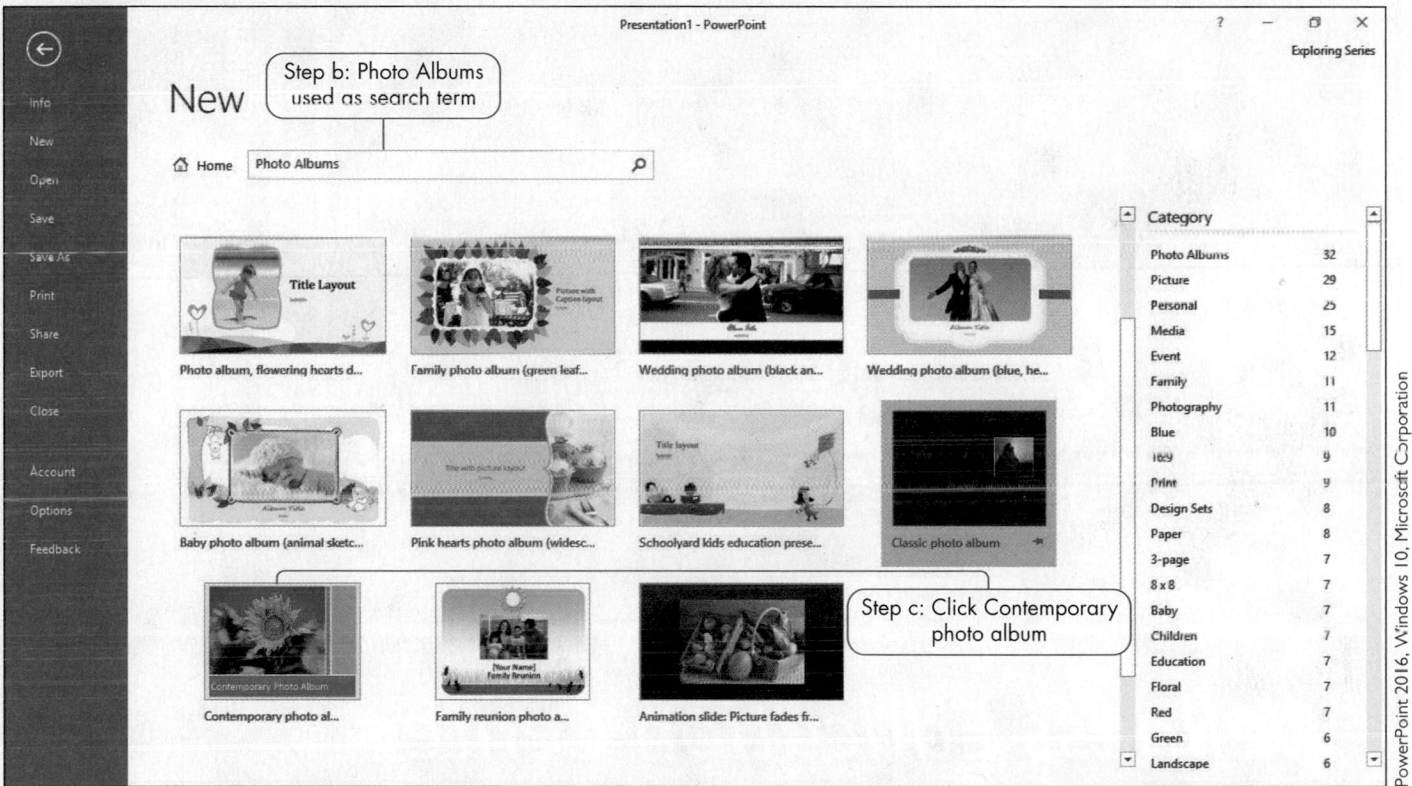

FIGURE 2.6 New Presentation Dialog Box

a. Start PowerPoint.

b. Type **Photo Albums** in the Search box and press **Enter**.

Thumbnails of sample Photo Album templates will display. The exact results may vary.

c. Scroll to locate, and then click **Contemporary photo album.** Click **Create** in the Preview window.

d. View the slide show and read each of the instructions included in the template.

Templates may include instructions for their use or tips on the content that may be added to create a specific presentation. For example, Slide 2 includes instructions to follow for adding your own pages to the album.

e. Click the **Insert tab** and click **Header & Footer** in the Text group. Click the **Notes and Handouts tab** in the Header and Footer dialog box. Create a handout header with your name and a handout footer with your instructor's name and your class. Include the current date. The page number feature can remain active. Click **Apply to All**.

f. Save the presentation as **p02h1Center_LastFirst**.

STEP 2 ›› MODIFY A PLACEHOLDER

The template you selected and downloaded consists of a Title Slide layout you like, but the text in the placeholders needs to be changed to the Wellness Education Center information. You edit the title slide to include the Center's name and slogan. You also modify the title placeholder to make the Center's name stand out. Refer to Figure 2.7 as you complete Step 2.

FIGURE 2.7 Edited Title Slide

a. Click **Slide 1**, select the text **Contemporary Photo Album** in the title placeholder, and type **Wellness Education Center**.

> **TROUBLESHOOTING:** If you make any major mistakes in this exercise, you can close the file, open *p02h1Center_LastFirst* again and then start this exercise over.

b. Select the title text, and click **Italic** and **Text Shadow** in the Font group on the Home tab.

You modify the template's title placeholder to make the title text stand out.

c. Click the **subtitle text**, *Click to add date or details,* and type **Dedicated to Promoting Healthy Lifestyles!**

d. Save the presentation.

The Contemporary Photo Album template includes many layouts designed to create an interesting photo album. Although the layout you selected conveys the warm feeling you desire, the layouts will be modified to fit your needs. You modify a section layout and add a new slide with the layout of your choice. You also delete unnecessary slides. Refer to Figure 2.8 as you complete Step 3.

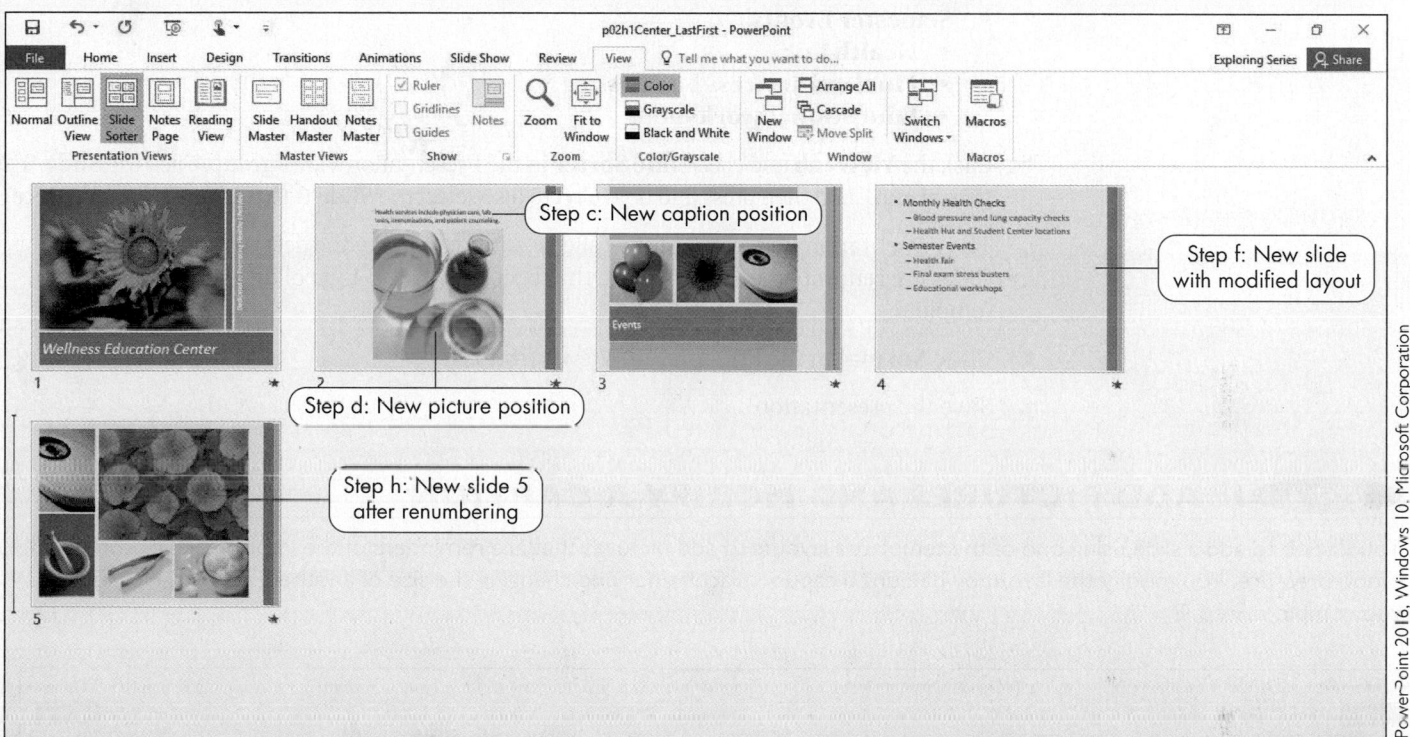

FIGURE 2.8 Title and Content Layout

a. Click **Slide 2**, replace the sample text with **Health services include physician care, lab tests, immunizations, and patient counseling.**

b. Click **Layout** in the Slides group and click the **Square with Caption layout**.

Note that the Contemporary photo album template has many more layouts than the default Office Theme template. The number of layouts provided with a template varies, so always check to see your options.

c. Select the caption, and drag it to the top of the picture (not above it).

As you drag, you will notice red line guides appear to help you as you move the object. You can press and hold Shift to constrain the movement of the caption as you drag for additional control.

d. Select the picture and drag the picture below the caption.

The location of the placeholder is modified to show the caption above the picture.

e. Click **Slide 3**, select the placeholder text **Choose a layout**, and type **Events**. Delete the subtitle text.

When you delete existing text in a new template placeholder, it is replaced with instructional text such as *Click to add subtitle.* It is not necessary to delete this text, as it will not display when the slide show is viewed.

f. Click the **New Slide arrow** and click the **Title and Content layout**.

> **TROUBLESHOOTING:** Clicking the New Slide arrow opens the Layout gallery for you to select a layout. Clicking New Slide directly above the New Slide arrow creates a new slide using the layout of the current slide.

g. Delete the title placeholder and drag the content placeholder to the top of the slide. Type the following information:

- **Monthly Health Checks**
  - **Blood pressure and lung capacity checks**
  - **Health Hut and Student Center locations**
- **Semester Events**
  - **Health fair**
  - **Final exam stress busters**
  - **Educational workshops**

h. Click the **View tab** and click **Slide Sorter** in the Presentation Views group. Click the **Slide 5 thumbnail**, and then press and hold **Ctrl** to also select the **Slide 6 thumbnail**. Press **Delete**.

The presentation now contains five slides. After you make the deletions, the remaining slides are renumbered, and the slide that becomes Slide 5 is a collage of images from the template.

i. Click **Normal** in the Presentation Views group.

j. Save the presentation.

STEP 4 》》 ADD PICTURES AND MODIFY A CAPTION

You decide to add a slide using one of the template's layouts to add pictures that are reminders of the importance of controlling blood pressure. You modify the layout by deleting a caption placeholder and changing the size of another. Refer to Figure 2.9 as you complete Step 4.

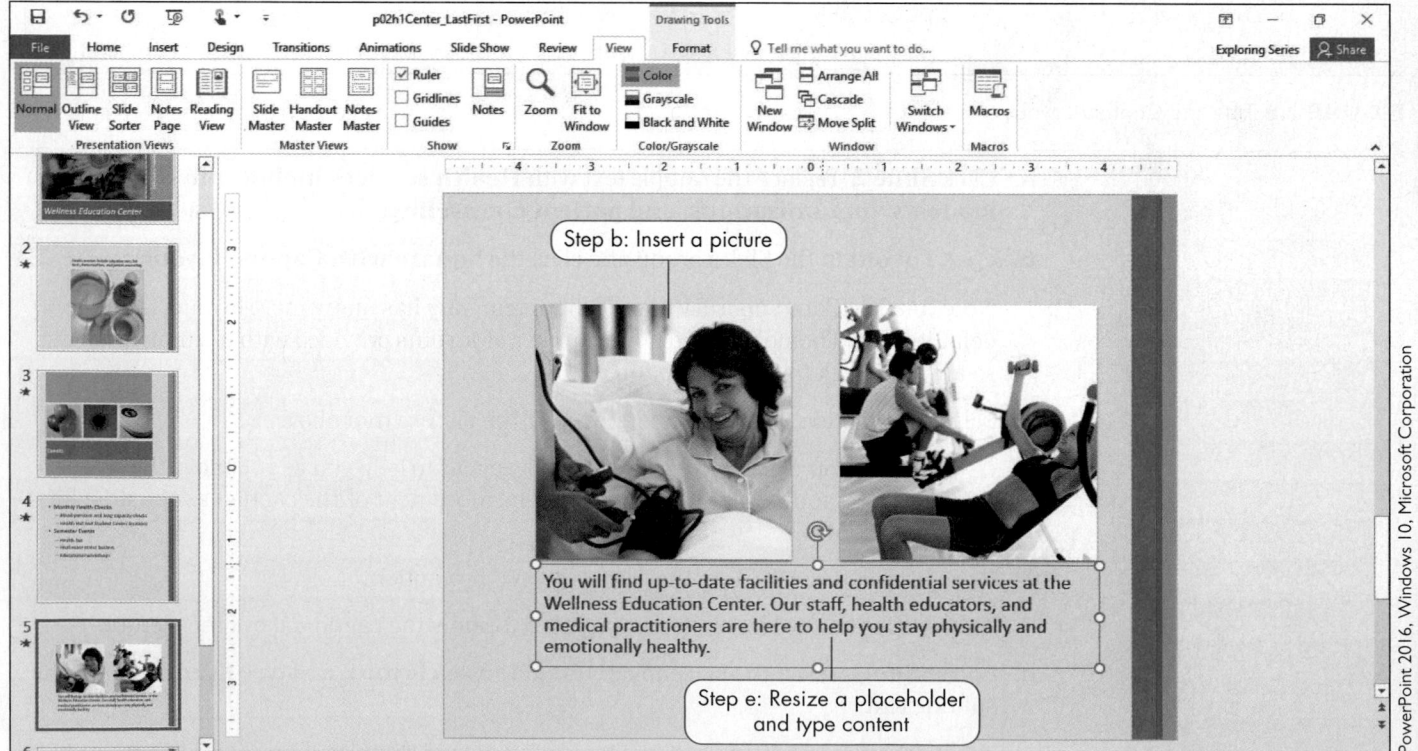

FIGURE 2.9 Edited Slide

a. Ensure that Slide 4 is the active slide, click the **New Slide arrow** on the Home tab, and then click **2-Up Landscape with Captions**.

A new slide is created. The layout includes two picture placeholders and two caption placeholders.

b. Select the **left picture placeholder** and click **Online Pictures** on the Insert tab. In the Bing Image Search box, type **blood pressure check**, press **Enter**, and then insert a picture of your choice.

The image is added to the placeholder.

> **TROUBLESHOOTING:** Clicking the icon in the center of the picture placeholder will open the Insert Picture dialog box. If this happens, click Cancel. Click somewhere in the white space around the icon to select the placeholder. Once the placeholder is selected, you will be able to continue with the instructions for adding an Online Picture.

c. Select the **right picture placeholder** and click **Online Pictures** on the Insert tab. In the Bing Image Search box, type **gym**, press **Enter**, and then insert a picture of your choice.

d. Delete the right caption placeholder and select the remaining caption placeholder. Click the **Format tab**. In the Size group, change the Width to **9"**. The caption placeholder is now the width of both pictures.

e. Type the following in the caption placeholder: **You will find up-to-date facilities and confidential services at the Wellness Education Center. Our staff, health educators, and medical practitioners are here to help you stay physically and emotionally healthy.**

f. Left align the text and then run the spelling checker. Save the presentation. Keep the presentation open if you plan to continue with the next Hands-On Exercise. If not, close the presentation, and exit PowerPoint.

Outlines

An *outline* organizes text using a *hierarchy* with main points and subpoints to indicate the levels of importance of the text. When you use a storyboard to determine your content, you create a basic outline. An outline is the fastest way to enter or edit text for a presentation. Think of an outline as the road map you use to create your presentation. Rather than having to enter the text in each placeholder on each slide separately, you can type the text directly into an outline, and it will populate into the slides automatically.

In this section, you will learn how to add content to a presentation using Outline view. After creating the presentation, you will modify the outline structure. Finally, you will print the outline.

Creating a Presentation in Outline View

To create an outline for your presentation you must be in Outline view. *Outline view* shows the presentation in an outline format displayed in levels according to the points and subpoints on each slide. There are two panes in Outline view, the outline and an image of the active slide. Instead of the slide thumbnails displayed in Normal view, the presentation is displayed as a hierarchy of the titles and text for each individual slide. Each slide is denoted by a slide number and a slide icon, followed by the slide title if the slide contains a title placeholder. The slide title is formatted as bold. Slide text is indented under the slide title. A slide with only an image (no text) will not have a title in the outline and will display only the slide number and icon.

Use Outline View

> **To change to Outline view, complete the following steps:**
> 1. Click the View tab.
> 2. Click Outline View in the Presentation Views group.

One benefit of working in Outline view is that you get a good overview of your presentation without the distraction of design elements, and you can move easily from one slide to the next. You can copy text or bullets from one slide to another and rearrange the order of the slides or bullets. Outline view makes it easy to see relationships between points and to determine where information belongs. Figure 2.10 shows a portion of a presentation in Outline view.

FIGURE 2.10 Outline View

Edit in Outline View

STEP 2 ▶▶ PowerPoint accommodates nine levels of indentation, although you will likely only use two or three per slide as a design best practice. Levels make it possible to show hierarchy or relationships between the information on your slides. The main points appear on Level 1; subsidiary items are indented below the main point to which they apply, and their font size is decreased.

You can promote any item to a higher level or demote it to a lower level, either before or after the text is entered, by clicking Increase List Level or Decrease List Level in the Paragraph group on the Home tab. When designing your slides, consider the number of subsidiary or lower-level items you add to a main point; too many levels within a single slide make the slide difficult to read or understand because the text size becomes smaller with each additional level.

TIP: CHANGING LIST LEVELS IN AN OUTLINE

As a quick alternative to using Increase and Decrease List Level commands on the Home tab, press Tab to demote an item or press Shift+Tab to promote an item.

Outline view can be an efficient way to create and edit text in a presentation.

Modifying an Outline Structure

STEP 3 ⟩⟩ Because Outline view shows the overall structure of your presentation, you can use it to move bullets or slides until your outline's organization is refined. You can collapse or expand your view of the outline contents to see slide contents or just slide titles. A *collapsed outline* view displays only slide icons and the titles of the slides, whereas the *expanded outline* view displays the slide icon, the title, and the content of the slides. You can collapse or expand the content in individual slides or in all slides.

Figure 2.11 shows a collapsed view of the outline displaying only the icon and title of each slide. When a slide is collapsed, a wavy line appears below the slide title, letting you know additional levels exist but are not displayed. The collapsed view makes it easy to move slides. To move a slide, position the pointer over a slide icon until the pointer changes to a four-headed arrow, and then drag the icon to the desired position.

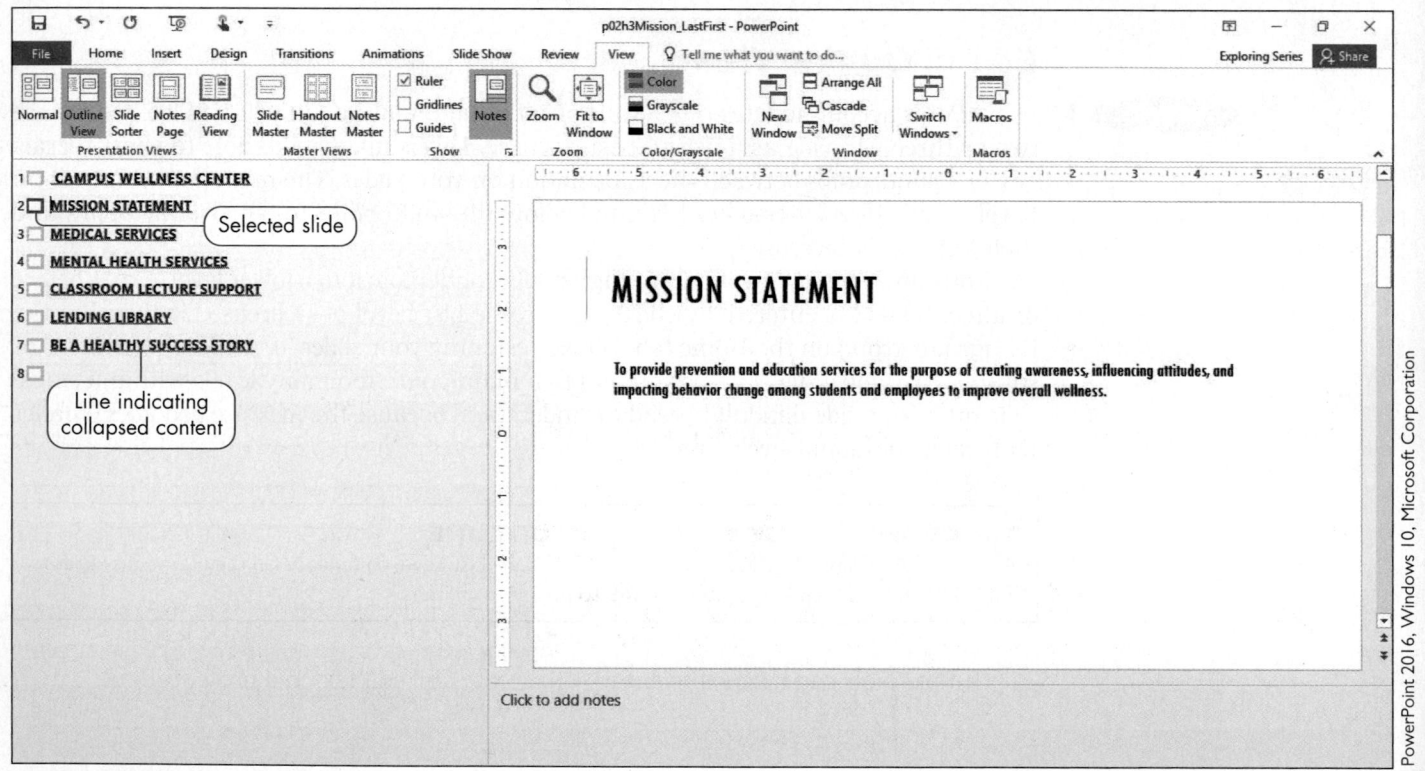

FIGURE 2.11 Collapsed Outline View

To collapse or expand a slide, complete the following steps:

1. Double-click the slide icon in the Outline pane. Doing this action collapses or expands the slide contents in the pane.
2. Right-click the text following an icon to display Expand or Collapse. Pointing to either will display the shortcut menu with options for collapsing or expanding the selected slides or all slides (see Figure 2.12).

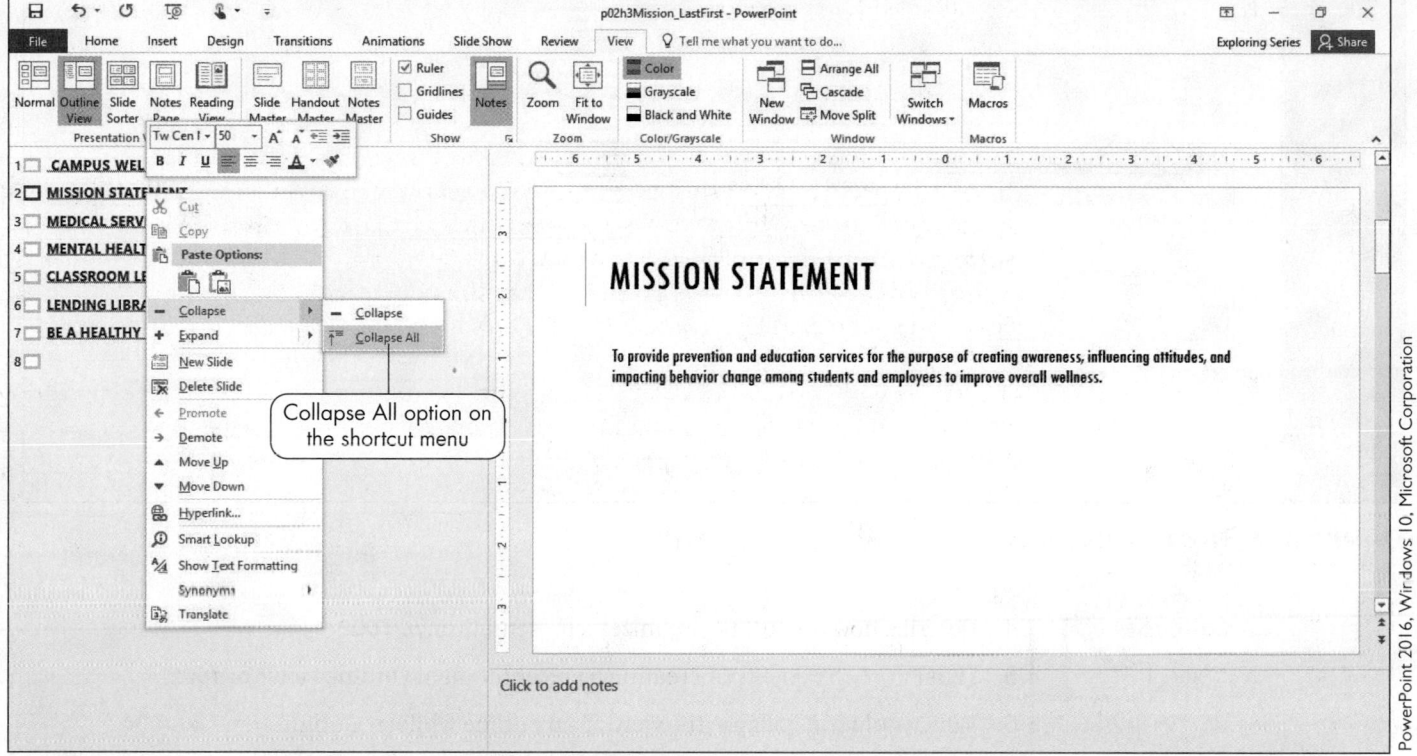

FIGURE 2.12 Collapse Outline Process

Printing an Outline

You can print an outline in either expanded or collapsed view. Figure 2.13 displays a preview of an expanded view of the outline ready to print. The slide icon and slide number will print with the outline.

To print the outline, complete the following steps:

1. Click the File tab and click Print.
2. Click Full Page Slides, Notes Pages, or Outline (whichever displays) to open a gallery of printing choices.
3. Click Outline.
4. Click Print.

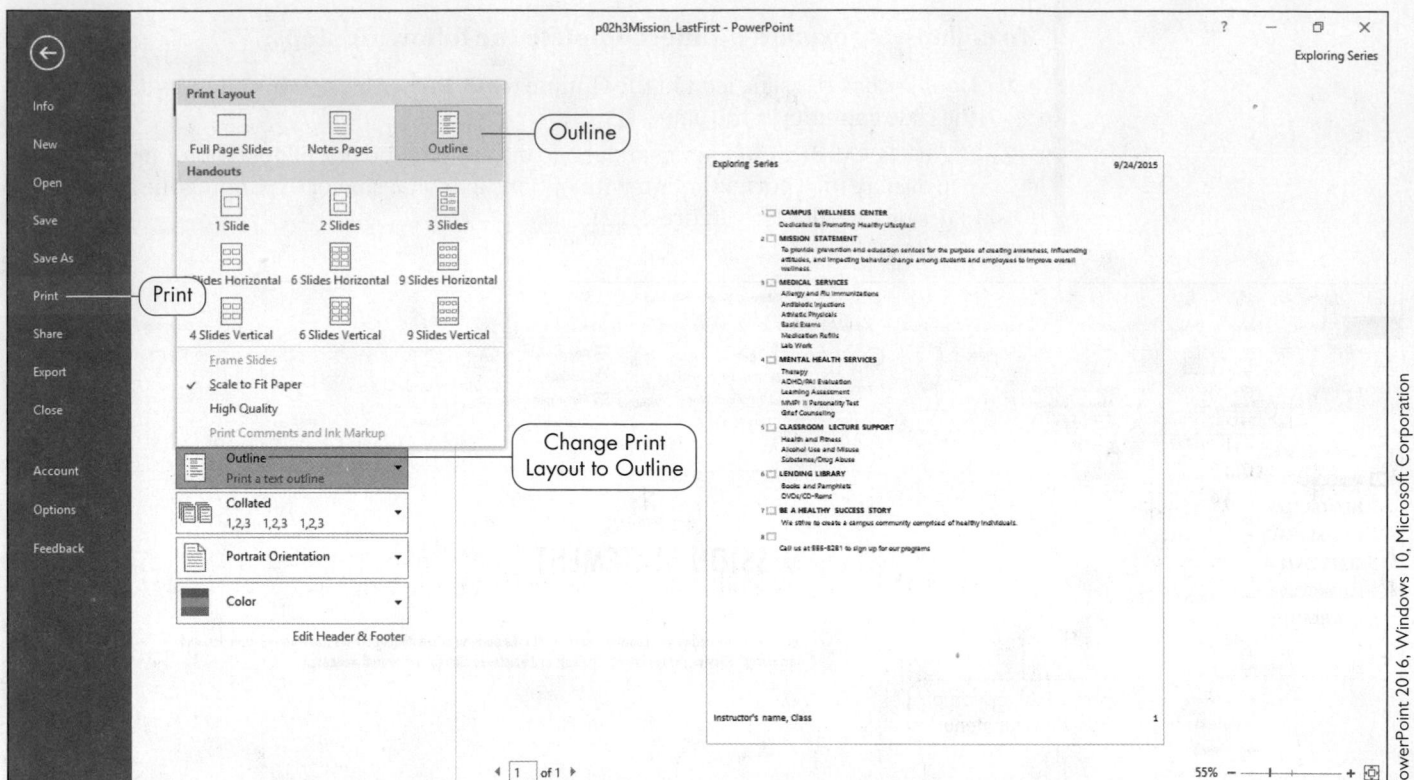

FIGURE 2.13 Outline Printing

Quick Concepts ✓

4. Describe how an outline organizes a presentation. *p. 1002*

5. What are two benefits of creating a presentation in Outline view? *p. 1002*

6. Why would you collapse the view of an outline while in Outline view? *p. 1004*

Hands-On Exercises

Watch the Video for this Hands-On Exercise!

MyITLab®
HOE2 Training

2 Outlines

The Wellness Education Center sponsors a Walking Wellness group to help campus members increase their physical activity and cardiovascular fitness. The director of the Wellness Education Center believes that joining a group increases a member's level of commitment and provides an incentive for the member to stay active. She asks you to edit the slide show you created in Hands-On Exercise 1 to include information about the walking group.

STEP 1 ›› USE OUTLINE VIEW

Because you want to concentrate on the information in the presentation rather than the design elements, you use Outline view. You add the information about the walking group as requested by the director. Refer to Figure 2.14 as you complete Step 1.

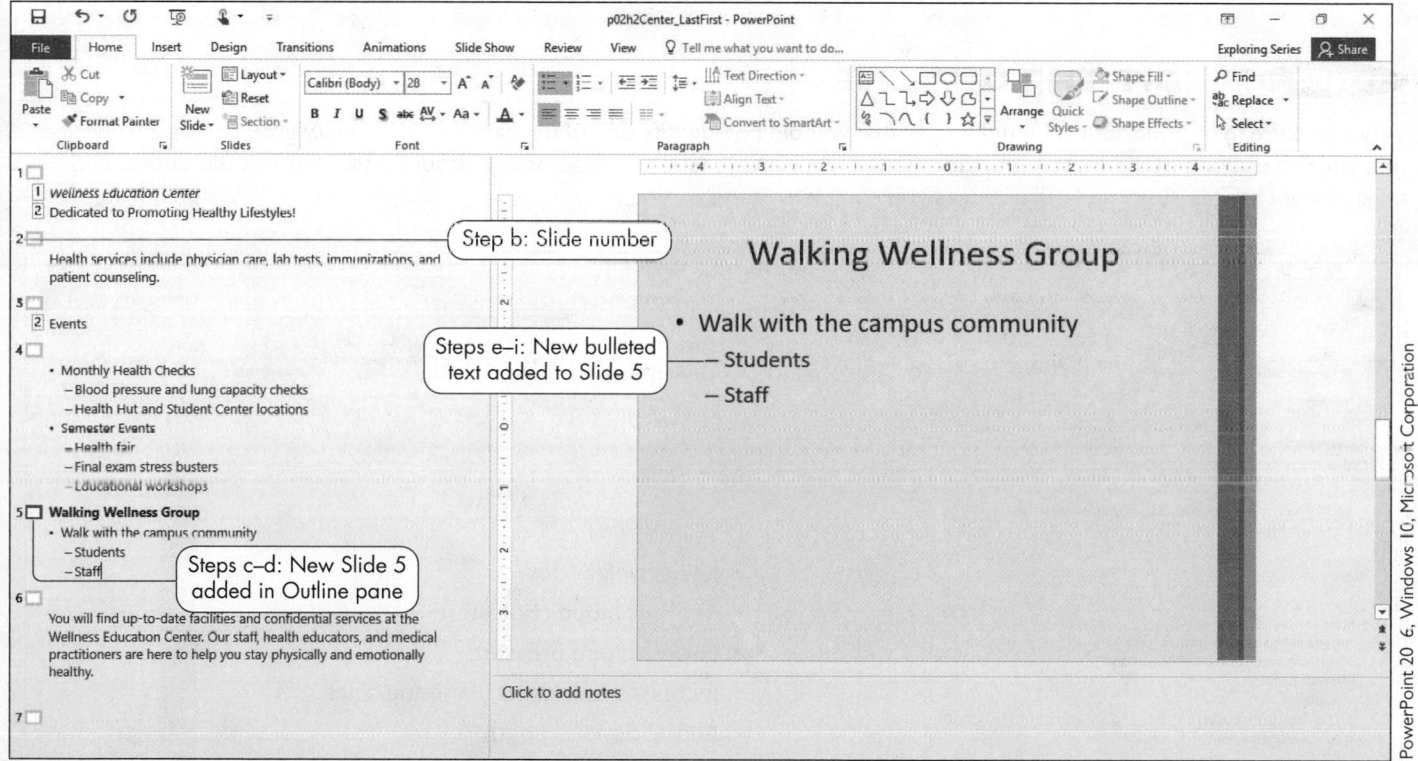

FIGURE 2.14 Revised Outline

a. Open *p02h1Center_LastFirst* if you closed it at the end of Hands-On Exercise 1, and save it as **p02h2Center_LastFirst**, changing h1 to h2.

b. Click the **View tab** and click **Outline View** in the Presentation Views group.

Note that each slide in the presentation is numbered and has a slide icon. Slides 1 through 5 include text on the slides. Slide 6 contains images only, so no text is displayed in the outline. None of the slides has a title. The text in the Outline pane on the left is also displayed on the slide in the Slide pane on the right.

c. Click at the end of the last bullet for Slide 4 in the Outline pane and press **Enter**.

The insertion point is now positioned to enter text at the same level as the previous bullet point. To create a new slide at a higher level, you must decrease the indent level.

d. Click **Decrease List Level** in the Paragraph group on the Home tab twice.

A new Slide 5 is created, the previous Slide 5 is renumbered as Slide 6, and Slide 6 is renumbered as Slide 7.

e. Type **Walking Wellness Group** and press **Enter**.

Pressing Enter moves the insertion point to the next line and creates a new slide, Slide 6. The title is bold in the Outline.

f. Press **Tab** to demote the text in the outline.

The insertion point is now positioned to enter bulleted text on Slide 5.

g. Type **Walk with the campus community** and press **Enter**.

h. Press **Tab** to demote the bullet and type **Students**.

Students becomes Level 3 text.

i. Press **Enter** and type **Staff**.

j. Save the presentation.

STEP 2 ⟫ **EDIT THE OUTLINE**

While proofreading your outline, you discover that you did not identify one of the campus community groups. You also notice that you left out one of the most important slides in your presentation: why someone should walk. You edit the outline and make these changes. Refer to Figure 2.15 as you complete Step 2.

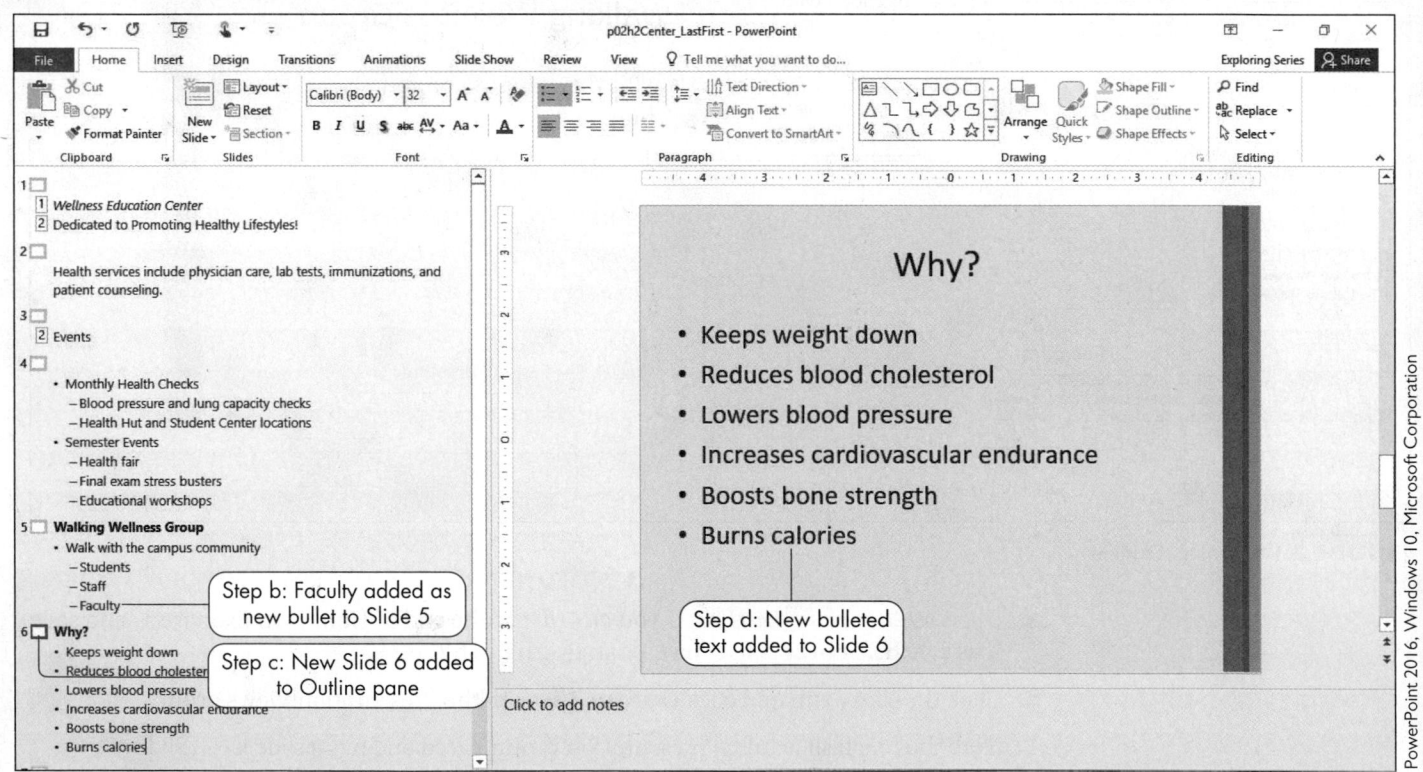

FIGURE 2.15 Edited Outline

a. Ensure that the word *Staff* on Slide 5 is selected in the outline.

b. Press **Enter** and type **Faculty**.

> **TROUBLESHOOTING:** If your text does not appear in the correct position, check to see if the insertion point was in the wrong location. To enter a blank line for a new bullet, the insertion point must be at the end of an existing bullet point, not at the beginning.

c. Press **Enter** and press **Shift+Tab** twice.

Pressing Shift+Tab promotes the text to create a new Slide 6.

d. Use the Outline pane to type the information for Slide 6 as shown below:

Why?

- **Keeps weight down**
- **Reduces blood cholesterol**
- **Lowers blood pressure**
- **Increases cardiovascular endurance**
- **Boosts bone strength**
- **Burns calories**

e. Save the presentation.

STEP 3 » **MODIFY THE OUTLINE STRUCTURE AND PRINT**

The director of the Wellness Education Center has reviewed the slide show and made several suggestions about its structure. She feels that keeping weight down belongs at the bottom of the list of reasons for walking and asks you to reposition it. Refer to Figure 2.16 as you complete Step 3.

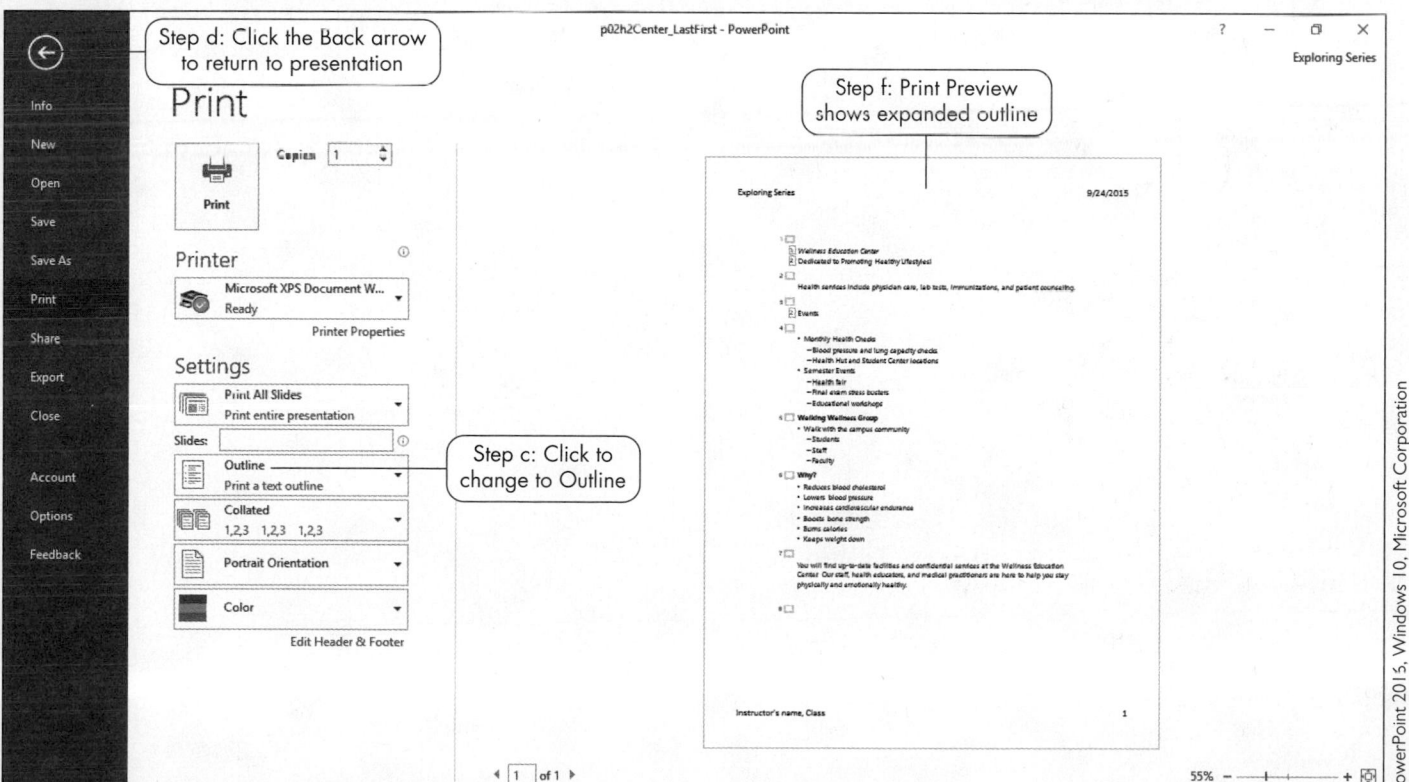

FIGURE 2.16 Expanded Outline in Print Preview

a. Position the pointer over the first bullet, *Keeps weight down*, on Slide 6 in the outline. When the pointer looks like a four-headed arrow, click and drag the text until it becomes the last bullet on the slide.

b. Right-click anywhere in the Slide 6 text, point to **Collapse**, and then click **Collapse All**.

Only the slide titles will be shown in the Outline.

c. Click the **File tab**, click **Print**, and then click the **Full Page Slides arrow**. Click **Outline**.

A preview of the collapsed outline shows in the Preview pane. Because so few slides contain titles, the collapsed outline is not helpful.

d. Click the **Back arrow** to return to the presentation.

The Outline pane is once again visible.

e. Right-click any text visible in the Outline pane, point to **Expand**, and then select **Expand All**.

f. Click the **File tab** and click **Print**.

The Outline Print Layout is retained from Step c and the expanded outline shows in the Preview pane.

g. Click the **Back arrow** to return to the presentation.

h. Check spelling in the presentation. Save and close the presentation. You will submit this file to your instructor at the end of the last Hands-On Exercise.

Data Imports

You can add slides to a presentation in several ways if the content exists in other formats, such as an outline in Word or slides from other presentations. PowerPoint can create slides based on Microsoft Word outlines (.docx or .doc formats) or outlines saved in another word-processing format that PowerPoint recognizes (.rtf format). You can import data into a slide show to add existing slides from a previously created presentation. This is a very efficient way to add content to a slide show.

In this section, you will learn how to import an outline into a PowerPoint presentation and how to add slides from another presentation into the current presentation.

Importing an Outline

STEP 1 ❱❱ Outlines created using Outline view in Microsoft Word can be imported to quickly create a PowerPoint presentation. To create an outline in Word, you must click the View tab, click Outline, and then type your text.

PowerPoint also recognizes outlines created in Word and saved in **_Rich Text Format (.rtf)_**, a file format you can use to transfer formatted text documents between applications such as word-processing programs and PowerPoint. You can even transfer documents between different platforms such as Mac and Windows. The structure and most of the text formatting are retained when you import the outline into PowerPoint.

> **To create a new presentation from an outline, complete the following steps:**
>
> 1. Click the New Slide arrow on the Home tab.
> 2. Click Slides from Outline.
> 3. Locate and select the file and click Insert.

Solve Problems While Importing Word Outlines

You may encounter problems when trying to import an outline. For example, a list using the numbered list or bullet feature in the Paragraph group on the Home tab in Word (that was not created in Outline view) will not import easily to PowerPoint.

If you import a Word document that appears to be an outline and after importing, each line of the Word document becomes a title for a new slide, the Word document is actually a bulleted list rather than an outline. These two features are separate and distinct in Word and do not import into PowerPoint in the same manner. Open the bulleted list in Word, apply outline heading styles, save the file, and then re-import it to PowerPoint.

PowerPoint also recognizes outlines created and saved in a **_plain text format_** (which uses the file extension **_.txt_**), a file format that retains text without any formatting. But because .txt outlines have no saved hierarchical structure, each line of the outline becomes a slide. Avoid saving outlines you create in this format. If you receive an outline in a .txt format, you can create a hierarchy in PowerPoint without having to retype the text by simply moving the text around to create the structure.

Reusing Slides from an Existing Presentation

STEP 2 ❱❱ You can reuse slides from an existing PowerPoint presentation when creating a new presentation without having to open the other file. The imported slides display in a pane on the right so that you can select the slides you want to import into your existing presentation. This feature can save you considerable time.

> **To import existing slides without having to open the other file, complete the following steps:**
>
> 1. Click the New Slide arrow in the Slides group on the Home tab.
> 2. Click Reuse Slides.
> 3. Click Browse, click Browse File, and then navigate to the folder containing the presentation that has the slides you want to use.
> 4. Click Open.
> 5. Select each slide individually to add it to the presentation. Or right-click any slide and click Insert All Slides to add all of the slides to the presentation.
> 6. Close the Reuse Slides pane.

By default, when you insert a slide into the presentation, it takes on the formatting of the open presentation. If the new slides do not take on the formatting of the open presentation, select the imported text in Outline view and click Clear all Formatting in the Font group of the Home tab. It will format the slides using the active theme. If you wish to retain the formatting of the original presentation, click the Keep source formatting check box at the bottom of the Reuse Slides pane, shown in Figure 2.17.

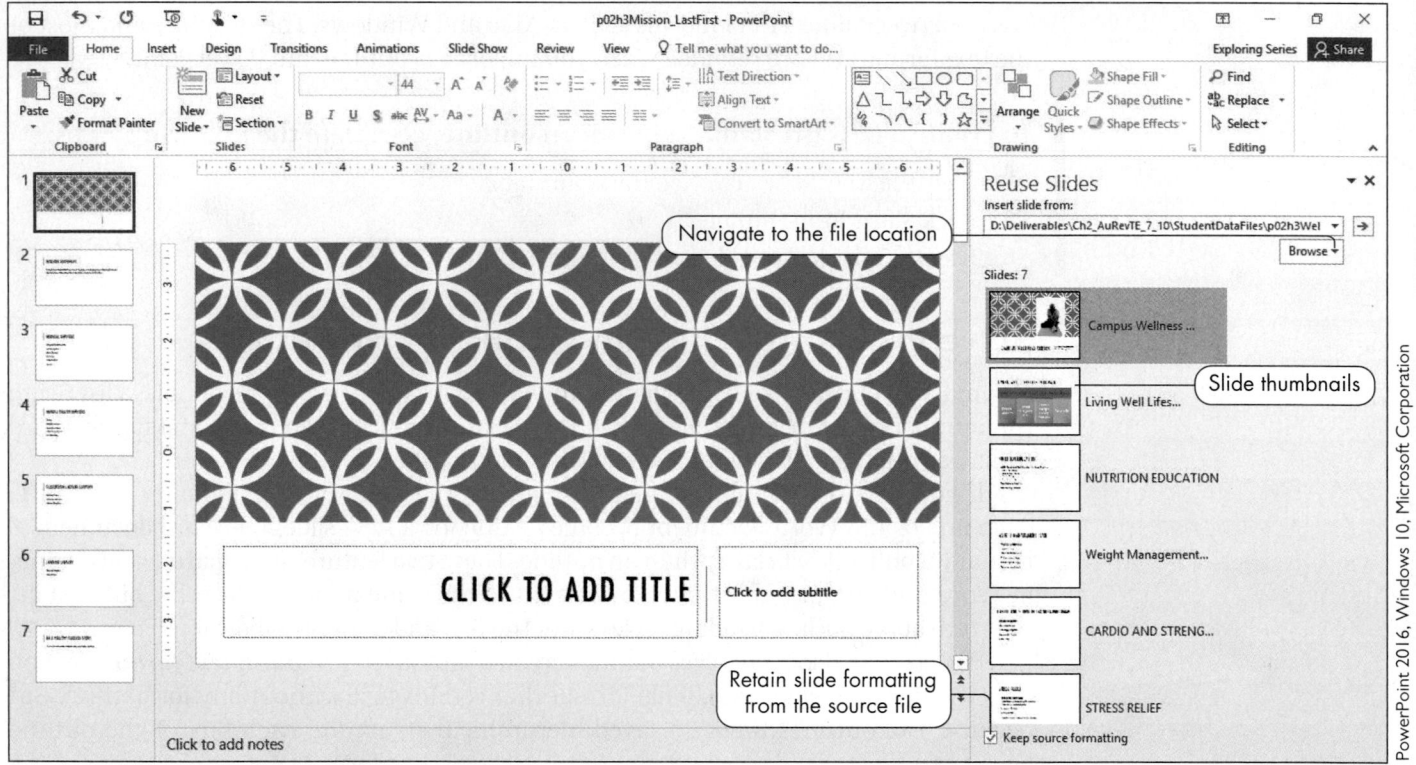

FIGURE 2.17 Reuse Slides Pane

Quick Concepts

7. Describe two problems and their solutions that you may encounter when importing an outline into PowerPoint. ***p. 1011***

8. Describe how you would use slides from another presentation in your current presentation. ***p. 1012***

9. When you insert a slide into a presentation, what formatting does it use? How would you change this default setting? ***p. 1012***

Watch the Video for this Hands-On Exercise!

MyITLab®
HOE3 Training

3 Data Imports

The director of the Wellness Education Center is impressed with the center's overview presentation you created. She gives you an electronic copy of an outline she created in a word-processing software package and asks if you can convert it into a slide show. You create a slide show from the outline and then supplement it with content from another slide show.

STEP 1 ›› IMPORT A RICH TEXT FORMAT OUTLINE

The director of the Wellness Education Center saves an outline for a presentation in Rich Text Format. You import the outline into PowerPoint to use as the basis for a presentation about the center, its mission, and the services it provides to students, staff, and faculty. Refer to Figure 2.18 as you complete Step 1.

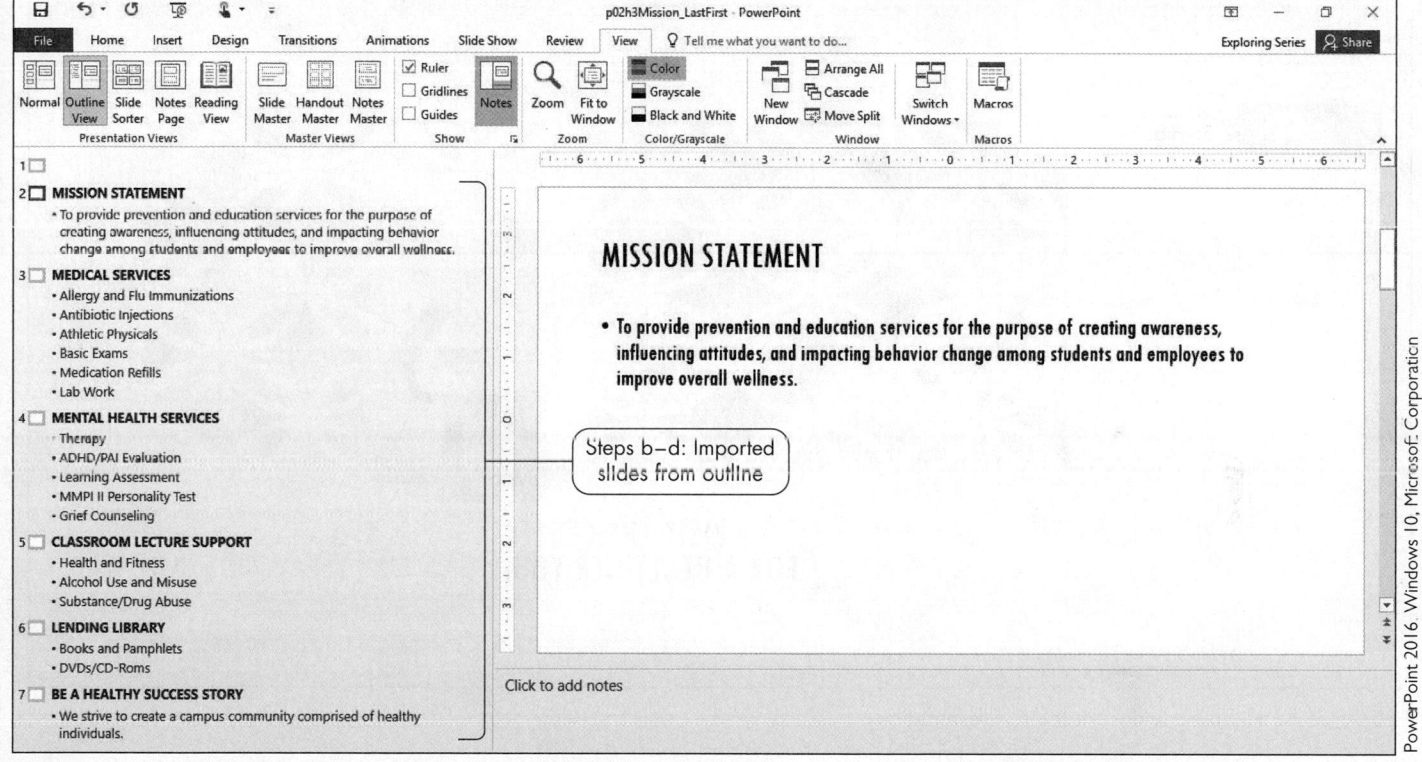

FIGURE 2.18 New Presentation Based on an Outline

a. Click the **File tab**, click **New**, and then double-click **Blank Presentation**. Save the presentation as **p02h3Mission_LastFirst**.

A new blank presentation opens and is saved.

b. Click the **New Slide arrow** on the Insert tab, click **Slides from Outline**, and then navigate to the location of your student data files.

c. Browse and insert file *p02h3MedOutline*.

The outline is opened and new slides are added to the presentation.

d. Click the **View tab** and click **Outline View** in the Presentation Views group.

Because the file was created in Word with heading styles applied and saved in Rich Text Format, the outline retains its hierarchy. Each slide has a title and bulleted text.

e. Create a handout header with your name and a handout footer with your instructor's name and your class. Include the current date.

f. Apply the **Integral theme** to all slides.

The Integral theme adds a subtle blue line next to the title.

g. Save the presentation.

STEP 2 ›› **REUSE SLIDES FROM ANOTHER PRESENTATION**

While reviewing the Wellness Education Center presentation, you realize you do not have a title slide or a final slide inviting students to contact the Center. You reuse slides from another presentation created for the Center containing slides that would fit well in this presentation. Refer to Figure 2.19 as you complete Step 2.

FIGURE 2.19 Reused Slides Added to Presentation

a. Switch to **Normal view**. Click **Slide 1**, click the **New Slide arrow** in the Slides group on the Home tab, and then click **Reuse Slides** at the bottom of the New Slides gallery.

b. Click **Browse**, click **Browse File**, and then locate your student data files. Select *p02h3Wellness*, and then click **Open**.

> **TROUBLESHOOTING:** If you do not see the *p02h3Wellness* file, click Files of type and select All PowerPoint Presentations.

c. Click to select the **Keep source formatting check box** at the bottom of the Reuse Slides pane.

With *Keep source formatting* selected, the images and design of the slides you reuse will transfer with the slide.

d. Click the **first slide**, *Campus Wellness*, in the Reuse Slides pane.

The slide is added to your presentation after the current slide, Slide 1.

e. Delete the blank title slide that is currently Slide 1.

The newly reused slide will be in the Slide 1 position to serve as the title slide of your presentation.

f. Select the **Slide 7 icon**, *BE A HEALTHY SUCCESS STORY*, in the Slides pane of the original presentation.

g. Click **Slide 7** in the Reuse Slides pane and close the Reuse Slides pane.

h. Save the presentation. Keep the presentation open if you plan to continue with the next Hands-On Exercise. If not, close the presentation, and exit PowerPoint.

Design

After you are satisfied with the content, then you can consider the visual aspects of the presentation. You should evaluate many aspects when considering the visual design of your presentation. Those aspects include layout, background, typography, color, and animation, as well as dividing the content into sections. Sections can help you effectively organize and manage the parts of the presentation.

In this section, you will work with tools that allow you to create well-designed presentations. Using these features, you can create a slide show using a professional template and themes and then modify it to reflect your own preferences. Before doing so, however, you need to consider some basic visual design principles for PowerPoint. Finally, you will customize the slide master and slide layouts controlled by the slide master.

Using Sections

STEP 1 ›› Content divided into *sections* can help you group slides meaningfully. This is similar to how tabs help to organize a binder. These sections provide organization to a presentation by giving a point at which to collapse or expand the slide hierarchy.

When you create a section, it is given the name Untitled Section. You will want to change this to a meaningful name, which enables you to jump to a section quickly. For example, you may be creating a slide show for a presentation on geothermal energy. You could create sections for Earth, plate boundaries, plate tectonics, and thermal features.

TIP: USING A SECTION HEADER

It is easy to confuse term *section* with *section header*. If you need to create a visual break in the presentation, such as stopping to pose questions for the audience, then you will want to use a section header slide instead of a section. Section header slides can be added through Slide Master view.

Use either Normal view or Slide Sorter view to create sections. Figure 2.20 shows a section added to a presentation in Normal view. Slide sections can be collapsed or expanded. The collapsed view makes it easier to move groups of slides around to reorganize a presentation.

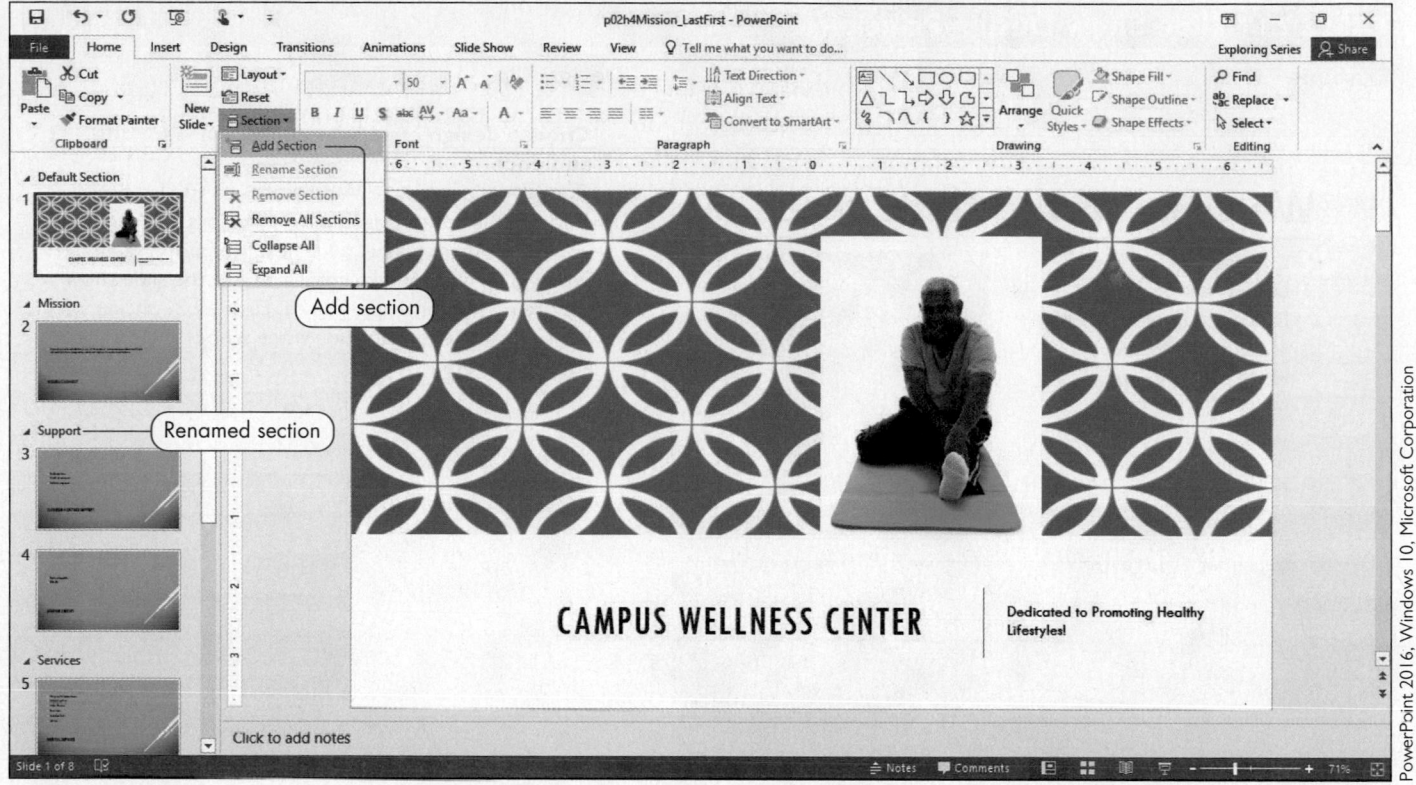

FIGURE 2.20 Using Sections

To create a section, complete the following steps:

1. Select the first slide of the new section.
2. Click Section in the Slides group on the Home tab.
3. Click Add Section.
4. Right-click Untitled Section and select Rename Section.
5. Type a new name for the section.

Examining Slide Show Design Principles

STEP 2 ›› When applied to a project, universally accepted design principles can increase its appeal and professionalism. Some design aspects may be applied in specific ways to the various types of modern communications: communicating through print media such as flyers or brochures, through audio media such as narrations or music, or through a visual medium such as a slide show. Table 2.1 focuses on principles that apply to slide shows and examines examples of slides that illustrate these principles.

TABLE 2.1   Slide Show Design Principles

Example	Design Tip
 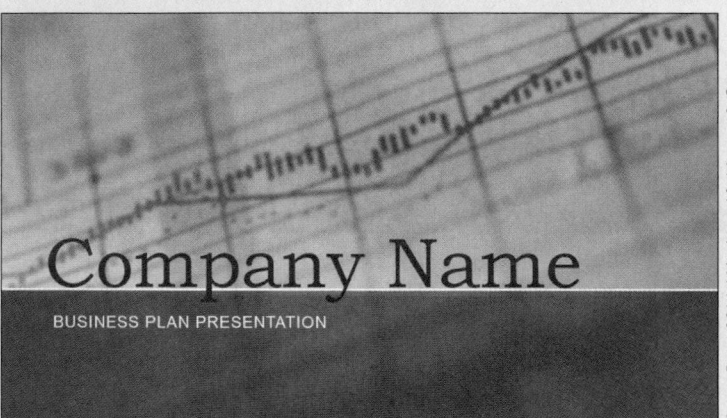 **FIGURE 2.21** Examples of Templates Appropriate for Different Audiences	• **Choose design elements appropriate for the audience.** Consider the audience. A presentation to elementary students might use bright, primary colors and cartoon-like images. For an adult audience, use photographs rather than cartoon-like images to give the slide show a more professional appearance. Figure 2.21 shows design examples suitable for grade school and business audiences, respectively.
 **FIGURE 2.22** Example of a Clean Design	• **Keep the design neat and clean.** Avoid using multiple fonts and font colors on a slide. Avoid using multiple images. Use white space (empty space) to open up your design. Figure 2.22 shows an example of a clean design.

PowerPoint 2016, Windows 10, Microsoft Corporation

PowerPoint 2016, Windows 10, Microsoft Corporation

TABLE 2.1 Continued

Example	Design Tip
 PowerPoint 2016, Windows 10, Microsoft Corporation	• **Create a focal point that leads the viewer's eyes to the critical information on the slide.** The focal point should be the main area of interest. Pictures should always lead the viewer's eyes to the focal point, not away from it. Images should not be so large that they detract from the focal point, unless your goal is to make the image the focal point. Figure 2.23 illustrates examples of an effective focal point.

FIGURE 2.23 Example of an Effective Focal Point

PowerPoint 2016, Windows 10, Microsoft Corporation

• **Use unified design elements for a professional look.** Visual unity creates a harmony between the elements of the slide and between the slides in the slide show. Unity gives the viewer a sense of order and peace. Create unity by repeating colors and shapes. Use images in only one style such as all photographs or all line art throughout the presentation. Figure 2.24 shows a disjointed and a unified design.

FIGURE 2.24 Example of Unified Design Elements

PowerPoint 2016, Windows 10, Microsoft Corporation

FIGURE 2.25 Sans Serif (left) and Serif (right) Fonts

• **Choose fonts appropriate for the output of your presentation.** If a presentation is to be delivered through a projection device, consider using sans serif fonts with short text blocks. If your presentation will be delivered as a printout, consider using serif fonts. Figure 2.25 displays an example of sans serif and serif fonts.

TABLE 2.1 **Continued**

Example	Design Tip
**Text Guidelines** • <u>Do not underline text.</u> • DO NOT USE ALL CAPS. • Use **bold** and *italics* sparingly. • Avoid text that leaves one word on a line on its own. • Avoid using multiple spaces after punctuation. Space once after punctuation in a text block. Spacing more can create rivers of white. The white "river" can be very distracting. The white space draws the eye from the message. It can throb when projected.	• **Do not use underlined text.** Underlined text is harder to read, and it is generally assumed that underlined text is a hyperlink. • **Avoid using all capital letters.** In addition to being difficult to read, words or phrases in all caps are considered to be "yelling" at the audience. • **Use italics and bold sparingly.** Too much emphasis through the use of italics and bold is confusing and makes it difficult to determine what is important. • **Avoid leaving a single word hanging on a line of its own.** Modify the placeholder size so that more than one word is on a subsequent line. Or use Shift+Enter to create a soft break. • **Use just one space after punctuation in text blocks.** Using more than one space can create distracting white space in the text block. Figure 2.26 illustrates these principles.

PowerPoint 2016, Windows 10, Microsoft Corporation

FIGURE 2.26 Appropriate and Inappropriate Text Examples

Pearson Education, Inc.

Remember that these design principles are guidelines. For example, the use of all capital letters is found for headings and titles in certain themes. You may choose to avoid applying one or more of the principles, but you should be aware of the principles and carefully consider why you are not following them. If you are in doubt about your design, ask a classmate or colleague to review the design and make suggestions. Fresh eyes can see things you might miss.

Modifying a Theme

STEP 3 ❯❯ Themes can be modified once they have been applied. You can change the variants, colors, fonts, and effects used in the theme. You can even change the background styles. Each of these options is on the Design tab, and each has its own gallery. Figure 2.27 shows the locations for accessing the galleries.

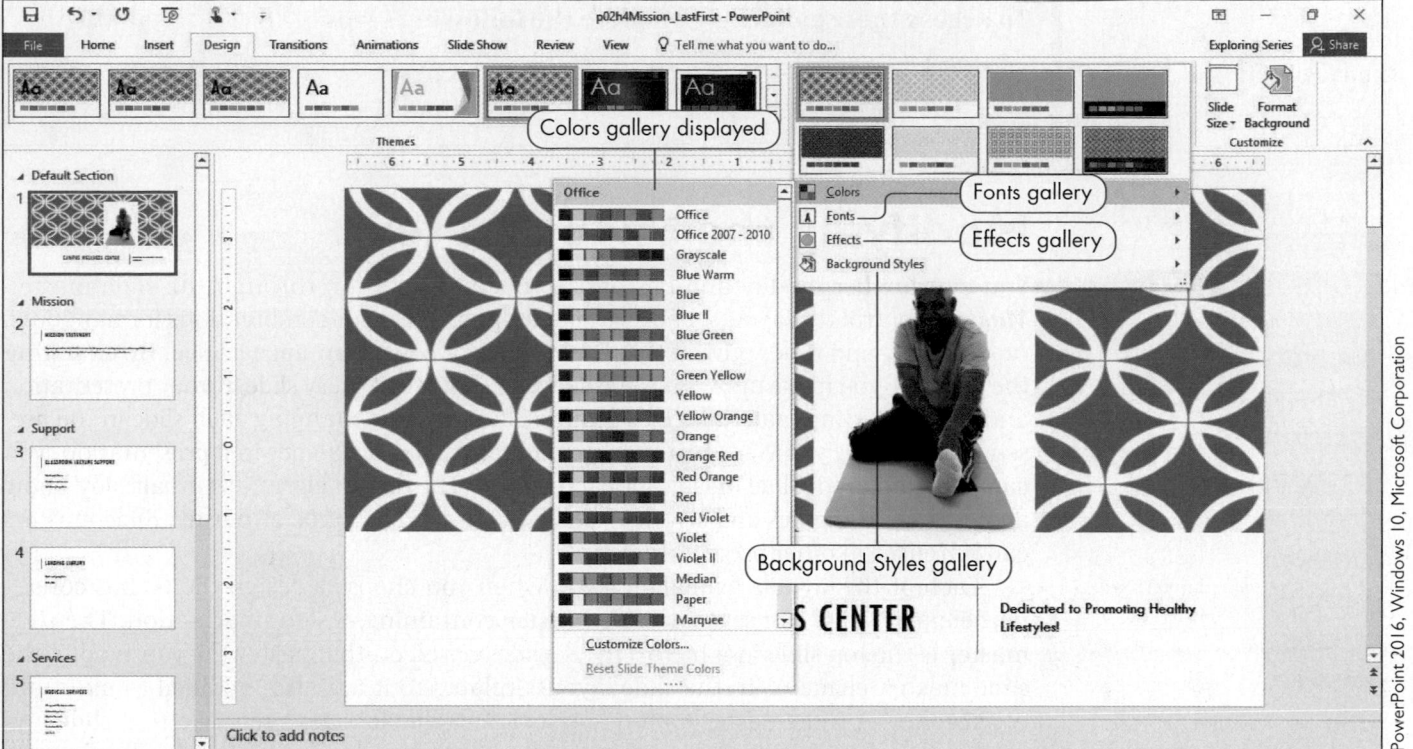

FIGURE 2.27 Design Galleries

Each PowerPoint theme includes a **Colors gallery**, a gallery that provides a set of colors with each color assigned to a different element in the theme design. Once the theme is selected, you can change the colors by displaying the Colors gallery. Use Live Preview as you move the pointer along the various color sets to see how each color theme applies to your slides. You can even customize one or more of the colors in each color set.

Selecting a font for the title and another for the bullets or body text of your presentation can be difficult. Without a background in typography, determining which fonts go together well is difficult. The **Fonts gallery** is a gallery that pairs a title font and a body font. Click any of the samples in the Fonts gallery, and the font pair is applied to your theme.

The **Effects gallery** displays a full range of special effects that can be applied to all shapes in the presentation. Using effects aids you in maintaining a consistency to the appearance of your presentation. The gallery uses effects such as a soft glow, soft edges, shadows, or three-dimensional (3-D) look.

You can change the background style of the theme by accessing the **Background Styles gallery**, a gallery containing backgrounds consistent with the selected theme colors. Simply changing your background style can liven up a presentation and give it your individual style.

Some of the themes include background shapes to create the design. If the background designs interfere with other objects on the slide, such as tables, images, or charts, you can select Format Background in the Customize group of the Design tab, and then click Hide Background Graphics by clicking so that the background shapes will not display for that slide.

Modifying the Slide Master

STEP 4 ▶▶ You can further modify and customize your presentation through the slide master. *Masters* control the layouts, background designs, and color combinations for handouts, notes pages, and slides, giving the presentation a consistent appearance. By changing the masters, you make universal style changes that affect every slide in your presentation and the supporting materials. This is more efficient than changing each slide in the presentation. When you want two or more different styles or themes in a presentation, you can add a different slide master for each theme. The design elements you already know about, such as themes and layouts, can be applied to each type of master. Slide masters can be reused in other presentations.

Each of the layouts available to you when you choose a design theme has consistent elements that are set by a *slide master* containing design information. The slide master is the top slide in a hierarchy of slides based on the master. As you modify the slide master, elements in the slide layouts related to it are also modified to maintain consistency. A slide master includes associated slide layouts such as a title slide layout, various content slide layouts, and a blank slide layout. The associated slide layouts designate the location of placeholders and other objects on slides as well as formatting information.

To modify a slide master or slide layout based on a slide master, complete the following steps:

1. Click the View tab.
2. Click Slide Master in the Master Views group.
3. Click the slide master at the top of the list or click one of the associated layouts.
4. Make modifications.
5. Click Close Master View in the Close group.

In Slide Master view, the slide master is the larger, top slide thumbnail shown in the left pane that coordinates with the Title and Content Layout. The Title Slide Layout is the second slide in the pane. The number of slides following it varies depending upon the template. Figure 2.28 shows the Integral Theme Slide Master and its related slide layouts. The ScreenTip for the slide master indicates it is used by one slide because the slide show is a new slide show composed of a single title slide.

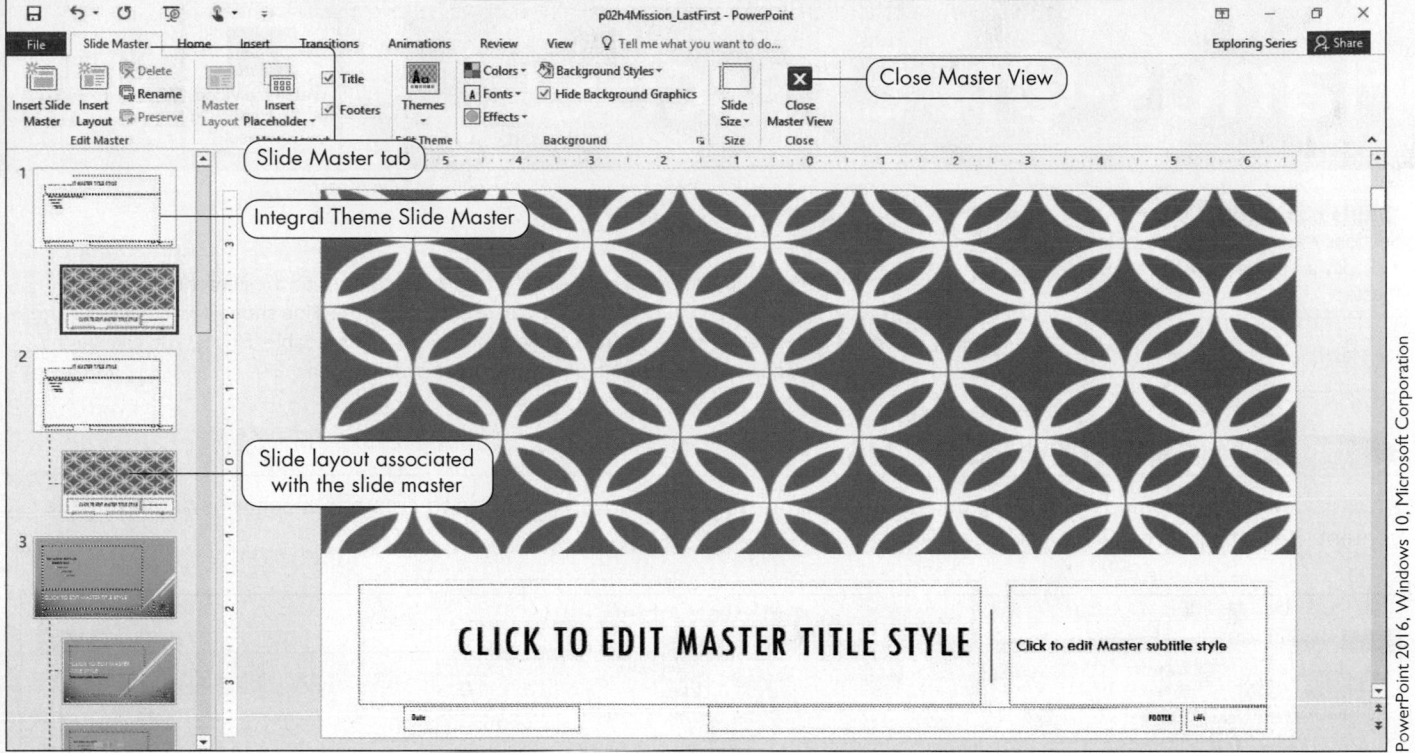

FIGURE 2.28 Slide Master View

The slide master is the most efficient way of setting the fonts, color scheme, and effects for the entire slide show. For example, you may wish to add a small company logo to the right corner of all slides. To set this choice, click the slide master thumbnail in the slide pane to display the slide master. The main pane shows the placeholders for title style, text styles, a date field, a footer field, and a page number field. Double-click the text in the Master title style or any level of text in the Master text styles placeholder and insert the logo.

You can move and size the placeholders on the slide master. The modifications in position and size will be reflected on the associated slide layouts. This may conflict with some of the slide layout placeholders, however. The placeholders can be moved on the individual slide layouts as needed.

Quick Concepts

10. How are sections in a presentation similar to tabs in a binder? *p. 1016*

11. Why is it important to have unified design elements in a presentation? *p. 1019*

12. Which elements of a theme can be modified? Where do you access these elements to make the change? *p. 1020*

13. In what ways can a slide master give a consistent appearance to presentations? *p. 1022*

Hands-On Exercises

Watch the Video for this Hands-On Exercise!

MyITLab®
HOE4 Training

Skills covered: Create Sections • Apply Design Principles • Modify a Theme • Modify a Slide Master

4 Design

The director of the Wellness Education Center plans to add more content to the center's mission presentation. To help her organize the content, you create sections in the slide show. You apply your knowledge of design principles to make the text more professional and readable. Finally, you change the theme and make modifications to the presentation through the slide master.

STEP 1 ›› CREATE SECTIONS

After reviewing the Campus Wellness Education Center mission slide show, you decide to create four sections organizing the content. Refer to Figure 2.29 as you complete Step 1.

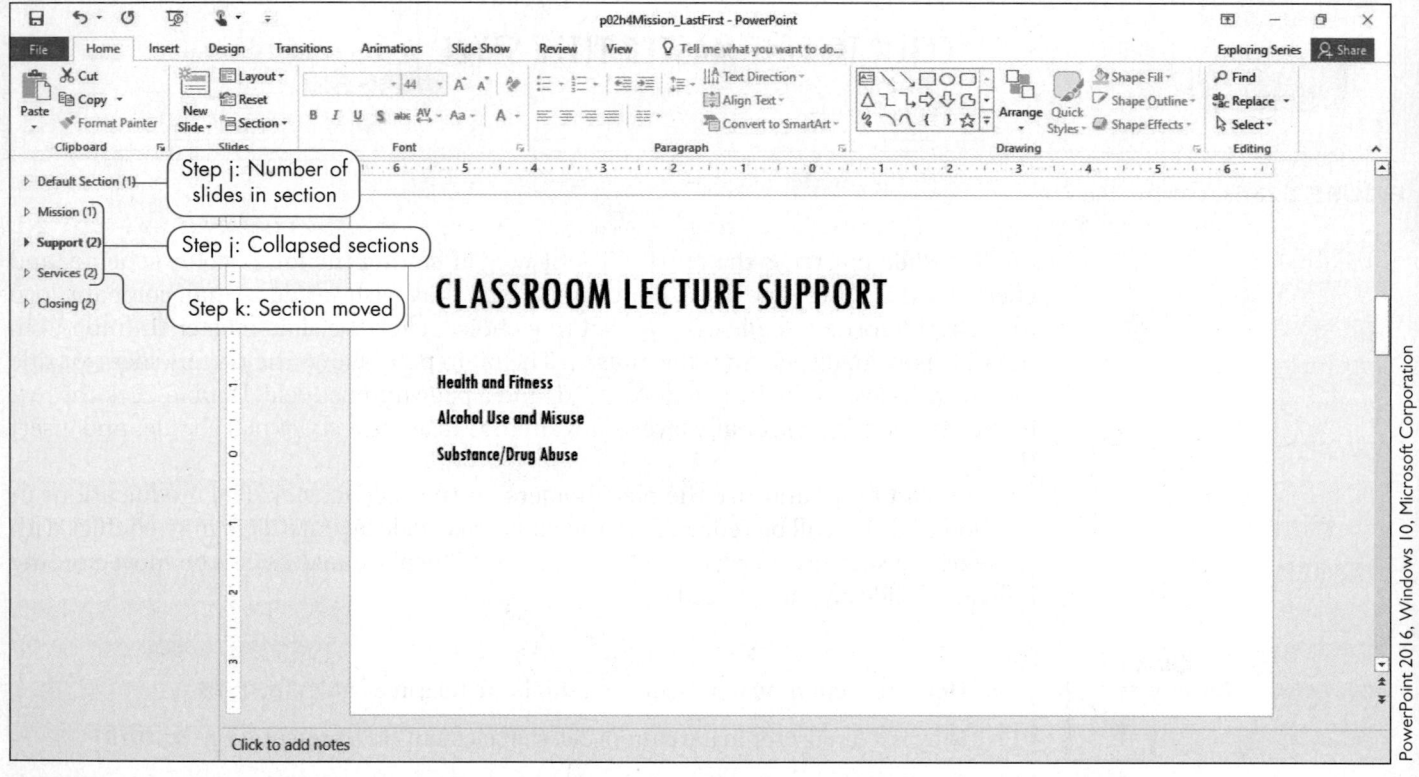

FIGURE 2.29 Content Divided into Sections

a. Open *p02h3Mission_LastFirst* if you closed it at the end of Hands-On Exercise 3, and save it as **p02h4Mission_LastFirst**, changing h3 to h4.

b. Click the **View tab**, click **Normal**, and then click the **Slide 2 thumbnail**.

c. Click **Section** in the Slides group on the Home tab and select **Add Section**.

A section divider is positioned between Slide 1 and Slide 2 in the Slides tab. It is labeled *Untitled Section*.

d. Right-click the **Untitled Section divider** and select **Rename Section**.

The Rename Section dialog box opens.

e. Type **Mission** in the Section name box and click **Rename**.

The section divider name changes and displays in the Slides tab.

f. Create a new section between Slides 2 and 3.

g. Right-click **Untitled Section**, click **Rename Section**, and then name the section **Services**.

h. Right-click between Slide 4 and Slide 5, click **Add Section**, and then rename the section **Support**.

i. Right-click between Slide 6 and Slide 7 and create a section named **Closing**.

The slide show content is divided into logical sections.

j. Right-click any section divider and select **Collapse All**.

The Slides tab shows the four sections you created: Mission, Services, Support, and Closing, as well as the Default section. Each section divider displays the section name and the number of slides in the section.

k. Right-click the **Support section** and click **Move Section Up**.

The Support section and all its associated slides are moved above the Services section.

l. Right-click any section divider and click **Expand All**.

m. Click the **View tab** and click **Slide Sorter** in the Presentation Views group.

Slide Sorter view displays the slides in each section.

n. Click **Normal** in the Presentation Views group. Save the presentation.

STEP 2 » **APPLY DESIGN PRINCIPLES**

You note that several of the slides in the presentation do not use slide show text design principles. You edit these slides so they are more readable. Refer to Figure 2.30 as you complete Step 2.

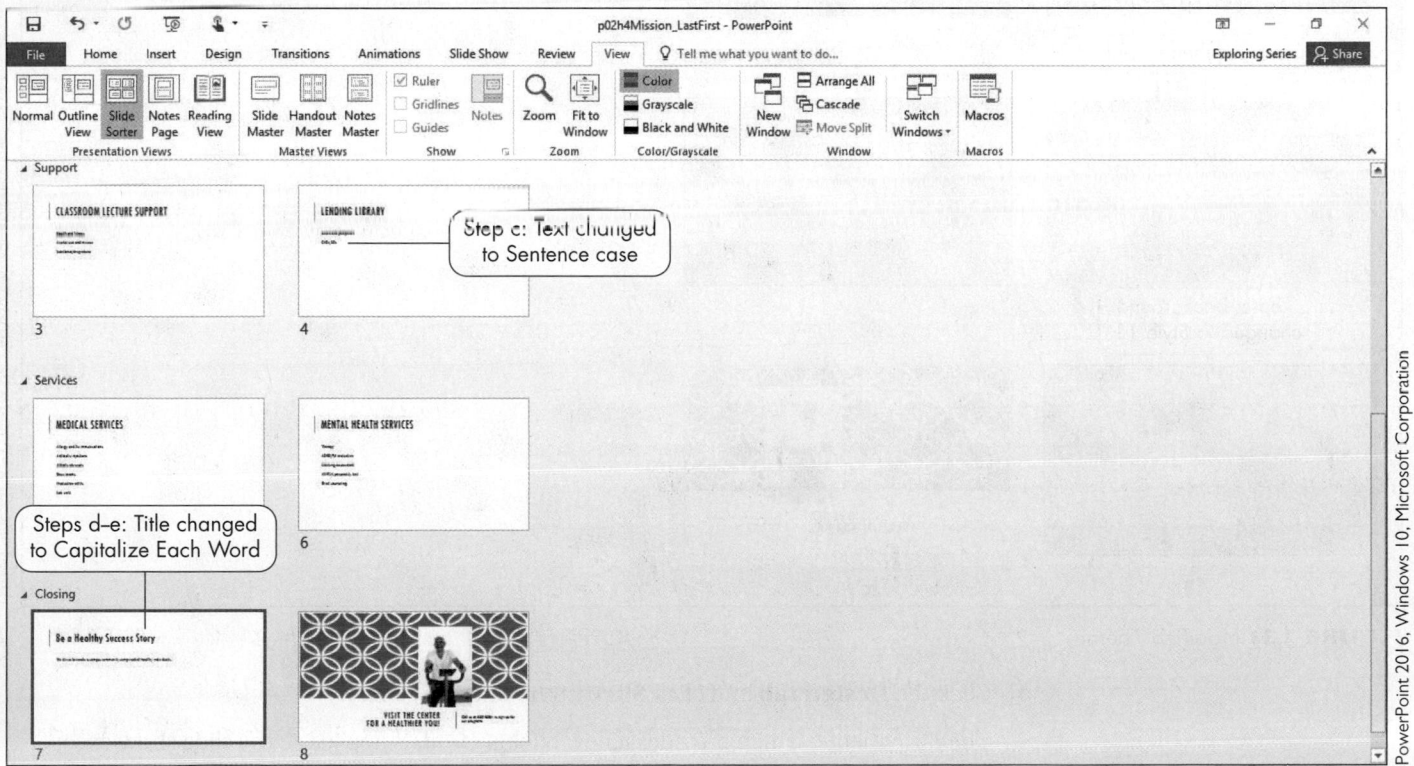

FIGURE 2.30 Portion of Slide Show in Slide Sorter View

a. Click **Slide 3**, select the text below the title placeholder, click the **Change Case arrow** in the Font group on the Home tab, and then select **Sentence case**.

The text now meets the guideline and is more readable.

b. Change the text below the titles in Slides 4, 5, and 6 to **Sentence case**.

c. Click **Slide 4**, change the second line to **DVDs/CDs**.

Always proofread to ensure that the case feature accurately reflects proper capitalization.

d. Click **Slide 7**, select the **title text**, click **Change Case** in the Font group, and then click **Capitalize Each Word**.

Each word in the title begins with a capital letter.

e. Change the uppercase *A* in the title to a lowercase *a*.

Title case capitalization guidelines state that only significant parts of speech of four or more letters should be capitalized. Minor parts of speech including articles and words shorter than four letters should not be capitalized.

f. Click the **View tab** and click **Slide Sorter** in the Presentation Views group.

Note the sentence case in the Services section.

g. Save the presentation.

STEP 3 ⟩⟩ MODIFY A THEME

Although you are satisfied with the opening and closing slides, you think the main body of slides should be enhanced. You decide to change the theme and then modify the new theme to customize it. Refer to Figure 2.31 as you complete Step 3.

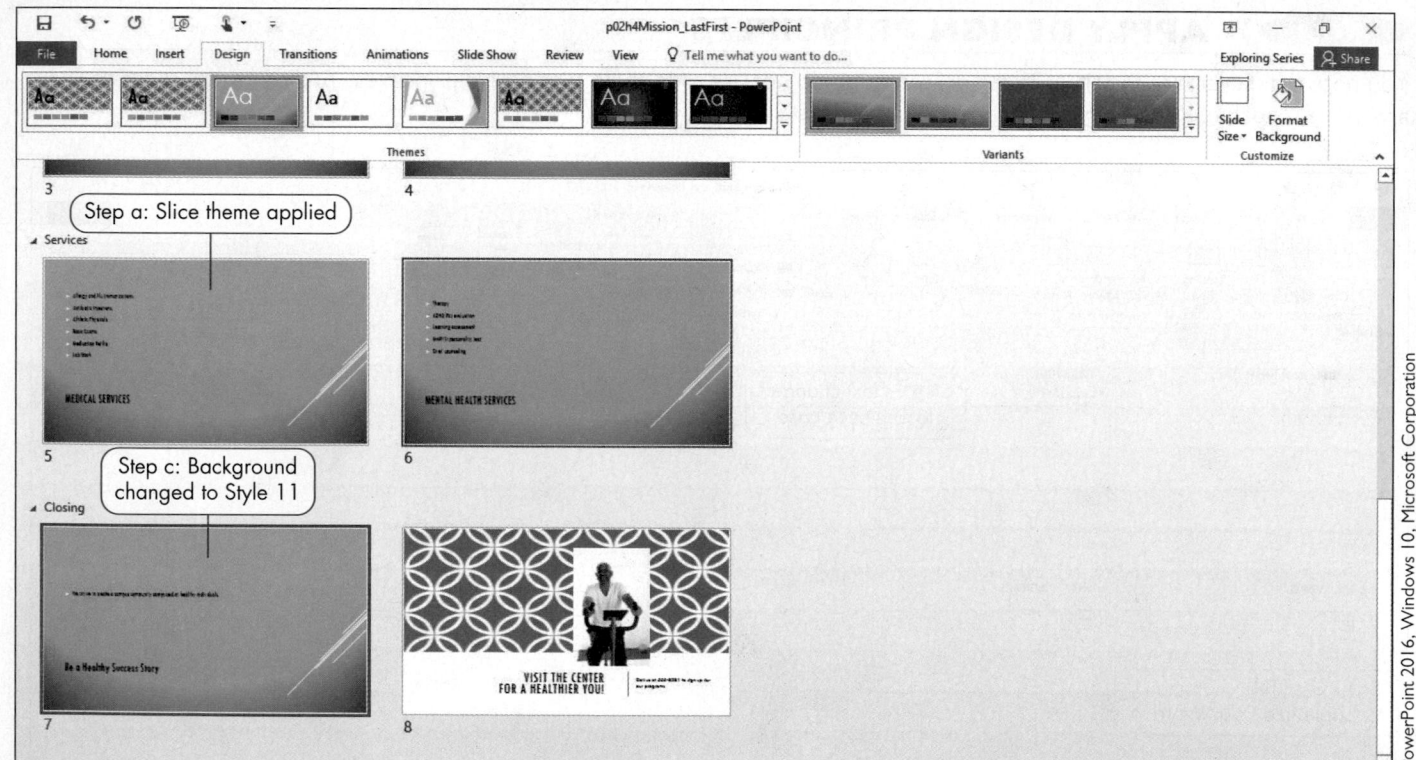

FIGURE 2.31 Modified Theme

a. Click the **Design tab** and click **Slice** in the Themes gallery.

The Slice theme, which provides a new background, is applied to the slide show except for the title and conclusion slides.

b. Click the **Design tab** and click **More** in the Variants group.

The Variants Gallery opens.

c. Select **Background Styles** and click **Style 11**.

d. Save the presentation.

You want to add the Wellness Education Center's logo to slides 2 through 7 using the slide master. Refer to Figure 2.32 as you complete Step 4.

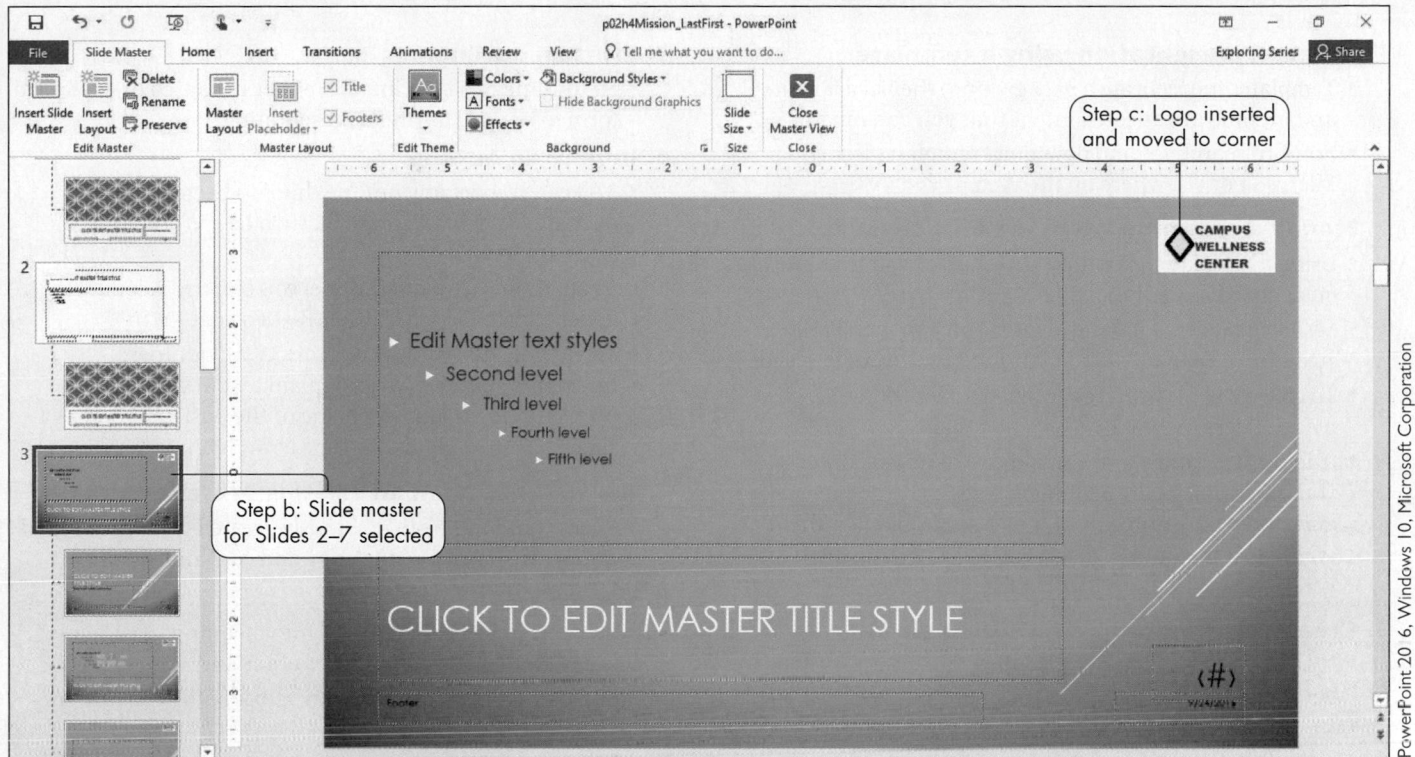

FIGURE 2.32 Modified Slide Master

a. Click the **View tab** and click **Slide Master** in the Master Views group. Scroll to the top of the slide pane.

Note the masters labeled 1 and 2. These masters control the first and last slides of the presentation.

b. Click the **slide master thumbnail** next to the number 3.

The third slide master controls slides 2 through 7.

c. Click the **Insert tab** and click **Pictures**. Locate the *p02h4Logo* picture file in the student files folder and click **Insert**.

The logo is inserted. The logo will display in the slide pane thumbnails and slide show, but not on the full slide in Normal view.

d. Move the logo to the top right corner of the slide master.

e. Click the **Slide Master tab**. Click **Close Master View** in the Close group.

Observe that the logo has been inserted on Slides 2 through 7 in the presentation.

f. Check spelling in the presentation. Save and close the file. Based on your instructor's directions, submit the following:

p02h2Center_LastFirst
p02h4Mission_LastFirst.

Chapter Objectives Review

After reading this chapter, you have accomplished the following objectives:

1. Create a presentation using a template.
- Templates incorporate a background, theme, a layout, and in some instances, content that you can modify.
- You can search for and download templates from Microsoft or elsewhere on the Web.

2. Modify a presentation based on a template.
- Using a template saves time and enables you to create a customized presentation.
- Modify a placeholder and layout: You can modify the structure of a template by changing the layout of a slide.
- To change the layout, resize placeholders or drag placeholders to new locations on a slide.
- Add pictures and captions: You can add visual interest to your presentation by adding pictures that you have taken and stored on your computer or by searching for them on the Internet and then saving and inserting them into your presentation.

3. Create a presentation in Outline view.
- When you use a storyboard to determine your content, you create a basic outline.
- Working in Outline view enables you to edit the presentation easily, and saves time because you can enter information efficiently without moving from placeholder to placeholder on slides.
- Use Outline view: Entering your presentation in Outline view enables you to organize the content of the presentation in a hierarchy of main points and subpoints.
- Edit in Outline view: Levels of indention makes it easy to show the relationships between information on the slide. You can promote or demote either before or after the information is entered on the slide.

4. Modify an outline structure.
- Because Outline view helps you see the structure of the presentation, you are able to see where content needs to be strengthened or where the flow of information needs to be revised.
- If you decide a slide contains content that would be presented better in another location in the slide show, use the Collapse and Expand features to easily move it.
- After collapsing the slide content, you can drag the slide to a new location and then expand it.
- To move individual bullet points, cut and paste the bullet points, or drag and drop them.

5. Print an outline.
- An outline can be printed in either collapsed or expanded form to be used during a presentation.

6. Import an outline.
- You can import any outline that has been saved in a format PowerPoint can read, such as a Word outline (.doc or .docx).
- In addition to a Word outline, you can use a common generic format such as Rich Text Format (.rtf).
- Solve problems while importing Word outlines: Importing outlines saved in plain text (.txt) can be problematic because each line of the outline becomes a slide instead of retaining the hierarchy.

7. Reuse slides from an existing presentation.
- Slides that have been previously created can be reused in new slide shows for efficiency and continuity.

8. Use sections.
- Sections help organize slides into meaningful groups of slides that can be collapsed or organized.
- Each section can be named to help identify the contents of the sections.

9. Examine slide show design principles.
- Using basic slide show principles and applying the guidelines make presentations more polished and professional.

10. Modify a theme.
- A template includes themes that define its font attributes, colors, and backgrounds.
- Using galleries, you can change a template's theme colors, fonts, effects and backgrounds.

11. Modify the slide master.
- A slide master controls the layouts, background designs, and color combinations associated with the handouts, notes pages, and slides in a presentation.
- By changing the slide master, you make changes that affect every slide in a presentation.

Key Terms Matching

Match the key terms with their definitions. Write the key term letter by the appropriate numbered definition.

a. Background Styles gallery
b. Collapsed outline
c. Colors gallery
d. Effects gallery
e. Expanded outline
f. Fonts gallery
g. Hierarchy
h. Master

i. Outline
j. Outline view
k. Plain text format (.txt)
l. Rich text format (.rtf)
m. Section
n. Slide master
o. Template

1. _____ A file that incorporates a theme, a layout, and content that can be modified. **p. 992**

2. _____ A method of organizing text in a hierarchy to depict relationships. **p. 1002**

3. _____ A method used to organize text into levels of importance in a structure. **p. 1002**

4. _____ A view showing the presentation in an outline format displayed in levels according to the points and any subpoints on each slide. **p. 1002**

5. _____ An Outline view that displays only the slide number, icon, and title of each slide in Outline view. **p. 1004**

6. _____ An Outline view that displays the slide number, icon, title, and content of each slide in the Outline view. **p. 1004**

7. _____ A Word outline saved in this format can be used when transferring documents between platforms. **p. 1011**

8. _____ A file format that retains only text but no formatting when transferring documents between applications or platforms. **p. 1011**

9. _____ A set of colors available for every theme. **p. 1021**

10. _____ A gallery that pairs a title font with a body font. **p. 1021**

11. _____ A range of special effects for shapes used in the presentation. **p. 1021**

12. _____ A gallery providing both solid color and background styles for application to a theme. **p. 1021**

13. _____ The top slide in a hierarchy of slides based on the master. **p. 1022**

14. _____ A slide view where the control of the layouts, background designs, and color combinations for handouts, notes pages, and slides can be set giving a presentation a consistent appearance. **p. 1022**

15. _____ A division to presentation content that groups slides meaningfully. **p. 1016**

Multiple Choice

1. A widescreen template that can be used for display on most screens and televisions is found in the category:
   (a) 4:3.
   (b) 11:17.
   (c) 16:9.
   (d) 20:20.

2. To add pictures to a presentation, you can:
   (a) Use your own photos.
   (b) Search for and insert pictures from Bing Image Search.
   (c) Use the default images that came with the template.
   (d) Use any of the above options.

3. What is the advantage to collapsing the outline so only the slide titles are visible?
   (a) Transitions and animations can be added.
   (b) Graphical objects become visible.
   (c) More slide titles are displayed at one time, making it easier to rearrange the slides in the presentation.
   (d) All of the above.

4. Which of the following is *true*?
   (a) The slide layout can be changed after the template has been chosen.
   (b) Themes applied to a template will not be saved with the slide show.
   (c) Placeholders downloaded with a template cannot be modified.
   (d) Slides cannot be added to a presentation after a template has been chosen.

5. In Outline view, levels of indentation showing the hierarchy of information *cannot* be created by:
   (a) Pressing TAB to demote a bullet point from the first level to the second level.
   (b) Pressing SHIFT+TAB to promote a bullet point from the second level to the first level.
   (c) Pressing ALT+TAB to demote a bullet point from the first level to the second level.
   (d) Pressing Decrease List Level to demote a bullet point from the first level to the second level.

6. Which of the following is the easiest method for adding existing content to a presentation?
   (a) Import an outline using heading styles created in Word.
   (b) Import a numbered list created in Word.
   (c) Import a bulleted list created in Word.
   (d) Import a document saved in plain text format.

7. How is formatting affected when reusing slides from an existing presentation?
   (a) The slide being reused takes on the formatting of the open presentation.
   (b) You can click Clear All Formatting to format slides using the active theme.
   (c) The original presentation's formatting can be retained by clicking Keep Source Formatting.
   (d) Any of the above may happen.

8. Which of the following is *not* true of sections?
   (a) Sections can be renamed.
   (b) Sections can be created in Normal view or Slide Sorter view.
   (c) Sections can be collapsed.
   (d) A slide show can be divided into only six logical sections.

9. Which of the following formats *cannot* be imported to use as an outline for a presentation?
   (a) .jpg
   (b) .docx
   (c) .txt
   (d) .rtf

10. You own a small business and decide to institute an Employee of the Month award program. Which of the following would be the fastest way to create the award certificate with a professional look?
    (a) Enter the text in the title placeholder of a slide, change the font for each line, and then drag several images of awards onto the slide.
    (b) Select a theme, modify the placeholders, and then enter the award text information.
    (c) Create a table, enter the award text in the table, and then add images.
    (d) Search for online templates and themes and download an Award certificate template.

Practice Exercises

1 Classic Photo Album

FROM SCRATCH You enjoy using your digital camera to record nature shots during trips you take on weekends. You decide to store these pictures in an electronic slide show that you can display for your family. You use the Classic Photo Album template. Refer to Figure 2.33 as you complete this exercise.

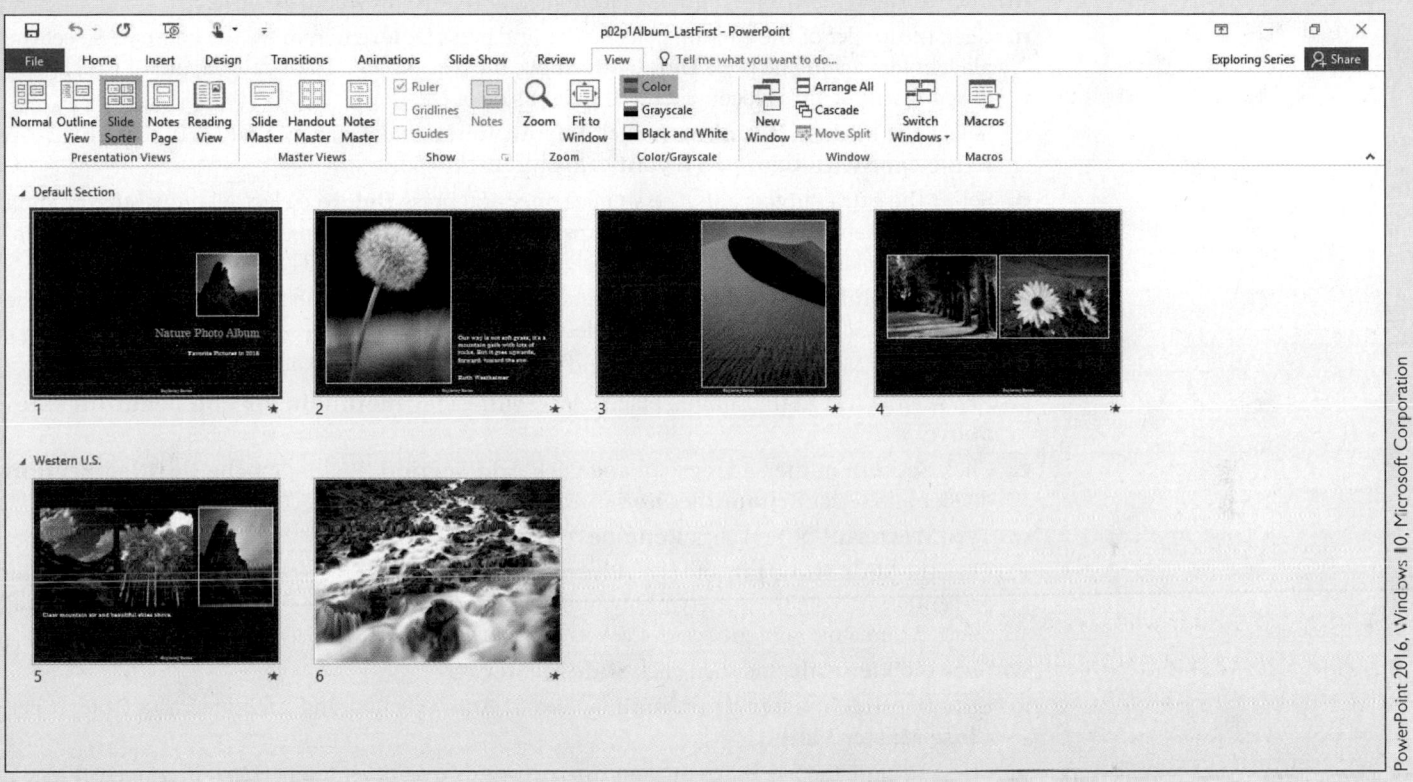

FIGURE 2.33 Classic Photo Album in Slide Sorter View

a. Start PowerPoint.

b. Type **Photo Albums** in the Search box and press **Enter**.
   Thumbnails of sample templates will display.

c. Click **Classic photo album** and click **Create**.

d. Save the presentation file as **p02p1Album_LastFirst**.

e. Create a Notes and Handouts header with your name and a footer with your instructor's name and your class. Include the current date set to update automatically. The page number feature can remain active. Click **Apply to All**.

f. Select the word **CLASSIC** in the title placeholder of the first slide and type **Nature**.

g. Change the case of the title to **Capitalize Each Word**.

h. Replace the text in the **subtitle placeholder**, *Click to add date and other details*, with **Favorite Pictures in 2018**.

i. Click the **New Slide arrow** to display the Layout gallery.

j. Click the **Portrait with Caption layout** to add a new Slide 2.

k. Click the **Picture icon**, locate the image *p02p1Nature* from your student data files, and then click **Insert**.

l. Click in the **caption placeholder** and type **Our way is not soft grass, it's a mountain path with lots of rocks. But it goes upwards, forward, toward the sun.** Press **Enter** twice and type **Ruth Westheimer**.

m. Click **Slide 3**, read the text in the placeholder, and click anywhere in the text.

n. Click the border of the caption placeholder and press **Delete** to remove the content. Select the placeholder again and press **Delete** to remove the placeholder. Modify the layout of the slide by dragging the picture placeholder to the right side of the slide.

o. Select the **Slide 4 thumbnail**, click **Layout** in the Slides group, and then click the **2-Up Landscape with Captions layout** to apply it to the slide.

p. Select the extra photograph (the smaller one) and press **Delete**. Select a border surrounding one of the caption placeholders and press **Delete**. Repeat selecting and deleting until all caption placeholders have been deleted. Delete the CHOOSE A LAYOUT placeholder.

q. Select the **Slide 5 thumbnail**, press and hold **Ctrl**, and select the **Slide 7 thumbnail** in the Slides tab, and then press **Delete** to delete Slides 5 and 7 entirely.

r. Ensure that Normal view is selected, and then click **Slide 5**.

s. Replace the text in the subtitle placeholder with **Clear mountain air and beautiful skies above.**

t. Click **Section** in the Slides group and click **Add Section**. Right-click the **Untitled Section** divider and select **Rename Section**.

u. Type **Western U.S.** and click **Rename**.

v. Click the **Slide Show tab** and click **From Beginning** in the Start Slide Show group to view the presentation. Note the variety of layouts. Proofread to ensure all text is in serif font and that Slides 2 and 5 use sentence case. Press **Esc** when you are finished viewing the presentation.

w. Click the **View tab**, and then click **Slide Master**.

x. Click the **slide master thumbnail** labeled 1. Add your first and last name as a footer. Click **Close Master View**.

y. Save and close the file. Based on your instructor's directions, submit p02p1Album_LastFirst.

Your community's Small Business Development Center (SBDC) asks you to provide training to local small business owners on preparing and delivering presentations. You create an outline and then supplement it by reusing slides from another presentation and by adding slides from an outline. Because the slides come from different sources, they have different fonts, and you change the fonts to match one of the design principles discussed in the chapter. You create sections to organize the presentation and then polish the presentation by adding and modifying a theme. Refer to Figure 2.34 as you complete this exercise.

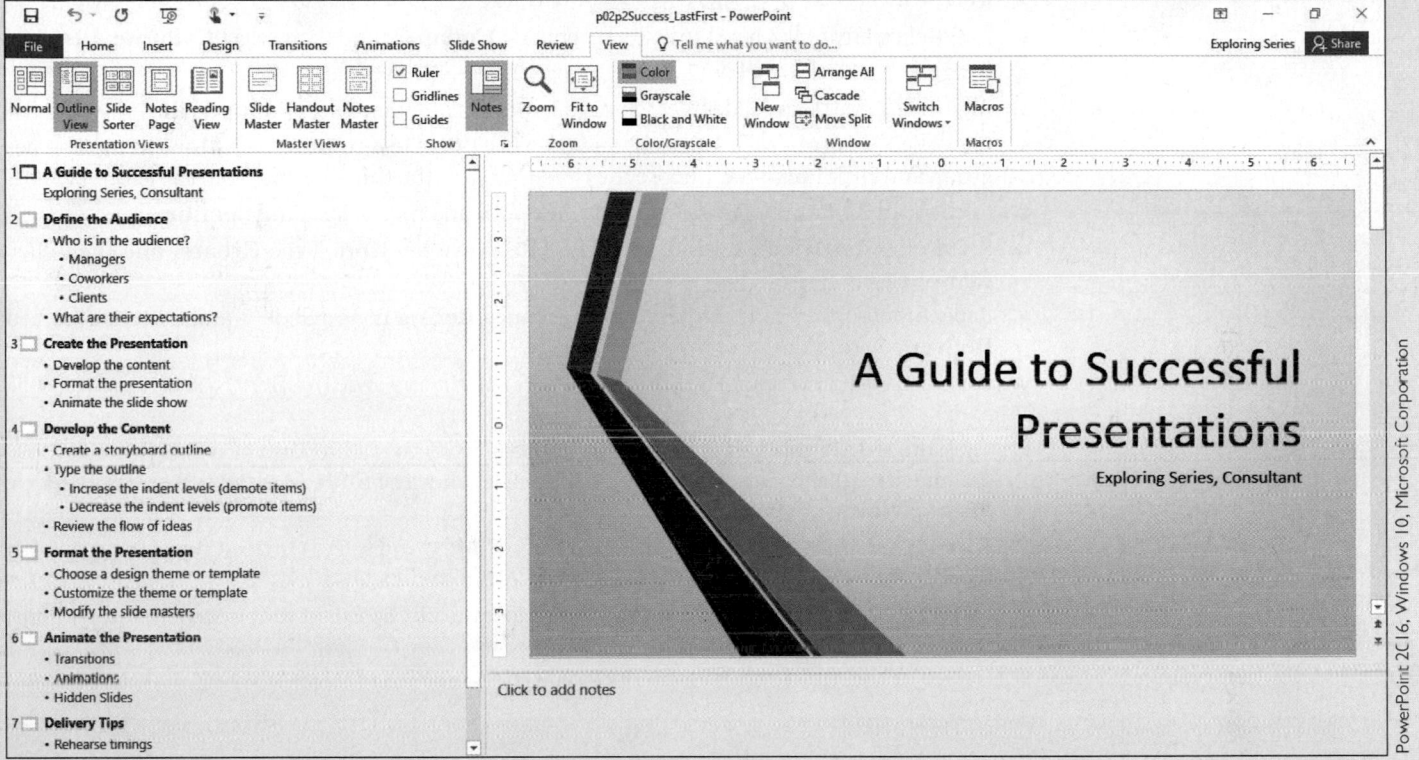

FIGURE 2.34 Presentation Created from an Outline and Reused Slides

a. Create a new, blank presentation. Click the **View tab** and click **Outline View**. Click next to the Slide 1 icon and type **A Guide to Winning Presentations**. Press **Enter** and press **Tab**. Type your name and add the title **Consultant**.

b. Save the new presentation as **p02p2Success_LastFirst**.

c. Create a Notes and Handouts header with your name and a footer with your instructor's name and your class. Include the current date set to update automatically. The page number feature can remain active.

d. Click the **New Slide arrow** in the Slides group on the Home tab, click **Slides from Outline**, locate *p02p2TipsOutline* in your student data files, and then click **Insert**.

e. Select the word **Winning** on Slide 1 while in Outline view, and type **Successful**.

f. Click at the end of the last bulleted text on Slide 3, press **Enter**, and then press **Shift+Tab** to create a new Slide 4. Type **Develop the Content** and press **Enter**.

g. Press **Tab**, type **Create a storyboard outline**, and then press **Enter**.

h. Type **Type the outline** and press **Enter**.

i. Press **Tab** to create a subpoint and type **Increase the indent levels (demote items)**. Press **Enter**.

j. Type **Decrease the indent levels (promote items)** and press **Enter**.

k. Press **Shift+Tab** to return to the previous level and type **Review the flow of ideas**.

l. Click at the end of the last bulleted text on Slide 4 and click the **New Slide arrow** in the Slides group.

m. Click **Reuse Slides** at the bottom of the gallery to open the Reuse Slides pane. Click **Browse**, click **Browse File**, select *p02p2Reuse*, and then click **Open**.

n. Double-click each of the slides in the Reuse Slides pane to insert the slides into the slide show. Close the Reuse Slides pane.

o. Press **Ctrl+A** to select all text in the outline, change the font to **Calibri (Body)**, and then deselect the text.

p. Right-click any bullet point to collapse, point to **Collapse**, and then select **Collapse All**.

q. Drag the Slide 5 icon below the Slide 7 icon.

r. Right-click one of the slide titles, point to **Expand**, and then select **Expand All**.

s. Click the **View tab**, click **Normal**, and then click the **Design tab**. Click **More** in the Themes group and click **Parallax**. Choose the Green variant (the third variant from the left).

t. Click **Slide 2**, click the **Home tab**, click **Section**, and then select **Add Section**.

u. Right-click **Untitled Section** and select **Rename Section**. Type **Create**, and then click **Rename**.

v. Repeat Steps t and u to create a section named **Refine** before Slide 5 and a section named **Deliver** before Slide 7.

w. Click the **View tab** and click **Slide Master**. Click the top slide (numbered Slide 1) in the slide pane.

x. Click the **Insert tab** and click **Pictures**. Locate *p02p2PresenterLogo* and click **Insert**. Move the image to the bottom-right corner of the slide. Click the **Slide Master tab** and click **Close Master View**.

y. Click the **File tab**, click **Print**, click **Full Page Slides**, and select **Outline**. View the outline in the Preview pane and then press **Back** to return to the presentation.

z. Check spelling in the presentation. Save and close the file. Based on your instructor's directions, submit p02p2Success_LastFirst.

Mid-Level Exercises

1 Nutrition Guide

You have been asked to help create a presentation for a local Girl Scout troop that is featuring good nutrition as its theme for the month. You locate a template online for nutrition that has some fun colors that you think the young girls will enjoy. Since you have given similar presentations, you decide to reuse basic slide content you have previously created on standard nutritional guidelines supported by the U.S. Department of Agriculture. Lastly, you modify the presentation using the slide master so all the changes are easily implemented to all slides.

a. Start PowerPoint, and in the *Search for online templates and themes* box, type **Nutrition**.

b. Select **Fresh food presentation** and click **Create**.

c. Save the presentation as **p02m1Food_LastFirst**.

d. Create a Notes and Handouts header with your name and a footer with your instructor's name and your class. Include the current date.

e. View the slides in Slide Show view.

f. Review the presentation, noting the several types of slide layouts.

g. Click **Slide 1**, replace the Title layout text with **Nutritional Guide**. Replace the subtitle with **June 2018**.

h. Click **Slide 6** and replace the title text with **Food!** Type **Make Good Choices** as the subtitle text.

i. Make the following changes to Slide 2:
- Replace Title of the Presentation with **Great Nutritional Choices**.
- Add three bullets: **Colorful fruits and vegetables, Fresh food over processed foods, Reasonable portions.**

j. Delete Slides 3 through 5 and then delete all remaining blank slides.

k. Click the **New Slide arrow** in the Slides group of the Home tab and select **Reuse Slides**.

l. Browse to locate and select the *p02m1Diet* presentation from the student data files in the Reuse Slides pane.

m. Select all seven slides in the Reuse Slides pane. Close the Reuse Slides pane.

n. Move Slide 3 so it becomes the last slide of the presentation.

o. Click the **View tab** and click **Slide Master** from the Master Views group.

p. Click the third slide in the left pane and make the following changes to the Title and Content Layout slide master:
- Select the five levels of text in the content placeholder, click the **Font Color arrow** in the Mini toolbar, select the **Eyedropper**, and then click the orange rectangle in the upper-left corner to select one of the colors found in the graphics.
- Select the text in the title **Click to edit Master title style**, click the **Font Color arrow** in the Mini toolbar, and then select **Dark Green, Accent 6** (theme color, last column).
- Increase the font size of the slide title to **40**.
- Close the Slide Master.

q. View Slides 2 through 9 to ensure the changes in the slide master are reflected in the slides.

r. Select Slide 10 and make the following changes:
- Replace *Food!* with **Food is fun for everyone!**

s. Run the spelling checker and proofread the presentation. Save and close the file. Based on your instructor's directions, submit p02m1Food_LastFirst.

2 Go Digital

CREATIVE
CASE
FROM
SCRATCH

The local senior citizens' center asked you to speak on photography. The center has many clients interested in learning about digital photography. You decide to create a presentation with sections on learning the advantages of a digital camera, choosing a camera, taking pictures with a digital camera, and printing and sharing photos. In this exercise, you begin the presentation by importing data from an outline and then complete it by reusing some slides from another presentation.

a. Create a new blank PowerPoint presentation and create slides from the *p02m2Outline* outline. Save the slide show as **p02m2Digital_LastFirst**.

b. Apply the **Wisp theme** to the slides.

c. Delete the blank Slide 1 and change the layout of the new Slide 1 to **Title Slide**. Add your name in the subtitle.

d. Review the presentation in PowerPoint's Outline view and add the following information as the last bullets on Slide 2:
   - **Instant feedback**
   - **Sharing**

e. Promote the text **Free Experimentation** on Slide 4 so that it creates a new slide.

> **TROUBLESHOOTING:** If you cannot select a bullet, place your insertion point at the end of the bullet and click to select the bulleted line.

f. Select all text in Outline view and click **Clear All Formatting** in the Font group on the Home tab.

g. Open the Reuse Slides pane and browse to locate and open the *p02m2Slides* presentation. Click the last slide in the original presentation in the Outline pane. Right-click any slide in the Reuse Slides pane and click **Insert All Slides**. The new slides should be inserted as Slides 6 and 7. Close the Reuse Slides pane.

h. Select **More** in the Variants Gallery on the Design tab and change the presentation font to **Corbel**. Using the Colors gallery, change the presentation colors to **Red**. Apply **Background Style 10**.

i. Return to Normal view.

j. Create a section between Slides 1 and 2 named **Advantages**.

k. Create a section after Slide 7 named **Choosing a Digital Camera**.

DISCOVER

l. Use the Web to research things to consider when purchasing a digital camera. Be sure to include the major types of cameras available.

m. Insert a new Slide 8 in the **Choosing a Digital Camera** section to explain your findings.

n. Create a Notes and Handouts header with your name and a footer with your instructor's name and your class. Include the current date.

o. Save and close the file. Based on your instructor's directions, submit p02m2Digital_LastFirst.

3 | Using Social Technologies for Ideas and Resources

COLLABORATION CASE

FROM SCRATCH

Social networking enables us to connect with others who share common interests via the Internet. Social networking also helps businesses connect with their customers. In this exercise, you will give an overview of some of the popular social media technologies such as Facebook, Twitter, LinkedIn, etc. and discuss how businesses can utilize them to engage their customers. Choose a business that interests you and discuss which social media technologies it uses and how they are used to connect with its customers. You will visit Microsoft's Office.com website, download a template from the Design Gallery, modify the template with your information, and then post the PowerPoint presentation you create to a location where others can view and comment on it.

a. Access the Internet and go to **http://templates.office.com**. Click **PowerPoint**. Click to see all available PowerPoint 2016 templates.

b. Click several of the thumbnails to see further details about the presentation.

c. Select one of the templates and download the slides to the location you use to store your files for this class. Save the file as **p02m3Resources_GroupName**. Open the saved slide show and modify the slides so they reflect your information and ideas. Be sure to follow the design principles discussed in the chapter. Your presentation should be approximately six to nine slides in length, including the title and credit slides. Delete any unnecessary slides found in the template. Make sure you create a final slide that credits the source for the template design. Provide the URL for the location from where you downloaded the template.

d. Load your edited presentation to an online location for others to review. Upload your presentation to your Microsoft OneDrive account or use another method for sharing your presentation with your instructor and classmates. (If you do not already have a OneDrive account, you can create a free account at https://onedrive.live.com.)

e. Invite three classmates to view the presentation you saved at the site, and then add a comment about your presentation. If using OneDrive to add comments, click the **Comment button** in PowerPoint Online. If you saved to another online storage location, share the location with three classmates and ask them to download the presentation. After viewing the presentation, ask them to email you with their comments.

f. Visit three of your classmates' presentations from their storage locations. Leave a comment about their presentations or email your classmates, sharing a comment about their presentations.

g. Review the comments of your classmates.

h. Save and close the file. Based on your instructor's directions, submit p02m3Resources_GroupName.

Beyond the Classroom

Social Media Marketing

You have a bright, creative, and energetic personality, and you are using these talents in college as a senior majoring in marketing. You hope to work in social media marketing. The Marketing 405 course you are taking this semester requires every student to create a social media marketing plan for a fictional company and to present an overview of the company to the class. This presentation should include the company purpose, the company's history, and past and present projects—all of which you are to "creatively invent."

Search http://templates.office.com for an appropriate template to use in creating your presentation. Save your presentation as **p02b1Marketing_LastFirst**. Research what a social media marketing campaign entails, and use what you learn to add your own content to comply with the case requirements. Add images, transitions, and animations as desired. Organize using sections. Create a handout header with your name and a handout footer with your instructor's name and your class. Include the current date and page number. Save and close the file. Based on your instructor's directions, submit p02b1Marketing_LastFirst.

Michigan, My State

Your sister spent a lot of time researching and creating a presentation on the state of Michigan for a youth organization leader and team members. She does not like the presentation's design and has asked for your help. You show her how to download the state history report presentation template from Office.com, Presentations category, Education subcategory. Save the new presentation as **p02b2State_LastFirst**. Reuse her slides, which are saved as *p02b2Michigan*. Cut and paste the images she gathered into the correct placeholders and move bulleted text to the correct slide. Resize placeholders as needed. You tell your sister that mixing cartoons and drawings with photos is contributing to the cluttered look. Choose one format based on your preference. Create new slides with appropriate layouts as needed. You remind her that although federal government organizations allow use of their images in an educational setting, your sister should give proper credit if she is going to use their data. Give credit to the State of Michigan's website for the information obtained from Michigan.gov (http://michigan.gov/kids). Give credit to the U.S. Census Bureau (http://www.census.gov) for the Quick Facts. Finalize the presentation by deleting unneeded slides, adding appropriate sections, modifying themes, checking spelling, proofreading, and applying transitions. Create a handout header with your name and a handout footer with your instructor's name and your class. Include the current date. Print the outline as directed by your instructor. Save and close the file. Based on your instructor's directions, submit p02b2State_LastFirst.

Capstone Exercise

You are developing a report for your sociology class about the roles of women in the science, technology, engineering, and mathematics (STEM) fields. After doing some research, you begin to see that throughout history, women have had very few opportunities in these areas for historical and societal reasons. You want to demonstrate to your classmates the key and increasingly important role women have played in STEM advances. You will use your PowerPoint presentation to inform them of some key contributors in the STEM areas. In this capstone project, you concentrate on developing the content of the presentation.

Design Template

You download a template from http://templates.office.com to create the basic design and structure for your presentation, save the presentation, and create the title slide.

a. Create a new presentation using one of the available templates. Search for the template using the search term **Technology** and locate and download the **Technology at work design slides template**.

b. Save the presentation as **p02c1Women_LastFirst**.

c. Type **Women in STEM** as the title on the title slide.

d. Type the subtitle **Science, Technology, Engineering, and Mathematics** and change the font size to 20.

e. Insert 6 blank new slides.

f. Create a handout header with your name and a handout footer with your instructor's name and your class. Include the current date. Apply to all slides.

Outline and Modifications

Based on the storyboard you created after researching women in STEM on the Internet, you type the outline of your presentation. As you create the outline, you also modify the outline structure.

a. Open Outline view.

b. Type **Name 3 women in STEM** as the title for Slide 2.

c. Type each of the following as Level 1 bullets for Slide 2: **My biology teacher**, **My computer applications teacher**, **My math teacher**.

d. Type **Think on a bigger scale** as the title for Slide 3. Enter each of the following as Level 1 bullets for Slide 3: **National names?**, and **International names?**

e. Add this speaker note to Slide 3: **These may be hard questions to answer quickly because there are relatively few women in these fields**.

f. Type **Here are some names to get you started** as the title for Slide 4.

g. Type each of the following as Level 1 bullets for Slide 4: **Sally Ride**, **Christa McAuliffe**.

h. Add this speaker note to Slide 4: **For different reasons, both of these women were important in the development of the aerospace industry.**

Imported Outline

You have an outline on women in STEM that was created in Microsoft Word and also a slide show on that topic. You reuse this content to build your slide show.

a. Position the insertion point at the end of the outline after Slide 4.

b. Use the **Slides from Outline option** to insert the *p02c1Stem* outline.

c. Delete Slide 5 and any blank slides.

d. Demote the last two bullets on the new Slide 5.

e. Click the first bullet on Slide 6. Cut and paste the text after the name and date from the bullet point to the Notes pane. Replace *She* with **Hypatia**. Repeat for the remaining two bullets.

f. Delete all text after *physics* for the first bullet of Slide 7. Replace the comma with a period.

g. Position the insertion point at the end of the outline.

h. Reuse Slides 2 and 3, using the same order, from *p02c1Work* to add two slides to the end of the presentation.

i. Modify the outline structure by reversing slides 8 and 9.

Design

The content of some of the imported slides does not fit well and the font colors are not uniform across all of the slides. You want to adjust the layout and font color to create a well-designed presentation. Then you decide to view a slide show to verify your changes.

a. Switch to Normal view. Change the layout of Slide 9 to Blank.

b. Check Slides 5–7 to ensure the title placeholder font is Arial Black (Heading) with the color set to Black, Text 2. Check the subtitle font to Arial Body with the color set to Grey 80%, Text 1.

c. Use the spelling checker and proofread the presentation.

d. View a slide show from the beginning.

e. Move Slide 5 to just before Slide 8.

Sections

To facilitate organization of the presentation and moving between the slides, you create sections.

a. Add a section before Slide 2 and rename it **Quiz**.

b. Add a section before Slide 5 and rename it **History**.

c. Add a section before Slide 7 and rename it **Reasoning**.

d. Print the outline as directed by your instructor.

e. Save and close the file. Based on your instructor's directions, submit p02c1Women_LastFirst.

Presentation Design

LEARNING OUTCOME   You will use shapes, diagrams, and objects to enhance a presentation.

OBJECTIVES & SKILLS: After you read this chapter, you will be able to:

CASE STUDY | Illustrations and Infographics Workshop

This summer, you are working with several IT interns. You want to introduce the interns to drawing using computer-based drawing tools, creating infographics, and working with online pictures. You decide to teach the concepts in a PowerPoint workshop because you want to introduce the participants to an application they all have access to and because PowerPoint has many tools for creating and modifying illustrations.

You begin training by teaching the participants how to create and modify lines and shapes, how to use shapes to create flow charts, how to use SmartArt diagrams, and how to modify online pictures to meet their needs. You also demonstrate WordArt manipulation as a creative way to enhance text used in illustrations and infographics. You conclude the workshop by showing the interns how to modify and arrange objects to better meet their needs.

Illustrations and Infographics

The Project Management Life Cycle

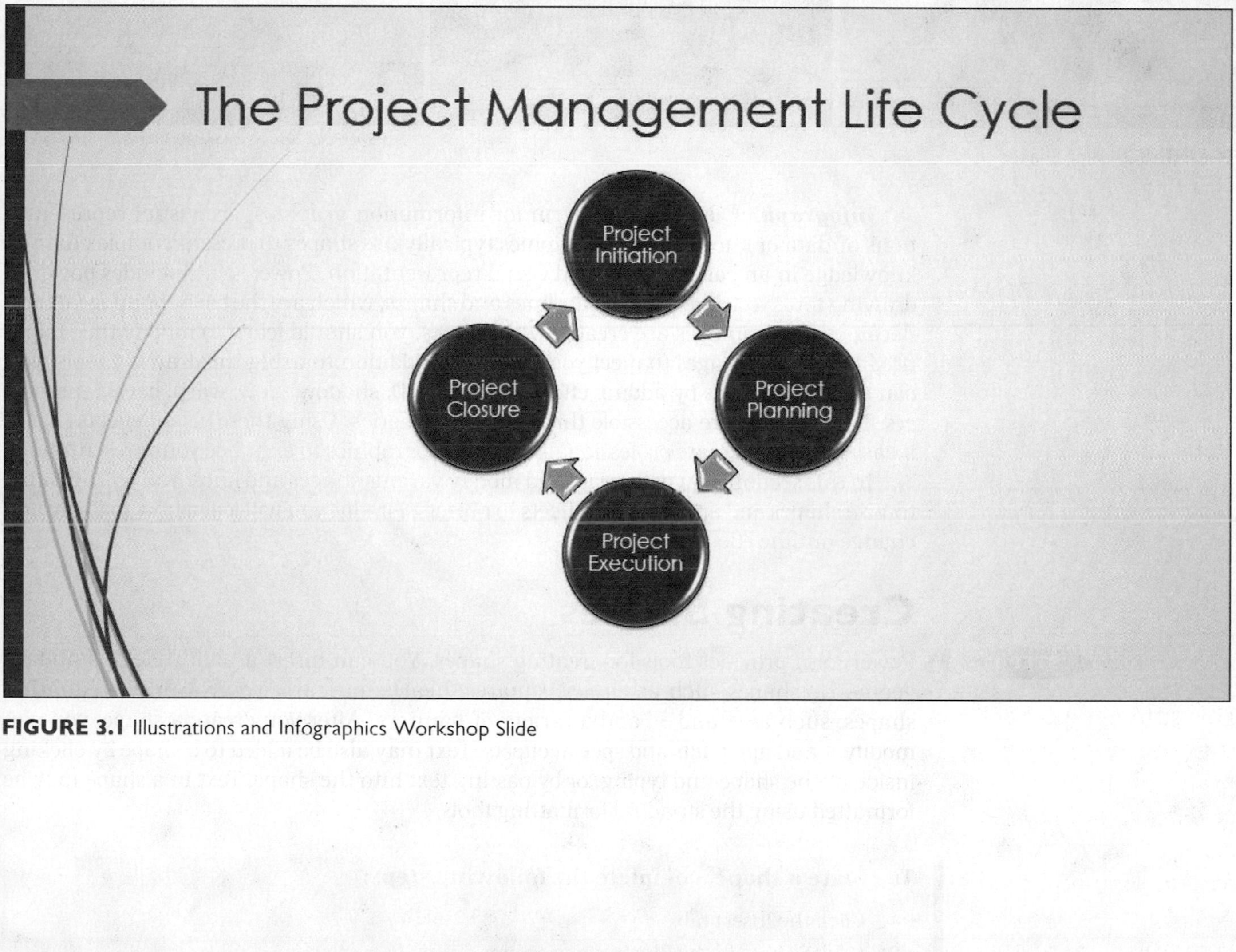

PowerPoint 2016, Windows 10, Microsoft Corporation

FIGURE 3.1 Illustrations and Infographics Workshop Slide

CASE STUDY | Illustrations and Infographics Workshop

Starting Files	Files to be Submitted
p03h1Project	p03h1Project_LastFirst
p03h2ProjectManagement	p03h3ProjectManagement_LastFirst

Shapes

Text can be very effective when giving a presentation, but sometimes an illustration or diagram can add additional clarity to the idea that is being presented. One type of visual element is a **shape**, a geometric or non-geometric object used to create an illustration or to highlight information. For example, you can create a quote inside a shape to call attention to it. You can also combine shapes to create complex images. Figure 3.2 shows three PowerPoint themes using shapes. The Berlin theme uses a rectangular shape to draw attention to the information in the title placeholder. The Vapor Trail theme uses curved shapes to create an interesting design. SmartArt in the Quotable theme uses rounded rectangles to emphasize each concept.

FIGURE 3.2 Using Shapes

PowerPoint 2016, Windows 10, Microsoft Corporation

Infographics, a shortened term for information graphics, are visual representations of data or knowledge. Infographics typically use shapes to present complex data or knowledge in an easily understood visual representation. PowerPoint includes powerful drawing tools you can use to create lines and shapes, which are the basis for infographics. Because drawn images are created with shapes, you should learn to modify the shapes used for drawn images to meet your needs. In addition to using the drawing tools, you can enhance shapes by adding effects such as 3-D, shadow, glow, warp, bevel, and others. These effects are accessible through style galleries. Using these visual effects makes it easy for you to create professional-looking infographics to enhance your presentation.

In this section, you will create and modify various shapes and lines. You will also customize shapes and apply special effects to objects. Finally, you will learn how to apply and change outline effects.

Creating Shapes

 PowerPoint provides tools for creating shapes. You can insert a multitude of standard geometric shapes such as circles, squares, hearts, or stars. You can insert equation shapes, such as + and ÷, and a variety of banners. After you create a shape, you can modify it and apply fills and special effects. Text may also be added to a shape by clicking inside of the shape and typing, or by pasting text into the shape. Text in a shape may be formatted using the standard formatting tools.

> **To create a shape, complete the following steps:**
>
> 1. Click the Insert tab.
> 2. Click Shapes in the Illustrations group.
> 3. Click the shape you want from the Shapes gallery.
> 4. Click the desired position in which to place the shape, or drag the cross-hair pointer to control the approximate size of the shape.

To resize the shape, drag any of the sizing handles that surround the shape after it is created. Figure 3.3 shows the Shapes gallery and the many shapes from which you can choose. Notice that the most recently used shapes are at the top of the list so you can conveniently reuse them.

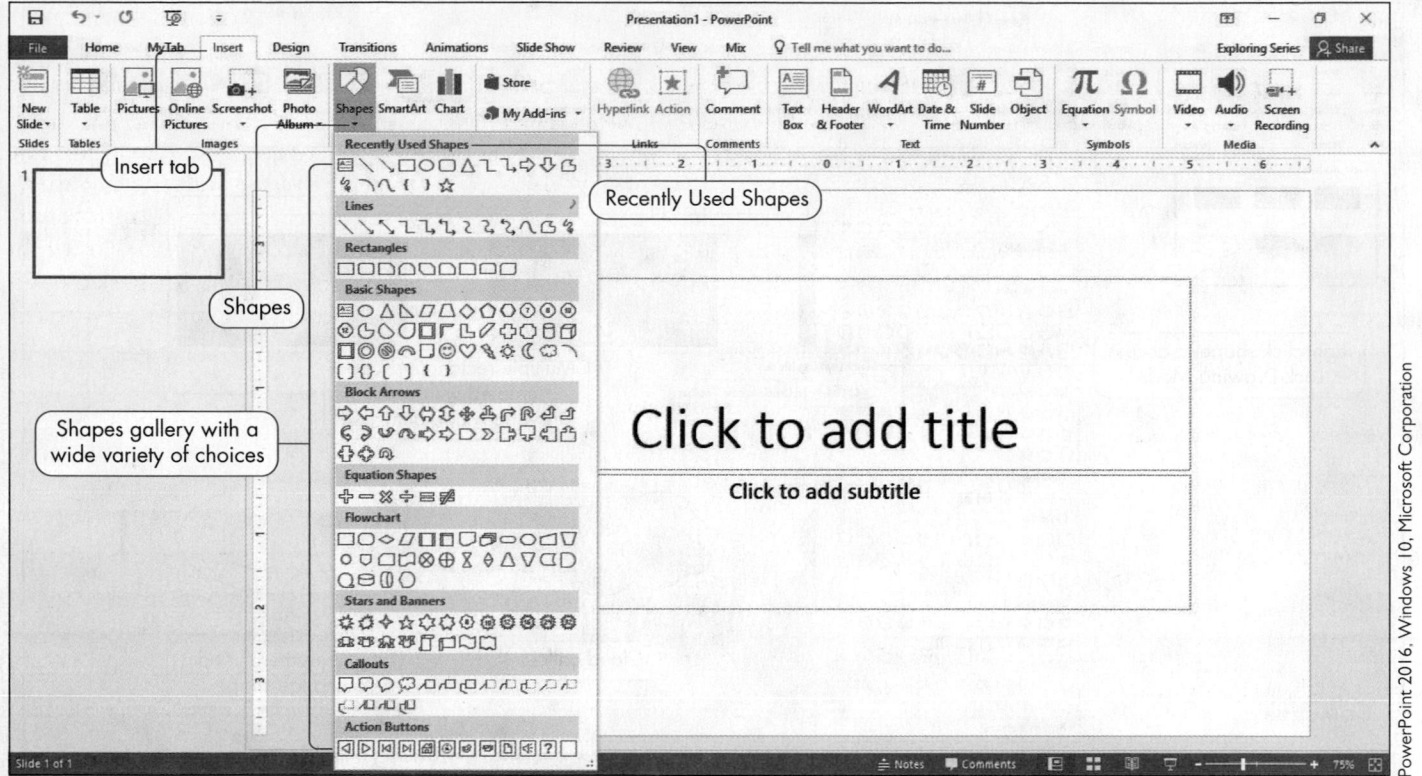

FIGURE 3.3 Shapes Gallery

TIP: USING THE DRAWING GROUP

You can also access the Shapes gallery from the Drawing group on the Home tab. The Drawing group enables you to choose a shape, arrange its order and position, apply a Quick Style, and then change properties of the shape. If you have a widescreen monitor or if your monitor is set for a higher resolution, the Drawing group displays individual shapes instead of one Shapes command. If you only see one shape, click the More button to open the Shapes gallery.

The Shapes command deactivates the selected shape after you draw it once, forcing you to reselect the shape each time you want to use it. By activating the *Lock Drawing Mode* feature, you can add several shapes of the same type on your slide without selecting the shape each time.

To activate Lock Drawing Mode, complete the following steps:

1. Right-click the shape you want to use in the Shapes gallery and select Lock Drawing Mode.
2. Click anywhere on the slide or drag to create the first shape.
3. Click or drag repeatedly to create additional shapes of the same type.
4. Press Esc to release Lock Drawing Mode.

Figure 3.4 shows a series of rectangles created with Lock Drawing Mode activated, a basic oval, and smiley face all of that are located in the Basic Shapes category in the Shapes gallery. In addition, a *callout* is shown that was created using the Cloud Callout located in the Callouts category. A callout is a shape that can be used to add text, often used in cartooning. Notice that the smiley face shape is selected on the slide. The sizing handles display around the shape. A yellow circle is located on the mouth of the shape. This is an *adjustment handle* that you can drag to change the shape. If you drag the adjustment handle upward, the smile becomes a frown. Some shapes have an adjustment handle, and some do not.

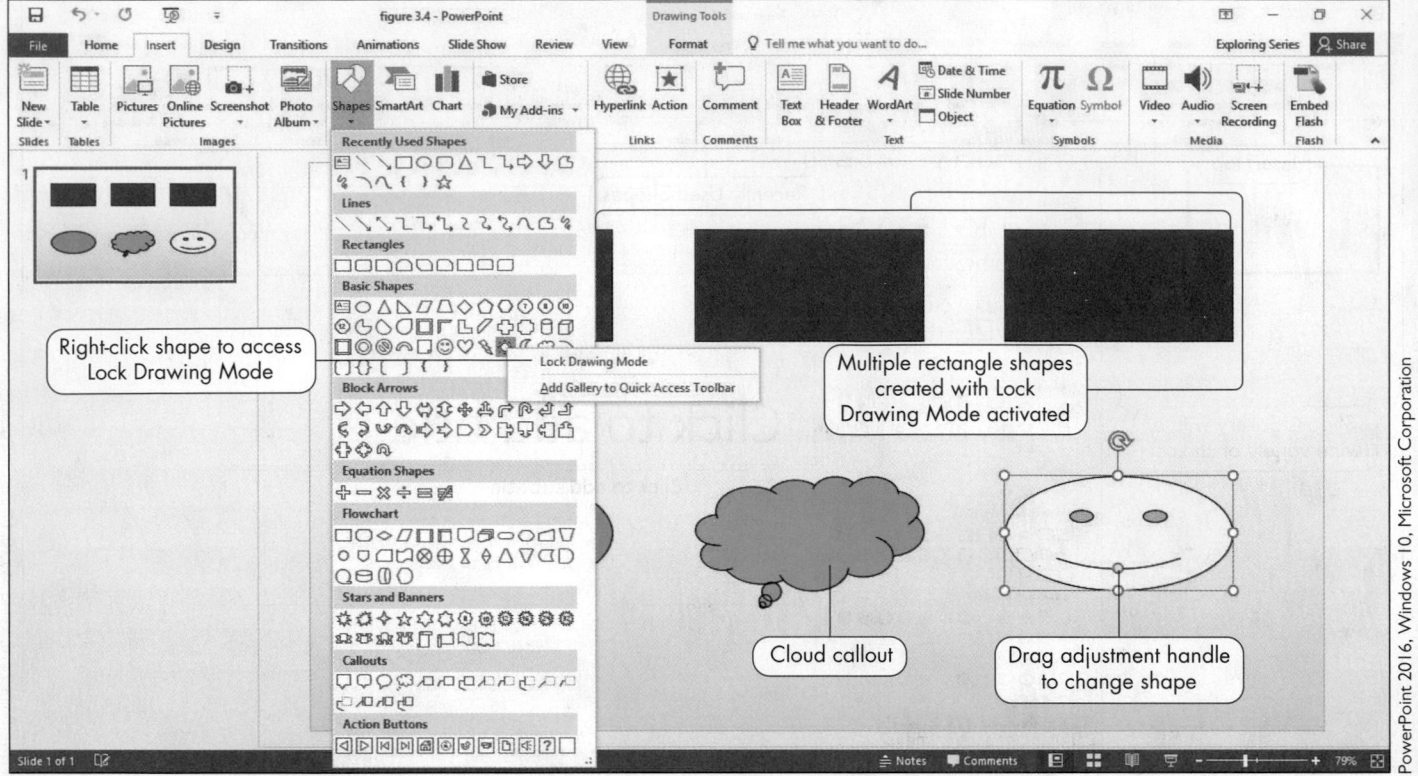

FIGURE 3.4 Basic Shapes

TIP: CONSTRAIN A SHAPE

A rectangle can be constrained or forced to form a perfect square, and an oval or ellipse can be constrained to form a perfect circle. To constrain a shape, press and hold Shift as you drag to create the shape. Or, if you click on the screen instead of dragging when you initially create the shape, you get a perfect 1-inch square or a perfect 1-inch diameter circle.

Draw Lines and Connectors

STEP 2 ▶▶ Lines are shapes that can be used to point to information, to connect shapes on a slide, or to divide a slide into sections. Lines also are often used in slide design.

To draw a straight line, complete the following steps:

1. Select Line in the Lines category of the Shapes gallery.
2. Position the pointer on the slide where you want the line to begin.
3. Drag to create the line. Hold Shift as you drag to constrain to a perfectly horizontal, vertical, or any multiple of a 45-degree angle line.

You can also create curved lines. These may take a little practice to get the curve you want.

To create a curved line, complete the following steps:

1. Click Curve in the Lines category of the Shapes gallery.
2. Click the slide at the location where you want to start the curve.
3. Click again where the peaks or valleys of the curve occur and continue to click and move the pointer to shape the curve in the desired pattern.
4. Double-click to end the curve.

As you click while creating the curve, you set a point for the curve to bend around. To draw a shape that looks like it was drawn with a pen, select the Scribble shape.

In addition to drawing simple lines to create dividing lines and waves, you may need **connectors**, or lines with connection points at each end. Connectors stay connected to the shapes or placeholders to which you attach them. Connector lines move with shapes when the shapes are moved. The three types of connectors are: line (to create straight lines), elbow (to create angled lines), and curved. Not all line shapes are connectors. To determine which line shapes are connectors, point to the line in the gallery and a ScreenTip will appear with the shape name, such as Curved Arrow Connector.

The first step in working with connectors is to create the shapes you want to connect with lines. Once the shapes are created, you can use connectors to join them.

To connect shapes, complete the following steps:

1. Create the shapes you wish to connect.
2. Select a connector line from the Lines category of the Shape gallery.
3. Move the pointer over a shape; circles appear around the shape. These are the locations where you can attach the connector.
4. Click one of the circles to connect the line and drag to the next shape, releasing the mouse button when you see the circle on the shape to which you want to connect. You can also drag to control the direction and size of the connector line.

If you move a shape that is joined to another shape using a connector line, the line moves with it, extending or shortening as necessary to maintain the connection. Sometimes when you rearrange the shapes, the connectors may no longer extend to the shape that was not moved, or the connectors may cross shapes and be confusing. If that happens, you can use the yellow adjustment handle located on the connector line to reshape the connectors. Select the connector lines and drag the handles to obtain a clearer path.

A **flow chart** is an illustration that shows a sequence to be followed or a plan containing steps. For example, you could use a flow chart to illustrate the sequence to follow when implementing a new product. Connector lines join the shapes in a flow chart.

The typical flow chart sequence includes start and end points shown in oval shapes, steps shown in rectangular shapes, and decisions to be made shown in diamond shapes. Colored shapes are optional, but be sure to be consistent when you apply color. Connectors with arrows demonstrate the order in which the sequence should be followed to accomplish the goal. Each shape in a flow chart has a label to which you can add text.

When you select a shape and type text in it or when you paste text into a shape, the text becomes part of the shape. Sometimes, however, it is necessary to add a text to a slide and you do not have a placeholder or shape in which to place the text. You can add a **text box**, an object that provides space for text. A text box can be more flexible than content placeholders and can be added to slides in which the chosen layout does not include a content placeholder, but text is still necessary. For example, use a text box to add a quote to a slide that is separate from the slide content placeholder. Text inside a text box can be formatted just as text in placeholders is formatted. You can even add a border, fill, shadow, or 3-D effect to the text in a text box. Figure 3.5 shows a basic flow chart created with shapes, connectors, and text boxes.

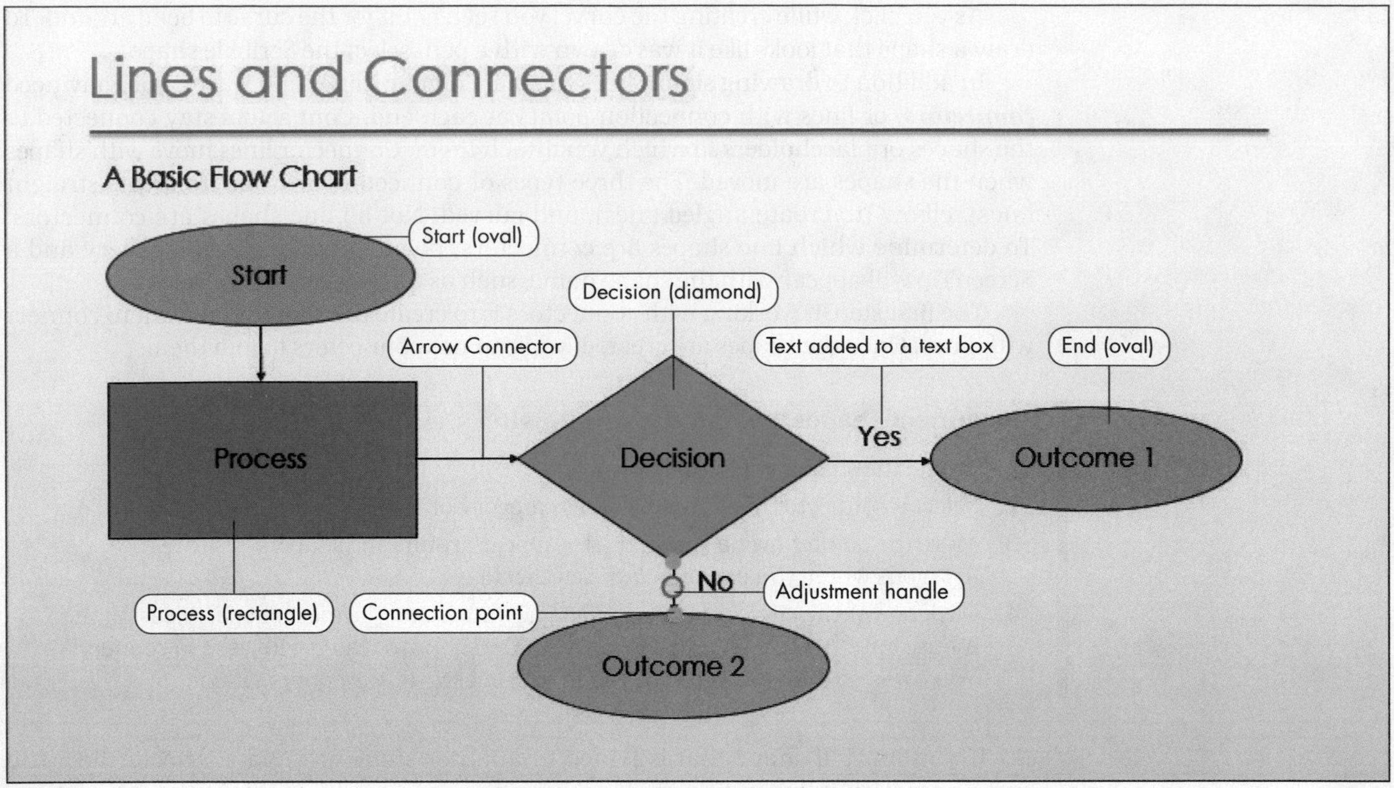

Lines and Connectors

A Basic Flow Chart

Start (oval)

Start

Decision (diamond)

Arrow Connector

Text added to a text box

End (oval)

Process

Decision

Yes

Outcome 1

Process (rectangle)

Connection point

No

Adjustment handle

Outcome 2

FIGURE 3.5 Basic Flow Chart

Create and Modify Freeform Shapes

A *freeform shape* is a shape that can be used to create customized shapes using both curved and straight-line segments. It enables you to draw whatever you want, like you would draw with a pencil on a sheet of paper. A freeform shape can be comprised of straight-line segments and curved segments. One use for the freeform tool is to trace a picture.

To create a freeform shape, complete the following steps:

1. Select the Freeform shape in the Lines category of the Shapes gallery and click the slide to set the starting point for the shape.
2. Click to draw straight lines and drag to create curves.
3. Double-click to end the freeform shape.

TIP: CREATE A CLOSED SHAPE
If you use the Curve, Freeform, or Scribble line tool to create a shape and end the shape at its starting point, the starting point and ending points join to create a closed shape. The advantage of joining the ends of the line and creating a closed shape is that you can include a fill, or interior content.

Sometimes, the freeform shape you have drawn is not exactly as you desired. You can modify the freeform shape to achieve the desired shape. This can be achieved through the help of a vertex. A *vertex*, also known as an anchor point, is a black square that controls a curved line segment and indicates where two line segments meet or end. You can control the shape by using these anchor points. Click a point to move and drag it to a new position or to modify the shape's line segment curve. A vertex can be deleted if you right-click the point and select Delete Point. Either moving a vertex or deleting it will redefine the object's shape. Figure 3.6 shows a freeform shape with its vertexes displayed. Figure 3.7 shows a selected vertex dragged to a new position. When you release the left mouse button, the freeform will take the new shape.

CHAPTER 3 • Presentation Design

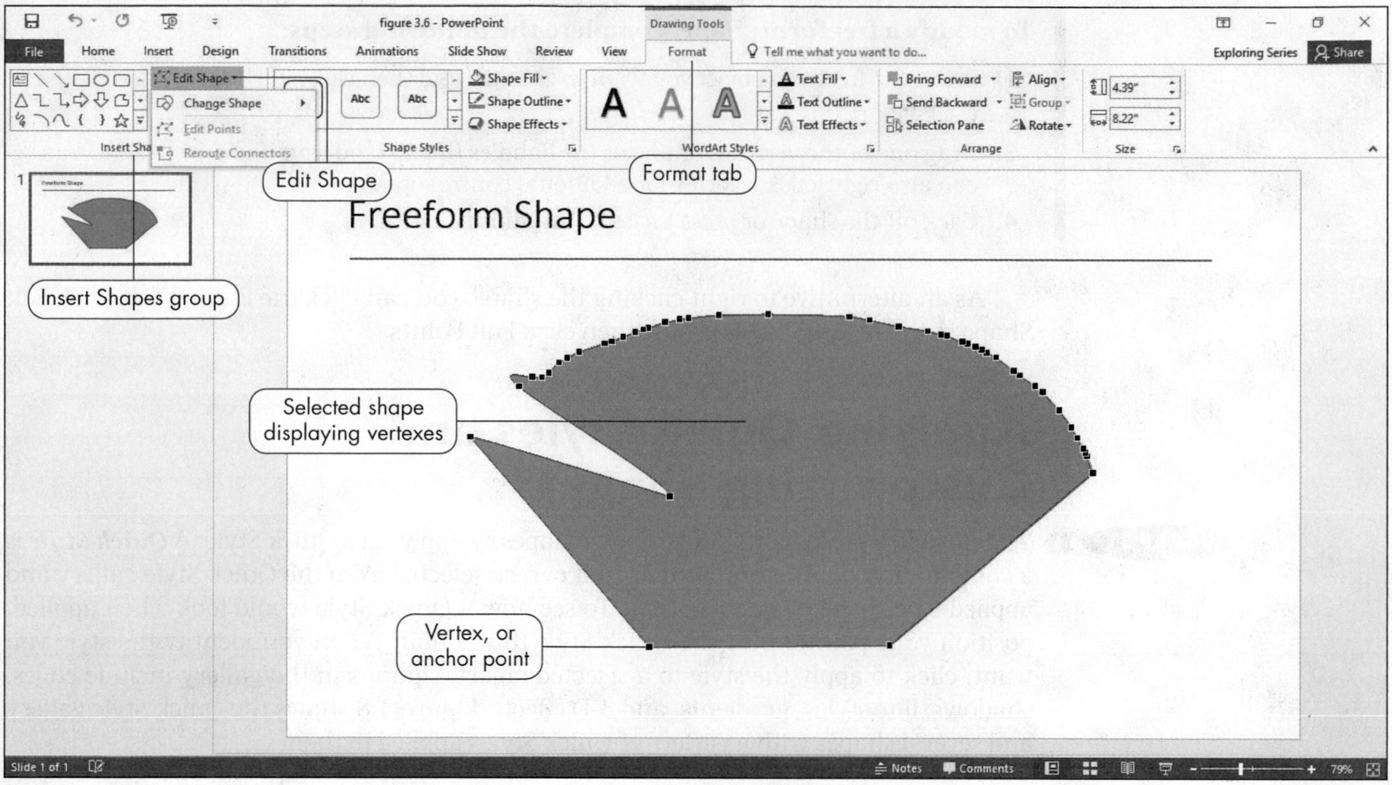

PowerPoint 2016, Windows 10, Microsoft Corporation

FIGURE 3.6 Modifying a Freeform Shape

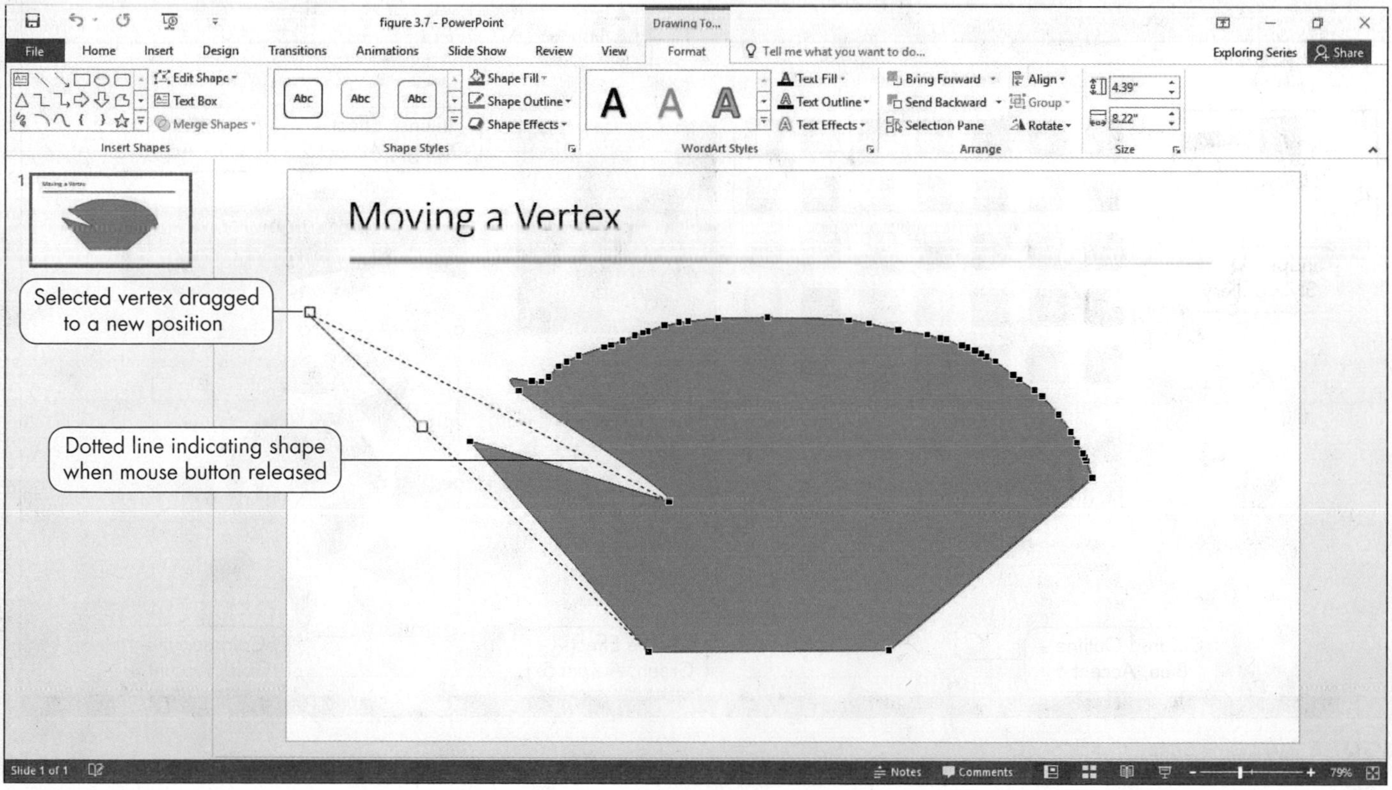

PowerPoint 2016, Windows 10, Microsoft Corporation

FIGURE 3.7 Moving a Vertex

As an alternative to right clicking the shape, you can click the Format tab, click Edit Shape in the Insert Shapes group, then click Edit Points.

Applying Quick Styles and Customizing Shapes

STEP 3 ▶▶ You can add a professional look to your shapes by applying a Quick Style. A **Quick Style** is a combination of different formats that can be selected from the Quick Style gallery and applied to a shape or other objects. To see how a Quick Style would look when applied, position your pointer over the Quick Style thumbnail. When you identify the style you want, click to apply the style to a selected object. Options in the gallery include edges, shadows, line styles, gradients, and 3-D effects. Figure 3.8 shows the Quick Style gallery and several shapes with a variety of Quick Styles applied to them.

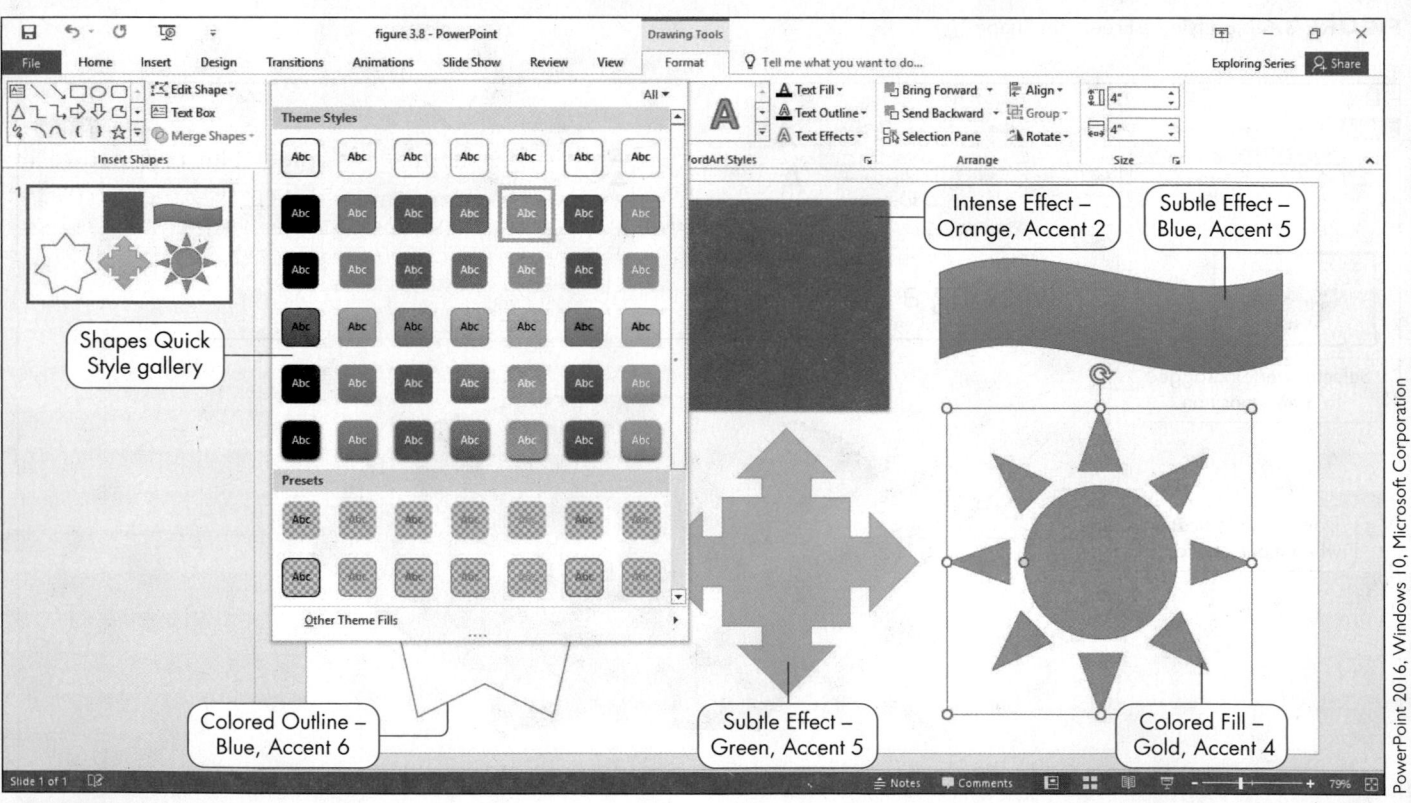

FIGURE 3.8 Using Shape Quick Styles

To apply a Quick Style to a shape, complete the following steps:

1. Select the shape and click the Format tab.
2. Click the More button in the Shape Styles group. This enables you to apply a Quick Style or to select the fill and outline of the shape manually and apply special effects.
3. Preview the styles in the Quick Styles gallery by moving the pointer over the various styles.
4. Click the Quick Style you wish to apply.

As an alternative to using the Format tab, you can click the Home tab and click Quick Styles in the Drawing group.

To apply a Quick Style to multiple objects, use a **selection net** or **marquee**. A selection net or marquee is a selection of multiple objects and is created by dragging a rectangle around all of the objects you want to select and ending the selection by releasing the mouse button. All objects contained entirely within the net will be selected. With the objects selected, you can apply a Quick Style to all the objects at the same time.

TIP: SELECTING MULTIPLE OBJECTS

If objects are difficult to select with a selection net because of their placement or because they are nonadjacent, press and hold Ctrl or Shift as you click each object. While the Ctrl or Shift keys are pressed, as you click each object it is added to the selection. When you have selected all objects, choose the style or effect you want, and it will apply only to the selected objects. If you click an object you do not want to include, simply click it a second time and it will be removed from the selection.

Change Shape Fills

One way to customize a shape is by changing the shape fill, or the interior format of the shape. You can choose a solid color fill, no fill, a picture fill, a gradient fill, or a texture fill. These options are available from the Shape Fill gallery in the Shape Styles group on the Format tab. The Shape Fill gallery provides color choices that match the theme colors or color choices based on standard colors. Figure 3.9 shows the Shape Fill options and a shape filled with the Theme color Gold, Accent 4.

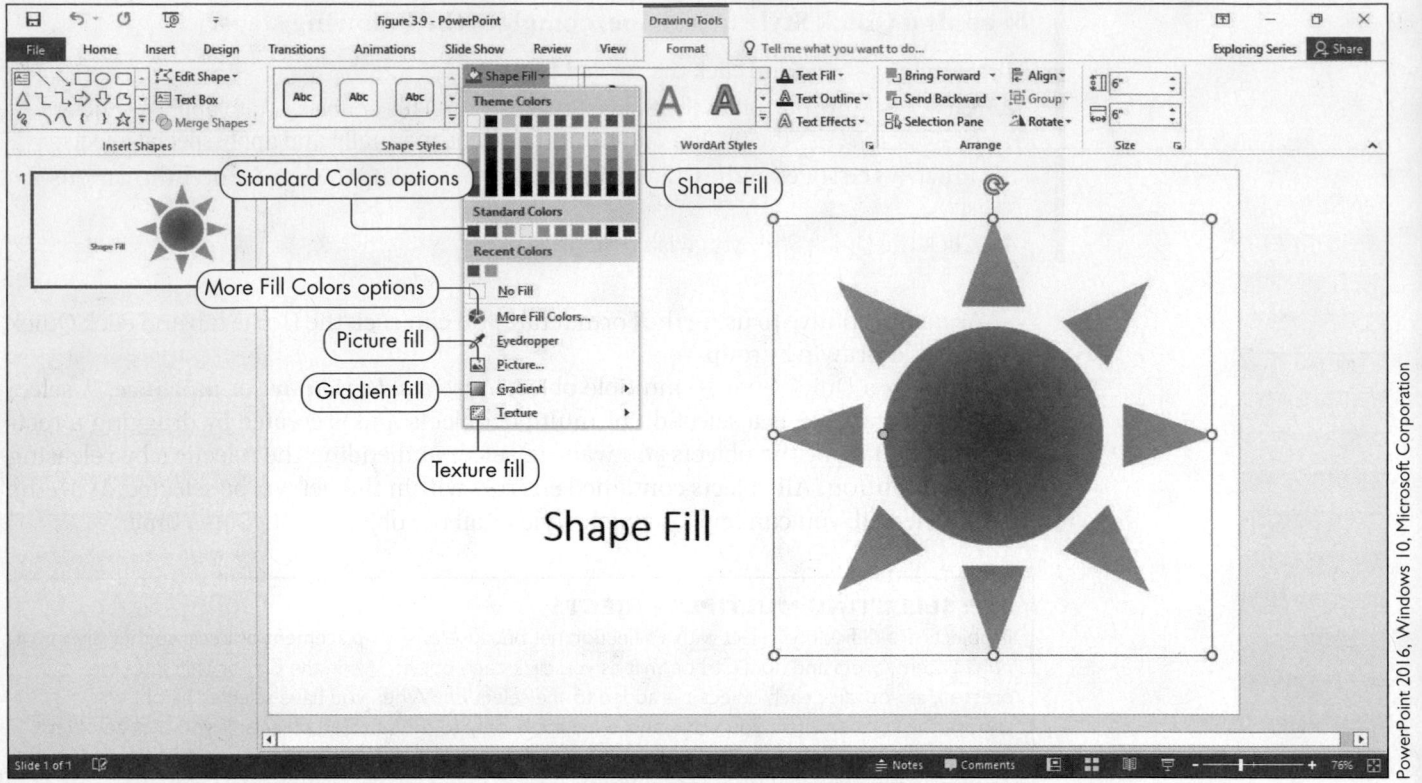

FIGURE 3.9 Shape Fill Options

To change the fill of a selected object, complete the following steps:

1. Select the shape and click the Format tab.
2. Click the Shape Fill arrow in the Shape Styles group.
3. Select the fill option you want.

You may want to recreate an exact color in another part of your presentation by using the *Eyedropper*. The Eyedropper enables you to match colors used in other slides to create a unified look to your presentation. For example, you want to re-create the yellow in a sunset used in the introduction slide of your presentation. Figure 3.10 shows a color picked up by the Eyedropper and applied to another object.

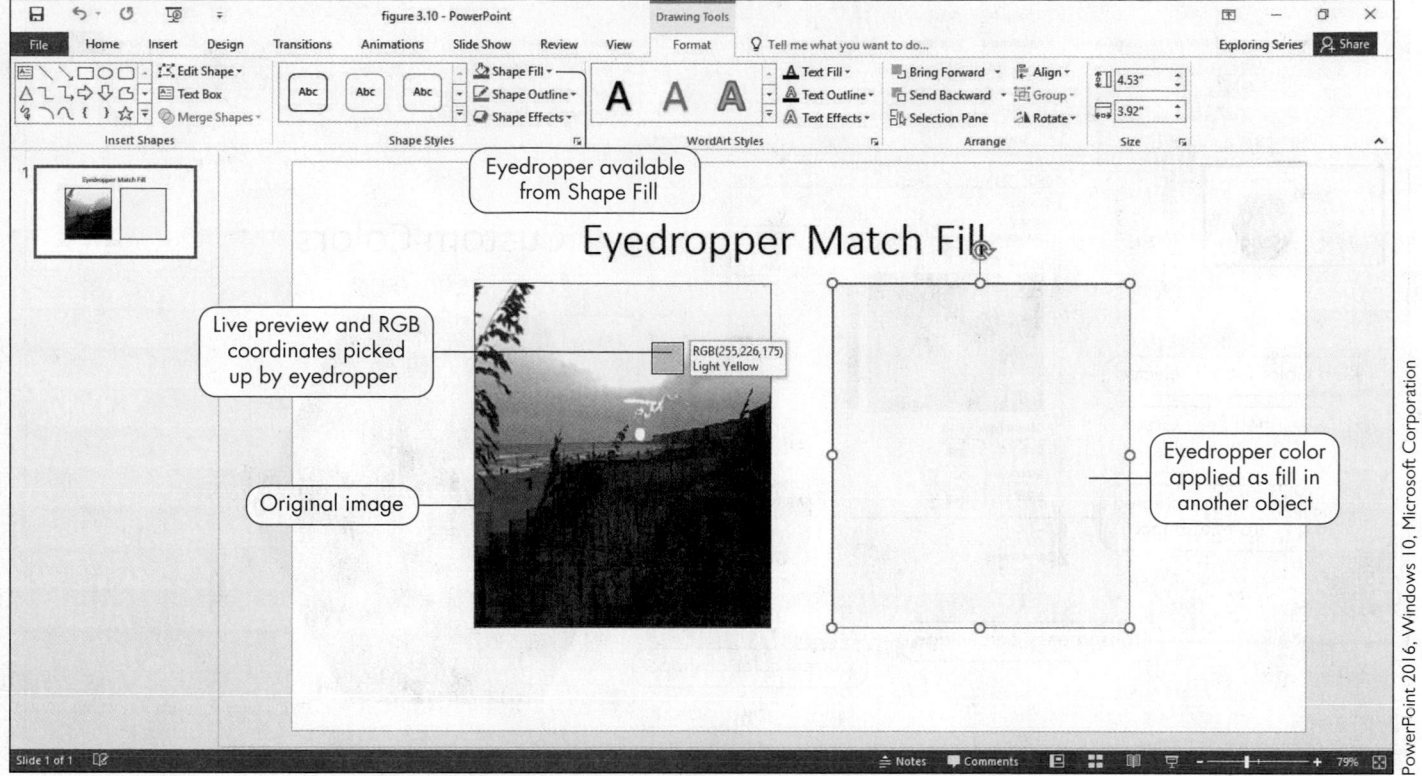

FIGURE 3.10 Using the Eyedropper

> ### To use the Eyedropper to match colors, complete the following steps:
>
> 1. Click the shape you want to fill, click the Shape Fill arrow in the Shape Styles group on the Format tab, and then select Eyedropper.
> 2. Point to the color you want to recreate. While pointing to different colors, you will see a Live Preview of the color aiding you in your decision of which color to select.
> 3. Click and the shape will fill with the color in the Eyedropper. If you decide you do not want to use the Eyedropper, press Esc.

Alternatively, you may also select More Fill Colors to open the Colors dialog box where you can mix colors based on an RGB color model (Red Green Blue) or an HSL color model (Hue Saturation Luminosity). The default RGB color model gives each of the colors red, green, and blue a numeric value that ranges from 0 to 255. The combination of these values creates the fill color assigned to the shape. When all three RGB values are 0, you get black. When all three RGB values are 255, you get white. By using different combinations of numbers between 0 and 255, you can create more than 16 million shades of color.

The Colors dialog box also enables you to determine the amount of *transparency*, or visibility of the fill. At 0% transparency, the fill is *opaque* (or solid), while at 100% transparency, the fill is clear. The Colors dialog box enables you to drag a slider to specify the percentage of transparency. Figure 3.11 shows the Colors dialog box with the RGB color model selected, Red assigned a value of 236, Green assigned a value of 32, Blue assigned a value of 148, and a transparency set at 0%.

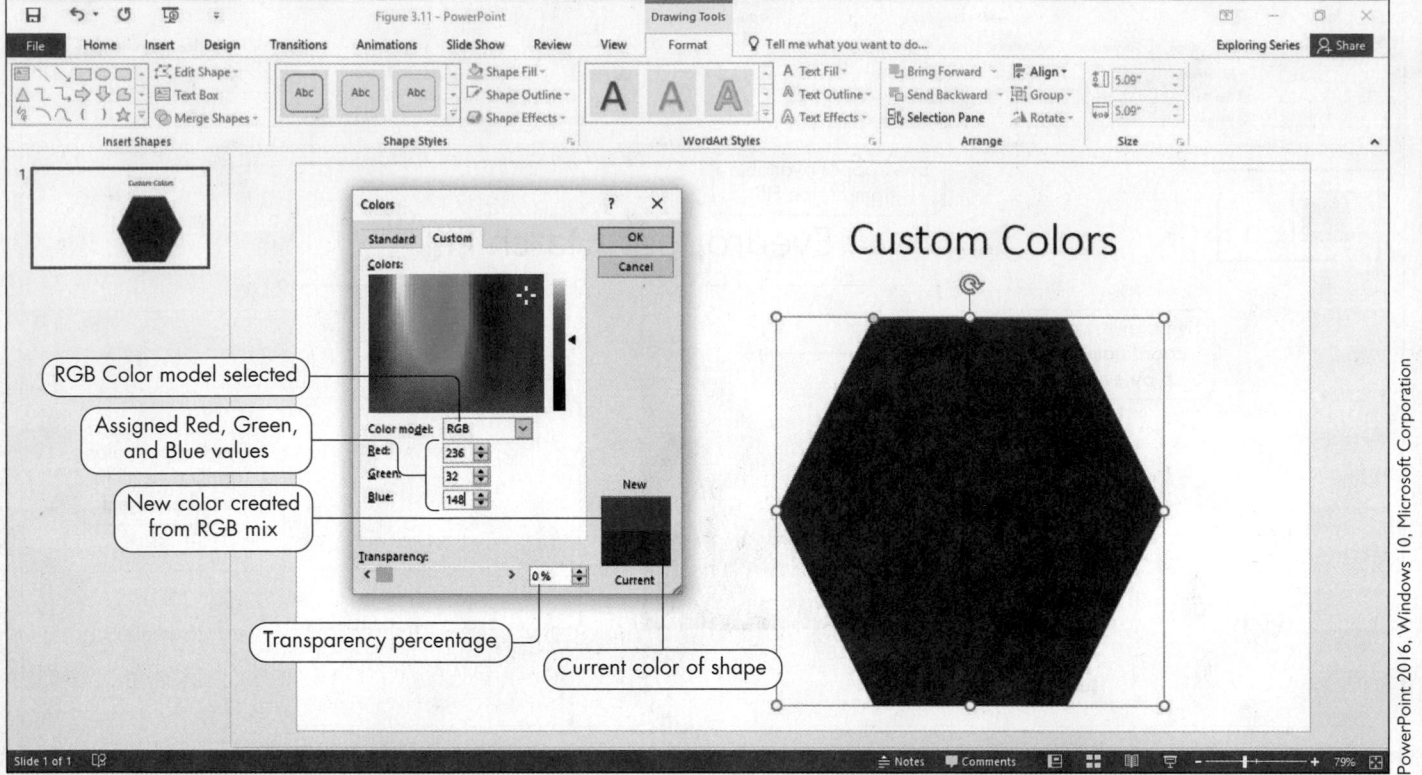

FIGURE 3.11 Colors Dialog Box

You can fill shapes with images using the *picture fill* option. This option enables you to create unusual frames for your pictures and can be a fun way to vary the images in your presentation.

To insert a picture as a fill, complete the following steps:

1. Click the shape you want to fill, click the Shape Fill arrow in the Shape Styles group on the Format tab, and then click Picture.
2. Click Browse to locate a picture from a file that you want to add and double-click the picture to insert it. To insert an online picture, click Search Bing to search the Web for a Bing image.

Figure 3.12 shows the 7-Point Star shape filled with a picture that was saved on the computer hard drive. The image is of a wildflower growing through snow that the presenter selected to enhance a presentation about perseverance.

PowerPoint 2016, Windows 10, Microsoft Corporation

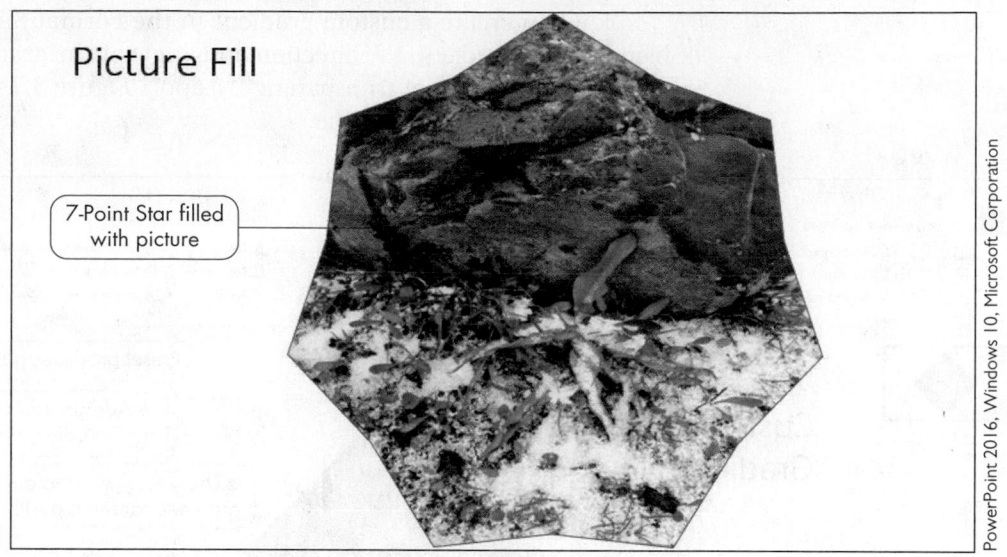

FIGURE 3.12 Shape Filled with a Picture

You can fill shapes with a ***gradient fill***, a blend of two or more colors. When you select Gradient from the Shape Fill gallery, another gallery of options opens, enabling you to select Light and Dark Variations that blend the current color with white or black in linear or radial gradients. Figure 3.13 shows the gradient options for a selected object.

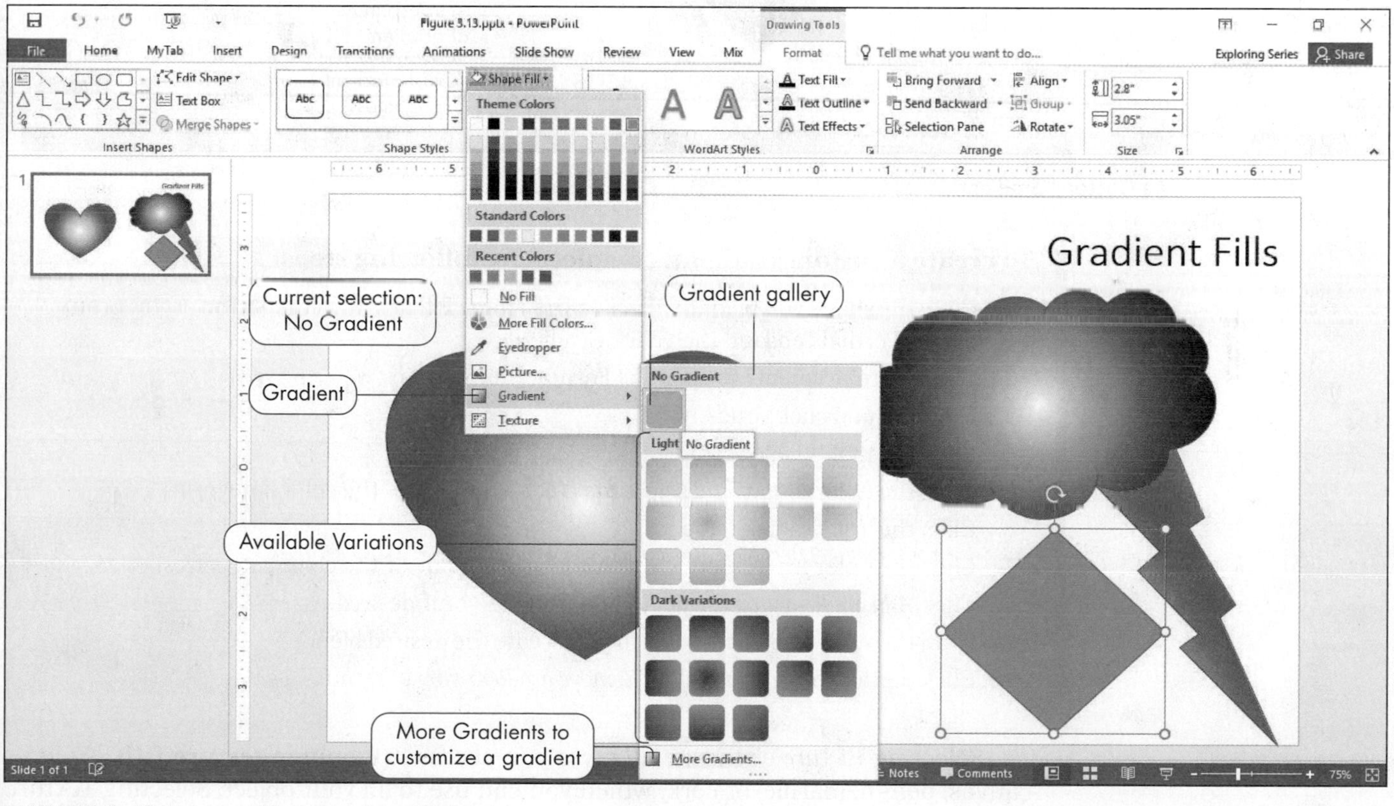

PowerPoint 2016, Windows 10, Microsoft Corporation

FIGURE 3.13 Light and Dark Gradient Variations

When you select More Gradients at the bottom of the Gradients gallery, the Format Shape pane opens. The Gradient fill option in the Fill section provides access to the Preset gradients gallery. This gallery gives you a variety of gradients using a multitude of colors based on the theme for the presentation.

You can create a custom gradient in the Format Shape pane. Select the colors to blend for the gradient, the direction and angle of the gradient, the brightness of the colors, and the amount of transparency to apply. Figure 3.14 shows a custom gradient created in the Format Shape pane.

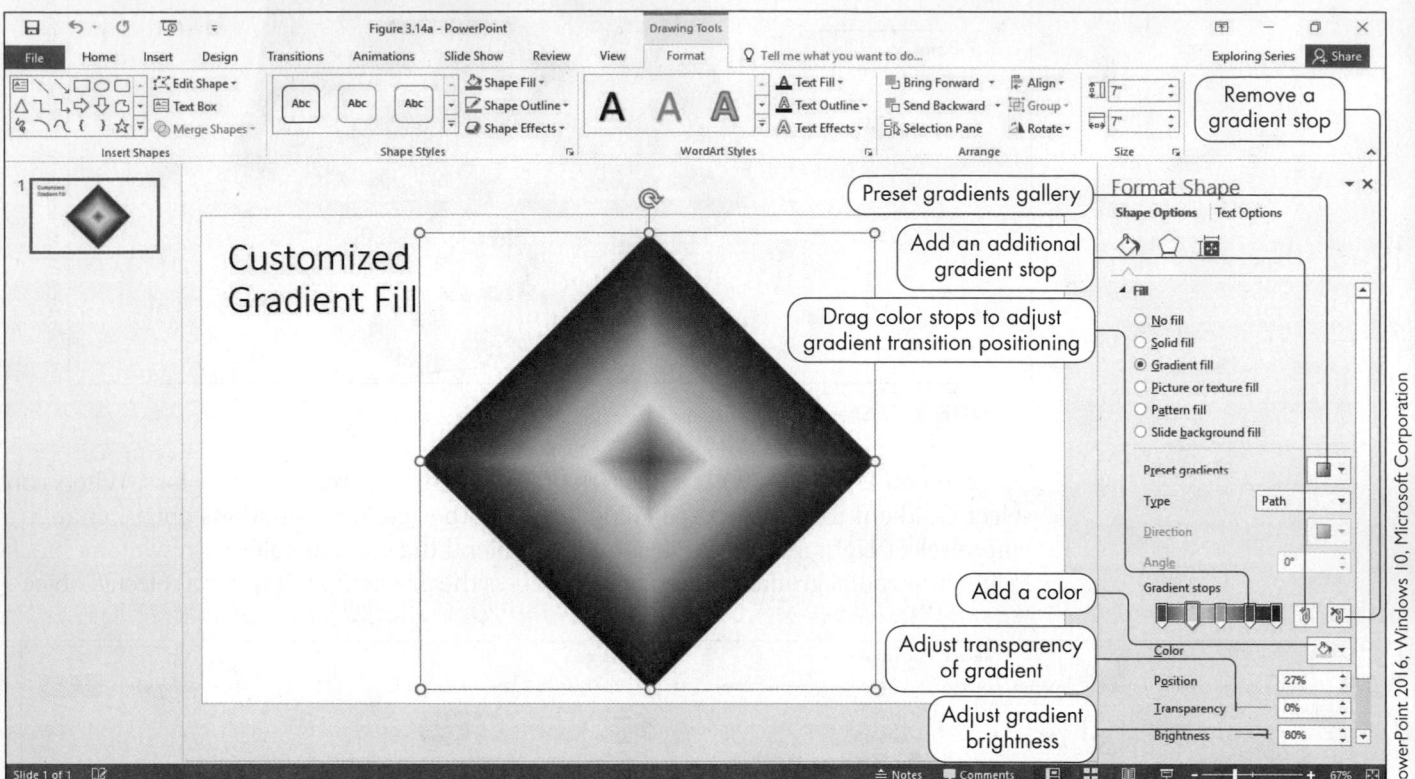

FIGURE 3.14 Creating a Custom Gradient

To create a custom gradient, complete the following steps:

1. Click the shape you want to fill, click the Shape Fill arrow in the Shape Styles group on the Format tab, and then click Gradient.
2. Click More Gradients to open the Format Shape pane.
3. Click Fill and click Gradient Fill.
4. Click the first Gradient stop.
5. Click the Color arrow and select the color from one of the color categories.
6. Click the last Gradient stop.
7. Click the Color arrow and select the color from one of the color categories.
8. Click *Add gradient stop* to add an additional color if desired.
9. Drag the new gradient stop until you create the desired blend.
10. Click a gradient stop and click *Remove gradient stop* to remove a color.

Selecting *Picture or texture fill* gives you access to common ***texture fills***, such as canvas, denim, marble, or cork, which you can use to fill your object. Selecting Texture opens the Texture gallery, with options for setting a transparency level and tiling. Tiled textures have seamless edges so that you cannot tell where one tile ends and another begins. Figure 3.15 shows the Texture gallery and a Plaque shape with an Oak texture applied. The first plaque is scaled at 100% while the second plaque Scale X was scaled to 75% and and Scale Y was scaled to 50%.

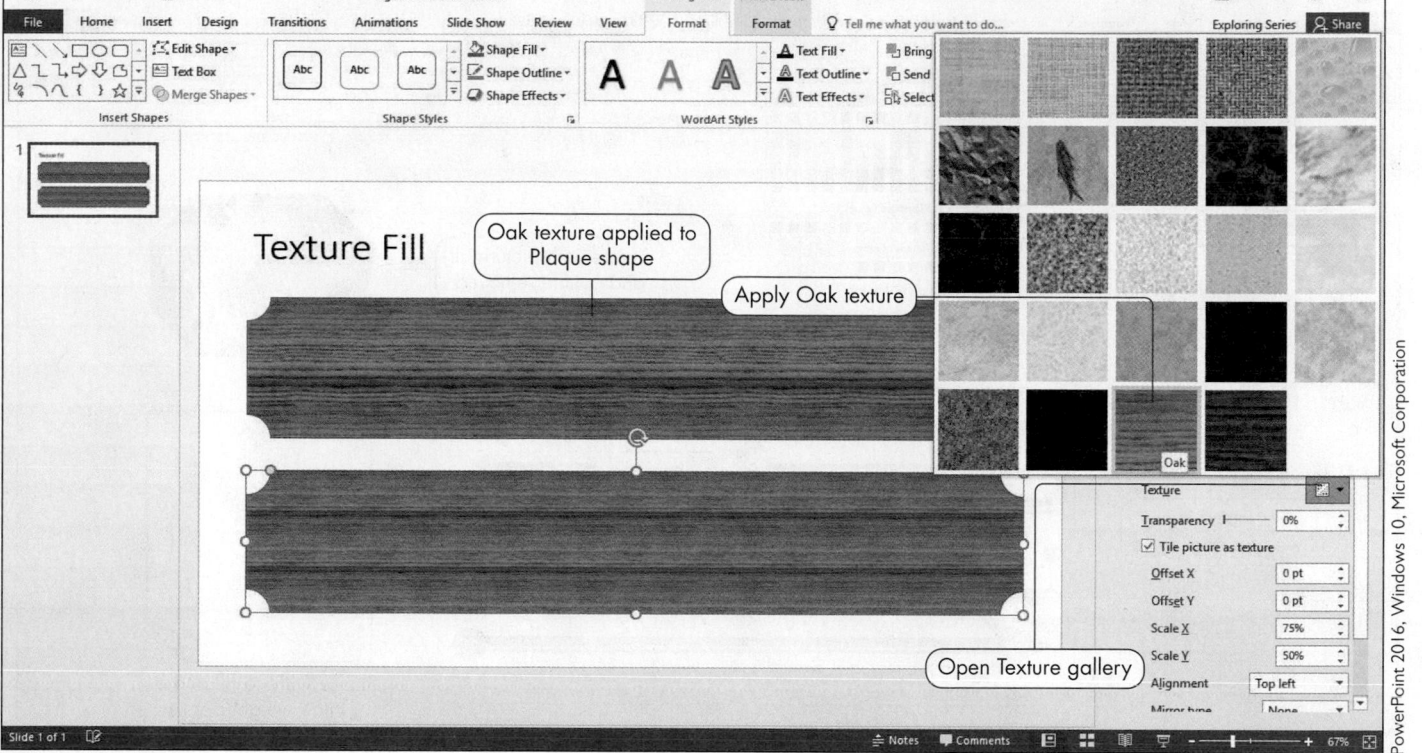

FIGURE 3.15 Texture Fills

To apply a texture fill, complete the following steps:

1. Click the shape you want to fill, click the Shape Fill arrow Shape Styles group on the Format tab, and then click Texture.
2. Select More Textures to open the Format Shape pane.
3. Click Picture or texture fill and then click the Texture arrow.
4. Click the texture you want to apply to your shape.
5. Select scaling, if desired.

Change Shape Outlines

By default, outlines form a border around a shape. You can modify a shape's outline by changing its color, style, or *line weight* (thickness). Figure 3.16 shows examples of each of these modifications. You can modify outlines by using the Shape Styles feature accessible in the Shape Styles group on the Format tab, or by clicking the Shape Styles Dialog Box Launcher to open the Format Shape pane. Click the Fill & Line icon and then click Line.

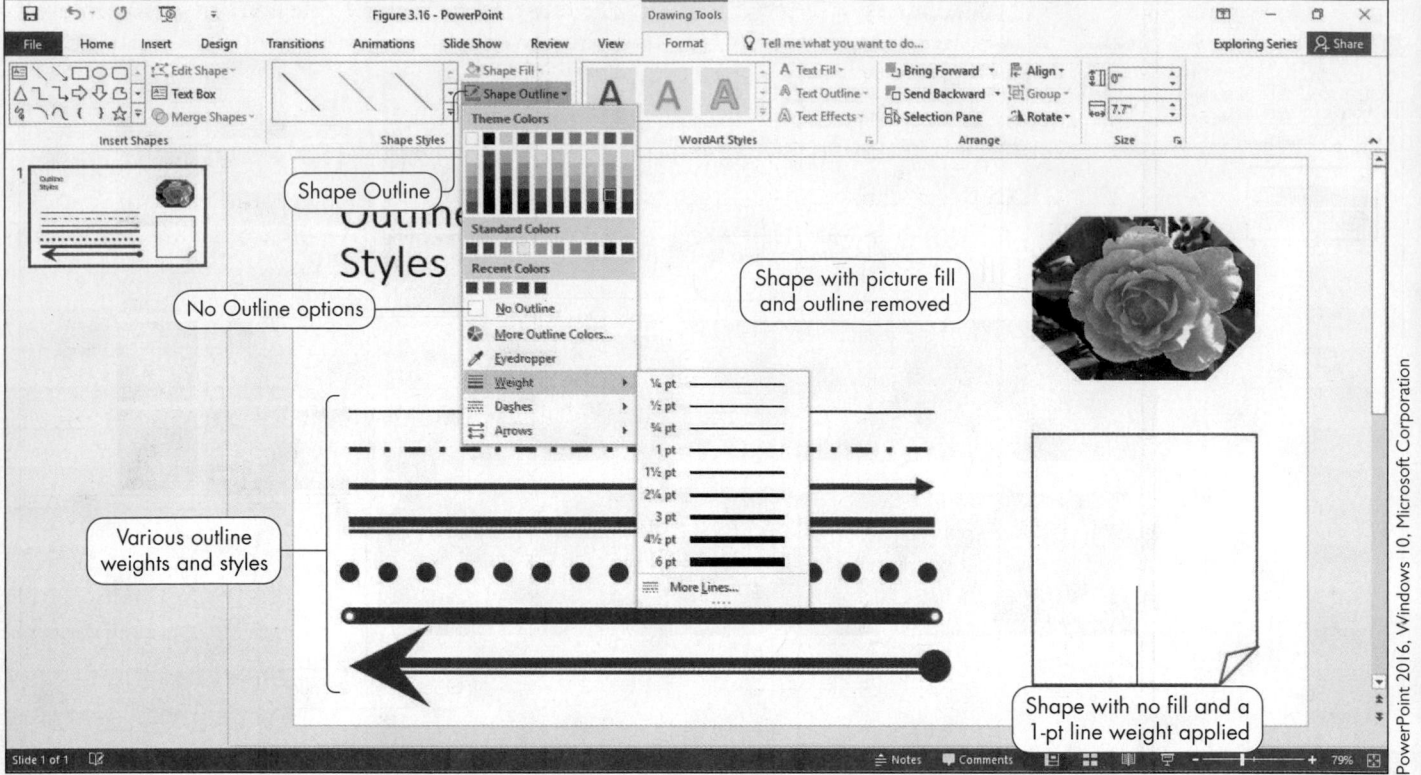

FIGURE 3.16 Outline Colors, Styles, and Weights

You can customize outlines using the Shape Outline gallery options available in the Shape Styles group or the Line options in the Format Shape pane.

To change an outline color, complete the following steps:

1. Click the shape you want to change the outline color of and then click the Shape Outline arrow in the Shape Styles group on the Format tab.
2. Select a theme color, a standard color, or a color from the More Outline Colors option.

The width or thickness of a line is measured in ***points*** (pt), the smallest unit of measurement in typography. One vertical inch contains 72 pt. If you do not want an outline around a shape, click No Outline in the Shape Outline gallery. See Figure 3.16 to see an example of a shape with a picture fill that has the outline removed so it does not detract from the image.

To set the line width, complete the following steps:

1. Select a line or an object with an outline and click the Format tab.
2. Click the Shape Outline arrow in the Shape Styles group, and point to Weight to display line weight choices from 1/4 pt to 6 pt.
3. Click one of the weight options or click More Lines.

Selecting More Lines opens the Format Shape pane with the Line options displayed. The Format Shape pane enables you to change the line weight using the spin arrows in the Width box or by typing the weight directly into the Width box. You can also use the Format Shape pane to create Compound type outlines, which combine thick and thin lines.

For variety, you can change a solid line to a dashed line. Dashed lines make interesting boxes or borders for shapes and placeholders by using round dots, square dots, and combinations of short dashes, long dashes, and dots.

To make a line or object outline dashed, complete the following steps:

1. Select a line or an object with an outline.
2. Click the Shape Outline arrow in the Shape Styles group on the Format tab, and point to Dashes to display dash options.
3. Click the desired dash style.

You can add an arrowhead to the beginning or end of a line to create an arrow that points to critical information on the slide. The Shape Outline feature enables you to create many different styles of arrows using points, circles, and diamonds.

To add an arrowhead, complete the following steps:

1. Select a line.
2. Click the Shape Outline arrow in the Shape Styles group on the Format tab, and point to Arrows to display start and end arrow options.
3. Click the desired arrow style.

Change Shape Effects

STEP 4 ▶▶ PowerPoint enables you to apply many stunning effects to shapes: preset three-dimensional effects, shadow effects, reflections, glows, soft edge effects, bevels, and 3-D rotations. Shape effects will change if you choose a new theme. Figure 3.17 shows an example of some of the shape effects available.

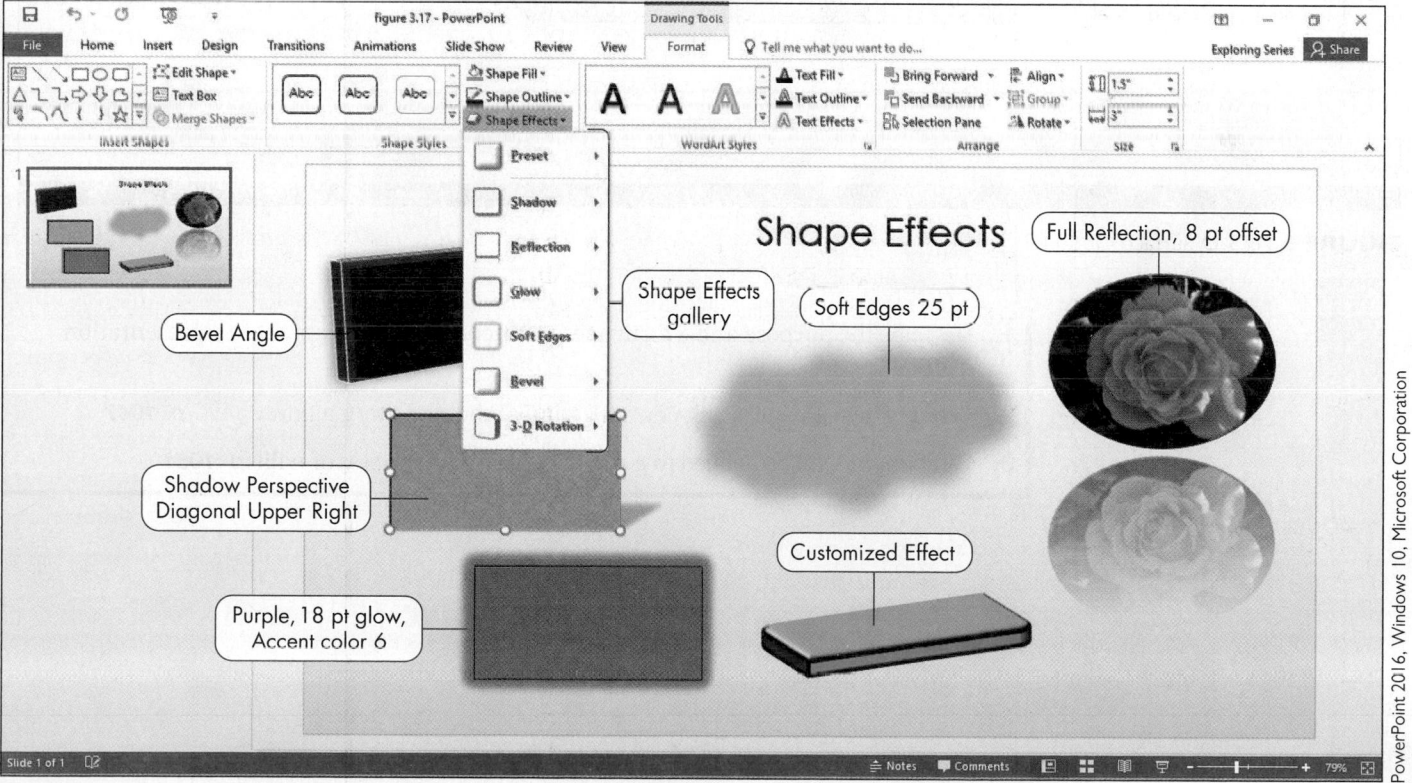

FIGURE 3.17 Sample Shape Effects

To customize an effect, click 3-D Options at the bottom of the Preset gallery to open the Format Shape pane, where you can define the bevel, depth, contour, and surface of the effect. Figure 3.18 displays the Format Shape options and the Material options for the surface of a shape.

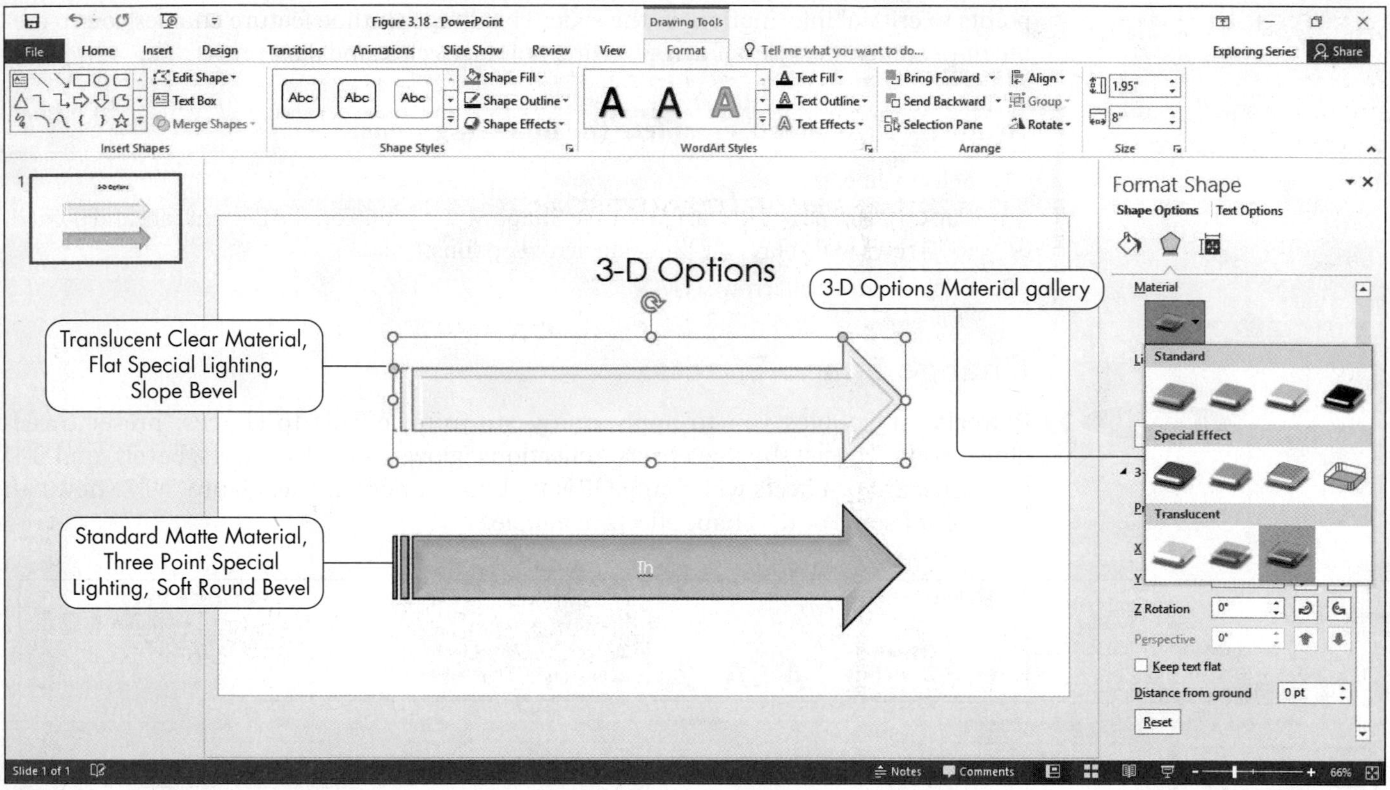

FIGURE 3.18 3-D Surface Options

Quick Concepts

1. Describe the purpose and effectiveness of incorporating shapes into a presentation. **p. 1044**

2. What is the value of using connector lines when creating a flow chart? **p. 1047**

3. Why might a fill be applied to a shape? Give two examples of a fill. **p. 1051**

Hands-On Exercises

Watch the Video for this Hands-On Exercise!

MyITLab®
HOE1 Training

Skills covered: Create Shapes
• Draw Lines and Connectors
• Apply a Quick Style and Customize
Shapes • Change Shape Effects

1 Shapes

You begin the illustrations and infographics workshop by having the interns work with a project status report. They will create basic shapes using PowerPoint's drawing tools. You also ask the group to customize the shapes by adding styles and effects.

STEP 1 ›› CREATE SHAPES

Knowing how to use a flow chart to diagram the processes or steps needed to complete a project or task is a valuable skill. To teach participants how to create multiple shapes using Lock Drawing Mode, you have them create several ovals as part of a project flow chart. Refer to Figure 3.19 as you complete Step 1.

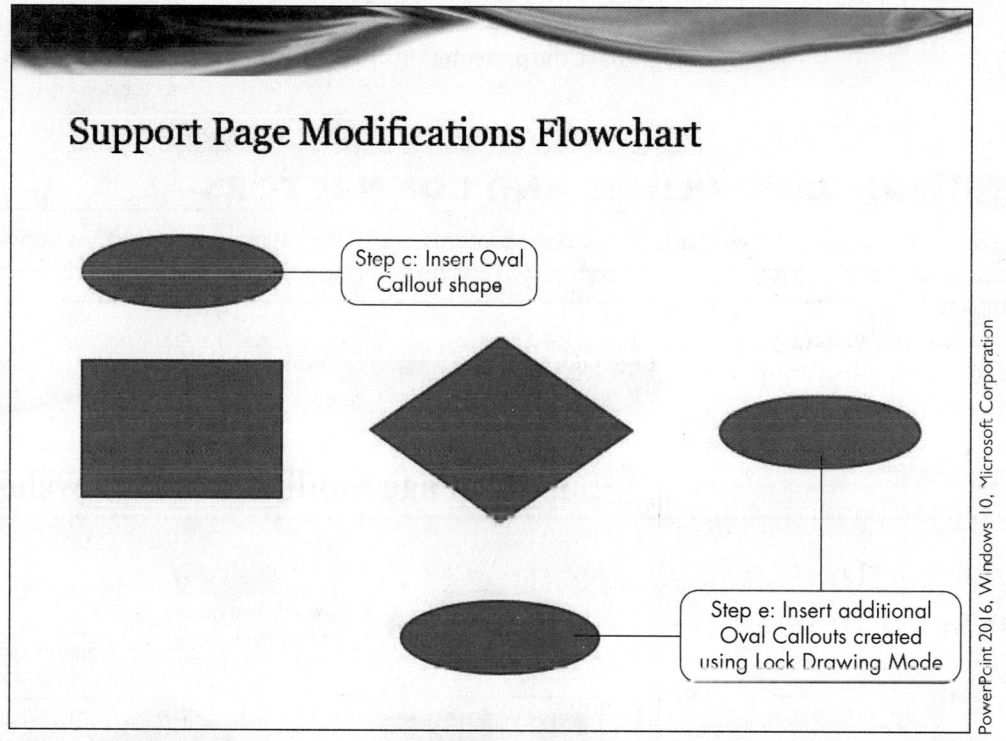

PowerPoint 2016, Windows 10, Microsoft Corporation

FIGURE 3.19 Basic Shapes

a. Open *p03h1Project*, and save it as **p03h1Project_LastFirst**.

> **TROUBLESHOOTING:** If you make any major mistakes in this exercise, you can close the file, open *p03h1Project* again and then start this exercise over.

b. Replace *First Name Last Name* on Slide 1 with your name. Create a handout header with your name and a handout footer with your instructor's name and your class. Include the current date. Apply to all.

c. Move to Slide 6, and click **Oval** in the Basic Shapes in the Drawing group on the Home tab. Position the pointer on the top-left side of the slide above the square shape and below the title and drag to create the shape.

> **TROUBLESHOOTING:** If you do not see the Oval shape, click More for the Basic Shapes or click the Insert tab and click Shapes in the Illustrations group.

Do not worry about the exact placement or size of the shapes you create at this time. You will learn how to precisely place and size shapes in the steps to follow.

d. Click the **Insert tab** and click **Shapes** in the Illustrations group. Right-click **Oval** in the Basic Shapes category and select **Lock Drawing Mode**.

You activate Lock Drawing Mode so that you can create multiple shapes of the same kind.

e. Position the pointer to the right of the diamond and drag to create an oval. Repeat this process below the diamond to mimic Figure 3.19.

f. Press **Esc** to turn off Lock Drawing Mode.

You created two additional Oval shapes.

g. Save the presentation.

STEP 2 ▶▶ DRAW LINES AND CONNECTORS

To continue building the flow chart, the workshop interns practice creating connecting lines between shapes. You also teach the group how to add a text box to a slide so they can add text, because the Title Only layout is being used. Refer to Figure 3.20 as you complete Step 2.

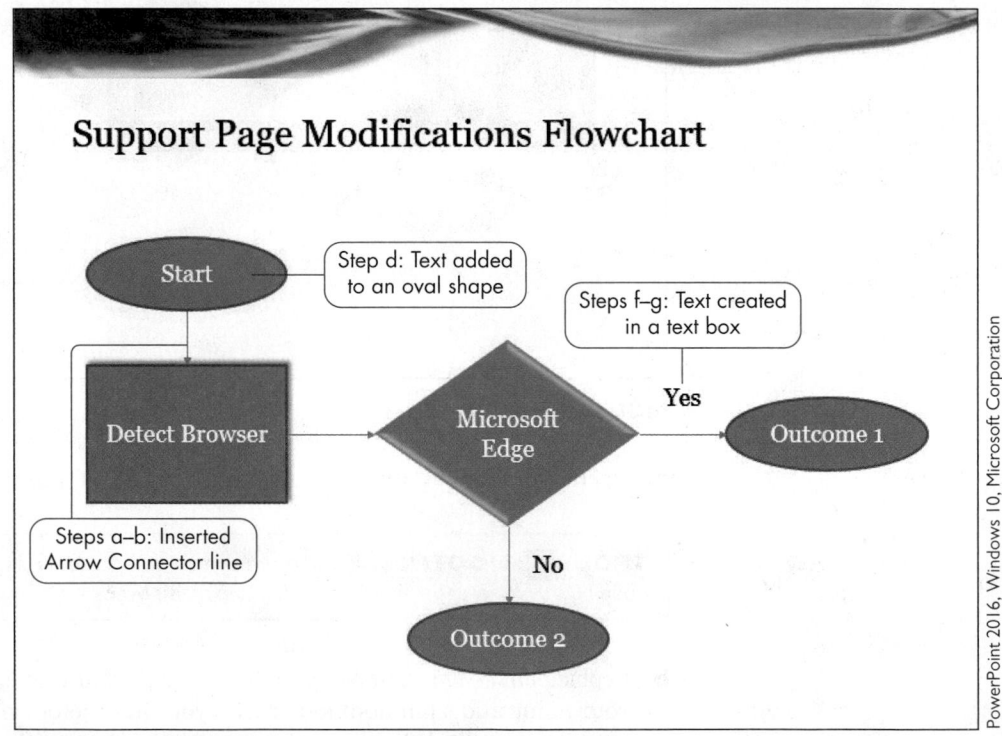

FIGURE 3.20 Basic Flow Chart

a. Click **Shapes** in the Illustrations group from the Insert tab, click **Arrow** in the Lines category, move the cross-hair pointer over the oval on the left side of the slide, and then position the pointer on the bottom-center handle.

The shape's connector handles appear when a connector line is selected and the cross-hair pointer is moved onto the shape.

b. Drag a connecting line that attaches the bottom-center connecting handle of the oval to the top-center connecting handle of the rectangle below it.

A connector arrow is placed between the oval and the rectangle. The default line weight is thin at 3/4 pt.

c. Click **Shapes** in the Illustrations group on the Insert tab, right-click the **Arrow**, and then select **Lock Drawing Mode**. Create connecting arrows using the technique just practiced that will attach the rectangle to the diamond and the diamond to the two remaining ovals, as shown in Figure 3.20. Press **Esc**.

d. Right-click the oval on the top-left of the slide, select **Edit Text**, and then type **Start**.

The text you typed becomes part of the oval shape.

e. Select the **square shape** and type **Detect Browser**. Use either of these methods to select each of the remaining shapes and type the text shown in Figure 3.20.

f. Click the **Insert tab** and click **Text Box** in the Text group.

Clicking Text Box enables you to create text anywhere on a slide.

g. Position the pointer above the connector between the Decision diamond and the Outcome 1 oval, click once, and then type **Yes**.

> **TROUBLESHOOTING:** If the text box is not positioned above the connector line between the Decision diamond and the Outcome 1 oval, click the border (not the sizing handle) of the text box and drag it into position.

h. Click **Text Box** in the Insert Shapes group on the Format tab, position the pointer to the right side of the connector between the Decision diamond and the Outcome 2 oval, click once, and then type **No**. Reposition the text box if necessary.

i. Save the presentation.

You encourage participants of the workshop to experiment with Quick Styles and to modify shape fills, but you ask them to set the shapes to styles of your choice in this slide show to demonstrate that they can meet specifications when asked. Refer to Figure 3.21 as you complete Step 3.

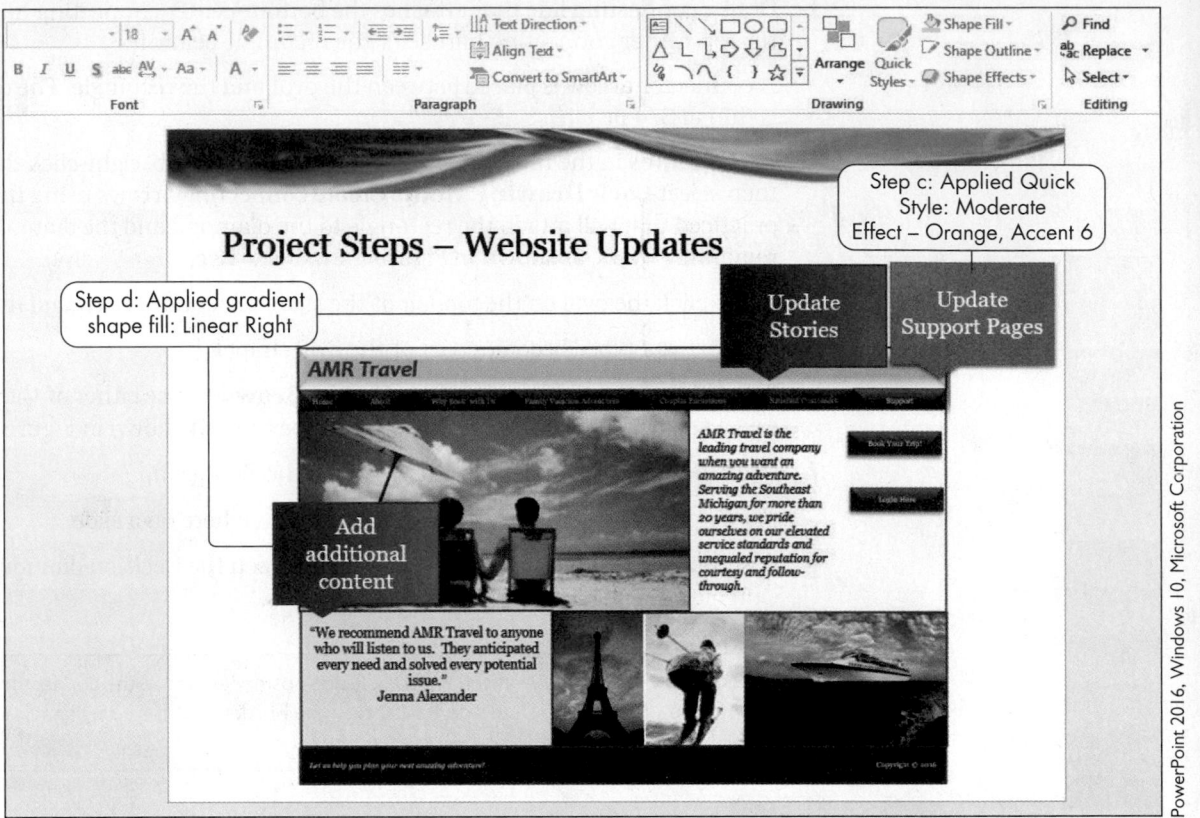

FIGURE 3.21 Quick Styles and Customized Fills

a. Click **Slide 5** and then select the far-right callout shape, **Update Support Pages**.

b. Click the **Format tab** and click **More** in the Shape Styles group.

The Quick Style gallery opens.

c. Move the pointer over the Quick Styles and note the changes in fill, outline, and effects to the shape as you do so. After you are through experimenting, click **Moderate Effect - Orange, Accent 6** (fifth row, seventh column). Click in an empty area to deselect the callout.

Live Preview shows the effects on the object as you move the pointer over the Quick Style options.

d. Press and hold **Ctrl** and click the remaining two callout shapes to select them. Click the **Format tab**, click **Shape Fill arrow** in the Shape Styles group, and then click **Blue, Accent 1** (first row, fifth column). Click **Shape Fill arrow** again, point to **Gradient**, and then click **Linear Right** under Dark Variations. Click **Text Fill arrow** in the WordArt Styles group and click **White, Background 1** to change the text to white.

You apply a gradient fill to more than one shape at a time.

e. Save the presentation.

PowerPoint provides many shape effects that you can use for emphasis. You ask the participants to apply effects to the flow chart shapes so they become familiar with the options available. Refer to Figure 3.22 as you complete Step 4.

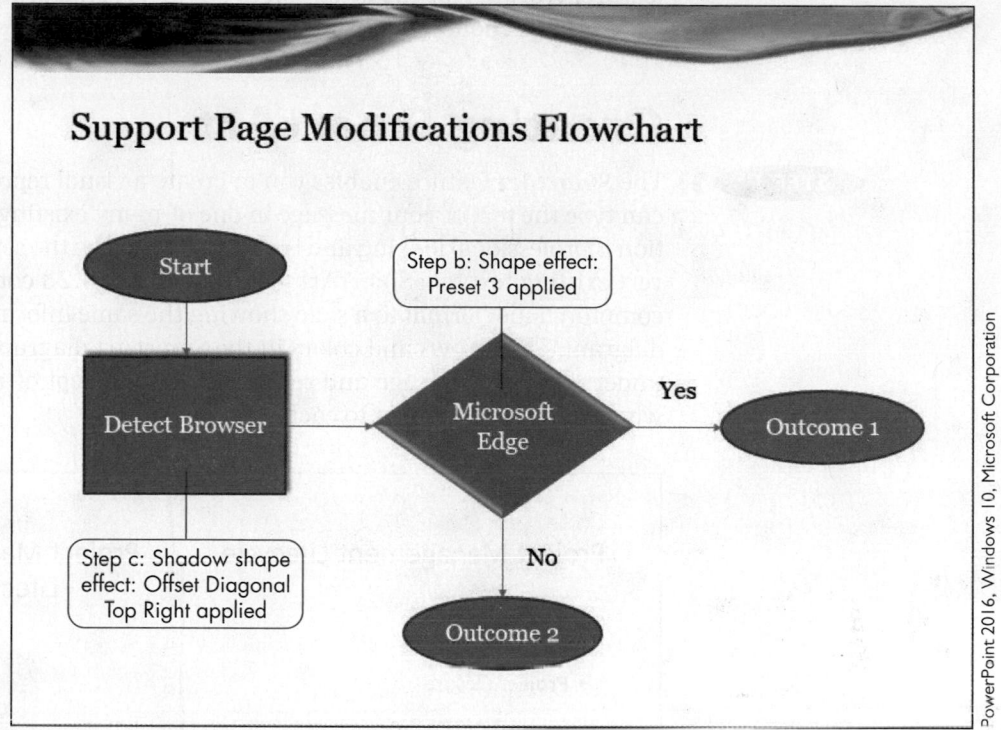

FIGURE 3.22 Shape Effects

a. Click **Slide 6** and click the **diamond shape**.

b. Click the **Format tab**, click the **Shape Effects arrow** in the Shape Styles group, point to **Preset**, and then click **Preset 3**.

Preset 3 combines a bevel type, a depth, contours, and a surface effect.

c. Select the **rectangle shape**, click the **Shape Effects arrow** in the Shape Styles group, point to **Shadow**, and then click **Offset Diagonal Top Right** (Outer category).

The Offset Diagonal option applies a soft shadow to the top-right of the rectangle.

d. Spell check and review the presentation.

e. Save and close the presentation. You will submit this file to your instructor at the end of the last Hands-On Exercise.

SmartArt and WordArt

Diagrams are infographics used to illustrate concepts and processes. PowerPoint includes a feature to create eye-catching diagrams: SmartArt. Another eye-catching PowerPoint feature, WordArt, draws attention to an infographic using text.

In this section, you will create and modify SmartArt diagrams and WordArt text.

Creating SmartArt

STEP 1 »» The *SmartArt* feature enables you to create a visual representation of information. You can type the text of your message in one of many existing layouts. The resulting illustration is professional looking and is complemented by the selected theme. You can also convert existing text to a SmartArt diagram. Figure 3.23 compares a text-based slide in the common bullet format to a slide showing the same information converted to a SmartArt diagram. The arrows and colors in the SmartArt diagram make it easy for the viewer to understand the message and remember the concept of a cycle. It is especially effective when you add animation to each step.

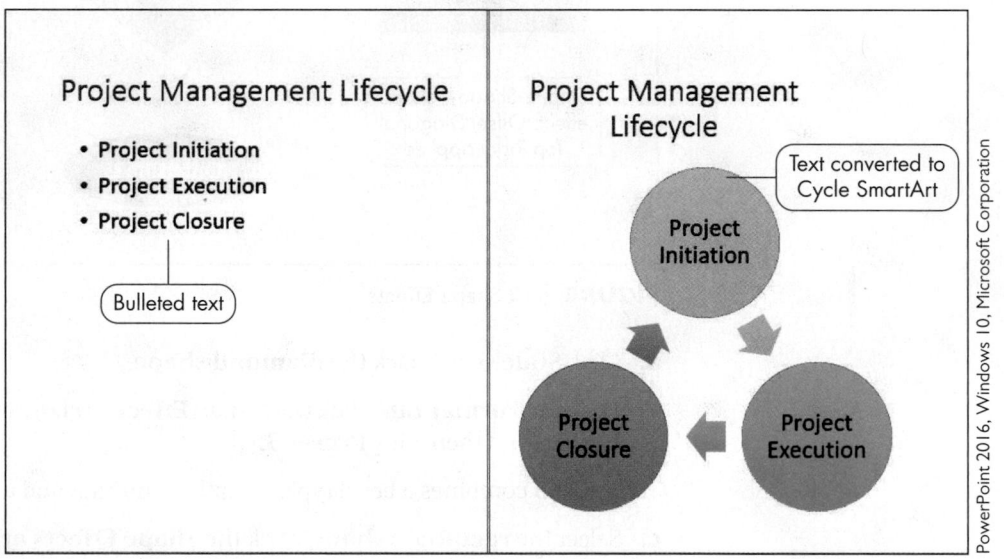

FIGURE 3.23

Choose a SmartArt Diagram Type

To create a SmartArt diagram, first choose a diagram type that fits your message. The SmartArt gallery has nine different categories of diagrams: List, Process, Cycle, Hierarchy, Relationship, Matrix, Pyramid, Picture, and Office.com. At the top of the list of categories is All, which you can click to display the choices from all categories. Each category includes a description of the type of information appropriate for the layouts in that category. The following Table 3.1 shows the SmartArt categories and their purposes.

TABLE 3.1 SmartArt Types and Purposes

Type	Purpose	Sample SmartArt
List	Show nonsequential information. For example, a list of items to be checked on a roof each year.	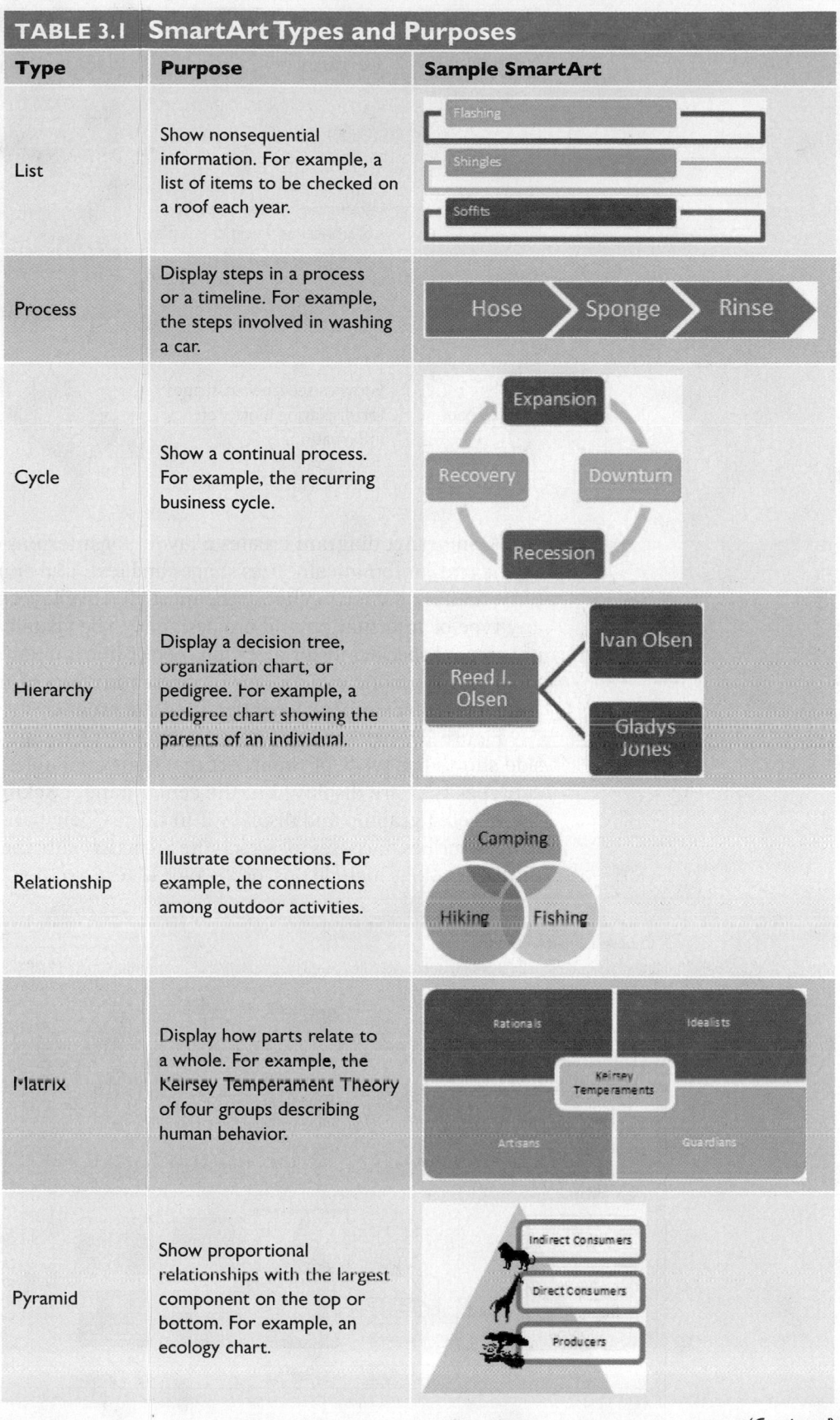
Process	Display steps in a process or a timeline. For example, the steps involved in washing a car.	
Cycle	Show a continual process. For example, the recurring business cycle.	
Hierarchy	Display a decision tree, organization chart, or pedigree. For example, a pedigree chart showing the parents of an individual.	
Relationship	Illustrate connections. For example, the connections among outdoor activities.	
Matrix	Display how parts relate to a whole. For example, the Keirsey Temperament Theory of four groups describing human behavior.	
Pyramid	Show proportional relationships with the largest component on the top or bottom. For example, an ecology chart.	

(Continued)

TABLE 3.1 Continued

Type	Purpose	Sample SmartArt
Picture	Display nonsequential or grouped blocks of information. Maximizes both horizontal and vertical display space for shapes.	Xeriscaping / Zeroscaping
Office.com	Show miscellaneous shapes for displaying blocks of information.	Images / Audio / Video

Pearson Education, Inc.

A SmartArt diagram creates a layout for information, provides a pane for quickly typing text, automatically sizes shapes and text, and enables you to switch between layouts, making it easy to choose the most effective layout. Some layouts can be used for any type of information and are designed to be visually attractive, while other layouts are created specifically for a certain type of information, such as a process or hierarchy. SmartArt types include options for presenting lists of information in ordered (steps to complete a task) or unordered (features of a product) formats.

Figure 3.24 shows the Choose a SmartArt Graphic dialog box. The pane on the left side shows the types of SmartArt diagrams available. Each type of diagram includes subtypes that are displayed in the center pane. Clicking one of the subtypes enlarges the selected graphic and displays it in the preview pane on the right side. The preview pane describes purposes for which the SmartArt subtype can be used effectively. Some of the descriptions include tips for the type of text to enter.

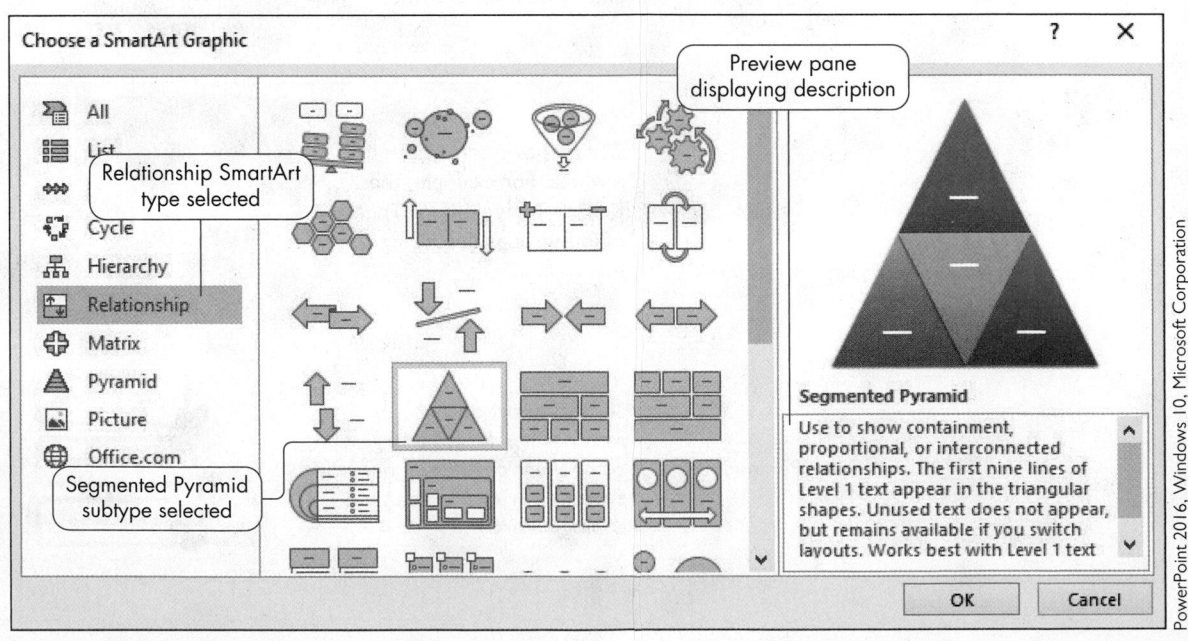

FIGURE 3.24 Choose a SmartArt Graphic Gallery

To create a SmartArt diagram, click the SmartArt icon on the icon palette of a layout, or complete the following steps:

1. Click the Insert tab.
2. Click SmartArt in the Illustrations group.
3. Click the type of SmartArt diagram you want in the left pane.
4. Click the SmartArt subtype you want in the center pane.
5. Preview the selected SmartArt and subtype in the right pane.
6. Click OK.

Use the SmartArt Text Pane

Once you select the SmartArt diagram type and the subtype, a *Text pane* opens in which you type text. If the Text pane does not open, click Text Pane in the Create Graphic group on the SmartArt Tools Design tab. The Text pane works like an outline—type a line of text, press Enter, and then press Tab or Shift+Tab to increase or decrease the indent level. The font size will adjust to fit text inside the shape, or the shape may resize to fit the text, depending on the size and number of shapes in your SmartArt diagram.

The layout accommodates additional shapes as you add text unless the type of shape is designed for a specific number of shapes, such as the Relationship Counterbalance Arrows layout, which is designed to show two opposing ideas. If you choose a diagram with more shapes than you need, you can delete the extra shapes; PowerPoint will automatically rearrange the remaining shapes to eliminate any blank space.

Some layouts are limited in the space available for text. Some layouts allow for points and subpoints. Read the description of the layout in the gallery for information relating to these limitations and special features. Figure 3.25 shows text typed into the Text pane for a Basic Cycle SmartArt diagram. Because four lines of text were typed, four shapes were created. The description for the Basic Cycle SmartArt diagram states that the diagram works best with Level 1 text only.

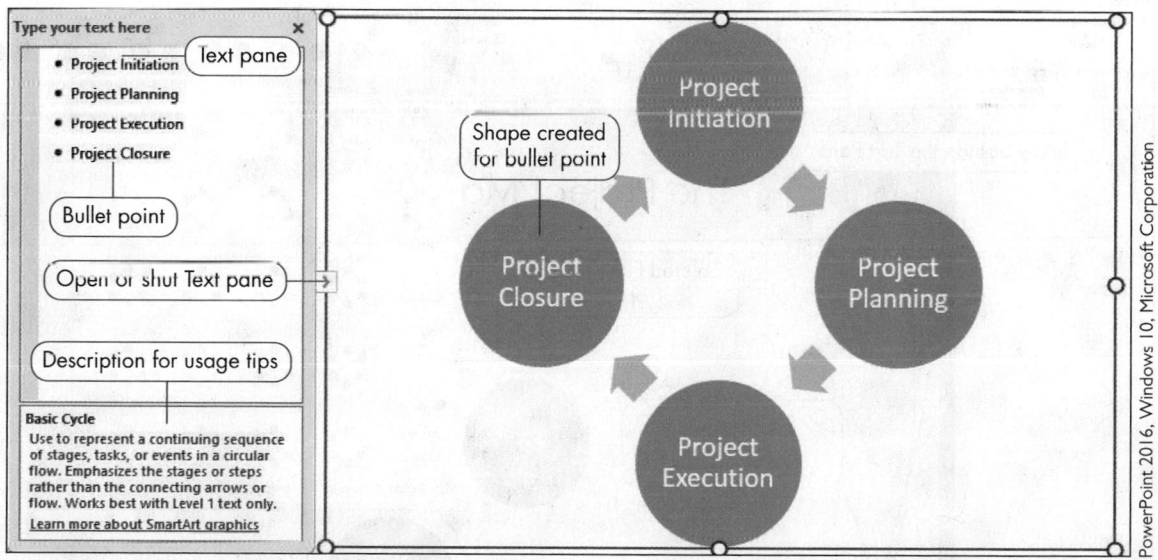

FIGURE 3.25 SmartArt Text Pane

TIP: TEXT IN SMARTART

Some SmartArt layouts allow only one level of text, while others are set up for one or two levels of text. So, if there are main and subpoints that need to be displayed, a SmartArt graphic that allows two levels of text is necessary. Be sure to keep the text short and limit it to key points to create a visually appealing diagram.

Modifying SmartArt

You can modify SmartArt diagrams with the same tools used for other shapes and text boxes. You can reposition or resize a SmartArt diagram by dragging its borders. You can modify SmartArt text in the Text pane just as if it were in a placeholder, or you can modify the text in the shape itself. If you need an additional shape, click to position the insertion point in the Text pane at the beginning or end of the text where you want to add a shape, press Enter, and then type the text. An alternative method for adding shapes is to use the Add Shape command.

> **To add a shape to the SmartArt, complete the following steps:**
>
> 1. Click an existing shape in the SmartArt diagram.
> 2. Click the SmartArt Tools Design tab.
> 3. Click the Add Shape arrow in the Create Graphic group.
> 4. Select an available option

SmartArt diagrams have two galleries used to enhance the appearance of the diagram, both of which are located in the SmartArt Tools Design tab in the SmartArt Styles group. One gallery changes colors, and the other gallery applies a combination of special effects.

Change SmartArt Theme Colors

STEP 2 ▶▶ To change the color scheme of a SmartArt diagram, click Change Colors to display the Colors gallery (see Figure 3.26). The gallery contains Primary Theme Colors, Colorful, and Accent color schemes. Click a color variation to apply it to the SmartArt diagram.

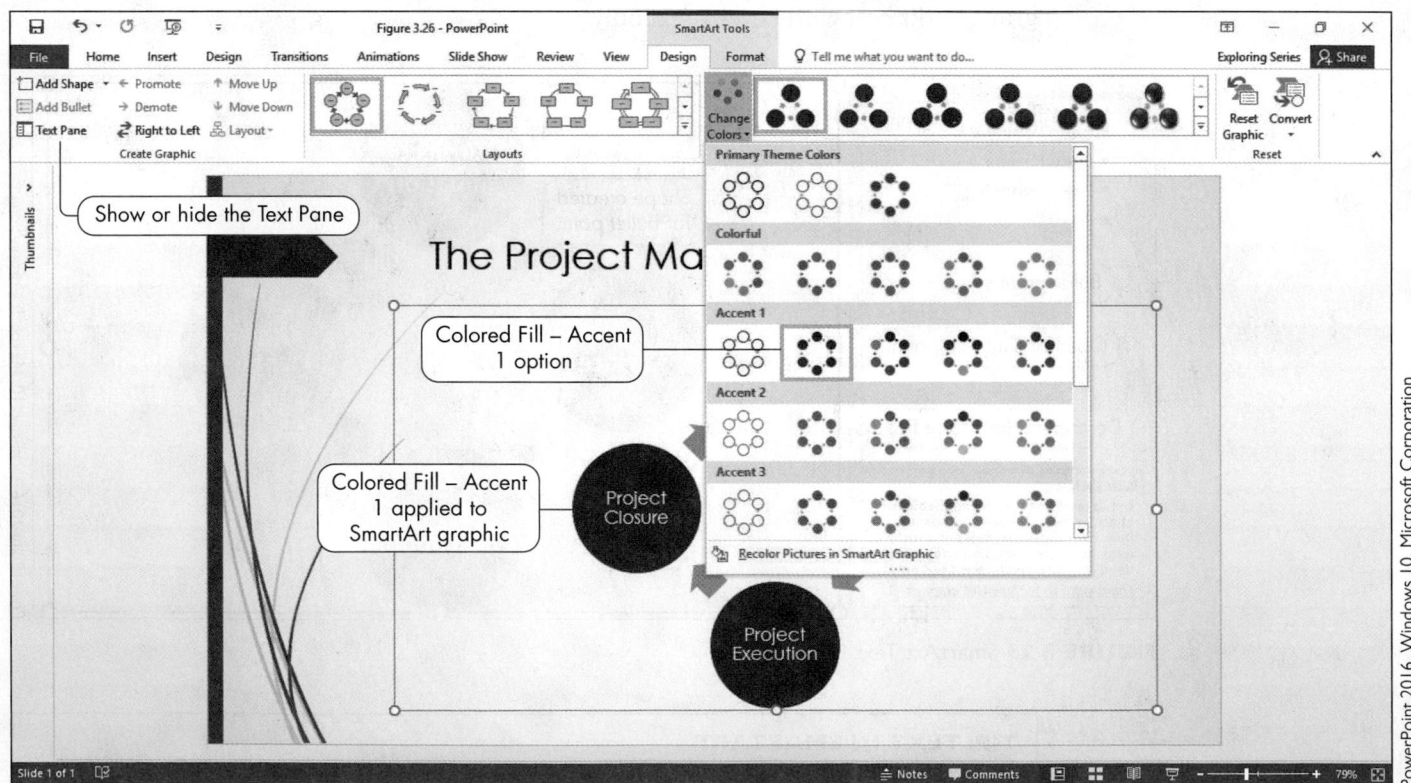

FIGURE 3.26 SmartArt Theme Color Options

Use Quick Styles with SmartArt

After creating the diagram, use SmartArt Quick Styles in the SmartArt Styles group to adjust the style of the SmartArt to match other styles you have used in your presentation. The style you select, however, should make the diagram easier to understand. The SmartArt Quick Styles gallery displays combinations of special effects, such as shadows, gradients, and 3-D effects that combine perspectives and surface styles. Figure 3.27 displays the SmartArt Quick Styles gallery.

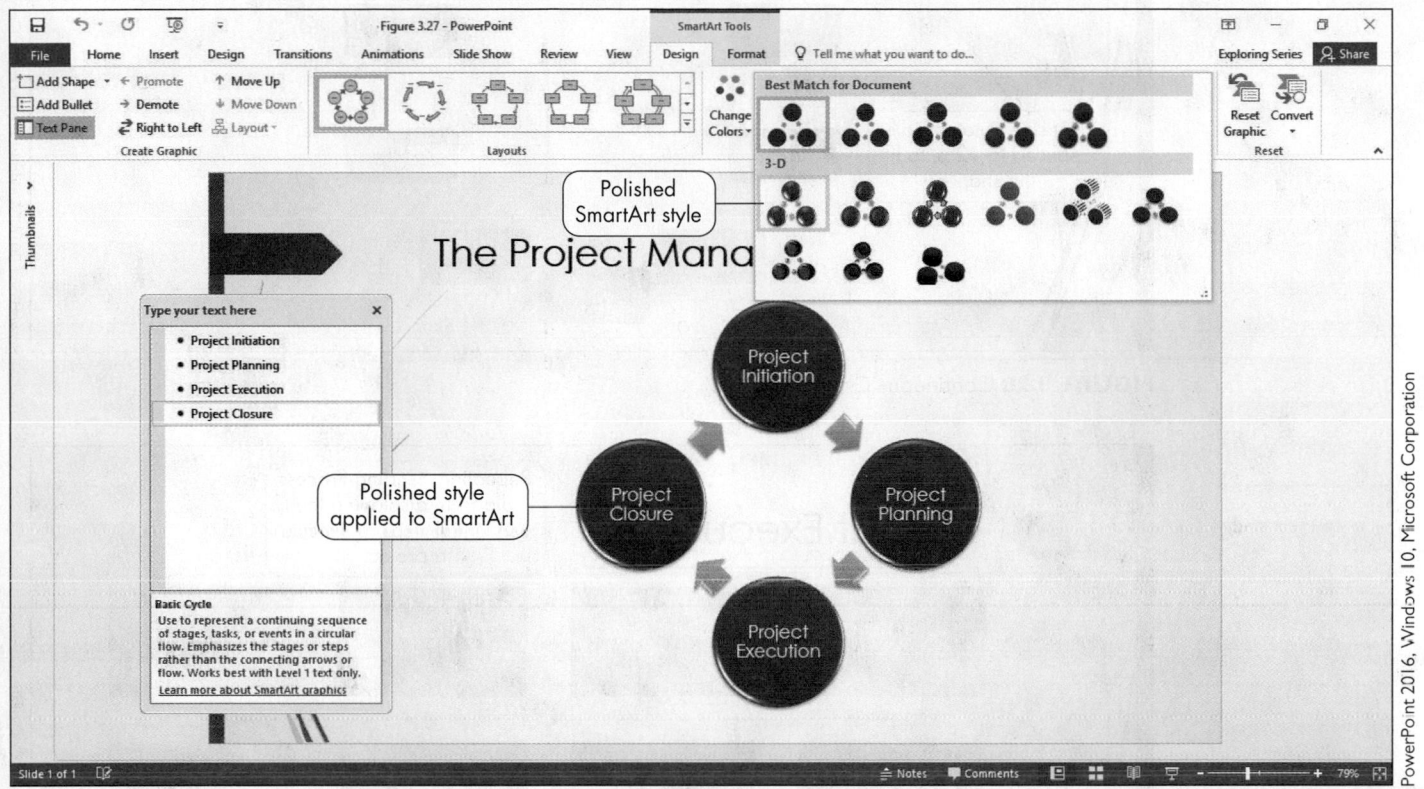

FIGURE 3.27 SmartArt Quick Style Gallery

Change the SmartArt Layout

STEP 3 ▶▶ After creating a SmartArt diagram, you may find that the layout needs adjusting. For example, as you type text, PowerPoint reduces the size of the font. If you type too much text, the font size becomes too small. Figure 3.28 shows a Process diagram displaying the sequential steps to execute a project. To allow the text to fit in the shapes of the diagram, PowerPoint reduced the font size to 12 pt making it difficult to read. By adjusting the layout, you can make the diagram easier to read. Figure 3.29 shows the same process from Figure 3.28, modified to utilize the Basic Bending Process layout.

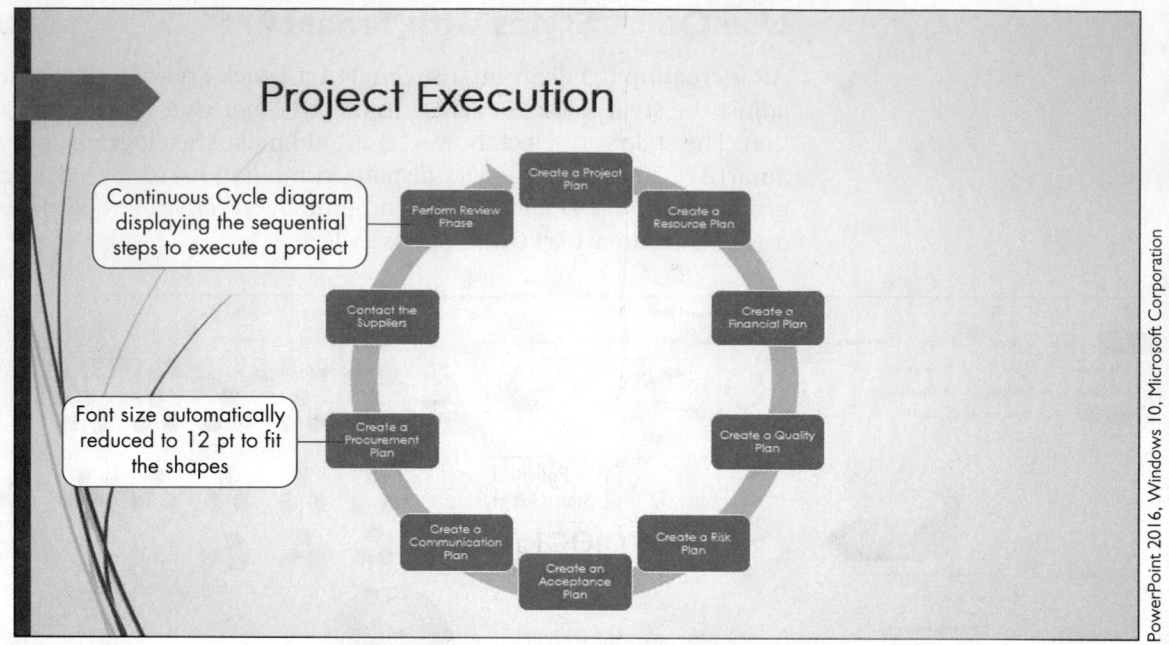

FIGURE 3.28 Continuous Cycle SmartArt

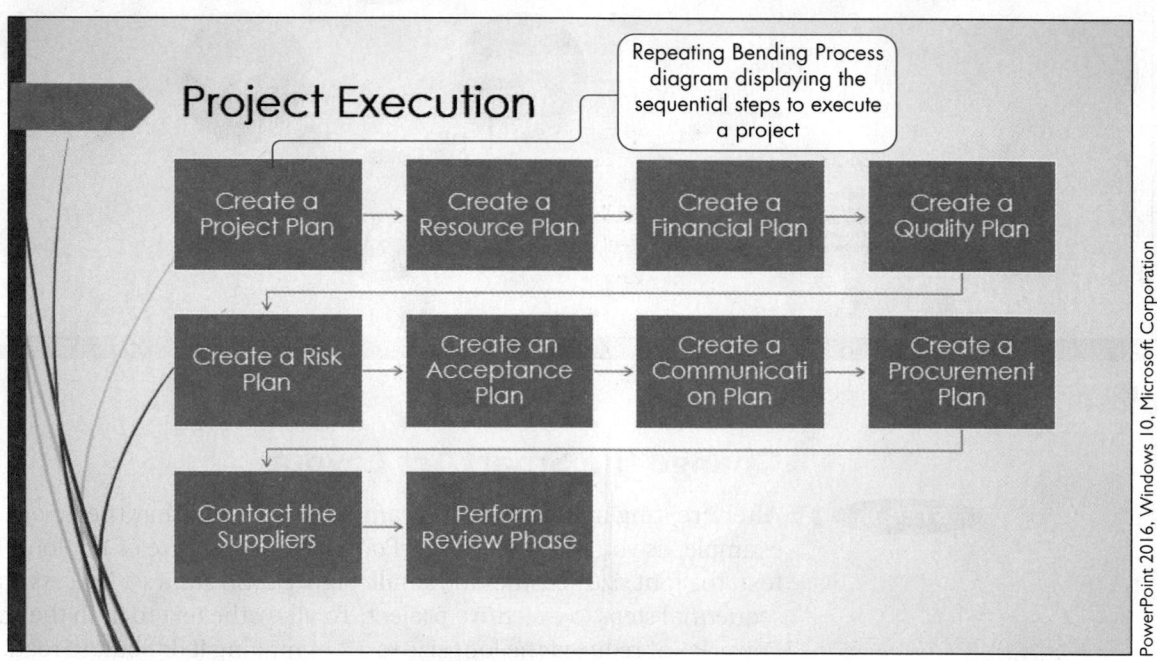

FIGURE 3.29 Modified SmartArt Layout

> **To change the layout of a SmartArt diagram, complete the following steps:**
>
> 1. Select the SmartArt diagram and click the SmartArt Tools Design tab.
> 2. Click More in the Layouts group to display the Layouts gallery.
> 3. Use Live Preview to determine which layout subtype presents your information in the best way.
> 4. Select the layout you want to use.

Change SmartArt Type

You can change the SmartArt diagram type if you decide a completely different type of diagram would be better. The process is similar to changing the SmartArt layout subtypes. Changing the diagram type may affect the audience's perception of your diagram.

For example, if you have created a list of unordered items, switching to a cycle diagram implies that a specific order to the items exists. Also, if you have customized the shapes, keep in mind that changes to colors, line styles, and fills will transfer from the old diagram to a new one. However, some effects, such as rotation, do not transfer.

> **To change the SmartArt diagram type, complete the following steps:**
>
> 1. Select the SmartArt diagram.
> 2. Click More in the Layouts group on the Design tab and click More Layouts. The Choose a SmartArt Graphic gallery opens, displaying all the layouts grouped by category.
> 3. Click the type and layout you want.

Convert Text to a SmartArt Diagram

You can also convert existing text to a SmartArt diagram by selecting the placeholder containing the text and clicking Convert to SmartArt Graphic in the Paragraph group on the Home tab. You can also select the text, right-click the placeholder, and then select Convert to SmartArt. When the gallery opens, click the desired layout for the SmartArt diagram. See Figure 3.30.

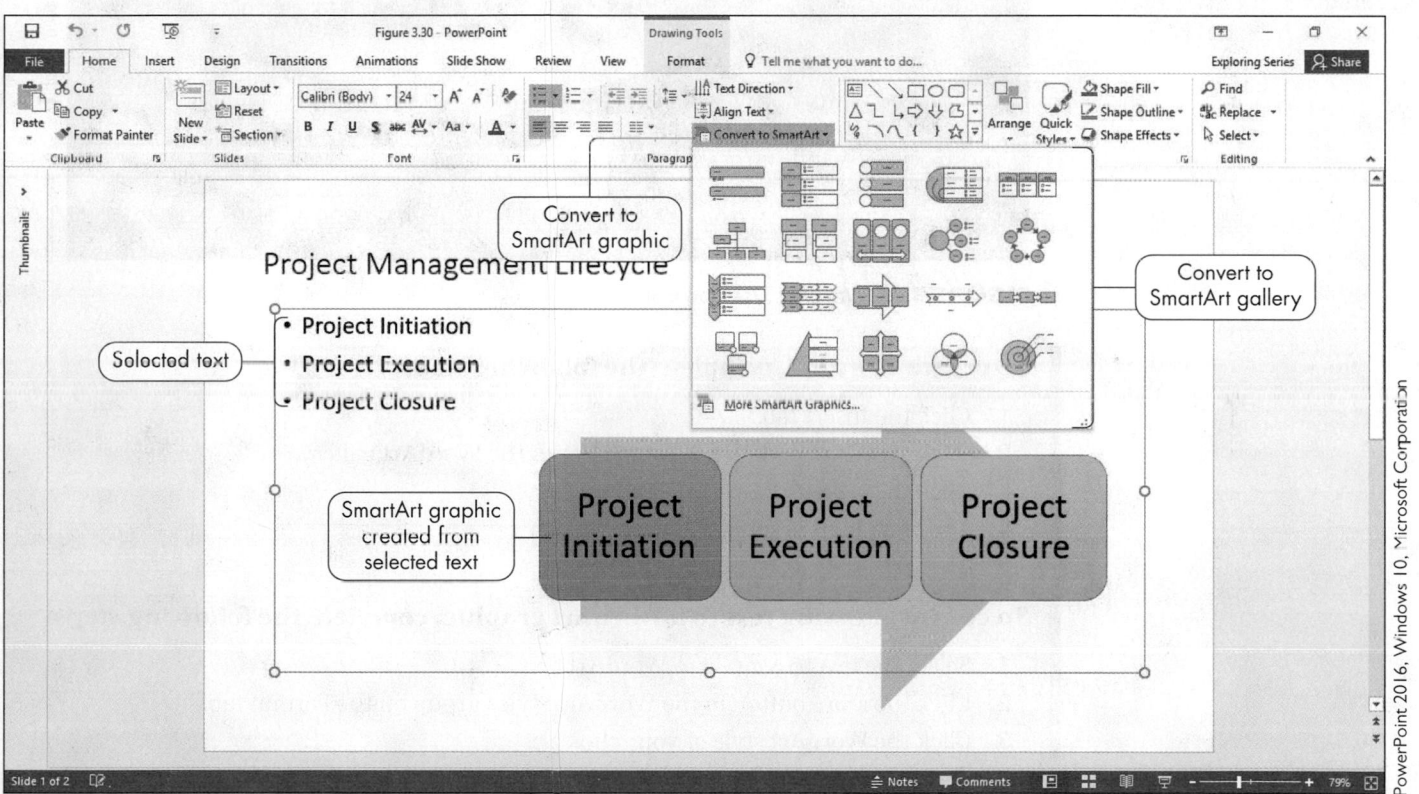

FIGURE 3.30 Convert to SmartArt

Creating WordArt and Modifying WordArt

STEP 4 ›› You may want to call attention to text on a slide by using WordArt. **WordArt** uses special effects based on text rather than a shape. In WordArt, special effects apply to the text itself, not to the shape surrounding the text. For example, in a WordArt graphic the text may have a 3-D reflection rather than the box surrounding the text. By applying special effects, such as curves or waves, directly to the text, you can create text that emphasizes the information for your audience.

Create WordArt

When you create WordArt, PowerPoint provides a gallery of WordArt styles that has a variety of text styles to choose from, as well as the option to change individual settings or elements to modify the style. You can convert existing text to WordArt text, or you can create a WordArt object and then type text. The colors depend upon the theme you have selected. Figure 3.31 shows a slide with a WordArt effect enhancing text on the slide.

FIGURE 3.31 WordArt Used on a Slide

To create WordArt, complete the following steps:

1. Click the Insert tab.
2. Click WordArt in the Text group to open the WordArt gallery.
3. Click the WordArt style of your choice.
4. Type text in the WordArt placeholder.

To convert existing text to a WordArt graphic, complete the following steps:

1. Select the text to convert to WordArt text.
2. Click the More button in the WordArt Styles group on the Format tab.
3. Click the WordArt style of your choice.

Modify WordArt

You can change the style of a WordArt object by clicking a Quick Style located in the WordArt Styles group on the Format tab. Alternatively, you can modify the individual elements of the WordArt by clicking Text Fill, Text Outline, or Text Effects in the WordArt Styles group. WordArt Text Effects includes a unique Transform option. Transform can rotate the WordArt text around a path or add a warp to stretch, angle, or bloat letters. Figure 3.32 shows the warp options available in the WordArt Transform category.

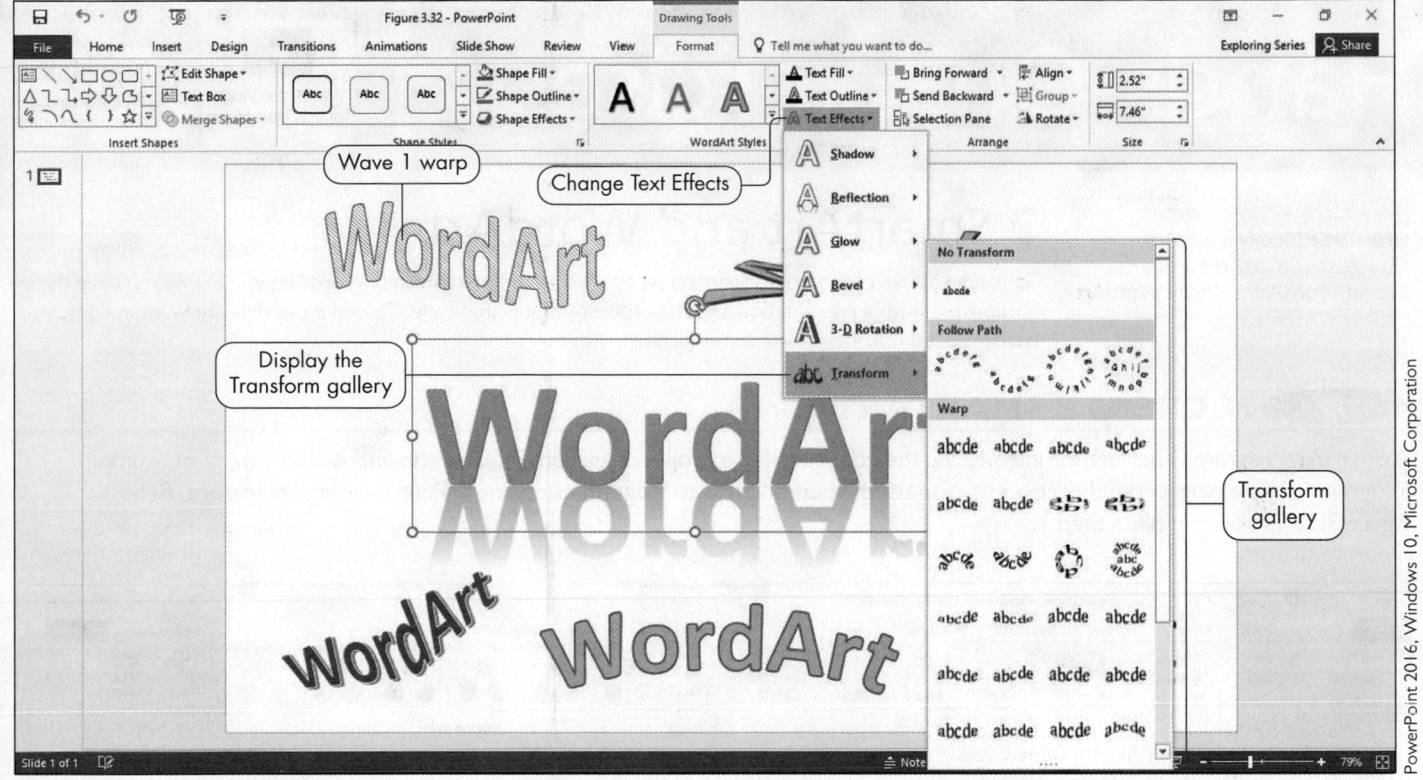

FIGURE 3.32 Warp Options

4. Which SmartArt diagram type would be most effective to show an organization chart or pedigree? *p. 1067*

5. How does typing text in a SmartArt text pane work like an outline? *p. 1069*

6. Why would you convert existing text to a SmartArt diagram? *p. 1066*

7. Why would you use WordArt on a slide? *p. 1073*

SmartArt and WordArt • PowerPoint 2016   **1075**

Hands-On Exercises

Watch the Video for this Hands-On Exercise!

MyITLab® HOE2 Training

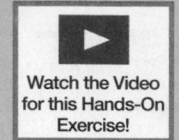

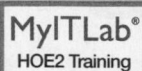

Skills covered: Create SmartArt • Modify SmartArt • Change the SmartArt Layout • Create WordArt • Modify WordArt

2 SmartArt and WordArt

To teach your workshop participants how to work with SmartArt and WordArt, you choose to have the group work with a presentation about a process—the water cycle. To make the slide show interesting, you have included fun, interesting water facts.

STEP 1 » CREATE SMARTART

A SmartArt diagram is perfect for introducing the concept of the project management life cycle and is an example of a simple infographic explaining a complex concept. You teach your students to diagram using PowerPoint's SmartArt feature. Refer to Figure 3.33 as you complete Step 1.

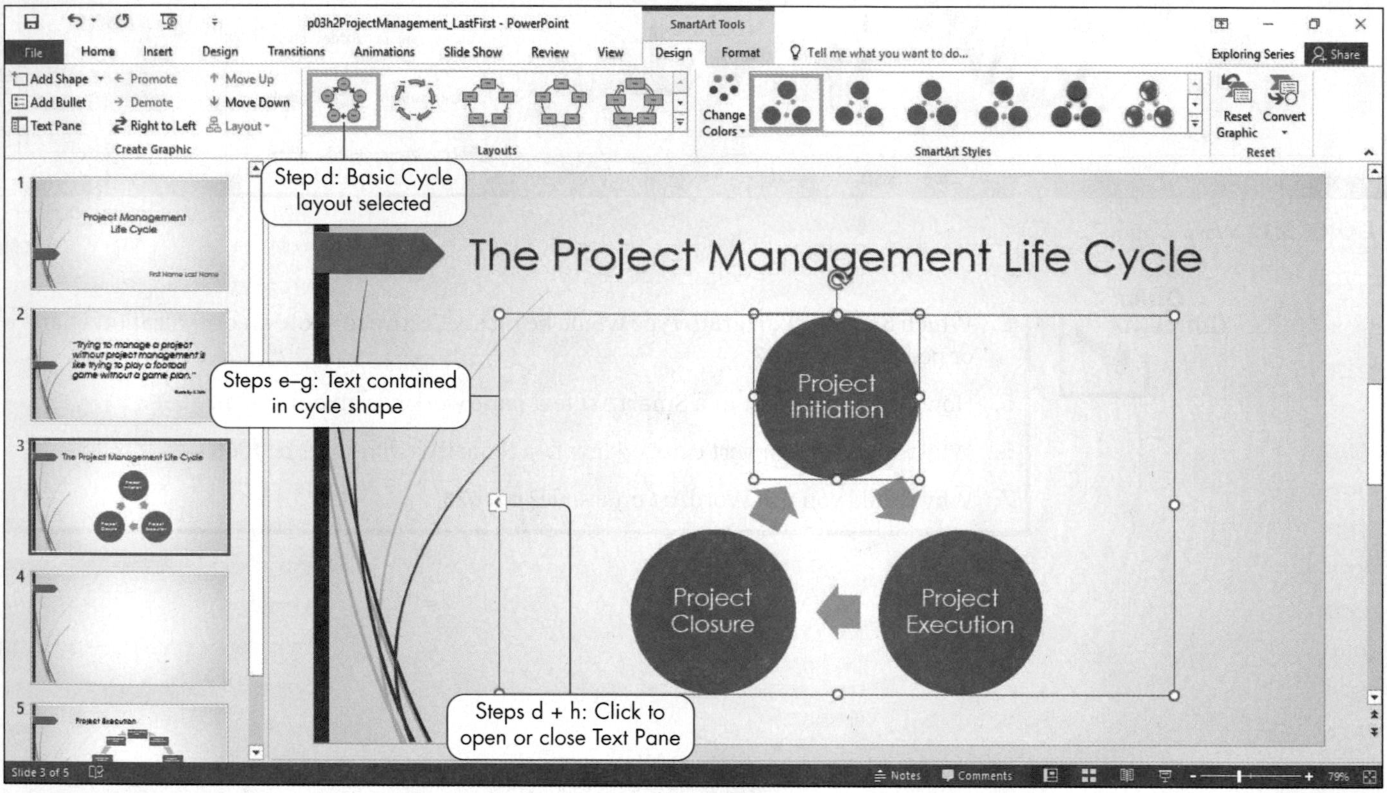

FIGURE 3.33 Basic Cycle SmartArt

a. Open the *p03h2ProjectManagement* presentation and save it as **p03h2ProjectManagement_LastFirst**.

b. Replace *First Name Last Name* with your name on Slide 1. Create a handout header with your name and a handout footer with your instructor's name and your class. Include the current date. Apply to all.

c. Click **Slide 3**. Click the **Insert tab** and click **SmartArt** in the Illustrations group.

The *Choose a SmartArt Graphic* dialog box opens.

d. Click **Cycle**, click the subtype **Basic Cycle**, read the description of the SmartArt diagram, and then click **OK**.

The Text pane opens with the insertion point in the first bullet location so that you can type the text for the first cycle shape.

e. Type **Project Initiation**.

As you type, the font size for the text gets smaller so the text fits in the shape.

f. Press ↓ to move to the second bullet and type **Project Execution**. Repeat this technique to add a third bullet and type **Project Closure**.

g. Press ↓ to move to the blank bullet point and press **Backspace**. Repeat to remove the remaining blank bullet point.

The extra shapes in the Basic Cycle SmartArt are removed.

h. Click **Open/Close Text pane** or **Close (X)** on the top-right of the Text pane to close it.

i. Drag the SmartArt object down so that it does not overlap the title.

j. Ensure that the SmartArt object is still selected. Click the **resizing handle** on the top-right corner of the SmartArt diagram, drag a corner of the object inward approximately an inch, and then reposition it so the object is approximately centered under the title (Refer to Figure 3.33).

k. Save the presentation.

STEP 2 ⟩⟩ MODIFY SMARTART

You need to modify the structure of the SmartArt diagram because a step in the cycle was omitted. The diagram could also be enhanced with a color style change. You teach your participants these skills. Refer to Figure 3.34 as you complete Step 2.

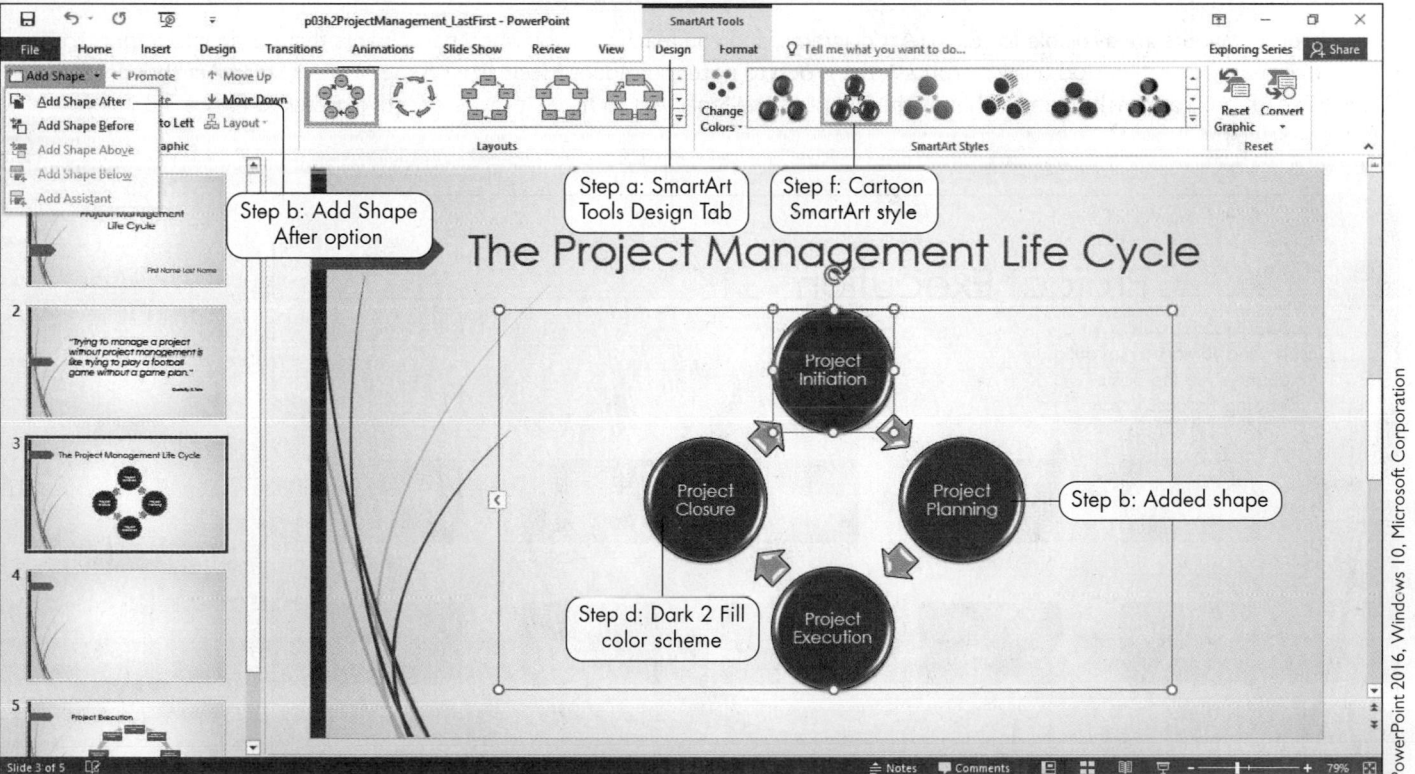

FIGURE 3.34 Modified SmartArt

a. Click the **Project Initiation shape** and ensure that the SmartArt Tools Design tab is selected.

b. Click the **Add Shape arrow** in the Create Graphic group and select **Add Shape After**.

You have added a new shape after *Project Initiation* and before *Project Execution*.

> **TROUBLESHOOTING:** If you had clicked Add Shape, you would have automatically added a shape after the selected shape. Using the Add Shape arrow gives you a choice of adding before or after.

c. Type **Project Planning** in the new shape.

d. Click the **SmartArt border** to select all the shapes in the SmartArt diagram, click **Change Colors** in the SmartArt Styles group, and then click **Dark 2 Fill** in the Primary Theme Colors category.

e. Click **More** in the SmartArt Styles group and move the pointer over the styles.

Live Preview shows the impact each style has on the shapes and text in the SmartArt diagram.

f. Click **Cartoon** in the 3-D category (first row, third column).

This choice makes the text readable and enhances the appearance of the SmartArt diagram.

g. Save the presentation.

STEP 3 ›› **CHANGE THE SMARTART LAYOUT**

Many different layouts are available for SmartArt diagrams, and you teach the workshop participants that for an infographic to be effective, it must be understood quickly. You ask the group to note the reduced font size on the process SmartArt showing the Project Execution. You teach them to change the layout of the SmartArt to make it more effective. Refer to Figure 3.35 as you complete Step 3.

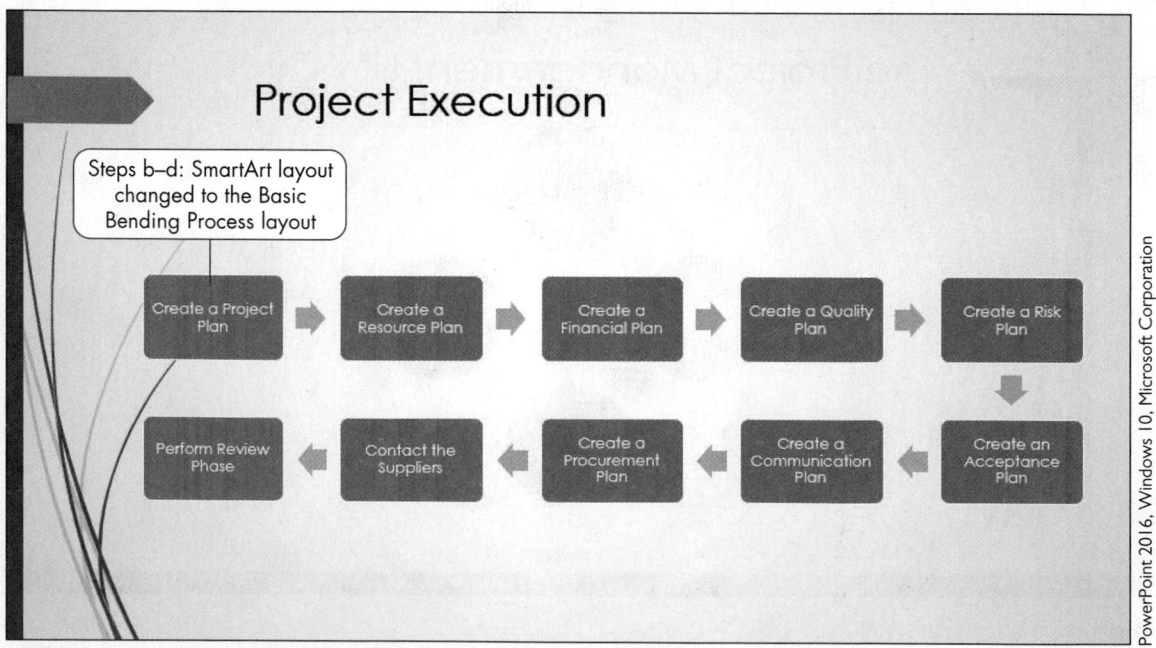

FIGURE 3.35 Basic Bending Process SmartArt

a. Click **Slide 6**. Select the **SmartArt Continuous Cycle shape** by clicking any shape.

b. Click the **SmartArt Tools Design tab**, click **More** in the Layouts group, select **More Layouts** at the bottom of the Layouts gallery, and then click **Process** in the left pane of the *Choose a SmartArt Graphic* dialog box. Click **Basic Bending Process** in the center pane and click **OK**.

c. Ensure that the SmartArt border is selected. Click the **Format tab**, type **4.03** in the **Shape Height box** in the Size group, and then press **Enter**.

d. Open the Size Dialog Box Launcher. Click **Position** and **type 1.6** in the **Horizontal Position box** and **2.44** in the **Vertical Position box**. Close the Format Shape pane. Deselect the SmartArt diagram by clicking outside of the SmartArt.

e. Save the presentation.

STEP 4 ›› **CREATE AND MODIFY WORDART**

You teach the participants how to use WordArt to call attention to text and how to modify Text Effects applied to WordArt. You also have them insert text in a text box so they can compare the options available with each method for adding text to a slide. Refer to Figure 3.36 as you complete Step 4.

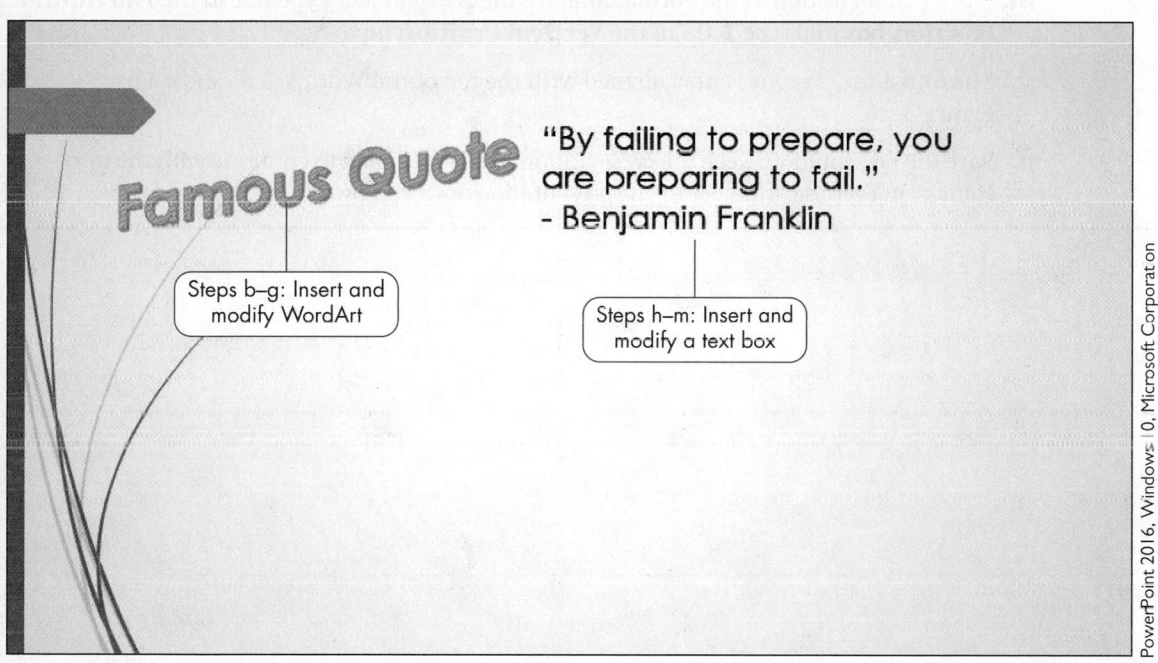

FIGURE 3.36 Modified WordArt

a. Click **Slide 4**. Click the **Insert tab** and click **WordArt** in the Text group.

b. Click **Pattern Fill - Orange, Accent 1, 50%, Hard Shadow - Accent 1 (**fourth row, third column).

A WordArt placeholder is centered on the slide.

c. Type **Famous Quote** in the **WordArt placeholder**.

d. Click **Text Effects** on the **Format tab** in the WordArt Styles group, and then point to **3-D Rotation**.

The 3-D Rotation gallery opens, showing No Rotation, Parallel, Perspective, and Oblique categories.

e. Click **Off Axis 1 Right** (under Parallel category, second row, second column).

f. Type **1.5** in the **Shape Height box** in the Size group and press **Enter**.

The height of the WordArt shape adjusts to 1.5.

g. Open the Size Dialog Box Launcher and ensure that Position is expanded so the options are available. Type **0.87** in the **Horizontal Position box** and **1.33** in the **Vertical Position box**. Close the Format Shape pane and deselect the shape.

h. Click the **Insert tab** and click **Text Box** in the Text group.

i. Click to the bottom-right of the WordArt shape and type **"By failing to prepare, you are preparing to fail." – Benjamin Franklin**.

The text box expands to fit the text, with the result that the text is contained in one long line that flows off the slide.

j. Click the **Format tab**, type **5.2** in the **Shape Width box** in the Size group, and then press **Enter**.

k. Click the **Size Dialog Box Launcher**, scroll down to see the Text Box options, click to expand and view the options, and then click the **Wrap text in shape check box**.

l. Click the **border** of the text box to select all the text. Click the **Home tab** and change the font size of the text to **28 pt**.

m. Ensure that Position in the Format Shape pane is expanded. Type **6.2** in the **Horizontal Position box** and type **1.08** in the **Vertical Position box**.

The top of the text box is now aligned with the top of the WordArt, as shown in Figure 3.36.

n. Save the presentation. Keep the presentation open if you plan to continue with the next Hands-On Exercise. If not, close the presentation and exit PowerPoint.

Object Manipulation

As you add objects to your slides, you may want to manipulate them by arranging them differently on the slide or recoloring them. Perhaps you have several shapes created, and you want to align them at their left edges or arrange them by their center points and then determine the order of the shapes. You may have inserted a drawn image, and then find that the colors used in the image do not match the colors of the theme of your presentation. You may have added a drawn image that includes something you do not want.

In this section, you will learn to modify objects. You will isolate objects, flip and rotate objects, group and ungroup objects, and recolor an image. You will also learn to determine the order of objects and align objects to one another and to the slide.

Modifying Objects

Many images are made from a series of combined shapes. You can modify existing drawings by breaking them into individual shapes and removing pieces you do not need, changing or recoloring shapes, rotating shapes, and combining shapes from several objects to create a new object. Figure 3.37 shows a picnic illustration available from Microsoft Office Online. In the bottom-right corner of the figure, the illustration was broken apart; the fireworks, flag, fries, and tablecloth removed; the hamburger, hotdogs, and milkshake flipped and resized; and the hamburger and chocolate milkshake recolored.

FIGURE 3.37 Modified Objects

Resize Objects

STEP 1 ❯❯ Resizing objects is the most common modification procedure, and it is important for you to know a precise resizing method for times when you need exact measurements. For example, you use PowerPoint to create an advertisement for an automobile trader magazine, and the magazine specifies that the ad must fit in a 2" by 2" space. You can specify the exact height and width measurement of an object or adjust to a specific proportion of its original size.

The controls to resize an object to an exact measurement are found in the Size group on the Format tab or the Format pane. The Size group contains controls to change the height and width of an object. The Format pane also contains boxes for typing exact measurements for shape height and width, but additionally allows you to use a precise rotation angle and to scale an object based on its original size (note that not all Online Pictures are added at full size). To keep the original height and width proportions of an image, make sure the *Lock aspect ratio* check box is selected. **Aspect ratio** is the ratio of an object's width to its height. Figure 3.38 shows the sizing options available on the Format Picture pane.

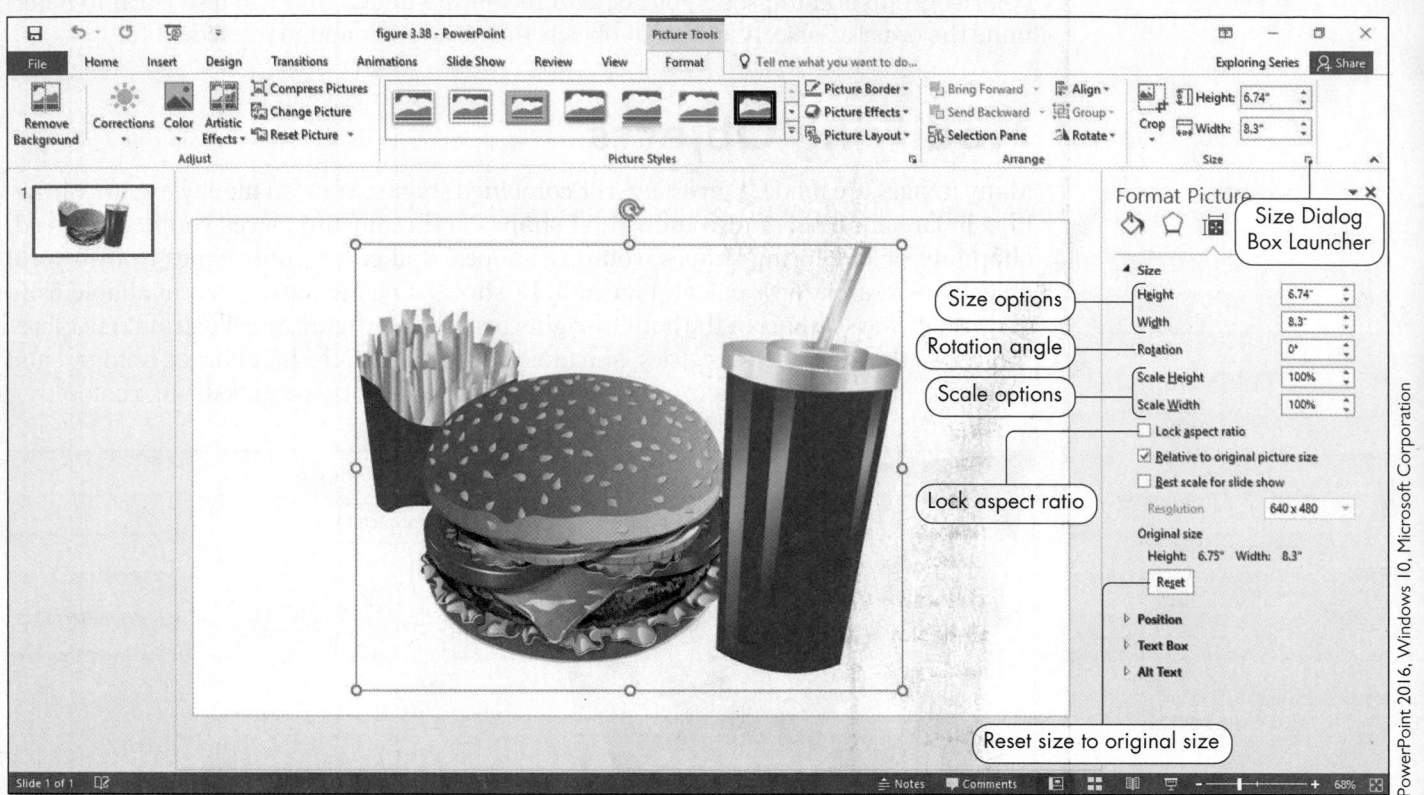

FIGURE 3.38 Sizing Options

Flip and Rotate Objects

STEP 2 ▶▶ Sometimes you will find that an object is facing the wrong way and you need to reverse the direction it faces, or **flip** it. You can flip an object vertically or horizontally to get a mirror image of the object. You may find that you need to **rotate** an object, or move the object around its axis. Perhaps you took a photograph with your digital camera sideways to get a full-length view, but when you download the image, it displays sideways. You can quickly rotate an object left or right 90°, flip it horizontally or vertically, or freely rotate it any number of degrees.

You rotate a selected object by dragging the rotation handle located at the top of the object in the direction you want it to rotate. To constrain the rotation to 15° angles, press and hold Shift while dragging. To rotate exactly 90° to the left or the right, click Rotate in the Arrange group on the Format tab. If you want a mirror image, click Rotate and select Flip Vertical or Flip Horizontal. You can also drag one of the side sizing handles over the opposite side to flip it. However, this method will cause distortion if you do not drag far enough to keep the height and width measurements proportional. Figure 3.39 shows the original and its flipped counterpart along with the rotate options.

FIGURE 3.39 Rotating and Flipping Options

Merge Shapes

The Merge Shapes feature enables you to take individual shapes that you have inserted and merge them together to create one image. There are five different merging options: Union, Combine, Fragment, Intersect, and Subtract. Figure 3.40 shows the five different merging option results of a square and a circle created using Shapes in the Insert Shapes group on the Format tab. The five merged objects are blue because in every case, the blue square was selected first.

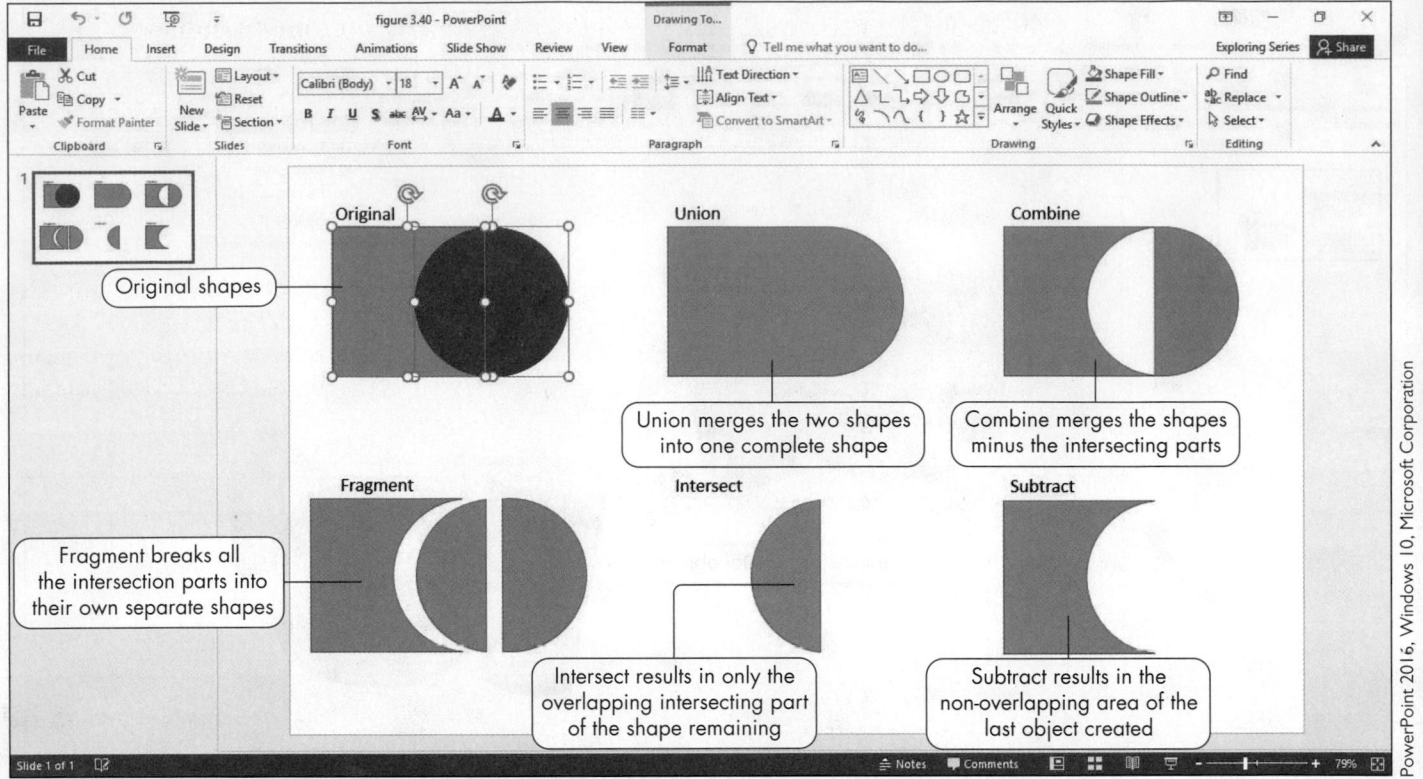

FIGURE 3.40 Merging Shapes

To merge shapes, complete the following steps:

1. Arrange the shapes so they overlap as desired.
2. Select the overlapping shapes.
3. Click the Format tab.
4. Click Merge Shapes in the Insert Shapes group.
5. Click the merge option of your choice.

> **TIP: USING SUBTRACT SHAPES**
> When applying the Subtract Shapes merging option, you will have a different result depending on the shape you select first. In Figure 3.40, the square was selected first, and the circle second.

Group and Ungroup Objects

STEP 3 ›› A drawn object is usually created in pieces, layered, and then grouped to create the final image. These images can be ***ungrouped***, or broken apart, so you can modify or delete the individual pieces. ***Grouping*** enables multiple objects to act or move as though they were a single object, whereas ungrouping separates an object into individual shapes. Grouping is different from merging a shape. Grouping simply makes it easier to move the newly grouped object or apply formatting, whereas merging may create a new object altogether.

Some images are typically created and saved as ***vector graphics***, which are math-based. Drawing programs such as Adobe Illustrator and CorelDRAW are used to create vector graphic images. The advantage of vector files is that they retain perfect clarity when edited or resized due to the fact that the computer simply recalculates the math. Vector files also use a smaller amount of storage space compared to their pixel-based counterparts such as photographs. Many company logos are vector graphics, which leads to another advantage of vector images.

To convert a vector graphic into a drawing object of grouped shapes, complete the following steps:

1. Right-click the image on the slide and select Edit Picture if the option is available. If the option is not available, the graphic cannot be converted into a drawing object.
2. Click Yes if after you select Edit Picture, a message opens asking if you want to convert the picture into a drawing object.

If a vector image is inserted, it is automatically a grouped image, and thus, the option to ungroup is available. This ability to ungroup (or group) the image enables you to separate the parts of the image and edit or adjust the image to tailor it to your needs. Some vector graphics that have been grouped have to be converted into drawing objects by ungrouping them.

> **TIP: AN IMAGE THAT WILL NOT UNGROUP**
>
> If your selected image will not ungroup for editing, it is not in a vector format. Often pictures from the Web are in .bmp, .jpg, .gif, and .png formats, which are not vector-based images and cannot be ungrouped.

To ungroup a drawing object, complete the following steps:

1. Right-click the drawing object on the slide.
2. Point to Group.
3. Select Ungroup to view the individual shapes.

Alternatively, you can ungroup an object using Group in the Arrange group on the Format tab. Select Ungroup to see each individual shape surrounded by adjustment handles. Click outside of the image borders to deselect the shapes.

Some images may have more than one grouping. The artist may create an image from individual shapes, group it, layer it on other images, and then group it again. If this occurs, the ungroup option will be available to repeat again. Figure 3.41 is an example of an image that has been ungrouped with some of the pieces selected.

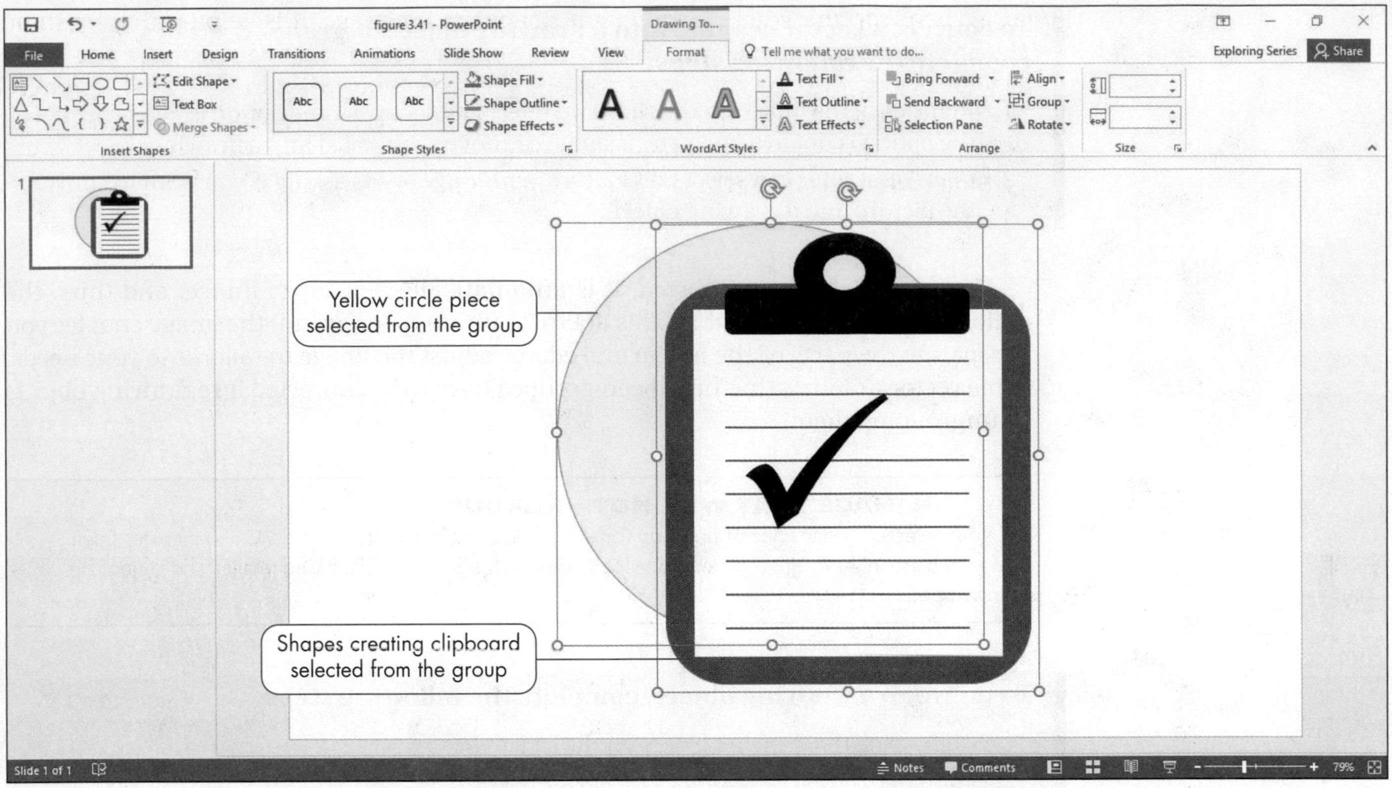

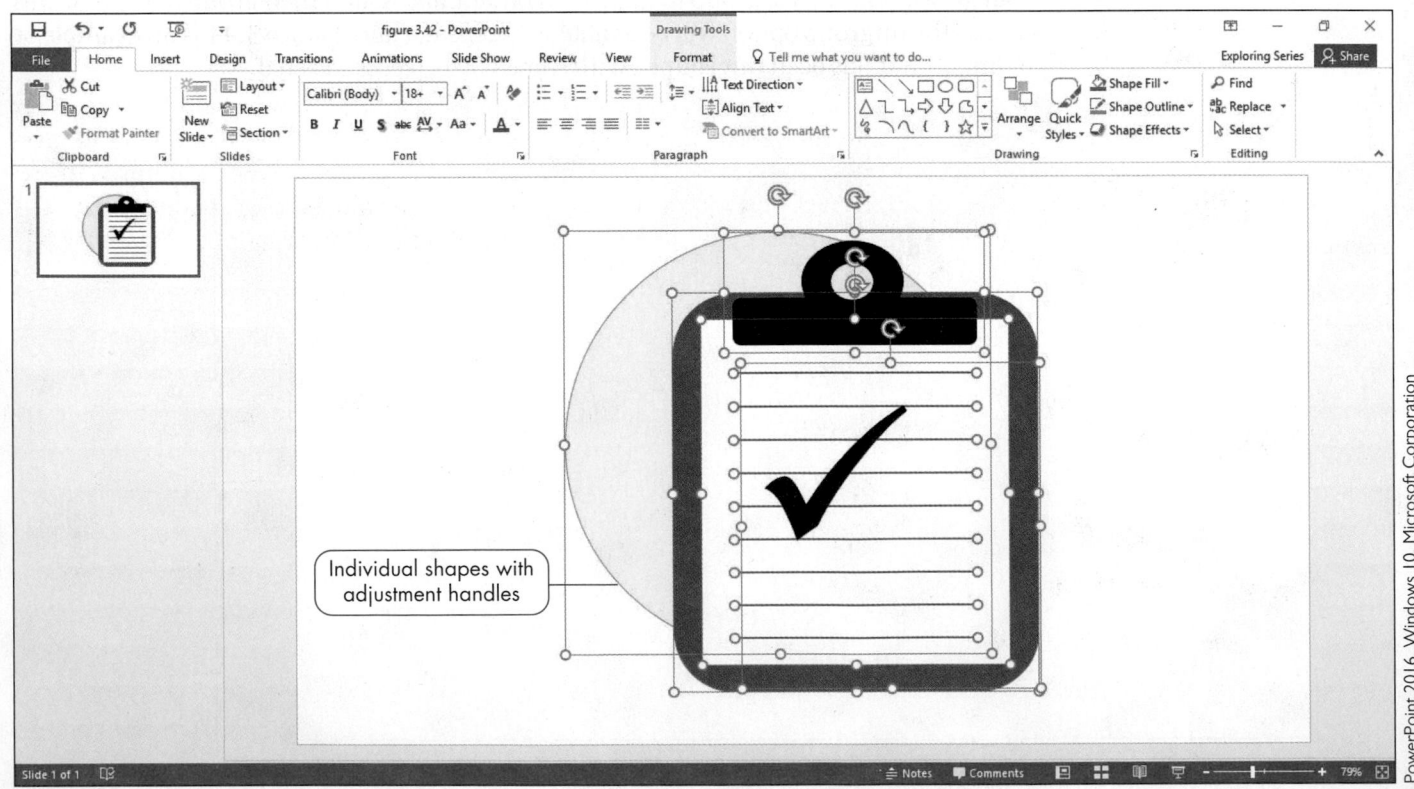

FIGURE 3.41 Modified Objects

If necessary, to continue ungrouping, select the image, right-click, click Group, and then click Ungroup as many times as necessary to break the image down to all shapes. Figure 3.42 shows a graphic that has been ungrouped to its lowest level. All of the individual parts are selected.

FIGURE 3.42 Ungrouped Complex Image

When working with the individual shapes of an image, it is helpful to zoom in on the image. Zooming helps you make sure you have the correct shape before you make modifications. Figure 3.43 shows a selected shapes (lines) that have their fill changed to a theme color. Once you have made all of your needed changes, drag a selection net around all the shapes of the image and group or regroup the image. If you do not group the image, you risk moving the individual pieces inadvertently.

FIGURE 3.43 Modifying Ungrouped Shapes

Recolor Objects

STEP 4 ▶▶ You can quickly change the colors in an image using the Recolor Picture option regardless of image file type, which enables you to match your image to the color scheme of your presentation without ungrouping the image and changing the color of each shape. You can select either a dark or a light variation of your color scheme.

You also can change the color mode of your picture to Grayscale, Sepia, Washout, or Black and White. Grayscale changes your picture up to 256 shades of gray. Sepia gives you that golden tone often used for an old-fashioned photo look. Washout is used to create watermarks, whereas Black and White is a way to reduce image color to black and white. Figure 3.44 shows two different file types of a dog with variations of color.

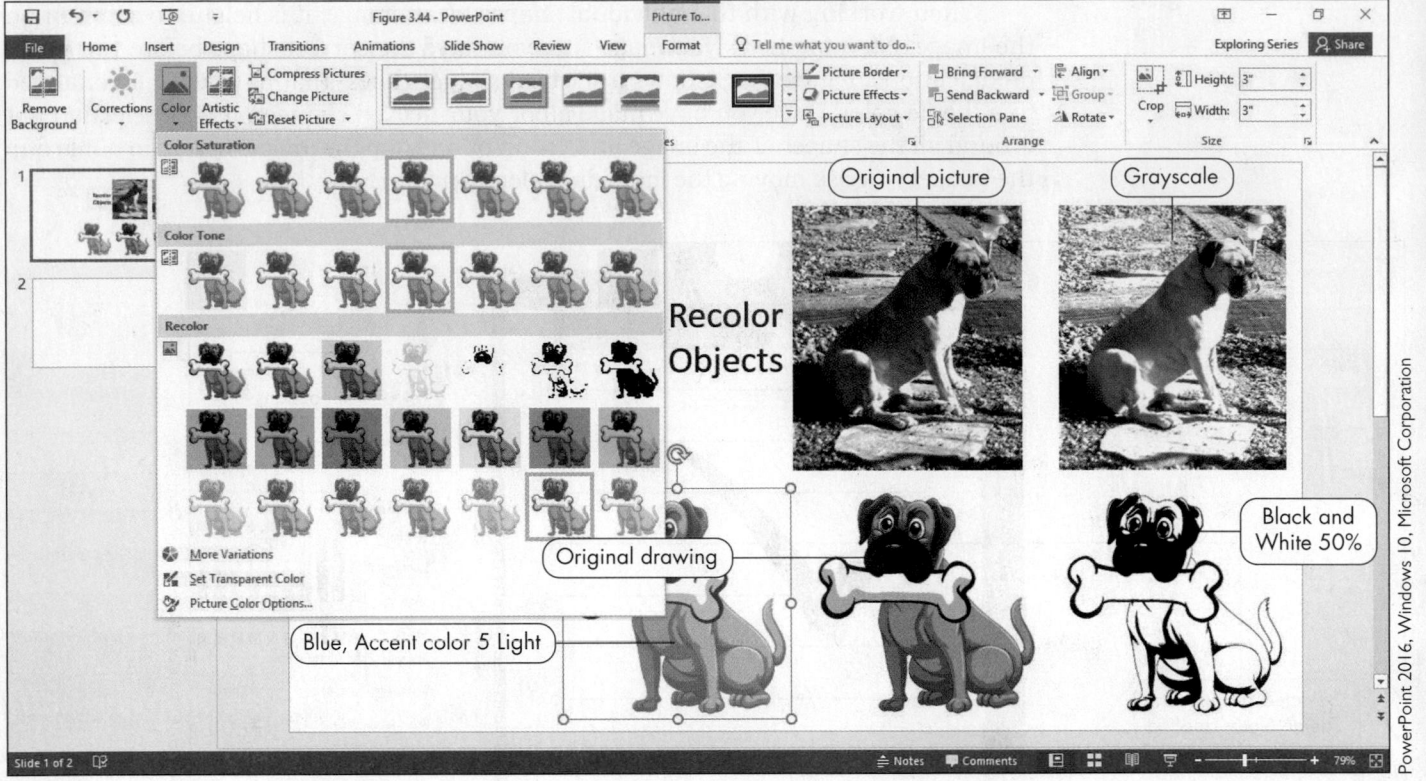

FIGURE 3.44 Recoloring Objects

To change the colors of an image, complete the following steps:

1. Select the image you want to change.
2. Click the Format tab.
3. Click Color in the Adjust group.
4. Click the color variation of your choice, or select More Variations to open the Theme Colors options and select a theme color.

You may want an image without a background, or decide that a portion of the image needs to be transparent. The Recolor gallery includes a Set Transparent Color option that is valuable for creating a transparent area in many pictures. In Figure 3.45 the black is set to transparent so the purple background shows.

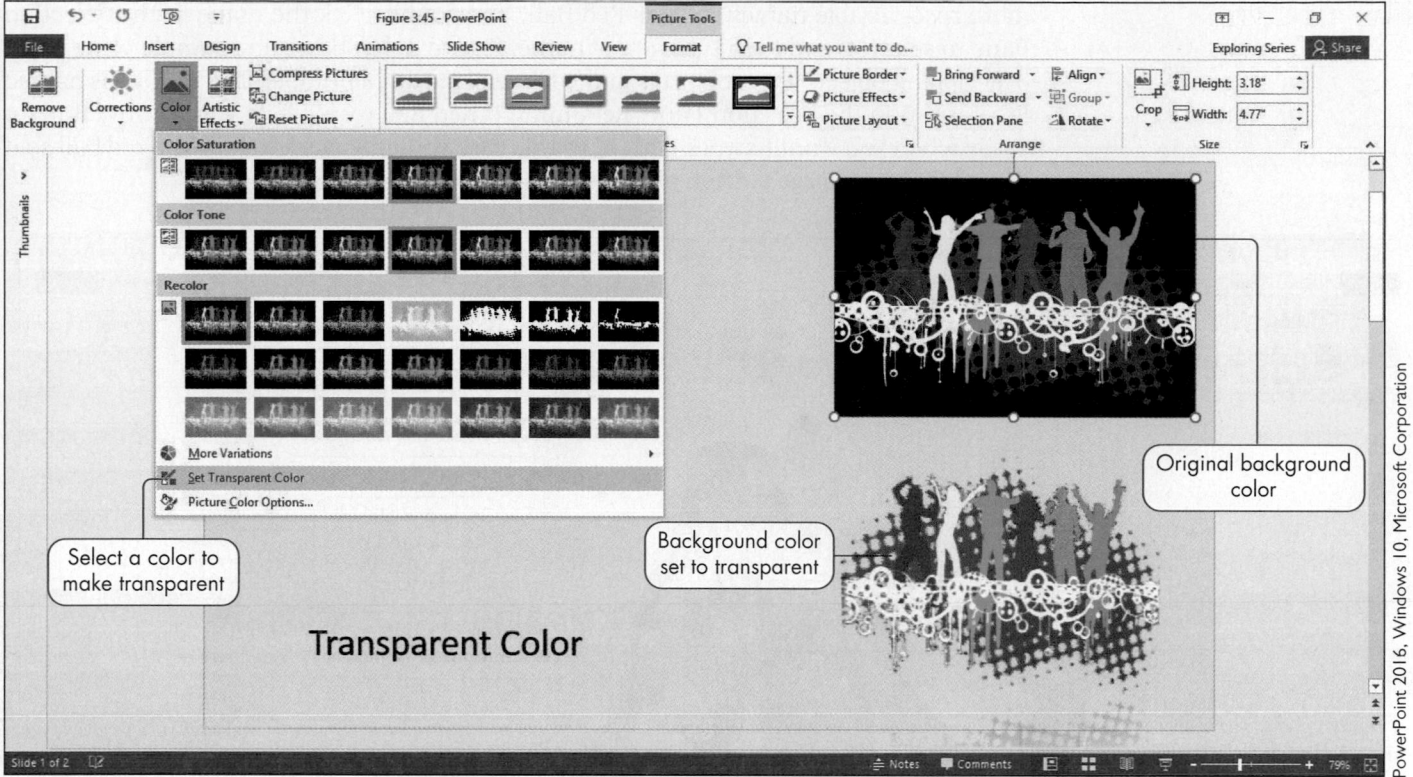

FIGURE 3.45 Set Transparent Color

To set a transparent color in your image, complete the following steps:

1. Select the image in which you want to set a transparent color.
2. Click the Format tab.
3. Click Color in the Adjust group.
4. Click Set Transparent Color and point to the color you want to make transparent.
5. Click to make the color transparent.

Arranging Objects

When you have multiple objects such as shapes, online pictures, SmartArt, and WordArt on the slide, it can become challenging and time consuming to arrange them. While Smart Guides are good for simple alignment, they do not work for all situations. For more complex situations, PowerPoint has several features to control the order and position of the objects, how the objects align to one another, and how they align to the slide. Before using any of these features, you must select the object(s).

Sometimes there are so many objects placed so closely together that it is difficult to select the individual object you need on the slide. You can select the object(s) by using the **Selection Pane**. The Selection Pane, found in the Arrange group on the Format tab, lists all objects on the slide and enables you to select, multiselect, show, hide, or change the order of objects on the slide. The Selection Pane is incredibly helpful when you are working with complex images comprised of overlapping objects. Every object displays on the pane and you can click through the objects to identify them.

The object you selected is highlighted in the Selection Pane. If an object is not selected, click the Home tab, click Select in the Editing group, and then select Selection Pane. Because the Selection Pane is so valuable, you may want to memorize the keyboard shortcut for opening it—Alt+F10—or add it to the Quick Access Toolbar.

If you have many objects of the same shape type listed in the Selection Pane, it might be difficult to identify which to select. In a case like this, you can rename objects with more recognizable names such as Red Ball. Just double-click the name in the Selection Pane to select it, and then type a new name. Figure 3.46 shows an example of multiple overlapping objects. Each object is named Freeform with a number. The red ball is named Freeform 6 in the Selection Pane. Renaming it Red Ball would help you identify it more easily when you want to work with it. In this case you may want to hide the red ball so it is not blocking a large portion of the image.

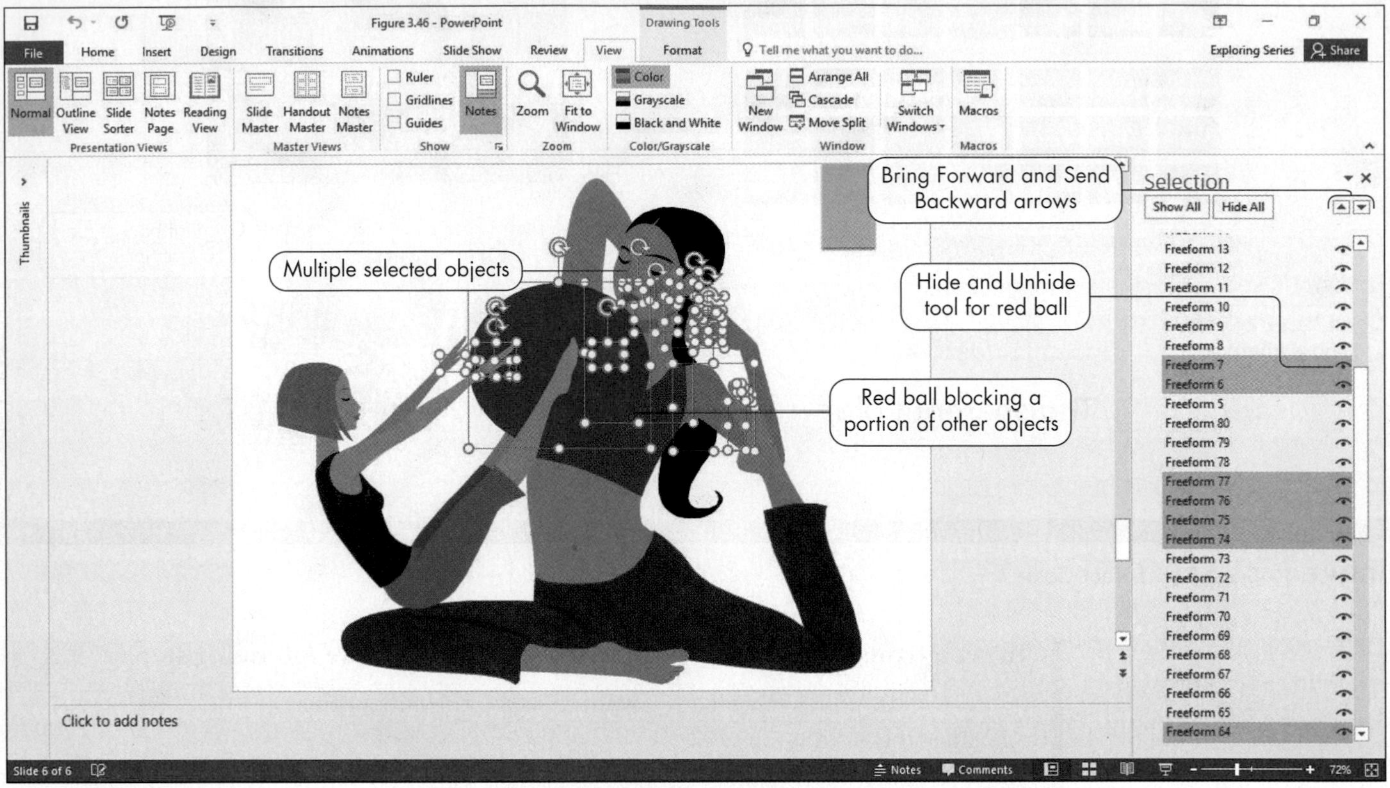

FIGURE 3.46 Selection Pane

If you are having a difficult time identifying objects, you can use Hide and Unhide (the eye) on the Selection Pane to identify objects: select an object on the list, and then click to hide it and click again to unhide it. An even more valuable use of Hide and Unhide, however, is to make objects invisible so you can work on the areas you need without objects getting in the way.

Order Objects

STEP 5 You can layer shapes by placing them under or on top of one another. The order of the layers is called the ***stacking order***. PowerPoint adds shapes or other objects in a stacking order as you add them to the slide. The last shape you place on the slide is on top and is the highest in the stacking order. Drawn images are comprised of shapes that have been stacked. Once you ungroup an image and modify it, you may need to change the stacking order. You can open the Selection Pane to see the order in which objects are placed. The topmost object on the list is at the top of the stacking order. You can use the Bring Forward and Send Backward arrows in the Selection Pane to change the order of the selected object. Figure 3.46 shows the location of the Bring Forward and Send Backward arrows in the Selection Pane.

The Arrange group on the Format tab also includes the Bring Forward and Send Backward arrows. Use the Bring Forward arrow to bring an object forward one layer or to bring it all the way to the front to become the top layer of a stack. Use the Send Backward arrow to move an object back one layer, or move it all the way to the back behind all layers. Figure 3.47 shows the results of reordering a circle at the back of a stack of objects to the top of the stacking order.

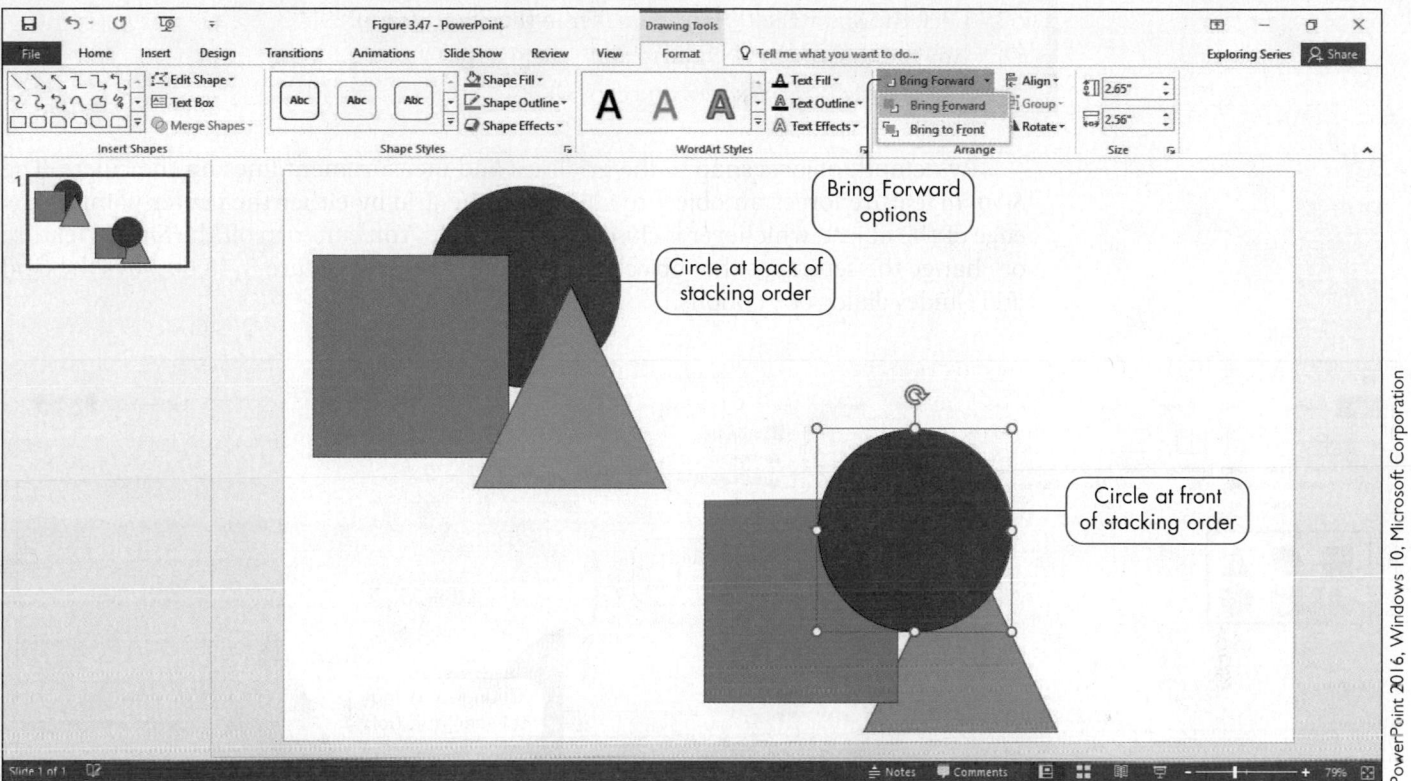

FIGURE 3.47 Changing Stacking Order

> **TIP: ORDERING SHORTCUTS**
> You can right-click a shape and select *Bring to Front* or *Send to Back*. Using this method, you can still choose whether to move one layer or all layers.

Align Objects

Dragging an object to position it on the slide is an easy way to position objects when you use Smart Guides. ***Smart Guides*** display when you drag an object on your slide to help you quickly align objects in relation to other objects. For example, you might want to align a series of rectangles at their tops or adjust the amount of space between the rectangles so that they are evenly spaced. PowerPoint has rulers, a grid, and drawing guides that enable you to complete the aligning process quickly.

Rulers provide you with visual cues that help you keep your objects aligned. They enable you to see the size of an object or the distance between shapes. PowerPoint provides both a horizontal ruler and a vertical ruler.

> **To view and then hide the ruler, complete the following steps:**
> 1. Click the View tab.
> 2. Click the check box for Ruler in the Show group.
> 3. Click the check box for Ruler again to turn off the Ruler.

Each slide can also display a ***grid*** containing intersecting lines, which, by default, are hidden. You can display the grid to align your objects and to keep them evenly spaced. When you activate the grid, you will not see it in Slide Show view, and it will not print.

To view the grid and change the grid settings:

1. Click the View tab.
2. Click the check box for Gridlines in the Show group.
3. Click the Show Dialog Box Launcher in the Show group.
4. Adjust the settings for Snap to and Spacing.
5. Click *Display grid on screen* and click OK.

By default, objects snap to the gridlines and measurement lines on the rulers. The *Snap to* feature forces an object to align with the grid by either the center point or the edge of the object, whichever is closer to the gridline. You can turn off the *Snap to* feature or change the setting so that objects snap to other objects. Figure 3.48 displays the Grid and Guides dialog box options.

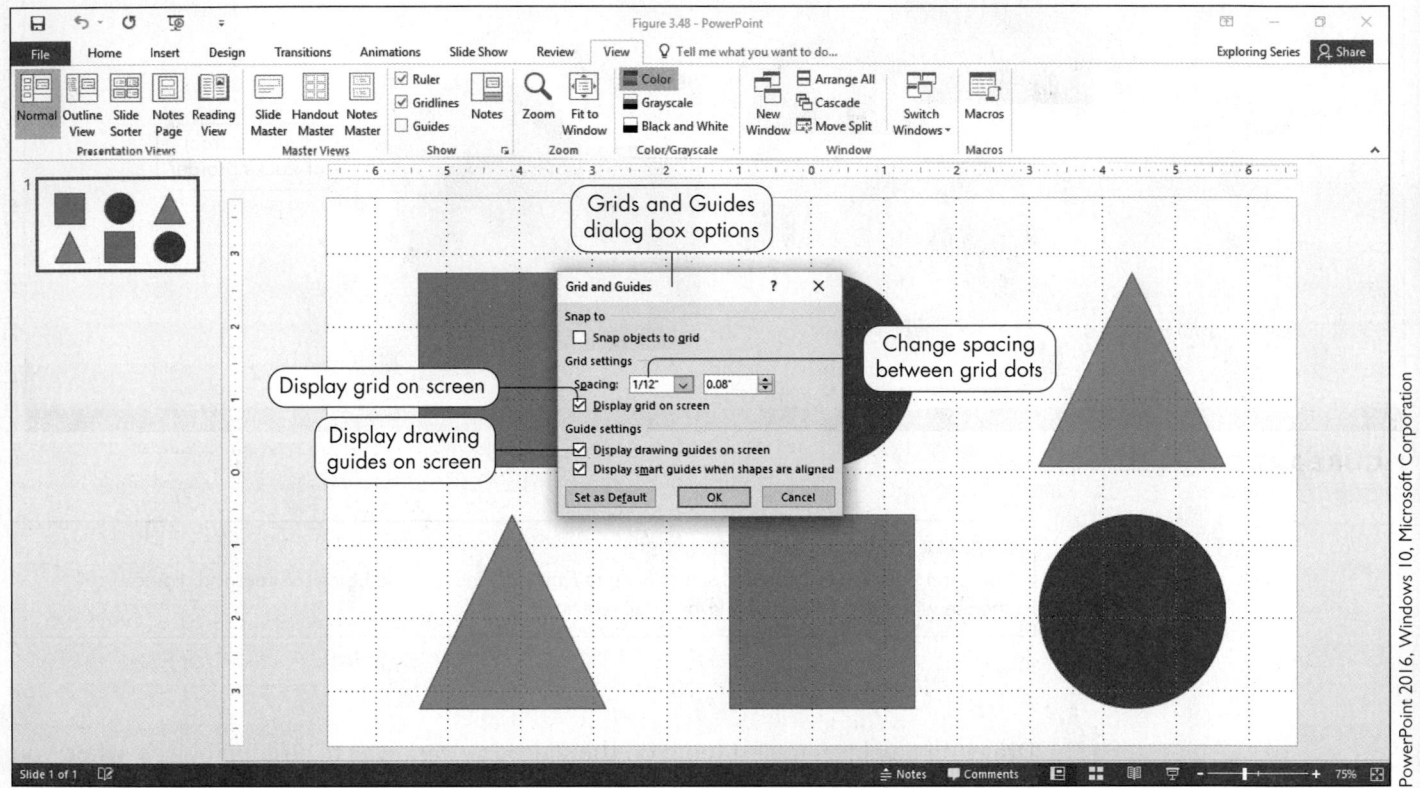

FIGURE 3.48 Grid and Guides Setting

Guides are nonprinting, temporary vertical or horizontal lines that you can place on a slide to help you align objects or determine regions of the slide.

To activate guides, complete the following steps:

1. Click the View tab.
2. Click the check box next to Guides.

When you first display the guides, you see two guides that intersect at the center of the slide (the zero setting on both the horizontal and vertical rulers). To move a guide, point to it and drag. A directional arrow will appear as well as a measurement telling you how far from the center point you are moving the guide. To create additional guides, press Ctrl+Shift while dragging. To remove guides, drag them off the slide. Figure 3.49 displays the default horizontal and vertical guides as well as two additional guides that were created to the left and the right of the zero point on the horizontal ruler.

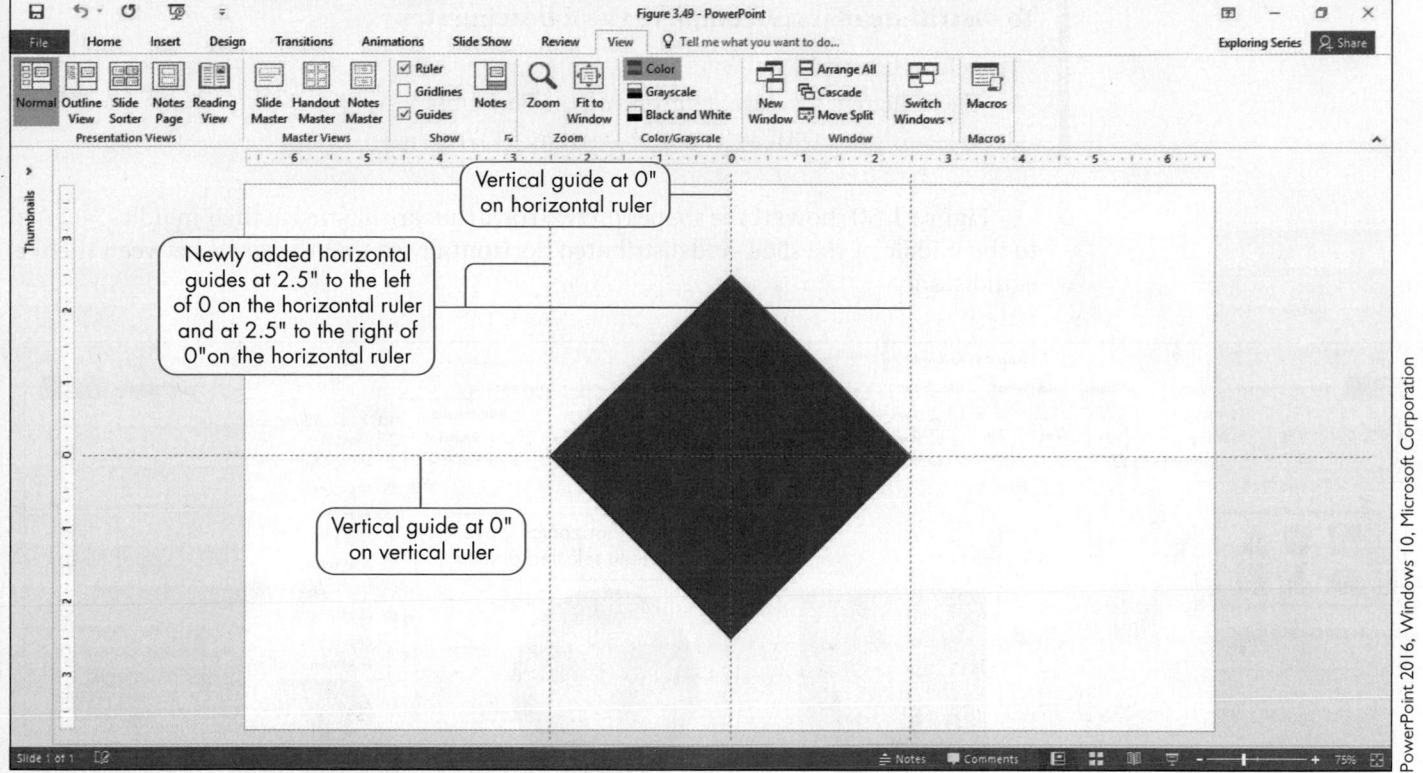

FIGURE 3.49 Creating a Guide

PowerPoint 2016, Windows 10, Microsoft Corporation

> **TIP: RULE OF THIRDS**
> Grids and guides can help you utilize the rule of thirds, a photography strategy that breaks a composition up into horizontal and vertical thirds to draw attention to part of the shot. Change the settings for your grid and guides to divide the screen into horizontal and vertical thirds and then place your objects accordingly. Generally it is easy to center the object on one of the guide intersections.

The **_Align_** feature makes it simple to line up shapes and objects in several ways. You can align with other objects by lining up the sides, middles, or top/bottom edges of objects. Or, if you have only one object or group selected, you can align in relation to the slide—for example, the top or left side of the slide.

To align objects, complete the following steps:

1. Select the objects you want to align.
2. Click Align in the Arrange group on the Format tab.
3. Select Align to Slide or Align Selected Objects depending on if you want to align the objects to the slide or align the objects to one another.
4. Click Align in the Arrange group on the Format tab. This step is not necessary if the option you want is already selected in Step 3.
5. Click one of the following: Align Left, Align Center, Align Right, Align Top, Align Middle, or Align Bottom.

The Align feature also includes options to **_distribute_** selected shapes evenly over a given area. Perhaps you have shapes on the page but they are unequally spaced and you want to have an equal amount of space between all the shapes. Use the distribute options to assign an equal amount of space between the shapes.

Figure 3.50 shows three shapes on two rows that are aligned at their middles, aligned to the middle of the slide, and distributed horizontally so that the space between them is equidistant.

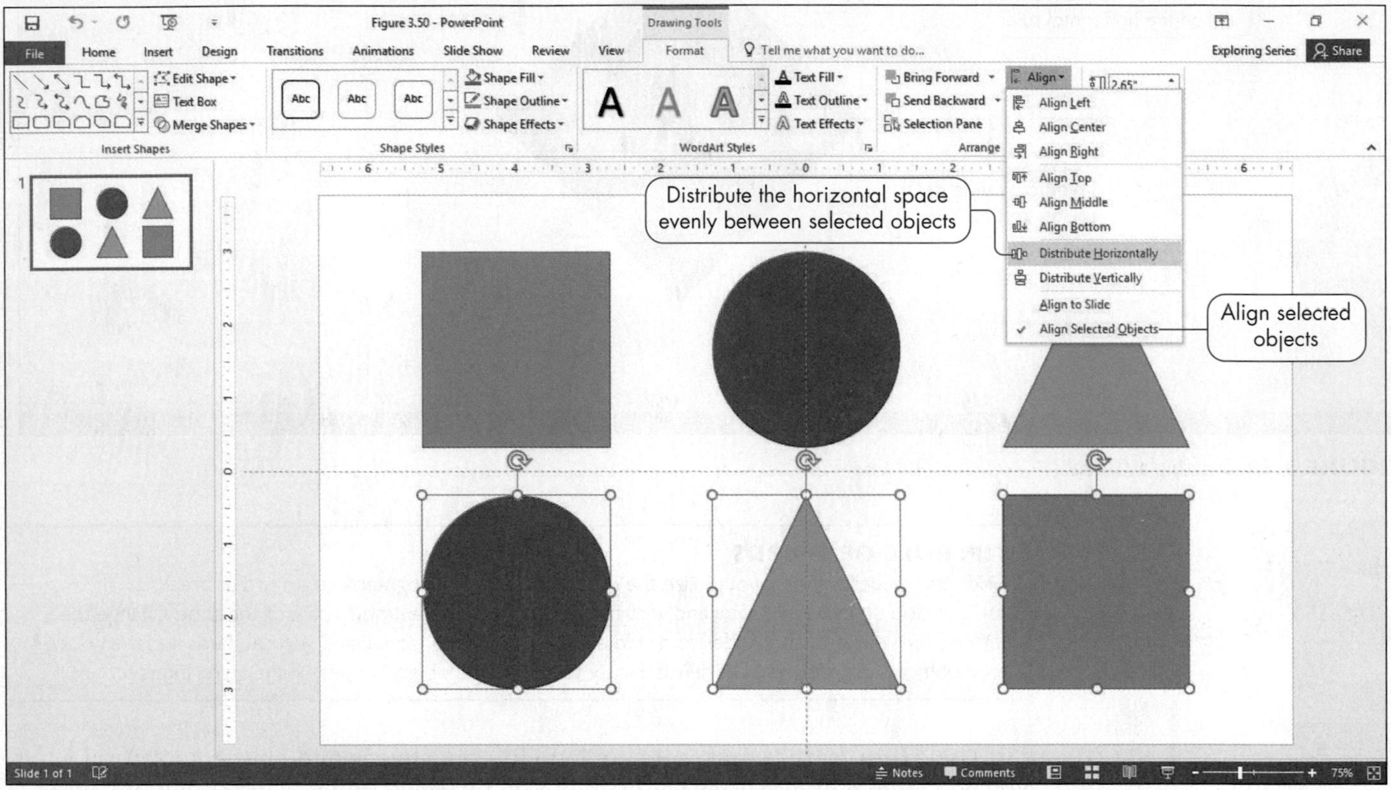

FIGURE 3.50 Alignment Options

8. Why would you ungroup a picture? *p. 1084*

9. Why is the Selection Pane useful? *p. 1089*

10. Why would you use the Recolor Picture tool? *p. 1087*

11. How are rulers, a grid, and drawing guides used when aligning objects? *p. 1091*

Hands-On Exercises

Watch the Video for this Hands-On Exercise!

MyITLab®
HOE3 Training

Skills covered: Resize Objects • Flip Objects • Group and Ungroup Objects • Recolor Objects • Order Objects

3 Object Manipulation

You teach the workshop participants how to size, position, align, ungroup, and use other object manipulation techniques to images. The ability to manipulate pictures by grouping and ungrouping, recoloring, combining, and using other techniques offers unlimited possibilities for creativity. You want your group members to have these skills.

STEP 1 ›› RESIZE OBJECTS

You teach your workshop participants to use the Size Dialog Box Launcher. You want them to be able to precisely size and position objects on the slide. Refer to Figure 3.51 as you complete Step 1.

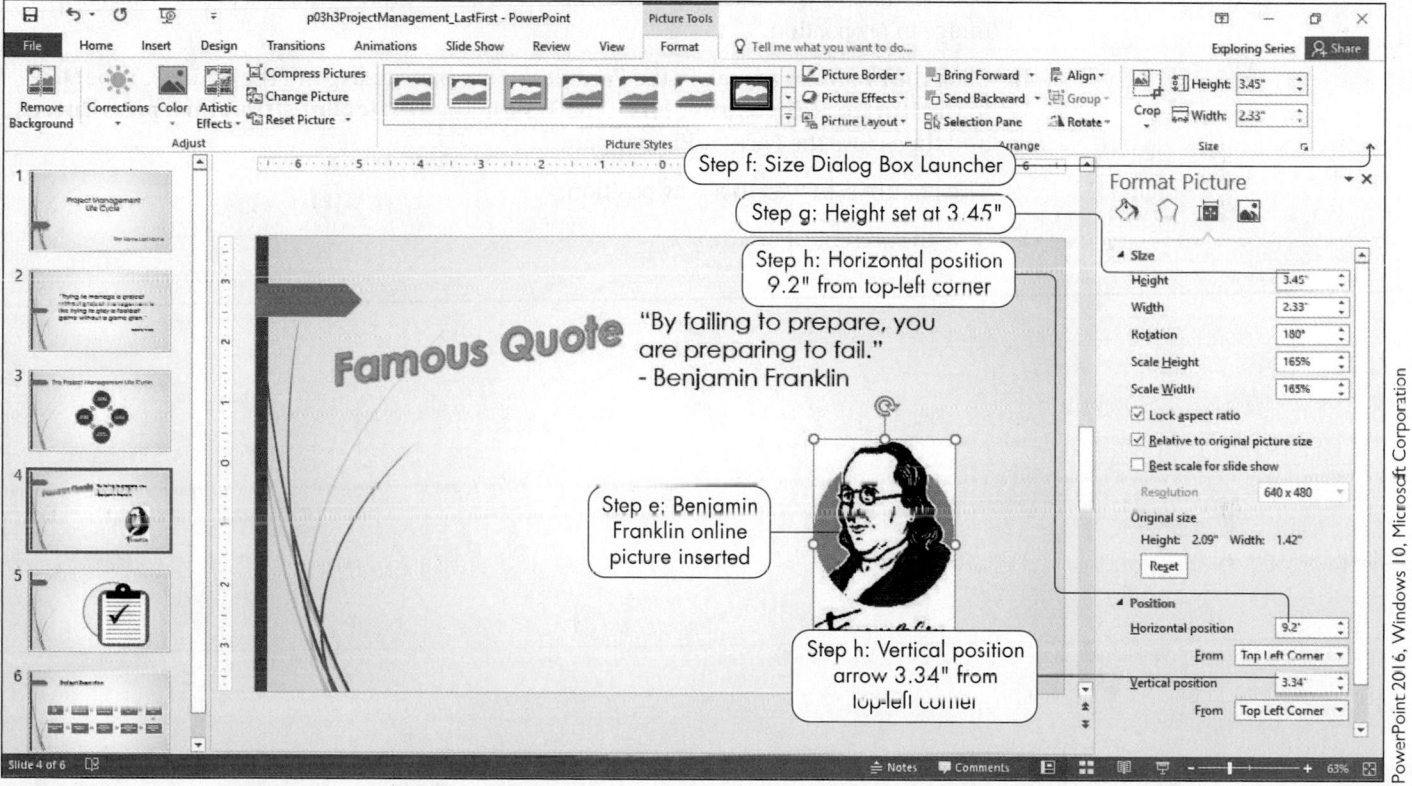

FIGURE 3.51 Size and Position Alignment Options

a. Open *p03h2ProjectManagement_LastFirst* if you closed it at the end of Hands-On Exercise 2, and save it as *p03h3ProjectManagement_LastFirst*, changing h2 to h3.

b. Click **Slide 4**. Click the **Insert tab** and click **Online Pictures** in the Images group.

The Insert Pictures dialog box opens.

c. Type **Benjamin Franklin** in the **Bing Image Search box** and press **Enter**.

The search results of Benjamin Franklin are images licensed under Creative Commons.

d. Click **Close** to close the Creative Commons Information Box.

e. Insert the image of Benjamin Franklin as shown in Figure 3.51.

You have inserted the image in the center of Slide 4.

f. Click the **Size Dialog Box Launcher** in the Size group on the Format tab.

The Format Picture pane opens with the Size option expanded.

g. Type **3.45** in the **Height box** and click in the **Width box**.

Because *Lock aspect ratio* is selected, the width of the image changes to 2.33, keeping the image in proportion.

h. Click the **Position arrow** in the Format Picture pane to expand the options. Type **9.2** in the **Horizontal position box**, type **3.34** in the **Vertical position box**, press **Enter**, and then close the Format Picture pane.

The picture is moved to a new position.

i. Save the presentation.

Rotating and flipping are both ways to angle an object on the slide. You can rotate using precise measurements or, for an imprecise method of rotation, you can rotate the object using the Rotation handle. You ask your participants to use these methods so that they are familiar with the benefits of each. Refer to Figure 3.52 as you complete Step 2.

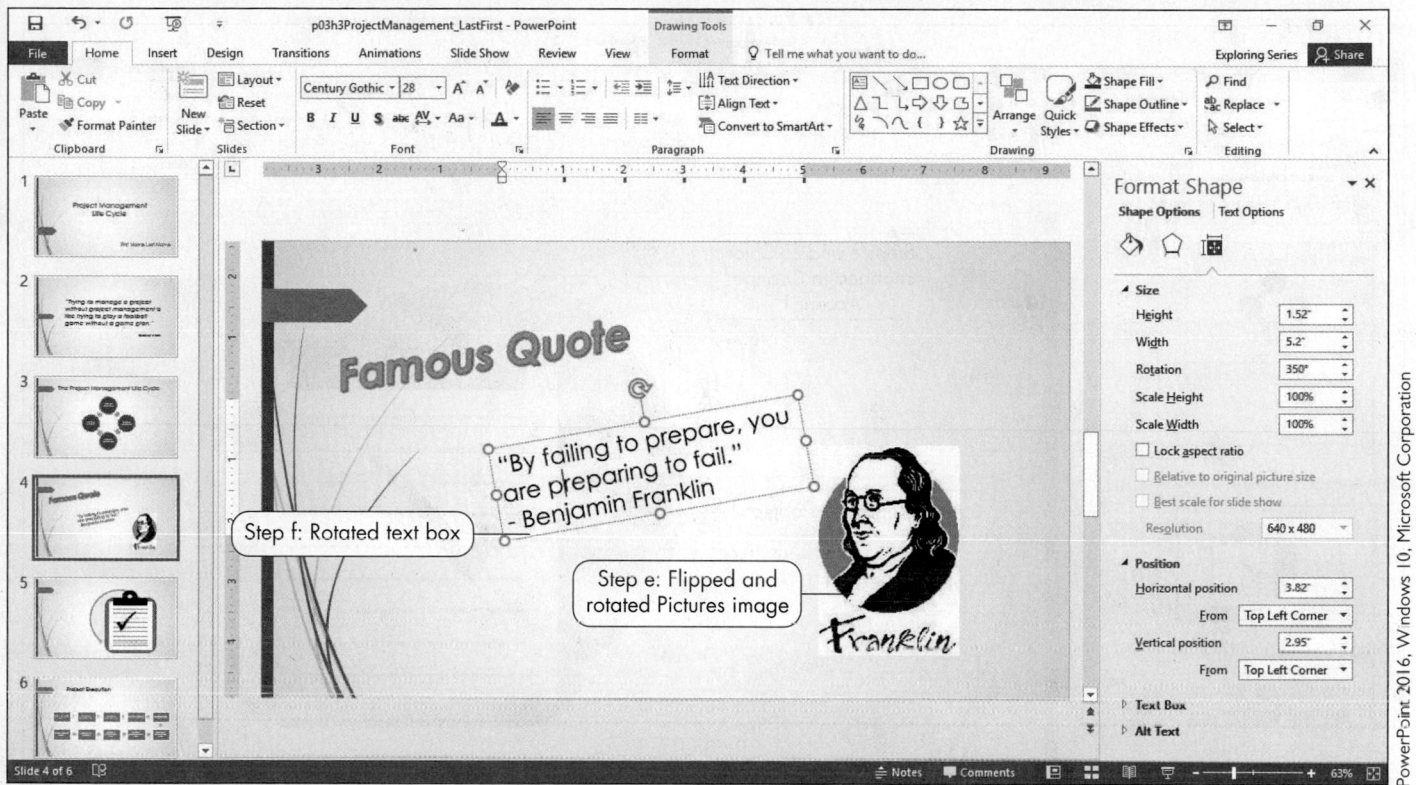

FIGURE 3.52 Flipping and Rotating

a. Click the **Benjamin Franklin image** and click **Rotate** in the Arrange group on the Format tab.

The rotate and flip options appear.

b. Click **Flip Horizontal**.

Benjamin Franklin now faces to the right side of the slide.

c. Click **Rotate** in the Arrange group and select **More Rotation Options**.

d. Type **180** in the Rotation box and press **Enter**.

The picture is rotated upside down.

e. Click **Rotate** in the Arrange group and select **Flip Vertical**. Close the Format Shape pane.

The Online Pictures picture appears to be in its original position, but the rotation angle is still set at 180°.

f. Select the text box in the top-right of the slide and drag it down and to the left to the approximate center of the slide using the Smart Guides to help you position the text box. Position the insertion point over the rotation handle and drag the rotation handle to the left until the text box is rotated to approximately match the slant in the *Famous Quote* WordArt.

> **TROUBLESHOOTING:** As you change the angle of rotation for the text box, you may need to reposition the text box on the slide so that it does not overlap the picture. An easy way to make small position adjustments is to press the arrow keys on the keyboard.

g. Save the presentation.

Being able to change colors, remove shapes, add shapes, and group, ungroup, and regroup images are important skills you want your participants to master. You ask the participants to ungroup an image, change the color of a portion of an image, and regroup the image. Refer to Figure 3.53 as you complete Step 3.

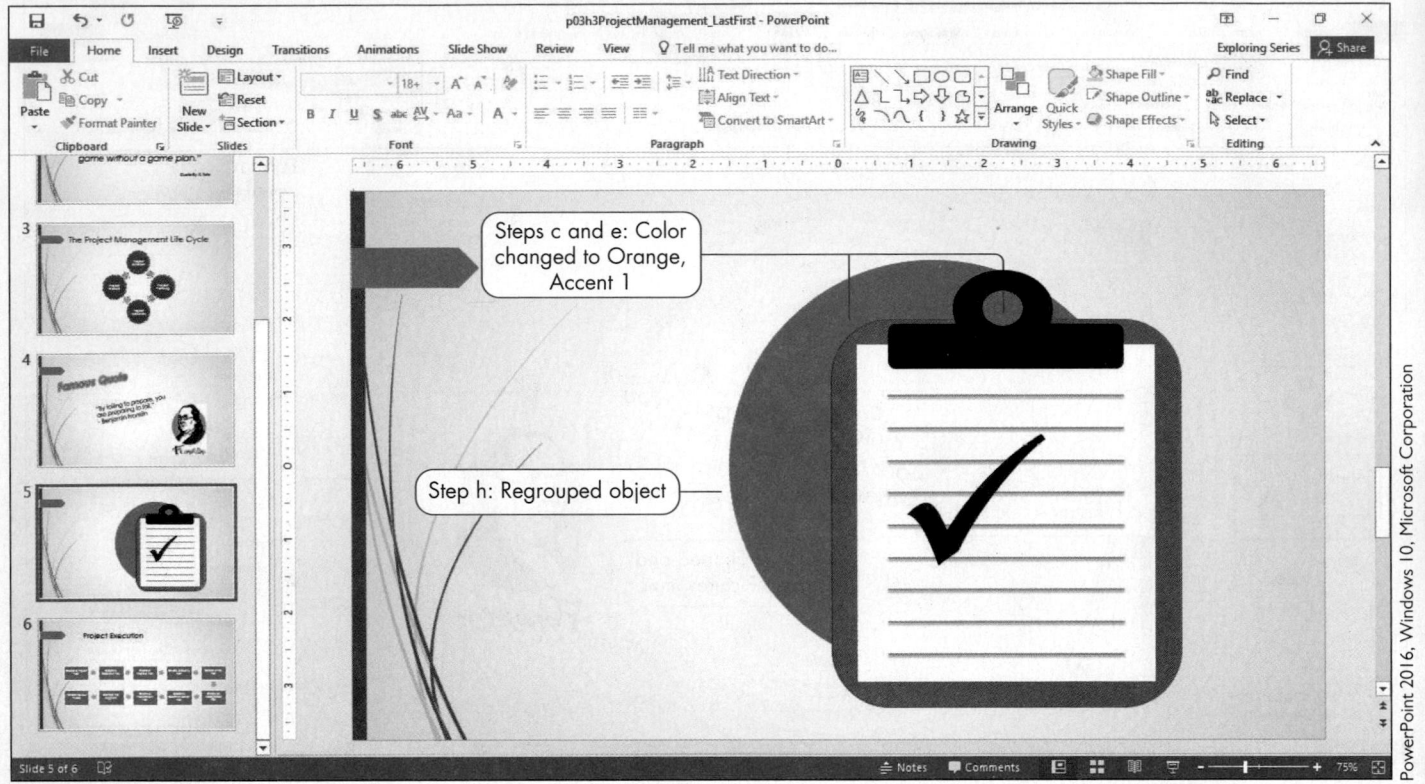

FIGURE 3.53 Grouping, Ungrouping, Regrouping

a. Right-click the **clipboard picture** on Slide 5, click **Group**, click **Ungroup**.

The picture breaks into two groups: a circle and a clipboard comprised of multiple shapes.

> **TROUBLESHOOTING:** If Group does not appear as an option when you right-click the picture, right-click another area of the picture.

b. Click the **Format tab**, click **Group** in the Arrange group, select **Ungroup**, and then click outside the picture border.

When you ungroup this time, objects are selected and surrounded with adjustment handles but there are still grouped shapes forming the clipboard. Clicking outside the border deselects the shapes so that you can select just the one you wish to modify.

c. Select the **large yellow circle**, click **Shape Fill** in the Shape Styles group, and then click **Orange, Accent 1** (first row, fifth column).

You change the harsh yellow fill to one of the theme colors of the presentation. You note, however, that the small circle on the clipboard handle is still yellow.

d. Select the **handle** of the clipboard, click **Group** in the Arrange group, and then select **Ungroup**. Click outside of the image again.

All of the shapes making up the clipboard handle have now been ungrouped.

e. Select the **small yellow circle**, and then click the **Shape Fill button** (not the arrow) to change the fill color to **Orange, Accent 1**. Click outside of the image.

The Shape Fill button will default to the last color selected.

f. Right-click the **clipboard picture**, click **Group**, and then click **Regroup**.

g. Drag diagonally from the lower-left and create a selection net around all the shapes used to make the clipboard picture and the background circle.

All the shapes are selected.

h. Click the **Format tab**, click **Group** in the Arrange group, and then select **Regroup**.

i. Save the presentation.

STEP 4 ›› RECOLOR OBJECTS

You teach your workshop participants to recolor a picture so that it matches the color scheme of the presentation. Refer to Figure 3.54 as you complete Step 4.

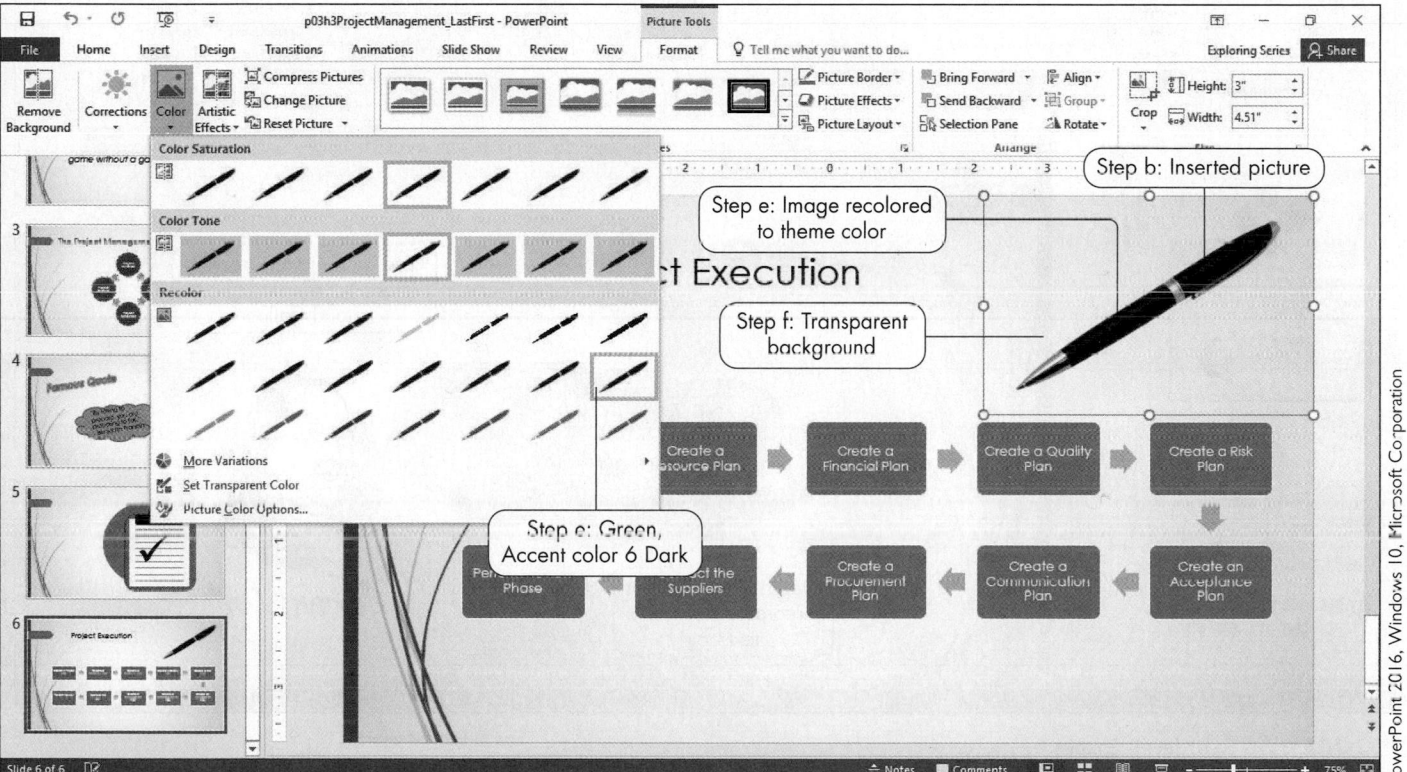

FIGURE 3.54 Recolored picture

a. Click **Slide 6**. Click the **Insert tab** and click **Pictures** in the Images group.

b. Locate *p03h3Pen* in your data files and click **Insert**.

c. Ensure the image is selected, and click the **Format tab**. In the Size group, change the height to **3**.

The width will change automatically.

d. Click **Align** in the Arrange group and select **Align Top** to move the object to the top of the slide. Once the picture is aligned to the top, click **Align** again and select **Align Right**.

The picture is now aligned to the top-right of the slide.

e. Click **Color** in the Adjust group and click **Green, Accent color 6 Dark** under the Recolor category (second row, seventh column).

The color of the image now matches the colors in the theme.

f. Click **Color** and click **Set Transparent Color**. Click anywhere in the background around the pen.

The distracting background becomes transparent leaving the pen.

g. Save the presentation.

STEP 5 ›› ORDER OBJECTS

Being able to create and reorder shapes allows you to be creative, enabling you to create backgrounds, borders, and corners. Refer to Figure 3.55 as you complete Step 5.

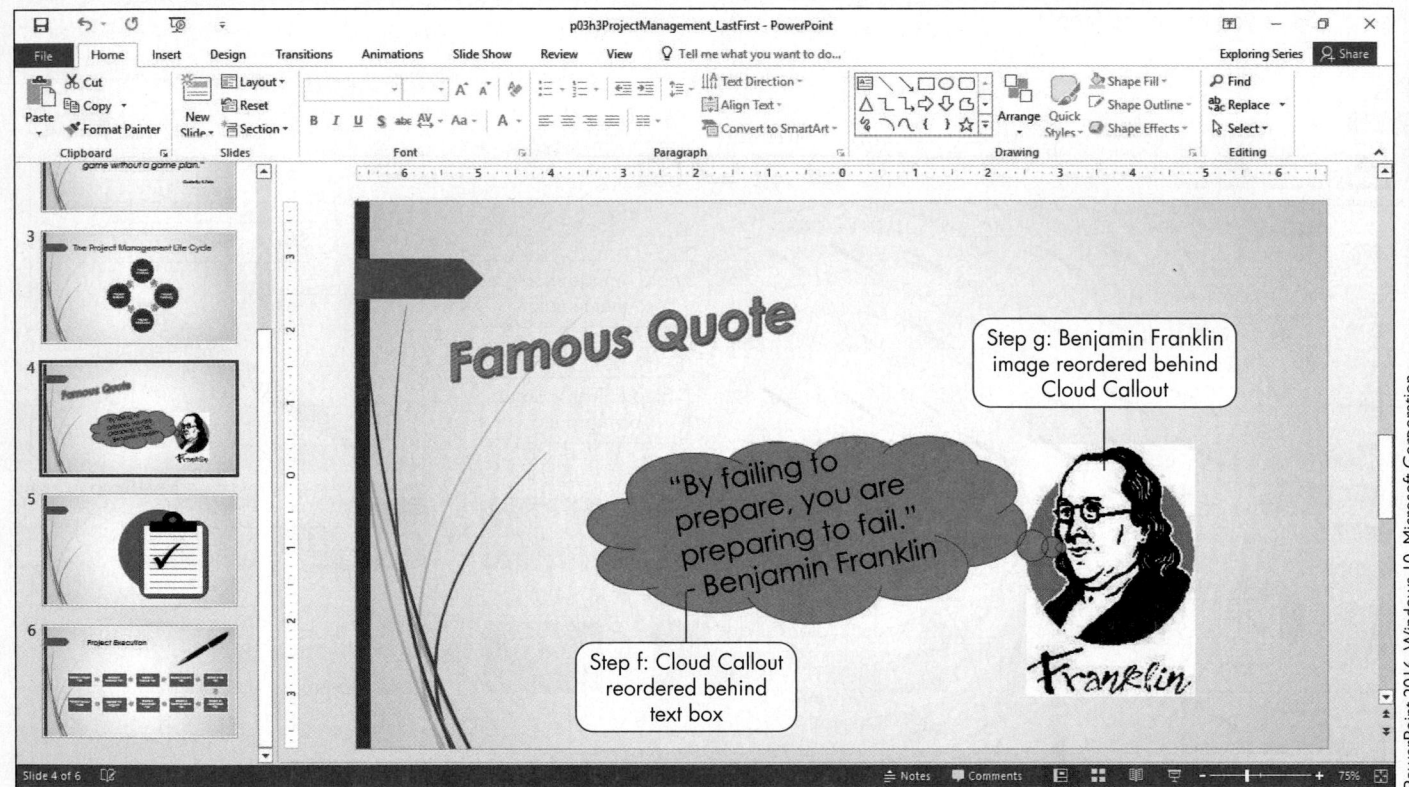

FIGURE 3.55 Reordered Shapes

a. Click **Slide 4**. Click the **View tab** and click the **Ruler check box** in the Show group to view the ruler if it is not currently displayed.

The horizontal and vertical rulers display.

b. Click the **Insert tab**, click **Shapes** in the Illustrations group, and then click the **Cloud Callout** in the Callouts category.

c. Position the cross-hair pointer on the slide so that the indicator on the ruler is at the **3.5" mark** to the left of the zero point on the horizontal ruler and the **0.5" mark** above the zero point on the vertical ruler.

This is the beginning point for the cloud callout.

d. Drag to the **2.5" mark** to the right of the zero point on the horizontal ruler and the **2" mark** below the zero point on the vertical ruler and release.

A large cloud callout shape in the theme color is created on top of the text box on the slide. You will use the cloud callout as a callout for the Online Pictures image. Currently, it is hiding the quote and must be reordered.

> **TROUBLESHOOTING:** Drag the top-left handle of the selected shape to adjust the starting point. Drag the bottom-right handle of the selected shape to adjust the ending point.

e. Drag the adjustment handle (yellow circle) at the bottom of the callout shape to the **3" mark** to the right of the zero point on the horizontal ruler and the **1" mark** below 0 on the vertical ruler until it looks similar to the position shown in Figure 3.55.

f. Click the **Format tab**, click the **Shape Fill arrow** in the Shape Styles group, and then click **Orange, Accent 1, Lighter 40%** (fourth row, fifth column). Click the **Send Backward arrow** in the Arrange group of the Format tab and select **Send to Back**.

g. Select the **Benjamin Franklin picture**. Click the **Send Backward arrow** in the Arrange group and select **Send to Back**. If necessary, move the text box into position as seen in Figure 3.55.

> **TROUBLESHOOTING:** Adjust position and the size of the text box to fit within the cloud callout if the text does not fit within the shape.

h. Save and close the file. Based on your instructor's directions, submit the following:

p03h1Project_LastFirst

p03h3ProjectManagement_LastFirst.

Chapter Objectives Review

After reading this chapter, you have accomplished the following objectives:

1. Create shapes

- You can use shapes to highlight information, as a design element, as the basis for creating illustrations, or to contain information in infographics.
- Draw lines and connectors: Lines are shapes that can be used to point to information, or to divide a slide into sections. Connectors are lines that attach to the shapes you create and move with shapes when the shapes are moved.
- Create and modify freeform shapes: PowerPoint provides tools for creating, sizing, and positioning shapes. You can modify a freeform shape to achieve the desired shape through the help of vertexes.

2. Apply Quick Styles and customize shapes

- A Quick Style is a format that can be applied to a shape or object to add a professional look.
- Applying a Quick Style enables you to apply preset options.
- Change shape fills: A shape can be customized by changing its default fill to another color, to a picture, to a gradient, to a texture, or to no fill.
- Change shape outlines: The shape outline color, weight, or dash style can be modified.
- Change shape effects: Special effects such as shadows, reflections, and glows may be added.

3. Create SmartArt

- SmartArt graphics are diagrams that present information visually to effectively communicate a message.
- Type text in an existing SmartArt layout or convert existing text into a SmartArt diagram.
- Choose a SmartArt diagram type: Select a diagram type from one of the nine categories of diagrams in the SmartArt gallery. Refer to the description of the layout to ensure that it is appropriate to the information type.
- Use the SmartArt Text pane: SmartArt diagrams include a Text pane which enables you to type text in the pane like you would type an outline.

4. Modify SmartArt

- Change SmartArt theme colors: SmartArt diagrams can be modified to fit nearly any color scheme.
- SmartArt can be modified to include additional shapes, to delete shapes, to apply a SmartArt style, to revise the color scheme, or to add special effects.
- The direction, size, and positioning of a SmartArt diagram can be changed.
- Use Quick Styles with SmartArt: After creating the diagram, you can use Quick Styles to adjust the style to match other styles you have used in your presentation or to make the diagram easier to understand.
- Change the SmartArt layout: Once a SmartArt diagram type has been chosen, it can easily be converted to another layout.
- Change SmartArt type: You can change the SmartArt diagram type if you decide a different type would be better.
- Convert text to a SmartArt diagram: Bullets and other text can be converted directly to a SmartArt diagram.

5. Create WordArt and Modify WordArt

- WordArt is text with decorative effects applied to draw attention to the text.
- Crcatc WordArt: Select a WordArt style and type the text you desire.
- Modify WordArt: WordArt can be modified by transforming the shape of the text and by applying special effects and colors. Special effects available include 3-D presets and rotations.
- Text created as WordArt can be edited.

6. Modify objects

- Resize objects: To precisely resize objects, specify the exact height and width measurement in the Size group on the Format tab or in the Format pane.
- Flip and rotate objects: An object may be flipped horizontally or vertically, or rotated by dragging its green rotation handle.
- Merge shapes: The Merge Shapes feature enables you to take shapes that you have inserted and merge them together. There are five different merging options: Union, Combine, Fragment, Intersect, and Subtract.
- Group and ungroup objects: Vector images can be ungrouped so basic shapes can be customized, and objects can be regrouped so they can be moved as one object.
- Recolor objects: Pictures can be recolored by changing their color mode or by applying dark or light variations of a theme color or custom color.

7. Arrange objects

- Objects are stacked in layers.
- The object at the top of the layer is the one that fully displays, while other objects in the stack may have some portions blocked.
- Order objects: The stacking order of shapes can be reordered so that objects can be seen as desired.
- Align objects: Features such as rulers, grids, guides, align, and distribute can be used to arrange objects on a slide and arrange objects in relation to one another.

Key Terms Matching

Match the key terms with their definitions. Write the key term letter by the appropriate numbered definition.

a. Adjustment handle   **k.** Infographic
b. Aspect ratio   **l.** Line weight
c. Callout   **m.** Lock Drawing Mode
d. Connector   **n.** Picture fill
e. Distribute   **o.** Selection net
f. Eyedropper   **p.** SmartArt
g. Freeform shape   **q.** Stacking order
h. Gradient fill   **r.** Texture fill
i. Group   **s.** Vector graphic
j. Guide   **t.** Vertex

1. _____ Inserts an image from a file into a shape. **p. 1054**

2. _____ A blend of two or more colors or shades. **p. 1055**

3. _____ A marquee that selects all objects in an area you define by dragging. **p. 1051**

4. _____ A yellow circle that enables you to modify a shape. **p. 1045**

5. _____ Enables the creation of multiple shapes of the same type. **p. 1045**

6. _____ A tool used to recreate an exact color. **p. 1052**

7. _____ A visual representation of data or knowledge. **p. 1044**

8. _____ A line shape that is attached to and moves with other shapes. **p. 1047**

9. _____ Diagram that presents information visually to effectively communicate a message. **p. 1066**

10. _____ A feature which keeps an object's proportion the same with respect to width and height. **p. 1082**

11. _____ Combines two or more objects. **p. 1084**

12. _____ Point where a curve ends or the point where two line segments meet in a freeform shape. **p. 1048**

13. _____ To divide or evenly spread shapes over a given area. **p. 1043**

14. _____ Inserts a fill such as marble into a shape. **p. 1056**

15. _____ A shape that combines both curved and straight lines. **p. 1048**

16. _____ An object that provides space for text anywhere on a slide. **p. 1045**

17. _____ The order of objects placed on top of one another. **p. 1090**

18. _____ An object-oriented graphic based on geometric formulas. **p. 1084**

19. _____ A straight horizontal or vertical line used to align objects. **p. 1092**

20. _____ The width or thickness of a line. **p. 1057**

Multiple Choice

1. Which of the following presents information as a diagram?

   (a) Text box

   (b) WordArt

   (c) Text pane

   (d) SmartArt

2. An object that provides space for text anywhere on a slide:

   (a) Text box

   (b) WordArt

   (c) Text pane

   (d) SmartArt

3. Which of the following is a reason for ungrouping a drawn object?

   (a) To resize the group as one piece

   (b) To move the objects as one

   (c) To add text on top of the group

   (d) To be able to individually change shapes used to create the composite image

4. Which of the following breaks all intersecting parts of selected shapes into their own separate shapes?

   (a) Fragment

   (b) Intersect

   (c) Subtract

   (d) Union

5. You have inserted a picture of a field with a dog on the right side. If you flip the picture vertically, what would the resulting image look like?

   (a) The image would show right side up, but the dog would be on the left side.

   (b) The image would be upside down with the dog's head pointing down.

   (c) The image would be rotated 270°, and the dog would be at the top.

   (d) The image would be rotated 90°, and the dog would be on the bottom.

6. You have items needed for a camping trip in a bullet placeholder. Which of the following SmartArt diagrams would you use to display the data as an infographic?

   (a) Hierarchy

   (b) Cycle

   (c) List

   (d) Relationship

7. Which of the following is *not* a layout available from the SmartArt gallery?

   (a) Information table

   (b) Horizontal bullet list

   (c) Process graphic

   (d) Cycle matrix

8. Which of the following might be a reason for changing the stacking order of shapes?

   (a) To show a relationship by placing shapes in front of or behind each other

   (b) To hide something on a shape

   (c) To uncover something hidden by another shape

   (d) All of the above

9. Which of the following SmartArt diagram layouts is used to illustrate connections?

   (a) Relationship

   (b) Matrix

   (c) Cycle

   (d) Pyramid

10. Which of the following may be used to precisely align objects?

    (a) Gridlines

    (b) Smart Guides

    (c) Ruler

    (d) All of the above

Practice Exercises

1 Hiring Flow Chart

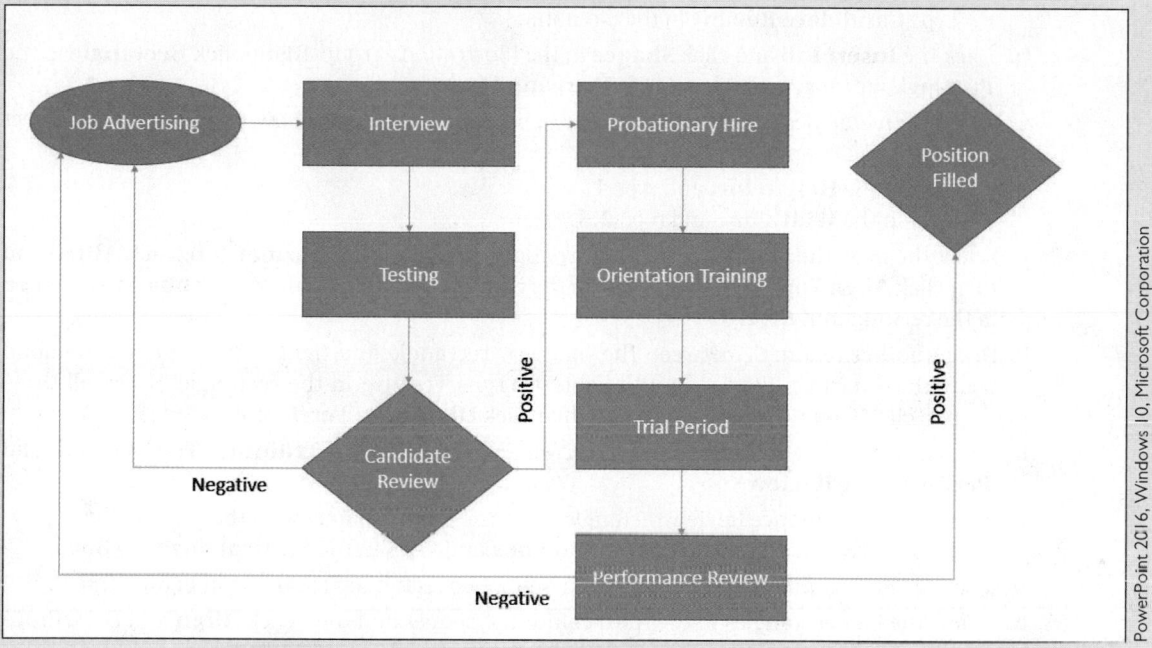

FROM SCRATCH To help explain the hiring process at your company, you create a Hiring Flow Chart. You want the flow chart to show the four stages of the hiring. Refer to Figure 3.56 as you complete this exercise.

FIGURE 3.56 Hiring Flow Chart

a. Open a blank presentation file and save it as **p03p1Hiring_LastFirst**. Create a Notes and Handouts header with your name and a footer with your instructor's name and your class. Include the current date.

b. Click the **Home tab** and click **Layout** in the Slides group. Select the **Blank layout**.

c. Click the **Insert tab** and click **Shape** in the Illustrations group. Click **Oval** in the Basic Shapes category. Drag to create an oval on the slide.

d. Change the size of the oval shape by doing the following:
   - Click the **Format tab** and click the **Size Dialog Box Launcher** to open the Format Shape pane.
   - Click in the **Height box** and type **1**.
   - Click in the **Width box** and type **2.5**.
   - Click the **Position arrow** and type **.3** in the **Horizontal position box** and **0.89** in the **Vertical position box**.
   - Type **Job Advertising** in the oval.

e. Click the **Insert tab** and click **Shapes** in the Illustrations group. Click **Diamond** in the Basic Shapes category. Drag to create a diamond on the slide.

f. Change the size of the diamond shape in the Format Shape pane by doing the following:
   - Click in the **Height box** and type **2**.
   - Click in the **Width box** and type **2.5**.
   - Click the **Position arrow** and type **10.03** in the **Horizontal position box** and **0.89** in the **Vertical position box**.
   - Type **Position Filled** in the diamond.

g. Create another diamond shape in the Format Shape pane with the following formatting:
- Click in the **Height box** and type **2**.
- Click in the **Width box** and type **2.5**.
- Click the **Position arrow** and type **3.54** in the **Horizontal position box** and **4.46** in the **Vertical position box**.
- Type **Candidate Review** in the diamond.

h. Click the **Insert tab** and click **Shapes** in the Illustrations group. Right-click **Rectangle** in the Rectangle category and select **Lock Drawing Mode**.

i. Draw six rectangles on the screen in the approximate locations shown in Figure 3.56. Select all six rectangles and:
- Click in the **Height box** and type **1**.
- Click in the **Width box** and type **2.5**.

j. Select the oval, the diamond, and the two top rectangles. Click **Format tab**, click **Align**, and then click **Align Top**. Type **Interview** in the rectangle on the left and type **Probationary Hire** in the rectangle on the right.

k. Drag another rectangle between the *Interview* rectangle and the *Candidate Review* diamond using the Smart Guides to align the objects. Type **Testing** in the rectangle. Select all three shapes, click **Format**, click **Align**, and then click **Distribute Vertically**.

l. Type the following in the remaining rectangles: **Orientation Training**, **Trial Period**, and **Performance Review**.

m. Select the Performance Review rectangle. Click the **Position arrow** in the Format Shape pane and type **6.78** in the **Horizontal position box** and **6.25** in the **Vertical position box**.

n. Use the Smart Guides to position the remaining two rectangles as shown in Figure 3.56.

o. Select the four rectangles in the third column of shapes and then click **Align** and **Distribute Vertically**.

p. Click the **Insert tab**, click **Shapes**, and then right-click **Elbow Arrow Connector** in the Lines category.

q. Position the pointer over the oval labeled *Job Advertising* to view the connecting points. Drag from the connecting point on the right side of the oval to the connection point on the left side of the *Interview* rectangle. Continue to connect shapes as shown in Figure 3.56. PowerPoint will automatically determine where to bend the arrow as you are dragging the line.

r. Click the **Insert tab** and then click **Text Box** in the Text group. Position the pointer below the connector line to the left of *Candidate Review*. Type **Negative**. Create the three remaining text boxes to complete the flow chart.

s. Save and close the file. Based on your instructor's directions, submit p03p1Hiring_LastFirst.

2 Principles of Pilates

You have created a slide show about Pilates for your Pilates instructor to show prospective students. You use infographics, shapes, and online pictures to share the message. Refer to Figure 3.57 as you complete this exercise.

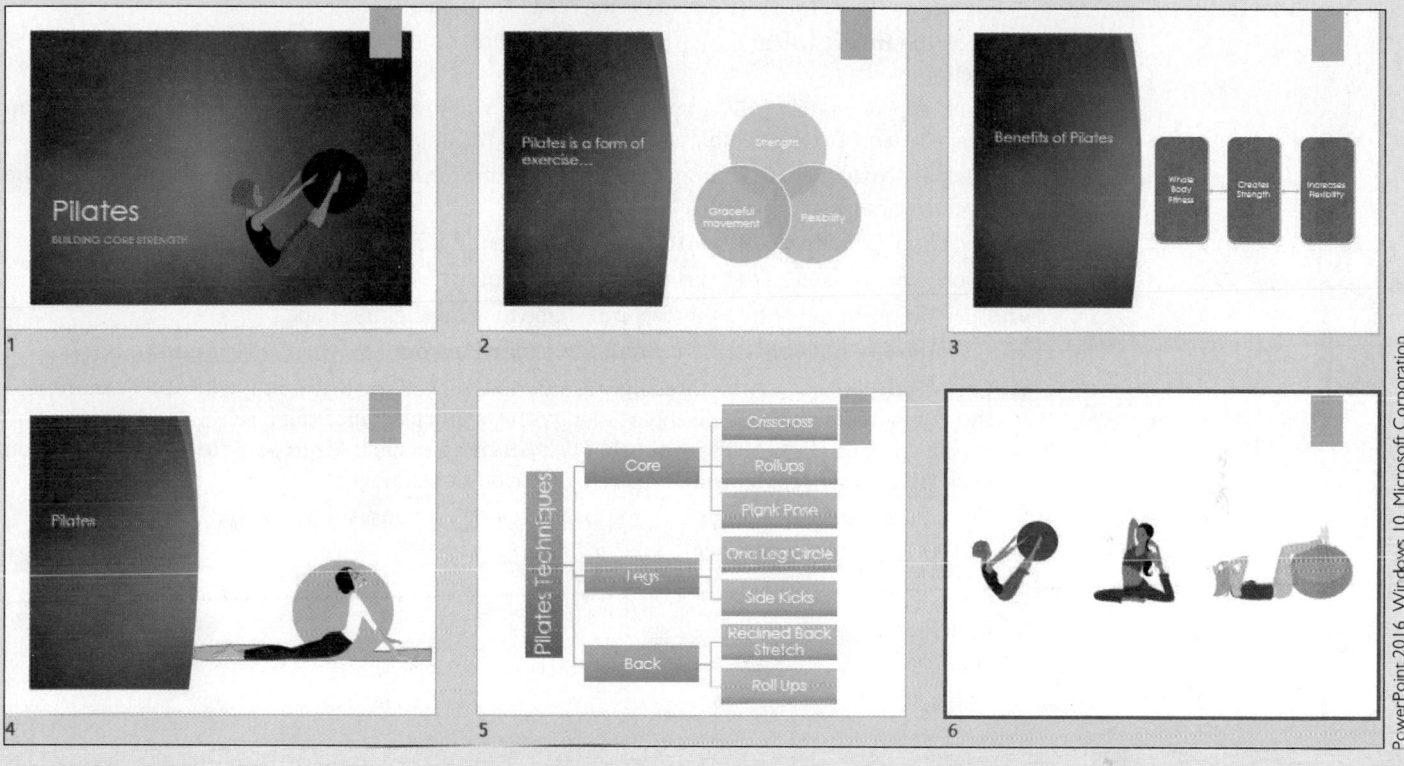

FIGURE 3.57 Pilates Presentation

a. Open *p03p2Pilates* and save it as **p03p2Pilates_LastFirst**.

b. Create a Notes and Handouts header with your name and a footer with your instructor's name and your class. Include the current date.

c. Click **Slide 2**. Click the placeholder containing the bullet points and click the **Home tab**.

d. Click **Convert to SmartArt** in the Paragraph group and click **Basic Venn**.

e. Click **Change Colors** in the **Design tab** in the SmartArt Styles group. Click **Transparent Gradient Range - Accent 1** in the Accent 1 section.

f. Click **Slide 3**. Click the **Insert tab**, click **Shapes** in the Illustrations group, and then select **Double Arrow** in the Lines section. Drag an arrow from the right-center connecting point on the Whole Body Fitness shape to the left-center connecting point on the Creates Strength shape. Repeat this step to create a connector between the Creates Strength shape and the Increases Flexibility shape.

g. Click **Slide 5**. Select the **Hierarchy SmartArt** and click the **SmartArt Tools Design tab**.

h. Select the **Core shape** and click the **Add Shape arrow** in the Create Graphic group. Select **Add Shape Below** and type **Plank Pose**.

i. Click **More** in the Layouts group on the Design tab and select **More Layouts**. Click **Horizontal Multi-Level Hierarchy** in the Hierarchy category.

j. Click **Intense Effect** in the SmartArt Styles group.

k. Click **Slide 1**. Select the image, click the **Format tab**, and then click **Color** in the Adjust group. Click **Sepia** in the Recolor variations category (first row, third column).

l. Click **Slide 4**. Right-click the image and select **Edit Picture**. Click **Yes** to convert the picture into a drawing object. Select the image again.

m. Click the **Format tab** and click **Group** in the Arrange group. Select **Ungroup**.

n. Click the **View tab** and click **Zoom** in the Zoom group. Select **200%** and click **OK**. Deselect the shapes and select the circle.

o. Click the **Format tab** and click **Shape Fill**. Select **Lime, Accent** 1 (top row, fifth column).

p. Click **Fit to Window** in the Zoom group.

q. Drag a selection net around all the shapes comprising the image, click the **Format tab**, click **Group** in the Arrange group, and then select **Regroup**.

r. Click the **Insert tab** and click **Shapes** in the Illustrations group. Click **Freeform** in the Lines section.

s. Click approximately **0.5"** from the foot of the woman to create the first point of a freeform shape you create to resemble a mat (see Figure 3.57).

t. Click approximately **0.5"** from the right hand of the woman to create the second point of the freeform shape.

u. Click approximately **1/4"** vertically and horizontally from the bottom-right of the slide.

v. Click approximately **1/4"** vertically and horizontally from the bottom-left of the slide.

w. Click the starting point of the freeform shape to complete the shape.

x. Click the **Format tab**, click the **Send Backward arrow**, and then select **Send to Back**.

y. Click **Slide 6**. Line up the three figures in a horizontal line beginning with the woman with the red ball and ending with the woman with the purple ball. Drag a selection net around all the images and click the **Format tab**. Click **Align**, then click **Align Middle**. Click **Align**, then click **Distribute Horizontally** to evenly distribute the images.

z. Save and close the file. Based on your instructor's directions, submit p03p2Pilates_LastFirst.

Mid-Level Exercises

1 SmartArt and Online Pictures Ideas

To help you become familiar with the SmartArt Graphic gallery and the types of information appropriate for each type of diagram, you create a slide show of SmartArt ideas. You also manipulate an image. In this activity, you work extensively with sizing, placement, and fills.

a. Open *p03m1Ideas* and save it as **p03m1Ideas_LastFirst**. On Slide 1, replace *First Name Last Name* with your name.

b. Create a Notes and Handouts header with your name and a footer with your instructor's name and your class. Include the current date.

c. Display the gridlines.

d. Click **Slide 2**. Insert a **Vertical Box List SmartArt diagram** (second row, second column in the List category) and make the following modifications:
   - Apply the **Subtle Effect** from SmartArt Styles.
   - Apply **Colored Outline – Accent 3** Color style.
   - Type the following list items into the **Text Pane**:
     - **List**
     - **Process**
     - **Cycle**
     - **Hierarchy**
     - **Relationship**
     - **Matrix**
     - **Pyramid**
     - **Picture**
   - Change the text font size to **20 pt**.
   - Size the SmartArt diagram to **7"** wide and drag it so that it is at the horizontal center of the slide using the grid to help you determine placement.
   - Align the bottom border of the SmartArt diagram with the last line of the gridline.

e. Click **Slide 3**. Convert the text to an **Upward Arrow Process SmartArt diagram** and make the following modifications:
   - Apply the **Simple Fill SmartArt Style**.
   - Change the height of the SmartArt diagram to **6.17"** and the width to **10"**.
   - **Align Center** the diagram. Then **Align Middle** the diagram.

f. Click **Slide 4**. Insert a **Diverging Radial SmartArt diagram** and make the following modifications:
   - Apply the **3-D Polished SmartArt Style**.
   - Change the SmartArt colors to **Colorful - Accent Colors** (first row, first column in the Color section).
   - Type **Residential College** as the center hub and type **Build Community**, **Promote Personal Growth**, and **Support Academic Success** as the spokes around the hub. Remove the extra shape.
   - Set the height of the SmartArt to **5.5"** and the width to **6.67"**.

g. Click **Slide 5**. Insert a **Horizontal Hierarchy SmartArt diagram** (third row, fourth column in the Hierarchy category) and make the following modifications:
   - Apply the **Flat Scene SmartArt Style**.
   - Type **School of Business** as the first-level bullet in the **Text Pane**. Type **M&M** and **DIS** as the second-level bullets. Type **Marketing**, and **Management** as third-level bullets under M&M, Type **MIS**, and **POM** as third-level bullets under DIS.
   - Click **Right to Left** in Create Graphic group on the SmartArt Tools Design tab to change the orientation of the diagram.
   - Drag the borders of the SmartArt graphic until it fits the page and the text is large enough to read.

h. Click **Slide 6**. Insert a **Basic Venn SmartArt diagram** (tenth row, fourth column in the Relationship category) and make the following modifications:

- Type the following as three bullets in the **Text Pane**: **Anesthesiology**, **Nurses**, and **Surgeon**.
- Insert a picture fill in the *Anesthesiology* shape using an Online Picture with **Doctor** as the key term.
- Insert a picture fill in the *Nurses* shape using an Online Picture with **Nurse** as the key term.
- Insert a picture fill in the *Surgeon* shape using an Online Picture with **Surgeon** as the key term.
- Recolor all images using the **Grayscale variation**.
- Format the SmartArt text with the **Fill - White, Outline - Accent 2, Hard Shadow - Accent 2 Style**.
- Set the height of the SmartArt to **4.5"** and the width to **5.5"**.
- Use the grid to center the Venn diagram in the available space.

i. Click **Slide 7**. Insert a **Basic Matrix SmartArt diagram** (first row, first column in the Matrix category) and make the following modifications:
- Apply the **Subtle Effect SmartArt Style**.
- Change the colors to **Colorful - Accent Colors**.
- Type the following text in the Text Pane:
  - **Urgent & Important**
  - **Not Urgent & Important**
  - **Urgent & Not Important**
  - **Not Urgent & Not Important**

j. Click **Slide 8**. Insert a **Basic Pyramid SmartArt diagram** (first row, first column in the Pyramid category) and make the following modifications:
- Apply the **Subtle Effect SmartArt Style**.
- Press **Spacebar** to create a blank space at the top pyramid level and add the following text to the remaining levels. You will add the text for the top pyramid level in a text box in a later step so that the font in the SmartArt is not reduced to a difficult-to-read font size.
  - **Esteem**
  - **Belonging and Love**
  - **Safety**
  - **Biological Needs**
- Drag the border of the SmartArt diagram until it fills the available white space on the slide. Deselect the pyramid.
- Create a text box on the top left of the slide and type **Self-Actualization** in the text box. Change the font size to **39 pt**. Drag the text box so it is centered over the top of the empty pyramid.
- Apply the **Fill – Dark Red, Accent 1, Shadow WordArt Style** to the text box *Maslow's Hierarchy of Needs*.
- Apply the **Deflate Transform Text Effect** to the WordArt text.

k. Click **Slide 9**. Ungroup the complex image until all grouping is undone. Make the following changes:
- Change the color of the bird so it is red.
- Regroup the pieces of the image.

l. View the slide show. Save and close the file. Based on your instructor's directions, submit p03m1Ideas_LastFirst.

2 The Arts

CREATIVE CASE

A presentation created for a local children's arts center can be improved by adding a theme, using shapes and SmartArt, and adding online pictures. You will update the presentation using the theme of your choice and the SmartArt style and colors of your choice.

a. Open *p03m2Perform* and save it as **p03m2Perform_LastFirst**. Create a Notes and Handouts header with your name and a footer with your instructor's name and your class. Include the current date.

b. Apply the theme of your choice to the presentation.

c. Click **Slide 3**. Select the bulleted text and convert it to a **Continuous Block Process SmartArt diagram** available in the Process SmartArt category. Apply the SmartArt colors and style of your choice.

d. Click **Slide 4**. Select the existing SmartArt diagram and change the layout to a **Segmented Pyramid** in the Pyramid SmartArt category. Change the height of the SmartArt to **6"** and the width to **10"**. Set its position at **0"** from the Top Left Corner both horizontally and vertically. Apply the SmartArt colors and style of your choice.

e. Click **Slide 5**. Insert a minimum of two online pictures of items that could be donated to the center. For example, you could add tables, musical instruments, easels, clay, chalk, etc. Adjust colors as desired.

f. Click **Slide 6**. Ungroup the images and change the fill color of several shapes to theme colors. Resize and position the image as appropriate. Regroup the image.

g. Save and close the file. Based on your instructor's directions, submit p03m2Perform_LastFirst.

3 Learning from an Expert

COLLABORATION CASE Video-sharing sites such as YouTube.com make it possible to learn from PowerPoint industry experts as well as everyday PowerPoint users. You can learn through step-by-step instructions or by inspiration after seeing others use PowerPoint. The video source may also refer you to a professional website that will provide you with a wealth of tips and ideas for creating slide shows that move your work from ordinary to extraordinary. In this exercise, you will view a YouTube video featuring the work of Nancy Duarte, a well-known PowerPoint industry expert. After viewing the video and related website, you will use shapes and animation to recreate one of the effects in Duarte's presentation. Finally, you will present your slides online to other classmates, and then use WordOnline to discuss the experience with your classmates.

a. Access the Internet and go to www.youtube.com. Search for the video *Duarte Design's Five Rules for Presentations by Nancy Duarte.* View the video, click the supporting link beneath the video (http://blog.duarte.com/), and note the additional resources available to viewers of the video.

b. Advance to 2:29 in the video clip on YouTube and rewatch Duarte's Rule 4—Practice Design Not Decoration.

c. Open *p03m3Duarte*, which contains the slide Duarte's Rule 4. Apply animations to the shapes and text contained in the file to reproduce the effect of Duarte's slide. Add a shape to the slide that applies Duarte's Rule 4. Save the file as **p03m3Duarte_LastFirst**.

d. Click the File tab, then click Share. Click Present Online and present your slide to another classmate. Have that classmate also present their slide to you.

e. Go to Office.live.com, and open a Word Online Blank document. Write a brief description of Duarte's rules, noting how you can apply Rule 4 to future presentations. Ask the classmate with whom you shared your Online Presentation to add his or her own thoughts about Duarte's rules to the Word Online document. Save the file as p03m3DuarteNotes_LastFirst_LastFirst (adding the Last and First name of you and your classmate).

f. Based on your instructor's directions, submit p03m3Duarte_LastFirst_LastFirst. Using the Share feature in Word Online, invite your instructor to view your document.

Beyond the Classroom

Human Rights

Plan a presentation about one or more human rights leaders you admire, such as Helen Keller, Martin Luther King, Jr., Thurgood Marshall, Nelson Mandela, Cesar Chavez, or Michelle Bachelet. Research the person or persons of your choice and sketch out a storyboard of at least four slides sharing information about the person or persons. Create the presentation and name it **p03b1Rights_LastFirst**. Include an appropriate title slide, key topic slides, and conclusion slide. Add text boxes and shapes to add emphasis to information, and a slide with SmartArt that shows a timeline or list of accomplishments. Include a slide with a quote enclosed by a shape and include the name of the person you are quoting. Type a speaker note for the introduction slide that summarizes why you admire this person or these people. Apply a design theme and modify it and other elements as desired to make your presentation interesting and informative. Apply a transition to all slides. In addition to the SmartArt, include several pictures in appropriate locations. Add transitions and animations to enhance the show. Include a Notes and Handouts header with your name and a handout footer with your instructor's name and your class. Save and close the file. Based on your instructor's directions, submit p03b1Rights_LastFirst.

Predators

Your friend who teaches in a middle school asked you to fix the presentation she created about sharks to make it more interesting for her students. Open *p03b2Predators* and save the new presentation as **p03b2Predators_LastFirst**. View the presentation and note visually jarring WordArt that was applied as well as images that are positioned poorly. Convert the bulleted text on Slide 2 into a pyramid demonstrating the food chain using a SmartArt diagram. Use the following levels from top level to bottom level: **Predators**, **Secondary Consumers**, **Primary Consumers**, and **Primary Producers**. The food chain is shown as a pyramid to show that meat-eating predators at the top of the food chain are rarer than plant-eating primary consumers, which are rarer than primary producers such as plants. Type a speaker note for the food chain slide that summarizes how the levels of the food chain work. After Slide 2, review the slides and edit layouts, fonts, and other style elements to make the slides readable and effective. Add at least three shapes, and add shape effects to them to present information located in the speaker notes. On the title slide, modify the WordArt so that it is legible. Add a transition and animations to enhance the show. Include a Notes and Handouts header with your name and a handout footer with your instructor's name and your class. Save and close the file. Based on your instructor's directions, submit p03b2Predators_LastFirst.

Capstone Exercise

You are working on a presentation about energy use in the home. You decide to incorporate shapes to demonstrate heat loss in a home and use the SmartArt feature to create infographics relating to energy use and efficiency.

Create a "Heat Loss" Illustration Using Shapes

You decide to create shapes to explain the concept of heat loss and insulation. You stack three oval shapes to create the zones, and you use a combination of text boxes and online pictures to create the landscape.

a. Open *p03c1Energy* and save it as **p03c1Energy_LastFirst**. Create a handout footer with a fixed date and time, a page number, your name and your class. Replace Student Name with your name on Slide 1.

b. Click **Slide 3**. Insert a Right Arrow shape from the Block Arrows category in the approximate center of the blank area to the left of the slide. This will be the shape containing the information about insulation. Apply the following modifications to the arrow shape.
  - Change the arrow shape size to a height of **1.75"** and width of **3.4"**.
  - Change the arrow shape position to a horizontal position of **0.4"** from the Top Left Corner and a vertical position of of **4"** from the Top Left Corner.
  - Change the Shape Fill, under More Fill Colors, to a custom RGB color: **Red:255**, **Green:255**, and **Blue:50**, and a **Transparency** of **10%**.
  - Change the Shape Outline to **Blue** in the Standard Colors category.
  - Type **Insulation can reduce heat loss by 2/3**. (Do not include the period.)
  - Change the text color to **Dark Blue** in the Standard Colors category.

c. Create an Arrow shape from the Lines category. Begin the arrow at the left center connecting point on the top circle and ending at the roof. Use Shift while dragging the arrow to ensure you create a horizontal line with no angle. Apply the following modifications to the arrow shape:
  - Change the arrow width of **1.45"**.
  - Change the arrow color to the theme color **Gray - 80%, Background 1**.
  - Change the arrow weight to **2 ¼ pt**.

d. Ensure that the arrow is still selected and press **Ctrl+D** three times to create three more arrows.

e. Ensure that the bottom (last) arrow is still selected and then activate the Selection Pane. Rename the selected object **Arrow 4**. Select the arrow above Arrow 4 on the slide and rename it **Arrow 3**. Continue this process to rename **Arrow 2** and **Arrow 1**.

f. Position Arrow 4 at **7.37"** horizontal position from the Top Left Corner and vertical position **6.68"** from the Top Left Corner.

g. Use the Selection Pane to select Arrows 1 through 4, and then use the Align feature to distribute the lines vertically. With the four arrows still selected, **Align Left**.

h. Ensure that the four arrows are still selected, and then bring the object to the front so the arrow heads are on top of the house.

i. Select the house and ungroup twice. Select the window on the left and press **Ctrl+D** to duplicate it. Drag the new window down, and using the Smart Guides, align the window on the left with the window above it and the top with the top of the windows on the door.

j. Regroup the house shapes. Select the house and the new window and then group them.

k. Move to **Slide 5** and insert a text box in the blank space at the bottom of the slide. Type **Change your lifestyle** inside the text box. Make the following modifications:
  - Change the font size to **44 pt**.
  - Align the text box to the center of the slide.

Convert Text to SmartArt

To add visual interest to slides, you review the slide show and convert some of the bulleted lists to SmartArt graphics.

a. Click **Slide 2**. Convert the bulleted text to a **Basic Venn SmartArt graphic**. Change the colors of the diagram to **Colorful Range – Accent Colors 3 – 4**.

b. Click **Slide 4**. Select the **Insulation Can Help bulleted text** and convert it to a **Target List SmartArt graphic**. Apply the **Moderate Effect SmartArt Style**. Change the colors of the diagram to **Colorful Range – Accent Colors 3 – 4**.

Create SmartArt

You have a list of three ways that someone could save that you decide would present well as a SmartArt list.

a. Add a new slide after Slide 2 using a **Title and Content layout**.

b. Type **What Can You Do** in the title placeholder.

c. Insert a **Vertical Picture Accent List SmartArt**. Type the following text in the following the Text Pane and then close the Text Pane:
  - **Conserve electricity**
  - **Change thermostat setting**
  - **Insulate**

d. Click the picture icon for the Conserve electricity shape and insert *p03c1Electricity*. Insert *p03c1Thermostat* in the picture shape for Change thermostat setting, Insert *p03c1Insulate* in the picture shape for Insulate.

e. Make the following modifications to the SmartArt diagram:
- Change the color of the SmartArt to **Colored Fill - Accent 3**.
- Recolor the three pictures to **Orange, Accent color 6 Dark**.

Convert Text to WordArt

You want to convert some of the text in the slide show to WordArt for emphasis. After converting text to WordArt, you will apply an animation scheme.

a. Click **Slide 4** and select **Heat Loss**.

b. Apply the **Fill - Blue, Background 2, Inner Shadow WordArt Style** to the text.

c. Apply the **Triangle Up Warp Transform effect**.

d. Click **Slide 6**. Select the placeholder for the **Change your lifestyle** text box and apply the **Fill - White, Outline - Accent 1, Glow - Accent 1 WordArt Style**. Apply the **Square Transform Text Effect**.

Apply the **Fly In animation** to the WordArt.

e. Check the spelling in the slide show and accept or correct all spellings on the slide.

f. View the slide show.

g. Save and close the file. Based on your instructor's directions, submit p03c1Energy_LastFirst.

Enhancing with Multimedia

LEARNING OUTCOME You will prepare a slide show featuring pictures, photos, video, and audio.

OBJECTIVES & SKILLS: After you read this chapter, you will be able to:

CASE STUDY | Engagement Album

Your sister was recently married. As a gift to the couple, you decide to create two memory slide shows to celebrate the occasion. The first slide show will feature images of the couple in a few engagement photos and on their honeymoon in Europe. The second slide show will display photos taken during a family vacation.

As you prepare the first slide show, you edit the images using PowerPoint's Picture Tools tab. Each slide in the first slide show is created individually, and each image is manipulated individually. You download an image from the Internet representing the couple's honeymoon and insert a video of fireworks recorded by the groom during the honeymoon. You insert a fireworks sound clip and music file to complement the fireworks display. Finally, you create the second slide show, a family vacation, using PowerPoint's Photo Album feature. You utilize the Photo Album options for image manipulation.

FIGURE 4.1 Engagement Photo Album

CASE STUDY | Engagement Album

Starting Files	Files to be Submitted
p04h1Memory **p04h1Memory_Media folder** **Blank PowerPoint presentation** **p04h4Album_Media folder**	**p04h3Memory_LastFirst** **p04h4Album_LastFirst**

CHAPTER 4

PowerPoint Rich Media Tools

Wavebreakmedia/Shutterstock

PowerPoint 2016, Windows 10, Microsoft Corporation

Pictures

Multimedia refers to multiple forms of media, such as graphics, sound, animation, and video, that are used to entertain or inform an audience. You can use any of these types of media in PowerPoint by placing the multimedia object on a slide. Multimedia graphics include images, objects created using drawing programs, diagrams and illustrations, scanned images, digital pictures or photographs, and more.

In this section, you will expand your experience with multimedia by inserting digital pictures and modifying their appearance, properties, or location on a slide.

Inserting a Picture

STEP 1 ⟩⟩ Pictures are bitmap images that computers can read and interpret to create a photorealistic image. Unlike ***vector graphics*** which are created by mathematical statements, ***bitmap images*** are created by bits or pixels placed on a grid or map. In a bitmap image, each pixel contains information about the color to be displayed. A bitmap image is required to have the realism necessary for a photograph. Think of vector graphics as connect-the-dots and bitmap images as paint-by-number, and you begin to see the difference in the methods of representation.

Each type of image has its own advantages and disadvantages. Vector graphics can be sized easily and still retain their clarity but are not photorealistic. Bitmap images represent a much more complex range of colors and shades but can become pixelated (individual pixels are visible and display square edges for a jagged effect) when they are enlarged. A bitmap image can also be a large file, so ***compression***, a method applied to data to reduce the amount of space required for file storage, may be applied. The compression may be lossy (some data may be lost when decompressed) or lossless (no data is lost when decompressed).

TIP: COMPRESSION: LOSSY VERSUS LOSSLESS

Depending on the image's use, you may want to choose a specific image format so that images do not appear pixelated when enlarged. Certain formats can be either lossy or lossless. Lossy compression reduces a file by permanently eliminating certain data, especially redundant data. This makes the file size smaller. However, when the file is uncompressed, only a part of the original data is still there. Pixelation may not even be noticeable for certain image uses, so it might not be an issue. The JPEG image file, a common format, is an image that has lossy compression.

Alternatively, with lossless compression, data that was originally in the file remains after the file is uncompressed. All of the information is completely restored. The Graphics Interchange File (GIF) image format provides lossless compression.

Figure 4.2 displays a pumpkin created as a vector graphic and one created as a bitmap image. Note the differences in realism. The boxes show a portion of the images enlarged. Note the pixilation, or jaggedness, in the enlarged portion of the bitmap image.

FIGURE 4.2 Types of Graphics

PowerPoint does not have to be all bullets; a good image can be more memorable than a simple list of words. You can accomplish this task by scanning and saving a photograph or piece of artwork, by downloading images from a digital camera or smartphone, by downloading an image from Bing Image Search or the Internet, or by creating an image in a graphics-editing software package like Adobe Photoshop™. Table 4.1 displays in alphabetical order by file extension the types of graphic file formats that you can add to a PowerPoint slide.

TABLE 4.1 Types of Graphic File Formats Supported by PowerPoint

File Format	Extension	Description
Bitmap	.bmp, .dib	**Device Independent Bitmap** A representation consisting of rows and columns of dots. The value of each dot is stored in one or more bits of data. Uncompressed and creates large file size.
Windows Enhanced Metafile	.emf	**Windows Enhanced Metafile** A Windows 32-bit file format.
GIF File	.gif	**Graphics Interchange Format** Limited to 256 colors. Effective for scanned images such as illustrations rather than for color photographs. Good for line drawings and black-and-white images. Supports transparent backgrounds.
JPEG File Interchange Format	.jpg, .jpeg	**Joint Photographic Experts Group** Supports 16 million colors and is optimized for photographs and complex graphics. Format of choice for most photographs on the Web. Uses lossy compression.
PICT File	.pict, .pic, .pct	**Macintosh PICT** Holds both vector and bitmap images. PICT supports 8 colors; PICT2 supports 16 million colors.
PNG File	.png	**Portable Network Graphics** Supports 16 million colors. Approved as a standard by the World Wide Web Consortium (W3C). Intended to replace .gif format. Uses lossy compression.
TIFF File	.tif, .tiff	**Tagged Image File Format** Best file format for storing bitmapped images on personal computers. Can be any resolution. Lossless image storage creates large file sizes. Not widely supported by browsers.
Windows Metafile	.wmf	**Windows Metafile** A Windows 16-bit file format.

There are multiple ways to add a picture that you have saved on your computer to a PowerPoint slide. You can use a placeholder or you can insert the image without a placeholder. Both methods have advantages and disadvantages.

To add a picture to a slide using a placeholder, complete the following steps:

1. Select a layout with a placeholder that includes a Pictures icon.
2. Click the Pictures icon to open the Insert Picture dialog box.
3. Navigate to the location of your picture files and select the picture you want to use.
4. Click Insert.

Figure 4.3 shows two examples of placeholders with Pictures icons. When you insert a picture in this manner, the picture is centered within the placeholder frame and is sometimes cropped to fit within the placeholder. This effect can cause unwanted results, such as the tops of heads cropped off. If this situation occurs, undo the insertion, enlarge the placeholder, and then repeat the steps for inserting an image. Avoid enlarging the placeholders when possible because any changes you make to the slide master or theme may not appear correctly once those changes are applied to the slide where you modified the placeholder.

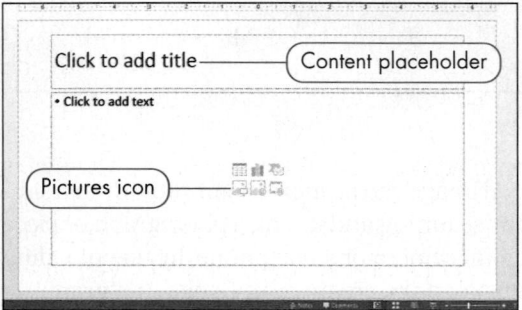
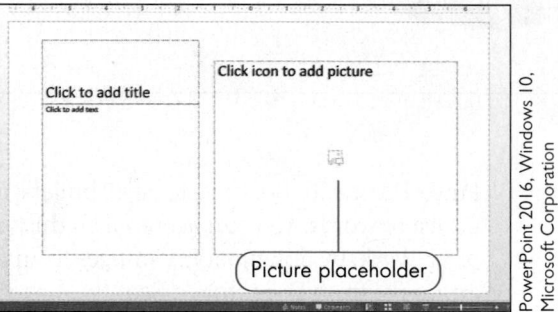

FIGURE 4.3 Insert Picture Using Placeholders

Another way to insert an image is to click Pictures on the Insert tab. The advantage of this method is that your image comes in at full size rather than centered and cropped in a placeholder, and you do not need a picture placeholder. You can then resize the image to fit the desired area. The disadvantage is the time you may spend resizing and positioning the image.

To add a picture using the Insert tab, complete the following steps:

1. Click the Insert tab.
2. Click Pictures in the Images group.
3. Navigate to the location of your picture files and select the picture you want to use.
4. Click Insert.
5. Adjust the size and position of the picture as necessary.

TIP: ADDING IMAGES USING FILE EXPLORER
If you are adding multiple images to a slide show, you can speed up the process by inserting images directly from File Explorer. Open File Explorer and navigate to the folder where the images are located. Position the File Explorer window next to the PowerPoint window and drag the images from the Explorer window onto the slides of your choice.

Transforming a Picture

Once you insert a picture onto a slide, PowerPoint provides tools that you can use to adjust the image. Found on the Picture Tools Format tab (see Figure 4.4), the Picture Tools tab is designed to adjust an image background, correct image problems, manipulate image color, or add artistic or stylized effects. You can also arrange, crop, or resize an image using Picture Tools tab. Additionally, when you right-click on the picture and select Format Picture, you will open the Format Picture task pane, where you can also access these same tools.

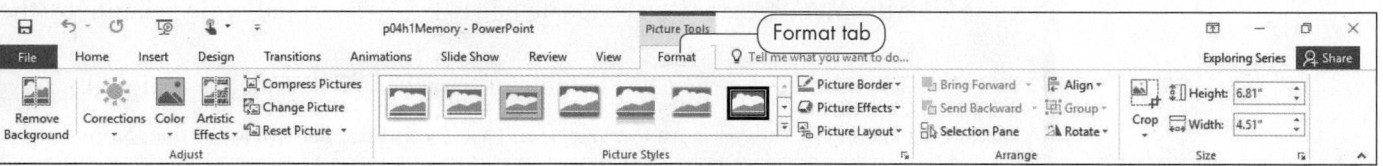

FIGURE 4.4 Picture Tools

PowerPoint 2016, Windows 10, Microsoft Corporation

Remove a Picture Background

The Remove Background tool in the Adjust group on the Format tab enables you to remove portions of a picture you do not want to keep. Rather than have a rectangle-shaped picture on your slide, you can have an image in the shape of the desired object on the slide. For example, if you remove the background in a picture of a flower, you can have a flower-shaped image on your slide instead. This can create a more interesting and creative look for your slide.

When you select a picture and click the Remove Background tool, PowerPoint creates an automatic marquee selection area in the picture that determines the *background*, or area to be removed, and the *foreground*, or area to be kept. PowerPoint identifies the background selection with magenta coloring. You then adjust PowerPoint's automatic selection by marking areas you want to keep, marking areas you want to remove, and deleting any markings you do not want. You can discard all changes you have made or keep your changes. Figure 4.5 shows a picture in which the Remove Background tool has created a marquee identifying the foreground and background.

FIGURE 4.5 Remove Background Marquee, Foreground, and Background

Once the background has been identified by the marquee, you can refine the marquee size and shape so that it contains everything you want to keep without extra areas.

> **To resize the marquee, complete the following steps:**
>
> 1. Select the picture and drag a marquee handle to indicate the desired foreground.
> 2. Refine the picture further by using the tools available on the Background Removal tab (see Figure 4.6):
>   - Use the *Mark Areas to Keep* tool to add to the foreground, which keeps the area.
>   - Use the *Mark Areas to Remove* tool to add to the background, which eliminates the area.
>   - To use both tools, drag a line to indicate what should be added or removed.
> 3. Press Esc or click away from the selection to see what the picture looks like. Note that the thumbnail also shows what the image will look like with the changes applied.

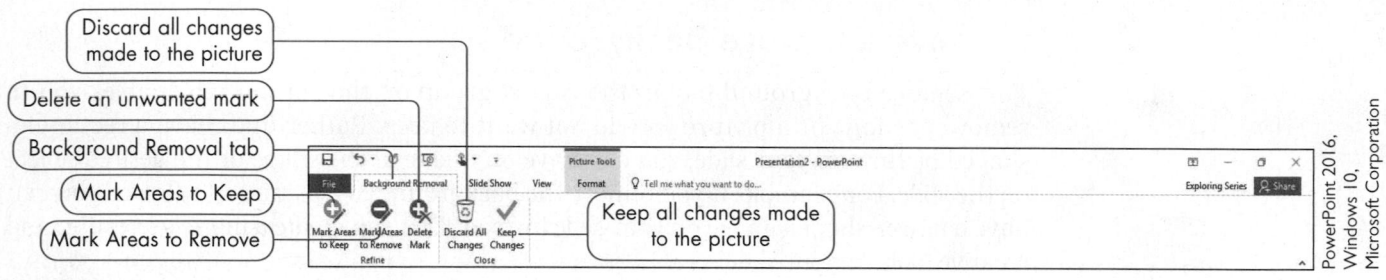

FIGURE 4.6 Background Removal Tools

You can make further changes by returning to Background Removal and continuing to work with your picture. Figure 4.7 shows a resized marquee with enlarged areas marked to show areas to keep and to remove. Figure 4.8 shows the flower picture with the background removed.

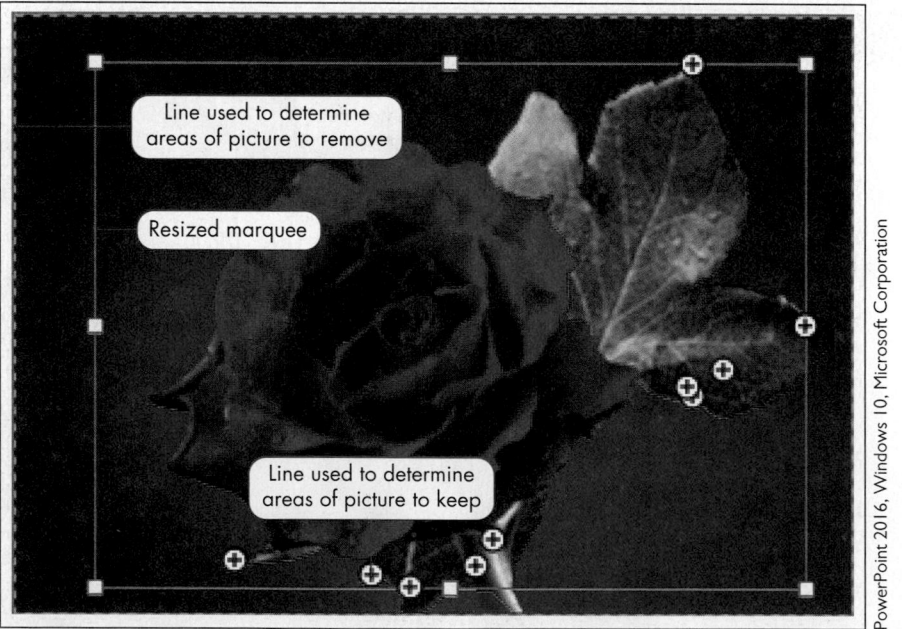

FIGURE 4.7 Background Removal Process

FIGURE 4.8 Background Removed from Flower

Correct a Picture

STEP 2 ▶▶ PowerPoint includes Corrections, a set of tools in the Adjust group. Corrections enables you to adjust brightness and contrast of an image and also soften or sharpen a picture. You can see what a correction will look like by previewing it in Live Preview.

You can enhance a picture by *sharpening* it—bringing out the detail by making the boundaries of the content more prominent. Or you may enhance the picture by *softening* the content—blurring the edges so the boundaries are less prominent. Sharpening a picture can make it clearer, but oversharpening can make the picture look grainy. Softening is a technique often used for a more romantic image or to make skin appear softer, but applying too much blur can make the picture difficult to see.

> **To sharpen or soften a picture, complete the following steps:**
>
> 1. Select the picture.
> 2. Click the Format tab.
> 3. Click Corrections in the Adjust group.
> 4. Point to the thumbnails in the Sharpen/Soften section to view the corrections in Live Preview.
> 5. Click the thumbnail to apply the degree of correction you want.

You can make fine adjustments to the amount of sharpness and softness you apply to a picture. To make adjustments, follow Steps 1–3 above and click Picture Corrections Options at the bottom of the gallery. The Format Picture pane opens. Drag the Sharpness slider or enter a percentage in the box next to the slider until the desired effect is obtained. Figure 4.9 shows the Corrections gallery, a picture that has been softened, and a picture that has been sharpened.

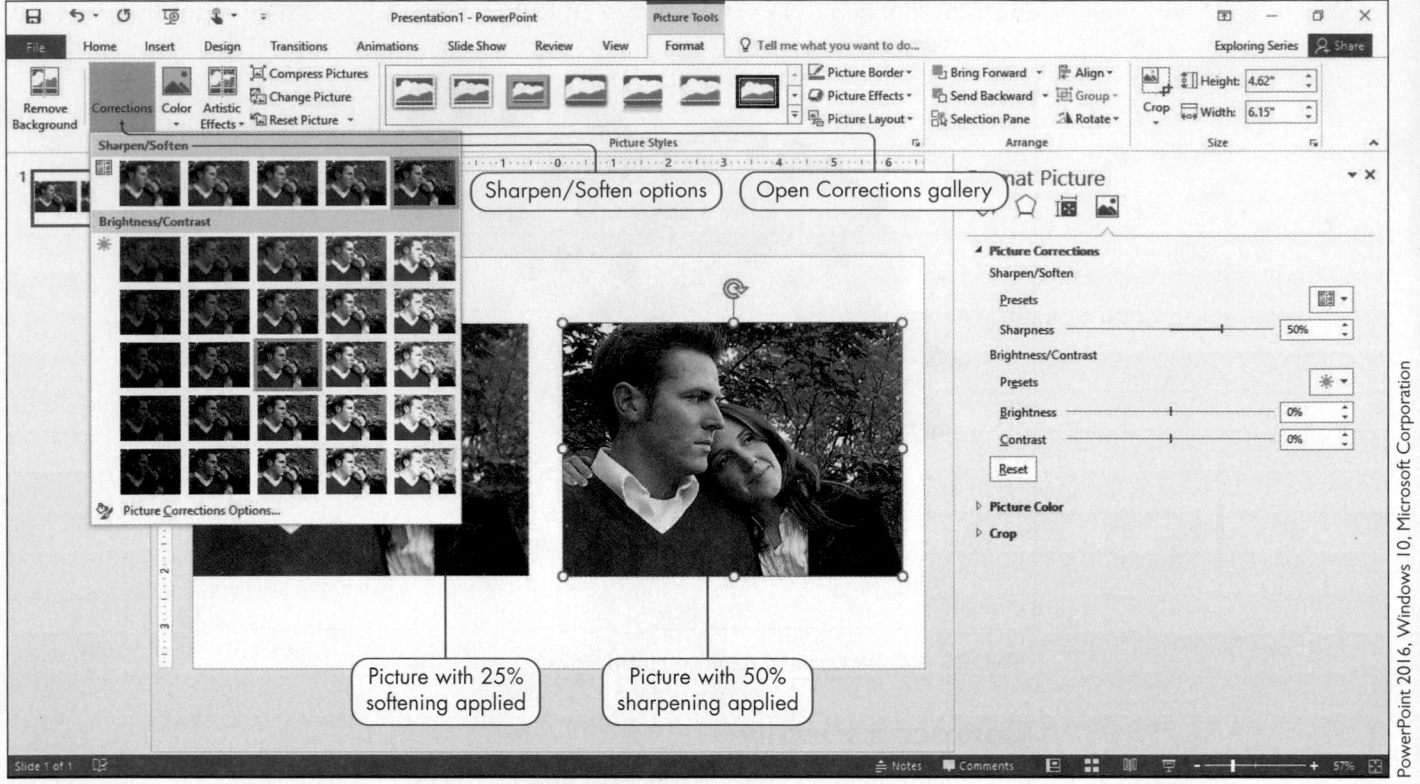

FIGURE 4.9 Corrections Gallery and Softened and Sharpened Pictures

The **brightness** (lightness or darkness) of a picture is often a matter of individual preference. You might want to change the brightness of your picture for reasons other than preference, however. For example, sometimes printing a picture requires a different brightness than is needed when projecting an image. This situation occurs because during printing the ink may spread when placed on the page, making the picture darker. Or, you might want a picture as a background and need to reduce the brightness so that text will show clearly on the background.

Contrast refers to the difference between the darkest area (black level) and lightest area (white level) of an image. If your picture has too little contrast, it can look washed out or muddy; too much contrast, and the light portion of your image will appear to explode off the screen or page. Your setting may vary depending on whether you are going to project the image or print it. Projecting impacts an image because of the amount of light in the room. In a very light room, the image may seem to need a greater contrast than in a darker room, and you may need to adjust the contrast accordingly. Try to set your control for the lighting that will appear when you display the presentation.

To adjust the brightness and contrast of a picture, complete the following steps:

1. Select the picture.
2. Click the Format tab.
3. Click Corrections in the Adjust group.
4. Point to the thumbnails in the Brightness/Contrast section to view the corrections in Live Preview.
5. Click the thumbnail to apply the degree of correction you want.

You can make fine adjustments to the amount of brightness or contrast you apply. To make adjustments, follow Steps 1–3 above and click Picture Corrections Options at the bottom of the gallery. The Format Picture task pane opens. Drag the Brightness and

Contrast sliders or enter percentages in the boxes next to the sliders until you get the result you want. Figure 4.10 shows the Corrections gallery displaying the same picture before and after it has been adjusted for brightness.

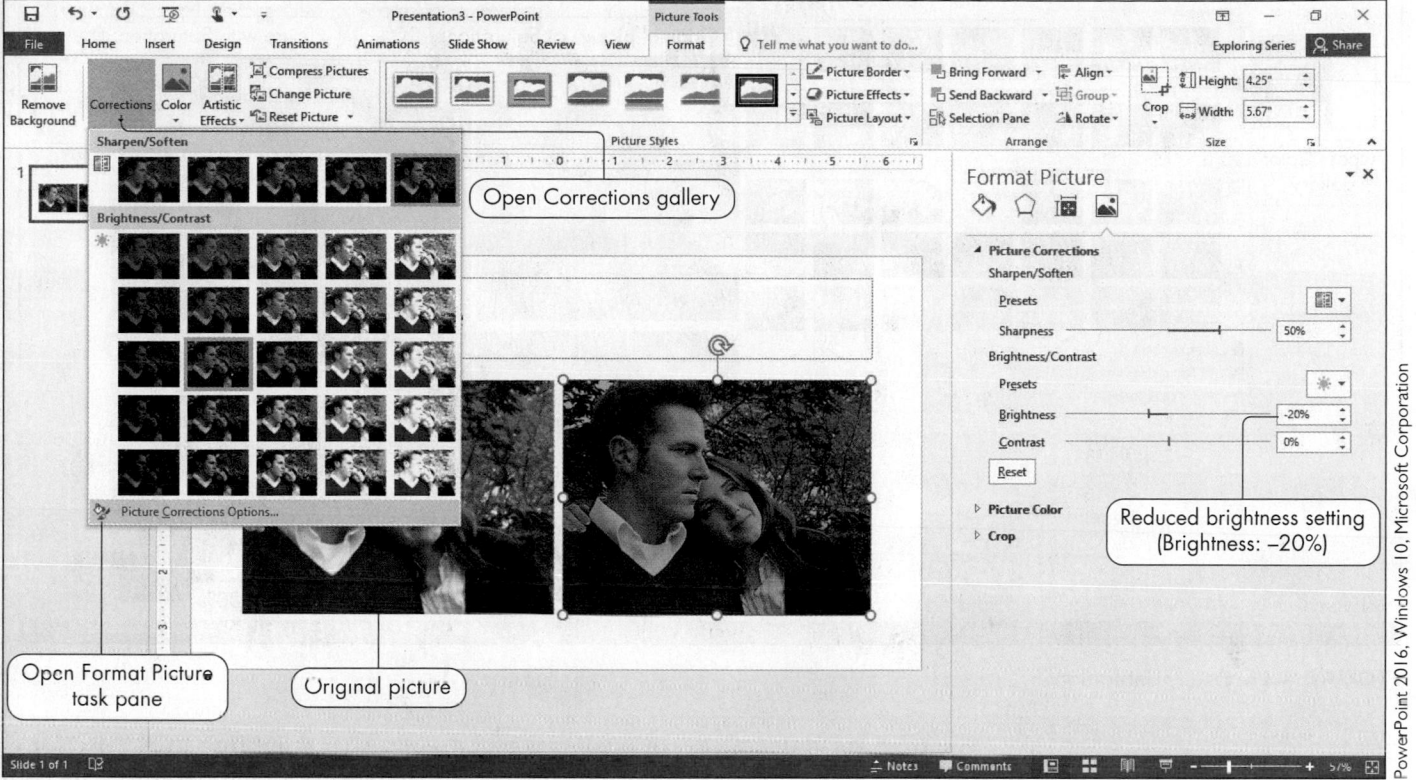

FIGURE 4.10 Format Picture Task Pane and Adjusted Picture

Change Picture Color

You can change the colors in your picture by using PowerPoint's color tools.

To access the color tools, complete the following steps:

1. Select the picture.
2. Click the Format tab.
3. Click Color in the Adjust group.
4. Point to the thumbnails in the gallery to view the corrections in Live Preview.
5. Click the thumbnail to apply the color effect you want.

You can change a picture's **saturation**, or the intensity of the colors in an image. A high saturation level makes the colors more vivid, whereas 0% saturation converts the picture to grayscale. Figure 4.11 shows a picture at its original (100%) intensity and with various levels of intensity.

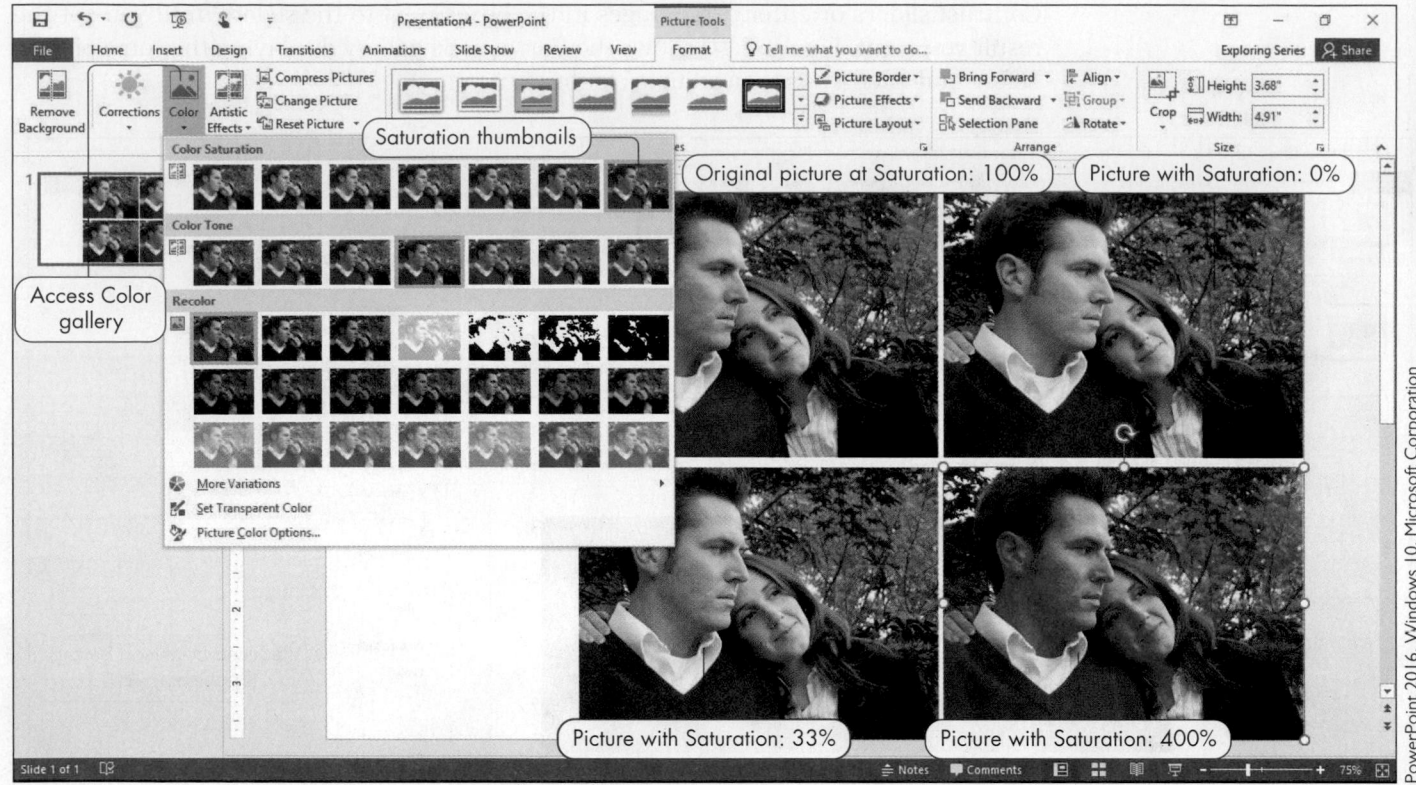

FIGURE 4.11 Picture Saturation

The *tone*, or temperature, of a color is a characteristic of lighting in pictures. It is measured in **kelvin** (K) units of absolute temperature. Lower color temperatures are cool colors and appear blueish white, whereas higher color temperatures are warm colors and appear yellowish to red. PowerPoint enables you to increase or decrease a picture's temperature to enhance its details. Point to a thumbnail to see the amount of temperature in kelvin units that would be applied. Figure 4.12 shows a picture with its original cooler tone and a copy of the picture at a higher temperature with a warmer tone.

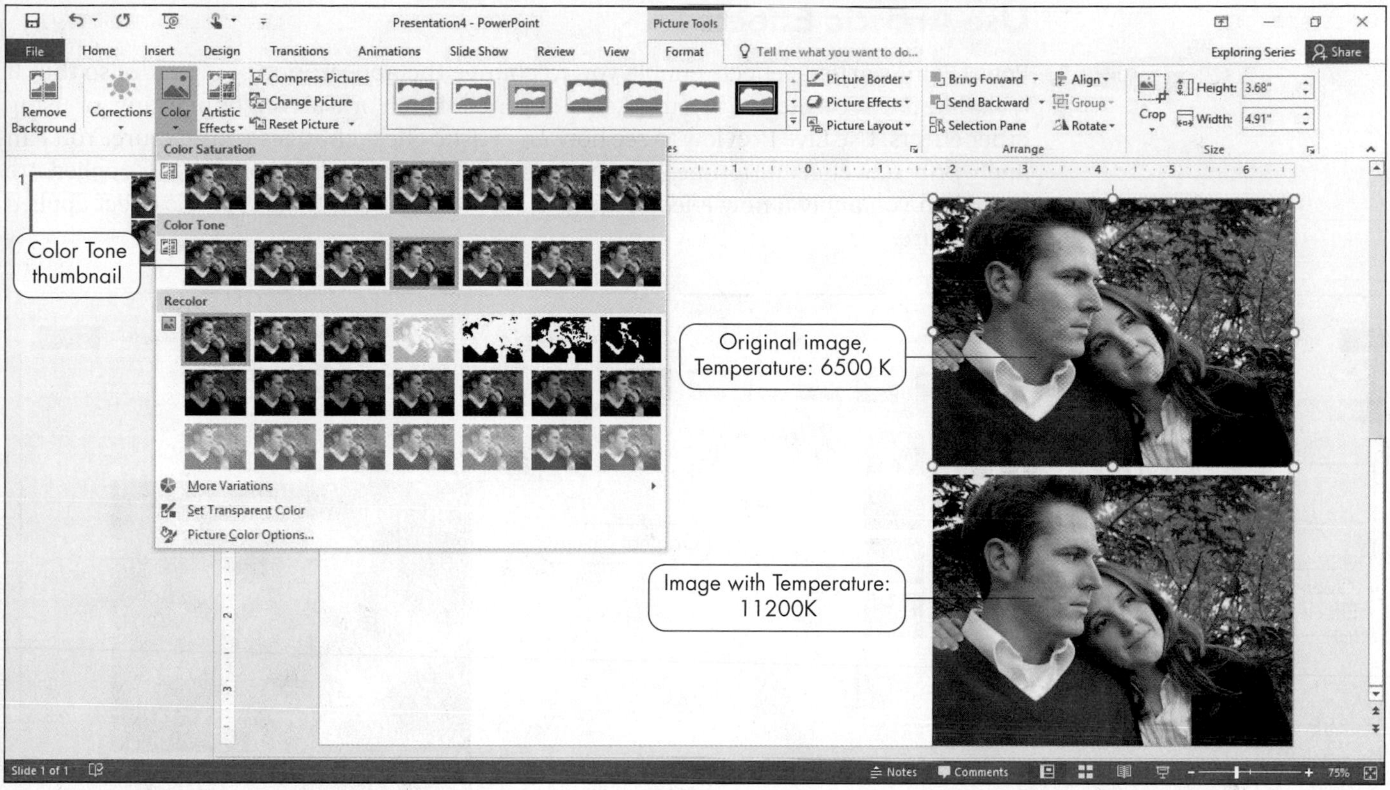

FIGURE 4.12 Picture Color Tone

In an earlier chapter, you ***recolored*** objects by using the Format tab. You can use the same process to change pictures by adjusting the image's colors. You can click a preset thumbnail from the gallery or click More Variations to pick from additional colors. To return a picture to its original color, click the No Recolor preset thumbnail under the Recolor section. Figure 4.13 shows a picture with the Sepia Recolor preset applied.

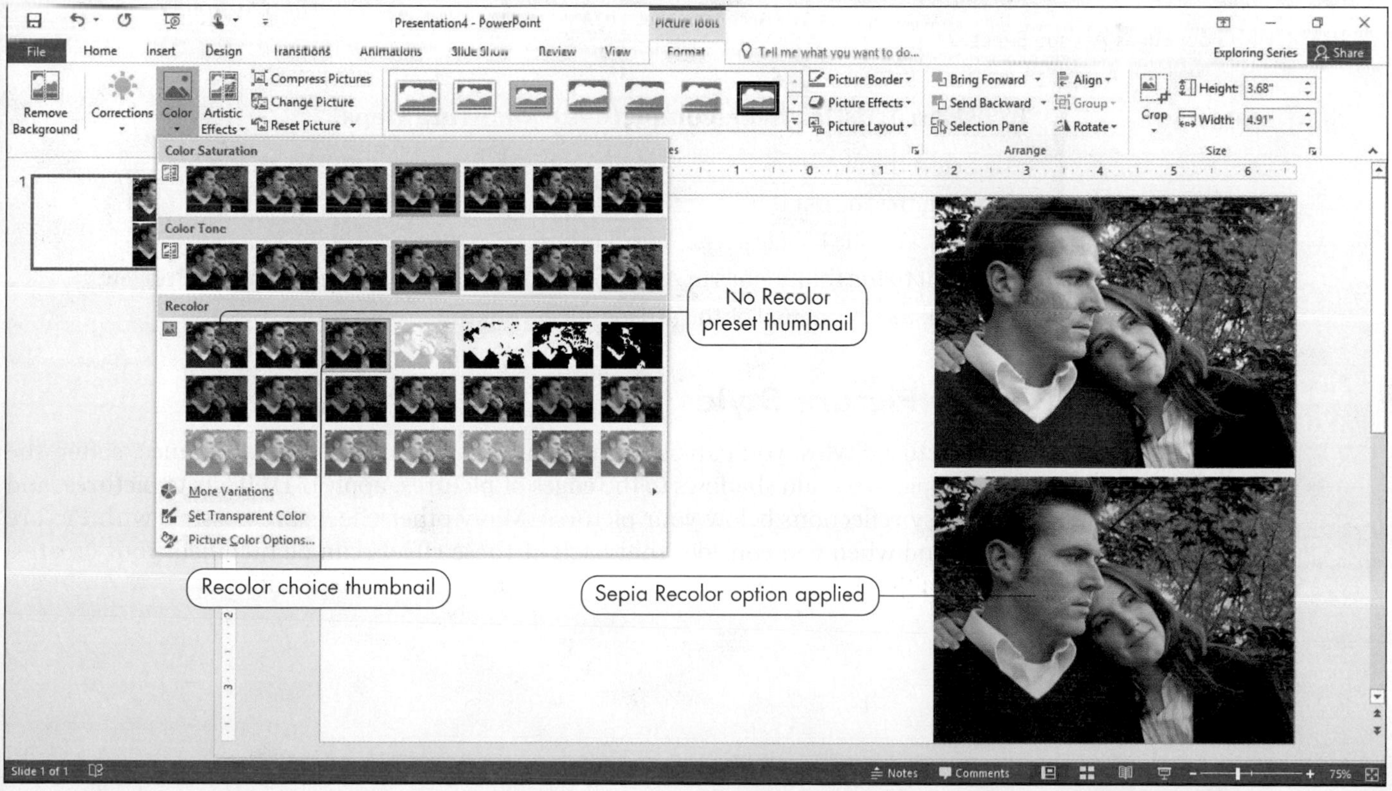

FIGURE 4.13 Sepia Recolor Preset

Use Artistic Effects

STEP 3 » PowerPoint's artistic effects enable you to change the appearance of a picture so that it looks like it was created with a marker, as a pencil sketch or watercolor painting, or using other effects. Use Live Preview to see how an artistic effect changes your picture. You can apply only one effect at a time. Any artistic effects that you have previously applied are lost when you apply a new effect. Figure 4.14 shows a Glow Edges artistic effect applied to a picture.

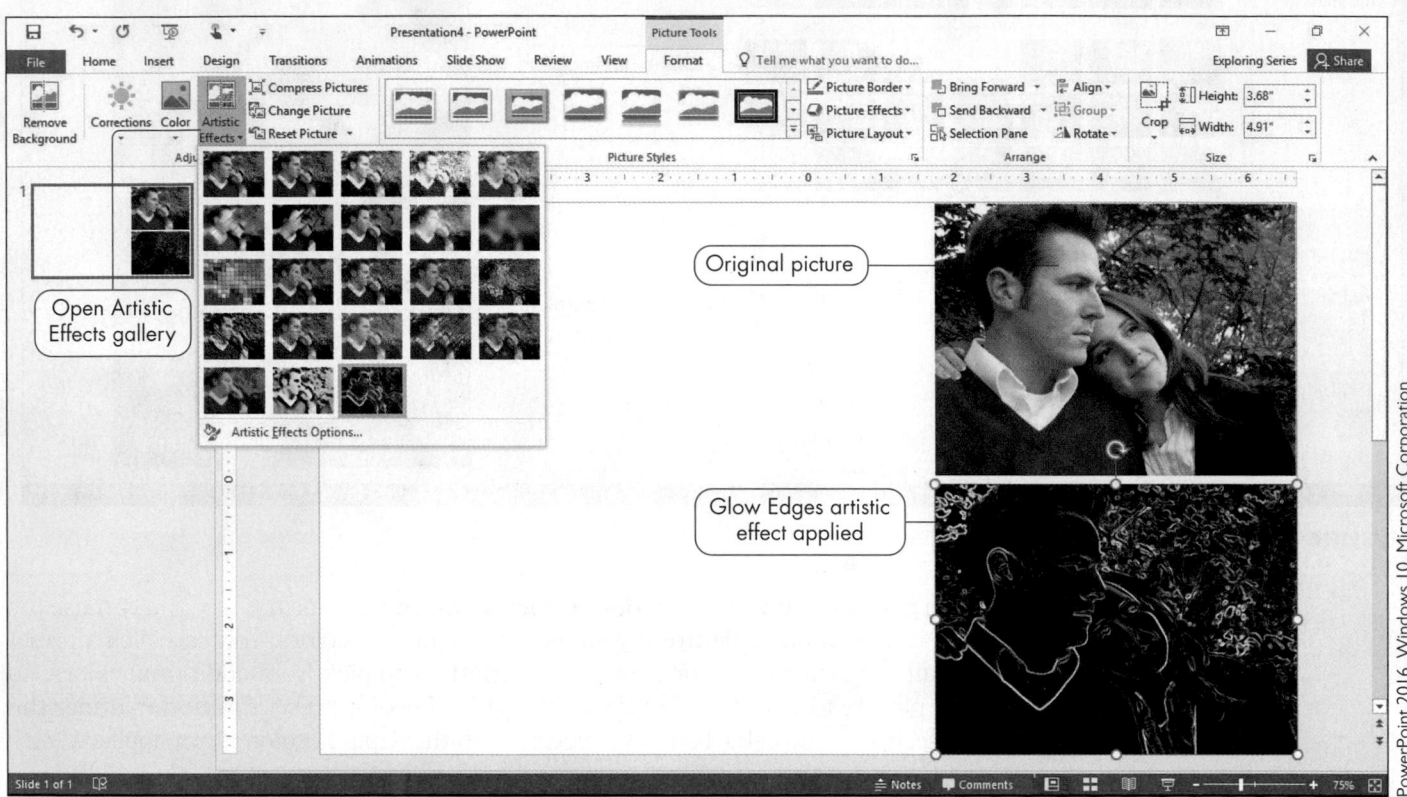

FIGURE 4.14 Glow Edges Artistic Effect

To use an artistic effect, complete the following steps:

1. Select the picture.
2. Click the Format tab.
3. Click Artistic Effects in the Adjust group.
4. Point to the thumbnails in the gallery to view the artistic effects in Live Preview.
5. Click the thumbnail of the artistic effect you want to use.

Apply Picture Styles

With Picture Styles, you can surround your picture with attractive frames, soften the edges of pictures, add shadows to the edges of pictures, apply 3-D effects to pictures, and add glossy reflections below your pictures. Many other effects are possible with Picture Styles, and when you consider that each of these effects can be modified, your creative opportunities are endless! Figure 4.15 shows a few of the possibilities.

FIGURE 4.15 Picture Style Applications

Labels in figure:
- Snip Diagonal Corner, White Picture Style applied
- Metal Oval Picture Style Applied
- Bevel Perspective Left, White Picture Style applied

PowerPoint 2016, Windows 10, Microsoft Corporation

To apply a picture style, complete the following steps:

1. Select the picture.
2. Click More in the Picture Styles group to open the gallery, then point to a style to see a Live Preview or click the style to apply it to the picture.
3. Apply additional image changes by completing one or more of the following steps:
   - Click Picture Border in the Picture Styles group to select the border color, weight, or dash style.
   - Use the Picture Effects option to select from Preset, Shadow, Reflection, Glow, Soft Edges, Bevel, and 3-D Rotation effects.
   - Select Picture Layout to apply your picture to a SmartArt diagram.

Resize or Crop a Picture

STEP 4 ❱❱ You can resize a picture by dragging the sizing handles for the image. You can also use the Format Picture task pane to change the size of the picture to a percent of the original. When *Lock aspect ratio* is checked, the image is resized proportionally.

To resize a picture, complete the following steps:

1. Click the Size Dialog Box Launcher in the Size group on the Picture Tools Format tab to open the Format Picture task pane.
2. Click in the Scale Height or Scale Width box, and then type the new size.

Cropping a picture using the Crop tool lets you eliminate unwanted portions of an image, focusing the viewer's attention on the most important part of the graphic. Remember that if you crop an image and try to enlarge the resulting picture, pixelation may occur that reduces the quality of the image. Figure 4.16 shows a picture with the areas to be cropped from view displayed in gray.

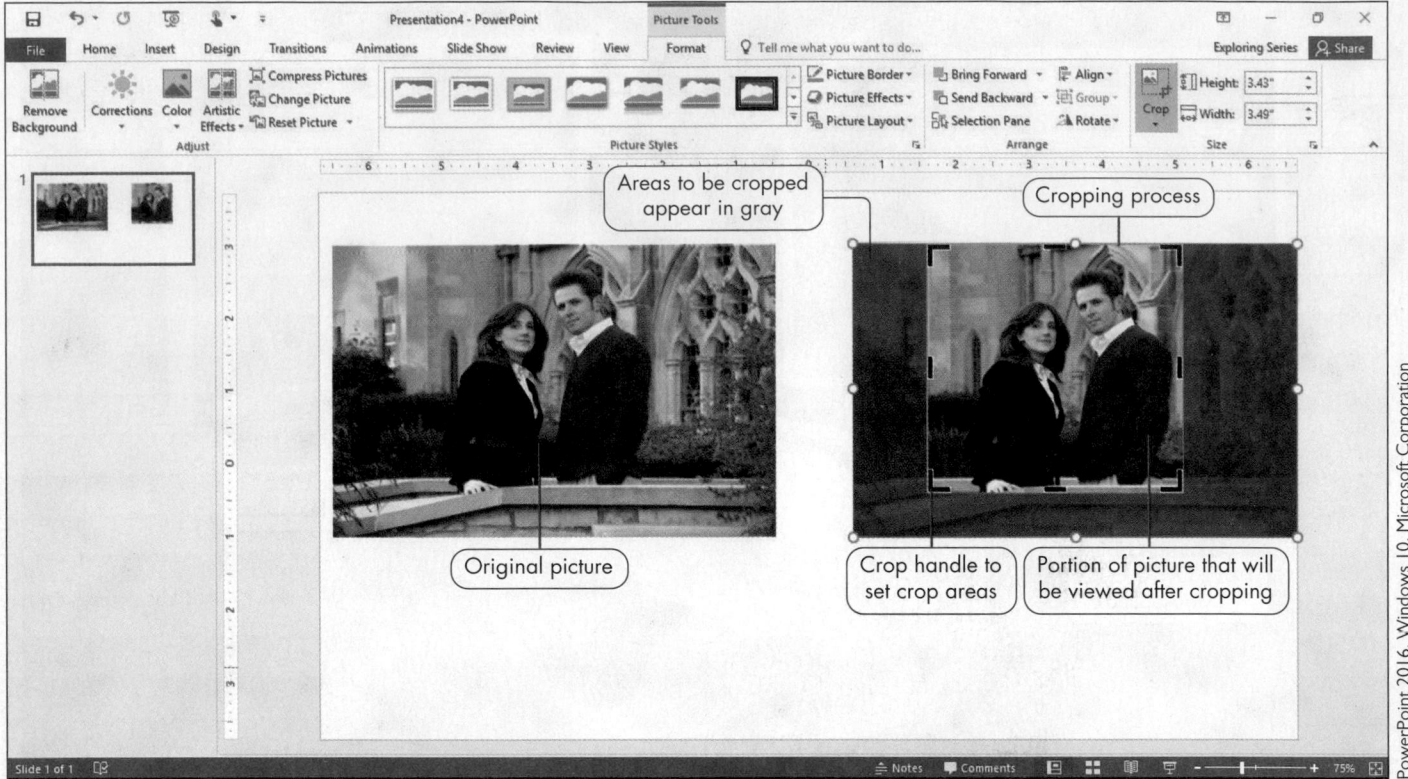

FIGURE 4.16 Use Crop to Focus Attention

To crop a picture, complete the following steps:

1. Select the picture.
2. Click the Format tab.
3. Click Crop in the Size group.
4. Point to a cropping handle and drag inward to eliminate the portion of the image you do not want to view. Use a corner cropping handle to crop in two directions at once.
5. Repeat Step 4 for the remaining sides of the picture.
6. Click Crop again to toggle it off.

When you crop a picture, the cropped portion does not display on the slide, but it is not removed from the presentation file. This is helpful in case you decide later to reset the picture to its original state. When you crop an image, because the unwanted portions of the image are not deleted, the file size is not reduced. Use the Compress Pictures feature to reduce the file size of the image, or all images at once, to reduce the file size of the presentation.

Compress Pictures

The Compress Pictures feature enables you to reduce file sizes by permanently deleting any cropped areas of a selected picture and by changing the resolution of pictures. When you add pictures to your PowerPoint presentation, especially high-resolution pictures downloaded from a digital camera, the presentation file size increases dramatically. It may increase to the point that the presentation becomes slow to load and sluggish to play. Use the Compress Pictures feature to eliminate a large part of this problem. The Compress Pictures feature is in the Adjust group on the Picture Tools Format tab.

By default, you apply compression to only the selected image. If you remove the check in the Compress Pictures dialog box, all pictures in the presentation are compressed. Figure 4.17 shows the Compress Pictures dialog box. You select the amount of compression applied by determining your output. Select 330 pixels per inch (ppi) for use on high-definition displays. Select 220 ppi to ensure that you will obtain excellent quality printouts. Select 150 ppi, however, if you will be displaying the slide show only onscreen or using it for a webpage. Select 96 ppi if you plan to share the slide show by email.

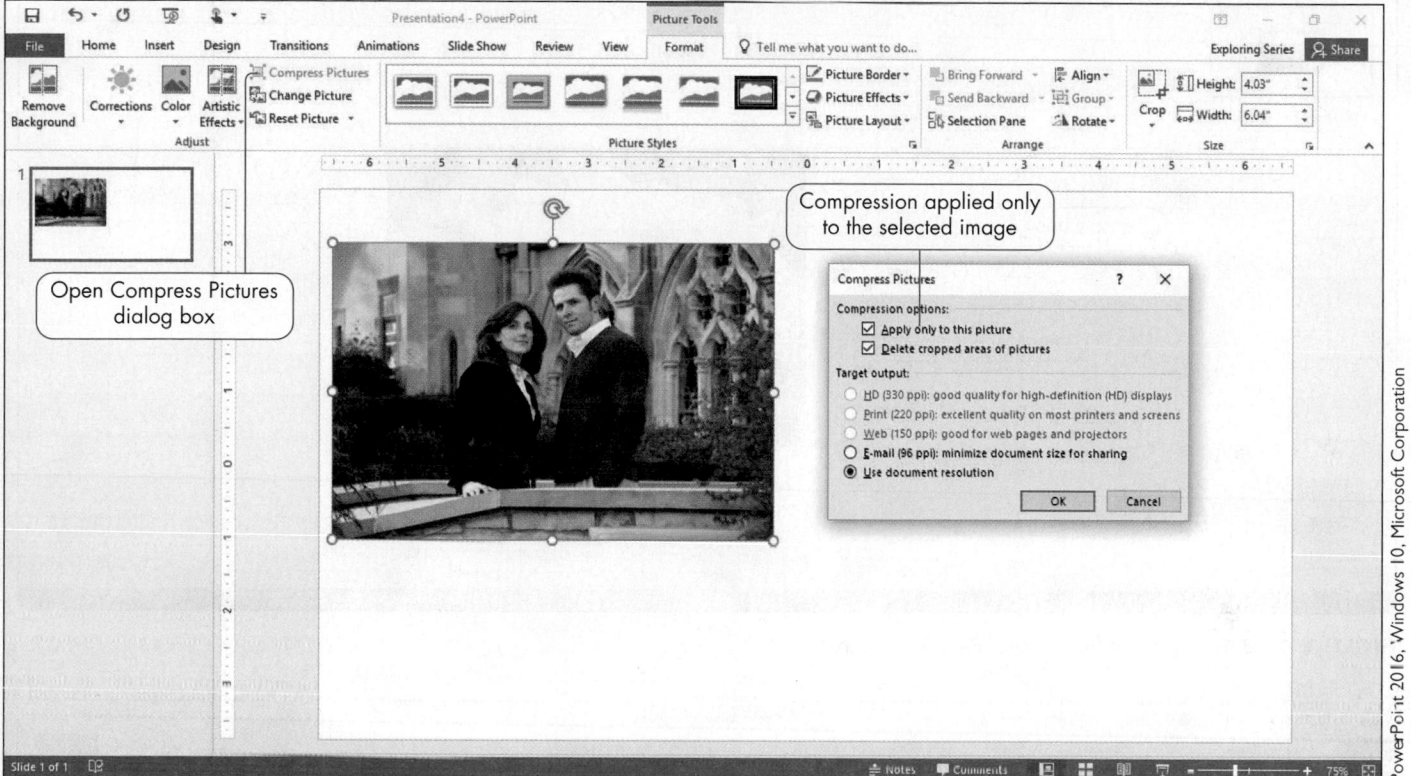

FIGURE 4.17 Picture Compression Options

Create a Background from a Picture

Pictures can make appealing backgrounds if they are transparent enough that text on top of them can be easily read. Picture backgrounds personalize your presentation. To use a photograph as a background, use the Format Background command on the Design tab rather than the Insert Picture feature. Using Insert Picture involves more time because when the picture is inserted it must be resized and the order of the objects on the screen has to be changed to prevent the photograph from hiding placeholders. Figure 4.18 shows an image inserted using Insert Picture that must be resized if it is to be used as a background. It hides the placeholders, so it needs to be positioned at the back and its transparency must be adjusted. Figure 4.19 shows the same picture as Figure 4.18, but in this figure, it was inserted as a background. It is automatically placed behind placeholders and resized to fit the slide, and the transparency is adjusted.

If the background image is too busy or not transparent enough, it can make the presentation difficult to read or distract the audience. Test several images and settings if its color does not contrast enough with the text.

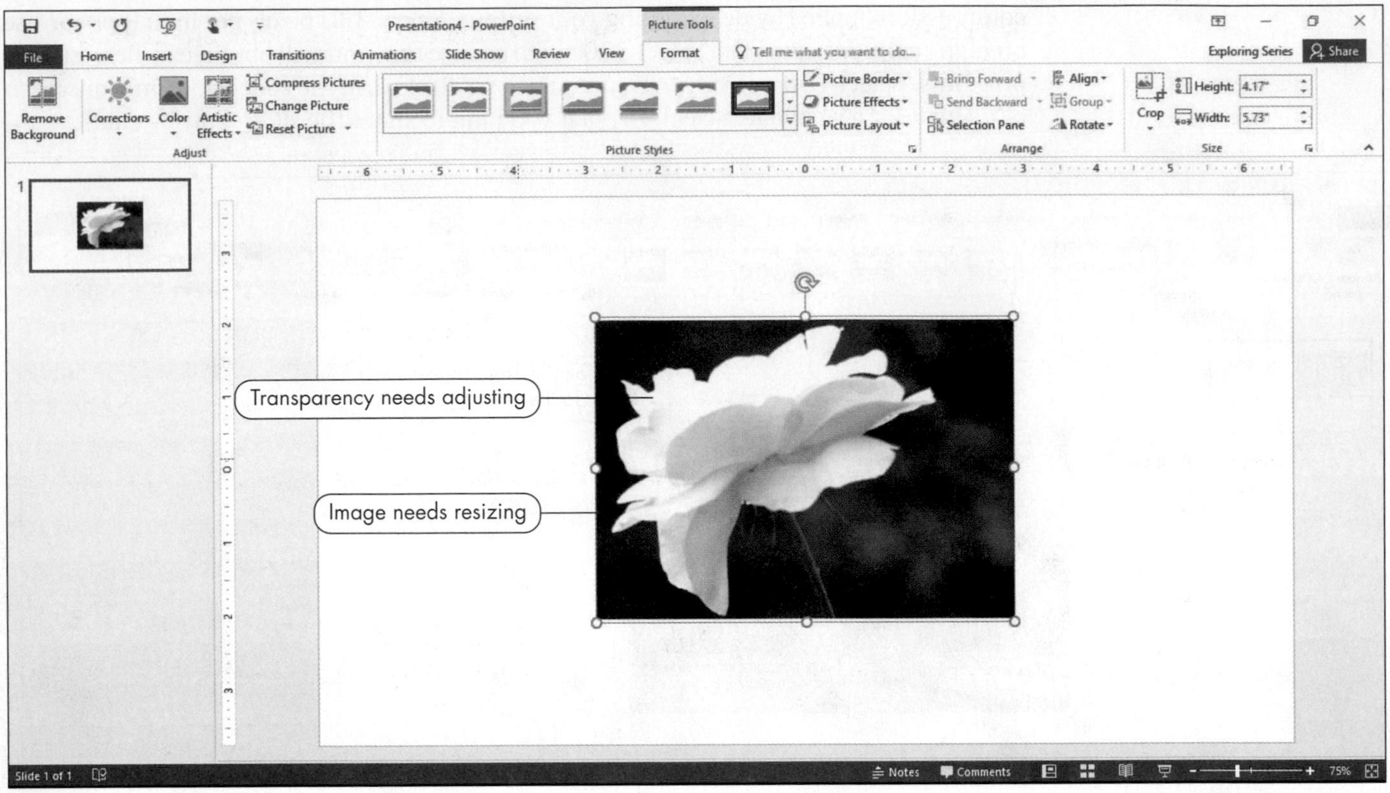

FIGURE 4.18 Background from Insert Picture Option

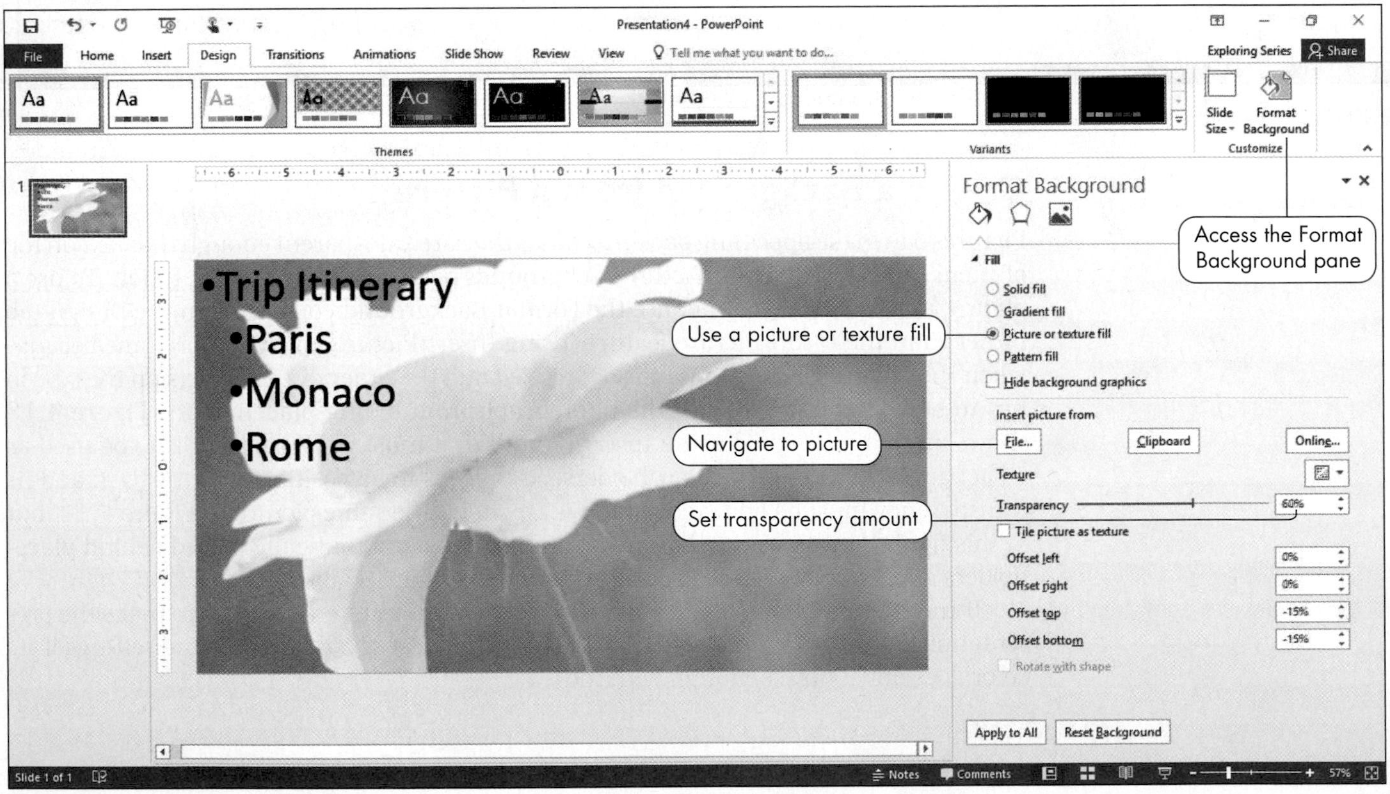

FIGURE 4.19 Background from Format Background Option

> **To create a background from a picture using the Background command, complete the following steps:**
>
> 1. Click the Design tab.
> 2. Click Format Background in the Customize group. The Format Background task pane displays.
> 3. Click Picture or texture fill.
> 4. Click File and navigate to the location where your picture is stored.
> 5. Click the picture file and click Insert.
> 6. Adjust the transparency for the picture by dragging the Transparency slider.
> 7. Click Close to apply the picture background to the current slide or click Apply to All to apply it to all slides in the presentation.

The task pane also includes options for moving the picture by offsetting it to the left or right or the top or bottom.

Using the Internet as a Resource

STEP 5 ›› You can use the Internet as a resource for pictures, video, and audio. PowerPoint interacts with the Internet in three important ways:

- You can download pictures, video, and audio from some webpages for inclusion in a PowerPoint presentation. Note, however, that some of these resources may not be used without permission or license from the creator.
- You can insert hyperlinks into a PowerPoint presentation and click those links to display the associated webpage in your browser provided you have an Internet connection during the presentation.
- You can convert any PowerPoint presentation into a webpage.

Regardless of how you choose to use the Internet for resources in your presentations, your first task is to locate the required resource. For example, if you want to use an image of a dolphin in your presentation on oceanography, you can use a search engine and a search term such as *dolphin images* and save the images to be inserted into the presentation. Or you could use Online Pictures in PowerPoint to access the Bing Image Search and insert them directly from the search results. You could also use a search engine to locate videos or audio of dolphins using *dolphin video* or *dolphin audio*. A search results page will display and you can review the list of results to see what you want to include in the presentation.

> **After you have found an image on the Internet, to save or copy the image, complete one of the following steps:**
>
> - Right-click the image to display a shortcut menu and select *Save picture* to save the file on your computer. (This command may vary among Web browsers.) Then, in PowerPoint, click the Insert tab and click Pictures in the Images group. Navigate to the picture and click Insert.
> - Right-click the image to display a shortcut menu and select Copy to copy the picture onto the Clipboard. Then, simply, paste it onto the slide.

Saving audio files from the Internet can be accomplished by right-clicking the link of the audio file and then selecting the command *Save Target As* from the shortcut menu. Note that different browsers may call the command differently. Videos are typically very large files, so you may want to link to a video by inserting a hyperlink to the resources website. You can click Insert Hyperlink in the Links group on the Insert tab to add it to your slide. Again, you need to be connected to the Internet during your presentation in order for the video to play. Some websites may provide instructions on how to embed a video into your presentation.

Understand Copyright Protection

A *copyright* provides legal protection to a written or artistic work, including pictures, drawings, poetry, novels, movies, songs, computer software, and architecture. It gives the author of a work the exclusive right to the use and duplication of that work. A copyright does not protect facts, ideas, systems, or methods of operation, although it may protect the way these things are expressed.

The owner of the copyright may sell or give up a portion of his or her rights; for example, an author may give distribution rights to a publisher and/or grant movie rights to a studio. *Infringement of copyright* occurs anytime a right held by the copyright owner is used without permission of the owner. Anything on the Internet should be considered copyrighted unless the site specifically says it is in the *public domain*, in which case the author is giving everyone the right to freely reproduce and distribute the material, thereby making the work owned by the public at large. A work also may enter the public domain when the copyright has expired. Facts themselves are not covered by copyright, so you can use statistical data without fear of infringement. Images are protected unless the owner gives his or her permission for downloading.

TIP: USING MEDIA ELEMENTS

Photographs, fonts, sounds, and videos available from Microsoft and its partners through Office.com are part of Microsoft's Media Elements and are copyright protected by Microsoft. To see what uses of Media Elements are prohibited, go to http://support.microsoft.com and search for *Use of Microsoft Copyrighted Content*.

The answer to what you can use from the Web depends on many things, including the amount of the information you reference, as well as the intended use of that information. It is considered fair use, and thus not an infringement of copyright, to use a portion of a work for educational or nonprofit purposes, or for critical review or commentary. In other words, you can use quotes, facts, or other information from the Web in an educational setting, but you should cite the original work in your footnotes, or list the resource on a bibliography page or slide. Table 4.2 presents guidelines for students and teachers to help determine what multimedia can be used in an educational project based on the Proposal for Fair Use Guidelines for Educational Multimedia created in 1996. These guidelines were created by a group of publishers, authors, and educators who gathered to interpret the Copyright Act of 1976 as it applies to educational and scholarly uses of multimedia. You should note that although these guidelines are part of the Congressional Record, they are not law. They can, however, help you determine when you can use multimedia materials under Fair Use principles in a noncommercial, educational use.

TABLE 4.2 Multimedia Copyright Guidelines for Students and Teachers

The following guidelines are based on Section 107 of the U.S. Copyright Act of 1976 and the Proposal for Fair Use Guidelines for Educational Multimedia (1996), which sets forth fair use factors for multimedia projects. These guidelines cover the use of multimedia based on Time, Portion, and Copying and Distribution Limitations. You can learn more about copyright at http://copyright.gov/.

General Guidelines

- Student projects for specific courses may be displayed and kept in personal portfolios as examples of their academic work.
- Students in specific courses may use multimedia in projects with proper credit and citations. Full bibliographic information must be used when available.
- Students and teachers must display copyright notice if copyright ownership information is shown on the original source. Copyright may be shown in a sources or bibliography section unless the presentation is being used for distance learning. In distance learning situations, copyright must appear on the screen when the image is viewed.
- Teachers may use media for face-to-face curriculum-based instruction, for directed self-study, in demonstrations on how to create multimedia productions, for presentations at conferences, and for distance learning. Teachers may also retain projects in their personal portfolios for personal use such as job interviews or tenure review.
- Teachers may use multimedia projects for educational purposes for up to two years, after which permission of the copyright holder is required.
- Students and teachers do not need to write for permission to use media if it falls under multimedia guidelines unless there is a possibility that the project could be broadly distributed at a later date.

Text Guidelines

- Up to 10 percent of a copyrighted work, or up to 1,000 words, may be used, whichever is less.
- Up to 250 words of a poem may be used, but no more than five poems (or excerpts) from different poets or an anthology; no more than three poems (or excerpts) from a single poet.

Illustrations

- A photograph or illustration may be used in its entirety.
- No more than 15 images may be used from a collection.
- No more than 5 images of an artist's or photographer's work may be used.

Motion Media

- Up to 10 percent of a copyrighted work or 3 minutes may be used, whichever is less.
- The clip cannot be altered in any way.

Music and Sound

- Up to 10 percent of a copyrighted musical composition or sound recording may be used, not to exceed 30 seconds.
- Alterations cannot change the basic melody or fundamental character of the work.

Distribution Limitations

- Multimedia projects should not be posted to unsecured websites.
- No more than two copies of the original may be made, only one of which may be placed on reserve for instructional purposes.
- A copy of a project may be made for backup purposes, but may be used only when the original has been lost, damaged, or stolen.
- If more than one person created a project, each person may keep only one copy.

Pearson Education, Inc.

Quick Concepts ✓

1. What is the difference between bitmap images and vector graphics? Name one advantage and disadvantage of each type of graphic. ***p. 1118***

2. Why would you compress an image? ***p. 1118***

3. List five ways to transform an image by using PowerPoint's Picture Tools tab. ***p. 1121***

4. What is infringement of copyright? What is "fair use"? ***p. 1134***

Hands-On Exercises

Skills covered: Insert Pictures
• Remove a Background • Correct
a Picture • Change Picture Color
• Apply an Artistic Effect • Apply a
Picture Style • Create a Background
from a Picture • Crop a Picture
• Compress a Picture • Insert a
Picture from the Internet

1 Pictures

You decide to create a memories slide show for your sister and her husband, who were recently married.
You include their engagement and honeymoon pictures.

STEP 1 ›› INSERT PICTURES AND REMOVE A BACKGROUND

You start the memory album with a picture from the couple's engagement. Because the Title Slide layout does not include
a placeholder for content, you add a picture using the Insert Picture from File feature. You then insert images into content
placeholders provided in the album layout. Refer to Figure 4.20 as you complete Step 1.

Steps e–f: Resized
and positioned

Step g–i: Image inserted and
background removed

AMY AND DAN   September 9th

Steps m–n: Images inserted
using content placeholders

PowerPoint 2016, Windows 10, Microsoft Corporation

FIGURE 4.20 Inserted Pictures

a. Open *p04h1Memory* and save it as **p04h1Memory_LastFirst**.

b. Create a handout header with your name and a handout footer with your instructor's name and your class. Apply to all slides. Include the current date.

c. Ensure that you are on Slide 1, click the **Insert tab**, and then click **Pictures** in the Images group.

You add a picture using the Insert Picture command because the Title Slide layout does not include a placeholder for content. The Insert Picture dialog box opens.

d. Locate the *p04h1Mem1* picture in the *p04h1Memory_Media* folder and click **Insert**.

The picture is inserted and centered on the slide.

e. Click the **Size Dialog Box Launcher** in the Size group on the Format tab to open the Format Picture task pane. Click in the **Scale Height box**, select **100**, and then type **96**. Press **Enter**.

Typing 96 in the Scale Height box automatically sets the Scale Width to 96% because the *Lock aspect ratio* check box is selected.

f. Click **Position** in the Format Picture task pane and set the Horizontal Position to **1.00"** from the Top Left Corner. Set the Vertical Position to **0.11"** from the Top Left Corner. Click the **Close** button for the Format Picture task pane.

g. Click the **Insert tab**, click **Pictures** in the Images group, and then locate and insert *p04h1Mem2*.

h. Click **Remove Background** in the Adjust group on the Format tab.

A marquee that includes most of the flower appears around the image. Some petals are cut off and need to be added back in.

i. Drag the left-center, left-bottom, and right-center sizing handles of the marquee as necessary until all petals and the stem are included in the picture (see Figure 4.21).

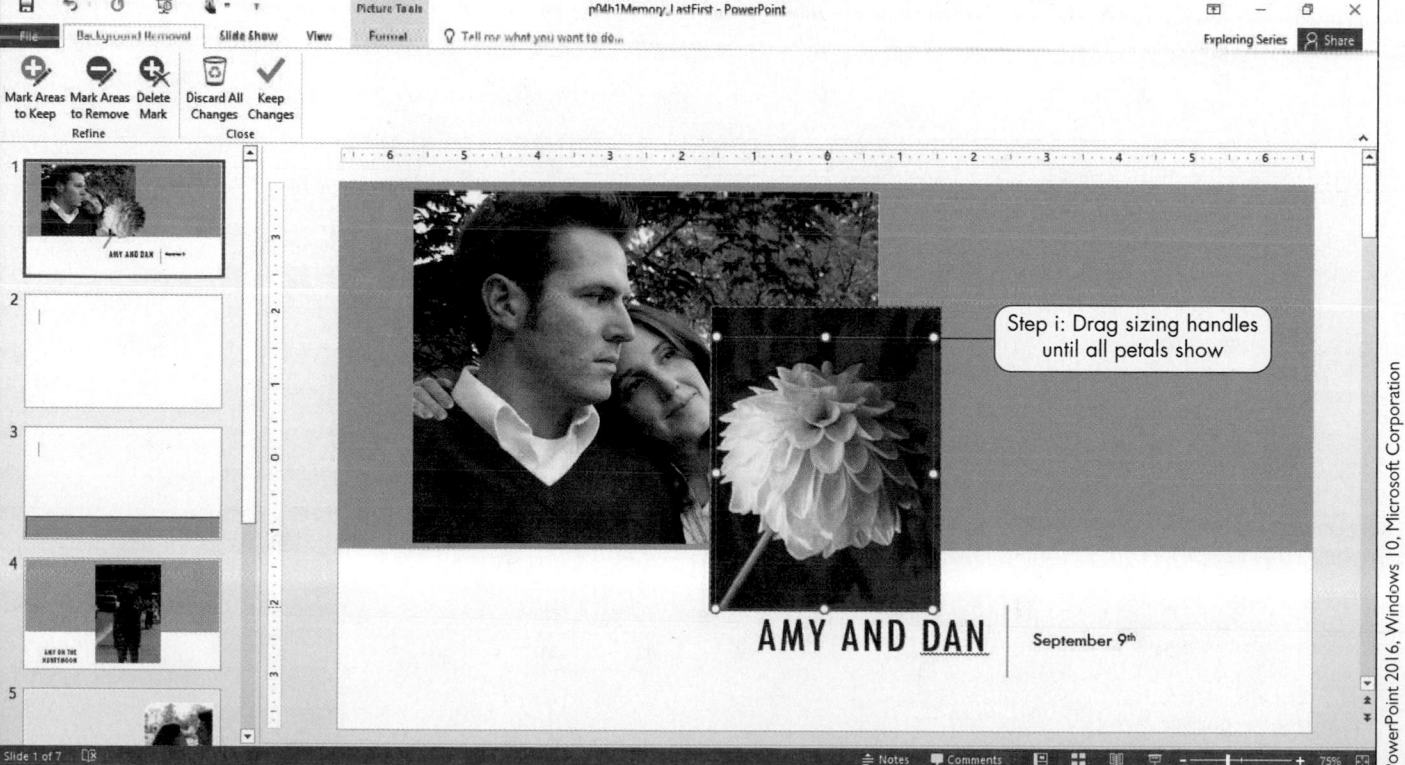

FIGURE 4.21 Adjusted Marquee

j. Click **Keep Changes** in the Close group on the Background Removal tab.

The background is removed from the flower.

k. Click the **Size Dialog Box Launcher** in the Size group to open the Format Picture task pane and click the **Relative to original picture size check box** to deselect it in the Size section. Click in the **Scale Height box** and type **50**. Press **Enter**.

l. Click **Position** in the Format Picture task pane and set the Horizontal Position to **11.59"** from the Top Left Corner. Set the Vertical Position to **4.79"** from the Top Left Corner. Close the Format Picture task pane.

The flower is now positioned in the lower-right section of the slide. Refer to Figure 4.20.

m. Click **Slide 2**. Click the **Pictures** icon in the large content placeholder on the left side of the slide. Click the *p04h1Mem3* file to select it and click **Insert**.

n. Use the Pictures icons in the two small content placeholders on the right side of the screen to insert *p04h1Mem4* into the top placeholder and *p04h1Mem5* into the bottom placeholder.

Note that the images were centered inside the placeholders.

o. Save the presentation.

You want to include two pictures of the couple in the memory presentation, but the pictures were taken in different lighting conditions. You decide to use PowerPoint's correction tools to enhance the pictures. You also change the color tone of a picture to warm it up to match the warm color of the background graphic color on the slide where it appears. Refer to Figure 4.22 as you complete Step 2.

Steps b–c: Apply Brightness/Contrast

Steps e–f: Adjust temperature and apply picture style

AMY ON THE HONEYMOON

PowerPoint 2016, Windows 10, Microsoft Corporation

FIGURE 4.22 Picture Correction and Color Tone Adjustment

a. Click **Slide 3**. Click the **Pictures** in the content placeholders to insert *p04h1Mem6* into the left placeholder and *p04h1Mem7* into the right placeholder.

b. Select the image on the left and click **Corrections** in the Adjust group on the Format tab. Click **Brightness: −20% Contrast: +20%** (fourth row, second column of the Brightness/Contrast section).

The image becomes slightly darker, and the increased contrast brings out the picture detail.

c. Select the image on the right and click **Corrections** in the Adjust group on the Format tab. Click **Brightness: −20% Contrast: 0% (Normal)** (third row, second column of the Brightness/Contrast section).

The brightness is reduced in the image.

d. Click **Slide 4** and select the picture of the woman.

e. Click **Color** in the Adjust group on the Format tab and click **Temperature: 11200 K** in the Color Tone gallery. Next, click **Corrections** in the Adjust group and click **Brightness: +40% Contrast: 0% (Normal)** (third row, fifth column).

The cooler tones in the image are converted to warmer tones, which casts a gold hue over the picture. The picture is also brighter, emphasizing the Colosseum in the background.

f. Click **More** in the Picture Styles group and click **Rotated, White**.

g. Save the presentation.

STEP 3 ›› APPLY AN ARTISTIC EFFECT AND A PICTURE STYLE

The title slide includes a picture of the couple that you want to stand out. The Artistic Effects gallery includes many picture effects, and the Picture Styles gallery includes a variety of Picture Border effects. You decide to experiment with the options available in the galleries to see the impact they have on the title slide picture. You also apply an artistic effect. Refer to Figure 4.23 as you complete Step 3.

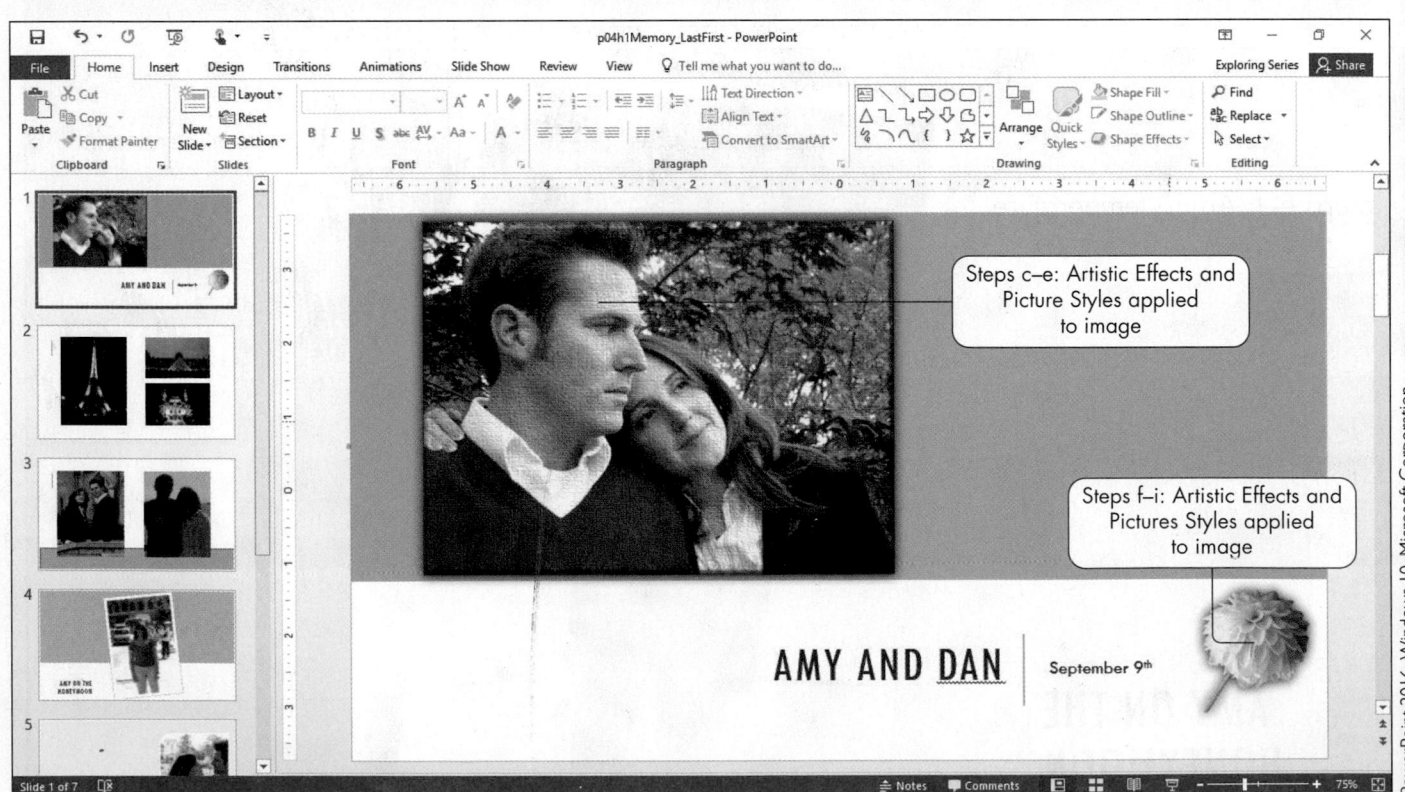

FIGURE 4.23 Applied Artistic Effect and Picture Styles

a. Click **Slide 1**, select the picture of the couple, and then click the **Format tab**.

b. Click **Artistic Effects** in the Adjust group on the Format tab.

The Artistic Effects gallery opens. Point to the effects and watch how each effect impacts the image.

> **TROUBLESHOOTING:** Some of the artistic effects involve extensive changes, so expect a slowdown as the preview is created.

c. Click **Texturizer** (fourth row, second column).

A light texture is applied to the picture.

d. Click **More** in the Picture Styles group.

The Picture Styles gallery opens. Point to the styles and watch how each style impacts the image.

e. Click **Center Shadow Rectangle**.

A gray shadow displays evenly around the picture.

f. Click the **Home tab**, click **Format Painter** in the Clipboard group, and then click the **flower picture**.

You copied the picture style, and applied it to the flower.

g. Select the picture of the couple again and click the **Format tab**.

h. Click **Picture Border arrow** in the Picture Styles group and click **Brown, Text 2** (first row, fourth column) in the Theme Colors section.

i. Click **Picture Effects** in the Picture Styles group, point to **Bevel**, and then click **Cool Slant** (first row, fourth column of the Bevel section).

The Bevel effect is applied to the outer edges of the picture.

j. Save the presentation.

The honeymooners stayed in a suite with a gorgeous view of a garden, and you want to include a picture of one of the flowers as the background setting of a picture of the honeymooners. Refer to Figure 4.24 as you complete Step 4.

FIGURE 4.24 Background from a Picture

a. Click the **Design tab**.

b. Click **Slide 5** and click **Format Background** in the Customize group.

The Format Background task pane displays.

c. Select the **Hide background graphics check box** in the Format Background task pane.

d. Click **Picture or texture fill** and click **File** to open the Insert Picture dialog box.

e. Select *p04h1Mem8*, click **Insert**, and then close the Format Background task pane.

f. Examine the picture on the far right of the slide.

g. Click the **View tab** and ensure that the Ruler is selected in the Show group.

Activating the ruler will make it easier for you to determine the area to crop.

h. Select the picture, click the **Format tab**, and then click **Crop** in the Size group.

i. Drag the top-left corner down and to the right until the vertical ruler reaches approximately the +2 1/2" mark and the horizontal ruler reaches approximately the +2" mark.

The resulting size of the image is 5.81" high and 4.25" wide—yours may differ.

j. Click **Crop** in the Size group again to crop the area from view and to turn off the Crop feature.

k. Select the cropped picture and ensure that the Format tab is selected.

l. Click **Compress Pictures** in the Adjust group.

The Compress Pictures dialog box opens.

m. Ensure that Use document resolution is selected in the Target output section.

n. Click the **Apply only to this picture check box** to deselect it.

You need to compress all the pictures you have used in the presentation to reduce the presentation file size, not just the selected picture.

o. Click **OK**.

The portions of the image that were cropped from view are deleted, and all pictures in the slide show are compressed.

p. Save the presentation.

STEP 5 ›› **INSERT A PICTURE FROM THE INTERNET**

The couple visited Rome, Italy, during their honeymoon, so you want to insert a picture of the Colosseum to end the slide show. You insert an image from Morguefile.com, a website that provides pictures free for personal or commercial use. Refer to Figure 4.25 as you complete Step 5.

FIGURE 4.25 Hyperlink to Morguefile.com

a. Click **Slide 6**. Click **Slide Show** view.

Note that the text *Morguefile* is a hyperlink. The hyperlink to Morguefile.com will display if you view the presentation in Slide Show view.

b. Click the link to launch the website in your default browser.

> **TROUBLESHOOTING:** If you are not connected to the Internet, the hyperlink will not work. Connect to the Internet and repeat Step b.

The Morguefile website displays a thumbnail of an image of the Colosseum in Rome.

c. Right-click the image, select **Copy picture**, and then close the browser.

The Copy picture command may be named something else depending on the Web browser you are using.

d. Press **Esc** to return to Slide 6 in the presentation. Right-click anywhere on Slide 6 and paste the image using the Picture paste option in the submenu.

e. Adjust the image size so that it covers the left half of the color block on the slide (see Figure 4.25).

Depending on the size of the image you insert, you may or may not need to do this step.

f. Drag the picture to position it on the left side of the slide, leaving the Morguefile text box visible.

The Morguefile website provides royalty-free images, but they ask that credit be given to the photographer. The text box should be visible to give credit to the image source.

g. Save the presentation. Keep the presentation open if you plan to continue with the next Hands-On Exercise. If not, close the presentation and exit PowerPoint.

Video

With video added to your project, you can greatly enhance and reinforce your story, and your audience can retain more of what they see. For example, a video of water tumbling over a waterfall would stir the emotions of a viewer far more than a table listing the number of gallons of water falling within a designated period of time. Anytime you can engage a viewer's emotions, he or she will better remember your message.

In this section, you will learn the types of video file formats that PowerPoint supports and where to search for videos. You will learn about different methods for adding them to your presentation. You will examine the options available when using video and insert a video clip into the memories presentation.

Adding Video

STEP 1 ⟫ Table 4.3 displays the common types of video file formats you can add to a presentation, listed in alphabetical order by file extension. Different file formats use different types of *codec* (coder/decoder) software, which use algorithms to compress or code videos, and then decompress or decode the videos for playback. Video playback places tremendous demands on your computer system in terms of processing speed and memory. Using a codec reduces those demands. In order for your video file to be viewed correctly, the video player must have the appropriate software installed and the correct version of the software. Even though your video file extension is the same as the one listed in Table 4.3, the video may not play correctly if the correct version of the codec software is not installed.

TABLE 4.3	Types of Video File Formats Supported by PowerPoint	
File Format	**Extension**	**Description**
Windows Media File	.asf	**Advanced Streaming Format** Stores synchronized multimedia data. Used to stream audio and video content, images, and script commands over a network.
Windows Video File	.avi	**Audio Video Interleave** Stores sound and moving pictures in Microsoft Resource Interchange File Format (RIFF).
MP4 Video	.mp4	**Moving Picture Experts Group 4** File format commonly used with video cameras. Supported by all browsers.
Movie File	.mpg or .mpeg	**Moving Picture Experts Group** Evolving set of standards for video and audio compression developed by the Moving Picture Experts Group.
Adobe Flash Media	.swf	**Flash Video** File format that can be used to deliver video over the Internet. Uses Adobe Flash Player.
Windows Media Video File	.wmv	**Windows Media Video** Compresses audio and video by using Windows Media Video compressed format. Requires minimal amount of storage space on your computer's hard drive.

Pearson Education, Inc.

When you add video to your presentation, you can *embed* the video and store the video within the presentation, or you can *link* to the video, which creates a connection from the presentation to another location such as a storage device or website. The advantage of embedding video is that a copy of the video file is placed in the slide, so moving or deleting the original video will not impact your presentation. The advantage of linking a video file is that your presentation file size is smaller. Another advantage of linking over embedding is that the presentation video is updated automatically if the original video object is changed. One caution for using a linked video from a file—the video is not part of the presentation. You can save the video file and the presentation file in the same folder and then compress the folder to help reduce its overall size. Having the two files in the same folder ensures that the link will still work in case the compressed folder is copied or transferred to a new storage location.

To insert a video in a presentation, complete the following steps:

1. Click the Insert tab.
2. Click Video in the Media group.
3. Click Video on My PC.
4. Browse, locate, and select the video you want to use in the presentation.
5. Click Insert to insert the video in your presentation or click the Insert arrow and select Link to File to link the video to your presentation.

PowerPoint has made it even easier to add online video, such as a video from YouTube, to a presentation. You can search for an online video from within PowerPoint, and the video will be inserted directly into your slide. You can then move the video to a different location on the slide or resize the video just as you would a photograph. Figure 4.26 shows the search box options for Online Video. Video can be inserted from your OneDrive account (if you have video saved there), YouTube, or a website where you have been given the embed code for the video.

Figure 4.27 shows the results of a whales video search. The search term *whales* in the YouTube Search box was used for the search.

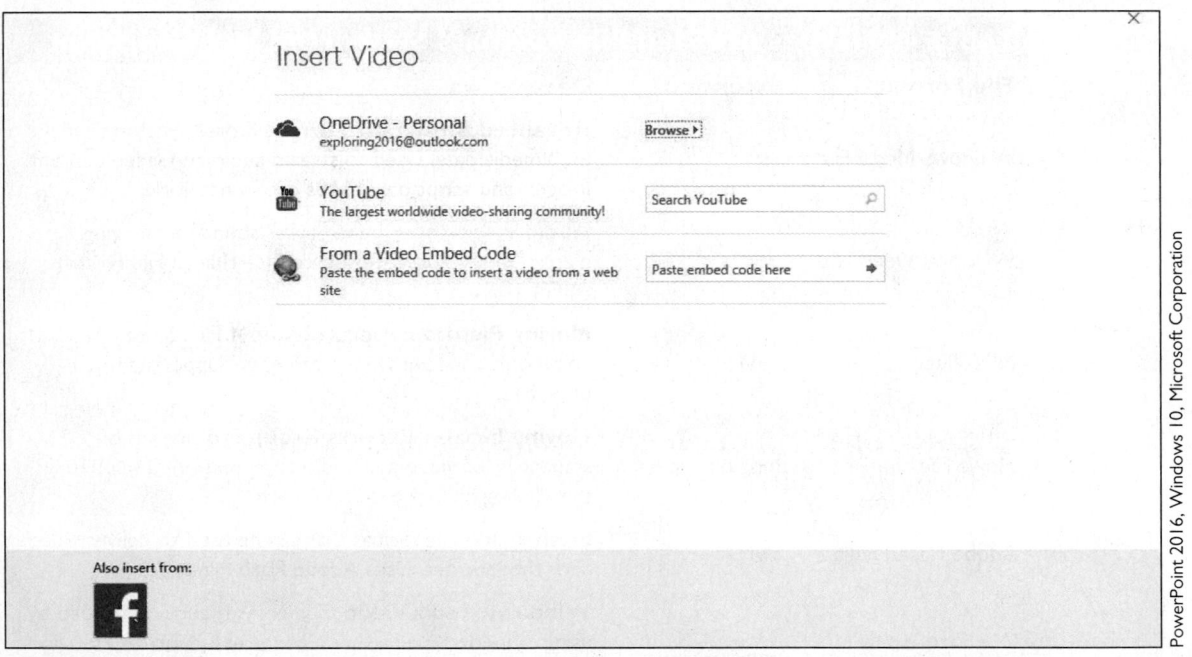

FIGURE 4.26 Online Video Search Options

FIGURE 4.27 Search Results for YouTube Search

To search for and insert an online video in a presentation, complete the following steps:

1. Click the Insert tab.
2. Click Video in the Media group.
3. Click Online Video.
4. Browse, locate, and select the video you want to use in the presentation.
5. Click Insert to insert the video in your presentation.

You can also embed video from an online website. When you embed video from the online site, you have to copy and paste the embed code from the site into the *From a Video Embed Code* box (see Figure 4.28). If you have embedded video from an online site, you must be connected to the Internet when you display the presentation.

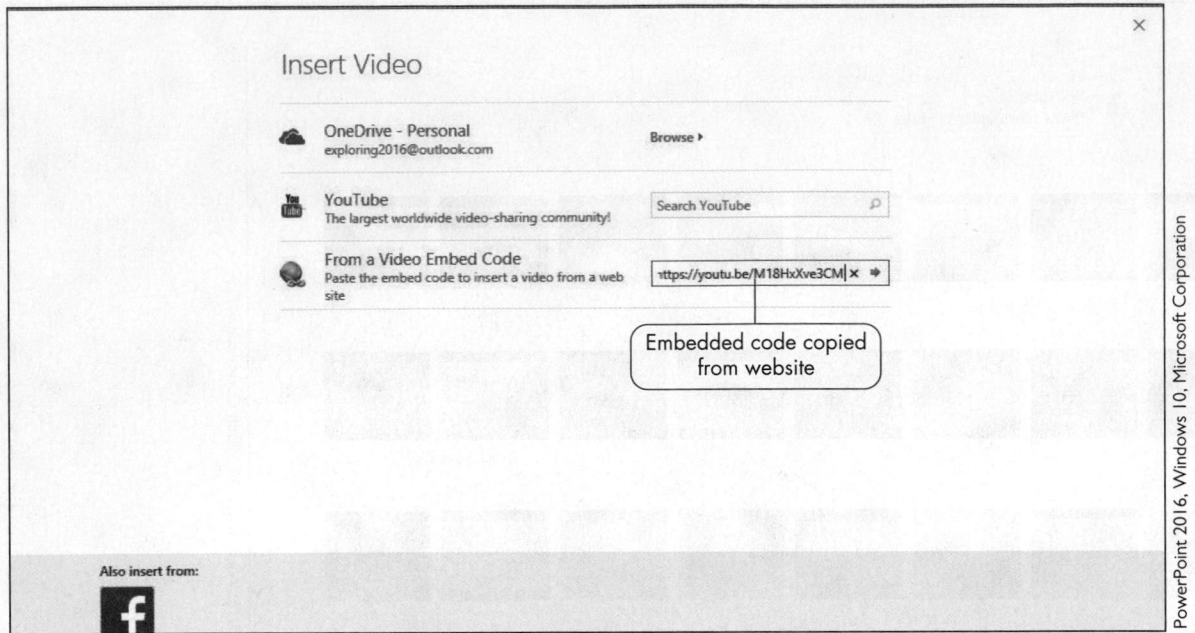

FIGURE 4.28 Embed Code from a Website in PowerPoint

To insert embed code from an online video site, complete the following steps:

1. Locate video on an online video site.
2. Copy the embed code.
3. Click the Insert tab in PowerPoint.
4. Click Video in the Media group.
5. Click Online Video.
6. Paste the embed code into the *From a Video Embed Code* box.
7. Click the Insert arrow at the right side of the box.

Whether you have inserted your own video or video from a website, the video will include a Media Controls bar with a Play/Pause button, a Move Back button, a Move Forward button, a time notation, and a Mute/Unmute control slider. The Move Back and Move Forward buttons aid you when editing your own video. However, these controls may auto-hide and become visible only when the pointer is moved. Additionally, videos inserted from websites may use their own control bars instead of the PowerPoint Media Controls bar shown in Figure 4.29.

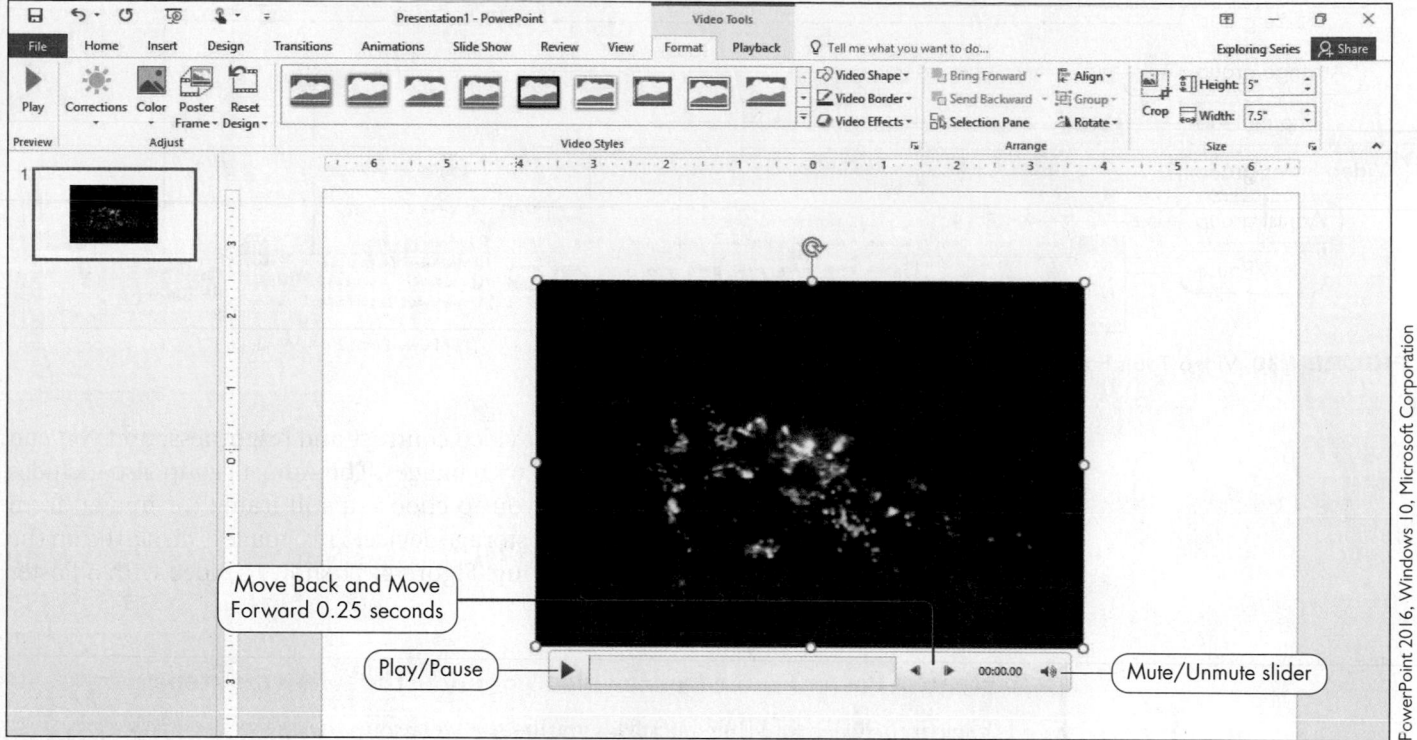

FIGURE 4.29 Media Controls Bar

Using Video Tools

PowerPoint includes tools for working with video. You can format the video's brightness and contrast, color, and style. You can apply most artistic image effects, add or remove bookmarks, trim the video, and set fade in or fade out effects. When you select an inserted video, the Video Tools contextual tab displays with two subtabs: the Format tab and the Playback tab.

Format a Video

 The Format tab includes options for playing the video for preview purposes, adjusting the video, applying a style to the video, arranging a video on the slide, and cropping and sizing the video. Figure 4.30 displays the Video Tools Format tab. Some of these tools will not work with embedded website videos.

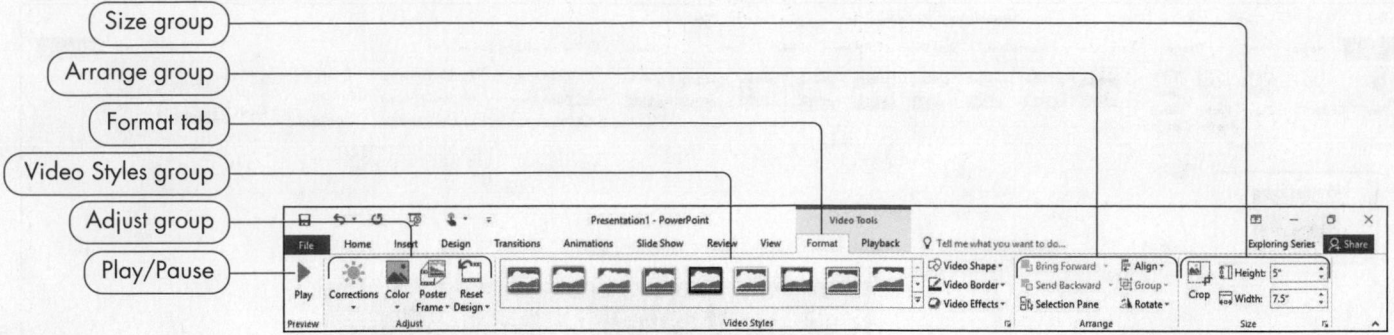

FIGURE 4.30 Video Tools Format Tab

PowerPoint 2016, Windows 10, Microsoft Corporation

Using the Adjust group, you can adjust video contrast and brightness, and you can recolor a video as you did when you worked with images. The Adjust group also includes the ***Poster Frame*** option, which enables you to choose a still frame (or image) from within the video or any image file from your storage device. This image is displayed on the PowerPoint slide when the video is not playing. Figure 4.31 shows a video with a Poster Frame option set to the current frame.

To create a Poster Frame from a video, complete the following steps:

1. Select the video and then click Play in the Preview group to display the video.
2. Pause the video when the frame you want to use as the poster frame appears.
3. Click Poster Frame in the Adjust group.
4. Click Current Frame.

To create a Poster Frame from an image stored in your storage device, complete the following steps:

1. Select the video and click Poster Frame in the Adjust group.
2. Click Image from File.
3. Locate and select desired image.
4. Click Insert.

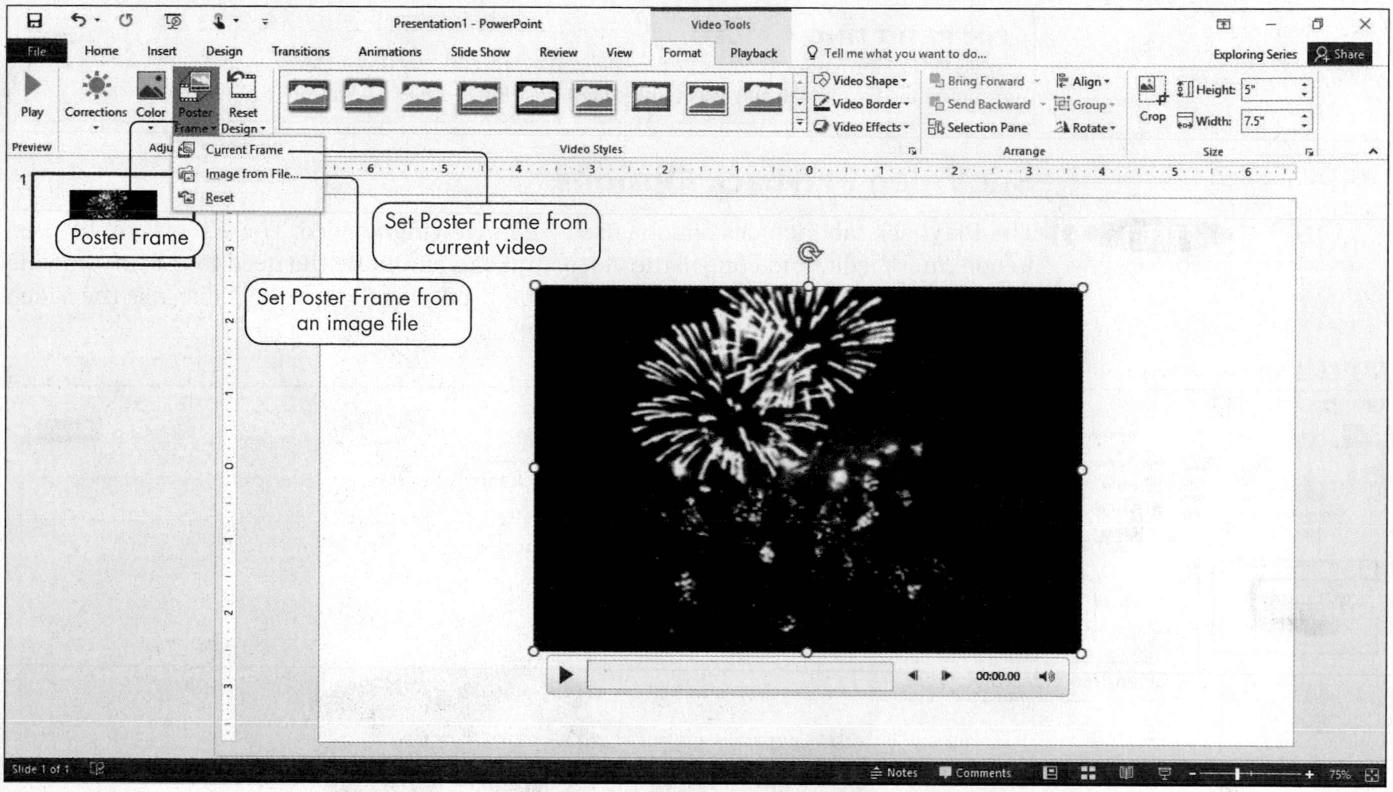

FIGURE 4.31 Poster Frame Option

The Style effects available for images are also available for videos. In addition to the styles in the Video Styles gallery, you can edit the shape of a video, change the border of the video, and add video effects such as Shadow, Reflection, Glow, Soft Edges, Bevel, and 3-D Rotation. Figure 4.32 shows a video formatted to fit a PowerPoint shape, with a gray border and reflection added.

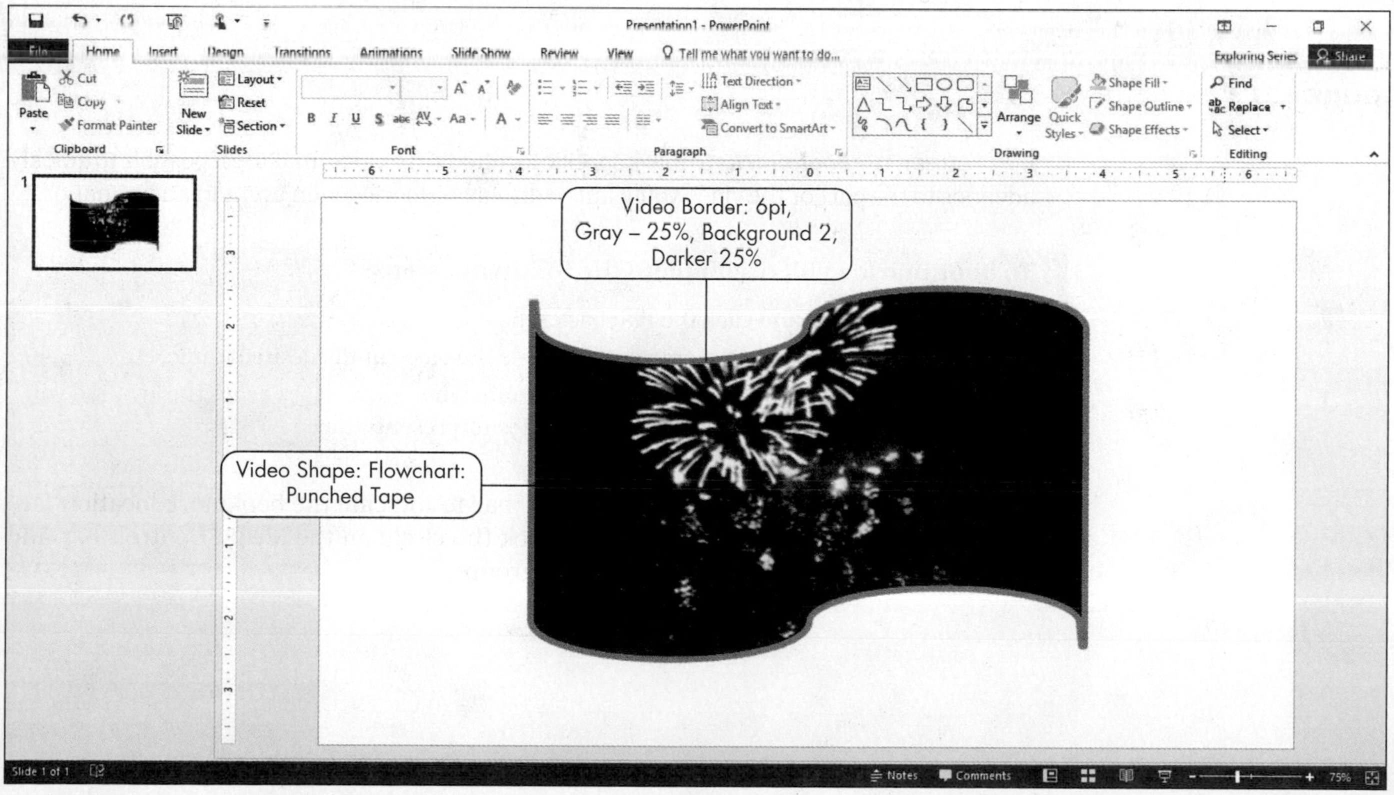

FIGURE 4.32 Video Styles

Set Video Playback Options

STEP 3 ▶▶ The Playback tab includes options used when viewing a video. These tools can be used to bookmark, edit, and control the video, and can eliminate the need to use any outside video-editing software for basic video-editing functions. Figure 4.33 displays the Video Tools Playback tab.

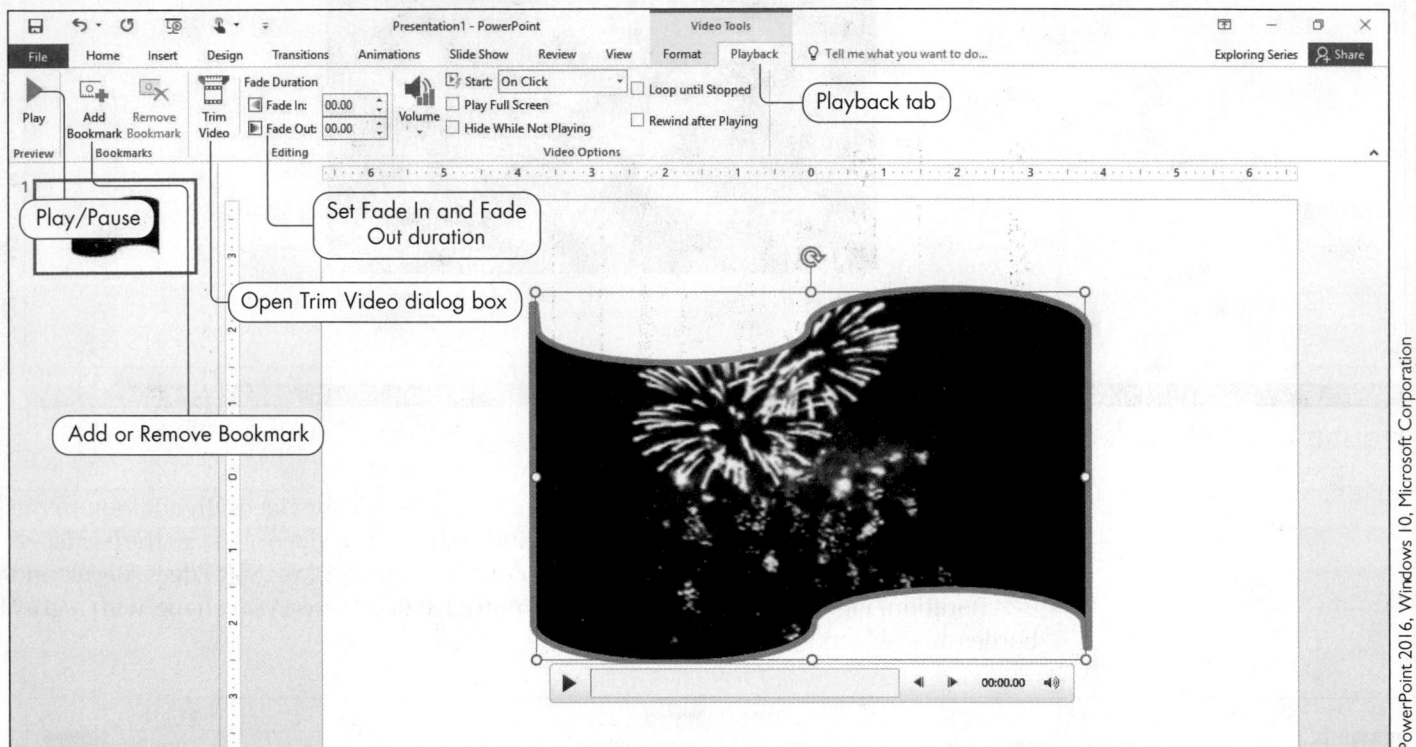

FIGURE 4.33 Video Tools Playback Tab

You can use ***bookmarks*** to mark specific locations in a video, making it possible to quickly advance to the part of the video you want to display or to trigger an event in an animation.

To bookmark a video, complete the following steps:

1. Select the video and click the Playback tab.
2. Click Play on the Media Controls bar. Pause the video at the desired frame.
3. Click Add Bookmark in the Bookmarks group when the video reaches the location you want to be able to move quickly to during your presentation.

A circle displays on the Media Controls bar to indicate the bookmark location (see Figure 4.34). To remove the bookmark, click the circle on the Media Controls bar and click Remove Bookmark in the Bookmarks group.

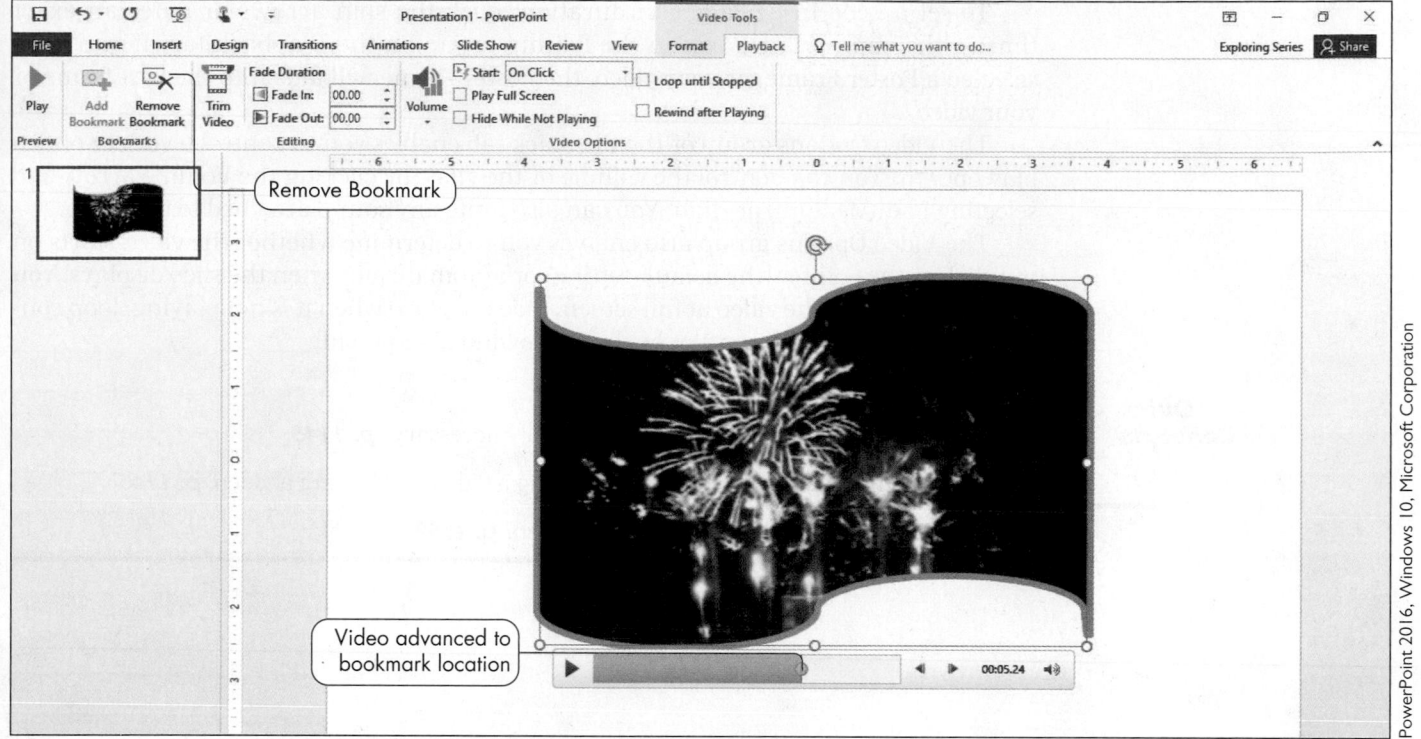

FIGURE 4.34 Bookmarked Video

PowerPoint provides basic video editing by enabling you to determine the starting and ending of a video and set a Fade In and Fade Out duration. In the Trim Video dialog box, which you access in the Editing group on the Playback tab, you can use the Trim option to specify the Start Time and End Time for a video, or you can drag the Start marker and the End marker on the Timing bar to select the time. The advantage to dragging the markers is that as you drag, you can view the video. Any bookmarks you set will also display in the Trim Video dialog box. Figure 4.35 shows the Trim Video dialog box.

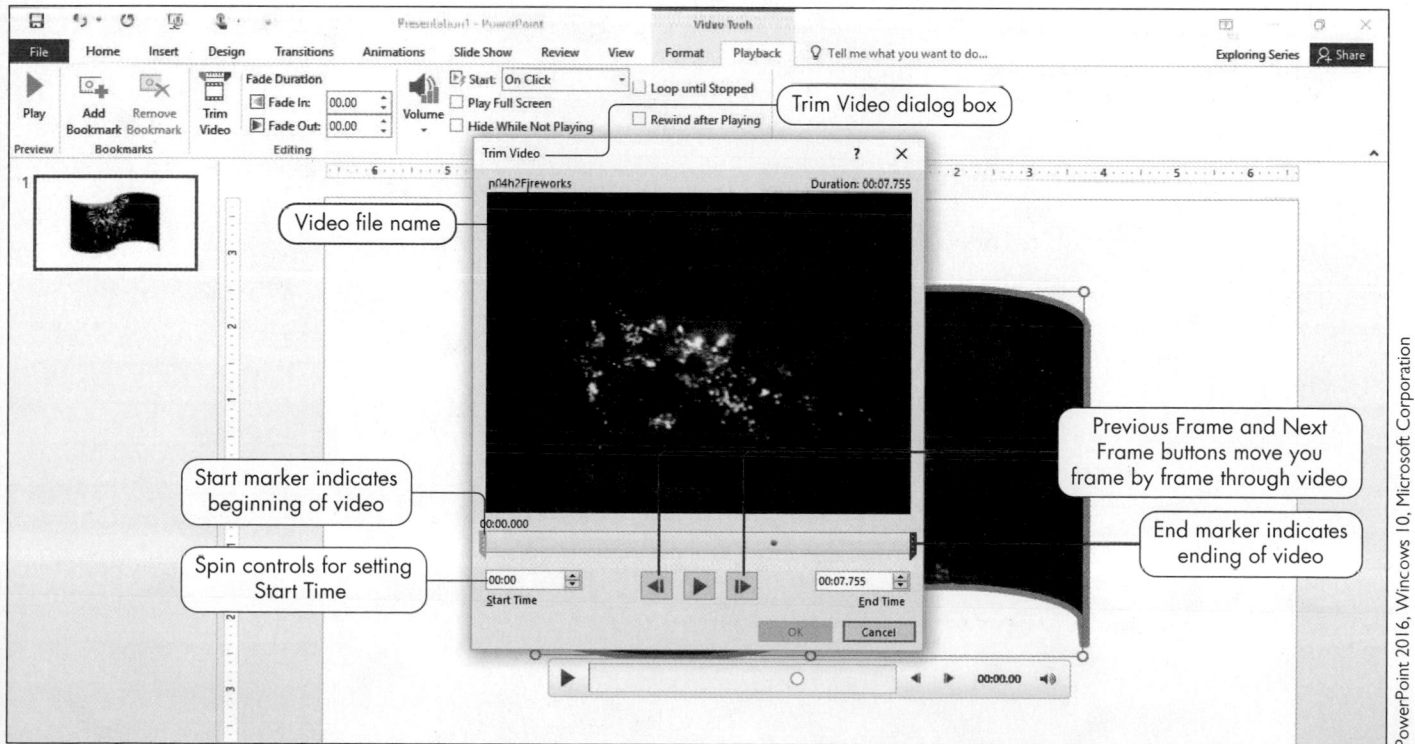

FIGURE 4.35 Trim Video Dialog Box

To set a Fade In or Fade Out duration, click the spin arrows or enter an exact time in the appropriate boxes in the Editing group on the Playback tab. If you have selected a Poster Frame for your video, the Poster Frame will fade into the first frame of your video.

The Video Options group of the Playback tab enables you to control a variety of display options. You can control the volume of the video by clicking the Volume arrow and selecting Low, Medium, or High. You can also mute any sound attached to the video.

The Video Options group also enables you to determine whether the video starts on the click of the pointer (the default setting) or automatically when the slide displays. You can choose to play the video at full screen, hide the video when it is not playing, loop continuously until you stop the playback, and rewind after playing.

Quick Concepts

5. What is a video codec, and why is it usually necessary? *p. 1145*

6. Explain the difference between embedding a video and linking a video. *p. 1145*

7. Why would you add a bookmark to a video? *p. 1152*

Hands-On Exercises

Watch the Video for this Hands-On Exercise!

MyITLab®
HOE2 Training

Skills covered: Insert a Video from a File • Format a Video • Set Video Playback Options

2 Video

In Europe, the couple recorded some fireworks displayed during a sports event. The groom gave you a copy of the fireworks video because you think it would be an excellent finale to the slide show. You insert the video, add a photo frame, and set the video playback options.

STEP 1 ›› INSERT A VIDEO FROM A FILE

You create a copy of the previous presentation and insert the fireworks video. Refer to Figure 4.36 as you complete Step 1.

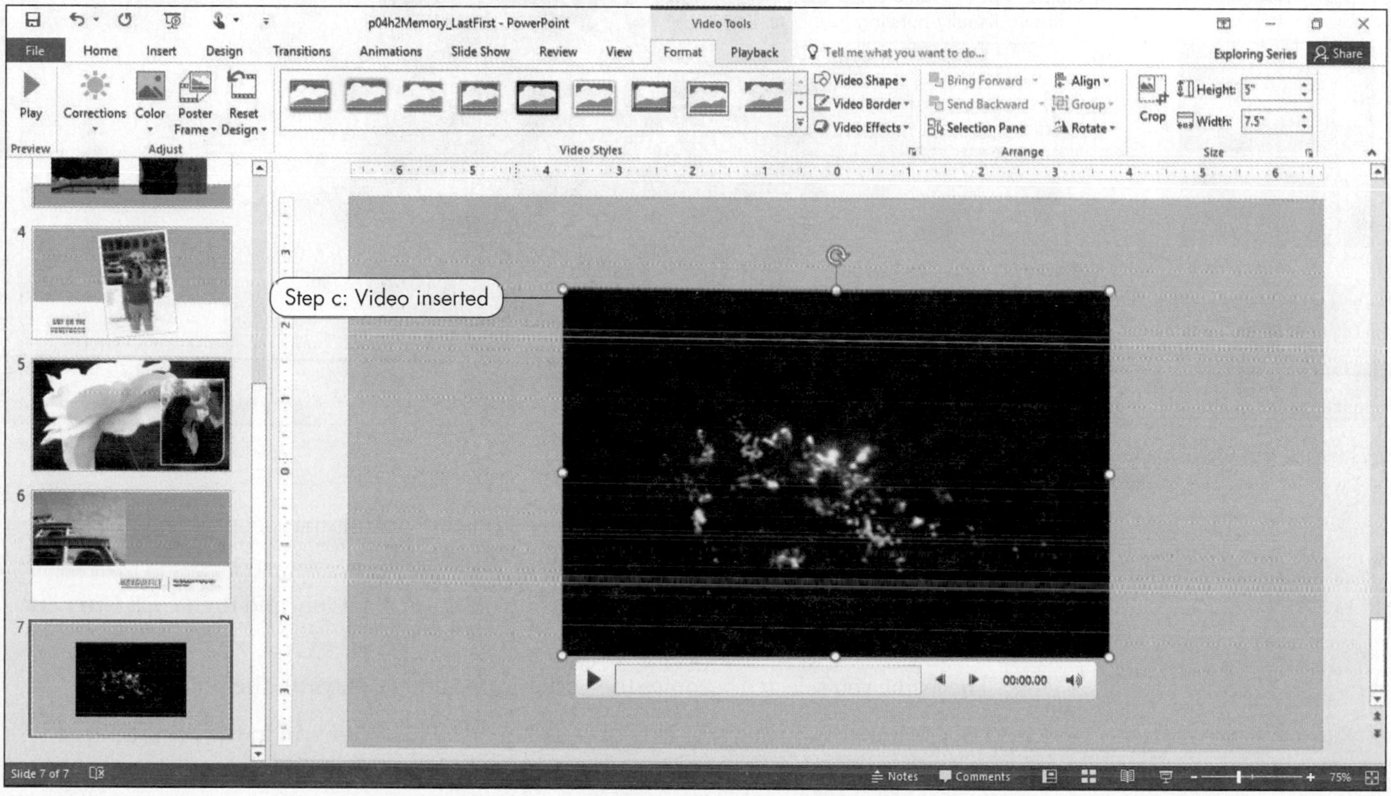

Step c: Video inserted

PowerPoint 2016, Windows 10, Microsoft Corporation

FIGURE 4.36 Inserted Windows Media Video File

a. Open *p04h1Memory_LastFirst* if you closed it at the end of Hands-On Exercise 1, and save it as **p04h2Memory_LastFirst**, changing h1 to h2.

b. Select **Slide 7**. Click the **Insert tab** and click **Video** in the Media group.

c. Click **Video on My PC**, open the *p04h1Memory_Media* folder, select *p04h2Fireworks*, and then click **Insert**.

d. Save the presentation.

The first image of the video shows the fireworks in the beginning stages. You decide to use a Poster Frame of the fireworks while they are fully bursting so the slide has an attractive image on display before the video begins. You also decide that a shape removing the edges of the video would be an improvement. Finally, you add a shadow video effect. Refer to Figure 4.37 as you complete Step 2.

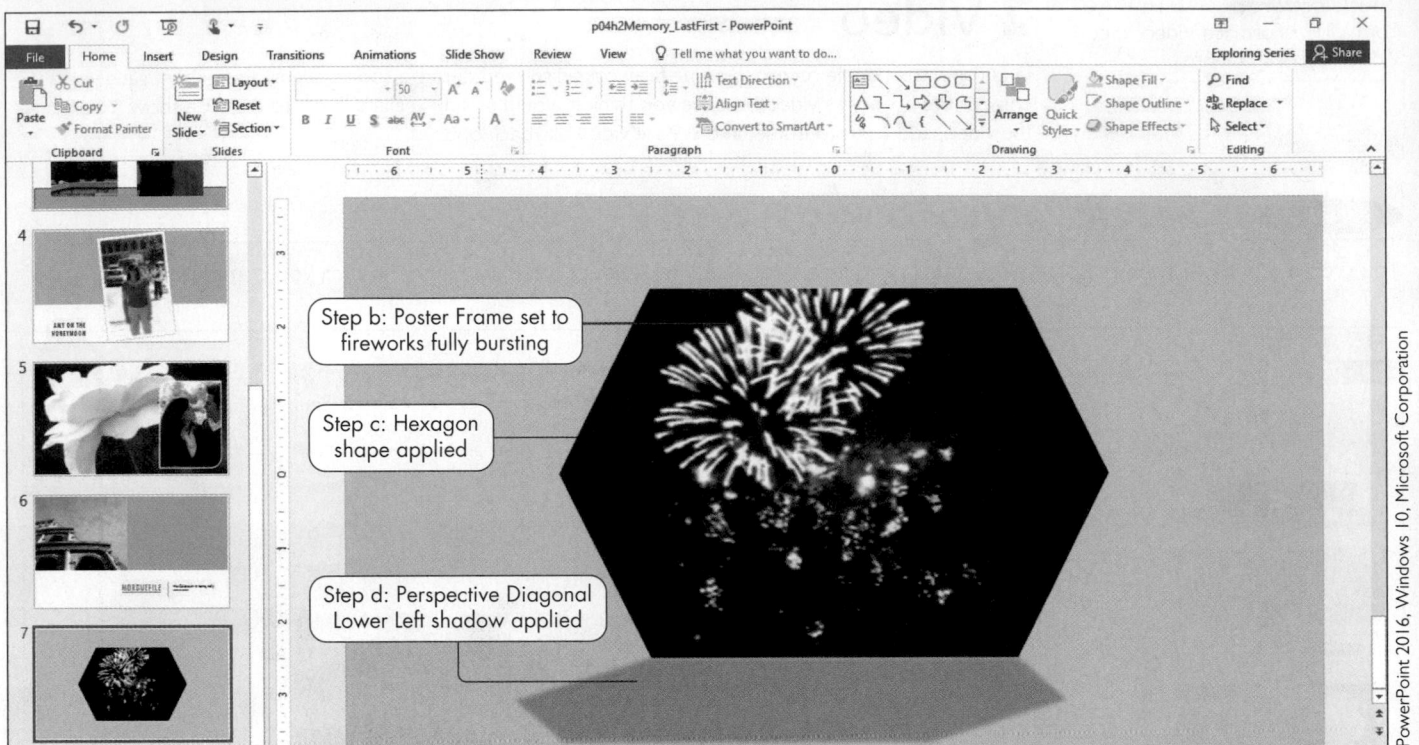

FIGURE 4.37 Formatted Video File

a. Click **Move Forward 0.25 Seconds** on the Media Controls bar located beneath the video to advance the video to the frame at 2.00 seconds.

b. Click the **Poster Frame** in the Adjust group on the Format tab, and then click **Current Frame**.

The frame you selected becomes the poster frame and displays on the slide.

c. Click **Video Shape** in the Video Styles group and click **Hexagon** in the Basic Shapes category.

The video shape changes to a hexagon.

d. Click **Video Effects**, point to **Shadow**, and then click **Perspective Diagonal Lower Left** in the Perspective category.

The shadow displays in a hexagon shape with a perspective view.

e. Click the **Slide Show tab** and click **From Current Slide** in the Start Slide Show group.

Slide 7 opens with the video displayed on the slide. The poster frame shows the fireworks at full cascade with the video shadow. Note that the Controls will display if you move the pointer to the bottom of the video.

f. Move the pointer to the bottom of the video to display the Media Controls bar and click **Play**. Press **Esc** when you are finished.

g. Save the presentation.

The last burst of fireworks does not finish its crescendo, so you decide to trim away this last portion of the video. Because you do not want the viewers of the presentation to have to click to begin the video, you change the start setting to start automatically. You decide to loop the video to play continuously until stopped because it is so short. Refer to Figure 4.38 as you complete Step 3.

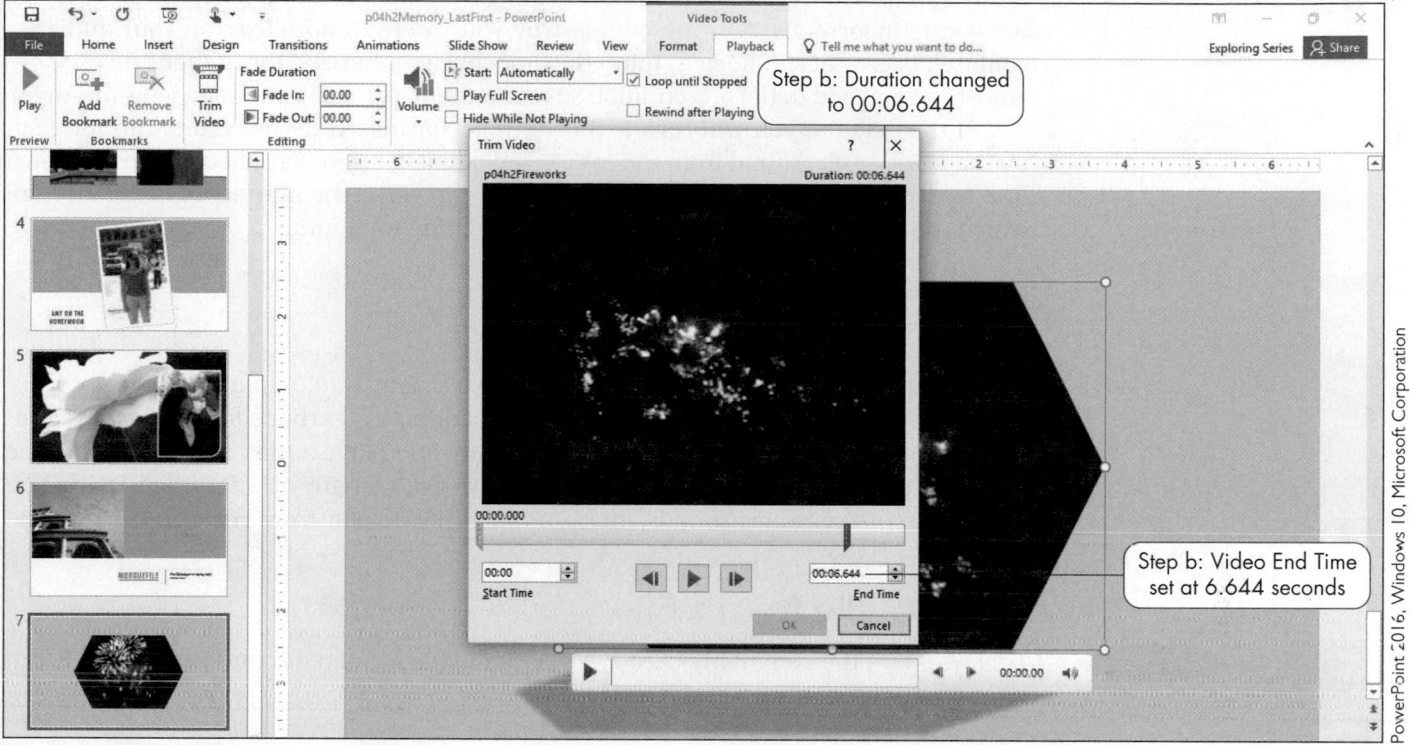

FIGURE 4.38 Video Duration Change

a. Select the video object, click the **Playback tab**, and then click **Trim Video** in the Editing group.

The Trim Video dialog box opens.

b. Drag the red **End Time marker** on the slider until *00:06.644* appears in the End Time box, or type **00:06.644** in the End Time box, and click **OK**.

The duration of the video changes from 7.755 seconds to 6.644 seconds.

c. Click the **Start arrow** in the Video Options group and select **Automatically**.

d. Select the **Loop until Stopped check box** in the Video Options group.

The fireworks video will continue to play until you advance to end the slide show.

e. Click the **Slide Show tab** and click **From Beginning** in the Start Slide Show group.

Advance through the slide show. Note that the video plays in the hexagon shape.

f. Save the presentation. Keep the presentation open if you plan to continue with the next Hands-On Exercise. If not, close the presentation and exit PowerPoint.

Audio

Audio can draw on common elements of any language or culture—screams, laughs, sobs—to add excitement, provide a pleasurable background, set the mood, or serve as a wake-up call for the audience. Harnessing the emotional impact of sound in your presentation can transform your presentation from good to extraordinary. On the other hand, use sound incorrectly, and you can destroy your presentation, leaving your audience confused or distracted. Keep in mind the guideline emphasized throughout this book—any object you add to the presentation should enhance, not detract from, your message.

In this section, you will review the methods for inserting sound and tips for each method. You insert sound from the Insert Audio dialog box or saved audio file and learn how to determine the number of times a sound clip plays, the number of slides through which the sound plays, and the method for launching the sound.

Adding Audio

Your computer needs a sound card and speakers to play audio. In a classroom or computer laboratory, you will need a headset or headphones/earbuds for playback so that you do not disturb other students. You can locate and play sounds and music from the Insert Audio dialog box, or from a hard drive, flash drive, or any other storage device. You can also record your own sounds, music, or narration to play from PowerPoint.

Insert Audio from a File

STEP 1 ▶▶ Table 4.4 lists the commonly used types of audio file formats supported by PowerPoint, listed in alphabetical order by extension.

TABLE 4.4 Commonly Used Audio File Formats Supported by PowerPoint

File Format	Extension	Description
MIDI File	.mid or .midi	**Musical Instrument Digital Interface** Standard format for interchange of musical information between musical instruments, synthesizers, and computers.
MP3 Audio File	.mp3	**MPEG Audio Layer 3** Sound file that has been compressed by using the MPEG Audio Layer 3 codec (developed by the Fraunhofer Institute).
Windows Audio File	.wav	**Wave Form** Stores sounds as waveforms. Depending on various factors, one minute of sound can occupy as little as 644 kilobytes or as much as 27 megabytes of storage.
Windows Media Audio File	.wma	**Windows Media Audio** Sound format used to distribute recorded music, usually over the Internet. Compressed using the Microsoft Windows Media Audio codec.

Pearson Education, Inc.

To insert audio from a file, complete the following steps:

1. Click the Insert tab.
2. Click Audio in the Media group.
3. Click Audio on My PC.
4. Browse, locate, and select the desired file.
5. Click Insert.

A gray speaker icon representing the file displays in the center of the slide with a Media Controls bar beneath it. The same controls are available when you select audio as when you select video.

TIP: HIDING THE SOUND ICON DURING A PRESENTATION

When audio is added to a presentation, the sound icon shows on the slide. You may not want the icon to display during the presentation, however. To hide the icon during a presentation, click the icon, click the Audio Tools Playback tab, and select Hide During Show in the Audio Options group.

Record and Insert Audio

Sometimes you may find it helpful to add recorded audio to a slide show. Although you could record music, *narration* (spoken commentary) is more common. One example of a need for recorded narration is when you want to create a self-running presentation, such as a presentation displaying in a kiosk at the mall or online. Rather than adding a narration prior to a presentation, you could create the narration during the presentation. For example, recording the discussion and decisions made during a meeting would create an archive of the meeting.

Before creating the narration, keep in mind the following:

- Your computer will need a sound card, speakers, and a microphone.
- Comments on selected slides may be recorded rather than narrating the entire presentation.
- Voice narration takes precedence over any other sounds during playback, making it possible for a voice to play over inserted audio files.
- PowerPoint records the amount of time it takes you to narrate each slide, and if you save the slide timings, you can use them to create an automatic slide show.
- You can pause and resume recording during the process.

To record narration, complete the following steps:

1. Click the Slide Show tab.
2. Click the Record Slide Show arrow in the Set Up group.

You can choose from Start the Recording from the Beginning or Start Recording from the Current Slide. The Set Up group provides other options to Play Narrations, Use Timings, or Show Media Controls.

Another example when you would want to include audio in your presentations is the creation of an association between words and an image on the screen for a presentation. This could be helpful for a group learning a new language and for helping young children build their vocabulary. These examples differ from narration because the audio is associated with a specific slide.

To record an audio clip, complete the following steps:

1. Click the Insert tab.
2. Click Audio in the Media group.
3. Click Record Audio.
4. Click Record (see Figure 4.39).
5. Record your message.
6. Click Stop.
7. Click Play to check the recording.
8. Type a name for the recording and click OK.

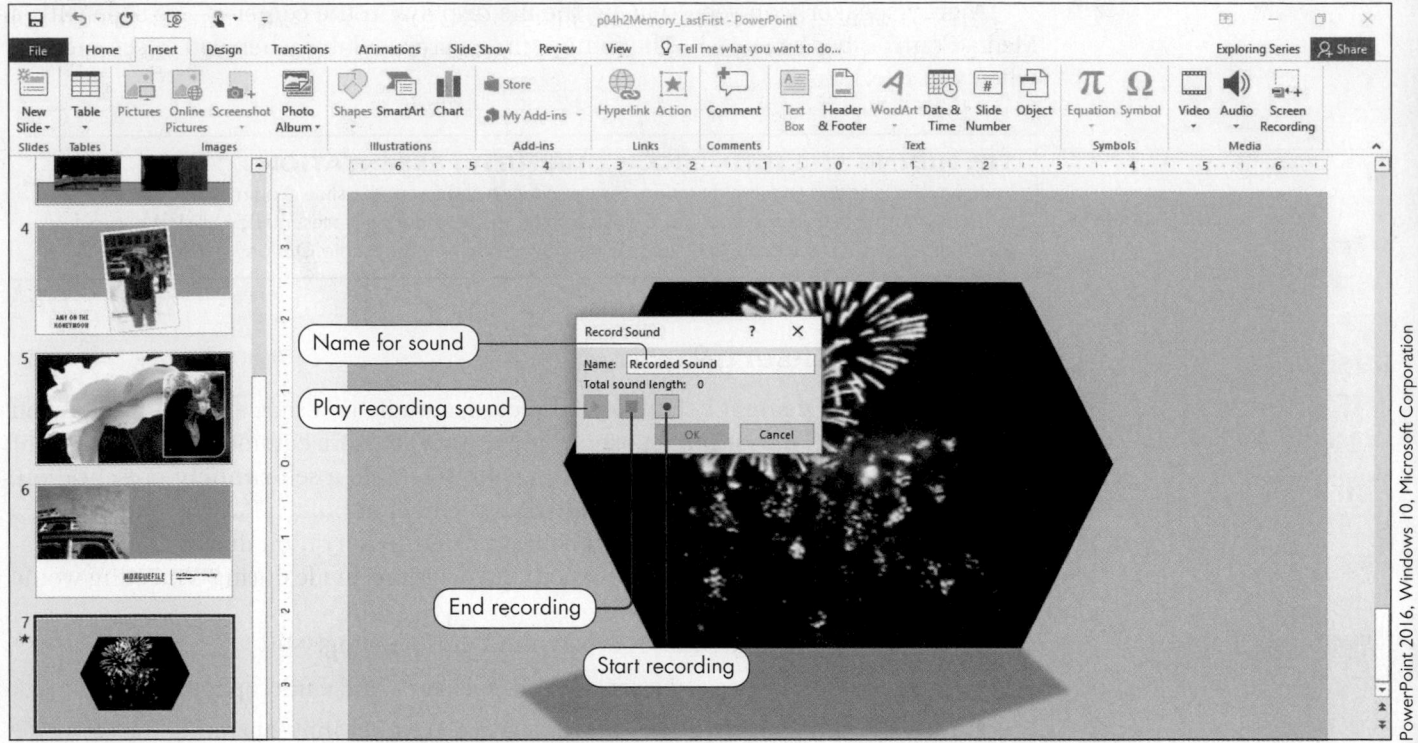

FIGURE 4.39 Record Sound Dialog Box

> **TIP: CREATE NOTES OF YOUR NARRATION**
> A transcript of your narration should be available for those in your audience who are hearing impaired. Providing the transcript lets this audience gain from your presentation, too. Put the transcript in the Notes pane and print the notes pages to provide a transcript.

Changing Audio Settings

When the icon for an inserted audio clip is selected, the Audio Tools contextual tab appears with two subtabs: Format and Playback. The Format tab provides options relating to the inserted sound icon. The Playback tab provides options for playing and pausing the audio clip, adding a bookmark, trimming, fading in and out, adjusting volume, determining starting method, hiding the audio icon while playing, looping, and rewinding after playing. All of these features work similarly to the video features, except that the Trim audio feature provides an audio timeline rather than a video preview window.

Animate an Audio Sequence

 >> Although the Playback tab gives you only two options for starting—On Click or Automatically—you have other options available through the Timing group on the Animations tab. You can choose whether the audio plays with a previous event or after a previous event; for example, you can have the audio play as a picture appears or after.

> **To set the audio to play with or after a previous event, complete the following steps:**
>
> 1. Select the sound icon.
> 2. Click the Animations tab.
> 3. Click the Start arrow in the Timing group.
> 4. Click With Previous or After Previous.

The Timing group on the Animations tab also includes a Delay spin box that you can use to delay the playback of an audio clip (see Figure 4.40).

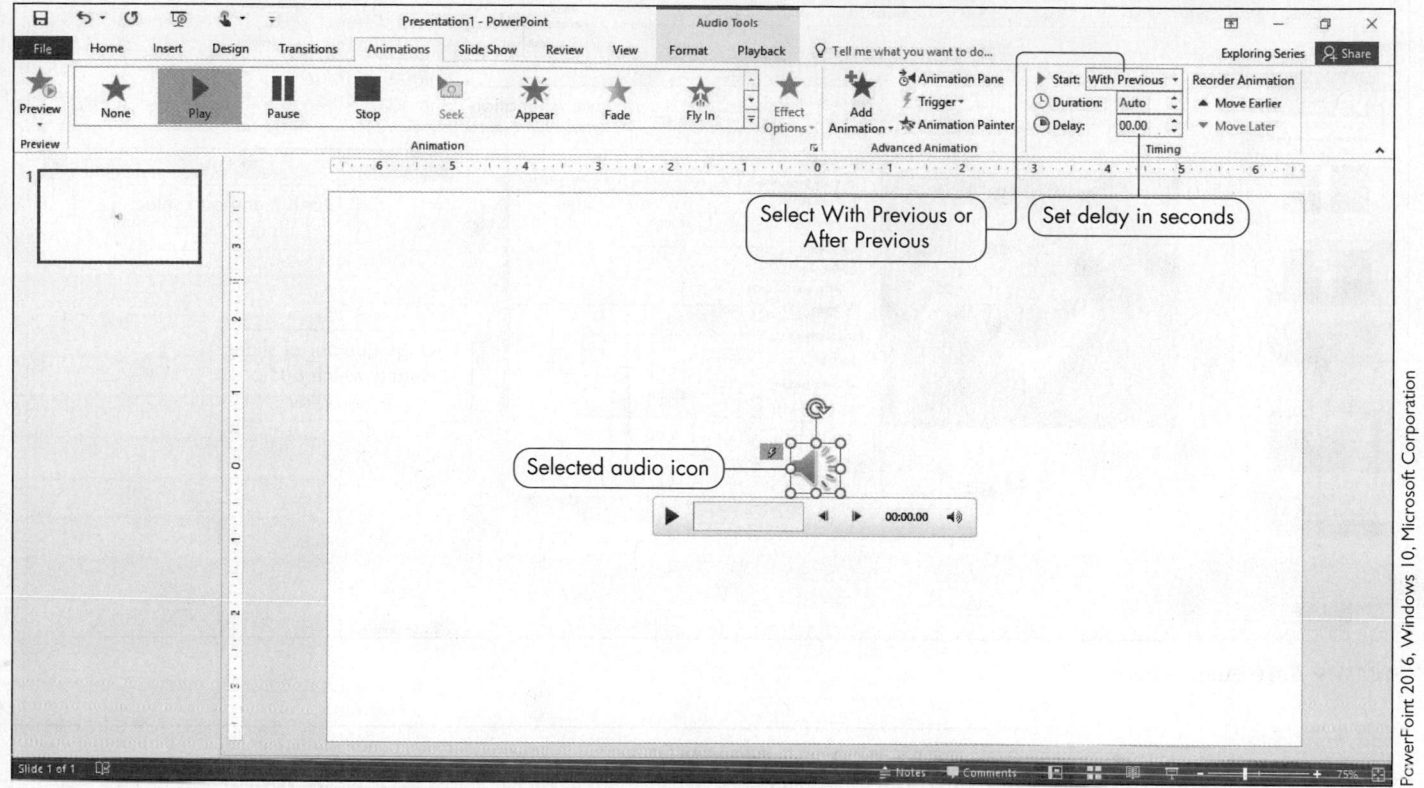

FIGURE 4.40 Audio Sequencing Options

Play a Sound over Multiple Slides

By default, audio plays until it ends or until the next mouse click. If you are playing background music, this means the music ends when you click to advance to the next slide.

To continue audio over multiple slides, complete the following steps:

1. Select the sound icon and click the Animations tab.
2. Click Animation Pane in the Advanced Animation group.
3. Select the sound you want to continue over multiple slides.
4. Click the arrow to the right of the sound.
5. Click Effect Options.
6. Click the After option in the Stop playing section of the Effect tab.
7. Enter the number of slides during which you want the sound to play (see Figure 4.41).

If the background music stops before you get to the last slide, use the Loop Until Stopped feature to keep the sound repeating. Click the Playback tab and click the Loop Until Stopped check box in the Audio Options group.

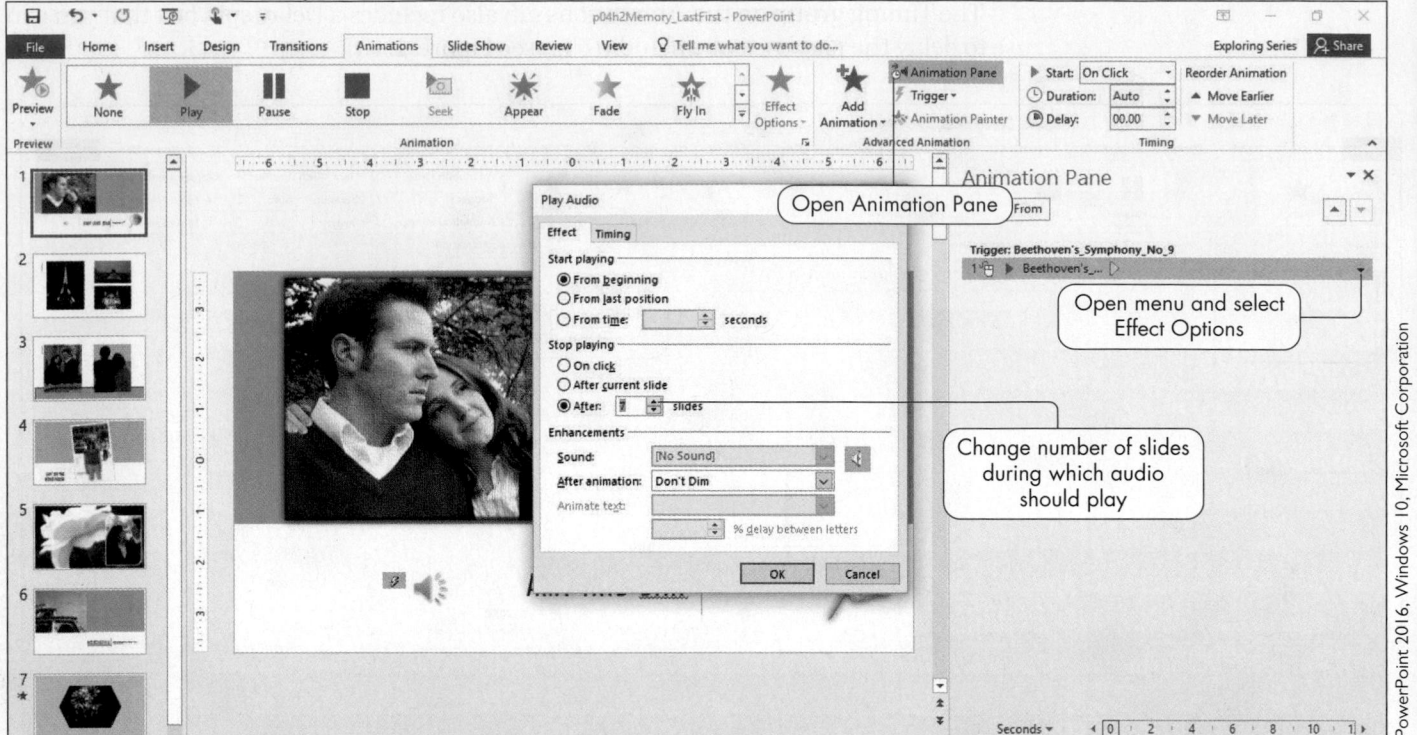

FIGURE 4.41 Audio Effects

TIP: PLAY ACROSS ALL SLIDES

You can set an audio clip to play across slides easily by clicking the Playback tab and selecting the Play Across Slides check box. This option does not let you set the number of slides over which you want the audio to play, however.

Quick Concepts

8. What are two methods for inserting audio into a presentation? *p. 1158*

9. Describe a situation where a narrated PowerPoint presentation would be advisable. *p. 1159*

10. What audio options are available from the Audio Tools Playback tab? *p. 1160*

Hands-On Exercises

Watch the Video for this Hands-On Exercise!

MyITLab®
HOE3 Training

3 Audio

You decide to create a background mood for the memories presentation by inserting a favorite audio clip of the bride—Beethoven's Symphony No. 9.

STEP 1 ›› ADD AUDIO FROM A FILE

The bride is a classically trained musician, so you decide to enhance the slide show with one of her favorite pieces. Refer to Figure 4.42 as you complete Step 1.

FIGURE 4.42 Slide 1 Audio Settings

a. Open *p04h2Memory_LastFirst* if you closed it at the end of the Hands-On Exercise 2, and save it as **p04h3Memory_LastFirst**, changing h2 to h3.

> **TROUBLESHOOTING:** To complete this exercise, it is best that you have a sound card and speakers. Even if this equipment is not available, however, you can still perform these steps to gain the knowledge.

b. Click **Slide 1**. Click the **Insert tab**, click **Audio** in the Media group, and then select **Audio on My PC**.

The Insert Audio dialog box opens.

c. Locate the *p04h1Memory_Media* folder, select *Beethoven's_Symphony_No_9*, and then click **Insert**.

The sound icon and Media Controls bar are displayed in the center of the slide.

d. Click the **Playback tab**, click the **Start arrow** in the Audio Options group, and then select **Automatically**.

e. Drag the **sound icon** to the top-right corner of the slide.

f. Click the **Hide During Show check box** in the Audio Options group.

g. Click **Play** in the Preview group.

h. Save the presentation.

STEP 2 ›› CHANGE AUDIO SETTINGS

Because PowerPoint's default setting ends a sound file when a slide advances, the Beethoven file is abruptly cut off when you advance to the next slide. You adjust the sound settings so the file plays continuously through all slides in the slide show. Refer to Figure 4.43 as you complete Step 2.

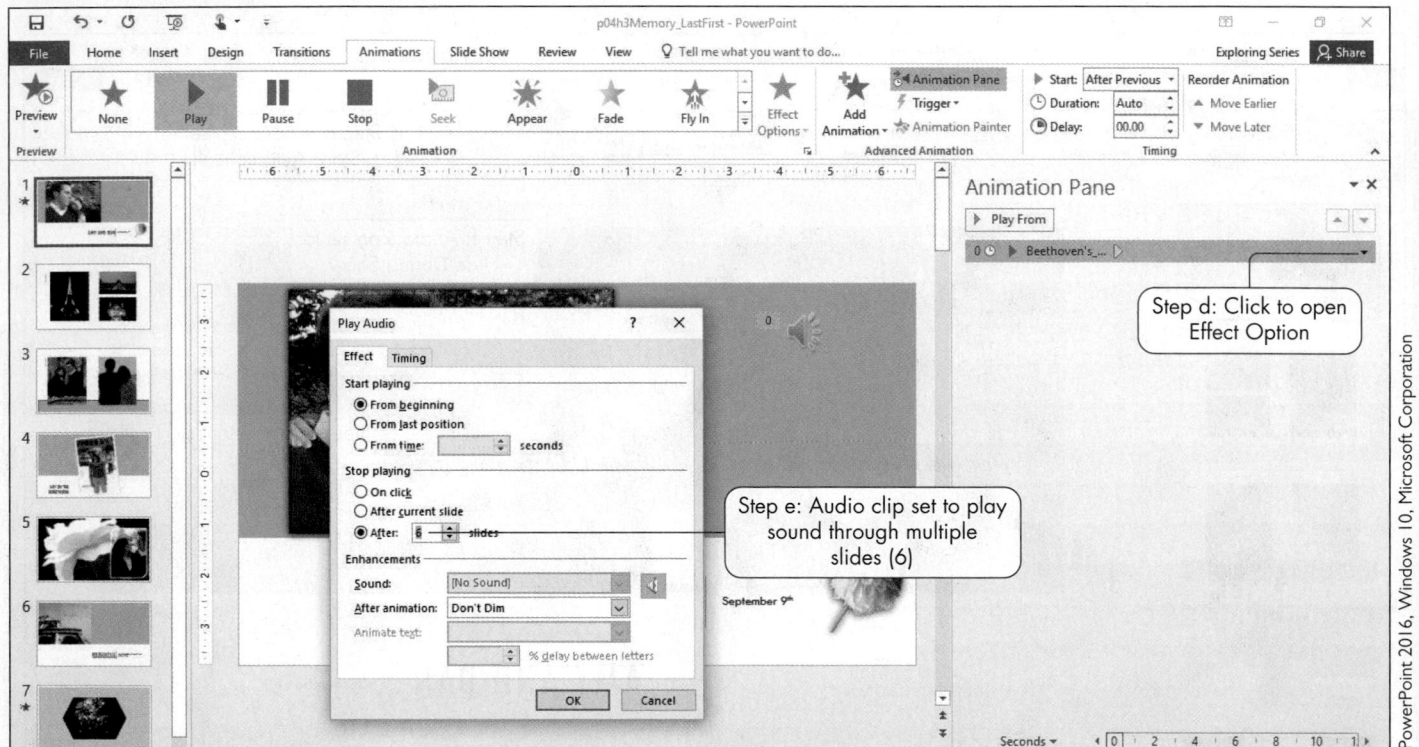

FIGURE 4.43 Play Audio Dialog Box

a. Click the **Slide Show tab** and click **From Beginning** in the Start Slide Show group. Advance through the slides and end the slide show.

Note that the sound clip on Slide 1 discontinues playing as soon as you click to advance to the next slide.

b. Select the **sound icon** on the top-right of Slide 1.

c. Click the **Animations tab** and click **Animation Pane** in the Advanced Animation group.

d. Click the **Beethoven's Symphony sound arrow** in the animation list and select **Effect Options**.

e. Click **After** in the Stop playing section, type **6** in the box, and then click **OK**. Close the Animation Pane.

f. Play the slide show and note the music plays through the sixth slide.

g. Save and close the file. You will submit this file to your instructor at the end of the last Hands-On Exercise.

Photo Albums

PowerPoint has a Photo Album feature designed to speed up the album creation process. This feature takes the images you select and arranges them on album pages based on selections you make.

In this section, you will use the Photo Album feature to create an album. Then you will use the feature settings to customize your album for picture selection, picture order, adjusting contrast and brightness, adding captions, and adjusting the album layout.

Creating a Photo Album

 A PowerPoint *Photo Album* is a presentation that contains multiple pictures that are imported and formatted through the Photo Album feature. Because each picture does not have to be formatted individually, you save a considerable amount of time. The photo album in Figure 4.44 took less than two minutes to create and assign a theme. Because a four-per-page layout was selected, images were reduced to fit the size of the placeholder. This setting drastically reduced the size of some images.

FIGURE 4.44 PowerPoint Photo Album

PowerPoint 2016, Windows 10, Microsoft Corporation

> **To create a photo album, complete the following steps:**
> 1. Click the Insert tab.
> 2. Click Photo Album in the Images group.
> 3. Click File/Disk.
> 4. Navigate to your pictures and select the pictures to include in the album.
> 5. Click Insert.
> 6. Repeat Steps 3–5 to add additional photos from other folders.
> 7. Select the Photo Album options you want.
> 8. Click Create.

If you click the Photo Album arrow, you may choose between creating a new album and editing a previously created album. When you select the pictures you want to include in the album, do not worry about the order of the pictures. You can change the order later. Once an album has been created, you can edit the album settings by clicking the Photo Album arrow in the Images group on the Insert tab and selecting Edit Photo Album.

> **TIP: CREATING FAMILY ALBUMS**
> After creating an album, add transitions and you have a beautiful presentation for a family gathering or special event. Loop the presentation to let it run continuously so that people can watch as they desire. Burn the presentation to a DVD/CD or save it on a USB to send it as a memento of the event.

Setting Photo Album Options

Using the photo album features can save you some time formatting and setting various design options. Several tools allow you to do things such as selecting picture order, rotating images, changing contrast and brightness, inserting captions for your photos, and finally selecting an album layout. Figure 4.45 shows the location of these tools. Each is discussed in detail in the following sections.

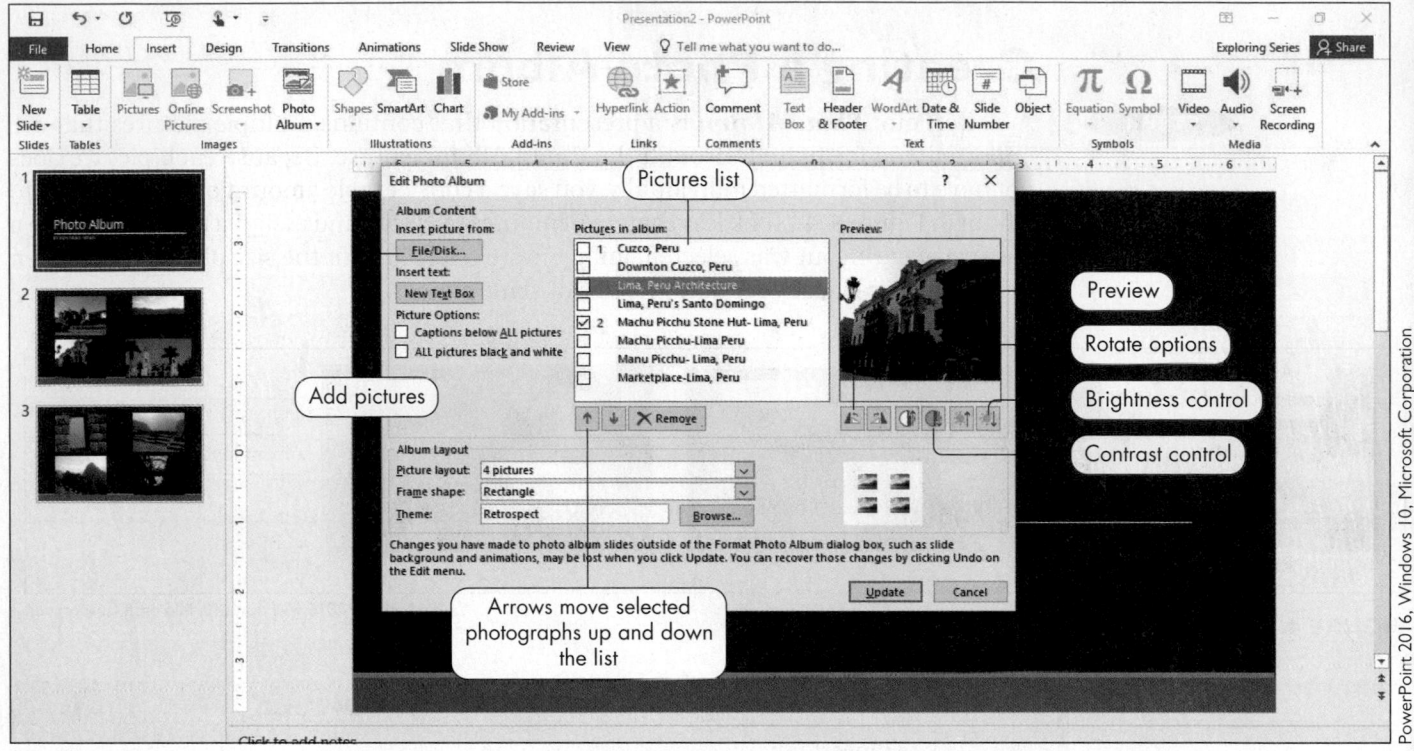

FIGURE 4.45 PowerPoint Photo Album Content Options

Select Pictures and Setting the Picture Order

After pictures are selected, they will display in a list in the Pictures in album section of the Edit Photo Album dialog box. Click the name of a picture to display a preview to help you determine the order of pictures in the album. Click the check box to the left of any picture to select or deselect it within the Pictures in album list.

> **To set the picture order, complete the following steps:**
> 1. Click the check box next to any image to select it, or use Ctrl or Shift to select more than one image.
> 2. Use the Move up arrow and the Move down arrow to reposition a selected photograph.
> 3. Delete any unwanted photographs by selecting them and clicking Remove.

If you have downloaded photographs from a digital camera, you may need to rotate some images. Select the photo you want to rotate and use the rotate left or rotate right button. Rotate buttons are included in the Album Content section under the image preview.

Change Picture Contrast and Brightness

STEP 2 ▶▶ Contrast and brightness controls enable you to fine-tune your pictures by enhancing details in over- or underexposed photos. Brightening the picture overall may make some details easier to see. Changing the contrast will increase the definition of the borders between light and dark portions of a picture.

> **To set the contrast or brightness, complete the following steps:**
> 1. Click the check box next to the photo you want to modify.
> 2. Click the contrast or brightness controls until the photo is modified as desired.

Insert Captions

The New Text Box button allows you to insert a text box with the photo caption in the album. The text placeholder is the same size as the placeholders for pictures. The *Captions below ALL pictures* option will not become available until you choose an album layout, which is discussed next. When this option is active, the file name of the picture displays as a caption below the picture in the album. You can modify the caption text once the album is created.

Set an Album Layout

STEP 3 ▶▶ The Album Layout section of the Photo Album dialog box gives many options for personalizing the album. First, you can select a Picture layout: a single picture fitted to a full slide; one, two, or four pictures on a slide; or one, two, or four pictures and a title placeholder per slide. When you select a single picture per slide, the image is maximized on the slide.

STEP 4 ▶▶ You can select from a variety of frame shapes in the Album Layout section. Options include rectangles, rounded rectangles, simple black or white frames, a compound black frame, a center shadow rectangle, or a soft edge rectangle.

STEP 5 ▶▶ You can apply a theme for the background of your album while in the Photo Album dialog box. This helps to personalize the album. If you are in a networked lab situation, it may be difficult to navigate to the location where themes are stored. If this is the case, create the album and in the main PowerPoint window, click the Design tab, click the More button in the Themes group, and then select a theme from the gallery.

Quick Concepts ✔

11. What advantages does the Photo Album feature offer? *p. 1165*

12. List two image transformation tools available in the Album Content section of the Photo Album dialog box. *p. 1167*

13. Describe one way to personalize an album. *p. 1167*

Hands-On Exercises

Watch the Video
for this Hands-On
Exercise!

MyITLab®
HOE4 Training

Skills covered: Create an
Album • Select and Order Pictures
• Adjust Contrast and Brightness
• Set Album Layout • Select Frame
Shape • Edit Album Settings • Apply
a Theme

4 Photo Albums

The bride and groom also took a trip to Peru, capturing photos of the gorgeous scenery. You prepare a photo album to help them preserve their memories. You take the time to improve the picture quality by adjusting the brightness and contrast. You also apply an album layout, apply frame shapes, and apply a theme to further personalize the album.

STEP 1 ❯❯ CREATE AN ALBUM, AND SELECT AND ORDER PICTURES

You have a folder in which you have saved the images you want to use for the vacation album. In this step, you add the images to the album and order the images by the date during which the trip was taken. Refer to Figure 4.46 as you complete Step 1.

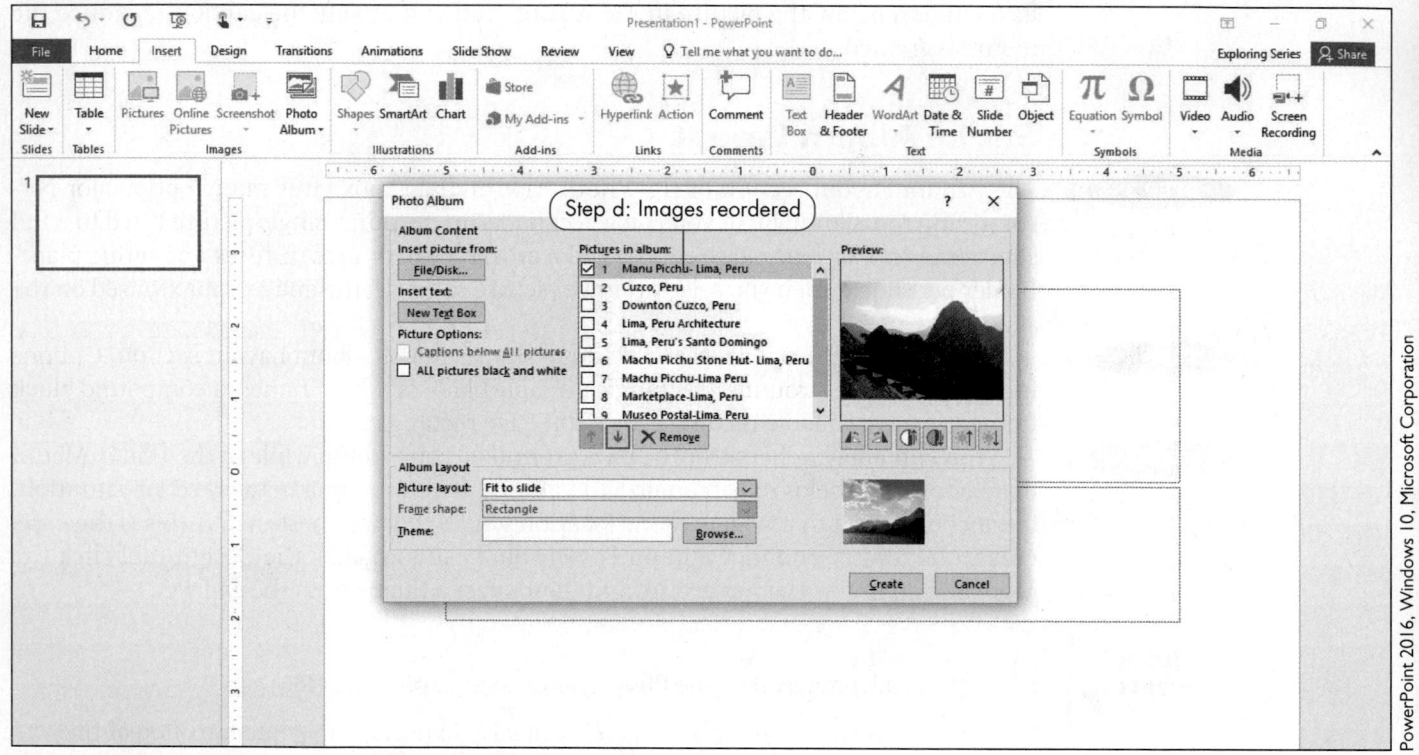

FIGURE 4.46 PowerPoint Photo Album Dialog Box

a. Open a new blank presentation. Click the **Insert tab** and click **Photo Album** in the Images group.

The Photo Album dialog box opens.

b. Click **File/Disk**. Open the *p04h4Album_Media* folder.

c. Click one of the files in the list, press **Ctrl+A** to select all pictures in the folder, and then click **Insert**.

The list of pictures displays in the *Pictures in album* box.

d. Click to select the **7 Manu Picchu - Lima, Peru** picture and click the **Move up arrow** to reposition the picture so that it is the first picture in the list. Refer to Figure 4.46 to ensure that the images are in the correct order and click **Create**.

The Photo Album feature includes buttons that enable you to adjust the contrast and brightness of images without having to access PowerPoint's Picture Tools tab. You use the Photo Album buttons to adjust the contrast in one of the Peruvian pictures. Refer to Figure 4.47 as you complete Step 2.

FIGURE 4.47 PowerPoint Photo Album Picture Tools

a. Click the **Photo Album arrow** located in the Images group on the Insert tab.

b. Select **Edit Photo Album**.

> **TROUBLESHOOTING:** If the list of photos does not display, you have selected the Photo Album button and not the Photo Album arrow.

c. Select **5 Lima, Peru's Santo Domingo** in the Pictures in album list.

d. Click **Increase Contrast** (third button from the left) four times.

e. Click **Increase Brightness** (fifth button from the left) twice.

The adjusted image can be viewed in the Preview window. If you had changed brightness only, the image would be washed out.

You change the layout of the album pages to four pictures per page. Then, to help identify the location the image was taken from during the trip, you include captions. Refer to Figure 4.48 as you complete Step 3.

FIGURE 4.48 Album Setup

a. Click the **Picture layout arrow** in the Album Layout section of the Photo Album dialog box.

b. Click one of the layouts and view the layout in the Album Layout Preview window on the right (below the larger Album Content Preview window). Then repeat to select **4 pictures**.

Clicking *4 pictures* will create an album of four pages—a title page and three pages with pictures.

c. Click the **Captions below ALL pictures check box** in the Picture Options section.

Captions below ALL pictures only becomes available after the layout is selected.

You decide to use a simple white frame to enhance the pictures taken during the trips. Refer to Figure 4.49 as you complete Step 4.

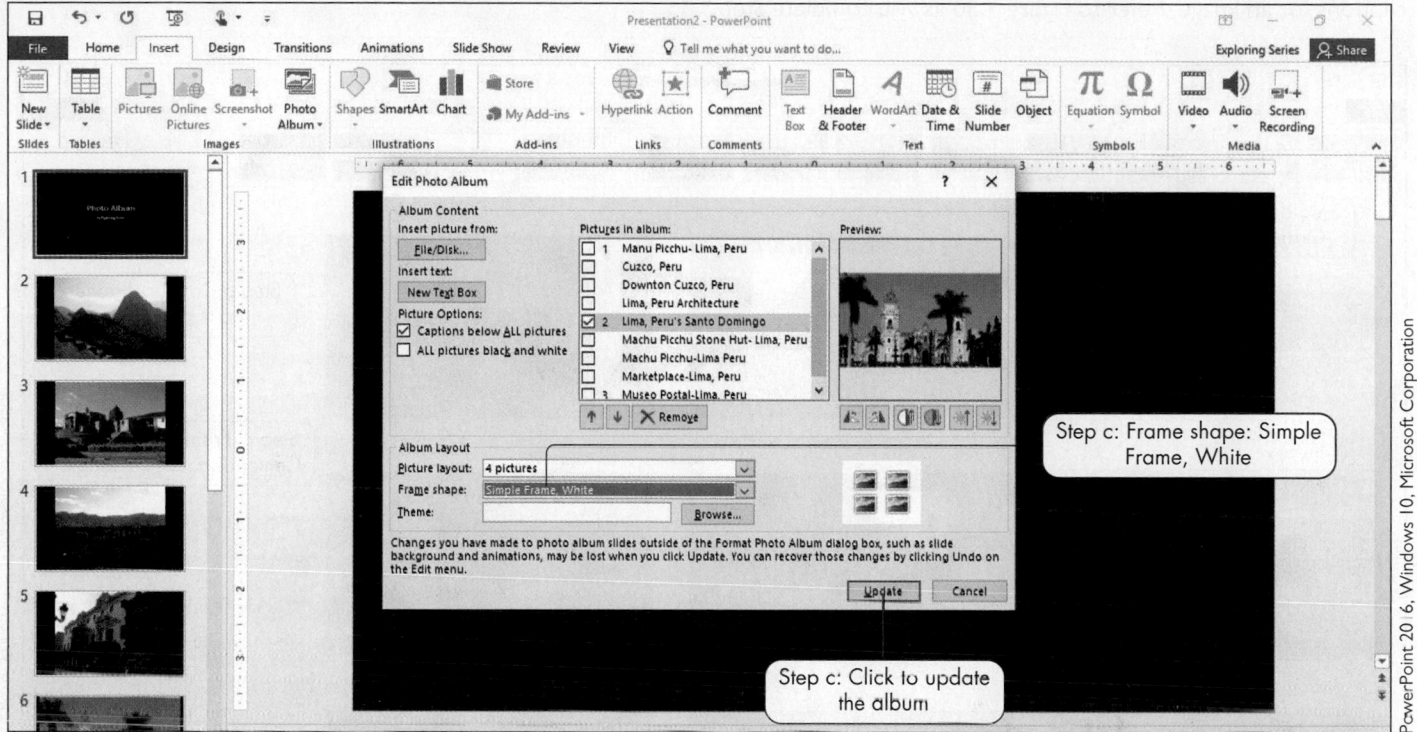

FIGURE 4.49 Frame Shape Selection

a. Click the **Frame shape arrow** in the Album Layout section.

b. Select each of the frames and view the layout in the Preview window on the right.

c. Select **Simple Frame, White** and click **Update**.

d. Create a handout header with your name and a handout footer with your instructor's name and your class. Include the current date.

e. Ensure that your name is in the subtitle placeholder on Slide 1.

f. Save the presentation as **p04h4Album_LastFirst**.

You decide to edit your album settings so that you include only one picture per page rather than four. This allows more space for the pictures to show more detail. You also change the frame shape and apply a theme to the album. Finally, you correct one of the captions for an image. Refer to Figure 4.50 as you complete Step 5.

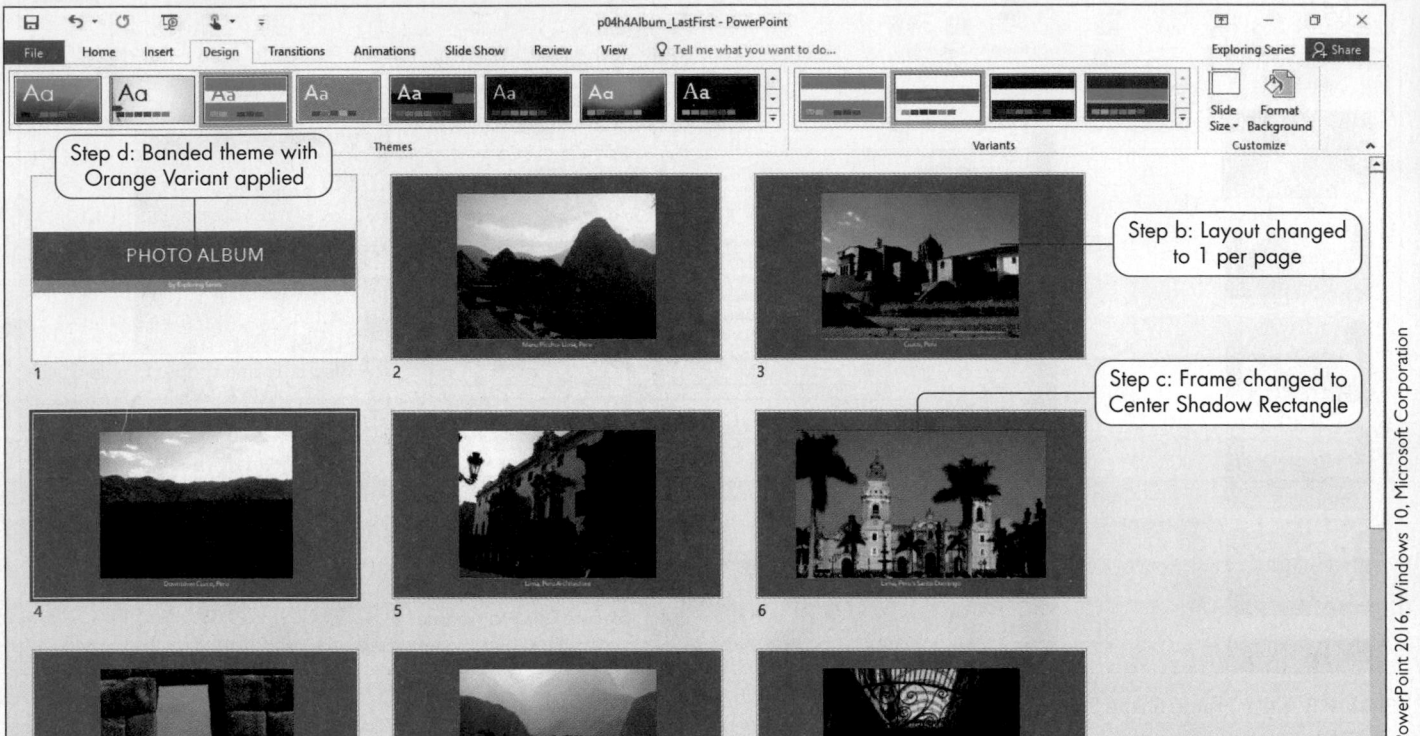

FIGURE 4.50 The Revised Photo Album

a. Click the **Insert tab**, click the **Photo Album arrow** in the Images group, and then select **Edit Photo Album**.

The Edit Photo Album dialog box opens displaying the current settings, which you may now change.

b. Click the **Picture layout arrow** and select **1 picture**.

c. Click the **Frame shape arrow** and select **Center Shadow Rectangle**. Click **Update**. Delete any blank slides from the album.

The pictures now display one per page.

d. Click the **Design tab**, apply **Banded theme** in the Themes group, and then click the **Orange Variant** in the Variants group.

e. Click **Slide 4**. Edit the text box to correct the spelling of *Downtown*.

The text box caption below the image has been corrected, since the picture file name was misspelled.

f. Save and close the file. Based on your instructor's directions, submit the following:

p04h3Memory_LastFirst

p04h4Album_LastFirst

Chapter Objectives Review

After reading this chapter, you have accomplished the following objectives:

1. Insert a picture.

- Bitmap images, represented by pixels placed on a grid, produce photorealistic portrayals.
- Pictures can be inserted using the Insert Picture option, which centers the image on the slide, or by using placeholders that center and crop the image inside the placeholder.

2. Transform a picture.

- Pictures can be transformed in a variety of ways, including removing the background, applying corrections, changing colors, applying artistic effects and picture styles, and cropping.
- Remove a picture background: The Remove Background tool enables you to remove portions of a picture you do not want to keep.
- Correct a picture: You can enhance a picture by sharpening or softening it, or you can increase or decrease a picture's brightness and contrast.
- Change picture color: Use the color tools to adjust the saturation and tone of your pictures.
- Use artistic effects: With artistic effects you can change the appearance of a picture so that it looks like it was created with a marker, as a pencil sketch, and more.
- Apply picture styles: You can surround your pictures with attractive frames, soften the edges of pictures, add shadows to the edges of pictures, apply 3-D effects to pictures, add glossy reflections, and more.
- Resize or crop a picture: You can resize pictures or crop them to remove unwanted portions of the image.
- Compress pictures: Pictures can be compressed to save file storage space.
- Create a background from a picture: Pictures can make appealing backgrounds when you adjust the transparency.

3. Use the Internet as a resource.

- The Internet can be extremely valuable when searching for information for a presentation.
- Understand copyright protection: Although students and teachers have rights under the Fair Use Act, care should be taken to honor all copyrights.
- Before inserting any information or clips into your slide show, research the copyright ownership.
- To be safe, contact the website owner and request permission to use the material.
- Any information used should be credited and include hyperlinks when possible, although attribution does not relieve you of the requirement to honor copyrights.

4. Add video.

- You can insert video located on your hard drive or storage device or YouTube, or embed coding from an online site.

5. Use video tools.

- PowerPoint includes video editing tools.

- Format a video: You can adjust the brightness and contrast, recolor, set a poster frame, select a style, and arrange and size a video.
- Set video playback options: You can also add a bookmark, trim, set a fade in and fade out effect, control the volume, determine how to start the video, set the video to play full screen, hide the video when not playing, loop until stopped, rewind after playing, and show media controls.

6. Add audio.

- Audio catches audience attention and adds excitement to a presentation.
- Take care when adding sound that it enhances your message rather than detracts from it.
- Insert audio from a file: PowerPoint supports many different audio file formats that enable you to include sounds with your presentation.
- Record and insert audio: You may find it helpful to add recorded audio to a slide show by using narration (spoken commentary) or record individual audio clips for individual slides.
- You can hide the speaker icon when not playing, loop until stopped, rewind after playing, and show media controls.

7. Change audio settings.

- Animate an audio sequence: You can add a bookmark, trim, set a fade in and fade out effect, control the volume, and determine how to start audio.
- Play a sound over multiple slides: By default, audio plays during one slide and stops when you advance to a new slide, but it can be set to play over multiple slides.

8. Create a photo album.

- When you have multiple images to be inserted, using the Photo Album feature enables you to quickly insert the images into a slide show.
- After identifying the images you want to use, you can rearrange the order of the pictures in the album.
- You also can choose among layouts for the best appearance.

9. Set Photo Album options.

- Select pictures and set the picture order: PowerPoint enables you to determine the order of pictures in the album.
- Change picture contrast and brightness: Album options for contrast and brightness enable you to make image changes without having to leave the Photo Album dialog box.
- Insert captions: File names can be turned into captions for the pictures.
- Set an album layout: A frame shape can be selected and a theme applied to complete the album appearance.

Key Terms Matching

Match the key terms with their definitions. Write the key term letter by the appropriate numbered definition.

a. Background
b. Bitmap image
c. Brightness
d. Compression
e. Contrast
f. Copyright
g. Cropping
h. Embed
i. Foreground
j. Link

k. Multimedia
l. Narration
m. Photo Album
n. Poster frame
o. Public domain
p. Recolor
q. Saturation
r. Sharpening
s. Softening
t. Tone

1. _____ An image created by bits or pixels placed on a grid to form a picture. **p. 1118**

2. _____ Spoken commentary that is added to a presentation. **p. 1159**

3. _____ Process of changing a picture by adjusting the image's colors. **p. 1127**

4. _____ A characteristic of lighting that controls the temperature of a color. **p. 1126**

5. _____ A characteristic of color that controls its intensity. **p. 1125**

6. _____ A technique that enhances the edges of the content in a picture to make the boundaries more prominent. **p. 1123**

7. _____ Legal protection afforded to a written or artistic work. **p. 1134**

8. _____ A method of storing an object from an external source within a presentation. **p. 1145**

9. _____ The difference between the darkest and lightest areas of a picture. **p. 1124**

10. _____ The process of eliminating any unwanted portions of an image. **p. 1129**

11. _____ The rights to a literary work or property owned by the public at large. **p. 1134**

12. _____ Method applied to data to reduce the amount of space required for file storage. **p. 1118**

13. _____ The portion of the picture that is kept, which is also the main subject of the picture. **p. 1121**

14. _____ Various forms of media used to entertain or inform an audience. **p. 1118**

15. _____ Presentation containing multiple pictures organized into album pages. **p. 1165**

16. _____ The portion of a picture that can be removed because it is not desired in the picture. **p. 1121**

17. _____ A connection from the presentation to another location such as a storage device or website. **p. 1145**

18. _____ The image that displays on a slide when a video is not playing. **p. 1150**

19. _____ A technique that blurs the edges of the content in a picture to make the boundaries less prominent. **p. 1123**

20. _____ A picture correction that controls the lightness or darkness of a picture. **p. 1124**

Multiple Choice

1. Which of the following are images that are created by mathematics?

   (a) Photography

   (b) Poster frame

   (c) Vector graphics

   (d) Bitmap images

2. Which of the following is *not* permitted for a student project containing copyrighted material?

   (a) The student markets the project on a personal website.

   (b) Only a portion of copyrighted material is used, and the portion was determined by the type of media used.

   (c) The student receives permission to use copyrighted material to be distributed to classmates in the project.

   (d) The educational project is produced for a specific class and then retained in a personal portfolio for display in a job interview.

3. Which of the following in the Picture Tools tab would help you manage large image files by permanently deleting any cropped areas of a selected picture and by changing the resolution of the pictures?

   (a) Brightness

   (b) Contrast

   (c) Recolor

   (d) Compress Pictures

4. Which type of compression reduces a file by permanently eliminating certain data?

   (a) Linked

   (b) Lost

   (c) Lossy

   (d) Lossless

5. Which of the following stores sound and moving pictures in Microsoft Resource Interchange File Format (RIFF)?

   (a) .gif

   (b) .wmv

   (c) .avi

   (d) .bmp

6. What is used to measure the tone of a color in pictures?

   (a) Saturation percentage

   (b) Kelvin unit

   (c) Contrast level

   (d) Aspect ratio

7. Which of the following is a *false* statement regarding recording a narration?

   (a) Narrations cannot be paused during recording.

   (b) Narrations can be created for presentations displayed in kiosks.

   (c) PowerPoint records the amount of time it takes you to narrate each slide.

   (d) Voice narration takes precedence over any other sounds during playback.

8. Anytime a right held by a copyright owner is used without permission is known as:

   (a) Duplication.

   (b) Infringement.

   (c) Public domain.

   (d) Fair Use.

9. Which of the following reduces the demand on your computer as it plays back a video?

   (a) The contrast

   (b) A bookmark

   (c) Added narration

   (d) A codec

10. Audio Playback tools enable you to do all of the following *except*:

    (a) Add a bookmark.

    (b) Fade the audio in.

    (c) Rewind after playing.

    (d) Change the saturation.

Practice Exercises

1 Geocaching Slide Show

The slide show in Figure 4.51 is designed to be used with a presentation introducing a group to the sport of geocaching. Geocaching became a new sport on May 2, 2000, when 24 satellites around the globe stopped the intentional degradation of GPS signals. On May 3, Dave Ulmer hid a bucket of trinkets in the woods outside Portland, Oregon, and the sport was born! Your geocaching presentation is designed to teach the basic geocaching skills of taking something, leaving something, and signing the logbook. Refer to Figure 4.51 as you complete this exercise.

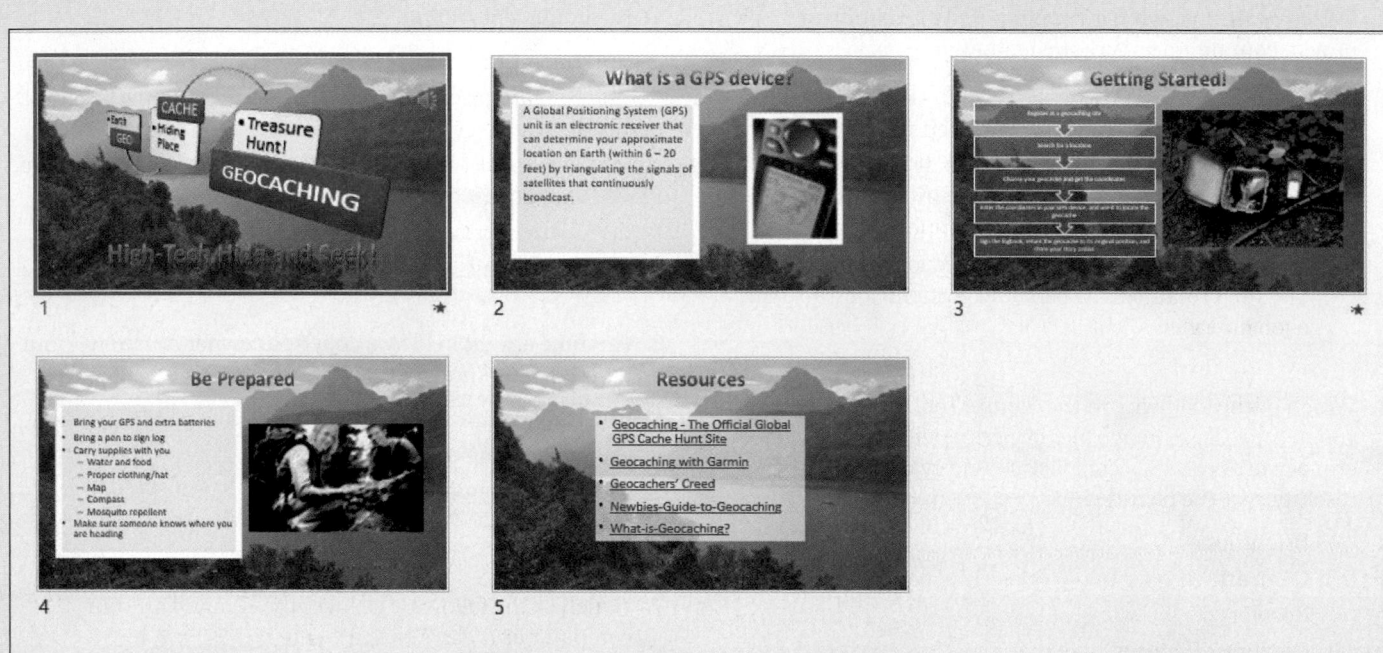

FIGURE 4.51 Geocaching Slide Show

a. Open the *p04p1Cache* slide show and save it as **p04p1Cache_LastFirst**.

b. Create a handout header with your name and a handout footer with your instructor's name and your class. Include the current date.

c. Click the **Design tab** in any slide and click **Format Background** in the Customize group to open the Format Background task pane.

d. Click **Picture or texture fill**, click **Online**, type **mountain lake** in the Bing Image Search box, and press **Enter**. Select the photo shown in the background of Figure 4.51 (or a similar photo) and click **Insert**. Drag the Transparency slider to **30%** or type **30** in the Transparency box. Click **Apply to All** and click **Close** to close the Format Background task pane.

e. Click **Slide 2**. Click the **Pictures button** in the right placeholder. In the *p04p1Cache_Media* folder, click and examine the *p04p1Gps* picture. Click **Insert** and examine the image on Slide 2 and note the resizing of the placeholder to keep the image in proportion.

f. Click **Color** in the Adjust group and change the **Color Saturation** to **0%**.

g. Click the border of the text box on the left side of the slide, click the **Home tab**, click **Format Painter** in the Clipboard group, and then click the **gps picture**.

h. Open your browser and type **morguefile.com/archive** in the address bar and press Enter to open the website. Search for a free photo using the search term *geocaching*. Right-click one of the resulting pictures and select **Save Picture**. Save the image as **p04p1geocache** to your student data folder for this chapter. Close your browser.

> **TROUBLESHOOTING:** If you are using Edge as your browser, you may get prompted to copy the image to a social media site. Click More actions in the upper-right corner of the browser and select Open with Internet Explorer to complete Step h. The Save Background As option is available in Internet Explorer. If you are using Firefox, select the image, and then right-click and save the image.

i. Click **Slide 3**. Click the **Pictures button** in the placeholder on the right. Locate the *p04p1geo-cach* image that you saved and click **Insert**. Crop or resize the picture as needed.

j. Click **Slide 4**. Click the picture of the geocachers and click the **Format tab**. Click **Artistic Effects** in the Adjust group and select **Paint Strokes**.

k. Click **Slide 1**. Complete one of the following steps:
- If you are able to record sound in your computer lab, click the **Insert tab**, click the **Audio arrow** in the Media group, and then select **Record Audio**. Click the red **Record Sound button** and read the Speaker Note at the bottom of Slide 1. When finished reading, click the blue **Stop button** and click **OK**. Proceed to Step m.
- If you are not able to record sound, proceed to Step l.

l. Click **Insert**, if you are not able to record narration in your computer lab. Click the **Audio arrow** in the Media group, and then select **Audio on My PC**. Locate *p04p1Speaker* in the *p04p1Cache_Media* folder and click **Insert**.

m. Click the **Playback tab** and select the **Hide During Show check box** in the Audio Options group. Drag the audio icon to the top right of the slide.

n. Click the **Start arrow** in the Audio Options group and select **Automatically**.

o. Click the **Animations tab** and click **Animation Pane** in the Advanced Animation group. The audio object displays on the Animation Pane. Click the **Re-Order up arrow** until the sound object moves to the top of the list.

p. Click the **Start arrow** in the Timing group and select **With Previous**. Close the Animation Pane.

q. View the slide show.

r. Save and close the file. Based on your instructor's directions, submit p04p1Cache_LastFirst.

2 Geocaching Album

FROM SCRATCH Geocachers are asked to share their geocaching experience in the geocache logbook. *Geocaching — The Official Global GPS Cache Hunt Site* includes some easy steps for logging a geocache find and even enables you to upload a photo with your log entry. Often, geocachers also put their geocaching stories, photos, and videos online in the form of slide shows using a variety of software packages. In this exercise, you create a geocache slide show quickly and easily using the PowerPoint Photo Album feature and add video and text to the slide show. Refer to Figure 4.52 as you complete this exercise.

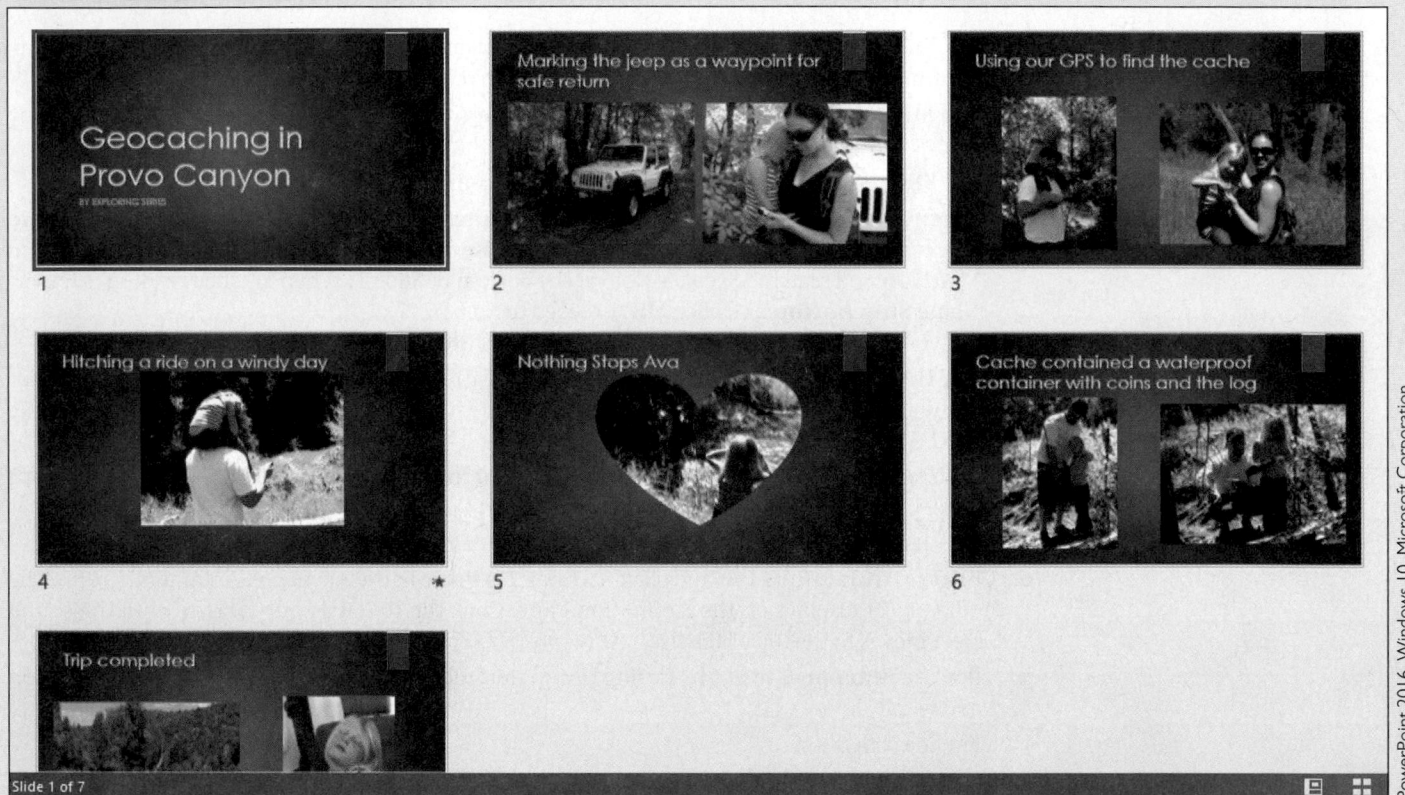

FIGURE 4.52 Geocaching Album

a. Open a new blank presentation. Click the **Insert tab** and click **Photo Album** in the Images group.

b. Click **File/Disk** in the Insert picture from section, open the *p04p2Geo_Media* folder, click one of the files, and then press **Ctrl+A** to select all pictures in the folder. Click **Insert**.

c. Click the check box for *p04p2Img3* in the Pictures in album section to select it and click **Rotate Right** (second option from the left). Click the check box again to deselect the picture after the rotation. Repeat to rotate *p04p2Img5* and *p04p2Img8* to the right.

d. Click the **Picture layout arrow** in the Album Layout section and select **2 pictures with title**.

e. Click the **Frame shape arrow** in the Album Layout section and select **Center Shadow Rectangle**.

f. Click **Create** and save the album as **p04p2Geo_LastFirst**.

g. Create a handout header with your name and a handout footer with your instructor's name and your class. Include the current date.

h. Ensure Slide 1 is displayed. Change the title to **Geocaching in Provo Canyon**. Ensure that the subtitle includes your name.

i. Click the **Design tab**, click **More** in the Themes group, and then click the **Ion theme**.

PowerPoint 2016, Windows 10, Microsoft Corporation

j. Enter the following slide titles:

Slide 2   **Marking the Jeep as a waypoint for safe return**
Slide 3   **Using our GPS to find the cache**
Slide 4   **Cache contained a waterproof container with coins
and the log**
Slide 5   **Trip completed**

k. Click **Slide 3**. Click the **Home tab**, click the **New Slide arrow**, and then select **Title Only**. Change the title of the slide to **Hitching a ride on a windy day**.

l. Click the **Insert tab**, click the **Video arrow** in the Media group, and then select **Video on My PC**. Click *p04p2Vid1* from the *p04p2Geo_Media* folder and click **Insert**.

m. Click the **Playback tab** and click **Trim Video** in the Editing group. Type **00:17.491** in the **Start Time box** and click **Play**. Type **00:22.337** in the **End Time box** and click **OK**.

n. Type **00.01** in the **Fade Out box** in the Editing group.

o. Click the **Start arrow** in the Video Options group and select **Automatically**.

p. Click the **Format tab** and select the video frame at 4.75 seconds. Click **Poster Frame** in the Adjust group and select **Current Frame**.

q. Insert a new **Title Only** slide, change the title to **Nothing Stops Ava**, and then insert *p04p2Vid2* from the *p04p2Geo_Media* folder.

r. Click the **Playback tab** and click **Move Forward 0.25 Seconds** on the Media Controls bar to advance the video to the frame at 14 seconds. Click **Add Bookmark** in the Bookmarks group.

s. Click the **Format tab**, click **Video Shape** in the Video Styles group, and then click **Heart** in the Basic Shapes gallery.

t. Select one of the images in your album, click the **Format tab**, click **Compress Pictures** in the Adjust group, and then click the **Apply only to this picture check box** to deselect it. Click **OK**.

u. View the slide show. On Slide 5, point to the Media Controls bar, click the **bookmark**, and then click **Play** to begin the video at the bookmark site.

v. Run the spelling checker. Save and close the file. Based on your instructor's directions, submit p04p2Geo_LastFirst.

Mid-Level Exercises

1 Impressionist Paintings

CREATIVE CASE

In this exercise, you will use the Internet to obtain images of paintings by some of the masters of the Impressionist style. The paintings may be viewed at the Web Museum (http://www.ibiblio.org/wm/paint) that is maintained by Nicolas Pioch for academic and educational use.

a. Open the *p04m1Painting* presentation and save it as **p04m1Painting_LastFirst**.

b. Create a handout header with your name and a handout footer with your instructor's name and your class. Include the current date. On Slide 1, change the subtitle *First Name Last Name* to your name.

c. View the slide show and click the hyperlink to *The Web Museum* on Slide 1 to open the Famous Artworks exhibition. Click the Impressionism (1860–1900) link on the Famous Artworks exhibition page.

d. Locate and click the link for each artist listed below. Review the paintings and locate the thumbnail of each title listed below. Click the thumbnail to enlarge it. Then right-click it and save the image to a new folder on your storage device named **Impressionist Paintings**. Ensure that the name of the file includes the last name of the artist and the first word of the title of the painting. Repeat this process until you have saved each of the images of the paintings shown in the table below and close the browser.

Slide #	Artist	Title
Slide 1	Alfred Sisley	*Autumn: Banks of the Seine near Bougival*
Slide 2	Claude Monet	*Impression: soleil levant (pink version)*
Slide 4	Edgar Degas	*Ballet Rehearsal*
Slide 5	Claude Monet	*Waterlilies, Green Reflection, Left Part*
Slide 6	Berthe Morisot	*The Artist's Sister at a Window*
Slide 7	Pierre-Auguste Renoir	*On the Terrace*

e. Return to your slide show. Insert the picture for Slide 1 as a background and insert each of the remaining pictures on the appropriate artist's slide. Resize and position the images as needed. Use picture styles. You do not need to compress the images, as they are already low resolution.

f. Change the font on the Slide 1 Subtitle Placeholder to **White Bold**.

DISCOVER

g. Insert an audio clip of your choice in Slide 1. As an alternative to recording your own audio clip, search for audio using the keywords **copyright free classical music** on the Internet. Save the file and then insert it in Slide 1.

h. Position the audio icon on the slide and hide it during the show. Loop the audio clip and set the song so it plays continuously across slides and does not stop with the next mouse click.

i. Check the spelling in the presentation but ignore any suggestions for the names of the artists. Save and close the file. Based on your instructor's directions, submit p04m1Painting_LastFirst.

2 Red Butte Garden

FROM SCRATCH

You visited Red Butte Garden, a part of the University of Utah, and enjoyed the natural gardens and the botanical garden. You want to create a Photo Album of the pictures you took that day.

a. Create a new Photo Album and insert all of the pictures in the *p04m2Garden_Media* folder.

b. Remove the *p04m2Img1* (Red Butte Garden & Arboretum) picture.

c. Locate *p04m2Img2*, increase the brightness six times, and then increase the contrast twice.

d. Locate *p04m2Img14*, increase the brightness twice, and then increase the contrast six times.

e. Apply a **2 pictures layout** and the **Simple Frame, White frame** shape style.

f. Create the album and save it as **p04m2Garden_LastFirst**.

g. Create a handout header with your name and a handout footer with your instructor's name and your class. Include the current date.

h. Edit the album so only one picture per page displays and click **Update**.

i. Insert *p04m2Img1* as the background for Slide 1 and remove the title and subtitle placeholders.

j. Move Slide 2 to the end of the slide show, select the image, and then apply the **Paint Brush Artistic Effect**.

k. Click **Slide 14**. Select the image and apply a **Sharpen: 50% correction**.

l. Apply the **Reveal transition** on any slide and set the advance to automatically advance after **00:02:00**. Apply to all slides.

m. Save and close the file. Based on your instructor's directions, submit p04m2Garden_LastFirst.

3 Collaborating on a Group Project

CREATIVE CASE

COLLABORATION CASE

In this exercise, you will collaborate with two to three students from your class to create a PowerPoint presentation advertising a product. Your group will determine the product you want to sell. Be inventive! Find an existing product that you can use as a prop to represent your new product (see example in second paragraph). Create a storyboard for that product and use a digital camera or cell phone to capture images for the product. You will upload your version of the pictures to a location all team members can access, such as a OneDrive account. You will then view your team's pictures, download the ones you want to use, and create a presentation based on the storyboard—each group member prepares his or her own storyboard and presentation. Only the images are shared. You will insert the images you want to use in the slides. You will edit the images as needed. You will create a final slide that lists all of the team members in your group. Finally, you will blog about your experience.

For example, after talking using chat technology, a group decides to use green mouthwash as their product. But rather than have it represent mouthwash, they are going to use it as a "brain enhancer." They create a storyboard that lists Slide 1 as a Title and Content slide using the image of the mouthwash and the name of the product—Brain ++. For the second slide, they illustrate the problem by having a picture of a person holding a test paper with the grade F plainly visible. For the third slide, they illustrate the solution by having the same person pretending to drink the Brain ++. The fourth slide demonstrates the result by showing the same person holding a test paper with the grade A plainly visible. The last slide lists all members of the group. Note: This exercise assumes you have done the Collaboration exercise for Chapter 1. If you have not completed that exercise, use OneDrive or another method for sharing your presentation with your instructor and classmates.

a. Create a group with two to three class members and exchange contact information so you will be able to message each other. For example, have each member create a Microsoft account, a Yahoo! account, a Facebook account, or use some type of text or video chat technology.

b. Determine, as a group, the product you will be advertising and its use. Discuss the story line for your product with the group, then each member should create a storyboard.

c. Each member should use a digital camera or cell phone to take pictures of the product.

d. Upload your images to OneDrive, which will enable all group members to access the pictures.

e. View all of the images your group uploaded, determine which ones you want to use in your presentation, and then download those images.

f. Create a PowerPoint presentation and insert the product images into slides following the storyboard you created. Edit the slides and images as needed. Enhance slides as desired. Save the presentation as **p04m3Product_LastFirst**.

g. Create a blog posting about this experience, or write an essay using Microsoft Word, answering the following questions: Was collaborating with others through a chat tool a good experience or was it difficult? What did you like about the experience? How could it have been improved? How easily did your group reach agreement on your product?

h. Save and close the file. Based on your instructor's instructions, submit p04m3Product_LastFirst.

Beyond the Classroom

Zeroscaping Versus Xeriscaping

GENERAL CASE

While on a trip through the Southwest, you took pictures of zeroscaping examples. You plan to use them in an existing slide show on waterwise landscaping. You also want to know more about xeriscaping, however, so you research xeriscaping online.

Open *p04b1Landscape* and save it as **p04b1Landscape_LastFirst**. Add a handout header with your name and a handout footer with your instructor's name and your class. Include the current date. Research zeroscaping and xeriscaping online and include the websites on a Resources slide at the end of the slide show. Please remember that giving credit to your source does not mean you are released from copyright requirements. Create several speaker notes with information you find during your research. Use the zeroscaping images located in the *p04b1Landscape_Media* folder where appropriate, and search the Internet to obtain images for the xeriscaping portion of the slide show. Use a xeriscaping picture for the background of the Title slide. You may change the template and add animations as desired. Add an audio clip and set it to play across all slides. Insert a related video on its own slide. Save and close the file. Based on your instructor's directions, submit p04b1Landscape_LastFirst.

Cascade Springs Ecosystem

DISASTER RECOVERY

You are working with another fifth-grade teacher to create slide shows for your science students. The other teacher visited Cascade Springs, took pictures, and created a PowerPoint Photo Album of the pictures. Open *p04b2Springs* and save the new presentation as **p04b2Springs_LastFirst**. Review the album and read the speaker notes created from National Forest Service signs available to hikers to help them understand the fragile ecosystem. Your role is to review the presentation created by the album and determine which slides and speaker notes to keep. When necessary, rotate images. You may also change the template or slides as desired. If it is possible to record sound clips in your classroom lab, read and record shortened versions of at least three speaker notes and add the audio files to the slides. If you are unable to record the narration, insert the audio files in the *p04b2Springs_Media* folder in appropriate locations. Set the audio files to play when the sound icon is clicked. This allows a teacher to determine if he or she wants to use recordings during the presentation or lecture himself or herself. Finalize the presentation by proofreading, applying transitions and animations, and testing sound icons to ensure that they work properly. Compress all images to Web Target output. Finally, create a handout header with your name and a handout footer with your instructor's name and your class. Include the current date. Save and close the file. Based on your instructor's directions, submit p04b2Springs_LastFirst.

Capstone Exercise

The Science Club at your school wants to raise awareness of the fragility of the world's oceans. You volunteer to create a slide show that can be used at promotional events put on by the club. You use a modified version of Microsoft's Classic Photo Album template. The album has been modified to use the Blue II Color theme. In this activity, you will create the content, insert the photos, modify the photos, add sound, and insert a video clip of the ocean floor. All media for this activity are located in the p04c1Ocean_Media folder.

Insert Pictures

Using template layouts and picture placeholders, you insert photos of the ocean. You modify template placeholders for better fit.

a. Open the file named *p04c1Ocean* and save it as **p04c1Ocean_LastFirst**.

b. Create a handout header with your name and a handout footer with your instructor's name and your class. Include the current date.

c. Ensure that Slide 1 is selected. Click the existing picture and delete it. Locate the *p04c1Ocean_Media* folder and insert *p04c1Ocean1* into the picture placeholder to replace the deleted image.

d. Change the Title placeholder to **Our Fragile Oceans**. Change the subtitle to your first and last name.

e. Click **Slide 2** and replace the existing image by inserting *p04c1Ocean2*. Replace the existing text with **Whales are amazing creatures**.

f. Insert a new **Slide 3** with the **Panorama** layout. Insert *p04c1Ocean3* in the picture placeholder and replace the caption text with **Colorful fish swim together**. Delete Slide 4.

g. Delete **Slide 4** with three picture placeholders.

h. Click the new **Slide 4**. Change the layout to **2-Up Mixed with Captions**.

i. Replace the text in the caption placeholder with **Fish live in coral reefs**. Insert *p04c1Ocean4* in the left picture placeholder and insert *p04c1Ocean5* replacing the existing image that is in the right placeholder.

j. Insert a new **Slide 5** with the Portrait with Caption layout. Replace the text in the caption placeholder with **A close-up of brightly colored coral**. Insert *p04c1Ocean6*. Delete **Slide 6** and **Slide 7**. Then insert *p04c1Ocean7* as a full page picture on the new Slide 6.

k. View and save the presentation.

Apply and Modify a Picture Style, Change Images

After viewing the presentation, you decide to make some modifications. The picture on Slide 1 would stand out better if it had the background removed. The picture on Slide 6 can be improved with an artistic effect. Some of the captions are too small.

a. Click **Slide 1**. Select the picture and remove the background. Resize the picture so image has a height and width of 3.66".

b. Click **Slide 6**. Apply the Artistic Effect **Plastic Wrap** to the picture (fourth row, last column).

c. Click **Slide 4**. Change the font to **UPPERCASE** and ensure the font size is set to **18**. Apply these same effects to the Slides 2 and 5. **Right-align** the text on Slides 2 and 5.

d. Save the presentation.

Adjust and Compress Images

The picture on Slide 2 needs the brightness, contrast, and color tones adjusted. You use the Picture Tools tab to adjust the pictures, and you apply compression to all of the photographs.

a. Click **Slide 2**, select the picture, and then increase the image sharpness **+25%**.

b. Set the saturation to **200%**, and then set the color tone to **4700 K**.

c. Compress all images using document resolution.

d. Save the presentation.

Insert a Video

You insert a video clip of the ocean and modify the settings. Finally, you add a clip of a whale song that plays on one slide.

a. Click **Slide 5**. Insert a New Slide using the **Blank** layout.

b. Search for and insert a YouTube video showing the ocean.

c. Set the video to play automatically.

d. Change the Video Options to **Hide While Not Playing** and to **Rewind after Playing**.

e. Check spelling in the presentation. Save the presentation.

Create a Photo Album

Your club wants to have something to use as handouts at the upcoming presentations. They ask you for a printed copy of all of the images. You prepare a photo album and print it.

a. Create a New Photo Album using the images in the *p04c1Ocean_Media* folder.

b. Rearrange the pictures so they appear in the following order: Ocean1, Ocean3, Ocean2, and then the remaining pictures in numerical order.

c. Edit the album using two pictures per slide and a **Simple Frame, White frame shape**.

d. Update the album and then save it as **p04c1OceanPix_LastFirst**.

e. Create a handout header with your name and a handout footer with your instructor's name and your class. Include the current date.

f. Change the title on the Title Slide to **Our Fragile Oceans**. Ensure that your name is in the subtitle.

g. Save and close the file. Based on your instructor's directions, submit the following:

p04c1Ocean_LastFirst
p04c1OceanPix_LastFirst

Word Application Capstone Exercise

You plan to participate in a research day at your university, in which students present research projects. You have completed research and composed a draft of a research paper related to the preparedness of young adults for war. Before you are accepted for competition, you must submit a draft copy of the research paper along with a brief resume. Before submitting the draft, you must format the paper, include citations, prepare a cover page, edit an abstract, and prepare a resume.

Use Mail Merge to Create Personalized Letters

You prepare a cover letter to accompany the research packet that you must submit to a faculty committee. You use mail merge to create a personalized letter to each committee member, introducing your project

a. Open *wApp_Cap1_Letter*. Save the document as **wApp_Cap1_Letter_LastFirst**.

b. Remove the comma and space after the words *United States* in the first paragraph and insert an em dash between the words *United States* and *a project*.

c. Select the inside address (3 lines) as well as the date. Set a 3" left tab stop, deselect the selected text, and tab each of the previously selected lines to begin at the 3" tab stop. Set a 3" tab stop for *Sincerely*, and *Student Name*, and ensure that both lines begin at the tab stop.

d. Change *Student Name* at the end of the letter and *Student Name* at the top of the letter to your first and last names. Check spelling and correct any errors. Ignore any suggestion that your name is misspelled.

e. Use the Step-by-Step Mail Merge wizard and this document to send the same letter to each committee member.

- The list of committee members is on Sheet 1 of the Excel file *wApp_Cap1_Committee*.
- Sort recipients alphabetically by last name.
- Insert Merge fields for each committee member's title and last name after the word *Dear* in the salutation.
- Merge all documents in a new document, then save the merged letters as **wApp_Cap1_MergedLetter_LastFirst** and close the document.
- Save **wApp_Cap1_Letter_LastFirst** and close the document.

Create an Abstract and a Cover Page

You prepare a one-page abstract summarizing your research. You also prepare a cover page to identify the research.

a. Open *wApp_Cap1_Research* and save it as **wApp_Cap1_Research_LastFirst**. Complete the following tasks:

1. Press **Enter** at the top of the document. At the top of the document, include a centered heading, **Abstract**. Ensure that the heading line does not include a first line indent. The heading should be formatted in **Times New Roman 12 pt** font size.

2. Check spelling and correct any errors.

3. Select the second, third, fourth, and fifth body paragraphs, beginning with *Are the young men and women*, and ending with *Do young adults possess the mental assuredness*. Number the selected paragraphs with the default numbering style, and begin each numbered paragraph at the left margin.

b. Ensure that nonprinting characters show. Insert a page break at the top of the document. At the top of the new page (page 1), change the font to **26 pt**. Set line spacing to **3.0**. Text should be centered. Press **Enter** and type the following lines, replacing *Student Name* with your first and last names.

Student Name

Phi Kappa Phi Research Competition

18 July 2017

The Preparedness of Young Adults for War

Create an MLA Research Paper

You continue to work on the research paper by inserting text to follow the abstract. After ensuring that the paper adheres to MLA guidelines, you check spelling and edit text. Finally, you add a header.

a. Insert a page break at the end of page 2. With the insertion point at the top of page 3, insert text from *wApp_Cap1_Paper*.

b. Ensure that the paper adheres to MLA guidelines in the following ways:

1. Double-space pages 3–5 of the document and change the font to Times New Roman 12 pt.

2. Add a first line indent of .5" to each paragraph on pages 3–5. Remove all paragraph spacing from those pages.

3. Adjust margins of the entire document to 1" on all sides.

c. Ensure that nonprinting characters show. Check spelling and correct all identified errors, with the exception of "more timely." Ignore that error.

d. Remove the second sentence in the last paragraph on page 2, beginning with *The commitment of time*, so that the abstract requires only one page.

e. Include a title at the top of page 3—**The Preparedness of Young Adults for War**. (Do not type the period.) The title should be centered, in Times New Roman 12 pt. It should not include a first line indent.

f. Press **Enter** at the top of page 3. Left-align the new blank paragraph above the title. Beginning at the new blank paragraph, type the following, ensuring that all lines are double-spaced. Replace *Student Name* with your first and last names.

Student Name

Phi Kappa Phi Research Competition

18 July 2017

g. Insert a header (select **Edit Header**) with your last name, followed by a page number. The page number should be **Current Position** and **Plain Number**. Right-align the header and ensure that it is in **Times New Roman 12 pt** font. The header should not display on the first page.

Add New Sources and Insert Citations

At various points in the paper, you need to cite research sources so that readers are aware of where you located information. You insert citations according to MLA style requirements, editing them as necessary.

a. Ensure that the writing style selected is MLA. In the last paragraph on page 5, insert a citation after the sentence containing the quote *"a long-term reaction to war zone exposure"*. The citation should be placed between the ending quotation mark and the ending period. The source is an article in a periodical.

Author: Matthew J. Friedman

Title: Post-Traumatic Stress Disorder in the Military Veteran

Periodical: Psychiatric Clinics of North America

Year: 2016
Month: June
Day: 25
Pages: 265-277
Volume: 17
Issue: 2

b. Insert a citation after the word **violence**, in the second paragraph on page 6. The sentence ends in *by chronic exposure to violence*. The citation should be placed before the period ending the sentence. The source is from a journal article.

Author: **Chris R. Brewin**

Title: **Meta-Analysis of Risk Factors for Posttraumatic Stress Disorder**

Journal: **Journal of Consulting and Clinical Psychology**

Year: **2017**

Pages: **748-766**

c. Edit the Brewin citation in the second paragraph on page 6 to include the page number **750** along with the author name.

d. Insert a citation, using the Brewin source, at the end of the next sentence on page 6, ending in *"... and childhood behavior problems"*. The citation should be placed between the ending quotation mark and the ending period. After inserting the citation, edit the citation to include page number **750**, but suppress the author name, year, and title.

Add a Table

Selected text in the paper is converted into a table so you are better able to organize and summarize data. Working with the table, you insert rows, add formulas, adjust column widths, and align the table. To identify the table, you add a caption.

a. Switch the order of the last paragraph on page 6 and the first paragraph on page 7 (one begins with *Opposing claims* and the other with *In addition.*).

b. Select the tabbed data on page 8, beginning with **Age** and ending with a blank paragraph mark at the end of the tabbed data. Convert the selected text to a table, accepting the default settings.

c. Adjust the width of all columns in the table to 1.5" and center text in row 1 (select **Align Center** in the Alignment group). Change the text in the third column of the first row to **Percentage of Total**. Using alignment commands in the Alignment group, apply **Align Center Right** alignment to the numbers in the middle column and **Align Center** alignment to text in the first column. Insert a hard return after the table.

d. Add a row at the end of the table, with the word **Total** in the first cell on the new row and a function in the second cell in the last row to total values in column 2. The format should be the same as the values above. Develop a formula in the last cell on the second row to divide the value in the preceding cell by the total in the last cell of the second column. Multiply the result by 100 to obtain a percentage. The format should be 0.00%. Enter a similar formula and format for Percentage of Total cells in the next two rows. Apply **Align Center Right** alignment to all percentages in the last column.

e. Insert a row above the first row. Merge cells in the first row and include the centered text, **U.S. Armed Forces Enlistees (2014-2017)**. (Do not type the period.) Apply the table style **Grid Table 4, Accent 5**. Align the table in the center of the page horizontally.

f. Include a caption below the table with the text, **Figure 1: Enlistees by Age**. (Do not type the period.) Modify the Caption style to be centered, not italicized, and with a font color of **Blue, Accent 5**.

Insert a Works Cited Page, Update a Source, Insert and Modify a Footnote, and Add Document Properties

A research paper includes a bibliography page, which is formatted as a Works Cited page in MLA style. You insert and modify the bibliography, and insert a footnote. The footnote should be formatted as text in the research paper, so you modify the footnote style accordingly. To identify the author and purpose of the document, you add document properties.

a. Insert a page break at the end of the document. Insert a bibliography at the top of the new page, with the centered heading **Works Cited**. Click Manage Sources on the References tab and update the Brewin source in the current document to include **pages 748–768**. The source should be updated in both the master list and the current document. Update the bibliography.

b. All text on the Works Cited page should be **Times New Roman 12 pt** and should be double-spaced. All sources should be formatted with a hanging indent. Ensure that there is no paragraph spacing on the Works Cited page.

c. Insert a footnote after the last sentence in the second-to-last paragraph on page 8 (ending with *imbue*). The footnote should be placed after the ending period. The footnote should be referenced with a superscript 1, with the text **The G.I. Bill, signed into law in 1944, provides tuition assistance for veterans.** (Include the period.)

d. Modify the footnote style to use **Times New Roman 12 pt** font.

e. Use Document Properties to include your name as the Author. Comments should include **Research for English 112, Spring Semester 2017**. (Do not type the period.)

Insert and Format a Resume Table

The research committee requires you to include a personal resume, providing a brief summary of your background. You insert a table that contains resume information, and then format the table to make it more attractive.

a. Insert a page break at the end of the document. Remove the First Line indent from the first line on the new page. At the top of the new page, insert text from *wApp_Cap1_Resume*.

b. Format table text as follows:
- Bold *Bachelor of Business Administration* in row 1.
- Remove the bullet from *Carnes State University* in row 3 and ensure that the text from which you removed the bullet is left-aligned under *Computer Information Systems Department*.
- Apply line spacing of 1.15 to all text in the second column of row 5.
- Ensure that all table text is **Times New Roman 11 pt**.

c. Delete the last three rows in the resume table.

d. Insert a row above the first row and merge all cells in the row. Text in row 1 should be **Times New Roman**. Center text both horizontally and vertically in the new row. Type the following, replacing *Student Name* with your first and last names. Your name should be bold, but all other text should not be bold. Leave a space after the parenthesis ending the area code.

Student Name
myname@csu.edu
1234 Main Street
Addison, MT 87964
(736) 555-1234

e. Right-click the email address and remove the hyperlink. Your name in row 1 should be 16 pt font size, with all other text in row 1 at 11 pt. Assign 12 pt paragraph spacing after the phone number and 12 pt paragraph spacing before your name in row 1. Remove all borders from the resume table.

Insert a Text Box, Add a Watermark, and Share a Document

A text box added at the end of the resume explains the purpose of the resume, providing an area for a brief comment. You indicate that the document is a draft copy (not yet final) by including a watermark, and you share the document with your instructor online.

a. Draw a text box at the end of page 11, with the centered text on two separate lines:

This abbreviated resume is provided as support for the preceding research.
Additional information is available upon request.

b. Ensure that the text box includes only two lines. Delete any additional paragraph marks that may display. The text box should be **5.5"** wide and **1"** tall. Center the text box horizontally on the page. Text in the text box should be **Times New Roman 12 pt** size. Format the text box with a shape fill of **Blue, Accent 5, Lighter 80%** and a shape effect of **Shadow, Offset Diagonal Bottom Right** (row 1, column 1 in the Outer section).

c. Include a watermark in the document that displays the word **Draft** in a diagonal format. The watermark should be colored in **Blue Accent 5**. The watermark will not display on page 1.

d. Share the document online and get an editing link. Include the link as a left-aligned footer in the document. (Select **Edit Footer**.) Format the footer as **Times New Roman 12 pt**.

e. Save and close the files. Based on your instructor's directions, submit the following:

wApp_Cap1_MergedLetter_LastFirst
wApp_Cap1_Research_LastFirst

Excel Application Capstone Exercise

You are a vice president for a publisher of software training books. Your division publishes three series that focus on Microsoft Office and Windows. You want to analyze the sales data and calculate author royalties. You will format the worksheet, insert formulas and functions to perform calculations, sort and filter data to review specific book sales, and prepare a chart that compares sales by series.

Format the Worksheet

Your assistant compiled the initial data and saved it in an Excel workbook. However, the column labels are hard to read because the full text does not display. You will use alignment and format options to make it easier to read the labels.

a. Open *eApp_Cap1_Publisher* and save it as **eApp_Cap1_Publisher_LastFirst**.

b. Select the **range A6:K6** on the Data worksheet.

c. Wrap the text and apply Center alignment to the selected range.

d. Change the row height to **30**.

Insert Formulas and Basic Functions

The Data worksheet contains the quantity of books sold, the number of books returned, and the unit price per book. You want to calculate the percentage of books that were returned from bookstores to your warehouse. Then you will also calculate the net sales, the amount of royalties to pay the authors, and the total author earnings. You want to insert functions to calculate the average, highest, and lowest net sales amounts. Use appropriate relative, absolute, and mixed references correctly in your formulas.

a. Click **cell F7** on the Data worksheet and insert a formula that calculates the percentage of books returned based on the number of books returned and the quantity sold. Copy the formula from cell F7 to the **range F8:F22**.

b. Click **cell H7** and insert a formula that calculates the net sales. This monetary amount reflects the number of books *not* returned and the unit price. Copy the formula from cell H7 to the **range H8:H22**.

c. Click **cell I7** and insert a formula that calculates the amount of the first author's royalties. An author's royalties are based on the Royalty Rate located in the Input Area and the respective Net Sales. Copy the formula from cell I7 to the **range I8:I22**.

d. Click **cell K7** and insert a formula that adds the first author's royalty amount to the bonus. Copy the formula from cell K7 to the **range K8:K22**.

e. Click **cell J2** and insert a function to calculate the average net sales.

f. Click **cell J3** and insert a function to calculate the highest net sales.

g. Click **cell J4** and insert a function to calculate the lowest net sales.

Move Data and Insert Functions

The legend that explains the abbreviations for each series would look better in a different location. You will insert a new column in the worksheet and insert a lookup function to display the full series names. Finally, you will replace the bonus with a function that calculates a bonus only if the return rate is less than 10%. Use relative, absolute, and mixed references correctly in your functions.

a. Select the **range L1:N2**, copy the selected data, and transpose the data when pasting it to **cell A2**. Delete the data in the **range L1:N2**.

b. Click **cell C6** and insert a column. Type **Series Name** in **cell C6**.

c. Click **cell C7** and insert a lookup function that identifies the series code, compares it to the series legend, and then returns the name of the series. Copy the function you entered from cell C7 to the **range C8:C22**.

d. Change the width of column C to **18**.

e. Click **cell K7** and insert an IF function that compares the percent returned for the first book to the return rate in the Input Area. If the percent returned is less than the return rate, the result is $500. Otherwise, the author receives no bonus. The only value you may type directly in the function is 0 where needed. Copy the function you entered from cell K7 to the **range K8:K22**.

Format Data

Most of the values were already formatted with Accounting Number Format, and when you inserted functions in the Net Sales area, Excel formatted the values for you because the source values were already formatted. However, you want to format the values in the Percent Returned and Bonus columns. In addition, you want to format the Series legend to match the other ranges at the top of the worksheet. You will merge and center the label and apply a border around the range.

a. Select the **range G7:G22** and apply the **Percent Style** format with one decimal place.

b. Select the **range K7:K22** and apply the **Accounting Number Format**.

c. Merge and center the label Series Legend in the **range A1:C1**.

d. Apply **Thick Outside Borders** to the **range A1:C4**.

Select Page Setup Options

Currently, the worksheet data would not fit on one printed page. You will change the orientation, scaling, and margins so that the data would fit on one page if you decide to print the worksheet.

a. Select **Landscape orientation**.

b. Adjust the scaling so that the data fits on one page.

c. Set **0.1"** left and right margins.

Insert a Table, Sort and Filter Data, and Apply Conditional Formatting

To preserve the integrity of the original data, you will work with a portion of the dataset in the Sales worksheet. First, you will convert the data to a table and apply a specific table style. Next, you will sort the data in a specific order and display the total net sales by series and within each series with the highest to lowest net sales. Then you will add a total row to display the total net sales. Finally, you want to apply a conditional format to focus on the book titles where 10% or more of the books were returned and then apply a filter to focus on the books with the lowest net sales.

a. Click the **Sales sheet tab** and convert the data to a table.

b. Apply **Table Style Light 9**.

c. Sort the data by Series Name in alphabetical order and then within Series Name, sort by Net Sales from largest to smallest.

d. Add a total row to display the sum of the Net Sales column. Change the column width to **14** for the Net Sales column.

e. Select the values in the Percent Returned column and apply conditional formatting to apply **Light Red Fill with Dark Red Text** for values that are greater than 9.9%.

f. Select the values in the Net Sales column and apply a filter to display only net sales that are less than $100,000.

Create a Column Chart

The Net Sales worksheet contains net sales organized by software and series. You will create a clustered column chart to compare the software sales across the series.

a. Click the **Net Sales sheet tab**.

b. Select the **range A3:D7** and create a clustered column chart.

c. Move the chart so that the top-left corner covers **cell A9**. Change the chart width to **4.66"** and the chart height to **2.9"**.

d. Link the chart title to **cell A1**.

e. Format the value axis to display whole numbers only.

f. Format the chart title, value axis, category axis, and legend with **Black, Text 1 font color**.

Create a Pie Chart

The Series Sales worksheet contains net sales organized by software and series. You will create a pie chart to determine the percentage of sales for each book within the Office Reference series.

a. Click the **Series Sales sheet tab**.

b. Select the **ranges A4:A7** and **C4:C7** and create a pie chart. Move the pie chart to a chart sheet named **Office Reference**. Move the Office Reference chart sheet to the right of the Series Sales sheet.

c. Change the chart title to **Office Reference Series**. Apply **bold** and change the font size to **18** for the chart title.

d. Apply the **Style 12** chart style and change the colors to **Color 4**.

e. Display data labels in the **Inside End** position. Display **Percentage** data labels; remove the Value data labels. Apply **bold**, change the font size to **18**, and then apply **White, Background 1** font color to the data labels.

f. Apply these fill colors: Excel data point **Green**, Access data point **Purple**, PowerPoint data point **Orange, Accent 2**.

Finish the Project

You want to insert a footer on each sheet.

a. Group the Data, Sales, Net Sales, and Series Sales sheet tabs.

b. Create a footer with your name on the left side, the sheet tab code in the center, and the file name code on the right side of each sheet.

c. Click the Office Reference chart sheet and create a footer with your name on the left side, the sheet tab code in the center, and the file name code on the right side.

d. Save and close the file. Based on your instructor's directions, submit eApp_Cap1_Publisher_LastFirst.

Access Application Capstone Exercise

You were recently hired by your local college to help with registering all transfer students. The college's Transfer Counseling Department is a one-stop location for transfer students to come with questions. They have been working with Excel spreadsheets generated by the Information Technology department, but they are hoping to do more with an Access database. They have had a number of problems, including employees putting information in the wrong fields, inputting information in the wrong format, and creating incorrect formulas. They are also hoping for more consistent ways of finding information, as well as being able to generate reports. Your tasks include importing an existing Excel worksheet as a table into your Access database; modifying the table; creating a relationship between two tables; creating queries with calculated fields, functions, and totals; creating a form for input; creating a report; and backing up the database.

Set Up the Database File and Import an Excel Worksheet

To start, you have been provided with a database the Information Technology department created. The database has one table and one form. You will be importing an Excel spreadsheet into a table and creating a primary key.

a. Open *aApp_Cap1_College* and save the database as **aApp_Cap1_College_LastFirst**.

b. Import the *aApp_Cap1_Transfer* Excel workbook into a new table named **Transfer Schools**. While importing the data, ensure that **StudentID** has a data type of **Short Text**, and select **StudentID** as the primary key.

Modify a Table

Now that you have imported the data from the spreadsheet, you will modify the field properties in the Transfer Schools table and demonstrate sorting.

a. Open the Transfer Schools table in Design view.

b. Set the StudentID field size to **10**.

c. Remove the @ symbol from the StudentID format property.

d. Change the AdmittingSchool field size to **75**.

e. Change the RegistrationFee and TuitionDue fields to have **0** decimal places.

f. Switch to Datasheet view. Resize the AdmittingSchool column by double-clicking on the border between AdmittingSchool and AdmissionDate.

g. Sort the Transfer Schools table on the CreditsTransferred field in ascending order.

h. Save and close the table.

Create Relationships

Now that the table is imported and modified, you will create a relationship between the Transfer Schools and Transfer Students tables.

a. Add the Transfer Schools and Transfer Students tables to the Relationships window.

b. Create a one-to-one relationship between the StudentID field in the Transfer Students table and the StudentID field in the Transfer Schools table. Enforce referential integrity between the two tables and cascade updates.

c. Save the changes and close the Relationships window.

Modify Data in a Form

You will demonstrate changing information in a form.

a. Open the Transfer Students Data Entry form.

b. Change the major for *Cornelius Kavanagh* to **Elementary Education**. Close the form.

Create a Query

Rey Rivera, a counselor in the center, would like your assistance in helping him find certain information. You will create a query for him and demonstrate how he can change information.

a. Create a new query using Design view. This query will access fields from both the Transfer Schools and Transfer Students tables. From the Transfer Students table, add the FirstName, LastName, Major, Class, and GPA fields. From the Transfer Schools table, add the AdmissionDate, TuitionDue, CreditsEarned, and CreditsTransferred fields.

b. Save the query as **Transfer Credits**.

c. Set the criteria in the AdmissionDate field to **8/1/2018**. Run the query (19 records will display).

d. Type **$1500** in the TuitionDue field for Diana Sullivan and type **3.51** as the GPA for Audrey Owen.

e. Save and close the query.

Create Calculated Fields

Now that you have created the query, you will create a second query for Rey that will calculate the number of credits students lost upon transfer, the tuition payments for which they will be responsible (assuming three payments per semester), and the due date of the first payment.

a. Create a copy of the Transfer Credits query. Name the copy **Transfer Credit Calculations**. Open the new query in Design view.

b. Remove the criteria from the AdmissionDate field.

c. Create a calculated field in the first empty field cell of the query named **LostCredits** that subtracts CreditsTransferred from CreditsEarned.

d. Create another calculated field named **TuitionPayments** that determines tuition paid in three installments. Using the Pmt function, replace the rate argument with **0.025/3**, the num_periods argument with **3**, and the present_value argument with the student's tuition payment. Use **0** for the future_value and type arguments. Ensure that the payment appears as a positive number.

e. Format the TuitionPayments calculated field as **Currency**.

f. Create another calculated field named **FirstPayment** after the TuitionPayments field. To calculate the due date, add **30** to their AdmissionDate. Run the query and verify that the three calculated fields have valid data.

g. Add a total row to the datasheet. Sum the TuitionDue column and average the TuitionPayment column. Save and close the query.

Create a Totals Query

Cala Hajjar, the director of the center, needs to summarize information about the transfer students for the 2018–2019 academic year to present to the College's Board of Trustees. You will create a totals query for her to summarize the number of transfer students, average number of credits earned and transferred, and total tuition earned by transfer institution.

a. Create a new query in Design view. Add the Transfer Schools table.

b. Add the AdmittingSchool, StudentID, CreditsEarned, CreditsTransferred, and TuitionDue fields.

c. Sort the query by AdmittingSchool in ascending order.

d. Show the Total row. Group by AdmittingSchool and show the count of StudentID, the average of CreditsEarned, the average of CreditsTransferred, and the sum of TuitionDue.

e. Format both average fields as **Standard**.

f. Change the caption for the StudentID field to **NumStudents**, the caption for the CreditsEarned average to **AvgCreditsEarned**, the caption for the CreditsTransferred average to **AvgCredits Transferred**, and the caption for the sum of TuitionDue to **TotalTuition**.

g. Run the query.

h. Save the query as **Transfer Summary**.

i. Close the query.

Create a Form

Hideo Sasaki, the department's administrative assistant, will handle data entry. He has asked you to simplify the way he inputs information into the new table. You will create a form based on the new Transfer Schools table.

a. Create a Split Form using the Transfer Schools table as the source.

b. Change the height of the AdmittingSchool field to be approximately half the current height.

c. Remove the layout from all the labels and fields. Shrink each field so it is approximately as large as it needs to be.

d. Click record **123455** in the bottom half of the split form. Make sure all values are still visible in the top half of the form. If not, adjust the controls so all values are visible.

e. Move the CreditsTransferred field so it is to the right of the CreditsEarned field on the same row.

f. Change the format of the TuitionDue field so the font size is **18** and the font color is **Red** (last row, second column in the Standard Colors section). Resize the field if necessary so the entire value displays.

g. Change the fill color of the StudentID field to be **Yellow** (last row, fourth column in the Standard Colors section).

h. Save the form as **Transfer Schools Form**. Save and close the form.

Create a Report

Cala is hoping you can create a more print-friendly version of the query you created earlier for her to distribute to the Board of Trustees. You will create a report based on the Transfer Credit Calculations query.

a. Create a report using the Report Wizard. Add the **Class**, **FirstName**, **LastName**, **Major**, **GPA**, and **LostCredits** fields from the Transfer Credit Calculations query. Do not add any grouping or sorting. Ensure that the report is in Landscape orientation.

b. Save the report as **Transfer Students Report** and view the report in Layout view.

Format a Report

Now that you have included the fields Cala has asked for, you will work to format the report to make the information more obvious.

a. Apply the **Wisp theme** (last row, first column) to this object only.

b. Group the report by the Class field. Sort the records within each group by LastName then by FirstName, both in ascending order.

c. Change the font size of the Class field to **16**.

d. Adjust the text boxes so the values for the Major field are completely visible.

e. Switch to Print Preview mode and verify that the report is only one page wide (Note: It may be a number of pages long).

f. Export the results as a PDF document using the file name **aApp_Cap1_Transfer_LastFirst**.

g. Save and close the report.

Close and Submit the Database

    a. Create a backup of the database. Accept the default name for the backup.

    b. Close all database objects and exit Access. Based on your instructor's directions, submit the following:

    aApp_Cap1_College_LastFirst

    aApp_Cap1_College_LastFirst_*CurrentDate*

    aApp_Cap1_Transfer_LastFirst

PowerPoint Application Capstone Exercise

You have worked hard to meet your goal of becoming a school teacher. You are excited to start teaching in the fall and want to be prepared. You began a slide show to introduce science to your students and now want to modify the original slide show to add additional information and visual impact. You will insert slides, change layouts, insert a picture and a video, add WordArt, insert a SmartArt diagram, reuse a slide, and create a table. You will also add a transition and animations.

Set Up Presentation

You open the original slide show, rename the file, and save it.

a. Open *pApp_Cap1_Science* and save the file as **pApp_Cap1_Science_LastFirst**.

b. Create a Notes and Handouts header and footer with the date, the page number, your name in the header, and your instructor's name and your class in the footer.

c. Replace *Student Name* with your name on **Slide 1**.

Use WordArt, Format a Background, Add a Video

You decide to enhance the presentation introduction by changing text to WordArt. In addition, you change the background to enhance the slide show. You add a video clip to a slide.

a. Click **Slide 2**. Select the text in the title placeholder and apply the WordArt style **Fill - White, Text 1, Outline - Background 1, Hard Shadow - Background 1**.

b. Select the title placeholder and change the shape fill to **Red, Accent 6, Darker 25%**.

c. Click the **View tab**, select **Outline view**, select the **subtitle placeholder** on Slide 2, and then type **The word "Science" means "knowledge" in Latin**. Switch to Normal view.

d. Insert a new slide after **Slide 2** using the **Two Content layout**. Type **Science is:** in the title placeholder. Type **A collection of knowledge that is used to explain the world around us.** in the left content placeholder and **A way of uncovering new pieces of knowledge.** in the right content placeholder.

e. Click the **Design tab** and click **Format Background**. Insert a picture fill using *pApp_Cap1_DNA*.

f. Select both content placeholders, then change the font size to **36 pt** and the font color to **Gray-80%, Background 2**.

g. Change the transparency of the background to **50%**.

h. Use the content placeholder on **Slide 4** to insert the video *pApp_Cap1_Questions*.

i. Add a speaker note that reads **Science explains what is happening in the world around us. Science uses the scientific method to do this.**

Add SmartArt and Shapes

You create a SmartArt graphic and shapes to explain The Scientific Method. After completing the diagram, you animate it.

a. Create **Slide 5** using the **Blank layout**. Insert a **Vertical Bending Process** SmartArt diagram.

b. Open the Text pane and type the following:
- **Ask a question**
- **Do research**
- **Construct hypothesis**
- **Test hypothesis**
- **Draw a conclusion**

c. Remove the four empty [Text] bullet points.

d. Close the Text Pane. Deselect the Draw shape, select the SmartArt, and then **Align Left**.

e. Select the *Draw a conclusion* shape and make two copies.

f. Position one copy of the *Draw a conclusion* shape at **8.9"** horizontally from the **Top Left Corner** and **0.84"** vertically from the **Top Left Corner**. Replace the *Draw a conclusion* text with **Try again**.

g. Select the remaining copy of the *Draw a conclusion* shape and replace the *Draw a conclusion* text with **Hypothesis is proven**. Drag the shape containing the *Hypothesis is proven* text to the right using the SmartGuides to align it with the center of the *Draw a conclusion* shape and with the left side of the *Try again* shape.

h. Create an arrow connecting the *Draw a conclusion* shape to the *Try again* shape. Change the weight of the arrow to **6 pt** and change the shape outline to **Red, Accent 6**.

i. Group the arrow and the *Try again* shape. Deselect the grouped shapes.

j. Create an arrow connecting the *Draw a conclusion* shape to the *Hypothesis is proven* shape. Change the weight of the arrow to **6 pt** and change the shape outline to **Red, Accent 6**.

k. Group the new arrow and the *Hypothesis is proven* shape.

l. Select the SmartArt and apply the **Float In** animation. Set the animation to start **With Previous**.

m. Select the *Try again* group and apply the **Wipe** animation with the **From Left** effect.

n. Select the *Hypothesis is proven* group and apply the **Wipe** animation with the **From Left** effect.

o. Add a speaker note that says **Trying again is not a failure. When results disprove a hypothesis the scientist has gained new knowledge.**

Add Content and Animation

You reuse a previously created slide to add content, and you modify the layout on the reused slide to make it easier to read and understand.

a. Select **Slide 3** and use the Reuse Slides feature to add the slide *pApp_Cap1_Fields* so that it becomes Slide 4. Close the Reuse Slides pane.

b. Change the slide layout to **Blank**.

c. Select the SmartArt and change the layout to **Organization Chart**.

d. Change the height of the SmartArt to **7.5"** and the width to **11.78"**.

e. Reposition the SmartArt so that it is in the **center** of the slide.

f. Select the **Biology shape**, click **Layout** in the Create Graphic group on the Design tab, and change the layout to **Both**.

g. Repeat Step f for the Chemistry and Physics shapes.

h. Change the SmartArt style to **Powder**.

i. Change the SmartArt colors to **Colorful Range – Accent Colors 5 to 6**.

j. Apply the **Wipe animation** (Entrance category) to the SmartArt. Change the sequence of the animation to the **One by One effect**.

Add a Table

You add a table to the slide show showing science disciplines that combine knowledge of all three fields of science to uncover facts.

a. Insert a **Title and Content** slide at the end of the slide show.

b. Add the title **Disciplines Requiring Combined Knowledge**.

c. Create a table with **4 columns** and **6 rows** in the content placeholder.

d. Type the following table:

Discipline	Biology knowledge	Chemistry knowledge	Physics knowledge
Biochemistry	X	X	
Genetics	X	X	
Forensic science	X	X	X
Geology	X	X	X
Nuclear chemistry		X	X

e. Select the cells with Xs as their content and change the paragraph alignment to **Center**.

Insert and Modify a Picture

You want to introduce the Applied Science section with a picture. You insert a picture and add a picture frame to the image.

a. Create a new slide, **Slide 8**, with the **Panoramic Picture with Caption** layout. Insert *pApp_Cap1_Structure*.

b. Apply the **Metal Oval** picture style.

c. Type **Applied Science** in the title placeholder. Delete the subtitle placeholder.

d. Select the title placeholder and change the shape fill to **Red, Accent 6, Darker 25%**.

e. Change the height of the title placeholder to **1.75"**.

f. Change the size of the font in the title placeholder to **96 pt**

Finalize the Presentation

To ensure the professionalism of the presentation, you review the presentation and make changes.

a. Check the spelling of the presentation and correct any misspelled words.

b. View the presentation in **Slide Show view** and note that Slide 4 does not appear in the correct order in the slide show. Close the slide show.

c. View the presentation in **Slide Sorter view**. Drag Slide 4 so it becomes Slide 6.

d. Apply the **Orbit transition** to all slides.

e. Change the transition timing so that all slides advance automatically after 8 seconds.

f. View the presentation in **Reading View**.

g. Save and close the file. Based on your instructor's directions, submit pApp_Cap1_Science_LastFirst.

Glossary

100% stacked column chart A chart type that places (stacks) data in one column per category, with each column the same height of 100%.

Absolute cell reference A designation that indicates a constant reference to a specific cell location; the cell reference does not change when you copy the formula.

Access A relational database management system in which you can record and link data, query databases, and create forms and reports.

Accounting Number Format A number format that displays $ on the left side of a cell, formats a value with a comma for every three digits on the left side of the decimal point, and displays two digits to the right of the decimal point.

Action Center A location in Windows 10, accessed by an icon in the Notifications area on the taskbar, that provides status information, notifications, and recommended actions for various maintenance and security settings.

Active cell The current cell in a worksheet. It is indicated by a dark green border, and the Name Box shows the location of the active cell.

Add-in A custom program or additional command that extends the functionality of a Microsoft Office program.

Adjustment handle A yellow circle on a shape that is used to change the shape.

Aggregate function A calculation performed on an entire column of data that returns a single value. Includes functions such as Sum, Avg, and Count.

Align A feature that enables you to line up shapes and objects. You can align objects by lining up the sides, middles, or top/bottom edges of objects.

Alignment The placement of data within the boundaries of a cell. By default, text aligns on the left side, and values align on the right side of a cell.

Alignment guide A horizontal or vertical green bar that appears as you move an object, assisting with aligning the object with text or with another object.

Alt text An accessibility compliance feature where you enter text and a description for an objective, such as a table or a chart. A special reader can read the alt text to a user.

AND condition A condition in a query, returns only records that meet all criteria.

Animation A motion applied to text and objects.

Annotation A written note or drawing on a slide for additional commentary or explanation

APA (American Psychological Association) A writing style established by the American Psychological Association with rules and conventions for documenting sources and organizing a research paper (used primarily in business and the social sciences).

Application part A feature that enables you to add a set of common Access components to an existing database, such as a table, a form, and a report for a related task.

Area chart A chart type that emphasizes magnitude of changes over time by filling in the space between lines with a color.

Argument A positional reference contained within parentheses in a function such as a cell reference or value, required to complete a function and produce output.

Aspect Ratio The ratio of an object's width to its height.

Auto Fill A feature that helps you complete a sequence of months, abbreviated months, quarters, weekdays, weekday abbreviations, or values. Auto Fill also can be used to fill or copy a formula down a column or across a row.

AutoComplete A feature that searches for and automatically displays any other label in that column that matches the letters you type.

AutoNumber A number that automatically increments each time a record is added.

AutoRecover A feature that enables Word to recover a previous version of a document.

AVERAGE function A predefined formula that calculates the arithmetic mean, or average, of values in a range of cells.

Axis title A label that describes either the category axis or the value axis. Provides clarity, particularly in describing the value axis.

Back Up Database A utility that creates a duplicate copy of the entire database to protect from loss or damage.

Background The portion of a picture that can be deleted when removing the background of a picture.

Background Styles gallery A gallery providing both solid color and background styles for application to a theme.

Backstage view A component of Office that provides a concise collection of commands related to an open file.

Bar chart A chart type that compares values across categories using horizontal bars where the length represents the value; the longer the bar, the larger the value. In a bar chart, the horizontal axis displays values and the vertical axis displays categories.

Bibliography A list of works cited or consulted by an author in his or her work.

Bitmap image An image created by bits or pixels placed on a grid to form a picture.

Blog The chronological publication of personal thoughts and Web links.

Bookmark A method used to mark specific locations in a video.

Border A line that surrounds a paragraph, page, or a table or table element.

Border (Excel) A line that surrounds a cell or a range of cells to offset particular data from the rest of the data in a worksheet.

Border Painter A feature that enables you to choose border formatting and click on any table border to apply the formatting.

Breakpoint The lowest value for a category or in a series.

Brightness A picture correction that controls the lightness or darkness of a picture.

Bulleted list A graphic element that itemizes and separates paragraph text to increase readability; often used to identify lists.

Calculated field A field that displays the result of an expression rather than data stored in a field.

Callout A shape that be can used to add notes, often used in cartooning.

Cancel An icon between the Name Box and Formula Bar. When you enter or edit data, click Cancel to cancel the data entry or edit, and revert back to the previous data in the cell, if any. Cancel changes from gray to red when you position the pointer over it.

Caption A descriptive title for a table

Caption property A property that is used to create a more understandable label than a field name that displays in the top row in Datasheet view and in forms and reports.

Cascade Delete Related Records When the primary key value is deleted in a primary table, Access will automatically delete all records in related tables that contain values that match the primary key.

Cascade Update Related Fields An option that directs Access to automatically change all foreign key values in a related table when the primary key value is modified in a primary table.

Category axis The chart axis that displays descriptive labels for the data points plotted in a chart. The category axis labels are typically text contained in the first column of worksheet data (such as job titles) used to create the chart.

Cell The intersection of a column and row in a table, such as the intersection of column B and row 5.

Cell address The unique identifier of a cell, starting with the column letter and then the row number, such as C6.

Cell style A set of formatting applied to a cell to produce a consistent appearance for similar cells within a worksheet.

Center alignment Positions text horizontally in the center of a line, with an equal distance from both the left and right margins.

Chart A visual representation of numerical data.

Chart area A container for the entire chart and all of its elements, including the plot area, titles, legends, and labels.

Chart element A component of a chart that helps complete or clarify the chart.

Chart filter A setting that controls what data series and categories are displayed or hidden in a chart.

Chart sheet A sheet within a workbook that contains a single chart and no spreadsheet data.

Chart style A collection of formatting that controls the color of the chart area, plot area, and data series.

Chart title The label that describes the entire chart. The title is usually placed at the top of the chart area.

Chicago Manual of Style A writing style established by the University of Chicago with rules and conventions for preparing an academic paper for publication.

Citation A note recognizing a source of information or a quoted passage.

Clipboard An area of memory reserved to temporarily hold selections that have been cut or copied and allows you to paste the selections.

Cloud storage A technology used to store files and to work with programs that are stored in a central location on the Internet.

Clustered column chart A type of chart that groups, or clusters, columns set side by side to compare several data points among categories.

Codec (coder/decoder) A digital video compression scheme used to compress a video and decompress for playback.

Collapsed outline An Outline view that displays only the slide number, icon, and title of each slide in Outline view.

Color scale A conditional format that displays a particular color based on the relative value of the cell contents to the other selected cells.

Colors gallery A set of colors available for every theme.

Column A format that separates document text into side-by-side vertical blocks, often used in newsletters.

Column chart A type of chart that compares values vertically in columns where the height represents the value; the taller the column, the larger the value. In a column chart, the vertical axis displays values and the horizontal axis displays categories.

Column heading The alphabetical letter above a column in a worksheet. For example, B is the column heading for the second column.

Column index number The column number in the lookup table that contains the return values.

Column width The horizontal measurement of a column in a table or a worksheet. In Excel, it is measured by the number of characters or pixels.

Combo chart A chart that combines two chart types, such as column and line, to plot different types of data, such as quantities and percentages.

Comma Style A number format that formats a value with a comma for every three digits on the left side of the decimal point and displays two digits to the right of the decimal point.

Command A button or area within a group that you click to perform tasks.

Comment A note, annotation, or additional information to the author or another reader about the content of a document.

Comment balloon A small balloon that displays on the right side of a paragraph in which a comment has been made and provides access to the comment.

Compact and Repair Database A utility that reduces the size of a database and fixes any errors that may exist in the file.

Comparison Operator An operator such as greater than (>), less than (<), greater than or equal to (>=), and less than or equal to (<=), etc. used to limit query results that meet these criteria.

Compressed (zipped) folder A folder created with the Zip feature, contains a file or group of files. A compressed folder uses less drive space and can be transferred or shared with other users more quickly.

Compression A method applied to data to reduce the amount of space required for file storage.

Conditional formatting A set of rules that applies specific formatting to highlight or emphasize cells that meet specific conditions.

Connector A line with connection points at each end.

Constant A value that does not change.

Contextual tab A tab that contains a group of commands related to the selected object.

Contrast The difference between the darkest and lightest areas of a picture.

Control A text box, button, label, or other tool you use to add, edit, and display the data in a form or report.

Copy A command used to duplicate a selection from the original location and place a copy in the Office Clipboard.

Copyright The legal protection afforded to a written or artistic work.

Cortana Microsoft 10's personal assistant that helps search the Web and your PC, and can also assist with reminders, tasks, and other activities.

COUNT function A predefined formula that tallies the number of cells in a range that contain values you can use in calculations, such as numerical and date data, but excludes blank cells or text entries from the tally.

COUNTA function A predefined formula that tallies the number of cells in a range that are not blank, that is, cells that contain data, whether a value, text, or a formula.

COUNTBLANK function A predefined formula that tallies the number of cells in a range that are blank.

Cover page The first page of a report, including the report title, author or student, and other identifying information.

Criteria row A row in Query Design view that determines which records will be selected.

Crop The process of reducing an image size by eliminating unwanted portions of an image or other graphical object.

Current List A list that includes all citation sources you use in the current document.

Custom Web app A feature which enables users to create a database that you can build and then use and share with others through the Web.

Cut A command used to remove a selection from the original location and place it in the Office Clipboard.

Data bar Data bar formatting applies a gradient or solid fill bar in which the width of the bar represents the current cell's value compared relatively to other cells' values.

Data label An identifier that shows the exact value of a data point in a chart. Appears above or on a data point in a chart. May indicate percentage of a value to the whole on a pie chart.

Data point A numeric value that describes a single value in a chart or worksheet.

Data redundancy The unnecessary storing of duplicate data in two or more tables.

Data series A group of related data points that display in row(s) or column(s) in a worksheet.

Data source A list of information that is merged with a main document during a mail merge procedure.

Data structure The organization method used to manage multiple data points within a dataset.

Data table A grid that contains the data source values and labels to plot data in a chart. A data table may be placed below a chart or hidden from view.

Data type Determines the type of data that can be entered and the operations that can be performed on that data.

Database A collection of data organized as meaningful information that can be accessed, managed, stored, queried, sorted, and reported.

Database Management System (DBMS) A software system that provides the tools needed to create, maintain, and use a database.

Database Splitter A utility that puts the tables in one file (the back-end database), and the queries, forms, and reports in a second file (the front-end database).

Datasheet view A grid containing fields (columns) and records (rows) used to view, add, edit, and delete records.

Deck A collection of slides.

Design view A view which gives users a detailed view of the table's structure and is used to create and modify a table's design by specifying the fields it will contain, the fields' data types, and their associated properties.

Desktop The primary working area of Windows 10 that contains objects such as windows and icons.

Dialog box A box that provides access to more precise, but less frequently used, commands.

Dialog Box Launcher A button that when clicked opens a corresponding dialog box.

Disk Cleanup An administrative tool in Windows that is used to remove unnecessary files from the computer.

Distribute To divide or evenly spread selected shapes over a given area.

Document Inspector Checks for and removes certain hidden and personal information from a document.

Document properties Data elements that identify a document, such as author or comments.

Document theme A set of coordinating fonts, colors, and special effects that gives a stylish and professional look.

Draft view View that shows a great deal of document space, but no margins, headers, footers, or other special features.

Effects gallery A range of special effects for shapes used in the presentation.

Embed A method of storing an object from an external source within a presentation.

Endnote A citation that appears at the end of a document.

Enhanced ScreenTip A small message box that displays when you place the pointer over a command button. The purpose of the command, short descriptive text, or a keyboard shortcut if applicable will display in the box.

Enter An icon between the Name Box and Formula Bar. When you enter or edit data, click Enter to accept data typed in the active cell and keep the current cell active. Enter changes from gray to blue when you position the pointer over it.

Error bars Visual that indicates the standard error amount, a percentage, or a standard deviation for a data point or marker in a chart.

Excel An application that makes it easy to organize records, financial transactions, and business information in the form of worksheets.

Expanded outline An Outline view that displays the slide number, icon, title, and content of each slide in the Outline view.

Exploded pie chart A chart type in which one or more pie slices are separated from the rest of the pie chart for emphasis.

Expression A combination of elements that produce a value.

Expression Builder An Access tool that helps you create more complicated expressions.

Eyedropper tool A tool used to recreate an exact color.

Field The smallest data element contained in a table, such as first name, last name, address, and phone number.

Field property A characteristic of a field that determines how it will look and behave.

File Explorer The Windows app that is used to create folders and manage files and folders across various storage locations.

File History A utility in Windows that continuously makes copies of your important files so that you can recover them if you encounter a file problem.

File management The means of providing an organizational structure to file and folders.

Fill color The background color that displays behind the data in a cell so that the data stands out.

Fill handle A small green square at the bottom-right corner of the active cell. You can position the pointer on the fill handle and drag it to repeat the contents of the cell to other cells or to copy a formula in the active cell to adjacent cells down the column or across the row.

Filter A feature which allows users to specify conditions to display only those records that meet those conditions.

Filter By Form A more versatile method of selecting data, enabling users to display records based on multiple criteria.

Filtering The process of specifying conditions to display only those records that meet those conditions.

Firewall A software program included in Windows 10 that helps to protect against unauthorized access, or hacking, to your computer.

First line indent Marks the location to indent only the first line in a paragraph.

Flash Fill A feature that fills in data or values automatically based on one or two examples you enter using another part of data entered in a previous column in the dataset.

Flip To reverse the direction an object faces.

Flow chart An illustration showing the sequence of a project or plan containing steps.

Font A combination of typeface and type style.

Fonts gallery A gallery that pairs a title font with a body font.

Footer Information that displays at the bottom of a document page.

Footnote A citation that appears at the bottom of a page.

Foreground The portion of the picture that is kept when removing the background of a picture.

Foreign key A field in a related table that is the primary key of another table.

Form A database object that is used to add data into or edit data in a table.

Form letter A letter with standard information that you personalize with recipient information, which you might print or email to many people.

Form tool A tool used to create data entry forms for customers, employees, products, and other tables.

Form view A view that provides a simplified user interface primarily used for data entry; does not allow you to make changes to the layout.

Format Painter A feature that enables you to quickly and easily copy all formatting from one area to another in Word, PowerPoint, and Excel.

Formatting The process of modifying text by changing font and paragraph characteristics.

Formula A combination of cell references, operators, values, and/or functions used to perform a calculation.

Formula AutoComplete A feature that displays a list of functions and defined names that match letters as you type a formula.

Formula Bar An element located below the Ribbon and to the right of the Insert Function command. It shows the contents of the active cell. You enter or edit cell contents in the Formula Bar for the active cell.

Freeform shape A shape that combines both curved and straight-line segments.

Freezing The process of keeping rows and/or columns visible onscreen at all times even when you scroll through a large dataset.

Fully qualified structured reference A structured formula that contains the table name.

Function A predefined computation that simplifies creating a complex calculation and produces a result based on inputs known as arguments.

Function ScreenTip A small pop-up description that displays the function's arguments.

Gallery An area in Word which provides additional text styles. In Excel, the gallery provides a choice of chart styles, and in PowerPoint, the gallery provides transitions.

Gradient fill A fill that contains a blend of two or more colors or shades.

Grid Intersecting lines on a slide that enable you to align objects.

Gridline A horizontal or vertical line that extends from the horizontal or vertical axis through the plot area to guide the reader's eyes across the chart to identify values.

Group A subset of a tab that organizes similar tasks together.

Group (PowerPoint) Multiple objects connected so they are able to move as though they are a single object.

Grouping A method of summarizing data by the values of a field.

Guide A nonprinting, temporary vertical or horizontal line placed on a slide to enable you align objects or determine regions of the slide.

Hanging indent Aligns the first line of a paragraph at the left margin, indenting remaining lines in the paragraph.

Header An area with one or more lines of information at the top of each page.

Header row The first row in a data source, which contains labels describing the data in rows beneath.

Hierarchy A method used to organize text into levels of importance in a structure.

Histogram A chart that is similar to a column chart. The category axis shows bin ranges (intervals) where data is aggregated into bins, and the vertical axis shows frequencies.

HLOOKUP function A function that looks for a value in the top row of a specified table array and returns another value located in the same column from a specified row.

Horizontal alignment The placement of cell data between the left and right cell margins. By default, text is left-aligned, and values are right-aligned.

Icon A graphical link to a program, file, folder, or other item related to your computer.

Icon set Symbols or signs that classify data into three, four, or five categories, based on values in a range.

IF function A predefined formula that evaluates a condition and returns one value if the condition is true and a different value if the condition is false.

Indent A format that offsets data from its default alignment. For example, if text is left-aligned, the text may be indented or offset from the left side to stand out. If a value is right-aligned, it can be indented or offset from the right side of the cell.

Index An alphabetical listing of topics covered in a document, along with the page numbers on which the topic is discussed.

Infographic Informational graphic that is a visual representation of data or knowledge.

Infringement of copyright A situation that occurs when a right of the copyright owner is violated.

Input area A range of cells in a worksheet used to store and change the variables used in calculations.

Insert control An indicator that displays between rows or columns in a table; click the indicator to insert one or more rows or columns.

Insert Function An icon between the Name Box and Formula Bar. Click Insert Function to open the Insertion Function dialog box to search for and insert a particular function.

Insertion point Blinking bar that indicates where text that you next type will appear.

Insights A pane that presents outside resources, such as images, definitions, and other references.

Jump List List of program-specific shortcuts to recently opened files, the program name, an option to pin or unpin the program, and a close window option.

Justified alignment Spreads text evenly between the left and right margins, so that text begins at the left margin and ends uniformly at the right margin.

Kelvin The unit of measurement for absolute temperature used to measure the tone of an image.

Label Wizard A feature that enables you to easily create mailing labels, name tags, and other specialized tags.

Landscape orientation A document layout when a page is wider than it is tall.

Layout Determines the position of the objects or content on a slide.

Layout control A tool that provides guides to help keep controls aligned horizontally and vertically and give your form a uniform appearance.

Layout view A view that enables users to make changes to a layout while viewing the data in the form or report.

Left alignment Begins text evenly at the left margin, with a ragged right edge.

Left indent A setting that positions all text in a paragraph an equal distance from the left margin.

Legend A key that identifies the color, gradient, picture, texture, or pattern assigned to each data series in a chart.

Line chart A chart type that displays lines connecting data points to show trends over equal time periods, such as months, quarters, years, or decades.

Line spacing The vertical spacing between lines in a paragraph.

Line weight The width or thickness of a shape's outline.

Link A connection from the presentation to another location such as a storage device or website.

Live Layout Feature that enables you to watch text flow around an object as you move it, so you can position the object exactly as you want it.

Live Preview An Office feature that provides a preview of the results of a selection when you point to an option in a list or gallery. Using Live Preview, you can experiment with settings before making a final choice.

Lock Drawing Mode Enables the creation of multiple shapes of the same type.

Logical test An expression that evaluates to true or false.

Lookup table A range that contains data for the basis of the lookup and data to be retrieved.

Lookup value The cell reference of the cell that contains the value to look up.

Macro A stored series of commands that carry out an action; often used to automate simple tasks.

Mail Merge A process that combines content from a main document and a data source.

Main document A document that contains the information that stays the same for all recipients in a mail merge.

Margin The area of blank space that displays to the left, right, top, and bottom of a document or worksheet.

Markup A feature to help customize how tracked changes are displayed in a document.

Marquee A selection of multiple objects created by dragging a rectangle around all of the objects you want to select.

Master A slide view where the control of the layouts, background designs, and color combinations for handouts, notes pages, and slides can be set giving a presentation a consistent appearance.

Master List A database of all citation sources created in Word on a particular computer.

MAX function A predefined formula that identifies the highest value in a range.

MEDIAN function A predefined formula that identifies the midpoint value in a set of values.

Merge field An item that serves as a placeholder for the variable data that will be inserted into the main document during a mail merge procedure.

Microsoft Office A productivity software suite including a set of software applications, each one specializing in a particular type of output.

Microsoft Word A word processing software application used to produce all sorts of documents, including memos, newsletters, forms, tables, and brochures.

MIN function A predefined formula that displays the lowest value in a range.

Mini toolbar A toolbar that provides access to the most common formatting selections, such as adding bold or italic, or changing font type or color. Unlike the Quick Access Toolbar, the Mini toolbar is not customizable.

Mixed cell reference A designation that combines an absolute cell reference with a relative cell reference. The absolute part does not change but the relative part does when you copy the formula.

MLA (Modern Language Association) A writing style established by the Modern Language Association, with rules and conventions for preparing research papers (used primarily in the area of humanities).

Module An advanced object written using the VBA (Visual Basic for Applications) programming language.

Multimedia Various forms of media used to entertain or inform an audience.

Multiple Items form A form that displays multiple records in a tabular layout similar to a table's Datasheet view, with more customization options than a datasheet.

Multitable query Results contain fields from two or more tables, enabling you to take advantage of the relationships that have been set in your database.

Name Box An element located below the Ribbon, which displays the address of the active cell.

Narration Spoken commentary that is added to a presentation.

Navigation Pane An Access interface element that organizes and lists the objects in an Access database.

Nested function A function that contains another function embedded inside one or more of it's arguments.

New sheet An icon that, when clicked, inserts a new worksheet in the workbook.

Nonadjacent range A collection of multiple ranges (such as D5:D10 and F5:F10) that are not positioned in a contiguous cluster in an Excel worksheet.

Normal view (Excel) The default view of a worksheet that shows worksheet data but not margins, headers, footers, or page breaks.

Normal view (PowerPoint) The default PowerPoint workspace.

Notes Page view Used for entering and editing large amounts of text to which the speaker can refer when presenting.

Notification area An area on the far right of the taskbar, that includes the clock and a group of icons that relate to the status of a setting or program.

NOW function A predefined formula that calculates the current date and military time that you last opened the workbook using the computer's clock.

Nper Total number of payment periods.

Null The term Access uses to describe a blank field value.

Number format A setting that controls how a value appears in a cell.

Numbered list Sequences items in a list by displaying a successive number beside each item.

Object An item, such as a picture or text box, that can be individually selected and manipulated in a document.

Object (Access) A component created and used to make the database function (such as a table, query, form, or report).

One-to-many relationship When the primary key value in the primary table can match many of the foreign key values in the related table.

OneDrive Microsoft's cloud storage system. Saving files to OneDrive enables them to sync across all Windows devices and to be accessible from any Internet-connected device.

Opaque A solid fill, one with no transparency.

OR condition In a query, returns records meeting any of the specified criteria.

Order of operations A rule that controls the sequence in which arithmetic operations are performed. Also called the *order of precedence*.

Outline A method of organizing text in a hierarchy to depict relationships.

Outline view A structural view of a document that can be collapsed or expanded as necessary.

Outline view (PowerPoint) A view showing the presentation in an outline format displayed in levels according to the points and any subpoints on each slide.

Output area The range of cells in an Excel worksheet that contain formulas dependent on the values in the input area.

Page break An indication of where data will start on another printed page.

Page Break Preview A view setting that displays the worksheet data and page breaks within the worksheet.

Page Layout view A view setting that displays the worksheet data, margins, headers, and footers.

Paragraph spacing The amount of space before or after a paragraph.

Paste A command used to place a cut or copied selection into another location.

Paste Options button An icon that displays in the bottom-right corner immediately after using the Paste command. It enables the user to apply different paste options.

PDF (Portable Document Format) A file type that was created for exchanging documents independent of software applications and operating system environments.

PDF Reflow A Word feature that converts a PDF document into an editable Word document.

Percent Style A number format that displays a value as if it was multiplied by 100 and with the % symbol. The default number of decimal places is zero if you click Percent Style in the Number group or two decimal places if you use the Format Cells dialog box.

Photo Album A presentation containing multiple pictures organized into album pages.

Picture A graphic file that is retrieved from storage media or the Internet and placed in an Office project.

Picture fill Inserts an image from a file into a shape.

Pie chart A chart type that shows each data point in proportion to the whole data series as a slice in a circle. A pie chart depicts only one data series.

Pin A process to add a tile to the Start menu or icon to the taskbar.

Placeholder A container that holds text, images, graphs, or other objects to be used in a presentation.

Plagiarizing The act of using and documenting the works of another as one's own.

Plain text format (.txt) A file format that retains only text but no formatting when you transfer documents between applications or platforms.

Plot area The region of a chart containing the graphical representation of the values in one or more data series. Two axes form a border around the plot area.

Pmt function A function that calculates the periodic loan payment given a fixed rate, number of periods (also known as term), and the present value of the loan (the principal).

Point The smallest unit of measurement used in typography, 1/72 of an inch.

Pointing The process of using the pointer to select cells while building a formula. Also known as *semi-selection*.

Portable Document Format (PDF) A file type that was created for exchanging documents independent of software applications and operating system environment.

Portrait orientation A document layout when a page is taller than it is wide.

Poster Frame The image that displays on a slide when a video is not playing.

PowerPoint An application that enables you to create dynamic presentations to inform groups and persuade audiences.

PowerPoint presentation An electronic slide show that can be edited or delivered in a variety of ways.

PowerPoint show An unchangeable electronic slide show format used for distribution.

Presenter view Specialty view that delivers a presentation on two monitors simultaneously.

Primary key The field (or combination of fields) that uniquely identifies each record in a table.

Print area The range of cells within a worksheet that will print.

Print Layout view View that closely resembles the way a document will look when printed.

Print order The sequence in which the pages are printed.

Print Preview A view that enables you to see exactly what the report will look like when it is printed.

Property Sheet The location where you change settings such as number format and number of decimal places.

Public domain The rights to a literary work or property owned by the public at large.

PV A predefined formula that calculates the present value of a loan.

Query A question about the data stored in a database answers provided in a datasheet.

Quick access A component of File Explorer that contains shortcuts to the most frequently used folders. Folders can be pinned and removed from Quick access.

Quick Access Toolbar A toolbar located at the top-left corner of any Office application window, this provides fast access to commonly executed tasks such as saving a file and undoing recent actions.

Quick Analysis A set of analytical tools you can use to apply formatting, create charts or tables, and insert basic functions.

Quick Style A combination of formatting options that can be applied to a shape or graphic.

Radar chart A chart type that compares aggregate values of three or more variables represented on axes starting from the same point.

Range A group of adjacent or contiguous cells in a worksheet. A range can be adjacent cells in a column (such as C5:C10), in a row (such as A6:H6), or a rectangular group of cells (such as G5:H10).

Range_lookup An argument that determines how the VLOOKUP and HLOOKUP function handle lookup values that are not an exact match for the data in the lookup table.

Rate The periodic interest rate; the percentage of interest paid for each payment period; the first argument in the PMT function.

Read Mode View in which text reflows automatically between columns to make it easier to read.

Reading View Displays the slide show full screen, one slide at a time, complete with animations and transitions.

Real Time Typing A Word feature that shows where co-authors are working, and what their contributions are as they type.

Real-time co-authoring A Word feature that shows several authors simultaneously editing the document in Word or Word Online.

Recolor The process of changing a picture by adjusting the image's colors.

Record A group of related fields representing one entity, such as data for one person, place, event, or concept.

Record source The table or query that supplies the records for a form or report.

Recycle Bin Temporary storage for files deleted from the computer's hard drive or OneDrive.

Referential Integrity Rules in a database that are used to preserve relationships between tables when records are changed.

Relationship A connection between two tables using a common field.

Relative cell reference A designation that indicates a cell's relative location from the original cell containing the formula; the cell reference changes when the formula is copied.

Report A database document that outputs meaningful, professional-looking, formatted information from underlying tables or queries.

Report tool A tool used to instantly create a tabular report based on the table or query currently selected.

Report view A view that enables you to determine what a printed report will look like in a continuous onscreen page layout.

Report Wizard A feature that prompts you for input and then uses your answers to generate a customized report.

Resource Monitor A feature that displays how the computer is using its key resources such as the CPU and RAM.

Revision mark Markings that indicate where text is added, deleted, or formatted while the Track Changes feature is active.

Ribbon The command center of Office applications. It is the long bar located just beneath the title bar, containing tabs, groups, and commands.

Rich Text Format (.rtf) A file format that retains structure and most text formatting when transferring documents between applications or platforms.

Right alignment Begins text evenly at the right margin, with a ragged left edge.

Right indent A setting that positions all text in a paragraph an equal distance from the right margin.

Rotate To move an object around its axis.

Row heading A number to the left side of a row in a worksheet. For example, 3 is the row heading for the third row.

Row height The vertical measurement of the row in a worksheet.

Sans serif font A font that does not contain a thin line or extension at the top and bottom of the primary strokes on characters.

Saturation A characteristic of color that controls its intensity.

Search box A feature located on the taskbar. Combined with Cortana, or used alone, it provides a convenient way to search your computer or the Web.

Section A division to presentation content that groups slides meaningfully.

Section break An indicator that divides a document into parts, enabling different formatting for each section.

Select All The triangle at the intersection of the row and column headings in the top-left corner of the worksheet. Click it to select everything contained in the active worksheet.

Selection Filter A method of selecting that displays only the records that match a criterion you select.

Selection net A selection of multiple objects created by dragging a rectangle around all of the objects you wish to select.

Selection pane A pane designed to help select objects.

Semi-selection The process of using the pointer to select cells while building a formula. Also known as *pointing*.

Serif font A font that contains a thin line or extension at the top and bottom of the primary strokes on characters.

Shading A background color that appears behind text in a paragraph, page, or table element.

Shape A geometric or non-geometric object, such as a rectangle or an arrow, used to create an illustration or highlight information.

Sharpening A technique that enhances the edges of the content in a picture to make the boundaries more prominent.

Sheet tab A visual label that looks like a file folder tab. In Excel, a sheet tab shows the name of a worksheet contained in the workbook.

Sheet tab navigation Visual elements that help you navigate to the first, previous, next, or last sheet within a workbook.

Shortcut An icon on the desktop designated with a small arrow in the bottom-left corner, that provides a link a program.

Shortcut menu A menu that provides choices related to the selection or area at which you right-click.

Simple Markup A Word feature that simplifies the display of comments and revision marks, resulting in a clean, uncluttered look.

Simple Query Wizard Provides a step-by-step guide to help you through the query design process.

Sizing handle A series of faint dots on the outside border of a selected object; enables the user to adjust the height and width of the object.

Sizing handles (Excel) Eight circles that display on the outside border of a chart—one on each corner and one on each middle side—when the chart is selected; enables the user to adjust the height and width of the chart.

Sleep A power saving state that puts work and settings in memory and draws a small amount of power to allow the computer to resume full-power operation quickly.

Slide The most basic element of PowerPoint, similar to a page in Word.

Slide master The top slide in a hierarchy of slides based on the master.

Slide show A series of slides displayed onscreen for an audience.

Slide Show view Displays the completed presentation full screen to an audience as an electronic presentation.

Slide Sorter view Displays thumbnails of presentation slides enabling a view of multiple slides.

Slide pane The main workspace in PowerPoint, that displays the currently selected slide.

Slides pane Pane on the left side of Normal view that shows the slide deck with thumbnails.

Smart Lookup A feature that provides information about tasks or commands in Office, and can also be used to search for general information on a topic such as *President George Washington*.

SmartArt A diagram that presents information visually to effectively communicate a message.

SmartGuide A guide that displays when an object is moved that helps align objects in relation to other objects.

Snip A screenshot taken with the Snipping Tool accessory application in Windows.

Softening A technique that blurs the edges of the content in a picture to make the boundaries less prominent.

Sort A feature which lists records in a specific sequence.

Sorting The process of arranging records by the value of one or more fields within a table or data range.

Source A publication, person, or media item that is consulted in the preparation of a paper and given credit.

Sparkline A small line, column, or win/loss chart contained in a single cell to provide a simple visual illustrating one data series.

Split form A form that combines two views of the same record source—one section is displayed in a stacked layout and the other section is displayed in a tabular layout.

Spreadsheet An electronic file that contains a grid of columns and rows used to organize related data and to display results of calculations, enabling interpretation of quantitative data for decision making.

Stacked column chart A chart type that places stacks of data in segments on top of each other in one column, with each category in the data series represented by a different color.

Stacked layout A layout that displays fields in a vertical column.

Stacking order The order of objects placed on top of one another.

Start menu A feature that provides the main access to all programs on your computer.

Status bar A bar located at the bottom of the program window that contains information relative to the open file. It also includes tools for changing the view of the file and for changing the zoom size of onscreen file contents.

Status bar (Excel) The row at the bottom of the Excel window that displays instructions and other details about the status of a worksheet.

Stock chart A chart type that shows fluctuation in stock prices.

Storyboard A visual plan of a presentation that displays the content of each slide in the slide show.

Structured reference A tag or use of a table element, such as a field label, as a reference in a formula. Field labels are enclosed in square brackets, such as [Amount] within the formula.

Style A named collection of formatting characteristics that can be applied to text or paragraphs.

Style manual A guide to a particular writing style outlining required rules and conventions related to the preparation of papers.

Style set A combination of title, heading, and paragraph styles that can be used to format all of those elements in a document at one time.

SUBTOTAL function A predefined formula that calculates an aggregate value, such as totals, for displayed values in a range, a table, or a database.

SUM function A predefined formula that calculates the total of values contained in one or more cells.

Surface chart A chart type that displays trends using two dimensions on a continuous curve.

Symbol A character or graphic not normally included on a keyboard.

Syntax A set of rules that governs the structure and components for properly entering a function.

Tab Located on the Ribbon, each tab is designed to appear much like a tab on a file folder, with the active tab highlighted.

Tab stop A marker that specifies the position for aligning text in a column arrangement, often including a dot leader.

Table (Access) The location where all data is stored in a database; organizes data into columns and rows.

Table (Excel) A structured range that contains related data organized in a method that increases the capability to manage and analyze information.

Table alignment The horizontal position of a table between the left and right margins.

Table array The range that contains the lookup table.

Table of contents A page that lists headings in the order in which they appear in a document and the page numbers on which the entries begin.

Table style A named collection of color, font, and border designs that can be applied to a table.

Tabular layout A layout that displays fields horizontally.

Task Manager A tool that displays the programs and processes that are running on your computer. It is also used to close a non-responding program.

Task pane A window of options to format and customize chart elements. The task pane name and options change based on the selected chart element.

Task view A button on the taskbar that enables the user to view thumbnail previews of all open tasks in one glance.

Taskbar The horizontal bar at the bottom of the desktop that displays open applications, the Notification area, the Search box, and pinned apps or programs.

***Tell me what you want to do* box** Located to the right of the last tab, this box enables you to search for help and information about a command or task you want to perform and also presents you with a shortcut directly to that command.

Template A predesigned file that incorporates formatting elements, such as a theme and layouts, and may include content that can be modified.

Template (Access) A predefined database that includes professionally designed tables, forms, reports, and other objects that you can use to jumpstart the creation of your database.

Text Any combination of letters, numbers, symbols, and spaces not used in Excel calculations.

Text box A graphical object that contains text.

Text box (PowerPoint) An object that provides space for text anywhere on a slide; it can be formatted with a border, shading, and other characteristics.

Text pane A pane for text entry used for a SmartArt diagram.

Texture fill Inserts a texture such as canvas, denim, marble, or cork into a shape.

Theme A collection of design choices that includes colors, fonts, and special effects used to give a consistent look to a document, workbook, presentation, or database form or report.

Thesaurus A tool used to quickly find a synonym (a word with the same meaning as another).

Thumbnail A miniature view of a slide that appears in the Slidespane and Slide Sorter view.

Tile A rectangular icon on the Start menu that allow you to access programs and apps.

Title bar The long bar at the top of each window that displays the name of the folder, file, or program displayed in the open window and the application in which you are working.

TODAY function A predefined formula that displays the current date.

Toggle commands A button that acts somewhat like light switches that you can turn on and off. You select the command to turn it on, then select it again to turn it off.

Tone A characteristic of lighting that controls the temperature of a color. See also *Kelvin*.

Total row (Access) A method to display aggregate function results as the last row in Datasheet view of a table or query.

Total row (Excel) A table row that appears below the last row of records in an Excel table and displays summary or aggregate statistics, such as a sum or an average.

Totals query A way to display aggregate data when a query is run.

Track Changes A word feature that monitors all additions, deletions, and formatting changes you make in a document.

Transition A specific animation that is applied as na previous slide is repladed by a new slide while displayed in Slide Show view or Reading view.

Transparency The visibility of fill.

Trendline A line that depicts trends or helps forecast future data in a chart. For example, if the plotted data includes 2005, 2010, and 2015, a trendline can help forecast values for 2020 and beyond.

Ungroup To break a combined grouped object into individual objects.

Unqualified reference The use of field headings without row references in a structured formula.

Value A number that represents a quantity or a measurable amount.

Value axis The chart axis that displays incremental numbers to identify approximate values, such as dollars or units, of data points in a chart.

Variant A variation on a chosen design theme.

Vector graphic An image created by a mathematical statement.

Vertex The point where a curve ends or the point where two line segments meet in a shape.

Vertical alignment The placement of cell data between the top and bottom cell margins.

View The various ways a file can appear on the screen.

View controls Icons on the right side of the status bar that enable you to change to Normal, Page Layout, or Page Break view to display the worksheet.

Virtual desktop A way to organize and access groups of windows for different purposes.

VLOOKUP function A predefined formula that accepts a value, looks the value up in a vertical lookup table with data organized in columns, and returns a result.

Watermark Text or graphics that display behind text.

Web Layout view View that displays the way a document will look when posted on the Internet.

Wildcard A special character that can represent one or more characters in the criterion of a query.

Windows app A program that displays full screen without any borders or many controls. It is designed to be best viewed and used on smaller screens such as those on smartphone and tablets.

Windows Defender Antispyware and antivirus software included in Windows 10.

Windows Update A utility in Windows that provides a means to initiate updates and modifications pushed to the user that enhances Windows security or fixes problems.

Word An application that can produce all sorts of documents, including memos, newsletters, forms, tables, and brochures.

Word Online An online component of Office Online, it is a Web-based version of Word with sufficient capabilities to enable you to edit and format a document online.

Word processing software A computer application, such as Microsoft Word, used primarily with text to create, edit, and format documents.

Word wrap The feature that automatically moves words to the next line if they do not fit on the current line.

WordArt A feature that modifies text to include special effects, such as color, shadow, gradient, and 3-D appearance.

Workbook A collection of one or more related worksheets contained within a single file.

Works Cited A list of works cited or consulted by an author in his or her work; the list is titled Works Cited.

Worksheet A single spreadsheet that typically contains descriptive labels, numeric values, formulas, functions, and graphical representations of data.

Wrap text An Excel feature that makes data appear on multiple lines by adjusting the row height to fit the cell contents within the column width.

Writing style Writing a paper as directed by a style manual such as MLA or APA.

X Y (scatter) chart A chart type that shows a relationship between two variables using their X and Y coordinates. Excel plots one coordinate on the horizontal X-axis and the other variable on the vertical Y-axis. Scatter charts are often used to represent data in education, scientific, and medical experiments.

X-axis The horizontal border that provides a frame of reference for measuring data left to right on a chart.

Y-axis The vertical border that provides a frame of reference for measuring data up and down on a chart.

Zoom control A control that enables you to increase or decrease the size of the worksheet data onscreen.

Zoom slider A feature that displays at the far right side of the status bar. It is used to increase or decrease the magnification of the file.

Index